BELLVM·INTER·COIP·AHAM·EFFRANCS

THE ILLUSTRATED
ENCYCLOPEDIA OF
MEDIEVAL
CIVILIZATION

THE ILLUSTRATED ENCYCLOPEDIA OF
MEDIEVAL CIVILIZATION

ARYEH GRABOIS

octopus

Designed by: A. Yuval.

First published in the U.S.A. in 1980
by Mayflower Books Inc.,
575 Lexington Avenue, New York City 10022

Originally published in England by
Octopus Books Limited, 59 Grosvenor Street,
London W1.

© 1980 G.G. The Jerusalem Publishing
House Limited, Jerusalem.
Printed in Israel.

Library of Congress Cataloging in Publication Data
Grabois, Aryeh, 1930 –
        The Illustrated Encyclopedia of Medieval Civilization
Bibliography: p.
Includes index.

        1. Civilization, Medieval – Dictionaries. I. Title.
CB353.G7   909'.1'03   79-13630
ISBN 0-7064-0856-X

Page 1: The coronation of Charlemagne; miniature from the Chroniques de France, *14th century*
Page 2: St. Ambrose crowning the artist Vulvinus, *detail from St. Ambrose Altar at Milan*

Contents

FOREWORD 7

LIST OF ABBREVIATIONS 9

SELECT BIBLIOGRAPHY 9

THE ILLUSTRATED ENCYCLOPEDIA OF MEDIEVAL CIVILIZATION 13

MAPS 737

TABLE 741

INDEX 746

ACKNOWLEDGMENTS 752

Foreword

Ever since Isidore of Seville completed his *Etymologicae* at the beginning of the Middle Ages, the production of encyclopedias and dictionaries, offering the intelligent layman a comprehensive summary of available knowledge, has not ceased. The division of modern arts and sciences into numerous fields of specialization makes the use of encyclopedias indispensable for scholars, students, and general readers in search of information. It was only natural that with the tremendous growth of modern culture the number of encyclopedias has increased to such an extent that the compilation of any bibliography has become a difficult enterprise in itself. In addition, to meet the needs of particular nations, a wide range of specialized encyclopedias and dictionaries on specific disciplines, subjects and periods has to be added. While many of these encyclopedias enhance our knowledge of the Middle Ages, none deals specifically with the medieval civilization as such, despite the impressive progress in medieval studies in the last hundred years.

The present volume is therefore a first attempt to fill this gap and provide a general reference book on the period. Like all pioneer efforts, it has both advantages and risks. Designed for the general public, this is not an academic work purporting to contain all medievalist knowledge — which would require several volumes, and would also risk being outdated by the time it is published — rather, it represents a selection of the essential data on medieval civilization. It is arranged in some 4000 entries, with illustrations and short bibliographies, according to the author's idea of history and concepts of the Middle Ages, in the light of modern research.

The traditional view of the Middle Ages, as reflected in most general encyclopedias, is confined to Western Europe in the years 500-1500, with slight extensions to neighbouring cultures. Such a view may be convenient, because it deals with a unity of cultural values: Christianity was the common religion, Latin the scholastic language and feudalism the common form of social organization. But the fact remains that most of mankind did not inhabit Western Europe, nor was civilization by any means confined to this part of the world. The Islamic culture, for example, reached a higher level of achievement than that of Western Europe before the 13th century, and cannot be ignored in an encyclopedia of the Middle Ages. Nor is it possible to leave out the great Oriental civilizations — those of India, China and Japan — which, isolated from the Western and Middle Eastern world, achieved great heights. While a similar compendium on the classical world can concentrate on the Mediterranean region, an encyclopedia of medieval civilization must be almost universal in scope. This entails certain difficulties. For example, the many existing transcriptions of Islamic and Oriental names, some of which are firmly rooted in Western literature, often cause problems of terminology.

Crusaders in battle against the Saracens; 13th-century miniature

In general, I have adhered to popular usage. A more fundamental problem is that the traditional chronological boundaries of the Middle Ages, based on Western history, impose an arbitrary break in the evolution of other civilizations.

The present volume reflects the author's view of history as the sum of the activities of *Homo sapiens,* from earliest times. Political history, therefore, with its events and the men who shaped them, is only a part of total history. Religion – especially in the Age of Belief, as the medieval world has been called – as well as social and economic factors, are legitimate parts of the historical saga. In addition, the history of literary and artistic creativity, and of the intellectual life, with its trends of thought, scientific and technological achievements, all belong in the total picture, and without them the meaning of history would be distorted. Perhaps there is no better way of demonstrating the universality of the medieval world than by studying the continuous inter-relationships in the intellectual and scientific fields, wherein, on the foundations of the classical heritage, Christians, Jews, Moslems and Orientals taught and learned from each other, despite their political and religious animosities.

For one man to undertake a work of so broad a scope may be considered presumptuous by some. But it was a challenge worth meeting, even in an age of narrow specialization, when team-work is almost always the rule. Its main advantage lies in the unity of conception. Wherever necessary, I relied on the well established authorities. I was several times reminded of the words of the 12th-century scholar, John of Salisbury, that "we are dwarfs on the shoulders of giants, but in that higher position we are able to enlarge the horizons of our sight" – in particular when I resorted to past authorities rather than more recent studies of a particular subject.

This encyclopedia offers the reader general articles on major, comprehensive topics, such as Feudalism, Medieval Art or Arabs; there are many shorter entries on specific terms, concepts and persons. Such entries vary immensely – a rapacious adventurer who also founded a respectable dynasty may be included beside a physician whose studies in physiology led to improvements in the diagnosis and the treatment of diseases. A system of cross-references (signified by asterisks in the text) furnishes the reader with a ready means of obtaining additional information. Illustrations and maps add a visual dimension to the text.

I am grateful to the many colleagues with whom I have exchanged views during the years, and whose assistance and advice have been invaluable; to Mr Zvi Baras, who wrote the entries in the letter "D"; Dr. Michael Toch (letters U-Z); my research assistant, Ms Irith Shai, and the staff of the Jerusalem Publishing House who were of cardinal help in the editing of the work.
Uxori vero, amplissimam.

Aryeh Grabois

LIST OF ABBREVIATIONS

AASS	*Acta Sanctorum*, ed. Bollandist Soc. (1643-present).
CEcH	*Cambridge Economic History*, ed. M. M. Postan, 3 vols. (1939-58).
CHI	*Cambridge History of Islam* (1970).
CMedH	*Cambridge Medieval History*, ed. H. M. Gwatkin, 8 vols. (1911-36).
CSEL	*Corpus Scriptorum Ecclesiasticorum Latinorum* (1866-present).
DACL	*Dictionnaire d'Archéologie Chrétienne et de Liturgie*, ed. F. Cabrol, 15 vols. (1907-53).
DHE	*Diccionario de Historia de España*, 1.
DHGE	*Dictionnaire d'Histoire et de Géographie Ecclésiastique*, ed. A. Baudrillart (1912-present).
DNB	*Dictionary of National Biography*, ed. L. Stephen and S. Lee, 21 vols. (1908-09).
DTC	*Dictionnaire de Théologie Catholique*, ed. A. Vacant, 15 vols. (1903-50).
EB	*Encyclopaedia Britannica*, 15th ed., 31 vols. (1973).
EC	*Encyclopaedia Catholica*, 12 vols. (1949-54).
EI	*Encyclopaedia of Islam*, 2nd ed., 7 vols. (1966-76).
EJ	*Encyclopaedia Judaica*, ed. C. Roth – G. Wigoder, 15 vols. (1972).
GAL	C. Brockelmann, *Geschichte der arabischen Literatur*, 5 vols. (1898-1942).
GE	*Grande Encyclopédie*, 32 vols. (1936-58).
Hussey	J. M. Hussey, *Byzantium* (*CMedH*, vol. IV, 2nd ed. 1964).
Manitius	M. Manitius, *Geschichte der Lateinischen Literatur des Mittelalters*, 3 vols. (1911-31).
Mansi	*Sacrorum Conciliorum Nova et Amplissima Collectio*, 31 vols. (1759-98).
Muratori	L. A. Muratori (new ed. by G. Carducci), *Rerum Italicarum Scriptora*, 344 fasc. (1900-1961).
MGH	*Monumenta Germaniae Historica*, ed. H. Pertz, 200 vols. (1825).
Niermeyer	J. F. Niermeyer, *Dictionary of Medieval Latin*, 12 fasc. (1954-73).
Nouvelle Clio	*Nouvelle Clio*, ed. R. Boutruche and P. Lemerle, 16 vols. (1963-present).
PG	*Patrologia Graeca*, ed. J. P. Migne, 162 vols. (1857-66).
PL	*Patrologia Latina*, ed. J. P. Migne, 221 vols. (1844-64).
RHC	*Recueil des Historiens des Croisades, 16 vols.* (1841-1906).
RHGF	*Recueil des Historiens des Gaules et de la France*, 24 vols. (1734-1904).
Rolls Series	*Chronicles and Memorials of Great Britain and Ireland during the Middle Ages*, 244 vols. (1858-1896).
SCFMA	*Société des Classiques Français du Moyen Age*, ed. M. Rocques (1911-present).
SRGMA	*Scriptores Rerum Germanicarum Medii Aevi*, 180 vols. (1880-present).

SELECT BIBLIOGRAPHY

The following list is a short selection on medieval history and civilization. While the bibliographical data accompanying the entries are not restricted to works published in English, and include a large number of monographs and scholarly publications in French, German and Italian, too, the general selection is based solely on books published in English. It consists mainly of recent and current works, or reissues of classical ones. The dates are generally those of the last editions.

CAMBRIDGE COLLECTIVE SERIES
The Cambridge Economic History, vols. I-III (1952-68).
The Cambridge History of English Literature, vol. I (1937).
The Cambridge History of Islam, 2 vols. (1970).
The Cambridge History of Poland (1950).
The Cambridge Medieval History, vols. I-VIII (1922 ff.; vol. IV-Byzantium, reiss. 1966).

SELECTION IN ALPHABETICAL ORDER
Artz, F. S., *A History of the Medieval Mind* (1967).
Atiya, A. S., *Crusade, Commerce, Culture* (1962).
Atiya, A. S., *The Later Crusades* (1934).
Baron, S. W., *A Social and Religious History of the Jews*, vols. IV-XII (1955-63).
Barraclough, G., *The Origins of Modern Germany* (1963).

Bloch, M., *Feudal Society*, 2 vols. (1961).
Bolgar, R. R., *The Classical Heritage and Its Beneficaries* (1964).
Bowsky, W. M. (ed.), *The Black Death* (1972).
Brown, P., *Augustine of Hippo* (1967).
Bury, J. P., *A History of the Later Roman Empire* (1957).

Butler, W., *The Lombard Communes* (1969).

Cochrane, C. N., *Christianity and the Classical Culture* (1944).

Cohn, N., *The Pursuit of the Millennium* (1957).

Crombie, A. C., *Medieval Science*, 2 vols. (1957).

Dawson, C., *The Making of Europe* (1932).

Dill, S., *Roman Society in Gaul in the Merovingian Age* (1970).

Duby, G., *Rural Economy and Country life in the Medieval West* (1968).

Duckett, E. S., *Alcuin, Friend of Charlemagne* (1965).

Duckett, E. S., *The Gateway to the Middle Ages*, 3 vols. (1961).

Dvornik, F., *The Slavs in European History* (1962).

Florinsky, M. T., *Russia; A History and Interpretation*, vol. I (1953).

Folz, R., *The Idea of the Empire in the West* (1967).

Ganshof, F. L., *Feudalism* (1965).

Geanakoplos, D. J., *Byzantine East and Latin West* (1966).

Geanakoplos, D. J., *Medieval Western Civilizations and the Byzantine and Moslem Worlds* (1979).

Genicot, L., *Contours of the Middle Ages* (1967).

Gilson, E., *Heloise and Abelard* (1960).

Gilson, E., *A History of Medieval Philosophy* (1955).

Haskins, C. H., *The Normans in European History* (1966).

Haskins, C. H., *The Renaissance of the Twelfth Century* (1927).

Havinghurst, A. F. (ed.), *The Pirenne Thesis* (1969).

Hitti, P. K., *A History of the Arabs* (1963).

Holmes, U. T., *A History of Medieval French Literature* (1948).

Huizinga, J., *The Waning of the Middle Ages* (1924).

Jones, A. H. M., *The Later Roman Empire*, 2 vols. (1964).

Jones, G., *A History of the Vikings* (1968).

Kantorowicz, E. H., *Emperor Frederick II* (1931).

Kempf, F., *The Church in the Age of Feudalism* (1970).

Laistner, M. L. W., *Thought and Letters in Western Europe, 500-900* (1957).

La Monte, J. L., *The World of the Middle Ages* (1957).

Leff, G., *Medieval Thought; From Augustine to Ockham* (1960).

Leff, G., *Heresy in the Later Middle Ages* (1967).

Le Goff, J., *The Intellectuals of the Middle Ages* (1968).

Lewis, B., *The Arabs in History* (1956).

Lewis, P. S., *Later Medieval France* (1968).

Loomis, R. S. (ed.), *The Arthurian Literature in the Middle Ages* (1959).

Lopez, R. S., *The Birth of Europe* (1972).

Lopez, R. S., *The Commercial Revolution of the Middle Ages* (1972).

Lopez, R. S., *The Tenth Century: How Dark the Dark Ages* (1959).

Lopez, R. S. and Raymond, I. W., *Medieval Trade in the Mediterranean World* (1967).

Lot, F., *The End of the Ancient World and the Beginnings of the Middle Ages* (1931).

Moss, H. S. L. B., *The Birth of the Middle Ages* (1964).

Mundy, J. H. and Riesenberg, P., *The Medieval Town* (1958).

O'Callaghan, J., *A History of Medieval Spain* (1975).

Painter, S., *French Chivalry* (1940).

Painter, S., *Medieval Society* (1951).

Painter, S., *The Reign of King John* (1949).

Panofsky, E., *Gothic Architecture and Scholasticism* (1956).

Perroy, E., *The Hundred Years' War* (1958).

Petit-Dutaillis, C., *Feudal Monarchy in France and England* (1964).

Pirenne, H., *Economic and Social History of Medieval Europe* (1956).

Pirenne, H., *Medieval Cities* (1956).

Pirenne, H., *Mohammed and Charlemagne* (1955).

Poole, A. L., *From Domesday Book to Magna Charta (Oxford History of England)* (1951).

Power, E., *Medieval People* (1963).

Powicke, F. M., *The Thirteenth Century (Oxford History of England)* (1953).

Powicke, F. M. and Emden, A. B., *Rashdall's History of the Universities of Medieval Europe*, 3 vols. (1936).

Prawden, M., *The Mongols* (1940).

Prawer, J., *The Crusaders' Kingdom* (1972).

Roover, R. de, *The Medici Bank* (1948).

Rorig, F., *The Medieval Town* (1967).

Runciman, S., *A History of the Crusades*, 3 vols. (1953).

Schevill, F., *Medieval and Renaissance Florence*, 2 vols. (1963).

Simpson, O. von, *The Gothic Cathedral* (1956).

Smalley, B., *The Study of the Bible in the Middle Ages* (1952).

Southern, R. W., *The Making of the Middle Ages* (1953).

Stenton, F. M., *Anglo-Saxon England (Oxford History of England)* (1947).

Strayer, J. R., *Western Europe in the Middle Ages* (1974).

Stuard, S. M., *Women in Medieval Society* (1976).

Sykes, P., *A History of Persia*, 2 vols. (1921).

Taylor, A. J., *The Course of German History* (1967).

Taylor, H. O., *The Classical Heritage of the Middle Ages* (1958).

Tellenbach, G., *Church, State and Christian Society at the Time of the Investiture Contest* (1970).

Thompson, E. A., *The Goths in Spain* (1969).

Tierney, B., *The Crisis of the Church and State* (1959).

Turbeville, A. S., *Medieval Heresy and the Inquisition* (1964).

Ullmann, W., *The Carolingian Renaissance and the Idea of Kingship* (1969).

Ullmann, W., *The Individual and Society in the Middle Ages* (1968).

Ullmann, W., *A Short History of the Medieval Papacy* (1972).

Van Cleve, T. C., *The Emperor Frederick II of Hohenstaufen* (1972).

Vasiliev, A. A., *A History of the Byzantine Empire* (1968).

Vernadsky, G., *Kievan Russia* (1953).

Waddell, H., *The Wandering Scholars* (1968).

Waley, D., *Later Medieval Europe* (1975).

Waley, D., *The Italian City-Republics* (1969).

Wallace-Hadrill, J. M., *The Barbarian West* (1962).

White, L., *Medieval Technology and Social Change* (1966).

Wilkinson, B., *The Later Middle Ages in England* (1969).

Wittek, P., *The Rise of the Ottoman Empire* (1971).

For Africa, China, India and Japan, see bibliographical data accompanying the respective articles.

The Madonna of all Saints *by Giotto di Bondone (c. 1305)*

A

AACHEN See AIX-LA-CHAPELLE.

ABACUS An accounting instrument, probably of Chinese origin, which was already known in classical Greece and Rome. The instrument was perfected in western Europe in about the 9th century, and consisted of a wooden panel with a number of "fields", upon which small wooden buttons were placed. An answer to the need for accurate accountancy, the A. was based on the currency, thus 12 *denarii* (pence) making 1 *solidus* (shilling); 20 *solidi* making 1 *libra* (pound). The "field" for pence had 12 coins, that of shillings 20; having made up 12 d., the accountant transferred them into 1 s. The 13th-century mathematician, *Leonardo Fibonnacci of Pisa, based his treatises on the use of the A., and became its theorist. By the end of the 15th century, the decimal system of accounting was adopted, and the instrument was adapted accordingly.

A. C. Crombie, *Science in the Middle Ages*, I (1952).

ABAGHA Mongol khan of *Persia (1265-81), son of *Hulagu, member of the Chingizide dynasty. After the defeat of the Mongols at Ain-Jalut (1261), he established the seat of his government in Persia, from which he also ruled Iraq and northern Syria. Being a Christian, A. established close relations with the remnants of the Crusader states, and based his government on *Nestorian Christians. Nevertheless, during his reign a strong Moslem influence spread in the khanate, led by his brother and heir Ahmad.

M. Prowden, *The Mongols* (1940).

ABBADIDS Arab dynasty of *Andalusia in the 11th century. Its founder, Abu Al-Kasim Muhammad Ibn Abbad, served at the beginning of the 11th century as *Kadi* (religious judge and mayor) of Seville. In 1023 he revolted against the caliphate of *Córdoba, declared Seville independent of it and established his own kingdom (1023-42). His son Abbad Al-Mutadid (1042-69) annexed the minor Arab kingdoms of western and northern Andalusia. Himself a poet, he patronized arts and culture at his court in Seville. Under his heir, Muhammad Ibn Abbad, Seville became the centre of Spanish Moslem culture. He tried to continue the expansionist policy of his father, and even occupied Córdoba temporarily. Concerned by the *reconquista* policy of King *Alfonso VI of Castile, and particularly after the latter's conquest of Toledo (1085), he allied himself with the Moorish *Almoravides, who turned against him and, in 1095, conquered Seville.

E. Lévy-Provençal, *Histoire de l'Espagne musulmane*, I (1950).

ABBA MARI HAYARKHI OF LUNEL (Provençal: 'N Astruc) Rabbi at Montpellier *c.* 1300, he was the leader of the traditionalist party of the Jewish community of Montpellier and southern France. His position was that Judaism is based on the faith in the unity of

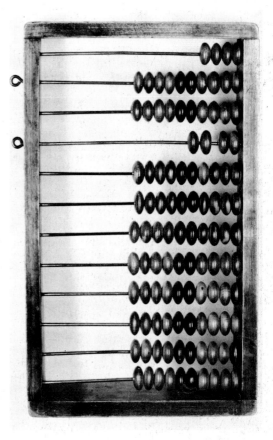

A Russian abacus

God and that philosophy and other lay studies, except medicine, could cause people to lose their faith. A. contested the philosophical books of *Maimonides and led the anti-Maimonidean party in southern France. Between 1305-08, he urged the excommunication of the Maimonideans and published the *Minhath Kenaoth* (The Offering of Zeal), the most vigorous polemic against Maimonides. After the expulsion of the Jews from France (1306), he settled at Perpignan, where he had to accept a compromise permitting people over 25 years of age to study the philosophical books of Maimonides.

Works, ed. Pressburg (1828).

ABBASIDS A dynasty of Moslem caliphs (750-1258) who reigned in *Baghdad. Originally, the A. were a *Shiite sect, its ancestor being Abbas, the uncle of the prophet *Mohammad. Their leader, the Imam, led the sect from Al-Humeimah in Transjordan, in opposition to the *Ummayad caliphs. The Imam's representatives were particularly active in southern *Iraq, from their centre at Kufa, which was established at the end of the 7th century. About 720 they were intensely active in *Khorasan (eastern Persia), where the non-Arab Moslems opposed the Ummayad regime because of its discrimination against them by the Arabs, which was manifested especially in the economic life and the imposition of taxes. At the same time, other Shiite groups, especially the tribes of southern Arabia, like Qalb and Yemen, who were deprived of their leaders, joined the opposition, led by the propagandist Abu Muslim, who rebelled in 747. The war against the Ummayads continued until 750, when the dynasty was defeated. The Caliph *Marwan II fled to Egypt, where he was murdered and the caliphate passed to the A., except for Spain, where the Ummayads founded an independent state. The Imam *Abu Al-Abbas Al Saffah was proclaimed caliph.

The A. later abandoned the religious principles of their revolt and adopted the *Sunnite rite, which was that of the majority. Abu Muslim and many other leaders of the revolution were put to death and the new dynasty established its seat of power in Iraq (from 762), where the new capital city of Baghdad was built. While the caliphate remained in the hands of Arabs, and the official language was Arabic, the A. gave equal status to non-Arab Moslems, appointing to the government viziers of Persian origin, who established an administration rooted in Persian tradition. As a result the caliph was isolated from his subjects, who had to deal with the viziers' bureaucracy and absolutist tendencies increased. The A. concentrated on the eastern part of the empire, abandoning the Mediterranean orientation of the Ummayads in favour of an Asian one. Attention was paid mainly to the development of trade with India, China and Central Asia.

The first hundred years of the A. caliphate are considered a glorious age of the Moslem civilization. It reached its height in the reign of *Harun Al-Rashid at the end of the 8th century and the beginning of the 9th. The court of Baghdad was then at its zenith, and the caliph became a legendary person, as reflected in the stories of the *Thousand and One Tales*. Islamic theology was then at its most creative, Arabs and Persians collaborating in its development. Literature and poetry flourished under the dynasty's patronage. A Persian-Arab style of building and abstract decoration (the arabesque) evolved in the caliphate and spread as far as Spain and north Africa.

The A. began to decline in the middle of the 9th century. The western provinces, particularly the Maghreb, where the dynasty's rule was never effective, rebelled under the leadership of the *Fatimids, and created a separate caliphate, which in the 10th century conquered Egypt and Palestine. In the east, Persian generals and governors became independent, although formally they remained subject to the caliph, who lost power even in Baghdad, though his religious authority grew. At the beginning of the 11th century, the A. caliphate ceased to exist, and the caliphs merely confirmed, by formal appointment, the political changes in the eastern states. They had to countenance the rise of the *Seljuk Turks, who, in 1055, conquered Baghdad

and established a new empire over the Asian provinces of the caliphate. Nevertheless, the A. continued to bear the title, and became even more ceremonious and the protocol in the "inner city" reflected their heightened religious prestige. Even the greatest rulers, such as *Saladin, paid their respect to the caliph and sought his appointments so as to legitimize their government.

In 1258 the *Mongols conquered Baghdad and abolished the caliphate. But their prestige was so great that the Mameluke Sultan Baibars appointed a member of the dynasty as caliph in Cairo.

C. Brockelmann, *History of the Moslem Peoples* (1954).

ABBEVILLE Town near the estuary of the Somme in northern France. It was built in the 9th century as the abbot's borough, to protect the subjects of the abbey of St. Riquier from the *Norman invasions. The town became the administrative centre of the abbey's possessions and, during the 12th century, a textile industry was developed in the area. In the 13th century, A. became the centre of a little county, the suzerainty of which was disputed between the counts of *Flanders and the kings of France and England. For a major part of the *Hundred Years' War, A. was under English rule. It was finally seized by France in 1452. After the devastations of the war, the city was rebuilt, and a new church, dedicated to St. Wulfran, was erected in its centre in the late Gothic style.

ABBEY Monastic institution. Although the term A. is commonly used as synonymous with monastery, it has had a distinct significance from the 9th century on. The establishment of monastic congregations, or confederations, in Catholic Europe, deprived some of the monasteries of their *abbots and made them dependent on "mother institutions". Thus, only the independent monasteries, governed by their elected abbots, are, correctly speaking, abbeys.

The A. is ruled by the monastic constitution, commonly the "Rule of St. *Benedict", of the 6th century, with its revisions. It is a monastic community whose members live together, pray and work and obey their abbot. The rule required the monks to retire from secular life and concentrate their activities within the A., which was closed to the outer world. Physically, the A. is a cloister, which enjoyed an immunity of the powers. It had four distinct units: the church, which was open to all the faithful attending services; the cloister itself, with the monks' cells built around an inner court; the *refectorium*, a hall for the common meals; the library and the *scriptorium*, where the members of the community copied manuscripts. The library and the scriptorium were the intellectual and scholarly heart of the A., and were generally open to students from outside. Other sections of the A. were: the administrative centre, with the abbot's palace with its seignorial (or manorial) activities, with the abbot acting as lord of his vassals and peasants; and the economic centre, with the stores and artisan workshops. Thus, from the 10th century until the end of the Middle Ages the A. was a feudal institution, owning estates and manors, and possessing political, as well as judicial and economical, power. The monastic rule made the assembly (*congregatio monachorum*) the supreme institution of the A., but its principal prerogative was the election of the abbot, who had unlimited authority in his A. In many cases, however, barons were privileged, as the founder's heirs, to recommend the candidate. The main exception was the case of the Cluniac As. which specifically obtained an exemption.

ABBO OF FLEURY, St. (945-1004) Born near Orléans, he entred the abbey of Fleury, and studied also in Paris and Rheims. He was one of the most cultivated men of his time. He was in charge of studies in the abbey and, in 985, directed its school at Ramsey in England. In 988 he was elected abbot and supported the *Cluniac reform. He published treatises defending papal authority within the church, and the freedom of monasteries from both episcopal and secular interference. Nevertheless, he tried to conciliate between the powers, recognizing a certain right of the king over the church. As a counsellor to King *Robert II of France, he developed the idea of cooperation between the throne and Rome. He also wrote on mathematics and astronomy and composed a short history of the papacy. A. was killed while reforming the priory of La Réole in Gascony.
Texts: *PL*, 139, 417-578;
DHGE, I.
ABBOT (Syriac: abba "father") The superior of an *abbey. The rule of St. Benedict gave the A. the authority of *Pater familiae*, i.e., the father of his community. Thus, he had full authority over his monks as well as the duty to direct their life in the correct way of salvation. Once elected by his community, the A. had to receive the benediction of the bishop, which was considered a form of consecration necessary to the spiritual rights. From the 7th century on the As. were admitted to the ecclesiastical councils. In Carolingian times, the As. were considered members of the nobility and, as such, took part in the deliberations of the court and were employed in the highest offices in the empire. In the 9th and 10th centuries, lay lords expropriated monasteries and, in some cases, appointed themselves lay As. Thereafter there is a distinct alteration in the life of the A., which came to resemble that of a feudal lord. Even after the abolition of lay As. the situation continued in most of the abbeys, where the As. lived in luxuriously-appointed palaces, contrary to monastic rule. Being engaged in the politics and the administration of his demesnes, the A. left the government of the abbeys to the prior, a monk appointed for that purpose. The Cluniac reform and the ascetic orders of the 12th century tried to change the situation, but with little success. At the end of the Middle Ages the As. were generally selected from the high nobility; in England they were considered peers, with membership in the House of Lords.
C. Butler, *Benedictine Monasticism* (1919).
ABD AL-MALIK IBN MARWAN (647-705) *Ummayad caliph (685-705). He began his reign at a difficult time for his dynasty, after the victory of the *Hejjaz tribes. In order to fight the Arabian rebels, he stopped the war with *Byzantium and was made to pay an annual tribute. He crushed the Hejjaz rebellion, but only after having attacked the *Kaaba at Mecca (692); the anti-caliph Abdallah Ibn Al-Zubair, who ruled in Mecca (683-92), was killed and the Moslem world was reunified. A. built the famous Dome of the Rock at *Jerusalem, held to be the third most sacred place for Islam, probably with the intention of providing an alternative focus of pilgrimage for devout Moslems. In his administration of the caliphate, he imposed the uniform use of the

Arabic language, instead of Greek, Syriac and Coptic, and issued the first Islamic gold coins.
F. Gabrieli, *Muhammad and the Conquests of Islam* (1968).
ABD AL-RAHMAN Arab governor of Spain (first half of the 8th century). He established the Arab domination over Spain after its conquest. In 731 he began the expansion towards the Pyrénées and entered Gaul. Pushing northward, he reached the region of *Poitiers. In 732-33 he met the Frankish army of Charles Martel between Poitiers and Tours and was defeated. The Battle of Poitiers is considered the end of Arab advancement through Europe.
E. Lévy-Provençal, *Histoire de l'Espagne musulmane*, I (1950).
ABD AL-RAHMAN I (731-88) *Ummayad prince, who fled Damascus after its conquest by the *Abbasids and found refuge in Spain. In 756 he founded the emirate of *Córdoba and, having crushed his opponents who sought the aid of *Charlemagne (777-778), established the independent Ummayad rule in Spain.
ABD AL-RAHMAN II (792-852) *Ummayad ruler of Spain (822-52). He fought against rebels and against the Normans, but failed to impose his rule on the Christian states in northern Spain. His reign is considered as the dawn of Islamic art and culture in Spain. In his palace at *Córdoba he introduced the protocol of the Baghdad caliphate, and imported theologians and architects from the East.
ABD AL-RAHMAN III (889-961) Caliph of *Córdoba (912-61), the most important ruler of Moslem Spain. At the beginning of his reign, he found the caliphate in a state of disintegration, and had to devote his efforts to the restoration of the realm. He also fought successfully against the Christian kingdoms in northern Spain. In 929 he took the title of caliph, the first one in Spain. A. ruled a powerful state, extending his government to north Africa. In his reign, Moslem Spain reached stability and cultural life flourished. His tolerant attitude to non-Moslems, particularly the Jews, led to the cooperation of the best talents of his realm, creating a regime of enlightenment.
E. Lévy-Provençal, *Histoire de l'Espagne musulmane*, I-III (1950-53).
ABELARD, PETER (1079-1142) French scholar and teacher. Born at the castle of Le Pallet in Brittany, A. was the pupil of *Roscelin, but after his studies at Tours continued to work independently of his master. In 1100 he settled in Paris, where he began to teach liberal arts, but very soon entered into conflict with the master of the cathedral school, *William of Champeaux. He left Paris and in 1102 founded a school at Melun, which, thanks to his educational talents, became famous and attracted many students. After the retirement of William of Champeaux to the new abbey of St. Victor, A. succeeded him as master of the Parisian cathedral school (1108). In his search for perfection in theology, A. went in 1113 to the school of *Anselm of Laon, the most famous philosopher of his time. But he was disappointed in Anselm's teachings and returned to Paris, where students from all of western Europe gathered to hear his lessons. His career was interrupted suddenly, by his elopement with *Heloise, the niece of Canon Fulbert (c. 1116), whom he secretly married and took to his family estate in Brittany. After the birth of their child,

Astrolabe, the two returned to Paris. A. was castrated by the vengeful Canon Fulbert and the couple separated. Heloise became a nun at Argenteuil, while A. resumed his teaching, concentrating on the problem of the Divine Unity and Trinity, trying to explain the Catholic faith in rational terms. His opponents, the pupils of Anselm of Laon, accused him of mistakes, and, in 1121, he was summoned to defend himself before the Council of Soissons. He was condemned and confined to the abbey of St. Denis. Here, despite the welcome extended him by the Abbot Adam, his criticism of *Dionysius the Areopagite (whose identity was confused with that of Denis of Paris, the patron saint of the abbey), created an atmosphere of hostility around him. A. left St. Denis and retired to Champagne to the deserted hermitage of Paraclet. His students followed him there and Paraclet became an important school; A.'s lessons produced the most important of his philosophical books, *Sic et Non* (Yes and No), using the scholastic method to settle contradictions. In 1125 he was elected abbot of the Breton abbey of St. Gildas, but, finding his monks too "barbarian" for his taste, he continued his work at Paraclet. In 1129, when the nuns of Argenteuil were expelled from their convent, he gave Paraclet to Heloise, and became the spiritual director of that community and the author of its rule. He finally left Brittany for Paris in 1132, where he resumed his teaching on the Left Bank of the Seine. His new school was the nucleus of what eventually became the University of Paris, and an important intellectual centre for western Europe. Several of his students later assumed high positions in the chuich, as bishops, cardinals and even popes. Others became in their turn masters of other schools; some became heretics, like *Arnold of Brescia. His teaching was severely criticized by his opponents, whose leader was *Bernard of Clairvaux. In 1140, the Council of Sens condemned his works and forbade him to teach. A. decided to appeal to the pope and went to Rome. On his way he stayed at Cluny, where he was persuaded by Abbot *Peter the Venerable to give up his struggle and remain at the abbey. It was there that he wrote his last book, the *Dialogue between a Jew, a Christian and a Philosopher*, a liberal interfaith discussion on monotheism. He died in 1142, before finishing the book, and was buried at Paraclet.

A.'s theology is based on the Catholic faith and the accusations of his critics were unfounded. Nevertheless, his attempts to provide a rational and humanist interpretation of the faith were too advanced for his times and considered as non-conformist. His activities as a scholar paved the way for the establishment of the universities. While, he was mainly known as a philosopher and a great scholastic, he also was a poet, author of satirical poems and a person of great sensibility, as his letters to Heloise show.

Works, *PL*, 178.

J. Monfrin, ed., Autobiography (*Historia Calamitatum*) (1962);

R. Thomas, ed., *Dialogue* (1967);

G. Sikes, *Abelard* (1932);

(Proceedings of Cluny Congress), *Pierre Abélard, Pierre le Vénérable* (1974).

ABRAHAM ABULAFIA (1241-c. 1292) Kabbalist and mystic. Born in Saragossa, he travelled in Spain, Palestine, Greece and Italy. He elaborated the method of the prophetic Kabbalah, which attempted to calculate the prophecies on the Salvation, reaching the truth of the spirit of the Scripture, as expressed by the letters of its text. In 1280 while in southern Italy, he came to the conclusion that the salvation of the Jews, which, to his mind, was tantamount to that of mankind, could be attained by the conversion of the gentiles to Judaism. He went to Rome, hoping to convert Pope *Nicholas III. He was arrested, and condemned to be burnt at the stake, but the pope's death prevented the execution and he escaped.

A. Abulafia, *Sepher Haoth* (The Book of the Letter) (1888);

G. Sholem, *Major Trends in Jewish Mysticism* (1945).

ABRAHAM BAR HIYYA (12th century) Mathematician, astronomer and philosopher at Barcelona, and one of the leading figures of the Jewish community in Catalonia. He served at the court of *Alfonso I of Aragon (1104-34). A.'s translations of scientific books from Arabic into Latin contributed to the transmission of the Greek-Arabic scientific heritage to Latin-Christian Europe. A major work, *Megillath Hamegaleh* (The Scroll of the Revealer), finished in 1129, was written in order to strengthen the Jewish faith. Adopting the position that Moslem rule was the most oppressive for Judaism, A. contended that Christianity has a role to play in the strengthening of Judaism and, therefore, the Jews have to see it as a catalyst for their salvation. He viewed the *Crusaders favourably, because they destroyed Moslem rule in Jerusalem. But, he maintained, the Crusaders' victory could not be total and their kingdom would finally collapse. This prediction, based on logical analysis, was unique in his times, and he even tried to calculate the date. In his view, the mutual destruction of Moslem and Christian powers would pave the way to Tradition), a historicophilosophical view of perpetuity and the unity of the Jewish people, even in dispersion. While the book is concerned with ancient times, it is an original and important document of his own age and a cardinal work on the idea of history.

G. Cohen, *Abraham Ben Daud's Book of Tradition* (1968).

ABRAHAM BEN DAUD OF TOLEDO (1110-80) Philosopher, historian, physician and astronomer. He studied at Córdoba and later settled in Toledo, where he wrote an apologia of the Jewish faith. In 1161 he finished his historical work, *Sefer ha Kabbalah* (The Book of the Tradition), a historiosophical view of the perpetuity and the unity of the Jewish people, even in dispersion. While the book is concerned with ancient times, it is an original and important document of his own age and a cardinal work on the idea of history.

G. Cohen, *Abraham Ben Daud's Book of Tradition* (1968).

ABRAHAM BEN DAVID OF POSQUIÈRES (Rabad; 1120-98) Talmudist and philosopher. Born and educated at Narbonne, A. settled at Posquières, a small town near Nîmes, where he was appointed the spiritual leader of the Jewish community, and where he headed a school whose influence spread beyond the province, through the rest of France and to Spain. He was one of the great masters of the Talmud of all times and the most important figure of the Jewish school of Languedoc and Provence. He wrote authoritative commentaries on the Talmud and his own *responsa*, wherein he interpreted actual problems of Judaism. But his most important works are his scholia, of polemical nature, which criticize the philosophical works of Alfasi, *Zerahia Halevi and especially *Maimonides, towards whom he adopted an attitude of respect and criticism.

I. Twersky, *The Rabad of Posquières* (1962).

ABRAHAM BEN ISAAC OF NARBONNE (1110-79) Talmudist and spiritual leader in Languedoc, the head of the Jewish school of Narbonne in the 12th century, and a student of Rabad (*Abraham ben David of Posquières), whose daughter he married. He also served as head of the rabbinical court of Narbonne and his verdicts, condensed in his book *Sefer ha-Eshkol* (The Book of the Cluster), became the basis of the jurisprudence of Jewish communities in southern France and in Spain, and were quoted until the end of the 13th century, being a contribution to the development of Jewish religious law and its underlying ideas.

S. Albeck, ed., *Sefer Haeshkol* (1926).

ABRAHAM BEN MOSES MAIMONIDES (1186-1237) Son of Moses *Maimonides, philosopher, exegete, physician and head of the Jewish community of Egypt. Taught by his father, he became the head of Egyptian Jewry at the age of 19, being already reputed for his science. He organized his communities, wrote verdicts on current problems, but his main activity was the defence of his father's philosophical works. He adopted Maimonides' methods in his own works, principally in his book *The High Ways to Perfection*, which is an encyclopedia of Judaica.

S. Rosenblatt, ed., *The High Ways to Perfection of A. Maimonides* (1927-36);

Freimann, ed., *Responsa* (1937).

ABRAHAM BEN NATHAN HAYARKHI (1155-1215) Talmudic scholar and traveller. Born in Lunel, he was educated in various schools in Languedoc. He continued his studies at Dampierre, in northern France. For most of his adult life he travelled through western Europe, paying attention to the customs of different nations and religions – particularly in the Jewish communities – and to synagogue usages. His *Sefer ha-Manhig* (The Book of Behaviour), is one of the first descriptions of popular customs and of folk tales.

ABRAHAM IBN EZRA (1089-1164) Jewish poet, grammarian, exegete, philosopher, astronomer and physician. Born to a poor family of Tudela (Aragon), he travelled for his education and was acquainted with many great Jewish figures of his day. At the age of 40 he settled in Toledo, where he practised medicine. There he became famous as a lyrical poet, writing both secular and sacred poetry, some of which was introduced into the Jewish liturgy. Much of his versatile work was written after 1140, when he left Toledo and, as a wandering scholar, travelled through Italy and France. He left biblical commentaries, based on both linguistic and philosophical methods, three books on grammar, including the translation of Arabic treatises into Hebrew as well as writings on astronomy. A. is one of the principal exegetes of Judaism, contributing to the diffusion of the Islamic-Jewish method of interpretation to the trans-Pyrenean Jewish communities and even, through his connections in Paris and Chartres, to the Christian exegetes. His philosophy, mainly expressed in the commentaries, was based on neo-Platonic and Aristotelian roots. A.'s wanderer's life and complex figure, with

its non-conformist features, made him a popular legend in his own lifetime.

M. Friedländer, *Abraham Ibn Ezra*, 4 vols. (1934).

ABSALON OF LUND (1128-1201) Danish statesman and prelate, a relation of King *Waldemar I, who helped to make him bishop of Roskilde (1158) and archbishop of Lund. A. contributed to the consolidation of the Danish monarchy and its independence from the Holy Roman empire. He also helped to strengthen Danish supremacy in northern Germany, initiating the wars against the Wends. He was the guardian of King Canute VI during his minority (1177-82). At the same time, A. continued his legislative activity at Lund, seeking to make it the ecclesiastical centre of northern Europe. He built the town of Havn (the future Copenhagen).

L. Musset, *Les Peuples Scandinaves au Moyen Age* (1961).

ABSOLUTION The formal act of a priest or bishop pronouncing the remission of sins to those who earned it by penance. The penitent had to confess his sins publicly or privately, before receiving A. In the Middle Ages the main form of A. was that of the public "sins" of rulers who had been involved in activities against the Church, or the established order, and *excommunicated. In such cases, the A. was a political act and was pronounced either by the pope, or on his behalf. The most famous A. in the Middle Ages was that of Emperor *Henry IV, pronounced at Canossa in 1077 by Pope *Gregory VII, and was a stage in the *Investiture contest. Having received the A., the penitent was reconciled with the Church and rejoined the community of the faithful.

DHGE, I.

ABU AL-ABBAS, AL-SAFFAH The first *Abbasid caliph (749-54). Proclaimed by the rebels led by Abu-Muslim, he opened his reign with the massacre of the entire *Ummayad family, only one of whom, *Abd Al-Rahman, escaped and fled to Spain. To consolidate his reign he converted to the Sunnite sect of Islam. Many of his supporters, including Abu-Muslim, were disgraced and murdered.

P. K. Hitti, *History of the Arabs* (1953).

ABU AL-FARAJ ALI AL-ISFAHANI (897-967) Arab poet, one of the members of the Abbasid literary school. Settled at Isfahan, Persia, he composed an anthology in 20 volumes of Arab poetry with music (*Kitab Al-Agani*), containing important biographical notes on poets and musicians of the first three centuries of Islam.

GAL, I, 146.

ABU AL-FIDA, ISMAIL IBN ALI IMAD AL-DIN AL-AYYUBI (1273-1331) Historian and geographer. A. was a prince of the *Ayyubid dynasty, ruler of Hama (Syria). He devoted himself to literary activity and wrote a world history (ed. Cairo 1907) dividing it into the pre-Islamic times, as the "Ancient History", and the "Modern Age", after *Mohammad. His historical work is of importance chiefly for the *Ayyubid period, where he introduces original evidence and as such is a source for the history of the *Crusades. A. also wrote a descriptive geography of the world, mainly the Moslem countries, and pointed out the achievements of the geographical science of his times.

GAL, II, 44.

ABU BAKR, UTHMAN IBN ABDALLAH The first caliph of *Islam (632-34). Member of a wealthy family of Mecca, A. was one of the first companions of Moham-

The port of Acre

mad, who married his daughter *Aisha. In 622 he accompanied Mohammad on the Hegira to Medina, and remained there as his closest disciple. After the Prophet's death, he was elected caliph (vicar of the Prophet). He crushed the last rebellions against Islam in Arabia, and began the Moslem expansion. He fought against the Persians, conquering Al-Hira, and against the Byzantines in Transjordan and southern Syria.

F. Gabrielli, *Muhammad and the Conquests of Islam* (1968).

ABU KHANIFA, AL-NUAMAN IBN THABET (699-767) Moslem theologian and lawyer, he lived in Iraq. He commented on the *Koran and is considered as one of the most important interpreters of Islamic faith in the spirit of *Sunnite orthodoxy. His method is based to a certain degree on inference, thus creating a new ground for commentaries. A. founded and led a school of Sunnite orthodoxy and his disciples became known as Khanafites.

GAL, I, 169.

ABU NUWAS, AL HASAN IBN HANI (c. 747-815) One of the most popular poets of the Abbasid period. *Harun Al-Rashid invited him to his court in Baghdad, where he remained until his death. A.'s poetry is connected with the genre of *diwans*, poems praising the great dignitaries and the aristocracy. He also wrote on the delights of life, food and wine. His poetry shows a great sensibility. His reputation earned him a mention in *The Thousand and One Tales*.

GAL, I, 75.

ABU SUFYAN *Ummayad leader of Mecca at the end of the 6th century and beginning of the 7th century. He was the head of the principal clan of the Quarish tribe. In 614-15 he opposed Mohammad and his group. Mohammad tried to win his favour by according the

central place in his new religion to the shrine of *Kaaba. A., as the leader of the conservative aristocracy, was concerned about the agitation of the new sect. In 622 he tried to have Mohammad arrested, charging him with plotting against the establishment. The migration of Mohammad to *Medina marks the official founding of the Moslem religion. A. commanded the Mecca expedition against Medina in 624, and was defeated at the Battle of *Badr.

F. Gabrielli, *Muhammad and the Conquests of Islam* (1968).

ABYSSINIA See ETHIOPIA.

ACCURSIO, FRANCESCO (1185-1263) Italian jurist, professor of law at the University of Bologna. His glosses to the *Code of Justinian contributed to the renovation of Roman law. His main work, *Magna Glossa* (The Great Glossary) was one of the most authoritative medieval interpretations of Roman law and jurisprudence.

Friedberg, ed., *Corpus Juris Civilis*;

G. Le Bras, *Sources et théories du Droit: l'âge classique* (1965).

ACRE (Acco, Ptolemais, Saint-Jean d'Acre) Port city in Palestine. The city, founded by the Phoenicians in the 2nd millennium BC, has a continuous history to the present time. At the beginning of the Middle Ages, the city, then called by its Hellenistic name Ptolemais, was a provincial harbour and the site of a Byzantine bishopric, of secondary importance to Caesarea and Tyre. In 640 it was conquered by the Arabs, who put an end to its Hellenistic character and brought in a Moslem population from other parts of the caliphate. The city declined during the 7th and 8th centuries, but became prosperous in the 9th century, under the Egyptian *Tulunid governors. The harbour was rebuilt to serve the maritime trade of Damascus. Under Arab rule the city resumed its ancient Semitic name, Acco – or Akka in the Arabic pronunciation. In 1104 the *Crusaders conquered A., which became the main harbour of the Latin kingdom of *Jerusalem and its second capital. The Crusaders granted the Italian cities, especially Venice, Genoa and Pisa, special rights in the city and its harbour, as they depended on their fleets. Thus, Italian settlements, linked to the mother-cities, were founded at A. They were granted the privilege of having their own quarters, with their own institutions and churches, exemption from certain taxes, and their own judiciary. Under the Crusaders, A. was the chief harbour of East-West trade, which was controlled by the Italian communes. Its prosperity attracted settlers of various nationalities and religions, and many settled in it. Of a cosmopolitan nature, the city was overcrowded from the 12th century. It was governed by a royal viscount, whose authority did not extend to the Italian communes. The viscount presided over the court of *Burghers, which was the supreme jurisdiction of the city, while in the harbour another court, the *Court of the Chain, was established under the authority of the viscount to deal with maritime affairs. This court, named after the chain which closed the entrance to the harbour from the sea during the night, played an important role in the formulation of the medieval maritime code. A. was one of the royal residences and the site of many assemblies of the nobility, the most famous being that of 1148, which gathered the leaders of the Second *Crusade, and which decided to attack Damascus.

In 1187 *Saladin conquered the city. It was besieged in 1192 by the forces of the Third *Crusade, led by *Richard I of England and *Philip II of France. After the capitulation of the city, the Moslem population was expelled and A. became the capital of the new Crusader kingdom. While the Italian influence was predominant, the military-religious orders, the *Hospitallers and *Templars, established their independent headquarters within the city, and a new commercial and residential quarter, Montmusart, was built in the north. Between 1233-44 A. was the theatre of a struggle between the imperial governor, Filanghieri, and the local nobility led by the *Ibelin family. The nobility, organized in the St. Andrew's commune, adhered to a theory of government based on the oligarchic power of the class, diminishing the power of the king. In 1250-52 the city was fortified by *Louis IX of France, who also attempted to bring the struggle to an end. But after his return to France, a new war, the St. Sabas War, between Venice and Genoa, weakened the Crusaders and increased the disorder in the city. Part of the nobility emigrated to Cyprus. From 1265, with the opening of a new route for commerce through the Black Sea and the Mongol empire, A. began to decline economically and the Italian cities were no longer so interested in its harbour. The nobility, ignoring the consequences of the rise of the *Mamluk power in Egypt, continued their chivalric style of life, of feasts, tournaments and feuds. While the Crusaders' city was the theatre of internecine wars, and in gradual decline, the Jewish community, already an important one in the 12th century, grew and attracted settlers from western Europe. Outstanding rabbis from France and Spain established a famous intellectual centre in the city.

In 1291 the Mamluk sultan *Qalawun conquered A., destroying the Crusader's kingdom and massacring some of its population, while others fled to Cyprus. Under Mamluk rule, in the 14th and 15th centuries, the city declined and became a mere fishermen's village. Some of the medieval structures of A. still exist, showing their beautiful Gothic architecture – chiefly the complex of the Hospitallers', remnants of Italian communes and, in the harbour, a tower called the *Tour des Mouches.*
E. Johns and K. Makhouly, *A Guide to Acco*;
J. Prawer, *The Crusaders* (1973);
B. Dichter, ed., *The Maps of Acco* (1972).

ACTA SANCTORUM The most authoritative collection of the lives of the saints, arranged in the chronological order of their feast days, which was begun by the *Bollandists in the 17th century and is still going on. The scope of the collection, as conceived by the Belgian Jesuit H. Rosweyde (d. 1629), was to collate all the sources pertaining to the lives of the saints, so as to establish an authoritative calendar of the Christian sainthood. While important for the study of hagiography, in its religious-liturgical and sociological aspects, the series is also an important example of the most popular literature of Christian Middle Ages and, as such, a precious source for the study of medieval mentality.
Bollandist Society Brussels, ed., (1643).

ADALBERON OF LAON (c. 947-1030) Bishop of Laon (977-1030). He supported *Hugh Capet in 987 against the last Carolingians, whose stronghold was the county of Laon. In 988 he was given the bishopric of Laon. Hugh Capet made him the tutor of his son

*Robert II. A., who was a gifted Latin poet, wrote in a satirical style. His most important poem, *Carmen ad Rodbertum regem* (A poem to King Robert), composed c. 1020, represents his theory of the three *estates, organic components of society – the clergy, warriors and peasants. He formulated the theory of feudal hierarchy and the mutual dependence of the social classes, with the king as moderator of the social order.
Works, *PL*, 151;
E. Huckel, *Les oeuvres satiriques d'Adalberon de Laon* (1903).

ADALBERON OF RHEIMS (c. 920-88) Descendant of a noble family from the Ardennes, he became archbishop of Rheims in 969. He reorganized the church of Rheims and its school and appointed Gerbert of Aurillac (see *Sylvester II) as its director. On excellent terms with Emperor *Otto I, Empress *Adelaide and Otto II, he was very active in the political life of France. He was one of the leaders of the movement which brought *Hugh Capet to the throne of France. At the Assembly of Noyon he spoke in Hugh's favour, but also for the principle of an elected monarchy, which he considered an office and not a dignity.
Richer, *Histories*, IV;
J. F. Lemarignier, *La France médiévale* (1975).

ADALBERT OF BREMEN (1000-72) Descendant of a noble Saxon family, he entered an ecclesiastical career and, in 1045, became archbishop of *Bremen-Hamburg. He promoted missionary activities mainly to the Nordic countries, and planned to become the patriarch of the North. In 1053 Pope *Leo IX appointed him legate to the Nordic nations. Being closely associated with Emperor *Henry III, he was appointed guardian of *Henry IV during his minority, and was granted rich properties. The jealousy of his enemies compelled Henry to dismiss him (1066), but he was recalled in 1069.
H. Gebhardt, *Deutsche Geschichte* (1960).

ADALGIS Lombard prince, son of *Desiderius, last king of the Lombards. He fought in his father's army against *Charlemagne, escaping from Pavia when the city was conquered by the Franks. In 775 he took refuge in *Constantinople, where he was granted the title of *patrice*, and prepared his revenge against his former brother-in-law Charlemagne. With a Byzantine army under his command, A. landed in Calabria and tried to unite the Lombards against Charlemagne. He failed in this attempt, because of the opposition of Grimoald, duke of Benevento (787) and retired to Constantinople.
R. Winston, *Charlemagne* (1956).

ADAM (LE BOSSU) DE LA HALE (c. 1240-85) A troubadour of Artois (northern France). A gifted poet and musician, he is considered the innovator of French secular theatre. He wrote satirical poems, such as *Jeu de la Feuillée, Le Congé, Jeu de Robin et de Marion* and *Jeu de Pèlerin*, in which he amusingly criticized church and society. He accompanied his lord, Count Robert of Artois, to Naples, where he was received at the court, and there he died.
Bossuat, *Histoire de la littérature française au Moyen Age* (1946).

ADAM OF BREMEN (d. 1076) Historian canon of the church of Hamburg. His work, *Gesta Pontificum Hammersburgensium* (The Deeds of the Archbishops of Hamburg), is not only an important history of the ecclesiastical metropolis of northern Germany from its establishment in 788, but also the main source for the history of the Nordic countries, including the Scandinavian and the Baltic peoples.

MGH, Scriptores;

Loenborg, *Adam von Bremen* (1897).

ADAM OF ST. VICTOR (c. 1112-92) Poet. Born in Brittany, he became a canon in the Victorine Abbey in Paris. He wrote poems on theological and mystical topics, combining a facility of style with liturgical austerity and doctrinal precision. Some of his poems are devoted to the Marian Cult (see St. *Mary).

Works, ed., C. Blume and H. M. Bannister (1915);

F. J. E. Raby, *History of Christian Latin Poetry from the Beginning to the Close of the Middle Ages* (1953).

ADAMNAN, St. (624-704) Descendant of a noble Irish family, he was educated by the monks of St. *Columba. In 650 he joined the Abbey of *Iona and, in 679, became its abbot. A. tried to introduce Roman observance in Ireland. In 697 he forbade taking women and children as prisoners of war; the interdiction was generally accepted in church legislation and is commonly called the Canon of St. Adamnan. A. wrote the Life of St. Columba whom he particularly venerated, describing the saint's prophecies, miracles and visions, and an account of the Holy Land (*De Locis sanctis*, ed. Geyer 1898).

DNB, I.

ADELAIDE, St. (931-99) Empress of the Holy Roman empire, she was the daughter of *Rodolph II of Burgundy, who married her to Lothair of Italy; widowed of her first husband, she was held prisoner by *Berengar of Friuli. Freed by *Otto I of Germany, who married her (951), A. became queen and, from 962, empress. She had an important influence at the court of her son, Otto II and of her grandson, Otto III, which she used to enforce the imperial authority. She was also active in support of *Hugh Capet in France, through *Adalberon of Rheims. After 985, she retired from the court, although she continued to influence it, and devoted herself to religious affairs, favouring the Cluniac reform (see *Cluny), and to founding and reforming abbeys in Germany and Lorraine.

Wimmer, *Kaiserin Adelheid* (1897).

ADELANTADOS Castilian nobles who, in the early Middle Ages, led military expeditions for the king; from the beginning of the 13th century they were also appointed by the sovereign to judicial and administrative positions over districts. During the reign of Ferdinand III (1217-52) an upper group was created among them, the *adelantados mayores*, who served as district appeal judges and were also responsible for organizing the army in their jurisdiction.

P. E. Russell, *Spain* (1973).

ADELARD (ADALARD) OF BATH (early 12th century) English scholastic philosopher. Studied at Tours and Laon and travelled in Europe, north Africa and Asia Minor. He translated scientific works from Arabic and, in his principal work, *De eodem et diverso* (On the Same and the Different), he developed a theory of the liberal arts and tried to reconcile the Platonic and Aristotelian doctrines, holding that in reality the universal and the particular were identical, their distinction existing only in the way they are apprehended by man.

F. J. P. Bliemetzrieder, *Adelhard von Bath* (1935).

ADHEMAR OF CHABANNES (c. 988-1034) Historian. A descendant of a noble family in Limousin, he studied at the cathedral of Limoges and was a monk at Angoulême. His principal work is his *Chronicle*, written in 1028 and divided into three books. The first two are actually a compilation of Frankish histories; the third one, however, dealing with the 10th and beginning of 11th century, is an original work, and the best source for the history of Aquitaine. A. went on a pilgrimage to Jerusalem, where he died.

J. Chavanon, ed., *Chronicle*, (1897).

ADHEMAR OF MONTEIL (d. 1098) Bishop of Le Puy. He was one of the leaders of the First *Crusade. A close friend of Pope Urban II, he was appointed at the Council of Clermont (1096) to be the papal legate, with full representative powers, among the Crusaders. A. was associated with the army of *Raymond of Saint-Gilles, but was also respected by the leaders of the other armies. During the expedition he played an important role as the unifying figure for the different armies and, in the difficult times, at Nicaea and Antioch, he fortified their spirits. After the conquest of Antioch he led the Crusade on its way to Jerusalem, but fell ill and died near Laodocaea (Latakieh).

S. Runciman, *A History of the Crusades*, I (1953).

ADOLPH OF NASSAU (c. 1250-98) Emperor of the Holy Roman empire (1292). He was elected emperor by the elements that opposed the Hapsburgs in the College of Electors (see *Germany), who feared the introduction of a new dynasty. As emperor he very soon became unpopular with the electors, on account of his independent policies – he tried to annex Thuringia and Meissen to his estates and allied himself with Edward I of England against Philip IV of France. The electors deposed him and transferred their allegiance to *Albert of Austria. A. fought against his rival, but was killed at the Battle of Gelheim.

E. Gebhardt, *Handbuch der Deutsche Geschichte*.

ADOPTIANISM A heresy, originating in Spain in the 8th century, which held that Jesus Christ, in his human form, was not the natural son of God, but His adopted son. The origins of the heresy are linked with the Arian schism and certain trends in the eastern churches, such as the *Nestorians, who had a certain influence in Spain after the Arab conquest. The main leader of the Adoptianists was Elipandus, archbishop of Toledo (*c.* 718-802), who organized the sect. His theory is based upon a metaphorical interpretation of the Scriptures, holding that the *Logos* (the Word), identified with God, adopted Humanity, represented by Jesus Christ. The Spanish bishops, who opposed Elipandus' theory, communicated the facts to the pope and to *Charlemagne, who, at the Council of Frankfurt (794), condemned the heresy. The excommunication of Elipandus was ineffective, because of the Arab rule at Toledo. The real theological dispute, therefore, was with his principal associate, *Felix, bishop of Urgel. After the formal condemnation of A. at Frankfurt, *Alcuin led the polemics on behalf of orthodoxy, and wrote a number of pamphlets, entitled *Contra Felicem* (Against Felix). In 799 Pope Leo III deposed Felix and called the Spanish Christians to fight against the heresy. After the death of Elipandus the Adoptianists, lacking leadership, dispersed and the heresy disappeared. Nevertheless, certain metaphorical ideas of the Adoptianist theory continued to manifest themselves in Catholic theology, in an orthodox form, mainly in the 12th and 13th centuries; but they were rejected by the majority of theologians as incompatible with Christology.

DTC, I.

ADRIAN I (d. 795) Pope (772-95). Member of a noble Roman family who held important positions at the papal court, and was active in Stephen III's policy of collaboration with the Frankish realm. On close terms with *Charlemagne, he had a part in the king's expedition against the Lombards, who were presented as the persecutors of the Roman see (774). He maintained close friendly relations with the king of the Franks, gave him religious support for his wars, which were represented as holy campaigns for the defence of the faith and helped him to enforce his rule in Italy. At the same time, he opposed the tendencies of interfering in theological and purely ecclesiastical affairs, such as the condemnation by the Synod of Frankfurt (794) of the decisions of the Council of Nicaea (787) in the *Iconoclastic controversy, despite their approval by the pope. A. also devoted himself to administration, restoring the ruins of the city of Rome and fortifying it.

Works, *PL*, vol. 96 and 98;

L. Duchesne, *Les premiers temps de l'Etat pontifical* (1913).

ADRIAN II (792-872) Pope (867-72). A native of Rome, he gradually entered the inner circle of the papal court during the pontificates of *Leo IV and *Nicholas I, whom he succeeded. He devoted his efforts to the security of Rome and its district, while the *Carolingian empire was in decline. He also encouraged missionary activities, mainly the missions of *Cyril and Methodius to the Moravians, gave Cyril a home in Rome and allowed the use of Slavonic liturgical books.

F. Dvornik, *The Slavs* (1956).

ADRIAN III (d. 885) Pope (884-85). A native of Rome, he had to deal with the disorders in Rome and Italy which were caused by the struggle between the claimants to the *Carolingian inheritance in Italy. His appeals for aid to *Charles the Fat were not responded to.

ADRIAN IV (Nicholas Breakspear; c. 1100-59) The only English pope (1154-59). He studied at Paris, joined St. Ruf's Abbey near Avignon and became its abbot. About 1150 he was appointed by *Eugene III cardinal bishop of Albano, and joined the papal court. A. was sent as papal legate to Scandinavia, where he reformed the church, erected the archbishopric of Trondheim (Norway) and laid the foundation for the cooperation between Church and State. As pope, he crushed the Roman revolt led by *Arnold of Brescia, who was executed (1155). He tried to impose papal supremacy over Christian Europe and is considered as one of the creators of the theocratic policy of the papacy. In 1155, he obtained from Frederick *Barbarossa an oath of allegiance, as a condition of crowning him emperor. His claim that the emperor held his crown as a *beneficium* from the pope, precipitated a quarrel with Barbarossa, who opposed it, and, at the Diet of Besançon (1157), declared the full sovereignty of the empire. A. tried to withhold recognition from *William I as king of Sicily, but having been defeated by him, was compelled to invest him with the kingship as vassal of the pope. He had good relations with the king of France, *Louis VII, whom he supported against the duke of Burgundy, and

*Henry II of England. He was believed to be the pope who gave the king of England authority over Ireland, but it is probable that the Bull *Laudabiliter*, which is the basis for this belief, was forged.

Works, *PL*, 188;

H. K. Mann, *Nicholas Breakspear* (1914);

W. Ullman, *Papacy* (1963).

ADRIAN V (Ottoboni Fieschi; d. 1276) Pope (1276). Member of the famous Genoese family Fieschi and a nephew of *Innocent IV, who brought him to the papal court, he belonged to the anti-French party, which supported *Gregory X. He died soon after his election.

ADRIAN "THE AFRICAN", St. (d. 709) Monk. Born in north Africa, he settled in Italy, near Naples, where he became head of an abbey. Though he declined the offer to be archbishop of Canterbury, he was sent to England, where he assisted Archbishop Theodore (668). A man of great learning, he established an important school at Canterbury and during 40 years he made it an Anglo-Saxon centre of scholarship.

Beda, *History of England*, IV, I;

N. K. Chadwick, *Studies in the Early British Church* (1958).

ADRIANOPLE City in Thrace, an important centre in the *Byzantine empire. As early as the 14th century it was a key position for the defence of *Constantinople. In 378 the Goths, having invaded the Balkans, met the imperial army of Valens in A., and won a celebrated victory, the first by a barbarian army against Roman legions. Many historians consider the Battle of A. the symbolic end of the ancient world and the beginning of the Middle Ages, one of the reasons being that the mounted Goths represent the decline of infantry and the advent of cavalry in medieval warfare. Valens' successor, Theodosius, re-established his rule in the city. In the 6th century, it became a religious centre. The cathedral, (which today is a mosque), was built in the style of *St. Sophia of Constantinople. From the 9th century, after the Bulgarian invasions and the establishment of the Bulgarian empire, A. became an important frontier-post, with a military character. In 1096 the *Crusaders passed through the city and looted it, which provoked a hostile reaction by the Byzantines and sharpened the disagreement between Eastern and Western Christians. In 1204 the city was conquered by the forces of the Fourth Crusade and became a part of the Latin empire of Constantinople (1204-61). Under the Byzantines it remained a provincial capital until 1361, when the *Ottoman Turks conquered it. A. was the capital of the Ottoman empire until 1453, when the Turks conquered Constantinople. Under Turkish rule, the city, called Edirne, gradually lost its Christian-Greek character.

N. H. Baynes, *The Byzantine Empire* (1943).

AEGELNOTH (AILNOTH) OF CANTERBURY (11th-12th centuries) Historian. Born at Canterbury, he left England after the Norman Conquest and settled in Denmark (*c.* 1085). His reaction against *William the Conqueror and the Norman repression of the Anglo-Saxons (1085) led him to venerate the memory of King *Canute II (St. Cnut), who had tried to invade England and was murdered in his own country. He wrote the *Historia sancti Canuti regis* (History of the King St. Canute), which expressed his feelings.

G. Langebek, *Scriptores Rerum Danicarum*, III (1776).

AELFRIC THE GRAMMARIAN (955-1020) Abbot of Eynsham. Educated at Winchester, he was one of the greatest scholars of Anglo-Saxon England and the literary leader of his generation. He composed homilies in Anglo-Saxon, as well as doctrinary works in Latin. His main work is *The Lives of Saints*, important both as an historical source as well as a liturgical document. While having a thorough knowledge of Latin culture, A.'s writings in Anglo-Saxon meant that doctrinal and liturcal works could reach the rural English clergy.

Works, ed., W. Skeat (1881-90);

S. H. Gem, *An Anglo-Saxon Abbot, Aelfric of Eynsham* (1912).

AENEAS, LEGEND OF (Chanson d'Enée) A romance in French, composed *c*. 1150 by one of the Breton poets. The romance is based on the classical *Aeneid* of Virgil, adapted to the knightly manners of the 12th-century courts. The adventures of A., represented as an ideal Christian knight, became very popular in aristocratic society in France and England. The poem had an important influence on the works of *Chrétien de Troyes and thus indirectly on the literature of the late 12th century and of the 13th.

Ed. J. J. Salverda de Grave, 2 vols. ('902-08);

U. T. Holmes, *A History of Old French Literature* (1946).

AFRICA The continent of A. was a third of the medieval world. As in ancient times, only a part of it was known in the Middle Ages, principally the northern and eastern parts, near the Mediterranean and Red Sea coasts. After the conquests of *Islam and the penetration of Moslem influence in eastern and central A., Arab travellers and geographers described a larger part of the continent, mainly Sudan and the Sahara. The real discovery of A. began only at the end of the Middle Ages and was carried out by Portuguese explorers. In the Middle Ages, therefore, the African continent should be divided into four distinct parts, according to our knowledge and the development of the historical civilization:

1) Northern A., from the Mediterranean shores to the Atlas Mountains, including the Valley of the Nile in Egypt and Sudan, which was a part of the classical heritage, with the highly developed Roman provinces of Egypt and A. From the 7th century on, it was an important part of the Islamic world, with major centres in *Egypt, *Kairwan and Morocco. Nevertheless certain ancient civilizations survived in the region, as that of the *Copts in Egypt.

2) Eastern A., with the independent Christian empire of *Ethiopia and certain Arab-Negro settlements, like the Somalis and the Swahili-speaking populations, as far as Zanzibar and the coastal part of present-day Tanzania.

3) The tropical region of Sahara and western Sudan, unknown to Europeans and only slightly to the Moslems, where, under the influence of north African elements and the Islamic civilization, certain Negro states emerged and developed their own civilizations, based on tribal traditions, such as the empire of *Ghana and *Mali.

4) The central and southern parts of the continent, representing most of A., were in the Middle Ages at a prehistorical stage of development. Entirely unknown to Moslems and Europeans, tribal civilizations evolved there, such as those of the Bantus. These civilizations were discovered only in modern times.

At the beginning of the Middle Ages, Christianity had reached the north African provinces and became established – mainly in Egypt, which became its major centre, and in the province of A., which was the most developed of the Latin part of the Roman empire. Carthage was a centre of Christian Latin literature, as well as of theology. In the early 5th century, it was enhanced by the personality of *Augustine of Hippo. In 429, the *Vandals conquered the province and established the capital of their kingdom at Carthage. They built a fleet, very active in western Mediterranean, which attacked Italy. The Byzantines under Justinian destroyed the *Vandal kingdom in 534 and established their rule in north A. The province enjoyed a period of cultural prosperity until the Arab conquest, which began with the conquest of Egypt in 640 and culminated in that of Carthage in 698. The conversion to Islam was relatively rapid and, under the rule of the *Ummayad caliphs (660-750), the African provinces knew economic prosperity. The *Berbers converted to Islam, as did the Nubians of eastern Sudan, where the discovery of gold mines at the end of the 7th century led to the direct intervention of the Damascus caliphs. With the *Abbasid revolution (750), the political and economic orientation of the caliphate turned eastwards. The court of Baghdad gradually lost interest in north A., where the local dynasties of emirs (governors) were autonomous, while formally recognizing their dependence on the caliph. In the 9th century a Shiite dynasty, the *Fatimids, revolted against the Abbasids and established an independent caliphate in *Kairwan. Pushing eastwards, they conquered Egypt, where they founded their own caliphate and built a new capital, *Cairo. Economic reasons, and particularly the search for Negro slaves, brought Arab merchants and missionaries to Black A., spreading Islam through the Sahara, Sudan and eastern A. Ethiopia, which had been converted to Christianity by Egyptian monks in the 5th century, and which was an important ally of the Byzantine empire in its wars against the Persians in the early 7th century, was thus isolated from the centres of Christianity by the Islamic expansion and developed independently. The scanty knowledge about this Christian state was the root of a popular legend in medieval Europe, namely the existence of the "kingdom of *Prester John". In the 11th century the most important force in A. was Islam, but it lost its unity. While the *Fatimids established their rule in Egypt (969-1171) and conquered Palestine and part of Syria, the western lands of north A. were divided among different local dynasties, the most powerful of which was the *Almoravides (1061-1163). The dynasties warred between themselves, making for political instability. The Arab element was challenged by the Berbers, who were more militant and fanatic in their faith. The quest for Negro slaves brought the Moslems into conflict with the Tuareg states of Sahara; the Empire of *Ghana (4th-11th centuries) was destroyed by these conflicts. From the cultural and artistic point of view, Moslem north A. was one of the centres of Islamic civilization. In the new city of Cairo the Fatimids established the famous school of Al-Azhar (970), which soon became the most important centre of Islamic studies in the entire Moslem world. Other important theological centres, at Kairwan and *Fes, also produced important religious art, mainly the decoration and ornamentation of liturgical objects. The most beautiful copies of the *Koran are originally from Kairwan. The first signs of decline of Moslem A. appeared in the 12th century. But while in Egypt the Fatimids were supplanted by the *Ayyubids (1171-1250), under *Saladin the country was the heart of Islam. The rise of the *Almohades (1147-1269) in northwestern A. opened an era of violence and oppression. The *Crusaders and the Italian cities tried to establish bases in Egypt and even to conquer it (1217 and 1247-48) and Tunis (1270), but they were unsuccessful and the Moslem power remained unchallenged. The decline was chiefly a result of internecine wars and of the rise of the Berber elements in the *Maghreb, while the *Mamluk rule in Egypt did not continue the policy of development followed by the previous dynasties. In the 14th and 15th centuries a series of plagues, such as the *Black Death of 1348, and famine ravaged north A., and particularly Egypt. These were also factors in the decline of the Moslem region, while the opening of the Mongol trade route to the Far-East caused an economic depression in the continent.

In the Middle Ages tropical A. developed separately. While the Christian empire of Ethiopia succeeded in preserving its independence against Arab attacks at the price of isolation, having lost coastal provinces (present-day Eritrea and Somalia), the tribal confederation and kingdoms such as Ghana and Mali, were more exposed to Moslem influence. A number of routes crossed the Sahara and the Sudan, serving the trade between Moslem north A. and the fetishist and polytheistic Negro tribes. The empire of Mali founded by Moslem leaders, was in the 13th and 14th centuries the most powerful of the Negro states. Its capital Timbuktu, described by Ibn Batuta, was a major market of salt, slaves and gold. It was reached in the 15th century by Italian merchants. The rise of the kingdom of Gao in the 15th century facilitated the contact between the Mediterranean civilizations and the Nigerian tribes, which evolved an important culture.

The other parts of the continent, from Nigeria to the southern countries, were still in the Stone Age. Their technical and artistic achievements show a fine skill in the use of stone tools. While the art appears to be original, at least in its motifs, some anthropologists believe that they were influenced by the Stone Age civilizations of the Middle East.

The Pelican History of Africa (1968).

AGAPETUS, St. (d. 536) Pope. Known as a strong defender of orthodoxy, he went to Constantinople after his election in 535, in order to lead the struggle against the *Monophysite Patriarch Anthymus. Despite the opposition of *Justinian, he succeeded and consecrated an Orthodox patriarch, Mennas.

Letters, *PL*, 66;
DHGE, I.

AGAPETUS II (d. 955) Pope (946-55). A native of Rome, he was appointed to the papacy by the all-powerful master of Rome, the senator *Alberic. While having to obey Alberic in Roman and Italian affairs, A. tried to make his authority recognized by the universal church. He intervened in the struggle in France between King *Louis IV and Duke *Hugh the Great, supporting the King's candidate to the archbishopric of Rheims (948-49). The Rheims affair led to an understanding between him and *Otto I of Germany, who was the ally of

Louis IV, and imposed order in Germany. However, when Otto came to Italy in 951 and defeated *Berengar, A. was compelled by Alberic to refuse to crown him as emperor.

Letters, *PL*, 132;
J. Haller, *Das Papsttum*, II (1962).

AGDE City in Languedoc (southern France). Conquered by the *Visigoths in 415, it became an ecclesiastical centre of their kingdom, where many councils were held. Of these, the most important was in 506, when problems of ecclesiastical organization, discipline and hierarchy were discussed, and the decisions guided the activity and organization of the Catholic Church through the Middle Ages. That council also dealt with the relations between the Church and lay society, providing ideological support for the aristocratic structure of society, ecclesiastical property and serfdom. In the 8th century A. was occupied by the Arabs, but in 754 *Pepin the Short conquered and attached it to the realm of the Franks. Under *Charlemagne a county was established in A., which became in the 9th century part of the great county of Toulouse. In the 12th century the *Albigensians were active there and, after the 13th-century crusades, it became part of the French *sénéchaussée* of *Beaucaire.

A. Castaldo, *L'Eglise d'Agde* (1970).

AGHLABIDS Arab dynasty of north Africa (c. 800-909). Founded by Ibn Aghlab, governor of Zab (Algeria), who was rewarded for his faithful services by *Harun Al-Rashid with the governorship of the whole province of Ifriqiya (present-day Maghreb) and obtained hereditary rights to his dignity in 800). The A. established their rule in Kairwan, which became the flourishing heart of an autonomous state, though officially a dependent of the Abbasid caliphs. They failed to impose their rule on Morocco, where a local dynasty, the Idrisids, declared itself independent (808-930). They conquered Sicily, after a long war which began in 830 under Ziyadatallah I and ended only in 865, and created a system of government based on the Arab traditions and Byzantine bureaucracy. The Aghlabid governor of the island was called Emir Al-Bahr (the Emir of the Sea), having control of the fleet as well as of other emirs. This title was adopted at the end of the 11th century by the *Norman conquerors of Sicily and given a French form (*Amiral*), which became the modern word "admiral". At the end of the 9th century the A. had to fight against *Berber uprisings, resulting in their repression. Some of the Berbers during pilgrimages to Mecca, joined the *Shiites of south Arabia, who led their open revolt. In 908 they succeeded in overthrowing the A., who fled to Baghdad, and a new dynasty, the *Fatimids, established an independent caliphate.

CHI, I.

AGILA King of the Visigoths (548-54). He was the first king of the Visigoths to concentrate his activity in Spain, abandoning the dreams of restoring the domination of Gaul. To strenghten his rule he seized Córdoba and Seville, causing the local Gothic lords to revolt with the help of the Catholics whom he persecuted. Under the leadership of a Visigoth noble, *Athanagild, the rebels defeated A., who was murdered at Merida.

Isidore of Seville, *Historia Gothorum*;
MGH, Auctores Antiquissimi, I;
R. Menendes-Pidal, *Historia de España* (1935).

AGILULF King of the Lombards (590-616). Duke of Turin, he was elected king in 590, and devoted his efforts to unifying the Lombard kingdom. He succeeded in checking the Byzantines at Ravenna and, after a short siege, received payment from Pope *Gregory I to leave Rome. Though he failed to reduce the independent Lombard dukes of Spoleto and Beneveto, he established a strong rule in northern Italy. He married a Catholic princess, Theodelinda of Bavaria, whose influence helped spread the Catholic faith among the Arian Lombards. A. himself remained an Arian, but he favoured *Catholic monasticism and permitted the foundation of the Irish monastery of *Bobbio.
Paulus Diaconus, "Historia Langobardorum", *MGH*;
F. H. Dudden, *Gregory the Great* (1905).

AGINCOURT Locality in *Artois, northern France, famous as the site of one of the principal battles of the Hundred Years' War (25 October 1415). The English army, composed mainly of infantry and archers and led by King *Henry V, took advantage of the conditions of the terrain and the driving rain, which forced the French cavalry under the Constable of Albret to dismount, and won a decisive victory, bringing northern France under English rule. The French cavalry was decimated and the Constable of Albret was killed in the battle.
A. H. Burne, *The Agincourt War* (1956).

AGOBARD (779-840) Archbishop of Lyons (816-40). One of the most interesting figures of the *Carolingian renaissance of the 9th century, A. was a scholar, theologian, poet and ecclesiastical writer. He was also a counsellor of Emperor *Louis the Pious. He devoted his efforts to securing the supremacy of the Catholic Church, in the belief that the existence of the empire depended on the support of the Church. He, therefore, opposed the *Adoptianists and the speculative liturgy of Amalarius of Metz, which he felt was endangering the unity. He also tried to discredit the Jews, who enjoyed imperial protection, and proposed that the Jews be put outside the law, forbidden to hold office in a Christian state, or to own land and employ Christian servants.
PL, 104;
A. Bressolles, *Saint Agobard* (1949).

AGRICULTURE By and large, A. was the mainstay of medieval economy and was, therefore, closely related to the political and social structures of the medieval state. Thus the study of the agrarian society and its structure is closely related to the study of *feudalism. From the methodical view point, therefore, there is a fundamental difference between west European A. and that of the Byzantine and Moslem empires. It is a commonplace that Roman technology and structures persisted for centuries after the fall of the Roman empire; nevertheless, the absence of slaves, particularly in the West, led to the development of new agrarian techniques, to serve the new social structures. Thus, in the Byzantine empire the great estates, belonging to the aristocracy and the Church, continued to be administered much like the old Roman *latifundia*, based on slave labour, producing a variety of crops and serving also the urban markets. But outside the great estates an important class of free peasants who cultivated their own plots of land emerged in the Balkans and Asia Minor. By the beginning of the 8th century this class was important enough, numerically and economically, to win the legal status which was affirmed in the Byzantine code of A., promulgated in 726 by Emperor *Leo I the Isaurian. This code, which, with some light changes, remained in force until the end of the Middle Ages, shows that feudal trends in Byzantine A. were confined to the estates, from which derived the great wealth of the society. From the economic view point, Byzantine A. was from the beginning subject to commercial and monetary practices.

The establishment of the Arab caliphate created a new concept of A. in the Moslem lands. The Arab conquerors preferred to settle in cities and engage in trade; they left the cultivation of the land to the conquered populations, which continued in their traditional ways. This continuity explains why the countryside was Islamized slowly, so much so, that in places like Syria and Egypt the peasants continued to use the Julian calendar until the end of the Middle Ages, as it was more adapted to the seasons and the organization of field labour. Nevertheless, landowners were compelled, from the 7th century on, either to become Moslems or to leave, since possession of land was allowed only to Moslems. The peasants had to pay taxes, not only to the state but also to the landowners. In the 11th century the introduction of the system of *Iqtaa introduced a certain feudalization of the Moslem A., but only from the fiscal aspect, the justice being administered by *kadis* appointed by the government. As in Byzantium, Moslem A. was based on commercial considerations. Persian influence was responsible for the great innovation of floriculture, which was brought to a unique level of perfection in the beautiful gardens of Persia, Mesopotamia and Spain.

Unlike the Byzantine and Moslem agrarian societies, west European A. had to face the growing shortage of slaves from the 4th century on. In the last century of the Roman empire, the free peasants were bound to the land and compelled to work on the estates of the aristocracy, so as to provide food for the army. In time, three classes of peasants emerged: the small class of slaves, the land-bound peasantry, and a certain number of free peasants. This division continued under the Barbarians in the 6th-8th centuries, but new techniques of *assolement*, in which one third of the land was left fallow each year, helped to solve the problem of the shortage of slaves. Another technological innovation from the Barbarian age, was the water-mill. Agrarian economy lost its commercial character, most of the produce being consumed on the estates, with a certain amount being exchanged between the *villae*. Beginning in the 9th century, feudal structures began to affect the agrarian society and economy. The estate became a *manor, ruled by a lord, who held it as a vassal-tenant of his own overlord, exercising jurisdiction over his petty vassals and peasants, who were compelled to yield their free lands to him. *Allodial lands became rare and, after the *Norman conquest of England, which put an end to the free Anglo-Saxon peasantry, they remained only on the margin of feudal A. The final disappearance of slavery in the 9th century, turned the mass of peasants into serfs, or into *villeins, who were deprived of rights. The manor estate was divided into: (a) the seignorial reserve or demesne, which contained the castle, lands cultivated by the peasants as part of their duties to the lord, the woods, the lakes, the mills, and a smithy and bakery. When heavy ploughs were introduced in the 11th century, permitting more intensive cultivation, they were part of the manorial inventory, given to the peasants for their work services; (b) lands alloted to the peasants, whose fields were arranged in longs strips, in order to accommodate the plough-team, which was made up of six to eight oxen and a number of peasants. A peasant had to give his lord a portion of his produce, pay poll-tax and supply work services, known as the *corvée*. From the 12th century, with the revival of commerce and the growth of towns, some of those obligations were commuted to monetary payments, thereby beginning the revival in the West of commercial agrarian economy. The peasant community became more autonomous and a number of peasants improved their situation and bought their freedom. This development was facilitated by the new colonization of waste lands by the churches and barons, who offered better conditions to peasants they wished to attract as colonists. In eastern Germany this process was managed by contractors (*schulteiss*), who recruited landless peasants from the overpopulated areas of the Rhineland and the Low Countries, organized them and established new villages. The commutation of peasant duties into fiscal obligations also led from the 13th century on, to the employment of hired servants to work on the manorial demesne. The manors were gradually transformed into farms, with certain capitalistic forms of exploitation, based on efficiency and profits from the sale of the produce. In the 13th century a number of manuals of husbandry were produced, the most important being that of the Englishman Walter of Henley (ed. E. Lamond). The great plagues and crises of the 14th century affected A.: the shortage of manpower caused the lords to demand the restoration of work services and to close off fields. The peasants revolted (in France between 1355-60, in England in 1381), but were crushed by the lords.

G. Duby, *Rural Economy and Country Life in the Medieval West* (1968).

AHARON BEN JOSEPH HALEVI (d. 1305) Spanish rabbi and statesman. Born at Barcelona, he studied at the school of *Nahmanides. In 1284 he accepted the position of rabbi of the Jewish community at Saragossa, which was then undergoing an internal struggle, at the personal request of the king of Aragon, *Peter III. Later he returned to Barcelona, where he continued his teaching and scholarly work, mainly in jurisprudence. His *Bedek Bayit* (Repair of the Home), is a book of rules concerning Jewish Law and conduct. Refusing all official positions, he was reputed to be a wise statesman, respected at the royal court and renowned among the Jewish communities in Spain and France.

Ed. Venice (1605);
I. Baer, *History of the Jews in Christian Spain*, I (1968).

AHARON BEN MESHULLAM BEN JACOB OF LUNEL (d. 1210) One of the foremost scholars of the Jewish centre at Lunel in southern France. His main scholarly work dealt with the interpretation of the Law, but he was also a poet and astronomer, and wrote an important treatise on the Christian and Jewish calendars. He was a warm supporter of *Maimonides'.

H. Gross, *Gallia Judaica*, 280.

AHARON OF LINCOLN (d. 1185) Jewish merchant, a prominent figure in the economic life of England in the 12th century. He was active mainly in the commerce be-

tween England, Flanders and northern France. After his death, his fortune was confiscated by the *Exchequer, and a special account (*scaccarium Aaroni*) was opened to administrate it. The oldest house in Lincoln is believed to have been his home.

H. Richardson, *The Jews in Angevin England* (1958).

AHMAD Khan of the Mongols of Persia (1281-84). Third son of *Hulagu, he became the khan at the death of his brother *Abagha. He adopted a pro-Islamic policy, thus ending the alliance between the Mongols and *Crusaders. As a result the Crusaders were isolated and weakened.

M. Prowden, *The Mongols* (1940).

AHMAD IBN BUWAYH (10th century) Persian general. A son of one of the rebels against the *Abbasid rulers of Persia, he founded a local dynasty in *Isfahan, A. intervened in the local struggles in Baghdad in favour of Caliph Mustakfi. He conquered Baghdad (945) and became the commander-in-chief of the caliph's army, a title which gave him full authority over the caliphate. From Persia he imposed his protégés as caliphs and practically ruled over Baghdad, leaving his title to his descendants.

C. Brockelman, *History of the Islamic Peoples* (1949).

AHMAD IBN TULUN (835-84) Governor of *Egypt (868-84). Of Turkish origin, son of a freed slave, A. entered the army and served the *Abbasids. In 868 he was appointed commander-in-chief of Egypt, where he deposed the civil governor and seized power. Revolting against the caliphate, he conquered part of Syria and, though formally recognizing the caliph's sovereignty, he created an independent state in Egypt and in the coastal region of Palestine. He encouraged economic reforms, building markets and repairing harbours such as *Acre. He founded the dynasty of the *Tulunids (868-905), which was also concerned with the development of the Nile Valley. Of their monuments, the mosque of Fustat (now Cairo), still stands.

C. Brockelman, *History of the Islamic Peoples* (1949).

AIGUES-MORTES City in southern France, near Nîmes. Built and fortified by King *Louis IX, it was his port of embarkation to the *Crusades of 1246 and 1270. The city was built on a rectangular plan, with straight intersecting streets. Deserted in modern times, it represents a type of medieval town as originally planned.

F. R. Hiorns, *Town Building in History* (1956);
P. Lavedan, *Histoire de l'Urbanisme*, vol. I (1926).

AILLY, PIERRE D' (Petrus de Alliaco; 1350-1420) French cardinal and theologian. Born in Compiègne, he studied at Paris, where he became a doctor of theology in 1381. He joined the University of Paris and, in 1389, became its chancellor, as well as confessor to King *Charles VI. A favourite of Pope *Benedict XII, he obtained many ecclesiastical benefices, as well as bishoprics. His main concern was to end the *Great Schism and, with that aim, he broke with Benedict XIII in 1408. He attended the councils of Pisa (1409), of Rome (1411) and of Constance (1414), where he supported the need for a general reform of the Church. A. also believed in the supremacy of the Council over the pope. He expressed the view that bishops received their jurisdiction directly from God, thereby opposing the infallibility of the popes – ideas which became widespread during the Reformation. His treaty, *Tractatus*

Aigues-Mortes – a well-preserved Crusader town in southern France surrounded by crenelated walls

super reformatione Ecclesiae (On the Reform of the Church), had a great influence, mainly in Germany and England. In 1412 he was created cardinal and then acted as papal legate to Emperor *Sigismund of Germany.

A. also studied astrology and geography and wrote a book *De imagio mundi* (The Image of the World), wherein he expressed the idea that the Indies could be reached by sailing westwards; this book was known to Columbus. Works, ed., E. Baron (1930);
L. Salembrier, *Pierre d'Ailly* (1886).

AILRED, St. (1109-67) Abbot of Rievaulx. Of Anglo-Saxon origin, he was in his youth at the court of David, king of Scotland. In 1133, he joined the *Cistercians and entered the abbey of Rievaulx, becoming its abbot in 1147. Under the influence of *Bernard of Clairvaux, he combined in his theological writings mysticism and speculative theology. His main works in that field were on charity and on spiritual friendship, which gave him the name of "the English St. Bernard". He also wrote the life of *Edward the Confessor.
Works, *PL*, 195;
DNB, I.

AISHA (614-78) Daughter of *Abu-Bakr and the favourite wife of the prophet *Mohammad at Medina. From 627 on she followed Mohammad in his battles and, after his death, was called "Mother of the Believers". Active in the political life of the first generation of Islam, she opposed Ali, the son-in-law of the Prophet. She tried to mobilize opposition to his elevation as caliph, and from Mecca and Basra (Iraq), she supported the *Ummayads, which led to the religious schism between *Shiites and *Sunnites.
N. Abbott, *Aishah* (1942).

AIX-EN-PROVENCE One of the oldest Roman cities in Gaul. It declined with the Roman empire and, until the 9th century, remained a small town without importance. With the division of the *Carolingian empire, A. was chosen to be the residence of the counts of *Provence, and began to flourish again in the 10th-11th centuries. When the county was inherited by the Catalan house of Aragon, it brought the city a new prosperity; in the 13th century it obtained its privileges and had an elected council to administer it. This council, whose statutes were approved in 1290 by the Angevin court, was original in that it included both nobles and burghers, which was closer to the Italian custom than to the trans-Alpine. In the 14th and 15th centuries the city became an important cultural centre for all of Provence.

AIX-LA-CHAPELLE (AACHEN) Town in the German empire, between the Rhine and the Meuse. The site with its hot springs was the centre of an estate belonging to the *Carolingian family. It was a favourite place of *Charlemagne, who built himself a palace there, and between 795 and 799 an imposing church, imitating the Byzantine Sacred Palace of the emperor. After the imperial coronation (800), A. became the real capital of the Carolingian empire and it was there that Charlemagne's son, *Louis the Pious, was crowned emperor in 814. In the 9th century a little city arose around the palace and the church. After the establishment of the *Holy Roman empire (962), the elected emperors were crowned, immediately after their election, at A., and bore the official title of King of the Romans, until their official coronation by the pope in Rome. With the proclamation of Charlemagne as saint by Emperor Frederic *Barbarossa in 1164, A. enjoyed a

period of prosperity thanks to the pilgrims who flocked to its church, which became a cathedral, containing in its original Carolingian part the shrine of the Holy Emperor. The development of a local market made it a commercial centre but, by the end of the Middle Ages, it declined in importance.
R. E. Dickinson, *The West European City* (1951).

ALA-AL-DIN MOHAMMAD Khwarizmian shah (1199-1120). The most important ruler of the *Khwarizmian kingdom, who brought it to the peak of its power and prosperity. He defeated the Turkish princes in Persia and planned to attack Baghdad so as to appoint there a caliph of his choice, one reputed to be a descendant of the Shiite family of *Ali. Only a plague, in 1217, prevented him from realizing his project. He conquered the major part of Turkestan, Persia and part of the coast of Arabia on the Persian Gulf. His capital, Gurgansh, became a wealthy and important commercial centre. He embellished it by building palaces, mosques and markets.
W. Barthold, *Turkestan down to the Mongol Invasion* (1928).

ALAIN OF LILLE (1128-1203) Theologian and philosopher. He studied at Paris, participated as theologian at the Third *Lateran Council (1179) and probably became a monk at *Cîteaux. He held a rationalist-mystical view of the relationship of philosophy and religion, maintaining that all the truths of the faith are discoverable by unaided reason. His mysticism was based on his philosophy, which is a mixture of Pythagoreanism and *neo-Platonism. The key to his system was his belief that nature mediates between God (*Verbum*) and matter (*Physis*). A. was also influenced by *Boethius. Made famous by his theologic works, which were based on the exegesis of the Scriptures, he was called *doctor universalis* and accredited with authorship of different treatises, which are now known to have been written by others.
Works, *PL*, 210;
E. Gilson, *Philosophy of the Middle Ages* (1952).

ALAMANNI (Allemanni) German tribes, called also Suevi or Suebi. Originally from the southern shores of the Baltic Sea, they began their migrations in the 1st century and came in contact with the Roman empire in the 3rd century, when they tried to invade Gaul and Italy. They settled between the Main River and Lake Constance and conquered Alsace. In 357 the Roman emperor *Julian defeated them, but after his death they reconquered Alsace. At the end of the 5th century they warred with the *Franks and were defeated in 496 by *Clovis, who annexed their territory to the Frankish kingdom. They preserved their ethnic and linguistic identity through the centuries; from the 9th century on the duchy of Alamannia (or Swabia) consolidated their position in southern Germany. To the French they represented the German nation, which in France is still called Allemagne.
K. F. Strohecker, *Germanentum und Spätantike* (1965);
E. Schwarz, *Die Herkunft der Alamannen* (1954).

ALANS Nomadic tribes of Iranian origin, who settled, probably in the 1st century BC, in what is today southern Russia. The invasion of the *Huns from central Asia forced the A. to migrate westwards. Some of them entered the service of the Huns and participated in *Attila's invasion of Gaul and Italy, but most of them crossed the Rhine in 409, together with the Germanic

The chapel of Charlemagne's palace at Aix-la-Chapelle

tribes of the *Suevi and *Vandals, went through Gaul and participated in the conquest of Spain. Pressed by the *Visigoths, they became the subjects of the kings of the Vandals and helped them to conquer north Africa in 1430. During the Barbarian invasions, the A. were a dependent people and did not have a kingdom of their own. Regarded as good fighters, they were assimilated mainly by the Vandals.
Jordanes, "Getica", *MGH*;
B. S. Bachrach, *The Alans* (1969).

ALARIC I (370-410) King of the *Visigoths. Descendant of the family of Balthi, one of the leading families of the Goths, he served as a commander in the Roman army under Theodosius. After the emperor's death (395), he was disappointed in his hope to obtain a more important position in the government of Arcadius. Elected by the Visigoths as their king (*c.* 397), he tried to invade the Balkans. Arcadius paid him to move towards Italy where, in 400, A. founded a Visigoth kingdom on the northern shore of the Adriatic. In 410 he occupied Rome and for several weeks the Visigoths sacked the city, which had not been conquered after the Gallic invasion in ancient times. The event caused a shock in the Roman world, and was seen as the end of its civilization. A. did not intend to establish an independent

kingdom in Italy and prepared to invade north Africa, but died in 410 before he could accomplish his design.
A. Piganoli, *Le Sac de Rome* (1964).

ALARIC II King of the *Visigoths (484-507), the son and successor of *Euric. When the *Franks, under *Clovis, conquered northern Gaul, he did not attempt to intervene. The opposition of the Gallo-Roman population of his kingdom to his Arian government grew after Clovis' conversion to Catholicism (497), and, to appease it, A. introduced a policy of tolerance toward the Gallo-Romans. He promulgated a code of law for them, based on the Roman, and known as the *Lex Romana Wisigothorum* or *Breviarum Alarici* (The Roman Law of the Visigoths or The Breviary of Alaric). Attacked by Clovis in 507, he left Poitiers to oppose the Frankish army, and was defeated and killed in Vouillé. Aquitaine was conquered by the Franks.
R. de Abadal, *Del Reino de Tolosa al reino de Toledo* (1960).

ALBAN, St. See ST. ALBANS.

ALBANIA Country in the eastern Balkans, on the Adriatic shore. Part of the Roman province of Illyricum in ancient times, its population became an ethnical entity during the Middle Ages, combining the Illyrian and Thracian elements. The Albanian tribes, while preserving their own language and traditons, did not achieve political independence or form a political organization. After the division of the Roman Empire (395), A. belonged to the *Byzantine empire, as a separate military province (*thema*), Dyrrachium, whose capital was Durrazzo. The penetration of the *Slavs into the Balkans in the 8th century isolated A. from the centre of the empire and screened it from the influence of Greek-Byzantine culture. The local tribes preserved their independence from the Yugoslavs and *Bulgarians, and remained under the rule of Byzantine governors, sent from Italian provinces of the empire. With the restoration of the Byzantine rule throughout the Balkans by *Basil II in 1014, A. was governed directly from the imperial court, becoming part of the province of Epirus. To the end of the 11th century, Norman adventurers from Apulia under the leadership of *Robert Guiscard and his descendants, repeatedly invaded the country. In 1097 the Norman participants in the First *Crusade, under Bohemond of Taranto, and Tancred, landed in A. on their way to Constantinople. In the 12th century, the influence of *Venice in Durazzo grew, and gradually Latin Catholicism spread through the country, whose western part became a Venetian protectorate. After the Fourth Crusade, A. was divided between the Byzantine overlordship of Epirus and Italian dependencies. Its central part was annexed to the kingdom of *Naples (1217-1380), and *Charles of Anjou, who conquered it, proclaimed himself king of A., the first to bear this title. In the 14th century, eastern A. was conquered by the Serbs, and became part of the empire of *Stephen Dushan. After his death the tribes revolted and freed themselves from the Serbian rule and, with the dissolution of the Neapolitan rule in the Balkans, the Angevin kingdom of A. disappeared. The coastline was annexed by Venice, with the cities of Skutari, Durazzo and Valona, in 1390. From 1430 on, the *Ottoman Turks began their conquest of A. A local leader, George Castriotes, called Skanderbeg, united the tribes in opposition to the Turkish attacks. Under his leadership, A.

achieved independence (1444-66). He became a national hero, and was also described as the champion of Christian Europe, having challenged the Turks. However, after his death Albanian resistance was broken and, in 1479, the country became a province of the Ottoman empire; about two-thirds of the population adopted the Islamic faith.
Thalloczy, ed., *Documents of Mediaeval Albania*, 2 vols. (1913-16);
C. Chekrezi, *Albania, Past and Present* (1949).

ALBERIC Senator of Rome (*c.* 915-54). Son of Duke Alberic of Spoleto and Marozia, and grandson of *Theophylactus, ruler of Rome. In 932 he led a revolt of the Romans against the projected marriage of his mother, mistress of the city and mother of Pope *John XI, with Hugh, king of Italy, who claimed the imperial crown. He succeeded in overthrowing his mother and took the title "Senator of Rome". He exercised full powers over the city and the papacy, appointing his own protégés. Nevertheless, A. was more liberal than his mother. In 951 he opposed an attempt to invite the king of Germany *Otto I to Rome, to offer him the imperial crown. Before his death he appointed his illegitimate son Octavian as heir to his secular dignity and future pope (*John XII).
W. Ullmann, *The Growth of Papal Government in the Middle Ages* (1955).

ALBERIC Count of Tusculum (*c.* 1003-15). A member of the family of *Theophylactus, he seized power in Rome (1012), where he appointed his brothers successively as popes; his family controlled Rome until 1046 and promoted the spread of *feudalism in central Italy.
G. Mor, *Storia d'Italia; l'Età Feodale* (1956).

ALBERIC OF MONTE CASSINO (11th century) Scholar. Born in Italy, he entered the famous abbey of *Monte Cassino, where he devoted himself to the study of classical Latin and theology. In 1079, in Rome, he challenged the ideas of *Berengar of Tours and obtained his condemnation. His main work was the *Ars dictaminis*, wherein he fixed the order of the alphabet and Latin charts style, on the basis of classical authorities. His manual was influential in the 12th century.
J. de Ghellinck, *L'Essor de la Littérature latine au 12e siècle* (1954).

ALBERT OF AACHEN (c. 1100) Historian. A. was a priest at the cathedral of Aix-La-Chapelle. He wrote a history of the First *Crusade and of the *Latin kingdom of Jerusalem until 1121 (*Historia Hierosolymitanae Expeditionis*). Although A. never visited the Holy Land, his book is an important source for the history of the Crusades. His information came mainly from veterans of *Godfrey of Bouillon's army, and letters sent from the kingdom of Jerusalem.
Ed. in *Recueil des Historiens des Croisades*, Occidentaux, IV;
B. Kugler, *Albert von Aachen* (1885).

ALBERT OF HAPSBURG (Albert I of Austria; 1250-1308) Son of *Rudolph of Hapsburg, Holy Roman emperor from 1298. In 1282, he received from his father the duchy of *Austria, where he imposed a strong government, fighting the nobility and imposing the ducal prerogatives. Upon his father's death (1292), the electors, afraid of his ambitiousness, elected

Adolf of Nasaau. A. took advantage of a general
revolt against Adolf to win the election as king of
Romans (1298). Having defeated his rival at the Battle
of Göllheim, he proceeded to suppress the revolts of the
princes of the Rhine, and imposed his authority over
Bohemia. He was the ally of *Philip IV the Fair, king of
France. Overruling the nobility, he promoted commerce
and the growth of the cities. A. is also known for his
repression of the Swiss cantons, which is the background of the legend of *William Tell. He was assassinated by his nephew, John Parricida.

E. Kopp, *König Albrecht und seine Zeit* (1862);
G. Barraclough, *Origins of Modern Germany* (1954).

ALBERT OF LIÈGE, St. (c. 1166-92) Son of Godfrey
of Lorraine. In 1191 he was elected bishop of *Liège,
against the wishes of Emperor *Henry VI, at whose
instigation he was murdered in 1192. He is regarded as a
national martyr by the Walloons, who gave his life for
their freedom.

H. Pirenne, *Histoire de Belgique* (1901).

ALBERT OF MAGDEBURG (d. 981) German prelate.
He had been a clerk of *Otto I, who promoted his
appointment as archbishop of *Magdeburg (966-81).
From this city, with its proximity to the Slavic tribes
east of the Elbe, he preached the Christian faith and
organized missions to the Slavs. A. was thus one of the
first prelates to introduce German influence to Poland.

J. W. Thompson, *Feudal Germany* (1928).

ALBERT "THE BEAR" (1100-70) First margrave of
*Brandenburg (1134). Son of *Otto the Rich and
member of the important Saxon dynasty of the Ascanians, he became lord of Anhalt in 1123. In recognition
of his help in Italy, Emperor *Lothair I, in 1134, appointed him ruler of the Northern March, which became
*Brandenburg. He fought the *Slavs, conquering terri-
tories as far east as the Elbe, and joining them to his
new dominion. In 1138 Emperor *Conrad III made
him duke of Saxony, in the belief that A., who was
faithful to the dynasty of *Hohenstaufen, would help
to impose imperial authority in northern Germany. But
he was expelled from Saxony by the *Welfs and returned
to Brandenburg only in 1143, and began its colonization
by Germans.

Krabbo, *Albrecht der Bär* (1906).

**ALBERT THE GREAT (ALBERTUS MAGNUS), St.
(1193-1280)** Theologian. Born in Germany, scion of a
noble family, he entered the *Dominican order in Padua
in 1223 and five years later was sent to Cologne to teach
theology. In 1245 he went to Paris, where he became
one of the foremost theologians at the university; his
most famous pupil was *Thomas of Aquinas. In 1248
the order sent him to reorganize the *studium* (school) at
Cologne and, when he had done that, he was appointed
the provincial (head of the order) in Germany (1254).
In 1260 A. was elected bishop of Ratisbon (Regensburg),
but, after two years, resigned to devote himself to teaching and writing. He preached in support of the Crusade
in 1263 and, as a reputed theologian, took part in the
Council of Lyons. A man of vast learning, which gained
him the titles "Great" and *doctor universalis*, A. tried to
reconcile theology with philosophy, mainly with Aristotelian thought, anticipating his pupil Thomas de Aquinas.
He was influenced by Jewish philosophy, mainly *Maimonides, whose method of seeking rational explanations
for the faith he adopted. His writings in theology and on

The Gothic cathedral at Albi, France

creation, as well as his commentaries on *Peter
Lombard's works, represented a new trend in scholasticism. Difficult to read, they are full of digressions and
lack the organic unity of Aquinas' works. He was also
interested in the sciences and medicine and wrote a
treatise called *The Secrets of Women*, which was a
popular textbook on pregnancy and childbirth in the
late Middle Ages.

Works, ed. B. Geyer, (1955 ff.);
H. Wilms, *Albertus Magnus* (1933);
E. Gilson, *Le Thomisme* (1951).

ALBI City in southern France, in the province of
*Languedoc. Founded probably in the 4th century by
the Romans, as a fortified outpost, it is mentioned in
early 5th-century documents as a bishop's see, a city of
the kingdom of the *Visigoths. Under the *Carolingians,
it became a county in the kingdom of *Aquitaine but,
in the middle of the 9th century, it was given to the
counts of *Toulouse, and remained until the 13th
century in the great county of southern France; then it
was annexed to the estates of the French monarchy.
During the Tolosan period it was governed by a local
feudal family, the Trancavel, who were vassals of the
counts of Toulouse. At the end of the 11th century, a
sect opposed to the Catholic hierarchy settled near the
city and grew into the heretical movement known as the
*Albigenses, which in the course of the 12th century
spread throughout southern France. During the *Albigensian Crusade, A. was devastated and part of its
population destroyed. To strengthen Catholicism a
new cathedral in Gothic style was built in the city,
with appropriate fortifications. It is one of the most
beautiful Gothic churches and the most important
monument of A.

E. Leroy-Ladurie, *Histoire du Languedoc* (1965).

ALBIGENSES A heretical sect, named after the city of *Albi, which arose in southern France in the 11th century. In other parts of Europe, they were often called the *Cathari. The sect believed in the principle of *Manichaean dualism, which attempted to reconcile the belief in two distinct powers, the good and the evil, with Christian religion. The A. retained the Old and the New Testament, but interpreted them allegorically, denying Jesus' corporeal sufferings, and attacked the Catholic Church for its literal interpretation of the Bible, which they considered a corruption of the faith, "the work of the Devil". For these reasons they rejected the sacraments and the liturgical role of the clergy, maintaining that the church cannot mediate between God and believer. They were opposed to the church's owning temporal property, such as lands and buildings and receiving income. Theirs was a strict doctrine forbidding marriage, and the consumption of animal products. But, aware that such austerity could not be expected from the masses, they recognized two classes of the faithful – the "perfect", or pure, who received the sacrament of *consolamentum*, and observed all the principles of the sect; and the believers, who led normal lives, and would receive the *consolamentum* at some point in the future. But even the believers had to live austerely, abjuring all external signs of wealth. The A. segregated themselves thus not only doctrinally but socially from Catholic society, and created their own communities.

During the 12th century the sect spread throughout southern France, its opposition to the Church establishment making it extremely popular. Repeated condemnations by Church councils and persecutions by the authorities, failed to keep it down, and even a part of the nobility joined the sect. In 1167 the A. were numerous enough to create a federation of the communities, teaching its own authorized text, called the "Cathar Bible". Under the influence of Bulgarian dualists, they created the "Albigensian bishopric" of the Val d'Aran, which was in effect a congregation of the sect's communities. Alarmed by their progress, the Church and the kings of France and England, *Louis VII and *Henry II, decided to repress the movement. In 1184 a council, assembled at Verona by Pope *Lucius III, dealt with the heresy and resolved to establish the *Inquisition, whose function would be to investigate suspected heretics and bring them to lay trial. But these measures were ineffective and the A. won even greater sympathy in the region, some of the greater nobles adopting an ambiguous position, which was interpreted as favouring the sect. Pope *Innocent III attempted to convert the A., and appointed monks, such as St. *Dominic, with special missions for that purpose. The missionary activity only aggravated the situation and, in 1208, the papal legate Peter of Castelnau, was assassinated. The pope now decided to launch a *crusade against the A., and called upon the faithful of northern France to extirpate the heresy by force of arms. Led by *Simon of Monfort, an army of French knights was assembled, and proceeded to commit great massacres, such as that of *Béziers (1208), where heretics and innocents alike perished. A coalition of southern forces, led by *Peter of Aragon and Raymond VI, count of Toulouse, tried to protect the local population, but Simon won the Battle of Muret in 1213 and became the master of the province until his death in 1218. Nevertheless, the A.

were not entirely crushed and the French crown-prince Louis lead a new crusade, which continued under his own rule (as *Louis VIII) until 1226. In 1229, his widow, *Blanche of Castile, negotiated the Peace of Paris, which settled the political aspect of the crusade in favour of French monarchy, with the annexation of part of the country of Toulouse (the *Sénéchaussée de Beaucaire*) to the royal demesne, and the marriage of the heiress of Toulouse to the king's second son, Alphonse of Poitiers. The remnants of the A. were left to the Inquisition, reorganized by Pope *Gregory IX and entrusted to the new *Dominican order. The bloody repression, culminating in the massacre of the A.'s last citadel Montségur (1244), succeeded in stamping out the sect, but traces of the heresy remained dormant until the 14th century.

Z. Oldenbourg, *Le Bûcher de Montségur* (1960) (Engl. trans. *Massacre at Montségur*);
Z. Oldenbourg, *A History of the Albigensian Crusade* (1961).

ALBIZZI *Ghibelline family in Florence. The family made its fortune in the 13th-14th centuries in the wool industry and in trade. In 1375, the head of the family, Peter (Piero degli A.), became the leader of the aristocratic party and the virtual ruler of Florence. In 1378 the wool artisans (the *Ciompi*) rebelled against him and joined the aristocratic opposition. Peter was murdered and his family exiled. In 1382 his nephew, Maso degli A., succeeded in establishing his own rule in Florence. He conquered Pisa, creating the basis of the Florentine principality of Tuscany. By the time he died, in 1417, he had attained an important position in Italian and European affairs, and promoted the prosperity of his city-state. His son Rinaldo, who had acquired experience as his father's foreign minister, failed in his attempt to conquer Lucca, and had to fight the opposition, led by the *Medici, which tried to exploit this failure. In 1433 he expelled Cosimo de' Medici from the city, but could not repress the opposition. In 1434 he himself was expelled by the Medici-led powers and died in 1442 in Ancona.

F. Schevill, *Medieval and Renaissance Florence*, II (1961).

ALBOIN (d. 572) King of the *Lombards (561-72). A noble who was elected king by the Lombard tribes on the Danube, A. led them to Italy, which they invaded in 568. Though his followers were not numerous, he was able to make use of the Italian opposition and the resistance to Byzantine rule, and threaten the empire's armies. Approaching from north-east, he took *Friuli and Aquilea, whose patriarch fled to the island of Grado (the future Venice). Having taken Verona, he made it his capital, then conquered Milan and began the assault on Pavia. He was assassinated at the instigation of his wife.

Paul the Deacon, *Historia Langobardorum* (ed. *MGH*);
C. Brühl, *Studien zu den langobardischen Königsurkunden* (1970).

ALBORNOZ, GIL ALVAREZ CARRILLO OF (1310-67) Cardinal. Born at Cuenca (Castile), he was educated at Toulouse and returned to his native country, where he was appointed to ecclesiastical dignities, including that of archbishop of *Toledo, the highest ecclesiastical position in Spain. He had close relations with King *Alfonso XI, and played an important role in

the state. At the court he represented the anti-Moslem
policy, counselling to renew the *reconquista. He opposed the expulsion of the Jews from Spain, emphasizing
their importance to the prosperity of Spain. His relations
with *Peter the Cruel, Alfonso's successor, were not
good, and he joined the papal court at Avignon, where
he was created cardinal. In 1353 *Innocent VI made
him his legate to Italy and governor of the papal state.
He reorganized the administration of Rome and its
region and promulgated a new constitution in 1357
(*Constitutiones Aegidianae*), which was changed only in
1816.

F. Filippini, *Il Cardinale Egidio Albornoz* (1933).

ALBUMASSAR Latinized form of Abu Ma'shar (Ja'ffar
Ibn Muhammad Al-Balhi), the greatest *astrologer who
wrote in Arabic. Originally from the city of Balh
(Khorasan), he settled in the middle of the 9th century
in Baghdad. His work was based on the heritage of
antiquity. Of his numerous books the best-known was
the *Introduction to Astronomy*, written shortly before
his death (886); it was translated into Hebrew and Latin
in the 12th century. Medieval western scientists such
as Roger *Bacon, frequently quoted his writings about
the correlation between the positions of stars and the
rise of religions.

F. J. Carmody, *Arabic Astronomical and Astrological
Sciences in Latin Translation* (1956);
EI, s.v. "Abu Ma'sher".

ALCALDE (Arabic: al Kadi)   Spanish mayor. During
the period of the *reconquista (12th-13th centuries),
the organization of the Spanish cities conquered
from the Moslems was based on the adaptation of Arab
local-government institutions. The Christian Spanish
conquerors found that the most important of the Moslem
officials in the cities had been the religious judge, i.e.
the *kadi*, who might even represent the local community
against the government. The kings of Castile retained the
institution, although its judicial function was entrusted
to a church official, and created the post of A. as a
court-appointed administrator.

P. E. Russell, *Spain* (1968).

ALCÁNTARA, ORDER OF   Military-religious order of
Spanish knights, created in 1156 by Suero Fernández
Barrientos, to defend the city of St. Julian del Ferriero
against the Moslems. In 1177 the order was recognized
by Pope *Alexander III, who approved its regulations,
which were adapted from those of the *Templar knights.
In 1213 King *Alfonso IX of Castile charged the order
with the defence of the newly-conquered city of Alcántara (in Arabic *Al-Kantara*, the bridge), on the Tagus
River, giving it the city and its lands as a pious donation.
During the 13th and 14th centuries the order took part
in the wars of the *reconquista and became one of the
wealthiest in Spain and Portugal. The Castilian kings
were closely interested in the order's policies, and even
decreed that its master should always be a royal prince,
who would be destined from youth to serve in it. In
1494 King Ferdinand the Catholic appointed himself
Great Master of A., thus affiliating it with the Spanish
crown.

P. E. Russell, *Spain* (1968).

ALCAZAR (Arabic: al-Kasr "the fortress")   During
the Moslem domination of Spain, the Arab and Moorish rulers built themselves castles near their capitals.
These structures combined the seat of government, the

An alchemist; from a 16th-century engraving

royal residence and the court with gardens, all in one
place. Most of these palaces were retained after Christian
conquest, and used by the kings, chiefly of Castile and
Aragon. These places continued to be known by the
Arabic name. Hispanicized as A. The most famous are
the As. of Seville, within the city which, after the 13th
century, was one of the favourite residences of the kings
of Castile, and the palace of *Alhambra at Granada.

P. E. Russel, *Spain*, (1968).

ALCHEMY (Arabic: al-Khimia "chemistry") A theoretical and pragmatic search, begun in late antiquity by
Hellenistic philosophers and naturalists, for a way of
transforming base metals into gold and silver. Practised
mostly by the Arabs and Europeans in the Middle Ages,
A. was developed by other civilizations, such as the
Indian and the Chinese, from the 3rd until the 18th
century, when it was supplanted by modern chemistry.
The philosophical foundation of A. was an interpretation
of Aristotle's philosophy of physics, which was based on
the Greek belief that four natural "elements", earth, air,
fire and water, made up everything in nature, including
metals. The repeated failure of the attempts to trans-
mute other metals into gold led medieval scholars to
believe in the existence of a mysterious substance,
known only to the initiates, and called the "philosophers'
stone" (*lapis philosophorum*). The search for that substance became the goal of A., practically and theoretical-

ly. Some alchemists believed that it was to be found in water, and that liquid gold would regenerate human beings and restore their youth. They aimed to produce an elixir of life (*elixirium vitae*). It was thought that the secret had been known to the ancient Egyptians, having been revealed to them by their gods.

While the early alchemists were *gnostics of the 3rd-4th centuries in Egypt, the most important treatises on the subject were written in Byzantium between the 7th and 10th centuries, and based entirely on the speculative method. However, medieval western Europe neglected the Byzantine manuscripts (which were brought to Venice only in the 16th century), and knew A. only through the Arabs, who had probably found *Coptic manuscripts in Egypt. In 1144, Robert of Chester translated an Arabic manuscript on A., under the title *Book of Alchemical Composition (Liber de Compositione Alchemiae)*, attributing it to a certain monk Marianus of Rum.

The most important Arab alchemist was the 8th-century Abu Musa Jabber Ibn Khiyan Al-Sufi, who tried to repeat the experimental methods of the gnostics. The Persian philosopher *Ibn Sinna opposed this mystical trend. From the beginning of the 12th century, these theories filtered through Spain and southern Italy into western Europe, where they were accepted as a distinct science and combined with a cosmological philosophy involving the four elements. As late as the 16th century, Francis Bacon showed that A. was a particular, semi-intuitive pursuit, as opposed to physics and astronomy, and thus helped to isolate it from scientific endeavour.

Although medieval laboratories did not produce gold, nor the *Universal Medicine*, they did make some important discoveries, such as alcohol, in the 12th century, and sulphuric acid in the 13th. The Church regarded A. as a science and in the 13th century, allowed such philisophers as *Albert the Great, *Thomas Aquinas and *Ramon Lull, to study it. However, it opposed the mystical trends combining A. with *astrology and, in 1326, Pope *John XXII condemned the "alchemical charlatans".

E. J. Holmyard, *Alchemy* (1957).

ALCIRA City in Spain, in the province of Valencia. In 711 it was conquered by the Arabs. In the 12th century it became the centre of an emirate, which was independent of Valencia. In 1242 *James I of Aragon conquered the city and annexed it to his kingdom.

ALCUIN (735-804) Anglo-Saxon monk, originally from York, the most famous scholar of the 8th century, the moving spirit of the *Carolingian renaissance. Educated at the cathedral school of York, he became its master in 766. While on a visit to Italy in 781 he met *Charlemagne, who invited him to join his court, and made him his chief adviser in religious and educational matters. A. founded the royal academy at the palace of *Aix-La-Chapelle, which attracted prominent scholars and literary men from all the empire. He played a leading role in the emergence of the imperial ideology, which he associated with the biblical idea of kingship; he even called Charlemagne "David". In 795 he contributed to the *Libri Carolini*, a theological-political treatise, which was attributed to Charlemagne. As a teacher he used the dialogue method for instruction and, through his manuals, made *Augustine, *Boethius and the grammarians the chief subjects of study. In 796 Charlemagne appointed him

abbot of St. Martin of Tours, where in his last years he established an important school and library. He revised the *Vulgate translation of the Bible, for which purpose he consulted rabbis in Italy. He also revised Gallic liturgical texts to bring them in line with the practices of the Roman Church. He wrote a treatise against the *Adoptionists, a history of the church of York and poems in Latin. His letters, which were assembled in the 9th century to serve as a textbook for the teaching of Latin composition, are an important source for the study of the Carolingian empire and its society.

Works, ed. *PL*, vols. 100-101 and additions in *Monumenta Alcuiniana* (1873);
E. S. Duckett, *Alcuin, Friend of Charlemagne* (1951).

ALEPPO City in northern Syria, one of the oldest in the world. At the beginning of the Middle Ages, the Hellenistic city was transformed by the *Byzantines into a Christian one. New fortifications in the 6th century protected the city from *Persian invasions (540 and 611). In 637, the city was conquered by the Arabs and became a provincial capital. It also grew in importance as a trade link between Asia and Europe, and as a locus of cultural contact between the Moslem and the Syrio-Christian civilizations. In 945 Sayf Al-Dawlah, the founder of the *Hamdanid dynasty, made A. the capital of his kingdom, which remained until its conquest by the *Fatimid caliphs of Egypt in 1015. During the 11th century, Beduin revolts disturbed the peace and, in 1024, a Beduin principality was settled in the city and its surroundings, acknowledging the sovereignty of the Fatimids. In 1086 the *Seljuk Turks conquered the city and established a Turkish principality. The city resisted attacks by the *Crusaders (1118, 1124) and became an important Moslem base against the Crusader principality of *Antioch. In 1128 *Zengi, the atabeg of Mosul, became the ruler of Aleppo. He created the important kingdom of northern Syria and Iraq, from which the Moslems launched their counter-attack against the Crusaders. His son, *Nureddin, moved the centre of the new sultanate to Damascus, which he had conquered in 1152. Under *Saladin, A. became the centre of an *Ayyubid principality, and enjoyed economic and cultural prosperity. In 1261 the *Mamluks conquered the city, which served them as a base against the *Mongols and, in the 14th and 15th centuries, against the *Armenian principalities and the *Ottoman Turks.

Following the Arab conquest (637), most of the Christian population converted to Islam. During the Middle Ages A. was one of the most important Islamic centres, where a religious philosophy was developed, combining the Hellenistic heritage with strict Moslem observance. The schools of A. were famous and by the 12th century, a pluralistic trend evolved, with the co-existence of *Sunnite and *Shiite educational institutions. This relative liberalism also favoured the growth of an important Jewish community whose scholarly achievements were famous throughout the Middle East. The "Keter Aram Zova" Torah scroll – the most ancient in the world, except for the Dead Sea scrolls – was kept in an A. synagogue for hundreds of years. Under Nureddin's reign, in the middle of the 12th century, there was a drastic change: the Shiite schools were closed and the philosophical method of education was regarded as endangering the faith; orthodox Sunnite schools were

established, based on the authoritative teaching of Islam and the method of learning by rote, excluding debates.
J. Sauvaget, *Alep* (1941).

ALESSANDRIA City in northern Italy (Lombardy), founded in 1168 by the *Lombard League, which was created to oppose Emperor *Frederick Barbarossa's designs in Italy. It was named after Pope *Alexander III, who inspired the League. The city resisted Frederick's attempts to conquer it and, in 1198, was recognized as a free city. During the 13th century the city enjoyed independence and economic prosperity. At the beginning of the 14th century it suffered, like most Italian cities, from the struggle between the aristocratic parties and, in 1348, was annexed to the duchy of Milan.
P. Munz, *Frederick Barbarossa* (1965);
D. Muir, *History of Milan under the Visconti* (1924).

ALEXANDER I Pope (105-15). According to ancient Roman tradition, he was the fifth pope, or bishop of Rome after St. Peter. No historical evidence about his life and activity remains.
Eusebius of Caesaria, *Ecclesiastical History* (*c.* 330).

ALEXANDER II (Anselm of Luca) Pope (1061-73). Born in Baggio near Milan, he was a disciple of *Lanfranc of Bec and then held important offices in the church of Milan, being also an influential leader of the *Patarines, especially in their pietistic trends. In 1057, he became bishop of Lucca and soon distinguished himself as one of the leaders of the church reform party (known as the *Gregorian reform). In 1061 he was elected pope with the support of Hildebrand, the future *Gregory VII. He refused to ask for imperial confirmation and as a result *Henry IV appointed an antipope (Honorius II); but A. was recognized by the Catholic world. He actively promoted the reform projects and, for that purpose, renewed the decrees requiring clerical celibacy and the banning of *simony and lay *investiture. He sent legates to Lombardy, Spain, France, England and Germany to enforce the decrees, and excommunicated some of the counsellors of Henry IV. In 1066 he gave his blessing to *William of Normandy's conquest of England and later approved the election of his teacher Lanfranc as archbishop of Canterbury.
EC, I.

ALEXANDER III (Rolando Bandinelli; c. 1105-81) Born at Siena, pope (1159-81). A scion of the aristocratic Bandinelli family of Siena, he studied canon law and, by 1140, was one of the foremost teachers of law at *Bologna. In 1150 he was made cardinal and was very influential under *Adrian IV, whose mainstay he was. After Adrian's death, a majority of the cardinals elected him as pope but, with the support of *Frederick Barbarossa, a minority chose an antipope, Cardinal Octavian, who succeeded in establishing himself in Italy with the help of the emperor, who destroyed Milan. A. fled to France, where he received the support of the Catholic clergy in the west and of kings *Louis VII of France and *Henry II of England. He managed to isolate Frederick and, in 1166, was strong enough to return to Italy, and lead the *Lombard League against the imperial domination of northern Italy. Neither party achieved its aim and, in 1177, they met at Venice and came to an understanding (Peace of Rialto), which ended the schism and recognized A. as the legitimate pope. In 1179 he assembled and presided over the Third *Lateran Council, which was the public manifestation of his posi-

tion as the leader of the Catholic world. Principally concerned with the struggle against the empire, he also was involved in the politics of his age: in France, he helped Louis VII to enforce his rule and bestowed on him the title of "Most Christian King"; in England, he tried to reconcile Henry II and Thomas à *Becket and, after the latter was murdered, forced the king to make public penance (1171); in Spain, he supported the *reconquista*. He also tried to create an international league under the emperor of *Byzantium and the king of France, to help the *Crusader kingdom of Jerusalem. As a scholar, A. wrote commentaries on the Decree of *Gratian and the *Sententiae Rolandi*, influenced by *Abelard's works. His scholarly works, decrees and political activities, aimed to create a theocratic regime, with the pope as the unchallenged leader of Christendom.
M. Pacaut, *Alexandre III* (1956).

ALEXANDER IV (Raynald of Segni) Pope (1254-61). Of an aristocratic Roman family, the counts of Segni, he was cardinal of Ostia under *Innocent IV. Though for a short time he protected Conradin, the grandson of *Frederick II, he later turned against the *Hohenstaufen dynasty and tried to mobilize a "crusade" against them. involving Edmund, son of *Henry III of England, in the Sicilian affair. In 1258, when the influence of the *Ghibellines grew in Rome, he fled to Viterbo. A. tried to reconcile the Catholic and Orthodox churches and to organize a crusade against the Mongols. He protected the *Franciscan order.
EC, I.

ALEXANDER V (Peter Philarges; 1340-1410) Born at Candia (Crete), pope (1409-10). In his youth, he joined the *Franciscan order and studied at Mantua, Oxford and Paris. In 1381 he became master of theology at Paris, and was later sent by the order to Lombardy, where he became successively bishop of Piacenza (1386), Vicenza (1387), Novara (1389), and archbishop of Milan (1402). In 1409, at the Council of *Pisa, assembled to end the *Great Schism, he was unanimously elected pope. His reputation as an eminent theologian and a strong personality aroused hopes that he would succeed in renewing unity of the Catholic Church, but he died after ten months. His treatise *Commentary on the Sentences*, which was begun in Paris and finished in Lombardy, is considered as more than a commentary, being a contribution to *nominalist philosophy.
F. Ehrle, *Der Sentenzenkommentar Peters von Candia, des Pisaner Papstes Alexanders V* (1925).

ALEXANDER I (c. 1078-1124) Son of Malcolm of Scotland and St. *Margaret. King of Scotland (1107-24). Under his mother's influence he introduced English customs into Scotland and fought against the autonomy of the clans.
E. W. Robertson, *Scotland under her Early Kings* (1862).

ALEXANDER II (1198-1249) Son of *William the Lion, king of Scotland (1214-49). In 1215 he intervened in the baronial revolt against *John Lackland in England, intending to annex Northumberland to his kingdom but, in 1236, after a series of unsuccessful attempts, was compelled to renounce his ambition. His reign was a time of prosperity for Scotland, where he sought to introduce *feudalism as a political and social system.
E. W. Robertson, *Scotland under her Early Kings* (1862).

ALEXANDER III (1241-86) Son of *Alexander II, king of Scotland (1249-86). During his minority, the

clans succeeded in regaining their strength and the kingdom was unsettled by their quarrels. In 1262 A. took power and succeeded in imposing his authority upon the clans. He seized the Isle of Man and the Hebrides from the Norse. His reign was a time of peace and justice in Scotland, and remained in the popular memory as the golden age of the kingdom. His death was widely mourned and the *Lament for Alisaunder*, in praise of his memory, is one of the oldest Scottish ballads.
DNB, I.

ALEXANDER NEVSKI (c. 1220-63) National hero of medieval Russia, grand-duke of *Vladimir and *Novgorod (1252-63). The son of *Yaroslav of Vladimir, he organized at an early age the defence of his principality against the *Mongols, who had conquered *Russia. However, concluding that the forces of the khanate of the *Golden Horde endangered the existence of the northern Russian principalities, he submitted and even paid tribute to the conquerors. At the same time he fought against the Swedes and the German order of Livonian knights, who tried to seize northwestern Russia. In 1240 he won a decisive battle against the Swedes on the Neva River, from which comes his name. In 1242 he crushed the Livonian knights on the frozen Lake Peipus, on the Estonian border, which enabled him to annex the principality of Novgorod and put an end to the spread of Catholicism in Russia. As a result, he was proclaimed a saint by the Russian Orthodox (Pravoslav) Church. Although he did not unite the Russian principalities, A. was accepted by all the Russian princes as their leader. After his death he became a legendary national hero of Russia's independence.
G. Vernadsky, *The Mongols and Russia* (1953).

ALEXANDER OF BERNAI (12th century) French poet, active at Paris. Destined to a clerical career, he became priest of La-Croix-en-Brie (second half of the 12th century). However, he devoted himself to profane literature and wrote some French *Fabliaux*, being one of the originators of the poems of the *Fox. His main work, however, was the rendering of the *Roman of Alixandre* in dodecasyllables, also called alexandrines.
Pauphilet, *Poètes et Romanciers du Moyen Age* (1952).

ALEXANDER OF HALES Philosopher and theologian (1170-1245). Born in Gloucestershire, England, he was educated at the abbey of Hales. He studied at Paris and was later appointed professor of theology at the university's *Franciscan college (1236). His teaching, combining the study of St. *Augustine, St. *Anselm and *Hugh of St. Victor with such Aristotelian method as was known to the Parisian masters, won him great fame and the title *Doctor Irrefragabilis*. A great number of works written by other Franciscan masters were attributed to him and published with his genuine works.
V. Douce ed. Works (Bibliotheca Franciscana Scholastica), (1951, ff.).

ALEXANDRIA City in Egypt and its harbour. Founded by Alexander the Great in 332 BC., A. enjoyed its greatest prosperity as a Hellenistic city and the capital of Egypt in ancient times. With the rise of Christianity in the 4th century, its role as a Hellenistic centre seriously declined. Nevertheless, at the beginning of the Middle Ages, it was the most important centre of the new faith, and the theological discussions, which took place there laid the foundation for the Christian dogma. The see of a patriarchate believed to have been founded by St.

Mark, it enjoyed an independent apostolic tradition. A., prospering economically, continued to be the capital of the Egyptian province of the *Byzantine empire and second only to Constantinople, being the pivot of trade between the eastern and western Mediterranean. The population lived in distinct ethnic quarters, notably the Greek, Coptic and Jewish. In the 7th century the city was devastated by invaders. Conquered in 616 by *Chosroes, king of Persia, who destroyed part of its Christian quarter, it was already in decline when the Arabs conquered it in 642. Many of its inhabitants fled and the Moslem colonization did not make up the loss in population. Although under Arab rule it continued to be the most important city in Egypt, the governorship was established in *Fustat (today the old city of Cairo). A. remained a commercial centre, as well as a religious and cultural one, where the Greek heritage was transmitted to Islam. After 968, when *Cairo was founded by the *Fatimids, A. lost its political importance and declined further. But the city and its harbour remained prosperous, serving the maritime commerce between Egypt, north Africa and Italy. The establishment of the Italian communes in *Acre during the *Crusades had a certain adverse effect on A., but, in the 13th century, its commercial activity revived, with resultant prosperity and a demographical increase in the city's four quarters: the Arab, Coptic, Greek and Jewish. The discovery of new commercial routes through the *Mongol empire, the *Black Plague (1348) and, finally, the discovery of the Cape route by the Portuguese at the end of the 15th century, caused its final decline and the reduction of its population to 4000-5000 inhabitants.
R. Taragan, *Alexandria* (1931).

ALEXIUS III, Angelus (d. 1210) Emperor of Byzantium (1195-1203). Member of the dynasty of Angelus, who were related to the Comneni, he rebelled against his brother *Isaac and succeeded him. His reign was characterized by dynastic conflicts and by the growing influence of Venice, which he failed to check. This was manifested by the Venetian support of Isaac and his son *Alexius IV, who succeeded in deposing A.
N. H. Baynes and H. S. L. B. Moss, *Byzantium* (1949).

ALEXIUS IV, Angelus (1182-1204) Son of *Isaac Angelus, emperor of Byzantium (1203-04). Supported by Venice, he led a revolt against his uncle *Alexius III, deposed him and proclaimed himself emperor, restoring his father and reigning together with him. In 1204 he himself was deposed, and during these upheavals, Constantinople was overwhelmed by the participants of the Fourth *Crusade, who founded the *Latin empire of Constantinople.
N. H. Baynes and H. S. L. B. Moss, *Byzantium* (1949).

ALEXIUS I, Comnenus (1048-1118) Founder of the dynasty of the Comneni, emperor of *Byzantium (1081-1118). A. became emperor following a revolution, which put an end to the ten-year long political anarchy in the empire during which the *Seljuks had conquered Anatolia. He re-established order and succeeded in maintaining the empire's power, by a series of battles against the *Normans of south Italy, the *Petchenegs and the Seljuks. A. had to contend with the participants of the First *Crusade, who assembled in Constantinople in 1096. Before sending them to fight the Seljuks in Nicaea – where they were crushed and decimated – he obtained their oath of allegiance and their help in restoring some of the Byzantine domination in Asia; but he failed to impose his overlordship over the new Crusader states in the Middle East.

N. H. Baynes and H. S. L. B. Moss, *Byzantium* (1949).

ALEXIUS II, Comnenus (1167-83) Emperor of Byzantium (1180-83). Son of *Manuel Comnenus and of Mary of Antioch, his reign was dominated by the regency of his mother, who was unpopular on account of her Latin background. The revolt of members of the imperial dynasty in 1183, led to the murder of Mary and A., and the appointing of a new regent, *Andronicus.

N. H. Baynes and H. S. L. B. Moss, *Byzantium* (1949).

ALEXIUS V, Dukas Son-in-law of *Alexius III. He led the revolt against *Alexius IV and deposed him. Proclaimed emperor of Byzantium, he tried without success to resist the Crusaders, and was killed while defending Constantinople (1204).

N. H. Baynes and H. S. L. B. Moss, *Byzantium* (1949).

ALEXIUS, St. (1293-1378) Metropolitan (archbishop) of Moscow, one of the fathers of the Russian Orthodox (Pravoslav) religion. Protector of St. *Sergius, he strengthened the supremacy of the Moscovite see in the Russian church. In the years 1359-62 he acted regent during the minority of *Dmitri Donskoi, suppressing the restless nobles and helping to establish the centrality of the Moscovite principality in Russia.

G. P. Fedotov, *The Russian Religious Mind* (1946).

ALFONSO I, el Batallador King of Aragon (1104-34). Having married Urraca, heiress of Castile, he claimed her inheritance and sought to proclaim himself emperor of Spain (1106). Urraca opposed her husband's ambitions and went to war against him. A. managed to penetrate Castile, but his main effort was directed against the Moslems who, in 1110, attacked his capital, Huesca. In a series of battles, from which derives his cognomen, he reached *Andalusia and conquered the important cities of Tudela (1115) and Saragossa (1118), extending his kingdom south of the Ebro. He imposed his suzerainty over the nobles of southern France and made of the minor kingdom of Aragon an important military power. A. was fatally wounded in battle at Fraga.

A. Castro, *The Structure of Spanish History* (1954).

ALFONSO II (Raymond; 1152-96) Son of *Raymond Berengar IV, count of Barcelona, and of Petronilla, granddaughter of *Alfonso I, heiress of Aragon. King of Aragon (1164-96). Together with *Alfonso VIII of Castile he fought against the Moslems and also against *Sancho VI of Navarre (1177). But his main concern was the pursuit of the traditional Catalan policy in Provence, where he fought against *Raymond V, count of Toulouse. A patron of poets and troubadours, he composed poems in the French Occitanian language.

H. J. Chaytor, *A History of Aragon and Catalonia* (1933).

ALFONSO III (1264-91) Son of *Peter III, king of Aragon (1285-91). His reign was marked by the war with France and its allies in the Balearic Islands. To win the allegiance of the nobles to his dynasty, he gave them large privileges, including the rights of making war and peace, of consent to taxation and the appointments of magistrates (1287).

H. J. Chaytor, *A History of Aragon and Catalonia* (1933).

ALFONSO IV (1299-1336) King of Aragon (1327-36). The son of *James II, in 1320 he conquered Sardinia for his father, and then led the war against *Genoa for the part of the island which was under Genoese rule. As king, he imposed a heavy taxation, particularly on the Jews (1333).

DHE, I.

ALFONSO I (693-757) King of *Asturias (739-57). He organized the small Christian kingdom of northern Spain after the Arab conquest and, taking advantage of the dissent among Moslem rulers, conquered and annexed the province of Galicia in northwestern Spain to his kingdom.

G. Jackson, *The Making of Medieval Spain* (1972).

ALFONSO II (757-842) King of *Asturias (791-842). He fought the Moslems and extended his kingdom as far as the Duoro River. Tradition attributes to him the establishment of the important religious centre of *Santiago de Compostela and the veneration of the shrine of St. James by all western Europe.

DHE, I.

ALFONSO III, the Great (838-910) King of *Asturias and *León (866-910). He fought the Moslems and enlarged his kingdom, becoming a legendary hero, to whom colonization activities have been wrongly attributed.

DHE, I.

ALFONSO IV, the Monk King of *Asturias and *León (924-27). A weak-minded person, he abdicated in favour of his brother Ramiro and chose monastic life. However, soon after his abdication he repented and rebelled against *Ramiro, who defeated him, blinded him and sent him back to his abbey in the Asturias, where he died in 932.

DHE, I.

ALFONSO V (994-1027) King of *Asturias and León (999-1027). On attaining his majority he found the kingdom in a state of anarchy and reorganized it around León and Castile. He supported the towns as a check against the nobles and was the first Spanish king to issue them charters of privileges (*fueros*). He fought the Moslems and was killed at the siege of Viseu (northern Portugal).

A. Castro, *The Structure of Spanish History* (1954).

ALFONSO VI (1030-1109) Son of *Ferdinand I. King of León and Castile (1072-1109). His father divided the kingdoms between his sons and A. was to receive León. A feud with his brother *Sancho II caused him to seek refuge in Toledo, which was under Moslem rule. When Sancho was killed in 1072, Alfonso was recognized as king of both Castile and León. He took advantage of the decline and disorder of the Moslem states in Spain to enlarge his dominions. In 1080 he besieged Toledo to help Alkadar, son of the Emir Al-Mamun, who gave him refuge. Then he invaded Andalusia, besieged Seville and threatened other Moslem centres, such as Granada. In 1085, after the Alkadar's renunciation of his right to Toledo, he took the ancient *Visigothic capital and made it the capital of Castile. His military victories led to the fall of the *Abbadids and to the conquest of Moslem Spain by the *Almoravides. These, under their leader *Yussuf Ibn Tashfin, defeated him in 1086 and 1108. After the conquest of Toledo A. titled himself "Emperor of all the Spains". He encouraged the settlement of French knights and burghers in his kingdom, and introduced the monastic reform of *Cluny. Despite his strong Catholic stand, he was tolerant towards his Moslem and Jewish subjects.

DHE, I.

ALFONSO VII (1105-57) Grandson of *Alfonso VI. King of Castile and León (1126-57). He took part in the war between his mother Urraca and his step-father *Alfonso I of Aragon, and won his inheritance by the Treaty of Tamara (1125). He managed to subdue the nobles, who had been restive during Urraca's reign, and was recognized as overlord by the kings of Navarre and Aragon and by the lord of Portugal. To celebrate the event he crowned himself in 1135 as emperor. Nevertheless, he failed to impose his rule on *Portugal, which became independent in his reign. He took part in the wars against the Moslems in Andalusia and even succeeded in temporarily seizing Cordoba and Almeria. He helped found the Order of *Alcántara in 1156.
DHE, I.

ALFONSO VIII, the Noble (1155-1214) King of *Castile (1158-1214). During his minority, the vassal kingdoms of Navarre and Aragon proclaimed their independence and *Ferdinand II of León tried to conquer Castile. In 1166 A.'s army seized Toledo and he was crowned king. In 1170 he married Eleanor, daughter of *Henry II, king of England, so as to secure the Angevin alliance against Navarre and León. The warring of the Christian states in Spain, which continued until 1196, benefited the Moslems, who defeated A. at Alarcos in 1195 and conquered Guadalajara and Madrid. After a peace treaty with *Peter II of Aragon, A. was able to concentrate his forces against the *Almohades, helped by the archbishop of Toledo, Rodrigo *Ximenes, who travelled to France, Germany and Rome to recruit help. In 1210 Pope *Innocent III called for a crusade in Spain. In 1212 A. crushed the Almohades at the Battle of Las Navas de Tortosa, considered the key victory of the *reconquista.
G. Jackson, *The Making of Medieval Spain* (1954).

ALFONSO IX (1166-1230) King of *León (1188-1230). His reign was marked by a prolonged conflict with the papacy, on account of his prohibited marriages with Theresia of Portugal and Berengaria of Castile, and he was repeatedly excommunicated by the popes. Although he was supported by the nobles and clergy of León, he was unable to resolve the problem of the inheritance of his throne and, in 1230, at his death, a general revolt broke out.
DHE, I.

ALFONSO X (1221-84) King of Castile and León (1252-84) emperor of the *Holy Roman empire (1267-72). He continued the wars against the Moslems, and even tried to invade Morocco. He completed the conquest of western Andalusia (1265), and with the help of the emir of *Granada, established his rule in the valley of Guadalquivir. By a series of marriages, he settled the disputes concerning Castilian claims to Gascony and Portugal, renounced them and obtained English and Portuguese alliances. In 1267 he was elected emperor of the Holy Roman empire, but never went to Germany to put his election into effect; after the election of *Rudolph of Hapsburg (1272), A. was compelled to renounce the title. From 1270 he had to face internal troubles. Led by the family of Lara, some of the nobles revolted, demanding the abolition of certain taxes and services. The revolt was suppressed only in 1275. When A.'s eldest son, *Ferdinand of La Cerda (1275), died, the younger, Sancho, claimed his place as heir to the kingdom, whereas A. decided to recognize Ferdinand's sons.

The rebellion forced him to give up the war against Morocco, and even to ally himself with the Moslems against Sancho and his followers. The devaluation of the currency in 1281 aggravated the troubles and the kingdom was split: the *cortes* of Valladolid resolved to depose him, while that of Seville declared Sancho a rebel (1282).

A. had a deep interest in literature and science, as well as in legislation. He promoted the translation into Castilian of Arabic books on astronomy and astrology by Arabs and Jews and the use of Castilian as a literary language instead of Latin, which helped its development. In the field of legislation, he sought to establish a common law for the kingdom, by the abolition of special privileges. In 1255 he published a codex of all the laws and appointed a committee of legislators to create the "Castilian jurisprudence" (1265). He also initiated the official historiography of Spain. In his court there were poets and troubadours, and some poems are attributed to him.
A. I. Solalinde, *Alfonso X el Sabio* (1922);
DHE, I.

ALFONSO XI (1311-50) King of *Castile and *León (1312-50). His childhood was marked by the dynastic troubles which began in Castile in *Alfonso X's time and which created general anarchy in the kingdom. In 1325 the *cortes* proclaimed his majority and the factions agreed to cease their hostilities. His marriage to Maria of Portugal was intended to secure internal peace, but A.'s preference for his mistress, Eleanor de Guzmán, rekindled the tensions, which obliged him in 1331 to suspend the war against the Moslem state of *Granada and concentrate on settling the internal issues. By way of checking the nobility, he gave privileges to the towns (1337) and was reconciled with his wife. Supported by knights from England, France and Navarre, and by Portugal, he renewed the war against Granada and Morocco and won a decisive victory in 1340, conquering the city of *Algeciras and besieging Gibraltar, thereby isolating the Moslems in Spain from their African backing. The *Black Death ravaged his kingdom in 1349-50 and A. himself was one of its victims.
DHE, I.

ALFONSO I (1110-85) King of *Portugal (1139-85), founder of the kingdom. Son of Henry of Burgundy and Theresa of Castile, he inherited the county of Portugal in 1112, though the power was exercised by his mother. In 1128 he rebelled against her and defeated her supporter *Alfonso VII of Castile. Taking advantage of this victory he severed his feudal ties with the kingdom of León. In a series of wars against the Moslems he conquered Santarem and Lisbon (1147). In 1139 A. was hailed by his soldiers as king of Portugal and, in 1179, the title was recognized by Pope Alexander III.
H. V. Livermore, *A History of Portugal* (1947).

ALFONSO II (1185-1223) King of *Portugal (1211-23). He defeated the Moslems at Alcácer do Sal, a key position south of the Tagus, thereby extending *Alfonso I's conquests. Principally concerned with internal problems and the administration of his realm, he clashed with the nobility and the clergy over taxes. In 1220 he ordered an investigation of the church property in the kingdom and was excommunicated by Pope *Honorius III for trying to expropriate the church incomes.
H. V. Livermore, *A History of Portugal* (1947).

ALFONSO III (1210-79) Second son of *Alfonso II. He became the king of Portugal after the deposition of his brother *Sancho II (1248-79). He went to war against the Moslems and, in 1249-50, conquered the province of Algarve, establishing the frontiers of Portugal. He moved the capital to Lisbon and, in 1254, reformed the constitution of the realm, including representatives of the cities in the *cortes*.

H. V. Livermore, *A History of Portugal* (1947).

ALFONSO IV (1290-1357) King of *Portugal (1325-57). He rebelled against his father, Denis, who preferred his illegitimate sons. He quarrelled with *Alfonso XI of Castile, who repudiated his wife Maria, but renewed the friendship with the Castilian king after Maria's return to the court, and helped him in the war against the Moroccans. In the last years of his reign his son Peter led a revolt in the northern provinces, when A. supported the murderers of Peter's wife.

H. V. Livermore, *A History of Portugal* (1947).

ALFRED THE GREAT (849-99) King of *Wessex (871-99). His brother Aethelred shared the government with him from 866, leaving him to conduct the war against the *Danes. A. defeated the Danes at Ashdown (871) and, despite some reverses, was able to stop them from invading Wessex. The Danes renewed the attempt in 875 and, in 878, A.'s army was crushed and the country was overrun by the invaders. He retired to Somerset, where he reorganized his army, defeating the Danes at Adington in the same year. As a result, England was divided between the independent, Anglo-Saxon part, dominated by Wessex and the Danish territories, northwest of the road between London and Chester (the *Danelaw). A. built up a strong system of defence, based on compulsory military service for all free-men of the kingdom, fortifications and a fleet. These measures proved themselves when the Danes again attempted to invade Kent in 893.

A. was the first Anglo-Saxon leader to stop the Scandinavian invasions of England. He could not free all the territories held by the Danes and bring all of England under his rule, but his achievements assured him a special place in English history. A national hero, he influenced the growing national consciousness of the Anglo-Saxons, and the historiography of his and later ages presented him as the defender of Christianity against the pagans. In the short periods of peace during his reign, A. also reformed the administration of the kingdom, imposing justice and unity. He established at his court a school for the sons of the nobility and patronized scholarship, including the translation of philosophical and theological works from Latin into Anglo-Saxon. For this purpose, he encouraged the monasteries as centres of culture and learning. A. himself wrote books on history and geography, and is considered the first writer of Anglo-Saxon prose. His endeavours promoted the evolution of Anglo-Saxon as a literary language.

Asser, *Life of Alfred the Great* (1904);

B. A. Lees, *Alfred the Great* (1915).

ALGARADE Spanish word, of Arabic derivation, meaning dispute. In medieval Spain, the term was used to indicate private and illicit wars between nobles.

DHE, I.

ALGARVE (Arabic: Al-Gharb) The southern province of *Portugal. Conquered by the Arabs in 711, it remained under Moslem rule until the 13th century. After the dis-

solution of the caliphate of *Córdoba in 962, the province became a petty principality, ruled by north African princes, who resided in southwestern Andalusia or on the Moroccan coast. In 1249-50 it was conquered by *Alfonso III and annexed to Portugal. In 1438 Henry the Navigator established at Sagres, in the southwestern point of the province, an institute for the search of navigational routes, which played an important role in the discoveries of the coast of west Africa and the Cape route to India.

H. V. Livermore, *A History of Portugal* (1947).

ALGEBRA A branch of arithmetic, designed to aid calculation by using symbols for unknown values in equations. While the name is Arabic, taken from the title of the book *Al-Gebr* and *Al-Mukableh* written in the 8th century by *Al-Hwarismi, the method is an ancient one, known to the ancient Egyptians and developed by the Greeks. It appears that Al-Hwarismi had a certain knowledge of the algebraic techniques of the Indians, which had reached the Arab world through Persia. The method, as used by the Arabs in Spain and southern Italy, was transmitted to Christian Europe by the Jews. At the beginning of the 12th century *Abraham Bar Hiyya of Barcelona wrote *The Book of Geometry and Algebra*, which was translated into Latin and prepared the way for the translation of Al-Hwarismi's classical work during the 12th century and its use at the school of *Chartres. The word A. was adopted by the Latin West to express the system of solving unknown equations. The system was perfected by the greatest medieval mathematician in the West, Leonardo of Pisa, and was used by his methods until the 18th century.

A. C. Crombie, *Augustine to Galileo; Science in the Middle Ages* (1959).

ALGECIRAS (Arabic: the island) City in southern *Spain, near Gibraltar. Built on the ruins of an ancient Roman town, A. was the first city in Europe to be conquered by the Arabs in 713. Part of the caliphate of *Cordoba and of the emirate of Andalusia, the city came in the 13th century under Moroccan influence. In 1344 it was conquered by the Castilians after a long siege, in which guns were probably used. But the Castilian rule was not solid and when, in 1369, the army of *Granada conquered the city, it was entirely destroyed. It was rebuilt in the 18th century by the Spanish government after the cession of Gibraltar to Britain.

L. Bertrand and C. Petrie, *The History of Spain* (1952).

ALGIERS (Arabic: Al-Jazair "the islands") City in north Africa, built in 944 by Bulukin ben Ziri, on the ruins of ancient Icosium, as the capital of his principality (the major part of today's Algeria). From 646 to the 10th century it was a part of the Arab province of *Africa. The Berber family of Ben Ziri ruled the principality under the suzerainty of the *Fatimid caliphs of Egypt. After Bulukin's death, a branch of the family, the Hamadids, seized power, and the Zirids were forced eastwards to Mahdia. The rivalries among the Berber dynasties and between Arabs and Berbers gave rise to the practice of piracy in the small ports of A. The Hamadids tried to strengthen their position by acknowledging the *Abbasid caliph of Baghdad, to which the Fatimid court reacted by sending an Arab expedition which ravaged the country in 1052. In 1070 the *Almoravids began their conquest of Algeria, deposing the Hamadids; in 1152 the entire country was conquered

The Court of the Lions at the Alhambra, Granada

by the *Almohades. But the Almohades' control was inadequate, and the Berber tribes remained semi-autonomous. In the 13th century they became independent and, after a series of wars, the country was divided into three parts, all ruled by Berber dynasties, until the 16th century, when parts of A. were conquered by Spain. Despite the divisions, the country called Barbary, was considered by the Europeans in the 13-15th centuries as one.

G. Gsell, G. Marçais, G. Yves, *Histoire d'Algérie* (1927).

ALHAMBRA The royal palace of the kings of *Granada, the most important architectural and artistic accomplishment of the Moslems in Spain. The site, southeast of Granada, on a hill which dominates the city, had previously been used by Romans, who built a fortress there. The building of the palace began in the second half of the 13th century, in the reign of Sultan Muhammad El-Ahmar and was completed in the 14th century. Part of the complex was destroyed in 1527 by Charles V, who built for himself a palace in the style of the Renaissance, but in the 19th century it was restored in part to preserve the original style. A complex of buildings around two courts, with great open halls, it was designed for the public life of the monarchs. The architecture, influenced by the majestic Moslem-Persian style, is embellished with rich decorations, including verses from the Koran.

F. P. Bargebuhr, *The Alhambra* (1968).

ALHARIZI, JEHUDAH BEN SALOMON (c. 1170-1235) Poet and translator. Born in Toledo, Spain, to a wealthy Jewish family, he studied in his native city. In 1190 he visited Provence and then spent many years in the Middle East, visiting and sojourning in Egypt, Palestine, Syria, Iraq and Persia. A. influenced the Oriental Jewish communities by introducing them to the cultural legacy of *Sephardic Jewry. He wrote most of his works during these years and probably returned to Spain towards the end of his life.

His most important book is the *Takhkemoni*, finished in 1229. He introduced the style of the *makama*, familiar in Arabic poetry, into Hebrew. Besides the literary importance of the book, considered as one of the classical works in Hebrew poetry, it has also an historical importance, being an autobiographical description of his journey and of the life of the Jews in the Middle East. Parts of it were translated into Latin. He also translated into Hebrew Arabic poems; but his most important translation was that of *Maimonides' *Guide of the Perplexed* into Hebrew. Though imperfect, it was used as a basis for a Latin translation in medieval Europe.

EJ, II.

AL-HASAN (625-70) Elder son of *Ali and Fatima, the daughter of *Muhammad. He participated in his father's war against *Muawiya and, after Ali's murder in 661, was elected caliph by the partisans of Ali, who had assembled at Kufa (Iraq) with a great army, ready to continue the war. A., who was disinclined to fight, abdicated and settled to a luxurious life at Medina. Rumours were spread that the *Ummayads had paid him to abdicate, while other rumours had it that he was poisoned by the Ummayads.

P. K. Hitti, *A History of the Arabs* (1953).

AL-HUSAYN (626-80) Younger son of *Ali and Fatima. After the death of his brother *Al-Hasan, he was considered the leader of the *Shiites. In 680 he went to Iraq with a small company and was met at Karkala by the *Ummayad governor of Kufa. The local Shiites were dispersed and A. was defeated and killed. A martyr of the Shiite sect of Islam, the day of his death (the 10th of Muharram) is marked as its traditional Day of Lamentation.

P. K. Hitti, *A History of the Arabs* (1953).

AL-HWARISMI, MOHAMMAD IBN MUSA (c. 780-845) Persian mathematician, astronomer and geographer, one of the great scientists of Islam, who created a synthesis between the Greek and Indian scientific heritages. His most important work, written in Baghdad, where he was one of the leading figures of the *Abbasid Academy, is his book of *Al-Gebr and Al-Mukabaleh*, in which the concept of *algebra first appeared. Its Latin translation by *Adelard of Bath in the 12th century became the standard text for the study of algebra in the Middle Ages. He also composed trigonometrical tables and his astronomical works deal with the *astrolabe and the solar year.

A. Mieli, *La science arabe* (1939).

ALI (Ibn Abu Taleb; c. 600-61) Cousin and son-in-law of *Mohammad, the fourth caliph (656-61). One of the first followers of the Prophet, he married his daughter Fatima and participated in his wars. In 632 he was considered by some Moslems as most eligible to succeed Mohammad, but the majority preferred the elder companions of the Prophet and A. was elected only after the murder of *Uthman. Having refused to disavow the murderer of Uthman, he became suspect in the eyes of the *Ummayads, who wanted to avenge their leader. They joined *Aisha, Mohammad's widow, who was A.'s foe, and who had prevented his accession to the caliphate in the previous elections. A. defeated Aisha and her partisans and, from Arabia, imposed his rule on Iraq; but he failed to gain Syria, whose governor, *Muawiya, head of the Ummayad clan since the death of Uthman, had an army of his own and proclaimed himself caliph in 660. A. was preparing a decisive war, when he was murdered in Kufa. The *Shiites considered A. the only legitimate caliph, by Mohammad's election and hereditary rights. A traditional Shiite celebration marks a particular day on which Mohammad supposedly chose Ali as his successor.

E. L. Peterson, *Ali and Muawiya in Early Arab Tradition* (1964).

ALICANTE City in southeastern Spain, and ancient Roman colony (Lucentum). Under the *Visigoths, it was the centre of a county which remained independent for some time after the Arab conquest of Spain. The city was taken and retaken by Moslems and Christians between 1097 and 1250, when *Alfonso X of Castile conquered it.

He developed the city by settling merchants and sailors in it and granting them privileges. A. was conquered in 1296 by *James the Conqueror, king of Aragon, who annexed it to his realm.

J. Pastor della Roca, *Historia general de la Ciudad y Castillo de Alicante* (1891).

AL-IDRISI Arab *geographer and traveller (end of 11th-second half of 12th century). Born at Ceuta of Spanish-Arab parents, he studied in Morocco and Andalusia and then travelled through the Moslem and Christian worlds, from England to the Middle East. Settling in the middle of the 12th century in Palermo, at the court of *Roger II, he wrote his *Geography*, which is a description of Christian and Moslem countries, with an emphasis on human and economic aspects.

ALIENOR OF AQUITAINE See ELEANOR.

ALLEGORY Medieval civilization inherited the Greek way of expressing ideas by images and developed it. Thus, the allegorical form was used in literature and poetry, philosophy, history, theology and exegesis. A. was formally adopted by *scholasticism as one of the four ways of interpreting biblical texts. "The Song of Songs" for example was interpreted as an allegorical expression of the love between Christ and the faithful, represented collectively by the Church. The exegetical influence was manifested from the 12th century even in secular literature, such as the *Roman de la Rose*.

M. D. Chénu, *La Théologie au XIIe siècle* (1957).

ALLODIUM In *feudal terminology, "outright ownership of land". Its ancient Germanic meaning was "without charges". The term came into use in the 10th century, when the political structures of the states were dissolved and the feudal lords undertook political and judicial responsibilities. In parts of Carolingian Europe some peasants and landowners managed to avoid swearing *homage to the lords and, in the absence of a royal administration, they were free of feudal obligations and taxes. The general trend in the 10th-12th centuries was to force the free peasants into the feudal system, even if it meant according them certain rights, particularly in taxation and the judiciary, such as the

right to testify in court. The A. system survived only in the farthest corners of feudal Europe. In England it was abolished after the *Norman Conquest (1066).

F. L. Ganshof, *Feudalism* (1965).

ALL SAINTS DAY A Catholic feast in honour of all the saints. With the multiplication of saints in the 6th century, the devotion of the faithful began to be expressed in different ways to various saints. To unify the cult, Pope *Boniface IV introduced in 609 a prayer to all martyrs and saints. The date of the feast was fixed by *Gregory III as 1 November, the day on which, in 740, a chapel in the Basilica of St. Peter's was consecrated to all the saints who had no particular chapels or altars.

H. Delehaye, *Sanctus* (1928).

ALMAGEST The Arabic name of Claudius *Ptolemy's treatise on astronomy, written in the 2nd century at Alexandria. The treatise was translated into Arabic in the 9th century and was the basis of the *astronomical knowledge in medieval times. It reached Christian western Europe through Spain, where it was used by Arabs and Jews and served also for the study of geometry and trigonometry. *Abraham Bar-Hiyya used it in his scientifical works and *Adelard of Bath introduced it into the schools of Paris and Chartres. The A. was very popular in scientific circles until the end of the Middle Ages. In the 12th-13th centuries it was considered as absolutely authoritative and, in the translation of Gerard of Cremona (1175), it was accepted north of the Alps as the normative astronomy.

R. Catesby Taliaferro, *Ptolemy; the Almagest* (1952).

AL-MANSUR (714-75) The second *Abbasid caliph (754-75). He suppressed the rebellions against the Abbasid authority (762) and sent his generals to the eastern borders of the caliphate to spread Islam. The land of Tabaristan (near the Caspian Sea) and the provinces of Afghanistan and Kashmir were conquered and annexed to the caliphate; but he lost Spain to *Abd-al-Rahman (756). He founded Baghdad in 762 and made it his capital, introducing Persian influence at his court.

T. Nöldeke, *Caliph Mansur* (1892).

AL-MANSUR, MUHAMMAD IBN ABU AMR (d. 1002) Member of an ancient Arab family which settled in the region of *Algeciras, Spain. In the 8th century, he served at the court of the last *Ummayad caliphs in *Córdoba as administrator and counsellor, being at the same time governor of Seville. In 977 he led military expeditions against the Christians in northern Spain, and became the chief vizier (prime minister) and the all-powerful leader of the Córdoba caliphate. In 985, he conquered Barcelona and, in 987, Santiago de Compostela, whose cathedral he destroyed. He preferred not to annex the conquered principalities, but to exact tributes from the Christian rulers. His title means "the victorious".

E. Lévi-Provençal, *Histoire de l'Espagne Musulmane*, II (1950).

ALMERIA City in southeastern Spain, in the Gulf of Almeria. Under Moslem rule (713-1489) it was a commerical centre, which traded with Italy and north Africa. In 1031, after the fall of the *Ummayads, A. became an independent principality, which maintained its independence until 1288, when it was annexed to the kingdom of *Granada, as a vassal emirate, until its conquest by the Spanish army in 1489.

E. Lévi-Provençal, *Histoire de l'Espagne Musulmane*, II (1950).

ALMOHADES (Al-Muwahadin) Moslem religious movement dynasty (12th-13th centuries) in north Africa and Spain. Founded by the *Berber leader Muhammad Ibn Tumart, an Islamic reformer, the movement sought to restore the original values of the faith. While its ideology was not new, Ibn Tumart gave it coherence and popular appeal. The refusal of the *Almoravides to accept his reform led Ibn Tumart to launch his movement and declare, in 1122, a holy war against the Almoravides. His followers proclaimed him *Mahdi* (orthodox leader) and rallied to his campaign. After his death, his disciple Abd Al-Mamun continued the war and, by 1145, had conquered Morocco and all of the Maghreb. To help the petty Moslem principalities in Spain, which were threatened by the Christian *reconquista*, he invaded Spain in 1150 and established the A. rule in Andalusia. In 1172, Moslem Spain was annexed to the new empire, which pursued a policy of extreme religious fanaticism, which was resented both by those Moslems who did not accept the Almohade principles, and by religious minorities, such as the Jews, who were no longer tolerated. The massacre which the A. organized in Morocco in 1147, whose victims were not only the Almoravides, but also Moors and Jews, culminated in the confiscation of properties in favour of the *Waqf* (the Islamic religious property authority) and enforced conversions, particularly of Jews, ending the Golden Age of Arab-Jewish civilization in Andalusia. A Jewish revolt in Granada in 1165 was savagely crushed by the A. By the end of the century, the A. leader Abu Yakub Yusuf (1184-99) had defeated the Castilian and Aragonese armies, conquered Madrid and established the boundary near the Tagus River. At the beginning of the 13th century the A. began to weaken and became rather less fanatical. Their defeat by the Castilians at Las Navas de Tortosa (1212) and the territorial losses in Spain were a symptom of this weakness, which made them more dependent on the merchant class and on trade. They liberalized their religious principles and, in 1220, permitted Jewish merchants to settle in Morocco. While they succeeded in maintaining their rule in the Maghreb, they failed to do so in Spain, where the *reconquista* reached Andalusia. In 1248 the Castilians conquered Seville and the principality of *Granada, the last important stronghold of the Moslems in Spain, and became an independent kingdom and an enemy of the A. empire. By that time, the process of dissolution affected even the Maghreb, where local leaders in Morocco and Algeria revolted and in the second half of the 13th century, reduced the A. state to a small principality, which was finally eliminated in 1296, with the creation of an independent kingdom in *Morocco.
R. Millet, *Les Almohades: Histoire d'une dynastie berbère* (1923).

ALMORAVIDES (Al-Murabitun) *Berber dynasty which ruled Morocco, parts of Algeria and Moslem Spain in the 11th and 12th centuries. The dynasty originated from the Sahara's Tuareg tribes, who had accepted the Moslem teachings of the Moroccan theologian Abdallah Ben Yassin. He established in the desert fortified mosques (*ribat*), which gave the name to the movement, where he taught the Moslem religion. At the beginning of the 11th century the A. controlled the commercial routes of the Sahara, including the passage of convoys carrying gold to the Maghreb. This made the leaders of the

Maghreb dependent on them and facilitated their conquest of Morocco and Algeria, where they destroyed the remnants of the *Fatimid regime. By 1082 they had taken the Maghreb, where *Yussuf Ibn Tashfin founded the city of Marrakesh and made it his capital. The A. were strong enough at that time to raise the hopes of the Moslem princes in Spain, who had been defeated by *Alfonso VI of Castile. After the loss of Toledo (1085) they appealed to Yussuf for help and the A. moved into Spain, where they defeated Alfonso at *Silaca (1086). Yussuf did not return to Morocco but began to annex to his kingdom the various Moslem principalities of Spain. At his death (1107) the A. empire was an important power, reaching from the frontiers of *Ghana in the Sahara to the Ebro in Spain. His successors failed to maintain control of the empire and the decadence of the dynasty began in the reign of his son, Ali Ben Yussuf (1107-43). Scholars attribute the decline to the moral and religious weakening of the dynasty in the 12th century, when it was no longer able to preserve the religious austerity of its nomadic ancestors and gave in to the luxurious life of the palaces. Another important factor was that the A. had based their empire on a tiny military clan, which was unable to sustain its administration and had to accept local elements with interests of their own. The rise of the *Almohades in north Africa and the *reconquista* in Spain compelled the dynasty to fight on two fronts. The A. first collapsed in north Africa, when, with the conquest of Marrakesh by the Almohades in 1146, their African kingdom passed to the new dynasty. In 1148 they lost their last strongholds in Spain, when the Moslem principalities gained their independence.
J. Bosch Vila, *Los Almoravides* (1956).

ALP ARSLAN Nephew and successor of *Tughril Beg, Seljuk sultan (1063-72). At the death of his uncle, he was recognized as leader of the Seljuk Turks, overran *Armenia and advanced into Anatolia. He won a decisive victory over the Byzantines at *Manzikert in 1071 and took Emperor *Romanus IV prisoner. Entrusting the conquest of Anatolia to one of his cousins, A. settled at Isfahan, which he made the capital of the Seljuk empire.
EI, I.

ALPHONSE OF POITIERS (1220-71) Second son of *Louis VIII of France and of Blanche of Castile, brother of *Louis IX and one of his closest supporters. He received the county of *Poitou as an apanage, as a check against the ambitions of *Henry III of England in Aquitaine and to press the Aquitanian barons into fealty to the French crown. In 1229 he was betrothed to the heiress of the county of *Toulouse, as part of the settlement of the *Albigensian question and, in 1249, he became count of Toulouse on behalf of his wife Joan. He was also given those Aquitanian territories, like Saintonge, which passed to the kingdom of France after the conclusion of the Peace of Paris (1258). Although he was the most powerful lord in France, A. did not try to establish an autonomous power of his own and was entirely devoted to his brother and to the French royal policy. He was mainly concerned with administration, which he centralized, thus playing an important role in the decline of the *feudal system.
E. Boutaric, *Saint Louis et Alphonse de Poitiers* (1870).

ALSACE Province of Gaul, situated on the Rhine. In the 4th century it was conquered by the *Alamanni, who settled there and gave the place its Germanic character. A part of the Alamanni kingdom, it passed to the *Franks in 496 and, after the 9th century, was part of the duchy of *Swabia. Particularist feudal tendencies caused it to be broken up into a number of baronies in the 11th century. One of them bore until the middle of the 12th century the title of county, though lacking any effective power. The most important feudal unit was that of the bishops of Strassburg, subject directly to the *Holy Roman emperor. In the second half of the 12th century certain towns, particularly Strassburg, obtained the status of free cities, making them independent of the feudal lords. In the 13th century the free towns formed an alliance against feudality and created the *Decapolis* (the federation of the ten cities). In the 11th century the *Hapsburg family had inherited lands in southern Alsace and, by the 13th century, it was the most powerful barony within the province, and part of the dynasty's vast demesnes in southern Germany and Switzerland. The Hapsburg influence became predominant in the province in 1272 when *Rudolph I was elected Holy Roman emperor.

From the 12th century on, A. was one of the most important centres of German culture and art; the Gothic cathedral of Strassburg was one of the outstanding examples of architecture and art in Germany. Towards the end of the Middle Ages, feudal power declined in the province, which was divided between the Hapsburg territories, the bishopric of Strassburg, with its centre at Saverne near Strassburg, and the free cities.

F. Dollinger, ed., *Histoire d'Alsace* (1972).

ALTAR Originally the *Eucharistic table of the ancient Christian congregations, it served in the Middle Ages to designate the tables at which the priests conducted the prayers and the sacrifices. The consecration of an A. opened a church or a chapel for religious service; from the 6th century on, it was associated with the presence of a shrine of *relics. The early As. were made of wood and only gradually were stone As. introduced, to become ubiquitous in the 9th century, with the exception of the Scandinavian churches, which continued to use wood. The A. was decorated, chiefly with gold; from the 10th century on, artists and goldsmiths ornamented As., generally with sculptures and inscriptions taken from the Bible. In the Catholic Church there were often several As., a main A. and others; in the Greek-Orthodox Church there was only one.

J. Braun, *Der christliche Altar* (1924).

ALVASTRA Abbey in Sweden, founded in 1143, the first abbey of the *Cistercian Order in that country. Thanks to the influence of St. *Bernard of Clairvaux, it was taken under the protection of the royal house and became an important focus of religious and cultural life of central Sweden. In the 14th century it was the retreat of St. *Birgitta of Sweden and the place where she wrote her "Revelations".

A. Mahn, *L'Ordre Cistercien* (1953).

AMALFI City in southern Italy on the Gulf of Salerno. in the 8th century, after the decline of *Byzantine rule in Italy, A. belonged to the duchy of Naples. With the development of its maritime commerce at the beginning of the 9th century, the ties which bound it to Naples weakened. *Lombard invaders conquered it in 836, and made it an independent duchy, until 839, when the city became independent. Its fleet was strong

The medieval town and harbour of Amalfi, Italy

enough to help Pope *Leo IV in his war against Moslem invaders. In the organization of its commerce in the western and eastern Mediterranean, A. was the first city-state of Italy, before the famous republics of *Pisa and *Genoa, and competed successfully with the Venetians for the east Mediterranean routes. By the 10th century A.'s commercial activity reached to the point that the city founded colonies in north Africa, Egypt and Palestine. In 1055 Amalfian merchants bought a plot of land and a church (St. John's church, near the Holy Sepulchre) in Jerusalem and founded a hospital. It was the beginning of the famous order of the *Hospitallers. In the second half of the 11th century, A. was one of the most important city-states in Italy and its population was estimated at 70,000 inhabitants, but the number seems to be exaggerated. A. still played an important role at the beginning of the *Crusades and founded colonies at *Acre and Latakia, but also continued to develop their trade interests at Alexandria in Egypt. In 1131, *Roger II of Sicily conquered the city and annexed it to his kingdom. The Norman conquest signalled the decline of A., which was aggravated by the plague. At the end of the century, its harbour was destroyed by a storm and much of its trade was taken over by Genoa and Pisa, Naples and Palermo.

In the 11th century the Amalfian authorities promulgated a series of regulations concerning maritime commerce and navigation, the *Tabula amalphitana* (Table of A.), which was accepted as the Maritime Law by Mediterranean cities until 1570.

Moretti, *La prima republica marinara d'Italia* (1904).

AMALRIC-ARNOLD (d. 1225) Abbot of Cîteaux (1192-1209), archbishop of Narbonne (1209-25). One of the most energetic prelates of his time, he was sent in 1204 by *Innocent III as papal legate to Languedoc to organize the repression of the *Albigenses. After the murder of his colleague *Peter of Castenau, he became the religious leader of the crusade against the Albigenses (1207). At the siege of *Béziers, he ordered the massacre of all the inhabitants without exception, exhorting the crusaders, according to tradition, with the words: "Kill them all, God will choose those who were innocent". After the conquest of Narbonne in 1209, he became its archbishop, the head of the Catholic hier-

Coin of Amalric I (top). Townsman's seal (below)

archy in southern France. He continued to lead the repression of the Albigenses, but also to fight his political opponents, such as *Raymond V of Toulouse.

Z. Oldenbourg, *Massacre at Montségur* (1968).

AMALRIC (Ayméric) I (1135-74) Second son of *Fulk of Anjou and Melisande of Jerusalem, he became after the death of his elder brother *Baldwin III, king of the *Latin kingdom of Jerusalem (1163-74). In his reign the Crusader kingdom reached its zenith, but at the same time the germs of its decline appeared. He led, with the help of Byzantium, three expeditions into Egypt (1164, 1167, 1168), which ended the *Fatimid rule in that country. But this achievement did not profit the Crusaders: *Saladin, a young officer sent by *Nureddin to Egypt, seized power and saved Egypt from the Crusaders. A. sought to strengthen his kingdom by an alliance with *Byzantium, and for that purpose repudiated his wife and married the Byzantine princess Maria Comnena. He also called upon the west European knights to help his kingdom. His efforts in that respect were not fruitful and he could not prevent Nureddin from conquering Banias (1164) and Saladin, from conquering Eilat, Daron and Gaza (1170). A. was a gifted administrator, who tried to discipline the nobility and maintain the royal prerogative. As a check against the growing power of the higher nobility he instituted the *Assize of Amalric*, by which all the nobles could attend the High Court of the realm, expecting that the minor nobles would vote with the king and isolate the greater lords. The system worked during his lifetime. After his death its deficiencies became evident, when the decisions by the High Court were blocked by a large number of members, and because the low nobility voted with their lords, upon whom they were economically dependent.

J. Prawer, *The Crusaders* (1973).

AMALRIC (Ayméric) II OF LUSIGNAN King of *Jerusalem and *Cyprus (1194-1295). Scion of the lords of Lusignan in Poitou he went to the Holy Land, where he married Eschive of *Ibelin, and having distinguished himself in the battles, was in 1179 appointed constable by *Baldwin IV. In 1180 he arranged the marriage of his younger brother *Guy with the king's sister and heiress Sybil. He was taken prisoner at the Battle of *Hattin (1187) and after a while released by *Saladin. In 1194 he inherited the kingdom of Cyprus after the death of Guy, and having married Isabella of *Courtenay, was proclaimed king of Jerusalem (1197) and crowned at Acre. He reorganized his kingdoms, taking advantage of the German crusade of *Henry VI (1198) to conquer *Sidon. He was one of the instigators of the Fourth Crusade, which turned against Byzantium without helping him.

J. Prawer, *The Crusaders* (1973).

AMANDUS, St. (d. 675) The *Merovingian apostle of Flanders. Born in Nantes, he studied at Tours and led an ascetic life. In 628 he was consecrated bishop without see at the behest of *Clotaire II and began his misssionary activity in Flanders. In 633 he founded two monasteries at Ghent and later one near Tournai, of which he was abbot; the locality is called Saint-Amand.

E. de Moreau, *Saint-Amand* (1927).

AMBROSE, St. (339-97) Bishop of *Milan, one of the fathers of the Latin Christian Church. The son of the Roman prefect of Gaul, he was born at Trier, and practised Roman law; in 370 he was appointed governor of Emilia-Liguria, centred in Milan. A Christian by belief, he had not been baptized until 374, when Auxentius, Arian bishop of Milan, died. The Catholics of the city asked A. to become their bishop, which he accepted after some hesitation, and was then baptized and ordained. He devoted himself to the study of theology, and proved to be a zealous defender of orthodoxy and an excellent preacher. Thanks to Milan's central position in the Roman empire, he had close relations with the emperors, particularly *Theodosius, who recognized Christianity as the official religion of the empire (381). A. combated paganism and argued in favour of destroying the most famous pagan monument of Rome, the *Ara Victoriae*, which symbolized the traditional Roman cult. He also fought Arianism, by preaching and by letters, and defended the independence of the Church against the civil authorities. He did not hesitate to excommunicate *Theodosius, after the massacre of the Christians at Thessalonica. His most important work, *De officiis ministrorum* (The Tasks of the Ministers), deals with the ethics of the priests, based on the ideas of Cicero. He also wrote on ascetics and composed liturgical treatises and hymns, adapting prayers from Greek for use in the Latin Church. His influence was felt in all the western provinces of the Roman empire and even in some of the eastern ones. He is considered one of the four Doctors of the Latin Church, whose works and letters remained authoritative throughout the Middle Ages.

Works, ed. C. Schenk, *Corpus Scriptorum Ecclesiae Latinae* (1902);

F. H. Dudden, *The Life and Time of St. Ambrose* (1935).

AMIENS City in northern France, on the river Somme in Picardy. Built by the Romans in the 1st century, its population converted to Christianity in the 4th century, and a bishopric was established there, linked to the mission of St. *Firmin. In the 9th century it was the centre of a county and of an episcopal seigneury. The counts of A. became strong feudal lords in the 11th century and maintained a careful balance between the king, the duke of Normandy and the counts of Flanders and Vermandois. At the end of the century, with the extinction of the dynasty, the county passed to the family of *Vermandois, which was related to the royal house. During the 12th century the city grew and fought for its liberties against the bishops and the counts. A first charter of liberties was granted to A. early in the 12th century, known only from its main charter of 1185. That year A. was annexed by *Philip II August to the royal demesne together with the Vermandois estates. The king granted the city, which became the provincial capital of Picardy, a charter of liberties to encourage the free development of its textile works and commerce. In 1220 the building of the famous Cathedral of A. was begun; the church was dedicated to the Virgin and its construction went on until the end of the century. The largest cathedral in France, it is one of the finest achievements of Gothic art: 143 m long and 43 m high, its tower is a soaring 109 m. It contains 3600 sculptures, most of them medieval. In 1263 *Louis IX arbitrated there between the king of England *Henry III, and the baronial opposition, led by *Simon of Montfort. His decision, known as the *Mise d' Amiens*, is an important document which defined the rights of the monarchy over the barons, in accordance with the *feudal concepts of the king of France, who believed that the power of the sovereign ensured the rights and privileges of his vassals. In 1329 *Edward III was summoned to A. to swear homage to *Philip VI, thereby recognizing the *Valois as legitimate king of France. The formal repudiation of the A. oath in 1337 signalled the beginning of the *Hundred Years' War. During the 14th century the city was ruled by the French and, in 1363, the *Estates General were assembled there to deal with the ransom of *John II and discus the administration of the kingdom by *Charles V. After the Battle of *Agincourt (1414), the city was conquered by the English, but passed in 1418 to the *Burgundians, who held it until the end of the Hundred Years' War. At the end of the 15th century, it was re-annexed to the French kingdom and was the seat of the royal bailiff of Picardy.

A. de Callonne, *Histoire de la ville d'Amiens* (1898);

AMRAM, Rabbi (d. c. 875) *Gaon (head of Jewish academy) of Sura. One of the leading scholars of Mesopotamia and world Jewry, A. became a gaon in the middle of the 9th century. His most important work was the composition of the Jewish prayer book, called in Hebrew *siddur* (order), which he compiled at the request of the Jewish community in Barcelona. His *siddur* was the basis of Jewish liturgy, which was augmented and diversified by different communities.

A. Marx, *Untersuchungen zum Siddur des Gaon R. Amram* (1908).

ANACLETUS II (Pietro Pietroleone, c. 1090-1138) Antipope (1030-38). He was the grandson of Leone, a Jewish moneylender of Rome, who converted to the Christian faith in the middle of the 11th century and became one of the leaders of Roman aristocracy. A. was destined for the church, and after a period of studies in Italy and in France, was created cardinal in 1120. He became one of the most influential diplomats of the papal court, and was sent on difficult missions to Germany and France, where he energetically imposed papal authority. Admired by some of the clergy, he was viewed with hostility by others. In 1130, after the death of *Honorius II, the cardinals failed to agree in their election of a new pope. The majority elected A., and his rival, *Innocent II, fled to France, where he obtained the recognition of the king, *Louis VI, as well as that of the leaders of the monastic orders *Peter the Venerable, the abbot of Cluny and *Bernard of Clairvaux. Their propaganda and polemics on his behalf gained him the support of Emperor *Lothair II and of *Henry I of England. Despite the power of the coalition and his excommunication by the Council of Pisa (1134), A. remained at Rome until his death, being supported by *Roger II, whom he recognized as king of *Sicily. The polemical literature characterized A. as the "Jewish pope", accused him of seeking to seize the treasures of the Church so as to distribute them to the Jews, and even used racial slurs to denigrate him.

J. Schmale, *Studien zur Schisma des Jahres 1130* (1964).

ANAN BEN DAVID (8th century) Founder of the *Karaite sect. He was a member of the dynasty of the *exilarchs of Babylonia, and, as such, believed to be a descendant of King *David. Little is known about his early life; after he finished his studies, it seems that he was candidate for the exilarchate, but, as in other cases in the 8th century, he was defeated by his opponents who accused him of heresy, and his younger brother was elected. He refused to accept his defeat and organized his supporters into a sect, which rejected the authority of the Oral Law (the Talmud), accepting solely the Old Testament as authority. By 754 the schism was completed, A. and his partisans having been excommunicated by the majority, whom the Karaites called Rabbanites. Between 762 and 767, he wrote *Sefer Hamitzvoth* (The Book of Precepts), which became the Law of the Karaites. His partisans founded communities in Iraq, Palestine, Syria, Egypt and Byzantium.

L. Nemoy, *Anan Ben David* (1947);

Z. Ankori, *Karaites in Byzantium* (1959).

ANASTASIUS I, St. Pope (399-401). One of the outstanding priests of the Roman *Church, renowned for his personal behaviour and his efforts to establish Christian rule in Rome, where a good part of the aristocracy remained pagan. His short pontificate did not allow him to extend the influence of the Western Church. He earned the praise of St. Jerome.

L. Duchesne, *Liber Pontificalis*, I (1886).

ANASTASIUS II Pope (496-98). A Roman by birth, he was the successor of *Gelasius I. But, unlike his predecessor, he showed favour to Emperor *Anastasius I, thereby arousing the opposition of the Roman clergy to the Greek influence in Rome.

L. Duchesne, *Liber Pontificalis*, I (1886).

ANASTASIUS III Pope (911-13). Of a Roman family, he was protected by *Theophylactus, who probably appointed him pope.

L. Duchesne, *Liber Pontificalis*, I (1886).

ANASTASIUS IV (Conrad) Pope (1153-54). Member of an important Roman family, he was elected pope after the death of *Eugene III, being the chosen candidate of the different parties of cardinals. His short pontificate continued the policies of his predecessor.

J. Haller, *Das Papsttum*, III (1953).

ANASTASIUS I (430-518) Emperor of *Byzantium (491-518). The son of a simple family of Durazzo (Albania), he served *Zeno I and after his death was chosen by his widow Ariadne, as emperor. He was suspected of being *Monophysite and was compelled to take an oath of fidelity to the Orthodox faith before his coronation. The *Isaurian bodyguards of Zeno, who lost their influence, revolted in Anatolia and A. suppressed them savagely (492-96). His reign was marked by the invasions of the Slavs and Bulgars in the Balkans. Unable to stop the invasions, A. fortified Constantinople and built a new wall around the capital. At the eastern boundaries, he succeeded in quashing the Persian attempts to conquer Armenia (502-06), and preventing the invasion of Arab tribes into Palestine, for which purpose he fortified the Island of Tiran at the entrance of the Gulf of Aqaba. He maintained friendly relations with the Germanic tribes, which had conquered the Western Roman empire and obtained their recognition of his nominal authority. He also tried to spread Greek influence in Rome, which led to conflict with Pope *Gelasius I. He improved the imperial administration, forbade the selling of offices, and encouraged commerce by abolishing arbitrary taxation. At his death, the treasury was well-filled, and despite the financial burden of the wars and fortifications, the empire underwent a period of prosperity. His last years were marked by religious strife and it seems that he returned to his old *Monophysite faith.

J. M. Hussey, *The Byzantine Empire* (1963).

ANASTASIUS II (d. 721) Emperor of *Byzantium (713-16). He was the chancellor of *Philipicus (711-13) and after his deposition succeeded him. A. failed to overcome the anarchy in the empire and, in 716, was deposed by a revolt led by *Leo I the Isaurian, and entered a monastery near Thessalonica. In 720 he made an unsuccessful attempt to lead a rebellion.

J. M. Hussey, *The Byzantine Empire* (1963).

ANASTASIUS BIBLIOTHECARIUS (9th century) Scholar. A native of Rome, educated by Greek monks, he became the best Greek scholar of his age in western Europe. In 855 he was proclaimed antipope (*Benedict III) by the imperial party, but after a month he was abandoned by his supporters and returned to his studies, becoming the librarian of the papal court. In 869 he attended the 8th *Oecumenical Council at Constantinople, and translated its acts into Latin.

L. Duchesne, *Liber Pontificalis*, I (1886).

ANASTASIUS THE SINAITE (d. c. 700) Abbot of the monastery of *St. Catherine on Mount Sinai and Byzantine theologian. He was a strong defender of the Orthodox faith and opponent of the *Monophysites at Alexandria, against whom he wrote his most important treatise, the *Hodegos* (The Guide). He also wrote commentaries on biblical texts, the "Questions and Answers".

PG, vol. 89;

G. Bardy, *La littérature polémique des Questiones et Reponsiones sur l'écriture sainte: Anastase le Sinaïte* (1933).

ANATHEMA Ecclesiastical term of Greek origin, meaning *excommunication. In the Middle Ages, it was generally used in reference to a church verdict of separating the infidels from the Christian community, mainly with regard to groups of heretics, but also in the excommunication of individuals.

DTC, I (1903).

ANATOMY The science of the human body. The Middle Ages inherited the Greek and Roman concepts of A., which were related to the philosophical system of the Greek science; they were introduced to west European society in the 10th-11th centuries through Moslem and Jewish science, mainly medicine. The *Talmudic knowledge of A. was independent of the Greek philosophic system and was related to pragmatic study of medicine and surgery. This view of the human body had an important influence on the development of A. in Islam, mainly in Syria, Sicily and Spain. It is now generally believed that the study of A. in the West began in southern Italy with the establishment of the medical school at Salerno in 1030, where Jewish physicians, among them *Sabetai-Isaac Donolo, taught alongside Christians. In the 11th century the Benedictine monk Constantine the African wrote in Salerno a book on the A. of pigs, which remained for centuries the standard textbook on A. in general. In the 12th and 13th centuries A. was related to surgery and was studied by separating bones from skin. From the beginning of the 14th century, it was a separate subject in the medical schools of Bologna, Padua and Montpellier, which became the most important centres of this science. In 1315 Modino de Liucci introduced at Bologna public courses in A., based on theory and on dissection of corpses. In his book, *Anatomia* (1316), he stressed the importance of the dissection of human bodies, because of the difference between them and animals. This concept was not universally accepted and in the 14th century it was still believed by many, mainly north of the Alps, that the study of textbooks was sufficient. As for dissection, the conservative school maintained that it was enough to use animals there being no need to "desecrate" human bodies. But Liucci's theories were gradually accepted and the first dissection of a man's body took place at Vienna in 1404; the use of pigs being reserved for the study of A. only when a human corpse was unavailable.

G. W. Corner, *History of Anatomy* (1930).

ANCONA City in central *Italy, on the shores of the Adriatic Sea. After the dissolution of the Western Roman empire (476), the city remained faithful to the Roman traditions. In 539 and 551 it resisted successfully the *Ostrogoths' attempts to conquer it, and became part of the Italian province reconquered by *Justinian. To the end of the 6th century, when the *Lombards conquered Italy, the city succeeded in remaining within the Byzantine empire, linked to Constantinople by its naval trade. A Moslem invasion in 848 destroyed the city but, during the second half of the 9th century, it was rebuilt and became a republic within the *Papal States. A., like Venice, developed its commerce with the East. The Jewish community of A., established in the 10th century, played an active part in this commerce,

The Romanesque cathedral of Angoulême, France, built in the 12th century

which brought prosperity to the city. A.'s fleet took part in the First *Crusade, transporting crusaders to the Orient. In the struggle between *Frederick Barbarossa and *Alexander III, the city supported the papacy and, in 1174, was besieged by the imperial army, but did not succumb. The emergence of the *Venetian empire in the 13th century, and the establishment of the *Latin empire of Constantinople, weakened A., by depriving it of much of its oriental trade. In 1355 the city was annexed to the Papal States, but still enjoyed a certain autonomy, which came to an end only in the 16th century. In the 11th-12th centuries, A. was also an artistic centre, where a particular style of architecture, combining *Romanesque and *Byzantine influences was developed, notably expressed in the structure and decoration of the Church of St. Cyriac.

G. Fasoli, *Dalla "civitas" al commune nell'Italia setten-trionale* (1969).

ANDALO, BRANCALEONE DEGLI (d. 1258) Italian soldier, member of an aristocratic family of Bologna, he took advantage of the struggle between *Frederick II and the papacy to recruit an army of his own, and became involved in Roman affairs. In 1252, he became the "captain of the people" and was elected senator, the first non-Roman to win this position, which put him in control of Rome. He fought against the power of the cardinals and destroyed their towers in the city. Pope *Alexander IV was forced to reside at Viterbo, while A. imposed an authoritarian regime at Rome. He was killed in 1258, at the siege of Corneto.

E. Dupré-Theseider, *Roma dal Commune di Popolo alla signoria pontificia* (1952).

ANDALUSIA Province of southern Spain, between the mountains of Sierra Morena and the Mediterranean. From ancient times it was one of the most developed and richest parts of Spain and of the Western Roman empire. At the beginning of the 5th century it was conquered by the *Vandals, who gave it its name. In 554 it was reconquered by *Justinian and annexed to the Byzantine empire, becoming an important cultural centre, which flourished even after its conquest by the *Visigoths. This flowering reached its peak, in the 7th century, at the time of *Isidore of Seville. In 711 the country was conquered by the Arabs, who established their Spanish capital at *Córdoba. Between the 9th and the 11th century A. was the heart of the Moslem and Jewish cultural heydey, known as the "Golden Age of Andalusia", which was so marked that Arabic sources refer to Moslem Spain as Al-Andalus. After the fall of the *Ummayad caliphate of Córdoba (1034), A. was divided into Moslem principalities, of which that of the *Abbadids was the most powerful. At the end of the 11th century it was conquered by the *Almoravides, and became the most important part of their Spanish-African empire. In 1150 it fell to the *Almohades and under their rule began the cultural decline of the province. In the 13th century the Almohades weakened and the province was split into independent Moslem principalities, and an important part of it was taken by *Castile, which established its rule in the valley of the Guadalquivir and annexed successively the most important cities, like Seville and Córdoba. Nevertheless, the Moslems maintained their rule in the southern part of the province, and founded the kingdom of *Granada (1258) which was their last stronghold in Spain until 1492,

when it too was conquered by Isabella and Ferdinand of Aragon and Castile.

W. M. Watt, *The History of Islamic Spain* (1965).

ANDORRA Peasant community in the Pyrénées. The origins of the community are unknown; from the 9th century it is mentioned as being an autonomous commonwealth of shepherds. It seems that its isolated position in the mountains created the conditions of autonomy, there being no feudal lord in the region interested in annexing it to his estates. The local priest was ordained by the *Catalonian bishop of Urgel. Following the feudalization of southern France, the counts of *Foix in the middle of the 13th century laid claim to A., but were contested by the bishops of Urgel, who asserted their spiritual rights. In 1278 a compromise was signed, which is still valid: the count of Foix and the bishop of Urgel were to be the joint suzerains of the community, which was granted the right to have its own council, elected by the six villages. The council elected officers, who had to be presented to the lords before taking office. Justice was administered alternatively by judges appointed by the count and the bishop, the latter having jurisdiction only in spiritual matters.

B. Neuman, *Andorra, Past and Present* (1931).

ANDREA PISANO (1295-1349) Sculptor and architect. Born at Pontedera, near Pisa, he settled at Pisa, from which his surname derives. His main creation was the renovation of the Baptistery of Florence, which marked the beginning of Renaissance art in Italy. His work was inspired by *Dante.

E. W. Anthony, *Early Florentine Architecture and Decoration* (1927).

ANDREAS CAPELLANUS Latin writer of the 12th century. He was probably born in France, but nothing is known about his origins, family and education, before his arrival in 1170 at the court of the counts of *Champagne, where he served as one of the chaplains of Countess Mary at Troyes. His signature on several documents of the court shows that he was still holding this position in 1186, after which there is no mention of him, nor any information about his death and place of burial. A. wrote *De arte honeste amandi* (The Art of Honest Love), which is a treatise on the art of courtly love, reflecting the life and manners of the knightly society in France in the second part of the 12th century. The work is influenced by Ovid's *Ars amatoria* (The Art of Love), but also by the Moslem-Spanish poetry on this subject. Nevertheless, his approach is original: he chose the form of a scholastic learned treatise, examining the attitude of different social classes to love, seen as a pattern of civilization and corresponding to the hierarchical views of the society of his time. Opposed to the erotic and carnal manifestations of love, the work served as a model for the *courts of love in the late 12th and 13th centuries.

J. J. Parry, *The Art of Courtly Love by Andreas Capella-nus* (1941).

ANDREI BOGOLUBSKI (1110-74) Prince of *Suzdal (1157-74). Son of *Yuri Dolgoruki, he continued his father's policy of challenging the authority of the princes of *Kiev over the Russian princes and, after the conquest and sack of Kiev (1169), he proclaimed himself "Great Prince". However, he refused to move, as required by tradition, to the ancient capital, and reigned at Vladimir, the capital city of Suzdal. This decision was

Mayan art: detail of a temple

The doors of S. Giovanni Baptistery at Florence by Andrea Pisano

to have consequences later: when Kiev and southern Russia were conquered by the *Mongols in 1240, *Vladimir, which was situated north of the routes that concerned the conquerors, remained independent and served as a basis for the emergence of a new Russia and of resistance to Mongol rule. A. established his capital with churches and monuments, some of which still exist. He endeavoured to establish new villages and estates in his principality, and develop its agriculture. His wars against the *Bulgars on the Volga led to the fall of this ancient principality and opened it to Russian colonization. He attempted to reduce the power of the feudal lords and impose his authority through the creation of a new aristocracy, with the result that in 1174, he was murdered during a revolt in which some members of his court participated.

G. Vernadsky, *Kievan Russia* (1948).

ANDREW, St. According to the Gospels, he was the brother of St. Peter, a fisherman on the Lake of Gennesaret and one of the Twelve Apostles. The cult of A. was very popular in the Middle Ages and many congregations made him their patron saint. The most important of these was the 13th-century brotherhood of A. in *Acre. It took its name from the assembly of the Crusading nobility in A.'s church in 1234, which met to oppose the attempts of Filangieri, the governor sent by *Frederick II to administer the Crusaders' kingdom, to curtail their privileges and liberties. The brotherhood, led by the *Ibelin family, espoused the idea of an oligarchical republic, whose monarch was merely the "chief lord of the kingdom", subject to the authority of the *Haute Cour*, of the entire nobility of the kingdom. The brotherhood's army fought against the imperial authority, and in the resulting anarchy the kingdom was unable to defend itself against the *Khwarizmians (1244). Its success in the struggle against Filangieri and Frederick II, was thus balanced by the disaster of Forbie, where the Crusaders were defeated by the Khwarizmians.

In the 14th century a knightly order of A. was created to mobilize knights to fight against the infidels, but it became merely another knightly society, distinguishing its members for their courage. The order adopted as its symbol the "Cross of St. Andrew", in form of "X", for the Greek initial letter of Christ.

DHGE, I;

J. Prawer, *The Crusaders* (1973).

ANDREW I King of Hungary (1047-61). Of the royal family of St. *Stephen. He succeeded to the throne after a period of unrest caused by German and Venetian interference in Hungarian affairs and a pagan uprising in 1046. He re-established the power of the monarchy, and beat back the Germans, regaining Hungarian independence. He married Anastasia, daughter of *Yaroslav of Kiev for the sake of the Kievan alliance. At the end of his reign he had to face the revolt of his brother *Bela, and sought a German alliance. He was murdered by Bela's partisans.

F. A. Eckhart, *A History of the Hungarian People* (1931).

ANDREW II (1175-1235) King of Hungary (1205-35). He favoured German colonization, as a measure of developing commerce and populating the kingdom. This brought him into conflict with the nobility, which revolted in 1213, while he was at war with the Russian principality of Galicia, and his German wife Gertrud was

murdered. In 1217 he led a Hungarian Crusade and with his knights reached Beth-Shean, but an *Ayyubid counter-attack surprised him and the Hungarian Crusaders were dispersed. His failure in Palestine was resented in Hungary, where the nobility compelled him to accord them extensive privileges, proclaimed in the *Golden Bull (*bulla aurea*) of 1220, which was the basis of the freedoms of the Hungarian nobility.

F. A. Eckhart, *A History of the Hungarian People* (1931).

ANDRONICUS I (Comnenus; 1122-85) Emperor of *Byzantium (1183-85). He was the cousin of *Manuel I and in 1180, after an aristocratic plot, he became co-emperor with the young *Alexius II. He instigated the murder of Alexius and became sole emperor. He tried to improve the administration and to reduce the expenditures of the court. He also tried to curtail the power of the aristocracy, which had grown during the 11th-12th centuries. He was murdered during an uprising at Constantinople.

F. Chalandon, *Les Comnènes*, II (1913).

ANDRONICUS II, Palaeologus (1260-1332) Emperor of *Byzantium (1282-1328). Son of *Michael VIII, he was opposed to the attempts to unify the Byzantine and Catholic churches, and restored Greek Orthodoxy at Constantinople. While primarily interested in religious affairs, he had to face the *Ottoman threat and to do so resorted to western mercenaries, who had interests of their own and weakened the empire. In 1295 he brought his elder son *Michael IX to share the government of the empire. When Michael died in 1320, his grandson *Andronicus III was appointed co-emperor and succeeded in blocking the western threat to the imperial authority. In 1325 plots at court created a conflict between A. and his grandson and, in 1328, the old emperor was deposed and sent to a monastery for his last years.

J. M. Hussey, *CMedH*, IV (2nd ed., 1965).

ANDRONICUS III, Palaeologus (1295-1341) Emperor of *Byzantium (1328-41). While still as the heir of *Andronicus II, he tried to restore imperial authority and managed to impose it on the western mercenaries and to conquer Chios and Lesbos from Genoa; but he failed to impose it on the *Serbs and *Ottomans. He was supported in his conflict with his grandfather by the aristocratic family of Cantacuzenus, whose influence became predominant during his reign. He spent his last years in brilliant courtly life, while the real power passed to *John Cantacuzenus.

J. M. Hussey, *CMedH*, IV (2nd ed., 1965).

ANDRONICUS IV, Palaeologus (1348-85) Emperor of Byzantium (1376-79). Son of *John V, whose reign was a time of anarchy, he rose against his father, deposed him and ruled with the backing of Genoa. In 1379 he was overthrown by John V supported by the Turks.

J. M. Hussey, *CMedH*, IV (2nd ed., 1965).

ANGERS City in northwestern France, capital of *Anjou. The medieval town was an extension of the ancient Gallo-Roman city. In the 9th century it was sacked by the *Normans and then rebuilt and fortified by the counts of Anjou, who made it the centre of their powerful county in the 10th-12th centuries. The castle, which was entirely rebuilt after the annexation of the city by the French monarchy (1206), was completed in 1238. The rebuilt *Gothic cathedral is in the so-called Angevin style.

The 12th-century castle at Angers. Some of the buildings are of the 15th century

A panel from the famous Angers Apocalypse *tapestry; 14th century*

C. Urseau, *Les monuments anciens d'Angers*, 7th ed. (1934).

ANGEVINS Technically, the inhabitants of *Anjou. The term was used from the 12th century to describe the different dynasties of Anjou, such as that of *Fulk of Anjou in the *Latin kingdom of Jerusalem, the kings of England from *Henry II to *Richard III (commonly named "Plantagenet"), and the kings of Sicily and Naples in the 13th-15th centuries. It also denoted the partisans of the dukes of Anjou in the 14th-15th-century France.

ANGILRAM (d. 791) Bishop of *Metz (776-91). Archchaplain to *Charlemagne. Member of a Frankish family of *Austrasia, he was one of the followers of Charlemagne and, as bishop of Metz, participated in the political life of the kingdom. Appointed archchaplain after the death of *Fulrad of St. Denis, he became one of the closest aides of the kings of the Franks with an important position in the kingdom. A. was one of the most learned persons at the court and contributed to the intellectual movement known as the *Carolingian Renaissance.

J. Boussard, *The Civilization of Charlemagne* (1971).

ANGLES Germanic tribe, originally from Schleswig (today Denmark and Germany). In the 5th century they, together with the *Saxons, invaded Britain and settled in the southeast. One of the *Anglo-Saxon kingdoms was a settlement mainly of the A. and perpetuated their name (East Anglia), but there is no real distinction between them and the Saxons.

ANGLO-SAXON CHRONICLE An historical compilation, made at Peterborough Abbey from the 9th to the 12th century in the Anglo-Saxon language, which became the national historical work of that people. It is an important source for the history of the Anglo-Saxon kingdoms until the Norman conquest of England, including the reaction of the populace to the conquest.

B. Thorpe, ed. (1861) (Rolls Series, 2 vols. Text and Translation);

G. N. Garmonsway, *The Anglo-Saxon Chronicle* (1960).

ANGLO-SAXONS The common name of the Germanic tribes of the *Angles, *Saxons and *Jutes, originating from Jutland and northern Germany. They invaded Britain in the 5th century, conquered most of the island from the Celtic *Britons, founded seven kingdoms (the *Heptarchy) and gave the country the name England. The most important of these kingdoms – which were not strong enough to exist as independent states – were *Wessex, *Mercia and *Northumbria. During the 9th century most of them were conquered by the Danes, who established a Scandinavian kingdom (the *Danelaw). Only Wessex, under *Alfred the Great, continued to be independent and absorbed the remnants of the Anglo-Saxon kingdoms. At the beginning of the 11th century Wessex was attacked by the Danes and in 1015 was incorporated in the empire of *Canute the Great. In 1042 it recovered its independence under *Edward the Confessor, who united A. England under his rule. His reign was marked by the introduction of Norman influence, as well as by the increasing power of the nobles, led by *Godwin, who became earl of Wessex. After the death of Edward a dynastic crisis led to the Norman invasion of 1066, under *William the Conqueror, who conquered England and abolished the A. state.

The A. in England were peasants. Their communities were called the *hundreds, from the groups of a hundred fighters, which had settled with their families in the areas assigned to them. The hundred became a territorial and social entity, with its own autonomous government, justice and finance, subject to the royal *sheriff. Besides the free peasants, the A. village also contained serfs, who worked in the manors and lands of the "thanes" (nobles) and of the lords. During the 9th century the tribal organization of the society was replaced by a pre-feudal system of peasantry dependent on the lords. However, unlike the Continent, most of the peasantry remained free until the Norman Conquest. Christianity, introduced in the 7th century, made a major impact on A. society and gave it a learned character, so that in the 8th century it influenced the Continent.

The A. language is part of the old Low-German linguistic group, which emerged as a cultural language in the 7th century, blending together the tribal dialects, with a small infusion of the local Celtic language. From the 7th century on, a number of Latin terms, particularly ecclesiastical ones, penetrated into the A. language, as well as some Greek and Hebraic biblical words. By the 12th century, the language sustained a well-developed culture, with its own literature and poetry, a wealth of official writing, such as laws, charters and jurisprudence, as well as chronicles and annals. Lay literacy was far more developed than in other European countries of the time, as the vernacular language was used in writing, Latin being confined to theological and clerical works, which interested only the ecclesiastical society. The Norman Conquest was a serious blow to the A. language, reducing it to the lowest class of society.

F. M. Stenton, *Anglo-Saxon England* (1962).

ANGOULÊME City in western France, in the duchy of *Aquitaine. In the 3rd century it became an episcopal city. In the 9th century it was devastated by the Normans and rebuilt in 868 as the centre of the new county of A. Being the highway between Poitiers and Bordeaux, and thus along the route of *Santiago de Compostela pilgrims, the city prospered in the 11th and 12th centuries. Its cathedral, built in a particular Romanesque style, is one of the most beautiful monuments of that period. The cathedral school was one of the main centres of learning in western France, containing one of the richest libraries of ecclesiastic and classical Latin works. The palace of the counts, situated in the centre of A., was rebuilt in the 13th century. Parts of it are incorporated in the modern town hall. In the middle of the 13th century the city was granted communal privileges. The county of A. was created in the 9th century as a feudal entity, a vassal of the duchy of Aquitaine. While recognizing the suzerainty of the dukes, the counts of A. managed to maintain a large degree of independence by political and familial alliances with other feudal lords in the vicinity. At the end of the 12th century Isabella, the heiress of the county, was betrothed to *Hugh of Lusignan, count of La Marche, who intended to establish a great feudal principality in the west-centre of France. But *John Lackland, king of England and duke of Aquitaine, prevented it by marrying her in 1200. Lusignan's complaint to the court of *Philip II of France led to a sentence disinheriting John of his French fiefs, thus reopening the war between the kings of France and

England. After John's death Isabella returned to A. and married Hugh of Lusignan in 1216. The new principality remained part of the duchy of Guyenne (Aquitaine) and resisted the French attempts on it. In 1258 it became a vassal of *Alphonse of Poitiers' estates, and after the extinction of the house of La Marche in 1302 was annexed to the royal demesne, and was given as apanage to princes of the dynasty. In 1360 the county passed to the English and remained under their rule until 1373, when it was reconquered by the French.

L. Mirot, *Manuel de géographie historique de la France* (1935).

ANJOU County in western France, on the banks of the Loire. The county was created in the 9th century, at the time of the *Norman invasions. In 861 *Charles the Bald gave it to *Robert the Strong, count of Tours, who halted the Scandinavian invasion in the Loire Valley. Robert installed in A. one of his vassals, *Fulk, who founded the first Angevin dynasty. His successors preserved the integrity of the county, which became in the 11th century one of the most powerful feudal principalities in France. In 1054 *Tours was annexed to Anjou and the counts controlled the route from northern France and Spain, which gave them a large income, and with the development of the trade the county became prosperous. The Angevin coinage, minted at Tours, was one the best currencies in western Europe. At the beginning of the 12th century the county of Maine (north of Anjou) was annexed to A., which led to conflict with the dukes of Normandy. Under the rule of *Fulk V (1109-26), the administration was improved and the count's control of the vassals was made more efficient, there being few great vassals in the county. New castles were built in strategic places and Fulk became an important personage, whose alliance was sought by both kings of France and England. In 1125 he concluded an alliance with *Henry I of England, which put an end to their rivalry over Maine and had an important consequence in medieval history: his son, *Geoffrey Plantagenet, married Henry's daughter *Matilda, widow of Emperor *Henry V, and the only living child of the king of England. Fulk gave the rule of Anjou to his son, as part of the agreement, and left Europe for the *Latin kingdom of Jerusalem, where he married *Melisande, daughter of *Baldwin II and heiress of Jerusalem, becoming in 1130 king of Jerusalem. Geoffrey Plantagenet was involved in the struggle for the heritage of Henry I and, in 1151, conquered Normandy on behalf of his wife and son, *Henry II. At his death in the same year, the county of Anjou ceased to be the centre of the estates of the dynasty, although it remained one of the central pivots of the "Angevin empire" created by Henry II, who, in 1152, married *Eleanor of Aquitaine and in 1154 became king of England. The social and administrative structure of the county of A., as established by Fulk V, assured the function of its government even in the absence of the count. In 1206 A. was conquered by *Philip II, king of France, who disinherited *John Lackland, and was annexed to the royal demesne. Nevertheless, its institutions continued to function as before, and the county was governed on behalf of the king of France by a royal seneschal. From the middle of the 13th century, it was an apanage given to the younger brothers of the king. Thus in 1246 *Louis IX gave it to his brother *Charles,

who founded the second dynasty of A. In 1268 Charles of A. became king of Sicily and his heirs reigned in *Naples until the end of the Middle Ages. The county itself was given as a dowry to Charles' granddaughter Margaret, when she married *Charles of Valois. In 1328, at the accession of Charles' son, *Philip VI, to the throne of France, A. returned to the royal demesne. In 1360 *John the Good made A. a duchy and gave it to his second son, *Louis (I of Anjou), who founded the third dynasty, which became related to the Angevin kings of Naples.

J. Boussard, "L'Anjou" in R. Fawtier (ed.), *Histoire des Institutions françaises au Moyen Age*, I (1957);
P. S. Lewis, *Later Medieval France* (1968).

ANNA COMNENA (1083-1148) *Byzantine empress, daughter of *Alexius I Comnenus and wife of Emperor *Nicephorus Briennios. When her husband failed to govern the empire, A. became a nun and began to write history. Her book, the *Alexiad*, deals with the history of her father's reign and is one of the most important sources for Byzantine history of the end of the 11th and beginning of the 12th century. It is of special importance in the historiography of the *Crusades, as it gives the Byzantine reaction to the First Crusade and to the establishment of the *Latin kingdom of Jerusalem. It is one of the best historical works by Byzantine historians, written by a talented woman with a good literary education as well as a perfect knowledge of Byzantine society and government.

Works, ed. B. Leib, 3 vols. (1937-45);
G. Buckler, *Anna Comnena* (1929).

ANNALS Historical writing in western Europe, in use from the early Middle Ages until the end of the 12th century. The A. are a short account of the main events of the year, as viewed by the writer, without entering into details or explaining motives. Most A. were written in monasteries and to a lesser extent in cathedral churches. Generally written by several persons in the course of many years, and not by one author, they lack a coherent conception of historical evolution. Nevertheless, they provide a good picture of the events, mostly of local interest, as seen by their contemporaries. Among the most important A., are the *Annales Regni Francorum* (The Frankish Royal A.), which give the official view of the *Carolingian court of the events from 741 to 829, covering the reigns of *Pepin the Short and *Charlemagne, and the major part of the reign of *Louis the Pious.

M. McCormick, *Les annales du Haut Moyen Age* (1975).

ANNONA A feudal tax in medieval western Europe It originates in the obligation of serfs to feed their lords by giving them part of their farm produce, which was converted into monetary payment.

M. Bloch, *Land and Work in Medieval Europe* (1967).

ANSEGIS, St. (d. 833) Abbot of Fontenelle (France). He was one of the learned men of the reign of *Louis the Pious and, while administering his abbey, took part in the imperial court's activities. His culture and deep knowledge of laws and policy gave him great influence in the interpretation of the imperial ordinances, the *Capitularies. In 827 he prepared a collection of capitularies, covering the reigns of *Charlemagne and Louis the Pious, which became an authoritative text of Frankish legislation. He was also a popular architect of religious buildings, and thus one of the leading figures of *Carolingian art. His masterpiece, the Abbey of Fontenelle, no longer exists.

J. Boussard, *The Civilization of Charlemagne* (1968).

ANSELM OF CANTERBURY, St. (1033-1109) Archbishop of Canterbury (1093-1109). Born at Aosta in Savoy, he went to France and, in 1059, entered the monastic school of *Bec in Normandy, headed by *Lanfranc, whose disciple he was. In 1063 he succeeded Lanfranc as prior. His strong personality and intellectual abilities gained him a great reputation as a teacher. He was one of the greatest philosophers of his age, who sought to provide a rational explanation of the faith, based on the dialectical method of inquiry. In 1078 he became abbot of Bec. He succeeded in gaining the confidence of *William the Conqueror, as well as of the Anglo-Norman nobility and the clergy. When Lanfranc died in 1089, A. was chosen to succeed him as archbishop of Canterbury, but refused to give up his spiritual independence. *William II Rufus refused to approve the election and A. was installed only in 1093; the king, being gravely ill, accepted him. Soon after William's recovery a long conflict began between them and the king, having tried in vain to force the archbishop to compromise, hoped to compel him to resign. The conflict can be described as the English version of the *Investiture contest. In 1097 A. left England and attached himself to *Urban II at Rome, where he was one of the Pope's staunchest partisans in the Investiture contest. After the death of William in 1100, he was recalled to England, but continued to stand on his principles and was soon at odds with *Henry I, and went again into exile in 1103. The more tolerant policies of *Pascal II helped to bring about a compromise, by which the king's right to consent to the election of bishops was recognized. A. returned to his see in 1107 and spent his last years in reforming the clergy. Both as theologian and philosopher, A. was one of the foremost *Scholastic thinkers and is considered as the most important figure between *Augustine and *Thomas Aquinas. He held that faith is a precondition of the use of reason: *credo ut intelligam* (I believe so as to understand), suggesting that revealed faith can be explained by reason, but only when the faith is universally accepted. He also dealt with the human form of God, attempting to explain the biblical text on Genesis (*Cur Deus homo*). Most of his writings date from his sojourn at Bec.

Works, ed. F. S. Schmitt (1946 ff.);
R. W. Southern, *St. Anselm* (1963).

ANSELM OF LAON (c. 1050-1117) Theologian. Educated at *Bec and one of the most distinguished disciples of *Anselm of Canterbury, he established a school at the cathedral of Laon, which became famous, particularly in exegesis, and attracted such students as William of Champeaux and *Abelard. His teaching consisted of commentaries of the Bible, taught in the *scholastical method and based on the combination of the literal and the allegorical interpretations of the text. Though only a book of Sentences remains from his writings, he had an important influence on the 12th-century standard commentaries of the Bible.

J. de Ghellinck, *Le Mouvement théologique au XIIe siècle* (1947).

ANSELM OF LUCCA, St. (1036-86) Bishop of Lucca (1071-86). He was the nephew of *Alexander II, who appointed him bishop. He accepted the *investiture by *Henry IV, but repented and retired to the *Cluniac abbey of Polirone. At the insistence of *Gregory VII, he returned to his see, where he disagreed with the chapter when he tried to impose rules of asceticism. Expelled from Lucca, he served as papal legate to Lombardy, where he fought against lay investiture. His main work is a famous collection of canons, which made him an outstanding ecclesiastical lawyer.

Works, *PL*, CXVIII;
R. Montanari, *La Collectio Canonum di S. Anselmo di Lucca e la Riforma gregoriana* (1941).

ANSKAR, St. (801-65) "The Apostle of the North". Native of Picardy, he became a monk at Corbie and engaged in missionary work. His activity in Schleswig was interrupted by the local pagans. He founded the first Christian church in Sweden and, in 832, became bishop of Hamburg and, in 848, the first archbishop of Bremen. In 854 he went back to Denmark and converted King Eric of Jutland, but after A.'s death the Scandinavian countries returned to paganism. It seems that he was venerated as a saint soon after his death.

E. de Moreau, *Saint Anschaire* (1930).

ANTELAMI, BENEDETTO (12th-13th centuries) Italian sculptor. A native of Parma, he was active in that city between 1178-1233. Considered the founder of the second school of Lombard sculpture, he was influenced by both the Provençal Romanesque style and *Gothic art. The combined influences can already be discerned in his early work, the *Descent of the Cross*, installed in the Parma cathedral in 1178. His finest work was in the new baptistery of Parma, begun in 1196, where he had the opportunity to create the entire sculptural element. His works are distinguished for the sense of movement in the figures, which was an innovation in his time.

A. O. Quintavalle, *Antelami sculptor* (1947).

ANTICHRIST The figure symbolizing enemies of Christ. Originating in the Epistle of St. John, the figure changed its identity through the generations. In early Christianity, Jews and Romans were referred to as A., the term designating the opponents of the faith. In the Middle Ages, it was represented as a diabolical figure, whose aim was to persecute Christianity and test Christians by ordeal. In its medieval form, it was unconsciously related to the dualist (*Manichaean) belief in the two great powers governing the world: the "Good", represented by Christ and the Church, and the "Bad", represented by the A. In the 10th century the belief was associated with the *Millenarian movement, which held that at the end of the world (i.e., the year 1000), a great world-wide war would break out between Christ and the A.; the victory of Christ, would be the signal for the ressurection of the dead. From the 11th century on the figure of A. was dissociated from actual events, and Roman emperor Nero, the first to persecute the Christians, became the prototype of the A., as the permanent foe of Christianity. Nevertheless, during the *Crusades the figure was once again concretized as an allegorical representation of the forces of Islam. With the growing criticism of the Church establishment in the 14th century, it was believed by some that the pope himself was the incarnation of A., as *Wycliffe expressed it. But the term began to be used also in political polemics. In the 15th century the *Hussites believed that the pope and the Catholic establishment were the real A., and the

Antichrist crowned by demons, bribing the faithful

good relations with the Byzantine empire. Under the rule of the Crusaders, A. was also an important centre of commerce betweeen East and West. It resisted attacks by *Nureddin and *Saladin in the second half of the 12th century. In 1268 it was conquered by the *Mamluks led by *Baibars, who exiled most of its population and destroyed the city, which thereafter declined rapidly and became a little provincial town, deprived of its commercial pre-eminence. Part of its ancient and crusader monuments still exist and are incorporated in the present-day town of Antakiya in Syria.

P. Jacqout, *Antioche* (1931);
K. M. Setton, *A General History of the Crusades*, II (1957).

ANTHONY OF EGYPT, St. (251?-356) The father of Christian asceticism. He retired from *Alexandria *c.* 285 and lived ascetically in the desert, isolated from the world. The holiness and the ordered discipline of his life attracted many disciples in Egypt and the entire Middle East, and he became the most popular religious authority on the 4th century. Anthony's solitude and asceticism made him one of the most popular saints in the Middle Ages, particularly in the Eastern Church. He was also popularly venerated in the Western Church, despite the *Benedictine rule, which did not accept individual solitary monasticism.

J. Décareaux, *Les Moines et la Civilisation* (1962).

ANTHONY OF PADUA, St. (1195-1231) *Franciscan monk. Born in Lisbon of a noble family, he was educated in Portugal and in 1220 began his missionary activity in Morocco. In 1221 he attended the Chapter General of the order at *Assisi, where he was noticed by (St.) *Francis. When his oratorical talents were discovered he was charged with preaching and teaching, and in 1222 became professor of theology at *Bologna. In 1224 he was transferred to Montpellier in France, where he remained for three years, and was then appointed provincial father of Emilia in Italy. He was later released from this post, at his own request, to devote himself to preaching. His sermons were directed against vice, usury and the exploitation of the poor. His defence of poverty as the ideal Christian life, made him the patron saint of the poor even in his own lifetime. He died in 1231 near Padua and his cult spread rapidly throughout western Europe.

R. M. Huber, *St. Anthony of Padua, Doctor of the Church Universal* (1945).

ANTWERP (Anvers) City in the Netherlands, which was annexed to the medieval county of *Flanders. There is no exact information about its origins, but the locality is already mentioned in 7th century documents. In 837 it was destroyed by the Normans, but because of its advantageous position at the estuary of the Scheldt, it was soon rebuilt. In the 11th century the town passed to the dukes of *Brabant, who protected its trade and encouraged the construction of churches, palaces and monuments, built in the *Gothic style. Its prosperity made A. a strong city, whose privileges were recognized in 1291, and it enjoyed autonomous rule. In 1315 it became one of the cities of the *Hanseatic League, rivalling *Bruges in importance. In 1337 *Edward III of England prohibited the export of English wool to Flanders, which had taken the French side at the beginning of the *Hundred Years' War, and estab-

*Taborites called on their followers to fight against the A. army.

W. Bousset, *The Antichrist* (1906).

ANTIOCH Hellenistic city in northern Syria, founded in the 4th century BC. At the beginning of the Middle Ages, A. was the capital of *Byzantine Syria and one of the foremost centres of the Christian religion, being one of the sees of the four patriarchates; and, after the establishment of a patriarchate at Jerusalem in the 5th century, one of the five sees. Its importance as a theological centre of Christianity was even greater and in the 5th and 6th centuries, most of the debates concerning the *Monophysite heresy were held in the city, whose schools were famous and second only to those of *Alexandria. The decline of A. began in the 6th century, when part of it was destroyed by earthquakes, and its commercial importance diminished. At the beginning of the 7th century it was conquered by *Chosroes, king of the Persians, and then reconquered by *Heraclius, emperor of Byzantium. In the middle of the century it became a frontier city, cut off from Syria, which was conquered by the Arabs (640). In 1084 it was conquered by the *Seljuks, who annexed it to the principality of *Aleppo. In 1098, after a siege which lasted five months, it was conquered by the *Crusaders, led by *Bohemund (Bohemond) of Taranto, who founded the Crusader principality of A. A Latin Catholic patriarch was appointed in the city and until 1268, its history was linked with the Crusades and characterized by prolonged wars with Aleppo. Its princes managed to maintain

lished a centre in A., for the distribution of English wool on the Continent. As a result A. became the most important port in Belgium and one of the biggest in western Europe. Its importance grew in the 15th century, when the Netherlands were united under the rule of of the dukes of *Burgundy, who had become the overlords in 1390. Under Burgundian rule A. was a very rich and prosperous city, and also a centre of the arts, known as Flemish art.

M. van de Velde, *Le port d'Anvers* (1930).

APANAGE Term, used mainly in France, to designate territories which were given to the younger sons of kings, assuring them estates of their own. With the decline of *feudalism in 13th-century France, the A. system began to be used in favour of the younger sons of *Louis VIII. The territory was given to the prince and his male descendants, with all the rights of government and administration of justice, and had to be surrendered to the crown with the extinction of the branch. The only restriction imposed on the holders prohibited the alienation of the A., wholly or in part, by sale or mortgage, or as a dowry. In the late Middle Ages the apanage princes possessed great power and exercised influence which often weakened royal authority and created conditions for civil wars.

L. A. Maffert, *Les apanages en France* (1900);
C. T. Wood, *The French Apanages and the Capetian Monarchy* (1966).

APULEIUS, LUCIUS (4th century) Roman botanist; he travelled widely in the western provinces of the Roman empire. His *Roman *Herbal*, a description of plants and their properties, became a model for the medieval herbals. Some of these, in the late Middle Ages, were attributed to A. and are known as "pseudo-Apuleius herbals". Until the 12th century they were used as guides in the planting of gardens in Benedictine monasteries.

A. C. Crombie, *Science in the Middle Ages* (1957).

APULIA Province in southeast *Italy. After the fall of the Western Roman empire, A. was ruled by Germanic leaders, until it was conquered by the *Ostrogoths (*c.* 500), and became a part of the realm of *Theodoric. The Ostrogothic rule was never well established in the province, which was one of the gateways for the *Byzantine attack on Italy in 535. The province was devastated during the twenty-year long war, while its links with *Constantinople were developed through the commercial relations of its ports with the capital of Byzantium. With the *Lombard conquest of Italy in 568 the northern part of A. was annexed to the Lombard duchy of *Benevento, while most of the province with the important cities, remained a Byzantine possession and the Greek influence increased. In 839 Moslem invaders appeared for the first time in A. and during the 9th century the country was fought over between them and the Byzantines, who gradually lost control of its main city, *Bari. In consequence, anarchy reigned in A., parts of it remaining under Byzantine rule through the 9th-11th centuries and parts under the Moslems. In 1017 the *Norman adventurers arrived in southern Italy and began the conquest of the province. In 1402 the county of A. became a Norman principality and its importance grew under the rule of *Robert Guiscard, who, in 1059, took the title duke of A. and made it the centre of his state, which soon included Sicily. In 1071 he conquered Bari and launched his eastern offensive against the Byzantine possessions in the Balkans. After his death (1075), the Norman state was divided and A. became an independent duchy, whose rulers took a keen interest in the *Crusades. In 1128 *Roger II of Sicily annexed the duchy and made it one of the provinces of his realm. At the beginning of the 13th century it was prospering under *Frederick II, and it became one of the most developed countries in Europe. Despite the wars in the second part of the 13th century, its prosperity continued thanks to the commercial activity of Bari. Nevertheless, it lost its political pre-eminence to *Naples and, in 1282, after the *Sicilian Vespers, followed Naples and remained under *Angevin rule until the end of the Middle Ages.

S. La Sorsa, *Storia di Puglia* (1953).

AQUITAINE French province which at its greatest extension occupied the entire territory between the Pyrénées in the south and the Loire River in the north and between the Bay of Biscay in the west and the rivers Rhine and Loire in the east. At the beginning of the 5th century the major part of the province was conquered by the *Visigoths, who established their kingdom at Toulouse. After the fall of the Western Roman empire, the remaining part of the province was annexed to the Visigothic kingdom. In 507, at Vouillé, *Clovis defeated the Visigoths and A. was conquered by the Franks, and became a province of the *Merovingian realm. However, the Frankish domination was nominal, and the southern part of the province, later known as Gascony, was autonomous. In the 8th century local dukes appeared and tried to free themselves from Frankish domination. *Pepin the Short and his sons, *Carloman and *Charlemagne, suppressed the Aquitanian revolt, and appointed Frankish counts to govern the country. In 778 Charlemagne created the kingdom of A. for his younger son, *Louis the Pious, who bore the title until he became emperor in 814. In 817 Louis gave the kingdom to his son *Pepin, who tried to reorganize and even to extend it (831). But his wars with his brother, *Charles the Bald, king of the western Franks (France), caused him to lose the southern provinces, such as Gascony and Toulouse, in 836. At his death in 838 his son, *Pepin II, inherited a weakened kingdom, in which the counts of Poitiers and Auvergne were very powerful. He was compelled to submit to the protectorship of his uncle, Charles the Bald, who abolished the royal title of A. after Pepin's abdication in 856, but was unable to establish his own authority over the new duchy. During the second half of the 9th century several feudal families struggled for the control of A., including the counts of Auvergne, Poitiers and Toulouse, and the dukes of Gascony. While the duchy of Gascony was dismantled during this conflict, the counts of Toulouse became increasingly involved in their Mediterranean policy. The new duchy was therefore reorganized on a smaller territory than the kingdom, and at the beginning of the 10th century was united under the counts of Poitiers (the dynasty of "Guillem", or *William, so called because the name was used by the family for generations). The dukes of A. succeeded in imposing their power over their vassals and created a strong feudal principality. In 1054 Gascony was annexed to the duchy. As a result, the dukes became more involved in Spanish politics and, at the same time, controlled the highway leading to *Santiago de Compostela, one of the major routes of pilgrimage in the Middle Ages and an important commercial artery. Made rich by the income from this source, the ducal court of *Poitiers was from the second half of the 11th century one of the most important centres of culture in western Europe. In addition to the scholastic institution in the city, the court was a literary centre, where the first *troubadours, led by Duke *William IX, who was a poet himself, created the first lay lyrical poems in Europe. Under William IX and his son, *William X, A. reached the peak of its development, politically and culturally. In 1137, at the death of William X, the heiress of A., *Eleanor, married the king of France *Louis VII and, until 1152, the duchy was linked with the French crown. During this period the local nobility grew stronger and a condition of anarchy began to be felt in the central part of the duchy, where several families, such as the *Lusignans, became more powerful. After Eleanor's divorce in 1152 and her marriage with *Henry II Plantagenet, A. became a part of the *Angevin empire and was governed by Henry's officers, although the ducal title continued to exist and was bestowed on Henry and Eleanor's second son, *Richard Coeur de Lion. Henry and Richard's rule over the duchy was marked by a continuing struggle against the nobility and a suppression of revolts; Richard met his death in such a revolt in 1199. Although the conflict between *John Lackland and *Philip II of France was caused by the complaint of Hugh of Lusignan against the king of England, who had married Isabel of Angoulême, A. remained faithful to its duke and by the Treaty of Chinon (1218) remained under English rule. Nevertheless, a great feudal principality was constituted within the duchy, under the Lusignan family, which at the end of the 12th and at the beginning of the 13th century incorporated parts of Poitou, La Marche and Angoulême, and played an important role in the conflict between the kings of France and England in the 13th century. During the reigns of *Louis VIII and *Louis IX, French influence grew in the northern part of the duchy, which was annexed to the crown and given as an apanage to *Alphonse of Poitiers, Louis IX's brother. The Peace of Paris in 1258, which marked the end of the feudal conflict between the two dynasties, consecrated the division of Aquitaine: its northern and eastern parts, namely Poitou and Auvergne, remained under French domination, while the southern part, including mainly Gascony and certain parts of the central A., remained under the rule of the kings of England. The new capital of the duchy, renamed Guyenne, was established in Bordeaux. At the end of the 13th and the beginning of the 14th century, conflicts between the officers of the two kings, mainly on questions of jurisdiction, intensified and became one of the causes of the *Hundred Years' War. Governed by *Edward the "Black Prince", Guyenne served as one of the bases of the English army during the war, climaxing at the Battle of Poitiers in 1358, when the French army was destroyed and King *John II was taken prisoner. The Peace of *Bretigny-Calais (1360) stipulated the unification of ancient A., but in the reign of *Charles V, the French gradually recovered their territories and, in 1383, English rule was confined to Guyenne. Moreover, certain counties in southern Gascony, such as Béarn and Albret, were annexed to the county of *Foix, which at the beginning of the 15th

century became an important principality, challenging the authority of the royal officers of France and England. Because of its internal divisions Guyenne did not actively participate in the last phases of the Hundred Years' War and the war was decided in northern France. In 1453 the French artillery played a decisive role at the Battle of Libourne, near Bordeaux, and the last vestige of English rule in Gascony came to an end, and with it the war.

Y. Renouard, "L'Aquitaine", in F. Lot and R. Fawtier, *Histoire des Institutions françaises au Moyen Age, I: Institutions seigneuriales* (1957).

ARABIA Peninsula in western Asia, bound by the Red Sea in the west, the Indian Ocean in the south, the Persian Gulf in the east and by Iraq, Syria and Palestine in the north. Most of the peninsula is a desert, inhabited from prehistorical times by Semitic nomadic tribes. From ancient times the southwestern corner of the peninsula (present-day Yemen); was its most developed part and was called in classical sources *Arabia Felix* ("Blessed Araby"). The important kingdom of Hemyar was established there, as well as other kingdoms, like Saba and Maan, which managed to resist the forces of the Hellenistic and Roman empires. Nevertheless, in the 3rd century AD these kingdoms began to disintegrate and were destroyed by *Ethiopian attacks; Christian Ethiopia tried to spread the Christian faith in southern Arabia, but without result. In the 5th century Persian influence began to be felt in the area. In northwestern A. the development of political structures was made possible by contacts with the Roman empire. From the first century BC Arab tribes left the desert and came into close contact with the countries of the Fertile Crescent. In the 4th century AD the tribes created two buffer states, the Ghasanids at the Syrian border and the Lakhmids south of Mesopotamia, to prevent attacks from the desert. The province of *Hejjaz began to develop only at the beginning of the Middle Ages. A settlement of Jewish refugees from Palestine favoured the development of trade and the growth of towns like Yatreb (Al-*Medina). One of the oldest cities in the Hejjaz, which had been a centre of a fetishist cult and the object of pilgrimages to a great stone in its midst, the Kaaba, was the city of Mecca. In the 5th century it became an important market-town, controlled by the tribe of Quraysh. Mecca's trade spread as far as Damascus and the city grew, becoming at the end of the 6th century the most important city in the Hejjaz. It was in Mecca, with its many pilgrims, that *Mohammad began to preach his new faith, *Islam, although he had not won over most of his own tribesmen, the Quraysh. Mohammad's exile to Medina in 622 (the *Hegira*) renewed the rivalry between the two major cities of the Hejjaz, which was concluded after the Battle of *Badr in favour of Medina, but mainly in favour of Islam, which, by 632, the year of Mohammad's death, had swept over all of A.

Under Mohammad's successors, the first four caliphs, A. became the core of the new faith, which spread rapidly throughout the Middle East (see *Arabs). The political and religious centres remained in the Hejjaz. Only in 661, the capital of the caliphate was moved to Damascus and A. became a mere province. Mecca and Medina continued to be the holy cities of Islam and their prosperity was assured by the *Hajj* (the pilgrimage of the faithful, prescribed by the Koran). The transfer of the political capital to Damascus unsettled the Hejjaz, where the tribes rebelled against the *Ummayad caliphs and elected an anti-caliph, Abdallah Ibn Al-Zubair (683-92), who was defeated by *Abd Al-Malik Ibn Marwan in 692. No further attempts were made to restore the caliphate in A., and the central power of the Ummayads and *Abbasids had little authority in Arabia, where the tribes continued to lead an independent existence. Two local dynasties of the *sherifs* of Mecca and Medina, descendants of Mohammad, ruled the holy cities autonomously, though formally recognizing the caliph's authority. In 960 the Meccan *sherif*, descendant of *Ali, recognized the *Shiite caliph of Egypt, but, in 1063, when the Hashemites became the *sherifs*, they turned to the *Sunnites and recognized the Abbasids. In the Yemen the Shiites succeeded in imposing their authority from the 8th century and they helped the Abbasids to overthrow the Ummayads; but with the conversion of the caliphs of Baghdad to Sunnite Islam, the division between the centre of the caliphate and the south Arabian province became more evident. In 820 the province's governor, Ziyyad, declared it independent and proclaimed himself imam of the country. Thus, while formally united under the rule of the caliphs, A. was divided until the 15th century and no central power had authority over the whole province. The situation enabled the tribe of the *Karmatians of Oman at the beginning of the 10th century to conquer most of the Yemen and create a powerful state in south A. In 930 they took Mecca and removed the holy black stone of the *Kaaba, which was restored only in 950 at the instigation of the Fatimids. Later they revolted against the Fatimids, who defeated them in 985. The last attempt in the Middle Ages to reunite A. was made by *Saladin after 1171. He succeeded in enforcing Sunnite Islam in the Hejjaz, and at the end of the 12th century, Egypt ruled the western part of the peninsula, from Aden to the Syrian border, and spread its influence over Hadramaut in the south. But after Saladin's death Yemen and Hadramaut recovered their independence, while the other parts of the country returned to a state of anarchy. Only the *Hashemite *sherifs* of Mecca continued to represent order and continuity, which lasted until 1922. This continuity was based on Mecca's position as the religious centre of Islam, and by the prestigious position in the Moslem world of the *sherifs* as guardians of the holy city.

A. S. Attiya, *The Arabs* (1955).

ARABS General name of the tribes originating from *Arabia (meaning desert), and the Near Eastern peoples, formed in the Middle Ages from the mixing of the local populations with their Arab conquerors. At the beginning of the Middle Ages most of the Arabian tribes were pagans (*jahili*), following various fetishist cults. Only at the frontiers of Arabia did religious influences penetrate from abroad, as certain Persian dualist beliefs in the east and the south, and Christianity in the north. While the Nabateans were assimilated by the Hellenist and Greek Christian civilization, the Ghaznavids adopted Nestorian Christianity in the 5th century. The appearance of *Mohammad was therefore a genuine revolution, not only in the history, but in the civilization of the A. He began in *Mecca to preach the new faith of *Islam, a strictly monotheistic belief in the almighty power of the unique

God, Allah. There he encountered the opposition of the traditionalist tribal leaders and was compelled to flee to *Medina in 622. The date of this event, the *Hegira*, is considered by the A. as the beginning of a new era, in religion, history and civilization. But in 622 Mohammad was a refugee at Medina, with a number of friends and supporters who had accompanied him from Mecca, and called him the Prophet. Only after he obtained power in Medina, and a long series of battles which lasted ten years, did Mohammad impose his religion upon the A. Consequently, war for the propagation of Islam is held to be one of the most important tenets of the faith. After the death of Mohammad, his followers elected a caliph, i.e., a vicar, as their leader; the first to be elected, in 632, was the prophet's oldest companion and father-in-law, *Abu Bakr. In 633 Abu Bakr launched the wars of religious expansion by sending Mohammad's general, *Khalid Ibn Al-Walid to the border of Iraq, where he conquered the state of the Lakhmids and the major part of the country. But the real challenge was the Byzantine army in Syria, and against it Khalid sent a second great general, *Omar Ibn Al-Aas, who defeated the Byzantines in Transjordan (634) and began the conquest of Syria. Meanwhile another Arab army penetrated southern Palestine and defeated the Byzantines near Gaza. The death of Abu Bakr in 634 and the election of *Omar Ibn Al-Khatib, who had also been a companion of the Prophet, gave the Arab expansion a new impetus. In 635, Damascus was conquered, with the complicity of the Syrian Christians, who had been persecuted as heretics by the Byzantine authorities. In 636 the A. won their greatest victory at the Battle of the *Yarmuk, near the Sea of Galilee, where the Byzantine army sent by *Heraclius was destroyed. In 638, after a short siege, Jerusalem was conquered, and Arab domination was proclaimed on Mount Moriah, which became a holy place, related with Koranic traditions. While the army led by Khalid completed the conquest of Syria and Palestine, Omar sent another army under *Saad Ibn Abu Waqqas to the Persian border, where in 637 he won a decisive victory on the Tigris, and conquered the western part of Persia. In 661 the Persian king Yzdegerd III was murdered and the Arab conquest of the kingdom was completed. Earlier in 640, Omar had sent an army commanded by Omar Ibn Al-Aas, to Egypt, and with the help of the *Copts won the richest province of the Byzantine empire; in 642 Alexandria fell, despite the numerical superiority of the defenders. All those conquests, accomplished within ten years of Mohammad's death, were achieved by relatively small forces, but, unlike their enemies, the A. were inspired by their faith and convinced that they were fighting a holy war, a *jihad*. They gained by the religious schism in the Byzantine empire between the Greek Orthodox and the Oriental Christian sects, and by the accelerated trend of conversion to Islam, mainly in Iraq, Syria and Egypt. For example, the Arab chronicles of the 8th century state that the army sent to conquer Egypt began the campaign with 4 000 soldiers and ended it with 10 000. Undoubtedly, too, an important reason for the Arab victories was the strong national feeling of the tribes united by Mohammad, and the expected material gains in the conquered territories. In effect, Omar was the founder of the Arab Moslem empire, and he organized it in his reign (634-44). Every conquered province had its military governor (emir), and a treasury official (*amal*) who was responsible for the collection of the capital and land taxes imposed on all non-Moslem subjects. At this stage there was no settlement of A. in the conquered lands, and the armies remained in garrisons, like Kuffa in Iraq and Fustat in Egypt, which only became bases of settlement a generation later. The status of non-Moslems was not yet fixed, but from Omar's time a distinction was made between the *dhimmi* (non-Moslems) of the monotheistic religion (Christians and Jews), who were tolerated as the "People of the Book" (the Bible), and the pagans, like the Persians, who were compelled to convert to Islam. After Omar's death in 644 the conquests were continued by the Arab generals, while a grave crisis around the caliphate was developing in Hejjaz. *Othman (644-56) was murdered and *Ali, who was Mohammad's son-in-law, quarelled with Othman's relatives and was murdered at Kuffa in 661. His murder opened the breach between Ali's partisans, who were called the *Shiites, and the majority, the *Sunnites; the latter were led by *Muawiyah, governor of Syria, who was proclaimed caliph in 661. Muawiyah established his capital in Damascus, thereby departing from the policy of the first four caliphs who had governed from Medina, and founded the *Ummayad dynasty (661-750). Under the Ummayads the A. settled in the conquered lands and thus began the trend of Islamization and Arabization of the caliphate. Nevertheless, the administrative structure of the states was still left to their former functionaries, while the Ummayads adopted the economic interests of their Mediterranean provinces. In the old centres of the Hellenistic-Byzantine culture, the ancient heritage began to be transmitted to the A. and its works to be translated into Arabic. The Ummayads expanded their empire in Asia, reaching the Indus River in 704; in Africa, where the Sudan and north Africa were conquered before the end of the 7th century; and in Europe, where the conquest of Spain began in 711. The Arab army reached Poitiers in France, where it was defeated in 732 by the Franks, led by *Charles Martel. Despite these successes, the Ummayads had great difficulties: in Arabia the tribes revolted, and in 683 an anti-caliph was proclaimed in Mecca and supported by the holy cities of Mecca and Medina; the *Shiites openly opposed the reigning dynasty and won support, particularly in Persia, where the forced Islamization created an opposition to Damascus. A Shiite uprising broke out in 750, proclaiming the *Abbasids as caliphs. The Ummayad family was massacred, with the exception of *Abd Al-Rahman I, who fled to Spain where he was recognized by the emirs. Under the Abbasids, who established the centre of the caliphate in *Iraq, the caliphate reached its zenith politically and culturally. At the same time (8th-9th centuries) important transformations took place in Arab society: the settlement in the fertile countries of the caliphate broke up the nomadic tribal structure of Arab society. A distinction arose between the Beduin desert tribes and the new society, which emerged as the conquered peoples, who converted to Islam and had to adopt the Arabic language, assimilated with their conquerors. The affinity of the Syrio-Aramaic language and Arabic facilitated the process, which was manifested primarily in the cities. The new society was until the 10th century mainly an urban one and new Arab cities

were founded, such as *Baghdad (Iraq), *Ramlah (Palestine), *Fustat (Egypt) or *Kairwan (Tunisia). There was also an occupational transformation, as the descendants of the warriors became, in the upper classes, government officials and landowners, and in the lower classes, tradesmen and artisans. Military service was left partly to the nomads, but largely to slaves, both Negro and Turkoman from the Asian steppes; in the western provinces, the army was composed mainly of Berbers. In the 10th century the army of the Abbasid caliphate was made up entirely of non-Arab elements, and it became the most influential factor in the empire; only the caliph's office and a number of religious functions, the *ulema*, remained Arabic. This process led to the decadence of the caliphate and to its eventual disintegration. The eastern provinces were governed by Turkish officials who, although Moslems, adopted the Persian culture, bringing about the revival of the Persian language and civilization. In north Africa the Shiite dynasty of the *Fatimids established its rule and broke with the Abbasids; the conquest of Egypt by the Fatimids in 983, put an end to Abbasid domination in Africa. In Syria Beduin tribes established their own principalities, notably in *Aleppo. Finally, at the beginning of the 11th century the caliph's real power was confined to Iraq, although he remained nominally the leader of the faithful all over the Moslem world, and formal recognition of his leadership was demanded by most of the independent rulers. With the invasion of the caliphate by the *Seljuk Turks and the conquest of Baghdad by *Tughrul Beg, the political history of the A. in the Middle Ages came to an end. The Arab caliphs retained only their religious dignity, while the political power passed to the Turks, who conquered successively Syria and Palestine and established their principalities, ruling over the A. The decline and the fall of the Fatimid caliphate of Egypt in 1171, placed even that country under the rule of a Kurdish officer, *Saladin. In the 13th century a military caste, the *Mamluks, came to power in Egypt and Syria, while Persia and Iraq fell to the *Mongols. Nevertheless, the process of Islamization and Arabization of the Middle East continued and permeated to the remotest rural areas. However, with the political downfall of the A. began their cultural decline.

Arab civilization was based on the religious roots of *Islam; the unity of the faith determined the unity of language and culture. The Arabic language belongs to the Semitic group and developed in the Middle Ages from the north Arabic dialect which was spoken in the Hejjaz, the language of Mohammad and of the Koran. With the great conquests of the 7th century and the spread of Islam, it was diffused to all parts of the A. empire, but the presence of pre-Islamic languages, as well as the assimilation of the conquered peoples, led to the development of local dialects, which differed from the classical written Arabic of the official version of the Koran, compiled in Othman's times (644-56). The study of the classical language was emphasized for religious reasons, although the spoken dialects diverged greatly from it. To preserve its purity Arab grammarians brought their discipline to a level that made it one of the main achievements of the Arabic culture. The growth of Moslem theology, the *Hadith*, from the 8th century on, and the desire to conserve the unity of the faith and its interpretation, helped create a cultural Arabic which, unlike the classical, became an analytic language, wherein each word has a single meaning. This linguistic development was also enhanced by the translation of Greek philosophical and scientifical works, as well as from Aramaic and Persian. These translations, in the 8th and 9th centuries, introduced the influence of the Greek philosophical system of the sentence, and contributed to the enrichment of the grammar. By the 9th century cultural Arabic was brought to such a degree of perfection that it became a creative language not only in philosophy, science and theology, but also in lay literature and poetry. The Abbasid period was a literary flowering – court poets wrote verses in praise of the virtues and deeds of the lords who engaged them. Compendia of such poems, known as *diwans* (from *diwan* – office, where receptions were given), also contain poems praising the nature and beauty of the lord's wives and daughters, viewed as his possessions, as well as love poetry. Scholars nowadays agree that the love poems of A. that circulated in Moslem Spain in the 10th-11th centuries, served as a model for Christian poets and influenced the development of lyrical and *troubadour poetry in western Europe, mainly Spain and France. By contrast the Ummayad period had left only theological writings and political poetry, which had continued the pagan poetical tradition, and differ in their structure from the *diwans*. The difference between the two literary ages expresses better than many treatises the transformation of Arab society from a nomadic and military one, as it had been in the Ummayad period, to the urban civil society of the Abbasids. The later culture was vividly portrayed in the most famous literary work of the Abbasid period, *The Tales of A Thousand and One Nights*, which is a good example of the development of Arabic prose, written after it was narrated to listeners. The style reflects a strong Persian influence, but through the ages it also assimilated other tribal traditions, such as those of the Berbers of north Africa.

Historical literature was one of the most advanced genres of Arabic literature in the Middle Ages. It began in 8th-century Egypt and was influenced by Byzantine historiography, which narrated the deeds of the heroes, but also sought to explain them, thereby acquiring a certain didactic character, associated with the propagation of religion. Arab historiography was the first one to attempt a methodical division of history into periods; the Hegira (622) was chosen as the turning-point between two ages: the pre-Islamic, i.e., the pagan era, which was considered ancient history, dealing with all civilizations; and the post-Hegira, i.e., the Islamic era, considered as the modern age. This division, based principally on the religious factor, imposed on Arab historians a particular attitude towards the events they related and interpreted, a view of the world as made up of Moslem and anti-Moslem units; no neutrality was allowed and evidence, which in certain cases is found only in the Arab histories, has to be seen by modern research in the light of that basic attitude. An important stage in Arabic historiography was the time of Saladin, the hero of all Islam, who was a Kurd. His biographers and the historians of his times, who were influenced by the great work of Al-*Tabari (d. 923), the first to write a general history of the caliphs, enlarged the scope and included all Moslems (even non-A.) in the historiography,

as well as excerpts from older historians. The greatest medieval historian who wrote in Arabic was *Ibn Al-Athir, who adopted the chronological method, dividing the work into a history of events, biographies of personalities and other phenomena, such as plagues. From the 14th century on Arab historiography produced also local and regional histories, the best-known of which being *Makrizi's *History of the Sovereigns of Egypt in the 15th century*.

Geography and travel literature was also a notable achievement of Arabic literature and science in the Middle Ages. Based on the heritage of Hellenistic geography, particularly on Ptolemy of Alexandria, Arab geography from the 9th century on described the world, introducing data from the writer's own travels and observations. Their descriptions included physical geography, human habitations, political divisions of countries and continents, as well as famous buildings, local traditions and economic resources. The most important Arab geographer, *Al-Idrisi, lived in the 12th century at the Norman court of Sicily. The A. also continued the Hellenistic tradition of cartography, and until the 14th century this field was entirely dominated by them; they specialized mainly in the Portolan maps, which gave the contours of coastlines and the location of harbours, and were an important instrument in navigation. The cartographers used their knowledge of astronomy, which Arab science had advanced. Associated with geography was the Arabic travel literature, which is the main source for medieval ethno-geography and ethno-history. In this context one may mention one work out of many, the important *Memoirs* of *Usamah Ibn Munqud, prince of Shaizar, in the 12th century, which combine an autobiography with descriptions of travels, mainly in the *Crusaders' kingdom of Jerusalem, and which give a very interesting picture of Crusader society in Palestine. Another was the travel book of Ibn-Batutta from the 14th century, which includes the first good description of Africa.

Arab music evolved during the Abbasid period (750-1258) as a synthesis of Arabic tradition with Persian, Byzantine and Gothic influences. These, in musicological methodology, are viewed as three distinctive regional heritages: the eastern, with its Iraqi-Persian centre; the central, with its origins in Syria and Egypt, and the western, emanating from Andalusia and north Africa. In the 12th-13th centuries, the eastern and central groups became so blended that the distinctions between them are merely of detail, while the western group became increasingly influenced by the Spanish romances. From the theoretical point of view, the A. studied the Greek musical heritage and adapted its philosophical classification and metre. The Aristotelian theory of music, as a part of the *Quadrivium*, was adapted in Arab musicology in the 9th century by *Ibn Farabi, in his *Great Book of Music*, which became the theoretical textbook for later musicologists, wherein a distinction is made between liturgical and lay music. As Islam forbade the use of music for pleasure, the liturgical songs, being more recitative, remained monotonous, whereas secular music, in contrast with Christian Europe, became the more advanced.

In the field of philosophy the Arabic language was used in the Middle Ages not only by A. and Moslems, but by people of all races and religions who lived under the rule of Islam, most notably the Jews. The principal trends in Arabic philosophical thought were the *Kalam*, i.e., the theology of Islam, which from the beginnings took on the character of apologetics, and pure philosophy, which built on the Greek and Hellenistic heritage, having a universalist character and form. The evolution of Arabic philosophy was tightly connected with the translation from Greek into Arabic of *Platonic and *Aristotelian treatises, which had been done chiefly by Eastern Christians in the 8th century at Alexandria and Antioch. In this field, too, the Abbasids took a great interest; at the beginning of the 9th century, the caliph *Mamun founded at Baghdad the "House of Wisdom", with the double goal of helping the translators and the teaching philosophy. The founding of his academy marked the inception of creative philosophical work in Arabic. The leading personality of the time was *Farabi, who had studied Greek thought and adapted it to the Islamic, and more broadly, monotheistic viewpoint. The Greek and Hellenistic concept of the interrelation between *Logos* (the Word), *Nomos* (the Law) and *Physis* (the Material) was adapted as a universal concept of the faith, which was to be explained in a rational way. Thus, the omnipotent God was identified with the Supreme Reason, which creates itself and projects its qualities onto the various material elements. This idea implies an hierarchical concept of the universe, faith and the human body. The Prophet is viewed as a philosopher, to whom the commands of the Supreme Reason was given by revelation. Farabi's work was the foundation of Arabic philosophy and he influenced both Moslem and Jewish thinkers, some of whom became more famous than he, as for example *Ibn Sinna and *Maimonides. The development of Aristotelian thought by Ibn Sinna is one of the most important contributions to medieval philosophy. Although his books were criticized, his influence was well established in Moslem Spain, where Arab philosophy was more widespread in the 10th-11th centuries than it was in the East. It passed from Spain to Christian Europe, where he was known as Avicenna. The Arab philosophical school reached its highest level in the 12th century in Moslem Spain, with on the one hand, *Ibn Rushd, the Aristotelian commentator (known in Christian Europe as Averroes), who developed Ibn Sinna's thought into a comprehensive philosophical approach to the Moslem faith and, on the other hand, the Jewish philosopher Maimonides. During the same period in the eastern countries, particularly Iraq and Persia, there was a certain revival of Platonic thought which combined with ancient Persian traditions to produce a new school, that of the "Wisdom of the Levant", which is the title of the book written by its founder, the Persian Shihab Al-Din Ihia Al-Suharawardi. This school, which was inclined to the idealistic and contained a strong mystical element, influenced the Moslem pietists, and was, therefore, highly popular, especially among the Persians and other Oriental Moslems.

Arab contribution to the development of scientific methods, and particularly to the transmission of the Greek heritage to the West, is of particular importance. The translation into Arabic of Greek scientific works in the 8th-9th centuries, was the basis of the growth of Arabic scientific thought to the end of the 11th century. Its foundation is a philosophical one, influenced by Aristotle's *Physics*. However, besides the Greek and Hellenistic ideas, it absorbed also Persian and Indian influences, and the ancient Mesopotamian heritage. An important scientific contribution of the A. was in mathematics, notably the field of algebra and the principles of geometry. Their mathematical theories, based on the works of Apollonius of Perge, were developed into a comprehensive theory, which was translated into Latin in the 12th century and remained in use until the modern era. Astronomy, based on mathematics, remained closely allied with astrology, combining the Babylonian and Greek heritages. Arab astronomers contributed to the fixing of astronomical tables, the most complete being that of *Alfonso X of Castile (1252). Arab contribution to the field of physics was in optics and the theory of magnetic fields. In addition to *alchemy, to which the A. contributed an important philosophical aspect, they were very active in the development of medicine, though the main contribution was that of Jewish physicians. The A. evolved from the cosmological ideas of Aristotle to a theory of an organic world, composed of the four elements, air, earth, water and fire, whose combination represent nature and life. (For Arab art, see *Art.)

CHI, 2 vols. (1970).

ARAGON Kingdom in *Spain, situated in the eastern part of the Iberian Peninsula, between France and Castile. Its origins lie in the Christian organization of the territories in northern Spain which had not been conquered by the Arabs. In the 9th century the county of A. was established by the kings of *Navarre around the city of Jaca, and was held by their vassals. In 1035 it was given by *Sancho-Garcia of Navarre to his third son, *Ramiro (1035-63), with the title of king. Ramiro is considered the founder of A., to which he annexed two neighbouring counties. After his death the situation was as yet unstable, and the kings of Navarre had to struggle to impose their rule over the new kingdom. A turning point for the independence of A. was the conquest of Huesca from the Arabs in 1096, and the establishment of the capital in that city, which belonged to Navarre. By the end of the 11th century the kingdom extended to the Ebro River, which became its frontier with the Moslem dominions. Under *Alfonso I, the wars of the *reconquista* were continued, with the participation of French knights. In 1118 Saragossa was conquered and became the principal city of the kingdom. The Battle of Fraga, in 1131, eliminated the danger of Moslem counterattacks and A. became a powerful state between Navarre in the north and the county of *Catalonia, its new rival, in the south. The marriage of the heiress of A., Petronilla, with *Raymond Berengar IV, count of Barcelona and Catalonia, created in 1154 the greater kingdom, which, for dynastic reasons, was oriented more in the direction of the *Provence and southern France than towards Spain. During the 12th century feudalism was introduced in A. and the king's council, the *fuero*, which was the assembly of the nobility, became an organ of government, dealing particularly with legislation and justice. Nevertheless, the feudal nobility did not become as powerful and influential as in France, since the throne enjoyed a large income from the commercial activities of the Catalan cities. The Catholic Church had a strong influence in the kingdom, which at the end of the 12th century became a vassal of the papacy. After the death of *Peter II, killed at Muret in France (1213), the kings of A. concentrated their interests in the affairs of Spain and the wars of the *reconquista. They conquered from the Moslems the plain south of the Ebro, the Balearic Islands (1229), and *Valencia and its principality (1238). Thus A. became an important power in Spain, second only to Castile. Often, during the 13th century, the rivalry between the two kingdoms led to wars. Catalan commercial interests in the Mediterranean and their rivalry with *Marseilles and Provençal shipping, brought A. into conflict with *Charles of Anjou, king of *Sicily. Taking advantage of a revolt in Sicily (the "Sicilian Vespers"), *Peter III conquered the island in 1282, and made it one of the most important possessions of the crown of A. The failure of *Philip III of France to avenge his uncle in an attack on the Pyrénées in 1285, enabled A. to establish its domination in the western Mediterranean, annexing *Sardinia and Montpellier in southern France. By the end of the 13th century A. became one of the major powers in western Europe, controlling international trade, and Barcelona even competed successfully with *Genoa. But the long wars compelled the kings to make concessions to the nobility so as to obtain the necessary resources. The fueros were replaced by a more powerful assembly, the *cortes wherein the clergy, high nobility, representatives of the knights (hidalgos) and of the cities sat together. In 1283 it obtained the privilege of discussing and approving taxes and, in 1289, it was even granted the right to appoint the king's counsellors; a chief justice was appointed to deal with conflicts between the king and the nobility. In the 14th century the kings managed to enforce their authority over the cortes. A. continued its expansion: between 1311-87 it ruled Athens in Greece. However, dynastic interests split the kingdom: the Balearic Islands were made into the kingdom of *Majorca, while a collateral branch of the dynasty reigned in Sicily. After the death of *Martin (1410), the last descendant of the Aragonese-Catalan dynasty, Prince *Ferdinand of Castile, was recognized as king of A. (1412), and restored the authority of the monarchy in the kingdom.

H. J. Chaytor, A History of Aragon and Catalonia (1933).

ARBOGAST *Frankish leader in the 4th century. Like many warriors of his nation he entered the service of the Roman empire, and rose to the military command of the Rhine boundary. In 387 Emperor *Theodosius appointed him magister militum (master of the army) in Gaul, and adviser to his young colleague, Valentinian II. A. beat the *Ripuarian Franks in 389, and succeeded in maintaining Roman power on the Rhine. The victory strengthened his position and, despite his fidelity to the pagan faith of his people, he became the virtual master of Gaul. He appointed many of his kinsmen and other Franks to high positions in the army and administration. After Valentinian's death in 392, he appointed a Roman palace official, Eugenius, as "Augustus of the West", and encouraged the pagan revival in the Western empire. In 394 he was defeated by *Theodosius, who restored the unity of the Roman empire, and committed suicide. In the 7th and 8th centuries the story of A. inspired the legends of the ancient tribal chiefs, who were seen as the fathers of the *Salic Law.

E. Stein, Histoire du Bas-Empire, I (1959).

ARCADIUS FLAVIUS (377-408) Son of *Theodosius, emperor of the Eastern Roman empire (395-408). A weak person, he was manipulated by his counsellors who were motivated by their own interests to perpetuate the division of the Roman empire and concentrate on the affairs of the Eastern empire. During his reign his empire was invaded by the *Visigoths and other Germanic tribes; to save it A. and his court bribed the invaders to divert them to the Western empire (401). A. conflicted with the Church and expelled from Constantinople *John Chrystostom, who had criticized Empress Eudoxia. Although A. did not contribute himself to its evolution, he is considered as the founder of the *Byzantine empire.

A. D. M. Jones, The Later Roman Empire, I (1963).

ARCHIPOETA Anonymous Latin poet of the second half of the 12th century; the name was the expression of the admiration felt for him by the *Goliards. He was one of the best known wandering poets, whose work praised love, women and wine. Judging from his songs, he originated from the Rhine country in Germany, and he followed *Raynald of Dassel, archbishop of Cologne to Italy and began to write verse about 1160. He adopted a satirical style and criticized the Church; his famous poem, Confession, deals with a poet who finds in vice, wine and women, the inspiration for his creation, which would pave his way to paradise. His verses, in which he prayed to die in a wine-cellar, were often quoted in the Goliardic poems of the 13th century.

H. Waddell, The Wandering Scholars (1935).

ARCHITECTURE Medieval A. was in many ways a continuation of the classical, but gradually it adopted new forms, corresponding both to the functional and social needs of the period and to the diversity of climate and civilization. Three categories were common to the different styles: religious buildings; palaces and monuments, and urban construction. From the chronological and stylistic points of view, medieval A. can be divided into five main groups: the early Christian building; the *Byzantine; the *Islamic; the *Romanesque, and the *Gothic, corresponding to the principal trends of medieval art.

Early Christian A. was, more than the others, a continuation of classical traditon, combined with the heritage of the ancient simple basilicae. From the 5th century on churches were built in the form of a cross, symbolizing the faith, but also for the practical purpose of separating the *altar and the space reserved for the clergy from that of the community of the faithful. The tradition of classical temples called for a façade with columns, which served as the base of the cross-shaped building and the entry to the church, and was generally called the galilee, to symbolize the entry to the Holy Land from the north, as did the European pilgrims. On the other hand, Oriental influence introduced by the early Christians brought in the hemispheric form, which broke the straight lines of the classical buildings and became the apse of the church, near the altar. Until the 10th century there was only one apse in the church, as the buildings were not very big. After the Roman empire bells were added, to call the faithful to prayer; they were located in a little tower, either in a separate building beside the church, or built on over the galilee. Beside the church, in the corner of one of the arms of the cross, a little rectangular yard was enclosed, in which members of the community were buried. The

The Wood Hall at Lavenham, Suffolk, built in the 15th century

A late medieval building at Queen's College, Cambridge

Minarets of Al-Azhar Mosque and University, Cairo, Egypt

The Papal Palace at Avignon, France, built in the 14th century

founder saint, certain members of the clergy and of
aristocratic families were buried in the crypt, which
was often dug under the floor. With the spread of
*monasticism from the end of the 6th century, the
cloister appeared, with the monastic buildings grouped
around a rectangular inner yard, linked to an arm of the
church building.

The secular A. of the age continued to be the classical one, the old buildings of the Roman period remaining in use, although they gradually deteriorated. North
of the Alps the new constructions were mainly in
wood, although stone was also employed in new buildings, which were no longer monumental, sometimes of
irregular shape.

Byzantine A. developed in its own way, being a compromise between the classical and oriental styles. The
development of Byzantine A. is closely associated with
the reign of *Justinian, whose monumental constructions introduced the style. The cathedral church of
*Hagia Sophia at Constantinople epitomizes this inno-
vation and is the culmination of the Byzantine Style.
The curves, the great cupolas and the apses, which were
the main novelty, were added to the regular forms of the
buildings. Great columns sustained arches which permitted the elevation of the buildings to a height previously
unknown. Another style of religious building was the
rotunda of hexagonal or octagonal form, as, for example,
the Church of the Holy *Sepulchre in Jerusalem. The
monasteries were built on an irregular plan, forming little
monastic cities, like that of Mount *Athos in Greece, or
St. *Saba in Palestine. Each building containing a number
of cells (*lavra*), was an independent entity, with its own
cupolas and bell-towers; the whole complex, grouped on
several levels around the monastic church, gave an impression of an urban concentration, and the illusion of a city
in the desert. Secular A. retained more of the Roman
heritage, but from the 6th century on, it copied the
imperial palace (trycline) of Constantinople. An important category in Byzantine A. was the fortress, built
on a rectangular plan of the outer walls. In the centre of
the courtyard, the church and the commander's house
represented the monumental part of the fortress, while
the other buildings within the yard were functional.
Another important Byzantine feature was the indoor
garden within the palace, a patio as an extension of the
hall. The Byzantine style of A., diffused throughout the
empire, influenced the Moslem world and, via Italy, the
A. of western Europe.

Islamic A. was primarily an expression of religious
requirements. The mosques, which initially, in the 7th
century had no established character, gradually became
religious monuments, whose composition of walls and
columns created the form of a temple. Under the
influence of Byzantine and Persian art, the columns,
cupolas and curves became in the 8th century an
essential part of the building, differing entirely from the
primitive structures of the Arabian desert. The bell-
towers of the Christian world were replaced in Islamic
A. by the minarets, from which the muezzines called
the faithful to prayer, and were designed for that
purpose: topped with a small dome, they included room
for the muezzine. The religious requirement of bathing
the extremities before prayer, which became a precept
in Islam, demanded the construction of a fountain near
the mosque. From the 9th century on, mosques became

Christ Church College at Oxford, built in the 14th century

Detail of a Gothic flying buttress at Bourges cathedral

Monastic architecture: Maria Laach church and abbey

The cathedral vaults of the Mezquita at Cordoba

imposing monuments, notably in Iraq, Persia, Syria, Egypt, Kairwan and Spain. Generally, the rectangular form remained, but under the influence of the building of the *Dome of the Rock in Jerusalem, octagonal forms were also used. Secular A. displayed strong Persian influence. Palaces stood inside great courts, with elaborately laid out gardens filled with fragrant plants and flowers. From the *Abbasid period on, some of the public life of the government was conducted in the gardens of the fortified palaces, or al-kasr (*alcazar) in Arabic. While in Damascus and Egypt Byzantine influence continued, Persian influence reached its apogee in the building of the caliph's palace at Baghdad at the end of the 8th century, in the reign of *Harun Al-Rashid, and from there spread to the western Moslem lands. The magnificent palaces included courtyards, public and private apartments, and bathrooms with a water supply system, based on wells and aqueducts. The most perfect examples of the Persian-influenced trend were the palaces of southern Spain, the alcázars, which were the seats of the government and, at the same time, the cultural centres of the principalities. The finest achievement of Islamic A. is the building complex of the *Alhambra, near Granada, completed in the 15th century.

In western Europe new architectural trends appeared during the *Carolingian renaissance. While the early Christian style continued in church building, the idea of the Empire led the architects of *Charlemagne to apply the Byzantine style in the construction of the imperial palace and church at *Aix-La-Chapelle, at the very end of the 8th century. But the decline of the Carolingian empire and the instability during the 9th century, produced a regression in the style of A., though the abbeys were still built in a grand style. The construction of castles throughout the empire and the need for defence, created the style of fortification. A castle was basically an enclosed courtyard surrounded by a moat, built of stone and earthworks with a tower as the main building, in which the lord and his family lived in cramped, insalubrious quarters. Only the changing political conditions in the second half of the 10th century, permitted new architectural developments, associated with the reign of *Otto I. The larger dimensions of public buildings, notably the churches, where greater numbers gathered to worship, called for the use of columns and vaults to support the higher roofs, and of buttresses to support the walls. Some vestiges of Byzantine influence remained, particularly in the domes and apses, but these changed gradually, climatic considerations being taken into account, A. evolved in the German empire, and the Low Countries, its perfect expression – known as the "Mosan Art", after the River Meuse – being found at *Liège. In the 11th century the style reached France, where it was adapted to new conditions and became known as *Romanesque A.* This style was perfected in the churches and cathedrals. The architectural principle was the division of the building into three parts, the nave (containing two floors) and two lateral aisles. Each of these parts ended with an apse, which meant at least three altars. Two rows of columns separated the three parts, while the aisles also served to buttress the structure of the nave. The high gable roof was devised to permit the drainage of rainwater, domes were gradually eliminated, and one or two bell-towers were built over the

The façade of Winchester cathedral

The Romanesque church of St. Mary Magdalene at Vezelay

galilee. However, the cruciform plan of the church still dominated the architectural conception of the building. The Romanesque churches were continuously developing in the 11th and 12th centuries, adding new chapels, which called for additional apses, or enlarging the buildings, to accommodate more worshippers, as populations increased. It resulted in a disproportion between the choir, reserved for the clergy and separated by the transept (with the arms of the cross) from the nave with the aisles, which were made longer and longer. This disproportion was less noticeable in monastic churches, where the choirs were constructed so as to allow room for the monk's stalls. The entry to the church was also made to correspond to the new architectural conceptions, which were the monumental embodiment of the Trinitarian doctrine. The three portals, corresponding to the nave and the aisles, were decorated with religious scenes, the central one depicting the Last Judgement and the Resurrection of the Dead (see *Art; *Romanesque). To support the higher elevation and permit the opening of windows, the columns were made more solid, supporting vaults and round arches, and sustaining the roof. Romanesque style was also used in the construction of castles, whose moats were eliminated, the towers becoming more elaborate buildings within the courtyards. Stone was a widely used material in Romanesque buildings, where the social conditions of manpower made it possible. The great stones of classical times disappeared, and were replaced by smaller ones, suited to the availability of peasant labour for a limited number of days in the year. The style was spread throughout western and southern Christian Europe, with some regional diversity of form. In many countries it remained in use even after the 12th century, either where buildings were restored, mainly in the Mediterranean countries, or in new churches. But generally speaking the Romanesque period ended in the second half of the 12th century, when it no longer correponded to the needs of society, particularly in the cities. Gothic A. was to serve growing city populations.

Gothic A. replaced the Romanesque, being basically an evolution of its conceptions. The first Gothic building was the abbey of *St. Denis near Paris, begun about 1140 by the Abbot *Suger, who reported that he was disturbed by the crowds that attended his abbatial church. While the cruciform and the tripartite plan of nave aisles remained in use, the problem was how to sustain the elevation of the building. It was solved by the construction of pillars, which were a development of the Romanesque columns, and by more solid vaults, which became more pointed and then lost their semicircular form. In order to preserve the proportion of the dimensions of the cross, the choir was enlarged and completed by an *ambulacrum*, giving access to the several chapels, devoted to the worship of different saints, and the use of donors. The bell-towers were adapted to hold the new bells, which were much heavier. Over the centre of the church, a pointed, arrow-shaped tower, emphasized the height of the building. In the second half of the 12th century and in the 13th, the Gothic style was adopted by the cathedral builders of northern France, England and Germany, and then spread throughout Catholic Europe. From the 14th century to the end of the Middle Ages the style was diversified in form and detail; it is called the Flamboyant Gothic to distinguish it from the original, and is preserved in Westminster Abbey in London, and the cathedrals of Cologne, Milan and Strassburg, while the classical Gothic is preserved in the cathedrals of Durham, Chartres and Amiens. In Spain the style was influenced by Islamic A., and in several places, where mosques were converted into churches, there are combinations of styles, as, for example, Córdoba, whose cathedral occupies part of an enormous mosque. The Gothic style was used in the building of palaces, which replaced the older feudal castles. The use of pillars and vaults made possible the halls, where the courtly social life of the knights brought about a renaissance of secular culture. The Gothic city remained a tight conglomeration of buildings with narrow streets, but in its centres the market-place became the monumental part of the city, with the town- or guild-hall dominating it.

E. Adam, *Baukunst des Mittelalters*, 2 vols. (1963).

ARENA Garden in the city of Padua in Italy, designed and planted at the beginning of the 14th century for the aristocratic family of the Scroveni. With its regular design and the diverse plants, it was considered as one of the great achievements of medieval gardening. A family chapel was erected in the garden in 1303, which is famous for 38 frescoes by *Giotto, including his master-pieces, the *Life of Christ* and *Life of the Madonna*.

O. Siren, *Giotto and Some of his Followers* (1917).

ARIBERT OF ANTERMINO (d. 1044) Archbishop of Milan (1021-44). Of an aristocratic family in Lombardy, he was elected archbishop with the support of the *capitanei*, the high aristocracy of the city. After 1022 he opposed the imperial intervention in Lombardy and succeeded in uniting the city against *Conrad II, who besieged Milan. He is considered as one of the founders of Milanese society.

C. Violante, *La Societá Milanese nell'eta precomunale* (1914).

ARISTOTELIANISM The philosophical and theological trends influenced by Aristotle's teaching in the Middle Ages. After Aristotle's death (322 BC), his work was somewhat neglected for 200 years, and only in the first century BC was the study of it revived in the Academy of Athens, which was a centre of A. until 529, when the school was disbanded by *Justinian, on the grounds that it was opposed to the Orthodox Church. However, the scholars fled to the East with their books and established new schools in Persia and, in the 7th century, in *Antioch and *Alexandria, where A. flourished again. The early Christians never formally excluded Aristotle and preferred *neo-Platonism as a comprehensive philosophy, which better fitted the needs of Christianity. On the other hand, the adoption of A. by the *Monophysite Syrians helped them to oppose Greek Orthodox centralist conceptions and, therefore, they concentrated on its study and interpretation, continuing under Arab rule at Antioch and Alexandria. From the 8th century on the first translations of Aristotle's writings into Arabic enhanced the development of the Arabic philosophical school, which was based on his thought, and used his ideas to evolve a rationalist view of the *Islamic religion. The school of *Baghdad in the 9th century was based entirely on that heritage, so much that every Greek philosophical work whose author was not known to them, was assumed to be Aristotle's. Only with *Ibn Sinna was a certain order brought to the study of A., and a

The Arena chapel of Padua, Italy, decorated by Giotto

classification of Aristotle's writings was made separating his moral and ethical thought and his philosophy of science, which was fundamental to the development of Arabic science. When Ibn Sinna's work reached Andalusia, A. passed to Spain, where it became the basis of Moslem and Jewish thought, culminating in the 12th century with the great school of *Córdoba, which gave birth to the two giants of Aristotelian philosophy, *Ibn Rushd and *Maimonides. Both philosophers used A. to build up a rationalist theory of the world and divine revelation and for an explanation of the faith, rooted in reason. Through *Toledo, which, though it was conquered by the *Castilians in 1095, remained one of the centres of Jewish and Arabic learning, Christian scholars became acquainted with A. at the end of the 12th century. They transmitted it to the French schools of *Chartres, where the scientific heritage was studied and developed, and to Paris, which was an important theological centre. Until the beginning of the 13th century some scholars of western Europe used Aristotle's ideas, taken from the translations of Boethius or from the new Aristotelian school of *Constantinople, but the real integration of A. as a method of thought was the work of *Thomas Aquinas and his teaching at Paris during the 13th century. Under the influence of Aquinas, A. became the common basis for Christian theology, assimilating the universal concept of natural law with the Christian belief in divine law, as given to humanity by the revelation of Christ. At the end of the

13th century, A. was discovered by the Italians and *Dante used it in his writings, thus helping to spread its ideas. From the 14th century on the University of *Padua adopted the study of Aristotle's writings and their commentaries and interpretations as an integral part of the philosophical education of students.

F. Van Steenberghen, *Aristotle in the West* (1955).

ARLES City in *Provence, on the delta of the river Rhône, one of the most beautiful sites of Roman Provence, whose ancient part testifies to the classical civilization of the province. At the beginning of the 4th century it was the residence of *Constantine, who made it the virtual capital of Gaul. Because of its importance in the last century of the Roman empire, it became one of the major Christian centres and the seat of an archbishop. A number of important councils were held at A., including that of 314, one of the first church assemblies in the West, in which the *Donatist heresy was condemned. In the 5th century A. fell under the rule of the *Visigoths and then the *Ostrogoths, and was conquered by the *Franks in 509. Under Frankish rule and the division of the realm it was one of the important cities of the *Burgundian kingdom. In 730 the Arabs conquered it for a short time, but *Charles Martel restored it to Frankish rule. The wars and the repeated conquests damaged the city, which lost its ancient splendour and began to decay. Nevertheless, it remained an important centre and in the 10th century, after the disintegration of the *Carolingian empire and of the kingdom of Provence, it was included in the new kingdom of Burgundy; in 933 it became its capital and the kingdom was named Arelate. At the end of the 10th century it was incorporated in the *Holy Roman empire and with the dissolution of the kingdom of Burgundy in the 11th century, it became an imperial city, enjoying autonomy and self-government.

This government was organized in the 12th century: the burghers elected a chief, *podesta,* while the archbishop appointed two *consuls.* The autonomy was contested in the late 12th century by the counts of *Barcelona and *Toulouse, who fought for the rule of Provence. In 1251 it was conquered by *Charles of Anjou, and incorporated in his county of Provence, but it declined in favour of *Marseilles, which controlled the trade of the whole country. Though under the *Angevins the city remained in decline, it also produced some of its finest artistic creations, the most important monument of the period being the Romanesque cathedral, built in the 12th century and decorated and embellished in the 13th-15th centuries. In 1485 A. was annexed to France, together with the rest of Provence, and became a small provincial town.

A. Benoît, *Arles, ses monuments, son histoire* (1927).

ARMAGH City and kingdom in northern *Ireland, named so in memory of Ard-Macha, a legendary Irish queen. In 445 St. *Patrick founded in A. an archiepiscopal see, which became the religious centre of Ireland. In accordance with Irish Christian custom, the archbishopric was also the see of the heads of the clan and a monastery, which in the 6th century included a flourishing school which was also attended by Anglo-Saxon students. The A. library was one of the most important in Ireland and its rich collection of sacred and secular works was put together in the 8th century and copied, in Irish and Latin, in a uniform format by Ferdommach

of A. in the 9th century. During the *Norman invasions, the counts of A. imposed their authority on the country (1021-1105) and on the church, which began to decline. The reforms carried out by its 12th-century bishops, mainly St. *Malachy, met a strong opposition and A. failed to be restored as the centre of the Irish church. Under English domination (from 1176) the city lost its importance and the church was dominated by English prelates

E. Curtis, *The History of Medieval Ireland* (1938).

ARMAGNAC County in southwestern France, created in the 10th century out of several feudal estates in Gascony, and united under the lords of A., a castle near Auch. In the 10th-13th centuries, the counts consolidated their county, conflicting with other feudal lords in Gascony particularly with the counts of *Foix. Under John I (1319-73), having inherited some estates near Rodez, they were powerful enough to enter French politics, taking part in the *Hundred Years' War. Under John II (1373-84) they helped *Charles V to recover the provinces conquered by the English. Their position was highest when Bernard VII of A. (1319-1418) became Constable of France by favour of *Louis of Orléans, brother of *Charles VI. After the murder of Louis at Paris (1407), Bernard became the head of the Orléans party and father-in-law of Louis' son, *Charles of Orléans. Supported by an important faction of the French nobility, he fought the *Burgundians, who had been responsible for the murder of Louis and were supported by the Parisians and by the university. His party, the *Armagnacs, sacked the capital and crushed the *Cabochien revolt (1413), whose radicalism drove the bourgeoisie to support him. Bernard became the virtual ruler of France, until his assassination by the Burgundians in 1418.

C. Samaran, *La Maison d'Armagnac au XVe siècle* (1907).

ARMENIA Country in Asia Minor, between the Eastern Roman empire and Persia, including a part of the Caucasus. At the end of the 4th century A. was divided between the Roman empire and Persia, but local petty kingdoms continued to exist under the two empires and maintained a certain autonomy. The Christianization of the country, beginning in the late 2nd century, was accelerated by the adoption of the Armenian language in the Christian rites. In 294 *Gregory "the Illuminator" established his metropolitan see at Etchmiadzin, near Mt. Ararat, and is considered as the true founder of the Armenian church, which was of great importance in sustaining Armenian national feelings, particularly after the disappearance of the last autonomous kingdoms in the 5th century. The creation of the Armenian alphabet by St. Mesrob at the beginning of the 5th century, and the translation of the Scriptures into Armenian, were the basis of the development of the language and culture of A., where religion and nationalism are closely linked. In 527 *Justinian conquered the Persian part of A., and until 639 the country was under Byzantine rule. During this period there was a migration of Armenians to the centres of the empire in Asia Minor and at Constantinople, where many of them held important economic, administrative and military posts. Two Byzantine emperors, *Leo V and *Basil I, in the 9th century, were of Armenian origin. In 639 the *Arabs, who had conquered Syria and Iraq, penetrated into A. and occupied the major part of the country. As in Syria and Egypt, the Byzantine government was hated for its religious intolerance and the Armenians favoured the Arab conquest. The new rulers did not interfere in local affairs, appointed Armenians to administrative offices in the country, and were content to collect the taxes. The position of landowners became stronger and some feudal structures appeared. Among the feudal families, the Bagratians, believed to be descendants of King David, reached an important position, due to their wealth and their devotion to the national-religious tradition. In 806 Ashot I was recognized by the *Abbasid court as prince of Armenia, and began to impose his authority over the local lords. His grandson, Ashot III, was granted in 860 the title of "prince of princes" of Armenia, *Georgia and the Caucasus and, in 886, he was elected by the clergy and nobility king of A. During his reign, the kingdom reached its greatest political development in the Middle Ages, and extended from the Caspian Sea to the Euphrates. It was also a time of cultural flowering and economic prosperity, due to the extensive commerce through the kingdom. However, in the 10th century the rivalries among the nobility curtailed the royal power and finally split the country into six separate kingdoms. Consequently A. was reconquered by the Byzantines at the beginning of the 11th century and was greatly weakened. In 1071 the *Seljuks, led by *Alp Arslan, conquered it and annexed it to the sultanate of Konya. During the 12th century, *Kurdish emirs governed A., and in 1240 it was conquered by the *Mongols and remained under their rule until 1349. The Mongol occupation was a time of devastation and decline, as a result of which many Armenians emigrated, including entire clans. Some of these, led by aristocratic families, settled in Cilicia, on the south coast of Asia Minor, where they were welcomed by the Byzantine authorities and allocated an underpopulated region. It was called "Little Armenia", and became a new kingdom (1080-1375). The basis of the new kingdom was the principality founded by a Bagratid noble, Rupen, in 1080, whose dynasty (the Rupenids) controlled the strategic passes of the Taurus, between Asia Minor and Syria. In 1098 the Rupenids extended vital aid to the participants of the First *Crusade on their way to the Holy Land. From the beginning of the 12th century the relations between the Crusader princes of *Antioch and the Rupenids were close and mutual cultural influences between the aristocracies of the two countries developed. In 1137 the Byzantines conquered Cilicia and, until 1145, the Armenian state was under their domination. The Rupenid restoration of 1145 coincided with the fall of *Edessa, and emphasized the importance of the independent Armenian kingdom on the passes of the Taurus, to assure the land route to the Crusader states. Under Leo II (1187-1219), Little A. reached its historical apogee. He took part in the Third Crusade and, in 1198, swore fealty to Emperor *Henry VI, who recognized him as king of Cilicia and A. Family ties connected the Armenian and Crusader aristocracies, and commercial privileges were granted in A. to the Italian cities, as they were in the Crusader states. The Armenian church even adopted some of the rites of the Catholic Church, and in the 13th century the country flourished economically and culturally. In the second half of the 13th century the Seljuks from Konya and after them the Mongols imposed their overlordship on

the Rupenid state, which also had to defend itself against the *Mamluks, who, after the conquest of Antioch in 1268, attacked Cilicia. To do this, the Rupenids allied themselves with the *Lusignan kings of *Cyprus by a series of marriages; this introduced Frankish and Catholic influence into the kingdom. These trends provoked uprisings by the local nobility, which made the dynasty more dependent on Cyprus. After the extinction of the Rupenids (1342), the kingship passed by inheritance to the Lusignan dynasty of Cyprus, which further increased the Western influence. A Catholic-Armenian church was established in the kingdom, acknowledging the supremacy of the pope, retaining the right to a certain autonomy. But it was not a theological split in the Armenian church, the differences being only in organization. Nevertheless, the opposition to the "Westerners" weakened the kingdom, and the Mamluks continued to seize parts of it. In 1375 they conquered the last Armenian stronghold, *Sis, which marked the fall of the last Armenian state. The nobility was massacred, while the lower classes were subjected to new lords. By the end of the 14th century, with the decline of the Mongol khanate of *Persia, local principalities emerged again in Great Armenia, but they had to submit to the ruling dynasties, Mongol or, from 1404, *Turkoman. A certain religious autonomy remained; negotiations with the Church of Rome continued, with the aim of bringing about a union.

H. Pastermadjian, *History of Armenia* (1947).

ARMORICA Peninsula in northwestern Gaul (France). In the Roman empire it was part of the province of Gaul, whose capital was *Tours. In the 6th century Celtic tribes from Britain, pressed by the *Anglo-Saxon invasion, found refuge in A. It was then named "Little Britain", which in time became *Brittany, or Bretagne (in French). However, the name A., or Armor, was used in Latin literature and, as a classical reference, in ecclesiastical sources.

ARNOLD OF BRESCIA (d. 1155) Revolutionary reformer of the Church. Born in Brescia (northern Italy), he studied at Paris, where he was a pupil of *Abelard until 1140, and one of his last supporters. After the condemnation of Abelard, he led a group of poor students at Paris and attacked personages such as *Bernard of Clairvaux. Expelled from Paris by order of *Louis VII, he returned to Italy, where he began systematically to attack the worldliness of the Church, maintaining that confession should be made not to a priest, but by one Christian to another, that the sinfulness of a priest destroyed the value of sacraments he administrated, and that the Church may not possess worldly goods or exercise temporal authority. Expelled from Brescia, he went to Rome in 1145, where he joined a local party that opposed the temporal dominion of the pope. In July 1148 he was excommunicated by *Eugenius III; but retaining his popular support, he was one of the leaders of the commune of *Rome, which embodied the revolutionary trend. After the accession of *Frederick Barbarossa to the empire in 1152, the commune was crushed, and A. was arrested by the imperial army, condemned to death and delivered to the prefect of Rome, who had him executed.

G. W. Greenaway, *Arnold of Brescia* (1931).

ARNOLD OF WINKELRIED (d. 1386) Swiss peasant of the canton of Unterwald. He fell in the Battle of

*Sempach and in the aftermath of the victory, he became a national hero, to whom the crushing victory over the *Hapsburgs was attributed. (See *Switzerland.)

ARNOLFO DI CAMBIO (1232-1301) Architect and sculptor. Born at Colle Valdelsa near Siena, he studied under *Nicola Pisano, and in the years 1266-69 served as his assistant in making the sculptures for the cathedral of Siena. After working for a period for *Charles of Anjou in Naples, he went to Perugia in 1277, where he decorated a number of monuments with sculptures. In 1285 he settled in Rome, where he built and decorated churches; among his works of that period was the sculpture of *Boniface VIII at St. Peter's in the Vatican. In 1296 he went to Florence, where he created his masterpieces, among them the design and building of the façade of the cathedral, and the council hall, the Palazzo Vecchio. In his works, both as architect and sculptor, he created the style called Florentine *Gothic, which reflects the transition from medieval to Renaissance art. It is a combination of Late Gothic art with some realistic elements, which heralded the new age.
V. Mariani, *Arnolfo di Cambio* (1943).

ARNULF (Arnoul), St. (c. 580-655) Bishop of *Metz (c. 614-55). A member of a noble Frankish family, he held important offices at the court of *Theodebert II, king of *Austrasia. Being one of the main supporters of *Clotaire II, he was rewarded with the bishopric of Metz, while continuing his activity at court. In about 630 he appears to have retired to a life of solitude. Popular tradition emphasizes this retirement as a model of meditation and prayer. Before being ordained he established a family; one of his sons, Ansegisel, married Begga, a daughter of *Pepin of Landen, and was thus an ancestor of the *Carolingian dynasty.
J. Boussard, *The Civilization of Charlemagne* (1968).

ARNULF (850-99) King of *Germany and emperor (887-99). He was the illegitimate son of Carloman, king of Bavaria, and grandson of *Louis the German. In 876 his father bestowed on him the land of Carinthia, and he won fame as a warrior, fighting against *Svyatopolk, duke of Moravia. Subsequently, he was elected king by the nobility, and having obtained an important victory over the *Normans near Louvain in 891, was recognized as overlord by the kings of France, Burgundy and Italy and, in 896, was crowned emperor.
J. W. Thompson, *Feudal Germany* (1928).

ARNULF (Arnoul) OF RHEIMS (965-1021) Archbishop of Rheims (989-91 and 998-1021). Bastard son of King *Lothair, he supported at Laon the pretensions of Lothair's brother, Charles of Lorraine against *Hugh Capet. In 989, after the death of *Adalberon of Rheims, he joined Hugh's party, so as to obtain the archbishopric of Rheims. In 991 he was accused of treason against the king and deposed. But the papacy never recognized the decision of the Council of St. Basil, which had pronounced the deposition and, in 998, *Robert II was compelled to restore him. After his restoration, A. abandoned the *Carolingian party and remained loyal to Robert.
G. Duby, R. Mandrou, *History of French Civilization*, I (1964).

ARNULF OF ROELX (d. 1118) Patriarch of Jerusalem (1099 and 1112-18). He was the chaplain of *Robert Curthose, duke of Normandy, and accompanied him on the First *Crusade. His personality was controversial, but he was recognized as one of the most eloquent preachers in the Crusaders' army. In July 1099 he was elected patriarch of Jerusalem; his election was, however, contested as uncanonical by his opponents of the southern French clergy and, after the arrival of *Daimbert of Pisa at the Holy Land, he was deposed and held office in the chapter of the Holy Sepulchre in Jerusalem. In 1112 he was again elected patriarch, this time without opposition, and was active in the organization of the Latin Church in the Crusader kingdom.
S. Runciman, *A History of the Crusades*, I (1953).

ARPAD (c. 850-905) Hungarian prince and the founder of the kingdom of *Hungary and its first dynasty, which reigned until 1301. He united the various Magyar tribes and under his leadership they settled in 895 in the ancient Roman province of Pannonia, an area corresponding to the present-day territory of Hungary. He provided military help to *Leo VI of Byzantium in his wars against the Bulgarians (892-4), and to Arnulf of Carinthia against the Moravians. A. was the subject of many legends as the founder of Hungary, but very little is known about his personality and his deeds.
C. A. Macartney, *The Magyars in the Ninth Century* (1930).

ARRAS City in northern France, the centre, and in the late Middle Ages, the capital of the county of Artois. In the late Roman empire, it became an important centre of wool industry, which was its main resource during the Middle Ages. In the 4th century a bishopric was established in the city. It declined after the Frankish conquest of Gaul, and in the 10th century became a part of the county of *Flanders, which it remained until 1180. A. was the first city in the county of Flanders to receive a charter of rights, at the beginning of the 12th century, by virtue of which the burghers were allowed to elect their own judges, who had previously been appointed by the count. In 1180 the city was given to *Philip II of France, as the dowry of his wife Isabelle of Hainault. In 1237 it was given as an apanage to Robert of Artois, son of *Louis VIII, and became the capital of the county. Its political history was from this period linked with that of *Artois. During the *Hundred Years' War and the wars between the kings of France and the Burgundian rulers in the 15th century, the city was devastated and suffered a recession. Nevertheless, its wool manufacture and trade continued for most of the period, and its revenues were an important income for its rulers. In the 14th century, after 300 years of agitation and struggles between the rich burghers and the textile workers, it came under the rule of the wealthy wool merchants. The Church had actually accused the workers of heresy in 1030 and in the second part of the 12th century, and thousands of them perished in the repressions. In the 15th century the real power passed to local officials of the dukes and of the kings.

In 1435 the representatives of the kings of France and England convened at A. to settle the conflict between them. The Treaty of A., concluded with the mediation of the pope, stipulated a French-Burgundian alliance, recognizing Charles VII as the legitimate king of France. Its reputation by England led to the renewal of the war and the loss of the *English possessions in France.
J. Lestocquoy, *Les dynasties bourgeoises d'Arras* (1945).

ARSUF Town in *Palestine, in the Sharon coastland. In the classical period it was a prosperous city, called Apollonia, but at the beginning of the Middle Ages the city lost most of its inhabitants, and after the *Arab conquest (636) it became a small town. Under the *Crusaders, it was fortified and became the centre of a seigniory, with a little harbour, built on the remnants of the ancient Roman port. In the 12th century the lords of A. were involved in the government of the *Latin kingdom of Jerusalem, and were related to the high nobility of the kingdom. In 1191 an important battle at A., between the participants of the Third *Crusade, led by *Richard Coeur de Lion and the Moslems, led by *Saladin, ended with the Crusaders' victory and opened the way to Jaffa and southern Palestine. In the 13th century the lordship of A. passed to the family of *Ibelin, which sold it in 1261 to the *Hospitallers. In 1265 the city was conquered by *Baibars and destroyed.
S. Runciman, *A History of the Crusades* (1953).

ART Medieval A. grew on the foundations of the classical age, but with the introduction of monotheistic motifs, the heritage of Judaism, Christianity and Islam. Except for Far-Eastern A. (see *Asia-Art) and that of pre-Colombian America, which evolved along different lines, the main trends and styles of medieval A., as manifested in *architecture, painting and sculpture, were in some way interconnected, although ideological, geographic and climatic conditions produced a variety in the artistic forms around the Mediterranean area and in Continental Europe. There are five primary divisions in medieval A.: Byzantine, Islamic, Romanesque, Gothic and pre-Renaissance.

Byzantine A., inherited the classical principles of design, but, from the 6th century on, under the combined influences of oriental (notably *Persian) forms and Christian ideology, it created its own style and spread through the eastern provinces of the empire, with extensions as far as Persia and *Ethiopia. The birth of true Byzantine A. is associated with the reign of *Justinian, and it also flourished under the Comneni (9th-11th centuries) and the Palaeologi (14th-15th centuries). The two main elements of Byzantine A. were the mosaics, which were in some way a continuation of classical technique and style, elaborated in the Middle East in the 1st century AD, and painting, with the introduction of icons. The development of Byzantine mosaics under Justinian was enhanced chiefly by the decoration of the floors of the churches and palaces, using symbols of the faith, besides motifs of flora and fauna, but also introducing iconographic elements of sainthood. Even temporal figures, such as the Emperor and the Empress *Theodora, were shown with the halo of sainthood around their heads. This mixture of imperial and saintly features, gave the representation of human figures a quality of immobility, or majestic posture, which was unrealistic but created a normative style. From the 6th century on the use of mosaics spread throughout Italy, the Balkans, Asia Minor and the Middle East. Their style influenced the painting of icons, which began in the 7th century in Asia Minor, replacing classical sculptures, and which were objects of worship. After the *iconoclastic dispute in the 8th century, icons became the leading expression of Byzantine religious A., representing the figures of venerated saints. The painting was done on wood, and the colours were of mineral

Moorish decoration at the Alhambra Palace, Granada

origin, with the important use of gold for the saintly nimbus. To maintain the freshness of the colours, exposed to the heat of thousands of candles, oil was used as a base. This technique was described and perfected at the beginning of the 12th century by a monk of Mount *Athos; this work was included in a manual compiled in the early 12th century by a German monk, Theophilus: *De diversis artibus* (On the Various Arts). The worship of icons in the Greek Orthodox church helped to spread the style, which was also introduced in the illumination of manuscripts, not only of Byzantium, but also Armenian, Coptic and Ethiopian, with diversifications based on their own artistic traditions.

Islamic A., unlike the Byzantine, was essentially non-figurative, as the Moslem religion forbade the representation of human or animal images. While the forms were influenced by the Byzantine style, the main influence on the development of Islamic A. was that of Persian artists. They introduced the decorative element of

Christin majesty, *Romanesque relief at the 12th-century church of St. Mary Magdalene at Vezelay, Burgundy*

12th-century tympanum at the cathedral of Bourges, France

Christ in majesty; *12th-century Romanesque relief*

Detail of a Mayan palace at Uxmal, Mexico

sculpture, as well as the use of plaster, which could be moulded. Non-figurative decoration was based on the use of verses from the *Koran, as well as other inscriptions, and abstract patterns known as "arabesques". During the *Ummayad and *Abbasid periods the use of mosaics continued, but their main decorative element was floral, while animal representation was developed under Persian influence in a more realistic fashion. In religious buildings floral design, together with inscriptions, was used decoratively, while in the palaces birds and animals, especially lions, were added. In the eastern provinces the finest extant examples of medieval Islamic A. are preserved at Isfahan in Persia, and in the *Dome of the Rock in Jerusalem; in the West, the most perfect is the *Alhambra palace in Granada in Spain. Pottery, too, was highly developed in Islamic A., used in the creation of domestic objects and for decoration. The illumination of manuscripts, notably the holy Koran, began in the 9th century, and was influenced mainly by the techniques of Byzantine and European artists, yet the style is purely Islamic, excluding human images. The use of the abstract arabesques and floral motifs was brought to perfection by the *Kairwan school of miniaturists, who worked largely for the upper classes.

The spread of Christianity in western and northern Europe in the 6th-10th centuries extended the influence of Byzantine A. In eastern Europe the influence was dominant due to the worship of icons, whereas in the west it was finally adapted only in Venice, where the Church of San Marco (built and decorated between 1071 and 1117) shows Byzantine style and technique. From the *Carolingian period on, mosaics were no longer used in western Europe and, there being no worship of icons, painting was mainly applied in the illumination of manuscripts. In this field important achievements were made in the 9th century, marking the independent evolution of the A. of the miniature in the West. It began in the monastic *scriptoria*, where monks copied books. A new style of handwriting was adopted, based on the cursive, the so-called Gothic lettering, which already had an artistic character. Initial letters were illustrated, as well as whole pages of parchment, not only with holy scenes, but also with pictures in praise of patrons. The Bible of Charles the Bald is the best example of the new *Carolingian A., which had freed itself from the Byzantine representation of saints, although it retained and adapted the majestic representation of sovereigns. Another important decorative element was sculpture, which was a return to classical expression. Carolingian sculpture revived the art and led to the emergence of a new school in the 10th century, in the *Holy Roman empire, called the Ottonian sculpture, which used columns for the representation of biblical figures. Another important form of sculpture was the reliefs, which also influenced the goldsmiths. Ottonian altars are the best examples of this form, depicting saints and other persons on the sides, either carved in the stone or moulded on the gold covers of the altars. The reliefs were more realistic, relieving the frozen majesty of the Byzantine and Carolingian styles and preparing the way, at the beginning of the 11th century, for the Romanesque.

Romanesque A. emerged in the 11th century in northern Spain and southern France, and rapidly spread throughout western Europe. It broke with the classical

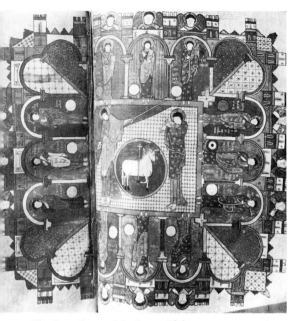

The Apocalypse of St. Sever; *12th-century manuscript*

to express this belief, and the entrance door decorated accordingly. The space under the arch and above the doors was reserved for reliefs representing the end of the world, the resurrection of the dead and the Last Judgment presided over by Christ, represented in majestic style. In depicting the execution of the judgments, the artists created realistic figures, putting an end to the frozen portrayal of human beings. The new trend of greater realism, combined with the superstition which introduced elements from the medieval bestiary as symbols of faith and punishment, was manifested not only in sculpture, but also in painting and illumination. Romanesque A. returned to mural painting and the revival of the fresco was one of its major achievements. In this field the Byzantine techniques were insufficient, because the artists had to paint the walls directly, rather than on wood. Having to solve the problem of humidity, compelled them to devise other combinations with oil to maintain the freshness of the mineral colours. As for the motifs, they were taken mainly from the lives of the saints, but also scenes from life, such as hunting and warfare, which were made to represent the struggle of good against evil. Motifs were taken from book illuminations, where they had been treated in miniature. The improvement of living conditions, the building of large churches and castles, also stimulated the development of other means of decoration, such as wall tapestries and stained-glass windows. The tapestry was an artistic creation involving both the composition of scenes and fine embroidery, executed by women at the feudal ladies' courts. Even when donated to a church or a monastery, the tapestry introduced secular A., and was often influenced by the popular epic songs, such as the *chansons de geste*. The most famous of these creations is the *Bayeux tapestry, ordered by Matilda, wife of *William the Conqueror, to commemorate the Battle of Hastings (1066) and the conquest of England by the Normans. Stained glass, introduced mainly in the Belgian province of *Liège, was used to decorate the larger windows of churches. At the beginning of the 12th century, it was not yet perfected as it was by the middle of the century, when it was used in Gothic buildings. Early Romanesque stained glass improved the technique, as attested by the German monk *Theophilus in his *De diversis artibus* mentioned above, by the production of colours and the preparation of the glass.

influence and developed its own motifs and techniques. The great medieval pilgrimages to Santiago de Compostela in Spain, to Rome and Jerusalem, bringing thousands of pilgrims to the most venerated shrines of the Catholic faith, were an important factor in the development and the fast spreading of the new style, that combined diverse customs and beliefs in an authoritative way. Although the artists worked for the aristocratic classes, lay and ecclesiastic, their creation was primarily an expression of popular beliefs, including a good deal of superstition. The Messianic belief in the *Millennium, the Last Judgment, was the dominant motif in the early Romanesque art. The portals of the churches were made

Adam and Eve; *from a 12th-century Catalan fresco*

Gothic A. was, as in architecture, an outgrowth of the Romanesque, beginning in the middle of the 12th century. The greater height of buildings and columns affected the sculptors and painters. In what is called the "Renaissance of the 12th century", Gothic artists worked on biblical themes, but also classical legends, such as that of Alexander the Great and the epic songs. At the portals of the cathedrals statues depicting prophets and kings of the Old Testament were ranged in majestic attitudes, leading up to representations of Christ and the Virgin. Other statues, inside the cathedrals or decorating their outer walls, were created in more natural postures, although their immobility gave an impression of grandeur and expressed the respect of the masses for holiness. Stained glass, however, was an innovation: the colours created an atmosphere of mystery and the window pictures presented scenes from the Bible, but also figures of ordinary people. The first great achievement in this field were the windows of the abbey of *St. Denis near

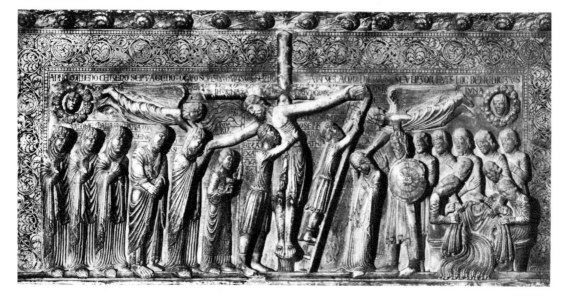

The Deposition from the Cross *by Antelami at the cathedral of Parma (1179)*

John the Baptist; *14th-century Angers tapestry*

Paris, where biblical figures and saints alternate with parables, such as the "Tree of *Jesse", representing the verse: "And there shall come forth a rod out of the stem of Jesse, and a branch shall grow out of his roots" (Isaiah 11:1), referring to the Davidic descent of Christ, or depicting the flight of the Holy Family to Egypt. The most perfect examples of stained glass are found at the cathedral of *Chartres (end of the 12th and beginning of the 13th century), where biblical and religious subjects alternate with secular. Here, besides kings and queens and nobles, are shown crafts-men and peasants with their tools. Thus, a humanist concept of society found its artistic expression, best symbolized in the main rose-window over the central portal, dedicated to the scene of creation, wherein the central figure is that of Adam. The same trend is to be found in the art of illumination, where the miniature was perfected in the 12th to 15th centuries. As learning became more widespread, and princely palaces acquired libraries, books were lavishly illustrated with both sacred and profane motifs. The *Livre des Heures* of the duke of Berry from the second part of the 14th century is the most beautiful of these, with its 12 illuminations corresponding to the months of the year. Illuminations were also made by Jewish artists and among their finest creations should be mentioned the *Prayer Book of Worms* (12th century), and the *Sarajevo *Haggadah* (14th century). The Gothic style also reached the goldsmiths and porcelain makers, such as those of Limoges, while in the palaces and churches cabinet makers applied it to furniture.

Pre-Renaissance A. began in northern Italy at the end of the 13th and beginning of the 14th century, evolving out of the Gothic style. The school of Pisa, led by *Andrea Pisano, marked the new trend of greater naturalism in sculpture, and was followed in Siena and Florence, where it was adopted in painting too. Certain Byzantine elements of colours and haloes were combined with the traditional western motifs and, together with the new approach to form, produced a more humanist artistic expression, heralding the coming Renaissance. In Italy the transition was chronologically uneven: in *Lombardy the Gothic style remained in use until about the middle of the 15th century, when the pre-Renaissance stage appeared for a short time and quickly made way for the Renaissance style. In central Italy, however, notably in Pisa, Siena, Florence, Rimini and to some extent Rome, the pre-Renaissance stage lasted longer, from the 14th to the middle of the 15th century, although certain elements of Renaissance A. appeared as early as the beginning of the 15th century. The *Black Death of 1348 had a significant impact on the transition: human suffering was vividly observed and the artists sought to represent figures expressing the gamut of human feelings, which caused them to break at last with the stiffly-elaborate Gothic majesty. Pre-Renaissance A. grew out of the Gothic also in the *Burgundian lands, especially in the Low Countries, in the 15th century. It evolved mainly in painting, in which, in contrast with Italy, sharp colours were used, but also in a realistic style of expression, which was favoured by the burgher class and the city magistrates.

Pre-Columbian A. in America developed indepen-dently of medieval Europe, out of the local civiliza-tions, the most important of which were the Aztec in

Mexico, the Maya in Central America, and the Inca in Peru. Mayan A. flourished in the 5th-7th centuries, when most of the extant monuments were built and decorated. While having a certain monolithic character, their sculpture and painting used human motifs in allegorical representation, combined with serpents, which were a religious symbol. The Aztecs inherited from the Maya much of their artistic conception, but in the 13th-15th centuries introduced motifs of their own faith, giving a dramatic expression to nature and the fear of death. The Incas, whose empire reached its zenith in the 12th-13th centuries, created an artistic style based on geometrical forms, both in architecture and the decorative arts. They made pottery in a very particular style, such as the *Aribal*, and specialized in metallurgy, including gold with which they decorated the temples of their capital Cuzco.

H. Gardner, *Art through the Ages* (1936);
A. Hauser, *The Social History of Art* (1952);
H. Focillon, *Art d'Occident* (1938).

ARTEVELDE, JAMES (Jacques) VAN (1290-1345) Flemish merchant and leader. Born at Ghent to a family of cloth merchants who imported wool from England, A. continued the family business. At the beginning of the *Hundred Years' War, *Edward III forbade the export of wool to *Flanders, as a punitive measure against its count, Louis I, who took the French side. The economy of Ghent was severely affected, and a revolt against the count united the population. A. became its leader and, in 1338, the count was expelled and he was chosen as captain of the city. He negotiated with the kings of England and France, and obtained their recognition of Flemish neutrality. The English prohibition was lifted and wool was again imported, restoring the prosperity to the city. The communes of Bruges and Ypres signed an act of federation with Ghent, recognizing A. as common leader. He ruled Flanders for seven years, trying to maintain the balance between the social classes. But with prosperity the conflicts between the merchants and artisans reappeared and in 1345, the workers rebelled. A. asked for the help of Edward III, and became unpopular with the democratic party. He was murdered in the uprising and the rule of the count was restored.

H. van Werveke, *Jacques van Artevelde* (1942).

ARTEVELDE, PHILIP VAN (1340-82) Son of James A., Flemish leader. In 1381 he led the uprising of Ghent against its count, Louis II, and like his father succeeded in uniting the social classes in the city. He organized an army and conquered Bruges. The revolt was viewed as a danger to the social order in France, and *Charles VI sent an army to support Louis II. In a battle at *Roose-beke the French army defeated the forces of Ghent, and A. was killed.

W. J. Ashley, *James and Philip Van Artevelde* (1883).

ARTHUR Legendary hero of the *Celtic Britons, around whose figure were woven many tales and literary works. While the legendary quality is obvious in chroni-cles of the 12th century and later, it seems that they had a historical foundation: in 540 the Celtic historian Gildas reported that, at the beginning of the century, a warrior named Arthur succeeded in halting the *Anglo-Saxon conquest of western Britain and won a number of battles, the most important having been that of Mons Badonis. In the 9th and 10th centuries chroniclers described A. as a Christian leader, whose fight against the pagan Anglo-Saxons was a holy war; it was said that he fell in battle in 537. From the beginning of the 12th century the figure was transformed into the mythological one of King A., whose youth was spent in wandering and marked by miracles, and who, as king, conquered European countries such as Spain and Italy. He held at his court a "round table", around which sat twelve knights, symbolizing the twelve apostles of Christ, representing the ideal of perfect chivalry. But his sister's son Mordred, who had taken his wife *Guinevere, rebelled and conquered his kingdom. A., severely wounded, found refuge in the island of Avalon, with his sister, the witch Morgain (Morgan le Fay), whose land could be seen from afar but never approached (hence "Fata Morgana" for mirage). He remained there for ages, waiting for the right time to return and save Britain from foreign conquerors — to whom the 12th-century chroniclers added the *Normans. This legendary account became from the 1160s the basis of a vast literary output in French, particularly at the court of the counts of *Champagne. King A. and his twelve knights were heroes of poems and romances glorifying the archetypes of French chivalry, eulogizing them as warriors, men of tested fidelity, wise and perfect Christians. The most important poet of the Arthurian cycle was *Chrétien de Troyes, who between 1160-70 wrote in praise of five Arthurian heroes: Erec, Cligès, Launcelot, Ywain and Percivale. Thereby he launched what became one of the most popular themes in mediaeval literature. At the end of the 12th and the beginning of the 13th century, the number of these poems increased and some were also composed in German. Important works were written about Arthurian heroes like Percivale and Tristram and became literary classics: e.g., Percivale (in German Parsival) was the subject of a religious myth, "The Quest of the Holy Grail", in which he personified fidelity and heroism. The adventures of *Tristram and Ysolde are still among the most beautiful romances of adventure, heroism and love. The Arthurian cycle was further amplified during the 13th century, and became very popular in England, where in 1470 Sir Thomas Malory composed its poetic synthesis in his *Morte d'Arthur*, which concluded the medieval cycle, bringing together in one great romance all the heroes of the various legends.

R. S. Loomis, ed., *The Arthurian Literature in the Middle Ages* (1959).

ARTHUR I OF BRITTANY (1187-1203) Son of Geoffrey *Plantagenet, grandson of Henry II. In 1199, after the death of *Richard I, a party of the nobility supported his claim to the English throne, but his uncle *John Lackland succeeded to it. A.'s cause was supported in 1201 by *Philip II of France, who, as suzerain, recognized him as legal heir of the *Angevin dominions in France. John had him put in prison, where he was murdered, probably by the king himself. The crime made the nobility on the Continent desert John's party, and Normandy and Anjou were conquered with little opposition by Philip II.

F. M. Powicke, *The Loss of Normandy* (1912).

ARTOIS County in northern France, corresponding geographically to the diocese of *Arras (established at the beginning of the 4th century). In the 9th century A. became part of the powerful county of *Flanders and remained under Flemish domination until 1180,

King Arthur and his Round Table

when it was given to *Philip II of France as the dowry of his wife Isabella of Hainault, niece of Philip of Alsace, count of Flanders. In 1237 the county was given as an apanage by *Louis IX to this brother Robert, who took the title count of Artois (1237-50), and followed his brother to the *Crusade of 1248. He was killed at Mansurah in Egypt. During the second half of the 13th century the administration of the county was organized on the model of the royal demesne; Count Robert II improved its financial organization and appointed officers (1293), breaking with the last forms of political *feudalism in the county. At the beginning of the 14th century the county was troubled by wars of succession, between Mahaut, the daughter of Robert II (1309-29), and Robert III, his grandson. Mahaut was recognized by the crown and finally Robert III went to England and allied himself with *Edward III, so as to strengthen his claim, having been suspected of the sudden death of Mahaut. The county also suffered from the devastations of the *Hundred Years' War and the *Black Death, but it seems that the ravages were comparatively minor, and in the second half of the 14th century prosperity was restored. In 1367, with the marriage of Margaret of Flanders, heiress of A., with *Philip the Bold, duke of Burgundy, the county was incorporated into the great Burgundian state and, in 1477, it was inherited together with the Low Countries by *Maximilian of Hapsburg.

C. Hirschauer, *Les Etats d'Artois de leur origine à l'occupation française, 1340-1640* (1923);

J. Lestocquoy, *Histoire du Pas-de-Calais* (1946).

ARUNDEL, THOMAS (1353-1414) Member of the important family of the earls of Arundel, he was destined to an ecclesiastic career. In 1374 he became bishop of Ely and, in 1388, archbishop of York. In 1396 he was transferred to Canterbury, becoming the chief ecclesiastic of the English Church. An influential politician, he was, together with his brother, among the leaders of the opposition to *Richard II. Impeached in 1397, he was restored to his see in 1399 by *Henry IV, who also appointed him chancellor. He opposed and persecuted the *Lollards.

K. B. McFarlane, *John Wycliffe and the Beginnings of English Non-Conformity* (1953).

ASAPH, St. (6th century) Welsh saint. He was one of the first organizers of the Catholic Church in Wales. About 570 he became abbot of Llanelli, later called St. Asaph, and is considered as the first (historical) bishop of the country.

DNB, Suppl. I (1901).

ASAPH "THE PHYSICIAN" (6th century) Jewish physician, who lived probably in Iraq or Persia, famous for a medical treatise written largely by his disciples and named after him. (Some of it is of later authorship, dating from the 7th to the 10th century.) Nothing is known about his life and activity, but the book, written in Hebrew, is a valuable source for the medical knowledge of his time. The attention given to the climate of Palestine and Syria, as well as the quotations in Aramaic and Persian, may indicate that he lived also in those countries. He was influenced by the Mesopotamian, Persian and Greek medical science, while there is no trace of Arab influence. His anatomy was merely a classification of parts of the human body, with particular attention to the blood. He also tried to describe some embryological phenomena, being interested in problems of procreation. His originality in this field is his adoption of the Talmudic idea of the importance of the first 40 days of the foetus. An important part of the treatise is devoted to the description of illnessess, from the viewpoints of prognosis, diagnosis, hygiene and pharmacology. A.'s approach to medicine was chiefly a preventive one, hence his attention to hygienic conditions, in relation to climate and food. For this reason he explained the practical character of Talmudic prescriptions. The treatise also contains translations from Greek works and was popular in Spain and, in 1279, was translated into Latin .

S. Muntner, *The Book of Medicine by Asaph* (1947).

ASCALON City in southern Palestine, on the Mediterranean coast. Under *Byzantine rule the ancient city began to decline, although its harbour was still in use. The decay was accentuated after the Arab conquest (636), when it became a provincial town in the *Jund* (province) of *Filastin*, whose capital was the new city of Ramlah. In the 10th century A. passed to the *Fatimids and became one of their strongholds in southern Palestine. Its population increased and a large Jewish community settled there. The importance of A. for the Fatimids increased after the foundation of the *Crusaders' kingdom of Jerusalem. In the first years of the Crusaders' kingdom, the plain between A. and Ramlah was the theatre of annual wars between the Egyptian army, based in A., and the Crusaders. To prevent more attacks *Fulk of Anjou built in 1136 four castles around the city, though its importance had diminished. In 1153 it was conquered by *Baldwin III and became the seat of a county which was given to the younger brother of the king. A. was conquered by *Saladin in 1187, who destroyed it before it was taken again by the Crusaders in 1191, under *Richard I of

England. The latter had to leave the city, which was reconquered by the Crusaders in 1239 and fortified again. In 1247 it fell to the *Ayyubids, but did not recover its prosperity. In 1270 *Baibars destroyed it to prevent a possible landing of the Crusaders and it remained ruined until the 20th century.

J. Prawer, *The Crusaders* (1973).

ASCETICISM Monastic term in the Middle Ages, from the Greek for "exercise". In early Christianity the term was used to indicate preparation for martyrdom, expressing the idea of moral exercise in the worship of God. In this sense the notion was adapted from the Stoics, meaning an act performed for the purification of the soul. With *Anthony of Alexandria, at the beginning of the 4th century, the term began to take on an added physical significance, such as isolation in the desert, abstinence, fasts and vigils. With the emergence of *Benedictine monasticism in the West, the term acquired a particular significance in Catholic monasticism, in which the trend of religious communities opposed the individual isolation of the East. Thus Western A. stressed penance and corporal suffering, in emulation of the sufferings of Jesus. In the 12th century the ascetic ideal found its expression in the new monastic orders, such as the *Cistercians, who established their abbeys in deserted places and farmed fallow lands. In the 13th century, with the advent of the *Mendicant orders, A. was identified with poverty and spiritual work, represented as the reaction to the worldliness of the Church and the materialism of society. A treatise such as *The Little Flowers of St. *Francis* represents this trend of A., as an imitation of Christ. At the end of the Middle Ages, particularly after the *Black Death, ascetic trends were an integral part of the works of the moralists, such as *Thomas à Kempis, combining it with mysticism.

J. de Ghellinck, *Patristique et Moyen Age* (1948).

ASHER BAR JEHIEL (ROSH) (1250-1327) One of the most important rabbinical exegetes of the Middle Ages. Born in Germany, the son of Rabbi Jehiel, a famous pietist, he studied at his father's school and then at Troyes in France. After his marriage he settled in Cologne and later went to Worms, where he studied under Rabbi Mayer of Rothenburg, the greatest figure of German Jewry. After his master's arrest, he became the leader of the German Jews, trying to fortify the spirits of persecuted communities. His decisions concerning the conduct of individuals and communities hurt by the persecutions were accepted by Jews everywhere. In 1303 he fled from Germany to avoid his master's fate, and wandered in Italy and Spain. In 1305 he was invited to be the rabbi of the community of Toledo, where he remained until his death. He introduced in Spain the teaching methods of *Ashkenazi Jews, and particularly the study of the *Tosafists. Though he was opposed to philosophy, he admitted the independent study of the sciences. His reputation became so great that questions were addressed to his court at Toledo not only from all the Jewish communities in Spain, but also from other European countries and as far as Russia. Besides decisions and legal treatises, wherein he also used authorities from Germany and France, and which represent a codex of Talmudic jurisdiction, he also wrote commentaries on the Mishnah and *Tosafist works.

A. C. Freimann, *Ascher Bar Yechiel* (1918).

ASHKENAZ Hebrew geographic term, which in the 10th-11th centuries referred exclusively to western Germany, and later to greater Germany. After the expulsion of the *Jews from England (1291) and from France (1306), the term Ashkenazi began to be used to indicate European Jews, except for those of Spain and Italy with the cultural significance, such as the use of Yiddish as a common language and the heritage of the French and German Jewry's methods of thought and learning.

ASHTORI HAFARHI (c. 1280-c. 1355) Jewish physician and geographer. Born in Provence, in a family of Spanish origin, he studied Talmudic exegesis and medicine at Montpellier. With the expulsion of the Jews in 1306 he left France and for a number of years wandered in Spain and Egypt. About 1310 he decided to move to Palestine and went to Jerusalem; but finding there a strong opposition to *Maimonides, he left the holy city and settled at Beth-Shean, where he practised medicine. He travelled through the country, studying its topography, flora and fauna. His systematic research was a pioneering work for the Middle Ages and is the first geographical study of the Holy Land, published in Hebrew under the symbolic title, *Kaftor Va-Perah* (Bud and Flower, meaning "wonderful"). He also wrote treatises on medicine, which he mentioned in this work, which are lost.

E. Grünhut, *Die Geographie Palästinas nach Estori Farchi* (1913).

ASIA The largest continent of the three known to the medieval world. Except in the northern plains of Siberia, which were cut off from the civilized world, there were great civilizations with major cultural and technological achievements in the continent, although they were not always known to one another. It is, therefore, impossible to use the historical divisions which apply mainly to European history, to the entire continent of A. The histories of its different civilizations must be divided in accordance with their independent evolutions. During the thousand years of the Middle Ages, only the 13th century, that of the *Mongol empire, can be described as a period of interrelation between them. While following the European periodization, as accepted by general history, four main cultural and historical groups, divided geographically, evolved independently between 500 and 1500:
1. Western A., with the *Byzantine, *Persian and *Arab empires, dominated by Islam from the 7th century on.
2. Central A., the country of the steppes and nomadic tribes, which played an important role in the great migrations in the 5th and 6th centuries, and then dominated by *Turkish and *Turkoman tribes until the emergence of the Mongol empire in the 13th century.
3. Southern A., including the *Indian subcontinent and its dependencies, whose history was untouched by outside events, such as the fall of the Roman empire, until it faced the Islamic penetration at the beginning of the 11th century and the Mongolian invasion at the end of the 15th. Thus Indian civilization emerged and grew independently of the classical and Islamic ones. 4. East A., including *China, *Japan, *Korea and Indo-China, dominated by the Chinese empire and its civilization.

R. Grousset, *Histoire de l'Asie* (1958).

ASKOLD (d. 879) Scandinavian chieftain, a follower of *Rurik. Very little is known about him; he probably settled in Novgorod with Rurik and, in 862, became one of his officers. Sent by his lord to impose his rule in the area of the Dnieper, he conquered *Kiev and imposed his dominion on the Slavs of the area, who had been paying tribute to the *Khazars. He was a prince of Kiev, as a vassal of Rurik's, until his death. It seems that he tried to establish an independent principality, but was killed by Rurik's heir *Oleg.

V. Nabokov, *The Song of Igor's Campaign* (1960).

ASPAR (d. 471) Alani chieftain, general of the Eastern Roman empire. He joined the army as a Barbarian officer under *Theodosius II, and fought for the integrity of what was to become the Byzantine empire. He became so influential that after the death of Theodosius, he secured the election of Pulcheria, the emperor's sister, having forced her to marry one of his associates, Marcian (450-57). When the latter died, A. again controlled the election and proclaimed a Dacian soldier, *Leo I, emperor. After he was defeated by the *Vandals in 470 he lost his influence, and was murdered by the Isaurian guard at Leo's order.

A. H. M. Jones, *The Later Roman Empire* (1964).

ASPERUKH (7th century) Khan of the *Bulgars. Grandson of the fabled leader of the Bulgars, *Kubrat, he led his tribe on its migration from the Don, where they had been displaced by the *Khazars, to the Danube. In 629 he supplied military aid to Emperor *Heraclius, and settled in Moesia (modern Bulgaria), establishing his capital at Pliska in Dobrudja. He began the Bulgarian expansion southwards in the Balkans.

S. Runciman, *History of the First Bulgarian Empire* (1930).

ASSASSINS (Hashishin) Radical Moslem sect in the *Ismaili faction of the *Shiites. Organized to fight the opponents of the Ismaili by any means, including murder and poisoning, they used to fortify their spirits with the aid of hashish (hence their Arabic name which means users of hashish, pronounced by the French-speaking *Crusaders as "assassin", which became synonymous with murderer). The sect was organized at the end of the 11th century by the Persian Ismaili leader Hasan-i Sabbah, who was fighting against the *Seljuk sultanate from his stronghold of Alamuth in northern Persia. The earliest activities of the A. were in 1090 in Persia, but very soon they spread to Iraq, Syria and Egypt and when Hasan-i Sabbah died in 1124, the sect numbered thousands of adherents in several countries, and was greatly feared on account of its fanaticism and violence. In the 12th century the sect spread in Persia and continued to fight the Seljuks, who proceeded to massacre thousands of Ismailis. At the beginning of the 13th century the Persian A. became somewhat more moderate, but soon they had to fight against the *Mongols and were destroyed by *Hulagu Khan. At the beginning of the 12th century the disciples of Hassan formed a powerful organization in Syria, mainly in Aleppo and Damascus. In 1126 the Damascus authorities invested the A. with the city of Banias, hoping to save the capital from their influence while using them to fight against the Crusaders. But after their repression in Damascus, the A. preferred to surrender Banias to the Crusaders and continue their activities against their Moslem foes. The Aleppo A., on the other hand, who had established a protectorate of the Shiite population of the city, had to fight against *Zengi and *Nureddin,

The cathedral and convent of St. Francis at Assisi

who, in 1152, imposed the *Sunnite faith in Aleppo. Most of the A. fled to Jebel Al-Summaq, the mountains between Aleppo and Homs, near the border of Antioch, where they built a stronghold. Under the leadership of Sinan Ibn Salman Ibn Muhammad, called Rashid a-Din, they founded a little state, which succeeded in maintaining its independence even in the time of *Saladin; attempts to murder him were probably made, but were not successful, and attempts to repress them were equally ineffective. Under Sinan the A. began to act against the Crusaders and, in 1192, two of them murdered King *Conrad of Montferrat. In order to stop their activities in the Crusader states, some tribute was paid to them during the 13th century. The Mongol menace induced the Syrian A. to cooperate with other Moslems against the power which massacred their Persian brethren. After 1261 *Baibars was powerful enough to make their state a protectorate and prevent their leaders from re-establishing its independence. At the end of the 13th century the realm of the "Old Man of the Mountain", as Sinan was called by his sect, was finally integrated in the *Mamluk sultanate.

B. Lewis, *The Assassins* (1970).

ASSISI Town in central *Italy which flourished in Roman times. In 545 it was conquered and destroyed by the *Ostrogoth king Totila and only a few vestiges remain of the ancient city. Later in the 6th century a bishopric was settled there, but the city had not yet recovered from the devastation. After the *Lombard conquest it was included in the duchy of Spoleto (7th-9th centuries). In the middle of the 9th century, it became the centre of a county, and was disputed between the bishops and a local feudal family. In 1197 it passed to the government of the bishops. In the 13th century,

A. reached the peak of its development, being the native city of St. *Francis and one of the centres of the Franciscan order. The Gothic church, built over the tombs of St. Francis and St. *Clare, became the object of one of the most popular pilgrimages in the late Middle Ages. At the beginning of the 14th century a commune was established in the city and its leaders, supported by Perugia, fought against the bishop's government. The city lost its independence and during the 14th-15th centuries was disputed between Perugia, Spoleto, the dukes of Milan and the church-state of Rome, which finally annexed it to the papal state. These wars did much harm to the city, which declined and became entirely dependent on the Franciscan pilgrimage. The cult of St. Francis made A. one of the artistic centres of pre-Renaissance Italy and beautiful frescoes were painted in its church.

F. Hermann, *Assisi, the City of St. Francis* (1928).

ASSIZES An Old French term, meaning laws. Used mainly to denote feudal legislation, either particular laws imposed by the king with the consent of the nobles (e.g., the Assizes of *Clarendon under Henry II of England), or the codification of laws, e.g., the *Assizes of Jerusalem, Assizes of Romania. In northern France the term also meant courts, whose verdicts were considered *customary laws.

ASSIZES OF JERUSALEM (Assises de Jérusalem) The feudal customary law of the Latin kingdom of *Jerusalem, compiled in French by *John of Ibelin, count of Jaffa, in the middle of the 13th century. The A. are a collection of all the laws, privileges and ordinances from the beginnings of the kingdom in the 12th century. They open with a "letter to the king", which is an important document expressing the views of the nobility on the regime of the Crusaders' state, showing the supreme authority of the *Haute Cour*, the organ of the nobility of the realm. The A. are divided in two parts: the first part, continuing the "letter to the king", is the law of the kingdom and the nobility, and the second, the *Assises aux Bourgeois*, deals with the legislation of the cities, trade and the burghers.

A. Beugnot, ed., *Les Assises de Jerusalem (Recueil des Historiens des Croisades, Lois)*;

J. Prawer, *The Crusaders* (1973).

ASSIZES OF ROMANIA (Assises de la Romanie) The feudal law of the Venetian possessions in the Balkans, including the provinces which belonged to feudal lords in the *Latin empire of Constantinople. Its first edition, in French, dates from 1325 and records unwritten laws and customs. In the 15th century the Venetian authorities issued two official editions (1423 and 1453). The A. are an important source for the study of the influence of Byzantine legal tradition on the basic structure of a colonial society.

G. Recoura, *Les Assises de la Romanie* (1930);

D. Jacoby, *La Féodalité en Grèce médiévale: les Assises de Romanie* (1971).

ASTROLABE Instrument for *astronomical observation and measuring the positions of the stars. The A. was developed in Moslem Spain, notably at Córdoba, by Arab and Jewish mathematicians and astronomers. The observations of Al-Bitrurgi in the second half of the 12th century, which were used in the composition of the Alfonsine Tables, prepared in 1253 by order of *Alfonso X of Castile, served also for the development of the A. In the 15th century the instrument was perfected and was used in navigation. In 1482, Abraham *Zaccutto revised its elements and produced an A., which served Columbus in his explorations.

P. H. van Cittert, *Astrolabes* (1954).

ASTROLOGY One of the oldest sciences of human civilization, based on the observation of the celestial bodies and their movements, and speculation on their supposed influence on human life and events. The origins of A. are rooted in the ancient Babylonian heritage, but medieval society developed a syncretic view of astrology, containing Persian, Indian and Greek elements, which were merged in a philosophical system based on the Hellenistic thought. Thus the Stoic philosophy, based on the theory of a universal rule of cosmic harmony, provided the theoretical ground of A. as the master-science of nature, represented by gods and stars, with their influence on each day of the week. Although A. was tolerated by Judaism, the Fathers of the Christian Church opposed it strongly, considering it a manifestation of paganism. A. was, therefore, neglected in medieval Europe for generations, especially between the 5th and 12th centuries, the only exception being its medical application (the influence of the stars on the health), which was studied in the 8th century by *Bede in England and in the 9th century by *Rabanus Maurus in Germany. On the other hand, it was studied and practised in Islam, both under Persian influence and of the many translations from the Greek in the 8th century. While Islam accepted the philosophical principles of the Stoics, it also adopted the astronomical and mathematical method of Ptolemy of Alexandria, whose *Almagest* was translated into Arabic. Between the 9th and 11th centuries several Jewish and Arab astrologers

published observations of the heavens and sought to define their influence on cosmic and human life, with the intention of foretelling events – this was the horoscope, which was based on the relative positions of the stars and planets during the 12 months of the year. The belief that the earth is the only planet which does not move remained axiomatic. The system was elaborated in the 9th century by *Abu Maashar (Albumassar) and by the Jews Sahel Ibn Bishar and Ma Sa Allah (Mesalla), and perfected in the 11th century by Ali Ibn Abi Al-Rajal (Abenragel); the latter's works were translated into Latin in the 12th century and helped the development of astrological studies in medieval Europe. While the theologians continued to oppose it, it was accepted by the scientists and after Roger *Bacon, towards the end of the 13th century, an ambiguous attitude towards astrology was adopted in Catholic Europe. At the beginning of the 14th century, with the appointment of official astrologers at the royal courts, and especially the papal court in *Avignon, the attitude became openly favourable. To counter the influence of Jewish astrologers, a new school of "Christian" astrology was founded in the West. It made use of the Latin translations from the Arabic, but also accepted Jewish contributions, ranging from *Abraham Bar Hiyya in 12th-century Catalonia, to *Gersonides of the early 14th century – the latter was, *inter alia*, the official astrologer of the papal court at Avignon. One of the most important teachings of Abraham Bar Hiyya was that A. is based on the divine pre-determination of human fate, revealed by the stars and, therefore, subject to certain rules; this idea was held also by *Yehudah Halevi and *Abraham Ibn Ezra. Gersonides, who adopted a critical-rationalist attitude towards astrology, believed that it represented pre-determination, but, he added, human knowledge of the cosmic system being imperfect, astrologers were liable to err in their interpretations of the astronomical observations. Moreover, the freedom of choice given to men by God could also have an influence on astrology. In the 15th century astrology was studied in Italy, and became part of a "good education" in the Renaissance.

R. Eisler, *The Royal Art of Astrology* (1946).

ASTRONOMY The science of the celestial bodies. Medieval A. was based on the Ptolemaic system, as transmitted to Europe in the *Almagest*, through the astronomers of the Arabic world. Because of the great attention paid to *astrology, A. did not develop as an independent science, but largely in relation to the former. Only in 12th-century Andalusia, with the development of trigonometry, did an important improvement take place in astronomical observation and measurement. The Persian Nasir al-Din al-Tusi (1201-74), who headed the observatory founded at Maragha by the Mongolian khan *Hulagu, produced the astronomical tables of 1272, called the Il-Khanian tables which, together with those of *Alfonso X of 1252, were the basis of measurements and were used in navigation. The translation of the *Almagest* into Latin by Gerard of Cremona in 1175, was followed by astronomical works written by West Europeans, but they remained dependent on Arab science for centuries. Under the influence of Cardinal Johannes Bessarion, in the 15th century, European A., led by the German Peuerbach (who published his *Theory of the New Planets* in 1472),

Arab with an astrolabe and astronomer with a sextant

absorbed fully the Ptolemaic methods, and paved the
way for the humanists to attempt new methods of
research, culminating with Copernicus in the Renaissance.
P. Doig, *A Concise History of Astronomy* (1950).

ASTURIAS Country in northern *Spain, between the
mountains of Asturia-León and the Bay of Biscay. At
the beginning of the Middle Ages it was part of the kingdom of the *Visigoths. The Arabs, who conquered
Spain in 711, failed in their attempt to take A. in 718.
Led by a local leader, Pelagius, the inhabitants defeated
the Arabs at Covadonga, and Pelagius became the first
king of A. In 765, Froila, the son of *Alfonso I, established his capital at Oviedo and continued his father's
wars against the Arabs. At the end of the 9th century
*Alfonso III succeeded in uniting almost all of Christian
Spain under his rule. When he died (910), his realm was
divided into three petty kingdoms: A., Galicia and
León, the last of which was the most important. In 925
an attempt to unite the states was made by the royal
court of León, but it did not last and A. survived as
little principalities, which were annexed to Castile in
1037. To commemorate its particular entity, the heir
to the throne of Castile was called, from 1388 on,
Prince of Asturias.
A. Castro, *The Structure of Spanish History* (1954).

ATABEG Turkish term meaning governor, or "acting
for the lord". In the tribal system of the 10th-11th
centuries, the A. was a veteran officer attached to the
house of the *beg* (prince), where he was entrusted with
administrative responsibility and, mainly, the education
of the prince's sons. After the *Seljuk conquest of the
Abbasid caliphate, the post of the A. became a political
one. The Seljuk princes of the vast Turkish empire
appointed As. to assist them in the government of their
principalities. In the first half of the 12th century, with
the extinction of Seljuk dynasties in Syria, and particularly at Damascus, Aleppo and Mosul, the As. seized
power and created their own states. The most famous
A. was *Zengi, who seized the government of Mosul
and Aleppo and created a powerful state.
EI, I.

ATHALARIC (516-34) King of the *Ostrogoths of
Italy (526-34). He was the grandson of *Theodoric
through his mother Amalasuntha. Upon Theodoric's
death he was proclaimed king and reigned at Ravenna
under the regency of his mother. In 533, attaining
majority, he appointed *Cassiodorus praetorian prefect
and continued his predecessor's policy between the
Ostrogoths and Romans.
J. M. Wallace-Hadrill, *The Barbarian West* (1967).

ATHANAGILD (d. 567) King of the *Visigoths (554-
67). Member of a noble Visigothic family from Andalusia, he rebelled against *Agila in 550 and sought the
help of *Justinian, who sent him a fleet and a very small
army to Spain, enabling him to defeat Agila at Seville
and proclaim himself king. He had to surrender Andalusia and part of the province of Cartagena to the Byzantines and, at that sacrifice, was able to consolidate
his own rule. He established his capital at Toledo, which
became the new centre of the Visigothic realm, fought
the Basques and pushed them back to Navarre, and prevented the Franks from further progress in *Septimania.
R. de Abadal y de Vinyals, *Del reino de Tolosa al reino
de Toledo* (1960).

ATHANARIC (4th century) *Visigothic leader. In 375,
pushed by the *Huns, he led his tribe into the Balkans
and attacked the Roman empire. In 376 he was allowed
to settle there with his tribe, but was dissatisfied with
the terms. He continued southward and, in 378, defeated the Roman army at Adrianople and killed the
Emperor Valens. This was the first time that Barbarian
cavalry defeated the Roman legions.
K. K. Klein, Frithigern, *Athanarich und die Spaltung des
Westgotenvolkes* (1960).

ATHANASIUS, St. (296-373) Bishop of *Alexandria
(328-73). He was the chief opponent of Arianism (see
*Church) at the First Council of Nicaea in 325, where he
composed the *Creed of Athanasius*, which is to this day
the basic confession of Orthodoxy and Catholicism. In
336 he was exiled by Emperor Constantine to Trier and
he returned to his see in 337. In 339 he was forced to
flee to Rome, where he won the support of the Western
Church. Restored in 346, he was again exiled in 356. He
was also exiled by Emperor Julian in 362, and only in
366 was finally restored and prepared the triumph of
the Nicaean party. In his several periods of exile, he
became acquainted with many church leaders, to whom
he wrote treatises in defence of his theses, and a great
number of letters. A. was a friend and protector of the
hermits of the Egyptian desert.
Mueller, *Lexicon Athanasianum* (1952).

ATHANASIUS OF MT. ATHOS, St. (920-1003) Byzantine monk. Born at Trebizond, he became a monk in
Bythinia and then went to Mount *Athos, where in 961
he established the first of its famous monasteries.
Although it was opposed by the hermits already established on the mountain, the monastery prospered thanks
to imperial support. He became abbot-general of all the
communities of the Mount, which counted 58 at his
death.
R. M. Dawkins, *The Monks of Athos* (1936).

ATHAULF (d. 415) King of the *Visigoths (410-15).
A brother-in-law of *Alaric, he was proclaimed king at
the latter's death. An admirer of Roman civilization, he
married Honorius' sister, Galla Placida, whom he had
captured at Rome. He led his people from southern

Italy to Gaul and Spain, where he founded a kingdom, whose capital he established at *Toulouse. Master of about half of Gaul and part of Spain, he distributed lands to his warriors, who settled chiefly in southern Gaul and in northern Spain.

R. de Abadal y de Vinyals, *Del reino de Tolosa al reino de Toledo* (1960).

ATHENS At the beginning of the Middle Ages, A. still epitomized the classical heritage, although it was merely a provincial city without any political importance. The symbol of antiquity was the Academy of Plato, considered an embodiment of the Hellenistic-pagan tradition. The *Byzantine influence, based on Christianity, began to be felt in the 5th century, but was not yet strong enough to overwhelm the vestiges of paganism, as it had done in the other places in the Roman empire. In the 6th century *Justinian took strong measures to extirpate paganism and impose orthodoxy throughout the empire; one of these measures was the abolition of the Athenian academy in 529. The city declined further, becoming a minor provincial town. In the 7th-8th centuries it was attacked by *Avars and *Slavs, but was saved by its ancient fortifications. The economic stagnation of the city was so marked that the Byzantine government established the provincial capital of Hellas in Thebes.

The seizure of Constantinople by the participants of the Fourth *Crusade in 1204, and the establishment of the *Latin empire of Constantinople, brought about a change of regime at A. The city and its surroundings were given as a fief to the *Burgundian knight Odo of La Roche, who made it a local principality, which became duchy in 1270. In 1311 the duke *Walter (Gauthier) of Brienne was defeated by the *Catalan adventurers, representing the merchants of Barcelona and other Catalan cities; they conquered the duchy and made it their commercial base, being formally dependent on the *Aragon kings of Sicily, who did not interfere in the affairs of the duchy. Their rule ushered in a period of economic prosperity for A., though it also involved it in the struggles over the Mediterranean trade. In 1387-88 the Italian competitors of the Catalans, supported by the *Angevin kings of Naples, attacked A. and their leader, *Ranieri Acciaiuoli, became the new duke. His descendants ruled A. until 1456, when it was conquered by the *Ottoman Turks. The 250 years of Latin, or Frankish, rule were a time of prosperity, thanks to the tolerant policy of the conquerors towards the local population and to its economic recovery.

F. Gregorovius, *Geschichte der Stadt Athen im Mittelalter* (1889);

K. M. Setton, *Catalan Domination of Athens* (1948).

ATHOS, MOUNT (The Holy Mountain) A mountain (2033 m high) in the centre of a peninsula in northern Greece, in the province of *Thessalonica. Hermits began to settle in A. in the 8th century, but the first monastery, the Lavra, was founded in 963 by St. *Athanasius. The place was declared to be holy and, with the support of the Byzantine emperors, many other monasteries were established there, observing the strict rule of St. *Basil. From the 11th century on, other Orthodox churches established monasteries on A., the first being a Russian abbey, founded in 1080 — but the majority was Greek. An abbot-general was elected by the monasteries to rule the mountain and to deal with the imperial

The monastery of St. Denis at Mount Athos, Greece

authorities. The monks of A., who were militant Orthodox, were persecuted under the *Latin empire of Constantinople (1204-61), and refused to accept its authority. In 1430 the monks submitted to the *Ottoman Turks and were granted religious autonomy and local rule. An unusual ancient rule forbids the access to Mount A. to any non-Christian, as well as any female, human and animal. Under the Byzantine regime the A. communities were richly endowed with lands in different parts of the empire, and the practice was adopted by other Orthodox rulers in Russia, Serbia, Bulgaria, Moldavia and Wallachia.

F. W. Hasluck, *Athos and its Monasteries* (1924).

ATOMISM The philosophical doctrine of small indivisible particles, inherited by medieval science from the Greek, which had applied it both in physics and geometry. The medieval thinkers received their idea of A. from the Platonic philosophy, which explained the role of the small particles in the organic creation of the universe. In the 12th century this theory was developed by the French philosopher *William of Conches, who believed in the indestructibility of matter and explained the properties of the elements in terms of the motions of particles. In the 13th century, under the influence of Arab theories of Aristotelian physics, A. was applied to *alchemy, as the theory of the decomposition of elements into atoms.

A. C. Crombie, *Science in the Middle Ages* (1952).

ATTILA (d. 453) King of the *Huns (434-53). Together with his brother Bleda, he ruled over the Hunnish
tribes from the Caspian Sea to the Rhine, their seat
being in Pannonia (modern Hungary). In 445 he murdered his brother and became the king of a vast empire. He
attacked the Balkans and forced the Eastern Roman
emperor, Theodosius II, to pay him tribute. In 450 he
asked the Western Roman emperor, *Valentinian III, to
give him his daughter Honoria as one of his wives, and
at his refusal decided to invade the Western Roman
empire. In 451 his army penetrated Gaul, destroying
everything in its way, and reached Orléans. He was
defeated on the Catalaunic plains (near Châlons), by a
Roman-Frankish-Gothic army, led by the Roman
general Aetius, after a prolonged and bloody battle. A.
left Gaul and, having reorganized his army, turned to
Italy, where he devastated the northeastern part of the
country. Refugees from his invasions fled to the northwestern shore of the Adriatic Sea and founded the city
of *Venice. A. continued his march to Florence, where
an epidemic decimated his army. The Roman authorities,
in terror at the news from the north, in 453 sent Pope
*Leo I to buy his withdrawal. A., who was unable to
continue his expedition, accepted the money and
returned to Hungary, where he died suddenly while
celebrating his marriage with the Burgundian princess
Ildico. Papal sources represented the outcome of the
interview at Florence as a miracle performed by the
pope, but it was achieved with the aid of enormous
quantities of gold and jewels. After the death of A., the
Hunnish empire disintegrated and fell; but his memory
remained imprinted in the minds of Europeans for
generations, because of his cruelty. For the moralists he
was the "scourge of God", sent to punish Christians for
their sins. A popular saying had it that "where A. set his
foot, the grass no longer grew".
E. A. Thompson, *A History of Attila and the Huns*
(1948).

AUBRI OF TROIS-FONTAINES (d. 1251) Historian.
A monk at the abbey of Trois-Fontaines in northern
France, he wrote a "universal chronicle" in which he
compiled the works of historians of previous eras together with his own accounts. He was one of the first
historians who, beginning in the 13th century, did not
limit themselves to stories and anecdotes, but also
introduced documents to support their accounts and
adopted a critical attitude towards the facts reported.
His chronicle is an important source for the events of
the first half of the 13th century.
J. W. Thompson, *History of Historical Writing* (1942).

AUGSBURG City in Germany on the river Lech, between Bavaria and Swabia. Founded by the Romans in
14 BC, A. was in the early Middle Ages one of the
centres of Christianity in Germany and the see of a
bishopric. In 497 it was annexed by *Clovis to his
Frankish kingdom, together with the whole country of
the Alamanni. In 955 it was attacked by the Hungarians,
who were decisively defeated by *Otto I near A., in
*Lechfeld. Between the 10th and the 13th century the
city, which belonged to its bishop, grew and became an
economic centre in southern Germany. In the 13th
century the burghers, conscious of their power, struggled
with the bishops, demanding autonomy and greater
freedom. A.'s position on the route between Venice and
northern Germany brought it not only prosperity, but

also political importance; in 1280 the burghers obtained
the status of an *imperial city, and were freed from the
rule of the bishops. In the 15th century A.'s prosperity
made it a major city in the German empire, and a branch
of the Fugger family settled there.
A. Gebhardt, *Handbuch der Deutschen Geschichte*
(1953).

AUGUSTINE, St. (Aurelius Augustinus; 354-430)
Bishop of Hippo and one of the Doctors of the Church.
While his life and activity belong to the classical age, of
which he is one of the last outstanding figures, his teaching and thought were of paramount importance in the
Middle Ages.
     Born in Tagaste (Munidia), to Monica, a devoted
Catholic, A. studied in his native town and in Carthage,
and in 373, began teaching rhetoric. He read the *Hor-
tensius* of Cicero in 373, and was attracted to the study
of philosophy. For nine years, he followed the Gnostic
doctrines of the *Manichaeans. Moving to Milan in 384,
A. was much influenced by Bishop *Ambrose. He converted to Catholicism and was baptized in 387. He returned to Africa the following year, and became bishop
of Hippo (modern Bône in Algeria) in 355.
     A.'s adoption of Platonic philosophy as a basis for
his own religious and political thought made it the
dominant philosophical system in western Europe.
He viewed the Christian religion as an organic system of
faith, which was to create the conditions for salvation
through the knowledge of God and the appropriate
behaviour of the faithful within the Church, which
represented the *corpus Christi* (the body of Christ); a
view which affected the ecclesiastical organization in the
Middle Ages, as well as the relations between Church
and lay society. His political ideas, as expressed in his
De civitate Dei (The City of God), were at the foundation of the medieval Christian state, which sought to
achieve the theocratic ideal regime, led by the Church
for the salvation of mankind. This was based on the
concept that the present is a mere phase on the way to
the ideal state, that of the kingdom of God, which
would come about some time in the future. Thus,
"political Augustinism", as the doctrine was called by
the political thinkers of the Middle Ages, implied the
acceptance by the Church of the social systems of
Christian states, with all their injustices, such as slavery,
or barbaric customs like trial by ordeal, on the condition that the lay ruler accepted the spiritual leadership
of the Church and its censure. The identification of the
state with Christian society (*Corpus Christi*) implied the
exclusion of non-Christians from the political body.
This exclusion was applied with extreme severity to
pagans, as demonstrated in the late 8th century by
*Charlemagne in Saxony ("convert or die"), whereas
Jews were tolerated and excluded only from public
office and the tenancy of lands. Moreover, lapsed
Christians, pronounced heretical by the Church, were also
excluded from the political body, but these had to be
punished for their sins, which were viewed as a form of
infectious disease. To prevent propagation of heresy
within the Christian body, the Church had to investigate
and extirpate the heretics. This Augustinian idea was the
basis for the establishment of the *Inquisition at the end
of the 12th century. Most medieval theologians and
thinkers did not know all the writings of A., which
were studied by a very small number of scholars. They

were familiar with the excerpts from his writings and the interpretations of his thought which were found in the works of St. *Isidore of Seville. This is particularly true of A.'s philisophical and theological works; his main political work, *The City of God*, was more widely known.

P. Batiffol, *A Monument to St. Augustine* (1930);
W. Ullmann, *A History of Political Thought: The Middle Ages* (1968).

AUGUSTINE OF CANTERBURY, St. (d. 604) Missionary and first archbishop of *Canterbury. Born in Italy, he was the prior of St. Andrew's Abbey in Rome. In 596 Pope *Gregory the Great sent him to propagate Christianity in England and to refound its church. In 597 he landed in Kent, where Queen Bertha, a Christian Frankish princess, received him. Her husband *Ethelbert formally adopted Christianity and imposed it on his people. A. was consecrated archbishop of Canterbury and began his dual task of propagating the faith and organizing the church. Shortly before his death he sent the bishops of London and Rochester to preach among the Saxons.

A. J. Mason, ed., *The Mission of St. Augustine to England* (1897);
H. Howorth, *Saint Augustine of Canterbury* (1913).

AUGUSTINIAN (AUSTIN) CANONS The name of a congregation of regular *canons who adopted a rule of common life, believed to be the rule prescribed by St. *Augustine of Hippo to his canons. The congregation and its rule were established in the second half of the 11th century in northern Italy and sanctioned by the Lateran Council of 1063. During the 12th century they spread rapidly through western Europe, where many churches adopted the rule. Among their numerous communities there was a number of independent ones, such as the *Victorines (1113) and the *Premonstratensians. They were popular in England and from the 14th century were known as the "Austin canons". The congregation suffered from the disasters and epidemics of the 14th century and declined at the end of the Middle Ages.

J. C. Dickinson, *The Origins of the Austin Canons and their Introduction in England* (1950).

AURAY, BATTLE OF (1364) One of the minor battles in the *Hundred Years' War, which was decisive for *Brittany. The army of John of Montfort, on the English side, defeated Charles of Blois, who was aided by *Du Guesclin. As a result the Montforts evicted the house of Blois from Brittany and forced the king of France, *Charles V, to recognize them as dukes of Brittany.

E. Perroy, *The Hundred Years' War* (1965).

AUSCULTA FILI ("Hear, my son") Papal bull, issued by *Boniface VIII in 1301, warning *Philip IV of France that the pope was above all kings. The French clergy was summoned to a council at Rome, where Philip's offences against the Church were to be judged. Representing the ideas of Boniface VIII on the supremacy of the Church in society, the bull had little effect at a time when the secular state was beginning to take shape.

T. F. Boase, *Boniface VIII* (1930).

AUSTRASIA The eastern part of the *Frankish-kingdom in the 6th-8th centuries. In the numerous divisions of the *Merovingian realm A., which included northeastern France, the Low Countries and western Germany, was one of the independent kingdoms and became a separate entity, wherein the Germanic ethnolinguistic element remained fairly constant. In the 7th century the Austrasian nobility became aware of its power, which increased as the Merovingian monarchy decayed. The union of the families of St. *Arnulf of Metz and *Pepin of Landen created an important Austrasian dynasty, which monopolized the office of *majordomo and is known as the *Carolingian dynasty. After the death of Charlemagne (814), the Austrasian entity diminished and, in 843, when the empire was divided at *Verdun, it ceased to exist, its western part having been Romanized and united with France.

AUSTRIA Country in the *Holy Roman empire, in southeastern Germany, on the Danube River. A German principality, which emerged and became established in the Middle Ages, it became, by the end of the era, the centre of the empire.

After the fall of the Roman empire, in the 5th century, the region was invaded by Slav tribes. In the 7th century these were pushed north by the *Bavarians in the West and the *Avars in the east, who between them conquered the major part of the country. In 798 the Avars were defeated by *Charlemagne, who annexed their kingdom and founded in 800 the Eastern March (Ostmark in German, hence the country's name). In the middle of the 9th century the march was devastated by the *Hungarians and the last Carolingian colonies were destroyed. Only after 955, when *Otto I defeated the Hungarians at *Lechfeld, was the Eastern March reestablished and began to flourish, with the development of trade and growth of towns, chief of which was *Vienna. In 976 *Otto II gave A. to the family of Babenberg, who ruled it until 1246. They expanded eastward and northward and, in 1046, the modern border between Austria and Hungary was determined. In the 11th century another branch of the family established the March of *Carinthia. Both marches were vassals of the dukes of Bavaria, a dependence which was not only political, but economic and social. The Bavarian migrations in the 11th and 12th centuries helped to populate the Austrian marches and strengthen their German character. In 1156 Henry II of Babenberg obtained from Emperor *Frederick Barbarossa, who wanted to diminish the Bavarian power in Germany, the title of duke, and A. became a duchy within the Holy Roman empire. In return, the dukes gave their support to the emperor and, in 1192, Duke Leopold V joined him on the Third *Crusade; after the emperor's death he led the German army to Acre, where he fought with *Richard I of England. In 1192 Leopold inherited Styria and established at Vienna one of the most brilliant courts in Germany; the epic of *Nibelungen is believed to have been composed there. In 1246, after the extinction of the Babenberg family, *Ottokar II of Bohemia inherited the duchy. He opposed the election of *Rudolph of Hapsburg to the imperial throne and, in 1278, was defeated at Marbach and killed. In 1282 Rudolph made his son *Albert duke of A., and from then until 1918 it was ruled by the *Hapsburg dynasty. After Albert's death, and until the end of the 14th century, the dynasty was chiefly concerned with Austrian affairs. In 1335, Carinthia was inherited and annexed to the duchy; in 1363, Tyrol was added, linking the family's estates in A. and Switzerland. In 1382 the conquest of Trieste gave A. a harbour on the Adriatic

Sea. The order established in the duchy favoured economic development and the prosperity of the towns. Vienna grew and became one of the great cities of central Europe.

E. Zoellner, *Geschichte Österreichs* (1961).

AUTHENTICA HABITA Privilege given by *Frederick Barbarossa in 1158 to the scholars and students of Bologna, allowing them the liberty of study and exempting them from lay jurisdiction, whether at Bologna or in their journeys to it. Although it was issued to the Bologna students only, and is considered as the foundation charter of the university, it had a general importance as model for university privileges in the Middle Ages.

C. O. Haskins, *The Rise of Universities* (1922).

AUVERGNE County in central France, traversed by the A. Mountains. In the 5th century, with the decline of the Roman empire in the West, many aristocratic families settled in A., which was conquered in 415 by the *Visigoths, who did not settle there. In 507 *Clovis conquered it and the country was attached to the kingdom of the Franks. A county family established itself in A. at the beginning of the 9th century, when the region became part of the kingdom of *Aquitaine. When that kingdom was abolished in 852 by *Charles the Bald, the counts of A. tried to take over the entire duchy of Aquitaine and fought against the counts of Poitiers, who had the same ambition. The prolonged wars led to the disintegration of A. in the 11th century, and a number of feudal families tried to establish their rule in the province. The bishops of Clermont and Le Puy created their own estates. In 1096 Pope *Urban II issued the call to the *Crusades at the Council of Clermont in 1096 and confirmed the privileges of the churches. At the beginning of the 12th century four main principalities were established in the province: two counties, subject to the dukes of Aquitaine, and the ecclesiastical seigniories, under the protection of *Louis VI of France. Local troubles in 1164 prompted a royal expedition to the region in 1166; *Henry II of England, as duke of Aquitaine, was compelled to give up his suzerainty in favour of the kings of France. In the 13th century A. was given to *Alphonse of Poitiers, brother of *Louis IX, as part of his great apanage and he tried to reorganize it. However, the counties continued to exist, but the closer royal control enforced the peace in the province, whose fidelity to the French crown was proved in the *Hundred Years' War.

G. Fournier, *Histoire de l'Auvergne* (1971).

AUXERRE City in central France, conquered by the Franks in the reign of *Clovis. In the 5th and 6th centuries A. was one of the great centres of learning in western Europe, famous for its monastic school. Among its students was St. *Patrick, who received his education there, before returning to *Ireland. The school flourished also in the 9th century, being one of the theological centres of the *Carolingian renaissance. In 1003 *Robert the Pious annexed the county of A., which had been a part of the duchy of Burgundy, to the royal demesne. In the 12th and 13th centuries the city was also one of the centres of Romanesque and Gothic *art.

J. Leboeuf, *Mémoires concernant l'histoire d'Auxerre* (1848).

AUXILIUM Feudal term meaning the military service and aid owed by the vassal to his lord. There were four

kinds of A. in feudal society: the defence of the lord's castle, the ransom of the lord, if taken captive, the costs of the knighthood of his eldest son and those of the marriage of his eldest daughter. In the 12th century another kind of A. was recognized, the participation of the lord in a crusade.

AVARS Turkish-Mongol tribes of Central Asia who, in the 4th century, replaced the *Huns in the Asiatic steppes. In 552 their kingdom in Asia was destroyed and the A. were pushed westward. In 558 they entered the service of the *Byzantine empire and fought against the Slavs, who had settled on the Danube and threatened the Balkans. The A. defeated the Slavs and created a large kingdom, whose centre was present-day Hungary, and which by the end of the 6th century ranged from the Black Sea to the Alps, ruling over Slavs and other tribes. Under their pressure the *Lombards left their territories on the Danube and invaded Italy (590). The A. attacked the neighbouring states and, in 624, even besieged Constantinople. They also fought against the *Khazars, north of the Black Sea, but failed to maintain their rule over them. In the 7th century the khanate was weakened by internecine wars between the branches of the royal family, who lived in "rings" (tent-cities arranged in circles of hierarchical order rising towards the centre, where the khan's tent was placed), in which they also kept their treasures and plunder. The Bulgars, Czechs and Moravians succeeded in freeing themselves at this time, but the A. were still powerful in the 8th century, when they threatened the Bavarians. In 791-803 they were defeated by *Charlemagne, their realm was destroyed, and the treasures of their "rings" were seized. The A. disappeared completely in the 9th century and were assimilated by the Slavs and Hungarians. Only a small tribe remained among the Khazars in Dagestan in the Caucasus.

A. Kollautz, *Die Awaren* (1954).

AVE MARIA (Latin: Hail Mary) The prayer to the Virgin Mary, based on the greeting of the angel Gabriel (Luke 1:28). The prayer was incorporated in the Mass in the 11th century, and became very popular as it expressed the belief that the mother of Christ could best intercede for repentant sinners. The popularity of the prayer left its mark on medieval music, and had an important place in medieval hymnology.

H. Thurston, *The Origins of Hail Mary in Familiar Prayers* (1953).

AVERROÉS See IBN RUSHD.

AVERROISM The philosophical trend in Christian western Europe, which was based on the theories of Averroés. The writings of *Ibn Rushd became known to scholars in Catholic Europe in the 13th century and became popular at the University of Paris when, in 1255, the Faculty of Arts prescribed the study of Aristotle. Of the scholars who adopted Averroist methods the most important was *Siger of Brabant, who taught at Paris. The accent put by A. on the human intellect and on its unity was recognized as dangerous to the Christian faith and, consequently, was attacked by St. *Albert the Great who, at the request of Pope *Alexander IV, wrote in 1256 a refutation entitled "On the Unity of the Intellect against Averroés", and by St. *Thomas Aquinas who, in 1257, attacked the Averroists in his *Summa contra Gentiles*. The influence of A. at the university prompted Pope *Urban IV to repeat, in

1263, the prohibition against the study of Aristotle and to condemn the Averroists. But they remained influential and attempted to show that their theories could be reconciled with the Church dogma. In 1270 they were again attacked by Thomas and, at his demand, their errors were formally anathematized and they were excommunicated by the bishop of Paris. The matter did not end there and, in 1277, a new condemnation was issued against the Averroists, and they disappeared from the University of Paris. Certain philosophers in the West continued to espouse A., as, for example, *John of Jandun, who taught it at Paris in the 14th century. In Italy, an Averroist school survived at Padua until the middle of the 15th century.

M. Grabmann, *Der Lateinische Averroismus des 13 Jahrhunderts und seine Stellung zur christlichen Weltanschaung* (1931).

AVICEBRON See IBN GABIROL, Salomon.

AVICENNA See IBN SINNA.

AVIGDOR COHEN-ZEDEK OF VIENNA, RABBI (1180-1255) One of the leaders of the Jewish community in Germany, reputed for his perfect knowledge of the Jewish Law, so that rabbis from all over Germany and from Italy addressed questions to him about their interpretations. His *Responsa* were considered authoritative in the first half of the 13th century, and his correspondence is an important source for the history of German and Italian Jews of his time.

I. Elbongen, *Germania Judaica*, I (1936).

AVIGNON Town in Provence on the Rhône River, one of the oldest in western Europe, having been a Celtic, Phoenician and Roman settlement. There were Christian and Jewish communities there from the 3rd century on. In the 5th century it was conquered by the *Visigoths and *Burgundians, who ravaged it and destroyed some of its classical monuments. In the 6th century it became a part of the *Frankish realm, but lost its importance. In the 9th and 10th centuries it was sacked several times by the Moslem pirates from Algeria. It began to flourish again only in the 11th century with the revival of its commercial activity. Disputed by the kings of *Arles and *Burgundy, A. was formally incorporated into the *Holy Roman empire with the county of *Provence. In the 12th century the city became politically autonomous and an influential *Albigensian community settled there. In 1226 *Louis VIII of France destroyed its fortifications, to punish it for its Albigensian attachment. In 1246 *Charles of Anjou, who inherited the county of Provence, abolished A.'s autonomy and appointed officers to govern it. In the second half of the 13th century the economic prosperity of the city made it an important focus of the west European trade. In 1309 Pope *Clement V settled in A., which was given to him by Countess Joan, and it remained a papal residence for 70 years. During this period, called the "Babylonian exile of the papacy", the city flourished and benefited from the wealth of the papal court. A monumental pontifical palace was built in its centre, as well as many splendid residences for the cardinals and officials. A new city wall, still in existence, was erected, as well as a new bridge on the Rhône. Even after the return of the popes to Rome, A. remained a papal possession and part of the Curia continued to function in the city, ruled by a legate, until it was annexed to France in 1791.

T. Okey, *The Story of Avignon* (1921).

AXUM City in *Ethiopia. From the 1st to the 6th century, A. was the centre of an Ethiopian kingdom, which was named after it; its kings reigned over a large part of northern Ethiopia and southeastern Sudan. In the 4th century a Christian community was established in the city, which became the religious centre of the country. Even after the fall of the kingdom, A. preserved its religious character and many churches and monasteries were built there; it also became the national focus of pilgrimages. Its religious character gave rise to a number of legends, among them the belief that the tablets of the Law, which had been kept in the Temple of Jerusalem, were brought to A. by King Menelik, a son of Solomon and the queen of Sheba.

J. T. Bent, *The Sacred City of the Ethiopians* (1893).

AYYUBIDS Moslem dynasty which ruled *Egypt, *Syria and parts of *Arabia in the 12th-13th centuries, originating the Kurdish tribes of Armenia. The founder of the dynasty, Ayyub Ibn Shaddi Ibn Marwan, was an officer in the army of *Zengi and, in 1154, was appointed governor of Damascus by *Nureddin and became one of his counsellors. His son, *Saladin, was sent in 1169 to help the *Fatimids in Egypt, who were under attack by the *Crusaders. In 1171, after the extinction of the Fatimid dynasty, Saladin became the ruler of Egypt and, in 1174, united it with Syria, succeeding Nureddin. Under Saladin (1171-93), the dynasty reached the zenith of its power and prestige, ruling also the Hejjaz and Yemen. In 1187 he conquered almost all of the *Crusader kingdom of Jerusalem, but could not prevent the Third Crusade and the restoration of the Latin kingdom in the coastal regions of Palestine. The Peace of *Ramlah of 1192, concluded with *Richard I of England, was the last event of Saladin's life. After his death, the Ayyubid empire was divided between members of the dynasty, who were rivals in the 13th century, particularly the sultans of Egypt and Damascus. The division and the repeated wars, weakened the A. states and their regimes. The Egyptian state tried to maintain good relations with the European Christians, in order to prevent the invasion of their country, as had happened in 1217 during the Fifth Crusade, and reached an agreement with Emperor *Frederick II in 1228, which conceded Jerusalem to the Christians. The Syrian A. had to fight not noly family feuds, but also the attacks of the *Khwarizmians and the *Mongols. In Egypt the family was overthrown by the *Mamluks in 1250; the Damascus branch ceased to rule in 1260. Only in Hama did the dynasty remain – until 1341, when the principality was conquered by the Mamluks. The A. were speedily Arabized and, from Saladin's time, their courts were centres of culture and learning. Many of them participated in the cultural activities of their courts. At the beginning of the 14th century the prince of Hama, Abu'l Fida, was a gifted geographer and historian. *EI*, I.

AZHAR, AL- A school in *Cairo, the most famous in the Moslem world. It was founded in 970 as the first mosque in the new city of Cairo by the *Fatimid caliph Al-*Muizz. In 988 the court set up a fund for 35 jurists and specialists in Islamic law at the mosque. This became the first academy of Islamic law and theology, and from the 12th century on the most important centre of studies in the Moslem world. The history of A. was written in the 15th century by the Mamluk historian Makrizi.

B

BABENBERG County in *Franconia (Germany). In the 9th century the counts of B. expanded their rule over eastern Franconia and fought for the ducal title. In 906 they were defeated by the *Salians of western Franconia, but remained an important family, around whose castle grew the city of Bamberg. In 976 *Otto II made Leopold of B. marquess of the March of *Austria, which the Bs. ruled until 1246.
K. Lechner, *Urkundenbuch zur Geschichte der Babenberger* (1950).

BABYLON In the Middle Ages the name lost its ancient geographical-historical meaning and was chiefly used in religious polemics, to signify evil and the enemy of Christianity. This sense had its origin in the writing of St. *Augustine of Hippo, who described B. as the "city of the devil", in contrast to the "city of God", and as a symbol of tyranny. In the 10th and 11th centuries west European pilgrims described B. as a city in Egypt, and at the time of the *Crusades it was generally identified with Cairo.

BACCALARIUS See BACHELOR.

BACHELOR Originally meaning "young man", the word came to designate a man of any age who did not marry and have a family. With the development of schools and universities in the 12th-13th centuries, the term referred to those clerics who, having finished their studies, did not teach but continued their studies or travelled before taking up their duties in the church. In the 14th century it became a title given to students who had finished their studies in the faculties of art, with the initials B.A. (*Baccalarius Artium*, or Bachelor of Arts). The title was no more than a symbol of general education but, until the end of the Middle Ages, it gave its bearer the privileges of a cleric, thus exempting him from secular justice.
P. Kibre, *Scholarly Privileges in the Middle Ages* (1962).

BACON, ROGER (1214-92) Philosopher and scientist. Born probably in Ilchester, he studied at Oxford. In 1236 he went to Paris, where he was the first to lecture on *Aristotle. It was there that he became interested in experimenting and, about 1247, retired from teaching to devote himself to science. He returned to England where, in 1251, he joined the *Franciscan order. In 1256 he returned to France, but being ill, had to give up his studies until the middle of the 1260s. At this stage of his life, Pope *Clement IV, who had heard about his works, asked him for an account of his theories. By 1268 B. had produced two long treatises, the *Communia Naturalium*, on science, and the *Communia Mathematicae*, which summed up the mathematical knowledge of his time. These treatises, together with a preamble, were complemented by two others, the *Opus Majus* and the *Opus Minus*, which were a kind of encyclopedia of a variety of subjects, including philosophy and theology, grammar, mathematics, geography, perspective, physiology and experimental science – the last called by him the *domina omnium scientiarum* (the Lady of All Sciences). He also sent to Rome a treatise on alchemy. The death of Clement IV in 1268 disappointed his hopes of a papal recommendation, and after a dispute with his Parisian superiors he returned to Oxford. Here he composed his Greek and Hebrew grammars, completed his encyclopedic works with the *Opus Tertium* and, in 1272, published a *Compendium Studii Philosophiae*, which contained a bitter attack on the vices and ignorance of the clergy. His last years were marred by conflicts, caused by his independent character. He died before he could finish his *Compendium Studii Theologiae*, in which he stressed the need to know Greek and Hebrew for the study of the Bible. B. was one of the most original scholars of his age – philosopher and scientist, he was in many ways a man ahead of his time; his stress on the experimental approach conflicted with the conventional methods and were a real challenge to the scholarly establishment of the age.
Works, ed., R. Steele (1905);
S. E. Easton, *Roger Bacon and his Search for a Universal Science* (1952).

BACULUM Staff and sceptre. In medieval ecclesiastical Latin the term signified the episcopal staff, symbolizing the pastoral authority of the bishop in his diocese. From the 10th century on, a newly-consecrated bishop received both the staff and ring (*annulum*) to symbolize his *investiture. The *Gregorian reformers opposed these practices of investiture and condemned them as lay interference in ecclesiastical affairs. The decoration of the B. was an expression of the art of the goldsmiths in the Middle Ages.

BADAJOZ City and province in southwestern Spain, near the Portuguese border. In 711 it was conquered by the Arabs and later became part of the *Ummayad caliphate of *Córdoba. In 1031, with the extinction of the dynasty, it became one of the independent Moslem kingdoms of the *Taifas. In 1064 *Ferdinand I of Castile threatened the emirate of B. and compelled the city to pay him a tribute. Nevertheless, the local dynasty succeeded in remaining independent until 1229, when it was conquered by *Ferdinand III of Castile. The city was fortified in the 13th century and a Gothic cathedral was built there. In 1267 the Treaty of B. fixed the boundary between Portugal and Castile.
A. Castro, *The Structure of Spanish History* (1954).

BADOER Venetian family, descendants of the leaders of the settlers in the islands in the lagoons. The family became prominent at the end of the 7th century and its members and relatives were among the dukes of Venice from 697 to 1032, when the dukedom was elective.
H. Kretschmayr, *Geschichte von Venedig*, I (1905).

BADR, BATTLE OF (624) Although this battle between Mohammad's partisans of Medina and his opponents of Mecca, led by *Abu Sufyan, was like many other tribal battles in Arabia and had no decisive results, it is held in Islamic tradition as an important turning-point in the rise of the new religion. It was Mohammad's first victory and strengthened his position against the old aristocracy of Mecca, which had tried to seize him in 622 and from which he was a fugitive.
F. Gabrielli, *Muhammad and the conquests of Islam* (1968).

BADR ED-DIN AL-AINI (15th century) Egyptian historian. Very little is known about his life and background. He lived at the court of the *Mamluk sultans and wrote an important history of their dynasty, based on the documents of the court.
EI, II.

BAGHDAD City in present-day Iraq. In the second millennium BC it was a Persian settlement. The city was founded in 762 by the *Abbasid Caliph *Al-Mansur, who made it his capital. From 812 on its eastern side was the seat of government and new palaces were built for the caliph's household and the viziers. In the 9th century the city became an important centre for the Far Eastern trade and that of the steppe tribes and eastern Europe as far as Scandinavia. The prosperity of the markets of B. attracted settlers, mainly Moslem, but also Jews, who migrated there from the little towns of the region. Its position as the capital of the Islamic world enhanced its growth as a centre of learning and culture, in which Persian tradition mixed with the Hellenistic heritage. The Academy of B. played an important role in the development of Arab philosophy and science, based on the Aristotelian system. The city continued to grow in the 10th century, when its northern quarters became the seat of government, known as *Dar al-Mamlaka* (the House of Kingship). After the *Seljuk conquest of 1055 the city lost part of its importance, as the conquerors established their capital in Persia, but its role as the city of the caliphs, and thus the religious capital of Sunnite Islam, prolonged its prosperity. In 1065 the vizier Nizam Al-Mulk founded in B. the famous school, known as the *Nizamiyah*. In the 12th century a new phase of building activity gave B. its medieval grandeur; among the new constructions were the city wall and the caliph's courts, which became an "inner city", described by *Benjamin of Tudela as one of the wonders of the world: three miles long, with a park, wherein grew trees from all over the world. *Ibn Jubair records 30 schools in the city at the end of the 12th century. The *Mongol invasion of *Hulagu-khan in 1258 devastated the city and many of its palaces were destroyed. Mongol rule, which lasted until 1411, was a period of stagnation for the city, its prosperity was over and it became an unimportant town in the Mongol khanate of Persia. In 1411 it was conquered by the Turkomans, who made it their capital, but their kingdom lacked the cohesion and stability needed for the recovery of the city.
G. Le Strange, *Baghdad during the Abbassid Caliphate* (1900).

BAHRITES Name of the first line of the *Mamluk sultans of Egypt (1250-1382). The name, meaning "river", is taken from the Mamluk garrison on the banks of the Nile in Cairo, where the first sultan, Aybeg, was stationed before he seized power from the last *Ayyubid sultan Al-Salih. The B. gave Egypt 24 sultans, among them the most famous Mamluk figures, such as *Baibars and *Qala'un. They were not a dynasty, with a direct order of succession, but a group of families, originally slaves of the Ayyubids.
S. Lane-Poole, *Egypt in the Middle Ages* (1925).

BAHYA BEN JOSEPH IBN PAQUDA (d. c. 1080) Jewish moral philosopher. He was born in Moslem Spain and lived in Saragossa, which was then still under Moslem rule. Little is known about his life and studies. By his own testimony it is known that he wrote poems, of which none survived. Only one of his works is preserved, *Duties of the Heart*, which was written in Arabic and was translated into Hebrew in 1161 by Judah Ibn Tibbon. He was influenced by Moslem mysticism, which sought to achieve spiritual integrity so as to reach the divinity. The book is divided into ten parts, devoted to the relations between mankind and God as seen from different aspects, and concluding with the love of God, which was one of the main ideas of his philosophy. Man has to prepare himself to be worthy to love God. B.'s book concentrates on the ways and means of this preparation, based on faith. It therefore has the character of a didactical work, whose aim is to teach how to avoid evil. The Hebrew translation of the book was widely distributed in the Jewish communities and influenced the mystical trends in Spain, France and Germany.
G. Vajda, *La théologie ascétique de Bahya ibn Paquda* (1947).

BAIBARS (1223-77) *Mamluk sultan of Egypt (1260-77). Of a Turkish family which had settled in southern Russia, he was sold as a slave-soldier (*mamluk*) to the *Ayyubids. In 1246 he was brought to Egypt and entered the guard of Sultan Al-Salah Ayyub, who made him a commander in the army. B. took part in the Mamluk revolution of 1250 and, after the murder of his colleague Qutuz, he became, in 1260, the fourth sultan of the *Bahri line. In order to win acceptance, he recognized the uncle of the last *Abbasid caliph, who was murdered by the *Mongols at Baghdad in 1258, and became a champion of *Islam against the Mongols. In 1261 he met and defeated the Mongolian forces at Ein Jalud, west of Beth-shan in Palestine. Although this was only part of *Hulagu's army of the Khanate of Persia, it was the first time that a Mongolian army was defeated in battle, and B. won considerable prestige and the sobriquet "Al-malik al-Zahir" (victorious king), and was recognized as the leader of Islam. Thanks to his victory Syria was saved from the Mongol invasion. B. consolidated it by conquering most of the Ayyubid states in Syria (Kerak, Damascus and Aleppo, 1262-63). Then he attacked the remnants of the *Crusader states and, between 1265 and 1271, conquered Caesarea, Arsuf, Safed, Antioch, Beaufort, Jaffa and Montfort. This was the virtual end of the Crusader states, of which only a number of fortified coastal cities including Acre, Beirut and Tripoli remained. He also attacked the Armenian kingdom of Cilicia and conquered a number of strongholds on the Taurus passes. B. was not only a gifted general, but also a clever statesman, who knew how to isolate his enemies by a series of alliances, and concentrate on his main objectives. He organized the army and the navy and encouraged economic development.
P. K. Hitti, *A History of the Arabs* (1953).

BAILIFF (French: bailli, bayle) An administrative position in the feudal estates in French-speaking Europe and medieval England. Originating in the duchy of Normandy in the 11th century, when the dukes and other great lords would appoint a steward to administer each of their estates, the post included the supervision of the lesser officers, financial management and, to some extent, the administration of justice. The Norman model was adopted in the 12th century by the kings of France, with adaptations that departed from the feudal custom of giving the land to a vassal in return for services. Thus, the royal Bs. became virtual governors of territories, representing the king and residing in one of the towns of their *baillage*. In the 13th century the Parliament of Paris controlled their judicial functions, and the *Cour des Comptes* their financial activities. The source of their power deriving entirely from the royal authority, the Bs. were very exacting in the exercise of all the rights of the king, even more than the monarchs themselves. In England the office of *sheriff was in many ways the equivalent of that of the French B. The English B. was a feudal officer in the great manors, but in the royal administration he was one of the assistants of the sheriff, commonly charged with the function of the courts of the shires (which has survived in the office of B. of the court). In the Mediterranean countries the office, called "bayle", was also used by the cities; e.g., Italian and Provençal cities were represented in the *Latin kingdom of Jerusalem by bayles, who governed their local citizens.

F. L. Ganshof, *Feudalism* (1965).

BALAQ, NUR AL-DAULA Emir of Aleppo (1122-24). Descendant of the Turkoman family of the Orthoqids who served the *Seljuks and governed Jerusalem in 1071, he was in charge of the family estates on the Euphrates in 1100, and fought against the *Crusaders at Edessa. In 1120 his uncle Il-Ghazi appointed him his lieutenant at Aleppo, and he distinguished himself in the battles against the Antioch Crusaders. In 1123 he took King *Baldwin II captive. During his short emirate he tried to organize an Orthoqid state in northern Syria, but was killed in battle near Menbij before he realized his ambition.

R. Grousset, *Histoire des Croisades*, I (1936).

BALDRIC OF BOURGUEIL (1046-1130) Poet and historian, archbishop of Dol (1107-30). He was the abbot of Bourgueil, where he led a Latin literary circle and tried to imitate the works of Ovid. His poems are simple and with a deep religious feeling. After settling in Dol, Brittany, he began writing his historical works. The first was a new life of St. *Samson; about 1110 he wrote the *Life of Robert of Arbrissel*, one of the best hagiographies of the 12th century. His main work as an historian is a history of the First *Crusade, which shows his literary talents.

J. de Ghellinck, *L'Essor de la Littérature latine au XIIe s.* (1954).

BALDWIN I (1171-1205) Emperor of Constantinople (1204-05). Count of *Flanders from 1198, he was one of the leaders of the Fourth *Crusade. After the conquest of Constantinople by the Crusaders, B. was elected emperor of the new *Latin empire of Constantinople (1204). He imposed his rule over Thrace and then tried to overcome his rival, *Boniface of Montferrat, who settled at Thessalonica. In 1205 the Greek population

Baibars' heraldic device on St. Stephen's Gate, Jerusalem

Seal of Baldwin I, Emperor of Constantinople

of Constantinople rebelled and the Slavs of Thrace joined the uprising, which was also supported by the *Bulgars. He was defeated in the Battle of Adrianople (1205), taken captive by the Bulgarians and died soon after.

W. Miller, *The Latins in the Levant* (1908).

BALDWIN II (1217-73) Last Latin emperor of Constantinople (1228-61). Nephew of Baldwin I, he was proclaimed emperor after the death of *Robert II of Courtenay, under the regency of *John of Brienne, whose daughter he married in 1234. He began to rule in 1237, after John's death, but had no effective power over the empire, which was divided among the great vassals; even at Constantinople, he had to share the rule with the Venetians. In order to improve his economic situation, he sold many relics and sacred objects to the West. Unable to prevent Michael *Palaeologus from reconquering the capital and restoring the Byzantine empire in 1261, B. fled to western Europe, where he tried to obtain support for a new crusade against the Byzantines. To this purpose he concluded an alliance with *Charles of Anjou, king of Sicily, in 1267.

W. Miller, *The Latins in the Levant* (1908).

BALDWIN I, of Boulogne (d. 1118) The first king of the *Latin kingdom of Jerusalem (1100-18), brother of *Godfrey of Bouillon. Having taken part in the First *Crusade in his brother's army, he went in 1097 with a small detachment to help the *Armenians in eastern Anatolia. He was adopted by the Armenian ruler of Edessa, Thoros, and when the latter was killed, became count of Edessa (1098), and founded a Crusader state east of the Euphrates. He succeeded in stopping an attack of the Mosul forces against the city, and extended the boundaries of his state. In 1100, after the death of Godfrey, the nobility of Jerusalem elected him king, despite the opposition of *Tancred, prince of Galilee and of the Patriarch Daimbert; B. having given Edessa to his cousin, Baldwin of Bourg, went to Jerusalem and, on 25 December 1100, was crowned at Bethlehem as the first king of Jerusalem. His immediate efforts were directed at repelling the *Fatimid attacks on his kingdom (1100-05), organizing the nobility and establishing the territorial cohesion of the kingdom. He was successful in all three aims; in the war against the Egyptians he showed courage and leadership, which united the nobility and the Church around his absolute rule. In 1102 his principal rival, Tancred, left the kingdom to govern Antioch, which enabled B. to organize the feudal structure of his kingdom under his own strong control. He proceeded with the conquest of the coastal cities of Palestine, including *Acre (1104) and Sidon (1110), thereby extending the kingdom over the entire territory between the Mediterranean and the Jordan River. To prevent an eventual coalition between Egypt and Damascus, he led an expedition to southern Transjordan, where he built the castles of Montreal and Val-Moyse, and the Ile-de-Graye on Jesirath Faraoun, an island near Aqabba in the Red Sea. He encouraged Crusader colonization of his kingdom, settling a Latin population at Jerusalem (1113), and giving privileges to the Italian cities, to develop the trade and the harbours, especially Acre, which became the main port of the kingdom. He also built a castle in the Golan, northeast of the Sea of Galilee, to prevent attacks from Damascus. To strengthen the Frankish population he encouraged the importation of Italian women as wives for the knights of his kingdom. In 1118 he led an expedition to Egypt and penetrated deeply into Sinai, but fell ill and died; the place is still called *Sabhath Bardawill* (the Lake of Baldwin). B. was the real founder of the Latin kingdom of Jerusalem and one of its greatest kings.

J. Prawer, *The Crusaders* (1973).

BALDWIN II, of Bourg (d. 1131) King of Jerusalem (1118-31). A cousin of *Baldwin I, he followed him to Edessa during the First *Crusade. In 1100 he became count of Edessa, where he fought against the Moslems and was captured by them (1104-08). In 1118 he was visiting Jerusalem, when his cousin died and he was elected king. He continued the policies of Baldwin I, but extended his activities to northern Syria, as the overlord for the Crusader principalities of Tripoli, Antioch and Edessa. In 1122 he was taken prisoner by *Balaq of Aleppo and held until 1124. During this time the kingdom of Jerusalem was ruled by the Patriarch Gormund, who, profiting from the presence of the Venetian fleet to defeat the Egyptians near Ascalon, also, with B.'s consent, conquered Tyre. B. led a number of expeditions to Transjordan, to block any attempts against his kingdom by Damascus, and established the Crusaders' rule in the Gilead. He sought to establish a true colonial society in the kingdom; at the Council of Nablus (1120) draconic laws were promulgated to bar mixed marriages between the settlers and the local population. In his last years the nobles grew more powerful and B., to strengthen the royal authority, married his daughter and heiress, *Melisande to *Fulk of Anjou, who settled in Jerusalem. With B.'s death the first generation of the founders of the Crusader state came to an end and a new generation, born in the Holy Land, took over.

J. Prawer, *The Crusaders* (1973).

BALDWIN III (1131-64) King of Jerusalem (1144-64), son of *Fulk of Anjou and Melisande. During his minority the kingdom was ruled by his mother as regent. This was a time of reverses for the kingdom, when cooperation with Damascus, cultivated by Fulk, changed to hostility, climaxing during the Second *Crusade, and as a result of which *Nureddin was able to conquer Damascus and unite Syria under his rule (1154). In 1152 B. rebelled against his mother, who refused to hand over the reins of government, and a civil war broke out among the Crusaders. His victory made him the sole ruler, but the upheavals had increased the power of the nobility. In 1153 he conquered Ascalon, completing the conquest of western Palestine, and fortified the frontier with Egypt, including Gaza and Daron. The main danger to his kingdom was the increasing might of Nureddin, who tried to conquer Banias in 1157. B. defeated him at Chastelet and maintained the boundary-line. To strengthen his kingdom he concluded an alliance with *Byzantium, and married Theodora Comnena, a relative of the emperor *Manuel. He died in Beirut while trying to help Antioch. During his reign the city of Jerusalem was enriched and the Church of the Holy Sepulchre reconstructed.

J. Prawer, *The Crusaders* (1973).

BALDWIN IV, the Leper (1160-85) King of Jerusalem (1173-85), son of *Amalric I and Agnes of Courtenay. He was able to rule despite his illness, which restricted his actions on several occasions and made heroic efforts to maintain the Crusader kingdom in

circumstances which would have tried an experienced statesman. In 1173 *Saladin seized power in Syria, being already governor of Egypt, and the kingdom of Jerusalem was for the first time encircled by a united Moslem power, which had a vital strategic interest in destroying it, so as to control the way between Egypt and Syria. Internally, the nobility, which had grown powerful during the second half of the 12th century, was attempting to control the kingdom. The situation was aggravated by the emergence of two parties among the nobility, one of which called for good relations with the Moslems and a moderate policy, while the other favoured an active, and even provocative policy. Seeking to impose a certain amount of discipline, B. several times had himself carried in a litter to preside over the assemblies. In 1177 Saladin attacked the kingdom from Egypt; B. called on the knights to join him at Ascalon, but they were cut off by Saladin's army, which had reached Ramlah. A battle was fought at Montgisard, near Ramlah, in which Saladin was defeated and had to flee to Egypt. The king appointed one of the heroes of the battle, Raynald of Châtillon, to be prince of Transjordan. This noble, who was the leader of the activist party, launched an independent policy which aggravated the conflict, notably in his naval expedition to the Red Sea, which gave Saladin an opportunity to annex Yemen and the Hejjaz and to call for a "holy war" (*jihad*). Between 1182 and 1185, the Moslem leader every year attacked the Transjordanian castles, and tried to invade the kingdom through the valley of Beth-Shean. Only the courageous resistance of B. saved the situation. Nevertheless, he was unable to prevent the doubtful marriage of his sister and heiress, Sybil, with an unknown knight newly arrived from France, Guy of *Lusignan. This marriage split the nobility and B. succeeded in postponing the conflict by proclaiming that the child of Sybil's by a previous marriage would be the heir of the kingdom. He stipulated that during the boy's minority the regency would be in the hands of the moderate party, whose leader, *Raymond III of Tripoli, was since 1183 the most important person in the kingdom, and had tried to come to an agreement with Saladin. But Raymond's authority was challenged by Guy, who was the ally of Raynald of Châtillon. Under the circumstances, anarchy spread through the kingdom and, in 1185, no accepted leader existed in the Latin kingdom.
W. Baldwin, *Raymond III of Tripoli and the Fall of Jerusalem* (1936).
BALDWIN V (1175-86) Son of Sybil of Jerusalem and William of Montferrat, he was proclaimed heir of the kingdom of Jerusalem in 1183; in 1185 he became king under the regency of *Raymond III of Tripoli and Joscelin III of Courtenay, leaders of the moderate party in the Crusader kingdom. The regency was contested by Sybil and Guy of *Lusignan and an open conflict broke out between the parties. B. died in 1186 at Acre, and there were rumours that he had been poisoned.
W. Baldwin, *Raymond III of Tripoli and the Fall of Jerusalem* (1936).
BALDWIN Name of nine counts of *Flanders:
Baldwin I, "Bras-de-Fer" (862-79) In many ways the founder of the county, he united under his rule feudal estates in the region and fought against the Normans. He married Judith, daughter of *Charles the Bald of France.

Baldwin II (879-918) Continuing his father's policy he became one of the most important lords of his time. His marriage with Elftrud, daughter of *Alfred the Great, began the association of the Flemish counts with England.
Baldwin III (959-62) Son of *Arnulf the Great.
Baldwin IV (988-1035) Son of Arnulf II. He imposed peace in the county and encouraged the development of the towns.
Baldwin V, of Lille (1035-67) Continuing the policy of his father, he allied himself with the Capets of France, marrying Adela, daughter of *Robert II. In 1059-65 he was regent of France on behalf of *Philip I.
Baldwin VI, of Mons (1067-70) Before becoming count of Flanders, he was marquis of Antwerp and count of Hainault, thereby enlarging the county and making it an important power in the Low Countries. He was on close terms with *William the Conqueror, who married his sister Matilda.
Baldwin VII (1111-19) Continuing the policy of his father, Robert II, he assured the prosperity of the county by encouraging trade and the cloth industry of the towns. Allied with *Louis VI of France, he fell at the Battle of Breteuil in 1119.
Baldwin VIII (1191-96) Count of Hainault and Flanders, brother to Philip of Alsace; in 1180, his daughter, Isabella, was married to *Philip II August of France.
Baldwin IX See BALDWIN I of Constantinople.
BALEARIC ISLANDS See MAJORCA, KINGDOM OF.
BALL, JOHN (d. 1381) Priest and social preacher. Little is known of his early life. In 1366, while living in Essex, he was summoned before the archbishop of Canterbury, accused of preaching the doctrines of *Wycliffe and forbidden to preach. He nevertheless continued to do so, condemning church property and teaching the equality of bondsmen and gentry. In 1376 he was arrested, but his popularity remained high and, in 1381, when the Peasants' Revolt broke out, he was freed and took an active part in the rebellion. Captured at Coventry, he was brought before *Richard II and executed as a traitor.
R. B. Dobson, *The Peasants' Revolt of 1381* (1970).
BALLIOL, ROUSSEL OF Norman adventurer. After a period of activity in southern Italy in 1070 he entered the service of the *Byzantine empire as a mercenary and was sent to fight the Turks in Asia Minor. In 1074 he tried to create an independent state in Anatolia. An army led by the emperor's uncle, John Ducas, was sent against him, but B. won him over by proclaiming him emperor. To crush the rebellion, Emperor *Michael VII joined forces with the *Seljuks. A combined attack led by the Byzantine general *Alexius Comnenus succeeded in crushing the revolt and killing B. (1076).
CMedH, IV.
BAMBERG City in Germany, in the ancient duchy of *Franconia. The city was founded towards the end of the 10th century, as a borough in the domain of the counts of *Babenberg. In 1004 a bishop's see was established in the city, which became the centre of an important ecclesiastical seigniory, with a beautiful Romanesque cathedral. In the 11th and 12th centuries the bishops of B. were on close terms with the emperors, who allotted them important estates. From the 13th century on they were princes of the *Holy Roman empire, the city being an important centre of learning

The Romanesque cathedral of Bamberg, Germany

and culture. In 1803 B. and its principality were annexed to the kingdom of Bavaria.

G. Barraclough, *Mediaeval Germany* (1953).

BANCHERIUS Latin word used in Genoa in the 12th century, meaning moneychangers. The term derives from *banca* (bench or counter), used by the moneychangers in the marketplace. In the 13th century the term was extended by the Lombard dealers to credit operations, and became synonymous with the business of money, i.e. banking. Thus, the origin of the modern word banker.

CEcH, II.

BANKING The term, meaning credit operations, was used in northern Italy in the 13th century; it was introduced by the Lombards and other Italian merchants who settled in the commercial centres of western Europe, into general European usage to denote the business of money. Some such activities had been practised since the beginning of the Middle Ages but, until the end of the 10th century, they consisted simply of borrowing money against a gage, or pledge. With the economic transitions of the 11th century, including the divisions of the estates among a greater number of heirs and the development of the money economy, recourse to credit became more frequent. Landowners needed money for particular enterprises or to make up the difference between their income and expenditure. In the 11th-12th centuries money was borrowed either from Jews, who could not invest their profits in real estate, or from certain great abbeys. The prohibition of usury (i.e. the charging of interest) led to the adoption of a system of gages: properties or a source of revenue (such as taxes) were pledged, or bonded, allowing the moneylender to collect the income, until the capital was repaid. Generally speaking, the pledge had to produce for the moneylender an income of about 45% per year on the capital, but certain monasteries received as much as 60%. In many of the cases, these conditions made the repayment of the capital impossible and, in the long run, many bonded lands passed to the moneylenders; apparent donations to monasteries frequently hid such credit operations, and the lower classes of the feudal society were thereby ruined. The credit operations of Jews were regulated by ecclesiastic and royal legislation, so as to prevent them from acquiring land by the way of forfeiture. Thus, while Jewish moneylending was known to be bearing interest and led to accusations of usury, their operations were limited to small capitals and the rate of interest they charged was controlled. In the 13th century, first in Italy and then in western Europe, the city merchants began to invest in moneylending, finance transactions and profiting from the money-change. While cash transactions were practised by the *bancherii*, who added an *agio*, corresponding to the rate of interest to the sum lent, the practice of the letter of credit was used by the kings and princes who participated in the Crusades, leaving it to their treasuries to repay. These letters of credit were negotiated among the bankers internationally; many Italian houses maintained associates in the main European ports and capitals, for example the Datini of Prato in the 14th century and the most famous bankers of the age, the *Medici of Florence.

CEcH, III.

BANNOCKBURN The site of a battle on the English-Scottish border in 1314, between the English army, led by *Edward II, and the Scots under Robert *Bruce. The Scottish pikemen defeated the English cavalry and the victory helped prolong the independence of Scotland.

BAPTISTERY The hall or chapel of the church reserved for baptismal ceremonies; in certain cases, even separate little churches, built in a round or octagonal form and placed under the patronage of St. John the Baptist. The Gothic B., mainly in Italy and France, was decorated with sculptures and reliefs depicting the life of John the Baptist. Towards the end of the Middle Ages and in the pre-Renaissance period, paintings were included.

J. G. Davies, *The Architectural Setting of Baptism* (1962).

BAR County and duchy (959-1480) in northeastern France, on the Meuse River; it was alloted to the Lotharingian kingdom in the Verdun partition of 843 and was annexed to Germany in 888. In 959 *Otto I made it a county, independent of the dukes of Lotharingia. In the 11th century the counts of B. were involved in French affairs, connected by marriages to the counts of Troyes-*Champagne. In 1151, the count of Champagne, Henry I, inherited B. and, for its eastern part, was vassal of the *Holy Roman emperor. In 1301, the western part, called thereafter the French B., was annexed to the French crown, together with Champagne, while another branch of the counts continued to rule the German, or imperial, B. In 1335 the county was made a duchy. In 1431 René of Anjou inherited it and Lorraine and, after his death in 1480, B. was attached to the duchy of Lorraine and became an integral part of it.

A. Martin, *Le pays Barrois* (1912).

BARBARA, St. According to early Christian tradition, she was the daughter of a pagan of Nicomedia who handed her over to the Roman authorities when she converted to the Christian faith, and was subsequently martyred. The cult of B. was very popular in western Europe in the 11th and 12th centuries, and was spread further by her inclusion in the *Golden Legend. She was the patron saint who protected from fire, and one of the most popular subjects in medieval art.

S. Peine, *St. Barbara* (1896).

BARBARIGO Aristocratic Venetian family, involved in the administration of the republic's possessions in Greece in the 13th-15th centuries. The most important of the B. were: Andrea B., bailiff of Negroponte (Euboea) in 1261-63, who stopped the conquests of *Michael VIII Palaeologus in Greece and, in cooperation with the family of *Villehardouin, preserved the independence of the duchy of Athens and of Negroponte; Andrea B. (1399-1449) several times bailiff of Negroponte and doge of Venice in 1448-49; he fought the *Ottoman Turks by sending mercenary armies to Greece.

F. Thiriet, *La Romanie Vénitienne au Moyen Age* (1959).

BARBO Aristocratic Venetian family in the 14th-15th centuries, whose fortune derived from the economic development of Greece. In 1464 the prestige of the family rose when Pietro B. became pope as *Paul II.

F. Thiriet, *La Romanie Vénitienne au Moyen Age* (1959).

BARCELONA City in northeastern Spain, capital of Catalonia and an important port. Conquered by the *Visigoths in 415, it was during the 6th century the capital of their kingdom. At that time it also became an important ecclesiastical centre. In 713 it was conquered by the Arabs, who made it the seat of the provincial governor (*wali*), but their cultural influence was not profound and gradually a local entity, the *Catalan, emerged from the conglomeration of Visigoth, Roman and Iberian elements. In 781 they were sufficiently aware of their national identity to rebel against Arab domination. In 801 the Franks, led by William of Gotha, *Charlemagne's commander of the expeditions in Spain, conquered B. and made it the capital of the *March of Spain. In 874 the March was divided into several feudal units, the most important being the county of B., which remained formally a vassal of the kings of France until the 12th century. During the 10th century the Arabs twice conquered the city (914; 986), but failed to hold it and the local dynasty, helped by knights from southern France, fought back successfully. During the 11th century B. was an important commercial port in western Mediterranean and the city began to prosper. This development increased the power of the local counts, who began to take part in the political struggle in southern France, inherited counties in Languedoc and Provence and competed with the counts of *Toulouse. In 1068 Count Rámon Berenguer promulgated the *Ustages, a code of law based on Catalan customs, which was a precedent in the history of law

The pulpit at the Baptistery of Pisa by Niccolo Pisano

and medieval constitutions. The union of *Aragon and Catalonia in 1137 under the counts of B., brought prosperity to the city, which was the real capital and the economic centre of the united realm. It became the most important Spanish port on the Mediterranean and its commercial connections spread far and wide. The substantial Jewish community in B. played an active role in its trade from the 10th century on. Jews were also involved in the establishment of trade-companies, notably the *"Catalan Company" which, after the Aragonese conquest of Sicily (1282), won a position of supremacy in the Mediterranean trade; during the 14th century it actually conquered the duchy of *Athens. The city appointed consuls in other ports to represent it and defend the interests of its merchants. In the 13th century Italian merchants settled in B. and introduced the banking methods that had been developed in northern Italy. The economic prosperity of the city rested on the large measure of autonomy which it enjoyed and on the liberal attitude to the Jewish community; the latter was ruled, until the 13th century, by a dynasty of patriarchs, who were on close terms with the counts and later, with the royal court. The merchants, growing in importance, became the dominant element in the Jewish community and, in 1241, were recognized by King *James I as an autonomous body. In 1359, when *Peter IV of Castile attacked the port of B., the entire population came to the aid of *Peter I of Aragon and defeated the Castilian fleet. In 1460

Elijah's seat *at the basilica of S. Niccola, Bari*

the city rebelled against *John II, who tried to impose a centralist regime, and compelled him to extend the local liberties. The establishment of the *Inquisition in B. in 1480, the forced conversions and subsequent expulsion of the Jews, marked the beginning of the city's economic decline, which became more noticeable in the 16th century, with the development of the Atlantic trade. In the 13th and 14th centuries B. was an important cultural centre, notably of *Catalan literature, whose outstanding figure *Ramón Lull, influenced the literature of western Europe.

Valls y Taberner, *Estudios d'Historia de Barcelona* (1929).

BARDI Merchants and bankers in Florence. In the second half of the 13th century the B., one of the oldest Florentine business families, went into international trade. By the end of the 13th century they were investing their profits in banking and had established a large company which, in 1310, lent money to the kings of *Naples and *England (from the latter they obtained lands in Devon as security). In 1337 *Edward III borrowed money from them at the beginning of the *Hundred Years' War. The economic crises of the 14th century hurt the B., but the diversity of their investments as well as the English victories helped them to remain in business when other Italian banks went bankrupt. In the middle of the 14th century they built the B. chapel at Florence, which is the family burial place,

and one of the finest examples of 14th-century art in that city. At the end of the 14th century they became associates of the *Medici and their fortune became linked with that of the ruling dynasty of Florence.

A. Sapori, *La crisi delle compagnie dei Bardi e dei Peruzzi* (1926).

BARDOWICK Market and trading post in northern Saxony, on the Elbe. In ancient times the Slavs used to exchange goods there with German tribes. At the end of the 8th century *Charlemagne established at B. one of the trading posts between the Frankish empire and the northern countries, including Scandinavia, where taxes were paid to a Frankish official. This function continued through the 9th and 10th centuries, until the establishment of the *March of the North, when the dynasty of the Billungs undertook the supervision of the border with the Slavs, and B. gradually disappeared. *CEcH*, II.

BARGELLO (Palazzo del Popolo) The palace of the government of the city of Florence. Its building was begun in 1255, after the victory of the democratic party, and it was conceived as a stronghold, to emphasize the power of the commune. Completed in 1260, it is one of the principal monuments of civil architecture in Florence.

F. Schevill, *Medieval and Renaissance Florence*, I (1936).

BAR HEBRAEUS (Abu'l Faraj; 1226-86) *Jacobite (Monophysite) Syrian bishop and philosopher. The son of a converted Jewish physician, he studied medicine at Antioch and Tripoli, before being consecrated bishop in 1246. In 1264 he became the Jacobite metropolitan of the East, residing near Mosul. His travels enabled him to visit libraries and acquire a great erudition, both in biblical exegesis and Aristotelian philosophy, wherein he followed the doctrines of *Ibn Sinna. His greatest work, *The Cream of Science*, is a vast encyclopedic work, wherein he summarizes many of his predecessors' writings. He also wrote a world history in Syriac, which is an important source for the history of the Middle East in the 10th-13th centuries.

A. Baumstark, *Geschichte der syrischen Literatur* (1922).

BARI City in southern Italy, capital of *Apulia. After the fall of the Roman empire, it declined with the rest of the province and, by the beginning of the 6th century, it was a minor town in the kingdom of the *Ostrogoths. In 536 it was conquered by the Byzantines, who made it their chief port in their war with the Ostrogoths. Its position depended on the port, with its connections with the Balkans and the East. After the conquest of Italy by the *Lombards, B. remained under Byzantine rule and from the 7th century on, it was the main port of southern Italy and one of the principal commercial links with Constantinople and the Moslem countries in the eastern Mediterranean. At that time, the relics of St. *Nicholas were brought there and B. became the centre of his cult, which spread rapidly through western Europe, where he became one of the most popular saints. In the 9th century it served Moslem and Jewish shipping, and the *Rhadanite merchants made it one of their bases in Europe; also in the 8th and 9th centuries, it was the port of embarkation for pilgrims to the Holy Land. In the 10th century it was attacked by the Moslems from Sicily, who held it for

The Patriarchs; *13th-century Gothic sculpture at Chartres Cathedral, France*

short periods, although finally it returned to Byzantine rule. In 1071 the *Normans, led by *Robert Guiscard, conquered it and the rest of Apulia, and made it a part of the kingdom of *Sicily; after 1282 it belonged to the Angevin kingdom of *Naples. After the Norman conquest, the city became an important religious centre and the seat of an archbishop. Its 12th-century Romanesque cathedral is distinguished for its form, which was influenced by Byzantine *architecture. Hebrew inscriptions found in B. confirm the presence of a major Jewish settlement there in the 9th-12th centuries.
F. Caraballesse, *Bari* (1909).

BARLAAM AND JOASAPH, Sts. Medieval legend. Based on Buddhist sources, the legend tells of an Indian prince named Joasaph, of whom it was prophesied that when he grew up he would become a Christian. His pagan father ordered him shut away in a palace, out of reach of everyone. But the prince escaped and met the hermit Barlaam, who taught him the Christian faith and converted him. The tale, which probably dates from the 8th century, was written to glorify Christian monasticism; written first in Greek, it passed to the West, where it became widely popular.
DHGE, VI.

BARON Aristocratic title (from medieval Latin *baro*). Originally meaning *vassal of a great lord, it was used in that sense until the end of the 11th century, in some countries even later. From the 12th century, with the division of the nobility into classes, the term came to signify the direct vassals of the king, namely the higher nobles, who did not bear other titles such as dukes or counts. The assemblies of the higher nobility in 13th-century England were known as "baronial assemblies", and all the Bs. were members of *Parliament.
M. Bloch, *Feudal Society* (1961).

BARTHOLOMEW OF BOLOGNA (d. c. 1294) Theologian. Born in Italy, he joined the *Franciscan order and studied theology at Paris, where he remained to teach and acquired a considerable reputation. He was then called to the university of Bologna, to head its school of theology. His main work, *De Luce* (On the Light), is a synthesis of the theological view of science in his age, based on the axiom that the truth is to be found wholly in the Scriptures. On this basis, he examined the theories of optics and tried to reconcile science with theology.
E. Longpré, *Bartholomeo di Bologna* (1923).

BARTHOLOMEW OF EXETER (d. 1184) Bishop of Exeter (1161-84) and canonist. Having been archdeacon at the church of Exeter he became its bishop under the patronage of *Theobald, archbishop of Canterbury. In 1164 he opposed Thomas à *Becket, but later changed his attitude and became one of his staunch supporters. He wrote a number of treatises concerning canon law and a "Dialogue against the Jews", in which he expressed his opposition to the prevailing custom of consulting Jewish authorities on biblical texts.
A. Morey, *Bartholomew of Exeter* (1937).

BARTHOLOMEW OF MESSINA (13th century) Judge and historian. Born at Neocastro (Sicily), he received a legal education and served as judge in Messina. In 1282 he was elected to the local Council of Four, which stood for the continuation of the rule of *Charles of Anjou. After the conquest of Sicily by the Aragonese he wrote an historical memoir of the events, which he tried to

put in a larger perspective of the Sicilian past and entitled *Historia Sicula* (The Sicilian History).
S. Runciman, *The Sicilian Vespers* (1958).

BARTHOLOMEW OF PISA (1260-1347) *Dominican friar and theologian. He joined the Dominican order in 1277, studied at Bologna and Pisa and taught in several Dominican houses. His main work, *Summa de Causis Constientiae* (The Treatise of the Causes of Constiency, 1338), is an alphabetically arranged concordance of the theological-moral problems that concerned his age; it was taught as an authoritative text at the universities in the late Middle Ages.
EC, II.

BARTOLUS (1314-57) Italian jurist. Born in Sassoferrato in central Italy, he studied at Bologna and, from 1343, taught at the University of Perugia. He specialized in Roman Law and its interpretation, becoming the greatest authority in the field – his writings were accepted in the courts as jurisprudence. One of his main concerns was the conciliation of Roman Law, which he believed to be universal, with particular laws, which he considered local customs. In dealing with the conflict between them he acknowledged that local customs depend on the sovereign will of the prince, thereby reaching a definition of sovereignty, which was his contribution to the political thought of the 14th century.
C. N. S. Woolf, *Bartolus of Sassoferrato* (1913).

BASIL I (812-86) Emperor of Byzantium (867-86), founder of the Macedonian dynasty. He was born to a peasant family which had emigrated from Armenia to Macedonia, and about 840 went to Constantinople, where he worked in the imperial stables. He showed great ability, married a maid-servant of Emperor *Michael III and became a personal attendant of the emperor's. In 866 he murdered Bardas, an uncle of Michael III, whom the emperor suspected of plotting against him, and was rewarded with a position in the government. In 867, fearing to lose the emperor's favour, he murdered him and proclaimed himself emperor. He turned out to be an energetic and skillful ruler. In 867 he tried to effect a reconciliation with the Roman Church and expelled the Patriarch *Photius, who was considered heretic by Rome. He fought to restore Byzantine supremacy in the Balkans and succeeded in imposing his authority over the Slavs. He reconquered *Bari in 871, and the Byzantine fleet defeated the Arabs in 880; but he was unable to prevent the conquest of Sicily by the *Aghlabids. In Anatolia he defeated the Arabs and consolidated the Byzantine rule. At the end of his reign his relations with Rome had deteriorated and Photius was recalled. B. distinguished himself also in the administration of the empire, re-ordering its financial system and improving the efficiency of its administration. He is also credited with having promoted the development of the law and particularly jurisprudence.
A. Vogt, *Basile I, Empereur de Byzance* (1908).

BASIL II, Bulgaroktonos (957-1025) Emperor of Byzantium (963-1025). The last emperor of the Macedonian dynasty, he was in his childhood co-emperor with his stepfathers, *Nicephorus Phocas (963-69) and *John Tzimisces (969-76). Even after Tzimisces' death he was unable to rule until 985, but had to struggle against his generals who, supported by the aristocracy, held the real power within the empire. He

fought against the Bulgarian Tsar *Simeon, who was trying to build an empire, but was defeated in 986 near Sofia. The defeat triggered a rebellion of the Byzantine aristocracy and B., aided by *Vladimir, prince of Kiev, crushed them in 989. He abolished the privileges of the nobility and subjected them to his authority, confiscating their lands and depriving them of public office. In 991 he began to prepare his revenge against the Bulgarians and their tsar Samuel, whom he saw as a personal enemy. However he had to interrupt his activities in the Balkans to respond to a *Fatimid attack on the borders of Anatolia. In 995 and 999 he defeated the Arabs near Aleppo, but was stopped at the eastern frontier. In 1001 he returned to the Balkans and began a methodical offensive against the Bulgarians; he defeated them in 1004 and again in 1014 but, infuriated by their resistance, blinded thousands of prisoners. He succeeded in destroying the Bulgarian empire and in Byzantine historiography is called "Bulgarian-killer".
S. Runciman, *A History of the First Bulgarian Empire* (1930).

BASIL BOJOANNES (10th-11th centuries) Byzantine general of *Basil II. One of the faithful servants of the emperor, he was sent by him to southern Italy at the head of the Byzantine army, with the title "Captain of Italy" (991). He tried to unite the southern Italian principalities under Byzantine rule, but his death (about 1020) marked the beginning of the decline of that rule and the appearance of the *Norman adventurers.
F. Chalandon, *Histoire de la domination byzantine en Italie méridionale* (1908).

BASIL DIGENIS AKRITAS Popular Byzantine epic poem, composed in the first half of the 11th century. It describes the Arab-Byzantine wars and life on the frontiers of Anatolia. The poem tells of an Arab emir who, while fighting against the Byzantine army, falls in love with a Christian princess, is converted to Christianity, and creates a small principality. His son, Basil, called Digenis (son of two races) and Akritas (border-wanderer), the hero of the epic, is a defender of the Empire and its values.
C. Diehl, "Le Roman de Digénis Akritis", in *Figures Byzantines* (1908).

BASIL THE GREAT, St. (c. 330-79) Born to an aristocratic Cappadocian family in Caesarea, he studied in his native city and travelled to Constantinople and Athens. In 356 he was baptized and converted to Christianity. Thereafter he visited Syria, Palestine and Egypt, where he was attracted by the ascetic forms of monasticism. He founded on one of his father's estates a monastic community, based on retreat and meditation together with physical labour. Opposed to the individual forms of anchorite monasticism, he extolled its communal form; he is therefore held as the father of Greek-Orthodox monasteries, which are governed by the "Rule of St. Basil". In 362 Eusebius of Caesarea invited B. to his city, where they collaborated on the polemics against Emperor Julian the Apostate. In 370 B. was elected bishop of Caesarea. He wrote a number of books and treatises on the Trinitarian ideology, as well as some exegetical works on the Bible and polemics against the Arians and his own opponents.
M. M. Fox, *The Life and Times of St. Basil the Great* (1939).

BASILEUS (Greek: king) Title of the Byzantine emperors. The complete title, *Basileus Romaion*, (Emperor of the Romans), used in the charters until the 10th century, and later in highly ceremonial documents, refers to the continuity of the Roman empire in Byzantium.
N. H. Baynes and H. S. L. B. Moss, *Byzantium* (1949).

BASILICA The early form of the building used for Christian worship. Continuing the style of the classical B., it was rectangular in form and subdivided by columns and arches. It was used by the congregation for prayer and study, but mainly for the Eucharist supper. The floors were decorated with mosaics, its motifs symbolizing the faith, especially in the form of fauna and flora. The altar was added later with an apse in front of it. In the 9th century the cruciform plan of church buildings prevailed and the B. fell into disuse. One of the basilicas which have been best preserved is the 5th-century church of St. Sabine at Rome.
J. G. Davies, *The Origin and Development of Early Christian Church Architecture* (1952).

BASILICA Byzantine code of laws, collected in the 9th century in the reign of *Leo VI. It includes all the imperial decrees promulgated after Justinian, except those which had been abrogated. Its underlying principle is that of absolute monarchy. It completes the elements of the Roman Law.
J. M. Hussey, *The Byzantine World* (1957).

BASILIDES A *Gnostic of Syrian origin who taught at Alexandria in the 2nd century, and claimed to possess St. Peter's secrets of the faith. Even where his works were unknown, his influence was felt in the heretical movements of the Middle Ages.
DHGE, VI.

BASILISCUS General of the Eastern Roman Emperor *Leo I. Unsuccessful in his campaigns against the *Ostrogoths, he was nevertheless able to retain his position thanks to the emperor's support and the fidelity of his mercenary troops. In 474, at the death of *Leo II, he proclaimed himself emperor, but was defeated and killed by *Zeno in 476.
A. H. M. Jones, *The Later Roman Empire* (1963).

BASLE (Basel) City on the Rhine, which in the Middle Ages was part of the *Holy Roman empire. Its name comes from *Basilica* (the stronghold), a Roman fortress in the locality, which is mentioned for the first time in 374. A few years later the Christian community which settled around the fortress was large enough for a bishopric. In 497 the city was conquered by the *Franks together with the kingdom of the *Allemanni. By the Treaty of *Verdun (843), B. went to the Middle Franconian kingdom of *Lothair and after its dissolution, became part of the *Burgundian realm (912) and later annexed with it to the Holy Roman empire (1032). The city with its environs was given to its bishop, who acted as its feudal lord. In the 12th century the city prospered as an important commercial centre, mainly for the Rhine trade. Gradually the merchant class acquired a strong position in the urban society and, during the 13th century, they fought the bishops for political rights. These were granted in 1350 by *Charles IV and the city became an *imperial city, free of the bishop's rule. From the middle of the 14th century to the end of the 15th B. flourished. In 1400, the commune bought from the bishop large tracts around the city which, in the 16th century, became the Swiss canton of B. During this period the centre of the city was richly rebuilt in the Gothic style. In 1460 a university was established in B., making it a major intellectual centre.

A. Heusler, *Geschichte der Stadt Basel* (1934);
P. Lazarus, *Das Basler Konzil* (1912);
B. Tierney, *Foundations of the Conciliar Theory* (1955).

BASQUES An ancient folk which settled near the Bay of Biscay, on either side of the Pyrénées. The Romans called them *Vascones*, and the name was retained in the Middle Ages, and applied also to other Iberian tribes, such as the Gascons in southern France and the Navarrese in northern Spain. In the 5th century, with the establishment of the *Visigoth kingdom, the B. preserved their autonomy and remained free of interference by the authorities. They adopted the Christian faith, but the religious ties did not bring them any closer to the Frankish kingdom. They resisted the attempts of *Charlemagne to conquer their country and defeated his army in 787 at *Roncesvalles. In the 10th century most of their country formed the kingdom of *Navarre, while the rest was little principalities which were vassals of the dukes of *Gascony; the most important of these was Béarn. In the 15th century these principalities were united under the counts of *Foix as feudal overlords while the B. themselves continued to enjoy a limited autonomy in their communities of peasants and shepherds.

J. Caro Baroja, *Los Vascos* (1949).

BASRA City in southern Iraq. Founded by the Arab conquerors of Iraq in 637, it was first a military camp near the site of an ancient city, which had been deserted at the end of the 6th century. A garrison for the army and its families, B. was a Beduin settlement, divided into quarters according to their tribes. In 657-61 it was one of the centres of the plots against the Caliph *Ali. Under the *Abbasids B. grew into a large city and the main harbour of Baghdad, as well as an important cultural centre. At the beginning of the 9th century a group of Negro slaves who had served in the army settled in the city. They were active in the conflicts which marked the decline of the caliphate. B. itself began to stagnate in the 11th century with the appearance of the *Seljuks and, in 1258, it was destroyed by the *Mongols.
CHI.

BASTIDES (French: boroughs) Name given in south-west France to the towns which appeared in the 12th-13th centuries, often as the villages developed, but also founded as such. The local lords, as was customary, granted the inhabitants of the *bastides* a limited autonomy and certain rights, mainly in financial matters and the public services, so as to attract population.

F. Rörig, *The Medieval Town* (1965).

BATTANI, MOHAMMED BEN GEBIR, AL (Albategnius; 858-929) Arab astronomer who lived in Iraq and worked at the Academy of Baghdad. His work, based on the treatises of Ptolemy of Alexandria, as well as on his own measurements and observations, was the most popular textbook on astronomy until the 16th century; it was translated into Latin in the 12th century. By accurate observations he improved astronomical constants and thereby the accuracy of the calendar.

F. J. Carmody, *Arabic Astronomical and Astrological Sciences in Latin Translations* (1956).

BATU-KHAN (1224-56) Khan of the *Golden Horde (1227-56), grandson of *Genghis-Khan. After the death of his father, Juji, he was given the western provinces of the *Mongol empire, between the Lake of Aral and the Ural mountains. There he began to reign under the regency of Subotai, Genghis-Khan's most gifted general, who had commanded the campaign in Persia. With the military leadership of Subotai, B. set out in 1236 to conquer Russia, which was to be his crowning achievement. In 1237 the old *Bulgar kingdom of the Volga was destroyed and annexed. Then, he attacked the Russian principalities. While the southern principalities led by Kiev were occupied, the northern, defeated, acknowledged his overlordship and paid him tribute. In 1241, having subdued Russia, the Mongols – called Tartars in Europe – pushed westwards and defeated the kings of Poland and Hungary, destroying their lands. They got as far as Silesia and Dalmatia, arousing alarm in central and western Europe. But in 1242 the great offensive came to an end when the great khan Ogodai died and B. hastened to Karakorum to take part in the election of the new great khan. Hungary and Poland were vacated and B.'s realm was based on his domination of Russia; its new capital, Sarai, was built on the Volga. B. became the most important of the Mongol khans and was the senior member of the dynasty; his influence was dominant in the elections of great khans, but he never took the title for himself. His government was based on the perfect organization of the army and an efficient administration. He favoured the development of commerce with the West and imposed strict order on the trade routes.

M. Prawden, *The Mongols* (1940).

BAUDOUIN DE SEBOURC French epic poem. The poem, which belongs to the cycle of the *Crusade epics, was composed by an anonymous poet in the last years of the 13th or the beginning of the 14th century, probably in Flanders or northeastern France. While the aim of the poem was to praise the family of *Godfrey of Bouillon and its antecedents in northern France, it includes long descriptions of knightly life, in the castles and at war, from the viewpoint of chivalrous conduct. The stories, all purely imaginary, of adventures from Scotland to Egypt and Palestine, illustrate the heroic deeds of the nobility common to Christian and Moslem warriors. Like other epics of the age, the poem also deals with love, which is always the better argument for conversion to Christianity than the preachings of the clergy.

E. R. Labande, *Etude sur Baudouin de Sebourc, chanson de geste* (1940).

BAUTZEN City in Germany, in the March of Lusatia. Its origins are Slavic; in the 10th century, it was a town of the *Wends, who called it Bodishin. In the 12th century the Slavs were exterminated and the place was settled by Germans. The lords of B., vassals of the dukes of *Saxony, built a castle with strong towers in the centre of the borough; there is also a fortified church from the same period near the castle. In the late Middle Ages the overlordship of B. was disputed between the kings of Bohemia and the dukes of Saxony, who succeeded in establishing their rule only in 1635.

J. W. Thompson, *Feudal Germany* (1928).

BAVARIA (Bayern) Duchy in the *Holy Roman empire, between the Alps and the Danube; founded at the end of the 5th century by the tribes of the Bavarians (Latin *Baiovari*), a Germanic folk which migrated from northern Germany and modern Bohemia and settled in the Roman provinces of Rhaetia and Norricum. During the 6th and 7th centuries the Bavarians, who became Christian, settled throughout the territory between the Alps in the south, the Lech in west and the valley of the Danube near present-day Vienna. In 560 the Agilolfinger family, which acknowledged Frankish suzerainty, united the Bavarian tribes and established an autonomous duchy, which eventually became independent of Frankish overlordship. The *Carolingians reimposed it and, in 757, *Pepin the Short compelled Duke Tassilo to pay him homage. *Charlemagne, who wanted an excuse to seize B., through which ran the route from Saxony to Italy, repeated his demands for homage (781 and 787), threatened a military expedition and, in 788, deposed Tassilo and annexed B. to his realm. A Frankish dynasty was installed in the duchy and B. was integrated in the Carolingian empire.

In 843, with the division of the empire, B. became the centre of the East Frankish kingdom, ruled by *Louis the German, who made it a kingdom and gave it to his son. At the end of the 9th century, when the *Hungarians invaded and ravaged the country, its Carolingian dynasty fell. In 907 Count Arnulf (907-36), succeeded in repelling the Hungarians and reuniting the duchy, In 947 *Otto I gave the duchy to his brother Henry and, after the victory of *Lechfield (955), augmented it with the Austrian territories as far as Italy. Henry II rebelled in 976 against *Otto II, who deposed him and divided the duchy into three parts: the *March of the East (Austria), the duchy of Carinthia, Friul and Verona, and B. itself, which was reduced and restored to Henry by Otto III. This Henry was a favourite of the imperial court and, after the death of Otto III, his son became Emperor *Henry II. In the 11th century the duchy was given to the sons of the Salian emperors, who held it until 1061, when it was given to the Saxon noble Otto of Nordheim. In 1070 B. was bestowed on *Welf I, the founder of the Welf (Guelph) dynasty, which ruled in the 11th and 12th centuries over B. and *Saxony and warred with the emperors of the *Hohenstaufen dynasty. The most important of the Welfs was *Henry "the Lion", the rival of *Frederick Barbarossa, who overthrew him only in 1180. The conflict was carried over to Italy, where the parties opposing the German emperors called themselves *Guelphs. After the long reign of Henry "the Lion", the duchy was given to Count Otto of *Wittelsbach, whose family was to reign in B. until 1918. Under the new dynasty, B. grew and prospered. One of its cities, Munich, which had begun as a small borough belonging to a monastic community, became in the 13th century the capital of the duchy. Other cities, particularly those on the Danube, prospered as well. However, the political evolution of B. was less serene: Duke Otto II (1231-55) divided the duchy, with the *Palatinate of the Rhine which he had inherited from his father, among his sons. *Louis IV, duke of Upper B., reunited the duchies and became the leading German prince of his times; in 1314 he was elected emperor. After his death (1347), B. was again divided, and at the beginning of the 15th century four rival

duchies shared the Wittelsbach principality, which was reunited again by Albert the Wise (1460-1508), duke of Munich. He established the law of primogeniture excluding younger brothers from the territorial inheritance.
B. Hubensteiner, *Bayerische Geschichte* (1952).

BAYAZID I, Ilderim (1347-1403) *Ottoman sultan (1387-1402). The son of *Murad he began to reign after his father was assassinated during the Battle of Kossovo. Having overwhelmed the *Serbians he proceeded to Anatolia, where he conquered the independent Turkish principalities. In 1391 he besieged Constantinople and, returning to the Balkans, invaded Bulgaria, Greece, Albany and Bosnia. The decisive speed of his movements, which won him the sobriquet of "Thunder", alarmed western Europe. In 1395, at the instigation of *Venice, concerned with the fate of its overseas possessions, the papacy called for a crusade; a great army of knights from all over Europe gathered at *Nicopolis in 1396, but was defeated by B., who became the master of the Balkans. The situation of Constantinople became precarious and the sultan prepared the final assault. But in 1400, when he was at the peak of his power, reigning over an empire from the Danube to the Euphrates, the *Mongols, led by *Timur Leng, invaded Anatolia. In 1402 B. was defeated near *Ancyra and was taken captive. Timur restored the independence of the Turkish states of Anatolia and divided the Ottoman empire between the sons of B., who died in prison in 1403.
P. Wittek, *The Rise of the Ottoman Empire* (1958).

BAYEUX City in Normandy (France). In 360 it was the seat of a bishopric, and became one of the Christian centres of the country. In the latter half of the 5th century it was conquered by the Franks and became part of the realm of *Neustria. Under *Charlemagne it was constituted as a county. In the 9th century the counts of B. were unable to prevent the county from being invaded by the Normans, who conquered it in 890, and the city became part of the duchy of Normandy. From the 10th century on its history is that of Normandy. The cathedral of B., parts of which date from the 8th-10th centuries, is an important example of medieval *architecture and its evolution until the 15th century; beside the Carolingian remnants, its Romanesque part is of interest for its distinctive Norman style. The famous Bayeux Tapestry, from the 11th century, is preserved in the municipal museum.

The tapestry, in pure Romanesque style, was executed by Queen Matilda, wife of *William the Conqueror, and her ladies, to illustrate the Battle of *Hastings and the Norman conquest of England (1066). It is 70.4 m long, 50 cm wide and depicts the expedition, from the preparations in Normandy to the sailing and the battle itself. Beside its artistic value, it is also an extremely valuable historical source for the art of war, arms, shipping, and tools.
F. M. Stenton, ed., *The Bayeux Tapestry* (1965).

BEAUCAIRE Town in Languedoc (France), on the Rhône River. The medieval borough is known from the 9th century, when it belonged to the kingdom of *Burgundy. In 1067 it was a commercial centre in the county of *Provence. In 1125 it was conquered by *Alphonse-Jourdain, count of Toulouse, and became an administrative centre of the county of Toulouse. The counts used to hold courts of chivalry in B., which

The Norman Conquest of England; *11th-century Bayeux tapestry, Normandy*

*troubadours performed; the feasts of the court of 1174 were remembered throughout the Middle Ages in the literary life of France. From 1168 on an annual fair was held in B., which attracted merchants from all over France, Spain and Italy, thanks to the tax exemption allowed during the fair. The substantial Jewish community in B. contributed to its economical prosperity. During the crusades against the *Albigensians, B. was a French base and, from 1229, was attached to the crown lands, as the centre of "royal Languedoc" and the residence of the royal governor, the seneschal.

R. Michel, *L'administration royale dans la sénéchaussée de Beaucaire* (1910).

BEAUFORT Family in late medieval England, a bastard branch of the Plantagenet dynasty. Its founder was *John of Gaunt, duke of Lancaster, third son of *Edward III, who lived at Beaufort in Anjou with his mistress Katherine Swynford. Of the four children of this union the most famous was the second son, Cardinal Henry of B. (1375-1447). Educated at Cambridge and Oxford, chancellor of the University of Oxford (1397), he became bishop of Lincoln in 1398. In 1403 he became chancellor of England and, in 1404, was transferred to the see of Winchester. He was a staunch supporter of his half-brother, *Henry IV. Later he also played an important role in the reign of *Henry V, to whom he lent money, the hidden interest on which enabled him to amass a fortune, which in turn made him indispensable to the crown. In 1417 he represented the English church at the Council of *Constance, where he threw his formidable influence into the efforts to end the *Great Schism of the papacy. In 1421 he was appointed one of the guardians of *Henry VI, and virtually ruled the realm until 1426,

when his dispute with the king's uncle, *Gloucester, forced him to retire from the court. He was then created cardinal and, in 1427, led an unsuccessful crusade against the *Hussites in Bohemia. In 1431 he crowned Henry VI at Paris as king of France, and took an active part in the negotiations of *Arras, believing that the continuation of the war would benefit only the French. But Gloucester prevailed and the negotiations failed (1435). The successes of the French army proved him right and, after the fall of Gloucester, he reached the height of his power as the "Grand Old Man" of English politics, although he gradually retired from public positions. He died in 1447. The descendants of the oldest B. brother, John, became dukes of Somerset; John's daughter, Jane B., married *James Stuart of Scotland, and his granddaughter, Margaret B., married Edmund Tudor, and was the mother of *Henry VII.

L. B. Radford, *Henry Beaufort* (1908).

BEAUJEU French barony in eastern France, near Lyons. The barony emerged as a feudal entity, which was dependent on the county of *Forez during most of the Middle Ages. In the 14th century the barons of B. became direct vassals of the king and distinguished themselves in the *Hundred Years' War. In 1400 the last baron of the local line, Edward II (1375-1400), sold B. to *Louis II of Bourbon, who had inherited Forez by his marriage with Ann of Auvergne (1371). The dukes of Bourbon would bestow the barony with the title to their sons, before acceding to the ducal title.

BEAULIEU *Cistercian abbey in Hampshire, England. Founded in 1204 by *John Lackland and dedicated in 1246, when its building was finished, it represents one of the finest examples of Gothic monastic architecture. In the 15th century the crown gave the guardianship of the abbey to the *Warwick family, which used it in the latter half of the century as one of its bases in the Wars of the *Roses.

H. Breakspear, *The Cistercian Abbey of Beaulieu* (1906).

BEAUMANOIR, JEAN DE (d. 1366) French knight in the service of Joan of Penthièvre, duchess of *Britany. In 1351 he distinguished himself as the hero of the "Battle of the Thirty", against the pro-English party in Brittany, in the first stages of the *Hundred Years' War. Although this battle did not change the course of the war, or prevent the establishment of the pro-English Montfort family in Britany, it was praised by French historians of the war as one of the French victories. The figure of B. and those of his companions became in the 14th-15th centuries models of perfect chivalry.

E. Perroy, *The Hundred Years' War* (1965).

BEAUMANOIR, PHILIPPE DE REMI DE (c. 1250-96) French jurist. Born in Paris, in a family of magistrates, he studied at the University of Paris and about 1275 became a royal officer. Sent as bailiff to Beauvais, in northeastern France, he worked to secure the rights of the crown in his province; he also conducted a methodical investigation of the local customs. About 1280 he published the results of his enquiries in a treatise, *Les Coutumes de la Beauvésie* (The Customs of Beauvais), which is the best textbook of feudal common law in France. Though his main object was to consolidate the royal prerogatives in the administration of justice and finance, he also determined the rights of the subjects as they had evolved through the centuries. While there are other such legal collections by French jurists, B.'s work is the best and has been a basic text for the study of medieval law and political theory. B. was opposed to absolutism: "Although the king can make any new laws, he must take special care that he makes them for reasonable cause and for the common good and by means of the great council and especially that they be not made against God and good custom".

Philippe de Beaumanoir, *Coutumes de Beauvésis*, ed. A. Salmon, 2 vols. (1899-90).

BEAUMONT An important family of *Norman barons who followed *William the Conqueror on his expedition to England in 1066; they settled on a great estate which they were given in central England. In the 12th century they inherited the earldoms of Leicester and Warwick and became one of the leading families of Anglo-Norman nobility. In the 14th and 15th centuries they were involved in the activities of the throne; in the Wars of the Roses the family, led by John of B., fought for the *Lancastrian party and suffered heavy losses.

J. M. W. Bean, *The Decline of English Feudalism* (1968).

BEAUNEVEU, ANDRÉ (c. 1330-1410) Architect, sculptor and miniaturist. Born at Valenciennes, in Flanders, he settled in Paris, where he began to work as architect and became famous for his realistic sculptures. In 1364 he was invited by *Charles V to come to his court and to create the tomb of *Philip V. His success as sculptor brought him more commissions from the king, including the tombs of Charles and of his wife Jeanne of Bourbon. The realistic representation of the royal couple opened a new era in French sculpture. After the death of Charles, he joined the court of his brother, the duke of *Berry; for him he created, among

other things, the famous illuminated Bible. As a painter, he applied to the art of the miniature the same realistic style he had introduced in sculpture.

R. de Lasteyrie, *Les miniatures d'André Beauneveu* (1896).

BEAUVAIS City in Picardy, northern France. Built in Celtic times on a promontory overlooking the Oise River, it dominated its surroundings. In the Roman period it was an important centre and stronghold, and its ancient walls served the medieval city. In the 9th century B. became the centre of a county; the counts' dynasty became connected with the houses of *Vermandois and *Troyes, which gave it a powerful position in the later *Carolingian France (10th century). In 1015, when the title passed to the counts of Troyes-Champagne, who had inherited the county, the city and its surroundings became the seigniory of the bishops, who took the title "bishop-count of B.", and in the 13th century were recognized as *peers of France. In the 11th century the remaining parts of the county were divided among several feudal heirs who, in the 12th century, became vassals of the kings of France. The city itself was organized as a *commune, probably at the end of the 11th century, which was recognized by *Louis VI after 1122. B. developed in the 13th century and, under *Louis IX, a royal bailiff was established there; the real power in the urban community went to the guilds of money-changers and goldsmiths. In 1358 the county of B. was the centre of the peasants revolt, the *jacquerie, which was crushed by *Charles V.

L. H. Labande, *Histoire de Beauvais* (1892).

BEC Benedictine abbey near Rouen in Normandy, founded in 1041. Under its founder and first abbot, Herlouin, B. became a centre of monastic studies, which attracted scholars such as *Lanfranc and, later on, St. *Anselm. In 1060 it was rebuilt on a much larger scale. Many of the bishops of England after the Norman conquest, had been monks at B. as well as the future pope, *Alexander II. The abbey enjoyed ducal and royal patronage; among its royal protectors were *Henry I and *Henry II. In 1263 most of the buildings burned down. Although it was reconstructed, the abbey began to decline, and never regained its former stature as a scholarly and intellectual centre.

A. A. Porée, *Histoire de l'Abbaye de Bec* (1901).

BECCHERIA Family in Pavia, Italy. It came to prominence in the Pavian commune in the 12th century, when it was one of the leading merchant families in the city, wealthy and well-supported. In the 13th century they fought for political control of the city; in the second half of the century and the beginning of the 14th they were in power, until the city fell under the control of Milan.

J. K. Hyde, *Society and Politics in Medieval Italy* (1973).

BECKET, THOMAS A (1118-70) Archbishop of Canterbury (1162-70). The son of Norman settlers in London, he studied in England and then went to Paris, where he studied arts and theology. In 1141 he joined the household of *Theobald, archbishop of Canterbury, who sent him to study law at Bologna and Auxerre and, in 1154, appointed him archdeacon of Canterbury. In 1155 *Henry II made him his chancellor; he became a close friend of the king and one of the most influential persons in the realm. He participated in the courtly life and helped the king in his politcal moves, even when they opposed the interests of the Church. In 1162, having been elected archbishop of Canterbury, he adopted a very austere style of life; he soon found himself in opposition to Henry about the taxation of the clergy. In 1164, when the Constitutions of *Clarendon were published, which gave the crown jurisdiction over churchmen, B. openly broke with the king. The following year B. was summoned by Henry to come to the Council of Northampton, but he fled to France, appealing for justice to *Alexander III. The pope, who was already at odds with Emperor *Frederick Barbarossa, preferred not to disturb his relations with the king of England and proposed to negotiate with him on the matter. Becket remained as an exile in France until 1169, carrying on a polemical war against the king, trying to bring about his excommunication and win the support of the clergy, whose prerogatives were threatened. Some of the bishops supported the king, but B. had the majority with him, and some talented polemists and thinkers such as his secretary *John of Salisbury, whose political treatise *Policraticus*, dealt with the subject of tyranny as embodied by the king. B. himself wrote hundreds of letters about his cause, which became a public issue. In 1170 the crowning of the heir to the throne, by the archbishop of York, although it was the right of the archbishop of Canterbury, led to a threat of papal interdict. A reconciliation was achieved and B. returned to England, where he was enthusiastically received. The conflict, however, soon reopened because of B.'s refusal to absolve the bishops who had assisted at the coronation, unless they swore obedience to the pope. On Christmas Day, 1170, he excommunicated them. Henry's rage incited four of his knights to assassinate B. in Canterbury Cathedral on 29 December. The murder provoked great indignation throughout Europe and, whether he had ordered it explicitly or only inspired it by intemperate words, the king was held responsible and had to make public penance at *Avranches to obtain pardon. B. became a sainted martyr overnight; miracles were soon reported at his shrine in Canterbury, which attracted pilgrims from all Europe until the end of the Middle Ages. He was canonized in 1173.

The conflict between B. and Henry II was of far greater significance than the actual dispute. From the point of view of the historical development of society, Henry's attitude represented a progressive idea, namely the authority of the state − as represented by the king − over all the subjects, including the clergy. B. stood for the exemption of a privileged class, namely the Church, with all its properties and people, as an independent entity within the state. Yet the originality of his thought, in the context of the 12th century, was in his seeing the privileges of the Church as a restriction of the absolutist ambitions of the crown. For a society which was concerned with the danger of tyranny, which is synonymous with absolutism, B. represented the idea of the limitation of power, an idea he found in the political system of the biblical kingdom, in which the prophets warned, taught and checked the kings by divine right. It was from this point of view that his ideas were seen by the masses in his times, which were centuries away from democracy and saw in such liberties the guarantees against tyranny.

The sacrilegious murder of B. was the theme of many works of art, music and drama; in modern times, the best-known work is *Murder in the Cathedral*, by T. S. Eliot (1935).
M. D. Knowles, *The Archbishop Thomas Becket* (1949);
R. Foreville, *Le culte de St. Thomas Becket* (1967);
A. Grabois, *L'idéal de la royauté biblique dans la pensée de Th. Becket* (1973).

BEDE (BEDA) THE VENERABLE (673-735)   English scholar. Born in Northumbria, he was sent at the age of seven to the monastery of *Wearmouth, where he was educated. In 692 he began to teach at the school of the monastery of Jarrow, writing for didactical purposes an alphabetical glossary on orthography, and a collection of Latin verse forms with explanations. Toward the end of the century he wrote *De temporibus* (On the Times), a computation of time for the use of the clergy, to simplify the Paschal calculation (the time of Easter) according to Roman usage. This work, together with *De Temporum Ratione* (The Reckoning of Time), which he wrote in 725, provided a method of dating events, from the birth of Christ, used throughout the Middle Ages. These works show that he had a fair knowledge of astronomy, which is also evident in his scientific treatise *De Natura Rerum* (On the Nature of Things), which is a cosmographical compilation based on *Isidorus of Seville and certain classical authors, such as Suetonius and Pliny the Elder. He produced the mass of his biblical works, mainly commentaries, in the early 8th century. He used previous authorities, especially the Latin Fathers of the Church, but also proposed original views, based on his own studies of the Vulgate, of ancient Latin fragments, Greek and possibly Hebrew texts. His most important works were the histories: his masterpiece, which earned him the surname of Father of English History, is the *Historia Ecclesiastica Gentis Anglorum* (The Ecclesiastical History of the English Nation), completed in 731. It is a primary source for early English history, of particular value thanks to his careful and methodical separation of facts from hearsay and tradition. (Its 1843 edition, with English translation, by J. A. Giles, pioneered the historical research of Anglo-Saxon England.) Later Anglo-Saxon chroniclers wrote continuations of B.'s history, and copied whole parts from it. With B., the Northumbrian school reached the peak of its fame, becoming a centre of learning of the west European society.
A. Hamilton-Thompson, *Beda, his Life, Times and Writings* (1935).

BEDFORD, JOHN OF LANCASTER, DUKE OF (1389-1435)   The third son of *Henry IV of England. In 1413 his brother *Henry V made him duke of Bedford and entrusted him with the administration of England while he was away fighting in France. At the death of Henry V (1422), B. was made regent of France on behalf of his nephew the infant King Henry VI. He continued the war against Charles VII and won a series of victories which helped to stabilize the English rule in northern France, and continued the close alliance with the *Burgundians. In 1429 he tried but failed to conquer Orléans, which was saved by Joan of Arc. His brother *Gloucester profited from this reverse to control the Council, reducing the influence of B. and Cardinal *Beaufort. B.'s interests in the Low Countries broke up the Anglo-Burgundian alliance and allowed the

French armies to make progress in the war. He appointed the judges of Joan of Arc and ordered the execution of her sentence. He died and was buried in Rouen in 1435. His death symbolizes the end of the English supremacy in the *Hundred Years' War.

A. H. Burne, *The Agincourt War* (1956).

BEGUINES, BEGHARDS The Béguines were a religious sisterhood, founded in the Netherlands in the 12th century. They lived austerely in communities, but were free to own property and to leave the community and marry. Their male counterparts were the Béghards. The names derive from Lambert le Bègue (the Stammerer), a preacher at Liège in the latter half of the 12th century. In the 13th century there were Béguine communities in France and in the Rhine Valley, devoted to philanthropic aims, such as helping the sick and the poor. Their work gave rise to social doctrines and, although they were not organized as an order and had no superior general, they were united; they accepted the guidance of the *Franciscans, who stressed the spiritual value of poverty. Suspected of heresy, their teaching was condemned by the Council of *Vienne of 1311. Many of the Béghards adapted to a more conformist position and were allowed to continue in existence by *John XXII in 1321. The Béguines, who suffered a century of persecutions by the ecclesiastical authorities, despite their popularity in the towns, became in the 15th century charitable institutions.

E. W. McDonnell, *The Beguines and Beghards in Medieval Culture* (1954).

BEHA ED-DIN (1145-1234) Moslem jurist and historian. He was educated in Syria and joined the court of *Saladin, who appointed him judge in the army. He took part in the battles against the *Crusaders and, in 1187, Saladin made him *Kadi* of Jerusalem. He wrote a well-documented biography of the sultan, which is not only the best description of Saladin's person and deeds, but also one of the best historical works by a Moslem historian.

CHI.

BEIRUT City on the eastern coast of the Mediterranean. At the beginning of the Middle Ages, B. was a Christian centre in the province of Tyre, and had a school of law. In 529 the city was destroyed by an earthquake and fell into decline during the 6th and 7th centuries; its school was transferred to Sidon. In 635 it was conquered by the Arabs. After the establishment of the caliphate at Damascus, B. became one of its principal ports and prosperity returned to the city and its traders. But in the 9th century it declined again and became a provincial town, neglected by the authorities of Baghdad. Towards the end of the 10th century it passed to the *Fatimids of Egypt, who appointed local emirs to govern the city. In 1100 the *Crusaders conquered the city after a siege of three months, and established a Latin bishopric and a feudal seigniory. The lords of "Baruth" (the city's name in the Crusaders' texts) were among the most important members of the feudal aristocracy of the *Latin kingdom of Jerusalem, and were related to the principal families of the kingdom. In 1187 *Saladin conquered B., but in 1196 the Crusaders of Emperor *Henry VI defeated its garrison and reestablished their rule. During the 13th century the city dwindled, until it was conquered by the *Mamluks in 1291. Under the Crusaders, B. served the trade with

the West, and Italian cities established communes in it; but it was relatively a minor port, which is why the Mamluks did not destroy it. In the 14th century it became the main port for the commerce between Cyprus and Syria. Subjects of the king of Cyprus had an autonomous quarter in the city administered by Cypriot officers, who also acted as protectors of the local churches and the Christian community.

S. Runciman, *A History of the Crusades* (1953).

BELA I King of *Hungary (1060-77). In 1058 he rebelled against his brother *Andrew, with the support of the nobility, which feared the German expansion. His reign was a period of compromise between the royal prerogative and the nobility.

BELA II, the Blind (d. 1141) King of *Hungary (1131-41). The son of *Almos, he was blinded during his father's revolt against *Stephen II. Exiled to Constantinople, he returned to Hungary at Stephen's death to be crowned king. Most of his reign was spent in contending with Prince Boris, Stephen's half-brother, who claimed the crown and was supported by the Germans. The nobility was behind him in the struggle to free Hungary from its dependence on the empire, and he was able to secure his position and the inheritance to his son Geza II without opposition.

BELA III (c. 1148-96) King of *Hungary (1173-96). The second son of Geza II, he fled in his youth to Constantinople, where he was brought up and educated by *Manuel II Comnenus, and was even proclaimed his heir presumptive. In 1173 he returned to Hungary and reorganized the administration of the kingdom on the model of the Byzantine government. He adopted a careful policy of friendship with both the *Holy Roman empire and Byzantium. However, after the death of Manuel in 1180, he felt free to pursue a policy of expansion in the Balkans, where he succeeded in conquering a part of Dalmatia, conflicting with Venice in 1181-88 and 1190-91. He helped the Serbs to free themselves from the rule of Byzantium. In 1188 he conquered eastern Galicia, but later had to withdraw from it.

BELA IV (1206-70) King of *Hungary (1235-70). Son and successor of *Andrew II, he managed to restrain the nobility and pacify the country after the troubles of his father's reign. In 1241 the *Mongols invaded the kingdom as far as Dalmatia, but then left the country, having devastated much of it, when *Batu-khan was called to Karakorum to the Great Khan's election. B. devoted his reign to reconstructing his kingdom and improving its economy. To do this, he encouraged the settlement of foreign colonists, notably Germans, particularly in the towns, which began to prosper. He also settled Jews in the cities and, in 1251, gave them the privilege of being direct dependents of the crown. In 1261 the Mongols again invaded Hungary, but B. defeated them near the border and saved the country from repeated destruction.

F. A. Eckhart, *A History of the Hungarian People* (1931).

BELGIUM At the beginning of the Middle Ages the Roman province of B. became the central part of the *Frankish kingdom (5th century), and ceased to exist as a separate political and administrative unit. In the 7th-8th centuries it was incorporated into the kingdom of *Austrasia. In the 9th century its territory was divided among several feudal units, some of which, like Rheims,

Picardy and Flanders, belonging to the kingdom of France; the rest became, in 843, the kingdom of *Lothair and in 889 was annexed to Germany as the duchy of Lower Lorraine. In the 11th century the ducal title passed to the house of Bouillon, but several provinces became dependents of the emperors, mainly the bishopric of Liège. When *Godfrey of Bouillon went on the *Crusade, the duchy of Lower Lorraine, corresponding roughly to present-day Walloon B., was split into several feudal units, such as the counties of Namur, Louvain, Hainault and Luxemburg, while its northern part, corresponding to the Netherlands, formed a group of feudal units depending directly on the emperors. In the 12th century Hainault was attached by dynastic ties to Flanders, and together they formed the western group of Belgian provinces, whose cities, trade and crafts were more advanced; the central and the eastern provinces remained divided. In the 14th century the house of Luxemburg acceded to the imperial crown and concentrated its territorial power and interests in Bohemia. Another important development of the 13th and 14th centuries was the constitution of the duchy of *Brabant, uniting several feudal entities, such as Louvain and the southern territories of modern Holland; this development corresponded with the growth of the cities of Antwerp and Brussels, which became the capital of the duchy. The marriage, in 1364, of *Philip the Bold, duke of Burgundy, with Margaret of Flanders, brought Philip the "Flemish group" of Belgian lands. In 1419 Brabant and Holland went to Duke *Philip the Good by his marriage with the heiress of the "Brabant group". The purchase of Namur and Luxemburg by Philip united B. under the house of Burgundy and it became the richest and the most powerful state in western Europe in the 15th century. With Antwerp as the main port in western Europe and Brussels as the ducal capital, centre of the textile industry and the residence of the most brilliant European court in the late Middle Ages, the country became an important cultural, intellectual and artistic centre, ushering in the northern Renaissance. The founding of the University of Louvain in 1426 gave the country its scholarly centre.

H. Pirenne, *Histoire de Belgique* (1901).

BELGRADE (Beograd) City in the Balkans, at the confluence of the Sava and Danube rivers. Its Roman name was Singidunum. At the beginning of the 5th century the Roman castle was destroyed by the *Huns and, during the 5th-6th centuries, it was conquered and ruled by Huns, Sarmatians, Goths and Gepids, who were defeated in 531 by *Justinian, who placed it under Byzantine rule, which lasted until the middle of the 7th century. The city was called *Alba Graeca* (White Greece) and was incorporated into the defence of the empire on the Danube. It did not, however, stop the penetration of Slavic tribes into its surroundings. When the *Avars settled in Pannonia they conquered B., which became populated with Slavs who changed its name into *Beograd* (the White Town). In the 9th century B. belonged to the *Bulgarian empire until its destruction in 1015 by *Basil II, who sent a Byzantine governor to B. to defend it from the *Hungarians; these nevertheless succeeded in conquering and destroying it in 1124. In 1154 the Byzantines reconquered the city and rebuilt it. In the last years of the 12th century B. passed back

to the Hungarians and then to the Bulgarians, who held it until the 14th century, when it was attached to the *Serbian kingdom. In 1403 King *Stephen established the capital of Serbia at B. In 1433 it fell again under the rule of the Hungarians, who made it a stronghold against the *Ottoman Turks. In 1456, John Hunyadi defeated the Turks near B. The wars and the repeated changes of rule made B. a fortified city of marked military character. Despite its ideal position for commerce on the Danube and with the Balkans, it did not prosper economically on account of its political instability.

H. W. V. Temperley, *History of Serbia* (1921).

BELISARIUS (c. 494-565) Byzantine general. A close friend of *Justinian even before his accession to the throne, he was, in 526, appointed by him commander-in-chief of the army, and sent to fight against the *Persians. His failure to produce successful results led to his dismissal. But when the *Niké riots broke out at Constantinople the emperor recalled B. and entrusted him with the suppression of the riots. His success in doing so was the starting point of his new career as general of the army and the commander of the Byzantine reconquest. In 533-34 he defeated the *Vandals of north Africa and conquered their country. In 535 he was sent to Italy to fight the *Ostrogoths. It was a long and difficult war and only in 541 did he succeed in conquering Rome and Ravenna, where he captured King Vitiges and brought him to Constantinople, together with the Ostrogoth treasury. But the completion of the conquest was entrusted to another general, *Narses, a man of political skill. B. was sent to fight the Persians, who had invaded the empire and penetrated into Syria. He defeated them and strengthened the imperial frontier on the Euphrates. Between 544 and 559 he fought several battles in Italy, Spain and the Balkans, but now his fortunes began to decline. Various accusations were made concerning the origins of his great fortune and, in 562, he was charged with treason. His property was confiscated and according to tradition he was reduced to begging in his last years, a victim of court plots and rumours, although he remained faithful to the emperor and had been one of the builders of the empire.

Pauly-Wissova, *Realencyclopedie*;
R. Graves, *Count Belisarius* (1968).

BELLS The introduction of B. in Christian churches corresponds with the beginning of the Middle Ages. According to tradition it was Paulinius, bishop of Nola in Campania, who first introduced them in the churches; in the late Middle Ages it was widely believed that the word *campanile* (Italian: bell-tower) derived from *Campania* and *Nola*. However, there is no etymological evidence to support this tradition. By the end of the 6th century, in the time of *Gregory of Tours, the use of B. was widespread, and he did not describe them as an innovation. From the 8th century on B. were blessed by a bishop in a ceremony called the baptism of B.; they were engraved with inscriptions in praise of benefactors and patrons. The B. were hung in special towers beside the churches – especially in Italy – but gradually they were incorporated in the church building itself; from the 10th century on, the bell-tower crowned the front of the Romanesque and Gothic churches. In the Gothic churches there were usually two towers, one of them housing the main, or the great bell, used for the most important ceremonies. In the 11th century it became customary for one of the B. to ring the hour, and it marked the time for people around. The bell of Durham Cathedral, for example, was recognized in the 12th century as an official instrument for measuring working time. With the introduction of public clocks in the 14th century, the monopoly of the church-B. as the official timepiece came to an end and gave place to expressions such as "the time of the church", "the time of the king", or of the feudal lord, and "the time of the city", all these having the right to set up public timepieces.

G. S. Tyack, *A Book about Bells* (1898).

BENEDICT I Pope (575-79). Though of Roman family, he did not interfere in Italian politics and accepted the superiority of Byzantium. He encouraged monasticism and maintained good relations with the communities of Subiaco.

BENEDICT II Pope (684-85). Of Roman family, he spent his short pontificate in building and restoring the churches of Rome, for which he was later canonized. He won from Constantinople an agreement that the recognition of a new pope would be given by the Byzantine *exarch of Ravenna, and not by the imperial court, which was a step towards freeing the papacy from its dependence on Byzantium.

A. Duchesne, *The Early History of Papal State* (1908).

BENEDICT III Pope (855-58). Born in Rome, he was from his youth at the papal court and was created cardinal by *Leo IV. At the latter's death he was elected pope and resisted the attempt of Emperor *Louis II to invalidate his election and appoint *Anastasius "the Librarian". He won the support of the cardinals, even those who had acted on behalf of the emperor. He sought to consolidate the independence of the papacy and prepared the way for his successor, *Nicholas I.

J. Haller, *Das Papsttum*, II (1943).

BENEDICT IV Pope (900-03). Promoted to the papacy by the support of his fellow Roman nobles, his main act as pope was the coronation of the last *Carolingian emperor, *Louis "the Blind" (900), whom he believed capable of fighting the *Hungarians, who had invaded northern Italy. The victory of *Berengar of Friuli, which eliminated Louis from the Italian scene in 902, reduced B.'s influence.

J. Haller, *Das Papsttum*, II (1943).

BENEDICT V (d. 966) Pope (964). Elected by the partisans of *John XII, despite the election of *Leo VIII and his recognition by *Otto I, who deposed and degraded him. Removed as a prisoner to Hamburg, B. died there.

BENEDICT VI Pope (973-74) Born in central Italy, he was the candidate of *Otto I in a disputed election. When news of the emperor's death reached Rome, riots broke out and B. was imprisoned and murdered, and Boniface VII was proclaimed pope. His election, however, was not recognized and he is considered an antipope.

L. Duchesne, *Liber Pontificalis* (1903).

BENEDICT VII Pope (974-83). Member of an important Roman family, he was bishop of Sutri before he was made pope by *Otto II. Enjoying imperial support, he succeeded in appeasing the Roman factions. B. carried out ecclesiastical reforms, encouraged the order of *Cluny and created new bishoprics in Germany. In 981 he held a council, with the participation of the emperor, in which he condemned the practice of *simony.

J. Haller, *Das Papsttum*, II (1943).

BENEDICT VIII Pope (1012-24). Born Theophilactus, son of Gregory, count of Tusculum, *Otto III's commander of the navy. B. inherited the county but, in 1012, left it to his brother Alberic and was elected pope. He was recognized by *Henry II, who left him a large authority at Rome. B. did all he could, acting as a feudal ruler, to restore the papal state in Italy. He made his brother Romanus duke of Rome, the better to control the city. B. had close relations with the abbey of Cluny and supported its reforming activities. In 1012, he went to Germany where he supported the efforts of the emperor to reform the church. In 1016 he led an expedition against the Arabs of north Africa, who had invaded the coast near *Pisa and conquered Sardinia; his victory over them gave rise to the maritime empire of Pisa. His expeditions in southern Italy against Byzantium were unsuccessful and the Byzantines remained in control of the area for another generation. In 1022, at the height of his prestige, he held the Council of Pavia, which was one of the first steps in the movement of ecclesiastical reform of the 11th century.

J. Haller, *Das Papsttum*, II (1943).

BENEDICT IX (Theophylactus of Tusculum; c. 1003-55) Pope (1033-45). The nephew of Benedict VIII, he was made pope by his family which was in complete control of Rome. His unseemly behaviour and inexperience led him into difficulties, which he tried to solve by an alliance with Emperor *Conrad II. Nevertheless he lost the respect and support of the people of Rome, and in 1044, the riots became an open revolt against him, until he was compelled to abandon the pontifical see to *Gregory VI.

R. L. Poole, *Benedict IX and Gregory VI* (1917).

BENEDICT X (John Mincius) Pope (1058). He was bishop of Velletri when, at the death of *Stephen IX, the Tusculum family, which tried to renew the custom of electing Italian popes, chose him to succeed. However, the opposition of Emperor *Henry III and of part of the clergy, made his pontificate impossible and he had to give it up in favour of the nominee of the emperor, *Nicholas II.

BENEDICT XI (Nicholas Boccasino; 1240-1304) Pope (1303-04). He was the general master of the *Dominicans from 1296, and a close collaborator of *Boniface VIII, whom he succeeded. His short pontificate was a year of transition before *Avignon.

BENEDICT XII (Jacques Fournier; d. 1342) Pope (1334-42). Of a humble family of Gascony, he became a *Cistercian monk and studied in Paris, where he became a master of theology. In 1311 he became abbot of Fontfroide and, in 1317, bishop of Pamiers in southern France. In 1327 he was created cardinal and took part in the dogmatic controversies of the time, especially the question of poverty. Elected pope, he introduced several reforms, particularly in the life of the clergy, where he fought nepotism and greed. He was also a zealous reformer of the religious orders. He attempted to moderate between the kings of France and England and proposed to launch a new *Crusade. But he failed in these efforts and it was during his pontificate that the *Hundred Years' War began. He was on bad terms with the emperor, *Louis of Bavaria, and his opposition to the declaration of the German electors, that the emperor's rights derive from his election by the princes, and not from the pope's recognition, did not improve matters. In the administration of the Church he succeeded in improving the finances of the *Curia*. B. began the building of the famous palace of the popes at Avignon.

G. Mollat, *The Popes of Avignon* (1923).

BENEDICT XIII (Pedro de Luna; d. 1423) The last pope of *Avignon (1394-1417). Of Spanish origin, he was doctor of canon law and won a reputation for great learning. In 1375 *Gregory XI created him cardinal and he took part in the election of *Urban VI; later, however, he became a partisan of the Avignonese pope, *Clement VII, whom he succeeded in 1394, promising to end the schism of the papacy by abdicating. But this he refused to do and the negotiations with the Roman popes, *Boniface IX, *Innocent VII and *Gregory XII failed to restore unity. He resisted a siege of his palace in Avignon, while his supporters began to abandon him. In 1409 the Council of *Pisa deposed him but, with the support of Aragon, Castile, Scotland and Sicily, he annulled the decision at the Synod of Perpignan. In 1417 the Council of *Constance deposed him again, and his last adherents left him. He retreated to his castle of Peniscola in Spain, where he tried to continue the struggle with a few number of clerics, whom he created cardinals.

DHGE, VIII.

BENEDICT BISCOP, St. (c. 628-89) Monk. Born in a noble Northumbrian family, he spent his youth at the court. After two visits to Rome he entered the Benedictine abbey of Lérins in 333. In 669 he returned to England and became abbot of the monastery of St. Peter and Paul at Canterbury. In 674 he returned to Northumbria and founded the monastery of Wearmouth and, in 682, that of Jarrow. Devoting his efforts to the liturgy, he also encouraged learning at the schools of the monasteries and received *Bede at Wearmouth. In a spirit of adoration, Bede wrote his biography.

DNB, II.

BENEDICT OF ANIANE, St. (750-821) Monk born in an aristocratic family which ruled in Languedoc, he served in the Frankish army under *Pepin the Short and *Charlemagne. In 773 he became a monk at the abbey of St. Seine near Dijon. In 779 he founded a monastery on his own property at Aniane in Languedoc, and it became the centre of a monastic reform in the Frankish kingdom. He was inclined to severe asceticism, although as abbot he often had to leave the monastery and visit the court. His reform received the official sanction of Charlemagne and of *Louis the Pious. The latter proclaimed his Rule, which was a revised version of the Rule of St. *Benedict, the official law of the empire in 817. B. is considered as the second father of *Benedictine monasticism.

J. Narberhaus, *Benedikt von Aniane* (1930).

BENEDICT OF NURSIA, St. (c. 480-550) The patriarch of western monasticism. Born in Nursia to an old Roman family, he was educated in Rome, where he encountered the licentious ways of contemporary society. Disgusted by the libertinism which violated the ideals of his childhood and youth, he retired to a cave at Subiaco, where he lived in complete isolation, in imitation of the Egyptian hermits. This retreat lasted a few years, and was broken by the gathering of disciples. Gradually a community was established there, which B. organized in 12 monasteries of 12 monks each, whose

St. Benedict by Perugino

abbots he appointed. Local jealousies grew with the organization, and it appears that B. found it difficult to control the community. In 525 he left Subiaco and established a new monastery at *Monte Cassino, southeast of Rome. It was here that he developed his idea of reforming monasticism and composed his Rule, which became the model for western monasticism.

The Rule of St. Benedict was traditionally attributed in its entirety to B., but modern research shows that only part of the extant document was his own, the rest having been added during the 7th-8th centuries. It is influenced by earlier Greek rules, but does not call for excessive austerity. The Rule gives absolute power to the abbot, who is elected by the community. The vow requires withdrawal from lay society and residence in the monastery, obedience and poverty. The principal task of the monk is the performance of the work of God (*opus Dei*), meaning labour (corporal and spiritual), study and prayer. All possessions are to be held in common, as are the meals, which are part of the spiritual work of the congregation.

F. Cabrol, *Saint Benedict* (1934).

BENEDICTINE ORDER During the pontificate of *Pelagius II, after the sack of *Monte Cassino by the *Lombards (580), the monks of St. *Benedict moved to Rome, taking with them their Rule, which had begun to be adopted by other monasteries, including that of *Gregory the Great. When Gregory became pope in 590, the monasteries which were governed by this Rule called themselves Benedictine. This was the beginning of the B., which during this pontificate spread to Gaul and Britain. Gregory encouraged it and employed its monks in missionary work, like the mission of St. *Augustine to Kent. The B. played an important role in shaping the population of western Europe: the abbeys, independently of one another, created centres of settlement in various regions, and the administration of their estates served as a model for lay estates. The obligations to study, imposed by the Rule, gave rise to the establishment of schools and libraries in the abbeys, which were thus the foci of scholarship in Europe until the 12th century. In the 8th and 9th centuries the abbeys also helped to spread books, which were copied by monks in the *scriptoria* of the monasteries.

C. Butler, *Benedictine Monasticism* (1924).

BENEDICTUS LEVITAS (9th century) Probably a pseudonym of a cleric who lived in France in the middle of the 9th century and who described himself as the deacon of the church of Mainz in Germany. He compiled a great mass of canon *law, based on the Decretals of *Isidore of Seville, including a great many false decrees and laws, which he attributed to Isidore but which are by their language easily recognized as a work compiled in France in the 9th century. The aim of the compilation was to revise the principles of canon law in favour of local bishops.

E. Seckel, *Studien zu Benedictus Levita* (1919).

BENEFICE (Latin: beneficium) The literal meaning of the word is "doing good", and it was originally used in Christian terminology. At the beginning of the Middle Ages, it also meant a donation of money or land, to the church, in return for which, the donor could expect the gift of divine grace for himself and his family. From the 8th century on, B. referred to the land given by a lord to his vassal and the permission to use its produce, in return for which the vassal would render either military or administrative service. The B. remained the property of the lord and was returned after the completion of service, usually upon the vassal's death. Under the *Carolingians, from the time of *Charles Martel, vassals were barred by law from transferring the B. in whole or in part, bequeathing it to their heirs, or from transferring peasants and animals from the B. to the vassals' own properties. By the time of *Charlemagne, during the 9th century, these laws were not always adhered to: more and more vassals came to regard the Bs. as family tenures, attempting to dispose of them as they saw fit – a process which accelerated with the decline and partition of the Carolingian empire and culminated in 875 in the official decision permitting the vassals to bequeath their Bs. to their heirs. Thus, the term B., which was still used in the charters, became synonymous with *fief. Gradually, the term disappeared from feudal documents, and from the 12th century, it was exclusively used by the Church to designate the perpetual income received by clergymen both while they were in office and after they retired.

M. Bloch, *Feudal Society* (1939).

BENEFIT OF CLERGY The term signifies the exemption from trial for a felony by a secular court, a privilege accorded to the clergy in west European countries in the Middle Ages. It was granted to all clerical ranks, including students in the universities. Complaints against clerics had to be addressed to an ecclesiastical court. The privilege caused many disputes between lay courts and the Church.

L. C. Gabel, *Benefit of Clergy in England in the Late Middle Ages* (1929).

BENEVENTO City in Campania (southern Italy). B. was destroyed by the *Ostrogoths but was shortly afterwards rebuilt by the Byzantines. In 570 the *Lombards conquered the city and made it the capital of their dominions in southern Italy, thereafter called the duchy of B. The dukes, related to the royal family, enjoyed a large measure of autonomy, and in the 8th century, became independent of Pavia. Duke *Grimoald succeeded in retaining his independence after *Charlemagne's conquest of the Lombard kingdom, although he formally recognized the authority of the Franks. In the 9th and 10th centuries the dukes of B. repulsed Byzantine and Arab attempts to conquer the duchy, which remained independent of the *Holy Roman empire. Nevertheless, the long fights weakened the ducal authority and, at the beginning of the 11th century, they lost their power. The duchy disintegrated into a number of principalities, most of which were conquered by the *Normans and became part of their kingdom of Sicily, while the city of B. itself was annexed to the *Papal state in 1054, remaining a part of it until 1860. Although Roman domination was a constant factor in Beneventan history, both politically and religiously, the city was in close economic cooperation with *Naples, and was an enclave within that kingdom in the 13th century. The cathedral of B., which was built in the 9th-12th centuries and was a masterpiece of southern Italian art, was destroyed in World War II.

F. Hirsch, *Il ducato di Benevento* (1968[2]).

BENJAMIN (BEN JONAH) OF TUDELA (12th cent.) Traveller. His book, *Itinerary*, told of his voyages between 1159 and 1172. Nothing is known about his childhood and education. As an adult, B. lived in Tudela in Aragon, where he was a gem merchant. His travels took him through Spain and France, Italy, the Byzantine empire, Cyprus, Syria, Palestine, Iraq, Persia, Egypt and Sicily. He was primarily interested in the Jewish communities of the cities he visited, but also in the gentile population and its life. His book, written after his return to Tudela, is therefore an informative and accurate guide to the life and customs of Jews, Christians and Moslems in the second half of the 12th century.

Ed. with Engl. trans. M. N. Adler (1907);
M. N. Adler, *The Journey of Benjamin of Tudela* (1907).

BENOIT DE SAINTE-MAURE (Saint Mor) French poet (12th century). In the years 1154-73 he composed the *Roman de Troie* in 35,000 verses, a history of Troy based on Greek mythology. The poem was one of the most popular epics in the courts of the 12th century, as was B.'s other romance of antiquity, the *Roman de Thèbes*. B. described the ancient world as a mirror of 12th-century knightly life, built around bravery in the field of battle, fine manners and courtly love. His works were known even outside the French-speaking countries – in the 13th century they were translated into German, Latin, Spanish and Italian and, in the 14th, into English and Greek.

R. K. Gordon, *The Story of Troilus* (1932).

BENTIVOGLIO Italian aristocratic family influential in Bologna from the 13th century. They led the city's anti-papal movement in the second half of the 14th century, intending to oust the governors installed by the popes. John I B., who led the movement at the end of the 14th century, seized power, and in 1401 became a lord of Bologna. Disputes with the *Visconti of Milan led to his assassination in 1402. His son, Anthony Galeazzo, a jurist, continued his father's policy until his death in 1435. Thereafter the city entered a period of decadence, with political-religious conflicts causing several leadership changes. Sante B. became lord of Bologna in 1446 and ruled until 1462. Reaching an agreement with the papacy enabled him to concentrate on restoring order. Under him the city flourished and the university, which he reorganized, regained its former fame. His successor, John II, was one of the most important personalities of the Italian Renaissance.

C. M. Ady, *The Bentivoglio of Bologna* (1937).

BENZO OF ALBA (11th century) Born in northern Italy, he maintained relations with the imperial court under *Henry III, and with Germany even after becoming bishop of Alba in 1060. Opposed to the election of *Alexander II in 1061, he became one of the leaders of the anti-*Gregorianists in the church. His opinions led to his expulsion from Alba in 1077, but in 1081 he returned to become head of *Henry IV's supporters. He developed his political-religious views in a treatise entitled *Liber ad Heinricum* (The Book to Henry), attacking the political concepts of the Gregorian reform, considered by him a movement of the devil, and exposing his concept of a strong Roman empire as the only way for Christian salvation. His book, criticized by *Peter Damiani, was one of the most important contributions to the ideological polemics of the *Investiture contest.

P. E. Schramm, *Kaiser, Rom und Renovatio* (1929).

BEOWULF Epic poem in Old English. While the oldest extant manuscript of the poem dates from the late 10th century, the poem was probably composed in the early 8th century. Its anonymous author, an Anglo-Saxon, is believed to have been a Christian, but one who was educated in classical traditions: pagan values and influences of *Virgil are reflected in the poem. B. concerns the Anglo-Saxons' Germanic ancestors of the 5th and 6th centuries, events of that period having presumably been kept alive by a rich oral history. The poem is divided into two parts, corresponding to the two stages of its hero's life: in the first B. is depicted as a young noble warrior, saving his country from a monstrous enemy, and in the second as an old king, who remained an excellent warrior and a wise leader. While the poem is an allegory on the triumph of good over evil, it also praises the heroic deeds, loyalty and devotion of the warriors, seamen and nobles and is an important source of information on early English society.

D. Wright, *Beowulf* (1956).

BERBERS The natives of northwestern Africa, of Indo-European and negro descent. Although subjugated by the Romans, Vandals and Byzantines, they managed to preserve a measure of autonomy, based on their tribal organization, language and culture. In the 7th century, opposing Byzantine attempts to introduce Christianity, they fought alongside the Arab general Uqbah Ibn-Nafi, and helped him conquer north Africa from the Byzantines in 667. But, when Uqbah tried to consolidate his conquests in the Atlas Mountains, they revolted and, under the leadership of Kusaylah, fought against the Arabs and killed Uqbah in 683. The Arabs, nevertheless, succeeded in retaining north Africa and the Berbers subsequently adopted *Sunnite Islam, albeit in a very superficial form. Despite their Islamization, they were treated by the Arabs as subordinates and subjected to tribute. The B. began a long series of revolts against the governors sent by both the *Ummayads and *Abbasids. In their fight against the *Aghlabids, they supported the Shiite *Fatimids in the 10th century. The B. were also employed in Moslem Spain, coming into contact with the more developed centres of Sunnite Islam. They brought Islam into the Sahara, where the Tuareg tribes adopted it in the 10th century; they supported the *Almoravides in the 11th century and became the main force of their empire. In the 12th century, the B. of what is today Algeria revolted against the Almoravides and established the *Almohade dynasty. After the fall of the Almohades, they set up a number of principalities in north Africa in the middle of the 13th century. Though they were the dominant element in north Africa during the 14th and 15th centuries – the Europeans called the region "Barbary" – rivalry between sectarian tribes prevented the establishment of a powerful state. The process of Arabization from the shores of the Mediterranean to the Atlas Mountains continued until the end of the Middle Ages, when the B. were pushed southwards.

G. Marçais, *La Berbérie musulmane et l'Orient au Moyen Age* (1946).

BERENGAR I (d. 924) King of Italy (887-924), emperor (915-24). Related through his mother to the *Carolingians, he was count of Friul, in northeastern Italy. He profited from the anarchy that prevailed in the Carolingian realms to enlarge his dominion and in 887 was elected king of Italy. His title was disputed by *Guy of Spoleto, who defeated him and even after he became the king in 898 he was challenged by nobles who weakened his power. After his defeat by the *Hungarians in 899, they proclaimed *Louis of Provence king of Italy. B. defeated Louis in 905 at Verona and blinded him. By this act he established his authority in Italy and reigned with the help of the clergy. In 915 Pope *John IX, requiring his protection at Rome, crowned him emperor, although his real authority was limited. In 923 he was defeated by *Rudolph, king of Burgundy, and murdered at Pavia a few months later.

O. Pastine, *Il regno di Berengario I* (1912).

BERENGAR II (d. 966) King of Italy (950-63). Grandson of *Berengar I and inheritor of the county of Friul. After an abortive attempt in 940 to conquer the realm of Italy from Hugh of Provence, he fled to the court of *Otto I of Germany, who helped him continue his struggle. He returned to Italy in 945 and defeated Hugh, who abdicated in favour of his son Lothair. B. became the most prominent prince in Italy and won the support of the nobility. In 950, at the death of Lothair (for which B. was probably responsible), he proclaimed himself king. His reign marked a period of anarchy that necessitated the intervention of Otto I. In 951 Otto compelled him to free Lothair's widow, Adelaide, who became Otto's wife. Otto deposed B. in 952 but after his return to Germany, B. again assumed the title of king. In 963, after the imperial coronation of Otto, the German army defeated B., holding him prisoner at Bamberg until his death in 966.

G. Barraclough, *Medieval Germany* (1955).

BERENGAR OF TOURS (Berengarius; c. 999-1088) Theologian and philosopher. Born in Tours (France), he studied at Chartres under *Fulbert. He became master of the school of St. Martin of Tours and in 1040 was appointed canon of Angers. His teaching, influenced by the thought of John Scot *Erigena, was considered heterodox by his contemporaries, who attacked his ideas on the Eucharist, seeing them as a denial of the sacrament. He was denounced as a heretic at the councils of 1050 and 1051 and his writings burnt. Although absolved from excommunication in 1054 and again in 1059, he remained suspect to the Church hierarchy and was compelled by *Gregory VII in 1079 to retract his later works. Disappointed, he lived his remaining years as a hermit. His thoughts were expressed in his main book *De Sacra Coena* (On the Sacred Supper), which was an answer to *Lanfranc's theories. He rejected the literal interpretation of the Eucharist – that bread and wine were transformed into the real flesh and blood of Christ after consecration in the Mass though without losing its outward appearance – and saw it only as a symbol, arguing that it is impossible to speak of a carnal return of Christ before the Last Judgement.

A. J. MacDonald, *Berengar and the Reform of Sacramental Doctrine* (1930).

BERGAMO City in Lombardy, north of Milan. The upper part of the city, fortified during the Roman period, served in the 7th-8th centuries as seat of a Lombard duchy and was an important political centre of northern Italy. Under the *Carolingians, the city declined, becoming at the end of the 9th century the centre of an autonomous seigniory, whose lords fought against the bishops for its mastery. Although economically dependent on Milan, B. in the 13th century began to resent its influence. This influence gave way to the official suzerainty of the *Visconti from 1264 until 1428, when B. was conquered by Venice. As part of the Venetian States in Italy, B. flourished; new quarters of a commercial character were built to constitute the lower part of the city. One of them, still called *Il-Ghetto*, became the Jewish community's settlement, but also served as financial centre of the whole city.

G. Antonucci, *Bergamo* (1946).

BERGEN City in Norway. Founded in 1075 in the Byfjord near an ancient Viking settlement it included a village of fishermen and a shepherd's settlement, which gave it its name (Bjorgvin). Rapid development in the 12th century made the city one of the most important ports in Norway and the centre of the international fishing trade. With the foundation of a bishopric (1158), B. also became a spiritual centre of central Norway. In 1350 the German *Hanse established a commercial enclave in B., eventually incorporating the city into their league, of which B. remained a member until the beginning of the 16th century. Political and commercial ties with the German states contributed in large measure to the growth of B.'s maritime trade and the concomitant economic boom.

H. Zimmern, *The Hansa Towns* (1889).

BERNARD (797-818) King of Italy (810-18). Son of Pepin of Italy, he was appointed king by his grandfather *Charlemagne at his father's death. After the death of Charlemagne in 814, his relations with the new emperor, his uncle *Louis the Pious, deteriorated, as Louis saw in B. a potential adversary. In 818 Louis accused him of felony and rebellion and sentenced him to death.

BERNARD I, of Saxony (d. 1011) Duke of Saxony (973-1011). He was a kinsman of Emperor *Otto II and one of his most devoted partisans. He helped him and *Otto III in their eastern policy, and initiated the German expansion eastward to the Elbe, where members of his family, the *Billung, obtained large estates.

BERNARD II, of Saxony (d. 1059) Duke of Saxony (1011-59) and son of Bernard I. His rule was initially obstructed by powerful vassals, who controlled a large part of the duchy, but an alliance with the bishops helped him restore his authority in East Saxony. B.'s rule of the Slavs there and their ready acquiescence brought him into conflict with *Adalbert of Bremen, who led a missionary group from his archbishopric to the Slavs of northern Europe and the Baltic in an attempt to win their loyalty. From 1044 on, the conflicts between Adalbert and B. worsened, leading in turn to friction between B. and Emperor *Henry III, Adalbert's protégé. These prolonged antagonisms led the duchy into a period of decline from which it recovered only after B.'s death in 1059.

J. W. Thompson, *Feudal Germany* (1928).

BERNARD GUI (1261-1331) Inquisitor. Born in Limousin (France) to a family of lesser nobility, he joined the *Dominican order in 1279 and studied theology at Montpellier until 1290. For several years he was a prior in various Dominican houses in southern France. In 1307, Pope *Clement V appointed him inquisitor, with headquarters in Toulouse. His chief task was to seek out and convict people suspected of heresy, mainly the *Albigensians. In 1324 he was appointed bishop of Lodève, where he died in 1331. B. was not only a devoted inquisitor, but also a prolific writer, particularly in history and theology. The most important of his works is *Practica inquisitionis heretice pravitatis* (The Conduct of the Inquisition of Heretical Depravity), also called *The Manual of the Inquisitor*. The book, based on his own experiences, was written when his term of office ended at Toulouse. He summed up some of the practices of the heretical sects whom he considered influential in his time: Cathars, Waldenses, "pseudo-Apostles", Béguines, Jews and sorcerers. He compiled materials from earlier sources to produce a systematic work which was to serve the Inquisition in the late Middle Ages.

C. Douais, *Le Manuel de l'Inquisiteur de Bernard Gui* (1886).

BERNARD OF ANHALT (d. 1212) Duke of Saxony (1180-1212). He was the youngest son of *Albert the Bear, who invested him with power over the county of Anhalt in 1170. One of the most devoted princes in Germany to *Frederick Barbarossa, he fought against *Henry the Lion, duke of Saxony (1178-80), and was invested with the dukedom by the emperor in 1180. Unable to exert his ducal authority, powerful vassals, such as the counts of Holstein, rebelled against him. During his rule, the great duchy of *Saxony lost part of its territory and began to concentrate in the southeast, the basis of modern Saxony.

G. Barraclough, *Origins of Modern Germany* (1947).

BERNARD OF CHARTRES (d. 1130) Philosopher, theologian, and prominent figure of the school of *Chartres, which he headed between 1117 and 1130. According to *John of Salisbury, B. arrived at philosophy through the study of grammar and logic. He was one of the most eminent teachers of *scholasticism whose methods were inspired by Plato's philosophy.

E. Gilson, *History of Medieval Philosophy* (1954).

BERNARD OF CLAIRVAUX, St. (1090-1153) Abbot, ecclesiastical writer. Born to a noble family at Fontaines near Dijon in Burgundy, he entered the monastery of *Cîteaux in 1113 together with 30 other young nobles. In 1115 he was commissioned by his abbot, *Stephen Harding, to found the monastery of the *Cistercian order at Clairvaux, whose abbot he remained until his death. He soon became one of the most active formulators of church policy, establishing his reputation as the leader of monastic reform of his age. He was at loggerheads with *Louis VI, king of France, whom he accused of opposing the reform, and with *Peter the Venerable, abbot of Cluny, who was both his friend and rival. Already enjoying great prestige in 1128, he was asked by the *Templars at the Council of Troyes to write their code of discipline, which was approved by the council. In one of his most important treatises, *De laude novae militiae* (In Praise of the New Knighthood) he inveighs against secular chivalry while praising the idealism of religious knights, who lost their private interests to fight against the infidels. To assure the recognition of Pope Innocent II in 1131, he used his polemical skills to disseminate adverse propaganda against the pope's rival, *Anacletus II. A champion of orthodoxy, he was to become the virtual dictator of Christendom in western Europe. He criticized the rationalism of *Abélard and had him condemned at the Council of Sens in 1140. He also attacked the Parisian scholars on the grounds that they constituted a new "Babylon". From 1141 to 1143 B. was opposed to *Louis VII's policy, but *Suger of St. Denis brought about a reconciliation between the two. B. was thus able to influence Louis' decision to lead a *Crusade. When his pupil was elected pope in 1143 B.'s influence increased substantially. He wrote a treatise, *De consideratione* (On Consideration), for the new pope, *Eugenius II, in which he argues for a theocracy, claiming that the rule of the Christian world is the prerogative of the pope alone, while it was the kings' and nobles' duty to fight the infidels. He was the spiritual leader of the Second Crusade, preaching for the fulfilment of the duty to protect the Holy Land and the Holy Sepulchre. While the pope advocated the crusade on both religious and political grounds B. saw it as solely a religious expedition, destined for the salvation of souls. Moreover, his spiritual concepts were at variance with the lay manners of the Crusaders themselves and, this led to the Crusade's failure. B. opposed the Crusade's anti-Jewish manifestations and his intervention saved the Jews of the Rhinelands from persecution. Towards the end of his life, B. was already regarded as a saint, his pupils attributing his activities to the Divine spirit and considering them as miracles. He was canonized after his death.

B. S. James, *St. Bernard of Clairvaux* (1957);
St. Bernard et son temps (1963).

BERNARD OF CLUNY (Bernard of Morval or Morlass; d. c. 1140) Probably of English origin, he became a monk at *Cluny under *Peter the Venerable. Famous author of sermons in the early 12th century, his most important work was a long Latin poem, *De Contemptu Mundi* (The Contempt of the World), in which he attacked the monastic disorders and stressed the transitoriness

St. Bernard of Clairvaux by Fra Filippo Lippi

of life on earth. This pessimistic approach to the world is complemented by an optimistic mystical view of celestial Jerusalem, symbol of what is to come at the end of time. The poem became a source for many hymns of the medieval liturgy.

F. J. E. Raby, *A History of Christian Latin Poetry* (1953).

BERNARD OF GORDON (d. c. 1310) Surgeon. Born in France, he studied at Montpellier and became famous as a surgeon. In the late 13th and the beginning of the 14th century, he was consulted by physicians on difficult cases: his answers (the *consilia*), many of which are preserved, show that he was also a fine diagnostician. In 1303, when consulted on a case of defective eyesight, he discussed the use of spectacles – one of the first references to such treatment.

E. Rieseman, *The Story of Medicine in the Middle Ages* (1935).

BERNARD OF GOTHIA (9th century) Son of a certain Count Bernard, he was one of the feudal adventurers, who caused trouble in the kingdom of France during the reign of *Charles the Bald. In 865 he was invested with power over the March of Gothia (*Languedoc), the subject of dispute between him and two other *Bernards (of Septimania and of Toulouse). His relations with the royal court fluctuated and reached their nadir in 878, when, held responsible for weakening the royal power and causing disorders in southern France, he was excommunicated at the Council of Troyes and deprived of his honours; the following year King Louis II banished him to Aquitaine, where he died in misery.

J. Calmette, *La question des Pyrénées et la Marche d'Espagne* (1947).

BERNARD OF MENTHON, St. (923-1009) Born at Menthon in Savoy, B. became a hermit in the Alps, where he was active in helping people pass through the mountains. He founded hospices for the pilgrims who travelled over the Mont Blanc range. He soon became an object of veneration among pilgrims for his help and rescue activities, and was considered a saint during his life-time. His name was given to the St. Bernard Pass between Switzerland and Italy, and to a breed of alpine dogs trained to rescue people.

BERNARD OF SEPTIMANIA (d. 844) Son of St. *William of Gelonne. In 820 he became duke of Septimania and of the Spanish March. Related to the *Carolingian dynasty, he was one of the most powerful and influential persons under *Louis the Pious, arousing the jealousy of the nobility. In 827 he succeeded in defending Barcelona from an Arab attack, even though the army sent to help him failed to arrive. In 829 Louis promoted him at the imperial court to the prestigious post of Chamberlain. His opponents accused him of being the lover of the Empress Judith, the mother of *Charles the Bald. After the revolt of Louis' son in 831, B. was forced to leave the court, but shortly afterwards returned to Septimania, where he continued to enjoy full authority. In 840, at the death of Louis, he allied himself with *Pepin II of Aquitaine against *Charles the Bald. But Charles was to retaliate: after the partition of the empire at Verdun (843), he went to Aquitaine, ostensibly to establish order, it being rumoured that B. intended to create an independent realm. B. was denounced as a traitor, sentenced to death, and his possessions were confiscated.

J. Calmette, *Le démembrement de l'Empire Carolingien* (1945).

BERNARD OF VENTADOUR (12th century) Poet. Born at the castle of Ventadour near Limoges, he became a well-known troubadour while still a youth. He composed the most famous love songs of his time at the court of *Eleanor of Aquitaine (c. 1151). B. took part in the coronation of *Henry II and Eleanor in England in 1154 and, after a while, returned to southern France, travelling through the various feudal courts. His poems are written with a delicate, lyrical skill and a perfect mastery of the Occitanian tongue, while his subject matter – extolling love – made him very popular.

H. Davenson, *Les Troubadours* (1963).

BERNARD OF VERDUN (13th century) Astronomer. One of the first experimentalists in western Europe. He was influenced by Arab astronomy, which he had learned through Latin translations. Concurring with the empiricism of Arab astronomy and its emphasis on observation, he challenged the Western school, which, under the influence of *Thomas Aquinas, sought to reconcile reason with faith.

A. C. Crombie, *Science in the Middle Ages* (1961).

BERNARD PLANTEVELNE (d. 885) Son of *Bernard of Septimania. Despite his family's opposition to *Charles the Bald, the king of France appointed him count of Autun and he sat among the king's vassals at the Assembly of Pîtres in 862. When his expectations of ascending to his father's rank in southern France were not met, he is believed to have revolted. Convicted of felony, he was ordered to surrender Autun, but for two years he resisted Charles' attempts to conquer the county. He was subsequently reconciled with the king, and appointed count of Auvergne, and in 868 was invested with the rank of marquis. While B. thus became one of the most prominent figures of the kingdom, he also remained a self-seeking adventurer. After the death of Charles, B. became adviser to his son *Louis, who entrusted him with the guardianship of his sons, *Louis

III and *Carloman before Louis' death in 879. He fell in battle in Vienne, on the Rhône, while commanding the army of Carloman in his fight against Boso's attempts to proclaim himself king.

F. Lot, *Naissance de la France* (1948).

BERNARD SILVESTRIS (c. 1150) Philosopher. Little is known about his life. Born at Tours, he probably studied at the school of Chartres and maintained excellent relations with its master, *Thierry. Until his death he was master of the school of Tours, where he taught his neo-Platonist philosophic method. A man of broad culture and a Latin scholar, he wrote a commentary on Virgil's *Aeneid*. But his most famous work is the *Cosmographia*, dedicated to his friend Thierry. His concept of the Cosmos, influenced by the neo-Platonism of the 3rd century, distinguishes between the *Macrocosmos* (Nature and the four basic elements – earth, fire, water and air – ordered by the Divine will), and the *Microcosmos*, the human world. The treatise is written in an elegant allegoric style and purports to explain the basic concept of nature and cosmography of his age.

E. Gilson, *Philosophy in the Middle Ages* (1951).

BERNE City in Switzerland. The ancient Roman settlement there was destroyed in the 5th century and the territory annexed to the realm of the *Allemanni. In the 6th century it formed part of the kingdom of *Franks and in the 9th century, after the division of the *Carolingian empire, was incorporated in the German duchy of *Swabia. In 1191, Duke Berthold V of Zhäringen built a castle on the site, which soon became a population centre. In 1218 the town was granted the status of *imperial city and subsequently it was to dominate the towns and villages of the neighbourhood. Its name derives from the colony of bears, the symbol of its liberation from the feudal lords of southern Swabia, against whom B. fought in the 13th and 14th centuries. B.'s victory in 1339 consolidated its independence and authority over the territory, known as the canton of B. It joined the *Swiss confederation in 1353 to become its most powerful member. Together with the other cantons, B. fought against the *Hapsburgs conquering their estates in the Aargau in 1415. In the 15th century, B. enjoyed a period of economic prosperity, reflected in the late Gothic architecture of the city's centre.

R. Feller, *Geschichte Berns* (1949).

BERNICIA Province of the Anglo-Saxon kingdom of *Northumbria. In 632, after the Britons attacked Northumbria from the Isle of Man, the earls of B., who were a branch of the royal family, proclaimed B. an independent kingdom, thereby splitting Northumbria in two. B. thrived under the rule of Oswald (633-41). In the second half of the 7th century, the history of B. is confused with that of Northumbria, because its kings entitled themselves kings of Northumbria.

F. Stenton, *Anglo-Saxon England* (1947).

BERNO (d. 926) First abbot of *Cluny (910-26). Born to a noble family in Burgundy, B. became a zealous monk at Autun. In 894 he founded the Abbey of Gigny, where he reformed the strict observance of *Benedictine rule. He was called to head the new monastic community of Cluny in 910, receiving the title of abbot of Cluny in addition to that of abbot of Gigny. His reformist activities won him prestige not only in France, but also at Rome. While he stressed monastic discipline and

Noah's Ark; 13th-century stained-glass window, France

prayer, B. was, on the whole, a moderating influence on the austerity of Benedictine rule.

L. Smith, *Cluny* (1930).

BERNWALD OF HILDESHEIM (d. 1022) Bishop of Hildesheim (992-1022). Born to a noble family of Saxony, he was educated at Corvey, where he developed an interest in Latin literature. *Otto II appointed him tutor for his son, the future *Otto III, who later made him his adviser. B., patron of arts and letters, also proved himself an energetic politician and was one of the members of the team which, together with the emperor, elaborated upon the theory of the universal Christian empire. After the death of Otto III, B. retired from political activity devoting himself to his duties as bishop. He enjoyed great prestige and in his last years was considered a saint.

F. J. Tschan, *St. Bernwald of Hildesheim* (1952).

BÉROUL (12th century) Poet. Very little is known about his person and life. His language and style indicate that he lived in Normandy and wrote between 1170-90. His most important poem is *Tristan*, which he based on oral traditions already crystallized in the *Arthurian legend. *Tristan*, which already includes must of the elements of the classical romance, is a poem of 4000 verses. It served as the source for *Tristan und Isolde* by Godfrey of Strassburg at the beginning of the 13th century.

R. S. Loomis, *Arthurian Literature in the Middle Ages* (1961).

BERRY Province in France. At the beginning of the Middle Ages, B. was part of Aquitaine and its main city, *Bourges, was the ecclesiastical capital of Aquitaine. In the 9th century, under *Charles the Bald, B. was detached from the kingdom and divided among several vassals, who quarrelled over it. In the 10th century, the eastern part of the duchy was united under the family of the viscounts of Bourges, and in 1101 it was sold by its last viscount, Eudes Harpin, to King *Philip I, who annexed it to the royal demesne. The western part of the province remained divided into many feudal seigniories, and eventually it fell under the suzerainty of the dukes of Aquitaine. During the 11th-12th centuries, however, most of the southwestern section came under the rule of the counts of La Marche, a powerful vassal family of the dukes. The kings of France, *Louis VII and *Philip II claimed the overlordship of western B., with the seigniories of Issoudun, Châteauroux and Graçay, but failed to obtain them from *Henry II of England. In 1199, Philip II negotiated the marriage of his son Louis with Blanche of Castile (the niece of *John Lackland) and obtained the estates as her dowry. During the 13th and the beginning of the 14th century, the royal administrators succeeded in reuniting the province, which became one of the most prosperous in France. In 1360, B. was proclaimed a duchy and given as an *apanage to *John of Berry (1360-1416) the third son of King *John II. John, who was one of the wealthiest princes in France and was known as a patron of arts and letters, set the foundations of a good administration, which assured the peace and prosperity of B. When the duchy was annexed to France under *Charles VI in 1416, after the death of the old duke, it extended her much-needed monetary aid. Under *Charles VII, B. was one of France's most faithful provinces supplying the king with aid against the English army in the *Hundred Years' War. After the war, the duchy of B. became one of the central provinces of France, keeping its own officers and courts, and was no longer given to a prince of the royal house.

M. Marion, *Histoire du Berry* (1934).

BERTHOLD OF CARINTHIA (c. 899-947) Duke of Bavaria (938-47). He was the younger son of Marquis Liutpold, who at the end of the 9th century, established a military command in southeastern Germany and who bequeathed Carinthia to B. In 938, *Otto I appointed him duke of Bavaria, having deposed B.'s nephew Eberhard, who refused to pay homage to the king. B. organized the duchy and maintained good relations with Otto until his death.

BERTRAND OF BORN (c. 1140-c. 1215) Poet. Born to a noble Aquitanian family and lord of Hauteford, he was compelled to leave the castle and became a troubadour after a quarrel with his brother. He befriended *Richard Coeur de Lion and his brother, Henry the Young. He composed many popular lyrics, in praise of love and friendship, wars and knightly tournaments.

C. Appel, *Bertrand of Born* (1933).

BERTRAND, PIERRE (d. 1361) Jurist and cardinal. At the beginning of the 14th century, B. studied law in Italy and France, specializing in Roman Law, and trying to determine its impact upon ecclesiastical jurisdiction. He taught law at Avignon, Montpellier and Paris and, having established his reputation as jurist, became bishop of Autun in 1326. In 1329, he argued for the independence of ecclesiastical jurisdiction on behalf of the clergy before *Philip VI of France. Pope *John XXII made him a cardinal at Avignon, a position which gave him legislative powers and made him a close counsellor of the popes.

G. Mollat, *The Popes of Avignon* (1952).

BERTULPH, St. (d. 639) A Lombard noble, he joined the monastery of *Bobbio in 613 and became the abbot. He attempted to reconcile Irish monasticism and St. *Columba's rule with *Benedictine rule. Under his guidance, special attention was given to education at Bobbio. He employed the monks in copying books and established one of the best libraries in Christian Europe.

D. Knowles, *Christian Monasticism* (1969).

BESANÇON City in eastern France. After the fall of the Roman empire, the city declined and only a few ruins from the ancient Roman city remained, in the centre of which a small Christian quarter emerged. In the 5th century, B. became part of the *Burgundian kingdom and remained under Frankish rule until the 9th century. In 843, B. was annexed to the kingdom of *Lothair and in 887, with the fall of the Lotharingian realm, it became one of the centres of the new kingdom of Burgundy, while suzerainty was given to its archbishops. In 1032 B. was annexed together with the Burgundian kingdom to the *Holy Roman empire. The German emperors supported the burghers' opposition to the archbishops' rule and in 1282 B. obtained the status of imperial city, freeing it from the suzerains. In 1360 the city and its province (Franche-Comté) were inherited by the dukes of Burgundy, and remained under their rule until 1477.

E. Droz, *Recherches Historiques sur la ville de Besançon* (1870).

BESSINUS (d. 530) King of the *Thuringians (c. 500-30). His actual name is unknown; the Latin form was

The Presentation of Christ at the Temple; *12th-century Romanesque relief at Moissac, France*

The Sacrifice of Isaac, *from the Psalter of York*

The Apocalypse, *from the Bible of the Poor*

recorded by the historian and poet *Venantius Fortunatus. B. was an ally of the *Lombards, his neighbours to the north and east, but at the same time he entered into close relations with *Theodoric, king of the *Ostrogoths and married his niece Amalaberga. In 506-07, he fought against the Frankish king, *Clovis, and succeeded in maintaining the independence of Thuringia. His alliance with Theodoric continued until the latter's death (524). B.'s last years were marked by weakness and disputes between his sons; the king tried to appease them by dividing his realm in such a way that it was the Franks who profited after his death.

H. Patze, W. Schlesinger, *Geschichte Thuringens* (1968).

BETHLEHEM Town in Palestine, the birthplace of Christ. With the spread of Christianity, the ancient town of Judaea rose from a little village at the beginning of the Middle Ages, to a centre of religious attraction. The first church built over the Crypt of the Nativity by Helen, mother of the Emperor Constantine (c. 330), was too small for the ever increasing numbers of pilgrims, and in the 6th century a new church with a beautiful mosaic pavement was built by *Justinian. Hermits gravitated towards the small settlement established near the church, and around which small monasteries sprung up. The proximity of Jerusalem hindered the development of the town, which declined under *Arab rule (636-1099). After the conquest of the town by the *Crusaders in 1099, B. became the see of a Latin

bishopric and from 1100, the kings of Jerusalem were crowned in the Church of the Nativity. Between 1160-70 the church was enlarged by Byzantine architects. In 1187, after the Battle of *Hattin, B. was conquered by the Moslems, who did not harm the church or the community. The bishops of B. continued to rule, and to assure them a regular income, they were granted estates in France, where the see was transferred at the end of the 13th century. In the late Middle Ages, B. continued to attract pilgrims from western Europe, even though the *Mamelukes neglected the town.

R. W. Hamilton, *A Guide to Bethlehem* (1939).

BEVERLEY Locality in Yorkshire, England. In 721, St. John of Beverley built a church which became the destination of local pilgrimages in Northumbria. In the 10th century a minster of secular canons was established on the site. After the destruction of the church by fire in 1188, a new building, one of the finest examples of Gothic architecture in England, was erected.

A. H. Thompson, *Collegiate Church of St. John, Beverley* (1931).

BEZIERS City in *Languedoc, southern France. Originally a Roman colony, B. was conquered by the *Visigoths in 412 and became part of their province of Septimania. In 720 it was conquered by the Arabs and in 733 annexed by *Charles Martel to the Frankish realm. *Pepin the Short founded the county of B. in 754, but the counts had to share the lordship with the bishops. Under *Charlemagne and during the 9th century, B. was part of the March of Septimania, and in the 10th century it became a fief of the counts of Toulouse. In the 11th century they appointed viscounts to manage it. The house of Trencavel, which administered the county of *Carcassonne, also took control of B.'s affairs, and in the 12th century they compelled the bishop to give them complete lay authority there. In the latter half of the 12th century the *Albigensians were allowed to settle in the city by the viscounts. B. was one of the first targets of the Crusade against the Albigensians in 1209 and the conquest of the city was followed by a cruel slaughter of the populace. A 13th-century author, Cesarius of Heisterbach, quoted the words of the legate: "Kill them all; God will recognize those who are His". B. was annexed to the new *sénéchaussée* of Carcassonne by *Louis VIII and was governed from 1224 by a royal officer.

E. Sabatier, *Histoire de la ville et des évêques de Béziers* (1854).

BIBLE The word "Bible" (Lat. *Biblia*, derived from the Gr. *Biblia*, meaning "books"), first used in the Septuagint, the term was later modified to mean the Holy Scriptures. While in medieval Judaism the Bible meant the 39 books of the Old Testament; for Christendom, the term denoted the Old and the New Testaments. The books of the Old Testament are divided into three groups: 1) the Torah (Pentateuch) with its five books: Genesis, Exodus,

Leviticus, Numbers and Deuteronomy; 2) the Prophets, divided into the historical group of Joshua, Judges, Samuel I, Samuel II, Kings I, Kings II and the Later Prophets, including Isaiah, Jeremiah, Ezekiel and the Twelve Minor Prophets; 3) the third group comprising the books of Psalms, Proverbs, Job, Song of Songs, Ruth, Lamentations, Ecclesiastes, Esther, Daniel, Ezra, Nehemiah, Chronicles I and Chronicles II. In the Greek translation of the Old Testament, known as the Septuagint this order was altered slightly. The later Latin translation, the Vulgate, adopted the Greek order. The New Testament includes the four Gospels: Matthew, Mark, Luke and John; the Acts of the Apostles, the Letters of St. Paul, as well as the seven Letters of James, Peter, John and Judas and the Apocalypse. The canon of the Hebrew Old Testament was established at the beginning of the 2nd century AD and that of the Greek New Testament dates from the middle of the same century.

By the 4th century many partial versions of the Bible, translated into Latin from the Septuagint, were widely disseminated in western Europe. But a complete Latin Bible was still lacking, and there were discrepancies between different versions. Therefore, St. *Jerome undertook a new translation of the Bible, which he called the Vulgate, at the beginning of the 5th century. He studied Hebrew and translated the Old Testament from the original, thus producing the authoritative text for the Latin Catholic Church. The study of the Bible

Initial of "The Prophecy of Joel" in the Winchester Bible

has, however, caused difficulties for both Jews and Christians, with regard to the proper understanding of the texts and their interpretation. More scholars engaged in biblical commentary in the Middle Ages than in any other historical period. The Jews were the first to do so, and their methods were to some extent borrowed by the Christians. According to Jewish scholars, the Scriptures could be interpreted on four different levels: the literal (Heb. *Peshat*); moral (Heb. *Remez* = allusion); historical (Heb. *Derash*); allegorical (Heb. *Sod* = mystery). While the literal and historical methods dealt with understanding and explaining the body of the text, the moral and allegorical methods attempted to find the spirit, or the underlying message of the *Divina pagina* (the divine page). Most of the Jewish biblical commentators belonged to two main schools: firstly, that of Spain, which emphasized the literal and moral-philosophical aspects, and which flourished in the 10th-13th centuries; it included scholars like *Dunash Ben Labrat, the grammarian, *Abraham Ibn Ezra, *David Kimhi, and *Nahmanides. Secondly, the school of *Ashkenaz, which concentrated on the literal and historical aspects of the Bible and which flourished in the 11th-14th centuries. The chief scholar was *Rashi, the greatest Biblical commentator of all ages. In the latter half of the 12th century, another school of biblical exegesis emerged in the Jewish communities of southern France and northern Spain which gathered around the mystical (*kabbalist) centre of Gerona, and concentrated on biblical allegory, aiming to figure out the *process* of messianic salvation.

Christian exegesis could be divided into three distinct phases: 1) the patristic period (the Fathers of the Church); continuing through the beginning of the Middle Ages, when, under the influence of Philo of Alexandria, a Jewish philosopher of the first century, and of St. Jerome, attention was given only to the literal and moral aspects of the Bible. Pope *Gregory I, *Bede and *Alcuin are all of this period. 2) The period of the 11th-13th centuries saw the growth of the school of *St. Victor at Paris, and the contribution of a number of individual exegetes. This period saw the introduction of the four senses in Christian exegesis, and commentaries took the form of glosses in the texts. Exegetes working on the literal and historical senses consulted with Jewish scholars on textual problems and some of them even learned Hebrew, but exegetes working on the moral and allegorical senses, such as *Bernard of Clairvaux, were less concerned with mere textual interpretation. 3) The 14th and 15th centuries were a transitional period: While many tendencies of the 13th century lingered, the period also contained the seeds of rationalism, humanism and the Renaissance. On the one hand, there was the mysticism of *Eckhart, and the asceticism of the *Franciscans, who produced the "Bible of the Poor"; on the other, rationalist tendencies, albeit in their embryonic stage, were already evident in the universities and schools of theology, where the Bible was usually interpreted in senses other than the mystical. Greek teachers in Italy brought the Septuagint to the attention of Western scholars. There was widespread dissemination of the Bible in the Middle Ages, which made it obligatory to keep it in the libraries of every cathedral and collegiate church as well as in every monastery. In the monastic *scriptoria* of the Middle Ages, the books were copied and special attention was given to the script;

initial capital letters of books and chapters were illustrated by artists. Illustrating the B. was begun in the West in the 9th century and was the source of the art of miniature painting on parchment. This phenomenon parallels the practice of illustrating the Koran, but, while the latter was decorated with abstract art, the biblical illuminations showed persons and animals against a floral background. At the end of the 13th and during the 14th-15th centuries, copies of the Bible were introduced into libraries of royal courts and great princes. The artists then used new motifs taken from secular and profane life, intending to glorify their rulers.

B. Smalley, *The Study of the Bible in the Middle Ages* (1964);

A. Grabois, *The Intellectual Relations between Jews and Christians in the 12th century* (1975).

BILL OF ATTAINDER (lit. to prove guilty) The B., used in England in the 15th century, was an efficient way of impeaching an enemy of the king or an unpopular minister without a court trial. A bill would be introduced in the parliament. When voted on, and approved by the king, it became law, and the person concerned was considered a criminal. It became an instrument in the hands of the king by which he could rule without having to resort to the judicial system, thus giving rise to many abuses.

B. Lyon, *A Constitutional and Legal History of Medieval England* (1960).

BILLUNG Dynasty of dukes of Saxony (10th-12th centuries). In the 10th century, the B. family held the eastern marches of Saxony. In 961, *Otto I, preparing his imperial coronation at Rome, renounced his ducal title and appointed his kinsman Hermann B. duke of Saxony. The B. governed the duchy until the dynasty's extinction in 1106. In the 11th century, they opposed the emperors, creating problems in Germany. After the extinction of the main branch of the family one of the secondary branches, the Ascanians, claimed B. as their heritage. They obtained *Brandenburg and in 1078 *Bernard of Anhalt became duke of Saxony, which was ruled by his descendants until 1432.

J. W. Thompson, *Feudal Germany* (1928).

BIRGIR MAGNUSSON (d. 1266) Regent of Sweden. He was a member of the powerful House of the Earls of Folkung, of Östergötland, who held an influential position at the royal court in the first half of the 13th century. He married the sister of King *Eric XI and from 1234 was, for all purposes, the real ruler of Sweden. In 1250, after Eric's death, B. proclaimed his son *Waldemar king while he himself continued to act as regent until his death. B. was an active legislator and imposed the supremacy of royal justice. He instituted revolutionary social and economic changes by suppressing the old nobles and establishing a new feudal aristocracy, more dependent on the king; abolishing serfdom; encouraging German colonists to settle in Sweden, and developing trade with Germany. He attempted to expand in the eastern Baltic and conquered Finland, but while trying to continue eastward, he was defeated by *Alexander Nevski on the Neva.

C. Hallendorf, *History of Sweden* (1929).

BIRGITTA (BRIDGET) OF SWEDEN, St. (1303-73) Daughter of one of the most powerful families in Sweden, B. married at the age of 13 and bore 8 children. In 1340, she developed a keen interest in religion and mysticism, and the following year made a pilgrimage to *Santiago de Compostela. Becoming a widow upon her return, she entered the *Cistercian abbey of *Alvastra in 1343, where she wrote the *Revelations*, a book of her visions. The book immediately became very popular, even outside Sweden. In 1346 she founded the order of the *Brigittines, and in 1349 she went to Rome to obtain confirmation for her order. She cared for the victims of the *Black Death in Rome and was regarded as a saint both in Rome and its environs.

J. Jorgensen, *St. Birgitta of Sweden* (1954).

BIRINUS, St. (d. 649) Of Italian origin, he was sent to *Wessex in 634 as a missionary. In 635 he converted King Cynegils, who granted him the bishopric of Dorchester. He founded the first church of Winchester and until his death he devoted his efforts to the Christianization of Wessex.

T. Varley, *St. Birinus and Wessex; From Odin to Christ* (1934).

BISHOP (Latin: episcopus) The highest order of ministers in the Christian Church. In the early Christian period, bishops were elected by the members of large communities to supervise the priests and to guide the faithful in the area. From the 4th century on, bishops were ordained in every *civitas* (city), the central locality of an administrative unit. Thus, the Christian church adapted its organization to the administrative structures of the late Roman empire. Bishops of provincial capitals were called metropolitan bishops, archbishops. They presided over provincial councils of bishops and ordained new bishops after their election. After the fall of the Roman empire in the West, when public authorities in the cities ceased to function, the bishops were not only spiritual leaders, ordaining priests, consecrating churches, leading synods and being responsible for the education of the faithful, but also acquired temporal power. In principle, they continued to be elected "by clergy and people" but, because of their political importance, the kings of the barbarian realms used to appoint their chaplains to the bishoprics. The dissolution of the *Carolingian empire had its impact on the feudalization of the bishopric; counts and other lay lords shared the practice of appointing bishops in their individual fiefs with the kings (10th century) and would reserve the episcopal dignities for one of their sons, even when he was not prepared for spiritual office. In many cases, candidates or their families bought the office; this practice was called *simony. *Otto I reformed the practice in Germany: all the bishops were bound to the emperor, who had the sole authority to approve the election of bishops and to invest them with the large estates given to them. The *Gregorian reform movement fought against the lay interventions in the church and opposed the lay investiture; the decrees of *Gregory VII forbade them, causing the *Investiture Contest – a conflict between the Church and the Empire. Finally, the *Concordat of Worms (1122) decided upon free elections of bishops by the clergy; approval by the emperor (or the king); consecration by the archbishop; and investiture of the estate by the emperor, provided that it would not be made by using the episcopal signs, the cross and the ring. This practice remained in force until the 14th century, although there were cases when kings compelled the cathedral chapters to elect their candidates. In the 14th century, the *Avignon popes appointed

A silver-gilt and enamel 15th-century bishop's crozier

bishops, either to assure offices for their clients, or in order to enjoy the revenues; free elections were exceptions. In the last two centuries of the Middle Ages, the appointment of bishops became a common privilege of popes and kings.

W. Telfer, *The Office of a Bishop* (1962).

BLACK DEATH The plague, believed to be bubonic, which, originating in the East, ravaged western and central Europe in 1348-50. Modern research has proved that other types of plague also manifested themselves and were probably responsible for part of the devastation. Nevertheless, the B. as it was called at the time, remains the name by which the pestilence is known. The germ of the epidemic was apparently brought by a Genoese ship from Pera (Crimea) in the late summer of 1347, spreading to the major Italian cities by autumn. The mortality rate swiftly rose and caused panic. In 1348 France, England, Germany and Spain were contaminated, while a second round began in Italy. Only east European countries were spared. The chroniclers of the time added to the feeling of catastrophe by exaggerating the effects of the plague and by

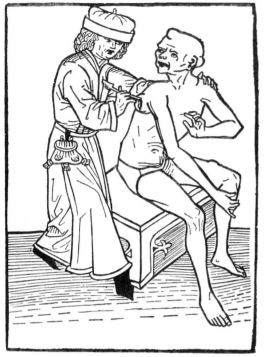

A plague doctor lancing a boil; 15th-century woodcut

describing entire regions filled with human corpses with no one to bury them since everyone was ill. More accurate research shows that the direct mortality in western and central Europe was about one third of the population (approximately 20 million people), while the indirect demographic losses were of course heavier. The losses were not compensated for until the end of the 15th century. The mass hysteria that ensued was sometimes manifested in a search for culprits: in various cities, hostilities were directed against Jews, who were accused of infecting the wells; elsewhere, mass move-

Penitents dancing and praying during the Black Death

ments for penitence held street-processions imploring divine mercy. The most important of these were the *Flagellants, originating in Germany, who decried the church hierarchy for having neglected its spiritual duties. Another repercussion of the plague was a crisis in the agrarian sector, where the lack of manpower gave rise to restrictions on the peasants against leaving their farms and a consequent return to conditions of *serfdom. This, in turn, led to peasant uprisings during the latter half of the 14th century, some of which, like the *Jacquerie in France or the *Great Revolt of 1381 in England, were cruelly repressed. The B. also had its impact on the *Hundred Years' War; the lack of manpower was felt both in the English and in the French armies and contributed to a change in the nature of warfare, especially after the Battle of *Poitiers.
F. Ziegler, *The Black Death* (1969).

BLACK FRIARS See DOMINICANS.

BLANCHE NEF (The White Ship) Name of a ship, fitted out at Barfleur in Normandy in 1120. On 25 November 1120, William Aetheling, son of *Henry I and heir to the English crown, embarked with his court to sail from Normandy to England. The ship was wrecked immediately after it set sail, William was killed and the problem of the English succession to the throne and the civil war of 1135-54, which broke out after Henry's death, ensued.
F. Barlow, *The Feudal Kingdom of England* (1961).

BLANCHE OF CASTILE (1188-1252) Queen of France. Daughter of *Alfonso the Noble of Castile and of Eleanor of England, and through her mother, granddaughter of *Henry II. She was betrothed to Prince Louis, heir to the French crown, as part of the Le Goulet peace settlement between her uncle *John Lackland and *Philip II August, king of France (1200). Educated at the French court, she was a woman of strong religious feelings, which she tried to impose upon her children. In 1223, when *Louis VIII became king of France, she continued to concentrate on the education of her children, divorcing herself from politics. Nevertheless, with the sudden death of Louis VIII in 1226, B. became regent on behalf of her minor son, *Louis IX. She remained regent until 1234, when Louis reached his majority, and, despite his lack of political experience, proved himself a great statesman. She subdued the conflicts between the factions of the high nobility, and in 1229, she brought about the Peace of Paris, which settled the *Albigensian problem and arranged for her second son *Alphonse of Poitiers to inherit the county of Toulouse. She succeeded in separating the Lusignan-La Marche lords of Aquitaine from Henry III, when he failed in his expedition to Brittany and negotiated with her his withdrawal to England in 1230. In 1232-34 she ensured French expansion in Aquitaine, imposing her authority on the lords, who were virtually defenceless without the support of the emperor. Even after Louis IX became king, B. continued to exert tremendous influence on his decisions. In 1247, when the king went on his *Crusade, she was again the regent, ensuring order during her son's absence. She remained the dominant force in France until her death in 1252.
E. Berger, *Histoire de Blanche de Castile, reine de France* (1895).

BLANCHE OF LANCASTER (d. 1369) Daughter of Henry, duke of Lancaster. In 1359 she married *John of Gaunt and brought him her heritage, the duchy of Lancaster. She bore a son, the future *Henry IV, founder of the royal branch of Lancaster. Both her beauty and strength of character inspired *Chaucer to write the *Book of the Duchess*.

R. Somerville, *History of the Duchy of Lancaster* (1953).

BLEMMYDES, NICEPHORUS (d. 1268) Byzantine philosopher and writer. His father, reputedly a learned man, left Constantinople in 1204 and established himself at Brussa, where he tried to give the best education possible to his son. B. studied under various Byzantine refugees in Bythinia, and in 1236 he moved to Nicaea, where Emperor *John Vatatzes appointed him head of the new imperial school and tutor of his son *Theodore II Lascaris. B. gathered Greek manuscripts while travelling in the Balkans and Anatolia and developed the study of philosophy at Nicaea, where his students became noted for their works. He expressed some of his ideas in his letters to Emperor Theodore Lascaris, revealing the impact of Aristotelian thought on his own ideas. In 1265 he wrote an autobiography, which is an important testimony to the intellectual life in the Empire of Nicaea.

A. Heisenberg, *Nicephorus Blammydas* (1896).

BLOIS City in France, on the Loire River, between Orléans and Tours. Its importance in late antiquity and during the Middle Ages lay in its being situated on a bridge linking northern–southern France. Its location had economical advantages and political consequences. From 584 the fortified *castrum* (camp) of the Roman period became the residence of a Frankish count who established his rule over the entire district. When the old line of the Frankish aristocracy died out in the 8th century, the *Carolingians appointed their own vassals in the castle. Between 830 and 840, B. was the subject of dispute between *Pepin of Aquitaine and *Charles the Bald, sons of *Louis the Pious. The Treaty of *Verdun in 843 ratified its allocation to the realm of France as a part of the northwestern province of Neustria. During the troubled period of *Charles the Bald and his successors, B. was dominated by various lords, until it became part of the duchy of *Robert the Strong in 887. In the 10th century it belonged to the *Capetian great fief. The dukes allowed their vassals to rule the city and its surroundings. But gradually the counts of Blois and Chartres established a dynasty in B. Although they began as adventurers, towards the end of the 10th century, under Count Eudes I, they became one of the most powerful feudal forces in France, also ruling the counties of Tours in the west and Troyes and Meaux in Champagne. In the 11th century the counts of B. even posed a threat to the royal authority, and in the latter half of the century, they allied themselves with the dukes of Normandy, who became kings of England. Their power, however, waned: they lost Tours to the counts of Anjou, and the possession of the counties in Champagne forced them to direct their efforts against the local nobility. In the 12th century it became obvious that the task was too difficult for one person and after the death of Thibaut II (·1151) their dominions were divided between the county of Champagne, bestowed on the senior branch of the family, and the county of Blois-Chartres, which started its own dynasty. Development of its trade in the 12th century made B. a prosperous commercial centre on the Loire. This affluence is reflected in the Gothic buildings erected in the second half of the century around the new count's palace. In 1177 the Jews of B. were accused of ritual murder of a Christian child, to "prepare with his blood the Passover bread", the first such accusation in France. By order of Count Thibaut, all the members of the community, including women and children, were murdered. In the 13th and 14th centuries the city continued to thrive, being spared the devastations of the *Hundred Years' War. In 1498 the County of B. was annexed to the crown estates and became a royal residence.

L. Lex, *Les comtes de Blois: Eudes II* (1892).

BLONDEL OF NESLE (12th century) Troubadour. Very little is known about his life and poems. At an unknown date, he joined the court of the king of England, *Richard Coeur de Lion and became one of his favourite poets. It was said that when Richard was taken prisoner while returning from the *Crusade, he was hidden in a secret castle by the emperor, and in his loneliness, used to sing songs of his own and of other troubadours. B., who travelled to Germany to seek his royal master, discovered him upon hearing one of their favourite songs, thereby making possible the opening of negotiations for the king's ransom. The tale, part of the romantic legend of Richard, is that of the 13th-century Minstrel of Rheims and, while it is historically inaccurate, it is another testimony to Richard's manners and to the role of Blondel, the troubadour of love.

E. N. Stone, *Three Old French Chronicles of the Crusades* (1939).

BOBBIO Abbey in northern Italy. It was founded in 612 by the Irish monk, St. *Columba (d. 615) who introduced *Irish rule. In 628, the monastery was exempted from the bishop's authority, and was dependent solely on the pope. Abbot *Bertulph introduced the reformed Benedictine rule which accorded with Irish practices. B. soon became a centre of learning, and in the *Carolingian period was one of the most important cultural centres of the empire, with the greatest collection of manuscripts in western Europe. When *Gerbert of Aurillac became its abbot in 983, he counted more than 700 early manuscripts, which he used in his works. He took some of them to Rheims, mainly books on mathematics. From the 11th century on, B. began to decline, with the monks being more attentive to the administration of their estates than to spiritual and cultural work. In the 12th century, the little borough founded near B. began to develop independently and a beautiful church was built there. In the 15th century, the *humanists realized the importance of B.'s library and, at the beginning of the 16th century it was transferred to the Library of the Vatican, where it still presents an impressive collection. Other manuscripts from the library are preserved in public libraries of Italy and France.

P. Collura, *La precarolina e la carolina a Bobbio* (1943).

BOCCACCIO, GIOVANNI (1313-75) Italian writer. Born in Paris into a Florentine merchant family. After his mother's death, his father, who had returned to Florence and married there, took him to his home where B. was maltreated by his stepmother. B.'s earliest stories praised his mother and described his own sufferings as a child. His father intended him to be a merchant, but he liked literature and studied Latin. In

Scene from Boccaccio's Decameron; *1518 edition*

1328 he was sent to Naples to study law and the business world. B. spent most of his time in the company of scholars and writers and was probably in contact with the poet *Cino of Pistoia, a friend of *Dante and *Petrarch. In 1336 he severed his ties with his father and devoted himself to his literary vocation. His love affair with Maria d'Aquino, illegitimate daughter of *Robert of Anjou, king of Naples, inspired his poetical works, which showed the influence of Roman poets. During this period (1336-40), he frequented the royal palace, where he saw the libertine conduct he later described in the *Decameron*. In 1340 he was reconciled with his father and returned to Florence, where he attained an honourable position as an intellectual and writer. He was appointed to the city council, and sent on diplomatic missions. He went to Naples to negotiate with Queen *Jane; to the Tyrol, to conclude a military alliance with the duke of Bavaria; to Ravenna, where he gave Dante's daughter a present from the city of Florence, and to Padua to offer Petrarch a position as professor at the University of Florence (he became a close friend of the poet's). He also visited the papal

Scene from Boccaccio's Decameron; *1531 edition*

courts of Avignon and Rome. In 1348 he began to write his most important work, the *Decameron*, which he completed in 1353. At this time, B.'s character and behaviour underwent a profound change. He became serious, preoccupied with religion, gave up his poetry and profane writing. In his autobiographical novel, *Corbaccio*, written in 1354, he wrote satirically about libertine and lay life and criticized the women he once adored. This charge became more accentuated after an illness and a prediction of a monk who filled him with fear of death. He gave up his humanist works and intended to burn all of his sinful writings, but was prevented from doing so by Petrarch. B. never returned to writing in the vernacular, and from 1363, all his works were composed in Latin. In his last years he settled in the little town of Certaldo, near Florence, where he lived in isolation. He died in 1375.

B. wrote many scholarly works, mainly on history. He also wrote critical interpretations of the important books of his age, such as Dante's *Divine Comedy*. But his longest-lasting creation is the *Decameron*. A collection of one hundred tales, it was written with a didactic purpose of teaching, through the adventures of the protagonists, the lessons of human wisdom. He dealt ironically with the different social classes, whose behaviour was belied by their beliefs. He particularly criticized the clergy and concluded that people have to depend upon their own judgement and wisdom.

T. C. Chubb, *The Life of Giovanni Boccaccio* (1930).

BODEL, JEHAN (John; c. 1170-c. 1210) Born in Arras, northern France, he was the herald of the city, and a poet. In 1204, he prepared himself to join the Fourth *Crusade, but contracted leprosy and was sent to the hospice of Meulan. On leaving his city, he composed a farewell poem, which became a model of this genre. A number of his works are preserved – shepherds' poems, an epic concerning the wars of *Charlemagne against the Saxons, and some fables. But his most famous work was *Jeu de Saint-Nicholas* (The Game of St. Nicholas), a dramatic work praising the miracles of St. Nicholas and describing the urban life of his times.

O. Rohnström, *Etude sur Jean Bodel* (1900).

BODONITZA Region in Greece, near the Thermopylae. In 1205, *Boniface of Montferrat, king of Thessalonica, conquered it from the Byzantines and created a marquisate, the overlordship of which he invested on Guido Pallavicini, one of his followers in the Fourth *Crusade. In 1236, the suzerainty of the marquisate was transferred to the princes of Morea, but they allowed the Pallavicini to rule it in their stead. Nevertheless, in 1258 Ubertino Pallavicini joined the coalition led by the lord of Athens, Guy I, against the expansionist tendencies of William of *Villehardouin, prince of Morea. Pallaricini was defeated at Karydi and was compelled to swear homage to his prince. Even after the fall of the *Latin empire of Constantinople in 1261, the Pallavicini continued to rule B. until the end of their dynasty in 1338, when the heiress, Guglielmina Pallavicini, married the Venetian noble Niccolo Giorgio, who became marquis of B. and ruled under the protectorate of Venice. The Giorgii maintained their rule in B. until its conquest by the *Ottoman Turks in 1414.

W. Miller, *Latins in the Levant. A History of Frankish Greece* (1908).

BOETHIUS, ANICIUS MANLIUS (480-524) Statesman and philosopher. Born to a noble family, he entered the service of *Theodoric, king of the *Ostrogoths, and in 510 was made consul. He rose in the king's favour and, in 522, was appointed Master of the Offices. In 524 he was suddenly suspected of treason and Theodoric ordered his arrest and execution. B. studied philosophy and science and was a man of ample means. His most famous work, *On the Consolation of Philosophy*, was written in prison. He employed the philosophical methods of Aristotle, acquainting the medieval philosophers with Aristotle through his *Consolation*. He also completed Aristotle's works on logic and intended to translate both Aristotle and Plato into Latin.

B. had a tremendous impact on medieval thought. His *Consolation* was very popular and, although it was not based on Christian ethics, was adopted by the Christian philosophers of the later generations as a part of the early church heritage. *Alfred the Great translated the treatise into Anglo-Saxon, but B.'s other works, including the *Commentaries on the Categories of Aristotle*, were studied in Latin. Through his works, B. contributed to the transmission of the classical heritage to the Middle Ages.

H. F. Steward, E. K. Rand, *De Consolatione* (1918);
H. R. Patch, *The Tradition of Boethius. A Study on his Importance in Medieval Culture* (1935).

BOGOMILES A dualist sect, believed to be an offshoot of the *Catharists. Their name probably derives from their founder, Bogomilus, a Bulgarian translation of the Greek name Theophilus, who taught between 927 and 950 in Bulgaria. The centre of the sect was Philipopolis in Thrace, whence it spread to Constantinople. In 1118 Emperor *Alexius Comnenus had their leader burnt and, in 1140, a synod ordered the destruction of their books. In spite of the persecutions, the sect continued to exist in the Balkans and Asia Minor, until their conquest by the *Ottoman Turks. The B. believed in a supreme god, the Father, whose son, Satanael revolted against him and was driven from heaven. Satanael created Adam; but as the Father supplied Adam's soul, man belongs to God as well as to Satan, who seduced Eve and was punished by being deprived of his creative power, though entrusted with the government of the world. As Man fell more and more under the power of Satan, the Father sent into the world his second son, Jesus, to conquer Satan. Jesus returned to heaven, leaving his creature, the Holy Ghost, to the only true Christians, the B., whose activity will bring salvation.

D. Obolensky, *The Bogomiles* (1948).

BOHEMIA Country within the *Holy Roman empire. At the beginning of the Middle Ages, the native inhabitants of B., the Boii, a Celtic people also known as the Baiovari, migrated to *Bavaria, and during the 6th and 7th centuries, Germanic tribes, such as the *Longobards, settled there. While migrating to Italy in the 8th century, Slav tribes, primarily of Czech origin, settled in the country, and established two small principalities, B. and Moravia. At the end of the 8th century, B. came under the Frankish sphere of influence and *Charlemagne established his protectorate over the country. This suzerainty had no practical effects, but it was maintained throughout the 9th century. However, in order to stabilize it, *Louis the German had to lead several military expeditions into B. between 846 and 855. As a

result, Christianity was introduced into the country. During this period, Moravia was the most important and powerful Czech state, while B. remained a small country. The Magyar invasions, which destroyed Moravia at the end of the 10th century, altered this situation. In 906 B. granted the Magyars passage through their land and in 911, B.'s leaders formally broke with the German overlordship. The leading Bohemian family, the Přemyslids, who ruled as patriarchs, tried to organize B. as an independent duchy. But in 929, *Henry I invaded B. and forced Duke Wenceslas to recognize his overlordship. But Wenceslas' brother, *Boleslav I, revolted, murdered his brother and reestablished independence. Not until 950 did *Otto I defeat him and impose German overlordship. Christianization of the country continued and in 975, the See of Prague was founded, dependent on the archbishops of Mainz in Germany. Several attempts were still made to maintain the independence of the duchy, but constant fights between the members of the dynasty over their hereditary claims, made the revolts unsuccessful. The state of anarchy tempted *Boleslaw the Great, king of Poland. He conquered B. in 1003, but was compelled to give up his conquest by *Henry II. Constant enmity between the Czechs and the Poles favoured the continuance of German overlordship and compelled the dukes to remain faithful to the emperors. Nevertheless, in the 11th century B. gained a special status within the empire; it was no longer considered an imperial fief and the emperors recognized the hereditary rights of the national dynasty. During the *Investiture contest, the dukes remained faithful to the emperors and *Henry IV rewarded Vratislav II for his help in the Italian expeditions by granting him the life-long title of king. In the 12th century, B. saw a period of economic prosperity, due to exploitation of its mines and to German colonization, mainly in the towns, which helped to develop trade. While its original constitution remained unchanged, marriages were contracted between members of the ducal dynasty and German princes, giving rise to its involvement in German politics. In 1157 *Frederick Barbarossa awarded Vladislav II the title of king, but in 1174, his heirs lost it, and the marquisate of Moravia was detached from the duchy, and came under direct imperial control. In 1198, after the death of *Henry VI, the royal title was restored to *Ottokar I (1197-1230), the builder of a secure state within the empire. In 1212 he obtained from Frederick II a Golden Bull, a charter which recognized the king of B.'s power and called for the transfer of B.'s bishoprics from imperial to royal authority. Ottokar also introduced the feudal system in B. and its archaic tribal structures were changed into a more efficient system, even as German cultural influence grew. During the interregnum in Germany (1254-72), B. became more powerful. *Ottokar II (1253-78) seized Austria and Carinthia upon the extinction of the *Babenberg dynasty, and was recognized as one of the seven *Electors of the Empire, after competing with the dukes of Bavaria for the position. In 1272, he was candidate for the imperial crown and fought against *Rudolf of Hapsburg, his rival. Rudolf defeated him and compelled him to surrender the Austrian territories, where the Hapsburgs then established the seat of their power. A subsequent campaign to regain the Austrian lands failed, and Ottokar was killed at the

Battle of Marchfeld. B. then turned eastward. In 1300 B.'s king, *Wenceslas II, also became king of Poland and candidate for the Hungarian crown, although the imperial opposition defeated him. In 1308, that last member of the Premyslid dynasty, Wenceslas III, was murdered, and for three years the B. crown was claimed by several German princes. In 1310 it was finally conferred on John of Luxemburg (1310-46), who established a new German-Czech dynasty which reigned in B. until 1437. Under the Luxemburgs, B. was opened to German colonization and the towns became Germanized. The villages, which remained Slavic, continued their traditional life under a nobility that succeeded in preserving its rights. Heretical trends due to a mixture of *Catharistic doctrines and opposition to the establishment, developed, and in the latter half of the century, the movement was led by a Czech, Jan (John) Milic, a forerunner of *Huss. *Charles IV of Luxemburg, who became emperor and king of B., was B.'s greatest king. Continuing the expansionist policy of his predecessors he annexed Silesia to the kingdom; in 1346 he succeeded in persuading the pope to elevate the see of Prague to the rank of archbishopric; and in 1348 he founded the University of Prague, which became the greatest intellectual centre of the empire and which, due to the influx of many German students, had the character of a German university rather than a Slavic one. The Caroline university was, however, the pride of the Czechs and, since its founding, was a centre of B. nationalism. Charles was also reputed as a legislator, and his *Majestas Carolina* was the Bohemian constitution until modern times. The basic concept of his constitutional theory was the participation of the estates in public life, each social rank having its own privileges and duties. Thus, the nobility shared in the government by its participation in the Diet, while rank in the royal family was strictly by birth. The peasants, however, were oppressed and their liberty restricted. Under Charles' successors, his sons *Wenceslas and *Sigismund, royal authority weakened to the benefit of the nobility, while the country became the scene of a religious reform movement, which culminated in the appearance of John *Huss. His thesis that the impoverishment of the country was the result of the excessive wealth of the church was enthusiastically accepted by people of all classes, who were so interested in receiving a share of that wealth, that they agreed to the theological implications. Thus, when Emperor Sigismund persuaded his brother King Wenceslas to convict Huss for heresy in 1415, a petition was signed by many of the aristocrats, attesting to his orthodoxy and good faith. The condemnation of Huss at the Council of *Constance and his subsequent execution caused a general uprising in B. S. Harrison Thompson, *Czechoslovakia in European History* (1953).

BOHEMOND I, of Taranto (1050-1111) Prince of *Antioch. Son of *Robert Guiscard, he took part in his father's battles against the Byzantines (1080-85) and was invested with the duchy of Taranto. In 1096 he joined the First *Crusade as leader of the group of south Italian Normans. He played a decisive role in conquering Antioch in 1098, and was subsequently proclaimed its prince, thus founding the first Crusader state in the Middle East. In 1100 he was taken prisoner by the Aleppo forces. Released in 1103, he quarrelled with

the Byzantines and in 1105 went to France and Italy to gather money and an army against Byzantium; his attack of Durazzo in 1108 failed and B. was compelled to sign a treaty recognizing the suzerainty of Emperor *Alexius Comnenus. The treaty was denounced by his nephew *Tancred, regent of Antioch.
R. B. Yewdale, *Bohemond I* (1925).

BOHEMOND II (1109-30) Prince of Antioch (1126-30). Son of Bohemond I, he was proclaimed prince upon reaching his majority. He came from Italy to his principality and married Alice of Jerusalem, daughter of *Baldwin II. He engaged in quarrels with his Christian neighbours from Edessa and Little Armenia, as he tried to regain land he had lost to them. In 1130 he was killed at the Taurus passes by a Turkish-Armenian army.
S. Runciman, *A History of the Crusades* (1953).

BOHEMOND III (1144-1201) Prince of Antioch (1162-1201). Son of Constance of Antioch and Raymond of Poitiers, and, through his mother, grandson of Bohemond II. He was proclaimed prince in 1162, when his stepfather, *Raynald of Châtillon, was held prisoner by the Moslems. His reign was marked by constant wars against *Nureddin, sultan of Aleppo, and Syria. In 1164 he was defeated and taken prisoner. His ransom was paid by the emperor of Byzantium, *Manuel Comnenus, who thereby acquired the right to set up a Greek patriarch at Antioch. B. fought a series of battles with the kings of Little Armenia, which were concluded only by the end of the 12th century through marriage arrangements destined to solve the problems of the succession in the two states. In 1188, he saved Antioch from conquest by *Saladin and he joined the Third *Crusade. After abortive attempts to conquer Laodicea he signed a peace treaty with Saladin in 1192. An imbroglio over succession rights in Antioch started during B.'s last years, and was to continue long after his death.
S. Runciman, *A History of the Crusades* (1953).

BOHEMOND IV (1175-1233) Prince of Antioch and count of Tripoli (1201-33). Son of Bohemond III, he fought for 20 years with the Armenians for the succession of Antioch; in 1222 a peace treaty was signed recognizing his rights. He also quarrelled with the *Templars and *Hospitallers.

BOHEMOND V (d. 1251) Prince of Antioch and count of Tripoli (1233-51). Son of Bohemond IV, he continued his father's policy and was in constant conflict with the Armenians. In 1244 the *Khwarizmians invaded, occupied his country, and compelled him to pay tribute. By his marriage with Alix, widow of *Hugh I of Lusignan, king of *Cyprus (1219), he was related to the royal houses of Jerusalem and Cyprus, creating the opportunity to claim his son's rights to the throne of the *Latin kingdom of Jerusalem.
S. Runciman, *A History of the Crusades* (1953).

BOHEMOND VI (1237-75) Prince of Antioch (1251-68) and count of Tripoli (1251-75). During his minority, the principality was ruled by his mother, Alix, as regent. She ended the long dispute with the Armenians by marrying him to Sybil, daughter of Hethum, king of Armenia. He maintained good relations with *Hulagu, the khan of the *Mongols in Persia, but the latter refused to provide military help, when B. asked him to support Acre against the attacks of *Baibars. In 1265 he fought against Baibars who defeated him and ultimately conquered Antioch in 1268, putting an end to the first state

of the *Crusaders. The great majority of the population was killed or taken captive. B. withdrew to Tripoli, where he reached a peace treaty with Baibars in 1271.
S. Runciman, *A History of the Crusades* (1953).

BOHEMOND VII (d. 1287) Count of *Tripoli (1275-87). In 1277, after the death of Baibars, B. tried to re-conquer Antioch, and for that purpose he organized a coalition with the *Hospitallers, Armenians and the Mongols. But in 1281 he was defeated by the new sultan of Egypt, Al-Malik Al-Mansur, and he lost Laodicea, re-maining the ruler only of the county of Tripoli.
S. Runciman, *A History of the Crusades* (1953).

BOHUN Aristocratic family of Norman origin, who settled in England after the Conquest. Their status rose during the reign of *William II when, in reward for the faithful services of Humphrey of B., they were given large estates in central England. In the 12th century they managed to increase their power and their estates, although they did not yet rise to the highest ranks of the nobility. Under *Henry II another Humphrey of B. was appointed constable of the realm and, after distin-guishing himself in the campaign against the Scots in 1175, he obtained the title earl of Hereford. The earldom became hereditary, and, during the baronial wars in the 13th century, the family's power grew. While Earl Humphrey (d. 1275) remained faithful to *Henry III and was taken captive at the Battle of *Lewes, his son, (also Humphrey) was a prominent leader of the barons' party and became a member of the Council of Nine, which ruled England after the Battle of Lewes. His opinions cost him his life when he was wounded at the Battle of Evesham (1265) and died soon after. The earl-dom passed to his son, Humphrey the Younger (1275-98), who gained an influential position during the reign of *Edward I. But his opinions were often at variance with Edward's and, in 1294-97, he led the opposition to the king. His son, Humphrey (1302-22), became a key figure in the government of *Edward II and the county of Essex. But having joined the Lancastrian party, his fate was linked with theirs, and in 1322 he was killed at the Battle of Boroughbridge. His successors, John (1326-36) and Humphrey (1336-61), served *Edward III faithfully. The last Humphrey of B. (1361-73) was a prominent figure at the royal court, where he represented the ideal of chivalry. He was granted the county of Northampton, previously held by another branch of the family. His daughter and heir, Eleanore, married Thomas of Woodstock, duke of Gloucester, the fourth son of Edward III. Humphrey's death marked the end of the B. family, whose rise from the Norman conquerors of the 11th century to the ranks of the nobility is so characteristic of medieval England.
J. H. Round - W. Page, *Family Origins and Other Studies* (1930).

BOILEAU, ETIENNE DE (d. 1270) French lawyer. Born in Paris, he studied at Paris University and obtain-ed his degree in Law. He entered the royal administra-tion and became provost of Paris under *Louis IX. He composed *Le Livre des Métiers* (The Book of Crafts), an annotated collection of customs and laws concerning the craft guilds of Paris at the time. The book was designed as an accurate legal text for lawyers on the rights and duties of guilds. But it is also an important document on the social and economic history of Paris-ian society in the 13th century.

Ed. 1879; E. Faral, *La Vie quotidienne au temps de Saint Louis* (1938).

BOINEBROCKE, JOHN (d. c. 1286) Merchant of Douai, Flanders. He belonged to a rich family of clothes merchants, which accumulated a large fortune in the second half of the 12th and the first half of the 13th century. B. increased the commercial activities of the family, also pursuing the food and luxury trade. At the same time, he invested his profits in textile workshops, thus controlling the production of cloth. In this manner, he created a multi-purpose enterprise – from the importation of wool, to control of production, where the workers and craftsmen were his employees, to the sale of the goods – which assured him a monopoly in the field. In this way he became one of the first capital-ists of the Netherlands in the 13th-14th centuries. He was also involved in banking and invested some of his profits in the purchase of estates. This type of invest-ment could not compare to commercial profits but, like many merchants of his time, B. was influenced by the school of thought which maintained that land was the safest investment.
G. Espinas, *Les Origines du Capitalisme: Sire Jehan Boinebroke* (1933).

BOIS, MANSART DU See DUBOIS, MANSART.

BOLESLAV I (d. 967) Duke of Bohemia (929-67). In 929 he led a national rebellion against his brother, St. *Wenceslas, and after murdering him, became duke. He succeeded in defeating Saxon and Thuringian armies sent against him until 950, when *Otto I personally led an expedition to Bohemia, defeated B. and compelled him to swear homage to the king of Germany. Although he was unable to secure the full independence of Bohemia, B. managed to organize a united state within the *Holy Roman empire.
S. Harrison Thompson, *Czechoslovakia in European History* (1953).

BOLESLAV II (d. 999) Duke of Bohemia (967-99). He supported the revolt of Henry of Bavaria against *Otto II, thus trying to secure the independence of Bohemia, but in 982 he submitted to the emperor and accepted the appointment of St. Adalbert to the see of Prague. Some of the chroniclers added the adjective Pious to his name.

BOLESLAV III (d. 1037) Duke of Bohemia (999-1003). His right to succeed to his father's title was contested by his step-brothers, Jaromir and Udalric, and as a result, Bohemia was torn by civil war. In 1003 the king of Poland, *Boleslaw Chrobry, profited from the anarchy, conquered Bohemia and took B. into lifelong captivity after blinding him.

BOLESLAW I (Chrobry; d. 1025) King of Poland (992-1025), son and successor of the first king of Poland, *Mieszko. He distinguished himself as a general who, by a long series of wars transformed the little Polish duchy into a great state, establishing its boundaries from the Baltic Sea in the north to the Carpathian Mountains in the south, and from the Elbe River in the west to Volhy-nia in the east. In 996 he first conquered Pomerania, and then the small town of Cracovia from Bohemia, annexing it to his kingdom. In 1000, *Otto III officially crowned him king of Poland in the Cathedral of *Gnieszno, which became the religious capital of the realm. In 1003, profiting from the death of Otto III, he invaded Germany and conquered territories on the Elbe, and subsequently invaded Bohemia, deposing the duke *Boleslav III and taking the ducal title. Thus he united all the West Slavic tribes under his rule, but in 1005 was compelled by the Emperor *Henry II to withdraw from Bohemia. He fought against the tribes of Volhynia on the eastern border. In 1018 he defeated *Yaroslav, the prince of Russia, and entered Kiev, but was unable to maintain his rule in the Russian capital.

The Cambridge History of Poland (1950).

BOLESLAW II, the Bold (d. 1082) King of Poland (1058-79). He tried to recover the provinces lost by Poland after the death of his grandfather, *Boleslaw I, but had only partial success. His wars against Bohemia were failures and made him dependent upon the clergy. In the east, he helped the Russian prince Yziaslav to seize power at Kiev (1069), receiving in return "Red Russia" (Galicia). His attempts to impose his authority on the nobles provoked civil wars and conspiracies. B.'s lack of political skill favoured the opposition, led by Stanislav, bishop of Cracow. The murder of the bishop during a prayer service was imputed to B. and in 1079, Pope *Gregory VII excommunicated him. He fled to Hungary with his sons and died there in 1082.

The Cambridge History of Poland (1950).

BOLESLAW III, Wry-mouthed King of Poland (1102-39). His reign was a period of continuous wars against Emperor *Henry V and Bohemia. Having defeated the German army near Breslau in 1107, he conquered Silesia and annexed it as a principality to his kingdom. In 1109 he imposed his rule on Pomerania, where he supported Christian missionary activity. But in 1120-24 his own vassals revolted and were supported by the Pomeranian tribes. B. cruelly repressed the revolts. The chroniclers related that 18,000 Pomeranians were killed during the repression and 9000 deported. Allowing room for exaggeration, the figures still symbolize the heavy losses sustained by this Slavic tribe which was practically destroyed, and the result of which was the German colonization of the country and its annexation to the German empire in the middle of the century. In his last years, B. fought unsuccessfully against Bohemia and Hungary. At his death he ordered that Poland be divided between his four sons.

The Cambridge History of Poland (1950).

BOLESLAW IV King of Poland (1146-73). Second son of *Boleslaw III. He succeeded his brother Vladislav II, whom he dethroned. Vladislav sought the protection of Emperor *Conrad III, who invaded Poland unsuccessfully. The only result of the invasion was the increasing support for B. in Poland. In 1157 *Frederick Barbarossa invaded Poland with a large army from Germany and Bohemia. Defeated, B. was forced to surrender Silesia — which was set up as a principality within Germany and granted to Vladislav's sons — and to pay homage to the emperor. He promised to pay tribute and to send an army to the emperor's expedition in Italy, but failed to keep his word.

The Cambridge History of Poland (1950).

BOLESLAW V King of Poland (1227-79). During his minority the nobles became powerful in the kingdom and when he came of age and began to reign in 1238, he found that the royal treasury was empty. In 1240 the *Mongols, led by *Batu-khan, invaded Poland but B. was unable to raise an army against them. The kingdom was overrun and, after the retreat of the *Mongols who

reached Silesia in 1241, it was left in ruins. B.'s efforts to improve the situation led to repressive economic measures against the peasantry. In 1260 he granted large privileges to the nobility to obtain its support. Thus, they became the real force in the kingdom: their advice and approval was considered necessary before any royal decision was taken and they were granted the right to elect the king.

The Cambridge History of Poland (1950).

BOLOGNA City in the province of Romagna, northern Italy. During the 5th-century invasions the Roman city of Bononia was conquered and ravaged by the *Ostrogoths. Its importance lay in its strategic site, commanding the Apennine passes. After the establishment of Byzantine rule in Italy in the middle of the 6th century, B. was one of the cities of the exarchate (province) of *Ravenna and it shared the capital's fate. Granted to the *Papal State by *Pepin the Short in 753 and by *Charlemagne in 774, B. enjoyed a measure of autonomy under the leadership of its archbishops who ruled it until the beginning of the 12th century. In the 11th century the city grew as commerce developed. With the establishment of its law school by *Irnerius, B. became a famous centre for the study of Roman *Law, attracting students from all over western Europe. In 1112 B. was granted the privilege of a "free city" and joined the *Lombard league. The city took part in the struggle between the papacy and the empire with its leaders supporting whichever side proved more convenient. In 1159 *Frederick Barbarossa granted the law school the *Authentica Habita*, which served as the university's charter, exempting it from secular jurisdiction and allowing its teachers and students to travel freely to and from B. In the 13th century anti-imperial feelings were strong and the opposition to the *Hohenstaufen (the *Guelph party) seized power. Between 1239 and 1242 the bastard son of *Frederick II was held in captivity at a palace in B. which is still called after his name. In the 14th-15th centuries two dynasties claimed the right to rule the city, the *Bentivoglio and the *Visconti of Milan. Under the Bentivoglio rule B. became a prestigious cultural centre of the Renaissance. The struggle between the dynasties proved beneficial for the papacy, which imposed its direct authority over the city in 1506. B. is a remarkable centre of Italian Gothic architecture. Its cathedral, built on the site of the Roman centre, is 13th- and 14th-century Gothic. It combines architecture with sculpture. The governor's palace, started in 1201, the city hall in 1290, and the merchants' guild hall in the 14th century, represent various stages of Gothic style. Near the merchants' house, in the old centre of the city, two towers (97 m and 42 m high), which were built for defence purposes at the beginning of the 12th century, stand as a reminder of the struggle for autonomy.

The University of B. was its most renowned medieval institution. It is one of the oldest universities in the world and some historians consider it the first. Its first department, the School of Law, was founded in 1088 by Irnerius, and in the 12th century it became the legal training-ground for all of Europe, both in Roman and in canon law. Among distinguished teachers who taught there in the first half of the 12th century, were *Gratianus and Roland Bandinelli (Pope *Alexander III). A college of liberal arts (*Studium Generale*) was

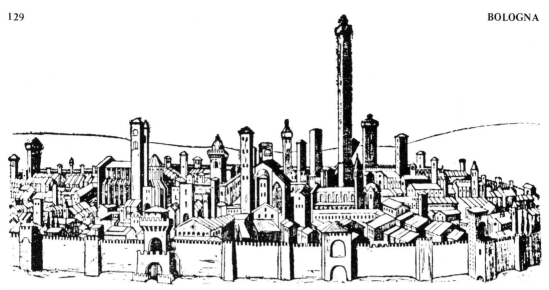

Medieval Bologna. Woodcut

established in the middle of the 12th century. In 1218, Pope *Honorius III granted the university self-government and instituted the practice of conferring degrees. During the 13th century a medical school was established and incorporated into the university. At the beginning of the 14th century, the practical study of anatomy, including the dissection of corpses, attracted students from abroad, thus it became a distinguished centre for the study of medicine. The university library, with its 5000 manuscripts, was, since its inception, one of the most important in the West.

G. Zucchini, *Bologna* (1914);

C. M. Ady, *The Bentivoglio of Bologna* (1937);

P. Kibre, *Scholarly Privileges in the Middle Ages* (1962).

The Purification, *relief by Jacopo della Quercia on the portal of the basilica in Bologna*

BONAVENTURA, St. (Giovanni di Fidanza; 1221-74)
Franciscan theologian. Born in Fidanza, Italy, he
entered the *Franciscan order c. 1240 and studied in
Paris, where he taught from 1248 to 1255. His teaching
was interrupted by the opposition of the secular professors to the *Mendicants; when they were restored in
1257, he was reinstated and obtained his doctor's degree.
In the same year he was elected minister general of his
order and in this capacity, he was responsible for settling internal friction in the order. In 1263 the order
approved his *Life of St. Francis* as the official biography
of the founder of the order, and in 1266 the general
chapter ordered that all other versions or legends be
destroyed. In 1271 he was instrumental in getting
*Gregory X elected to the papacy, and in 1273 he was
created cardinal-bishop of Albano.

As a theologian, B. remained faithful to the methods
of St. *Augustine and had little sympathy for the
*Aristotelian trends of thought, which had developed in
his time. He therefore opposed *Thomas Aquinas.
He emphasized that human wisdom was folly when
compared with the mystical illumination which God
sheds on faithful Christians. This argument was developed into a mystical theory of knowledge in his most important work, *Itineratius Mentis in Deum* (The Itinerary
of the Reason to God).
Ed. with Engl. trans., *The Franciscan Vision* (1937);
E. Gilson, *The Philosophy of St. Bonaventure* (1938).

BONCOMPAGNO DI SIGNA (c. 1165-c. 1240) Scholar
and rhetorician. He was educated at the University of
*Bologna and taught rhetoric there from the beginning
of the 13th century. His book, *Antiqua Rhetorica* (The
Ancient Rhetorics), is based on the Ciceronian tradition
of rhetorical art and was praised as one of the best contributions to the revival of Latin. In 1215, the University
of Bologna awarded him the laureateship for scholarship
and in 1266 he was bestowed the same honours by the
University of Padua.
A. Sorbelli, *Storia della Università di Bologna*, I, (1944).

BONIFACE, St. (680-754) The apostle of Germany.
Originally called Wynfrith, he was born to a Saxon
family at Crediton in Devon. He became a monk before
700 and joined the missionary activities of the Anglo-
Saxon monks. In 715 he went to *Frisia, but his mission
had little success. In 717 he went to Rome and in 719,
armed with a papal writ, he began to preach in Germany
among the Hessians and Thuringians, where he made
many converts. Invited by *Gregory II to visit Rome in
722, he was met there by a full papal delegation, and
tradition has it that on that occasion, his name was
changed to Boniface. On his return to Germany, his
mission met with great success and B. began to organize
the German church, assuming the title of archbishop of
Mainz. In 741, after the death of *Charles Martel, he
was commissioned to reform the Frankish church. He
entered into close relations with *Pepin the Short,
obtaining Frankish armed support for his missionary
activities which, thereby, also acquired political significance – and he promoted the elevation of the *Carolingians to kingship. In 751 he supported the dethronement of the last *Merovingian king *Chilperic III, and
the election of *Pepin, whom he crowned in 752. In
753 he founded the Abbey of *Fulda in the centre of
the land whose inhabitants he had converted. He became its first abbot. In 754, he gave up all of his dignities

and went on a missionary journey to the Frisians, where
he was killed, thus becoming Germany's saint and
martyr.
Works, *PL*, vol. 89;
W. Levison, *England and the Continent in the 8th century* (1946).

BONIFACE I Pope (418-22). B. was a priest at Rome
before his election and, although elderly, he was elected
by the majority of the clergy, who opposed the archdeacon Eulalius. But because of friction with those in
favour of Eulalius, B. could only assume his position
with the support of Emperor Honorius and his wife
Galla Placida. He tried to impose the supremacy of the
Roman see on the churches of the Western Roman
empire.

BONIFACE II Pope (530-32). He maintained good
relations with the *Ostrogoth court of Ravenna and
limited his activities essentially to the Church of Rome.

BONIFACE III Pope (607). Member of an important
Roman family, he represented the papacy at Constantinople and after his return became a close collaborator of
*Gregory I. During his short period in office, he ordered
a 3-day intermission between the funeral of a pope (or
bishop) and the election of his successor.

BONIFACE IV (St.) Pope (608-15). Born in Marsia,
Italy, he devoted himself to monastic life and employed
his family's wealth to help the poor. *Gregory I called
him to the papal court and, after the death of Boniface
III, he was elected pope. His pontificate was devoted to
the building and consecration of churches and to the
development of the cult of saints, particularly that of
St. Mary. B. instituted the feast of *All Saints on
1 November.
L. Duchesne, *The Early History of the Papal State*
(1922).

BONIFACE V Pope (619-25). Born in Naples, B. dealt
with legal and administrative problems. He was concerned with the organization of the Church of England after
the first generation of missionary activities in the Anglo-
Saxon realms. In Rome, he introduced the term "papal
notary", destined to replace "imperial notary". This
innovation was of paramount importance for the West,
as Roman Law required that all legalization of private
contracts be done by public notaries appointed by the
imperial court. Candidates for the position of notary
(whose primary importance was in Italy where the wills
continued to be written according to Roman Law), had
to apply to the Byzantine exarch of Ravenna for an
appointment as imperial notary. This implied the recognition of Byzantine sovereignty in the West. By appointing papal notaries, this link was broken to the benefit of
the papal authority.
EC, II.

BONIFACE VI Pope (896). A priest of the Roman
Church who, during the disturbances of the Eighties was
twice deposed and reinstated. At the death of Pope
*Formosus, a popular movement brought him to the
papal see, where he died after only 15 days in office.

BONIFACE VII (Franco) Pope (974; 984-85). After
the death of *Otto I, an anti-imperial reaction in Rome
was led by Count *Crescentius. Pope *Benedict VI was
murdered and the priest Franco was installed on the
papal see, taking the name of B. The intervention of the
German forces led B. to flee to Constantinople, where
he sought the protection of Emperor *Basil II. In 984,

after the death of *Otto II, he returned to Rome, probably with the consent of the Byzantine emperor. There B. was hailed pope, while the incumbent Pope *John XIV was imprisoned and died in captivity. But his pontificate ended abruptly when he died suddenly in 985.

J. Haller, *Das Papsttum* (1950).

BONIFACE VIII (Benedetto Gaetani; 1234-1303) Pope (1294-1303). Born in Anagni as a scion of the noble family of the Gaetani, he studied Roman and canon law in various Italian schools, culminating in *Bologna. As a jurist, he made a valuable contribution to canon law in his *Liber Sextus* (The Sixth Collection), in which he described the development of canon law from 1234 down to his own pontificate. In 1281 he was made cardinal and was sent on diplomatic missions to Germany and France, thereby acquiring first-hand knowledge of the conditions in the principal Catholic states. After the abdication of *Celestine V, he was elected pope. He was energetic, self-confident and, as so many of the popes had done favoured his own family and relatives whose estates were enlarged. He aimed to restore the preponderance of the papacy in political affairs, bring peace to Europe and renew the *Crusades. For practical purposes it was in his interest to continue the *Guelph policy of his predecessors, which consisted of an alliance with the king of France and his relatives, the *Angevin kings of Naples. But his relations with *Charles II of Anjou-Naples were bad as B. feared Charles' Italian ventures. Thus, he tried to isolate Naples by an alliance with the kings of Aragon, but this only further embroiled him in conflict with the Neapolitans and the French allies. In Germany, he had more luck. *Albert of Austria, at loggerheads with the *electors, came to an agreement with B., recognizing the, sole right of the pope to crown the emperor. B. was at odds with Florence over his territorial claims in Tuscany. He entered into open conflict with the powerful family of *Colonna, whose interests were opposed to those of the Gaetani and who contested the legitimacy of his election, claiming that the abdication of Celestine V was illegal. The Colonna allied themselves with the Spiritual Brethren, a left wing offshoot of the *Franciscan order who preached against wealth and in favour of extreme poverty, and who were already condemned by Pope *Nicholas III in 1279, in a pontifical letter, composed by B. himself. All of these conflicts prevented B. from realizing his goal, of bringing peace to Europe through papal arbitration and instead, made him a party to the conflicts. Moreover, they further embroiled him in a major conflict with *Philip IV the Fair, king of France. The history of his relations with Philip is divided into three phases: a period of cordial relations, between 1294 and 1296, when his Italian interests dictated a rapprochement with France, manifested in his efforts to better the relations between the kings of France and England, the key condition to lauching a Crusade: the period of the "gathering storm", when the pope intervened in the conflict between Philip and the French church, concerning the taxation of the ecclesiastical estates (1296-1303); and a period of open conflict (1301-03), when B. opposed the king's claims of sovereignty with his own theory of the universal supremacy of the pope in Christian society. The first period was short and uneventful; the second period opened with B.'s reaction to the

Pope Boniface VIII; sculpture by Arnolfo di Cambio

complaints of the French clergy who were forced by the royal administration to pay taxes on their estates. In a famous bull *Clericis laicos* in 1296, B. expressed his view that taxation of the clergy is illegal, if consent of the pope was not previously obtained. He even threatened the secular authorities with excommunication. But he could not maintain this extremist view; the Italian conflicts made him dependent on Philip, and forced him to adopt a more moderate attitude. He recognized that in certain emergency cases, the king could ask the clergy for grants for the defence of the realm. But this attitude appeased neither the French court nor the clergy, who upheld the theory of the "Gallican liberties", minimizing the right of the papacy to interfere in such cases. In 1298, B. succeeded in defeating Colonna and was able to live undisturbed at Rome. He prepared the feasts of the jubilee year of 1300, which were to bring pilgrims from all over Europe to Rome and to display the prestige of the pope as head of Christian society. The feast increased B.'s self-confidence and made him anxious to apply his theories on papal supremacy. In 1301, his close friend Bernard Saisset, bishop of Pamiers, was arrested by French officers and charged with treason. B. protested to Philip about what he called "the breach of clerical immunity", and his successive letters showed his growing anger. The last letter, the famous bull *Unam Sanctam*, was not only a threat to the king of France, but also a document of principles, stating that the authority of the Church was higher than that of the State and that every Christian should be subject to the apostolic authority of the pope. He thus expressed the core of theocratical principles, which were never fully accepted even in previous centuries. In response to the bull, Philip gathered the *Estates General of the kingdom, where his jurists prepared their arguments on royal sovereignty. B. was accused of heresy, and a motion was passed to summon a general council to judge him. This decision of the Estates General of 1303 was sent to the pope through a delegation headed by William of Nogaret, Philip's influential counsellor. On his way to the papal palace of Anagni, Sciarra Colonna, B.'s enemy, joined the delegation. When the pope threatened the king with excommunication and deposition, Nogaret assaulted him and took him prisoner. Although he was released by the people, he died at Rome a few weeks later, a broken man.

The conflict between B. and Philip was not merely between two adversaries; it was one between two different ideologies: the universal supremacy of the papacy vs. the national sovereignty of kings. The former ideology was already expressed by *Gregory VII, *Alexander III and *Innocent III. B.'s letters were intended to be public manifestos, and they were written for large circles of contemporaries. In them B. censures the national sovereignty of the "king of France who does not recognize any superior authority in his realm". He also rebukes the Estates General – representing the three orders of French society, clergy, nobility and the masses – who participate in the exercise of sovereignty. The social and political evolution of the 12th and 13th centuries tended to favour the national monarchies, while universalist theories were already outdated. Therefore, the efforts of B. – who was unaware of this change – were doomed to failure.

T. S. R. Boase, *Boniface VIII* (1933);
C. T. Wood, *Philip the Fair and Boniface VIII* (1967).
BONIFACE IX (Pietro Tomacelli; c. 1345-1404) Pope (1389-1404). Born in Naples, B. was a practical politician whose career coincided with the return of the popes to Rome (1378) and the beginning of the *Great Schism. Although he was young, he was elected as the second pope in the Roman line, with the hope that his skills would bring an end to the schism. While he succeeded in imposing his authority in Italy and in recovering the Papal States in 1400, he failed to reunite the Church, with the supporters of the *Avignon line of popes rejecting his authority. Concerned with political and administrative problems, he also tried to restore the finances of the Roman court by imposing heavy taxes and selling *indulgences to the faithful.
W. Ullman, *The Origins of the Great Schism* (1967).
BONIFACE OF CANOSSA Marquis of Tuscany (1030-52). Born to a Franco-Italian family which settled at Modena in the 9th century and established their feudal rule from their castle of *Canossa in the Apennine passes. In 1030 Emperor *Conrad II appointed him marquis of *Tuscany and married him to Beatrix, daughter of Frederick, duke of Lorraine. B. was one of the most energetic princes of his time in northern Italy. He imposed order in his marquisate and concentrated on developing the cities, particularly Florence, Siena and *Pisa, which became one of the main harbours in Italy. His daughter was the famous Countess *Matilda.
D. B. Zema, *The Houses of Tuscany and of Pierleone in the Crisis of Rome in the 11th Century* (1944).
BONIFACE OF MONTFERRAT Marquis of Montferrat (1188-1204), king of Thessalonica (1204-07). B. was the

son of William of Montferrat, a high-ranking noble in northern Italy, and of Sophia, daughter of *Frederick Barbarossa. In 1204 he was elected leader of the Fourth *Crusade. Under Venetian influence, he accepted the digression of the crusade towards Constantinople and was among the conquerors of the city. He was a candidate for the new title of *Latin emperor of Constantinople, but fearing his power, the electors chose *Baldwin of Flanders for that post, while B. became king of Thessalonica and was promised the rule of Greece and other territories in the Balkans yet to be conquered. His conflict with Emperor Baldwin over the extent of independence to be allowed the new kingdom in the empire was subdued by the Venetians. In 1205, B. conquered most of the territories allotted to his realm, extending to Athens, the rule over which he invested on one of his vassals, Guy de La Roche. Attacked by the Bulgarians in 1207, he was killed at the Battle of Mossynopolis.
W. Miller, *The Latins in the Levant* (1908).
BONIFACE OF SAVOY (d. 1270) Archbishop of Canterbury (1241-70). Son of Thomas, count of Savoy, he became the uncle of Queen Eleanor, who was married to *Henry III of England through his sister Beatrice, countess of Provence. While he was bishop of Belley in Burgundy, Henry called him to England, assuring him the post of archbishop of Canterbury. As a foreigner to the kingdom, he met with opposition from clergy and barons, and left England several times. In 1269 he accompanied Prince Edward (the future *Edward I) on his crusade, but fell ill and died, while they sojourned in Savoy. B. was an ardent supporter of Henry III during the baronial revolts, but his activities as archbishop hardly left an imprint.
DNB, V.
BONVESIN DE LA RIPA (c. 1240-1314) Italian writer and historian. Born and educated at Milan he was absorbed in the grandeur of the city. His writings are a major source of Lombardian history towards the end of the 13th century. His most important work, *De magnalibus urbis Mediolani* (On the Greatness of the City of Milan), contains a brief history of the city from ancient times until the 14th century, and an original description of its population, traditions, manners, and activities, destined to prove its greatness during the writer's life. He included countless details, such as the following passage: "Six hundred butchers provide meat for the city every day. They slaughter 70 large cows and an innumerable quantity of sheep and chicken. The dogs of Milan eat more bread every day than the whole population of Lodi". The book provides interesting testimony to an affluence that permeated every stratum of Milanese society at the beginning of the 14th century.
G. Bertoni, *Il ducento* (1930).
BOOK-KEEPING Until the 12th century, medieval B. existed only in a rudimentary form, practised mainly by ecclesiastical institutions, who recorded their incomes and expenses, but without detailed accounting. With the development of international commerce in the 12th century and the constitution of mercantile partnerships, B. became essential for efficient control of operations. Among the oldest examples of medieval B. are those which were developed in the Italian cities, such as Venice and Genoa. The B. was entrusted to *notaries, thus having an official character. On ships, a

special crew man, the scribe, was entrusted with the B. and like notaries was sworn in. In the 13th century, merchant and credit houses in Italian cities did their own B. and, c. 1250, the system of double-entry B. was invented, facilitating the full record of debits and credits. In larger firms with branches in Italy and abroad, the system was constantly improved upon during the 14th century. According to the documents still available, the best examples were the *Medici Bank at Florence and the Datini House at Prato near Florence. The system was described by Luca Pacioli, whose treatise, published in 1494, helped spread the practice to all other European countries in the 16th century. It continued to be employed without changes until the 19th century. Some of the Italian book-keepers in the 14th and 15th centuries even recorded depreciation of equipment, although it did not have the same importance to the economy as it had from the time of the Industrial Revolution. In other European countries, B. was not as developed as in Italy, and the *Hanse traders used the simple forms of the 12th century, despite the fact that they had contact with Italians through places like London and Bruges.

CEcH, III.

BOOK OF THE PREFECT A Byzantine code of the late 9th century, enacted by Emperor *Leo VI the Wise. This is a book of rules on the practices of commerce and handicraft, as they existed in the empire. Its mainstay is the rigid functioning of the *guild system in every branch of economic activity, guaranteed by the intervention of the state. The guilds were empowered to regulate production, quality, and price and to determine the place and time of the sales. The book is by far the best and most complete evidence of the functioning of an organized medieval economy controlled by the state. The statutes of the west European guilds represent a later development, which from the 13th century on was similar in many ways to the B. but which did not include state intervention.

E. H. Freshfield, *Roman Law in the Later Roman Empire* (1938).

BORDEAUX The main city of *Aquitaine, in western France. The Roman city of Burdigala had been devastated at the beginning of the Middle Ages, and though rebuilt, it declined under the *Visigoths (418-507) and the *Franks, becoming an insignificant town though the seat of an archbishopric. In 732 it was conquered by the *Arabs, but in 735, *Charles Martel recovered it and made it a stronghold of his actions against the Moslems. Under *Pepin the Short and *Charlemagne, it was fortified against the attacks of the "Vascones". Nevertheless, B. remained a small, insignificant town until the 11th century, when it became an important station on the pilgrims' route to *Santiago de Compostela. Commerce developed, and the dukes of Aquitaine stayed there with their courts for short sojourns. In 1137, the marriage of *Louis VII with *Eleanor of Aquitaine was celebrated at B. and on that occasion Louis granted the churches of Aquitaine the same privileges they enjoyed in the kingdom of France. Upon the second marriage of Eleanor with *Henry II Plantagenet (1152) and the coronation of Henry as king of England (1154), B. entered an era of prosperity. The city became the main port for the exportation of Gascon wines to England and its economic interests demanded good relations with England. In the 13th century, after the loss of Poitiers by *Henry III, B. became the capital of the duchy of Guyenne, the part of Aquitaine which remained under English rule. Its commercial life prospered and the city became an important administrative centre, with the nobility and magistrates gathering around the ducal government. B. remained faithful to the English crown during the *Hundred Years' War.

C. Higounet, *Histoire de Bordeaux au Moyen Age* (1969).

BOREL (Burrelus) Count of Vich (8th-9th centuries). Born in Septimania (southern France), he distinguished himself in the wars with the Moslems of Catalonia. In 898, *Louis the Pious, then king of Aquitaine, appointed him count of Vich in Catalonia and entrusted him with the campaigns, which saw the conquest of the March of Spain.

BOREL Count of Barcelona (947-92). B. reorganized the administration of the county and encouraged the establishment of resident scholars from Moslem Spain at Barcelona including mathematicians and astronomers. He became known as a patron of learning and was instrumental in the transmission of Arab science to Latin Europe. The most famous young student to benefit from B.'s patronage was Gerbert of Aurillac, the future Pope *Sylvester II.

R. Walzer, *Arab transmission of Greek thought to Mediaeval Europe* (1945).

BORGHESANO, FRANCESCO (13th century) Italian engineer. In 1272 at Bologna B. invented a machine for throwing silk. This invention was one of the most important trade secrets at Bologna, so much so, that it remained unknown even in the neighbouring Italian cities until the end of the Middle Ages. The machine was described by the scientist Zonca who reported on B.'s work in 1600.

C. Singer and E. J. Holmyard, *History of Technology*, II (1956).

BORGOGNONI Family of physicians in 13th-century Bologna. Hugh B. (d. c. 1255) established a laboratory for the preparation of drugs. Together with his son, Theodoric (1205-98), who continued his work after his death, he made regular use of chemicals, such as arsenic oxide, antimony and mercury salts, pioneering modern pharmacopoeia.

J. R. Partington, *Origins and Development of Applied Chemistry* (1935).

BORH Anglo-Saxon term meaning security. From the 7th century on, it was customary in the peasant communities of the Anglo-Saxon kingdoms for every freeman to procure a pledge from a well-known person who would appear in court as his security. Those peasants who were subjects to lords were exempt from a particular B., the lord being their pledge. In later centuries, the kings compelled all free-men to have their own B. These regulations became a burden on the lords, who tried to impose the duty on the communities themselves. The kings, particularly those of Wessex, viewed the B. as a means of preventing people from escaping justice, but the result was the introduction of feudalism into the realm. After the *Norman Conquest, the B. was gradually transformed into the frankpledge which was imposed on the free-men of the kingdom by *Henry I in 1130 and was the basis of the shire-court administration.

B. Lyon, *A Constitutional and Legal History of Medieval England* (1960).

BORIL Tsar of Bulgaria (1207-18). The nephew of *Kaloian, B. usurped the throne after his uncle's death. In 1208 he concluded a peace treaty with *Henry, the Latin emperor of Constantinople, and married his daughter. B.'s dependence on the Latin empire aroused the opposition, which broke out in open revolt in 1218, and was supported by the *Russian princes. B. was dethroned by his cousin, *John Assen the son of Kaloian. He was blinded and died in prison. With B.'s deposition, the aspiration of the Catholic Church to convert the Bulgarians was ended.

BORIS I (d. 907) Khan of the Bulgarians (852-89). B. tried to consolidate the *Bulgarian state in the Balkans, but was not able to impose his authority on all the southern Slavic tribes. In 865 he converted to Christianity, as a result of the mission of *Cyril and Methodius. His godfather at the baptism was the Byzantine Emperor *Michael III. Nevertheless, he opposed the efforts of the Byzantine church to integrate the Bulgarian territories into the Greek administrative system, obtaining in 869, the establishment of an independent archbishopric for the Bulgarians at *Tirnovo, while accepting the dogmatic and theological teachings of the Greek Orthodox Church. He promoted missionary activities in Bulgaria and surrounded himself with monks and priests. In 889 he abdicated and retired to a monastery.
S. Runciman, *The First Bulgarian Empire* (1932).

BORIS II (949-79) Tsar of Bulgaria (969-72). He reigned during a troubled period of conflict with the Byzantine empire. Despite his efforts to maintain peace on the borders of the empire, he was not successful, having been compelled by internal state problems to reverse his alliances. In 972 Emperor *John Tzimisces forced him to abdicate.

BORIVOJ (d. 902) Duke of Bohemia (892-902). In 894 he was converted to Christianity by the *Moravian mission of *Methodius and was the first Christian prince of Bohemia. He fought against Emperor *Arnulf, hoping to free his country from German rule. Under B.'s rule, Bohemia was opened to the political influence of the kingdom of Moravia and the cultural influence of the Eastern Church.
G. Barraclough, *Medieval Germany* (1938).

BORNA (d. 821) Duke of the Croats. He led his tribe, belonging to the group of southern Slavs, to the territory between the Drava River and the Adriatic Sea, where his leadership was challenged by one of his kinsmen, Duke *Ljudevit. In 818 he fought a series of minor battles with the Frankish empire of *Louis the Pious, and established his rule in present-day Croatia and Dalmatia.
F. von Šišič, *Geschichte der Kroaten* (1917).

BORNHOLM Island in the Baltic Sea. Archaeological evidence and tradition establish the island as the land of origin of the *Burgundian tribes, dating back to the 2nd century AD. From the 3rd to the 9th century, prosperous *Viking settlements existed, and the island became an independent principality. In the 10th century, it came under Swedish control and, with the spread of Christianity in Scandinavia, became dependent on the archbishops of *Lund. In the 12th century a number of round, Scandinavian-type fortified churches were built in the island, and are still standing. From the end of the 12th to the end of the 15th century, B. belonged to the kingdom of *Sweden, but in the 14th century a *Hanse colony was established there, and at the end of the 15th century (between 1490 and 1501), the island came under the control of the Hanseatic League.
L. Musset, *Les Peuples Scandinaves au Moyen Age* (1951).

BOROUGH (Burg, Burgus, Burh, Bourg) Synonymous with town. Originally the term referred to a small locality fortified by a surrounding wall and moats and usually around a monastery or castle, which was founded in the Germanic countries during the 9th and 10th centuries. From the late 10th century on, the term began to be used to designate new towns founded in the Middle Ages, which had no Roman roots and therefore were distinguished from the *civitas* (city) which was rooted in the classical tradition. Nevertheless, not all medieval settlements were called B., or contained this term in their name (such as Edinburgh), and some continued to use terms similar to the Roman *castrum* or castle to signify their origin. The various towns named Chester in Anglo-Saxon England, or Château, Castel, etc. in French-speaking countries are examples of such. With the development of medieval towns in the 12th century the term B. began to signify those which enjoyed certain liberties and privileges; and those of their inhabitants who were allowed to participate in public life were known as burghers, meaning they owned their own houses. Bs. had their own councils and gradually acquired the right to collect taxes, thus obtaining the *firma burgi* (the "farm" of the B.). The B. paid a lump sum to the Treasury, and was free to set revenues as it wished. In some of the Bs. this status also included responsibility for the judicial system. The king's officials and magistrates were maintained within the B. at its expense and the inhabitants benefited from the courts in their towns. Although technically the distinction between city and B. continued to be observed in medieval documents (the city being the seat of a bishop so that upon the creation of a new episcopal see, a town was elevated to the rank of city), for all practical purposes they were identical. The real distinction was that between the privileged town (commune or incorporated B.) and the regular town, which was under the authority of a lord.
J. Tait, *The Medieval English Borough* (1936);
F. Rörig, *The Medieval Town* (1967).

BOROUGHBRIDGE, BATTLE OF The main battle in the clash between *Edward II, who took up arms on behalf of the *Despensers, and the ordainers, where the royal forces defeated the Lancastrian party in 1322.

BOROUGH-ENGLISH Term designating the English custom of ultimogeniture, meaning that all land was inherited by the youngest son. This form of succession was primarily used by unfree peasants in *Anglo-Saxon England, and remained a popular custom in the English boroughs after the *Norman Conquest. In 1327 in Nottingham, ultimogeniture was officially recognized in England, as opposed to the French custom of primogeniture and division of the inheritance among the heirs. The English custom persisted until the 20th century, when it was abolished.
J. E. A. Jolliffe, *The Constitutional History of Medieval England* (1961).

BOSO King of Provence (879-87). Originally from a noble Frankish family of Lotharingia, B. was the brother of Richildis, the second wife of *Charles the Bald (870).

He married Ermengarde, daughter of Emperor *Louis II. His brother-in-law elevated him to high positions in France, such as governor of *Aquitaine in 871 and count of *Bourges in 875. He followed Charles to Italy, where he ruled the kingdom on his behalf. One of the most important counsellors of King *Louis II, B. was appointed in 879 to the regency-council, thus assuring the coronation of the king's sons, *Louis III and *Carloman. In autumn 879, for reasons unknown, he suddenly left the young kings, and went on to conquer Vienne, the capital of the *Carolingian kingdom of Provence, where he proclaimed himself king despite the fact that he was not a member of the Carolingian dynasty. Although attacked in his new capital by King Carloman and *Bernard Plantevelue, his rival at the Frankish court, he maintained his rule until his death in 887. B. was a political adventurer whose fortunes improved with the decline of the Carolingian empire. He founded a new dynasty and his son *Louis the Blind, succeeded him and became emperor.

L. Halphen, *Charlemagne et l'Empire Carolingien* (1950).

BOTANY Medieval B. was deeply influenced by the works of Greek scientists and by the *Natural History* of Pliny the Elder (1st century AD), which stressed the classification of plants and their properties. In the early Middle Ages, B. was studied through the works of *Isidore of Seville and *Bede, and through the *Herbal* attributed to Pseudo-*Apuleius in the 6th century. The study of plants and herbs concentrated on their medicinal properties and therefore, the science remained at a rudimentary stage in western Europe until the 13th century. The only valuable western contribution up to that time was the Herbal of *Rufinus of the 9th century, whose structure exemplifies the scientific methods of the time, a great part of it being simply a repetition of earlier authorities. Until the 13th century, the most impressive progress was achieved by Arab botanists, like Akhmad Ibn Wukhashieh of the 10th century, who produced valuable lexicographies on plants and herbs, linking their own observations to the achievements of the ancient Greek school of botany. With the discovery of *Aristotle by the Latin-speaking West in the 13th century, valuable progress was made; the Latin translation of the pseudo-Aristotelian *Liber de Plantis or de Vegetalibus* (The Book of Plants or Vegetables) in 1217 became the authority in the field. Roger *Bacon and particularly *Albertus Magnus contributed the results of their observations of the study of B., and the second Herbal of Rufinus, published in 1287, marked a step toward accurate representation of plants and herbs. Nevertheless, important consideration continued to be given to the medicinal qualities of herbs, and botanists of the 13th and 14th centuries remained closely associated with the work of pharmacists.

H. W. K. Fischer, *Mittelalterliche Pflanzenkunde* (1929).

BOUCHARD, WILLIAM (13th century) French goldsmith, originally from Paris. In 1254, a delegation sent by *Louis IX to the court of the great khan of the *Mongols met B. at Karakorum where he had established his workshop. He produced many gold vases and jewellery at the Mongolian court, where he was well treated.

R. Grousset, *L'Empire des Steppes* (1952).

BOUCIQAUT, JEAN (Jean Meingre; d. 1367) Marshal of France. He was one of the commanders of the French army under the reign of King *John II and took part in his campaigns in the *Hundred Years' War. In 1360-62, he negotiated the peace treaty of *Bretigny on behalf of the French court.

BOUCIQAUT, JEAN (II) (1366-1421) Son of Jean le Meingre and marshal of France in 1391. Having been educated for a military career as the heir to his father's charge he took part in the Battle of *Roosebeke in Flanders in 1382, where he was noted by the king's uncle, *Philip the Bold of Burgundy. In 1396, he joined the Crusade of *Nicopolis, but was taken captive. Recovering his freedom, he organized an expedition to help Constantinople, then besieged by *Bayazid I. After his return to France, he was appointed governor of Genoa (1401-09), where he proved himself as an administrator. In 1415 he took part in the Battle of *Agincourt and was again taken prisoner. In 1421 he died while in captivity in Yorkshire.

A. S. Atyia, *The Crusade of Nicopolis* (1934).

BOUILLON Duchy of the *Holy Roman empire. The origins of the duchy lay in a small feudal seigniory, established in the 8th century around the castle of B., near the French frontier of Belgium. Until the 11th century the lords of B. were vassals of the dukes of Lower Lotharingia, and under Emperor *Henry IV, they became direct vassals of the emperor. In 1093 Henry created the duchy of B. on behalf of his faithful vassal, *Godfrey of B. In 1096, when Godfrey left his country to paticipate in the First *Crusade, he passed the duchy to the bishops of Liège in Belgium and it remained part of their principality until the end of the 15th century. During the 15th century, the lords of La Marck acquired part of its estates and obtained the ducal title in 1483.

J. F. Ozeray, *Histoire de la ville et du duché de Bouillon* (1864).

BOULOGNE Town in northeastern France, on the shore of the English Channel. B. was founded on the site of a Gallo-Roman locality named Gesoriacum, of which only the Bononia castle, built in the 4th century, remained at the beginning of the Middle Ages. Under Frankish rule it had little importance and was better defined as a fishing village. In the 7th century, legends about miracles wrought in its church by a depiction of the Virgin *Mary, brought pilgrims to B. and contributed to the growth of its population. Under *Charlemagne the castle was rebuilt to defend the coast from *Norman invasions. Charlemagne himself showed interest in this strategic point and visited B. several times. In 812 he issued a *Capitulary there, concerning military problems of the empire. With the decline of the *Carolingian empire, B. fell under the suzerainty of the counts of *Flanders, although it formed a separate county in the Flemish principality. B.'s family of counts reached a distinguished position in the latter half of the 11th century, when one of its members, Godfrey, inherited the duchy of Bouillon and became one of the leaders of the First *Crusade. His brother, *Baldwin, became king of *Jerusalem and founded the first dynasty of the Latin kingdom of Jerusalem. Another branch of the family, headed by Count Eustache, became related to the English monarchy in the 12th century. In the later centuries of the Middle Ages, suzerainty over B. was disputed between England and France and several of the battles in the *Hundred Years' War were concerned with that controversy. The town, however, grew and became one of the main ports connecting England and the Continent.

H. Pirenne, *Histoire de la Belgique* (1901).

BOURBON Seigniory and, later, duchy in central France; also, dynasty.

The seigniory of B. was created in the 10th century in the southeastern part of the county of *Bourges, in a woody area divided by the main road between northern France and Auvergne. Its lords built a castle, Bourbon-L'Archambault, which became the centre of the seigniory. Towards the end of the 11th century and in the 12th century, B.'s population grew as a result of the arrival of new immigrants from the surrounding provinces, who settled in the deforested estates. B.'s agrarian development in the 12th-13th centuries enriched both the lords and the population and in the 13th century the former became important personalities in the French feudal hierarchy. In 1327 the seigniory was elevated to the rank of duchy. Its urban development, which began later than in the surrounding areas, took place primarily in the borough of Moulins, a provincial centre of trade and the administrative seat of the ducal court.

The house of B., usually refers to a branch of *Capetian princes who reigned in France from 1589. But in a more exact sense, the house constituted several families which succeeded one another, until it was transferred by marriage to the *Capetian princes.

a) The first house of B. was that of the lords of B.-Archambault and was founded by Aymard in the last years of the 9th century. Like many of the great nobles of France, his ancestry is unknown; through the analysis of his name it seems that he was originally from Aquitaine, where the name Aymar, Aymard and Adhémar is common. Through services rendered to the viscounts of Bourges, the feudal lords of the province, he was granted the seigniory, where he and his successors established themselves. In the 10th century, Archambault of B., having sworn homage to King *Lothair, became a direct vassal of the king of France. The first house of B. lasted until the end of the 12th century; after its extinction, Guy of Dampierre, one of the faithful vassals of *Philip II Augustus, inherited the seignory by marriage.

b) The second house of B. was founded by Guy of Dampierre in 1198. He and his son, Archambault, took part in the royal campaigns in Auvergne and governed that country on behalf of the crown. Under the Dampierre branch the seigniory prospered and its lords became members of the highest aristocracy of France, marrying their daughters off to the sons of the most important barons, such as the dukes of Burgundy. In 1258, Odo of Burgundy became the titular lord of B., and the seigniory was ruled by his brother, John. At John's death in 1267, it was inherited by his daughter Beatrix and transferred to *Robert of Clermont, son of King Louis IX upon their marriage in 1276.

c) The third house of B. was a royal one. It began with Beatrix's marriage to Robert of Clermont. Their son, *Louis I was made duke of B. in 1327 and his descendants continued to inherit the duchy until the end of the Middle Ages (see genealogical list).

F. Lot, R. Fawtier, *Histoire des Institutions Françaises au Moyen Age, Institutions seigneuriales* (1957).

BOURGES City in central France, capital of the province of *Berry. The ancient Roman city was surrounded by walls, part of which are still preserved in the medieval buildings at its centre. At the beginning of the 5th century it was conquered by the *Visigoths and annexed to their kingdom, but the actual rulers were the archbishops of B., who inherited the Roman administration. Their regime continued after 507, when the *Franks, led by *Clovis, conquered the city and it lasted until the end of the 8th century. In 782 B. was transferred to the kingdom of Aquitaine, established by *Charlemagne on behalf of his youngest son, *Louis the Pious. There it remained until 856, when *Charles the Bald annexed it to the kingdom of France. During the period of the *Norman invasions, Charles appointed local counts to defend B. from attacks and in 871, he gave the city and its country to his brother-in-law, *Boso. In 878 the Normans sacked the town, and destroyed much of it. Towards the end of the 9th century, a family of viscounts settled there and began to reconstruct its ruins. The last of the viscounts, Eudes-Harpin, sold it to King *Philip I of France, in order to finance his Crusade, and the city was annexed to the royal demesne. In the 12th century the walls were rebuilt and the city began to prosper as a centre of commercial activity in central France. The kings and archbishops beautified it and a cathedral, one of the masterpieces of Gothic architecture, was built there in the course of the 13th-15th centuries. Under the rule of John, duke of *Berry (1360-1418), the city reached the height of prosperity and many of the richest burghers of France settled there seeking peace and shelter from turbulent Paris. They built houses in the Flamboyant Gothic style.

L. Raynal, *Bourges et ses antiquités* (1899).

BOUVINES, BATTLE OF (1214) The decisive battle in the war between the French army of *Philip II Augustus and the English army of *John Lackland which had begun in Normandy in 1202. It also marked the end of the dispute between *Frederick II of Hohenstaufen and *Otto IV of Brunswick over the imperial crown, the latter having lost. The French, utilized their topographical position in the field, situated in Flanders, to better advantage. Their victory allowed them to finalize the conquests of Normandy, Anjou and Touraine, and created domestic difficulties for John in England, so that upon his return home he was confronted with a rebellion by the barons and was compelled to issue the *Magna Carta in 1215. As to the competition for the imperial crown, John's nephew, Otto of Brunswick, was dethroned, while Phillip's ally, Frederick II, who had come from Sicily to inherit his father's position (1212), became emperor, thus renewing German dependence on Italian politics.

G. Duby, *Le Dimanche de Bouvines* (1973).

BOVARIUS (Bouvier) Technically, the word means "ox-driver". From the 10th century on, with the growing importance of the plough in the feudal manor in western Europe, the ploughmen and the B. became men of key positions in the village communities. The custom in the 12th century of keeping the plough-teams in the lord's reserve, and allocating them to the peasants in return for boon works and other payments, made the B. one of the most important servants in the lord's farm as well as one of the more distinguished members of the peasants community on the manor.

G. Duby, *Rural Economy and Coutry Life in the Medieval West* (1968).

BRABANT Province in the centre of Belgium. It constituted a duchy in the *Holy Roman empire. B. is first mentioned as a separate entity in a document of 870, dealing with the fate of the kingdom of *Lothair II as a province (*pagus*). When the duchy of Lower Lotharingia was established in the 10th century, B. became part of it. It was thus ruled by the counts of *Louvain who acquired all its territories in the 11th century and annexed the port of *Antwerp in the west and the county of Limburg in the east in the 12th century. In 1106 the Emperor *Henry V made Godfrey of Louvain duke of Lower Lotharingia, but this term was an anachronism since Lower Lotharingia had ceased to exist in the 11th century, and the autonomous counties did not recognize the authority of the house of Louvain. Therefore the title was eventually changed into the duchy of B. In the 12th century B. knew economic prosperity as a result of the development of towns such as Brussels, Louvain and Antwerp, where the textile industry became the main source of wealth. The house of Louvain ruled B. until 1355, and at the death of John III, the duchy was inherited by his daughter Joan, who was married to Wenceslas, duke of Luxemburg, the youngest brother of Emperor *Charles IV. They granted broad privileges to the Assembly of the Estates, including the right to set taxes and offer grants. The Assembly was composed of the high clergy, the nobility and the representatives of the cities. It met near the ducal palace at Brussels. The ducal couple tried to have the inhabitants of their country fill the public offices. Nevertheless, knights continued to serve in the hired armies of the western kingdoms, just as they had done since the 12th century, and for many centuries the word Brabançon was synonymous with mercenary. At the same time the governing of the city shifted to the local oligarchies of the textile guilds (La guilde de la Draperie), which included the produces and the merchants. After Wenceslas died without leaving any descendants in 1388, B. became the property of a branch of the house of *Burgundy. In 1430, the main branch of the family inherited the duchy and made it the centre of its power in the Low States. From the end of the 14th century, the history and civilization of B. having reached its peak in the 15th century, was intermingled with that of *Burgundy. Its Assembly of the Estates continued its influence in the 15th century compelling every new duke to make a festive "entry" at Brussels, where he was forced to swear his loyalty to the charter of 1355. The Assembly survived until modern times.
M. Martens, *L'administration du domaine ducal en Brabant au Moyen Age* (1954).

BRACTON, HENRY OF (d. 1268) English legal writer. B., who was originally from a family of the lower nobility in England, was appointed judge in 1245. He served in the royal high court, where he was an itinerant *justiciary, mainly in the southwestern counties of England. In 1267, he was made a member of a committee of bishops, nobles and judges, which was appointed to hear the complaints of the supporters of Simon of *Montfort, whose estates had been confiscated after the repression of his rebellion. Between 1250-58 B. wrote *De Legibus et Consuetudinibus Angliae* (On the Laws and Customs of England), a work which has assured him fame through the centuries and which justified his being called the "Father of the Common Law of England"

The treatise is divided into five parts, and deals with all the problems facing the English jurisdiction of his time. Although influenced by Roman Law, especially by the school of Bologna, B. proves his perfect knowledge of feudal law and of local English customs, dating from the Anglo-Saxon period throughout the *Norman conquest. His book is a primary source for the constitutional history of medieval England and for the history of English law. It also became a manual of precedents which was taken into account in the English courts in the Middle Ages and was in use until the 18th century.
B. Lyon, *A Constitutional and Legal History of Medieval England* (1960).

BRADWARDINE, THOMAS (1290-1349) Archbishop of Canterbury (1349). Born at Chichester, he was educated at Oxford and in 1335 became chaplain to Richard of Bury, bishop of Durham. This position enabled him to come into contact with the highest authorities in England, and in 1337 he became confessor to *Edward III, whom he accompanied on his travels in France. In 1346 he was one of the commissioners who tried to establish peace between England, France and Scotland. A few months after his consecration as archbishop of Canterbury, he died of the *Black Death. B. was held in great esteem by his generation for his learning, especially in mathematics and theology. His theological works were based on determinism, and he paved the way for Nicholas of Autrecourt's and John *Wycliffe's concept of predestination. In mathematics he used arithmetic, in speculative geometry and in proportions.
S. Hahn, *Thomas Bradwardine und seine Lehre von der menschlichen Willenfreiheit* (1905).

BRAGA City in Portugal. An ancient Roman colony, B. declined under the rule of the *Suevi and the *Visigoths at the beginning of the Middle Ages. In 712 it was conquered by the Arabs, and became part of the caliphate of *Córdoba. In 1040 it was reconquered by the Castilian army and became a county within the kingdom of León, which together with the county of Oporto, became the kingdom of Portugal in 1130 and B. was made its first capital.

BRANDENBURG March and principality in Germany, situated between the Elbe and Oder Rivers. Its original inhabitants were the Germanic tribe of the Semnones, mentioned in Roman sources up to the 2nd century AD. It is probable that, mixed with other tribes, these migrated to the Rhine and Danube boundaries in the 3rd-5th centuries. Their place was occupied by Slavs, among whom the *Wends were the dominant tribe, maintaining their independence until the 10th century, the beginning of the era of German expansion eastwards. The Wends established their capital in the little town of Branibor (after which B. is named), where a small fair brought the Slavs and German merchants together. In 983, from this centre, the Wends succeeded in restoring the independence they had lost, but the northwestern part of their country remained under German rule and *Otto II established a feudal county there, related to the duchy of Saxony, known as the Nordmark (the Northern March). In 1134 the Emperor *Lothair of Supplinburg gave the March to one of his relatives, *Albert the Bear of the Ascanian family. Albert founded the dynasty of B. which ruled until 1320. Under the Ascanians, the Nordmark expanded eastward; Albert himself began a series of wars against the Wends and during the 12th century the Ascanians reached the Oder. In 1170 the Wends were either massacred or became assimilitated into the new German settlements in the country. Branibor underwent a complete ethnical change and was renamed B. The defeat of *Henry the Lion, duke of Saxony and Bavaria, by *Frederick Barbarossa, also left its impact on the evolution of B. Its margraves were freed from the lordship of their powerful neighbours and instead, were made vassals of the emperor, thus becoming "princes of the empire" (see *Germany and *Holy Roman empire). Their power and influence continued to grow in the 13th century and, during the *Interregnum (1254-72), when the college of seven princes (empowered to elect the emperor and therefore called electors) was constituted, the margrave of B. was among them. With the foundation of the new city of *Berlin, the eastern part of B. was colonized by German settlers and by the end of the 13th century, the last Slav tribes were assimilated and the Germanization of the country was completed. With the extinction of the Ascanians in 1320, Emperor *Louis of Bavaria appointed his son Louis of *Wittelsbach margrave of B. His rule was troubled; being a stranger to the country, he found himself in conflict with the local nobility and at war with the neighbouring princes. Their interference in the relations between the Baltic states made the Wittelsbach princes of B. dependent upon the nobles. During the 14th century, B. was in a state of turmoil, which reduced it to devastation and civil war. In 1373, Otto of Wittelsbach tried to rule B. from 1351 but had to hand over the government to the emperor for six years in 1365 when he was compelled by *Charles IV to abdicate. He was allowed to maintain his title during his life-time. Charles granted B. to his younger son, *Sigismund of Luxemburg, who succeeded in bringing order to the country with his father's support. The government of Sigismund (1378-1411) marked a period of restoration of order and prosperity to the country, but at the same time, B. became a province in the vast semi-German, semi-Slav conglomerate of the estates of the house of Luxemburg. Its interests became secondary to those of the central lands of the dynasty, such as Bohemia and Hungary, particularly after Sigismund's election to the Hungarian throne in 1401. When Sigismund became emperor in 1411, he granted B. to his friend, the burgrave of Nuremberg, *Frederick of Hohenzollern.

H. Bauer, *Die Mark Brandenburg* (1954).

BRANIMIR (9th century) Duke of the Croats. Descendant of the family of *Borna, he succeeded in uniting the Croats under his rule and promoted the dissemination of Christianity. He continued the conquest of Dalmatia from the Byzantines, where he fought against the archbishops of Spalato (Split), who remained faithful to Byzantium. In order to overcome their opposition, he sent a delegation to Rome in 879 to negotiate the adoption of the Catholic faith. A long discussion concerning the language of the liturgy – the Croats wishing to maintain the Slavonic while the papacy required the introduction of Latin – prevented him from obtaining immediate results. B. is considered the father of Catholicism in Croatia and the eventual consequence of his conversion was the religious breach between the Croats and Serbs.

BRAULIO (6th-7th centuries) Bishop of Saragossa (c. 630). Of noble origin, he was a pupil of *Isidore of Seville and became bishop of Saragossa as a result of the intervention of Julian, archbishop of Toledo, who wished to raise the prestige of the bishops in the *Visigothic kingdom. B. is known as one of Isadore's closest collaborators and he prepared the final version of some of his works. His introduction to the works of Isidore is not only a testimony of B.'s vast culture, but also an important statement on the cultural activities of the Spanish clergy in the 7th century. His commentaries on Isidore's *Etymologies* are of particular importance since Isidore did not finish this work, and B., who divided it into 20 parts, explained several possibly confusing passages.

J. Fontaine, *Isidore de Séville et la culture classique dans l'Espagne wisigothique* (1959).

BREISGAU County in southwestern Germany. The area was part of the realm of the *Allemanni in the 4th-5th centuries and was annexed to the kingdom of the *Franks by *Clovis in 497. In the 10th century B. became a county within the duchy of *Swabia and was given to the family of *Zähringen, which turned it into one of the bases of its power in feudal Germany of the 12th-13th centuries. The ruins of their feudal castle, which dominated the entire region, testify to the family's power. Under Zähringen rule, the county developed, and a new town, Freiburg, which still retains its original character, was built. In 1272, *Rudolf of Hapsburg annexed B. and the county became a large estate during the dynasty. It remained part of the Hapsburg estates until 1801.

K. S. Bader, *Der deutsche Südwesten in seiner territorialstaatlichen Entwicklung* (1950).

BREMEN City in northern Germany, at the beginning of the estuary of the Weser River. The territory was part of the Saxon state in the 8th century and was conquered by *Charlemagne and the *Franks before 787, at which time Charlemagne established a bishopric there. In the 9th century, B. served as a religious centre for the north, and its bishop *Anskar led a Catholic mission to the Scandinavian countries. In 845 the bishopric of B. was raised to the rank of archbishopric, as befitting the "Metropolis of the North", In 967 *Otto I invested the archbishop with the county of B., thus creating an ecclesiastic principality in the heart of the duchy of *Saxony. At the same time, the papal court defined the jurisdiction of the archbishop, to include Denmark, Sweden, Norway and Iceland, and later extended it to include Greenland. The spiritual authority granted the archbishops of B. also lent them strong political influence within the *Holy Roman empire. The city itself, which had not been of major importance between the 8th and 10th centuries, began to develop as a commercial centre in the middle of the 10th century. In 965, a market was established in the 11th century and the harbour began to develop. The 12th century marks one of the most important periods of B.'s evolution. The creation of national archbishoprics in the Scandinavian countries deprived the city of its importance as a spiritual centre, but the development of its maritime trade in the North and Baltic seas promoted the rise of a merchant class which, conscious of its power, struggled for its liberties with the archbishops, whose power had begun to decline. In 1186 *Frederick Barbarossa granted the city certain economic privileges and allowed the burghers to form their own municipal institutions. This was the first step towards the independence of the city, a process which culminated in the 13th century when the archbishops were compelled to give up their temporal rule in the city and content themselves with the lordship of the rural surroundings. In 1276 B. joined the *Hanse and became one of the principal cities of its western group. As a free city, it was governed by the aristocratic guild of the sea merchants, who kept the other city corporations out of the council. Their rule, however, led to the rise of opposition, and in 1285 a democratic revolution brought about a new regime. A new constitution granted participation in the council to all merchants and craftsmen. The Hanse reacted emphatically and B. was excluded from the confederation, thus hurting its commerce. But attempts to restore the aristocratic government failed until 1358, when disputes between the guilds allowed the "patricians" to seize power and to change the constitution. The city was again made a member of the Hanse and its trade prospered. The centre was rebuilt and substantial Gothic buildings attest to its prosperity. Internal troubles continued, however, and several generations later the "democratic" guilds again fought to obtain their rights. In 1427 they succeeded in seizing power and B. was again excluded from the Hanse until 1433, when the aristocratic party returned to the government. In the 15th century the city expanded, new quarters were added on and a new city wall was built. Artists were called from abroad to work on monuments and public buildings, among them the city-hall built in the Late Gothic style. An interesting statue was erected in the market and dedicated to a German version of the knight *Roland, the hero of the Charlemagne epic.

H. Tiedemann, *Abriss der Geschichte Bremens* (1954).

BRESCIA City in northern Italy on the road between the Brenner Pass and Lombardy. The Roman city of Brixia was destroyed by the *Huns in 452. The little town named B., rebuilt on its site in the 7th century, served as the centre of a *Lombard principality, which was converted into a county during the *Frankish rule (9th century). In the 12th century, B. joined the Lombard league and played an active part in the political events of northern Italy, including the struggle against *Frederick Barbarossa, But in the 13th century, when the league dissolved and its great cities fought amongst themselves for supremacy, B. became a second rate city, fighting merely to maintain its independence. From 1258 on, *Verona and *Milan, B.'s powerful neighbours, strove to obtain overlordship and in 1426 B. was conquered by *Venice and became part of its empire. Its political decline in the last centuries of the Middle Ages was in some measure compensated for by economic expansion, especially in the crafts, such as silk production and glass-works, as an important part of B.'s trade was based on the exportation of these goods. In the 15th century, B. also became a centre of the arts, due mainly to the establishment of its famous school of painting, which earned great fame during the Renaissance.

Bettoni-Cazzago, *Storia di Brescia* (1909).

BRESLAU (Wroclav) City in the *Holy Roman empire, capital of *Silesia. The site was populated from ancient times, but there is no evidence as to the identity of the original inhabitants. In the 8th century, Slavic tribes settled on the site, and at the end of the 9th century,

a castle named Wrotitzla was built there and became the centre of the new town which was founded under the rule of the dukes of *Bohemia. *Boleslaw I Chrobri conquered it at the end of the 10th century and annexed it to *Poland, to which it belonged until the middle of the 12th century, being one of the cities of the royal demesne of the *Piast dynasty. In 1139, *Boleslaw II, in his famous partition of the realm, assigned B. to his elder son Ladislav. When Ladislav was dethroned in 1146 by his brother *Boleslaw IV, he requested help from *Frederick Barbarossa, who, in 1157, compelled the Polish king to surrender Silesia and the city of Wroclav. Frederick granted the city to Ladislav's sons, and they founded a Piast principality under the lordship of the emperors. But in the 12th century, the city had already lost its Polish character and it became a German city. Its Slavic name was changed into the German B. During the 13th century, German colonization spread and the city became a commercial and industrial centre on the Upper Oder. In 1241 the *Mongols conquered it and burned its old wooden houses, but soon after their retreat, the city was rebuilt and its prosperity rapidly restored. In 1261, B. was granted the *Magdeburg charter of liberties, which allowed its burghers to form a municipal council and to enjoy self-government. When B. joined the *Hanse in 1294 its trade flourished as it linked the Baltic Sea with eastern Europe. After the death of the last of the Piast princes of Silesia, the city was annexed to the kingdom of *Bohemia in 1335 by *Charles IV, who furthered its development. The centre of the city was entirely reconstructed by the Luxemburg kings of Bohemia. Only the 13th-century cathedral remained as a monument of the earlier period. The new city-hall, built during the 14th-15th centuries, is a fine example of late German Gothic architecture.

F. Landsberger, *Breslau* (1925).

BRETAGNE See BRITTANY.

BRETHREN OF THE COMMON LIFE An association founded in the 14th century by Gerard de *Groote (d. 1384) to foster a higher level of Christian life and devotion. He preached against clerical abuses and called people to repentance. The B. were not asked to take any particular vow. They laid great stress on teaching, and they founded schools throughout the Low Countries, the Rhineland and north Germany. They engaged in the copying of manuscripts and, in the second half of the 15th century, in printing, in order to supply books for their schools. Thomas à Kempis, Pope Adrian VI and Gustav Biel were among their members and one of their famous students was Nicholas of Cusa.

A. Hyma, *The Christian Renaissance* (1925).

BRETHREN OF THE FREE SPIRIT A mystic movement within the Catholic Church, which appeared in France and the Netherlands in the middle of the 13th century, and whose members professed to be independent of ecclesiastic authority and to live in accordance with the free spirit of piety. Some of their opponents in the Catholic hierarchy attacked them as a heretical sect, but it seems difficult to describe them as such because of their individualism. Their appearance and teachings were a manifestation of nonconformism which preceded the greater and more important protest movements, such as that of *Wycliffe and his followers, and some of the *Hussites.

R. E. Lerner, *The Heresy of the Free Spirit* (1972).

BRETIGNY, TREATY OF (1360) The B. marked the end of the first stage of the *Hundred Years' War, after the French defeats at *Crécy and *Poitiers. It was negotiated by the representatives of England and France when the two kingdoms were exhausted by their war efforts and the consequences of the *Black Death. While the representatives of *Edward III tried to exploit the English victories and the captivity of King *John II the Good of France, the representatives of the dauphin (*Charles V), attempted to obtain the best possible conditions for France, having already denounced the Treaty of London, negotiated by John in prison. The final agreement, concluded in May 1360 and ratified at *Calais in October, stipulated Edward's renunciation of his claims to the French throne, but it recognized his full and free ownership of *Aquitaine, as well as the districts of Ponthieu, Guines, Montreuil and the city of Calais in the north. The ransom for King John was established at 3,000,000 Crowns.

E. Perroy, *The Hundred Years' War* (1965).

BREVIARY (Latin: breviarium "abridgment") Since the Middle Ages the term had been used in its liturgical sense, meaning the book of prayers selected to be recited in the Divine Service of the Catholic Church. The original service consisted almost exclusively of Psalms and Scriptural lessons. In the 6th century, the Hymns of St. *Ambrose and of St. *Benedict were added to the service, which was divided into daily prayers, and Sunday and festival (primarily Easter) prayers. In the 8th century, the cycle of hours was introduced and the B. came to include the Matins recited in the midnight service, the Compline for the day service and the Vespers, for the evening prayers. In several Bs. of the later Middle Ages, excerpts from the Lives of Saints were also introduced.

EC, III.

BREVIARY OF ALARIC The name was given to Theodosius II's abridged code of Roman Law, which was written in the *Visigothic kingdom in the 6th century and originally titled *Lex Romana Visigothorum* (The Roman Law of the Visigoths). The code officially promulgated by *Alaric II in 506 at the Council of *Agde and thereafter known as *Breviarium Alarici*. The B. contained several imperial edicts and a number of civil legal precepts, and its use spread rapidly in all the western provinces of the Roman empire. It was used to determine the legal status of the "Roman" population, including all elements not of Germanic origin, and also contained certain laws prohibiting marriage between Romans and non-Romans, and especially between Christians and Jews.

F. Lot, *The End of the Ancient World and the Beginning of the Middle Ages* (1951).

BRIDGET, St. (of Sweden) See BIRGITTA, St.

BRIENNE County in Champagne, eastern France. B. was founded in the 9th century, when the *Merovingian *pagus* (area) of Brenois, was divided into several feudal units. Its beginning can be traced back to 853, when it was ruled by a feudal family which received a number of *benefices from *Charles the Bald. In the 10th and 11th centuries, the counts of B. lost much of their power and, although they preserved their title, fell under the lordship of the counts of Troyes, becoming their vassals. In the 12th century, the counts of B., whose castle was near Troyes, succeeded in imposing their rule on estates

which had been lost by their ancestors in the 10th century. They obtained additional power as vassals of the counts of *Champagne, whom they accompanied to the *Crusades. Their participation in the Crusades brought the family great fame. *John of B. (1148-1237) became king of Jerusalem in 1210, and reigned at Acre until 1225. In 1231 he became emperor of Constantinople. In the 14th century, other members of the family, *Walter V and Walter VI, became dukes of Athens.

F. Lot, R. Fawtier, *Histoire des Institutions Françaises au Moyen Age: Institutions seigneuriales* (1957).

BRIGITTINE ORDER Monastic order of the Salvation, founded in 1346 by St. *Birgitta of Sweden. Its innovation lay in the existence of twin communities of women and men, who used the same chapel and lived in separate wings of the same monastery. Although the members of the order, like all religious orders, were required to live a life of denial, they were allowed to possess a number of books for study. In the second part of the 14th century and the beginning of the 15th, they spread out into western Europe and established additional monasteries in Scandinavia, Germany, England, the Netherlands, Italy and Spain.

B. Williamson, *The Brigittine Order* (1922).

BRINDISI Port in *Apulia in southern Italy. Situated at the southern end of the Roman *via Appia*, B. was a prosperous harbour in the 5th and 6th centuries, when it fell under Byzantine rule. Its maritime relations with Greece and Constantinople were uninterrupted until the 9th century, when it was attacked and destroyed by the Arabs in 839. It practically ceased to exist until the beginning of the 11th century, when the Byzantines rebuilt it. In 1071, *Robert Guiscard conquered it and the city became part of the *Norman duchy of Apulia. The *Crusades had a great impact on its growth and prosperity, and its port served as one of the Crusaders' points of embarkation in the 12th century, second only to *Bari. The prosperity of the city is also reflected in its 12th-century Romanesque churches, which were influenced by the Byzantine style and are richly ornamented. When the kingdom of *Sicily was founded at the end of the 11th century, B. became part of it, and, in 1282, when the *Angevins returned to the Continent and founded the kingdom of *Naples, B. became one of its important cities. In 1456, B. was destroyed by an earthquake.

F. Ascoli, *Storia di Brindisi* (1936).

BRITTANY Province in northwestern France, the bulk of which is a peninsula between the English Channel and the Gulf of Biscay. Originally it was the Gallo-Roman country of Armorica, but as a result of the immigration of Celtic Britons who had been expelled from Britain by the *Anglo-Saxons in the 6th century, the name was changed to B. or *Britannia Minor* ('The Lesser B.'). The great forest which, at the beginning of the Middle Ages, covered the territory of Maine, east of B., isolated the Britons from the *Franks and allowed them to retain their customs, preserve their own language, and develop their own Christian traditions. Between the 6th and the 8th century, the story of their migration and settlement acquired a legendary form, as expressed in the Latin *Life of St. *Samson*. In this period, only the church united the various clans which continued to be ruled by their own chieftains. Gradually, one of the dynasties, the lords of the northeastern area of Dol, which was the

Page from an illuminated Catalan 15th-century breviary

site of St. Samson's activities, acquired a certain influence over the other chieftains, and by the end of the 8th century, became the rulers of the entire country. They succeeded in maintaining their independence against *Charlemagne, who failed to conquer B. Under the leadership of *Roland, Charlemagne established the March of B., which also included a small area near Nantes conquered from the Britons. Although they officially accepted Charlemagne as overlord, the Britons limited their relations with the *Carolingian court to external expressions of loyalty, which had little effect on their daily lives.

In the 9th century, B. reached the zenith of its power. Prompted to action by the invasions of the *Normans, in 826, the Britons elected the count of Vannes, *Nominoë, as their duke. He organized the defence of the country and took the royal title. In 840 he fought against *Charles the Bald, whom he finally defeated at Ballon in 845. By the time of his death in 851, he had conquered the counties of Nantes and Vendôme, having thus annexed a great part of the Frankish *Neustria. His son, Erispoë (851-66) completed his father's conquests and was formally recognized as duke of Vendôme. Under his successor, Salomon, the western part of what was later to be *Normandy was attached to the state, but the eastward advancement of the Britons was stopped by *Robert the Strong, count of Tours and duke of the Franks. During the 9th century, the kings of B. established the boundaries of the country, which included the counties of Nantes and Rennes, the latter becoming the state's capital. But the great efforts required to fight both Normans and Franks were too heavy a burden for the Britons who were not men of war. Further Norman invasions in the 11th century caused the collapse of the realm and the fall of the dynasty of Nominoë. The counts of Rennes became dukes of B., renouncing all expansionist policy and even became vassals of the dukes of Normandy. Nonetheless, when *William the Conqueror tried to realize his suzerainty by an invasion of B. in 1085, Duke Alan Ferjean succeeded in preventing the country's conquest. In the 12th century, internal conflicts became common to B. A rift was created between the eastern counties of Rennes and Nantes, where French ethnical and cultural influence was dominant, and the "Cornish" counties of the peninsula, where the Celtic traditions remained pure. In addition, the rivalry between the houses of Rennes and Nantes led to civil wars, which weakened the duchy. The dukes were forced to seek foreign aid and in 1165, Duke Conan IV turned to *Henry II Plantagenet and, in order to obtain the help of the king of England, swore him homage and married his daughter, heiress to Henry's son, Geoffrey, who was proclaimed heir of the duchy. In 1171, at Conan's death, Geoffrey became duke of B. and the country was included in the vast *Angevin empire. When Geoffrey died in 1196, his son *Arthur, named after the legendary King Arthur, became duke, and in 1199 was declared candidate for the English throne by a part of the nobility who sustained his right over his uncle *John Lackland. The hostility between them brought about the intervention of *Philip II, king of France, in B.'s affairs. The murder of Arthur by John in 1203, brought a new dynasty to power when the ducal title passed to the *Capetian prince, Peter of Dreux, through his marriage to Arthur's sister, Alix.

The second half of the 12th century, particularly after the Angevin intervention, was a period of economic prosperity for B. Naval activities, in ship-building, maritime trade, and in fisheries, were developed and led to the growth of the harbours. Demographic development led to land reclamation and to the founding of new agrarian settlements. In 1171, when the Assize of Geoffrey was proclaimed, the social and administrative structures of the empire of Henry II, were applied in B. From the point of view of the country's development, this was a social revolution, leading to the feudalization of the duchy within an efficient administration, which began to work through the *inquest procedure. This procedure was known in Normandy and England, but was not in use in France until the 13th century. The inquests allowed the ducal officers to fix the rights and the duties of several social classes in the different counties, and granted them the right to judge the claims of free-men juries in the courts. Moreover, the nobility was included in the administrative system, which prevented a recurrence of troubles of the previous regime and directed the nobles' energy to the service of the ducal court.

In this respect, no radical changes were made upon the accession of the Dreux dynasty to the ducal rule, where an immediate succession saved the country from dynastic rivalry until 1341. The influence of French culture, introduced in the 12th century by bishops such as *Marbodius and Stephen of Fougères at Rennes, continued and grew; the Celtic population became considered "barbarian" and French became the language of the ducal court, of the nobility and of the notables (a term synonymous with gentry in England). Bishops and abbots of French origin, or Bretons who had studied in Paris, were frequently appointed to the duchy and they not only introduced French culture, but also adopted practices of the French administration. But this phenomenon ended in 1341, when John III died childless. Inheritance of the duchy was then disputed between the houses of Montfort and Penthièvre, relatives of the Dreux. The *Hundred Years' War complicated the issue, the pretenders to the ducal role having requested the help of the kings of England and of France; thus, John of Montfort was protected by *Edward III, while Charles of Blois, the husband of Joan of Penthièvre, obtained the support of *Philip VI. The dynastic wars lasted until 1365, when an agreement between the two branches assigned the duchy to the house of Montfort, which governed until the end of the dynasty in 1491. The dukes were loyal to the French crown and under *Charles V B. supplied France with knights and generals, the most famous of them being Bertrand *Du Guesclin. The government adopted new French practices, such as the Estates General, when the ducal council became the government of the country and the cities were allowed to participate in the councils' deliberations. The judiciary was reorganized into two different sections, the French and the Celtic (Briton). In 1414 a university was founded at Nantes and was transferred at the beginning of the 16th century to Rennes.

E. Durtelle de Saint-Sauveur, *Histoire de Bretagne* (1946).

BROEDERLAM, MELCHIOR (c. 1328-1410) Painter. Born at Ypres, he studied with French and Italian masters, but gradually adopted his own style and is considered the father of the Flemish school. He painted for the last counts of Flanders and was appointed ducal painter by Philip the Good, duke of *Burgundy. His masterpiece is the collection of paintings of the Champnol Abbey, part of which are preserved at the Museum of Dijon. The figures are naturalistic, and are of an entirely different style than the French miniaturists. The special use of colours, as is characteristic of Flemish painting, marked new trends in art.

J. Lassagne, *La Peinture Flamande* (1957).

BROWN, THOMAS (12th century) Official of the *Exchequer. Born in England, before 1120, into a Norman family of burghers, he chose an ecclesiastical career and was employed as a cleric in the administration of the *Exchequer. In the middle of the century, he went to Sicily where he was employed at the court of King *Roger II as administrator of finances. He helped to transform the Byzantine and Arab offices of the Treasury into an organization similar to the Anglo-Norman Exchequer. He reached the position of proto-notary, corresponding to the highest official rank in the Byzantine hierarchy. He returned to England around 1160 and was reinstated by *Henry II in the administration of the Exchequer serving as almoner. He gained the king's confidence and acquired general esteem for his skills. It is reported that he died soon after 1175.

A. L. Poole, *From Domesday Book to Magna Charta* (*England in the 12th Century*) (1955).

BRUCE Scottish family of Norman origin. Its founder, Robert Brus, was a Norman knight, who followed *William the Conqueror to England in 1066 and, after the conquest, was granted estates in the northern provinces of the kingdom. His son, also named Robert, settled in Scotland during the reign of *David I (1124-53) and was given vast estates in the county of Dumfries in southwestern Scotland. His descendants increased their power and influence and, by the end of the 13th century, became one of the most important families in the kingdom. While Robert VI B. tried, unsuccessfully to seize the royal power in 1290, his descendants, *David and *Robert reigned in Scotland in the 14th century. Robert, who defeated the English army of *Edward II at Bannockburn in 1314 is considered the national hero of Scotland.

A. M. Mackenzie, *Robert Bruce, King of Scots* (1934).

BRUGES City in Flanders. In the 7th century, the *Franks built a fortress on the site of the city, later named *Municipium Brugense*, which from the 9th century on served as one of the castles of the counts of *Flanders. The *borough, which was an extension of the first settlement around the castle, gained importance in 867, when Count Baldwin II built its walls. Commercial activity was expanded beginning in the 10th century, when its harbour became one of the most important in the North Sea. In the 11th century, B. served as one of the main centres of the English wool trade with the Continent and the development of this trade led to the establishment of the textile industry in the city. From the beginning of the 12th century, B. also became an important trade centre between the Middle East and northern Europe, and many Italian merchants settled in the city. The counts of Flanders, who encouraged its development, granted its merchants broad privileges, and in 1190 the city was allowed to establish its own municipal institutions. Its freedoms were extended during the 13th century, when the merchants,

The Presentation at the Temple *by Broederlam*

who were the leading force in the "Flemish Hanse", seized power in the city. In 1240, the "Flemish Hanse" obtained trade privileges at London and in addition to being an economic power, became an important political organization. The city flourished and reached the peak of its prosperity, monopolizing the international trade. Towards the end of the 13th century it was named "Venice of the North" and maintained close relations with the German *Hanse and the Italian cities. But the patrician government of the merchants was opposed by the "democratic" guilds of the craftsmen, who felt themselves oppressed, and at the beginning of the 14th century, problems were widespread at B. In order to avoid a revolution, the patricians allied themselves with *Philip IV the Fair, king of France, and surrendered the city to him in 1301. However, the royal policy in Flanders caused the craftsmen to revolt and on 18 May 1302 (*Matins of Bruges) 4000 French soldiers were killed. Although the French did not recover their position at B., the agitation continued even after a compromise was reached allowing both merchants and craftsmen to govern the city. The prosperity which continued until the beginning of the *Hundred Years' War contributed to a certain degree of concord between local leaders, and during this period much urban construction was

The Town Hall of Bruges built in the 14th century in the Gothic style

undertaken. The most important of these projects was the design of the city market, with its Gothic square, municipal tower and city hall.

The beginning of the Hundred Years' War marked the decline of B. The ordinance of *Edward III, which forbade the exportation of wool to Flanders and established the staple of *Antwerp, led to the revolt of the Flemish cities, but the leadership and initiative came from Ghent, where *Artevelde organized the rebellion. The decline of B. gradually led to the prosperity of Antwerp in the 15th century; in 1488, the foreign merchants left B. to settle there.

M. Letts, *Bruges and its Past* (1926).

BRUNHILDA (548-613) Frankish queen. Daughter of *Athanagild, king of the Visigoths she was married to *Sigebert I, king of the Austrasian *Franks in 567. She induced him to fight against *Chilperic I, king of *Neustria, whose mistress, *Fredegund, she accused of the murder of her sister, queen of Neustria. After the murder of Sigebert in 574, B. continued the war against Fredegund and her party, and she succeeded in ruling Austrasia on behalf of her son and grandson until 613. She fought against the nobility in order to impose royal power, but in 613, her guard revolted and allied with *Clotaire II, Fredegund's son, and B. was killed.

F. Lot, *Naissance de la France* (1952).

BRUNO, St. (925-65) Archbishop of Cologne (953-65). He was the youngest son of *Henry I, king of Germany and was prepared by his father for the church. In 941 he was ordained deacon and appointed abbot of the monasteries of Lorsch and Corvey by his brother *Otto I. Despite his youth, he proceeded energetically to reform his abbeys and organized their schools, where he trained the future clerks of the imperial court. In 950, his brother appointed him archchancellor and he became Otto's closest associate and political adviser. In 953 he was appointed archbishop of Cologne and secured overwhelming influence for himself in ancient Lotharingia. As archchancellor for Italy, he prepared Otto's imperial coronation in 962. B. was an important statesman, aiming at the political and spiritual renewal of the empire of *Charlemagne. With the help of his sisters who were married to *Lothair, king of France, and to Duke *Hugh the Great, he intervened in French politics, maintaining the pre-eminence of the emperor, whose policy he supported. He was the patron of learning in the new empire and is considered the father of the Ottonian Renaissance. At his death, he was venerated as a saint, and honoured as a German patriot.

H. Schrörs, *Erzbischop Bruno von Köln* (1917).

BRUNO, St. (1032-1101) The founder of the *Carthusian order. Born at Cologne, Germany, he was educated in his native city and at Rheims. After being canon at Cologne, he was appointed *scholasticus* (master of the school) of the cathedral-school of Rheims, one of the most important institutions of learning in his time. The future Pope *Urban II was among his pupils at Rheims. After a long dispute with Archbishop Manasses, B. left Rheims and became a monk at Solesme under St. *Robert (who was later to found Cîteaux). In 1084 he left Robert and, together with six other monks, founded a monastery in the desert mountains of Grenoble, under the protection of the Archbishop Hugh. Thus was the *Carthusian order founded. In 1090 he was summoned to Rome by Urban II to act as his counsel, but after a while, he decided to leave the papal court and retire to the wilderness of Calabria, where he founded the monastery of La Torre and later died.

H. Loebbel, *Der Stifter des Karthäuser-Ordens, der heilige Bruno aus Köln* (1899).

BRUNO OF LONGOBURGO (13th century)   Surgeon. He was educated at Padua in northern Italy. After several years of practice, he returned to his university and was appointed professor in its medical school, which contributed much to its fame. He wrote a treatise, *Chirurgia*, on his speciality, which became the most authoritative textbook on surgery until the 15th century. B. was aware of the problems of infections and insisted upon cleanliness and sterilization as a prerequisite for healing wounds and for performing amputations.

R. A. Leonardo, *A History of Surgery* (1942).

BRUNO OF QUERFURT, St. (974-1009)   Born at Querfurt in *Saxony into a noble family, he was educated at Magdeburg and in 995 was already a member of the chapel of *Otto III. He became one of Otto's faithful counsellors and accompanied the emperor to Rome in 997. Under the influence of *Adalbert of Prague, he left the court in 998 to become a monk. When Adalbert died while on a mission to the Prussians, B. decided to go in his place, and he obtained the approval of Pope *Sylvester II, who appointed him head of a new mission. Wars between Germany and *Boleslaw I of Poland forced him to postpone the beginning of the journey and to remain at the court of *Henry II. While waiting to start out on his mission, B. wrote the biography of St. Adalbert and of the five brethren who helped him. With the support of Prince *Vladimir of Kiev, he preached to the *Petchenegs. Disappointed with the German and Polish governments, who continued their wars, he began his mission to Prussia in 1009, but at the very beginning of their journey, he and his 18 companions were killed.

D. H. Voigt, *Bruno von Querfurt* (1907).

BRUNSWICK   City in *Saxony. Founded in 961 as a *borough on the Ocker River, it served as a small centre to the surrounding area. In the latter half of the 12th century, *Henry the Lion, duke of Saxony, built a castle in the enlarged borough, and controlled part of the trade of Westphalia. The city was granted autonomous privileges and in the 13th century it joined the *Hanse. Thus, its autonomy was reinforced and its economic prosperity gave it influence in northern Germany. Its 14th-century city hall reflects the pride of B.'s citizens, who built it in the form of a semi-castle so as to correspond to the 12th-century ducal castle. In the 15th century, B. reached the zenith of its development, when the commercial activity between the Rhine Valley and

the North and Baltic Seas flourished. At this time many of its rich burghers built themselves grand houses.

BRUNSWICK (BRAUNSCHWEIG)   Duchy in northern *Saxony. Named after the city, the duchy was created in 1180, when *Frederick Barbarossa accused *Henry the Lion of felony, had him convicted and compelled him to cede Saxony. Henry was allowed to maintain his family's estates in northern Saxony as well as the ducal title, which was officially changed to B. in 1235 when Henry's grandson Otto "the Child", was created its duke by *Frederick II. After Otto's death, the duchy was divided into several feudal principalities (1252). This division was the beginning of the duchy's decline in the later Middle Ages, in sharp contrast to the growth of the city of B.

O. Hochstein, *Geschichte des Herzogstums Braunschweig* (1908).

BRUSSELS (BRUXELLES)   City in the duchy of Brabant. Its most ancient part, the borough of Bruocsella, was founded in the 10th century and is first mentioned in a document of *Otto I concerning Lower *Lotharingia (966). At the end of the 11th century it belonged to the estates of *Godfrey of Bouillon and, after his departure to participate in the *Crusades, it became part of the county of Louvain (1096). When the counts of Louvain were given the title dukes of *Brabant in the 12th century, the centre of their power moved southward to Brussels. They built a castle near the town, on the *Coudenberg* (the site of the Place Royale in present-day Belgium), an area through which ran the trade route between Bruges and Cologne in Germany. The building of the castle, which assured peace in the area, enhanced the economic development of B. Textile industries were established and rapidly prospered. The town grew in the 13th century into an industrial and commercial centre and new quarters were built, which were called the upper city. At the same time the Gothic church of St. Gudule was built and became B.'s spiritual centre. During the 14th century the two "towns" were united and fortified by a wall, built between 1357-79. B. came to be the most important city of Brabant and, in 1383, the capital of the duchy was moved there from Louvain. The establishment of the ducal court in the city was followed by an influx of nobility and court officials who became integrated into the urban society. Nevertheless, the merchants' guild continued to rule the city, forcing each new duke to recognize its privileges before his "festive entry" into the city. Under the dukes of Burgundy, B. reached the peak of its prosperity and became the capital of the Low Countries. The craftsmen were granted representation in the local government in 1421, and the town hall, situated in the *Grande Place*, with its beautiful guild-halls, became the symbol of the city's self-government. The ducal court also gained renown as one of the country's cultural and artistic centres. It is estimated that the population of B. included 45,000 inhabitants in 1455.

M. Schmitz, *Bruxelles* (1945).

BRYENNIUS, NICEPHORUS (d. 1079)   Byzantine general. B. belonged to an established aristocratic family, whose members rose to important military positions in the 10th and 11th centuries. In the middle of the 11th century, B. was commander of the Balkan army and his influence grew during the anarchic period of the Ducas emperors (see *Byzantium). As duke of Durazzo, c. 1070, he fought against the *Normans of southern Italy. In 1072, he suppressed a revolt of the Slavs and became the most important general in the European part of the empire. Five years later, he revolted against *Michael VII Ducas and proclaimed himself emperor in his native city of Adrianople. At the same time, however, other generals from Asia Minor sought to win the imperial crown, and B. was defeated in 1078. He was killed by *Alexius Comnenus.

G. Ostrogorsky, *History of the Byzantine Empire*, (1954).

BRYENNIUS, NICEPHORUS CESAR (d. c. 1120) Historian. Son of General *Bryennius, he became reconciled with *Alexius Comnenus through the intervention of the Empress Irene, who brought him to the court. There he married Princess *Anna Comnena, the great historian. B. won the general esteem of the court as an intellectual, and particularly that of the empress, who tried in 1118 to persuade Alexius to proclaim him his heir. After the death of Alexius, his wife led a revolt against her brother, *John, in order to obtain the throne for him, but B., who lacked the courage to lead the revolt, retired from the court and the revolt failed (1118). B. is noted for his history of the early period of the House of Comnenus up to the time of Alexius, which is an important source for the Byzantine history of the 11th century.

C. Diehl, *Figures Byzantines* (1908).

BUCCELARIUS (Butcher) The term had two meanings in the Middle Ages: 1) Between the 6th and 9th century the B. was one of the officials of the royal palace in the "Barbarian" realms, charged with supplying meat to the royal table. As such, he was responsible for the administration of the herds and of the forests. The office disappeared gradually in the 9th century and records of its last traces appeared in the 11th century. 2) With the development of urban society in the 11th and 12th centuries, the B. became one of the most important guilds of the cities. It was located in specific quarters and was, therefore, involved in the local government until the end of the Middle Ages. Frequently, the guild led the democratic parties of the towns and its leaders had great influence on the populace.

CEcH, III.

BUCELIN (6th century) Duke of the *Allemanni. He emerged as one of the local leaders of the Allemanni in 536, when the territory of Rhaetia, where they lived under the protectorate of the *Ostrogoths, was conquered by the *Franks. His main achievement was the union of the Allemanni counties under his rule, which was recognized by the Franks. In 552 he fought against the Byzantines in Italy. B. established the centre of his duchy near the Lake of Constance, in southwestern Germany, where he organized an aristocratic government of heads of clans under Frankish sovereignty.

M. Lintzel, *Grundfragen der alemannischen Geschichte* (1961).

BUCELLARII Name given to the mercenaries engaged in the army of the Eastern Roman empire until the end of the 6th century. They played an important role as bodyguards under *Justinian.

BUCH, CAPTALS OF Feudal family in Gascony, whose ancestors were known as local leaders in the southwestern part of the duchy from the 11th century. The family became notorious in the 14th century, when the Captals entered the service of the kings of England as dukes of Guyenne and obtained positions of military command in the country. The most eminent among them was Jean de Grailly (d. 1369), who served in the army of *Edward, the Black Prince, and distinguished himself in the Battle of Poitiers (1358). Later on, he joined the army of *Gaston of Foix and helped to crush the rebellion of the peasants in the Parisian area (the *jacquerie). He married Rose of Albret and became related to the most prominent noble families of southern France. His wars provided him with such wealth that he became one of the richest nobles in Gascony. Upon the disappearance of the family line in the 15th century, its estates were inherited by the counts of Foix.

R. Boutruche, *La Crise d'une Société; Seigneurs et Paysans du Bordelais pendant la Guerre de Cent Ans* (1947).

BUDA City in Hungary (from 1872, part of Budapest). The city of B. was built on a hill on the eastern bank of the Danube, on the ruins of the Celtic and Roman town, Aquincum. In the 5th century, *Attila, the king of the Huns established his palace there and the town received its name, which is of Hunnish derivation. In the 6th century and until the 10th century, Slavs settled in the area. The *Hungarians arrived in the 10th century and changed the city's ethnic character. They built a castle on top of the hill around which the little village developed. In 1241, B. was destroyed by the *Mongols, but after their retreat, the Hungarian king, *Bela IV, rebuilt both the castle – making it into a royal palace – and the city, where German and Jewish merchants and craftsmen established themselves. In the 14th century the city became the capital of Hungary and in the second half of the 15th century, the royal palace was rebuilt and the city fortified by *Matthias Corvinus. A university was founded in the city in 1389, but it had closed by 1465.

E. Lévai, *Budapest, An Historical Geography* (1949).

BUILDING The building techniques of the classical world became inapplicable to western Europe beginning in the 5th century. The common explanation of this decline, which was accepted until the 20th century, i.e. the "barbarization" of classical manners, is by now considered as only part of the answer, while the main explanation is related to the decline of slavery and the resultant lack of manpower which had been previously employed in construction. Thus, in the new "barbarian" states, great and monumental buildings ceased to be erected, stone was no longer cut as previously and a greater number of buildings were built of wood. The stone buildings generally had thick walls, which were supported from the exterior by *ante-muralia* (buttresses). Until the 11th century these usually served as religious buildings, such as churches and monasteries. The great majority of civil buildings, but also a considerable number of churches, were constructed of wood during the high Middle Ages, with the exception of buildings in Italy and part of Spain, where the use of stone material was current. Destroyed and abandoned classical structures served as an important source for stone material which was then re-employed in the new buildings. With the exception of the palace of *Charlemagne at Aix-la-Chapelle, which was built of stone, palaces and castles were generally constructed of a combination of stone, wood and earth, which also served for the construction of the moats, frequently used for defence purposes in the 9th century. The demographic changes of the 11th century, leading to a significant increase in manpower, made possible the return to the use of stone as the main material of construction of churches and castles, which allowed architects to design large buildings, as well as to provide for their elevation through the use of vaults and columns. Thus the Romanesque style of *architecture was introduced. In the 12th century the use of the flying buttress in northern France allowed builders to reduce the thickness of the walls, a technique which is significant in the transition from Romanesque to Gothic architecture. This development enabled the opening of large windows, thus introducing the use of glass. The dimensions of the new buildings posed some technological problems for the architects and masons in the fields of geometry and statics. Because of the lack of writings on masonry in the Middle Ages, the degree of technical training available to masons is indeterminable. It seems, however, that in the majority of the cases, their knowledge was purely empirical. Even architecture was learned through apprenticeship. Nevertheless, the notes of one of the greatest architects of the 13th century, *Villard de Honnecourt, indicate that he had a good understanding of statics and a certain knowledge of geometry. From the 13th century on, with the development of cities and their economic prosperity, town buildings also came to be erected in stone and their design was entrusted to architects who had to solve problems of construction within urban agglomerations. For these reasons, civil architecture of the later Middle Ages was connected with the development of urbanism, including the designing of squares within the cities.

D. Knoop and G. P. Jones, *The Mediaeval Mason* (1933).

BUKHARA City and principality in eastern Turkestan. The city, which is first mentioned in the 7th century BC, was founded in a fertile oasis at the confluence of the Zerawshan and Koshka-Darin rivers. From ancient times it served as a junction point of the trade routes from Persia to Samarkand and Tashkent and from the Caspian Sea to China; thus, B. controlled the main routes of all of central Asia, including the "silk route" between China and the West. The city's name is a result of the corruption of the Sanskrit, *Vihara*, which means "the hidden". The Turks conquered the country in the 1st century AD and destroyed the ancient principality of Sogdiana, which had belonged to the Hellenistic realms of the Orient since the conquests of Alexander Macedon. The Turks founded a state ruled by a Buddhist clan, which granted religious freedom to all sects and faiths. In 709 B. was conquered by the Arabs, who annexed it to the province of *Khorasan, where it formed a distinct administrative unit, known as Transoxiana, until 874. The inhabitants were forced to convert to Islam, but they continued to follow their own customs and to maintain relations with the Persians, so that they did not become assimilated into the Arab ethno-culture. The decline of the *Abbasid caliphate and the establishment of local dynasties in its eastern countries brought about the foundation at B. of a local dynasty, the Persian *Samanids, who seized power in 874 and ruled over a vast area for 145 years. The most eminent ruler of this period was the Emir Ismail (892-907), who removed Transoxiana from Khorasan sovereignty and conquered vast territories up to the borders of the central Asian steppes and parts of Persia. At the beginning of the 11th century, the *Seljuk Turks conquered Central Asia and in 1004 they established their rule at B. Under Seljuk rule (1004-1133), power was actually entrusted to a local Turkish dynasty of emirs, belonging to the Uigur tribes, which developed the principality and promoted its prosperity. At this time there were three official languages — Arabic, used as cult-language, Persian, serving as vernacular and commercial language, and Turkish, spoken and written by the rulers and administration. In addition, the government was noted for its liberalism. The Uigurs maintained their rule even after the fall of the Seljuks, but had to fight the *Khwarizmians, who became the major power in Transoxiana and in the central Asia steppes. The continuous wars weakened the dynasty and also negatively affected the city's prosperity. In 1220 *Genghis-Khan conquered B. and destroyed it, selling what was left of its population into slavery. The devastation was so great that the city did not regain its previous prosperity, even when it became the capital of the khanate of Genghis's son *Chaghatai in 1224. Under the Chaghatai khans, the Persian element disappeared and the Uigur Turks became the dominant part of the population. The city's decline was accentuated by the transfer of the capital to *Samarkand under the reign of *Timur-leng (Tamerlane) in 1369. By the end of the Middle Ages, B. had become a minor city in the Timurid empire and it is only through some of its monuments, such as the tomb of Emir Ismail (10th century) and the Kalian Mosque of the 12th century, that its glorious past is attested.

V. Barthold, *Turkestan down to the Mongol Invasion* (1927).

BULAN (8th century) Legendary khan (king) of the *Khazars. According to Jewish and Moslem traditions, he decided to adopt a monotheistic religion. Having consulted Christian, Moslem and Jewish scholars at his court, he chose to convert to Judaism, together with his family and nobles. The legend recalls the conversion to Judaism of some of the Khazars, including members of the royal family, which took place over a period of several generations in the 8th and 9th centuries. See *Khazars.

D. M. Dunlop, *The History of the Jewish Khazars* (1954).

BULGARI (BOLGAR) City on the Volga River, near the mouth of the Kama River. The city was founded by the *Bulgars in the 5th century and was the capital of their khanate. In the 7th century, when the Bulgars were divided into "White" and "Black", B. was conquered by the latter who, after the migration of the White Bulgars, became known as the Bulgars of the Volga and founded a prosperous state, through which ran the main roads of trade in eastern Europe. The city was visited in 922 by the Arab traveller Ibn Fadlan, who described it as an important commercial centre and estimated its population at 10,000 people, a figure which, in comparison with the west European cities of the period, represented a very great city. In the same year the khan of B. converted to Islam and, for nearly 300 years, the state was the most advanced stronghold of the northern Moslem world. In 1237 *Batu Khan conquered and destroyed the city and annexed the Bulgar state to his *Golden Horde. In the 14th century it was rebuilt by the Mongols and became one of the *Tatar cities in Russia. In 1413, the prince of *Moscow, Vassili, destroyed it, and not long after, it was conquered by *Timur-leng. The major part of the population left the city and towards the end of the century, the city of Riazan flourished as a result of its decline. Among several medieval ruins found on the site, a number of Chuwashi inscriptions of the 5th century are an important source for the study of the Bulgars' language.

B. F. Smolin, *Studies on Ancient Bulgari* (1926).

BULGARIA Country in the Balkan peninsula between the Danube and Thracia, B. was the realm of the Bulgarians, founded on territory conquered from the Byzantine empire in the 9th century. The Bulgarians were the descendants of the "White Bulgars", who left their territory on the Volga and migrated southward. At the period of their move they were still a Finno-Mongol tribe, distinguished by their ethnical character from the Bulgarians. Internal disputes brought several groups to leave B., and, beginning in the 5th century, they appeared on the Danube frontiers of the Byzantine empire within larger tribes which had invaded from eastern Europe. But only in the 7th century, when the "White Bulgars" left the Volga state, did migration reach a massive scale. Under the leadership of *Kubrat Khan, they settled in western Ukraine, by the mouth of the Danube. Kubrat helped the Byzantines fight the *Avars and obtained the title "Patrice". In 679, under his son, *Asperuch Khan, the Bulgars crossed the Danube and conquered territory which reached to the Balkan Mountains. In the 8th century the Bulgars were assimilated into other Slavic tribes in the Balkans, lost much of their Finno-Mongol character and adopted a Southern Slavic tongue. From this melting-pot of the Bulgars and Slavs, plus certain local elements of the Byzantine Moesia, the Bulgarian nation was created. The settlement of these people on both banks of the Danube was, however, not well-enough organized, although all of their leaders accepted the authority of the khan, who belonged to Kubrat's family.

The 9th century marked the period of the foundation and organization of the medieval Bulgarian state. The Khan *Krum (802-15) attacked Byzantium and in 812 defeated Emperor *Nicephorus I, who was killed at the Adrianople Battle; his head served as a wine cup for the feast banquets of Krum. After a second defeat, the Emperor Michael prevented the conquest of Constantinople by paying a tribute. But while the Bulgarians were a constant danger to the Byzantines, the process of their assimilation continued and under *Boris I, they converted to Christianity. Although both the Roman Catholic and the Orthodox Churches led missions, the Greeks succeeded in converting them to the Orthodox faith, while allowing them ecclesiastical autonomy and the use of the Slavonic liturgy of *Cyril and *Methodius. The conversion of the Bulgarians contributed to a long period of assimilation in which they lost their original character. Only certain traditions remained. Boris' son, *Simeon, was the greates tsar of medieval B. During his reign (893-927), the country reached the "three seas", the Black to the east, the Aegean to the south and the Adriatic to the west; in 918, he was crowned "tsar of the Bulgarians and the Greeks" and a Bulgarian patriarchate was established at Preslav, the capital of the new empire. After Simeon's death, B.'s power was weakened by dynastic rivalry, which divided the nobility. The military intervention of the prince of Kiev, *Svyatoslav, in 967 and 969, who acted as an ally of Byzantium, seems to

have brought about the fall of B. But the Kievan danger alarmed the Byzantines; in 971 the Emperor *John Tzimisces defeated Svyatoslav, freed *Boris II from captivity and, after having used his services as an ally, deposed him and annexed eastern B. to the Byzantine empire. With the dethronement of Boris II, the dynasty of Korbat came to an end, but western B. remained independent. Its tsar, *Samuel (980-1014) of the Sisman house, reorganized the realm, conquered Serbia, Bosnia and Dalmatia and resumed war against Byzantium. He was defeated and killed in 1014 by *Basil II, who crushed the Bulgarians and annexed their kingdom in 1018. In order to further weaken the Bulgarians, the emperors of Byzantium encouraged the settlement of *Petcheneg tribes in the country.

In the latter half of the 12th century, some princes of the Sisman house took advantage of the difficulties of Byzantium and its wars with Hungary in order to try to restore their independence. In 1186, Prince Assen was successful in doing so, and his brother, *Kaloian (1197-1207), reigned over a restored Bulgarian kingdom. His victory over *Baldwin I, the Latin emperor of Constantinople (1205) consolidated the second Bulgarian kingdom, which recovered most of the territories of the first kingdom in the 13th century. But in the latter half of the 13th century, the country was again troubled by dynastic rivalry and by invasions, such as those of the *Mongols. B. lost most of its conquests, including Macedonia and Wallachia, where independent principalities were founded. The growth of the kingdom of *Serbia in the 14th century threatened the independence of B. and its princes were compelled to recognize the overlordship of the Serbian kings and to pay them tribute. After the Battle of Kossovo (1366), where the *Ottoman Turks crushed the Serbians, large parts of the Bulgarian territory were occupied by the Turks. In 1393, *Bayazid I conquered their capital Tirnovo and, after the failure of the crusade of *Nicopolis in 1396, the rest of the country was conquered and annexed to the Ottoman empire. The nobility and the urban upper classes were killed or compelled to convert to Islam, and, from the 15th century on, the Bulgarian patriarchate was abolished and the church was submitted to the Greek Orthodox hierarchy.

G. Songeon, *Histoire de la Bulgarie* (1913);
S. Runciman, *The First Bulgarian Empire* (1930).

BULGARUS (d. 1167) Jurist. He studied law at *Bologna under *Irnerius and, from 1125 until his death, continued the work of his master. He is considered one of the four great founders of the legal studies at Bologna. His specialty was the impact of Roman *Law on the problems of his time. In 1158 Emperor *Frederick Barbarossa invited him to the Diet of Roncaglia as counsellor, asking his advice on the framework of the document in which the principles of imperial sovereignty over Italy were formulated. B. was mainly a teacher; his lessons, in which he commented on Roman Law, were attended by students from all over western Europe. His teaching and opinions were often quoted in the later works of his students.

S. Mochi Onory, *Fonti Canonistiche dell'Idea Moderna dello Stato* (1951).

BULL (Latin: bulla) Term meaning the seal of the public authority which issued documents. The notion of "public authority" in the Middle Ages included sovereign

The Lady and the Unicorn; *15th-century tapestry of the Burgundian School*

Madonna and Child *by Dirk Bouts, 15th century*

(emperors, kings and princes) as well as ecclesiastical courts. As distinguished from feudal seals, the Bs. were made of metal, according to the following classification: lead seals (*bulla plumbea*) for regular documents, which was the most common; silver seals (*bulla argentina*), for important acts and the Golden B. (*bulla aurea*), used in festive imperial and papal documents. Over the ages, the name was also given to documents sealed by the B., especially regarding papal documents. Certain imperial documents are also called B., like the *Golden Bull of *Charles IV. The study and research of the B. is an independent discipline called Sigillography.

P. Ewald, *Siegelkunde* (1914).

BUONSIGNORI Family of bankers of Siena (Italy) who, at the beginning of the 13th century, invested the profits from their estates in commercial transactions and political activities, specializing in credit activities. In the latter half of the 13th century Orlando B. enlarged the activities of his bank to include Catalonia, France and England; and his *gran tavola* (great table) became the centre of the financial transactions of a great part of western Europe. He helped finance the expedition of *Charles of Anjou to Sicily and southern Italy in 1268, making enormous profits from the transaction. At the beginning of the 14th century, the B. bank had some difficulties, like a great number of other Italian credit institutions, caused by the economic crisis in western Europe. The bank was unable to handle such difficulties and, after its bankruptcy, the B. family lost its privileged social position.

M. Chiandano, *I Rothschild del ducento, la gran tavola di Orlando Buonsignori* (1935).

BURCHARD I Duke of Swabia (917-26). He was the son of B. of Rhaetia and at his father's death, inherited his claims to the duchy. In close relations with the new king of Germany, *Henry I, whom he had aided in fighting the separatist tendencies of the German nobility and particularly *Arnulf of Bavaria, he was appointed duke of Swabia, where he established order and imposed his authority over the nobility and the bishops. In 922 he forged an alliance with *Rudolf II of Burgundy, giving him his daughter in marriage and supporting his Italian policy. In 926 B. was killed while participating in an expedition to Italy.

G. Tellenbach, *Königtum und Stämme in der Werdezeit des deutschen Reiches* (1939).

BURCHARD (BOUCHARD) D'AVESNES (c. 1190-1243) Lord of *Beaumont. Member of the famous family of the lords of Beaumont in northern France, he had been prepared for an ecclesiastical career. Once he became deacon, he was sent to Flanders, where he met Princess Margaret, heiress of the county. In 1212 he secretly married her. When news of the marriage was divulged at court, B. was excommunicated, but refused to render his wife and children to the Countess Joan, even at the price of his liberty. In 1243, Joan ordered his arrest, and he was executed a few months prior to the countess' death, which was followed by the accession of his wife Margaret to Joan's title.

H. Pirenne, *Historie de Belgique* (1901).

BURCHARD OF MONTMORENCY see MONTMO-RENCY.

BURCHARD OF RHAETIA (d. 916) Marquis of Rhaetia. He was one of the feudal princes in southwestern Germany whose accession in the last years of the 9th cen-

tury was the result of the political anarchy of the last German *Carolingian kings. At the beginning of the 10th century, he laid claim to the duchy of Swabia, proclaiming himself duke, and was recognized by King *Conrad I. Defeated by a military man who shared his pretensions (Erchanger), he lost the duchy, but never renounced his claim.

BURCHARD OF URSBERG (d. 1231) He was provost of the Premonstratensian abbey of Ursberg (1215-31), where he distinguished himself as historian. He continued the *Annals* of *Ekkehard of Aura from 1125 to 1225. The most valuable part of his *Universal Chronicle* is that covering the last years of the 12th and the beginning of the 13th centuries, which is his original contribution. He had many sources of information, having often travelled to Rome and to the imperial court.

O. Holder-Egger, *Die Chronik des Propstes Burchard von Ursberg* (1916).

BURCHARD OF WORMS (965-1025) Bishop of Worms (1000-25). Distinguished by his studies at the court of *Otto III, he was appointed bishop of Worms, where he was very active in the reorganization of the bishopric, in the foundation of new parishes, in the reform of the clergy and in imposing his authority on lay vassals. He soon became one of the most influential bishops of his time. B.'s main work is his *Decretum* (1012), which is a compilation of the canon laws and decrees of ecclesiastical authorities up to his day. The *Decretum* came to be the most authoritative text in ecclesiastical jurisdiction, until it was superseded at the end of the 11th century by more updated works.

PL, vol. 140; *EC*, II.

BURCHARD OF WÜRZBURG (d. 753) He maintained a close relationship with *Pepin the Short, who appointed him bishop of Würzburg in 742. As a counsellor to the Frank, B. helped Pepin to arrange the revolution of the dynasty in 751. In 749 he led the delegation sent by Pepin to Pope *Zacharias at Rome, with the famous question: "Who should reign? He who holds the royal dignity by ancestral heritage but is unable to rule or he who reigns effectively?". The Pope's answer led to the dethronement of the last *Merovingian, *Chilperic III and to Pepin's coronation.

R. Folz, *Le Couronnement impérial de Charlemagne* (1964).

BURGHER Literally the term signifies any inhabitant of a *borough. But from the 11th century on, as evident through its use in documents (Latin: *Burgensis*) the original meaning of the word was altered to express the notion of "citizen of the borough" (city). Because of the great diversity of urban charters and privileges, even that definition had various interpretations, according to the nature of the urban "liberties". The most common is synonymous with the possessor of a house, granting such a person the rights to participate in urban activities. Towards the end of the Middle Ages, and closely related to the development of aristocratic constitutions in the cities, which excluded craftsmen and other guilds from urban institutions, the term came to have a new meaning, parallel to the older one, by which the Bs. were honourable members of the city, wealthy enough to employ others to work for them, and free to seek good investments for their money and to participate in public activity.

M. Weber, *The City* (1958).

BURGOS City in northern ("Old") Castile. B. was founded in 884 by *Alfonso III, king of Asturia. Its name derives from the castle (*burgus, al-burj*) built at the top of a hill which dominates the city. Its foundation was part of the king's strategic plan to attack the Moslems in the Valley of Duero and to enlarge the Christian dominions southward. In the 10th century B. became the capital of a county ruled by one of the branches of the royal family. In the 11th century (1037-87) it became the capital of the united kingdom of Castile and León, and remained a royal residence even after the establishment of the capital at Toledo. In 1097 a bishopric was established in the city. In the 12th-15th centuries it was a prosperous commercial centre of the northern part of Spain and served as a junction of the trade routes of the realm. Its prosperity was closely connected with its Jewish community, which was one of the most important in Castile. The city began to decline in the 14th century, when its population diminished as a result of the plagues and particularly the *Black Death. Nevertheless, it remained an important centre of the wool trade. With the expulsion of the Jews from Spain in 1492, B. declined economically, remaining an aristocratic provincial city. Of its medieval monuments, the most noted are its Gothic cathedral (built between the 13th and 15th centuries); a number of palaces, where the tradition of Castilian chivalry and the *Reconquista* wars are perpetuated in reliefs and paintings; and its rich archives, where important, ornately-decorated manuscripts have been preserved.

P. J. Pérez de Urbel, *Historia del Condado de Castilla* (1945).

BURGUNDIANS Germanic people. The oldest traces of the B. are in the Island of Bornholm in the Baltic Sea and it seems that their original country was there. In the 2nd century the B. left Bornholm to settle the area between the Vistula and Oder Rivers, in what is now western Poland. Pushed in the 3rd century by the *Goths, who had invaded the territory from Scandinavia, they began their migration westwards and settled in the area of the Main. In the year 400 and shortly afterward, they were allowed to settle as *foederati* (allies) of the Roman empire on the Rhine, in the areas of Worms and Mainz. For unknown reasons, their good relations with the Roman authorities were broken off and in 436 they were attacked by the Roman general Aetius. Their king Guntaric and many of his men were killed by the Hunnish mercenaries during this clash; this episode served as the background for a national epic, the Song of the *Nibelungs. Aetius settled the remnants of the B. in the mountains of Savoy, near Geneva. There they adopted the Catholic faith and restored their kingdom. In the latter half of the 5th century the B. were strong enough to attack the Romans left in Gaul and succeeded in extending their kingdom to include the entire area between the Alps, the Rhône, the Saône and the Mountains of Jura; they established their capital at Lyons. The country they had conquered received the name of *Burgundy, which perpetuated their name (later on it was changed to Great Burgundy, to distinguish it from the historical Burgundy, which is in the northern part of that realm). Their leader, *Gundobald, was strong enough to intervene in the crisis of the Roman empire, appointing Glycerius as Emperor of the West in 473. When Gundobald became sole king of the B. in 480, the growth of the *Franks caused him concern; therefore, he concluded an alliance with *Clovis, who married his niece Clotilda. In 501 he promulgated the first B. laws (*Loi Gombette*), but was not able to maintain his independence. After his death, the kingdom of the B. was conquered by the Franks and annexed to their own sovereignty, although it preserved its name throughout the various divisions of the realm by the *Merovingian kings. The B. became assimilated by the Franks and eventually lost their own ethnical character.

R. Guichard, *Essai sur l'Histoire du Peuple Burgonde* (1965).

BURGUNDIO OF PISA (d. 1193) Jurist and translator. Born at Pisa, he distinguished himself as a lawyer and served as judge in his own city, where he was highly esteemed. He travelled on behalf of the city, visiting Constantinople in 1135-36 and again in 1171, and frequently visiting Sicily and Dalmatia. Besides his judicial activity, he was involved in the translation of texts from Greek into Latin, which gained him fame as a humanist. In 1140, he translated the Greek quotations of the legal *Digestae*, but his most important translations were in the field of philosophy and theology, among them *The Orthodox Faith* of John of Damascus and *The Human Nature* of Nemesius (in 1150 and 1159). He translated medical works including those of Hippocrates and Galen. *DHGE*, IX.

BURGUNDY (Bourgogne) Name of a kingdom, duchy and county in western Europe. In the Middle Ages applied to the last Burgundian kingdom, later called the kingdom of *Arles, and to the countship of B. later known as Franche-Comté.

The kingdom of B. After the division of the *Carolingian empire in 843, the ancient lands of the Burgundians were divided by the kingdom of France, where they were organized into the duchy of B. and the states of *Lothair. At Lothair's death in 855, he left those territories to his second son, Charles (855-63), with the title of king of Provence. Charles, however, was unable to rule, as the nobility brought about total anarchy. Nevertheless, at his death they were united in their opposition to an eventual annexation of the kingdom to the other Carolingian kingdoms. The state of anarchy lasted until 879, when Count *Boso succeeded in conquering the city of Vienne and proclaimed himself king. At the same time, the northern counties of the realm were united under the leadership of *Rudolf I, who proclaimed himself king of B., reigning in the country corresponding to what are now the western Swiss cantons (888). The two kingdoms continued their struggle for independence, but were also involved in Italian affairs. Several of their kings, such as *Louis the Blind, the son of Boso and *Rudolf II, the son of Rudolf I, even laid claim to the imperial throne. In 934 Rudolf II united the realms and founded the kingdom of Arelate, named after the new capital, *Arles, in Provence. Thus, during the 10th century the Burgundian counties became subject to outside rule. The court became more open towards Mediterranean society. The kingdom lost its cohesion, however, when the *Ottonians re-established the empire and began to gain influence in B. When *Rudolf III died in 1032 without issue, the crown of B. was inherited by the German emperors, but the kingdom continued to be considered a separate entity within the empire. The various counties were grouped in the 11th century into three main groups, northern (Higher B.), central (Lower B.) and Provence. From the end of the 11th century the last was claimed by both the count of Toulouse and the count of Catalonia. The efforts made by *Frederick Barbarossa in the 12th century to consolidate the imperial power through the unification of the realm and the creation of an administration dependent on the emperor did not reap the expected results and of the entire Burgundian kingdom, only the county of High B., whose capital was the city of Besançon, continued to bear the name of B.

The duchy of B. In 843 the Burgundian territories included in the kingdom of France were divided into various counties, the most important of them having been that of Autun, given in 875 by *Charles the Bald to his brother-in-law, *Boso. After Boso's death in Vienne in 887, his son Richard named the Justician, inherited Autun, which was separated from the kingdom of Provence, given to his brother *Louis the Blind. Richard extended his power in 893, when he acquired the territories around Dijon and laid the foundations of the duchy of B. His son *Raoul (Ralph), who married Emma, the daughter of *Robert I of France, acquired a great number of counties in eastern France and was elected king in 923, in place of the deposed *Charles III, as heir to his father-in-law. After his death (937), the ducal title was disputed between relatives, who belonged to the Robertian dynasty. When this dynasty died out in 1015, the duchy was inherited by King *Robert II, who was compelled by the nobility to maintain it as a distinct entity, separate from the royal demesne. However, he did annex part of its northwestern territories, including the city of Sens, to royal sovereignty. At his death in 1032, he appointed his younger son, Robert, duke. Robert was the founder of the *Capetian House of B., which reigned in the duchy until 1361.

Like the senior royal branch the Capetian dukes proved themselves to be good administrators and devoted their efforts to establishing an efficient government in the duchy. During the 12th century they imposed their authority on their vassals and, with the collaboration of the church, they established order in the country. The revival of commerce brought prosperity, and ducal favours to the abbeys contributed to their development and to the flourishing of religious and intellectual life in the duchy. In the 11th century the monastic school of Dijon was one of the most prominent in western Europe. Masters like William of Volpiano and his pupil *Lanfranc taught there and brought the achievements of Italian scholars to western and northern Europe. The order of *Cluny particularly flourished in B. and at the beginning of the 12th century, the *Cistercians also founded a monastery in the duchy. The duchy was also a very important centre of the Romanesque and Gothic styles of art, so much so that there are special Burgundian variations of these styles. The fidelity of the dukes to the royal dynasty strengthened their authority and helped maintain peace in the duchy. An efficient judiciary administration imposed order in the country and was responsible in part for the flourishing of its economy. Unlike other French provinces, B. was spared the devastations of the *Hundred Years' War, being outside of areas of the campaigns. Nevertheless, its nobility took an active part in the battles within the French army. In 1330 the county of B. (also known as

Franche-Comté) was inherited by Duke Eudes IV, who also became vassal of the *Holy Roman emperor for the county. Thus the duchy became a powerful principality in the middle of the 14th century, whose leader, Duke Philip of Rouvres was expected to inherit Artois and Flanders. At his death, having left no successor from the Capetian dynasty of B. (1161), the duchy was taken over by the king of France, *John II.

The great duchy of B. In 1363 John II granted B., as an *apanage, to his younger son *Philip. Philip married Margaret, the daughter and heiress of *Louis de Male, count of Flanders. His inheritance included the *Artois estates, among them, the county of Artois in northeastern France and Franch-Comté. Philip, who governed B. through officers and the ducal *Estates General* of Dijon, resided at the royal court at Paris and, after the death of his brother *Charles V (1380), acted as regent for his nephew *Charles VI. He used the royal army to crush a revolt in Flanders after the death of Louis de Male (1383) and after his victory at *Rosebeke, took possession of the Flemish principality. In 1390 he purchased the county of Charolais in southern B. and at the beginning of the 15th century laid the grounds for the inheritance and annexation of Brabant and the Low Countries, through the marriage of his son, John, to Margaret of Holland. By his death, in 1404, the major part of Belgium and Holland had come under Burgundian influence and direct rule. Philip was known as a patron of the arts and the forty years of his reign were not only a period of political growth, but also marked the beginning of the "Golden Age of B." (from 1383 the term B. was used to designate all the possessions of its duke), a period of flourishing culture and of economic prosperity. His son *John the Fearless (1404-19), continued his policy and was also active at the French court, where he opposed the duke of Orléans and was accused of his murder, an act which sparked the battle between the *Armagnac and *Bourguignon parties in Paris. John was very popular at Paris and, after the Battle of *Agincourt in 1415, tried to reconcile *Charles VI and *Henry V, through a dynastic union, intended to exclude the Dauphin Charles from the royal succession. John's murder in 1419 brought the support of his son and heir Philip the Good (1419-67) to the English party, where it remained up to the Peace of Arras in 1435.

R. Poupardin, *Le royaume de Bourgogne, 888-1032* (1907);

J. Richard, *Les ducs de Bourgogne et la formation territoriale du duché* (1954);

A. Cartellieri, *The Court of Burgundy* (1929);

J. Huizinga, *The Waning of the Middle Ages* (1924).

BURIDAN, JOHN (1300-c. 1366) Born at Béthune. in northern France, he was a student of William *Ockham and became one of the leading thinkers of late *Scholasticism. In 1328 he was elected rector of the University of Paris and taught there until 1358. Although he adopted Ockham's *nominalistic methods, he criticized some of his master's views, and in 1340 formally condemned them as unorthodox. He opposed the view that abstract universalistic notions represent reality and claimed that science is based only on actual facts and elements. In his development of the theory of the absence of free choice, he formulated the famous example of 'Buridan's ass', which his rationalist opponents used against him. B. criticized the physical theories

of Aristotle, as well as Ptolemaic cosmology. His works in this field, in which he stressed the importance of air as an autonomous force, became an important source for the development of the physical theories of Galilei and Copernicus in the Renaissance period. The Parisian chronicles of the 14th century describe B. as an important philosopher and teacher, but also mention the rumours of his love affair with Princess Ann of Bavaria.
G. Leff, *Paris and Oxford Universities in the 13th and 14th Centuries* (1968).

BURIDS Turkish dynasty which reigned in Damascus (1117-54). The B. rose to power from the rank of *atabeg* (military governor, appointed to aid and educate the *Seljuk princes). At the end of the 11th century, when the Seljuk prince *Duqaq, became sultan of Damascus, his *atabeg*, Toghtekin, governed the principality and fought against the *Crusaders. He founded a dynasty named after his son, Taj-al Din Buri, who succeeded him in the office of *atabeg* and in 1117, at the extinction of the Seljuk dynasty, became emir of Damascus. The B. established an alliance with the kings of Jerusalem, and especially with *Fulk of Anjou, which contributed mainly to the development of the trade between East and West through Damascus and Acre. The break in the alliance by the participants in the Second *Crusade, who attacked Damascus without success, brought about the decline of B. and led to the conquest of the city by *Nureddin in 1154.
EI, II.

BURLEY, WALTER (d. after 1360) Mathematician and scientific thinker. He was educated at the Merton College, at Oxford, where he discovered and adopted the teaching tradition of Robert *Grosseteste. He remained to teach at the college, which flourished between 1320-60 as one of the most important centres for the study of science in western Europe. Like his Parisian contemporary, John *Buridan, B. was concerned with criticism of the Aristotelian theories of physics, and especially of the origins and physiological movements of animals. His commentaries on Aristotle's treatises led him to formulate physical theories on movement, which served as a basis for further research in modern times.
G. Leff, *Paris and Oxford Universities in the 13th and 14th Centuries* (1968).

BYZANTIUM (Byzantine empire) The East Roman empire, derived from the ancient name of Constantinople. It was the only state whose existence covered the whole of the Middle Ages (395-1453). During this long period, B. developed its own history, social evolution, and material and cultural civilization, concentrated in a specific legal, institutional and religious way of life.
History The history of B. begins in 395 at the death of *Theodosius I, who divided the Roman empire into Western and Eastern empires, bequeathing to his son Arcadius office at the imperial palace of Constantinople. But the period until the end of the 6th century had more of a transitory nature, with many traces of Roman influence, as well as the use of Latin as the official language, so that historians consider it the Later Roman empire. The beginning of this period was marked by continual Germanic invasions in the Balkans. The Goths, who became divided toward the end of the 4th century into *Visigoths and *Ostrogoths continued to threaten the empire and its centres in the Balkans. Arcadius had to bribe the Visigoths in order to obtain their departure

to Italy, which allowed him time to reorganize the defence of his empire. Other tribes were considered to be "allies" of the empire, their chieftains were given honorific Roman titles and some of their men were hired to serve as mercenary troops in the imperial army, employed in the defence of the borders. *Theodosius II (408-50) continued his father's efforts to establish peace on the borders and to reorganize the administration. The Western Roman empire had dissolved entirely; thus, Theodosius II imposed his authority on the Balkans, Asia Minor, Syria and Palestine, Egypt and Pentapolis (the eastern part of Libya). In order to assure the necessary resources for military expenses, he stressed the role of the bureaucracy in the imperial administration, including the ecclesiastical hierarchy; a codification of the Roman Law (bearing the name of *Codex Theodosianius* "The Theodosian Code") imposed the unification of the legal and institutional system of government and was a valuable instrument with which to assure survival of the empire. The autonomy of the Church, which led to some conflicts in the second half of the 5th century, was also limited and with the enactment of the *Henotikon, by Emperor *Zeno (474-91), the church became integrated into the administrative structure of the state and subordinated to the emperor. The protests of the Western bishops and the famous treatise of Pope *Gelasius I, who called for the religious independence of the Church, proclaiming a clear division between the two worlds, only enlarged the breach between the Latin West and Greek East in the ecclesiastical domain. The conquest of Italy by the Ostrogoths led to the elimination of the last power which could have threatened the empire in the Balkans. Thus, by the end of the 5th century, B. had become consolidated as a centralist state. Its main difficulties were internal and they entailed disputes between factions of the aristocracy mainly at Constantinople. In 518, *Justinus, a career soldier who became general, seized power in an attempt to restore order. His goal was realized by his nephew and successor, *Justinian (527-65), who was the greatest emperor of B. Together with his wife, Theodora, a former actress, he imposed order at Constantinople and cruelly crushed the Niké riots in 532, which threatened his reign. He was thus able to concentrate for a long period on foreign policy, whose first stage was the defence of the eastern borders from Persian invasions and the building up of his forces in hopes of realizing his great aim, the reunification of the Roman empire. Aided by a great general, *Belisarius, Justinian won north Africa from the *Vandals (534) and began the conquest of Ostrogoth Italy in 536; only after 20 years of wars was General Narses able to complete the conquest begun by Belisarius. At the same time the southern part of Spain was won from the Visigoths and so the Mediterranean became once more a "Roman" sea, *Mare Nostrum*. But while such efforts were undertaken in the West, the Persians still presented a threat at the eastern borders, and on the Danube frontier, an infiltration of Slavs began to be felt. Moreover, revolts of Jews and Samaritans in Palestine, which were cruelly repressed, were signs of unrest in the eastern provinces. Justinian tried to impose his authority by a bureaucratic unity of the empire, the compilation of the Roman Law, named *Codex Justinianus* and the publication of new laws, were part of this policy, which was crowned by the issue of the *Corpus*

Juris Civilis (The Collection of the Civil Law - see *Law, Roman). The administration was improved and the new provinces of the West were governed by exarchs, who were high officials, awarded military and civil power in their areas. Justinian also intervened in the religious policy of the empire; in this area, too, he acted according to his interpretation of the concept of the imperial function and the responsibility he felt for order. The compelling of his subjects to be faithful was a precondition for their salvation. The Greek Orthodox dogma was considered the sole way to express fidelity; the famous Academy of *Athens, considered a promulgator of pagan philosophy was therefore closed. The long dispute concerning the *Monophysite heresy, which represented God, the Father, and Jesus as the same matter, became by his intervention a political issue. He ordered the persecution of the Monophysites whose repression caused the non-Greek eastern provinces much difficulty, so that religious opposition became an anti-Greek movement, and Syrians and Egyptians found themselves hereties. Nevertheless, until Justinian's death the effects of the repression were barely felt and the positive achievements of his reign were foremost.

After the death of Justinian the situation changed. The *Lombards invaded Italy and conquered most of it. In the Balkans, the penetration of the Slavs became massive and at the eastern borders, the Persians renewed their attacks and were supported by the local population. The establishment of a faithful hierarchy in the Eastern Churches was met by total opposition on the part of the population, which remained obedient to its religious leaders and called the new bishops *Melkites* (in Armenian: the men of the king). Thus, the Greek character of the empire and of the imperial administration was accentuated and the last traces of the Roman empire disappeared. With the extinction of the Justinianean dynasty in 602, the Later Roman empire became replaced by the Greek Byzantine state. A military revolt led by General Phocas, who proclaimed himself emperor (602-10) did not improve the situation; the Persians, under *Chosroes II, penetrated Asia Minor and anarchy reigned. Only the cruel repression of all opposition undertaken by Phocas prevented the final division of the empire.

In 610 a plot led by *Heraclius, the son of the exarch of Cartago put an end to Phocas' reign. The new emperor (610-41) enjoyed the support of the clergy, headed by the Patriarch *Sergius, as well as of the army. He fought successfully against the *Avars in the north. The Persians, who conquered Jerusalem in 613 and attacked Constantinople in 626 were also controlled. Heraclius sent his army to penetrate Persia, while his fleet fought in the Red Sea and Indian Ocean against the Persian ships. In 629 he defeated the Persian army and put an end to the *Sassanid dynasty; revolts of the Syrians and Jews who supported the Persians were cruelly crushed. In the Balkans, the emperor subjugated the Slavs and by 630 it seemed that the imperial authority was restored. But Heraclius had ignored the revolutionary change which had taken place in the Arabian Peninsula, nor had he recognized the importance of the rise of *Mohammad and Islam. He was unable to prevent the Arab attack on Transjordan and Iraq, and in 636 his army was severely defeated by the Arabs on the *Yarmuk River. The consequences of the religious split,

Christ Pantocrator; *Byzantine mosaic at Monreale*

which brought the Eastern Christians to an open conflict with the empire, were disastrous for Heraclius. Syria, Palestine, Egypt and Iraq were lost before his death and later in the century B. lost the African provinces and Spain. The Arab fleet even attacked Constantinople in 673, which was saved by the use of *Greek fire bombs, a new warring device. At the end of the 7th century, B. lost the majority of its territories and resources of wealth; only Asia Minor and the Balkans remained under its authority. Despite this blow, B. remained cohesive, becoming a Greek state, by means of its ethno-social and religious structure. Nevertheless, the dynastic dispute of the beginning of the 8th century and the revolts against Justinian II (685-711) weakened the empire, which was not able to suppress the *Bulgarian invasion of the Balkans and the establishment of their realm south of the Danube.

After a period of anarchy, power was seized by an Anatolian dynasty, the Isaurians (717). The founder of the dynasty, *Leo III (717-41), was able to rectify the military situation and to agree with the Arabs to established borders at the Taurus mountains. However, the empire was faced by a new crisis, this time on religious grounds, i.e., the issue of *Iconoclasm. In 726, Leo III published a decree forbidding the cult of images, which he considered idolatry. The core of the opposition came from the monasteries and the masses, which considered icons as a necessary part of their worship. The conflict reached an end only in 843, when the cult of the images was fully restored. Although the decree of 726 had had such an important impact, the result of which weakened the empire, it was only one of the reform activities of Leo III, who proceeded to completely reorganize the administration. He divided the empire, for purposes of defence, into *themes* (military provinces), which were required to procure the appropriate resources for the maintenance of the army, thus subordinating the civil administration to the military commanders. The theme system's results were immediately positive; the army became much more efficient. But in the long run, the system led to the establishment of a military aristocracy and granted overwhelming influence to generals. Moreover, the economy became subordinate, for fiscal reasons, to military needs, which brought about the intervention of the state in economic activities through legislation and administrative measures, as is outlined in the *Book of the Prefect*. Leo's reforms were completed by the issue of the *Ekloge*, a new collection of laws and ordinances, which consummated the legislative activity from the times of Justinian I. The impact of the iconoclastic conflict was seriously felt after Leo's death and weakened the empire in the Balkans, where the Bulgarians and the Slavs gained power. In Italy, B. lost its last positions in the centre of the peninsula and Ravenna, the capital of the Italian exarchate, was conquered by the Lombards in 749. While *Charlemagne conquered Italy and began to prepare for the establishment of his empire, B. was troubled by a dynastic dispute between the Empress *Irene and her son *Constantine VI, who finally was blinded and overthrown by his mother in 797. The various rivalries and the reign of the generals at the beginning of the 9th century allowed for the establishment of Great *Bulgaria.

The situation was rectified with the ascension of the Macedonian dynasty (867-1057). The Emperors *Basil I and *Basil II reached their fame as military leaders against the Bulgarians; *Leo VI, on the other hand, was considered one of the great B. legislators. His *Basilica revised and consummated the works of his predecessors in the field of legislation. Upon this work was based the code which remained in effect until the end of the empire. The Macedonian emperors tried to re-establish the rule of B. over territories lost to the Arabs in the 7th century. *Nicephorus Phocas and *John Tzimisces attacked Aleppo and invaded Syria and Palestine, but lacking logistic support, they were unsuccessful. Nevertheless, the 10th and 11th centuries marked a period of renewed military activity on the Islamic border, reflected in the B. epics, such as *Basil Digenis Akritas*. The great Macedonian renaissance of the empire was also felt in the religious sphere. An important evolution in the scholarly system (see B. civilization) was apparent in missionary activities among the Slavs. The mission of St. *Cyril and St. *Methodius, which brought the Orthodox faith to the Moravians and the southern Slav tribes, was based on the concept that the liturgy language had to be taught in their native tongue; for that purpose an alphabet, still in use among the Slavic nations, was invented (adapted from the Greek). It was given the name Cyrillic and liturgical and theological writing was thus translated into 'Slavonic'. The most important achievement in the area of religion was the conversion of the *Russians at the end of the 10th century, which expanded Orthodox Christianity northwards, compensating for the Islamization in the Near East countries. At the end of the 9th century, relations with the Roman Catholic Church became more difficult. Although theological disagreements were insignificant, differences in the mentality and the organization of the churches created a gap, which gradually became wider. In the latter half of the 9th century, the popes accused Patriarch *Photius of

Constantinople of heresy; the 'Photian schism' thus opened the way for the Great Schism of 1054, when Pope *Leo IX and Patriarch *Michael Cerularius excommunicated one another and the two churches became totally separated.

During the last years of its reign, the Macedonian dynasty weakened and the imperial throne was disputed between factions of generals, who revolted frequently, and landed aristocracy, whose influence grew in the 11th century. A period of anarchy, which was accentuated in 1057, after the death of Empress Theodora II, characterized B. history until 1081. During this period, the empire suffered its most serious blow: in 1071, the *Seljuk Turks, entering through Persia, penetrated Anatolia, defeating the imperial army at *Menzikert, where Emperor *Romanus IV Diogenes was killed. Within a period of a few years, the Turks had conquered almost all Asia Minor, where they founded the Sultanate of *Rum or Konya. B. was unable to resist and a desperate appeal to the West brought no support. For a period of ten years generals continued to fight amongst themselves for power, while the empire was attacked in the Balkans by the *Normans of south Italy. The period of anarchy came to an end only in 1081, with the ascension of *Alexius I Comnenus, who founded a new dynasty, which reigned until the end of the 12th century.

The new period was characterized by reorganization of the empire, now concentrated mostly in the Balkans. It was also the time of the *Crusades, which had an important impact on the history of B. Alexius took advantage of the First Crusade, whose leaders passed through Constantinople, to reconquer a part of Asia Minor, including all of the coastal provinces of the peninsula. The passage of Crusaders through Constantinople brought about a mutual hate between East and West, based on the latter's envy of the rich 'Greeks' and, the former's distaste for the 'barbaric' manners of the Westerners. Thus, when dynastic rivalries concerning the succession of the last Comneni erupted at Constantinople, the Angeli princes sought help in the West. The Fourth Crusade (1204), directed by the Venetians to intervene in the dispute at Constantinople, ended with the Crusaders' conquest of the capital and the establishment of the *Latin empire of Constantinople (1204-61) and of other Crusader principalities in Greece. The B. thus collapsed, but points of resistance remained. The Orthodox clergy continued to oppose the 'Latins' within their lands. Three independent B. states were established: the empire of *Nicaea, under the Lascarid generals, the empire of *Trebizond on the Black Sea, and the 'despotate' of Epirus, consisting of the surviving B. possessions in the Balkans. The Lascarids succeeded in reorganizing the empire at Nicaea, where the old B. traditions were maintained; the renaissance of schools there allowed the empire to prepare for reconquest and proved the vitality of its civilization. In 1261 Emperor *Michael VIII Palaeologus (1259-82) took advantage of the disputes at Constantinople and, after imposing his authority on the despots of Epirus, recaptured the capital and re-established the empire, which now extended only over a minor part of the ancient empire of the Comneni, i.e. the western part of Asia Minor, the area of Constantinople, Adrianople, Thrace and part of Greece. In the northern part of the Balkans, the *Serbian and Bulgarian realms were entirely independent, while southern Greece (Athens and Morea) remained under the rule of the "Latins" and the overwhelming influence of Venice.

The restored empire, under the Palaeologi (1259-1453), had to struggle for its independence. Michael VIII devoted his efforts to dismantling a western coalition, led by *Charles of Anjou, king of Sicily, who hoped to restore the Latin empire and to create a great Mediterranean state under his rule, including the Crusaders' possessions in Palestine and Syria. In combating this threat, Michael neglected the protection of the Eastern boundaries, where the *Ottoman Turks established a principality between the Seljuk sultanate of Rum and B. In the last years of the 13th century the Ottomans attacked the Asian provinces of the empire, a situation which the heirs of Michael VIII were unable to handle; instead they struggled amongst themselves. At the beginning of the 14th century, under the Sultans *Osman and *Orkhan, the Turks began to systematically conquer B. provinces. In 1326, they conquered Brussa and in 1329 Nicaea. In 1354, *John Cantacuzenus, who hoped to receive their support in a court quarrel at Constantinople, allowed them to settle at Gallipoli (in Europe). But Orkhan had his own plans, and Gallipoli was to serve him as a means of further expansion into Thrace. There the Turks conquered Adrianople, which became the capital of their empire (1365) until 1453. Constantinople was thus surrounded and isolated from the rest of the empire. In addition, the Ottoman advances in the Balkans were spectacular. *Murad I (1359-89) fought the Serbians and the Bulgarians and, after the Battle of Kossovo (1389), the two kingdoms were conquered. The fact that B.'s government was unable to take any initiative alarmed the west Europeans; thus, a crusade was proclaimed by the papacy at the instigation of Venice, but its participants were crushed by *Bayazid I at *Nicopolis (1396). Constantinople was besieged and saved only by the courage and self-confidence of the French marshal *Boucicaut (1397-99). The *Mongol invasion of Anatolia, led by *Timur-Leng, and the defeat inflicted upon Bayazid in 1402, was used skillfully by B. diplomacy to allow the empire a half century of respite. Nevertheless, under Murad II (1421-51), the Ottomans renewed their attacks and, although confronted by the resistance of Constantinople, they conquered the major part of B.'s possessions in Greece, attacked Albania and defeated another crusade at Varna in 1444, which was led by the Hungarian hero John Hunyadi. Finally, under a new sultan, Muhammad II, they attacked Constantinople in 1453 with great force and heavy artillery. The city was conquered and the last B. emperor, Constantine XI died heroically leading the defence of the city, which was all that remained of the former empire.

Civilization During the 1000 years of its existence, B. developed its own particular civilization, based on classical traditions and expressed in the Greek language, which was used both for learned and vernacular culture and influenced by the Greek Orthodox Christian faith.

Literature B. literature was a continuation of the classical Greek, in form if not in content. The authors felt bound to the ancient style, which limited their expression. For the first 300 years, the poetry was in transition — the classical pagan motives of the Hellenic and Hellenistic heritage being interwoven with Christian ideas. Works such as the *Dionysiaca* by Nonnos, written in the 5th century, foreshadowed the transformation which began in the 6th century with the introduction of long descriptive poems (*ecphraseis*), in which Christian virtues were brought in confrontation with paganism. The aim was to praise the great wisdom of the constitution, where Church and State were seen as the two poles which served to maintain the ideal life of B. In the 7th century, the Greek historical epic was revived, becoming, through the court poet George Pisides, a poetry of praise, intended first of all to honour the emperor, his actions and his victories. This courtly epic poetry prevailed until the 12th century. But, at the same time, attention was given to "holy poetry", consisting of hymns and liturgical songs, which, through the use of idioms from the spoken language and introduction of changes in the style, came to be a new genre, the most original B. literature. The so-called holy poetry reached perfection through the composition of the canon, which included an entire work of short and long poems, primarily for liturgical use, but also meant for devotion to and praise of the saints. The iconoclastic controversy was responsible in part for the development of holy poetry, whose importance was considerable not only in terms of the literary history of B., but also for the emergence and development of Slav poetry.

In the 11th century B. lay, holy and epic songs were revived. The development of schools under the Macedonian dynasty contributed to the renaissance of literature, under the influence of the Hellenistic heritage. Without surrendering religious aspects, satirical motifs were thus introduced in the poems, and the epic was no longer based on the courtly model. The poem *Basil Digenis Akritas* marked the new trend; its popularity is proved by the great number of copies, most being partially revised versions, which appeared until the 14th century. This revival of the epic was followed in the 12th century by the introduction of romances, which were in some ways similar to the *Arthurian romances of the West, but entirely different in the choice of heroes and traditions, which were peculiar to the Greek and B. heritage.

As distinct from poetry, B. prose did not concentrate on *belles-lettres*, but had a learned character from its beginnings, expressed in its theological, historical and hagiographical nature. B. theology was founded on the writings of the Greek Fathers of the Church and was influenced by the works of *Gregory of Nyssa of the 4th century, who summed up the tradition of the ancient Church. Under the influence of his work, attention was given to the defence of strict orthodox thought and to the ethical behaviour of the faithful. Therefore, there was little room for original thought, and the polemical aspect became dominant from the 7th century. The iconoclastic dispute had, in that respect, an important influence on the development of theological works. Among the prose works of that period, the most important were those of *Theodore of Studios, who considered iconoclasm heresy and of *John of Damascus, monk at the monastery of St. *Saba in Palestine, who composed *The Source of Knowledge*, where he added a philosophical dimension to the theological views of the dogmatic orthodoxy. He based his work on Aristotle and, thus, brought Aristotelian thought to medieval society. The treatise became one of the fundamental

A Lady of Rank; *6th-century Byzantine marble sculpture*

and the aim was to defend the independence of Greek orthodoxy.

The historical literature of B. consisted of chronicles, composed from the 6th century by monks, and of histories, written as a result of the combined influence of ancient Greek historiography and Christianity. An example of the latter is found in the work of Eusebius of Caesarea, who wrote a biography of Constantine in the 4th century. His work served as a model for B. historiography, which flourished from the 6th century, as part of the cultural renaissance during the rule of Justinian. *Procopius of Gaza, linking evidence with personal experience, composed the history of the wars of Justinian. In this masterpiece Procopius combined a description of the facts with his opinion as an historian. From the 7th century, scholarly historiography declined, although historic works continued to be composed. Chronography took its place, the best chronicle of the period, that of *Theophanes, compiled at the beginning of the 9th century, which related the history of the Isaurian dynasty; written in popular Greek, the chronicle contributed to a further development of the language. Under the Macedonian dynasty historical writing, like other cultural activities, was revived; this was evidenced by the works of Michael *Psellos and the members of his generation. But the best achievement of the revival period was the *Alexiad* of *Anna Comnena in the 12th century. The school of Nicaea in the 13th century looked to past glory, seeking consolation for the disasters that had befallen them. They aimed to prepare the public for the restoration of the empire and, after 1261, composed important compilations, which, although certainly lacking descriptive vitality, gave evidence of the scholastic trend of the learned medieval historiography.

The B. hagiography consisted of a vast amount of works describing the lives of saints, meant for use in worship and for the religious education of the masses. The iconoclastic controversy had an important impact on the development of the B. hagiography, which opposed the iconoclasts and offered material to be used for the worship of the icons. In the 10th century, hagiographical collections were compiled in accordance with the liturgical calendar.

Art and Architecture See *Architecture, Byzantine; *Art, Byzantine.

N. H. Baynes & H. S. L. B. Moss, *Byzantium, An Introduction to East Roman Civilization* (1953); *CMedH*, IV.

works of medieval dogmatism and was translated into Latin in the 12th century by *Burgundio of Pisa. From the end of the 9th century B. theologians were involved in polemics with the Catholic Church, either through development of their own thought, such as *Photius had done, or by opposition of the Roman Catholic faith. From the 13th century on, this trend was accentuated

C

CABOCHE, SIMON (d. c. 1420) Parisian leader. A member of the butchers' guild, he became its leader in 1412, openly expressing his sympathies for the *Burgundian party. In 1413 he led the populace against the court and the *Armagnacs, inspiring terror in the city. His faction, the Cabochiens, imposed its reign in Paris, under the protection of *John the Fearless, duke of Burgundy, who tried to hold the movement in check. The Cabochiens were the radical group of the *Bourguignons and, during 1413, C. was the actual leader of the city. By intimidating the court and through the use of terror and violence, he imposed a general reform of the royal administration, promulgated as the *Ordonnance Cabochienne* (The Cabochian Ordinance). However, his violent attitude persisted and C. maintained his control over Paris by daily executions, which ultimately led to the uniting of the opposition. In 1414 the court, the Parliament and the high bourgeoisie united under the leadership of John Juvenel d'Oursins and, with the support of the *Armagnacs, C. was overthrown. He reappeared on the public scene in 1419, during the troubles caused by the Peace of Troyes, but won little support.
A. Coville, *L'Ordonnance Cabochienne* (1888).

CADIZ City in southern Spain, near the mouth of the Guadalquivir River. Founded as an ancient Greek colony, it flourished under Carthagenian and Roman rule. It was conquered by the *Vandals in 401, who used its harbour. The city later declined under the *Visigoths and the Byzantines, who annexed it to their province of Andalusia. In 711 C. was conquered by the Arabs and, in the middle of the 8th century, became part of the caliphate of Córdoba. When the caliphate fell in 1032, an independent emirate was founded in the city and its surroundings; its rulers, the *Taifas, were able to maintain their independence from the *Abbadids. While they acknowledged the overlordship of the *Almoravides and *Almohades, the Taifas continued to be independent, their resources based on the prosperity of the city's harbour, which was one of the most important points of commercial trade with Morocco. In 1250, *Ferdinand III of Castile conquered the city and annexed it to his kingdom.
W. M. Watt, *A History of Islamic Spain* (1965).

CAEDMON (d. c. 680) The earliest known English poet. He was a monk at the monastery of Whitby, where he learned the Scriptures. According to *Bede, who is the principal source on C., he used to convert Scripture texts into verse. He is mainly known, however, as a writer of popular religious poetry, meant to be read by the laity. Of all his poems which are quoted by Bede and other sources, only one hymn has survived, which presents him as a poet inspired by his dreams.
DNB, IV.

Interior of the Abbaye aux Hommes *at Caen*

CAEN City in Normandy. It was founded by the Normans in the 10th century and developed around a ducal castle. In the 11th century it became the residence of the dukes of Normandy, who founded two abbeys there, the Abbey for Men (*l'Abbaye aux Hommes*) and the Abbey for Women (*l'Abbaye aux Dames*), to which *William the Conqueror made a rich endowment. Their churches are important monuments to Norman Romanesque architecture. In 1202, C., together with the duchy of Normandy, came under French royal rule, although some of the provincial assemblies continued to be held there, symbolizing its traditional role as ducal city. The capital, however, remained at Rouen. In 1419 the city was conquered by the English army and remained under

Part of the Crusader citadel wall at Caesarea

English rule until towards the end of the *Hundred Years' War. In 1432, the duke of Bedford, as regent for King Henry VI of England, founded the university at C., which was officially recognized in 1452 by *Charles VII.
A. de Bourmont, *La Ville et l'Université de Caen* (1885).

CAESAREA The ancient Herodian and Roman city of Palestine, which remained the provincial capital under Byzantine rule at the beginning of the Middle Ages. In the 6th century it became a Greek city, and the non-Greek part of its population was assimilated by the Greek element. After the Arab conquest of Palestine, C. resisted and was besieged by the Arabs. It fell only in 640, when it was conquered by *Mu'awiyah, the governor of Syria. Under Arab rule, the city rapidly declined. The majority of its Greek inhabitants left, its maritime trade diminished and the provincial capital was transferred to Ramlah. In 1100, it was conquered by the *Crusaders, who restored its archbishopric and founded a seigniory, which was amongst the most important in the Latin kingdom of Jerusalem. C. was conquered in 1187 by *Saladin, but in 1191, the Crusaders recaptured it. In 1250 *Louis IX of France reconstructed its fortifications, but could not prevent its conquest and destruction by the Mamelukes in 1268.
S. Runciman, *A History of the Crusades* (1953).

CAESARIUS, St. (470-542) Archbishop of Arles (502-42). In 489 he entered the monastery of *Lérins, where he received his spiritual education. Being on good terms with the *Visigothic king *Alaric II and with *Theodoric the Great, king of the *Ostrogoths, he succeeded in having Arles made the primatial see of Gaul. He played an important part in the ecclesiastical administration of the country and was also respected by the *Frankish court after 507. C. led the struggle against heretical trends and movements in his time, which assured him

a leading position in the whole Western Church. A celebrated preacher, he wrote sermons and compiled a collection of canons. In the last years of his life he was already venerated as a saint.
S. Cavallin, *Studien zur Vita Caesarii* (1934).

CAESARIUS OF HEISTERBACH (1180-1240) Historian. Born near Cologne, he entered the *Cistercian monastery of Heisterbach on the Rhine in 1199. Of his many works the most important are the *Dialogus Miraculorum* (The Dialogue of the Miracles), written about 1223, historical anecdotes for the edification of novices, to which were later added the eight volumes of the *Miracles*. His books, which include many supernatural incidents, cover the historical events of the 12th and 13th centuries as he interpreted them, and a description of popular beliefs in his time. There are also important testimonies on the heretical movements, primarily the *Albigenses and the beginnings of their repression.
A. E. Schönbach, *Über Caesarius von Heisterbach* (1902).

CAESARO-PAPISM A term used to describe the political system of the *Byzantine empire, whereby the emperor ruled over the church. It means that the sovereign is emperor and pope at the same time. Devised by modern historians, the definition is shown by current historical research to be too generalized, and requires a more thorough comprehension not only of institutional imperial supremacy, but also its legal and theological aspects.
N. H. Baynes and H. S. L. B. Moss, *Byzantium* (1953).

CAETANI (Gaetani) Aristocratic Roman family, which from the 12th century on owned large estates in the area and was involved in the political life of the city and the papacy. Its influence grew in the 13th century, when members of the C. family were created cardinals and competed with the *Colonna and *Orsini for control of the city and the papal office. With *Boniface VIII on the papal throne, the family reached the peak of its influence. They enlarged their estates and became counts of Anagni, one of the papal residences. In the 14th century, while popes were installed at *Avignon, the C. were powerful in Rome and manipulated Italian politics. The return of the papacy to Rome in 1378 limited their ability to act and they were seen as troublemakers of the pontifical state. In 1400 they were defeated by a coalition of their rivals and lost the county of Anagni, after which they declined.
G. Caetani, *Domus Caietana; Storia documentata della famiglia Caetani* (1927).

CAFFARO (1081-1166) Genoese historian. As an official of the city of Genoa, he had access to state documents. From 1099 until he died he wrote the annals of the city, wherein he summarized the events of the year. The importance of *Genoa in international politics makes his chronicle a very important source, not only for the history of his city, but of northern Italy, the papacy and the Genoese colonies in the Mediterranean Sea. It is also a significant source for the history of the *Crusades.
Ed. *Fonti per la Storia d'Italia*, I-II (1887).

CAHORS City in southwestern France (Aquitaine). In the last century of the Roman empire, it became an important centre of the Christian faith for the whole region. After the fall of the Roman empire, it belonged to the *Visigothic kingdom and its economic importance diminished. In 507 it was conquered by the *Franks and a count was appointed to govern it and its surroundings; but by the middle of the 6th century, it had already been taken over by its bishops. In the 8th century it was often attacked and conquered by the dukes of Aquitaine and in 763, *Pepin the Short re-established Frankish rule. Although the direct feudal lordship of the city remained in the hands of its bishops, C. belonged to the kingdom of Aquitaine and, after its dissolution in 858, to the county of Toulouse. From the 11th century the country was peaceful and the city's location on the banks of the Dordogne encouraged the revival of commerce and the establishment of fairs, which attracted merchants from all over the area. The economic prosperity of the time is evidenced by the city's churches and monuments, built according to a particular style of Romanesque art. In the 13th century, C. became a centre of international business and Italian merchants came to its fairs; as a result of several financial transactions, the city became renowned as a banking centre. The Cahorsins became noted moneylenders in several cities, but the term Cahorsin does not exclusively imply men of C. In the *Hundred Years' War, claim to the city was disputed between the English lords of Guyenne and the counts of *Armagnac. The latter annexed it to their duchy at the beginning of the 15th century.

Ph. Wolff (ed.), *Le Quercy (Provinces et Pays de France)* (1971).

CAIRO Capital of Egypt. The city was founded in 969 by the *Fatimid Caliph Al-Mu'izz and its name is actually a contraction of a longer one, *Al-Qahirah Al-Mu'izziyah* (The Victorious City of Mu'izz). Its site on the Nile incorporated the elder Arabic city of *Fustat, founded in the 7th century, which became known as Old Cairo. The city was designed and planned as an urban agglomeration of distinct quarters for Arabs, Berbers, Jews, Greeks, Kurds and Negroes; and each community was run by its own autonomous local institutions. The city's importance grew rapidly with the establishment of the Fatimid government over all of Egypt and with its conquest of large territories in Palestine and Syria. The building of the Mosque of Al-Azhar in 970, where a number of Moslem schools of theology were to be housed, helped make C. a spiritual centre of Islam. Al-Azhar thus became an academy where Islamic theology was discussed and studied, and the scholars' conclusions were generally accepted in the Moslem world. The city was also an important economic centre, especially regarding the trade between the Far East and the Mediterranean. Merchandise unloaded in the Red Sea harbours was transported to C., and shipped to Alexandria via the Nile. The late 19th-century discovery of the archives of the old Jewish community in Cairo, which were called *Genizah*, provided extensive documentation on these commercial activities during the 10th-13th centuries. During the 12th century the city continued to develop, but an open space remained between the old quarters of Fustat and the aristocratic city of C., as has been related through the stories of Moslem travellers and in the correspondence of *Maimonides. With the extinction of the *Fatimids and the ascension of *Saladin (1170), the importance of C. as the great centre of Islamic civilization, as well as of Jewry in the Islamic countries, grew considerably. In the 13th century, new quarters were built and a garrison of Mameluke

The Cairo Citadel built by Saladin in 1179

soldiers was set up on the bank of the Nile (the *Bahri Castle). In 1250, the Bahri Mamelukes revolted against the last *Ayyubids and established their rule in Egypt and C. The city benefited from their conquests; for example, pillars from Caesarea were used in the building of the Great Mosque. In the 14th century, the city was troubled by social revolts, which rapidly developed into religious movements, led by preachers and rulers, against the *dhimmis*; the Christian and Jewish communities suffered and some of their members emigrated. This caused a certain decline in commercial activities. In the middle of the century, plagues, including the *Black Death, also contributed to the city's decline. In the 15th century the situation was somewhat improved, although C. did not regain the state of prosperity it had known in the 13th century until the modern period.
CHI (1970).

CALABRIA Province in southern Italy, marking the southwestern point of the Italian peninsula, between Naples and Sicily. After the fall of the Western Roman empire, C., located away from the great centres and reputed for its relative poverty, remained removed from the great historical events of the time. Its development largely followed that of its neighbouring provinces. Thus, at the beginning of the 6th century it belonged to the *Ostrogothic kingdom and, after its conquest by the Byzantines, remained under the rule of Byzantium until the 11th century. In its mountains, which were suitable for seclusion, many monastic communities were founded and flourished as reform centres of Christianity. In the middle of the 11th century, Norman adventurers penetrated the country and conquered it from the Byzantines. In 1054 it was part of the state founded by *Robert Guiscard and served in the succeeding years as a base for the Norman conquest of Sicily (1060-71).

The Norman settlement along the roads which connected Sicily and Naples gave the province added importance, although the mountain area continued to be inhabited by small villages of sheep rearers. After the *Sicilian Vespers (1282) and the subsequent establishment of two separate kingdoms at Sicily and at Naples, C. became part of the Angevin kingdom of *Naples, where it constituted a separate province. It was elevated in the 14th century to the rank of duchy and was given to one of the sons of the king of Naples.

E. Pontieri, *Il Medioevo Calabrese* (1957).

CALAIS City in northeastern France. Until the 12th century, C. was a small fishermen's village in the county of *Flanders, whose development was connected with that of *Boulogne. Gradually its harbour grew and became active in the naval trade between England and Flanders, and the village became a borough, whose importance increased in the 14th century, when trouble in the Flemish cities made it one of the most suitable places for the importing of English wool. In 1345, after their victory at *Crécy, the English army attacked C., which resisted more than six months of siege. *Edward III, who decided to establish a secure position in France, both in order to continue the *Hundred Years' War and to control the export of English wool, forced C. to capitulate unconditionally. Eustache de St. Pierre, who led the resistance, together with five other burghers, was killed, but the city was spared and fell under English rule until 1558. In 1347, Edward signed a truce with the representatives of France, which put an end to the first stage of the war. A staple where wool sent from England was sold to those cities which declared themselves allies of the king, was established at C. in 1345, assuring its prosperity. Thus, under English rule, the city flourished economically and was fortified. An effort was made to change its ethno-cultural character through the settlement of English burghers in the city, but, despite the establishment of an English bourgeoisie, the change was superficial.

E. B. Fryde, *Edward III's War Finances* (1953).

CALATRAVA, ORDER OF The order originated in 1158, when the monks of the *Cistercian monastery of C., north of the Sierra Morena, together with a number of knights organized the defence of their monastery and borough. They adopted the form of the *Templars and organized a religious-chivalric order, intended to fight the Moslems. In 1164 they were given the support of Pope *Alexander III, and the Castilian kings often granted them the use of castles and territories on the Andalusian borders. They remained affiliated to the Cistercian order and their leader (Great Master) was often invited to the meetings of the order in the 13th century. In the 14th and 15th centuries they became involved in the internal political struggles of *Castile and became a powerful and rich organization within the state. In 1482, the order became attached to the crown by Ferdinand and Isabella.

R. Altamira, *A History of Spain* (1949).

CALENDAR Medieval society used religious Cs. Thus, those of the Jewish and Moslem communities were based on the cycles of the moon. The Christians, however, adopted the Roman civil C., the Julian, which was used in the later Roman empire. While it served most needs, the Julian C. posed problems in liturgical life, especially regarding the fixing of Christian holidays which were related to the Jewish origins of Christianity. The various systems of computation continued to be discussed in the early Middle Ages. Important progress was made with the establishment of the tables by *Bede, by which the dates of Easter and Pentecost could be fixed according to the calculation of the beginning of spring. While in the Byzantine empire and in the Slavic countries, which converted to Orthodox Christianity, the Julian C. continued to be used, in western Europe two different systems were adopted from the 9th century: the "Pisan C.", used mainly in the Mediterranean countries and in the *Holy Roman empire, based on the Christmas cycle (meaning that the year began on 25 December); and the Easter cycle, used mainly in England, France and northern Europe, as well as in the Netherlands and certain German provinces, in which Easter – a movable feast – was the beginning of the year. In the countries where the Easter cycle was used, dates were fixed according to the liturgy of the saints; for example, payment of certain taxes were due at Michaelmas and not on 29 September.

H. Grotefend, *Zeitrechnung des Mittelalters und der Neuzeit* (1891).

CALIMALA The name of the guild of wool craftsmen at Florence. The C. became a very important association in the 13th century, when its members controlled the production and prices of the wool industry in Italy. Its economic importance gained it political power and its leaders were active in the political life of Florence in the latter half of the 13th century; in 1273, they established one of the five major parties of Florence, consisting of a federation of the seven major guilds under their leadership. Their power began to decline in the 14th century, although they maintained their economic influence, forming the association of the *Arte della Lana*, which continued until the constitution of the *Medici principality.

F. Schevill, *Medieval and Renaissance Florence* (1961).

CALIXTUS I, St. (155-222) Pope (218-22). A descendant of slaves, his life and pontificate are subjects of controversy between his Roman adversaries and his venerators. The catacombs in San Callisto at Rome are named after him.

EC, II.

CALIXTUS II (Guido of Vienne; 1060-1124) Pope (1119-24). He was a descendant of the counts of *Burgundy and thus related to Emperor *Henry V and the king of France, *Louis VI, as well as to other royal houses in western Europe. In 1088 he became archbishop of Vienne and was active in the *Gregorian reform movement. In 1112 he took part in the Council of Lateran, where he influenced Henry V's condemnation. He was elected pope at Cluny, where his predecessor *Gelasius II had died as a refugee. Having gained the support of the French and English clergy and kings, he excommunicated Henry V at the Council of Rheims, where lay *investiture was proclaimed heresy. Thus he provoked a civil war in Germany, which was ended by the intervention of the assembly of German princes, who compelled the parties to come to a peaceful solution of the Investiture controversy. C. negotiated a settlement and the terms were recorded in the document known as the Concordat of *Worms (1122), which was promulgated at the Council of Lateran in 1123, the first ecumenical council of the Catholic Church. C. organized the government of the Church in a centralist manner, giving papal legates of various countries authority over the local hierarchy, even when their ecclesiastic rank was lower; he based his move on the grounds that the legates were representatives of the sovereign pontiff.

U. Robert, *Histoire de Calixte II* (1891).

CALLINICUS (7th century) Byzantine engineer. Born in Syria, of a Greek family, he took refuge in Constantinople after the Arab conquest of Syria (640). Employed at the imperial arsenal, he invented the *Greek fire bombs, which were successfully used in the naval battle of Constantinople in 674. The Arab fleet was destroyed by these bombs which were launched from Byzantine vessels.

G. Zenghelis, *Le Feu grégeois et les armes à feu des Byzantins* (1932).

CALLISTUS (d. 1363) Patriarch of Constantinople (1350-54; 1355-63). He belonged to the conservative party of the Byzantine clergy, which opposed union with the Catholic Church. Brought by this party to the see of the ecumenical patriarchate, he found himself involved in the political struggle at Byzantium and opposed the government of *John Cantacuzenus, who deposed him in 1354. After the fall of Cantacuzenus and the restoration of *John V Palaeologus, his position was restored, but he opposed the emperor's political understanding with Rome. C. worked to gain recognition of the Greek patriarch of Constantinople as privileged over the autonomous patriarchs of the *Bulgarians and the *Serbs; he was largely successful in establishing his primacy. He negotiated further agreements with the Serbs, intended to unite the Orthodox churches of the Balkans against the *Turks, but died before they came into effect. Thus, at the same time that the *Byzantine empire was weakening, the Orthodox Church was becoming strengthened.

S. Zankov, *The Eastern Orthodox Church* (1930).

CALTABELLOTTA Town in southern Sicily where a peace treaty was signed between *Charles of Valois and the Aragonese in 1302. The former had invaded Sicily on behalf of his cousin *Charles II of Anjou, king of Naples, and was defeated in his attempt to reconquer the island from the Aragonese army, who had established their rule there after the *Sicilian Vespers (1282). According to this treaty, Aragonese rule in Sicily was recognized.

S. Runciman, *The Sicilian Vespers* (1958).

CAMALDOLESE, ORDER OF A religious order founded in 1012 by St. *Romuald at Camaldoli, near Arezzo, in central Italy. Its ideal was the barest minimum of communal ties. The order was organized in hermitages and the monks were required to live the life of *hermits. The primitive severity was gradually relaxed in the 12th century and the monks of C. came to be employed in the service of the Church, noted as one of the most ascetic monastic congregations.

DHGE, XI.

CAMBRAI City in Flanders. The Gallo-Roman town of C. was conquered by the Salian *Franks *c.* 430 and became the capital of an insignificant kingdom, whose kings were allied with those of Tournai. In 490, the city came under the sovereignty of *Clovis and in the 7th century, its bishopric was attached to that of Arras. In the 10th and 11th centuries the city grew and became an important economic centre in the Flemish county, reputed for its cloth industry. Its prosperity caused the

emperors, who were formally its sovereigns, to establish an independent bishopric there in an attempt to impose their authority through the influence of the bishops. The burghers, however, succeeded in maintaining their privileges, based on their resources. Thus, the government of the city was divided between three authorities: the township, the imperial bishops and the counts of Flanders. The power of the counts diminished in the 13th century, and they were compelled to recognize the jurisdiction of the bishops. At the beginning of the 15th century the "free bishops" of C. fell under the authority of the dukes of *Burgundy. As a ducal city, C. became attached to Flanders and under *Charles the Bold it was ethnically and economically integrated into French-speaking Flanders. Its Gothic cathedral, designed by *Villard de Honnecourt, is one of the most interesting achievements of 13th-century Gothic architecture.

A. Dubrulle, *Cambrai à la fin du Moyen Age* (1904).

CAMBRIDGE City in England. Its origins go back to Celtic times and its urban organization dates from the Roman period. After the *Anglo-Saxon conquest of Britain the city declined. Its claim was disputed between the East Anglia and Mercia kingdoms and gradually its importance grew because of its bridge on the Cam River, which was one of the points of traffic to the Midlands. In the latter half of the 9th century C. was conquered by the *Danes several times and, after a short period of English rule under *Alfred the Great, it remained in the

Queen's College, Cambridge, built in the 15th century

An aerial view of Cambridge

*Danelaw, becoming the administrative centre of Cambridgeshire. In the 10th century the town prospered as a trade centre, to which merchants came from the Continent and from Ireland. In the years following the *Norman Conquest (1066) a castle was built near the city by *William the Conqueror, in order to assure the conquest of the northern provinces. The city further developed in the 12th century and was granted a charter of privileges by *Henry I in 1122, who allowed it a monopoly over the naval trade in the shire. During the period of anarchy which reigned under *Stephen, C. was one of the fields of battle and became, temporarily, an autonomous earldom. Under *Henry II the city flourished again and became a monastic and cultural centre. Due to a conflict at Oxford in 1209 a number of teachers and students migrated to C. where they founded a school. This later became the university established by *Henry III in 1229. From that date, C. became famous as a university-city, second to Oxford; colleges were established in the city and at the end of the 15th century their number rose to 15. In 1381 C. was one of the centres of the great peasants' rebellion (see *England), and its repression led to the ruin of the wealthy burghers who took part in the rebellion, led by their mayor.

J. Tait, *The Medieval English Borough* (1936).

CAMEL, BATTLE OF (656) The first war among the Moslems, between *Ali and his supporters, and *Aisha, the widow of *Mohammad, who was supported by the Mecca tribes. The battle was won by Ali, while Aisha fled on a camel, hence the name of the battle. The outcome marked the end of Meccan supremacy in the Islamic world, and the capital of the caliphate was transferred by Ali to *Kufa in Iraq. Nevertheless, the battle did not settle the dispute between the *Ummayads and Ali, which brought about the schism of the *Shiites.

E. L. Peterson, *Ali and Muawiya in Early Arab Tradition* (1964).

CAMPAGNA, CAMPANIA COMMUNIS Latin terms designating arable fields, which were generally cultivated by the communities of medieval villages. As distinct from private fields, they were under the supervision of one of the lord's servants, or rented by the mayor on behalf of the village. See *Agriculture.

CAMPALDINO, BATTLE OF (1289) The last of a series of wars between the *Guelph leaders of *Florence and its *Ghibelline neighbours. The Florentine victory assured the superiority of Florence in Tuscany, and was the basis for the establishment of the principality of Florence in central Italy.

F. Schevill, *Medieval and Renaissance Florence* (1961).

CAMPANIA A fertile plain in central Italy, south of Rome and north of Naples. It formed a province in the last century of the Roman empire, whose capital was *Capua. C. was one of the centres of food supply to Rome and, therefore, the conquerors of Italy at the beginning of the Middle Ages tried to secure possession of the area, which passed from the *Ostrogoths to the Byzantines and finally to the *Lombards. In 774 *Charlemagne granted it to the papal state, to which it belonged until 1859. But from the end of the 8th century C. was divided into several counties and only the northern part of it, which continued to bear the name of the province, belonged to the papal state. Capua became the capital of a Lombard duchy, which fell in the 10th century under Byzantine rule. In the 11th century, with the establishment of the *Normans in southern Italy, the major part of C. was attached to their state and became part of the kingdom of Sicily and later (from 1282) became part of the kingdom of Naples. The area's northern part, named Roman C., remained under papal rule.

E. R. Labande, *Naples et la Campanie* (1953).

CAMPIN, ROBERT See FLEMALLE, MASTER OF.

CAMPUS MAURIACUS, BATTLE OF (451) A field near Troyes (eastern France), identified with the modern village of Moirey, where the Roman general *Aetius, together with *Visigothic and *Frankish troops, defeated the Huns, led by *Attila. The victory freed Gaul from Hunnish conquest and destruction, but, despite the prestige of Aetius, could not prevent the decline of Roman authority in Gaul and the rise of the Barbarian realms.

E. A. Thompson, *A History of Attila and the Huns* (1948).

CANALE, MARTINO DI (d. c. 1290) Venetian historian. He wrote a history of Venice, covering the period from the foundation of the city up to his own days. Regarding the earlier periods, the work is a compilation of various chronicles, but beginning in 1250 and up to 1275, the chronicle is based on the author's own memories and on documents he was able to gather. This latter part is a valuable source of information about the development of the Venetian empire in the Mediterranean and in Italy. C. was one of the first historians to write in French, this language being the most pleasant and expressive of his time.

J. W. Thompson, *History of the Historical Writing* (1943).

CANON Originally a Greek word meaning a straight rod or bar. The term was adopted into the ecclesiastic vocabulary, both Greek and Latin, where it had several meanings. The oldest, borrowed from the metaphorical use of the original, was the authoritative list of the Holy Books, or Scriptures, containing the Old and the New Testaments, the liturgical books and the writings of the Fathers of the Church. Later on, the term also signified some orders of hymns and, from the 6th century, it was also used to indicate ecclesiastic legislation, as opposed to civil law. Thus, all decisions and decrees of the ecclesiastic councils were named Cs. until the 15th century, when a distinction was introduced between legislative and other documents. The term C. was used to refer to the former. Another meaning of the term is the title conferred to members of specific parts of the clergy.

The term as an ecclesiastical title was particularly used in this sense in the Westen Church. Until the 10th century it was used to designate all of the secular clergy, excluding monks and private chaplains; every C. had a share in the revenues of the Church, a prebend or a stipend. From the 11th century, the term was redefined more precisely to signify the clergy which had official positions in the cathedral churches and were allowed to elect the bishop. The C. body was organized as an autonomous college, governed by a dean, administrating that part of the Church patrimony which was granted to them by the bishop. This autonomy implied adoption of a certain rule (*regula*) concerning their manner of living, which was generally approved by the papacy, and mainly concerned their behaviour and the administration of their share, the *mensa capituli* (the revenue of the Chapter). A large portion of the colleges of Cs. adopted rules of communal living, later called *Augustinian C. Under the influence of the *Gregorian reform, certain colleges of Cs. were established in the late 11th and 12th centuries in separate monasteries, where the members (regular C.) lived communally. Of the several orders of regular C., the most important were the *Premonstratensians, founded in 1119. In the last centuries of the Middle Ages, the C. title was generally reserved for the upper clergy in the cathedral churches; these were frequently absent from their pastoral duties, either because they also fulfilled duties in the royal and princely courts, or because they were appointed to that dignity by papal decrees, merely to assure them suitable revenues for activities on behalf of the papacy.

The sources of C. law were the Bible, decrees of the councils and the writings of the Fathers of the Church and similar authorities. In the 6th century the C. law was codified under *Justinian as a part of the imperial law, and the C. law of the Eastern Church remained part of the imperial legislation in the Byzantine empire until the 15th century. In the Catholic Church, however, the development of the C. legislation was independent of the state, particularly after the death of Justinian. Under *Charlemagne, an attempt was made to legislate C. under the imperial authority, but, from the middle of the 9th century, the councils became entirely independent of the sovereigns. While the Bible, the decrees of the councils and the writings of the Fathers, were common sources of the C. law in both Eastern and Western Churches, the latter also recognized papal decisions as a source of law. Nevertheless, no official *corpus* of C. existed in the West and the various collections were private. In the middle of the 9th century, such a collection, which came to be called the Frankish Decretals or the Pseudo-*Isidore C., was compiled in France and Germany. It included a number of false Cs. At the beginning of the 11th century, *Burchard of Worms compiled a more authoritative collection, which he called *Decretum*. During the Gregorian reform movement, this collection was added to in Italy by *Anselm of Lucca, but the best compilation was that of *Ivo of Chartres (codified *c.* 1100), who divided the vast material into sections. Besides his *Decretum*, which suited learned circles, he also produced an abridged form of the collection, the *Panormia*. The most authoritative collection of C. law, however, was that of the Bolognese jurist, *Gratian, whose *Concordantia Discordantium Canonum* (The Concordance of the Discordant Canons), or *Decretum Gratiani* (1139-40) codified the earlier C. and established a recognized body of ecclesiastical law.

Henry IV, Matilda and Hugh of Cluny at Canossa

Gratian's collection was discussed and commented upon in universities and was later revised by generations of jurists in the late Middle Ages. Beginning in the latter half of the 12th century, papal decretals, which were issued on different occasions, were added to C. law.

The C. law consisted of several aspects of legislation: it dealt with the governing of the church, including Cs. regarding the rules of ecclesiastical life, both for secular and regular clergy, and specifying their duties and privileges; relations between Church and State, including the degree of independence of ecclesiastical jurisdiction and the immunity of the clergy to lay jurisdiction (for example, a clerk, who had murdered someone, had to be tried according to the C. law and, if convicted, was reduced to lay status, in which case he was brought to trial for the murder in a lay court); and the moral and spiritual life of the laics, also including such aspects as marriage, family life, the legitimacy of children, etc.
DHGE, XII;
Corpus Juris Canonici, ed. E. Friedberg (1879);
P. Fournier - G. Le Bras, *Histoire des Collections Canoniques en Occident depuis les fausses Décrétales jusqu'au Décret de Gratien* (1931-1932).

CANONIZATION The procedure in the Catholic Church of declaring saints. Until the 12th century, no formal procedure existed and saints were proclaimed generally by the veneration of the faithful masses. Nevertheless, even then certain rules were observed and, with the exception of the personalities of the Scriptures and the Fathers of the Church, it was required that miracles be shown to have taken place at the saint's tomb. From the 12th century on, the privilege to declare saints was solely reserved to the pope, who allowed the C. only after an investigation based on the biography of the saint, which had to include miracles occurring during his life and after his death.
E. W. Kemp, *Canonization and Authority in the Western Church* (1948).

CANOSSA Castle in northern Tuscany, near Reggio, which belonged to the marquises of Tuscany. In 1077, *Matilda of Tuscany offered hospitality to Pope *Gregory VII there. The pope was on his way to Germany to join the rebels against *Henry IV, whom he had previously excommunicated. Henry, who tried to prevent this meeting, came in the winter and made public penance before the lodgings of the pope, abasing himself by standing in the snow for three days. Although the excommunication had political overtones, Gregory could not refuse to grant absolution to the emperor, who thus regained moral authority over his rebellious subjects and placed the pope in an unfavourable light. This incident, which was really a great victory for the emperor, became the basis of the expression "To go to Canossa", i.e., to humiliate oneself, to beg pardon for one's sins.
A. J. Macdonald, *Gregory VII* (1932).

CANTERBURY City in southeastern England, the see of the primate of the English Church. The town existed in the Roman period under the name *Durovernum Cantiorum*, and from the 6th century it became the capital of the kingdom of *Kent. In 597, St. *Augustine settled there and began to propagate the Christian faith in England. From 601, C. became the diocese of the archbishops, whose authority was imposed on all the bishops of the southern part of England. Its ecclesiastic character became more accentuated in the 8th century, when it became the religious centre of Anglo-Saxon England, and churches were built in the city. The ancient cathedral there was often rebuilt and enlarged in accordance with current styles of architecture, its major part being Romanesque and Gothic. One of the most ancient buildings, partially constructed at the beginning of the 7th century, is the Monastery of Sts. Peter and Paul, intended to provide burial places for the archbishops and the kings of Kent. The cloister church of the monastery was dedicated in the 8th century to St. Augustine, whose tomb is still venerated there. In the 12th and 13th centuries its monks challenged the privileges of those belonging to the order of regular canons of Christchurch. The city of C. remained the religious capital of England in the late Middle Ages, but, from the 13th century, the archbishops began to reside at London, in Lambeth Palace.

F. R. H. DuBoulay, *Canterbury* (1966).

CANTILUPE, St. THOMAS OF (c. 1218-82) Bishop of Hereford (1275-82). Born to a noble family of Hambleden, he was educated at Oxford, Paris and Orléans. In 1262, he became chancellor of Oxford University, and in that capacity supported the baronial revolt against *Henry III. With the barons' victory at *Lewes, C. became chancellor of England, but after their subsequent defeat he retired to Paris, where he taught at the university. He returned to England in 1272, resuming his post at Oxford. In 1275 he was elected bishop of Hereford and became a close adviser to *Edward I. He fought against nepotism and for the rights of his see, entering into conflict with the archbishop of Canterbury, John *Peckham, who excommunicated him in 1282. C. appealed to the papal court, but died before judgement was passed. Despite the excommunication, he was widely regarded as a saint and miracles were said to have occurred at his tomb. He was canonized in 1320.
DNB, VIII.

Remains of a Crusader vaulted street at Caesarea

CANTIMPRÉ, THOMAS OF (c. 1228-44) Born in Brabant, he was a scholar who dedicated himself to natural history. Like Roger *Bacon, he produced works on botany and zoology based on his own observations, summed up in his *De Natura Rerum* (On the Nature of Things). This treatise is of a lower standard than the works of Bacon, but was more popular.
A. C. Crombie, *Science in the Middle Ages* (1957).

CANUTE IV, St. (1040-86) King of Denmark (1080-86). Son of Sweyn Esthrithson, he conducted military expeditions to England and the Baltic, but at the same time had deep religious feelings. As king, he fought against the power of nobles, supporting the establishment of churches, which he also intended using for his internal policy. His administration imposed heavy taxes on farmers, who therefore often revolted. In 1086 a general revolt compelled him to flee to Odense, where he took refuge in the priory of the Evesham monks which he had established, but was murdered there. In 1101 he was proclaimed a saint.
P. G. Foote and D. Wilson, *The Viking Achievement* (1970).

CANUTE VI (1163-1202) King of Denmark (1182-1202). Son of *Waldemar Knudsson and his successor. He reigned with the aid of his brother and successor *Waldemar II and of *Absalon, archbishop of Lund. Having married the daughter of *Henry the Lion, duke of Saxony, he refused to submit to the overlordship of Emperor *Frederick Barbarossa, Henry's rival. He supported Absalon's expeditions to Pomerania and Mecklenburg in northeastern Germany, where a number of cities were conquered. To celebrate the conquests, C. added King of the Slavs to his royal title. He subsequently conquered Holstein, Hamburg and Lübeck and established Danish domination in the Baltic Sea. His main achievement was the establishment of a feudal monarchy in Denmark, putting an end to the Viking age.
P. G. Foote and D. Wilson, *The Viking Achievement* (1970).

CANUTE (KNUT) I, Eriksson (d. 1195) King of Sweden (1168-95). He succeeded his uncle Charles VII. After many years of dynastic strife in Sweden, his reign marked a period of peace. Having had his father, *Eric, canonized, he established his cult at Uppsala, which became the political and spiritual capital of the realm. C. fought against the raids of Estonian pirates and fortified the country with a series of strongholds, the most important of them having been the foundation of Stockholm.
I. Andersson, *A History of Sweden* (1952).

CANUTE (KNUT) LAVARD (c. 1096-1131) Danish prince, nephew of King Niels. His personality and his successful expeditions against the *Wends made him very popular, particularly in Schleswig and southern Jutland. He appeared to be most fit to succeed Niels according to the Viking custom of elective kingship. The king murdered him in 1131. The murder created a wave of hostility against Niels and his son and heir Magnus, which brought C.'s son, *Waldemar I, to the throne and led to the foundation of a new dynasty. C. became a legendary figure of medieval Denmark.
P. G. Foote and D. Wilson, *The Viking Achievement* (1970).

CANUTE THE GREAT (Knud, Knut; 995-1035) King of Denmark (1018-35), England (1016-35) and Norway

(1028-35). Son of King *Sweyn, C. completed the Danish conquest of England begun by his father and in 1016 was proclaimed its king, establishing an equitable rule over his Anglo-Saxon subjects. In 1018, he succeeded his brother *Harald to the throne of Denmark and established a powerful empire of the North, to which he annexed Norway – where anarchy reigned – in 1028. C.'s rule was based on respecting the traditions and institutions of his realms. He built a powerful fleet, securing his domination in the northern seas. He maintained friendly relations with Emperor *Conrad II and introduced Danish influence in Schleswig.
L. M. Larson, *Canute the Great* (1912).

CAPELLA PALATINA An impressive church in the palace of the Norman kings of *Sicily, at Palermo. Built during the reign of *Roger II in the 12th century and completed by his successors, its architecture combines Arab, Byzantine and Romanesque architectural and decorative elements, creating a unity of conception. It served as the chapel of the Sicilian kings until 1860.

CAPETIANS The third royal dynasty in France, named after *Hugh Capet (987-97). A famous ancestor of the C. was *Robert the Strong, count of Tours and duke of the Franks, who defeated the *Normans when they invaded the Loire Valley in 867. His descendants alternated with the last *Carolingians as kings of France in the late 9th and early 10th century. With the election of Hugh Capet, the C. established their dynasty, but, until the 12th century, they were virtually powerless, even having to defend their domains, from Paris to Orléans, against small vassals (see *France, History). In the 12th century, profiting from economic and social circumstances and gaining the support of the church and the towns, they crushed the small vassals and increased their power. With *Louis IX (St. Louis), the dynasty reached the peak of its authority and prestige. From the 14th century on, they built the structures of a centralist government. In 1328, with the death of *Charles IV, who had no sons, the direct C. line ended and the kingship was inherited by a collateral branch, the Valois, descendants of the younger son of *Philip III, Charles of Valois. His son, *Philip VI, founded the Valois branch of the C., which reigned until 1498. Other branches of the dynasty ruled over French provinces, either by the marriage of younger sons of dynasty members with heiresses of feudal principalities, or by the establishment of *apanages in their favour. Among the most important of those branches were the dukes of *Burgundy (of both families, direct C. and Valois), the *Anjou and the *Bourbon.
R. Fawtier, *The Capetian Kings of France* (1957).

CAPITANO DEL POPOLO (Head of the People) Title given to leaders of craftsmen's guilds in Italy in the 13th and 14th centuries. The C. were recognized as the democratic party, in opposition to the aristocratic governments. During the latter half of the 13th century they seized power in the majority of city-states in Italy, with the exception of Venice where aristocratic rule continued unabated. In most of the cities concerned, the government of the C. alternated with that of the aristocracy and, when the latter was in power, they led the opposition. With the establishment of aristocratic dynasties and principalities in the 14th century, the C. began to decline; in the 15th century, it no longer existed.
F. Niccolai, *Città e Signori* (1941).

French ship leaving for the Crusade; page from a 14th-century manuscript

CAPITULARY The written form of the ordinances pronounced in court assemblies *(placitum)*, used particularly in the *Carolingian period (9th-10th centuries). Organized in chapters, C. is derived from the Latin word *Caput* (chapter). They were intended to be diffused over the realm or empire and, in certain cases, in the provinces concerned, by the *missi dominici* (the lord's delegates). The C. are divided into three main categories: legislative, publishing laws or amending them; administrative, containing regulations, ordinances and provisions of general and local interest; declarative, informing the subjects on royal and imperial decisions and actions on matters of principle. In certain cases, the C. combined materials of an administrative and a declarative nature, although those of legislative character always appeared separately. About 830, certain abbeys copied and preserved the C. in special registers and such collections were the sources of the modern editions.
F. L. Ganshof, *Recherches sur les Capitulaires* (1958).

CAPPADOCIA Province in Asia Minor which belonged to the Byzantine empire until the end of the 11th century, when it was conquered by the *Seljuk Turks. The historical importance of C. resides in its having been a centre of Christianity in the 4th-6th centuries under the leadership of the Cappadocian Fathers, St. *Basil, St. *Gregory of Nanzianus and St. *Gregory of Nyssa, whose teachings and works had a major impact on medieval theology. C. also was the province where the Greek-Orthodox form of monasticism was instituted by St. Basil. Only after the establishment of Byzantine centralism, during the reign of *Justinian, did its importance as a religious centre began to decline.
N. H. Baynes and H. S. L. B. Moss, *Byzantium* (1949).

CAPUA City in central Italy, between Rome and Naples, on the famous Roman Appian Way. Founded by the Etruscans, the ancient city of C. declined in the 6th-8th centuries, when it became part of the *Lombard principality of *Benevento. During the Moslem invasions in Italy in the 9th century, C. was attacked several times and in 840 completely destroyed. In 856, the Lombards of Benevento built the new city of C., 4 km north of the Roman site, which became the capital of a duchy bearing the same name. Disputes over the duchy between its Lombard rulers and the Byzantines during the latter half of the 10th century left C. open to incursions and the interference of *Otto II, who imposed his suzerainty over the dukes. In the 11th century, C. was attacked by the *Normans who settled in southern Italy, and conquered in 1058 by Richard of Aversa, a Norman chieftain. Under Richard, C. continued to be a semi-dependent city with formal links to Pope *Nicholas II. The Aversa family ruled C. until 1139, when *Roger II, king of Sicily, conquered it and annexed it to his kingdom. C. eventually lost its political importance and its history became that of the kingdom of Sicily and, from 1282, of Naples. In the 12th century it became an economic centre, famous for its textile industry; in 1231, *Frederick II granted its Jewish population a monopoly over the dyeing of textiles. In the 14th and 15th centuries, the city was a financial centre of the kingdom of Naples, but, towards the end of the Middle Ages, it declined into a small town.
M. W. Frederiksen, *Capua* (1959).

CAPULETTO A powerful *Ghibelline family in Verona, northern Italy, influential in the city and its surroundings in the 14th and 15th centuries. The C. fought for the rule of Verona with the Guelph family of *Montague, and both families alternated in seizing power. After the conquest of Verona by Venice in 1432, their importance – already checked by the ascension of the *Scaligeri, who seized the overlordship of the city – diminished. The C. were immortalized in Shakespeare's famous drama *Romeo and Juliet*.
H. Spandenberg, *Cangrande I Della Scala und Verona* (1895).

CARCASSONNE City in the province of Languedoc, southern France. Conquered by the *Visigoths in 419, it became part of their kingdom until its collapse in 711. After a period of turmoil it was conquered by the *Franks under *Charles Martel in 735. In the 9th century, C. and the county of which it was part were ruled by a local noble family, under the nominal suzerainty of the counts of *Toulouse. Through a series of marriages, the countal title passed to the counts of Barcelona in the middle of the 11th century. Unable to impose their authority over the feudal lords of C., they were compelled to accept the domination of the Trencavel family of Béziers, which took the title of viscounts of C. Under the Trencavels, C. flourished, due to its economically advantageous location on the main road between Toulouse and the shores of the Mediterranean. C. was conquered along with the other Trencavel dominions by the Crusaders, led by *Simon of Montfort in 1210, despite the fact that *Albigensian settlement in the region was marginal. In 1229 it was annexed to the French royal demesne becoming the seat of a royal seneschal. The city was fortified in the 13th century and its impressive walls are still extant, as is its cathedral, built in the Gothic style. In the last centuries of the Middle Ages, C. became a provincial town within the 13th-century walls.
J. Poux, *La cité de Carcassonne, Histoire et description* (1922).

CARDINAL Dignitary of the Roman Catholic Church. In ancient times and at the beginning of the Middle Ages, the Cs. were the deacons (administrators) of the seven historical hills of Rome, forming the core of the papal administration. From the 7th century on, popes appointed priests of the city's main churches as Cs., especially those who were employed in the papal government, and these churches were thus entitled C.-churches. The seven bishops of Roman suburbs who were employed in the papal government and were often present at the papal court, joined the assemblies of the Cs. In the 11th century, the college of Cs. was established as the supreme council of the papacy and was composed of three orders: C.-bishops (6: Albano, Ostia, Porto, Preneste, Sabina, Tusculum); C.-priests; C.-deacons (7). Their main duty, according to the decree of *Nicholas II in 1059, was the election of a new pope, which was to be by secret vote – thus the elective assemblies of Cs. were called conclaves. The appointment of Cs. was and remains a prerogative of the pope, who could employ them in political and administrative charges, either permanent or temporary. Although a C. sent by the pope to accomplish a mission remained hierarchically inferior to the bishops, he was considered during his mission as the representative of the pope, which gave him authority over the established church hierarchy. Until the end of the 13th century a C. resided at Rome, or accompanied the pope

The 13th-century walls and fortifications of Carcassonne, Languedoc

on his journeys. From the 14th century on, certain prelates of the main Catholic states were appointed Cs. (with the rank of C.-priests), continuing to reside in their own countries and entitled Princes of the Church. *EC*, III.

CARDINAL VIRTUES A term used by the medieval church, which borrowed the classification from Plato and Aristotle. The four C. are prudence, temperance, fortitude and justice, which, according to St. Augustine, lead the faithful to perfection. They complement the four "theological virtues": faith, hope, continence and charity, which lead to salvation. *EC*, III.

CARIBERT I (d. 567) Son of *Clotaire I and king of the *Franks (561-67). He ruled over Paris and *Neustria — the new provinces acquired by the *Merovingians in the 6th century — which were shared by his brothers after his death.
J. M. Wallace-Hadrill, *The Long-Haired Kings* (1962).

CARIBERT II (d. 632) Son of *Clotaire II and king of the *Franks (629-32). He was considered mentally deficient and was only given a nominal kingship over a few cities around Toul without any real power. His period marked the decline of the *Merovingians and the ascension of the "mayors of the palace".
J. M. Wallace-Hadrill, *The Long-Haired Kings* (1962).

CARINTHIA Province in the southeastern part of the German kingdom (now Austria). In the 5th-8th centuries C. was populated by Slavs and became part of the kingdom of the *Avars. In the latter half of the 8th century Christian missionaries from Bavaria were active in C. and their activity was facilitated after its conquest by *Charlemagne in 794, who annexed it to Bavaria. In the 9th century, the Germanization of C. began to be felt, particularly under the reign of *Carloman, the son of *Louis the German, who was appointed king of Bavaria.

In 876 Carloman created the duchy of C., investing it on his son, the future Emperor *Arnulf. In the 10th century C. was devastated by Hungarian raids, but restored after the victory of *Otto I at Lechfeld in 954, and reunited to Bavaria in 989. In an attempt to reduce the power of the Bavarian dukes, the Emperor *Henry II detached C. from Bavaria, making it an independent duchy. At the beginning of the 11th century he appointed a local count, Adalbero of Eppenstein, as duke. Emperor *Henry III preferred to rule the duchy directly. After his death in 1056, his widow Agnes, seeking the support of the nobility, invested it on a Swabian count, Berthold of *Zähringen. Until the 13th century, no dynasty was established in C., and the dukes were appointed by the emperors, even where sons were to inherit their father's office. In the 13th century, Austria and C. enjoyed close ties, with the duchies cooperating in the economical development of the Danube area. After 1272, when *Rudolf of Hapsburg became emperor and established the Hapsburg's rule in Austria, members of the family were appointed as dukes of C. Thereafter, C. became part of the hereditary Hapsburg states, despite the formal continuation of its autonomous existence.
J. W. Thompson, *Feudal Germany* (1928).

CARLISLE Capital of the earldom of Cumberland, northern England, and part of the Anglo-Saxon kingdom of *Northumbria. It was conquered by the Danes in the 9th-10th centuries, and lost much of its importance, but after the *Norman Conquest in 1066, it became a stronghold on the Scottish marches. In 1092, *William II created the earldom of C. — which included the Cumberland and Westmorland counties — for defence purposes. In 1133 *Henry I made C. into a bishopric and a community of *Austin canons settled there. This settlement contributed to the development and prosperity of C. Under the *Plantagenets in the 14th and 15th centuries, princes of the royal dynasty replaced the bishops as rulers of C.

J. Wilson, 'Carlisle' in *Victoria Counties History*, II (1955).

CARLOMAN (715-54) Son of *Charles Martel. At his father's death, he and his brother *Pepin the Short, became *mayors of the palace and rulers of the Frankish kingdom of *Austrasia (741-47). A man of deep religious feeling, C. left the real power to his brother, resigning in 747, to become a monk at Monte Cassino in Italy, where he died.

L. Halphen, *Charlemagne et l'Empire Carolingien* (1947).

CARLOMAN (751-71) Son of *Pepin the Short, king of the Franks (768-71). At the death of Pepin, he shared the kingdom with his brother Charles (*Charlemagne). He undertook the struggle against the separatist trends in *Aquitaine, but shortly afterwards entered into conflict with his brother. In 771 he was forced to flee, taking refuge at the court of the Lombardian king, Desiderius. He died on his way to Pavia. The event was exploited by Charlemagne for his expedition of 774 against Desiderius and the conquest of Italy.

L. Halphen, *Charlemagne et l'Empire Carolingien* (1947).

CARLOMAN (828-80) Son of *Louis the German, king of Bavaria (865-80). After the division of the *Carolingian empire (843), he was chosen by his father, the king of Germany, to govern Bavaria. With the aid of his brothers, he compelled Louis to bestow on him the royal title in 867. He concentrated on developing the eastern marches, *Carinthia, *Carniola and *Austria, and on fighting against the *Moravians but failed to impose his authority over the *Croats. From 870, C. became involved in the affairs of Italy, with his father trying to assure his succession to Emperor *Louis I. But instead Pope *John VIII crowned *Charles the Bald, the king of France, emperor in 875. Disappointed, C. returned to his kingdom, where he was faced with anarchical trends, accentuated after his father's death in 876, which threatened Bavaria's position as the most powerful kingdom in Germany and paved the way for the reunification of Germany by his brother, *Charles the Fat, after C.'s death.

G. Tellenbach, *Königtum und Stämme in der Werdezeit des deutschen Reiches* (1939).

CARLOMAN (866-84) King of France (879-84). At the death of his father, *Louis II, he was chosen to reign jointly with his elder brother, *Louis III, and given particular responsibility over the southern part of the realm. Despite his young age, he besieged *Boso in the city of Vienne and, when his brother died in 882, repulsed the Norman invasion in the north. His courage and leadership won him the esteem of the warriors and inspired the French epic *Gormond et Isembert*. After his victory in 884, he was killed in a hunting accident.

R. Folz. *De l'Antiquité au Monde Médiéval* (1972).

CARMELITE ORDER (The Order of Our Lady of Carmel) Monastic order founded in 1154 by St. Berthold on Mount Carmel in Palestine. The first monks claimed to be the heirs of the hermits who had lived on the Mount in ancient times, and even to be the direct descendants of the prophet Elijah and the "Sons of the Prophets". Initially they advocated extreme asceticism: absolute poverty, abstention from meat and solitude. After the *Crusades they migrated to western Europe, where the C. was reorganized in the 14th century by St.

Simon Stock along the lines of the *mendicant friars. Carmelite monasteries were established throughout western Europe, their rule being contemplation, missionary work and the study of theology. In 1452, an order of Carmelite nuns was founded in the Low Countries and rapidly spread through France, Italy and Spain. It followed the same rule as the male order, but the nuns were perpetually cloistered.

L. van den Bosche, *Les Carmes* (1930).

CARMINA BURANA Collection of Latin songs, composed by students and wandering scholars during the late 12th and early 13th century in France and Germany. The extant collection was compiled between 1225 and 1250 by an anonymous editor either in the Moselle Valley or in the abbey of Benedictbeuren in Bavaria, a famous literary centre in the 13th century. The C. comprises songs on wine, women and love, satirical songs against the social and religious establishment, as well as songs in praise of nature, youth and student life. They were popular in the universities of the late Middle Ages and considered a mirror of university life.

A. Hilka and O. Schumann (ed.), *Carmina Burana* (1930).

CARNIOLA County and march in southeastern Germany (Austria). Settled by Slavs in the 6th-7th centuries, C. belonged to the kingdom of the *Avars until its conquest by *Charlemagne at the end of the 8th century. In the 9th century, it was contested by Germany and the Croats, and in 865 became part of the kingdom of Bavaria, as a distinct march. From the 11th century on, marquises of C. were direct vassals of the *Holy Roman emperors. Due to C.'s frontier position, its rulers were not involved in the political struggles within Germany but concentrated instead on fighting against the Croats and Hungary. A large part of the population remained Slavonic, but the northern part of C. was colonized by Germanic peoples expanding from Bavaria, Carinthia and Austria during the 12th-14th centuries — who founded the city of Klagenfurt. From the 14th century on, C. was part of the *Hapsburg estates, and was annexed to Austria at the end of the Middle Ages.

J. W. Thompson, *Feudal Germany* (1928).

CARNIVAL Festival preceding Lent which, originating in the western Mediterranean countries, spread northwards during the Middle Ages. The term is derived from the Latin expression *carne vale* (farewell flesh), referring to the Christian prohibition of consuming meat during Lent. The C. is rooted in ancient pagan festivities, which were held for three days, usually in February, to symbolize the end of winter and the approach of spring. At the beginning of the Middle Ages the Christians turned it into a religious feast, while preserving the ancient customs. The C. was thus considered as the last rejoicing before the solemn period of public penance corresponding to the 40 days of Lent. In the late Middle Ages processions, which were an essential part of the C., were exploited for ridiculing the religious and political establishment.

J. Evans, *Civilization in France in the Middle Ages* (1934).

CAROLINE BOOKS (Libri Carolini) A treatise compiled *c.* 792-94, attributed to *Charlemagne (therefore named "Caroline"), but probably the work of *Alcuin, a theologian at his court. The C. contain a criticism of the

*Iconoclastic Council of Nicaea of 754, which forbade the cult of images, and the Second Council of Nicaea of 787, which allowed the veneration of icons. Its attribution to Charlemagne is probably linked to the attempts of the royal Frankish court to break with the Greek-Byzantine authority within the Church, and to discredit the Empress *Irene, thus paving the way for the imperial coronation of Charlemagne.

Leges, Text ed. *MGH* III (1924);

H. Bastgen, *Die Libri Carolini* (1934).

CAROLINGIAN CYCLE OF POEMS Epic poems of the 12th-15th centuries, often based on historical fact, composed in the vernacular. Centring on Charlemagne, they embody legends about wars or chivalric deeds by heroes who acted on his orders. In general, these heroes were placed in an active role, while Charlemagne himself was depicted as a majestic old king, with a very long beard, seated on his throne. The most important poems are those devoted to *Roland (in French, German, Norse and Italian) and to *Girart of Vienne and his family (mostly in French). The poems extol the virtues of perfect knights and justice, or else their theme is the holy war, with the Saracens depicted as the enemy. The Carolingian heroes are represented as the prototypes of princes and feudal lords of the 12th-14th centuries, creating thus a sort of legitimacy for new dynasties. For example, Roland is represented as the count of Anjou, insinuating thus that the counts of Anjou of the 12th century, the *Plantagenet kings of England, should be his heirs. The poems mirror the ideals of chivalry of the age of their composition, without any historical ties to the period of Charlemagne, and, as such, are related to other cycles of poems, such as the *Arthurian and the *Crusade cycles.

U. T. Holmes, *A History of the Old French Literature* (1948).

CAROLINGIAN EMPIRE The empire created by *Charlemagne at the end of the 8th century and that ruled by his descendants (the Carolingians) in the 9th and 10th centuries. The history of the C., which extended over France, western Germany, Austria, Switzerland, the Low Countries and the major part of Italy, consists of three distinct periods: the formative period (753-800); the united empire (800-43); the division and decline (843-951).

The formative period. With the coronation of *Pepin the Short, a new dynasty acceded to the throne of the Frankish kingdom, receiving its legitimization from the Church. The event marks the development of the idea of a Christian monarchy – built on the concepts of the biblical realm of King *David – to supersede the tribal, barbarian realms. Ideally, the monarchy was to have supremacy over all Christendom. Thus, the Church encouraged the spread of Christianity to non-Christian peoples. The concept of a *feudal society and state subservient to the monarch was generally accepted in the Frankish kingdom under Pepin (753-68), who created the appropriate military and administrative structures for its realization. The missionary activities of Anglo-Saxon monks in Germany and the Friesland (northern Netherlands) helped spread Frankish influence and expanded the Frankish kingdom northwards and eastwards. But the predominant figure of the formative period was Charlemagne, Pepin's son. In a long series of wars, he conquered *Lombardy in 774, being hailed at

Pavia as King of the Lombards in addition to his own royal Frankish title; he annexed *Bavaria, having convicted its duke, *Tassilo, of perjury and began a long war with the *Saxons, which lasted over 30 years and ended with the conquest of the whole of northern Germany. Following the Spanish campaign of 787, during which Charlemagne's army overran *Roncesvalles, he decided to change the structure of his realm in 789, modelling it on the biblical monarchy. The wars against the *Avars culminated in the conquest of the Danube territories in 798. At the same time, Charlemagne had his eyes on the imperial throne and circumstances augured well for his acceding to it. The Roman imperial title – held by *Irene at Byzantium – was considered by the West as vacant, because Christianity barred a woman from ruling. Moreover, the weakness of the papacy compelled Pope *Leo III, to depend on the support of Charlemagne. When Charlemagne asked the pope to change his title Patrice of the Romans, which gave him temporal power, into an imperial title, the pope acceded to his request. On Christmas Day, 800, at St. Peter's Church of Rome, the pope crowned him "Emperor of the Romans". This was not the title Charlemagne had sought, and he never used it in official documents, being disappointed in his ambition to be hailed as "Emperor of the Christians".

The period of the united empire. After the imperial coronation, Charlemagne organized his empire, combining the religious ideals of the biblical monarchy and feudal reality. He instituted an administrative system whereby each state was governed by counts – each count responsible for a specific province – as vassals of the emperor. Control was exercised by annual inspections of the *missi dominici* (the delegates of the lord), composed of groups of counts and bishops or abbots, who heard appeals and reported to the emperor. The emperor's sons were appointed kings to aid him: Pepin in Italy, Charles at the court and Louis in Aquitaine, where he led the campaigns in northern Spain and established imperial rule in Barcelona and Catalonia. To alleviate the burden of controlling so vast an empire, Charlemagne decided in 806 to divide it among his sons, but was prevented from doing so by the deaths of Pepin and Charles. The empire was subsequently inherited by *Louis the Pious in 814. The difficulties which arose under Charlemagne were exacerbated in the reign of his son, who was faced not only with the problem of controlling the counts, but also with preserving the unity of the empire, which conflicts among kings threatened to disintegrate. The increasing importance of the church served to balance the centrifugal trends. The execution of his nephew, King *Bernard of Italy, in 818, who was convicted as a traitor, did not put an end to the conflicts. The emperor was compelled to assign kingdoms to his three sons. The birth of a fourth son, Charles, in 822, which implied a further division of power within the empire, led his three older sons to revolt. The promise of the imperial title to the eldest son, *Lothair, and his coronation at Rome failed to appease him. In 829, an open revolt was staged against the emperor, who had to ask the clergy for support. The last years of Louis' reign were a period of open revolts, when imperial unity all but disappeared, with its only remnant being the annual councils of the bishops. His sons ruled their own kingdoms: Louis, the territories of the Eastern Franks (the future Germany), Charles Neustria, Pepin Aquitaine, while Lothair had many provinces from the Low Countries to Italy. In the meantime, cultural and ethnographical changes created new realities, which made the old *Merovingian divisions of the Frankish kingdoms obsolete. By 840 a linguistic barrier separated the East-Franks, who spoke a Germanic tongue, from the West-Franks, whose language was already Romanized. When Louis and Charles agreed to unite against their brothers in 840 and met with their armies at Strassburg, they had to swear the oath of alliance in both languages so as to be understood by their respective vassals. The division of the C. was almost complete.

The period of division and decadence. At the death of Louis the Pious, a war broke out between his sons, which lasted three years and ended with the Treaty of *Verdun (843), the impact of which still survives on the political map of western Europe. The C. empire was finally divided: Lothair, the emperor, obtained the kingdoms of Italy and Central Francia (comprising the Low Countries, Lorraine, the province later named after him, and Provence); Louis was recognized as king of Eastern Francia (*Germany); Charles, who received Western Francia, with authority over the autonomous kingdom of Aquitaine, founded the kingdom of France. Nevertheless, the treaty failed to achieve peace and stability. Invasions by Normans, Arabs from north Africa and Hungarians, compelled the monarchs to invest territories on warriors, to build castles and ensure the defence. This led to revolts by counts and other vassals, who perceived a threat to the heredity of their charges and lands, and who, at the same time, wanted to increase their power. Frequent wars between the Carolingian brothers, seeking to profit from their neighbours' troubles and to revise the Verdun treaty in their favour, made the kings dependent on their vassals. Lothair divided his kingdom among his sons, and it was never reunited; Louis the German divided Germany into three kingdoms, but it was reunited in 880 by his son *Charles the Fat. While the kingdom of France persisted as such, it was divided into small feudal units and extremely weakened at the death of *Charles the Bald. While in reality the C. no longer existed by the middle of the 9th century, the idea of the empire remained one of the big theoretical questions of the age. The imperial title was still held by the Carolingians, even if the emperor's power was only nominal. Thus, after the death of *Louis II, Lothair's son, Pope *John VIII, proclaimed Charles the Bald emperor (875) and after his death the title was given to his German nephew Charles the Fat. At the end of the 9th century the title passed to small princes, the last direct Carolingian to bear it having been *Arnulf of Carinthia. In the 10th century, Italian princes of Frankish origin, who claimed to belong to the dynasty by marriage, took the crown. The emperor was no more than a figurehead until 951, when *Otto I, king of Germany, deposed *Berengar II.

R. Folz, *Le Couronnement Imperial de Charlemagne* (1964).

CAROLINGIAN RENAISSANCE The cultural revival in western Europe in the 8th and 9th centuries. Whether it can properly be called a renaissance was the subject of much debate by historians. The C. refers to the activities of Anglo-Saxon missionaries on the Continent, the founding of a school of history at the abbey of *Monte Cassino in Italy, where classical works were copied, and the work of several Spanish churchmen, who held prestigious positions in Charlemagne's empire. A prominent figure was *Alcuin of York, who settled at Charlemagne's court in 782 and was active at the court academy, established at Aix-la-Chapelle. Writers, poets and historians gathered at the academy, creating a cultural centre where Latin classical tradition was revived. They even gave themselves classical names, reserving the name of David, king of Israel, for Charlemagne. Academy leaders also strove to improve the "barbarian" Latin of their own age and to copy the style of classical writers. But more important was the reform of the education system. After the fall of Rome (476), the West had no consistent education policy. As cities declined, so did their schools – a heritage of antiquity – until they disappeared in most towns, with some exceptions in Italy. A monopoly over education was eventually held by the church. Most abbeys founded monastic schools, some of them on a high standard modelled on the 5th-century school of *Cassiodorus. But not before 787 – when Charlemagne issued his first *capitulary ordering each monastery and cathedral to have its own school – was a systematic policy designed. Later capitularies dealt with curricula, based on the study of the seven liberal arts, prayers and some theology. Alcuin himself established a monastic school at St. Martin's of Tours, while the Spaniard *Theodulf (bishop of Orléans), an eminent leader of the C., founded the cathedral school at Orléans. While most cathedral and monastic schools remained on an elementary level, they contributed to the spread of literacy. Some of the schools, like those of Orléans, Rheims, Fulda, Corbie, Ferrières, St. Riquier, St. Wandrille and St. Gall were to become prestigious centres of learning in the first half of the 9th century. Originality of thought, however, never figured prominently in the Carolingian schools: emphasis was on reviving and conserving their classical heritage and developing it along the lines of the founding fathers. But there were some notable exceptions.

The systematization of education created the need for books. An original achievement of the C., was the introduction of a new calligraphic type of handwriting, using uncial characters (Gothic handwriting). The production of books, by copying ancient or new works, was organized in monasteries, where the *scriptorium* was introduced. A group of monks wrote, by the dictation of one of them, the text of a book intended for dissemination. These copies, corrected and illustrated, were sent to libraries of abbeys and cathedrals, but also to courts, where, like the famous Bible of Charles the Bald, they were of artistic and iconographic interest. The *scriptorium*, although connected with the monastic school, was not a part of it. Its sole purpose was the copying of books on parchment. (In the 8th century papyrus was scarce and had to be imported from Egypt.) While the *scriptoria* played an important role in disseminating Roman classical works, they saw little need for producing new, original works.

The revival of the ancient heritage stimulated new developments in the 9th century, mainly in theology, poetry, history and philosophy. A prominent philosopher of the period was John Scot *Erigena.

W. Ullmann, *The Carolingian Renaissance* (1969).

CARRARA Family in Padua (Italy), which seized power in the city in the 13th century and, during the 14th and 15th centuries, ruled it as tyrants. As in many other Italian cities, the family of C. rose to power by maintaining its strength during local contests between *Guelph and *Ghibelline families. In 1318 Jacopo da C. imposed his rule on the city and its surroundings and thwarted the attempts of the *Scaligeri of Verona to annex Padua to their principality. After a brief period of troubles during which the C. lost Padua, they reconquered the city in 1350. Jacopo's son, Francesco da C. (d. 1393), fought against Venice and its territorial aspirations on the Continent. During the late 14th and early 15th century, the C. sided with Milan in her conflicts with Venice. In 1407, when Venice conquered Padua, the C.'s domination came to an end.

P. P. Vergerio, *De principibus Carrariensibus et gestis eorum liber* (1925).

CARTHAGE City in north Africa. In the 5th century, C. was the second city of the Western Roman empire and its most important cultural centre. Conquered by the *Vandals in 431, C. became the capital of their kingdom and one of the most active ports in the western Mediterranean. In 543 C. was conquered by the Byzantines under *Justinian, remaining the capital of north Africa until its conquest by the Arabs in 657. Frequent wars with the *Berbers, and attempts by the Christians to maintain relations with Constantinople weakened Arab rule. But when the Arabs defeated the Berbers a trend to Islamization developed, accentuated by the foundation of the new capital, *Kairwan. As a result, some of the population emigrated from Kairwan, which had a deleterious influence on the city. With the foundation of the city of Tunis in the 13th century C. was deserted.

K. Brockelmann, *A History of the Islamic Peoples* (1953).

CARTHAGENA City in Spain, in the province of Murcia, situated on the shore of the Mediterranean. The ancient Roman city was successively conquered by the *Vandals at the end of the 4th century, the *Visigoths, who destroyed a major part of it, in the 5th century, and by the Byzantines in the middle of the 6th century. The Visigoths' attempts to conquer it in the 7th century failed, despite a weakened Byzantine rule. In 711, the Arabs conquered the city establishing an emirate ruled by governors, and later by the caliphs of *Córdoba. In the middle of the 13th century, the city and the province, were conquered by the Castilians.

L. Suarez Fernandez, *Historia de España: edad media* (1970).

CARTHUSIAN ORDER A monastic order founded by St. *Bruno in 1084 at the Grande Chartreuse (whence its name). At its start, the C. had no particular rule, but dictated humility, renunciation of worldly goods and silence. In accordance with Bruno's instructions, each monk lived in a separate *cell within the monastery, where he worked and prayed in solitude. The monks met only at Mass and ate communally only on feast days. At the beginning of the 12th century, the C. attracted many converts and the order spread rapidly so that new monasteries were founded. In order to maintain uniformity of behaviour, Guigues of Châtel, the prior of the Grande Chartreuse compiled a rule in 1127. During the 12th-13th centuries the rule was amended several times, attenuating the strict austerity of the original C. Nevertheless, the C. preserved its ascetic character to a large extent, combining the customs of *Benedictine monachism and hermitic asceticism. By the end of the Middle Ages, the C. had been established in all of Catholic Europe, and the order was one of those least affected by the decline of monasticism in the late Middle Ages. This was largely due to the fact that the C. had survived a crisis which had divided the Charterhouses at the end of the 14th century.

E. Baumann, *Les Chartreux* (1928).

CASALE City in Piedmont, northern Italy. Situated on the banks of the Po River, C. developed in the 12th century when it became part of the *Lombard League. As was the case with other Italian cities of the 13th century, authority over C. was disputed between Guelph and Ghibelline families. In the 14th century, it suffered such a decline that the principalities of Milan, Montferrat and Savoy rivalled over control of the city. C. was barely able to defend itself. Only because its powerful neighbours were unable to destroy the balance of power did it succeed in maintaining its independence until the end of the 15th century.

A. Visconti, *La biscia Viscontea* (1929).

CASAMENTUM *Feudal Latin term regarding relations between lords and vassals. Throughout the 8th-11th centuries, the C. signified a lord's investiture of a house, together with its estate, to his vassal, after the latter had sworn him *homage. Thus, a *rassus casatus* was a vassal who ceased to live in his lord's *castle, thereby enjoying a large degree of autonomy. The practice of the C. led to the division of great feudal estates into a maze of small anarchical units, most of them lacking a proper political and economic foundation. With the reorganization of society and the establishment of principalities and monarchies in the 12th and 13th centuries, the practice of C. declined and was replaced by rents and the indenture system.

M. Bloch, *The Feudal Society* (1961).

CASIMIR I, the Restorer (1016-58) King of Poland (1039-58). Son of *Mieszko, C. was educated for an ecclesiastical career. On bad terms with his brother, *Boleslaw, C. fled to Germany in 1034. During the same period, a general revolt in Poland brought the country to a state of anarchy, facilitating its invasion by the *Bohemians. In 1039, C. was called upon to reign and, with the help of Emperor *Henry III, restored order and royal authority. He established the capital of the Polish kingdom at Cracow.

P. David, *Casimir le Moine et Boleslav le Pénitent* (1932).

CASIMIR II, the Just (1138-94) King of Poland (1177-94). He was the youngest son of *Boleslaw III, who granted him control over the principality of Sandomiersz. However, C.'s actual rule began only some years later in 1166. During a period of revolts on the part of the nobility, C. seized the Polish throne (1177), having obtained the support of the prelates, to whom he offered land and privileges. His hereditary right to kingship was recognized and confirmed by Pope *Alexander III and Emperor *Frederick Barbarossa. C. was responsible for beginning Poland's eastward expansion.

Cambridge History of Poland (1950).

CASIMIR III, the Great (1310-70) King of Poland (1333-70). Son of Wladyslaw I, he showed political expertise soon after his coronation despite his youth. C.'s

main aim was to develop and peacefully assert the power of Poland. He was largely successful, as his reign brought Poland great prosperity. To reach his goals, C. allied himself with *Charles Robert, king of Hungary and *John of Luxemburg, king of Bohemia. Within his own kingdom he obtained the support of the nobility of Little Poland and of the towns. Furthermore, aware of the Jews' contribution to the economic development of the kingdom, he granted them certain privileges in 1334, thus mustering their support as well. In 1345 he issued the Constitution of Wislicze, which was an attempt to centralize the government and unify the kingdom's legislative system, opposing the separatism and provincialism of the feudal aristocracy. He expanded upon the practices of *Magdeburg law, which already served as a basis for a good number of city charters. He attempted to develop this system and apply it to Poland. Consequently, he established the Magdeburgian Law Court, which specialized in urban jurisprudence, at Cracow in 1356. In the area of foreign policy, he renounced Poland's claims to Silesia (1343) thus allowing John of Luxemburg to stake his claim. In return, he obtained control of the Czech counties surrounding Cracow. In the same year, he signed a peace treaty with the *Teutonic order, which required that both parties relinquish their territorial claims. C.'s foreign policy enabled him to expand eastwards, where he annexed the city of Lwow (1340), the principality of Halicz (1345) and large territories in the Ukraine. Thus, he doubled the size of the Polish kingdom during his reign. C. encouraged cultural and scientific development in his realm and, in 1364, at the height of his international fame, founded the University of Cracow. The opening ceremony was attended by Emperor *Charles IV and King *Louis I of Hungary, who accepted C. as mediator of their disputes.
Cambridge History of Poland (1950).

ČASLAV Town in Bohemia, known as one of the centres of the *Hussites as well as a centre of the nobility's opposition to the houses of Luxemburg and Hapsburg during the 15th century. At that period, the town embodied the Czech character of the kingdom. Modern Czechoslovakia therefore looks upon it as a symbol of the Czech struggle against Germanization.

CASSEL Town in southern *Flanders and the site of two important battles. In 1071, the Flemish army, led by Count Robert, defeated *Philip I, king of France; the result was the increase of local power in Flanders and the limitation of the royal rights within that county. In 1328, King *Philip VI of France defeated the popular army of the Flemish cities. By means of the pro-French dynasty of the counts in Flanders, royal control was imposed.

CASSIAN, JOHN (360-435) Monk. There are no explicit data concerning his origin and childhood. As a young man, he entered a monastery at *Bethlehem, but, after several years, went to Egypt where he studied monasticism. After 385, he became a deacon of the Church of Constantinople and, at the beginning of the 5th century, visited Rome and settled in the West. In 415 he founded two monasteries near Marseilles in Provence and there, using information he had gathered in Palestine and Egypt, wrote his two books, the *Institutes* and the *Conferences*, which deal with the monastic way of life, including its search for perfection as a step towards salvation. The books had a great influence on the emer-

gence and ideological development of monastic thought in the West and were largely used by the *Benedictines in the elaboration of their rule.
Ed. *PL*, vols. 49-50;
O. Chadwick, *John Cassian* (1950).

CASSIODORUS, FLAVIUS MAGNUS AURELIUS (485-580) Author and high official. Born to a noble Roman family, he became *consiliarius* (legal assessor) to his father in his youth. In 507 he was quaestor at Rome and in 514 consul. He later entered the service of *Theodoric, king of the *Ostrogoths, who appointed him chief of the civil service (*magister officiorum*) in 526. After Theodoric's death, C. continued to serve at court and became praetorian prefect in 533. C. devoted his adult life to mitigating the rivalry between the Romans and the Ostrogoths, despite the fact that the latter were Arians, in the belief that the two peoples could create a powerful Italy. In 540 he retired from public life and founded two monasteries of the *Benedictine type on his estates in southern Italy, at *Vivarium. Having tried in vain to establish in Rome a theological school modelled on that of *Alexandria, he himself became a monk at Vivarium and made his monastery into a centre of learning, where religious and secular study and the copying of manuscripts of antiquity were encouraged. Through these activities, C. established a tradition of scholarship among the monks, which served to preserve the classical culture of Europe during the Middle Ages. C. is also known for his writings. Some of his works concentrated on legal issues, and his 12 volumes of imperial edicts served as a model for the medieval chanceries. His book, *De anima* (On the Soul), which established his ideas about the spirituality of the soul, was not recognized by the philosophers of his time. The book serves as a bridge between his secular and religious writings. The most important of his works, however, was *Institutiones Divinarum et Saecularium Litterarum* (The Divine Institutions and Secular Literature), influenced by St. *Augustine, in which he defended his conceptions of a Christian education based on a mixture of sacred and profane studies. The book also encouraged the adoption of the *Seven Liberal Arts as the basis of the curriculum. This suggestion was one of his most important contributions to the methods of learning.
Ed. *PL*, vols. 69-70;
G. Bardy, *Cassiodore et la fin du monde ancien* (1945).

CASTEL SANT'ANGELO *Castle on the eastern bank of the Tiber in Rome, near St. Peter's Basilica. It was built in the 9th century to protect *Rome from *Saracen raids and, if necessary, to serve as a refuge for the Vatican. From the 10th century on, the castle also served the *Holy Roman emperors and their garrisons and was later used as a prison for the enemies of the popes.

CASTILE Kingdom in medieval Spain and the most important of the realms of the Iberian Peninsula, which served as the basis for the realization of a united Spain at the end of the Middle Ages. Located in the central part of Spain, its territory included the high Iberian plateau, and it was divided into two sections — Old C. in the north and New C. in the south — by the Tagus River. The area was conquered by the *Visigoths in the 5th century, becoming the core of their kingdom in the following century, the city of Toledo serving as their capital. In the 8th century the entire country was conquered by the Arabs (711-18). The remnants of the Christian population were driven north, where at the end of the 8th century they founded the *Asturian kingdom. In the 10th century the leaders of Asturia and León conquered the territory around *Burgos from the Moslems. There they built numerous *castles, whence the name C. Under *Ferdinand Gonzales (930-70), the importance of C. became at least as great as that of León and the county was made a kingdom. In the 11th century, under the rule of *Ferdinand I, C. became the central realm of Christian Spain, annexing the territories of León and Asturia, although kings bore double titles and, temporarily, the realms were divided among the sons of kings. The territorial growth of C. was linked with the *reconquista wars and in 1064, still under Ferdinand I, it began to expand south of the Duero River. In 1090, with the conquest of Toledo, the ancient Visigothic capital and the primatial see of Spain, its border was established on the Tagus. The annexed territories were populated by migrants from southwestern France, while the *hidalgos* (fealty) were composed of various ethnic elements from France, northern Spain and Provence, and enjoyed wide privileges. Nevertheless, royal power was strong enough to check that of the nobility until the reign of *Alfonso VI, when feudal customs became predominant and the nobility began to receive a share in the government, participating in the meetings of the *Cortes* (the royal High Court). During the same period, the Burgundian counts of Oporto declared their independence and established the kingdom of *Portugal in the western part of C. A dynastic crisis developed after the death of Alfonso VI (1109), aggravated by the marital union of C. and Aragon through the marriage of Alfonso's daughter Urraca to *Alfonso I of Aragon. The situation developed into a civil war, which ended only with the expulsion of Alfonso I and the recognition of the independence of Portugal in 1118. The crisis weakened C. so that the Moslems, under the *Almoravides and the *Almohades, were able to invade its territories, temporarily reconquering Toledo. Nevertheless, in the middle of the 12th century, the *Reconquista* wars were renewed and C. continued its southward expansion. This was facilitated by the foundation of new military orders, those of *Calatrava and *Alcantara, whose knights took part in the campaigns under the orders of the kings. The proclamation of several *crusades, which mobilized knights from all over western Europe to fight in holy wars against the Almohades, reinforced the kingdom's power. In 1177 *Alfonso VIII won a strategic battle at Cuenca, which gained him passage to Andalusia and the city of *Córdoba. But the greatest victory was won in 1212 at *Las Navas de Tolosa by a concentrated effort of the Spanish kingdoms with reinforcements from France and Provence. This brought about a radical change in the kingdom's status: the Almohade power was broken and C. became the greatest monarchy in Spain.

The victory was exploited by *Ferdinand III who systematically conquered southern Spain. Beginning with Badajoz, captured in 1228, he moved on to annex Córdoba in 1236, Seville in 1248 and Cádiz, thus reaching the coast. Only *Granada remained in Moslem possession. Ferdinand also reorganized the kingdom and, in 1230, formed a permanent alliance with León. His son, *Alfonso X, continued his father's policy, increasing the power of the *Cortes* and the nobility. Moreover, the conquests made by his father had caused a radical

change in the structure of the realm. With the new territories, an important Moorish and Jewish element became subject to C., enhancing the role of commerce and manufacturing. They also made a significant cultural contribution entirely different from the rather rural, feudal old C. Arabic was heard at court and in the principal cities. This change in economic and social structure brought prosperity to the kingdom, but also created problems of legal pluralism. Alfonso X, who was a great legist, tried to standardize the laws; he enacted the *Siete Partidas,* a code of various laws, including both moral and legal maxims. He also promulgated the *Fuero Real,* a code of old Castilian laws, which became the offical law of the realm until the end of the Middle Ages. By 1281, four years before Alfonso's death, C. virtually became a state, although its name continued to recall its origins; the kingdom's new status was strongly felt when dynastic troubles concerning its inheritance erupted, leading to civil war at Alfonso's death in 1284. The parties sought not only the support of the nobility, but also that of the Moslem states, such as Granada and *Morocco; Moorish soldiers fought on both sides and the policy of *Reconquista* was halted for a century, thereby preserving the existence of Granada until 1492. In order to retain their authority, the kings were forced to concede more privileges to the *Cortes,* where the nobility held strong influence. As early as the 12th century, the kings had encouraged the participation of city dwellers in the *Cortes,* in an attempt to check the power of the nobility. The cities therefore obtained wide privileges and were allowed to create brotherhoods, known as *hermandades* – organs of self-government, which obtained particular privileges (*fueros*). The *hermandades* developed into city confederations whose representatives at the *Cortes,* could balance the power of the nobility. With the outbreak of civil wars between the royal line and the branch of *La Cerda, which lasted from the end of the 13th century to the second half of the following century, the *hermandades* also became associations working for the preservation of peace in the kingdom, thus becoming an important political entity in the realm. Nevertheless, the kingdom was continually weakened by civil war, which broke out once more on the death of *Alfonso XI in 1350. The reign of *Peter the Cruel and his disputes with his half-brother, *Henry of Trastamare, led not only to anarchy, but also to the intervention of England and France, thereby extending the *Hundred Years' War to Spain. Thus, the victory of Trastamare in 1369 was also considered a French victory.

The last century of C.'s history as an independant state began with the decline of the monarchy accompanied by growth in the political power of the nobility and the towns. The kings had to rely on the support of the church and the military orders, with their zealot trends, to transform the society into a Catholic one. Thus, from the end of the 14th century, Jews and Moslems were persecuted and, after the anti-Jewish riots in 1391, forced conversions multiplied. This alliance of church and throne was also supported by the *Mesta,* the great association of sheep-growers organized to regulate the wool trade, which was the major product of Castilian export.

A. Castro, *The Structure of Spanish History* (1954).

CASTLE The term was used in medieval Latin in two different forms, with different meanings: 1) *castrum* (whence in English "chester" and in Spanish "castro") was inherited from Roman times, when it signified a military camp. Gradually the term began to be used to designate a fortified *borough containing its own C. The C. was owned by its lord, the *dominus castri*, and inhabited by his knights. In such a form, the *castrum* was integrated into the *feudal system. With urban development in the 12th-13th centuries, the *castrum* became an anachronism, preserved in city names, but without any actual significance. 2) the term *castellum* was also inherited from the military vocabulary of ancient Rome, where it signified a small fortress. The term continued to be used in the same sense in the late Middle Ages, becoming in vernacular use *castel* or *chastel* in all the Romanic countries; this term was used to designate localities which developed around the *castel*. From the 9th century, the term began to be used to mean the fortified house of a feudal lord, built on an elevated portion of his estate, and used as a means of defence. The word also began to be used in vernacular French as *château* (whence "C." in English was derived). In the 9th and 10th centuries, the C. was rather primitive in structure. Surrounded by a moat, it contained a tower, in which the lord and his family resided and where the treasury was located. A number of buildings in the court were reserved for the knights, who lived permanently in their lord's C., and there were also quarters for servants and buildings where food was stored. Living conditions in the towers were difficult, as they lacked windows. Only in the 12th century did the classical feudal C. appear, which dominated western Europe until the end of the 14th century, when the introduction of firearms entirely changed the situation. The feudal C. of the 12th-14th centuries was a fortified complex of buildings, surrounded by walls and including numerous towers where watchmen and guards were posted. The C. also contained the main court, in which the most important and impressive building was the lord's palace. There his family was lodged, but the palace was also used for social and government functions. The earlier tower was transformed into a hall (*aula*), where assemblies, receptions and feasts were held. Thus, the C. became a cultural centre, where poets presented their epics and romances. From the latter half of the 12th century, it became customary for the lady to be responsible for the activities in the hall, while her husband assumed the roles of warrior, hunter and judge. The halls of the Cs. became the centres of courtly life, imposing criteria of behaviour and manners which were considered fitting to the social standing of nobility. This new mentality is illustrated in the *Livre des manières* (The Book of Manners) written c. 1170 by Stephen of *Fougères, chaplain of *Henry II of England and bishop of Rennes, in which a code of noble life is presented.

J. Levron, *Le château-fort et la vie au Moyen Age* (1963).

CASTRACANI, CASTRUCCIO (1281-1328) Lord of Lucca (Italy). An adventurer, he became influential at Lucca at the beginning of the 14th century, despite his youth, due to his qualities as warrior and politician. With the collapse of the popular government of Lucca, he aided Uguccione della Faggiuola, who proclaimed himself absolute ruler of Pisa in 1314. C. took advantage of this alliance to seize power in his own city. A skilled statesman, he began a policy of expansion which brought him into conflict with *Florence, a city which had been weakened by civil wars. Conquering Pistoia and Prato,

he encircled Florence and, in 1325, defeated the Florentine mercenaries, but was unable to exploit his success by actually conquering Florence. In 1327 Emperor *Louis of Bavaria appointed him duke of Lucca, investing him with an imperial dignity in Tuscany.

F. Winkler, *Castuccio Castracani, Herzog von Lucca* (1897).

CATACOMBS This term was used for the subterranean, early Christian burial places located in various cities of the Roman empire, the most famous and extensive being those of Rome. Since Roman legislation considered every burial place as sacrosanct, Christians could use the C. for ritual purposes in times of persecutions, and their practices there were rarely disturbed. According to Roman tradition, burial was forbidden within the towns; therefore, the C. are situated outside city walls, along the roads leading from the town. The most impressive are those of St. Callistus, along the Appian Way. The consist of labyrinths of galleries and chambers, generally arranged on two to four levels. During the 5th century, use of the C. gradually ceased and several tombs were even transferred to churches within the city. While the C. were not used in the Middle Ages, they influenced the medieval Christian tradition of crypt-burial under the church. *EC,* III.

CATALAN GRAND COMPANY Originally an association of merchant-adventurers, involved in the trade activities between Barcelona, Sicily and other Italian provinces, was gradually put under the control of mercenaries, hired to protect the trade. At the end of the 13th century, it changed its nature and became a band of Catalan *Almogavares* (light-armed infantry), which won a great reputation for its military efficiency and served under *Frederick of Sicily in his wars against the *Angevins of Naples. After the Peace of *Caltabellotta (1302), their presence in Sicily became unnecessary. Consequently they moved eastwards and were engaged by the emperor of Byzantium, *Andronicus Palaeologus. While serving the empire and fighting the *Ottoman Turks, they pursued their own interests at Constantinople, where they massacred Italians. Sent in garrison to Gallipoli, they began to raid all of Thrace and Macedonia, devastating the country and establishing a great slave market at Gallipoli, where their captives were sold to the Moslems. During this time, *Walter of Brienne, duke of Athens, engaged them to conquer Thessaly on his behalf (1310). Because of a dispute with Walter concerning their wages, they turned against him and, in 1311, conquered the duchy. They settled down in the province, marrying the widows of their former enemies and established themselves as rulers of the land, under the sovereignty of the Catalan kings of Sicily. In 1377, they accepted the sovereignty of the kings of Aragon. During their rule, which lasted until 1388, they established their capital at Thebes and turned the province into a "little *Catalonia": the *Utsages de Barcelona* became its official law, Catalan institutions were adopted and their language was imposed as the official tongue of the duchy. But the transformation from military camp life to governing a state had its effect upon them. Many, due to their mixed marriages, became semi-Hellenized; in addition, the possession of land often led them to quarrel with one another, so that their power was significantly weakened in 1378, when the Navarrese Company appeared in Greece.

K. M. Setton, *Catalan Domination of Athens* (1948).

CATALAN WORLD ATLAS An atlas of the world, drawn in 1375 at *Majorca in the Balearic Islands, by the Jewish cartographer Abraham ben David, one of the leading members of the Majorcan school of cartography. The atlas was presented to *Charles V of France. The maps were drawn according to "Portolan cartography" (see *Geography) and contain valuable information on Europe, the Middle East and north Africa. The C. also contains fictitious maps of the Far East, the country of "Gog and Magog".
M. Destombes, *L'Atlas Catalan de 1375* (1967).

CATALOGUS BARONUM (The Barons' Inquest) Prepared in 1152 under the orders of *Roger II of Sicily, the C. is a record of the inquest undertaken to determine the services due the king by his barons. The barons of Sicily had heavier duties than other western European feudal lords, including military service of 40 days with the addition of castle guard and coast guard. The detailed register is an important source of the history of Sicily and of the study of its noble class.
C. Cahen, *Le régime féodal de l'Italie normande* (1940).

CATALONIA Province in northeastern Spain located between the Pyrénées and the Ebro River. The area was conquered in 418 by the *Visigoths and remained under their rule until 711, when it fell with their kingdom to the Arabs. During that period, C. was much more closely connected with Septimania, its neighbour to the north, than with the surrounding Spanish province. Thus, C. developed an ethnic and linguistic character distinct from Spain, the language of its population being Catalan. Under Arab rule, a governor of the province (named in the 8th century the *vilayeth*) was established at Barcelona, the capital of C. From 778, the Frankish armies of *Charlemagne penetrated the region; however, only at the very beginning of the 9th century, under the nominal leadership of his son, *Louis the Pious, then king of Aquitaine and under the command of William (Guilhem) of Toulouse, marquis of Gothia, was the systematic conquest of C. accomplished with the foundation of the March of Spain (801). During the latter half of the 9th century, the march was divided into several counties, a division from which the Arabs profited, as they attacked Barcelona several times and even succeeded in temporarily reconquering it. Local rivalries strongly divided the march, and, of the many counties, Barcelona became the most important, so that its counts succeeded in uniting the province under their rule at the beginning of the 10th century, at which time they recognized themselves as vassals of the kings of France. But those feudal ties remained formal, due to the weakness of the French kingship, so that the counts were practically independent. They profited from their strategic location between Moslem Spain and Christian Europe, so that the area's trade and culture developed. Thus, their court became an important cultural and scientific centre, where students from France could learn Greek philosophy and science through the Arabs. This was particularly the case of Gerbert of Aurillac, a student of Barcelona who became the most important teacher of western Europe in the latter half of the 10th century. In the 11th century, C. remained an important cultural centre, and the revival of maritime commerce granted its counts great power. Thus C. began a policy of expansion. In 1068, the count Ramon Berenguer I issued a local code of laws, the *Utsages de Barcelona, written in Catalan, which was a

codification of customary or common laws, and was considered the basis of the "Catalan liberties", limited to the nobles and burghers. He began the territorial expansion of C. into *Languedoc (France), where he inherited the county of *Carcassonne. At the beginning of the 12th century, the counts of Barcelona conquered *Provence, at which time a long struggle with the counts of Toulouse began over rule of the Provençal area. In the meantime, *Ramon Berenguer IV married Petronille, the heiress of *Aragon (1137), and, in 1154, was crowned king of Aragon, uniting the two states. Although the political history of C., from the latter half of the 12th century, was closely interwoven with that of Aragon, the former's social and economic evolution is of particular interest. Being the most developed part of the realm, C. had commercial interests in the Mediterranean, whose profits were the most important source of royal wealth and had, therefore, an important influence on Aragonese politics. The struggle in Provence continued and grew, at the beginning of the 13th century, with the clash in *Languedoc, where *Peter I was killed during the Battle of Muret (1214). Commercial competition also led to a dispute between the Catalans and the *Angevins, both of which were interested in the trade of Marseilles and later of Italy. The seamen and maritime merchants of Barcelona, who had been granted important privileges codified in the *Consulado de Mar*, brought the Aragonese crown to intervene in 1282 in the *Sicilian Vespers, which enabled them to conquer Sicily and to establish their influence in Sardinia. Catalan fighters, hired by the *Catalan Grand Company, took part in the battles of Sicily. Until the end of the 14th century, C. prospered as a result of its influence in the Mediterranean. Moreover, the kings respected the province's liberties. However, the 15th century was a period of crisis. The accession to the throne of Aragon by a Castilian dynasty caused opposition in C., especially when the policy of the new kings proved to be centralistic. A number of revolts ended with the confirmation of C.'s rights, but at the same time Catalan commerce was badly hurt.
J. Carrera Pujal, *Historia Politica y Economica de Catalunia* (1946).

CATECHISM The term, related to *catechumen, was used in the Middle Ages to mean oral instruction about the Christian faith given to new converts. From the 12th century, the content taught began to be methodized, and, in certain countries, even employed a systematic training which, according to the decisions of the Lambeth Council of 1281 (provisions for England), was entrusted to a special cleric. From the 16th century, the C. ceased to be exclusively oral and manuals bearing this name were written.
W. C. E. Newbolt, *The Church Catechism* (1903).

CATECHUMEN In the early Church, this Greek word, meaning disciple or student, was used to designate those people who prepared themselves for Christian baptism, undergoing a period of study in which they learned the principles of the faith. In times of persecution, until the 4th century, the term also signified a period of observation by the community of the faithful, which preceded acceptance of the new candidate's conversion. At the beginning of the Middle Ages, a convert was called C. from the period of his conversion until his baptism, which was a time of learning and of penance. In the majority of countries, this period was established before

Panel of the altarpiece by Luis Borassa at the cathedral of Vich, Catalonia

Easter, and therefore Lent became a customary time for C.

EC, III.

CATHARS See ALBIGENSES.

CATHEDRA In a strict sense, the bishop's chair or throne in his church, situated in the centre of the apse behind the high altar. The bishops used these chairs when preaching on festive occasions. Such sermons, dictated *ex C.*, were considered teachings in orthodoxy and, when given by popes, were not to be challenged. In the 12th century, the term was extended to include the teacher's place in medieval universities.

CATHEDRAL Literally, the church which contains a cathedra; the term signified, from the Middle Ages, the main church of a *diocese, that of an archbishop or bishop. As the seat of the bishop could be placed in only one church, it was customary that each diocese contain only one C.; nevertheless, at Rome there were two – St. John's of Lateran, in the vicinity of the medieval papal palace and St. Peter's of the Vatican. Another famous exception was the status of C. granted to the church of Aix-La-Chapelle, the palatial church of *Charlemagne. During the early Middle Ages, the C. was generally dedicated to the saint who had founded the Christian church in the diocese, or to a famous Christian martyr, hence the name St. Peter's at Rome, and the several Cs. dedicated to St. Stephen, the first martyr of Christianity. Certain Cs., however, were not dedicated in such a way – for example, the Church of the Nativity at Bethlehem, the Holy Sepulchre at Jerusalem, the Church of the Patriarchs, or of St. Abraham, in the Crusaders' city of Hebron, and the Church of St. Sophia (Wisdom) at Constantinople. By the year 1000, with the growth of St. *Mary's cult, many Cs. changed their original dedication to that of St. Mary, the *Madonna*, the Virgin, or *Notre-Dame*, including among the chapels one dedicated to the saint founder of the church. This practice, however, was not compulsory. In the earlier Middle Ages, the C., which was always located near the bishop's residence, was under his charge. He was assisted by a number of priests and acolytes, and administration of the C. was handled by the deacons. But with the development of the communities and the growth of political duties of the bishops in the 8th and 9th centuries, the small churches were replaced by impressive buildings, such as the Romanesque and Gothic Cs. The bishops, therefore, began to pray in private oratories within their palaces, coming to the C. only for the great feasts or processions. The C. was then entrusted to a corporation of priests and deacons, who formed *chapters. As *canons, they were in charge of worship and administration of the C. In the great majority of Cs. the chapters were made up of secular clergy. However, there were, from the end of the 11th and until the 13th century, some chapters composed of regular canons, such as the *Augustinians (Austins) or *Premonstratensians. In certain Cs., the chapters were similar to a monastic community. The bishops had the prerogative to appoint the chapter's dean, who was responsible for activities in the C. Nevertheless, under the impact of the *Gregorian reform, the canons in a great number of Cs. obtained the right to elect a dean from amongst themselves.

E. W. Benson, *The Cathedral* (1878).

CATHERINE OF SIENA, St. (1347-80) *Dominican nun. Caterina Benincasa was the daughter of a dyer from Siena. From her childhood, she was reputed as having mystical visions and leading a life of humility. In 1360 she joined the Third Order of the *Dominicans and devoted herself to contemplation, service to the sick and poor, and the conversion of sinners. She was soon surrounded by a large number of followers and venerators coming from different social strata. In 1376 she undertook a journey to *Avignon to plead with *Gregory XI on behalf of Florence, and persuaded him to return to Rome. When the *Great Schism in the papacy broke in 1378, she actively supported *Urban VI and urged cardinals and monarchs to submit to his authority. She was canonized in 1461.

R. Fawtier, *Sainte Catherine de Sienne*, 2 vols. (1921-30).

CATHOLIC The word is derived from the Greek *katholikos*, meaning "general" or "universal". As used by the Greek Fathers of the Christian church it had the double meaning of universality of the faith and its "orthodoxy", i.e. the true faith, as opposed to the false ones. Thus, after the First Council of *Nicaea (325), the church used the form: "the Orthodox-C. Church". The double term was inherited by the early medieval church and was used both in Greek and Latin documents. From the 7th century on, the Latin creed in the West emphasized the "C.", while the Greek favoured the term "Orthodox", both of them bearing the double meaning. Thus, the Latin Western Church is named the Roman C. and Apostolic Church, and, with the split between the Latin and Greek Churches, the term C. was used to signify the faith of and obedience to the Roman Church.

CATHOLICOS An *Armenian title, first used in secular administration to designate high officials of finance. In the Armenian Church it was applied first to the head of a number of monasteries located in the same city and was gradually changed to the title of the higher ecclesiastical hierarchy. From the 7th century, it was restricted to the two patriarchs of the Armenian churches, the Orthodox-Armenian and the *Nestorian. The Armenian C. were considered leaders of all Armenians, whether at home or dispersed abroad.

A. Fortescue, *The Lesser Eastern Churches* (1913).

CATTLE In the agrarian-feudal system of the West, C. was considered one of the most important resources of the lord, and, from the 8th century on, particular attention was given to it. When it belonged to the village or was looked after by the villagers, the C. was permitted to use the lord's reserve, the pasturage. As for the C. owned by the lord, a special service was set up in the manor which managed the equipment, and held the prescribed number of animals, as well as being responsible for the pasturage. *Charlemagne instructed the reeves (stewards) of the imperial demesnes to pay particular attention to the C., both as to quantity and quality. In medieval official records, such as the *Domesday Book in England, C. and pasturage were carefully inventoried. From the 12th century on, the peasants had to hand over to their lords the best of their C. as part of their taxes; this custom spread through all feudal countries, although the amounts and dates of payment varied. In late medieval England, as a consequence of the *Black Death, the sytem of *enclosures was introduced in order to preserve the pasture for the lord's C.

G. Duby, *Rural Economy and Country Life in the Medieval West* (1968).

CAUSE In the medieval vocabulary the Latin word *causa* was used in two senses: in the language of *canonists and theologians, it signified the systematic discussion of a particular topic, framed in the form of a question, which was part of a broader subject being treated. In this debate, sources of authority were cited so as to eventually reach an answer to the topic in question. In the vocabulary of the theorists of scientific thought, the term had the same meaning until the end of the 12th century. In the 13th century, the element of reason was introduced under the influence of Aristotelian philosophy. Thus, in the generation between Alexander *Neckam and *Albertus Magnus, the C. came to mean the scholastic discussion of the reasoning behind physical, astronomic and geologic phenomena, where facts, such as the characteristic properties of the element studied, were interspersed with moral and even mystical explanations.

A. C. Crombie, *Science in the Middle Ages* (1957).

CEDD (Cedda), St. (d. 664) Bishop of the East Saxons. Educated at *Lindisfarne, he was sent, after his ordination as priest (653), to convert the Middle Angles. A year later, he was called back and sent to Essex for the same purpose, where he was consecrated bishop of the East Saxons of Essex. He founded many churches and monasteries. In 664, at the Synod of *Whitby, he accepted the Roman calculations regarding the correct date for Easter, opposing the Irish tradition, which was current in England. Shortly afterwards he died of the plague and was venerated as one of the first generation of the Anglo-Saxon leaders of the church, disciples of the missionaries sent by Rome to evangelize the island.

DNB, IX.

CELESTINE I, St. (d. 432) Pope (422-32). Born and educated in Rome, he was elected pope after the death of *Boniface I, whose policy he continued, developing the theory that the pope, as successor of St. Peter, is by definition the expression of orthodoxy. He fought heretical trends, condemning *Nestorius and charging St. *Cyril of Alexandria with the carrying out of his excommunication and deposition. Despite his doctrinal claims, his actual authority was limited and contested by Western bishops, like those of Africa, who demanded respect of their rights. His power at Rome was checked by the functionaries of the Western Roman empire. He left his successors the legacy of the primacy of St. Peter's See, which became the basis of the papal apostolic authority.

DTC, II.

CELESTINE II (Guy of Tuscany; d. 1144) Pope (1143-44). He was one of the leading moderate cardinals and was elected pope as a compromise candidate between the conservative "Gregorianists" and the militants in favour of a papal theocracy. He died before he could establish his own views on the papal see.

CELESTINE III (Hyacinth Bobo; 1106-98) Pope (1191-98). Member of the important Roman family of *Orsini, he studied at Paris, where he attended *Abelard's lectures in philosophy. In 1141, he openly defended Abelard and opposed the decisions of the Council of Sens, which forbade his master to teach. In 1144 he was made cardinal and urged a policy of compromise between Church and State, both in the papal conflict with *Frederick Barbarossa and in that between Thomas *Becket and *Henry II. Elected pope at the age of 85, he showed

much vitality. However, he failed in his attempts to prevent *Henry VI from conquering *Sicily. In his relations with other European monarchs, he firmly insisted on the honouring of matrimonial laws, and forced *Alfonso IX of León and *Philip II of France to abandon their projects, which opposed ecclesiastical laws. He was also active in the preparations of a new *Crusade and confirmed the rule of the new *Teutonic order.

J. Leinweber, *Caelestinus III* (1905).

CELESTINE IV (Geoffrey of Castiglione; d. 1241) Pope (1241). Member of the Lombard family of the lords of Castiglione, he was one of the collaborators of *Gregory IX, whom he succeeded, but died after a few months of his pontificate.

CELESTINE V, St. (Peter Morrone; 1215-96) Pope (1294). In 1232 he joined the *Benedictine order, but his love of solitude caused him to retire to Monte Morrone in the Abruzzi Mountains, where he established an ascetic monastery, the nucleus of the *Celestine order. His reputation for sanctity led to his election as pope, as a result of an impasse at the Conclave. Naive and ignorant of all procedure and political problems, he became a tool in the hands of *Charles II of Naples; his supporters forced him to abdicate and his successor, *Boniface VIII, imprisoned him in the castle of Fumone, where he died.

EC, III.

CELESTINE ORDER A branch of *Benedictine monks, founded in 1250 by Pope *Celestine V, at Monte Morrone in Italy. The C. introduced more severe discipline in Benedictine monasticism and was influenced by ascetic trends. From the end of the 13th century, the order became very popular, and, by the end of the Middle Ages, it had established 150 monasteries in Italy, Spain, France and the Low Countries, as well as other Charterhouses in Germany, Poland, Bohemia, Hungary and England.

F. X. Seppelt, *Monumenta Coelestiniana* (1921).

CELL The word was used in medieval Latin in the monastic vocabulary to mean the private room where a monk or nun slept. There were two types of Cs.: a hermits' C., built as an individual lodging, isolated from any other place of residence, and a monastic C., located within a monastery. The latter was actually a small bedroom, which also played a special role in monastic life; several orders imposed a period of penance and meditation upon their members which took place in the C. Thus, the room also often became a place of study.

CELTS An Indo-European people, who settled in central and western Europe in the 10th century BC, characterized by Greek historians and geographers as a distinct ethnic and linguistic group. While the majority of the C. were conquered and assimilated by the Romans, a considerable portion of them continued their separate way of life at the beginning of the Middle Ages. The most important of these were the Britons, situated in what is now England. Other Celtic groups and tribes were established in Ireland and Scotland, and certain tribes and clans continued to exist in northwestern Gaul, such as the Armoricans. The Anglo-Saxon invasion of Britain in the 5th century brought them into conflict with the Britons, who were gradually pushed westwards. Some of the battles became legendary and were immortalized in the *Arthurian romances of the Middle Ages. At the beginning of the 6th century, the Britons were finally defeated and forced to leave their country. Some of them settled in Wales and Cornwall, where they became assimilated into the local Celtic (Gaelic) tribes, while a considerable number migrated to the Continent and settled in Armorica, which changed its name to *Brittany. They converted to Christianity, but continued to speak their own language, the main dialects of which were Welsh and Breton. In Ireland, the C. maintained their primitive social system even after their Christianization and continued to live in their clans until the English conquest in 1172; the ecclesiastical organization was adapted to this structure and aided in preserving the system in the 9th and 10th centuries against the Viking raids. The English conquest and the introduction by *Henry II of the feudal and ecclesiastical administration caused clans to be abolished (see *Ireland), but the population continued to maintain its ethno-linguistic character. In *Scotland, the C. combined the tribal and clan organization with the establishment of an independent kingdom where the southern parts gradually adopted the feudal structure of Anglo-Norman England, while in the north, the original clan structure of the Caledonian C. was preserved.

N. K. Chadwick, *The Celtic Realms* (1967).

CENSUALES In medieval Latin, the term signifies that part of the population which had to pay the tax of the *census*. Thus it generally signified a considerable portion of the peasantry.

CENSUS In the Middle Ages the term used to designate a tax corresponding to the sum imposed on the peasants by their lords. In the 8th century the C. became synonymous with capital tax, and free-peasants were, therefore, exempt from paying it. With the feudalization of society, the vassals, who received lands and had to render military service, also became exempt. The amount of the C. diminished through the centuries, becoming more a symbol of servitude than a real burden, while the major part of taxation was imposed through indirect taxes.

M. Bloch, *Feudal Society* (1953).

CERDA County in *Castile. In 1270 C. was given by *Alfonso X to his eldest son, Ferdinand, who married Blanche, daughter of *Louis IX of France. At Ferdinand's death in 1275, while his father was still living, an important part of the Castilian nobility, together with the king himself, supported the rights of Ferdinand's sons, the *Infantes de La C.*, to the throne. Alfonso's second son, *Sancho IV, however, contested their rights, aiming to claim the throne for himself. At the death of Alfonso, a civil war broke out in Castile. The La C. party received the support of the pope and the royal houses of France and Morocco. The rivalry continued into the 14th century and weakened the royal authority in Castile. The claims of the La C. branch of the dynasty were gradually disregarded, and they became part of the Castilian nobility.

A. Castro, *The Structure of Spanish History* (1954).

CERDAGNE County in the Pyrénées, on the shores of the Mediterranean Sea between France and Spain. C. was established as a county dependent upon the march of *Bernard of Gothia during the reign of *Charles the Bald, c. 850. During the 10th century, it became dependent on the counts of Barcelona and was one of the

units of the state of *Catalonia. This status was legalized in 1258 by the Treaty of Corbeil, when *Louis IX of France renounced French claims on C., allowing *James I of Aragon to lay his claim. The county's history was interwoven with that of Catalonia, while its social structure evolved on the same pattern as that of the neighbouring counties of *Languedoc. It was ceded in 1468 by John II of Aragon to Louis XI in order to gain French assistance against the rebels who challenged his reign. In 1492, as part of the transaction through which Charles VIII of France married Ann of Brittany, the land passed to Spain.

P. Wolff, *Le Languedoc* (1968).

CEREMONIES, BOOK OF A treatise written in the first half of the 10th century by the Emperor *Constantine VII, Porphyrogenetus. It deals with customs and ceremonial, both of the Byzantine court and church. The author used a historical approach to the subject, citing ancient authorities and customs in an effort to discover the roots of the rigid Byzantine protocol – which he preferred to a dynamic legislation. The C. became an important authority for later generations and was used as a practical guide for the Byzantine ceremonies until the fall of Constantinople in 1453.

A. Vogt (ed.), *De ceremoniis*, 3 vols. (1935-40).

CESLAV Serbian leader of the 10th century. He led the struggle of the *Serbs for independence when under the Bulgarian rule of *Simeon. In 927, after Simeon's death, he succeeded in uniting the Serbs under his rule. In order to preserve his people's independence, and to save them from conquest by the Bulgarians and the Croats, he recognized the supreme authority of the Byzantine emperors.

H. M. V. Temperley, *A History of Serbia* (1919).

CHAGHATAI (d. 1242) The second son of *Genghis-Khan. During his father's lifetime, he was appointed the chief justice of the Mongol army, responsible for the maintenance of the *yassak* (strict military discipline), and proved himself a faithful executor of his father's orders. In 1226 he was appointed khan of the Transoxianian provinces in Central Asia, under the authority of his younger brother, *Ogodai who ruled the western part of the steppes. His descendants ruled the *Mongol khanate of Transoxiana, which remained a minor state within the Mongol empire.

M. Prawden, *The Mongols* (1940).

CHAGHATAI, KHANATE OF The *Mongol state in Transoxiana, inherited in 1226 by *Chaghatai and named after him. The khanate reached the height of its development in the 13th century. It began to decline in the following century because of its division between various Mongol princes and because of the claims of the Persian branch of khans.

CHAIN (CATENA) In the Middle Ages, the harbours, especially those of the Mediterranean region, were closed at night and at times of attack by Cs. In the 11th century, a special official was made responsible for the C., and was charged to deal with problems concerning the security of the harbours. In the city of *Acre at the time of the *Crusaders' rule (12th and 13th centuries), this office was entrusted to the royal viscount of the harbour. The viscount presided over a court whose duty it was to judge cases of conflict in the harbour and, eventually, cases of maritime jurisdiction. This institution, *curia catenae* (the *Court of the C.) thus became the first maritime court; its decisions were largely diffused and incorporated into medieval codes of maritime law.

J. K. La Monte, *The Latin Kingdom of Jerusalem* (1931).

CHAISE-DIEU *Benedictine abbey, founded in the last decade of the 11th century by St. *Robert, who introduced a stricter discipline. Its 12th-century church is one of the most original buildings of Romanesque architecture. The abbots of C. were active in the political and feudal affairs of 12th-century Auvergne, and favoured the establishment of French royal authority in the area of Brioude (Auvergne), where the abbey was located.

G. Fournier, *Le Peuplement de l'Auvergne au Moyen Age* (1964).

CHALCEDON City in northwestern Asia Minor, in the vicinity of Constantinople. It was famous for the assemblies of prelates of the Christian church held at its imperial palace. The most important of these assemblies was the Fourth Ecumenical Council, held in 451 upon the request of Emperor *Marcian. About 600 bishops, mostly from the East, attended the council. Its purpose was to deal with heretical movements in the Church. Its main achievement was a definition of the faith, entitled the C. Definition, which condemned the various heresies and established rules of orthodoxy in the Church. The council also adopted a resolution concerning the patriarchates, establishing the primacy of five sees: Rome, Constantinople, Alexandria, Antioch and Jerusalem.

H. Bacht, *Das Konzil von Chalcedon* (1954).

CHALICE (CUP) The term was originally reserved to signify that cup containing the wine which symbolized Christ's blood (i.e. used in the Eucharist). The earliest Christian Cs. were of glass, but from the 5th century, they came to be made of gold or silver. As a result of its liturgical importance, artistic forms were developed and, from the 9th century, Cs. were richly ornamented. They also became a theme of poetry, such as the case of the *Grail in the *Arthurian romances.

DTC, II.

CHÂLONS-SUR-MARNE City in eastern France (Champagne). The ancient Roman city of C. lost its importance at the beginning of the Middle Ages and only its bishopric remained as the nucleus of a new urban centre. In the 9th century, the major part of the land belonging to the county became the property of the bishops, who took the title of counts in the 10th century. Despite their feudal position as lords, the bishops had to accept the infeudation of a great part of their estates to the dukes of *Burgundy and the counts of *Troyes, who recognized themselves as vassals of the bishops. By the rules of inheritance and dowry, the estates passed in the 13th century to the counts of *Champagne, who were, in effect, the lords of the county and imposed their rule over the other vassals of the area. Despite the loss of actual power, the bishops of C. were recognized as *Peers of France in the 13th century, being among the six ecclesiastic lords to bear this title. With the development of commerce, the city of C. grew to become one of the provincial centres of eastern France.

A. de Barthélemy, *Châlons-sur-Marne* (1889).

CHÂLON-SUR-SAÔNE City in Burgundy (eastern France). The Gallo-Roman city of C. declined at the beginning of the Middle Ages into a small agglomeration around the cathedral. It existed as such until the 10th century, when the city and its surroundings formed a feudal county under the suzerainty of the dukes of Burgundy. Friction between branches of the countal house allowed the lower-ranking vassals to free themselves from countal authority. The bishops soon after succeeded in establishing their control over C., assuming at the same time the countal title. In the 12th century, when the dukes of Burgundy imposed their rule upon C., the county ceased to exist as such. Under the Burgundians, the city grew into an important commercial centre on the Saône River, assuring its prosperity in the late Middle Ages.

J. Richard, *Le duché de Bourgogne* (1953).

CHÂLUS Castle in Limousin (western France), belonging to a local feudal family. C. was the site where *Richard Coeur-de-Lion died in 1199, when he attacked the castle in a feud with the lords of C.

CHAMBELLAGE The term, used in feudal courts of France, England and Spain in the 12th-15th centuries, referred to the *Chamberlain's revenues, which came from a tax paid by peasants and later on by burghers, who required his services. This fiscal aspect of the term was inherited by the modern period and was abolished only by the French Revolution of 1789.

R. Boutruche, *Seigneurie et Féodalité* (1968).

CHAMBER (Latin: camera) The term emerged in the feudal vocabulary of the 9th and 10th centuries, meaning the treasury of the feudal lord. The C. was located in the lord's private residence as part of his wardrobe, containing also the jewellery of his wife, and was administered by an official, the *Chamberlain. With the emergence of feudal principalities and monarchies, the C. was transferred from the private residence and became one of the most important offices at the court, administering the king's or prince's estates and responsible to the direct subjects of the ruler. In Germany, all non-noble subjects of the emperor were considered as the "subjects of the C." (the Jews, for example, had the status of *servi camerae*, the serfs of the C.). From the 13th century on, the C. and the treasury became two separate entities.

M. Bloch, *Feudal Society* (1953).

CHAMBERLAIN (Latin: camerarius) The officer in charge of the *chamber. Until the 10th century, the C. was a steward in the royal household, who, in the larger feudal estates, was attached to the service of the lady. In the 11th century, however, with the development of the chamber, the C. was appointed from the lower ranks of the nobility of a feudal principality and was one of the four main officers of the court. From the 13th century on, the C. became the head of a large bureaucratic service, an office corresponding to finance minister. He was aided by a number of officers, the *chambellans*, some of whom administered the private treasury of the lord or king. In England the C.'s office remained attached to the royal household, administering the king's private treasury, as distinct from the *exchequer, which was the public royal treasury.

B. Lyon, *A Constitutional and Legal History of Medieval England* (1960).

CHAMBRE DES COMPTES An organ of financial administration in late medieval France. It originated at the end of the 12th century as an office at the royal court that controlled the financial activities of the *baillifs and in the 13th century was modelled on the

English *exchequer. At the beginning of the 14th century it was organized under *Philip IV as a court of accounts, charged with verifying the accounts of provincial governors. The court was composed of a number of magistrates and clerks and kept its own records, containing the fiscal rights of the crown.

F. Lot and R. Fawtier, *Histoire des Institutions Françaises au Moyen Age*, II (1957).

CHAMP DU MENSONGE (The Camp of Betrayal) A field in Alsace, south of Colmar, named after the "betrayal" by a major part of *Louis the Pious' vassals, who deserted him in 833, when he tried to suppress a revolt by his sons. His defeat was considered as a judgement of God in favour of his sons and accentuated the decline of imperial authority in the *Carolingian empire.

K. F. Morrison, *The Two Kingdoms* (1964).

CHAMPAGNE Province and county in eastern France, on both banks of the Marne River. One of the richest wine-producing areas in Gaul and situated at the crossroads between north and south, and east and west, C. prospered when it belonged to the Roman empire province of *Belgium. In 483 it was conquered by the *Franks under *Clovis, becoming an important part of the Frankish kingdom of *Austrasia. The foundation of an abbey, vested with large estates in the province, caused its division into many feudal baronies in the 8th and 9th centuries. The name C. thus lost its significance and was no longer mentioned until the 12th century. During the 9th and 10th centuries, the region was claimed by powerful neighbours, *Vermandois in the north and *Burgundy in the south. Part of its ecclesiastical estates developed into seigniories and feudal principalities, such as *Rheims, where archbishops took the countal title. An important step towards the revival of C. was the establishment of the county of *Troyes at the beginning of the 11th century and its inheritance in 1014 by Count *Eudes of Blois. Although vassals of the dukes of Burgundy, for the county of Troyes, the counts of Blois and Troyes were able to establish a powerful rule at Troyes, posing a threat to the kings of France in their demesne of Paris and Orléans, and becoming their most bitter foes. They inherited the county of Meaux before 1050 and, with the revival of trade in the second half of the 11th century, established the Fairs of Champagne at Troyes, Provins and Lagny (near Meaux), to which merchants from all over Europe gathered and which were the basis of their wealth. At the end of the 11th century the branch of Troyes became the most powerful of the Blois family and at the beginning of the 12th century they imposed their rule upon all the family's dominions. By the marriage of Adèle, daughter of *William the Conqueror, with Count Stephen of Blois, they became relatives of the kings of England. While their younger son, *Stephen, became king of England (1135-54), the elder, *Thibaut, was the founder of the county of Champagne. He was allied with his uncle, *Henry I of England, against *Louis VI of France, who fought energetically, but unsuccessfully against him. Thibaut protected the famous philosopher *Abelard and granted him the hermitage of *Paraclete in 1122, which became a famous intellectual centre in France. In 1135, he left his political and military activities, concentrating instead on the administration of C. and supporting the churches and monastic establishments. In 1141-42, he fought against *Louis VII on dynastic issues, but failed to prevent the conquest of the village of Vitry, where the church was burnt by the French royal army. Married to Mary of Burgundy, he acquired great prestige in western Europe and, during the Second *Crusade (1147-49), was one of the "wise old men", who established stability and order in France. His son, *Henry the Liberal, a colourful "perfect" knight, was a prominent figure in the second half of the 12th century. His court of Troyes became the cultural centre of Europe, where a new style of knightly life was presided over by his wife, Mary of France, daughter of *Louis VII. The greatest poets of the age, among them *Chrétien de Troyes, gathered at his court and composed romance poems, part of the *Arthurian cycle. They praised the virtues of *chivalry, the new "manners" of the nobility and love. A skilled politician and related to the three sovereign houses of Europe – *Frederick Barbarossa, *Louis VII and *Henry II – Henry the Liberal was a key figure in diplomatic affairs of the 12th century. He also capitalized on the awakening of *Carolingian popularity in 12th-century Western society, claiming *Carolingian heritage through female descendants of the counts of Vermandois, who were considered descendants of *Charlemagne; thus, the marriage of his daughter, Adèle, to King Louis VII of France, was considered as the reconciliation of the Capetian and Carolingian dynasties. The participation of the nobility of C. in the *Crusades spread its culture to the East; his son, Henry, who took part in the Third Crusade, became king of Jerusalem (1192-97). Henry's son and successor, Thibaut III, married Blanche of Navarre and his son, Thibaut IV, who became count of C., also assumed the kingship of Navarre (1234-53). In the 13th century, C. lost some of its importance. The growth of royal power in France under *Philip II, Adèle's son, and *Louis IX, made the counts more dependent on the French kings, despite the counts' insignificant Spanish knightship. In 1284, *Philip IV the Fair married Joan of Navarre, heiress of C., and united C. with the royal demesne. Thereafter the history of C. became that of France. The last two centuries of the Middle Ages were a period of decline for C.: the economic crisis at the beginning of the 14th century affected its fairs and it also suffered the consequences of the *Black Death.

R. Crozet, *La Champagne* (1946).

CHAMPMOL *Carthusian Charterhouse near Dijon in *Burgundy. Founded in 1383 by *Philip the Bold, duke of Burgundy, to serve as his dynasty's burial house. The Charterhouse was richly decorated with artworks by Flemish artists, the most interesting of which are the sculptures of Claus *Sluter.

O. Cartelliery, *The Court of the Dukes of Burgundy* (1939).

CHANCELLOR (Latin: cancellarius) Officer at the medieval courts, responsible for correspondence, drawing up official documents and keeping court records. During the early Middle Ages the Roman institution of notary was still in use at barbarian courts. But with the decline of the ancient lay-municipal schools in the West, notaries were gradually replaced by churchmen, who had the necessary education to deal with clerical matters. In the 8th century clerical service was put under the supervision of a bishop or abbot, who was entitled C. During the reign of *Charlemagne, the institution was organized:

daily clerical work was done by the king's (later emperor's) chaplain and by a bishop during festive assemblies. In the *Carolingian realms of the 9th century, the C. continued to be a high-ranking prelate, and his office was gradually separated from the court. From the 10th century on, the office became a mere ceremonial dignity, like the coronations, entrusted to the highest ranking prelate of the realm (the archbishop of Mainz in Germany; that of Rheims in France); but in practice a lower-ranking cleric was appointed C. From the 12th century on, the C. became a permanent officer, running his own department, which developed into the most important office at the court, the *chancery. At the same time, bishops appointed Cs. to their own courts. The episcopal C. was responsible, among other things, for the administration of schools and the appointment of teachers, granting them the *licentio docendi* (teaching licence). With the establishment of medieval universities, the episcopal C. became the head of the *university. In many cases he transferred his residence to its quarters, thus becoming more identified with the university than with the episcopal court. The C. at the papal court was one of the cardinals.

R. L. Poole, *Lectures on the History of Papal Chancery* (1915).

CHANCERY (Latin: cancellaria) The office headed by the *chancellor in medieval courts. Until the 12th century, the C. was very rudimentary; the chancellor, if he exercised his powers to the fullest, was assisted by the royal chaplain and by one or two monks or clerics, the *scribes,* called clerks because of their clerical origin. From the 12th century on, the C. developed into an important office, supplying clerical services to all the court's activities. Thus, its personnel increased; in some courts the charge of vice-chancellor was created. The C. was divided into departments, among the most important of which was that dealing with the sealing of documents, which was entrusted to a high official. While in German courts the chancellor himself kept the seal, in England, France and other countries, the Keeper of the Seal was the head of the C.'s department that legalized official documents. In modern times this department evolved into the Ministry of Justice. At the end of the 13th century, many charges of the C. were entrusted to men with a legal background, acquired at the universities. Some of them developed their departments as magistracies enjoying a measure of independence, especially on procedural issues. In the 14th century, some department heads were named secretaries to the king or secretaries of state, having taken the oath to keep their king's secrets in the fields of their activity. The C. thus formed the nucleus of future ministerial offices; the first of these was the Foreign Office where, in the late Middle Ages, correspondence with foreign courts was prepared and minutes of decisions on foreign relations were kept.

T. F. Tout, *Chapters in the Administrative History of Medieval England* (1920).

CHANDOS, SIR JOHN (d. 1370) English captain. Born to a family of poor knights. He entered the English army, distinguishing himself in the first phase of the *Hundred Years' War, to the extent that *Edward III personally promoted him. He led part of the army at the Battle of *Poitiers (1346) under the *Black Prince, winning the reputation of a "perfect" knight. In 1348,

Edward III granted him the Order of the *Garter, as one of its founding members, together with the Black Prince and the Earls of Salisbury, March and Warwick. As the closest adviser to the king and to the Black Prince, he was appointed a member of the Council of Gascony, where he was involved in all decisions concerning the war with France and the campaign in *Castile.

Caxton's Book of the Ordre of Chivalry, ed. A. T. P. Bayles (1926).

CHANSON DE GESTE (epic poem) The name given in the 13th century to the poems (mostly in French) praising the *geste* (heroic deeds) of real or legendary heroes, who exemplified the virtues and glory of chivalry. It is not known who composed the earliest extant versions of these poems. They are believed to have been recited by their authors in assemblies of warriors or at festive ceremonies of courts. A famous example is the *Chanson de *Roland,* which, according to tradition, was recited on the eve of the Battle of *Hastings (1066) to warriors of *William the Conqueror's army. Generations of poets added passages to the C. until they received their final form in the 12th and 13th centuries. The authors were inspired by two main events: the emergence of the *Carolingian empire and the *Crusades — around which the two most important cycles of epic poems centre — but also by particular incidents or heroes, such as the *Nibelungs and the Spanish *Cid.

U. T. Holmes, *A History of Old French Literature* (1948).

CHANSON DE ROLAND See ROLAND, CHANSON DE.

CHANTILLY Village in France, between Paris and Senlis. In the 11th century it served as the capital of the dominions of the *Montmorency dynasty, and an impressive feudal castle was built nearby. With the growth of the family's importance through their service to the *Capetians in the 12th and 13th centuries, the castle of C. was embellished and became an important artistic centre in northern France, where precious items, such as war trophies and knights' equipment, were kept. A Gothic church, which originated as a private chapel, was added to the castle in the 14th century.

J. Levron, *Le Château-fort et la vie au Moyen Age* (1962).

CHANTRY The mass for the souls of the founder of a church or abbey, and his friends. It also referred to the small *chapel in which the mass was usually celebrated. The creation of a C. was considered a private enterprise until the 13th century, when rules concerning it were formulated. It required an endowment for its erection and allocation of funds for upkeep, the permission of the local bishop and the consent of the crown or the lord for the alienation of lands.

G. H. Cook, *Mediaeval Chantries and Chantry Chapels* (1947).

CHAPEL The term, introduced in the 7th century, is derived from *cappella,* the little room where the *Merovingians housed St. Martin's cape (Latin: *cappa*), considered a sacred relic. From the end of the 8th century on it was applied to shrines containing other relics, and then to places of worship which in various ways were subordinate to churches. They include the following:

Imperial or royal Cs. which were private oratories in an imperial or royal palace used by the monarch, his family and court members. The first such C. in the

West was built in the palace of Charlemagne at Aix-La-Chapelle. Under Byzantine influence, an imposing chapel-church, which was later to become a cathedral, was built within the palace. The C. served the emperor and his family, who sat in the upper stage, while court members and servants had their places on the main floor. Priests were specially appointed to officiate at the imperial and royal Cs.; they were also employed as scribes or secretaries to the monarch. The chaplains were bound to the person of the monarch and, because of their fidelity to him, were often promoted to bishop-rics. (In England, for example, the kings would assemble the canons of a vacant bishopric in the royal C., where they proceeded to a controlled election of a new bishop, who was often a royal chaplain.) The C. also served as the place where, until the 14th century, new vassals swore *homage to their lord.

Episcopal Cs. Private oratories built within the palaces of popes, bishops and abbots, who were too occupied to take part in the prayers of their cathedral-churches, except for the holidays. Such Cs. were dedicated to a saint to whom the bishop was particularly devoted. From the 12th century on, these Cs. developed into impressive, richly decorated halls, where members of the episcopal court took part in prayers. The most famous of them is the Sistine Chapel in the Vatican Palace at Rome, built at the end of the Middle Ages and completed during the Renaissance.

Cs. of institutions, such as colleges, hospitals and certain religious orders. Designed to serve large assemblies of the faithful employed in these institutions, these Cs. were often of imposing dimensions, and eventually were attached to the institution's main building. Chaplains – approved by the institutions but appointed by the local bishop – were in charge of these Cs.

Feudal Cs. The Cs. in feudal castles for the lords, his family and servants. These Cs. belonged to the lord, who appointed the chaplain, in many cases a bastard son of the family.

Church Cs. Small private oratories within the church, mostly under the windows around the main altar, dedicated to various saints, where private prayers for aristocratic families were said. These and other ceremonies were not attended by the masses. Such Cs. also served as burial places for bishops and abbots and for members of their families, who funded their upkeep. The Gothic churches contained Cs. on both sides of the church.
EC, II.

CHAPLAIN The priest in charge of a *chapel. An ordinary cleric without parochial duties, the C. served the chapel's owner, by whom he was appointed upon consent of the local bishop, who ordained the C. While in feudal chapels, the Cs. were of the lower classes and, in certain cases, illegitimate sons of the aristocrats, in most imperial and royal chapels they were learned clerics and sons of noble families, who saw their service as a spring-board to the episcopate or to higher charges at the court, such as *chancellors. In the *Carolingian states, emperors and kings appointed a chief C., the arch-chaplain, who was one of their closest advisers.

CHAPTER (Latin: capitulum) The term had many meanings in the ecclesiastical vocabulary of medieval western Europe:

1) A section of monastic rule, read during daily services in monasteries.

2) The assembly of the monks of a monastery called to hear the reading of the C. and, later on, to deal with monastery business, elect a new abbot, and establish regulations on questions submitted to them by the abbot. The C. also referred to assemblies of abbots of a certain monastic order or their representatives, either within a province (the provincial C.) or the whole order (general C.).

3) The body of canons of a cathedral church. Originally such Cs. were assembled to hear the bishop's instructions or to elect a new bishop, when the see was vacant. From the 11th century on, the C. became more independent of the bishops, obtained part of the revenues of the church and dealt with their administration. They chose their dean and divided the income (*prebend) among the canons. The C. had a special place (stalls) in the centre of the cathedral, on both sides of the main altar, and in festive ceremonies accompanied the bishop in processions and in his entry to the church. From the 12th century on, the C. were granted a number of church estates administered by a provost, who was in charge of the vassals and peasants. By a papal provision of the 14th century, the popes claimed the right to appoint a number of canons to the various Cs. These canons assigned prebends to their personnel and were exempted from the routine duties of C. members.

4) In the last two centuries of the Middle Ages, the term referred to the assemblies of chivalric orders, such as the Order of the *Garter, the *Golden Fleece, etc.
Dictionnaire de Droit Canonique III.

CHARLEMAGNE (Charles the Great; 742-814) King of the Franks (768), emperor (800-14). Son of *Pepin the Short and Bertha, he was crowned king, together with his brother *Carloman, in 753. At his father's death the realm was divided between him and his brother, but soon after they were at loggerheads with each other. At the death of Carloman in 771, C. became sole king. He eliminated Carloman's family and used the alliance between them and *Desiderius, king of the Lombards, as a pretext for invading Italy, ostensibly to extend military help to the Roman Church. In 774, he conquered Pavia and was crowned king of the Lombards. Pope *Adrian I also granted him the title Patrice of the Romans – which he bore in addition to his two royal titles – authorizing him to intervene in the temporal affairs of Rome, under the formal authority of the pope. Returning to his realm, C. embarked on a war against the *Saxons, led by his most powerful enemy, *Widukind, which lasted more than 30 years, until 804. Saxony was conquered step by step, and its population was forcibly Christianized. In his ordinance of 777 (the *Capitulary to Saxony), draconic measures were prescribed, including the death penalty for opposing conversion. In 787 he responded to a call of Moslem rulers in northern Spain, who were fighting against the *Ummayads of Córdoba, and led a raid into Spain. The only practical results of this expedition were the destruction of Pamplona, capital of the Christian kingdom of *Navarre, and the retaliation by the *Basques, who wreaked havoc on the rear-guard of his army in the pass of *Roncesvalles. C. had to use all his skills to prevent the defeat from provoking a general revolt by the Saxons. Having crushed his opponents, C. proceeded to change the structure of his kingdom: in 789, he promulgated the Capitulary of Herstal, a decree aimed at realizing the ideal Christian kingdom, based on the biblical concepts of the "Holy People and Sacred Monarchy". The Franks were represented as the heirs of ancient Israel and the Chosen People, while C. was portrayed as a new King David. His subjects were ordered to swear allegiance to him, every revolt or sign of infidelity being considered as an offence against religion. The Church was incorporated in the royal system, as part of the government subservient to the monarch.

Among C.'s conquests were the duchy of Bavaria (788), the march territories of Brittany and the Slavs on the Elbe; but, these conquests were incomplete, and C. contented himself with imposing his overlordship. From 797 to 799 he attacked the *Avars and conquered their kingdom, enriching his treasury with the booty. After many conquests and achievements, the idea of a Christian empire was broached at C.'s court, where one of his main counsellors was the Anglo-Saxon theologian, *Alcuin. The idea was first given public expression at the council held in 794 at Frankfurt, where many decisions on ecclesiastical and lay reform of the kingdom were taken, according to the principles of the Capitulary of Herstal. The condemnation of the *Adoptionist heresy in Spain and that of the decisions of the Council of *Nicaea II concerning images, presented C. as the leader and defender of Christianity, while the publication of the *Caroline Books was intended to discredit Byzantium and Empress *Irene, and also to create a new status for C. After the death of Adrian I, C. recognized the new pope, *Leo III, and in a letter to him attempted to clarify the division of power, limiting the pope to prayers. A revolt against Leo, which compelled him to flee from Rome, served C.'s intentions. He received the pope at his camp at Padeborn, where the army was mobilized against the Saxons, and promised to come to Rome "to clarify the situation". In 799, after having seen to the completion of his palace at *Aix-La-Chapelle – which was modelled on the Byzantine imperial palace – he led an expedition to Rome, intending to arbitrate between the pope and his accusers. Leo skillfully prevented his intercession by purging himself of the accusations, and put himself on an equal position with C. At the Christmas Mass of 800, he crowned C. Emperor of the Romans, to the great disappointment of the Frankish king, who sought a more general title, such as Emperor of the Christians (see *Carolingian empire). In 802, C., who was never to return to Rome, began to organize his empire on the religious principles of the Capitulary of Herstal, but also taking into account the *feudal structures of society. He tried to win recognition of his imperial title by the Byzantine *Basileus, obtaining it only in 812. His conflict with Byzantium led him to develop relations with the Caliph *Harun Al-Rashid of Baghdad; they exchanged embassies and presents.

The last years of C.'s reign marked the beginning of his empire's disintegration. As his empire lacked an appropriate administrative structure, C. tried to govern by obtaining his vassals' and counts' fealty. But this system was not very efficient and signs of local particularism emerged – despite the emperor's great prestige. Moreover, the long and continuous wars ruined the free peasants, who began to shirk their military duties.

The first Scandinavian raids were disastrous for the counties along the coast of northern France and the Low Countries.

C. was an unusual man. He adopted the lifestyle and customs of his German ancestors, speaking the Frankish idiom of Austrasia and wearing traditional clothes. A patron of arts and letters, he encouraged the spread of learning throughout his empire, despite the fact that he did not know Latin. He gathered scholars and intellectuals at his palace of Aix-La-Chapelle; was responsible for the *Carolingian Renaissance; took an active part in discussions of the palace academy, and thus became the patron saint of learning and of the universities. While demanding a perfect moral life from members of his family and shutting in monasteries those who sinned, he continued to entertain concubines. He became a legendary figure through the centuries, to the point that all the good deeds of his dynasty were associated with his personality.

R. Folz, *Le Couronnement impérial de Charlemagne* (1967).

CHARLES II, the Bald (823-77) King of France (840-77), emperor (875-77). Son of *Louis the Pious and Judith of Bavaria, his birth created a problem concerning his future share in the empire, partition of which was already decided on in 818, causing his three brothers to revolt and civil wars (see *Carolingian empire). Despite his youth, he took part in campaigns and, in 840, when Louis died, his authority was recognized by the Western Franks, who supported him at the Conference of *Strassburg. In 843, by the Treaty of *Verdun, his rule in France was officially recognized. C. was faced with the problems of organizing the kingdom, overcoming the particularism of the *Aquitanians and subduing the revolts of vassals, who wanted more lands. *Norman raids accelerated, adding to the trend of anarchy. To maintain his power, he sought the support of the church. Aided by *Hincmar, archbishop of Rheims and his main counsellor, and by many prelates – who were devoted to the idea of a biblical kingship and tried to adapt it to the realities of the times – he continued *Charlemagne's tradition of annual councils to manifest the existence of the empire at a time when social and political structures all but disintegrated. While he succeeded in repressing revolts and punishing certain vassals, such as *Bernard of Gothia, he was compelled to accept the rise of adventurers, such as *Boso, *Bernard Plantevelue and *Robert the Strong, the ancestor of the *Capetians, who helped him overcome a major crisis in 865-67: a Norman invasion in the Loire Valley coupled with revolts and threats by his brother, *Louis the German. To assure his vassals' fidelity, he gave them official permission, at the assembly of *Quierzy in 875, to bequeath their *benefices to their heirs, completing thus the establishment of *feudalism. Despite the troubled age, he supported scholars and artists, and his reign was one of the last periods of the *Carolingian Renaissance. In 875, he responded to the appeals of Pope *John VIII, who invited him to come to Italy to receive the imperial crown and establish order. Shortly after his imperial coronation, he fell ill and died. C. was the last Carolingian monarch to have effective authority over the entire kingdom, despite frequent rebellions.

P. Zumthor, *Charles le Chauve* (1957).

CHARLES III, the Simple (879-929) King of France (898-923). He was the third son of *Louis II. When his brother *Carloman died in 884, he was too young to reign and the nobles chose his German uncle, *Charles the Fat as king. C. was elected king in 898 and began to reign after the death of the Robertian king, Eudes (Odo). His reign was marked by troubles and revolts. To put an end to the Norman raids, he recognized *Rollo, duke of the Seine Normans, as his vassal, granting him the duchy of *Normandy in 911. This renewed revolts by Frankish nobles, led by Duke *Hugh the Great, who defeated C. and deposed him in 923. C. fled to England, taking refuge in *Wessex, where he died in 929.

E. J. Knapton, *France* (1971).

CHARLES IV, the Fair (1294-1328) King of France (1322-28). He was the third son of *Philip IV and succeeded his brother *Philip V, who had no sons and whose daughters were barred from inheriting the royal title. His reign was marked by troubles in *Flanders and in *Gascony, where his officials tried to impose royal authority; these troubles are considered as preliminaries of the *Hundred Years' War. Leaving only daughters at his death, he was the last direct *Capetian to reign in France.

R. Fawtier, *The Capetian Kings of France* (1960).

CHARLES V, the Wise (1338-80) King of France (1364-80). Son of *John II, he became regent of the kingdom in 1356, when his father was taken prisoner at the Battle of *Poitiers. His regency coincided with the hostilities of the *Hundred Years' War and the raids of the *Grandes Compagnies, which were linked to the revolt of *Charles the Bad of Navarre, who was allied with the English and claimed the throne; that of the burghers in Paris led by Etienne *Marcel; and that of the peasants, the *Jacquerie, who suffered the consequences of the *Black Death. At the same time, he had to negotiate with *Edward III the ransom for his father and conditions of peace. C., who sought the support of the *Estates-General (national assembly), succeeded in isolating the rebels, defeating the Parisian army, and compelling Charles the Bad to retreat to Normandy. The negotiations with England led to the Peace of *Bretigny-Calais, by which nearly half of the realm was ceded to the English in 1362. He also had to respect the liberalities of his father, who created large apanages for his younger sons, despite the fact that this weakened the kingdom. C. began his own reign in 1364 in better circumstances, due to his achievements during his regency. With the help of a Breton adventurer, Bertrand *Du Guesclin, he fought against the *Grandes Compagnies*, and, having appointed Du Guesclin as *connétable, reorganized the army and sent it to Castile, where it defeated the English. The return to order and the imposition of discipline over family members helped him to recover part of the territories ceded to England and to pacify the realm. The finances were reorganized and a new tax on salt, the *gabelle, provided the treasury with the necessary revenues for expenditures. Towards the end of his reign, France enjoyed prosperity, the city of Paris grew and a circle of walls was erected to contain new commercial quarters, as well as a new aristocratic centre, the *Marais*, where palaces were built. While the nobility found its expression in the revival of *chivalry, C. was a patron of learning, founding the royal library for scholars and, jointly with his brothers, protecting artists. In his ecclesiastical policy, he supported the popes of *Avignon, even after the election of a new Roman pope in 1378. His cognomen the "Wise", was given to him by one of the most learned women of his times, *Christine de Pisan, who wrote his biography.

J. Calmette, *Charles V* (1945).

CHARLES VI (1368-1422) King of France (1380-1422). He was the son of *Charles V and, during his minority, the kingdom was in effect ruled by his uncles, particularly the dukes of *Burgundy and *Berry, who used their influence for their own interests and wasted the money in the treasury left him by his father. Upon reaching his majority, C. called to his palace the old counsellors of his father, the *Marmousets, who tried to put order into the finances. A hunting accident in 1392 caused his madness and he ceased to reign in practice, while the kingdom was troubled by feuds among family members. To add to his political troubles, rumours circulated about the moral behaviour and conjugal fidelity of his wife, Isabel of Bavaria. At the beginning of the 15th century, the realm was rent by rivalries between C.'s brother, *Louis of Orléans, and his uncle, *Philip of Burgundy. Violence and active participation of the Parisian mob (the *Cabochiens) in the struggles led to murders and culminated in a major civil war between the *Armagnacs and *Burgundians which further divided and weakened the kingdom. When *Henry V of England reopened the *Hundred Years' War and won the Battle of *Agincourt, C. was compelled to accept the Treaty of *Troyes, proclaiming Henry as his legitimate heir in 1419.

M. Rey, *Le Domaine du Roi sous Charles VI* (1965).

CHARLES I (Charles Robert; Carobert), of Anjou 1291-1342) King of Hungary (1308-42). He was the son of *Charles Martel and renewed his father's claims to the crown of Hungary. In 1307, he succeeded in obtaining the support of an important part of the nobility and conquered Croatia. An assembly of magnates of the realm proclaimed him hereditary king and he was crowned in 1308. His reign opened with a struggle against the nobility, which lasted 15 years, until the power of the various dynasties was broken. He subsequently imposed a centralized royal government, into which he integrated the lower-ranking nobles (*banderia*), who served in the local government. The cities retained their previous privileges. With the establishment of a royal court of justice in 1324, he stopped convening parliament, the organ of the high-ranking nobles. C. also reformed the finance system, establishing a new currency, the *florin*, and organizing financial administration, which brought prosperity to Hungary.

D. Sinor, *History of Hungary* (1959).

CHARLES II King of Hungary. See CHARLES III, king of Naples.

CHARLES I, of Anjou (1226-85) King of Sicily and Naples (1266-85). He was the tenth son of *Louis VIII of France, who left him the county of *Anjou as an apanage. By his marriage with Beatrix, heiress of Provence, he also became count of Provence in 1246. Supporting the economic and maritime policies of *Marseilles, he became involved in Italian politics. In 1266, he was offered the throne of *Sicily by Pope *Clement IV and with the consent of his brother, King *Louis IX of France, he fought against Manfred

of *Hohenstaufen and conquered Sicily. C. tried to establish a hegemonic Mediterranean kingdom, with Sicily as its capital, acquiring also succession rights in the Balkans and the *Latin kingdom of Jerusalem. Under his influence, Louis IX organized the *crusade against Tunis, where the king of France died. C.'s policy instigated an open revolt against the Angevin magistrates in the island of Sicily which was supported by the Aragonese; the *"Sicilian Vespers" of 1282 were the high point of the revolt. C. lost Sicily and established his seat at Naples, reigning over the kingdom's mainland provinces.
S. Runciman, *The Sicilian Vespers* (1958).

CHARLES II (the Lame), of Anjou (1248-1309) King of Naples and count of Provence (1285-1309). He was the son of *Charles I and continued his father's policy. He introduced the French style of government in Naples, combining royal autocracy with feudal organization of the countryside. He became influential at Rome and was involved in papal affairs. His efforts to conquer Sicily led to a long war with Aragon, forcing him to accept the realities of the *Sicilian Vespers' results. The Peace of *Caltabellotta of 1302 separated the two kingdoms. To compensate his cousin, *Charles of Valois, for his help in the war, he ceded him the counties of Anjou and Maine, the Angevin apanages in France.
S. Runciman, *The Sicilian Vespers* (1958).

CHARLES III, of Anjou-Durazzo (1345-86) King of of Naples (1381-86) and Hungary (1385-86). Member of a cadet branch of the Anjou dynasty, he inherited the duchy of Durazzo in Albania, where he was active in Greek politics. In 1381, when Naples was troubled by a revolt against Queen *Joan I, C. was called by Pope *Urban VI to the kingship. Commanding a Hungarian and Albanian army, he invaded Naples and was crowned king by the pope. He also became king of Hungary in 1385.

CHARLES I King of Navarre (1322-28). Third son of *Philip IV of France and Joan of Navarre, he inherited the crown of Navarre in 1322 and also that of France (see *Charles IV of France). The Navarrese heritage customs gave priority to male heirs of a king. But as C. had no sons, he recognized the rights of his niece, Joan, daughter of his brother Louis X, as heiress of Navarre.

CHARLES II, the Bad (1332-87) King of Navarre and count of Evreux (1349-87). Grandson of *Louis X, he was brought up in France and was mainly interested in French affairs. After the Battle of *Poitiers (1356), he was allied with *Etienne Marcel and led a revolt in Paris against the dauphin, claiming maternal rights to the crown of France. Failing at Paris, he returned to Normandy, where he continued his revolt; in 1364, however, he was defeated by *Du Guesclin at Cocherel and compelled to flee to his kingdom, where he continued to be an ally of the English.
S. Honoré-Duvergier, *Charles le Mauvais, Roi de Navarre* (1969).

CHARLES III, the Fat (839-88) King of Germany (876), emperor (881-88). Son of *Louis the German, who granted him the kingdom of Swabia in 865. After the death of his father and of his uncle, *Charles the Bald, he became active in Italian affairs and in 880 was offered the imperial crown by Pope *John VIII. At the

same time, his two brothers, *Carloman, king of Bavaria, and Louis, king of Saxony, died, enabling him to re-unite Germany under his rule. In 881 C. was crowned emperor, but shortly after left Italy, having done nothing to counter the Moslem raids. In 884, after the death of the king of France, *Carloman, the French vassals elected C. king, expecting him in return to mobilize his forces against the *Norman raids. C. reigned over *Charlemagne's empire but, unlike its founder, was an incompetent ruler. He did nothing to repulse the Normans, enabling them to invade France in 887 and besiege Paris without any opposition. As a result, the French nobles revolted and dethroned him. A year later, he died, leaving the empire in total disorganization.
R. Folz, *De l'Antiquité au Monde Médiéval* (1972);
L. Halphen, *Charlemagne et l'Empire Carolingien* (1947).

CHARLES IV, of Luxemburg (1316-78) Holy Roman emperor (1347-78). Son of John of Luxemburg, king of Bohemia, he was regent on behalf of his blind father, whom he succeeded in 1346. As leader of the opposition to Emperor *Louis of Bavaria, who lost the princes' confidence, C. was elected emperor in 1346, but seized power only after Louis' death in 1347. He loved and supported *Bohemia, making a great effort to assure its prosperity. He founded the University of Prague, annexed Silesia to his kingdom and proclaimed a new constitution for Bohemia. Although his primary concern was with Bohemia, he tried to restore order and peace in Germany, encouraging the local peace associations, the *Landfrieden*. He fought against the powerful family of *Wittelsbach, dukes of Bavaria and marquises of Brandenburg, weakening them and paving the way for a new organization of Brandenburg and northern Germany. His reign was affected by the disastrous consequences of the *Black Death in Germany, where he was neither able to check popular revolts nor prevent anti-Jewish riots. He was crowned emperor at Rome in 1355, profiting from his journey to Italy to sell imperial dignities to local adventurers. His most important achievement in Germany was the issue of the *Golden Bull in 1356, which became the empire's new constitution. It dealt with the procedures for imperial elections, creating the body of the seven prince-electors, comprising the king of Bohemia, the duke of Saxony, the prince of the Rhine Palatinate, the marquis of Brandenburg and the archbishops of Mainz, Cologne and Trier. The electors were granted many privileges, which made them quasi-independent within the empire. His struggle against the free cities was unsuccessful, although some of them were ruined economically and were thus annexed to territorial principalities.
B. Jarrett, *The Emperor Charles IV* (1935).

CHARLES-CONSTANTINE OF VIENNE (d. 963) Count of Vienne (930-63). Son of *Louis the Blind, he claimed the kingdom of Provence, but extreme feudal division of the kingdom limited his rule to the county of Vienne, seat of his grandfather *Boso. During the period of his rule, the *Carolingian kingdom of Provence declined and disappeared.
R. Poupardin, *Le Royaume de Provence* (1910).

CHARLES DE LA CERDA (d. 1354) Constable of France. Castilian prince, of the house of La *Cerda, he established himself in France in 1346 and became one of the favourites of King *John II, who used his military talents in his army. In 1351, he was appointed *connétable* (constable), obtaining thus the high command of the French army. He was murdered in 1354 by *Charles the Bad of Navarre, who broke with John.

CHARLES MARTEL (690-741) Frankish mayor of the palace (716-41). He was an illegitimate son of *Pepin II (of Herstal). Since his youth, he showed military skills and leadership qualities. At his father's death, he fought against his half-brothers and other members of the Pepin family, who disputed his heritage, succeeding in imposing his rule. In 716, he defeated the *Neustrians and united the three *Merovingian kingdoms of Austrasia, Neustria and Burgundy. Later on, he compelled Eudo, duke of Aquitaine, into submission. To impose his authority, he reorganized the Frankish army, creating units of horse-mounted warriors (the future chivalry). He based military service on *feudal grounds, granting lands as lifetime *benefices to the fighters, who became his vassals. These lands were confiscated from the churches' estates. His new army proved itself in 732 when it defeated a Moslem invasion from Spain in the Battles of *Poitiers and Tours. The Battle of Poitiers gave him great prestige, having been considered as the greatest victory of Christianity over Islam since the time of *Mohammad, halting Moslem progress in Europe. Although his role was exaggerated, C. was praised as the champion of Christianity, who saved European civilization from Moslem "barbarism". He profited from his victory to conquer Provence and advance in southern France. Although maintaining friendly relations with the Roman see, he refused to respond to the popes' invitation to come to Italy to continue the holy war against the enemies of the papacy.

L. Halphen, *Charlemagne et l'Empire Carolingien* (1947).

CHARLES MARTEL OF ANJOU-SICILY (d. 1295) He was the eldest son of *Charles II, king of Naples and, through his mother, Mary, grandson of *Stephen V, king of Hungary. When the direct line of the *Arpad dynasty came to an end in 1290, he claimed succession rights, but was defeated by Andrew III. His claims were renewed after his death by his son, Charles-Robert.

CHARLES OF BLOIS (d. 1364) Duke of Brittany (1341-64). Member of the countal house of Blois, he married Joan, daughter of Guy of Brittany. In 1341, when the succession of Brittany was open, he claimed the duchy. He was recognized by the French-speaking sector of the duchy, while the Bretons recognized his rival, *John of Montfort. Supported by the French royal court, he was able to maintain his rule at Rennes. In 1364, he was defeated by John and killed in battle.

E. Durtelle de Saint-Sauveur, *Histoire de la Bretagne* (1935).

CHARLES OF CALABRIA (d. 1328) Son of King *Robert of Naples, who granted him the duchy of Calabria. C. was very active on his father's behalf in the affairs of Italy, where he tried to impose *Angevin influence. He thus supported *Florence in its wars against Pisa. His premature death, during his father's lifetime, opened a dynastic crisis at Naples, since he left only one daughter, the future Queen *Joan I.

E. G. Léonard, *Les Angevins de Naples* (1954).

CHARLES OF LORRAINE (953-91) Duke of Lower Lorraine (977-91). He was the younger son of *Louis IV of France and among the last *Carolingians. In 977 he was appointed duke of Lower Lorraine (now Belgium) by *Otto II, and was active in German politics until 987. At the death of his brother's son, *Louis V, he

claimed the crown of France, but his claims were rejected on the grounds that his service to the emperor made him unworthy of the kingship. He fought against *Hugh Capet, invading France in 978, but was taken prisoner in 990 and died. With the death of his son Otto, the Carolingian dynasty came to an end.

F. Lot, *Les Derniers Carolingiens* (1891).

CHARLES OF NEUSTRIA (d. 811) The eldest son of *Charlemagne. From 784 on, he was involved in the affairs of the Frankish kingdom and, as commander of the army, played an active role in the wars against the *Saxons and the *Danes. He governed *Neustria on behalf of his father. In 806, he was promised the major part of the Frankish kingdom as his share after the death of his father. His death in 811 annulled plans for dividing the *Carolingian empire.

L. Halphen, *Charlemagne et l'Empire Carolingien* (1947).

CHARLES OF PROVENCE (d. 863) King of Provence (855-63). He was the youngest son of Emperor *Lothair I, who bequeathed him the kingdom of Provence. He proved an incompetent ruler, the country being effectively ruled by Girard, count of Vienne, while his brothers and uncles attempted to annex it to their realms.

L. Halphen, *Charlemagne et l'Empire Carolingien* (1947).

CHARLES OF VALOIS (d. 1325) Count of Valois (1284-1325). He was the younger son of *Philip III, king of France, and the founder of the *Valois branch of the *Capetian dynasty. C. was a gallant knight, very ambitious but lacked political skill. As a reaction to the *Sicilian Vespers, Pope *Martin in 1284 called for a crusade against *Peter III of Aragon, offering C. the kingdom of Aragon in exchange for French support. Philip III thus organized a military expedition in 1285, but failed. C. was subsequently active in Italy on behalf of *Charles II of Anjou-Naples, trying to reconquer Sicily, but met with little success and received in compensation the county of Anjou. In 1301, he was active in Italy on behalf of his brother *Philip IV, claiming the title Latin Emperor of Constantinople. Although supported by his brother, he failed to become the *Holy Roman emperor. He commanded Philip's army in Flanders, where he imposed royal authority. His son, Philip, became king of France in 1328.

R. Fawtier, *The Capetian Kings of France* (1960).

CHARLES THE CHILD (l'Enfant; 847-66) King of *Aquitaine. He was the second son of *Charles the Bald, who appointed him king of Aquitaine in 855, to appease the Aquitanians, who claimed their kingdom. In 862, he revolted against his father, at the instigation of the local nobility. Defeated in 865, he was subsequently restored to the throne, but died a few months later. C. was the last king of Aquitaine.

CHARLES THE GOOD (1081-1127) Count of Flanders (1119-27). He was son of *Canute IV the Saint, king of Denmark, and of Adèle of Flanders. After his father's murder in 1086, his mother returned to Flanders, where C. was educated. In 1119, he inherited the county of Flanders from his cousin *Baldwin VII. He was a skilled administrator, trying to impose justice and to face the growth of the cities, which threatened to disrupt the feudal order. He was murdered at Bruges.

F. L. Ganshof, *La Flandre sous les Premiers Comtes* (1949).

CHARNY, GEOFFREY OF (d. 1356) French knight and writer. Originally from the county of Auxerre in

The Visitation; *13th-century Gothic sculpture at the cathedral of Chartres, France*

central France, he entered the service of King *John II. He was the bearer of the oriflamme at the Battle of *Poitiers, at which he died. In 1352, he wrote a long treatise to the king, who had instituted the chivalric Order of the Star. Entitled *Demandes* (Requests) the treatise summarized the main aspects of knightly life, such as jousts, tournaments and war, and contained a codification of military laws from the knights' point of view.

A. Piaget, *Le Livre de Messire Geoffroy de Charny* (1897).

CHAROLAIS County in central France, at the western boundaries of the duchy of Burgundy. It originated as a number of feudal seigniories, which were gradually united into a county and incorporated into the duchy of Bur-

gundy in 1316. The dukes bequeathed it to their heirs, entitled counts of C.

CHARROUX Monastery in Poitou, western France, founded during the reign of *Charlemagne in 772. A reason for its establishment was to enforce *Frankish rule in *Aquitaine. Charlemagne granted C. large estates. In 987, an assembly of bishops proclaimed the *Peace of God at C. The C. document served as model for peace associations in the 11th century.

A. Richard, *Histoire des Comtes de Poitou* (1898).

CHARTERS OF FRANCHISE The term referred to feudal documents granting the franchise (liberty), to a serf in western Europe whom the lord elevated, usually in administering justice. From the 12th century on, the

Pedlar at work *from the Codex Manasse, 14th century*

A 15th-century gold coin from the mint of Cologne

term also applied to the freedom granted to the inhabitants of a town or borough. In such cases, the issue of the C., which freed the town from servitude to feudal lords, was a precondition to its incorporation into the urban community.

F. Rörig, *The Medieval Town* (1963).

CHARTERS OF LIBERTIES The term referred to the documents granting "liberties", i.e., privileges to the upper classes of society. During his coronation ceremony, a king usually issued such a charter swearing to preserve the privileges of churches and nobles. Following vassals' revolts, the king usually reissued such a charter, which was more specific than the original, detailing the nature of the privileges granted. The most famous C. was the *Magna Charta Libertatum* (Great Charter of Liberties), issued by King *John of England in 1215, which laid the foundations for the political liberties and constitution of England.

CHARTRES City in northern France, 96 km west of Paris. After its conquest by the Franks in 483, C. declined into a small ecclesiastical centre. In the 9th century it became the seat of a county, which the powerful counts of *Blois annexed to their estates in the 10th century. The cathedral school of C. became famous at the beginning of the 11th century, during the pontificate of Bishop *Fulbert (a pupil of Gerbert), who developed it into an important centre of learning, which specialized in philosophy and science. The school flourished in the 11th and 12th centuries, producing many notable scholars, who travelled to Spain and southern Italy and brought back the essence of Arabic learning and scientific knowledge. Only in the second half of the 12th century did the school of C. begin to be eclipsed by the centre at Paris, and it declined with the establishment of the *University of Paris. At the peak of its development in the early 12th century, the school of C. was the cradle of medieval humanism, putting man in the centre of the *microcosm. During the late 12th and 13th centuries, C. became famous for its cathedral, a masterpiece of Gothic architecture. Besides its architecture and sculpture, which dictated the style of religious art in western Europe, its stained-glass windows were an original creation, not only for their iconographic motifs, but also for their technical perfection, among which the "Chartres blue" was a composition of colours never to be reproduced. In the late Middle Ages C. declined to a provincial town, whose main attraction remained a religious one: the annual Virgin Mary pilgrimage, to which large crowds gathered.

M. Aubert, *La Cathèdrale de Chartres* (1952).

CHÂTEAU-GAILLARD Castle at the borders of Normandy and Ile-de-France commanding the valley of the Seine River. Built as a feudal stronghold in the 12th century, it was rebuilt and fortified by *Richard Coeur-de-Lion in 1196. After the conquest of Normandy by *Philip II in 1204-06, the castle lost its strategic importance and gradually was ruined.

CHÂTELET (the little castle) Name given to a number of strongholds built in the 11th and 12th centuries to defend the bridges on the Seine in Paris. Of these, the most important were the "Grand C." on the right-bank and the "Petit-C." on the left bank, commanding the high road from north to south. In the 13th century the "Grand C.", later called C., became the seat of the royal provost of Paris, and his offices, including the court of

The Romanesque portal at the cathedral of Chartres

police, became one of the most important judicial institutions of medieval and modern France. C.'s archives are a major source of information on the administrative and legal history of France.

F. Olivier-Martin, *Le Châtelet de Paris* (1914).

CHAUCER, GEOFFREY (1340-1400) English poet. He was the son of a London vintner and served as a page at the court of *Edward III, whom he followed in his campaigns in France. Taken prisoner in 1359, he was freed by the king, who paid his ransom. After his return to England, he resumed his service at Edward's court in various capacities, among them diplomatic missions. He continued to serve in minor posts under *Richard II. His greatest work, which gave him posthumous fame, is the *Canterbury Tales*, written between 1386 and 1390. The tales were conceived as a true and fair representation of

The Cloth Market at Florence; *14th-century manuscript illumination*

English life in the second half of the 14th century, focusing on a pilgrimage to St. Thomas *Becket's shrine at Canterbury, where typical representatives of various classes meet and tell stories. The Tales emphasize the new lay spirit of the times, while they are also a fine criticism of clericalism.

Ed. F. N. Robinson (1933);

H. S. Bennett, *Chaucer and 15th-Century England* (1947)

CHAUVIGNY Abbey in Poitou. As a part of the school of *Poitiers, it was an important cultural centre in the 11th century, influencing the revival of classical studies, particularly in rhetoric and the study of Cicero.

A. Richard, *Histoire des comtes de Poitiers* (1908).

CHELLES Abbey in Champagne. One of the oldest monasteries in western Europe. Founded in the 7th century, it is commonly associated with the activities of King *Dagobert, but was probably established after his death. The monastery was richly endowed with estates and revenues by the last *Merovingians and the *Carolingians. In the 12th and 13th centuries the abbots of C. were highly esteemed, and the monastery regarded as embodying the monastic ideal of life and spirituality.

J. Leclercq, *La Spiritualité de Pierre de Celle* (1946).

CHEMISTRY Medieval C. began as an empirical art, rooted in the theory and practice of *alchemy. By the 13th century, the many extant chemical theories made it possible to begin developing a system of explaining qualitative and substantive changes in inanimate matter in everyday life. The chief sources of practical C. in 13th-century Europe were Latin translations of Arabic and Greek treatises on the art of dyeing, painting, glassmaking, but also on medicine, mining and metallurgy. These works served as guides to the respective *artists* (the term scientists was not yet applicable); but they also elaborated on an ancient Greek chemical theory, according to which the four elements − air, fire, water and earth − were the basis of all matter. The four elements were considered primary and all other matter secondary, being derived from their interaction. This theory persisted until the 17th century. Aristotle perpetuated it, and it was further developed and analysed in the Middle Ages. In the 10th century the Arab alchemist *Rhazes gave the primary elements a quasi-atomic form. The philosopher *Ibn Sinna (Avicenna) made substantial progress, dealing primarily with the geological side of mineralogy. Scientists of the 13th century − such as *Albertus Magnus, Roger *Bacon and Bartholomew − developed a more scientific theory of C., related to the natural sciences and freed of alchemy. Under their influence, the chemists developed new laboratory methods for distillation, which were used both in pharmaceutics and in the preparation of alcohol. In the last two centuries of the Middle Ages, C. focused on what were considered the six basic metals, gold, silver, lead, tin, copper and iron. Chemists studied and described their qualities, trying to establish laws concerning their weight, by using the balance as an essential laboratory tool. Nevertheless, there was as yet no clear dividing line between alchemy and chemistry, as evidenced by the *Ordinall of Alchimy*, whose author, Thomas Norton (*c.* 1477), one of the last medieval theorists, considers the two arts as one.

A. J. Holmyard, *Makers of Chemistry* (1931).

CHERBOURG Harbour in Normandy, on the northern coast of the Cotentin peninsula. C. was founded by the *Normans and in the 11th and 12th centuries was an important harbour, maintaining connections between Normandy and England. With the growth of the town and of the commercial activities in western Normandy and Brittany, it eventually became second to *Rouen. Its strategic importance was emphasized during the *Hundred Years' War, when C. was conquered by the English in 1345, but recovered shortly afterwards by the French. Between 1346 and 1366 it was part of the estates of *Charles the Bad of Navarre, who ceded it to the English. C. remained under English rule until the end of the Hundred Years' War and was fortified during that period.

M. De Bouard, *Histoire de la Normandie* (1956).

CHERNIGOV City in medieval Russia, north of *Kiev, on the main road between *Novgorod and Kiev. C. was assured prosperity as an important commercial centre of the Russian state founded by *Rurik at the end of the 9th century. The merchants of C. also travelled to Constantinople in the south and Novgorod in the north. In the middle of the 11th century, C. became a principality, considered second to Kiev, and ruled by a branch of the Rurik dynasty. With the division of Russia into many principalities in the 12th century, C. remained among its main cities, but dynastic divisions diminished its relative importance. In 1240 *Batu Khan conquered C. Under Mongol rule, it became part of the khanate of the *Golden Horde and, after an initial period during which it suffered destruction, it remained a tributary provincial town. With the growth of *Moscow in the 15th century, C. was conquered by Ivan III in 1485 and annexed to the new Muscovite Russia.

M. T. Florinsky, *Russia* (1947).

CHERSON City and province in Crimea, southern Russia. The ancient Greek city of C. became the capital of a Roman province on the northern shore of the Black Sea. As such, it was also a province of the *Byzantine empire, which maintained it as a centre of commerce with the Slav and Ugro-Mongol countries. Its economic and strategic importance lay in its location, commanding the mouths of the Don and Dnieper rivers. In 987, C. was conquered by the Russian prince of Kiev, St. *Vladimir. In 922 Byzantine emperor *John Tzimisces recognized the conquest as dowry for his daughter Ann, who married Vladimir. C. thus became part of Kiev and its importance gradually declined. In 1238 it fell to the *Mongols and lost its character, and in the 14th and 15th centuries was part of the khanate of *Crimea.

G. Vernadsky, *Kievan Russia* (1943).

CHESS The game was introduced in the Middle Ages by the Persians, who improved the original Chinese version. The Arabs diffused the game in the 8th century, when it was known at the court of *Harun Al-Rashid. C. was introduced in western Europe in the 9th century, being played at royal courts and using real people instead of pieces. In the late Middle Ages, C. pieces were art objects, most of them being made either of precious metals or carved in stone.

J. Huizinga, *The Waning of the Middle Ages* (1924).

CHESTER City in England, on the coast of the Irish Sea. An ancient Roman settlement which preserved its Latin name Castrum, C. was conquered by the Anglo-Saxons in the 5th century and attached to the kingdom of Mercia. In the 7th century an episcopal see was established in the city. C. saw a temporary decline in the 9th-10th centuries; however after the restoration of the

Anglo-Saxon kingdom of *Edward the Confessor, the town flourished due to the development of its trade. *William the Conqueror sanctioned its communal rights and liberties in 1081. The city's strategic position on the border of *Wales led to the establishment of a Norman earldom there. The earldom was granted by William the Conqueror to Hugh I, of the family of the viscounts of Avranches. The earls of C. maintained their position until the 13th century, when royal sheriffs began to be active in the county.

J. Tait (ed.), *The Cartulary of the Chester Abbey* (1923).

CHICHESTER City in Sussex, founded in the 5th century by the Anglo-Saxons on the site of the ancient Roman town of Regnum. During the Anglo-Saxon period, C. remained a small town and provincial capital. Its prosperity developed with the *Norman Conquest and the establishment of a bishopric in 1075. The cathedral of C., built in the 12th-13th centuries, is one of the most beautiful Gothic structures in England.

A. S. Duncan-Jones, *The Story of the Chichester Cathedral* (1933).

CHILDEBERT I (d. 558) Son of *Clovis, he became king of the *Franks in 511 and reigned over Paris. His rule marked a period of consolidation and organization of the central Frankish kingdom.

CHILDEBERT II (570-96) King of the Franks. He was the son of *Sigebert I and Brunhilda. Upon his father's death, he was proclaimed king of Austrasia (575) and in 593 also became king of Burgundy and Orléans. His reign was marked by a series of disputes and wars, caused mainly by the intervention of his mother.

J. M. Wallace-Hadrill, *The Long-Haired Kings* (1962).

CHILDEBERT III (683-711) King of the Franks (695-711). Son of *Thierry III, he was one of the last *Merovingians. He was proclaimed king of all the Frankish realms by the mayor of the palace, *Pepin II of Herstal, who, in actuality, ruled over the kingdom.

CHILDERIC I (c. 436-81) King of the *Salian Franks (457-81). He devoted his reign to the strengthening of his kingdom of Tournai and to the imposition of his overlordship upon the minor realms of the Salian Franks, established in the Low Countries. His achievements paved the way for the great conquests of his son and heir, *Clovis. C. is considered as the real founder of the *Merovingian dynasty, which was named after his father, Meroveus (Merowing).

C. Verlinden, *Frankish Colonization* (1954).

CHILDERIC II (650-75) King of the Austrasian *Franks (656-75). Son of *Clovis II, he inherited his father's title at the age of six. During his reign, the Pepin-Arnulf family (see *Carolingians), which had already obtained the rank of mayors of the palace, became the most powerful force in *Austrasia and in actuality governed the realm.

J. M. Wallace-Hadrill, *The Long-Haired Kings* (1962).

CHILDERIC III (d. 754) King of the Franks (743-51). He was the last *Merovingian monarch. Elevated to the throne, which had been long vacant, by *Charles Martel, he was proclaimed king by *Pepin the Short and *Carloman, but did not reign effectively. In 751 he was deposed by Pepin, with the consent of Pope *Zacharias, tonsured and sent to a monastery, where he died.

L. Halphen, *Charlemagne et l'Empire Carolingien* (1947).

CHILDREN'S CRUSADE A mystical movement in France and the Low Countries, in which, under the impact of the propaganda for a new *Crusade, children of various social classes began to take the cross in 1212. A substantial group of children left their homes in order to fight the Moslems and recover Jerusalem. A similar group was formed in Germany. It seems that the movement included a total of about ten thousand participants, among them a substantial number of adults. While the great majority of children returned home at the insistence of the authorities, others died in shipwrecks in the Mediterranean, and several were sold as slaves in Egypt and North Africa. The C. was the result of a pietist movement, which spread in northern France, the Low Countries and Germany. Its existence was a source of astonishment to 13th-century Europe.

G. Z. Gray, *Children's Crusade* (1898).

CHILPERIC (d. 480) King of the *Burgundians. Brother of King Gundioc, he acquired prestige among the Burgundians as the military leader who had taken a decisive part in the conquest of the country between the Alps and the Rhône River and who had distinguished himself in the war against the *Suevi. Upon his brother's death, he was proclaimed king of the Burgundians. During his reign, he conquered some northern provinces in modern Switzerland and Burgundy.

O. Perrin, *Les Burgondes* (1968).

CHILPERIC I (539-84) King of the Soissons Franks (561-84). He was the son of *Clotaire I and married *Fredegund. His reign, marked by numerous troubles caused by his wife's ambition, signalled the beginning of the decline of the *Merovingians, although the dynasty continued to govern effectively.

J. M. Wallace-Hadrill, *The Long-Haired Kings* (1962).

CHILPERIC II (670-721) King of the Neustrian Franks (715-21). He was the last king of Neustria and reigned under *Charles Martel.

CHINA A vast empire in eastern Asia, which extended over all the fertile lands between the shores of the Pacific Ocean and the countries of the steppe tribes. Separated from other civilizations by chains of mountains in the south and the west and deserts in the north west, C., which was known to western medieval civilization as **Cathay**, emerged as an independent ethnic, historical and social entity, whose development was not affected by western civilizations. As a result of this distinction, the western chronology of the Middle Ages does not suit the evolution of Chinese history and civilization, which have their own distinct character and periodic divisions. The period covered here, between the 5th and the 15th centuries, reflects the general historical point of view.

History After the fall of the **Han** dynasty (220), the political unity of the empire was broken, although the Han culture continued to serve as a unifying factor. In the 3rd century, three great kingdoms were formed in C., Wei, in the northern part, **Chu-han** in the southwest and **Wou** in the south. Their rulers fought one another and brought the empire to anarchy, which prepared the ground for the emergence of the feudal nobility, whose power was based on their large estates. Some Turkish-Uigur tribes took advantage of the situation to invade C. and to settle in its territory, fighting in the service of the rival kings and nobles. At the same time, Chinese influence grew in neighbouring countries, through the emigration and settlement of Chinese in Burma, Thailand and Indochina, as well as by the

The Tribute Horse; *Chinese painting in ink and colour on silk of the Sung dynasty period*

development of trade, which brought C. economic supremacy in the Far East. This polarity between expansion abroad — together with economic prosperity — and political anarchy was stressed in the 4th century, when *Hunnish tribes invaded C. from the Altai Mountains and took part in the civil wars, conquering large territories within the empire.

The southern kingdom of Wou, which had been spared from the invasions, reached a higher degree of organization than the other kingdoms in the 5th century. Attempts by Tibetan tribes to invade the realm had been quashed in 383 and the civil wars, which had led to a general peasant uprising against the lords in 400, reached an end in 420 with the rise of General Liu-yu to the imperial throne. Liu-yu founded the Sung dynasty (420-78), which symbolized the revival of order and of the efforts to reunite C. Nevertheless, stability was not yet achieved; four dynasties continued to rule the country successively until 598.

In the northern realms anarchy was a constant threat, and Uigur tribes of the Turkestan steppes played an important role in the civil wars and the destruction of political structures. In the 5th century these Uigur-Turkish tribes practically conquered the Wei realm, but were unable to establish their rule, since they were constantly warring amongst themselves. In 351, a Tibetan leader, Fu-chin, succeeded in establishing his authority over this conglomeration of tribes and temporarily founded an empire which extended from Korea to

Turkestan (351-84). He organized an army, composed of Chinese infantry and Turkish cavalry, and entrusted the administration to Chinese officials. At his death, the empire was divided into eight kingdoms, the most important of them being that of Northern Wei. By the 5th century the nomadic tribes had become considerably assimilated and, despite political anarchy, the Chinese element became dominant in the north.

The reunification of C. was undertaken by Swei, a southern general who seized power in 589 and succeeded in conquering the northern countries. He fought against individualist claims to power and imposed a strong central government, based on a well-organized administration and a strong army, which was employed to repress any rebellion. The Swei emperors were able to successfully unify the area only by imposing a cruel despotic rule, a fact which eventually led to their downfall in 618. Nevertheless, the impact of their policy was felt even after their fall. The Swei period was an age of prosperity in terms of agricultural and commercial development. In addition, new schools were established, and the *Confucians came to play a dominant role in these institutions. Moreover, the Swei reform of the bureaucracy, in which the system of recruitment through examination was introduced, brought about the emergence of the civil service, which served to maintain the unity of the empire.

The successors of the Swei, the Tang dynasty (618-907) benefited from these reforms and, under Emperor

Tai Tsung (627-49), one of the greatest rulers of C., the empire, based on Confucian philosophy, reached its highest period of stability and prosperity. The emperor extended his rule over *Mongolia and Turkestan and took control over the trade routes to Persia and India. His descendants attempted to conquer Tibet and Korea, but had to content themselves with the overlordship of these countries.

In the 8th century, C. was faced with Moslem invasions in central Asia; in 751 at the Battle of Talas the Chinese lost Turkestan to the Arabs. In the same year, a second defeat in Thailand signified a decline in Chinese power and the revival of anarchy. In order to regain internal cohesion, the emperors were compelled to abandon Manchuria, Mongolia and Turkestan and to renounce their suzerainty over Tibet. In 763 the administration was able to subdue anarchical trends and to impose a revival of the Tang government. In the 9th century, however, the empire was weakened by rivalry between the *Buddhist monks and the Confucians, which led to a general struggle in the second half of the 9th century. As a result, the dynasty declined. The wars caused the destruction of the agricultural and irrigation systems and the peasants suffered starvation. It was the famine which finally caused the fall of the Tangs.

The Swei and Tang periods had been among the most prosperous in the history of C. The imperial organization, devoted to the idea of Chinese unity, and based on a professional and hierarchical administration, was able to check the powers of the nobility. The political duties of the nobles were withdrawn and were given to the gentry of estate owners in the provinces. A second innovation was the development of an irrigation system which caused agricultural development. This made agriculture the backbone of the Chinese economy. In addition, the expansion of political authority and influence brought about the development of commerce, as goods were exported to Moslem and European markets. Moreover, the Tang period was the age of two important Chinese inventions, namely printing (in the 7th century) and gunpowder, used for fireworks in the 9th century.

In the 10th century, the fall of the Tang dynasty led to complete anarchy with a power struggle between several military leaders. As a result, the empire was divided into ten realms. Turkish and Mongol mercenaries were employed, and these were able to seize power in several kingdoms; this, in turn, further accentuated the political instability. It was not until the 11th century that the empire was reunited by the **Northern Sung** dynasty (960-1126). Despite this achievement, a portion of the territories remained in foreign hands and the imperial treasury was forced to pay tribute to the "barbarians", in order to prevent new invasions (1042). The dynasty imposed an administrative reform and based its rule on small estate-owners. The emperors were great patrons of the arts. However, their rule collapsed when an agricultural crisis, leading to famine, in addition to heavily-imposed taxes, led the peasants to revolt at the beginning of the 12th century. The **Southern Sung** dynasty (1127-1279) succeeded in rectifying the situation by reforming the administration. They introduced a council of high officials, who were to head the government. These were given the power to determine long-term policies. Towards the end of the 12th century, this system led to plotting, creating, to an extent, a breach

of unity, especially in the northern provinces, where the government of "southerners" was considered a foreign one. The Sung dynasty opposed an active foreign policy, concentrating on internal affairs, and particularly on the development of a system of social welfare. However, this dependence on a defensive foreign policy was ultimately fatal to C. The government was unable to foresee the consequences of changes taking place in the steppes, where the Mongol tribes had organized and begun a policy of expansion. The northern provinces thus became detached from the empire, and the great khan of the Mongols, *Genghis-Khan, was also able to conduct his conquests of northern China (1211-15), culminating in the conquest of Hanbalik (Peking), the capital of the realm of Kin, one of the states originally belonging to the Sung empire. The conquest was continued by Genghis' son *Ogodai (1229-41), while in 1251, the great Khan Mongka, began the conquest of the southern Sung empire, which was achieved by his brother, *Kublai-Khan (1276). Thus, C. lost its independence and became part of the Mongol empire, which extended over the major part of Asia and Russia. West European travellers, who came to the court of the Great Khan, became acquainted with Cathay for the first time, and their descriptions enlightened the west European public. The most famous of these travellers was Marco *Polo.

In 1279 Kublai-Khan transferred his capital to Peking and shortly afterwards the Mongol dynasty began to be assimilated to the point that it was called the **Yuan** dynasty (1279-1368). The new capital contained the "inner city", where the sacred palace of the khan stood and the administrative machinery, largely adopted from Chinese practices, was based. The "inner city" was forbidden to foreigners. Although considered a Chinese dynasty, the Yuan emperors employed foreigners in their administration, most of them Mongols and Persians, but also *Nestorian Christians, who were appointed by the emperor, despite the civil service examination system, which was reintroduced only in 1315. The first emperors continued the Mongol tradition of a strong, cruel and disciplinary government, as well as the policy of conquests, which brought them to Indochina, Burma and even Java (1292). In the 14th century, their power declined and the Chinese character of the empire became accentuated. In the same century the Great Khanate was divided into several states, which were ruled by the descendants of Genghis-Khan. In this way, the Mongol empire lost its dynastic solidarity and was further weakened. The rulers of Peking were thereby deprived of a constant stream of Mongols into their court and army and were compelled to rely on Chinese officials. This structural change in the government personnel of the empire occurred at the time of one of the most difficult economic crises in 14th-century C. In order to ensure the income of the treasury, currency was depreciated, a fiscal measure which eventually led to greater economic difficulties. In 1340 a number of secret societies, with the aim to rebel against the government, emerged. The rulers could no longer rely upon the Mongol army, which had previously camped in the cities. Chu-Yuan-Chang, a farmer from the province of Nanking, who led the secret society of the "White Lotus", succeeded in uniting the opposition groups in 1351, and in 1356 these groups conquered Nan-king, where Chu proclaimed himself emperor and established his capital. In 1368 the last Yuan forces surrendered at Peking and the new **Ming** dynasty (1368-1644), was formally established. Chu restored the ancient Chinese practices and devoted his reign to reforming the economic structure of the empire. The fruits of his economic policy were apparent in the 15th century, which was a period of prosperity and stability in Chinese history. Politically, the Chinese expansion into southern Asia was renewed: in 1433 Indochina was conquered and annexed to the empire, and 50 cities and principalities on the coast of the Indian Ocean, as far as Persia and Aden, recognized the suzerainty of the emperor as a result of a massive Chinese fleet which sailed there. The dynasty, which re-established its capital at Peking in 1421, attained the highest prestige and power in Asia. In the latter half of the 15th century, efforts were directed towards a northern expansion; Manchuria and the major part of Mongolia were conquered and the Chinese protectorate over Korea was restored.

Society Basically, Chinese society of the 5th-15th centuries was characterized by an agrarian structure. The peasants not only made up the majority of the population, as was true elsewhere in the Middle Ages, but also were given special treatment by the upper classes. Nevertheless, the peasantry was not a homogeneous class and the villages had a complex social structure. Aside from people who owned no land and were therefore reduced to slavery on the estates of landowners, there were millions of free peasants who possessed small tracts of land, but were forced to pay taxes to and provide services for the estates of the aristocracy; such groups were comparable with the European peasants of the 5th-6th centuries. Their existence created the conditions under which feudal structures and manorial systems emerged and developed. The upper class in the village was that of the free farmers, who possessed enough land so as to be independent of the lords. During the **Sung** period some of these attained high economic status and performed important civil duties, as notables, in their villages. Others had developed ties with estate-owners during the **Tang** period and formed a lower class of the nobility. During the periods of anarchy, the nobles, especially those who possessed the largest estates, became politically active and established ties with the class of military leaders. However, the great majority of the Chinese nobility in the 7th-15th centuries corresponded to the gentry in the European later Middle Ages. They were groups of wealthy landowners, respected in their provinces, who had a certain influence on local business and were employed in various advisory capacities in the local government. As distinct from European nobles, the Chinese nobility had relatively little political influence as a class, even those of its members who dedicated their life to a military career.

While the urban classes were a relatively small minority in C., the demographic dimensions of the country were such that urban areas enjoyed a status superior to that found in European cities of that time. The Chinese town, whose population was continuously supplemented by migrations from the countryside, was made up of a conglomeration of inhabitants, most of whom were craftsmen or merchants. The foreign policy of the empire depended, in many cases, on the economic interests of the urban population, especially with respect to southeastern Asia. Chinese territorial expansion was in reality the growth of the urban classes, because these town dwellers emigrated or due to their business interests which required increased government influence upon neighbouring countries. Despite the economic importance of Chinese towns, these never attained the autonomy of European cities and boroughs – whether in regard to communal institutions or foreign policy. The Chinese cities were ruled by government officials and by military governors, who represented the imperial government and, during the periods of anarchy, by the regional dynasties.

The most singular class of Chinese society was that of the officials; this bureaucratic class found its roots in the ancient traditions of the **Han** period; its administrative system was based on a hierarchical organization of governmental activities. The difficulties created by the Chinese system of writing prevented the uneducated from gaining access to the class. Through the political reforms of the **Swei** and **Tang** dynasties, the officials became the real machinery of the empire's administration and were well organized in the various departments through the system of recruitment on the basis of examinations. Thus, from the 8th century on, they gained not only the power granted them by the imperial court, but also a great deal of autonomy. Established in the capital and in the cities, they became the real élite of the Chinese society, whose interest in the unity and prosperity of the empire was related to the desire to preserve their social status. Moreover, certain positions were becoming hereditary.

Language and literature The Chinese language, in effect, comprised a group of distinct dialects, or even languages, which often differed from province to province. The historical and political divisions during the Middle Ages were, in a certain measure, the result of linguistic particularism and antagonism between the north and the south; political boundaries often followed linguistic frontiers. Nevertheless, linguistic unity was the result, not only of the common origin of the various dialects, but also of the cultural unity imposed by the Chinese script and manifested in cultural and literary activities. One of the oldest in the world (the most ancient inscriptions are from the 14th century BC), the Chinese system of writing is a development of a pictographic method to express ideas, each character being a symbol of an actual notion. Gradually, characters came to be grouped together, creating a great number of possible combinations, based on thousands of characters. The most complete lexicon of Chinese script contains 50,000 characters, but most of these are variants and the Mandarin language (used by the officials in the Middle Ages) contained about 10,000 characters.

The literary legacy of C. is one of the most ancient in the world and, through a conservative tradition of writing, was preserved and developed in the Middle Ages. Some of the most important pieces of literature were historical works, which not only related a narrative of events, including deeds of the emperor and political occurrences, but also contained long dialogues, satirical inserts and stories. During the Tang period, the prose was enriched by moral and religious treatises and literary criticism. Urban development and the emergence of the bureaucratic class led to the composition both of material with a moral and didactic purpose, and of works meant for leisure and diversion. A great number of literary works during the **Tang**, **Sung** and **Yuan** periods, namely the romances, dealt with the life of particular individuals and also with popular traditions, rooted in the Chinese past. Books were greatly diffused beginning in the 7th century as a result of the invention and utilization of the presses. Printing thus served as an important factor in the unification of the Chinese cultural heritage.

Poetry was also developed in medieval Chinese literature. While the ancient poems were on the whole epic works, the Tang poetry was mainly lyrical, and an important poetic theme was nature. Many poets emphasized the mystical aspects of contemplation in their works. Poetic activity was also found in the theatre, especially the puppet theatre, where the texts were recited in verse. This branch of art reached its peak in the 12th-14th centuries. Drama emerged as an independent branch of literary expression in the 12th-14th centuries, but only towards the end of the 15th century did theatrical literature begin to be more consistent and expressive.

Arts As was the case in Chinese history and literature, it is difficult to distinguish periods of art history which correspond to the Western division. The continuity of artistic creation imposed a certain unity of motif, style and techniques, which did not correspond to that found in Western civilizations. One innovation of 5th-century art was the adoption of the Indian style of representation of gods. This was influenced by the penetration of *Buddhist ideas and religious practices and by the total absence of such a representation of anthropomorphic divinities in Chinese art. An important development in the theory of art, which had a tremendous impact on artistic achievement, were Chiehho's treatises on the arts (6th century). Chieh established six principles of painting: 1) the spirit of life concerning the painter's subject; 2) the technique of painting and the correct use of tools; 3) realism in design and figure; 4) the correct mixing of colours; 5) the exact division of the space painted; and 6) the study of motives by execution of previous models, considered classical. These principles were fully implemented by the painters of the **Tang** period, beginning with Li Su Chow (7th century), who was the great master of the Chinese naturalist school of painting, which flourished until the 13th century. The Mongol conquest brought about a decline in painting, and only in the second half of the 14th century did a revival of the previous traditions prepare the way for the artistic renaissance of the **Ming** period. Sculpture, which reached its height in Chinese art upon the penetration of Buddhism, was developed mainly in the 5th-9th centuries. Pottery was one of the most interesting forms of Chinese decorative arts; its technical and artistic work, with a superlative elegance of style, was produced mainly in the **Sung** period, but its artistic value remained highly regarded during Mongol rule, when the technique of producing a combination of white and blue colours was brought to perfection.

In the field of architecture, the concept of the harmony between the structure and its surroundings was the fundamental premise upon which architects designed their buildings. The horizontal plan of the houses, conceived in the ancient periods, remained unchanged during the Middle Ages, while religious monuments, such as pagodas, were built in a gradual elevation, adopting the triangular design. The greatest architectural innovations appeared with the Mongol conquest and the building of the "inner city" of Peking, designed as a complex of palaces, temples and administrative services, enclosed by a wall. Under the Ming emperors of the 15th century this structural design reached its perfection, when the capital was re-established at Peking.

Philosophy and religion The religious and moral thought of classical C. was influenced by the philosophy of Confucius, who lived in the 6th century BC and laid the religious foundations of the Chinese faith, based on deistic ideas and entirely opposed to an anthropomorphic divinity. It primarily emphasized the moral qualities of men and preached the pursuit of human perfection. Although discussed and even opposed in ancient times by other philosophical trends and schools, such as Taoism, the Confucian system of thought became the heritage of the ancient periods and was adopted in the Middle Ages as a religion. However, in the 5th century, Buddhist ideas penetrated from India and Tibet and became influential in C. This was especially due to the establishment of Buddhist monasteries, which were not only places of retreat and meditation, but also centres of an intensive missionary activity. Buddhist philosophical conceptions were largely accepted by the Taoist thinkers and during the 6th-7th centuries a certain conceptual syncretism was apparent although religious practices remained distinct. During the **Tang** period a revival of Confucian philosophy developed. Its arguments became crystallized through a polemical fight with Buddhism, begun by Han Yu (768-824), who is considered the founder of the neo-Confucian school. In the 11th and 12th centuries this school developed its ideas in an attempt to derive a rationalist and metaphysical system of dualism, in which spirit (Li) and matter (Chi) were at the heart of every creation and idea. According to neo-Confucian conceptions, divinity, nature and human qualities could only be understood through the study of interaction between Li and Chi. Despite its appeal among intellectuals and members of the bureaucratic class, the Confucian philosophy, represented in the religious field by certain liturgical practices, was not able to wipe out Buddhism. Although attempts were made in the 8th and 9th centuries to suppress Buddhism, it remained a popular religion whose system of faith and worship was largely accepted by the masses.

W. Eberhard, *A History of China* (1969);

E. T. Z. Sun and J. De Francis, *Chinese Social History* (1956);

W. Willets, *Foundations of Chinese Art* (1965);

Yu-lan Feng, *A Short History of Chinese Philosophy* (1947);

C. K. Yang, *Religion in Chinese Society* (1961).

CHINDASWINTH (d: 653) King of the *Visigoths (642-53). He was elected king after a revolt of the nobles and began his reign by violently repressing the opposition, killing the leaders of the nobility and reducing the others to slavery. By 646 peace had been gained in the kingdom and C. summoned a council at Toledo. This marked the second phase of his reign, entirely different in character from that of the first. Not only was it a period of peace, it was also an epoch dedicated to the passing of legislation. A new Visigothic code was prepared to serve as the fundamental law of the kingdom.

E. A. Thompson, *The Goths in Spain* (1968).

CHIOGGIA Village in Italy, near Venice. In 1378, during a long war between *Genoa and *Venice (1338-80), the Genoese fleet, allied with Sicily, Padua and Hungary, attacked the village and occupied it. The War of C. lasted until 1380, when the arrival of the Vatican fleet from the eastern Mediterranean made a counter-attack possible. The Genoese fleet was crushed and the defeat led to the decline of Genoa.

H. Kretschmayr, *Geschichte von Venedig* (1935).

CHIONIADES, GREGORY (d. 1332) Byzantine poet and astronomer. Born at *Trebizond, he was educated at the palatial academy there. At the beginning of the 14th century he proved himself to be one of the academy's most outstanding members. He composed religious poems, most of them hymns, which were used in the liturgy. His correspondence is one of the most important testimonies of the cultural life of the empire of Trebizond. Interested in astronomy, C. journeyed to Persia on behalf of the academy and gathered treatises and other materials of the Persian astronomers. In this way, he was able to teach his Greek students the Persian methods of astronomical observation.

W. Miller, *Trebizond: The Last Greek Empire* (1926).

CHIOS Island in the Aegean Sea. One of the most important possessions of Byzantium and a commercial centre, C. was attacked and conquered by the Arabs in 669. The Byzantine fleet, armed with shells containing *Greek fire bombs, defeated the Arabs in 678, recovering the island. It remained in Byzantine possession until 1204. In the 12th century, the Venetians conquered the island several times. Although C. was recovered by the Byzantines, the Venetians retained their influence and their commercial rights to C. were recognized. In 1204, C. was given to the *Latin emperor of Constantinople and in 1225 was reconquered by *Theodor Lascaris, emperor of Nicaea. In 1261, Genoa was granted the privileges to C. which had been formerly reserved for Venice. In addition, Genoa was allowed to establish a settlement on the island, and in 1304 this became the basis of Genoese territorial domination in C., which lasted until the 16th century. Although attacked by Turks, Byzantines and Venetians during the 14th century, the Genoese succeeded in maintaining their domination over the island, which became the seat of the powerful commercial company of the Giustiniani family, the "Mahonna", which had a powerful fleet at its disposal. In the 15th century, C. was made a staple of Genoese commerce with Crimea in the Black Sea and became an important economic base, bringing prosperity to the city. The "Mahonna" also created an administrative system based on the Byzantine model.

Ph. P. Argenti, *The Occupation of Chios by the Genoese* (1958).

CHIVALRY Social class and manner of life in medieval western Europe. The emergence of C. is related to technical developments, and to the subsequent employment of mounted warriors in the army of *Charles Martel, at the beginning of the 8th century, in the Frankish realms. The introduction of the stirrup, of Chinese origin, in western Europe, permitted the warrior to fight while mounted. This called for increased investment in equipment, which was beyond the means of a peasant soldier. In addition, the training necessitated a longer period of service than that of the infantry. Thus, the mounted warriors received as *benefices larger estates, corresponding to at least 12 *mansi (peasant-family units) of land. As vassals of their *Carolingian lords, the importance of this class grew with the expansion of the Carolingian state under *Pepin the Short and *Charlemagne and the foundation of the empire. The C. served as its main military force; in fact, in medieval Latin the word *miles* (soldier) became synonymous with knight. From the 9th century on, the C. became the basis of the feudal nobility, although the process was not uniform. In France they were integrated into the nobility, while, in Lorraine and Germany, a certain distinction was made between knights and nobles — until the 12th century the knights being considered the lowest rank of the aristocratic class, dependent on the lords who enjoyed jurisdiction. With the increased participation of

The lord of the manor at his table, *from the Luttrell Psalter, 14th century*

French and Burgundian knights in the wars in Spain, and other expeditions in the 11th century, a certain ethos began to distinguish C. from other social classes, based on the pride in its fighting ability, particularly for the Christian cause against the Moslems and pagans. This ethos, based on the epic songs (the *Chansons de Geste*), in which knights were attributed perfect qualities of warriors, implied a number of qualities, such as gallantry, boldness, loyalty to one's lord and comrades in battle, and readiness to sacrifice one's life.

To acquire these qualities, the knight had to be of appropriate background, which was a condition for access to the class in the 12th century, and also to be correctly trained for his task. Thus, a system of education, intended to play a vital role in forming the character of the future knight, was set up in western Europe between the 11th and 13th centuries. Training began in childhood, when the future knight served at the court of a famous lady. There he was expected to acquire the style of "noble behaviour" practised in the castle. Later the youth began to learn not only warfare, but also "chivalric" behaviour under the direction of an elder knight. At the end of the formative period the young man was "ordained" a knight in a special ceremony combining religious and secular elements. The knight was expected to prove not only his military abilities, but also to act in accordance with his social status. He participated in hunting parties, tournaments and the courtly life, as distinguished from urban and rural society. The term "villein", designating peasants, was used by knights to denote simple, crude people, whose way of life contrasted with the fine manners of the knights. Beginning in the 12th century, the ideals of C. found their expression in medieval poetry. The revival of the legendary past, both in the cycles of epic poems, such as the *Carolingian epic and that of the *Crusades, the lyric songs of the *troubadours and the *Arthurian romance, and many other tales of real or legendary heroes, reflected feudal C. as it was perceived by its contemporaries. This literature formed part of a continuous education imparted at the court assemblies to young and mature knights alike. Modelled after the life at the courts of *Aquitaine and the perfected style of the court of *Champagne in the second half of the 12th century, the chivalric style of life was adopted at royal and princely courts elsewhere in Christian medieval Europe. While at the beginning of the 11th century, C. had not always been synonymous with nobility, and a knight was not necessarily a nobleman, at the beginning of the 14th century, C. was more highly esteemed and only an educated nobleman could become a knight.

An important aspect of medieval C. was its religious code, which in some ways resembled the ideals of monasticism. Religious C. found its roots in the *Crusades at the beginning of the 12th century, when it was practised by the order of the *Hospitallers. This order served as a model of the religious code in which emphasis was placed upon unremitting battles with the Moslems, and upon an ascetic-monastic life in the castles. The foundation of the order of the *Templars in 1119, and the establishment of its rule in 1129, stressed this combination of C. and monasticism, which was idealized by St. *Bernard of Clairvaux, in his treatise *De laude novae militiae* (In Praise of the New Knighthood). Religious C. spread to Spain in the second half of the

Late medieval knight armed with sword and shield

12th century with the foundation of the orders of *Calatrava, *Alcantara and *Santiago, and to Germany, towards the end of the 13th century, where the order of the *Teutonic Knights was founded with the aim of providing German knights to serve in the *Crusaders' kingdom of Jerusalem. However, from the 13th century, in northern Germany and the Baltic countries, these Teutonic Knights served primarily as a means of imposing Christianity upon Prussia and *Livonia, and were also responsible for the Germanization of these countries.

Religious C. represented the ideal of the perfect knight, who was expected to concentrate all his efforts upon fighting for Christianity and was to be entirely detached from the secular life of the courts and from family ties.

In the 14th century kings and other princes founded chivalric orders to epitomize the perfect warrior and gentleman. Such was the Order of the *Garter, established by *Edward III in England to commemorate an incident of chivalrous conduct towards a lady at the royal court. The most brilliant of these orders was the Golden Fleece at the court of *Burgundy in the 15th century. The new orders were organized on a semi-ecclesiastical model, their members being congregated in "chapters", but their actual character was entirely secular. The king or the prince, who headed the order, would choose members from among the most famous and "gentle" warriors of the time. Their assemblies were great occasions for literary and musical performances,

Knights exhibiting their banners before a tournament; from a 15th-century illuminated manuscript

and made a lasting impression on Western civilization. Their impact was felt in the mores of society, in fashions, the arts, architecture and warfare. Several treatises were written in the 14th and 15th centuries, in which the qualities of C., as the highest and most civilized class of society, were praised.

In 13th-century England, a particular form of C. emerged with the knights of the *shire, a lower rank of the nobility which was employed in the administration of the counties and shires and was separate from the main body of C. This category also emerged in Germany, where the knights, who were called *junker* (young lords), devoted themselves to government of the states.

E. Prestage, *Chivalry* (1928).

CHOIR (Latin: cor "heart") The term was used to describe the part of the church around the main *altar, which was considered the heart, on the basis of the symbolic meaning of the church as the Christian body. The seats of the clergy were situated in the C. from the beginning of the Middle Ages. From the Romanesque period on, the C. became the object of particular attention on the part of architects, who introduced the notion of an elevated part of the church building. In the Gothic period, it became separated by a circular semi-wall from the deambulatory, which gave access to the C.-chapels and was richly decorated by reliefs and sculptures. By extension, the body of singers, monks and canons, who assisted in the divine service, was also designated by this name. This group had already existed as far back as the 4th century, but was organized at the end of the 6th century, when Pope *Gregory I established it under the name of *Schola Cantorum*. In the Middle Ages the Cs. of cathedrals and monasteries were almost the sole places where music was taught, first orally and from *c*. 1100 with the help of written Gregorian notes. Up to the 15th century, most of the musical activity in the churches was vocal and therefore C.-singing was an indispensable part of the service.

F. Blume, *Musik in Geschichte und Gegenwart* (1949).

CHOPINEL, JEAN See JOHN OF MEUNG.

CHOSROES I, Nushirwan King of Persia (531-79). Son of Cawad I, he repealed his father's reforms (see *Persia) and restored family life and private property. His legislative reforms, on the basis of which he was dubbed the Persian *Justinian (the emperor being his contemporary), were also directed at the fiscal structure of the kingdom and at its agrarian way of life. The army was also reformed and *chivalry became its main unit. C. invaded Byzantium in 540, a war which waged until 561. The battles were held in the Caucasus, Armenia, and Syria, while the Persian fleet attacked and conquered Yemen, thus severing communication between the Byzantines and the Christian realm of Ethiopia. Although the war came to an end without important territorial changes, the peace treaty of 561 required that Byzantium pay tribute to Persia. A second war with Byzantium was begun in 572 and was still in full force when C. died in 579.

A. Christensen, *L'Iran sous les Sassanides* (1944).

CHOSROES II, Parviz King of Persia (590-628). Grandson of *Chosroes I, he was proclaimed king by the council of the realm, when General Varhran revolted against his father and conquered the capital of Ctesiphon. He fought against the rebels and, with the help of Emperor *Mauricius of Byzantium, was able to repress the revolt in 591. In 602, after the murder of Mauricius, he renewed the war with Byzantium. Within the course of a few years, his army had conquered Armenia and penetrated Asia Minor to the Sea of Marmara. A second army conquered Antioch in 611 and Palestine in 614, where the Jews revolted against the Byzantines. In 619 Egypt was conquered and C. was acclaimed as *Parviz* (the "Victorious") and restorer of the ancient Persian monarchy. But when the Byzantine emperor *Heraclius reorganized his army and led a counter-attack, Persia lost all its conquered territories, and even its capital, Ctesiphon. C. was murdered while in flight. The Persian king had been cruel and had reigned with great power, being the last great *Sassanid ruler. His army, reorganized by his grandson, proved its efficacity. Although he distinguished himself as a military leader, C. did not have the qualities of a statesman, which might have helped him to accept other priorities over his war objectives.

A. Christensen, *L'Iran sous les Sassanides* (1944).

CHRÉTIEN DE TROYES (c. 1135-83) French poet and writer. Little is known about his early life and education. Born to a family of poor knights, he spent his youth at the court of the counts of Flanders and, reaching fame as a poet, was received at the court of *Champagne, the most important literary centre of western Europe in the second half of the 12th century. There Countess Mary discovered his talents and became his patron. C., who became one of the leading personalities at court, praised *chivalry and knightly virtues in his works. He was a prolific author of romances and contributed to the development of the *Arthurian legend. Influenced by *Tristan and Isolde, he praised the capital virtues of an ideal knight: pride, courage, fidelity and love. He innovated the genre of the *roman courtois*, in which he tried to depict a combination of religious, moral and lay behaviour; thus, he created the *femme-dame* type, representing the married woman, devoted to her husband and family, and the lady who imposed her own wishes and caprices. His main works are *Erec et Enide* (1165), the first French novel; *Cligès* (1165-70); *Lancelot* (1170); *Yvain* (1175) and *Perceval* (1180), unfinished at his death. Under the influence of his romances, notions such as the "Round Table" were introduced in the political and social life of the princely courts. In fact, C.'s representation of King Arthur sitting at the round table with his twelve perfect knights was behind the foundation of the institution of the twelve *Peers of France. C. is considered as the greatest 12th-century French poet who had considerable influence on the literature of England and Germany.

R. S. Loomis, *Arthurian Tradition and Chrétien de Troyes* (1949).

CHRISM (Greek: chrio "to anoint") A mixture of olive oil and balsam, used in the Church to anoint the faithful from the early times of Christianity. The C. reflected the tradition of the Old Testament, symbolizing the anointment of King David, believed to be the ancestor of Jesus Christ. From the beginning of the Middle Ages it was used for the *sacraments, the consecration of churches and the anointment of kings at their coronation. Once the mixture was prepared, it could be used only when consecrated, a duty which was the exclusive right of the bishops.

EC, III.

CHRISTINE DE PISAN (1364-1430) Poet and historian. Born at Venice, her parents settled in France when she was a child. In 1372 she married Etienne Castel, a Picardian noble. After her husband's death in 1389, C. began to work in the literary circles at Paris and became a well-known poet in France. She composed lyrical and didactic poems such as *Cent ballades d'amant et de dame* (Hundred ballads of a lover and his lady), in which allegory and imagery alternated on the background of mystical love. Her most important achievement was, however, the *History of Charles V*, which represents her particular approach to historical biography. In this work she brought out the moral lessons to be learned from the events treated. She wrote *The Book of the Three Virtues*, a manual for the education of women, on the same lines. In the last year of her life, C. praised the vision of Joan of Arc and composed a poem dedicated to her leadership at Orléans. C. was one of the most important intellectuals during the troubled times of *Charles VI and Charles VII; her literary and historical works were published in a critical edition in three volumes (1886-96).

J. M. Pinet, *Christine de Pisan* (1927).

CHRISTOPHER I (1219-59) King of Denmark (1252-59). The third son of *Waldemar the Victorious, he was elected king during a period of unrest, after the death of his elder brothers. In order to improve the state of the royal treasury, he attempted to tax the clergy, whereby he entered a struggle with the church, which later developed into a civil war. At his death, C. was excommunicated and Denmark was placed under an interdict.

L. Musset, *Les peuples Scandinaves au Moyen Age* (1951).

CHRISTOPHER II (1276-1332) King of Denmark (1320-26; 1330-32). Brother of *Eric VI, he rebelled against him; and, when Eric died childless in 1319, C. was elected king by the nobility. In order to obtain his election, he was compelled to grant the feudal nobles wide privileges, among them the power to assemble annual parliaments, which limited royal power. As a result of his attempt to levy taxes, civil war broke out, causing C.'s deposition in 1226. Although he was recalled in 1330, his reign marked a period of decline of the Danish monarchy.

L. Musset, *Les peuples Scandinaves au Moyen Age* (1951).

CHRISTOPHER, St. One of the most popular legendary saints in the Middle Ages. According to one of the ancient Byzantine sources, he was a Roman soldier who converted to Christianity and died a martyr during the persecutions of Emperor Decius in 250. Another legend made him the son of cannibals, who had heads of dogs. As in the first legend, C. converted to Christianity and was martyrized. This second legend was adopted by medieval artists, who represented C. as a saint with a dog's head. The cult of C. spread in Byzantium and, in the 5th century, reached western Europe, where C. was made the patron saint of travellers. In the Romanesque churches of Switzerland many frescoes depict the various legends concerning him. Chapels dedicated to C. were erected in most countries of western Europe.

J. De La Maduère, *St. Christophe* (1955).

CHRISTOPHORUS OF MYTILENE (11th century) Byzantine poet. Originally from Mytilene in the island of Lesbos, he joined the imperial court at Constantinople, where he became famous as a poet. In his epigrams he combined sacred and profane verses. His poems were considered by his contemporaries, the protagonists of the cultural Byzantine renaissance of the 11th century, as models of elegance of style. His work won him fame which was recognized by succeeding generations.

F. A. Wright, *The Poets of the Greek Anthology* (1928).

CHRODEGANG, St. (d. 766) Bishop of Metz (742-66). Closely associated with *Charles Martel and *Pepin the Short, C. acted as secretary at their courts and was one of their intimate counsellors. He retained his position at court even after his appointment as bishop of Metz. In that dignity, he distinguished himself as one of the most active ecclesiastical reformers of his time, founding new monasteries and introducing Roman liturgy and chant in his diocese. His most famous reform was the establishment of the regular *canons at his cathedral and his drawing up of their rule (c. 755), which bears his name and served as a model for the chapters of regular canons. *DHGE*, XII.

CHRONICLES The C. were one of the main sources of medieval history and the most popular form of historical writing in the Middle Ages. The term is of Greek origin, meaning history presented in a chronological form, and the style was transmitted to the Latin West through translations of the Bible. The Books of Chronicles in the Old Testament were in effect the model for the medieval C. From the beginning of the Middle Ages, both Byzantine and west European chroniclers borrowed earlier material, beginning with a short résumé of biblical (sacred) and Roman history, as well as longer excerpts of other sources. Only a portion of the C., generally that which corresponded to the events that took place during the lifetime of the narrator, was an original contribution. The C. were divided into universal, national and local histories. In Byzantium, the C. of *Procopius of Gaza, which dealt with the period of *Justinian, concentrated upon the imperial court. These C. became the model of the universal form of historical writing. In western Europe, the C. of *Gregory of Tours (late 6th century) and of *Bede the Venerable (7th century) became the model for later chronographies. These were written by churchmen and monks who were therefore not dependent upon the royal courts and enjoyed a certain degree of freedom in their evaluation of political events and personalities. On the other hand, the ecclesiastical authorship not only incorporated the ideological aspect of the interpretation into the work, but also was responsible for the didactic character of the C., written to teach succeeding generations a lesson through the good and evil deeds of the heroes. Thus, the C., and especially the universal and national ones, contained a certain amount of critical writing aside from the narrative description. A major problem in chronicling was the verification of information which was based merely on hearsay, and generally somewhat exaggerated and distorted by the chronicler's sources. Moreover, the authors showed no interest in the economic and social aspects of the subjects treated. Only a few of them used authentic documents which were an objective testimony of related deeds.

While the Byzantine chronography forms a distinct group by the character of the works, the variety of the western C. permits internal classification. Besides the C. of the early Middle Ages (6th-8th centuries), western chronography includes a German group, which emerged with the Ottonian C. and reached its perfection with the works of *Otto of Freising in the 12th century. The aim of these C. was to provide a universal view of society, concentrated about the *Holy Roman empire. The French and the Anglo-Norman C. of the 12th to 14th centuries, were of only local interest; however, some of them, such as the C. of Matthew *Paris, have a broader viewpoint. The *Crusades were the subject of important chronographical works, written either in the West or the Latin kingdom of Jerusalem. The C. of *William of Tyre were one of the best examples of historical thought. The Italian chronography had a local character, while the C. of the late Middle Ages, written in the vernacular languages, reflected national views.

K. H. Krüger, *Die Universalchroniken* (1976).

CHRONIQUES DE SAINT-DENIS (Grandes Chroniques de France) A collective historical work, composed at the abbey of *St. Denis, near Paris, and covering the period of the 12th-15th centuries. A great number of historians, some of them anonymous and others well-known, contributed to the work, composed of *chronicles corresponding to the reigns of the French kings. The C. were begun in Latin, but those dealing with the 14th-15th centuries were written in French. The authors were well informed, some of them having held official positions at the royal court.

J. Viard, *Les Grandes Chroniques de France*, 10 vols. (1920-53).

CHRYSOLORAS, MANUEL (c. 1355-1415) Byzantine scholar. Born to a noble family of Constantinople, he was trained for a diplomatic career, but also studied Greek and Byzantine literature. His description of the city of Constantinople, praising the *Palaeologue emperors for their capital, was a masterpiece of literary elegance and style. After a number of visits to Italy on several diplomatic missions, C. settled in Florence (1395), where he was appointed to teach the Greek language and alphabet. His teaching was one of the channels through which the Greek heritage was transmitted to the West and, as such, he was one of the forerunners of the Renaissance.

G. Cammelli, *Manuele Crisolara* (1941);

D. J. Geneakoplos, *Byzantine East and Latin West* (1966).

CHRYSOSTOM, St. JOHN (347-407) Bishop of Constantinople and Doctor of the Church. He was educated at Antioch to practise law, but having studied theology under Diodoros of Tarsus, turned instead to the ecclesiastical life and rapidly gained wide fame as an orator, preacher and scholar. In 398 he was called, against his will, to Constantinople and made patriarch by Emperor *Arcadius. His zealous reform activities in the capital made him many enemies, among them Empress Eudoxia, who found herself censured by his moral reform. In 403 he was condemned at a council set up by Eudoxia's followers and removed from his see. His unyielding attitude caused his banishment to Antioch and later to Pontus, where he was murdered.

Supported by Pope *Innocent I and by the whole Western Church (among whom St. *Augustine was one of his firmest defenders), C. was one of the last leaders of a united Christianity. His preaching and church activities became a model for both the Greek-Byzantine and

Roman Catholic churches and was influential in the Middle Ages.

Works, ed. *PG*, vols. 47-64;

D. Atwatter, *St. John Chrysostom* (1959).

CHURCH The term signified both the institution of the Christian religion, and the building wherein Christian worship took place. It was derived from the Greek word *Ekklisia*, which meant assembly, and was borrowed by the early Christians to denote their congregations. The Latin *Ecclesia* was based on the Greek term but, by the 4th century, its meaning had been expanded to include all the faithful. While in ancient Christianity, the body of the faithful was somewhat heterogeneous, despite the fact that it used to exclude persons convicted of *heresy, the institutional foundations of the C. were laid down in the 4th century and particularly at the Council of *Nicaea, where the definition of the faith was adopted and the official hierarchy of bishops became its government, under the imperial authority (325). The establishment of the ecclesiastical institution was a result of the Arian schism, which began as a theological discussion at Alexandria, Egypt between the priest Arius and Bishop *Athanasius. Arius maintained his thesis of a distinction between God the Father and Son (Jesus Christ), while Athanasius expounded his trinitarian doctrine of the equality of the Divine substance. The theological discussion led to disputes in the city and the question was discussed at the Council of Nicaea, where the doctrine of Arius was condemned as a heresy, while the thesis of Athanasius, sustained by the great majority of the hierarchy, became the basis of the articles of faith, described as "Orthodox and Catholic" (The true and universal faith). The Arians, however, refused to give up their beliefs and, during the 4th century, the dispute continued. The Arian cause was alternately accepted and rejected, especially in the eastern provinces of the empire. When at last the Arians were defeated, they turned to the Germanic tribes and spread their faith among them, creating a new division between Orthodox-Catholic Romans and Arian Germans. These conflicts had a strong impact on the C., which organized itself and created the *canonic authority, based on that of the Bible, the Fathers of the C. and the decisions of councils. At the second ecumenical council, held at *Constantinople in 381, when Christianity was recognized as the official religion of the Roman empire, the C. became a part of the imperial establishment and the hierarchical organization was completed with the setting up of the patriarchates at Rome (the See of Peter), Constantinople (the New Rome), Alexandria (the See of Mark) and Antioch (founded by Peter and Paul). In the 5th century the patriarchate of Jerusalem was added to this collegial government, but its influence remained minor. This structure was perpetuated in the Middle Ages, when both the institutional and theological concepts of the Christian body of the faithful, as had been defined at the beginning of the 5th century by St. *Augustine, were adopted as the basis for the term, C.

The Greek-Orthodox C. Rooted in the traditions of the Greek Fathers of the Ancient C., the Greek-Orthodox C. became an integral part of the *Byzantine empire in the 5th and 6th centuries. Under the high rule of the emperor (creating the regime of *Caesaro-Papism) and of the patriarch of Constantinople, known, from the 7th century, as the "Ecumenical Patriarch", its main distinguish-

Service at Westminster Abbey

ing features were its use of Greek liturgy and its imperial organization. Later on, the cult of icons also came to characterize the faith, even after the practice developed into the *Iconoclastic Controversy. Together with the political situation of the time, such differences in belief gradually led to the C.'s separation from its Latin counterpart in the West. But at the same time, theological disputes in the Orthodox C. itself caused a split between the Greek and the Semitic and Coptic faithful. The latter groups organized themselves in separate churches in the 6th century, using their native languages in the liturgy and adopting their own canonic rules. Considered heretics by Byzantium, the Eastern Christians cooperated with the Arabs in the 7th century against the Byzantine empire. The Orthodox C., on the other hand, expanded its missionary activities to include the *Slavs and, in the 8th-11th centuries, the great majority of the Slavic peoples in eastern Europe were converted to Orthodoxy, being allowed to use the Slavonic language with its Greek-derived alphabet in the liturgy. In the meantime, the gap between the Greek and Latin C. became wider. While theological differences remained minor, it was the institutional organization which broadened the gulf, accentuated by the issue of supremacy claimed both by the popes and the patriarchs of Constantinople. In 1054, when Patriarch *Michael Cerularius excommunicated Pope *Leo IX, the final separation of the two Cs. was achieved and all efforts to bring about a new union at the end of the Middle Ages failed. Although, for politi-

Ecclesia and Synagoga; *Gothic sculpture on the portal of the cathedral of Strassburg*

cal reasons, the 15th-century Byzantine emperors were interested in recreating unity, the Greek-Orthodox clergy opposed all attempts. The decline of Byzantium in the 13th century led to a similar loss of authority of the Greek-Orthodox patriarch of Constantinople. Independent patriarchates were established in the Slavic kingdoms, and although based on the unifying factors of faith and worship, they were autocephalous (with their own head) in terms of their organization.

The Roman Catholic C. The development of the Roman Catholic C. corresponds to the decline and fall of the Western Roman empire. Deprived of the strong political infrastructure which continued to exist in the Byzantine East, the C. represented the last remnant of the ancient heritage. Moreover, the spread of Arianism in the new Germanic kingdoms contributed to the accession of the C. hierarchy to a position of leadership over the Romanic population. The most significant process in this trend was the emergence of the papacy and the formation of a centralistic government of the Roman Catholic C. In the period between the pontificates of *Leo I (middle of the 5th century) and *Gregory I (beginning of the 7th), the bishops of Rome gained full authority over the ecclesiastical hierarchy in the West, based on the Petrine doctrine, which claimed the pope to be the vicar of St. *Peter, who was given primacy over the faithful by Jesus Christ. The conquest of the Western provinces by the Germanic tribes in the 5th century led to a total decline of the cultural centres in the West and made the bishops more dependent on Rome. Even after the conversion of the *Franks to Catholicism (*c.* 500) the papal authority was maintained, despite the conquest of Italy by the Byzantines in the middle of the 6th century, and their attempt to dominate the papacy. The political events in western Europe and the loss of Italy to Byzantium allowed the Catholic C. a greater degree of liberty than in the East, and the phenomenon of Caesaro-Papism remained unknown in the Catholic world. Thus, even during periods of a strong imperial power, such as the times of *Charlemagne, *Otto I or *Otto III, when the papacy was entirely dependent on the emperor and the C. was integrated into the political system of government, the Roman Catholic C. never lost its spiritual independence. In the 9th century the process of *feudalization also affected the C., whose properties were considered part of the share which could be divested by feudal lords and granted to their families and younger sons, who were appointed to ecclesiastical dignities. Thus, while missionary activity helped to spread the Roman Catholic faith to northern Europe, the C. knew a period of spiritual decline in the 9th-11th centuries; dignities were sold (the sin of *simony) and clergymen enjoyed a secular way of life, neglecting their duties. Only a certain number of monasteries, such as *Cluny, maintained the purity of their ideals.

The 11th-century reorganization of the C., known as the Gregorian reform, attempted to radically alter the situation, both through change in the ecclesiastical way of life and through the abolishment of the lay *investiture, intended to put an end to interference of the laity in the appointment to ecclesiastical dignities. A long struggle between C. and State, the *Investiture quarrel (1076-1122), ended in a compromise. The papacy succeeded in imposing its centralist government within the C. and began to struggle with the *Holy Roman empire

over supremacy within the Christian body (1150-1250). Both the empire and the papacy turned out to be the victims of this long controversy, which paved the way for the rise of national monarchies, the sovereign states. Thus, in the last centuries of the Middle Ages, the papacy declined, its prestige hurt by the rise of popular movements. As a result, the new monarchies, such as that of *Philip IV of France, were able to impose their sovereignty over the clergy. Moreover, the *Avignon "captivity" of the papacy, followed by the *Great Schism, led to the emergence of non-conformist trends within the C., and to the rise of the lay religion.

The Roman Catholic C. knew non-conformist and dissident trends from its beginnings and condemned them as heresies from the 5th century onwards. Ecclesiastical councils were assembled, like in the East, in order to defend the C. organization from this challenge, caused only partially by theological disputes. Many of the heretical movements of the 12th-13th centuries, the most important being the Albigensian heresy, were the result of social uprisings, and these movements had to define their opposition to the aristocratic hierarchy in terms of their own doctrines. The C. made use of three main courses through which it repressed such movements. Firstly, it established the *mendicant orders, charged with the task of preaching the true faith. A second method was to use the *Crusade movements against the heretics. Thus, although the Crusades had been instituted with the aim of fighting Islam and liberating the Holy Land, they were now also turned against "bad" Christians and became, in the 13th century, a political tool in the hands of the papacy. The third important institution established to fight heresies was the *Inquisition, founded in 1184 by *Lucius III and developed in the 13th century in southern France. However, despite such efforts, the repressions were largely unsuccessful; at the end of the 14th century, *Wycliffe openly contested the C. establishment, while the *Hussite movement in Bohemia was never destroyed.

The Eastern Cs. In the 5th century a number of bishops in the eastern part of the Byzantine empire, succeeded in challenging their official condemnation by the councils and established Cs. on the borders of the empire which were supported by non-Greek faithful. While in *Armenia a national C. emerged and developed its own independent history, which was integrated in the history of the Armenian people, comparable with the evolution of the *Ethiopian C., other sects had lesser congregations. The *Nestorians, who spread eastward and reached the Mongolian steppes, settled small communities in China, while the *Jacobites and Assyrians had a more local congregation in Syria and Mesopotamia. In Egypt, the Coptic C. emerged as a result of the persecutions of *Justinian and became the national C. of the non-Greek element in the valley of the Nile, with its own institutions and structures similar to the Orthodox C. In the 12th century, a sect headed by the priest Maro, founded the *Maronite C., which became united with the Roman Catholic C., and was allowed to maintain its Syriac rite and liturgy.

D. Stone, *The Christian Church* (1905);
B. C. Butler, *The Idea of the Church* (1962).

CID CAMPEADOR (Ruy Diaz de Bivar; 1043-99) Hero of the Spanish epic. Born to a family of the lesser nobility of Burgos in Castile, he entered the service of King

*Alfonso VI, who sent him on a diplomatic mission to Seville to collect tribute. In 1081 the king exiled him on the basis of charges concerning his mission. Bivar then offered his services to the Moslem king of Sarragossa and earned great fame in the battles against Christians and particularly against Raymond Berengar II, count of Barcelona, whom he twice made captive. During this period, he began to be surnamed *Cid*, a derivation of the Arabic title *sidi* (lord). In 1093 he left his Moslem allies and organized his own army. With it, he conquered Valencia in 1094, and there proclaimed himself lord. He died in that capacity as a venerated and respected head of a Christian state. His life and heroic adventures were the subject of the most famous epic poem of medieval Spain, *Cantar de mio *Cid.*

R. Menendez Pidal, *La España del Cid* (1956).

CID, CANTAR DE MIO Castilian epic poem, by an anonymous author, composed at the very beginning of the 13th century. The poem deals with the adventures of Ruy Diaz de Bivar, the *Cid Campeador, who had already become immortalized as the greatest Spanish hero. The historical facts known to the author are mixed with a long series of legends and anecdotes, not only representing the Cid as exhibiting the courage and pride of a perfect knight, but also as being a very pious Christian, who devoted his life to the crusade against the infidels. Thus, all the qualities of religious *chivalry are praised in the poem, which traces the virtues of *sapientia et fortitudo* (wisdom and heroism).

C. Smith, (ed.), *Poema de Mio Cid* (1972).

CILICIA Province in the southeastern part of Asia Minor, between the Mediterranean Sea and the Taurus Mountains. C. was part of the Byzantine empire and prospered in the 5th-8th centuries, due to its location on the trade routes between Constantinople and Syria. In the second half of the 7th century, the Arabs attacked it several times and gradually conquered a major part of the province at the beginning of the 8th century, when an *Ummayad governor ruled the country. In 962, Emperor *Romanus II led a Byzantine effort to reconquer C., and in 964 his son, *Basil II, succeeded in regaining Adana. But Byzantine rule lasted only for one century. In 1071, *Seljuk armies invaded the province and established a Turkish principality at Tarsus. At the same time, Armenians, seeking refuge, founded a number of principalities in C., known from the beginning of the 12th century as Lesser *Armenia. From the end of the 11th to the 14th century, the history of C. is interwoven with that of Lesser Armenia. In 1359 the province was conquered by the *Mamluks, who annexed it to their Egyptian State. It was later conquered by the Ottoman Turks in 1515.

W. M. Ramsay, *Historical Geography of Asia Minor* (1890).

CIMABUE, GIOVANNI (1240-1302) Florentine painter. Little is known of his life and works, but he had already attained great fame in the 13th century, as is mentioned by *Dante in the *Divina Commedia.* He painted in the various churches of Florence and Assisi, the most impressive of his works being his *Crucifixion* and a monumental *Madonna and Child*, in the church of St. Francis of Assisi. He also executed, in the last years of his life, the mosaics of the Cathedral of Pisa, where his *Christ in Glory* is a masterpiece of late medieval mosaic art.

CINO OF PISTOIA (1270-1337) Born at Pistoia, in Tuscany, C. studied law at Siena and was noted for his wide knowledge and his abilities of legal interpretation of jurisdiction. He taught law at the universities of Siena and Perugia, where he expressed his admiration for Emperor *Henry VII, whom he wished to see more active in Italian affairs. While teaching law at Bologna, he became a close friend of *Dante and had a great influence on young *Petrarch. King Robert of Naples invited him to settle in his capital and C. spent the last part of his life at Naples, teaching law at the university and writing poetry in which he praised women and love in a new, realist style.

G. N. Monti, *Cino da Pistoia* (1924).

CINQUE PORTS A confederation of five harbours in southeastern England, established in 1051 and recognized by *Edward the Confessor. The king granted the men of Sandwich, Dover, Fordwich, Romney and Hastings the profits of the courts of justice in their boroughs, on the condition that they supply the necessary ships and seamen for the royal fleet. The confederation survived the Norman Conquest and its privileges were confirmed by *William the Conqueror and by *Henry II, who recognized their leader as a baron of the kingdom (1171). Their barons were included among those recognized by King *John in the *Magna Charta and they played an active role in English politics during the 13th century. During the *Hundred Years' War, their fleet assured the English naval supremacy.

K. M. E. Murray, *The Constitutional History of the Cinque Ports* (1935).

CIOMPI A popular association in Florence, founded in 1343, and including the lower classes of society; its name seems to be of French origin, a corruption of the word *compère*. In 1378 the members of the C. took advantage of the rise of Salvestro de *Medici, who tried to seize power in the city, to revolt and to impose their rule through the use of violence and by threatening their adversaries. The C. was at last repressed and destroyed by a counter-attack of the guilds.

F. Schevill, *Medieval and Renaissance Florence* (1961).

CIRCUMSPECTE AGATIS Statute of *Edward I of England, issued in 1285. Its aim was to regulate the royal jurisdiction and control over the church in England. The major part of the statute is simply a reconfirmation of previous texts of *William the Conqueror and *Henry II. However, Edward was able to establish royal prerogatives on the basis of his new system of government which comprised integration of the church.

B. Lyon, *A Constitutional and Legal History of Medieval England* (1962).

CISTERCIAN ORDER A monastic order in western Europe, named after the abbey of *Cîteaux (*Cistercium*) and established by St. Stephen *Harding *c.* 1120, and by the congregation of Cîteaux and its daughter monasteries. The order, originally a French one, spread rapidly in western Europe, attaining its strongest influence under St. *Bernard of Clairvaux, in the middle of the 12th century. Representing an ascetic trend of monasticism, the C. founded its monasteries in deserted places and worked towards land reclamation. Noted for their white mantles, they were named the white monks, as opposed to the traditional black of the *Benedictines. The C. succeeded in placing its monks in episcopal chairs, and in 1145 St. Bernard's disciple, *Eugenius III, became pope. The order was governed by the annual assembly of the abbots of all its houses, who formulated appropriate statutes for its administration and were presided over by the abbot of the founding monastery of Cîteaux. The C. actively imposed the authority of the church, especially in the fight against heresies. The order was supported by many kings and feudal lords. Under the influence of St. Bernard, chivalric orders, affiliated to the C., were established. These included the *Templars, the knights of *Calatrava, *Alcantara and *Santiago, all of which introduced in their respective rules principles taken from the C. constitution, the *Charta Caritatis* (The Charter of Love), which had been issued in 1119 by Stephen Harding, and which remained the basic rule of the order. In the 13th century the members of the C. began to gradually surrender some of their ascetic manners and the order, although still influential in the church and in west European society, began to decline.

The art of the C. is a particular style of Gothic architecture and ornamentation. As the order was opposed to the richness of Gothic structures and ornaments, it developed a style of abstract elements, based on simplicity.

J. B. Mahn, *L'Ordre Cistercien et son Gouvernement* (1945).

CÎTEAUX   Abbey at the borders of Burgundy and Champagne in eastern France, founded in 1098 by St. *Robert of Molesme, who sought, together with a small number of monks of the *Benedictine monastery of Molesme, to establish a more ascetic form of monasticism. While Robert was compelled by a papal order to resume his post as abbot of Molesme, the community continued to exist and attracted a number of monks from several provinces and countries. Its first years were precarious and only the energy of its abbot, St. Stephen *Harding, saved the small community. The abbey became prosperous in 1112 when St. *Bernard, a novice from Burgundy and later the founder of *Clairvaux, came to C., bringing with him many members of his family. During the following years, C. became the mother-house of the *Cistercian order.

DHGE XII.

CIVIDALE   City in northern Italy, in the march of Friul. In the 7th century the town was one of the cultural and artistic centres of the *Lombard kingdom and an impressive temple was erected there. In the 9th century, it became part of the march of Friul and, after the establishment of the *Holy Roman empire, became part of German duchies and marches of Bavaria and Carinthia. Later on, the city belonged to the domains of the patriarch of Aquileia, whose impressive title did not represent any real authority. In 1415 it was conquered by Venice and annexed to its Italian patrimony.

J. K. Hyde, *Society and Politics in Medieval Italy* (1973).

CIVITATE   Town in southern Italy, near Benevento, famous for the battle of 1053, when the papal army, led by Pope *Leo IX, was defeated by the Normans. The pope was taken prisoner and compelled to recognize the rule of *Robert Guiscard in southern Italy.

CLAIRVAUX   *Cistercian abbey founded in a deserted valley in the county of Châlons (Champagne) in 1115 by St. *Bernard, who named the area *Clara vallis* (the "Clear Valley"). Under Bernard's administration (1115-53), the abbey knew a period of prosperity and was considered one of the most prestigious monasteries in western Europe, so much so that *Alfonso I, king of Portugal, declared his kingdom in 1143 as vassal of the abbey, and undertook to pay an annual tribute. In the 13th century, C. continued to be considered one of the most important centres of Cistercian monasticism where monks came to learn the rule and the manners of observance. An extensive library was established at the monastery and served as a centre of studies. At the end of the 13th century, however, discipline slackened and the abbey knew a period of spiritual decline.

A. A. King, *Clairvaux and its Elder Daughters* (1954).

CLARE, St. (1194-1253)   Foundress of the "Poor Clares". In 1212, inspired by the teachings of St. *Francis, she gave up all her possessions in central Italy to lead a life of poverty along the *Franciscan lines. Followed by a group of women (the Poor Clares or *Clarisses) she joined St. Francis and became abbess of the separate community of Franciscan nuns at *Assisi in 1215. The order spread rapidly with the founding of daughter-houses, and in 1229 it was recognized by Pope *Gregory IX. C. was buried in the crypt of the Franciscan cathedral of Assisi and her cult rapidly spread all over Europe.

E. Gilliat-Smith, *Saint Clare of Assisi* (1913).

CLARENDON   English royal residence, where *Henry II used to gather his court. C. became famous in English constitutional history due to several ordinances issued there and named after it. The most important among them are:

1) *The Constitutions of C.* (1164). A document issued in January 1164, after a dispute between Henry II and Thomas *Becket, the latter having contested royal authority over the church. Most of the provisions were a brief reminder of the legislation issued by *William the Conqueror and *Henry I. These included articles which required royal consent prior to the excommunication of royal vassals and those which restricted appeals to Rome by requiring the preliminary approval of the king. An important innovation was in the field of church jurisdiction over clerics. The clause stated that investigations were to be made by royal officers and, while the ecclesiastical justice would continue to be exercised, the hearing was to be conducted in the presence of a royal justice who would control the procedure. Moreover, the convicted cleric had to be handed to the royal justice for his punishment. Although the constitutions of C. served to deepen the great conflict between Becket and the king, the latter refused to abolish them.

2) *The Assize of C.* (1166). Issued with the consent of the Great Council, the Assize is one of the most important pieces of legislation produced by Henry II and one of the fundamental laws of England concerning criminal procedure. It called for a general inquest, at the sheriff's court or before an itinerant royal justice, of all the crimes committed and as yet untried. The Assize created the institution of the Great Jury, which required the participation of men of the county and the boroughs.

B. Lyon, *A Constitutional and Legal History of Medieval England* (1960).

CLARRISSES or POOR CLARES   The order of *Franciscan nuns, founded in 1215 by St. *Clare of Assisi.

CLEMENT, St. (c. 97)   Pope. According to the papal tradition, he was a disciple of St. Peter's and the third bishop of Rome. In the Middle Ages, some apocryphal writings, attributed to him, made him part of the apostolic tradition in the West. This literature was used as a

basis for the papacy's claim of supremacy in the church.
L. Sanders, *L' Hellénisme de St. Clément de Rome et le Paulinisme* (1943).

CLEMENT II (d. 1047) Suitger of Bamberg; pope 1046-47). An important German clergyman, he became bishop of Bamberg in 1040. There he distinguished himself by his ecclesiastical work. Appointed pope in 1046 by Emperor *Henry III, whom he crowned in the same year, he was the first of the "German popes" of the 11th century, who paved the way for the reform of the church. later known as the *Gregorian reform.
J. Haller, *Das Papsttum* (1953).

CLEMENT III (Paul Scolaro; d. 1191) Pope 1187-91. Member of a Roman family, he distinguished himself at the court of *Alexander III and, after the death of *Gregory VIII, was elected pope. During his pontificate he tried to organize the Third *Crusade, reconciliating the kings of England and France, *Richard I and *Philip II. From 1189, he was involved in the *Sicilian heritage, supporting the claims of *Tancred of Lecce against those of Emperor *Henry VI.
J. Haller, *Das Papsttum* (1953).

CLEMENT IV (Guy Foulcauld; d. 1268) Pope 1265-68. Member of a French family of lesser nobility, he studied law at Paris and served at Toulouse under *Alphonse of Poitiers. His loyalty to Alphonse brought him in close relations with the royal family and *Louis IX appointed him his counsellor. In 1265, he was elected pope. C. continued the efforts of the papacy against *Manfred, the son of *Frederick II and supported *Charles of Anjou, whom he proclaimed king of Sicily in 1266. He helped finance Charles' expedition to Sicily. C. encouraged the efforts of the *Teutonic knights to conquer Prussia and Livonia and called for a new *crusade against the Moslems in Spain.
E. Jourdain, *Les Régistres de Clément IV* (1945).

CLEMENT V (Bertrand de Got; 1264-1314) Pope 1305-14. Member of an influential French family of Gascony, he studied law at Toulouse, Orléans and Bologna, before becoming bishop of Comminges in 1295. In 1299 he was appointed archbishop of Bordeaux, where he earned the esteem of the kings of England and France. After the death of *Benedict XI, he was elected pope and crowned at Lyons in the presence of *Philip IV, king of France, who exercised an overwhelming influence over him. In 1309 C. settled at *Avignon and established the seat of the papacy there. He abolished the order of the *Templars, proclaiming them heretics and leaving their fate to the secular authorities (1311), as he was requested to do by Philip IV. He also took the side of the English monarchy of *Edward I and *Edward II against the Scots. He introduced the practice of nepotism into the papal administration, appointing many of his relatives and southern France clerics to the charges of his Avignon court. C. supported scholarship and, as a jurist, contributed to the development of the *canon law.
G. Mollat, *The Popes of Avignon* (1952).

CLEMENT VI (Peter Roger; 1291-1352) Pope 1342-52. Born to a family of French magistrates, he entered the abbey of Chaise-Dieu at the age of ten and later studied and taught at Paris. In 1326 he was appointed abbot of Fécamp in Normandy. Soon after he became bishop of Arras (1328), and was then promoted archbishop of Sens in 1329, and of Rouen in 1330. In 1338 he was created cardinal and settled at Avignon, where he was elected

pope in 1342. As declared adherent of *Philip VI of Valois, he failed to restore peace between France and England, despite the short truce of 1343, which ended with Edward III's invasion of France. Regarding imperial affairs, C. continued the struggle against *Louis of Bavaria and supported the claims of Charles of Luxemburg (*Charles IV) to the imperial throne. In 1347 he secured the obedience of William of *Occam and the *Franciscans, who had been condemned by *John XXII. C. disregarded Italy, establishing the services of his court at Avignon, which he purchased from *Joan I of Naples in 1348. Though strongly inclined towards nepotism and prodigality, he helped the poor during the *Black Death, trying to minimize its consequences. Nevertheless, political demonstrations against the papacy and the court of Avignon became a common phenomenon in the last years of his pontificate.
G. Mollat, *The Popes of Avignon* (1952).

CLEMENT VII (Robert of Geneva; 1342-94) Pope at Avignon 1378-94. Born to the family of the counts of Geneva, he was created cardinal at Avignon despite his youth. In 1378 the French cardinals, who opposed the return of the papacy to Rome, elected him pope. He was recognized by the king of France, *Charles V, as well as by other west European monarchs, but was excommunicated by the Roman court, and is considered an antipope. His residence at Avignon precipitated the *Great Schism of the papacy.
G. Mollat, *The Popes of Avignon* (1952).

CLEMENT III (Guibert of Ravina; d. 1100) Antipope 1084-1100. As archbishop of Ravenna, he supported Emperor *Henry IV against *Gregory VII and was appointed pope by the emperor but did not receive recognition by the clergy and the western monarchs. The support of the imperial army enabled him to set up court in Rome, which compelled *Urban II to seek refuge in France.
J. Haller, *Das Papsttum* (1953).

CLEMENT THE SCOT (d. c. 830) Grammarian. Of Irish origin, C. settled at the beginning of the 9th century in the Frankish empire and taught at the imperial academy at *Aix-La-Chapelle during the reigns of *Charlemagne and *Louis the Pious. A specialist in Latin literature, he distinguished himself as a teacher and contributed to the revival of the Latin language, being thus one of the principal characters in the *Carolingian Renaissance movement. He also wrote poetry which was devoted to religious themes.
M. L. W. Laistner, *Thought and Letters in Western Europe* (1957).

CLEMENTINES The term is used to denote the material added to *canon law by Pope *Clement IV. These revisions were undertaken during a period (late 13th to the beginning of the ¾14th century) in which canonic legislation was in its stages of development.

CLEONI Family of aristocratic origin in Bergamo (Lombardy). In the 13th century they assumed control in the city and led a long struggle for its independence, first against the imperial governors of Lombardy (until 1250) and then against Milan. Their attempts to establish a principality at Bergamo failed at the end of the 13th century due to their rivalry with the *Soardi family also of that city, and also because they were unable to weaken the power of the *Visconti of Milan, who finally conquered Bergamo in 1349.

J. Luchaire, *Les sociétés italiennes du XIIIe au XVe siècle* (1933).

CLEPH (d. 574) King of the *Lombards. He was one of the chieftains of the Lombard tribes during their migration to Italy and took part in their conquests. In 572, after the murder of *Alboin, he was elected king. He confiscated the estates of the remnants of Roman nobility and divided them between the heads of the clans, the *farae*. While trying to impose his authority so as to organize the new kingdom, he was murdered by a group of rebellious nobles (574).

C. Brühl, *Studien zu den langobardischen Königsurkunden* (1970).

CLERGY (Latin: clerici) The term designates the members of the ecclesiastical order in the Middle Ages. In the late Roman empire only those ordained as priests and bishops had held a privileged position in society, and even they had been considered subjects of the empire who had to submit to the jurisdiction of the state. From the beginning of the Middle Ages, however, this situation changed, and in western Europe the church obtained special status for certain members of the body who were considered the *familia episcopi* (the bishop's dependents) and were subject to the jurisdiction of the bishop. Gradually (in the 7th-8th centuries), the churches obtained *immunities, which exempted their personnel from the jurisdiction and taxation of the king or the feudal lord. Such immunities, which had first been granted to particular churches or monasteries, became a general immunity under the *Carolingians;

Portrait of an ecclesiastic; *drawing by Jean Fouquet*

thus, from the 9th century, the C. became a privileged order within the society, exempt from the authority of the state. The political theorists of the 9th century sought, however, a means to integrate the C. into the political body. From the times of *Hincmar of Rheims to those of *Adalberon of Laon, in the 11th century, it was established that the C. was the first Estate in the realm, above the nobility and the peasants. The "benefit of the C." was extended to all ecclesiastical personnel and from the 11th century the Latin term, *clericus,* had a double meaning: culturally, it signified those people who knew Latin and were able to draw up a document in that language; and in that respect, it designated the C. and also the personnel in the offices of royal and feudal courts. In the latter sense, the term was a forerunner of the English "clerk". Secondly, the Latin term signified the lower echelon of the C., such as those who were not ordained and, from the 12th century on, also the students of the universities. The lower C. enjoyed the immunities, even in criminal and civil cases, but were not granted the privileges of the C. as a political body. These rights were reserved for the prelates, such as bishops and abbots.

In England the C. was integrated into the political structure after the Norman Conquest. From the times of *William the Conqueror, the ecclesiastical courts were placed under the high authority and control of the king, although they continued to judge according to the *canon law. This integration was developed in the 12th and 13th centuries through the legislation of *Henry II and *Edward I, which stressed the sovereignty of the state over the C. Towards the end of the Middle Ages, such concepts also began to be adopted on the Continent, but the autonomy of the church jurisdiction still allowed the C. a special status within the society.
EC, III.

CLERICIS LAICOS A bull issued by *Boniface VIII on 25 February 1296, in order to protect the clergy of England and France against the fiscal exactions of the secular powers. It forbade clerics to pay ecclesiastical revenues to laymen without the permission of the Roman See, and forbade laymen to receive such payments. The vehemence of its language aroused the fierce opposition of *Philip IV the Fair and *Edward I. As a result, the dispute between the pope and the king of France developed into a major conflict.
T. R. S. Boase, *Boniface VIII* (1933).

CLERMONT City in central France, in the county of *Auvergne. C. was one of the last Roman strongholds in 5th-century Gaul, before it became part of the kingdom of the *Visigoths. In 507 C. was conquered by the *Franks, but its Roman character continued to be emphasized until the end of the 6th century. During the 8th-9th centuries, it was one of the cities belonging to the kingdom of Aquitaine. Under the reign of *Charles the Bald, the Frankish dynasty of *Bernard of Auvergne settled there and shared the government of the city with the bishops. While the counts were the vassals of the dukes of Aquitaine, the bishops remained faithful to the kings of France. Repeated conflicts between the counts and the bishops finally led to the intervention of the kings of France, *Louis VI and *Louis VII, who, at the bishops' request, introduced the royal authority over C. in the 12th century. In the following century, the city and the county were given as an *apanage to

*Alphonse of Poitiers, brother of *Louis IX; under his authority, a local feudal family, the dynasty of Clermont, established a small county, which developed at the end of the Middle Ages into an important principality.

The city of C. achieved its fame due to the Council of C., held in 1095 by Pope *Urban II, in which bishops and abbots of France, Spain, England and Germany played an active role. The number of participants (about 200) made it one of the most important councils of the Roman Catholic Church. The council confirmed the regulations of the *Truce of God and promulgated a series of decisions concerning the rights of the faithful and the hierarchy of the church; but the most important of its decisions was the pope's proclamation of the *Crusade. The famous speech of Urban II, calling upon Western knighthood to go forth to Jerusalem, was given at the end of the council and is considered a turning point in the history of the Middle Ages.

G. Fournier, *Le Peuplement de l'Auvergne au Moyen Age* (1965);

G. R. Grégut, *Le Concile de Clermont en 1095 et la Première Croisade* (1895).

CLEVES County in the Rhineland (Germany). Following the dissolution of the duchy of Lower Lorraine, C. emerged in the 12th century as an autonomous feudal unit, dependent upon the emperors. Nevertheless, the county remained a minor feudal unit until the 14th century, when its counts gained power by means of advantageous matrimonial arrangements. In 1368 the counts of C. inherited the county of Marck and created an important principality in the Rhineland. Allied with the dukes of Burgundy in the 14th century, they then took part in the development of the Low Countries, preserving their autonomous position within it. Their frequent visits to the court of Brussels assured them a higher standing, both in the empire and at the Burgundian court.

F. L. Carstens, *Princes and Parliaments in Germany* (1959).

CLISSON, OLIVIER DE (1326-1407) Constable of France. Born to a noble Breton family. He was a friend of *Du Guesclin and, during the reign of *Charles V, helped him reconquer most of the French territories lost to the English in the first phase of the Hundred Years' War. He succeeded Du Guesclin as constable, but during the initial period of *Charles VI's reign his power waned. In 1388 he became a leader of the *Marmousets*, who tried to restore the form of administration practised by Charles V, and had a major influence on the king's decisions. In 1392, however, when Charles VI was struck by madness and Charles V's brothers returned to power, he was deprived of his office and exiled to Brittany.

E. Perroy, *The Hundred Years' War* (1959).

CLOCK The use of a C. as an instrument for measuring time dates from ancient times. Water Cs., such as the clepsydra, were used by the Egyptians and the Greeks and perfected by the Arabs. But they astonished the West when *Harun Al-Rashid presented one to *Charlemagne in 802. In the 10th century, the water C. was used in churches and monasteries of western Europe, with a monk being appointed watchman to check its proper functioning and adjust it according to the position of the stars. But until the 14th century, the sundial or canonical C. was the most popular device for measuring time. The hours were unequal, varying with the

The Belfry of Bruges with the city clock

seasons. Bells rang on the hour, conveying the time to the population. According to this system, the measurement of time began with the morning sunshine, and the ninth hour (*nona*) – from which the word "noon" is derived – corresponded with lunch-time in the abbeys. From the 12th century on, there were also bells announcing the working hours. But as these bells also signalled wage-units, the sundial proved inefficient. The way was thus paved for the invention of a mechanical C., adapted in the 13th century from Oriental models. A mid 13th-century book, written for *Alfonso X of Castile, describes a C. operated by a falling weight controlled by the passage of mercury through small apertures. Such mechanical Cs., some of them artistically ornamented, were introduced in cathedrals, like those of Strassburg, the Rhine Valley and Lund. Kings and feudal princes introduced mechanical Cs. in their courts, imposing on their subjects the "royal hour", fixed through astronomical observations. With the diffusion of mechanical Cs. in the 14th and 15th centuries, they became smaller in size. Borough-corporations began using them as status symbols. The city hall's tower, for example, was equipped with a C. showing local time. Despite the improvement of mechanical Cs. with the development of physics, the earlier water Cs. were still more precise at the end of the Middle Ages.

A. P. Usher, *A History of Mechanical Inventions* (1954); J. Le Goff, *Temps de Travail et Temps de l'Eglise* (1965).

CLODION (CHLODION)   Chieftain of the Salian *Franks. According to Frankish historiography of the late 6th and 7th centuries, he lived in the 5th century and was the ancestor of the *Merovingians.

E. Lavisse. *Histoire de la France* (1901).

CLOPINEL, JEAN   See JOHN OF MEUNG.

CLOTAIRE I (497-561)   Merovingian king of the *Franks (511-61). The youngest son of *Clovis, he was proclaimed king of Soissons at his father's death. He helped his brothers in their military expeditions from Spain to Germany and annexed *Thuringia. After the death of his elder brothers in 555, he became sole king, imposing Frankish overlordship on *Bavaria, whose first duke, Grimoald, paid him tribute. C. was an energetic person and a good administrator, but could also be very ruthless: in 560, when his son Chram revolted against his authority, he did not hesitate to have him burned. He supported the settlement of Jews and Syrians in his kingdom.

J. M. Wallace-Hadrill, *The Barbarian West* (1952).

CLOTAIRE II (584-629)   Merovingian king of the *Franks (584-629). Son of *Chilperic I, he was raised as king of Neustria by his mother *Fredegund, after the murder of his father. Dynastic feuds forced him to defend his kingdom against *Brunhilda and her sons. In 613, after the death and murder of the other members of the *Merovingian dynasty, he became sole king of the Franks. He put Brunhilda to death, charging her with the murder of "ten kings", among them those he himself had killed. C.'s intensive legislative activity put him in the ranks of the most important Frankish kings. In 614, at a council of clergy heads and leaders of the nobility held in Paris, he issued an edict reforming the realm. He legalized the office of mayor of the palace in each of the four traditional Frankish realms: Neustria, Austrasia, Burgundy and Orléans. The appointment of *Pepin of Landen, one of his closest aides, as mayor of

the palace of Austrasia had historical significance, being the origin of the *Carolingian dynasty. He recognized the privileges of the nobility in their estates, creating thus the conditions for the emergence of *feudalism. The clergy obtained the right of *immunity, both personal and on their estates. C. supported the activities of the *Irish monks on the Continent and granted the abbeys large estates.

J. M. Wallace-Hadrill, *The Long-Haired Kings* (1964).

CLOTAIRE III (d. 673)   Merovingian king of Neustria (657-73). He succeeded his father, *Clovis II, to the kingship of Neustria and Burgundy and reigned as a puppet king under the effective rule of the mayor of the palace, *Ebroin, symbolizing thus the decadence of the *Merovingians.

CLOTAIRE IV (d. 719)   Merovingian king of the Franks (718-19). He was proclaimed king by *Charles Martel, but was recognized only in Austrasia.

CLOTH MANUFACTURE   Medieval C. developed on different bases in the East and the West. The Byzantine and Moslem civilizations continued the traditions of the late Roman empire and of the Oriental world, based on urban crafts and using raw materials such as linen, silk and wool and the ancient techniques of dyeing. In the West, however, the decline of the cities led to the ruin of its craftsmen. Thus, in the high Middle Ages, ceremonial attire, such as that of prelates and monarchs, had to be imported from Byzantium. But in general,

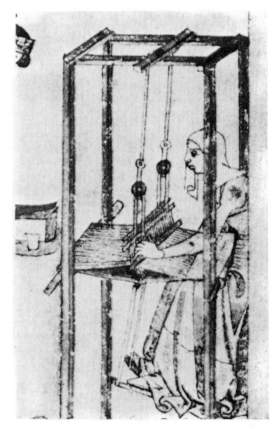

Weaving cloth; *from a 15th-century English manuscript*

Dyeing cloth; from a 15th-century English manuscript

cloth was manufactured on the estates by the wives of peasants, as part of their compulsory labour services, in the house of the estate's owners and under the supervision of the landlady. In the 11th century, however, with the revival of towns in the West, the cloth crafts returned to the cities, especially in Flanders and northern Italy, and were organized on a business scale; wool, the main raw material, was imported from the

Fragment of a 15th-century Flemish tapestry

countryside and, when local production was insufficient, – as was the case in Flanders in the second half of the 11th century – even from abroad, especially from England. The production was then exported and sold by merchant-guilds. *Hugh of St.-Victor has classified, in the first half of the 12th century, the manufacture of C. as one of the mechanical arts of his times. During the same period, C. was organized on a large scale; besides a number of qualified masters, who formed the core of upper guilds in the Low Countries and Italy, thousands of workers were employed in the related works and, in the 13th century, were considered as the lower guilds. As a result of the *Crusades, silk manufacture was brought to western Europe and developed, especially in Lombardy. The economic importance of C. had its impact on politics. Thus, Flanders' economic links with England became more important than its political relations with France. When, at the eve of the *Hundred Years' War, the counts of Flanders remained faithful to *Philip VI of France, *Edward III proclaimed an embargo on the export of English wool to Flanders, establishing staples to control its sale. This measure instigated revolts in the Flemish towns – but it also had a major impact on the development of the manufacture in *Brabant, where it became a highly important branch of economic activity.
CEcH, III.

CLOTILDA, St. (474-545) Frankish queen. She was a niece of *Gundobald, king of the Burgundians, and in 492 married *Clovis, king of the Franks, as part of a scheme of alliance between the heads of the Germanic kingdoms in the West. Brought up as a Catholic, she tried to persuade her husband to convert to the Roman Catholic faith. She supported the clergy, bringing to her court *Remigius, the bishop of Rheims, who succeeded in converting Clovis. After the death of her husband, she retired to the abbey of St. Martin of Tours, where she became famed for her piety and good deeds.
G. Kurth, *St. Clothilde* (1898).

CLOVIS (466-511) King of the *Franks. At the death of his father, *Childeric I, he inherited the realm of the Salians, which extended over part of present-day Belgium, with its capital at Tournai. He united the Frankish tribes under his rule and in 486 attacked the Roman general Syagrius, who had established his rule at Soissons and governed northern Gaul. The defeat of Syagrius and the conquest of Soissons enabled C. to annex the territory between the North Sea and the Loire River. He founded the Frankish kingdom, establishing his capital at Paris. Continuing his wars eastward, he united the Ripuarian Franks, on the Rhine, to his realm and began expanding towards Germany. His quarrel with the Burgundians, who threatened his southern boundaries, ended by his marriage with *Clotilda, niece of the Burgundian king *Gundobald. At the same time, he established an alliance with *Theodoric the Great, king of the *Ostrogoths, who had conquered Italy, giving him his sister as wife. This system of alliances allowed C. to extend his rule in Germany, where he defeated the *Thuringians and fought against the *Allemanni in 596 in a struggle so difficult that his victory was later attributed to a divine miracle. C.'s prayer to the "God of Clotilda" and his promise to convert to the Roman Catholic faith in the case of a victory is a testimony to the difficulties. His victory enabled him to annex the Allemanni realm to his kingdom. His subsequent conversion was the result of a combined effort of persuasion by Clotilda and the bishop of Rheims, Remigius. The event has a unique importance in European history, because C. was the first Germanic king to convert to Catholicism, while the other rulers were Arians. He thus won the fidelity and support of the Gallo-Roman population, which was Catholic. Moreover, religious unity allowed the emergence of peaceful relations between the conquerors and the conquered and created the conditions for their mutual assimilation, which led to the founding of France and the birth of the French people. C.'s achievements climaxed with his war against the *Visigoths, who ruled the territories south of the Loire. In 507 he defeated them at Vouillé and began the conquest of *Aquitaine and Tolouse, the capital of the Visigoths.

C. is often credited with the establishment of Frankish and particularly *Salic Law, but this is an error. Besides his military and political achievements, he proved his organizational skills by enforcing rigorous discipline in his army, controlling the distribution of booty and rewarding the army chiefs. For that purpose, he confiscated public lands, giving them as estates to his followers (the *leudes*), who became the new nobility of his kingdom. He did not, however, expropriate private property and was thus able to integrate the Gallo-Roman aristocracy in the ruling class of the kingdom, although on a basis of subordination to the Franks.

G. Tessier, *Le Baptême de Clovis* (1964).

CLOVIS II (635-57) King of Neustria and Burgundy (639-57). He was the younger son of *Dagobert and began the line of indolent *Merovingian kings, who left the real power to the mayors of the palace. At the same time the influence of the nobles increased. C. married an Anglo-Saxon princess, Bathild, who tried to restore royal power and was famed for piety and her alliance with the church.

J. M. Wallace-Hadrill, *The Long-Haired Kings* (1964).

CLOVIS III (d. 675) King of the Franks (675). Belonging to the Austrasian line of the Merovingians, he was proclaimed king in 675, but was dethroned by Ebroin and killed.

CLOVIS IV (682-95) King of Neustria (691-95). He was the eldest son of *Thierry III and at his father's death was made king of Neustria by the mayor of the palace of Austrasia, *Pepin II of Herstal, who was his tutor and the effective ruler of Neustria.

CLUNIAC REFORM Monastic reform in the 10th-11th centuries introduced under the influence of the abbey of *Cluny. The C. does not only refer to those monasteries which adopted the Rule of Cluny and became part of the order, but also to hundreds of houses which accepted its principles, while maintaining their independence.

CLUNY Abbey in southern *Burgundy. *William the Pious, duke of Aquitaine, founded the abbey in 910, endowing it with his estate, by the same name. He put C. under the direct protection of the papacy, formally expressing his will, that it neither be controlled by a bishop or feudal lord, nor by an advocate. The monastic community was established by Abbot *Berno (910-27), who imposed on it an austere *Benedictine rule and commuted the obligation of manual work to prayers and meditations. His successors, all outstanding person-

The abbey of Cluny represented in a 17th-century engraving

alities, among them St. *Odo, Majolus, Odilo and Hugh, also enforced rigorous discipline, and struggled successfully against lay and ecclesiastical influence on the monastery. C.'s power within the church and over lay circles grew. By promoting the belief that the monk sought not only his own salvation through retirement from the secular world, but also that of the faithful by praying for the remission of their sins, the abbey acquired numerous donations of lands, incomes and private monasteries. The donations enabled the abbots to build the church of C., which became a model of Romanesque *architecture. In the 12th century C. underwent a crisis under the rule of Abbot Pons (1122-26), who engaged in an open conflict with some of his monks and with the papacy. Pons was deposed, and abbatial authority was restored by his successor, *Peter the Venerable (1126-51), the last great abbot of C. Nevertheless, the dispute had economic repercussions on the abbey, which suffered deficits. At the same time, the emergence of large feudal principalities and monarchies made C. dependent on secular authority. While the abbots, until the death of Peter the Venerable, exercised tremendous influence on west European policy, placing their monks in bishoprics and even on the papal see and imposing their spiritual leadership on emperors and kings, their successors were compelled to depend on royal defence. C. thus declined — but retained its prestige as witnessed by the splendid, Gothic-style abbatial palace built at Paris for the sojourn of C.'s abbots.

The order of C. was a group of abbeys and priories which accepted Cluniac reform and introduced Cluniac rule. They spread first in France and Italy, where many famous monasteries accepted C.'s authority and their monks acquired prominent positions in the church: among them were Popes *Gregory VII, *Urban II and *Paschal II. In the 11th century, under the rule of St. Hugh (d. 1109), the order numbered about 1000 monasteries, extending from Spain — where they played an important role in the *Reconquista process — to the Holy Land, as well as in all the Catholic countries of central and northern Europe.

J. Evans, *Monastic life at Cluny* (1931);
G. de Valous, *L'Ordre de Cluny* (1935).

COBLENZ City in Germany, at the confluence of the Moselle and Rhine Rivers. Julius Caesar, recognizing the site's strategic importance, built there a castle, Confluentes, which was to serve as the medieval town's headquarters. In the 6th century the *Merovingians fortified C., which became one of their connecting bases to Germany and, later on, one of the main demesnes in the Frankish kingdom of Austrasia. With the division of the *Carolingian empire in 843, C. was granted to *Lothair, but after 860 it was incorporated into the German kingdom. With the revival of trade on the Rhine, C. evolved into a thriving commercial centre, over which the counts of neighbouring areas fought. It was eventually granted to the archbishops of *Trier in 1018 and annexed to their principality. C.'s prosperity in the 13th-15th centuries led the archbishops to establish their court there. They embellished the city, and, in 1343, erected an impressive bridge in the Rhine Valley.

B. Gebhardt, *Handbuch der deutschen Geschichte* (1930).

CODE OF JUSTINIAN The most comprehensive codification of Roman Law. It was compiled by a committee of jurists, appointed in 528 at the instigation of *Tribonian, a reputed jurist and close counsellor to *Justinian. The C. consists of four parts: the Code proper — comprising the constitutions and laws issued between the middle of the 5th century and 529; the Digest — a treatise issued in 534 and based on the *Theodosian Code of 438 containing the old Roman laws; the Institutes — a manual for law students, which became the authority on teaching law, issued in 532; the Novels — a compendium of new ordinances and laws issued by Justinian and collected by Tribonian until the year of his death, 545. The four works comprise the *Corpus Juris Civilis* (The Body of Civil Law), which is the basis of civil law in medieval and modern Europe.
Ed. E. Friedberg, *Corpus Juris Civilis* (1886).

COIMBRA City in Portugal. C. was part of the kingdom of the *Suevi, but fell to the Arabs in 711, remaining a frontier city of Moslem Spain until the 11th century. Conquered by *Ferdinand I of Castile and León, C. was annexed to the country of Oporto which, in 1137, became the kingdom of Portugal. In 1187, C. became the kingdom's capital, and knew a period of prosperity until the middle of the 13th century, when the capital was transferred to Lisbon. Part of *Alfonso III's court remained in the city, which, during the second half of the 13th century, was a renowned cultural centre. When the University of Lisbon was founded in 1290, many of its masters preferred teaching at C. During the 14th and 15th centuries, the seat of the university alternated between the two cities, until it was finally established at C. in 1515.
H. V. Livermore, *A History of Portugal* (1947).

COINAGE The origin of medieval coinage lay in the currency reform by the Roman emperor Diocletian, at the end of the 3rd century. He established the gold basis of C. The new standard gold-piece was the *solidus*, 20 of which were minted from one *libra* (*c*. 408 g) of gold. As silver had 1/12 the value of gold, the *solidus* was worth 12 *denarii* of silver. This currency-system was adopted by the medieval world and continued to exist in Britain until quite recently, when it was superseded by the centesimal system. The real value of the coins fluctuated with changes in economic realities. While in *Byzantium fluctuations in the gold/silver rates were relatively minor, in western Europe the economic crisis, marked by the decline of cities and their commercial activities, caused a flow of gold eastward, provoking thus a radical change in the rates of the two precious metals: the *solidus* was sold for 40 *denarii* of silver in the 7th century. The Moslem world adopted the Byzantine system of gold C. and, until the 12th century, the Islamic *dinar* had a course analogous to that of the Byzantine *besant*. The concentration of gold in eastern markets caused a scarcity of silver in Moslem countries at the beginning of the 8th century. But gradually the gold/silver rate stabilized at around 1/18. With the *Carolingian monetary reform silver became the basis of C., remaining as such in western Europe centuries later. Minting was entrusted to goldsmiths, but also to vassals, particularly those in prominent positions, such as dukes and counts. Precious metals were officially marked by the treasuries, hence the term *mark*, which came into the monetary language first as the expression of legal weight of the metal and, at the very end of the Middle Ages, to designate a particular coin.

While in Byzantium and the Moslem world, C. was subject to imperial control and standardization, even when the minting was local or entrusted to *entrepreneurs,* there was no such overall control in 9th-12th centuries' western Europe. Feudal mints produced coins of various weights or proportions of precious metals and therefore there were fluctuations in the coins' value and in the extent of their circulation. Money-changers, who sat either on bridges of rivers near towns, or by the city entrances, played an important role in determining the currency's real value, basing it not only on the coin's weight and quality, but also on its economic strength. Important trade fairs also affected a currency's value. The Fairs of *Champagne, for example, which attracted merchants from all over western Europe, increased the value of the coins minted at Provins in Champagne, and enlarged the area of their circulation. On the other hand, the *solidus* minted by the small counts of Melgueil, in the Languedoc, was highly esteemed for its quality and correct weight and was universally accepted as the standard money of southern France and northern Spain.

The revival of trade in the Mediterranean and the *Crusades had a revolutionary effect on C. The Crusaders and Italian merchants discovered the gold basis of currency in the East. To facilitate the payments' system, they minted a local currency, the *bisantinus,* modelled on the Byzantine coin (*bisantinus sarracenatus*), which in turn was modelled on Moslem money. When they returned, they introduced the gold basis of currency to western Europe. With the decline of feudalism in the 13th century, gold again became the standard basis, according to which the value of silver coins was computed. New gold coins minted under sovereign authority

The Mint of Ury, Switzerland; 16-century miniature

replaced those that were produced in feudal mints. The economic reforms in France under *Louis IX and the establishment of strict principles governing the minting of gold coins, provoked a demand for the *livre tournois,* the French royal coin, minted at Tours. This coin, later known as the *louis,* was the standard coin of northern Europe in the 13th and 14th centuries. At the same time, the growing importance of Florence and of Italian money-lenders, helped the local gold piece, the *florin,* to be accepted as a valid currency outside of Italy. Characteristic of the 13th-century C. was the use of heraldry, to symbolize the sovereign authority of the state. Some of the coins were even named after such symbols, such as the *scudo,* the *crown,* etc.

The economic crisis of the 14th century had its effects on C. To assure ordinary revenues, the royal courts began depreciating the money, by diminishing the proportion of gold or silver in the coins. Such steps, (only symbolic in the fiscal policy of *Philip IV le Bel, king of France), engendered rumours in the public and among merchants that the court was "counterfeiting" money. The minting both of "bad" and "good" currency in the 14th century created a chaotic situation in the exchanges of money and of goods. While the crisis of the *livre tournois* affected all of northern Europe, French monetary theorists were discussing conservative means of returning to the "good" C. of *Louis IX. A result of the 14th-century economic crisis was the emergence of

The New Art of Coinage; *16th-century engraving*

national C. in the 15th century. In England Edward III minted a more stable *livre*, the sterling, while in the Low Countries the *florin* replaced the *livre tournois*. Some Italian currencies, such as those of Florence, Venice and Milan, gained international acceptance.

C. M. Cipolla, *Money, Prices and Civilization in the Mediterranean World* (1954).

COLA DI RIENZO (1313-54)   Roman popular leader. C. was the son of a poor publican and aspired towards a better career ever since childhood. An autodidact, he reached the position of notary, becoming involved in public affairs. In 1343 he was sent on a diplomatic mission to Pope *Clement VI at Avignon. Impressed by the young man, the pope appointed him notary of the Apostolic Chamber at Rome, one of the most influential positions of the city. After his return to Rome, C. began to dream about ways of restoring Rome's greatness under his leadership. In 1347 he proclaimed himself tribune of the people, according to the ancient Roman tradition. Within a few months he succeeded in heading a popular movement, and, styling himself master of the city, proclaimed the unity of Italy. He won wide support, especially in central Italy, where cities sent him armies to realize his dream. At the height of his ambitions, he proclaimed himself "August" and summoned the pope to Rome. A counter-revolution led by the aristocracy forced him to flee. He went to Avignon, where he was imprisoned, but was freed in 1353 by Pope *Innocent VI, who sent him to Italy with the army led by Cardinal Albornoz, to reconquer the lost states of the papacy. Appointed senator, C. succeeded in imposing his rule on Rome in 1354. To secure his position, he repressed the population, which in turn revolted, causing his final defeat and death.

H. Vielstedt, *Cola di Rienzo, die Geschichte des Volks-tribunen* (1936).

COLCHESTER   City in England. Built and fortified by the Romans, C. was annexed to the kingdom of Essex after the Anglo-Saxon conquest of England. In 936, it was conquered by Athekstan, king of Wessex, who made it one of the seats of his court. At the beginning of the 10th century it was a stronghold of the *Danes of East-Anglia and resisted Anglo-Saxon counter-attacks, which destroyed its Roman walls. After the Norman Conquest, a castle was built in C. with bricks of the Roman buildings and the city became the capital of the county of Essex, which was part of the kingdom of Essex.

The Victoria History of the Countries of England (1898).

COLLEGE   The term was originally used in ecclesiastical terminology to designate a body of clergymen, having a special status. The most frequent use was in reference to a C. of canons, living together communally. Hence a "collegiate church" served by such canons. The most important of these Cs. was the C. of *cardinals of the Roman Church. In the second half of the 12th century, the term began to signify a group of students and their masters who lived in a foundation. In 1188 an English knight returning from Jerusalem fell ill at Paris and, when he recovered, made a donation for establishing the "C. of the 18", designed to lodge 18 poor students. In the 13th century such pious donations multiplied, and gradually new Cs. with lecture halls were established. The most famous of the Parisian Cs. was that of the *Sorbonne, which became a renowned centre for the study of theology. The Cs. were the basic units of the English universities at Oxford and Cambridge. Founded in the 12th century by royal or private donations, they were richly endowed to cover the costs for teaching and stipends for room and board for the masters and students. The medieval C. was organized as a chapter, where the masters had the right to coopt their colleagues and elect a principal, who had to be confirmed by the university's chancellor. The student body was allowed to participate in decision-making on economic problems of the C. and was requested to take part in group activities, such as meals, prayers and processions.

H. Rashdall, *The Medieval Universities* (1935).

COLLEGIATE CHURCH   The churches which were served by a college of canons, headed by an elected dean, who was approved by a bishop. The term also referred to chapels and churches in university colleges.

COLOGNE (Köln)   City in Germany, situated on the Rhine. C. was founded by the Romans as Colonia Agrippinensis and survived the Germanic invasions. From the end of the 4th century, the city became an important Christian and Jewish centre as part of the Ripuarian *Franks' dominions, which were annexed to the Frankish kingdom by *Clovis. With the stepped-up activities of Christian missionaries in 8th-century Germany, C.'s bishopric was elevated to the rank of archbishopric by *Charlemagne. At the beginning of the 9th century, when the archbishops' estates extended over the entire Rhine province, C. became an ecclesiastical seigniory. The archbishops were considered second in rank only to those of *Mainz and were granted the prerogative of crowning the German kings at *Aix-La-Chapelle. Because of C.'s status, Emperor *Otto I appointed his brother *Bruno archbishop of C. and Bruno's successors played important political roles in the *Holy Roman empire. The revival of trade in the 11th century contributed to C.'s growth and led to the establishment of a burgher aristocracy, led by the merchant guilds. In the 12th and 13th centuries these guilds developed trade with the Low Countries and England. The burghers' commercial interests dictated a policy of friendship towards England and the towns of the Rhine, which did not always accord with the interests of the archbishops. In the 13th century, repeated conflicts between C.'s burghers and archbishops caused the latter's power to wane. But under Archbishop Conrad of Hochstaden, who began the building of C.'s impressive Gothic cathedral in 1245, the religious character of C. was again accentuated and its important *Dominican community, exemplified by *Albertus Magnus, made the city a prestigious centre of learning. However, in 1288, when the burghers seized power in C., the archbishops were compelled to grant them a charter of liberties, which nevertheless recognized the lordship of the archbishop. The *Golden Bull of *Charles IV (1348) gave the archbishops the title of Prince-Electors, but the real power was left to the "patricians", the burghers' aristocracy. C. joined the Confederation of the Rhine (see *Germany) and the *Hanse. In 1388 the city-council founded its university, the first to be established by townsmen. As the archbishops' power declined, the craftsmens' guilds became the most powerful body in the city in 1396, and in the 15th century they shared power with the merchants. While the dominions of C.'s electors, extending over the

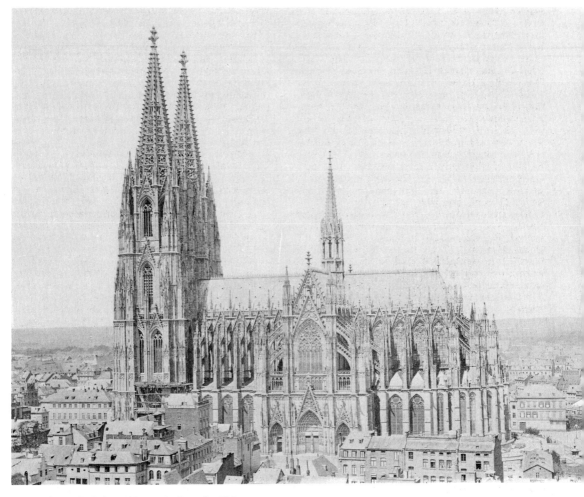

The Gothic cathedral of Cologne, built in the 13th century

countryside, were incorporated into a vast principality in western Germany, C. itself became a free *imperial city in 1475.

R. Koebner, *Die Anfänge des Gemeindewesens der Stadt Köln* (1922).

COLOMBINI, GIOVANNI (1300-67) Founder of the order of Gesuati. Born to an aristocratic family of Siena, he received a secular education, married and served in public affairs. The reading of the *Life of St. Mary of Egypt* influenced the course of his life: he divorced his wife, devoting himself to the sick and poor. Exiled from Siena, he was followed on his journeys in Italy by many disciples, who were very active and useful during the *Black Death. At Siena, the epidemic was considered a divine punishment for his exile and he was recalled to found a monastery dedicated to the service of Jesus, hence the "Gesuate brothers". His letters were a major contribution to the spiritual and mystical awakening in Italy after his death, particularly among those who opposed the Renaissance trend in the 15th century.

G. Pardi, *Il Beato Colombini di Siena* (1927).

COLONATE The term used in the 4th and 5th centuries to designate the free peasants of the Western Roman empire, who had the legal status of Roman citizens and whose ancestors were granted lands in the "colonies" (agricultural settlements) after their military service. Under Emperor *Constantine the Great they were compelled to remain on their lands and to furnish food and work for the Roman army and were put under the supervision of big landowners, even though they were considered free citizens by law. Entering thus into a close dependence on the landlords the C. was part of the *villa of the early Middle Ages. They were eventually identified with the serfs, although their juridical freedom was maintained. From the 6th century on, as the C. became assimilated with free peasants of Germanic origin, it lost its Roman character.

M. Bloch, *Feudal Society* (1948).

COLONNA A distinguished Roman family which played a prominent role in papal and European politics between the 12th and 18th centuries. As vassals of the popes, they held large estates around Rome and became influential in the city itself at the end of the 12th century, when members of the family were appointed *cardinals. In the 13th century they supported the pro-imperial *Ghibellines, entering into a drawn-out conflict with the *Orsini, their greatest rivals. This conflict culminated in an open clash with Pope *Boniface VIII, who excommunicated them in 1297 and attempted to deprive them of their estates. But they allied themselves with Florence, and their head, Sciarra C., helped *Philip IV, king of France, attack Agnani and take the pope captive. When the popes were at *Avignon, they seized power at Rome, while also imposing their power on the *Papal States. In 1417, Oddo C. was elected pope and took the name Martin V. After his death the family's power declined and their old quarrel with the Orsini caused continuous troubles in Rome during the second half of the 15th century. Among the most important members of the family are:

1) **Giovanni C. (d. 1216)** He was created cardinal by *Celestine III. He was praised for his virtues and was one of the first protectors of St. *Francis of Assisi.

2) **Giovanni C. (d. 1244)** Nephew of the former, he was created cardinal in 1212, took part in the conquest of *Damietta in Egypt (1219), and later assisted *Frederick II against the popes.

3) **Giacomo C. (d. 1318)** Nephew of the former, he was created cardinal in 1278 by *Nicholas III (an Orsini) in an attempt to reconcile the two families. He was a zealous opponent of *Boniface VIII, who excommunicated both him and his nephew Peter, also a cardinal, in 1297. Both were reinstated by *Clement V in 1305.

4) **Sciarra C. (d. 1334)** "Captain of the People". A military leader, he avenged the family for their excommunication by *Boniface VIII in 1297 and the ruin of their castles in Rome and its vicinity. In 1303, he conquered Agnani, and helped William of *Nogaret, Philip IV's counsellor, take Boniface prisoner. In 1305 he seized power at Rome and eventually defeated the Orsini. Chosen "Captain of the People", he crowned *Louis of Bavaria emperor in 1328, leading thus the opposition to Pope *John XXII.

5) **Stefano C. (d. 1347)** Senator of Rome and leader of the family after the death of Sciarra. He was a close friend of *Petrarch, whom he received at Rome and crowned with laurels. He led the counter-attack on *Cola di Rienzo in 1347, despite his very old age.

P. Colonna, *I Colonna dalle origine all'inizio del secolo 19* (1927).

COLOPHON The inscription often found at the end of medieval manuscripts giving information about authorship, sources, date and sometimes the scribe himself.

COLUMBA, St. (c. 521-97) Abbot and missionary. Born to a noble Irish family, he was educated in Irish monasteries and subsequently founded churches and monasteries in his native country. In 563, impelled by missionary zeal, he left his homeland and founded a monastery on the island of *Iona, off western Scotland. The twelve companions who joined him constituted the first Iona community, which spread Christianity to Scotland and helped found a number of monasteries. Among his converts were Brude, king of the Picts, and Dal Riada, the new king of the Scots, who came to Iona in 574 to be crowned by him. C. was highly esteemed both in Scotland and in Ireland, where his abbey was regarded as a centre of learning.

W. D. Simpson, *The Historical St. Columba* (1927).

COLUMBAN, St. (c. 550-615) Abbot and missionary. Born in Ireland, he went through England to Gaul, where he settled in 590 and founded a monastery of a very strict rule at *Luxeuil, in the wilderness of the Vosges Mountains. His attempts to introduce Irish monasticism met with strong opposition, but he defended himself vigorously, both in Rome and before a synod of the Frankish court in 603. While he had close relations with King *Clotaire II, he extended his activities throughout the Frankish realm. But in 612, when his monks were expelled from their Burgundian monastery, he engaged in missionary activities among the *Allemanni and later founded the monastery of *Bobbio in northern Italy, which became a prestigious centre of learning.

Works, ed. with biography, G. S. M. Walker (1957).

COMITATUS *Carolingian term referring to the territory governed by a *comes* (count). Until the second half of the 9th century the C. was a district corresponding more or less with the late Roman *civitas* and, in Germany, with the traditional *gau*. The C., which included the estates of individuals, of the church and of the *vassals, was considered part of the royal or imperial realm. C. thus also signified the attributes of royal authority within a specific territory, in the administrative, fiscal and jurisdictional fields. The decline and the fall of the Carolingian empire and kingdoms led to the dislocation of the C. in the 10th century and the establishment of the new *feudal type of *country, which no longer fell under direct royal jurisdiction. For the primitive meaning of the term, see *Feudalism.

J. R. Strayer, *Feudalism* (1965).

COMMANDERY Term used in the 13th-15th centuries to designate the estates of the military orders of *chivalry (*Hospitallers, *Templars, etc.) within a certain province in Europe, which were governed on behalf of the order by a commander. The commander was responsible for the estate's subjects and for the administration of the lands and revenues.

M. Melville, *La Vie des Templiers* (1951).

COMMENDATIO *Feudal term applied to the act of recommendation, whereby a subject sought the protection of a landlord. Until the 8th century, in the C. ceremony, the subject conceded his lands (*commenda*) to the lord, whereupon he became the lord's vassal, swearing fealty to him and agreeing to serve him especially in his army. In return he received these lands as a *benefice and was given the lord's protection. After the 8th century, the land concession remained a symbolic gesture, while the most important part of the ceremony was the swearing of *homage.

F. L. Ganshof, *Feudalism* (1965).

COMMERCE Medieval commerce was generally considered as a marginal activity of society, rooted in agrarian structures in western Europe. Contemporary research, however, by the historian Henry *Pirenne and others after him, allows a more balanced judgement on the role of C. in the Middle Ages. After the fall of the Roman empire, commercial activities continued in the East, where the Byzantines and, from the 7th century, the *Arabs developed individual and collective forms of C. The existence of the state-structure and political authority were conducive to the maintenance of roads, used by caravans, transporting goods between Europe and the Middle East, and Central Asia and the Far East. The main roads of the great invasions, such as those of the *Huns, *Avars, *Turkish and other *Mongol tribes, were primary trade routes. Maritime trade also continued on the Mediterranean and the Black Sea, as well as along the Indian route, traversing the Red Sea and the Indian Ocean. In western Europe, however, the decline of cities in the 5th-9th centuries led to a lessening of trade activities, but these revived somewhat in the 6th and 7th centuries with the establishment of *Syrian and Jewish quarters in Italy and Gaul. The slowdown in commercial activities in the West had its repercussions on East-West trade: the export of goods to the East was severely curtailed while the deficit of gold in the West limited the import of luxury products from the East. Nevertheless, international C. never came to a complete standstill: Mediterranean harbours maintained their structures and activities, and there was intensive trade activity between western Europe and Scandinavia and, along the Russian steppes and rivers, between Scandinavia and Byzantium and the Arab caliphate. Until the 9th century local trade was based on nomadic merchants and small fairs at the confluences of rivers or near the economic-agrarian centres of estates, where goods were exchanged and craftsmen's wares sold to peasants and to the inhabitants of manors.

Towards the end of the 9th century, the volume of trade increased, particularly in Italy and in the Low Countries, while the exchange of goods between Germany and the Slav tribes led to the development of staples on the Elbe and Danube Rivers. The growth of C. activity marks the revival of towns and the foundation of *boroughs, where local and regional markets were established. The sporadic character of trade by nomadic merchants gave way to a more permanent form of C., still based on the exchange of goods. While Mediterranean trade was still virtually monopolized by the Byzantines and the Arabs, the decline of the *Abbasid caliphate led to the development of maritime companies, which had not only to organize the transport of goods, but also to protect the vessels against piracy. One of the first organized companies was that of the Jewish *Rhadanites, who organized tours in the Mediterranean in the 9th and 10th centuries. The Jews were active in international C.: the fact that Jews everywhere adhered to Talmudic jurisprudence allowed them to create partnerships with the dispersed communities in various countries. The documents of the Genizah of Cairo show such partnerships at work, on the great route between southern Europe and north Africa, through Egypt, where goods were transferred to the Red Sea vessels, to Aden, India and China (and vice versa). Some Italian cities began to organize trade on a collective basis. In *Amalfi, merchant associations were formed and appropriate defence measures, which included arming the crews, were adopted. The city also established an overseas colony, which controlled the area and evolved into a *fundacco* (from Arabic *funduq*, a caravanserai), with accommodations for traders, warehouses and a religious and administrative centre. The model of Amalfi was perfected in the 11th century by *Venice and also adopted by cities such as *Pisa and *Genoa. The Venetian system was based on the collective ownership of ships by the city and this boosted trade development. The *Crusades allowed the Italian cities to reach supremacy in international trade in the 12th century, obtaining the privilege of autonomous communes in

Trade at Bruges in the 15th century

Crusader states. These states were governed by consuls or bailiffs sent from the mother-city and enjoyed substantial exemptions, financial and juridical. The Italians held the monopoly of trade until the end of the Middle Ages. In the 13th and 14th centuries, the conflicts between Venice and Genoa figured more prominently than their trade ties with the Byzantine or Moslem

Merchants counting money; *woodcut by Jost Amman*

world. The decline of Genoa at the end of the 14th century left Venice the most important Italian commercial city, but new centres, such as Florence and Milan, arose.

With the growth of trade north of the Alps, towns developed around a market-place as did the ecclesiastical centre around the cathedral. The market was connected to streets leading to the gates, where various craft-guilds settled, while the market-place itself was surrounded by communal buildings, among them the Guild Hall, which symbolized the importance of C. in town life. The development of large-scale C. among all the countries of western Europe was facilitated by the establishment of permanent fairs, at which merchants from various countries and provinces exchanged merchandise. Most famous were the fairs of Champagne (at Troyes, Provins and Meaux) – at their zenith in the 12th and 13th centuries – where merchants from Italy, the Low Countries, England, France and Germany converged. Other important trade-routes were that from Venice, through northern Italy, the Rhine Valley, to the Low Countries and England, and the famous route of St. Jacques (Santiago de *Compostela), named after the great pilgrimage, which linked northern and central Europe, through Paris, the Loire Valley and western France, with Spain. Of lesser importance were the routes of the wine C. linking the Rhineland, Champagne and other French provinces, with northern Europe and England. An important step in the development

of northern European C. was the foundation of the German *Hanse, whose centre was established in the second half of the 12th century at Lübeck and which grouped in the 13th and 14th centuries most Baltic and North Sea ports, as well as a number of German cities. Its trade covered northern Germany, the Scandinavian countries and all of northern Europe, from London to Novgorod in Russia. Composed of a number of free cities, the Hanse evolved into a potent political force in northern Europe, imposing its mercantile policy on the kingdoms and on its own member-cities with the help of an important fleet in the North and Baltic Seas. The German towns in the Rhine Valley organized themselves on the same model, but their league was of lesser importance. In the 13th century they established the Confederation of the Rhine, imposing their own police to compel the feudal princes to respect the *Landesfrieden* (the peace of the country). Such peace associations, but on a much smaller scale, already existed in 11th- and 12th-century France, where they were led by the bishops and specifically included the merchants in the Peace and *Truce of God associations.

In the late 13th century, international commerce flourished after the conquests of *China and Russia by the Mongols and the establishment of the Mongol empire. The great roads of Eurasia were reopened and the invention of the *post by the Mongols facilitated traffic, to the advantage of the merchants. Italians visited the Mongol capitals of Karakorum and Peking and numerous Oriental goods were brought by caravans to the Black Sea ports and the mouths of the Danube, whence the Genoese distributed them to western Europe. This spurred the revival of C. in central Europe, where cities began to be Germanized and organized according to customs of German towns. These cities were granted the equivalent of the Magdeburg Charter, which granted merchants tremendous influence in the city. The dissolution of the Mongol empire in the late 14th century and the establishment of independent khanates had an impact on international C: roads began to move southwards and sea-commerce developed. Italian and Portuguese merchants began to explore the Atlantic, and set out to find the road to India, an attempt which led to major geographical discoveries.

The development of C. and its techniques, such as financing, credit, accountancy, etc., led in the 14th and 15th centuries to the emergence of schools on economic theory. Commercial schools were founded in Italian cities, where a number of treatises on commerce – mainly summaries of mercantile activities – were written and diffused in other commercial centres of Europe.

CEcH, vols. II and III;
R. L. Lopez and I. R. Raymond, *Medieval Trade in the Mediterranean World* (1955).

COMMODIAN Christian Latin poet. Very little is known about his life. Some scholars believe he lived in the 3rd century in Africa, while according to others he was a Gaulish pagan who converted to Christianity in the 5th century. He belonged to non-conformist trends in the Roman Catholic Church and most of his poems were condemned by the church in the 6th century. One of his extant poems, a polemic against the gods of the pagans and an apology of Christianity, was widely used, although unquoted, in the Christian hymns of the early Middle Ages.
H. Brewer, *Die Frage um das Zeitalter Kommodians* (1910).

COMMUNE (Latin: communitas) Until the end of the 11th century the term signified groups of clergymen, such as communities of *canons. In the 11th century it also referred to associations for maintaining the *Peace of God, whose members, including churchmen, nobles and burghers, swore fidelity to the "articles of peace". In the late 11th and 12th century the term was applied to the associations of burghers, who struggled against ecclesiastical and feudal lords of cities and boroughs to obtain self-rule within the town. (In this context the term had negative connotations, from the ecclesiastical point of view.) During the 12th century, such Cs. used to buy or obtain by contractual agreement the monarch's recognition of its privileges and his consent to self-government – and were thus directly dependent on him. The difference between the C. and other privileged towns lay not in the nature of the privileges granted, but in its solidarity. The C. was a *communio jurata* (sworn community), each of its members pledging allegiance to it. This type of C. – which mainly developed in France, England, the Low Countries and Italy (in northern Italy it also included the nobility) – played an important role in the 13th century. In England, the C. of London was a corporation recognized in the *Magna Charta. With the emergence and development of Parlia-

ment, the C. was called on to participate in its works, and, in the 14th century, convened in a special chamber, the Chamber of the C. In Italy, the Cs. profited from the struggle between the papacy and the empire, to gain independence. They created city-states, which, at the end of the 13th century, fell under the rule of local oligarchies. In France, the growth of royal authority in the 13th century, and especially during the reign of *Louis IX, weakened the C. The royal government capitalized on the C.'s internal dissent, granting the privilege of *bourgeois du roi* to some of the most important burghers, thereby enticing them to switch loyalties. But the economic importance of the towns instigated *Philip IV to call them, as the "Third Estate", to the assemblies of the Estates General, whether on a national, or on a provincial basis. The French example was adopted during the 14th century by the other European realms enabling the Cs. to exercise political influence in such assemblies.
J. M. Tait, *Borough and Town* (1935);
C. Petit-Dutaillis, *Les Communes Françaises au Moyen Age* (1948).

COMMUNITAS REGNI (The Community of the Realm) Constitutional term used in 13th-century England to designate the general representation of the country. The C. was the embryonic form of the *Parliament. In 1215, the barons who compelled King *John to issue the *Magna Charta considered themselves the spokesmen for the whole realm. During the 13th century they regarded their assemblies as representative of the community and thus did not find it necessary to call upon other social classes to join. This concept prevailed in the Provisions of *Oxford (1259) and in the revolt of Simon of *Montfort. The kingship, on the other hand, which required the support of the lower classes in its struggle against the barons, since 1213 convened assemblies of delegates of the knights of the shires and representatives of the towns (the Commons) to discuss judicial issues. In 1255 such an assembly was summoned to discuss the grant of aid and, in the 1260s it joined the assemblies of barons and clergy. The assembly summoned by *Edward I in 1275 was the core of the English Parliament.
B. Lyon, *The Constitutional and Legal History of Medieval England* (1961).

COMO Town in northern Italy, on the coast of Lake Como, on the road between the St. Gotthard Pass and Milan. Contested by the Allemanni and the Lombards, who finally conquered it, C. was a gateway of Frankish and German invasions of Italy. In the late 12th century, it was annexed to the city-state of Milan.

COMPASS An instrument, based on the use of a magnetized needle, which, when suspended freely, will point towards the North and South poles. Of Chinese origin, the C. was adopted by Moslem sailors and was already known in western Europe in the 12th century, when its existence was mentioned by Alexander *Neckam in his *De Naturis Rerum*. Physical and astronomical achievements in the 13th century permitted a description of its magnetic qualities by Petrus *Peregrinus of Maricourt in 1269. During this period and until the end of the Middle Ages the C. was used by the Portolan cartographers for map-drawing.
E. O. von Lippmann, *Geschichte der Magnetnadel bis zur Erfindung des Kompasses* (1932).

COMPIÈGNE Town in northeastern France, at the confluence of the Oise and Aisne Rivers. The *Merovingians built a palace there, which was subsequently used by *Frankish rulers on their sojourns to C. In 757, at a council held at C., *Pepin the Short established the principles of an ecclesiastical reform of the kingdom. In 833 a council of bishops assembled at C. decided to depose Emperor *Louis the Pious. C. continued to belong to the domains of the last *Carolingians and the *Capetians, but was administered by the abbots of St. Corneille, a local abbey. In 1431, Joan of Arc was taken prisoner while defending the town.
A. de Barthélemy, *L'Abbaye de Sainte-Corneille de Compiègne* (1889).

COMPOSITIONES AD TIGENDA (Composition for dyeing) An anonymous treatise, written in 8th-century Italy, in Latin, dealing with the preparation of pigments and other chemical substances. Until the end of the 13th century it served as an important guide for dyers.
A. C. Crombie, *Science in the Middle Ages* (1957).

COMPOSTELA See SANTIAGO DE COMPOSTELA.

COMPURGATION Judicial procedure originating in Germanic law in the early Middle Ages and adopted in *feudal law. C. was the trial and purgation by oath of an accused. This type of legal defence was limited to men of good birth and reputation. The defendant had to produce at least two witnesses − persons of good standing − who would swear that he was telling the truth. Should the claimant bring co-accusers, the defendant had to produce an equal number of supporters.
M. Bloch, *Feudal Society* (1952).

CONCILIAR MOVEMENT Movement at first mainly among intellectuals and in the universities, urging the convening of a council, to reunite the papacy. During the *Great Schism which began in 1378, two popes were elected, at Rome and at Avignon. When negotiations failed, the movement won general support and the pressure it exerted led to the convening of the council at Pisa in 1409. It was followed by the *Ecumenical Council of *Constance in 1417, which deposed both popes and elected a new pope, *Martin V. The theologians gathered at the council put forth a doctrine on the superiority of the Council to the pope, which was further discussed by the Council of Basle. Nevertheless, the lack of unity of the participants and the long discussions of details, allowed Pope *Eugenius IV to redress the papal authority and dissolve the council. The C. continued to manifest itself until the middle of the 15th century.
B. Tierney, *Foundations of Conciliar Theory* (1968).

CONCLAVE (Latin: cum clave "with a key") Since the late 13th century the term referred to the closed room where the College of *Cardinals congregated to elect a new pope; by extension, it meant the whole session. In 1271, after an election which lasted three years, Pope *Nicholas decreed the C. procedure, according to which the cardinals were to remain in closed session until they elected a pope.
L. Lector, *Le Conclave; origines, histoire, organisation* (1894).

CONCORDAT An agreement between the ecclesiastical and lay authorities upon matters of vital concern to both parties. Among the numerous Cs. in the West between the papacy and emperors or kings, the most famous is the C. of *Worms of 1122, which ended the *Investiture Contest by compromise.

CONDOTTIERI Italian word, meaning mercenary generals and captains. The word derives from *condotta* (lance). The C. appeared in northern and central Italy in the late 14th century, when communal authorities hired military leaders, primarily for their defence, and, in the 15th century, for offensive and defensive purposes. The C. hired their own soldiers and officers and, besides their *solde* (privileged treatment), also received part of the booty. Contracts were made either for a specific war or for long-term service. In the small city-states, the C. gained political power; they became the virtual leaders, and even, in certain cases during the 15th century, they were tyrants who founded local dynasties. In the larger city-states, such as *Florence and especially *Venice, the rebublic was strong enough to impose its orders upon the C.
O. Browning, *The Age of the Condottieri; A Short History of Mediaeval Italy, from 1409 to 1530* (1895).

CONFIRMATION OF THE CHARTERS The statute issued by *Edward I of England in 1297. It confirmed the *Magna Charta and the Charter of the Forest as part of Common Law and made taxation subject to the approval of the "community of the realm". The ordinance was issued to appease the clergy and barons, whose agitation threatened to erupt into an open revolt following the energetic fiscal measures introduced by the royal court.
B. Lyon, *A Constitutional and Legal History of Medieval England* (1961).

CONFIRMATION, SACRAMENT OF The rite at which Christian children, upon reaching their majority, confirm the vows made on their behalf at the sacrament of Baptism. Late Roman and early medieval theologians stressed the fact that infants are baptized − and thus bestowed the Grace of God − without free choice and therefore the administration of the first sacrament had to be confirmed at an age at which children can understand their religious responsibilities. This practice, of Oriental origin, had already been developed in Judaism and was adopted by Christianity. As in the earlier practices, the age of C. coincides with the age of puberty, between 12 and 13, for both sexes.
C. R. Thornton, *Confirmation. Its place in the Baptismal Mystery* (1954).

CONNAUGHT Tribal kingdom in western Ireland. Like other Irish realms, C. was a confederation of Gaelic clans, which were better organized in the 6th century, as a result of the Christianization of the country by St. *Patrick. The O'Connor clan succeeded in imposing its authority over the others and maintained the realm's independence during the *Viking raids in the 10th century. In the 12th century, the O'Connors were the high kings − a figurehead position with only nominal power, but to which the other Irish kings were subservient. Under the reign of Rory O'Connor, they resisted the attempts of *Henry II to conquer Ireland. Rory, who remained the national leader after the English conquest of Dublin, eventually came to terms with Henry: by the Treaty of Windsor, he was recognized by the English as high king, and agreed to pay tribute. Feuds among the independent tribal kingdoms weakened his rule. The turbulent state of the C. kingdom at his death in 1198, facilitated the penetration of the English though, initially, under the cover of a local prince appointed by the king of England (1205).

E. Curtis, *The History of Medieval Ireland* (1938).

CONNÉTABLE See CONSTABLE.

CONON I (d. 992) Count of Rennes, duke of *Brittany (987-92). he was head of the countal dynasty of Rennes, which, during the 10th century, fought against the counts of Nantes, claiming the ducal title of Brittany. In 987 C. succeeded in imposing his rule and uniting the duchy, hitherto rent by internal anarchy. He was the founder of the last Breton dynasty, which ruled Brittany until 1169.

E. Durtelle de Saint-Saveur, *Histoire de Bretagne* (1946).

CONON II (d. 1066) Duke of Brittany (1040-66). He devoted his efforts to impose order in the duchy and to fight against *William the Conqueror, duke of Normandy, who tried to expand towards Brittany.

CONON III, the Fat (d. 1148) Duke of Brittany (1112-48). He became duke, while still a minor, after his father, Alain Fergent, abdicated. During his youth, Brittany was divided by civil wars between factions of the nobility, which he was able to suppress only with the help of the count of Anjou, *Geoffrey Martel, who introduced Angevin influence in the duchy.

E. Durtelle de Saint-Saveur, *Histoire de Bretagne* (1946).

CONON IV (d. 1171) The last Breton duke of Brittany (1156-69). Grandson, through his mother, of Conon III. He was supported by the nobility of western Brittany in his efforts to maintain the duchy's independence from *Henry II, king of England, duke of Normandy and count of Anjou, who sought to obtain the suzerainty over the duchy. C.'s attempts failed and he was compelled by Henry to agree to the marriage of C.'s daughter and heiress, Constance, with Henry's third son, Geoffrey. In 1169 Henry deposed him and proclaimed Geoffrey duke of Brittany, but only after C.'s death, was the Angevin government able to rule the duchy.

E. Durtelle de Saint-Saveur, *Histoire de Bretagne* (1946).

CONON DE BÉTHUNE (c. 1150-1219) Lyric poet. Born to a noble family of the county of *Artois. One of his most famous poems was his lamentation on the conflict between his religious duty to take part in the Crusades, and his love for a lady of his native county. He took part in the Third and Fourth *Crusades, in the latter holding a high-ranking post in the army of *Baldwin of Flanders. In 1216, at the death of Emperor *Henry of Hainault, he was appointed regent of Constantinople, a post he held until his death.

G. Cohen, *La vie littéraire au Moyen Age* (1953).

CONQUES *Benedictine abbey in Aquitaine (France). It was founded by *Louis the Pious to celebrate the cult of St. Foy, and rebuilt in the 9th-12th centuries. During that period, it was a thriving centre for the decorative arts, attracting goldsmiths and other craftsmen. C. stands as one of the most beautiful monuments of Romanesque architecture.

"CONQUESTE DE JERUSALEM" An epic poem, composed during the 13th century in northern France. Dealing with the conquest of Jerusalem by the *Crusaders in 1099, the C. relates the deeds of a number of knights and other popular "leaders" of the Crusade, emphasizing their courage, pride and wisdom. The historical leaders of the First Crusade are given background roles, while other participants, even some of ill repute – such as *Thomas de Marle, who in actual

fact fled from Antioch in 1098 and returned to France where he was branded a brigand and excommunicated – are represented as the heroes of the day. Modern scholars suggest therefore that the poem may have been composed to please some of these "heroes' " descendants, who rose in social status in the 13th century and thus wanted to "repaint" the image of their ancestors.

S. Duparc-Quioc, *Le Cycle de la Croisade* (1955).

CONRAD I (d. 918) King of Germany (911-18). He was a member of a western Franconian countal family, the Conrads. After the extinction of the *Carolingian dynasty in Germany, the nobles elected him king, despite the opposition of the *Lotharingian nobility, who preferred *Charles III the Simple, as a symbol of Carolingian continuity. He devoted his efforts to suppressing Lotharingian separatism and trying to impose royal authority on the "tribal" dukes. He failed in his attempts to create a dynasty, even though he was supported by the bishops.

G. Tellenbach, *Die Entstehung des deutschen Reiches* (1943).

CONRAD II (990-1039) *Holy Roman emperor (1024-39). Son of Henry, count of Spires, he was elected king at the extinction of the *Saxon dynasty in Germany, founding thus the Salian dynasty. Having pacified Germany, he went to Italy in 1026, imposing his rule on Lombardy. He was crowned emperor the following year. In 1032 he inherited the kingdom of *Burgundy and annexed it to the empire. His activities on the eastern frontier of Germany opened the way to German expansion east of the Elbe River and to German influence in Poland, Bohemia and on the Slav tribes between the Elbe and the Oder. To consolidate his authority and improve his administration in Germany, C. promoted the *ministeriales* (officials of low birth) and granted his vassals full suzerainty over their subordinates, thus establishing *feudalism in Germany. He returned to Italy in 1038 to repress a revolt by Milan, but an epidemic decimated his army, forcing him to lift the siege of the city.

K. Hampe, *Deutsche Kaisergeschichte in der Zeit der Salier und Staufer* (1949).

CONRAD III, of Swabia (1093-1152) Holy Roman emperor (1138-52). He was the son of Duke Frederick of Swabia and Agnes, daughter of *Henry IV, and the founder of the *Hohenstaufen dynasty in Germany. In 1117 he was appointed duke of Franconia by *Henry V. He became a leader of the opposition to Emperor *Lothair III, but was reconciled with him in 1135. C. was elected emperor after Lothair's death in 1138. His election provoked a rebellion by *Henry the Proud, duke of Bavaria and head of the *Welf family, and was the root of the Hohenstaufen-Welf rivalry that was a constant factor in German political history of the 12th and 13th centuries. The conflict was transplanted to Italy, where factions in the cities fought as Guelphs (Welfs) or Ghibellines (which derives from Weiblingen, the original castle of the Hohenstaufen in Swabia). While C. had some success in his struggle against Henry, he was forced to acquiesce the inheritance of Saxony by the Welfs and to grant privileges to the princes, who became a potent force in Germany. To neutralize their power, C. used the services of the *ministeriales*. In 1147 he took part in the Second *Crusade, despite the objection of Pope *Eugenius III, who wanted him to repress the rebellion of *Arnold of Brescia in Rome. The Crusade failed with a great part of C.'s army being destroyed in Asia Minor, either in battles against the *Seljuks or by epidemics. C. arrived in Acre with the remnants of his army in 1148 and took part in the war against Damascus, which, too, failed. On his return, C. and his ally, Emperor *Manuel Comnenus of Byzantium, geared themselves for attacking *Roger II, king of Sicily, whom C. held responsible for the failure of the Crusade. But on hearing of renewed uprisings by the Welfs in Germany, he returned home to pacify his realm.

W. Ohnsorge, *Kaiser Konrad III.* (1958)

CONRAD IV (1228-54) Holy Roman emperor (1250-54), king of Jerusalem (1228-54). Son of *Frederick II of Hohenstaufen and Isabel of Brienne, queen of Jerusalem, he was proclaimed king of the Latin kingdom of Jerusalem at his birth, but never reigned over the Crusaders' realm. At the request of his father, he was crowned king of the Romans (i.e. of Germany) in 1237 to assure the succession. When Frederick died C. was unable to meet the challenges to his rule in Germany. He went to Sicily, which he had also inherited, ruling it from 1252 until 1254 under the tutelage of his half-brother, *Manfred. His death in 1254 put an end to the rule of the Hohenstaufen dynasty.

E. Kantorowicz, *Frederick the Second* (1957).

CONRAD V (1252-68) Also named Conradin (Conrad the Younger); nominal king of Germany, Sicily and Jerusalem (1254-68). Son of *Conrad IV, he was recognized in Germany by supporters of the Hohenstaufen family. He was crowned at Palermo at the age of two, reigning under the regency of his uncle *Manfred. In 1266, after Manfred was defeated by Charles of Anjou and died in battle, C. led the Ghibellines – who called him from his duchy of Swabia – against the pro-papal *Guelphs, but was defeated at the Battle of Tagliacozzo in 1268. He was executed by Charles on charges of treason.

S. Runciman, *The Sicilian Vespers* (1958).

CONRAD I (d. 993) King of Burgundy (937-93). Son of *Rudolf II, he was proclaimed king, despite the opposition of Hugh of Arles, who considered C. too young to rule. When Hugh sought to displace C., the latter fled to the court of *Otto I of Germany. With the emperor's support C. was able to return to his kingdom in 942 and reign under German influence.

CONRAD BUSARUS (13th century) Jurist, counsellor to Duke Louis of Bavaria. In 1260 he was sent by the duke to the papal court to win support for *Conradin against *Manfred of Sicily. While his mission had no practical results, it generated a split in the *Ghibelline party in Italy. His treatise on the legitimate succession rights of the Hohenstaufen dynasty helped discredit Manfred, but profited the *Guelphs and *Charles of Anjou.

K. Hampe, *Geschichte Konradins von Hohenstaufen* (1894).

CONRAD CAPECE (d. 1270) Leader of the Ghibelline party in Tuscany. He entered the service of *Manfred of Sicily, who appointed him vicar of Ancona, Tuscany and Sicily. In 1267, he called *Conradin to Italy and, after the Battle of Tagliacozzo, led the opposition against *Charles of Anjou in Sicily. He was taken prisoner in 1270 and executed by the king's order.

K. Hampe, *Geschichte Konradins von Hohenstaufen* (1894).

CONRAD OF ANTIOCH (d. 1290) Illegitimate grandson of *Frederick II. He was vested with lands in the Abruzzi Mountains, central Italy, where he became a leader of the *Ghibelline party after 1260, aided by his uncle *Manfred. In 1266 he managed to retain the Abruzzi strongholds despite the defeat and death of Manfred. Thus, he went to Germany and escorted *Conradin to Italy, where they fought against the *Guelphs. C. was taken prisoner at the Battle of Tagliacozzo (1268), but escaped. He led the opposition to *Charles of Anjou in Italy, and became an ally to the Aragonese in 1282 playing an important role in the *Sicilian Vespers.

S. Runciman, *The Sicilian Vespers* (1958).

CONRAD OF BAVARIA (d. 1055) Grandson of Emperor *Henry III, he was appointed duke of Bavaria in 1049. His attempts to establish his rule in the duchy prompted a violent quarrel with the bishop of Ratisbon, who was protected by the emperor. From 1053 until his death, he led the opposition to Henry III, who accused him of breaking imperial peace.

G. Tellenbach, *Die Entstehung des deutschen Reiches* (1943).

CONRAD OF CARINTHIA Name of three dukes of *Carinthia in the 11th century:
Conrad I, the Elder (1104-11) Related to the Saxon imperial dynasty, through his mother Liutgarde, daughter of *Otto I. He governed his duchy as an obedient tool of *Henry II.
Conrad II, the Young (1036-39) Son of C. I. On the refusal of Henry II to grant him Carinthia in 1011, he retired to Franconia and entered into close relations with the Salians; in 1036, *Conrad II appointed him duke of Carinthia, where he favoured trends of Germanization, and was active in imperial policy.
Conrad III (1056-61) Nephew of C. II. Reputed as a good administrator of his duchy, where he encouraged the establishment of towns and favoured German immigration.

G. Tellenbach, *Die Entstehung des deutschen Reiches* (1943).

CONRAD OF HOCHSTADEN (d. 1261) He was one of the greatest archbishops of Cologne (1238-61) and influential in political affairs. In 1240 he deserted the cause of *Frederick II and played a prominent role as leader of the opposition and in the elections of anti-kings. During the German *Interregnum (1250-75), he was one of the chief electors of various kings, among them *Richard of Cornwall. He exploited his position to gain recognition of his rule over the principality, which, in addition to Cologne, included the strip of land on the west bank of the Rhine. He favoured the establishment of a *Dominican school at Cologne, where he was in close contact with *Albertus Magnus and built the famous Gothic cathedral of the city.

M. Kettering, *Kölner Erzbischof Konrad von Hochstaden* (1951).

CONRAD OF MARBURG (c. 1180-1233) Papal *inquisitor in Germany. Native of Marburg, he probably studied at Bologna, and subsequently lived an ascetic life. In 1213 he preached the *Crusade proclaimed by *Innocent III. Charged with missions in Germany, he became the spiritual guide to St. *Elisabeth, wife of

Louis of Thuringia. In 1231 *Gregory IX appointed him inquisitor of heresies in Germany, and he was directly answerable to the pope. His ruthless attitude led to his denunciation by a court of bishops assembled at Mainz, where he was accused of condemning suspects on insufficient evidence. On his way to Marburg, he was assailed and murdered by the populace.

B. Kaltner, *Konrad von Marburg und die Inquisition in Deutschland* (1882).

CONRAD OF MAZOVIA (d. 1238) Duke of Mazovia (northern Poland). Descendant of the royal dynasty. His main concern was to defeat the pagan Prussian tribes and to effect that end he called the *Teutonic order to Prussia in 1230.

CONRAD OF MONTFERRAT (d. 1192) King of Jerusalem (1190-92). Uncle of the infant king *Baldwin V. He left Constantinople before the Battle of *Hattin and arrived in Palestine after the Crusaders' disaster. C. organized the defence of Tyre, the last stronghold of the kingdom, and was proclaimed its lord (1187). He thus refused to recognize King Guy of Lusignan and adopted an independent policy, taking part in the siege of Acre. By marrying Princess Isabel, heiress to the throne, in 1190, C. became king of Jerusalem, but was murdered by an *Assassin emissary in 1192.

S. Runciman, *A History of the Crusades* (1953).

CONRAD OF URSLINGEN (d. 1201) Duke of Spoleto (1183-98). Member of a family of Urslingen lords. He distinguished himself in the service of *Frederick Barbarossa, who sent him to Italy. In 1183 he was appointed duke of Spoleto, central Italy, to keep an eye on Rome. *Henry VI, finding in C. one of his most devoted men, appointed him his vicar in *Sicily and, in 1197, entrusted him with the guardianship of his son, *Frederick II. C. was compelled to submit to Pope *Celestine III in 1198, and to give the child-king to Constance, widow of Henry VI. *Innocent III forced him to surrender Spoleto, which was annexed to the papal state.

K. Hampe, *Deutsche Kaisergeschichte in der Zeit der Salier und Staufer* (1949).

CONRAD OF WITTELSBACH (d. 1200) Archbishop of Mainz. Member of the noble family of Wittelsbach, he was appointed archbishop of Mainz (1163) by *Frederick Barbarossa, who counted on his fidelity. C. tried to reconcile the emperor with the papacy, urging him to recognize *Alexander III. At Frederick's refusal, he fled to the papal court and was deprived of his see. He was transferred to the see of Salzburg in 1176 and subsequently allowed to return to Mainz, where he became a prominent leader of the German church. He took part in the *Crusade of *Henry VI. After his return to Germany, he sought to unify the realm, an aim which, he believed, could be realized by the *Hohenstaufen dynasty; therefore, after the death of Henry, he favoured the claims of Henry's brother, *Philip of Swabia to the German crown and tried to win the support of *Innocent III, who was opposed to the candidacy.

K. Hampe, *Deutsche Kaisergeschichte in der Zeit der Salier und Staufer* (1949).

CONRAD OF WÜRZBURG (c. 1225-87) German poet. In his youth, he travelled throughout the Rhine Valley, particularly in Strassburg and Basle, where he acquired a vast theological and legal knowledge. His popular poetry, in German, was esteemed by the aristocracy and clergy of the Rhine area. His work contains epic poems, moral verse and lyrics.

P. Schröder (ed.), *Die goldene Schmiede, Konrad von Würzburg* (1969).

CONRAD OF ZÄHRINGEN See ZÄHRINGEN.

CONRAD THE GREAT Margrave of Meissen (1124-56). Member of the Saxon family of Wettin, he was appointed margrave in 1124 by *Lothair of Supplinburg, the future emperor, against the explicit order of *Henry V, who had his own candidate for the office. C. introduced an efficient government in the march and was a leading figure in the German expansion east of the Elbe.

J. W. Thompson, *Feudal Germany* (1928).

CONRAD THE RED (d. 955) Duke of *Lotharingia. He was a member of an influential Franconian family. In 944 *Otto I appointed him duke of Lotharingia and married him to his daughter, Liutgard. C.'s main task was to pacify the large duchy, where pro-*Carolingian feelings still prevailed. In 951 he was sent on a mission to Italy, where he concluded an agreement with *Berengar II. Shortly after, the good relations with Otto turned into rivalry. In a conspiracy against the king, C. allied himself with other German malcontents and with the *Hungarians. He was forced to surrender and lost the duchy, which was subsequently divided into two parts: Upper Lotharingia (Lorraine) and Lower Lotharingia, which included the Low Countries.

G. Tellenbach, *Königtum und Stämme in der Werdezeit des deutschen Reiches* (1939).

CONRAD THE SALIAN (d. 1101) Son of Emperor *Henry IV, he was made duke of Lorraine by his father. He was sent to Italy, vested with the royal title, in 1086 to implement Henry's policy against the papacy. Instead, once there, he revolted against his father, who deposed him in 1100 and deprived him of his succession rights. He died in Florence.

G. Tellenbach, *Church, State and Christian Society at the Time of the Investiture Contest* (1959).

CONSECRATION The Christian rite, in which a person or thing is dedicated to divine service. In the Middle Ages, there were three forms of C. within the church.

1) C. of the *Eucharist, by which bread and wine became the body and blood of Christ, which could be effectuated by a priest;

2) C. of bishops, by which they are ordained after their election as prelates of the church; the ceremony had to be presided over by the archbishop, with the participation of two other bishops;

3) C. of a new church, or altar, or Eucharistic vessels, a rite reserved for bishops.

The C. was materialized by anointing with sacred oil the person or thing consecrated. Thus, by extension, the anointment of a king was considered consecration, although not in the theological sense.

EC, III.

CONSILIUM (Counsel) The debates at the lord's court in which his vassals participated when requested to do so as one of their elementary duties to him. The decisions taken, either military or juridical, were binding on the vassals. The duty to attend the C. was also a privilege, as the imposition of taxes or grants to be paid to the lord was subject to previous discussion and consent by the vassals.

F. L. Ganshof, *Feudalism* (1965).

CONSISTORIUM (Consistory) The term is of Roman origin and in the Roman empire meant the antechamber of the imperial palace, where the emperor administered justice. In the Middle Ages, however, the term was integrated into ecclesiastical vocabulary, with different meanings, according to the Greek-Orthodox and Eastern Churches or to the Roman Catholic. In the East, it designated the bishop's court of justice, where cases belonging to *canon law were judged, in the Roman Catholic Church, it gradually was reserved for assemblies of cardinals in the presence of the pope, either in public meetings, for solemn affairs, or in private, when the pope summoned the cardinals for advice on a specific issue.
EC, III.

CONSOLAMENTUM The sole sacrament of the *Albigensians which was deemed highly important and by which the faithful who received it became "pure" and were expected to live in rigid asceticism. The C. could only be administered once in a lifetime and therefore was the expression of an ideal purity, rather than a daily ceremony. In the second half of the 12th century, it was taken only by those who felt their death was imminent.
A. Borst, *Die Katharer* (1958).

CONSTABLE (Latin: constabularius, French: connétable) The officer at feudal courts, commanding the army in the king's or lord's absence. The term derives from *comes stabuli,* the "count of the stable" who was responsible for cavalry at the *Carolingian court. The post became more important in the 9th and 10th centuries with the C. undertaking the command of the army in person when the monarch was unable to do so for reasons of health or age. From the 11th century on, the C. was put in charge of the army unit or detachment considered unsuitable for royal command. High-ranking vassals, such as dukes or marquises, created similar offices at their own courts. With the growth of royal power and domains in the 12th century, a king would appoint several Cs. according to the number of provinces or other territorial divisions of his realm. In England, after the Norman Conquest, the office of C. never acquired the same importance as on the Continent. Cs. became royal officials at sheriffs' courts, who were in charge of the police within the shire, arrested people and guarded the prisoners. In 14th-century France, however, the post became the most important military charge in the kingdom. The *connétable* was invested with a royal sword, symbolizing his office; during important ceremonies, such as royal coronations, he stood near the king and held up his sword. The charge was therefore granted to the highest-ranking nobles. The few exceptions, such as the appointments of *Du Guesclin and *Clisson by *Charles V, met with some disapproval by members of the royal family and other aristocrats. While the Cs. still enjoyed great prestige in the late Middle Ages, their importance declined with the introduction of fire-arms and infantry.
M. Bloch, *Feudal Society* (1952).

CONSTANCE City on Lake Constance, southwest Germany. C. was an episcopal see since the 6th century and governed by the bishops of the *Holy Roman empire. In the 10th-13th centuries it was vested with large estates. The city is famous for the Council of C. (1414-18), convoked by Pope *John XXIII, under pressure from Emperor Sigismund, after repeated demands to put an end to the *Great Schism. The most prominent figure at the Council was French Cardinal Pierre d'*Ailly, who, supported by the emperor and the theological authority of John *Gerson, proposed the deposition of the three popes, John XXIII, *Gregory XII and *Benedict XIII. In 1415 the Council, by a vote of all nations represented on it, adopted the famous Four Articles of Ailly, which exposed the essence of the *Conciliar theory: it proclaimed itself a General Council, which derived its authority directly from God and whose decisions were binding on all Christians, even the pope. Although the Italians rejected the articles, they were duly promulgated by the Council, with the active support of the emperor. John and Benedict were deposed (in 1415 and 1417), while Gregory resigned, paving the way for the election of a new pope, as proposed by Henry *Beaufort, bishop of Winchester. It was decided that the conclave to elect the pope be composed of the 23 cardinals and 30 deputies of the Council, who elected Odo *Colona as Pope *Martin V in 1417. The Council also discussed the problem of heresies, condemning the doctrines of John *Wycliffe and John *Huss. Huss — who came to C. to defend his theses, with a safe-conduct of the emperor — was handed over to the secular authority to be burned for heresy. The Council dispersed without coming to effective decisions on church reform and its failure was one of the causes of the 16th-century Reformation.
H. Finke (ed.), *Acta Concilii Constantiniensis,* 4 vols. (1928);
E. F. Jacob, *Essays on the Conciliar Epoch* (1945).

CONSTANS I Emperor of Rome (337-50). At the death of his father, *Constantine the Great, he inherited the provinces of Italy, Africa and Illyricum. In 340 he defeated his brother, Constantine II, emperor of Gaul, Spain and Britain, and annexed his provinces, which constituted the Western Roman empire, to his realm.
A. H. G. Jones, *The Later Roman Empire* (1964).

CONSTANS II (630-68) Emperor of Byzantium (641-68). Son of *Constantine III he was proclaimed emperor by a popular uprising at Constantinople. In 649 he issued the *Typos,* an imperial ordinance designed to pacify the *Monophysites, which brought him into conflict with the Orthodox and Catholic elements in the empire. He expelled Pope *Martin I from Rome, thereby deepening the breach with the Catholics. His reign coincided with the period of spectacular conquests by the Arabs: Egypt, Libya, Cyprus and Rhodes were conquered with little resistance; moreover, the Byzantine fleet was severely defeated in 655. Religious opposition forced C. to leave Constantinople in 660. He planned to transfer his capital to Sicily and settled in Syracuse, but was assassinated there in 668.
J. B. Bury, *A History of the Later Roman Empire* (1889).

CONSTANTINE (d. 766) Patriarch of Constantinople (754-66). Of monastic background, he was appointed patriarch by Emperor *Constantine V at the end of the Council of Constantinople, which forbade the worship of images. His particular task was to impose the *iconoclastic policy of the emperor within the church.
N. H. Baynes and H. S. L. B. Moss, *Byzantium* (1949).

CONSTANTINE City in North Africa (present-day Algeria). The Carthaginian and classical city of *Cirta* was destroyed in 311 by the Roman emperor Maxentius. *Constantine the Great ordered it rebuilt in 312 and the new city took his name. It became a provincial capital and survived the various conquests of the *Vandals and *Byzantines. C. was conquered by the Arabs in 710 and annexed to their province of Africa (*Ifriqyia*). C.'s history in the 8th-11th centuries coincides with that of Africa. Toward the end of the 11th century, a local Moslem dynasty seized power in C. and its environs, ruling until 1140, when the *Almohades conquered the city and annexed it to their empire. C. became a prosperous harbour-city and in the second half of the 13th century reached its independence under a Berber dynasty, which reigned until the 16th century.

R. H. Idriss, *La Berbérie Orientale* (1962).

CONSTANTINE I, the Great (Flavius Valerius Constantinus Magnus; c. 270-337) Emperor of Rome (306-37). While the period of his reign belongs to the Classical era – because C. is regarded as perhaps the last great emperor of Rome – some scholars consider it a transition to the Middle Ages. Two major factors support their thesis: the recognition of Christianity as a legal religion in the empire and the hierarchical organization of the *church; his regulations concerning the attachment of the *colonate to the soil, creating thus the dependence links which were the basis of *feudalism. C. was the son of Emperor Constantius I and (St.) *Helena, daughter of a Christian innkeeper. He grew up in army camps, commanding the Roman army in Britain. In 306, he was given the title Caesar, and embarked on a career which brought him from York to Constantinople. In 312 he defeated his rival Maxentius in a struggle over the supremacy of the West. His victory at the Milvian bridge over the Tiber River was not only the decisive point of his political career, but also a key event in the history of Christianity. His biographer, Bishop Eusebius of Caesarea, relates that C. had a dream on the eve of the battle, in which a sign, then common to Christians, appeared in the heavens, while a voice declared: *In hoc signo vinces*! ("With this sign, thou shalt win!"). C. then ordered that the sign be put on the soldiers' shields. (The major part of the army had already adopted Christianity, despite the fact that he and the officers still adhered to the cult of the sun.) In 313 he issued the Edict of Milan, which legalized Christianity in the empire and granted Christian freedom of worship and organization. C. exploited his Christian sympathies to win the support of the large Christian population in the eastern provinces of the empire, which enabled him to defeat his rival Licinius, the co-emperor in the East (316-24) and become sole emperor. He used the Christian sign, the *lavarum*, on the official flag of the army; moreover, he granted the bishops a status similar to that of imperial officials, allowing them, in 318, to use imperial carriages. He thus had at his disposal a faithful chain of informants, who could watch the activities of the pagan administration and directly report to him. This policy gave the church a hierarchical structure. For C., discipline carried more weight than theological arguments: any discussion between a priest and a bishop always ended in the latter's favour. He intervened in the theological conflict at *Alexandria between the patriarch *Athanasius and the priest Arius by convening the Council of *Nicaea in 325. The Council – comprising the bishops of the empire and presided over by C. – condemned the heretical doctrine of Arius (see *Church) and adopted the official creed, as drafted by Athanasius – this despite C.'s ignorance of the nature of the dispute. But when Arianism won the bishop's support, C. tolerated the movement. Under the influence of his mother, who went to Jerusalem, he encouraged the construction of a church on the site venerated as the tomb of Christ – the church of the *Holy Sepulchre – contributing a large grant towards its erection.

C.'s social and economic legislation was a prelude to the future medieval society. In 326, he made offices and trades hereditary, to assure the function of institutions and economic activity. He ordered that the colons (free peasants) and serfs be bound to the soil and put under the control of the owners of large estates, so as to put an end to the trend of emigration from the West to the East. The measure was also necessitated by the need to procure food for the army and manpower for the maintenance of roads and bridges.

A. H. M. Jones, *Constantine and the Conversion of Europe* (1949).

CONSTANTINE II Emperor of Rome (337-40). Son of Constantine I, he inherited the empire of Gaul, Spain and Britain. C. was murdered by his brother *Constans in 340.

CONSTANTINE I (d. 715) Pope (708-15). Born to a family of Syrian merchants established at Rome. Distinguished by *Sergius I, he was active at the papal court at the beginning of the 8th century. As pope, he entertained good relations with Byzantine Emperor *Justinian II and reinforced papal authority in Italy.

L. Duchesne, *Early History of the Christian Church* (1909).

CONSTANTINE III (612-41) Emperor of Byzantium (641). He succeeded his father, *Heraclius, but fell ill and died shortly after his coronation.

CONSTANTINE IV, Progonatus (654-85) Emperor of Byzantium (668-85). Son of *Constans II. During his reign, the use of *Greek Fire enabled the Byzantine fleet to regain naval supremacy and to put an end to the attacks by the Arabs, who had penetrated Asia Minor and had threatened Constantinople (672-78). C. also fought against the *Bulgars, who had crossed the Danube. His illness, however, left the army without effective leadership, compelling him to recognize the regime of Khan *Asperuch in 680. Under C., Greek replaced Latin as the language used in administrative and legal activities and in official documents. He imposed his authority on high-ranking officers and limited the powers of vice-emperors. In 680 he convoked and presided over the 6th Ecumenical Council of the Church at Constantinople, which put an end to tolerance of the *Monophysites and restored religious peace to the empire.

A. A. Vasiliev, *History of the Byzantine Empire* (1952).

CONSTANTINE V (718-75) Emperor of Byzantium (741-75). Son of *Leo III. He was the most fanatic of the *iconoclast emperors. On his initiative, an ecclesiastical council held in 754 at *Nicaea prohibited the use of icons. He executed many who supported icon-worship and clashed with the monks – most of whom worshipped icons – confiscating their estates and dispersing their communities. He defeated the Bulgarians and the Arabs, who invaded Armenia and Mesopotamia.

A. A. Vasiliev, *History of the Byzantine Empire* (1952).

CONSTANTINE VI (771-805) Emperor of Byzantium (780-97). He was the son of *Leo IV and reigned under the tutelage of his mother, *Irene. In 790 Irene arrested him and, when he tried to revolt against her domination, a civil war broke out in the empire. Irene was recalled in 792 as co-empress, and in 797 she had him dethroned and blinded.

CONSTANTINE VII, Prophyrogenitus (905-59) Emperor of Byzantium (913-59). Son of *Leo VI. He reigned under the regency of his mother, Zoe, and of *Romanus I. In the initial period of his own rule, he enjoined the landowners to return to the independent peasants their estates, but the order went unheeded. He fought against the *Hamdanites in Syria and spread Byzantine influence to Russia. C. was a learned man, who played an active role in the cultural awakening of *Byzantium in the 10th century. He was a patron of learning and an able writer. His works, which include *Ceremonies, The Imperial Administration* and *The Themes* (on provincial administration), are authoritative descriptions of the various aspects of Byzantine life.

A. A. Vasiliev, *History of the Byzantine Empire* (1952); N. H. Baynes and H. S. L. B. Moss, *Byzantium* (1949).

CONSTANTINE VIII (960-1028) Emperor of Byzantium (1025-28). Son of *Romanus II. He was proclaimed co-emperor with his brother, *Basil II in 963. Preferring a life of pleasure, C. left the government to his brother. After Basil died, he became sole emperor. His reign represents little more than the continuity of the empire and of the Macedonian dynasty.

A. A. Vasiliev, *History of the Byzantine Empire* (1952).

CONSTANTINE IX, Monomachus (d. 1054) Emperor of Byzantium (1042-54). Member of a noble family of Constantinople, he was a high civil official and later on, senator. By marrying Empress Zoe in 1042 he became emperor. His accession, representing the elevation of the civil aristocracy, instigated military revolts in 1043 and 1047. C. succeeded in repressing them, but to diminish the generals' political influence dismissed soldiers and thus weakened the army. The results were immediate: the empire suffered defeats in the Balkans, in southern Italy and on the eastern borders. C. was a sensitive person and a patron of letters, supporting scholars of the Constantinople academy, among whom *Psellus was prominent. His lack of energy was manifest, when he failed to intervene in the quarrel between Pope *Leo IX and Patriarch *Michael Cerularius, which ended in the schism of East and West and the separation of the two Churches in 1054.

A. A. Vasiliev, *History of the Byzantine Empire* (1952).

CONSTANTINE X, Ducas (d. 1067) Emperor of Byzantium (1059-67). Member of the noble Ducas family of Constantinople. He was proclaimed emperor by a joint revolt of the church dignitaries and the civil nobility headed by *Psellus, which led to the deposition of *Isaac Comnenus and his military government. C. weakened the army despite the grave consequences of this step, reinforced the senatorial class and gave a large number of burghers of Constantinople access to the Senate.

A. A. Vasiliev, *History of the Byzantine Empire* (1952).

CONSTANTINE-CYRIL See CYRIL.

CONSTANTINE KEPHALAS (CEPHALAS) (10th century) Byzantine poet and satirical writer. Brought to the imperial court and protected by *Constantine VII, he developed the Greek epigram. His *Anthologia Palatina* is the largest collection of epigrams, containing about 3700 entries and poems, many of them on love and secular life.

W. R. Paton, ed., *The Greek Anthology*, 5 vols. (1916-18).

CONSTANTINE THE AFRICAN (c. 1020-87) Physician and translator. According to tradition, he was born at Carthage, in northern Africa, to a Christian family, living under Moslem rule. He travelled throughout Asia and Africa, acquiring the medical knowledge of the Arabs and learning from their books. He settled at Salerno, southern Italy, (c. 1040), where the first medical school in Christian Europe was established. During his sojourn at Salerno, he was appointed secretary to *Robert Guiscard, the Norman leader of southern Italy, and became acquainted with the members of the school. In the middle of the 11th century he became a monk at *Monte Cassino, where he devoted his time to translating Arabic medical books into Latin. As the Arabic works were essentially translations of 2nd-century Greek treatises, C. thus brought the Greek medical heritage to the medieval western world.

M. Steinschneider, *Konstantinus Africanus und seine arabischen Quellen* (1866).

CONSTANTINE TICH Tsar of *Bulgaria (1257-77). He was a member of a family which opposed Tsar Michael Assen, against whom he rebelled and whom he dethroned. C. married Irene, daughter of *Theodor II, emperor of Byzantium. This alliance allowed him to establish his reign in Bulgaria and to try to expand his power in the Balkans. After the Palaeologi seized power in Byzantium he concluded a treaty with *Charles of Anjou in 1270.

F. Doelger, *Bulgarien und Byzanz* (1940).

CONSTANTINOPLE The capital of the Byzantine empire, on the European side of the Bosporus and the Marmara Sea. The ancient city of Byzantium was chosen by *Constantine the Great as the Roman empire's new capital, to which he transferred the seat of his government in 330, changing its name to C. This shift led the Roman aristocracy from the West to settle in C., thus making it a bilingual capital. Only after the 6th century did Latin disappear and did C. acquire a Greek character. In building the "New Rome" Constantine sought to imitate the original capital: C. was built on seven hills, divided into 14 quarters, and its palaces and urban institutions paralleled those of Rome. Like their Roman counterparts, the inhabitants of C. were given a free supply of bread. From its founding, C. had a Christian character and its bishops were considered second to those of Rome The *Oecumenical Council of C. in 381, contributed to its development as one of the most important centres of the Christian Church. With the final division of the Roman empire in 395, C. became the capital of the Eastern empire, or *Byzantium. The growth of the city was considerable in the 4th and 5th centuries and, in 413, the wall of Constantine was demolished and a new wall erected by Theodosius II, which doubled the urban area. Immigration from the Latin West and from the countryside made C. a cosmopolitan centre, but it also led to antagonism among the heterogeneous populace. During the reign of *Justinian, its institutions were reformed and the city was embellished. The building of the cathedral of *Santa Sophia and of the collossal imperial palace mark the rise of Byzantine architecture. The city school, founded in 425, was transferred to new grounds near the imperial palace. After 529, when Justinian dissolved the famous Platonic Academy of *Athens, the school of C. became the empire's most important educational institution. Trade development in the empire made C. the greatest economic centre in the Mediterranean world in the 6th century.

C.'s fortifications aborted the attempts of the *Persians (616), Avars (626), *Arabs (669, 672-78, 717) and the *Bulgars to conquer it. But the city suffered damages by the frequent revolts and clashes between the principal factions of the military and civil nobility after the death of Justinian. The loss of the eastern provinces to the Arabs in the 7th century and the decline of the "barbarian" West were factors in strengthening the Greek element in the city and even in its becoming an economic, cultural and religious centre. C. reached its zenith in the 10th century and particularly during the reign of *Constantine VII Porphyrogenitus, when the cultural and artistic renaissance of the empire was essentially that of its capital city. The political and administrative centralism of the Byzantine empire also had its effects on the development of C. The senatorial class, composed of high officials and landowners, settled in the city and contributed to its architectural and artistic flourishing. Moreover, in 1082, when the Venetians were granted trade privileges and their own quarter, C. developed into a thriving commercial centre, expanding out of the Galata quarter on the northern side of the Golden Horn (an arm of the Bosporus). C.'s greatness and opulence made a striking impression on foreigners, especially the *Crusaders. The latter's quarrels with its inhabitants, whom they wished to subordinate to their feudal nobility, according to Western customs, created a gap between East and West. The West blamed the "perfidy of the Greeks" for their failures against the Moslems.

The participants in the Fourth *Crusade (1204) conquered C. and wreaked havoc on the city. After three days of virtual genocide and destruction, what remained of C. was made the capital of the *Latin empire of Constantinople (1204-61). C.'s commerce was handled by Venice, its Orthodox churches were Catholicized and its Greek school was closed. The Byzantine restoration of 1261 under the *Palaeologi was in a sense a renaissance for C., but the city was never to reach its former glory. It remained one of the greatest cities in the world, attracting Italian merchants and visitors from Europe and Asia. But with the advances of the *Ottoman Turks at the end of the 14th century, C. became a frontier city. It fell to the Turks in 1453.

D. A. Miller, *Imperial Constantinople* (1968).

CONSTITUTIO IN FAVOREM PRINCIPUM (The Constitution in favour of the Princes) Constitutional document issued in 1231 by *Frederick II in favour of the German princes. It confirms the feudal rights of the higher nobility (princes), who enjoyed full government powers in their respective territories, to the point that Germany was divided into hundreds of semi-indepen-

dent principalities. The document thus marked a setback in the policy of the *Hohenstaufen in Germany, after nearly a century of efforts by *Frederick Barbarossa, *Henry VI and Frederick himself, to impose a central government, based on a powerful imperial demesne and collaboration with the cities. It was issued after a period of abuses by Prince Henry, Frederick's son and representative in Germany, which led the nobles to rebel against him.

E. Kantorowicz, *Frederick the Second* (1929).

CONSTITUTIONES AEGIDIANAE A code of law issued in 1357 by Cardinal *Aegidius Albornoz for Rome and the Papal States in central Italy after he restored order and papal authority, on behalf of the court of *Avignon. The ordinances, named after him,

Santa Sophia Cathedral, Constantinople

The Contarini Palace at Venice

concerned the administration of papal territories, and were to remain in force until the beginning of the 19th century.

F. Filippini, *Il cardinale Egidio Albornoz* (1933).

CONSTITUTIONS OF CLARENDON   See CLARENDON.

CONSTITUTIONS OF MELFI   See MELFI.

CONSUBSTANTIAL   The literal meaning of the word is "of one and the same substance or being". The term was used from the 4th century in Orthodox and Catholic theology to express the eternal relationship between the components of the Holy Trinity – God the Father, Jesus Christ the Son, and the Holy Spirit – believed to be the same substance.

W. C. Wand, *The Four Great Heresies* (1955).

CONSUL   The term originated in ancient Rome, where it designated the highest office in the republic. It continued to be used in the Middle Ages, but gradually its meaning changed: while, in the transition era (5th-6th centuries), it referred to the high dignity conferred by Byzantine emperors upon Germanic kings, in the 7th century it lost its connection with the classical term. In Italy, southern France and Christian Spain, the Cs. were a college of urban leaders (8-12 persons), who ruled the city and represented its interests before the political authority. In the Latin medieval chronicles of the 9th-13th centuries, the word is synonymous with *count.

H. Pirenne, *Medieval Cities* (1925).

CONTADO   Italian word meaning county. In feudal Italy (9th-13th centuries), the term was applied both to the territory that fell under the jurisdiction of a count and to the government privileges vested in it. Through the process of marriages, inheritances and pious donations, the *Carolingian C., which had been a complete administrative unit, was divided among aristocratic families who settled in the cities of northern and central Italy. At the end of the 11th century, the rural C. and the urban C. were two different entities; the former carried on the feudal form of government, while the latter was the basis of the autonomous Italian city-state of the 12th-13th centuries.

J. K. Hyde, *Society and Politics in Medieval Italy* (1973).

CONTARINI   Venetian aristocratic family, influential in the 12th century. The family, which acquired its wealth through commerce with the East, gave the Republic many doges (chief magistrates) and members of the High Council. In the 14th century they were active in exploring trade routes with China and India and in establishing commercial relations with the *Mongol empire. Its members also held important posts in the Venetian administration of the *Latin empire of Constantinople and Greece. Their palace, on the Grand Canal in Venice, became an artistic centre of the Renaissance in the 15th century.

H. Kretschmayr, *Geschichte von Venedig* (1920).

CONVERSI   The term, used in the Middle Ages and particularly in monastic society, to designate those who elected the monastic way of life but had not yet taken vows. By extension, it meant the lay brothers in the monasteries and in the military-religious orders. The legal relationship between the C. and the regular members of monastic communities varied, according to the institutions.

COPENHAGEN (medieval Danish: copmandshavn "merchants' harbour")   City in Denmark, on the island of Zealand, on the Oresund Strait, separating Sweden from Denmark. C. was a small fishing village until the 11th century, when it began to develop into a commercial centre. The fortification built in 1167 by archbishop *Absalon of Lund, as a defence against piracy, is considered the basis of the new city. In 1254 the merchants' community was granted privileges, among them the "urban liberties", of self-government. The 13th and 14th centuries were a period of continuous wars with the German *Hanse, with C. being burnt and reconstructed several times. Its proximity to the capital and religious centre of Denmark, Roskilde, led the kings to develop an interest in C. C. became the capital of Denmark in 1443.

S. Andersen, *Copenhagen in the Middle Ages* (1949).

COPTS   The descendants of the ancient Egyptians who continued to manifest their ethnical and cultural identity after the Hellenization of Egypt. The C. converted to Christianity in the second half of the 3rd century, and, in the 4th century, developed the tradition that the Coptic Church was founded by St. Mark. This tradition is maintained in the official title of their religious leader: "Pope of Alexandria and Patriarch of the See of St. Mark". Their adoption of *Monophysitism in the 5th century was considered an expression of their identity against the orthodoxy of the Greeks. After the condemnation of the Monophysites by the Council of *Chalcedon in 451, they set up their own church and were oppressed by the Byzantine authorities, particularly under *Justinian, in the 6th century. Their loyalty to the Byzantine empire thus diminished and, in 641, they welcomed the Arab conquest of Egypt as a liberation. The Moslems granted them religious freedom, with the restrictions of the statute of *dhimmi. In the 7th and 8th centuries, some persecutions and fiscal burdens favoured a trend of Islamization among them. This decreased their number, but also created greater solidarity amongst the remnants, organized in communities under the spiritual government of the *abbuna* "father", corresponding to abbot. The C. established an ecclesiastical hierarchy under the supreme leadership of the Coptic patriarch of Alexandria. The economic pros-

The cathedral of Durham, England, built in the 12th century

perity of Egypt under the *Fatimids also affected the C., who became an important community in *Cairo and other cities.

The C. developed their liturgy and theological works in their own language, translating the Bible and the early writings of the Church Fathers into Coptic, which had become a written language in the 1st century, using the Greek alphabet with additional vowels. In the 5th century their cult spread to *Ethiopia. An autonomous Ethiopian Church, with formal ties to the patriarch of Alexandria, was eventually established.
W. H. Worrell, *A Short Account of the Copts* (1945).

CORBEIL Town near Paris, one of the royal residences in the 11th-13th centuries. The town is famous for the Treaty of C. of 1258, concluded between representatives of *Louis IX, king of France, and *James I of Aragon, whereby the problem of the *Carolingian march of Spain, formally under the suzerainty of the French kingdom, was resolved. While the French monarchy relinquished its claims over the march, and recognized the independence of the Catalonian part of Aragon, the kings of Aragon abandoned their claims to Languedoc, with the exception of the city of Montpellier.
C. Petit-Dutaillis, *Feudal Monarchy in France and England* (1952).

CORBIE Famous *Benedictine monastery, founded on the *Merovingian estate of C., in Picardy, near the city of Amiens. Its first community, composed of monks of *Luxeuil, settled there in 660. The abbey became a literary and intellectual centre in northern France, with one of the greatest libraries north of the Alps in the early Middle Ages. Its monks helped propagate Christianity in Saxony during the reign of *Charlemagne, and contributed to the *Carolingian renaissance of the 9th century.
P. Riché, *Education et Culture dans l'Occident Barbare* (1962).

CORBINIATUS, St. (d. 730) Born at Melun, France. He was active in the Christian mission to Germany under *Pepin II. Sent to Bavaria, he founded the bishopric of Freising and was consecrated its first bishop. C. brought the clergy with him and expanded Frankish influence in Bavaria.
R. Bauerreiss, *Kirchengeschichte Bayerns* (1958).

CORDOBA City in Andalusia, Spain. The ancient Roman city of C. declined at the beginning of the Middle Ages and after its conquest by the *Visigoths became an insignificant provincial town. C. was conquered by the Arabs in 711, and became the seat of government of Moslem Spain in 719. The city flourished, reaching its zenith under the *Ummayad caliphs (755-1031), when it was an important political, cultural and economic centre and one of the most prosperous cities of western Europe. Its leather products were sold in Europe as well as in Africa, but its silk industry and its goldsmiths also contributed to its fame. With the decline of the Ummayad caliphate, the city fell under the rule of Berber governors (1013) and it declined from the middle of the 11th century, although it continued to be one of the most important centres of the Arabic and Jewish renaissance in Spain. Its school was among the most prestigious scientific and philosophical centres in the West and the most famous centre of *Aristotelianism. Its eminent teachers and thinkers included *Ibn Rushd (Averroes) and *Maimonides. Under the

Fragment of a 5th-century woven Coptic textile

*Almoravides, C. knew a period of prosperity and its most splendid Ummayad monuments, the mosque and the Alcazar – considered in the West masterpieces of Moslem art – were completed. When the *Almohades conquered the city in 1148 and destroyed its school, some of its Moslem, Jewish and Christian intellectuals fled. But C. still remained one of the largest cities in Europe, with its population variously estimated at between 100,000 and 500,000 (the lower figure is probably more correct). In 1236, C. was conquered by King *Ferdinand III of Castile, who built a Catholic cathedral within its great mosque. Its importance declined and, after a series of plagues culminating in the *Black Death, its population decreased; in 1408 it was estimated at 70,000 persons – which still represents a large city for the period. C. was one of the most flourishing artistic centres in Spain. Its mosque-cathedral, the *Mezquita,* with its 850 columns, is one of the best examples of Arab and Christian architecture and design of the 10th-14th centuries.
M. S. Hierro, *Cordoba* (1963).

CORFU Island in the Ionean Sea, near the western coast of Greece. C. belonged to the Byzantine empire, as part of the province of Epirus. In 1078 it was attacked and invaded by the Normans of southern Italy under *Robert Guiscard and, after his death, the conquest of C. became one of the strategic goals of the Norman and Sicilian kings. When C. was conquered by the army of the Fourth *Crusade, the island passed to Venice, but continued to be disputed between the Venetians, the Byzantines, who held Epirus, and the kings of Sicily-Naples. At the beginning of the 14th century, it became part of the Venetian empire.
A. A. Vasiliev, *History of Byzantium* (1952).

CORINTH City in Greece, in the northeast Peloponnese. C. belonged to the Byzantine empire and, until the 12th century, was a small provincial town. In 1147 it was attacked and ravaged by *Roger II of Sicily,

The Mezquita *at Cordoba, Spain, built in the 10th century*

whose attempt to conquer it was part of his eastern expansionist policy. In 1204 it fell to the Crusaders who turned it into a Catholic bishopric within the principality of *Morea. During this period C. became a cultural centre, where Greek and Latin intellectuals gathered and transmitted the classical heritage to the West. C. was conquered by the *Ottoman Turks in 1430.

W. Miller, *The Latins in the East* (1913).

CORLEONE Town in Sicily, south of Palermo. C. was an autonomous Christian enclave when the Arabs ruled Sicily in the 10th and 11th centuries. Under the Normans the local leaders continued their autonomous life. But in 1282, during the *Sicilian Vespers, the inhabitants of C. followed those of Palermo in revolting against the Angevin government under *Charles of Anjou. They proclaimed C. a popular commune, which was later recognized by the Aragonese government.

S. Runciman, *The Sicilian Vespers* (1958).

CORONATION OATHS The oaths taken by an emperor upon being crowned. With the spread of feudalism and the growth of power of the church in 9th-century western Europe, the Byzantine custom of C. – according to which a new emperor swore at his coronation that he would be a faithful Christian – was adapted, with important changes. Under the influence of *Hincmar, archbishop of Rheims, who imposed the oath on *Louis II in 877, the king had to swear, before his anointment in the cathedral church, to maintain liberties and privileges of the churches and of his vassals. The oath, pronounced during the coronation ceremony, was accompanied by the issue of a "charter of liberties" – the monarch's first official act. The custom spread throughout western Europe, and was considered not only a part of the coronation ceremony, but also a constitutional act, binding the monarch to respect laws and customs of the realm. In England, from the 13th century, particular reference was made to the *Magna Charta in the C.

B. Wilkinson, *The Coronation in History* (1953).

CORPUS CHRISTI (Latin: the body of Christ) In Christian theology, from the time of St. *Augustine, the term was applied to the whole community of the faithful, considered as the body of Christ. In medieval thought it expressed the organic concept of society, primarily as a religious body. In the 13th century, the feast of C. was instituted, following the vision of St. Juliana, a nun of Liège, who, in 1230, asked that it be celebrated together with the feast of the Holy *Eucharist, on the Thursday after *Trinity Sunday. The feast's liturgy was established in the 14th century, but most of it had already been composed in the 13th century by St. *Thomas Aquinas.

EC, III.

CORPUS JURIS CANONICI The most comprehensive body of *canon law of the Roman Catholic Church, composed of: 1) the *Decretum* of *Gratian, a systematic compilation of canons until 1140; 2) the *Decretals of Pope *Gregory IX, composed as a supplement to the *Decretum* by St. Raymond of *Peñafort, at the request of the pope, and promulgated in 1230; 3) the *Sext*, a compilation of decretals, added by *Boniface VIII; 4) the *Clementines*, of *Clement IV, promulgated in 1317 by *John XXII; 5) the *Extravagantes,* a compilation of canons and decretals of John XXII,

published in 1325; 6) the *Extravagantes Communes,* canons and decretals covering the period between 1261-1471.

Ed. E. Friedberg, *C.I.C.* (1880).

CORPUS JURIS CIVILIS See CODE OF JUSTINIAN.

CORRECTORIUM A book compiled in the 13th century containing a set of variant readings, to "correct" the corrupted texts of the Latin *Vulgate. During the 13th century several universities and monastic orders compiled their own *correctoria,* the most important of which were those of the *Dominicans and *Franciscans.

H. Denifle, *Die mittelalterlichen Correctoria* (1892).

CORSICA An island in the Mediterranean Sea, north of Sardinia and west of Italy. As a province of the later Roman empire, C. was invaded and conquered in 430 by the *Vandals, who established there a provincial government of their kingdom. In 552 it was conquered by the Byzantines and annexed to their empire. With the empire's decline in the 8th century, C. passed to the *Lombards and became part of their kingdom of Italy. *Pepin the Short promised the island to the Papal State, a commitment made good by his son *Charlemagne in 774. Papal rule proved ineffective, with the island being several times invaded and devastated by the Arabs and Berbers of north Africa in the 9th and 10th centuries. In the 11th century C. was contested by Genoa and Pisa, and in 1077, Pope *Gregory VII granted it as an estate to the archbishop of Pisa. But Genoese influence continued to be felt, despite the religious authority of the Pisan church, and, in the 12th century, the overlordship of C. was divided between the two city-states of Italy. The Genoese victory at the Battle of Melloria in 1284, made Genoa the sole ruler of the island. While the townsmen and peasants remained faithful to Genoa, the rural landowners revolted, turning for support to King James II of Aragon. In 1296 the Aragonese king, with the consent of Pope *Boniface VIII, conquered the island. After a long war, C. was redivided between Genoa and Aragon, but the rule of the latter was weak. In 1420 a new war broke out. The Aragonese won, consolidated their government, and compelled the Genoese to withdraw, despite the large support Genoa enjoyed among the populace. But in 1434 the Genoese expelled the Aragonese army.

P. Arrighi, *Histoire de la Corse* (1971).

CORTENUOVA, BATTLE OF During the war between *Federick II and the towns of the Lombard League, the imperial army attacked and defeated the urban militia at C. in 1237. This victory led to the dissolution of the League; most of the cities involved surrendered to Frederick, who imposed his rule in northern Italy through the appointment of an imperial governor in Milan.

E. Kantorowicz, *Federick II* (1932).

CORTES (Courts) The name given to the assemblies of nobles and city representatives in the kingdoms of León and Castile. While such assemblies were sporadic until the 13th century and were mainly convened to approve special taxes, they became a common government organ, including the participation of the high clergy, from the 13th century on. Rooted in the feudal practice of the *consilium,* the C. were regularly summoned to discuss constitutional and political matters as well as fiscal problems of the realm. Their influence varied according to the character of the monarch of the time and to the unity of the nobility, which reached its peak in the 14th and 15th centuries. Even after the establishment of the powerful monarchy of *Ferdinand and *Isabella, the C. continued to meet, however, much of their influence was lost.

P. E. Russell, *Spain* (1973).

CORVADA (Corvée) In the Romanic tongues, and later in French, the term meant request or demand. It was used to express the requisition of the compulsory work peasants had to undertake on their lord's demesne, as part of the duties due to the lord. The C. was set down on the basis of the number of days this work was to be done. The amount varied from 3 days per week to 21 days per year, according to need, custom and status of the peasant (free-man being less burdened than the serf). The C. entailed a variety of activities, the most common being field work on the *manorial demesne, or the maintenance of the plough equipment. Work within the castle or the manorial court was also included: women worked under the supervision of the lady of the castle. In the second half of the 12th century, the large number of peasants involved became a burden to the lords, who had to put them to use and feed them: therefore, the C. commuted into tax payments, part of which were used to hire field workers, the *famuli,* whose employment was more profitable. After the demographic losses of the 14th century and especially the *Black Death, the lords tried to reinstate the C. practice, this, however, led to peasant revolts. The most famous was the *Jacquerie* in France and the great revolt of 1381 in England.

G. Duby, *Rural Economy and Country Life in the Medieval West* (1948).

CORVEY Abbey in Saxony, founded after 778. *Charlemagne established a community of monks from *Corbie there (hence the name) with the aim of Christianizing the conquered territories of *Saxony. In the 9th and 10th centuries the abbey became a very important artistic and literary centre in Germany and, under *Otto I, its monks contributed to the renaissance of the imperial ideology.

R. Folz, *L'Idée de l'Empire en Occident* (1958).

COSMAS AND DAMIAN, Sts. The patron saints of physicians. There is no definite information available about their lives, and it seems that their legend was taken from the mythological story of the *Dioscuri.* According to the tradition developed from the 5th century, they were twin brothers who practised medicine without claiming payment from their patients. Both are said to have been martyrs. Their cult first developed in the Byzantine empire and later (from the 6th century) spread to the West and became very popular.

L. Deubner, *Kosmas und Damian* (1907).

COSMAS INDICOPLEUSTES (Greek: Indian navigator) Sixth-century geographer. C. was an Alexandrian merchant who travelled to India. His *Christian Topography,* in 12 volumes (*c.* 547) was written on the basis of his travel notes, after his conversion to monasticism. It contains important information about the Indian peninsula, Ceylon and the neighbouring countries. In it, C. attacked the Ptolemaic system (see *Geography), favouring several fantastic astronomical doctrines, which were in accord with a literal understanding of the Bible.

E. O. Winstedt, *The Christian Topography of Cosmas Indicopleustes* (1909).

COSMAS MELODUS (of Maïuna) Poet; born probably at Jerusalem, about 700, he was educated by a monk named Cosmas, under whose influence he entered the monastery of St. *Sabas in Judaea in 732. Nine years later, he became bishop of Maïuna, near Gaza. He was famous for his liturgical poems, especially canons composed for the great feasts. His poetry is brilliant in form and was inspired by biblical language.

H. M. Stevenson, *Cosmas Melodus* (1885).

COSMAS OF PRAGUE (1045-1125) Historian. Born in Bohemia, he studied at the cathedral school of Liège at a relatively late age and was ordained a priest in 1099. At the beginning of the 12th century he returned to his native country and became dean of the episcopal chapter of Prague. He was the first Czech historian and began the *Chronicle of Bohemia* at the age of 75, keeping it up to date until his death. As a historical work, it was influenced by the chroniclers of Lorraine and the Moselle region, with whom he had probably been acquainted during his formative years. The information included is entirely original, as no other sources on Bohemia were extant at the time. The chronicle is written in Latin, but includes several Slavic expressions. These Slavic terms have proven useful in the study of the early Bohemian language. In the later generations, C. was named the "Herodote of Bohemia".

MGH, Scriptores, IX.

COSMOLOGY The medieval C. is rooted in the biblical view of creation as interpreted by the Christian Fathers of the Church, in Greek philosophy and natural sciences, and in Arab studies. The Greek achievements were adopted through the writings of Pliny the Elder on natural history and those of St. *Augustine. However, the most important source of medieval C. was the biblical view of creation, which emphasized that the Cosmos was divinely created out of nothing, according to God's will. According to this medieval C. there is no logical arrangement of cosmic elements, they are to be perceived as they are. The understanding of the cosmic order is rooted, rather in divine revelation. This view was accepted as the official doctrine of the Church. It was formulated by St. Augustine, who denounced the attempts of Clement of Alexandria (2nd century) to explain creation through the existence of a particular divine substance, which was the basis of the four elements: earth, water, fire and air. In 1215 the Fourth *Lateran Council promulgated this view as the canonical C. of the Roman Catholic Church and *Thomas of Aquinas supported it by an argumentation based on his philosophical method. Thus revelation was integrated in the Christian doctrine of C. On the other hand, from the 13th century, under the influence of Arabic science, astronomers developed a scientific cosmological view, named by Thomas of *Cantimpré the "Aristotelian" C. This view, based on the observations of natural phenomena, already undertaken by Roger *Bacon, developed the 12th-century theory of the existence of the "Macrocosmos", which is beyond human approach and can only be explained through revelation, and the "Microcosmos", to be sought and studied by human beings. These views lasted until the establishment of the Copernican theories during the Renaissance.

A. D. Sertillanges, *L'Idée de la création et ses retentisse-ments en Philosophie* (1945).

COUCY A feudal castle in Picardy, northern France, built in the late 11th century and rebuilt in typical Gothic fashion in the 13th century. The lords of C. rose to an important stature in the 11th century thanks to the decline of the counts of *Vermandois, whose vassals they were. They took advantage of the feudal anarchy in the province to acquire new estates and accumulate wealth through every possible means, including brigandage. Thomas de Marle, who imposed terror in Vermandois and Picardy, was a typical case. He took part in the First *Crusade, leaving in 1098 after the siege of Antioch. As a result of his behaviour, Thomas was excommunicated by church councils, being convicted as a peace-breaker. In addition, King *Louis VI personally conducted two wars against him, until the latter was defeated and put to death (1130). The later generations of the family of C. became integrated in the ranks of the higher nobility of France; in the 13th and 14th centuries, they faithfully served the monarchy and were rewarded with large estates and military charges at court. They tried to change the image of their predecessors and, when the participation of an ancestor in the Crusades became a symbol of higher social status, they developed a new epic-type, that of *Thomas de Marle, who was transformed by epic poetry into one of the heroes of the Crusade and the conqueror of Jerusalem. During the *Hundred Year's War, the family distinguished itself in the French army.

T. Du Plessis, *Histoire de la ville et des seigneurs de Coucy* (1728).

COUNCIL (Latin: concilium) The term denotes ecclesiastical assemblies convened by legitimate authority to discuss current problems, theological, canonical, or disciplinary, which concerned the Church. While in Eastern and Greek-Orthodox *Churches the Greek term *synod*, i.e. congregation, prevailed, the Roman Catholic Church used the term C. The *canon law specifies four categories of Cs.:

1) the diocesan C.: convoked by the bishop, with the participation of the abbots and the priests of the diocese, and dealing with local affairs and the implementation of discipline and the canons;

2) the provincial C.: convoked and presided over by the archbishop, with the participation of bishops, abbots and other members of the ecclesiastical hierarchy, and dealing with provincial affairs and the reviewing of complaints;

3) the general C.: convoked by the pope or in his name, and including the participation of the prelates of one or several countries; its decisions, named *canons, had a legislative, as well as an operative authority. The most famous of the general Cs. was that of *Clermont, in 1096, where the *Crusade was promulgated. The decisions of general Cs. were pending the approval of the pope, when he did not participate in person;

4) the oecumenical (world) C.: the highest authority of the Church, convoked by the emperor (in Byzantium) or by the pope (in the Roman Catholic Church), and dealing with problems concerning the principles of faith. The first oecumenical C., that of *Nicaea of 325, was assembled by *Constantine the Great and defined the creed of the Orthodox-Catholic faith. The first eight oecumenical Cs. (325, 381, 431, 451, 553, 681, 787

and 869, all of which were assembled in the East), are recognized both by the Orthodox and Catholic Churches, while later Cs. are considered oecumenical only by each particular church. The Roman Catholic Church resumed the practice of the oecumenical C. only in the 12th century, when the 9th C. (*Lateran I), was assembled by Pope *Calixtus II in 1124. Until the end of the Middle Ages only twelve Cs. assembled in the West were considered oecumenical. While an oecumenical C. was considered legitimate only when convoked by the pope, it was not clear whether or not the C. had supremacy over the pope. The issue was explicitly developed by the *Conciliar movement in the late 14th and in the 15th century, but it was not accepted by the papacy. Participation in oecumenical Cs. was generally limited to the episcopal rank and some great abbots, qualified as the Fathers of the C., however, distinguished theologians were also included. The decisions of the oecumenical C. became part of the canon law.

S. J. Hefele - H. Leclerc, *Histoire des Conciles* (1913).

COUNCIL, KING'S See KING'S COUNCIL.

COUNCIL OF THE TEN A Venetian organ of government, established in 1310. Its members, drawn from the Great Council of the Republic, had wide powers, especially regarding the administration of justice. Their deliberations were kept secret and their decisions were final.

G. Maranini, *La Constitutione di Venezia* (1931).

COUNT (Latin: comes) In the later Roman empire, the term to designate the commanders of military units. It was adopted in the early Middle Ages by the Germanic tribes to denote the close companions of the king, among whom were chosen the highest government officials. During the reign of *Charlemagne the C. was the appointed governor of a territorial district (the *comitatus*, or *county), where he represented the emperor and held public authority, including military command, administration of justice and fiscal prerogatives. Nevertheless, some of the king's companions in the imperial palace continued to bear the title *comes palatinus* (the palatine C.) and were charged with political, juridical and administrative duties. In the 9th and 10th centuries, the Cs. seized public power (through the regalian privileges) and authority over their disintegrating counties became hereditary; on similar lines, the *earls emerged in Anglo-Saxon England. With the reorganization of the feudal principalities of western Europe in the 11th century the C. became one of the highest members of the nobility. The title, however, was attached to the historical counties of the 9th century, even when it no longer represented the same territory in actuality. Thus, for example, the C. of Alsace ruled only over one part of the ancient county, but continued to bear the title, while other lords, whose estates were larger, were not allowed to bear it (e. g. the lords of Bourbon). In the 13th and 14th centuries, with the hierarchical organization of the nobility, the rank of C. was made second to the duke; kings interested in promoting nobles to the rank of C. began to establish new counties.

G. Duby, *Hommes et structures du Moyen Age* (1973).

COUNTY The feudal C., as it emerged and developed in western Europe in the 11th century, was formally a continuation of the *Carolingian *comitatus. But in nature, very little of the earlier organization was preserved, especially concerning its identity with public authority over a specific territory. By the year 1000, the assemblies of free-men (the *mallus*), which used to be convened by the *counts on behalf of the king, were replaced by assemblies of vassals of the count, whose jurisdiction did not necessarily correspond with the ancient boundaries of the *comitatus*. Thus, with some exceptions, the most notable being the organization of the *shires in England, the new Cs. represented the quasi-autonomous power of the count. In many cases, feudal divisions limited the count's power and, during the 11th century, only strong historical traditions preserved the term. In other cases counts were able to impose their rule on greater territories and founded real states with full economic, social and political activity (such as *Flanders, *Barcelona, *Toulouse-Languedoc, *Savoy, etc.). The reorganization of the feudal principalities in the late 11th and 12th century, transformed the C. into a political and economical reality, with its own institutions (developed from the assemblies of the vassals), administration and judicial system. In the late Middle Ages many counts were compelled to allow their vassals and the boroughs to establish "Estates" which became representative assemblies, voting on the taxes and dealing with the administration.

In England the C. had a different nature. With very few exceptions, such as Chester, which was granted to a feudal family, the C. as a unit was a royal district, administrated by the *sheriff in his capacity as royal official. While the greater vassals (the barons) were directly linked to the kingship and the royal court, the lesser vassals (the knights) and the representatives of boroughs and of the *hundreds, were put under the jurisdiction of the sheriff.

F. L. Ganshof, *Feudalism* (1965).

COUR DES COMPTES See CHAMBRE DES COMPTES.

COURT (Latin: curia) The Latin term *curia*, with juridical meaning, was adopted by medieval society with many changes, under the influence of traditions of the Germanic tribes. In the Germanic concepts, the primary duty of a ruler was to administer justice, whether through leading the army or in his estate (German: *hufe*, later *hof*, Latin: *curtis* = C.). Thus, in the early medieval kingdoms, the C., which included a number of members of the royal household (noble men, clerks and servants), became an organ of government exercising political, administrative and juridical powers. With the spread of *feudalism in the 9th century, the term was no longer used to distinguish the sovereign's government, but also served to indicate assemblies of vassals of various lords. Thus, the word was used in the church (the pope and every bishop having his *curia*), in the great feudal estates (such as the Cs. of dukes, counts, etc.), as well as in the royal administration (*curia regis*). Gradually the great vassals, who were occupied in their own estates, appeared less frequently at the royal C., limiting their participation in the Council (see *King's Council), and the daily work at the C. was done by lesser vassals and by servants (*ministeriales* in Germany). Until the end of the 12th century the distinction between the public (i.e. sovereign) character of the C. and the private one (the household) was superficial, and only in the 13th century was the royal C. reorganized as an organ of the government, with the notable exception of England. There constitutional development had anteceded that of Continental Europe; the public

nature of the royal C. was already in existence after the Norman Conquest of 1066.

The development of the administrative and government activities in the 13th century led to an increase in the number of personnel at the C. "Plenary C." corresponded with assemblies of the barons or the high nobility and were named "High C." or "Haute Cour", but the real work was done by specialized personnel in the various chambers. The four high offices of the feudal C. (the *Sénéschal, responsible for the administration of justice on behalf of the sovereign, the *Constable, commanding the army, the *Steward, responsible for the administration of the estates, and the *Chamberlain, in charge of the treasury) became complex services, with their own Cs. supervised by the *Chancellor and his C. Moreover, the employment of specialists, as, for example, people with legal training, led to the establishment of specialized Cs., such as that of Parliament (in Continental Europe, the High C. of Justice) and the C. of Accounts (*Cour des Comptes), which functioned without the actual presence of the king. Thus, in the 14th century, the term C. had various meanings, whose precise definition required a qualification. Moreover, the notion of the royal C. was extended to the multitude of noblemen and ladies, who lived at the royal palace together with poets, artists and entertainers. Such Cs. originated in the 12th century in some feudal castles, where the lords used to gather the nobility and men of letters, in accordance with the code of *chivalry. The C. of the counts of Champagne in the second half of the 12th century became the model of such high-society gatherings and was introduced in the royal and princely Cs. at the end of the Middle Ages.

R. Fawtier, *Histoire des Institutions Françaises au Moyen Age*, II (1958);
J. Huisinga, *The Waning of the Middle Ages* (1922).

COURT OF CHAIN Maritime courts, which convened in that building of the harbour in which the chain, which closed off the entry to the harbour at night, was kept (whence its name). The decisions of the C. were made on the basis of some maritime codes, such as the Rhodian, for Byzantium and the East, the Amalfian and Barcelonese for the western Mediterranean, or the Customs of Oléron for western France and England (see *Law, Maritime).

COURT OF PIEPOWDERS Borough courts established in 13th-century England to judge cases of merchants who came to fairs and needed a quick trial. The word "piepowders" derives from the French *pieds poudrés*, which referred to wanderers who had no time to brush their shoes.

A. Harding, *The Law Courts of Medieval England* (1973).

COURT OF THE EXCHEQUER See EXCHEQUER.

COURTENAY A French family from the Ile-de-France, whose estates were concentrated near Orléans. The knights of C. took part in the First *Crusade. Upon their return, the head of the family, Joscelin, became closely associated with the royal court. His younger son, Joscelin, maternally related to *Baldwin of Bourg, count of Edessa, was granted the county in 1118 upon Baldwin's election as king of Jerusalem. Joscelin I was thus the founder of the Crusaders' branch of the House, which ruled *Edessa until its conquest by *Zengi in 1144. After the loss of Edessa, Count Joscelin

II retired to the kingdom of Jerusalem, where the family received an important barony in western Galilee. With the marriage of his daughter, Agnes, to the future king *Amalric I in 1157, then count of Jaffa and Ascalon, the family reached the height of its influence and maintained it despite the divorce of Amalric, at the request of the barons, when he inherited the crown in 1161. Agnes was the mother of *Baldwin IV, and as a result, the C. family played a major role in the political activities of the kingdom of Jerusalem between 1173-87. Her brother, Joscelin III, was the Senéschal of the kingdom and in 1187 commanded Acre, which he surrendered to *Saladin. With his death, the Crusaders' branch of the C. became extinct.

In France, however, the lords of C. became related with the *Capetian dynasty through the marriage of Isabel of C. to Peter I, the fourth son of King *Louis VI. He became lord of C. and founded the Capetian branch of the family, which received the county of Nevers in 1184. His son, *Peter II, became Latin emperor of Constantinople in 1217.

Another branch of the family settled in England.

P. Anselme, *Histoire Généalogique de la Maison de France* (1736).

COURTOIS (Courtly) A term denoting the manners and conduct of *chivalry and the nobility. Among its expressions were courtly love, literature, poetry and romance. These were meant to set examples of behaviour to society according to the ideals of chivalry, as formulated in the 12th century, and which reached its height in the 15th century. The noun "courtesy" (*courtoisie*) derived from this adjective.

S. Painter, *French Chivalry* (1940).

COURTRAI Town in *Flanders. C. became famous in the 14th century, when the French army, sent by *Philip IV to repress the burghers' party of the county, was defeated by the local militia. As result of this humiliating loss, the French monarchy lost control of Flanders, where pro-English feelings prevailed. Increased tensions eventually led to the *Hundred Years' War, although this battle was not its main cause.

S. T. Wood, *Philip the Fair and Boniface VIII* (1973).

COURTS OF LOVE The C. were developed as a part of the feudal *courts, being a form of feminine *chivalry. They began in southern France, especially in the duchy of *Aquitaine, and found their perfect expression in the second half of the 12th century in the court of *Champagne, whose model was imitated elsewhere. A "court" was a social gathering presided over by the lady of the castle, the assembled knights and ladies behaving in their most "gentle" manner, listening to and composing love songs. The ideal form of love was platonic, and always hopeless. The knight was expected to be the champion of his beloved lady (always a married woman of high status), to fight for her honour and to recite love songs praising her beauty and ideal qualities. The poets and artists who gathered at the C., made some of them into important literary events. Their rules of conduct were established in a famous charter of *Mary of Champagne, c. 1170.

S. Painter, *French Chivalry* (1940).

COUTUMIERS (Customary) The term defines the local usages, which were codified during the 15th century as provincial and local laws. The C. were established through inquests of royal officers, from the 13th

Courtly love; 15th-century Flemish parade shield

century on, the most famous of them having been Philip of *Beaumanoir's *Coutumes de la Beauvésie*. Although for generations they were considered private handbooks for the use of magistrates, their official codification gave them the power of law, but only in the particular district for which they were specified.

J. Ellul, *Histoire de Institutions Françaises au Moyen Age* (1966).

CRACOW City in southwestern Poland. Founded in the 9th century by Slav settlers of Little Poland, the city became a political and religious centre under the influence of Great *Moravia. In the 10th century the land was disputed by the dukes of Bohemia and Poland, but from the reign of *Boleslaw I, Polish domination was affirmed and C. became one of the most important cities in the realm. Under *Boleslaw III (1102-38), who divided the kingdom between his sons, C. came to be a great commercial centre serving Germany and the Slavic countries. In addition, the city was the seat of one of the four principalities of Poland and, in the second half of the 12th century, its princes took the title of "Great Princes". Its development in the late 12th century was interrupted by its conquest in 1241 by the *Mongols, who destroyed it. After their retreat at the beginning of the 14th century, C. was rebuilt and its ancient centre, including its new Gothic cathedral, churches and palaces, became one of the most beautiful in Europe. The development of crafts and trade attracted German and Jewish settlers and under *Wladyslaw IV (1305-33), the city practically became the capital of the kingdom. It officially reached this status during the reign of *Casimir III, at which time the high court of the realm was moved to C. and the city was granted the status of *commune, by the adoption of the *Magdeburg Charter of urban liberties. In 1364 Casimir founded the university at C., thus making the city the cultural centre of the kingdom as well.

The Cambridge History of Poland (1950).

CRÉCY, BATTLE OF (1346) One of the decisive battles of the *Hundred Years' War. The battle, which took place near the village of C. in Picardy, opposed the French chivalry and the English and Welsh bowmen and infantry of *Edward III. The discipline of the latter contributed to the defeat of the French. The English victory led to their conquest of *Calais as well; but of equal importance was that northern France was now open to further English attacks. The heavy losses suffered by the French impaired their morale and weakened the power of France.

E. Perroy, *The Hundred Years' War* (1965).

CREED In the ecclesiastical vocabulary, the C. means a concise, formal and authorized statement of important points of Christian doctrine. Thus the Nicene Creed is the formal statement of the faith, as elaborated and developed by the Council of *Nicaea in 325. The C. was taught to converts and recited in the prayers of important feasts.

O. Cullmann, *The Earliest Christian Confessions* (1949).

CREMONA City in northern Italy (Lombardy). After a long period of decadence at the beginning and late Middle Ages, C. began to develop in the 11th century under the influence of Milan. In the 12th century, the city was ruled by aristocratic families and supported the imperial party, especially during the reign of *Frederick Barbarossa. This attitude became a pro-Ghibelline policy in the 13th century. After the defeat of *Manfred of Sicily at Benevento in 1267, the Guelphs of Lombardy invaded C., which had lost its traditional leadership and was troubled by civil wars. Despite its efforts to maintain its independence, the city was gradually integrated into the state of Milan at the end of the 14th century.

E. R. Labande, *L'Italie de la Renaissance* (1954).

CRESCENTIUS Noble family of Rome which undertook the leadership of the city aristocracy in 966. The head of the family, C., had been active in the 966 riots, which had been appeased by *Otto I. He now headed the revolt against *Otto II in 972, and in 980 seized power with the title of consul. After his death (984), the family and the city was led by his son John C. (984-98), who opposed *Otto III and elected his own popes; defeated by the emperor in 996, he was decapitated after being convicted of treason. His son, John II C. took advantage of Otto's death to seize power in Rome (1002-12). He is considered the leader of the Roman "national" party against the Germans.

P. Brezzi, *Roma e l'Imperio Medioevale* (1947).

CRESCENZI, PETER OF (14th century) Italian naturalist of the 14th century. C. was educated in central and northern Italy, where he became acquainted with classical Latin works on agriculture. In 1306 he wrote his *Ruralium commodorum opus* (The Book of Rural Commodities), which is a compilation of the information available to him on plants and animals, as well as on gardens and agriculture. That part which deals with agriculture is considered the best medieval treatise on the subject. C. borrowed a large portion of his information from Roman writers such as Cato the Elder, Varro and Pliny, as well as from 13th-century medieval scientists of the school of *Albertus Magnus.

A. C. Crombie, *Science in the Middle Ages* (1957).

CRETE The largest island of the Greek Aegean archipelago. A province of the Byzantine empire, C. was under the authority of the emperor's prefect of naval administration. In 804 the island was conquered by the Arabs and, as a result, became a base for Moslem and other pirates, whose raids ravaged Greece and disturbed the maritime traffic in the eastern Mediterranean. In 963 C. was reconquered by the Byzantines and became a monastic centre. The monasteries were granted a large part of the island estates, especially those in the mountains. In 1204, during the Fourth *Crusade, the island was conquered by the Venetians, who made it a colony of their empire. They set up their administration and commercial centre in the city of Candia, whose fortifications are a reminder to this day of the Venetian rule that prevailed until the 16th century. During the Venetian occupation no serious attempt was made to introduce Catholicism in the island. Rather, C. became one of the most important centres of painting of Byzantine icons.

W. Miller, *Essays on the Latin Orient* (1921).

CRIMEA Peninsula to the north of the Black Sea. An ancient Roman province, C. came under Byzantine rule, becoming a separate *thema* (military province), but in the 7th and 8th centuries, the northern part was gradually conquered by the *Khazars. They maintained good relations with the Byzantines, who continued to hold the coastal region and the ports. As a result of these relations, the trade route from China, which passed through the steppes of Central Asia and southern Russia and ended in C., remained open. This assured C.'s ports relative prosperity, compensating for Constantinople's loss of control over the maritime routes. In 989 *Basil II, in need of military support of the Russian prince of Kiev, *Vladimir, surrendered the province to him as dowry for his sister

Ann. Under the domination of Kiev, C. lost much of its importance, the China trade having been disrupted. This condition continued until the peninsula's conquest by the *Mongols in 1240. The Mongol period was one of the most prosperous in the province's history; the trade routes were reopened and Genoese merchants were granted wide privileges in the town of Caffa, which became one of the most active centres in eastern Europe of the 13th-15th centuries. An important province of the *Golden Horde, C. reached a position of autonomy in 1395, when a local Mongol family took advantage of the victories of *Timur-leng to disobey the khan. Nevertheless, only in 1430, under a descendant of *Genghis-Khan, Hadjiz-Gerei, was the independent khanate of C. established at Bahchi-sarai, the Mongol capital of the province. The Gereid khans maintained their good relations with the Genoese colony of Caffa until its conquest by the *Ottoman Turks in 1477. Although the khans continued to rule the interior part of the peninsula, they did so as vassals to the Ottoman emperors.

V. O. Kliuchevskii, *A History of Russia* (1960).

CROATIA Country in the northwestern part of the Balkans, corresponding to the ancient Roman province of Illyricum. It was so named after the Croats, a Slavic tribe, originally of the region of Cracow, who invaded the country at the beginning of the 7th century and were permitted to settle there in 620 by the Byzantine emperor *Heraclius, in order to create a barrier against the *Avars. In the 8th century the Croats expanded their settlements in the direction of modern Austria, but they were divided into several principalities, some of which acknowledged the overlordship of Byzantium, while others were dependent on the Avars. After the destruction of the Avar state by *Charlemagne in 798, Frankish influence penetrated into C., where two princes, *Borna and *Ljudevit, disputed the hegemony. Ljudevit's victory (819) coincided with his revolt against Frankish suzerainty and the attempt to establish a Croat realm, including Dalmatia, Carniola and Austria. Having been defeated in 822 by an army sent by *Louis the Pious, he was also attacked by the Bulgars. While the Franks, and in the second half of the 9th century the Germans, were able to conquer the northwestern Croatian possessions and to establish the march of *Carniola, the attempts of the margraves of Friuli to restore Frankish influence in Balkan C. failed, and the country continued to enjoy a great deal of autonomy under the formal rule of the Bulgars and, from the 10th century, under the suzerainty of Byzantium. The Croats opposed Byzantine interference in their affairs and, in order to preserve their independence, adopted the Roman Catholic faith. Under the rule of Prince *Branimir (879-92), the negotiations with the papal court led to the recognition of the Croat episcopate, although discussions concerning the adoption of the Latin liturgy did not end before the pontificate of *John X. John recognized the royal title of *Tomislav (910-28), the actual founder of the Croatian state, in 925. Allied with Byzantium against the Bulgarians, the kings of C. maintained their independence and under *Stephen Držislav (969-97), C. became an important kingdom in the Balkans, ruling over other Slavic tribes, such as the Serbians, and gaining control over the Adriatic coast as a result of its annexa-

tion of Dalmatia. In the 11th century the kingdom fought for its independence against the Hungarians, who eventually conquered the country in 1097.
S. Guldescu, *History of Mediaeval Croatia* (1964).

CRUSADE, CYCLE OF POEMS The popular name for a number of epic poems of the 13th-14th centuries, written in French and dealing with the *Crusades, mostly concentrating on epic episodes. One such cycle, the "cycle of Godfrey of Bouillon", includes poems which made him into a legendary figure with a mythical ancestry. The heroism of his family is also praised; their adventures with Moslem princesses introduced an exotic element in medieval French literature, leaving much room for imaginary events presented as "fiction-history". Other poems deal with the great events of the First Crusade, the conquests of Antioch and Jerusalem and with the passage of the army through Asia Minor (*Les Chétifs*). While the historical leaders remained in the background, the poets put the emphasis on persons of lesser origin, who were depicted as real heroes. In this respect, the great leaders were treated with a reverence due their majesty, making them, as in the *Carolingian epic, immutable figures, while the qualities and weaknesses of the simple knights made them better heroic models.
S. Duparc-Quioc, *Le Cycle de la Croisade* (1955).

CRUSADES A broad historical movement (1096-1291) which originated in western Europe with the aim of liberating the *Holy Sepulchre from the Moslems and defending possession of it. The name, which was coined subsequent to the events, derived from the sign of the cross, which distinguished the participants (*Crucesignati*). While motives behind the C. could be discerned and attributed to individuals and groups, the movement as a whole was the result of the combined effects of various causes and immediate factors. These causes were religious, political, social, demographic and economic.

a) The religious factor was connected with the spread of biblical learning and preaching in Catholic Europe, which emphasized the spiritual link to the holy places in Palestine, as the Land of Israel, and that of the life and Passion of Christ. These feelings were made concrete through pilgrimages, which became numerous in the 11th century, as well as by stories of the pilgrims, which gave a realistic setting to the more abstract themes which had been preached and expounded by priests. Thus, places like Jerusalem, Nazareth, Bethlehem, Galilee and Judaea, became familiar to the large masses in western Europe.

b) The political reasons behind the movement were twofold. Firstly, in the East, the spectacular conquests of the *Seljuk Turks, who, in 1071, captured Jerusalem and defeated the Byzantines at *Menzikert, conquering Anatolia, led Byzantium to turn to the West in a desperate appeal for help. The image of the "Eastern brethren" subjugated by the Moslems and suffering persecution, was thus connected with the spiritual attachment to the holy places. Secondly, in the West, the *Investiture controversy and the great quarrel between the papacy and the *Holy Roman empire, where both claimed universal hegemony, brought Pope *Urban II, compelled to flee from Rome by the Emperor *Henry IV, to seek support from the knights. He mobilized them to fight the holy war against the infidels, with the aim that the ideal of peace within the Christian world would serve to weaken the emperor. Moreover, by leading a universal military expedition the papacy could obtain real secular power to back its claim to universal hegemony.

c) The social and demographic factors underlying the C. were related particularly to the kingdom of France and French-speaking countries, where *feudal development brought about the emergence of anarchy and the creation of particularist policies, leading to a state of continual war. The demographic changes in the 11th century, which were not accompanied by technical improvement of labour, created land and work shortages. Although a portion of the peasantry was settled in new estates and another part migrated to the towns, the major part of the lesser nobility was compelled to emigrate. Some had already participated in the *Reconquista* wars in Spain and settled there, while others, particularly of northern France, had taken part in the Norman conquest of England in 1066 and settled there. Nevertheless, at the end of the 11th century, thousands of "errant knights" were still in search of land, fortunes and adventures, while a great number of former peasants were still unsettled and lacked the means to provide basic nourishment.

d) The economic factors involved were related to the policy of the Italian harbours, which were already interested in commerce with the Orient and needed a political backing for their bases in the East. Although their fleets had already become an important factor in the Mediterranean Sea, they were dependent on political stability in the Middle East, which had been upset by the Seljuk conquest.

On the whole, the C. were general, regional or local movements, according to specific cases and circumstances. Their classification and numeration is an arbitrary one, established by historians in the early Modern Era who did not take into consideration the fact that there was hardly a year without a Crusade within the period mentioned and concentrated their attention upon nine Crusades, which can be considered as the most important ones:

The First Crusade was the result of Pope *Urban II's appeal at the Council of *Clermont in 1095, which completed a preparatory stage, already begun in Italy and continued by his negotiations with French feudal princes. The speech at Clermont, which initiated the Crusade had, however, a larger appeal then intended and brought about immediate organization of the popular Crusade preached by *Peter the Hermit, with a multitude of participants, including some poor knights. The zeal of the participants impaired their military organization. They attacked Jewish quarters in the French and German cities, murdering and plundering, and by the time they had reached Constantinople, they had already gained a reputation as an anarchic movement. Transported by the Byzantine emperor *Alexius I to Anatolia, they were severely defeated by the Seljuks at Nicaea, where many of them were killed.

The Crusade of the barons, however, was better planned. *Raymond of St. Gilles, count of Tolouse, led the Provençal knights; Godfrey of Bouillon headed the contingent of Lorraine, German and Belgian knights; *Bohemond of Taranto and Tancred headed the southern Italian force and *Robert, count of Flanders, *Hugh, duke of Vermandois and *Robert, duke of Normandy, had followings as well. The participants arrived at Constantinople in 1097, where Emperor *Alexius I demanded that they swear him fealty. This provoked antagonism between the Crusaders and the Byzantines, which later had its impact on the C. The Crusader victory at *Dorylaeum in Asia Minor over the Seljuks allowed the Byzantines to reconquer the western part of Anatolia and to weaken the sultanate of Konya. Despite the difficulties, the Crusaders traversed the Anatolian peninsula and in 1098 attacked *Antioch, which was conquered and became the first Crusader principality in the East, under Bohemond. At the same time another army conquered the province of Edessa, on the Euphrates, where *Baldwin of Bologne, the brother of Godfrey of Bouillon, founded an independent county. The major part of the army, joined by the remnants of the popular Crusade, continued to Palestine. In April 1099 they conquered the city of Ramlah, which was abandoned by its defenders, and advanced to Jerusalem, conquered in July 1099. The First Crusade ended officially with the establishment of the Crusader state of Jerusalem.

The Second Crusade, proclaimed by Pope *Eugenius III after the conquest of Edessa by *Zengi in 1144, was preached by St. *Bernard of Clairvaux. It was led by Emperor *Conrad III and *Louis VII, king of France. The choice of the terrestrial route along the Danube and through Asia Minor, considered as the way of the alleged Pilgrimage of Charlemagne to Jerusalem, created military difficulties, as the armies lost part of their effective force in the arid Anatolian plateau. In 1148, at an assembly held at Acre, it was decided to attack Damascus, the former ally of the Latin kingdom of Jerusalem, but the Crusaders failed to conquer the Syrian city. The results of the Second Crusade were the conquest of Damascus by *Nureddin, who thus realized the union of Syria, and the strategic weakening of the Latin states in the East.

The Third Crusade was a European reaction to the *Hattin disaster of 1187. Under the leadership of Emperor *Frederick Barbarossa, King *Philip II of France and King *Richard I of England, an extremely imposing army left Europe to restore the Latin kingdom of Jerusalem. Frederick chose the terrestrial route and died in Anatolia (1189); the Western kings on the other hand sailed the Mediterranean in 1189. The Anglo-French rivalry continued on their journey East, so that in Sicily, and later on in the Holy Land, Philip and Richard quarreled quite openly. The real leader of the Crusade was Richard, who conquered Cyprus on his way eastwards; the island came to a new Crusader kingdom established in 1192 under *Guy of Lusignan, the former king of Jerusalem. In 1191 Acre was besieged and conquered by the Crusaders and subsequently, the kingdom was restored along the coastal strip until Jaffa (1192).

The Fourth Crusade, proclaimed by *Innocent III in order to consolidate the weak kingdom of Acre, was led by *William of Montferrat and *Baldwin of Hainault, who sailed with their followers in Venetian ships. The Crusade was detoured towards Constantinople by the Venetians, who used it to protect their own interests. In 1204, the Crusaders attacked the capital of the Byzantine empire and conquered it, thus settling to their own advantage the dynastic conflict between the *Angelus

the aristocracy which maintained its ancient tribal C., or that of minorities, such as the Jews. In the late 8th and 9th century, *Charlemagne codified these C. as the *Leges Barbarorum,* ("The Laws of the Barbarians"), representing the tribal phase of these traditions. The diversity of C. in the feudal period led to the distinction between "bad C.", or abuses, and "good C." which were generally attributed to the wisdom of ancestors. In England, this system led to the establishment of the Common Law, which was a codification of the current C. In continental Europe, from the 13th century on, C. were compiled by jurists in the form of *coutumiers.*

H. M. Cam, *Lawfinders and Lawmakers in Medieval England* (1962).

CYNEWULF (c. 750) Anglo-Saxon poet. Nothing is known about his life, aside from the connection made between him and C., bishop of Lindisfarne (d. 783) which has not been proven. His poetry, religious in content, was inspired by his devotion to the Christian mysteries and the cult of the saints. It reveals considerable knowledge of theological and historical aspects of Christianity.

C. W. Kennedy, *The Poems of Cynewulf translated into English Prose* (1910).

CYPRUS Island in the eastern Mediterranean Sea. At the beginning of the Middle Ages, it belonged to the Byzantine empire, forming a specific province under the authority of the "Count of the Orient", whose seat was at Antioch. Subordination was also present in the ecclesiastical domain, despite the opposition of the local clergy, who claimed an autonomous status on the basis of the fact that Cypriot Christianity had emerged as a result of the apostolic activity of Barnabas, one of the disciples of Christ. This claim was accepted by the council of *Ephesus in 341 and ecclesiastical autonomy was promulgated by Emperor *Zeno in 488. The result was that the relations with the authorities of Antioch were weakened and, in the 6th century, C. became directly dependent on Constantinople. This period was a time of prosperity for the island, whose trade was developed and which became an important cultural centre in the empire. Such prosperity, however, saw its end in the middle of the 7th century. Following the Arabic conquest of Syria, *Muawiya, its new governor, headed a raid into C. and imposed the payment of a tribute on its inhabitants (647). In 653 an Arab army invaded C. and the island was divided into two. One part was occupied by Arabs while the countryside remained under Byzantine control. During this time and up to the 10th century, the church wielded a great deal of power. In fact, the bishops and abbots became the secular lords of the Greek side of the island. In 965 C. was reconquered by *Nicephorus II Phocas, who restored Byzantine rule. The island's strategic location led to the appointment of governors of the highest rank, among them relatives of the emperors. Although the church lost its political power, it remained the largest landowner and was very influential in C.'s social and economic life. During the 10th-12th centuries, the monastic movement flourished and many new abbeys were founded and richly endowed. During the First *Crusade, the governor of C. aided the Crusaders, providing them with food during the siege of Antioch in 1098, and even military

support, given to *Raymond of Saint-Gilles in 1101 to establish the county of *Tripoli. However, the relations were broken when, in 1156, *Raynald of Châtillon, then prince of Antioch, invaded the island and took its governor prisoner. This raid, followed by an earthquake in 1157, left its mark on C. and the period of stability came to an end. In 1183 *Isaac Comnenus, governor of Cilicia and relative of the Byzantine emperor, seized power and proclaimed himself emperor of C. (1185). Because of the heavy taxes he imposed to finance his revolt, he was hated by the population. This tension facilitated the conquest of C. in 1191 by *Richard I, king of England, who had entered a dispute with Isaac during his stay at Famagusta and was able to defeat him without Greek opposition. Richard sold C. to the *Hospitallers, but not having received the price agreed upon, regained the island in 1192.

In order to settle the dynastical crisis in the Latin kingdom of Jerusalem, Richard granted the island to *Guy of Lusignan, who then abandoned his claim to the crown of Jerusalem (1192). In 1194 C. was inherited by Guy's brother, *Amalric of Lusignan, who swore fidelity to Emperor *Henry VI, thus legitimizing the royal title of the Crusader rulers of the island. Amalric was the actual founder of the "Frankish" kingdom of C., which was run on a feudal basis similar to the Latin kingdom of *Jerusalem. The Greek-Orthodox Church lost its central position as a result, and a Catholic archbishop was established at Nicosia. A great part of the Greek church estates was confiscated and given to the new ruling class. Nevertheless, the efforts to impose the Catholic faith in the island remained unsuccessful; the Greek population, deprived of a political position, continued to remain faithful to its ecclesiastical leadership, which retired to monasteries. The island's nobility was imported from the Latin kingdom; as such, C. was not a reinforcement to the Crusader states in the East, but rather weakened them by drawing a portion of their leaders. This migratory trend continued throughout the 13th century, bringing the settlement of some of the most important families of the Latin East. One such case was the *Ibelin family, who won a decisive victory against other factions of the nobility in 1233 and became second only to the royal dynasty of Lusignan. Even when the kings of C. were also made kings of Jerusalem, as was true in the case of *Hugh III, this migratory trend continued and was accentuated by internal rivalries in the continental principalities. After the fall of the Latin states (1291), the survivors settled in C., which became at the end of the 13th century a "little France of the East". Its government tried to administer political institutions according to the feudal codes and to impose the ideal behaviour of "French *chivalry". Economically, the island was mainly under the control of *Genoa from 1233 but also had to resist Venetian pressure.

In the 14th century the kings of C. were among the most active participants in the later *Crusades, fighting the *Mamelukes in Egypt and the Turks in Asia Minor. While they received support from the Hospitallers and the kings of Lesser *Armenia, the nobility of the island was opposed to their actions. After the death of *Peter I, the last powerful Lusignan monarch (1369), a political crisis erupted; Genoa imposed its rule in Famagusta, the main harbour, while the nobility was divided amongst themselves. The civil war allowed the Mamelukes to intervene and impose their protectorate over the island in 1426. The crisis came to a halt only in 1460, when the archbishop of Nicosia, James of Lusignan, an illegitimate member of the royal dynasty, seized power, expelling the Mamelukes and defeating the Genoese in 1464. He gained Venetian support in his wars and, in order to maintain this alliance, married Catherine Cornaro. After his death, in 1473, Catherine continued to rule the kingdom with the help of Venetian advisers until she gave up the throne and C. became annexed to the Venetian empire.

The Lusignan period was one of the most prosperous in the history of C. Conditions were present for the development of trade and the growth of cities, especially Famagusta. The Western manner of life, which was introduced in the kingdom, revealed itself through the development of Late Gothic art in religious institutions, palaces and fortifications.

G. Hill, *A History of Cyprus*, II-III (1944-52).

CYRIL AND METHODIUS, Sts. The "Apostles of the Slavs". They were brothers from a noble Greek family of Thessalonica. The younger brother, Constantine (826-69), had a strong influence upon his brother, M. (815-85), guiding him towards an ecclesiastical career. The two studied and were ordained together. They then settled in Constantinople, where Constantine, who distinguished himself by his theological knowledge, became librarian of *St. Sophia. They were sent to the realm of the *Khazars and in 862, by permission of the Emperor *Michael III, they began their missionary activity in *Moravia, where they taught the Slavs the principles of the Christian faith in the vernacular. Constantine, who took the monastic name of C. during the mission, was keenly interested in the Slavic language which he was able to adapt to the Greek alphabet (see *Cyrillic), thus becoming the founder of Slavonic literature and liturgy. The two brothers developed the Christian liturgy in Slavonic and circulated a Slavonic version of the Scriptures. In 868 they journeyed to Rome, where C. died. After his death, M. was consecrated Bishop of the Moravs (869) by Pope *John VIII, who sent him to continue his mission. Despite papal authority, M. had trouble with German bishops, who imprisoned him; his release was obtained through papal intervention, although permission to use Slavonic as the liturgical language was withdrawn. While the eastern Slavs and southern Slavs (or Yugoslavs) continued to employ the Slavonic language in liturgy and religion, the western Slavs were compelled by the 872 "privilege" (the release of M.) to accept the liturgy in Latin.

F. Dvornik, *Les Légendes des Sts. Constantin-Cyrille et Méthode vues de Byzance* (1933);

F. Grivec, *Konstantin und Method, Lehrer der Slawen* (1960).

CYRIL OF ALEXANDRIA, St. (d. 444) Patriarch of Alexandria (412-44). C. was one of the most important leaders of the Orthodox trend in the Church and vigorously fought non-conformist attitudes. In 430 he

contested the views of the patriarch of Constantinople, Nestorius, on the theological interpretation of the word *Theotokos* ("Mother of God"), given to the Virgin Mary. Rivalry within the Church led to the expansion of the conflict into social and ethnic spheres. Nestorius' views were adopted in the East, having been sustained at Antioch, while Rome, on the other hand, supported Cyril's criticism. The issue was discussed at the Third *Oecumenical Council at Ephesus (431), where C. dominated the debates and obtained a formal condemnation of *Nestorianism. C. was one of the greatest theologians of his time, and his view that the Virgin Mary was the mother of the human Christ was a fundamental belief of both Greek-Orthodox and Roman Catholic Churches in the Middle Ages, although only among the theologians. The masses of faithful were not able to distinguish between the subtle theological interpretations and neither accepted nor rejected C.'s theology.

EC, III.

CYRIL OF SCYTHOPOLIS (6th century) Byzantine monk and hagiographer. Born at Scythopolis (Beth-Shean) in Palestine, C. was influenced, while still a child, by St. *Sabas (d. 572). In 543 he became a monk at Jerusalem, but opted for the isolated life of an anchoret on the banks of the Jordan. In 557 he joined the monastic community of *Mar Sabas, where he wrote of the lives of the Palestinian saints. Written in popular Greek, these accounts rapidly spread throughout the Byzantine empire and became a model for Byzantine hagiographical literature during the Middle Ages.

E. Migne, *PG*, vol 114;

F. A. Wright, *A History of the Later Greek Literature* (1932).

CYRILLIC Alphabet invented by St. *Cyril, the "Apostle of the Slavs", and based on the adaptation of Greek symbols to Slavonic phonetics. The C. was used in the liturgical writings of the Slavonic peoples of the Orthodox church. The modern Slav alphabet is derived from it.

CYRUS Patriarch of Alexandria (631-42). Appointed by Emperor *Heraclius to this high dignity, he tried to reconcile the various heretical sects and the orthodoxy, in order to bring religious union. His attempts caused him much trouble; the Orthodox, led by *Sephronius, patriarch of Jerusalem, attacked him as heretic and tried to depose him, while the *Copts of Egypt were distrustful of his motives. C. was also the last Byzantine civil governor of Egypt. He was aware of the impossibility of opposing an Arab invasion of the country which took place in 640, and in 642 he signed an act of capitulation, surrendering Alexandria to the Arabs.

A. A. Vasiliev, *History of the Byzantine Empire* (1952).

CZECHS Common name of the western Slavs, including *Bohemians and *Moravs, as well as of lesser tribes, which were assimilated by them. In the Middle Ages, the term C. had no political significance, because of the development of Moravia and Bohemia, but rather denoted the ethnic and linguistic entity of these Slavs. From the 12th century, both in Bohemia and Moravia, local dialects were united to form one Czech language.

D

DACIA The Latin name, erroneously used during the Middle Ages to designate Denmark and other Scandinavian provinces. Originally the name D. was applied to a Roman province north of the Danube River, situated in what is now Rumania. This mistake, first discernible at the beginning of the 11th century (*c*. 1020) in the Frenchman, Dudo of Saint Quentin's chronicle *Historia Normanorum*, continued into the succeeding century, when the term was broadened to include all of Scandinavia. In the 13th century D. became a popular term, as the mendicant orders, especially the *Dominicans and *Franciscans, called the recently evangelized Scandinavian countries – Denmark, Norway, Sweden and Finland – *provincia Daniae*.

A similar province was also established by other orders such as the *Carmelites, the Knights of Malta etc. In fact, the Scandinavian friars of the Dominican order were known as *de Dacia*, meaning they were from Denmark, although they actually came from other countries. Likewise, is the case of the *Collegium Dacicum*, also named after the province, which was in fact one of the most ancient colleges of medieval Paris.

J. Gallén, *La Province de Dacia de l'ordre des frères prêcheurs* (1946).

DAGOBERT I (605-39) Merovingian king, son of *Clotaire II, one of the last kings of that Frankish dynasty to rule over a united and prosperous kingdom. In 623 he became king of Austrasia, and in 629, on his father's death, marched against the magnates of Neustria and compelled them to recognize him as king of the entire realm. For better and effective control over the empire, D. moved his capital to Paris. But to calm the Austrasians' resentment he appointed his son, Sigebert, as their king (634). But D. was not averse to using force to obtain order and peace and in this way he crushed the revolts of the Bretons (636) and the Gascons (637). His foreign policy was equally successful. He signed a treaty with the Byzantine emperor, Heraclius (629), and pacified the Saxons and the Wends. D.'s administration of justice was carried out through a series of visits throughout his realm, which won him the reputation of a righteous king.

D.'s prosperous reign witnessed the establishment of many ecclesiastic foundations and the spread of learning. He particularly favoured the abbey of *St. Denis, which he endowed with many rich donors. He also worked to revise the old Frankish law, and was a patron of arts and letters.

R. Barroux, *Dagobert, roi des Francs* (1938).

DAGOBERT II, St. (650-79) Frankish king (656-79), Being a child at the death of his father, Sigebert III, D. was entrusted to the guardianship of *Grimoald, the mayor of the palace. In 660 he was exiled by Grimoald, who installed his own son, Childebert, in his place. Only after a span of 15 years, during which Austrasia was governed by *Childeric II (622-75), was D. brought back to the throne (676) with the help of the Austrasians.

The Neustrian opposition led by the mayor of the palace plotted against him and arranged his assassination while he was hunting in the woods. Because of his cruel murder, D. was proclaimed a martyr.

F. Lot, *The End of the Ancient World and the Beginning of the Middle Ages* (English trans.) (1961).

DAGOBERT III (699-716) Merovingian king of Neustria (711-16). The son of Childebert III, he began his reign as a boy. His rule was in fact controlled by *Pepin II of Herstal, the powerful mayor of the Austrasian palace.

DAIMBERT (Dagobert; c. 1050-1107) Patriarch of Jerusalem and a major figure in the early days of the Crusader kingdom of Jerusalem. As archbishop of Pisa (1092) he accompanied Pope *Urban II to the Council of Clermont (1095), where the First *Crusade was proclaimed. In 1098 D. acted as papal legate in Spain, and at the death of *Adhemar of Monteuil, the legate of the First Crusade, he was appointed successor by Urban. Heading a Pisan fleet, D. sailed for the Holy Land (end of 1098) and, upon his arrival in the East, became the friend and ally of *Bohemond of Antioch. At Bohemond's instigation D. deposed Arnulf, the patriarch of Jerusalem in 1100, claiming his election to have been uncanonical. He subsequently secured his own election as patriarch, at which time he made *Godfrey of Bouillon and Bohemond his vassals. However D. was not content with theoretical overlordship; he sought real power and demanded from Godfrey a considerable share of land and power of government (over Jaffa and part of Jerusalem) – claims that bring to mind those of Pope *Gregory VII. D.'s intrigues and political ambitions soon led him to an open and bitter conflict with *Baldwin, Godfrey's brother and successor, who brought about D.'s deposition and banishment from Jerusalem (1102). D. turned for support to *Tancred, another ally who ruled Antioch during Bohemond's captivity. Threatening Baldwin with his withdrawal of military aid, Tancred demanded D.'s reinstatement. D. resumed office temporarily, but was soon tried, found guilty and deposed by a legal synod headed by the new papal legate. In 1105 D. sailed to Italy where he appealed to the new pope, *Paschal II. When Baldwin failed to answer D.'s charges, the pope retracted the deposition on grounds of civil interference. While en route to resume his patriarchate, D. died at Messina.

S. Runciman, *A History of the Crusades* (1952-54).

DALMATIA A province on the Adriatic shore, named after the Dalmatae, an Illyrian tribe, who had settled there by the 4th century BC. Governing the Adriatic Sea, D.'s favourable location made it a prime target for

appeal to Hungary and Venice for support. Upon the union established between D. and Hungary (1102), King *Koloman recognized D.'s autonomous rule and its municipal privileges. However, from a commercial point of view, the alliance with Venice seemed more favourable. Unlike Hungary, Venice had no interest in territorial expansion, but was rather intent upon building its maritime power, and found the coastal cities of D. essential for that purpose. Hungary, on the other hand, had supporters among farmers and merchants who traded in D.'s interior. Thus, the area soon became the source of rivalry between Hungary and Venice and some 21 wars were waged in a constant struggle over D. (1115-1420). In the course of the 13th century, rule over D. passed through many hands. In 1202 Zara was occupied by the troops of the Fourth *Crusade at Venice's instigation. A Mongol invasion occurred in 1241-42, and in the mid-14th century, southern D. was conquered by *Stephen Dushan, and then, for a while (1389-90), came under the control of Stephen Tvrko, king of Bosnia. At the beginning of the 15th century, when Hungary was troubled by rivalry over succession and weakened by the Ottoman attacks, Venice gained the upper hand in D. The turning-point came in 1409 when D. was sold to Venice by Ladislas of Naples, king of Croatia, in order to finance the Hungarian succession campaign. Later, in 1420, Venice conquered the whole of D. Its long domination (1420-1797) was marked by constant warfare against the Turks.

L. Vojnović, *Histoire de Dalmatie* (1934);

P. Digović, *La Dalmatie et les problèmes de l'Adriatique* (1944).

DAMASCUS (Arabic: Dimashq as Sham) An ancient city in southern Syria, of great importance primarily for its favourable location. Situated near a major junction commanding both the desert and the river routes, D. naturally grew into a centre of trade between Arabia, Palestine and Mesopotamia and the Fertile Crescent. For many centuries despite the vicissitudes of politics and regimes D. retained its military, administrative and commercial predominance. After the division of the Roman empire (395) the church of D. assumed considerable importance. Its delegates were already present at the Council of Nicaea (325). By *Arcadius' order, the pagan temple of D. was converted into a Christian church dedicated to St. John the Baptist. D. suffered from the constant wars between the Byzantines and the Parthians. In 613 D. was occupied by the Parthians and in 635 the Arabs entered the city. In 650, when Caliph *Muawiya transferred the seat of the caliphate to Mesopotamia, D. became its new capital. Under the *Ummayad dynasty (667-750), D. prospered commercially and culturally. Its fine textiles and metal crafts were known throughout the world. However, its wealth also attracted raiders, such as the *Karmathians and *Seljuks. In the reign of *Walid I the church of St. John the Baptist was converted into a mosque, known as the Great Mosque, which is one of its most impressive buildings. From the 9th century D. nominally belonged to the ruling dynasty of Egypt. In 1076 it was seized by the Seljuk Turks. The *Crusaders attacked it in 1126, but could not control the city, although they dominated the countryside for a short while. From 1154 D. was ruled by *Nureddin, and his successor *Saladin made it his main base during his prolonged wars against the

Entrance-way to the Ummayad Mosque at Damascus

attack and, therefore, it saw numerous battles over the years. With the decline of the Western Roman empire, D., after a short period as an independent state (c. 460-76), fell into the hands of *Odoacer and *Theodoric, and remained in their control until 535. During the 6th century D. served as battleground in the dispute between the Goths and *Justinian. The latter eventually incorporated the province to his empire. In the following century, D. was invaded by the Avars and other barbarian tribes. Some of these tribes — the Croats in the north and the Serbs in the south — were called upon by *Heraclius to invade D., remove it from control of the Avars, and settle the country. These incursions caused a certain crystallization of the population. While the Slavs settled in the countryside, the former Roman inhabitants concentrated themselves in the safe coastal towns which they had founded. Not only an ethnic division but also a religious distinction separated the Orthodox Slavs and the Catholic urban population. The Slavs recognized Byzantine suzerainty, which officially lasted some 600 years (535-1102), but was in fact more nominal than actual. In 806, during the conflict between *Charlemagne and the Byzantine emperor, D. came under Frankish domination for a short while, after which it was raided by the Saracens (829). In 998 D. suffered a naval defeat inflicted by the Venetian doge, Pietro Orseolo II, who took the title duke of D. without offending the Byzantine nominal suzerainty. Because of its physical distance, D. could not depend upon Byzantine aid to relieve the growing pressure of the Croat state, which imposed an annual tribute. The coastal cities in particular, which suffered from corsair and Norman raids (1073), turned to Italy for support. During the 12th century, unable to stand alone, D. had to

rbis ſitū

dico aggredior
ipediti9 opus
et facūdie
nudiunie a
pꝰ v. Coſtat
eiu fere qꝰ
tuū latoꝝ
noibz et eoꝝ
perplex ſa
tis ordie que
pſeq̄ longa e
magis qm̄ bem
uia inatia. Ver
ſpia tū cauioſtriq̄
digniſſimū. ꞇ quod
ſiue ope iterem ora
tis ac ipa ſiu con
tēplatioe precuū ope

attēdentur abſoluut · idica tū aliae plura et expatius
ſur aut ut q̄cūq̄ uut clariſſima et ſtricti · ac pmo
quide q̄ ſit forma tra9 q̄ maᵫe partes q̄ ſingle modo
ſur · vt q̄ hⁱtzentur expedia. deinde rurſus ora om̄iu
et litora ut intra eoꝛ̄ q̄ ſur atq̄ ut ea ſubit ac cir
cūfluit pelag9 addicis q̄ ī naturā rⁱmouiū ieol · ꝛꝛ̄ nue
moꝛadi ſur. Id q̄ facili9 ſtari poſſie atq̄ recꞓpi paulo al
ti9 ſuua repetatur. Otiue igr hoc quicq̄d eſt ciu uni
di cali q̄ nouiē ındıdiūꞇ uni d̄ e · ꞇ uno ābitu ſp
circa q̄ aplectitur. ꝑartibz diſſert unde ſol oritur

Franks. In 1260 D. was occupied by Mongol invaders but was liberated by the Mameluke sultan Kotuz. Subsequently the city was ravaged and put to the torch by the furious *Timur-Leng (Tamerlane), who also captured most of the metal and textile artisans of the city.
P. K. Hitti, *Syria: A Short History* (1962).

DAMASUS I, St. (305-84) Pope from 366. D. was the protégé of Pope *Liberius (352-66). Upon the latter's death in 366 a controversy arose over the election of his successor. The supporters of the antipope Felix elected Ursius (Ursicinius), while the majority of the clergy chose D. as pope. The struggle between the rival popes and their factions lasted until 381, when Emperor Valentinian intervened in D.'s favour and exiled his opponent. The pontificate of D. was marked by his indefatigable activity in suppressing heretic doctrines such as Arianism and *Donatism. D. also strengthened the position and role of the papacy. In response to Constantinople's claims of pre-eminence in the church on political grounds (Council of Constantinople I, 381), D. affirmed the supremacy of Roman bishops, as being the true heirs and successors of St. Peter (Council of Rome, 382).

D. was concerned with liturgical and administrative reforms. He made Latin the official liturgical language of Rome, and introduced improved administrative methods in the papal chancery. In addition, D. appointed his private secretary, St. *Jerome, to revise the Latin translations of the Gospels. This work was to be a part of what came to be known as the Vulgate version.
A. Fliche and V. Martin (eds.), *Histoire de l'Eglise depuis les origines jusqu'à nos jours*, III (1955).

DAMASUS II (d. 1048) He was bishop of Brixen (Bolzano) and a close friend of Emperor *Henry III. As supporter of the reform movement in the church he played an important role in the reform councils. In 1047 he was nominated by Henry as successor to Clement II; however, his coronation was postponed until 17 July 1048, when the deposed pope Benedict IX was expelled from Rome under the emperor's orders. D.'s pontificate lasted only 23 days. He died of malaria.

DAMIETTA (Arabic: Dumyat) An ancient town in Lower Egypt on the eastern part of the Nile delta, situated near the Mediterranean Sea. Owing to its advantageous position, D. was a prosperous commercial centre in ancient times in competition with Pelusium. But the rise of Alexandria (332 BC) on the western bank of the Nile, led to its decline. In the middle of the 7th century, D. came under Arab domination and soon became an important port and textile centre, after which is named a special kind of cloth (called *dumyaty* or *dimity*). Considered the heart of Egypt's wealth, D. later became one of the targets of Crusader attacks. It was the main area of battle of the Fifth *Crusade. In 1218 the city endured a long siege of one and a half years that ended with its surrender (1219). The Christians controlled D. until 1221, when it was liberated by Al-Kamil after a long campaign. In 1249 King *Louis IX of France sent the Sixth *Crusade to Egypt and occupied D. without difficulty. But when he was defeated and taken prisoner at Mansura (1250), D. returned to Moslem hands as part of the ransom agreement. Because of its non-strategic position, and in order to prevent further attacks, the Mameluke sultan *Baibars destroyed D., blocked off the river mouth and moved the city inland to its present site. D. served as a place of exile during the Mameluke and Ottoman periods.

DANCE OF DEATH (French: danse macabre) A medieval motif in literature, drama and the arts, signifying the inevitability of death, regardless of wealth, social rank or power. The D. motif is usually depicted as a procession of living persons representing the entire social hierarchy, from emperor and pope down to child, monk and simple man, with a skeleton leading them to the grave. It should be borne in mind that death was an everyday and highly visible occurrence in medieval life, due to the prolonged wars (e.g., *Hundred Years' War), famine and the recurrent epidemics such as the *Black Death. The D. was probably associated with a morality play, in which the dance was mimed. But the origin of this motif is to be sought in the 13th-century French moral poems known as *Les dits des trois morts et des trois vifs*, a dialogue between three young nobles and three skeletons, who reveal their inevitable fate and describe the power of death. The earliest examples of the *danse macabre* motif are in 14th-century French drama, and the painting cycle from the cemetery of *Les Innocents* (c. 1425), reproduced in the woodcuts of Guyot Marchant (1485). As a moral reminder and exhortation to repent, the D. motif was employed by the clergy, and it spread rapidly during the 15th century.
L. Dimier, *Le danses macabres et l'idée de la mort dans l'art chrétien* (1902);
F. Carco, *La Danse de morts* (1948).

DANDOLO A distinguished patrician family of Venice whose members held prominent positions from the 11th century, including four Venetian doges, and several lords of Venetian maritime colonies.
Enrico D. the best known doge (1193-1205), enjoyed a successful career as a diplomat and an administrator. Although an elderly man when elected doge, he remained active and contributed to the constitutional and economic development of the Venetian republic. His main concern was to regain control over *Dalmatia and to override Byzantine refusal to renew its grant of special economic privileges. His solution to the latter problem was to direct the Fourth *Crusade towards Constantinople, the consequence of which was the collapse of the Byzantine state and the rise of the *Latin empire of Constantinople.
Giovanni D. became doge (1280-89) at a crucial period. Venice lost much of her prestige and power with the fall of the Latin empire of Constantinople (1261). Furthermore, her maritime hegemony was seriously challenged by the growth of her rival, Genoa, which also inherited Venice's trade privileges. Giovanni utilized his military expertise to strengthen the city's armed and naval forces, and thus prepared it for long-term conflict with Genoa.
Francesco D.'s dogeship (1329-39) was marked by a sudden change of tactics. Instead of the traditional maritime policy he adopted an attitude of continental expansion, which brought Venice in conflict with Verona, as the latter blocked the way to the European commercial centres. Francesco occupied Treviso and other areas, thus extending Venice's possessions in the hinterland.
Andrea D. was doge (1343-54) during the long and bitter war with Genoa. He subdued the rebellious town

The Three Continents, *world map showing Europe, Africa and Asia; from a 15th-century manuscript*

of Zara and defeated the Hungarians (1345) who had instigated its revolt. Subsequently he confronted Genoa, which had attacked Venetian territories, and gained a great naval victory at Lojera in 1353. Andrea was not only a wise and competent statesman (*Petrarch had a high opinion of his integrity), but also a man of letters. A former law student, he collected and published a code of law (1346), but is best known as a historian, whose *Annals* and collection of documents, *Liber albus*, are a primary source of Venetian history.

DANDOLO (DEGLI ANDOLO), BRANCALEONE (13th century) A Bolognian senator who became the podesta of the Roman capital as a result of a sudden popular rebellion in 1252. To put an end to the chaos prevailing in Rome since the previous popular insurrection during the papal vacancy (1241-43), the Romans and the great patrician families called upon D. and granted him unlimited dictatorial powers. D. used his authority to initiate a civic reform of the Roman guilds, to restore public order and safety and to limit the temporal power of the papal curia. These measures of civic autonomy had to be accepted even by the popes, such as *Innocent IV and *Alexander IV. However, his greatly advanced social programmes brought about a negative public reaction and ultimately led to his deposition in 1255. D.'s contribution was commemorated by the erection of a special column in his honour.

DANEGELD A tax imposed by Anglo-Saxon kings in the 10th century as a means of financing the tribute owed to *Danish invaders since the days of King Ethelred II (987-1016). The D. generally consisted of two shillings per hide, although there were periods when four shillings or more were required. Although the tribute had been paid since 991, the term D. was unknown before the Norman Conquest.

D. is not to be confused with the *Heregeld*, which was an annual tax imposed between the years 1012-51, first to pay the Danish mercenaries and later to maintain a standing army. Anglo-Norman kings, especially William the Conqueror and Henry II, continued to levy the D. until 1162, and used the revenues for special war efforts or to meet extraordinary expenses.

F. M. Stenton, *Anglo-Saxon England* (1947).

DANEHOF The name of the Danish parliament, which emerged in the middle of the 13th century. Originally it was an aristocratic assembly, formed as a result of a struggle against the crown, and was meant to restrict King *Eric V's arbitrary rule. The church's attack on the crown, led by the archbishop *Erlandsen, played a considerable role in this conflict, since it weakened the royal position and drove the king to accept the aristocracy's constitutional demands. In 1282 the authority of the D. was legally recognized and the king's powers limited by a special royal charter, which also instituted the annual convention of the D.

DANELAW (DANELAGH) (Old English: Dena lagu "Danes' law") The name of those districts in the northern and eastern parts of Anglo-Saxon England settled by the invading *Danes in the 9th century. The D., which included the kingdoms of Northumbria and East Anglia, and the five Danish boroughs, formed a distinctive region in which customs and laws of Danish origin prevailed.

DANEWERK (Danevirke; Dannevitke) A medieval system of earth-work fortifications in Denmark. The D. is

actually a 17 km-long rampart, the most extensive piece of construction of medieval Scandinavia, built over a period of 350 years (9th-12th centuries). Its purpose was to defend the land from the south. The earliest section of the D. goes back to the year 808 when the Danes became involved in a conflict with *Charlemagne. In response to Charlemagne's establishment of a march at the border of Jutland, the D. was constructed to protect the town of Hedeby (Schleswig). Although the D. seems to have been more of a symbol than a real defence system, it nevertheless proved impregnable during the 10th century. During the reign of Waldemar I (1157-82), a brick wall, named after him (*Waldemarmauer*), was added.

DANIEL OF GALICIA (Danilo Romanovich; 1202-64) Prince and later king of Galicia and Volhynia (modern Poland and Ukraine). During his long minority (1205-21) under his mother's regency, the principalities were troubled by numerous pretenders to the throne and by incessant feudal wars. By 1221 D. had gained control of Volhynia, but only in 1238 did he succeed in imposing his rule over Galicia. From 1235 until his death, the two principalities, which had been united by his father, prospered and developed thanks to the trade between East and West that passed through them. D. encouraged immigrants to settle in his lands and built new cities (e.g., Chelm, Lvov). During the Mongol invasion (1240-41) D. was forced to acknowledge the khan's overlordship. In 1245 he gained a decisive victory over the Poles and the Hungarians, becoming the mightiest ruler in central Europe. D. sought support from western powers to throw off the Mongol yoke. He negotiated with Pope *Innocent IV, accepted the Catholic faith and was awarded the title of king (1253). In 1256, when the promised crusade did not materialize, he marched against the Mongols alone and succeeded in driving them out of Volhynia. A few years later (1260), however, he was again forced to accept Mongol suzerainty.

M. Hrushevsky, *A History of Ukraine* (1941).

DANIEL OF KIEV (Danil Igumen; 12th century) Russian travel writer. He was the abbot (*igumen*) of a monastery in Little Russia, who journeyed to Syria and Palestine about 1106-07. His narrative begins at Constantinople, continued in Cyprus, and then turns to a description of the Holy Land. D.'s visit in Palestine took place during the reign of *Baldwin I, shortly after the Crusader kingdom of Jerusalem was established. He stayed in Jerusalem for more than a year, during which time he journeyed on three separate occasions, thus acquiring personal knowledge from his own experience. His account of his travels contains not only topographical and historical details of the holy places, church services, their rituals and liturgy, but also depicts social and economic conditions in Jerusalem and elsewhere. The pilgrimage narrative is considered a valuable medieval document as it is an eyewitness account more detailed and accurate than previous itineraries. His Old Russian narrative has been translated into modern languages.

B. de Khitrovo, *Itinéraires russes en Orient* (1889); *Palestine Pilgrim's Text Society*, IV (1895).

DANIEL OF MORLEY (Morilegus) Astronomer, natural scientist and philosopher, of the late 12th century. D. studied at Oxford and Paris but was disappointed with the teaching methods, complaining that his teachers knew very little about natural sciences. He later went to study at *Toledo, then an important centre of learning and science, and became acquainted with the advanced research undertaken in physics and astronomy. With scholars such as Adelard of Bath and Robert of Chester, also Englishmen, D. shared the pioneer task of translating Arabic philosophical books into Latin. This project, undertaken at the Toledo school of translation, also enlisted the cooperation of Jewish, Greek and Arab scholars. D. brought back many translated books on *astronomy, the natural sciences and philosophy from Spain, which were later copied and considerably circulated in England.

D.'s teachings are compiled in *Philosophia magistri Daniel de Merlac*. He also wrote the *Liber naturis inferiorum et superiorum*.
C. H. Haskins, *Studies in the History of Medieval Science* (1924).

DANIEL OF MOSCOW (Daniel Nevski; end of 13th century) Prince and founder of the principality of Moscow and of the dynasty of the Moscow Grand Princes. D. was the youngest son of *Alexander Nevski (d. 1263), who had in his time obtained from the Mongol khan of the *Golden Horde the title and office of deputy in Russia. D. also secured his appointment from the khan and, as prince of Moscow (1280-1303), he built up his authority against rival Russian princes. He brought in many colonists and merchants to develop the country, which had an advantageous commercial position near the Moscow River. From a small settlement in the Rostov-Suzdal principality, Moscow grew into a prosperous and important centre.
G. V. Vernadsky, *The Mongols and Russia* (1953).

DANTE (DURANTE) ALIGHIERI (1265-1321) Italian poet. Born to an ancient Florentine family. At an early age, he showed a great talent for poetry. He studied grammar and rhetoric, but his poetic creativity gained considerable impetus through his social contacts and friendship with poets like Latini and Cavalcanti, who were among his early instructors. His first important work in the Italian vernacular was the *Nuova Vita* (The New Life), written *c.* 1293, in which he described in prose and verse his reflections on the various phases of his devoted and courtly love for Beatrice – a young lady who had captured D.'s heart since he was nine years old. The death of Beatrice (1290) was a traumatic experience in D.'s life, but soon afterwards he married and engaged himself in study. He attended the mendicant schools of the *Franciscans and the *Dominicans, where he read classical and contemporary poetry and showed great interest in philosophy, logic and theology, subjects that enriched his cultural outlook and are reflected in his later poetry. In 1295 D. began his political career, at a time when *Florence was troubled by disputes between rival factions within the *Guelph party: the Blacks and the Whites. The Blacks, with the backing of *Boniface VIII, pursued a policy of territorial expansion in Tuscany, which was the cause of internal intrigues in Florence. D., who remained neutral, soon assumed an important role in city affairs as administrator and diplomat, being elected *priore*. As a means of enforcing peace and public order, D. banished the leaders of both factions and later became the leader of the Whites, opposing the pope's policies. When *Charles I of Valois, who invaded Tuscany at the pope's request, threatened Florence, D. was sent to appease Boniface, but all was in vain. After Charles

entered the city, the Blacks had the upper hand, taking revenge on the Whites, whom they labelled *Ghibellines. The latter were tried in court and expelled. D. was also tried and when he failed to appear, being outside of Florence, he was condemned to death.

Thus D. began a lifetime of wandering, travelling through Verona (1303, 1316), Bologna (1304-06), Lucca (1308) and Ravenna (1318-21), where he held various diplomatic posts. In the first years after the Blacks' successful attack, D. took part in the Ghibellines' schemes to recover Florence. However, he soon disagreed with the Whites' policy of petty revenge and withdrew, but remained a true patriot of his native city.

During his years of exile, D. produced some of his best works. While at Bologna he wrote *Il Convivio* (The Banquet) and *De vulgari eloquentia* (On Vulgar Eloquence), both unfinished works, which reflect his return to philosophical and rhetorical studies. The latter work shows a deep concern for the Italian vernacular which he regarded not only a nationalistic expression, but as a genuine language of poetry. The *Convivio* hints at D.'s idea of imperial authority, which was later systematically developed in his Latin treatise *De Monarchia* (On Monarchy). In this work, D. expounded his conviction that a universal monarchy ruled by a secular emperor authorized by divine right was the only remedy for the Christian world and for divided and tormented Italy. D. spent his last years in Ravenna, where he wrote his greatest poetic work, *La Divina Commedia* (The Divine Comedy), on which he laboured many years (1307-21). The work consists of three parts: *Inferno* (1310); *Purgatorio* (1314); *Paradiso* (1315-21), and describes in fine poetry D.'s allegorical journey into the afterlife. Guided by Virgil, D. is led through the dark Inferno, where he meets sinful historical figures (from ancient to his own time), including emperors, popes, churchmen, politicians and women, to Purgatory. At the entrance to Paradise, Beatrice comes to escort him and leads him through all ten heavens to the highest one, where, through the intervention of St. Bernard, he is granted a short glimpse of divinity. Besides its aesthetic and poetic value, *The Divine Comedy* also has historical importance as a contemporary work reflecting the medieval world, in which the author passes judgement on contemporary figures and events.
B. Croce, *The Poetry of Dante* (1922);
J. A. Mazzeo, *Medieval Cultural Tradition in Dante's Comedy* (1960).

DANZIG (Polish: Gdansk) Medieval city and port on the Baltic Sea at the mouth of the Vistula River; member of the *Hanse. The earliest record of D. dates from 997, when the city was evangelized by *Adalbert, bishop of Prague and missionary of the Slavs. During the 11th century D. developed from a small town built around a seignorial castle into a city port. With the expansion of shipping activities eastwards, G. became the trade centre of Pomerania. By 1227 a market of German merchants from Lübeck was founded in the city. In 1260 G. was granted municipal autonomy. For a long period, it belonged to the dukes of Pomerania. In 1294, when no heir remained, the duchy, together with D., was bestowed on the great duke of Poland. In 1308 D. was captured by the *Teutonic order as part of its conquest of central Europe. Even the defeat of the Teutonic Knights at Grunwald in 1410 did not alter the situation. During the 13th and 14th centuries D. came to play an important part in the trade which took place between the cities of the Hanse. Its commercial ties were with cities throughout Europe and in particular with the eastern Baltic ports.

F. Dvornik, *The Slavs in European History and Civilization* (1962).

DAUPHINÉ Ancient province in southern France whose borders were *Provence and *Comtat Venaissin to the south and *Savoy to the north. Its name derived from the cognomen of one of its earliest counts, Guigues IV Dauphin. The name Dauphin came to be a title designating his successors and later designating the heir to the French crown.

D. is mentioned relatively late in the history of medieval France (13th century). Its origins lay in the county of Vienne, given as a fief (1029) to Guigues I de Vion, count of Alban, the ancestor of Guigues IV Dauphin (1133-42). Guigues I and his heirs considerably expanded the domain during the 12th century. Further territories were added by ruling families, of the house of

King David playing the Harp; *in the Psalter of Siegbury*

Burgundy (1162-1282), and the house of La Tour du Pin (1282-1349), who inherited D. through marriage. This expansion inevitably led the Dauphins to a series of wars with the counts of Savoy, exhausting their financial resources. It was Humbert II, the last Dauphin (1333-49), and one who contributed much to the province's development and organization, who was forced to face this situation. The lack of funds for his war expenses and other internal projects, and the fact that he remained heirless on the death of his sons, induced him to sell his province to the king of France, Philip VI. In 1349 a treaty was signed by which D. was transferred to Charles, grandson of Philip VI and the future King Charles V, for 200,000 florins. D. was not incorporated into the royal domain and became the traditional domain of the eldest son of the French king, the heir apparent.

G. Le Tonnelier, *Histoire du Dauphiné* (1958).

DAVID King of Israel. The personality of King D. was extremely popular in the Middle Ages, both in Jewish and Christian societies. In Judaism, the Messianic belief was connected with the descent of D. and, as such, he gained an important place in the liturgy. Moreover, the attribution of the Psalms to him contributed to his popularity, drawing Jews to visit his tomb on Mount Zion at Jerusalem during their pilgrimages to the holy places. To belong to the Davidic dynasty also had a social impact. The leaders of the Jews in Mesopotamia, the exilarchs, were considered a dynasty descended from D., and their prestige was paramount until the 13th century. Moreover, various leaders of communities in the West emphasized their Davidic ancestry as well. Among them were the heads of the community of Narbonne in France, who established a dynasty (9th-14th centuries) which was recognized as descending from the biblical king even by Christian circles, who officially entitled them "the Jewish kings of Narbonne".

In Christian society, both Christology — emphasizing the prophecy of Isaiah about the Virgin's child "Emmanuel" and Mary's descent from the Davidic dynasty — and the liturgical influence of the Psalms contributed to D.'s popularity. The idea of the biblical monarchy and its representation in the Christian empire were related with the person of D. as being the model monarch. Thus, in the 8th century, the title D. was given to *Pepin the Short and then to *Charlemagne, represented as a new D. in the palace academy of *Aix-La-Chapelle. The political thinkers of the *Carolingian Renaissance saw King D. as a symbol of both justice and piety (the king-poet); this figure became an exemplary type of monarch and during the Middle Ages certain kings, such as *Louis VII of France, were hailed as D.

A. Grabois, *Le souvenir et la légende de Charlemagne dans les textes hébraïques médiévaux* (1966).

DAVID, St. (Welsh: Dewi; c. 520-c. 601) The national patron saint of Wales. Very few facts concerning his life have been substantiated. His earliest biography, the *Life,* by Bishay Rhygyfarch or Ricimas, dates from the 11th century and was written with the intention of establishing the pre-eminence of the Welsh see of St. David over the Norman see of Canterbury.

According to tradition, D. was of noble birth, was ordained a priest and studied with St. Paulinus of Wales for some time. Later he began his missionary work, in the course of which he founded monasteries and settled

at Mynyw or Menevia, an abbey which became a religious and spiritual example of Welsh monasticism. As a monk, D. led an ascetic life, hence his cognomen of "water drinker" (*aquaticus*). D. is said to have played a important part in two synods, that of Brefi (in 560) and the *Synod of Victory (in 589, convened to combat Pelagianism). Among the legends told about D. is the story of his pilgrimage to Jerusalem where he was created archbishop by the patriarch of Jerusalem. D. was canonized by Pope Calixtus II (1120) and his cult spread rapidly throughout Wales. In works of art, D. is generally represented with a dove on his shoulder.
N. K. Chadwick *et al., Studies in the Early British Church* (1958).

DAVID I (c. 1084-1153) King of Scotland (1124-53). The youngest son of *Malcolm III and. Margaret, he spent many years at the court of *Henry I of England, who was married to his sister. Upon the death of his brother Edgar, king of the Scots (1107), D. received the southern parts of Scotland, while another brother *Alexander I won the north and the crown. His possessions were increased by his marriage to Matilda (1113), who brought him the earldom of Huntington. In 1124, when Alexander I died, D. succeeded him as king of Scotland. His involvement in English affairs was due to his fealty oath (1127), in which he recognized *Matilda as heir of Henry I. When *Stephen usurped the throne in 1135, D. took up arms, invaded England and fought a series of battles on Matilda's behalf. In 1136 D. got Cumberland, while the earldom, and later also Northumberland (1139), were given to his son Henry. In 1141 D. again fought Stephen on behalf of Matilda and her son (the future *Henry II, whom D. knighted in 1149); he was captured, held for a short while and escaped. Thereafter he stayed in Scotland and devoted himself to secular and ecclesiastical affairs. D. established a central administration and a strong government, and was the first king to strike royal coins. D. furthered the process of feudalism by receiving in his service a new Anglo-Norman aristocracy which was to play a predominant role in the political and cultural history of Scotland. D. was a noted ecclesiastical patron, reorganized the church according to European models, established five bishoprics and founded 12 abbeys and numerous churches. His reign is considered an epoch of greatness for Scotland.
W. C. Dickinson, *Scotland from the Earliest Times to 1603* (1961);
R. L. Mackie, *A Short History of Scotland* (1962).

DAVID II, the Bruce King of Scotland (1324-71). Son of *Robert I the Bruce, who, in accordance with the terms of the Anglo-Scottish treaty, was married at the age of four to Joanna, the sister of the future king *Edward III. He spent most of his reign outside Scotland, either in exile or in prison. D. first left his country as the result of the success of his rival, Edward Balliol, who was the vassal of Edward III and the actual ruler of Scotland. D. spent seven years (1334-41) in France, where he was offered hospitality by Philip VI, and fought with the French against Edward III in the early campaigns (1339-40) of the *Hundred Years' War. In 1341 after his supporters gained the upper hand with French backing, D. returned to Scotland, where he became engaged in a series of wars with England. In 1346 Philip VI was fighting the English at Calais, and in response to his appeal for aid, D. invaded England but

was defeated and captured at Neville's Cross. Subsequently he spent 11 years in a London prison. In 1357 he was released for an enormous ransom of 100,000 marks, which after a few payments proved beyond the country's resources. D., being childless, offered to recognize Edward or one of his descendants as his successor, in return for the cancellation of the ransom. This proposal, opposed by his nephew and successor, *Robert II, was also rejected by the Scottish parliament, who ultimately paid the entire ransom. D.'s last years were marked by the parliament's opposition to his extravagant expenditures.
R. L. Mackie, *A Short History of Scotland* (1962).

DAVID BEN ZAKKAI (d. 940) Jewish Babylonian *exilarch of Sura, Iraq (917), appointed by the head of the Jewish academy (*rosh yeshiva*) of Sura, a few years after his uncle had been removed from his position by his antagonist, the *Rosh Yeshiva* of Pumbedita. D.'s office coincided with a period of struggle over the Jewish leadership in Babylon. As exilarch, D. tried to maintain his hereditary office, which was disputed by a party of wealthy citizens, who wanted to abolish the position altogether. D. proved himself a determined leader and administrator and, in order to save the Sura academy from decline, appointed *Saadia Gaon as its head (927). A few years later (930), a bitter dispute arose between the two concerning matters of leadership and authority, and each took steps to reduce the other's power. Saadia and his supporters announced D.'s deposition, appointing his brother in his place; whereby D. responded by appointing a new gaon of Sura. The dispute was brought before the caliph, who ruled in D.'s favour and Saadia was removed from his position and expelled. Only in 937 were D. and his opponent reconciled; but three years later the former died. D.'s long struggle secured the prestigious position of the traditional exilarchate despite the attempts to usurp its leadership.

DAVID KIMHI (Radak or Maistre Petit; c. 1160-1235) Jewish exegete and philologist. A member of the Kimhi family of scholars, exegetes and grammarians. D. was a teacher in Narbonne, and active in the *Maimonidean controversy (1232) defending the memory of the great Jewish scholar. His main philological work was the *Michlol* (Compendium), comprising grammatical and lexicographical sections. The latter part became known independently as the *Book of Roots* (1480). As an exegete D. combined the Spanish speculative and philological traditions of *Ibn Ezra with the rabbinical Midrashic method and with the simple interpretations of *Rashi. His commentaries on Prophets, Chronicles and Psalms reveal his philosophical inclination and reflect the rationalism of *Maimonides. They also contained important polemical material which denounced Christological as well as allegorical interpretations by Christians. The polemical fragments were collected and published separately under the title *Teshuvot ha-Nozerim* (Christian *Responsa*). His exegetic and lexical studies, associated with a deep interest in the correct text of the Bible, influenced the Christian Hebraists and humanists of the Renaissance.
F. Talmage, "R. David Kimhi as Polemist", *HUCA*, 38 (1967);
Idem, "A Hebrew Polemical Treatise", *HTR*, 60 (1967).

DAVID OF AUGSBURG (c. 1200-72) German preacher, theologian and mystic. At an early age he joined the

*Franciscans in Regensburg, where he studied and later became teacher and master of novices (1235-50). In 1246 he was appointed visitator at Augsburg, and from 1250 made a number of journeys for the purpose of spreading the faith. He became famous as a great preacher and spiritual thinker, who laid more stress on practical aspects of humility and complete obedience than on pure and speculative contemplation. D. preached against the *Waldenses and wrote the tractate *De haeresis pauperum de Lugduno*. Some of his Latin works, which have been erroneously attributed to St. *Bernard or St. Bonaventura, include *De exterioris et interioris hominis compositione*; *Tractatus de oratione*. D. is also the author of eight German spiritual exhortations and mystical works. His clear mystical theology influenced later spiritual circles such as *Devotio Moderna* and the German mystics.

DAVID OF DINANT (c. 1160-c. 1210) Early scholastic philosopher. D. taught at the University of Paris (c. 1200) and lectured on Aristotle, relying on Erigena's interpretation incorporated in *De divisione naturae*. Like Erigena, D. held to the pantheistic view, which divided reality into matter (bodies), intellect (souls), spirit (eternal substance), and identified God with Aristotle's primary matter. This doctrine was condemned as heresy by the Council of Sens at Paris (1210) and at Rome (1215), and D. himself was exiled from Paris. All copies of his main work *De Tomis, id est de divisionibus*, probably identical with his *Quater nulli*, were burned publicly. Some of his views are preserved in the writings of philosophers like *Albert the Great, *Thomas Aquinas and *Nicholas of Cusa, who combatted and repudiated his pantheistic doctrine.
E. Gilson, *History of Christian Philosophy in the Middle Ages* (1955).

DEACON The lowest rank of church office, below that of bishop and presbyter (priest); an old institution which came into being with the organization of the primitive Christian community. The D.'s earliest function was the collection and distribution of alms. In the apostolic age the D. also read the Epistle and assisted the priest in the mass. In time, the practical and administrative duties soon made the D., and in particular the archdeacon of the diocese, the bishop's managing officer. In addition to taking care of the poor, the sick, widows and orphans, the D. was in later times also entrusted with supervising church property and managing its finances. In Rome the D. assumed a predominant role by his close relationship with the pope, and often served as papal messenger on important missions. His duties and power led to abuses, often criticized in church councils. During the Middle Ages the D.'s influence and importance declined.
J. Colson, *La fonction diaconale aux origines de l'église* (1960).

DEACONESS A term in the early church designating a woman who performed functions similar to those of the *deacon. In the early days the D. was an older woman who took care of poor and sick women, was present when females were interviewed by higher clerics, kept order in the women's section of the church and instructed the female catechumens. The D. was connected in particular with the baptism of women, where her assistance was necessary as the priest could not perform this sacrament by himself. This led to other priestly duties, such as administering the Eucharist to women and read-

ing the Scriptures, especially in the schismatic churches and communities. The position gradually lost its importance when adult baptism fell into disuse, and the office was cancelled by two church councils in the 6th century. In certain places it survived, although in a moderated form, until the 11th century.
C. H. Turner, "Ministries of Women in the Primitive Church. Widow, Deaconess and Virgin in the Four Christian Centuries" in *Catholic and Apostolic* (1931).

DEAN (Latin: decanus) Originally the title of a monk responsible for the supervision of ten monks or novices. Generally, a minor church official who functions as the head of a group. There were: a) the D. of a cathedral, who is the head of the *chapter and figures next to the bishop. He is charged with the regulation of services and administration of the cathedral. The importance of the D.'s function is illustrated by the fact that in some cathedrals the bishop himself is the D. and the D.'s post is filled by a provost; b) a D. appointed by an archbishop, in charge of ten or more parishes, who also acts as head of the chapter; c) the D. of the Sacred College of the Roman Church, always a cardinal bishop.
Some of the D.'s offices were not entirely ecclesiastical and therefore held by laymen, such as: a) the D. of a college or a university; b) the D. of Arches, who performed legal and juridical functions, and was the only lay judge who could pass sentence on a person in holy orders.

DE ARTE VENANDI CUM AVIBUS (The Art of Falconry) A treatise written by Emperor *Frederick II (c. 1248), after 30 years of preparation, which included personal observations, research and accumulation of data. The treatise, divided into six books, is more than a manual for training birds or taming falcons for the hunt. It is regarded as a zoological study written from a scientific and methodological point of view, revealing broad knowledge and an investigative approach. Frederick used as references several biological and zoological works available in his time, especially those of *Aristotle and *Ibn Sinna, most of them translated from Arabic by *Michael Scotus at Frederick's request. But a large portion of the book was based on his personal research and observation of birds.
D. was completed in 1248 but was lost in battle near Parma. The revision made by Frederick's son, *Manfred, is the main source for the printed editions.
C. A. Wood and F. M. Fyfe, trans. and ed., *The Art of Falconry* (1943).

DECIMA NOVALIUM (Latin: new tithes) Tithes granted to monasteries from newly-cultivated lands and distinguished from field tithes. Although the D. tithes had already been mentioned in the 9th century at the Council of Tribur (895), they remained unimportant until the 12th century. During the gradual expansion of that century, when more and more waste lands were being cleared for cultivation, especially at the frontiers, marches, forests and swamps, these tithes assumed great economic importance. The D. was regarded as a form of property, and became a disputed question within the church which preoccupied the best legal minds and ecclesiastical lawyers.

DECRETALS Papal decisions, precepts or rulings on various matters of canonical discipline. Originally the D. were pontifical letters sent to bishops in response to questions, reports or appeals. The first known D. stem

from the 4th century. Since they had the binding authority of law, they were assembled into collections, which later became part of the *canon law. Among the earliest and most influential collections, prior to that of *Gratian, were the Roman compilation, *Dionysiana Collectio*, which in the 8th century became the well-known *Dionysio-Hadriana Collectio*; the Frankish *Collectio Corbeiensis* (c. 524) and *Collectio Andegavensis* (c. 670); and in particular the Spanish *Hispana Collectio* (c. 600), mistakenly attributed to *Isidore of Seville. Beginning in the middle of the 9th century, the circulation of *False Decretals, which included many spurious letters stressing the supremacy of papal authority, added special significance to the development of decretal codification. As a result, many fictitious D. were incorporated into the systematic compilation known as *Decretum Gratiani*. However, from the 1170s, the time of Pope *Alexander III, a new stage in the tradition of canon law began. Its main characteristic was that the systematic compilations of D. employed mostly recent or contemporary canonical decisions. These collections, initially mere appendices to Gratian's Decretum, were entitled *libri decretalium* or *libri extravagantium*. Best-known among them were the *Quinque Compilationes Antiquae* (Five Antique Compilations), which replaced most preceding collections. Later on, in the middle of the 13th century, the *Quinque* was superseded by the Gregorian D. (1234). This very systematic work, compiled by *Raymond of Peñafort at Pope *Gregory IX's request, became the main source of canon law. The D. of Gregory were supplemented by other authoritative collections, mainly the *Liber Sextus* (1298) published by *Boniface VIII and the *Constitutiones Clementinae* (1317) of John XXII, which formed the official *Corpus Iuris Canonici*.
C. Duggan, *Twelfth-Century Decretal Collections and Their Importance in English History* (1963);
G. Le Bras *et al.*, *L'Age classique, 1140-1378. Sources et théorie du droit* (1965).

DECRETUM GRATIANI A collection of *Decretals assembled by *Gratian c. 1140-41, whose full title is *Concordantia Discordantium Canonum*. This codex contains some 4000 references to numerous ecclesiastical sources: apostolic constitutions, patristic texts, canons of councils and papal decretals, both genuine and spurious, dating from early centuries to Gratian's own time, even including the decrees of the Lateran Council of 1139. All these sources, dealing with church discipline, were systematically arranged according to scholastic methods in such a manner as to make the contradictions between different church authorities seem to agree in reference to a specific subject. The D. was soon regarded as a textbook of *canon law, particularly at the law schools of Bologna, Paris and Oxford, and it served as an authoritative reference work in courts throughout Europe. The collection attracted many commentators from the 12th century onward, among them, the future Pope *Alexander III. It constitutes the first part of the *Corpus Iuris Canonici*.
G. Le Bras *et al.*, *L'Age classique, 1140-1378. Sources et théorie du droit* (1965).

DE DONIS CONDITIONALIBUS Also known as the Second Statute of Westminster. An act passed by *Edward I in 1285 which made possible the entailing of estates. Accordingly, a person could prevent the alienation or transfer of his estates to anyone other than his immediate legitimate heirs. The statute put an end to the prevailing practice in the 13th century which interpreted the law to mean that as soon as a person had an heir of his own he was free to dispose of the property as he wished, or transfer it to whomever he pleased. The new act declared such an interpretation contradictory to the intention of the grantor. It achieved a double purpose, preventing the disinheritance of direct successors, and ensuring that, in the event of there being no immediate issue, the estate would return to the king.
G. B. Adams, *Constitutional History of England* (1963).

DE HERETICO COMBURENDO (On the burning of a heretic) An act passed by the English Parliament in 1401, intended to suppress the heresy of the *Lollards. The initiative for this statute came from the bishops, who, alarmed by the spread of John *Wycliffe's doctrines throughout England, won the support of King *Henry IV. The act condemned the preaching or teaching of opinions contrary to the Catholic faith, and authorized the arrest and trial of persons holding such heretical views before an ecclesiastic court. Convicted heretics, namely those who refused to repent or guilty of returning to heresy after recantation, were handed over to the secular authorities to be publicly burnt, an act meant to serve as a deterrent for others .
There was much opposition to the act, which led to popular unrest. The Lollards demanded its modification, and the Commons, who sought a safeguard against such arbitrary arrests, required that the role of the Church be minimized. Ultimately a compromise was reached in 1414, whereby the arrest of heretics was entrusted to the secular authorities, while church jurisdiction was maintained during the trial.
K. B. MacFarlane, *John Wycliffe and the Beginning of the English Nonconformity* (1953).

DEIRA The southern Anglo-Saxon kingdom, which later became incorporated into the kingdom of Northumbria. D.'s northern border was the Tees River. Its capital was York, which served as the nucleus of many ancient Anglo-Saxon settlements. Archaeological finds have indicated that these settlements existed long before the second half of the 6th century, the date given by the earliest records of the kingdom, which mention the first king, Aelle, Aelli or Ella as having ruled about 560. After Aelli's death D. was governed by Aetnelfrith, who is considered the founder of the Northumbrian kingdom. Later, the two kingdoms were ruled by Edwin (617-32), son of Aelli. From that time onwards, the fate of D. and its rulers was largely dependent upon Northumbrian policy.
F. M. Stenton, *Anglo-Saxon England* (1947);
P. Hunter Blair, *An Introduction to Anglo-Saxon England* (1959).

DELHI City and sultanate in northern India. An ancient city, D. was ruled for many centuries by a series of Hindu dynasties. In 1193 the last Hindu king was killed when D. was captured by the Moslem, Mohammed of Ghor. Kutb Al-Din Aybak, who was left in charge, imposed a Moslem character on the city and, in 1206, declared it autonomous. In 1211 D. became the capital of the sultanate under Itutmish (1211-36), who consolidated his rule against other generals of Mohammed of Ghor. After a period (1236-46) of internal struggle for the throne, Ghiyas Al-Din Balban gained control and D.

enjoyed many years (1246-87) of stable government, avoiding direct confrontation with the Mongols. But it was the Khalji sultans (1290-1326) who turned D. into a great power, subduing other Hindu kingdoms in the south. During this time they also succeeded in defeating the Mongol army several times. At the end of the 14th century the sultanate was seriously threatened by the invading *Timur-Leng (Tamerlane) (1398-99), and D. was besieged and plundered. Thereafter the power of the sultanate, which was under the Sayyids (1414-51), declined considerably and D. became an insignificant principality.

A. M. Husain, *Le gouvernement du Sultanat de Delhi* (1936);
P. Spear, *Delhi: A Historical Sketch* (1945).

DELLA FAGIUOLA, UGUCCIONE (1250-1319) A Ghibelline leader, soldier and statesman, who held positions of authority in various cities. Beginning in 1297, when he fought at the head of a band of military adventurers, he became a Ghibelline partisan. In 1303 he was made podesta of Arezzo, but was soon expelled. He was later appointed leader and chief of the Ghibellines in Tuscany. In 1313 he was elected podesta of *Pisa, and a year later became lord of Lucca, but his despotic rule brought about his expulsion (1316). Afterwards he found refuge with Cangrande della Scala, the imperial vicar of Verona, who was in the process of building a Ghibelline state in northern Italy. D. was therefore put in charge of the Ghibelline forces and later appointed podesta of Venice (1317).

DELLA TORRE A noble Italian family whose members ruled *Milan during the 13th and the beginning of the 14th century. The family rose to prominence in the 13th century when Pagano D. became leader of the popular party and sided with the *Guelphs (1240). But the most impressive figure of the family was Martino, who became ruler of Milan in 1247. Two years after the defeat of the *Ghibellines (1257) Martino was elected podesta. He shared the power with Pallavicini, whom he appointed captain. From that time, Martino was re-elected annually until his death. He was succeeded by his brother Filippo, who dismissed Pallavicini and ruled alone for a short period (1263-65). Filippo's rule was followed by that of his nephew, Napoleone, or Napo (1265-73). When the rival Visconti returned to power, Napo appealed to *Charles of Anjou who named him imperial vicar (1273). But the bitter conflict dragged on and ended with Napo's defeat and the restoration of the Visconti.

At the beginning of the 14th century the D. regained control of Milan when the Guelphs retaliated. They remained in power for a few years (1302-11) until *Henry VII's invasion of Italy put an end to their rule and reinstated their opponents, the Visconti.

DEMETRICIA (DEMETRITZES), BATTLE OF (1185) The site in Macedonia of a battle fought between the Normans and the Byzantine army where the latter was victorious. The Normans had advanced into Greece, when their leader, *William II of Sicily declared war on *Andronicus (1185), taking advantage of the internal struggle between *Isaac Angelus, who succeeded Andronicus, and the pretender to the throne, *Alexius Comnenus. After conquering Thessalonica and Serres, the Norman army was divided into small groups which wandered and ravaged the countryside. The Byzantine

general, Alexius Branas, who recruited a fresh army and gained several victories over these wandering bands, confronted the Norman army at D. Here, Branas broke the truce which had been agreed upon between the parties. His sudden attack kept the Normans from gaining reinforcements and resulted in their complete defeat. Among the captives were Alexius Comnenus and two Norman generals. The victory of D. put an end to Norman attempts of expansion in Greece.

DEMETRIUS King of *Croatia (1076-89). D. married into the family of the Hungarian rulers of *Arpad. This, together with the support of the Latin faction and his close relations with Pope *Gregory VII, brought him to the throne. D. was crowned by the papal legate in Split (1076), thus inheriting the kingdom from Kresimir (1058-74), who had brought the Croatian kingdom to the peak of its prosperity. In 1089 D. planned an extensive campaign against the Seljuks, counting on the new pope's cooperation. At an assembly which he convened in order to gain the support of his subjects, he was accused by the Croatian nobles of being the pope's vassal and was condemned to death.

DEMETRIUS OF MONTFERRAT King of *Thessalonica (1207-22). Son of *Boniface of Montferrat, he inherited the kingdom while still an infant. During most of his reign, the kingdom fell under the regency of his mother. At the outset, he was confronted with a baronial revolt. The Lombard barons, led by D.'s guardian, Hubert of Biandrate, refused to recognize the suzerainty of *Henry of Flanders, the Latin emperor of Constantinople. They therefore rebelled against D., who supported Henry, offering his kingdom to his half-brother, William of Montferrat. In 1209 D. was crowned by the emperor himself, who crushed the revolt, thus establishing his suzerainty over young D. and his kingdom. From the time of the emperor's death (1216) his kingdom was seriously threatened by *Theodore, the Greek despot of Epirus, who invaded it in 1222. D. fled to Italy, where he appealed to Pope *Honorius III to organize a Crusade. But the crusaders arrived too late and, in the meantime, Thessalonica fell to the Greeks in 1224.
CMedH, IV – *The Byzantine Empire* (1964).

DENIS, St. (3rd century) Bishop of Paris and patron saint of France. Little is known of his life. In the 6th century, *Gregory of Tours wrote that D. was one of the seven bishops sent to evangelize Gaul during the reign of Emperor Decius, and that after becoming the first bishop of Paris, he suffered martyrdom during the Valerian persecution (258). In 626 his relics were brought to their present site, the Benedictine abbey of St. Denis, near Paris, which was founded by *Dagobert. Subsequently D.'s cult spread rapidly. His grave at St. Denis' abbey became a revered shrine, and the abbey became the burial place of the kings of France. During the 9th century, D. was mistakenly identified with *Dionysius the Areopagite, and therefore believed to be the author of the Pseudo-Dionysian writings. Adoration of D. as patron saint contributed significantly to the consolidation of French national consciousness during the Middle Ages. His name was used as a battle-cry by French knights and the oriflamme banner of the D. abbey was adopted by the kings of France.
H. Delehaye, *Les origines du culte des martyrs* (1933);
R. J. Loenetz, "La Légende parisienne de S. Denys l'Aréopagite", *Analecta Bollandiana*, 69 (1951).

DENMARK A Scandinavian kingdom comprising the peninsula of Jutland and a group of islands. Although inhabited since prehistoric times, and mentioned in early literary sources (see *Beowulf), D.'s earliest documented history begins with the Vikings. In the early Middle Ages D. was conquered by Danish tribes from the East, who kept their tribal organization. For a long time D. had virtually no dealings with the rest of Europe, its close association with it beginning in the early 9th century, with the conquests of *Charlemagne. The Danes, under their kings Godfred and Hemming, managed to halt the Frankish expansion and established the border on the Eider River by a treaty signed in 811. Throughout, the Danes, with the Frisians, were active in the north European trade with the Near East, and actively sought new markets. Together with other northern Vikings they went on raids and voyage-conquests in Friesland, England, France and Russia.

These activities brought them into close contact with Christian Europe. The first missionaries had entered D. in the 8th century, but made little headway. The effort to Christianize the Danes was somewhat more successful when led by *Ebbo of Rheims and by St. *Anskar, the papal legate for the North and later bishop of Hamburg. He had not only the political support of *Louis the Pious, but also the cooperation of the newly converted Danish king (Harald Klak). It was, however, only in the middle of the 10th century that D. officially adopted Christianity, with the conversion of King Harald Blaatland (960), who promoted the evangelical mission and organized the church. Harald also laid the foundations for a consolidated kingdom. His conquests in Norway were carried further by his successors: Sweyn I, who conquered England in 1013, and *Canute, in whose reign the Anglo-Scandinavian kingdom, including parts of Sweden, saw its hey-day. In his reign, too, ecclesiastical and monastic establishments multiplied, with the help of churchmen inspired by the reform ideas of *Cluny. By the middle of the 11th century the Danish church had eight sees and hundreds of churches and monasteries all over the country.

After the death of Canute (1035) began the disintegration of his great kingdom, and D. was again merely a Scandinavian power for one hundred years, for a time dominated by Norwegian rulers. Attempts were occasionally made to reunify the kingdom, especially by Sweyn II and his sons (1074-1134). This critical period was marked by internal struggles for the throne, some of the kings accepting their land in fief from the Holy Roman emperor. The weak central rule enabled feudal nobility to strengthen its position, but the church was regarded as a stabilizing factor. In 1104 it became a national church, when Pope Urban II recognized D. as an independent northern province under the metropolitan of Lund. The political unrest came to an end at the middle of the 11th century, when *Waldemar I (1157-82) overcame his rivals, reunified the kingdom and established Danish independence for almost two hundred years. He organized a strong army and an efficient governmental system, with statesmen-churchmen such as *Eskil (1138-77) and *Absalon (1177-1201), who cooperated in building a strong and flourishing state and an authoritative monarchy.

This period is considered the golden age of the Danish church. It was a time of intense church building

Viking tombstones in Denmark

(over 2000 churches), and cultural creativity expressed in philosophy, theology and historiography, coinciding with the "early Renaissance" of 12th-century Europe. Important chronicles, biographies and works on the natural sciences were produced in monasteries by Danish scholars, the best known of whom are: Saxo Grammaticus, whose *Gesta Danorum* is a valuable source for the history of D.; Boethius of D., the philosopher; Peter of D., who wrote on mathematics and astronomy; Anders Sunesen, who wrote the *Xexameron,* a Latin work in hexameter on philosophy and theology.

Under *Waldemar II (1202-41) D. expanded her rule to the Baltic and the Slav countries. In a series of wars marked by a crusading spirit, D. achieved the conversion of the Wends, and gained control over Pomerania (1169) and Estonia (1219). Because of the weakness of Germany, the emperor in 1214 had to recognize Danish suzerainty over the Slav lands north of the Elbe. This drive eastward, however, drained D.'s resources and weakened her. This was aggravated by the tendency of King Waldemar II to distribute great feudal apanages, which soon threatened the unity of the kingdom.

Now followed a period (1241-1340) of decline and dissolution. A violent struggle among the heirs to the throne and the internal conflict between church and the crown exacerbated the process. The nobility also took advantage of the weakened royal authority, and became a threat to the crown. Later the barons cooperated with the church, under the leadership of Archbishop Jacob Erlandsen, and compelled the king to recognize the establishment of the *hof, the Danish parliament (1250), and the charter by which the national assembly limited the king's authority (1282). Attempts by Eric VI to resume power and authority made things worse, as the king was compelled to mortgage large territories in order to raise funds, and this played into the hands of the aristocracy who resisted the monarchy. In 1340, after the throne had been vacant for eight years, Waldemar IV managed to reorganize the kingdom and built a central authority, based on a strong national army and an efficient administration. At the national assembly of Kalundborg (1360) he gave a legal definition to the respective rights of the people and of the king. The following year he was driven out of the country by a coalition of the feudal nobility and the *Hanseatic League. To maintain his throne, Waldemar had to accept the great commercial privileges granted to the league.

With Waldemar's death the direct line came to an end, and D. was ruled by the privy council, which elected as king, *Olaf, the young son of Margaret, daughter of Waldemar and queen of Norway. Thus D. became a part of the Scandinavian union, dominated by Margaret (1387-1412), who was officially recognized as sovereign of D. and Norway.

A. Olrik, *The Heroic Legends of Denmark* (1919);
J. H. S. Birch, *Denmark in History* (1938);
L. Krabbe, *Histoire du Danemark, des origines jusqu'à 1945* (1950);
J. Bailhache, *Danemark* (1957).

DERBY, DERBYSHIRE Town and county in central England, whose earls played an important role in the baronial resistance. The name D. is a corruption of the Danish *Dearaby*. The entire region was subjected to Danish raids in the 9th century. D. later became one of the Danish burghs until 918, when it was conquered by Aethelflaed. It fell again into Danish hands to be recovered in 941-42 by *Edward the Elder. D. became a shire in the course of the 9th century, but was long associated with Nottinghamshire. During the 12th century D. received various privileges from *William I and *Henry I. The first earl of D. was Robert de Ferrers, granted the title by King *Stephen in 1138. His descendants retained the title until 1236 when Robert was dispossessed and deprived of his earldom, after having revolted against *Henry III. The estates were transferred to the king's son, Edmund, and to his grandson, who made himself earl of Ferrers. In 1337 Henry, Edmund's grandson, was made earl of D., and the title was later conferred on *John of Gaunt and on his son the future King *Henry IV as well. In 1485 the earldom of D. was held by the Stanley family.

J. P. Yeatman *et al.*, *Victoria County History of Derbyshire*, I-II (1905-1907);
P. L. Linton (ed.), *Sheffield and Its Region* (1956).

DESCHAMPS, EUSTACHE (c. 1346-c. 1406) French poet. D. was educated at Rheims by his uncle Guillaume de Machaut, and later studied law at Orléans. He joined the service of King *Charles V and travelled in central Europe as the king's messenger. Later he held various offices as bailiff of Valois and Senlis. D. witnessed many events of the *Hundred Years' War. His house was burned down by the English. Many of these events, and his hatred of the English in particular, are reflected in his works. In his later years he was appointed to other offices by *Charles VI, but his release from office as bailiff of Senlis displeased him and he became embittered, often complaining of poor health. D. devoted much of his time to poetry, which he had learned from Guillaume de Machaut. His works include more than 1000 ballads and poems. D. is considered the master of ballads in which he portrayed vices of clergy and officials in a satiric manner. His verses also reflect the anarchy in France and the situation that prevailed in his time. Among his works are the *Fiction du Lion* (1382), an allegorical description of the king's duties, addressed to the young Charles VI; *Miroir du mariage* – some 13,000 verses mocking women, two comic plays and the *Art de dictier* (1392), a treatise on poetics, considered the earliest and most important work on the subject.

E. Hoepffner, *E. Deschamps, Leben und Werke* (1904);
D. Poirion, *Le poète et le prince* (1965).

DESIDERIUS King of the *Lombards. Duke of Tuscany and, from 756, king of Lombardy. He was connected by marriage to the Frankish crown, his two daughters having wed *Pepin's sons, *Charlemagne and Carloman. When elected king, D. acknowledged papal domination over the lands granted him by Pepin. However, his independent policies brought him into direct conflict with *Hadrian I and later into an inevitable confrontation with Charlemagne. D.'s relations with Charlemagne had already begun to deteriorate in 771, when the latter disregarded the claim of Carloman's heirs, D.'s grandchildren, and appropriated Carloman's domains. When D.'s daughter fled to his court for his support, D. recognized his grandchildren as legitimate Frankish kings and pressed the pope to crown them. In response to the appeal of Hadrian I, Charlemagne invaded Lombardy and besieged Pavia (774). D. surrendered and was deposed and banished for the remainder of his life. His kingdom became part of the empire of Charlemagne.

F. Lot, *Les Destinées de l'empire en Occident de 395 à 888* (1940).

DESPENSER Name of an English family whose members distinguished themselves in state and baronial affairs during the 13th and 14th centuries. The name may be a derivation of *dispensator*, the office of steward that they held. Distinguished members of the family included:
1) **Hugh Le D.** (c. 1232-65), a leader of the baronial opposition to *Henry III. He was a member of the council appointed by the Oxford parliament (1258), and a justiciar, and he served as mediator of several delicate disputes between the king and the barons (1264), and between *Simon of Montfort and Gilbert of Clare, earl of Gloucester.
2) **Hugh Le D., the Elder (1261-1326)**, son of D.(1), who became active in Parliament in 1295, fought with *Edward I against France and Scotland and served as the king's emissary. From 1312 he was *Edward II's chief adviser and the object of the barons' jealousy. As a result the barons secured his temporary deposition in 1315. In 1322 he was made earl of Winchester.
3) **Hugh Le D., the Younger (d. 1326)**, son of D.(2). From 1318 he served as chamberlain to *Edward II. In 1321 he and his father were accused by a strong baronial opposition of abusing their positions to gain land and influence. The king reluctantly consented to their banishment, but soon reinstated them (1322). D.(3) was a competent and ambitious administrator who tried to make the king's chamber an autonomous department with its own seals, funds and private income. These methods were greatly resented and made him many enemies. During the revolt of Queen Isabella and *Roger Mortimer, the D. family remained loyal to the king. Both father and son were captured, tried and executed in 1326.

R. F. Treharne, *The Baronial Plan of Reform* (1932).

DESSAISINE (Dessaizine) A French term of feudal procedure meaning deposition. The term was usually used in the expression *dessaisine-saisine* or *vest-divest*, with regard to the feudal custom of transferring property and particularly to the alienation of fiefs.

D. was the act of handing a fief or property over to the lord from whom the tenant had received it, accompanied by a proper declaration of property restitution. Thus, the lord could invest a new vassal with the fief. However, from the 12th century onwards this act was replaced by the tacit consent of the lord to the alienation procedure.

R. Boutrouche, *Seigneurie et féodalité*, I (1959).

DEUSDETIT I (ADEODATUS) Pope (615-18). A Roman priest, who was elected to the papal throne. His pontificate coincided with a period of great anarchy in northern Italy, where the Byzantine exarchate of Ravenna was unable to control the Lombards, who revolted and killed the exarch. During this confrontation D. remained faithful to the emperor, thus saving Rome the retribution of the new exarch. D. is noted for restoring to the secular clergy the respect and high position which his predecessors, Boniface IV and Gregory I, had accorded the monks. During his pontificate Rome suffered from a serious earthquake and later from a plague. D. was proclaimed a saint of the Roman Church.

H. K. Mann, *The Lives of the Popes in the Early Middle Ages* (1932);

D. Bertolini, *Roma di fronte a Bisanzio e ai Longobardi* (1941).

DEUSDEDIT II (ADEODATUS) Pope (672-76). A Roman monk who succeeded Pope Vitalian. D. is known for his determined attitude in the *Monothelitic controversy that divided Christianity in the 7th century. He rejected Monothelitism, which he regarded as a heretical conception contrary to the orthodox faith. He was a generous pope and, as a Benedictine, favoured his own order, bestowing many gifts upon its monastery of St. Erasmus, where he had lived before his election.

DEUTZ Eastern quarter of *Cologne, situated on the eastern bank of the Rhine. D. commanded the Rhine bridge and, as such, was considered an important stronghold since early times. In the 4th century it was known as *Castellum Divitia* and fortified by *Constantine the Great (310). D. kept its strategic position as late as the 10th century. It is also known for the Benedictine abbey founded there in 1002 by Archbishop Heribert with the help of *Otto III. The original church, demolished by an earthquake (1019), was replaced by a great church famous for its long chancel. D. abbey became prominent in the controversy concerning the Benedictine way of life, which was defended by its abbot *Rupert during the second decade of the 12th century.

DEVIL (Hebrew: Satan, Greek: diabolos "accuser") The chief of the fallen angels who rebelled against God. The D. as the embodiment of evil, known by many names in the Old and New Testaments (Satan, evil, tempter, Lucifer etc.), is conceived as a spiritual being whose object is to tempt men and induce them to sin. The concept of D. in the early church was greatly influenced by the apocryphal literature and, in particular, by the Book of Enoch (6-11), according to which the demons were the offspring of the fallen angels and human females. The Church Fathers conceived of the D. as a spiritual being like other angels, who was expelled from heaven because of his ambition to seize divine power and be like God. They differed, however, as to the nature of the D.'s sin. Some – e.g., Tertullian, *Cyprian and *Clement – held that it was envy, while others – such as *Augustine, *Origen – believed it to have been pride.

In the Middle Ages the D. and the idea of evil preoc-

The Mouth of Hell *by Jacobus de Teramo; 1473*

cupied many great minds. It was part of scholastic speculation and intensely debated in the mendicant schools. *Albertus Magnus and *Thomas of Aquinas held that the D., like all other angels, was created in a state of grace and chose to sin, for, otherwise, God himself would have been the source of evil. The idea of the D. played a considerable and mysterious role in the thinking and imagination of the common people. The D. was portraited in church morality plays and in the plastic arts as an ugly, horned being with a tail, a menacing, treacherous creature, always out to tempt men and lead them through sin to hell. The church, however, claimed to have the power of control over the D., and of strengthening men's resistance against the D.'s temptations by means of the sacraments.

G. Bazin, *Satan* (1948);

H. Colleye, *Histoire du diable* (1945);

G. Papini, *The Devil* (1955).

DE VIRIS RELIGIOSIS A statute passed by *Edward I in 1279 dealing with church property found in the state of *mortmain* (dead hands). The statute forbade the granting of estates and landed property to the church without special permission from the king. This act, adopted first in England and later throughout Europe, was in response to the fact that the church, unlike lay tenants, was a corporate unit which would not die, marry, or commit a felony, and therefore the king was unable to collect certain revenues from it, such as feudal benefits and reliefs or to enjoy its privileges of escheat, wardships etc. The act resulted from a dispute which arose between Edward and the archbishop of Canterbury, but was not meant to encroach upon the privileges of the clergy. In fact, it did not prevent further grants to churches, but only made it necessary that special payments be made to the crown in return for the grants.

G. B. Adams, *Constitutional History of England* (1963).

DEVOLL, TREATY OF A treaty signed near the Devoll River (Balkan) in 1108, whereby the Norman *Bohemond of Antioch recognized Byzantine overlordship in *Antioch. The rivalry between the Normans and the Byzantine emperors, once restricted to southern Italy, had spread with the First *Crusade to the Near East. Ever since Bohemond's capture of Antioch and his establishment of an independent government there, he was a bitter enemy of the Byzantine emperor, *Alexius I. When Bohemond returned to Italy in 1104, after a long period of captivity in Moslem hands, during which Antioch was ruled by *Tancred, he raised a new army, invaded the Byzantine province and attacked Avlona. Alexius had the upper hand and Bohemond was compelled to sign the D., which included not only recognition of Alexius' suzerainty but also the reinstatement of a Greek patriarch in Antioch. However, the D. was not implemented since *Tancred, who was acting as regent in Antioch, refused to accept the terms.

DEVON, DEVONSHIRE A county on the southwestern coast of England. Its name was derived from the British Dumnonii, who survived the Saxon invasion of the late 7th century, remaining in England. D. became a shire in the mid-8th century, was incorporated into the kingdom of Wessex and formed part of the Sherborne diocese until 909. In 1050 the see of D. was moved to Exeter. During the Danish invasions D. suffered from many raids (851-1003). Its citizen were hostile towards *Harold, and later towards *William I, who conquered it and granted many fiefs to his Norman barons. Among the earls of D. in the 12th century were members of the de Redvers family, but in the following century the title passed to the Courtney family. D. took an active part in the civil war between *Stephen and *Matilda (the castles of Exeter and Plympton being held by Baldwin de Redvers against Stephen) and again in the Wars of the Roses. The county sent two delegates to Parliament in 1258 and 1290, and from 1295 was continuously represented there. Some monastic foundations, mostly of the Benedictine and Cistercian orders, were created during the 12th and 13th centuries.

W. C. Hoskins. *Devon* (1954).

DEVOTIO MODERNA A term designating the movement or school of revived religious spirituality which emerged in the Netherlands towards the end of the 14th century and then spread to France, Spain and northern Germany. The movement laid special stress on the deepening of spiritual life, on contemplation and on the reading of devotional writings, thus distinguishing its new modern spirituality from the older scholastic and speculative trend. The D. originated from *Groote's circle in Deventer, and soon was adopted by laity and clergy alike, who were eager to lead a true Christian life, to emphasize religious introspection rather than ritual. and to contemplate and follow the moral examples of such great spiritual guides as *Augustine, *Bernard, *Bonaventura etc. The laity was organized into independent associations of men and women, who adopted a religious way of life without taking vows, known as the *Brethren of the Common Life. Clergical members, who had a set way of life of their own, were known as the Regular Canons of Windesheim. The movement encouraged special spiritual exercises to strengthen will power. It regarded self-knowledge as a starting point for perfection, which was attainable through the practice of virtues, and through solitude, silence and mystic meditation.

Among the members of the movement were writers who dedicated special treatises to methods of spiritual and mystical contemplation and to asceticism. These authors included G. Groote, F. Radewijns, G. Peters, Mombaer and H. Mande. But the best-known and the most representative of them was *Thomas à Kempis, whose *Imitatio Christi* (Imitation of Christ) is regarded as an important guide to attain higher spirituality.

A. Hyma, *The Christian Renaissance. History of the 'Devotio Moderna'* (1925);

S. Axters, *De Moderne devotie 1380-1550* (1956).

DHIMMIS An Arabic term (*dhimma*) designating non-believers living in Islamic states, who were tolerated and accorded protection or hospitality in return for their recognition of the Islamic authority and payment of taxes. The concept's justification lies with the cardinal precept of the *Koran (IX, 24) which instructs the Moslems to fight infidels until they pay the poll-tax (*djizya*). Such a policy was based on the earlier attitude of Mohammed towards Jews and Christians, with whom he concluded agreements of submission and protection at the time when Islam was spreading to neighbouring countries.

DIALOGUS DE SCACCARIO A treatise written *c.* 1179 by Richard *Fitzneale, bishop of London and treasurer of King *Henry II. In the form of a dialogue between narrator and layman, the work attempts to explain to the latter the complicated business of running the exchequer. It describes in detail the methods and procedures used in the king's treasury, initiated by the author's father, Nigel, bishop of Ely and treasurer of *Henry I. According to the treatise, the exchequer consisted of two distinct departments; the lower (*inferius scaccarium*) was a permanent office whose principal agents were the treasurer, the clerk, two chamberlains and two assisting knights. This branch dealt with receipt and payment of money, using the tally system for accounting, and was charged with preserving the *Domesday Book. The upper department (*superius scaccarium*) was a council or court which convened twice a year, at Easter and Michaelmas, to check the accounts submitted by the sheriffs, using the *abacus. Its members were called Barons of the Exchequer. The D. is considered one of the earliest and most important references for Henry II's administrative reforms.

C. Johnson (ed. and trans.), *Dialogue of the Exchequer* (1950).

DICTATUS PAPAE The name was commonly reserved for the draft, or list dictated by *Gregory VII in the early days of his pontificate, which laid down his governing policy and theocratic conceptions. It contains 27 short entries, most of them dealing with church matters, which illustrate Gregory's policy concerning the papal authority in church and state. The D. proclaimed the spiritual supremacy of the pope in Christendom and his temporal command over clergy and lay rulers as well. Firstly, it affirmed that, as bishop of Rome, the pope had supreme judicial, legislative and administrative authority in the church. Secondly, it claimed that the pope had the right to depose emperors and absolve subjects from loyalty to unjust and arbitrary rulers. The intentions of the D. are much disputed. Some consider it to be only a short private memorandum without binding authority, while others see it as a list of headings and titles for a planned collection of *canon law. Still others regard the D. and, in particular, those articles concerning the secular princes, as the result of the conflict between Gregory and Emperor *Henry IV.

K. Hofman, *'Dictatus Papae' Gregors VII* (1933).

DIDIER The name of several French saints, of whom the better known are:

D., bishop of Cahors (630-55), son of a noble family who held various positions at the court of the Merovingian kings *Clotaire II and *Dagobert. His brother had preceded him as bishop of Cahors and upon his murder in 630, D. was elected to take his place, although still a layman. D. is described as a devoted churchman, who assembled local synods, built churches and founded monasteries, among them the abbey of Moissac and the monastery of St. Géry at Cahors, where he was buried. D. is credited with having written a monastic rule.

D., bishop of Vienne (595-606). A learned and able man who, after refusing many ecclesiastical positions, accepted the bishopric of Vienne in 595. He had an interesting correspondence with *Gregory I and offered his hospitality to St. *Augustine, who was on his way to evangelize England. D. was deposed and exiled by the Council of Chalon-sur-Saône (602-03), at Queen. *Brunhilda's instigation, on grounds of immoral conduct. A few years later D. was reinstated as bishop of Vienne, but as he continued to reproach *Theodoric II, Brunhilda's son, for improper conduct, he was arrested in his own church and later murdered by hired assassins. D. was declared a martyr and saint. The church of St. Didier-sur-Charlaronne, built near his grave, is dedicated to his memory.

A. Butler, *The Lives of the Saints* (1956).

DIES IRAE (Day of wrath) The opening words of the well-known hymn forming part of the office of the dead and the requiem Mass used in the Roman Catholic Church. The sequence has traditionally been attributed (since the end of the 14th century) to the Franciscan *Thomas of Celano. However, modern research holds that parts of it were written prior to that time, and reflect earlier hymns and motifs. It is therefore assumed that Thomas of Celano only revised an earlier work or compiled several texts. Originally, the hymn was not intended for liturgical purposes, as is evident from its personal tone and from the fact that it is written in the first person.

R. Gregory, *"Dies Irae" in Music and Letters* (1953).

DIETRICH OF FREIBERG (1250-1310) German theologian, scholar and philosopher. He studied and taught at the Dominican school of Freiberg, and later completed his studies in Paris. D. was a versatile scholar who wrote about philosophy, science, logic and theology. He was influenced by the Platonic philosophy of Plotinus and Proclus, whose works had been translated and widely circulated at the time. His scientific work included studies of geometry and optics. He explained how the rainbow is seen by the human eye. He also worked with lenses and magnifying glasses. In his major work *De intellectu et intelligibili* (On the Intellect and the Intelligible), D. tried to reconcile the classical pagan philosophy with Christian doctrine. He believed Proclus' concept of "One", i.e., the source of all things, to have intellectual value. He understood creation as an intellectual emanation from the primary cause – God – who had created the entire world. D.'s Platonic views with regard to creation and emanation had a great influence on the later German mystical school. He is also regarded as a forerunner of *Eckhard and *Tauler.

E. Gilson, *History of Christian Philosophy in the Middle Ages* (1955).

DIGENES AKRITES See BASIL.

DIGEST (PADECTS) (533) The title of the second part of *Justinian's *Corpus juris civilis* issued in 533. The D. is a collection of juristic opinions of the greatest Roman jurists. The work, compiled by *Tribonian and a special committee, consists of 50 books arranged according to titles and subjects. Because of its value as a source of legal decisions, it immediately received a binding authority and became a prominent reference book. In the 12th century, with the revival of Roman law, the D. was regarded as the main source of jurisprudence, and became the basic text for law studies at the universities. It also served as a source for political theory, since it granted emperors theoretical and legal support in their claim of supremacy over the popes.

DIJON An ancient city in eastern France and capital of the dukes of *Burgundy. Its name was derived from the Latin *Divio* or *Castrum Divionense*, which appeared in the 6th century. D. was originally a Roman camp which subsequently became fortified. After the Germanic invasions, D. assumed considerable importance as a fortified city, commanding an important road junction, and as a religious centre. In 525 the abbey of St. Bénigne was founded and a borough emerged in the area. The older castle and the new borough were soon united. When the *Capetians founded the duchy of Burgundy in the 10th century, D. became their capital. The great fair of D. contributed much to the commercial and trade development of the entire region, and was a major source of income for the Burgundian dukes. When Burgundy was united with the kingdom of France, in the late 14th century, D. managed to maintain its position as a provincial capital.

P. Quarré - P. Gras *et al.*, *Le Diocese de Dijon, histoire et art* (1957).

DIMITRI DONSKOI (1350-89) Grand duke of Vladimir and Moscow, son of *Ivan Ivanovich, who succeeded his father at an early age. In 1362 he was acknowledged duke of Vladimir by the Tatar khan. He fortified Moscow by building the *Kreml* citadel. D.'s reign was marked by a long and ultimately successful struggle to establish Moscow's hegemony over the Russian principalities. Although D. encountered the opposition of Tver backed by the Lithuanians, who attacked Moscow several times, he was able to force their retreat. In 1371 he gained the support of the Great Khan, and the following year defeated the Lithuanians. By 1375 he was recognized as national leader and the head of the Russian princes. After several campaigns against the Tatars who had raided Russian lands, he turned his efforts to the removal of Mongol domination. In 1380, in the plain of Kilokovo, D. defeated the allied armies of the Lithuanians and the Tatars. However, his victory was soon avenged (1381) by Tokhtamysh, *Tamerlane's general, who invaded Russia, captured Moscow and reinstated the Mongols. Although D. was compelled to accept Mongol suzerainty, he maintained his hegemony and bequeathed a powerful dukedom to his son.

DINANT Ancient town in the province of Namur (modern Belgium) famous for its artistic metal work. In the 7th century D. was a small borough belonging to the bishop of Tongres, and from the 10th century the fief of the bishop of *Liège. A citadel was built there in 1040. During the 14th and 15th centuries D. was a prosperous town with a highly-developed copper industry. Because of the skilled work of its artisans, its name was given to a type of brass ware, known as *dinanderic*, produced in the neighbourhood of the town. The city declined after 1466.

DINIZ (Dinis; 1261-1325) King of Portugal (1279-1325). Son of *Afonso III and an illegitimate daughter of *Alfonso X of Castile. In 1282 he married Isabella of Aragon. D. succeeded in establishing a permanent border between Portugal and Castile. He was a competent king, who strengthened the authority of the crown and restricted the power of the nobility and church. D. did not hesitate to start a long struggle with the church, by reducing its land. This conflict was ended in 1290 through a special concordat with the papacy. D. initiated agricultural, economic and commercial development in Portugal by means of afforestation, land clearance, ship-building and the extension of trade relations with European countries. D. was a patron of the arts and literature, himself being a gifted poet. He encouraged the use of the vernacular, and secured its position by making Portuguese the official language of the judiciary. Upon his orders, the legal code of *Siete Partidae* was translated into the vernacular.

A. Livermore, *A History of Portugal* (1947);
E. Prestage, *Royal Power and the Cortes in Portugal* (1927).

DIOCESE (Greek: dioikesis "administration") The territorial administrative unit of a bishop. Originally, the D. was a secular term introduced by the Roman administrative reforms of Diocletian and Constantine I, whereby the empire was divided into Ds. and provinces. The church adopted this administrative division and placed a bishop at the head of each D., assisted by the curia, made up of various officials and clergy, while a province made up of several Ds. was governed by a metropolitan. These terms, however, were not entirely exclusive and their meanings became fixed only during the 13th century. The D., which only the pope could establish, divide, combine or abolish, was further divided into parishes and deaneries.

DIONYSIO-HADRIANA A collection of church *canons sent by Pope *Adrian I to *Charlemagne in 774, when he was in Rome. The basis of this compilation was the *Dionysiana collectio,* a corpus of canon laws written in the mid-6th century by Dionysius Exiguus, a Roman canonist. The D., which contained the canons of the councils of Nicaea, Constantinople, Chalcedon and others, became widespread as a disciplinary code, and during the 7th and 8th centuries it was considerably expanded. Its canons stressed the supremacy of the Roman Church as reflected by the council decrees, avoiding reference to those canons which attributed to the bishop of Constantinople powers equal to those of the bishop of Rome. The collection was officially recognized by the Frankish church in 802. It later served as a basis for other collections, and was frequently quoted in 11th- and 12th-century canonical collections.

C. de Clercq, *La Législation religieuse franque* (1936).

DIONYSIUS See DENIS, St.

DIONYSIUS THE AREOPAGITE Bishop of Athens, converted by St. Paul. In the 9th century D. was confused with St. *Dionysius of Paris. He was also erroneously considered the author of the Pseudo-Dionysian writings, a collection of texts from Syria, written *c.* 500, in which *neo-Platonism was combined with Christianity. These served as a point of reference in the *Monophysite controversy and had a decisive influence on medieval mystical theology. The corpus deals with the process by which the soul can achieve mystical union with God. According to it, the soul has to pass through three phases: the purgative, illuminative and unitive stages of spiritual life before it can be united with God. First the soul has to rid itself of sensual perception and intellectual reasoning, and then to enter a stage of obscurity in the course of which it will be illuminated towards ascension to the unitive stage. The corpus, written in Greek and in a very obscure style, was gradually recognized as authoritative in the Eastern as well as in the Western Church. Pope *Gregory I's and *Martin I's reference to the work, and its Latin translation by *Erigena (858), earned it a large circulation in the West. Theologians like *Hugh of St. Victor, *Albertus Magnus, *Thomas Aquinas and *Bonaventura wrote commentaries on these writings, and great mystics such as *Eckhard, *Tauler and *Rolle of Hampole found them a source of inspiration.

The authenticity of the writings was questioned as far back as the Middle Ages, but such doubts were completely rejected by the humanist Lorenzo Valla and by scholars of the 16th century. Only modern research has established with certainty that these writings were forged, but the identity of the author has remained an enigma. Recently it was suggested that the author may have been the Monophysite Peter the Iberian (5th century).

E. Honigmann, *Pierre l'Ibérien et les Ecrits du Pseudo-Denys l'Aréopagite* (1951);
V. Losky, *The Mystical Theology of the Eastern Church* (1957).

DIR (d. 879) A Viking soldier and leader whose career is associated with *Kiev. In the middle of the 9th century D. and another Norse leader, Askold (Höskuld), fighting for Rurik, the Scandinavian ruler of Novgorod, conquered Kiev, which had been held by the Khazars. This was another landmark in the progressive expansion of the Scandinavians in their search for new markets, Kiev being situated on the main water route of their trade with Asiatic tribes and Byzantium.

D. is one of the early, near-legendary princes of Kiev, who in 860 launched the first Russian campaign against Constantinople. Although it failed, modern historians believe that it was not the disaster that the Byzantine sources describe. The outcome of D.'s attack was a Byzantine effort to isolate Kiev diplomatically, and subsequently to Christianize the Russians.

D. was assassinated by Oleg, another Norseman who came to Kiev from Novgorod.

F. Dvornik, *Les Légendes de Constantin et des Méthodes vues à Byzance* (1933).

DIYARBAKIR (Arabic: "The land of the Bakr tribe") A town and province in northern Mesopotamia. Originally D. was a Roman colony (*c.* 230) called Amida. It was extended by Constantius II, but was soon captured by the king of *Persia. D. was a battlefield during the prolonged wars between the Romans and the Persians and therefore changed hands frequently. In 502, during the reign of Anastasius, D. was again conquered by the Persians, and remained under their domination until the Arab conquest. In 638 D. was taken by the Arabs, but actually retained a semi-independent government under the leadership of local dynasties (9th century). Even when the Seljuk empire was established (11th century) D. remained a principality, since it served as a buffer state between Byzantium and the Seljuk states. Although annexed in the middle of the 11th century, D. soon regained its special autonomy under the *Urtukids (12th century), a Seljuk dynasty, during whose reign D. enjoyed remarkable prosperity. The rivalry of the *Ayyubids over the province culminated in 1241 with their conquest of D. After the *Mongol invasion in 1260 D. was forced to recognize their suzerainty. Later on, D. frequently became the prey of nomadic tribes whose attacks against Christians contributed to the Islamization of the entire province. At the end of the 14th century D. suffered from *Timur-Leng's destructive invasion. For a few years D. returned to Persian hands (1505) but was conquered by the Ottomans in 1515.

DJEBAIL (Djubayl) An ancient port south of Tripoli (distinct from the northern Djabala (Jabala), located south of Lattakiya) known as Byblos or Gebal in the biblical period. It was a commercial and maritime centre which enjoyed great prosperity during the Roman domination, and was the see of a bishop in the early Christian era. D. declined rapidly after the Arab conquest (7th century); a Moslem garrison was kept there until the 11th century. In 1103 D. was conquered by the *Crusaders with the help of the Genoese, who received control of the greater part of the city. Thus D. became one of the first Genoese colonies in the East. It was given in fief to the Genoese Embriaci who took the title of "lords of *Gibelet". Their descendants held D. until 1187, when it was captured by *Saladin. Ten years later, D. was regained by the Franks, who retained control until *Baibars' offensive of 1266-67. Once recovered, D. was fortified and made part of the Mameluke district of Beirut and ruled by its governors.

DOBERAN (c. 1171) A Cistercian abbey in Mecklenburg, northern Germany. It was one of the earliest Cistercian foundations in northern Europe. Established in 1170 by Bishop Berus of Schwerin, D. was soon destroyed (1179) by the heathen Wends. in 1186 D. was reconstructed and gradually became the cultural and religious centre of the entire area. During the 13th century D. encouraged monastic expansion and served as motherhouse of several new settlements. Among its earliest daughter-abbeys was the monastery of Dargun. The modest Romanesque church built in D. in 1232 was later replaced (1294-1368) by a large Gothic church.
A. A. King, *Citeaux and Her Elder Daughters* (1954).

DOL (Dolum) Ancient city in *Brittany. According to tradition, its origins are connected with St. Samson's monastery, founded in the 6th century (c. 550) by a group of Bretons from Ireland. Later D. became the see of a bishop and by the middle of the 9th century it rose to the rank of metropolitan see of Brittany, reflecting the desire of the kings and dukes of *Brittany to have their own ecclesiastical centre. This led to a long, bitter conflict with the archbishops of Tours, who refused to recognize its metropolitan rank. In 1199 the case was brought before *Innocent III who decided in favour of Tours, and D. was reduced to a simple bishopric. During the 9th and 10th centuries D. suffered from the invasions of the Normans who passed through that part of Brittany. It was unsuccessfully attacked by *William I, and later captured by *Henry II (1164). It remained in the hands of the *Plantagenets until 1206 when, together with the rest of the duchy, it was conquered by *Philip II Augustus. During the 12th century

D. was a cultural centre of learning and among its outstanding bishops was the poet and chronicler, *Baldric of Bourgueil. The cathedral church of St. Samson, built in the 13th century, and the episcopal palace are D.'s most remarkable buildings.
Ch. Robert, *Guide du touriste archéologue à Dol-de-Bretagne* (1948);
E. Durtelle de St. Sauveur, *Histoire de Bretagne*, II (1957).

DOLCE STIL NUOVO A style of Italian love poetry adopted by a school of Florentine poets towards the end of the 13th century. The term was used by *Dante in his *Purgatorio,* to describe different styles of poetry. The D. is characterized by a refined and delicate expression, which regards love as a noble, elevated and spiritual cause of inspiration. The pioneer of the new style was Guido Guinizelli, but better known were poets like Guido Cavalcanti and *Dante.
J. H. Whitfield, *A Short History of Italian Literature* (1960).

DOM (Latin: dominus "master") The title of professed monks of the *Benedictine, *Cistercian and *Carthusian orders, and of some regular canons such as the *Premonstratensians.

DOME OF THE ROCK (Arabic: Kubbet es-Sahra) Mistakenly called the Mosque of Omar. Moslem shrine in Jerusalem on the Temple Mount, known in Arabic as *Haram ash-Sharif,* the noble temple. It is built over the sacred rock which religious tradition considers the centre or heart of the world. The Jews believe it to be the stone on which Isaac was to be sacrificed by Abraham, and the Moslems claim it to be the rock from which *Mohammad ascended to heaven. The D., actually not a mosque, was erected as a shrine by Caliph *Abd Al-Malik in 691, to replace the wooden structure built 50 years earlier by *Omar. The great golden dome is raised by a drum, pierced by windows and rests on columns arranged in a circle which constitutes the centre of a double octagon. The D., one of the earliest Moslem shrines, richly decorated and orna-

Interior of the Dome of the Rock, Jerusalem (detail)

mented by colourful mosaics, is considered one of the marvels of Islamic art.

K. A. C. Creswell, *Early Muslim Architecture*, I-V (1932-40).

DOMESDAY BOOK (Domesday) The popular name of the great survey of England completed in 1086 and undertaken at *William I's order. Originally it was known as a *descriptio* or the *liber de Wintonia* (Book of Winchester), but it eventually gained the title of D., derived from the fact that no appeal could be made against its assessment. Actually, the D. was a summary of the extensive survey carried out by several delegations of royal officers, dispatched to different districts, where they held a public inquiry in every hundred of each county. Through their investigations, they were able to draw up lists of royal estates and the holdings of the king's direct tenants-in-chief. These records were brought to the royal treasury at Winchester, where they were abridged, and arranged systematically to form the D.

The primary purpose of the survey, which had covered almost all counties except those of northern England (Northumberland; Durham; Westmorland; Cumberland) and some major cities (London; Winchester), was the king's desire to know the precise extent and value of royal lands and those of his immediate vassals.

The D. consists of two volumes. The first, called the *Great Domesday,* contains the abridged records of all counties surveyed except eastern Essex, Norfolk and Suffolk, whose unabridged lists form the second volume, the *Little Domesday.* The D. is classified according to fiefs, although the survey lists referred to holdings according to hundreds. The D. lists of each county opens with a reckoning of the king's estates, then enumerates the holdings of churchmen (archbishops, bishops) or religious institutions, followed by the possessions of the king's direct barons or earls and closes with a record of estates held by women and the king's sergeants. Each fief is precisely described with regard to size, boundaries, amount of arable land, and the number of its resources, such as pastures, woods, fishponds etc. The D. refers to tenants holding fiefs in 1086 which had been previously owned in 1066, a detail of major importance, as it served as a basis for researching the history of the Norman Conquest. The D., in itself an important administrative achievement, is considered a primary source for the study of social, economic and demographic rural history of medieval England as well as a reference for topographic and genealogic research of that area.

F. W. Maitland, *Domesday Book and Beyond* (1907);
H. C. Darby and I. B. Terrett, *The Domesday Geography of Midland England* (1954).

DOMINIC OF CALARUEGA, St. (Domingo de Guzman; 1170-1221) Founder of the Friars Preachers known as the *Dominicans, D. was born in the village of Calaruega, near Burgos, Spain and studied theology at Palencia. At an early age, he exhibited great sympathy towards the poor and the suffering. He is said to have once sold his valuable collection of books in order to help the needy. In 1199 D. joined the canons of the cathedral of Osma, where he was introduced to the apostolic life and discipline and soon became head of the community. In 1203, while accompanying the bishop of Osma on a mission, he became aware of the *Albigensian heresy in southern France. Three years later (1206) he met the papal legates sent to oppose the Albigensians, and engaged in a preaching campaign. It was then that he developed the concept of mendicity. D. claimed that in order to convince the Albigensians, who despised worldly possessions, the preachers themselves had to set an example by going barefoot and adopting a life of poverty.

In 1206 he also founded a nunnery at Prouille (in Albigensian territory) with the purpose of converting heretic women. During the following years, which coincided with the Albigensian *Crusade, D. and several followers attempted to win the heretics back to the church. In 1215, with the bishop's consent, D. founded a religious house in Toulouse (which had been recently recovered from the Albigensians) for preaching and defending the faith. A year later D. received the approval of *Innocent III in Rome, although formal recognition of the order was given in the bulls of 1216-17 by *Honorius III. Between 1217 and 1221 D. devoted his time to the organization and expansion of his order. He travelled widely, founding new houses in Paris, Bologna, Madrid, Rome and Toulouse, seeing to it that the friars were busy with studies, teaching and preaching. In 1220 he summoned the first general chapter of the order in Bologna. D. was a modest person who declined many dignities offered to him but he was also a zealous preacher who did not hesitate to put his life in danger for his cause. He was proclaimed a saint in 1234.

B. Jarrett, *The Life of St. Dominic* (1934);
M. H. Vicaire, *L'imitation des apôtres* (1963).

DOMINICANS (Ordo Praedicatorum; Friars Preachers) An order founded by St. *Dominic, whose main objectives were preaching and study in the service of the church. The order emerged during a turbulent period, at a time when the *Albigensian heresy in southern France presented a serious threat to the unity of the church. The order, its name, rule and purposes, were formally recognized by Pope *Honorius III in the bulls of 1216 and 1217, but the two general chapters, held at *Bologna in 1220 and 1221, determined the order's ultimate character.

The D. adopted the rule of St. Augustine and a quasi-monastic regime. They accepted the principles of poverty and mendicity, whereby they were to beg for their living, and to own no property other than their churches and houses. The founders of the order also promoted evangelism, whereby the D. were to lead a humble life, wandering and preaching the true faith. Because of these aims the D. abandoned the physical work which was generally practised by other religious orders, and stressed the importance of study, education and teaching. The D. were therefore mainly active in urban centres and cities. The order spread rapidly throughout Europe during the 13th century and the D. set up schools in every priory and town, which soon became centres of study and education. The highest ranking school of the Dominican system was the *Studia Generalia,* which was mainly attached to a university and whose teachers served as professors of theology. The D. were known throughout the Middle Ages as leading thinkers and university teachers. The contributions of *Albertus Magnus, *Thomas of Aquinas and

The Eastern Gate of Genoa, built in the 13th century

The fortress of Najac, southern France, built in the 13th century

Robert Kilwardby to science, philosophy and theology were enormous, and further promoted the high reputation of the order. Not less notable were the achievements of the canonist *Raymond of Peñafort, the orientalist Raymond Martini, and the inquisitor *Bernard of Guy.

The D. were directly subordinate to the pope and, due to their training and complete obedience, served the papacy in various missions; they were selected to preach in favour of the Crusades, to collect and levy taxes, to undertake diplomatic tasks and to preach against heretics. The D. soon extended their ministry to include missionary activity directed against Jews, Moslems, Mongols and others. They also filled the ranks of the *Inquisition and because of their activity were nicknamed *Domini canes* (the Lord's watchdogs).

The order was divided into provinces and priories, and its supreme authority was the general chapter, which also elected the Master General. The general chapter, held annually (until 1370), consisted of priors and deputies chosen from every province. It is believed that the representative system of the Dominican organization inspired the convocation method of the English Parliament.

The D. had a Second Order of nuns who lived in convents and adopted a similar rule as the friars, and a Third Order of lay tertiaries who lived in accordance with the Dominican spirit. The D. order spread under the leadership of Dominic's able successors, Jordan of Saxony, Raymond of Peñafort and Humbert of Romans. By the middle of the 14th century, before the Black Death, the D. order numbered 21,000 members in over 630 priories throughout Europe.

G. R. Galbraith, *The Constitutions of the Dominican Order 1216-1360* (1925);
W. A. Hinnenbuch, *Early English Friar Preachers* (1951).

DOMINIUM A legal term prevailing in the feudal system and in particular in relation to land tenures and fiefs. The D. designates the legitimate ownership of property. However, a clear distinction was drawn between the *D. directum,* the direct ownership of a possession leased or granted to another, and the *D. utile,* by which the holder of the land had the right to exploit and cultivate the land leased to another.

F. L. Ganshof, *Feudalism* (1961).

DOMINUS See LORD.

DONATION OF CHARLEMAGNE The grant of *Charlemagne to Pope *Adrian, given on several occasions, which confirmed the *donation of Pepin and recognized papal domination over certain territories in central Italy. The first D. was granted at Easter in 774 in Rome, when Charlemagne, called in by Adrian against *Desiderius, renewed his father's donation and, in return, was awarded the title of Patrician of Rome. At Easter in 781, and again in 787, Charlemagne increased the original donation, granting the pope considerable territory in the east (Sabina, Narni) and north (Terracina), which later became known as the papal patrimony.

W. Ullmann, *Growth of Papal Government in the Middle Ages* (1962).

DONATION OF CONSTANTINE (Constitutum Constantini) A false document probably fabricated in the middle of the 8th century, according to which Emperor *Constantine I transferred his capital to Constantinople, granting Pope *Sylvester I the rule of Rome, Italy and the Western empire. The emperor's move was allegedly in return for his conversion and his miraculous recovery from a dangerous illness. During the Middle Ages the D. served the papacy as a legal basis for governmental claims and in particular in the disputes between popes and emperors. It was first used by *Stephen II in 754 to induce *Pepin to act against the Lombards, who had conquered papal territories and endangered Rome. Stephen also used it to strengthen the independent status of the papacy in the face of Byzantine refusal to recognize the pope's primacy. The D., which relies on a 5th-century legend (*Legenda s. Silvestri*), is therefore believed to have been composed in the papal chancery. The document's validity was strongly attacked by medieval lawyers and secular authorities, who suggested that the emperor had overstepped his powers and had illegally alienated authority and territory by giving the pope such grants.

The fabrication of the D. was proven in the 15th century by Nicholas of Cusa and Lorenzo Valla.

W. Ullmann, *Growth of Papal Government in the Middle Ages* (1962);
S. Williams, "The Oldest Text of the Constitutum Constantini", *Traditio*, 20 (1964).

DONATION OF PEPIN A document, no longer extant, drawn up by *Pepin in 755. It enumerated the territories held by the *Lombards which he intended to liberate and hand over to the papal government. These areas included the exarchate of Ravenna, Ancona and 23 other cities. Thus, the document laid the early foundation of the Papal States. The D. was the result of cooperation between Pepin and Pope *Stephen II. The latter had crowned Pepin as king of the Franks and made him Patrician of Rome (754). In return, Pepin promised to restore the exarchate of Ravenna and the other territories, together with the rights unlawfully usurped by the Lombards, to the Roman Church.

DONATIST HERESY A movement whose theological conception caused a schism in the unity of the north African church in the 4th and 5th centuries. It originated from its members' refusal to accept the spiritual leadership of the *traditores*, those bishops who had handed sacred books over to the authorities during the Diocletian persecution (303-05). The movement set up rival bishops, one of the most famous being Donatus, bishop of Carthage (313-47), after whom the movement is named. Although an investigation undertaken under the orders of the bishop of Rome (313) ruled against the Donatists, the heresy gained momentum and withstood coercion by several emperors (Constantine I in 316; Constantius II in 347; Julian in 361).

The Donatists believed that sanctity and grace could be found only in their own church, and that contact with sinners was defiling. They also claimed, referring to the teaching of *Tertullian and *Cyprian, that sacraments administered by the unworthy were invalid, and therefore rebaptized those joining their sect. The D., whose greatest opponent was *Augustine, declined after 411, but the sacramental controversy was an important phase in the development of medieval theology.

W. H. C. Frend, *The Donatist Church* (1952);
J. Kelleher, *St. Augustine's Notion of Schism in the Donatist Controversy* (1961).

DOON DE MAYENCE (13th century) A baron and the protagonist of an old French epic cycle named after him – *Geste de Doon de Mayence.* This cycle is part of the *Charlemagne legends, the *chansons de geste,* which relate the deeds and revolts of Charlemagne's rebellious vassals. Though this epic reflects a rebellious tradition among the Mayence family, it is generally believed that the baron's antagonistic attitude and insolence were directed not so much against Charlemagne, the great emperor, but rather his incapable successors. The first part of the cycle, dealing with D.'s romantic childhood, is purely fictitious, but the latter part, describing battles fought in Saxony, related certain historical events.

J. Crosland, *The Old French Epic* (1951);
M. de Riquer, *Les Chansons de Gestes françaises* (1957).

DORESTAD (Dorstad) A Merovingian town on the northern Rhine, where the river divides into Lek and Kromme Rijn. In its early stages, D., consisting of fishing villages, served as an area of trade established by Frisian merchants (*Friesland). Gradually, with the foundation of Frisian colonies along the Rhine River, D.'s commercial relations were extended. Thus, the town contributed to the foundation of the merchant city of Mainz, where the Frisians had established themselves (866).

D. became a flourishing trade centre towards the end of the Merovingian period. It controlled most of the northern commerce carried out by the Frisian merchants, and was known as the "city of forty churches". However, the city declined during the 9th century. Its commercial activity was gravely disturbed by the Norse incursions. Even more damaging to D. was the diversion of the trade route to another river branch, which led to the rise of a rival city (Tiel on the Waal).

DORIA (D'ORIA), THEODISIO (end of 13th century) Genoese merchant. He belonged to the great house of Doria, whose members enjoyed high standing and held responsible positions in Genoa from the 12th to the 14th century.

Theodisio was the son of Lamba Doria, the captain who had defeated the Venetian fleet at Curzola. D. owned several galleys which were engaged in profitable trade in the eastern Mediterranean. In 1291 he set up a commercial association and raised the necessary funds to man and furnish two vessels. Under Vivaldi, a well-known Genoese navigator, these ships sailed out to discover the riches of India. It is traditionally believed that one of the galleys managed to reach Ethiopia, but was detained there by its ruler.

E. H. Byrne, *Genoese Shipping in the Twelfth and Thirteenth Centuries* (1930);
R. S. Lopez - I. W. Raymond, *Medieval Trade in the Mediterranean World* (1955).

DORPAT (Tartu) A Russian town in Estonia, originally called Tartu, which became important with the building of the fortress of Yuryev there in 1030 by the prince of Novgorod, *Yaroslav I, as a stronghold against the Finns. When the *Teutonic order expanded its territories along the Baltic shore, both Germans and Russians claimed domination over D. In 1224 it was seized by the Teutonic knights, assumed the new German name of D., and became the seat of an archbishop. D. became an important land station of the *Hanse, which controlled the trade of the Novgorod region, and enjoyed great prosperity. D. remained under German domination until 1558 when it was captured by the Russians.

DORTMUND (Throtmania) German town in Westphalia, whose advantageous position made it important from the 9th century, when it was known as Throtmania (885). Emperor *Henry II convened both his ecclesiastical council (1005) and the imperial diet of 1016 at D. The town was fortified in the 12th century by the construction of a fortified wall. In 1220 D. became an independent imperial city and by the middle of the 13th century it had joined the *Hanse and thus enjoyed considerable prosperity, as it was able to trade with countries such as England, Scotland, Poland and Russia. Some of D.'s merchants were engaged in money-lending and even the kings of England figured among their clients.

DORYLAEUM (Dorylaion; Arabic: Darubiyya) Ancient town in northwestern Anatolia (hence the modern name of Eskisehir, "old town") and a prosperous Phrygian city in classical times. During the Byzantine rule it served as a rallying point for the Byzantine army during the eastern campaigns led by the emperors. At the beginning of the 8th century (708) D. was conquered by the Arabs. The town's strategic position made D. and the surrounding area a frequent battle site. Thus, in 1097 the *Crusaders, on their way to the Holy Land, defeated the Seljuks near D. and penetrated southward into Syria. But the use of D. as a passageway to surrounding areas was halted in 1147 when the Crusaders, led by *Conrad III, were defeated there. In 1175 D. was fortified by Manuel I Comnenus, but it soon passed into the possession of the Seljuks. In 1240 *Urtoghrul, the Seljuk general, settled the area near D. This region, which his son *Othman received (1289) as a fief, gradually became an independent state (14th century), later known as the cradle of the Ottoman Turks.

CMedH, IV – *The Byzantine Empire* (1964).

DOUAI (Latin: Duacum) Flemish town, south of Lille. D. originated from a Roman camp or fortress, which, as early as the 7th century included a castle, *castrum Duacense,* which was the core of the fortified town. D. was an important trade centre of Flemish textiles and belonged to the counts of Flanders. During the 12th and 13th centuries the town gradually acquired communal privileges. In 1228 its autonomy was confirmed by a special charter which was subsequently renewed. During the second half of the 13th century D. was troubled by social tension and internal struggle between the patriciate, who wished to control the government, and an active group of merchants led by *Boinebroke. The conflict led to many revolts (1280). D.'s actual decline, however, was a result of the Hundred Years' War and the subsequent influx of English wool. D. fell into the hands of the French kings several times. In 1384 D. was passed through marriage to the dukes of Burgundy and later (1477) came under Austrian rule. The town is renowned for its Notre Dame Church (12th-14th centuries), the Gothic belfry, built in 1380, and the city hall of the 15th century.

V. Bufguin, *Histoire de la ville de Douai* (1951).

DOUGLAS, WILLIAM (d. 1298) Member of a noble Scottish family, and the first to assume the title of Lord of Douglas. His abduction of and subsequent marriage to a noble lady aroused *Edward I's ire. D. was forced to recognize *Balliol as king of the Scots, and to pay homage to Edward (1291). When the Scottish barons rebelled against Edward, D. commanded the fortified Berwick Castle, but in 1296 the city was sacked and D. was taken prisoner. He was released after renewing his fealty oath to Edward, but nevertheless lost his English possessions. Shortly after his release (1297) he joined the revolt of Wallace against Edward, but he was soon captured and sent to the Tower of London, where he met his death.

DOVER An ancient seaport in southern England, situated on the English Channel, being the port closest to the Continent. D.'s history antedates the Roman invasion. During the Roman period it was known as Dubris. In the 4th century D.'s harbour was protected by a strong fortress which constituted part of the Saxon defence of the coast. By the time of the Norman Conquest (1066), D. had become one of the greatest ports of England. *William I regarded it as an important link between Normandy and England, and therefore increased its fortification. In the *Domesday Book, D. figures as a town which received a certain amount of authority in return for its naval service to the crown. During the 11th century D. became one of the *Cinque Ports – a federation of five English ports (Hastings, New Romney, Hythe, Sandwich and D.) which were to supply ships and men for the king's service – and was thus vital to the English fleet. A joint charter granted in 1278 gave D. (and the Cinque Ports) communal liberties in return for their service. D.'s rights were extended during the 13th and 14th centuries. Its naval importance declined after the 14th century.

DRACONTIUS BLOSSIUS AEMILIUS (5th century) Latin poet of Africa. D. was born into a wealthy Carthaginian family, probably of Spanish origin. His occupation was the practice of law. After the Vandal invasion, D. was imprisoned and his property confiscated because of his panegyric poem praising the emperor rather than the Vandal king. He obtained his freedom by writing a poem of praise, the *Satisfactio,* addressed to the king. His most important work is *De laudibus Dei* (On the praises of God) or *De Deo* (on God), a poem containing some 2300 hexameters in three volumes. The poem describes the Creation, the Fall and God's benevolence towards mankind as demonstrated mainly through the Redemption. The first book, dealing with Creation, was circulated separately under the title of *Hexaemeron,* which was edited in the 7th century by Eugenius, bishop of Toledo. D. is also said to be the author of *Orestis tragoedia.* His poetry reveals D.'s remarkable background in biblical and Roman literature.
F. Chatillon, "Dracontia", *Revue du Moyen Age Latin,* 8 (1952).

DRAMA Medieval D. originated in the monastic orders in the 9th century, as a form of religious rite. It began as a mimed performance showing the "Easter story", i.e., the death and resurrection of Christ, immediately after the Mass. According to a contemporary English account describing this custom, it included the recitation or chanting of psalms and hymns, as well as mimed dialogues performed by monks or priests as part of the Divine Office. Gradually the repertoire came to include other events in the Holy Scriptures, related to feasts other than Easter. A type of liturgical D. developed, which soon included Christmas, Epiphany and tales of the Nativity, such as the Procession of the Prophets or the Adoration of the Magi. Performed in Latin until the 13th century, these liturgical Ds. gradually evolved into vernacular mystery plays, of which the earliest known is *Le Mystère d'Adam* (1175).

In time the plays became more elaborate, and laid greater stress on the secular aspects, the comical element and mimicry. Performed by laymen in public squares outside the churches, they were still connected with religious feasts, though not with Christmas and Easter.

From the 13th century on, the plays were generally associated with the *Corpus Christi procession (a feast commemorating the gift of the Holy Eucharist, officially instituted by Pope Urban IV in 1264), and gradually developed into a cycle of 30 to 40 plays. It covered the entire story of Salvation, and included scenes such as the Garden of Eden, the Fall of Man, the Nativity, the Passion of Christ, the Resurrection, Antichrist and the Last Judgement. Corpus Christi cycles differed slightly from country to country. Later, non-biblical subjects were also introduced in plays such as the *Invention of the Holy Cross,* and the legends and miracles of the saints, which paved the way for the morality plays of the late Middle Ages.
K. Young, *The Drama of the Medieval Church,* I-II (1933);
G. Frank, *The Medieval French Drama* (1954);
O. B. Hardison Jr., *Christian Rite and Christian Drama in the Middle Ages* (1965);
V. A. Kolve, *The Play called Corpus Christi* (1966).

DRESDEN A German town on the Elbe River, and the capital of Saxony. It was originally a Slav village on the eastern bank of the river, inhabited by "forest dwellers" (*Dresdane*). The town expanded as a result of German colonization which took place when Margrave Dietrich built a neighbouring town on the western bank (1216), later known as the Old City (Altstadt). Situated on an important water route, D. soon developed a prosperous trade and became a mining centre. By 1270 D. had become the official capital of Henry the Illustrious, margrave of Meissen. However, the city changed hands several times after his death. In the 13th century it belonged, for a short while, to *Wenceslas I, king of Bohemia, and later to the margrave of Brandenburg. In the 14th century D. returned to the possession of Meissen's margraves. In 1485, when Saxony was divided, D. came into the hands of the Albertine line.

DREUX Town and county, northwest of Chartres, which gave its name to the dynasty of counts related to the royal *Capetian line. (The area had been the ancient capital of the Gallic tribe of Durocasses, known as Drocae in the Roman period.) D. was the major town in the county and had a strong castle as far back as the 10th century. Half of the county came into the possession of Odo II, count of Chartres, as part of the dowry he received upon marrying the daughter of Richard I, duke of Normandy. Towards the end of the 10th century, Odo ceded D. to the king of France, *Robert the Pious. By 1135 the county of D. was given to Robert I, son of *Louis VI, who founded the dynasty of the counts of D. In 1184 the county was passed to Robert's first successor, Robert II (1184-1216). Although, four years later, D. was attacked and captured by Henry II of England, it was soon recovered by *Philip II Augustus. From that time, the county remained in the hands of the D. dynasty, who ruled successively until the end of the 14th century:

Robert III(1216-34); John I (1234-48); Robert IV (1248-82). In 1377, however, the county of D. passed through marriage to the Thonars family.

The town of D. had received communal privileges in 1159. Aside from its fortress it also boasts several beautiful churches, in particular the chapel of St. Louis and its Gothic church, built in the 13th century.

P. d'Espezel, *Memorial de la premiere famille de France. La chapelle de Dreux* (1957);

Ch. Moullier, *Dreux et le pays drouais* (1958).

DRISTRA (Drystra, Dorystolum, Silistria) A fortified town in Bulgaria, on the bank of the Danube. Having been a Roman military camp (*Durostorum*), it remained an important strategical position. Under the Byzantine empire D. was an administrative centre, and in the Bulgar kingdom the seat of a patriarch. In 971 D. witnessed the greatest campaign between the Byzantine and the Russian armies. On a plain near D Emperor John I Tzimisces defeated the Russian prince Svyatoslav, who had invaded Bulgaria and sought refuge in the fortress of D. The town was besieged for three months, at the end of which Svyatoslav surrendered and agreed to evacuate Bulgaria. Consequently, Bulgaria's Tsar Boris abdicated and the kingdom was annexed to the Byzantine empire. Later on D. was an important stronghold against the repeated attacks of the Ottomans, and after the fall of Bulgaria became a Turkish fortress.

S. Runciman, *A History of the First Bulgarian Empire* (1930);

F. Dvornik, *The Slavs: Their Early History and Civilization* (1956).

DROGO OF METZ (801-55) Bishop and prominent figure responsible for church reform carried out during the reign of *Louis I, the Pious. D. was the illegitimate son of *Charlemagne. In 818 he lost the favour of Louis I and was sent to a monastery. Five years later (823), D. won back the emperor's grace and was created bishop of Metz and later chief chaplain to the emperor, thus becoming a close and influential adviser. In 813 D. was elevated to the rank of archbishop and was put in charge of the ecclesiastical affairs of the kingdom. He contributed to the consolidation of church reforms aimed at improving the spiritual life of the clergy and its congregation. In 844, at Emperor *Louis I's request, D. was the head of a committee which investigated and certified the validity of Pope Sergius II's election. D. was later appointed papal vicar in the Frankish kingdom, mainly in Lothair's domain. In 885 he drowned near Luxeuil.

P. Viard, *Catholicisme*, III (1948).

DRUZE (Arabic: Duruz, Durzi) A community named after its first leader, Al-Darazi, who formulated his creed towards the end of *Al-Hakim's reign (1017). The Fatimid caliph plays a central theological and supernatural role in the D.'s faith. Hamza, a leader who gave the movement its definitive form, regarded Hakim not only as the head of Islam, but also as the incarnation of a cosmic principle, the One, which is the eternal epitome of intellect, which is beyond good or evil. After the disappearance of Hakim and Hamza, the D., under the leadership of Al-Muktana, developed a certain eschatological expectation. They believed that Hakim had not died and would return triumphantly to judge the world and make them its rulers. The D. also believe in reincarnation which is repeated until a state of perfection is reached, at which point they ascend to heaven.

The D. have kept their doctrines secret and forbid their followers to intermarry with other sects or practise conversion. Thus they gradually became a close-knit group dissociated from others and united by religious precepts and ethnic solidarity. The D. are concentrated mainly in the hilly areas of Syria and Lebanon. The D. community is divided into "sages" (*'ukkal*) and "ignorants" (*djuhhal*). Only the sages, from whom the *sheikhs* are recruited, are permitted to read their holy scriptures and participate in the secret ritual. The D. religion prescribes seven commandments, among which the precept to defend their faith ranks highly. In order to keep the secret of their faith, the D. have even outwardly accepted the religion and customs of a superior power. It is because of these characteristics that the D. have survived as a close and distinct community despite numerous political upheavals.

P. K. Hitti, *The Origins of the Druze People and Religion* (1938);

F. Massey, *Druze History* (1952).

DRYBURGH Scottish Premonstratensian abbey, south of Edinburgh, founded in 1150 by Hugh of Moreville, the constable of Scotland, on the site of an ancient Celtic monastery. The new abbey, situated on the Scottish border, became established in 1152 when the Premonstratensian canons of Alnwick joined it. In 1322 D. was burned by *Edward II during his campaign in Scotland. It was subsequently rebuilt and then destroyed a second time in 1385 by *Richard II. Among its outstanding abbots were Adam Scotus (*c.* 1388), the Premonstratensian spiritual preacher, who gained his fame in France, and the scholastic philosopher Ralph Strode (*c.* 1354).

D. G. Manuel, *Dryburgh Abbey in the Light of Its Historical and Ecclesiastical Setting* (1922);

J. S. Richardson and M. Wood (eds.), *Dryburgh Abbey* (1948).

DUANA A fiscal institution of Moslem origin introduced into the administration of Norman Sicily by *Roger II. the D. was the central financial department of the kingdom, which kept written records and registers of the state revenues. It was part of the royal *curia* known by the Arabic name *diwan*, the Greek *secretos* or the Latin *duana* or *secretum*. The person in charge was called *secreton*, and employed a large staff of (Moslem) clerks, divided into two departments. The *duana de secretis* dealt with all royal incomes and revenues, and kept up-to-date registers of royal lands, with their description and area, lists of serfs and tenants and their debts to the royal exchequer.

It also kept a record of every sale of land and the amount paid. The other department, the *duana baronum*, kept a record of feudal holdings, sub-infeudated lands, and the exact services due to the king. One of the products of this section was the *catalogus baronum* (compiled *c.* 1152), in fact a roster of the king's vassals in every province and services they owed their monarch. The similarity between the function and procedures of the D. and the Anglo-Norman *exchequer is explained by their mutual influence, effected by officials of English origin, such as Robert of Selby and, notably, Thomas Brown, who was fiscal officer under Roger II, and later served in *Henry II's exchequer. The D. in Norman Sicily, however, was an amalgam of Arabic, Byzantine and Norman elements.

F. Chalandon, *Histoire de la domination normande en Italie et en Sicile, 1009-1194*, I-II (1907); C. H. Haskins, *Studies in Norman Institutions* (1918).

DUBLIN City in Ireland, capital of the county of D. and a seaport on the estuary of the Liffey River. D. has a long history going back to prehistoric times and tradition has it that there Christianity was introduced into Ireland by St. *Patrick (*c.* 450). However, nothing certain is known about D. until the 9th century, when D. was conquered by the Danes, who settled there with their first king Thorkel I (832). Danish supremacy was not seriously challenged until the beginning of the 11th century. At intervals, between 1014 and 1136, the Irish would attack the Danes. D. became Christian before the 11th century, was made a metropolitan see in 1152, its bishops being consecrated at Canterbury. In 1171 the Danes were finally driven out by *Henry II of England, who entrusted the government of D. to Hugh de Lacy. Subsequently D. became the capital of the English domains in Ireland and its archbishops from then on were Anglo-Normans. Periodically conflicts broke out between the Irish and the Anglo-Normans, and the kings tried to pacify the parties. D. got several charters (1207, 1216) determining her jurisdiction, boundaries and government. During the 13th century the city became a major centre, rivalling *Armagh in importance. Its high ecclesiastical lords, who were at the same time the king's magistrates, secured its immunity and some of them assumed the title of primate. In the 14th century D., supported by the Irish church, successfully repelled the invasion (1315) of Edward Bruce. In 1394 *Richard II raised D. to the rank of marquisate and entrusted it to Robert de Vere.
D. Cosgrave, *North Dublin – City and Environs* (1932); D. Guiness, *Portrait of Dublin* (1967).

DUBOIS, PIERRE (Petrus a Bosco; 1250-1321) French lawyer, and political pamphleteer. D. studied at Paris and was a successful lawyer in Coutances, Normandy, where in 1300 he became a royal advocate. His favourable attitude to royal politics attracted attention during the conflict between *Philip IV and *Boniface VIII. D. wrote several pamphlets anonymously, which supported the king's attitude towards the pope. These pamphlets were supposed to represent the people's voice, thereby justifying royal policy. In 1302 and 1308 D. represented his town at the Estates General assembled by Philip IV in order to gain the people's support. His views are best reflected in his important treatise *De recuperatione Terre Sancte* (On the Recovery of the Holy Land) written *c.* 1306. Although dealing with the realization of a crusade, the work actually expounds his general outlook on political, social and church issues. D. believed that the strengthening of the royal authority was vital for peace in Europe and for carrying out necessary radical reforms in education, law, administration and the church. D. proposed transferring the church patrimony into secular hands and compensating the church by an annual pension. In his works, D. promoted the bestowal of the higher and more prestigious roles in the Christian affairs of Europe, usually reserved for the Holy Roman emperors, upon the kings of France.
W. I. Brandt, *The Recovery of the Holy Land* (1956).

DU GUESCLIN, BERTRAND (c. 1320-80) French soldier and commander who distinguished himself during the first stage of the *Hundred Years' War. D. was of a

Bertrand du Guesclin in full armour; woodcut

noble family and gained his military expertise during the prolonged wars between the French and the English. At first he was in the service of Charles de Blois and from 1357 he served the royal house. It was during the siege of Rennes (1357) that D. became noted for his bravery. He succeeded in penetrating the city and reinforcing its defence so that it was able to withstand the siege for a considerable period of time. In 1357 he was made captain of Pontorson. D. was captured and the king agreed to pay a huge ransom for his release. In 1360 he was appointed by *Charles V to fight the mercenary troops who were plundering Normandy and Maine. As captain general of Normandy he drove the troops of Charles II of Navarre out of Mantes and Meulun (1364). In 1365 D. led the expedition to Spain, sent by Charles V to support Henry of Trastamare against *Pedro I. D. was defeated and captured by Edward the Black Prince, who had intervened on Pedro's behalf (1367). However, a second expedition led by D. proved successful. In 1370 D. was appointed constable of France by Charles V, and, as such, conducted many military operations against the English in Guienne (1374), Cherbourg (1378) and other places. Recognizing the superiority of the English army, D. recommended cautionary tactics, such as wearing out the enemy and attacking him by surprise. D. was regarded as a brave knight of rare courage and was the hero of many poems and songs.
M. Dulud, *Du Guesclin* (1958); R. Maran, *Bertrand Du Guesclin de l'épée du roi* (1960).

DUNASH BEN LABRAT (c. 920-c. 980) Hebrew poet and linguist. D. was born in Baghdad where he was a student of *Saadia Gaon. He continued his studies in *Fez, Egypt and later settled in *Cordoba, where he became involved in the study of linguistics and in a philological controversy with *Menahem ben Saruk. D. severely criticized Menahem's dictionary (*Mahberet*) and his biblical interpretation, claiming that it led readers astray in matters of belief. The violent argument which ensued between the supporters of each party aroused vivid interest in Jewish scholarly circles of his time and contributed to the development of Hebrew grammar and philology. D.'s arguments are often quoted in the works of *Rashi, *David Kimhi and others. D. wrote secular and religious verses, and was the first to adopt Arabic meter in Hebrew poetry, thus laying the foundation for medieval Hebrew poetry. D. was highly appreciated by Solomon ibn *Gabirol. Among his best known religious poems is his Sabbath song, *Dror Yikra*.

H. Hirschfeld, *Literary History of Hebrew Grammarians and Lexicographers* (1926);

D. Merowsky, *Hebrew Grammar and Grammarians* (1955).

DUNS SCOTUS, JOHN (c. 1264-1308) Famed scholastic philosopher and theologian, often called *Doctor subtilis* or *Doctor maximus*. D. was born in Scotland, and educated by the Franciscans. At the age of 15 he joined the order and was ordained priest in 1291. About that time he was sent to Oxford and Paris to study theology. In 1302 he was in Paris, studying and lecturing on theology, but had to leave because in the dispute between *Philip IV and *Boniface VIII the Franciscan order took the pope's side. In 1304, back in Paris, he wrote his *Quaestiones quadlibetales*, and a year later received his doctor's degree. D. lectured on the *Sentences* of *Peter Lombard at Oxford (1297-1301), Paris (1302-05) and Cologne (1307-08), continuously revising his notes. These notes, known as *Ordinatio* or *Opus Oxoniense*, together with the *Quaestiones quadlibetales,* are the major texts of his philosophy. He also wrote a *Tractatus de primo principio,* and many commentaries on Aristotle. D.'s thought, which was formed after the *Averroist condemnation of 1277, combines philosophy and theology, and is a synthesis of *Augustinian and *Aristotelian elements. According to him, the primary object of the intellect is pure being (*esse*), without which nothing is comprehensible. D. accords the prime role not to reason and knowledge, but to love and will. He stressed the free will of God, upon which natural law depends. Though God may change or suspend a certain course of things, He never acts arbitrarily or contrary to His reason. D. regarded the freedom of Man as the highest value and perfection of human nature. His theological thought emphasized the practical, rather than the speculative aspect. The purpose of theology, according to D., is to perceive that God, as an infinite being, is love and that therefore everything is originated in love — thereby going beyond *Anselm's proof of God's existence. God's love, manifested in the incarnation and redemption, proves His intention of redeeming mankind. These concepts led D. to the doctrine of the Immaculate Conception, according to which the Virgin Mary and Christ were united in the Incarnation; thus through Christ's grace, the Virgin was free of the original sin. This issue was much debated in scholastic circles, but D.'s attitude, for which he was called *Doctor Mariamus*, was accepted and declared a doctrine of faith.

D. was considered one of the greatest scholastic thinkers and a major authority, to whom many spurious works were later ascribed. His authentic writings have been published in a critical edition by the Vatican since 1950.

E. H. Gilson, *History of Christian Philosophy in the Middle Ages* (1955);

B. de Saint-Maurice, *John Duns Scot: A Teacher for Our Times* (1955);

J. K. Ryan and B. M. Bonansea (eds.), *John Duns Scotus 1265-1965* (1965).

DUNSTAN, St. (909-88) *Benedictine abbot, archbishop of Canterbury. He was educated at Glastonbury, which he joined as a monk, and later became its abbot (940). D. introduced the Benedictine rule, reformed the monastery and made it a cultural centre. He himself led an ascetic life and divided his time between study and practical work (the illumination and copying of books, silversmithery and metalwork). D. served as minister and counsellor to several kings. His collaboration with King *Edgar (957-75) brought about basic reforms in church and state affairs. In 957 D., summoned from exile on the Continent, was appointed bishop of Worcester and London, and in 970 was made archbishop of Canterbury. He is credited with the restoration of monastic life in England and the introduction of monastic reforms on the Continent. It was through his influence that the Synod of Winchester (970) promulgated the *Regularis concordia*, a code of monastic regulations based on the Continental model, to be observed by all monasteries in England. D. is considered the patron saint of metal workers.

E. S. Duckett, *Saint Dunstan of Canterbury* (1955).

DUPPLIN MOOR (MUIR) Battle site of 1332, southeast of Perth, famous both in Scottish history and for the warfare tactics employed. On this site, *Balliol, the claimant to the Scottish throne, and his partisans overcame the greater forces of *David II, led by his regent, Donald, earl of Mar. The importance of this battle lays in the new tactics used by Balliol which were later adopted by *Edward III in the *Hundred Years' War against France, and which gained the latter victory at the battles of *Halidon Hill (1333) and *Crécy (1346). According to this new war strategy, all men dismounted and formed a thick phalanx, while archers were placed at either flank. Thus, when the enemy attacked, they were caught in the centre, with archers shooting arrows from either side. This, of course, led to numerous casualties and disorder in the enemy lines.

C. W. C. Oman, *The Art of War in the Middle Ages* (1963).

DUQAQ, SHAMS AL-MALIK Ruler of *Damascus (1095-1104) on the eve of the First *Crusade. D. belonged to a Seljuk ruling family who bore the title of *Malik* – i.e., king. His father, Tutush of Damascus (d. 1095) had claims on the Seljuk sultanate, and his brother, Ridwan, was the lord of *Aleppo. D. was the emir of southern Syria, his authority reaching as far as the land of Suwat, east of the Sea of Galilee.

In 1098 D. was among the first emirs to confront the Crusaders who besieged Antioch. His expedition, sent to rescue Yaghi-Siyan, the lord of Antioch, was halted and defeated by Bohemond before it reached the city. His later departure from Antioch, due to the danger the *Fatimids posed to his southern territories, no doubt facilitated the Crusader victory there. In 1100 D. ambushed Bohemond and Baldwin on their way from the coronation procession in Jerusalem to their domains, but his attack near Baalbeck was unsuccessful. During the following year D. tried in vain to maintain his overlordship in the Suwat, which was ravaged by *Tancred and *Godfrey. His attack on Tancred brought about a fierce retaliation and a demand from the prince of Galilee to convert to Christianity. His evasion of an open campaign ultimately cost him the loss of Suwat, whose emir agreed to accept Crusader suzerainty. His attempt to attack Baldwin (1101) on his way to succeed his brother as king of Jerusalem ended in his utter defeat at the Dog River, and in his paying Baldwin an enormous ransom for the captives of that battle. D.'s expansion toward the coast led him to a confrontation with Raymond. In 1101 his sizable forces suffered a defeat in the hands of Raymond's smaller Crusader army outside Tripoli. In 1103 D. took control in *Homs, which was being threatened by Raymond, appointing his loyal counsellor, Toghtekin, in the city. D.'s death in 1104 virtually led to the dissolution of one of the Moslem forces which posed a threat to the young Crusader establishments in Syria and Palestine.

DURANDUS OF SAINT-POURÇAIN (de S. Porciano; c. 1275-1334)

Theologian and philosopher. D. joined the *Dominicans at Clermont and studied theology at Paris. There he taught and commented upon the *Sentences* of *Peter Lombard, attacking the teachings of *Thomas Aquinas, which were accepted as official by the Dominicans. D.'s teaching and writings were criticized, examined by a Dominican commission and censured. In 1313 he became theological lecturer at the papal court at Avignon, and subsequently bishop of Limoux (1317) and Meaux (1326).

D., known as *doctor resolutissimus*, and a strong opponent of Thomism, is regarded as a nominalist and the forerunner of *Ockham. He reflected the reality of mental entities, namely the universals, claiming that only individuals exist. D. held that there is a sharp contrast between reason and faith. Reason has its own authority to support it, but the truths of faith are independent of reason and rational arguments. His major works are a commentary on the *Sentences* of Peter Lombard (1313-27), which he corrected and modified three times, guided by the critical comments of his superiors; *De origine potestatum et jurisdictionum* (1329), dealing with a jurisdictional dispute between Pope *John XXII and King *Philip VI; *De visione Dei quam habent animae sanctorum ante judicium generale* (1333), a treatise written upon the pope's request concerning the beatific vision of just souls before the Last Judgement. D.'s work was highly valued in the 15th and the 16th centuries and is considered to have influenced later theologians and reformers.

E. Gilson, *History of Christian Philosophy in the Middle Ages* (1955).

DURANDUS, WILLIAM, The Elder (c. 1230-96)

Canonist, administrator and bishop of Mende in Languedoc. An outstanding student of law at Bologna and Modena. In 1260 he served Cardinal Hostiensis at Rome, and later was appointed *auditor* at the papal court, that is, one of the judges who heard the appeals brought to the pope. In 1274 he attended *Gregory X at the Second Council of Lyons and drafted the decrees of that council. From 1278 he held various high administrative positions in the territories (Bologna and Romagna) newly added to the Papal States. In 1285 he was elected to the see of Mende, however, he did not assume office until 1291.

D. was a leading canonist in his own time, and gained the esteem of his peers through his comprehensive treatise on judicial procedure. His *Speculum judiciale* (1276, 1289-91), which give him his cognomen "speculator", became an authoritative textbook, widely studied and followed by ecclesiastical courts. He also wrote a *Repertorium sive Breviarium* on canon law and a commentary on the decrees of the Second Council of Lyons. In addition D. contributed significantly to the study of divine worship and liturgy. His revision of the *Pontificale Romanum,* completed at Mende, became a model for the official text of prayers later published by *Innocent VIII (1488). His *Rationale divinorum officiorum* (1285-91), a treatise on church liturgy and its symbolism also became a reference.

L. Falletti, "Guillaume Durand", in *Dictionnaire de droit canonique*, V (1953).

DURANDUS, WILLIAM, The Younger (c. 1271-1330)

Bishop of Mende in Languedoc. D., nephew of *D. the Elder, whom he succeeded in 1296 when he was appointed bishop by *Boniface VIII. In 1305 he led a delegation sent by Pope *Clement V to pacify Italy and restore order to the Papal States. As an able lawyer and leading churchman, D. was appointed (1308) a member of the committee charged with the investigation of the accusations against the *Templars. He prepared a long treatise for the Council of Vienne, which was summoned by Clement in 1311 to discuss several issues dealing with the Templars, church reform and a new crusade. In his *Tractatus de modo concilii generalis celebrandi*, D. particularly criticized the growth of the papal curia's power at the expense of the episcopate rights. D. also wrote a memorandum about the launching of a new crusade; its exact date of composition is still debated. As a prominent adviser to the royal court, D. was sent in 1329 on a mission to the Near East and died in Cyprus on his way home.

P. Viollet, *Guillaume Durant le Jeune, évêque de Mende, Histoire littéraire de la France* (1921).

DURAZZO (Dyrrachium) (Serbian: Drac, Albanian: Durrës)

The name of a seaport on the Adriatic shore in Illyria (modern Albania), opposite Bari and Brindisi. Its Italian name is derived from the Roman Dyrrachium, the name given to the port of Epidamnus, founded by the Greeks in the 7th century BC. After recovering from an earthquake in 314 D. became capital of the province Epirus Nova. Due to its importance D. soon became (449) the see of an archbishop. With the partition of the Roman empire D. came into the possession of the eastern emperors, who turned it into a base from which to eliminate piracy in the Adriatic Sea. D. suffered from various barbarian invasions: in 481 it was seriously threatened by *Theodoric, king of the Ostrogoths, and it was attacked by the Bulgarians during the 10th and 11th centuries, but during most of the Middle Ages it remained incorporated in the Byzantine empire as a distinct *theme. In 1082 D. was occupied by the Norman *Robert Guiscard, after a decisive battle against *Alexius' army. Robert held the city until his death in 1085, when the inhabitants of D. drove out the Normans and restored Byzantine rule. Subsequently D.

passed from hand to hand. In 1202, at the time of the Fourth *Crusade, the Western Romans became head of Constantinople, and D. came under Venetian domination. In 1258 D. passed, as dowry, to the possession of *Manfred of Sicily and later to *Charles of Anjou. D. was destroyed by an earthquake in 1273, but was soon rebuilt and became an independent duchy under John of Anjou, the ancestor of the house or dukes of D., which was a branch of the *Angevin family. From 1336 to 1355 D. was held by the Serbian king Stephen Dushan, and later (1358) came into the hands of the Albanian family, Topias. Towards the end of the 14th century (1394) D. returned to Venetian control under which it enjoyed a long period of prosperity until it was captured in 1501 by the Ottomans.

DÜREN An imperial town on the Rur River. D. was originally a Frankish palace and the town developed around it. The town was favourably located in the heart of the land and connected *Aachen to *Cologne. During the Carolingian period several state diets were convened by *Charlemagne and his successors in D.'s Duria or Dura Square. In the 12th century D. came to play an important economic role and developed into a trade centre of grain, corn, cattle, livestock and textiles. In 1236 *Frederick II pledged D. to Count William of Jülich, who incorporated it into his county.

DURHAM (Latin: Dunelmensis) Cathedral city and county in northern England. The see of D. was founded in 995, when the relics of St. *Cuthbert were transferred to its church, built on an easily defendable peninsula. The present cathedral (the church of Christ and Blessed Mary) was first built in 1093 by Bishop William of St. Carilef, who also replaced the Saxon clergy with a *Benedictine community. The cathedral, considered a typical example of Norman architecture, was the destination of many pilgrimages. Besides the shrine of St. Cuthbert, it also contained the relics of St. *Bede, dating from the 12th century, for which the Galilee chapel was built. D.'s strategic location far in the north, close to the Scottish border, contributed to its growing importance. The bishops of D. were also great feudal lords and commanded armies of their own. Entrusted with the defence of northern England they soon became Palatinate counts. Best known among them are Hugh du Puiset (1153-95), Anthony Bek (1284-1311), Richard of Bury (1333-45), Thomas Hatfield (1345-81). These prince-bishops not only had ecclesiastical authority, but were also invested with wide powers of civil jurisdiction over the county and were often involved in state and national affairs.

N. Pevsner, *County Durham* (1953);

P. A. White, *Portrait of County Durham* (1969).

E

EADMER (c. 1066-c. 1130) Historian. E. was educated at the monastery of Christ Church in Canterbury where, in 1093, he became St. *Anselm's chaplain, secretary and close friend. There he gathered material for the biography of St. Anselm and wrote a history of his own time, the *Historia Novorum*. In 1121 E. was appointed bishop to the see of St. Andrews, which he left shortly afterwards, disappointed by church policy. E. returned to Canterbury to continue his hagiographical work on the lives of early English saints, such as *Dunstan and Wilfrid. He also wrote a treatise defending the doctrine of the Immaculate Conception. His works are collected in J. P. Migne (ed.), *Patrologia Latina* (1844-64).
R. W. Southern, *Saint Anselm and his Biographer* (1963).

EALDORMAN (Alderman) The term was used in Anglo-Saxon England to designate notables who were called upon to participate in the councils of *hundreds and other local governments. Towards the end of the Anglo-Saxon period, it came to specifically denote the members of the city councils, and in that sense continued to hold after the Norman Conquest. The Es. were charged with administrative and fiscal tasks of their respective boroughs during the 12th and 13th centuries. Boroughs had councils of 12 or 24 Es., depending on their size.
B. Lyon, *A Constitutional and Legal History of Medieval England* (1960).

EARLS Members of the highest rank of the Anglo-Saxon nobility and corresponding to the Continental *counts. Until the *Norman Conquest of 1066, the E. were entrusted with the government of a district, roughly corresponding to a shire. During wartime the E. commanded armies under the high authority of the king. The Anglo-Saxon feudal system did not recognize the jurisdiction of the E. and their status was solely based on their social rank, being kinsmen of the royal families, as well as on their membership in the *witan. After the Norman Conquest, earldoms no longer corresponded to shires, and the latter were governed by royal officers, the *sheriffs. The E. thus became the highest rank of the Anglo-Norman nobility, most of them being members of younger branches of the royal dynasty.
B. Lyon, *A Constitutional and Legal History of Medieval England* (1960).

EAST ANGLIA One of the seven kingdoms of the Anglo-Saxons, situated in the eastern part of Britain, northeast of London. The Angles, who settled in the area during the 5th century, organized their realm *c.* 500 and were able to maintain their independence for nearly two centuries, However, in the 7th century E. finally fell under the influence of the neighbouring

kingdom of *Mercia, although it continued to maintain its political entity as a vassal kingdom. In the 8th century Mercian influence became paramount and E. was incorporated into the great realm of King *Offa. From the end of the 8th century, the area became a distinct province which, like Mercia and *Northumbria, was conquered by the *Danes and was made part of the *Danelaw in the 10th century.
F. M. Stenton, *Anglo-Saxon England* (1947).

EBERHARD Duke of Bavaria (935-39). Son of Duke Arnulf, he was proclaimed duke by his father and, after the latter's death, received the fealty of the vassals. Claiming his authority as hereditary and "by the election of the people", he refused to swear fidelity to King *Otto I of Germany and revolted against him in 937, entering an alliance with several dukes and nobles. Defeated, he was deposed in 939; up to the time of his death (*c.* 966) he made several unsuccessful attempts to recover his legacy.
G. Tellenbach, *Königtum und Stämme in der Werdezeit des deutschen Reiches* (1939).

EBROIN (d. 680) Mayor of the palace of *Neustria. E. was a member of a family which had risen through its service at the royal palace and which had no connection to the old Frankish nobility. In 657 he became mayor of the palace and exercised total authority over the realm of Neustria, oppressing the nobility. Defeated by an alliance of *Austrasian forces with the Neustrian nobility, he was sent to the monastery of Luxueil (673), but returned after two years and recovered his power. His repressive policy incited a renewed war with Austrasia, and he was defeated by *Pepin II of Landen and killed by a Neustrian official.
J. M. Wallace-Hadrill, *The Long-Haired Kings* (1963).

ÉCHEVIN See SCABINUS.

ÉCHEVINAGE Tax in medieval France levied for the maintenance of the office of the local *échevins*. Its amount varied from locality to locality. In the 13th century it became one of the resources of the royal treasury.

ECKHART, MEISTER (c. 1260-1327) German *Dominican mystic. Born to a noble family of Thuringia, he entered the Dominican convent of Erfurt. In 1302 he acquired his master's degree at the University of Paris and in 1304 was appointed provincial of the order in Saxony. He was sent to teach in Paris in 1311 and, after a short period, returned to Germany and settled at Cologne, where he became a very famous and popular preacher who mixed learning with the study of mysticism. Accused of heretical teaching, he was tried at the court of the archbishop of Cologne and convicted in 1326. He made an appeal to the pope, but died during the proceedings. In 1329 Pope *John XXII condemned some of his sayings as heretical and dange-

rous, but this in no way lessened the veneration of his disciples. His works, written both in German and Latin, were the subject of several interpretations and some scholars even considered him a forerunner of Luther. Actually, E.'s mystical conception of the world led him to elaborate a pantheistic view of the Divinity.
J. M. Clark, *The Great German Mystics* (1949).

ECOUAGE See SCUTAGE.

ECTHESIS See MONOTHELITISM.

EDDA Scandinavian mythological figure, the mother of the slaves in the Nordic societies. She was a subject of Scandinavian mythological poetry, the oldest version being known as the Eddaic verse. At *c.* 1220 E., as the "great grandmother", was immortalized in the Rigsthula saga, a mythological version of the origins of the Scandinavian social classes.
P. G. Foote and D. Wilson, *The Viking Achievement* (1970).

EDESSA City in the north Mesopotamian plain, between the Euphrates and Tigris rivers (present-day Turkey). At the beginning of the Middle Ages E. was one of the important centres of Syrian culture. Conquered by the Arabs in 640, it became a frontier city near the Byzantine borders. E. declined under Arab domination, although it remained a centre, containing a large Christian population of Syrians and Armenians and a relatively small number of Moslems. In 1098 the city and its surroundings were conquered by a group of participants in the First *Crusade, led by *Baldwin of Boulogne, brother of *Godfrey of Bouillon. The Crusaders established a principality, called the county of E. When Baldwin succeeded his brother to become king of Jerusalem in 1100, he left the county of E. to his cousin, *Baldwin of Bourg who, in many respects, is considered the real founder of the state. The latter fortified the city and built a number of fortresses controlling the passes of the Euphrates. In 1118 he inherited his cousin's kingship and E. was given to the *Courtenay family, whose younger son, Joscelin I, became the founder of its Crusader branch. The Courtenays, who sought to create a territorial link with the other Crusader states, engaged in constant wars with the Moslem rulers of *Aleppo. The country's distant location and the ineffective size of its fighting units posed a serious threat. In 1143 *Zengi, the atabeg of Mosul and Aleppo, finally captured E. from the Crusaders. The fall of E. was one of the reasons underlying the Second Crusade, but the participants of that Crusade never took steps to recover the county.
S. Runciman, *A History of the Crusades* (1953).

EDGAR THE PEACEFUL (944-75) King of *Wessex, *Mercia and *Northumbria (959-75). Nephew of King Eadred, he was proclaimed king of Mercia and Northumbria in 957 and, upon his brother Eadwig's death, was elected king of Wessex by the *witan. He made use of his peaceful reign to revive the Anglo-Saxon culture. Praised for his wisdom, he reformed the administration of the realm, including that of the *Danelaw, which was allowed to preserve its own laws. His administrative achievements are concentrated in a compilation of the "Laws of E.", of which only a part were his own legislation, the rest being ordinances promulgated by Anglo-Saxon kings. His main achievement was the reform of the Anglo-Saxon church and the revival of its learned monasticism. E. was highly

renowned in Britain, so much so that several Celtic kings met him at Chester in 973 and swore him allegiance.
F. M. Stenton, *Anglo-Saxon England* (1947).

EDINBURGH City in *Scotland and one of its royal residences prior to its becoming the capital in the late Middle Ages. The first settlement in E. was built under Roman rule and inhabited by the *Picts. The site was conquered by the *Northumbrian Anglo-Saxons in the 7th century and the foundation of the city is attributed to *Edwin, king of Northumbria, who gave it its name. Edwin built a fortress on top of the city's principal hill, which was later the site of E.'s famous royal castle. During the 9th century the city was invaded and destroyed several times by the *Vikings, and in the 11th century it became part of the kingdom of Scotland. After the *Norman Conquest of England (1066), Anglo-Norman influence began to be felt in E. and, by the first half of the 12th century, it had reached its peak. The royal castle became the residence of Queen Margaret, who built a chapel in 1076 in the Norman Romanesque style. Under her influence, Holyrood Abbey was founded and lavishly built in 1128. The city grew in the area lying between the castle and Holyrood Abbey, the centre of which was occupied by St. Giles' Cathedral, built in the Gothic style in the 13th and 14th centuries. The wars with England in the late 13th and 14th centuries accentuated the strategic importance of E. and kings came to spend more of their time in the city. During the 14th century parts of Holyrood Abbey were transformed into a royal residence and gradually into a palace. The palace became the official royal residence in 1498, when E. was made the official royal capital of Scotland by *James IV.
J. S. Richardson, *Edinburgh* (1949).

EDMUND I (c. 922-46) King of Wessex (939-46). Shortly after E. succeeded his brother Athelstan as king, he was threatened by a Norse invasion and lost control of Mercia and Northumbria. Due to his courage and statesmanship, E. was able to recover the northern territories and, in 944, established his rule over all of England and invaded the Celtic realm of Strathclyde. In 946 he prepared a military expedition to France to help his nephew, King *Louis IV. His plans were interrupted by his death, the work of a criminal.
F. M. Stenton, *Anglo-Saxon England* (1947).

EDMUND II, Ironside (c. 980-1017) King of England (1016-17). Son of King Eadric of Mercia, he rebelled against his father's policy and, in 1015, was recognized by the Anglo-Danes of the *Five Boroughs as their lord. His opposition to the Danish invasion led by King *Canute earned him popularity in the country and, in 1016, at the death of King *Ethelred of Wessex, he was hailed king of Wessex and recognized by all of Anglo-Saxon England. Despite E.'s initial successes near London, neither he nor Canute were able to attain a decisive victory. Only after E.'s death in 1017 was Canute recognized as king of England.
F. M. Stenton, *Anglo-Saxon England* (1947).

EDMUND OF ABINGTON, St. (c. 1180-1240) Archbishop of Canterbury (1233-40). Born at Abington to pious parents, he earned a reputation of austerity and learning as a youth. At the beginning of the 13th century and until his election to the see of Canterbury, he taught logic at Oxford, where St. Edmund Hall, which was supposed to have been built on the site of his residence, commemorates his association with the university. As archbishop, he boldly attempted to check royal mismanagement and papal exactions. Failing in his efforts, he retired to Pontigny, France, where he died in self-imposed exile. In 1247, upon popular request, Pope *Innocent IV proclaimed him a saint of the church.

A. B. Emden, *An Oxford Hall in Medieval Times* (1927).

EDMUND OF LANGLEY (1341-1402) Fourth son of *Edward III. Born at Langley (hence he was known as E.), he was made earl of Cambridge by his father in 1368. He supported his nephew, *Richard II, who granted him the duchy of York in 1385 and entrusted him with the government of the realm. E. was the founder of the house of York (1385-1485).

F. R. H. du Boulay and C. M. Baron, *The Reign of Richard II* (1971).

EDMUND THE MARTYR, St. (c. 840-70) King of East Anglia (855-70). Son of a Saxon noble who became king of East Anglia, E. succeeded his father in 855. He was renowned for his just rule, which lasted until 870, when the *Danes invaded the kingdom, murdering E. upon his refusal to share his kingship with their pagan chieftain. The cult of his martyrdom started almost immediately, and in the 10th century the monastery of Bury St. Edmund's was founded on his grave site.

F. Hervey, *The Story of King Edmund the Martyr and the Early Years of his Abbey* (1927).

EDUCATION With the exception of the Far Eastern civilizations, medieval E. was a religious matter in all three monotheistic faiths. At the beginning of the Middle Ages, what remained of the educational system of classical antiquity gradually declined and in the 6th and 7th centuries its disappearance was symbolized by the closing of the Platonic academy of Athens in accordance with the edict of *Justinian in 529. Nevertheless, medieval E. continued the legacy of classical E., as it was based on the study of the seven liberal arts (the *Trivium and the *Quartrivium*), and professional training was acquired through apprenticeship.

The religious primacy of E. was first developed in Byzantium, where the ancient model of the urban school continued to exist, but came under the supervision of the church. The lay academies were replaced by an important institution of higher learning established at Constantinople under the patronage of the imperial school; the members of the teaching body at this academy became state officials. The academy offered the study of liberal arts as well as of advanced work in the fields of law, theology and history. Particular emphasis was placed on juridical studies, meant to train students for work within the administration of the empire, and also to promote the development of jurisprudence. The 10th century was an important era in terms of Byzantine E. and culture; schools were reformed and the entire system was put under state control. Programmes were made rigid and uniform; classical authors were studied and their books were copied. The imperial court became the core of higher E.

The Byzantine educational structure suffered a grave blow when Constantinople was captured by participants in the Fourth *Crusade. As a consequence, Greek schools within the Latin empire of Constantinople (1204-61) were made into monasteries, which then became centres of Orthodox theological training. The state system was preserved and developed at *Nicaea where, in order to challenge the Latin Catholic establishment of Constantinople, particular attention was paid to the development of philosophy and theology, rooted in the Greek philosophical legacy and orthodox practices. This not only stimulated the Greek-Orthodox clergy to oppose unification with the Catholic Church, but also (and mainly) inspired an intellectual revival, which enabled the emergence of the Renaissance in the West.

In the Moslem world, E. originated from studies of the commentaries on the *Koran and of philology, the latter subject concerning the linguistic rules of Arabic. In the 8th century under the influence of the Greek and Persian schools, philosophical and scientific dimensions were added to the Moslem schools that had been established in cities of the caliphate. The Moslem educational system reached its maturity at the beginning of the 9th century when the Academy of Baghdad was founded by the Caliph *Al-Mamun. The school attracted the best scholars of the caliphate and became the centre of studies of Aristotelian philosophy and of the sciences, including mathematics, physics, astronomy and astrology. During the second half of the 9th century and in the 10th century, the scholarly centres spread and important academies were founded at *Kairwan and in Moslem Spain (where studies came to be concentrated at *Cordoba). Furthermore, the construction of the Mosque of *Al-Azhar at Cairo (974) and the concentration of stipended scholars in its midst formed the basis for the development of its academy where, originally, Islamic theology and jurisprudence were studied. By the beginning of the 12th century, it was the Moslem educational system which was the most progressive, both in its organization and content of study, and its achievements were accepted by other civilizations. The Egyptian academy began to decline in the second half of the 12th century, due to *Nureddin of Syria, who closed the traditional philosophical-scientific schools and created the system of the *medressa*, aimed to produce propagandists of *Sunnite Islam and, at the same time, to train government officials. The teaching method adopted in the *medressa* was based on the authoritative and normative study of the law and religion; as such, rote, rather than the analytic method, was used. With the gradual spread of the *medressa* in the 13th century and the *Mongols' destruction of the intellectual centres in Persia and Iraq, Moslem E. surrendered its creativity in the late Middle Ages.

In western Europe the fall of the Roman empire was followed by a rapid decline in social structures and the educational system, which affected the urban schools. The church's monopoly on E. was based on monastic schools, according to the system elaborated by *Cassiodorus at the beginning of the 6th century. These schools, which spread through Italy, Spain and Gaul, were introduced at the end of the 6th century in Ireland and in the 7th century in Anglo-Saxon Britain. Irish monasticism afforded a high level of learning and, when Irish monasteries were settled in Continental Europe, traditional studies were revived in the West (7th century). The Anglo-Saxon achievements were introduced to the kingdom of the *Franks by *Alcuin of York at the end of the 8th century. Since he wielded much influence at the court of *Charlemagne, he was allowed to found an academy, which eventually became the institution of higher learning in the *Carolingian empire. Moreover, he was responsible for the educational reform of Charlemagne, which demanded the establishment of a school in every bishopric and monastery of the empire where clergy would be trained through a normative method. As a result of these measures and the Carolingian Renaissance, theological learning and *scholasticism emerged in the 9th-11th centuries. The programmes were enriched by the influence of the Arab schools of Spain, by translations of scientific works from Arabic into Latin, and by the development of philosophical debates in the schools. In the second half of the 10th century the teaching of Gerbert at Rheims stimulated the emergence of new schools, which spread to Lorraine and the Low Countries, as well as to western France. At the same time the monastic schools developed their teaching systems, which flourished in northern Italy, eastern France and Normandy in the 11th century. Such achievements eventually led to the establishment of the most original feature of medieval west European E., the *universities, which first emerged in the 12th century at *Bologna and Paris and then spread throughout the Continent during the 13th century. Thus a pluralist system of E. emerged from 12th-century Renaissance, ranging from elementary E. in cathedral schools to the universities and monastic schools. The adoption of Aristotelian philosophy and interest in the sciences were responsible for new teaching methods, based on the analytical system of instruction.

Judaism created its own educational system, which was based, at the beginning of the Middle Ages, on the great Talmudic academies of Mesopotamia. These establishments were the sole institutions of higher E. in the Jewish world up to the end of the 8th century, and they emphasized the study of the law and interpretation of the holy books. Geo-political conditions caused reputed teachers to migrate to other countries, and communities began to found their own schools, directed by local rabbis. The diversification within the school system led to differences regarding emphasis in the Jewish schools of the 10th century; while the Spanish (*Sephardi) group was influenced by Arab E. and concentrated on philosophical, scientific and linguistic topics; other schools, such as those of the Franco-German (*Ashkenazi) group, developed the legal and exegetic studies.

A. O. Norton, *Readings in the History of Education* (1909).

EDWARD I (1239-1307) King of England (1272-1307). Son of *Henry III, he was active in governmental affairs during his father's reign and extended English domination in Wales. In 1265 he defeated an alliance of barons led by Simon of *Montfort and, later on, led a *Crusade to Palestine (1270-71). E. began his reign by uniting the nobility and the knights of the shires, establishing a new administrative structure in the kingdom (1274). He also entered a long series of wars against Scotland, aiming to impose his overlordship upon the northern kingdom. Despite military success, he did not achieve his aim, due to the revolts of the Scottish leaders *Wallace and *Bruce.

Imaginary likeness of Edward II of England

E. earned the reputation of the greatest legislator among the English kings and was named "the English Justinian". His reforms were intended to create a centralistic royal administration, based on the sovereign rule of the law and on the participation of barons and *community representatives in the government, by means of Parliament. His legislative activity covered a wide range of juridical and administrative problems, and the statutes he issued formed the basis of the English constitution in the late Middle Ages. His *Confirmation of the Charters*, issued in 1297, had important political implications, as it gave Parliament the sole right to impose taxes and offer grants, thus requiring the elaboration of budgetary practices.

F. M. Powicke, *Oxford History of England* (1955).

EDWARD II (1284-1327) King of England (1307-27). Son of *Edward I, he was proclaimed prince of Wales in 1301, thus inaugurating the precedent that the heir apparent of England be given this title. He began his reign over England, following the powerful regime of his father, by appointing favourites, such as *Gaveston and the *Despensers, who were hated by the barons. He was also faced with opposition by the Scots who, led by Robert *Bruce, reconquered the territories lost to Edward I and took possession of large areas in northern England, defeating E. at *Banockburn in 1314. As a result, the baronial opposition rose against the king and E. was compelled to dismiss his favourites, who were impeached by Parliament. In 1327 his wife, Isabelle of France, joined the rebels and allied herself with *Mortimer, the enemy of the Despensers. Captured, E. was compelled to abdicate in favour of his son, Edward III, and was later murdered by his wife's agents.

M. McKisack, *Oxford History of England* (1959).

EDWARD III (1312-77) King of England (1327-77). Son of *Edward II and of Isabelle of France (daughter of King *Philip IV), he began his reign in 1330, after putting an end to his mother's regency. Educated at his mother's court, E. became not only a brilliant knight, but also a great statesman. He opposed the inheritance claims of *Philip VI of Valois as king of France, asserting his own rights as grandson of Philip IV. This dispute, together with conflicts with the French administration in Flanders and in *Guienne, eventually led to the *Hundred Years' War. E.'s response to France was the imposition of an economic blockade upon Flanders, preventing the export of English wool, and the creation of a staple at *Antwerp, which brought prosperity to the cloth industry of Brabant. E. led the war against France (which began in 1337) with brilliant military skill, but also made use of diplomacy in an attempt to isolate France from the Low Countries and the German Rhenish principalities. His naval victory at Sluis (1340) established English maritime supremacy and enabled him to land in northern France with massive armies, among them the Welsh archers, whom he successfully employed against the French cavalry. The result was a decisive victory at *Crécy (1346), followed by the conquest of *Calais, which was transformed into an English town. E. made *Brittany his protectorate, supporting the house of Montfort and, c. 1350, gained strong influence in northern France. Meanwhile he sent his son, *Edward the Black Prince, to Guienne as lieutenant and commander-in-chief of the Anglo-Gascon armies. The Battle of *Poitiers (1356), which led to the collapse of the French army, crowned E.'s military successes and allowed him to secure a peace settlement favouring England. Negotiated with the dauphin *Charles V, the Treaty of *Brétigny-Calais, which ended the first stage of the Hundred Years' War, granted E. domination over about half of the French territory and imposed a heavy ransom for the release of the French king, *John II. During this period E. was at the height of his power and prestige. His court became one of the most brilliant of western Europe and his establishment of the Order of the *Garter signified a new stage in the development of chivalric behaviour. However, after the coronation of *Charles V (1365) and the renewal of the war, E. suffered a number of reversals. The extension of the war to *Castile, begun with the victory of the Black Prince at *Najera, ended with the fall of his ally, King Peter the Cruel (1369, while the guerilla war led by *Du Guesclin in France ended with the loss of the major part of the territories acquired through the Brétigny-Calais treaty. Moreover, constant warfare and the consequences of the *Black Plague had had a devastating impact on the royal finances. As a result, E. became more dependent on Parliament, which was gradually divided into two houses, the Lords and the Commons. The financial burdens created a troubled situation in England and led to opposition along religious lines from among the scholars of Oxford, led by *Wycliffe. This group openly contested papal policy and the right of the church to possess wealth. Only E.'s prestige and the Parliament's support prevented open clashes.
M. J. Hewitt, *The Organization of War under Edward III* (1966).

EDWARD THE BLACK PRINCE (1330-76) Son and heir of *Edward III, he was proclaimed prince of Wales and, in 1350, his father sent him to *Gascony and *Guienne as his lieutenant. One of the most brilliant knights of his age and a gifted commander, he quickly earned the respect of the Gascon nobles who enrolled in his army. In 1354-56 he commanded several military expeditions in southern France and, in 1356, gained a reputation by defeating the French army at *Poitiers, taking *John II captive and sending him to the Tower of London. In 1367 at *Najera, E. defeated the French army commanded by *Du Guesclin as well as the supporters of *Henry of Trastamare, pretender to the throne of Castile. Under the cognomen "the Black Prince" he became the symbol of the 14th-century chivalrous knight.
M. J. Hewitt, *The Black Prince's Expedition of 1354-56* (1958).

EDWARD THE CONFESSOR, St. (1003-66) King of England (1042-66). Son of King *Ethelred II of Wessex and of Emma of Normandy, he was sent by his mother to Normandy in 1013 and was educated at the court of his uncle, Duke Richard. In 1042, after the death of *Hardicanute, his half-brother, he was summoned to England and proclaimed king, which put an end to Danish domination. E.'s reign was peaceful but it was also marked by the increasing influence of Norman clergy, whom he had brought to England, and of the local nobility, led by *Godwin and his son *Harold, earls of Wessex. E. himself was mainly occupied with religious matters (his cognomen, the Confessor) and became famous for his piety. He built *Westminster Abbey, consecrated in 1065. The lack of political authority held by the king caused succession to be disputed and eventually led to the *Norman Conquest. E. was canonized in 1161.
T. J. Oleson, *The Reign of Edward the Confessor* (1955).

EDWARD THE ELDER (d. 924) King of Wessex (899-924). Son of *Alfred the Great, he fought against the Danes, defeating them several times, and began the reconquest of the *Danelaw, assisted by a Mercian army. In c. 920, he reorganized the bishoprics of his kingdom and integrated them into the political system of Wessex, employing the bishops in his administration. He also regulated trade as a result of the emergence of towns in his kingdom. The regulations he adopted are known as the "Laws of E".
F. M. Stenton, *Anglo-Saxon England* (1947).

EDWIN (c. 585-633) King of Northumbria (617-33). The son of Aella, king of *Deira, who had lost his kingdom to the dynasty of *Bernicia, E. was a refugee for many years. He wandered through northern Wales, Mercia and East Anglia in an attempt to obtain help to recover his kingdom. In 617, assisted by King Redwald of East Anglia, his kingdom was restored and, after a few years' time, E. united the kingdoms of *Northumbria, conquering the country from the Lottian *Picts. His territory corresponded to southeastern Scotland and there he built the fortress of *Edinburgh, named after himself. In 725 he married Ethelburga, sister of the king of Kent and a Christian, bringing her chaplain, Paulinus, to the royal court. E. then converted to the Christian faith and appointed Paulinus as first bishop of York. His wars with Mercia ended with his defeat in 633 by *Penda, the heathen Mercian king, at Heathfield. E. died of his battle wounds and the realm of Northumbria fell apart after his death.

F. M. Stenton, *Anglo-Saxon England* (1947).

EGBERT THE GREAT (c. 775-839) King of Wessex (802-39). Son of Ealhmund, who reigned in Kent, and member of the Wessex royal dynasty, E. was exiled during his childhood by *Offa, king of *Mercia, who conquered his father's realm, and spent his youth at the court of *Charlemagne. In 802 he was proclaimed king of Wessex, which recovered its independence from Mercia. Up to 820 he worked to consolidate his government and then launched a long series of wars, facilitated by the disintegration of the Mercian kingdom. E. systematically conquered the southern Anglo-Saxon kingdoms, making himself ruler over all of Anglo-Saxon England (825). In 829 he conquered Mercia and added its royal title to that of Wessex. During the last ten years of his reign, E. organized his vast kingdom and worked to increase the influence of Wessex.

F. M. Stenton, *Anglo-Saxon England* (1947).

EGICA King of the *Visigoths (687-700). His reign was a troubled period in the history of Spain. E. persecuted both the noble families and the Jews, whom he accused of appealing to foreigners to invade Spain (694), alluding to the Arabs. His tyranny caused the clergy of his realm to join the nobles in their plots against the government. Such conspiracies grew more frequent during the last years of E.'s reign. The king's repressive measures greatly weakened the Visigothic kingdom of Spain.

A. K. Ziegler, *Church and State in Visigothic Spain* (1950).

EGIDIUS ROMANUS See GILES OF ROME.

EGINHARD See EINHARD.

EGYPT Country in the eastern part of north Africa. At the beginning of the Middle Ages (395-614), E. was one of the most prosperous provinces of the *Byzantine empire and one of its most important cultural and religious centres. The patriarchs of Alexandria enjoyed great prestige as leaders of the Greek-Orthodox Church. However, after the constitutional reforms of *Justinian (6th century), which centralized the church government in *Constantinople, the authority of the patriarchs of Alexandria declined. This incited a certain degree of opposition, resulting in the emergence of different religious groups, such as the *Monophysites and *Monothelites, and of the distinctly Egyptian and autonomous *Coptic church. The attempts of Emperor *Heraclius to achieve religious unity through the issuance of his *Ecthesis (673) did not bring the expected results and, on the eve of the Arab invasion, all of E. was opposed to the imperial power. This split enabled the Arabs, who invaded E. in 640, to conquer the country without difficulties and, by 641, Byzantine domination in E. was at an end.

The Arab conquest created not only political changes, but also ushered in a socio-cultural evolution, which transformed E. into an Arab and Moslem country. From their camp at *Fustat, south of the Nile Delta (*Cairo), the conquerors imposed Islam upon the majority of the populace, although important minorities of Coptic and Greek Christians, as well as Jews, continued to exist in the country. E. thus became a province of the *Ummayad and *Abbasid caliphates, and the process of Islamization brought the conquerors in contact with the important Greek learning centre of Alexandria (7th-9th centuries). In consequence, the Arabs assimilated much of the classical and Hellenistic Greek heritage into their culture, translating the Greek philosophical and scientific works into their own tongue, and E. became one of the centres of Arab science. Under the *Tulunid governors (9th century), E. experienced economic development and prosperity, based both on Mediterranean trade and on the relations with Sudan and west Africa. The decline of the Abbasid caliphate at the end of the 9th century allowed the governors of E. a large degree of autonomy, but also deprived them, together with the other rulers of north Africa, of support from the central government of the caliphate.

The *Fatimids took advantage of this situation to conquer E. in 974, founding the new city of Cairo, which became the capital of their caliphate. E. thus became an independent state and attained a central position in the Moslem world, due to the *Shiite allegiance to the Fatimids. The latter had also conquered and established their overlordship over large territories in Palestine, Syria and Hedjaz. The building of the *Al-Azhar mosque at Cairo, which became an important centre of Moslem learning, made E. one of the most important centres of Islamic studies, as well as one of scientific work. Its geo-political position also contributed to the country's development in the 10th and 11th centuries, as it served as the middleman in trade between the Mediterranean world and the Far East. This brought it economic prosperity, enhanced by its control over Syrian and Palestinian ports. The arrival of the *Seljuk Turks in the Middle East (1071) dealt a blow to the Fatimids, who lost the major part of their provinces, together with Jerusalem, to the Seljuks, maintaining their rule over the littoral cities of Syria and Palestine, which were taken at the beginning of the 12th century by the *Crusaders, and over the coastal provinces of Syria. Attempts by the Fatimids to recover the territories lost to the Crusaders (1100-10) were unsuccessful, causing the dynasty to decline. This development left the military viziers to serve as the actual rulers of E. The establishment of the Crusaders' merchant communities at Acre, Tyre and Antioch, which gave the Italian city-states a monopoly over the trade between East and West, dealt a serious blow to the Egyptian economy and also figured in the Fatimid decline in the middle of the 12th century. This situation prompted the Crusaders to attempt the conquest of E. and, in 1169, the armies of *Amalric I reached the Nile. The failure of the Crusaders to actually conquer the country was due to the arrival of a supporting army under the command of *Saladin, sent by *Nureddin of Syria. In 1170 Saladin put an end to the Fatimid dynasty and, establishing the *Ayyubid dynasty, became governor of E., which he united with Syria in 1174. He was able to restore the central position once held by E. in the Moslem world, even though the centre of his government was in the Syrian provinces.

After Saladin's death, the Ayyubid empire was divided and E. gained its independence under the rule of Al-Adil, Saladin's brother (1194). The Ayyubid sultans, however, were involved in disputes with the Syrian branches of the dynasty and sought control over the Palestinian territories, thus neglecting the administration of their own country, which they considered only as the basis of their power and resources. At the same time, the Crusaders took renewed interest in E., hoping to recover the kingdom of Jerusalem by means of control over it. Thus, some of the Crusades of the 13th century were directed towards the Nile Delta, and the conquest of *Damietta, located at the eastern mouth of the Nile, became one of their goals. Although such attacks enabled only a temporary conquest of Damietta, they caused the Ayyubid sultans to become dependent, to a large extent, on hired *Mameluke soldiers, who had risen from servile positions to high command and who became a permanent military force, camped on the borders of the Nile at Cairo. In 1252, after the failure of the Crusade of King *Louis IX, the Mamelukes seized power in E.

The Mamelukes reigned until the 16th century. Being a military caste, they were primarily interested in wars against the Syrian Ayyubids and the Crusaders; the latter they repeatedly defeated, conquering their castles and principalities and destroying their kingdom in 1291. They also successfully opposed the *Mongols and established their rule in Palestine and Syria as far as the Taurus Mountains on the Anatolian frontier. In terms of internal affairs, they left the civil government to local officials, who were expected to raise taxes and tributes. E. therefore suffered during their rule. Its decline was reinforced by the *Black Death (1347-50) which, with other diseases, ravaged the country and eliminated most of the urban population.

S. Lane-Poole, *A History of Egypt in the Middle Ages* (1936).

EIGENKIRCHE (Private Church) Modern German term, adopted by the historians to signify the proprietory status of many churches in the 9th-12th centuries, which belonged to feudal lords. (The term does not include chapels built in castles or palaces.) Legally, the possessor of an E. owned the building and its appendages, whether they be lands or houses, and was given access to the income of the church, such as the tithes. He had the right to appoint the priest, who was ordained by the bishop. Because he took over the church's resources, he was required to provide for the priest's necessities. The Gregorian *reform opposed the practice, considering it to be an extension of the lay investiture.

G. Tellenbach, *Church, State and Christian Society* (1953).

EINHARD (Eginhard; c. 770-840) Historian. Born in *Franconia, he was educated at the abbey of *Fulda and later at the palace academy of *Charlemagne, where he became a friend of the emperor. He also enjoyed the favour of *Louis the Pious, who granted him large estates in Germany. E. wrote the biography of Charlemagne, modelled after *The Twelve Caesars* by Suetonius. The work is one of the most remarkable biographies of the Middle Ages, presenting a physical and moral portrait of the emperor and relating his deeds. E.'s letters, which dealt with the administration of his estates in Germany, serve as important evidence of the feudalization of German society in the 9th century. E. retired from the imperial court in 830 and then settled in his estates.

L. Halphen (ed.), *Eginhard, La Vie de Charlemagne* (1923).

EKKEHARD (910-73) Monk of St. Gall. E. was one of the most gifted Latin poets of the 10th century. His most famous work, the *Waltharius,* was a Latin version of an ancient German epic, from which he expurgated all pagan allusions. He wrote the work in hexameters in imitation of the poetry of Virgil. The poem deals with the adventures of Waltharius, son of the king of Aquitaine, who was a captive at the court of *Attila the Hun. There he met Hiltikundis, daughter of a Burgundian king. Attila is represented as a peaceful king, who educated and loved the couple. However, their love for their homelands was stronger then their attachment to Attila and they fled, taking with them a large portion of the Huns' booty. Frankish knights attacked them, attempting to rob this treasure, but Waltharius, despite losing his hand in the battle, defeated them. Returning home, he became king and made Hiltikundis his queen.

S. Strecker (ed.), *Waltharius* (1907).

EKKEHARD (d. 1002) Margrave of Meissen. Member of a distinguished Saxon family which was related to the *Ottonian dynasty, he gained important military experience while fighting the Slavs under *Otto III. Upon Otto's death, he was named one of the candidates to the imperial throne, but was murdered by personal enemies and his march was attacked by King *Boleslaw of Poland.

R. Folz, *La Naissance du Saint-Empire* (1968).

EKKEHARD OF AURA (d. c. 1130) Monk and later abbot of the German monastery of Aura, he took part in the abortive Crusade of 1101. After his return to his monastery, he became acquainted with the historical works of its library and, in 1115, he wrote a history of the First Crusade. During that time, he was requested to edit the annals of Aura; this he did until 1125. On the basis of these annals, he wrote a continuation of the universal history of *Hermann the Lame, particularly covering the years 1099-1125.

J. W. Thompson, *History of Historical Writing* (1943).

ELBING City in *Prussia on the lower Vistula. It was founded in the 14th century by the order of the *Teutonic Knights, who built a castle overlooking the town. Populated by German settlers, it became an important trade centre in the 15th century. In the middle of the century, troubles arose in the city, owing to the refusal of the order to grant privileges to its inhabitants and, in 1454, it joined the "Prussian Union" of German settlers who opposed the order. In 1466 it was conquered by King *Casimir IV of Poland and became one of the centres of "Royal Prussia", which belonged directly to the Polish crown.

The Cambridge History of Poland, I (1960).

ELEANOR OF AQUITAINE (Alienor, Eléonore, Eonor) Daughter of the last duke of Aquitaine, *William X (1122-1204). After the death of her father, who left her in the custody of *Louis VI of France, she was married to *Louis VII (1137) and became queen of France. She accompanied her husband on the Second Crusade, during which she lost the great influence she had had over him, and they quarrelled. In 1152 the Council of Beaugency pronounced the separation of the royal couple, annulling their marriage. E. returned to her court of Poitiers and married *Henry II Plantagenet, who became king of England, and annexed Aquitaine

Eleanor of Aquitaine

to his vast domains in France. She intervened in her husband's government and encouraged their sons to rebel against him. A person of great energy, she tried to save *John Lackland, and only after her death in 1204 did the Angevin empire begin to collapse. She patronized poets and artists at her court. She was buried in an artistic tomb at the abbey of *Fontrevault near her husband Henry II and beloved son *Richard the Lion-hearted.

She was a controversial personality to her contemporaries. Respected in Aquitaine and known as patron of arts and letters, she was also accused by French chroniclers of being an intriguer, an unfaithful wife and even a witch.

A. Kelly, *Alienor of Aquitaine* (1952).

ELEAZAR HA-KALIR (8th century) Jewish poet. Little is known about his life and personality. He wrote his poems in Palestine in the century following the Arab conquest. E. is considered the greatest Hebrew poet of the early Middle Ages and thus one of the revivers of Hebrew poetry. His works were incorporated in the Jewish liturgy, especially in the elegaic prayers. His main theme was a lamentation over the destruction of the Temple and the subjection of the Jewish people to the "Gentiles". In his 150 known poems he used a particular style which was later adopted by the Hebrew religious poetry of the Middle Ages and became characteristic of the liturgical poetry of the various Jewish communities.

S. W. Baron, *A Social and Religious History of the Jewish People*, IV (1957).

ELEAZAR OF WORMS (1165-1238) Jewish mystic and pietist. Born at Mainz, he belonged to the family of *Kalonymus, which was highly esteemed by the Jews of Germany and France. He studied in the best schools of

the Rhenish Jewish communities before fleeing from his native city, where a persecution of the Jews broke out in 1188. He settled at Worms and, in 1196, when *Crusaders gathered in the city, two of them entered his home and murdered his wife and two daughters in his presence. This event had a lifelong impact upon him. In 1201 he became the rabbi of the Jewish community of Worms and directed its famous school. E., who already in his youth was initiated to the mystical love of the "secrets of God" (see *Kabbalah), devoted himself to this field of study and was the first in *Ashkenazi Jewry to make them known to the general public. In his treatise entitled *Commentary on the Prayers and their Secret Message*, he claimed that an oral tradition concerning their mystical significance had been transmitted from Mesopotamia to Italy and, through his family, to Germany. He proposed a mystical interpretation of the characters and verse of the Scriptures and a spiritual interpretation of the Divinity. This subject was treated in his chief work, *Misraf le-Hohmah* (The Purgatory of Wisdom). In order to explain his theory, he adopted a method based on both the philosophical ideas of *Saadia Gaon and on the pietist practices of his master, *Jehudah the Hasid. This method led him to present a cosmological theory of the Divinity in which rationalistic and mystical elements were blended. His most popular work, *Rokeah* is concerned with pietist practices and religious behaviour.

G. Scholem, *Ursprung und Anfänge der Kabbalah* (1962).

ELIGIUS, St. (c. 590-c. 660) Bishop of Noyon and patron saint of metalworkers. Born in Aquitaine, his work on precious metals brought him to the court of *Clotaire II, king of the Franks. Employed by the king at the royal mint, he was made master of the mint at Marseilles. Clotaire's son, *Dagobert I, made him his chief counsellor (629-39). He was employed in ransoming captives, founding monasteries on behalf of the king and in pious works. In 641 he became bishop of Noyon and proved himself a zealous pastor, active in missionary work in Flanders.

P. Parsy, *Saint Éloi* (1907).

ELIZABETH OF HUNGARY, St. (1207-31) Daughter of King *Andrew II of Hungary, in 1211 she was sent to Thuringia with a view to making a future political marriage. In 1221 she was married to Landgrave Louis IV, but under the influence of the *Franciscans, showed an interest in the ascetic life and donated large sums of money to charities. In 1227, after her husband's death, she was driven away from the court by her brother-in-law, *Henry Raspe, on the pretext that her charities were exhausting the state finances. She settled at Marburg, gave up her children and lived a life of great austerity, practising physical mortifications and devoting her energies to visiting and caring for the sick and poor. Thus, she gained a reputation for saintliness and was canonized in 1235.

W. Canton, *St. Elizabeth of Thuringia* (1913).

ELY, ISLE OF On the bank of the Ouse River, between *East Anglia and *Mercia. In 673 St. Ethelreda founded there a double monastery. granting it dominion over the island. Destroyed by the *Danes in 870, in 970 it was restored as a monastery and abbey by King *Edgar. In 1109 it was transformed into the bishopric of E. Endowed with rich territories in Cambridgeshire, it became

The high Gothic vaults at the cathedral of Amiens, France, built in the 13th century

a mainstay of royal authority under the *Norman and Plantagenet kings.

E. Miller, *The Abbey and Bishopric of Ely* (1951).

EMMA OF NORMANDY (d. 1044) Daughter of Duke *Richard of Normandy, she married *Ethelred II, king of Wessex, to whom she bore two sons, Alfred and *Edward the Confessor. In 1015, after the Danish conquest of England and the death of her husband, she married *Canute the Great, becoming the mother of *Hardicanute. In 1036, after Canute's death, she was exiled to Flanders, where she supported the claims of her younger son to the throne.

F. M. Stenton, *Anglo-Saxon England* (1947).

EMMANUEL BEN SALOMON, the Roman (Manoello Romano; 1261-1336) Jewish poet and scholar. Member of an aristocratic Jewish family of Rome, he was educated in both religious and liberal studies. In *c.* 1295, having lost his wealth, he left his native city and wandered as a poor poet in the various communities of Italy. In 1328 he settled at Fermo and began to compile *The Notebook of E.,* a collection of his Hebrew poems. He also wrote sonnets in Italian. His work reveals the influence of *Dante, but there is no evidence that they met. This influence is particularly evident in a group of poems in which E. described a journey in Purgatory and Paradise. His poetry includes a satirical commentary on the manners of his age, applicable to both Christians and Jews, with a strong erotic emphasis, unusual in the Jewish society of the period. But apart from this satirical element, many of his poems are concerned with a historical approach to the Jewish fate in the Diaspora. As a scholar, E. wrote a treatise on the literal form of the Bible and Talmud and commentaries of the Bible.

M. D. Cassuto, *Dante e Manuello Romano* (1936).

EMPHYTEUSIS System of land-tenure practised in the later Roman empire and Byzantium. Tracts of unreclaimed land were granted to individuals, with the understanding that for a number of years the estate would be exempted from taxes in view of the cost of settling and colonizing the territory.

M. Bloch, *Feudal Society* (1952).

EMPIRE, IDEA OF The medieval E. was a fusion of the Roman imperial ideology and the biblical idea of the elected nation. In the first centuries of the Middle Ages, the idea was based on the universal legacy of the unity of Rome, as expressed by its continuation in the Byzantine empire. It implied the full sovereignty of the empire, while the independent Germanic kingdoms in the West were recognized by the grant of honorific Roman titles (such as consul) to their kings. In practice, however, this unity was broken by the foundation of the empire of *Charlemagne (800), based on the biblical concept of the Christian E. (an interpretation of the idea of the elect nation), but at the same time being officially named the Roman empire, like Byzantium. This universalistic concept again found expression in the *Holy Roman empire, conceived as the superior political organization of the Catholic world, with the emperor as the formal head of Christian society. As such, it contested the papal claims to absolute authority and power, countering it with the theory of the universal sovereignty of the emperor. The result was the dispute between the empire and the papacy which lasted for 200 years (1059-1254) and led to the weakening

of both forces and the decline of the universalistic theories. In the late Middle Ages, the idea was successfully contested by the rise of the independent monarchies, based on nationhood and territorial sovereignty. In practice, though not in theory, this view finally also affected the E., and facilitated its transformation into the German E.

R. Koebner, *Empire* (1961).

ENCLOSURE Agricultural practice in the estates of later medieval England, resulting from the *Black Death. The shortage of manpower in the second half of the 14th century led many of the lords to transform a large part of their estates into pasture for sheep, which required less manpower, with the aim of exporting wool. These pasturelands were enclosed and thus forbidden to the peasants, who lost their source of cultivation. In the last third of the 14th century the spread of the E. led to a troubled atmosphere in the country, culminating in the great Peasants' Revolt of 1381. After the repression of the revolt, the system was maintained through the 15th century.

E. Lipson, *The Economic History of England*, I (1937).

ENGLAND The southern and central part of the island of Britain, the most fertile and populated section of it. The name E. (Latin *Anglia*) derives from the *Anglo-Saxon tribes who conquered and settled it, creating a distinct civilization with a language belonging to the Germanic family.

The last Roman holdings in Britain were abandoned at the beginning of the 5th century; from 407 the country was left to disunited, partially Romanized *Celtic tribes and clans. The weak political and military organization of Britain enabled the *Anglo-Saxon and Jute tribes to invade the island in the mid-5th century and to establish permanent settlements, particularly in the area of Kent, which became the base for their further expansion in the island. The Britons' attempts to organize a defence proved ineffective, having been initiated too late. After a series of battles, including that of Mount Badon (495), won by the Britons, the Celts were compelled in the 6th century to the western edge of the island, where they continued to enjoy independence in their principalities of Wales and Cornwall and along the coast of the Irish Sea, while some of them migrated to the Continent and settled in *Brittany. While the main lines of these developments are clear, there are many interpretations of the details, which became the basis for legendary stories, the most famous being those of *Arthur. However, the Anglo-Saxons completed their conquest and settlement only by the middle of the 6th century, when they founded their first kingdoms in E., headed by descendants of the original invaders.

In the 6th and 7th centuries, the political organization of the Anglo-Saxon kingdoms lacked stability, and some of them, such as Lindsey, Deira or Bernicia, were short-lived. Gradually, the number of states was reduced to the seven of the Anglo-Saxon *Heptarchy: *Kent, *Essex, *Sussex, *Wessex, East Anglia, *Mercia and *Northumbria. This concept, however, was largely theoretical and the "Heptarchic" system never really existed in practice. Among the multitude of small kingdoms, the chief ones were Northumbria in the north, Mercia in the centre, and Wessex and Kent in the south. The geo-political situation of Kent and

Bronze 14th-century statuette of a French knight

its continued relations with the *Frankish kingdom favoured its development and, at the end of the 6th century, the realm was the best organized among the Anglo-Saxon kingdoms. Thus, the Christian mission to E., led by St. *Augustine, entered the island through Kent, and in 601 he was consecrated archbishop of *Canterbury and primate of E. Nevertheless, and despite its cultural and religious influence, Kent remained a little kingdom, and in the 7th century the political centre moved northwards to the kingdoms of Northumbria and Mercia, which disputed the hegemony between them. The founding of the Northumbrian realm, which spread under *Edwin to southern Scotland, was followed in the 8th century by the establishment of a cultural and scholarly centre at *York and the surrounding area, which produced such scholars as *Bede and *Alcuin, who became intellectual leaders of western Europe. In the 8th century, however, the political ascendancy of Northumbria was successfully challenged by Mercia. Under the leadership of a series of kings, including the heathen *Penda and the Christian *Offa, the Mercians imposed their suzerainty on the petty kingdoms, some of which they conquered and, by the end of the 8th century, Offa succeeded in uniting almost the whole of E. under his rule and negotiated as an equal with his contemporary, *Charlemagne. After his death, dynastic disputes weakened Mercia and, in 802, Wessex recovered its independence, becoming the most important Anglo-Saxon kingdom in the 9th century. Under *Egbert (802-39), the supremacy of Wessex was recognized by the other kingdoms, some of which joined it, creating a permanent bastion of Saxon rule in southern E..

Under Egbert's successors, Scandinavian tribes, particularly the *Danes, began to invade E. In the mid-9th century, the sporadic raids turned into massive invasions, ending with settlements in 855. The northern kingdoms, Northumbria, Mercia and East Anglia, were destroyed and conquered (866-70), and Wessex itself was threatened. The reign of *Alfred the Great, however, proved to be a turning-point in English history. He waged protracted wars against the Danish chieftain *Guthrum and, achieving supremacy at sea, was able to impose on him a treaty dividing E. into two parts, with "Watling Street", the road from London to Chester, as the border. Thus, the country south and west of "Watling Street" belonged to Wessex, while that to the north and east, including Essex, East Anglia, part of Mercia and Northumbria, was recognized as the *Danelaw, belonging to Guthrum. This agreement (878) created not only a political, but also a legal division of E., which, despite changes in the political situation, remained solid until the *Norman Conquest of 1066. Its major achievement was the consolidation of the leadership of Wessex and of Anglo-Saxon culture. In the 7th and 8th centuries the Anglo-Saxons were in close association with the *Irish monks, opened schools in the new monasteries, where studies revolved mainly around ecclesiastical Latin culture and, as a result, produced missionaries and scholars who were active in the Frankish kingdom and in Germany. The 9th century, culminating in the reign of Alfred, was the great age of Anglo-Saxon culture expressed in the vernacular, which was used both for literature and learned treatises, as well as for official purposes.

In the 10th and 11th centuries, political conditions changed. The Danish kingdom of Guthrum was weakened by dynastic struggles and by the creation of *Norse principalities, and finally collapsed. Most of it was conquered and annexed by Wessex, whose monarchs reigned over a double kingdom: the "Saxon" one and the Anglo-Danish "Danelaw". In 1015 the situation changed radically. *Canute the Great, king of Denmark, invaded and conquered E., creating the "Empire of the North", which consisted of Denmark, Norway, England and parts of Sweden. During his reign (1015-36) Canute evolved his own form of government, regarding himself as the "national" monarch and ruling with the active participation of both Danes and Anglo-Saxons. His empire of the North, however, did not outlast his reign. After his death, the kingdoms were separated and his sons, *Harold and *Hardicanute, failed to preserve their father's heritage. In 1042 the national monarchy of the Wessex dynasty was restored and *Edward the Confessor became the last Anglo-Saxon king of E. His reign (1042-66), however, was a period of transition. While the local nobility, led by *Godwyn, earl of Wessex, was influential in political affairs and in the *witan, Edward brought over churchmen and knights from Normandy. The Anglo-Saxon tradition, which had developed continuously from the 6th century and was represented by institutions, both at the level of local government (that of the *hundreds, with their courts of free-men) and of the central government (represented by the witan, the supreme council, composed of nobles and royal counsellors), reflected the social structure of the kingdom and greatly influenced its constitution. In that respect, the Norman influence was slight, but it introduced elements of the feudal system, which were important for the future. When Edward died childless (his nephew, *Edgar Aetheling being too young to claim the throne) the succession was disputed between two men, representing the two traditions: *Harold, son of Godwin, the champion of Anglo-Saxon liberties and *William, duke of Normandy. Harold, who defeated a Norse invasion at York, appeared to be a strong king and was supported by the witan. But William's invasion, supported by Pope *Alexander II, changed the direction of English history. At *Hastings, his cavalry destroyed the Anglo-Saxon infantry and Harold was killed in battle. William became the new king of E., through conquest, but he also sought and obtained a formal election by the witan (1066).

The Norman conquest of E. opened a new period in the history and civilization of the country. The Anglo-Saxon nobility and clergy were driven out and destroyed. William introduced the Norman version of feudalism into E., granting lands to his vassals and creating the Anglo-Norman nobility, whose language and culture were entirely French. The administration of the realm was entrusted to royal officers, the viscounts or *sheriffs. The destruction of the Anglo-Saxon nobility and clergy was followed by the elimination of their language from the administration and courts, where it was replaced, as a written language, by Latin and, as a spoken language, by French. On the other hand, in the villages and hundreds, local government continued to function according to Anglo-Saxon legal traditions, but with the significant difference that the free peasants (the "sokemen") were gradually reduced to *villeinage.

Anglo-Saxon revolts were cruelly repressed (1070-72) by *William the Conqueror, who founded his government on this combination of the two systems. The lands register, known as the *Domesday Book, compiled in order to provide the royal administration with full data on the taxes levied in the Anglo-Saxon period, enabled the new government to establish its authority. The despotic reign of *William II, in which the conflict between Church and State appeared in England, brought no structural changes in the regime instituted by the Conqueror. Under the reign of his youngest son, *Henry I, the process of fusion continued and the new institutions created by his administration were characteristic of English feudalism (1100-35). The territories, which the Anglo-Norman nobility possessed both in the kingdom of E. and the duchy of Normandy, made Henry undertake the conquest of the duchy where he was formally a vassal of the king of France (1107) and to play an active part in French politics. This interest and his concern for the succession to the throne, jeopardized by the accidental death of his son William (1120), caused Henry to enter into an alliance with the house of *Anjou. In 1126 the alliance was sealed by the marriage of Henry's daughter, Matilda, widow of Emperor *Henry V, with *Geoffrey Plantagenet, heir of the county of Anjou.

On Henry's death in 1135, a troubled period began in E. Many of the nobility supported the claims of his nephew, *Stephen of Blois, while the supporters of Matilda opposed him. A civil war broke out, causing anarchy and weakening the royal power, until an agreement was reached in 1152, recognizing the succession of Matilda's son *Henry II, who was already duke of Normandy, count of Anjou and, by his marriage with *Eleanor of Aquitaine, duke of Aquitaine, and thus the ruler of the major part of France. When Henry was crowned in 1154, he ruled over an empire which extended from the Scottish frontier to the Pyrénées.

Henry II, who continued the policy of his grandfather, was the architect of the feudal monarchical system in E. His desire for royal supremacy, which brought him to an open conflict with Thomas *Becket and the church, caused him to establish his government by legislation and inquest, based on a tight control of the administration both by the *justiciars and the royal court and by trial by grand *jury, selected from among the local gentry. An efficient administration permitted a strengthening of the monarchy, which disposed of resources and was able to plan budgets through the manipulation of the *Exchequer. These resources made the king less dependent on feudal military service and allowed him to hire mercenaries. The vitality of the system proved itself during the reign of Henry, who was able to let his justiciars govern the kingdom during his wars on the Continent and carry on the conquest of *Ireland. Moreover, it revealed its effectiveness in the time of *Richard I, who was absent from E. for most of his ten-year reign. The Angevin period was also one of economic development and the growth of cities, which enjoyed a measure of self-government through the *firma burgi* (the delegation of administrative powers to the city councils). The reign of King *John was a continuation of this system, but there were also innovations. His character earned him the enmity of the barons and created an unstable administration, while

his repeated defeats on the Continent not only led to the loss of Normandy and Anjou, but also to a draining of resources. After his defeat at *Bouvines (1212), the barons became unruly and rose against him, compelling him to issue the *Magna Charta (1215), with the aim of putting an end to the arbitrary rule of the king and creating a council of barons, the *Community of the Realm, which was empowered to bring grievances before the king and to demand the implementation of necessary reforms.

The 13th century was thus an age of innovation in the system of government. The attempts of *Henry III to free himself from the obligations imposed by the Magna Charta aroused opposition from the barons who, despite their French origins and culture, felt themselves to be part of the kingdom and objected to the influx of the new French nobles from Poitou and Provence. The struggle between the royal party and the barons generally proved favourable to the baronial party, which compelled the king to confirm the Magna Charta, to issue the Provisions of *Oxford (1258), where he agreed not to raise new taxes without the consent of the Community of the Realm and, finally, to give up his claims of arbitrary rule after his defeat at the Battle of *Lewes. The restoration of royal authority in the last years of Henry's reign was due to the energy of his son, *Edward I, whose system of government was based on a respect for the royal promises. Edward's reign was in this respect was the culmination of the evolutionary trends of the century. The institution of *Parliament introduced the barons and representatives of the shires into the machinery of the government, while his legislation enabled the executive power to rule through the administration of justice. The conquest of Wales and his wars against the Scots were major steps towards the unification of Great Britain, despite the fact that the Scottish desire for independence did not allow him to attain his objectives.

The 13th century was also a period of awakening of English scholarship. While in the 12th century English scholars were active in France, the establishment of universities at Oxford and Cambridge encouraged local scholarly activities, particularly in the sciences. Men like Robert *Grosseteste and Roger *Bacon fostered the development of Aristotelian studies and of sciences in E.

The later Middle Ages was a period of crisis in the history of E. The troubles began in the reign of *Edward II (1307-28), due to the personal incapacity of the king and his attempt to reign through favourites. His defeats in the war against the Scots and the unpopularity of his favourites aroused an opposition among the nobility, who finally deposed the king in favour of his son, so creating a precedent. The reign of *Edward III, however, was an exception to the general decline, due to the spectacular victories of the English armies in France in the *Hundred Years' War. These victories not only enhanced royal prestige, but also created a major source of revenue for the crown and nobility which took part in the campaigns, so that the full impact of the crisis of the middle and second half of the 14th century, which was aggravated by the *Black Death (in which 66% of the population was estimated to have perished), was not felt during the lifetime of Edward. Its full impact was felt only under *Richard II, who had to fight a turbulent nobility, popular unrest and the Peasants' Revolt of 1381, which began as a protest against the reintroduction of feudal duties in the manors and developed into a rebellion against the ruling power. The non-conformist trends which originated with *Wycliffe and the *Lollards, and which arose amongst the educated classes, also grew into a popular movement directed against the clergy. The repression of the Peasants' Revolt and the intellectual non-conformists alike failed to resolve the crisis, but made the king more dependent on the nobility, leading finally to a general uprising and the deposition of the monarch by Parliament on grounds of tyranny.

With the proclamation of *Henry IV as king, the *Lancastrian branch of the *Plantagenet dynasty rose to power. Henry's skills made him the natural leader of the nobility and clergy and enabled him to restore royal authority and to prepare for a renewal of the war with France. His policy paved the way for his son *Henry V, who invaded France, won a decisive victory at *Agincourt (1415) and became master of the northern part of the French kingdom, by the Treaty of *Troyes, being appointed heir presumptive to the French crown.

The late Middle Ages was the formative period of English culture. While at the beginning of the 14th century French and Latin continued to characterize the civilization of the upper classes, and Anglo-Saxon remained the spoken language of the peasants and lower classes, the situation changed radically in the middle and second half of the 14th century. The rise of a military nobility which made its fortune in the French wars and had no blood connection with the Anglo-Norman nobility, facilitated the revival of the English language, based mainly on Anglo-Saxon, but with a large addition of French words, integrated into the language during the long period of intercourse with the feudal nobility. With *Chaucer and his Canterbury Tales, the new English emerged as a literary language, and the Lollards were influential in spreading it throughout the realm. In the 15th century the English language won its position as the national language of the gentry, while the decline and, finally, the fall of the traditional nobility made it the official language of the realm. The proceedings of Parliament (especially the House of Commons) were held in English from 1433.

J. E. Morpugo (ed.), The Pelican History of England:
D. Whitelock, The Beginnings of English Society (1952);
F. M. Stenton, English Society in the Early Middle Ages, III (1952);
A. R. Myers, England in the Late Middle Ages, IV (1956).

ENZIO OF HOHENSTAUFEN (1220-72) King of Sardinia (1238-49). He was an illegitimate son of Emperor *Frederick II. In 1236 he became one of the commanders of the imperial army in central Italy, effectively aiding his father against Pope *Gregory IX and the *Guelphs. In 1238 his father made him king of *Sardinia, which was a papal dominion under the imperial authority. He succeeded in preventing Gregory IX from assembling a council in Rome to depose Frederick II by capturing the participants at Ostia in 1239. Later, he fought the Guelphs in northern Italy, but in 1249 was captured by the army of *Bologna and held prisoner until his death.
E. Kantorowicz, Frederic II (1932).

EPHESUS City in Asia Minor, situated on the coast of the Aegean Sea. The ancient Greek city, which was one of the major centres of the classical period, was burnt down by the *Goths in 263 and, although immediately rebuilt, never regained its ancient importance, but remained a provincial centre of the Eastern Roman empire. As one of the most ancient Christian communities, E. enjoyed special honour after the recognition of the Christian Church as the official religion of the empire. In 431 the Third Oecumenical *Council was assembled at E., and among the decisions that were taken, the cult of St. *Mary was proclaimed there, under the influence of the local clergy. This proclamation was hailed by the population, still under the impact of the pagan cult of Artemis and, unwittingly, strongly encouraged the process of conversion to the Christian faith. In 449 another council condemned the *Nestorians and its decisions were the basis for the deliberations of the Council of *Chalcedon. The administrative reorganization of the *Byzantine empire and the establishment of new centres in Asia Minor in the 6th century, led to the decline of the city, which was gradually deserted by its inhabitants in the 7th century and became an insignificant village.
W. M. Ramsay, Excavations at Ephesus (1908).

EPHRAIM BEN ISAAC (Rabbi E. the Great; 1110-75) Exegete and Jewish poet. Born at Ratisbon in Germany, he travelled in his youth and studied in the Rhenish schools and in France. He acquired a great reputation for his learning. In 1136 he finally settled at Ratisbon as leader of the community. He wrote commentaries on the Talmud and legal interpretations which were widely disseminated and appreciated for their concise lucidity. Many of his poems were incorporated in the Jewish prayer-books and are considered to be some of the greatest medieval Hebrew poetry written outside Spain.
S. W. Baron, A Social and Religious History of the Jewish People, VI (1959).

EPHRAIM BEN JACOB OF BONN (1132-97) Jewish exegete and poet. He studied in his native city, where he became head of the rabbinical court. His legal decisions are important not only juridically, but also as interpretations of Talmudic literature. A gifted Hebrew poet, he wrote elegies on the persecutions of the communities of the Rhine Valley during the Second *Crusade which, at the same time, are a major source for the history of the Jewish communities in the 12th century.
S. W. Baron, A Social and Religious History of the Jewish People, VI (1959).

ERFURT City in *Thuringia (Germany). It was founded in the 8th century and, in 741, St. *Boniface established there a bishopric intended as a base for missionary activities in Saxony. In 755 the see was abolished and *Pepin the Short gave it as an estate to the archbishops of Mainz. In 805 *Charlemagne established there a market-place for trading with the Slavs. The commercial activities were a major factor in the development of the city as a trade centre between the eastern and western parts of Germany, and E. prospered in the 12th and 13th centuries. In 1378 a university was established in the city which, in the late Middle Ages, became an important cultural and academic centre. In 1483 it was incorporated in the electorate of Saxony.
K. Beyer, Geschichte der Stadt Erfurt (1935).

ERIC Name of 13 kings of medieval Sweden, from the 8th to the 15th century. Some were obscure *Viking chieftains who reigned over petty kingdoms in the central and eastern part of the country. Among the most significant were:

Eric the Victorious   King of Sweden from *c.* 980 to 1000. He reigned at Uppsala and became famous after his victory over a rival prince, Styrbjörn, which allowed him to unite the Swedish principalities and to impose his suzerainty over the Danes in southern Sweden.

Eric the Saint   King from 1156. Little is known about his life and reign. In 1160 he was murdered by members of the nobility and, soon after his death, came to be regarded as the patron saint of Sweden. His life grew into a legend elaborated on by later generations, who ascribed to him all the good deeds associated with an ideal monarch. He founded the dynasty of the "Erics", which reigned in Sweden until 1250 and died out with E. XI.

Eric of Pomerania (1382-1459)   King of Norway, Denmark and Sweden. He was adopted by his great-aunt, Margaret, regent of the three Scandinavian kingdoms and elected king by the clergy and nobility, who created the Union of *Kalmar in 1397. In practice, however, he began to reign in 1412 after Margaret's death. E. based himself in Denmark and rapidly became unpopular in his kingdom owing to his protection of German clerks and nobles, to whom he gave high positions at his court. In Sweden and Norway, he promoted Danes who, together with Germans, obtained the chief appointments. Despite the opposition of the nobles, E. was able to maintain his authority in the first 25 years of his reign due to the prosperity which German and Danish investments brought to the Scandinavian cities. A crisis in the copper-mines in central Sweden, however, brought about an uprising of the mineowners led by Engelbrekt Engelbrektsson (1439), which was joined by the peasants and exploited by the nobility. This revolt was followed by revolts of the nobility in Norway and Denmark and, in 1442, E. was compelled to abdicate in favour of his nephew Christopher.
L. Musset, *Les Peuples Scandinaves au Moyen Age* (1951).

ERIC V, Glipping (c. 1249-86)   King of *Denmark. Upon his father's death in 1259 E., still a child, ascended the Danish throne. The kingdom, governed by his mother, was troubled by a grave conflict between the state and the church: the throne was placed under an interdict as a result of his father having imprisoned Archbishop Erlandsen, the leader of the ecclesiastical anti-royal party. Although he had been released, the archbishop refused to crown the new king. In 1261 the Danish army was defeated and E. and his mother taken prisoner by a league led by Erlandson, which favoured the accession of E.'s cousin, the duke of Schleswig, to the throne. Only after the intervention of the pope and the German princes was E. reinstated. In 1266 E.'s actual reign began, but his arbitrary rule aroused strong baronial opposition. E.'s struggle with the magnates led to the issuing of the royal charter of 1282 in which the king gave in to the demands of the aristocracy. The charter protected the latter from being arbitrarily imprisoned, limited the king's power and recognized the *Danehof as a legal aristocratic institution which was to convene once a year. E. also reluctantly agreed to further reforms in the areas of foreign policy and government administration.

ERIC THE RED (c. 940-1010)   Norse chieftain and traveller. Born in the province of Jaeder in southwest Norway, he was exiled from his country for manslaughter and settled in Iceland. In 982 he was banished from Iceland for the same reason and sailed westwards with his vessel. He discovered *Greenland and passed the time of his banishment in prospecting the southeastern coast, preparing for the future settlement of the island and giving it its name. In 986 he led an expedition of 25 vessels to Greenland and founded the first Scandinavian settlement, consisting of individual farms constructed around the Eiriksfjord, where he also built his own farm.
H. Fogh, *Erik the Red's Greenland* (1967).

ERIGENA, JOHN SCOT (c. 810-77)   Philosopher. Born in Ireland, he settled in France and won the favour and patronage of *Charles the Bald, who appointed him head of the palace school in Paris. He played a major role in the theological disputes of his age, debating both with *Gottschalk and *Paschasius Radbert. E.'s philosophy was an attempt to reconcile the neo-Platonic idea of emanation with the Christian view of creation. Accordingly, he developed a hierarchical view of nature as a synonym of the cosmos, fully expounded in his greatest treatise, *De divisione naturae* (On the Division of Nature). He divided nature into four categories: 1) nature which creates and is not created, i.e., God; 2) nature which is created and creates, or the world of the primordial causes of the Platonic ideas; 3) nature which is created and does not create, i.e., things; 4) nature which neither creates nor is created, or God, to whom all things must finally return. Thus, the world was held to begin and end with God, source of all the elements. This concept was supported by his adoption of the celestial hierarchy of *Dionysius the Areopagite, whose Greek works he translated into Latin. E.'s last years were obscure and one tradition reports that he went to England, where *Alfred the Great may have invited him to teach his ideas at the abbey of *Malmesbury.
Works, *PL*, vol. 122;
M. Cappuyns, *Jean Scot Erigena* (1933).

ERWIN OF STEINBACH (1244-1318)   Architect. Born in the village of Steinbach in Alsace, he worked on the construction of Gothic churches in the Rhine Valley and, towards the end of the 13th century, gained a considerable reputation when he was entrusted with building the cathedral of *Strassburg. He developed the Gothic style and began the period of monumental Late Gothic architecture.
K. Clark, *The Gothic Revival* (1950).

ERZURUM   One of the most ancient cities of *Armenia, in eastern Anatolia. In 422 it was conquered by the Byzantines who invaded it from Persia, and became the capital of the Byzantine duchy of Armenia. In 530 it was fortified and a castle was built there. In 642 the Arabs conquered E., but were not able to retain control of the city and, during the second half of the 7th century, it was regained by the Byzantines. From 1050 to 1070 it was attacked several times by the *Seljuks and destroyed, but at the end of the 11th century its inhabitants returned and the city was rebuilt, now belonging to the Seljuk sultanate of Konya. Conquered during the 12th century by the *Georgians, E. became a strategic point in Anatolia, changing hands between the Georgians and the Turks. In 1224 it was invaded and again destroyed by *Ghengis-Khan, and became part of the *Mongol empire until 1241, when it was regained by the Turks of Konya. Conquered by *Timur-Leng (Tamerlane) in 1387, it remained under Timurid rule until 1514, when it was annexed to the Ottoman empire.

EI, vol. II.

ESKIL (d. 1181) Archbishop of Lund (1158-78). Member of a noble Danish family, he was educated at *Hildesheim in Germany, where he became acquainted with the *Cistercians. During his travels, he had the opportunity to develop a friendship with *Bernard of Clairvaux, who greatly influenced his thinking. In 1143 he became bishop of Roskilde and took part in the political life at the court of Denmark. At the same time he was an active reformer of the church and introduced the Cistercians in Scandinavia. In 1158 he became archbishop of Lund and his period of office as head of the Danish church was characterized by continuous struggles with King *Waldemar I. In 1160 he recognized Pope *Alexander III and this action, contrary to royal policy, compelled him to retire to *Clairvaux until 1167, when Waldemar supported Alexander. In 1170 he crowned *Canute IV and exerted a great influence at the court. In 1178 he gave up his position and retired to Clairvaux, where he died a simple monk.

L. Musset, *Les Peuples Scandinaves au Moyen Age* (1951).

ESSEX Anglo-Saxon kingdom, situated on the northern bank of the Thames, east of London. It was founded at the end of the 5th century by immigrants from Saxony who preserved their dynastic traditions and their particular dialect. Its historical development is obscure and the petty realm maintained its independence more because of the rivalry between its stronger neighbours than through its own powers. During the 6th century it spread westwards and included London, which became its main city. In 652, under the influence of the sovereigns of *Northumbria, the royal family converted to Christianity and the bishopric of London was restored. In the 8th century E. declined and lost most of its territories, including London, to *Mercia; its kings recognized the Mercian overlordship and, under the reign of *Offa, king of Mercia, they lost their independence. In 824 *Egbert, king of Wessex, conquered E. and annexed it to his realm. E. never recovered its independence and, in the second half of the 9th century, was conquered by the Danish chieftain, *Guthrum, becoming part of the *Danelaw. Under *Edward the Confessor, E. became a minor earldom of the kingdom of England and, after the *Norman Conquest (1066), the title earl of Essex was conferred upon various Norman lords, being merely a symbol of status until the end of the Middle Ages.

F. M. Stenton, *Anglo-Saxon England* (1947).

ESTABLISSEMENTS DE SAINT LOUIS (The Institutions of St. Louis) French legal code, compiled at the end of the 13th century and containing a number of laws and customary procedures. It was attributed to King *Louis IX, hence its great authority, but only some of the texts originated with him. Most of the compilation was a selection of various traditions by French legists in the reign of *Philip IV the Fair.

P. Viollet, ed., *Les Etablissements de Saint Louis* (1881).

ESTATES Name given in the Middle Ages and early modern period to the social classes in western Europe.

The term derived from the Latin word *status*, which denoted the place of a given class within the social system and derived from the concept developed in the 10th and 11th centuries of the division of society into three distinct groups: the clergy who prayed, the nobility who fought, and the peasantry who worked. This division was reflected in the duties and privileges of the various groups within feudal society, but the emergence of the urban class in the 12th and 13th centuries brought about a change in the nature of the third estate, which now included the wealthy burghers as well as the peasants, whose role was passive. The early medieval practice of the participation of the free-men in the assemblies where political and legal decisions were made, and the feudal assemblies of vassals convened to give counsel to their lord, led to the appearance of representative assemblies in the 12th century, reaching their full development under *Henry II in England, and enjoying much political power, as in the English Parliament in the 13th and 14th centuries or the *Cortes in the Spanish kingdom. The first Estates General met in France in 1302.

In the late Middle Ages the system of representative assemblies was developed by the creation of the Estates-General in France under *Philip IV the Fair, summoned by the king in order to support the monarchy and to deal with taxation. This system was adapted in the various European countries, with the personal participation of the prelates and barons (i.e., the First and Second Estates) and of elected representatives of the lesser nobility and burghers, which became the Third Estate on the Continent and, in England, the "Commons". While in England, Spain, the Scandinavian countries and eastern Europe, such assemblies became regularly summoned permanent bodies, in France and Germany the E. were summoned sporadically and became a government organ with various rights but no executive authority.

A. Marongiu, *Medieval Parliaments* (1968).

ESTE Family of *Ferrara (Emilia). Members of the feudal aristocracy, which settled in the city in the 11th century. In the 12th century they became one of the leading families of the city and, in 1196, Azzo VI became podesta of Ferrara and established his rule over a group of towns in the delta of the River Po. In 1208 he eliminated rival families from the local government and became *signore* (lord) of Ferrara, ruling over the Emilian state. In the 13th century the E. adopted an anti-imperial policy, becoming one of the leading *Guelph dynasties in northern Italy and, from 1240 onwards, fighting successfully against *Frederick II. Azzo VIII, who led the army, took advantage of his victory over *Ezzelino da Romano to create a powerful state, whose alliance was sought in 1266 by both *Manfred of Hohenstaufen and *Charles of Anjou. His son Obizzo strengthened the E.'s authority in Ferrara, encouraging economic development and destroying the power of the *Arti* (the guilds of craftsmen), the sole obstacle to the absolute power of the E. In the 14th century they were able to consolidate their state by becoming the papal representatives in Emilia and fighting against Venice, which several times attempted to conquer Ferrara. Towards the end of the century Ferrara became one of the most brilliant courts in Italy, in which the cultural and artistic revival was encouraged, so that it came to play a leading role in the Renaissance in the 15th century.

J. K. Hyde, *Society and Politics in Medieval Italy* (1973).

ETHELBALD King of *Mercia (716-57). Member of a junior branch of the royal family of Mercia, he spent his youth in exile, before he was called to reign when the senior branch became extinct. An energetic military leader, he organized a strong army and imposed his rule in Mercia, without consideration for the noble families. In 726 he began a series of wars in the south, seizing London and imposing his suzerainty upon the neighbouring Anglo-Saxon kingdoms, including *Kent and *Wessex. These, however, preserved their own kings and institutions, though accepting the primacy of Mercia, and its king as overlord. E. was able to maintain his power for 30 years until he was murdered by his bodyguard as a result of feuds with the Mercian nobles over whom he ruled tyrannically.

F. M. Stenton, *Anglo-Saxon England* (1947).

ETHELBERT, St. King of Kent (560-616). A descendant of *Hengist, the founder of the realm in the 5th century, he extended his authority over large areas in southern England, becoming the most important Anglo-Saxon monarch of his age. By his marriage with Bertha, daughter of *Caribert, king of the Franks, he gained great prestige, and opened his kingdom to Frankish influence. Through the queen's influence, Christian missionaries settled in Kent and, in 597, E. welcomed St. *Augustine, was converted by him and granted him *Canterbury, where an archiepiscopal see was established in 901. E.'s association with St. Augustine made Kent the spiritual centre of England. E. was also a legislator and issued the "Dooms" of Kent.

F. M. Stenton, *Anglo-Saxon England* (1947).

ETHELBERT, St. (d. 793) King of the East Angles. He reigned under the suzerainty of *Offa, king of *Mercia. It seems that he attempted to recover the independence of his kingdom and, failing, was killed by his overlord. A later tradition, expressing the sentiments of the East Anglians, described his death as a treacherous murder, making him a martyr and venerating his tomb at the cathedral of Hereford.

F. M. Stenton, *Anglo-Saxon England* (1947).

ETHELHARD (d. 805) Archbishop of Canterbury. Member of a noble Mercian family, he was appointed archbishop of Canterbury by *Offa, king of *Mercia, in 791. The nomination met with open opposition from the Kentish clergy and nobles, who protested against the nomination of a Mercian prelate to the primary see of England. Thus, only in 798 was E. able to take up his office, which he devoted to restoring Canterbury's greatness. In 802 he obtained from Pope *Leo III the abolition of the Mercian archbishopric of Lichfield established by Offa. His work, supported by his friend *Alcuin, was an important step towards the unity of Anglo-Saxon England.

F. M. Stenton, *Anglo-Saxon England* (1947).

ETHELRED King of *Wessex (865-71). The third son of *Ethelwulf, he acceded to the throne on the death of his brother *Ethelbert. He was faced with the task of resisting the *Danish invasions which, in 865, had destroyed the kingdom of *Northumbria and now threatened Wessex. Helped by his younger brother *Alfred, he attempted to consolidate the defences on the Thames and, in 870, fought against the Danes at Reading. Although officially an Anglo-Saxon victory, the Battle of Reading was not decisive and, at E.'s death, Wessex was still threatened.

ETHELRED II (965-1016) King of *Wessex and England (978-1016). He was the second son of *Edgar and was proclaimed king after the murder of his elder brother, Edward the Martyr. Although recognized by the whole Anglo-Saxon nobility as the legal king, the murder of his step-brother, of which his mother was accused, seriously harmed the prestige of the crown and, from the beginning of his reign (984), he had difficulty in imposing his authority. In 1002 he married *Emma, daughter of *Richard I, duke of Normandy, and tried to raise his prestige by this Norman alliance. In 1014 he had to face a new Danish invasion, led by King *Sweyn of Denmark, who conquered London and proclaimed himself king of England. Supported by the old Wessex nobility, E. retired to that country and led the resistance against the Danes. In 1015 he was able to recover his authority over England, but in 1016 was defeated by Sweyn's son, *Canute and died shortly afterwards, while his kingdom fell to the Danes and his widow married the new conqueror.

F. M. Stenton, *Anglo-Saxon England* (1947).

ETHELWULF King of *Wessex and *Kent (839-58). Son of King Egbert, in 836 he was given the sub-kingdom of Kent and, after his father's death, inherited all his possessions. E. showed a predilection for Kent and neglected Wessex so much that the old nobility of the West-Saxon kingdom openly opposed him. His reign was an anti-climax after the greatness of his father's reign, despite his military success in resisting the *Danish invasions and his attempt to establish his government on a personal basis through the creation of a great royal domain. During his journey to Rome in 855, while he was staying at the court of *Charles the Bald, king of France (whose daughter Judith he married), Wessex revolted and, in 856, he gave the kingdom to his eldest son, Ethelbald, while still retaining the kingdom of Kent.

F. M. Stenton, *Anglo-Saxon England* (1947).

ETHIOPIA Country in East *Africa dominating the southern passage to the Red Sea. Populated by a variety of Negro and Hamitic tribes, E. also comprised various linguistic groups, the most important being the Geez in the north and the Swahili in the south and east.

History At the beginning of the Middle Ages, most of the country was united by the kings of *Axum, who established their kingdom under Hellenistic influence, and in the 4th century converted to Christianity. In the 6th century the kingdom of Axum became one of the most important states in Africa and, despite the *Monophysite rite of the Ethiopian Church, influenced by the *Coptic monks who immigrated from Egypt, the Byzantines sought its alliance against Persia. Under the leadership of King Kaleb, E. invaded Yemen and, in 525, destroyed and conquered the Yemenite Jewish kingdom of Hemyar. The event was historically important, not only because it made E. the dominant power in the Red Sea and compelled Persia to divide its army between two areas, the Byzantine and the Ethiopian, but also because of the adoption by the royal dynasty of Axum of a legend representing them as the descendants of King Solomon and the Queen of

Sheba. During the 6th century E. continued to be involved in Asia; in 570 an attempt to conquer *Mecca failed and was followed by maritime defeats by the Persian fleet, with the result that, at the end of the century, E. lost its possessions in Yemen. On the other hand, the rise of *Islam and the Arab conquests (622-42) isolated E. from the Byzantine and the Christian world and, in the 7th century, caused its political and cultural decline. The northeastern territories, among them Eritrea, were conquered by the Arabs in the 8th century, and the Moslem faith spread into large areas of E., reaching the eastern and southern territories populated by Somali tribes. The kingdom of Axum collapsed and its Semitic dynasty settled in the mountains in the central part of the country.

In the 10th century tribal revolts and an anti-Christian reaction led to general anarchy, which lasted until the 12th century. In 1137 a successful attempt to restore the unity of the state was made by the tribal dynasty of Zagwe, whose members were pious Christians. Their success led to the union of the mountain tribes and the restoration of Christianity as the national religion (1137-1270). The Zagwe achievement, however, failed to satisfy traditional dynastic requirements. Their legitimacy was contested by the church itself on the grounds that the legal ruler could only be a descendant of Menelik, the legendary son of King Solomon and the Queen of Sheba. He alone was entitled to bear the title *negus* (king). Thus, a coalition of prelates and monks with some noble families finally led to the revolt of Yekuno Amlak, who claimed the legitimate descent and founded the Solomonic dynasty, which reigned until 1855. His descendants, who reigned with the support of the church, imposed a theocratic regime, based on the support of the wealthy monasteries and a strict protocol of legitimacy which was finally fixed in the 14th century in a document entitled *Kebara Nagast* (The Splendour of Kingship). The kings, who received biblical names, fought against the Moslem penetration, which was dominant in the eastern half of the country, strove to preserve the independence of the kingdom and, in the 14th and 15th centuries, succeeded in their aims, establishing a powerful monarchy and breaking the power of both the Moslem princes and the local tribal chieftains. Rumours of these achievements spread to western Europe where, in the 14th century, the legend of Prester *John and his kingdom became identified with E. and its *negus*.

Civilization The ethnic and linguistic variety of E. was reflected in its civilization. From ancient times, the country was divided into two main groups: a nomadic society roughly corresponding to the Swahili-speaking peoples in the east and south of the country, and an agrarian society, established in the mountains and plateaus of the central and northern parts, who founded the political organization of E. In both groups, the typical social patterns throughout the Middle Ages were tribal ones, which facilitated a division of the population according to religion. The sedentary tribes consisted of Christians and a group of Jews, the *Falashas*, while the pagans and partially Christianized nomads were finally converted to Islam.

Thus, among the sedentary part of the population an original civilization came into being under the influence of Hellenistic and early Christian culture. The isolation of the Ethiopians, however, and their adoption of Monophysitic ideas, led them to develop their culture in the national languages and to create their own alphabet, adapted from the script of Hemyar in the 5th century. It consisted of 26 characters, which at Axum became the sacred script of all E.'s languages and served mainly for liturgical and religious purposes. Preserved in the monasteries, where it was further developed, the Ethiopian alphabet was also used for profane literature, such as epic poems and historical treatises. Religious elements, however, were dominant in literature as well as in the arts, which developed at Axum and later in the monasteries. Architecture included impressive buildings and obelisks, with wooden and stone sculpture. Especially interesting is the development of painting, expressed in the miniature art of book-illumination and frescoes, in which gold dust mixed with vegetable oils served as a basis for the colours.

A. H. M. Jones-E. Monroe, *A History of Ethiopia* (1960).

ETSI DE STATU Bull issued by Pope *Boniface VIII in 1297, whereby he revoked the provisions of the Bull *Clericis laicos* after receiving the reactions of the French and English courts and churches. He sought a compromise between his principle that the clergy should not be taxed and the pragmatic needs of the state. The bull stipulated that the clergy should contribute taxes for the defence of the realm in cases of emergency and with papal consent.

EUBOEA Island in the Aegean Sea near the coast of Greece, facing *Thessalonica. In the Middle Ages it was also named Negroponte, after its main city. Until 1204, E. belonged to the Byzantine empire. Conquered by the participants in the Fourth *Crusade, it was given to *Venice, as stated in the treaty of alliance which preceded the conquest of Constantinople. The Venetian administration established there one of its chief centres of government in the Greek territories, controlling the trade in the Aegean Sea. After the fall of the Latin empire of Constantinople (1261), E. became the centre of the Venetian government in the East, headed by members of the major Venetian families who had been serving in the home government. In 1497 it was conquered by the *Ottomans.

F. Thiriet, *La Romanie Vénitienne au Moyen Age* (1959).

EUCHARIST (Greek: "thanksgiving") The central rite of Christian worship, consisting in the consumption, after Mass, of bread and wine, symbolically transformed into the body and blood of Christ. Recalling the events of the Last Supper, the E. was practised from early Christian times. The doctrine of the E. received its final theological form in the 13th century.

E. Masure, *The Christian Sacrifice* (1934).

EUDES (875-98) King of France (888-98). He was the son of *Robert the Strong and became count of Paris during the reign of King *Louis II of France. In 887-88 he distinguished himself at the defence of Paris against the *Normans. Following the deposition of *Charles III, the French nobles elected him king despite the fact that he did not belong to the Carolingian dynasty. His legitimacy, however, was contested and he was compelled to accept the Carolingian prince *Charles the Simple as his heir.

E. Favre, *Eudes, Comte de Paris et Roi de France* (1893).

EUDES Count of Blois (995-1037). Son of Count Eudes I, a faithful vassal of *Hugh Capet, E. was one of the most powerful feudal lords in France. He endeavoured to enlarge his territories and, at the beginning of the 11th century, he was continually in conflict with the counts of *Anjou over the control of the Loire Valley. Defeated in 1017 by *Fulk Nerra, he turned eastward and his claims to the lordship of Troyes brought him into military and judicial conflict with King *Robert II. In 1023 he obtained satisfaction by expressing his fidelity to the king in one of the most remarkable letters of the feudal period. His success virtually deprived the king of the right to seize fiefs on the grounds of felony and created a serious problem for the *Capetian kingship by facilitating the union of Blois and Champagne, thus encircling the royal domain. From 1026 he claimed, as nephew of *Rudolf III, the inheritance of the kingdom of Burgundy against the claims of Emperor *Conrad II and, in 1032, he seized power at Arles. In 1034, however, he was compelled to give up his claims before the imperial army.

L. Lex, *Eudes, Comte de Blois* (1892).

EUDES The name of four dukes of Burgundy:

Eudes I, Borrel (1079-1102) In collaboration with the abbots of Dijon, he imposed his authority as duke in central Burgundy. He participated in the First *Crusade.

Eudes II (1142-62) He was one of the greatest dukes of Burgundy, succeeding in imposing his rule over the duchy. In order to do so, he fought territorial enclaves within the duchy, particularly the bishops of Langres. At his death he left Burgundy a consolidated feudal principality.

Eudes III (1193-1218) He took part in the *Albigensian wars and supported *Philip *Augustus against *John of England.

Eudes IV (1315-50) Involved in the dynastic struggle in France after the death of King *Philip IV the Fair, he supported the principle of the male inheritance of the crown. From 1328 onward he was a faithful ally of *Philip VI of Valois, whose daughter Joan he married. In 1330 he inherited the imperial county of Burgundy (Franche-Comté), laying the foundation of the future great Burgundian duchy of Valois. He was one of the most powerful barons in France of his time.

J. Richard, *Les Ducs de Bourgogne et la formation du Duché* (1953).

EUDES (ODO) OF DUEIL (d. 1162) Historian. Little is known about his origins and early life. A native of Dueil, near Paris, he became a monk at the monastery of *St. Denis, where he attracted the notice of Abbot *Suger. In 1147 he was appointed chaplain of King *Louis VII and accompanied him on the Second Crusade. After his return in 1149, he returned to his monastery and was active in its administration. In 1152 he succeeded Suger as abbot, but his election was contested and he was accused of ill-treatment of Suger's family. During the Crusade, at Suger's request, he took notes concerning the expedition, which were intended for a book on Louis VII, planned by Suger. The notes, however, became an independent historical account, *De profectione Ludovici VII in Orientem* (The Journey of Louis VII to the East), which is one of the major sources for the Second *Crusade.

Ed. and trans. V. G. Berry (1948).

EUDES OF MONTREUIL (c. 1220-89) Architect. He began his career working on the abbey church of *St.

Denis, continuing the work of his teacher, Peter of Montreuil, and completing the present Gothic building. He then became architect to King *Louis IX, following him on the *Crusades, where he was active in the fortifications of *Caesarea and *Jaffa and, after his return to France, worked in Paris and the surrounding area.

EUGENIUS I, St. Pope (654-57). Little is known about his family and early career. He was elected pope in 654 but, like his predecessor *Martin I, he declined to recognize the *Monothelite patriarch of Constantinople. He died before sanctions were taken against him.

EUGENIUS II Pope (824-27). Member of a wealthy Roman family. As pope, he crowned *Lothair I, the eldest son of *Louis the Pious, emperor.

EUGENIUS III (Bernard Pignatelli; d. 1153) Pope (1145-53). Born at Pisa, he joined the *Cistercian order, becoming a monk at *Clairvaux in 1135. Singled out by St. *Bernard, after a short stay at Clairvaux he became abbot of St. Anastasio at Rome. In 1145 he was elected pope but, refusing to recognize the sovereignty of the Roman senate, had to flee and established his court at Viterbo. At Christmas 1146 he called for a crusade and, in 1147, went to France where he asked his master, St. Bernard, to preach. At this period he had to repress a rebellion in Rome, led by *Arnold of Brescia, whom he excommunicated. In 1149 he returned to Rome, but the unrest resumed and he had to leave, returning only in 1153 with the support of *Frederick Barbarossa. He was an active reformer of clerical morals, acting on the advice of St. Bernard of Clairvaux, who wrote for him his famous treatise *De Consideratione*.

H. Gleber, *Papst Eugen III* (1936).

EUGENIUS THE ADMIRAL (12th century) Scholar and great civil servant. Born at Palermo of a Greek noble family whose members served at the royal court of Sicily, he gained the title of "Admiral" (*emir*, "head of office") at the court after 1153. Besides his official functions at the court of *Roger II and *William I, he used his profound knowledge of Greek, Arabic and Latin to translate scientific works into Latin. His most famous translation was that of the *Optics* of Ptolemy from the Arabic. He was also a poet and left Greek poems, some of which were eulogies of King William I, while others, written in prison after his disgrace under *William II, describe his love of solitude in the company of the classics.

E. Jamison, *Admiral Eugenius of Sicily* (1957).

EULENSPIEGEL, TILL (c. 1300-c. 1350) Peasant of northern Germany, who died near Lübeck shortly after the *Black Death. In contemporary sources, he was represented as a wanderer who served his lords and, with his engaging personality, was able to make good for himself. This figure later inspired popular legends and folklore, which made him either a grotesque or a satirical stereotype. The oral materials were gathered together in 1483, when the first story of E. was published, with a comic-heroic treatment of the hero.

W. Kablec, *Untersuchungen zum Volksbuch von Eulenspiegel* (1916).

EURIC King of the *Visigoths (466-84). He seized power after murdering his brother *Theodoric II, and began a policy of expansion against the last remnants of the Western Roman empire, particularly in Gaul. He conquered most of Roman Gaul and, in 475, established

the frontiers of his kingdom on the rivers Rhône and Loire. After the fall of the Western Roman empire (476), he extended his authority over Provence, and his kingdom – which spread over Spain, most of Gaul and Provence – was the most powerful western state in the latter half of the 5th century. His court at Toulouse became one of the major political centres in Europe, his alliance being sought by the Eastern Roman empire, the Persians and other Germanic realms. Besides his military skills and political achievements he was a good ruler, reorganizing the system of government of his kingdom. He also published a code of Roman laws for his Roman subjects. Among these, an ordinance allowed the Gothic conquerors to claim a third of the lands conquered from their Roman owners. E. was an Arian and it seems that he adopted this position for political rather than religious reasons. Arianism, in his view, enabled him to express his independence of the universalism claimed by the Roman Church.
K. F. Stroheker, *Eurich, König der Westgothen* (1937).
EUSTACE Count of Boulogne (1087-1126). The eldest brother of *Godfrey of Bouillon, he inherited the county of Boulogne from his father, as well as estates in England granted to his father, who fought in the army of *William the Conqueror. Married to Mary of Scotland, he was also related to the Anglo-Saxon dynasty of England. In 1096-99 he participated in the First *Crusade, where he was one of the leaders of the Lotharingian army headed by his brother, took part in the conquest of Jerusalem and returned home after the Battle of Ascalon. Brother-in-law to *Henry I, he became involved in English politics. In 1125 he gave his only daughter Matilda in marriage to *Stephen of Blois, the future king of England.
F. M. Stenton, *The First Century of English Feudalism* (1949).
EUSTACHE OF SAINT-PIERRE (c. 1287-1371) Burgher of Calais. He was one of the chief defenders of the city besieged by *Edward III in 1347. When Calais was captured and Edward wished to slaughter the inhabitants, he led the delegation which begged for mercy for the population at the price of their own lives. Pardoned by the king at the request of Queen Philippa, his wife, for the remainder of his life E. became a legendary figure.
E. Perroy, *The Hundred Years' War* (1958).
EUTHYMIUS ZIGABENUS (12th century) Byzantine theologian. A monk in Constantinople, he was introduced into the imperial court, where he preached. Highly praised for his orthodoxy, he was ordered by Emperor *Alexius I Comnenus to write a treatise condemning all the heresies. His book *Panoplia Dogmatica*, became a standard work of orthodoxy, containing the history of all heresies, which he systematically refuted. Of particular interest is the passage concerning the *Cathar Bogomils, which is our main source of information about them. He also wrote commentaries on patristic works and books of the Bible.
S. Runciman, *The Medieval Manichee* (1945).
EVIATHAR BEN ELIJA HACOHEN (1040-1109) The last Palestinian *gaon and historian. Son of the gaon Elija, he was educated by his father and was praised for his wide knowledge. When the *Seljuks conquered Jerusalem in 1071, he followed his father to Tyre and helped him preserve the Jewish spiritual

centre in Palestine. In 1048 he was appointed gaon of Haifa and defended the primacy of the Palestinian centre, contested by the leader of the Cairo community. As part of the polemic, he wrote his *Roll of Eviathar*, a history of the Palestinian gaonate. After the conquest of Palestine by the *Crusaders he fled to Syria, where he died.
J. Mann, *The Jews in Egypt and Palestine* (1924).
EVREUX City in Normandy, France. The ancient Gallo-Roman town of E. became one of the centres of the Catholic Church in the kingdom of the Franks and, in the 6th century, a bishopric was established there. In the 9th century *Charles the Bald fortified it against the Norman raids and a countal family settled there. The counts were able to enjoy a certain degree of autonomy due to their position, E. being between French and Norman rule. Vassals of the dukes of Normandy in the 11th-12th centuries, they came under the rule of the kings of France in 1204. The feudal dynasty became extinct in the 13th century and, in the 14th century, the county of E. became an apanage of the kings of *Navarre. Its importance grew in the middle of the 14th century when it served as a centre for *Charles the Bad of Navarre. Its Gothic cathedral (12th-15th centuries) is decorated with beautiful stained-glass windows, which reflect this period of prosperity.
L. Mirot, *Manuel de Géographie Historique de la France* (1935).
EXCHEQUER Name given to the administration of finances in Anglo-Norman England and Norman Italy. Its origins lay in the practice of some feudal courts of using a chequered table on which peasants would deposit a token representing their duties to the lord. The system, however, reached its full development in England at the beginning of the 12th century, when the sheriffs would set down their accounts on the table. Under *Henry I, the system was adapted to the financial needs of the kingship and a special court of the E. was established where the taxes to be paid by the shires were recorded, and a number of clerks were employed to verify the accounts of the sheriffs. Some of the members of the feudal *curia regis specialized in hearing the cases connected with the accounts and they became the "Barons of the E.". Unlike the Treasury, the E. became an administrative office, with its specialized personnel and its scrolls in which the accounts were recorded. In the latter half of the 12th century, one of its masters, Richard *Fitzneale, wrote a treatise, *Dialogus de Scaccario* (The Dialogue of the E.), which is a detailed description of the institution, its organization and functions.

King *Roger II of Sicily introduced the English practice of the E. in his realm, making use of an English specialist, Thomas *Brown, for the purpose. The peculiarity of the Sicilian E. was that it was grafted onto Greek and Moslem administrative practices, adapting them to the feudal mentality of the Norman barons of the kingdom.
B. Lyon, *A Constitutional and Legal History of Medieval England* (1960).
EXCOMMUNICATION Term signifying the exclusion of a Christian, by a competent ecclesiastical authority, from the community of the faithful on account of his sins. In common usage, it is often confused with the *Interdict, owing to a misunderstanding of the terms. E.

was pronounced against an individual, depriving him of the right to administer or receive the *Sacraments and of all intercourse with other Christians. E. was not an exclusion from the church, but merely a suspension from it, intended to encourage the subject to confess his sin and to do penance, so as to be reintegrated in the community. The papacy's use of E. as a political weapon against its adversaries, particularly from the time of the *Investiture contest and the great struggle with the *Hohenstaufen emperors, diminished its effectiveness from the 12th century onwards.

W. Ullmann, *A Short History of the Papacy in the Middle Ages* (1972).

EXEGESIS (Greek: exegious "explanation") Term used in western Europe from the 12th century to refer to the commentaries on the Bible and other sacred books, such as the works of the Church Fathers. Unlike the gloss, which was also applied to profane and ecclesiastical writings after the patristic period, the strict meaning of E. was an explanation of the holy texts on four different levels: the literal, the historical, the allegorical and the mystical.

B. Smalley, *The Study of the Bible in the Middle Ages* (1952).

EXETER City in southwestern England. The ancient Roman settlement there was deserted at the beginning of the 5th century and the Celts ruled the area, which was attached to the British principality of Cornwall. During the 6th century, it was conquered by the Anglo-Saxons and belonged to *Wessex. In *c.* 685 an abbey was founded on the site and became the centre of the new settlement. Shortly after the foundation of the monastery, E. became a major centre of scholarship and St. *Boniface was among its students. In the 9th century the development of trade brought prosperity to the area, and the city with its harbour grew and prospered. As a result, a bishopric was established there. After the *Norman Conquest, *William the Conqueror became aware of its strategic importance and housed his administration in its castle. Under the Norman and *Angevin kings, E. prospered, becoming an ecclesiastical and administrative centre of southwest England, as well as one of its chief harbours.

F. Barlow, *Feudal England* (1967).

EXILARCH Title borne until the 13th century by the heads of the Jewish community in Mesopotamia (Babylonia). Held to be descendants of the dynasty of King David, the Es. were considered "princes of the exile" and, thus, leaders of the Jewish community in the Diaspora. Their authority rested on the rights granted them by the Persian kings and Arab caliphs as the representatives, before the sovereign and his court, of the Jewish communities, responsible for the collection of taxes and internal administration. Outside Mesopotamia, the E. enjoyed high prestige but had no real function; inside Mesopotamia, however, they possessed large domains and shared power with the *gaonim, being jointly responsible for the appointment of office-holders.

S. W. Baron, *A Social and Religious History of the Jews*, IV (1957).

EXPEDITIO (Expedition) Feudal term for a military campaign. The E. was one of the essential duties which vassals owed their lords, connected with the obligation of military service. Originally unlimited, under *Charlemagne the E. became an economic burden due to the expansion of the empire and the long distances to be travelled before engaging in battle. The terms were therefore limited: the vassal had to serve his lord in E. at his own expense for 40 days per year while, if the period of service was longer, the lord had to cover the expenses. In the 12th century, with the appearance of mercenaries, the practice of exemption from the E. began to be accepted and a special tax, the *scutage*, was levied in its place.

F. L. Ganshof, *Feudalism* (1965).

EZZELINO DA ROMANO (1194-1259) Tyrant of Verona and *Ghibelline leader in Italy. Member of the aristocratic Romano family of northern Italy, in 1233 he entered the service of Emperor Frederick II, carrying with him the support of the cities of Treviso and Vicenza dominated by his family. He supported the imperial army not only for political reasons, but also because of their common enemies, the Lombard cities and the house of *Este. He was a skilled military leader and ruthlessly fought his adversaries. In 1242 he was appointed imperial vicar of the march of Treviso and its province, where he acted independently and seized Verona. After the death of Frederick II (1250) and the fall of the Ghibellines in northern Italy, he was able to maintain his authority, until defeated by a coalition led by the Este at Cassano, where he was mortally wounded.

H. Stieve, *Ezzelino von Romano* (1909).

St. Francis preaching to the birds, *fresco by Giotto at the Church of St. Francis at Assisi*

F

FAIRS The medieval F. emerged in the early Middle Ages during a time when towns and commerce were in a state of decline. Originally, they were occasional gatherings of peasants and merchants at cross-roads and near bridges and water confluents, where peasants exchanged their products for goods which were not produced in their own villages. The Carolingian F. were a development of these primitive gatherings and included, to a certain degree, international trade, especially at the eastern and northeastern borders of the empire. The invasions and civil wars of the 9th century created the necessity to hold the F. in fortified places and they were gradually transferred to neighbouring cities and new boroughs. The demographic and economic developments of the 11th and 12th centuries had a great impact on the establishment and development of the F. in western Europe: the F. of the high Middle Ages (11th-14th centuries) became great seasonal commercial events, including the participation of merchants, money-changers and bankers from distant countries. As such, they became of interest to the authorities, who began to grant privileges in the hopes of attracting clientele to the F. One important concession was the establishment of speeded judicial procedures which led to the creation of special courts, such as the Court of Piepowders, the predecessor of the commercial court. The granting of freedom of movement to persons en route to F. anticipated the abolishment of *serfage in the 12th and 13th centuries.

Among the medieval F., the most famous were those of *Champagne, which flourished in the 12th-14th centuries and brought about a wide exchange of goods between the Mediterranean area and northern Europe. Not only was merchandise traded, which had its impact on craftsmanship quality, but social relationships also developed as a result of human contacts both during the negotiations and in the taverns during free time. Popular tales, bawdy stories, etc. were mixed with exchanges of news. The F. were in this respect an important factor in the development of a uniform civilization in western Europe. Moreover, F. led to the foundation of merchant associations which allowed the introduction of the "bill of exchange", intended to facilitate the financing of transactions on an international scale.

Some F. became more specialized. The *St. Denis F., near Paris, promoted the textile trade, while other F. specialized in the sale of wines. The F. began to be visited by great commercial companies in the 13th century; among them was the German *Hanse which co-opted cities to join it in expeditions through northern Europe where each maintained regular counters in various great F. In the Rhineland, the F. were run by the cities of the Confederation of the Rhine (see *Germany), which were responsible for policing the roads and administer-

Opening ceremony at the St. Denis Fair; *14th-century*

ing justice. In the 14th and 15th centuries, Italian traders and banking companies took an active part in many F. established throughout western Europe.

CEcH, III.

FAITH The term was used in the Middle Ages in at least two distinct meanings in Christian thought: the objective F., or the "Body of the Truth", as found in the *Creeds in the *canons of councils, the teaching of the Fathers of the Church and, above all, the biblical revelation. It was defined as "that which one believes" (*fides quae creditur*); the subjective F., which was qualified as the first of the theological virtues, containing hope and love, as set down by the teachings of St. Paul. It was the human response to divine truth and was defined as "that by which one believes" (*fides qua creditur*). For the theologians this last meaning was by far the most important: the Christian could make an act of F. only by virtue of God's action upon his soul. Therefore, the majority of medieval theologians taught that F. was a divine grace, granted only to those who were worthy of it, through the *Sacraments and the purity of their hearts. Through F., the faithful were able to acquire the truth comprehensible to the human intellect, or that which could be attained only through F. itself, such as the belief in the Holy Trinity. Thus, the notion, explained in the late 11th century by St. *Anselm of Canterbury, created the schema of "F. seeking the intellect" (*fides quaerens intellectum*), which was given its highest reasoning by *Thomas

Aquinas in the 13th century. In the late Middle Ages, a distinction was also made between the F. which could be learned, as explained by *scholasticism, and the mystical F.

St. Thomas Aquinas, *Summa Theologica*, II (ed. 1963); W. R. Inge, *Faith* (1909).

FALIERO Aristocratic family of Venice, whose members held important offices on behalf of the republic in the Middle Ages. Among them were:

Vitale (d. 1096) Doge in 1084. He attacked and succeeded in subverting the expansionist policies of *Robert Guiscard, the leader of the Normans of southern Italy.

Ordelafo (d. 1118) Doge (1102-18). One of the most active Venetian leaders at the beginning of the 12th century, he enjoyed the confidence of the aristocracy. He led the Venetian expansion into Dalmatia and was among the builders of naval power.

Marino (d. 1355) As doge (1354-55), he felt slighted by the fact that the constitution had established the *Council of the Ten, leaving his own position virtually powerless. Consequently he plotted to restore his power. The conspiracy was discovered, however, and he was arrested, tried by the "Ten" and beheaded.

H. Kretschmayer, *Geschichte von Venedig* (1934).

FALSE DECRETALS A collection of ecclesiastical law, attributed to *Isidore of Seville (7th century), but actually compiled in northern France, *c.* 850. Its aim was to defend the rights of the bishops against their metropolitans and, to a lesser extent, to support the papal claim to supremacy. The author, who was probably *Benedictus Levitas, had access to archives and his arrangement of material reveals great skill. In 865 Pope *Nicholas I made use of these decretals in the interests of the papacy. In later generations, the F. were considered a genuine document of high authority. Only in the 16th century was it proven to be a forgery.

Text, Migne, *PL*, vol. 130; J. Haller, *Nikolaus I und Pseudoisidor* (1936).

FALUN Town in central Sweden, west of Stockholm. At the beginning of the 12th century, its copper mines began to be systematically exploited. During the 12th-14th centuries, the copper was used to produce jewellery in the borough. The town was famed for its copper industry and artistic achievements not only within Sweden, but outside the country as well.

P. G. Foote, *The Viking Achievement* (1969).

FAMAGUSTA City in the southeastern part of *Cyprus. Situated on the coast, near a large bay, it had all the natural resources to make it an important harbour and, in fact, by the 12th century, the city had become the most important harbour of the island of Cyprus. But its real epoch of prosperity and greatness came during the rule of the *Lusignan kings, who developed F. and built its imposing fortifications. The city declined under the economic influence of *Genoa in 1233, and in the 14th century, the Ligurian city-state established its dominion over the city.

FAMINES F. were a constant factor in the social history of the Middle Ages, both in the East and in the West. In the Far Eastern countries, such as *China and *India, F. were endemic. Although in the central Asian steppes they were more sporadic, they had a stronger impact on the history of mankind, causing the great migrations of the steppe tribes between the 4th and the 13th century. These tribes attacked settled agricultural countries, thus bringing about political change and social revolts from China to the Middle East and western Europe. In Europe, on the other hand, F. were of lesser gravity, but the chronicles prove their constant manifestation, either as a result of plagues – due to natural phenomena, such as climate – or of raids and wars which destroyed the majority of crops. In the 14th century F. became more frequent and had a harsh effect on the population of western Europe, eventually leading to the *Black Death. It is now commonly accepted that these F. were a direct result of changes in climate which occurred at the beginning of the 14th century, causing an imbalance in the rate of precipitation. Of the major F. in Europe, those occurring in 1314-15 and 1316-17 had the worst effects. France and the Low Countries were particularly affected, and thousands starved. The situation in the cities was particularly critical as there were not enough people to bury the dead. The result was a series of plagues, which spread to the neighbouring countries. So many people were struck that some began to believe the calamity to be a divine punishment. As a result, penitents' movements and reformers emerged who rose up against the ecclesiastical and social establishment and provoked a period of political agitation, especially felt in Flanders.

H. S. Lucas, *The Great European Famine of 1315, 1316 and 1317* (1930).

FAMULUS In medieval Latin the term means a hired labourer in the manors. Such labour began to be used in western Europe in the late 12th century, replacing the peasants' *corvées* (*corvada) which were commuted into taxes. The F., which supplied most of the manpower in the agricultural sector during the 13th century, were recruited among widows, who left their family's strip of land to their married sons, or the *cottarii*, inhabitants of cottages at the village borders, whose lands were not large enough to produce the minimum crops for their subsistence; and who therefore sought an additional revenue as hired labourers. Two main groups of F. can be distinguished on the basis of employment conditions: the daily workers, hired for a single day, and labourers hired for a season. In both cases the F. were poorly paid, and they received no protection from their lords in cases of sickness or famine.

CEcH, I.

FARABI, AL- (Mohammed Ibn Mohammed Abu-Nasr Al-Farabi; 873-951) Moslem philosopher. Born at Farab, in central Asia, he studied at Khorasan and at Baghdad, where he discovered Aristotelian thought and adapted it to Moslem philosophy. His works on Aristotle and Plato were known to west European philosophers of the 13th century, who called him "Avennasar". After many years at Baghdad, F. settled in Aleppo, where he was received at the court of *Saif Al-Dawlah in 942. He tried to adapt his philosophical and political ideas, largely influenced by both Aristotle and Plato, to the reality of the Moslem caliphate, aiming to be its leader in the capacity of philosopher and prophet. Such a figure could achieve, in his opinion, human perfection, both through reason and through faith. The idea of reason as a cardinal virtue, combined with understanding and knowledge, was developed from Aristotelian philosophy.

R. Hammond, *The Philosophy of Al-Farabi and its Influence on Medieval Thought* (1947).

FARGANI, AL- (Abu Al-Abbas Ahmad Ibn Mohammed Al-Fargani; 9th century) Arab astronomer. He lived in Iraq and distinguished himself at the Academy of *Baghdad, where he was protected by the *Abbasid caliphs, to whom he was related. F. was the most important interpreter of Ptolemaic cosmology, and his book *On the Wisdom of Astronomy and the Movement of Celestial Elements,* which was very popular in the Middle Ages, was translated into Latin and remained the most important authority in the field until Copernicus. In 861 he was commissioned to build a "Nilometer", an observatory on the Nile, in Egypt.

A. Mieli, *La Science Arabe* (1966).

FATIMA (d. 633) Daughter of the prophet Mohammad and his first wife, Khadija. F. accompanied her father in his travels and was married to *Ali, Mohammad's nephew and one of this first followers. In the 9th century the *Shiite leaders of north Africa, the *Fatimids, claimed to be her descendants.

P. K. Hitti, *A History of the Arabs* (1953).

FATIMIDS Moslem Shiite dynasty (909-1071). Originally from northern Syria, where the Ismaili branch established a principality under the authority of their own mahdi. At the end of the 9th century, Abu Abdullah, one of the leaders of the movement, settled in north Africa, where he won the support of the Berber tribes, who revolted against the *Aghlabids. In 909 he conquered *Kairwan, where the Mahdi Ubaydullah joined him to establish an independent *Shiite state. Abdullah took the title of caliph and built a new capital, Mahdia. The F. purported to be descendants of *Fatima, daughter of Mohammad (hence their name), and claimed authority over the whole Moslem world. After the establishment of their north African state, they began a policy of expansion, supported by the Berbers. Missionaries were sent to Egypt and Arabia to prepare the way for their military expedition. The decline of the *Abbasid caliphs facilitated their task, and in 969, the F. conquered Egypt under the caliph Al-Muizz (d. 975). In order to mobilize his resources to take control over Egypt, Al-Muizz granted the north African province to a loyal family, the Zirids, who ruled the Maghreb on behalf of the F. until 1047. In the meantime, the F. established their government in Egypt, where they founded a new capital, *Cairo, and began to expand to Hedjaz, Palestine and Syria, which they conquered from the Abbasids. The conquests themselves were accomplished with the help of the Berbers, and the establishment of the F. empire was facilitated by their liberal attitude towards the *dhimmi (Jews and Christians), who were numerous in Egypt and had been persecuted by the Abbasid governors. This tolerance, which had a practical purpose, was also the result of the theological views of the Ismailis who believed that religious perfection could only be reached by a qualified minority, while the others (among them the *Sunnites), had to be considered equals on the basis of common monotheistic principles. Thus, they were able to govern Egypt, Palestine and a great part of Syria, despite the Sunnite majority, granting a large autonomy to the Jewish and various Christian communities. With the exception of the reign of Caliph Al-*Hakim (966-1021), who was recognized as mentally insane, the F. caliphs were able to maintain these principles and to .profit from their policy. They achieved economic prosperity, making their empire the centre of Mediterranean and Indian trade in the second half of the 11th century.

The conquest of the *Seljuks led to the loss of Syria and of the major part of Palestine in 1071. The counterattacks of the F. in the Asian provinces made them more dependent on their military leaders and, from the end of the 11th century, the vizier commanding the army became quite powerful, even imposing his authority on the caliphs. The *Crusaders who came to Palestine dealt another blow to the F. They gradually conquered the last strongholds the F. maintained in Asia, the Palestinian and Syrian coastal cities. Egyptian counterattacks, which were conducted in the area between Ramlah and Ascalon (1100-05), were unsuccessful. Moreover, *Baldwin I led a raid into Egypt, and only his death in northern Sinai prevented an invasion of the Delta. In 1136 *Fulk of Anjou, king of Jerusalem, prepared the conquest of Ascalon, accomplished in 1153. This event coincided with the decline of the caliph's power in Egypt as the caliphate had become· totally subordinate to the. viziers. The Crusader invasion of Egypt under the leadership of *Amalric I thus precipitated their fall, and led to the rise of *Saladin, who was sent to help Cairo and suppressed the Fatimid caliphate in 1171.

L. E. O'Leary, *A Short History of the Fatimid Caliphate* (1923).

Gold dinar *of the Fatimid Caliph Al-Mustansir; 1046*

FÉCAMP Monastery in Normandy. Founded as a nunnery by the *Merovingians in the 7th century it was destroyed in the 9th century during the Norman invasions. In 990 a community of regular canons was established in the ancient monastery. William of Vulpiano was elected as abbot, a dignity he held together with that of St. Bénigne of Dijon, Burgundy. Under his guidance, F. became an important scholarly centre, which flourished in the 11th-12th centuries; in 1101 a community of monks renovated the monastery.
J. F. Lamarignier, *Etudes sur les Abbayes normandes* (1937).

FELIX (d. 818) Bishop of Urgel, Spain. He was one of the leaders of the *Adoptionists. Charged as a heretic at the Council of Ratisbon in the presence of *Charlemagne (792), he publicly recanted before Pope *Adrian I, but upon his return to his see, continued to express his views. *Alcuin then criticized his doctrines and brought about a renewed condemnation at Frankfurt in 794. Upon a second recantation of the heresy, F. was allowed to maintain his dignity, but remained under the supervision of the archbishop of Lyons until his death.
EC, V.

FELIX I (d. 274) Pope (269-74). He was firm in his conviction of maintaining the cohesion of the Christian community of Rome during anti-Christian persecutions.

FELIX II (d. 365) Pope (355-65). He was elected after the deposition of Pope Liberius in 355. To many theologians of his time, the act was considered illegal, but F. secured the support of the Roman Church and was able to obtain imperial recognition.

FELIX III (d. 492) Pope (483-92). He distinguished himself for his independence. He refused to accept the *Henotikon*, the religious ordinance of the East Roman Emperor *Zeno, promulgated to restore ecclesiastical peace after the *Monophysite dispute. In 484 he assembled a synod at Rome, where he condemned the *Henotikon* and summoned Acacius, the patriarch of Constantinople, a supporter of the ordinance. F. excommunicated him for his lack of obedience to himself as the hierarchical head of the universal church.
L. Duchesne, *Ancient History of the Church* (1913).

FELIX IV (d. 530) Pope (526-30). Originally of northern Italy, he became pope through the influence of *Theodoric, king of the *Ostrogoths, despite the open opposition of the Roman clergy. As pope, he opposed the *Pelagians and promulgated St. *Augustine's doctrine on grace as the official teaching of the church. He converted the ancient pagan temples of Rome into churches and he consecrated the church of Sts. *Cosmas and Damian.
L. Duchesne, *Ancient History of the Church* (1913).

FELONY In medieval law, a F. was considered a transgression of the feudal *customs, meaning a breach of obligations. From the 9th century on, custom recognized certain circumstances where a vassal had a legitimate right to commit a F. This was the case when a lord failed to protect his vassal from an enemy's attack, refused to do him justice by hearing his complaints at his court, or conducted himself in a dishonourable manner, striking or beating his vassal. In such cases, it was the lord who was considered responsible for the F. and the vassal was relieved of his obligations.
M. Bloch, *Feudal Society* (1961).

FERDINAND I, of Antequera (1380-1416) King of Aragon (1412-16). Grandson of *Peter IV of Aragon through his mother Eleanor, and younger son of *John I, king of Castile, he was elected king of Aragon after the death of his uncle *Martin I (1410). His short reign was marked by his attempts to impose his rule in *Catalonia, where anti-Castilian feelings were openly manifest. He succeeded only after he swore to maintain the "Catalan liberties".
H. J. Chaytor, *A History of Arágon and Catalonia* (1933).

FERDINAND I, the Great (c. 1017-65) King of Castile and León (1035-65). He was the son of *Sancho III, king of Navarre, who appointed him count of Castile in 1029. In 1035 he proclaimed himself king and reigned over a part of Castile, while the other part remained under the dominion of the realm of Navarre. In 1037 he inherited León and at the Battle of Tamarón defeated the nobility and imposed his rule over the kingdom. Shortly after the consolidation of his authority, F. resumed the *Reconquista* wars against the Moslems and conquered large territories between the Duero and Tage Rivers. In 1054, having defeated the Navarrese army, he annexed the Castilian territories of Navarre. Assuming the title of emperor, he reigned over nearly half of the Iberian peninsula.
A. Castro, *The Structure of Spanish History* (1954).

FERDINAND II (1137-88) King of León (1157-88). Son of *Alfonso VII of Castile and León, he inherited the latter kingdom and fought against the powerful nobility, imposing royal authority. He successfully combatted the *Almohades and conquered the provinces of Extremadura, where he initiated a project of colonization intended to replace the population of Moslem peasants which had been expelled. In order to maintain the independence of his kingdom, he fought against the neighbouring areas of Castile and Portugal. In 1158 he granted royal protection to the new order of *Calatrava in an attempt to attract the knights to León, and in 1175 he allowed the foundation of the military order of *Santiago.
A. Castro, *The Structure of Spanish History* (1954).

FERDINAND III, the Saint (1199-1252) King of Castile (1217) and León (1230-52). He was the son of *Alfonso IX of León. In 1217 he inherited the crown of Castile from his uncle, *Henry I, but was forced to defend himself against his father, who had invaded Castile. After his father's death, F. permanently united the two kingdoms. He devoted himself to suppressing the power of the nobility and to the organization of the kingdom. In the latter case, he took it upon himself to reform the laws of the land, promulgated in the form of a compilation called *Codigo de las siete partidas* which became the Castilian civil code. In 1239 he founded the University of Salamanca. His main achievement was, however, the revival of the *Reconquista* process, taking advantage of the decline of the *Almohades. After his victory at Jeres in 1233, he began a systematic conquest of *Andalusia; in 1236 he conquered Cordoba, in 1242, Murcia, in 1245, Jaen and in 1248, Seville, the last becoming one of the royal residences. Only the kingdom of *Granada remained an independent Moslem realm.
P. L. Fernandez de Retana, *San Fernando III y su época* (1941).

FERDINAND IV (1285-1312) King of Castile (1295-1312). He succeeded his father, Sancho IV, at the age of six with his mother as regent. His minority was marked by continuous rebellions and conspiracies mounted by the Castilian nobles and supported by Portugal and Granada. He succeeded in halting the rebellions through an alliance with *Aragon.

A. Castro, *The Structure of Spanish History* (1954).

FERDINAND I (1345-83) King of Portugal (1367-83). Son and heir of *Peter I, he attempted to intervene in the dynastic crisis of Castile, claiming its throne after the death of *Peter the Cruel in 1369. F. allied himself with *John of Gaunt against Castile and Aragon. His struggle with *Henry II of Castile had no positive results and only succeeded in weakening Portugal.

H. V. Livermore, *A History of Portugal* (1947).

FERDINAND DE LA CERDA (d. 1275) He was the eldest son of *Alfonso X, king of Castile. Married to Blanche, daughter of King Louis IX of France, he was made count of La Cerda as heir apparent. His death during his father's lifetime led to a struggle over the succession of Castile.

FERDINAND DE LA CERDA (the "Infante de La Cerda"; d. 1296) Son of *Ferdinand and Blanche, he claimed the succession of Castile during the last years of his grandfather, Alfonso X (1282-85). While the old king supported his claims, the majority of the nobles supported *Sancho IV, the younger son of Alfonso. Although F. was supported by France, he could not prevent Sancho's accession to the throne. After years of civil war, he fled to France, although he never surrendered his claim to the Castilian crown.

A. Castro, *The Structure of Spanish History* (1954).

FERDINAND OF MAJORCA (d. 1316) Son of *James II, king of *Majorca, he claimed the succession of the Frankish principality of *Morea in 1313, on the basis of the rights of his wife, a descendant of the family of *Villehardouin. In 1315 he conquered Morea and was proclaimed prince. But in 1316, another pretender, Louis of Burgundy, reached the principality and defeated and killed F. at the Battle of Manolada.

W. Miller, *The Latins in the Levant* (1913).

FERRAND (FERDINAND) OF PORTUGAL (1186-1233) Count of Flanders (1211-33). Son of *Sancho I, king of Portugal, he married Joan, heiress of Flanders and as a result was made count. In 1212 he became allied with *John Lackland, king of England and joined the English and German camp at the Battle of *Bouvines, where he was taken prisoner by *Philip II, king of France. F. was released only after having made territorial concessions to Philip. As a result, he lost much of his authority and power.

G. Duby, *Le Dimanche de Bouvines* (1973).

FERRARA The main city of the province of Emilia (northern Italy). In the early Middle Ages, F. was a small town under the influence of the governors of *Ravenna. Its own history begins with the Lombard conquest in 753, when it was detached from Ravenna and became the centre of a Lombard county. In 774 *Charlemagne gave the city to the pope, but papal rule was ineffective and in the late 9th and 10th centuries, F. was ruled by local families. In 998 it was conquered by the counts of Canossa, remaining under their rule until the death of Countess *Matilda of Tuscany (1102). During the 12th century the city again gained

independence and joined the *Lombard League. After its temporary conquest by *Frederick Barbarossa in 1158, government of the city was disputed between the *Ghibelline family of Salanguerra and the *Guelph Adelardi. The latter's rights to city leadership were inherited in 1184 by the counts of *Este, who thus became a prominent family. In 1240 the house of Este finally became rulers of the city under Ezzo VII, an ally of the papacy. Under the family's rule (who in 1471 reached the rank of dukes), the city prospered and became one of the most important political, literary and artistic centres of northern Italy, containing important buildings and art treasures of the late medieval and Renaissance periods. Attempts by Milan and Venice to conquer F. in the 15th century were unsuccessful.

R. Jannucci, *Storia di Ferrara* (1958).

FEUDALISM The term was derived by early modern historians from the adjective *feudalis*, already employed in medieval documents. It originated from the old Germanic word *feh* or *feo*, meaning cattle. F. denotes the relations of dependence between lords and their vassals, based on the tenure of land (*fief). Despite the fact that such relations were existent in various countries during the Middle Ages and that the term is broadly used, historical F. emerged and was developed in western Europe. F., which denotes the evolution of dependency in the agrarian society, had its foundation on two levels: the infrastructure of the demesne or manor, concerning the peasants and their landlords; and the feudo-vassalitic relations, based on the oath of fealty and *homage, in return for the *investiture of an estate.

The relations of dependency in the framework of the demesne date from the later Western Roman empire (4th and 5th centuries), when a major portion of public authority was passed to the great landowners, who found themselves responsible for the *colons*, bound to their lands by the legislation of *Constantine the Great. These free peasants were controlled by the aristocracy of the owners of *latifundia*, and they were forced to pay them taxes in terms of produce and manpower for public labour. With the decline and fall of the Roman empire, the free and freed peasants sought protection and services at the centre of the great estate, the *villa*, where the local lord resided and where the services of craftsmen and public utilities were found. In return for the use of their services, the lord demanded that the peasants work on his estates a certain number of days per year (an amount which varied from region to region). Moreover, the peasants had to supply the lords with part of their produce and cattle. Gradually, and in direct relation with the disappearance of the last remnants of the Roman functionaries (6th-7th centuries), the lords of the *villae* took responsibility for the jurisdiction of their peasants and thus, in the 8th century, the *villa* became a seigniory. At the same time, with the abolition of ancient slavery, the major portion of the peasants in the demesne became bound to the manor as serfs. Only those peasants who had larger properties (the *allods) at their disposal continued to be free and depend directly on the court of the *count, who represented the king until the end of the 9th century. The rest of the peasants were considered tenants of a *mansus* (the family land unit), whose status accorded to their juridical standing.

It was through this agrarian infrastructure that the links of dependence emerged and developed. They were based on the old Germanic practice of the *comitatus, a community of fighters which attached itself to a military leader. Through the foundation of the Germanic kingdoms in western Europe, the *comitatus* lost its primitive significance and was replaced by groups of free-men loyal to a king or a noble, who provided for their needs in return for their military service. Residing at court, these warriors could expect some remuneration, either by the gift of estates or by appointment to administrative and governmental offices. They were the beginnings of the new nobility in the Germanic kingdoms. In the 7th century, however, some of these aristocrats were unable to retain their independence in the state of constant war and had to seek the protection of the more powerful lords. Thus, they commended themselves to such lords, surrendering their own estates so as to receive the status of tenants. In this capacity, they were required to serve their lords as *vassi, particularly regarding military service, and to bind themselves by an oath of fealty to the lord. Among the lords who took advantage of the vassalage in order to increase their power, the most famous were the *Pepin-Arnulf mayors of the palace of Austrasia, the ancestors of the *Carolingians. These became the most important landlords in the Frankish kingdom, controlling a significant number of vassals, who served in their army and helped them to become, under *Pepin II of Herstal, the real rulers of the kingdom.

An important modification of the system occurred in the 8th century under *Charles Martel and *Pepin the Short. The technological advance which allowed the use of horses in military operations led to the introduction of the *chivalry in the Frankish army. The new fighters, who were expected to supply their own horses and equipment, were in need of greater resources. Consequently, Charles Martel confiscated church lands and granted them to his vassals as a *beneficium so that they could equip themselves and be free for warfare. The first to benefit from the new system were the remnants of the court vassals, called *vassi casati* (vassals with a fief). While their estates technically continued to belong to the church and they were bound to pay tithes to the ecclesiastical owners, they were required to take an oath of homage, making them the personal vassals of the mayor of the palace. The system of the *beneficium* spread widely during the 8th century.

Under Pepin the Short, the oath was made a religious act, and the homage was also used for political purposes; thus, *Tassilo III, duke of Bavaria, was compelled to swear homage to the Frankish king in 758 and in return was invested with his duchy, which he held as a tenant of the king. Under *Charlemagne, the principle of "no land without a lord" was held, imposing the practice of vassalage in the empire, while counties were invested on the members of the great families, creating the political framework of the feudal regime. Thus the distinction between the *beneficia* was clearly established: a vassal bound to military service was invested with up to 12 *mansi, becoming the lord of the peasants settled on the manor, while the counts and other high officers were granted larger *beneficia,* according to the dignity of their office.

The *Carolingian practice continued into the 9th century, but with an important change: the vassals were allowed to pass their benefices to their heirs. Such a development, defined in the great assembly of the vassals of *Charles the Bald at Kierzy (875), was a result of the decline of royal power, which created confusion regarding the ownership of estates and the tenure of benefices. Such a measure also implied the inheritance of the public charges and authority on the territory of the benefice, the *regalia. In the 10th century, the term *beneficium* lost its significance and a new term, the *fief (*feodum*) was used to denote the tenures.

The fall of the Carolingians brought about the rise of individual power, held in the 10th-11th centuries by those vassals who were strong and rich enough to build and defend a castle. Only some of the counties and duchies were able to maintain their cohesion and that was generally the case where the tenants of castles were too weak to impose their own authority, such as in Normandy, Flanders, and the German duchies. Moreover, the partition of fiefs between the descendants of lords led to the disintegration of F. at the end of the 11th century. This situation created the appropriate conditions for the establishment of feudal principalities, which was the last stage of political F.

The establishment of feudal principalities allowed the revival of royal authority in France and England, based on the creation of the royal demesne in the 12th century. The establishment of royal officers gradually led to the restoration of the administrative monarchy, which used F. as a means of imposing its authority. A decisive factor in this process was the revival of *commerce and the establishment of non-feudal resources in the royal treasuries. Moreover, while the disintegration of the vassalage system led to a plurality of homages, meaning that a vassal might swear fealty to several lords, from the 12th century it usually became the practice that when one of those lords was also the king, he became the main lord, without consideration of the nature of the fief held by the vassal. Thus, assignation of rents by monarchs altered the character of the vassalage system and was a factor in the emergence of the *indenture system, which replaced political F. in the 13th century.

In the late Middle Ages, F. regained its social and economic character, based on the exploitation of the seigniory and the manor. Although royal justice, administrated by specialized, legally-trained magistrates, was paramount, several lords maintained their courts. By royal grant, they were invested with "high" or "low" justice, the former being the right to judge capital crimes within their fiefs. In England, however, the justice was a royal prerogative, administered by justiciars and sheriffs and including the participation of a jury selected from among the free-men.

With the revival of the state, in the 12th-13th centuries, F. lost its vitality in western Europe and remained a system used by lawyers, as verified by the numerous treaties compiled in the 13th century. On the other hand, the eastward expansion of western Europe as a result of the *Crusades led to the implantation of feudal practices, both in the Latin states of Palestine and Syria, and in the Latin empire of Constantinople and Frankish Greece. Although the feudal infrastructure of the demesne was not transferred to the East, political F. became an ideal of the Eastern nobility, which became

an oliogarchic body with large control over the kingship.
M. Bloch, *Feudal Society* (1958);
R. Boutruche, *Seigneurie et Féodalité* (1962-68);
D. Herlihy, *A History of Feudalism* (1970).

FEZ (FES, FAS) City in the Maghreb (Morocco). F. was founded in 789 by Idris I, who established the Idrisid dynasty in *Morocco and made the city his capital. In the 10th century F. became a battlefield between the *Fatimids and *Ummayads of Spain, who finally conquered it in 980. Under the Ummayads the city thrived and, until 1012, its history is related to that of the Ummayad caliphate of *Cordoba. After the fall of the Ummayads, F. fell to *Berber tribes and was divided into two main boroughs, in continuous rivalry. Under the *Almoravides – who conquered the city in 1070 and established there an important military garrison – and the Almohades who displaced them in 1143, F. was a centre of commerce and industry, especially of textiles and leather. New walls were erected and splendid palaces and mosques were built in the west Moslem style, typical of Andalusian art. After the fall of the Almohades (1269), F. was contested by local dynasties. The Banu Marin made it the capital of Morocco (1270-1465) and an important religious centre for northwest Africa.
R. Le Tourneau, *Fès in the Age of the Marinides* (1961).

FIBONACCI, LEONARDO (d. c. 1240) Mathematician. Born at Pisa (hence his cognomen "Leonardo of Pisa") to a family of merchants, he made business trips to north Africa in the late 12th century. At Algiers he became acquainted with Indian calculus and after his return to Pisa wrote a treatise on the *abacus (*Liber abaci,* published in 1202). The revised manuscript, published in 1228, included materials gathered during his travels to Egypt, Syria, Sicily and Provence. His book was instrumental in introducing the use of Arabic numerals to Christian Europe. Besides summarizing Greek and Arabic mathematics, it also included F.'s own work on algebra. The treatise and a second book, written *c.* 1220 on practical geometry and trigonometry (*Practica Geometriae*), won him fame in learned circles of Italy. Emperor *Frederick II invited him to join his court at Sicily, where he was a central figure at discussions on mathematics.
D. J. Struik, *A Concise History of Mathematics* (1948).

FICINO (FACINO) CANE (c. 1360-1412) Italian *condottiere.* Originally from the county of Vercelli, he entered the service of the dukes of Milan in 1386 and distinguished himself during the rule of Gian Galeazzo *Visconti. He became an eminent general of the period and in 1401 defeated the German army near Brescia. After the death of Gian Galeazzo, F. began to look after his own interests, conquering a large seigniory for himself, including the cities of Alessandria, Novara and Piacenza. He also sought to impose his overlordship on Genoa, where he defeated the French in 1409. F. aspired to the title captain of Milan, but was considered too dangerous and Duke Gian Maria Visconti prepared for war against him. However, both F. and the duke died in 1412.
N. Valeri, *La Vita di Facino Cane* (1940).

FIDELITY (Latin: fidelitas) The term denoted faithfulness to the Roman Catholic Church. With the emergence of *feudalism in the 7th century it also meant a vassal's loyalty to his lord. The religious and secular definitions merged during the reign of *Charlemagne. In 789 he ordered all Christian men of his kingdom to take the oath of F. to him – and thereby to the Roman Catholic Church, since he regarded himself as a religious ruler. From 802 the oath had to be taken by all males aged 12 and over. It was primarily a pledge not to betray the emperor nor allow enemies to enter his territory. The active form of F. included serving in the army or administration and paying taxes. In the 9th century the term was restricted to the oath of loyalty to the monarch, in contrast to *homage to the lord, which implied mutual obligations. With the decline of the Carolingian states and the disappearance of the notion of the state in feudal Europe, the lords enjoined their vassals and free-men residing in their counties to take the oath of F., which in this case was synonymous with homage.

The religious sense of F. revived in the 10th century, when a monarch had to swear F. to the Roman Catholic Church as a precondition for his coronation. Later on, such an oath was also taken by other dignitaries upon assuming their posts.
F. Bloch, *Feudal Society* (1958).

FIDES (Latin: faith) The term, used in a theological context, meant faith in the Christian religion as established in the *Creeds of the Councils (i.e., *The Fides Damasi,* "Faith of Pope Damasus", *c.* 380, adopted by the Western Church). The term was also used in a legal sense: in his defence, a free-man, accused of a crime, swore that he acted *bona fide* (in good faith). To have him convicted, the plaintiff had to prove the *male fide* (bad faith) of the accused.
H. Niermeyer, *Medieval Latin Dictionary* (1957).

FIEF (Latin: feudum or feodum) In feudal law, the estate held by a vassal from his lord. (The variants *feo, feos, fedum, feum, feus, feuz, fevum,* were also used in some medieval documents.) The F. was given to a vassal after he swore *homage to his lord. It was considered "noble tenure", vesting the vassal with the right to administer the land, with authority over his own subordinates and with the privilege of rendering "noble" services to his lord, such as *consilium and *auxilium. The F. was governed by precise laws, but in practice these differed from one estate to another. With the different forms of feudalism from the 13th century on, the term acquired various meanings. *F. de bursa* (money-fief) referred to the fee paid by kings or high-ranking lords to their vassals for military service. A *felony led to the immediate forfeiture of payments. *F. de camera,* another form of money-fief, denoted the revenues of the royal chamber, administered by the *chamberlain. *F. de dignité* (F. of honour) originated in the 9th century as a benefice granted to public officials and from the 13th century, was given to various dignitaries at courts and government officers. *F. francum* (free fief) exempted the vassals from certain services to the lord. *F. ligium* designated the land held by a vassal from the "main lord" (where he held land from more than one lord), to whom he was compelled to give priority in military or other services in case of conflict of interest.

From the 13th century on, any land held from the king, regardless of size or importance, was considered *F. ligium. F. loricae* or *F. militum* (the knight's F.) was a small piece of land given to a knight, the income from which was deemed sufficient for acquiring a coat of mail. *Feodum solis* (fief of the sun), synonymous with the *allod, signified the absolute ownership of land, not under a feudal lord. *Feodum vavassoris,* used especially in Germany, implied the fief of the small vassal who generally was vested only with land, and had no say in the jurisdiction over it. *Fio,* used in the 13th century in Italy, designated the payment for an honourable service and lost all connection with the granting of land. In the 14th century, the term spread to Germany and England, where it is still used in the form of "fee".

M. Bloch, *Feudal Society* (1958).

FIERABRAS Late 12th-century epic poem, written by an anonymous author. F. is the name of a Moslem giant, who seized the relics of the Passion when Rome was conquered by the Barbarians. The poem relates the exploits of a group of knights who devote their lives to recovering the relics and emphasizes their courage, thereby extolling the ideals of Christian *chivalry.

U. T. Holmes, *A History of Old French Literature* (1948).

FILIOQUE, DISPUTE OF The Latin term *filioque,* meaning "And from the Son", was added by the Roman Catholic Church to the *Creed of Nicaea after the sentence "The Holy Ghost proceedeth from the Father". The Eastern Churches rejected the revision, and it was the subject of major theological disputes between the Latin and Greek Churches from the end of the 10th century. At the Council of Florence in 1439, the Greek Church was compelled to accept the doctrine as a condition for reunion with the Latin Church. The Orthodox Church continued to reject it.

S. Runciman, *The Eastern Schism* (1955).

FINLAND Country in northern Europe, on the northeastern coast of the Baltic Sea. At the beginning of the Middle Ages, the settlement of the country by groups of Finno-Ugric tribes was already completed. "Finland" derives from Fenni, the name given to the tribes by Tacitus in the 2nd century. In the 6th-11th centuries, the tribes founded three kingdoms. The two in the north and east lacked cohesion, while the third, in the south and southwest, the *Suomi,* was better organized and gave its name, in Finnish, to the whole country. It prospered by the fur trade with neighbouring countries and even with Byzantium and the Arab caliphate of Baghdad. Nevertheless, the Suomi's political organization was rudimentary and, in the middle of the 12th century, King *Eric IX of Sweden had no difficulty in conquering the kingdom by a military expedition proclaimed as a crusade. Christianity was introduced in 1156 by Archbishop Henry of Uppsala, and it spread rapidly. Another series of crusades in the second half of the 13th century led to the conquest of the rest of the country. With the conquest of Karelia in 1293, the whole of F. became Swedish, despite the opposition of the Russian princes of *Novgorod, who were compelled to recognize Swedish rule in F. in 1323.

Under the Swedes, F. developed rapidly, with towns being founded, particularly along the Baltic coast. The large settlement of Swedes contributed somewhat to a change in the ethnic character of F., especially in the coastal area. But the Finns were not reduced to a state of serfdom, as were the Baltic tribes conquered by the German knights of *Livonia. Moreover, they were allowed to participate in the self-government institutions of cities and counties. In 1362 F. became a duchy within Sweden. The Swedes and Finns of the duchy had their own assembly of estates, with representatives of the nobility, clergy, towns and countryside.

E. Jutikkala, *A History of Finland* (1962).

FIRDUSI (Abu Al-Kasim Mansur; c. 935-1020) The greatest Persian epic poet. Born in the area of Meshed (northeast Persia), he lived at the court of Sultan *Mahmud of Ghazni, where he composed his great poem, *Shah-Nama* (Book of Kings). Although little is known about his life, legends abound concerning his maltreatment by Mahmud, and possible disgrace, which motivated him to compose satirical poems against the sultan. The *Shah-Nama* is the product of 35 years of work and was completed in 1010. It praises the glory of Persia from mythological times to the eve of the Arab conquest. The poem, consisting of 60,000 verses, was designed to give a picture of the Persian kings – at war, at the palace or at the hunt and other sports. But it is also a mirror of major Persian achievements in religion, the sciences, arts and crafts, through Persian history. As in all epic poems, the stories are built around heroic figures, whom F. places in the historical background of his work. F. was one of the chief protagonists in the revival of the Persian language.

V. Minorsky, *The Older Preface to the Shah-Name* (1956).

FIREARMS While F. were first used in the Middle Ages, the explosive properties of a mixture of saltpetre, sulphur and charcoal were already known in China (the motherland of F.) between 500 and 700. In the West other inflammable mixtures were used in the 7th century, such as the Byzantines *"Greek fire", a mixture of quicklime, naphtha and sulphur. The use of gunpowder spread from China only in the 12th century and was introduced to western Europe in the late 13th century, probably by the *Mongols. The earliest extant Western formula for gunpowder is in a Latin manuscript of *c.* 1300, the *Liber Ignium* (The Book of Fire), attributed to a certain Mark the Greek, about whom very little is known. While the West lagged behind China in the use of gunpowder, it took the lead in the manufacture of weapons. The first canons, employed between 1311 and 1345, were made of metal, by a process similar to that used for making bells. In the *Hundred Years' War these canons appeared both in the English and French armies – although the warfare ideals of *chivalry made the French more reluctant to use them. The *Ottoman Turks also learnt the use of F., and, with the help of artillery, won the Battle of Kossovo (1368), which led to Turkish domination of the Balkans. The use of artillery spread throughout Europe, and in the 15th century gunpowder was widely employed as missile-propellant.

H. W. L. Hime, *The Origin of Artillery* (1915);
W. Ling, *On the Invention and Use of Gunpowder and Firearms in China* (1947).

FIRMIN DE BELLEVAL (14th century) French astronomer. He proposed reforming the calendar, based on the *Alfonsine Tables – an improvement of Ptolemy's planetary tables – completed in the mid-13th century at the court of *Alfonso X of Castile. In 1345 he came to Avignon, at the request of Pope *Clement VI, and presented a detailed report on calendar reform, which was the basis for the 16th-century Gregorian calendar.

A. C. Crombie, *Science in the Middle Ages* (1957).

FISCUS The Latin term, used in the 5th-8th centuries, was applied to the kings' estates in the various realms of western Europe. The term was originally used by the Romans to designate state property in contrast to the emperor's personal property. With the fall of the Roman empire, this distinction disappeared. The F.'s revenues were considered as belonging to the monarchs, their families and attendants.

F. L. Ganshof, *Feudalism* (1965).

FITZNEALE (FITZNIGEL), RICHARD (d. 1196) Treasurer of England. In 1155 he entered the service of *Henry II and in 1158 became treasurer, a post purchased for him by his father, Nigel, bishop of Ely, and which he held until his death. In 1159 he also became bishop of London, and was a prominent figure in the government of *Richard I. In 1179 he completed a treatise *Dialogus Scacarii* (The Dialogue on the Exchequer), which is the most comprehensive description of the English *exchequer of the period. The book, written in the form of a dialogue, is divided into two parts. The first describes the structure and functions of the exchequer, the staff and its work, the *pipe rolls and writs, the accounting system, the tallies and system of weighing; the second part deals with exchequer procedure.

C. Johnson (ed.), *The Course of the Exchequer by Richard, son of Nigel* (1950).

"FIVE BOROUGHS" A confederation of the boroughs of Leicester, Lincoln, Nottingham, Stamford and Derby, the strongholds of which were built by the *Danes in the 9th century to keep the part of England they occupied in subjugation. The Danes sent delegates to a general assembly that constituted a high court, which promulgated Danish law in England. In the 10th century the kings of *Wessex converted the confederation into shires.

B. Lyon, *A Constitutional and Legal History of Medieval England* (1960).

FLAGELLANTS Group of Christians who scourged themselves in public processions, as a penance for the sins of the world. Flagellation was first practised in 13th-century Italy. The best known were the F. of 1348-49, who saw the *Black Death as a punishment for sins and called for public penance. The most radical of them, the F. of Germany, accused the Jews and the church establishment of being responsible for the plague and were condemned for heresy.

A. Hübner, *Die deutschen Geisslerlieder* (1931).

FLAMBARD, RANULF (d. 1126) Of a humble Norman family, he became clerk at the ducal court of Caen, Normandy, and subsequently held some minor ecclesiastical offices in England. In 1083 he became chaplain

A procession of the Flagellants, 17th-century engraving

Panel of the The Hardwick Hunting Tapestry; *15th-century Flemish School*

to *William the Conqueror and clerk to the chancellor of England. In 1087, *William II appointed him justiciar, which, in the late 11th century, signified not only the position of chief justice, but also that of the most powerful minister. He imposed the royal will in the realm, and the government machinery he installed was highly efficient for the time. But his unscrupulous methods made him many enemies and in 1100, at baronial request, *Henry I imprisoned him in the Tower of London. He soon escaped and won royal grace in 1101, becoming bishop of Durham (1101-26).

R. W. Southern, *Ranulf Flambard and Early Anglo-Norman Administration* (1933).

FLANDERS County in the Low Countries and part of the kingdom of France in the Middle Ages; now divided between Belgium, France and the Netherlands. In 358, when the Romans allowed the *Franks to settle in the empire as their allies, F. became the centre of the *Salian Franks. They established in F. a number of tribal kingdoms, the most important of them having been that of Tournai, the first capital of the Merovingians in the 5th century. As the Gallo-Romans left, and the Franks – later to become the Flemings – imposed their dialect and customs on F., the ethnic character of the country changed. After the conquest of Gaul by *Clovis, the kingdom of Tournai ceased to exist as such. In the 6th century F. became a Frankish province, with part of its estates being granted to the monasteries founded in the 6th-8th centuries. The abbeys developed sheep-breeding and the wool industry emerged. The peaceful age of F. was broken in 820, when the *Normans sacked the country, which lacked effective leadership for organizing its defence. During the 9th century attempts by various adventurers to build castles and counter the raids were abortive. *Charles the Bald, who became king over the West Franks by the Treaty of *Verdun (843), established the county of F. in 862. He appointed his son-in-law, *Baldwin I, count and marquis of F. Baldwin succeeded in checking the Nor-

mans and, with the help of the monasteries, established his authority over the vassals. His son, *Baldwin II (879-918), completed his father's work, organizing countal rule and favouring the founding of boroughs, such as Bruges, around his castle.

The counts of the 10th and 11th centuries devoted their efforts to consolidating the county and extending its bounderies. They annexed the neighbouring counties of *Artois in France, and *Hainault and Waes in the Holy Roman empire. Although vassals of the French kings, the counts enjoyed a substantial measure of independence. The revival of trade spurred the growth of towns, which became centres of the *cloth industry. F. evolved into one of the most prosperous counties in western Europe. With F.'s dependence on the import of English wool as raw material for its main industry, F. and England developed close relations, reinforced by marriages between English and Norman royal members. Under *Robert II (1087-1111) F. reached the zenith of its power, enjoying naval supremacy in the North Sea. While Robert took part in the First *Crusade as one of its most important leaders, the counts were left to face internal agitation during the 12th century. *Baldwin VII (1111-19) succeeded in repressing the revolts of the nobility, but failed to do so in the towns, where certain social movements were condemned as heresies. Under the rule of his heir, *Charles the Good, the revolts intensified and led to his murder in 1127. The king of France, *Louis VI, intervened and installed *William Clito of Normandy as count, attempting thus to impede the good relations between F. and England. But William failed to impose his authority, and the cities and the nobility recognized *Thierry of Alsace, who founded the second dynasty of counts. He and his son *Philip succeeded in imposing their authority and in maintaining good relations with both the kings of France and those of England. F. continued to thrive in the 12th century, despite the repression of the textile workers, who were condemned as heretics and many of whom were killed. Philip of Alsace married his niece, Isabelle of Hainault, to King *Philip II of France, giving her Artois as dowry – and thus, the active involvement of France in Flemish affairs from 1194. Philip intervened in the disputes concerning the succession of F. When *Baldwin VIII, his brother-in-law, took part in the Fourth *Crusade (1204), he sought to impose a count who was likely to pursue his policy. He thus influenced the marriage of the heiress Joan to *Ferrante of Portugal (1211) who succeeded to the county. But the new count championed the interests of the towns, which favoured an alliance with the English, and joined *John Lackland in a coalition against Philip. After Philip's victory at *Bouvines (1214), he arranged the marriage of Margaret, sister and heiress of Countess Joan, to his loyal vassal, William of Dampierre.

In the 13th century countal authority declined somewhat, despite French support, while the power of the cities grew. Rapid industrialization brought with it class struggle. Merchant guilds ("patricians") were at loggerheads with craftsmen ("democrats"), both vying for their share in government. When prosperity gave way to economic stagnation and crisis in the late 13th century, the atmosphere was conducive to revolt. Class conflict was aggravated by the struggle between France and England, the patricians siding with the former, while the democrats supported the latter and resented French influence in F. The democrats succeeded in seizing power at Bruges and Ghent and, in the *"Matins of Bruges" in 1302, decimating the French garrison in the city. In the same year they also defeated the army sent by *Philip IV at *Courtrai and F. resumed its relations with England. But urban agitation continued and the patricians returned to power. Moreover, Count *Louis of Nevers (1322-46), who was faithful to France, recalled the French, who defeated the cities in 1328 at *Cassel. The French reimposed their influence in the county, which adopted an anti-English policy, against the interests of the towns.

With the beginning of the *Hundred Years' War (1337), *Edward III of England proclaimed an embargo on the export of wool to F. He established a staple at *Antwerp, which caused the textile industry of *Brabant to flourish, while F. was hit by a severe crisis. The democrats revolted and, under the leadership of James of *Artevelde, of Ghent, seized power and renewed their alliance with the English, who resumed the supply of wool. In 1345 the parties convened to proclaim the neutrality of F. But civil war continued and F. suffered from the *Black Death. The return of the patricians to power did not remedy the situation. The dynastic contest finally ended by the marriage of *Philip the Bold, duke of Burgundy, to the heiress of Count *Louis of Mâle (1367). Philip, who obtained the military support of his nephew, King *Charles VI, defeated the army of Philip van *Artevelde at *Roosebeke in 1382, imposed his rule on Flanders and annexed the county to his duchy of *Burgundy. The history of F. thereafter becomes that of Burgundy.

J. Lestocquoy, *Histoire de la Flandre et de l'Artois* (1949).

FLEMALLE, MASTER OF (c. 1378-1444) Identified as Robert Campin, Flemish painter. He settled at Tournai in 1406 and taught Rogier van der Weyden. He was one of the founders of the Flemish school of

The 12th-century castle of the Counts of Flanders, Ghent

painting in the 15th century, and executed frescoes in the cathedral of Tournai, where his work was inspired by biblical themes. His fame, however, derives from the *Flemalle altar-piece,* executed for the monastery of F. near Liège. His work, realist in style, marks a break with the Gothic tradition.

E. Panofsky, *Early Netherlandish Painting* (1953).

Madonna and Child *by the Master of Flemalle*

FLETA Treatise on English law dating from the late 13th century and written in Latin. Its author is anonymous, but the F. is believed to have been named after him. It summarizes the great treatise of *Bracton and, in the late Middle Ages, was considered an authority on English law.

T. F. T. Plucknett, *Early English Legal Literature* (1958).

FLEURY-SUR-LOIRE Benedictine monastery in France, founded in 651. It owes its fame to the alleged transfer of the remains of St. *Benedict from Monte Cassino to F. in the late 7th century, after the *Lombards ravaged Italy. The monastery, which became a shrine of the founder of the Benedictine order, changed its name to St. Benoît-sur-Loire. Embellished under the *Carolingians, F. became an important monastic centre of learning in the 10th-12th centuries, when its Romanesque abbey church, still extant, was built.

A. Vidier, *L'historiographie à St.-Benoît-sur-Loire et les miracles de Saint Benoît* (1965).

FLODOARD OF RHEIMS (894-966) Frankish priest and chronicler. Born at Epernay in *Champagne, he was educated at Rheims and became a clerk and later a *canon of the archbishopric. Involved in the political affairs of the first half of the 10th century, he travelled to Rome and Germany and was acquainted with a great number of ecclesiastical and lay personalities of his time. Prominent among his works are the *History of the Church of Rheims,* praising the glory of the see, and the *Annals,* the most important chronicle of 10th-century France, covering the years 918-65. His personal involvement as well as his access to documents, allowed him to produce an accurate history, which is the best source of information on the later *Carolingians and the feudal conditions of France of his age. F. also wrote poetry.

P. Lauer (ed.), *Les Annales de Flodoard* (1906).

FLORENCE City in central Italy, capital of Tuscany, on the Arno River. The ancient Roman colony Florentia was often invaded in the 4th and 5th centuries. With the fall of the Roman empire in the West and the resultant political instability in 6th-century Italy, F. was dominated by various rulers until it became the seat of a *Lombard duchy in the late 6th century. F. was ruined in 774, when the Lombard kingdom of Italy was conquered by *Charlemagne. Although legend attributes its rebuilding to Charlemagne, it was probably the work of his grandson, Emperor *Lothair I, who in 825 established its cathedral school, one of the nine still extant in Italy. The Carolingians favoured the foundation of monasteries in F. and its environs and endowed them richly. In the second half of the 9th century, F. became the capital of the march of Tuscany, whose counts were promoted to the ranks of margraves. In the 10th century the counts and margraves left F. and established their residence at the castle of *Canossa, but continued to rule the city through their officials, who shared their authority with the archbishops. At the death of Countess *Matilda, and as a reward for its fidelity to the pope in the *Investiture contest, F. gained autonomy in 1115.

The city's establishment as an independent *commune coincided with the beginning of its economic development, based on the production of textiles, the quality of which reached international fame in the 12th and 13th centuries. Its commerce flourished, even though its economy began developing later than that of other Tuscan cities, such as *Pisa and *Lucca. F.'s rapid progress had an impact on its demography already in the early 12th century. The immigration of peasants to the city was an important factor in the growth of its population, and was accompanied by the weakening of the feudal nobility who had moved to F. from neighbouring areas. Demographic changes influenced the system of government. The constitution of 1138, which created a committee of consuls (from six to eight), and a council of 100 notables as the government of the city, gave representation to both the nobles and the guilds. The struggle for power between the *torri* (nobles) and the *arti* (guilds) was to a certain extent related to the broader conflict in Italy between papal and imperial parties. The struggle gave way to civil war at the beginning of the 13th century. The traditional parties lost much of their original character: in the guilds, the division between merchants and craftsmen led to the emergence of a new aristocracy, combining nobles and merchants; the *arti* split up into privileged and popular guilds (the future *calimala*). To impose order, the constitution was changed. In 1193 the office of podesta, as sole leader, was created, and to prevent conflicts it was decided in 1207 that the podesta should not be a citizen of F.

Nevertheless, violent rivalry continued unabated, with F. being divided into *Guelphs and *Ghibellines. The long series of wars weakened the nobility and strengthened the guilds, which contributed immensely to making F. a prosperous commercial centre of international importance.

In 1252 its mint produced the golden florin, which soon became esteemed in European markets and helped boost international trade. Banking became one of F.'s major economic activities in the second half of the 13th century. The decline of the nobility and the growth of guilds had political repercussions. It gave rise to a popular party, under the leadership of the *capitano del popolo* and his council of aldermen, who governed together with the aristocratic podesta. The popular party split up into upper guilds – bankers, merchants, cloth craftsmen and the liberal professions – and "democratic" guilds of less important *arti.* The latter fought for a share in government and in 1293, the "Ordinances of Justice" (*Ordinamenti di Giustizia*) recognized their right to representation on the council. Executive authority was entrusted to a new official, the *gonfaloniere di giustizia,* who ruled together with a small council of officials from the upper guilds. Until the end of the 13th century, F. expanded in Tuscany and some of the surrounding cities fell under its authority. But in contrast to other Italian republics, F. was weak, exerting little influence on Italian politics. It was also subordinate to the papacy, France, the *Angevins of Naples, the *Colonna of Rome, and other influential dynasties.

F. reached its zenith in the 14th century. The city flourished and was among the largest in Europe, with its population estimated at 100,000 inhabitants. Its fine textiles were exported throughout western Europe and its banking houses became the most important in Europe, despite the crisis which brought some of them to bankruptcy. Even as the city prospered and systematically conquered the Tuscan towns, with the exception of the littoral cities, internal conflicts never ceased.

The Guelphs, who seized power at the end of the 13th century, were soon divided into White and Black Guelphs. The latter gained control of the party in 1301 and banished their opponents, among whom was *Dante, who died in exile. The Black Guelphs, led by the large banking houses, held power until 1339, when the banks of *Bardi and *Peruzzi went bankrupt, and the duke of *Athens, Walter of Brienne, became tyrant of the city. In an attempt to win the support of the masses to consolidate his power, he drafted a new popular constitution, which gave power to the "small" guilds (*popolo minuto*). The upper guilds revolted in 1343 and expelled the tyrant, but a popular revolt in 1344 brought the small guilds back to power. In 1378 F. stood against Pope *Gregory XI, who sought to annex Tuscan territories to the papal states. Allied with Bernabo *Visconti, duke of Milan, F. became a political power in Italy. The aristocrats attempted to change the constitution, but a popular revolt of the *ciompi* led to the election of Salvestro da *Medici as *gonfaloniere*. While the revolt of the *ciompi* was repressed, the workers' guilds were recognized and, for the first time in Italian history, were allowed to join the democratic government. Nevertheless, in 1382 the ordinances of 1378 were annulled and the Albizzi family seized power, leading an oligarchy whose main concern was foreign policy. Pisa was conquered in 1406, followed by Livorno in 1421, and Tuscany was thus united under Florentine rule. F. deployed a powerful fleet, enabling it to further develop its commerce. The opposition, led by a rich family of bankers, the *Medici, who were supported by the democrats, seized power in 1423 and, after a short period of troubles in 1433-34, expelled the Albizzi and established their hereditary rule in F. Patrons of the arts and scholars, the Medici made F. the cradle of Italian Renaissance, developing and favouring the new trends which first emerged in the late 14th century.

F. Shevill, *Medieval and Renaissance Florence* (1963).

FLORENCE OF WORCESTER (d. 1118) Chronicler. He was a canon of the cathedral of Worcester and compiled a history of England from the Anglo-Saxon period to his own time. While the 13th-century manuscripts under his name cover the period until the end of the 12th century, modern research shows that the history of the period after his death was written by three anonymous writers. F. used Anglo-Saxon sources for the first part of his chronicles and his original contribution is limited to the reign of *Henry I (*c.* 1100-18). His work is marked by clarity of style and accuracy, with F. providing documentary evidence for his assertions. Much of his material was embodied in the major historical compilations of the 13th century and particularly in the universal chronicle of *Matthew Paris.

The Chronicle of Florence of Worcester, ed. and trans. T. Forester (1854).

FLOTTE, PIERRE (d. 1302) French jurist. Born in Languedoc, he studied at the universities of Toulouse and Paris. His legal and administrative skills were recognized by *Philip IV the Fair, who appointed him keeper of the seal and chancellor. He was one of the closest advisers of the king in his quarrel with *Boniface VIII over royal vs. papal supremacy. In 1302 he was sent with the French army to repress the revolt at Flanders, and was killed at the Battle of *Courtrai.

F. J. Pegues, *The Lawyers of the Last Capetians* (1962).

FOIX County in southern France founded by the feudal lords of the castle of Foix, who were vassals of the counts of Toulouse. They gradually established their authority over other vassals in the Pyrénées Valley of Ariège and profited from the rivalry between the counts of Barcelona and those of Toulouse, whom they served faithfully, to obtain the countal title, as well as a number of fiefs and seigniories. In the 12th century F. grew into an important commercial town and in the early 13th century its counts wielded great power. They supported the count of Toulouse in his opposition to the *Albigensian Crusade by troops from northern France. (The Albigenses had settled in most parts of southern France, including F.) In 1229 they had to countersign the Peace of Paris, which settled the Languedoc-Toulouse inheritance in favour of the royal dynasty. The last Albigenses converted to Catholicism in F., whose counts remained faithful vassals to the king of France following a brief attempt to acquire independence in 1270, which was repressed by *Philip III. F. prospered in the 13th century and its counts began a policy of territorial expansion in the area and in Gascony. In 1290 Count Roger-Bernard III, by marrying Margaret of Béarn, inherited the principality of Béarn, laying the foundations for the most important noble house of southern France in the late Middle Ages. In the 14th century the family inherited through marriages other important seigniories in southern France and established one of the most prestigious courts in France. The counts remained faithful to the kings of France in the *Hundred Years' War, while enjoying a large measure of autonomy, especially manifest in their relations with *Aragon. The direct line of F. counts ruled until the death of Gaston-Fébus in 1391, when a collateral branch, the lords of Castelbon, inherited their principality.

P. Tucoo-Chala, *Le Vicomté de Béarn et le problème de sa souveraineté des origines à 1620* (1961).

FOLGORE OF SAN GIMIGNANO See SAN GIMIGNANO.

FOLIOT, GILBERT (d. 1188) Bishop of London (1163-88). Of a Norman family, he became monk at *Cluny, where he distinguished himself for his learning, eloquence and austerity. In 1139 he was elected abbot of Gloucester in England, and became prominent in the English church. In 1148, he became bishop of Hereford and played a prominent role in the ecclesiastical and political affairs of England. F. supported *Matilda against *Stephen of Blois and acted as a confidential adviser to the archbishop of Canterbury, *Theobald. In 1162 he opposed the election of Thomas *Becket to the see of Canterbury and remained his rival. In 1163 he was transferred to the see of London by *Henry II, who sought its independence from the archbishops of Canterbury. F. supported the king in his struggle with Becket and represented Henry in the talks with Pope *Alexander III. In 1169 Becket excommunicated F., but the sentence was ineffective and the bishop defended himself in a series of polemical letters. In 1170 he took part in the coronation ceremony of young Henry, Henry II's son, who was crowned by the archbishop

The cloister at the Cistercian abbey of Fontenay, built in the 12th century in the Romanesque style

of York, an act for which F. and the other bishops who attended were excommunicated. After the return of Becket to Canterbury, F. fled to Normandy, seeking the protection of the king. He returned to London only after the murder of Becket by supporters of Henry. He was absolved in 1172, and continued to play a prominent role in the ecclesiastical affairs of England.

D. Knowles, *The Episcopal Colleagues of Archbishop Thomas Becket* (1951).

FONDACCO DEI TEDESCHI See VENICE.

FONTENAY *Cistercian abbey, founded in 1118 by *Bernard of Clairvaux. Its church, built between 1130 and 1147, is a significant monument of Romanesque architecture. It is distinguished for its sober lines and abstract ornaments.

L. Genicot, *Contours of the Middle Ages* (1961).

FONTENOY, BATTLE OF (841) Decisive event in the division of the *Carolingian empire. It was fought between a coalition of *Louis the German and *Charles the Bald, against Emperor *Lothair, who contested the Oaths of *Strassburg of the previous year. The victory of Charles and Louis over their brother led to the partition of the empire by the Treaty of *Verdun (843).

L. Halphen, *Charlemagne et l'Empire Carolingian* (1947).

FONTEVRAULT, ORDER OF A "double order" of monks and nuns, living in separate convents, but under the rule of one abbess. It was founded in 1100 by *Robert of Arbrissel at Fontevrault, in *Anjou, prescribing more austere rules than those of the regular *Benedictine abbeys. The order prospered under the protection of the counts of Anjou, who were kings of England from 1154. During the 12th and 13th centuries dependent houses were established in France, England and Spain. An abbey church – a masterpiece of late Romanesque architecture – was built in the mother-house at F. Cherished by *Henry II and *Eleanor of Aquitaine, it became the burial place of the Plantagenets: Henry and Eleanor were buried there, as well as *Richard Coeur-de-Lion and his wife, Berengaria of Navarre. The order reached its zenith in the 14th century, when it was one of the richest monastic houses in western Europe. It declined in the 15th century.

L. F. Bosseboeuf, *Fontevrault* (1890).

FORCHHEIM Town in *Franconia (central Germany). Due to its location at the cross-roads in Germany, it was the site of many assemblies of German princes from the 10th century convened for various purposes, such as the election of kings. The most famous of these gatherings was that of 1077, when the princes opposed to *Henry IV, who had been excommunicated by Pope *Gregory VII, assembled and elected *Rudolf of Swabia anti-king. They invited the pope to come to Germany to support their revolt. But the pope had already absolved Henry at *Canossa. The revolt was crushed by Henry.

W. Ullmann, *The Growth of Papal Government in the Middle Ages* (1955).

FORFEITURE (Latin: foriscacere "to forfeit") The term, used in feudal justice in the Middle Ages, referred to a vassal's having to surrender his fief to his lord, should he be convicted at the lord's court. The most famous illustration of F. in feudal justice, was the confiscation of *John Lackland's fiefs in France in 1200 for failing to appear at the royal court upon being summoned by his lord, *Philip II, king of France. The summons was issued after a complaint by Hugh of Lusignan, one of John's vassals in Aquitaine, who felt aggrieved at John's marrying Isabel of Angoulême after she had been promised to Hugh.

R. Boutruche, *Seigneurie et Féodalité* (1970).

FORMOSUS (816-96) Pope (891-96). After a long period of service in the church of Rome, he was created cardinal bishop of Porto in 864 and was sent by successive popes on diplomatic missions to the *Carolingian kings and to Byzantium. After his election to the papal see, he adopted an intransigent policy towards the Eastern Church, quarrelling vehemently with the patriarch of Constantinople, *Photius, whom he excommunicated, and refusing to accept as priests those who were ordained by the patriarch. Although the condemnation of Photius and his doctrines was largely accepted, F.'s extremism led to the rise of an opposition at the papal court which refused to break with Byzantium. After his death, the opposition elected *Stephen VI as pope. F. was posthumously charged with usurpation of the papal see and his pontificate was annulled. In 897 his body was exhumed and mutilated. The sentence was reversed by succeeding popes.

DTC, VI.

FORTUNATUS VENANTIUS See VENANTIUS FORTUNATUS.

FOUAGE (French) Feudal tax, paid on *feu* (fire), i.e., a hearth-tax. Until the 13th century, it was imposed by lords on their vassals, its amount varying according to local customs in western Europe. The lords eventually abandoned the practice. But in 1362 *Charles V, king of France, imposed the F. on his subjects to raise funds for the recovery of his kingdom. The F. was extremely unpopular and was cancelled by Charles in 1380.

J. Favier, *Finance et Fiscalité au Bas Moyen Age* (1971).

FOUNTAINS ABBEY A *Cistercian monastery in Yorkshire, founded in 1132. F.'s community grew rapidly and, in the middle of the 12th century, the abbey became the mother-house of eight other monasteries in England. During the latter half of the 12th century, it played a major role in the agricultural development of northern England.

G. Hodges, *Fountains Abbey* (1904).

FRA DOLCINO (d. 1307) *Franciscan friar in northern Italy. Little is known about his life and teachings

before he joined the Spiritual Franciscans movement at the beginning of the 14th century. F. preached the virtues of poverty and inveighed against the opulence of the townsmen and the church. In 1305 he tried to found a movement for poverty in the province of Novara, but was convicted of heresy by the authorities of the cities of *Novara and Vercelli, who feared the social consequences of his activity.

T. Labande-Jeanroy, *Les Mystiques italiens* (1919).

FRAGA Town in Catalonia, north of the Ebro River. F. was the site of a decisive battle in 1134, between the *Almoravides and a large Christian coalition led by *Alfonso I of Aragon, the counts of Barcelona and Toulouse and other feudal lords of southern France. The defeat of the Christians caused a dynastic crisis in Aragon and brought the *Reconquista* advances to a halt for a generation.

H. J. Chaytor, *History of Aragon and Catalonia* (1933).

FRANCE The country occupies the major part of Roman Gaul and is named after the *Franks, who conquered it under *Clovis. In the early Middle Ages its history is that of the Frankish kingdom, which also covered parts of Germany and the Low Countries. Under the *Merovingians and the early *Carolingians (until the reign of *Louis the Pious), there were no clear ethnical divisions between the various provinces of the kingdom. But cultural and linguistic differences began to manifest themselves in the 7th and 8th centuries. The province of *Austrasia was predominantly Germanic, while other provinces were to a large extent Romanized. Among these provinces, *Aquitaine became a distinct ethno-linguistic unit, especially its southern part, where the French *langue d'Oc* (the Occitanian tongue) developed. By the 9th century ethnographical division was complete: in 840, when *Louis the German and *Charles the Bald, accompanied by their vassals, met at Strassburg and agreed on the division of the *Carolingian empire, they had to pronounce their oaths in Germanic and Romance languages to make themselves understood to their respective vassals. The Treaty of *Verdun (843) made France a separate kingdom, and the frontiers delineated by the pact remained the boundaries of medieval F., with minor changes. In the north and the west, the sea formed a natural frontier; in the south the Pyrénées Mountains marked another natural, but unstable, border with Spain; in the east, the four rivers — Rhône, Saône, Meuse and Escaut (Scheldt) — separated F. from *Lotharingia and later on from the *Holy Roman empire of Germany. Even within these frontiers, the country lacked unity. The three great historical duchies — Francia in the north, Burgundy in the east and Aquitaine in the southwest — were still in various degrees a melting-pot of Gallo-Roman peoples and Germanic tribes.

The 9th-11th centuries saw the disintegration of the kingdom. The raids of the *Normans in the north and west and those of the Moslems in the south, coupled with the appearance of feudal adventurers, brought with them instability and the weakening of the kingship in the 9th century. Moreover, the feuds among the nobles in the late 9th and 10th centuries hastened the disintegration of the Carolingian administrative system and the establishment of the *châtelennies* (estates dominated by a *castle), as basic units of government.

The revival of *Breton ethnical separatism in the 9th century and the settlement of the Normans in *Normandy (911), added to the trend of anarchy. Royal authority ceased to make itself felt beyond a limited area in Picardy and Champagne (northeast F.), where the last Carolingians had their estates.

The last Carolingian king, *Louis V, died as a child in 987, and an assembly of prelates and nobles of northern F., presided over by *Adalberon, archbishop of Rheims, elected *Hugh Capet, duke of Francia, as king. He seized the opportunity of the appearance of a mission, sent by the count of Barcelona to seek help against the Moslem threat, to make his son *Robert co-ruler and thus obtain recognition for the succession of the throne. The precedent of installing an heir as co-ruler was an important one, as until the end of the 12th century it prevented contests concerning royal succession rights. Nevertheless, the Capetians' rule was marked by a constant struggle for authority over the nobles. The feudal system generated a permanent state of civil war at the end of the 10th and first half of the 11th century, which led to the disintegration of the kingdom. Attempts to restore order, such as the establishment of the *Peace of God, were initiated and carried out by the church, while the kingship was ignored. Moreover, the appearance of new social and economic conditions in the 11th century favoured the emergence of feudal principalities, such as Normandy, Flanders, Blois and Troyes, Anjou, Burgundy, Aquitaine and Toulouse-Languedoc, whose organization impeded the liberty of action of the royal power. The *Capetians, aware of their limitations, preferred to concentrate on establishing their direct rule over their counties of Paris and Orléans. This attitude – which was inconsistent with feudal practices, according to which a king was obliged to vest his domains on other vassals – saved the dynasty and created the conditions for the emergence of F. as a nation. The creation of the royal demesne, comprising Paris and Orléans, was a first step towards the organization of the royal principality, the Ile de France. The 11th-century kings were faced with an uphill battle, not only against some of the powerful feudal princes, such as the counts of Blois and Troyes who encircled the royal domain, but also against their small vassals, whose castles obstructed their freedom of movement from Paris to Orléans. Royal authority was restored only in the first half of the 12th century, by *Louis VI (1108-37), who defeated the small feudal lords by using the *Truce of God to his advantage. Moreover, by granting privileges and liberties to the *communes of northeastern F. he weakened the powerful feudal lords.

While the period of the 10th-12th centuries was one of division and weakness, it also saw the emergence of French culture and civilization, which to a large extent centred around the church. Latin culture developed in the abbey and cathedral schools. Centres such as the Burgundian and Norman abbeys, Auxerre, Poitiers, Laon, Rheims, Tours and especially Chartres and Paris, flourished, and the fame of French scholarship – particularly in theology and philosophy – spread. But the age also witnessed the birth of French popular culture in the spoken languages, with its legends of sainthood and miracles, and epic poetry in praise of *Charlemagne and his heroes, personified in the great noble families of F. National-religious feeling found its expression in the ideals of the nobility and chivalry. These ideals spread throughout the Continent and England in the 11th century. They were brought to Spain by French knights, who fought in the Reconquista wars and influenced the course of Spanish civilization. These knights returned to France with accounts of the battles against the Moslems, which were later embodied in epic poems. Norman expansion in southern Italy and the conquest of England in 1066, led to the establishment of French culture in those countries, where French became the language of the aristocracy and the courtiers. French culture was integrated into the local traditions of the empire's French-speaking territories, from Provence to Walloon Belgium. The *Crusades, in which F. played a leading role, brought French culture to the Levant, where it was adopted by the upper classes of the Crusader states. F. also developed the artistic concepts behind Romanesque architecture, the style which flourished in Europe in the 11th-13th centuries.

Although *Louis VII (1137-80) is considered by some modern historians as a weak monarch, he paved the way for the transformation of the feudal kingdom of F. into a strong monarchy. His constant wars with *Henry II prevented the Plantagenet king from imposing his rule on F. and caused dissent even in Henry's own family. Louis thus attained the respect and obedience of the kingdom's powerful vassals and enjoyed more international prestige than any of his predecessors. In collaboration with the papacy, he strengthened his authority over the churches; in 1163 Pope *Alexander III granted him the title of "most Christian king", which was to remain the hereditary title of the kings of F. until 1789. He profited from the economic development resulting from the revival of trade and growth of the cities to enrich his treasury. His son, Philip, born in 1165 from Louis' third marriage with Adèle of Champagne, was hailed as a descendant of Charlemagne, putting an end to theoretical disputes on the legitimacy of *Capetian rule. Building on the foundations laid by his father, Philip was to make France a leading power. He organized the administration; overcame his dangerous rival *John Lackland, king of England and conquered Normandy, Anjou and a large number of counties on the Loire River that were under the suzerainty of Anjou, annexing them to the royal domain. His victory at *Bouvines (1212) consolidated the conquests and extended his influence to Flanders. His consent to the participation of the barons of northern F. in the *Albigensian crusade proclaimed by Pope Innocent III, freed him of some turbulent elements in the area he was mainly interested in. By sending his son, *Louis VIII, at the head of a military expedition in the south in 1218, he was able to reap the fruits of the crusade and expand in Languedoc. Under *Louis IX, the French monarchy reached the peak of its power and influence. The efficient centralized government he installed imposed its authority on the provincial administration, leaving him to exert his influence elsewhere. He adopted the principles of feudal monarchy laid down by Philip II, who opposed the interference of the church in the political affairs of state. Louis is considered the founder of the "religion of the monarchy" in F. By the Peace of Paris (1258), he recognized Henry's lordship of *Gascony – but as a vassal of the king of F.

The Peace of Corbeil in 1259, renouncing the feudal lordship of *Catalonia, settled a long conflict with *Aragon and made Louis the arbiter of Europe.

Social and economic trends of the period favoured the monarchical system of government at the expense of feudalism. Economic prosperity brought about the rise in importance of the burghers. Their growing share in commercial activities and wealth weakened the feudal nobility, which began to depend on royal pensions. The period also saw the emergence of the *noblesse de robe*, officials who settled in the cities and studied in law schools or universities. Serfdom virtually disappeared as the peasants, too, profited from the economic boom by selling their products to the growing towns. But even as the benefits of a thriving economy accrued to all classes − except for the former feudal nobility, the main victim of the evolution − social stratification became even more pronounced. The class-consciousness of the once-powerful nobles was heightened by their practice of chivalry. And the hierarchical structure of French society in the 12th and 13th centuries lacked the social mobility that existed in England.

F. flourished not only economically but also culturally. *Scholasticism found its highest expression in the 12th-century schools of Chartres and Paris and, with the foundation of the University of *Paris in the late 12th century, it reached the peak of its influence. The convergence of students and teachers from all over Europe to Paris in the 12th century enhanced the university's prestige to the extent that it was exempt from the local bishop's authority (1231). The revival of *Aristotelian philosophy at the university and the prominent scholars who taught there, such as *Thomas Aquinas, made it the intellectual centre of Europe in the 13th century, on which other universities were modelled. Popular culture also developed. French became a learned, written language, used all over western Europe by nobles and knights. In some countries, such as England, Sicily and the Latin kingdom of Jerusalem, it even became the legal language of the courts. The burgeoning of epic poetry, which mirrored the ethos of *chivalry, and lyric poetry, developed by *troubadours in southern and western F., were important factors in the laicization of French culture. But the nucleus of French culture was 12th-century Champagne, the motherland of the romances and of the *Arthurian cycle which dominated French literature in the 13th century. Mysticism also developed under the impact of monastic reform by such personalities as *Bernard of Clairvaux. In the artistic domain, it was the age of French Gothic, which expanded from Paris to western Europe.

But economic and cultural growth gave way to stagnation and crisis in the late 13th and the 14th centuries. F., like most of Europe, was affected by a series of epidemics, the most devastating of which was the *Black Death, that caused great mortality and disrupted the economy. The crisis had political repercussions. Under *Philip IV the Fair (1285-1314) the trend of centralization persisted and Champagne was annexed to the royal domain, but the king adopted some draconian measures to replenish the treasury: he debased the coinage, and expelled the Jews (1306) and the *Templars, whose properties he confiscated. His attempts to tax the clergy brought him into conflict with the papacy, and particularly with *Boniface VIII. Philip convened the Estates General to justify his doctrine of royal sovereignty, and won its support. The dynastic crisis after Philip's death led to the establishment of rules governing French succession. According to these rules, later to be known as *Salic law, only males descended from the male line of the ruling family, were permitted to succeed to the crown. By this law, the *Valois dynasty succeeded to the throne, and the claims of the king of England, *Edward III, on behalf of his mother, Isabel, daughter of Philip IV, were a contributing cause to the *Hundred Years' War

The war broke out in 1337 and had disastrous consequences on F. The first stage, the battles of *Crécy (1345) and *Poitiers (1356), saw major English victories, culminating in the capture of French King *John II at Poitiers. The French defeats coincided with the havoc wreaked by the Black Death of 1348. Under the regency of the dauphin Charles, half of the realm was conquered by the English, while the other half was threatened by disbanded companies of soldiers, the *Grandes Compagnies*, who sought to obtain the revenues of which the cease fire had deprived them, by robbery. Revolts by the nobles, led by *Charles the Bad of Navarre, by the Parisian bourgeoisie, led by Etienne *Marcel, and by the peasants, the *jacquerie*, were the most dangerous aspect of the disaster. The necessity of

French or Flemish bronze candlestick; 14th century

raising money for the ransom of the king in such conditions, led Charles to adopt unpopular measures. He nevertheless surmounted the difficulties, and having concluded the Treaty of *Bretigny (1362), was able to deal with internal problems. The reign of *Charles V (1364-80), who continued his policy as dauphin, was a period of recovery for F. Helped by his general, *Du Guesclin, he sent the Grandes Compagnies to *Castile, where they took part in the civil war between *Peter the Cruel and *Henry of Trastamare. He replenished the treasury by revenues from the annexed provinces of the empire (Lyons in 1301 and Dauphiné in 1349), and by levying two new general taxes, the *gabelle and the *fouage. Most of the provinces lost to the English were patiently recovered by Du Guesclin and Olivier of *Clisson and economic activity was revived. During Charles' reign F. knew a period of tranquillity and relative prosperity that was to continue during the first years of the reign of his son, *Charles VI. But the king's uncles, who obtained large apanages from John II, exerted great influence and depleted the treasury for their own interests, such as supporting *Philip the Bold, duke of Burgundy, to establish his power in the Low Countries, and the duke of *Berry, the great patron of artistic revival. The madness of the king caused the struggle between various factions at the court and even outside. In the early 15th century, the rivalries between *Armagnacs and *Burgundians degenerated into open war, with political murders and Parisian uprisings. The civil war eventually became part of the Hundred Years' War. The Burgundians allied themselves with *Henry V of England who invaded F. in 1415. The English routed the French at *Agincourt, and Henry became the virtual master of northern F. He compelled Charles VI to sign the Treaty of *Troyes (1419), which recognized him as heir to the throne by his marriage with Catherine, Charles' daughter. While the Parisian parliament and the university endorsed the settlement, the opposition, led by the dauphin (later Charles VIII), renounced it. At the death of Charles VI in 1422, the dauphin was proclaimed legitimate king in Bourges, central France. After the death of Henry V, his brother and regent, the duke of Bedford, commanded the English army, which continued to advance, while Charles VII adopted a passive attitude. But the tide of the war turned with the appearance of Joan of Arc. In 1429 she lifted the siege of *Orléans and conquered Rheims, where Charles was ceremoniously crowned. Her military achievements raised the morale and national consciousness of F. Thus, despite the "maiden of Orléans" ' defeat near Paris, and her captivity and trial, which culminated in her being burned at Rouen, the French successes continued. When Bordeaux was captured in 1453, all of France was liberated, with the exception of *Calais, which remained under English rule even after the end of the Hundred Years' War.

G. Duby-R. Mandrou, Histoire de la Civilisation Française (1958).

FRANCIS OF ASSISI, St. (1181-1226) Founder of the *Franciscan order. F. was born at Assisi, in central Italy, to the rich merchant, Pietro Bernardone. Until the age of 20, F. assisted his father in his business. During a war between Assisi and Perugia in 1202, F. was taken prisoner. Returning home, he decided to abandon

St. Francis of Assisi, detail of a 14th-century fresco

his worldly life and devote himself to helping the poor. His ideals took a more concrete shape after a pilgrimage to Rome. As a result, he founded in 1208 a small congregation at Assisi, whose aim was to minister to lepers. F. drew up a simple rule of life for the community (the regula primitiva) which was approved in 1209 by Pope *Innocent III. The congregation was organized by an assembly of disciples, who called themselves "minor friars" (fratres minores), to stress their humility. In 1212 their ideals were accepted by St. *Clare, a noble woman of Assisi who had founded a similar society of women. In 1214 F. travelled through southern France and Spain, seeking to convert the Moors, but illness prevented his reaching Africa. His travels led to the organization of the Franciscan order (1217) into provinces, with superiors appointed by the General Chapter. In 1219 F. preached a "spiritual crusade" in eastern Europe and Egypt, aimed at converting the Moslems. During that journey, F. gave up the direction of the order and never resumed it, feeling that he lacked the necessary skills for its administration. He remained the spiritual leader of the Franciscans until his death; his generosity, his simple and unaffected faith, his love of nature and his deep humility caused him to be venerated as a saint within his own lifetime. In 1228, just two years after his death, F. was officially proclaimed saint by the Church.

Works, ed. and Engl. trans. P. Robinson (1906); T. S. R. Boase, Saint Francis of Assisi (1936).

FRANCIS OF MEYRONNES (d. 1326) Scientist. Born in Provence, he studied at Paris, where he was one of the first disciples of *Duns Scot. He was among the first scientists in the West to express his beliefs, adopted from Aristotelian thought, on the existence of an earth sphere, distinct from that of the heavens. In his later years he was called by Pope *John XXII to Avignon and became actively involved in the determination of papal policy. During this period, he tried to apply his scientific concepts to the field of political theory, where he opposed Dante's belief in the universal monarchy. F. established his theory of the pope's universal dominion over a Christian society, which was divided into sovereign monarchies.

P. Duhem, *François de Meyronnes* (1913).

FRANCISCAN ORDER (Ordo Fratrum Minorum)

Founded in 1209 by St. *Francis of Assisi. The order was established to allow its founder and his followers to concretize their ideal of poverty. Such an ideal had already been expressed by various Catholic reformers from the 11th century, based on the aim to return to the way of life adopted by the "Apostolic Fathers" of the Church. The F., however, tried to implement it in their daily life through their rule, *regula primitiva*. With the growth in the number of friars and the spread of the order throughout the Catholic countries, the rule was amended to suit new conditions; in 1221, St. Francis and his friend Elia da Cortona drew up the *regula prima*, which was approved by Pope *Honorius III in 1223 and became the order's constitution. According to its stipulations, neither the order nor its individual members were allowed to possess any kind of wealth; the friars were expected to preach to the people and to subsist from the donations of the faithful (hence their name *"mendicants"). The ideal of poverty prevented them from establishing monasteries and the order was organized in provinces, corresponding to the countries, with houses in the principal towns. Nevertheless, this organization implied a certain detraction from the principles of extreme poverty, and St. Francis, who no longer felt suited to run the order, passed on its direction to Cortona. Under Cortona, the interpretation of the rule led to long discussions and two main trends emerged within the F.: the Conventuals accepted reality and made attempts to reach a compromise with the established church, while the Spiritual Franciscans refused to surrender any of the primary ideals of extreme poverty. After the death of St. Francis, the conflict threatened to split the order. It was the leadership of St. *Bonaventura which brought both trends to coexist.

The F. rapidly gained popularity within Christian society as preachers and fighters for a pious cause; some, such as St. *Anthony of Padua, were venerated for their missionary activity. Their greatest fame, however, was acquired through their scholarly activity in the universities, where they taught theology and entered into the study of philosophy and science. Figures such as St. Bonaventura, *Duns Scot (at Paris) or *William of Ockham (at Oxford) became intimately connected to the development of the universities and of learning, thus contributing to the glory of the order. Their prestige brought further growth of the F., which led to the establishment of new houses and provinces throughout the entire Catholic world.

The dispute between the "conventuals" and "spirituals" was revived at the beginning of the 14th century, when the latter contested the order's policy. The teaching of the Spirituals was considered subversive and dangerous to the social order, and the *fraticelli* (the Italian Spirituals) were condemned by the ecclesiastical authorities. In 1318, the Avignon papacy openly supported the Conventuals; bulls, which allowed the F. to held collective possessions, were issued. Moreover, Pope *John XXIII condemned the Spirituals as heretics and ordered the burning of four of their leaders. Despite the repression of the Spirituals, their ideas continued to be adopted in various forms by members of the order and, during the 14th century, requests for reform were made. The dispute eventually led to the order's decline in the 14th century; many of its members were then criticized for their irregular life by such writers as *Boccaccio and *Chaucer and by thinkers such as *Wycliffe. In the 15th century the F. again flourished, but the order was split into many groups, the most important being that of the Observants, who attempted to conform to the original rule. In the 14th and 15th centuries, the Franciscans represented the Catholic Church in the Holy Land, where they established a convent on Mount Zion at Jerusalem.

J. R. Moorman, *A History of the Franciscan Order* (1968).

FRANCO OF COLOGNE (13th century) Musicologist.

He was a canon of the cathedral of Cologne, in charge of the *schola cantorum*. His musical treatise, *Ars Cantus Mensurabilis* (The Art of Measuring Chants), was the most remarkable of the period. In it he summed up the changes made during the first half of the 13th century. F. laid down the rule whereby the ear is the judge of dissonance and consonance. Perfect harmony is attained, in his judgement, when two tones blend so well that they can hardly be distinguished, while imperfect consonance occurs when two tones are sounded together, each maintaining its independence.

G. Reaney, *Medieval Music* (1960).

FRANCONIA Country in central *Germany located

between the Fulda River (to the north) and the Neckar River (to the south); its name recalls the 7th-century Frankish conquest and settlement. In 720 F. was annexed to the royal demesne of *Austrasia and became a base for the further conquests of the *Carolingians in Germany. The first urban centres of Germany – Mainz, Spires, Worms and Würzburg – were located in F. In the 8th century these centres were the bases for the expansion of Christianity over all of Germany. In 840, with the establishment of the kingdom of Germany by *Louis the German, F. became one of its duchies. Two families of counts, the *Babenbergs, in the valley of the Main River and the Conrads, counts of Worms, struggled for the ducal title (840-906); but no real ducal power was acquired in F., where the *Carolingians enjoyed strong influence. In 906 the Conrads won the long struggle; with the election of their leader, *Conrad I, as king of Germany (911-18), the duchy of F. was granted to his brother Eberhard, who organized it and attempted to rule it independently. In 939 Eberhard revolted against *Otto I, denying his royal title, but was defeated and killed. Otto then divided F. into several units, granting a great part of its territory to the bishops and to some important abbots. The remaining portion, together with the ducal title, was granted to a related branch of the Conrads, the *Salian dynasty, whose leader, *Conrad the Red, married Otto's daughter, Liut-

Late medieval houses at Frankfurt am Main

gard. From 1027, when the duke of F., *Conrad II, was elected emperor, until 1125, the Salians reigned over the empire. During this period, F. became the stronghold of the imperial power, but at the same time, it lost its historical character. Although the ducal title was temporarily granted to some of the relatives of the emperors, the major portion of its lands was given to the churches and to vassals. In addition, several towns were granted the status of *imperial cities. In 1168 *Frederick Barbarossa granted the ducal title to the bishop of Würzburg, whose successors held it until 1803. However, it no longer represented any real power, and F. was split into two large areas. In the west, the counts of the *Palatinate of the Rhine founded a principality, while the eastern section was divided up between the bishops of Würzburg and the counts of Babenberg. The Rhine cities obtained their own rights and, at the beginning of the 13th century, established the "Confederation of the Rhine", which became a state within the German state. During the *Interregnum* in Germany (1250-72), F. was further split into numerous principalities.

R. Schmeidle, *Franconia und das Deutsche Reich im Mittelalter* (1930).

FRANGIPANI Aristocratic family of Rome. In the second half of the 11th century members of the family imposed their authority over the city, controlling some of the cardinals. In the 12th century their power was contested by the *Pierleone, but the latter were un-

able to weaken their authority. In 1130 the F. succeeded in gaining the support of an important party of the cardinals for the election of Pope *Innocent II. With the support of the transalpine church, Emperor *Lothair III, and the kings of France and England, *Louis VI and *Henry I, the family continued to impose its rule. In the latter half of the 12th century, the family's power, although still considerable, began to decline. This trend continued into the 13th century, when the families of *Colonna and *Orsini acquired their position as leading figures of the Roman aristocracy.

P. F. Palumbo, *Lo Scisma del 1130* (1942).

FRANKALMOIN See ALLODIUM.

FRANKE, MEISTER (15th century) German painter. Probably born in the Low Countries, he worked at Hamburg, where he produced realistic paintings with religious subjects, among them figures of saints. In 1424, F. painted his *Sailors to England,* part of the Thomas Becket Altar-piece in the church of St. John's of Hamburg. Influenced by the Burgundian school, he developed the Late Gothic style of painting in northern Germany.

B. Martens, *Meister Franke* (1929).

FRANKFURT AM MAIN City in Germany. A fortress was first built at F., near the Main River, by the *Franks in the 7th century. *Charlemagne built a palace on the site, where he often resided with his court. In addition, he convened councils of the clergy and nobility there, the most important being that of 794, which condemned

Louis IX (Saint Louis), king of France; 14th-century reliquary at Notre Dame, Paris

† HAS · PRESVL · X̄PI · VITÆ · SOCIAS · HABVISTI ·

the canons of the Second Council of *Nicaea concerning the *Iconoclastic policy and the *Adoptionist heresy in Spain. During the 9th century F. was one of the capitals of *Franconia. The town began to grow in the 12th century under the rule of an imperial burgrave; in 1311 the city was granted full liberties and a municipal council was established. In the 13th and 14th centuries, several assemblies of German princes were held at F., and the centre of the city became the residence of rich merchants, who settled among the aristocratic palaces. *Charles IV provided in the *Golden Bull of 1356 that F. be the place of election of the emperors. The city continued to grow and the ancient Jewish quarter was annexed to it and placed under its jurisdiction. It reached the status of "free imperial city" in 1375. In the 15th century F. was one of the most prosperous cities in Germany.

F. Bothe, *Geschichte der Stadt Frankfurt-am-Main* (1966).

FRANKFURT AN DER ODER City in Germany, on the western bank of the Oder River. Founded at the beginning of the 13th century by *Franconian settlers, at the cross-roads between *Brandenburg and Poland, it developed on the basis of its location and its role in the control of trade. The city received communal privileges in 1253 and was granted self-government. In the 14th century its constant development and prosperity brought it in close relations with the *Hanse, to which it was accepted as a member in 1368. The electors of Brandenburg nevertheless imposed their authority on the city, which became part of their state in the 15th century. In 1506 a university was founded at F. on the site of its ancient synagogue.

H. Bauer, *Die Mark Brandenburg* (1954).

FRANKS A group of Germanic tribes which conquered the Roman province of Gaul in the 5th century, giving it their name, *France. The group probably originated in Pomerania on the Baltic Sea, although some historians locate their first settlements in the Danish islands of the Baltic. The earliest precise information concerning these tribes dates from the 3rd century. According to it, they were settled northeast of the Rhine and were divided into two branches: the *Salian and the *Ripuarian F. At the beginning of the 4th century, the F. crossed the Rhine and Meuse Rivers, some tribes as allies, and others as enemies, of the Roman empire. After their defeat in 358 at the hands of the Roman emperor Julian, the F. submitted to imperial authority. They were allowed to settle in Belgium, in order to protect the frontier from other Germanic tribes. There they founded a number of small tribal realms, the Salians settling the northwestern districts, while the Ripuarians established themselves at Cologne and in the region between the Rhine and Moselle. The settlement was a massive one as the Gallo-Roman peoples had left the country deserted. Among the minor Frankish kingships, the most important was that of *Tournai, whose kings, serving in the Roman army, gained status above that of the other tribal monarchs. In 451 the Salians, commanded by the Tournai king, Merovech or Merowing, took part in the Battle of *Châlons-sur-Marne, led by the Roman general Aetius against the Huns. In the following years, they expanded their territory southwards to the Somme River. In 481 *Clovis inherited the kingdom of Tournai and

imposed his authority over the Salian tribes. He defeated Syagrius, the last Roman governor of northern Gaul in 486, conquering the capital of *Soissons and extending his realm to the Loire River. Clovis then sought the allegiance of the Ripuarians with the aim of unifying the Frankish tribes. His success, together with an alliance concluded with the *Burgundians and *Theodoric, king of the Ostrogoths of Italy, enabled him to successfully fight the *Allemanni (496) and the *Visigoths, whom he defeated at Vouillé in 507, annexing the major part of *Aquitaine. The F. converted between 496-506 to Christianity, thereby enjoying the sympathy and aid of the Christian population of Gaul, which helped them against the Arian Visigoths.

At the time of Clovis' death (510) the Frankish kingdom was the most powerful in western Europe, extending over a great portion of Gaul and over large territories in Germany, part by direct rule and part, like the Allemanni, through dependent dukes. Clovis' sons annexed the Burgundian kingdom in 536, thus completing their father's great conquests.

The *Merovingian descendants of Clovis divided the kingdom between their sons. The Salian family customs were considered the fundamental law of the kingdom and were gradually codified in the 6th and 7th centuries, representing the concepts of a tribal and agrarian society. However, the kingdom did not have a monolithic law. The F. recognized a pluralistic legal system, allowing tribes such as the Ripuarians, Burgundians and Alemanni, to live according to their own legal customs, but also required the observance of Roman law. The Jewish communities were also allowed to maintain their own law, (i.e. the Talmud), which made them dependent on the great Jewish centre of Mesopotamia. The pluralist juridical system led to the establishment of personal law, whereby every free-man could be judged in accordance with his law, while the peasant classes were subjected to the laws of their landlords. The F. brought their agrarian traditions, which were more advanced than Roman agriculture, to Gaul; thus, they made use of the "three fields" (*agriculture) which provided them with an adequate solution for the lack of slaves, and they introduced the first water-mills in the 6th century. Politically, the divided kingdoms were rivals and the history of the Merovingians is marked by constant strife between the kings and their armies. Thus, during the 6th and 7th centuries, the old nobility of the pre-conquest and conquest period disappeared, together with a great many members of the dynasty. At various intervals, the kingdoms were reunited and again divided. The last union, that of *Clotaire II at the beginning of the 7th century, marked the period of the codification of the Frankish constitutions. In this respect the edict of 614 marked a turning-point leading to the pre-feudal practices of government.

Clotaire's son, *Dagobert I, was the last Merovingian monarch to effectively rule the realm. The dynasty, weakened by feuding, became dependent on a new aristocracy, which issued from the servants of the royal palaces and the bodyguards of the *antrustiones,* who served the kings and were rewarded by grants of lands from the royal demesne. The leaders of this new aristocracy were the *mayors of the palace who, in the 7th century, became powerful in the traditional Frankish kingdoms of *Neustria, *Burgundy and *Austrasia, governing the country and the kings, although the monarchs continued to be considered sacred and were symbolically distinguished by their long hair. Among the mayors of the palaces, the most important were those of Austrasia, who belonged to the Arnulf-Pepin family, later known as the *Carolingians.

In 689 the mayors of Austrasia, under *Pepin II, united the kingdoms of the F. and ruled them under their own power, disregarding the last Merovingian kings. *Charles Martel obtained the power and prestige necessary to rule the kingdom and, after the victory of *Poitiers (732), he was considered the untitled king, and he divided the kingdom between his sons, *Pepin III and Carloman (741). Pepin III went even further to dethrone the last Merovingian, *Chilperic III and proclaim himself king, with the assistance of the papacy (751). The last phase of the kingdom of the F. corresponds thus with the rise of the *Carolingian empire, being a period of political and military expansion and of social revolution, i.e., the emergence of *feudalism. Within the empire of *Charlemagne, the F. were not only leaders, but they also continued to express their identity and traditions. From the times of Charlemagne, this task was undertaken by the Frankish church, which did not share the universal views of the papacy. *Louis the Pious (829-40) tried to represent and realize the idea of the unity of the F., but was unable to prevent the outbreak of civil wars and the division of the empire, caused not only by dynastic concerns, but also by ethno-linguistic factors.

J. M. Wallace-Hadrill, *The Long-Haired Kings* (1962).

FRATICELLI In the latter half of the 13th century, this name was one of those given in Italy to the *Franciscan friars. At the beginning of the 14th century, it became synonymous with the Spiritual Franciscans, who contested the direction of the order and its conformism to the established trends of the church. In 1317, after the condemnation of the Spirituals by Pope *John XXII, the Italian friar Angelo Clareno (d. 1337) organized the F. as a separate mystical Franciscan trend.

FREDEGAR (7th century) Chronicler. Little is known about his life. Of Frankish origin, he lived in Austrasia and was employed at the court of the mayors of the palace. His book, *Historia Francorum* (The History of the Franks), is divided into three parts, the first of them summarizing *Gregory of Tours' Chronicle, while the other two describe Frankish history up to his own time. His view was that history was based on the feats of the *Franks, whom he considered the chosen people. F.'s influence was great in the 8th century. An anonymous historian completed his book by adding a fourth part, *The Chronicle of Pseudo-Fredegar*, which relates the rise of the *Carolingian dynasty.

MGH, ed. B. Krusch (1888);

J. M. Wallace-Hadrill, *The Fourth Book of the Chronicle of Fredegar* (1960).

FREDEGUND (c. 545-97) Frankish queen. Mistress to *Chilperic I, king of Soissons, she was considered responsible for the death of Galswintha, the *Visigothic wife of the king. Her marriage to Chilperic in 573 began a long feud, directed against her by *Brunhilda, queen of Austrasia and sister to Galswintha. F. was responsible for the murder of several Frankish kings, including Sigebert, and of certain nobels.

J. M. Wallace-Hadrill, *The Long-Haired Kings* (1962).

FREDERICK (d. 1189) Duke of Bohemia (1173-89). Son of *Vladislav II, he became duke through the abdication of his father. *Frederick Barbarossa, who opposed the inheritance, instead appointed F.'s cousin, Sobieslav II, who was unable to maintain authority. As a result, the emperor agreed to enfeoff F., although he reduced the duke's power by supporting *Conrad-Otto as margrave of Moravia and declaring the bishopric of Prague to be directly dependent on the empire (1187).

B. Bretholz, *Geschichte Böhmens und Mährens bis zum Aussterben der Premysliden* (1912).

FREDERICK Archbishop of Cologne (1099-1133). He was chosen by Emperor *Henry IV for this position because of his loyalty to the empire during the *Investiture controversy, but in 1114 changed his stand to support the papacy against *Henry V, whom he defeated at Andernach. He later fled to Saxony, laying an *interdict on Cologne. F. took advantage of the Investiture conflict to annex some new estates to his principality; he was successful despite the emergence of the urban movement for liberties in the diocese. In 1125 he supported the candidacy of *Lothair of Saxony as emperor.

T. Ingen, *Die Entstehung der Städte des Erzstifs Köln* (1902).

FREDERICK Archbishop of Mainz (938-54). Member of a feudal family of western Franconia, he repeatedly opposed the policy of *Otto I in Germany and was one of the turbulent feudal prelates who characterized the church hierarchy in the first half of the 10th century in Germany. Isolated after the failure of the Franconian rebellion against Otto, F. made his peace with the king and was sent in 951 to represent him in Italy. The stand he adopted concerning *Berengar II was one of compromise, which did not satisfy Otto. After his return to Germany, F. again came into opposition with Otto and an open confrontation between them was prevented only by the archbishop's death in 954.

H. Beumann and H. Buttner, *Das Kaisertum Ottos d. Groessen* (1963).

FREDERICK I, Barbarossa (1123-90) *Holy Roman emperor (1152-90). The son of *Frederick, duke of Swabia, and a member of the *Hohenstaufen dynasty. In 1147 he became duke of Swabia and accompanied his uncle, Emperor *Conrad III, on the Second *Crusade. In 1152, with Conrad's support, he was elected king of Germany, and in 1155 was crowned emperor. F. was described by contemporary sources as a beautiful young man and the incarnation of the ideals of *chivalry. Aware of the dignity of his position, he was determined to restore it to the standards of *Charlemagne. He officially proclaimed this intention in 1164 at Aix-La-Chapelle, on the occasion of the 350th anniversary of Charlemagne's death. In order to realize his ideal, he was determined to impose imperial rule over the German princes and to overcome the opposition of the papacy, which had developed its own theory of universal leadership from the time of *Gregory VII. His first important step was to proclaim the superiority of the empire at the Diet of Besançon (1156), claiming that the nobility's rights and privileges were granted by the emperor, the sole possessor of the "regalian prerogatives", a concept which, in the feudal vocabulary, was synonymous with sovereignty. In 1158, F. came to

Italy, where he fought to subjugate the independent *Lombard cities, and mainly Milan. At the Diet of *Roncaglia he promulgated constitutions aimed at imposing imperial authority over Italy. Among other things, he granted the privileges of the University of *Bologna, a precursor of future academic freedoms. His policy led him into an open war in northern Italy, but in 1162 Milan was conquered and destroyed. The Italians, however, did not give up and, with the support of the papacy and the *Welf opposition in Germany (hence the *Guelphs), organized open opposition in the form of the *Lombard League, which resisted F.'s attacks and in 1176 defeated the imperial army at *Legnano.

A more serious confrontation separated F. and the papacy. After the Diet of Besançon, Pope *Adrian IV had reiterated the principles of papal universalism, which had been expressed by his representative, Cardinal Bandinelli. When, in 1159, Bandinelli was made Pope *Alexander III, conflict became inevitable. F. attempted to impose his own candidate on the papacy, and Alexander was compelled to leave Rome and seek the support of the kings of France and England. F.'s efforts to bring the church and the monarchs to recognize an antipope failed, and in 1166 Alexander was able to return to Rome. The struggle, however, continued until 1177, when a compromise was signed at Venice; the settlement opened the way to an armistice with the Lombard League and finally to the Treaty of Constance, which recognized the urban liberties of the northern Italian cities (1182).

In Germany, F. maintained his territorial basis of Swabia and in 1156, through his marriage with the heiress of Burgundy, annexed the kingdom of *Burgundy. Throughout his reign, F. was able to obtain the cooperation of the German clergy and, with the help of his chancellor, *Raynald of Dassel, archbishop of Cologne (d. 1167), imposed his authority over the German church and the towns. Moreover, he made use of the *ministeriales in the administration in an attempt to check the power of the feudal nobility. His most pressing problem, however, was the growing power of the Welf dynasty, to whom he was related through his mother. In 1157 he invested the duchy of *Bavaria upon *Henry the Lion, duke of Saxony and head of the Welfs, while *Austria, separated from Bavaria and constituting a distinct duchy, was granted to the dynasty of *Babenberg. This move was reversed, however, after the Truce of Venice, when F. brought Henry the Lion to trial, according to feudal custom, for his refusal to serve him in the Lombard war in 1176, causing his defeat at Legnano. In 1180 sentence was pronounced by the court, depriving Henry of all his imperial benefices for felony. The remainder of the lands of the Welfs, located in the region of *Brunswick, were made to constitute a duchy, thus dividing Saxony.

The last years of F.'s reign marked the most glorious period of his rule. He was able to assert his authority in Germany, and the good relations he enjoyed with the papacy created the illusion that the great conflict between Church and State had finally come to an end. In 1184 F. met with Pope *Lucius III at Verona, where they discussed steps to be taken against heretical movements; the *Inquisition was established as a result. In 1186 F. concluded the marriage of his son and heir, Henry, to Constance, heiress of Sicily. He assumed lea-

Frederick Barbarossa and his sons; *12th-cent. miniature*

dership of the Third *Crusade (1189), but drowned in Cilicia (Asia Minor) en route to Palestine.

The figure of F. rapidly became a legendary one; he was considered the restorer of the Holy Roman empire and actual heir to Charlemagne. During the 13th century a German cult emerged which refused to accept his death; stories were told of the "old emperor with his red beard" held captive in a cave by "demons", who, it was believed, would escape and restore the "Reich" to its former greatness and splendour for another thousand years.

P. Munz, *Frederick Barbarossa* (1964).

FREDERICK II (Frederick Roger; 1194-1250)   *Holy Roman emperor from 1212, king of Sicily (1197-1250) and of Jerusalem (1226-50), also nicknamed *stupor mundi* ("the amazement of the world"). Born in Sicily, he was the son of *Henry VI and Constance of Sicily, and grandson of *Frederick I Barbarossa. At his father's death, he was proclaimed king, being three years old; in 1198 his mother also died and F. reigned under the guardianship of Pope *Innocent III and the regency of his father's German and Sicilian counsellors. Educated at Palermo, he considered himself an Italian, despite the fact that he belonged to the German *Hohenstaufen dynasty. One of the most intelligent men of his generation, F. was praised for his vast knowledge and scholarship. He was deeply influenced by the cultural background of Sicily, where Latin, Greek and Arab heritages met. Thus, he became one of the 13th-century protagonists of philology, philosophy and science, as well as of the lay spirit of learning.

In 1212, when Innocent III excommunicated Emperor *Otto IV, he sent F. to Germany to claim the throne. After his election, F. defeated Otto at *Bouvines, as the ally of *Philip II of France. F. was compelled to make concessions for his election, both to the church and to the princes, since such a union between the empire and Sicily contradicted the traditional policy of the papacy. One such concession was the Golden Bull of Eger, which recognized the privileges of the German princes and paved the way for the feudalization of Germany. Only after the issue of the Bull was F. crowned King of the Romans at Aix-la-Chapelle in 1215. Further negotiations with the papacy, together with his promise to conduct a crusade, led to his imperial coronation in 1220. His elder son, Henry, was parallelly crowned king in Germany at the age of nine, and was left to rule, guided by a council of princes and prelates. After his coronation, F. delayed his departure to the crusade and rushed to Sicily. There he crushed a feudal revolt and established a centralistic government, based on the bureaucratic service of royal officials. In 1231 he initiated constitutional reforms and issued the Constitutions of *Melfi, which made Sicily the most advanced state of medieval Europe. In the meantime, the relations between the emperor and the church had radically changed. His policy in Sicily and Italy had proven that Innocent III's hopes to control him had been unrealistic and that the papal state had become encircled by a powerful monarch. Consequently, beginning in 1225, the papacy encouraged the *Guelph elements in the Italian cities to revolt against F., while pressure was also placed on the emperor to carry out his promise of a crusade. In order to arouse F.'s interest, Pope *Honorius III arranged a second marriage for him to Isabella of Brienne, the heiress of the *Crusader kingdom. Once the marriage was secured, F. ordered Isabella's father, King *John of Brienne, to remain in Italy and to leave him the government of the kingdom of Jerusalem (1126); a special delegate was sent to Acre for this purpose. Brienne thus became another enemy of F. in Italy.

Pope *Gregory IX decided to bring the relations with F. to a head; in 1228, he excommunicated the emperor, thus giving full legitimacy to revolts against him in Italy, where the Lombard League had been revived. As a result, F. decided to carry out his projected crusade and in 1229 sailed to Acre, but not before a secret negotiation with the *Ayyubid sultan of Egypt, Al-Malik Al-Kamel was made, allowing the Christians the civil government of the holy cities of Jerusalem and Nazareth. The crusade was an unusual event since it was led by an excommunicated person for the first time; consequently, the French-speaking nobility of the kingdom of Jerusalem refused to approach F. and the same attitude was maintained by the religious and military orders of the *Hospitallers and the *Templars, while the church hierarchy, the patriarch of Jerusalem at its head, openly condemned him. F. was supported only by the German crusaders, a group of Italians and the *Teutonic order. Nevertheless, the expedition reached Jerusalem, where his opponents kept their distance and, in the church of the Holy Sepulchre, F. crowned himself king of Jerusalem. His diplomatic crusade had achieved more than any other of the 13th century, but F. had

begun it at the expense of leaving his kingdom divided and in a state of anarchy. Upon his return, he repressed the revolts in Italy and resumed his position of leadership through the Treaty of *San Germano, having been absolved by the pope.

In Germany, Henry's government had come to be entirely under the influence of the nobility, and in 1233 Henry rebelled against his father. F. came to Germany, repressed the revolt and dethroned Henry (1234), placing his son in prison for the remainder of his life. The emperor also took advantage of his stay in Germany to reorganize the imperial constitution in favour of the princes, who were called upon to assist his second son, *Conrad IV, the new king. Returning to northern Italy, F. defeated the Lombard League at *Cortenuova and, in 1238, his power seemed solidly established. He appointed his illegitimate son *Enzo as king of Sardinia and was practically the sovereign of all Italy. Gregory IX, who feared for the independence of the papacy, again excommunicated him. This struggle between F. and the church reopened the hostilities in northern Italy; in 1245, Pope *Innocent IV added a sentence of deposition and officially proclaimed any revolt against F. as legitimate; even the organization of a crusade against F. was planned. In Germany, the Thuringian Count *Henry Raspe was hailed as anti-king, but he died in 1246 and the new leader of the opposition, Count *William of Holland, fought against Conrad IV unsuccessfully. In Italy, the Lombard League again revolted in 1247 and defeated F. near Parma and then Enzo at Bologna (where the latter was taken prisoner). Even F.'s old counsellor of Sicily, Peter of Vigna, plotted to murder him, but was arrested and committed suicide while in prison. During those difficult years, F. was helped by another illegitimate son, *Manfred. In 1250 the emperor died in his palace near Luccera and was buried in the cathedral of Palermo.

Despite his full political and military life, F. also found time for intellectual occupations and ran one of the most brilliant courts of Europe. The way of life adopted at his court was based on his rationalist views. It was cosmopolitan in character and was not restricted to Christians; Moslem and Jewish intellectuals were invited to take part in activities, which followed the Renaissance style. F. also wrote a treatise on falconry, *De arte venandi cum avibus, and some Italian poems. His political and religious liberalism and tolerance were unusual for a medieval ruler and aggravated his conflicts with the church establishment.

E. Kantorowicz, *Frederick the Second* (1932);

T. C. van Cleve, *The Emperor Frederick II of Hohenstaufen* (1972).

FREDERICK I King of Sicily. See FREDERICK II, Holy Roman emperor.

FREDERICK II, of Aragon (1272-1337) King of Sicily (1296-1337). The third son of *Peter III, king of Aragon, and Constance of Sicily, he was appointed king of Sicily in order to allow the crown of Aragon to withstand the pressures of the papacy and France. With the help of the *Catalan companies he defeated *Charles II of Anjou, and in 1302 the Treaty of *Caltabellotta recognized him as the legitimate king of Sicily. He dedicated his reign to the organization of the government of the island.

S. Runciman, *The Sicilian Vespers* (1958).

FREDERICK III of Aragon (1342-77) King of *Sicily (1355-77). He began his reign under the regency of his elder sister Euphemia (d. 1359), at a time when the influence of the nobility was growing. In an effort to maintain the island's independence and repulse the repeated attempts of the Angevins of *Naples to reconquer it, he adopted a policy of cooperation with the nobility, which weakened the kingship.
S. Tramontana, *Michele da Piazza e il potere baronale in Sicilia* (1963).

FREDERICK II, of Babenberg (d. 1246) Duke of Austria (1230-46). He was the last duke of the *Babenberg dynasty in Austria. Nicknamed "the Quarrelsome", his rule was characterized by repeated wars against the neighbouring states, especially Bohemia and Hungary. In 1234 he took part in the revolt of *Henry, the son of *Frederick II; a Bohemian army sent by the emperor to dethrone him did not achieve its aim and Frederick was forced to personally lead a war against him, conquering Vienna and confiscating the duchy. After the emperor's return to Italy, F. succeeded in reversing the alliances, conquering Vienna (1239) and making his peace with the emperor. In 1245 he took part in the rebellion of *Henry Raspe, but before he was able to endanger the imperial authority, he was killed in a battle with the Hungarians.
E. Jordan, *L'Allemagne et l'Italie aux XIIe et XIIIe siècles* (1939).

FREDERICK OF MEISSEN Landgrave of Thuringia (1253-1311). Son of Henry of Meissen, landgrave of Thuringia, and Margaret, the daughter of Emperor *Frederick II, he was proclaimed candidate to the throne of Sicily in 1268, after the death of *Conrad V, being the closest kin of the *Hohenstaufen dynasty. Supported by the Italian *Ghibellines, he promised in 1270 to come to Italy; however, despite repeated commitments, nothing materialized. In 1272 the Hohenstaufen party made him their candidate for emperor, but *Rudolf of Hapsburg was elected. F. returned to Thuringia, where he ruled peacefully, annexing the march of Meissen to his principality in 1301.
J. Kempf, *Geschichte des Deutschen Reiches während des grossen Interregnums* (1893).

FREDERICK I (d. 1105) Duke of Swabia (1079-1105). F. belonged to the south German family of Büren. In 1077 he built a castle, Staufen, in his county (whence the name *Hohenstaufen, given to the entire dynasty). F. remained faithful to *Henry IV during the rebellion of the dukes of Bavaria, Carinthia and Swabia; thus, when Henry deposed Rudolf of Swabia in 1079, F. was appointed duke and was married to the king's daughter, Agnes. F.'s fidelity to the emperor was strengthened by the claims of Rudolf's son, Berthold of *Zähringen, to his duchy. Berthold was compelled to abandon his claims in 1098. In the meantime, F. established his rule in Swabia, governing it together with his servile officers, the *ministeriales.
Mediaeval Germany, ed. G. Barraclough (1961).

FREDERICK II (1084-1147) Duke of Swabia (1105-47). Son of *Frederick I, he remained a close ally of Emperor *Henry V, his uncle, but preferred to concentrate his efforts upon the affairs of his duchy, where he established a strong central government. In 1125 at Henry's death, he supported the claims of his younger brother *Conrad to the crown, but after the election of

The 14th-century clock tower at Freiburg im Breisgau

*Lothair of Supplinburg, he recognized the new emperor, although he continued to stake claim to Henry's Franconian lands. Lothair's refusal to recognize such claims ignited a long war between the emperor and F., which began with the conquest of Nuremberg and of the Rhine estates by the Hohenstaufen brothers. Despite his Bavarian alliance, Lothair was unable to seize the lands in 1128, and only in 1132 did he obtain a few limited victories, among them the conquest of Nuremberg and of a part of the western Franconian estates at Spires. However, he was forced to accept the rising authority of the Hohenstaufen family. In 1137 at Lothair's death, F. supported the election of his brother Conrad III, as emperor.

FREDERICK III Duke of Swabia. See FREDERICK I, Barbarossa.

FREIBURG IM BREISGAU City in southwestern Germany, it was founded in 1120 by Duke Berthold of *Zähringen as the commercial centre of the county of Breisgau. Due to its location at a cross-road, F. rapidly prospered during the 12th century. In 1218 it was annexed to the estates of the dukes of Urach, and in 1368 it passed to the *Hapsburgs, who made it the centre of their demesnes in western Germany. The city flourished in the 13th century, its prosperity signified by the construction of its Gothic cathedral, whose tower is 115 m high. In 1457 a university was founded in the city.
F. Laubenberger, *Freiburg-im-Breisgau* (1963).

FREQUENS Decree issued by the Council of *Constance in 1417, considered the key constitutional document of the *Conciliar movement. The F. ordered that a general council be held five years after the close of the Council of Constance, and that councils should be held regularly thereafter at stated intervals. The frequency (hence the name of the decree) of the meetings was meant to express the superiority of the council.

H. Finke, *Acta Concilii Constanciensis* (1896);

B. Tierney, *Foundations of Conciliar Theory* (1968).

FRESCOBALDI Family of bankers and traders at Florence. During the 13th century they became *Guelphs and, as such, opposed the *Hohenstaufen dynasty, especially after the death of *Frederick II (1250). In 1266 they helped *Charles of Anjou to finance his expedition to Sicily and in return, they obtained commercial privileges in the Angevin kingdom. They continued to hold these privileges in the kingdom of Naples at the beginning of the 14th century, when they became associates of the mints of Naples. At the end of the 13th century they began financing English exports and became bankers of the royal house. The crisis of 1340 dealt a terrible blow to the family, which suffered bankruptcy. Some members of the F. family were gifted writers and poets. Giovanni F. (d. 1337), having received valuable experience in England, composed a short treatise in Italian verse entitled *Some Advice to those who Cross to England,* which sums up his opinions of Italian trade with England.

A. Sapori, *La Compagnia dei Frescobaldi in Inghilterra* (1946).

FRETEVAL, BATTLE OF (1194) The battle of F., near Vendôme, west of Paris, was the first clash between the French royal army and the English and Norman-Angevin troops after the return of *Richard I, king of England, from the *Crusade and after his captivity in Germany. Richard severely defeated *Philip II, king of France, who fled, leaving behind all his baggage, documents and seals of the royal chancery. As one of the consequences of the battle, Philip decided to establish his archives at Paris, in the tower of the Louvre.

FRIARS The common title of the members of the mendicant orders, derived from the Latin *frater* "brother". The title was given especially to the *Dominicans and the *Franciscans, who were distinguished also by their mantles, respectively the Black and the Grey F. In the 14th century the *Carmelites were named the White F.

FRIDESWIDE, St. (d. c. 735) Patron saint of the city and university of *Oxford. Very little is known about her, and what genuine information there is has been mixed with 12th-century legends. F. was the daughter of a king of Mercia, who took a vow of virginity and, in order to avoid marriage with a neighbouring prince, fled to Oxford, where she lived alone for three years. There she founded a nunnery. From the end of the 12th century and until the 16th century her shrine became a place of pilgrimage. With the establishment of the university, it became customary for members of the institution to visit the shrine twice annually. In 1434 Archbishop Chichele ordered F.'s feast to be observed as that of patroness of the university.

F. M. Stenton and E. F. Jacob (eds.), *St. Frideswide Papers* (1953).

FRISIA The country of the Frisians, located on the coast of the North Sea, between the mouths of the Weser and Rhine rivers. The Frisians, who belonged to a western group of the Germanic tribes, had settled in the country since prehistoric times and had developed an independent civilization, with its own language and traditions. They were particularly involved in fishing and shepherding. In the 1st century they established contact with the Romans, who had conquered Gaul, and tried to impose their rule over F. Roman influence was only superficial and even the military service of the Frisians in the imperial army did not cause the Romanization of the country. Contact with the Romans did, however, aid in the development of commerce and F. became an important base of trade between Roman Gaul and Scandinavia. After the fall of the Roman empire, the Frisians expanded to the north of the Rhine, into the modern Netherlands, and created Great F. (5th-8th centuries), a prosperous country with a developed textile enterprise. In the 7th century Christian missionaries, mostly Anglo-Saxons, attempted to convert the Frisians, but they were opposed and some were even killed. Consequently, the missionaries sought the help of the *Franks and *Pepin II, mayor of the palace, agreed to send an army to protect them. His death and the ensuing civil war postponed the execution of the project and only in 734 was *Charles Martel able to resume the conversion activities. He also conquered "Great F." and annexed it to the Frankish kingdom. Under *Charlemagne, both political and missionary activities were continued in the northern part of F. In 802 Charlemagne ordered the compilation and promulgation of the Frisian laws. In the middle of the 9th century Norman raids isolated F. from the other lands of the *Carolingian empire, but from the 10th century on the Frisians were reintegrated into the empire of *Otto the Great.

The feudalization of F. was part of imperial policy and led to continuous confrontations with the Frisians, who were strongly attached to their tribal heritage and their village communities. Whereas the German counts of Emden succeeded in imposing their rule over East F., where a process of Germanization had begun in the 11th century, the attempts of the counts of Holland and of the bishops of Utrecht, as well as those of their vassals, to impose their rule over West and Central F., led to long wars which ended in failure. The Frisians were able to preserve their old customs and retain the self-government of their villages, although they acknowledged the overlordship of the emperors. During the 12th-14th centuries they built dykes in order to protect their villages and fields from the sea. A popular proverb of the late Middle Ages reveals the extent of their activity: "God created the sea and the Frisians the shore".

B. H. Slicher van Bath, *The Economic and Social Conditions in the Frisian Districts from 900 to 1500.*

FRIULI Country in northeastern Italy, situated between Venice and Istria. In the early Middle Ages, it was used by invading tribes as a main means of passage into Italy. Attacks were begun by the Visigoths in the 5th century and continued up to the invasion of the *Lombards in 568. The country was sacked by the *Avars in the 7th and 8th centuries. The Lombards established a duchy in F. in order to defend the country, but ducal administration was inefficient. After *Charlemagne conquered Italy in 774, he created the *march of F. and granted the new margrave, Eric, large territories in northern Italy, trying to establish a powerful unit which could be used to supervise both *Bavaria and the Avars. *Louis the Pious used the march as the instrument of his policy towards the *Croats and the

Slavs (819) and added new territories to the jurisdiction of its margrave. The importance of the march within the Carolingian empire was evident by the margraves' relationship with the imperial family. Eberhard of F. married the daughter of Louis the Pious, Gisela, and later played an active role in the negotiations between *Lothair, *Charles the Bald and *Louis the German, his brothers-in-law, which led to the division of the empire at Verdun (843). In the later years of the 9th century his descendants were among the pretenders to the crown of Italy and the imperial title; *Berengar I even imposed his rule over Italy, while similar attempts by *Berengar II brought the intervention of *Otto I of Germany. After the establishment of the *Holy Roman empire (962), F. lost its importance. Divided into seignories, it came to depend more and more upon the German emperors, until the 15th century, when it was gradually annexed to Venice.
J. K. Hyde, *Society and Politics and Medieval Italy* (1973).

FROISSART, JEAN (JEHAN) (1335-1405) Chronicler. Born at Valenciennes in Flanders, he was educated at the count's court, where he became acquainted with the manners of *chivalry and became informed about politics. In 1361 he went to England, where he served as secretary to Queen Philippa, wife of *Edward III. In this capacity he began to gather material for his chronicles and travelled to several princely courts in western Europe. His main work was his *Chronicles,* written over a long period of time and covering the period 1127-1400, the time of the *Hundred Years' War. These proved to be one of the most valuable sources for the history of western Europe in the 14th century, despite the fact that the work was not systematic nor was any distinction made between principal and secondary facts. A great part of the book contains various stories on knights and their adventures, as well as court gossip. Although such fragmentary information is of little importance for the historical evolution of France, England and the Low Countries, the material is useful for the study of everyday life amongst the nobility of the 14th century. The chronicles have been edited by S. Luce, G. Raynaud and A. L. Mirot (1869-1957).
H. Wilmotte, *Froissart* (1958).

FUERO Spanish term which originally meant charters of liberties or privileges, issued by kings or other great territorial lords in order to encourage the resettlement of territories conquered from the Moslems in the 10th-12th centuries. While the term, usually in the form of *F. Real* (Royal Charter), continued to be used in this way in Castile during the 13th and 14th centuries, it came to be used in the kingdom of *Aragon to designate assemblies convened by the kings, which dealt particularly with economic affairs, such as the raising of taxes. In the 15th century, it became synonymous with the assemblies of the estates.
P. E. Russell, *Spain* (1973).

FUJIWARA One of the most ancient and powerful feudal dynasties of *Japan. The founder of the dynasty, Kamatari, of the house of the priests of Shitu, was made a noble in 669 as a reward for his services to the empire in the capacity of minister of the imperial court. The F. became one of the five noble families which were allowed to marry into the imperial family, and they took advantage of their kinship with the emperors to increase their political power. From the 9th century, when Yosiphusa F. became prime minister (852), to the 12th century, they practically governed Japan. The family reached the height of its power under Mitchinaga F., who governed the country tyrannically (996-1028). In the 12th century their power was contested by other feudal families and they began to decline, but nevertheless maintained great influence until the modern epoch.
R. K. Reischauer, *Early Japanese History* (1937).

FULBERT, St. (960-1028) Bishop of Chartres (1007-28). Born in Italy, probably near Rome, he studied under *Gerbert of Aurillac at Rheims and, after Gerbert's departure from Rheims, moved to Chartres, where he was appointed chancellor of the bishopric and principal of the cathedral school (990). As a result of F.'s work, the school became the most famous in Europe, attracting scholars interested in the sciences, which were taught at Chartres on the basis of Arab studies. F. himself was famous for his broad knowledge, which extended to all the sciences studied in his days. When he became bishop of Chartres, he continued to concentrate his efforts on the development of the school, but also paid attention to political issues, becoming a distinguished statesman, and enjoying the confidence of the king of France, the duke of Aquitaine and the count of Blois and was sent on diplomatic missions to Rome. He arbitrated many local conflicts and, upon the request of the duke of Aquitaine, defined, in a famous letter, the principles of *feudalism, especially the mutual obligations of lords and vassals. He also proved himself a notable builder and constructed the cathedral of Chartres, of which only the crypt remains, while the other parts were replaced by the extant Gothic building.
Works, *PL,* vol. 141;
H. Johnstone, *Fulbert of Chartres* (1926).

FULCHER OF CHARTRES (1058-1127) Chronicler. Born in the county of Chartres, he studied at the cathedral school of Chartres where he later became a clerk. In 1095 he attended the Council of *Clermont and took part in the First *Crusade as chaplain to *Baldwin of Boulogne, whom he accompanied to Edessa and later (1100) to Jerusalem, where Baldwin was crowned king. While maintaining his position at the royal court, F. became canon of the Holy Sepulchre, where he retired after Baldwin's death. He wrote a chronicle of the First Crusade and of the first generation of the Latin kingdom of Jerusalem, which is one of the most important sources today. His work concerning the first 25 years of the kingdom of Jerusalem is especially valuable, being the sole eyewitness acount of the events.
H. S. Fink (ed.), *Fulcher of Chartres, A History of the Expedition to Jerusalem 1095-1127* (1969).

FULDA The *Benedictine abbey of F., located in northern Franconia, was founded in 744 by St. *Boniface and his disciple St. Sturmius, to assist in missionary work in Saxony. The site of Boniface's tomb, the monastery attracted many pilgrims and it became one of the richest abbeys in Germany. Under Abbot *Rabanus Maurus (822-42), F. became one of the most important intellectual centres in Europe. Its library was famed for its rare manuscripts, some of which are the sole extant copies of certain classical and medieval texts. In the late 10th century, the abbots of F. were given certain rights over the Benedictine monasteries of Germany. A borough emerged near the monastery and gradually became an important town.

P. Lehmann, *Fuldaer Studien* (1925).

FULK I, the Red Count of Anjou (909-45). He was a feudal adventurer, one of the vassals of *Hugh the Great, duke of Francia, who established his rule over Anjou, having conquered Nantes. He fought against the neighbouring lords and sought the recognition of Hugh. In 919 he lost Nantes and concentrated his efforts on firmly establishing his rule in Anjou.

FULK II, the Good Count of Anjou (c. 945-60). Heir of Fulk I, he maintained relations with *Hugh the Great and was noted as protector of the abbeys of Anjou.

L. Halphen, *Le Comté d'Anjou au XIᵉ siècle* (1909).

FULK III, Nerra Count of Anjou (987-1040). Son and heir of Geoffrey I Grisegonelle (Grey Tunic), he is considered as the real founder of the *Angevin feudal state in the Middle Ages. Taking advantage of the election of his lord, *Hugh Capet, as king of France and of the dissolution of the duchy of *Francia, F. annexed a number of seignories in western France, which had previously been dependent on the dukes, to his county and founded a mighty principality. During the same period, he was active in Aquitaine, where, by means of inheritance, family claims and conquests, he enlarged the county of Anjou and established an Angevin seignory at Saintonge. He was lord-guardian of many great abbeys in northwestern France, including the richly endowed abbey of *Vendôme, where he enjoyed the rights of founder. As such, he controlled their large estates and used their vassals. In his last years he entered into a prolonged conflict with the counts of Blois. As ally of King *Henry I, he aimed to conquer the county of Tours. While he achieved the conquest of a part of the county, the city itself fell only after his death.

L. Halphen, *Le Comté d'Anjou au XIᵉ siècle* (1906).

FULK IV (Foulques le Réchin) Count of Anjou (1068-1109). Younger son of Count *Geoffrey Martel, he inherited the Angevin possessions in Aquitaine upon his father's death (1060). Involved in local feudal conflicts, he lost authority over Saintonge. He subsequently travelled to Anjou, where he rebelled against his brother, Geoffrey le Barbu, imprisoned him (1067) and in 1068 became count. Although contested by King *Philip I, the duke of Aquitaine and the count of Blois, who were intent on profiting from F.'s illegitimate seizure of power, F. compelled them to finally recognize him as count. In 1094 he made his peace with the church, obtaining from Pope *Urban II the absolution of his excommunication. He destroyed some of the vassals within the county, reintroducing order, and he fought *William the Conqueror, king of England and duke of Normandy, for the suzerainty of the county of Maine. In 1100 he succeeded in annexing Maine, which compensated for the loss of the Saintonge estates. In 1103 his elder son, Geoffrey, with the support of the duke of Aquitaine, rebelled against him. Only the death of Geoffrey in 1106 prevented the county from being divided again. Aside from his political activity, F. was also a literary man and a chronicler; he wrote *The Deeds of the Counts of Anjou*, in which he relates his conquests to support his claims.

O. Guillot, *Le Comte d'Anjou et son entourage au XIᵉ siècle* (1972).

FULK V (1095-1143) Count of Anjou (1109-28), king of Jerusalem (1131-43). Son of *Fulk IV and Bertrade of Montfort, he was taken by his mother to the royal court where she became the mistress of King *Philip I. Sent to Anjou by the duke of Aquitaine in 1101, he was imprisoned for some years before being released in 1108. His father entrusted him with the government of Anjou. As count, F. was concerned with the organization of the administration and the defence of his county. He built fortresses and castles to maintain peace and devoted his efforts to asserting his rule over the various parts of the Angevin county. His patient work led to the creation of a powerful state in western France, which became the best organized feudal principality in western Europe. His main concern was with the relations with Normandy, since he feared the great power of King Henry I of England, duke of Normandy. He therefore supported the claims of *William Clito, Henry's nephew, but after 1125 reversed his policy and began to negotiate with Henry. The king of England, who was concerned with the fate of the succession to the throne after the loss of his son William Aetheling in 1120, decided to remarry his childless daughter, Matilda, widow of Emperor *Henry V. F. and Henry agreed to the marriage of Matilda to his son, *Geoffrey Plantagenet, stipulating that the couple would immediately receive the county of Anjou and be declared heirs of England and Normandy. Thus, F. laid down the basis of the Angevin, or Plantagenet empire, which was to be realized by his grandson *Henry II. After the death of his first wife, F. went to the Holy Land on a pilgrimage. In 1128, having abdicated his county to his son, he decided to spend the remaining years of his life in the Crusader kingdom.

F. arrived in Jerusalem in 1129, at a time when inheritance to the crown was in dispute; since *Baldwin II had no sons, his heiress was his daughter *Melisande, whom he gave in marriage to F. in order to avoid feuds of the local barons. The marriage was secured despite the great difference in age between them and despite Melisande's inclination for the count of Jaffa, and F. was proclaimed heir. In 1131 F. was crowned king of Jerusalem. He began his reign by crushing a revolt of the nobles, led by Count Hugh of Jaffa, whom he expelled from the Holy Land (1132). He imposed his authority over the barons of Jerusalem and over the northern principalities, which he protected against the rising power of the Moslem princes of Mosul and Aleppo. F.'s reign marked the zenith of the Crusader kingdom. He kept the peace, maintaining good relations with Damascus, a policy which allowed him to consolidate and organize the realm. F., experienced in the building of fortresses, also created a system of defence for the kingdom by constructing several fortresses in southern Palestine. F also organized the administration of justice in the high court.

H. E. Mayer, *Studies in the History of Queen Melisande* (1972).

FULK OF BENEVENTO (12th century) Chronicler. A monk at the monastery of St. Sophia of Benevento, he was responsible for writing its annals and running its library. His chronicle presents the history of the Norman conquest of southern Italy up to the foundation of the kingdom of Sicily by *Roger I. The numerous bits of harsh criticism directed at the Norman leaders in his text indicate F.'s antagonistic attitude toward the Norman conquerors.

Rerum Italicarum Medii Aevi Scriptores, ed.
L. Muratori (1778).

FULK OF MARSEILLES (c. 1151-1231) Bishop of Toulouse (1205-31). Born to a family of rich merchants of Marseilles, he remained in the family business, frequently travelling to Italy. Also a gifted poet, he became a *troubadour and composed love songs in Provençal. In 1195 he abandoned secular life and became a monk at the monastery of Thoronet. Transformed into a very pious man, he made remarkable progress in theology and was elected abbot of the monastery. In 1206 he was appointed bishop of Toulouse. In that capacity he attacked the count of Toulouse for his tolerance of the *Albigenses. F. was one of the most energetic opponents of the Albigenses and gave his support to the Crusaders. He was responsible for making the University of Toulouse a scholarly centre of the Catholic faith.

J. Laffont, *Foulque, évêque de Toulouse* (1948).

FULK OF NEUILLY (d. 1202) Preacher. F., of humble origin, was the parish priest of the village of Neuilly-sur-Marne near Paris. Interested in intellectual pursuits, he often visited the Parisian schools, where he became a student of Peter the Cantor. His teacher discovered his talent for preaching and encouraged him to make use of it throughout the country. He became famous in 1195 and his sermons began to attract large audiences. In 1198, Pope *Innocent III appointed him to arouse a French following for the Fourth *Crusade. Despite his low rank in the church hierarchy, he was allowed to choose his own assistants from the religious orders. F. envisioned the crusade as a spiritual activity and preached that participation would lead to penance and the adoption of a pure religious way of life.

P. Alphandéry-A. Dupront, *La Chrétienté et l'Idée de Croisade* (1959).

FULRAD (d. 784) Abbot of *St. Denis. F. was a member of *Pepin the Short's court and became his chaplain *c.* 749. In 750 he was sent to Rome, together with Bishop *Burchard of Würzburg, to prepare the proclamation of Pepin as king of the Franks. Although abbot of St. Denis, he continued to be a counsellor of the king, who sent him in 755 to Italy to restore Pope *Stephen II, who had fled from the Lombards. In 756 he was responsible for the election of Desiderius, who was loyal to Pepin, as king of the Lombards. After Pepin's death, F. continued to enjoy the confidence of *Charlemagne, who maintained him as chaplain of the kingdom. F. took advantage of his high position to obtain donations in Alsace, Franconia and Bavaria for his monastery. He used the revenue to build a new abbey church, which remained intact until the 12th century; parts of the church can still be found in the Romanesque and Gothic basilica.

L. Halphen, *Charlemagne et l'Empire Carolingien* (1947).

FUSTAT City in Egypt, on the Nile, part of the old city of modern *Cairo. The town originated from a military camp established in 642 by Amr-Ibn-Al-Aas, the Arab general who conquered Egypt. The camp, organized according to the tribal division of the Arabs which existed in the early times of Islam, also served as the government centre and gradually developed into a city. In the 8th century the tribal make-up of F. disappeared and new inhabitants, among them Islamized Egyptians, *Copts and Jews, settled there. Under the *Tulunid governors of Egypt, the city flourished; new aristocratic quarters were built and the centre of the town became an important market-place, where merchandise from the Far East, brought to Egypt via the Red Sea, was shipped westward via Alexandria.

M. Hassan, *Les Tulunides* (1933).

FYRD Anglo-Saxon term which denoted the military service of the free-men and, by extension, the popular militia of the kingdoms in England. The F. was organized within the shires, each *hundred being obligated to provide military service. *William the Conqueror maintained the institution after the *Norman Conquest of 1066, using it mainly for fiscal purposes.

B. Lyon, *A Constitutional and Legal History of Medieval England* (1960).

G

GABELLE Medieval French term originally denoting any form of indirect tax. The term seems to be of Sicilian origin, deriving from the Arabic *qabala* (tax) and not, as usually suggested, from the Latinized German *gavalus* (a tax on corn due from arable land). As early as the 13th century, the G. appeared in France as a tax on consumption goods. From the 15th century onward it applied to the tax levied on salt consumption, since salt was used by all parts of the population for preservation of food, making it an ideal object of taxation. In some regions in France the G. meant the compulsory purchase of salt from the state monopoly. The clergy, the nobility and other privileged persons were exempt. One of the most hated institutions of the *Ancien Régime*, the G. was abolished only in 1790.

G. Dupont-Ferrier, *Etudes sur les institutions financières de la France à la fin du Moyen Age*, II (1932).

GABES Harbour in Tunisia, in the Gulf of G. The ancient town was used by the *Vandals as a port and also became a Byzantine naval base in the exarchate of Africa (533). Conquered by the Arabs in 648, it was used as an important military base for their further expansion into the northwestern parts of Africa. The harbour also served the Arab fleet, which attacked Sicily in 667. In a later period, G. became an important commercial centre, and its harbour was used by pearl fishermen. Claimed by the kings of Sicily, it was conquered by *Roger II in 1148.

CHI (1970).

GABIROL SOLOMON BEN JUDAH, IBN (c. 1020-c. 1058) Jewish poet and philosopher, also known in Arabic as Abu Ayyub Suleiman Ben Ihiya Ibn Gabirol and in Latin as Avicebron. Born at Malaga, in southern Spain, he was educated at Saragossa, in Aragon. Being of ill health, he concentrated his efforts on intellectual work, and especially on poetry. In 1045 he wandered through the cities of Moslem Spain, residing at Granada and then Valencia, where he died at the age of 38. During his short life, G. wrote about 20 volumes of poetry and philosophical treatises, the most important being the *Book of the Perfection of the Soul*, which was translated into Latin as *Liber de Anima* and became very popular in Europe. A second important philosophical treatise was his *Source of Life* (*Fons Vitae*), preserved only in the 12th-century Latin translation. G. made use of the Socratic dialogue, although he avoided the Platonic method of discussion; much of his work indicates the influence of Aristotelian thought. The core of G.'s philosophy was that the various things existing in the universe are made up of a combination of matter and form, which are harmoniously arranged into the Great Form. Spiritual forms, which are superior, influence matter by means of the radiation of reason, which emanates from the soul. While the forms are related to the study of their effects, they are created and determined by the development of the Great Form, which directly emanates from the divine will. Faith, leading to revelation, can aid in the understanding of actions of the sovereign divine will.

While the philosophical works of G. were written in Arabic, his poetry was composed in Hebrew, probably as a result of biblical and Talmudic influence. He composed both lay and religious poems, including praise of his friends and patrons, elegies for great personalities, and the praise of nature. G.'s religious poems became very popular and were introduced into the Jewish liturgy.

Poems, ed., in Hebrew, H. Schirmann (1953);
Philosophical works, ed., with Engl. trans., S. Wise (1902);
J. Millas-Vallicrosa, *Selomo ibn Gabirol como poeta e filosofo* (1945).

GABRIEL RADOMIR Tsar of the *Bulgarians (1014-15). Son of Tsar *Samuel, he tried unsuccessfully to organize the Bulgarians after their defeat. The Byzantine Emperor *Basil II continued to apply pressure and, as a result, a group of Bulgarian nobles arranged for him to be murdered.

S. Runciman, *The First Bulgarian Empire* (1932).

GADDESDEN, JOHN OF (d. 1361) Surgeon. Born in England, he practised dental surgery and developed new instruments for extracting teeth. Well versed in Byzantine and Arab work undertaken in this field, he is considered the father of west European dentistry.

C. J. S. Thompson, *The History and Evolution of Surgical Instruments* (1942).

GAETA City in Italy, located between Rome and Naples, being an important port at the beginning of the Middle Ages. Conquered by the *Ostrogoths at the end of the 5th century and by the Byzantines in the middle of the 6th century, G. enjoyed a great deal of autonomy, although it was influenced by the Byzantine system of local government. The city was entrusted to a group of oligarchic families, which appointed the town officials. G. was able to organize its own fleet and to fight off Arab invaders during the 7th to 9th centuries. During the same period, the port became one of the commercial centres connecting Italy, Byzantium and the Moslem world. During the 9th century, the city was attacked by Moslems from north Africa and its overlordship was contested between the papacy, the Byzantines and the Lombard nobles. The nobles seized the countryside, establishing feudal forms of government. In 877, a local family, related to one of the collateral branches of the Lombard dynasty of dukes of *Benevento, seized power in the city and formally recognized Byzantine overlordship. During the 10th century, the lords of G. conquered the countryside and proclaimed themselves dukes.

13th-century marble statue of St. Genevieve, now at the Louvre, Paris

At the beginning of the 11th century, they became closely related, through a series of marriages, to the Lombard princes of southern Italy. They were able to check the process of feudalization, due to their profits from the prospering commercial activities of the city. In 1073, G. was conquered by the *Normans, but preserved its autonomy under the counts of Aversa until 1136, when *Roger II of Sicily annexed it to his kingdom. In 1225 Emperor *Frederick II rebuilt the 8th-century fortress in order to control the city, where a pro-papal party had become active. During the 13th and 14th centuries, the city was disputed between the papacy and the kings of Sicily and Naples. It was annexed to the kingdom of Naples in 1435 by the Aragonese king, Alfonso V.

O. Gaetani di Aragone, *Memori Storici della Citta di Gaeta* (1879).

GAETANI See CAIETANI.

GAINAS Gothic leader (4th century). He commanded the invasion of the Goths in the Balkans at the end of the 4th century and, after the death of Emperor Theodosius (395), became the virtual ruler of the Eastern Roman empire, appointing Gothic officials and Arian priests in the Balkans. In an attempt to overthrow G., Emperor *Arcadius allied himself with the *Huns, calling on them to move westwards from the steppes of modern Ukraine. G. was defeated by the Huns in 401 and killed in battle.

E. A. Thompson, *A History of Attila and the Huns* (1948).

GAISERIC See GENSERIC.

GALATA The commercial quarter of *Constantinople, on the northern shore of the *Golden Horn. Until the 11th century, G. was isolated from the city itself and developed as a settlement of Italian merchants within the capital of the Byzantine empire. During the 12th and 13th centuries the influence of the *Venetian colonies was dominant in the quarter but, after 1261, the *Genoese colony obtained privileges and was allowed self-government under one of the consuls of the city. In 1453, G. was conquered, together with Constantinople, by the *Ottoman Turks, who transferred the Greek-Orthodox patriarchate there.

G. Young, *Constantinople* (1945).

GALICIA Russian principality in the Middle Ages. The territory, located north of the Carpathian Mountains, between the upper Vistula and upper Dniester rivers, was settled in the 6th-9th centuries by Slav tribes, some of whom had emigrated to the west and south. The country was named after the fortified town of Halitch, which, in the earlier Middle Ages was a trade centre for the tribes. At the beginning of the 10th century, G. was conquered by the Poles and became part of the state of Poland, despite the ethnic difference between the Polish tribes and the local Slavs. In 981, the prince of Kiev, *Vladimir the Great, conquered the country and annexed it to his state. After his death, the country became a scene of war between the Polish state and the Russian princes; it changed hands frequently until it was finally conquered by the latter in 1087. According to the division of Russia between the princes of the dynasty of *Rurik, G. was given to the sons of Vladimir (son of *Yaroslav I of Kiev). These divided the principality amongst themselves, under the authority of Prince Rurik, who settled at the beginning of the 12th century

at Halitch. A state of anarchy reigned in the country until the beginning of the 13th century, when Roman, the son of Prince Mstislav of Kiev, representing another branch of the dynasty of Rurik, was granted G. by the council of princes. He imposed his authority over the Ruthenian princes and founded a powerful state bordering Kiev, Poland and Hungary. His son Daniel proclaimed himself king of Vladimir-Halitch and was able to maintain his power after the Mongol invasion, led by *Batu-khan (1241-42). G. preserved its independence until 1340, when the dynasty of Rurik died out. During this period, the country developed and cities were founded, among them Lvov, which became the commercial centre of G. and, in the 14th century, the residence of the princes. Annexed to Poland, G. was inherited in 1370 by *Louis, king of Hungary, constituting a separate principality in the kingdom of *Hungary. At the beginning of the 15th century, it was inherited by *Jagiello of Lithuania.

B. D. Grekov, *Kiev Rus* (1959).

GALICIA Province in the northwestern part of the Iberian peninsula. In the 5th century the country was conquered by the *Suevi, a Germanic tribe which settled in the valleys of the Miño River and its confluents. In the 7th century G. was annexed to the *Visigothic kingdom, remaining under its rule until the Moslem conquest of 711. The Arabs, however, did not conquer G., where independent principalities emerged during the 8th century. In the 9th century these regions were united as part of the kingdom of *Asturia. During the 9th and 10th centuries, G. was subjected to Norman raids which destroyed the political unity of the principality. The *Ummayad vizier of Cordoba, *Al-Mansur, took advantage of the disorder to conquer the country in 997; however, he was unable to maintain his rule in a hostile environment and, at the beginning of the 11th century, his army was compelled to withdraw. G. became one of the bases of the Spanish *Reconquista and knights who departed from its territory conquered the areas of the kingdom of *León, which encircled G. The supposed "discovery" of the bones of St. James in the small town of Compostela in G. attracted masses of pilgrims from all over western Europe and, in the 11th and 12th centuries, the pilgrimage of St. James became one of the most important, so that Compostela grew and its name was changed to *Santiago. During the 11th to 13th centuries, when the Spanish kingdoms were not yet united, G. unsuccessfully struggled for its independence. Only occasionally, such as in 1063-72, did its nobility attain the degree of freedom reached by the neighbouring realm of León. The country was eventually included in the kingdom of *Castile, becoming an integral part of it in the 13th century.

P. David, *Etudes historiques sur la Galicie* (1947).

GALILEE Province of northern *Palestine, lying between the Mediterranean Sea and the Jordan River; while the Litany River was its northern boundary, its southern borders were not fixed, and during certain periods the province included the Plain of Esdraelon. Under Byzantine rule, G. was part of the province of ancient Palestine, whose capital was Tyre. It included a prominent Jewish settlement, inhabiting its cities and villages, whose centre was the city of Tiberias. The non-Jewish population was converted to Christianity and churches were built in the holy places, such as *Nazareth and the area of the Lake of Gennesaret, at Capernaum and Tabiha. The Jews fought for their independence and periodical revolts broke out against the imperial power. The rovolt of 529 was cruelly repressed by *Justinian and a great part of the Jewish settlement was destroyed. Nevertheless, the Jews' supply of provisions continued to be very important in the country and sustained the *Persians against the Byzantines. In 614, when King *Chosroes invaded the country, the Jews helped him militarily. After the Byzantine reconquest by *Heraclius, a large part of the Jewish population was massacred. In 636, the Arabs conquered the country, which became part of the province of Jordan (*Jund Al-Urdun*), establishing their capital at Tiberias. In the latter half of the 7th century and during the 8th century, a strong trend of Islamization was evident in the province, although the Christian and Jewish populations continued to be of significance. In 1071, the *Seljuks conquered the interior of the province, while the coastal area continued to belong to the *Fatimid caliphate of Egypt.

The *Crusaders appeared in G. in 1099. *Tancred, a Norman prince of south Italy, conquered the interior of the country, together with Tiberias, and established the "principality of G.". The coastal cities were conquered later and were kept separated from the principality; they were generally taken over by the royal demesne, such as in the cases of *Acre (conquered 1104) and *Tyre (1123), or they were granted to feudal barons (as was Haifa, in 1100). The principality of G. was organized as a feudal barony, granted by the kings of Jerusalem. After the departure of Tancred to *Antioch (1102), it was enfeoffed to a family of knights, originally of St. Omer in Flanders, which was faithful to King *Baldwin I. The princes concentrated their power in Tiberias, while other cities were granted to their vassals. The churches and abbeys were also granted important estates, especially the *Cluniac monastery of Mount Tabor (1102). The location of the principality required the building of a great number of castles; some of these were given to the orders of the *Hospitallers, *Templars and *Teutonic knights. In the latter half of the 12th century the principality was inherited by the counts of *Tripoli, who fortified Tiberias. *Raymond III (1163-87) was the most distinguished leader of the moderate barons of the Latin kingdom of Jerusalem and tried to reach an understanding with *Saladin. The negative attitude of the extremist party of barons, led by *Raynald of Châtillon, prince of Transjordan, caused his attempts to fail, and the repeated wars led to the decisive defeat of the Crusaders at *Hattin (1187). Thus, G. was conquered by Saladin and, even after the establishment of the second kingdom of the Crusaders (1192), the principality was not re-established. With the help of the European participants in the Crusades at the beginning of the 13th century, a part of the country was restored to the Crusaders, but this area did not extend further than Tiberias and its surrounding localities. The most important city in 13th-century G. was Safed, where the Templars built a great citadel. In the latter half of the 13th century, the *Mamelukes gradually conquered G., making Safed the capital of their provincial government in the 14th and 15th centuries.

M. W. Baldwin, *Raymond III of Tripoli and the Fall of Jerusalem* (1936).

GALILEE In medieval cathedrals and abbey churches the outer portal of the building, together with an entrance hall, was called the G., since it symbolized the entrance to the *Holy Land. It was customary to erect a chapel within the G., where penitents were brought before being admitted to the main church.

GALL, St. (550-645) Missionary. Born in *Ireland, he was one of the 12 disciples who accompanied St. *Columban to Gaul, where he was one of the founders of Luxeil. In 612, he left St. Columban and Luxeil and devoted himself to the conversion of the Swabian people to the Christian faith, working in the area which is now the German-speaking part of Switzerland. In his later years, he became a hermit and lived, according to tradition in St. Gallen, which was named after him. G. was symbolically portrayed in medieval art as a bear.

B. Krusch, *MGH, Scriptores Rerum Merovingicarum*, IV (1902).

GALLICANISM The collective name for the body of doctrine which asserted, to a greater or lesser extent, the freedom of the Roman Catholic *Church, especially in France, from the ecclesiastical authority of the papacy. While the definition of G. was realized in modern times, its foundations lay in the Middle Ages. Such doctrines were taught at the *Sorbonne from its inception in 1257, and they supported the claims of the French church for a privileged position in its relations with the papacy. Such claims were expressed at the beginning of the 14th century by the lawyers of King *Philip IV the Fair, in his quarrel with Pope *Boniface VIII, as *libertés de l'Eglise gallicane*, meaning, primarily, the prerogative of the king to assemble the clergy and employ it for the sake of the state without the interference of the pope. During the *Great Schism and the *Conciliar period (1378-1439), the theory also received a theological form; theologians such as John *Gerson and Peter d'*Ailly asserted the rights of the assemblies of the Gallican church, on the basis of historical traditions, to discuss problems of dogma and to establish rules, without need of specific approval from the pope. This view did not, however, prevail and, in the 15th century, G. came to mean the right of the king to nominate or accept bishops. Thus, the medieval form of G. tended to express the notion of the sovereignty of the kings of France and of its church.

V. Martin, *Les Origines du Gallicanisme* (1939).

GANDERSHEIM Monastery of nuns in Saxony, founded by *Otto I the Great. Under imperial patronage, the abbesses were appointed from the Saxon dynasty. The convent became one of the most highly reputed cultural centres of the Ottonian Renaissance in Germany. The literary works composed by the nun *Hrosvitha testify to its cultural level.

F. G. E. Raby, *A History of the Christian Latin Poetry* (1927).

GAOL DELIVERY A writ of *Edward I, king of England, commissioning justices to the prisons ("gaols") of the kingdom, in order to return captives who had been unjustly imprisoned. The justices were usually assisted by local notables, such as knights and prominent burghers of the shires.

B. Lyon, *A Constitutional and Legal History of Medieval England* (1960).

GAON (Hebrew: "the Illustrious") Title granted to the great masters of the Jewish Talmudic academies. Although the term was originally employed as a personal title granted to the most outstanding masters, it became institutionalized in 6th-century Mesopotamia to designate the heads of the Talmudic academies of Sura and Pumbedita, who were recognized as the supreme religious authority for all Jewry. The G. was appointed by the members of the academy with the approval of the *exilarch. The gaonate helped to maintain the unity of the Jews in the Diaspora, both through its legislation and through interpretation of the precepts, which was carried out by the *responsa (answers) to questions sent to the G. by various communities. These responsa were decided upon by means of discussions carried out within the academy. The Mesopotamian gaonate reached the height of its prestige in the 10th century – the age of *Saadia Gaon, but the political split in the Islamic world at this time created difficulties of communication between the western communities in both Moslem and Christian countries. Through the growth of rabbinical centres in Spain, north Africa, Egypt, Italy and the countries of the *Carolingian empire, the academies of Mesopotamia became less consulted and the gaonate declined. At the beginning of the 11th century, *Sherira Gaon (d. 1004) composed a historical treatise on the gaonate for western communities. His son, *Hai Gaon, was the last great G. (d. c. 1040). The development of the Palestinian academy, first at Tiberias and, in the 11th century, at Jerusalem, led to the establishment of Palestinian Gs., although their authority never achieved the same degree of prestige as that of their Babylonian colleagues. After the decline of the gaonate, the title was occasionally given to certain great rabbis.

S. W. Baron, A. Social and Religious History of the Jews, V (1957).

GARCIA Name of several kings of *Navarre in the 9th to 12th centuries. Among them, the most important were:

Garcia IV (1035-54) The second son of *Sancho III the Great. While his elder brother, *Ferdinand, received *Castile, G. inherited the family's realm of Navarre. He organized the kingdom and its institutions and took part in the *Reconquista wars against the Moslems, leading campaigns in the upper valley of the Ebro River. Ferdinand made war on him to recover the territories annexed from Castile and G. was killed in battle.

Garcia V (1134-50) Son of Prince Ramiro, grandson of *G. IV, he managed to restore Navarre's independence from the crown of Aragon at the death of his cousin, King *Alfonso I. His reign was dedicated to the consolidation of his realm, which was isolated from the Moslem part of Spain by the Aragonese possessions and remained a small state in the northeastern part of the Spanish peninsula.

A. Castro, The Structure of Spanish History (1954).

GARIOPONTUS (11th century) Physician. He practised in southern Italy and taught at the medical school of Salerno (c. 1030-c. 1050). Through his relations with Jewish, Arab and Greek physicians in Sicily, he learned of the achievements of anatomy and medicine. With the aid of the material he gathered, he composed a treatise on medicine, among the first in Latin, in which he largely quoted from Hippocrates, although he used such quotations loosely, linking them to the oral tradition.

J. J. Walsh, Medieval Medicine (1920).

GARLAND, JOHN OF (d. 1252) Born in France as a member of the noble family of Garland, he moved to England in his youth and studied at Oxford (probably before 1209) under John of London. Some years later, he settled at Paris, where he taught grammar at the university. A distinguished moralist, he wrote the Morale scholarium (The Morals of the Scholars) and Parisiana Poetria (The Parisian Poetry), in which he described the society of teachers and students at the university, criticizing their behaviour in a fine satirical style. His books are also an important testimony of the curriculum adopted at the Parisian university.

Two Medieval Satires on the University of Paris, Works, ed. L. J. Paetow (1927);
G. Leff, Paris and Oxford Universities in the 13th and 14th Centuries (1968).

GARLANDE, STEPHEN OF (d. 1150) Chancellor of King *Louis VI of France. Member of a feudal family in the Ile-de-France, whose importance grew through its service to the kingship. He became a canon of the cathedral of Paris in 1101 and chancellor of Louis VI in 1106, serving in this capacity until 1137, with the exception of 1127-29. He took advantage of his charge and the influence he had over the king, to elevate the status and increase the possessions of his family. His main achievement was the organization of the French royal chancery as a public office, which foreshadowed the revival of the notion of state in the 12th century.

A. Grabois, Le Personnel de la Chancellerie capétienne au XIIe siècle (1973).

GARTER, ORDER OF THE Chivalric order, instituted by King *Edward III of England in 1348, following the famous incident occurring during a ball held at Calais, when the countess of Salisbury dropped her garter and the king picked it up and bound it on his knee, adopting it as the badge of the new order. The G. was modelled on the ideal fellowship of the knights of *Arthur's round table. The code of *chivalry of the Arthurian fellowship, which was integrated in the statutes of the G., taught that the first duty of a knight was to serve his lord loyally and to uphold justice. Another requirement was the display of gallantry and correct behaviour. Appointments as "knights of the G.", under the direct leadership of the king, were reserved for those nobles who had earned heroic fame as fighters and who had attained the reputation of leading an ideal life. The assemblies or the "chapters" of the order came to be occasions of major feasts in the court during the 14th and 15th centuries. During such meetings, knighthood was bestowed upon important political personalities, such as the dukes of *Burgundy, who received their status for political reasons.

K. B. McFarlane, The English Nobility 1290-1521 (1972).

GASCONY Duchy in southwestern France, situated between the Pyrénées, the Garonne River and the Bay of Biscay. G. was part of the historical kingdom and duchy of *Aquitaine. Its original population, the Vascones (Gascons), was related to the neighbouring Basques, but gradually assimilated into the Romanized population and adopted the Aquitanian French dialect (langue d'Oc). In the 10th century, G. constituted a distinct duchy. The ducal authority, however, was checked by powerful local dynasties, some of which had adopted the feudal system of life, while others were in control of important *allodial demesnes, being

practically independent. In 1053, through the marriage of the heiress of the duchy, G. was annexed to Aquitaine and, until the middle of the 13th century, its history corresponded to that of Aquitaine, being ruled by the *Plantagenet kings of England (from 1152). According to the peace treaty of Paris of 1258, King *Henry III of England was recognized as duke of *Guienne and, in that capacity, as vassal of the king of France. The main part of the duchy was G. itself, but only its western part was administered by officials sent from London, while the interior of the duchy remained under the rule of powerful lords, such as the counts of Comminges, the viscounts of *Béarn and the lords of Albret and *Armagnac. At the end of the 13th century and at the beginning of the 14th century the lords frequently alternated their fidelity between the kings of France and England, causing a state of permanent anarchy and war in the country, which eventually escalated into the *Hundred Years' War. During this war (1337-1453), G. was one of the most important bases of the English government in France, although the authority of the English government was often limited. Thus, lords like the Armagnacs supported the French party, others remained neutral, while an important part of the Gascon lords, such as the captal of *Buch in the 14th century, were faithful to the English. The southern part of the duchy became united during this period under the authority of the counts of *Foix, through a series of marriages and inheritances.
S. Dartigue, *Histoire de la Gascogne* (1951).

GASTON III, Phoebus (1331-91) Count of Foix (1343-91). Son of Gaston II and Eleanor of Comminges, he began to rule under the regency of his mother. Until 1352, his government had to face problems of integrating the two large units under its authority. The one, the county of *Foix, was traditionally linked to French policy, while the administration of the other, Béarn, whose viscounts demanded independence, meant dealing with the English dukes of *Gascony. The *Hundred Years' War complicated the issue and G. had to prove his political skills in order to maintain the unity of his lands. For that purpose he imposed a strong government and created an administration dependent on the dynasty. In 1352, he became loyal to the English side, becoming an ally of the Black Prince, although at the same time he developed independent trends through an alliance with *Aragon. After the English victory at *Poitiers (1356), G. kept his distance from the English government and in 1359 even helped the dauphin, *Charles V, to maintain his authority. In the same year he crushed the revolt of the peasants (the *Jacquerie*) at Meaux. His main concern after 1360 was to maintain his power in the south; as a result there was constant war between him and the lords of *Armagnac, whom he defeated in 1360 at Launac. His victory allowed him to create a powerful state in southern France, whose alliance was sought both by the Black Prince and by the duke of *Berry, governor of Languedoc on behalf of his brother, Charles V. G. established what has been described by *Froissart as one of the most brilliant European courts.
P. Tucoo-Chala, *Gaston-Fébus et la Vicomté de Béarn* (1960).

GASTON VII (1129-1290) The last viscount of Béarn. His rule began with a family regency during his minority,

which weakened his authority. By 1240, he began to govern himself and devoted his efforts to the restoration of the county, which he transformed into one of the great feudal powers in southwestern France. He imposed his authority over feudal families in surrounding areas and struggled with the lords of *Armagnac for the overlordship of the counties of Bigorre and Comminges. His marriage in 1240 with the heiress of Marsan brought him an important territorial gain, allowing him to set up a united principality of Garonne. His only daughter and heiress, Margaret, married Roger-Bernard II, count of *Foix; at G.'s death, the principalities became united (1290).
J. P. Laborde, *Précis d'Histoire du Béarn* (1942).

GASTON-PHOEBUS (1362-81) Son of Count *Gaston III of Foix. He headed a plot of the nobility of Béarn in 1380-81, with the support of *Charles the Bad, king of Navarre. The conspiracy was against his father, who uncovered the plot and beat his son to death. The story was related by *Froissart and became an episode in the chivalric and romantic stories of the late 14th century, where the figure of Charles of Navarre became a diabolic one, conspiring and inducing the young prince to poison his father. The punishment was also transformed in the story into a fatal accident.
J. Huizinga, *The Waning of the Middle Ages* (1924).

GAVESTON, PIERS (d. 1312) Earl of Cornwall. A younger son of a knight of Béarn, he entered the service of *Edward I in *Gascony and, at the end of the 13th century, reached the court of England, where he was made squire of Prince Edward, heir to the crown. His influence on the prince caused the king to banish him from the court. In 1307, upon the accession of *Edward II to the throne, G. became a favourite of the king, who granted him the earldom of Cornwall, considered one of the counties worthy of a king's son. Arrogant and a stranger, G. became unpopular with the upper nobility, which requested his banishment from the court. However, he continued to enjoy the king's favour, having married Margaret of Gloucester, Edward's cousin. In 1309, he commanded part of the army against the Scots. With the appointment of the Ordainers, G. was officially deprived of his lands and exiled. Yet, the king later recalled him, aiming, with his help, to restore royal authority. The Ordainers succeeded in capturing G., and he was executed in 1312.
T. F. Tout and H. Johnstone, *The Place of the Reign of Edward II in English History* (1936).

GAZA City in southern Palestine, on the ancient *via maris* (The Maritime Road), at a cross-road connecting the Arabian desert and the Negev. Due to its location, G. was a prosperous city and an important port at the beginning of the Middle Ages. Its importance declined after the conquest of *Palestine by the Arabs (636) and it became merely a provincial town which, in the 9th century, was ruled by officers of the governors of Egypt. Conquered by the *Crusaders (*c.* 1130), it was fortified by *Fulk of Anjou in 1136 and given to the *Templar knights. The remnants of its 12th-century castle were destroyed during the First World War. In 1187, it was conquered by *Saladin and became the seat of a governor, dependent on Egypt. In 1239 the Crusaders, led by *Thibaut of Champagne, tried to reconquer it, but were severely defeated by the Ayyubid army and compelled to retreat. In 1244 the *Khwarizmians, after the conquest of Jerusalem, marched to G; at Ascalon, while en route, they defeated the Crusaders, who compared the disaster to the Battle of *Hattin. The defeat caused the king of France, *Louis IX, to decide to undertake a Crusade. In 1252, before returning to France, Louis signed a treaty at G. with the *Mamelukes, which brought some years of peace to the kingdom of Acre. Under the Mamelukes, G. became one of the provincial capitals of Palestine; however, the city was never able to recover the state of prosperity it had enjoyed during the Byzantine period.

M. Meyer, *History of the City of Gaza* (1913).

GDANSK See DANZIG.

GEBHARD OF SALZBURG (d. 1088) Archbishop of Salzburg (1060-88). Born of a noble family in Swabia, he studied in France at Chartres and Rheims. In 1055 he was ordained a priest and became a chaplain of Emperor *Henry III. While he was one of strong supporters of the reform movement in the church and fought against *simony, he tried to avoid conflict between Church and State and adopted a moderate attitude in the controversy of the *Investiture. After the excommunication of *Henry IV by *Gregory VII, he recognized *Rudolf of Swabia as anti-king and maintained his fidelity to him even after the *Canossa reconciliation of 1077. After Rudolf's death in 1080, he attempted to reconcile Henry and Gregory, but his efforts failed. In 1081, he became the leader of the Gregorian party in Germany and expressed his ideas in a letter addressed to *Hermann, bishop of Metz, which was meant to be a political manifesto arguing the papal case. Quoting the authorities, the manifesto emphasized the prohibition against contact with excommunicated persons; it was intended to isolate the emperor and to legitimize a revolt against him.

L. Spohr, *Die politische und publizistische Wirksamkeit Gebhards von Salzburg* (1890).

GEDYMIN Grand duke of Lithuania (1316-41). Head of the tribal dynasty, he unified the *Lithuanian tribes, creating a powerful state between the lands of the *Teutonic order and Muscovy and founded a new capital at Vilna. He took advantage of the weakness of the Mongol *Golden Horde to expand his territory towards the basin of the Dnieper River, conquering Polotsk, Minsk and Kiev. G. maintained good relations with Poland and, through the marriage of his daughter Aldona with King *Casimir III of Poland, laid the foundations for the union between Lithuania and Poland, realized by his grandson *Jagiello.

Cambridge History of Poland, I (1950).

GELASIUS I, St. (d. 496) Pope (492-96). Born in Rome, he served in the Roman Church and became one of the closest associates of Pope *Felix III. He was elected to succeed the pope at his death. G. strongly maintained the primacy of the Roman see, based on the Petrine tradition, which considered the pope as successor to St. Peter, the "prince of the apostles". This view brought him in conflict with Acacius, patriarch of Constantinople, whose teachings he condemned in a treatise on the dual nature of Christ. He was most famous for the letter he wrote to Emperor *Anastasius of Constantinople, in which he fiercely attacked the *Henotikon of *Zeno, censuring the concept that the emperor had any say in doctrinal and theological disputes within the church. He developed the "theory

of the two swords", based on biblical precedents, according to which the independence of both the kingship and the priesthood denied the emperor the right to intervene in doctrinal affairs of the church. This concept was further discussed and developed in the West as the Gelasian theory.

Works and Letters, ed. *PL*, vol. 59;

H. Koch, *Gelasius im kirchenpolitischen Dienste seiner Vorgänger der Päpste Simplicius und Felix III.* (1935); *EC*, V.

GELASIUS II (John of Gaeta; c. 1058-1119) Pope (1118-19). One of the most active cardinals of *Pascal II, he was elected pope at the latter's death, but was compelled to flee from Rome, where Emperor *Henry V had imposed *Gregory VIII as antipope. G. took refuge at the abbey of Cluny in France, where he died.

J. Haller, *Das Papsttum* (1953).

GELLÉE, JACQUEMART (second half of the 13th century) Writer. Born at Lille in Flanders to a bourgeois family, he displayed a keen interest in the literature of the *fabliaux* and in the personification of animals, especially the fox, which was popularly used as a satirical device in the moralistic literature of his time. In 1288 he completed his book, *Renard le Nouvel* (The New Fox), in which his clever fox criticized the morals of the established upper classes in a fine allegorical style.

G. Cohen, *La Vie Littéraire au Moyen Age* (1953).

GELLONE Benedictine monastery in Languedoc (southern France), near *Aniane. Founded at the end of the 8th century by Count *William of Toulouse, who led the campaigns in *Catalonia and founded the *Carolingian march of *Spain, it became related with his family's traditions. In 806, William himself retired from public life and became a monk at G., which was also known, several years after his death, as St. Guilhem-du-Désert. The abbey was richly endowed and possessed a substantial library; among the manuscripts preserved there until the abbey's decay in the 17th century, was the *Sacramentary of G.*, written c. 772, a primary source of the history of the early Roman liturgy.

P. Tisset, *L'Abbaye de Gellone au diocèse de Lodève des origines au XIIIe siècle* (1933).

GELMIREZ, DIEGO (d. 1139) Archbishop of *Santiago de Compostela (1100-39). Descendant of a noble family of *Galicia, he was educated to be a clerk of the cathedral church of Compostela and was devoted to the cult of St. James. After his election as bishop, he strove to raise the status of his church and did so by promoting a great building campaign; the result of his effort was a basic alteration of the cathedral's structure. On the basis of the tradition which declared St. James of Compostela to be none other than the brother of Jesus, and that his remains had been brought to Galicia by 12 of his disciples, G. attempted to create a *cardinal college in his cathedral. While the papacy refused to recognize this innovation, reserving cardinals for the Roman Church, G. obtained papal permission for his see to be raised to the rank of archbishopric in 1120. At his instigation, a *Guide of the Pilgrim to Santiago of Compostela* was composed and falsely attributed to Pope *Calixtus II, as part of his efforts to claim his church's primacy in Spain.

W. M. Whitehill, *Liber Sancti Jacobi. Codex Calixtinus* (1944).

Remains of the Crusader fortress of Montfort in Galilee, built in the 12th century

GENEVA County located between the Alps and the Jura, which acquired its name from the city of G., situated on the Rhône River at the tip of the Lake of G. Founded by the Romans in Gaul, the city and its territory were conquered by the *Burgundians in the 5th century. In 532, the *Franks conquered it, and the city, which remained an ecclesiastic centre containing a bishopric, declined until the 8th century. With the growth of the interests of the *Carolingians in Italy in the 8th century, G. became an important way station for the armies of *Pepin III the Short and *Charlemagne en route to Italy. Its renewed prosperity was also a result of the 9th-century revival of commerce, since G. served as a cross-road connecting France and Lotharingia to Italy and linking Germany with the Mediterranean, along the Rhône. With the establishment of the kingdom of *Burgundy in 888, the county and city of G. became part of its realm and local counts were appointed to govern it. The bishops, who were richly endowed, also wielded a large share of authority over the city. In the 11th century, the counts of *Savoy established their suzerainty over the local counts. The bishops became subject to the emperor from 1032, according to the *Ottonian constitution, and in 1162 were granted the status of "princes of the empire". This division of the public authority led to many conflicts between the bishops and the counts, weakening both parties and facilitating the increasing authority of the counts of Savoy in the 13th century. Moreover, the burghers took advantage of the conflicts to acquire privileges and rights of self-government. The city corporation was established in 1309 and, during the 14th century, it became a close ally of the bishops against the house of Savoy. But when the centre of interests of the *Luxemburg emperors was moved, from the time of *Charles IV, to Bohemia and the East, the influence of Savoy, whose rulers had been granted the ducal title, became overwhelming in G. In the 15th century, authority over the city was divided between the dukes of Savoy, the counts, who still enjoyed certain privileges, the prince-bishops and the common people. The last group was split between a pro-Savoyard party and a "patriotic" one, the latter aiming for the city's independence and its attachment to the *Swiss cantons. The "patriotic" party was supported by the guilds of the rich merchants and the bankers; however, despite their rule in city-hall, whose new building was a measure of their wealth, they were unable to realize their goals by the end of the 15th century.

R. Montadon (ed.), *Histoire de Genève,* I (1951).

GENEVIÈVE, St. (422-500) Patron Saint of Paris. According to tradition, she decided to become a nun at the age of seven and was blessed by St. *Germain of Auxerre. At 15 years of age, she realized her profession of faith and founded a nunnery at Paris. In 451, when the *Huns, commanded by *Attila, were approaching Paris, she left the nunnery in order to intercede on behalf of the city, which was saved. The same tradition credits her with saving the city from atrocities when the *Franks fought to conquer Paris. Her fame was well established at the beginning of the 6th century and became the basis for a popular cult in Paris; her intercession was often invoked on behalf of the city. In the 7th and 8th centuries, she was worshipped as one of the popular saints of the Frankish kingdom, aside from her following at Paris, where a famous abbey was built on her tomb.

M. Reynès-Monlaur, *Sainte Geneviève* (1924).

GENGHIS- (CHENGHIZ) KHAN (1155-1227) The founder of the *Mongol empire and its great khan (1203-27). Son of the chieftain of a nomadic tribe, Yeysugai, he was named Temuchin. Upon his father's death in 1165, he was reduced to poverty and his tribe dispersed. Refusing to accept defeat, G. began, at the age of 13, to reorganize his tribe in the eastern Mongolian desert. He worked to prove his skills as a warrior in order to regain his father's authority. During 30 years of continuous wars, G. proved to be an able warrior and leader, surpassing his ancestors. By 1203, he reigned over eastern and central Mongolia and, by 1206, all the Mongol tribes had recognized his rule. At an assembly held at Karakorum, proclaimed his capital, the chiefs of all the Mongols swore unconditional allegiance to his person, entitled G. ("the overlord"). He organized his army in units of tens, hundreds and thousands, including a personal bodyguard, composed of Mongol nobles; discipline was strongly imposed upon all the troops. In terms of administration of his realm, G. ordered the collection of Mongol customs into a coherent code, the *Yassak,* which was promulgated as the sole law of the state. This code formed the basis for a strong political organization of centralist tendencies, giving the great khan full authority over his subjects.

In 1211, G. began his impressive conquests, attacking *China and conquering its northern and western parts, more than half of the empire, by 1216. In 1215, the northern capital, Peking, had been conquered and some of the Chinese armies joined his own forces. In 1216, upon returning to Karakorum, G. learned of a revolt of the northwestern nomads, who accepted the rule of the Kirgiz leaders. A campaign was undertaken against them, which led to the conquest of the *Turkestan areas in central Asia in 1218. A minor incident expanded the war and the empire of the *Khwarizmians was also attacked and conquered. In 1220, the conquest of central Asia was achieved with the capture and destruction of the great and rich cities of Bukhara and Samarkand. G. continued his attacks and, during 1220-22, his army conquered Khorasan and Afghanistan, destroying the cities and massacring their inhabitants. His faithful general, *Subodai, attacked Persia and, by means of a rapid march south of the Caspian Sea, attacked and destroyed the realm of *Georgia, conquering the Caucasus region. The *Russian princes, who attempted to oppose the march, were severely defeated on the banks of the Kalka River (1223). Another Mongol army penetrated Baluchistan, destroying the country as far as the Indus, and some units also attacked the Indian realm of Punjab. In 1225, G. returned to Karakorum, his capital city, to prepare a war against the Siberian Tangut tribes; it was at this time that he died. Before his death, G. proclaimed a constitution of his enormous empire, imposing the hereditary rule of his dynasty. According to it, the great khan was to be chosen from among his four sons or their descendants, while all others were to obey him unconditionally in the government of the empire.

G. was the greatest conqueror known in history;

The cathedral of Monreale, built in the 12th century in the Norman-Romanesque style of Sicily

Genoa harbour depicted in a 16th-century engraving

from chief of a poor, insignificant tribe, he rose to become the absolute ruler of an empire which encompassed the major part of China and central Asia, parts of Persia and Afghanistan, reaching to the Indus, while, in the West, it reached as far as the Dnieper River. Aside from his leadership and military skills, he proved himself a great statesman, organizing his empire and imposing a uniform legal and administrative system. However, on the other hand, he retained the mentality of a nomad; therefore, his reign was marked by the destruction of towns and of economic activity, his treasury being filled by the products of plunder and booty. The great massacres of the conquered population, especially in the Moslem countries, brought about the destruction of certain civilizations in central Asia.

C. C. Walker, *Jenghiz (Genghiz) Khan* (1939).

GENOA City in northern Italy (Liguria). The ancient Ligurian and Roman city continued to be a provincial town at the beginning of the Middle Ages under *Ostrogothic and *Byzantine rule. In 640, G. was conquered by the *Lombards and declined to the status of a fishing village. The archbishops of the city established their seignory around the cathedral and were granted important estates in the province in the 8th and 9th centuries. The city began to develop as a commercial and maritime centre in the 10th century, after its inhabitants and sailors successfully defended it against the raids of the *Fatimid north African navy (931-35) and fortified the harbour. In the middle of the century, Genoese ships began to counter-attack the Moslem forces and were able, in the latter half of the century, to defend the Ligurian and Provençal coasts. In the 11th century, these fleets landed in *Corsica and *Sardinia where,

together with that of the *Pisans, they compelled the Moslems to retreat, establishing their own colonies in their place. When the Genoese fleet captured *Mahdia in north Africa in 1088, G. became the central naval power in the western Mediterranean.

During the same period, the city received complete autonomy within the *Holy Roman empire. The last *Carolingian counts had already lost power in the city in 888, when the *Campagna* (the association of freemen wielding weapons) had been established. In the middle of the 11th century, the consulate was established as the executive power in the city, the consuls having been elected by the *Campagna*, which had itself expanded to include the vassals of the archbishops. The counts in the Ligurian estates lost what was left of their power to the consuls, who were virtually independent of the imperial rule. In 1098, the city officially became a free commune, a term corresponding with the notion of city-state.

The greatness of G. developed at the same time that the *Crusades were in progress. The Genoese and Pisan fleets took part in the First Crusade, bringing provisions to the Crusaders at the decisive time of the siege and conquest of Jerusalem (1099). In 1105, G. obtained a privilege allowing it to possess and administer its own quarter in Acre, with special tax exemptions and permission to trade freely in the harbour; thus, the first of the Italian communes was created in the kingdom of the Crusaders and it became a model for others – Venetian, Pisan, Provençal and Catalan. Its monopolization of eastern trade with western Europe brought wealth to the city of G. which became an important political and economic power in the Mediterranean world. Becoming the capital of an empire, the city grew rapidly in the 12th century and its population was estimated at 100,000 inhabitants. The entire province of Liguria was annexed to the city and formed its hinterland. A conflict with Pisa over the domination of *Corsica ended in favour of G., which also conquered the island of Elba and obtained trade privileges in the Norman kingdom of Sicily. The city itself fell under the rule of a group of aristocratic and wealthy merchant families, including the *Doria and *Spinola families, who began to influence city policy. G. also played an important role in Italian and European policy of the 12th century and it benefited from the conflict between the empire and papacy. In the latter half of the 12th century, the city supported *Frederick Barbarossa and obtained commercial privileges in Germany. In 1187, prior to the *Crusaders' defeat at Hattin, the city owned a series of colonies in the Latin kingdom, at Jerusalem, Acre, Jaffa, Tyre, Arsuf, Caesarea, Haifa, Tripoli and Antioch, which were governed by consuls sent from the mother-city to the Levant. The city imported and distributed textiles, glass, perfumes, indigo, sugar and other "eastern" products in the West. Its craftsmen learned to manufacture glass and silk, and factories were established at G.

The prosperity of G. continued in the 13th century, when it became the strongest power of the western Mediterranean and, during the first half of the century, it had strong influence on the trade in Sicily. Moreover, the ancient rivalry with Pisa was finally settled in 1284, when the Genoese fleet destroyed that of Pisa near the island of Meloria. In the eastern Mediterranean, on the other hand, G. was rivalled by *Venice and, therefore, did not wield quite as much influence as it did in the West. The rivalry between these two Italian powers was also felt in the Crusaders' states, where the nobility was divided according to its relations with either city. In 1256, as result of the "War of St. Sabbas", concerning the possession of a house located at the entrance of the harbour of Acre, the Venetian fleet inflicted a severe defeat upon that of G. in the Bay of Acre and the Genoese ships were driven out of the Levant. G. avenged this loss through an alliance with the Byzantine empire of *Nicaea, an enemy of Venice; as a result, upon the reconquest of Constantinople in 1261, G. obtained privileges in *Galata, as well as in islands in the Aegean Sea, the most important among them being *Chios, which became a Genoese colony. From Constantinople, G. crossed the Black Sea and established an important colony in Crimea, where the city of Caffa became the centre of their trade operations with the Mongol empire. In addition, G. controlled the mouth of the Danube River. At the end of the 13th century, the city obtained control over the trade in the Lusignan kingdom of *Cyprus, thus becoming an important power in the eastern Mediterranean as well. Moreover, G.'s achievements in the East compensated for its losses during the last decades of the 13th century in the West, where the development of *Aragon and of the Catalan maritime trade led to a decline in Genoese influence in Sicily and the establishment of Aragonese authority in Sardinia and Corsica (1282).

By 1300, when the Genoese empire had reached the peak of its expansion, the first signs of decay were beginning to be felt in the city of G. itself. The oligarchic rule of the aristocratic-merchant families was challenged by the popular party, a struggle which led to a compromise in 1310, through which a council of 13 members was created – 6 were of the aristocratic party, 6 of the popular party and the final representative was the "Abbot of the People". The compromise collapsed in 1311, and the city was forced to acknowledge the seignory of Emperor *Henry VII (1311-13). The internal struggle continued, however, during the fluctuations between independence and foreign domination, such as the condominium of Pope *John XXII and *Robert of Anjou, king of Naples (1318-35). Moreover, the city became involved in Italian affairs, paying special attention to *Milan, which sought to rival its influence in Lombardy. The Mediterranean empire of G. gradually declined and Venice took advantage of this fact to attack, and severely defeated the Genoese fleet at Chioggia in 1379; the resulting loss of part of the Genoese colonies aggravated the city's inner conflict. The once prosperous city suffered a serious financial crisis, being unable to pay its *condottieri. In 1396, G. became the subject of *Charles VI, king of France, and was ruled by French governors until 1409. The recovery of its independence did not end its social troubles and the drawn-out conflict between the aristocratic and popular parties continued to weaken G. The rise of the *Ottoman Turks and the fall of Byzantium in 1453 led to the decline of the Genoese empire in the East and, at the end of the 15th century, only Corsica remained under Genoese authority.

The centre of the city, with its Gothic buildings of the 13th century, among them the cathedral of St. Lawrence (begun in the 12th century and completed in the 16th century), is a monument to the former greatness and prosperity of G. The university, founded in 1243, attracted scholars and students from East and West during the period of Genoese glory.

N. Zambroghia, *Storia di Genova* (1942);
G. I. Bratianu, *Recherches sur le Commerce des Génois dans la Mer Noire* (1929);
R. F. Lopez, *Storia delle colonie Genovesi* (1938).

GENSERIC (GAISERIC) King of the *Vandals (428-77). G. became king when the pressure of the *Visigoths compelled the Vandals to retreat to southern Spain (*Andalusia). G. organized the tribe and in 429 invaded north Africa. Within the course of a year, the Vandals succeeded in defeating the Romans and the Mauretanians and conquering the territory from Gibraltar to the Libyan borders. Only a few cities, although besieged, remained under Roman rule, but by 439 they had been conquered and, with the capture of Carthage, G. was able to establish a capital for his new kingdom, which was recognized in 442 by the Roman emperor *Valentinian III. With the conquest of the coastal cities, the Vandals acquired their fleets and G. rapidly adapted them to seafare. He controlled the western basin of the Mediterranean, intercepting the food supply of Rome from Sicily. He also practised piracy, using the booty to replete his treasury, thus enabling himself to rule without the backing of the council of the nobles, to whom he granted land. In 455, he sacked Rome, capturing Empress Eudoxia, widow of Valentinian III, whom he gave in marriage to his elder son, *Huneric. Aside from his military and naval success, G. proved to be a skilled statesman, a fact which challenges his accepted image as a fierce pirate. He organized his kingdom, distinguishing it from other Germanic realms, where division of the kingdom between the sons of the deceased monarch was common, by establishing inheritance based on primogeniture, provided that the eldest son of the king was of age and able to rule. In this sense, he adopted the Roman concept of the state as a public body and not the private property of the royal family. While the estates of the Roman nobility and the church were expropriated and given to the conquerors, part of the landed aristocracy was allowed to maintain their estates after the payment of a redemption tax. As an Arian, G. persecuted the Catholic Church, especially through confiscation of its properties. He encouraged the development of crafts and trade.

C. Courtois, *Les Vandales et l'Afrique* (1955).

GEOFFREY Name of several counts of *Anjou in the 10th -12th centuries:

Geoffrey Grisogonelle Count 960-87. Son and heir of *Fulk the Good, he was a faithful vassal to *Hugh Capet. He dedicated the major part of his rule in organizing the county, basing his power on the great abbeys which, in return for his protection and wardship, supplied him with military resources and counsellors.

Geoffrey Martel (1006-60) Count 1040-60. Son of *Fulk Nerra, he became part of his father's government in 1030 and was granted the county of Vendôme. Upon receiving the rank of count, G. became one of the most important feudal lords in western Europe; he gave his step-daughter Agnes in marriage to Emperor *Henry III, and the resulting kinship helped to raise his prestige. He also allied himself with King *Henry I of France against *Thibaut of Blois, the most dangerous enemy to the crown. In 1044 he conquered Tours, thus removing the influence of the house of Blois from the county of Touraine; this conquest made him one of the most important rulers of the Loire Valley and allowed him to control the main roads of France, from east to west and from north to Aquitaine and Spain. G. also reaped additional resources from the trade and the mint of Tours, one of the most important in Europe. His relations with the king of France were dictated by his interests; at times he allied himself with the French, and at other times he took advantage of a state of war to expand his possessions or to spread Angevin influence, such as was the case in the county and bishopric of Maine. G. was childless and therefore chose Geoffrey and Fulk, the sons of his sister, Ermengard, and the count of Gâtinais, as his heirs.

Geoffrey the Bearded Count 1060-68; nephew of G. Martel. He had already succeeded his father as count of Gâtinais in 1046, and had displayed a poor leadership. His period of rule in Anjou was equally unsuccessful; defeated by the dukes of Aquitaine and Normandy, he lost much of the authority and his attempts to violently impose his power over the churches brought him into a clash with the church and led to his papal excommunication. His brother, *Fulk IV, revolted against him in 1068. G. died as prisoner to his brother at the castle of Chinon in 1096.

O. Guillot, *Le Comte d'Anjou et son entourage aux XIe siècle* (1972).

GEOFFREY OF MANDEVILLE See MANDEVILLE.

GEOFFREY OF MONMOUTH (1100-54) Welsh writer and chronicler. Little is known of his early life and origins. In 1129 he settled at Oxford, where he remained as a clerk until 1151. Elected bishop of *St. Assaph, he returned to his motherland (Wales) and was one of the ecclesiastical leaders of the Welsh principality until his death. His main work, written in Latin between 1136 and 1139, is the *Historia Regum Britanniae* (The History of the Kings of Britain), which deals with the early history of Britain up to the settlement of the *Anglo-Saxons. G. mentions an earlier British version of the book which he had discovered at Oxford, but it seems that this particular source was a fictitious one. His work praises the British Celts and the author expresses his pride in belonging to that nation. In his work, G. mixed historical facts with legends, handling the latter as if the events they described were true. For example, he treated as factual the legend of the Trojan origins of the Britons, as descendants of a certain Brutus (or Brito), grandson of Aeneas the Trojan; the tales about the "prophet" Merlin are also dealt with as historical facts. The most important sections of G.'s book are dedicated to King *Arthur, represented as the hero of the British resistance to the Anglo-Saxon invasion. These stories became very popular and contributed to the development of the Arthurian romance in the latter half of the 12th century. In 1150, G. composed in Latin verse a *Life of Merlin*, which is both a romantic history and a didactic poem.

Works, ed. J. Hammer (1951);

J. S. P. Tatlock, *Legendary History of Britain* (1950).

GEOFFREY OF PARIS (14th century) Chronicler. Born and educated at Paris, where he was an official at the royal court under the last direct *Capetians and *Philip VI of Valois, he wrote a rhyming chronicle on the reigns of the sons of *Philip IV the Fair, covering the period between 1314-28. His chronicle is not merely an eyewitness testimony, but also the author's views on the realm of France and especially on the primacy of the *raison d'état* over dynastical concerns.

RHG, XXII.

GEOFFREY PLANTAGENET, the Fair (1113-51) Count of Anjou (1128-51). The son of *Fulk V (Fulk of Jerusalem). After his marriage to Empress *Matilda, daughter and heiress of *Henry I, king of England, he received the counties of Anjou and Maine, where he administrated according to his father's policies. His main innovations included the establishment of noble officials, a framework which allowed him to impose his rule over the vassals and to introduce a central administration. In 1135, at the death of Henry I, he claimed the crown of England on behalf of his wife, but when *Stephen of Blois seized the kingship, G. left Matilda to fight in England with her allies. At the same time, he began to besiege Normandy, whose domination was closer to his own interests. After conquering Normandy, he assumed authority as duke, imposing his rule upon the nobility. G. was the founder of the Plantagenet dynasty, which ruled England from 1154 to 1485.

J. Chartrou, *L'Anjou sous Geoffroi le Bel* (1928).

GEOFFREY PLANTAGENET (1158-86) Duke of *Brittany (1166-86). Fourth son of *Henry II, king of England, he married Constance, daughter of *Conan IV, duke of Brittany, and ruled the duchy nominally, while effectively it was governed by his father. He often rebelled against his father but ultimately submitted to him, although he continued to nurture a close friendship with *Philip II of France. He died in an accident, before the birth of his son *Arthur.

J. Boussard, *Le Gouvernement d'Henri II Plantegenêt* (1956).

GEOGRAPHY Medieval G. was based on the achievements of the Greeks and especially on the Hellenistic school of Egypt, although gradually the systematic methods of Ptolemaic geographical research were forgotten and G. became merely a description of various lands. In the early Middle Ages (5th-8th centuries) the Hellenistic traditions were still strong in Byzantium and western Europe; the works of men such as *Cosmas "Indicopleustas" in the 6th century continued the traditions of the school of Ptolemy, and those of *Bede the Venerable in England were also oriented towards a search of astronomical data. Although such adopted material was developed to a degree, the major part of the geographical data of this period was conservative, tending to be a compilation and summary of the classical achievements, interpreted in accordance with the Christian faith. Philosophers and theologians such as St. *Augustine opposed the Greek teaching of the Antipodes and thus had a stagnating effect upon geographical knowledge. This decline was expressed in the 5th century in the historical book of *Orosius, *Adversus Paganos* (Against the Pagans) which, according to the classical tradition, opens with a geographical description of the empire compiled entirely from ancient sources. The great encyclopedic work of *Isidore of Seville in the 7th century, the *Ethymologiae*, contains two volumes on cosmography and G., which also summed up the classical achievements. While its importance in the spread of such knowledge in the Middle Ages was considerable, the compilation was largely responsible for the emergence of the normative method of geographical study in the West until the 13th century. Thus, from the 8th century, no progress was made.

For the Christian geographers of the early and high Middle Ages, the concept of the earth as a disc, whose axis was the Mediterranean and whose central point was Jerusalem, remained an axiom rooted in the faith. The outer boundaries of the disc were purported to be countries of fantasy, such as the lands or realms of *Gog and Magog. The Ptolemaic tradition was preserved among the eastern Christians in Persia and Syria, where dissident sects were not bound to the dogmatic attitude of the western and even Byzantine church. A translation into Syrian of the Ptolemaic system, together with further developments, was completed in 555 and preserved in a curious volume, *Scariphos D'Tevel* (Description of the World), which served as the basis for new works in the East. The most important among such works were those of *James of Edessa, who divided the world into seven climatic regions and developed research on climatology as a geographical discipline. His conclusions made possible the development of the popular theory, based on the north-south axis of the earth. Such progress in the study of G. was inherited by Islam and the Arabs who, as in other fields of philosophy and science, continued and developed the Greek heritage. Arab activity in this field began during the reign of Caliph *Al-Mamun (813-33), who ordered the preparation of new astronomical tables and geographical maps based on accurate measurements. While the Ptolemaic system continued to be the source of new works, more attention was given to a study of the East, an approach represented in the 9th century by the research of Al-Farghani. Climatic data were studied on the basis of latitudinal lines; demographic G. (the study of towns) was arranged on a longitudinal basis, from east to west.

Arab and Persian G. was developed on the basis of descriptions of travellers from memory, both with regard the physical and demographic data. Contemporary Christian travellers were particularly and almost exclusively interested in "Holy G.", and thus described holy places and religious sanctuaries in an attempt to actualize the biblical past, without any consideration of the changes which had occurred between biblical times and their own. Arab and Persian travellers of the 9th-14th centuries, on the other hand, paid primary attention to physical aspects. The works of Al-Mukkadassi in the 10th century, of Al-Bakhri and of Nazim Al-Khosroes in the 11th, and especially of *Yakut in the 13th, are good descriptions and geographical lexicographies.

Besides descriptive G., the Arabs also developed new trends of astronomical G., which helped them to make important progress. *Al-Idrissi, who was employed by King *Roger II. of Sicily, was the pioneer of this study, his book on the subject appearing in 1154. *Abu'l Fida added a critical and methodical analysis in his 14th-century work, while *Ibn Battutah combined description with astronomical elements.

Under the impact of the works of Al-Idrissi, G. be-

gan to be studied as a science in Christian Europe from the end of the 12th century. In 1188 Guy of Pisa wrote a historical compilation of G. which, although based on the *Ethymologiae* of Isidore of Seville, differed from that of his predecessors; it included a new interpretation of Bede, on the basis of which he developed ideas about the global form of the earth. Such an approach, which was quite advanced, also led him to learn of the conclusions of Al-Idrissi. This work was the first step towards revised geographical studies, first through the rejection of astrological fictions and then by the establishment of a systematic study of astronomy and nature under the impact of the revival of *Aristotelianism. Such developments led to new conclusions, including those of Roger *Bacon on physical geography and of Nicephorus *Blemmydes in Byzantium, who defended the view of the globality of the earth. At the end of the 13th century, astronomic G. became a basic means for drawing maps and for analysing the various components of the earth; its achievements were of prime importance in the emergence of large-scale navigation and prepared the tools for geographical discoveries. With the establishment of the school of navigation by *Henry the Navigator (15th century), G. began to be studied as a systematic school of thought in Portugal and later on in Spain.

C. R. Beazley, *The Dawn of Modern Geography* (1906); J. K. Wright, *Geographical Lore at the Time of the Crusades* (1925).

GEORGE, St. Martyr and patron saint of England. Very little is known about his life. It seems that he lived at the end of the 3rd century, probably in Palestine, and was put to death at Lydda. From the beginning of the Middle Ages, his story became interwoven with many legends, part of them adapted from classical

St. George and the Dragon; *late 15th-century painting*

mythology (e.g., G. fighting the dragon). From the 8th century on, his cult was particularly popular in England where, in the 13th century, he became the patron saint of the realm, at first together with St. *Edward the Confessor and then, in the 14th century, alone. G.'s arms (the red cross on a white background) were introduced in the English army during the *Hundred Years' War and, with the establishment of the Order of the Garter by *Edward III, G. was proclaimed the order's patron. The cult of G. was also very popular among the *Crusaders in the Latin kingdom of Jerusalem. The Crusaders attributed their victories against the *Fatimids (1099-1105) to his intercession. The name of the town of Lydda, of which only the cathedral remained standing in the 12th and 13th centuries, was changed under the Crusaders to G. (spelled *Saint Jorje*).

G. J. Marcus, *St. George of England* (1939).

GEORGE I, Terter Tsar of *Bulgaria (1280-92). Of Cuman origin, he was one of the leaders of the Bulgarian nobility who rebelled against *John Assen III. He allied himself with *Charles of Anjou, king of Sicily, against the Byzantines, who protected John Assen. The *Sicilian Vespers of 1282, which immobilized Charles, compelled him to abandon his plans of expansion and led him to deal with the internal problems of his kingdom, where the influence of the landed nobility had become preponderant.

W. N. Slatarsky, *Geschichte der Bulgaren*, I (1918).

GEORGE Kings of *Georgia, in the Caucasus Range. Among them, the most important were the kings of the Armenian dynasty of Bagration:

George II (1156-84) He fought the autonomous leanings of the nobility, since *feudalism had been gaining ground during the 12th century, and he imposed his authority over the upper classes. In 1180, he gained an important victory over the *Seljuk princes in northern Persia and Asia Minor and enlarged the boundaries of his realm southwards.

George IV, the Illustrious (1212-23) His reign was considered the golden age of Georgia. He ruled over an expansive realm, including the whole of the Caucasus, from the Black Sea to the Caspian, together with the major part of "Great" *Armenia. Georgian civilization within his state reached its apex both in literature and in artistic achievement. During his last year of reign, he was confronted by *Mongol invasions.

George VI (1299-1346) He began to rule as a vassal of the Turks and of the Mongols and took part in their wars. G. succeeded in freeing himself of the alien overlordship in *c.* 1306 and, after a long series of defensive wars, was able to recover Georgian independence. He ruled under the influence of the monastic clergy and maintained close relations with the Georgian monastery at Jerusalem.

W. E. D. Allen, *A History of the Georgian People* (1932).

GEORGE-GREGORY OF CYPRUS Patriarch of Constantinople (1281-89). He was one of the firmest opponents to the policy of union between the Orthodox and Catholic churches, and was appointed patriarch of Constantinople so as to impose pure orthodoxy upon the Byzantine clergy. A distinguished theologian, G. wrote a *Tome of the Faith* and a treatise on the *Procession of the Holy Spirit,* in which he developed his orthodox ideas; he also composed an excellent autobiography. Opposition to him caused Emperor

*Andronicus II to order his deposition and G. retired to a monastery for the remainder of his life.

W. Lameere, *La tradition manuscrite de la Correspondance de Gregoire de Chypre,* (1937).

GEORGE SYNCELLUS (c. 800) Byzantine historian. In his youth he lived in Palestine and then moved to Constantinople, where he served in the office of the patriarch. He wrote an important *Chronicle* which covers the period from creation to the end of the 8th century; in his work he expressed his ideas of the historical succession of nations.

Chronicle, ed. W. Dindorf (1828);

GEORGIA Kingdom in the Middle Ages, in the Caucasus Mountains; now the Georgian Soviet Socialist Republic. The medieval realm of G. was established on the ruins of the ancient kingdom of Iberia, which had been destroyed by the *Sassanid Persians in the 3rd century. One of the branches of the Sassanid dynasty established an autonomous principality in G. at the beginning of the 4th century and was converted to Christianity. In the 5th century the princes of G. won their full independence in cooperation with the church which, like that of *Armenia, became a national one. King Wakhtang I who, according to tradition, was responsible for gaining national sovereignty, founded his capital in the city of Tblisi (Tiflis) in 455. The Georgian realm was a perpetual scene of war between Byzantium and Persia, and under *Justinian it was divided into two areas of influence. The wars caused the disintegration of the realm into numerous feudal principalities, whose rulers accepted the overlordship of the great powers (6th-8th centuries). In 643 the Arabs conquered eastern G. and Tblisi became the seat of an Arab governor (emir), who ruled the country on behalf of the caliph. In the 10th century the Armenian noble family of Bagration, which had settled in G. in the previous century and acquired a distinguished position, succeeded in unifying the country and founding the medieval kingdom. Bagrat III (d. 1014) founded the new capital, Kutais, and ruled together with the lesser nobility, the knights. G. was attacked by the *Seljuk Turks between 1064-72 and remained in a state of anarchy until the reign of David III (the Renewer, 1090-1125), at which time its independence was restored. David's descendants, and mainly *George III, fought feudal trends and established a monarchic rule, which became known as the golden age under Queen Thamar (1184-1212) and her son *George IV. The *Mongol invasions in 1234-42 caused destruction and ruin of the kingdom, which surrendered its independence. The monarchy became weak, and the great landowners became powerful. Until the beginning of the 15th century, the country was a vassal realm of the Mongols and Turks, despite a short period of independence under the kingship of *George VI. After the fall of the empire of *Tamerlane, G. remained a weak state, where the influence of the Ottoman Turks and of Persia led to the division of the kingdom and the Islamization of a part of its population.

Culture Georgian civilization and culture is closely related with the Christian faith. The first literary works date from the 5th century and deal with popular Christian tales, among them stories about the saints. These were composed in the national language, using a particular 38-letter alphabet – the "alphabet of the church" – specially adapted for such writings. The alphabet was revised in the 12th century and the new writing system was named "the knights' alphabet". The translations of the Bible into Georgian, whose first versions date from the 5th century, also contributed to the literary development of the language. This work was perfected in the 11th century, with the revised translation of the Bible by St. George, a monk who lived on Mount Athos. From the 9th century on, Georgian civilization was influenced by the Byzantines through the Georgian monasteries established on Mount Sinai, Mount Athos and later on at Jerusalem. Through the monks, the theological achievements of the Greek-Orthodox Church were transmitted and formed a foundation for the theological and dogmatic treatises in Georgian. At the end of the 12th century and the beginning of the 13th century, during the reign of Queen *Thamar, Georgian culture reached its golden age. Poetry, which had previously been confined to hymns and liturgical chants, was developed into the literary form of the Georgian epic. Thamar patronized arists, among them the greatest Georgian poet, Shote Rustaveli, who wrote the national epic song, *The Man in the Panther's Skin,* which praised the heroes of the wars of independence and became the symbol of G.'s national and social ideals, combining faith, pride and love of the motherland. The Mongol invasions in the latter half of the 12th century led to the decline of Georgian culture, which saw its revival only in the 17th century.

Arts The artistic development of medieval G. was influenced by Byzantine-Christian art. Until the 7th century this influence, based on direct contact with monasteries in Palestine, Syria and Mount Sinai, was overwhelming, although the quality of Georgian work did not equal that found in the Byzantine sanctuaries. The Arab conquest of Syria and Palestine terminated the link with Byzantium, and Georgian art developed independent trends. In architecture, the style which prevailed and was brought to perfection was that of simplicity, harmony within the landscape and moderation. Ecclesiastical architecture was based on the form of the cross, above which rose an octagonal tower. The most significant piece of Georgian architecture is the monastery of Gelati, built in the 12th century. Concerning the plastic arts, Byzantine influence was merely technical. Georgian art imitated the Byzantine forms of frescoes, icons and sculpture, but the motifs used indicate an independent national style. The figures of kings and heroes were based on Caucasian types, which were also used in the representation of saints. The goldsmiths remained free of outside influence and developed their own techniques of producing gold and jewels for both sacred and secular ornaments. From the 9th century, illustration and illumination of books was also developed, at first in the copies of the holy books and, in the 12th and 13th centuries, in books of poetry. In an attempt to attain harmony, colours were used which suited the natural lighting of the region.

W. E. D. Allen, *A History of the Georgian People* (1932); J. Karst, *Littérature Géorgienne Chrétienne* (1934).

GEPIDS Germanic tribe, related to the *Goths and originally from Scandinavia. In the 4th century they settled in Dacia, together with some other tribes, but lost their independence with the arrival of the *Huns. The G. took part in the invasion of *Attila (451), recovering their independence after his death. In the 6th century

they attempted to invade the Balkans, but were severely defeated by *Justinian and remained in Dacia (modern Rumania). A portion of them followed the *Lombards to Italy in 568, where they became assimilated with the conquerors; those that remained in Dacia lost their independence upon the arrival of the *Avars. The G. were thus gradually absorbed into the population of the Avar empire. Mention of their separate existence is last found in the 9th century.

H. Sevin, *Die Gebiden (Gepiden)* (1955).

GERALD OF BARRI See GIRALDUS CAMBRENSIS.
GERARD (GIRARD) Count of Vienne (851-70). Appointed by *Lothair I to this dignity, he created a powerful principality for himself on the Rhône. In 855, he became the protector of the weak *Carolingian king, *Charles, son of Lothair, who had inherited the kingdom of Provence. In 870, he was defeated by *Charles the Bald, king of France, who deprived him of his county. G. became the literary hero of 12th-century epic poems and his figure and his supposed deeds became very popular among knights.

R. Louis, *De l'Histoire à la Légende (Girart de Roussillon)* (1946).

GERARD OF BORGO SAN DONNINO (d. c. 1260) Spiritual *Franciscan. Born in Italy, where he joined the order, he studied at Paris and preached a life of poverty. His studies gained him knowledge of the doctrines of *Joachim of Fiore, from whom he adopted apocalyptical ideas to prove that the Spiritual Franciscans were established according to biblical prophecies. In 1254 he wrote his *Introduction to the Eternal Gospel,* revealing his ideas. This immediately caused a scandal at the University of Paris as well as within the order. Brought before Pope *Alexander IV, he was condemned to imprisonment at Anagni, while his teaching was proclaimed heretical. He died in prison shortly after his condemnation, but his teaching continued to be diffused among the Spirituals.

P. Glorieux, *Les Polémiques contra Geraldino* (1935).

GERARD OF CREMONA (1114-87) Translator. Born at Cremona, in Lombardy, he travelled in Spain, where he discovered Arab science and, during a long sojourn at Toledo, became acquainted with philosophy and astronomy books in Arabic. Among the works which he translated were those of *Alfarabi and the *Almagest* (translated in 1175). His translations became the foundation of the development of astronomical studies in Latin western Europe.

C. H. Haskins, *Studies in the History of the Medieval Science* (1927).

GERBA Island and city near the southern shore of Tunisia. Conquered in 439 by the *Vandals, it became one of their naval bases in the Mediterranean until it fell to the Byzantines in 533. In 655, the Arabs conquered G. and those of its Christian inhabitants who did not emigrate, converted to the Moslem faith. In the 9th century, *Berber settlers established themselves in the island. In the 12th century, the Sicilian Normans attempted to conquer G., attacking it several times. The Aragonese succeeded in capturing the island in 1238 and built a fortress, which they held until the 16th century. An important part of the population of medieval G. was Jewish, and it was this community which established a trade route from the western Mediterranean to Egypt via their city. The synagogue, dating back to the 11th century, is the island's most impressive building.

N. Slouschz, *Travels in North Africa* (1927).

GERBERT OF AURILLAC See SYLVESTER II.

GERHOH OF REICHERSBERG (1093-1169) Reformer and polemist, he was one of the principal agents of the *Gregorian reform in Germany. After studying at Freiburg and Hildesheim, he became head of the cathedral church of Augsburg in 1119. In 1121, he was forced to leave his post due to his quarrel with bishop Hermann, whom he accused of being a *simoniac. In 1122, after the official acceptance of the Concordat of *Worms, he became reconciled with the bishop and resumed his post. G. took part in the *Lateran Council in 1123, where he presented a programme entailing reform of the clergy. Since his proposals were rejected, he entered the congregation of the *Augustinian Canons at Rottenbuch in 1124, and wrote his *Liber de Aedificio Dei* (The Book of God's Building), which includes his ideas on church discipline (1130). In 1132, he was appointed provost of the Augustinian Canons of Reichersberg. There he continued his reform efforts and was quite active in public affairs, travelling to Rome and preaching throughout Germany. His activity won him many supporters, but also gained him much hostility to the point that he was even accused of heresy, despite the fact that he strongly defended the orthodox teaching. In 1166, upon his refusal to recognize the antipope, he was banned by Emperor *Frederick Barbarossa, against whom he had written *De Investigatione Antichristi* (On the Investigation of the Antichrist) in 1161. In this work he advocated a clearer distinction between the papal and imperial spheres of power.

Works, *PL*, vol. 193-94;
H. Fichtenau, *Studien zu Gerhoh von Reichersberg* (1938).

GERMAIN OF PARIS, St. (c. 496-576) A native of Autun, he became a monk and gained a wide reputation for his generosity towards the poor. In 555, he became bishop of Paris and sought to check the licentiousness of the Frankish kings and to put an end to the perpetual civil wars. Legends developed with regard to his activity and "prophecies" were attributed to him. In the 7th century, G. was venerated and worshipped as a saint and a monument was built over his tomb, which later became the oldest part of the church of *St. Germain-des-Prés.

A. Wilmart, *Saint Germain de Paris* (1924).

GERMANS Common name given to a number of tribes and ethnic groups belonging to the Indo-European race and having a common ethnic and linguistic origin. From ancient times, the Germanic peoples were spread out over large territories north of the Danube and east of the Rhine. They were commonly divided into several groups, primarily those of Teutonic and Scandinavian origin. The Teutonic G., who were known to the Romans from the 1st century BC, gradually disappeared in the 3rd and 4th centuries, when the Germanic world completed its primitive and prehistoric stage. Tribes which migrated from Scandinavia and the Baltic shores spread into central and eastern Europe from the 2nd century on, and were divided into several groups of tribes, generally classified according to their geographical settlements. The western group included the *Franks, *Burgundians, *Alamanni and *Anglo-Saxons; the

southern, or central, group included the *Bavarians, Thuringians and numerous lesser tribes; the eastern group consisted of the *Goths (Visigoths and Ostrogoths), *Vandals, *Gepids and *Lombards, while the northern group consisted of the Scandinavians proper, or the *Viking tribes. In the 4th century, all these Germanic tribes began to move southwards and westwards, crossing into the frontiers of the Roman empire. Some attacked the Romans and were considered dangerous enemies, such as the Goths who, in 372, defeated the Roman army at *Adrianople. Others received permission to settle on the Roman frontiers and were considered *foederati* (allies). They served in the Roman army in the 5th century and attained high military positions, especially in the Western empire. During the 5th century, the G. conquered the Western Roman empire, but generally became assimilated into the local populations, creating a great number of realms, most of which had only a temporary existence. The Germanic invasions of Rome came to an end in the late 6th century, with the conquest of Italy by the Lombards. Among the states founded by the G., the most important were the Anglo-Saxon kingdoms, the Frankish kingdom, and the states of the Visigoths, the Vandals and the Lombards. The other states, the most important being the Ostrogothic kingdom of Italy, knew a very short period of existence.

L. Musset, *Les Invasions; Les Vagues Germaniques* (1969).

GERMANUS, St. (634-733) Patriarch of Constantinople (715-30). Descendant of a noble Byzantine family, he became a clerk at the cathedral of St. Sophia in 668, having previously received the best education possible of his time. He distinguished himself as one of the most energetic defenders of orthodoxy and was promoted to the metropolitan see of Cyzicus in *c.* 700. In 715 he was elected Patriarch of *Constantinople and worked to impose the Greek-Orthodox faith upon the empire and to fight heretical movements. When, in 725, Emperor *Leo III issued his edict against the veneration of icons (*Iconoclastic controversy), G. became a fierce opponent of the iconoclasts. In 730 he was forced to resign his position and retired to the monastery of Platonium. There, despite his old age, he continued to lead the opposition and wrote his treatise on the *Heretics and Synods*, in which he laid down the basis of his faith. The Latin translation of this treatise is the sole extant piece of his work, the others having been destroyed by the iconoclasts. According to his 8th-century biographers, G. also wrote many theological and liturgical works, as well as a *Mystical History of Christianity*. He was venerated as a saint by his followers and was officially recognized in the 8th century by both Orthodox and Catholic churches.

Acta Sanctorum, Mai, III;
E. J. Martin, *A History of the Iconoclastic Controversy* (1934).

GERMANUS II Patriarch of Constantinople-Nicaea (1221-40). He actively reorganized the Orthodox Church from the imperial seat of Nicaea, and he worked to impose unity upon the clergy of Greece and Cyprus. At the same time, he also negotiated with Pope *Gregory IX to re-establish the unity of the churches, although the negotiations ultimately failed in 1232. G. was a patron of learning and founded an important high school at Nicaea, which continued the traditions of that of Constantinople.

S. Zankov, *The Eastern Orthodox Church* (1930).

GERMANY Country in central Europe, populated by Germanic tribes, whose borders varied, at the end of the Middle Ages including the territories ranging from the Alps to the shores of the North and Baltic seas and from the Meuse (Maas) River in the west to Poland in the east. The country received its name from the Romans in the 1st century, although at that time the term designated the area east of the Rhine, next to the Roman *limes* (fortified frontier), named *limes Germaniae*. The name was perpetuated in Tacitus' description of the country and its people in his book *Germania* (2nd century). However, its inhabitants called their country *Deutschland* (after the Thioi tribes, the *Tedeschi* in Italian). The French, on the other hand, named the country after the tribe of the *Alamanni, whence *Allemagne*, the name which is still in use in contemporary France.

At the beginning of the Middle Ages, the territory of G. had no defined political status. Part of the Germanic peoples which populated it had left the country in the 4th-6th centuries to settle in the ancient provinces of the Western Roman empire. The remaining Germanic tribes inhabited the western parts of the country, while the territories situated east of the Elbe River, including the Bohemian plateau and modern Austria, were settled by Slavic tribes. At the beginning of the 6th century, western G. was divided into several political units: the Saxons and *Frisians became entirely independent, while *Thuringia, *Bavaria and *Alamania-(later named *Swabia), fell under the protectorate of the *Franks, who granted them a large degree of autonomy. The Franks conquered and settled a large area in the central part of the country, on both banks of the Main River, which they named *Franconia. Division of the country remained unchanged until the rise of the *Carolingians, the first dynasty to unify G. (8th century). Under *Pepin the Short, the Franks imposed their direct rule over Alamania and Frisia and established the country's religious unity in cooperation with St. *Boniface, who established his see at Mainz and was recognized as primate of all G. (751).

Unity was achieved by *Charlemagne, who conquered and attached to his realm the territories of Saxony (774-804), Bavaria (792) and the *Carinthian and *Austrian marches, captured from the *Avars (798-99). At this time, however, the term G. had not yet acquired political or ethnical meaning. In fact, in 806, when the emperor decided to divide his empire among his three sons, the partition of G. was considered.

The history of G. as a distinct entity begins in the 9th century with the creation of the kingdom of *Louis the German, one of the sons of *Louis the Pious. Louis obtained the territories east of the Rhine, named *Francia Orientalis* (Eastern Francia) in 829 and, a little over ten years later, they were recognized as one linguistic entity at the Assembly of Strassburg. In 843 the kingdom was officially recognized by the Treaty of *Verdun, when the Carolingian empire was finally divided. Louis and his sons extended their authority westwards, annexing the major part of the kingdom of *Lotharingia, including *Provence. Nevertheless, the idea of unity was not given consideration and the three principal

components of the kingdom, Saxony, Bavaria and Swabia were granted at Louis' death in 876 to his sons, *Louis, *Carloman and *Charles the Fat, respectively. The death of the first son enabled Charles, who received the imperial title in 881, to unify the country, and he succeeded in restoring the empire of Charlemagne in 887, although only for the span of one year. In 888 *France ı gained its independence, while *Burgundy and Provence became independent kingdoms. During the reigns of the last German Carolingians (888-911), the kingdom of G. remained nominally united, but in actuality duchies were set up in the territories of the ancient tribal realms, where a strong ethnic and legal tradition continued to exist. Thus the kingdom became a confederation of "national" duchies – Saxony, Lotharingia, Franconia, Swabia and Bavaria – which also extended over the marches of Carinthia and Austria and held a nominal overlordship over *Bohemia. However, the realm itself lacked a centre, as the royal authority declined, despite the regular elections of kings during the first half of the 10th century. Moreover, G. was weakened by *Norman raids, which affected Saxony and Lotharingia, and by *Hungarian invasions, which wreaked havoc on Bavaria and ruined its marches.

Restoration of royal power and political unity was effected by *Otto I the Great, whose reign had the strongest impact on the historical evolution of G. in the Middle Ages. Otto's power was based on his strong army – the major part of which was composed of forces from his hereditary duchy of Saxony – which was reputed for its victories over the Hungarians, crowned by the great victory of *Lechfeld (955). Additional power was procured from Otto's domination of northern Italy, a result of his expeditions of 951 and 962, the latter trip being the occasion of his coronation as emperor. All these factors allowed the king to impose his authority over the German duchies and to introduce radical changes in the political structure of G. Whenever a ducal office was left vacant, Otto would appoint members of his own family and thus was able to fight local separatism. Moreover, he granted large estates, taken from the duchies, to the bishops and imposed royal (and after 962, imperial) control upon the bishoprics of his kingdom. About a third of the territory which represented the ecclesiastical estates was put directly under the control of the kingship, allowing him to be less dependent on the dukes, so that he was able to curb ducal power. In addition, so as to suppress the strong sentiments towards the Carolingians which existed in Lotharingia, Otto's brother, *Bruno, archbishop of Cologne, divided the duchy, which he ruled on the king's behalf, into two (965), Lower and Upper Lotharingia (the latter comprising modern *Lorraine). Furthermore, *Carinthia, which was regained from the Hungarians, was made a duchy and separated from Bavaria. In 962, following his imperial coronation, Otto established the "*Holy Roman Empire of the German Nation", thus uniting G. with Italy and creating a universal empire based on the rule of German emperors (see *Holy Roman empire). The "Ottonian constitution" of G. formed the basis for the development of *feudalism in the country, which, as distinct from France, was more hierarchically structured; dukes, margraves, counts and bishops constituted the class of the "princes", while the lesser vassals, who wielded power on their own estates, were much more dependent on their lords than was the case in France and Italy.

Under Otto's successors, G. began to expand eastwards; Poland temporarily accepted the German protectorate, while Bohemia actually became a duchy within the kingdom. German bishops and other missionaries influenced the Slavic tribes located between the Elbe and Oder rivers, which helped to prepare the annexation of their territories to G. As a result of such expansion, G. became a multi-national state at the end of the 10th century, and three of the four "nations" constituting the empire, according to the conceptions of *Otto III, were included in the realm of G. (the Germans, the Slavs and the French).

After the extinction of the *Ottonian dynasty, G. was ruled by the *Salians (1024-1125), a Franconian dynasty. Under *Henry III royal authority was strong. With intentions of effecting church reform, Henry appointed bishops who were faithful to him. In this way he was able to compel the dukes and counts to be faithful executors of his policy. The public character of the ducal charge was enforced and the king appointed dukes of his own choice and dismissed those who were disloyal. Nevertheless, he was compelled, for the sake of imperial policy, to concede more power to the princes and vassals. Following Henry's death, G.'s involvement in Italian politics and the subsequent conflict with the papacy, known as the *Investiture controversy, led to a decline in imperial authority and to the rise of the German princes. The reign of his son *Henry IV was affected by revolts which reflected local separatism in Saxony and Swabia and led to the election of anti-kings in 1076-80. A state of quasi-anarchy marked the last years of Henry IV's reign and that of his son, *Henry V. The emperors were compelled to personally suppress frequent revolts and had to rely on the princes, whose loyalty was generally bought through the concession of privileges, such as the inheritance of duchies. Aware of their power, the German princes convened assemblies, or diets, during the years 1119-20, in which they elaborated the conditions for a solution of the Investiture contest, which was finally achieved by the Concordat of *Worms (1122).

The Salian period was also marked by the development of the cities in the Rhine Valley; originally ecclesiastical centres, they grew and prospered as a result of the revival of *commerce. The demographic "revolution" of the 11th century in western G. led to the beginnings of German expansion eastwards, particularly into Austria and Carinthia, which were Germanized. In that respect, and with the exception of the reconciliation between the church and the empire, the reign of *Lothair III of Supplinburg was a continuation of the social and economic policy of his Salian predecessors.

The age of the *Hohenstaufen dynasty (1137-1254) was the greatest period of medieval Germany. Their authority based in their duchy of Swabia, the emperors attempted to impose their rule over all of G. This was done by means of a non-feudal administration made up of the *ministeriales, officials of servile origin who were raised to this important political position, and by the development of feudal structures in such a way so as to weaken the power of the great princes. Imperial policy was elaborated at the Diet of Besançon by

*Frederick Barbarossa (1156). He proclaimed imperial sovereignty and expounded the royal rights of the regalia (governmental prerogatives, such as the administration of justice, taxation, and the maintenance of public order, which were exercised by the feudal lords in the name of the emperor). The most important consequences of Frederick's policy were the dissolution of the historical duchies and the division of G. into numerous feudal units of various sizes. This change was realized only after a long and difficult struggle between the emperor and the *Welf family, the latter ruling over Bavaria and Saxony, with its heads, *Henry the Proud and his son *Henry the Lion, acting as sovereigns. To weaken their influence, Frederick first worked to diminish the power of Bavaria. Raising Austria to the rank of a duchy which was directly dependent upon the emperor, he invested it to the loyal Franconian family of *Babenberg. Carinthia, too, was separated from Bavaria, while the royal title was granted to the dukes of Bohemia. In this way the Bavarian stronghold was encircled by Frederick's supporters. The emperor also made use of feudal procedures of justice at the Diet of *Gelnhausen to convict Henry the Lion of felony and to confiscate his fief of Saxony, which was subsequently divided into three separate duchies (1180). In addition, vassal units east of the Elbe were made direct vassals of the empire. Thus, the Diet of Gelnhausen marked a radical change in the political structure of medieval G. and its impact was felt up to 1864, when Bismarck reunited northern G. under Prussian rule.

The latter half of the 12th century was the Golden Age of German expansion eastwards, known as Drang nach Osten (The March Eastwards). Led by princes, such as Henry the Lion, the conquests led to the annexation of the territories between the Elbe and the Oder. The new territories were then settled by German colonists and those Slavs who were not killed were forcibly Germanized. In 1157 Frederick Barbarossa also annexed *Silesia, won from Poland, and began the process of its Germanization, together with that of the Slav country of Pomerania, located on the shores of the Baltic Sea. The success of the Germanization process was reflected in the spread of eastern European cities modelled along the lines of the German type (the Saxon city of *Magdeburg being the original model). The "Charters of Magdeburg", which had already been adopted in Poland and Hungary, became the symbol of urbanization in eastern Europe.

In the long run, the achievements of Frederick Barbarossa weakened imperial authority and also affected the unity of G. His poor relations with the papacy and Italy led to an alliance between the pope and the defeated Welfs, and with *Innocent III's support, the crown was transferred to *Otto of Brunswick, the son of Henry the Lion. Only when the pope saw that the new emperor meant to continue the policy of his predecessors, did he call upon his Sicilian ward, *Frederick II, convincing him to fight Otto for his rightful crown (1214). When a Hohenstaufen-*Capetian alliance defeated the Welf-English league at *Bouvines, a new era began for G. This was largely due to Frederick's interests in Italy and Sicily; the constitution he issued in favour of the princes, granting them privileges, was meant to win their fidelity. In addition, the absence of the emperor from G. (with the exception of some short visits), not only allowed the high nobility to act quasi-independently, but also left the country without a central government. Frederick's sons, *Henry (who revolted against his father in 1234), and after him *Conrad IV, lacked the necessary prestige, despite their royal titles, to regain control. The struggle between the papacy and the emperor, which lead to repeated excommunications, gave religious legitimacy to revolts in G.; in 1246 an anti-king, *Henry Raspe, was elected but failed to maintain his authority. In 1254, upon the death of Conrad IV, the princes were unable to agree on a candidate for the imperial throne; several princes, such as *Alfonso X of Castile, *Richard of Cornwall (brother of King *Henry III of England) and William, count of Holland, sought election, but without positive results. Anarchy continued in G. during the "Great Interregnum" (1254-72), and several counts and margraves were able to attain power to a degree previously unknown. The class of princes was enlarged to include all lords, who now wielded the prerogatives of government over greater territories than before. The cities, on the other hand, struggled for autonomy. Urban confederations emerged with the intention of defending the interests of the cities and their trade. Noted among these was the "Confederation of the Rhine", composed of the cities between and including Basle and Cologne, which created its own government and hired armies to impose peace. More important was the *Hanse, which became an international power in the 13th-15th centuries, extending from London to Novgorod in Russia. Thus, even though G. was in a state of political anarchy, this period was a most prosperous one, as reflected by the buildings and urban centres of the 13th century.

The election of *Rudolf of Hapsburg as emperor in 1272 marked the beginning of the last period of medieval G. Surrendering the imperial dreams of his predecessors of the high Middle Ages, he inaugurated a new policy which concentrated on G. itself. His need to constitute a basis for the imperial government led him to establish the territorial principality of the house, which included Austria, Styria and Carinthia. Gradually, the centre of German political life moved from the valley of the Rhine to that of the Danube, and Vienna was made the capital city. The revolt of the Swiss cantons, which deprived the Hapsburgs of their ancestral lands and castles, accelerated this trend. However, the princes, who looked out for their own interests and were jealous of the Hapsburg fortune, refused to accept the establishment of a new dynasty. After the death of *Louis of Bavaria, the imperial crown passed to *Charles of Luxemburg, king of Bohemia, whose dynasty reigned until 1437. Charles IV, who was aware of the anarchic trends of the princes, issued the *Golden Bull after his election, creating the college of the seven electors. These men, who had sole responsibility for the election of succeeding emperors, were selected from among the highest ranks of the princely class of G. Charles paid particular attention to his own kingdom of Bohemia, which became the most prosperous region in G.; as a result, he neglected the western parts of the country and, under the Luxemburg dynasty, the centre of the empire was moved eastwards to Prague. In the interests of Bohemia, the emperors became more involved in Polish and Hungarian affairs than in those of G. With

minor exceptions, such as imperial interventions in Bavaria and Brandenburg, the latter being enfeoffed to the faithful vassals belonging to the house of *Hohenzollern, the Luxemburg emperors confined themselves to the role of heading a vast confederation of principalities. Within each principality itself, the princes acted as independent sovereigns. One result of this policy was the establishment, without any real resistance from the emperor, of the *Burgundian state at the end of the 14th and the beginning of the 15th century. In this state, the entire block of the Low Countries, including the family's original principality, the county of Luxemburg, were united. Burgundian interests nearly led to the detachment of G. from the territories of modern Belgium, the Netherlands and Luxemburg.

Language The German language emerged gradually from the various dialects of the Germanic tribes, which reached a certain degree of unity towards the end of the Middle Ages. Although also related to other Germanic tongues, the historical evolution of G. eventually united these particular dialects into one German language. During the Carolingian period, the following groups of languages were spoken in G.: Old-Saxon, whose first literary texts date from the 9th century; Low-Frankish, from which emerged the Dutch language; High-German (*Hochdeutsch*), including the Rhine Frankish tongue, famous for its use in the Oath of Strassburg of 840, and in a translation of the anti-Jewish treatise of *Isidore of Seville, dating from the last years of the 7th century; the East-Frankish and Thuringian tongues, which merged in the 9th century; Bavarian, which included certain Latin words and whose first literary texts, including homilies and translations of sacred books, date from the 8th and 9th centuries; Alemannic, still spoken in the German part of Switzerland, which became a literary language in the 9th century, when the Psalms were translated into it by Notker. In the 11th century, these linguistic groups began to merge and gradually High-German became the most popular of the tongues and served as the literary language of G. But oral traditions continued to be maintained over the generations and some Latin and German documents still contain certain idioms from the various dialects.

Literature As in the other west European countries, the learned society of G. used Latin as their written language, in both scholarly and historical treatises and works, as well as in the production of official documents of the courts and authorities. On the other hand, popular literature, including popular religious texts, such adaptations of the lives of Jesus Christ, the apostles, several translations of the Holy Books and popular stories of saints, was written in the various Germanic tongues of the 8th and 9th centuries. Some prayers in the vernacular, such as particular requests for Divine Grace, were added to the Latin prayers in the 9th to 11th centuries. Also in German were the epic poems of the 11th-13th centuries, which dealt with adventures of knights. Among these was the *Rudolieb* (11th century), which included popular tales and fables. Also important was a group of moral texts in German, based on the lives of saints and historical episodes taken from Latin writings. These works and their Latin counterparts characterized the literature of the Ottonian and Salian periods, when the

Sts. Christopher, Eustace and Erasmus; *15th-century German wood sculpture by Hans Riemenschneider*

religious impact on literature was quite strong and the monasteries were the main sources of inspiration and writing. The Investiture contest and the ensuing struggle between the church and the empire had their impact both on theological-historical works and on polemical literature. In addition, this situation led to the emergence of lay literature in German which recalled the ancient classical tradition; it dealt with the lives of the emperors, adapted after Suetonius, and included German versions of the *Alexander the Macedonian romances (c. 1150). The epics of the *Carolingian era also merit mention, although they do not reach the same degree of quality and quantity as in the French language. The golden age of German medieval literature was that of the Hohenstaufen period. Based on the ideals of *chivalry, its authors, such as *Gottfried of Strasburg, contributed to the *Arthurian cycle or adapted classical motifs taken from Virgil; *Wolfram of Eschenbach worked largely in the latter mode, although his most famous poem, *Parzival*, earned him a distinguished place among the Arthurian poets of the 13th century. The most important work of the German literary school of the period was rooted in the national pagan epic tradition of the Germanic tribes, the *Song of the Nibelungs*, which became the motto of German pride and the symbol of tragedy. The poem greatly influenced the development of anti-papal feelings in G. and served as a model for the legends which praised German heroes, such as Emperor Frederick Barbarossa, "the prisoner of the papalists and of the foes of the German Reich". Lyrical songs which praised the virtues of knights and courtly love were popular in the valleys of the Rhine, Main and Danube, and were spread by the *minnesinger* (singer of love songs), the German minstrel. Another important type of 13th- and 14th-century literature was the scholarly treatise, written both in Latin and German verse. The vernacular was generally intended for the use of the upper urban society. These writings provided standards for a moral life rooted in the faith.

The last centuries of the Middle Ages, marked by the foundation of the German universities, were a time of learning. Theological works abounded, such as those of *Albertus Magnus, who wrote and taught at Cologne. His writing is noted not only for its Aristotelian method, but also for its scientific orientations. Mysticism was another subject for works in both Latin and German, such as those of Meister *Eckhardt and other *Dominican preachers. The impact of the *Black Death was strongly felt in this mystical pietism. Because of their content, these works were attacked by both the ecclesiastical and the lay establishments. Towards the end of the 14th century a new trend of lay literature, in German, emerged. It included the lyrical pedantic songs composed for the upper urban society and the courtly tales written for the entertainment of the nobility. The 15th century brought with it the emergence of German humanism, rooted in the moralistic treatise of John of Tepla (c. 1370-1430), *The Labourer of Bohemia*. Although a medieval moralistic work, it introduced notions which were later developed by the Renaissance humanists of the late 15th and 16th century.

Arts The various artistic expressions in G. were in accordance with the major trends of medieval art in the various periods. Still, German art revealed certain unique trends, such as was the case during the Ottonian Renaissance. The majesty of the new empire found its expression in the *architectural trends of the latter half of the 10th century; churches were built in accordance with the Byzantine style combined with elements which later developed into Romanesque architecture of the 11th century. Structures built along these lines include the monasteries of the valleys of the Rhine, Moselle and Meuse, the best example of these being the *Maria Laach abbey church, and those of Nivelles and of Worms. During Salian rule, the Romanesque style was dominant, but still with impressive dimensions of formality, such as the creation of the imperial box in churches, which were specifically German. In Lower Lotharingia, the plastic arts developed at the end of the 11th and the beginning of the 12th century, when the beginning of Gothic art appeared. Influenced by the Low Countries, the German Gothic style was somewhat developed in the Hohenstaufen period, although the main expressions of Gothic art remain those of France and England. At the end of the Middle Ages, an important school of painting flourished in western and northern Germany. Begun under the influence of the Flemish school, it eventually became independent, producing work in a realistic style.

G. Barraclough, *The Origins of Modern Germany* (1956); G. Waterhouse, *A Short History of German Literature* (1947).

GERONA City in *Catalonia (Spain), on the main road between Spain and France. In the 5th century it was conquered by the *Visigoths who did not interfere in local affairs, leaving actual authority to the bishop. Under Visigothic rule, certain Councils of the Church assembled there. In 713 the Arabs conquered the city, but Arab impact was also barely felt. In 785 the Arabs surrendered control of G. to *Charlemagne and the city came under the administration of a Frankish count, who was dependent on the margrave of Spain (see *March of Spain). In the middle of the 9th century the title of count became hereditary and the counts became assimilated into the Catalan aristocracy; they became vassals of the counts of *Barcelona and lost their connection with the kings of France in the 10th century. In 1135, when Catalonia became united with the kingdom of *Aragon, the county was abolished and the city was granted municipal privileges and the right to self-government by its municipal council; in addition, two of its delegates were given seats in the Catalan *cortes*. The granting of municipal privileges helped the city to develop into a prosperous commercial centre of northeastern Spain. Such growth continued despite the attacks of the French army under *Philip III of France (1270-85), who conquered the city for a few months in 1285. At the beginning of the 14th century G. was a flourishing city in the realm of Aragon. However, in 1348 the *Black Death took its toll and about two-thirds of the city's population were killed. As a result, G. declined and became a small provincial centre, which lost many of its privileges in 1351, when King *Peter IV granted it as a duchy to his son John.

G. was an important Jewish centre in Spain; in the 11th century a separate Jewish quarter, the Montjuich (The Jewish Mountain), was built in the city, and in the 13th century Jews were appointed to posts

within the city government. The community's fame
is connected to the mystical circles which sprang up
in the 12th century, making the city of G. the nucleus
of the *Kabbalistic movement.

J. P. Cargol, *Girona historica* (1947).

GERSHOM ("The Light of the Exile"; c. 960-1028)
Rabbi. Born at Metz, he was educated at the great rabbinical school of Mainz, where he became the school's
most famous teacher and one of the greatest rabbis of
German and *Ashkenazi Jewry. His works concentrated
on the interpretation and the jurisprudence of the
Talmud, and he was often quoted by his pupils and by
the greatest rabbinical authorities. In the 12th century
an eclectic collection attributed to G. began to circulate
under the title *Herem de'Rabbenu G.* (The Constitution
of our Rabbi G.). One of the most important legal
documents of European Judaism, these enactments
prohibited polygamy and limited the husband's right
of arbitrary divorce, strengthened the couts of law and
introduced the principle of majority rule into the community legislation. Modern research considers the
source of the legislation to have been several authorities
because of the work's eclectic nature. It was originally
attributed to G. because of his uncontested prestige.

Besides legal works, G. also composed liturgical
poems, especially for penitential prayers.

S. Eidelberg, *Responsa of Rabbi Gershom* (1956).

GERSON, JEAN DE (Charlier; 1363-1429) French
theologian. Born in the county of Rethel, he began his
studies in 1377 at the College of Navarre in Paris. There
he studied under Peter d'*Ailly, who remained his intimate friend. In 1394 G. was made a doctor of theology
and, in 1305, chancellor of the cathedral of Notre Dame
and of the University of Paris. Between 1397 and
1401 he retired to Bruges in Flanders, where he wrote
a treatise calling for church reform and putting an end
to the *Great Schism. Entitled *On the Manner of
Behaving in a Time of Schism*, the work exhorted
clergy and laity faithful to either pope (of Rome or
of Avignon) to recognize each other's sacraments. In
1398 he wrote a treatise *On the Restitution of Obedience*,
urging the people of France to renew their loyalty to
Pope *Benedict XIII of Avignon. Later G. became
convinced that only a general council could bring about
unity of the Church; thus, he approved the decisions of
the councils of *Pisa (1409) and Rome (1413), which
he had not attended. He was one of the leading personalities at the Council of *Constance (1415), where
he asserted the superiority of a general council over
the pope. He also demanded that doctors of theology
have a deliberate and definitive voice in such a council,
together with the bishops. In addition, G. condemned
John *Hus and denounced the theories of tyrannicide
advanced by John *Petit. The attitude created hostility
between the theologian and the court of Burgundy,
which he held responsible for the murder of the duke of
Orléans. The conflict was so heated that G. felt unable
to return to Paris, which was under Burgundian influence.
He therefore retired to the abbey of Melk near Vienna,
where he wrote his treatise on the *Consolation of
Theology*, modelled after the work of *Boethius. In
1420 he returned to France, spending the last years of
his life in seclusion at Lyons.

The work of G. has three main aspects: the theological, where he held that nothing was sinful in itself,
since any activity, good or bad, depended solely upon
the Will of God; the political, where he militated in
favour of church unity and the *Conciliar theory and
was one of the champions of *Gallicanism; and the
mystical, based on the views of St. *Augustine, and
also on those of *Dionysius the Areopagite, St. *Bernard.
the *Victorines and St. *Bonaventura. Even after his
own lifetime, his beliefs strongly influenced 15th-
century thought.

Works, ed. L. E. Dupin (5 vols.) (1706);
J. L. Connolly, *John Gerson, Reformer and Mystic*
(1928).

GERTRUDE THE GREAT, St. (1256-1302) German
mystic. Of a noble Thuringian family, she was educated
at the abbey of Helfta in Germany. At the age of 25 she
became a nun and began to lead a life of contemplation.
She composed a treatise on *Divine Piety*, which is one
of the finest literary expressions of Christian mysticism.
In her work, G. maintained that devotion was the only
way to understand the message of the divine will. G.
also wrote a collection of prayers, entitled *The Spiritual
Exercise*.

Works, ed. by the Benedictines of Solesmes (1875);
W. Lampen, *St. Gertrude the Great* (1912).

GERVASE OF CANTERBURY (d. c. 1200) Historian.
He was a monk at the Christ-church of Canterbury and,
in the last two decades of the 12th century, was the
librarian of the congregation. Having access to many
documents containing abundant information on the
court and the archbishopric see, he wrote a detailed
chronicle dealing with the last years of the reign of
*Henry II and especially concerning the reign of
*Richard I (1189-99).

Gervase of Canterbury, *Historical Works*, ed. W. Stubbs
(1880).

GESTES DE CHIPROIS (The Deeds of the Cypriots)
An anonymous history in French, written in Cyprus
in the early 14th century. It deals with the last generations of the *Latin kingdom of Jerusalem (1243-91)
and provides a history of the Crusaders' realm of
*Cyprus. The chronicle appears to be simply a com-
pilation of the work of several authors.

Ed. G. Raynaud (1887).

GEZA I Duke of the Hungarians (970-97). Member of
the *Arpad dynasty, G. imposed his rule on the various
Magyar tribes and united Hungary, fighting and destroying the tribal aristocracy. He fostered relations with
Emperor *Otto II which facilitated the introduction of
Christianity into his country, in 996 he himself converted to the Christian faith.

M. Hellman, *Die Ostpolitik Kaiser Ottos II.* (1956).

GEZA II King of Hungary (1141-61). During his minority, the kingdom fell into a state of anarchy, and the
crown was disputed between several Arpadian princes
supported by foreign powers, such as Byzantium and
the German *Welfs. G. began his actual rule in 1146
and was able to restore peace to the country, where
German influence had begun to be felt, particularly in
the towns. In order to maintain Hungary's independence,
G. fought the emperor of Byzantium, *Manuel Comnenus, whom he compelled to sign a peace treaty in
1155, which recognized him as sole sovereign of his
people.

F. A. Eckhart, *A Short History of the Hungarian People*
(1931).

GEZALIC King of the *Visigoths (507-11). He was an illegitimate son of *Alaric II and was proclaimed king at Narbonne, after his father's death. He fought the Franks who, under *Clovis, penetrated Aquitaine, but was unable to defend it. In 510 when *Theodoric the Great, king of the *Ostrogoths, supported G.'s half-brother, *Amalric, he lost control north of the Pyrénées and fled to Spain, where he died.

R. de Abadal y de Vinyals, *Del Reino de Tolosa al reino de Toledo* (1960).

GHANA Empire in Black Africa in the basin of the Niger River. In the 3rd century the tribes situated near the modern city of Timbuktu were united under the rule of the G. clan, whose members rode in caravans, passing through Sudan and the Sahara on the way to the frontiers of the Roman empire. The state of G. gradually developed and the dynasty imposed its rule over the tribes of western Sudan in the valley of the Senegal River. While very little is known of its history, archaeological and historical evidence proves that the empire achieved a high degree of civilization in the 8th century. The Arab conquest of north Africa, however, caused Berber tribes to migrate southwards and, in the 9th and 10th centuries, these peoples posed a threat to G., causing its emperors to organize a fierce defence. The clashes were generally favourable to G., which began to expand northwards, conquering the Berber principalities of Sudan. In 990 the empire reached the zenith of its expansion with the conquest of the Berber principality of Audaghost (modern Mauritania), where a black governor was appointed. The entire western Sudan consequently fell under Ghanian rule, marking the victory of the sedentarians over the nomads. According to the testimony of the Arab traveller, Al-Bekri of Cordoba, agriculture was developed in the 11th century within the empire, as was the trade of gold, elephants and slaves, sold to the Islamic countries. The development of commerce brought G. in close relations with the Moslem world and led to the penetration of Islam into the country. In the middle of the 11th century the empire was attacked from the north by the *Almoravides, who gained the capital city, G., in 1076.

R. Oliver and J. D. Face, *A History of Africa* (1964).

GHAZNI City in the province of Khorasan in eastern Persia (now Afghanistan), south of Kabul. Founded in the 10th century around a castle, the city served as the capital of an important Moslem state up to the 13th century. During its period of prosperity, the city was reputed for its palaces and gardens and for its developed irrigation system. G. was destroyed by the *Mongols in the 13th century, although it was partially rebuilt in the following century into a small provincial town. The city gave its name to the kingdom of G. and to its dynasty (10th-11th centuries).

The sultanate of G. was created by a Turkish *Mameluke, *Mahmud, who served in the *Abbasid army in the latter half of the 10th century and eventually acceded to military command. In 994 he was appointed governor of Khorasan and settled at G. In 997 and 998 he drove out his Persian and Turkish rivals and created his own realm, which extended, up to 1026, over a large territory covering parts of India, Persia and Turkestan. His embellished and developed capital became a centre of Hindu and Persian art, as well as a cultural centre of the Moslem-Persian civilization. Among those who gathered at his court was the greatest Persian poet, *Firdusi, who composed the great Persian epic, *Shah-Nama* (The Book of Kings) in his honour. Mahmud's son and successor, Massud, was unable to maintain his father's empire. Dynastic struggles facilitated the penetration of Turkish tribes from the Turkestan steppes, led by the *Seljuk family. In 1040 Massud lost control of Khorasan, and in the middle of the 11th century the Ghaznavid dynasty fell and was replaced by the Ghorids, who ruled the shrunken principality of G. until 1221, when it was conquered by *Genghis-Khan and the Mongols.

The Ghaznavid dynasty was founded by a Turkish slave, Subuktigin, who rose to the rank of military governor of G. (660) under the formal suzerainty of the *Samanid rulers of Persia. Upon his death, he was succeeded by his son Mahmud, who founded the state of G.

C. E. Bosworth, *The Ghaznavids* (1963).

GHAZZALI, AL- (Abu Khamad Muhammad Ibn Muhammad Altusi Alshaf'i; 1058-1111) Moslem scholar. Born in the city of Tus, Khorasan, he became involved from his youth in the struggle between the *Sunnites and their opponents, both *Shiites and philosophers. He studied at Nishapur, where he achieved great fame as a theologian. In 1091 he was appointed to teach theology at the new school founded by the *Seljuk vizier, Nizam Al-Mulk, at Baghdad. After the murder of his patron (1092), G. became deeply influenced by the mystical views of the *Sufists; in 1095 he left Baghdad and lived as a nomad *derwish* for 12 years. This period was most fruitful in terms of his creativity and he reached the position of the highest spiritual and scholastic authority in the Moslem world. Legends were spread about his life and deeds. In his writings G. developed a trend which combined sophisticated Islamic scholasticism with non-rational contemplation of the mystics and was based on practice of the faith. Among his numerous works, the most popular was an encyclopedia of the Islamic faith. His works rapidly spread through the Moslem world and were commented on by philosophers, among them *Ibn-Rushd. Through their commentaries, his works, under the name "Algazel", became known to the western Latin philosophers of the 13th century.

W. M. Watt, *The Life and Practice of Al-Ghazzali* (1953).

GHENT (GAND) City in *Flanders (Belgium). In 630 St. *Amandus founded two monasteries there, around which a borough gradually developed; it became a town in the 8th century. In the following century *Norman raids destroyed the major part of the town. In the last quarter of that century, the counts of *Flanders fortified the borough, and in 900 a castle was built for its defence. During the 10th and 11th centuries the counts alternated their visits between the castles of *Bruges and G. As a result, an administrative quarter grew around the borough's castle. The town subsequently developed and a wool and cloth industry was established there, making it an important economic centre. From the end of the 11th century, G. was dependent on England for the importation of wool. During the 12th century the city expanded and prospered, becoming one of the greatest western European centres north of the Alps. As a result, the counts became increasingly interested

The castle of the Counts of Flanders at Ghent (detail)

in the city and therefore visited it more frequently. As the ancient castle no longer served their needs, a new castle, *s'Gravensteen* (The Count's Rock) was built in 1180 by *Philip of Alsace. An impressive building, situated on top of a great rock, the castle still stands today.

Despite their renewed interest, the counts did not interfere in the internal affairs of the city, which had already been granted the right to self-government at the beginning of the 12th century. According to its constitution, the right to govern was reserved for the "Council of the 39", composed of patricians, members of wealthy merchant families. This system led to the establishment of close relations with England for economic reasons. The penetration of French influence into the county in 1302 had its effect upon the city as well. A democratic party composed of the leaders of the craftsmen contested the patrician government. In 1337, when Count *Louis aligned himself with the French party and King *Edward III of England responded with an embargo on wool exports, the democratic party, led by James of *Artevelde, revolted, seized power and imposed its authority over the Flemish cities. Artevelde then signed a treaty with England. After his death, troubles were renewed and the power of the counts was threatened. A fresh uprising, led by Philip van Artevelde in 1379, was directed against the counts and was crushed in 1383 by a combined French, Burgundian and noble army, led by the new count, *Philip the Bold, duke of Burgundy and uncle of *Charles VI, king of France. G. lost many of its privileges although it became an important city in the Burgundian state. In order to affirm their domination over the city, the dukes proclaimed themselves "first citizens of G." as counts of Flanders, and governors

were appointed to rule the city on their behalf. The city, which continued to prosper in the first half of the 15th century, became an artistic centre and a Flemish school developed there. The centre of the city was restored and large homes of nobles and burghers were built. These buildings, which have been preserved, reflect the city's wealth at that time.
J. Dhondt, *Ghent* (1948).

GHIBELLINES A common name of certain parties which emerged in the cities of northern and central Italy; originally it meant urban pro-imperial leaders. The name is Italian for Weiblingen, the castle in Swabia from which the *Hohenstaufen dynasty emerged. The term first appeared at the end of the 12th century, and in the 13th century it was associated with the supporters of *Frederick II and his decendants. While the G. were generally opposed to the *Guelphs, who were pro-papal, this ideological and political distinction was only one aspect of the struggle which divided the leadership of the Italian cities in the 13th and 14th centuries. Local affairs also played an important role in the emergence and development of the G. party. In fact, due to the local aspects of communal politics, the term continued to be used in Italy even after the fall of the Hohenstaufen dynasty, when German affairs had little to do with the *Holy Roman empire. Only at the end of the 14th century, when the failure of the communal regime in Italy was definitive and local tyrannical dynasties seized power, did the term become an anachronism.
J. K. Hyde, *Society and Politics in Medieval Italy* (1973).

GIANO DELLA BELLA (d. 1305) Florentine politician. Descendant of a wealthy *Guelph family, he was the leader of the *Calimala*, the oldest and richest of the aristocratic trade guilds. A conflict with his fellow-nobles caused him to join the democratic party and become the leader of the guilds of the *Arti Minori* in a revolt against the government (1290). In 1292 he seized power and reformed the constitution of the city through the issuance of the "Ordinances of Justice". In 1293 he was elected prior (head of the city), and he created a strong government with which to fight the aristocracy. Accused of breaking his own laws, he was victimized by a coalition of Pope *Boniface VIII, the local aristocracy and *Charles of Anjou, king of Naples, which brought about his exile. G. retired from the political scene in 1295 and resided in France for the remainder of his life.
F. Schevill, *Medieval and Renaissance Florence*, I (1961).

GIBELET (Jubail, Byblos) City in Lebanon. The Byzantine city of Byblos was destroyed in 565 by an earthquake and was reconstructed a century later by the Arabs, who also developed its harbour. Conquered by the *Crusaders in 1101, who gave it the name G., it was made a barony belonging to the county of *Tripoli. The lords of G. were one of the most important noble families of Crusader society.
S. Runciman, *A History of the Crusades* (1953).

GIHAD (JIHAD) "Holy War" in Islam. According to the teachings of the *Koran and the first caliphs, G. was considered one of the most important precepts of the Moslem faith. Moslem theology distinguished between two different senses of the term: the first, the spiritual G., had a sub-division of its own; the "small" G. was the physical fight for the spread and defence of the Islamic faith, while the "big" G. was a moral theology of the 8th and 9th centuries, meant to prepare Moslems, through appropriate teaching and spiritual exercises, to be worthy of the G. and Paradise. In its second sense, G. was merely a reform movement, related to politics, which aimed to create the ideal religious state. The existence of such a state was considered a necessary condition for preparation towards the spiritual G.

EI, III.

GILBERT DE LA POREE (Gillebertus Porretanus; 1076-1154) Scholastic theologian. He studied at Chartres under Meister *Bernard and, after completing his studies, became head of the cathedral school of Poitiers; in 1142 he became the city's bishop. In his theological studies he adopted the doctrine of universals, although he attempted to avoid pantheistic views. As a result, he came to consider divine nature, which he regarded as a concept of the human mind, claiming that only the persons of the divinity were real. His theory provoked strong criticism from St. *Bernard of Clairvaux, who charged him with heterodoxy at the Council of *Rheims of 1148, but his doctrines were not formally condemned. G. also wrote commentaries on the philosophical works of *Boethius, which granted him a distinguished place in the 12th-century Renaissance. Works in *PL,* vols. 64, 188;

N. M. Haring, *The Case of Gilbert de La Porée* (1951).

GILBERT FOLIOT See FOLIOT, GILBERT.

GILBERT OF SEMPRINGHAM, St. (c. 1093-1189) Founder of the Gilbertine order. He was a parish priest at Sempringham, in the diocese of Lincoln, where he encouraged women to convert to monasticism. Gradually their numbers grew and further foundations were established; in 1139 the Gilbertine order was set up. In 1148 G. travelled to *Cîteaux, seeking an incorporation of his nunneries into the Cistercian order, but when the chapter refused to accept authority over communities of women, G. returned to England and composed his own rule for the order. He was proclaimed a saint in the 13th century.

R. Foreville, *Un procès de canonization à l'aube du XIIIe siecle; Le Livre de St. Gilbert de Sempringham* (1943).

GILDAS, St. (c. 500-c. 570) The first British historian. Information about his life may not be reliable, since it is based on a biography, written in Brittany in the 11th century, which contains many legends. According to tradition, G. was a monk, forced to flee Wales after the *Anglo-Saxon raids in England. He subsequently visited Ireland, Rome and Brittany, where he died. He wrote a history of the Anglo-Saxon conquest of Britain, an important Celtic testimony of his people's national tragedy, covering the period from the Roman conquest of the 1st century to his own time. The book, written in Latin, became very popular and, in the 12th century, provided historical background for the *Arthurian legend and romance.

Ed. L. A. Giles (1885);

DNB, XXI.

GILES OF ROME (Aegidius Romanus; 1247-1316) Philosopher. Born at Rome, perhaps of the *Colonna family, he studied at Paris under *Thomas of Aquinas (1269-71). In 1295 he became archbishop of Bourges. His philosophical works consist of commentaries on Aristotelian philosophers, whose ideas he attempted to adapt to the Catholic dogmas. His most important works were two treatises. *De Regimine Principum* (On the Rule of the Princes) was written for his pupil, *Philip IV the Fair, king of France, upon his coronation in 1285. The second treatise, *De Summi Pontificis Potestate* (On the Power of the Pope) expressed his views on the superiority of the papal authority in the Christian world and was the basis for *Boniface VIII's famous bull, *Unam Sanctam.*

G. Bruni, *Le opere di Egidio Romano* (1936).

GIORDANO RUFFO (13th century) Scientist. Member of a family of Calabrian knights, who served at the court of *Frederick II Hohenstaufen, he reached the rank of marshal in the Sicilian kingdom. Interested in the mounted military service, he wrote, at the orders of the emperor, a book concerning the diseases of horses, which was completed after Frederick's death. The treatise was the first book on veterinary medicine to be written in the Middle Ages.

Ed. Molin (1818);

L. Moulé, *Histoire de la Médicine Vétérinaire* (1898).

GIOTTO DI BONDONE (1266-1377) Painter. Born at Cole near Florence, he worked in Florence, Rome, Naples and other Italian cities. In 1330 King *Robert of Naples appointed him *familiaris regis* (member of the royal household). He left the court of Naples in 1334 when the city of Florence offered him the post of director of artistic works. His mural paintings, inspired by biblical themes, were used to decorate numerous Italian churches, especially in Florence. Pope *Boniface VIII appointed him to paint a mural for St. Peter's Church at Rome. Aside from his frescoes, G. also painted on wood and developed new techniques for the preservation of colours on the wooden plates. He initiated a new era in painting, abandoning the Byzantine style and trying to focus attention on a more realistic presentation of his human subjects, as was in keeping with his *Franciscan ideals. In order to achieve this, he worked on spatial features, and was the first to produce spatial effects, although there was not yet any serious attempt to deal with perspective, a technique reserved for the Renaissance school. While G. was influenced by the *Gothic style of art, his work began a transitory period which led to the 15th-century Renaissance. His fame was so great in his own time, that *Dante mentioned his name in the *Divine Comedy.*

O. Siren, *Giotto and Some of His Followers* (1917).

GIOVANNI DE SAN GIMIGNANO (d. 1323) *Dominican preacher. Originally of San Gimignano in Tuscany, he was popular as a preacher at the beginning of the 14th century and was invited to preach penance and moral conduct throughout Italy. G. composed a manual for preachers in which he revealed the fruits of his experience. Written in encyclopedic form, the booklet provides examples for use in sermons, describing numerous technical subjects: agriculture, windmills and water-mills, ships, painting and limning, fortification, arms, *Greek fire, smithing, glass-blowing weights and measures. The manual is thus a valuable testimony of technological knowledge in the first quarter of the 14th century.

B. Gille, *Esprit et Civilisation technique au Moyen Age* (1952).

GIOVANNI PISANO (c. 1245-1314) Artist. Son of

The Adoration of the Magi, *painting by Giotto at the Arena Chapel, Padua*

Nicola Pisano, he studied in his father's workshop and was influenced by his work. G. is noted for his sculptures, especially those found in the cathedral of Pisa. His work was an expression of his dramatic feelings; he also introduced innovations, breaking ties with the majestic style of the Byzantine tradition and introducing the late Gothic form of sculpture to central Italy.

A. Venturi, *Giovanni Pisano* (1927).

GIRALDUS CAMBRENSIS (1147-1223) Welsh historian. Born in Pembrokeshire, he studied in Paris and, upon his return to England, became archdeacon of Brecon (1175). A year later, he was nominated as bishop of St. David's in Wales and was renominated in 1198, although he failed to be elected by the archbishops of Canterbury, who feared entrusting the see to a Welshman. In 1188 he preached the Third *Crusade in Wales. As a historian, he was interested in Anglo-Celtic relations and wrote a history of the English conquest of Ireland. His geographic books, concerning the topography of Ireland and a description of Wales, also contain important historical material.

Works, ed. J. S. Brewer, 8 vols. (1861-91);
F. M. Powicke, *Gerald of Wales* (1935).

GIRART DE ROUSSILLON French epic poem of the 12th century. The work deals with a legendary hero who fought for *Charlemagne, and whose reputation was gained through his pride and as a result of his victories over the Moslems in Spain. At the peak of his glory, the hero proves himself to be a pious man and builds the church abbey of Madeleine at *Vezelay; the poem is thus both an epic and ethical work.

J. Bédier, *Les Légendes Epiques* (1929).

GIRART DE VIENNE Epic poem of the 12th century. The anonymous poet created a legendary hero in *Charlemagne's army out of the historical figure of *Gerard, count of Vienne, during the latter half of the 9th century. The hero of the work gloriously fights the Moslems and, conscious of his noble rank, defends his peers against the persecutions of Charlemagne. The epic thus reflects the feudal nobility's consciousness and assertion of its dignity, its privileges and its social status.

R. Louis, *Girart de Vienne; de l'Histoire à la Légende* (1947).

GIUSTINIANI Genoese family. The G. were one of the most important merchant families of Genoa and, in the 14th century, they controlled the Mahonna, a trade company operating in the eastern Mediterranean. With the establishment of the Mahonna at *Chios in 1346 the Gs. were the actual rulers of the Genoese possessions in the Aegean Sea and rose to a position of political importance in *Genoa itself. The most famous of the family members was Giovanni G., admiral of the republic in 1450, who commanded the fleet sent by the papacy and Genoa to help Constantinople in 1453. He distinguished himself during the defence and was mortally wounded when the *Ottoman Turks conquered the Byzantine capital.

G. Héers, *Gênes au XVe siècle* (1961).

GLABER, RALPH (d. c. 1050) Historian. His origin is uncertain, but it is known that he became a monk when very young. His monastic life was rather unstable and, from the beginning of the 11th century, he resided at several different Burgundian monasteries. At St. Bénigne of Dijon, he drew near to the circle of *William of Volpiano, with whom he remained associated until the latter's death (1030). In 1031 G. joined *Cluny, where he won the favour of Abbot *Odillo, to whom he dedicated his *Histories* in 1048. He next went to Auxerre, where it is presumed that he died. G.'s expansive histories contain various kinds of information, into which he wrote stories and legends. G. was not systematic in his work, and he did not distinguish between principal and secondary facts, nor between actual and legendary events. However, his book is the best source available regarding the social attitudes in western Europe at the end of the 10th century and the beginning of the 11th century.

Ed. M. Prou (1886);

E. Pognon, *L'An Mille* (1947).

GLANVILLE, RANULF (d. 1190) Justiciar. Member of an Anglo-Norman family, he entered the service of *Henry II. In 1163 he was royal reeve at York, and later became sheriff of Lancashire. As sheriff he earned a great reputation in the administration of justice and finances. In 1147 he repulsed the Scottish invasion of his county; Henry then promoted him to the position of justice and attached him to the royal court. In 1180, G. became justiciar of the kingdom, a position second only to the king himself. He remained in that post until the king's death. In 1190 he accompanied *Richard I on the Crusade and died en route. G. wrote a *Treatise on the Laws and Customs of England*, completed in 1188, which was the most important legal work written in England prior to that of *Bracton. The treatise, based on his own experience and discussing royal statutes, was intended to be a practical manual for judges and royal officials. In his work, G. distinguished between criminal and civil cases. His main theme was the role of the royal court as administrator of justice, and he promoted the conception that royal prerogatives are supreme in the legal system of the realm.

Ed. G. E. Woodbine (1932);

B. Lyon, *A Constitutional and Legal History of Medieval England* (1960).

GLASS Like many other technological achievements, the art of G.-making was well-known in antiquity and continued to be developed in the Byzantine empire and the Moslem world. In those countries, G. was used not only for windows, but also for vessels and ornaments. In the Balkans and Asia Minor, minerals, mixed with sand and potassium carbonate, produced coloured G. in various shades of red and green while, in the Moslem world, most famous were the crafts of Tyre and Andalusia. Until the end of the 11th century, west European production was poor in quality and used exclusively for windows. Important progress was made, however, at the end of the 11th century and the beginning of the 12th century. This was largely the result of Romanesque *architecture, which required that a much larger surface be reserved for windows in the new churches. A problem therefore arose of how to produce the necessary quantity and quality of G. The problem was solved in the early 12th century, and a detailed account of the answer in found in the treatise of crafts by *Theophilus the Priest. According to this work, the new technique required that G. be blown; the materials, sand, carbonate and red lead were melted together in a furnace and, when the mixture had

15th-century German green glass beaker

cooled enough so as to become viscous, a blob was placed on the end of a long rod and rotated or blown, until the desired shape was obtained. Dexterity, speed and control of the temperature to which the cooling G. was exposed were essential, as these factors controlled the strength of the final product, which was of chief interest to the G. industry.

In the 12th century, G.-making again took a step forwards. By means of a mixture of minerals, such as copper and iron, stained G. was produced. Towards the end of the century, the technique was perfected to such an extent that the production of blue stained G. — or the *bleu chartrain* (Chartres blue) in northern France and the Low Countries, named after the windows of the cathedral of Chartres — has remained a technological secret, never successfully reproduced in later ages.

From the 13th century on, G. was used more frequently in domestic vessels, both in the West and in the East. As a result of the Crusades, the techniques of the Tyre industry were brought to Europe, and Venice became the centre of delicate G.-making, concentrated in the island of Murano. At the end of the 13th century, G. was used for spectacles, first introduced in 1285. From the 14th century, the neutral properties of G. in chemical experiments were recognized, and laboratory tools of G. began to be introduced.
E. B. Haynes, *Glass* (1948).

GLASTONBURY ABBEY The oldest monastery in England, of Celtic origin. In 708 it was turned into a Saxon abbey. Destroyed by the Danes in the 9th century, it was restored by King *Edmund in 944 and began to flourish. In the 12th century it became the scene of pilgrimages to the tombs of King *Arthur and St. Dunstan, which it was believed to contain. Many legends emerged concerning its place in the Arthurian romance, and also in connection with Joseph of Arimathaea and St. *Patrick. Another series of legends arose around the "Glastonbury Thorn", a kind of Levantine hawthorn, which flowered there twice a year, around Christmas and in May.
J. A. Robinson, *Two Glastonbury Legends: King Arthur and St. Joseph of Arimathea* (1926).

GNIEZNO (GNESEN) City in western Poland. In the 10th century the town of G. was the centre of the estates of the *Piast family, the founders of Poland and, at the beginning of the 11th century, it became the capital of the realm and the see of the Polish archbishops. An impressive cathedral was built at the end of the 11th century in the Romanesque style. Up to 1320 the city's history is closely related to that of Poland, since G. was the country's political capital before it was replaced by *Cracow. G. was also the religious centre of the country and in 1420 its archbishops were recognized as primates of the kingdom. The urban development of Poland in the late Middle Ages did not affect G., which preserved its noble and religious character.
M. Jedlicki, *La Création du premier archevêché polonais à Gniezno* (1933).

GNOSTICISM The term was derived from the Greek *genosis*, meaning knowledge. In early Christianity the movement, whose origin was pagan, was oriented towards a search for the knowledge of God, which was rooted, according to its followers, in a secret message found in the writings of the apostles and revealed only to true believers. In the 3rd century, the priest *Mani developed the theory of a dualist force; his teachings, which were renounced by the church hierarchy, served as a basis for the Manichaean theories. Although proclaimed heresy by the established church, the movement persisted at the beginning of the Middle Ages, particularly in Syria, Iraq and Asia Minor. In the 10th century, G. began to spread westwards to the Balkans. However, the overall movement was never consistent in belief and form. Adopted in the 11th century by the Bulgarians, Manichaeism was then passed to western Europe and, in the 12th century, was adopted by the *Albigensians.
S. Runciman, *The Medieval Manichee* (1949).

GODEFROY DE BOUILLON See GODFREY OF BOUILLON.

GODFRED King of Denmark (800-10). Chief of the Danish tribes of Jutland, and successor of King *Sigfrid, he continued his predecessor's policy of supporting the *Saxons against *Charlemagne. His confrontation with the Frankish monarch was largely indirect by means of his attack upon the Abrodites and the capturing of their king. Between 803 and 806 G. directly attacked the Franks in Saxony and commanded maritime raids in Frisia and the Low Countries. G. also made innovations in the field of fortifications in Scandinavia. He constructed a strong defence line in the Schleswig Isthmus, which bore his name. Its site is now occupied by the Kiel Canal.
G. Jones, *A History of the Vikings* (1968).

GODFREY IV, the Bearded Duke of Upper Lorraine (1044-45), of Spoleto (1057-70), of Lower Lotharingia (1065-69). Son of Gozelo, who had united the two Lotharingian duchies, he inherited only Upper Lotharingia. In an attempt to obtain the whole of his inheritance, he revolted against *Henry II, who had appointed his younger brother, Gozelo, as duke of Lower Lotharingia. His revolt failed and he was imprisoned. Later reconciled with the emperor, he was restored as duke of Lorraine in 1046. In 1047 he again revolted and Henry had to fight fiercely in order to effect his criminal sentencing. G. went to Italy and in 1054 married Beatrice, the widow of Marquis *Boniface of Canossa, ruler of Tuscany. Thus, by breaking the feudal code, he became the virtual master of Tuscany. Henry, who could not accept this situation, appeared in Italy and G. fled to Lorraine (1055). The sudden death of the emperor in 1056 allowed G. to dominate central Italy, while his brother Frederick was made Pope *Stephen X (1057). G. seized the duchy of Spoleto and was instrumental in the election of Pope *Nicholas II, without the emperor's permission, in 1059. He took advantage of the decline in imperial power during the minority of *Henry IV to add the duchy of Lower Lotharingia to his possessions (1065).
G. Tellenbach, *Königtum und Stämme in der Werdezeit des deutschen Reiches* (1939).

GODFREY OF BOUILLON (1060-1100) The first ruler of the *Crusader kingdom of Jerusalem (1099-1100). Member of the family of the counts of Boulogne and Ardennes, he inherited the duchy of Lower Lotharingia in 1076, and ruled it from the castle of *Bouillon. Although an important prince of the *Holy Roman empire under *Henry IV, his authority weakened when the power of the counts increased within the duchy. As a result, only the central part of his territory, later called *Brabant, remained effectively under his control. In 1096 G. took the cross and was one of the most important leaders of the First *Crusade. Crusaders coming from various provinces of the empire joined his army and followed him through the Danube, Constantinople, Asia Minor, Syria and Palestine. At the siege of Jerusalem, he commanded the northern section of the besiegers, composed of his own men together with troops from northern France and a Norman, south Italian contingent, commanded by *Tancred of Hauteville. As commander of the troops which first penetrated Jerusalem, G. was offered the crown by the Crusaders who had assembled at the church of the Holy Sepulchre. However, he refused the royal title, choosing to be "Advocate of the Holy Sepulchre", meaning the secular head of an ecclesiastic state. After most of the Crusaders had departed for their own countries, G. and Tancred, with the aid of the Venetian fleet, worked to defend the realm from an Egyptian counter-attack and from the conquest of the littoral cities. In the summer of 1100 G. became ill and died prior to the conquest of Haifa. G. was a man of deep religious convictions, which made him a poor politician. His ideal of founding an ecclesiastical state in Palestine was entirely unrealistic, considering the political and military conditions of the time; on the contrary, there was need for a strong lay authority in the new frontier state between Christianity and Islam. G.'s role as the founder of the kingdom of Jerusalem was exaggerated by later generations and his figure became the basis of legends; one such tale, *Roman du Chevalier au Cygne* (the "Swan Knight"), became a popular poem dealing with the royal origins of his family.

M. Lobet, *Godefroi de Bouillon* (1943).

GOG AND MAGOG According to biblical tradition, Gog and Magog were two peoples under the domination of Satan, and their great war of the "end of the world" was destined to be the prelude of Messianic times. The tradition was cultivated in the Middle Ages, and various legends emerged in western Europe which designated the peoples as giants. Such were they represented in the various styles of medieval art as well. From the beginning of the year 1000 G. became a central topic of popular sermons. In the late Middle Ages, the location of their country was fixed in the Far East, north of China.

N. Cohen, *The Pursuit of the Millenium* (1958).

GOLDEN BULL (Bulla Aurea) The term designated several documents of great importance, which were sigillated with a *bull of gold. Medieval protocol reserved them for imperial documents, such as those of Byzantium, and from Byzantium the practice was adopted in the *Holy Roman empire. Among the Gs. two are of particular historical importance:

The G. of Eger Issued in 1213 by *Frederick II, it granted wide privileges to the church and the German nobility in an attempt to win their support in the struggle against *Otto IV. The privileges offered recognition of a large degree of autonomy wielded by the German princes, who were given full military and jurisdictional authority over their vassals and subjects. Thus, the issuance of the G. of Eger was, in effect, the act which divided *Germany into a large number of principalities, under the authority of the emperor.

The G. of 1356 Issued by Emperor *Charles IV, it served to organize imperial elections in Germany through the establishment of the college of Seven Electors who were: the archbishops of Mainz, Trier and Cologne, the king of Bohemia, the duke of Saxony, the margrave of Brandenburg and the count-palatine of the Rhine. Upon the death of an emperor, the electors were to meet at Frankfurt and elect a successor. The electors were granted regalian rights, which made them virtually independent rulers in Germany and placed them at the top of the social and political hierarchy of the country. Thus, the pope's claim to examine rival candidates was ignored.

G. Kantorowicz, *Frederick II* (1931);
B. Jarret, *The Emperor Charles IV* (1935).

GOLDEN HORDE Mongol khanate in Russia and northern Turkestan, founded in 1241 by *Batu-khan; it formed the western part of the *Mongol empire of the *Genghis-khanid dynasty. The southern and eastern parts of the G. were made up of a number of territories under direct Mongol rule. These included the Ukraine (together with the ancient Russian principality of Kiev), the steppes of the Volga as far as *Bolgar and *Riazan, the northern parts of Caucasia, as well as some territories east of the Ural Mountains. The G. also indirectly dominated the Russian principalities, whose princes had to receive confirmation of their rule from the khan and were made to pay him heavy tributes, although they were allowed to rule autonomously. In 1242 Batu-khan began to build the capital of the G. on the lower Volga at Sarai. The project was completed by his brother and heir, Barka-khan (1257-66), who organized the kingdom and secured its virtual independence from the great khans of Karakorum and Peking. Barka-khan also granted *Genoa commercial privileges in Crimea, where the Genoese colony of Caffa (Kaffa), was situated, and in this way trade between the Asian steppes and the Black Sea was developed. Barka-khan converted to Islam and the G. itself became Islamized under his heirs. This change separated the Mongols and their Turkish subjects (grouped together and called *Tatars by the Europeans) from the Russians. As a result, the G. was the only Mongol state not assimilated in the surrounding civilization (as distinguished from the khanates of China and Persia).

Dynastic troubles in the last quarter of the 14th century facilitated the uprising of the Russian princes of *Moscow, who had obtained the title of great princes from the khans. In 1380 Prince *Dimitri "Donskoi" defeated the Mongol army at Kulikovo and proclaimed his independence. Victory, however, was not definitive and the new khan, *Tuktamish, invaded the Russian territories, destroyed the principal cities and imposed G. rule for another century. The Mongol state had nevertheless weakened, and in 1395 it was annexed to the empire of *Timur-leng (Tamerlane). Although restored at the beginning of the 15th century, the G. never regained its former stature. The western provinces were conquered by the dukes of Lithuania and annexed to the new great duchy while, in the north, the princes of Moscow again worked to consolidate their own state. Moreover, the foundation of new hordes led to the establishment of two new khanates at *Crimea and *Kazan, which lessened the authority of the monarchs of Sarai under the reign of Kuchuk Muhammad (1423-

59). In 1480, the great prince of Moscow, Ivan III, formally repudiated any allegiance to the G. and proclaimed the independence of Russia. The combined pressure of Russia and the dissident khanates, together with family troubles, finally led to the destruction of Sarai and the collapse of the G. in 1502. What little remained of it was attached to the khanate of Astrakhan in the 16th century.

G. Vernadsky, *The Mongols and Russia* (1953).

GOLDEN LEGEND (Latin: Legenda Aurea) A manual, consisting mainly of lives of the saints and short treatises of the Christian festivals, composed by *Jacob of Voragine between 1255-66. The book was arranged according to the church calendar year. Its purpose was to instil piety and the author made use of a great number of anecdotes and curious tales. The book became popular in northern Italy and had spread from Lombardy to all of western Europe by the end of the 13th century; in fact, it came to be called *Lombardica Historia* (The Lombardian History). In the 14th and 15th centuries it was translated into various languages and its Latin original became one of the first texts to be printed at Ulm in 1469.

P. Butler, *Legenda Aurea – Légende Dorée – Golden Legend* (1899).

GOLDEN ROSE A medal of distinction which the popes awarded to kings and princes, from the 12th century on, in recognition of their extraordinary activities on behalf of the faith. It was customary to bestow the G. only once a year and to a single person.

GOLIARDS A name given by 12th- and 13th-century Latin chroniclers of western Europe to a group of nomadic poets, considered the "sons" of a certain Golias, a legendary, learned bishop. The appearance of their work is related to the emergence of the urban schools and universities. The G., who were intellectuals, were known to praise nature, love wine and women and to criticize the ecclesiastical establishment. *Abelard is considered one of them because of the nature of his poems, although the form he used was not characteristic of this type. While the majority of the G. remained anonymous, the most famous among them was the *Archipoet, patronized by *Raynald of Dassel, archbishop of Cologne and chancellor of *Frederick Barbarossa. Among the collections of Goliardic songs, the most famous are the *Carmina Burana* from the beginning of the 13th century. The most exhaustive collection was compiled at the Bavarian Abbey Benedictbauren, and is now located at the National Library of Munich.

H. Waddell, *The Wandering Scholars* (1935).

GOMBETTE (Law) The popular name of the *Burgundian laws, issued before 500 and named after King *Gundobald, their supposed author. The code contains many oral customs and especially concerns private and family traditions of the Burgundian tribes, as well as customs concerning property, cattle and jurisdiction.

H. F. W. D. Fischer, *Leges Barbarorum* (1956).

GONDOBALD King of the Burgundians. See GUNDOBALD.

GONZAGA Aristocratic family of Mantua in Lombardy. It attained a position of importance in the city at the end of the 13th century when, due to his wealth, the head of the family was able to obtain popular support. On the basis of such support, the members

of the family claimed authority over the city and, in 1328, they succeeded in seizing power. Luigi was proclaimed hereditary captain general (1328-60) and, through a series of coalitions with Lombard tyrants, he imposed his authority over the county and subdued the power of the lords of Milan. His son, Guido, succeeded him (1360-69) and had no difficulty in retaining his power; he was actively involved in Italian politics. Under the rule of his grandson, Francesco I (1382-1407), the G., who became allied to the *Visconti of Milan, received the title of count and became key rulers of northern Italy.

W. F. Butler, *The Lombard Communes* (1906).

GORM THE ELDER King of Denmark (c. 936-50). One of the most active of Danish chieftains, he seized power over Jutland at a time when it was in a disorganized state, after the successful attack of King *Henry I of Germany in 934. G., a heathen, successfully repulsed the Christian missionaries from Germany. From his ornate capital, he was able to impose his authority over the various Danish chieftains, and to unite Denmark into a powerful state which included Scania. G. was the founder of a dynasty famous for its great achievements; one of his descendants, *Canute the Great, founded the great empire of the North.

G. Jones, *A History of the Vikings* (1968).

GOTHIC ART See ARCHITECTURE, GOTHIC; ART, GOTHIC.

GOTHS A Germanic people, originally from Scandinavia (southern Sweden), who gave their name to the island of Gotland. In the 1st century BC they crossed the Baltic Sea and settled in the country corresponding to modern Prussia, where they remained for 200 years. Pushed by migrations of other Germanic tribes, as well as by demographic expansion, they moved southwards and, in the 3rd century, settled in a very large territory, corresponding to modern Ukraine and Rumania. There they were divided into two tribal groups, the *Ostrogoths, who settled between the Don and the Dniester, and the *Visigoths, who settled between the Dniester and the Danube. During the 3rd century these groups clashed with the Roman empire and attacked its Danube frontier. In the late 3rd and the 4th century their raids in the Balkans became frequent and they posed a threat to the empire. In the middle of the 4th century a Gothic colony composed of merchants and warriors (among them prisoners and hostages) was established at Constantinople. Some of their chieftains were educated there and became influenced by the Arians (see *Church); one of their leaders, *Ulphilas, was ordained "Bishop of the G." and preached the Arian version of Christianity among the Gothic tribes. Conversion of the G. was facilitated by the translation of the Bible into Gothic. Incidentally, the affinity of the Gothic language to other Germanic tongues was an important factor in the conversion of many Germans to Arianism. In 376 the G. were pushed westwards by the *Huns, who conquered the Ukrainian steppes. The G. invaded the Balkans and won a decisive victory over the Romans at *Adrianople, where Emperor Valens was killed and the Roman legions were destroyed by their mounted troops. *Theodosius' recovery of the empire caused them to retreat but, after his death, they became Rome's most dangerous enemy. Between 376-400, the G. were divided into two distinct peoples. Their history

Knights in search of the Holy Grail, *from a 14th-century illuminated manuscript*

ceased to be common to both groups when the Visigoths invaded Italy (405).

E. A. Thompson, *The Early Germans* (1965).

GOTTFRIED OF STRASSBURG (13th century) Poet. Little is known about his life; born probably to a burgher's family of Strassburg at the end of the 12th century, he was educated in Germany and France; his broad cultural background is reflected in his poems, many of them concerning his unrequited love for a certain lady. Written in German, the form and style of his poetry make him one of the greatest German poets of the Middle Ages. His masterpiece, however, is the romance of *Tristan und Isolde* (written *c.* 1200-10), which he created on the basis of French *Arthurian legends. Containing 20,000 verses, this poem is one of the finest achievements in the genre relating the adventures of Tristram. G. also developed the art of description, criticizing his contemporary, *Wolfram of Eschenbach, the author of *Parzival,* for his obscure style.

G. Weber, *Tristan und Isolde* (1949);
G. Weber, *Tristan und die Krise des hochmittelalterlichen Weltbildes um 1200* (1953).

GOTTHARD, St. (d. 1038) Bishop of Hildesheim (1022-38). Born in Bavaria, he became a monk (990) and later the abbot at the Nieder-Altaich abbey. Distinguished for his vigorous rule and piety, he was called to the court of Emperor *Henry I. After his successful activity as a reformer of monasteries in Germany, G. was appointed bishop of Hildesheim. The St. G. (Godard) Pass in the Alps takes its name from a chapel on the summit which has been considered to be one of the places of his retirement.

O. G. Blecher, *Der heilige Gotthard* (1931).

GOTTSCHALK (c. 805-68) Monk and theologian. A son of the Saxon count Bruno, his father forced him to enter the abbey of *Fulda. He fled the monastery in 829, but was recalled by its abbot, Rabanus Maurus, and transferred to the monastery of Orbais, near Soissons in France. There he devoted himself to the study of theology and, on the basis of St. Augustine's writings, developed a theory of double divine predestination, which was attacked as heterodox by *Hincmar of Rheims. His teaching was condemned in 848 at the council held at Mainz and again in 849 at the Quierzy

assembly of the Frankish church. G. was deprived of his priesthood and held prisoner at the abbey of Hautvillers, where he continued his dispute with Hincmar, whom he accused of heresy. Aside from his work as a theologian, G. was also a distinguished Latin grammarian.

C. Lambot, ed., *Oeuvres Théologiques et Grammaticales de Godescalc d'Orbais* (1945).

GOUGH MAP A map of England, drawn by an anonymous cartographer between 1325-30, which is notable for its detail. It includes, for example, the exact position of roads together with their mileage as estimated by travellers. The G. has been preserved in the Bodleian Library at Oxford.

L. A. Brown, *The Story of Maps* (1951).

GOWER, JOHN (c. 1325-1408) English poet. He was one of the first poets in England to mark the transition from Latin and French to English. His earlier poems, which were written in Latin and French, are scholarly in their character and indicate his vast knowledge. In his later years, he wrote the *Confession of the Lover* (*Confessio amantis*) in English; this work is a collection of stories, largely derived from Ovid's *Ars Amandi*.

C. S. Lewis, *The Allegory of Love* (1936).

GRADENICO, PETER Doge of Venice (1289-1311). He was one of the most important reformers of the Venetian supreme authority, the *"Great Council". At the beginning of his term of office, the Council was disorganized and its membership had dropped. G. issued a series of laws (1297) by which families who could prove a paternal ancestor in the council since 1176, were elegible for membership. This law, commonly known as the "Closing of the Great Council", led to the establishment of a register of all births in any families eligible for membership, and it affirmed the aristocratic government of the republic. In 1310, after the attempt of Bajamonte *Tiepolo to overthrow G., the latter established the famous *Council of the Ten, which reached decisions secretly, as the supreme organ of the Venetian government. G. also began the territorial expansion of Venice in northern Italy.

H. Kretschmayr, *Geschichte von Venedig* (1920).

GRAIL, THE HOLY In medieval romances, a vessel which was believed to be the cup used by Jesus Christ at the Last Supper, and later possessed by Joseph of Arimathea. According to legend, the G. continued to exist and possessed spiritual qualities which could bring mystical benefits to its beholders; as a result, it was often sought after. The G. figures first in French literature, particularly in *Perceval* of *Chrétien de Troyes, and was incorporated into the *Arthurian romance. In the 13th century the search for the G. characterized the knights who aimed to reach perfection.

R. S. Loomis, *Arthurian Literature of the Middle Ages* (1959).

GRAMMAR Medieval G. was inherited from antiquity in various forms. In the Byzantine empire, G. was used to maintain the rules of classical Greek, and thus made the language rigid and created a gulf between written and spoken Greek. In western Europe, the Latin tongue declined during the first centuries of the Middle Ages and its G. was used in a very free form. The Arabs, on the other hand, were interested in the development of G. as a creative field of linguistics. The Arab grammarians of the 8th and 9th centuries laid the foundations for its renewal in other languages, the first among them being Hebrew. With the exception of the short period under *Alcuin and the *Carolingian Renaissance, these achievements were not imitated in western Europe prior to the 12th century, which was the epoch of the revival of Latin G. Then G. began to be studied at schools and universities of western Europe as a part of the liberal arts programme.

R. R. Bolgar, *The Classical Heritage* (1954).

GRAN (Esztergom) Religious centre of Hungary. Situated on the Danube, north of Budapest, the town of G. was founded in the last quarter of the 10th century. In 995 St. Adalbert of Prague settled there and founded a monastery where Prince Waic (*Stephen) was baptized in 996. During the time of his pupil Anastasius, who continued the missionary activity in Hungary, an archbishopric was established at G. (1000) and its primacy over the church of Hungary was asserted. Its proximity to Buda, the political capital of the kingdom, kept G. a small religious town, entirely dominated by its great cathedral.

C. A. Macarney, *The Magyars in the Ninth Century* (1930).

GRANADA City in southern Spain, at the foot of the Sierre Nevada. A small provincial town, noted for its temperate climate, G. was in the possession of the *Vandals,the Byzantines and the *Visigoths between the 5th and 8th centuries, and was finally conquered by the Arabs in 711. The city developed under Arab rule and became the summer residence of the *Ummayad caliphs of *Cordoba. In 1031, after the downfall of the caliphate of Cordoba, G. gained its independence and became capital of a minor emirate of the *Taifas. Conquered by the *Almoravides at the end of the 11th century, G. was integrated into their state and was governed by Moorish officers, who were subordinate to the provincial governors of *Jaen. This regime later continued under *Almohade rule. In 1230 the Taifas of Arjona in western Andalusia revolted against the Almohades and, in 1237, their leader, Al-Nasir, conquered G. He proclaimed himself emir, assuming the name *Muhammad I, and established the Nasirid dynasty, which continued to rule what was to be the last Moslem state in Spain until 1492. Up to 1250 Muhammad took advantage of the collapse of the Almohades and of the feuds between the Taifa emirates of southern Spain to conquer Almeria and the whole littorial strip up to Gibraltar. After that point, the Nasirids concentrated on the organization of their territories, which allowed the conquest of the other Andalusian principalities by the *Castilians. In 1270 G. was the last Moslem kingdom in the territory of Spain. As its capital, the city of G. flourished. Muhammad I began the construction of his palace,

General view of the Alhambra, *Granada*

the famous *Alhambra, which became the most important complex of Moslem art in Spain. Muhammad II (1302-09) built the city's great mosque and created the gardens of Alhambra. Until the 13th century the city had been cosmopolitan, containing some very important Jewish and Christian communities, but after the expulsion of its Jewish and Christian inhabitants in 1232 its Moslem character was accentuated. This was particularly due to the rule of the Nasirids, who claimed to be descendants of the prophet Mohammad. In the 14th century the city attracted emigrants from Morocco, who developed crafts and who enjoyed the luxuries of the Nasirid court. In the 15th century the power of the realm was weakened by disputes between the Banu Al-Sarraj (Abencerrages) and Thagri (Cegries) branches of the dynasty. The Nasirids gradually lost the major portion of their territories, including Almeria and the western strip of Gibraltar, and their kingdom was reduced to the neighbourhood of G. itself. Mohammad XI (known as Boabdil) sought the alliance of the Catholic sovereigns of Aragon and Castile. Nevertheless, G. was subjected to a long siege and capitulated in 1492. Mohammad XI, the last Moslem king of G. fled to Morocco. G. was united with the rest of Spain.

E. A. Peers, *Granada* (1929).

GRAND ASSIZE, THE A law issued by *Henry II of England in 1179, whereby claims concerning tenure of lands could be settled by a trial before a jury of 12 knights in a royal court. This procedure replaced the practice of the trial by battle; as such, the G. was one of the fundamental reforms of English common law.

B. Lyon, *A Constitutional and Legal History of Medieval England* (1960).

GRAND JURY Judicial institution of medieval England, established in 1166 by *Henry II in the Assize of *Clarendon. Each shire was appointed 12 jurors whose duty it was to indict all men having committed, or suspected of having committed, any criminal action. Only after indictment could the accused be brought to trial at the royal court. Since the 13th century the G. has been constantly developed and has become one of the fundamental institutions of English legal procedure.

B. Lyon, *A Constitutional and Legal History of Medieval England* (1960).

GRANDE ORDONNANCE OF 1357 A document issued at the Assembly of the French *Estates General, convened after the defeat of Poitiers (1356) and during the captivity of King *John II. It called for the levying of a heavy tax for royal needs, but also provided for the extensive reform of the state, requiring that all royal officers be responsible to the Estates. One of its most interesting features was the constitutional concept that the king's authority was shared with his counsellors and officers. The repression of the revolts of 1358-60 by *Charles V made the G. void and application of its "modern" constitutional concepts was delayed for a number of centuries.

R. Delanchenal, *Histoire de Charles V* (1909).

GRANDES CHRONIQUES DE FRANCE An extensive historical compilation composed by the monks of the abbey of *St. Denis near Paris. This history of the kings of France was begun in the 12th century by Abbot *Suger and was continued and kept up-to-date by monks until the end of the 15th century.

Ed. J. Viard, 10 vols. (1920-53).

GRANDES COMPAGNIES Bands of hired soldiers in the English army during the first stage of the *Hundred Years' War. After the Battle of *Poitiers (1356) they were discharged. They remained in France, where they became brigands and threatened public order during the regency of the dauphin (*Charles V). With the intention of removing them from French soil, Charles commissioned *Du Guesclin to enlist the G. in his army, which was to be sent to Spain to fight *Peter the Cruel, king of Castile (1369).

E. Perroy, *The Hundred Years' War* (1958).

GRANDMONT, ORDER OF Monastic order established in France in the 12th century by Stephen of Muret (c. 1054-1124), who founded a community which strictly observed the *Benedictine rule at Grandmont (Normandy). Its rule was drawn up in 1143, when several monasteries of western France and England joined the congregation. From 1184 disputes arose between the monks and the order began to decline in France, but continued to flourish in 13th-century England.

R. Graham, *The Order of Grandmont and its Houses in England* (1936).

GRATIAN (d. c. 1179) Canonist. Despite the fame of his work, which constituted a turning-point in medieval law and scholarship, very little is known about G.'s life and nothing is available concerning his origins. An Italian monk, he studied and taught canon law at *Bologna (c. 1140), where the law school had already become a reputed authority. Under the influence of Roman law, which was revived at Bologna during his time, G. wrote a vast compilation of ecclesiastical laws, the *Concordantia Discordantium Canonum* (The Concordance of Discordant Canons), better known as the *Decretum Gratiani.* The work was a systematic compilation of all legal materials concerning canon law, methodically arranged by subject and set in a framework of questions and answers. G. relied on earlier authorities, among them the Fathers of Church, the Councils (up to 1140) and the decrees of emperors and popes. The concordance was completed c. 1150 and immediately became a standard textbook of canon law. Pope *Alexander III created G. cardinal.

Corpus Juris Canonici, ed. E. Friedberg (1878).

GREAT COUNCIL (Venice) See VENICE.

GREAT REVOLT OF 1381 Also called the "Peasants' Revolt". One of the most serious social uprisings in England, the revolt presumably broke out in response to the poll tax imposed upon the population; however, its roots were much deeper. The situation of the peasantry had worsened after the *Black Death, when the landlords, short of manpower, attempted to renew the work duties of the peasants and also enclosed a great number of fields reserved for pasture. The disturbances of the G. were constant, particularly in southeastern England and the London area. There popular preachers, having studied the formulations of *Wycliffe and the Oxford *Lollards criticizing the ecclesiastical establishment, developed the doctrine of the ideal of the poor clergy and its affinity to the lower classes. The heterogeneous movement was led by such preachers, including John *Ball and Wat *Tyler. After initial successes in Kent, Sussex and neighbouring counties, the rebels marched into London where, for a short period in summer 1381, they imposed their rule, but without a constructive programme. An alliance made between the nobility and the burgher classes led to the organization of a counter offensive and, due to the poor organization of the rebel movement, the G. was repressed.

R. B. Dobson, *The Peasants' Revolt of 1381* (1970).

GREAT SCHISM, THE (1378-1417) A period during which the papacy was split in two, with popes at Rome and at Avignon, and the Catholic world divided in its obedience. In 1378, when *Gregory XI died at Rome before his return to Avignon, public pressure was applied on the cardinals, most of whom were French, to elect an Italian pope who would remain at Rome. *Urban VI, originally of the kingdom of Naples, was elected but, when he refused to go to Avignon, his election was declared void and a new pope, *Clement VII, was installed at Avignon. The two popes excommunicated each other and appealed for the obedience of the Catholic world. The positions of the various states and churches were rather flexible; they rallied with either pope according to political interests and advantages and were even known to switch their loyalties. The mutual excommunications of the Roman and Avignon popes only served to discredit the papacy in the public's eyes. Moreover, an important trend of thought, expressed by theologians and university professors of Paris, such as John *Gerson and Peter d'*Ailly, developed into the *Conciliar theory, which required that a general council be summoned to bring an end to the schism. An attempt to bring about the resignation of the popes of Rome (*Gregory XII) and of Avignon (*Benedict XIII), in order to allow the election of a new pope, ended in a deadlock. Both popes agreed to resign on the condition that the other do so first. A group of dissident cardinals, from both Avignon and Rome, finally decided to call for a general council at Pisa (1409), where they elected *Alexander V as pope; but the refusal of Gregory and Benedict to resign only created a wider schism entailing three papal contenders. The G. was finally brought to an end at the Council of *Constance, where the conciliar movement, supported by Emperor *Sigismund, triumphed. All three popes were deposed and *Martin V was elected as sole pope in 1417.

W. Ullman, *The Origins of the Great Schism* (1967).

GREAT WALL An imposing fortification in northern China, built in the 3rd century BC, intended to defend China from raids of the Turkish and Mongol tribes of the steppes. Beginning north of Peking, its length is about 3000 km. The G. was constantly rebuilt and developed and, in the 15th century, when the Ming dynasty acceded to imperial rule, it was entirely restored. See *China, History.

GREECE The name G. had several meanings in the Middle Ages. In terms of culture and civilization, it was synonymous with *Byzantium, and was applied as such in western sources. In the religious sphere, the term designated the *Orthodox Church. The third sense of the term was political. Up to 1204 G. designated the Byzantine empire (also called the Empire of the Greeks). Afterwards the various parts of G. became distinct political units. The country was united in 1460 by the *Ottoman Turks and became part of the Ottoman empire until the 19th century.

Under Byzantine rule (395-1204), G. had limited importance within the empire and, with the exception of

the rich province of *Thessalonica, became a backward area. The frequent invasions of Germanic and Slav tribes (5th-8th centuries) led to the emigration of the upper classes, and parts of the ancient villages were deserted; as a result, a great part of the land in northern and central G. ceased to be cultivated. The Slavic settlements in the 8th century somewhat compensated for the demographic losses; the new settlers, who had converted to Orthodox Christianity, became assimilated with the remaining portion of the Greek population and together they formed the *groemium* of the modern Greek nation. In the 9th and 10th centuries the Arabs attacked G. several times and conquered Crete (823-961); the province's western areas, and particularly *Epirus, were attacked by the Normans of southern Italy in the 11th and 12th centuries. While the classical centres of G. completely declined, Thessalonica, which became the city second in importance in the Byzantine empire, and its surrounding areas, were prosperous for a time. Commercial ties developed with the Balkan states and the cultural level was high.

The Fourth *Crusade, which destroyed the unity of the Byzantine world, had a tremendous impact on the history of G. The country was split into two areas in 1204; the Greek half continued to exist as a Byzantine entity, known as the despotate of Epirus, and the second area, the Latin states of G., were more or less dependent on the *Latin empire of Constantinople, although they were actually under Venetian influence. The despotate of Epirus (1204-1336), containing the major part of western G., from Albania to the Gulf of Corinth, was founded by Michael Angelus *Comnenus, a member of the imperial dynasty dethroned at Constantinople, who was able to organize a resistance in the territories he governed. In 1224 his brother and heir, Theodore, conquered the Latin kingdom of Thessalonica and proclaimed himself emperor; however, the Comneni were unable to maintain their authority and, in 1246, Thessalonica was conquered by the *Nicaean army. After the restoration of the Byzantine empire in 1261, the original despotate of Epirus continued to exist as a tributary state of the empire, until it collapsed in 1336 under the attacks of the *Serbs in the north and the Byzantines, who conquered its central parts.

Among the Latin states, the most important in G. was the kingdom of Thessalonica, ruled by the Italian family of *Montferrat (1204-24). Its existence, however, was ephemeral, both because of the constant rivalry between its king, who claimed the imperial title of Constantinople, and the Latin emperor, and because of the attacks by the Bulgarians and the Greek despots of Epirus, who conquered it in 1224 and attached it to their state. The duchy of *Athens (1205-1460) was founded by the Burgundian knight, *Odo of La Roche, who recognized himself as vassal of Boniface of Montferrat, king of Thessalonica; the duchy gained independence after the fall of the Thessalonican kingdom. After the extinction of its Burgundian dynasty, Athens was ruled by *Catalans and Italian princes (see *Athens). The principality of Achaia or *Morea (1205-1429) was the most important of the "Frankish" states in G. It was founded by William of *Champlitte, a vassal of the Montferrat kings of Thessalonica; however, the real power behind the state were the members of the French family of *Villehardouin, originally from Champagne.

Under the Villehardouin, Morea was organized as a feudal principality, where a specifically Frankish culture emerged and developed, combining local and western heritages. At the end of the 13th century most of the principality passed to the *Angevin princes of Naples, while another part of it was held by the *Navarrese company, which claimed full authority over the principality. The struggle between Naples and the Navarrese weakened Frankish Morea, and the Byzantine army gradually began to penetrate the principality, and conquered it in 1429.

An important portion of G. had also been placed in Venetian hands after 1204; some of this territory, such as Crete and Euboea (with the city of Negropont), were directly administered by Venetian officials, while other parts, such as the duchies of Naxos, Cephalonia and the Ionian islands, were held by aristocratic families of the republic. On the coast of the Aegean Sea, *Genoa developed an important colony, ruled by the powerful commercial association of the Mahonna, whose centre was established at *Chios.

The restoration of the Byzantine empire in 1261 affected G. only partially, since its major part remained under the rule of the western princes; in the last years of the 14th century these ruling princes were all Italian and were influenced by the great centres of Venice, Naples and Florence. The Byzantine reconquest did not change the situation of the country, since G. was not made a central part of the restored empire; as a result, it was gradually conquered by the Ottoman Turks.

CMedH, I, IV (1966).

GREEK FIRE A chemical compound of naphtha and sulphur which could burn on water. Invented and developed at Byzantium (whence the name G.) in the latter half of the 7th century, it was thrown in buckets or casks from catapults. The chemicals ignited on the water and burned ships. The G. was first employed in 674-77 (during the siege of Constantinople) against the Arab fleet, which was destroyed.

G. Zenghelis, *Le Feu Grégeois et les Armes à Feu des Byzantins* (1932).

GREENLAND Largest island of the world. Eskimo tribes from the west settled in the island between the 5th and 9th centuries. The remains of their earliest settlements, belonging to the Neolithic culture, show that they settled in the western and eastern coastal regions, and in the central region, the Thule. Towards the end of the 10th century, *Viking sailors arrived in G. from Iceland, and gave it its name. Under the leadership of *Eric the Red (982-86) they established several settlements south of the Eskimo areas, which had their own councils and survived as an independent commonwealth until the 13th century. In 1261, they accepted the sovereignty of *Norway, and royal governors were sent regularly to G. until the middle of the 14th century. During this period, the Scandinavians, who remained separate from the Eskimo stock, accepted Christianity, and a bishopric of G. was established in 1126. It is generally believed that in the 13th century the population numbered about 3000 souls, settled in about 300 "courts" or yards, the basic economic and demographic unit in G. In the second half of the 14th century, a series of plagues and wars affected the Scandinavian population, which diminished and began to emigrate. An important cause of this decline was the Norwegian

authorities' lack of interest in G., as a result of *Hanse influence in Norway, which produced a change in Norwegian policy. Thus, by 1400, the Scandinavian population had left the island. The memory of the G. adventurers was perpetuated only in the Icelandic sagas.

R. Tving, *A Thousand Years of Greenland Shipping* (1944).

GREGORIAN The term designates political and cultural movements named after the popes "Gregory". Of the many phrases which include the term, the most frequently used are G. *Music, the G. Reform and the G. *Calendar of the 16th century.

GREGORY I, the Great, St. (540-604) Pope (590-604). He was the fourth and last "Doctor of the Latin Church" and the founder of the papal state. Son of a senator and heir of large estates in Sicily and Rome, he became prefect of the latter city in 573; after a time, he decided to abandon the lay life and to sell part of his properties in order to help the poor. In 574 he founded seven monasteries, six in Sicily and one at Rome. He entered the last as a monk, imposing upon himself a very austere life. In 577 he left the monastery in accordance with a papal order and became one of the seven deacons of Rome. In 578 *Pelagius II appointed him *apocrisiarius*, in charge of the embassy at the imperial court of Constantinople. In this role, he acquired broad knowledge of the Byzantine court and church and received important diplomatic experience. Upon his return to Rome (585), he became abbot of his own monastery and remained attached to the papal court, where his influence grew. In 590 he was elected pope. In this position he was confronted with anarchy at Rome and in central Italy, where famines, floods and threats of the Byzantine Lombards led to poverty and internal conflicts. G. supplied Rome with food from his own Sicilian estates, and placed the St. Peter's insignia on the walls of the city as a form of defence against the Lombards. In return, he won wide powers of authority there. Thus, he successfully founded a papal state at Rome and made it independent of the Byzantine exarch of Ravenna, who had been deprived of direct contact with the city because of the foundation of the Lombard duchy of *Spoleto. The conclusion of a peace agreement between the papacy and the Lombards in 592 brought about recognition of the papal state. In his relations with Byzantium, G. adopted a firm position; he recognized the imperial civil authority, but demanded the independence of the church in spiritual and dogmatic matters and the supremacy of the Roman see over all other churches. His claim was matched by that of the patriarchs of Constantinople, who proclaimed themselves "Oecumenical Patriarchs". This conflict brought about a separation between the Orthodox and Catholic *churches, and the pope was recognized in the West as the supreme administrative and dogmatic authority of the church. In this role, G. denied the "barbarian" kings of the West any authority over the church. He employed the monastic movement in the service of the papacy; the most important step taken in this direction was the mission led by *Augustine of Canterbury, commissioned to convert the Anglo-Saxons of England (600).

G. was also an important author who adopted a practical rather than a speculative approach in his theological works. His *Liber Regulae Pastoralis* (The Book of the Pastoral Rule) sets out directives for the pastoral life of the bishops, whom he regarded mainly as shepherds of the soul; this book became the textbook of the medieval episcopate. The *Dialogues* (593) tell of the lives and miracles of the saints and reflect the uncritical credulity of the age; they became a model for medieval hagiography. G.'s commentaries on the Book of Job are not only an exegetical work, but also form the basis for a mystical explication of the Bible which served G. in his later works on the Gospels. G. followed the teachings of St. *Augustine of Hippo, whose ideas he accommodated to the mentality of his contemporaries. He instituted important liturgical changes and is considered the author of the Gregorian Sacramentary. He also made innovations in music and introduced the Gregorian Chant (see *Music).

Works and Letters in *PL*, vols. 85-88;

P. Batiffol, *St. Grégoire le Grand* (1928).

GREGORY II, St. (669-731) Pope (715-31). Member of a noble Roman family, he became deacon of the Roman Church and in 710 followed Pope *Constantine I to Constantinople, where he became acquainted with the *Iconoclastic controversy. As pope, he opposed the iconoclastic policy of Emperor *Leo III, an attitude which widened the gap with the Greek Church. In Italy, he defended the papal state against the Lombards and the Byzantine exarchs of Ravenna. He protected the German mission of St. *Boniface, appointing Boniface bishop of Mainz.

A. Dahmen, *Das Pontificat Gregorius II* (1886).

GREGORY III, St. (d. 741) Pope (731-41). Member of a Roman family, he served at the court of *Gregory II and succeeded him. He continued the policy of his predecessor, particularly with regard to Byzantium. In 739 he addressed himself to *Charles Martel, vainly seeking Frankish help against the Lombards. His pontificate at Rome was distinguished by the building and restoration of churches.

L. Duchesne, *Les Premiers Temps de l'Etat Pontifical* (1913).

GREGORY IV (d. 844) Pope (827-44). Of a noble Roman family, he was elected pope with the consent of Emperor *Lothair. He intervened in the dynastic struggle of the *Carolingian empire, particularly in the revolt of the sons of *Louis the Pious against their father (829-33). G. adopted this mediatory role in an attempt to diminish his dependence on the emperor.

GREGORY V (Bruno of Carinthia; 973-99) Pope (996-99). Son of Otto, duke of Carinthia and grandson of Liutgard, daughter of *Otto I. He was appointed pope by his cousin, Emperor *Otto III, despite his youth (23) in order to impose imperial authority upon the papal throne. Only with the help of the imperial army was he able to maintain himself at Rome, where local factions fiercely opposed him.

W. Ullmann, *A Short History of the Papacy in the Middle Ages* (1972).

GREGORY VI (John Gratian; d. 1048) Pope (1045-46). Originally of Rome, he earned the reputation of being a fine scholar in his youth. He was accused of simony, charged with buying the papal throne from *Benedict IX. Emperor *Henry III intervened and dethroned him; G. was subsequently exiled to Germany.

W. Ullmann, *A Short History of the Papacy in the Middle Ages* (1972).

GREGORY VII (Hildebrand; 1021-85) Pope (1073-85). Born to a poor family at Sovana in Tuscany, he became a monk in a Cluniac monastery in his native country and was educated at Rome. In 1045 he entered the service of *Gregory VI and later accompanied him in his exile to Germany. Upon his return to Rome in 1048, G. aroused the interest of Pope *Leo IX, who attached him to the service of the papacy. Between 1048 and 1073, G. collaborated closely with the successive popes and was very active both in the reform movement of the church (later destined to be named after him, the *Gregorian Reform) and in the diplomatic activity of the Curia, where he represented the popes in delicate missions to France and Germany. In addition, he was created cardinal. In 1073 he was elected pope and vigorously resumed the activities already begun. He adopted both the moral and the political aims of the reform movement; important issues involved the purging of the church of corrupted clergy; the struggle for priestly chastity by opposing their marriage, as well as "nicolaism" (their living with women); the battle against simony (the buying of ecclesiastical offices); attempts to restore unity with the Orthodox Church; and the holy war against the Moslems, aimed at freeing Spain and Palestine from Moslem rule. In order to achieve his aims, G. publicly proclaimed his *Dictatus Papae* (The Pope's Dictate) in 1075, a document which revealed the political scheme of his pontificate. It implied that: 1) the Roman pontiff was the sole and universal pope; 2) he alone was entitled to depose bishops or forgive them for their sins; 3) only he could wear the imperial insignia; 4) he had the prerogative to depose an unworthy emperor; 5) no ecclesiastical source could be taken into consideration in the church's internal disputes, if not in accordance with the sovereign will of the pope; 6) no person could judge the pope; 7) the Roman Church could never fail in its deeds and doctrines; 8) those who did not obey the Roman Church were not Catholics. In order to implement the claims stated in the document, G. appointed legates who would represent him in various countries, and who were given full power to intervene in local affairs and to depose unworthy bishops and abbots. G. thus established a centralist papal government within the church, based on the full sovereignty of the pope and the delegation of authority to the legates, placed in a position superior to that of the ecclesiastical hierarchy. In addition, G. forbade the lay *investiture, which he and his fellow reformers considered an expression of simony. The *Dictatus Papae* and the decree on investiture were in open opposition to the current practices in Germany, rooted in the Constitution of the *Holy Roman empire. Therefore Emperor *Henry IV denounced these proclamations in 1076, and intensive polemical activity began between the empire and the papacy.

In January 1076 Henry IV formally deposed G., whom he convicted of being a rebel against the imperial authority. G. responded with the excommunication of the emperor and by breaking the fidelity oath owed to him by his subjects. This step legitimized a revolt of Saxon nobles, who elected Rudolf of Swabia as antiking and called the pope to join them in Germany. G., who already was assured of the collaboration of the Normans of southern Italy and of Countess *Matilda of Tuscany, advanced towards Germany, where the emperor's situation had become difficult. Henry, however, took advantage of the ecclesiastical procedure of penance to break up this coalition. In 1077 while the pope was staying at *Canossa, Henry hurried to Italy, made penance and requested absolution in accordance with the ecclesiastical practice. G. was thus beaten with his own weapons; his allies, the German rebels, no longer had a legal basis upon which to oppose their emperor and were left to his mercy. As a result, the pope lost the upper hand in Germany; Henry was able to defeat the rebels and to reaffirm his authority (1080). To save face, G. attempted to assume the role of judge between the emperor and his vassals; upon Henry's refusal, he again excommunicated him, but this time the excommunication was ineffective. Henry invaded Italy, appointed an antipope, Clement III, and in 1081 besieged Rome. In 1084 when repeated excommunications proved ineffective, G. was compelled to flee Rome and to take refuge at Salerno, where he died the following year.

Despite his failure against Henry IV, G. was one of the greatest medieval popes. His reformatory programme was adopted in the major part of the Catholic countries, where he proved more flexible in his relations with their monarchs. In fact, the investiture controversy had only affected his relations with the German emperor. G.'s major achievement was the creation of a centralist government within the church, where the papacy emerged as its supreme organ of government.

Works and Letters, ed. E. Caspar, *MGH*, 4 vols;
E. Bernheimer, *Quellen zur Geschichte der Investiturstreites* (1930);
R. Morghen, *Gregorio Settimo* (1945).

GREGORY VIII (Alberto de Morra; d. 1187) Pope (1187). He spent his entire career in the papal Curia, where he was made cardinal in 1156. In 1178 he was appointed chancellor of the papal court. He was elected pope when the news of the defeat of the *Crusaders at *Hattin (July 1187) reached Europe. His sole action as pope was to proclaim the Third *Crusade; he died two months after his election.

G. Klemann, *Papst Gregorius VIII* (1913).

GREGORY IX (Ugolino di Segni; 1148-1241) Pope (1227-41). Member of the powerful Roman family of the counts of Segni, he served at the papal court from his youth. He was promoted by his kinsman, *Innocent III, to higher dignities and was eventually made cardinal. Elected pope at the age of 78, he proved active despite his years and continued the policies of *Gregory VII, *Alexander III and Innocent III, in a struggle for the supremacy of the papacy. He fiercely combatted Emperor *Frederick II, excommunicating him several times and calling for a revolt against his authority. He compelled the emperor to leave Italy for his *Crusade, believing that he could profit from his absence and thereby reaffirm papal authority. However, upon Frederick's return from Palestine, G. was compelled to make peace with him, having lost the support of the Lombard cities, defeated by the imperial army; the Treaty of *San Germano (1230) was essentially a repetition of Frederick's commitments to Innocent III in 1212; the pope did not gain any further advantage. Therefore, the agreement merely bought time so both forces could reorganize. In 1237 the struggle was renewed and G. again excommunicated the emperor; never-

theless, Frederick's victory at *Cortenuova, where he crushed the Lombard cities, endangered G.'s position. The imperial army invaded the Papal States, and G. failed to inspire renewed revolts in Germany and Italy. G. called together a council, in 1240, with the intention of deposing Frederick; however, the council never convened as the participants were captured by the imperial army. G. died in the following year, leaving the Roman see in a difficult situation.

Aside from his struggles against Frederick, G. was also very active in different fields of church politics, also with the intention of establishing papal supremacy. He therefore granted a privilege to the University of Paris (1231), which exempted it from the bishop's authority; he also favoured the *Mendicant orders and entrusted the *Inquisition, which he reorganized, to the *Dominicans. He intensified the activity of papal legates in western Europe and controlled the ecclesiastical hierarchy. Furthermore, he promulgated addenda to the *canon law, known as the Decretals, which included material from the time of the Decree of *Gratian to that of his own pontificate.

L. Auvray, *Régistres de Grégoire IX*, 3 vols. (1896-1910);
E. Kantorowicz, *Frederick II* (1931).

GREGORY X (Tebaldo Visconti; 1210-76) Pope (1271-76). Born at Piacenza in Lombardy, he filled a long series of ecclesiastical roles in France and England. In 1270 he accompanied *Edward I in his *Crusade. Upon his arrival in Acre, his election as pope was announced. The decision had taken three years. In order to avoid such long *conclaves, G. issued a decree concerning papal elections, which compelled the cardinals to remain together under lock and key until a pope was elected. G. actively encouraged a new Crusade, but was largely unsuccessful in this respect. In 1275 he presided over the Second Council of *Lyons, where he tried to find a formula for the reunion of the Catholic and Orthodox churches. G. supported the candidacy of *Rudolf of Hapsburg to the imperial crown.

J. Müller, *Studien zur Geschichte Gregorius X* (1929).

GREGORY XI (Peter Roger de Beaufort; 1329-78) Pope (1370-78). Born in Limousin (central France), he studied law at Perugia. The nephew of Pope *Clement VI, G. was appointed to various dignities at the papal court of Avignon. After his election as pope, he moved to Avignon, where he made efforts to reconcile the kings of England and France. He also actively encouraged missionary activity. When Florence backed a revolt in the Papal States in Italy in 1376, G. put an interdict on the city and travelled to Italy to restore his authority. His arrival broke up the Florentine coalition. Before his return trip to Avignon, which he intended to undertake despite the opposition of Roman circles, G. died, being the last pope before the *Great Schism.

G. Mollat, *The Avignon Popes* (1954).

GREGORY XII (Angelo Corrèr; 1335-1417) Pope of Rome (1406-15). Born at Venice, he became pope during the *Great Schism. He was elected on the condition that he resign when his counterpart, the Avignon pope, *Benedict XIII, would do the same, and thereby allow the election of one common pope. When no progress was made towards bridging the schism, G. began to lose support, some of his cardinals joined a party of Avignon cardinals to elect a third pope, *Alexander V, at Pisa in

1309. After Alexander's death in 1410, these cardinals elected *John XXIII, who was considered an antipope. G. refused to give up his dignity, claiming to be the legitimate pope. During the Council of *Constance, he was compelled to resign so as to allow the council to elect a new pope. G. was then appointed papal legate in the march of Ancona and died in the small town of Recanati.

W. Ullmann, *A Short History of the Papacy in the Middle Ages* (1972).

GREGORY OF TOURS (c. 540-95) Historian. Born into an aristocratic Gallo-Roman family in Auvergne, he embraced the religious life and in 573 was made bishop of Tours. He then became involved in the dynastical feuds of the *Merovingian kings, and acquired a thorough knowledge of the Franks. In 576, he began writing the most important historical work of the early Middle Ages, *Historia Francorum* (The History of the Franks). Influenced by biblical and Roman historiographies, he began his work with the creation, and the first four books relate biblical history and the early history of the Frankish people. Books V-X are a faithful account of his own period until 591. Narrative and detailed in his approach, the purpose of the history was didactic, gathering all available material on the good and evil actions of the Franks for the instruction of the faithful. Beside his history, G. wrote eight books on saints and martyrs, in which he described their lives and miracles.

History, ed. and English trans. by O. M. Dalton, with biography and studies on his minor works.

GREGORY PALAMAS (1296-1359) Greek theologian. He was born in Constantinople to a noble Anatolian family; his widowed mother, brothers and sisters all embraced the religious life. In 1318, he went to Mount *Athos, where he studied theology according to the teaching of the *Hesychasts. In 1326 he was ordained priest at *Thessalonica, but in 1331 returned to Athos, where he became one of the leading exponents of the Hesychast doctrine. His vigorous treatises in its favour brought him the censure of the established Orthodox Church and, finally, excommunication and forced retirement in 1344. In 1347, when *John Cantacuzenus seized the imperial throne, G. was released and appointed bishop of Thessalonica, which he was able to enter only with the military support of the emperor. In 1351, the orthodoxy of his teaching was recognized and in 1368, after his death, G. was canonized as a "Father and Doctor of the Church".

PG, vol. 150.

GREGORY THE SINAITE (14th century) Byzantine monk. Little is known of his life and origins. At the end of the 13th century he left the monastery of Mount *Sinai and led a nomadic life in the provinces of the Byzantine empire, where he originated and taught the *Hesychastic doctrine of ascetic and contemplative monasticism. His teaching was enthusiastically accepted by the monks of Mount *Athos, which became the centre of Hesychasm.

J. Bois, *Grégoire le Sinaite et l'hésichasme à l'Athos au XVe siècle* (1902).

GRENOBLE City in *Dauphiné (southeastern France). Founded in 379 by the Roman Emperor Gratianus and named Gratianopolis after him, it was a provincial centre in late antiquity. In the mid-5th century, it was conquered by the *Burgundians and was incorporated in their kingdom; in 543 it was annexed by the *Franks and, in the various divisions of the *Merovingian kingdom, always belonged to the realm of Burgundy. In 843, it was acquired by *Lothair, eldest son of *Louis the Pious and, in 888, was included in the kingdom of *Burgundy until 1032, when it was incorporated in the *Holy Roman empire. During this period, G. grew and became an important ecclesiastical centre. The crypt of the cathedral, dating from the end of the 9th century, is a surviving example of post-*Carolingian architecture. In the 13th century, the Delphins made the city the capital of their principality and gradually established their independence of the emperors. They built a fortress, the *Bastille*, on a mountain overlooking the city, and founded the University of G. in 1399. In 1343, it was sold to the king of France and remained a provincial capital, with its own *parliament.

R. Blanchard, *Grenoble; Etude de Géographie urbaine* (1936).

GRIMOALD King of the Lombards (662-71), previously duke of *Benevento. He struggled against the independent duchies and imposed his authority over the duchies of Spoleto, Friuli and Benevento. He successfully resisted the attempts of the Byzantine Emperor *Constans II to reconquer Italy and defeated him in 663 and 668, consolidating Lombard domination over most of Italy.

N. Aberg, *Lombard Italy* (1945).

GRIMOALD III Lombard ruler, duke of Benevento (787-806). The son of Duke Arichis, *Charlemagne allowed him to inherit the duchy of Benevento in order to create a friendly Lombard state in southern Italy which could oppose the coalition between *Adalgis, son and heir of *Desiderius of Pavia, and the Byzantines, who ruled Apulia, Calabria and Naples. Although G. swore fidelity to Charlemagne, he enjoyed much independence and created a Lombard state which survived until the 11th century.

W. Braunfels (ed.), *Karl der Grosse* (1965).

GROOT, GEERT OF (1340-84) Mystic. Born of a rich family of Deventer in Holland, he studied in Paris, where he learned theology, medicine, astronomy and canon law. He then travelled in the Rhine Valley and visited Avignon. In 1374, he returned to his home town and devoted himself to study and prayer. In 1380, he began to preach in the vernacular, urging the people to return to the simple life of the early Christians and criticizing both the sins of the masses and the abuses of the church establishment. He founded the confraternity of the Brethren of the Common Life with the aim of imitating Christ. His influence brought him the censure of the church and, before his death, he was forbidden to preach on the grounds that he had not been ordained. In the 15th century, he was named Gerardus Magnus.

J. van Ginneken, *Geert Groote's Levensbelt* (1942).

GROSSETESTE, ROBERT (c. 1175-1253) Scholar and bishop of Lincoln (1235-53). Born into a poor family in Suffolk, he became a cleric and studied at Oxford and, according to some authorities, in Paris. At the beginning of the 13th century he began to teach at Oxford and was active in transforming the school into a university. In 1224 he joined the new *Franciscan College at Oxford, despite the fact that he did not belong to the order, and taught there until he was elected bishop of

Lincoln. During this period, he was also chancellor of the university. As bishop of Lincoln, he devoted himself both to reforming the churches of his diocese, which was the largest in England and included Oxford, and to scholarly activities. He opposed the appointment of Italian clerics in England and upheld this position at the Council of Lyons (1245) and at Rome (1250), where he made his famous speech, *De corruptelis Ecclesiae* (On the Corrupters of the Church), pleading for the reform of the church and condemning nepotism and the abuses of over-centralized government. As a scholar, G. had a wide range of interests, including Aristotelian and Hellenistic philosophy, which he translated into Latin. He was also deeply interested in mathematics, astronomy, optics and the natural sciences, in which he conducted experiments. In his studies of natural phenomena, he was influenced by the philosophical ideas of St. *Augustine and of Arab neo-Platonists, in addition to Aristotelian thought. One of the best examples of his approach was his treatise on light, which he considered a very subtle corporeal substance and the first form of primary matter to be created, out of which all else developed according to immutable laws. Among his philosophical and theological works, the most important are his treatises on the soul, truth and free will.

L. Baur, *Die philosophischen Werke des Robert Grosseteste* (1912);

D. A. Callus, *Robert Grosseteste, Scholar and Bishop* (1955).

GUELPHS An Italian political party of the 12th-14th centuries, named after the *Welf dynasty in Germany, which was opposed to the *Hohenstaufen (*Ghibelline) emperors. The term was used to indicate the factions in the Italian cities which opposed the imperial rule of *Frederick Barbarossa and, in the 13th century, of *Frederick II. Accordingly, the G. were considered allies of the papacy. After the death of Frederick II (1250), the term lost its original significance, but G. parties continued to flourish, and were one of the commonest features of community life in the Italian cities. Thus, *Florence was traditionally governed by G., who were divided into several groups. In its new significance, the meaning of the term varied from city to city according to its constitution and political interests. With the decline of the Italian communes and the rise of tyrant dynasties, the party declined, and it disappeared at the beginning of the 15th century.

J. K. Hyde, *Society and Politics in Medieval Italy* (1973).

GUERRIC OF IGNY (d. 1154) Preacher and abbot. Born in the region of Tours, he was educated in Flanders and became canon and master of the cathedral school in Tournai. Under the influence of St. *Bernard of Clairvaux, he joined the *Cistercian order and entered the abbey of Clairvaux in 1131. There he became a close associate of St. Bernard and a successful preacher. In 1138, he founded the Cistercian abbey of Igny, near Rheims, becoming its abbot. G. continued to preach, and his sermons were widely disseminated. A collection of 50 sermons is still preserved.

Works, ed. *PL*, vol. 155;

D. de Wilde, *Guerricus d'Igny* (1935).

GUESCLIN, BERTRAND DU See DU GUESCLIN, BERTRAND.

GUI, GUIDO See GUY.

GUIBERT OF NOGENT (1052-1130) Abbot and historian. Born into a noble family in Picardy, he lost his father in childhood and was educated by his mother, who hired private tutors. He continued his studies as a monk in the abbey of St. Germer, where he became interested in classical literature and history. In 1104, he became abbot of Nogent and, while directing the monastery, wrote his three most important works: *Gesta Dei per Francos*, a history of the First *Crusade (1104) based on memories of the participants, which is one of the best historical works of the 12th century: *De Vita Sua*, an autobiography in the style of an Augustinian confession (1115), which is not only a good self-analysis, but also an interesting account of French society at the beginning of the 12th century; *De Pignoribus Sanctorum*, a treatise on popular faith and the cult of relics.

J. F. Benton, *Self and Society in Medieval France* (1970).

GUIENNE Duchy in southwestern France. The name is a popular French contraction of *Aquitaine and, until 1258, the two terms were used interchangeably. From 1258, when the division of Aquitaine was recognized at the Peace of Paris, G. signified the southern part of the duchy (including *Gascony), which remained under the rule of the kings of England, as vassals of the kings of France. Its centre was established at Bordeaux, where a governor appointed by the king of England represented him in France. The frontiers of the duchy changed radically after the death of *Louis IX, when the French officials penetrated into G. and attempted to impose the French royal authority. Thus, counties like Angoulême were detached from G. and subjected to the direct rule of the French king. In the *Hundred Years' War, G. was an important English base and, under the leadership of *Edward, the Black Prince, the English and Gascon armies defeated the French, notably at the decisive Battle of *Poitiers (1356). At this period, the internal history of G., was closely connected with that of Gascony, its most important component. At the beginning of the 14th century, the ducal title was given to the eldest son of the king of France, although the real power was vested with English and Gascon officials.

H. Stein, *Charles de France, frère de Louis XI* (1921).

GUIGUES I (d. 1137) Prior of the *Carthusian order (1109-37). A native of Dauphiné, he joined the Great Chartreuse after its establishment and became the leader of the order. His period in office was characterized by an organization and codification of the Carthusian rule. He stressed necessity of intellectual work by the monks and the organization of well-equipped libraries in the Charterhouses.

Works, *PL*, vol. 153:

A. Wilmart, *Le Recueil des Pensées de Guigue le Chartreux* (1936).

GUILDS Corporations of merchants and craftsmen in medieval cities. The origins of the G. lay in the tradition of professional corporations in the Roman empire and their continuation in the Byzantine empire. But unlike those of Byzantium, the western European G., which emerged in the latter half of the 11th century and developed in the 12th century, were not organizations controlled by the state. They were founded because of a need to organize professionals in the cities, to establish standards of work and to foster professional ethics. With the development of cities in western Europe, their corporative structure made the G. an important and vital element in the internal self-government of the cities. Thus, the corporation was not only a professional organization, but was also entrusted with authority over its members, whom its leaders represented in the city councils. The medieval custom of concentrating members of a specific profession in one quarter or street in the city, also forced G. to be responsible for the organization of civic life in the area inhabited by its members. The most important activities of the G., however, were economic; thus, the G. regulated the status of "masters", workers and apprentices, as well as the division of the work among its members, fixed prices and wages, and decided on the number of craftsmen required in a specific craft. In the 13th century, the G. were divided into "aristocratic" ones, such as merchants and certain crafts, like goldsmiths, and "plebeian" or lower G., generally consisting of craftsmen. The former would seize power and monopolize the civic government, while the latter were denied any share in it. This happened in many cities, causing uprisings, and led to rebellions and changes in the civic constitutions in the 14th century. The rebellions and counter-rebellions weakened the cities and finally resulted in direct royal or princely intervention in civic affairs or, as was the

A guild master with craftsmen; *15th-century miniature*

case in Italy, in the seizure of power by tyrants. The organization of the professional G. was not affected by these changes and the G. continued to be professional corporations, which also developed standards of behaviour for their members. The impact of religion reflected in the G.' adoption of patron saints, in religious celebrations and in processions of members on feast-days also contributed to the development of social customs, concentrated in the guild-hall, the centre of the social activities of the G.
CEcH, III.

GUILLAUME, GUILHEM, GUILLELM See WILLIAM.
GUILLAUME D'ORANGE Epic poem. Composed in northern France in the 11th century, it became one of the most popular **chansons de geste*, being the original of a whole cycle of poems dedicated to its hero and his supposed family. The poem's hero is *William, marquis of Gothia and Toulouse who, under the nominal authority of *Louis, third son of *Charlemagne, king of Aquitaine and future emperor, commanded the campaigns in Catalonia and founded the march of Spain. The poet represented him as brave knight, hero of the wars against Islam and protector of the monarchy.
U. T. Holmes, *A History of French Literature in the Middle Ages* (1948).
GUILLAUME LE MARÉCHAL A 13th-century French chronicle in verse, relating the adventurous life of *William Marshal. The poem reflects the chivalrous manners of the times, courtly life and the ideals of knightly conduct.
Ed. P. Meyer (1891);
S. Painter, *William Marshal* (1933).
GUINEVERE Legendary queen. In the Arthurian romances, she is the wife of King *Arthur and, as such, is a literary representation of the ideal feudal queen. Chief woman at the court, she shares the responsibilities of ruling the kingdom with her husband.
GUNDOBALD (GUNDOBAD) King of the *Burgundians (480-516). A younger son of King Gundioc, he entered into the service of the Western Roman empire and his uncle Ricimer appointed him commander of the army in Gaul. He later succeeded Ricimer as the supreme authority in the whole empire and appointed Glycerius as emperor. After Glycerius' defeat by Emperor Nepos, G. returned to Burgundy, where he succeeded his brother *Chilperic as king. He maintained the independence of his kingdom by an alliance with *Clovis, king of the Franks, to whom he gave his niece, *Clotilda, as wife. In 501, G. began to collect the customs of his people which were recorded by a number of scribes; in 506, he promulgated the laws of the Burgundians, known by the popular title, *Loi *Gombette.*
O. Perrin, *Les Burgondes* (1968).
GUNTRAM (c. 545-92) King of the Franks (561-92). Son of *Clotaire I, his father bequeathed him the kingdom of *Burgundy. He profited from the dynastic quarrel between *Brunhilda and *Fredegund to increase his influence in the Frankish realm, protecting his nephews and incurring the hatred of the two queens, who attempted to kill him. At his death, the kingdom was completely disorganized by civil war.
J. M. Wallace-Hadrill, *The Long-Haired Kings* (1963).
GUTHRUM (d. 880) Danish chieftain. In 874, he was one of the leaders of the Danish invasion of England. Elected king by his men, he led the raid of 875 into

central and southern England, occupying a large part of *Wessex. Defeated by *Alfred the Great, he was compelled to retire from Wessex and, by the peace treaty of 877, accepted Christianity and was recognized as king of East Anglia, which he conquered and whose Anglo-Saxon dynasty he replaced.

F. Stenton, *Anglo-Saxon England* (1947).

GUY I, of La Roche   Duke of *Athens (1225-63). Nephew of Odo of La Roche, the founder of the Frankish duchy of *Athens, he inherited his uncle's Greek domains when Odo returned to France. During his long period of rule, he fought for the independence of Athens against the princes of *Morea and, although he was obliged to swear an oath of allegiance recognizing them as overlords (1258), he was able to consolidate his state.

GUY II, of La Roche   Duke of *Athens (1287-1308). Grandson of Guy I, he was the last Burgundian duke of Athens. After reaching majority he ruled the duchy vigorously (1294-1308) and increased its influence in Thessaly. Despite his poor health (he died at the age of 28), he was very active and at Thebai established the most brilliant court in Greece.

W. Miller, *The Latins in the Levant* (1908).

GUY, BERNARD   See BERNARD GUI.

GUY-GEOFFREY (1030-87)   Duke of Aquitaine (1058-87), also known as William VIII. He was the grandson of *William the Great and from his mother, Sanchia, inherited the title of duke of *Gascony (1044), re-establishing the union between Gascony and *Aquitaine. As duke, he imposed his rule upon his turbulent vassals and created an efficient administration at Poitiers which, under his rule, became a brilliant city and the capital of the united duchy. In 1063, he led a Crusade to Spain, defeating the *Almoravides.

A. Richard, *Histoire des Comtes de Poitiers, ducs d'Aquitaine* (1908).

GUY (GUIDO) OF AREZZO (c. 990-1050)   Musician. Born at Arezzo (Italy), in his younger years he lived in France, where he was a monk at the abbey of St. Maur near Paris. He returned to Italy *c.* 1030, and lived in the Benedictine monasteries of Ferrara and Fonte Avellana where he died. G. was not only a musician but also a very important theoretical writer. His place in the history of music is assured by his invention of solmization, a six-tone system, with a half-tone between the third and fourth tones, each one being indicated by syllables. He thus reformed Gregorian *music.

W. Apel, ed., *Harvard Dictionary of Music* (1950).

GUY OF BAZOCHES (d. 1203)   Chronicler. Born to a noble family in Champagne, he was educated by his uncle, Bishop Haymon of Châlons-sur-Marne (d. 1153), who made him a priest in his cathedral. Later, he studied at Paris and took part in the Third *Crusade. Among his works, the most important are a *Cosmographia*, a detailed description of the world, in which some historical information was included as well as geographical. The *Apologia contra malignos* (Apology against the Envious), is a curious treatise in which morality is mixed with historical and geographical notions. The best of his works, however, is the *Chronographia*, a universal history from the creation of the world until 1199. The book is not only a compilation of ancient chronicles and histories as used by the medieval chroniclers, but also an exposition of his view of history, which was influenced by classical literature. His personal approach is demonstrated by some of his letters as well as by his historical writings.

Works, ed. A. Wattenbach (1893-98), completing the Chronographia (ed. *MGH, Scriptores,* vol. 26); J. de Ghellinck, *L'Essor de la Littérature Latine au XIIe siècle* (1955).

GUY OF CHAULIAC (d. c. 1360)   Surgeon. Born at Chauliac in southern France, he studied medicine at Montpellier and in Italy, where he became acquainted with the teaching of anatomy and autopsies at Bologna. In 1344 *Clement VI appointed him physician of the papal court at Avignon. He left a description of the *Black Death as he saw it in the Avignon region and, before his death, composed a treatise on surgery, *Chirurgia Magna*, in which he discussed the theories of the ancient Roman physician Galen and summed up the practices of his own age. As a partitioner, he also initiated the use of powders for skin diseases and prescribed spectacles for short sight.

H. E. Sigerist, *A History of Medicine*, I (1951).

GUY OF LUSIGNAN (1129-94)   King of Jerusalem (1186-92) and Cyprus (1192-94). A member of the house of the lords of *Lusignan in Poitou, he arrived in the *Crusader kingdom as an adventurer and in 1179, at the instigation of his brother *Aymeri, married Princess Sybil, sister of King Baldwin IV. He was endowed with the county of Jaffa and Ascalon and, despite the opposition of the moderate barons, who considered him unworthy of the throne, was crowned king with the support of the activist barons after the death of the child king, *Baldwin V. His ineptitude as a military leader led him into a conflict with *Saladin and defeat at the Battle of *Hattin (1187), where he was captured. Released, he attempted to recover his royal title, but was not admitted to Tyre by its ruler, his rival *Conrad of Montferrat. In 1192 *Richard I of England forced him to renounce his claim and gave him *Cyprus, which became the realm of the Lusignan dynasty.

S. Runciman, *A History of the Crusades* (1953).

GUY OF SPOLETO   Emperor (891-94). Son of Duke Guy of Spoleto and of Rothildis, daughter of *Lothair I, he was a member of a Frankish family which ruled Spoleto in the 9th century and became increasingly important through its ties with the *Carolingian dynasty. In 880, he became duke of Spoleto and, after the death of *Charles the Fat (887), began to establish his authority in Italy, claiming the right to his grandfather's crown through his mother. In 891, the Frankish leaders in Italy elected him emperor and imposed him on the papacy.

C. G. Mor, *L'Etat Féodal* (1952).

GUYENNE   See GUIENNE.

GUYOT DE PROVINS (d. c. 1230)   Poet and moralist. In his younger years, he belonged to the literary circle of the count of *Champagne, where he became acquainted with *Chrétien de Troyes and the Occitanian lyrical heritage. Among his lyrical works, a version of Perceval connects him with *Arthurian romance. However, he is mainly famous for his *Bible de Guiot*, a moralistic work in which he criticized the various social groups and particularly the monks, castigating their excesses, materialism and lack of charity. The "Bible" became a model for satirical works of the 13th-14th centuries.

A. Luchaire, *Social France at the Time of Philip Augustus* (1967).

Subterranean water reservoir in Ramla, built by Harun Al-Rashid in 789

H

HAAKON I, the Good (c. 925-61) King of *Norway (947-61). Youngest son of King Harold, he grew up as a Christian prince in England. After his father's death, he left England and, profiting from the civil wars between the Norwegian nobles, seized the throne. He won the title "Good" for his legislation, which aimed at creating a just system of government in accordance with the traditional laws of the people. In 960 he defeated a Danish invasion of his country and attacked Denmark. His capital, Trondheim, became an important city during his reign.
G. Jones, *A History of the Vikings* (1968).

HAAKON IV King of Norway (1217-63). Son of Haakon III, his reign was marked by economic prosperity and a long period of peace in Scandinavia, which allowed him to establish one of the most brilliant courts in northern Europe. He systematically expanded his authority over tne Scandinavian settlements in the west, such as the Faroe Islands, and imposed direct rule on the autonomous states of *Greenland (1261) and *Iceland (1262-64), which became territories of the Norwegian kingdom.
G. Jones, *A History of the Vikings* (1968).

HAAKON V King of Norway (1299-1319). He attempted to recover the royal authority, which was opposed by a powerful coalition of the German *Hanse and the landed nobility, seeking the support of the church. In 1308 he appropriated all fiefdoms and abolished the feudal powers, but the nobility was not decisively defeated and, in the absence of a male heir, its position with regard to the succession reinforced its authority.
K. Gierset, *A History of the Norwegian People* (1915).

HAAKON VI King of Norway (1343-80). Youngest son of *Magnus II, king of Sweden and Norway, he inherited the Norwegian throne, but continued to seek the Swedish crown in addition. His marriage to Margaret of Denmark paved the way for the union of the Scandinavian states.

HADRIAN See ADRIAN.

HAFIZ, SHAMS AL-DIN MUHAMMAD (c. 1325-89) Persian poet. Born in Shiraz, Persia, to a poor family, he lost his father as a child and worked as a hired worker in a bakery. In his free time he studied the Persian and Arabic languages and literature as well as theology, and began to write. His works (693 poems, most of them dealing with love, women, wine and beauty) were appreciated in his lifetime, mainly because of their brevity, their clear and beautiful language and the richness of their imagery, and he was recognized as one of the greatest and most popular Persian poets. H., however, was persecuted by the *Shiite religious leaders of the city for his poems on wine − forbidden by Islamic law − to such a degree that after his death they at first refused to allow him a funeral. His poetry indicates that he opposed the political-religious establishment and hated the Arab domination of Persia. After his death a mausoleum was erected on his tomb at Shiraz and his poems were gathered in a *Diwan* (collection of songs).
M. Farzaad, *Hafiz and his Poems* (1949).

HAGGADAH A collection of prayers, excerpts of tales and songs commemorating the Exodus of the ancient Israelites from Egypt, intended for recitation in Jewish communities at the festive Passover supper. The H. was gradually composed by various anonymous authors, and its authoritative text, used by Jews throughout the world, dates from the Middle Ages. The oldest manuscript (the *Saadia Gaon H.), dating from the 10th century, is followed by an Egyptian manuscript (the *Maimonides' H.) and one from western Europe (the Vitry H.), both of the 12th century. From the 13th century onwards manuscripts of the H. were richly decorated by Jewish artists with miniatures and ornamentation. Among the most beautiful examples are the Sarajevo H., of Spanish origin, the Birds'-head H., of German origin (14th century), and the Hamilton H., of Spanish origin (15th century), while the Rothschild manuscript of the late 15th century represents a Jewish version of Italian Renaissance art.
F.L. Stein, *The Influence of Symposia Literature on the Literary Form of the Pessah Haggada* (1957);
F. Landsberger, *New Studies in Early Jewish Artists* (1943-44).

HAGIA SOPHIA See SANTA SOPHIA, cathedral of Constantinople.

HAI GAON, RABBI (939-1038) *Gaon of *Pumbedita in Mesopotamia, and one of the greatest religious authorities in Judaism. He was the son of *Sherira Gaon and in 986 became his deputy, with the rank of Head of the Rabbinical Court. In 998 he became *gaon,* having been recognized for his knowledge and scholarly activities. In the 40 years of his *gaonate,* Pumbedita experienced a great spiritual awakening and students came to his school from various countries of Europe, Asia and Africa. His *Responsa* were universally recognized as authoritative so that about one-third of all the *responsa* of the *gaonic* period (6th-11th centuries) are his. His range of interests was wide, but his main concern was to maintain the unity of the Jewish people in the Diaspora. He therefore emphasized the importance of the courts of the local communities and of uniformity in the interpretation of Talmudic law.
E.E. Hildesheimer, *Mystik und Agada im Schrifttum d. Geonen R. Sherira und R. Hai* (1931).

HAINAULT Medieval country, most of which is in present-day Belgium. Established in the 10th century, it owed allegiance to the duchy of *Lotharingia, which was part of the German empire. The counts intermarried with their neighbours, the counts of *Flanders and,

Passover; from the 14th-century illuminated Haggadah *of Sarajevo*

from the 12th century, the history of H. is closely connected with that of Flanders, but the distinction between them and Hainault's allegiance to the *Holy Roman empire was always recognized. In order to avoid difficulties arising from plurality of *homage, a separate, junior branch of the counts of Flanders was given the title of counts of H. In the 14th century, through a process of marriage, the dynasty of the counts was replaced by a family which ruled Brabant, Holland and Zealand. By the marriage of Margaret of Holland, who inherited these areas, with *John the Fearless, duke of Burgundy (1404), H. was united with the Low Countries.

H. Pirenne, *Histoire de Belgique* (1922).

HAKIM, BIAMRALLAH AL- *Fatimid caliph of Egypt (996-1021). He is considered one of the most cruel of Islamic rulers, tyrannical and capricious. H. attempted to follow extreme *Shiite principles in governing Egypt, and this policy brought him into conflict with the *Sunnite Moslems and also with the Christians and Jews, whom he persecuted. After a great rebellion had broken out in Egypt, he initiated several repressive measures, including a series of decrees against the Sunnites in Egypt and the destruction of the church of the *Holy Sepulchre at Jerusalem (1011). The open rebellion against his government in Egypt, Palestine and Syria finally pro-

duced a radical change in his policy and in 1017 he issued a law of tolerance. At the same time, he claimed to be a god and sent out preachers to proclaim his divinity to the masses. One of them, Al-Durzi, preached to the people of southern Syria, where a group of believers, the *Druzes, accepted the doctrine.

EI, II.

HALES, ALEXANDER OF See ALEXANDER OF HALES.

HALLE City in southeastern *Saxony, on the banks of the Saale River. It developed from a fortress established by *Charlemagne in 806. The city's date of foundation and early history are unknown. By 1064, however, it was already an important commercial centre in the principality of the archbishops of *Magdeburg. Its economical prosperity was due to trade with the eastern provinces and Poland, as well as with the northern German cities. In the 13th century the city was also one of the centres of the *Dominican order in Germany, and the church is a typical example of Saxon Gothic architecture. In the latter half of the 13th century the city established its own municipal institutions and joined the *Hanse in 1281. As a Hanse city, H. flourished and became one of the most prosperous cities of Germany; the exploitation of the coal mines began at the beginning of the 15th century. In 1478, as a result of local troubles, the city lost its independence and was reincorporated in the principality of the archbishops of Magdeburg.

J.W. Thompson, *Feudal Germany* (1928).

HAMADAN City in western Persia on the main road from Baghdad to Teheran. One of the most ancient cities of the Persian empire, at the beginning of the Middle Ages it served as summer capital of the *Sassanid kings of Persia. In 644 it was conquered by the Arabs, who imposed Islam on its inhabitants. As in most of Persia, at the end of the 7th century its inhabitants embraced the *Shiite branch of Islam and supported the *Abbasid revolution of 750. The city flourished until the middle of the 9th century, being one of the commercial centres between Baghdad and central Asia. The decline of the Abbasid caliphate and the rise of autonomous rulers in Persia brought instability to the city which, despite losing part of its prosperity, still remained a cultural centre and one of the most attractive cities in Persia. The great Persian philosopher *Ibn Sinna was buried there in 1037. After the conquest of Persia by the *Seljuks, H. became one of the capitals of the Turkish principalities established in the 12th century and, until the end of the 12th century, was a seat of the Seljuk dynasty. The city experienced a period of development, marked by the construction of palaces, mosques and gardens, representing a high-point of Persian-Moslem art. The *Mongol conquest in 1221 brought calamity; the city was burnt and the major part of the population slain. In 1225, however, some of the displaced inhabitants resettled the city, which again began to prosper, but in 1386 a new Mongol raid, led by *Tamerlane, brought its destruction. The city remained in ruins and did not recover until the end of the Middle Ages.

P. Schwarz, *Iran im Mittelalter* (1936).

HAMBURG City in northern Germany, at the confluence of the Elbe and Alster rivers, at the mouth of the Elbe by the North Sea. It was founded by *Charlemagne in 804 as a fortress to defend the empire against the incursions of the Slavs and Danes. A borough grew up around the castle and was important enough for a bishopric to be established (835), which was richly endowed by *Louis the Pious. One reason for its establishment was to create a centre from which to missionize the Slavs to the east of the Elbe and the Scandinavian peoples. Its first bishop, *Anskar, was mainly occupied with this activity. The Norman and Slavic raids damaged the city and, in the latter half of the 9th century, the archbishopric was moved to *Bremen. Nevertheless, the city continued to develop in the area between the Elbe, the Alster and the Bille rivers, and is still named the *Altstadt* (Old City). Under *Otto I, peace was restored in the area and the archbishops began to return to H., although the see was shared with Bremen. The city became an important commercial centre for northern Europe, especially from the 11th century when it served as a base for missionaries who finally brought Christianity to Scandinavia. The pontificate of Archbishop *Adalbert (1043-72) was the turning-point of this development. While the city came to be known as "the metropolis of the North" and reached a very important position in the Scandinavian world, the antagonism with the dukes of *Saxony led to the establishment of an independent county, controlled by the archbishops, who sought to attract a population and develop the country.

The continuous growth of the city was accentuated in the 12th century, both by the policy of the archbishops, who lost their ecclesiastical control over Scandinavia with the establishment of independent archbishoprics in Denmark, Norway and Sweden and sought to consolidate their principality, and by other German colonization activities. Thus, in 1188 Count Adolf III of *Holstein founded the *Neustadt* (New City) in the neighbourhood of H. It became commercially important, and the two cities were united in 1215. This period of continuous growth fostered the development of relations between the merchants of H. and those of *Lübeck. H. became one of the most important members of the *Hanse, taking part in all its commercial activities. Nevertheless, the rule of the city remained divided between the archbishop and the lord of Holstein, which restricted its trade and facilities. In the 13th century there was a continual struggle for internal civic autonomy. In 1301 an agreement was reached, and the lords granted the city certain privileges of self-government which were gradually increased with the establishment of a local "Senate", composed of members of rich merchant families which ruled the city, whose area was enlarged. The impressive Gothic Senate Hall, built in the 14th and 15th centuries, symbolized not only the prosperity of the city, but also its new status, as described in its documents: *Freie und Hansestadt Hamburg* (The Free Hanseatic City of Hamburg).

B. Studt and H. Ohlsen, *Hamburg, die Geschichte einer Stadt* (1951).

HAMDANIDS Arab dynasty, which ruled in northern Syria and Iraq in the 10th century. At the end of the 9th century, its founder, the Beduin leader Hamdan Ibn Hamdun, became governor of Mardin in northern Iraq. In 905 his sons profited from the decline of the *Abbasids to seize power at *Mosul, and gradually increased their authority. In 944, their chief leader, Ali *Saif Al-Dawlah, conquered *Aleppo and created a powerful state (944-67), which was able to fight successfully against the Byzantines. At Aleppo he established a brilliant court, which continued to be famous under his successors. In 1003 the dynasty was dethroned by an uprising of local officials.

M. Canard, *Histoire de la dynastie des Hamdanites* (1953).

HANSE Originally a medieval German term meaning a trading company, it denoted groups of merchants living and trading abroad. Until the 13th century the term was used loosely and referred to various commercial associations of German merchants, but from that time it designated only the Hanseatic League, an association of German cities in northern Germany and in the Baltic. The entry will deal only with H. in its latter meaning.

The origins of the H. are probably connected with an association of German merchants in London which existed in the 11th century and established a council in 1157. The Rhenish elements in the company gradually gave way to merchants from northern Germany. It established connections with the company founded at *Lübeck in the previous year to trade with the merchants of Gotland who obtained a charter of privilege from *Henry the Lion, duke of Saxony. The granting of this charter is considered the foundation of the H., although the name does not figure in the document. The foundation of the company of Lübeck was, nevertheless, most important in the evolution and development of the H. Their associates in *Visby, Gotland, were already deeply involved in the Baltic Sea trade and perpetuated the ancient trading relations of the Swedes with Russia. The colonization activities in eastern Germany during the latter half of the 12th century brought manpower to Lübeck, which became active in Baltic trade; by 1200, a guild named "The Merchants of the Holy Roman Empire" imposed its rule on Lübeck and became the leading trading company, while the merchants of Visby gradually became its junior associates. In the same year, they established trade links with *Novgorod in Russia, and in 1201 they founded a settlement of German merchants at *Riga, then still a pagan town in Livonia. In the 13th century, the H. of Lübeck began to be active also in the West, in *Denmark, *Norway, *Bruges and London, at first through association with other companies, such as those of Hamburg, Bremen and the cities of the Elbe and the Weser valleys, but also through trading activities. The companies were very active and energetic agents for German merchant colonization, particularly in the Baltic area, where they founded new cities: *Wismar (1226), Rostock (1218), *Stralsund (1234), *Stettin (1243) and others, and helped to Germanize cities like Elbing, Braunsberg, *Danzig, Memel and Riga. In 1270 the various companies, among whose leaders those of Lübeck, Hamburg and Bremen were prominent, merged into the "German Hanse", which established its headquarters at Lübeck. Its constitution was modelled on the league of 1241 between Lübeck and Hamburg, which created a political as well as a commercial association with the purpose of protecting trade.

With the establishment of the political-commercial league, the H. entered into its golden age of prosperity. A large number of cities joined the association, which imposed "aristocratic" constitutions on all the associate cities, excluding the guilds of craftsmen and lesser merchants from the city councils. At the 1347 assembly, 160 cities participated, among them cities of the Netherlands such as Groningen, Nijmegen and Arnhem, Stockholm in Sweden, Bergen in Norway, Breslau and Cracow in Poland. The assembly issued a new constitution, based on a hierarchical organization of the League. Thus, the delegates of the member cities discussed and decided the policy of the H. at the annual assembly, while it was implemented by the permanent council at Lübeck. A member city which would not conform to the decisions was expelled and its merchants deprived of the protection given by the H. to its members. Such action virtually implied the commercial ruin of the expelled city, whose merchants were not only deprived of use of the establishments which belonged to the H. in various cities from England to Russia, but also no longer enjoyed the monopolistic privileges granted to the H. by monarchs. The assembly also decided on the creation of a fleet, which became the most important naval power in the Baltic and North seas.

The aims of the H., however, were economic and not political. Politics were regarded as being subordinate to economics. Thus, the war fleet was used only when trade privileges were restricted or a state attempted to annul them. Such was the case in the great war with Denmark, when King *Waldemar IV (1340-75) refused

to renew the privileges of the H. at Bergen and forbade its ships to pass the Sund. In 1367 the assembly of Kiel decided to declare war on Denmark and allied with Sweden. The H. fleet conquered *Copenhagen and Waldemar was compelled to restore all the privileges of the H. in his realms by the Peace of Stralsund (1370). At the end of the 14th century the H. reached the peak of its power, and was the most important political and economic organization of northern Europe, including large areas of Germany within its sphere.

HAPSBURG (HABSBURG) German dynasty which attained the imperial crown in 1273. Its name comes from the family seat, Habichtsburg (The Hawk's Castle), situated on the eastern bank of the Aare River, today northern *Switzerland. The founder of the dynasty was probably Guntram the Rich, who possessed large estates in southern Alsace in the middle of the 10th century. His grandson *Radbot, brother of Werner, bishop of Strassburg, built the castle and enlarged the family's domains in the Swabian territories between the Rhine and Are rivers. In 1090 the Hs. are mentioned as counts and were considered members of the middle group of nobility in the empire. Their increased importance in the 12th century was due to their services to the *Hohenstaufen dynasty. From 1135, they held the hereditary title of landgrave of Alsace and after 1170 added that of counts of Zurich, in both cases representing the imperial authority. At the beginning of the 13th century they became one of the most powerful and wealthy families in southwest Germany, extending their territorial possessions over large parts of Alsace and northern Switzerland. *Rudolf I, count of H. established the H. principality and, during the Interregnum (1254-73) in *Germany, his influence grew to the point that many members of the nobility followed his leadership. In 1273 he was elected emperor after a disputed election with *Ottokar II, king of Bohemia. The war between the two personalities which followed the election ended with the defeat of Ottokar, who was compelled to surrender the duchies of Austria and Styria (1278), which Rudolf bestowed on his son *Albert in 1282. Thus, he laid the territorial foundations of the dynasty, which moved to its new capital, Vienna. The acquisition of Austria compensated for the loss of the family's Swiss estates, where the revolt of the cantons against Albert could not be repressed and led to the independence of Switzerland. In the 14th century the family, failing to maintain the imperial crown, concentrated on its own interests and increased its Austrian possessions by successive inheritances and by the annexation of *Carinthia and Carniola (1335), *Tyrol (1363), parts of Istria (1374), Vorarlberg (1376) and the city of Trieste, giving access to the Adriatic Sea (1382). When Duke *Albert II died in 1397, this collection of principalities, corresponding in size to major realms, was divided between his two sons, *Albert III, who inherited Austria and the areas to the east, and Leopold, who inherited Carinthia and the areas to the west. Thus, the dynasty was divided into two branches, the Albertines and the Leopoldines.
R. A. Kann, *The Hapsburg Empire* (1957).

HARALD See HAROLD.

HARDICANUTE (1018-42) King of Denmark (1035-42) and England (1040-42). He was the only legitimate son of *Canute the Great and in 1026 was sent to Denmark to represent his father. In 1035 he succeeded to the Danish throne, but was unable to prevent *Norway from gaining its independence or the coronation of his half-brother *Harold I in England. After the death of Harold, he attempted, with the support of his mother, the Anglo-Norman Queen *Emma, to seize power in England, but proved himself incapable of ruling and died, probably of alcoholism.

G. Jones, *A History of the Vikings* (1968).

HAROLD I, Harefoot King of England (1035-40). An illegitimate son of *Canute the Great, a party of the Danish nobility proclaimed him king of the English possessions in the Danish empire. He was able to maintain his authority in England, despite the counter-attacks of his half-brother *Hardicanute, who inherited Denmark, thus causing the division and fall of the great Nordic empire of Canute.

F. M. Stenton. *Anglo-Saxon England* (1947).

HAROLD II, of Wessex (c. 1022-66) King of England (1066). Son of the Anglo-Saxon Earl Godwin, who was appointed earl of Wessex by *Canute the Great. H. inherited the earldom from his father in 1053 and was the most influential person in England in the reign of *Edward the Confessor. After Edward's death, H. was proclaimed king by the Anglo-Saxon earls, who opposed the claims of *William, duke of Normandy. H. defeated a Norse invasion in Yorkshire but, turning southwards to defend the country against the Norman invasion, was defeated by William the Conqueror and was killed at the Battle of *Hastings. He was the last Anglo-Saxon king.

F. M. Stenton, *Anglo-Saxon England* (1947).

HAROLD I, Fairhead (c. 850-930) King of Norway (860-930). Member of a Swedish noble family which ruled the territories around present-day Oslo, he was proclaimed king in 860. He began a long series of wars and, between 866 and 872, imposed his authority over most of the Norse tribes and founded the Yngling dynasty, which ruled until the 14th century. Many of the defeated chieftains preferred exile rather than surrender to his rule and attacked the west European countries within the context of the Norman raids at the end of the 9th century, while some attempted to invade Norway. H. organized his kingdom on the basis of personal authoritarian rule and won the support of the seamen. In 890 he led an expedition to the Orkney and Shetland islands where he had powerful opponents; he defeated them and imposed his rule over the Norwegian settlements in those islands, as well as in the Faroes. At the beginning of the 10th century he crushed revolts of the landed nobility, who rebelled against the high taxes he imposed on them. His last years, when he also became powerful in the Scandinavian settlement in England, were a period of family troubles and his sons, estimated as numbering 20, fought for their heritage. At the age of 80 he left the throne to his son Eric but, after his death, his other sons revolted and Norway fell into a period of anarchy.

P. G. Foote, *The Viking Achievement* (1971).

HAROLD II, Hardruler King of Norway (1047-66). A younger brother of King *Olaf II, he became an adventurer. In 1030 he travelled to Russia and subsequently went to *Byzantium, where he served in the *Varangian guard, winning the respect of his fellows and superiors, and also becoming wealthy. In 1045 he returned to Scandinavia, settling in Sweden, where he became an ally of King Amund, who used him to further his political

objectives in Norway. In 1047, when his nephew *Magnus I died, he proclaimed himself king imposing a strong rule upon the country, which gave him his nickname "Hardruler". In 1066 he attempted to profit from the troubled situation of England after the death of *Edward the Confessor and invaded it. Defeated by *Harold II of Wessex at Stamford Bridge, near York, he was killed in the battle.

G. Jones, *A History of the Vikings* (1968).

HAROLD BLUETOOTH King of *Denmark (950-86). Son of *Gorm the Elder, he was the first Danish king to reign over the whole of Denmark. He also conquered Norway. He fought unsuccessfully against Emperors *Otto I and *Otto II in an attempt to impose his rule over the territories between Jutland and the Elbe. In 960 he converted to Christianity and attempted to impose his faith on his subjects. His efforts met with fierce resistance from the nobility, which continued to worship its ancestral gods, and even his son *Sweyn joined the opposition. In 986 a general revolt led by Sweyn compelled H. to abdicate; he fled to the *Wends where he died some years later.

G. Jones. *A History of the Vikings* (1968).

HARUN AL-RASHID (766-809) *Abbasid caliph (786-809). Son of Al-Mehdi, he was trained from his early years for a political career. In 782, he nominally commanded an Arab army which defeated the Byzantines, and was appointed governor of the west Asiatic provinces of the caliphate, where he was counselled by Ihia the Barmakian, a skilled administrator and politician, who helped H. to become the sixth Abbasid caliph and was appointed chief vizier, becoming the most powerful person in the caliphate until the fall of his family in 803. The reign of H. is considered the most brilliant period of the Arab caliphate and there are many legends about his personality and government. Very little of this, however, has any real connection with the caliph, who established a system of government through viziers, which restricted access to him. His reign, which in general was a long period of peace, was marked by economic prosperity and the development of international trade, both in the Mediterranean and in the north, as far as the Baltic Sea. The wealth which was brought to Baghdad allowed the establishment of a splendid court, described in the tales of *A Thousand and One Nights*. The increasing preoccupation of the Arabs with trade and administration, which they shared with the Persians, forced them to seek soldiers among the African slaves and the Turks of the steppes. H. was not able to reimpose the caliph's authority in Spain, where the *Ummayad emirs ruled independently, and the frequent "wars" with the Byzantines were merely frontier incidents involving local commanders. In order to intimidate his Ummayad and Byzantine rivals, H. allied with *Charlemagne; the main result of this alliance, however, was the development of trade with the Frankish kingdom.

The legendary figure of H. is based on the image of majesty as depicted by the authors of the *Thousand and One Tales,* where he is described as the promoter of public welfare, whilst the viziers are an image of madness. His visits to fairs in disguise are praised as a means of controlling the administration and the execution of his orders, but at the same time leave the impression of a new kind of head of state who reigns rather than rules.

H. S. J. B. Philby, *Harun Al-Rashid* (1934).

Harun Al-Rashid dispensing justice; 13th-century miniature, Baghdad school

HASAN IBN ALI See AL-HASAN.

HASAN IBN AL-SABBAH (d. 1124) Leader of the *Assassins. Born at Kum in Persia to a rigid Shiite family said to have originated in Yemen, he was educated at Ravy (now Teheran), where he became acquainted with Ismaili books. In 1072 he was ordained by emissaries of the *Fatimid court as "preacher of the faith". After a journey to Egypt he returned to Persia, where his activities brought him the persecution of the *Seljuks and he was compelled to flee from Isfahan to the mountains of the northeast Persian provinces. In 1090 he seized the castle of Alamuth, on a rock which protected it from attack, and made it the headquarter of his sect. He sent missionaries to win more converts and seize castles. In order to achieve the purposes of Ismaili Islam, he urged the use, when necessary, of murder of political and religious opponents, demanding absolute obedience from the members of his sect.

H. was both a political-religious leader and a thinker and writer. He had a wide knowledge of philosophy, astronomy, mathematics and magic, which he used to develop his ideas. He advocated a Moslem-Shiite society where the sole source of authority would be Islamic theology, both in political life and in private conduct, giving a personal example: one of his sons was put to death on his orders, on suspicion of drinking wine.

B. Lewis, *The Assassins* (1967).

HASDAI CRESCAS (c. 1340-1410) Jewish philosopher and rabbi in Spain. He was educated in Barcelona, and c. 1380 settled at Saragossa (Aragon), where he became the leader of the community. He developed a philosophical view of Judaism based on his opposition both to the philosophy of *Maimonides and to rabbinical concepts as formulated by the followers of *Asher. His main argument was that the interrelationship of faith and reason, emphasized by Aristotelian thought, has no real existence and that the sole truth is that of divine revelation, which is the only basis for reasoning. His book, *The Light of God*, where he developed his ideas, was finished after 1391, when many Spanish Jews were killed by persecutions – among them his only son. H.'s conclusions are influenced by this event, which made him emphasize that God's intentions and deeds are unfathomable. He also wrote a polemical book in Spanish, against Christianity, which he composed to strengthen the faith of local Jewry.

I. Baer, *Die Juden im Christlichen Spanien* (1956).

HASDAI IBN SHAPRUT (10th century) Jewish politician and man of letters. Born to a rich family at Jaen, he was educated at *Cordoba, studied medicine and entered the service of the *Ummayad caliph of Spain, *Abd-Al-Rahman III (912-61). His learning and knowledge of languages allowed him to be distinguished at the caliph's court and brought him promotion. He was appointed head of a department of the Treasury and was also employed in diplomatic missions to Christian countries (958). H.'s political eminence caused him to be recognized as the leader of the Jewish communities in Spain. In that capacity, he contributed to the development of the Golden Age of Spanish Jewry, supporting intellectuals and scientists who worked for the revival of the Hebrew language. His activities encouraged the emergence of an autonomous Jewish religious centre in Spain, which became less dependent on the academies of Mesopotamia (see *Jews).

H. is also famous for a letter he wrote to Joseph, king of the *Khazars, in which he reported the situation of the Jewish communities in Spain, asking him about his Jewish kingdom and offering his services. The king's answer, which is considered a spurious document composed in Spain in the late 11th century, is a description of the conversion of the Khazars to Judaism.

E. Ashtor, *Histoire des Juifs en Espagne Musulmane* (1969).

HASHEMITES Arab dynasty of Mecca, belonging to the clan of Banu Hashim, the family of Mohammad. After the establishment of the *Ummayad caliphate at Damascus (660) and the settlement of the most important families of Mecca in Syria and Iraq, the H. became the local leaders in the Hedjaz and in the 8th century attained the rank of governors, *Sherifs* of Mecca, a rank which they held with few interruptions until 1922. Despite their great prestige as members of the prophet's family, their real power and influence was limited. See *Arabia.

HASHISHINS See ASSASSINS.

HASTINGS Town in southeast England, on the coast of the English Channel. It is famous for the battle of 1066, when the Normans, led by *William the Conqueror, defeated the Anglo-Saxons, killing their king, *Harold II of Wessex. The result of the battle was the conquest of England by the Normans. H. belonged to the federation known as the *Cinque Ports.

HATTIN Hill in eastern *Galilee, near Tiberias. It is famous for the battle of 4 July 1187 between the Moslems and the *Crusaders. The Moslems, led by *Saladin, defeated the Crusaders, led by *Guy of Lusignan, king of Jerusalem. The victory of Saladin was important because of its results. While most of the Crusaders were killed or taken prisoner, the kingdom of Jerusalem remained without defenders and almost all of it, including the capital, Jerusalem, and its major city, Acre, fell into the hands of Saladin and his army. When the news of the defeat at H. reached western Europe, the Third *Crusade was proclaimed.

S. Runciman, *A History of the Crusades* (1953).

HAUTEVILLE Norman dynasty in southern Italy and Antioch. They originally came from *Normandy, where they belonged to the lesser nobility and in the 10th century held the estate of H. Tancred of H., the head of the family at the beginning of the 11th century, encouraged the emigration of his numerous sons. The eldest, led by *William "Iron-arm", were among the Norman adventurers who invaded southern Italy in 1118. After some initial successes, William called his younger brothers to join him. Among them were *Robert Guiscard, who led the family after the death of William and *Roger, later count of Sicily. Under Robert, duke of Apulia (1057-85), the family conquered the lands of southern Italy and *Sicily, thus creating the Norman state of southern Italy which, in the 12th century, became the kingdom of Sicily. After Robert's death, the leadership of the family passed to his youngest brother Roger, while Robert's descendants ruled the duchy of Apulia until 1127, when it was inherited by *Roger II of Sicily. In 1096 Robert's son *Bohemond joined the First *Crusade as head of Italian-Norman group. He conquered *Antioch in 1098, where he was proclaimed prince, and his descendants ruled the principality until 1268, when it was conquered by the *Mamelukes. Thus, at the beginning of the 12th century, the dynasty was split into two main branches: the Sicilian, which reigned until 1194, when Roger II's daughter Constance, the wife of Emperor *Henry VI, passed it to the *Hohenstaufen; and that of Antioch, which ruled in the Latin states of the East.

C. Cahen, *Le Régime Féodal de l'Italie Normande* (1940).

HAWKWOOD, JOHN (d. 1394) English adventurer. He arrived in Italy c. 1360 and became captain of a private army, selling his services to the cities. In 1361 he was the *condottiere* of Pisa and participated in its wars with other Tuscan cities, among them Florence. Despite a defeat in 1364, he reached great fame and, through an alliance with Milan, became one of the most eminent political and military figures in Italy. In 1377 he entered the service of Florence and, until his death, commanded its armies, thereby bringing Tuscany under the domination of the city. An impressive tomb was erected in the cathedral of Florence for *Giovanni Acuto*, as he was called in Italian.

G. T. Leader, *Giovanni Acuto, Storia di un condottiere* (1899).

HEBREW The common language of the Jewish people. While it was practically unspoken in the Middle Ages, the written tongue experienced a revival and flourished after hundreds of years of the influence of Aramaic, which was used in the Talmud and even in the liturgy. The revival began on Palestinian soil in the 6th and 7th centuries and was closely related to the development of poetry. The poems, on Messianic and other religious themes, resulted in the emergence of popular moralistic tales, the *Midrashim*, intended to comfort the people of Israel at a time of persecution and continued exile, but also to improve individual conduct. One of the most important consequences of the revival of Hebrew was the return to the use of the language in the liturgy, resulting in the compilation of the Jewish prayer-book, the *Siddur*, and the study of the language by large sections of the Jewish poeple. Under the influence of Arabic linguists, the study of H. encouraged the development of a philological school which flourished mainly in Palestine and Spain, where it reached its greatest height. Thus, the "grammar of Tiberias", which was the starting point of this evolution in the 8th century, led in the 10th to 12th centuries to the elaboration of philological treatises during the golden age of Jewish culture in *Cordoba and *Toledo.

The linguistic revival in Spain was followed by a revival of poetry, which was written exclusively in H. and dealt with religious and secular topics. Medieval H. poetry, which reached the height of its perfection in Spain, became a major source of liturgical hymns and songs, but it was also an expression of the desire to see the salvation of the Jewish people and its return to Zion. In contrast to European literatures, no epic themes were developed and medieval H. poetry remained primarily lyric in style, even in satirical poems and *Diwans*, collections of songs in praise of a patron. Most of the poets were also recognized philosophers and scientists. However, while poetry and liturgical literature were written in H., philosophical and scientific works were composed in Arabic, even when they were theological treatises.

In Christian Europe, however, where Arabic was unknown, the Jewish intellectuals used H. in their interpretations of the Bible and Talmud, as well as in correspondence. This language, rabbinical H., was influenced by the writings of the Mesopotamian sages and, therefore, the use of Aramaic words was widespread. But under the impact of the philological treatises coming from Spain through Languedoc and Provence, an intermediate style gradually evolved from the 11th century. Thus, H. was the language of the liturgy as well as of scholars. From the 12th century, works written in Arabic in Spain, north Africa and Egypt were systematically translated into H. at *Narbonne and *Montpellier and spread to the *Ashkenazi Jewish communities.

The Jewish historical literature was written entirely in H. This genre of literature was influenced more than others by the historical books of the Bible, both in their form and style. At the same time it proves the existence of an interaction between the poetic and rabbinical forms of H.

A. Altman, *Biblical and other Studies* (1963).

HEBRIDES Archipelago northwest of Scotland. At the beginning of the Middle Ages it was populated by *Picts and Scots of *Celtic stock. In the 9th century, the H. were several times invaded by Norwegian *Vikings, who established a settlement and continued their raids to Ireland. Until the 12th century, they remained under Norwegian overlordship, but in practice the Norse and Celtic population merged and became part of the kingdom of Scotland.

HEDEBY (HAITHABU) *Viking city in southeast Jutland, near present-day Kiel. It was probably founded in the 8th century, comprising two or three settlements of fishermen and scamen and, c. 800, became one of the major commercial centres of northern Europe. Most of its trade was directed eastwards, to the Baltic countries and, via the great rivers of Russia, to Byzantium and the lands of the caliphate. But another important artery led from the Scandinavian countries to the *Carolingian empire. At the beginning of the 9th century it was fortified by a circular wall, said to have been built by King Gottfried. The town was divided into separate fishermen's, seamen's and merchants' quarters. During the 9th and 10th centuries its wealth caused the kings of Denmark and other Scandinavian princes to struggle for overlordship of the city, which grew, owing to the incorporation, before the 10th century, of a new Saxon settlement named Slesvik, within its new and enlarged fortifications. Its importance gradually declined in the 11th century, when it was disputed between the kings and the *jarls* of Denmark and Norway, as well as by the *Wends of eastern Gemany. The city was burnt c. 1050, probably by *Harold "Hardruler", king of Norway, and its inhabitants dispersed.

H. Jankuhn, *Haithabu, ein Handelsplatz der Wikingerzeit* (1963).

HEDJAZ (HEJJAZ) Province in western *Arabia, along the Red Sea coast, extending from Mecca to Idumaea. At the beginning of the Middle Ages, H. was populated by nomadic Beduin tribes, some of whom founded a number of small towns such as Mecca and Yathrib (later Medina), which were commercial centres. Among these tribes, there were also Jewish refugees from Palestine who settled mainly in the towns, adopted the Arabic language and social practices, but continued to observe their faith. In the 6th century, daily contact brought the Arab tribes under the influence of Jewish monotheism, but it was not consistent until the days of *Mohammad. Mohammad's activities had a revolutionary impact on the history of H. His success in imposing the new faith, *Islam, and in defeating his heathen opponents, resulted in the unification of the province (628), which became the centre of the Moslem faith. The Jewish settlers were compelled either to convert to Islam or to leave the country. H. Became the holy land of Islam and the two holy cities, *Mecca and *Medina, became centres of pilgrimage (Hajj) for Moslems from all over the world. But the great wars which spread Islam in the 7th century, resulted in the emigration of the leading families of the province; and, after the establishment of the Arab caliphate at Damacus (660), H. remained a distant province, dominated by caliphs resident in Damascus, Baghdad or Cairo. Several uprisings, aiming at restoring the province as the centre of Moslem government, failed in the later Middle Ages and its history was merged with that of Arabia.

P. K. Hitti, *A History of the Arabs* (1953)

HEGIRA (Hajira: the emigration) Name given to the flight of *Mohammad and his followers of Mecca to *Medina in 622. This event is considered the beginning of the Moslem era, which is counted from the H.

HEIDELBERG Town in western *Germany, on the Neckar River. The town was probably founded in the latter half of tne 12th century and was first mentioned in a document of 1196, as one of the towns of the bishopric-principality of *Worms. In the middle of the 13th century it was annexed to the county of the *Palatinate, to which it belonged until 1803. The electors of the Palatinate resided in the city and built a castle at its centre. In 1386 the Elector Rupert (d. 1390) founded its university, the third in Germany, which became one of the most important scholarly centres of the empire, attracting scholars and students from all the German countries.

H. Schrade, *Heidelberg* (1936).

HEINRICH See HENRY.

HELENA, St. (d. 330) Mother of Emperor *Constantine the Great. Born of humble parents, she was raised as a Christian and became the wife of Caesar Constantius Chlorus, to whom she bore Constantine (274). When Constantine became emperor, she was raised to a position of great honour and zealously supported the Christian cause. In 326 she went to the Holy Land, where she founded the churches on the Mount of Olives and in Bethlehem. There are various traditions about her activities in Jerusalem in her later years, among them the finding of the Holy Cross. Her journey in Palestine attracted the attention of the Christians to the Holy Land and gave an impetus to pilgrimages to the holy places and to the development of Christian worship there. For this reason H. was venerated in the Middle Ages, when she became a legendary figure related to the Holy Land. Some of the legends made her a native of England, daughter of a Celtic king, "Old King Cole" of Colchester. Another legend resulted in the emergence of the cult of H. at the abbey of Hautvillers, near Rheims in France, while pilgrims to Jerusalem during the Middle Ages were taken to her "palace" in the city. The popularity of her cult resulted in the development of motifs depicting or connected with her in Byzantine and Western art.

J. Maurice, *Sainte Hélène* (1929).

HELMHOLD (HELMOLD) (c. 112-1177) Historian. Born in northern Saxony, he became a monk at the Benedictine monastery of Neumünster, which he left in 1155 in order to become priest at Bosau. In 1172 he finished his great work, *Historia Slavonum* (History of the Slavs), an important account of the German colonization of northeast Germany, which he interpreted as a crusade against the heathen Slavs, hailing their destruction. H. saw this activity (between 1147-72) as part of the long historical process of the Christianization and Germanization of northern Germany, from the time of *Charlemagne to his own age.

Ed. in *MGH, Scriptores rerum germanicarum in usum scholarium* (1906).

HELOISE (1101-64) Abbess of Paraclete and *Abelard's beloved. Born in Paris, she was the niece of Fulk, one of the most influential canons of the cathedral of Notre Dame, who supervised her education. H., who showed a keen interest in intellectual life and study, was educated by Peter Abelard, who was her private tutor. Their love affair was described by Abelard in his *Historia Calamitatum*. Pregnant, she fled with Abelard to his family home in Brittany, where she bore their son Astrolabe. Then she persuaded him to give up family life and resume his work as philosopher and teacher, while she became a nun at Argenteuil. In 1229 when the community of Argenteuil was dispersed, Abelard gave her his country retreat at Paraclete in Champagne, where she founded and directed a nunnery. Abelard, who was appointed spiritual director of the nunnery, wrote its Rule, which was approved by Pope *Innocent II. H. is famous for her letters to Abelard, which show her firm character, piety and encouragement to her lover. In recent years, doubts have been expressed about the authenticity of the correspondence, but it appears that even if the letters, in their present form, were composed in the 13th century, when their love affair had become idealized, their substance is original, as is corroborated by the letter of consolation written to her by the abbot of Cluny, *Peter the Venerable, after Abelard's death in 1142. From the 13th century, H. became a legendary figure of the ideal beloved. Her tomb, near that of Abelard, in the abbey church, was visited by poets and admirers.

E. Gilson, *Héloïse et Abélard* (1946).

HENGIST AND HORSA (5th century) According to the tradition, which was adopted by *Bede, they were two brothers who led the Anglo-Saxon invasion of England, responding to the call of a British king whom they later defeated when they conquered Kent.

F. M. Stenton, *Anglo-Saxon England* (1947).

HENOTIKON A decree issued by the Byzantine Emperor *Zeno in 482, containing a theological formula elaborated chiefly by Patriarch Acacius of Constantinople in order to secure a union between the Orthodox and *Monophysites. The document reasserted the articles of the Creeds of *Nicaea and Constantinople, condemned *Nestorius and his followers, but omitted any reference to the "natures" of Christ as a major concession to the Monophysites. While the H. was widely accepted in the East, it met with strong opposition in Rome, resulting in the elaboration of the doctrine of "the two swords" by Pope *Gelasius I, who advocated the independence of the Roman Church.

Text, ed. *PG*, vol. 86.

HENRY I (c. 876-936) King of *Germany (919-36). Son of Duke Otto the Illustrious of Saxony, he became duke on his father's death in 912, and in 919 the Saxon and Franconian nobles elected him king of Germany. He had to fight against the German dukes in order to compel them to recognize his royal authority (921). After a long war against *Charles the Simple and *Ralph, kings of France, he restored German authority over the duchy of Lotharingia (925). H. was chiefly interested in Saxon politics and neglected those of Germany. Under his reign, Saxony began the Geman expansion northwards and eastwards as a result of a long series of wars against the Danes and the Slavic tribes.
W. Mohr, *König Heinrich I* (1950).

HENRY II, St. (972-1024) Emperor of the *Holy Roman empire (1002-24). A member of the Saxon dynasty, he was the son of Duke Henry of Bavaria, who had intended him for an ecclesiastical career. In 995, however, he became duke of *Bavaria and was one of the closest associates of his cousin, Emperor *Otto III. After Otto's death, he was elected emperor and reverted to the policy of his great-grandfather, *Otto I. His main interest was German internal affairs, and he sought to impose peace with the support of the church. In 1005 he signed a peace treaty with *Boleslaw I of Poland, which secured peace on the eastern frontiers of the empire. H. went to Italy three times (1004, 1014 and 1021-22), attempting to impose his authority on the country and to reform the papacy. In Germany he was preoccupied with ecclesiastical reform, appointing bishops and abbots whom he regarded as worthy of their positions. He encouraged the order of *Cluny. In 1007 he founded the bishopric of *Bamberg, which he intended as a missionary centre for the Slavs.
L. Mikoletzky, *Heinrich II und die Kirche* (1946).

Christ crowning Henry II; *11th-century miniature*

HENRY III, the Salian (1017-56) Emperor of the *Holy Roman empire (1039-56). Son of *Conrad II, he was the greatest emperor of the *Salian dynasty. His father had associated him with his rule in *c.* 1035 and he had already gained great experience when he inherited the empire. H. established peace within Germany and compelled the dukes of *Bohemia to accept his authority. In 1042-45 he fought against the Hungarians, who recognized his overlordship. In the West, however, he had difficulties with *Godfrey, duke of Lorraine, who attempted to organize a coalition against him and transferred the conflict to Italy, where he married the heiress of Tuscany, Beatrice. In his ecclesiastical policy, H. was a firm supporter of ecclesiastical reform and particularly of the order of *Cluny, and promoted many monks from the Cluniac monasteries to bishoprics within the empire. The decadence of the papacy, which fell under the influence of the Roman families, brought him to formulate the principle that the emperor's duty was to impose reform of the papal see through the appointment of suitable popes. His expedition to Italy in 1046 was conceived according to this principle: after the conquest of Rome, he deposed the rival popes and successively appointed German bishops in their place. During his reign, no papal election was valid without his having approved the candidates. By the middle of the 11th century H. had attained a unique position in western Europe, comparable only with those of *Charlemagne and *Otto I, as the unchallenged leader of Western society. His sudden illness and death at the age of 39, when he left as heir a son aged seven, therefore had considerable impact on the history of *Germany, the Holy Roman empire, the papacy and Italy.
T. Schieffer, *Heinrich III (Die grossen Deutschen)* (1956).

HENRY IV (1050-1106) Emperor of the *Holy Roman empire (1056-1106). Son of *Henry III, his reign began with the regency of his mother, Agnes of Poitou, who was unacquainted with German politics and was aided by a council of bishops. During the period of his minority the princes increased their power and profited from the weakness of the imperial government to strengthen their authority in the duchies. The papacy also profited from the regency to free itself from imperial control. In 1058 Pope *Nicholas II did not wait for imperial confirmation of his candidature and, in 1059, issued the decree on the papal elections, which proclaimed the exclusive prerogative of the College of *Cardinals in this area. H. began his personal reign in 1065 and, during the first ten years, fought against the princes in order to impose imperial power through the appointment of new dukes, some of them his kinsmen. In 1075 when Pope *Gregory VII issued his *Dictatus Papae*, H. opposed the new papal policy and, after a short dispute in writing, clashed openly with the pope, thus beginning the *Investiture contest. The name, however, only expresses the formal problem – the real issue of the contest being the problem of the sovereignty of the emperor.

However, this clash and his excommunication by the pope were the sign for a new rebellion of the princes, who chose an anti-king in the person of *Rudolf of Swabia, and requested that Gregory join them in Germany. H. decided to divide his adversaries. He rushed to Italy, met the pope at *Canossa (1078) and, making penance, was absolved. The German rebellion became illegitimate and he was able to crush the opposition with the help of the bishops (1080). The Canossa "humiliation" was, in fact, a victory for the emperor, who was now free to renew his dispute with the pope. In 1083 he conquered Rome, while Gregory fled to Salerno and appointed an antipope, *Clement III, who was not recognized by the clergy and the western states. The contest continued and, during the pontificate of *Urban II, Germany was again in upheaval. Urban favoured the the monks of *Hirsau, who became his close allies in Germany and raised public opinion against H., while rebellions affected his own family. In 1093 his eldest son *Conrad revolted, and only in 1098 was his revolt crushed. Conrad was sent to Italy, where he died in 1101. In 1105 his second son and heir *Henry, revolted and called for the deposition of the old emperor. H. died in 1106, in the midst of the war against his son.

H. F. Haefele, *Fortuna Heinrici IV Imperatoris. Untersuchungen zur Lebensgeschichte des dritten Saliers* (1954).

HENRY V (1081-1125) Emperor of the *Holy Roman empire (1106-25). Son of *Henry IV, his reign began in a chaotic situation, due to revolts in which he had participated. Only in 1110 did he succeed in pacifying Germany and he then travelled to Rome. In response to the request of Pope *Paschal II that he give up the lay *Investiture, he imprisoned the pope (1111) and thus obtained his acquiescence. But this action earned him the general opposition of the church and the Investiture contest began again. In 1119 the negotiations with Pope *Calixtus II, his kinsman, failed to reach a solution and a civil war devastated Germany. In 1121 the German princes, who organized themselves during his reign, imposed a compromise on the pope and emperor, known as the *Concordat of Worms (1122), which put an end to the Investiture conflict. In the last years of his reign H. tried to restore imperial authority, but without success. In 1124 he organized a military expedition to the Low Countries, which were considered a threat against France, which had supported the pope in 1119. He died childless in 1125 during an expedition against Liège. With his death the Salian dynasty came to an end.

H. Banitza, *Die Persönlichkeit Heinrichs V.* (1927).

HENRY VI (1165-97) Emperor of the *Holy Roman empire (1190-97), king of Sicily (1194-97), son of *Frederick Barbarossa and his heir from 1169. In 1186, at his father's request, he married Constance, daughter of *Roger II, king of Sicily, and was crowned king of Italy in Milan. Regent at the time of his father's departure for the Third *Crusade, he became emperor after his death in Asia Minor. From 1189 he was involved in the struggle for succession to the Sicilian throne which began with the death of *William II, whose heiress was Constance, his wife, as the nearest in succession. The Sicilian nobles' opposition to rule by a foreigner, however, gave rise to wars. In 1192 H. returned to Germany to deal with the local situation and with the captivity of *Richard I, king of England. In 1194 he pacified Germany and returned to Sicily, where the successive deaths of Norman princes enabled him to inherit the throne. In 1196 he led a *Crusade of the Germans, granting the royal title to the rulers of *Cyprus and conquering Sidon. He died of fever at Messina in 1197 leaving an infant son, the future *Frederick II.

J. Haller, *Heinrich VI* (1944).

HENRY VII, of Luxemburg (c. 1269-1313) Emperor of the *Holy Roman empire (1309-13). Son of Count Henry of Luxemburg, he was educated by French tutors; in 1288 he inherited the estates of the Luxemburg family in the Low Countries. His election to the imperial throne was due to the influence of his brother Baldwin, archbishop of Cologne. In 1310 he profited from a vacancy in the throne of *Bohemia to appoint his son *John as king, marrying him with the heiress to the throne. H. was concerned with Italian affairs and sought an imperial coronation at Rome. In 1311 he went to Italy, where he was hailed by *Dante as the new hope for the restoration of peace and order. In 1312 two papal legates, who arrived in Rome from Avignon, crowned him as Holy Roman emperor. H. failed in his attempts to restore order in Italy and became involved in the wars between the Italian cities. In 1313 he became ill and died near Siena.

F. Schneider, *Kaiser Heinrich VII, Dantes Keiser* (1940).

HENRY VII See HENRY OF HOHENSTAUFEN, son of Frederick II.

HENRY I (1204-17) King of *Castile (1214-17). Son of *Alfonso VIII and of Eleanor of England, he inherited the crown at the age of ten and, until his death, Castile was ruled by his brother-in-law, *Alfonso IX of León.

HENRY II, of Trastamare (1333-79) King of *Castile (1369-79). Illegitimate son of *Alfonso XI, he led the revolt against *Peter the Cruel, his half-brother. In order to overcome the royal power, he allied with the kings of Aragon and France and was helped by the French decision to send abroad the *Grandes Compagnies which *Du Guesclin hired for the Castilian war. Despite his defeat at *Najera (1367), he succeeded in defeating and personally killing King Peter, whom he succeeded in 1369. He was compelled to alienate large royal estates in order to recompense his supporters and to mobilize them against the claims of the English Prince *John of Gaunt, who married Peter's daughter. H.'s reign was a period of weakening of the royal power in Castile, but he was able to found a dynasty which reigned in Castile until the end of the Middle Ages.

A. Castro, *Periods of Spanish History* (1954).

HENRY III (1379-1406) King of *Castile (1390-1406). Grandson of *Henry II, he established peace within his kingdom. His marriage with Catherine of Gaunt, daughter of *John of Gaunt and Constance, daughter of *Peter the Cruel, effected a reconciliation between the two branches of the dynasty and allowed him to strengthen royal power. In 1391 he began a persecution of Jews and Moors, which caused severe economical damage to the country, deprived of its most productive urban inhabitants. During his reign the influence of the clergy became dominant in the state.

A. Castro, *Periods of Spanish History* (1954)

HENRY I (1068-1135) King of England (1100-35). He was the third son of *William the Conqueror and received a broad education, which won him the title *Beauclerc*. In 1100 he became king of England on the death of his brother, *William II. His reign was characterized by a return to the practices of his father's government, based on the administration of justice and enforcement of royal authority. In 1106 he defeated his elder brother *Robert, duke of Normandy, at Tinchebray and annexed the duchy of Normandy to England. Allied with the houses of Blois and Anjou in France, he was in a state of continuous rivalry and conflict with *Louis VI, and in 1120 forced the French king to accept him as his royal vassal for Normandy. In England, he improved the administration and employed members of the lesser nobility in the government. He developed the financial administration and centralized it by establishing the *Exchequer. His legal activities are summarized in a compilation named *Leges Henrice Primi* (The Laws of Henry I). In 1120 his only son died in a naval accident and H. was concerned with the problem of the succession. After the death of his son-in-law, Emperor *Henry V, he gave his widowed daughter, Matilda, to *Geoffrey Plantagenet of Anjou, with the understanding that she would inherit him. But, at his death, a civil war broke out between *Matilda and her supporters, and *Stephen of Blois, who also claimed the throne.

A. L. Poole, *From Domesday Book to Magna Charta* (1951).

HENRY II, Plantagenet (1133-89) King of England (1154-89). He was the son of *Geoffrey Plantagenet, count of Anjou, and of *Matilda. At his father's death in 1151, he inherited Normandy, Anjou, Maine and Touraine and claimed the rights of his mother in England. In 1152 he married the divorced queen of France, *Eleanor of Aquitaine, and seized her duchy. Thus, he became the master of more than two-thirds of the territory of the *Capetian realm. In 1154, at the death of *Stephen of Blois, he was recognized and crowned king of England, thus founding the *Angevin empire. H. was one of the most active and greatest kings of England. His reign was characterized by the monarch's continuous movement between his English and French dominions and by his conflicts with King *Louis VII of France, who did all in his power to withstand his dangerous vassal, who added *Brittany to his French possessions in 1168. This struggle forced H. to organize the government of his empire, so that he could find the resources necessary to maintain his position. He took into account the variety of local feudal customs of his principalities in France as well as the administrative and legal heritage of his grandfather, *Henry I, in England.

As king of England, H. created the system of the bureaucratic feudal monarchy, theoretically based on respect for the feudal laws but, in practice, ruled by an administration dependent on the king and governing according to the *Common Law of the country. In order to impose respect for legal practices, H. issued a long series of constitutions and *Assizes, based on the superiority of the royal authority and administration. The administrative organization of the government was based on the local communities, governed by sheriffs representing the crown. The central government was empowered to control the sheriffs and the courts of the shires by itinerant judges and by *justiciars, who became powerful royal officials. He introduced trial by jury as a means of imposing the peace and respect for law in the country with the active participation of the local communities. His attempt to impose royal sovereignty brought him into a protracted conflict with the church, led by the archbishop of Canterbury, his former chancellor, Thomas *Becket. For 14 years (1156-70), H. was compelled to struggle, not only against the exiled archbishop and his supporters, but also to reckon with external forces, such as the papacy and the French monarchy so as to stave off a general

conflict. In such a context, the murder of Becket, of which H. was morally accused, forced him to make some partial concessions. He profited from the conflict in order to conquer Ireland, ostensibly to spread the authority of the church, but in reality for political reasons. H.'s last years were troubled. His sons, *Henry, *Richard and *Geoffrey, who were given Normandy, Aquitaine and Brittany under his control, revolted against him with the support of the kings of France, Louis VII and *Philip II. Nevertheless, these revolts proved the solidity of the system of government he had established and he was able to repress them with resources provided by the English *Exchequer and Treasury. In 1189 he decided to take part in the Third *Crusade with Emperor *Frederick Barbarossa and *Philip II, king of France; but in the midst of preparations a new revolt, led by his sons Richard and John, compelled his attention in the Loire Valley, where he died.

J. Boussard, *Le Gouvernement d'Henri II Plantegenêt* (1956);

H. A. Davies, *Henry II Plantagenet* (1967).

HENRY III (1207-72) King of England (1216-72). Son of *John Lackland, his reign began in the difficult situation of his father's defeats on the Continent and the signing of the *Magna Charta in England. Until 1232 he reigned under the regency of *William Marshal, earl of Pembroke (d. 1219) and Hubert of Burgh, whom he dismissed in 1232, when he began his personal reign. In 1236 he married Eleanor of Provence and introduced some Provençal nobles in his court. This step aroused the opposition of the insular Anglo-Norman nobility, which criticized the appointments of foreigners to high offices in the government. Moreover, his defeats in France (1241), where he lost Poitou and Angoulême and his use of the English royal house to support papal policy against the *Hohenstaufens, sending his second son Edmund to Sicily (1255) and his brother, *Richard of Cornwall, to Germany as candidate for the imperial throne (1257), caused a general revolt of the nobility in 1258. The barons compelled him to issue the Provisions of *Oxford, reconfirming the Magna Charta and imposing on him a government controlled by the nobility. In order to continue his struggle, H. signed the Peace of Paris (1258) with *Louis IX, having been recognized as duke of *Guienne and *Gascony. When he refused to execute the Provisions of Oxford, the nobility, led by *Simon of Montfort, again revolted, defeating the royal army at *Lewes (1264), where H. was taken prisoner. The revolt was broken by Prince *Edward, H.'s son, who brought his army from the Welsh borders and crushed the barons in 1265, imposing on them the *Dictum of *Kenilworth*.

F. M. Powicke, *King Henry III and the Lord Edward* (1947).

HENRY IV (1367-1413) King of England (1399-1413). Son of *John of Gaunt and, thus, grandson of *Edward III and of *Blanche, heiress of Lancaster. He was the founder of the house of *Lancaster. Famous for his pride, he fought with the *Teutonic knights in Livonia (1390), travelled to Italy and Palestine and, after his return to England, supported *Richard II, but joined his critics in 1396. He was proclaimed king by Parliament after the revolution of 1399. He defeated his opponents in England and Wales and ruled with the support of the church. H. adopted a strict Catholic attitude and persecuted the *Lollards although, on the other hand, *Chaucer received his protection.

J. D. G. Davies, *King Henry IV* (1935).

HENRY V (1387-1422) King of England (1413-22). Son and heir of *Henry IV, he gained military experience in his father's campaigns. In 1414 he severely crushed a *Lollard revolt and destroyed their movement. His main concern, however, was with France, where he wished to restore English influence, profiting by the insanity of *Charles VI and the war between the *Burgundians and *Armagnacs. In 1415 he invaded France, renewing the hostilities of the *Hundred Years' War and destroying the French army at *Agincourt. He allied with *John the Fearless, duke of Burgundy, and in 1417-19 conquered Normandy and besieged Paris. In 1420 he signed the Treaty of *Troyes with the representatives of Charles VI, who gave him his daughter Catherine and the right to inherit the French crown after his death. H. planned a great *Crusade to be carried out by the united forces of England and France after his royal coronation, but died at Vincennes in 1422, leaving an infant boy as the heir of the two kingdoms.

E. F. Jacob, *Henry V and the Invasion of France* (1947).

HENRY I (1008-60) King of France (1031-60). Son of *Robert II the Pious, he inherited the crown of France on condition that the duchy of *Burgundy would be separated from the royal domain and given to his younger brother Hugh. During his reign, the royal power gradually weakened and the king's authority was limited to his domain in the Ile de France, between Paris and Orléans. His greatest difficulties arose with the union of the counties of *Blois and *Troyes under the rule of his enemy, Eudes of Blois, who encircled the royal domain. In order to overcome them, H. sought an alliance with the counts of *Anjou, who conquered Touraine from the family of Blois, and with the church, favouring the reform programme of the papacy and the establishment of monasteries, particularly of the order of *Cluny.

J. J. Lemarignier, *Le Gouvernement royal aux Premiers Temps des Capétiens* (1965).

HENRY I, of Lusignan (1217-53) King of *Cyprus (1218-53). Son of *Hugh I, he was proclaimed king as an infant of nine months, under the regency of his mother Alix and his uncle, Philip of *Ibelin. His minority passed in continuous struggles between the Ibelins and their opponents, supported by Emperor *Frederick II. Having reached his majority, H. attempted to free himself from imperial overlordship, allying himself with the Ibelin party. In 1248 he accompanied King *Louis IX of France on his *Crusade to Egypt and took part in the conquest of Damietta.

G. Hill, *History of Cyprus,* II (1944).

HENRY II (1271-1324) King of *Cyprus (1284-1324) and of Jerusalem (1285-91). Son of *Hugh of Antioch, he was a sickly child, incapable of continuous activity. As the last Crusading king of Jerusalem, he was unable to mobilize the forces of the kingdoms and lost *Acre and the last *Crusaders' strongholds in Palestine. The real authority lay in the hands of his younger brother, Aymeri, who seized power in the island in 1306 and compelled H. to go into exile in *Armenia. After Aymeri's murder in 1310, a civil war broke out in Cyprus and the loyalist party recalled H., who fought vigorously against the *Ibelins and destroyed this famous family, symbol of Frankish *feudalism in the Levant.

G. Hill, *History of Cyprus,* III (1948).

HENRY II, Jasomirgot Duke of *Austria (1141-77) and *Bavaria (1143-56). He inherited the march of Austria on the death of his brother, Leopold IV. Known as a faithful ally of Emperor *Conrad III, the latter appointed him duke of Bavaria after the death of *Henry the Proud, whose widow he married. He joined the emperor on the Second *Crusade, where he distinguished himself and married *Theodora Comnena, a Byzantine imperial princess. When *Frederick Barbarossa decided to reconcile himself with the *Welf dynasty in 1156, H. was compelled to surrender Bavaria but, as a reward, was created hereditary duke of Austria, which he held as an imperial fief. Faithful to the *Hohenstaufen dynasty, he devoted his reign to the development of the new duchy, which became Germanized. During his reign, the city of Vienna grew and became one of the important cities in Germany.

J. W. Thompson, *Feudal Germany* (1928).

HENRY II, the Wrangler (951-95) Duke of *Bavaria (955-76; 985-95). Son of Henry I, he ruled under the regency of his mother, Judith. In 975 he revolted against *Otto II in an attempt to obtain the duchy of Swabia; allied with the dukes of Bohemia and Poland, he threatened the imperial throne. Otto deposed him but H. continued to be a danger, raising opposition against the emperor. He attempted to govern during the minority of *Otto III and seized the boy, but was compelled to return the young king to his mother *Theophano. In return he was restored as duke of Bavaria, which he ruled peacefully during the last ten years of his life.

G. Barraclough, *Origins of Modern Germany* (1951).

HENRY IX, the Black Duke of *Bavaria (1120-26). He was the brother of Duke Welf II, whom he succeeded as duke and head of the *Welf dynasty. In the last years of Emperor *Henry V he became one of the leading German princes, and was opposed to the house of *Hohenstaufen. In 1125 he was a major supporter of the election of *Lothair of Supplinburg as emperor. By his marriage with Wilfild, daughter of Duke *Magnus of Saxony, he laid the foundations for the union of Bavaria and Saxony under the rule of the Welf dynasty.

S. Ritzler, *Geschichte Bayerns* (1927).

HENRY X, the Proud (1108-39) Duke of *Bavaria (1126-38) and *Saxony (1137-39). He inherited the large estates of the *Welfs in Germany and Italy and in 1127 married Gertrud, only daughter of Emperor *Lothair. As a member of the imperial family, he was the chief opponent of the *Hohenstaufens in Germany and helped Lothair resist the attacks of *Frederick of Swabia and *Conrad, his brother. In 1137, before his death, Lothair appointed him duke of Saxony and H. became the most powerful of the German princes; but his hopes of being elected emperor were not realized and his adversary, Conrad, became the new sovereign. Conrad III deprived him of the duchy of Bavaria, which he gave to his faithful allies, the *Babenbergs.

S. Riezler, *Geschichte Bayerns* (1927).

HENRY XII, the Lion (1129-95) Duke of *Bavaria (1156-80), of *Saxony (1142-80) and of Lüneburg (1180-85. Son of *Henry the Proud, he inherited Saxony from his father. In 1154 he was reconciled with Emperor *Frederick Barbarossa, who granted him the duchy of Bavaria as part of their political settlement (1156). His Saxon interests allowed him to enjoy good relations with the emperor, whose interests were directed towards Italy. H. is regarded as the father of the *Drang nach Osten,* the eastwards expansion of Germany. He fought and defeated the Slavic tribes to the east of the Elbe, where he led seven military campaigns between 1157 and 1177. A large part of the population between the Elbe and the Oder was slaughtered, while the rest submitted to Germanization. He brought German colonists from the West and settled them in the conquered lands, granting them generous privileges. Lübeck and Munich were among the cities he founded. In 1162 he married *Matilda, daughter of King *Henry II of England, and became one of the most powerful princes in Europe, whose alliance was sought everywhere.

In 1176 he refused to take part in the planned expedition of Frederick Barbarossa to Italy and this defection was considered a reason for the failure of the imperial army in Lombardy. In 1180 the emperor summoned him to be judged by the princes, accusing him of a breach of duty. He was deprived of his duchies of Bavaria and Saxony, but his extensive family estates in northern Saxony, in the area of Lüneburg and Brunswick, were left to him and, having submitted to the emperor, he was allowed to keep the ducal title to these estates. While Saxony was divided into several units, H. established the hereditary dynasty of Brunswick.

K. Hoppe, *Die Sage von Heinrich den Löwen* (1952).

HENRY I, the Liberal Count of Champagne (1152-81). From his father, *Thibaut of Blois, he inherited the counties of Troyes and Meaux as well as other estates, which he united as the county of *Champagne. He married *Mary, daughter of King *Louis VII of France and of Eleanor of Aquitaine. A skilled politician, he was an important ally of the king, negotiating on his behalf with Emperor *Frederick Barbarossa. H. proved himself a great administrator and he organized the governmental system of the county, which allowed the count and his agents to control his vassals and to use the resources of the county efficiently The *Fairs of Champagne, which reached their peak under his government, brought prosperity to the cities of Troyes and Provins, as well as to the whole county. At Troyes, H. established the most brilliant court of his time, where his wife patronized poets and men of letters, making it the centre of literary activities in the 12th century. The court became a model of the *chivalric ideal and an example to the whole of the West.

J. F. Benton, *The Court of Champagne as a Literary Center in the 12th century* (1960).

HENRY OF BLOIS (d. 1171) Bishop of *Winchester (1129-71). Brother of King *Stephen of Blois, he was brought up at Cluny. In 1126 *Henry I gave him the monastery of Glastonbury and in 1129 appointed him bishop of Winchester. In 1135 he crowned Stephen and became his firmest supporter in England. In 1139 Pope *Innocent II appointed him his legate to England, where he became one of the most powerful personalities of the time. After Stephen's death (1154), H. supported *Henry II and adopted a position of compromise during the king's dispute with Thomas *Becket. He built Glastonbury Abbey and embellished Winchester Cathedral. He was a great benefactor to Cluny and gave financial assistance to the monastery, which was in economic difficulties in the middle of the 12th century.

M. D. Knowles, *The Episcopal Colleagues of Thomas Becket* (1951).

HENRY OF BURGUNDY (1057-1114) Prince of *Portugal (1097-1114). Member of the house of *Burgundy, in 1096 he led an expedition of French knights to Spain, to secure the release of the king of Castile, *Alfonso VI, who was defeated and captured by the *Almoravides. In 1097 he married Urraca, Alfonso's daughter, and was granted the county of Oporto, recovered from the Moslems. He organized his principality and secured for it a large degree of independence. H. was the founder of *Portugal.

H. V. Livermore, *A History of Portugal* (1947).

HENRY OF CARINTHIA (d. 1335) King of Bohemia (1307-10). Duke of Carinthia and Tyrol, in 1307 he inherited the throne of Bohemia. His incapacity made him unpopular in the duchy, and in 1310 Emperor *Henry VII, who sought to acquire Bohemia for his family, deprived him of the kingdom and gave it to his son *John. H. returned to his estates.

F. Schneider, *Kaiser Heinrich VII* (1928).

HENRY OF CHAMPAGNE King of Jerusalem (1192-97). Son of *Henry the Liberal, count of Champagne, he was one of the leaders of the Third *Crusade, enjoying great prestige as the nephew of both the kings of France and England. After the death of *Conrad of Montferrat, *Richard I proposed him as king of the *Crusaders' realm. He married Conrad's widow Isabella, thus becoming the legal heir to the dynasty. H. reorganized the kingdom of Acre, consolidating it during the period of peace which followed the Treaty of Ramlah of 1192.

S. Runciman, *A History of the Crusades* (1953).

HENRY OF GHENT (d. 1293) Theologian. In 1267 he became a canon of Tournai and was later promoted to the position of archdeacon of Bruges and Tournai. In 1280 he was active in Paris in defence of *Augustinianism, as one of the chief representatives of the secular clergy. In 1282 he fought against the privileges of the *mendicant orders, attacking *Thomas of Aquinas. His most important theological works are the *Quodlibeta* and an unfinished *Summa Theologica,* where he attempted to combine the old Augustinian doctrines with Aristotelian theories. They won him the title *Doctor solemnis.*

J. Paulus, *Henri de Gand* (1938).

HENRY OF HAINAULT (1176-1216) Latin emperor of *Constantinople (1206-16). Brother of Emperor *Baldwin, he became regent in 1205 when his brother fell captive to the *Bulgarians and, after his death, became emperor. He redressed the military situation of the young empire and defeated the Bulgarians and *Theodore Lascaris, emperor of *Nicaea. Between 1208 and 1211, he imposed his authority over the Latin principalities in Greece and, owing to his military skills, was able to maintain the frontiers of the empire. He developed a policy of collaboration with the Greek population of the empire, understanding that the "Latin" or "Frankish" conquerors could not rule over a hostile population. For that reason, he showed tolerance to the Greek-Orthodox clergy, opposing Pelagius, the papal legate, who attempted to compel them to join the Roman Catholic Church.

W. Miller, *The Latins in the Orient* (1908).

HENRY OF HESSE (1325-97) German physician. He was known for his skill in identifying new diseases, which he cured with herbs. Besides enriching the contemporary knowledge of medicinal herbs, he also indulged in speculation about the origins of species and their mutations, which was a contribution to the study of biology in the late Middle Ages and early modern period.

C. Singer, *A Short History of Anatomy and Physiology from the Greeks to Harvey* (1957).

HENRY OF HOHENSTAUFEN (1211-42) Eldest son of *Frederick II. In 1220 his father brought him to Germany to represent the imperial authority, with the title "King of the Romans", and put him under the guardianship of Engelberg, archbishop of Cologne. He governed Germany from 1229, and attempted to restrict the prerogatives of the princes. In 1234 he revolted against his father, who repressed his revolt in the following year. He was brought to Italy as a prisoner and died in 1242, probably committing suicide.

E. Kantorowicz, *Emperor Frederick II* (1931).

HENRY OF LANCASTER See LANCASTER, HOUSE OF.

HENRY OF LANGENSTEIN (d. 1397) Theologian. Educated at Paris, he taught philosophy there in 1363. From 1376 he gave theology lectures at the *Sorbonne, remaining there until 1383, the year of his appointment to the University of Vienna, where he taught until his death. He wrote commentaries on the works of *Peter Lombard, and on Genesis, as well as composing a number of scientific treatises. From 1378 he was concerned with the *Great Schism, and called for the assembly of a General Council to settle it. He is, thus, closely connected with the *Conciliar movement.

E. Gilson, *Medieval Philosophy* (1963).

HENRY OF LAUSANNE (d. c. 1145) Medieval sectarian. He was a French monk who left his monastery to preach at the end of the 11th century. His first appearance as a preacher was at Le Mans in 1101. His attacks on the worldliness of the clergy and insistence on the ideal of absolute poverty made him extremely popular, at the same time bringing him persecution from the ecclesiastical establishment. He went to *Languedoc, where he continued preaching and was accused by St. *Bernard of Clairvaux of denying the objective efficacity of the *Sacraments. In 1135 he was arrested and forced to recant at the Council of Pisa, but soon resumed his anti-clerical preachings. In 1145 he was again arrested and died in prison. H. is considered the precursor of the *Waldensians.

H. C. Lea, *History of the Inquisition in the Middle Ages* (1888).

HENRY OF SEGUSIO (SUZA) See HOSTIENSIS.

HENRY RASPE (d. 1247) Landgrave of *Thuringia from 1242, anti-king of *Germany from 1246. In 1244 he joined the revolt of the German princes against *Frederick II and was proclaimed anti-king by *Conrad of Hochstaden, archbishop of Cologne. In 1246 Pope Innocent IV urged the German princes to elect H. as king in place of *Conrad IV, recently deposed by papal decree. H. defeated the army of Conrad IV at Frankfurt on the Main and prepared an expedition to Swabia,

the strongold of the House of *Hohenstaufen, but exhausted by his exertions, he died before the attack.

E. Kantorowicz, *The Emperor Frederick II* (1931).

HENRY SUSO (1295-1366) German mystic. Educated at the *Dominican monastery at Constance, he joined the order and immediately began his speculative mystical exercises as "Servant of the Eternal Wisdom". His booklet, *Das Büchlein der ewigen Weisheit*, written in 1328, became the most widely read work of meditation in Germany in the 14th and 15th centuries and influenced Thomas à Kempis.

Work, ed. K. Bihlmeyer (1907);

C. Groeber, *Der Mystiker Heinrich Seuseg* (1941).

HENRY THE YOUNG (1155-83) Son of King *Henry II of England. In 1170 he was crowned king by the archbishop of York in accordance with his father's orders, and was granted the duchy of Normandy. In 1173 and 1183 he revolted against his father but was defeated and compelled to submit. His death from dysentery in 1183 opened the way for the accession of *Richard I.

HEPTARCHY The collective name of the seven *Anglo-Saxon kingdoms in England in the 5th-9th centuries; these were Wessex, Sussex, Essex, Kent, East Anglia, Mercia and Northumbria. Although not all the kingdoms enjoyed independence throughout the four centuries, the term H. symbolizes the fact that they were in existence during the same period. See *England, History.

HERACLIUS I (575-641) Byzantine emperor (610-41). A native of Cappadocia, he earned the reputation of a successful military leader. In 610 he fought the usurper *Phocas, and upon his victory was proclaimed emperor, founding a dynasty which continued to reign until 717. During his rule, *Byzantium was attacked on all its frontiers. The *Visigoths gained possession of all Spain, and the Persians, under *Chosroes II, invaded Asia Minor and Syria and conquered Jerusalem (614). Only in 629, after an alliance with the Ethiopians, who supported the Byzantine fleet in the Red Sea and the Persian Gulf, was the situation redressed and the Persian threat removed, although both empires were left in a weakened state. From 634 the empire was attacked by the *Arabs, who conquered Syria; in 636 the Byzantine army was severely defeated on the Yarmuk, near its confluence with the Jordan River, and Palestine fell. H. was unable to raise up his army and prevent the conquest of Egypt (640-42). After his defeat at Yarmuk, H. vainly attempted to win the support of his non-Greek subjects by restoring the religious unity of the empire; but his decree of 638, which aimed to bring about a conciliation, came too late.

A. A. Vasiliev, *History of the Byzantine Empire* (1952).

HERACLIUS II (Heracleonas; 618-45) Byzantine emperor (641). Second son of *Heraclius I, he was proclaimed emperor upon his father's death, but was overthrown by *Constans II.

HERALDRY A branch of medieval historical science dealing with the symbols of recognition of noble houses, realms and city-states. Its beginnings are connected with the study of feudal banners, whose symbols, taken from flora and fauna, belonged to a certain family and were adopted by all its branches. For example, the coat of arms of the house of the *Angevin counts was that of three lions; when *Henry II Plantagenet became king of England (1154), this symbol became part of the royal heraldic device, but also continued to be used by the collateral branches of the Plantagenet house. Incidentally, the relation between certain branches of some families has been determined solely on the basis of similar heraldic symbols. From the late 12th century heraldic symbols were painted on the shields of knights and engraved on their coins. Not only was there a knightly and noble branch of medieval H., there was also an ecclesiastical one. Bishops had their own symbol made up of that of their see together with their particular family coat of arms. Until the 14th century heraldic symbols varied, especially in the families of the lower nobility. From the 14th century on, in accordance with the code of *chivalry, their usage became established, a development which symbolized the crystallization of nobility as a class.

W. H. Rüdt de Collenberg, *Héraldique Médiévale* (1972).

HERBALS (Latin: herbarius) Botanical manuals widely used in the Middle Ages for the description of plants. Medieval H. were largely derived from the botanical manuals of classical antiquity, such as the Pseudo-Aristotelian (in Greek) and Pseudo-Apulean (in Latin) H., in which plants and herbs were classified and described both morphologically and in terms of their medicinal and practical value. The Arabs, and particularly the botanical research of *Rhazes added to the classical heritage. While the Byzantine botanists continued to use and improve the Pseudo-Aristotelian H., western Europe was dependent, until the 13th century, on the Pseudo-Apulean H., which was studied by *Carolingian naturalists interested in the medicinal qualities of plants and herbs. This H. was translated, with some additions, into Anglo-Saxon in the 11th century. The translation dealt with some 500 plants and was one of the most important achievements in the Anglo-Saxon culture prior to the Norman conquest of England. The development of medical studies in western Europe in the 12th century, as well as translations from Arabic into Latin, acquainted western scientists with the Arab and Greek H. The materials gathered enabled a degree of development in the natural sciences of the 13th century, especially by such men as Roger *Bacon in England and *Albertus Magnus in Germany. These achievements were adopted by *Rufinus in his H., which is one of the best botanical works of the Middle Ages, including a wide range of plants and herbs which are described from the morphological and physiological aspects, as well as in terms of their medicinal properties. The development of medicine and surgery, together with the belief physicians held in the healing qualities of herbs — whether in their natural form or through distillation and the creation of elixirs — led to continued improvement of the H. in the late Middle Ages. From the end of the 13th century the H. were illustrated by artists who worked in collaboration with the naturalists.

A. Arber, *Herbals* (1938).

HERBERT II, of Vermandois (902-42) Count. H. was one of the most turbulent feudal lords in France in the first half of the 10th century. Ruling over a large territory in northeastern France, he attempted to expand his authority by dominating the archbishopric of Rheims; he did so by making members of his family archbishops. Although allied with *Charles III the Simple, H. did not hesitate to deliver him to the king-elect of the feudal nobles, *Ralph of Burgundy, in 924, and to become

the latter's ally. His disputes with Ralph of Cambrai served as the background for the 12th-century epic *chanson, Raoul de Cambrai.

K. F. Wernwer, *Untersuchungen zur Frühzeit des französischen Fürstentums* (1958-90).

HEREFORD MAPPA MUNDI A *geographical map drawn in England in 1314 by an anonymous geographer, and preserved at Hereford Cathedral, whence its name. The map details the world known to west European geographers at the beginning of the 13th century. Its most interesting feature is its accordance with the ecclesiastical practice of giving priority to the holy places and ecclesiastical sees and devoting little attention to the other physical and demographic elements. This map is therefore a late example of the distortion common to the science of *geography in the high Middle Ages.

L. A. Brown, *The Story of Maps* (1951).

HEREM HAYISHUB (The Ban of the Community) A juridical notion which emerged in the 10th century in the Jewish communities of the Rhine Valley and northern France, and which eventually spread to the whole of the *Ashkenazi communities in medieval Europe. The H. gave the community courts the right to expel certain persons from the collective body, as well as from its territory. The H. was placed on community members who refused to accept the jurisdiction of its court or to execute a verdict pronounced by it. The practice of the H. often differed from community to community and was constantly the subject of *Responsa of the highest rabbinical authorities in the Jewish medieval world. The rabbis who were involved with the use of this measure sought the appropriate means to act in the interest of the community as a whole, while protecting the individual from possible juridical tyranny.

E. L. Rabinowicz, *Herem Hayishub* (1945).

HERESY The term designates the formal denial or doubt of any defined doctrine of the Catholic and Orthodox faiths. It originated from the ancient Greek word *haeresis,* meaning choice, which was used to denote the tenets of specific philosophical schools which disagreed with the general trends. Early Christianity adopted this meaning to designate teachers of the faith who did not conform to the accepted teachings of the Scriptures. The polemical debates with the *Manichaeans led to a broader definition of the term in the 3rd century, while the *Trinitarian dogma confronted the ecclesiastical establishment with its opponents for the first time. The definition of the articles of the faith at the Council of *Nicaea (325) clarified the situation in this respect by providing the normative rules of Orthodoxy. The number of cases of H. was large in the Middle Ages: among the heretics were the *Pelagianists, the *Donatists and the *Adoptionists in the early Middle Ages, the *Albigenses and *Waldensians in the high Middle Ages and the non-conformist trends in the late Middle Ages. Besides being used to designate movements and organized opposition to the church, the term H. was also used against any particular person or group which threatened the establishment. Thus, textile workers in *Flanders and northern France who made appeals for social rights were condemned as heretics.

H. was considered both as a sin and an illness, and it was the responsibility of the established church to heal the Christian body of it. Therefore, H. was condemned and heretics were excommunicated. The submission and penance of offenders was sought through the preaching of the true faith. Only when such means were ineffective were heretics persecuted and, in many cases, burnt at the stake or otherwise killed, so as to extirpate the H. In 1184 the *Inquisition was established and charged with conducting an inquiry on H. and bringing heretics to trial; this institution became one of the most important tools of the church in its struggle against nonconformists.

W. L. Wakefield and A. P. Evans, *Heresies of the High Middle Ages* (1969).

HERIBERT See ARIBERT.

HERIMAN See HERMANN.

HERMANDAD (Castilian: brotherhood) Name given to armed urban associations which emerged in Spanish cities from the 12th century. Their aim was to ensure peace on the roads and within the towns in order to allow the normal development of trade. The first H. was established at *Toledo under the reign of King *Alfonso VIII. It was organized like other medieval corporations: its basic body was the assembly of the sworn members or "brothers", who elected commissioners in charge of dealing with the problems of the H. and specifically of choosing members to man look-out posts. Other Hs. were modelled after that of Toledo, with minor differences. They were common in the kingdom of *Castile, and some associations were interurban. In 1295 the Hs. were recognized as official corporations in Castilian law and were considered an integral part of the feudal system. In 1325 King *Alfonso IX abolished them, fearing that their wide privileges would present an obstacle to his government. *Henry II, seeking to overcome the supporters of *Peter the Cruel, attempted to reorganize the Hs. and gain their support for his kingship (1369). During this time, Hs. were also established in *Aragon; in both kingdoms the crown attempted to form an alliance with the burghers against the nobility and to use their militia to strengthen the royal armies.

P. E. Russell, *A Companion to Spanish Studies* (1967).

HERMANN BILLUNG (d. 973) Related to King *Henry I of Germany, he inherited the county of the Billungs in northern Saxony. In 940 he was appointed commander of the Saxon army and fought the Slavs. He was one of the firmest supporters of *Otto I, who appointed him duke of Saxony in 961.

R. Folz, *La Naissance du Saint-Empire* (1968).

HERMANN OF CARINTHIA (the Dalmatian; first half of the 12th century) Born in *Carinthia of Slavic origin (hence his cognomen), H. wandered in western Europe and studied at Chartres. His teacher *Thierry of Chartres, strongly influenced his inclination towards Platonic thought. Around 1138 H. travelled to Toulouse and Spain, mostly with a group of western scholars who were interested in Arabic. During his stay at Toledo, he began to translate philosophical and scientific works from Arabic into Latin. In 1141 his talents were discovered by *Peter the Venerable, abbot of Cluny, who asked him to translate parts of the *Koran into Latin. Among his many translations, the most important was that of Ptolemy's *Planisphere,* completed in 1144, which he dedicated to his former teacher, Thierry of Chartres.

C. H. Haskins, *Studies in the History of Mediaeval Science* (1924).

HERMANN OF KAPPENBERG (d. 1198) Polemist. He was born at *Cologne as a Jew, his original name being Godfrey. In 1128 while at Mainz on a business trip and after a discussion with local clerks, Godfrey converted to Christianity and became a *Premonstratensian canon. In 1140 he wrote a *Story of his Conversion,* a polemical treatise attacking Judaism. H. also contribued to the fictitious *Dialogue of *Rupert of Deutz* and continued to compose polemical pamphlets against the Jewish religion up to his election as abbot of Scheida.

J. de Ghellinck, *La Littérature Latine* (1947).

HERMANN OF METZ Bishop of *Metz (1073-90). He was one of the firmest supporters of Pope *Gregory VII in Germany and leader of the reform movement in western Germany and Lorraine. H. became famous as the recipient of Gregory's letters on the *Investiture problem, which were written as manifestos meant to receive wide public attention.

G. Tellenbach, *Church, State and Christian Society at the Time of the Investiture Contest* (1959).

HERMANN OF REICHENAU See HERMANN THE LAME.

HERMANN OF SALM (d. 1088) Anti-king of *Germany (1081-82). Count of Salm in Lorraine, he was elected anti-king by the opponents of *Henry IV and was blessed by Pope *Gregory VII. After an unsuccessful attempt to conquer *Swabia, H. retired to Lorraine, but his supporters abandoned him and he returned to obscurity.

G. Barraclough, *Origins of Modern Germany* (1952).

HERMANN OF SALZA (d. 1239) Of *Thuringian origin, he joined the *Teutonic order, becoming its leader in 1209. He was one of the most important political personalities of Europe and developed the east European policy of the Teutonic knights. In 1211 he accepted the offer of King *Andrew II of Hungary to found a settlement in Transylvania in order to fight the Cumans, but when full sovereignty over the territory granted to the order was refused, he ordered his knights to leave the country (1225). The following year he entered into negotiations with *Conrad, the Polish duke of Mazovia, in collaboration against the Prussians, with the express condition that the order be granted the conquered country; he obtained *Frederick II's confirmation of this treaty, which became the juridical basis for the German settlement of *Prussia. In 1229 H. accompanied the emperor on his *Crusade and took part in the coronation ceremony at Jerusalem. During his stay at the Crusaders' kingdom, he began the construction of the castle of *Montfort, which became the centre of the Teutonic knights in the Holy Land.

H. Heimpel, *Hermann von Salza* (1955).

HERMANN OF THURINGIA Landgrave (1190-1217). He took advantage of the civil war in Germany between the *Welf and *Hohenstaufen dynasties to increase his territories. H. built the famous castle of Wartburg, one of the country's most important literary centres, where poets and artists used to gather.

HERMANN THE LAME (Herimannus Contractus, Hermann of Reichenau; 1013-54) Poet and chronicler. He was educated at the monastery of *Reichenau, where he became a monk. Despite his physical disability, he had a brilliant mind and wrote extensively on a wide range of subjects including mathematics, astronomy, history and poetry. H.'s writings prove his high intellectual abilities and serious approach to his subjects, qualities which made his works valuable contributions in their particular fields.

Works, ed. *PL,* vol. 163;

H. Hansjacob, *Hermann der Lahme* (1875).

HERMIT (Greek: heremos "desert") One who, for religious reasons, decides to leave society and to adopt a solitary life of prayer, meditation and contemplation. The first Hs. were found in 3rd-century Egypt; they retired to the desert — hence their name. In the 4th and 5th centuries the practice spread to Palestine and Syria, and whole areas, such as Sinai and the Judaean desert, became populated with Hs. who lived in caves and were considered saints by society. Even after the establishment of monastic rules in the East, it was commonly accepted that a monk retire for a given period to a cave or small primitive structure near his monastery. Western Christianity did not know of the monastic eremitic way of life until the 8th century, when Hs. appeared in the so-called "deserts" of Italy, southern France and England. Only then did the practice spread in the West and become relatively common in the 11th and 12th centuries. As distinct from the Hs. of the East, the retirement of the western Hs. was not total. The latter would preach to gatherings of the faithful who lived in their surrounding areas. At the end of the 11th century eremitic communities began to emerge and constituted

new monastic orders, such as the *Carthusians and, in the 12th century, the *Carmelites. Other Hs. founded congregations of Benedictine monasteries or of regular canons who performed services in churches and parishes but otherwise lived a solitary life. Their popularity in western society and the degree of their holiness is reflected by the way the H. was represented in vernacular literature, as, for example, in the *Arthurian romances, where the H. was depicted as a good wise man.

DTC, VI.

HERRADE OF LANSBERG (1125-95) Abbess of Hohenburg in *Alsace and a writer. Born to the family of of the lords of Landsberg, she was educated in the monastery of Hohenburg, where she later became abbess. Her studies gave her in-depth knowledge of Latin classical literature, enriched through readings of medieval Latin poetry and prose. From her favourite authors H. compiled the *Hortus Deliciarum* (The Garden of Delights), a book intended for the moral and intellectual formation of her nuns. The book became famous, however, and shortly after its completion (*c.* 1175) was disseminated in the learned circles of the West. It became one of the most beloved subjects of lecture in cloisters and among the aristocratic families.

Ed. A. Struab and G. Keller, *Strassburg* (1899);

R. Will, *Le climat religieux de l'Hortus Deliciarum* (1937).

Hermits at work; fragment of a fresco; Pisa, 14th century

HERSTAL (HERISTAL) The centre of a large estate on the Meuse River, north of Liège (now Belgium). It was one of the residences most preferred by *Charlemagne, particularly before he established himself at *Aix-La-Chapelle. In 789, after his defeat at *Roncesvalles, he issued at H. the famous *capitulary which reformed the structure of the Frankish realm.

HERULI Germanic tribe which was established north of the Danube until the 5th century. In the middle of the 5th century the tribe was divided into clans which joined several other Germanic tribes in their invasions of the Roman empire. Some of the H. attached themselves to the *Vandals and settled in north Africa, others joined the *Alemanni and *Bavarians, while the main group of clans, under the leadership of their king, *Odoacer, joined other tribes to invade Italy. In 476 this group dethroned the last Western Roman emperor, Romulus Augustulus, putting an official end to that empire. The H. were then dispersed, and joined together with other, better-organized tribes, which caused their rapid assimilation and eventual disappearance. By the middle of the 6th century they had become entirely assimilated into the larger tribes.
J. M. Wallace-Hadrill, *The Barbarian West* (1967).

HESSEN Country in central *Germany named after the Hessians, a Germanic tribe which first settled in the region prior to the 2nd century. The Hessians were attacked by the *Franks in the 6th century, but successfully resisted the *Merovingians; only in the 8th century were they defeated by the *Carolingians. *Charlemagne sent Franks to settle in the southwestern parts of the country, which were considered some of the most strategic points of his realm, lying between Saxony and Bavaria. The monasteries of *Fulda and Hersfeld were founded in the country in order to spread the Christian faith. In the 9th century H., as a distinct duchy, was attached to *Franconia, of which it remained part until the death of *Henry V (1 25). During the 12th century it passed to the landgra es of *Thuringia. In 1264 it was granted, together with the title of count, to Henry, son of the duke of Brabant and grandson of St. *Elizabeth of Thuringia. Henry founded the duchy's dynasty, which continued to rule from his capital at Cassel until 1918.
H. Blumme, *Das Land Hessen und seine Landschaften* (1951).

HESYCHASTS A group of mystic monks residing on Mount *Athos in the 14th century. Their chief tenet was that man was able, by means of an elaborate system of ascetic practices involving perfect tranquillity of body and mind, to arrive at the vision of the increate light of the Godhead. Their ideas were formulated in a doctrine which became very popular among the Mount Athos communities in 1339. This doctrine was severely criticized by the Calabrian monk, Barlaam, who had been trained on Mount Athos; and in 1339 he denounced it as superstition. His opponent, George Palamas, defended hesychasm and prevented its condemnation in 1341. In 1342, however, the writings of Palamas were condemned and until 1347 the H. were persecuted. Emperor *John Cantacuzenus' belief in the theory and the support he offered to Isidore (a close friend of Palamas), whom he appointed patriarch of Constantinople, led to the spread of hesychasm within the Byzantine empire; during the latter half of the 14th century the doctrine was widely accepted by the Greek Church, despite the opposition of the conservative Orthodox circles. The fact that the doctrine of the H. was radically opposed to Latin doctrine widened the gulf between the Greek and Roman churches.
I. Hausherr, *La Méthode d'Oraison des Hésichastes* (1927).

HETHUM I (d. 1273) King of *Armenia (1226-69). Son of Constantine of Lampron, the leader of a baronial conspiracy in Lesser Armenia, he was proclaimed king by his father and founded the Hethumid dynasty of Armenia. One of the most skilled administrators of his age, he organized the kingdom after a period of trouble and civil war and, aware of the *Mameluke threat, allied himself with the principality of *Antioch through the marriage of his daughter Sybil to *Bohemond VI (1254). H. realized the importance of the *Mongol presence in the Middle East as far back as 1247 and allied himself with *Hulagu-khan, whom he aided in his campaigns in Syria (1258-60), destroying the *Ayyubids. The Mongol defeat at Ain-Jalud in 1261, which caused H.'s allies to leave Syria, brought the army of *Baibars to the proximity of the Armenian frontiers; in 1266 H.'s army was defeated at Darbsack and the cities of the realm were ravaged by the Mamelukes. H. was forced to abdicate and spent the remainder of his life as a monk. The Armenian king was also a gifted historian and wrote a history of the Christian states in the East.
F. Tournebise, *Histoire politique et religieuse de l'Arménie* (1900).

HETHUM II (d. 1307) King of *Armenia (1289-1301). He was made king against his will, being strongly inclined towards a monastic way of life. However, he was unable to realize his wishes to retire to a monastery due to the *Mameluke and *Mongol threats. Only in 1301 was H. able to abdicate, although he continued to counsel his nephew, *Leo IV, until his death.

HEURES DU DUC DE BERRY The name of two famous prayer-books prepared at the end of the 14th and the beginning of the 15th century for John, duke of Berry, uncle of King *Charles VI of France. The first, *Les Belles H.*, was richly illustrated by the miniatures of *Jacquemart of Hesdin in 1384. The second book is a most important artistic achievement, and was illustrated by the brothers of *Limburg; it has been preserved at the Museum Condé at Chantilly. Its most beautiful illustrations are those representing the seasons and months of the year.
P. Durrieu, *Les très riches Heures du Duc de Berry* (1904).

HIDE See HYDE.

HIERONYMUS, St. See JEROME, St.

HILALI (Banu Hilal) A Beduin tribe sent *c.* 1050 by the *Fatimid caliph Al-Mustansir to eastern north Africa to repress local rebellions. The atrocities they committed caused the extermination of the Nubian population and led to the Arabization of part of northern Sudan.
CHI (1970).

HILDEBERT OF LAVARDIN (1056-1133) Bishop of Le Mans (1096-1125), archbishop of *Tours (1125-33), poet and canonist. Born at Lavardin (western France), he was educated at the cathedral school of Le Mans and in 1096 became its bishop; he was elected despite the opposition of King *William II Rufus of England, who took him captive in 1099. Freed in 1100, H. travelled to Rome, where he was confirmed by Pope *Paschal II in his office. He returned to his see and built the new cathedral church. He was an ardent defender of the liberties of the church in accordance with the *Gregorian approach. In 1125 he was elected archbishop of Tours, and became involved in a dispute with King *Louis VI of France concerning his (H.'s) prerogatives. In 1130 he supported *Anacletus II as pope and, as a result, lost much of his influence. H. was chiefly famous for his literary works. A gifted poet, he mastered Latin better than any of his contemporaries; the elegant style of his Latin poems became a model for sacred and profane works. The same style is also found in his canonical interpretations.

Works, ed. *PL*, vol. 171;

F. X. Barth, *Hildebert von Lavardin* (1906).

HILDEBOLD (HILDEBALD) Archbishop of *Cologne and archchaplain of *Charlemagne (791-815). Descended from an important Frankish family of *Austrasia, he was raised at the Frankish royal chapel and assisted by Charlemagne, who appointed him archchaplain in 791. In 796-97 he was involved in the negotiations with Pope *Leo III, whom he received at Padeborn on behalf of the king. He was an intimate companion of Charlemagne during the period which preceded the latter's imperial coronation and probably had much influence on the king's elaboration of the idea of the *Carolingian empire.

W. Ullmann, *The Carolingian Renaissance and the Idea of Kingship* (1971).

HILDEBRAND See GREGORY VII.

HILDEBRANDSLIED An epic poem composed *c.* 800, the first *German literary work known; the present-day version of the poem actually dates from the beginning of the 11th century, although earlier parts have been discerned. The epic, composed in alliterative verse in a style similar to the Anglo-Saxon poems, tells of the adventures of an old warrior, Hildebrand, reputed for his courage and loyalty; so loyal was he that he even fought against his own son. The poem emphasizes the tragic plight of the faithful warriors.

J. G. Robertson, *History of the German Literature* (1947).

HILDEGARD OF BINGEN, St. (1098-1179) Visionary. Born to a noble family at Böckelheim, she was reputed for her religious visions from childhood. In 1116 she became a nun and, in 1136, she was made abbess of the *Benedictine community of Rupertsberg near Bingen. At this period she began to record her visions, which were published between 1141-51 as the *Scivias* (The Knowledge of the Ways) and received the approval of Pope *Eugenius III. H. exercised wide influence over certain personalities of her age, including St. *Bernard of Clairvaux and Emperor *Frederick Barbarossa. Her visions contain denunciations of vice and enigmatic prophecies of disaster. H. was also highly scientifically educated and displayed a keen interest in the natural sciences and medicine. Her medical treatises reflect a degree of scientific observation unusual in medieval times; they also prove her encyclopedic knowledge.

Works, ed. J. B. Pitra, *Analecta Sacra* (1882);

H. Liebeschütz, *Das allegorische Weltbild der heiligen Hildegard von Bingen* (1930).

HILDERIC (d. 532) King of the *Vandals (523-31). Son of King *Huneric and the Byzantine princess Eudoxia, H. lived in Constantinople and, upon becoming king, attempted to introduce Roman customs – including the Catholic faith – to the realm. This policy caused revolts on the part of the Vandal nobility and, in 531, his cousin *Gelimer dethroned and imprisoned him.

E. Courtois, *Les Vandales et l'Afrique* (1955).

HILDESHEIM City in *Saxony, south of Hannover. The history of the city begins in a fair, established *c.* 700 by the Saxons between the Rhine and the Elbe Rivers; in the 8th century the small burgh of H. was founded on the fair's site. Conquered by *Charlemagne in 787, the city became one of the bases of missionary activities in Saxony. In 815 a bishopric was established in the city, whose importance grew under St. *Bernwald (993-1022). In the 11th and 12th centuries H. became an important architectural centre and had its own particular style of building and ornamentation, called Saxon Romanesque. The city was governed by its bishops who, themselves, were subjects of the dukes of Saxony and *Brunswick until the 13th century. In 1235 Emperor *Frederick II freed the bishops from the rule of the dukes and authorized them to establish a market and impose taxes upon the burghers. The struggle between the dukes of Brunswick and the bishops continued, however, and, in the latter half of the 13th century, the dukes aided the burghers in their revolt against the episcopal authority. In 1300 the urban corporation attained autonomy and was granted wide privileges, which were gradually enlarged until it gained full independence in 1486 and joined the *Hanse.

G. H. Gebauer, *Aufsätze zur Hildesheimer Geschichte* (1938).

HILDUIN (806-42) A monk at *St. Denis, H. succeeded Abbot *Fulrad and entered the circle of the favourites of *Charlemagne; at this time, he also became one of the contributors to the *Carolingian Renaissance, particularly in the field of history. In 822 H. was appointed archchaplain of the empire by *Louis the Pious and held the dignity of abbot of *St. Germain-des-Prés and of St. Médard of Soissons as well as of St. Denis. In 829 H. supported *Lothair in his revolt against Louis the Pious; subsequently, the emperor dismissed him from his offices and sent him as prisoner to Padeborn. In 831 he was released and the monastery of St. Denis was restored to him. He devoted the last years of his life to his abbatial functions and translated the works of *Dionysius the Areopagite from the Greek in an attempt to prove his relation to St. Denis of Paris. Of particular importance among his historical works is the *Life of King Dagobert*, written to emphasize the role of the monastery of St. Denis as the main sanctuary of the Frankish realm. H. attracted an important circle of learned monks to his monastery. These monks were the principal cultivators of the 9th-century intellectual Renaissance.

M. L. W. Laistner, *Thought and Letters in Western Europe, 500-900* (1947).

HILLEL BEN SAMUEL OF VERONA (c. 1220-91) Jewish philosopher of Italy. He belonged to a family of rabbis and was educated in Talmudic studies and philosophy; he also studied medicine, which he practised in southern Italy. During his formative years, he apparently travelled to southern France and Catalonia. His philosophical methods were influenced by Christian *scholasticism and were in opposition to the Aristotelian *Averroist methods. H. defended the works of *Maimonides and greatly influenced the decisions of the Italian rabbis in the latter's favour. Among his works, the most important was his treatise on the soul and its divine attributes; in this work he expressed his preference of the philosophical, or rationalist faith, which he saw as superior to the simple faith.

I. Elbogen, *Hillel da Verona e la lotta per M. Maimonide* (1935).

HIMYAR Arab state in southern *Arabia (part of present-day Yemen). The Hs., who, according to their own tradition, were the descendants of the kingdom of Saba mentioned in biblical literature, reorganized their realm in the 4th century, making it one of the most important in southern Arabia. They were in constant clashes with the people of *Ethiopia and, in the 5th century, many of their tribes were converted to Judaism; in the 6th century they allied themselves with the Persians against the Ethiopian-Byzantine coalition. The H. kingdom was ravaged during the long periods of war (550-629) and severely declined. After 626 some of the H. tribes converted to Islam and proclaimed their allegiance to *Mohammad, who conquered the kingdom shortly before his death. (c. 630).

P. K. Hitti, *A History of the Arabs* (1953).

HINCMAR (806-82) Archbishop of *Rheims (845-82). He was educated at the monastery of *St. Denis by Abbot *Hilduin; from 822 he became one of Hilduin's followers and was brought to the imperial court. He gradually gained influence by his own merit and, in 830, intervened between *Louis the Pious and his abbot. In 834 he entered imperial service and, after Louis' death, served *Charles the Bald faithfully; in return, the latter appointed him archbishop of Rheims. H. worked to reorganize his diocese and became one of the most important leaders of the Frankish church, whose union was – in his opinion – the symbol of the unity of the *Carolingian kingdoms. Towards this purpose he assembled annual synods of the bishops of the three kingdoms of *Francia and imposed an authoritarian government upon the bishops and abbots of his own province. H. was also one of the most skilled politicians of his time and loyally supported Charles the Bald. In 876 he secured Louis II's succession to the throne, becoming one of his chief counsellors and regent for his sons.

H. was not a speculative theologian, although he did participate in the theological discussions of his time and opposed, in particular, the views of *Gottschalk. He was aided in that respect by his friend and former companion from St. Denis, John Scot *Erigena. In ecclesiastical affairs, H. was merely a canonist. Among his works are some historical pieces dating from his St. Denis period, as well as a treatise on the *Ordination of the Palace*, in which he examined the systems of government in the Frankish kingdom.

Works, ed. *PL*, vols. 125-26;
J. Beckmann, *Hincmar von Reims* (1933).

HINDUISM See INDIA.

HIRDH Scandinavian term meaning companionship. In the 9th to 11th centuries the term was used to signify the king's bodyguard, composed of young fighters of the realm together with adventurers. These men formed the core of the army and were rewarded monetarily and by appointment to various offices.

G. Jones, *A History of the Vikings* (1968).

HIRSAU (HIRSCHAU) Monastery in southwest Germany. Founded in 830, it became one of the most important monastic institutions in *Swabia and was richly endowed by the *Carolingian kings and the dukes of Swabia. The monastery began to decline in the 11th century until 1069, when a monk called *William, who had been educated at *Cluny, was elected to the position of abbot (1069-91). William introduced the rule of Cluny and created an affiliation with that order. Under his leadership, a great movement of monastic reform, directed from H., spread throughout Germany, creating the order of H. which remained connected with Cluny. William supported the *Gregorian party against Emperor *Henry IV and sent monks into Germany to preach against the emperor and his associate bishops. The influence of the congregations of monks from H. reached its peak during the pontificate of *Urban II, when their activity in the polemical struggle became intensive and created breaches in the imperial party. In the 12th century H. became one of the centres of artistic revival in Germany, and a specific style of Gothic *architecture. the "H. Gothic", emerged there and spread to the monastic churches of Gemany.

B. Hoffmann, *Hirsau und die Hirsauer* (1950).

HISHAM I (757-96) *Ummayad caliph of *Cordoba. son of *Abd-Al-Rakhman I, the founder of the Ummayad dynasty of Spain, he became emir of Cordoba in 788; in 789 he defeated his elder brothers who had ruled at Toledo, and became the sole ruler of Moslem Spain. He organized the government of his realm and was responsible for the building of many structures in Cordoba, including the great mosque.

HISHAM II (c. 964-1013) Caliph of *Cordoba (976-1013). During his minority the realm was ruled by viziers, who imposed their will on the caliph and continued to be influential even after he reached his legal majority. In 981 one of his ministers, *Al-Mansur, became the virtual ruler of Moslem Spain while H. merely retained his title.

HISHAM III (975-1036) Caliph of *Cordoba (1027-31). Descendant of a collateral branch of the Spanish *Ummayads, he was proclaimed caliph by the Moslem leaders of Cordoba. He did not show any interest in the government of the caliphate, which he left to his ministers. In 1031 he was dethroned by a plot of Moslem emirs of Andalusia and fled to Lerida, where he died. H. was the last caliph of Cordoba.

E. Lévi-Provençal, *Histoire de'l Espagne Musulmane* (1944).

HISHAM IBN ABD-AL-MALIK Tenth caliph of the *Ummayad dynasty. H. was considered by medieval Arab historians as one of the three great rulers of his family. Under his reign (724-43),the Arab caliphate achieved its greatest territorial expansion, reaching from India to southern France. But portents of its impending division were already in evidence; there were recurrent revolts of the *Berbers in north Africa and of the *Shiites and the *Abbasids in Persia and other eastern provinces. H., being a peaceable man, devoted the major part of his reign to the repression of these revolts and, by 742, brought peace to the caliphate. He also led a number of military expeditions into Byzantium (739-40), but

Mosaic pavement at Hisham's palace in Jericho

failed to capture *Constantinople. In 723 he sent a military force from Spain to France which reached as far as *Poitiers; however, the detachment was defeated by the Franks, led by *Charles Martel. H. was also a skilled administrator who reorganized the government of the caliphate, directing much attention to the efficiency of the government machinery. Under his reign, important economic development was evident both in the cities, with regard to trade, and in the countryside, with regard to agriculture.
F. Gabrielli, *Il Califato di Hisham* (1935).

Wall surrounding the pool at Hisham's palace in Jericho

HISPANA CANONS A compilation of canons and decretals probably undertaken in 6th- or 7th-century Spain, which was erroneously attributed, from the 9th century, to *Isidore of Seville, whence the name *Isidoriana*. The H. are arranged according to the countries and regions in which they originated. They served as one of the chief sources for the *False Decretals in the 9th century and were therefore widely spread.
Ed. *PL.*, vol. 84.

HISPERICA FAMINA An anonymous *Celtic poem written in the 6th century in southwest England. The poet invented a language, combining Latin, Celtic, Greek and Hebrew words or parts of words, which he used in his work. The title itself is taken from *hesper* (the evening star, signifying the West) and *famina*, coined to mean "speech", which combine to mean "Western (or Latin) Speech". The 612 lines of the work actually comprise several poems, which might suggest the existence of a local school where a number of monks may have engaged in such linguistic exercises. The work itself deals with various aspects of social life and is therefore a source of information about Britons living in areas such as Cornwall and southern Wales at the period of the Anglo-Saxon conquest. In addition, the poem reflects their learned character, which disappeared when the society was destroyed by the Germanic invasion.
F. H. Jenkinson, *Hisperica Famina* (ed.) (1908).

HISTOIRE D'ERACLES A French chronicle composed by several writers of the *Crusaders' kingdom between 1228 and 1275. The work begins with a description of the reign of the Byzantine Emperor *Heraclius in Palestine, hence its title. With regard to the periods up to the Third *Crusade, the chronicle is a compilation and summary of various other sources and, specifically, of the Chronicle of *William of Tyre. Its information about the Crusader generations between 1187 and 1275 is of great value.
Ed. *RHC*, "Occidentaux".

HISTORIOGRAPHY The art of historical writing was one of the most popular and most widely spread in the civilizations of the Middle Ages. Its wide use is explained not only by the curiosity of individual historians or by the desire of certain rulers to have themselves immortalized in historical works, but also by the influence of ancient traditions, which considered historical writing to be a didactical tool through which one could learn from the experience of past generations and with which to educate people towards proper behaviour. For specific information about Far Eastern H., see *China and *India, and for the H. of the *Arab world and of *Byzantuim, see their respective entries

The H. of western Europe was based on the Roman and biblical concepts of history. Thus, from the 5th century, special emphasis was placed on the influence of divine will on human behaviour although, at the same time, man's freedom to choose between good and evil actions was critically examined and was considered an important factor in the rise and fall of states. In that respect, the influence of St. *Augustine of Hippo was of primary importance. The writings of Orasius, one of the best interpreters of the rise and fall of Rome, became a model for later medieval Hs. However, it was actually the work of *Gregory of Tours at the end of the 6th century, which included

A typical Scandinavian church in wood at Borregaard Norway, built in the 12th century

his observations, information from documents, and a full critical account of various supernatural phenomena, such as miracles and popular superstitions, that set the characteristic form of medieval Hs. The finest piece of early medieval H. was the work of *Bede the Venerable, which concentrated on the history of the Anglo-Saxons.

Due to the fact that learning was mainly engaged in in the church establishments, the writing of Hs. was generally undertaken by clerks and especially by monks. Thus, medieval histories written in western Europe often neglected the social and economic aspects. In the latter half of the 8th century historiographers concentrated on the composition of *annals, which became the most popular expression of historical writing until the 10th century. Although chronological order was maintained, the summary of yearly events led to a rigid selection of material in accordance with the author's perspective; such works did not allow the historian to take the overall picture into account, nor did they lend themselves to the analysis of specific events. In that respect, the *Historia Francorum*, composed at the *Carolingian court, exemplify the official H., which neglected to include data which might not be favourable to the government. Such information could only be retraced through critical analysis of the text and its comparison with other available sources.

The *Ottonian revival in Germany and the foundation of the *Holy Roman empire led, first in Germany and later on in France, to renewed interest in *chronicles, which became the popular form of H. in the high Middle Ages. Such works can be divided into "universal" histories, chronicles dealing with a particular country and local chronicles, the last being the most common. All three types of chronography were primarily didactic, written with the intention of teaching both of the virtues and sins of men of achievement; the wrongdoings were treated so readers could learn from past mistakes. Such conceptions were based on two ideas fundamental to medieval H.: firstly a static view of historical development which would not accept any change in circumstances or the appearance of new factors unknown to previous generations; and secondly, focus on the actions of the individual, emphasizing a particular personality's impact on history, and thus being an expression of the historical cult of the hero. The latter approach was the result of the influence of epic songs and poems, such as the *chansons de geste* and the sagas, in which the heroic cult was exalted. As in the earlier Middle Ages, the authors mixed realistic narratives with supernatural tales dealing with worship of saints, miracles and phenomena, such as the appearance of comets, thunderbolts, and the like, which were considered portents of later events.

A number of historical schools, classified according to their field of interest, may be discerned in medieval H. In Germany attention was naturally attracted to the empire and universal policy. *Otto of Freising, for example, writing in the middle of the 12th century, proffered a well-developed universal view of history, which was shared by some of his colleagues such as *Sigebert of Gembloux and Helinand of Froidmont, both in Germany and in the Low Countries. But even while describing the Scandinavian and Slavic countries or dealing with a particular province, German historians tended to be subject to imperial influence. The French

historical school, on the other hand, displayed greater interest in local events and only gradually expanded its attention to include the entire realm. In the Anglo-Norman area particular attention was paid to the deeds of kings and, thus, their activities on both sides of the Channel were described. As a result, the Anglo-Norman school had a somewhat enlarged vision; some of its historians, like *Matthew Paris of the 13th century, displayed a keen interest in universal aspects of history. An outgrowth of the French and German schools developed in the latter part of the 12th century into a distinct *Crusader historical school, which focused its attention on the *Holy Land. With the work of *William of Tyre, this school came to express a kind of "national religious" history. In the 13th century its writers turned to the use of the French language, which paved the way for the composition of Hs. in vernacular tongues. This practice came to an end in western Europe with the fall of the Anglo-Saxon kingdoms. At the papal court a special kind of H. developed with the official composition of the *Liber Pontificalis*, a work which gathered biographical material about the popes from the 7th century on.

Biographies were yet another form of medieval H. Beginning in the 9th century with *Einhard's *Life of Charlemagne*, they came to deal with the deeds of a principal personality or were devoted to the period in which he lived. An important branch of H. related to the biography was the genealogy, which emerged towards the end of the 12th century; generally written at the request of high-ranking families, such works were used to prove their noble origins.

In the late Middle Ages, a type of H. appeared which placed some emphasis on the spoken language. This form was found in chronicles containing a collection of stories and anecdotes, together with the usual descriptions of political events; these were large compilations, usually based on national or regional histories. While the scholarly methods of writing history were not put to use until the middle of the 15th century, the technique of uncritically compiling various interpretations, including excerpts of historical works from previous generations, was common. This approach led to a certain loss of originality in works composed in the late Middle Ages. However, certain authors, such as George Chastelain, presented cohesive works, and some chronicles, such as those of *Froissart and Commynes, are important in that they reflect the chivalric ideas of their times.

J. W. Thompson, *History of Historical Writing* (1943).

HITTIN See HATTIN.

HOHENSTAUFEN German dynasty which ruled the *Holy Roman empire in the 12th and 13th centuries, and whose reign is considered the greatest period of medieval German history. The name is taken from their castle Staufen in *Swabia (modern Württemberg). Originally (in the 10th century), the Hs. were counts of *Weiblingen (whence their Italian name *Ghibellines) and belonged to the middle sector of German nobility, wielding a certain influence within the duchy of Swabia until the middle of the 11th century. In 1079 the head of the family, *Frederick I, married Agnes, Emperor Henry IV's daughter and was appointed duke of Swabia after crushing the princely revolt led by Duke *Rudolf of Swabia, who had been elected anti-king. Frederick

(Previous pages) The Book of Genesis, *11th-century fresco at St. Savin Abbey, France*
(Opposite page) The King and the Young Man; 13th century stained-glass window, now at the Musée Marmottan, Paris

was a faithful companion to his father-in-law, and his sons, *Frederick II and *Conrad, continued to prove their loyalty to *Henry V up to his death (1125). They led the opposition to *Lothair of Supplinburg, and won enough influence to prevent their deposition by the emperor. Moreover, the younger brother *Conrad, who was their candidate for the imperial throne, was able to obtain wide backing in Germany. Among his supporters was the *Babenberg family of Austria, his half-brothers through the remarriage of his mother Agnes to Margrave Liutpold of Austria. In 1137 Conrad III acceded to the imperial throne and, after his death, his nephew, *Frederick III Barbarossa, inherited the imperial crown (1152). Aware of the importance of their duchy of Swabia in the assessment of imperial power, the Hs. held on to their ducal status. Under Frederick Barbarossa, the H. dynasty reached the peak of its power in Germany and Italy. Giving the duchy to his elder son *Frederick IV, Barbarossa also ensured the family's inheritance of the realm of *Sicily through the marriage of his second son and heir, *Henry VI, to Constance, daughter of King *Roger II. The scheme was realized in 1194 when Henry became king of Sicily; but his premature death, leaving an infant child, *Frederick II, led to the first split in the dynasty and gave rise to a contest over the imperial title.

Although Henry's brother *Philip, duke of Swabia, was elected emperor, he met with the opposition of Pope *Innocent III, who feared the great power of the Hs. and, in 1202, called upon the German princes to hold another election, in which he supported *Otto, duke of Brunswick, the heir of the *Welfs. The civil war which broke out in Germany weakened the H. dynasty and, in 1208, after the death of Philip, it seemed that the extinction of the German branch would also cause the dynasty's loss of the empire. However, the conflict which developed between the pope and Otto IV brought Innocent to support *Frederick II of Sicily in 1212, with the hope of manipulating the young ruler. Frederick came to Germany, won the fealty of H. supporters and finally defeated Otto IV at Bouvines, restoring the great empire of his father's time. In 1220 he left the government of Germany to his eldest son *Henry and concentrated his efforts in Italy. Henry's revolt in 1234 brought Frederick to hand the German kingship to his second son, *Conrad IV, who was already heir of Sicily and of the *Crusaders' kingdom of Jerusalem. But the long clash between Frederick and the papacy caused many revolts in Germany. When he died in 1250 Conrad did not have full control over the situation in Germany, where civil war continued. In Italy, the illegitimate sons of Frederick, especially *Manfred, continued to fight the papacy and its allies, but the death of Conrad, who left an infant child *Conradin, brought the reign of the dynasty to an end. With the death of Manfred in 1266 and the murder of Conradin in 1268 by *Charles of Anjou, following the former's unsuccessful last attempt to achieve his inheritance, the house of H. became extinct, leaving both Germany and Italy in a state of anarchy.

J. Büchler, *Die Hohenstaufen* (1925).

HOHENZOLLERN German dynasty which acceded, at the beginning of the 15th century, to the rank of princes as electors of *Brandenburg. Its members were originally from *Swabia, where they were lords of the castle of

Zollern and its surroundings. The first known family member was Frederick, lord of Zollern, who served the duke of Swabia, Frederick of *Hohenstaufen, at the beginning of the 12th century. The family's loyal service to the Hohenstaufens in the 12th century earned them land and honours and, under *Frederick Barbarossa, they built a new castle on the summit of the Zollern mountain and named it Hohenzollern. In 1191 Lord Frederick III married the heiress of the burgrave of *Nuremberg and established his dynasty in *Franconia. Before his death he divided the estates between his two sons (1204), creating two branches – the Franconian and the Swabian. The Franconian line was the most important; its members settled at Nuremberg and gained political importance during the Great Interregnum in Germany. Burgrave Frederick IV (1220-97) was a firm supporter of *Rudolf of Hapsburg in 1272 and attained an influential position in the empire, which paved the way for the acquisition of the counties of Ansbach and Bayreuth at the beginning of the 14th century, making the Hs. a powerful family in Germany. Their alliance with the emperors of the *Luxemburg dynasty in the latter half of the 14th century provided an important means of support for the imperial authority and was a source of profit to the Hs. In 1415 Emperor *Sigismund rewarded Burgrave *Frederick VI for his support, granting him Brandenburg with the title of elector (Frederick I of Brandenburg).

R. Schneider, *Die Hohenzollern* (1953).

HOLLAND County belonging to the duchy of *Lotharingia, which covered part of the territory of western *Frisia, between the Rhine and Amstel rivers. The county was established at the beginning of the 10th century by a Frisian leader, Dirk, who organized territory reconquered from the *Normans and, in 922, was created count of H. by *Charles the Simple, king of France. His descendants ruled the county, which gradually grew, both through the reclamation of land previously inundated by the sea, and by matrimonial alliances with the families of the counts of *Zeeland and *Flanders. Under Count *William II (1234-56), H. gained powerful influence in feudal Germany, so that William was elected anti-king in 1147 by the German princes who rebelled against *Frederick II and *Conrad IV. The count's attempts to seize power in 1254 failed, and he returned to H., where he died two years later. In 1296 the Frisian dynasty died out and H. was inherited by John of Avesnes, count of *Hainault, who ruled as imperial prince over an important group of counties in the Low Countries. Under the counts of the Avesnes family and those of the Bavarian house of *Wittelsbach (1296-1417), the county knew a period of prosperity, due to the development of trade.

B. H. Slicher van Bath, *The Economic and Social Conditions in the Frisian Districts, 900-1500* (1965).

HOLSTEIN County in northern Germany between the Elbe and the Danish frontier. The territory was inhabited by the Obodrites, a Slavic tribe which resisted *Charlemagne and remained H.'s dominant population until the 12th century. Under the *Ottonians, the Germans became overlords of the province, which was also sought by the Danes, and the territory was attached to the northern march of the *Billungs. At the beginning of the 12th century the Germans carried out missionary activities which were supported by German colonization and the establishment of the county. In the mid-12th century, under the rigorous rule of Count Adolf (d. 1162), the Slavic elements were Germanized or destroyed. Adolf was killed in a battle against Niclot, the *Wendish leader in the area, but his policy was continued by *Henry the Lion, duke of Saxony, who imposed his overlordship over the county. In 1169 he granted freedom to the city of *Lübeck, detaching it from the county. Danish influence penetrated in the latter half of the century and, in 1180, *Frederick Barbarossa granted it special privileges in order to overcome his Welf rival. In the 13th century, this Danish influence became an indirect rule, subject to a vague imperial authority, and the relations between H. and Denmark brought it increasingly within the sphere of the Danish crown in the last centuries of the Middle Ages, until it was formally annexed, by the accession of the counts of H. to the Danish throne.

J. W. Thompson, *Feudal Germany* (1928).

HOLY CROSS Supposedly a relic of the cross on which Christ was crucified, preserved, from the 4th century, at the church of the Holy Sepulchre in Jerusalem. In 614 it was captured by the Persians, against whom the Byzantine emperor *Heraclius continued to fight until it was regained. Parts of the H. were later distributed as relics to churches in the West, where they served as objects of worship.

HOLY LANCE A relic, believed to be the lance used by a Roman soldier to pierce Christ's dead body. It was first mentioned in the 6th century and was located in the church of Mount Zion in Jerusalem. Captured by the Persians in 614, it was brought to Constantinople, where it was preserved at the cathedral of St. Sophia. In 1241 it was given to King *Louis IX of France, who placed it in his church of *Sainte-Chapelle in Paris. Another part, recorded in Jerusalem in the 7th century, was sent by the Turks to the pope as a gift after its capture in 1492.

F. de Mély, *La Sainte Lance de Constantinople* (1904).

HOLY MARTYRS A group of 14 auxiliary saints whose common characteristic was their *martyrdom. They included Sts. Achatius, Giles, George, Christopher, Blaise. Cyriac, Denis, Erasmus, Eustace, Pantaleon, Vitus, Barbara, Catherine and Margaret. Throughout the whole of the Middle Ages each one was venerated individually as patron saint of a particular country or *guild but, in the late Middle Ages, a common cult of the group emerged in northern France and spread throughout western Europe, expressing itself in popular literature and art. It seems that the impressive character of their images contributed to this development.

J. Huizinga, *The Waning of the Middle Ages* (1924).

HOLY ROMAN EMPIRE (The Holy Roman Empire of the German Nation) A political organization created in 962, when the king of Germany, *Otto I, was crowned emperor. Its main characteristic was its universalistic orientation, in that for medieval political thought it represented the heritage of both the Roman and the Christian empires. Another characteristic was the perpetual union of Germany and northern Italy under one rule, regarded as sovereign and "multi-national". In the reign of *Otto III this concept was elaborated into that of the empire of the "four nations": Germany, Italy, Gaul and the Slavs. The foundation of the empire

The Emperor and his subjects; *11th-century relief (detail)*

was connected with the idea of the protection of the universal Catholic Church by the emperors, which gave them a special prerogative over the papacy. This prerogative did not imply, as in *Byzantine tradition and practice, a control and sovereignty over the popes, but merely an interdependence, according to various interpretations of the *Gelasian theory of the "two swords". Thus, no king of Germany could become emperor without papal consent, expressed by his coronation at Rome while, on the other hand, no person could be elected pope without imperial consent. Even when the equilibrium was broken in imperial favour (as in the period before the death of *Henry III), in cases when emperors in fact appointed the popes, the fiction was still respected. The existence of such a political arrangement and the exercise of imperial prerogatives implied continual involvement of German sovereigns in Italy, where they had to fight against the independent aspirations of the Italian cities and waste their efforts in long campaigns on Italian soil. These necessities led to a certain neglect of German affairs, so that the emperors sought the support of the German nobility, gradually granting it privileges.

The period of *Henry IV's minority was a suitable occasion for the emancipation of the papacy from the imperial yoke. The decree of Pope *Nicholas II of 1059, which made the election of popes an exclusive prerogative of the College of *Cardinals, changed the situation and, for the first time since the foundation of the H., opened the way to a contest between the empire and the papacy, as two universal powers struggling for the sovereignty of the Christian world. The *Gregorian reform, prohibiting the lay investiture (1075) was mainly aimed against the imperial prerogative to control the episcopal elections by the investiture of their lands. The impossibility of any emperor accepting such a situation, which deprived him of his most important resources in Germany, led to the *Investiture contest, which generated a long series of wars between the two powers, bringing troubles both for the papacy and the emperors. The end of the Investiture contest through the compromise solution known as the Concordat of *Worms (1122), solved the technical problem, but did not bring any solution to the basic conflict for the supremacy of the Christian world. This conflict began after the *Hohenstaufen dynasty was raised to the imperial throne and came into the open under *Frederick Barbarossa, who attempted to restore imperial prerogatives. The resistance of the papacy, in close alliance with the monarchies of England, France and the Lombard cities of northern Italy, caused a general war, which ravaged the imperial forces, but also the resources of the papacy. Even the attempt of Pope *Innocent III to impose his authority and dictate to the German princes whom to elect emperor, was an incident, and the clash renewed under *Frederick II, who was almost constantly at war with the papacy and the Italian cities. His death in 1250 resulted in a long interregnum in the H. and in the fall of the Hohenstaufen dynasty, but at the same time in a weakened papacy, exhausted by the long wars and dependent on France.

After the election of *Rudolf of Hapsburg as emperor in 1272, a new period began in the history of the H. While the emperors conserved their universal title (which lasted until 1806, when it was abolished by Napoleon Bonaparte), they now focused their attention on Germany, so that the empire became a confederation of principalities, and its rulers were chiefly emperors of *Germany. With few exceptions, they renounced imperial

coronation at Rome and demonstrated their sovereignty in Italy through the appointment of local potentates as imperial representatives with honorific titles. Thus, Italy was left in a chaotic condition, which could not be redressed by the weakened papacy and caused views to be expressed in the favour of a revival of imperial power by such men as *Dante and *Marsiglio of Padua. The chaotic state of Italy finally resulted in the collapse of the communes and the rise of local tyrants, forerunners of the princes who established their power in the 15th century. The real beneficiaries from the long conflict involving the H. and from its collapse as a universal power, were the national kingdoms, either those in the West, such as France, England and the Spanish monarchies, or those in northern and eastern Europe, whose establishment brought into being the theory of royal sovereignty over a defined area of territory.

G. Falco, *The Holy Roman Republic* (1964).

HOLY SEPULCHRE The cave in Jerusalem where, according to an early tradition, Christ was buried and rose from the dead. The tomb was discovered in the 4th century by St. *Helena, who built a church on the site. It became one of the most important Christian shrines and the object of pilgrimages to the Holy Land. The church was rebuilt by *Justinian, and the patriarchs of Jerusalem established their cathedral there. Under the *Crusaders, the Latin patriarchate of Jerusalem was established there and the church was governed by a *chapter of canons, richly endowed both in the Latin kingdom of Jerusalem and in western Europe. The Crusaders used the third building, completed *c*. 1050, built on the ruins of the church destroyed by the *Fatimid caliph *Hakim. At the beginning of the 14th century the church achieved its final form and was opened to all Christian cults. The church itself is built in two parts. The western part, built in a circular form around the crypt containing the tomb of Christ, serves as a centre of pilgrimages. In the eastern part, a basilical structure was adopted, showing the strong influence of Byzantine *architecture.

W. Harvey, *Church of the Holy Sepulchre, Jerusalem* (1935).

HOLY YEAR A year during which the pope granted a special indulgence, called the *Jubilaeum*, to all pilgrims who came to Rome. It was instituted by *Boniface VIII in 1300 in order to demonstrate the solidarity of the faithful with the papacy, so gaining support in his political struggles. He decreed its celebration once every 100 years. In the 14th century, however, this period was changed to 50 and then to 33 years and, in 1470, Paul II fixed it at once every 25 years. One of its major features is the initial ceremony of opening the Holy Door at *St. Peter's by the pope.

H. Thurston, *The Holy Year of Jubilee* (1900).

HOMAGE See HOMINIUM.

HOMINIUM (Homage) *Feudal term denoting the oath taken by a vassal to signify his relationship with his lord. The H. implies a list of obligations undertaken by the vassal in return for the lord's protection and help. Among them is the performance of military service and participation in the lord's court as well as other forms of assistance. Until the 8th century, the H. was not clearly institutionalized and could either be an oral declaration of a certain free-man that he would be the "man" (Latin: *homo*) of a particular lord, or a written

contract. From the 8th century it became an oath, taken in a public ceremony, usually in the *chapel of the lord's palace, where the vassal swore on the relics of a venerated saint. The nature of the obligation was defined only in the 11th and 12th centuries but, from its very beginning, unlike the oath of *fidelity, it was a contractual oath, binding both parties. From the 11th century the ceremony, which became one of the most important ceremonies of the feudal courts and which was attended by other vassals and knights, included a religious section, the oath itself, when the kneeling vassal put his hands into those of the lord, swearing allegiance; a "kiss of peace", given by the lord to his new vassal; and the investiture of the land or estate held by the vassal as a tenure of his lord. In the 13th century a written document was added to the oral oath.
M. Bloch, *Feudal Society* (1952).

HOMO (man) The Latin word was used in the Middle Ages both in its literary sense and as a *feudal term, synonymous with vassal. i.e., "such a lord's man". This use was derived from the term *H. de corpore*, meaning an unfree subject, either slave or serf.

HOMS City in *Syria, on the eastern bank of the Orontes River. It was conquered by the *Arabs in 636 and its Byzantine character gradually disappeared. In 855 the process of Islamization led to a revolt of its Christian inhabitants, who were cruelly repressed by the *Abbasid government. The churches were destroyed and those Christians who were not killed, fled or were forced into exile. In 1070 the *Seljuks conquered the city and, at the beginning of the 12th century, a Turkish emirate was established there. After the First *Crusade and the creation of the county of *Tripoli (1102), H. became a Crusader city on the frontiers of Moslem Syria. In order to defend the county, the Crusaders built one of their most important strongholds, the *Krak des Chevaliers*, on the western bank of the Orontes. In 1150 *Nureddin, sultan of Aleppo and Mosul, annexed H. to his realm and the independent principality of H. was incorporated into the *Zengid and later on into the *Ayyubid state of Syria. After the Mongol defeat in 1281, it was conquered by the Mamelukes.
EI, II.

HONAN Province of *China, in the Hoang-ho River valley. Its central position between northern and southern China made it one of the territories most coveted by the various dynasties. At the beginning of the 13th century it belonged to the Kin empire and was conquered by the *Mongols under *Genghis-Khan. Its importance for the domination of China caused the Mongols to appoint as governors members of the ruling dynasty. In 1253 one of the grandsons of *Genghis-Khan, *Kublai-Khan, was appointed governor of H. In the following five years he conquered southern China, destroying the Sung empire as well as overrunning large parts of Indo-China, among them the empire of Annam. On the death of his brother *Mangu (1257), he proclaimed himself great khan in H. and made it the centre of the Mongol empire.
R. Grousset, *L'Empire des Steppes* (1946).

HONNECOURT, VILLARD DE See VILLARD OF HONNECOURT.

HONORIUS I (d. 638) Pope (625-38). Of a noble family of the Roman Campagna he entered the papal court during the pontificate of *Gregory I. H. intensified missionary activity in Anglo-Saxon England and was active in imposing his authority over the Italian clergy, part of which recognized the authority of the patriarchs of Aquilea, who sought to be independent. His struggle against the Aquilean separatism caused him to become dependent on Emperor *Heraclius of Byzantium, whose help was needed in order to assert his power. In theology he accepted the direction of Patriarch *Sergius of Constantinople, thus entering into conflict with *Sophronius, the patriarch of Jerusalem, who opposed the doctrine of the dual nature of Christ, the divine and the human. H., however, insisted on the idea, even after his correction by Sergius, and was anathematized after his death by the Council of Constantinople (681).
J. Chapman, *The Condemnation of Pope Honorius I* (1907).

HONORIUS II (Lambert Scannabecchi; d. 1130) Pope (1124-30). When cardinal, he collaborated with Pope *Calixtus II and proved himself a skilled negotiator, especially in arranging the compromise which resulted in the *Concordat of Worms (1122). Elected pope in 1124, he had to fight against the growing influence of the great Roman families and of *Roger II of Sicily. While his relations with Emperor *Lothair II were correct, he had to face growing opposition from the reform party in the church, which demanded a more active policy. On the eve of his death, even the College of *Cardinals was split.
J. Haller, *Das Papsttum* (1952).

HONORIUS III (Cencio Savelli; d. 1227) Pope (1216-27). A native of Rome, he became papal chamberlain in 1188 and was created cardinal in 1193. In 1197 Pope *Innocent III entrusted him with the education of the infant *Frederick II. Successor to Innocent III, he pursued the same policy as his predecessor, but less vigorously. In 1220 he crowned Frederick II emperor, on the understanding that he would immediately undertake the *Crusade planned by H. from the very beginning of his pontificate. He was active in his European policy, arbitrating between kings in an endeavour to bring peace to the Christian world, so as to mobilize all resources for the Crusade. He encouraged the monastic orders, especially the new ones, and granted privileges to the *Dominicans, *Franciscans and *Carmelites. As chamberlain of the papal court, in 1192 he composed the *Liber Censuum*, which is an important record of the papal revenues in his period. Another important achievement was the composition of the "Coronation Order" of the *Holy Roman emperors, in which he developed a coronation liturgy.
A. Keutner, *Papsttum und Krieg unter dem Pontificat des Papstes Honorius III* (1935).

HONORIUS IV (Giacomo Savelli; 1210-87) Pope (1285-87). Member of a Roman family, he was created cardinal in 1261 and contributed to the development of the *Angevin state in Italy. After the death of *Martin IV, he was elected pope despite his bad state of health and tried to pacify *Sicily by supporting the claims of the Angevins of Naples.
J. Haller, *Das Papsttum* (1953).

HONORIUS AUGUSTODUNENSIS (early 12th century) Scholastic and popular writer. Little is known about his life and origins. Some scholars wrongly thought that he came from Autun, France, but he was probably a hermit living near Ratisbon in Germany. His many treatises on theology, philosophy, natural sciences and history are compilations of earlier writings. Among them, the most popular were the encyclopedic *Imago Mundi* (Image of the World) and the *Elucidarium*, a popular exposition of Catholic theology which greatly influenced artists.

M. T. d'Alverny, *Le Cosmos Symbolique du XIIe siècle* (1954).

HORMISDAS, St. (d. 523) Pope (514-23). He took an active part in the theological discussions with the Eastern Church, attempting to arrive at an authoritative interpretation of the *Orthodox creed. In Italy he endeavoured to reach an understanding with the *Ostrogoths and to maintain good relations with their king *Theodoric.

L. Duchesne, *L'Eglise au VIe siècle* (1925).

HORMISDAS King of Persia (579-90). He was the son and successor of King *Chosroes I. His policy was based on peaceful relations with Byzantium, required for the consolidation of the kingdom and its expansion into the Caucasus. In internal affairs, his main concern was to reform the government and diminish the influence of the nobility. H. was unable to carry out his reforms, as he faced revolts from his generals. In 589 his authority received a serious blow with the rebellion of General Vahran, who succeeded in imposing his power over the provinces and, in 590, dethroned H.

A. Christensen, *L'Iran sous le Sassanides* (1944).

HORSE The chief non-human source of power in the Middle Ages, the H. was the most important animal in medieval civilization, closely connected with warfare and the nobility. Its use by *Germanic tribes for armed expeditions at the beginning of the Middle Ages created a revolution in the art of war but, until the 8th century, Germans and Huns used it for transportation only, dismounting in order to fight. In the 8th century *Charles Martel introduced mounted combat, the first manifestation of *chivalry in western Europe. The importance of the H. for military purposes caused it to be raised with special care and increased its value relative to other animals, such as cows and oxen, used for work and transportation. At the end of the 8th century mounted warriors were granted 12 *mansi of land, as compared to infantrymen, who were granted only four. This special care was also apparent at the royal court, where a high official of countal rank was put in charge of the stables – the *comes stabuli* (later *Constable). From the 10th century, Hs. were the symbol of knighthood and, as such, were a favourite subject of epic literature. From the 12th century on, they were also used for ploughing, where they replaced the oxen, and for drawing vehicles. Two kinds of Hs. were now bred: those intended for warfare and those intended for work purposes.

L. White, *Medieval Technology and Social Change* (1962).

HOSEBONDRIES Treatises dealing with the management of manors and farms, written in England from the 13th century. Among them the most famous, frequently copied and widely diffused, was the *Hosebondrie* by Walter of Henley (*c.* 1250), written in Anglo-French for the use of reeves who superintended farms. It contains a detailed description of Henley's manor with interesting botanical data. An important part is devoted to the cultivation of cereals and plants and the management of the manor.

Walter of Henley, *Hosebondrie*, ed. E. Lamond (1890).

HOSPITALLER KNIGHTS A religious-military order which became famous during the *Crusades. Their origin is connected with the care of sick pilgrims to the Holy Land and Jerusalem. While some theories try to trace their origins to the period of *Charlemagne, it is certain that the first brotherhoods of H. began to be active in Jerusalem in the first half of the 11th century. The acquisition, by a group of *Amalfi merchants, of the church of St. John the Baptist in Jerusalem in 1050, and the establishment of a hospital for pilgrims in the same building, resulted in the foundation of the order under the patronage of St. John (hence, they were also known as the Johannites). At the end of the 11th century, the order was based in Jerusalem and, besides the brothers who took care of the ill, a group of knights was employed to defend them and the pilgrims. With the conquest of Palestine by the Crusaders, the order underwent a radical change of character and organization. The *Domus Infirmorum* (The Sick House) still remained a basic foundation of its constitution, but it became entirely subordinated to the warriors, who enlarged their activity as defenders of the holy places and of the kingdom. As a result of this change, the knights were established in fortresses along the borders of the kingdom and knights were recruited in western Europe. Grants of lands and revenues in Europe followed and enabled the order to build its castles and maintain the knights.

In the mid-12th century, the H. became one of the most powerful organizations of the Crusader lands, possessing many of the most important castles and some seignories. Although integrated into the military system of the kingdom, they enjoyed practical independence, being exempted from obedience to the kings and patriarchs and under the direct authority of the pope. This situation led to a lack of discipline, causing defeats to the Crusader army. The kings had to negotiate with the order their participation in the fighting and only kings with exceptional prestige were able to impose discipline upon them. In the 13th century the H. established their centre in the city of Acre, where they built an impressive complex of halls, including a church, refectory and "sick house". Thanks to their revenues from Europe they were able to acquire seignories such as Mount *Tabor in Galilee and *Arsuf and to pursue their own policies. The order also established assizes in *Cyprus. After the fall of the Crusader kingdom, the H. settled in the island of *Rhodes (1309), which became their headquarters until its conquest by the Turks in 1522. Here they became purely military in character, while drawing their reserve of manpower from France. In 1530 they moved to Malta and became known also as the "knights of Malta".

J. Riley-Smith, *The Knights of St. John in Jerusalem and Cyprus, c. 1050-1310* (1967).

HOSPITALS In the Middle Ages H. became exclusively associated with monasteries. With the spread of monasticism in the West, it was commonly accepted that among the duties of the monks, and particularly of nuns, was care of the ill. A part of the hostelry where pilgrims were accommodated, was set aside for that purpose; thus, the Latin word *hospitium* was used to mean both a

The Knights' Hall in the Hospitallers' castle at Acre

hostelry and a hospital. Until the 12th century, the church authorities were opposed to the practice of medicine by monks, and only later was medical assistance part of the care. In the latter half of the 12th century, as a result of the growth of cities, urban H. were founded through the donations of private individuals who left their possessions or income to the H. They were situated near the cathedral or some other church and a *chapter was established to administer them. The most famous was the hospital of the *Quinze Vingts* (The Three Hundred) in Paris, which received the protection of King *Louis IX of France. A number of monastic orders devoted themselves to the care of contagious diseases, such as the Lazarists, who concerned themselves with the lepers. During the *Hundred Years' War the H. suffered damage but at the same time gained a new function, serving as alms-houses for wounded soldiers.

R. M. Clay, *The Medieval Hospitals in England* (1909).

HOSPITES Latin term used from the 12th century to designate free *peasants settled in new villages founded in ancient forest lands or on reclaimed land. In order to attract them, the lords taxed them very lightly, generally imposing only a house-tax, and they were usually relieved of compulsory labour for their lord.

G. Duby, *Rural Economy and Country Life in the Medieval West* (1968).

HOSTIENSIS (Henry of Suza; d. 1271) Italian legist. He studied law at *Bologna, where he became professor, after some years of lecturing on canon law at Paris. H. is considered one of the greatest canonists of the 13th century and his *Summa aurea*, composed *c*. 1250, became the most authoritative account of ecclesiastical legislation in the late Middle Ages. He emphasized the full authority of the pope in the interpretation of the divine law.

EC, VII.

HÔTEL-DIEU Famous *hospital in Paris, founded in 1162 near the cathedral of Notre Dame. Administered by the chapter of the cathedral and richly endowed by the burghers of the city, it also served as an alms-house for poor elderly people, who were maintained there by public charity. Its revenues came from lands and houses in the city which were rented to tenants. From the 14th century, it was customary for queens of France and other princesses to make ceremonial visits to the ill, thus emphasizing the obligation of charity.

L. Brièle, *Le Hôtel-Dieu de Paris* (1893).

HOTEL DU ROI A section of the French royal administration dealing with the king's household. It originates from the latter half of the 13th century, but only during the reign of *Philip IV (1285-1314) was it organized as a special ministry, administering lands and revenues which were set aside to meet the expenses of the king's household. As a result, in the 14th century a distinction came to be made between the state administration and that of the royal house (the palaces and the persons attached to the king's service). Its establishment marked the end of the feudal concept of the state, in which there was no distinction between the king and the realm.

F. Lot and R. Fawtier, *Histoire des Institutions Françaises* (1958).

HRABANUS MAURUS See RABANUS MAURUS.

HROSWITHA (10th century) German poetess. Of a noble Saxon family, she became a nun at the abbey of Gandersheim in Saxony, where she attained a wide knowledge of classical Latin literature as well as of the writings of the Church Fathers. An inspired and gifted poetess, she modelled her poems on classical Latin authors such as Terence. Opposing his views on the frivolity of women, H. laid emphasis on the chastity of Christian virgins and penitents. Many of her poems are devoted to lives of saints, while others deal with the continuous struggle between spirit and flesh and the spiritual superiority of the Christian faith.

PL, vol 137;

J. Schneiderhan, *Roswita* (1912).

HUBERT OF BURGH (d. 1243) Justiciar of England. He began his career in the royal administration in the reign of *Richard I and was promoted by *John to higher positions at the court. In 1205-06 he was in charge of the defence of Chinon Castle on the Loire, until its fall to the French. After his return to England, he was one of the most faithful followers of King John and supported him in the struggle against the barons. Appointed justiciar, he was influential during the minority of *Henry III and, from 1219, was regent of the kingdom. As justiciar and regent, he put order into the administration and legal system and was one of the most skilled English politicians of his time. In 1232 he was dismissed by Henry III, who regarded him as responsible for the defeat in Brittany (1229-30).

C. Ellis, *Hubert de Burgh. A Study in Constancy* (1952).

HUBERT WALTER (d. 1205) Justiciar of England and archbishop of Canterbury (1193-1205). He began his career as chaplain to *Glanville and gained considerable experience in administration. In 1180 he became bishop of Salisbury. H. accompanied *Richard I on the Third *Crusade and upon his return was appointed justiciar. Through the influence of Richard, he was elected archbishop of Canterbury and, after Richard's departure to the Continent in 1194, was entrusted with the government of the realm. He provided for the king's financial needs and served him faithfully, leaving a sound administration.

J. Appleby, *England Without Richard* (1969).

HUCBALD (c. 840-930) Musician and humanist. Of noble Lotharingian origin, he became a monk at the monastery of St. Amand in northern France and was elected abbot there at the beginning of the 10th century. He devoted his time to the monastic school of his abbey, where he taught the *quadrivium* and was interested in liturgy. As a result of this interest, he came to concern himself with the musical aspects of prayer, such as harmony. H. learned the classical heritage of musical theory, which he used to develop his own views, expressed in his four treatises: *De harmonica Institutione* (On the Rules of Harmony), *Musica Enchiriadis*, *Scholia Enchiriadis* (Revising the Greek Heritage) and *De alia Musica* (The Other Music). He applied the system of transcription of the eight modes with intervals, laying the foundations of medieval musicology.

E. Wellesz, *Eastern Elements in Western Chant* (1947).

HUESCA City in *Aragon, between the Pyrénées and the Ebro River. It belonged to the *Visigoths from the beginning of the 6th century and under their government became a provincial centre. Conquered by the Arabs in 718, it belonged to the province of Saragossa. In 787 it was captured by *Charlemagne, but at the end of the 8th century it again passed to the Moslems. In

1096 King *Peter I of Aragon conquered it and made the city the capital of Aragon until 1118. From that period it was one of the royal cities where kings frequently resided. In 1354 *Peter IV established there the university of the kingdom.

R. del Arco, *Huesca* (1950).

HUGH I, of Lusignan (1195-1218) King of Cyprus (1205-18). Son of *Aymeric I, he reigned under the guardianship of Walter of Montbéliard, his brother-in-law, who imposed a harsh rule upon the island. H. continued this policy when he assumed power, but died at the age of 23 before it could bear fruit.

HUGH II, of Lusignan (1253-67) King of Cyprus. Son of *Henry I, he became king on his father's death, when only a few months old. He reigned under the regency of his uncle, Hugh of Antioch.

HUGH III, of Lusignan-Antioch (d. 1284) King of Cyprus (1267-84) and of Jerusalem (1269-76). Grandson of *Hugh I of Cyprus and of *Bohemond IV of Antioch, he became regent of Cyprus in 1262 on behalf of his nephew *Hugh II and, in 1267, inherited the kingdom as the nearest of kin. Also regent of the Crusader kingdom of Jerusalem, he was proclaimed king and crowned at *Acre in 1269. His attempts to unite both kingdoms in order to save the remnants of the Crusader state failed, as it encountered a growing opposition, both in Acre, where the military orders and part of the nobility refused to accept his leadership, and in Cyprus. In 1276 he left Acre disappointed and renounced the kingship of Jerusalem, claimed by *Charles of Anjou, king of Sicily. In 1284 he landed at *Tyre, summoned by the nobility, in a last effort to save the kingdom from *Mameluke attacks, but died almost immediately.

S. Runciman, *A History of the Crusades*, III (1953).

HUGH IV, of Lusignan-Antioch (d. 1359) King of Cyprus (1324-59). Nephew of *Henry II, he was a wise ruler, who brought peace and prosperity to the kingdom of Cyprus. While allying himself with the papacy and Venice against the Turks in Anatolia (1343) and helping in the conquest of Izmir (Smyrna), he succeeded in establishing peaceful relations with Egypt, which boosted Cypriot trade.

G. Hill, *History of Cyprus*, III (1948).

HUGH Name of five dukes of the *Capetian dynasty of *Burgundy, among them:

Hugh II, the Pacific (1102-43) He was one of the most important dukes of medieval Burgundy, pacifying the country and establishing a strong rule from his new centre, Dijon. H. supported the great Burgundian monasteries, which enabled him to impose his authority over his vassals.

Hugh IV (1218-72) He began his rule under the regency of his mother, Alice of Vergy and, after reaching his majority, was a faithful retainer of Kings *Louis VIII and *Louis IX, whose policy he supported. H. was considered an ideal knight of his time, and his court at Dijon was one of the most brilliant in western Europe.

J. Richard, *Les Ducs de Bourgogne* (1953).

HUGH CAPET (941-96) King of France (987-96). Son of *Hugh the Great and of Hedwig, sister of Emperor *Otto I, on his father's death in 956 he became duke of the Franks and, as such, the most powerful feudal lord in France. In 978 he entered an alliance against King Lothair with his cousin, Emperor *Otto II, and *Adalberon, archbishop of Rheims. After the death of *Louis

V, the nobles of the kingdom elected him king against the candidacy of the last *Carolingian, *Charles of Lorraine. Crowned by Adalberon, he had to face a revolt of Charles' supporters within the nobility and the church, as well as to gain recognition from various feudal lords. He succeeded not only due to his merits, but also to the incapacity of his rivals, who were unable to unite against him. H. was the founder of the *Capetian dynasty.

E. Pognon, *Hugues Capet, Roi de France* (1966).

HUGH ETERIANUS (d. 1182) Theologian and translator. Born at Pisa. he studied dialectics in France and, in 1160, was sent as member of the Pisan delegation to Constantinople, where he became acquainted with Greek scientific and theological works. He entered into serious polemical debates with the Orthodox clergy, and wrote a number of treatises in Latin, in which he accused them of errors of doctrine. In 1173 he finished a treatise on the nature of the soul, including large excerpts from Greek philosophers, which he composed at the request of his city's clergy. His treatise *De Sancto et Immortali Deo* (On the Holy and Immortal God), dedicated to Pope *Alexander III in 1177, is a defence of the Latin faith and a full refutation of the Greek-Orthodox doctrines. The book was widely disseminated and H. became famous as one of the most skilled theologians of his time. In 1181 he was created cardinal by *Lucius III.

C. H. Haskins, *Studies in Medieval Science* (1924).

HUGH OF ARLES (d. 947) King of Italy (923-46). Grandson of the *Carolingian monarch *Lothair II and son of Count Thibaud of Arles. He became the most influential person at the court of his cousin *Louis the Blind, king of Provence, and inherited the kingship in 927. In 923 he claimed the Italian throne and invaded *Lombardy, where he was crowned in 927, but had to fight rival kings of the houses of *Spolato and *Burgundy. In order to assure his position, in 933 he ceded Provence to *Rudolf II of Burgundy in return for Rudolf's renunciation of his claims to the kingdom of Italy, and married Marozia, daughter of *Theophylactus, senator of Rome. His tyrannical rule in Italy caused his overthrow by *Berengar II of Ivera in 946. H. fled to Arles, where he died.

G. Fasoli, *I Re d'Italia* (1949).

HUGH OF AVRANCHES (d. 1098) Earl of Chester, son of Richard, viscount of Avranches, *Normandy, he was one of the major followers of *William the Conqueror. In 1066, while the Normans attacked England, he was entrusted with the guardianship of Normandy, and settled in England after the conquest. In 1070 William the Conqueror created him earl of *Chester near the Welsh frontier, granting him large estates. H. was one of the leaders of the Anglo-Norman penetration into Wales, where he founded cities and fought against the Welsh resistance to *William II, whom he supported faithfully.

D. C. Douglas, *William the Conqueror* (1966).

HUGH OF BLOIS Count of *Champagne (1090-1125). His long period of rule was one of continuous stability, permitting the emergence of the famous *Fairs of Champagne, which resulted in a revival of international trade. H. took part in the *Crusades and died in Jerusalem during his third pilgrimage.

A. Luchaire, *Louis VI, roi de France et son Règne* (1892).

HUGH OF LUSIGNAN The name of 12 lords of Lusignan, western France, heading the senior branch of the house of *Lusignan, whose junior branch founded the royal dynasty of *Cyprus. Among them, the most important were:

Hugh IX, the Brown (d. 1219) In 1198 he was betrothed to Isabella, heiress of Angoulême and *La Marche in central France. The marriage, however, did not take place, owing to the intervention of his lord, *John Lackland, king of England and duke of Aquitaine, who married Isabella himself. This breach of the feudal code resulted in John's conviction at the royal court in France and enabled *Philip II to forfeit his French fiefs. Participating in the Fifth *Crusade, he died at Damietta.

Hugh X (d. 1254) Son of Hugh IX by a former marriage, in 1219 he married Isabelle of Angoulême, his father's bride, widow of John Lackland. H. was a powerful count in central France and, after submitting to King *Louis VIII of France in 1226, he attempted, with the encouragement of his wife, to recover his freedom during the regency of *Blanche of Castile. His revolts, culminating in that of 1241-42, failed and he was defeated by King *Louis IX and compelled to accept the king's brother, *Alphonse of Poitiers, as his overlord. A large section of the Lusignan territories was seized by the crown. H. joined the king of France in his *Crusade (1247-52).

S. Painter, *Feudalism and Liberty* (1961).

HUGH OF ORLÉANS (Hugo Primas; 1093-1160) Satirical poet. Little is known about his life and career. From the few personal allusions, we learn that he studied at Paris and led a life of wayfaring in France, with long sojourns at Orléans, whence his title. He wrote poems devoted to love, women and wine, but also a long series of satirical songs criticizing the ecclesiastic and lay establishments of his age. Although he knew classical poetry well and even used motifs as allegorical themes in his songs, he did not, unlike his contemporaries, attempt to imitate the classical Latin poets, but developed a style of his own. Thus, he became the most original Latin poet of the Middle Ages, nicknamed by his followers *Primas* ("the first"). His poems continued to be recited after his death and inspired *Goliardic poetry.

H. Waddell, *The Wandering Scholars* (1932);
F. J. E. Raby, *A History of Secular Latin Poetry* (1934).

HUGH OF PAYNS (c. 1070-1136) Templar. Originating from Champagne, France, he settled as a *Crusader in the Latin kingdom of Jerusalem. Dissatisfied with the religious discipline of the *Hospitallers, he founded the order of the *Templar knights at Jerusalem in 1119, combining an ascetic monastic ideal with the fighting spirit of *chivalry. The order suffered from extreme poverty until it gained the notice of St. Bernard of Clairvaux who, at H.'s request, wrote their rule and encouraged them in a famous treatise, *On the Praise of the New Knighthood* (1128). H. became the first Great Master of the Templars and, under his leadership, the order began to prosper.

S. Painter, *French Chivalry* (1944).

HUGH OF PUISET See PUISET, FAMILY.

HUGH OF ST. VICTOR (1096-1141) Scholar and theologian. Born in Flanders. he was educated at Halverstadt in Germany. In 1118 he joined the abbey of St.

Victor in Paris, where he rapidly gained eminence in the learned community. In 1133 he became abbot of the monastery which, under his leadership, became one of the most important centres of learning in the West. As a theologian, H. attempted to reconcile mystical interpretations of the faith with Platonic philosophy. This endeavour brought him to a classification of knowledge described in his *Didascalion* (Scholastic Introduction), by which knowledge is divided into three categories: theoretical, comprising theology, mathematics and physics; applied, comprising morals, politics and economics; and "extraordinary sciences", such as mechanics, crafts and arts. He regarded logic as a comprehensive science unifying the various branches of knowledge. H. was also an outstanding exegete. He attempted to interpret the Bible by verifying its Hebrew sources and therefore entered into relations with Jewish scholars. While he approached the mystical sources of faith in a spirit of acceptance, he nevertheless tried to explain mystical thought in a rational manner, applying the methods of *Abelard, but without the disputation and polemics which characterized the work of his colleague.

B. Hauréeau (ed.), *Les Oeuvres de Hugues de Saint-Victor* (1886);
J. P. Kleinz, *The Theory of Knowledge of Hugh of St. Victor* (1944);
J. Taylor, *The Origin and Early Life of Hugh of St. Victor* (1956).

HUGH OF SEMUR, St. (1024-1109) Abbot of Cluny (1049-1109). Member of the family of the counts of Semur in France, from his childhood he displayed deep religious feelings and, at the age of 14, entered the monastery of *Cluny, where he soon rose to eminence in the community. At the age of 25 he was elected abbot and leader of the order of Cluny, becoming one of the chief protagonists of ecclesiastical reform in the Roman Church. He devoted himself to the reorganization of the order, which reached its zenith under his long tenure of office. He promoted the election of monks of Cluny to episcopal offices in various countries and enjoyed good relations with monarchs and princes. His prestige resulted in the appointment of monks of the order at the papal court, among them three future popes, *Gregory VII, *Urban II and *Paschal II. He encouraged the monks of *Hirsau to introduce reform in Germany and was involved in the establishment of monasteries belonging to the order in the countries conquered from the Moslems, in Spain and in the Levant, where the monastery of Mount Tabor was founded as a Cluniac institution. At his death, the order of Cluny numbered about a thousand monasteries and priories in all the Christian countries. The prestige of the order also attracted large pious donations, making it one of the greatest possessors of land in western Europe. H. was also concerned with improving the liturgical practices of the monasteries, basing himself on the concept adopted at Cluny, that prayer was the monk's work. H. is considered the greatest abbot of Cluny. He built the Romanesque abbey at Cluny, consecrated in 1090 by Pope Urban II, a former monk of the community, which became a model for church architecture in the West.

Letters, *PL*, vol. 159;
A. L'Huilier, *Vie de Saint Hugues, Abbé de Cluny* (1888).

HUGH OF TRIMBERG (c. 1230-1313) German poet. After a formative period in monastic schools, in 1260 he became a tutor in the cathedral school of *Bamberg. His Latin works include manuals for preachers, arranged according to the annual feasts and dealing with a wide range of topics, especially morals. His most important work, however, was a poem of 25,000 verses written in German, *Der Renner* (The Runner). The poem is a long series of reflections on human salvation and the ways of attaining it, advocating moral conduct of the faithful.
H. Berendt, *The Ethical Teaching of Hugh of Trimberg* (1926).

HUGH OF VERMANDOIS (1054-1102) Younger son of King *Henry I of France, he was married on the orders of his brother, *Philip I, to Adèle, heiress of the county of Vermandois. From 1075 he successfully ruled the county in northeastern France, providing an effective support for his brother. In 1096 he joined the First *Crusade and participated until the siege of *Antioch (1038). Sent to Constantinople for discussions with Emperor *Alexius Comnenus, he returned to France. In 1101 he again participated in the Crusade, but died at Tarsus in 1102.
S. Runciman, *A History of the Crusades* (1953).

HUGH, St. (1140-1200) Bishop of *Lincoln (1186-1200). Son of the count of Avalon in Burgundy, he joined the *Carthusian order *c.* 1160. His character and personality were known to *Henry II, king of England, who, in 1175, founded an English priory of the order with H. as prior. He became one of the most intimate friends of the king, who finally persuaded him to accept the bishopric of Lincoln. As bishop, he devoted himself to the administration of his diocese and proved himself to be an independent spirit, defending popular rights against the royal administration. He particularly opposed *Richard's financial demands, thus attracting great veneration among the people. After his death, his tomb became a centre of pilgrimage, second in importance in England to that of Thomas à *Becket.
J. Clayton, *St. Hugh of Lincoln* (1931).

HUGH THE ABBOT (d. 886) Feudal adventurer. Member of the *Welf family of Bavaria, he was a kinsman of Empress *Judith, last wife of *Louis the Pious. He was destined for a church career and entered into a close relationship with *Lothair II of Lotharingia who, in 864, appointed him bishop of Cologne. Deprived of his functions in 866, he went to France, where his relative *Charles the Bald appointed him count of Tours and lay-abbot of a large number of monasteries. He married the heiress of the county and, after the death of *Robert the Strong, was appointed duke of the Franks and charged by the king to fight the Normans. One of the closest counsellors of *Louis II, he faithfully supported his sons.
F. Lot, *La Naissance de la France* (1946).

HUGH THE GREAT (d. 956) Duke of the *Franks. H. was the son of King *Robert I and, on his father's death (923), inherited all his possessions between the Seine and Loire (*Neustria), including the counties of Paris, Orléans and Tours and the overlordship of powerful vassals, such as the counts of Blois and Anjou. His power and influence in France grew with his marriage to Hedwig, daughter of *Henry I of Germany. In 936 he was able to seize the royal title, but preferred to elect the Carolingian *Louis IV, while remaining the real master of the kingdom. His attempts to impose his authority on King Louis IV and *Lothair brought him into continuous alliance with his brother-in-law, *Otto I of Germany.
R. Pognon, *Hugues Capet, Roi de France* (1966).

HUGO (d. 1171) Legist. He was one of the most distinguished pupils of *Irnerius at Bologna and became one of the four great 12th-century experts on Roman *law. Irnerius praised his profound understanding of the spirit of the law. From 1158 H. was one of the legal counsellors of Emperor *Frederick Barbarossa.
M. Clagett, G. Post, R. Reynolds, *Twelfth-Century Europe and the Foundations of Modern Society* (1966).

HUGOCCIO (d. 1210) Canonist. He studied *law at the University of *Bologna and, after a short sojourn in Paris, returned to teach at his own university, where he interpreted *Gratian's teachings. His students came from various European countries and were destined for high ecclesiastical office. Among them was the future Pope *Innocent III. Elected bishop of Ferrara in 1190, he continued his canonist activities and wrote a *Summa* (commentary) on Gratian in which he developed his ideas on theocracy as a political and social system. H. also tried, under the influence of *Isidore of Seville, to explain legal and political ideas by an etymological study of the texts. He developed a theory of the hierarchy of the sources of law which became widespread in the 13th century and influenced theological and political thought.
G. Le Bras, *Histoire du Droit et des Institutions de l'Eglise en Occident,* IV (1965).

HUGOLINO (12th century) Canonist. Little is known of his life and origins. In the middle of the 12th century he began to teach canon *law at Bologna and achieved a reputation as a skilled interpreter of legal documents. His teaching, which appeared in the generation after *Gratian, was widely disseminated by his students, who came from various countries of Christian Europe, and was incorporated in their works.

HULAGU (1217-65) *Mongol khan of Persia (1251-65). Grandson of *Genghis-Khan, in 1251 he was entrusted by his brother, the Great Khan *Mangu, khan of Persia, with the mission of destroying the *Assassins. He conquered their stronghold Alamuth and imposed his rule over the various Persian provinces. In 1258 he began his march eastwards; he conquered and destroyed Baghdad, putting an end to the *Abbasid caliphate (1258) and annexing Iraq to his khanate. Then he conquered Syria and invaded parts of Palestine, destroying the city of Beth-Shean. While his army prepared to fight the *Mamelukes, he was summoned to the *kuraltai* (the assembly of the Mongol princes) at Karakorum, where his brother died. In his absence, the Mamelukes defeated his army at Ain-Jalut (Palestine), saving Egypt from Mongol attack. H., who was a Buddhist married to a Christian-Nestorian wife, was a firm opposer of Islam and favourable to Christianity. He received the allegiance of the king of Armenia and the prince of Antioch, as well as the embassies of King *Louis IX of France and the papacy. He founded the dynasty of the Mongol khans of Persia, which ruled until the end of the 14th century.
M. Prawden, *The Mongols* (1940).

HUMBERT OF SILVA-CANDIDA (d. 1061) Ecclesiastical reformer and statesman. Born in Lorraine, he

joined the monastery of Moyenmoutier and followed Bishop Bruno of Toul to Rome. When the latter became Pope *Leo IX, H. was employed by him at the papal court as one of his principal advisers in his projected ecclesiastical reform and, in 1050, he created him cardinal of Silva-Candida. H. wrote a treatise *Adversus Simoniacos* (Against Simony), which was a vigorous denunciation of the evils of the church, which he believed to originate in the selling of offices and in appointments by lay authorities. In 1054 H. was sent to Constantinople by the pope to discuss problems of church unity with Patriarch *Michael Cerularius. His conviction that no lay authority could be imposed on the church and that Byzantine *Caesaro-papism was a source of the evils he denounced, made him pronounce an excommunication of the patriarch on behalf of the pope, resulting in the final breach between the Catholic and Orthodox churches.
Works, *PL*, vol. 153;
W. Ullmann, *The Growth of the Papal Government in the Middle Ages* (1962).
HUMILIATI (the Humble) An order of penitents, founded in the mid-12th century, whose members followed the *Benedictine rule. They devoted themselves to a life of mortification and care for the poor, becoming very influential with the populace. At the beginning of the 13th century, they played a prominent part in the combat against the *Albigenses. In the late Middle Ages they declined, but some of them were active in movements advocating poverty such as the Spiritual *Franciscans and the various brotherhoods of the 15th century.
DTC, VII.
HUMPHREY Duke of Gloucester (1391-1447). Third son of King *Henry IV of England, he became regent of England in 1422, on the death of his brother *Henry V, while his elder brother, the duke of *Bedford, ruled France. He gradually expelled his brother's counsellors, especially the cardinal of *Beaumont, and imposed a policy of continuing the *Hundred Years' War. His claim to inherit *Holland brought him the enmity of Duke *Philip of Burgundy, who signed the Treaty of Arras (1435) with Charles VII of France. Thus, he destroyed the main political achievement of his brother, based on an alliance with *Burgundy which allowed the English to control northern France, and he opened the way for French victories in the war.
E. Perroy, *The Hundred Years' War* (1958).
HUNDRED Originally, the term was used by *Germanic tribes to signify a group of 100 warriors, together with their families and cattle, who lived together and fought as one unit. During the period when these tribes invaded western Europe, each H. settled in a specific area and was ruled by its own leader, who was called a *centenarius*, the Latin form of the Germanic term in continental Europe. Due to assimilation, the Hs. of continental Europe disappeared by the 8th century, when they were replaced by *feudal social systems. However, in *Anglo-Saxon England the structure of the H. persisted, although it lost its numerical significance, and became the territorial basis of the administrative system. The H. came to denote a community of free-men in a given area, roughly a sub-division of the *shire, with its own court of justice and military obligations. When England became organized according to a feudal system after

the *Norman Conquest, the administrative structure of the H. was adopted. It served fiscal and juridical purposes and was the basis for the representation of the communities. From the reign of *Henry II, the *sheriff was the royal representative who governed the H. and was responsible before the royal justiciar for its administration. The sheriff's clerks kept records pertaining to each H. and these rolls are an important source of demographic, legal, social and economic data on medieval English society.
H. Cam, *The Hundred and the Hundred Rolls* (1930).
HUNDRED YEARS' WAR The name commonly given to a series of wars between England and France, between 1337 and 1453, which had an impact on the political map of Europe at the end of the Middle Ages. Its immediate and direct cause was the claim of *Edward III to the French crown as the grandson of King *Philip IV, but the source of the conflict was actually more complex than a dynastic clash between the *Plantagenets of England and the *Valois house of France. The difficulties emerged from the English hold over *Guienne, in accordance with the resolutions of the 1258 peace treaty of *Paris. The complexity of feudal customs in an age of sovereign states made the situation of the king of England, who was also duke of *Aquitaine, a difficult one, not only because he owed *homage to the king of France for his duchy, but mostly because the jurisprudence of the sovereign courts of justice allowed French officials to intervene in the affairs of Guienne at the request of any dissatisfied feudal lord in the duchy. The situation led to an increasing number of incidents which exploded from time to time into open wars, even if of a local character. Such clashes affected the relations between the two kingdoms, which became aggravated by their economic rivalry in *Flanders. While the county belonged to the kingdom of France, its cities were dependent on exported English wool as raw material for their cloth industry. French expeditions in Flanders and uprisings in Flemish towns escalated the tension between France and England which had begun when Edward III inherited the English crown and made his dynastic claims. The arrangements made between the two kings in 1328, when *Philip VI of Valois acceded to the French throne, did not solve the basic conflict.
Together with a denunciation of his homage in 1337, Edward began the war by imposing an economic blockade upon Flanders and establishing an English wool staple at *Antwerp. This move caused an economic crisis in Flanders. A number of subsequent naval battles ended in the defeat of the French fleet. The intervention of both kings in a dynastic rivalry in *Brittany in 1340 weakened the French and made conditions ripe for an English invasion of northern France. Beginning at Normandy, the English army intended to cut Paris off from Flanders; moreover, under the leadership of James of *Artevelde, the Flemish townsmen drove out their pro-French count in order to obtain English wool. This stage of the war came to a close with the spectacular English victory at *Crécy (1346), where the French cavalry was decimated by Welsh bowmen, followed by the siege and capture of *Calais, and its transformation into an English city. Epidemics and particularly the *Black Death, led to a cease fire in northern France, while the administration of Guienne by Edward's son,

the Black Prince, drew hostilities southwards. The mediation of the *Avignon popes was unsuccessful and, after several raids, the Anglo-Gascon army met the French, led by King *John II, at Poitiers (1356) and defeated the city. The French chivalry was destroyed and many knights were taken prisoner, among them King John himself.

While both countries were weakened by the Black Death, the situation in France was the worse. A major part of its territory was now occupied by the English who, after attaining victory, had discharged their mercenaries; the latter, having lost their source of income, organized themselves as the *Grandes Compagnies and ransacked the French territories. Moreover, a series of revolts threatened the government of the realm, left to the young heir, Dauphin *Charles. Part of the nobility supported *Charles I the Bad of Navarre, who held extensive possessions in Normandy and claimed the throne as a descendant of King *Philip IV; the burghers, on the other hand, demanded a general reform of the kingdom and a share in the government, as a condition for paying their taxes; and at Paris the merchants, led by Étienne *Marcel, rose up against the royal government. The situation was complicated by an uprising of the peasants, the *Jacquerie, which threatened social order. The dauphin succeeded in restoring order and in paying ransom for his father, who nevertheless died in prison at London (1364). His negotiations with England ended with the signing of the peace treaty of *Bretigny-Calais (1362), which left a considerable portion of France (practically all the southwestern territories) to the English. *Charles V's real problem, however, was to restore that part of his country which was left to him. His most pressing task was to eliminate the Grandes Compagnies. The civil war in Castile, where France supported the claims of *Henry of Trastamare against *Peter the Cruel, ally of the Black Prince, was a suitable occasion to do so. Thus Charles hired the Grandes Compagnies for the Spanish campaign; and while the French, commanded by *Du Guesclin, were initially defeated at *Najera (1367), they eventually succeeded in crowning Henry king, and Castile became an ally of Charles V (1369). The English were weakened as a result, and Du Guesclin was able, through the use of guerilla tactics, to recover most of the territories conquered and held by the English in 1362. By the end of Charles' reign (1380) France had recovered both economically and militarily, while England was affected by internal troubles. However, the English had still not been completely driven out of France.

The reign of *Richard II marked a crisis period in England, where the Peasant's Revolt of 1381 and religious troubles immobilized the government and undermined royal resources. The establishment of the Burgundian finally led to the accession of the house of *Lancaster (1399). However, this impasse did not aid France, since the reign of the mad *Charles VI was taken advantage of by his uncles, who sought to augment their own estates and wealth. Of particular importance was the activity of *Philip the Bold, duke of Burgundy. who imposed his rule in Flanders and in the Low Countries, aided by royal resources. The establishment of the *Burgundian state had an important impact on the further development of the war at the beginning of the 15th century. The quarrel between the Burgundians and the Armagnacs led to a chaotic state of affairs at Paris and to a civil war amongst the nobility. It also eventually led to an alliance between the Burgundians and the English.

The third stage of the war, begun with an invasion of France by *Henry V (1414), led to a decisive defeat of the French army at *Agincourt (1415) and to the entrance of the Anglo-Burgundians into Paris. The peace treaty of *Troyes (1419) seemed to favour the English cause; Charles VI was compelled to disinherit his son Charles, while the marriage of his daughter Catherine to Henry V made the English king his heir. Northern France was thus entirely under English control, while the supporters of the Dauphin Charles, who settled at *Bourges in central France, were disorganized. After the deaths of both Charles VI and Henry V, *Charles VII, proclaimed king at Bourges, was in a hopeless position, and the major part of French nobility seemed to be paralysed. Despite the organization of the government of Bourges and the fidelity of southern France to its king, the English, led by the duke of *Bedford, regent of the young proclaimed king of England and France, Henry VI, easily advanced to the Loire Valley. In 1429 they besieged *Orléans, whose lord, Charles' cousin, had been captive in England since the Battle of Agincourt. Under such conditions, a popular movement of resistance emerged in France, related to the appearance of Joan of Arc, a maiden originally from a peasant family of Domrémy in Lorraine. She succeeded in raising the morale of the French army and, by mystical visions which expressed the awakening of a French national feeling, was able to deliver Orléans from the siege and to reconquer Champagne. This enabled the coronation of the king at *Rheims, an action which represented the legitimacy of his government. Nevertheless, Joan failed in her attempt to conquer Paris and was made prisoner by the Anglo-Burgundian armies. Accused of witchcraft and convicted by a court presided over by Bishop Peter Cauchon of Beauvais, she was burnt at the stake at Rouen in 1433.

However, Joan's efforts ultimately had their effect; the growth in national feeling enabled Charles to mobilize his armies, and the Burgundian party was put in a delicate situation. Duke Philip, who already had differences of opinion with *Humphrey of Gloucester, the regent of England, decided to negotiate and proposed a peace conference of the three parties at *Arras; while the English delegation was opposed to a settlement, the treaty signed between the French and Burgundian delegates (1435) was a determining factor in the last stage of the war. It enabled Charles VII to take the initiative and, after a long series of battles, to reconquer northern France and especially Normandy. In addition, after Bedford's return to England, the English army collapsed, lacking a united and decisive command. The conquest of Normandy freed the French armies to man the southern front, where the English still held Bordeaux and Gascony. In 1453 the French secured a decisive victory at Libourne, which enabled them to conquer Bordeaux and to put an end to the English domination of Gascony.

The H. began as one of the many feudal wars of the high Middle Ages, fought by chivalry and bowmen; it ended with the emergence of national states and of professional armies using artillery.

E. Perroy, The Hundred Years' War (1958).

HUNERIC King of the *Vandals (477-84). He was the son of King *Genseric, who married him to Eudoxia, widow of the Western Roman emperor *Valentinian III. H. repressed a revolt of the *Mauritanian tribes and consolidated the Vandal kingdom. In 484 he issued an edict which prohibited the presence of Catholic clergy in his realm, applying the same measures the clergy had enacted against the Arians (see *Church).

C. Courtois, *Les Vandals et l'Afrique* (1955).

HUNGARY Country in central Europe in the plains of the Danube River, bounded by the Alps, the Carpathian Mountains and the Balkans. It originally formed the Roman province of Pannonia, which was devastated at the beginning of the 5th century by barbarian tribes. In the middle of the 5th century the *Huns, led by *Attila, conquered the country and made it the centre of their realm. After the fall of their empire, Slavic tribes settled in the plains, but they submitted to the *Avars, who had established a powerful kingdom in H. At the end of the 8th century, when *Charlemagne defeated the Avars and destroyed their kingdom, H. was split into several parts; its western section, between the Danube and the modern-day Austrian frontier, was attached to the *Carolingian empire and belonged to the Austrian *march, although Frankish influence was quite superficial there. In the other parts of H., the Slavic elements integrated with the vestiges of the Avar population, but these groups were not united and did not establish political organizations like those of their neighbours, the *Moravians in the north and the *Croats in the south. H. was thus vulnerable to invasions of Asiatic tribes from the east and fell under the influence of the *Bulgarians, the dominant element during the 9th century until the arrival of the Magyars (the Hungarians).

The Magyars were a Finno-Ugric nomadic tribe, originally of northeastern Europe or western Siberia. In the 8th century they settled in the Don area, where they belonged to the realm of the *Khazars. At the beginning of the 9th century they established a "Confederation of the Ten Tribes", their first political organization. Under pressure from the *Petchenegs in the latter half of the 9th century, they began to march westwards and, in 862, their first known raid on the German frontiers was undertaken. But the Magyars were mainly concerned with the Slavic tribes between the Carpathians and the Danube, areas where the Slavs had contact with the Bulgarians. In 895 the Byzantine emperor *Leo IV hired the Magyars to fight the Bulgarians and they began to systematically conquer the Tisza and Danube valleys, where they finally settled under the leadership of Prince *Arpad in 896. After eliminating the Bulgarian influence in H., the Magyars became notorious for their frequent raids into Germany and even as far as France and Italy, during the first half of the 10th century. However, they were defeated in 955 at *Lechfield by *Otto I of Germany and compelled to return to H., where the Arpadian rulers began to organize their realm. H. gradually came under the western influence of the *Holy Roman empire. Under *Geza I, Christian missionaries from Germany made important progress, the king himself becoming a convert (975). But the real founder of the kingdom of H. was Geza's son, *Stephen I the Saint (997-1038). Married to Gisela, daughter of Emperor *Henry II, he organized the kingdom after the German model and, in 1001, was recognized as king

by Pope *Sylvester I, who sent him a crown, symbolically named the "Crown of St. Stephen".

The direct line of the Arpadian dynasty lasted until the end of the 11th century. The monarchs imposed their strong authority over the nobility, supported by the church and richly endowed with land and revenue. At the end of the 11th century they began to follow a policy of expansion, resulting in the conquest of *Slovenia, *Croatia and *Dalmatia (1091-1105). This trend created tension between H. and Byzantium, which in turn had its impact on the Hungarian dynastic struggles of the 12th century. Only under the reign of *Bela III (1172-96) were the Byzantines driven out of the northwestern Balkans and was H. able to impose its sovereignty over Croatia and Dalmatia, becoming the most important state of southeastern Europe. At this time, H. imposed the Catholic faith upon the Slavs included in its territories. Bela III also devoted his efforts to the economic development of the realm, encouraging trade on the Danube and the founding of cities, where Jews and Germans became dominant elements. This policy was continued by 13th-century sovereigns, who were challenged by the growth of the upper nobility, the magnates. In order to check their power, *Andrew II issued a Golden Bull in 1220, which granted broad privileges and land to the middle and lower nobility. In the long run, results were other than expected; the feudal nobility actually strengthened its power and was able to check the royal authority. The feudal privileges of the nobility, which included participation in government, remained part of Hungarian law until the 19th century. But for the time being, the measures allowed the kingship to control the magnates. Under the long reign of *Bela IV (1235-70), this policy proved its efficacity. The king was able to maintain unity even during the crisis of 1241, when H. was conquered by the *Mongols, and to restore order after their retreat. His wise policy brought the realm prosperity, based on the growth of cities and the development of commerce. The colonization activities during his reign created pluralism in Hungarian society; while the various noble classes were Magyars, the peasantry, reinforced by settlement of Cuman, Rumanian and Slavic elements, was heterogeneous; the towns, on the other hand, had been Germanized by German immigrants and by the establishment of municipal institutions modelled after the *Magdeburg Charter.

After the death of Bela IV, royal power declined and the last Arpadian kings were unable to impose their authority over the nobles; at the beginning of the 14th century a civil war over succession to the throne divided the country. In 1308 Prince *Charles-Robert (Carobert) of *Anjou-Naples won the support of the nobility and founded the Angevin dynasty of H., which reigned until 1382. The Angevin period was one of economic prosperity and cultural development, due to the influx of Italians and Frenchmen to the royal court of *Buda, which became one of the cultural centres of Europe. The Hungarian Angevins were interested in the Balkans, which separated them from their mother country and frequently intervened in the crises of the kingdom of Naples. As a result, they were made aware of the Turkish advancement in the Balkans; in 1377 King *Louis the Great was able to check the Turkish raids, mobilizing all the forces of his kingdom by an appeal for a war of Christianity against Islam. Thus the idea of the *Crusade was renewed and west European chivalry was called upon to participate in the defence of Christianity.

D. Sinor, *History of Hungary* (1958).

HUNS A nomadic people of Turkic-Uighur affiliation, originally from the Altai region in central Asia. Described in ancient Chinese sources of the Han period as a ferocious nomadic tribe which threatened the Chinese empire, the H. set up their first political organization in Mongolia at the beginning of the 3rd century, and rapidly spread southwards and westwards. But their empire had an ephemeral existence and, after their clash with China, they were divided into two groups. The eastern H. continued to dominate Mongolia under the Chinese protectorate, while the western H. were pushed to the central Asian and east European steppes. It appears that the H. had raided the Russian steppes in the 2nd century, but only in the 4th century did these invasions lead to an actual migration. About 370, under the leadership of their king, Balamir, they crossed the Volga River and attacked the *Goths, pushing them towards the Roman empire. At the beginning of the 5th century the H. conquered the Roman province of Pannonia (modern *Hungary), where they established the centre of their empire. Their kings founded the "ring", a circular city of tents, with the royal residence at the centre. From this base, they effectuated raids as far as central Asia, wracking desolation and destruction, and returned with booty and captives who were reduced to slavery. The Eastern Roman empire paid the H. an annual tribute in order to avoid such raids. In 446 *Attila, their most famous king, organized the realm over an enormous territory covering the valleys of the Danube, Dnieper, Don and Volga, as well as central Asia as far as the Chinese and Persian frontiers. However, during his unsuccessful attempt to invade Gaul (451) he was defeated by a Roman-Frankish army, led by *Aetius, the Roman governor of Gaul. In the following year, Attila invaded Italy, where he was met by Pope *Leo I (at Florence) and his retreat was bought at a dear price.

Attila's failure in Gaul marked the beginning of the H.' decline. The *Gepids revolted and, although their revolt was crushed (454), Attila was killed in the battle. His death caused a split in the empire, as his sons divided their inheritance. They were unable to quell a renewed uprising of the Gepids and so were forced to leave Hungary; The *Kotrigurs and *Utrigurs, European vestiges of the H., settled in the Ukraine, where they remained until the 6th century.

Another branch of the H., called the White H., were a part of Attila's realm and were concentrated in central Asia. In the latter half of the 4th century, they were pushed southwards by other Turkish tribes and thus began attacks on *India. In 485 they invaded the country, reached its centres and destroyed the Gupta empire. They then established a kingdom there, which lasted until the middle of the 6th century. At this time they turned their attention towards Persia. In 557 King *Chosroes I of Persia defeated them and the H. fled to the steppes, where they became assimilated with other Uighur and Turkish tribes. The eastern H. were integrated into the *Mongol population.

F. Altheim, *Geschichte der Hunnen* (1959).

HUNTING One of the most important sports of medieval nobility. Originally a basic occupation of the Germanic tribes, as it provided meat and furs, it was an integral part of their husbandry until the 8th century. From the 9th century it became restricted to the nobility, as one of the fields of their activity, second in importance to warfare. As such, H. became reserved exclusively for men, and from the 11th century it became considered part of the knightly training. From the late 12th century the sport also attracted noble ladies and became diversified, including falconry and bird H. As a noble sport, it lent itself to the composition of treatises, the most famous being that of *Frederick II on falconry.

M. Bloch, *Feudal Society* (1952).

HUON DE BORDEAUX French epic poem composed in the 12th century and belonging to the literary cycle of *Charlemagne. The hero, a certain Huon (Hugh) of Bordeaux, is represented as one of the faithful knights who served Charlemagne and proved himself in the long wars against the Saracens. Huon was also a wise counsellor and knew how to defend his family's honour. The

Hunting the stag, *from Queen Mary's Psalter*

poem provides information on the ethos of *chivalry as it was developed in 12th-century France.

J. Bédier, *Les Légendes épiques* (1929).

HUSAYN IBN ALI See AL-HUSAYN IBN ALI.

HUSS (HUS), JOHN (c. 1369-1415) Reformer and Czech religious leader. Born in the small town of Husinec, which gave him his surname, he was a poor member of the lower urban class. He graduated from the faculty of arts at the University of *Prague in 1393, obtaining his degree in theology three years later. In 1400 he was ordained priest but continued to teach at the university. The following year he was elected dean of the faculty of arts. During this time, H. preached in the vernacular in one of Prague's churches. He also became the leader of the Czech national movement at the university,

which had an essentially German character. After a long struggle, H. succeeded in changing the statutes of the university which, according to the foundation charter of 1378, had granted foreign professors three times the voting power of the Bohemians. The new statute of 1409 rendered the majority of votes to the latter. At this time H. was elected rector of the university and attained the height of his influence.

H.'s theological activity was influenced by the writings and doctrines of *Wycliffe. He maintained that the real church was the body of the faithful, whose conduct made them worthy of divine grace. As a result he faced the opposition of the church establishment. In 1403 H. published a defence of Wycliffe's theses, which had been officially condemned by the church. In 1409

A hawking party depicted on a French 14th-century sculptured ivory mirror case

he attacked the sale of *indulgences, which brought him into open conflict with the emperor, who had a share in the profits. His criticism gained him the enmity of the papacy and, in 1411, he was excommunicated. H. was compelled to leave Prague and found shelter amid the Bohemian nobles. In 1413 he reacted to the papal censure in a treatise, *De Ecclesia* (On the Church), in which he challenged the concept of papal infallibility, charging the pope with having sinned, and claimed the supremacy of the Bible in any dispute concerning faith. In 1414 H. was summoned to appear before the Council of *Constance to defend his theories. The Emperor *Sigismund assured him safe conduct and promised he would be allowed to speak freely and to return to Czechoslovakia following the debates. But after his arrival at Constance, H. was arrested. He refused to refute his views and was brought to trial, condemned and burned as a heretic. His letters from prison to his followers in Bohemia bolstered their spirit and aided in the organization of the *Hussite movement.

M. Rubiczek, *Warrior of God; the Life and Death of John Hus* (1947).

HUSSITES A Bohemian revolutionary movement in the 15th century, founded by the followers of John *Hus. The H. began to organize as a religious community during Hus' lifetime, and were distinguished by their "Holy Suppers", where they partook of bread and wine, symbolizing the body and blood of Christ, a practice opposed to the Catholic tradition. On that basis they were also called *Utraquists*, from *utraque specie* (both kinds). Their original aim was to reform the church and, up to the death of Hus, they were only a religious movement. In 1415-16, however, the movement was gradually transformed into a nationalist and social cause, which continued to maintain its religious tenets. The indignation in Bohemia at the arrest of Hus developed into a broad protest movement led by the Czech nobility and burghers; in 1417 the University of Prague sanctioned the *Ultraquist* practice and thus symbolically joined the H. In 1419 the Bohemian lay leaders threatened to reject the claims of Emperor *Sigismund to the Bohemian crown unless he agreed to implement the religious demands of the H. Upon his refusal an open revolt broke out in Bohemia (1420), aggravated by the joint proclamation by pope and emperor of a *Crusade against the H. During this time, the heterogeneous movement was split into two parties: the high nobility and the university professors stressed the need for religious reform and demanded recognition of the national rights of the "Crown of Bohemia", while a radical party, supported by the poor, expressed revolutionary ideas in both the religious and social fields. The latter, the *Taborites, gathered on a mountain near Prague, which they called Mount Tabor. Under the leadership of John *Zizka, both parties fought the Crusaders and defeated them in 1422, 1426, 1427 and 1431. Zizka's successor, *Prokop, one of the Taborite leaders, even began to attack neighbouring countries and, in 1432, Hussite knights reached the shores of the Baltic Sea. But as far back as 1424 the disputes between the two parties had degenerated into civil war, as the nobles were ready to came to an understanding with Emperor Sigismund. Zizka had defeated the nobles and had continued to lead a united movement in which the Taborite influence was dominant. After Zizka's death (1424),

John Hus

however, only military unity was preserved, while the religious and social differences widened. The *Utraquists* (the term now designating the aristocratic party) sought to reach an understanding with the church establishment; they proposed their articles of faith to the Council of *Basle, where many of the participants were in favour of a compromise. These negotiations had their impact upon Bohemia, where the burghers began to support the moderate line. In 1434 civil war again broke out and the nobles severely defeated the Taborites, felling Prokop in the Battle of Lipani. The destruction of the radical party enabled a compromise to be reached and approved by the Council of Basle in the following year.

F. G. Heyman, *John Zizka and the Hussite Revolution* (1956).

HYDE (HIDE) (Latin: hida) An *Anglo-Saxon unit of land, corresponding to a peasant's family estate, which was supposed to provide for his own needs, as well as for the taxes he owed to his lord. The size of the H. varied according to the nature of the land and the degree to which the soil was developed. After the *Norman Conquest the H. became a sub-division of the feudal *manor. The unit also served fiscal purposes, and was used to assess the feudal tax of hydage, imposed in the 12th and 13th centuries.

B. Lyon, *A Constitutional and Legal History of Medieval England* (1960).

HYGELAC (6th century) A famous Scandinavian leader and the first known chieftain to attack the kingdom of the *Franks. According to *Gregory of Tours, he was king of the Geats, a people in Jutland. He commanded a powerful fleet, led raids on the coasts of northern France and was killed during an attack against the

*Frisians (c. 565). His figure was immortalized in the Anglo-Saxon epic *Beowulf.

G. Jones, A History of the Vikings (1968).

HYMNS Sacred poetry set to music and sung in the course of public worship. Christianity inherited the Jewish practice of singing the *Psalms, which became the basis of hymnology in both the Greek and Latin churches. H. were composed by the Fathers of the Church and, from the 4th century on, their use became general and they were meant for particular feast-days. They were especially widespread in the Greek-Orthodox Church, which adopted them much earlier than the Roman Catholic Church. From the time of Pope *Gregory I, the H. were made part of the liturgy and codified to create liturgical unity (see Gregorian *Music). In the 9th century H. were introduced in the Mass. In addition they were collected into hymnals, which circulated in both East and West, and were also to be found in prayer-books.

C. Blume and G. M. Dreeves, eds., Analecta Hymnica Medii Aevi (1886-1922);

F. J. E. Raby, A History of the Christian-Latin Poetry, from the Beginnings to the Close of the Middle Ages (1927).

Detail of the entrance to the Church of the Holy Sepulchre, Jerusalem

I

IACOPONE DA TODI (1230-1306) Poet. Of noble origin, he was born at Todi, north of Rome, took up a secular life and married. He was involved in the political struggles at the end of the reign of *Frederick II. Continued contacts with the *Franciscans, however, influenced him deeply, causing him to develop mystical ideas. In 1268, after his wife's death, he joined the order and rapidly became one of the leaders of the Spiritual Franciscans. Pope *Boniface VIII ordered his arrest and, during his years in prison, he composed his religious poems, the *Laudi*.
L. Olschi, *The Genius of Italy* (1949).

IBELIN Crusader family which rose to the highest social station in the *Latin kingdoms of Jerusalem and *Cyprus. Despite the legend which related them to the viscounts of *Chartres in France, it is now accepted that their ancestor, Barisan, took part in the *Crusades and, while in Palestine, entered the service of Hugh of Puiset, lord of *Jaffa. He became constable of the county of Jaffa and, by his marriage with Helvis, the heiress of *Ramlah, became one of the most influential barons of the kingdom of Jerusalem. In 1132 he supported King *Fulk against his own master, the lord of Jaffa, and was granted the estates of Yabneh (Ibelin), where he built the castle from which the family derived its name (1136). Known as "Balian the Old of Ibelin", he owned lands extending from the hills of Samaria to the approaches of Ascalon. His sons married daughters of the major families of the kingdom and, in the middle of the 12th century, the Is. became one of the most powerful houses of the Crusader nobility. In 1175 his youngest son, Balian, married the widow of King Aymeri, *Maria Comnena, a Byzantine princess. In the reign of *Baldwin IV, the Is. became the leaders of the moderate wing of the barons of the kingdom and were actively involved in its government. By 1180 they were related to most of the Crusader nobility through marriage. Their dominions were considerable and, besides the lands of the elder branch in southwestern Palestine, included the area around Ramlⁱh, Samaria and the barony of *Beirut. After the Thⁱrd *Crusade, their power increased considerably and they became leaders of the nobility at Acre. Under the leadership of John the Old, lord of Beirut, the family was extended and, at the beginning of the 13th century, one of John's sons, Philip, settled in Cyprus, where he held large territories, and became regent during the minority of King *Hugh I of Lusignan. The other members of the family became famous for their opposition to *Frederick II Hohenstaufen as the leaders of the "Commune of St. Andrew" at Acre (See Latin kingdom of *Jerusalem). As defenders of the privileges of the nobility, they advocated government by an aristocratic oligarchy in which the king was reduced to the status of chief lord of the kingdom. This concept underlay the famous legal treatise *Assises de Jerusalem*, written in 1245 by *John of Ibelin, count of Jaffa. In the 14th century, they declined and the male line died out. The female line, on the other hand, intermarried with the greatest princes of Cyprus and Latin Greece, including the royal dynasty of *Lusignan.
W. H. Rüdt de Collenberg, *Les Premiers Ibelins* (1965).

IBN AL-ATHIR (1160-1233) Historian. Born at Mosul, where he was educated, he wrote a *History of the Atabegs of Mosul*, dealing with the emergence of the *Zengid dynasty. His admiration for the "national" Turkish dynasty of Mosul are also reflected in his second historical work, a universal chronicle of the years 1098-1230, in which he described the greatness of the Zengids, while also providing important information on the history of the *Crusades.
F. Gabrielli, *Arab Historians of the Crusades* (1969).

IBN BAJJAH (Avempace; d. 1138) Physician. Born in Andalusia, he was educated at *Seville, where he settled and practised medicine. His experimental clinical studies served as a basis for a number of treatises which gave him an important place in medieval Arab medicine. His works were also translated into Latin and he was known in western Europe as Avempace.
A. Castiglioni, *History of Medicine* (1947).

IBN JUBAYR, MUHAMMAD IBN AHMAD (1145-1217) Arab traveller. Born at Valencia in Spain, he was educated in various cities of Andalusia. Attracted by the personality of *Saladin, whose fame extended to Spain, in 1183 he travelled to the eastern Islamic countries. Upon his return, he wrote a descriptive book, *The Travels of I.*, containing interesting descriptions of Egypt, Syria and Palestine, and of a pilgrimage to Mecca, as well as expressions of admiration for the personality of Saladin. He went twice more to the Orient and died at Alexandria in 1217.
W. Wright (ed.), *The Travels of Ibn Jubair* (1907).

IBN KHALDUN, ABD AL-RAHMAN IBN ABDALLAH (1332-1406) Historian. Born of a *Yemenite family which settled in Seville in the 9th century and emigrated to Tunis in the latter half of the 13th century, he was conscious of his past. I. received a broad education, which enabled him to make a career as a high dignitary in the various Moslem courts of Spain, north Africa and Egypt. In Cairo he wrote a universal history, which is interesting both as a source of information on the events in the Islamic world, and because of its long introduction, which constitutes a methodological treatise in itself. I. attempted to formulate a historical view of society, based on a critical analysis of its development and not exclusively on religious considerations.
M. G. de Slane, *Prolégomènes d'Ibn Khaldoun* (1863).

IBN ROSHD, ABU AL-WALID MUHAMMAD (Averroes; 1126-98) Philosopher. Born at Cordoba in Spain, he studied in his native city. In 1169 he was appointed *kadi* of Seville and, in 1171, of Cordoba. In 1182 the *Almohade sovereign Abu Yaakub Yussuf invited him to become royal physician at his court at Marrakesh. During a period of persecution he had to leave the city, but he was later recalled to Marrakesh. His wide culture and knowledge of sciences led him to study *Aristotelian philosophy, and he commented on most of Aristotle's treatises. The commentaries, however, were merely preparatory to his own philosophical work, in which he attempted to present a correlation between philosophy, society and religion. As a man of faith, he claimed that a philosopher, in order to attain perfection, has to accept the primacy of religion, but that the study of philosophy can lead to a better understanding of the divine revelation. He concluded that a philosopher has to be active in society and the state. This interrelation of religion and philosophy in his thought resulted in a logical understanding of religion, without dependence on a mystical interpretation. He opposed the influence of religion on philosophy, believing that the study of Aristotle's methods could produce a correct understanding. On these grounds, he rejected the thought of *Ibn Sinna, which had prevailed in Islam until his time. His works were translated into Latin and he was known in Christian Europe as "Averroes". From the beginning of the 13th century, his works had a great influence in the universities and were an important factor in the discovery of Aristotelianism and its development in western Europe. At the University of Paris, a group of philosophers led by *Siger of Brabant developed "Averroist" ideas during the 13th century. In 1270, however, they were condemned by the Catholic Church.

G. Leff, *Medieval Thought* (1958);
L. Gautier, *Ibn Rochd* (1948).

IBN SINNA, ABU ALI AL-HUSSAYN (Avicenna; 980-1037) Philosopher and physician. Born in Buchara, in his childhood he was influenced by *Ismaili preachers who visited his father's home. He studied medicine and philosophy and became a metaphysician under the influence of his study of *Alfarabi. He spent his life wandering in various courts of Persia, and died at *Hamadan. His philosophical researches led him to study the philosophical interpretations of nature advanced by the Greek thinkers, especially the neo-Platonists, who attempted to discover the relationship of the physical and chemical elements in the universe. His contribution in this field was coloured by his religious feelings, in that he considered God as the source and incarnation of the ideal reality. This doctrine had some pantheistic implications, but I. particularly stressed the mystical unity of creation. Under the influence of Aristotle, he added to his doctrine some reflections on the place of man within this system, and especially on that of the individual within the social body. He created a system of thought which had a tremenduous influence on Moslem medieval Christian thought, based on the religious approach to philosophy. His works were translated into Latin, and he was known in the West as "Avicenna".

As a physician, he summarized his knowledge in a basic manual, *The Laws of Medicine,* which became authoritative in medieval medical studies in Moslem, Jewish and Christian circles. He gave particular attention to the study of drugs and their medical use. The manual was translated into both Hebrew and Latin in the 11th and 12th centuries, and was used in the normative teaching of medicine.

G. Leff, *Medieval Thought* (1958).

ICELAND Island in the north Atlantic Ocean, between Norway and Greenland. It was unpopulated until the 7th century, when Irish monks came and established a number of small hermitages which were destroyed on the arrival of Scandinavian settlers in the latter half of the 9th century. The great majority of these settlers came from Norway and arrived in I. between 870 and 930. It would appear that many of them fled Norway because of the tyranny of *Harold Finehair – as related in the 12th-century sagas. The colonization was an agrarian one and large farms were established near the bays, which served for landing. The settlers grew corn and raised cattle, while others continued to be seamen, but one of the characteristic features of I.'s development was its dependence on Norse seamen, who controlled most of the maritime connections of the island. Nevertheless, the western routes and the extension to Greenland and North America were pioneered by Icelandic seamen. From the social point of view, the settlers were free-men who had been used to settling their local affairs in community meetings in their land of origin, and they adopted this system of government in the new country. At the beginning of the 10th century, the isolated farmers began to organize themselves into communities which dealt with public affairs and, c. 1030, a man called Ulfljot was sent to Norway to learn its laws and adapt them to local conditions.

The free-men of the island gathered in an annual assembly which became a legislative organ, while the executive remained in the hands of local chieftains. The assembly was also a judicial court. An increase in the population, as well as the emergence of a group of wealthy landowners, produced a need to modify the constitution, the general assembly becoming impractical. In 1065 the constitution was altered and I. was divided into quarters, each of which possessed its own assembly and an executive of three *gothar* (chieftains). The 36 *gothar* would convene to discuss the public affairs of the island, thus constituting the *Althing,* the oldest parliament in the Western world. Another characteristic feature was the absence of a central executive power in the island, which encouraged the growth of local government but, on the other hand, left the country in a state of official dependence on the kings of Norway. Such a system was an obstacle to the rise of a nobility and an imposition of feudal patterns of society. On the other hand, the introduction of Christianity in the island was a centralizing factor and was fostered by royal support. It began with a mission sent by King *Olaf Tryggvason in 996, which bore results in 999, when they successfully preached to the *Althing.* The conversion began as a compromise, the population being compelled to accept Christianity openly, but being allowed to practise pagan worship in private. For this reason the progress of the Christian church was slow. The first local bishop, Isleif (1056-80), was educated in Germany and was consecrated bishop after his wife's death. With him and his son and successor, Gizur (1082-1118), Christianity in I. was finally organized and gave I. its first permanent institution.

In the 11th century, there was the beginning of a cultural awakening, reflected in the sagas, Scandinavian epic poems which related the traditions of the Norse Vikings (11th-13th centuries), and which were gradually absorbed into the Norse, German and French epic traditions. In the 12th century Latin literature flourished, and Ari the Wise, who wrote on the settlement of I. and its institutions, was one of the best chroniclers in the Western world.

In the late Middle Ages, I., like the Scandinavian countries, became part of the Union of *Kalmar.
P. G. Foote and D. M. Wilson, *The Viking Achievement* (1970).

ICONOCLASTIC CONTROVERSY The controversy concerning the use of *icons agitated the Greek-Orthodox Church from 725 to 842. At the end of the 7th century, influences hostile to the worship of icons gained ground in the Byzantine empire and particularly in Asia Minor, where *Manichaeism and a revival of faith in abstract monotheism appeared in circles close to the Isaurian family. The outbreak of the controversy was caused by Emperor *Leo III the Isaurian (717-40), who thought the cult of icons a major obstacle to the conversion of Jews and Moslems. In 726 he issued an edict declaring all images idols, and ordering their destruction. The edict was opposed by the monks and a large part of the hierarchy, led by the Patriarch *Germanus who was deposed in 730, when a systematic persecution of the defenders of icons by the iconoclasts ("image-breakers") began. At the same time, Pope *Gregory III condemned the iconoclasts. This policy was pursued by the emperors Leo III, *Constantine V and *Leo IV, who imposed their will on the secular clergy within the empire, but failed to win over the monks, who continued to oppose it fiercely and were supported by the masses. In 780, when Leo IV's widow, *Irene, became regent of the empire, persecution ceased and, in 787, at the Seventh Oecumenical Council which met at *Nicaea, a certain degree of veneration of icons was approved and the Council decreed their restoration.

Iconoclasm, however, remained strong in the army and the controversy was renewed after Irene's death, at the beginning of the 9th century. In 814, when General *Leo the Armenian was proclaimed emperor by the army, the iconoclastic policy was revived and the foremost defender of icon worship, St. *Theodore of Studium, was sent into exile. The persecutions continued under Leo's successors until 842, causing violent riots in the empire. In 843 the controversy was brought to an end by Empress Theodora, helped by Patriarch Methodius, a former monk. She abolished the I. legislation and a great feast was instituted in honour of the icons, known in the Eastern Church as the "Feast of Orthodoxy".
E. J. Martin, *A History of the Iconoclastic Controversy* (1930).

ICONOGRAPHY Medieval I. in Europe and the Middle East was deeply influenced by religion. Its subjects were the pictorial or symbolic representation of ideas, persons and history. While in Moslem and Jewish society, symbolism was chosen in order not to violate the commandment forbidding the use of images, which encouraged the development of abstract forms such as *arabesques, Christian I. was solely figurative. Its main concern was the representation of Christ, the saints and biblical themes, which became a part of the artistic trends of painting in the Byzantine world as well as of

western Europe. In the Eastern churches I. was connected with the liturgy, especially as a result of the *iconoclastic controversy and, as one of its consequences, it became stiff and rigid. In the Roman Church, I. remained freer from liturgical connections and, with the exception of Christ, the artists represented other figures from their imagination. Thus, artists executed works of such popular subjects as the "Last Supper". Western I. had an important didactic purpose, to teach the faithful what was considered good and virtuous and to denounce evil. In the 14th century mystical trends had a great influence on I. but, at the same time, the first signs of secular I. which was to prevail during the Renaissance appeared, leading to the gradual disappearance of didactic themes.
L. Réau, *Iconographie de l'Art Chrétien* (1955-58).

ICONS Images of saints, painted mainly on wood, which became popular in the Greek-Orthodox and Eastern Churches and which were the object of worship. Owing to their role in Christian worship, the *Byzantine artists conformed to certain rules in depicting saints, such as a static representation of the figures, whose heads were crowned by gilded haloes. The early I. (until the beginning of the 7th century), were painted in the late classical tradition and the hieratic style adopted during the reign of *Justinian. The *Iconoclastic controversy, however, produced a rigidity in the rendering and made the painting of I. an exclusively sacred art, practised only by monks.
I. Dirks, *Les Saintes Icones* (1939).

IDRISI See AL-IDRISI.

IGNATIUS (d. 877) Patriarch of Constantinople (847-58; 867-77). Son of Emperor *Michael I, he was sent to a monastery after his father's dethronment in 813 and was famous for his zeal and his defence of icon-worship. Created patriarch in 847, he opposed the iconoclasts and was one of the closest advisers of Empress Theodora. In 858 he was deposed by Emperor *Michael III and sent to the monastery of *Studion. A major part of the Byzantine church, however, refused to recognize his deposition, as did the new patriarch, *Photius, and they were supported by Pope *Nicholas I. Emperor *Basil I restored him to his office. During his second pontificate, I. faithfully followed imperial policy and consecrated the first *Bulgarian metropolis and bishops. He allowed a large measure of autonomy to the Bulgarian Orthodox Church, which served as a precedent for the other churches in the Slavic countries.
J. B. Bury, *The Imperial Administrative System in the Ninth Century* (1911).

IGOR Prince of Kiev (912-45), son of *Rurik of Novgorod. As a child, he was brought to Kiev by one of his kinsmen, *Oleg, whom he succeeded as prince of *Kiev in 912. During his long reign, he fought against the Byzantine empire and was gradually recognized by the various *Varangian leaders as prince of Rus, being the first leader of medieval Russia. In 945 he was killed during an expedition against Slavic tribes from whom he wanted to extort heavier tribute than was customary.
G. Vernadsky, *Kievan Russia* (1948).

IMMUNITY (Latin: immunitas) An area or group of men exempted from the jurisdiction and taxation of the state. The practice began in the *Frankish kingdom in the late 6th century, when kings would grant the privilege of I. to churches and monasteries on the grounds that the patrimony of a saint owed no duties to the state. In the 7th century, the practice was applied to all ecclesiastical property in western Europe. In the 9th century, it was adopted in the countries of the *Carolingian empire also for seignories, and became one of the bases of *feudalism, which substituted the lord's jurisdiction and taxation for that of the royal court.

F. L. Ganshof, *Feudalism* (1965).

IMPERIAL CITIES Name given to a number of cities in *Germany which were granted urban privileges by emperors and recognized the emperor as their sole lord. The beginnings of the practice are related to the granting of charters of privilege to cities in the Rhine Valley by the *Salian emperors in the 11th century. It was developed as a state policy by Emperor *Frederick Barbarossa in the latter half of the 12th century, an attempt to create imperial enclaves within the duchies and other feudal units of Germany. In order to symbolize imperial authority, an official, generally the burgrave, was appointed by the court as governor of the city. In most cases, the privileges granted autonomy to the cities, but in many others, authority was given to the burgraves, who established dynasties, such as that of the *Hohenzollern at Nuremberg.

G. Barraclough, *Medieval Germany* (1954).

IMRE King of Hungary (1196-1203). Son of *Bela III, he devoted his reign to imposing Hungarian authority in *Croatia, and tried to profit from the weakness of the *Bulgarian empire in order to expand towards Belgrade and its surrounding area. So as to realize his aims, he conceded wide privileges to the nobility, resulting in a diminution of royal power.

D. Sinor, *History of Hungary* (1958).

INDIA Peninsula, forming a sub-continent in southern Asia, separated by the Indus River from Persia, by the Himalayan Mountains from Tibet and China and by the Brahmaputra River from Burma and southeast Asia. In this great area, populated by various races and ethnic groups, a pluralist form of civilization developed around several centres, most of them in the northern part of the country, which includes the fertile and populated valleys of the Ganges and Indus Rivers. At the end of antiquity, the country was already characterized by this political, ethnic, religious and cultural diversity.

History In the 5th century, I. was divided into two main political groups. The southern territories were dominated by the Satawhana, a powerful dynasty from the Deccan, which succeeded in uniting the principalities of southern and central I. The north, however, was united by the Gupta dynasty, whose centre was in the Ganges Valley. The Gupta empire extended its boundaries to southern I. and, in the reign of Budha-Gupta, the last monarch of the dynasty, the Deccan principalities paid tribute to the empire (496). The empire began to decline after his death and feudal nobles rose against the central authority. In 530 the White *Huns began their raids into I. and the remainder of the Gupta empire fell before 550. From the Indian point of view, the Gupta period remains one of the most glorious, despite the fact that it was a short one, because the unity of the sub-continent was achieved by a national dynasty.

After a short period of raids and dominimination by the *Huns, I. was divided among many kingdoms which fought between themselves and created an age of anar-chy (6th-8th centuries). The political scene was characterized by the instability of the kingdoms, out of which there emerged three empires in the 8th century: the Rastrakuta in the south, the Rajputana in the northwest and Bengal in the northeast. The equilibrium achieved in the 8th century was merely temporary, because of the endemic wars between them, and the continuous revolts of princes attempting to gain their independence. The situation was ripe for the penetration of foreign influences, either from the northeast, where there was an infiltration of the Buddhist Chinese, or from the northwest, where the *Arabs established their strongholds on the Indus in 704 and began the conquest of territories along the frontier. Moreover, *Turkish tribes, converted to the Brahmanic religion, settled along the northern frontier and established their own rule in Punjab. At the end of the 10th century, I. was again divided into ten realms and principalities and particularist tendencies encouraged a return to anarchy. Thus, the attacks of *Mahmud of Ghazni, at the end of the 10th century and the beginning of the 11th, met a weakened country and permitted the *Ghaznavids with little resistance to conquer the northeastern part of the sub-continent, where the confederation organized by the Hindu princes of Punjab and Rajputana collapsed (1021). His raids covered most of the Indian continent, creating total disorganization in the country, except in the Deccan, which was shared by two dynasties. Mahmud also began Islamization of the northeastern territories annexed to the Ghazni state, and continued the process along the Indus. Thus, the foundations of present-day Pakistan were laid at the beginning of the 11th century. The impact of the Moslem conquest was felt in Sind and Punjab even after the fall of the Ghaznavid empire (1050).

In the Hindu territories, and particularly in Bengal and the Deccan, some of the kingdoms were reorganized in the late 11th century, and freed themselves from subjection to the sultans of Ghazni. In the 12th century Bengal was reunited under a local dynasty, the Chahamana. Their greatest king, Pritthawiraja III (1177-92), succeeded in uniting all the kings (*rajahs*) of northern I. and fought against the Turkish Ghorid rulers of Ghazni. After some initial successes, he was defeated and killed in battle, and the way was open for the Moslem conquest of I. The Turkish general Kutb Al-Din Aybak continued the Ghorid raids, and in 1206 conquered Delhi, which he made the capital of his state, the sultanate of Delhi, which existed until the 16th century, when I. was conquered by the Mongols. Aybak and his sons achieved the conquest of the whole of northern India, including Rajastan and Rajaputra in the west and Bengal in the east (1252). They attempted to convert their Hindu subjects to Islam and, for that purpose, established theological centres at Lahore and Delhi, which became one of the most prosperous cities of I. Their efforts were successful only in eastern Bengal, where the city of Dacca became a Moslem stronghold. In the 14th century, under the rule of Muhammad Taglak, the last great sultan of Delhi, his army penetrated into central and southern I. Taking advantage of the weakness of the Deccan monarchies, he conquered their territories, and in 1334 achieved the unification of the sub-continent, with the exception of three Hindu states which remained independent in the southern corner of the peninsula.

His efforts, however, resulted in the weakening of the sultanate, which, at the end of the 14th century, was divided into hundreds of principalities, more or less subservient to the sultans of Delhi. The 15th century witnessed a renewal of anarchy under regional leaders, who fought between themselves. The administrative reforms of the vizier Muhammad Gawan (1405-84), aiming at reuniting I., resulted in a certain concentration of power, but the princes continued to wield the real authority and, after his death, I. continued to be a divided country where anarchic tendencies paralysed any possibility of union or resistance to the attacks of the *Timurid Mongols.

Ethnography and society The ethnic diversity of the Indian population was one of the major factors in its historical evolution. Through a process of racial and ethnic amalgamation, two main groups had already crystallized at the beginning of the Middle Ages: the Hindu group, concentrated mainly in the north, and the Dravidian group in the south and centre. While even these groups were not homogeneous and it would be difficult to describe them as peoples, like their neighbours the Persians, Tibetans or Chinese, they nevertheless created a division between the northern empires and the southern, despite the continuous migration of Hindu elements southwards, where they formed part of the upper classes of society. Besides these main groups, in medieval India there were also hundreds of tribes of varied origins, some indigenous and others who had immigrated and belonged to various races. Most of these tribes did not evolve politically and formed part of the various states which emerged in I. In many cases, such as those of the Negroid and Malaysian tribes in the southern part of the Deccan or the Mongoloid tribes in the northeastern areas, they enjoyed a considerable measure of autonomy. Others founded principalities and little kingdoms which became part of the political maze of the Indian sub-continent and, whenever one of the greater empires declined, they were the first to win their independence. On the other hand, some of the tribes, especially those in the Himalayan region, achieved a powerful socio-political structure and were able to establish independent states, among them Sikkim and Nepal.

The ethnic diversity was complemented by the variety of languages which broke even the unity of the two main ethnic groups. Without mentioning the thousands of dialects, many of them still in existence, the linguistic division of I. could be based on the two great families, the Hindi and the Dravidian. At the beginning of the Middle Ages, the Hindi linguistic group was already divided between Sanskrit and Middle Hindi, but among them a variety of languages emerged. While Sanskrit was the classical language, that of the Brahmans (see Religions), Pali, enjoyed a particular prestige, not only in the west of the sub-continent, but also elsewhere as the language of Buddha and the first Buddhist texts. On the eve of the Ghaznavid invasions (end of the 10th century), the linguistic character of I. was highly diversified owing to the decline of Sanskrit and Middle Hindi. The Hindi languages were: Hindustani, Sindhi, Marathi, Bengali, Assamese, Bihari, Oriya, Gujarati, Nepali and Sinhalese. While they were related in their proto-Hindi origins, their differences increased to the point where the different peoples could understand one another only by means of translations. The Dravidian

group included Tamil, Kannada, Telugu and Gondi. On the other hand, the alphabet was more unified, being based on Sanskrit characters. A major exception was the Urdu language, developed in the late Middle Ages, which borrowed the Arab alphabet and characters.

The most original feature of the Indian society in the Middle Ages was the continuation of the ancient caste-divisions. Classical Hinduism imposed a division of society into four castes: the *Brahmans* (priests), *Kśattriya* (warriors), *Vaiśya* (merchants) and *Sudrya* (workers). This system was different from the class division in other civilizations, being based on a rigid separation of the castes and a strict hierarchy, which continued to exist until the Moslem conquest. Another characteristic feature was the "untouchables", the lowest social group. The caste system remained unchanged throughout the Middle Ages and was in large part sanctioned by the religious structure of the country. But regional developments resulted in a diversification. In the 9th century, the castes in the northern empires multiplied and in certain provinces there were 15-20 castes, most of them sub-divisions of the four essential castes.

The Moslem conquest in the 11th and the 13th centuries did not affect this structure, although conversions to Islam altered the system in the new Moslem territories, but these remained a minority in Indian society. For the Indian sub-continent as a whole, it only created a superstructure of Moslem lords and their followers, which came into being with the establishment of the sultanate of Delhi in 1209. Likewise, the immigration and settlement of non-Indian elements, especially in the great maritime cities and border regions, created a social group outside the caste system.

Religions Religious life in medieval India was on the whole a continuation of the ancient indigenous Brahmanic and Buddhist religions. In ancient times, the Brahmanic religion reached a synthesis between the polytheistic cult of the old Indian gods and a philosophy mainly based on contemplation. This syncretism introduced into Brahmanism an abstract element, as in the representation of the god Brahma as an impersonal divinity. Already in late antiquity, the theosophy of Brahmanism, which implied the existence of an exclusive caste of priests, became the dominant religious philosophy of I. through the medium of the Sanskrit language. There were no significant changes in Brahmanism during the Middle Ages and this unchangeability was primarily due to the caste system, which prevailed despite the great political changes during the medieval millennium. Moreover, the Brahmanic religion spread into territories where Buddhism had been dominant in antiquity, supplanting it completely in Bengal, which became the holy land of Brahmanism, as well as along the Ganges River, which became its holy river. Riverside cities such as Benares were the centres of Brahmanic worship.

At the beginning of the Middle Ages, large territories in northwestern I. were populated by devotees of the Persian Zoroastrian cult. During the first centuries of the Middle Ages, this faith in a duality of divine forces spread southwards, and after the conquest of Persia by the Arabs and its Islamization, the area between the Indus and Bombay became the centre of the dualist cults, whose main characteristic was their diversity. The penetration of Islam into I. was a blow to the Persian

sects, most of which became Islamized, while the remainder, in Gujarat and Bombay, were mainly confined to the Mazdaist and Zoroastrian cults.

The Islamization of I. began intensively in the 11th century. While the conquerors were Sunnites, the faith was mainly propagated by *Shiite elements from *Khorasan, who introduced various *Ismaili practices. As a result, Islam in I. was of a special kind, permitting a compromise between religious practice and the use of Arab characters on the one hand, and the national languages on the other, so that the conditions were created for the emergence of a local Islamic organization, independent of the caliphate and the Arab character of the Sunnite Moslems.

The Christian and Jewish religions, although present in India from the beginning of the Middle Ages, had no importance in the sub-continent. The existence of a Christian-Syrian community was known, however, in the West and was the origin of various legends, many of them related to the "kingdom of *Prester John".

Civilization Indian civilization is always connected with religion, even when it assumes a secular form. Medieval Indian literature was mainly written in Sanskrit and was therefore monopolized by the Brahmans, whether it was prose or poetry, expressed in epic or lyric form. The Golden Age of this literature was the Gupta period, and it continued until the 9th century. Some of the poets, such as Bharavi (6th century), Magha (7th century), Bhartrhari (7th century), are among the greatest in Indian literature. In the late Middle Ages (13th-15th centuries) Marathi literature flourished and developed new themes on classical foundations. In southern India, a Dravidian literature, influenced by the older and more sophisticated works in Hindi, attained an independent status in the Middle Ages (especially the 9th-12th centuries), developing its own poetry.

The main achievements of Indian philosophy belong to the ancient period, and little was added in the Middle Ages. The ancient heritage, however, was exploited by medieval thinkers, both in the sphere of abstract speculation and in that of scientific thought. Speculative philosophy contributed much to the growth of a tradition of quietism, particularly in an ascetic form, brought to perfection in the teachings of Sankara (9th century) and Ramanuja (11th century). They were concerned not only with the nature of deity (in its trinitarian form, Krishna, Vishnu and Shiva), and the meaning of the abstract spiritual concept of Brahma, but also with problems of phenomenology and the relationship of soul and body. The spread of quietistic ideas among the populace led to a policy of passive resistance to the Moslem conquest. At the beginning of the Middle Ages, Indian scientific thought spread to Persia, where it was adopted by the Arabs, who used it especially in the development of experimental sciences such as alchemy.

Medieval Indian art was deeply influenced by the Brahmanic and Buddhist religions. Architecture developed in the Ganges Valley, where in the 6th to 9th centuries the temples took a pyramidal form, adorned with sculptures of gods on the outer walls. The use of columns in the interior not only supported the roofs, but also created halls for the use of the various Brahmanic orders. The sculpture, even the colossal statues of the great temples, particularly emphasized movement. The originality of Indian medieval art lay in the naturalism with which human scenes were depicted, even when combined with non-human forms of the body, such as multiplication of hands. Even when gods were represented in majesty, there was no rigidity, as in Buddhist or Christian art. Indian painting came into existence in the 3rd century in the form of murals closely related to the reliefs in the temples. It developed in an independent form until the 10th century, when its character, style and subject-matter changed under the influences of Tibetan and Chinese painting, reaching its fullest development in miniatures and book illumination.

I. Prasad, *History of Medieval India* (1928);
V. A. Smith - P. Spear, *The Oxford History of India* (1958);
R. Mukerjee, *The Culture and Art of India* (1958);
C. Sharma, *A Critical Survey of Indian Philosophy* (1959).

INDULGENCE In the Roman Catholic Church, the term signified the granting of forgiveness of sins. Until the 11th century, I. was given to the faithful who made penance before going to fight for the church against the infidels, in order to assure salvation of their souls should they fall in battle. The prerogative was limited to popes, who, as successors of St. Peter, were held to possess the keys of heaven. At the time of the *Crusades, however, I. was automatically granted to those who participated. In the 13th century it was gradually extended also to people who, unable to participate directly on account of age or sickness, donated funds. In the late Middle Ages this principle was further extended, and came to include those who paid for the construction of a church. In the late 15th century, popes began to appoint agents to distribute Is. to such people, a practice known as the "sale of Is.", which was criticized by moralists and reformers.

A. H. M. Lepicier, *Indulgences* (1928).

INE (689-726) The greatest of the early kings of *Wessex. He imposed his authority upon the kingdom, fought the opposition of the great nobles (among them members of the royal family) and successfully fought the kings of Essex and Sussex, who offered asylum to the political refugees of his realm. His main achievement, however, was his organization of the kingdom and its institutions. In 694 he issued the first Anglo-Saxon body of law, codifying the traditional oral laws and customs. He instituted the *witan as the supreme council of the realm and organized the administration of justice, based on the principle of the participation of free-men in the courts. He also organized the church of Wessex, which constituted the diocese of Winchester.

F. M. Stenton, *Anglo-Saxon England* (1947).

INEFFABILIS AMORIS Bull of Pope *Boniface VIII, issued in 1396. It was a compromise between his principle that clergy should not be taxed and the strong reaction of King *Edward I of England and King *Philip IV of France. He conceded, "by his great love", that clergy should contribute to the financial needs of the realm when its defence required them to do so.

INGE THE OLD (d. 1110) King of *Sweden (1066-90). His reign was a period of struggle for the Swedish crown. According to the sagas, he killed 12 kings in order to seize power at Uppsala, among them members of his own family. Only in 1083 was he able to rule over the whole kingdom, but the atrocities he committed

6th-century bronze statuette of standing Buddha

provoked continuous opposition to his rule. In 1090 the nobles conspired and deposed him, and he was compelled to flee from Uppsala and remained a refugee until his death.

G. Jones, *A History of the Vikings* (1968).

INNOCENT I, St. (d. 417) Pope (401-17). A man of great ability, firm resolution and high moral character, he asserted the supremacy of the papacy. He insisted that major disputes be brought before the pope and, on those grounds, intervened in the theological disputes of the Eastern Church. I. was supported by the bishops of the Western *Roman empire, among them such noted personalities as St. *Augustine of Hippo.

J. Haller, *Das Papsttum,* I (1943).

INNOCENT II (Gregorio Papareischi dei Guidoni; d. 1143) Pope (1130-43). Descendant of an important Roman family, he began his career at the papal court under *Calixtus II, who appointed him cardinal; under Calixtus and *Honorius II, I. was sent on diplomatic missions to France and England, and there became acquainted with the leaders of the Western churches and especially with those of the great monastic orders, the *Cluniacs and the *Cistercians. In 1130 he was elected pope by a minority of the cardinal college in a dubious election. Failing to receive recognition at Rome and in Italy, where his adversary, *Anacletus II, enjoyed strong support, he turned to France. There he received the backing of *Peter the Venerable, abbot of Cluny, *Bernard of Clairvaux and King *Louis VI. Aided by the monastic leaders, I. gained the recognition of King *Henry I of England and Emperor *Lothair of Germany, followed by that of the other monarchs in the West. In 1134, with Lothair's military aid, he was able to return to Italy and formally assume office. It was then that he proved to be a difficult man, refusing to be reconciled with the former partisans of Anacletus and persecuting them, despite the advice of his firm supporters. His policy led to conflicts within the church and induced a long dispute with *Louis VII. According to many sources, I.'s death was considered a sign of reconciliation in Christendom.

F. J. Schmale, *Studien zum Schisma des Jahres 1130* (1961).

INNOCENT III (Lotario di Segni; 1160-1216) Pope (1198-1216). A member of the noble family of Segni, which was among the highest-ranking in the Roman aristocracy, I. studied theology in Paris and law in Bologna before entering the papal court, where he was rapidly distinguished for his intelligence and efficiency. At the age of 30 he was consecrated cardinal and, during the pontificate of *Celestine III, became one of the most influential persons in the Roman curia. Elected pope in 1198, despite his relative youth, he worked to implement the canonist theory of *plenitudo potestatis* (the full authority of the papal see) in Christian society. Thus he was one of the formulators of the concept of theocracy, interpreted in feudal notions as the superiority of papal power. The particular circumstances of his age, a time when the imperial throne was disputed, allowed I. the opportunity to attempt to put his ideas into practice. However, it must be noted that his notion of theocracy departed from the usual interpretation, as it did not incorporate the concept of universal rule.

As suzerain of the kingdom of Sicily, I. became tutor of the infant king, *Frederick II, soon after his election.

He used his influential position to expel the German officials and armies planted by Emperor *Henry VI from southern Italy. This step conformed with his unwavering policy to separate *Sicily from the *Holy Roman empire, considering their union to be a serious threat to the independence of the papacy. As such, I. intervened in imperial elections, the prerogative of the German princes, and opposed the election of *Philip of Swabia, younger brother of Henry VI and head of the *Hohenstaufen dynasty. However, his support of the *Welf candidate, *Otto of Brunswick, was equally motivated by purely ecclesiastical concerns; in his bull *Venerabilem,* he stated that, although the privilege of electing an emperor lay with the German princes, the pope had the right and authority to ensure the worthiness of the person elected (*principaliter et finaliter*) – *principaliter,* since the transfer of the empire from Greeks to Romans was accomplished through the pope, by the *Donation of Constantine, and *finaliter* because the blessing, coronation and investiture of the emperor were the responsibility of the pope. Thus, at least in theory, I.'s insistence on papal intervention was based on ecclesiastical doctrine. However, I.'s support of Otto and his subsequent backing of Frederick II when, after Philip's murder in 1208, Otto became too powerful and attempted to carry on the policy of the Hohenstaufen emperors in northern Italy, were politically motivated. I. nurtured the claims of the adolescent *Frederick II, expecting his pupil to become a faithful tool of the papal supreme government, since, prior to his imperial election, Frederick agreed to his request to formally maintain a distinction between Germany and his inherited kingdom of Sicily. I. died before Frederick's ideas about the universal empire, as opposed to the universal power of the papacy, were crystallized, thus, the clash between Church and State was postponed to subsequent pontificates.

In areas outside the empire, I. had wide success in enforcing his authority. Under his pressure, the kings of Sicily, Aragon and Hungary recognized themselves as papal vassals. In England, after a long dispute with *John Lackland, which had begun when the pope nominated Stephen *Langton for the archbishopric of Canterbury, I. took advantage of the English king's defeat in France to obtain his oath of homage. I. was also responsible for the reconciliation between King *Philip II of France and his wife, Ingeborg of Denmark (1202), but his demand that the decisions of feudal courts be placed under ecclesiastical jurisdiction, *ratione peccati,* was firmly opposed by the French king, who proffered his own idea of royal sovereignty so that I. was forced to abandon his claim (1205). Like his predecessors, I. also had an interest in the *Crusades. To aid the Crusader states in the East, he proclaimed a Fourth Crusade in the first year of his pontificate, and organized it in 1204. At first, he opposed the attempts of *Venice to employ the Crusaders against Christian states; but, after the conquest of *Constantinople in 1205 and the foundation of the Latin empire, he reversed his stand, viewing the Crusaders' attacks as a means of solving the dispute between the Roman Catholic and Greek-Orthodox churches in favour of the former, and of imposing papal authority in the Balkans and over the Greek clergy.

I. was firm in his resolution to combat heresy. In

order to extirpate the *Albigenses in southern France, he appointed legates to preach there. After the murder of *Peter of Castelnau, he proclaimed the Crusade against the Albigenses, allowing the use of force and the introduction of the *Inquisition in southern France. He recognized the new order of *Dominicans, charged with preaching and with acting as inquisitors and, thus, under his patronage a campaign of destruction and desolation of the Languedoc was carried out.

The Fourth *Lateran Council of 1215 was the culminating event of I.'s pontificate. It brought him the support of both the laity and the clergy of the Catholic world and its decrees reflected the broad sphere of his concerns. As a result, it is commonly accepted that his pontificate was the climax of the medieval papacy and I. himself was hailed as Vicar of Christ, rather than the usual Vicar of St. Peter.

Works, *PL*, vols 214-217;
A. Luchaire, *Innocent III,* 6 vols. (1904-08);
J. M. Powell, *Innocent III, Vicar of Christ or Lord of the World* (1963).

INNOCENT IV (Sinibaldo Fieschi; c. 1195-1254) Pope (1243-54). Originally from Genoa, he acquired fame as professor of canon law at the University of Bologna. His scholarly traits brought him into contact with the papal court, and in 1227 he was made a cardinal. After the long vacancy which followed the death of *Gregory IX, he was elected pope as a compromise candidate. I. initially tried to find a solution to the conflict between the papacy and *Frederick II, but after having failed, renewed the dispute and convened the Council of *Lyons in 1245, where the emperor was deposed and the way was paved for the election of an anti-king in Germany. I. is also known for having developed the institution of the *Inquisition, which he made directly dependent on the pope, in hopes of crushing the *Albigensian heresy. In 1252 he issued the bull *Ad extirpandam,* which allowed the inquisitors the use of torture.

G. von Puttkamer, *Papst Innocens IV* (1930).

INNOCENT V (Peter of Tarentaise; 1225-76) Pope (1276). Originally from Savoy, I. became archbishop of Tarentaise and was renowned for his diplomatic achievements and his patronage of the monastic orders. He died soon after his papal election.

INNOCENT VI (Etienne Aubert; d. 1362) Pope at *Avignon (1352-62). Born in *Limousin (western France), I. studied law and became professor of canon law at the University of Toulouse, where he was chief justice of the city. In 1342 he was made a cardinal and remained at the papal court at Avignon. Elected pope in 1352, he attempted to reaffirm papal authority over the cardinals, who had become too powerful under his predecessors. He also took measures against the Spiritual *Franciscans, ordering a reform of the order. His attempts to reconcile the kings of France and England failed, and the renewal of the hostilities resulted in the Anglo-Gascon victory of Poitiers (1356). One of I.'s most important concerns was the papal treasury, which had lost sources of revenue as a result of the *Black Death. His administrative reform of the Avignon treasury had important consequences. The last years of his pontificate were affected by the raids of the *Grandes Compagnies,* against whom he proclaimed a crusade.

G. Mollat, *The Popes of Avignon* (1954).

INNOCENT VII (Cosimo de' Migliorati; 1336-1406) Pope (1404-06). Born in Naples, where he spent the major part of his career, he was created cardinal by his countryman, *Urban VI, who reorganized the Roman line of popes at the beginning of the *Great Schism. His short pontificate was dedicated to the repression of a rebellion at Rome.

W. Ullmann, *The Origins of the Great Schism* (1967).

INNOCENTS' DAY (Childermas, Feast of the Holy Innocents) Festival celebrated in the Roman Catholic Church associated with the New Testament story regarding the massacre of the Holy Innocents. In the late Middle Ages, the Parisian church dedicated to the Holy Innocents, became one of the city's most important popular institutions. The church's courtyard, designed in late Gothic style complete with an impressive fountain, became the seat of a popular tribunal which had a degree of influence upon Parisian social life.

M. Poëte, *Paris, La Vie d'une Cité* (1925).

INQUEST A method of government investigation in medieval Europe, whereby royal officials conducted inquiries into the revenues owed to the king. The system was institutionalized in Normandy in the 11th century and reached its final form of development in England. The most famous I. was that ordered by *William the Conqueror in 1081-87, which resulted in the writing of the *Domesday Book. Under *Henry II, the I. was legally established and became part of the judicial administration; it was carried out by the *sheriff in the presence of a jury.

B. Lyon, *A Constitutional and Legal History of Medieval England* (1960).

INQUISITION The name of a papal judicial institution that combated heresy. It derives from the medieval *inquest system of government. At first, the church combated heresy and punished heretics by *excommunication, a practice which prevailed up to the latter half of the 12th century. Cases of persecution and even coercion of heretics which occurred at this time were a result of the church's handing over of the *excommunicated to the lay authorities. In the latter half of the 12th century, when uprisings of textile workers in Flanders and northern France threatened to destroy the social order and undermine the role of the church in society, Archbishop Henry of Rheims, supported by King *Louis VII and the local counts, ordered a number of inquiries (1163-66) into the "heretic" activities of the persons involved; convicted heretics were to be brought before the executive power and put to death. At the time, these measures were considered excessive, basically because they were responsible for thousands of executions, and church authorities still preferred persuasion through preaching. Only after 1180, when it became obvious that such moderate measures had no preventive effect upon the spread of such heretical movements as the *Albigenses, *Waldenses and others, did the idea of conducting inquiries gain acceptance at the papal court. In 1184 Pope *Lucius III met with Emperor *Frederick Barbarossa at Verona, and together they decided to create the institution of the I.

Until the beginning of the 13th century the new institution was operated by bishops. The proclamation of a crusade against the Albigenses was followed by a papal decision to entrust its work in southern France to the new *Dominican order. In 1232 *Frederick I issued an imperial edict appointing state officials to seek out heretics and, from that point, the I. became a universal institution. However, fearing the emperor's political ambitions, Pope *Gregory IX demanded that inquisitors be taken solely from the church and appointed several of the Dominicans to fill the positions. These inquisitors surveyed the country, exhorting those guilty of heresy to voluntarily recant. When a confession was obtained, a form of penance, such as a fast or pilgrimage, was imposed, but those who did not recant within the period of grace were summoned to a trial. The inquisitor was usually assisted by a jury of sorts, composed of both clerics and laymen and evidence of the heresy was established on the basis of testimony given secretly by witnesses. Beginning in 1252, the inquisitors were allowed to use torture to obtain confessions. Sentence was pronounced, after consultation with the jury, at a *sermo generalis* or *auto da fé* (act of the faith), which encompassed a solemn affirmation of the true faith. The penalties in serious cases included confiscation of property, imprisonment or delivery to the secular arm, the last meaning death at the stake. The I. was directed only against Christian heretics; action against non-Christians was prohibited.

H. C. Lea, *History of the Inquisition in the Middle Ages* (1888).

INTERDICT An ecclesiastical punishment used by the Roman Catholic Church, which excluded faithful from participation in spiritual activities, although it did not deprive them of Communion: The personal I. was only placed upon individuals, but was rarely used in the Middle Ages, having often been confused with *excommunication. The I. of a particular locality forbade sacred activities in that area. It was put into effect when a community indirectly supported heretics, as a means of pressuring them to denounce the heresy, and when an excommunicated emperor or king visited a certain locality, the latter type of I. being valid only for the duration of the ruler's stay. The general I. was pronounced by popes upon an entire realm with the intention of compelling the population to rise up against an excommunicated sovereign.

E. J. Coran, *The Interdict* (1930).

INVESTITURE CONTROVERSY The name given to a particular stage in the conflict between the papacy and the feudal states (particularly the *Holy Roman empire) in the period between 1075 and 1122. While the real issue of the dispute was the problem of supremacy in Christian society, as defined by Pope *Gregory VII and Emperor *Henry IV, the controversy was technically linked to the practice whereby a lay monarch could invest a bishop or abbot, using the religious symbols of the cross and the ring. The practice had been taken from the feudal system of the lord's investiture of a fief to his vassal, which meant the transfer of authority from the lord to his liegeman, in return for military service and the performance of fiscal duties. Indirectly, investiture also meant the right of the lord to accept a vassal, which, in the church, signified the appointment of bishops and abbots by the lay monarchs. Such a situation was unacceptable to the Gregorian reform movement, but no monarch was willing to renounce his privilege to invest, as this act was a symbol of belonging to the realm and a means of procuring service.

Thus, after Gregory VII's issuance of the decree forbidding lay investiture (1075), a clash was inevitable. The struggle was particularly strong within the empire, basically because the roots of the conflict were deeper there. In other Christian states, the papacy was content to elaborate its principles, supported by polemic treatises. Imperial opposition to the decree caused the excommunication of *Henry IV (1076), encouraging the German princes to revolt; the result was the election of *Rudolf of Swabia as anti-king. The overthrow of the Salian emperor was prevented by Henry's humble act at *Canossa (1078), which compelled the pope to offer his absolution; but the recantation was general in nature and avoided specific mention of the I., so that that issue remained unresolved. Henry's subsequent victory, which caused Gregory to flee from Rome, gave the emperor the upper hand in the I. within the empire, despite the constant opposition of Gregory's successors, among them *Urban II, who succeeded in gaining new allies in Germany and renewed the clash both in northern Italy and in Germany itself.

The disputants seemed to have arrived at a compromise at the beginning of the 12th century during the pontificate of *Paschal II. The agreements reached with *Henry I of England (1105) and *Philip I and his heir *Louis VI of France (1107), illustrate the concessions made; the practice of investiture was to continue – which allowed the king intervention in episcopal elections – but without the use of the ecclesiastical symbols. However, within the empire the struggle continued. In 1111 *Henry V captured Paschal and compelled him to agree that, while the emperor would not interfere in episcopal elections, bishops and abbots would not be endowed with estates by ecclesiastical authorities. This settlement was attacked by the papal court and the great majority of the ecclesiastical hierarchy, and the privilege of investiture was abolished by a council convened in 1112 at *Lateran. The I. then regained force and became a most passionate polemic which divided the church into papal and imperial supporters. Moreover, the conflict degenerated into an open civil war in Germany and northern Italy.

The election of Archbishop Guy of Vienne (*Calixtus II) to the papal see (1119) demonstrated the desire of the Gregorians to end the controversy. Calixtus, a relative of the emperor, enjoyed high esteem and prestige among the German princes, and this was considered an important weapon against the emperor. The pope's attempt to reach a solution at the Council of Rheims (1119) failed, however, and Germany was faced with a chaotic civil war. In response, an assembly of the princes of the empire at Wurzburg forced both the emperor and the pope to negotiate a compromise which would suit "the dignity of the empire" (1120). The settlement, called the Concordat of *Worms (1122), stipulated that the emperor renounce the use of the staff and ring in granting an investiture, but allowed him to continue to bestow the temporalities; in addition, in accordance with German tradition, he was to receive the *homage of the elected bishops before their consecration. In other parts of the empire, such as Italy and Burgundy, he was entitled to such homage only after the consecration. Thus, in Germany proper, the emperor maintained his influence on episcopal elections.

A. Fliche, *La Querelle des Investitures* (1946).

IONA (HY) A small island of the Inner Hebrides, near the western coast of Scotland. In 563 St. *Columba landed there with a few companions, and founded a monastery which became the centre of Celtic Christianity. From this monastery, missionaries were sent to Scotland and northern England with the task of converting heathens and founding daughter-houses. Columba established an important learning centre at I., which flourished after his death and spread the *Irish Christian doctrine to England and continental Europe in the 7th century. I. was a most important pilgrimage centre until the 9th century when it was ravaged by Norsemen.
T. Hannan, *Iona and Some of its Satellites* (1928).

IQTA'A The Moslem form of *feudalism, established under the *Abbasid caliphs. Unlike western feudalism, the I. was not based on personal relations between lord and vassal, but on the bestowal of landed income to army commanders in return for military service. Developed in Persia in the 9th and 10th centuries, the I. system reached its peak in the 11th and 12th centuries under the *Seljuk Turks. Territory was granted to a military commander, who enjoyed its revenues and, in return, maintained the necessary forces to guard the castles; he was also responsible for raising a certain number of soldiers to fight for a given period of service for his prince. The system declined in the 13th century with the rise of the *Mamelukes.
CHI (1970).

IRAN See PERSIA.

IRELAND Island situated west of Britain and separated from it by the Irish Sea. At the close of antiquity, I. was populated by *Celtic (Gaelic) tribes who had settled there in the 4th century BC. Although their social organization was based on clans, they established five kingdoms in the country: Ulster, Northern Leinster, Southern Leinster, Munster and *Connaught. In the 4th century the fifth realm imposed its overlordship upon the others and its kings became the chief rulers of I. During that period the Celts attacked Roman Britain and, at the beginning of the 5th century, established areas of influence there. This was also a time when some of I.'s inhabitants, converts to Christianity, travelled to Gaul to study at the Christian centres. In 432 one of those students, St. *Patrick, was sent back to I. to preach Christianity. He won the support of the royal families and his mission was a complete success; after his death he became the patron saint of I. One of his most important achievements was the foundation of monasteries, organized on tribal and regional lines, which became the framework for the ecclesiastical organization of the island. St. Patrick and his disciples adapted themselves to the social structure of I. and as a result, kings gradually combined their political dignities with the offices of bishops and abbots. However, piety and learning were also stressed, thus creating the model of Irish monasticism, which was subsequently perfected by St. *Columba.

Politically, the confederative union under the Connaught kings collapsed in the 6th century and I. of the early Middle Ages was a scene of constant warfare between the kings and chieftains. This weakened the country, causing the establishment of more and more realms, many of them ephemeral in nature. Parallelly, the peoples of I. began to migrate to northern Britain and imposed their rule over the *Picts of *Scotland. But the chaotic conditions in the country allowed the *Normans to attack the island in the 8th and 9th centuries and to gain important victories, the Danes conquering the south and the Norsemen taking possession of the rest of the island. Norwegian domination led to the foundation of the town of Dublin, which became the capital of Norse I. The Celts fiercely opposed their conquerors and were able to maintain their independence in the island's interior. In 1014 they defeated the Scandinavians at Clontarf and freed I. from Norman domination – with the exception of the Norse enclave at Dublin. The ancient kingdoms were restored although their centres were moved to the new cities founded by the Norse conquerors, such as Cork, Limerick and Waterford. After the Norman Conquest of England (1066) a degree of Norse influence began to be felt in I., where castles were built in the Norman fashion. Several Irish princes were educated in England and brought back new fashions. The earlier political struggles continued, however, accompanied by constant warring and feuds between princes of the royal families.

In 1168 *Henry II took advantage of the Irish civil war to begin his conquest of the island. He defended his intervention in Irish affairs as an attempt to spread Christianity, and particularly Roman Catholicism, in the Celtic countries and obtained papal benediction for his military expedition (1170). During a long war, which caused I. to unite under the kings of Connaught, Henry's generals conquered the island and established a feudal regime. Dublin and its surroundings became part of the royal domains, and most of the rest of the country was granted to English barons. A part of the island remained under the rule of those Gaelic kings who had surrendered and become Henry's vassals, the most important among them being the king of Connaught. Under the reign of *John Lackland, English domination increased and a new nobility was formed under the leadership of Anglo-Irish families. In the first half of the 13th century the local population was reduced to serfdom, and a great number of Irish perished as a result of the repressive policy of the government. *Edward I imposed a centralized government upon I. through the appointment of a viceroy, whose seat was established at Dublin. A local parliament was convened in 1297, and the English nobility was allowed to participate. The church was put under the control of an archbishop who resided at Dublin and the Celtic Church was deprived of its estates and subjugated.

The English conquest and domination was not able to destroy the Irish social structure. The organization into tribes and clans continued to exist in the 14th century and these groups attempted to revolt several times, particularly during the reign of *Edward II. The English repression of such attempts caused the desolation of the country and led to the creation, beginning in the mid-14th century, of three distinct societies: the English high nobility, who ruled vast estates and were supported by an English urban middle class; the "Anglo-Irish" nation, the result of the integration of the lesser English nobility with Irish, being a privileged class, but restricted from high office in the country; and the Irish, reduced to serfdom, some of whom were grouped into autonomous clans.
A. J. Otway-Ruthven, *A History of Medieval Ireland* (1968).

IRENE (c. 752-803) Byzantine empress (797-802). Born into a noble family of Athens, she married Emperor *Leo IV and, upon his death (780), was the regent for their son, *Constantine VI. In 784 she ordered the re-establishment of the cult of icons. An *iconoclastic military reaction in Asia Minor succeeded in driving her from the palace, and proclaimed Constantine VI sole emperor (790). In 792 I. was recalled by her weak son, whom she had blinded in 797, and then assumed the imperial title. The papacy used this action as a pretext for attacking Byzantium, and encouraged the proclamation of *Charlemagne as emperor. In 802 a palace revolution cause I.'s dethronement and *Nicephorus I was made emperor in her stead.

W. Ohnsorge, *Das Zweikaiserproblem im früheren Mittelalter* (1947).

IRMINON Abbot of *St. Germain-des-Prés, near Paris (806-29). His name is closely linked with the *Polyptic of I.*, one of the most important documents concerning the agrarian economy and society of the 9th century. The document, composed under I.'s order, contains a thorough description of the estates held by the monastery, and of the taxes owed to the monastery by the peasants and their families.

A. Longnon, *Polyptique de l'Abbaye de Saint-Germain-des-Prés* (1886).

IRNERIUS (d. c. 1130) Lawyer at *Bologna. Little is known of his life and origin. He taught law at Bologna at the end of the 11th century and became famous as a great scholar in matters of jurisprudence and commentaries on Roman law. Employed at the court of Countess Matilda of Tuscany and, later on, at those of Emperors *Henry V and *Lothair, he is considered one of the founders of the legal school and University of Bologna.

H. Rashdall, *The Universities of Europe in the Middle Ages* (1936).

ISAAC I, Comnenus (c. 1005-61) *Byzantine emperor (1057-59). He belonged to the military aristocracy in Asia Minor and became general in the course of his long military career. In 1057 he led a revolt of the generals against the civil aristocracy of Constantinople and, supported by the church, he compelled Emperor *Michael VI to abdicate. His reforms, which favoured the military aristocracy, incited a palace revolution by civil officials, and in 1059 he was dethroned and sent to the monastery of *Studion, where he died in 1061.

A. A. Vasiliev, *History of the Byzantine Empire* (1952).

ISAAC II, Angelus (1155-1204) *Byzantine emperor (1185-92; 1203-04). Kinsman of the Comneni, he was proclaimed emperor after the death of *Andronicus Comnenus. In terms of internal affairs, he was a weak ruler and unable to control the administration; however, he proved himself capable of fighting the Serbs and Bulgars. In 1192 he was dethroned and blinded by his brother, *Alexius III; but in 1203, supported by Venice and the participants in the Fourth *Crusade, his throne was restored. His son, *Alexius IV, attempted to impose his reign until both died at the beginning of 1204.

A. A. Vasiliev, *History of the Byzantine Empire* (1952).

ISAAC BEN ASHER HALEVI (d. 1133) One of the greatest exegetes of Rhenish Jewry, known also as "Riba". He studied at Troyes and Mainz and then spent a period of time travelling as a merchant. Through his travels he was introduced to several European countries and chose to settle at Spire, where he became famous as a teacher and exegete. I. is renowned for his juridical commentaries on Talmudic law.

G. Kisch, *The Jews in Germany* (1954).

ISAAC BEN JACOB ALFASI (1013-1103) One of the greatest scholars and exegetes of medieval Jewry. Born at Kal'ath-Hamad in Algeria, he studied at the famous Jewish school of Kairwan and c. 1040 settled at *Fès in Morocco (whence his surname Alfasi). There he taught until 1088, when, at the age of 75, he was forced to flee to Spain. He then settled at Lucena and continued to teach until his death. I. wrote numerous *responsa, which became juridical interpretations of Talmudic law, and was an authority during his own lifetime. He also wrote the *Sefer Hahalahoth* (The Book of the Canons), based on Talmudic jurisprudence. For that purpose, he made use of revelant Talmudic legislation so as to furnish the Jewish religious courts with a concise and systematic manual of jurisprudence. I. also sought to diffuse Talmudic learning to the Jewish public through this book by presenting his material in a simplified form and classifying his subject matter on a rational basis. The text was complemented by commentaries, which explained difficult words and notions and clarified legal precedents. The book was greatly popular and was widespread among the Jewish communities. I.'s digest was the forerunner of the great codes of *Maimonides and of *Joseph Karo.

S. W. Baron, *A Social and Religious History of the Jews*, IV (1957).

ISAAC BEN JOSEPH OF CORBEIL (d. 1280) One of the greatest Jewish scholars in 13th-century France. I. studied at Paris and then settled at Corbeil, where he served as rabbi of the community. In this role he became aware of the problems involved in teaching religious practice to the masses, whose occupations left them no time to study the law. For that purpose, he composed the *Sefer Miswoth Katan* (The Little Book of Precepts), in which he condensed the ritual precepts of the religious daily practice. His work became well known and was widely studied.

R. Chazan, *The Jews in Northern France* (1971).

ISAAC BEN SAMUEL OF DAMPIERRE (Rabbi Isaac the Elder; 12th century) Jewish scholar. He studied in the middle of the 12th century at Troyes under the direction of Rabbi *Tam. Prior to 1150 he settled at Dampierre in northern France, where he founded an important school of French *Tosafists. His works are interspersed with those of his students, who adopted his method of making religious practice a part of the social life of the Jewish community.

L. Rabinowicz, *The Social Life of Jews in Northern France in the 11th and 12th centuries* (1936).

ISAAC COMNENUS (d. 1192) Emperor of *Cyprus (1185-91). Member of a branch of the imperial Comneni dynasty, he was appointed governor of Cilicia by his kinsman, Emperor *Andronicus of Byzantium. In 1185 he attacked Cyprus in a rebellion against *Isaac Angelus, and proclaimed himself emperor. Having introduced a powerful regime and having amassed an ample treasury, he was hated by the Cypriots. In 1191 he was defeated by *Richard I of England, who took him prisoner and put an end to Byzantine domination of Cyprus.

G. Hill, *A History of Cyprus* (1944).

ISAAC IBN EZRA (d. 1121) Jewish poet. Born at Granada, he served the local government as one of the highest officials of the court until the conquest of the city in 1090 by the *Almoravides. He then settled at Toledo, where he became one of the founders of the Jewish cultural and philosophical centre in Castile. His poetry, written in Hebrew, is distinguished by the purity of its language and by its praise of nature.

I. Baer, *A History of the Jews in Christian Spain* (1966).

ISAAC OF NINEVEH (d. c. 700) *Nestorian bishop of Nineveh. Originally from Kurdistan, he became a monk and gained fame as a theologian in the Nestorian communities of northern Iraq and Syria. His works on asceticism were disseminated among the monastic communities of the *Ummayad caliphate and some were translated into Greek. I. is considered one of the leading personalities of eastern Christendom, his main achievement being the laying of a theological foundation, while under Moslem rule.

A. J. Wensinck, *Mystic Treatises of Isaac of Nineveh* (1923).

ISAAC OF STELLA (de l'Étoile; d. 1165) *Cistercian preacher. Originally from England, he became a monk at *Cîteaux in 1145. Distinguished by his preaching ability, he was made abbot of La Stella in Poitou, where he composed his sermons as well as exegetical works. His most important work, *De Officio Missae* (On the Office of the Mass), is an attempt to reconcile the mystical trends of Cistercian monasticism with scholarly theological works of his time.

W.Meuser, *Die Erkenntnislehre des Isaac von Stella* (1934).

ISABELLA OF BAVARIA (1371-1435) Queen of France. I. was married in 1385 to *Charles VI and became very influential at court after the insanity of her husband became apparent. Although she attempted to make use of the conflicts between the princes of royal blood to consolidate her authority, she lacked support and eventually came under the influence of the *Burgundians, being hated by the *Armagnacs, who discredited her conduct. A woman of frivolous ways, she was suspected of conjugal infidelity and rumours were spread about the paternity of some of her sons, among them the Dauphin Charles. In 1418-19 she played an important role in arranging the marriage of her daughter Catherine to *Henry V, convincing her husband to proclaim Henry heir to the crown of France and disinheriting her own son, Charles (afterwards Charles VII). After her husband's death, I.'s influence waned and she became a hostage of the English government in France.

E. Perroy, *The Hundred Years' War* (1957).

ISAURIANS Byzantine dynasty, originally from the central plateau of Asia Minor. Its organization was along tribal lines. The I. gained renown in the Byzantine empire during the 7th century as military leaders. They commanded the defence of the eastern borders of the empire, checking Arab penetration. The head of the family, *Leo III, acceded to the imperial throne in 717 and the dynasty reigned until 802. The period of their rule coincided with the *Iconoclastic controversy. The I. secured peace on the frontiers, checking the *Bulgars and the *Avars in the Balkans through their alliance with the *Khazars; while in Asia Minor they maintained stability along the Taurus Mountains and the Armenian borders.

CMedH, IV (1964).

ISFAHAN City in western *Persia, along the main route between the Caspian Sea and the Persian Gulf. Its origins are legendary, but there is some basis to the story that it was founded in the 5th century BC by Jewish exiles, settled by Nebuchadnezzar on an ancient site. The new city, including the two quarters of Jay and Iahudiyah, was founded, however, by the Moslem governors of Persia in the 10th century. I. was a provincial capital until 1055, when the *Seljuk Turks established one of their centres there. It then prospered as a political and administrative centre and was reputed for its trade and crafts, including the making of rugs. In 1222 I. was conquered by the *Mongols under *Genghis-Khan, who destroyed the city, killing thousands of its inhabitants. Gradually rebuilt, it recovered its importance and prosperity in the latter half of the 13th century under the rule of the Mongol dynasty of *Hulagu. In 1387 it was again destroyed by *Timur-leng, who put its population to death. I. remained a small town in the 15th century, having lost much of its earlier importance, and became an important centre of the *Shiites.

A. U. Pope, *A Survey of Persian Art*, II (1938).

ISIDORUS, St. (Isidore of Seville; c. 560-636) Bishop of Seville. Born to a noble family he was orphaned at a tender age and was educated by his brother *Leander, who directed him towards monasticism. During this period he acquired encyclopedic knowledge and became interested in the spread of knowledge, aiming to check barbarism in Spain to defend the Catholic faith against the Arians, who were still influential figures in the *Visigothic kingdom. In 600 I. became bishop of Seville, succeeding his brother. As such, he became involved in political life and worked to attain the triumph of Catholicism and to achieve the conversion of the Jews, an important portion of the population in Spain. His broad knowledge and his personality made him the most important leader of the Spanish church and, in his later years, he even presided over its councils at Toledo.

I. was one of the most prolific authors of his age and his works earned him the nickname of the "last of the Western Fathers of the Church". The most important of his works was the *Ethymologiae*, an encyclopedia relating the universal knowledge of his time. In it he summed up the heritage of classical learning, as well as the early Christian writings. The book's importance lies not only in its content, but also in I.'s presentation of ideas. His material was used by succeeding generations of writers who could no longer avail themselves of classical sources, especially works written in Greek. In that sense, I. may also be considered the last classical author in the West. I.'s concept of encyclopedic knowledge was the result of his analytic nature, which resulted in a thematic presentation of the entries, such as the earth, population etc., divided into 20 main categories.

I.'s other works were concentrated in the theological, canonical and historical fields. As a theologian, he was deeply influenced by the doctrines of St. *Augustine and Pope *Gregory I. He prepared a selection of canons, which became the basis for later falsified laws and caused the *False Decretals of the 9th century to be attributed to him. I. also wrote two histories. The first was the *Chronica Maiora*, a compilation of historical works, being a history of mankind from creation until 615; the passages concerning Spain are his original contribution. His other historical work, the *History of the Kings of the Goths, Vandals and Sueves,* has become the principal source of Spanish history from the fall of the Roman empire to his own day; it is actually a history of the Visigothic kingdom, and became a model for medieval *historiography.

Works, ed. *PL,* vols. 71-74;

J. Fontaine, *Isidore de Séville et la culture classique dans l'Espagne Wisigothique* 2 vols. (1959).

ISLAM (Literally, "surrender to God's will") The name given to the religion founded by *Mohammad, counting its beginning from the *Hegira (622). The basic foundation of I. is the revelation of the Word of God to the Prophet, as expressed in the *Koran. This revelation implies the transmission of the divine will, which is sovereign and has to be executed by the faithful (Moslems). The doctrine of I., based on the Koran itself and the *Sunna i.e., the "tradition" of Mohammad and his immediate successors, the caliphs), contains Arabic, Jewish, Christian and *Gnostic elements. Its central dogma is the absolute unity of God (Allah), who has predestined all things. At several periods of history, God has sent prophets, such as Moses, Jesus Christ and Mohammad himself, the last being the most important, to reveal His Word. The obligatory duties of I., which were established in the early period of the religion are: reciting the profession of faith in God and Mohammad, His prophet; ritual prayer five times a day; alms-giving; fasting during the month of Ramadan; the pilgrimage to Mecca, to be undertaken at least once in the lifetime of every Moslem; and the paying of the *zakat* tax.

Political reasons, related to the dynastic struggle between *Ali and the *Ummayads (see *Arabs), led to a schism in I. The *Sunnite sect accepted the continuous tradition of the faith as revealed through the caliphs, while the *Shiites, the partisans of Ali, focused their faith on the Koran. Sunnite I., which was accepted by the majority of Moslems, developed its dogma by authoritative interpretation, the Hadith (8th-9th centuries). Its elaboration was widely influenced by the Moslems' acquisition of the Greek philosophical heritage and it led to the elaboration of Islamic canon law, taught by the *Uleimah* (the wise men of the religion). Mystical movements were accepted by Islamic dogma, but did not bring about the foundation of Moslem monasticism; mystics were mainly involved in displaying piousness.

The Shiites developed their own practice of faith, which was more greatly influenced by Gnostic and mystical trends and which continued to be manifest in Persia and eastern parts of the caliphate. After the death of Ali's sons, they were deprived of a dynastic succession of caliphs, and attempts were made to discover indirect descendants of the Prophet, such as the *Fatimids, to serve as leaders. Their geo-political dispersion and varying degrees of enmity with official Sunnite I. caused splits within the Shiite sect in the 9th century. One such splinter group was the *Ismaili, who were more active in political and social life than other Shiite movements having a solely spiritual and mystical character.

T. W. Arnold and A. Guillaume (ed.), *The Legacy of Islam* (1931).

ISMAILISM *Shiite sect which emerged in the 9th century and was named after Isma'il Ibn Jafr Al-Sadek, one of the descendants of *Ali, and nephew and son-in-law of *Mohammad. The I. believed that the office of the imam, the "vicar" of the prophet whom they worshipped as a divine spirit, was reserved for Isma'il's descendants and particularly for Mohammad, his son. They believed Mohammad to be hidden away and destined to return to his faithful followers some time in the future. Influenced by Persian Gnostic theories, as well as by Eastern mysticism, the I. interpreted the *Koran in an allegorical way, considering spiritual exercises to be more important than sacred practices. Their religious and political radicalism caused them to organize themselves secretly and to develop efficient techniques of preaching. In the 10th century they defeated some of their opponents in Persia, Iraq and Arabia, when the *Karmatians, who converted to I., created a powerful state. During the same period another, less radical, Ismaili group, the *Fatimids, established an empire in north Africa and conquered Egypt in 969, ruling it until 1171 as caliphs. The I. were united until the 12th century, and after the fall of the Karmatians recognized the Fatimids as the true imams. Nevertheless, an Ismaili sect in Persia developed its own theology at the end of the 11th century and opposed the Fatimids and their supporters, the Nizamids, on the grounds that their conformism was incompatible with Ismaili radicalism. This extremist sect was the forerunner of the *Assassins (12th-13th centuries), a group who employed murder in diffusing their faith. I. spread during the 12th century over large territories of the Moslem world, especially in the East, but it lacked unity and its numerous sects became independent of one another.

B. Lewis, *The Origins of the Isma'ilism* (1940).

ITALY Peninsula and country of southern Europe, bordered on the north by the Alps and in the west, south and east by the Tyrrhenian, Mediterranean and Adriatic seas, respectively. Due to its history as the core of the Roman empire in antiquity and the centre of the Roman Catholic Church, I. was one of the most important centres of medieval civilization, and its historical, economic and cultural evolution was deeply connected with developments in Europe and the Mediterranean area. During the Middle Ages I. was conditioned by the universal trends of medieval civilization as well as by particularist tendencies which damaged its historical unity. Thus, throughout the Middle Ages there were few occasions where I. formed a political entity; most of the time it was sectioned into several parts, each having its own history and independent of its historical capital, Rome, which became the seat of the universal papacy.

After the fall of the Western Roman empire (476), I. was dominated by several Germanic tribes, some of which had settled in the country under the last Western emperors. At that time the chieftain of the Heruli, *Odoacer, served as an official, but ineffective, overlord on behalf of the Eastern Roman emperor. In 490 the *Ostrogoths, led by *Theodoric the Great, invaded I., besieged Odoacer at Ravenna and, upon his surrender and death in 493, made I. an Ostrogothic realm. Theodoric established a kingdom based on cooperation between the Gothic conquerors and the Italian population; the latter was invited to participate in the government and the cultural development of the realm. Reigning like an enlightened despot, he made his regime entirely different from that of the other barbarian kingdoms of western Europe. However, after Theodoric's death (525), the weaknesses of his system became apparent and the kingdom was weakened by struggles over succession. Such a situation drew Emperor *Justinian to attempt to conquer I., with the intention of working to restore Roman unity in the Mediterranean. Generals *Belisarius (533) and *Narses were commissioned for the task, and the latter succeeded in 555. I. then became a province of the *Byzantine empire and was rule by an exarch, seated at the new capital of Ravenna, near the mouth of the Po River. Rome, like other provincial centres, was governed by a Byzantine duke and became secondary in importance. The Byzantine regime was unpopular, as it imposed heavy fiscal burdens on the population, and the Italians felt no loyalty towards foreign lords from the East. The populace therefore remained passive when the *Lombards invaded their country in 568.

The Lombard invasion and conquests led to the first basic division of I. at the end of the 6th century. The Byzantines succeeded in maintaining their rule in Ravenna and its surroundings, as well as in large parts of southern Italy, such as *Apulia, *Naples, *Calabria and *Sicily. Pope *Gregory I took advantage of the Lombard threat to proclaim papal sovereignty at Rome (5900, laying down the basis for the Papal States in the centre of the peninsula. However, the major part of I. was occupied by the Lombards, who established an elective kingdom with a northern centre around their new capital of *Pavia. The northern part of the country thus came to be called Lombardy. The Lombard kingdom was weak and royal authority was mainly exercised in the north. Elsewhere semi-independent Lombard duchies were formed and had their own historical evolution; these included *Benevento in the south, *Spoleto in the central region and *Friuli at the extreme northeast. The 8th-century *iconoclastic controversy at Byzantium lent the papacy occasion to emancipate I. from Byzantine overlordship. In the middle of the 8th century the exarchate of Ravenna collapsed and Byzantine rule in northeastern I. was brought to an end. To avoid the consolidation of the Lombard state, the papacy appealed to the *Franks. Under *Pepin the Short, who recognized the territorial claims of the popes over the regions between Rome and Ravenna (755), the Franks began to infiltrate I. Moreover, Arab raids in Sicily weakened Byzantine rule in that part of the country.

Under Pepin the Short, Frankish influence was felt only politically. Marriages negotiated between the royal families created a balance of power, but this was destroyed by the alliance of Pope *Adrian I and *Charlemagne. The latter conquered the Lombard kingdom (744) and the duchies — with the exception of Benevento, where the local dynasty was allowed to maintain its government as vassals of the king. These conquests made the majority of I. a part of the *Carolingian realm and (from 800) empire. Charlemagne, having appointed one of his sons, *Pepin, as king of I., employed Frankish and Allemani counts in the administration. These nobles ruled over the kingdom, which became a Frankish dependency. Thus, the foundation of the Carolingian em-

pire had its impact on the historical evolution of I. Charlemagne, his son, *Louis the Pious, and his grandson, *Lothair, reigned from their palaces north of the Alps, interfering in papal affairs and appointing members of a turbulent nobility to govern parts of the country. In consequence, 9th-century I. was threatened by anarchy and particularism. A city like *Venice became an independent maritime republic; northern provinces, such as Verona, were alternately attached to and detached from German duchies; and Lombardy and the central part of the peninsula were disputed between Frankish dukes and relatives of the Carolingian dynasty. The Lombards of Benevento followed the same trends and their duchy was divided into several principalities. Arab raids reinforced anarchic trends and led to the conquests of Sicily and Apulia by the north African *Aghlabids. The remaining Byzantine enclaves at Naples, Salerno and their surroundings became autonomous. At the end of the 9th century and during the 10th, when Carolingian kings ceased to claim the imperial crown and most of the dynasty's branches became extinct, the dukes of Spoleto and Friuli, as well as the kings of Provence, struggled amongst themselves over the imperial crown. At the same time, aristocratic families, and especially the house of *Theophylactus, imposed their rule over the papacy.

The intervention of *Otto I, which began in 951 and increased after his imperial coronation in 962, led to the establishment of German rule in I., politically uniting the country to the rest of the *Holy Roman empire. Until the beginning of the 11th century the Ottonian emperors were able to impose their authority over northern and central I., including the Papal States, while anarchy prevailed in the south. The establishment of the Holy Roman empire caused a decline in importance of many of the feudal families, which, beginning at the close of the 9th century, divided the counties of northern and central I. amongst themselves. Parts of these families became integrated, through marriage and inheritance, with German noble families, while others began to settle in the cities.

Urban settlement increased in northern I. during the 11th century, bringing about the rise of the cities as political centres, a trend which differed from the evolution of feudal Europe north of the Alps. The rise of the cities, where landed aristocracy and wealthy merchants gained power, contributed a new divisive factor to a badly split I. However, at the same time new forces, opposed to imperial rule, began to emerge and to form into communal movements. Uprisings of cities (particularly *Milan) seeking independence prompted emperors, such as *Conrad II and *Henry III, to organize military expeditions against them. However, this only intensified the opposition to the empire in northern Italy. Until the middle of the 11th century, however, the communal movement was still in its infancy. The development of international trade in the Mediterranean encouraged the growth of the cities of northern Italy and by the latter half of the century, the institution of the city-state, with its fleet, armies and communal leadership, began to spread throughout the country. Thus, cities like *Genoa, *Pisa and *Amalfi gained their independence, while economic interdependence with cities in the interior brought the communal movement in I. to political maturity — which was not yet the case in other European countries. Furthermore, the *Investiture controversy between the empire and the papacy encouraged the spread of communal particularism in northern I. since the cities benefited from the struggle, which destroyed most of the remaining feudal principalities, such as the marquisate of *Tuscany. Only at the northwestern border of I. did feudal principalities such as *Savoy, *Montferrat and other small counties, continue to exist in the 12th century.

While northern and central I. of the 11th and 12th centuries was faced with disunity and disintegration the south, after experiencing a period of anarchy at the beginning of the 11th century, became united under the *Normans. The Norman bands first landed in the country in 1018, coming from Normandy in France; the adventurers gradually formed their own principality and, under the leadership of *Robert Guiscard, united the whole country, which became the principality of the house of *Hauteville. Between 1060 and 1071, Sicily and Apulia were conquered from the Arabs and Byzantines respectively, and the Norman realm was organized at the end of the 11th century by *Roger I, Robert's brother. In 1130 his grandson, *Roger II, became ruler of Sicily and established a powerful kingdom in southern I.; his realm became the most prosperous state of 12th-century Europe. It was organized along feudal social structures which were integrated into a strong royal administration, modelled after the Byzantine and Arab systems of government.

The century of *Hohenstaufen rule (1137-1268) was one of the most significant periods in the history of I. The dynasty's attempt to restore the universal empire caused its members to clash with the papacy in a struggle for supremacy in Europe. I. was the main battlefield, precisely because the realization of the Holy Roman empire implied the exercising of imperial authority in I. The principles elaborated in 1158 at the Diet of *Roncaglia by *Frederick Barbarossa incited the cities into open opposition, as their freedom was threatened. Frederick's military campaign, which ended in 1161 with the destruction of Milan, marked only the completion of one stage of the struggle. The cities reacted by forming a confederation of the *Guelph *Lombard League, supported by the papacy. Battles raged for twenty years and neither the league nor the emperor was able to obtain a decisive victory. A compromise was eventually reached which granted the cities a large degree of autonomy under imperial sovereignty, but this did not resolve the conflict. Meanwhile, *Henry VI, heir to the imperial throne, was married to Constance of Sicily, daughter of Roger II, and the peninsula was politically united under his rule, which was a blow to the papacy. The fact that Henry died leaving an infant son, *Frederick II (1198), allowed Pope *Innocent III to attempt to separate Sicily from the Holy Roman empire by encouraging the election of *Otto IV of Brunswick as emperor. Otto, however, revealed himself to be a supporter of the Hohenstaufen policy in I. and the pope was forced to seek out young Frederick and convince him to contest the German election. His hopes that the new emperor would be a tool of the papacy proved unfounded and Frederick became the most dangerous foe of the papacy, attempting to unite I. under his own rule. He was able to defeat the cities several times, as internal struggles had emerged there, dividing the city lea-

ders into Guelph and *Ghibelline factions. The emperor's death in 1250 put an end to the dreams of the unification of I.; the country was split into a multitude of city-states which fought amongst themselves. Sicily was invested to *Charles of Anjou, who established a new dynasty in the south, but following the Sicilian *Vespers (1282) he was compelled to retire to Naples and the island became an *Aragonese realm. This division continued until the end of the Middle Ages, and it led to Aragonese intervention in Italian affairs. The papacy itself was weakened by its long struggle with the empire and fell under French influence, which finally caused it to be relocated at *Avignon in southern France (1305).

The complete independence of the cities in northern and central I. in the latter half of the 13th century and at the beginning of the 14th brought about internal political and social warfare, creating conditions of instability. Political thinkers and intellectuals, such as *Dante and *Marsiglio of Padua, openly expressed their desires for a restoration of the empire in reaction to the failure of the communal regime. On the other hand, the economic prosperity of the cities led, to some extent, to the development of a conservative policy meant to prevent and repress social uprisings. For these reasons, foreign mercenary captains, the *condottieri, were hired in the 14th century. The age of the *condottieri was characterized by the rise of new oligarchies. New principalities were created, many of them under the rule of the condottieri themselves, others governed by local dynasties such as the *Visconti at Milan. While most of the principalities were short-lived, some imposed their overlordship upon the surrounding provinces and used the mercenary armies to create real states; their brilliant courts became artistic and intellectual centres of 15th-century Renaissance I. Among these central principalities, the most important were Milan, Florence, Venice (which established its rule over northeastern I.), Genoa, Este and Ferrara. In the northwestern part of the country, the counts (later dukes) of Savoy created a powerful principality in Piedmont. The *Papal States continued to be an ecclesiastical state, ruling large provinces in central I., while, in the south, the kingdoms of Sicily and Naples remained separated.

J. K. Hyde, *Society and Politics in Medieval Italy* (1973).

ITIL City on the Volga River, north of the Caspian Sea. Situated on the ancient trade and invasion routes between Central Asia and Europe, from the 4th century, the city served as a station for merchants. The *Khazars rebuilt it, making it their capital in the 7th century. During this period the city prospered and was the most important settlement in eastern Europe, serving also as the cross-roads of the empire. Although destroyed by the *Russians during their raid of 965, I. was reconstructed, but it did not regain its past prosperity. It gradually declined and was deserted in the 12th century.

Ibn Khordadbeh, *The Book of Roads and Countries,* ed. M. J. de Goeje (1889).

ITINERANT JUSTICES Judicial practice in medieval England, developed as part of the activities of the royal court. During the reign of *Henry I, royal officials were sent to courts of the shires to hear pleas and to administer the king's justice. The institution was further developed in the reign of *Henry II. The judges dealt also with administrative tasks, such as checking up after the sheriffs and inquiring into local conditions.

B. Lyon, *A Constitutional and Legal History of Medieval England* (1960).

IVAN I, Assen (Kalojan; d. 1207)   Tsar of *Bulgaria (1197-1207). Member of the Assen dynasty, he renewed Bulgaria's independence from the Byzantine empire. Cruelty, coupled with military skills, allowed him to revamp the political organization of the Bulgarians along the Danube. He was crowned tsar in 1197 and, defeating the Byzantines and the Serbs, recovered the provinces of the first Bulgarian empire, destroyed in 1014. In 1203 he entered into relations with Rome and received a legate from Pope *Innocent III, who consecrated a Bulgarian archbishop, a move destined to symbolize Bulgaria's independence from Constantinople. He defeated the participants in the Fourth *Crusade and, while on his way to besiege *Thessalonica, was murdered by one of his officials who acted at the instigation of his wife.

W. N. Slatarski, *Geschichte der Bulgaren* (1918).

IVAN II, Assen (d. 1241)   Tsar of *Bulgaria (1218-41). Nephew of Kalojan, he fled after his uncle's murder and was brought up by the Cumans (inhabitants of what is today Rumania). His claims to the throne, occupied by *Boril, were supported by *Manichaeans and other dissident factions and he was thus denounced by the church hierarchy. Capitalizing on the rising unpopularity of Boril and supported by Russian soldiers, he conquered the capital, Tirnovo, in 1218 and was proclaimed tsar. He was one of the greatest monarchs of Bulgaria, making Tirnovo an important cultural centre, reorganizing the administration and finances, bringing internal peace and, thereby, economic development and prosperity. His external policy was marked by a series of alliances with *Hungary, the empire of *Nicaea and *Epirus. But he would break these alliances when it suited him. He fought against Epirus, and after his victory at Kolonitsa in 1230, enlarged his territories from the Carpathian Mountains in the north to the Aegean Sea in the south. In continuous rivalry with the papacy, he separated the Bulgarian patriarchate from Rome.

W. N. Slatarski, *Geschichte der Bulgaren* (1918).

IVAN I (Kalita; 1304-41)   Prince of Moscow (1328-41). A descendant of the dynasty of *Rurik, he inherited the principality of Moscow from his father, Daniel, and swore fealty to the overlord, the *Mongol khan of the *Golden Horde. Together with his investiture, he obtained the privilege to collect the tribute owed by the Russian princes to the Mongols, which put him in a strong position, and made Moscow the central principality in Russia. Strictly observing the rules of the khans, I. devoted himself to developing his principality, encouraging settlement and economic activity. As a result, he is considered the founder of Muscovite power in Russia.

G. Vernadsky, *The Mongols and Russia* (1953).

IVAN II (1326-59)   Prince of Moscow (1353-59). Second son of *Ivan I, he succeeded his elder brother, Simeon, and continued his father's policy. At his death, Moscow was the most powerful of the Russian principalities.

IVANKO BESARABA   Prince of *Wallachia (1310-30). Member of a rich family in the Carpathians, he organized the principality of *Wallachia, situated between the Danube and the Carpathians, and successfully fought the Hungarians, who had claimed suzerainty over the country. I. ensured Wallachian independence by adopting the Bulgarian social system; even the church was organized according to Bulgarian Orthodox practices.

IVO, St. (1040-1116)   Bishop of Chartres (1090-1116). Born in northeastern France, he was educated at Paris and Bec (Normandy) and gained fame as a great *canonist. Prior of the collegiate abbey of St. Quentin at Beauvais, he began to interpret canon law, and continued his work at Chartres after his election as bishop. Involved in the policy of Church and State, he opposed King *Philip I.'s adulterous marriage. I., who was a moderate Gregorian, was an important papal counsellor who encouraged a relationship of understanding between Church and State, which he attempted to implement during the reign of King *Louis VI. He was the greatest canonist before *Gratian and composed two authoritative canonical collections. The *Decree,* a work containing 17 volumes, incorporated the texts of canon law which were arranged according to subject. Special importance was attached to the principles of the interpretation of canon law, on which I. elaborated in his *Prologus* to the *Decree.* These principles were adopted by Catholic canonists and were taught in schools and universities. The second collection, *Panormia,* an analytic summary of canon law, was a manual for use by ecclesiastical judges. It freed them from the need to refer to the original texts in clear-cut cases where interpretation was not required.

Works, ed. *PL*, vols. 161-162;
R. Sprandel, *Ivo von Chartres und seine Stellung in der Kirchengeschichte* (1962).

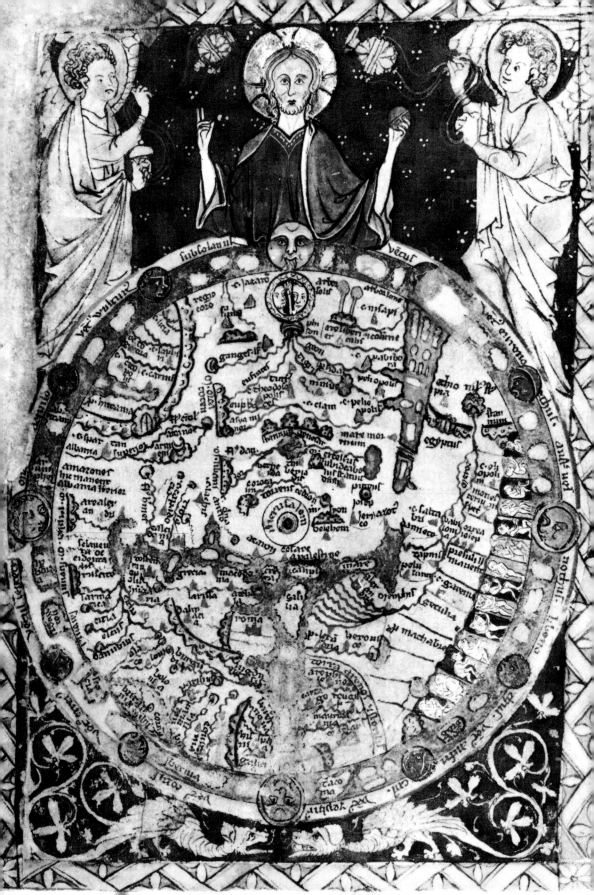

J

JACOB ANATOLI (d. 1237) Jewish philosopher and translator. Born and educated in Spain, where he became closely acquainted with Arabic sources, he settled in Provence and there earned a reputation for his translations of *Ibn Rushd into Hebrew. In 1132 he was invited to join the court of *Frederick II in Sicily and to translate Ptolemy's *Almagest* for the emperor. He also collaborated with *Michael Scot and was one of the most prominent translators of Arabic philosophy and science into Latin and Hebrew.
C. H. Haskins, *Studies in the History of Medieval Science* (1927).

JACOB BARADEUS (c. 500-78) The founder of the *Jacobites. Born at Tella in northern Mesopotamia, J. became a *Monophysite monk. In 528 he was sent to Constantinople to plead their cause before Empress Theodora. He remained there until 540 and by that time had been consecrated bishop of Edessa. J. fled the capital in disguise to avoid arrest. He spent the rest of his life wandering and founding Monophysite communities in Syria, Egypt and Mesopotamia.
A. Kugener, *Jacob Baradeus* (1902).

JACOB BEN ASHER (c. 1270-1340) Jewish exegete. Son of *Asher ben Yehiel, he was born in Germany and received his education at his father's school. In 1304 J. followed his father to Spain and settled at Toledo, where he became reputed for his commentaries on the Bible and on Talmudic treatises. He also compiled his father's *Responsa. J. was an active moralist who tried to unite the *Ashkenazi and *Sephardi heritages regarding Jewish ethics.
A. Freimann, *Ascher ben Iechiel* (1918).

JACOB BEN MEIR TAM (1100-71) The greatest Jewish scholar in France of the 12th century. J. was educated at the school of *Rashi, his grandfather, at Troyes and, after his formative years, settled in the small town of Ramerupt (*Champagne). There he prepared and sold wine and was also active in money-lending. His business associations brought him into close contact with county authorities as well as with large portions of the population. As a result he developed skills for bargaining and negotiating. J. had become a wealthy man by the time he left Ramerupt in 1146 to settle at Troyes. There he became leader of his community and devoted his time to scholarly activity. He wrote a series of commentaries on the Talmud and was mainly concerned with demonstrating the concurrence of the authorities, as opposed to discussing the varied ideas of the many sources. J.'s scholarship became well known and he was consulted by the greatest rabbis of his time on various topics concerning the daily life of Jews within their communities and their relations with their Christian neighbours. His *Responsa, which became authoritative, are scholarly treatises offering answers based on earlier interpreta-

tions. His grandfather's important library of authorities was, in that respect, greatly beneficial to his activities. From 1160 until his death, J. presided at assemblies of delegations of the Jewish communities, first only of Champagne and then of all of northern France. Such assemblies generally dealt with everyday business. J.'s decisions were binding and recognized by the communities of France, Lorraine, the Rhine Valley and England. Aside from the numerous activities mentioned above, J. wrote biblical commentaries and hymns.
L. Finkelstein, *Jewish Self-Government in the Middle Ages* (1924).

JACOB OF EDESSA (640-708) *Monophysite scholar and exegete. In 684 he became bishop of Edessa, but in 690 left his dignity and devoted himself to scholarly activity. His main achievements were commentaries on the Syriac version of the Bible. He used Greek and older Syriac sources, as well as the Hebrew text of the Old Testament for this purpose. J. also wrote a continuation of the Chronicle of Eusebius of Caesarea (4th century), which was a history of the Syriac churches. He is also known as the composer of a number of liturgical hymns.
E. Tisserant, *Jacques d'Edesse* (1924).

JACOB OF VORAGINE (c. 1230-98) The author of the *Legenda aurea* (*Golden Legend). Born at Varazze near Genoa, he entered the *Dominican order in 1244 and, after completing his education, devoted himself to preaching. In 1267 J. became provincial of Lombardy, an office he held until 1285. He was made archbishop of Genoa in 1292. J. wrote a Chronicle of Genoa, describing ancient times up to 1296, as well as sermons for the ecclesiastical year, but was most famous for his Golden Legend.

JACOBITES An eastern Christian church which united with the *Monophysites in the 6th and 7th centuries, taking its name from *Jacob Baradeus. The J. were persecuted by the Greek-Orthodox establishment for their Monophysite beliefs and by the Byzantine authorities for their Syriac particularism. Imperial persecution could not repress their activity, however, and, thanks to their monks, they became a powerful organization which lost all interest in the defence of the Byzantine empire. They therefore remained passive and even helped the Arabs to conquer Syria and Egypt (636-41). After the Arab conquest, religious persecutions came to an end; however, the process of Islamization took its toll and the movement decreased in number. In the 8th century internal divisions weakened the Jacobite church and further reduced the number of followers, who were mainly concentrated in northern Syria, around Edessa and in Palestine.
D. Attwaker, *The Dissident Eastern Churches* (1937).

JACOPO DA LENTINO (d. c. 1250) Sicilian poet. Born at Lentino in eastern Sicily, he distinguished himself by his poems and sonnets. He was received at the court of Emperor *Frederick II at Palermo and became one of the monarch's secretaries. His poems of that later period contain a number of courtly verses praising the emperor.

C. H. Haskins, *Studies in Medieval Science* (1927).

JACOPONE DA TODI See IACOPONE DA TODI.

JACQUEMART OF HESDIN (14th century) Painter. Born at Hesdin (Flanders), J. came to Paris *c.* 1370 and worked there under the guidance of André *Beauneveu, who introduced him to the royal court. Patronized by the duke of *Berry from 1380, J. specialized in miniatures and became famous for his illustrations of the *Grandes *Heures.* His work was inspired by the realism of Late Gothic painting.

R. de Lasteyrie, *Les Miniatures d'André Beauneveu et de Jacquemart de Hesdin* (1896).

JAQUERIE Peasant uprising in *France. The term derived from Jacques, a name commonly associated with the French peasant. The revolt broke out in 1358 in northeastern France in reaction to the social and economic changes which the nobility had imposed upon the peasants following the *Black Death. However, it was also connected with the difficulties France was experiencing after its defeat at the Battle of *Poitiers (1356). New taxes had to be raised and it was the peasant who was most heavily burdened. The nature of the J. was sharply violent. Under their leader, Guillaume Cale, the rebels attempted to attack Paris, expecting to join in the burghers' revolt headed by Etienne *Marcel. The J. only succeeded in uniting the nobility and the burghers and, as a result, the revolt was cruelly crushed.

G. Duby and A. Mandrou, *History of the French Civilization* (1963).

JAEN City in northern Andalusia, Spain. J. prospered under Arab rule and became an important commercial centre connecting southern Spain and Toledo. After the collapse of the caliphate of *Córdoba (1011), the city became the capital of an independent Moslem emirate. The local dynasty survived until the 13th century and enjoyed a large degree of autonomy under the *Almoravide and *Almohade sultans. After the defeat of the Almohades at *Las Navas de Tolosa (1211), J. became a frontier state between Moslem Spain and *Castile and gradually lost its northern territories. In 1246 King *Ferdinand III of Castile conquered the city and annexed it to his kingdom.

A. Castro, *The Structure of Spanish History* (1954).

JAFFA City and harbour in *Palestine. Under *Byzantine rule, J. was a small fishing settlement largely dependent on *Caesarea, the great capital and harbour. After the Arab conquest (640) and the decline of Caesarea, J. became the main harbour of the new capital, *Ramlah, and of *Jerusalem and was frequented by pilgrims. Its population grew and its commerce prospered as a result. In 1099 J. was conquered by the *Crusaders. It became the main base of provisions and logistic supply for the *Pisan fleet and was indispensable in the siege and conquest of Jerusalem. Despite difficulties of access to its rocky harbour, J. remained the main point connecting the Crusader realm to western Europe until the conquest of *Acre in 1104. Even afterwards J. continued to be a major harbour of the kingdom and was enfeoffed to the *Puiset family of France, whose members bore the title, counts of J. In 1132 J. was annexed

to the royal demesne by King *Fulk of Anjou and given as an *apanage to his younger son. In 1187 it was conquered by *Saladin, but regained by *Richard I of England in 1191, when it became one of the principal fiefs of the second Latin kingdom of Jerusalem. The county was then granted to the *Ibelin family, who held it until 1268, when it was conquered by the *Mamelukes. Under the Mameluke government, the city declined and lost its urban character.

A. Abel, *Géographie de la Palestine* (1928).

JAGIELLO Grand prince of *Lithuania (1377-1401) and king of *Poland (1386-1434). J. was one of the most powerful leaders of the Lithuanian aristocracy and, after seizing the ducal title, extended the country's territories to Ukrainian soil. In 1386 he converted to Christianity, married Jadwiga, heiress of Poland and became king of Poland as Wladyslaw II, and founded the Jagiello dynasty.

JALAL AL-DIN Shah of *Khwarizm (1220-31). Son and heir of *Ala Al-Din Muhammad, he attempted to resist the *Mongol invasion of *Genghis-Khan. Having lost the countries of Khwarizm and *Khorasan, he seized *Ghazni in 1221 and confronted the Mongol army. Defeated on the Indus (1223), he fled to Delhi. After recruiting Turkish mercenaries, he returned to fight on the Indus and in southern Persia and was killed there in 1231. His death marked the end of the Khwarizmian empire.

CHI (1970).

JALAL AL-DIN AL-RUMI (1207-73) *Persian poet and thinker. Born in Khorasan, his family left their homeland in fear of *Mongol invasions (1218) and settled at Konya in Anatolia. J. became famous for his Persian courtly poems, composed until 1244. At that date he met the philosopher Shams Al-Din, who encouraged him to pursue mysticism and *Sufi spiritualism, to which he then dedicated his creative work.

A. Iqbal, *The Life and Thought of Jalal Al-Din* (1964).

JAMES I, the Conqueror (1208-76) King of *Aragon (1212-76). Son of *Peter II, he reigned under the guardianship of his mother, Mary of *Montpellier, and a regency council until 1227, when he reached his majority. J. concentrated his efforts on the *Reconquista wars and became famous for his conquests, which included the *Balearic Islands, *Valencia, *Murcia and the territories south of the Ebro. He was also skilled diplomatically and came to an understanding with King *Louis IX of France. Through the Treaty of Montpellier (1258), he renounced his claims in *Languedoc, with the exception of Montpellier, his maternal heritage. J. was also active in domestic affairs and worked to protect the cities and Catalan trade through the improvement of the administration and the issuance of a new maritime code. He also established the *Cortes of Aragon, an assembly of the clergy, nobility and city representatives.

F. Soldevilla, *Life of James I the Conqueror* (1968).

JAMES II (1264-1327) King of *Aragon (1291-1327). Second son of *Peter III, he was proclaimed king of Sicily upon his father's death (1285). In 1291, when his elder brother *Alfonso III died, J. inherited the crown of Aragon as well. His power was weakened by the wars waged against the *Angevins of Naples, and in 1296 he renounced Sicily and worked to reassert royal power and revive the economy of Aragon. In 1297 J. conquered *Sardinia, which he annexed to the Aragonese crown. He was also proclaimed overlord of *Corsica, but his power there was challenged by the Genoese.

A. Castro, *The Structure of Spanish History* (1954).

JAMES I King of Cyprus (1385-98). Uncle to King *Peter II, he was captured by the Genoese in 1274, while defending Famagusta. To regain his freedom and the kingship, he was compelled to concede Famagusta to Genoa and to pay a heavy tribute. His reign was marked by economic dependence upon Genoa.

G. Hill, *A History of Cyprus* (1945).

JAMES I King of *Majorca (1276-1311). The younger son of *James the Conqueror of Aragon, he was given the royal title of Majorca, together with the Balearic Islands, Roussillon and *Montpellier (where he established his capital), on his father's death. J. assumed a neutral stand in the struggle over Sicily between the elder branch of the house of Aragon and the house of *Anjou. This earned him the enmity of the kings of Aragon.

JAMES II King of *Majorca (1324-49). The major part of his reign was devoted to dynastical struggles with the kings of Aragon, during which he lost parts of his kingdom. Prior to his death, he sold *Montpellier to King *Philip VI of France. The rest of his territory passed to the crown of Aragon after his death. Thus, J. was the last king of Majorca.

JAMES OF MOLAY (c. 1243-1314) The last grand master of the *Templars. He organized the order in Europe after the loss of Palestine and, from his centre at Paris, administered its valuable possessions. It seems that he and some of his knights became interested in the occult. From 1306 he was repeatedly accused of witchcraft and heresy by the legists of the French crown, who denounced him to Pope *Clement V. The real motive for such action, however, was the desire of the royal court to dissolve the wealthy order and to confiscate its property. In 1311 J. was formally condemned of heresy and, refusing to confess, was burned at Paris in 1314, pleading his innocence.

M. Melville, *La Vie des Templiers* (1951).

JAMES OF VENICE (first half of the 12th century) Translator. Born in Venice, he journeyed in the Byzantine empire and learned the Greek language. He then translated Aristotle's treatises into Latin. No data on his life and work is available. His translations date from 1128 and 1136.

C. H. Haskins, *Studies in Mediaeval Science* (1927).

JAMES OF VITERBO (d. 1308) Political theorist. Born at Viterbo, Jacopo Capocci became an Augustinian canon and was one of the students of *Aegidius Romanus. He began his literary work by summarizing his master's teachings. In 1301 he wrote a treatise of his own, *De regimine Christiana* (On the Christian Regime), in which he expressed his views on society. His main belief was that Christian society was to be led by the church, whose main task it was to offer wisdom and correct behaviour.

M. Grabmann, *Die Lehre des Jakob von Viterbo* (1930).

JAMES OF VITRY (c. 1170-1240) Historian. Born at Vitry, near Paris, J. became a teacher at the University of Paris. In 1209 he left his homeland to settle in *Acre, the capital of the Crusader realm. There he became bishop and also bore the title of patriarch of Jerusalem. In 1229 J. was summoned to the papal court and made cardinal by Pope *Gregory IX. As a historian,

J. is famous for his *Historia Occidentalis* and *Historia Orientalis* (the Histories of the West and East). In these works he expressed his disappointment in the decadence of the former and the renewed vigour of the latter (due to the efforts of the Crusaders). J. gathered material on both societies, which provides valuable information for the history of the late 12th and early 13th century.

J. W. Thompson, *History of Historical Writing* (1943).

JAPAN Island empire in eastern Asia. The country began to develop after the union of the Japanese peoples under the rule of a legendary dynasty of emperors, the "Sons of the Sun". The ancient period of Japanese history is masked by legends. It was not until the 4th century, with the rise of the Yamato empire, that historical sources can be considered accurate. The Yamato emperors imposed their rule over the numerous Japanese tribes and even began to expand towards Korea. There they became influenced by *Chinese patterns of political and cultural evolution. The empire was organized in 593 by Prince Shotoku, who acted as prime minister. He entered into relations with China and modelled the empire's administration along the lines of the Chinese system of government. In 604 he issued his constitution which organized the empire as an aristocratic state and granted the nobility political privileges. The other social classes were bound by the injunctions to obey their rulers. Chinese influence brought a cultural awakening in the 7th-9th centuries, when the Chinese system of writing and the Buddhist religion were introduced to J. This period was one of economic prosperity; however, imperial power was weakened as the nobility rose in stature and the empire became a sort of confederation. In 646 Prince Taikwa fought these trends by creating a stronger central government on behalf of the emperor, who was worshipped, but did not effectively govern.

In 858 Fujiwara was appointed regent for the young emperor, Seiwa. From that time his family virtually ruled the empire until 1159. They induced the emperors to marry their daughters, and established a strong aristocratic regime based on authority granted to the great landowners, who were exempted from taxes in return for military service. As a result, a special type of feudalism emerged in J., based on the private armies of the landowners, generally composed of peasants.

The rule of the Fujiwara collapsed in 1159, when one of the large landowning families, the Taira, conquered the capital Kyoto and imposed its rule over the country. The empire entered a period of civil wars between the most important noble families, and rule was imposed by the military-feudal class. With imperial consent, the constitution was amended in 1185 and real power within the state was granted to the shogun (the supreme commander of the army), who was to be appointed by the emperor. The shogunate was established in 1192 as a military government, which had supremacy over the civil one, the latter being confined to dealing with administrative and financial affairs. Thus, a new dual regime was established which lasted for 700 years. The emperor, considered a divine symbol of union, continued to wield illimitable authority, but it was the shogun who actually governed. The latter office was generally hereditary and formed the top rung of a rigid hierarchical system, in which provincial governors were considered vassals. Officers, too, who swore fealty to the shogun, were awarded the same position. The system was intended to secure political stability in the country, but did not prevent civil wars between candidates to the shogunate. Such disputes were frequent in the 13th century and a class of knights (the samurai), which emerged from the wealthy peasants, rose up. The samurai developed a code of honour and way of life based on ethical behaviour. This code, considered a means of attaining a perfect life, was largely diffused by writers and poets. The samurai reached a highly prestigious position after subduing two *Mongol attempts to invade J. in 1274 and 1281. But the internal life of the country continued to be characterized by military anarchy.

In 1318 the new emperor, Daigo II, attempted to restore imperial power. He won the support of a large portion of the samurai and in 1331 imposed direct imperial rule, which lasted for five years. At that time a reformed shogunate was established. The dignity was divided into northern and southern courts, intended to reduce the power of the shogun. The reform, however, was merely temporary; in 1392 Yoshimitsu of the Ashikaga house reunited the shogunate and imposed his rule, held by his dynasty until the 16th century. To ensure his power, he created a new military charge, the *daimyo,* large landowners who provided an army able to check the power of military provincial governors.

Civilization. Japanese civilization, based on ethnolinguistic unity, developed its native language and preserved its cultural patterns despite the introduction, in the 7th century, of the Chinese system of writing. A national literature therefore emerged in the 8th century and was concentrated at the imperial court. Such literary works, including both poetry and prose, dealt with worship of the emperor and praised moral values. From the 13th century the bulk of Japanese literature was written at the shogunate and its main concern was with the ethical values and honourable behaviour of the samurai. Some of J.'s greatest poets flourished at this time, among them Yoshimutu (1320-88).

The evolution of medieval Japanese art was greatly influenced by China. Up to the 13th century this was generally expressed in architectural developments, which also made use of indigenous features, as well as in sculpture, where gold was widely used. In the 14th century the first silk paintings appeared and were essentially the work of Buddhist monks. As in the case of the arts, medieval Japanese religion and philosophy were also strongly influenced by Chinese thought.
G. B. Sansom, *A History of Japan,* I (1958).

JAUFRE RUDEL (12th century) French troubadour. Born in the county of Blaye, near Bordeaux, he became famous for his pathetic verse and was admitted to the literary court of Poitiers by Duke *William X of Aquitaine. His poems about his *Far-away Love* gave rise to a popular legend. In literary circles, he was known as the "Prince of Blaye".
H. Davenson, *Les Troubadours* (1967).

JAVA Indonesian island. Since antiquity, J. was under the influence of Indian traders, who set up colonies and introduced their various cultures and religions. Indian merchants established the first political organizations in the 7th century, breaking the tribal system of the Malayans. These principalities, first established in the coastal area and based on trade, gradually expanded to the hinterland, where a Hindu-Malayan aristocracy emerged and became the ruling class of J. In the 8th century, the Sailendra (The Kings of the Mountains) dynasty unified the inner parts of the island and developed an advanced civilization, based both on local traditions and Sanskrit culture, while Buddhism became the dominant religion. The coastal principalities' spice trade made J. famous in southern Asia and the Mediterranean area. In 1293, after a period of war and anarchy which divided J. into the eastern and western states, the Mayapahit dynasty reunited the island and founded a powerful empire, which controlled the spice trade and was able to check Mongol-Chinese attempts to conquer it during the second half of the 14th century. The empire fell to the Moslems in the 16th century.
D. G. E. Hall, *A History of South-Eastern Asia* (1955).

JEAN, JEHAN, JOANNES, JOHANNES See JOHN.

JEANNE See JOAN.

JEHAN DE PARIS Anonymous French novel. It was composed in 1494 in honour of the marriage of *Charles VIII with Anne of Brittany. French civilization is depicted as superior to that of England, reflecting the national consciousness that emerged at the end of the *Hundred Years' War. The king of France, disguised as the burgher J., is portrayed as more refined than the king of England, in their bid to win the hand of a Spanish woman.
M. Wickersheimer, *Le Roman de Jehan de Paris* (1923).

JEHUDAH BAR KALONYMUS (d. 1200) Jewish exegete, poet and mystic. Born at Mainz, Germany, he studied at Spires and, after his return to his native city, became famous for his mystical interpretation of the Talmud. In 1189-93, he headed the Jewish community at Mainz and worked to maintain its cohesion during the Third *Crusade. J. was one of the fathers of the mystical trends that developed among German Jewry and out of which the 13th-century *Kabbalah movement arose.
G. Scholem, *Major Trends in Jewish Mysticism* (1954).

JEHUDAH BEN MEIR (Leo Leonte; 10th century) Jewish exegete. Little is known about his life, besides the fact that he was the head of the Italian Talmudic school, which, under his direction, was emancipated from the direct influence of the Babylonian *gaonim. His commentaries on legal problems of the Talmud were widely disseminated throughout western Europe.
S. W. Baron, *A Social and Religious History of the Jewish People,* IV (1957).

JEHUDAH HALEVI (1075-1141) Jewish poet and philosopher. Born at Toledo, Spain, into a rich family, he received a broad education, both in Hebrew and Arabic. He completed his studies in *Córdoba and *Granada while spending several years in *Andalusia, where he befriended prominent Jewish scholars and spiritual leaders, notable being the famous poet *Avraham Ibn Ezra. Distressed by the intolerant regime of the *Almoravides, who conquered Moslem Spain in 1090, J. returned to his native city in Christian Castile in 1096. In Toledo, he was honourably received, worked as a physician and was appointed personal physician of King *Alfonso VI. But disillusionment was to set in, with acts of violence perpetrated against Jews by Christian Spaniards, including the murder of a distinguished statesman, Solomon ibn Feruzziel in 1108. J. eventually returned to Córdoba in Moslem Spain. Although he himself lived in relative prosperity and his fame as physician, poet and thinker was well established, J. decided to leave Spain and settle in Palestine, which he envisaged as the homeland of the Jewish people. Such a decision was a natural result of his *Ode to Zion* and the apologetic treatise, the *Kuzari,* in which he developed the religious and national ideas of Judaism. In 1137 he left Spain; after a short sojourn in Egypt, he began his journey to Palestine, but died on his way in 1141, probably killed by a Moslem brigand.

J. was one of the greatest Hebrew poets of all generations. His religious and secular poetry, written in a lyrical style, shows a mastery of the Hebrew language. In his famous *Ode to Zion,* he expresses his yearning for Zion and describes the complexity of his life as a rich wanderer, a stranger everywhere. He developed his philosophy of divine revelation in a treatise, the *Kuzari,* written in Arabic in the form of an imaginary dialogue between the *Khazar king, seeking the true religion, and a learned Jew, who converts him to Judaism. In his view that religious truth arrived at through intuition transcends that acquired through logic, he was a neo-Platonist. His treatise, however, also shows an acquaintance with the *Aristotelian trends of Arabic philosophy. His method of rationalizing the Jewish faith accorded with the achievements of Jewish scholarship in Spain in the 11th and 12th centuries.

S. D. Goitein, *The Biography of Rabbi Jehudah Halevi in the Light of the Cairo Geniza Documents* (1959).

JEHUDAH IBN TIBON (1120-90) Translator. Born in Moslem Spain, he fled to southern France after the conquest of Andalusia by the *Almohades and settled in Lunel. There he devoted his efforts to translating from Arabic into Hebrew the philosophical treatises of prominent Jewish scholars from Moslem countries, beginning with *Saadia Gaon. He thus made their works accessible to the Jews who lived in Christian countries and did not read Arabic.

S. W. Baron, *A Social and Religious History of the Jews,* IV (1959).

JEHUDAH THE HASID (d. 1217) Jewish moralist and mystic. Born and educated at Speyer, he settled in Ratisbon, *Bavaria, at the end of the 12th century. Little is known about the events in his life, as he instructed his contemporaries not to divulge them. He devoted himself to exegetical work, but later acquired a keen interest in the mystical aspects of Judaism. The mysticism he developed differed from that of other Jewish thinkers in that the emphasis is on the everyday problems of Jewish existence rather than on ecstasy. J. believed that the process of salvation could be speeded up by strict moral conduct, a belief he developed in his works, among them *The Book of Responsa Concerning Morals, The Book of Honour* and a commentary on the prayers, which is lost. But the essence of his thought is contained in the *Sefer Hasidim* (The Book of Pietists), a manual of conduct which was later widely used by German Jews. His mystical ideas were adopted after his death by the founders of the *Kabbalah movement.

G. Scholem, *Major Trends in Jewish Mysticism* (1954).

JEROME OF PRAGUE (c. 1380-1416) *Czech religious reformer and disciple of John *Hus. He studied theology under Hus' direction at the University of Prague and, influenced by *Wycliffe's works, continued his studies at Oxford in 1398. Between 1401 and 1406 he travel-

led to various European universities disseminating his ideas on church reform and, according to his testimony, made a pilgrimage to Jerusalem. On his return to Prague, he took an active part in the religious disputes of 1407 and became one of the leaders of the Czech nationalist movement at the university. From 1410 he was suspected of heresy and persecuted. In 1415 he followed Hus to *Constance, where he was sentenced to burn at the stake in 1416.

R. R. Betta, *Jerome of Prague* (1947).

JEROME, St. (c. 342-420) Biblical scholar. Born in northern *Italy, he was educated at Rome, ordained priest and was a popular preacher in aristocratic women's monasteries. In 381 he left Italy and after several years of travelling in Christian centres of the East, settled in a cave near *Bethlehem, where he translated the Old Testament into Latin using the original Hebrew text. The translation, called the *Vulgate, became the authoritative Latin Bible in the Middle Ages and was widely diffused. His text was altered by copyists throughout the ages and among the variant versions that appeared, the Monte Cassino and the Gallican Vulgate were held to be most faithful to J.'s translation. From the 9th century on, various scholars produced amended versions, each claiming his to accord with J.'s original translation.

EC, VI.

St. Jerome's cell at Bethlehem

Seal of the Crusader kings of Jerusalem showing Jean de Brienne (obverse) and the city wall (reverse)

JERUSALEM Capital of *Palestine and holy city for Jews, Christians and Moslems. After a period of decline (2nd-5th centuries), when the city was named *Aelia Capitolina* and was controlled by officers sent by the Roman governors of *Caesarea, J. became one of the important religious centres of the Byzantine empire. The cult of the holy sites, the pilgrimages and the establishment of a patriarchal see in the city were important factors in its development, accentuated by the Byzantine buildings during the reign of *Justinian in the 6th century. This prosperity came to an end in 614, when the city was conquered by the *Persians and suffered extensive damage. Byzantine rule was restored in 628. Emperor *Heraclius began a reconstruction campaign and appointed a new patriarch, *Sophronius, who was entrusted with governmental authority. In 638 J. was conquered by the Arabs, who introduced fundamental changes during the 7th and 8th centuries. Its Christian character was preserved only in the quarters of the church of the *Holy Sepulchre, while Mount Moriah became a Moslem sanctuary, *Haram ash-Sharif*, where two important mosques, the *Dome of the Rock and Al-Aqsa, were built and became holy places of *Islam. A Moslem theological school was founded in the centre of the city, attracting Moslem immigrants and Eastern Christians who converted to Islam. Jews were allowed to settle near the Wailing Wall and they set up their own community. While J. was the religious centre of Palestine, its administrative capital was established at *Ramlah.

The 10th and 11th centuries saw the conquest of Palestine by the *Fatimids and Beduin uprisings. With the collapse of *Abbasid rule and repeated wars, many of J.'s inhabitants emigrated, while European pilgrims were finding it ever more difficult to reach J. and to stay within its walls. A process of decline began in the early 11th century, caused by the repressive measures of the *Fatimid Caliph Hakim and accelerated by an earthquake. At the same time, a trend towards Christianization was developing. An influx of Christian pilgrims

resulted in the establishment of Roman Catholic monasteries and their hospitals by religious orders, with funds coming from western Europe. The most important was the hospital of St. John, established in 1055 by the *Amalfi merchants. These pilgrimages continued after the *Seljuk conquest of J. in 1071, but, as the coastal area of Palestine remained under Fatimid rule and communication with J. became more difficult, they slowed down considerably.

On 15 July 1099 the *Crusaders conquered J. and proclaimed the *Latin kingdom of J. The Jews and most Moslems were murdered; those Moslems who managed to survive were expelled. J. became the capital of the new kingdom, but remained unpopulated. In 1113, an ordinance of King *Baldwin I prescribed the colonization of the city by Christians, including those of Eastern sects. While the royal government was concentrated around the Tower of David, East J., power was vested mainly in the churches and religious houses, under the authority of the patriarch. Under the new regime, economic activity was marginal, with resources coming primarily from pilgrims and pious donations. The Crusaders' impact on J.'s topography is manifested by religious buildings in the north, among them the Romanesque church of St. Ann, as well as by additions to already existing churches and mosques, which were converted into Catholic churches. With the kingdom's growth in the 12th century, J. prospered, despite the fact that the centre of economic and social activity was in the coastal area, where most of the Crusaders' settlements were established. Crusader authorities gradually opened J.'s doors to Jews and Moslems, whose work as craftsmen helped boost the economy. In 1187, after the Crusaders' defeat at *Hattin, J. was conquered by *Saladin, who allowed Jews to settle in the city.

J. became an *Ayyubid state. Attempts to recover it by the Third *Crusade (1187-91) failed. The Latin kings made *Acre their capital, to which most of the Christians who had settled in Jerusalem moved. A few abbeys remained in J. and they were looked after by monastic communities. In 1229, Emperor *Frederick II obtained the city from the sultan of Egypt, *Al-Kamel, through a diplomatic arrangement, whereby it was to be demilitarized and Moslems were to be given free access to the *Haram ash-Sharif*. After his coronation in the church of the Holy Sepulchre, the emperor returned to Italy, while J. remained a relatively unimportant town of the kingdom of Acre. In 1244, the *Khwarizmians, pressed by the *Mongols, stormed J., devastating the city and dispersing its inhabitants. It lay in ruins for 20 years, until its conquest by the *Mamelukes, who reconstructed its wall and renewed settlement. Under Mameluke rule (14th-15th centuries), J. was divided into four main quarters: Moslem, Christian, Jewish and Armenian.

H. Vincent-F. M. Abel, *Jérusalem Nouvelle* (1926).

JESSE-WINDOW The name given to stained-glass windows in the churches of western Europe, depicting the descent of Jesus from the royal line of *David. The motif, first used in mid-12th-century Gothic churches, took the shape of a tree springing from Jesse, David's father,. and ending in the Virgin or Jesus. It reached its highest form in the cathedral of *Chartres, which served as model for the 13th-century windows.

A. Watson, *The Early Iconography of the Tree of Jesse* (1934).

JEU D'ADAM (French: play of Adam) Anonymous 12th-century play written in the dialect of northern France. Apparently inspired by the text of Genesis relating the creation of Adam and Eve and their life in paradise, the author developed a scenario of *courtly love, in which the devil is represented as a seducer, who exploits the weakness of woman, to entice her to commit the first sin.

G. Cohen, *Le Jeu d'Adam et Eve* (1935).

JEWS See JUDAISM.

JIHAD See GIHAD.

JOACHIM OF FIORE (c. 1132-1202) Mystic. Although little is known of his life, legends about him abound. It is believed that in his youth he made a pilgrimage to Jerusalem, which supposedly influenced his conversion to religious life. On his return, he entered the *Cistercian order and in 1177 became abbot of Corazzo. He resigned a few years later, devoting himself to writing and contemplating the apocalyptic visions, which influenced his mystical thought. His residence at Fiore, Calabria, attracted many disciples, who were interested in his visions and doctrine. J. divided history into three main periods: the Father, or the Old Testament; the Son, or the New Testament, characterized by divine grace and the Holy Spirit; and the "monastic order", which would begin in the future and would be a synthesis of both former periods. J. calculated its beginning in 1260, when a new "spiritual order" would bring about the conversion of the entire world and salvation. Although J. himself never advanced his views of the third period as a danger to the ecclesiastical hierarchy, his disciples developed his Messianic theory into a political and social prophecy, which became widely spread in the 13th century and, under the title "Joachinism", was adapted to various political needs, among them those of the Spiritual *Franciscans.

M. Reeves, *The Influence of Prophecy in the Later Middle Ages; A Study in Joachinism* (1969).

JOAN Legendary female pope, whose reign supposedly coincided with the decay of the papacy in the 8th-9th centuries. According to the legend popularized during the 13th century, Joan donned male clothes, became a distinguished scholar, was elected pope and took the name John. After reigning for two years, she bore a child during a procession to the Lateran and died immediately.

J. J. J. Dillinger, *Die Papst-Febeln des Mittelalters* (1863).

Detail of the Tree of Jesse Window; *13th-century stained-glass window at the cathedral of Amiens*

JOAN I, of Anjou (1326-82) Queen of *Naples from 1343. She inherited the county of *Provence (1340) at the death of her father, Charles of Calabria, and in 1343 succeeded her grandfather, *Robert, to the throne of Naples. She married successively *Andrew of Hungary, *Louis of Tarento, *James II of Majorca and Otto of Brunswick. In 1347, she presented the city of *Avignon and its surroundings to the papacy, in return for which Pope *Innocent VI exonerated her from charges of having murdered her first husband. She reigned through favourites, some of them having been her lovers, a policy that led to continuous revolts in Naples and economic ruin. In 1371, when a revolt, led by her cousin and heir, *Charles of Durazzo, broke out, J. was imprisoned and killed in the castle of Muro.
E. Léonard, *Histoire de Jeanne I, reine de Naples, comtesse de Provence* (1937).

JOAN II, of Anjou (1371-1435) Queen of *Naples (1414-35). Daughter of King *Charles III, she was proclaimed queen at her brother *Ladislas' death. She reigned with the help of her lovers, whom she appointed to high offices, but their incompetence led to anarchy and decline. During her reign, the French house of *Anjou and that of *Aragon in Spain were at loggerheads over her domain. Vacillating in her alliances, she at times recognized Spanish claims to the Neapolitan crown, choosing Alfonso V as heir, and at times French claims, adopting Louis III. While she managed to maintain her realm's independence, her policies paved the way for foreign intervention.
E. Léonard, *Les Angevins de Naples* (1935).

JOCELIN OF BRAKELOND (d. 1215) Historian. In his boyhood he entered the monastery of Bury St. Edmunds and became chaplain under Abbot Samson (1182-88). He wrote a chronicle of the abbey covering the period 1173-1202. Of main interest is his juxtaposition of local and national history, especially during the reigns of *Henry II, *Richard I and the first years of the reign of *John Lackland.
J. W. Thompson, *History of Historical Writing* (1943).

JOHN I (470-526) Pope (523-26). Of a noble Roman family, he entered the service of the papal court in 484 and was promoted by Pope *Gelasius I, who appreciated his skills as theologian and diplomat. Until 519, he spent several years as papal emissary to the imperial court of *Constantinople, where he settled the conflicts between the popes and patriarchs. Elected pope in 523, he was sent to Constantinople in 525 by King *Theodoric the Great to obtain the abrogation of an edict by Emperor Justin I against the Arians. Failing in his mission, J. was arrested by Theodoric and starved in prison.
L. Duchesne, *Studies in the Early Church History* (1923).

JOHN II (Mercurius; 470-535) Pope (533-35). He was the first pope to change his name on election. At the request of Emperor *Justinian, he condemned the *Nestorians.

JOHN III (Catelinus; d. 574) Pope (561-74). Born at Rome, his pontificate coincided with the *Lombard invasion of Italy in 568. He persuaded *Narses to defend Rome in 571, but local opposition to the Byzantine governor compelled him to retire to the catacombs until Narses' death in 573.

JOHN IV (c. 580-642) Pope (640-42). Educated at the papal court, he was a Roman archdeacon before his papal election. As pope, he approved the Greek-Orthodox dogma against the *Monothelites.

JOHN V (d. 686) Pope (685-86). Active at the papal court, he was sent in 680 as papal legate to Constantinople, where he was esteemed as a man of learning and peace. As pope, he issued a decree concerning donations to the poor.

JOHN VI (d. 705) Pope (701-05). Member of a Greek family which settled at Rome, he was noted at the papal court for his wide knowledge of theological sources, both in Latin and Greek. As pope, he had to face attempts to conquer Campania by the Lombard duke, Gisolfo of *Benevento.

JOHN VII (d. 707) Pope (705-07). Of Greek origin; noted for his devotion to the Virgin *Mary and his restoration of Roman churches.

JOHN VIII (c. 820-82) Pope (872-82). Of a noble Roman family, he entered the service of the papal court under Pope *Leo IV and, as deacon of Rome, was active in the political life of the papacy and its struggle against Moslem raids in Italy. As pope, he was concerned with the defence of Italy and sought an emperor among the *Carolingian monarchs. In 875, he crowned *Charles the Bald of France as emperor and after his death, *Charles the Fat of Germany. The incompetence of the *Carolingians induced him to appeal to the knights for service in the papal army, the "militia of St. Peter", promising the remission of their sins to those who died in the holy war. He also created a papal fleet. On the other hand, he adopted a conciliatory policy towards Byzantium, recognizing *Photius as patriarch of Constantinople. He was murdered in 882 in a conspiracy at Rome.
A. Lapôtre, *Le Pape Jean VIII* (1895).

JOHN IX (840-900) Pope (898-900). His pontificate was troubled by the rise of an opposition within the Roman Church. To overcome it, he sought the support of lay authorities by renewing the privileges granted them by Emperor *Lothair I (824).

JOHN X (840-928) Pope (914-28). Born in Verona, he became archbishop of Ravenna in 905 and was elected pope by the influence of the powerful ruler of Rome, *Theophylactus. He crowned *Berengar of Friuli emperor, using his support in order to strengthen his position. In 915 he led the papal army against the Arabs, defeating them at Garigliano. J. returned to papal activity in the Catholic world, exerting his influence in Germany and France. Among his actions for church reform was his approval of the rule of the order of *Cluny. His alliance with *Hugh of Provence, whom he crowned emperor, enraged *Marozia, daughter of Theophylactus. Perceiving the alliance as a threat to her position, she had J. arrested and murdered.
W. Ullmann, *A Short History of the Papacy* (1975).

JOHN XI (906-35) Pope (931-35). Illegitimate son of Pope *Sergius III and *Marozia, he was appointed pope by his mother to consolidate her rule at Rome. In 933, an uprising led by his half-brother, *Alberic II of Spoleto, ended in the arrest of mother and son. J. died in prison two years later.

JOHN XII (Octavian; 937-64) Pope (955-64). His election at the age of 18 was ordered by his father, *Alberic II of Spoleto. His lack of experience led to the papacy's decline and made him an instrument of skilled politicians at Rome and abroad. In 962 he crowned Otto I emperor. But when J.'s role in the *Holy Roman empire turned out to be marginal, he rebelled against the emperor, who had him deposed and replaced by *Leo VIII in a synod convoked in 963. J. did not give up. When Otto left Rome, he convened a council which deposed Leo and reinstated J., who continued to be pope until his death.

JOHN XIII (d. 972) Pope (965-72). Bishop of Narni, Italy, and noted for his piety and integrity, he was chosen pope by Emperor *Otto I. Otto's steps to overcome the Roman nobility's opposition to the election marked the beginning of the Holy Roman emperors' active intervention in papal affairs.

JOHN XIV (d. 984) Pope (983-84). He was bishop of Pavia, northern Italy, when Emperor *Otto II elected him pope. The Crescentii, a powerful Roman family, opposed the election and appointed *Boniface VII as antipope. J. was murdered during an uprising àt Rome.

JOHN XV (d. 966) Pope (985-96). Member of a Roman aristocratic family, he became pope after the troubles of 984-85 – the murder of popes *Benedict VI and *John XIV by the antipope *Boniface VII – and attempted to conciliate the opposition. On the other hand, he filled the top positions at the papal court with his relatives. While his power at home was restricted by *Crescentius II, who took advantage of the minority of Emperor *Otto III to impose his authority, J. was an active leader of the Catholic Church in Germany, France and England.

W. Ullmann, *A Short History of the Papacy* (1975).

JOHN XVI (Giovanni Philagatus; d. 1013) Antipope (996-98). A Calabrian of Greek origin, he was elected antipope by *Crescentius after Emperor *Otto III left Rome and Pope *Gregory VI was deposed. When the emperor returned, J. was mutilated, and sent either to prison or to a monastery, where he died.

JOHN XVII (Giovanni Siccone; d. 1003) Pope (1003). Chosen by *Crescentius after the death of *Sylvester II, he died a few months after his consecration.

JOHN XVIII (Giovanni Fasano; d. 1009) Pope (1004-09). Born in Rome, he became pope by the influence of the *Crescentii. He was a docile instrument of the powerful family, and of Emperor *Henry II on matters concerning changes in the organization of the German church.

JOHN XIX (Romanus of Tusculum; d. 1032) Son of Count Gregory of Tusculum, he became Roman senator and governor in 1015, maintaining this secular post until the death of his brother, *Benedict VIII (1024), when he was elected pope. His pontificate was a period of papal decline with bribery being used to acquire ecclesiastical dignities.

JOHN XXI (Peter Juliani or Petrus Hispanus; c، 1220-77) Pope (1276-77). Born in Portugal, he studied at Paris and Siena (1240) and became physician and philosopher. After 1240 he taught medicine at Siena and was appointed personal physician to Pope *Gregory X. In 1272, he became archbishop of Braga, Portugal, and in 1273 cardinal. Elected pope in 1276, he died before realizing his goal of reconciling the Roman Catholic and Greek-Orthodox churches. As a philosopher, his main contribution was in the field of logic and his treatise, *Summulae Logicales,* was widely used in the universities of the later Middle Ages.

G. Leff, *Medieval Thought* (1958).

JOHN XXII (Jacques d'Euse; 1249-1334) Pope (1316-34). Born at Cahors, he studied at Paris and other French universities. In 1300 he became bishop of Fréjus and was transferred in 1310 to Avignon. Pope *Clement V created him cardinal in 1312. Elected pope in 1316, he established his court at *Avignon. In 1317 he condemned the Spiritual *Franciscans and their espousal of absolute poverty. His quarrel with Emperor *Louis of Bavaria, whom he condemned in 1324 as heretic, evolved into the broader conflict of papacy v. empire. J. found little public support for. his views. Prominent among his critics was *Marsilius of Padua, who wrote a treatise, *Defensor Pacis,* in favour of the emperor. J. was a capable administrator, reorganizing the Curia of Avignon, putting the papal finances on a sound basis and strengthening the Catholic Church hierarchy. But he also practised nepotism, appointing members of his family and men of his province to prominent posts at his court, among them twelve cardinals.

G. Mollat, *The Popes of Avignon* (1957).

JOHN XXIII (Baldassare Cossa; c. 1370-1419) Antipope (1410-15). Descendant of a *Neapolitan noble family, he was destined for a military career. After studying law at Bologna, he was created cardinal in 1402 and played a prominent role in papal policy. A party of cardinals elected him pope in 1410, but the validity of his election was contested, despite the support he won in Italy. In 1413 he called the Council of *Constance, at which he promised to abdicate if his rivals would. But he refused to fulfil his promise and fled Constance in 1414, hoping to bring about the council's disintegration. Captured by Emperor *Sigismund, he was imprisoned and deposed by the council.

E. J. Jacob, *Essays in the Conciliar Epoch* (1963).

JOHN I (1350-95) King of *Aragon (1387-95). Son and successor of King *Peter IV, he conquered *Sardinia and, after establishing his government, allied with *Charles VI, king of France, thereby introducing French influence in his realm.

A. Castro, *The Structure of Spanish History* (1954).

JOHN I, Tzimisces (925-76) *Byzantine emperor (969-76). Member of a noble Armenian family, he served in the army under general (and later emperor) *Nicephorus Phocas, distinguishing himself in the wars against the Arabs in Asia Minor and the Taurus Mountains. Coveting the imperial crown, he took part, together with his mistress, Theophano, in a plot that led to the murder of Nicephorus in 969. J. was proclaimed emperor on condition that he make penance. He subsequently broke his relationship with Theophano and had her confined to a monastery. In 971 he defeated the Bulgarians and the Russian army, led by Prince *Svyatoslav of Kiev, consolidating his northern frontiers. Continuing Nicephorus' war against the Arabs, his army penetrated Syria in 974-75, but, lacking logistical support, was compelled to retreat.

CMedH. IV.

JOHN II, Comnenus (1088-1143) *Byzantine emperor (1118-43). Son of *Alexius Comnenus, he dedicated his efforts to the recovery of territories lost to the *Seljuks in Asia Minor and to the reform of imperial finances. To realize the latter aim, he abolished *Venice's trading privileges in the empire; but the result was a blow to commerce and, in 1122, he was forced to renew those privileges. J.'s reign was characterized by campaigns against neighbouring states. In 1120 he defeated the Hungarians and fortified Belgrade and the northwestern frontiers. From 1130 he engaged in continuous wars against Sicilian King *Roger II, who attempted to establish his domination in Albania, Epirus and the Ionian Sea islands. His campaigns in Asia Minor contributed considerably to the weakening of the Seljuk principalities of Anatolia.

C. Diehl, *La Société Byzantine à l'époque des Comnènes* (1919).

JOHN III, Vatatzes (1193-1254) *Byzantine emperor at *Nicaea (1222-54). Member of an aristocratic Byzantine family which settled at Nicaea in 1205, he married Irene, daughter of Emperor *Theodore I Lascaris, whom he succeeded in 1222. After repressing a civil war at Nicaea, he dedicated his efforts to restoring the Byzantine empire. He enlarged his possessions in Asia Minor and in 1225 defeated the armies of the Latin empire of *Constantinople and of *Epirus. Allied with Bulgarian Tsar *John II Assen, he besieged Constantinople in 1235, but failed to conquer it. In 1241-42, he conquered territories in Epirus and *Bulgaria and prepared another attack on Constantinople. In domestic policy, he reformed the administrative structure of the empire, encouraged economic and cultural development and granted assistance to the poor.

CMedH, IV.

JOHN IV, Lascaris (1250-1300) *Byzantine emperor at *Nicaea (1258). Son of *Theodore II, he was proclaimed emperor at his father's death, under the regency of George Muzalon. During riots at Nicaea, Muzalon was murdered and the regency was entrusted to General *Michael Palaeologus, as co-emperor. After Michael conquered Nicaea, J. was imprisoned and died in prison.

JOHN V, Palaeologus (1332-91) *Byzantine emperor (1341-54; 1355-76; 1379-91). Son of *Andronicus III, he reigned as co-emperor under the regency of *John VI Cantacuzenus. He was deposed in 1354 after an abortive attempt to seize power with the support of *Venice; a year later the coalition defeated Cantacuzenus and J. was restored. During the second period of his reign, he failed in his efforts to defend the empire against the *Ottoman Turks and to check their advance in the Balkans. His appeals to Rome and his willingness to end the schism between the Byzantine and Latin churches, antagonized the Greek-Orthodox clergy, which supported the revolt of his son, *Andronicus IV, in 1376. J. was deposed and imprisoned, but in 1379 recovered his power, with the aid of the Turks, who forced him to recognize their overlordship, imposed on him a heavy tribute and compelled him to give them his son Manuel as hostage. In an attempt to recover his freedom during the last years of his reign, J. built new fortresses around Constantinople, but they were destroyed by the Turks.

CMedH, IV.

JOHN VI, Cantacuzenus (1293-1383) *Byzantine emperor (1341-55). A general in the army, he became chief adviser to Emperor *Andronicus III and the most influential person in the empire during his reign. In 1341 he became regent for *John V and took the imperial title. During his expedition against the *Serbs, he was accused of treason by the empress dowager, Ann of Savoy, having married his daughter to the *Ottoman Sultan *Orkhan in 1345. With the help of the Turks, he seized power in Constantinople in 1347. When he pro-

claimed his son Matthew co-emperor (1354), John V rose against him and was deposed. But in 1355 John V recovered imperial authority, and Cantacuzenus was forced to abdicate and retired to a monastery at Constantinople, where he distinguished himself as a historian. Among his works the most interesting is the history of the empire during the period 1320-57.

CMedH, IV.

JOHN VII, Palaeologus (1366-1408) *Byzantine emperor (1391-1402). Son of *Andronicus IV, he was *Bayazid's candiadate for the throne of Constantinople at the death of his grandfather *John V in 1391, but was compelled to submit to his uncle *Manuel II. In 1399 he ruled as regent while Manuel travelled to the West, to try to win support against the Turks. He energetically defended Constantinople against Bayazid. On Manuel's return, J. was appointed governor of Thessalonica, where he died.

CMedH, IV.

JOHN I (1358-90) King of *Castile (1397-90). Son of *Henry II of Trastamare he attempted to establish his reign by dynastic ties. Having married Beatrice of Portugal, he invaded that realm in 1383 and proclaimed himself king of Portugal. A national revolt, however, forced him to abdicate. He then sought the support of Aragon, marrying the daughter of King *Peter IV, Eleanor.

A. Castro, *The Structure of Spanish History* (1954).

JOHN I (d. 1285) King of *Cyprus (1284-85). Eldest son of King *Hugh III. Already ill when he inherited the throne, he died a few months later.

JOHN I (1316) King of *France. Posthumous son and heir of *Louis X, he died eight days after his birth.

JOHN II, the Good (1319-64) King of *France (1350-64). Son of *Philip VI of Valois, he was educated in the spirit of the *chivalric ideal — as a perfect knight rather than a king. His reign was troubled by the *Black Death and the *Hundred Years' War. In 1356 he was defeated at *Poitiers by *Edward the Black Prince, captured, and imprisoned in the Tower of London while the French army was decimated and a large ransom imposed on France. He was released in 1363, and sent his son Philip as hostage, but on hearing that Philip had fled, returned to prison, where he died.

E. Perroy, *The Hundred Years' War* (1957).

JOHN I, the Great (1357-1433) King of *Portugal (1385-1433). Illegitimate son of King *Peter I, he became in 1383 the leader of the nationalist party, which opposed the marriage of Queen Eleanor with *John I of Castile and the crowning of the Castilian king as king of Portugal. Supported by the burghers, he became king in 1385 and defeated a Castilian invasion, assuring Portugal's independence. He devoted his efforts to Portuguese expansion, which began in 1415 with the conquest of Ceuta, Morocco, and continued with naval explorations in the Atlantic. His policy was crowned by the discovery of the Azores archipelago in 1432 and its settlement by the Portuguese.

H. V. Livermore, *A History of Portugal* (1933).

JOHN (1340-1416) Duke of *Berry (1360-1416). Third son of *John II, king of France, he received from his father the duchy of Berry as an *apanage in 1360. He was active in helping his brother, King *Charles V, reorganize the French government. As regent during the minority of his nephew, *Charles VI, he crushed a revolt by the new officers at the court in 1381. During Charles' madness J. attempted to reconcile the two rival parties, the *Burgundians and the *Armagnacs. His influence was significant, but never preponderant. His is known primarily as a patron of the arts.

F. Lehoux, *Jean de France, duc de Berry* (1966).

JOHN The name of six dukes of Brittany:

John I Duke 1237-86. Son of *Peter Mauclerc, he was a faithful vassal of French King *Louis IX and reformed the duchy's administration according to that of France.

John II Duke 1286-1305. Son of J. I. He consolidated the ducal power.

John III, the Good Duke 1312-41. He reorganized the duchy's judicial system, imposing its administration on a number of ducal *seneschals, who replaced the old feudal administrators. He also reformed the fiscal administration. J. was involved in the preliminary stages of the *Hundred Years' War, although his policy was to keep the duchy neutral.

John IV of Montfort (1293-1345) Duke 1341-45. Younger brother of J. III. He was the rival of *Charles of Blois for the ducal title. Supported by *Edward III, king of England, whose army conquered part of Brittany, J. became duke, against the will of *Philip VI, king of France, who supported Charles of Blois. The civil war that ensued involved Brittany in the Hundred Years' War.

John V Duke 1364-99. Son of J. IV, he was recognized as duke after several wars against *Charles of Blois, having been supported by *Edward III, who appointed him to a commanding position in the English army. In 1364, before Charles died, an agreement was reached, whereby France recognized J.'s claims. After his ducal coronation, he dedicated his efforts to restoring the unity of the duchy, imposing internal peace and reforming the administration.

E. Durtelle de Saint-Sauveur, *Histoire de Bretagne* (1946).

JOHN BALLIOL (d. 1315) King of Scotland (1292-96). Son of Count John of Harcourt and descendant, by the female branch, of King *David I, he was proclaimed king of Scotland with the support of King *Edward I of England, who intended to be the overlord of *Scotland. J. took advantage of Edward's Welsh wars to secure his independence. But in 1296, Edward defeated him, conquered a large part of Scotland and held him captive in England. The "independent" Scots, however, refused to accept his deposition and continued to recognize him as legitimate king. A regency was thus established in northwestern Scotland, which acted until 1306, when *Robert Bruce was proclaimed king.

G. W. S. Barrow, *Robert Bruce* (1965).

JOHN LACKLAND (1167-1216) King of *England (1199-1216). Fourth son of King *Henry II and *Eleanor of Aquitaine, and the only one not to be granted a duchy – hence his title. Henry did make various land provisions for him but they were aborted by revolts of his brothers. He was Henry's favourite son and initially sided with him. However, in 1189, for reasons which are unclear, he was involved with his brother *Richard in a plot against the royal authority, just before his father's death. But he was later to conspire against Richard, who acceded to the throne, especially when the king went on the Crusade and during his captivity. J.'s intran-

sigence made him extremely unpopular among the nobility, who were educated in the spirit of *chivalry. At Richard's death, he was proclaimed king of England, duke of *Normandy and *Aquitaine and count of *Anjou. His marriage with Margaret of Angoulême, who was betrothed to *Hugh of Lusignan, brought him into conflict with the family of *Lusignan, who appealed to the court of French King *Philip II, J.'s overlord in France. J.'s refusal to appear in court meant, according to feudal law, the forfeiture of his fiefs. Philip, although aware of the difficulties involved in executing the sentence, supported the claims of *Arthur of Brittany, J.'s nephew, to the French fiefs. In the ensuing battle, *Arthur was captured, imprisoned in Normandy and murdered. This aroused the indignation of the nobility in Normandy and Anjou, which made it possible for Philip to conquer these territories in 1204-06 almost without opposition. J. was also in conflict with the papacy because he opposed the appointment of Stephen *Langton as archbishop of Canterbury. As a result, Pope Innocent III laid an *interdict on England. But J. – who could ill afford to be at loggerheads with the papacy at a time when he needed its support to regain Continental land and to quash domestic opposition – surrendered to the pope's terms and agreed to become his vassal. The interdict was relaxed, and with papal support, he was able to overcome baronial opposition in England (1208), to maintain his authority in Aquitaine and to prepare an expedition against Philip. He allied with his nephew, Emperor *Otto IV, while Philip supported *Frederick II Hohenstaufen. At the Battle of *Bouvines (1214), John was defeated and fled to England. The defeat and its economic repercussions, made him unpopular in England and led to a general uprising in the city of London. J. was forced to issue in 1215 the *Magna Charta, designed to ensure the liberties of the *community of the realm in England and which became the basis of the English parliamentary constitution.

S. Painter, *The Reign of King John* (1949).

JOHN MAUROPUS (11th century) Byzantine poet. He was the last poet to specialize in the epigrammatic style. His work combines pagan and Christian motifs.

A. S. Way, *Greek Anthology* (1939).

JOHN OF BRIENNE (1148-1237) King of *Jerusalem (1210-25), *Latin emperor of Constantinople from 1231. Count of Brienne in Champagne, he befriended *Philip II, king of France, whom he joined on the Third *Crusade. By marrying Mary, queen of Jerusalem, at Acre in 1210, he became king of the Crusaders' realm. Devoting his energy to consolidating the kingdom, he took part in the Fifth *Crusade at the Egyptian port of Damietta (1218-20), where his counsels against adventure went unheeded. In 1225, he arranged the marriage of his daughter Isabella with *Frederick II, hoping to retain his regency of the kingdom of Jerusalem. But Frederick ordered him to abdicate the kingship and vested him with lands in Italy, where J. became one of his adversaries. As one of the most experienced men of his time, he was called to Constantinople in 1228, to act as regent for young *Baldwin II and, at Baldwin's death, was elected emperor. In old age, he fought against the Bulgarians, maintaining the empire intact.

S. Runciman, *A History of the Crusades*, III (1953).

JOHN OF CHELLES (13th century) Architect. Born at Chelles, in northeastern France, he worked in the

Parisian area, specializing in the building of Gothic cathedrals. He contributed to the development of rec-.angular columns, which made possible the erection of higher buildings.

L. Male, *The Gothic Image* (1963).

JOHN OF DAMASCUS, St. (675-749) Greek theologian and Doctor of the Church. Born at *Damascus, he succeeded his father as a finance official in the caliphate, and also became the representative of the Christian community at the caliph's court. He abandoned public life in 716 and became a monk at the monastery of St. *Sabas in Palestine, where he wrote a treatise (c. 730) in defence of *icon worship. His most important work was, however, the *Fount of Wisdom,* divided into three parts, of which that dealing with the Orthodox faith made him famous and recognized as Doctor of the Church. The book attempts to reconcile Aristotelian philosophy with Christian faith and contains a comprehensive résumé of the teachings of the Greek Fathers of the Church, including the discussion of the *Trinitarian doctrine. The book was widely diffused during his lifetime and became one of the most important manuals of the Orthodox Church in the Byzantine empire. It was translated into Latin in the 12th century.

J. Nasrallah, *St. Jean Damascene* (1950).

JOHN OF GAUNT (1340-99) Duke of *Lancaster. Third son of *Edward III, he became duke of Lancaster in 1362 and one of the wealthiest English princes. He took part in the *Hundred Years' War, fighting under the command of his father and his brother, *Edward, the Black Prince. J. was the most powerful person in England during the last years of his father's reign and in the first years of the reign of his nephew, *Richard II. He repressed the peasants' revolt in 1381, but later broke with Richard and left the court. His claims for the kingship of Castile (1386-88), as husband of Constance, daughter of King *Peter the Cruel, were never realized. In 1389, he returned to England and mediated between the king and his brother Thomas of *Gloucester. His death left Richard without support in the realm.

S. Armitage-Smith, *John of Gaunt* (1904).

JOHN OF IBELIN The name of several members of the house of *Ibelin in the Latin East. The most famous among them were:

John, the Old Sire of Beirut Head of the house of Ibelin from 1192, he was appointed lord of *Beirut in 1197. In 1225 he was the leader of the Crusader nobility of the kingdom of Jerusalem-Acre and remained, until his death in 1236, the head of the baronial opposition to *Frederick II. During the years 1218-28, he acted as regent for *Henry I in Cyprus, laying the basis of the Ibelin barony in the island.

John, Count of Jaffa (1247-66) Legist. Born in Cyprus, he was the son of Philip of *Ibelin, the younger brother of the lord of Beirut. In 1247, he followed King *Henry I of Cyprus to Acre and was appointed count of Jaffa. Between 1254 and 1256 he was bailiff of the kingdom. He compiled the *Assizes of Jerusalem,* a legal code reflecting ideal feudal law and designed to govern the Crusader kingdom of Jerusalem.

J. L. la Monte, *John d'Ibelin* (1937).

JOHN OF JANDUN (1286-1328) Philosopher and scientist. He studied at the University of Paris and became a teacher of *Aristotelian philosophy at the College

of Navarre, Paris (c. 1310). He commented on Aristotle's treatises on animal life, adding the results of his own observations. Aristotle's political ideas influenced his criticism of the papal attitude in the conflict between Pope *John XXII and *Louis of Bavaria and his support of the ideas of *Marsilius of Padua. He was excommunicated by the pope in 1327.

G. Leff, *Paris and Oxford Universities in the 13th and 14th centuries* (1968).

JOHN OF LANCASTER See BEDFORD.

JOHN OF LA ROCHELLE (d. 1245) Theologian. Born at La Rochelle, western France, he joined the *Franciscan order and, after studying in Paris under *Alexander of Hales, taught theology at the Franciscan College of Paris until his death. His treatise, *On the Soul and Spirit,* attempts to reconcile Aristotelian rationalism with *Augustinian spiritualism.

G. Manser, *Johan von Rupella* (1912).

JOHN OF LUXEMBURG (1296-1346) King of *Bohemia (1310-46). Son of Emperor *Henry VII, he inherited Bohemia and *Luxemburg, while his attempts to obtain the imperial crown failed. Educated by French tutors, J. was an enthusiastic supporter of France and a frequent visitor at the *Valois court. As king of Bohemia, he was interested in its territorial expansion and between 1327 and 1330 conquered Silesia. After 1324, he was an ally of Pope *John XXII against Emperor *Louis of Bavaria. Despite the loss of his sight, he went to Paris in 1344, leaving the government of Bohemia to his son *Charles IV. In 1346 he took part in the Battle of *Crécy, fighting in the French army, and was killed.

R. Cazelles, *Jean l'Aveugle* (1947).

JOHN OF MATHA, St. (c. 1160-1213) Founder of the *Trinitarian order. Born in Provence, he was educated at *Aix-en-Provence, became a hermit and studied theology at Paris. In 1197 he founded a monastic community in Picardy, whose main aim was to free Christians held captive by the Moslems. He died at Rome in 1213.

N. Schuhmacher, *Der heiliger Johannes von Matha* (1936).

JOHN OF MEUNG (c. 1240-c. 1305) French writer. He studied at the University of Paris, where he took part in the disputes against the *Mendicant orders. He wrote the second part of the *Roman de la Rose* (c. 1279), continuing, though in a different style, the work of *William of Lorris. His main contribution was a realist interpretation of nature, according to the scientific achievements of the 13th century. He criticized the clergy, especially the Mendicants, and the bourgeois class, praising common sense and science.

G. Paré, *Les Idées et les Lettres au XIIIᵉ sciècle; Le Roman de la Rose* (1947).

JOHN OF PARIS (1225-1306) Political theorist. A *Dominican friar, he studied theology at the University of Paris under the direction of *Thomas Aquinas. He later taught at the university, defending the works of his teacher. His main interest lay in the relationship between Church and State, and he later advanced a doctrine which advocated the separation of their powers. He was condemned in 1289 for his ideas, but after his explanations, was absolved and allowed to continue lecturing. In his main work, *De Potestate Regia et Papali* (On Royal and Papal Power), completed in 1302, he argues that a council is superior to the pope, and that the pope

Tournament; miniature by Jean Fouquet

should be authorized to direct royal activities where moral issues are involved.

J. Leclercq, *Jean de Paris et l'ecclésiologie au XIIIe siècle* (1942).

JOHN OF PARMA (1209-89) Franciscan minister general. He taught logic at Parma, where he converted to the Franciscan order in 1233. Sent to Paris to continue his studies, he became a popular teacher and preacher and in 1247 was elected minister general of the order. He travelled to many of the order's houses in an attempt to restore discipline and the simplicity of St. *Francis' times. Accused of heresy, he resigned in 1257. J. managed to escape condemnation and retired to the hermitage of Greccio. He died in 1289 on his way to Constantinople, where he was sent on a mission on matters concerning the reunion of the Byzantine and Latin Churches.

R. de Nantes, *Le Bienheureux Jean de Parme* (1906).

JOHN OF PIANO-CARPINI (d. 1252) Traveller. A *Franciscan friar, he was sent on a mission in 1237 to try to convert the Mongols. After a journey to the court of the great khan at *Karakorum, he visited Russia and in 1240 went to Kiev, before returning to Italy. At Piano-Carpini, he wrote a book on his travels, which contains one of the first descriptions of the Mongol empire.

A. P. Newton, *Travel and Travellers of the Middle Ages* (1926).

JOHN OF PROCIDA (1210-99) Physician and *Sicilian patriot. Born at Salerno, where he studied medicine, he became the personal physician of *Frederick II and entered into close relations with the *Hohenstaufen dynasty. At the same time, he was on good terms with the papal court, where he cured cardinals and other dignitaries. After the conquest of Sicily by *Charles of Anjou (1266), he was forced to flee and dedicated his life to revenge. When his attempt to bring *Frederick of Thuringia to Sicily failed, he turned to Aragonese King *Peter III, who appointed him his chancellor in 1276. J. is considered one of the prime movers of the 1282 *Sicilian Vespers, which he instigated by diplomatic skill. In the last years of his life, he played an active role in reconciling the Aragonese and Anjou-Naples dynasties.

S. Runciman, *The Sicilian Vespers* (1958).

JOHN OF SALISBURY (c. 1115-80) Philosopher and historian. A native of Salisbury, he studied at Paris and Chartres between 1130 and 1140 and taught *liberal arts. From 1145 to 1153 he served at the papal court and in 1154 returned to England, where he was secretary to *Theobald and Thomas *Becket, archbishops of Canterbury. He was a faithful supporter of Becket in his conflict with King *Henry II and followed him to exile in France. He served as missionary in Paris and was an active propagandist among the French clergy for Becket's cause. J. returned to England after Becket and Henry were reconciled, but left after Becket's murder (1170) and settled in France, where he became bishop of Chartres in 1176. An accomplished Latinist and man of letters, J. was a leader of the 12th-century cultural *Renaissance. Influenced by Aristotle's writings, he wrote the *Metalogicon*, in which he combines logic and metaphysics. In his second important book, the *Policraticus*, he expresses his view of the church, as the organ of social and political pluralism and the guaran-

tor of liberty against royal despotism. He also elaborated on the theory of medieval tyranny. J.'s historical work, in the form of memoirs at the papal court, gives a detailed description of the period. His letters, of immense literary value, also serve as a good source of information on the Becket affair.

Works, ed. C. C. J. Webb (1909-29) and R. L. Poole (1927);

H. Liebeschütz, *Medieval Humanism in the Life and Writings of John of Salisbury* (1950).

JOHN OF SPAIN (Johannes de Luna, John of Seville; d. 1157) Translator of Jewish origin, he remains an enigmatic figure. Although some scholars continue to identify him with *John Ben Daud of Toledo, a converted Jew, it has been established that they were two different people. J. translated astronomical treatises from Arabic into Latin, which were used as official texts on the subject in medieval western Europe.

M. Alonso, *Juan Sevillano* (1953).

JOHN SCOT ERIGENA See ERIGENA, JOHN SCOT.

JOHN OF TOLEDO (d. 1166) Translator. Born into the Jewish Ben Daud (David) family of Toledo, he converted to Christianity (c. 1140), became a clerk at the archbishopric of Toledo and later bishop of Segovia. He translated Arabic philosophical works into Latin, from the Castilian translation. Among his translations are works of *Ibn Sinna and Ibn *Gabirol. He also developed some mystical ideas and used astronomical signs to calculate the end of the world, which he put at the end of the 12th century.

M. Steinschneider, *Die europäischen Übersetzungen aus dem Arabischen* (1904).

JOHN OF VIENNE (c. 1341-96) French admiral. A knight of Vienne, on the Rhône, he came to the court of King *Charles V in 1365 and, having distinguished himself in the campaigns of *Du Guesclin, was appointed by Charles admiral of France. He was charged with reorganizing the French fleet, destroyed during the first stages of the *Hundred Years' War. During 1373-77, he commanded successful maritime operations along the coasts of Normandy and Poitou, which diminished the English possessions in France. His influence grew during the reign of *Charles VI.

E. Perroy, *The Hundred Years' War* (1957).

JOHN OF WORCESTER (12th century) Historian. He wrote a chronicle of England, narrating the events from 1117 to 1141 and focusing on the court of King *Henry I.

JOHN OF WÜRZBURG (d. c. 1170) Traveller. Canon of the bishopric of Würzburg, Germany, he went on a pilgrimage to the Holy Land in 1160 and wrote an interesting account of his journey, describing *Crusader Jerusalem and its holy sites.

A. Grabois, *Le pélerinage de Jean de Wurzbourg* (1973).

JOHN THE FEARLESS (1371-1419) Duke of *Burgundy (1404-19). Son of *Philip the Bold, he was granted the county of Nevers in 1384, and, upon reaching maturity, was associated with the government of his domain. At the beginning of the 15th century, he governed the Low Countries on behalf of Philip. As duke, he was primarily involved in French politics. He won the support of the Parisian burghers (the *Burgundians) and was involved in their conflict with the rivals, the *Armagnacs. This contest brought him into an alliance with *Henry V, king of England, whom he helped at the Battle of *Agincourt and during the negotiations

(Previous pages) Santa Sophia, Constantinople
(Opposite page) 6th-century Byzantine mosaic at S. Vitale, Ravenna

which led to the conclusion of the Peace of Troyes (1418). J continued the organization of the estates and the administrative system created by his father and held one of the most brilliant courts in western Europe. He was assassinated in Montereau in 1419, at a meeting with the dauphin, the future *Charles VII.
R. Vaughan, *John the Fearless* (1966).

JOINT STOCK COMPANIES The emergence of associations with limited liability is connected to the development of Italian trade with the Near East during the *Crusades. In the late 11th and 12th century, a merchant entrusted either money or goods to a cargo vessel's master, who carried them to the East, sold them and reinvested the money in Asiatic wares, which he brought to Italy, where the merchant and sailor divided the profits equally. The practice was perfected in the middle of the 12th century by the distribution of wares among several vessels, to diminish the risks. It led to the establishment of merchants' associations, which chartered ships and divided activity among the associates. Initially, these associations dissolved after the sailing season, but from the 13th century, they were established on a permanent basis. The associates received shares according to the volume of their investment, while the company possessed ships and warehouses and was directed by officers. The largest J. in the Middle Ages was the St. George Bank at *Genoa, which possessed *Corsica in the 15th century and exerted considerable political influence. The Italian model spread throughout western Europe in the 15th century and was adopted by the German *Hanse and other commercial organizations.
CEcH, III.

JOINVILLE, JEAN DE (1224-1319) Historian. Member of the family of the lords of Joinville in Champagne, he entered French royal service as knight in 1241 and followed *Louis IX on his *Crusade. During the Crusade and the Egyptian captivity, he became a close friend of King Louis IX. Later on, he became *seneschal of Champagne, but continued to visit the court frequently. He wrote the *History of St. Louis* in 1314, one of the best biographies of the Middle Ages.
Jean de Joinville, *Histoire de Saint Louis*, ed. N. de Wailly (1879).

JONAH IBN JANAH (c. 990-1050) Philologist. Born in Andalusia, he was educated in Morocco and *Córdoba, where he became acquainted with Arab grammarians. Although he studied medicine, he dedicated most of his time to analysis and research of the Hebrew language. Among his works, his book on the *Complement* and *Manual of Exact Investigation*, made him one of the most distinguished philologists of the Hebrew language.
S. W. Baron, *A Social and Religious History of the Jewish People* (1957).

JONAS OF ORLÉANS (d. 843) Political thinker. Known for his scholarship, he became bishop of Orléans under Emperor *Louis the Pious and established a famous school in the city. Involved in the political life of the *Carolingian empire, he dominated the Council of Paris (829), which dealt with the revolt of Louis' sons against their father. He composed the decisions of the council and, in 834, developed them in a treatise, *De Institutione Regia* (On the Royal Institution), which became one of the basic political treatises of the Middle

Ages. He developed the Gelasian doctrine of the "two swords", as well as the theory of the "Christian monarch", who, to exercise full authority over his subjects, would have to be governed by the church on moral issues (see *Gelasius I).
E. Réviron, *Jonas d'Orléans et De Institutione Regia* (1900).

JONGLEURS Popular entertainers in the French-speaking countries of the Middle Ages. They recited popular tales, accompanied by songs and skits. In the 13th century they became an integral part of the *chivalric courts and feasts.

JORDAN Prince of *Capua (1058-91). Son of the *Norman adventurer *Richard of Aversa, he became duke of Gaeta in 1058 and in 1062, proclaimed himself prince of Capua. J. was a constant adversary of *Robert Guiscard and *Roger I of Sicily over the lordship of southern Italy. His political interests caused him to ally with Emperor *Henry IV against Pope *Gregory VII, who supported the *Hauteville brothers.
F. Chalandon, *Les Origines de la Domination Normande en Italie du Sud* (1908).

JORDANES (6th century) Historian. Of Gothic origin, he lived in a Roman province on the Danube and learned Latin. In 551, he began to write his history of the Goths (*Gethica*), which is an interesting description of the Germanic tribes, especially the *Goths. While the first part of his history abounds in legend and is of no historical interest, the part covering the events of the 5th century, from the invasion of the *Huns until the death of *Theodoric the Great, is an invaluable historical source, both for its data and for his interpretation of it.
J. W. Thompson, *History of Historical Writing* (1943).

JORDANUS NEMORARIUS (d. 1220) Mathematician. Little is known of his life. He was a *Dominican friar in Germany, who dictated the results of his research to his pupils. Influenced by the Greek school, he acquired an interest in mechanics and discovered the rules of weights. His works were taught until the 17th century.
E. A. Moody and M. Clagett, *The Medieval Science of Weights* (1952).

JOSAPHAT (JOASAPH), St. See BARLAAM.

JOSEPH KARO BEN EPHRAIM (d. c. 1130) Jewish exegete. He was a pupil of *Rashi and became an exegete in his own right at Paris, where he commented on the Bible. By his intellectual relationship with the members of the school of *St. Victor, he became familiar with the Christian interpretations of the Bible and attempted to refute them in his works. St. Victor scholars, however, accepted some of his interpretations of the Pentateuch.
B. Smalley, *The Study of the Bible in the Middle Ages* (1952).

JOSEPH KASPI (1279-1340) Jewish philosopher and exegete. Born into a rich family in Provence, he travelled, after completing his studies, to France, Spain, Egypt and Morocco, seeking the sources of Jewish philosophy, and especially that of *Maimonides. His philosophical works were primarily influenced by Maimonides' ideas, but also by *Aristotelian rationalism, although they lack the strictness of the philosophical method. In his exegetical commentaries, influenced by

*Abraham Ibn Ezra and Maimonides, he developed the antithesis as a method of criticism. J. also dealt with the problem of Jewish salvation, arguing that the return of the Jews to the Holy Land would be a political process and not a Messianic one. His views were attacked by his contemporaries.

W. Bacher, *Joseph Kaspi* (1906).

JOST (1351-1411) Margrave of *Moravia. Nephew of Emperor *Charles IV, he was granted *Moravia in 1376 and became a leading personality in the German political scene in the last quarter of the 14th century. After the death of Charles IV, he became the most powerful member of the *Luxemburg dynasty, annexing to his domain *Brandenburg and the county of Luxemburg, and exerting overwhelming influence on Emperor *Wenceslas. His activities accelerated the organization of Germany into a loose federation of principalities over which the emperor presided.

F. L. Carsten, *Princes and Parliaments in Germany* (1959).

JOUARRE Monastery in France, near Meaux (Champagne). Founded in 624, it is among the oldest *Benedictine abbeys in France and was one of the most important *Merovingian shrines. J. was put under the direct patronage of the Merovingian and *Carolingian kings and its abbots played an important political role until the 12th century. In the 11th century a borough was founded and fair-site established around the abbey.

F. Lot, *Naissance de la France* (1945).

JUDAISM J. refers to both the Jewish civilization and its history. The Judaic way of life was based on common tenets of faith and religious observance which had crystallized in antiquity. These precepts continued to be observed by the Jewish communities throughout the Middle Ages. Another cardinal factor in the historical development of J. at this time was the lack of a state or central political organization, together with the dispersion of the Jewish people in the Diaspora (Asia, Africa and Europe). Consequently, medieval J. was marked by the voluntary acceptance, by individuals and groups ("communities"), of the spiritual leadership of the masters of the law (later known as rabbis), who interpreted the Talmud. Furthermore, the communities were self-governed on the basis of such legislation. Such a collectivist system was able to develop in medieval society due to the pluralism of *law which was commonly part of the system of government and the corporative organization of the social body. Such communities were, in fact, granted charters of privileges by their respective rulers. The Jewish communal system had already been recognized in the late Roman empire and was the sole form of existence for any Jew who chose to maintain his faith.

At the beginning of the Middle Ages, the hegemony of J. was exercised by the Babylonian centres, located in Mesopotamia. Under the secular authority of the *exilarch, the Mesopotamian communities maintained two academies, at Sura and Pumbedita, where Talmudic legislation was interpreted and whose heads, the *gaonim, were recognized until the 10th century as the spiritual leaders of the entire Jewish world. Attempts made by the Palestinian academy and its gaonim to contest that authority in the 9th and 10th centuries failed, due to the higher standards of the Babylonian institutions. As a result of the fall of the *Umayyad caliphate in 750 and the establishment of an independent Arab government in Spain, where a substantial number of Jews lived, autonomous centres of J., founded by Babylonian scholars, emerged in western Europe and north Africa. The new centres, which were established at the end of the 8th century and the beginning of the 9th, developed their own schools and organizations; however, up to the beginning of the 11th century, they continued to address major issues to the Babylonian gaonate. The decline of the *Abbasid caliphate and the establishment of the *Fatimids in Egypt broke down communication and caused the final decline of the gaonate.

The new European and north African centres, together with those which emerged in Egypt, developed their own traditions. Thus, from the 11th century, there was no central religious leadership; however, works of jurisprudence were diffused among and commonly accepted by the different communities. This served to maintain unity, which even defied the historical split between the *Sephardi and *Ashkenazi Jews, a division which was not only socio-geographical, but also reflected ways of thought and methods of learning.

Sephardi Jewry, which developed in the 11th-13th centuries (the "Golden Age of J."), was moulded in a Hebreo-Arabic framework. Sephardi linguists laid down the foundation for the revival of Hebrew, which was used in liturgy and poetry, continuing the Palestinian tradition of the 6th-8th centuries; Hebrew literature reached its peak in the religious and secular works of Sephardi poets, especially *Jehudah Halevi. Arabic, on the other hand, was used in theological and philosoophical treatises, as well as in works of science and medicine. This use of Arabic was the result of the Moslem philosophers and scientists and of the Aristotelian translations into Arabic. Exegetical methods were adapted to the rationalist interpretation of Jewish law, especially by such philosophers as Ibn *Gabirol and *Maimonides. The same was true in fields of science, especially in astronomy. From the 13th century on, a mystical Jewish trend emerged in Christian Spain, as a result of which the *Kabbalah developed. A parallel centre of Jewish mysticism and learning arose in Languedoc-Provence and flourished during the 11th-13th centuries. Works were published in Arabic and translated into Hebrew so they could be diffused among the European communities.

In France and Germany, Sephardi traditions and philosophy were not accepted and the jurisdictional interpretations and exegesis of Babylonia prevailed. The pattern of the Ashkenazi communities was organized under the leadership of *Gershom, "the Light of the Exile" (11th century), while the commentaries of *Rashi provided an authoritative interpretation of the holy texts. The activity of the French *Tosafists worked along the same lines. With regard to communal government, that of Ashkenazi Jewry was better organized than in Spain. From the 12th century, inter-communal groups provided new systems of government under an aristocratic leadership.

The persecutions that began in western Europe with the Crusades consolidated the Ashkenazi communities, but also dealt a terrible blow to their economic activity. Thus, the 13th century was marked by a decline in the traditional Jewish communities of the West and the beginning of emigration eastwards. After the expulsion of Jews from England (1291) and France (1306), the trend of emigration to eastern Europe (especially Poland and Hungary, where Jews were granted wide privileges), caused a radical change in the demography of the Jewish people. The Rhine Valley lost its central position and was overshadowed by the communities of the Danube Valley. With regard to Sephardi Jewry, the *Reconquista* wars led to riots and Jewish persecution in the 14th century, when the economic aid of the Castilian Jews was no longer sought by the Christian monarchies. After the persecutions of 1381 Sephardi Jews migrated to north Africa. The final expulsion from Spain (1492) was followed by Jewish settlements in Italy, the Ottoman empire and the Middle East.

A. W. Baron, *A Social and Religious History of the Jewish People*, vols. IV-XIII (1952-64).

JUDITH OF BAVARIA (800-43) Empress. Daughter of Count Welf of *Bavaria, she married Emperor *Louis the Pious in 819, despite the opposition of his sons from his first marriage. In 822 she bore *Charles the Bald. Louis' attempts to give Charles a share of the empire were attributed to her influence. The opposition at the court accused her of having relations with high dignitaries. She was arrested and sent to a nunnery during a revolt against the emperor in 830, but was recalled by Louis in 831.

L. Halphen, *Charlemagne et l'Empire Carolingien* (1947).

JULIAN OF NORWICH (c. 1342-1413) English mystic. Little is known of her life except that she spent many years outside the walls of St. Julian's Church, Norwich. From 1373, she claimed to have received a series of revelations while in a state of ecstasy. She described these visions in *The Revelations of Divine Love*, written in 1303. In the book, which shows neo-Platonist influences, she formulated a mystical theory of divine love as the panacea for all existential problems.

P. Molinari, *Julian of Norwich: the Teaching of a 14th-century English Mystic* (1958).

JURY TRIAL The common system of administering justice in the Middle Ages. The practice emerged among Germanic tribes and their kingdoms in western Europe, and was based on the participation of free-men in assemblies, at which the accused were tried. Such assemblies – called *mallus* or *placetum* – were summoned by the chieftain or the king and, from the 8th century on, by the count. With the feudalization of western Europe in the 10th-11th centuries, assemblies were replaced by feudal courts, at which the lord and his vassals acted as judges. In England, however, the ancient system prevailed even after the *Norman Conquest, with justice administered by popular assemblies of the shire and the *hundred. During the 12th century, attendance at assemblies was restricted to a limited number of free-men who, according to the statutes issued by *Henry II, had to take an oath before the *sheriff, as the royal representative. These free-men were thus named jurors and the body a jury. Judicial decisions taken at the J. on the acquittal or the sentencing of an accused served as the basis of Common Law.

B. Lyon, *A Constitutional and Legal History of Medieval England* (1960).

JUSTIN I (c. 450-527) *Byzantine emperor (518-27). Born to a peasant family of Illyrian stock, he joined the imperial guard in 470. During his 40 years of service, he rose through the ranks, to become general with the title of count. In 518 he was proclaimed emperor. During his reign, he defended Orthodoxy against the *Monophysites and the Arians. In his struggle against the *Persians, he allied himself with the Ethiopians and built an impressive fleet in the Red Sea. Throughout his reign J. had the help of his gifted nephew and successor *Justinian I, whom he named co-emperor in 527.

A. H. M. Jones, *The Later Roman Empire* (1965).

JUSTIN II (d. 578) Byzantine emperor. He began his reign on a note of tolerance, adopting a more liberal attitude towards the *Monophysites and introducing tax reform. But after suffering successive defeats from the outside, he instituted the repressive fiscal and religious policies that characterized the reign of his predecessor, his uncle *Justinian. In 568, he failed to prevent the *Lombards from invading Italy, was defeated by the *Avars on the Danube and was compelled to pay them tribute in 574. He became insane, and from 573 on his nephew *Tiberius was the virtual ruler.

A. H. M. Jones, *The Later Roman Empire* (1965).

JUSTINIAN I (483-565) *Byzantine emperor (527-65). Nephew of *Justin I, who appointed him his heir in 525, he was one of the greatest rulers of the Middle Ages. Married to a former circus-artist, Theodora, he associated her to the government and was greatly influenced by her religious views. J. continued his uncle's repressive ecclesiastical policies, and, to impose Orthodoxy, ordered the closing of the famous Hellenistic Academy of Athens in 529, a move that marked the end of the classical period. His policy led to riots and he cruelly repressed the Niké revolt at Constantinople in 532. He appointed a committee of legists, led by *Tribunianus, to codify Roman law; the result of their work was the Justinian Code, issued in 534. It became the constitutional basis of the empire, which was governed by a hierarchical, military and civil bureaucracy. J.'s reign was also a period of continuous wars, both in the East and the West. He fought against the *Persians, enlarging his rule in *Armenia and creating a defensive network on the eastern frontiers. He also began a campaign in the West in 533 to reconquer Roman territory lost to the *Vandals and *Ostrogoths. Aided by his generals, prominent among them *Belisarius and *Narses, he defeated the Vandals and annexed to the empire their realm in north Africa and the west Mediterranean islands. From 535 Belisarius and Narses commanded expeditions to Italy, destroying the Ostrogothic kingdom and finally annexing Italy. They also reconquered southern Spain (*Andalusia). The same search for unity brought J. to fight the *Monophysites; the struggle led to the religious and ethnical division of the empire in the East, where the Monophysites gained supporters among the non-Greek-speaking population, who were consequently severely persecuted. J.'s attempts to break the Monophysites for the most part failed: only a minor part of the Syriac-speaking population accepted the authority of the Eastern Orthodox hierarchy, named the *Melkite* (imperial) church.

J. was one of the great patrons of the artistic revival, and during his reign Byzantine art and architecture achieved their highest expression. Among the numerous buildings he sponsored, most characteristic are the cathedral of St. Sophia at Constantinople, the churches of the Nativity at Bethlehem, of the Holy Se-

Emperor Justinian and his court; 6th-century mosaic at San Vitale, Ravenna

pulchre at Jerusalem, of San Vitale at Ravenna, as well as the monastery of St. Catherine on Mount Sinai.

R. Browning, *Justinian and Theodora* (1971).

JUSTINIAN II (669-711) *Byzantine emperor (685-95; 705-11). An agreement with the *Arabs in 685 allowed him to devote his efforts to fight the Slavs, who invaded Thrace. His victory of 688 enabled h'im to reconquer part of the Balkans. His position became precarious after his defeat in 692 by the Arabs, who conquered Armenia, and he was deposed and exiled to Crimea in 695. He fled from prison, spent several years with the *Khazars and the *Bulgars, and, with their help, recovered imperial power (705). His repressive policy led to his murder in 711.

CMedH, IV.

JUTLAND Peninsula north of Germany, comprising the continental part of *Denmark. At the beginning of the Middle Ages, it was populated by the Jutes, a Germanic people who gave it their name, the *Angles and the *Saxons. After the Anglo-Saxons emigrated and settled in England, J. was populated by Scandinavian tribes, among whom the *Danes were the dominant element. They developed both agriculture and naval trade from their towns, situated in the north, near Aarchus, and south, *Hedeby. The runic stones of northern J. attest to the emergence of a political organization in the 8th century. At the beginning of the 9th century, J. became part of the kingdom of Denmark, under the rule of King *Godfred.

G. Jones, *A History of the Vikings* (1970).

The Kaaba *at Mecca*

K

KAABA The most sacred Moslem shrine, located at *Mecca. The K. is a large black, cube-shaped stone. It was a shrine and a centre of pagan worship from earliest times and was held in veneration by the *Arab tribes. Pilgrimages to the stone increased the importance of Mecca, and contributed to the wealth of the city. *Mohammad adopted the practice of worshipping the K. and incorporated it in his new faith. Mohammad considered the *Hajj*, i.e., pilgrimage to the K., as one of the most important duties of *Islam.
Philip K. Hitti, *History of the Arabs* (1953).

KABBALAH (Tradition) The term was employed by *Jewish mystics, beginning in the 12th century, to denote the esoteric manner of theosophical contemplation, whether in search of salvation, the "practical" aspect of K., or of the secrets of creation and of divine revelation. According to Judah Ben-Barzillay (c. 1130), an eyewitness, certain sages used to introduce their disciples to these secrets in a lowered voice, relating the oral traditions, hence the name of the mystical trend. It appears that the Kabbalistic trend developed out of certain Jewish practices in Palestine and Egypt at the eve of the Christian era, under the influence of both Hellenistic and Eastern concepts. Such ideas were not developed into a formal framework until the 12th century, but they appeared in several Jewish works before that time and served as a foundation for the development of Jewish apocalyptic literature, which included some theosophical ideas as well as *gnostic thought. Only with the emergence of pietist movements (Hasidism) among the Jewish communities in France, Germany and Spain in the 12th century, did mysticism and allegorical interpretation of biblical texts become more common; and as a result, conditions became ripe for the Kabbalist movement.

The movement emerged in southern France among rabbis of Languedoc and Provence. Various circles were established at Narbonne, Lunel and Posquières, where philosophical and theosophical premises of Jewish mystics were taught and organized systematically. The publication of the treatise *Sefer Habahir* (The Book of Enlightment) towards the end of the 12th century signalled the crystallization of these ideas. The book itself, revised and edited in the 12th century in Languedoc, is of more ancient origin, as it contains a substantial amount of mythological and gnostic excerpts. To these mythical tales concerning creation and the nature of God was added a scientific dimension – a translation of the Greek theory of cosmic spheres developed by the neo-Platonists. Led by Rabbi *Jacob the Monk of Lunel (in medieval Hebrew, the term "monk" signified those people who left their secular occupations to devote themselves to the study of the Scripture and to contemplation, but married and lived

with their families), the circle of Kabbalist students grew rapidly and gained an audience among the communities of southern France and Spain. The activity of the circle became more intensive under the leadership of Isaac Sagi-Nahor (d. 1235), the first of the Jewish scholars to devote his entire time to mysticism. Modern researchers consider him the real founder of the K. movement. He was also responsible for its widespread diffusion facilitated by the aura of Messianic hope which developed after the anti-Jewish persecutions in western Europe at the beginning of the 13th century. Isaac brought to the K. the philosophical background of neo-Platonism, using it for his commentaries on the Scripture, and also attempted to introduce a mystical system based on Hebrew philology. His disciples brought Kabbalistic ideas to several circles in Spain, where many rationalist thinkers and scientists became interested in the new doctrine.

The most important among these circles was that of *Gerona in Catalonia, which became the centre of the Kabbalist movement in the 13th century. Led by Azriel of Gerona and *Nahmanides, it served to diffuse the achievements of the Kabbalist circles of southern France, and also contributed a complex theory of its own, encompassing the Divinity, the Cosmos and Judaism. The discussions of this group were recorded in treatises, which were to be disseminated and which conveyed the "Truth", another symbol of the movement. According to this Kabbalist circle, the cosmological theory of creation implied not only the acceptance of the theory of the spheres, but also the development of a doctrine of interrelation between the soul and the body, enlivened by the divine aeons, the essence of the souls, which were therefore immortal. In addition, the mythological and gnostic ideas were incorporated into a historical explanation of the K., according to which it was the Prophet Elija who revealed the K. to the sages of the Mishna, and particularly to Rabbi Simon Bar-Yokhai during his 13 years of reclusion in a Galilean cave. The overall theory of K. was perfected by Moses De Leon in Guadalajara (Castile), where he composed the most popular work of Kabbalistic literature, the *Zohar* (c. 1280-85), which came to be the movement's fundamental text. The book, which reflects the mysticism of Spanish Jewry, was written in an archaic style, using Aramaic and Chaldean so as to reflect the ancient wisdom of its message and to support its claim to be the work of Simon Bar-Yokhai of the 2nd century. The rapid spread of the *Zohar* among the Kabbalist circles contributed to the further development of the movement. While the mythological-gnostic teaching received greater emphasis than the philosophical system that had been developed at Gerona, a synthesis of the two was achieved at the beginning of the 14th century when the movement reached Italy. The persecutions against the Jews in Spain at the end of the 14th and the beginning of the 15th century created a split in the movement between the traditionalist trend, which continued to seek the secrets of the divinity, cosmic phenomena and the historical fate of Israel through mythology and philosophy, and the "practical" Kabbalists, who devoted themselves to speculation about Messianic times and the salvation of Israel. According to the latter trend, the time of redemption, which was to come into being as a result of a holocaust, could be calculated through the position of the cosmological spheres, the aeons, and the behaviour of the people.

G. Scholem, *Major Trends in Jewish Mysticism* (1954); Idem, *Ursprung und Anfänge der Kabbalah* (1962); A. Safran, *La Cabbale* (1972).

KABUL City in *Afghanistan and its present capital. The city developed thanks to its favourable location on the main trade route between India and Turkestan. In the 5th and 6th centuries it belonged to the White *Huns and, after their defeat by *Chosroes I, was conquered by the Persians. Under Arab rule, it became a provincial capital of eastern *Khorasan (8th century). After the establishment of the empire of *Mahmud of Ghazni, the growth of a new capital at Ghazni hastened

its decline. Conquered in 1223 by *Genghis-Khan, the city endured some Mongol attacks, but in the 14th century it again became an important centre. In the 15th century it was made one of the capitals of the *Timurid Mongols.

R. Grousset, *L'Empire des Steppes* (1947).

KAIRWAN City in the *Maghreb (Tunisia). Founded in 664 by the Arab general Ibn Naff'a, it served as headquarters for the Arab army during its conquest of north Africa and was also the administrative centre of the area's caliphate. K. was attacked several times by the *Berbers; in 801 (until 909) it became the capital of the *Aghlabids. During this period, the city became an important economic centre, reputed for its textiles and carpets. In addition, the construction of the city's two mosques, "The Great" and "The Three Gates", which are among the finest examples of Moslem architecture, made K. an important religious centre, a king of holy cities in Moslem *Ifriqia* (north Africa) which attracted many pilgrims. The Aghlabids encouraged scholars to settle in the city and K. became an important theological centre towards the end of the 9th century; its school also attracted philosophers and scientists, as well as artists who developed the art of miniature painting and were renowned for their ornamentation

The Great Mosque at Kairwan, built in the 10th century

of the *Koran. Such books are the most beautiful exemplars that have been preserved. In 909 the *Fatimids conquered the city, which remained an important centre, despite the fact that the capital had been transferred to *Mahdia, until 969 when the Fatimids conquered Egypt. In 969 a local dynasty, the Zirids, seized power at K. and established an independent principality. in the 11th century, after attacks by Beduin and Berbers, the city began to decline and under the *Almohades, who conquered it in 1139, it became a small but prestigious provincial town, which continued to be renowned for its religious structures.
P. Penet, *Kairouan* (1911).

KALMAR City in southeastern *Sweden, on the shores of the Baltic Sea. It was founded in the 12th century and became a prosperous harbour in the Baltic, successfully resisting attacks by the *Hanseatic League. The city is famous for its connection with the "Union of K." (1397), reached between *Denmark, *Norway and *Sweden, which lasted until 1523.

KALONYMUS An important dynasty of *Jewish scholars in the 9th to 12th centuries, whose members were among the most distinguished rabbis in northern Italy and the Rhine Valley. According to its own tradition, the family was originally from Mesopotamia and its earliest ancestor, Aharon ben Samuel, came to Lombardy, bringing with him the secrets of creation as transmitted from father to son, and settled at Lucca (end of the 8th century). Among the family's most famous members were:

Moses Son of Kalonymus (9th century), renowned for his liturgical songs. He lived at Lucca and was reputed as a specialist in Talmudic jurisprudence. He probably died in 926.

Kalonymus The son of Moses (above). He was widely acclaimed for his scholarship and was invited to found the Jewish scholarly centre in the Rhine Valley in Germany. His journey to Germany was later attributed to the efforts of *Charlemagne, "who brought him to Worms, in order to establish there a Jewish school". This legend, similar to other Carolingian tales developed in Germany and France, expressed the importance of the foundation of the Talmudic centre in Germany. Kalonymus apparently settled in Germany from c. 950.

Meshullam (d. 976) Son of Kalonymus (immediately above) A poet and exegete. The major part of his artistic and exegetical activity was undertaken in Italy. M. commented on Mishnaic books and wrote a polemic treatise attacking the *Karaites of Byzantium.

Meshullam, son of Moses (d. 1095) He was one of the most important exegetes of the famous Jewish school of Mainz and maintained relations with Palestinian scholars. He also distinguished himself as a historian of Jewish learning and wrote *Maase Geonim* (the Deeds of the *Gaonim), one of the most authoritative sources on the gaonate of Mesopotamia and Palestine.
S. Eppenstein (ed.), *Germania Judaica,* I (1963).

KALONYMUS Name of several Jewish leaders and scholars belonging to the Nassi dynasty of Narbonne in the 10th to 13th centuries. Among them, the most important were:

K. the Great (c. 1040-c. 1130) His ancestry was traced to an ancient family whose members were considered to be descendants of King David. He was the leader of the Jewish communities in Provence and

Languedoc, and was called "king of the Jews" by the Christians. Besides being a political leader, K. also composed liturgical poems and was considered an authority on Talmudic jurisprudence.

K. II, ben Todros (d. c. 1200) Grandson of K. the Great, he owned a large number of estates in the area of Narbonne and was known as "king of the Jews", one of the three lords of the city (the other two being the viscount and the archbishop). The Jewish school of Narbonne reached the height of its fame during his time and his *Edicts* were sought by the communities of northern Spain, France and Germany.
A. Grabois, *L'Ecole Juive de Narbonne* (1977).

KALONYMUS BEN KALONYMUS (1286-1328) Jewish scholar and writer. Descendant of a distinguished family in Provence, he was born at Arles. After spending his youth in his native city, K. adopted a nomadic way of life, and travelled between Spain and Provence. While at Barcelona, he studied under the great rabbis of the city and wrote to his family criticizing the manners of the Provençal Jews. His most reputed book *Even Habokhan* (Touchstone), dealt with moral life and is an excellent description of the Jewish communities in southern France. During his travels he learned many languages and earned a reputation as a translator. As a result, *Robert of Anjou, king of Naples, invited him in 1324 to settle at his court and employed him to translate Arabic texts into Latin. In 1326 K. settled at Rome, where he translated Jewish scientific books written in Arabic into Hebrew; he became a venerated member of the Roman Jewish community.
M. Steinschneider, *Gesammelte Schriften,* I (1925).

KAMA-SUTRA (The Rules of Love) An Indian treatise in Sanskrit, composed in the time of the Gupta empire (5th-6th centuries) and dedicated to Kama, the god of love. While the anonymous work, written in the form of a learned treatise, is filled with erotic descriptions of love, the book is also an important source of information on Indian society. See *India.

KAMIL, MALIK AL- (1180-1238) Sultan of Egypt (1218-38). Nephew of *Saladin, he became sultan of Egypt upon the death of his father, Malik Al-Adil. K. secured the retreat from Egypt of the participants in the Fifth *Crusade. His moderate political attitude led *Francis of Assisi to attempt his conversion to Christianity, thus begining a spiritual crusade, which also failed. K. fought his relatives, the *Ayyubid sultans, and became the head of the dynasty. In order to prevent a renewed crusade, K. made a treaty with *Frederick II, agreeing to grant the emperor control over Jerusalem and Nazareth, while Frederick promised to demilitarize the holy cities and to allow the Moslems freedom of worship at Jerusalem (1229). In 1237 K. conquered Syria and added to his title that of sultan of Damascus.
CHI (1970).

KARAITES Name of a *Jewish sect which emerged in the 8th century and spread mainly in the Near Eastern countries. The sect originated out of one of the frequent dynastic struggles in the house of the *exilarchs in Mesopotamia. The exilarchs were the descendants of the royal dynasty of King *David and ruled the Jews in the Moslem caliphate. When the claims of *Anan ben David to the dignity were not accepted (765), he rose up against the establishment and especially the *gaonate; thanks to his rhetorical abilities, he was able to attract a large following. Among his supporters were groups who rejected the authority of the Talmud, claiming that only the Old Testament (Hebrew: *Mikra,* hence their name) contained the divine word and had full authority. Such doctrines were influenced by the Islamic *Shiite movement, which combined the dynastic claims of the Alid dynasty with its opposition to the authority of the *Hadith. Anan united his followers and developed their ideas into a comprehensive theory, later expanded on by his successors and disciples. The Ananite movement spread in Mesopotamia, Syria, Palestine and Egypt and had become quite important by the end of the 8th century. When its members were excommunicated by defenders of the Talmudic authority, headed by the gaonim, they organized themselves as a distinct sect, with separate communities and leadership. The K. attached particular importance to the Jewish settlement of Palestine, where one of their groups, the *Avele Zion* (Mourners of Zion), developed an ideology of poverty and mourning until Messianic salvation.

Under the leadership of Benjamin Hanahondi (800-50), the K. doctrine was established and the dynastic aspect of the movement, which had been accentuated under Anan and his immediate descendants, gave way to an ideology which required a literal interpretation of the biblical precepts and, as a consequence, very rigid observation of the law. Due to their constant and sometimes successful struggle against Talmudic Judaism, the K. were forced to remain a sect, open only to those who accepted asceticism in accordance with their ideology. In the 9th century they established a new centre in the Byzantine empire, with an important community at Constantinople, and spread to the Crimea. In order to continue their struggle with the "Rabbanites", they trained popular preachers who were opposed to the sophistication of the Talmudic establishment. In the 10th century the K. were faced with the attacks of a strong personality, *Saadia Gaon, who took the initiative in the polemic struggle and gained significant victories for Orthodox Judaism. The sect therefore lost many of its supporters, but continued to exist, particularly in Palestine, where the K. had their own synagogues in Jerusalem, and also in Egypt and the Byzantine empire. Their original Mesopotamian and Persian centres, however, were greatly weakened and gradually disappeared.

Z. Ankori, *The Karaites in Byzantium* (1965).

KARMATIANS Beduin tribes, originally from eastern *Arabia, who revolted at the beginning of the 9th century against the *Abbasid caliphs and adopted the *Ismaili form of *Shiite Islam. They were notorious for their attacks on caravans of pilgrims to Mecca. Towards the end of the 9th century the K. threatened the Abbasid strongholds in Iraq and Hedjaz. Under the leadership of their chieftain Abu-Saad (894-913), they founded a state in the Bahrain area and began the systematic conquest of Arabia, even threatening the centre of Iraq (927). In 929 they attacked Mecca and carried off the Black Stone of *Kaaba. The act created a scandal in the Moslem world, and the K. were declared infidels by both *Sunnite and Shiite Islam. At the end of the 10th century the K. controlled the major part of the Arabian peninsula and established their government at Mecca. In 951 they restored the Black Stone and profited from the revenue it brought from pilgrims. In

constant war with the *Fatimids, the K. began to decline in the 11th century, when they lost *Hedjaz to Fatimid overlordship.

M. Farsi, *Le Qarmatisme* (1960).

KASHMIR Province in northern India. At the beginning of the Middle Ages, it belonged to the Gupta empire, and was one of the strongholds of the Indo-Aryan civilization. Conquered by *Mahmud of Ghazni *c.* 1000, it was made part of the Ghaznavid state until the latter's fall in 1044. During this period the province was greatly Islamized, which changed its ethnic character. In the 11th to 14th centuries, K. became an independent kingdom which was destroyed by *Timur-leng in 1398.

KAZAN City in *Russia, near the confluence of the Volga and Kama rivers. It was founded at the end of the 13th century by the *Mongols near the ruins of the ancient city of *Bulgar, and became one of the principal cities of the *Golden Horde. K. prospered in the 14th and 15th centuries, becoming an important commercial centre of the Mongol empire. In 1445 a Mongol prince of the Genghis-Khan dynasty, Ulu-Muhammad, whose claim to the khanship of the Golden Horde had been rejected, established an independent Mongol khanate in the city. Its independence, however, was short-lived, and in 1487 Ivan III of Moscow took advantage of dynastic disputes to reduce it to the status of a Russian protectorate.

R. Grousset, *L'Empire des Steppes* (1952).

KEMAL ED-DIN (1192-1262) Historian. Born in Aleppo, he was educated in his native city and in Mesopotamia, where he became acquainted with Arab historical works. He wrote an important history of *Aleppo, covering the 12th and 13th centuries, which is also an important source of information on the northern principalities of the *Crusaders. After 1254 he came to Egypt, where he was employed at the court of the *Mamelukes.

F. Gabrieli, *Arab Historians of the Crusades* (1969).

KENILWORTH Castle in central England in the earldom of Leicester. It was there in 1265 that Prince *Edward (later Edward I) defeated the army of *Simon of Montfort, earl of Leicester, thereby crushing the baronial rebellion against his father, *Henry III. In 1267 he issued the *Dictum de Kenilworth* there, an act of amnesty which forgave the barons and laid the basis for a reconciliation under royal authority. It was there that *Edward II was made to resign the crown in 1327.

F. M. Powicke, *King Henry III and Prince Edward* (1947).

KENT County in *England and one of the seven Anglo-Saxon kingdoms. One of the most Romanized areas in Britain, K. served as the gateway for the *Anglo-Saxon invasion of the island in the middle of the 5th century. The dominant tribes in the realm were the Jutes, originally from Jutland, who settled in Britain and became integrated with the Anglo-Saxon population. In the 6th century the kingdom was the most powerful Anglo-Saxon state in southern England, and its kings were recognized as overlords of the other Saxon realms, such as Essex and Sussex. King *Ethelbert of K., who married a Frankish princess, wielded influence over the realms south of the Humber. Under the influence of his wife, Ethelbert agreed to receive a Christian mission led by St. *Augustine and to convert to the Christian faith, allowing Augustine to establish himself at *Canterbury (603) as the first archbishop in England; thus, K. became the religious centre of England. In the middle of the 8th century, K. was conquered by *Offa, king of Mercia, but regained its independence after his death. Nevertheless, its glorious times were over and the kingdom fell under the influence of *Wessex, becoming a province of the latter in 825.

F. M. Stenton, *Anglo-Saxon England* (1947).

KHADIJA (d. 619) First wife of *Mohammad. A rich widow of a Meccan merchant, she originally employed young Mohammad to lead her caravans. She then married him at the beginning of the 6th century. K. was the first convert to the new faith he preached, which later developed into the Islamic religion. She exercised a large degree of influence over her husband and his companions.

Philip K. Hitti, *History of the Arabs* (1953).

KHALID IBN AL-WALID (d. 641) Arab general. Member of a distinguished Meccan family, K. fought *Mohammad and the men of Medina. After the Battle of *Badr, he converted to Islam; he became one of the most important commanders in Mohammad's army and was granted the cognomen *Saif Allah* (The Sword of God). In 633 he crushed a revolt of Arab tribes against Caliph *Abu Bakr. He was then sent to lead the war against the Persians, whom he defeated at Hira in the following year, also conquering the major part of Iraq. In 636 K. went to Palestine to fight the Byzantines. Under the high command of Caliph *Omar, he severely defeated their army at the Battle of the *Yarmuk, immobilizing their military forces and conquering Palestine. In 637 he was disgraced and so was appointed governor of Homs in Syria, where he died in 641.

Philip K. Hitti, *History of the Arabs* (1953).

KHARADJITES Members of a puritan and radical Moslem sect, originally followers of *Ali, which emerged as a result of their opposition to Ali's negotiations with *Muawiyah in 658. One of their numbers murdered Ali for committing this "sin". The K. organized themselves as a dissident sect under the *Ummayads; they preached strict observance of the Islamic religion and did not hesitate to employ force against their opponents. Their main supporters were found in north Africa, where the sect expanded in the 8th century on the boundaries of the *Abbasid strongholds. The K. were opposed to all the caliphs, recognizing only the authority of *Abu Bakr and *Omar. They chose their own imam (vicar) as leader on the basis of his worthiness; this was determined by his conduct and not by his origin or social status. Any Moslem sinner, in their opinion, was an infidel and subject to death. A moderate group of intellectuals from among the K. developed a pietist philosophy, and expressed their belief through poetry, prayer and sermons.

EI, III.

KHAYYAM OMAR See OMAR KHAYYAM.

KHAZARS A *Turkish people, originally from the central Asian steppes, who were part of the *Petchenegs. They lived under the authority of the *Huns until *Attila's death, at which time they gained independence. In the last years of the 6th century, the K. began to expand westwards to the valleys of the Volga and Don rivers. In 627 they allied themselves with *Heraclius, emperor of Byzantium, and fought the Persians. They were particularly active in the Caucasian areas, where their leader, Khagan Yabgu, established his headquarters. According to a Chinese source, Yabgu imposed his authority over a "multitude of tribes" and *c*. 640 reigned over a territory stretching from the Chinese frontiers to the Don River. During the 7th century the K. continued their westward expansion, ruling over the modern-day territories of the Ukraine and pushing the *Bulgarians southwards. They moved their capital to Itil, a city on the Lower Volga, and were thereby able to control the trade between East and West and between northern Europe and the Black Sea and Mediterranean areas. Besides the obvious economic advantages of such a move, it seems that it was also occasioned by their war with the Arabs (*c*. 650), who had conquered Persia and threatened their Caucasian centre. The Arabs however, were unable to defeat the K., failing a second time in 727-37. During this period, the K. expanded northwards and gained power over the kingdom of *Bulgar on the Volga and Kama rivers. Due to their enmity with the Arabs, the K. entered into an alliance with Byzantium, which expressed itself through intermarriage. In the 8th century the K. were known to frequently visit Constantinople, while Byzantine merchants often journeyed to their country as well. The strategic position of the K. kingdom encouraged both the Byzantines and the Moslems to enter into commercial transactions with them, and their influence gradually began to penetrate the vast kingdom of the steppes, whose rulers began to fear for their independence.

It seems that this fact underlay the royal family's decision to convert to Judaism, an undertaking which was later said to be the result of a theological debate, held before Khagan *Bulan, between Christian, Moslem and Jewish sages. The conversion, which occurred in the latter half of the 8th century, was not total, apparently including only the royal family and part of the nobility. In any case, none of the Turkish and Finno-Ugric tribes, who formed the majority of the population of the realm, embraced the Jewish faith. In the 9th and 10th centuries the empire was a multi-ethnic and multi-religious state, ranging from fetishists and shamanistic Mongols to pagans, and Christian, Moslem and Jewish believers. The royal family's conversion had not affected the political regime nor the social structure of the kingdom. The K. continued to conform to their ancient laws and to be organized on primitive tribal lines. They were led by the khagan and the beg, the latter being a type of prime minister; although appointed by the former, he enjoyed full power as the military leader of the state.

In the 9th century the K. began commercial transactions with Norsemen, the *Varangians, who penetrated the rivers of eastern Europe, moving towards Constantinople. The competition between the two peoples eventually degenerated into clashes and ultimately, when the Norse clan, *Rus, led by *Rurik, established their principality at *Novgorod, to open war. The power of the Russians (as the new inhabitants were called) was particularly strong in the Dnieper Valley, where they set up their centre at *Kiev at the end of the 9th century. Kiev's growth marked the decline of the K. empire, and in 965 the Kievan prince *Svyatoslav inflicted a severe defeat and destroyed the K.' capital at Itil. At

The great Temple of the Khmer period at Angkor Wat

the beginning of the 11th century the kingdom of the K. fell as a result of attacks by the Russians from the west and the *Polovtsi from the east; what was left of their population was converted to Islam.

D. M. Dunlop, *The Khazars* (1966).

KHMER Empire in southeastern *Asia, founded in the 8th century (in present-day Cambodia). The kingdom of K. was organized on social and religious lines by King Jayawarman II (802-50), who established his capital at Angkor, proclaimed himself god and made holy shrines of the royal palaces. Aided by a caste of Brahmanic officials who had immigrated in the previous centuries from India, he introduced a caste system in the country, with Khmerian nobles and Indian Brahmins as rulers of the civil government. He began a policy of expansion, which was continued by his successors in the 9th to 10th centuries and brought the greater part of southeastern Asia under Khmerian rule. During this period, Angkor flourished and became one of the most important art centres in Asia, where royal worship and the Indian culture influenced the development of a unique style of architecture and sculpture of colossal dimensions. In the 12th century the penetration of Buddhism into K. diminished the power of the Brahmanic element, and in the following century the kings themselves adopted Buddhism, which became the state religion. During this time the empire continued to hold sway over Indo-China. However, the removal of the Brahmanic officials had important effects on the empire's stability, which was already threatened by dynastic rivalries between the nobility. The situation led to frequent civil war in the 14th century, which enabled the Thai and Annamese subjects to revolt, while the Mongols of *China destroyed the political unity of the K. empire, causing its decline and fall in the 15th century.

L. P. Briggs, *The Ancient Khmer Empire* (1951).

KHORASAN The eastern part of *Iran, which, in the Middle Ages, included eastern Persia, Afghanistan and the northern areas inhabited by the Iranian population as far as the Aral Sea. The kings of Persia of the *Sassanid dynasty imposed their authority over the Iranian peoples of K., and at the beginning of the 6th century the country belonged to the Persian empire. In 650 it was conquered by the Arabs and Islamized. Opposition to the Arab caliphate took a religious shape with the spread of the *Shiites in the country at the end of the 7th century. The *Abbasid revolt against the *Ummayads was initiated in K. in 743, and many of the Iranian officials and scholars who settled at Baghdad and held office at the Abbasid court were originally from K. At the end of the 10th century the different sections of K. were united under the rule of *Mahmud of Ghazni; during the reign of the Ghaznavid dynasty (980-1044) K. attained political independence and flourished as the centre of the Persian-Moslem civilization and its cultural awakening. This period came to an end with the *Seljuk conquest of the country, which led to the establishment of an independent dynasty in Afghanistan and a split in K. Under the *Seljuks and the *Khwarizmians, K. continued to enjoy economic prosperity and was one of the most developed areas of their empire. However, this situation ended in 1220 with the *Mongol conquest of *Genghis-Khan, who wreaked destruction on the country. Under the Mongol khans of *Persia, the country began to recover and flourished again in the 14th century. Towards the end of the century (1398) *Timur-leng captured the country and again reduced it to a state of ruin.

C. Brockelmann, *History of the Islamic Peoples* (1954).

KHOSAU See CHOSROES.

KHWARIZM Country in central *Asia along the Amu-Daria River, inhabited by an Iranian people of the same name. In 712 it was conquered by the Arabs, who replaced its ancient Iranian culture with an Islamic one. A local dynasty, which was converted to Islam, continued to govern the country, although it did so under Arab authority, which was held by the governors of *Khorasan. The decline of the *Abbasid caliphate brought about a revival of local traditions, and in 995 the emir Mamun proclaimed his independence and encouraged the development of a Persian Islamic culture. In 1017 K. was conquered by *Mahmud of Ghazni, who attracted Turkish elements to the country, gradually changing the Iranian character of the population. After the death of Mahmud, his sons continued to reign over K., although Turkish local emirs acceded to semi-independence; but this situation came to an end in 1043, when the *Seljuks conquered the country. Although included in the Seljuk empire, K. was granted a large degree of autonomy under the leadership of local dynasties. In 1199, upon the dissolution of the Seljuk state, the K.-Shah family proclaimed its independence. Under the leadership of *Ala Al-Din Muhammad (1199-1220), the Khwarizmians founded a powerful state. They conquered a great part of Turkestan, gaining authority over *Turkish and Turkoman tribes, and continued conquests in Persia and along the eastern coast of Arabia, establishing the most powerful Moslem state of the beginning of the 13th century. After the death of Ala Al-Din, the empire collapsed under the *Mongol raids of *Genghis-Khan. In 1221 the Mongols conquered the country of K., and in the following few years destroyed the entire K. empire. The remnants of the population were pushed westwards into Iraq and Syria. In 1244 they conquered and destroyed the *Crusader kingdom of Jerusalem, and severely defeated the Crusader army at Forbie (between Gaza and Ascalon); but the Khwarizmians' attempt to conquer Egypt failed and they were dispersed among the other Turkish peoples of the Middle East.

W. Barthold, *Turkestan Down to the Mongol Invasion* (1928).

KHWARIZMI, MUHAMMAD IBN MUSA AL- (780-845) Scientist. Born to an Iranian family at Khwarizm, he was interested in mathematics, astronomy and geography. He became acquainted through his studies with the Persian and Greek heritages and earned his fame by effectuating their synthesis. His renown gained him an invitation to the Academy of *Baghdad, and Caliph Al-Mamun displayed his interest in his work by richly rewarding him. K.'s contributions to mathematics led to the development of algebra and a theory of numerals. In the field of astronomy, he was one of the developers of the astrolabe and prepared astronomic tables, based on a revision of the *Ptolemaic works. He also established trigonometric tables of the sine and tangent functions. His works continued to be reputed and studied in the 12th century, when they were translated into Latin.

C. Brockelmann, *Geschichte des Arabischen Literatur,* I (1943).

KIEV City on the Dnieper River and *Russian principality in the Middle Ages. The site was populated from ancient times and became a stronghold of the *Goths in the 3rd century. In the 7th century it belonged to the *Khazars, who established an important commercial town there, naming it Kuy-Ev (The Shore of the River). Another tradition concerning the city's origin was recorded in a Russian chronicle of the 12th century; it attributes the city's settlement to three Slavic chieftains, the name of one of them being Kiye. Modern historians, however, support the theory of a Khazar settlement. In the 9th century K. became one of the most important commercial towns of eastern Europe, as it was a central point in the trade route connecting Scandinavia and northern Europe with Constantinople and the Mediterranean world. Byzantine and *Varangian merchants settled there and the Khazar influence diminished. After the establishment of the *Russian state of *Novgorod by *Rurik, K. became subjected to Russian attacks. In 882 Prince *Oleg conquered the city, establishing his capital there. The Khazar influence was eliminated and the city became Slavic in character.

In the 10th century the house of Rurik established its centre in K. After the collapse of the Khazars in 965, the princes of K. became the most powerful rulers of eastern Europe. Gradually the Christian missionaries, who came from the Byzantine empire, converted the population to the Orthodox rite, allowing the use of the Slavonic language in the liturgy. In 998 Prince *Vladimir the Saint converted to the Christian faith and became the closest ally of the Byzantine empire. Under *Yaroslav the Wise, K. attained the peak of its political power in eastern Europe (1019-1154), imposing its domination over all the Slavic principalities east of Poland. Yaroslav's fame reached western Europe and his daughter Ann married *Henry I, king of France. The Russian constitution he adopted aimed to maintain the unity of the state, despite its division between the sons of the prince, by establishing a "brotherhood" of heirs. However, the constitution could not prevent civil war, which weakened the Russian state. Only in the 12th century, under *Vladimir Monomach (1113-25), was a central authority restored; and at that time, K. experienced a second period of prosperity. After Vladimir's death, however, conflicts arose among the Rurikian princes and the central role gradually passed northwards to the branches of *Smolensk and *Suzdal. But the prestige of K. was retained, and only those princes who held actual authority in the city were proclaimed grand princes of Russia. In 1240 K. was conquered by the *Mongols, under *Batu-khan. Most of the city was destroyed and annexed to the *Golden Horde khanate. Only the cathedral of St. Sophia (1037), the "Golden Gate" of the 11th century and some monasteries were left standing.

O. K. Kassimenko, *History of Kiev* (1960).

KILWARDBY, ROBERT (d. 1279) Theologian. He studied at the University of Paris, where he joined the *Dominicans, and taught theology at Paris and Oxford. In 1261 he became the provincial prior of the English Dominicans and became famous for his commentary on the *Sentences,* in which he challenged the Aristotelian methods of his colleague and friend, *Thomas Aquinas. In 1273 he became archbishop of Canterbury and devoted himself to the organization of a charitable enterprise. During this part of his life, he also displayed interest in metaphysical theories and wrote treatises in the field, which remain unpublished. In 1278 he was created cardinal-bishop of Porto and settled in Italy, where he died the following year.

E. M. F. Sommer-Seckendorf, *Studies in the Life of Robert Kilwardby* (1937).

KIN EMPIRE See CHINA.

KING'S BENCH, COURT OF It was originally a small court, dating from the latter half of the 12th century, which enabled the king to render justice without the participation of the plenary royal court. In the 13th century it developed into a permanent court of justice,

Krak des Chevaliers

headed by the king or his personal representative, its purpose being to hear appeals from lower courts. Its efficiency made it one of the most important organs of justice and government in medieval England.

B. Lyon, *A Constitutional and Legal History of Medieval England* (1960).

KING'S COUNCIL (England) See COURTS.

KIPCHAK A confederation of *Turkish tribes in Central Asia, which also included a number of *Mongol tribes. In the 11th century they spread over territories held by the *Khazars; among them, the most famous were the *Polovtsi, who settled between the Urals and the Don. In 1237 the K. was defeated by the Mongols, and joined their ranks. Under the leadership of *Batu-khan, they became a particular *horde* (army) within the *Golden Horde, and were characterized by their Moslem faith.

KNIGHTS OF THE SWORD OF LIVONIA A military-religious order founded in 1204 at the initiative of Pope *Innocent III, who assigned them the task of imposing Christianity in *Livonia. The knights came mainly from Germany and established their headquarters at Riga. They then began to systematically annihilate the pagan tribes and the atrocities they committed earned them the general enmity of the native population; in 1236 they were disastrously defeated. In 1237 the K. merged with the *Teutonic order.

KNOWLES (KNOLLES), SIR ROBERT (c. 1325-1407) English general. He began his career in the campaigns of the *Hundred Years' War in *Edward III's army. He so distinguished himself that he was knighted, despite his humble origins. Having extensive possessions in Brittany, he became one of the heroes of the small mounted bands in France (the *chevauchées*) and in 1370 he and his men threatened Paris. During the revolt of 1381 he commanded the loyalist army in England, which crushed the rebellions at London, Essex and Kent.

M. H. Keen, *England in the Later Middle Ages* (1973).

KNUT, KNUD See CANUTE.

KOLOMAN King of *Hungary (1095-1114). Son of *Ladislas I, he adopted his father's policy of an authoritarian government within the realm and of expansion into the Balkans. In 1096-97, he was confronted by participants of the First *Crusade who passed through Hungary. He proved his wisdom by providing means for their rapid passage. In 1101 he conquered *Croatia and in 1105 *Dalmatia, imposing the Catholic rite upon the Slavs. His last years were marked by dynastic troubles, when his brother *Almos, backed by Byzantium, claimed the kingship.

D. Sinor, *History of Hungary* (1957).

KÖNIGSBERG City in *Prussia on the shores of the Baltic Sea. It originated around a castle built by the *Teutonic knights in 1255. German settlers, brought to the site during the latter half of the century, developed it, and in 1286 K. became a city. In 1340 K. joined the German *Hanse and became one of its influential members. The Teutonic knights took control over the city in 1451, establishing there the centre of their order and the capital of their Prussian province.

G. Barraclough, *Origins of Modern Germany* (1954).

KONUNGSKUGGSJA (The King's Mirror) A mid-13th-century Norse description of the northern countries, including Iceland and *Greenland. Written with the intention of attracting colonists, it presents a somewhat idealized description of Greenland, its soil, nature and climate.

G. Jones, *The Vikings* (1968).

KORAN The holy book of *Islam. It consists of the oral revelations by God to *Mohammad, as the Prophet related them to his disciples from 613. Based on biblical and other stories, the K. developed the principles of Moslem monotheism. It is divided into chapters (*suras*). The K. was only compiled after the death of Mohammad, the first compilation dating from the time of his immediate successor, *Abu Bakr. The text used today is the revised compilation prepared *c.* 655 on the orders of Caliph *Uthman. This version, which superseded all other variants and is accepted by *Sunnite Islam, was contested by the *Shiites, who complained of the expurgation of all the prophet's precepts concerning *Ali. It contains an introductory prayer and 114 *suras,* arranged according to length, the longest coming first and the shortest last. The K. is in prose, much of it rhymed, written in a powerful style.

A. J. Arbery, *The Koran Interpreted* (1963);
R. Bell, *Introduction to the Quran* (1953).

KRAK *Crusader stronghold in Transjordan, east of the Dead Sea. It was fortified by the Crusaders in 1143 and included a small town and an impressive castle. It become the capital of the Crusader principality of Transjordan, one of the great baronies of the Latin kingdom of Jerusalem. Its main importance lay in its control of the main route from Syria to Egypt via the Hedjaz. After the accession of *Saladin to the thrones of Egypt and Syria (1174), he became aware that K. was the main obstacle to the union of his states, and he attacked it several times. K., however, resisted and was conquered only in 1189 after a long siege, two years after the fall of Jerusalem. In the 13th century the stronghold was used as a prison for enemies of the *Ayyubid rulers of Egypt, and as an apanage for minor princes of the dynasty (1229-45).

S. Runciman, *History of the Crusades* (1953).

KRAK DES CHEVALIERS One of the greatest fortresses of the *Crusaders in the Middle East. It was situated on the western bank of the Orontes River in the county of Tripoli, and faced the major city of *Homs. Its building began in 1142, when the *Hospitallers were given the site, where an ancient Byzantine and Moslem castle already existed. The fortress, which completely changed the character of the place, is one of the best surviving examples of Romanesque military architecture. The order held it until 1271, when the *Mameluke sultan of Egypt, *Baibars, conquered it after a short siege.

S. Runciman, *History of the Crusades* (1953);
P. Deschamps, *Le Krak des Chevaliers* (1936).

KRUM Khan of the *Bulgars (802-14). He led the great Bulgarian invasion from their territories in Dobrudja (between the Danube and the Black Sea) into the Balkan peninsula and founded a powerful state in the area of present-day Bulgaria. This invasion involved him in continuous war with *Byzantium (805-14). While, in the first stages of the war, the Byzantine armies had some successes and even destroyed Pliska, his capital, K., who proved himself a good organizer, was able to keep his people united and in 811 inflicted a severe defeat on Emperor *Nicephorus I, which opened the way to Constantinople for him. He destroyed most of the

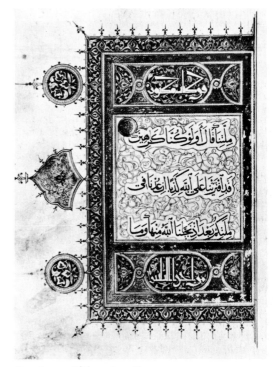

Page from a 13th-century Koran

cities between the Balkans and Constantinople and twice besieged the capital of the Byzantine empire (in 813 and 814); he died during the second siege. K. is considered the founder of the Bulgarian state.

S. Runciman, *The First Bulgarian Empire* (1930).

KUBLAI KHAN (1215-94) Founder of the *Mongol empire of China (1260-94). He was one of the grandsons of *Genghis-Khan and was sent by his uncle, the Great Khan *Ogodai to China, as governor of *Honan (1240). There he proved his military skills, which enabled him to complete the conquest of northern China, begun by Genghis-Khan, destroying the remnants of the Kin empire. Under the authority of his brother, *Mangu, he attained a considerable degree of independence and began the conquest of the Sung empire in southern *China. In 1259, on the death of Mangu, he claimed the title of great khan, but obtained recognition only in 1260, through the support of his brother *Hulagu in Persia. He moved his capital to Peking, breaking thus with the other Mongol khanates, and founded a Mongol-Chinese empire, proving himself to be a skilled politician, gaining the cooperation of the Chinese. He completed the conquest of southern China and expanded to Indo-China. His government was favourably described by Marco *Polo, who visited Peking.

R. Grousset, *L'Empire des Steppes* (1952).

KUFA Military camp and city in *Iraq, founded by the Arabs. Its origins are connected with the establishment, by Caliph *Omar in 638, of a garrison to control the conquered country of Iraq. He settled south Arabian tribes there. With the settlement of Iranian Moslems, employed in the administration of the country, the camp was rapidly transformed into a city. In 655 its governor and population proclaimed *Ali, son-in-law of *Mohammad, caliph, as against Caliph *Uthman and Mohammad's widow, *Aisha. The city became Ali's capital until his murder in 661 and one of the centres of the *Shiites. With the establishment of the *Ummayad caliphate, the importance of K. declined and the city once more became a provincial capital, where, at the request of the Ummayad governors, the Shiites were excluded. With the success of the *Abbasid revolution, K. became the capital of the caliphate until the building of Baghdad (649-63). The founding of *Baghdad caused its decline, which was accelerated in the 10th century when the *Karmatians invaded it in 924, 927 and 937 and robbed its population, whose remnants fled to Baghdad and settled there.

Philip K. Hitti, *History of the Arabs* (1953).

KULIKOVO-ON-THE-DON Locality on the upper Don in *Russia, famous as the site of a battle in 1380 between the Russians and *Mongols. Led by Mamay, khan of the *Golden Horde, the Mongols invaded Russia when Prince *Dmitri of Moscow refused to pay tribute. The Russian victory was a decisive event in their struggle for independence, and although it was not yet complete freedom from Mongol domination, it symbolizes the establishment of the new Russia under the leadership of *Moscow.

G. Vernadsky, *The Mongols and Russia* (1953).

KURALTAI The *Mongol term for the assembly of the princes of the royal dynasty. In the constitution of the Mongol empire, as laid down by *Genghis-Khan, the K. was the highest authority of the empire. It was convened at Karakorum, the capital of the empire, for the purpose of electing the great khan upon the death of the previous office-holder, or whenever the great khan decided to convene it to decide on legislative and administrative problems. The members of the dynasty were expected to attend the K. under all circumstances. The compulsory nature of this obligation was strikingly demonstrated by the decision of *Batu-khan to terminate his invasion of Europe after the conquest of Poland and Hungary in 1241, and to retreat with his forces in order to be present at the K. convened to elect a heir to his uncle *Ogodai.

M. Prawden, *The Mongols* (1942).

KURDISTAN The country of the *Kurds, in the mountains of western Iran, north of the Tigris River. Mentioned by the ancient Greek historians, the Kurds were semi-nomadic tribes of Iranian origin. Until the Middle Ages, all data concerning them is vague. In the 3rd century, when the *Sassanids seized power in Persia, the Kurds were dominant in their army and distinguished themselves as warriors. Despite their military importance in Sassanid Persia, they were not involved in the political life of the empire and continued their tribal organization and manner of life. Conquered by the Arabs in 640, they converted to Islam and were allowed to preserve a certain degree of autonomy. The *Abbasid caliphs employed them in the army and in the 9th century they formed the major part of it, together with Turkish recruits. Under the influence of *Baghdad, Moslem forms of culture were gradually adopted in K., where the national language continued to be used, but written in Arab characters from the 11th century. Thus, a Kurdish culture emerged and developed, including poetry, both epic and lyric, such as that of the sensitive poet Ali Hariri. A number of chieftains established their own courts, modelled after those of the Persian governors. The Kurds allied with the *Seljuk sultans and took part in their wars against the *Fatimids and the Byzantines. In the 12th century some of their leaders left the country and settled in the centres of the Seljuk emirates in Syria, Persia and Anatolia. Among them, the famous family of their Emir Al-Ayyub played a major part in the military and political life of northern Syria. In the latter half of the 12th century, his grandson *Saladin became the principal leader of the Moslem world and the "hero of Islam", uniting Syria and Egypt and defeating the *Crusaders. Nevertheless, the *Ayyubids, as well as other Kurdish families who left K. and settled in Syria, rapidly became Arabized, while their co-nationals in the mountains continued their tribal life and developed their national culture. The Kurds distinguished themselves in their resistance to the Mongol invasions, and in 1251 defeated *Hulagu-khan. Until the end of the Middle Ages, they continued their autonomous life in K., though without creating an independent realm.

H. Arfa, *The Kurds; A Historical and Political Study* (1966).

KYRENIA City on the northern coast of *Cyprus. It was a major naval base of the *Byzantines, who fortified the city and constructed its harbour. Under *Frankish rule, K. was one of the royal cities of the kingdom and its fortifications were rebuilt in the Gothic style. During the 13th century the castle of St. Hilarius, one of the chief strongholds of the island, was built near the city.

G. Hill, *History of Cyprus,* III (1949).

KYRIOTES, JOHN (John Geometres; 10th century) Byzantine poet. Employed at the imperial court at *Constantinople, he gained a reputation for his epigrams. One of the main features of his writing was the mixture of sacred with profane and pagan subjects. His epigrams deal with emperors and dignitaries, as well as Plato and Aristotle and the Fathers of the Church.

A. S. Way, *Greek Anthology* (1939).

L

LADISLAS I, St. (1040-95) King of *Hungary (1077-95). L. annexed large territories in Transylvania to Hungary, extending his realm's frontiers to the Carpathian Mountains. In 1091 he turned southwards and conquered *Croatia, where he introduced Catholicism. L. supported *Gregory VII against *Henry IV in the *Investiture controversy. During the last years of his reign, he was concerned with internal reforms which brought economic prosperity to Hungary.
D. Sinor, *History of Hungary* (1958).

LADISLAS II King of *Hungary (1162). He seized power after a civil war and deposed the legitimate king, *Stephen III, but died shortly after his coronation.

LADISLAS III King of *Hungary (1204-05). L. reigned under the regency of his uncle, *Andrew II.

LADISLAS IV (1262-90) King of *Hungary (1272-90). During his minority the country was divided by civil wars, and not until 1278 was L. able to impose his authority over the Hungarian magnates. In the same year, he allied himself with Emperor *Rudolf of Hapsburg against King *Otakar II of Bohemia. In 1282 he fought against the Cumans and conquered their lands in *Moldavia. During the war, he fell in love with a Cuman princess and left his wife, Isabella of *Anjou-Naples. As a result, he changed his life-style and surrounded himself with Cuman nobles, to the point that he was called the Cumanian. In 1288 Pope *Nicholas IV called for a *Crusade against L., which again sparked civil war in Hungary. The king was murdered by his Cuman guard in 1290.
D. Sinor, *History of Hungary* (1958).

LADISLAS (c. 1376-1414) King of Naples (1390-1414). Son of *Charles III of Durazzo-Hungary, his rights were contested by *Louis II of Anjou, and the struggle between the two parties lasted until 1404, when L. established his government. L. then allied himself with *Florence and strongly imposed his influence upon Rome so that it became a second capital of his state. After 1409 L.'s influence in Italy grew due to his statesmanship and the army that backed him. He thus began to express ideas of reviving the Italian realm. His plans were cut short by his death and his inheritance passed to his sister, *Joan II.
A. Cutolo, *Re Ladislao d'Angio-Durazzo* (1936).

LADISLAS Kings of Poland. See WLADYSLAW.

LAHORE City in northwestern *India. Founded in the 3rd or 4th century, L. first received mention in the sources as a commercial centre in the 7th century. At the beginning of the 11th century it was conquered by the sultans of *Ghazni and became one of the flourishing centres of the Ghaznavid and *Ghorid empires. Its population became Islamized and the impact of Moslem culture can be seen in the architectural plan of the Old City. In the 13th century the *Mongols despoiled much of L. In 1398 *Timur-leng destroyed the city, but it was rebuilt in 1422 as the capital of Mubarak Shah, one of the *Timurid monarchs.
EI, III.

LAMBERT, St. (635-700) Missionary. Member of a noble family of *Austrasia, he was prepared for an ecclesiastical career and became bishop of Maastricht. In 675 he left his see for political reasons and worked to spread Christianity in the Low Countries. L. had a serious dispute with the mayor of the palace, *Pepin II, and was murdered. He became the patron saint of *Liège. His cult was popular in the Middle Ages and was represented in medieval art.
G. Kurth, *Le Vita Sancti Lamberti* (1919).

LAMBERT OF HERSFELD (c. 1024-77) Historian. Benedictine monk at Hersfeld in Germany from 1058, L. was entrusted with the annals of his abbey. He recompiled these works, adding much valuable information from several sources and transforming them into a history of the (Christian) world. That material which covers the years 1040 to 1077 is original and contains much important data on the onset of the *investiture controversy. His work provides a close look at the feudal society of Germany in his time.
J. W. Thompson, *History of Historical Writing* (1943).

LAMBERT OF SPOLETO Emperor (894-98). Son of *Guy of Spoleto, he inherited his father's title, but was deposed by Pope *Formosus when *Arnulf of Carinthia invaded Italy and claimed the imperial crown. In 897, after Arnulf's return to Germany, L. defeated his rival, *Berengar of Friuli, and restored his crown. However, he died an accidental death in the following year.
C. G. Mor, *L'Eta Feudale;*
Storia Politica d'Italia, I (1952).

LAMBETH HOUSE The palace of the archbishops of *Canterbury at London. Situated on the southern bank of the Thames River, it was acquired in 1185 by Archbishop Baldwin II, who set up his office there. Beginning in the 13th century the palace became one of the most prominent cultural and political centres in London and became famous for its library, in which many illuminated manuscripts have been preserved.
S. R. Maitland, *Lambeth Palace* (1932).

LANCASTER County in northern *England. After the *Norman Conquest of 1066, the knight Roger of Poitou built a castle there, around which developed the city of L. In 1193 King *John granted the city its privileges and in the 13th century it was incorporated into a county. The title count of L. was granted to junior branches of the royal dynasty.

LANCASTER, HOUSE OF Junior branches of the *Plantagenet royal dynasties of England, named after the county of Lancaster. The title first appeared in

1267, when Edmund, the younger son of *Henry III, was granted the earldom together with the counties of Leicester and Derby. The house became extinct after the death of his grandson, Henry (d. 1361). In 1351, on the occasion of the marriage of Henry's daughter, Blanche, to *John of Gaunt, the fourth son of *Edward III, Lancaster was made a duchy and John founded the second L. His son, *Henry, became king of England in 1399 and the Lancastrians reigned until 1471. Their symbol was a white rose.

R. Somerville, *History of the Duchy of Lancaster* (1953).

LANCE, THE HOLY See HOLY LANCE.

LANCELOT, ROMANCE OF One of the most popular among the *Arthurian romances of the Middle Ages. Until the beginning of the 13th century, the character Lancelot was simply portrayed as a model knight residing at the court of King *Arthur. However, soon this figure aroused special interest and was made the hero of a separate romance. Lancelot became the symbol of fidelity towards his lord, a loyalty which was even stronger than the love he felt for his mistress.

R. S. Loomis, *Arthurian Literature of the Middle Ages* (1955).

LANDFRIEDEN See PEACE OF GOD.

LANFRANC (1005-89) Archbishop of *Canterbury (1070-89). L. was born at Pavia in northern Italy, where he studied law. In 1035 he went to France, studied theology at Dijon and settled in 1039 in Normandy, where he founded a school at Avranches. In 1042 L. entered the abbey of *Bec and in 1045 became its prior and the head of its monastic school. Under his tutelage the school became one of the most famous in Europe. After a brief contention with Duke *William, L. became one of his most trusted counsellors (1053). In 1070 William appointed him archbishop of Canterbury with the task of reorganizing the Church of England. L. nurtured harmonious relations both with the king and the papacy. He was one of the most distinguished scholars of his generation and, besides fulfilling his duties as archbishop and teacher, he also wrote a treatise on the sacrament and a commentary on the *Benedictine rule and monastic behaviour.

A. J. Macdonald, *Lanfranc* (1944).

LANGLAND, WILLIAM (1332-1400) Author. Born in Shropshire, L. was prepared for an ecclesiastical career. His studies probably influenced his writings, which are based on religious allegories. L. composed numerous poems rooted in the biblical tradition and praised monastic figures, such as *Bernard of Clairvaux, whom he found an inspiration to his ascetic way of life. *Piers Plowman*, the greatest English poem of the Middle Ages, has been attributed to L.

J. Lawlor, *Piers Plowman; An Essay in Criticism* (1962).

LANGRES City in eastern *France. The former Roman city declined at the beginning of the Middle Ages and was merely an episcopal centre during the *Carolingian period. From the 12th century on the city began to develop under the rule of the dukes of *Burgundy, who held L. as vassals of the bishops. In medieval times the bishops of L. were given the title of peers of the realm. The town suffered greatly from the *Hundred Years' war.

LANGTOFT, PETER (d. 1307) Historian. L. was canon of the *Augustinian abbey of Bridlington and was its treasurer from 1271-86. He wrote a history of Eng-

land, the most important parts of which deal with the last years of *Henry III and the reign of *Edward I.

J. W. Thompson, *History of Historical Writing* (1943).

LANGTON, STEPHEN (c. 1150-1228) Archbishop of *Canterbury (1207-28). Born in England. L. studied theology at the University of Paris and in 1181 began to teach there. At this time, he became the close friend of Lotario de Segni, later to be *Innocent III. During his 25 years at the university, L. earned wide fame as a theologian and for his exegetical commentary on biblical texts; a dictionary of Hebrew biblical terms numbers among his many compositions. In 1206 Innocent made L. cardinal and in 1207 appointed him archbishop of Canterbury despite the opposition of King *John. The ensuing dispute between the pope and king delayed L.'s entrance into England until 1213. The archbishop was sympathetic to the baronial revolt, although he did not play an active part, and was among those who advised John to grant the *Magna Charta. From 1216 L. firmly supported the regency of *Henry III. L. actively established discipline within the English church and imposed the primacy of the Canterbury see. In 1222 he issued a series of statutes of the Church of England, which included the decrees of the Fourth *Lateran Council.

F. M. Powicke, *Stephen Langton* (1928).

LANGUEDOC Province in southern *France. The Roman province of Narbonensis was conquered at the beginning of the 5th century by the *Visigoths. It remained under their rule until the 8th century. During that period it was also called *Septimania. After the collapse of the Visigothic realm, parts of L. were conquered by the *Arabs; however, their rule in the area was not well established. Thus the *Franks, under *Charles Martel and *Pepin the Short, reconquered the province in 754, calling it Gothia, and incorporated it into their kingdom. Under *Charlemagne the country became a base for wars against Spain and, when the *march of Spain was founded in 810, L. was made a part of it. During the 9th century the march was split in two and L. temporarily became the march of Gothia. In 924 it was finally united with the county of *Toulouse.

Under the rule of the counts of Toulouse the province was divided into a number of feudal units, the most important among them being the county of Melgueil (which included the seigniory of *Montpellier), the viscounty of *Narbonne and the seigniories of the house of Trencavel. The Trencavels became a major political power in southern France in the 12th century. This period was marked by economic prosperity and cultural development in L., especially as regarding secular literature, including the poetry of the *troubadours. In the 12th century the *Albigenses won much support in L., and at the beginning of the 13th century they became a powerful force in the country and received the backing of lords, including the Trencavels. The *Crusade against the Albigenses seriously harmed L. and introduced radical changes in its political and social structure. The power of the local dynasties, especially of the counts of Toulouse and the lords of Trencavel, was weakened and a large part of the country was annexed to the royal demesne, forming the *sénéchaussée* of Beaucaire. Other territories were annexed to *Aragon, while the remaining areas were placed under the lordship of *Alphonse of Poitiers, brother of King *Louis IX (1249). Moreover, the *Dominican order, founded in the province in 1215, was given the authority to seek out and punish heretics. After Alphonse's death (1270), L. was annexed to the lands of the crown and administered by a royal governor.

P. Wolff (ed.), *Histoire du Languedoc* (1968).

LAON City in northeastern *France. From the 5th century L. was essentially an episcopal see. It did not gain much importance until the 10th century, when it became the seat of the last *Carolingian kings of France. In 987 *Hugh Capet granted the royal palace to the bishop, who assumed the title of count, and the city became the centre of an important ecclesiastical seigniory. In 1113 the burghers revolted against the bishop and demanded communal rights. The revolt was repressed by *Louis VI, who nevertheless recognized and confirmed the city's communal status in 1128. Consequently the city enjoyed a large degree of autonomy.

S. Martinet, *Laon* (1965).

LAS NAVAS DE TOLOSA, BATTLE OF (1212) Fought at the gates of *Andalusia between a united Christian front (the kings of Castile, Aragon, Navarre and Portugal and some French knights) and the *Almohades. The victory of the Christians was a decisive step in the *Reconquista wars and marked the ultimate decline of Moslem power in Spain. The battle also paved the way for the conquest of Andalusia by Castile.

LATAKIA (Laodicea) City in northern *Syria, on the shores of the Mediterranean Sea. It had a prosperous harbour under Byzantine rule, but after the Arab conquest in 638, the city declined and its commercial activity was taken over by *Antioch. In 1103 L. fell to the *Crusaders, who placed it under the lordship of a family of vassals to the counts of *Tripoli. Conquered in 1188 by *Saladin, the city was recovered by the Crusaders in 1198, who ruled it until 1268, when the *Mamelukes annexed it to their empire. The city's impressive 13th-century Gothic cathedral is one of the most interesting structures of the medieval period.

J. Richard, *Le Comté de Tripoli à l'époque des Croisades* (1943).

LATERAN COUNCIL Religious councils convened in the *Lateran Palace. Of these, four were oecumenical:
First L. (1123) Convoked by *Calixtus II after having established peace with the emperor (the Concordat of *Worms), it was the first oecumenical council of the Roman Catholic Church to be held in the West.
Second L. (1139) Convoked by *Innocent II for the reformation of the church, it condemned the supporters of *Anacletus II and the theories of *Arnold of Brescia.
Third L. (1179) Convoked by *Alexander III after the peace treaty he made with *Frederick Barbarossa, it was meant to display church unity. The issues discussed included certain procedures concerning the majority needed for papal elections and a canon providing for the establishment of schools.
Fourth L. (1215) The most important of the Ls., not only because it was presided over by *Innocent III, but also because of the wide range of topics discussed. The issues held ramifications for theology, the liturgy and canon law. An important place was also given to the problem of the repression of heresies.

E. Josi, *San Giovanni in Laterano* (1953).

LATERAN PALACE Church and papal palace at Rome, built on the ruins of the ancient palace of the Laterani family, which was given by Emperor *Constantine I to the bishops of Rome. From the middle of the 4th century and until 1305, the L. became the offical residence of the popes. Its church, known as the cathedral of Rome, was rebuilt and dedicated to John the Baptist in the 10th century, after the earlier basilica had been destroyed by an earthquake. In the 14th century the church was damaged several times by fire, but was rebuilt. The L. was the site of many councils; although most were of a local or provincial nature, such meetings were given special significance since they were presided over by popes. In one such council (1059) the procedure for papal elections by the cardinals was established.

LATIN EMPIRE OF CONSTANTINOPLE, THE The political organization established in 1204 by the participants in the Fourth *Crusade, after the conquest of Constantinople and the destruction of the *Byzantine empire. Under the leadership of *Baldwin of Flanders the new empire formally included all Frankish conquests in Greece, namely the kingdom of *Thessalonica, the duchy of *Athens and the principality of *Morea. In actuality, however, these territories were independent of the emperors and the empire proper extended over the territories of Thrace. L. was largely dependent on *Venice; thus it established a Venetian quarter in 1204 and also allowed the city a commercial monopoly and domination over the harbours.

L.'s history was marked by constant wars with the *Bulgarians and the emperors of *Nicaea, the latter aiming to reconquer the capital of Byzantium. Moreover, aside from outside agitation, the local population also entered constant struggles with their conquerors, especially regarding religious issues. The empire was Latin in character and was obedient to the pope; in addition, Thomas *Morosini, a Venetian, was appointed patriarch. This aroused the fierce opposition of the Greek Orthodox clergy and especially the monks, who rejected union with Rome and preached against the conquerors. In 1261 Emperor *Michael Palaeologus of Nicaea reconquered Constantinople with the help of the *Genoese and restored the Byzantine empire.

Despite the extinction of L., the imperial title continued to pass, through marriage and inheritance, to several Italian princes, especially of the house of *Anjou-Naples, until the end of the Middle Ages.

J. Longnon, *L'Empire Latin de Constantinople* (1946).

LATINI, BRUNETTO (1220-94) Scholar and politician. Born at Florence, where he was educated, L. became a leader of the city's *Guelph party and distinguished himself as a radical politician. In 1260, when his party lost power in the city, he was driven out and took refuge in France. In1266 he returned to Florence and was elected to the city council. L. wrote an Italian adaptation of Cicero's rhetorical works, *La Rettorica*, a number of mystical poems in the Tuscan dialect and *Li Livres dou Trésor*, composed during his stay in France, which was considered an encyclopedia of contemporary scientific, philosophical and theological knowledge. L. was among the first western scholars to use the vernacular for scientific purposes.

F. J. Carmody, *Brunetto Latini's Tresor; Latin Sources on Natural Sciences* (1937).

LATIUM Province in central *Italy near Rome. At the beginning of the Middle Ages, L. was not a distinct entity and successively belonged to the *Heruli, *Ostrogoths and *Byzantines. With the foundation of the *Papal States under *Gregory I (590), L. became the core of the new political organization and was administered by papal counts. In the late 9th century the feudal system was adopted by the local nobility and a number of dynasties emerged from the landowners. These families built castles and imposed their authority over vassals and peasants. Among them, the most important were the counts of *Tusculum, the lords of *Anagni and others. In the 10th and 11th centuries such dynasties became strong enough to impose their authority upon the papacy; their power was not suppressed until they were defeated and destroyed by Emperor *Henry III. Even after this defeat, the feudal regime continued to prevail in the country, however, the new lords were Roman families who possessed estates in the province.

G. Falco, *The Holy Roman Republic* (1956).

LAUDS The traditional morning prayer of the Roman Catholic Church; the L. call for the intercession of God and the saints. From the 8th century it was the custom to recite L. for the popes, emperors, kings and princes. Such prayers were a sign of a certain area's loyalty to their monarch or lord.

E. Kantorowicz, *Laudes Regiae* (1954).

LAURA The name given to a colony of ascetic monks who lived in the desert.

LAUSANNE City on the northern shore of Lake Geneva. The former Roman settlement was conquered in the 5th century by the *Burgundians and made part of their kingdom. In 590 a bishopric was created in the borough and the city developed rapidly. In the 10th century the bishops imposed their rule over the city and its county, and from 1032 they held a large temporal principality of the *Holy Roman emperors. In 1159 *Frederick Barbarossa granted the bishops of L. the title, "princes of the empire", which they held until the end of the Middle Ages. In the 14th century their power began to decline, however, and much of their land passed to the counts of *Savoy.

G. A. Chevallaz, *Lausanne* (1960).

LAW In the Middle Ages L. was considered the basic framework of the social and political body; without it society could not exist. It was believed to be dictated by divine will and revealed to the wise men. From the early Middle Ages, legal practices were largely associated with more ancient Ls. In fact, in western Europe, it was believed that an ideal lawmaker was one who discovered the most ancient legal customs.

In the *Byzantine empire the Roman heritage was the basis of medieval legislation. Consequently, Byzantium continued the practices of Roman (or civil) L., and from the 6th century the issuance of new legislation became the prerogative of the emperor. The groundwork for this policy was laid by *Justinian and his jurists, who codified Roman L. in the articles of the *Corpus Juris Civilis;* and the concept continued to manifest itself in later legal codes until the 12th century. Consequently, the superiority of state L. over other legal authorities was recognized. This included the sovereignty of imperial edicts over those of the *Church.

In the West, religious and state L. were independent and two parallel systems of jurisdiction emerged. The latter system resulted from the codification of *Germanic tribal customs (distinct in nature from Roman L.) in the new realms of the early Middle Ages. Tribal L.,

codified between the 6th and 9th centuries and known as the *leges barbarorum* (The L. of the Barbarians), was rooted in ancient traditions. The most famous among such codes was the "Salic L." of the *Franks. The diversity of the legal codes encouraged pluralism and the principle of personal L. was also recognized. Thus, for example, a *Burgundian in southeastern France lived according to Burgundian L., while the native population respected the Roman L.; Frankish settlers, on the other hand, were ruled by the Salian or *Ripuarian L. The *Jewish communities were allowed to govern themselves according to the Talmud.

Legal pluralism facilitated the introduction of feudal L. in the 9th century, which came to replace the earlier tribal system. *Feudalism, too, was based on the pluralist concept; the vassal adopted the legal traditions of his lord. The relation of feudal ties to land grants led to the establishment of a territorial legal system, described by 19th-century legal theorists and known as the *Landrecht*. This system functioned together with the *Lehnrecht*, the feudal code proper. Feudal L. was territorially restricted and characterized by diverse traditions and customs, from which developed the concept of privileges. However, some practices were more widespread then others and became the common heritage of western Europe, such as military L. and the *chivalric codes.

As stated earlier, the Church developed its own legal system, the *canon L. As distinct from civil, tribal and feudal Ls., this system was considered an expression of divine will, based on its revelation to the faithful and its confirmation in the Holy Scriptures. Divine authority was complemented by the writings of the Fathers of the Church, the decrees of the councils and the ordinances of the popes. Canon L. was codified in the 11th and 12th centuries; the most notable work done in this field was by *Gratian. Ecclesiastical L. was applied to the clergy, who were exempt from the jurisdiction of civil and feudal authorities by the *privilegium fori*. Its impact was also felt by certain groups comparable to the clergy, especially teachers and university students. On the other hand, canon L. had authority over the entire community of faithful with regard to marriage and other such areas related to the administration of *sacraments.

Medieval legal thought was closely connected to politics and theology. It emerged from the theories of St. *Augustine, who arranged L. hierarchically according to three levels: 1) divine L., being the supreme authority and incontestable; it was revealed to the faithful and accepted on the basis of both faith and reason; 2) natural L., whose basic precepts could be understood by all creatures, and which lacked the perfection of faith, but could be improved by philosophy; and 3) temporal L. (particularly the Roman) which was man-made; its importance lay in the decisions made regarding the common wealth and service and, as such, the Church required that its ordinances be observed by the faithful when they did not contradict divine or canon L. This hierarchical view of L. was perfected by *Thomas of Aquinas in the 13th century.

The revival of Roman L. in the West began in *Bologna in the late 11th century, when *Irnerius taught his students to interpret the Code of *Justinian and to adapt it to the needs of their own time. The influence of Roman L. became strong by the beginning of the 12th century and Gratian himself found a need to refer to it when he prepared his canon code. He adopted the view that imperial ordinances were a source of authority when they did not oppose canon L. Roman L. also influenced the jurists of *Frederick Barbarossa in preparing the constitutional groundwork for the *Holy Roman empire. Despite the opposition of the feudal realms and churchmen, such as St. *Bernard of Clairvaux, who claimed that "the place where Justinian penetrates, St. Peter has to leave", Roman L. became rooted in western Europe, and in the 14th century it served as a model for secular legislation in the West.

Another important area of legislation was that of maritime L. Based on classical precepts, medieval maritime codes were enacted to regulate naval trade. Such codes were first issued in the 11th century with reference to the Mediterranean Sea. From the 14th century, maritime L. also concerned activities in the Atlantic. Such codes called for the establishment of special courts to try cases. The most prestigious among these was the Court of the *Chain at *Acre.

F. Kern, *Kingship and Law in the Middle Ages* (1939).

LAYAMON (d. c. 1200) English poet. According to his testimony, L. was a parish priest in Worcestershire. He wrote a rhymed version of the *Roman de Brut* of William *Wace, a History of Brutus of Troy, who was recognized as the first legendary king of *Britain. L.'s romance-chronicle, the *Brut,* deals with the legendary establishment of the Trojan dynasty in England. The Trojans were intended to lend more importance to the Britons and were considered ancestors of the legendary King *Arthur. The poem was consequently incorporated into the Arthurian cycle and was a source for 13th-century romances.

R. S. Loomis, *Arthurian Literature in the Middle Ages* (1959).

LAZARUS, St. A beggar in Christ's parable of the "Dives". In the Middle Ages, L. was venerated as the patron saint of lepers. A monastic order was founded in his name in the 11th century with the aim of treating lepers. This order founded hospitals for lepers in the main centres of western Europe, as well as in *Palestine. In Palestine the order also established a chapter of the "knights of L." in the second half of the 12th century.

LAZARUS (1329-89) King of *Serbia (1387-89). A member of the Serbian royal dynasty, L. was a vassal of the kings of *Hungary for the major part of his life, but enjoyed a large degree of autonomy, which he used to enlarge his principality. In 1387 he proclaimed the independence of Serbia. L. fought against the Turks and was killed at the Battle of *Kossovo; his death marked the end of the Serbian kingdom.

H. W. V. Temperley, *History of Serbia* (1919).

LEANDER, St. (c. 550-600) Bishop of *Seville (584-600). The elder brother of *Isidore of Seville. L. was sent to represent the Spanish church in Constantinople at the imperial court in 582. There he became acquainted with Pope *Gregory I and acquired his friendship. Upon his return, L. was appointed bishop of Seville and rapidly became the leader of the Spanish church. He played an important role in the conversion of the Visigothic king, *Reccared, to the Catholic faith. In 589 L. presided over the Council of Toledo, where he laid the groundwork for the organization of the church in the *Visigothic kingdom.

H. Ward, *St. Leander of Seville* (1882).

LECHFELD, BATTLE OF Fought between the *Hungarians, who advanced to the banks of the Lech River in Bavaria, and the Germans, led by King *Otto I (955). Otto's victory signalled an end to Hungarian raids into Germany. It also considerably increased the king's prestige, which allowed him to rule Germany uncontested and paved the way for his imperial coronation.

LEGATE (Latin: legatus) A personal representative of the pope sent on a mission and granted papal authority. Until the 11th century the Ls. were members of the Roman clergy who worked at the papal court and were sent on specific missions. *Gregory VII (end of 11th century) was the first to appoint permanent Ls. to a province or country; these representatives were chosen from among proven allies of the papacy who resided in the particular county in question. Both systems continued to function from the 12th century on, the first being called *legati a laetere* to distinguish from the second, the *legati nati*. A third kind of L. was the prelate, such as the archbishop of *Canterbury, who obtained the title in addition to his ecclesiastical dignity or office.

W. Ullmann, *A Short History of the Papacy* (1972).

LEGER (LEODEGAR), St. (616-78) Bishop of Autun (663-78). One of the most distinguished prelates of the *Merovingian Franks, he began his career at the court of King *Clotaire II and, after the king's death, was appointed archdeacon of Poitiers. In 663 he became bishop of Autun and was politically active. He was one of the leaders of the opposition to *Ebroin, the *mayor of the palace of *Neustria. Ebroin was responsible for L.'s murder in 678.

J. M. Wallace-Hadrill, *The Long-Haired Kings* (1965).

LEGNANO, BATTLE OF (1176) Decisive battle fought in a fortified town north of Milan, between *Frederick Barbarossa and the cities of the *Lombard League. The former's defeat led him to negotiate peace with Pope *Alexander III and to focus his efforts on his German rival, *Henry the Lion, whom he held responsible for the battle's outcome.

LEIDRADE (736-816) Archbishop of *Lyons (798-814). Counsellor to *Charlemagne, who appointed him archbishop of Lyons, L. was active in the repression of the *Adoptionist heresy. After the death of Charlemagne, L. retired to the abbey of St. Médard at Soissons, where he wrote a *Life of the Emperor*.

L. Halphen, *Charlemagne et l'Empire Carolingien* (1947).

LEIF ERICSSON (c. 970-1021) *Viking leader. Son of the Norwegian chieftain, *Eric the Red, L. was sent *c.* 1000 to the court of King *Olaf I of Norway to represent the settlers of *Greenland. In Norway he was converted to the Christian faith and sent by the king to spread Christianity in Greenland. En route, he deviated from his established course and landed in what he named Vinland. Thus he was actually the first to discover North America.

H. Ingstad, *Western Way to Vinland* (1969).

LEINSTER, KINGDOM OF Kingdom in southeastern *Ireland. It was founded in the 8th century by the union of Celtic clans under the rule of the Ui-Neill dynasty, whose members reigned until the middle of the 9th century. Conquered by *Norse Vikings, L. became a Scandinavian principality in the 9th-11th centuries and was then recovered by the Irish clans. In 1171 L.

was conquered by King *Henry II of England and became an earldom under the English government.

A. J. Othway-Ruthven, *A History of Medieval Ireland* (1968).

LEIPZIG City in *Germany founded by German colonists in 1015 on the site of the former Slavonic town, Lipsk. The city grew gradually and in 1170 was granted a charter and local autonomy. Its location at the crossroad of trade routes brought it prosperity in the 12th and 13th centuries and contributed to its development in the 15th century.

LELIAERTS A political party in 14th-century *Flanders which endorsed allegiance to France. The party included noble families and some members of the urban upper middle-class. It originated as a result of the campaigns of King *Philip IV of France in Flanders. The L. was not a homogeneous party and its influence was diminished by the uprisings of popular parties in the cities, who favoured a pro-English orientation due to their economic interests.

LENSES The use of L. spread from the 13th century due to experimental achievements in optics, which developed out of the work of Greek scientists and philosophers. The achievements of the Arab optician Alhazen (965-1039), who noted irradiation through glass, were used by *Grosseteste in the 13th century, who developed their theoretical and practical application. Grosseteste's pupil, Roger *Bacon, further explored the theories of irradiation, which made it possible to create L. both for the improvement of sight and for astronomical purposes, as developed by *Levi Ben Gerson at the beginning of the 14th century.

A. C. Crombie, *Robert Grosseteste and the Origins of Experimental Science* (1953).

LENT The fast of 40 days before Easter, prescribed by the Christian churches to prepare the faithful for the main feast of the liturgical year. It originated from the fasts prescribed for catechumens or new converts preparing for baptism (which took place in the early church on the eve of Easter). In the Middle Ages L. was strictly observed and only one meal was allowed during the day. Due to a pagan tradition, however, the fast came to be broken for one day to celebrate the carnivals.

H. Thurston, *Lent and Holy Week* (1904).

LEO I, the Great, St. (d. 461) Pope (440-61). Born at Rome, where he was deacon of the Roman Church, L. was the first to establish the supremacy of the papacy. He wielded a great deal of influence over Emperor *Valentinian III, one of the last emperors of the Western Roman empire, obtaining from him confirmation of the primacy of the Roman see over the churches in the empire. This act formed the basis for the unity of the Catholic Church and its subordination to the pope. In 453 L. met *Attila the *Hun at Florence, and secured his retreat from Italy in return for a large sum of money. The feat was considered a miracle and L. was praised as the man who spared Italy from the raids of the Huns. L. was also active as a theologian and sent delegates to the Council of *Chalcedon with instructions to defend Orthodoxy against the *Monophysites. His treatise, the *Tome,* made him the leader of Orthodoxy within the church. L. is venerated as a saint by both the Roman Catholic and Greek Orthodox Churches.

T. G. Jalland, *The Life and Times of St. Leo the Great* (1941).

LEO II Pope (682-83). L.'s pontificate was influenced by the Byzantine imperial court which, by means of the exarch of *Ravenna, forced him to adopt a policy favourable to the Greek Orthodox Church.

LEO III, St. (750-816) Pope (795-816). Of humble origin and born in Rome, L. became a priest. His virtuous character won him the confidence of Pope *Adrian I, who promoted him at the papal court. In 795, after Adrian's death, L. was elected pope, but his election was contested by members of the Roman aristocracy, who accused him of murder and a life of sin. In 796 an uprising at Rome led to L.'s arrest and he fled to the Frankish count at *Spoleto. L. went to meet *Charlemagne at *Padeborn in Saxony to exonerate himself (797) and was then recognized as pope and restored by a Frankish army. Nevertheless, the king was to come to Rome and review the charges brought against L. The pope mustered all his skill to avoid having judgement passed upon himself by a lay ruler; he honourably received Charlemagne at Rome and sat with him in council, declaring his innocence and requesting the punishment of his adversaries. L. crowned Charlemagne emperor (800) and, in this way, reaffirmed his position, since the pope alone could confer the imperial crown in the West. L. was able to ensure the spiritual independence of the papacy and also was successful in preventing the alienation of the Greek Orthodox Church.

L. Halphen, *Charlemagne et l'Empire Carolingien* (1947).

LEO IV, St. Pope (847-55). L. was a *Benedictine monk, employed at the papal court by *Gregory IV; he succeeded *Sergius II, who had made him a cardinal. L. worked to rebuild the ruined Rome; he erected a new wall and built a fortress dominating the Tiber River and defending the church of *St. Peter. The restored area was known as the *Leonine city. To repulse the Arab raids, L. summoned *Louis, the eldest son of Emperor *Lothair I, to Rome and crowned him emperor (850). Nevertheless, L. had to organize the defence of Rome and its surroundings by himself; for this purpose, he fortified Civitavecchia, and placed papal guards on the coast of Latium (854).

J. Haller, *Das Papsttum,* II (1952).

LEO V Pope (903). The two months of L.'s pontificate were marked by trouble at Rome; as a result, he was deposed and died soon afterward.

LEO VI Pope (928). L. was appointed pope by the mistress of Rome, *Marozia, who chose him from among the cardinals due to his experience in church affairs and fidelity to her family. He died after a pontificate of seven months.

LEO VII Pope (936-39). L. was a *Benedictine monk who was elected to the papal see due to his piety and the will to bring peace to Rome. He invited St. *Odo, abbot of Cluny, to assist him in his duties and proclaimed a reform of the church, particularly in Germany.

LEO VIII Pope (963-65). L., although a layman, was elected pope through the influence of Emperor *Otto I, who deposed *John XII. L. found it necessary to fight off the attempts of John and his supporters to return and had to rely on the military aid of the emperor until his death.

LEO IX (Bruno of Toul; 1002-54) Pope (1049-54). A native of *Alsace, he was prepared by his father, Lord Egishiem, for an ecclesiastical career and was sent to study at Toul. In 1026 he became bishop of Toul and distinguished himself as a church reformer and a leading supporter of the *Cluny order. His activities brought him to the court of *Henry III, where he found favour in the eyes of the emperor. In 1048 Henry nominated L. pope and in 1049 he was consecrated. L. became a leader of the reform movement and helped raise the prestige of the papacy. He initiated his activities by convening the Council of *Rheims (1049), attended by a great number of prelates from western Europe. There his reform policy was presented. To gain the papacy's independence from Roman families, L. summoned counsellors from Germany, whom he made cardinals. He did the same with distinguished monks of the Cluniac order, among them Hildebrand (the future *Gregory VII). L. took a firm stand against the Greek Orthodox Church, which eventually led to the schism of 1054 and the separation of the churches. L. fought against the *Normans in southern Italy, but after having been captured, recognized *Robert Guiscard as his vassal and as overlord of *Apulia and the southern Italian countries.
L. Sittler, *St. Léon IX, le Pape Alsacien* (1950).

LEO I King of *Armenia (1129-37). Brother of *Thoros I, he worked to strengthen the kingdom founded in Cilicia (see *Armenia). As a result of his efforts, he conquered the cities of Mamistra, Adana and Tarsus (1132) from the Byzantines, thus enlarging the territory of his kingdom.

LEO II, the Great King of *Armenia (1187-1219). L. was the greatest king of Lesser *Armenia. He consolidated the realm by improving foreign affairs and reforming internal social and religious structures. L. received the royal crown from *Henry VI, the *Holy Roman emperor, promising in return the union of the Armenian church with Rome. Thus, he made a final break with Byzantium and established a Catholic patriarchate of Armenia, which had wide autonomy, especially with regard to liturgy. L. was an ally of the *Crusaders and married a Frankish princess. Nevertheless, he opposed any intervention in Armenian affairs and even attempted to impose his authority upon Antioch.
S. Der Nersessian, *Armenia and the Byzantine Empire* (1945).

LEO III King of *Armenia (1269-89). L. fought against the *Mamelukes, who had invaded his kingdom during the last years of his father, *Hethum's, reign. In order to confront the enemy, L. allied himself with the *Mongols of Persia and took an active part in their raids into Syria. However, L. was defeated by the Mamelukes, who destroyed Adana and Tarsus.

LEO IV King of *Armenia (1301-07). L. fought against the *Mamelukes, but in 1307 was defeated and killed by the Mongols of Persia, who had allied themselves with the victors.

LEO V (1310-41) King of *Armenia (1320-41). Up until 1329 the Armenian kingdom was ruled by a regency council. Upon L.'s majority, he spent most of his time in war with the *Mamelukes and *Mongols, who ravaged the country. To acquire resources for his defence, L. allied himself with the *Lusignan kings of *Cyprus, promising them the heritage of Armenia were

he to die childless. In 1341 L. was murdered by local nobles who opposed his pro-Cypriot policy.

LEO VI, of Lusignan (d. 1393) King of *Armenia (1374-75). L. was elected king by the Armenian barons after the major part of the realm had been conquered by the *Mamelukes. His calls for a new *Crusade went unheeded and, lacking an army, he was unable to maintain himself at Sis, the capital of his kingdom. In 1375 he had to surrender Sis to the Mamelukes and thus the independent state of Armenia came to an end. Wounded, L. was imprisoned in Cairo and remained there until 1382, when the ransom required was paid through the sale of his lands in Cyprus. L. then went to France and was received at court. A circle of his supporters spread the tradition of the Armenian court in France, as was described by L.'s secretary, John Dardel.
A. Kohler, *La chronique de Jean Dardel* (1906).

LEO I *Byzantine emperor (457-74). Born in Thracia, he was a general of the East Roman empire prior to his imperial coronation. He fought against the *Vandals and was supported by the commander of the Gothic guard, *Aspar, whom he murdered in 471, fearing his heightened influence.

LEO II Byzantine emperor (474). Son and heir of *Leo I, he was murdered by his guard.

LEO III, the Isaurian (675-740) *Byzantine emperor (717-40). L. was originally from the central provinces of Asia Minor and was the founder of the Isaurian dynasty. A skilled general, he was proclaimed emperor by his army and had to virtually conquer Constantinople in order to begin his reign. L. reorganized the empire, issued the *Ecloga*, a new legal code, and reformed the administration. In 725 he issued a decree condemning the worship of icons, which led to the start of the *Iconoclastic controversy at Byzantium. L. successfully fought against the Arabs in Asia Minor.
CMedH, IV.

LEO IV, the Khazar (750-80) *Byzantine emperor (775-80). Son of *Constantine V and a Khazar princess, he was forced to repress a dynastic revolt and received aid from *Telerig, the khan of the *Bulgars (776). At the beginning of his reign, he adopted a liberal stand towards the iconoclastic controversy, but at the request of his army, returned to the traditional policy of the Isaurian dynasty.
CMedH, IV.

LEO V, the Armenian (d. 820) *Byzantine emperor (813-20). Of Armenian descent, he was a general in the Byzantine army and distinguished himself in the wars against the Arabs. At the beginning of the 9th century he wielded strong influence in Constantinople and gave his support to prospective emperors. In 813, after a campaign against the *Bulgarians, L. proclaimed himself emperor. Two years later he reissued the *Iconoclastic decrees and deposed the patriarch Nicephorus. L. was murdered by supporters of his predecessor, *Michael I, whom he had deposed.
CMedH, IV.

LEO VI, the Philosopher (866-912) *Byzantine emperor (886-912). L. succeeded Emperor *Basil I, his purported father. Educated by the patriarch *Photius, he was one of the most learned men of his times and wrote theological and philosophical dissertations even after his imperial coronation. L. gathered scholars and intellectuals at his court, and thus laid the foundations for the By-

zantine renaissance of the 10th century. L. is mostly noted for his legislative work, consisting of individual laws and a code, the *Basilicae,* which brought imperial legislation up-to-date. L.'s weakness lay in his foreign affairs; he was repeatedly defeated by the Arabs and Bulgarians and his empire greatly declined as a result.
CMedH, IV.

LEÓN City and kingdom (914-1230) in northwestern *Spain. Originally a Roman camp, the city was conquered by the *Visigoths at the beginning of the 6th century and declined under their rule. From 716 until 850 it fell to the *Arabs. It was then conquered by the Christian knights of *Asturias, who made L. the capital of a county, granted to younger sons of the royal dynasty. In 914 King García I established his capital in the city and founded the kingdom of L. From the 10th century, the history of L. is interwoven with that of *Castile. The latter was originally one of the counties in L. and gradually became the most important part of the realm. Until the 13th century the crowns of L. and Castile were considered separate, although the majority of kings ruled both realms. In 1230 L. was formally united with Castile.
A. Castro, *Structure of Spanish History* (1954).

LEONINE CITY The part of *Rome on the right bank of the Tiber which was fortified by Pope *Leo IV in 842. The L., now part of the Vatican, included the church of St. Peter and the castle of St. Angelo.

LEONTIUS (d. 705) Byzantine emperor (695-98). L. was the commander of the Byzantine army in Asia Minor. In 695 he was among those that led the revolt against *Justinian II. Taking advantage of the anarchy at Constantinople, he proclaimed himself emperor. He was deposed in 698 by *Tiberius III and retired to a monastery near the capital. He was decapitated in 705 under the orders of Justinian II when the Illyrian emperor was restored to his throne.
CMedH, IV.

LEONTIUS OF BYZANTIUM (485-543) Theologian. At the beginning of the 6th century L. became a monk at Constantinople and travelled in Italy; *c.* 510 he distinguished himself as a theologian at Rome. In 520 L. settled at Jerusalem. Influenced by the writings of *Cyril of Alexandria, he abandoned his pro-*Nestorian views and adopted an anti-*Monophysite ideology. He was also called Hierosolymitanus and Scholaticus.
B. Altaner, *Der Griechische Theologe Leontius* (1950).

LEOPOLD The name of three margraves and one duke of *Austria belonging to the *Babenberg dynasty. The most important among them were:
Leopold III Margrave 1096-1136. He supported Emperor *Henry V and married his sister Agnes. As margrave he worked mainly to reorganize the social and administrative structures of Austria. He also was known for his religious institutions and for founding a number of abbeys.
Leopold V Duke 1177-94. He participated in the Third *Crusade and became the leader of the German camp after the death of *Frederick Barbarossa. His conflict with King *Richard of England during the attempts to lift the siege of *Acre is well known. It ended with his taking Richard prisoner when the latter was en route to England (1192). L. annexed Styria to the duchy of *Austria in 1192 and developed Vienna as his capital.
J. W. Thompson, *Feudal Germany* (1928).

LEOPOLD OF HAPSBURG Name of two dukes of *Austria:
Leopold I (1293-1326) Duke 1308-26, grandson of Emperor *Albert I. While his elder brothers competed for the imperial crown, L. devoted his efforts to the administration of the family lands. In 1315 he fought unsuccessfully against the Swiss.
Leopold III (1351-86) Duke 1365-86, founder of the Leopoldine line of the *Hapsburg dynasty. L. ruled the duchy together with his brother *Albert until 1379, at which time they divided the lands between themselves. L. received *Carinthia, *Styria, *Tyrol, *Alsace and Istria. He fought against *Venice, conquering *Trieste, which became the main harbour of the Hapsburg lands. His attempts to restore the family's rule over the Swiss failed and in 1386 he was killed in the Battle of *Sempach.

LEOVIGILD Visigothic king (568-86). L. was the last Arian king of the *Visigoths. His main achievement was to unite the Iberian peninsula under his rule by conquering the realm of the *Suevi and wielding authority over the *Basques. His attempt to impose the Arian faith upon the Hispano-Roman peoples of his kingdom incited a general revolt in southern Spain. Ironically, his cruel repression of the uprising (580) won many adherents to the Catholic faith among the Visigoths.
K. F. Stroecker, *Leowigild* (1939).

LÉRINS, ABBEY OF Founded in 410 by St. Honoratus on a desert island in the Mediterranean, near Cannes (Provence), it became a famous Latin cultural centre in the early Middle Ages. Many of the great missionaries in western Europe received their education at L. in the 5th and 6th centuries. In 660 the abbey adopted the *Benedictine rule. In 732 the Arabs conquered L. and the surviving monks were dispersed. The monastery was rebuilt in the 10th century.
L. H. Labande, *L'Abbaye de Lérins* (1923).

LETTERS OF THE SEPULCHRE The first legal code of the *Latin kingdom of Jerusalem, composed by an anonymous author at the beginning of the 12th century. It included, in epistolary form, a number of feudal customs adapted to the needs of the kingdom.
J. L. la Monte, *The Latin Kingdom of Jerusalem* (1932).

LETTONIA Country on the eastern coast of the Baltic Sea. Medieval L. was founded by four ethnic groups: the Letts, the Semigallians, the Livonians and the Kurs. They became organized into tribes during the 6th century. Following numerous long wars between the clans, a confederation was established (7th century), but its centre was not definitively fixed. In the 10th century the state was destroyed by the *Novgorod Russian princes. The tribes gained their independence, but became subject to attacks by their neighbours. In the 12th century German missionaries and colonists settled in L., and in 1201 the city of Riga was founded in Livonia. The *Knights of the Sword ruled the country, which was subject to German influence until the end of the Middle Ages. In 1282 *Riga joined the *Hanse and became one of its prosperous members. The other parts of L. were divided between the bishops of Riga and the *Teutonic order.
A. Spekke, *History of Lettonia* (1951).

LEVANT (French: east) In medieval French the term denoted the countries along the eastern shore of the Mediterranean Sea. It was introduced in the 12th century in the Venetian dialect (*levante*) with reference to trade with the *Crusader lands. In the 13th century the meaning of the term was expanded to include all the territories from Greece to Egypt.

LEVI BEN GERSHON (GERSONIDES) (1288-1344) Scientist, philosopher and Jewish exegete. Born and educated at Montpellier, L. settled at Orange (Provence) and later established himself at *Avignon, where he was employed as an astonomer at the papal court. His observations, based on the works of earlier Moslem and Jewish astronomers allowed him to calculate cosmic dimensions. For that purpose, he developed the mathematical systems and the field of trigonometry in particular. As a philosopher, L. was a strict *Aristotelian, as is exemplified both by his theological beliefs, meant to express the rationality of the Jewish faith, and in his commentaries on *Ibn Rushd (Averroes). His main work was the *Wars of the Lord*, written in 1317-29, in which he utilized the *scholastic method to prove the rationality of divine revelation and the Jewish faith. L. also wrote a treatise on logic in Hebrew. His commentaries on Ibn Rushd, written in Latin, were published as part of the *corpus* of Aristotle's writings. His exegetical works consist of commentaries on biblical and Talmudic books. L. wrote his astronomical treatises in Hebrew, but due to their importance, he was requested by Pope *Clemens VI to provide a Latin version (1342). Only his main astronomical work was translated at the time, however.

N. Alderblum, *A Study on Gersonides* (1926).

LEWES Town in Sussex, *England. In the middle of the 11th century the town grew as a commercial centre and a Norman castle was erected for its defence. L. became famous as the site of the battle of 1264, when *Simon de Montfort and the baronial party defeated the royal army of *Henry III and took the king prisoner.

F. M. Powicke, *The Thirteenth Century* (1952).

LIBER PONTIFICALIS (Book of the Popes) An official compilation of papal biographies, written in Rome. The biographies were begun in the 6th century and continued in a regular pattern, meaning that there were many stereotyped formulas. Its first part, compiled under *Boniface II (530-32), is largely legendary in nature and covers the history of the papacy from St. *Peter to the 6th century. The most detailed and best biographies are those of *Gregory I and the popes of the 8th century. The original compilation of the L. closes with an account of *Stephen V (891). However, later biographies were also added to the collection.

Liber Pontificalis, ed. L. Duchesne (1886-92) including a study of its historical value.

LIBERTAS (Latin: freedom) The word was used by 11th- and 12th-century theologians in two senses: 1) *L. Ecclesiae* (freedom of the *Church) to express the struggle of the reformers and *Gregorian thinkers against the domination of the Church by lay rulers, especially the emperors; 2) in a purely theological sense, according to which liberty could be reached only within the Church and by complete obedience to its precepts. Its use in the second sense led to elaboration of the concept of the pope's supreme authority in the Church and, by extension, of his primary place in Christian society.

G. Tellenbach, *Libertas* (1936).

LIBRARIES The decline of the secular culture at the beginning of the Middle Ages and the church's monopoly on education had their impact on the development of medieval L. In the Byzantine empire, imperial L. continued to exist; however, important books were also gathered in churches and monasteries, where they were copied and richly illustrated. In western Europe lay L. disappeared in the 5th century and were replaced by monastic ones. These grew due to the fact that copying books was considered one of the basic duties of the monk. The most important L. of the early Middle Ages were those of *Lérins, *Monte Cassino, *Seville, *Iona and *York. With the spread of learning during the *Carolingian period, medieval L. continued to develop. The establishment of *scriptoria* in the most prominent monasteries provided the L. of new abbeys with additional copies of holy and classical books, as well as contemporary secular material. Among the most important and richly endowed L. of the Carolingian and post-Carolingian periods were those of *Bobbio, *St. Gall, *Fulda and *St. Denis. From the 10th century on cathedral schools, such as those of *Rheims, *Mainz and *Chartres, also contained their own L. By the beginning of the 12th century, most of the centres of western Europe were equipped with their own library collections, located either in monasteries or cathedrals. Translations of philosophical and scientific works from the Greek and Arabic into Latin, undertaken in the 12th and 13th centuries, were added to the library collections, especially those of the newly-founded *universities of Italy, France and England. In the 13th and 14th centuries books were copied and richly illustrated by the order of prelates and some lay princes; the latter established their own L., as had been customary in classical times. The most important of such private L. was that of *Charles V of France, opened to scholars in 1376. In the 15th century private L. in lay palaces became common.

N. Ker, *Medieval Libraries* (1941).

LIBRE DE L'ORDRE DE CAVALLERIA See LULL, RAMON.

LIBRI CAROLINI (The Caroline Books) A treatise compiled *c.* 791 and attributed to *Charlemagne, but actually the work of a skilled theologian, probably *Alcuin. The L. was an attack on the *Iconoclastic council of 754 and on the Council of Nicaea of 787. It attempted to prove that the theological attitudes adopted by the Greek Orthodox Church were erroneous.

MGH, III.

LICHFIELD City in *Mercia (England). Founded in the 7th century, it became an important ecclesiastical centre in the following century. In 786 King *Offa established an archiepiscopal see, concurrent with *Canterbury and meant to symbolize the religious independence of his realm. The see was removed in 803, but the bishopric remained one of the most important in England during the Middle Ages despite its removal to Chester and Coventry after the Norman Conquest.

A. B. Clifton, *Lichfield and its Cathedral Church* (1898).

LIÈGE City in the Low Countries (Belgium) on the Meuse River. Founded as a small commercial town in the 6th century, an episcopal see was established there in the following century and the city rapidly developed under the last of the *Merovingians and the first *Carolingians. *Pepin the Short granted L.'s bishops lordship over the city and its surroundings. In 843 it became part of *Lotharingia and prospered. In the 10th and 11th centuries, the town's cathedral became an important educational and art centre, whose influence was felt in East and West alike. After the fall of the duchy of Lower *Lorraine and the departure of *Godfrey of Bouillon to the *Crusade, the bishopric grew considerably, and in the 12th century the bishops became princes of the empire. However, they found themselves in constant conflict with the burghers who demanded a charter of liberties.

T. Gobert, *Liège* (1926).

LIEGNITZ, BATTLE OF (1241) Fought between the *Mongol army of *Batu-khan and an alliance of Poles and *Teutonic knights under the Duke of Silesia which had been organized after the Mongol invasion of *Cracow. The Mongol victory at Liegnitz enabled them to further advance into central Europe, but their plans were abandoned due to the sudden departure of Batu, who had to be present at the *kuraltai* of Karakorum.

LILLE City in *Flanders. In the early Middle Ages L. was a village. In 1030 Count *Baldwin IV of Flanders fortified it and established a provincial administration to govern the southern parts of his county. In the 11th-13th centuries L. became a prosperous textile centre, but its trade was destroyed at the beginning of the 14th century, when it became one of the battlefields of the *Hundred Years' War and was conquered successively by the French, English and Flemish armies. In 1383 L. became part of the *Burgundian state of Duke *Philip and was rebuilt. In the 15th century the county prospered under the Burgundian dukes.

A. Mabille, *Lille-en-Flandre* (1951).

LIMBURG The name of three brothers of the Hennequin family of L. (Flanders), Pol, Hermann and Jan, who became famous painters and miniaturists. They were active between 1386-1416. Following their training, including familiarization with the late Gothic style, they entered the service of *Philip the Bold, duke of Burgundy (1401) and were court painters for his son, *John. In 1411 the brothers entered the service of John, duke of *Berry and, under his patronage, created their most famous piece, the *Heures du Duc de Berry*, considered the greatest miniature work in the late Gothic style.

J. J. Rorimer, *The Belles Heures of Jean, duke of Berry, Prince of France* (1958).

LIMERICK City in southwestern *Ireland. The centre of a Gaelic-Irish clan, L. was conquered by Norse *Vikings in 812 and became the capital of a Scandinavian kingdom in Ireland. At the end of the 10th century the Irish hero Brian Boru recovered the city. L. changed hands often during the 11th century, until it became the capital of the Thomond kings (1106-74). Conquered by *Henry II in 1174, the city was then governed by English nobles. In 1197 L. was granted a charter of liberties by *Richard I. At the beginning of the 13th century King *John gave L. to the justiciar *William de Burgh, who brought English settlers into the city.

E. Curtis, *The History of Medieval Ireland* (1938).

LIMOGES City in western *France, the centre of *Limousin. The Gallo-Roman city of L. continued to exist at the beginning of the Middle Ages, but was basically a religious centre. In the 9th century, with the foundation of the abbey of St. Martial, L. began to grow. At that time it was governed by a feudal dynasty of

viscounts, vassals of the dukes of *Aquitaine. It also prospered thanks to its being one of the most prominent centres of goldsmiths and cloth in the the West. L. was best known, however, for the work of its enamellers, whose creations were sought by most of western Europe during the 12th-15th centuries. As a result of such prosperity, the city became an important art centre. Its notable place was maintained despite the city's political instability and the constant warfare to which it was subjected.

A. Perrier, *Limoges* (1939).

LIMOUSIN City in western *France. Conquered in the 6th century by the *Merovingian Franks, it became part of the duchy and kingdom of *Aquitaine in the 8th century. In the 10th century the title passed to the dukes of Aquitaine, while the land itself was divided into a great number of feudal seigniories. A secular culture developed there and reached its peak in the 12th century, when the county was called the "land of the troubadours". Feudal anarchy caused the dukes to expend much effort on instilling their authority in L. This situation continued and *Henry II Plantagenet, who gained suzerainty following his marriage to *Eleanor of Aquitaine, was forced to bring in hired English troops to quell the anarchists. In 1173 the task of bringing peace to L. was entrusted to Henry's son, *Richard, who was crowned duke of Aquitaine at Limoges. In 1199 Richard was killed while trying to impose his authority over the lords of Le-Chalus. In the 13th century L. was disputed between the kings of France and England. Meanwhile, the power of the feudal lords grew and was crushed only after their defeat at the hands of *Alphonse of Poitiers, who reorganized the county. During the *Hundred Years' War, L. changed hands several times. It finally fell to France in 1386.

L. Perche, *Limousin* (1960).

LINCOLN City in *England. L. developed around a Roman castle which controlled central Britain; in the 6th century it was conquered by the *Mercians. Under their rule, L. developed as an ecclesiastical centre and an episcopal see was established there. Conquered by the *Danes, the city became one of the five fortified cities of the *Danelaw (876). From the 11th century on the city was one of the most important centres of the wool trade in England. Its cathedral, in the Norman Romanesque style, was begun in 1083. Together with the Norman castle (1068), it is one of the oldest structures of Norman England. In 1154 the city received a charter of liberties, granting it the same privileges offered to *London. In 1216 Prince *Louis (VIII) of France invaded England and concentrated his army at L., where he was defeated by *William Marshal. From the 13th century the bishops of L. were the formal heads of the University of Oxford. In 1254 the prosperous Jewish community of L. was raided and its leaders were charged with the ritual murder of a Christian child and arrested. Although acquitted the following year, the Jewish community of L. continued to be persecuted.

J. N. F. Hill, *History of Lincoln* (1966).

LINDISFARNE Island in the North Sea near the shores of Yorkshire. L. became famous for its fortified monastery, founded in 635 by St. Aidan and intended to serve as a missionary centre for *Northumbria. In 875 L. was destroyed by Danish invaders and its monks settled at Durham. The monastery was rebuilt in 1082.

L. became a pilgrimage site and was called the Holy Island.

J. Wordsworth, *Lindisfarne* (1899).

LIONEL Duke of Clarence (d. 1368). L. was the second son of King *Edward III of England. Active at court, he took part, under his father's command, in the battles of the *Hundred Years' War. His descendants in the 15th century claimed the succession to the throne as dukes of *York.

LIPPE County in northwestern *Germany. It originated around a castle built by *Otto I in southern Saxony and granted later to a vassal, who also possessed land surrounding the valley of L. in southern Westphalia. The family rose gradually in status and in 1100 *Henry IV granted its members the title of count so as to weaken the ducal power in Saxony. *Lothair III withdrew the title, but the lords of L., nevertheless, became a powerful feudal dynasty in Germany and from 1180 were direct vassals of the emperor. In 1270 they became princes of the empire. In the 14th and 15th centuries L. prospered and was noted for the court of its princes, who became famous patrons of the arts.

E. Kittel, *Geschichte des Landes Lippe* (1957).

LISBON City and capital of *Portugal. The Roman city was conquered by the *Suevi in 468 and was part of their realm until the 7th century, when the *Visigoths attached it to their kingdom. In 717 the *Arabs conquered L. and changed its name from Felicitas Julia to Al-Ushbuna. This eventually was corrupted to Lishbona or L. Under Arab rule, which lasted until the middle of the 12th century, the city became a prosperous commercial centre, concentrating in its natural harbour the trade of the whole western part of the Iberian peninsula. In 1147 L. was conquered by a Portuguese army and fleet, aided by English and Scandinavian Crusaders. In 1256 King *Alfonso III established his capital at L. In 1290 a university was founded, but in 1357 it was transferred to *Coimbra. The 15th century was one of L.'s most prosperous periods; the city became the base of Portugal's maritime expansion and the port of departure for many great geographic expeditions.

T. D. Kendrick, *Lisbon, Past and Present* (1957).

LITANY (Greek: supplication)   A form of prayer consisting of a series of petitions and invocations and used in both the Eastern and Western Christian Churches. The L. was a favourite form of private prayer which invoked those saints venerated by the supplicant, his family and feudal kin. It was also used in some great and solemn feasts of the liturgical calendar and then bore the character of public supplication.

A. Baumstark, *Liturgie Comparée* (1953).

LITHUANIA Duchy in eastern Europe. The Lithuanians were a Baltic tribe which, until the 10th century, was closely associated with the *Prussians and the *Letts. By the beginning of the 11th century the Lithuanians had become organized into a tribal principality, mentioned in the German annals of Quedlinburg. They continued to practise their pagan cult and reject eastern and western Christian missionaries. In the 12th century they successfully resisted the attacks of Russian princes. At the end of the century the tribe began to expand eastwards and southwards and conquered Grodno. Throughout the 13th century they had to face attacks by the *Teutonic knights. This struggle led to the emergence of the state of L., which was consolidated with

the help of refugees from Prussia and *Lettonia. The founder of the state was Mindaugas (*Mindovg), who converted to the Christian faith in 1251. Mindaugas took advantage of the *Mongol conquest of Russia and of the decline of the Teutonic order to adopt an expansionist policy. He centred his attention on the southeast and conquered the major part of White *Russia. His successors fought the Teutonic knights, the *Poles and the *Mongols and were able to strengthen their state. Under *Gedymin (1316-41), L. became a powerful state and its capital was established in the newly-founded city of *Vilna. Despite a dynastic war, which broke out after Gedymins' death, the state continued to develop. His son, *Olgierd, conquered from the Mongols the territories between the Dnieper and Bug Rivers, thereby reaching the Black Sea and creating a powerful principality east of Poland. Olgierd's brother, Kestutis, who governed L. proper, was unable, however, to resist the attacks of the Teutonic knights, who conquered Kovno (Kaunas) in 1362. In 1377, at Olgierd's death, his son *Jagiello claimed suzerainty over all of L. In 1382 he defeated and killed his uncle Kestutis in an attempt to unite the state. But his cousins contested his rights and were aided by the Teutonic knights.

Threatened by the Teutons, Jagiello nevertheless refused to adopt the Orthodox faith and league himself with *Moscow. Instead he chose to ally himself with Poland. In 1386 he married Jadwiga, the heiress of Poland and thus gained its kingship, as well as the duchy of L. Although the two states remained independent and were governed by separate administrations, according to their own customs, the mere fact of his ruling both entities won him great power in eastern Europe. From the end of the 13th century the grand duchy of L. contained many ethnic groups; the Lithuanians were a minority, while the great majority of the population was of Slavic origin (Russians, Ukrainians and Ruthenians). The territory was equally divided along religious lines and included Roman Catholics, Orthodox and pagans. The dukes were able to efficiently govern their state thanks to their religious and political tolerance. In addition, an efficient taxation system enabled them to maintain a strong army, based on a mobile cavalry, ready to intervene when necessary. *Feudalism in its strictest form was not introduced in L. and the dukes allowed the landed aristocracy of the conquered territories to rule their estates, but without any political privileges.

C. R. Jurgela, *History of the Lithuanian Nation* (1948).

LIUDOLF Duke of *Saxony (850-66). Nephew of *Widukind, he was one of the tribal leaders of the Saxons in the 9th century. By his marriage to a Frankish princess, he attained a prominent position in Germany and was, from 840, loyal to *Louis the German. In 850 he was granted the title of duke of the eastern Saxons and founded the Liudolfing dynasty, which included kings of Germany (including *Henry I, his grandson).

J. W. Thompson, *Feudal Germany* (1928).

LIUTPRAND King of the *Lombards (713-44). Member of a princely house, he was recognized by the Lombard dukes as king after leading a rebellion which put an end to a succession of weak rulers. He reorganized the royal administration and the army and revised the Lombard code of law. Capitalizing on an uprising (727) against Emperor *Leo III the Isaurian, he conquered most of the Byzantine provinces in central Italy. He attacked Rome several times between 730 and 742, causing the popes to appeal for Frankish help.

G. Bonfante, *Latini a Germani in Italia* (1965).

LIUTPRAND OF CREMONA (912-72) Statesman and historian. Born to a noble Lombard family, he grew up in the court of *Hugh of Provence, entered a monastery and was ordained priest. *Berengar II appointed him his chancellor and in 949 sent him to Constantinople to negotiate an alliance with Byzantium. After a quarrel with Berengar in 956, he left Italy and entered the service of *Otto I of Germany, who appointed him bishop of Cremona in 961. He was a devoted supporter of Otto and helped him in his Italian policy. He was sent to Constantinople in 963 to negotiate the marriage between Otto's son, the future *Otto II, and Byzantine princess Theophano. L. wrote a history of Italy covering the period 890-950 and a chronicle of his mission to Constantinople, vividly describing the court and manners of the Byzantine empire.

M. Litzel, *Studien über Liutprand von Cremona* (1933).

LIVONIA Region, comprising modern Estonia and northern Latvia, and inhabited by the Livs, a people of Finno-Ugric stock. Until the 12th century, the Livs were organized as a tribal confederation, and succeeded in checking Scandinavian and Russian attacks. In 1160, the merchants of *Lübeck founded a colony on the Dvina River, which served as a base for Christian expansion into L. But the German mission began to work systematically in the region only at the end of the 12th century, with the foundation of the order of the *Knights of the Sword of Livonia. The order conquered L., and formed a powerful confederation which also included southern Latvia.

R. Wittram, *Baltische Geschichte* (1954).

LJUDEVIT (d. 823) Duke of the *Croats. Leader of the Pannonian Croats, he revolted in 819 against Emperor *Louis the Pious, united the Croat tribes, and helped them win independence from the Frankish empire.

LLEWELYN Name of two Welsh princes, who governed northern *Wales:

Llewelyn I, the Great (1174-1240) Prince from 1194. He took advantage of the troubled reigns of *John I and *Henry III to strengthen his power, uniting the *Celtic principalities of northern Wales.

Llewelyn II Prince 1246-82. From 1254 on, he fought against English attempts to conquer Wales, initiated with the appointment of Henry III's son, *Edward, as prince of Wales. To preserve Welsh autonomy, he agreed to become Edward's vassal in 1256, but revolted frequently. His death in a battle against the English signified the end of Welsh independence.

J. E. Lloyd, *History of Wales to the Edwardian Conquest* (1939).

LOBBES Abbey and town in *Belgium. Founded in 640, it developed into a seat of culture and population centre in the Frankish kingdom of *Austrasia. The abbey adopted the *Benedictine rule in the 9th century. Its library, until the 12th century, housed one of the largest collections of manuscripts.

E. Moreau, *Histoire de l'Eglise en Belgique* (1936).

LODI City in the province of *Milan, northern Italy. The ancient Roman city knew a period of prosperity in the 8th century, as a commercial centre, under Lombard

kings. Strategically located on an elevated plateau dominating Lombardy, L. became a *Carolingian county after 774. Countal power passed to the local bishops in the 9th century. From the end of the 11th century the wars with Milan became a constant factor in L.'s history. Twice destroyed by Milanese armies, in 1111 and 1158, the city was rebuilt by *Frederick Barbarossa in 1161, but in 1174, when the *Guelphs took over its government, it joined the *Lombard League against him. Party struggles during the 13th century led to its decline and eventual conquest by Milan at the beginning of the 14th century.

L. Cremascoli, *Lodi* (1955).

LOLLARDS Name given in the late 14th century to the followers of John *Wycliffe and, by extension, to the critics of the church establishment. The L. emerged from a group of Oxford University intellectuals, who were organized by Nicholas of Hereford, one of Wycliffe's disciples. They preached his teachings and won many followers from various English counties. The L. were discredited after the repression of the peasants' rebellion of 1381, having been considered by the upper classes as the instigators of the revolt. Although persecuted by the Church from 1382 on, they became popular among the burghers and the commoners. The movement lost its influence after a L. rebellion led by John Oldcastle in 1414 was severely repressed by *Henry V.

K. B. McFarlane, *John Wycliffe and the Beginning of English Nonconformity* (1952).

LOMBARDS (Longobardi) *Teutonic tribe originating in northeastern Germany. In the 4th century they began migrating southwards. They first went towards *Bohemia, where they organized their tribal kingship, and in the 5th and 6th centuries annexed large parts of *Austria to their realm. Pressed by the *Avars, the L. left their territories and, under the leadership of King *Ebroin, invaded Italy in 568, conquering most of the *Byzantines' northern and central provinces. The local population offered little resistance, as they felt oppressed by Byzantine rule. The Byzantine domain in Italy was thereafter confined to isolated strips of land around *Ravenna and in the south, while the papacy set up an independent state comprising *Rome and *Latium. It took several generations for the L. to integrate with the Romans. In the meantime, they were considered as foes of the papacy because they adopted the Arian faith. The L. kingdom, with its elective monarchy, was ruled according to tribal customs and was divided into administrative entities called duchies. These in turn were divided into smaller units, both familial and military, known as *farae*. A great number of duchies around the royal demesne (*Lombardy), with its capital at *Pavia, enjoyed a large measure of autonomy, the most important of them having been *Benevento, *Spoleto and *Friuli. Some of the dukes, who were related to the royal dynasty of Ebroin, were elected kings in the 7th century, when royal authority declined and a form of *feudalism was introduced. The kingdom, reorganized by *Liutprand in the early 8th century, became an important European power. The L., although they had already converted to Catholicism, continued to threaten the papacy by their attempts to complete their conquest of Italy. The popes' frequent appeals for Frankish help resulted in an alliance between the papacy and *Pepin the Short, who recognized papal sovereignty over Bologna in 757. In 774, called by Pope *Adrian I, *Charlemagne invaded Italy, defeated King *Desiderius and annexed the L. kingdom to his realm. Benevento, however, remained a Lombard duchy until the 11th century. Frankish rule in Italy accelerated the L.' integration into Roman society. Out of this fusion, the Italians emerged.

J. M. Wallace-Hadrill, *The Barbarian West* (1952).

LOMBARD LEAGUE An association of north *Italian communes and cities, organized in 1164 to resist *Frederick Barbarossa's imperial policy. Animated by the leaders of *Milan and supported by Pope *Alexander III, the L. mobilized financial resources and mercenaries to fight against the emperor. In 1166, they founded the city of *Alessandria, named for the pope, to fortify the access to the Po Valley. The L. achieved several defensive successes until 1177, when the emperor and the pope came to an agreement. Frederick's attempt to destroy the L. backfired. Defeated at *Legnano (1179), he was forced to agree to the consolidation of the communal autonomies in northern Italy. In 1208 the L. was renewed against *Otto IV, but dissolved after his departure from Italy. In 1226, when *Frederick II intervened in the affairs of northern Italy, the L. was again revived. Despite defeats, it remained the most powerful force of the *Guelphs. At the emperor's death in 1250, when independent city-states emerged, internal struggles and inter-urban rivalries led to its final dissolution.

D. P. Waley, *The Italian City Republics* (1969).

LOMBARDY Province in northern Italy, L. is named for the *Lombards, who in the late 6th century conquered most of Italy and divided it up into duchies. In the 7th and 8th centuries the name was restricted to the northern and central parts of Italy, which were ruled directed by the king. L.'s capital was *Pavia. The kingdom was annexed to *Charlemagne's empire in 774.

LONDON Capital of *England. In the Middle Ages L. was situated on the north bank of the Thames. The Roman city declined in the 5th century, but it seems that from the 6th century it began to revive. Trade brought growth and prosperity to L., which, by the 7th century, was the capital of the earldom of *Middlesex, in *Essex. During the 8th century L. was contested by the kings of Essex, *Kent and *Mercia, and was finally conquered by the latter. It passed to *Wessex in the 9th century. As one of the most important harbours in England, L. was subject to Danish raids and destruction during the second half of the 9th century. In 886 *Alfred the Great conquered the city, rebuilt its fortifications and restored its prosperity. Thereafter, L. saw constant growth, becoming, in the middle of the 11th century, England's largest city. Factors in its development were the establishment of *Edward the Confessor's court at the neighbouring borough of Westminster and the erection of the Tower of L. by *William the Conqueror after the *Norman Conquest. The charter of liberties William granted L.'s inhabitants was the basis of municipal autonomy. These privileges were extended by *Henry I in 1133, who granted the city, led by wealthy merchants, the right to have their own police and an independent judicial system. The mayor of L., considered in 1215 as one of the lords of the realm, was among those who were granted the *Magna Charta, in which a special paragraph provided for the respect of the city's

privileges. L. sided with the barons in their uprisings against *Henry III and was a stronghold of *Simon de Montfort. Trade with the Rhine Valley and northern Germany favoured the establishment of a *Hanse colony in the city in the 13th century. Population growth led to territorial expansion on both banks of the Thames. L. also included a number of Middlesex villages such as Soho. With an estimated 35,000 inhabitants in 1377, L. was one of the largest European cities. In the 15th century the city became the sole capital of England, with the king residing mainly at *Westminster.

I. J. C. Brown (ed.), *A Book of London* (1961).

LONGBOW Weapon believed to have originated in *Wales and used by Welsh warriors in the 13th century against English cavalry. The 1.8 m L., shooting arrows at a range of up to 180 m, was effective in that it avoided a face-to-face confrontation, in which the knights had the advantage of heavy weaponry and iron garments. *Edward I adapted it to the needs of the English army and, under *Edward III, it was a common weapon in infantry. It was efficiently used in the *Hundred Years' War.

C. W. C. Oman, *The Art of War in the Middle Ages* (1953).

LOPEZ DE AYALA (1332-1407) Statesman, poet and chronicler (1332-1407). He began his political career at the royal court of *Castile, serving as captain in the navy (from 1354), ambassador to France (from 1379) and royal chancellor (from 1398). In his last years, he devoted much of his time to writing. Among his most famous works are *Rimado de Palacio,* a narrative verse satirizing contemporary society; a treatise on falconry and a chronicle, which is an invaluable source for the Spanish history of the second half of the 14th century.

A. D. Deyermond, *The Middle Ages. A Literary History of Spain* (1971).

LORD (Latin: dominus or senior, Anglo-Saxon: hlaord) In the Middle Ages, the term was mainly used in the *feudal sense. The L. was anyone who had vassals and held lands, cultivated by dependent peasants. Such a L. could be the vassal of a higher L. The feudal ideals, as expressed in the *Assizes of Jerusalem, conceived of a series of Ls., with the king as the chief L. of his kingdom.

J. Strayer, *Feudalism* (1964).

LORDS APPELANTS The title assumed in 1388 by the heads of the baronial opposition to *Richard II in England, led by the duke of *Gloucester, the king's uncle. They seized control of the government and impeached Richard's ministers. In 1389 they were dismissed by the king, with the help of his uncle, the duke of *Lancaster.

LORDS ORDAINERS See EDWARD II, king of England.

LORENZETTI The name of two brothers, Ambrogio (*c.* 1290-1348) and Pietro (*c.* 1280-1348), both painters of the Sienese school. They developed new techniques of oil-painting which they applied in their frescoes, many of them at Siena, Florence and other Tuscan cities. Their main interest lay in the painting of altarpieces, the most famous of which is the triptych, *The Birth of the Virgin,* by Pietro, in the Uffizi, Florence. Ambrogio's painting of the *Peace Hall* at Siena indicates an individual expression of the late Gothic style.

C. Brandi, *Pietro Lorenzetti* (1958);
E. Borsook, *Ambrogio Lorenzetti* (1966).

LORRAINE Historical region between France and Germany, in the 9th century comprising the Low Countries and modern *Alsace-Lorraine. Part of the *Frankish kingdom, it was given by the Treaty of *Verdun (843) to Emperor *Lothair, eldest son of *Louis the Pious, and was known as *Francia Media. At Lothair's death (955) it passed to his son, *Lothair II and was renamed Regnum Lotharii (kingdom of Lothair) or Lotharingia. From 869 on it was contested by the kings of France and Germany. In 925 it became a duchy of *Germany, and then of the *Holy Roman empire. The strong particularism of the Lotharingians, who claimed to be the real descendants of the Franks, gave rise to a long series of revolts, led by the dukes, against the German kings. *Otto I, who crushed a revolt in 956, gave the duchy to his brother, *Bruno, archbishop of Cologne, in an attempt to stem the separatist current. Bruno divided L. into two duchies, Lower L. in the north, and Upper L. or L. proper. They both lacked political stability in the last years of the 10th century and at the beginning of the 11th century, with dukes being appointed at the emperors' convenience. Thus, *Otto II appointed a French *Carolingian, *Charles, brother of King *Lothair, as duke of Lower L. Powerful counties emerg-

"Falconer" water container; Lorraine, 14th century

ed, weakening ducal power. In an attempt to restore ducal authority, the family of Verdun-Ardennes, who ruled Lower L. in the 11th century, fought against the counts of *Louvain, *Hainault, *Namur and *Luxemburg, as well as against the powerful bishops of *Liège. They also revolted against the emperors and attempted, unsuccessfully, to create a principality in *Italy, by marriage contracts with the margraves of Canossa-Tuscany. When the last duke of Lower L., *Godfrey of Bouillon, went on the First *Crusade, his duchy was divided among the counts.

In Upper L., ducal power was restored in 1055 by Gerard of Châtenois, who founded a dynasty that was destined to govern L. until the 15th century. The duchy's influence, however, was diminished by the establishment of large ecclesiastical seignories — among them the bishoprics of Metz, Toul and Verdun, and many abbeys — which depended on the emperor. The counts of Luxemburg, Bar and Alsace also freed themselves from ducal authority. To maintain their power, the dukes of L. relied on the emperors, and proved themselves faithful vassals. In the 14th century French influence in L. became preponderant. The dukes were related to French princely families and even served in the French army. Nonetheless, they made efforts to preserve their independent status. The ducal court at Nancy, one of the most brilliant of western Europe, was open to the cultures of both France and Germany. In 1431, at the death of Duke Charles, a constable in the French army, the duchy was inherited by his son-in-

Italian merchants at work; fresco by Ambrogio Lorenzetti

law, René of Anjou. He and his son, John, who became duke in 1453, made every effort to oppose *Burgundian plans to annex L. to the great state which included the Low Countries.

J. Schneider, *Histoire de la Lorraine* (1951).

LORSCH Monastery in Franconia, Germany. Founded in the 8th century, it served as a base for missionary activity among the Thuringians and Saxons. Under the *Carolingians, it became an important imperial institution. Its abbey church was embellished in the 9th century, while the monastery became the burial place of the Carolingian kings of Germany. The prestige of L. gave it a place in popular literature. In the German epic *Nibelungen*, for example, it is mentioned as the burial place of the hero Siegfried.
DHGE.

LOTHAIR I (795-855) Emperor (840-55). The eldest son of *Louis the Pious, he was destined to inherit the imperial title and from 818 assisted his father in government. He revolted against his father in 828 and defeated him in 831. The first years of his reign as emperor were marked by struggles with his brothers, *Louis the German and *Charles the Bald, until an agreement was reached at Verdun (843), whereby the empire was divided. In addition to the imperial title, L. received Italy and a strip of land between Provence and Friesland, called *Francia Media. He divided his domains among his three sons shortly before his death.

L. Halphen, *Charlemagne et l'Empire Carolingien* (1947).

LOTHAIR II (825-69) King of *Lotharingia (855-69). Second son of *Lothair I he received the territory between the Jura Mountains and the North Sea. His domain, Lotharingia, was named after him. He fought against his uncles, the kings of France and Germany, and was at loggerheads with the papacy, which refused to sanction his divorce. He died childless.

LOTHAIR III, of Supplinburg (1075-1137) *Holy Roman emperor (1125-37). Member of the Saxon countal family of Supplinburg, he became duke of *Saxony in 1106 and was elected emperor in 1125. L. had to fight the opposition of *Frederick of Hohenstaufen, who claimed hereditary succession rights to the imperial crown. Aided by the Welf dukes of *Bavaria, he succeeded in imposing his rule in Germany. In 1130, he supported Pope *Innocent II against Pope *Anacletus II and in 1133 conquered Rome for the former. L. also encouraged German expansion east of the Elbe.

K. Hampe, *Deutsche Kaisergeschichte im Zeitalter der Salier und Staufer* (1959).

LOTHAIR I (941-86) King of *France (954-86). Son of *Louis IV, his reign was under the influence first of *Hugh the Great, duke of the Franks, and then of Emperor *Otto I, his father-in-law. Under L., the French *Carolingians lost their authority, being practically confined to the northeastern provinces of France. The feudal nobility exercised most power.

F. Lot and L. Halphen, *Annales du règne de Lothaire* (1899).

LOTHAIR OF PROVENCE King of *Italy (937-50). Son of *Hugh of Provence, he was proclaimed king after his father's return to Provence. L. was prevented from ruling, despite his alliance with King *Rudolf of Burgundy, who gave him his daughter Adelaide as wife. His claims were contested by *Berengar of Friuli, who probably murdered him in 950.

Marble statuette of a seated king; Lorraine, 14th century

LOTHARINGIA See LORRAINE.

LOUIS I, the Pious (778-840) *Carolingian emperor from 814. The youngest son of *Charlemagne, he was destined from childhood to become king of *Aquitaine, but the sole son to survive the emperor, he inherited the whole empire. L. clamped down on all opposition, even putting to death his nephew, the Italian King *Bernard, who revolted against him in 815. But the empire he inherited was by no means easy to govern. In a state of decline since the last years of Charlemagne's reign, it was beset by internal anarchy and external pressure, such as the *Norman raids. His empire threatening to disintegrate, L. sought the support of the high clergy, which still represented the idea of unity. in return, he gave extensive privileges to the churches, diminishing the royal demesne. According to the precedent set by his father in 806, L. divided the empire among his three sons, *Lothair, *Pepin and *Louis (the German), whom he associated with his government. The birth of a fourth son, *Charles, from a second marriage (822) and the subsequent change in the partition plan to give Charles a part of the empire, led to a series of revolts by the elder sons, who were supported by the turbulent nobility. By 829, the empire was in total disarray, with the governmental and administrative structures established by Charlemagne no longer functioning. His rebellious sons succeeded in deposing him twice, in 830 and again in 833. Supported by churchmen and nobles, L. recovered the imperial title, but was compelled to concede effective power to his sons in their respective realms. At his death, the *Carolingian empire disintegrated. Despite the opinion of some historians that L. was a weak monarch responsible for the empire's division, it is generally acknowledged that he was an energetic leader, who was prevented by external circumstances from maintaining a centralized government. L. encouraged intellectual and scholarly activity, and, during his reign, the Carolingian Renaissance reached its peak.

P. Charanis, *Son of Charlemagne* (1965).

LOUIS II (825-75) *Frankish emperor from 855. Eldest son of *Lothair I, he was made king of *Italy by his father in 844 and chosen as heir to the imperial title. He failed in his attempts to impose his authority on Italy, and Popes *Leo IV and *Nicholas I largely recovered their independence. Meanwhile, the *Saracens were making inroads to his realm. At his death, as he had only a daughter, the imperial title was contested by *Carolingian monarchs, and Italy's disunity worked to the advantage of feudal families.

G. Mor, *Italia nell'eta Carolingiana* (1951).

LOUIS III, the Blind (880-928) *Frankish emperor (901-05). Son of *Boso, he became king of *Provence in 888. Claiming the imperial crown in 901, he went to Italy, where he fought against another claimant, *Berengar I of Friuli. Defeated, he was taken captive and blinded before his return to Provence, where he reigned nominally until his death.

LOUIS IV, the Bavarian (1287-1347) *Holy Roman emperor (1328-47). Member of the house of *Wittelsbach, dukes of Bavaria, he was elected king of *Germany in 1314, following his victory over the house of *Hapsburg at Gammelsdorf in 1313. The Hapsburgs refused to recognize L. and appointed *Frederick III anti-king. L.'s defeat of Frederick at Muhldorf (1322) silenced Hapsburg opposition. But at the same time, L. entered a struggle against Pope *John XXII, who would acknowledge neither L.'s election nor his claims over Italy. The polemic dispute that erupted in 1324, when L. was excommunicated by the pope, was largely an extension of earlier quarrels between the papacy and the Holy Roman Empire over sovereignty of the western world, without regard for the new realities of the 14th century, when sovereign states emerged. Supported in Italy by the influential *Ghibellines, L. was crowned emperor at Rome in 1328 – in a lay ceremony – by Sciarra *Colonna, who represented the Roman populace. He was supported by many contemporary political thinkers, among them *Marsilius of Padua and William of *Ockham. The dispute continued until the death of the pope, whose intransigence brought the German electoral princes to support the emperor. In 1338, at the Diet of Rhens, the princes decreed that an emperor could be chosen by the *electors without papal confirmation. The last years of L.'s reign were dedicated to protecting the interests of the house of Wittelsbach. He annexed *Brandenburg, Lower Bavaria, *Tyrol and *Carinthia to his family's dominion. His attempt to appoint a Wittelsbach count in Holland antagonized the princes, who feared the growth of his power. In

1346, the electors chose *Charles of Luxemburg, king of Bohemia, as emperor. L. died the following year.

O. Bornhack, *Staatskirchlichen Anschaungen und Handlungen Ludwigs der Bayer* (1933).

LOUIS II, the Stammerer (846-79) King of *France (877-79). Son and heir of *Charles the Bald, he reigned under the influence of the clergy, led by *Hincmar of Rheims, and lay magnates, who obtained wide privileges for their families.

LOUIS III (863-82) King of *France (879-82). Son of *Louis II, he reigned together with his brother *Carloman. L. had to face a revolt by the nobles, who called King *Louis II of Germany to reign in France, because they felt that L. was too young to provide appropriate leadership against the Norman raids. He came to an agreement with the nobility, giving up his claims to *Lotharingia, and concentrated his efforts against the *Normans, whom he defeated in 881 at Saucourt. The victory made him a hero of epic poems, both in German (the *Ludwigslied*) and in French (*Gormond et Isembart*). He died in a hunting accident.

L. Halphen, *Charlemagne et l'Empire Carolingien* (1947).

LOUIS IV, d'Outremer (921-54) King of France (936-54). Son of *Charles III, he was brought up in England, hence his title, meaning "from overseas". After the death of King *Raoul, he was elected king by the magnates, led by Frankish Duke *Hugh the Great, who exercised the real influence in the realm. L. granted the magnates many privileges, to the extent that his reign saw the emergence of feudal principalities in France.

P. Lauer, *Le règne de Louis IV d'Outremer* (1900).

LOUIS V (967-87) The last *Carolingian king of France (986-87). Son of *Lothair I, he died in a hunting accident a few months after his coronation.

LOUIS VI, the Fat (1081-1137) King of *France (1108-37). Son of *Philip I, he was associated with his father's government in 1100. During the last years of his father's reign and after his own coronation, he aborted attempts by feudal lords to gain independence, thereby consolidating royal authority in his realm. L. had the active support of the church, and used the "Truce of God to enforce obedience by rebellious vassals. He also took advantage of the urban awakening in northern France to extend his authority, granting charters of *commune to various cities. He supported the papacy against Emperor *Henry V and was thus hailed as *Charlemagne's heir. In 1124, threatened by German troop movements, he ordered a general mobilization of the army, acting as king of the whole realm. Although his intervention in *Flanders following the murder of Count *Charles the Good (1127) had only minor results, it increased his prestige, and helped him win support for Pope *Innocent II, whom L. was the first monarch to recognize (1130). L. was assisted by a group of able counsellors and ministers, including his friend, Abbot *Suger of Saint-Denis. His power reached its zenith in 1137, when Duke *William X of Aquitaine made him guardian of his daughter *Eleanor and the duchy. Shortly before he died in Spain, L. arranged her marriage with his son and heir, *Louis VII.

A. Luchaire, *Louis VI le Gros* (1890);
A. Grabois, *De la Trève de Dieu à la Paix du Roi* (1966).

LOUIS VII, the Young (1120-80) King of *France (1137-80). Second son of *Louis VI, he was proclaimed heir at the death of his elder brother Philip in 1131. In 1137 he married *Eleanor of Aquitaine and began his reign both as king of France and duke of Aquitaine. The first years of his reign were a period of instability. Influenced by his wife, he dismissed his father's counsellors and entered into a series of conflicts with the papacy and some of the feudal lords, notably *Theobald, count of Champagne. But he was induced to revert to his father's policy in 1143 when his army, in retaliation, burned the village of Vitry in Champagne. L. was a leader of the Second *Crusade (1147-49) and, despite his military failures, he proved himself a perfect knight. His government, based on justice and a good relationship with the clergy, won him the respect of the nobility. In 1152 he divorced Eleanor (who bore him two daughters), and, thereby, lost Aquitaine to her second husband, *Henry of Anjou, the future king of England. A major part of France, extending from the English Channel to the Pyrénées, thus came under the rule of a powerful vassal, who also proved himself an able politician. In the long series of wars between the two monarchs, L. had the support of other vassals and the cities, as well as of the church. He supported Pope *Alexander III against *Frederick Barbarossa and in return was proclaimed "The Most Christian King", which became a hereditary title of French kings. L. was a patron of learning. During his reign the schools of Paris developed into a prestigious university, which made Paris the centre of west European culture.

M. Pacaut, *Louis VII et son royaume* (1965).

LOUIS VIII, the Lionheart (1187-1226) King of *France (1223-26). Son of *Philip II, he married *Blanche of Castile in 1200, as part of a political settlement between the kings of France and England. From 1212, he was active in royal policy and commanded the army. His attempt in 1216 to conquer England, claiming succession rights, failed and he returned to France to launch the Crusade against the *Albigenses. He resumed the Crusade after his coronation, annexing *Languedoc to the royal demesne.

C. Petit-Dutaillis, *Louis VIII* (1899).

LOUIS IX (St. Louis; 1214-70) King of *France (1226-70). He began his reign under the regency of his mother, *Blanche of Castile, who educated him as a pious Christian. He subdued a baronial revolt in central France in 1241 and enlarged the royal domain, of which he gave large *apanages to his brothers. In 1244, after the *Khwarizmians conquered Jerusalem and the Egyptians seized Damascus, he launched the Seventh *Crusade, conceived as a religious and moral expedition, to save the beleaguered Christian kingdom of the East. For that purpose, he ordered the building of a new harbour, *Aigues-Mortes. With a large fleet and logistical support, he attacked Egypt; after initial successes, he was defeated and, together with a large part of his army, was taken prisoner at Mansura (1249). Released for a heavy ransom, he went to *Acre, and subsequently devoted himself to fortifying the Christian cities. Recalled to France as a result of the *Pastoureaux troubles, he directed the building in Paris of the *Sainte Chapelle, a splendid monument of Gothic architecture. L. was not the typical statesman of his times. His actions were guided by two ideals – the religious and the feudal. While under his reign the *Parliament of Paris was organized as the high court of justice, he felt himself a

stranger in a court of lawyers with their procedures. Popular legend has him administering justice under the oak tree in the gardens outside his *Vendôme castle, his favourite retreat. The many ordinances he issued were codified in the *Establissements de St. Louis*. L. treasured peace, and towards that end he would make generous territorial concessions. In 1258 he signed the Treaty of Paris with *Henry III of England, enlarging Henry's possessions, in return for which the English king agreed to become L.'s vassal in *Guienne. In 1259, he signed the Treaty of Corbeil, bringing peace with *Aragon. His reputation as an equitable ruler, guided by the idea of the divine rights of kings made him the arbiter of disputes in Europe that did not necessarily involve France. An example of this is his attempt to negotiate peace between Henry III and the baronial party of England. L. was, however, to some extent influenced by the practical policies of his brothers, especially *Charles of Anjou, who persuaded him to support his expeditions to Italy and Sicily in 1266. In 1270, also influenced by Charles, he proclaimed a Crusade against Tunis, where he died. Jean de *Joinville's biography on L.'s life, deeds and character served as the basis for the emergence of the monarchical cult in France.

J. Levron, *Saint Louis ou l'apogée du Moyen Age* (1969).

LOUIS X, the Stubborn (1289-1316) King of *France from 1314. He inherited a troubled kingdom from his father, *Philip IV. To appease the nobles, he granted baronial charters to most French provinces.

LOUIS the German (804-76) King of *Germany from 843. Son of *Louis the Pious, he was assigned Bavaria in 817 and began to rule the country effectively on his father's behalf in 826. He later joined his brothers *Lothair and *Pepin of Aquitaine in their revolt against their father (829-33). But at their father's death in 840, when Lothair acceded to the imperial throne and claimed suzerainty over the whole empire, L. allied with *Charles the Bold against Lothair and defeated him. By the Treaty of Verdun (843), whereby the empire was partitioned between Lothair and Charles, L. became the leader of the East Franks, obtaining the territories of the Saxons, Franconians, Bavarians and Swabians which were later to become Germany. L. divided his kingdom among his sons while he himself was active in a series of unsuccessful attempts to conquer *Lotharingia and France. Despite his patrimonial concepts, as manifested in his division of the kingdom among his sons and in his attempts to restore the *Carolingian empire to his advantage, L. is considered as the founder of the medieval state of Germany.

L. Halphen, *Charlemagne et l'Empire Carolingien* (1947).

LOUIS II, the Younger (822-82) King of *Germany from 876. Son of *Louis the German, he was assigned *Saxony, *Franconia and *Thuringia in his father's division of the kingdom. He helped his father in his attempts to conquer *Lotharingia, annexing its eastern part to his kingdom in 876. That year he inherited the crown, but respected his father's arrangements for the division of Germany. In return for his brothers' help in Lotharingia, which he annexed to Germany by the Treaty of Ribemont, he supported the candidacy of *Charles the Fat for the imperial crown in 880.

L. Halphen, *Charlemagne et l'Empire Carolingien* (1947).

LOUIS III, the Child (893-911) He was the last *Carolingian king of Germany (900-11), reigning under the regency of Haithon, archbishop of Mainz. His reign was a period of anarchy, caused by *Hungarian raids.

LOUIS I, of Anjou (1326-82) King of *Hungary (1342-82) and *Poland (1370-82). Son of *Carobert, he was the greatest monarch of the Anjou-Naples dynasty of Hungary. He collaborated with the nobility and confirmed their privileges, but also managed to assert his authority. While this cooperation brought internal peace to Hungary and assured the economic prosperity of its cities, it created the conditions for oppressing the peasants. L. fought against *Venice and, after an initial defeat at the Adriatic port city of Zara in 1347, he conquered most of Venice's Dalmatian towns in 1358 and practically all of *Dalmatia in 1381. From 1351, he was active in supporting the *Serbs and Bulgarians against the Ottoman *Turks, but despite some victories, failed to check their advances in the Balkan peninsula. In 1347 he began to intervene in the affairs of *Naples, supporting the opposition against Queen *Joan I. His army occupied Naples in 1350 and again in 1378. In 1370 he was adopted by King *Casimir III of Poland and was elected king of Poland at Casimir's death.
A. Sinor, *A History of Hungary* (1958).

LOUIS I, of Anjou (1339-84) Titular king of *Naples (1383-84). He was granted the duchy of *Anjou by his father, King *John II of France, and was the founder of the third house of Anjou. He helped his brother *Charles V to restore royal authority in France, but also sought to enlarge his possessions. At the death of Queen *Joan I of Naples (1383), he entitled himself king of Naples, but his sole achievement was the conquest of *Provence, which he annexed to his territories.

LOUIS II, of Anjou (1377-1417) Titular king of *Naples (1384-1400). Son of *Louis I, he was proclaimed king at his father's death and was supported by the opposition to *Charles III. Brought to Naples in 1386, he was defeated by *Ladislas of Durazzo and deposed in 1400. L. returned to France, where he ruled the duchy of Anjou.

LOUIS, duke of Orléans (1372-1407) Second son of King *Charles V of France, he became active in French political affairs after 1392, when his brother *Charles VI was intermittently insane. He opposed the influence of Queen Isabella of Bavaria and her counsellors. While this policy brought him into conflict with *John the Fearless, duke of Burgundy, and many Parisians, it won him the support of a significant section of the nobility, led by Bernard of *Armagnac. From 1405 France was in a state of political turmoil. L. was murdered at Paris in 1407.
E. D'Avout, *La Querelle des Armagnacs et des Bourguignons* (1951).

LOUIS OF MALE (1330-84) Son of *Louis of Nevers, he was the last count of *Flanders (1346-84). His reign was marked by uprisings in the towns and economic crisis. To obtain support against the rebels, he gave his daughter Margaret in marriage to *Philip the Bold, duke of *Burgundy (1369), thus laying the basis for the union of Burgundy and Flanders.

LOUIS OF NEVERS (c. 1304-46) Count of *Flanders (1322-46). Member of the countal family of Nevers, he inherited the county of Flanders at the extinction of the house of Dampierre. He was supported by the French royal court in his attempts to overcome the opposition of the Flemish cities. His pro-French policy brought King *Edward III of England to impose an economic blockade against Flanders (1337). A serious crisis to the Flemish cloth industry, it was followed by urban uprisings.
H. Pirenne, *The Early Democracies in the Low Countries* (1914).

LOUIS OF TARANTO (1320-62) King of *Naples (1347-62). Member of a cadet branch of the Anjou dynasty of Naples, he married Queen *Joan I in 1347. L. fought against his kinsman *Louis I of Hungary, who invaded the kingdom to avenge the murder of his brother Andrew, Joan's first husband. L. and his wife fled to Avignon, where they received the support of Pope *Clement VII and, with the help of their vassals of Provence, attempted to reconquer his realm (1352). In 1359 he invaded *Sicily, but his conquest of Palermo was shortlived, because a revolt by the nobles at Naples compelled him to return. He died shortly after repressing the revolt.
E. Léonard, *Les Angevins de Naples* (1954).

LOUVAIN City and county in the Low Countries. It was founded in the early 9th century around a fortress built by *Charles the Fat against the Normans. The lords of L. were vassals of the dukes of Lower *Lotharingia. Their power gradually increased and, in the 11th century, they were granted the countal title and were among the dukes' chief vassals. During the same period, L. saw rapid economic expansion, situated as it was on the main roads of the Low Countries. After *Godfrey of Bouillon went on a *Crusade and the duchy of Lotharingia split up, the counts of L. became direct vassals of the emperors. In 1106, Count Godfrey was bestowed with the ducal title, which thereafter became hereditary. In 1190, L. became the basis of the duchy of *Brabant. The dukes established their capital at *Brussels in the 13th century, while L. itself remained a prosperous provincial city, where a textile and *cloth industry was established. In 1379, when the burghers' demands for communal privileges were rejected by the dukes, who had the support of the nobility, a popular uprising led to the murder of 17 nobles and to the proclamation of a *commune. The commune was abolished in 1383 by the ducal army and in 1405 L. was annexed to the Burgundian state. With the establishment of the first university in the Low Countries at L. in 1426, the city was transformed from an industrial centre to a seat of learning which attracted scholars and students from all over the Low Countries and northern Germany.
H. Pirenne, *Histoire de la Belgique* (1904).

LOUVRE 14th-century *Parisian palace. It originated as a fortress built by King *Philip II of France in 1195 on the right bank of the Seine River. The structure was enlarged, with the establishment of the royal archives at the L. in the 13th century.

LÜBECK City in northern *Germany, on the shores of the Baltic Sea. Originally a small Slavic town, L. was conquered by *Henry the Lion, duke of Saxony, in 1143. He rebuilt L. as a German city, and granted extensive privileges to its new German inhabitants. During the second half of the 12th century, the merchant guild of L. became the city's most powerful organization, with the guild's association, the *Hanse, highly influential in Baltic Sea trade. In 1226, Emperor *Frederick II granted L. the status of "free city", recognizing the privileges of the aristocracy. During his reign, L. flourished, becoming, in 1230, the headquarters of the Hanse. In the 14th century the city reached the peak of its growth and development, heading one of the greatest merchant empires of the late Middle Ages. Prosperity led to the rebuilding of the city centre, and splendid dwellings of rich merchants sprang up around the market-place and city hall.

F. Rörig, *The German Towns in the Middle Ages* (1957).

LUCCA City in *Tuscany, Italy. The ancient Roman city declined after the fall of the Roman empire and lacked importance under the successive governments of the *Heruli, *Ostrogoths, *Byzantines and *Lombards. In 774, it became the seat of *Frankish counts, who in the 9th and 10th centuries became the margraves of Tuscany. They were involved in power struggles with their powerful Tuscan neighbours and in the late 10th century the margravate passed to *Florence. In the 11th century, a conflict with the local bishops over the government of L. and its environs culminated in the establishment of a *commune by the burghers in 1088 and the rise of a new leadership, comprising mainly prominent merchants. The *charter of liberties granted L. in 1181 by Emperor *Frederick Barbarossa was the nucleus of its independence, attained during the 13th century. In the 12th and 13th centuries, L. was one of northern Italy's most prominent centres of Gothic art, especially sculpture.

J. K. Hyde, *Society and Politics in Medieval Italy* (1973).

LUCERA City in southern *Italy. The ancient Roman town was destroyed by the *Lombards in 663. On its site, near the frontiers of the Papal States, Emperor *Frederick II built a new city around his castle in 1233, and settled there some of his Moslem subjects. After the fall of the kingdom of Sicily, L. resisted for many years before it was conquered by *Charles of Anjou. Most of the Moslem inhabitants were murdered, while those who survived were forcibly converted to Catholicism.

LUCERNE City and canton in central *Switzerland. It originated as a fishing village whose inhabitants were serfs of the *Benedictine abbey of St. Leodegard, founded in the 8th century. In the 10th and 11th centuries the settlement grew into a prosperous town on the trade routes between Germany and Italy. To boost trade development, the abbots granted privileges to L., which were extended in 1178 in its *charter of liberties, allowing the inhabitants to establish their own council. In 1291, L. was sold to *Rudolf I of Hapsburg, despite the opposition of the city council. Its inhabitants joined the Swiss cantons in their revolt against the *Hapsburgs and in 1332 allied with the *Swiss Confederation. After the Battle of *Sempach (1386), L. gained its independence, becoming the capital of the canton by the same name.

CMedH, VIII.

LUCIUS II (Gerard of Bologna; d. 1145) Pope from 1144. Born in Bologna, Italy, he joined the papal court and was created cardinal. His advanced age and his position as chancellor of Pope *Innocent II were factors in his election during a troubled period for Rome.

J. Haller, *Das Papsttum* (1951).

Scene from the life of St. Nicholas in a Romanesque relief on the portal of the cathedral of Lucca, Tuscany

LUCIUS III (Ubaldo Allucingoli; c. 1097-1185)   Pope (1181-85). Born in Tuscany, central Italy, he entered the *Cistercian order and in 1141 was created cardinal by Pope *Innocent II. Promoted in 1159 to the bishopship of Ostia, he was elected pope in 1181 but was forced to flee to northern Italy when the Romans proclaimed the city a republic. In 1184, at a meeting with Emperor *Frederick Barbarossa at Verona, he established the *Inquisition.
W. Ullmann, *A Short History of the Papacy* (1972).

LUDOLF OF SAXONY (Ludolf the Carthusian; c. 1300-78)   Spiritual writer, about whose life little is known. In 1340 he joined the *Carthusians at Strassburg and became prior of the charterhouse at Coblenz in 1343. From 1348 on, he devoted his time to prayer, meditation and writing. Among his works, the most popular was *The Life of Christ*, conceived as a manual of moral and spiritual instruction for the faithful. The book was widely spread as early as 1474.
L. M. Rigollot (ed.), *La Vita Christi de Ludolf le Chartreux* (1870).

LULL, RAMON (1232-1316)   Scholar and mystic. Born in Catalonia, he entered the service of King *James I of Aragon and married at the court. At the age of 30 he suddenly left the court and became a *Franciscan monk, devoting himself to converting Moslems to Christianity. His missionary activity took him to north Africa and Asia, as far as the frontiers of India. In the intervals between his travels, he studied and taught at Montpellier, where he developed his neo-Platonic views on the unity of faith and moral values, refuting the *Averroist teachings. He travelled to Moslem countries in 1315, and legend has it that he was stoned at Bougie, Algeria, where he died. L.'s literary activity, in Latin, Catalan and Arabic, was prodigious. Influenced by the *Augustinian teachings, he wrote the *Ars Magna* (The Great Art), in which he attempted to explain universal knowledge on an encyclopedic basis, according to his conception of absolute truth. He formulated a method by which all possible knowledge could be reduced to, or derived from, certain first principles. As a mystic, he developed the ideal of contemplating divine perfection by the purification of memory, understanding and will. Such contemplation, he felt, would result in action for the greater glory of God. Besides his theological and mystical works, L. also wrote poetry. His poems in Catalan gave him a prominent place in Catalan literature. He wrote a treatise on chivalry, designed to combine his moral and religious ideals with the lay practices of knighthood. The book was widely spread and translated into several languages, serving as a manual for the education of young knights.
E. A. Peers, *Ramon Lull, A Biography* (1929).

LULLUS, St. (d. 786)   Bishop of *Mainz. Born in England, he was associated with St. *Boniface and followed him as a missionary to Germany, where he became his closest collaborator and his successor. His correspondence is an invaluable source for the history of the *Frankish kingdom, the papacy and missionary activity in 8th-century Germany.
MGH, Epistolae, III;
W. Levison, *England and the Continent in the 8th Century* (1946).

LUND   City in the province of Skäne (corresponding to modern southern Sweden). It was founded in 1020 by Danish King *Canute the Great as the capital of the Danish territory of Skäne. In 1060 it was made a bishopric and in 1103 was elevated to the rank of archbishopric for all of Scandinavia. Its 12th-century cathedral is one of the most interesting adaptations of Romanesque architecture in Scandinavian countries.
E. Newman, *Lund and its Cathedral Church* (1946).

LUPUS, SERVATUS (c. 805-62)   Abbot of Ferrières, France. Born in the province of Sens, he became a monk at an early age and studied at Fierrières and *Fulda, where his teacher was *Rabanus Maurus. In 836 he returned to Ferrières and won the favour of Emperor *Louis the Pious. In 840 he became abbot of Ferrières, which he made one of the centres of the *Carolingian renaissance. A humanist rather than a theologian, L. introduced classical studies at his abbey's school. He was also active in political life, attempting to maintain the unity of the *Carolingian empire. His collection of 132 letters are an invaluable source for the history of his times.
Works, ed. *PL*, CIX;
C. H. Beeson, *Lupus of Ferrières* (1930).

LUSATIA   Marquisate in *Germany, on the east bank of the Elbe River. Populated in the 8th and 9th centuries by the Sorbs, a Slavic people, L. was conquered in 928 by the Germans, who were organized as a march, dependent on Saxony. In 1002, King *Boleslaw I annexed it to Poland, but in 1033 the Germans reconquered it. With the settlement of Germans in L., it was subjected to German influence. Eventually divided between the marches of *Brandenburg and *Meissen, it lost its political identity.

LUSIGNAN   Feudal family of *Poitou, western France. They took their name from a 10th-century castle in western Poitou. As lords of L., they were vassals of the dukes of *Aquitaine. The founder of the dynasty, *Hugh L., was vested with extensive lands around the castle in the middle of the 10th century. His successors gradually increased their fortunes. By the middle of the 12th century, the lords of L. were a powerful dynasty in western France, related to the counts of La Marche. Two members of a cadet branch of the family participated in the *Crusades to the Latin kingdom of Jerusalem in the second half of the 12th century. Both distinguished themselves, especially *Amalric, who became the constable of the kingdom. He called his younger brother, *Guy, to join him and arranged his marriage with Princess Sybil, sister and heiress of King *Baldwin IV. In 1186 Guy became king of Jerusalem and after his defeat at *Hattin, transferred his capital to *Cyprus, where the L. family founded the royal dynasty, which was to reign until the 15th century. In the meantime, the heads of the family in France continued to develop their principality. *Hugh X sought to annex Angoulême to his county of La Marche by marrying Countess Isabella, heiress of Angoulême. But in 1098, his lord, King *John of England, aborted his plans by marrying Isabella himself. The Ls. turned to *Philip II, king of France, with whom they allied against John. After John's death, in 1216, Hugh's son, *Hugh XI, married Isabella. To maintain his power he had to fight both against *Henry III of England and *Louis IX of France. Defeated in 1241 by Louis IX, the Ls. declined.
S. Painter, *Feudalism and Liberties* (1949).

LUTTRELL PSALTER   See PSALTERS.

LUXEMBURG County in the southern part of the Low Countries. The territory was given by *Lothair II to the abbey of St. Maximin of Trier, and in the 9th and 10th centuries the abbots governed it as feudal lords. To fortify the area, a castle was built at Lutzelburg, hence the county's name. In 963 a German knight, Siegfried, acquired the abbey's castle and was vested by *Otto I with the countal title, under the authority of the emperor's brother, Bruno, archbishop of Cologne and duke of *Lotharingia. Siegfried's descendants took advantage of the decline in ducal power in Lower Lotharingia to consolidate their authority. In the 12th century they became princes of the *Holy Roman empire, having been related to highly prominent families in the Low Countries and Germany. In 1308 Count Henry IV was elected emperor and founded, under the name of *Henry VII, the L. dynasty (see *genealogy), which was to reign as emperors until the 15th century. The dynasty transferred its capital to *Bohemia while L. was given to cadet sons. In 1354, *Charles IV gave L. to his brother Wenceslas and elevated it to the rank of duchy. In 1411, as a result of the marriage between Elisabeth of Moravia, heiress of L., and Anthony of Burgundy, the duchy passed to Burgundian rule. In 1441, under the rule of *Philip the Good, duke of *Burgundy, L. was annexed to the Low Countries, becoming part of the Burgundian state of the later Middle Ages.

J. W. Thompson, *Feudal Germany* (1928).

LYONS City in Gaul. Founded as a Roman colony in 43 BC, the city became, under Roman rule, the capital of Gaul and, in the Middle Ages, continued to be considered as such by the church organization; the archbishops of L. were entitled "Primates of Gaul". Conquered by the *Burgundians in the second half of the 5th century, the city declined under Burgundian and then under *Frankish rule, remaining mainly an ecclesiastical centre. At the division of the *Carolingian empire in 843, L. was given to *Lothair I and became part of *Francia Media. At the end of the 9th century, when the kingdom of *Lotharingia was dissolved, L. became a Burgundian city with its archbishops as the effective rulers. In 1032, it was annexed to the *Holy Roman empire, together with the kingdom of Burgundy. Trade revival and L.'s favourable location at the cross-roads between France and Italy, and the North Sea and the Mediterranean, led in the 11th and 12th centuries to continuous growth and prosperity; the city expanded on both banks of the Rhône River and of its confluent, the Saône. *Frederick Barbarossa granted it extensive privileges, which favoured the development of trade and the establishment of a cloth industry. The special status of its archbishops, who continued to be the lords of the city, and the decline of imperial authority in Provence and Dauphiné, made L. virtually autonomous. The popes' influence was sufficiently large for L. to became the site of two ecumenical councils, in 1245, concerning the *Inquisition, and in 1274. After 1250, French influence became paramount: L.'s burghers entered into close relations with France and a large movement within the city requested French protection. In 1307, *Philip IV the Fair formally annexed L. to France, abolishing the archbishops' independence and their status as lords of the city. Under French rule, the city continued to prosper, a trend that was accelerated with the establishment of its trade *fairs in the 15th century, when L. became the second city in France, after Paris.

R. Fédou, *Lyon et les Foires du Lyonnais* (1964).

Minaret of the White Mosque in Ramlah, built by the Mamelukes in 1318

M

MACARIUS, St. Bishop of *Jerusalem (313-34). He attended the Council of *Nicaea, where he became acquainted with the imperial family and was appointed confessor of St. *Helena, the mother of Emperor *Constantine. In 326, after St. Helena's reputed discovery of the *Holy Cross, he was commissioned to build the church of the *Holy Sepulchre at Jerusalem, so laying the foundations of the cult of Christian holy places.
L. Duchesne, *History of the Early Church* (1923).

MACBETH King of the *Scots (1044-57). Grandson of King Kenneth II, in 1031 he inherited the earldom of Murray in northern Scotland from his father. In 1040 he revolted against his cousin, King Duncan I and, having killed him, claimed the kingship for himself, but actually attained the throne after four years of civil war. His reign was marked by civil war and dynastic strife. The opposition, supported by the Anglo-Saxons, was led by *Malcolm III, the legitimate claimant of the throne. In 1057 M. was murdered by Malcolm's troops. M. was the subject of a great classic tragedy by William Shakespeare.
W. C. Dickinson, *Scotland, from the Earliest Times to 1603* (1961).

MACEDONIA Province in the Balkan peninsula. After the barbarian raids of the first half of the 5th century, M. was regained by the *Byzantines and became a province of their empire. In the second half of the 6th century, however, invasions of *Slav tribes produced a change in the area's ethnic structure. The northern parts of the country lost their Greek character, while the southern part, including the capital, *Thessalonica, did not. This change did not immediately affect the political fate of the country, however. In the 9th century, when the *Bulgarians settled in the Balkans and established their empire, the Slavic portion of M. was conquered and annexed to the Bulgarian realm. In the second half of the 9th century, due to the successful mission of *Cyril and Methodius, the Slav population converted to Orthodox Christianity and an ecclesiastical centre was established at *Ochrida in the northwestern part of the country. In 971, after the fall of Bulgaria, the Bulgarian prince *Samuel seized power in M. and proclaimed himself "tsar" at Ochrida. Thus, M. became the centre of the new Bulgarian state, which existed until 1014, when the Byzantine emperor, *Basil II, destroyed it and annexed the province to his own empire. The imperial administration of Byzantium encouraged the immigration of Greeks and other groups who merged with the Macedonian people.

In 1204, after the collapse of the Byzantine empire, M. was again divided. While Thessalonica was conquered by the *Crusaders, who established the Latin kingdom of *Salonica, most of the province was regained by the Bulgarians, who attempted to reconquer the whole country. After a short period of domination by the despots of *Epirus, Thessalonica was conquered by the empire of *Nicaea (1246) and returned to Byzantine rule, while the northern part of the country was disputed between the Bulgarians and *Serbians. The latter succeeded in conquering it in 1345 and established their capital at Skopje. Serbian rule lasted only a short time, since the *Ottoman Turks invaded the Balkans and systematically conquered the peninsula. By 1371, the Turks had conquered the hinterland and only Thessalonica and its neighbourhood remained of the Byzantine province. In 1423 the Turks conquered the remaining areas and made M. part of the Ottoman empire.
E. Barker, *Macedonia and Its Place in Balkan Power Politics* (1950).

MACHAUT, GUILLAUME DE See WILLIAM OF MACHAUT.

MACLOU (MALO), St. (d. c. 640) *Breton saint. According to tradition, M. was either of Welsh or Breton descent and became one of the spiritual leaders of the Breton settlement in Armorica, later to become *Brittany. M. settled at Aleth, where he adopted an ascetic life, while opposite his place of residence his followers founded the city of St. Malo.
F. Lot, *Mélanges d'Histoire Bretonne* (1907).

MÂCON City in eastern *France. The Gallo-Roman city of M. fell to the *Burgundians in the middle of the 5th century. Following the conquest of the Burgundian kingdom (535), it passed to the Franks and became a major ecclesiastical centre. In the 9th century M. became a county and was annexed to the kingdom of France by the Treaty of *Verdun (843). It was claimed by the dukes of Burgundy in the 10th century, causing its counts to struggle for their independence. However they grew dependent on their vassals and the latter eventually usurped their power. The county was then divided into a number of seigniories and during the 11th and 12th centuries fell into a state of anarchy. Of the many seigniories, those of *Cluny (est. 910) and of the bishops of M., who became lords of the city, were the wealthiest. In 1166 the state of anarchy was curbed by the intervention of the French monarchy, and under *Philip II the whole region was incorporated in the French royal domain.
G. Duby, *La Société aux XIᵉ et XIIᵉ siècles au Maconnais* (1953).

MADELEINE, St. See MARY MAGDALENE, St.

MAGDALENES The word was often used to denote reformed prostitutes, who repented and corrected their ways in medieval nunneries. In a stricter sense, the term came to be applied, from the 13th century on, to those nunneries whose virtuous members worked actively, particularly in the cities, to curb prostitution. See *Mary Magdalene, St.

MAGDEBURG City in *Germany, lying on the left bank of the Elbe River. Its existence is recorded for the first time in 805, when it served as a Frankish outpost for trade with the Slavs settled east of the Elbe and as the seat of a Frankish governor, entrusted by *Charlemagne with control of commercial activities. The *Carolingian fortress gradually became a city and reached a state of prominence under *Otto I (936). In 968 Otto established an archbishopric in the city, which became the centre of colonization activities in northeastern Saxony and eastern Germany, as well as a central point for propagation of the Catholic faith among the Slavs and Poles. In 973 *Otto II granted M. a charter of liberties, which also referred to a Jewish quarter of the city. Under the rule of its archbishops, the city was transformed into a prestigious commercial and political centre of northeastern Germany. However, development came to a halt in 1188, when a fire destroyed the wooden houses occupying the major part of the city. Rebuilt in stone in the 13th century, M. flourished rapidly and during the first half of the 13th century its burghers obtained from the archbishops a number of privileges, among them *communal autonomy. At the end of the 13th century M. joined the *Hanse, becoming one of its principal members and an important trading centre between the North Sea and central and eastern Europe.

In c. 1250, the privileges of M. became the basis for the M. law, a code of municipal government which was adopted in most of eastern Europe (Poland, Bohemia, Hungary, Lithuania and Russia). The adoption of the "M. charter" often signified the Germanization of those cities, whose communal courts judged in accordance with the "laws of M." and, when necessary, made appeal to the municipal court of M.

F. Rörig, *Magdeburg's Entstehung und die ältere Handelsgeschichte* (1952).

MAGHREB ("the West") Name given from the *Abbasid period (8th century) to the western provinces of the caliphate. In its wider sense, it included both Spain and the north African provinces west of Egypt, but as Spain did not recognize Abbasid authority and remained under the rule of the *Umayyads, the term was actually confined to the countries which now form Morocco, Algeria, Tunisia and the western part of Libya. At the beginning of the 9th century M. was synonymous with Ifriquia, the ancient Byzantine areas of Africa, but with the collapse of the *Aghlabid dynasty, the term lost its geopolitical sense.

EI.

MAGIC The occult sciences by which men attempted to harness supernatural forces for the welfare of individuals or a group. Medieval society inherited the idea from ancient fetishistic practices as well as from eastern occults. Fought as a form of paganism and witchcraft by the established monotheistic religions, M. nevertheless infiltrated the religious sphere. It manifested itself in the cult of *relics and other practices based on transcendental mystical theories, which were meant to explain miracles. From the 7th century Arab scientists, influenced by Egyptian achievements, developed a theory of the transmutation of elements and its application to *alchemy. On the popular level, this expressed itself in belief in the magical properties of certain phenomena such as talismans and various elixirs, among them *aquavitae* (elixirs of life) or special potions for love, protection, etc. Popular belief accepted the validity of old wives' and witches' brews, and all classes had recourse to them, as is attested in the vernacular literature. In contrast to its attitude to alchemy, the church fought the practice of M. and denounced it as satanic.

G. Parrinder, *Witchcraft, European and African* (1963).

MAGNA CHARTA LIBERTATUM (The Great Charter of Liberties) The most important of feudal documents, issued by King *John Lackland of England in 1215. The barons of the realm compelled him to grant it by threatening to depose him and incite a general revolt. The barons were opposed to John's arbitrary rule and that of his officers and were further aroused at the king's defeats on the Continent. Thus, at their meeting at Runnymede near London they forced him to concede and confirm certain privileges, many of them in accordance with feudal traditions, which limited the power of the monarchy. What made the M. different from other medieval *charters of liberties was the addition of a clause stipulating the right of the community of the realm to remonstrate with the king and to establish a council of barons to deal with reparation of grievances. In this way, the M. laid the foundation for the English Parliament and was an innovation in medieval legal practice. The importance of the M. also lies in the fact that during the whole of the 13th century the barons of England continued to regard it as their basic charter of liberty, frequently sought its reconfirmation and put the clause concerning the convening of the council into effect, even rebelling against *Henry III in order to do so. After the confirmation of the charter by *Edward I in 1277, the question of its validity was no further discussed. Thus, the M. became the foundation of the English constitution and the council of barons was later transformed into Parliament.

W. S. McKechnie, *Magna Charta* (1914).

MAGNATES (Latin: magnus "great") The term was used in the Middle Ages to designate members of the highest ranks of the *nobility. In the early and high Middle Ages it signified the important persons in the realm, including the higher officers of the crown who did not necessarily belong to the higher nobility. From the 12th century to the end of the Middle Ages, the term became strictly attached to the highest noble class. At that time the M. of central Europe enjoyed wide political prerogatives, such as election of kings and participation in councils, which weakened royal authority, particularly in Hungary and Poland.

MAGNUS I, the Good (c. 1024-47) King of *Norway (1035-47). Son of St. *Olaf, he was expelled from Norway together with his father by *Canute the Great, king of Denmark and England, and spent his childhood with the Russian Vikings. After Canute's death, he was recalled and proclaimed king of Norway, reigning under the tutelage of his uncle, *Harold III. In 1042 he was proclaimed king of *Denmark as well, succeeding *Hardicanute. While he enjoyed great popularity in Norway, M. had to fight particularistic tendencies of the Danish nobility. He was killed in 1047 in one of the battles fought in Denmark.

G. Jones, *A History of the Vikings* (1968).

MAGNUS King of *Norway (1066-69). Son of *Harold III, he reigned together with his uncle, Olaf III, until his death.

MAGNUS II, Bareleg (1073-1103) King of *Norway (1093-1103). Son of Olaf III, he renewed the Norse tradition of expansion, leading a series of expeditions to the *Hebrides and Orkney Islands, as well as to *Wales and *Ireland. At the time of his death, the result of an accident in Ireland, his sovereignty extended over the entire Norse world in the Atlantic, from Greenland and Iceland to the Norse settlements in northern Scotland and in Ireland. In 1102 he made his son Sigurd head of a maritime expedition sent to Palestine to aid the new kingdom of the *Crusaders.
G. Jones, *The History of the Vikings* (1968).

MAGNUS III, the Blind King of *Norway (1130-35). He reigned under the regency of his uncle, *Harold IV. In 1135 he abdicated due to poor health and died in 1139.

MAGNUS IV King of *Norway (1162-84). His reign, following a turbulent period of dynastical disputes, was a peaceful one.

MAGNUS V, the Lawmender (1238-80) King of *Norway (1263-80). In 1266 he concluded a peace treaty with *Alexander III, king of Scots, ceding the Hebrides and the Isle of Man, thus bringing Norse domination in Britain to a close. His main achievement was the reform of Norwegian law; in 1274 he issued a new legal code, abrogating the provincial customs, which created constitutional unity in the realm. This was followed in 1277 by a series of ordinances, aiming to establish a united administration in Norway. In the same year, M. reached an agreement with the church, which surrendered its prerogatives in the royal elections in exchange for affirmation of independent ecclesiastical law.
L. Musset, *Les Peuples Scandinaves au Moyen Age* (1951).

MAGNUS VI, Ericsson (1316-74) King of *Norway (1319-43) and *Sweden (1319-65). He was a descendant of the kings of both Norway and Sweden and inherited the two crowns in 1319, being three years old, under the regency of his mother, Margaret. In 1330 he began to reign on his own, after being challenged by particularistic trends in both kingdoms, especially on the part of the nobility. He devoted most of his time to Sweden (where he was known as Magnus II the Good) and neglected Norwegian affairs. In 1343 the Norwegian nobles revolted and demanded the creation of a separate Norwegian government under his son, *Haakon VI; M. nevertheless continued to exercise high authority over Norway as regent for his son until 1355, when Haakon reached his majority and began to reign. In 1350 M. attempted to unite his kingdoms by issuing a common law for them and creating the assembly of the "Four Estates", namely the church, the nobility, the burghers and the peasants. His aim was to impose his authority over the country through an alliance with the lesser estates, but his legislation only heralded a new series of rebellions. In 1365 the Swedish nobles revolted and deposed him. He was captured and held prisoner until 1371, when he was released. He then settled in Norway, where he died in 1374.
L. Musset, *Les Peuples Scandinaves au Moyen Age* (1951).

MAGNUS LADULAS (1240-90) King of *Sweden (1277-90). M. was proclaimed king after leading a successful revolt against his brother, *Waldemar. He based his rule on an alliance with the church and the lesser nobility against the magnates, whom he attempted to deprive of their political privileges. In 1280 he issued an ordinance exempting mounted soldiers from taxation. This measure, which aimed to bring him the support of the knights, had its impact on the development of feudalism in Sweden.
L. Musset, *Les Peuples Scandinaves au Moyen Age* (1951).

MAGYARS See HUNGARY.

MAHDIA City in northern Tunisia, on the Mediterranean coast. Founded in 912 by a settlement of *Ismailis and owes its name to their leader or *mahdi*. In 921 M. became the capital of the *Fatimids and remained their stronghold and political centre until the conquest of Egypt and the foundation of *Cairo (969). From 973 M. became a provincial capital and was neglected by the Fatimids. As a result, it gradually declined up to the end of the 11th century, when the Zirid governors of the *Maghreb restored it. In this period the city had one of the most important harbours in north Africa. In 1150 King *Roger II of Sicily conquered M. and established a Norman-Sicilian dominion over the city. Although Sicilian rule lasted until the end of the Middle Ages, the city began to decline, its commerce having been ruined by constant warfare and rivalry with the Italian cities, which maintained direct relations with the Moslem centres.
EI, III.

MAHMUD (967-1030) Sultan of *Ghazni (998-1030). Of servile Turkish origin, he inherited his father's governmental duties in *Khorasan, but freed himself of *Abbasid allegiance and became the most important ruler of Asia of his time. From his capital of Ghazni he led a series of raids into India (999-1020), conquering its northwestern territories, which became the basis of Moslem *India (modern Pakistan). He also ruled over *Afghanistan, *Khorasan and large parts of central Asia as far as the Aral Sea. M. also proved himself a skilled administrator and an enlightened ruler. His court attracted poets, thinkers and men of letters, who contributed to the blossoming of the Persian Moslem culture and to the revival of the Persian language.
C. E. Bosworth, *The Ghaznavids* (1963).

MAHZOR (Hebrew: cycle) The term designates the *Jewish prayer-book, containing the services for the principal feasts of the year; its name derives from its cyclical arrangement. The most ancient exemplars of Ms. date from the 9th century, a time when their text was not yet finalized. Up to the 13th century prayers were added, and final versions were accepted only at the end of the Middle Ages. Despite the dispersion of the Jewish communities, the major part of the Ms. contains a common liturgy, but some of the prayers and particularly hymns differ from place to place. From the 11th century certain exemplars of M. were illuminated. The most beautiful extant specimen of a medieval M. is that of Worms.
S. W. Baron, *A Social and Religious History of the Jews*, VI (1959).

MAILLOTINS Name given to the Parisian mob which rose up in 1382 in protest of a new tax imposed by the government of *France. The M. employed violence against court officials and burghers, but they lacked organization and so the outbreaks did not develop into an actual revolt. The compromise reached between the uncles of King *Charles VI and the burghers of Paris

appeased the mob and enabled the royal police to arrest their leaders.

M. Rey, *Les Finances Royales sous Charles VI* (1965).

MAIMONIDES, MOSES (1135-1204) *Jewish philosopher and physician, also known as *Rambam* (initials of Rabbi Moses ben Maimon). Born at Córdoba in Spain, he was educated by his father, a reputed Talmudist. During anti-Jewish persecutions which followed the conquest of Córdoba by the *Almohades (1149), M., rather than be compelled to become an apostate, fled to *Fez in Morocco, where he wrote his treatise on *Apostasy*, attacking the Moslems and offering the Jews of Spain spiritual strength in the face of persecution. In 1165 M. was compelled to flee Morocco and, after a short stay in Palestine, he settled at *Fustat-Cairo, where he became the physician of *Saladin and of the court as well as the head of the Jewish communities in Egypt (1169). After arriving in Egypt he completed his commentary on the *Mishna*, begun at Fez, which is one of the most important works of scholarly exegesis. The philosophical methods used in that work were later employed in his *Mishne Torah* (in Hebrew, completed *c.* 1180), which is a Talmudic code, arranged by subject, consisting of a classification of Jewish religious doctrines, their interpretations by legal experts, and their moral and philosophical implications. In 1190 his *Guide for the Perplexed* was completed; his principal treatise, written in Arabic, and later translated into both Hebrew and Latin, it won him the reputation of the greatest Jewish philosopher, and was considered one of the most valuable Aristotelian works of the 12th century. M.'s goal was to achieve a working harmony between reason and faith. His "Guide" was divided into three parts: the first dealt with the concept of God; the second provided arguments supporting His existence, His manifestations, the incorporeal world, creation of the world in time and prophecy; finally, the last part treated the interpretation of the prophet Ezekiel's visions, the problem of evil, the end of creation, divine providence and divine knowledge.

M.'s aim to reach a synthesis between faith in divine revelation and the findings of human reason as proposed by Aristotle launched one of the most difficult polemics in Judaism, which lasted until the beginning of the 14th century and divided the Jewish world. His antagonists claimed his views to be heterodox, at the very least. The polemic ended with the conclusion that he remained within the boundaries of orthodoxy, but to avoid misinterpretation, his "Guide" was forbidden to young men.

As the leader of the Jews of Egypt, M. wielded strong political influence, which he used to improve the situation of the poor members of his community. He also attained wide prestige, and questions concerning religious practice and behaviour were put to him by various communities. Among his responses, the *Letter to the Yemenite Jews* (in Hebrew) is a masterpiece of spiritual counsel and messianic expectation. M. also reached a place of great authority and influence with regard to Moslem and Christian thought; men like *Albert the Great and St. *Thomas Aquinas made use of the Latin translation of the "Guide" for their own work.

Engl. trans. of works, A. Cohen, *The Teachings of Maimonides* (1927);

Traditional portrait of Maimonides. Woodcut

L. Roth, *The Guide for the Perplexed; Moses Maimonides* (1948);
B. Z. Bokser, *The Legacy of Maimonides* (1950).

MAINE French province, which had existed as a Gallo-Roman unit in ancient times. Conquered by the Franks under the reign of *Clovis (483), it became part of *Neustria. *Charlemagne attached it to his march of Brittany, but in the 9th century it became a separate county and a local family seized power as counts of M. from 890. In the 11th century authority over the counts was disputed between the dukes of *Normandy and the counts of *Anjou, and the latter eventually annexed M. to their state (1101). In the second part of the 12th century M. was one of the principal provinces of the Angevin empire, being the cross-road connecting England and Normandy to Anjou and Aquitaine. In 1206 it was conquered by *Philip II and annexed to the French royal demesne. According to the last will of King *Louis VIII, M. was granted, together with the county of Anjou, as an *apanage to his son, *Charles. Until 1481, when it was re-annexed to the royal domain, its history and institutional and social life corresponded with those of Anjou.

R. Philippe, *Le Maine et le pays manceau* (1976).

MAINMORTE Feudal term, originating from spoken French, which was adopted in the 12th century in documents written in both French and Latin. It referred to the serf's land which was given to the lord on the death of the subject tenant when there were no direct descendants.

F. L. Ganshof, *Feudalism* (1965).

Opening of the Heavenly Gates of Mercy; *page from the 13th-century* Mahzor *of Worms*

MAINZ City at the confluence of the Main and Rhine Rivers in *Germany. The original Roman settlement, *Moguntium,* was abandoned in the 4th century and the site was later occupied by the *Burgundians and the *Alemanni before it was finally annexed to the kingdom of the *Franks in 497. In the 6th century the settlement was re-established as a trade centre of the eastern province of the Frankish kingdom (later *Franconia). In 747 a bishopric was erected by St. *Boniface, who made it the ecclesiastical metropolis of Germany in 755. Twenty years later *Charlemagne granted the city and its neighbourhood to the archbishops, who later become the *electors of M., and the area served as the centre of their principality. In the second half of the 10th century, during the reigns of *Otto I and *Otto II, the city became an important cultural centre, influenced by the establishment of the *Holy Roman empire. Cultural activity was also at a peak in the Jewish quarter of the city, which became the scholarly and exegetical centre of *Ashkenazi Jewry, as exemplified at the beginning of the 11th century by the activity of Rabbi *Gershom, "The Light of the Exile". During the 11th century the city prospered and had its share in the development of the Rhine trade. The population grew and a burgher class emerged, which demanded autonomy. In 1118 M. was granted a *charter of liberties allowing the formation of a municipal council and a local court, which would, however, remain under the control of the archiepiscopal officials. Due to its privileges, the city rapidly developed during the 12th century, and from the beginning of the 13th century its leaders struggled to oust the archiepiscopal government. In 1244 the citizens took advantage of the civil war in Germany to obtain the status of a "free city", exempt from archiepiscopal dominion, and joined the confederation of the cities of the Rhine. In 1254 the central board of the confederation was established at M. During the Interregnum in Germany, the confederation became a powerful political organization, having its own army and jurisdiction, which imposed peace in the area. This development culminated in the middle of the 14th century, after which the *Black Death caused demographic and economic ruin and was followed by social unrest. The troubles continued into the 15th century, when a party within the city, seeking a stronger authority, supported the return of the archiepiscopal government. Consequently M. lost its liberties (1462) and the city declined in the last decades of the Middle Ages.
K. H. Esser, *Mainz* (1961).

MAJORCA The largest island of the Balearic archipelago in the western Mediterranean, near the Spanish coast. First conquered by the *Vandals, it became part of the *Visigothic kingdom in the 7th century. In 713 it was conquered by the Arabs and remained under Moslem rule until 1229, when King *James I of *Aragon conquered and annexed it to his kingdom. Under his reign, M. was made a Catalan province. However, prior to his death (1276), James divided his realm and gave M., together with the royal title, to his younger son, James, who was also lord of Roussillon, Cerdagne and Montpellier. The independent existence of the dynasty was constantly challenged by the elder branch, which ruled in Aragon. In 1344 during one of the battles between the two kingdoms, King *James II of M. was defeated by *Peter IV of Aragon and killed. With his

death the kingdom of M. disintegrated. M. itself and the counties of Roussillon and Cerdagne were annexed to the crown of Aragon, while Montpellier was returned to France. M. became one of the prosperous provinces of Aragon; it also became a commercial and cultural centre, and kept close relations with Barcelona.
H. J. Chaytor, *History of Aragon and Catalonia* (1933).

MAKRISI, AHMAD IBN ALI (1364-1442) Egyptian historian. After completing his studies, M. became a preacher in Cairo and founded a school in the city, where he taught *Hadith. His reputation earned him invitations to head similar schools in Syria, but he soon returned to Egypt. There he was employed by the *Mameluke government as chief inspector of the markets of Cairo, and thereby gained important experience. During this period he began to write; his description of Egypt first appeared at the beginning of the 15th century. The work was widely read and praised as the best manual of historical topography written about the country. Many of M.'s ancient sources were subsequently lost and are known of only through the excerpts in his book. M.'s most important work, the history of Egypt from the time of Saladin to 1436, is an important source for the period of the later *Ayyubids and the Mamelukes.
Works, ed. Quatremère (1874).

MALACHY, St. (1094-1148) Archbishop of *Armagh and primate of Ireland (1129-48). He was one of the foremost figures of Ireland in the Middle Ages. A strong supporter of the Roman practices within the church, he became involved in a long struggle with the supporters of traditional Irish customs. In 1139 he went to Rome to receive the *pallium* from Pope *Innocent II and while en route met St. *Bernard of Clairvaux, who became one of his closest friends. Under Bernard's influence, he introduced the *Cistercians to Ireland. In 1148, while on his way to Rome, he died at Clairvaux. St. Bernard then wrote his biography, gathering the material for his sainthood. A document, probably composed in 1590 and entitled the *Prophecies of M.,* is an apocryphal work attributed to the archbishop and sums up the popular beliefs regarding his prophetic skills.
A. Ghinato, *St. Malachy* (1951).

MALAGA City in southern *Andalusia, on the coast of the Mediterranean. Situated along a small gulf, the town prospered during the Middle Ages due to its harbour and exports, among them its own grapes and wine. Conquered by the *Vandals in the 5th century, M. passed to the *Visigoths, who established a provincial government there. In 711 the Arabs conquered the city, which rapidly grew and attracted Moslem immigrants from north Africa (*Moriscos*), who made up the principal part of its population. With the decline of the caliphate of *Córdoba, an independent emirate was founded at M. (1015). The emirs were able to maintain their autonomy under the supreme rule of the *Almoravides and *Almohades, paying them a tribute so as to enjoy full local authority. In 1253 the emirate became dependent on the kingdom of *Granada and was gradually annexed to it, serving as the main harbour of the last Moslem kingdom in Spain. This period marked the city's greatest prosperity. In 1487 M. was conquered by the armies of Castile and Aragon.
A. Castro, *The Structure of Spanish History* (1954).

MALATESTA Family in *Rimini (in the Papal States, Italy). The rise of the M. is related to the struggle between the *Ghibellines and the *Guelphs over the government of Rimini in the second half of the 13th century. At that time, members of the M. family were leaders of the Guelph faction. In 1295 M. da Verruchio seized power in the city and became its *signore*. By the beginning of the 14th century, the power of the family had been well established in the city; they had freed themselves of dependence on municipal institutions and imposed a tyrannical regime. After the establishment of the papacy at *Avignon, the Ms. began the systematic conquest of the province and founded a large principality covering part of the northern areas of the Papal States. Defeated in 1353 by Cardinal *Albornoz, the family was compelled to surrender the major part of its conquests, but its members continued to rule Rimini and its principality as papal vicars. In this capacity they were involved in the wars of northern Italy (late 14th to 15th century), and some served as *condottieri* in the armies of the *Visconti, lords of Milan.
P. J. Jones, *The Vicariate of Malatesta of Rimini* (1952).

MALCOLM I King of the *Scots (943-54). Son of King Donald IV, he became king of Albany (912) and fought against his cousin Constantine, whom he defeated and dethroned in 942, seizing supreme authority over the Scottish clans. Allied with the Anglo-Saxon king, *Edmund of Wessex, he enlarged his realm by conquering Cumberland from the Scandinavians as well as large parts of the Lothian territories in southern Scotland.
W. C. Dickinson, *Scotland, from the Earliest Times to 1603* (1961).

MALCOLM II King of the *Scots (1005-34). He began his reign by renewing the policy of southward expansion initiated by the Scottish kings of the 10th century and besieged Durham. His grave defeat in 1006 forced him to retreat northwards and he lost part of the Lothian county. M. attempted to resume his previously unfruitful activity after *Canute the Great's conquest of England by recognizing the king as his overlord. He was, however, unsuccessful, and after his defeat at the hands of the English earl Siwurg, the Tyne River was fixed as the border between England and Scotland.
W. C. Dickinson, *Scotland, from the Earliest Times to 1603* (1961).

MALCOLM III (1031-93) King of the *Scots (1058-93). Son of King Duncan I, his throne was seized by *Macbeth, and from 1049 he led the legitimist Scottish party, claiming the crown. After establishing his government, he became involved in English affairs and in 1066 accepted many Anglo-Saxon refugees into his realm, among them the members of the royal family of *Edgar Aetheling, whose sister Margaret he married. After the failure of the last Anglo-Saxon revolt in England, M. was compelled to recognize *William the Conqueror as his overlord (1072), but refused to assume feudal obligations and led five military expeditions to England against *William II. On his last expedition in Northumbria, he was killed by the king.
W. C. Dickinson, *Scotland, from the Earliest Times to 1603* (1961).

MALCOLM IV (1141-65) King of *Scotland (1153-65). He inherited the crown from his grandfather, *David I, at the age of twelve. His reign began with a series of rebellions and intrigues, which enabled *Henry II of England to extend his authority over the northern counties previously under Scottish rule. In 1157 M. renounced his claims over the disputed territories and became a faithful vassal of Henry. M.'s cognomen, "the Maiden", signified his chaste life.
W. C. Dickinson, *Scotland, from the Earliest Times to 1603* (1961).

MALETOTE Tax on goods, imposed from the 13th century in France, the Low Countries and England by the royal governments or by great territorial princes. Its amount varied according to the region and period, as did the specification of the goods taxed. In England, the M. was a tax on wool. The popular name, which prevailed in the documents, implies that it was considered a bad custom and a burden. In 1287 *Edward I of England decided not to impose the M. without the consent of Parliament.
CEcH, III.

MALI *African empire (13th-17th centuries) concentrated around the banks of the Niger River. It developed from the confederation of Malinke tribes, a Negro people, in the upper region of the Niger. In 1230 they were united by their chieftain, Sundiata, who established a strong government, supported by the gold merchants. By the time of his death in 1255, he had conquered the neighbouring tribes and begun to expand northwards as far as the Sahara Desert, with the aim of reaching a state of hegemony in western Africa. This development continued under his descendants, and at the beginning of the 14th century the major part of western Africa, together with the countries of the Gambian Valley, was incorporated into the empire, where Moslem missionaries introduced *Islam. During the reign of Mansa-Musa, the greatest ruler of M. (1312-37), the empire reached the peak of its power and prosperity and dominated all the routes of the gold trade between Black Africa and the Mediterranean. Mansa-Musa's visit to Cairo in 1324, during his pilgrimage to Mecca, marked the height of his influence and brought M., as an Islamic country, to the attention of the Moslem world. Mansa set up his government on the basis of a unified royal Malinke clan and employed slaves in the administration and the army.

At the beginning of the 15th century internal struggles and constant revolts weakened the empire. The revolt of two of its main cities, Gao and Timbuktu (1400 and 1431, respectively) was followed by a general revolt of the northern tribes and the establishment of the realm of Songai. At the end of the 15th century only the southwestern part of the empire continued to belong to M., whose decline continued into the 16th century, until its dissolution and tribal division in the 17th century.
N. Levtzion, *Ancient Ghana and Mali* (1972).

MALIK SHAH (1055-92) The third *Seljuk sultan (1073-92). The beginning of M.'s reign coincided with the last of the great Seljuk conquests in Asia Minor and Syria. Thus he was faced with the task of creating an administrative system. M. established his centre in western Persia, and after suppressing several revolts of the Turkish and Turkoman tribes in *Khorasan, he worked to develop a government system, based on the participation of the members of the dynasty. They were to be provincial governors and would receive the aid of a Turkish commander, the *atabeg*, appointed by the

Bridge built by the Mamelukes in Palestine in 1273

sultan. Under M.'s high authority, the system proved to be efficient, but in the long run, it led to feudalization and division of the Seljuk empire as well as to the rise in power of the *atabegs*. M. extended his rule to *Hedjaz, including the holy cities of Mecca and Medina, and established his capital in the city of *Isfahan, where his court became a brilliant cultural centre. His death in 1092 was followed by civil war, which effected the division of the empire and facilitated the penetration of the *Crusaders into the Middle East.
EI.

MALINES (MECHELEN) City in modern *Belgium. A settlement existed at the site as early as the 6th century, when it was the centre of a large estate in the kingdom of the *Franks. In 915 it was granted to the bishopric of *Liège and during successive centuries grew to become a prosperous town, having a successful textile industry and exporting goods throughout western Europe. Economic development brought the city into close contact with *Flanders, and during the 13th century Flemish influence was also politically manifested. In 1333 M. officially became a city of the county of Flanders, and during this period its centre was entirely rebuilt and the church of St. Romuald (later a cathedral) was constructed in the Gothic style of the Low Countries. Together with the county of Flanders, M. became part of the Netherland territories of the duchy of *Burgundy and flourished under the ducal regime of the 15th century. In 1473 M. also gained political importance through *Charles the Bold's establishment of the ducal high-court of justice within the city walls.
A. Cartellieri, *The Court of the Great Dukes of Burgundy* (1933).

MALMESBURY Town in northwestern *Wessex, which grew around a famous monastery, founded in 635. The abbey was one of the most important monastic and scholarly centres in England and was richly endowed by King Ethelstan in the 10th century. The borough grew due to its market, which, from the 8th century, became one of the most important trade points between Wessex and Wales. M. continued to serve this purpose after the *Norman Conquest of England, when the monastery was reformed and Norman abbots were appointed to rule it.
F. M. Stenton, *Anglo-Saxon England* (1947).

MALOUEL, JOHN (c. 1370-1419)   Dutch painter. Born at Nimeguen, he studied in Flanders and *c.* 1400 arrived in Paris, where he joined the court of Queen Isabella of Bavaria, wife of *Charles VI. In 1412 he left Paris and settled at Dijon, where he worked for the ducal court of *Burgundy. Among his works is the portrait of Isabella of Bavaria, one of the masterpieces of late medieval Flemish art.
L. Réau, *L'Art du Moyen Age* (1951).

MALTA Island in the Mediterranean, between Sicily and the Tunisian coast. Conquered by the *Vandals in 535, the island became part of their kingdom and served as an important maritime base for their raids. In 533 the *Byzantine fleet defeated the Vandals and M. became part of its empire, being attached to the province of Sicily. In 870 the Arabs of north Africa, led by the *Aghlabid emirs, conquered the island and formed a north African Moslem colony there. This settlement had a large degree of influence on the subsequent ethnic and linguistic character of the Maltese population. In 1091 *Roger I of Sicily conquered M., and under the rule of the Norman kings of *Sicily the island became a prosperous commercial centre, while local government institutions were developed. In 1220 Emperor *Frederick II ordered the expulsion of the Moslem inhabitants and, subsequently, the Maltese became Christians. In 1282 after the *Sicilian Vespers, M. was conquered by the Aragonese army and separated from the Sicilian realm. It thus became a province of *Aragon and part of the royal demesne.
B. Blouet, *The Story of Malta* (1967).

MALTA, ORDER OF See HOSPITALLERS.

MAMELUKES (MAMLUK) Name given to the soldiers of servile origin who served in the *Abbasid army from the 9th century. By extension, it also denoted Turkish mercenaries, who acceded from the middle of the 9th century to commanding positions in the caliph's army. In the 13th century the term was revived in *Egypt to designate the hired Turkish and Turkoman armies of the *Ayyubid sultans. In 1250 the M. camped at Cairo, on the bank of the Nile, and became the most important military force in the country. Employed in a military plot, they seized power and founded their own state in Egypt (1252).

The M. state was ruled by a military regime interested only in its conquests. The civil government was left to the local officials, who were responsible for raising money for the military budget. Under the rule of their greatest sultan, *Baibars, the M. began to systematically conquer Palestine and Syria. Baibars earned fame and prestige as leader of the Moslem world after his victory over the *Mongols at *Ain Jalud (1261), which enabled him to impose his rule over the last Ayyubid principalities in Syria and to conquer the major part of the *Crusader principalities. His work was completed in 1291 by *Qalawan, who conquered the last Crusader stronghold in *Acre. At the beginning of the 15th century the M. established their administrative system; it was based on the division of Egypt, Palestine and Syria into provinces which were to be governed by a M. military governor, residing in a fortified city or castle. The M. army was largely based on cavalry, and its mobility kept it well prepared for rapid military intervention. In Egypt, the M. built up a powerful fleet, needed for their wars with the Latin kingdom of *Cyprus, which they invaded several times. Their lack of interest in the economic development of their state caused a period of recession, aggravated by the crises which followed the *Black Death. As a result there was a sharp overall decline in the Middle East in the 14th and 15th centuries.

D. Ayalon, *Gunpowder and Firearms in Mameluk Egypt* (1956).

MAMUN, ABU AL-ABBAS ABDALLAH, AL- (786-833) *Abbasid caliph (813-33). In 813 he headed a conspiracy against his brother, Al-Amin, conquered *Baghdad and was proclaimed caliph. He attempted to stabilize his government through an agreement with the different Moslem factions, aiming to obtain internal peace. The endeavours, a result of his liberal ideas of rationalist faith, were opposed by most of the factions. His liberalism also motivated him to support the Academy of Baghdad, which became the world's most important centre of learning during his time. He invited the most important philosophers and scientists of the Moslem world there and engaged them in translation and expansion of Greek and Eastern works and also encouraged them to develop their own ideas.

CHI, I (1970).

MANANTS French *feudal term, derived from the Latin verb *manere* (to stay) and employed to designate those peasants who were obliged to reside on manorial lands and could not leave the villages without the consent of their lords. Generations of students of feudalism used to consider the term synonymous with the whole of medieval peasantry, but later research came to distinguish between two groups of peasants, classifying the M. as those villeins who, according to law, were attached to manorial estates.

F. L. Ganshof, *Feudalism* (1965).

MANDEVILLE English feudal family. Its founder, Geoffrey of M., was a Norman knight who followed *William the Conqueror and settled in England, where he was appointed reeve of the Tower of London and granted a title in the county of Essex. Services offered to the Conqueror and to *Henry I were rewarded with land and income grants, and in 1135 at the time of Henry's death, Geoffrey of M., grandson of the founder, was one of the most influential barons in England. By switching his support during the civil war between *Stephen of Blois and *Matilda, he obtained the title of earl of Essex, thereby firmly establishing the power of his family. His descendants maintained their title and high position in the realm and were close associates of Kings *Henry II and *Richard I. In 1214 Geoffrey of M., earl of Essex, was one of the leaders of the baronial revolt against *John Lackland and was part of the group which compelled the king to issue the *Magna Charta. In the 13th century the importance of the family declined.

J. H. Round, *Geoffrey of Mandeville* (1892).

MANDEVILLE, SIR JOHN (d. c. 1372) English writer. According to his own testimony, M. was born at St. *Albans and, after a formative period, began a life of wandering in Europe and the Middle East (1322). He kept notes of his travels and later used them to write a book (1366) describing areas he had visited. M.'s work was actually more than a travel account; he employed earlier authorities and included many historical and sociological descriptions. He also related a number of stories and legends and the book was considered one of the most lively descriptions of the world. Immediately after publication, the book became very popular in England, France and the Low Countries. After his death it was entitled the *Travels of M.*

M. C. Seymour, *Mandeville's Travels* (1967).

MANEGOLD OF LAUTENBACH (c. 1045-1103) Polemist. Born in Alsace, he studied in France (1070-80) and became a monk at the Alsatian monastery of Lautenbach. There he distinguished himself as a theologian whose advice was sought by bishops and abbots. M. firmly supported Pope *Gregory VII's position regarding investiture and, as a result, was forced to flee Alsace when the Gregorians were expelled in 1086. He spent his exile in Bavaria, where he wrote a treatise, in the form of a letter to Archbishop *Gebhard of Salzburg, in which he developed Gregorian ideas and polemized with the supporters of Emperor *Henry IV. He viewed the episcopal office not as a dignity, but as a purely spiritual function, and for that reason, considered any subjection to the state of a lay authority as a diminution of its worth. While his argument was cohesive in spiritual terms, it did not adequately deal with the problem of lands possessed by the church, which caused the incorporation of ecclesiastical affairs into those of the state and the feudal system. In 1090 M. returned to Alsace and founded the abbey of Marbach, which became one of the centres of Gregorian propaganda. Arrested in 1098 by Henry IV, he was released after a short spell in prison. Upon his death, M. was praised as one of the most important Gregorian propagandists.

T. A. Stead, *Manegold of Lautenbach* (1914).

MANESSE, MANUSCRIPT OF One of the most important compilations of German *Minnesänger poems, it was undertaken at the beginning of the 14th century at Manesse, in the Rhine Valley. It is presently located at the University Library of Heidelberg. The importance of the manuscript lies in its 138 miniatures, a masterpiece of 14th-century Gothic painting, which represent various aspects of the social structure of the time.

E. Jammers, *Das königliche Liederbuch des deutschen Minnesangs. Eine Einführung in die sogennannte Maneschische Handschrift* (1965).

MANFRED OF HOHENSTAUFEN (1232-66) King of *Sicily (1258-66). An illegitimate son of Emperor *Frederick II, he played a prominent part in the last wars of his father against the papacy, and from 1246 commanded the imperial army in central Italy. In 1250 Frederick appointed him regent of Sicily, a post he was supposed to hold until the arrival of his half-brother, *Conrad IV. As regent, M. led the imperial party in Italy and fought the *Guelphs and *Charles of Anjou. When Conrad's son, *Conradin, remained in Germany, M. had himself proclaimed king of Sicily (1258) by the barons of the realm and by the Hohenstaufen supporters in Italy; consequently, he attained international distinction as the virtual head of the dynasty. He concluded an alliance with *Peter III, king of Aragon, who married his daughter Constance and then laid claim to the Sicilian throne. In 1266 M. was defeated and killed by the army of Charles of Anjou at the Battle of *Benevento.

E. Momigliano, *Manfredi* (1963).

MANGU (MONGKE) KHAN (1208-59) Great khan of the *Mongols (1252-59). Grandson of *Genghis-Khan. Ruling from Karakorum, he was the last khan to be re-

Aerial view of Haddon Hall, Derbyshire, built in the 12th-15th centuries

cognized by all the members of the dynasty and the various *hordes of the Mongols. During his reign, his brothers, *Kublai-khan and *Hulagu commanded the greatest military expeditions of their generation. Kublai conquered all of China while Hulagu took possession of *Persia (1256), Iraq and Syria (1258), and put an end to the *Abbasid caliphate of Baghdad.

M. Prowden, *The Mongols* (1942).

MANICHAEAN HERESY The heresy was named after Manes, a priest in Mesopotamia in the 3rd century who attempted to introduce into the Christian faith the *Persian belief in the supernatural forces of light and darkness, signifying good and evil. Despite his condemnation as a heretic by the official Church, his teachings spread among Christian communities and served in various forms as an ideological basis for medieval heretical movements, among them the *Paulicians, the *Bogomiles and the *Albigenses, all of which were formally condemned both by the Orthodox and Catholic Churches.

S. Runciman, *The Medieval Manichee* (1947).

MANOR A feudal estate, deriving from the Latin *mansus*. Actually, the feudal estate on the European continent developed into the seigniory, so that the term M. is technically to be applied only to England,

where, after the *Norman Conquest, the manorial system prevailed. The M. was made up of lands worked by the peasants and the lord's demesne, containing the manorial court surrounded by his landed reserve, where the appropriate equipment, such as ploughs, working animals and the necessary workshops, was concentrated. The peasants' obligations, whether they be compulsory work or the payment of taxes, were carried out in the manorial court. The M. was administrated by a reeve on behalf of the lord, who often held more than one M. In fact, the lord's wealth was determined in the 11th-13th centuries by the number of his estates. In the English M. the lord's jurisdiction was limited by the development of the royal courts of the shires and the *hundreds, and this was the distinguishing factor between the M. and the continental seignory, as the lord of the latter had wide powers of jurisdiction.

H. S. Bennett, *Life on an English Manor* (1962).

MANSOURAH Town along the Nile River, north of Cairo, where King *Louis IX of France was sorely defeated and captured by the *Ayyubid army (1248). See *Crusades.

MANSUR, ABU-JAFAR, AL- (714-75) The second *Abbasid caliph (754-75). M. was the true founder of the Abbasid caliphate and established its system of government and administration. The first years of his reign were devoted to his struggle with his adversaries, the supporters of the *Umayyads and the *Shiites. To overcome his foes he cruelly suppressed their uprisings and killed their leaders. By 762 his authority was accepted throughout the caliphate, with the exception of Spain where the Umayyad *Abd Al-Rahman I was able to found an independent state. At this point M. began his administrative reforms and built a new capital for the caliphate in the city of *Baghdad. M. set up a regime based on Persian administrative traditions and having a strong bureaucracy.

T. Nöldeke, *Caliph Mansur* (1892).

MANSUR, MUHAMMAD IBN ABI AMIR, AL- (938-1002) Arab-Spanish general and statesman. Descendant of an ancient and distinguished Arab line which settled in *Spain at the beginning of the 8th century, he rose to important positions in his native city of Algeciras and in 967 was called to the court of the caliphate of *Córdoba, where he was charged with the administration of estates. Besides demonstrating his bureaucratic skills, he proved himself a victorious general and was chosen as one of the regents during the minority of Caliph *Hisham II. In 977 he led a successful military expedition against the Christian realms of northern Spain and, after his return, was able to depose his colleagues and to seize power in the caliphate, while virtually imprisoning the caliph in his own palace. Backed by a hired army of *Berbers and Christian mercenaries, M. then imposed himself as the sole ruler of Moslem Spain and called for the renewal of the holy war against the Christians. In 985 he conquered Barcelona and in 987, Santiago de Compostela in northern Spain, but left them to their Christian princes, who were thereafter compelled to pay an annual tribute. As a strict observer of Islam, M. imposed Moslem rites in his state, built a number of mosques and enlarged the great mosque of Córdoba, and burned lay books located in the caliph's library in Córdoba.

E. Lévi-Provençal, *Histoire de l'Espagne Musulmane* (1950).

MANSUS Latin term derived from the verb *manere* (to remain), which was used in the 4th century to denote the parcels of land of adscripted *colons, who were attached to their M. by *Constantine the Great. In western Europe the term became the common name of the basic unit of land, within the estate, whose produce could maintain the peasant and his family, after the payment of taxes and duties to the lord. The M. was a stable unit which did not change through the centuries; therefore, even more so than in the case of persons, its legal status was maintained, so that its tenants were divided into social categories in accordance with the type of M. they belonged to: the inhabitants of the M. *servilis* had to pay the duties of serfs; those living on the M. *liberis* paid duties of free peasants and the tenants of the M. *lidilis* fulfilled the obligations of the freed serfs. This led to the establishment of the taxation system in the early and high Middle Ages graded in accordance with the distinction between Ms. With the emergence of *feudalism in the *Carolingian period, the estates granted to the vassals came to be calculated by the number of their M., as military obligations were determined by this unit of measure.

M. Bloch, *Feudal Society* (1952).

MANTUA City in Lombardy, in the Po River valley. Devastated by the *Visigoths under *Alaric (409), M. was subsequently conquered, together with the surrounding country, by the *Ostrogoths, *Byzantines and *Lombards. After *Charlemagne's conquest of the Lombard kingdom (774), M. became the centre of a feudal county and gradually fell under the influence of neighbouring feudal princes. In 1012 it was conquered by *Boniface, marquis of Canossa and Tuscany and subsequently remained under the rule of his family until the death of Countess *Matilda (1115). Once freed of rule by feudal lords, M. gained communal liberties and became a free city (12th century). In 1167 it joined the *Lombard League and took part in its struggle against *Frederick Barbarossa. In the 13th century the city was divided into *Guelph and *Ghibelline factions, and, as a result of the civil wars, lost its communal liberties. Power was seized in 1276 by the family of Bonacolso, which imposed a tyrannical regime. In 1328 Luigi of Gonzaga defeated the Bonacolsos and assumed control of the city. M. became the capital of the principality of *Gonzaga and became involved in the political struggle in northern Italy, particularly opposing Milan. Under the dynasty's rule, the city prospered and became a flourishing cultural centre in the 14th and 15th centuries.

R. Quazza, *Mantova attraverso i secoli* (1953).

MANUEL I, Comnenus (1122-80) *Byzantine emperor (1143-80). Son and heir of *John II. After his coronation, aware of the power of the Norman kingdom of *Sicily, he fought diplomatically and militarily against *Roger II. For that purpose, he allied himself with *Conrad III, marrying the emperor's sister-in-law, Bertha. He attempted to halt the Second *Crusade, but after the departure of the German and French monarchs, had no other recourse than to try and isolate them from Roger. In 1149 he reconquered the territories captured by the Normans in Greece and in 1155 landed in Italy, conquering Ancona and Apulia. Sicily was saved by *Venice, which felt threatened by the possibility of Byzantine control over the Adriatic Sea. The naval victory of the joint fleets of Venice and Sicily (1157) near Brindisi brought an end to Byzantine western expansion and the Italians took advantage of the situation to produce a climate of distrust of the "Greeks". After the failure of the Second Crusade, M. was the only power to protect the Crusader states. He allied himself with King *Baldwin III, who married his sister Theodora, and supported the Crusader campaigns in Egypt. He also enlarged his possessions in Asia Minor and was recognized as overlord of the Crusader principalities. While M.'s relations with Venice continued to be poor, he intervened in the Balkans, where he exercised overlordship upon the *Bulgarians and the *Serbs and took advantage of the weakened state of *Hungary to conquer Croatia, Bosnia and Dalmatia in 1167. In an attempt to restore the greatness of the Byzantine empire, M. decided to take advantage of the civil wars in the *Seljuk sultanate of Konya to effect its conquest (1175). Such a feat would have brought him in the direct vicinity of the Crusader states and also enabled him to attack the Syrian state of *Nureddin from the north. However, his defeat at Myriocephalum by the Seljuk sultan, Kilij-Arslan (1176), put an end to his dream.

F. Chalandon, *Les Comnène* (1912).

MANUEL II, Palaeologus (1348-1425) *Byzantine emperor from 1391. Son of *John V he was placed in the government by his father and was involved in the wars against the Turks. A vassal of *Bayazid I, M. acceded to the imperial throne with the Turkish ruler's consent. In 1399 M. visited western Europe and requested aid against the Turks. The defeat of Bayazid by *Timur-leng gave him some years of peace which M., a literate man, took advantage of to delve in theological studies. In 1422, however, the Turkish threat was renewed by *Murad II and after three years of struggle, M. abdicated and retired to a monastery.

J. W. Barker, *Manuel II Palaeologus* (1969).

MANUUM IMMIXTIO (Latin: the joining of the hands) One of the symbolic acts performed in the ceremony of *homage in feudal Europe. The vassal, in approaching his lord, would place his hands in those of his liege, thus symbolizing his submission as well as his need for the protection and defence of his lord.

F. L. Ganshof, *Feudalism* (1965).

MANZIKERT Town in eastern Anatolia (*Armenia). It became famous for the Battle of M. (1071), in which the *Seljuks fought the Byzantine army, commanded by Emperor *Romanus IV. Under the leadership of *Alp-Arslan, the Seljuks destroyed the Byzantines, captured the emperor and advanced without opposition through Asia Minor, which fell into their hands. The defeat of M. provoked terror in Constantinople, where the empire was disorganized. An appeal for help was sent to western Europe, which eventually sparked the idea of the *Crusade.

CHI (1970).

MAPS See GEOGRAPHY.

MARBODIUS (1035-1123) Bishop of Rennes (1096-1123). A native of eastern Brittany, he studied at the famous school of *Angers and remained there to teach liberal arts. A gifted poet, he wrote in Latin hexameters; his principal work, *Liber de Gemmis* (The Book of Jewels) was completed at Rennes after his episcopal election. The book, in poetic form, treats the subject matter (jewels) in a symbolic manner, allegorically representing the best in nature.

Works, *PL*, vol. 171;
J. de Ghellinck, *L'Essor de la littérature latine au XIIe siècle* (1954).

MARCEL, ETIENNE (c. 1317-58) Parisian leader. Born to a rich burgher family of Paris, he was a cloth merchant and became the leader of the merchants' guild in Paris. In 1355 he opposed the new taxes, imposed by the royal government in order to finance the war with England, and following the French defeat at *Poitiers (1356) rose against the government. As the representative of Paris at the *Estates General convened by the dauphin *Charles (V) in 1357, M. proposed the dismissal of unfit officials and Estate control of the government in return for the raising of taxes to free King *John II. On Charles' refusal, he joined the revolt of *Charles the Bad of Navarre and incited the populace of Paris against the dauphin. In 1358 he agreed to join the peasants' revolt, the **Jacquerie*, but such an extremist position was opposed by the burghers of Paris. This enabled the dauphin to counter-attack and to penetrate Paris. M. was killed during the royal army's reconquest of the capital.

E. Perroy, *The Hundred Years' War* (1957).

MARCH Term used in western Europe, beginning in the *Carolingian period, to denote a frontier territory. The "count of the M." or margrave (later marquis in the western states) was invested with wide authority in either military or administrative affairs and was responsible for defence of the borders of the empire. Ms. retained their original ethnic character, especially when the local population was faithful to the empire: but in the majority of cases, settlements of Franks or Germans were established by the empire to protect the M. *Charlemagne created a number of Ms., among them the M. of the *Avars (corresponding to present-day Austria), also called the M. of the East; the M. of *Bohemia, on the eastern borders of Bavaria; the M. of Brittany, which included the counties of *Anjou, *Maine and *Nantes; the M. of *Gothia and Toulouse, overlooking the Pyrénées at the border common to Moslem Spain; the M. of Lusatia, on the upper Elbe; the M. of the North, later (12th century) called *Brandenburg; and the M. of Spain, or northern *Catalonia. In the 9th and 10th centuries new Ms. were created, especially in Germany and northern *Italy. Although they depended on the territorial dukes, their subjection was usually a formal one and there was a general trend, during the process of feudalization, for the M. to be freed of ducal dominion. In the later Middle Ages the M. no longer signified a frontier territorial unit and title to it was granted like any other to certain sectors of the nobility.

M. Bloch, *Feudal Society* (1952).

MARGARET OF DENMARK (1353-1412) Daughter of King *Waldemar of Denmark, she inherited the kingdoms of Denmark, Norway and Sweden in 1387 and ruled them as regent for her nephew, *Eric of Pomerania. Her belief in Scandinavian unity was implemented by the Union of *Kalmar, which joined the crowns, but left each country under its own government. M. was highly valued for her statesmanship.

L. Musset, *Les Peuples Scandinaves au Moyen Age* (1951).

MARGARET OF SCOTLAND, St. (1045-93) Wife of *Malcolm III, king of the Scots. In 1066 she and her family fled from England to Scotland, where she later married Malcolm (1070). She defended the interests of the English population conquered by the Scots in the previous century. A deeply pious woman, she was active in the reform efforts of the Scottish church and promoted the foundation of monasteries in the realm. Venerated by her people as a saint, she was formally canonized in 1250.

T. R. Barnett, *St. Margaret of Scotland* (1925).

MARIA LAACH *Benedictine abbey, about 24 km northwest of Coblenz. Founded in 1093 by Emperor *Henry IV, it became famous for its fine Romanesque church, containing five towers and a dome (completed in 1156). This church is considered one of the most beautiful and original Romansque structures.

A. Schippers, *Das Laacher Münster* (1927).

MARICOURT, PETER OF See PETER, THE PILGRIM OF MARICOURT.

MARIENBURG Town in *Prussia. Founded in 1236 by the *Teutonic knights, it rapidly became one of the centres of German settlement in Prussia. In 1276 the town was granted *communal privileges, while its castle, which remained under the direct lordship of the order, was fortified and became one of the most impressive fortresses in eastern Europe. After the defeat of the knights in 1457, M. was annexed to the kingdom of Poland.

E. Maschke, *Der deutsche Orden und die Preussen* (1928).

MARIGNOLA, GIOVANNI DA (c. 1290-c. 1356) Traveller and chronicler. Born at Marignola in Italy, he joined the *Franciscan order and in 1338 was sent as papal legate to the *Mongol emperor of China, Togon Temur. During his journey (1338-53) he visited many Mongol khanates in Russia, central Asia, China, India and Ceylon. Upon his return to Avignon, he wrote an account of his travels, which became one of the most informative descriptions of that area to be circulated in the West. In 1354 Emperor *Charles IV invited M. to join his court at Prague as imperial chaplain. During the two years he spent there M. revised the *Annals of Bohemia* under the title *The History of the Bohemian Kingdom*.

H. Yule, *Cathay and the Way Thither* (1866).

MARIGNY, ENGUERRAND DE (1260-1315) French minister. After completing his law studies, he was employed at the French royal court, where he held several offices of distinction; in 1302 he was promoted by King *Philip IV to the rank of chief chamberlain and became one of the closest of the king's advisers in both foreign and economic affairs. M. was not only a faithful executive of the royal orders, he also participated in the policy-making of the crown. He was among the group of French jurists who developed the theory of the complete sovereignty of the king of France (1302-08). M. was hated by members of the royal family, as well as by large sections of the nobility. After Philip's death, he was disgraced, charged with high treason and (in 1315) hanged. However, later generations revived his memory and he was considered one of the great royal ministers of France.

G. Pegues, *The Lawyers of the Last Capetians* (1953).

MARIOLOGY The systematic study of the person of St. *Mary and her cult.

MARITIME CODES See LAW, MARITIME.

MARKWARD OF ANWEILER (d. 1202) Regent of *Sicily. Of servile origin, he was one of the *ministeriales of *Frederick Barbarossa and served the emperor's son, *Henry VI, in Italy. The emperor promoted him to the dignity of count of the Abruzzi and margrave of Ancona. In 1197, after the death of Henry, M. assisted Empress Constance in the administration of Sicily and in 1198, after her death, became the virtual regent of the infant king, *Frederick II, despite the opposition of Pope *Innocent III and the plots organized against him by papal agents.

E. Kantorowicz, *Emperor Frederick II* (1932).

MARMOUSETS Derisive name by which the ministers of *Charles V of France who served during the minority of *Charles VI were called. Their efforts to maintain the standards of efficient administration and the regular activity of the treasury that had been established during the reign of Charles V were challenged by the princes, who demanded a larger share of power and resources.

MARMOUTIER *Benedictine abbey at Tours, the site of the tomb of St. *Martin, one of France's patron saints. Founded in the 4th century, it became one of the most venerated places in France and was a pilgrimage spot. The Benedictine community was reformed during the reign of *Charlemagne, who appointed his friend *Alcuin as abbot (796). In the second half of the 9th century powerful lay lords seized the abbatial dignity and took over the administration of its large estates. The community itself was ruled by a prior at that time. *Hugh the Great, duke of the Franks, was M.'s lay abbot in the middle of the 10th century, and he passed the title to his son and heir, *Hugh Capet. Upon the latter's accession to the French throne in 987, the title passed to the royal dynasty, which thereby held a seignory separating the lands of the counts of *Anjou and of *Blois. Thus the site became an important strategic spot in the 12th century, when royal authority reasserted itself.

L. de Grandmaison, *L'Abbaye royale de Marmoutier* (1889).

MARONITES A Christian community of *Syrian origin, named so after the 5th-century St. Maro, who is traditionally believed to be their founder. The sect itself emerged in the 7th century during the *Monothelite controversy, following the schism of eastern Christianity, and was considered heretical by the Orthodox. During the *Crusades the M. allied themselves with the Catholic clergy and, beginning in 1181, they were recognized by and became affiliated with the Roman Catholic Church. However, they retained their separate ecclesiastical structures and Syriac liturgy. In the 13th century they established a hierarchy of their own, headed by a patriarch subordinate to the pope, and including a number of bishops who reside in the community centres in Lebanon and the Galilee.

D. Attwaker, *The Catholic Eastern Churches* (1935).

MAROZIA (c. 886-932) Roman woman. Daughter of *Theophylactus, she became the mistress of Pope *Sergius III, to whom she bore a son. After her father's death (911), she ruled Rome by utilizing the armies of her successive husbands and by placing candidates of her choosing in the papal dignity. In 931 she had her son by Sergius appointed pope (*John XI). After her marriage to Hugh of Provence (932), her second son, *Alberic, led an uprising of the Roman populace against his new step-father. During the clash, M. was killed. Her activity symbolized the evils and vices of the papacy in the 10th century.

B. Hamilton, *Marozia, Daughter of Theophylactus* (1955).

MARSEILLES City in *Provence and one of the greatest ports in the western Mediterranean. The ancient city of M. was conquered by the *Visigoths in 480, led by their king *Euric. At the end of the 5th century it fell to the *Ostrogoths of Italy, and in 543, upon the collapse of their kingdom, it was conquered by the *Franks. The city declined and its trade diminished under Frankish rule. There was a certain revival of harbour activity in the 8th and the beginning of the 9th century, but the Moslem raids of the mid-9th century destroyed much of the city and ruined its trade. In the 11th century M. became the most important port in Provence and engaged in commercial activity with Barcelona and other Italian cities. As a result, it was patronized by the counts of Provence, who obtained a great part of their resources from its trade. The city continued to prosper during the *Crusades, as it had a hand in the eastern trade and founded colonies in the Crusader states. Due to this development its harbour was reconstructed and fortified in the 13th century. Under the rule of *Charles of Anjou, count of Provence, the city obtained *communal privileges and became autonomous (1258). Thus, M. was a flourishing commercial city in the late Middle Ages. In 1482 it was annexed, together with the rest of Provence, to France.

R. Busquet, *Histoire de Marseille* (1945).

MARSILIUS OF INGHEN (d. 1396) A native of Inghen in western Germany, he studied in Paris, where he learned philosophy from *Buridan and became an important Aristotelian. After a teaching career at Paris, he was summoned to Heidelberg (1385), where he became the first rector of the new university. Due to his studies M. came to reject the idea of a vacuum in physics, and to distinguish between a logical (or mathematical) proof, which could not validate the existence of God, and the metaphysical method, which could. His theory led him to the conclusion that faith was most important and could be strengthened through metaphysical means.

G. Ritter, *Marsilius von Inghen und die okkamistische Schule in Deutschland* (1921).

MARSILIUS OF PADUA (c. 1275-1343) Italian political thinker. A native of Padua he studied medicine there and then went on to Paris, where he studied and taught philosophy and theology. In 1313 he became rector of the University of Paris. He later returned to Italy where political conditions, together with the establishment of the papacy at *Avignon, awakened in him deep reflections about the European system of government. He expressed his views in his *Defensor Pacis* (The Defender of Peace), which was completed in 1324. M. adopted a firm anti-papal attitude, on the grounds that peace was the main goal of society and the sole means of salvation. He therefore supported strong imperial rule, and backed *Louis of Bavaria in his struggle with Pope *John XXII. M.'s beliefs were rooted in a legal view of the origins of power, which fundamentally rejected the medieval doctrine of a division of power between ecclesiastical and civil authorities. M. thus forged a new trail in political thought, which germinated the modern idea of the state.

A. Gewirth, *Marsilius of Padua: The Defender of Peace* (1956).

MARTIN I, St. (d. 655) Pope (649-55). Member of the papal court, he was renowned for his theological knowledge and was elected pope during the *Monothelite controversy at Byzantium. He firmly condemned the teaching as a heresy and denounced the *Typus* of *Constans II, claiming the emperor had no right to interfere in theological matters. This attitude led to his arrest, ordered by Constans. Brought to Constantinople, where he was judged as having attempted to oppose the imperial majesty, he was exiled to the Crimea and died there in 655. He was venerated in Rome as a saint and martyr.

L. Duchesne, *History of the Early Church* (1923).

MARTIN II (Marinus; d. 884) Pope (882-84). Of noble Roman origin, he was active in the papal court and in 869 represented the papacy in the discussions at Constantinople concerning the teachings of *Photius. During his term as pope, he continued to oppose the Photians.

MARTIN III (Marinus; d. 946) Pope (942-46). Appointed by *Alberic II, the virtual master of Rome, he was a docile instrument in the hands of the powerful senator. During his reign the papacy fell to its lowest political ebb. However, M. is to be noted for his support of monastic reforms.

J. Haller, *Das Papsttum*, III (1951).

MARTIN IV (Simon of Brie; 1210-85) Pope (1281-85). He studied at the University of Paris and later became one of its patrons. Upon completion of his studies, he was employed at the royal court of France; *Louis IX appointed him chancellor of France (1260) and member of the royal council. In 1261 he was made cardinal. After his election as pope, M. firmly supported *Charles of Anjou, which led him into a conflict with Byzantium and caused a rupture in the negotiations concerning unification of the churches. After the *Sicilian Vespers (1282), M. adopted a policy aimed at restoring Charles of Anjou to Sicily and at isolating *Aragon by means of excommunication and political activity.

W. Ullmann, *A History of the Papacy in the Middle Ages* (1972).

MARTIN I King of *Aragon (1395-1410). Son of *Peter IV, he inherited the realm in a time of economic crisis, which especially affected the *Catalan provinces, whose trade decreased radically and, as a result, led to a shortage in royal resources. M. tried to increase his revenues by turning to the agrarian sectors of the kingdom, but his attempts only created social unrest.

P. Vilar, *La Catalogne dans l'Espagne Moderne* (1962).

MARTIN, St. (d. 397) Bishop of *Tours and a patron saint of France. Originally a pagan, he served in the Roman army until his conversion to Christianity and in 360 went to Gaul to preach the faith. In 372 he became bishop of Tours and was responsible for the foundation of several monasteries. After his death, he became the object of popular veneration and miracles were reported to have been performed near his tomb. As a result, his cult became very widespread in the Frankish kingdom of the early Middle Ages and churches and monasteries were dedicated to him. His cape became a relic in the 8th century and was placed in a chapel named after him.

A. Régnier, *Saint Martin de Tours* (1907).

MARTINI, SIMONE (1284-1344) Painter. M. worked in his native city of Siena and by the beginning of the 14th century had already become one of the most important Gothic painters. His *Maestà* of 1315 earned him a fine reputation and he was invited to the Angevin court of Naples. After some years of travel across Italy and France, he settled at Avignon (1340), and there was received at the papal court. At Avignon he became acquainted with *Petrarch, who had a strong influence on the work of his later years, as illustrated by his later use of brighter colours and his choice of realistic forms.

M. C. Gozzoli, *L'Opera Completa di Simone Martini* (1970).

MARTYR (Greek: witness) The term was used in the first centuries of Christianity to denote those who bore witness to the Christian faith by suffering persecution and giving up their lives rather than deny their belief. The term was retained in the Middle Ages to signify those who died for their faith through the persecution of infidels, except when death resulted from an armed defence. Ms. were the object of a particular cult, which was integrated within the cult of saints and spread due to numerous legendary accounts. In the Roman Catholic liturgy, Ms. rank before other saints.

H. Delehaye, *Les Origines du Culte des Martyrs* (1912).

The Annunciation, *painting by Simone Martini*

MARWAN II (688-750) The last *Umayyad caliph (744-50). M. served in the army in his youth and was appointed governor of *Armenia. In this post he acquired useful administrative and military experience. After becoming caliph he applied this training in an attempt to reorganize the Arab empire. His most important measure was to transform tribal troops into a regular army. M. was defeated and killed by the *Abbasid rebels in Iraq in 750, and the members of his dynasty shared his fate.
CHI (1970).

MARY, St. The mother of Jesus, also called the Blessed Virgin, *Madonna, Notre Dame.* M. was accorded a high place in medieval Christian devotion and theology due to her position as mother of the Redeemer. It was also believed that she served as intercessor for sinners and could bring pardon and salvation. The cult of M., which was widely diffused among Christian communities beginning in the 5th century, combined such beliefs with some pagan practices adopted by the church. In 431 the Council of *Ephesus defined this cult and gave it the official sanction of the Church. Both the Eastern and Western Churches accorded M. pre-eminence among the saints and, up to the 6th century, she held a

supreme place in the liturgy, as well as in the popular rituals of piety, and was second only to Christ himself. The cult of M. had its impact on the arrangement of the medieval calendar, since her feasts were among the most popular of the year. Processions and gatherings of faithful took place in those areas where her cult was most developed during such feast-days, and this eventually caused political and administrative meetings to be set for those dates, the feast of the Assumption in particular (15 August). Beginning in the 10th century such rituals multiplied in number and their connection with *Millenarianism contributed to the further development of the cult, based on belief in M.'s salutary function and her role as intercessor on the Day of Judgement. Many cathedrals in western Europe were dedicated to M. and Romanesque artists granted her a most important place in their work. Thus her cult had a tremendous influence on the cultural and artistic life of western Europe between the 10th and 15th centuries.

Popular legends also reflected the cult, as legendary accounts about M. were found in hagiographical works or she was indirectly mentioned, generally in connection with her role as intercessor, in part of a literary piece. The popularity of M.'s cult is also revealed by the

The Church of Mary, Jerusalem, built by the Crusaders

development of private prayers to her in the vernacular, which became part of colloquial speech at the end of the Middle Ages. With regard to the upper classes, M.'s cult had its effect on *chivalric manners, as well as on the *monastic way of life.

J. Guitton, *La Vierge Marie* (1949; Engl. trans., 1952);
A. B. Jamesson, *Legends on the Madonna As Represented in the Fine Arts* (1852).

MARY OF CHAMPAGNE (1145-98)   Eldest daughter of *Louis VII. M. married *Henry the Liberal, count of Champagne, in 1164 and established one of the most significant cultural and literary centres of western Europe at her court. A patron of writers, poets and artists, she had a strong impact on the development of medieval literary life, as well as on courtly and chivalric manners.

G. Cohen, *Chrétien de Troyes et la vie littéraire à la Cour de Marie de France, comtesse de Champagne* (1948).

MARY OF FRANCE   Poetess. She lived in the middle of the 12th century, but biographical data about her life is not existent. It is only known that she lived for some years at the court of *Henry II Plantagenet, where she composed a poem beginning, "My name is Mary and I am of France", whence her name. M. wrote lyrical poems in French, in praise of love and composed lays inspired by the Breton tradition. She is considered the first French poetess.

R. Baum, *Recherches sur les Oeuvres attribuées à Marie de France* (1968).

MARY MAGDALENE, St.   Born in the village of Magdala in the Galilee, she was a disciple of Jesus Christ. Due to her image as the repentant sinner miraculously healed by Christ, as well as her description in the New Testament, M. became one of the most popular venerated saints in medieval Christendom. According to a tradition already existent in the West in the 6th century, she spent her later life in prayer and solitude in Provence. Her cult spread rapidly, beginning in the 5th century, both in the Greek-Orthodox and Catholic churches. Pope *Gregory I wrote a treatise about her as a person and saint, which was the basis of the western cult. Con-

sidered a patron saint of penitents and particularly ex-prostitutes, many churches and monasteries were erected in her honour, the most important of them being that of *Vézelay in Burgundy. As Madeleine, a Frenchified version of her second name, M. became the object of a popular cult in the 12th century. In a number of western European cities associations of *Magdalenes were founded to help wayward women abandon their evil ways. M. was also a subject of Christian medieval art, especially in painting and sculpture.

V. Saxer, *Le Culte de Marie Madeleine en Occident, dès Origines à la fin du Moyen Age* (1959).

MASS (Latin: missa "dismissal")   Originally part of the formula (*ite, missa est*) used in the Roman Catholic liturgy to dismiss the faithful at the end of the service. Its use in this sense is attested to by the sources until the 8th century. Later on, the meaning of the term was expanded in the popular vocabulary, and it finally came to denote the entire service where *sacraments were administered.

A. Fortescue, *Liturgy of the Mass. A Name and Definition* (1910).

St. Ursula and the virgin martyrs; *Flemish wood sculpture*

MASTER OF THE GOTHIC MAJESTY An anonymous painter of miniatures who worked in northern France in the second half of the 12th century. His illustrations of liturgical books proved him to be the first to work towards adaptation of the Gothic style in miniature art.

W. von den Steinen, *Homo Coelestis* (1965).

MATHEMATICS Medieval M. were based on the accomplishments of the ancient Greek scientists, which were widely studied in Asia and developed into three independent schools in *China, *India and the *Arab world, the last being the most important. The Arab school of M. began to develop in the late 8th century at *Baghdad, where translations of Greek, Persian and Indian works were undertaken. Most noteworthy of such works was *Khwarizmi's elaboration of earlier studies, written in manual form and entitled *Al Jaber* or algebra (825). Arab mathematicians were interested in calculation of size and produced a series of tables, relevant to geometry, astronomy and trigonometry. They were especially responsible for the development of algebra during the 9th and 10th centuries, this field being one of the youngest branches of M. In addition, they also developed the decimal system.

The achievements of the Arab mathematical school were introduced to western Europe in the 10th century via Spain and southern Italy and they were spread through Latin translations and original works. Gerbert of Aurillac (see *Sylvester II), who studied in Spain, was one of the first great western European mathematicians. Due to his interest, the *abacus was developed in Europe and used for calculations. The translations from Arabic into Latin multiplied in the 11th and 12th centuries and were responsible for further development in M. in western Europe. The works undertaken up to the end of the 12th century were included within the *Quadrivium. The school of *Chartres played an outstanding role in this development, although other centres, in Germany, Lotharingia and Italy, were also active. With the development of the physical and natural sciences, M. became an object of study and new centres, such as that of *Oxford, flourished in the 13th and 14th centuries. The Arabic and European achievements were summed up in the late 13th to early 14th century by Leonardo of Pisa (*Fibonacci) in his *Liber abaci* (The Book of the Abacus), which had a great influence on the adoption of Arabic numerals in Europe. Further progress was made by Nicholas *Oresme (14th century) in the study of functions and their graphic representation.

C. B. Boyer, *History of Mathematics* (1968).

MATILDA OF ENGLAND (1102-67) Also called the Empress Maud. Daughter of King *Henry I of England, she was married in 1114 to Emperor *Henry V and in 1125, after his death, returned to her father. In 1128 she married *Geoffrey Plantagenet, count of Anjou and bore in 1131 the future *Henry II. In 1135 Henry I made her his heiress, but a large sector of the English barons opposed the reign of a woman and supported *Stephen of Blois. M., however, laid her claims to the throne and led a civil war. The struggle ended with her personal failure, but with the expectation that her son, Henry, would inherit the crown. She then retired from politics and devoted herself to pious activity.

F. Barlow, *The Feudal Kingdom of England* (1961).

MATILDA OF FLANDERS (d. 1083) Daughter of *Baldwin V, count of Flanders, she married *William the Conqueror in 1051 and fifteen years later became queen of England. During the Norman invasion of England in 1066, she governed Normandy. She became famous for the *Bayeux Tapestry, also called the Tapestry of Queen M., which portrays her husband's conquest of England.

D. C. Douglas, *William the Conqueror* (1964).

MATILDA OF TUSCANY (1046-1115) Countess of *Tuscany. Daughter of Margrave Boniface, she inherited the county after her father's murder in 1052. Following the death of her step-father, *Geoffrey of Lotharingia (1069), she became countess of Tuscany, having married his son, Geoffrey. During her long reign, she assumed a constant anti-imperial stand and was the most faithful ally of the papacy and particularly of *Gregory VII. In 1077 she hosted the pope at the castle of *Canossa, when he was on his way to Germany, and witnessed the submission of Emperor *Henry IV. With the renewal of the conflict between the empire and papacy, M. supported the latter financially, militarily and diplomatically and encouraged the opposition to Henry IV and *Henry V in Germany.

W. von den Steinen, *Canossa, Heinrich IV und die Kirche* (1957).

MATINS OF BRUGES The May 1302 revolt of the common people in *Bruges (Flanders) against the local urban aristocracy, the *laeliarts*. During the uprising, the members of the aristocracy and the French garrison of the city were massacred.

H. Pirenne, *Early Democracies in the Low Countries* (1915).

MATTHEW OF AQUASPARTA (c. 1240-1320) *Franciscan philosopher. Born in Umbria (Italy), he became a Franciscan and was sent to study in Paris. In 1281 he became general of his order and in 1288 was made cardinal. In the latter position he became one of the closest associates of Pope *Boniface VIII. His written works included sermons and biblical commentaries, but the most important were his critical treatises of *Aristotelianism. He defended the *Augustinian theory of cognition, which he elaborated in great detail.

Works, ed. V. Doucet (1935);

M. Grabmann, *Die philosophische und theologische Erkenntnislehre des Kardinals Matthaeus of Aquasparta* (1906).

MATTHEW OF EDESSA (12th century) Chronicler. Little is known of the man except that he was an Armenian Christian living at *Edessa under the *Crusaders. His religion and origins have been determined through analysis of the chronicle he wrote (c. 1140). The work describes Syria during the period 950-1130. It criticizes the Byzantines, whom he hated, relates the events of the First Crusade and tells of the county of Edessa.

Works, ed. E. Dulaurier (1858).

MATTHEW OF PARIS (c. 1199-1259) English annalist. M. joined the monastery of *St. Albans in 1217. Due to his talents as an expert scribe and illuminator, he became the annalist of the abbey in 1236. His main work was the *Chronica Maiora*, which described world history from creation up to 1259. This chronicle is the most important historical work of the 13th century. The sections dealing with early history are actually a compilation of information taken from former historians; however, his own age is methodically described, and this part of the work is characterized by its critical evaluation and interpretation, as well as by the inclusion of contemporary documents.

Works, ed. H. R. Luard, 7 vols. (1872-83);
R. Vaughan, *Matthew Paris* (1958).

MAUR (MAURUS), St. (6th century) A disciple of St. *Benedict of Nursia. According to legend, he travelled to Gaul, founded a monastery at Glanfeuil on the Loire, which was named after him, and thereafter led a life of solitude and study. In the 9th century his cult began to spread in France, as a result of a forged biography, and many monasteries were founded in his memory. The Maurists emphasized study and their monasteries were cultural centres of the late Middle Ages.

H. Delehaye, *Les Légendes Hagiographiques* (1923).

MAURICE (539-602) Emperor of *Byzantium (582-602). An officer of the Byzantine army, he was appointed general of the eastern provinces in 578, and fought successfully against the *Persians. His victories induced Emperor *Tiberius II to make him his heir. As emperor M. continued to fight on all frontiers, especially against the Persians, the *Avars and the *Lombards, but he was unable to prevent the conquest of the major part of Italy by the last. His attempts to reform the administration were directed towards the imposition of new taxes as a means of covering military expenditures. Such measures were unpopular, and in 602 he was subject to a military overthrow, led by *Phocas.

A. A. Vasiliev, *History of the Byzantine Empire* (1952).

MAURITANIA Ancient Roman province in north Africa, conquered by the *Vandals in 429-30. During the period of Vandal domination (up to 533), the country was divided into two parts. In medieval times, M. proper consisted of the inland portion, located near the Sahara Desert and populated by the *Berbers. The Arab conquest had little effect on the local population and *Islam was gradually adopted in the territory during the 8th-10th centuries.

MAXIMUS THE CONFESSOR, St. (580-662) Byzantine theologian. A member of the old Byzantine aristocracy, he became imperial secretary under *Heraclius, but left the court to become a monk (*c.* 614). Threatened by a Persian raid, he took refuge in Africa, where he became an active adversary of the *Monothelites. In 653 he was brought to Constantinople in an attempt to force him to accept the *Typus* of *Constans II; on his refusal, he was exiled to Thrace. A second attempt to compel his submission through physical torture also failed (661) and he was exiled to the Caucasus Mountains, where he died. M. was a prolific writer on all ecclesiastical subjects. His theology was based on the purely Orthodox doctrine of the incarnation of Christ.

Works, ed. *PG*, vols. 90-91;
P. Sherwood, *The Earlier Ambigua of St. Maximus the Confessor* (1955).

MAYEUL, St. (c. 906-94) Fourth abbot of *Cluny (954-94). A native of Avignon, he entered Cluny during his youth and was distinguished for his piety and oratory skills. As abbot, he continued the reforms of his predecessor, Odo and, during the 40 years of his administration, was responsible for the expansion of the abbey and the creation of its order.

J. Smith, *The Order of Cluny* (1930).

MAYOR OF THE PALACE (Latin: majordomus) *Frankish official. The office, held by a servant in charge of domestic duties, was instituted in the 7th century by the *Merovingian kings. The M. was responsible for the administration of the "palace" (i.e., the king's court). During the 7th century the office gained political significance; and the M. came to act as a prime minister. After the death of *Dagobert and the decline of the Merovingian kingship, the M. attained an influential position, and served as tutor to the king, acting as the virtual master of the Frankish kingdom. At this time, the office became hereditary. The Ms. of *Austrasia sucessfully imposed their authority on the nobility and increased their territorial possessions, and, from the time of *Pepin of Landen, they became the most powerful lords of the Frankish kingdom. After the defeat of *Ebroin, mayor of *Neustria, by *Pepin of Herstal, the Austrasian dynasty of Ms. (known as the *Carolingians), seized control over the entire Frankish kingdom. In the middle of the 8th century, they laid claim to the royal title, which was given to *Pepin the Short in 753.

F. L. Ganshof, *Frankish Institutions* (1972).

MAZOVIA Region in central *Poland, near the Vistula River. Conquered and annexed to Poland in the 10th century, it became one of the most important territories of the Polish kingdom. In 1138 *Boleslaw III made it one of the four duchies of the country. During the second half of the 13th century, M. was divided into a great number of feudal units. At that time it was caught in a state of anarchy, which facilitated the penetration of the *Teutonic knights of Prussia into its northern parts. Only after 1350 was the royal government able to impose its dominion over the province.

Cambridge History of Poland (1950).

MEASUREMENT, UNITS OF Medieval society adopted, to a certain extent, the Roman system of M., which was based on the foot (for distance) and standard pottery (for measuring capacity). In the Byzantine empire this legacy of the ancient world was totally preserved. In the West, however, the lack of a central authority caused a degree of variation in standard measures. In fact, in feudal society, lords imposed their own measures, which differed radically amongst themselves. The rise of the cities and their attainment of autonomy in the 11th and 12th centuries led to the establishment of communal M., which were necessary for trade in the markets and fairs. Once these towns adopted certain M., they worked to have them recognized by other political or commercial groups. Thus, the Italian communes imposed their own M. on the authorities of the Latin kingdom of Jerusalem and other *Crusader states. With the development of *mathematics and *astronomy in the 13th century, ideas on means of standard measurement were expounded. Furthermore, the use of standard M. was spread through cartography and *geography, as well as by the establishment of astronomical tables. In the 14th century Nicholas *Oresme proposed the first principles of standard measures, which eventually led to the creation of the modern metric system.

A. E. Berriman, *Historical Metrology* (1953).

MEAUX City in *Champagne (France). In the 9th century M. became the centre of a county and passed by marriage and heredity to the counts of *Troyes (late 10th century). In this way it became part of the great

Pilgrims at the Kaaba, Mecca

county of Champagne. In the 11th century fairs were held regularly in the city, whose proximity to Paris and central position on the Marne River make it an ideal spot for trade. In 1229 the officers of the royal court and those of *Raymond VI of Toulouse prepared the Treaty of M., which ended the *Crusade against the *Albigenses and led to the annexation of Languedoc to the crown.

R. Crozet, *La Champagne* (1953).

MECCA City in *Hejjaz and the most holy site of the *Islamic religion. In ancient times it was a commercial and religious centre, the latter being the case due to its possession of the *Kaaba. The native city of *Mohammad, M. was the scene of his activities between 610-22. However, the opposition of the leading families of the city eventually compelled the prophet to flee to *Medina. In 624 Mohammad proclaimed M. a holy city and imposed the duty of the *Hajj:* all Moslems were obligated to undertake a pilgrimage to its shrine. He also required prayer to be directed towards M. In 630 Mohammad conquered the city, which became the religious capital of Islam (although Medina continued to be its political capital until 657). The establishment of the caliphate at Damascus in 661 created anarchy in M. and led to revolts against the *Umayyads, which caused the city's decline. In 930 it was conquered by the *Karmatians, who took possession of the "Black Stone" until 950. At the end of the 10th century a local dynasty of *sherifs* (descendants of Mohammad) established its rule in the

city and amassed a fortune from the revenues brought in by the Hajj.

Emel Esin, *Mecca the Blessed* (1963).

MECHANICS They were defined in ancient times as the science dealing with the motion of physical bodies. This definition was perpetuated in the Middle Ages, and Aristotle's *The Physics* and *On The Heavens* were important reference works for the medieval study of M. Up to the 13th century, ancient principles of M. were developed by Arab scientists and philosophers influenced by the activity of the *Baghdad Academy in the 9th century. Their findings, as well as other philosophical and scientific treatises, were translated into Latin in the 11th and 12th centuries. Beginning in the 13th century most important progress was made in western Europe by *Albertus Magnus and the Oxford school, which gathered at Merton College and continued the research activity of Roger *Bacon. Based on their observation of the motion of birds, they emphasized the two main types of motion found in Aristotelian M., i.e., the "linear", that of the four basic elements (earth, water, fire and air), and the "circular" or perfect motion, which was infinite. The theories of this school were applied in 14th-century technology, by the extension of the use of the wheel in machinery.

S. F. Mason, *A History of Sciences* (1953).

MECKLENBURG Duchy in northern Germany on the shores of the Baltic Sea. Up to the 7th century the area was the temporary home of a number of Germanic

A 15th-century doctor's office.

tribes on their way to settle in the countries of the Roman empire and in Germany. After the departure of the *Lombards, Slavs penetrated the area (7th century) and established the principalities of the Obodrites and Liutizi, which were later attacked by the Danes, Saxons and *Carolingians. In the 10th century Danish influence was dominant in the area, but by the beginning of the 12th century German colonists had begun to settle there and missionaries actively spread the Christian faith. In 1160 the Germans, led by *Henry the

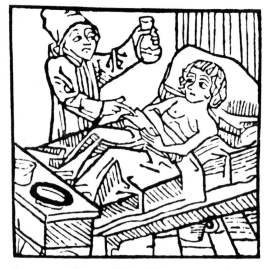

Doctor prescribing medicine; 15th-century woodcut

Lion, caused a radical change in the ethnic and religious character of the province. They defeated and killed the Obodrite prince, Niklot, and Henry made his son, Pribislav, his vassal and had him convert to Christianity. Pribislav was the founder of the dynasty of M. In the 13th century the different branches of the dynasty divided the country amongst themselves and the areas of M. became dependent on neighbouring countries, with *Denmark retaining a significant degree of influence. In 1436, after a long series of wars against Denmark, the M. branch succeeded in reuniting the province and assumed the ducal title, which had been bestowed on the counts of M. in 1348 by Emperor *Charles IV.

O. Vitense, *Geschichte von Mecklenburg* (1920).

MEDICI, HOUSE OF One of the most famous families of late medieval *Italy, which reached the height of its power in the Renaissance period. Their origins can be traced back to notable cloth traders in *Florence of the late 12th century. During the 13th century they expanded their business outside of Florence and became bankers. Although their bank was not the largest in the city, they survived the early 14th-century crisis which had led other houses into bankruptcy, and developed their credit business throughout western Europe. Their success was due to a division of their investments, which allowed them to absorb unprofitable deals. Besides being the bankers of the papacy and of the kingdom of Naples, they maintained branches in the major Italian cities, as well as at Bruges, London, Geneva and Avignon. At the beginning of the 15th century the house also dealt with the trade of iron and aluminium. Their economic power enabled them to become involved in the political life of Florence from the end of the 13th century. However, it was not until the mid-14th century that the first member of the family was to hold an important office. Salvestro (1331-88) became the *gonfaloniere* of Florence in 1351, as head of the city's democratic party. His power was greatest in the late 1370s, when he proved to be the only figure able to establish peace after the revolt of the *Ciompi*. However, in 1382 he was exiled by the oligarchical party and the family lost its political influence. Another Medici, Giovanni (1360-1429), who was responsible for much of the family's fortune, entered the political race in 1427 and made use of his wealth to fight the oligarchy. His son, Cosimo the Elder (1389-1464), realized Giovanni's goals; following his victory over the Albizzi (1434), he became the uncontested ruler of the Florentine republic and was involved in Italian politics.

R. A. de Roover, *The Rise and the Decline of the Medici Bank* (1966);

N. Rubinstein, *The Government of Florence under the Medici* (1966).

MEDICINE The study of M. in the Middle Ages was essentially an extension of developments begun in classical times. In the West medical traditions were handed down through the authoritative works of *Isidore of Seville. In the East the writings of Greek physicians, such as Hippocrates, were translated into Arabic. These texts, together with Persian, Indian and Jewish sources on anatomy and diseases, formed the basis of the study and development of the medical sciences. Certain 10th-century physicians and philosophers of the East, such as *Haly Abbas, *Ibn Sinna and *Rhazes, synthesized the ancient heritage with their own experience in their writings. Beginning in the 11th century these achievements became known to the West and to southern Italy in particular. Beforehand, the practice of M., although a basic part of the daily activity in Western monasteries, had been confined to surgical treatment and the healing of wounds. With the establishment of the medical school at *Salerno (c. 1030) medical science began to be systematically studied in the West, and treatises in Arabic were translated into Latin. Jewish physicians living in the West and trained in the study of anatomy contributed to the dissemination of medical knowledge in the western European centres of the 12th century. It was not until the 13th century, however, that M. became part of the university curriculum in the West and that new trends of study, favouring experimentation over normative theories, were developed. The practice of performing dissections, which offered greater knowledge of the human body, became part of the work and study programme at the medical schools of Italy and of *Montpellier in southern France in the 14th century. This practice also became common north of the Alps at the end of that century. The 13th- and 14th-century developments in chemistry and other branches of the natural sciences contributed to pharmaceutical studies and prompted systematic research on the healing properties of plants, herbs and chemicals.

A delineation was made at this time between scientific and popular M. The latter had an impressive tradition and was widely accepted in western medieval society. Despite its connection to superstition and *magic,

Craniotomy, *from an illustrated manuscript of 1335*

it remained very popular even among the upper classes, especially in such cases where scientific M. did not achieve the required results. Popular M. was practised by *hermits and village women (known as *bella donna* or *sage femme,* i.e., "wise women"). The church establishment, fearing the spread of popular cults, accused such women of witchcraft and had them persecuted (from the beginning of the 14th century).

In the late Middle Ages related branches of M., such as dentistry and optics, were also developed. Among the innovations made was the introduction of spectacles.
H. E. Sigerist, *A History of Medicine* (1951).

MEDINA City in *Hedjaz (Arabia). Originally called *Yathrib,* M. was a very prosperous centre whose merchants rivalled those of *Mecca. In 622 *Mohammad, fleeing Mecca, took refuge in the city and preached the *Islamic faith to its inhabitants. He proclaimed it sacred and changed its name to M., making it second only to Mecca. The city became the capital of the Arab caliphate and retained this position until 661, when the see was transferred to Damascus. Revolts then broke out in protest of the court's departure and these were severely repressed by the *Umayyad army in 683. As a result of such events, the city declined.
CHI (1970).

MEIR BEN BARUCH OF ROTHENBURG (Maharam; 1215-93) Rabbi and leader of German Jewry. Born at Worms, M. studied at Jewish schools of the Rhine Valley and France. In 1242 he settled in Rothenburg (Bavaria) and earned a great reputation as teacher and

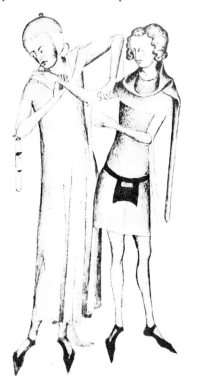

Pulse taking, from "Anatomy" by G. Vigerano, 1345

scholar. A merchant by day, M. dedicated his nights to his scholarly pursuits. His exegetical works made him the greatest authority of Jewish law of his time.

Although M. did not assume any official position, he was recognized as the virtual leader of the Jewish communities in Germany. Some time after 1272 he defended the rights of the Jews at the court of *Rudolf I of Hapsburg, an act which aroused the emperor's enmity. In 1286 he fled Germany with the intention of settling in Palestine; however, while in Lombardy, he was identified and arrested. In exchange for his release, the emperor demanded a large contribution from the Jewish communities of Germany, but M. forbade them to pay his ransom. He died in prison in Alsace.

I. A. Agus, *Rabbi Meir of Rothenburg* (1947).

MEISSEN City and *march in Germany, on the western bank of the Elbe. The city was populated by the *Misni,* a Slavic tribe which was Germanized in the 10th century. In 929 a German settlement was established and M. received its municipal charter from *Henry I. In 965 it became the centre of the march of M., founded by *Otto I. Under the rule of the margraves, the city became an important economic centre and the home of a reputable porcelain industry. During the 11th-13th centuries the march was a powerful feudal principality, ruled by the Wettin dynasty, one of the most important ruling families of late medieval Germany.

J. W. Thompson, *Feudal Germany* (1928).

MELFI City in Apulia (southern *Italy). The inhabitants of M. had been ruled by the *Byzantines from the 6th century and by the 10th century the city had become a site in which Byzantine and Western civilizations merged. In 1063 it was conquered by the *Normans and made the capital of their southern Italian principality. In 1071 M. was superseded by Palermo, but remained one of the favourite retreats frequented by the *Sicilian kings (12th and 13th centuries), who had a royal palace built there. In 1231 *Frederick II assembled the estates of the kingdom in the city and drew up the Constitution of M., which established strong monarchical rule.

E. Kantorowicz, *Frederick II* (1931).

MELISANDE (1110-61) Queen of *Jerusalem. Daughter of King *Baldwin II, she was married to *Fulk of Anjou in 1129. Two years later she and her husband were crowned queen and king. Following Fulk's repression of the revolt of *Hugh du Puiset (1132), who was suspected of being her lover, M. was allowed a role in the government and became extremely active in the political affairs of the *Crusader states. In 1144 she became regent for her son, *Baldwin III and, as leader of the state, played an important part in the Second Crusade. In 1150 Baldwin attempted to establish his own rule, and M.'s refusal to relinquish her power launched a civil war. Defeated in 1152, she was expelled from Jerusalem and sent to Nablus, where she established her court. She continued to wield a certain degree of influence from her new base, up to her death in 1161.

S. Runciman, *A History of the Crusades* (1953).

MELKITES (Syrian: royalists) Name given to certian *Syrian congregations of the 6th and 7th centuries who accepted the religious authority of the Byzantine emperors and became affiliated with the Orthodox *Church.

MELUN City in *France, south of Paris, intersected by the Seine River. Originally a borough built around a royal castle (11th century), the city grew and prospered during the 12th-15th centuries, as it was a favourite site frequented by royalty. In the late 14th and the 15th century it also became an important art centre, patronized by the court.

MELUSINE The name of a French poem and its mythological heroine, half woman and half serpent. According to a fairy tale which can be traced back to the late 12th century, M. was actually the daughter of a certain Albanian king. Her partial transformation into a serpent every Saturday was the result of a punishment inflicted on her. M. came to France and married Duke *Raymond of Poitiers for whom she built many castles. One Saturday he came to see her and discovered her secret; as a result, M. disappeared forever. Her spirit remained, however, and was said to safeguard her descendants, the lords of *Lusignan.

C. S. Lewis, *The Allegory of Love* (1937).

MENAHEM BEN SARUK (10th century) Hebrew grammarian and lexicographer. Born at Tortosa in Spain, he settled in his youth at Córdoba. There he was placed under the patronage of *Hasdai ibn Shaprut and served as his secretary. M. was the author of the *Mahbereth,* a dictionary of biblical Hebrew terms, including grammatical analyses. Written in Hebrew, the work rapidly became known in western Europe. From the 11th century, it was utilized by the Jewish scholars of Italy, Germany and France.

H. Hirschfeld, *Literary History of Hebrew Grammarians and Lexicographers* (1926).

MENANDER PROTECTOR (6th century) Byzantine historian. M. was employed at the court of Emperor *Maurice, who commissioned him to write a history of the empire covering the 6th century. The work, which concentrates on the period 558-82, is valuable due to its approach and its inclusion of important ethnographic material.

CMedH, IV.

MENDICANT FRIARS Name given to the *Dominican and *Franciscan friars in the 13th and 14th centuries, alluding to their mendicity.

MERCANZIA Italian term meaning a court dealing with trade disputes. The institution began to operate in several cities during the 13th century. At first, it was only a private court, established by the *guilds, but in the 14th century it became official and was responsible to the communal authorities. The important M. of Florence, recognized in 1307 by the civil authorities, served as a model for other such institutions in several Italian cities and west European countries.

CEcH, III.

MERCATORES See MERCHANTS.

MERCENARIES Name given in the 14th century to hired soldiers. M. were considered the "merchandise" (Latin, *merces*) of their captains, since they were not loyal to any particular lord or country but served the man who offered the best wages. They were looked down upon by the nobility, who highly regarded the feudal tradition of *fidelity.

MERCHANTS The term was used in the early and high Middle Ages to denote itinerant petty traders who sold their merchandise (*merces*) to peasants and at crossroads. The M. were distinguished from the Roman *mercatores,* who were sedentary traders. In the 12th century the two kinds merged into one and the medieval

Mendicant Friar preaching; *from a 14th-century manuscript*

Latin term was used in the vernacular to denote both types. Like medieval craftsmen, the M. were organized into professional corporations or *guilds. From the 13th century they formed the upper class of the urban community.
CEcH, III.

MERCIA *Anglo-Saxon kingdom, situated in central England, north of the Thames River. Founded in the 6th century by the Angles, the territory was extended to the north and east in the late 6th and early 7th century, and, as a result, the Britons were pushed towards Wales. Under the leadership of its last pagan king, *Penda (d. 654), M. became one of the most powerful realms of the *heptarchy. After his death, Christianity gained ground in the country, further reinforcing the influence the kingdom wielded over the rest of England. M. reached the peak of its power in the 8th century. Its kings, *Ethelred and *Offa, conquered London and imposed their rule on the other Anglo-Saxon realms, parts of which they conquered and annexed to their own kingdom. Offa, who virtually ruled over all of England (from `the Channel to the Humber River) was equated with *Charlemagne. He was noted for establishing a prominent cultural and scholarly centre at his court. After Offa's death, M. was troubled by a series of dynastical wars, which enabled the kings of *Wessex to attain independence and later to become the dominant kingdom of England (9th century). From 858 M. endured Danish raids, and in 877 it was split into *Danish and Anglo-Saxon sections, the dividing line being Watling Street, the road separating London and Chester. The Danish part of M. was included in the Viking kingdom established in England, while the Anglo-Saxon section was annexed to Wessex. M. thereby ceased to exist in its own right.
F. M. Stenton, *Anglo-Saxon England* (1947).

MERINIDS (Banu Marin) *Berber dynasty which ruled Morocco (1269-1472). Its founder, Abd Al-Hack, took advantage of the *Almohades' defeat at *Las Navas de Tolosa (1212) to establish a principality in western Morocco. His son, Abu Yussuf, fought the Almohades and

conquered their capital of *Marrakesh in 1269, proclaiming himself sultan of the Maghreb. The M. dominated Morocco, as well as large portions of Algeria, until 1358, and they were considered the protectors of the Moslem emirs in Spain. During this period they promoted trade development and economic growth. Their profits were used to build elaborate palaces in the royal cities, especially at Marrakesh, where a brilliant court was established. Dynastic conflicts and civil wars erupted in Morocco after 1358 and led to the immediate loss of Algeria. These wars continued into the 15th century and the M. declined; in 1472 the dynasty became extinct.
J. Brington, *Histoire du Maroc* (1968).

MERLEE, WILLIAM (14th century) English meteorologist. M. taught at the University of Oxford and became famous for his techniques of forecasting the weather. Records of his monthly observations, undertaken from 1337-44 in the Oxford district, have been preserved. They indicate a revolutionary attempt to predict the weather, partly on the basis of the state of heavenly bodies, but also according to such signs as the deliquescence of salt, the fact that the sound of distant bells carried and increased pain of wounds, all of which he considered indicators of greater humidity.
A. C. Crombie, *Science in the Middle Ages* (1957).

MERLIN One of the most popular characters in the medieval *Arthurian legend. The figure can be traced back to *Celtic mythology, where it represented a popular prophet and miracle maker. In the Arthurian romances, M. is an enchanter to whom many political prophecies are ascribed. He is an enigmatic figure with a strange ancestry, half man, half demon.
R. S. Loomis, *The Arthurian Literature of the Middle Ages* (1957).

MEROVECH (d. 457) King of the Salian *Franks (448-57). One of the Frankish chieftains who served in the Roman army, he became famous for the part he played in the wars against the Huns and in the defeat of their king, *Attila. While M. did not actually lead the army, as later legends have claimed, he did possess the skill and prestige to impose his rule over the Tournai

Franks. As their leader, he was the founder of the *Merovingian dynasty.

S. Hill, *Roman Society in the Last Century of the Western Empire* (1923).

MEROVINGIANS Frankish dynasty named after King *Merovech. In the middle of the 5th century the M. ruled the Salian kingdom of Tournai in Flanders. Merovech's son, *Chilperic, organized the kingdom and laid the foundations of the dynasty's power. His son, *Clovis, imposed his authority on the other Frankish tribes, conquered Gaul and founded the kingdom of the Franks, which was ruled by his descendants until 751. Like the other tribal kings, the M. had a patrimonial sense of state and used to divide the realm between their sons. However, the kingdom was reunited on a number of occasions in the 6th and 7th centuries due to the early deaths of certain members of the dynasty. The M. effectively ruled the kingdom up the death of King *Dagobert in 639. Beginning in the middle of the 7th century, however, the real power passed to the *mayors of the palace, while the kings were made puppets. Due to the great prestige of the family and the well-known legends concerning its origins, no one thought to dethrone the kings until the middle of the 8th century, when the mayor of the palace negotiated a change of dynasty with the papacy (751).

J. M. Wallace-Hadrill, *The Long-Haired Kings* (1962).

MERV City in *Khorasan (eastern Persia). The ancient city of M. was in a state of decline at the beginning of the Middle Ages. After the Arab conquest (660), however, it was rebuilt and became capital of Khorasan. The city served as a base of Arab expansion into central Asia. Under the *Abbasids an important Moslem school was established at M. and the city flourished, both commercially and culturally. In 1118 the *Seljuk sultan, Sanjar, made it his capital and the city prospered until 1221, when it was destroyed by the *Mongols.

CHI (1970).

MESHULLAM BEN KALONYMOS OF LUCCA (Rabbi M. the Great; 11th century) Jewish exegete. M. lived at Lucca (Tuscany), where he founded an important Talmudic school and became one of the greatest authorities in the Jewish world of his time. His advice was accepted as law by west European Jewry. At the beginning of the 11th century M. accepted an invitation to settle in the Jewish community of Mainz. There he became the leading figure in the Rhenish school. M. was the author of a number of religious poems which have been included in prayer-books.

C. Roth, *The World History of the Jewish People: The Dark Ages* (1966).

MESOPOTAMIA See IRAQ.

MESSINA City in *Sicily. After the fall of the Western Roman empire, the classical city of M. continued to be a prosperous centre. It was ruled by the *Vandals and later by the *Byzantines, and in 842 it was conquered by the *Arabs. In 1061 *Robert Guiscard took possession of the city and made it one of the most important commercial centres of the kingdom of Sicily.

MESTA, THE An association of sheepowners in *Castile, founded during the 13th century to defend their economic interests. The M. originated from provincial organizations of a similar nature. It was recognized by King *Alfonso X in 1273 and established on a general basis for the whole kingdom. The M. wielded control

A blacksmith; *from Caxton's "Game of Chess"*

over both the shepherds and the wool trade of the realm, and in the 14th and 15th centuries the organization became one of the most powerful in the kingdom and even held political power.

K. Klein, *The Mesta* (1964).

METALLURGY Medieval M. was basically associated with the production of iron. In parts of western Europe (north of the Alps) classical techniques of the Mediter-

Ironsmith's workshop; *late medieval woodcut*

ranean world were adopted in the early Middle Ages. In addition, iron ore mines were developed in Germany and the Low Countries, as the abundance of wood available provided adequate fuel. To the East, India's method of improving the quality of iron was adopted at the beginning of the Middle Ages in Persia, and in the 8th century steel was produced in central Asia and Damascus. The M. of the Arabs was thus the most developed of the medieval world until the 12th century, when furnaces began to be employed in western Europe as well. Coal began to be used in the 13th century and contributed to further developments. In the 14th century iron and steel of a finer quality were produced in the furnaces of Italy, Spain and Germany and were used to create better weapons, among them new kinds of swords. Such achievements were also applied to the production of copper and precious metals.

A. C. Crombie, *Science in the Middle Ages* (1957).

METAPHYSICS The medieval philosophical term was borrowed from the title of Aristotle's treatise, a study of certain topics written subsequent to the *Physics*. In medieval philosophy the concept signified the study of primary states. Both in regard to nature and to the mind, M. implied the study of abstract notions, many of them considered "secrets of creation" which could be revealed through divine grace to believers. From the 13th century the term was largely employed by theologians.

E. Gilson, *Philosophy in the Middle Ages* (1951).

METROPOLITAN The bishop residing in a metropolis (capital of a province), who wielded a certain degree of authority over the other bishops of his province. Beginning in the 9th century, the M. was given the additional title of archbishop.

METZ City in *Lorraine. The Roman site, built at the confluence of the Seille and Moselle Rivers, was one of the most prosperous cities of Gaul prior to its destruction by the *Huns in 451. In the 6th century M. was rebuilt as an episcopal see and Frankish royal residence. In the following century it became the capital of *Austrasia and an important political and cultural centre. Upon the division of the *Carolingian empire (843), M. was included in the kingdom of *Lotharingia, and in 870 it was annexed, together with the rest of the duchy, to Germany. In the 10th century M. was ruled by its bishops and became the centre of their powerful seigniory, which withstood ducal attempts to annex it to Lorraine. Under its bishops the city grew, and during the 12th century communal institutions were established under the rule of the urban aristocracy, which excluded craftsmen from taking part in the government. Economic prosperity led to cultural development and, in the 13th and 14th centuries, the centre of the city was remodelled and Gothic buildings were erected.

P. Schneider, *La ville de Metz aux XIIIe et XIVe siècles* (1950).

MICHAEL I, Rhangabe (d. 840) *Byzantine emperor (811-13). M. succeeded his father-in-law, *Nicephorus I, and fought the *Bulgarians led by their khan, *Krum, following their attack on Constantinople. Despite his victory in 813, M. was overthrown by a *coup d'état,* led by General *Leo the Armenian. Sent to a monastery near Constantinople, he spend the remainder of his life as a monk.

MICHAEL II, the Amorian (d. 829) *Byzantine emperor (820-29). Of humble origins, M. was promoted in rank during his military service on the basis of his achievements. By the beginning of the 9th century he had become one of the most powerful generals in the empire. In 813 he backed the revolt of his colleague, *Leo the Armenian, and was rewarded with the position of commander-in-chief of the army. M.'s influence grew and made him suspect to Leo, who therefore imprisoned him in 820. A military revolt resulted in his accession to the throne. After crushing internal rebellions (820-23), M. worked to find a compromise solution to the *Iconoclastic conflict. With regard to external affairs, he was unable to prevent the loss of Crete to the Arabs (826-29).

A. A. Vasiliev, *History of the Byzantine Empire* (1951).

MICHAEL III, the Drunkard (838-67) *Byzantine emperor (842-67). Proclaimed emperor at the age of four, he reigned under the regency of his mother, Theodora. In 855 he claimed his right to govern and, following a clash with Theodora and the murder of her minister, Theoctistus, M. began his own rule in 856. Although his reign was marked by a number of successful battles against the Arabs and the Russians, his power was weakened by religious troubles caused by his ambiguous relations with Patriarch *Photius, whom he appointed and later (863) deposed. Beginning in 860 M. fell under the influence of *Basil the Macedonian, who was appointed co-emperor in 866 and wielded a great deal of influence over the empire. In 867 Basil murdered M. and became sole emperor.

CMedH, IV.

MICHAEL IV, the Paphlagonian (d. 1041) *Byzantine emperor (1034-41). Although of humble origins, M. built a brilliant military career fighting the Bulgarians. In 1034 he was married to Empress *Zoe and proclaimed emperor. In this role, M. concluded a peace agreement with the *Fatimids of Egypt (1037). This act enabled him to concentrate his efforts on Sicily and to conquer Messina (1037) and Syracuse (1040).

MICHAEL V, Calaphates Byzantine emperor (1041-42). Nephew of *Michael IV, the Empress Zoe made him her husband's heir. In order to consolidate his rule, M. had Zoe placed in exile, but his opponents rose up and blinded him. M. was then sent to a monastery where he spent the remainder of his days in obscurity.

MICHAEL VI, Stratioticus (d. 1059) *Byzantine emperor (1056-57). M. was adopted and proclaimed emperor by Empress Theodora, but was unable to impose his authority over the generals, who elected *Isaac Comnenus, the commander of Asia Minor, in his stead. Deposed, M. was sent to a monastery, where he died in 1059.

MICHAEL VII, Ducas (1059-78) Byzantine emperor (1071-78). Son of *Constantine X, he reigned from 1068-71 as co-emperor with his step-father, *Romanus IV. After Romanus' defeat at *Manzikert, M. was proclaimed sole emperor. He attempted to rectify the situation in the empire by building a new army which would reconquer Asia Minor from the *Seljuks. For such purposes, he imposed heavy taxes, which made him unpopular. This difficult situation was aggravated by revolts on the part of the generals. M. thus decided to abdicate and become a monk (1078). He died shortly thereafter.

CMedH, IV.

MICHAEL VIII, Palaeologus (1224-82) *Byzantine emperor from 1258. Born to a distinguished family at *Nicaea, M. became emperor in 1258 and founded the dynasty of the *Palaeologi. As emperor he concentrated his efforts on regaining control over the Latin empire of *Constantinople. In 1261 he was successful and transferred his capital to the ancient city of Constantine. His efforts to restore the Byzantine empire brought him into a prolonged conflict with *Charles of Anjou, who had conquered part of Greece. As a result, M. established relations with the West and negotiated a union of the churches with the papacy (1274). This step met with the opposition of the Byzantine clergy, who aborted the attempt.
D. J. Geneakoplos, *Emperor Michael Palaeologus and the West* (1959).

MICHAEL IX, Palaeologus (1277-1320) *Byzantine emperor (1295-1320). M. was made co-emperor by his father, *Andronicus II, and charged with defeating the *Ottomans. For that purpose he hired the *Catalan company in 1303, but found their presence a more concrete threat than that of the Turks. Consequently he sent them to Greece in 1305, but not before they had ravaged Thrace.

MICHAEL I, Angelus Comnenus Despot of *Epirus (1204-15). Member of the Byzantine imperial dynasty, he was governor of Epirus when Constantinople was conquered by the participants in the Fourth *Crusade (1204). M. then founded an independent state in Epirus and claimed to be the legitimate successor to the Byzantine empire. He worked to consolidate his state by fighting against the Crusader kingdom of *Thessalonica.

MICHAEL II Despot of *Epirus (1237-71). After his accession, M. was forced to withstand attacks made by the *Bulgarians and the emperors of *Nicaea, who also claimed supremacy in the Byzantine empire. Between 1250-61 he lost most of his land and accepted the overlordship of *Michael VIII.

MICHAEL CERULARIUS (c. 1000-58) Patriarch of *Constantinople (1043-58). While building a political career, M. was affected by his brother's suicide in 1040 and decided to become a monk. During his retirement he studied theology and attacked the practices and dogmas of the Roman Catholic Church. In 1043 he was appointed patriarch and wielded a great deal of influence at court. His anti-Catholic attitude led to a renewed conflict with the papacy. The papal reform party, led by Pope *Leo IX and Cardinal *Humbert of Silva-Candida, was intent on avoiding imperial interference in papal affairs and therefore denounced the Byzantine practices as heretical. A delegation led by Humbert was sent to Constantinople in 1053 to force a settlement in the pope's favour. Upon M.'s refusal to concede, Humbert had him excommunicated (1054). This step sparked the final separation between Orthodox and Catholic Churches. M. assumed the title of ecumenical patriarch and refused to acknowledge the supremacy of the papal office.
S. Runciman, *The Eastern Schism* (1955).

MICHAEL SCOT (d. 1235) Astrologer and translator. Born in Scotland in the late 12th century, M. was educated in England. He then travelled to Spain, where he studied Arabic and became acquainted with the Aristotelian treatises on astronomy. In 1223 he went to Italy and served at the papal court. There he won the

favour of *Gregory IX, who recommended him to fill the archbishopric of Canterbury. After a stay in Pisa, where he became interested in mathematics, M. joined the court of *Frederick II and was appointed the emperor's astrologer. Besides translating from Arabic and Hebrew, M. also conducted a study on the volcanic Lipari Islands, based on his personal observation.
C. Haskins, *Studies in the History of Mediaeval Science* (1927).

MICHAEL THE ARCHANGEL, St. One of the four archangels mentioned in the New Testament, M. was the symbol of justice. His cult originated in Phrygia (Asia Minor), where he was venerated as a healer, and in the 5th century it spread to the West. Numerous churches and monasteries were dedicated in his name. Michaelmas Day (29 September), created in his honour, became one of the most popular feasts of the Catholic Church. M.'s figure, decked with a sword and battling a dragon, a symbol of justice destroying evil, was a common subject of medieval art.
O. Rojdestvensky, *Le culte de St. Michel et le Moyen Age latin* (1922).

MIDDLESEX *Anglo-Saxon kingdom. Founded at the end of the 6th century, it included the city of London. In the 7th century it fell under the dominion of the kings of *Essex, and at the beginning of the 8th century it was annexed to *Mercia. From the time of its annexation, M. lost its political independence and was reduced to an earldom, dependent on Mercia and later (in the 9th century) on *Wessex. As London developed, the power of its earls decreased. After the *Norman Conquest of 1066, M. became a shire, but in 1130 King *Henry I granted London the privilege of appointing its sheriff. With the exception of some royal enclaves, of which Hampton Court was the most important, M. was dominated by the mayor and aldermen of London.
F. M. Stenton, *Anglo-Saxon England* (1947).

MIESZKO I (930-92) Duke of *Poland (963-92). M. is considered the founder of the Polish state since he united the principal Polish tribes under his rule. In 966 he converted to Christianity but, in order to resist German influence, invited missionaries from Rome.
Cambridge History of Poland (1954).

MIESZKO II (990-1034) King of Poland (1025-34). Son of *Boleslaw I, he was unable to maintain control over the lands conquered by his father and lost large territories in the southeast to Bohemia and Germany.

MILAN City in northern Italy. M. had been an important political and ecclesiastical centre of the Roman empire and retained this position up to the 5th century, when it was attacked by the barbarians. During the 5th and 6th centuries, the city, like the rest of Italy, was conquered by the Huns, the Heruli, the Ostrogoths, the Byzantines and the Lombards. These rapid shifts in power led to the city's decline. The situation was worsened when the Lombards established their capital in the neighbouring *Pavia, while M. was left to the rule of its archbishops. Under the *Carolingian emperors and kings of the 9th century, the archbishops of M. became the feudal lords of the city and its surroundings. Attempts on the part of other feudal lords in Lombardy to gain influence and power in the city were checked by the archbishops and the local populace. In 936 a new wall was built around the city to keep out the feudal lords, with the exception of those who had already

Courtyard of Lateran Church, Rome, built in the 15th century

settled in M. and had created an urban aristocracy. In the 10th and 11th centuries this aristocracy joined itself with the rich merchants of the city. The merger led to the revival of trade and crafts and caused the city to grow. Prosperity awakened social discontent and led to the emergence of a popular party, the *Pataria,* which demanded a share in the government and ecclesiastical reform. The city's importance became apparent to the *Holy Roman emperors in the 11th century, and they attempted to conquer it and impose their dominion on its archbishops and inhabitants. M. was thus besieged several times, but without serious consequences. It continued to enjoy a large degree of autonomy.

As a result of external pressures and inner tensions, authority over the city was divided between the archbishops and the local commune in the late 11th and the 12th century. The privileges and economic resources of the latter enabled its leaders to become the actual rulers of the city. In the middle of the 12th century, M. gained great influence over the Lombard cities and became a provincial centre. To avoid granting M. the constitution of a principality, which would have been favourable to Pope *Alexander III, Emperor *Frederick Barbarossa besieged the city in 1162 and conquered it, destroying its fortifications. Nevertheless, M. was rebuilt in 1167 and became the core of the *Lombard League, which eventually defeated the imperial army at Legnano in 1176. Under its *Guelph government, M. was a centre of opposition to *Frederick II between 1226-50. But this long struggle, together with civil wars and social discontent, weakened the communal institutions.

As early as 1246 one of the local aristocratic families, the *Visconti, had begun to manifest its power, although the Guelph family of Della Torre was still the most influential. In 1277 the archbishop Ottone Visconti defeated his rivals and proclaimed himself *signore* of the city, appointing members of his family to key positions in the local government. The commune was abolished and the Visconti principality was established at M. towards the end of the century. As a result, M. became the most important city in northern Italy and the capital of a state. This extended its domination over the major part of Lombardy, and at the end of the 14th century even the powerful republic of *Genoa was conquered. During this period the Visconti were deeply involved in Italian affairs and switched alliances in accordance with their interests. They were alternately allied with Venice, Florence, Savoy, the papacy and other Italian principalities. Under the Visconti M. became famous for its silk industry, trade and banking, and its population grew steadily in the 14th and 15th centuries. Wealth was concentrated within its walls, which provided the Visconti with great resources. Thus, they were able to hire one of the most powerful armies of the time.
A. Bosisio, *The Story of Milan* (1960).

MILIČ, JOHN (Jan)   Czech preacher and reformer (d. 1374). Born and educated at Prague, M. was a popular preacher whose sermons, given in the Czech language, called for moral conduct on the part of the clergy and laymen. Although he included mystical themes in his sermons, M. was also a practical man. Some time after 1360 he founded a reformed community in Prague. His activities gained him the enmity of the established clergy and he was forced to make several visits to the papal court of Avignon to justify himself. M. was one of the precursors of the *Hussite movement.

MILITIA CHRISTI (Latin: "Christ's army")   The term denoted those knights who fought for the Christian church, especially against the Moslems. Included among them were the French knights who fought in the *Reconquista* wars in Spain, knights who waged war in Italy and the *Crusaders. Beginning in the 12th century the term was applied only to members of the military religious orders, such as the *Hospitallers, the *Templars and the *Teutonic knights.

MILITES   See KNIGHTS.

MILLENARIANISM   A mystical Messianic movement which spread throughout western Europe in the second half of the 10th century. Its members believed that the year 1000 would mark the end of the earthly world and usher in the Day of Judgement and the beginning of the heavenly realm. Its supporters preached reformed behaviour, especially as concerning the lay society, whom they believed should adopt a monastic way of life. The movement also espoused peace among the faithful. M. had a direct impact on artistic developments, on mystical thought and on the revival of pilgrimages to the *Holy Land.
H. Focillon, *The Year 1000* (1969).

MILLS   At the beginning of the Middle Ages the construction of water-M. became common in continental

A water-mill; from the Luttrel Psalter

(Previous pages) The Mongol Imperial Palace at Peking
(Opposite page) Viking ship found at Oseberg, Norway

Minstrels; *detail of a painting by Simone Martini*

Europe. This phenomenon was related to the decline of slavery and the subsequent lack of manpower to operate the stone wheels and grind the corn. Water-M. were thus seen as viable substitutes. The M. were monopolized by the *feudal lords, who compelled their peasants to use the seigniorial M. From the 8th century on, the water-M. were the most common type used in Europe, since a multitude of rivers allowed many to be built. Such a solution could hardly be implemented in arid countries, such as Persia, however, and from the 10th century windmills were used there. This new type of mill gradually spread westwards to north Africa and Spain; in 1167 it also appeared in western Europe, where it was generally located on the top of a hill. In the 13th century windmills became an everyday part of the landscape in several European nations, especially in the Low Countries, and they were improved by the addition of mechanical wheels.

C. Singer and E. J. Holmyard, *History of Technology,* II (1966).

MINDOVG (1219-63) Great duke of Lithuania. Son of a tribal chieftain, he united the *Lithuanians and founded their state, establishing his capital at Vilna. His attempts to expand westwards were checked by the Russian prince, *Alexander Nevski, who defeated him in 1258. He was more successful against the *Teutonic knights, whom he defeated in 1260, annexing *Livonia to his state. M.'s expansion southwards ended with the conquest of some parts of White Russia.

Cambridge History of Poland (1950).

MINING Ancient methods of M. were retained at the beginning of the Middle Ages and were practised mainly in trans-Alpine Europe. The many waterways in the area, however, made the digging of mines, begun in the 8th century, a complicated affair. It was necessary to line the mines with cement while digging and to employ systems of water evacuation. Such systems became more efficient in the 13th century when manual pumps were introduced. Important developments in M. activities were made following the creation of specific professional *guilds, which established professional standards. In the 13th century the experience that had been gained from the extraction of metals was applied to the production of coal, one of the most important energy sources of the later Middle Ages.

C. Singer and E. J. Holmyard, *History of Technology,* II (1966).

MINISTERIALES (Latin: servants) The term was used in Germany during the 11th-13th centuries to denote the class of imperial officials. The M. were originally of servile origin and rose in rank through their work at the court. They were rewarded for their services by land grants and gradually acceded to the nobility. With the rise of the *Hohenstaufen dynasty, the M., whose fidelity to the emperor was unconditional, were appointed to key positions in the government, both in Germany and in Italy. Some of the M. rose at the end of the 12th and the beginning of the 13th century to the highest ranks of the nobility.

G. Barraclough, *Medieval Germany* (1961).

MINNESÄNGER See MINSTRELS.

MINSK City in *Russia. The name first appears in documents in 1067, when M. was a provincial capital of White Russia. In 1101 the city became the seat of one of the Russian principalities and was vassal to *Kiev. After the collapse of the Kievan state in 1240, M. was spared conquest by the *Mongols and its princes paid tribute to the khans of the *Golden Horde. Ravaged by the raids of *Mindovg, the great duke of *Lithuania, M. lost its independence and in 1301 was annexed to the Lithuanian state. In the 14th and 15th centuries it was an important commercial centre.

A. Florinsky, *Medieval Russia* (1954).

MINSTRELS The name derived from the German *Minnesänger,* meaning "love poets". The M. wandered among the *chivalric courts and, in the tradition of the Provençal and French *troubadours, sang love songs and lyrical pieces composed for certain occasions. They were particularly active in the second half of the 12th and during the 13th century. In the late Middle Ages the name (*ménéstrel* in French) was given to all poets who sang about courtly love, superseding the Old French term, *jongleurs.*

R. J. Taylor, *The Art of the Minnesinger* (1968).

MIRACLE Medieval society believed in acts of marvel. Ms. were accorded a central place in literature (such as in the *Thousand and One Tales*) and in historical sources. The M., in its strictest sense, was a Christian manifestation, created by divine intercession and having a religious purpose. It could be directly produced by God, as a phenomenon of nature, or by means of the saints, either during their lifetime and on the site of their tombs or through relics. Most of the Ms. have been recorded in the *Lives of the Saints (Acta Sactorum),* a work which served to popularize the cult. The most important category of Ms. were those that involved healing hopeless invalids.

C. S. Lewis, *Miracles. A Preliminary Study* (1947).

MISE OF AMIENS See AMIENS.

MISE OF LEWES See LEWES.

MISNIA See MEISSEN.

MISSI DOMINICI (Latin: "the envoys of the Lord") Government institution in the *Carolingian empire. The M. were delegations of counts, bishops and abbots annually sent by *Charlemagne (from 789 on) to visit the provinces of the empire and to supervise the activities of the counts and the local administration. Other duties included proclaiming imperial laws and ordinances throughout the counties, assembling the freemen (*mallus*) and investigating charges of injustice. In many cases the M. were authorized to administer imperial justice. Upon their return to the court, they made a report of their travels to the emperor. As such, they were called his "eyes and ears". The institution continued to function even after the death of Charlemagne, but after 820 it was used less frequently and often the counts connived with the M. After the rebellion of the Louis the Pious' sons (829) the M. virtually ceased to exist.

F. L. Ganshof, *Carolingian Institutions* (1970).

MISTRA City in *Morea (Greece). Conquered in 1204 by *Crusaders, M. became part of the Frankish principality of Morea. A fortress was built on the site, near Sparta, and dominated the area. In 1262 M. was conquered by the *Byzantines and became the seat of their provincial government. The fact that the Byzantines appointed governors of the imperial Cantacuzeno family (1348-80) and then of the *Palaeologi (1382-80), indicates the city's importance. Under the Palaeologi, M. became a prominent political, cultural and artistic centre, where the final developments of Byzantine civilization were achieved. After the fall of *Constantinople (1453), M. remained the last Byzantine stronghold. It was conquered by the *Ottoman Turks in 1460 and began to decline.

M. Khatchidakis, *Mistra* (1956).

MOCENIGO *Venetian family. From the 12th century on, the M. was one of the most powerful aristocratic dynasties of the republic. It took an active part in the government and cultural life of Venice. Among its members, the most famous was Tommasso M., who held the office of doge between 1413-23. Tommasso fought the Turks and expanded Venetian power, gaining possessions along the Adriatic coast.

H. Baron, *The Doge Tommasso Mocenigo* (1952).

A miracle play at Coventry; from an old print

MODENA City in northern *Italy. Following the city's destruction by the *Huns in 453, M. was partially reconstructed. It was successively dominated by the Heruli, the Ostrogoths, the Byzantines and the Lombards. During this period it remained a town of minor consequence. In the 9th century M. was rebuilt by its bishops and became the centre of their seigniory. A *commune was established there in 1115, following the development of neighbouring cities. In the second half of the 12th century, internal struggles divided M.'s principal families, and in the 13th century it was used as a battlefield by the *Guelphs and *Ghibellines. Such events led to its decline and collapse in 1289, when it was conquered by the lords of *Este. The city remained under Este rule until the end of the Middle Ages.
G. Bertoni, *Storia di Modena* (1934).

MOHAMMAD (MOHAMMED, MUHAMMAD) IBN ABDULLAH IBN ABD AL-MUTTALIB (c. 570-632) The founder of *Islam. A member of the *Hashemite family of the Meccan Quraish clan, M. was orphaned in early childhood. He was entrusted to his uncle's care, and taught to be a tradesman. M. then entered the service of a rich widow, *Khadija, as the head of her caravan. In this capacity he wandered through *Hedjaz and visited Syria, which gave him occasion to meet many kinds of people and to learn of their beliefs and traditions. In *c.* 600 he married Khadija (who was then 40 years old), despite the fact that she was 15 years his elder; she bore him six children, among them *Fatima. M. became wealthy, but nevertheless devoted time to meditation in a cave near Mecca. His thoughts focused on the social situation of Mecca and on religious beliefs. By 610 he had begun to express his views publicly and to preach a monotheistic faith, which he believed had been revealed to him by the voice of God. Khadija and a small group of his friends accepted his revelations, and became the nucleus of *Islam. On the other hand, the Meccan aristocracy, led by the *Umayyad clan, opposed the Moslems and accused M. of challenging the city's ancient customs. As a result, many of his followers emigrated to the city of Yathrib. The antagonism between M. and his adversaries became aggravated after the death of Khadija (619) and in 622 an order was given for his arrest. The Prophet had no choice but to take refuge in Yathrib, which he renamed *Medina. M.'s "emigration", known as *hegira* in the Moslem tradition, marked the birth of the new religion.

M. attained a leading position in Medina and served as mediator between the local tribes. There he developed his ideas into a coherent faith, based on his revelations, the *Koran and moral precepts. He also raised a strong army and was able to defeat his enemies, the Meccans, at *Badr in 624. A fresh attack by the Meccans at the Khandak of Medina (627), in an attempt to win back their authority, restore Mecca's commercial prosperity and ensure the continuation of pilgrimages

Lazarus and the Miser; *12th-century relief at the abbey of Moissac*

to the *Kaaba, was equally unsuccessful. A year later, Mecca was conquered and M. became the undisputed Prophet and leader of Hedjaz. The Islamic faith rapidly spread throughout the Arabian deserts. With hopes of even greater expansion, M. planned an attack on the Byzantine territories of Transjordan. The victories were officially consecrated by the great *Hajj* (pilgrimage) to the Kaaba, which became one of the sacred precepts of Islam. In 632, while at Mecca, M. fell ill and died shortly thereafter.

W. M. Watt, *Muhammad at Mecca* (1953);
Idem, Muhammad at Medina (1956).

MOHI, BATTLE OF (1241) A battle fought between the *Mongols, led by *Batu-khan, and King *Bela IV of Hungary, in which the latter was utterly defeated. As a result, Pest was laid open to the Mongols and the major part of the Hungarian realm was destroyed.

MOISSAC Town in southern *France, near Toulouse. M. was originally a borough surrounding a famous monastery. This abbey underwent reform in 1076 and joined the order of *Cluny. The town's monastery was an important educational and cultural centre and contained one of the largest libraries in Europe up to the 12th century. In the late 11th and 12th century the abbey church and cloister were rebuilt in the Romanesque style and contained some of the finest specimens of Romanesque sculpture and iconography.

M. Aubert, *Cathèdrales et Abbatiales Romanes de France* (1965).

MOJMIR Duke of *Moravia (830-46). M. was a Czech chieftain who began a long struggle with other tribal and family leaders in 830. Ten years later he succeeded in unifying Moravia and establishing a powerful duchy there. M. also fought against *Louis the German, although he formally recognized him as overlord. In 846 Louis deposed the duke and appointed his nephew, *Rostislav, in his stead.

K. Boll, *Das grossmährische Reich in den politischen Welt des 9. Jahrhundert* (1966).

MOLDAVIA Rumanian principality situated on the lower Danube, between the Dniester River and the Carpathian Mountains. During the early and high Middle Ages the country was ruled by the *Goths, the *Avars, the *Cumans and other tribes. The area served as a westward passageway for invading tribes from the Asian and Russian steppes. In 1359 a group of "Vlaks" (Rumanians), having come from the Carpathian Mountains, established a principality under the rule of their *vojvod* (prince), Bogdan, on the banks of the Moldava River. In 1360 Bogdan revolted against his overlord, King *Louis of Hungary and gained his independence. Subsequent rulers of M. successfully withstood Hungarian and Polish attempts to conquer the country. In fact, they extended their dominion in the direction of the mouths of the Danube and Dniester Rivers. The principality of M. was organized by Alexander the Good (1400-32), who reigned in cooperation with the great landowners (the *bojars*) and put particular emphasis on commercial development.

R. S. Setton-Watson, *A History of the Rumanians* (1934).

MONACO Principality in *Provence. The ancient temple of Heracles Monoecus became the centre of the Roman settlement of M. at the beginning of the Middle Ages. The Romans attempted to maintain their ancestral traditions while under *Visigothic and *Frankish rule. From the 8th century, however, they became assimilated with the neighbouring population, and in the 9th century the town was included within the county of *Nice. Conquered by *Genoa in the middle of the 11th century, it was governed from 1070 by members of the Grimaldi family, who established a feudal seigniory there. At the end of the 11th century the Grimaldis became vassals of the counts of Provence. In 1297 the lords of M. took advantage of the wars between the *Angevins of Naples-Provence, Genoa and Aragon to free themselves of feudal ties and to proclaim their independence under the protection of the republic of Genoa. In the later Middle Ages the Grimaldi dynasty worked to develop the small principality.

F. de Bernardy, *Princes of Monaco* (1961).

MONASTICISM Christian M. originated in *Egypt at the end of the 3rd century. The practice of retiring to the desert was adopted due to the desire of pious men to devote themselves to the worship of God and to withdraw from secular affairs. Whether done individually or as a group, this form of M. was the common one until the 6th century and it spread to *Sinai and Palestine. M. of that period implied prayer and meditation, with no physical activity on the part of the monks.

Late medieval Burgundian stone statuette of a monk

Byzantine and Roman Catholic forms of M. were different in nature. Monastic groups became organized into communities, where monks studied theology and other subjects and were employed in the service of the church, serving as missionaries, theologians, etc. The withdrawal from society was merely physical, as the minister retained close ties with the laymen. M. of that time also required strict celibacy, although no such obligation was imposed on the rest of the clergy as yet. With the establishment of the monastery of *Subiaco and then of *Monte Cassino by St. *Benedict of Nursia, the aims of M. were defined by the Benedictine rule. Based on the desire to lead a life of perfection and sanctification, it required personal poverty, withdrawal from family life and society, physical and intellectual work and obedience to one's abbot.

In the Greek-Orthodox and Eastern Churches, it was the Byzantine type of M., which stressed the place of the individual within the monastic community, which prevailed. In the Roman Catholic Church, on the other hand, Benedictine M., based on the collectivity of the congregation, became the common form at the end of the 8th century. With the foundation of *Cluny in 910, a reformed Benedictine M. began to spread. It placed greater emphasis on prayer and living according to the monastic rule, which would bring salvation, not only to the monk, but also to all of Christian society. At the end of the 11th century reform movements, such as the *Cistercians, *Carthusians and other minor orders, stressed asceticism. From the 13th century on, with the foundation of the *Mendicant orders, an important change occurred in the structure of western M. Monks became involved in daily social life, especially in the cities and universities. With a few exceptions, such as the desert monasteries in Palestine or Sinai (St. Catherine, Mar Saba, etc.) and the Mount *Athos monasteries in Byzantium, M. failed to attain its ideal of withdrawal from earthly affairs. Through grants of estates, the monasteries came to possess large areas of lands and were integrated into the feudal society, while abbots and other dignitaries became involved in political life and were promoted to secular ecclesiastical dignities.

E. C. Butler, *Benedictine Monasticism* (1919);
D. Knowles, *Christian Monasticism* (1969).

MONASTIR City in *Macedonia. In the 7th century the Greco-Byzantine city of M. became Slavic in character. From the 9th-13th centuries dominion over the city was disputed between the Byzantines and *Bulgarians. The latter established a provincial centre around the local abbey, after which M. was named. At the beginning of the 14th century the city became part of the *Serbian kingdom, and in 1366 it was conquered by the *Ottoman Turks.

CMedH, IV.

MONDEVILLE, HENRY OF (d. 1325) Surgeon. A native of France, M. studied in Bologna. At the beginning of the 14th century he returned to his homeland and became a medical officer in the army. During his service he invented tools with which to extract arrows from wounded soldiers. In *c.* 1308 M. was appointed to teach medicine at *Montpellier. There he became famous for the dissections he made. His findings contributed considerably to the study of anatomy and of the nervous system in particular. A French annotated translation of his book on surgery was published in 1893.

E. Nicaise, *Maître Henri de Mondeville, Chirurgie* (1893).

MONGOLS The common name of Asian tribes, also known as Tartars, who wandered among the steppes north and west of China until the 13th century. Most of these tribes were of Uigur-Altaic origin, some were of *Turkish descent and only a number of tribes made up the M. proper. Information on the early history of the M. is only partially available. It has been extracted from Chinese sources and from material on the *Huns. The religious practices of the M. were shamanistic on the whole, but some of the population also accepted Buddhist, Christian-Nestorian and Islamic beliefs. The tribal structure included two upper classes: the priests, who enjoyed special privileges, and the warriors and chieftains.

In the early Middle Ages the Mongolian tribes joined the Uigur-Altaic and Turkish tribes in invasions of Europe and the Middle East. The eastern tribes periodically attacked China and sometimes entered the service of its emperors. It was not until the late 12th century, with the rise of *Genghis-Khan, that the M. were united and a capital was established at Karakorum. A series of military expeditions, raids and conquests ensued at the beginning of the 13th century. Victories were followed by massive plunder, murder and destruction.

By the time of his death, Genghis had become the supreme ruler of central Asia, China, Persia and the Caucasus. He left a well-organized empire to the collective rule of his descendants, who were bound to elect a great khan or supreme ruler in a special *Kuraltai* held at Karakorum. The descendants of Genghis" four sons continued his policy of expansion in the middle of the 13th century. *Batu-khan conquered Russia and invaded Poland and Hungary to found the *Golden Horde; other grandsons continued invasions in China and Turkestan. Still another grandson, *Hulagu, conquered Persia and Iraq, felling the *Abbasid caliphate in 1258 and reaching as far as the borders of Syria and Palestine until his army was defeated at Ain Jalut by *Baibars, the *Mameluke sultan of Egypt.

The Mongolian empire reached the peak of its power under *Kublai-khan (1259-94), who succeeded in conquering all of China and extending his influence into Indo-China, Korea, Japan and Java. Under his rule, west Europeans were permitted to visit Mongolian territories, and one such traveller, Marco *Polo, provided detailed descriptions of the countries, people and customs. In addition, Kublai moved his capital from Karakorum to Peking, and the court of the great khan was thereby subject to the influence of the Chinese civilization. The empire's strong organization and its control of the trade routes between East and West helped bring prosperity to the M. Yet, on the other hand, the colossal dimensions of the Mongolian territory, which extended from the Pacific Ocean to the Danube, led to its division at the end of the 13th century. The original Mongolian state remained a nomadic realm, while independent empires or hordes were founded in China, Persia, central Asia and Russia. In the 14th century the dynasty of China gradually adopted the Chinese culture. The Persian khanate gradually declined and its rulers adopted the Moslem faith. In Turkestan, the various hordes were contantly engaged in conflicts, although the Golden

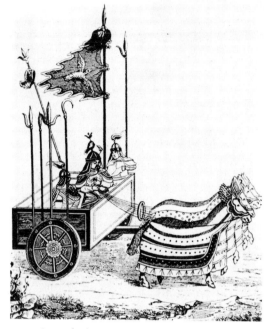

Mongol war chariot

Horde maintained its prominent position until the end of the 14th century.

The last phase in medieval Mongolian history began with the rise of the Timurids at the end of the 14th century. Under the leadership of *Timur-leng (Tamerlane), attempts at rebuilding the empire, in the style of Genghis-Khan, were made. Timur successfully imposed his rule in Persia and central Asia, and, following his victory at Angora over the Ottoman sultan, *Bayazid (1301), he became overlord of all the Mongolian khanates, with the exception of China. As in the time of Genghis-Khan, atrocities were committed and Persia and Iraq were laid to waste. Timur's descendants (the Timurids) ruled Persia in the 15th century and frequently raided India, which was conquered in the 16th century.

Generally speaking, the M. empire declined after Timur's death. The Golden Horde lost its control over the once dependent Russian princes, who won their independence under the leadership of the princes of *Moscow. In addition, the grand dukes of *Lithuania gained power in the Ukraine and conquered Kiev. Internal wars brought the collapse of the Golden Horde, China regained its independence and two independent khanates were established in Crimea and at Kazan.

B. Spuler, *Geschichte der Mongolen* (1968).

MONOPHYSITISM Christian heresy. Based on the doctrine of a single, divine nature of Christ, as opposed to the Orthodox teaching of a double nature (divine and human), M. emerged among various sects of the Middle East in the 5th century and gained ground among the eastern churches in the 6th century. In response to the firm opposition of the established Greek-Orthodox and Roman Catholic Churches, as well as the repressive activity of *Justinian, the Monophysites expressed their anti-Byzantine feelings and began a struggle for

self-identity by creating their own churches in the East. The *Coptic, *Jacobite and many other eastern churches adopted Monophysite ideas as the core of their dogmas.

A. A. Luce, *Monophysitism, Past and Present* (1923).

MONOTHELITISM A 7th-century heresy in the *Byzantine and eastern churches maintaining that Christ had but one will. An extension of *Monophysitism, M. was basically a political manifestation against the Byzantine establishment. Although at first condemned by Emperor *Heraclius, M. developed in Egypt. Under the pressure of Arab conquests, the emperor then vainly attempted to find a compromise solution (638).

V. Grumel, *Recherches sur l'histoire du Monothélisme* (1928).

MONREALE City in *Sicily, near Palermo. The site, which was unpopulated prior to the 12th century, became a religious centre under the *Norman kings of Sicily. In 1174 King *William II founded a Benedictine abbey, which became the nucleus of the town, and in 1182 the see of the archbishop of Sicily was established there. The monastery's cathedral, built in the 12th century, is one of the most beautiful structures of Sicilian art, combining Romanesque, Byzantine and Arabic styles of architecture and ornamentation. The Benedictine cloister, also dating from the late 12th century, is yet another fine example of Sicilian art.

E. Kitzinger, *The Mosaics of Monreale* (1960).

MONS LACTANTIUS Site near *Naples (Italy). It became famous as the site of the battle of 552, in which the Byzantine army, commanded by *Narses, defeated the *Ostrogoths and destroyed their kingdom in Italy.

MONTANIST HERESY One of the earliest heretical movements in the Christian Church, founded by the prophet Montanus in the 2nd century. The Montanists believed that the divine word was revealed through prophets who thereby paved the way for the second coming of Christ. The movement spread at the beginning of the Middle Ages, despite its having been condemned by the Church and councils. It retained its po-

Church at Monreale, built in the 14th century

The Benedictine monastery of Monte Cassino, founded in the 6th century – it was rebuilt several times on the same site

pularity into the 6th century, but, following Emperor *Justinian's attempts to combat it, the movement lost most of its following and eventually ceased to exist.

P. de Labriolle, *La Crise Montaniste* (1913).

MONTAPERTI Site of the battle of 1260 in which the *Ghibellines of *Siena defeated the *Guelphs of Florence. The Ghibelline victory enabled Siena to become the dominant power in Tuscany up to the 14th century. As a result, the city became a great economic and cultural centre.

MONTE CASSINO Benedictine monastery in central Italy, southeast of Rome. M. was founded in 529 by St. *Benedict of Nursia and built on the ruins of an ancient Roman temple. The monastery became the model of Benedictine *monasticism; the Benedictine rule was composed there and M. became the mother-church of the order. Its famous library contained copies of rare classical manuscripts which would have been lost if not for the labour of its monks. In the second half of the 11th century the abbey reached the peak of its power and prosperity. It possessed large estates in Italy and

wielded control over the economic activity of the region between Rome and Benevento. Economic resources were utilized for an intensive building campaign and the establishment of a monastic school, which flourished in the 11th and 12th centuries. M. began to decline in the 14th century, but its abbots continued to wield a certain degree of political influence.

D. Knowles, *Christian Monasticism* (1969).

MONTEFELTRO Aristocratic family in *Urbino (Italy). In the second half of the 12th and during the 13th century the M. led the *Ghibelline party in the city and fought papal officials. Their domination of Urbino gave the family the necessary resources to enlist the aid of hired armies. In the 14th century the M. established a vast principality and were deeply involved in the political struggles of central Italy. At this time the family became associated with prominent aristocrats in Italy. Under Federigo II (1422-82) the M. reached the peak of their influence and power.

R. de La Sizeranne, *Le vertueux condottiere: Federigo de Montefeltri* (1927).

MONTEIL, BATTLE OF (1369) See HENRY II, OF TRASTAMARE.

MONTE MORRONE Ascetic hermitage of the Spiritual *Franciscans, founded in the 11th century. Situated on the Apennine Mountains of central Italy, the hermitage became the site of a community of Spiritual Franciscans (1262), who retired there to meditate. One of its members, Pietro, who was renowned for his ascetic way of life and personal realization of the ideal of poverty, became Pope *Celestine V in 1294.

J. Moorman, *A History of the Franciscan Order* (1968); A. Frugoni, *Celestiana* (1954).

MONTFERRAT Marquisate in northwestern *Italy. It developed from a castle built by a Frankish family (late 9th century) on the southern bank of the Po River, dominating the road between Milan, Genoa and Torino. The castle was built at a time when the *Carolingian empire was in its decline, and its lords took advantage of the anarchic state of Italy to proclaim themselves counts in 943 and to impose their rule over a vast territory, covering the eastern part of modern Piedmont. In 954 *Otto I of Germany created M. as a march and in 967 the hereditary title of margrave was granted to the lords as vassals of the *Holy Roman empire. During the 11th-13th centuries the marquisate continually developed and its ruling family attained a prominent position within the empire, particularly after the marriage of *William IV of M. (1140-88) to Sophia, daughter of *Frederick Barbarossa. William's sons, *Conrad and *Boniface, took part in the *Crusades, the former becoming lord of *Tyre and king of *Jerusalem (1192) and the latter, who was leader of the Fourth Crusade, becoming king of *Thessalonica (1204-07). The family's influence continued to grow in the 13th and 14th centuries through a series of marriages with their neighbours from *Savoy, the Spanish dynasties and the *Palaeologi of Byzantium, and the marquises were recognized as princes of the empire. At the end of the 14th century, however, their power began to decline and, so as to defend themselves against the attacks of the *Visconti of Milan, they fell under the influence of the dukes of Savoy and Mantua.

A. Bozzola, *Il Monteferrato* (1923).

MONT-JOIE SAINT DENIS! The French battle cry of the Middle Ages. It originally summoned the vassals of the *St. Denis Abbey to battle (12th century), but from the 13th century on, it was adopted by the royal French army and indicated a proclamation of war.

MONTMORENCY French feudal family. The descent of the M. family has been traced back to the 10th century when a feudal castle was constructed north of Paris by its earliest members. In the 11th century the lords of M. promoted anarchy in the area and challenged the authority of the kings of France. The family acquired large territories and rose to the ranks of the higher nobility. After their defeat in 1102 by King *Louis VI, the M. accepted his authority and entered the royal service. They thereby became prominent barons in the kingdom.

A. Duchesne, *Histoire Généalogique de la Maison de Montmorency* (1657).

MONTPELLIER City in Languedoc (southern France). Founded in the 8th century as the stronghold of the Guilhems, a minor feudal family of the county of Melgueil, it began to grow and gain importance in the 10th century, when it became a commercial and finan-cial centre. In 1141 the burghers of M. rose up against their lord and attempted to establish a commune, but were defeated. The lords of M. thus became a powerful dynasty in Languedoc. Beginning in the second half of the 12th century the city's commerce flourished and included trade with the Crusader kingdom of Jerusalem. In 1204 M. was inherited through marriage by the kings of Aragon and the city became an episcopal see. In 1229 a *university was founded there and soon became famous for its medical school. Many of its teachers were Jews, who constituted an important part of the city's population; in fact, the Jewish community of M. was reputed as one of the most important cultural centres in southern France of the 13th century. In 1276 M. became the capital of the kingdom of *Majorca, and in 1349 it was acquired by King *Philip VI and annexed to France.

L. J. Thomas, *Montpellier* (1936).

MONTREAL Castle in the Latin kingdom of *Jerusalem. Built in 1113 by King *Baldwin I, it became the base of *Crusader expansion in Transjordan and held control over the areas south of the Dead Sea, as well as of the main road between Syria, Hedjaz and Egypt. The castle was strongly fortified during the 12th century, and *Saladin succeeded in conquering it only after a siege of four years (1190). The town of Al-Shaubak was built by Arab settlers on its ruins in the 13th century.

MONT-SAINT-MICHEL Island and abbey off the coast of *Normandy and Brittany. In the 8th century a chapel was built there and dedicated to the cult of St. *Michael the archangel. In 966 *Norman monks settled at M. and founded a *Benedictine abbey, which became an important spiritual centre and a pilgrimage site. Its buildings contain a mixture of Romanesque and Gothic art, the latter style having been added in the 13th century (1203-64).

G. et V. de Miré, *Le Mont-Saint-Michel* (1953).

MONTSÉGUR Castle in southern *France on the Pyrénées Mountains. In 1203 it became populated by *Albigenses fleeing the *Crusaders. The site was conquered and destroyed in 1244 by the French royal army, which struck the final blow to the Albigenses.

MONTSERRAT Mountain dominating the city of *Barcelona. It became famous due to a series of legends which claimed that the "Castle of the Holy *Grail" was located there. A Benedictine monastery was esta-

Mont-Saint-Michel, Normandy

The Benedictine monastery at Montserrat, Spain, built in the 12th century

blished on the site in the 10th century and a Romanesque church, a fine specimen of Catalan art, was built in the 12th century and housed the famous portrait of the Madonna of M., traditionally held to be the work of St. Luke. Following a period of decline, the monastery of M. was reformed in 1410 and the abbey became a prominent educational centre of Spain.

M. Muntados, *Montserrat* (revised ed.) (1967).

MORAVIA Country in central Europe, situated in the eastern part of the Czech plateau. After a period of temporary settlements by the migrating *Germanic tribes, M. became populated by Slavs, who fell under the domination of the *Avars at the beginning of the 7th century. In 822 the Slavic chieftains took an oath of fidelity to Emperor *Louis the Pious, but Frankish sovereignty was solely formal in nature. The tribes of M. were united in 840 under Prince *Mojmir, who initiated a struggle for independence from the *Carolingian rulers of Germany. His successor, *Rostislav, although appointed by King *Louis the German, continued the struggle and supported the mission of *Cyril and Methodius, in an attempt to prevent the country's Germanization. Following the death of Methodius (885), however, the Bavarian church forcibly replaced the Slavonic texts with the Roman Catholic liturgy.

Rostislav was succeeded by *Svatopluk, the greatest Moravian leader of the 9th century. Taking advantage of the anarchic state of Germany, Svatopluk was able to gain independence and by 880 had conquered the whole of Czech territory and of Slovakia, as well as large areas of southern Poland, founding Great M. The Moravian empire became one of the most influential political powers in central Europe at the end of the 9th century. Its control over the trade route between western and eastern Europe provided it with abundant resources and economic prosperity. However, the empire lacked an administrative structure and the tribal traditions, which remained strong, weakened the state. After Svatopluk's death (894), Great M. began to decline and lost its territories in *Bohemia. In M. proper a civil war between his sons divided the country. Thus, the *Hungarian invasion of 906 destroyed the state, most of which was annexed to Bohemia. From that date the history of Moravian civilization became linked with that of Bohemia.

K. Bosl, *Das grossmährische Reich in der politischen Welt des 9. Jahrhunderts* (1966).

MOREA Frankish principality in *Greece. The *Byzantine province of the Peloponnese was conquered by the *Crusaders in 1205. *Boniface of Montferrat, king of Thessalonica, granted it as a fief to *William of Champlitte. Geoffrey of *Villehardouin, Champlitte's associate and heir, gained independence for the province and established its first princely dynasty. A feudal regime was established in M. in the 13th century; it adopted the western concepts of nobility and chivalry but maintained the Byzantine system of land holding, which was highly respected by the local peasant population. In the second half of the 13th century the restored Byzantine empire began to apply pressure on the principality, which was forced to surrender the castle of *Mistra and a part of the Peloponnese. The remaining territory of M. fell under the influence of *Charles of Anjou, king of Sicily. Marriages between the last Villehardouin princes and the Angevins of Naples led to the establishment of Neapolitan rule at the end of the 13th century. *Venice acquired large parts of M. in the 14th century and became the most influential power in the principality at that time. Meanwhile, Navarrese companies of hired soldiers conquered another portion of the province in 1383. Thus, at the beginning of the 15th century, M. was divided into Neapolitan, Venetian and Navarrese areas, although the French-speaking nobility continued to maintain the fiction of a feudal French (Frankish) principality, governed in accordance with the *Assizes of Romania. In 1430 the Byzantine governors of Mistra conquered Frankish M. and united the country. In 1460 it fell to the *Ottoman Turks.

J. Longnon, *L'Empire Latin de Constantinople et la Principauté de Morée* (1949).

MORGARTEN, BATTLE OF   One of the main battles in the *Swiss struggle for independence, fought in 1315 between the Swiss cantons and *Leopold of Hapsburg, duke of Austria. The Swiss victory allowed the cantons of Schwyz and Uri to reaffirm their independence.

MORIMOND *Cistercian monastery in Champagne. Founded in 1115 as the fourth daughter-house of *Cîteaux, it became one of the most active monasteries of the order within a few years. Its monks wielded great influence in Germany and during the 12th and 13th centuries the German Cistercians accepted the authority of its abbot, who became their superior. The abbey's influence was also extended into Poland and the Scandinavian countries.

J. B. Mahn, *L'Ordre Cistercien et son Gouvernement* (1951).

MOROCCO (Maghreb: "the West")   Country in northwest *Africa. Under Roman domination M. formed the principal part of the province of Mauritania. However, Roman influence was superficial and apparent only in the Mediterranean coastal area; the interior of the country was inhabited by the Moors and *Berber tribes who did not recognize external authority. The *Vandal conquest of 429 did not affect this structure, which remained unchanged during the *Byzantine period (534-680); the Byzantine governors wielded purely formal authority in the country. It was the *Arab conquest, begun in 680 but achieved only in 790 due to the fierce opposition of the Berbers, which caused the most basic change in local structures. But even after the actual conquest, Berber revolts were frequent and the *Umayyads found Islamization of the country to be a most difficult task. A revolt in 740 developed into a general uprising against the caliphate, and the army sent to repress the rebels was defeated in 742. Berber particularism had found its expression even within the Islamization process, as some of the tribes

converted to *Kharijism. Thus, after the defeat of the Umayyad caliphate, a Berber principality was established in eastern M. by the Banu-Madrar family (771-958), based on the doctrines of Kharijite Islam. On the other hand, orthodox Islam also gained ground under the leadership of the Idrisid dynasty (788-985), which governed the main part of M. In 791 Idris II founded the city of *Fez and established his capital there, accepting the sovereignty of the *Abbasid caliphs of Baghdad, but, for all practical purposes, enjoying a large degree of independence. Islamization was achieved in the 10th century, when the country began to enjoy economic prosperity as a result of the gold trade passing through the Sahara Desert.

During the 10th century domination over M. was disputed between the Spanish Umayyads and the *Fatimids. Their struggles for power only succeeded in destroying the local political structures and bringing the country to a chaotic state in 985. The ultimate victors were the *Almoravides, who conquered M. at the end of the 10th century and made it the centre of their expansive empire. This conquest led to a number of changes in the country's social and cultural structure. The Berbers were pushed to the mountains and countryside and the urban dwellers adopted the orthodox Islamic beliefs of their conquerors. The settlement of the *Hilali Beduin tribes in the western part of the country caused Arabization of the population, especially in the cities. Major cities, such as Fez and *Marrakesh, became not only places of worship, but also centres of learning and of architecture and ornamentation.

In 1243 the Almoravides were defeated by a rival dynasty, the *Almohades. Although they established the centre of their African and Spanish empire at Algeria, the rulers often visited Marrakesh and Fez, and by the end of the 13th century the Almohades had shifted their centre to M. The Marinid dynasty of the Almohades was defeated in Tunisia in 1348 and lost the actual power of government to their viziers, the Watassi, although they retained the royal title until 1415. The Watassi then assumed power and became the last Moroccan dynasty of the Middle Ages. They were faced with the influence of Portugal and Spain, which established colonies in the main harbours. The sultans of the 15th century thus concentrated their power in the interior, while Iberian influence was paramount in the coastal areas.

H. Terrasse, *History of Morocco* (1965).

MOROSINI Aristocratic Venetian family. One of the oldest families of *Venice, the M. entered the political arena in the 10th century. At this time they won great esteem as defenders of Venetian independence from the *Ottonian emperors. During the 10th-14th centuries, members of the M. family held several offices in the state and distinguished themselves as politicians, generals and scholars. The most important among them were: Domenico M., doge (1148-56), who established Venetian domination in the Adriatic Sea and extended the authority of the republic into Istria, Dalmatia and parts of Albania; Michele M., doge (1382), who made peace with Genoa and was one of the most influential Italian politicians of his time; Antonio M. (1366-1434), historian, who wrote a documented history of Venice; and Tomasso M., the first Latin patriarch of Constantinople (1205-11).

H. Kretschmayr, *Geschichte von Venedig* (1920).

MOSAICS See ART, BYZANTINE.

MOSCOW City and *Russian principality. M. was first mentioned in the Old Russian Chronicle of 1147. In 1156 Prince *Yuri Dolgoruky built a castle (the Kremlin) on the site, so as to control the trade between *Novgorod and the Volga area. This castle contributed to M.'s growth and development. In the late 12th and the 13th century, it served as the strategic centre of the southern borderland, *Suzdal-Vladimir. In 1228-29 M. was destroyed by the *Mongols, but was rebuilt a few years later. After the fall of the Kievan Russian state in 1240, M. was one of the cities to be granted autonomy in return for a considerable annual tribute paid to the *Golden Horde. The relations between the Muscovites and the khans were good, on the whole, but in the late 13th century the former attempted to rebel and the city was destroyed for a second time in 1293. A year later the *Rurikid prince Daniel (d. 1303) rebuilt M. and proclaimed it a principality independent of Suzdal. The princes of M. took it upon themselves to raise the tribute to the Golden Horde on behalf of the autonomous Russian principalities. Thus, M.'s importance grew during the 14th century, especially under the rule of *Alexander Nevski, one of the heroes of medieval Russia. In 1326 the metropolitan see was transferred from *Vladimir to M. and the latter became the religious capital of Russia. In 1328 Prince *Ivan I conquered Suzdal, took the title of grand prince and made M. into a major Russian power. His successors continued to annex Russian principalities and struggled against the Lithuanians and Mongols. The Russian victory at the Battle of *Kulikovo, ensured the country's supremacy under *Dmitri Donskoi, who made M. its capital.

G. Vernadsky, *Medieval Russia* (1953).

MOSES BEN MAIMON See MAIMONIDES.

MOSES BEN NAHMAN See NAHMANIDES.

MOSES DE LEON (c. 1240-1305) *Kabbalist. Born at León, M. belonged to a rich Jewish family and received a higher education from private tutors. When M. displayed interest in philosophy, his father ordered a special copy of *Maimonides' treatises for him (1267). Later M. became interested in kabbalistic views, as they were developed in *Gerona. He absorbed the multitude of kabbalistic ideas and in 1286 compiled a variety of sources on Jewish mysticism. This famous work, the *Zohar*, written in an Aramaic dialect so as to suggest its antiquity, became the manual of the kabbalists. M. also composed a series of treatises interpreting the "ancient" *Zohar*.

G. Scholem, *Major Trends in Jewish Mysticism* (1954).

MOSES IBN EZRA (1055-1135) Hebrew poet of Spain. Born in Granada, M. received a comprehensive Hebrew and Arabic education and was employed as an official of the Moslem government in his native city. In 1090, when the *Almoravides conquered Granada, M. lost his position and wealth and soon fled to Castile, where he wandered. During this period M. composed the great bulk of his poetry, which included religious hymns and secular pieces. The works reflect his state of mind and his disappointment in his fellow man, as well as his faith in divine salvation and his love of nature. These poems are masterpieces of medieval Hebrew verse, due to the author's mastery of the art and his thorough knowledge of the Hebrew language.

H. Brody, *Introduction to the "Select Poems of Moses Ibn Ezra"* (1943).

MOSES IBN TIBON (c. 1190-1250) Translator. Son of *Samuel ibn Tibon, he helped his father translate philosophical and scientific treatises from Arabic into Hebrew. His reputation grew after his father's death, when his own merits were recognized. He was especially noted for his translation of the works of *Ibn Rushd.

H. Blumberg, *Moses Ben Samuel Ibn Tibbon* (1954).

MOSES KIMHI (1120-90) Grammarian. M. was one of the most prominent Hebrew grammarians in the 12th century and taught at the Academy of *Narbonne. His main interest was in the study of verbs. He published a series of treatises in which he attempted to logically explain Hebrew conjugation.

J. B. Sermonetta, *Il Libro delle forme verbale* (1967).

MOSES OF BERGAMO (12th century) A native of Bergamo in northern Italy, where his brother was provost of an ecclesiastical chapter, M. settled in the Venetian quarter of Constantinople. By 1130 he had been employed as secretary of Emperor *John Comnenus. M.'s position brought him wealth, which he used to buy rare Greek manuscripts during his journeys to Thessalonica and in the Balkans. M. was reputed for his thorough knowledge of both Greek and Latin, which he employed to translate Greek theological works into Latin.

C. H. Haskins, *Studies in the History of Mediaeval Science* (1927).

MOSUL City in northern Iraq. Founded by the Persian *Sassanids on the bank of the Tigris River, M. controlled the trade route between Persia and Syria and thus developed rapidly. On the eve of the *Arab conquest (641) it was one of the most important Christian centres in the East. After the Arab victory, many of the soldiers and their families settled in M. In the 8th century the city became the capital of northern Iraq. It also became one of the most important textile centres of the caliphate, and its muslin cloth was renowned throughout western Europe as well. Beginning in the 10th century local dynasties established their rule in M. under the nominal authority of the *Abbasid caliphs. In 1095 the *Seljuks conquered the city and appointed *atabegs to govern it. One such *atabeg*, *Zengi, proclaimed his dependence in 1127, and established a most powerful *Turkish principality, which became the base for the counter-offensive against the *Crusaders. As part of the Zengid and the *Ayyubid empire, M. continued to flourish in the 12th and 13th centuries until it was conquered by the *Mongols under *Hulagu-Khan. The city was destroyed and although subsequently rebuilt, remained a poor provincial town in the 14th and 15th centuries.

H. A. Foster, *The Making of Modern Iraq* (1935).

MOUNT ATHOS See ATHOS, MOUNT.

MOUSKES, PHILIP (d. c. 1241) French chronicler. A clerk in the cathedral of Rheims, M. used to accompany the archbishops on their visits to the royal court. There he became acquainted with prominent personalities and learned of contemporary events. On the basis of such information and the documents he worked with, M. wrote a *Rhymed Chronicle of France*, which covered the first half of the 13th century, up to 1241.

A. Molinier, *Les Sources de l'Histoire de la France Médiévale* (1906).

MOZARABS The name given to the Christians of Spain, who lived under Arab rule but preserved their own liturgy and rites, observing their faith as they had done at the beginning of the 8th century before the fall of the *Visigothic realm. Upon the reconquest of large parts of Castile and Aragon (11th century), the practices of the M. were condemned as heterodox, since they had lost contact with the established Church. During the 11th and 12th centuries, Mozarab bishops and other clergy were removed from their dignities and an intensive campaign was carried out to curtail their semi-Arabic practices.

A. Castro, *Periods in Spanish History* (1954).

MSTISLAV Grand prince of *Kiev (1125-32). The eldest son of *Vladimir Monomach, M. was able to impose his authority over his Russian kinsmen after continuous warfare. He also defended his country against the raids of the *Polovtsi tribes of the steppes. During his lifetime, Kiev was the centre of the Russian state, but his heirs were unable to retain their supremacy and Kiev's prominent place was lost to *Suzdal in the second half of the 12th century.

G. Vernadsky, *Kievan Russia* (1952).

MSTISLAV THE BRAVE Prince of *Smolensk (1167-1204). Descended from a younger branch of the *Rurik dynasty, which was granted the principality of Smolensk, M. was involved in the dynastical struggles over *Kiev (second half of the 12th century). His rival was *Mstislav the Daring; in 1204, they were both defeated and killed by the *Mongols at Kalka.

G. Vernadsky, *Kievan Russia* (1952).

MUAWIYAH IBN ABI SUFYAN (c. 603-80) Caliph (661-80). M. belonged to the aristocratic clan of the Meccan *Umayyads. After Mohammad's conquest of Mecca in 626, M. converted to Islam and joined his army. Under the reign of Caliph *Omar, M. distinguished himself as a skilled general and was entrusted with the command of the Syrian front. In 640 he became governor of the area. After the murder of his kinsman, Caliph *Uthman, M. fought against *Ali, whom he defeated in 661. M. was then proclaimed caliph and established his capital at Damascus, where he founded the Umayyad dynasty. During his reign, the caliphate adopted the Byzantine administrative system, which enabled M. to impose strong central control over his expansive empire. M. fought the Byzantines, but was unable to conquer *Cyprus or Constantinople. However, he is credited with conquests in *north Africa and eastern *Persia.

CHI (1970).

MUHAMMAD (MEHMET) (1380-1421) *Ottoman sultan (1413-21). The youngest son of *Bayazid I, he was able to reunite the independent Turkish principalities which had been dismembered after his father's defeat at the hands of *Timur-leng (1402). In 1413 M. became sultan of the renewed empire. His major achievement was the consolidation of the empire in Anatolia and the Balkans.

P. Vittek, *De la Défaite d'Ankara à la Prise de Constantinople* (1939).

MÜHLDORF Village in *Bavaria, famous as the site of the battle of 1322 between Emperor *Louis IV of Bavaria and *Frederick of Hapsburg, rivals for the German kingship and the imperial throne. Louis' victory allowed him to reign uncontested in Germany and to annex the march of *Brandenburg to the *Wittelsbach dominions. Moreover, the *Hapsburgs were consequently kept out of the imperial race for over a century.

MUNDEBURDIUM Term used in the *Frankish kingdoms of the 7th century to signify the protection and defence offered by a lord to the free-man (*mundeburdis*). In return, the free-man accepted his lord's sovereignty and granted him his estates. The M. was a primitive form of *feudal relations between a lord and his vassal; it was a forerunner of the oath of *homage.

F. L. Ganshof, *Feudalism* (1965).

MUNICH (München) City in *Bavaria on the western bank of the Isar River. Founded in 1158 on one of the main cross-roads of Bavaria, M. became a commercial centre and sponsored a fair. In 1255 the *Wittelsbach dynasty, which had been ruling Bavaria since 1180, made M. the capital of its duchy. The city developed rapidly as a political and administrative entity and, with the establishment of a bishopric, also became an important religious centre. In the 14th century the city's centre was rebuilt in the Gothic style and was dominated by a new cathedral. The ducal court became a prominent gathering place for artists during the 14th and 15th centuries and there the "Bavarian" style of late Gothic art developed.

E. Larsen, *Munich* (1967).

MÜNSTER City in Westphalia (Germany). The *Saxon town of Mimigernaford was conquered by *Charlemagne in 787 and became one of the Frankish strongholds in Saxony. In 804 the emperor founded a bishopric in the city, which had its name changed to M. The town developed into a trade centre and prospered in the 11th-13th centuries. In 1137 Emperor *Lothair granted its burghers a *charter of liberties, allowing them to establish communal institutions. In the 12th and 13th centuries trade developed with England, bringing M. great prosperity and eventually earning it membership in the *Hanse. The city's burghers took advantage of the situation to assert their power over that of the bishops.

W. Hager, *Münster in Wesftalen* (1961).

MUNTANER, RAMON (1265-1336) Born at Perelada in Catalonia, M. was employed at the royal court of *Aragon. His *Chronicle of the Kings of Aragon,* covering the 13th and the first part of the 14th century, is a classic work of Catalan literature.

E. Pears, *Catalonia Infelix* (1937).

MURAD I (c. 1319-89) *Ottoman sultan from 1359. M. began Ottoman expansion in the Balkan peninsula. His campaign achieved spectacular results and altered the map of Europe. In 1360 M. invaded Thrace and conquered *Adrianople, making it his capital. The Byzantine emperor, *John V, was compelled to pay him tribute, which enabled M. to hire soldiers and strengthen his army. In 1371, after recovering Gallipoli, M. continued his advance into the Balkans and defeated a coalition of Serbian and Bulgarian princes, seizing most of the *Macedonian towns. In 1385 he conquered *Sofia and reduced the Bulgarian rulers to vassalage. Although the Ottoman advance into the Balkans continued, M. turned to Asia Minor and attacked the Seljuk principalities in central Anatolia, obtaining territory as far as *Ankara. In 1388 he returned to Europe with fresh forces and defeated a Serbian coalition at *Kossovo but was killed on the battlefield.

P. Wittek, *The Rise of the Ottoman Empire* (1938).

MURCIA City in southeastern *Spain. A small provincial town under the *Visigoths, M. developed into a prominent city under Arab rule. After the fall of the caliphate of *Córdoba, a Moslem principality was founded in the city and its surroundings. Attempts by the *Almoravides to conquer M. were resisted until 1170, when the local population rose up against its emir and capitulated. In 1238 King *James I of Aragon conquered the city; a few years later it came under Castilian rule. In 1272 King *Alfonso X of Castile granted M. its municipal status, but stipulated the division of the city into three distinct quarters (Christian, Jewish and Moslem). A bishopric was established in the city and in 1285 construction of a cathedral was begun on the site of a former mosque.

A. Castro, *The Structure of Spanish History* (1954).

MUSIC The central part played by religion and the church liturgy in everyday medieval life was greatly responsible for the development of medieval M. In accordance with the Greek heritage, M. was one of the disciplines of the *Quadrivium, a sub-division of the *Seven Liberal Arts, and was studied as a metrical science. The highest place was accorded to vocal, and especially choral, M., which was studied in the *Scholae Cantorum* of the cathedrals. In the early Middle Ages it was the plainsong which was most commonly sung in such schools. The Western Church attempted to standardize the M. taught in the *Scholae Cantorum* and thus the Gregorian chant was introduced. This development is associated with Pope *Gregory I, who codified the M. The melody of the Gregorian chant (some 3000 are known) is based on a limited scale and may sound monotonic to the inexperienced ear. Use of the Gregorian chant spread throughout the *Benedictine monasteries in the 7th-9th centuries and attained canonic status. This is indicated in the *Capitularies of *Charlemagne, which prescribed the strict observance of its rules so as to attain salvation. The introduction of the first organs in the 9th century provided Gregorian M. with appropriate instrumental accompaniment. Beginning in the 10th century plainsong was also used in the liturgical drama; in the 12th and 13th centuries it was sung by the *Goliards and in the *Carmina Burana and was thus adapted to secular lyrics. Secular vocal M. was sung in the vernacular by the *jongleurs, *troubadours and *minstrels; their songs also laid the basis for the emergence of the first ballads in the 12th century. Because the Goliardic and vernacular M. was performed by wandering singers, it could not be accompanied by the organ and substitutes, such as the flute and zither, were used in western Europe, although no orchestral M. had developed as yet.

Polyphonic M. began to emerge in the 9th century during the *Carolingian renaissance. It was developed in the 11th and 12th centuries by such musical theorists as *Guy of Arezzo, Leonin and Perotin (1180-1226). The polyphonic song developed together with the organ and reached its peak in the Middle Ages through the theoretical work of *Franco of Cologne (13th century). However, the addition of voices to the *cantus firmus* (main melodic line) provoked the opposition of the Gregorians, who favoured the "ancient" art (*ars antiqua*) over the "new" one (*ars nova*) which was spreading rapidly in France and Italy. At the beginning of the 14th century the opposition won ground in the ec-

clesiastical hierarchy, and in 1324 Pope *John XXII issued an ordinance forbidding the use of additional voices. This decree made polyphony attractive to the lay circles and it came to be used more and more in secular M. Moreover, even ecclesiastical M. had been influenced by the new trends and during the 14th century the Frenchman *William of Machaut (c. 1305-77) composed a complete *mass for four voices. In Italy early 15th-century polyphonic compositions of Francesco Landino paved the way for Renaissance M. The *ars nova* was responsible for the emergence of orchestras which provided musical accompaniment. The great variety of instruments used contributed to the development of harmony.

A. T. Davison and W. Apel, *Historical Anthology of Music* (1964).

MUSSATO, ALBERTO (1261-1329) Italian politician and historiographer. Born in Padua to an aristocratic family, M. was knighted in 1296. In 1299 he began his political career, becoming a member of his native city's council as well as one of the leading personalities of the *Guelph party. M. represented Padua at the court of Pope *Boniface VIII in 1302 and appeared before Emperor *Henry VII in 1311. The political situation in Italy caused him to switch his loyalties to the emperor, whose presence in the country he deemed advantageous. Such ideas were also expressed in his writings, among them a history of Henry VII's military expedition into Italy and its aftermath, which is an important chronicle of northern Italy at the beginning of the 14th century. In addition to his success as a historiographer and politician, M. was also a gifted poet.

I. Siciliano, *Medioevo e Rinascimento* (1936).

MUSTAIN AL- *Abbasid caliph (862-66). After having been proclaimed caliph at Samarra under Turkish guard, M. attempted to free the caliphate of their control and fled to Baghdad. Intercepted by his guards he was compelled to return to Samarra, where he set up a puppet government controlled by the Turkish officers.
CHI (1970).

MUTASIM AL- *Abbasid caliph (833-42). The younger son of *Harun Al-Rashid M. was proclaimed caliph after the death of his brother, Al-*Mamun. His reign began with a series of palace intrigues and attempts by the viziers to seize power. To bring such conspiracies to a halt, M. hired Turkish guards from Transoxiana; these soldiers aroused the hatred of the army and civilians of Baghdad, who rose up against them. In 836 the Turkish guard was expelled from Baghdad, but on leaving they took the caliph with them. They settled in the city of Samarra and made it their headquarters. M. lost all influence during the last years of his reign.
CHI (1970).

MUTASIM AL- *Abbasid caliph (1242-58). M. was the last caliph of Baghdad. Having already been denied any true political power, he was deposed in 1258 by the *Mongol khan, *Hulagu, who conquered Baghdad and destroyed the Abbasid caliphate.

MUTAWAKKIL, AL (822-61) *Abbasid caliph (847-61). Son of Al-*Mutasim, he was educated at the Academy of *Baghdad, where he displayed a keen interest in theological discussions. After his accession to the throne, and despite the control the Turkish guard had over his activity, he played an independent role in the religious policy of the caliphate, favouring the ascension of the *Sunnites. M. persecuted the *Shiites, as well as the Christians and Jews. He proposed legislation discriminating agianst the *dhimmi* (855), which became the fundamental law of the caliphate and the basis of the trend towards religious intolerance within Islam. The freedom he was granted in determining religious policy, together with the constant wars faced by Byzantium, led M. to believe he could govern alone, but his hopes were crushed by the opposition of his Turkish guard at Samarra, who revolted and assassinated him.

CHI (1970).

MYSTERY AND MIRACLE PLAYS M. were the common form of religious drama in medieval Christianity. Performed in front of the main doorways of cathedrals and churches, these plays were basically dramatical representations of New Testament scenes and were generally related to specific feasts. Already in practice in the 11th century, the M. developed into complete units in the following century. Among them, the most important were the Passions, performed on the eve of Easter.

G. Cohen, *Le Théatre religieux au Moyen Age* (1947).

MYSTICISM The term implies an immediate knowledge of God attained through personal religious experience. It is primarily achieved in a state of prayer and there are different degrees of communion, ranging from short, temporary mystical states to a permanent union with God, the so-called "mystic marriage". M. was practised in most of the medieval religions, both polytheistic, such as Buddhism, Taoism and *Hinduism, and monotheistic, as in *Islam (e.g., the Sufists), *Judaism (the *kabbalah) and *Christianity. Distinctive of the Christian form of M. is its emphasis on two elements often absent in other religions. Christian M. recognized that the reality which it penetrated transcended the soul and cosmos. In place of all notions of absorption of the soul into the divine, it posited that the union was one of love and will, in which the distinction between creator and creature was permanently retained.

Christian M. gave rise to early Christian *monasticism and passed from the ascetic fathers of the 3rd and 4th centuries to the established Church, both the Greek-Orthodox and the Roman Catholic. Psycho-physical phenomena, such as dreams, trances, visions and states of ecstasy, frequently accompanied the mystical experience, and were often a means of attaining pure spirituality. The ascetic monastic movements, such as the *Cistercians in the 12th century (especially *Bernard of Clairvaux) and the *Franciscans of the 13th and 14th centuries, adopted the mystical experience as an integral step on the path to salvation. A number of visionary women also played an important role in the development of medieval M. The occurrence of the *Black Death sparked a revival in mystical experience in the second half of the 14th and the 15th century, manifested in the works of Master *Eckhart in particular.

H. Thurston, *The Physical Phenomena of Mysticism* (1952);

Evelyn Underhill, *Mysticism* (1911).

N

NAFELS, BATTLE OF (1388) A battle fought between the *Hapsburgs and the Swiss people of Glarus, the latter intent on securing the independence of their canton. Glarus had joined the *Swiss Confederation in 1352, but overlordship of the territory had been recovered by the Hapsburgs in 1355. Attempts by the latter to restore the feudal administration provoked frequent uprisings in the canton. When the revolt reached major proportions, Duke *Albert III of Austria sent a large army to repress the rebels. The Swiss victory at N. allowed the return of Glarus to the Confederation and was a decisive step in its attainment of formal independence.

G. R. Potter, *History of Switzerland* (1952).

NAHMANIDES (Rabbi Moses Ben Nahman, Ramban; 1194-1270) Jewish philosopher, exegete, poet and physician. Born at Gerona in Catalonia, N. came from a family of rabbis and scholars. He studied at the school of Gerona, basically learning the mystical teachings of the *Kabbalah and medicine, the latter later becoming his source of income. N.'s exegetical works brought him fame among the Spanish Jews. In 1232 his advice was sought at the court of King *James I of Aragon. N. also became the spiritual leader of the Jewish communities of Catalonia and took part in the disputes concerning the teachings of *Maimonides which had split the Jewish communities. N. adopted a moderate attitude, trying to bring about a reconciliation between the disputants. In 1263 N. defended Judaism in a public debate against Christian theologians (among them the converted Jew, Pablo Christiani) at Barcelona. His resolute apology earned him the king's respect, but at the same time his position became delicate and he was attacked by the *friars, who accused him of blasphemy and obtained a formal petition from Pope *Clemens IV for his prosecution (1267). N. was forced to leave Spain and settled in Palestine. There he worked to revive the Jewish settlement in Jerusalem and attempted to promote the idea of establishing a Jewish entity in Palestine, based on widespread immigration. N. died at Acre in 1270.

Among his works, that of particular importance is his biblical commentary, which is basically in keeping with the Spanish exegetical school, but was also influenced by the French *Tosafists. N. based his conclusions on the philosophical method of the *Aristotelians, trying to prove the logical aspect of faith. His poetry, on the other hand, reflects his unconditional faith and contains some of the mystical ideas he absorbed from his education at Gerona. N. did not, however, develop mystical works; he was rather the representative of the realistic trend of Jewish thought in the 13th century.

H. Chone, *Nahmanides* (1930).

NAJERA (NAVARRETTE), BATTLE OF (1367) One of the main battles in the civil war between *Peter the Cruel, king of Castile and *Henry of Trastamare, pretender to the throne. It was fought near the town of Najera in northeastern Castile. A French army, commanded by Bertrand *Du Guesclin, supported Henry while an Anglo-Gascon army, under the command of *Edward the Black Prince, backed the forces of Peter. The English force was victorious and Du Guesclin was taken prisoner; however, the battle did not bring about any basic changes in the fate of Castile, since Henry successfully gained the Castilian throne in 1369.

E. Perroy, *The Hundred Years' War* (1957).

NAMUR City in *Belgium. An administrative centre in the *Carolingian period, N. belonged to *Francia Media (843), later the kingdom and duchy of *Lotharingia. In 908 the city and its surroundings became a county, its counts becoming direct vassals of the *Holy Roman emperors in the 11th century. In 1420 N. came under the rule of the dukes of *Burgundy, the heirs of the counts of N. The castle of the counts of N., which dominated the valley of the Meuse River, was improved in the 15th century.

L. Genicot, *L'Economie Namuroise au Moyen Age* (1935).

NANCY City in *Lorraine. The borough developed in the middle of the 11th century around a feudal castle built by the dukes of Lorraine. During the 12th century the town grew and walls were built. The dukes of Lorraine settled and established their capital in N. in 1180. The city was burnt in 1218 by Count Theobald of Bar, but was later rebuilt. It grew as an administrative centre, being the base of the ducal court.

C. Pfister, *Histoire de Nancy* (1902).

NAPLES City in southern *Italy. After the fall of the Roman empire, N. remained one of the greatest cities of southern Italy, although it began to decline. Conquered by the *Ostrogoths in 493, it was one of the main objectives of the Byzantine reconquest of Italy and fell to *Belisarius in 536. In 543 the Ostrogothic king Totila seized N., which remained under Gothic rule until 553, when the Byzantines reconquered the city and its surroundings. The Byzantine administrative system was introduced in the territory and N. became the capital of a duchy, whose heads, high Byzantine dignitaries, were appointed by the imperial court from 661 to 755. In 763 the duchy gained its independence and local dynasties ruled it until 1027, resisting the invasions of the *Lombards, the *Normans, and the Byzantines. In the 9th century the city was attacked by *Arabs from north Africa, who destroyed its harbour, badly harming its commerce. In 1027 the duchy was united with the principality of Capua and was ruled by a dynasty of Byzantine origin, which continued to reign in

Gerard of Vaudemont and his wife; 12th-century sculpture at the Chapelle des Cordeliers, Nancy

Castel Nuovo, Naples, built in the 13th-15th centuries

accordance with the precepts of the Byzantine constitution. In 1139 N. was conquered by *Roger II, the Norman king of *Sicily, and remained part of the Sicilian kingdom until 1282. During this time, N. gradually became the centre of Sicily's continental possessions, and a royal castle (*Castel dell'Ovo*) was built in the city in the second half of the 12th century. *Frederick II founded a university at N. in 1224, which became an important cultural and scholarly centre. He also began the construction of a new royal castle (*Castello Nuovo*), completed after his death. This castle dominates the harbour and is one of the finest specimens of Gothic architecture. Conquered in 1266 by *Charles of Anjou, the city became the capital of the Angevin kingdom of N. in 1282. Under Angevin rule, N. became one of the most prosperous cities of Italy and numerous royal structures were erected. The city was noted by *Boccaccio for its beauty and splendour, but also for the wanton behaviour of its population.

G. Doria, *Napoli, Storia di una Capitale* (1958).

NAPLES, KINGDOM OF   N. was established in 1282, after the *Sicilian Vespers, due to the split in the kingdom of Sicily. The mainland territories of southern Italy, which had belonged to the Sicilian kingdom and which remained under the rule of *Charles of Anjou, were united around the new capital of Naples. Up to the beginning of the 14th century the efforts of the Angevin kings were principally devoted to the struggle against the *Aragonese, who were intent on reuniting the kingdom of Sicily. It was not until 1302 that peace was obtained and N. was recognized as a distinct political entity. Under King *Robert (1309-43), N. became a powerful realm in Italy, influencing the policy of Rome and the northern Italian states. In addition, the Neapolitan kingdom continued to exercise influence over Greece and the Balkans, in accordance with the principles of the eastern policy established by Charles of Anjou. Robert's kinship with the Angevin branch in *Hungary enabled him to expand his interests in the Balkans and N. rivalled Byzantium, Venice and Aragon. During the first half of the 14th century the court of N. was one of the most splendid in Europe, attracting

nobility, scholars, writers and artists. However, N.'s foreign wars and the lavish expenses of the court contributed to the poverty in the kingdom, which lacked the means to develop its economy. There was no strong local middle class in N. and all commercial activity was handled by foreign businessmen, particularly of Tuscany, Venice, Genoa and Marseilles. During the reign of Robert's daughter, *Joan I (1343-82), and her favourites, dynastical struggles erupted. Thus, the kingdom suffered from civil wars and total anarchy. If not for certain external circumstances, such as the *Great Schism of the papacy and the lack of stability in central Italy, King *Ladislas (1399-1414) could hardly have restored Neapolitan influence in Italy and royal power in his kingdom. After Ladislas' death, anarchy again reigned and N. was disputed between certain princes who sought the inheritance of *Joan II, especially *René of Anjou-Lorraine-Provence and *Alfonso of Aragon.

B. Croce, *Historia dell Regno di Napoli* (1953).

NARBONNE   City and religious centre of *Languedoc. Conquered in 417 by the *Visigoths, N. served at one time as their capital (ultimately established at Toledo in Spain). Following the collapse of the Visigothic kingdom of Spain, N. was conquered by the *Arabs (719), but Moslem rule was weak and the real power over the city remained in the hands of the Visigothic aristocracy. In 757 *Pepin the Short conquered the city and province and annexed it to the *Frankish kingdom. Its prominent Jewish community was granted wide privileges, an unusual phenomenon in western Europe; in fact, leaders of the community were known as "Kings of the Jews" by the Christian population. Under *Charlemagne, N. became part of the march of *Gothia and in the 9th century belonged to the counts of *Toulouse, who were considered territorial princes in Languedoc. In the 11th century the viscounts of N. (vassals of the counts) seized power in the city; this placed them in constant conflict with the archbishops, who also claimed control of N. The viscounts reached the height of their power in the 12th century as a result of their relations with the counts of *Barcelona and their allegiance to King *Louis VII of France. During the Crusade against the *Albigenses, N. was conquered by Simon of *Montfort (1212) and in 1218 became the possession of the French royal crown. Its trade continued to prosper and the harbour, built at the mouth of the Aude River, played an active part in Mediterranean commerce. However, at the beginning of the 14th century the water currents changed and the mouth of the river moved northwards. As a result, N.'s harbour became filled with sand and the city subsequently declined and was replaced by *Montpellier.

E. Carbonnel, *Histoire de Narbonne* (1923).

NARSES (c. 478-568)   Byzantine general. N. was employed in the financial management of the imperial palace of Constantinople. In 532 he took part in the repression of the Niké revolt. His success gained him access to a great military career and, after winning the confidence of *Justinian, N. was appointed governor of Alexandria and charged with repressing religious rebellions (535). In 538 he was sent to Italy to assist *Belisarius and in 552 replaced him as commander-in-chief. N. defeated the *Ostrogoths and annexed their kingdom to the Byzantine empire. From 555 he was the governor of Italy and imposed a strong rule in the country, exercising both civil and military authority. He was recalled by Justinian II in 567.

J. W. Barker, *Justinian and the Later Roman Empire* (1966).

NASIR, AL-MALIK AL- (1284-1340) *Mameluke sultan of the Bahri Mamelukes of Egypt. Son of *Qulawun, he was proclaimed sultan upon his father's death (1293), but was dethroned by a palace revolt led by his father's slaves in 1294. Restored in 1298, he reigned until 1308, when a second palace revolt, led by Baibars II, compelled him to abdicate. In 1309 his throne was again restored; at this point, N. dedicated his reign to economic reforms, which eventually brought prosperity to Egypt. In 1323 he reached a peace agreement with the *Mongols of Persia, which allowed him to reinforce his authority in Syria.

CHI (1970).

NATIONES (Latin: nations) A special organization within the medieval *universities. First created at Paris at the beginning of the 13th century, the purpose of the N. was to gather together teachers and students originating from the same country. The N. generally dealt with practical matters, such as the distribution of funds, lodgings and social conventions. The organization was related, to an extent, to earlier gatherings of English teachers and scholars held at Paris from the second half of the 12th century. The first N. to be established at the University of Paris were the Anglo-German, the French, the Norman and the Picardian (which included citizens of the Low Countries). The N. were often assembled to make decisions concerning current business and the administration of their possessions; and officers were elected to preside over the meetings. These organizations became a constitutional part of the university and were consulted in the election of rectors. Gradually, colleges were founded by the N. and their officers began to offer instruction. The Parisian model was eventually adopted by other medieval universities.

P. Kibre, *The Nationes in the Medieval Universities* (1948).

NATURAL LAW See LAW.

NAVARRE Kingdom in northeastern *Spain, lying between the Pyrénées on the upper Ebro River. The realm originated as a result of the strong particularistic attitude of the *Basque and Ibero-Romanized populace of the city of *Pamplona and its surroundings, who rebelled against the *Visigoths in the 5th and 6th centuries. The latter had never actually achieved real power in the country. In the 8th century the local population opposed the Arab advance and defeated the armies sent against them. Thus, the realm maintained its independence. This small Christian country also repulsed the attempts of *Charlemagne to conquer it (787). Although the emperor had succeeded in destroying the walls of Pamplona, the population attacked the Frankish rearguard and defeated it at *Roncesvalles. However, the country of N. lacked organization and was merely an anarchical confideration of clans, tribes and small townships. It was not until the 9th century that the lords of Pamplona, who had attained a leading position, gradually united the various groups. Unification was completed during the reign of *Sancho I (905-25), who became the first king of N. His successors fought the Moslems and took part in the first *Reconquista* wars. The kingdom reached the peak of its power

under *Sancho III (1000-35), who conquered *Castile (1029) and introduced the *Cluny order to N., thereby involving it in the reconstruction of Christian Spain. Following Sancho's death, dynastical wars broke out and N. lost possession of Castile; in addition, *Aragon gained its independence, becoming a separate kingdom. As a result, the territory of N. was reduced to the area north of the Ebro and the kingdom lost all direct contact with Moslem Spain, remaining a small realm situated between France, Aragon and Castile. Moreover, Aragonese influence came to be felt in N. and between 1076-1134 the realm was ruled by the kings of Aragon. Garcia V (1134-50) renewed its independence and gained the kingdom's support. The particularistic spirit was salient again in 1234, upon the death of *Sancho VII, who had attempted to appoint *James I of Aragon as his successor. A local uprising annulled the will and the crown was offered to a member of the collateral branch, Count *Thibaut of Champagne. Under its French kings, who continued to reside in northern France, N. became a distant province. The French Estates played a part in their government and the kingdom itself was involved in the French dynastical struggles, due to the marriage of the heiress of N.-Champagne to King *Philip IV of France. As it was the custom in N. to recognize inheritance of the crown through women, the Estates refused to recognize the *Valois kings of France as their rulers and elected the descendants of *Charles IV, the counts of Evreux. Their involvement in the French dynastical struggles, especially those of *Charles the Bad, weakened the realm, whose resources were wasted by its kings. *Charles the Noble reformed N. and brought it prosperity. The marriage of his daughter, Blanche, to King *John II of Aragon reunited the two kingdoms (1425-79). The union, however, only served to revive the earlier antagonism and, for a while, N. became independent.

A. Castro, *The Structure of Spanish History* (1954).

NAVARRETTE See NAJERA.

NAVE The central part of the *church where the faithful sit during prayers. The N. is separated from the choir by a screen or by an elevation of the floor and from the aisles by columns or pillars. It derives its name from the Latin *navis* (ship), since Christianity was symbolized as a ship sailing in foreign waters.

NAVIGATION ACTS A series of ordinances proclaimed by the kings of England, beginning in the 14th century, which were meant to protect English maritime trade. The N. of 1381, issued by *Richard II, is the first comprehensive legislation in the field, giving priority to English vessels in the transport of goods to and from the realm's harbours. The act had no immediate repercussions, due to the lack of English vessels; however, at a later date, it contributed to the development of the English commercial fleet.

B. Lyon, *A Constitutional and Legal History of Medieval England* (1960).

NAZARETH City in southern *Galilee. The village became famous as the home of Mary, Joseph and the child Jesus. As early as the beginning of the Byzantine period, shrines were established in N., which became one of the most popular pilgrimage sites in the *Holy Land. The earliest shrines were destroyed after the Arab conquest in 637, but the constant influx of pilgrims and the growth of hagiographical legends led to their recon-

Capital from the remains of the Crusader Church of the Annunciation at Nazareth

struction. Under the *Crusaders, the village grew into a city, where a Romanesque cathedral was built. In 1263 N. was conquered by the *Mamelukes under *Baibars and destroyed.

C. Kopp, *Beiträge zur Geschichte Nazareths* (1948).

NECKAM, ALEXANDER (1157-1217) English scholar. N. was trained for an ecclesiastical career at Paris; c. 1180 he began to teach theology there. In 1186 N. returned to England, where he became an *Austin canon although he continued to teach. In 1213 he was made abbot of Cirencester. While N. wrote commentaries on the Bible, his chief works were *De Naturis Rerum,* in which he summed up contemporary knowledge of the natural sciences, and *De Nominibus Utensilium,* a catalogue of instruments and their technical usage. The information for the latter book was obtained through his observations at London and Paris.

C. H. Haskins, *Studies in History of Medieval Science* (1927).

NEDAO, BATTLE OF Fought between the sons of *Attila in 454, N. was followed by an uprising of the Germanic tribes subjugated by the *Huns. As a result, the empire of the Huns was destroyed.

NEIDHART OF RENNENTHAL (1180-1250) German poet. Born to a family of knights, N. began to write satirical poetry in German at the beginning of the 13th century. He introduced the *Hæfische Dorfpoesie* (courtly village poetry), an adaptation of French poetry of courtly love set in the German village. This type of poetry focused on praise of nature rather than of love for ladies. N. introduced the naturalistic style to poetry, which made him one of the major and most popular German artists of the *Hohenstaufen period.

M. O. Walshe, *Medieval German Literature* (1962).

NENNIUS (9th century) *Anglo-Saxon historian. A monk at the York minster, N. produced a detailed description of the history of *Northumbria. His main work, *Historia Britonum,* deals with the customs and legends of the Britons, prior to and during the conquest of England by the Anglo-Saxons. N. was the first to mention King *Arthur, who later became the hero of the medieval Arthurian legend.

R. S. Loomis, *Arthurian Literature in the Middle Ages* (1957).

NEO-PLATONISM See PLATONISM.

NEPOTISM The term as used in the Middle Ages referred to irregular appointments within the church, whereby family members were promoted to high ecclesiastical offices. While the feudal concept of kinship and familial solidarity caused N. to be considered a positive quality – and even a sacred duty – in lay society, the practice was attacked in the Church, where promotion was to be decided on the basis of spiritual qualities. The *Gregorian reform linked the practice to simony, but was unable to rid the Church of N. Abbots, bishops and popes often appointed their nephews to various dignities. Such practices at Rome allowed the rise of families such as the *Caietani, the *Colonna and the *Orsini. N. was most widely implemented during the *Avignon period of the papacy in the 14th century. At that time considerable numbers of relatives were appointed cardinals, officials at the papal court and bishops.

W. Ullmann, *A Short History of the Papacy in the Middle Ages* (1972).

NESTORIANS Heretical Christian sect. Based on the doctrine that there are two separate persons in the incarnate Christ, one divine and the other human, it opposed both the Orthodox and the *Monophysite dogma. The founder of the sect was Nestorius (d. 451), a native of Syria, who became patriarch of Constantinople in 428. His teachings provoked open opposition at Constantinople and the criticism of Patriarch Cyril of Alexandria, the leader of the orthodoxy. Also condemned by the Church of Rome (430), Nestorius was summoned before the Council of *Ephesus, which condemned his teachings, deposed him (431) and banished him to Upper Egypt. Some bishops in the East refused, however, to abide by the condemnation and they organized themselves into a separate church, whose centre was in *Persia and northern *Mesopotamia. In the 5th and 6th centuries the N. were active missionaries and the sect spread to central Asia. Under Moslem rule, they enjoyed religious freedom and in 775 their patriarchate was moved to Baghdad. The patriarchs were considered high dignitaries of the caliphate. In the 9th-13th centuries, Nestorian missionaries reached *China and the Mongol territories; in the Byzantine empire, however, they were persecuted and executed. Generally speaking, the N. remained a small, loose sect and their influence in Iraq declined during the 9th century. While some members of the *Genghis-khanid dynasty embraced Nestorianism, the Islamization which took place among the Mongols during the second half of the 13th century dealt a serious blow to the sect.

A. R. Vine, *The Nestorian Churches* (1937).

NEUSTRIA *Frankish province and realm. In the 6th-8th centuries, its territory largely corresponded to the northwestern part of the *Frankish kingdom, between the Somme and Loire Rivers, its centre being in Paris. The repeated divisions of the Frankish kingdom gave N. a separate political identity. The area had its own *Merovingian kings and *mayors of the palace; the last of

the mayors, *Ebroin, was defeated by *Pepin II, who reunited the Frankish kingdom. During the 9th and 10th centuries N.'s frontiers were established between the Seine and Loire Rivers, and it became a duchy within the kingdom of France. Its dukes called themselves "dukes of the Franks". The northern part of N. was conquered by the *Normans and later became part of Normandy. After the accession of the *Capetian dukes to the throne of France (987), N. ceased to exist as a distinct unit and was divided among feudal counties and seigniories.

F. Lot, *Naissance de la France* (1953).

NEVA, BATTLE OF (1240) A battle in which the *Novgorod army, led by Prince *Alexander, defeated a strong *Swedish force which had attempted to conquer northwestern *Russia and *Novgorod. The fighting took place on the banks of the Neva River in northwestern Russia. Alexander's victory (thanks to which he earned the cognomen "Nevski") is considered one of the most important events in the making of Russia. It signified the successful defence of both the Russian soil and Orthodoxy and, in this way, compensated for the fall of Kiev and its conquest by the Mongols of *Batu-khan. Alexander, the hero of the day, became the grand prince of *Vladimir in 1246. He laid the foundations for the revival of Russian power in the northern principalities of Vladimir-Suzdal and *Moscow.

G. Vernadsky, *Medieval Russia* (1953).

NEVERS City in central France along the western border of *Burgundy. In the 11th century N. became the centre of a powerful county. The local dynasty became associated with the Capetian dukes of Burgundy in the 13th century and the dukes of *Bourbon in the following century. This made the counts of N. members of the highest French aristocracy in the late Middle Ages and they established relations with the most prominent European royal houses.

P. S. Lewis, *Later Medieval France* (1968).

NEWCASTLE UPON TYNE City in northern *England on the Scottish frontier. N. was originally the site of a castle, built in 1080 by *William the Conqueror to defend England's northern border. The borough emerged in the 12th century in the area of the castle. *Henry II promoted the development of northern territories, and, as a result, N. became an economic centre which controlled the trade between eastern England and Scotland. In 1172 a new castle was built near the bridge on the Tyne River and the centre of N. was likewise relocated. In 1216 the city was granted a *charter of liberties, establishing self-rule on the part of the burghers. Wool manufacture and trade developed in northern England during the 14th century and consequently N. became one of the major commercial centres of the country.

E. Carus-Wilson, *Medieval Merchant Venturers* (1954).

NEW TESTAMENT See BIBLE.

NIBELUNGENLIED (The Song of the Nibelungs) Anonymous German epic. Composed *c.* 1200, it is one of the greatest works of medieval *German literature. The poem is based on the rich folklore traditions of the German tribal period, as well as on historical events which became legendary over the centuries. The hero of the epic, the Netherlandish prince Siegfried, had seized the treasure of the Nibelungs and become king of the Rhine. This treasure later passed to the *Burgundian kings, after which time the Nibelungs were called Burgundians. Following is a short synopsis of the plot. Siegfried falls in love with Kriemhild, sister to King Gunther of the Burgundians and helps Gunther to defeat Queen Brunhilde so as to win his sister's hand in marriage. Brunhilde decides to take revenge and hires the knight, Hagen, to murder Siegfried. The widow Kriemhild then marries *Attila the Hun in hopes of avenging the memory of her beloved first husband. All-out war ensues and the treasure of the Nibelungs is sunk in the Rhine. Attila is represented in the poem as a loyal Christian knight, fighting for the honour of his wife. The legend is based on popular traditions concerning the invasion of the Huns in central Europe and the defeat inflicted on the Burgundians in 436 near Worms.

N. Thorp, *The Study of the Nibelungen* (1940).

NICAEA City in northwestern Asia Minor and one of the Roman imperial residences before the establishment of the capital at Constantinople. N. became famous as the seat of the First *Oecumenical *Council of the Church, convened by Emperor *Constantine in 325. There the Arian heresy was condemned and the Orthodox-Catholic creed was adopted. Under Byzantine rule N. remained an important centre. It was conquered in 1075 by the *Seljuks, but *c.* 20 years later was regained by Emperor *Alexius Comnenus, aided by the participants of the First *Crusade. In 1204, when Constantinople was conquered by the Crusaders, part of the Byzantine leadership fled to the city and founded the empire of N. (see below).

NICAEA, EMPIRE OF (1204-61) The N. was founded by *Theodore I Lascaris, who concentrated what remained of the Byzantine administration, Orthodox church and nobility in the city of Nicaea and its surroundings. Theodore's claims to supremacy in the Byzantine world were disputed by the despots of *Epirus and the emperors of *Trebizond and only gradually was the primacy of N. recognized. This occurred due to the establishment of the Greek Orthodox patriarchate in the city, making N. an important cultural centre whose impact was felt throughout the Greek Orthodox world. Theodore and his successors made numerous attempts to destroy the Latin empire of Constantinople. By 1230 they had begun the reconquest of Thrace and parts of *Greece, but they kept their capital at N. despite its rather non-central location. The independence of N. was strongly promoted by the leaders of the Greek Church, whose increasing anti-Catholic feelings caused them to define their theological position and oppose any compromise with the papacy, whom they held responsible for the persecution of the Orthodox clergy at Constantinople and in Greece. This leadership influenced the cultural patterns of the later Byzantine civilization which developed at N. In 1261 Emperor *Michael VIII Palaeologus succeeded in regaining Constantinople; thereafter the capital was restored to the prestigious centre of the Byzantine empire and N. was reduced to a provincial town. In 1329 it was conquered by the *Ottoman Turks.

A. Gardner, *The Laskarids of Nicaea* (1912).

NICEPHORUS, St. (758-829) Patriarch of *Constantinople (806-15) and historian. Member of a noble family of Constantinople, N. became a high dignitary at the imperial palace. In 787 he represented the emperor at the Council of *Nicaea where a settlement of the *ico-noclastic controversy was elaborated. After the council ended, N. withdrew from public life and founded a monastery. In 806 he was appointed patriarch, but refused to accept the iconoclastic policy of Emperor *Leo V, whom he had crowned and who deposed him in 815. Many of N.'s writings deal with the iconoclastic controversy and are of a polemical character. N. also wrote a history of the Byzantine empire, covering the years 602-770, which was highly praised for its accuracy.

P. J. Alexander, *The Patriarch Nicephorus of Constantinople* (1958).

NICEPHORUS I (d. 811) *Byzantine emperor (802-11). A general in the Byzantine army, N. was proclaimed emperor after a successful uprising against Empress *Irene His throne, however, was threatened by the revolts of other army generals. In 806 N. was defeated by an army sent to Asia Minor by *Harun Al-Rashid and was thereafter compelled to pay a large tribute. From 807 N.'s efforts were concentrated on protecting Constantinople from the raids of the *Bulgarians. His initial victories motivated an unwise decision to invade Bulgaria; he was defeated and killed in 811 during the battle.

CMedH, IV.

NICEPHORUS II, Phocas (913-69) *Byzantine emperor (963-69). member of an aristocratic family, N. distinguished himself as a general; in 955 he was appointed commander-in-chief of the eastern army which fought the *Moslems. In 963 N. married *Theophano, the widow of Emperor *Romanus II and was proclaimed emperor. His reign marked a brilliant period in Byzantine history. In 961 N. captured *Crete, restoring Byzantine supremacy in the Mediterranean Sea. Four years later he also reconquered *Cyprus and began to prepare a military expedition into *Syria, intending to recover the former Byzantine provinces which had been lost to the Arabs in the 7th century. In 969 N. seized Antioch and Aleppo. His offensive was interrupted, however, due to a palace plot; the emperor was murdered by *John Tzimisces, his rival for the favours of the empress.

CMedH, IV.

NICEPHORUS III, Botaniates (d. 1082) *Byzantine emperor (1087-81). A general of Asia Minor, he was proclaimed emperor by rebels opposing the reign of *Michael VII Ducas. Supported by the *Seljuks, he came to Constantinople and defeated two other rivals, but was unable to restore order and in 1081 retired to a monastery.

NICETAS STETHATOS (1000-80) Byzantine theologian. N. became a monk at the famous monastery of *Studion and there pursued his ideas of mystical orthodoxy. In 1053-54 he actively supported Patriarch *Michael Cerularius in the disputes with the delegation sent to Constantinople by Pope *Leo IX. His writings, which contain anti-Latin theological arguments, bear a sharp polemical character but also display great theological knowledge.

S. Runciman, *The Eastern Schism* (1947).

NICHOLAS, St. (4th century) Though one of the most popular of saints in both Orthodox and Catholic churches, little is known about his life other than that he was bishop of Myra (Asia Minor) and took part in the Council of *Nicaea in 325. Numerous traditions and legends have been connected with his life and offer much spurious information. The cult of N. spread in the 6th century, and in 565 *Justinian participated in a procession in his honour, which marks the first great official manifestation of his cult. In the 11th century a legend grew regarding the transference of his relics to the West; in this way N.'s cult was introduced into Italy, where pilgrimages were made from 1087 to his supposed burial site at *Bari. N. is considered the patron saint of sailors and of children (thanks to a legend according to which he delivered presents to the poor children of Myra). He became very popular in the latter respect as "Santa Claus". N. was also proclaimed patron saint of Russia. His feast-day is 6 December. N. was the subject of many artistic medieval works. The transformation of N. into Father Christmas or Father January took place later, first in Germany.

E. Crozier, *The Life and Legends of Saint Nicholas* (1949).

NICHOLAS I, St. (c. 800-67) Pope (858-67). Born to a noble family of Rome, N. entered the service of the papal court in 845 and was gradually promoted, becoming one of the most influential members of the Curia. After his election as pope, he led a long struggle with the eastern church, refusing to recognize the deposition of Patriarch Ignatius of Constantinople and his replacement by *Photius. In order to emphasize his supremacy, N. sent a mission to convert the Bulgarians, who were actually subject to the religious authority of the patriarch of Constantinople. Photius responded by excommunicating the pope in 867. In the West N. attempted to reinforce papal authority over the Frankish church and to strengthen his spiritual supremacy over the *Carolingian kings.

J. Haller, *Nikolaus I und "Pseudo-Isidor"* (1936).

NICHOLAS II (c. 980-1061) Pope (1059-61). Born in Burgundy, the monk Gerhard became bishop of Florence and in 1059 was elected pope without imperial consent. N. assembled a Lateran council and there issued a decree concerning the papal election, making it the sole right and responsibility of the cardinals and denying imperial interference. The bull was ineffectively attacked in 1061 by the German bishops and it came to officially dictate the conditions for papal elections.

A. Clavel, *Pape Nicolas II, son oeuvre disciplinaire* (1906).

NICHOLAS III (Giovanni Gaetano Orsini; 1220-80) Pope (1277-80). Member of the powerful Roman family of *Orsini, N. entered the service of the papal court and in 1244 was made cardinal. N. was realistic concerning political affairs. He aimed to enlarge the·pope's authority over secular matters in Italy as well as to create a new political balance between *Charles of Anjou (whose influence in Italy threatened papal authority) and Emperor *Rudolf of Hapsburg.

J. Haller, *Das Papsttum,* IV (1954).

NICHOLAS IV (Girolamo Masci; 1227-92) Pope (1288-92). A native of Ascoli, Italy, N. became a *Franciscan friar. In 1272 he was sent to Constantinople to negotiate the union of the Latin and Greek churches and, after his return, became general of the Franciscan order. In 1281 he joined the papal court and was made cardinal. In 1288, following a long dispute between French and Italian cardinals, N. was elected pope as a compromise candidate. He supported the *Colonna family and appointed its members to high dignities in the papal court. N. was responsible for reaching a compromise between France and Aragon. Beginning in 1291, when news of the fall of *Acre reached him, N. began to organize a new *Crusade. For that purpose, he sent a mission to the *Mongol court in China.

D. Waley, *The Papal State in the 13th century* (1961).

NICHOLAS OF BASLE (d. 1395) Heretic. N. was a *Beghard who preached in the district of Basle. He claimed that those who followed his teachings were free of sin and directly inspired by God. Arrested by the *Inquisition, N. was brought to Vienna, tried and burnt.

H. C. Lea, *The Inquisition of the Middle Ages* (1898).

NICHOLAS BREAKSPEAR See ADRIAN IV.

NICHOLAS OF LYRA (c. 1270-1340) *Franciscan scholar and exegete. Born at Lire in Normandy, N. joined the Franciscan order and was sent to study at Paris. In 1308 he became professor of theology and focused on the study of the Bible. He learned Hebrew so as to become directly acquainted with the Hebrew commentaries. His work became widely known and brought him fame as the foremost exegete in the western Christian world.

B. Smalley, *The Study of the Bible in the Middle Ages* (1952).

NICHOLAS OF ORESME See ORESME, NICHOLAS.

NICOMEDIA City of Asia Minor. One of the imperial residences of the later Roman empire, N. later became a provincial capital of the *Byzantine empire. The city gradually declined and became a small town in the high Middle Ages.

NICOPOLIS A town in *Bulgaria, the site of the battle between the *Ottoman Turks under *Bayazid and the west European crusaders (1396). The latter had joined the fight in response to the appeal of the Byzantines and the papacy, who called for the deliverance of Constantinople from the Turkish siege. The Ottoman victory allowed Bayazid to continue his attacks on Constantinople and his advance in the Balkans. The Crusader defeat dealt a serious blow to the idea of the Crusade.

A. S. Atiya, *The Crusade in the Later Middle Ages* (1938).

NICOSIA Capital of *Cyprus. The city of N. was a small provincial capital while under Byzantine and Arab domination. It grew and prospered under the rule of the *Crusader Lusignan dynasty. The Lusignan kings built numerous Gothic structures in the city, among them the cathedral church (built 1209-1325) in which Gothic themes are interwoven with elements of Byzantine architecture. The establishment of the royal court at N. caused the Frankish (French) and Greek cultures to merge in the 13th and 14th centuries. This, in turn, led to the emergence of the "overseas" nobility, mainly characterized by its cosmopolitan lifestyle.

G. Hill, *A History of Cyprus* (1950).

NIELS King of *Denmark (1104-34). The fifth son of *Sweyn Estrithson he was elected to his throne, which was threatened by the rise of feudal trends among the nobility. N.'s main concern was to make the crown hereditary and for that purpose he plotted the murder of his nephew, *Canute Lavard. N. was killed during a general revolt in the kingdom, while in flight to Schleswig.

P. G. Foote and D. M. Wilson, *The Viking Achievement* (1970).

NIKITA (11th century) *Cathari leader. Of Bulgarian origin, N. was one of the leaders of the *Manichaeans in the Balkans and resided in Constantinople for a time. In 1167 he came to *Languedoc, where he organized the *Albigenses and presided over their Council of St.

Felix, in which the heretical movement was organized.

S. Runciman, *The Mediaeval Manichee* (1946).

NIKLI Town in *Morea. N. became famous for the Parliament of Dames held there in 1260 by the Frankish nobility of Greece. The meeting was convened so as to negotiate peace with Emperor *Michael VIII following his victory at *Pelagonia. The fact that the majority of lords had fallen or been captured at Pelagonia and could not attend granted the ladies a paramount role in the meeting.

W. Miller, *The Latins in the Levant, A History of Frankish Greece* (1908).

NILUS OF GROTAFERRATA (c. 910-1005) Hermit. Born in Calabria to the noble family of Rossano, he became a monk and was noted for his ascetic life and his learning. N. attempted to reconcile Byzantine and *Benedictine monasticism. In 995 he left the monastic community to become a hermit and adopted a severely ascetic way of life at Grotaferrata. His learning and saintliness won him many disciples, as well as the veneration of aristocrats and royal figures, who sought his advice, among them Emperor *Otto III.

J. Décarreaux, *Normands, Papes et Moines en Italie Méridionale* (1974).

NINEVEH, BATTLE OF (628) Battle fought between the Byzantine army of Emperor *Heraclius and the Persians, under *Chosroes II, near the Persian capital of Ctesiphon on the Tigris River. The battle marked the peak of the Byzantine counter-offensive, which compelled the Persians to withdraw from Syria and Palestine and isolated their army in Asia Minor. Heraclius' victory brought anarchy to Persia but also weakened the Byzantine empire. Thus, it actually contributed to the destruction of the two powers in the Near East and facilitated Arab expansion and conquest of the area.

CMedH, IV.

NISH City in northern *Macedonia. Until the 8th century it was a provincial capital of the Byzantine empire, although it was gradually inhabited by *Slavs, who changed its ethnic character. In 817 the city was conquered by the *Bulgarians and was part of their kingdom until its recovery by Byzantium in 1014. N. served as a passageway for the participants in the First *Crusade in 1096. In the 13th and 14th centuries, it belonged to the Bulgarians and the *Serbs and was one of the great centres of the Serbian realm. In 1386 it was conquered by the *Ottoman Turks.

H. W. V. Temperley, *History of Serbia* (1919).

NISHAPUR City in *Khorasan (eastern Persia). Founded as a royal city and residence in the 3rd century, N. became a provincial centre after the Arab conquest of Khorasan (660). In the 9th and 10th centuries it was the capital of local Iranian and Turkish dynasties. In 1037 the city was conquered by the *Seljuks, whose leader, *Tughril Bek, made N. the capital of his state. Under Seljuk rule the city flourished and became a great economic centre. Moreover, vizier *Nizam Al-Mulk founded a prominent academy, which was renowned throughout the eastern Moslem states. During the 12th century the city was devastated by earthquakes and in 1221 was ravaged by the *Mongols.

G. le Strange, *The Lands of the Eastern Caliphate* (1905).

NISI PRIUS Legislation issued in 1285 by King *Edward I, intended to improve judicial procedure in medieval England. The statute stipulated that cases which were supposed to be brought before the central court of justice could also be dealt with by the *sheriff and jurors of the shire, who would hold trial on a certain date. The exception to the rule occurred when the judges of *assize arrived in the county prior to that date.

B. Lyon, *A Constitutional and Legal History of Medieval England* (1960).

NISSIM BEN JACOB (c. 990-1062) *Gaon of Kairwan. N. was the spiritual leader of the north African Jews and became universally recognized for his scientific and exegetical works on the Bible and Talmud, in which he summarized the work of the Jewish Babylonian school and of the north African rabbis. His writings rapidly earned notice in north Africa, Italy and Spain and were widely quoted in rabbinical courts. N. is also known by his Arabic name, Ibn Shahin.

J. Oberman, *The Arabic Original of Ibn Shahin's Book of Comfort* (1933).

NITHARD (d. 844) *Frankish chronicler. N. was a nephew of *Charlemagne through his mother, Bertha. He was brought up in the abbey of *St. Riquier in northern France. During the reign of *Louis the Pious, N. often appeared at court and was intimately involved in the political life of the empire. He wrote a four-volume chronicle outlining the history of Louis' reign.

R. Rau (ed.), *Quellen zur Karolingischen Reichsgeschichte* (1955).

NIZAM AL-MULK (Abu Ali Al-Hasan Ibn Ali; c. 1018-92) Persian politician and *Seljuk vizier. N. began his career as an official at the court of the sultans of *Ghazni, but after the Seljuks conquered Persia (mid-11th century), he entered their service. In 1072 N. became chief vizier (prime-minister) of Malik Shah. He organized the Seljuk state and its administrative structure and implemented the *Iqta'a feudal system in the realm. N. wrote a treatise on *The Art of Government*. He was also very active in the theological and cultural domains and attempted to reconcile orthodox Islam with Turkish practices. N. founded institutions of higher learning called (after himself) *Nizamiya, the most famous among them being that of Baghdad. In 1092 N. was murdered by the *Assassins, whom he had persecuted.

B. Lewis, *The Assassins* (1965).

NIZAMI, HAKIM JAMAL AL-DIN (1140-1214) *Persian poet. An orphan from childhood, N. wandered among the courts and wrote poetry which he dedicated to governors and princes, who became his patrons. N. wrote five epic poems, collected after his death under the title *Hamsah* (The Five), which dealt with the court life of the *Sassanid kings of Persia. N. introduced many mystical and ascetic ideals of Islam, as well as motifs of courtly love into his poetry. He also wrote lyrical pieces in which he combined contemporary Persian with the archaic style (which he was responsible for reviving), a device he used to express his emotions.

E. G. Browne, *A Literary History of Persia* (1951).

NIZAMIYA The name of the institutions of higher learning founded in the Seljuk empire in the late 11th and 12th century, modelled after the schools established by *Nizam Al-Mulk. The N. were founded in a number of provincial capitals, but the most famous among them was that of Baghdad. Their main purpose was to educate young officials in the spirit of orthodox Islam and to prepare them for an administrative and juridical position in the Seljuk principalities. Strong emphasis was therefore placed on the practical aspect of study, so that contemplative thought was largely left undeveloped. The N. were designed to counter the *Ismaili schools.

CHI (1970).

NIZHNI NOVGOROD City in *Russia at the confluence of the Oka and Volga Rivers. Founded by the princes of *Suzdal in the 13th century, the city sponsored a popular fair in the 14th century and became famous for its fur and timber trade. Burnt in 1378 by the *Mongols, it was regained and rebuilt by *Dmitri Donskoi, great prince of *Moscow, who annexed it to his principality.

G. Vernadsky, *Medieval Russia* (1954).

NOBILITY The upper social class in medieval civilization. Its character varied according to time and place. The common feature among the members of the N., however, was their military and administrative background, the fact that they owned land and the functions they carried out within the state. In the *Byzantine empire, the N. closely served the empire, which was structured on the basis of strictly civil and military ranks beginning in the 6th century. Land possession was generally a secondary feature and usually came about due to inheritance or through the purchase of estates; owning land, in itself, was not essential for acquiring access to the class. The Byzantine N. was an open class; imperial appointments to offices offered access to a number of ranks. However, with time it became the custom for sons of noble families to have priority to the offices which would grant their high ranking.

In the *Arab caliphate and Moslem states, the tribal aristocracy and military command of the conquest period (7th century) made up the N. But from the 8th century on, high dignitaries and wealthy proprietors of land joined the class, while other members relinquished their status. From the 10th century on military leaders not of Arab origin also joined the N. and became its most important part. The frequency of military revolts and political assassinations produced a great deal of mobility within the class.

In western Europe, the extinction of the ancient Roman aristocracy and the rapid changes in the *Germanic tribal leadership ushered in a transitional period. It was not until the 9th century that certain high rulers and others were considered "noble" (*nobilis vir*, a noble man in the sense of a gentleman). The N. was consolidated in the West in the 9th century when *feudalism emerged and it became the practice to inherit fiefs. Thus, the character of the members of the class was conditioned by land-tenure and by their military and governmental duties. The fact that the title was hereditary, and passed on by blood ties, made the western N. a closed class. While it did not reach the rigidity of the *Indian caste system, it did create a series of regulations which prevented or presented obstacles to access within its ranks. The decline of feudalism and the emergence of the centralist bureaucratic states (13th century) accentuated the trend of closing the ranks of the N. On the other hand, a new, parallel aristocracy of government officials, the *noblesse de robe,* emerged at that time.

T. Reuter, *Medieval Nobility* (1978).

NOMINALISM A theory of knowledge which denies universal concepts. N. emerged in western Europe in the 11th century and developed through debates between philosophers who initially held, according to Platonic realism, that universals, such as genus and species, had a separate existence apart from the particulars attributed to them. N.'s criticism of universalism, first expressed by *Roscelin, carried the denial of the unity of species to a point which led Roscelin to tritheism. In the 12th century *Abelard produced a more moderate theory of N. which only criticized the doctrine of the separate existence of universals.

E. Gilson, *History of Medieval Philosophy* (1951).

NOMINOE (d. 851) King of *Brittany (841-51). Leader of a Breton clan, N. rose in Brittany by defeating rival groups during the reign of *Louis the Pious. He took advantage of the civil wars which wracked the Frankish empire to establish his own rule during 833-40; after the accession of *Charles the Bald, he proclaimed his independence and took the royal title. N. attempted to enlarge his possessions eastwards and seized the counties of Nantes and Maine.

E. Durtelle du Saint-Sauveur, *Histoire de la Bretagne* (1946).

NORBERT OF XANTEN, St. (c. 1080-1134) Archbishop of *Magdeburg. Born to a noble family of Xanten, Germany, N. was prepared for an ecclesiastical career. After some years in several clerical and canonic offices, he adopted the monastic lifestyle (1115) and began to preach. In 1118 Pope *Gelasius II granted him permission to preach church and lay reform and he soon became famous for the sermons he gave in the cities and villages of France. In 1120 N. founded the *Premonstratensian order of regular canons at Prémontré near *Laon. In an effort to combat the heresy of *Tanchelm in the Low Countries, he travelled and founded daughter-houses there. In 1126, after having obtained recognition of his order from Pope *Honorius II, N. was appointed archbishop of Magdeburg and won the favour of Emperor *Lothair II.

E. Maire, *St. Norbert* (1932).

NORMANDY Duchy in northern *France located at the mouth of the Seine River. Up to the 9th century the territory was part of the *Frankish kingdom and belonged to *Neustria. During the second half of that century it was frequently invaded by the *Normans and both Norsemen and Danes began to settle (temporarily) along the coast, close to their ships. At the end of the century such settlements became permanent and threatened the kingdom of France. In 911 King *Charles III was compelled to accept *Rollo, the Norman leader of Rouen, as his vassal and duke of N. Rollo himself converted to the Christian faith and organized a strong duchy in which the Norman invaders merged with the local population.

During the 10th and 11th centuries, N. became the best organized feudal principality in Europe. The dukes held strong public authority which their weak vassals were unable to check. Even the reign of Duke *William (the Conqueror), an illegitimate son whose accession to the throne in 1035 provoked an uprising, was not marked by change in the basic structure of the government. William was able to repress his unorganized opposition and to renew the expansionist policy of the dukes, aiming to conquer the provinces of *Vexin (between Rouen and Paris) and *Maine, although challenged by the kings of France and the counts of Anjou. William was also involved in English affairs, where Norman influence had begun to be felt since 1051; in 1066, using the resources and manpower of the duchy, he conquered England and became its king, granting the Norman nobility estates on both sides of the Channel.

The Anglo-Norman monarchy had a unique character due to the status of the duchy of N. as a fief of France. Thus, while the monarch was sovereign in England, he continued to be vassal of the king of France. Aware of such difficulties, William saw to it that his countries be divided among his sons upon his death (1087); the eldest, *Robert, was given N., while the second eldest, *William II, inherited England. This settlement, however, was contrary to the interests of the nobility, who rose up against Robert and in 1107 supported his youngest brother, *Henry I, already king of England, enabling the latter to reconquer N. While the reunion of the two lands promoted the commerce of the duchy, it also opened the way for the historic rivalry between England and France in the Middle Ages, which was accentuated under the *Angevin Plantagenets (mid-12th century). Under *Henry II, N. became the corner-stone of a powerful state and its political structures served as models for the king's entire empire. Only the grave mistakes of King *John, and especially the murder of his nephew, *Arthur of Brittany, brought an end to the social solidarity and enabled King *Philip II of France to conquer N. (1204). Under the rule of the French kings, N. no longer had its own dukes, but was governed by royal officials. Its administrative structures, however, were preserved and largely adopted by the French in other provinces.

The privileges of the nobility and the cities were recognized by the French kings of the 13th and 14th centuries; as a result, the duchy enjoyed a period of prosperity up to the beginning of the *Hundred Years' War. N. was often invaded in the course of that war and passed from hand to hand several times. In accordance with the agreement reached at *Brétigny (1360), it was given to France, but at the beginning of the 15th century it was reconquered by the English, who ruled it until 1450.

R. Musset, *La Normandie* (1960).

NORMANS (Latin: nortmanni "men of the north") The common name given by the *Carolingian chroniclers of the 9th century to the Scandinavian peoples. It generally referred to the *Norse and *Danes, whose raids during the 9th century threatened the *Carolingian empire and hastened its dissolution. Therefore, historians tended to treat the N. as a people to be feared, and they exaggerated their importance and cruelty. In actuality, Norman invasions were carried out by small bands of seafarers who had left their native countries due to local feuds or over-population in certain areas. They raided the Carolingian countries from Germany to Bordeaux through their waterways. The empire's lack of a fleet and of efficient political and military organization made defence difficult. Thus, while actual damage was not serious, the frequency of the raids created an atmosphere of terror. The invasions continued into the second half of the 9th century, at which time small Norman settlements were established along the mouths of rivers, such as the Loire and Seine. *Normandy emerged out of the most developed of them — that settlement situated on the Seine.

In the 10th century the meaning of the term N. changed. It now came to be applied to the leading class of Normandy. These N., although they had become feudal landowners, continued to seek adventure. At the beginning of the 11th century bands of Norman knights arrived in southern Italy and eventually founded the powerful kingdom of *Sicily under the *Hauteville family. Another wave of migration, headed by Duke William, led to the Norman Conquest of England in 1066 and earned the duke the title *William the Conqueror. Expansion into both Italy and England was carried out by a people who had become Frenchified. Thus, the French language and culture, as well as the political, social and administrative system of Normandy were introduced in England and Italy.

(Coll. vol.), *I Normanni e loro espansione in Europa* (1969).

NORTHAMPTON City in central *England. Situated on Watling Street, it became an important commercial centre between London and Chester. A royal palace with a beautiful Romanesque church were built there after the *Norman Conquest. During the 12th-14th centuries, royalty resided there during the hunting season and assemblies of the court were convoked in the palace. In 1460 an important battle between the *Yorkists and *Lancastrians was fought at N. Despite the Yorkists' total victory, Henry VI was allowed to continue his reign.

NORTHUMBRIA *Anglo-Saxon kingdom. Situated north of the Humber River on the Scottish frontier, N. was the largest realm of the *Heptarchy. It was founded by the union of *Bernicia and *Deira at the beginning of the 7th century. Its first known king, Aethelstan, of the royal house of Bernicia, had also conquered a number of Celtic and Pictish provinces near the mouth of the Clyde River. His son, *Edwin, who converted to Christianity, conquered the Yorkshire province and established his capital at *York. His successors, *Oswald and *Oswy (d. 670), fought against *Mercia and brought the realm to the peak of its power. Under their patronage, monasteries were founded and schools were established, thus making N., especially under such men as *Bede the Venerable, the centre of European culture and learning at the end of the 7th and during the 8th century. Distinguished scholars were educated in the schools of N., the most important among them having been *Alcuin, who later settled at the court of *Charlemagne and promoted the *Carolingian Renaissance. In the 8th century the realm began to decline. It was finally conquered by the *Danes in 867 and became their centre in England.

F. Stenton, *Anglo-Saxon England* (1947).

NORWAY Scandinavian country, situated along the Atlantic coast of the peninsula. Populated by Germano-Scandinavian tribes, the Norsemen, it was one of the centres of *Viking civilization from prehistoric times. Up to the 9th century, the country was loosely structured into numerous tribes and clans. During the 9th century tribal wars became frequent and the defeated groups were forced to migrate. These events caused the colonization of the north Atlantic islands (such as Orkney, Shetland, Faroe and Iceland), as well as frequent raids and invasions, carried out in conjunction with the *Danes of England, Ireland and *Carolingian Europe. As a result of internal wars, the first political organizations were created in the country. These had the character of tribal confederations and included assemblies of warriors under the leadership of local kings. The most important rulers were the kings of the *Oslo fjord and of the southeastern area. At the end of the 9th century, King *Harold I united the various confederations and founded the kingdom of N. But civil wars erupted between Harold's sons after his death (940) and lasted until the end of the 10th century, when *Olaf I (995-1000) reunited the realms and introduced Christianity into the country. Olaf estabished his capital at *Trondheim, in the northern part of the country and fought against the Danes, who had conquered some of the southern provinces. He fell in the war and N. came under the rule of the Danish king (1000-16). The country regained its independence under *Olaf II, but in 1028 King *Canute of Denmark and England conquered it. After the death of Canute (1035), the Norse revolted against their Danish governors and *Magnus I restored the country's independence.

Magnus' reign was one of peace. He concentrated his efforts on organizing the kingdom and its institutions and expanding Norwegian control to the Atlantic islands. The Norse settlements in those islands were brought under the control of the kingship, although they were allowed self-government. Despite dynastic strife, the political and social cohesion of the kingdom was attained in the 12th century. With the establishment of the archbishopric of Trondheim (1152), N. also reached ecclesiastical autonomy and cohesion. Under *Haakon IV (1217-63), the country became a powerful state, flourishing both culturally and economically. However, commercial development, which occurred as a result of a number of treaties made with the *Hanse, made German influence dominant in the country and N. became economically dependent on the league. *Bergen, the economic centre, became a Germanized city and German merchants were granted wide privileges there. Thus the royal treasury was largely dependent on good relations with the Hanse and it became obligatory for the Norwegian kings to continue granting privileges to foreign merchants. This situation was not altogether unacceptable to the monarchy since such measures checked the power of the nobility and prevented the rise of feudalism in the country. However, German influence in Bergen did induce King *Haakon V (1299-1319) to move his capital to Oslo.

The age of Norwegian stability ended with the death of Haakon V. As direct descendants were lacking, the crown was disputed between relatives. *Haakon VI (1343-80) was the last national king of N. He married Margaret, heiress of Denmark and thus paved the way for the union of the kingdoms, achieved by the Union of *Kalmar (1387). The union made Denmark the dominant part of the new monarchy and N., the poorest of the realms, was, for all intents and purposes, annexed to the Danish crown. Administration of N. was entrusted to Danish nobles in the 15th century. Danish thus became the country's official language, while Norwegian was used by the population.

T. K. Detty, *A Short History of Norway* (1968).

NORWICH City and port in East Anglia. Mention is first made of the city in documents of 1004, when N. was devastated by the *Danes. After the *Norman Conquest it became a royal city and one of the centres of the English wool trade. In 1093 construction was begun of its Romanesque cathedral, built in the Norman style. A Norman castle was erected in the 12th century (and is now a museum). In 1144 the Jewish community of N. was accused of the ritual murder of a boy, and persecutions were begun. Beginning in the 13th century, N. became one of the centres of the cloth industry in England.

B. Green, *Norwich, The Growth of a City* (1963).

NOTARY Legal official in western Europe. At the beginning of the Middle Ages the Roman practice, which had also been adopted in *Byzantium, was preserved in the West. N. were public officials at the courts, whose duty it was to issue and care for official documents. From the 10th century on the nature of the office changed and Ns. settled in cities. There they took written note of private transactions, such as the drafting of wills, agreements and contracts. According to Roman custom, the N. had to be certified by the public authority, meaning either the *Holy Roman emperor or the *papacy. He was considered a legal officer and therefore his notes were admissible evidence. From the 13th century on the office became hereditary.

C. Stepheson, *Medieval Institutions* (1923).

NOTKER, St. (940-1008) Bishop of Liège (972-1008). Born to a noble Swabian family, N. was educated at *St. Gall. In 969 Emperor *Otto I appointed him imperial chaplain for Italy and, in 972, bishop of Liège. N. was one of the most devoted imperial officials, even after his promotion to the episcopal see. He sought to strengthen imperial authority in Italy and Lotharingia. After Otto's death, N. concentrated his efforts on his own diocese and paved the way for the pre-eminence of the bishops of Liège. He was famous as the founder of the important scholarly centre of Liège.

G. Kurth, *Notker de Liège at la Civilisation du Xe siècle* (1905).

NOTKER BALBULUS (The Stammerer; c. 840-912) Scholar. In his youth, N. entered the monastery of *St. Gall (Switzerland), where he studied and taught. In 890 he became librarian of the abbey and dedicated his life to writing. Among his works are some treatises dealing with the liturgy, including certain of its musical aspects, a poem on the life of St. Gall and a legendary history of *Charlemagne.

J. M. Clark, *The Abbey of St. Gall as a Centre of Literature and Art* (1926).

NOTKER LABEO (950-1022) Monk of *St. Gall. After completing his studies at the monastery's school, N. became its master and taught Latin literature. So as to make the classics more accessible to his pupils, he translated some works into German. He was the first in Europe to undertake such translations. Among his works was the first text of the German Psalter. N. also wrote a treatise on choral music in German and a series of short treatises in Latin on liturgical themes. He was a forerunner of German prose in the Middle Ages.

I. Schröbler, *Notker III of St. Gallen als Ubersetzer* (1953).

NOVARA City in western *Lombardy. The small town, situated on the road between *Milan and Turin, grew in the 11th century and became a prominent commercial centre bordering the march of *Montferrat. Due to

St. Sophia Cathedral, Novgorod, built in the 11th century

its commercial interests, it entered into long conflicts with Milan during the 12th century and, as a result, the *Ghibelline party became strong and the city collaborated with *Frederick Barbarossa. In the 13th century Spiritual *Franciscans made N. one of their strongholds. The city was annexed to the *Visconti principality of Milan at the beginning of the 14th century.
J. K. Hyde, *Society and Politics in Medieval Italy* (1973).
NOVGOROD City and principality in northwestern *Russia. Founded by Scandinavian merchants at the beginning of the 9th century, its name signified the "New City", as opposed to the "Old City", a Swedish settlement on Lake Ladoga. The founders of N. merged with the Slav population which had settled in the area, and by the middle of the 9th century the city had become Slavic in character. N.'s location along the waterway linking the Baltic and Black Seas made it a flourishing commercial centre which traded with Scandinavia, Constantinople and the Moslem world. In 862 the Swedish leader, *Rurik, belonging to the Rus tribe, founded an independent state in the city bearing his

name (Russia). From N., Rurik, his brothers and their kin began to expand southwards. In 912 the capital of the principality moved to *Kiev, but N. remained one of the major cities of Russia and was considered its second capital. Economic prosperity and the social development of the city led the urban class to seek self-government. In 1136 Prince *Vsevolod was dethroned by a local uprising and municipal institutions were established in the city, which came to be known as "The Great N. Lordship". The republic extended its lordship over the major part of northwestern Russia, from the shores of the Baltic Sea to those of the White Sea. Its trade became diversified and from the 13th century the city became one of the principal members of the German *Hanse. Like the western cities, N. included *guilds of merchants and craftsmen, whose officers were active in the institutions of the "Lordship". The highest institution of the republic was the assembly of the people, which convened regularly to elect the magistrate, the chief executive of the "Lordship".

The Rurikid princes of *Suzdal attempted to recover their power at N., but failed, and in 1169 the republic's army defeated that of Suzdal. Despite their second defeat in 1216, the members of the dynasty gained some influence in the city during the 13th century and became members of the "Lordship". The most important of them, *Alexander Nevski, was even elected prince and chosen to command the Novgorodian army, defeating the Swedes on the *Neva River in 1240 and the *Teutonic knights at Lake Peipus in 1242. However, when Alexander became prince of Suzdal in 1252, he surrendered his position in N., which remained independent. Although the city was not affected by the *Mongol conquest of Russia, towards the end of the 13th century it began to decline. The assembly of the people continued to function, but beginning in the middle of the 14th century true power passed from the guilds to the landed proprietors (the *boiars*), who exercised rigid control over the magistrate. In 1416 the *boiars* seized power and established an aristocratic council, presided over by the archbishop and including the former magistrates. Such a change could not help but hasten the decline of the principality.
M. W. Thompson, *Novgorod the Great* (1967).
NUREDDIN, MAHMUD Sultan of *Syria (1146-74). The second son of Imad Al-Din *Zengi, he was the most important monarch of the *Zengid dynasty. Upon his father's death he was proclaimed *atabeg of *Aleppo, while his elder brother, Shams Al-Din, was given control over *Mosul. Backed by two Kurdish officers, Shirkuh and Ayyub, N. consolidated his government at Aleppo and then conquered Mosul (1152). He also took advantage of the Second *Crusade to annex the Turkish Syrian emirates (1150-52) and in 1154 conquered *Damascus, becoming sultan of a united Syria. N. imposed a strong government in the state, as a preparatory stage for the holy war (*gihad*) against the Crusaders. He therefore reformed the religious and social structures of his kingdom and set up a strictly *Sunnite regime; the *Shiites were persecuted and an educational reform put an end to philosophical and scientific study in the Moslem schools. The new *medressa* (schools) were based on an orthodox teaching of Islam through rote (analytical thought was not developed). Military organization and mobilization of resources was aided by the introduc-

tion of the feudal practices of the *Iqta'a. N. fought the Crusaders in 1157, but his attempted invasion of the Galilee was unsuccessful. In 1163, however, he conquered Banias, opening a serious breach in the Crusader's defence of the Jordan. He also attacked *Antioch, but failed to conquer it due to a serious illness. In 1169 he sent a unit to Egypt, under the command of *Saladin, to help the *Fatimids resist a Crusader attack on Cairo. The Crusaders were compelled to retreat and Saladin, acting on behalf of N., dethroned the rulers of the Fatimid empire and became governor of Egypt. N. was aware of the increasing power of his Kurdish officer, but his illness did not allow him to act. Thus, upon his death, the Zengid state fell into the hands of *Saladin.

V. Eliséeff, *Nur Ad-Din* (1966).

NUREMBERG City in northern *Bavaria (Nordgau). It originated around a castle built in 1040 near the older town of Fürth. The borough surrounding the castle eventually began to develop into a commercial city and sponsored a renowned regional *fair. After the power of the *Welfs had been destroyed, Frederick Barbarossa granted N. the status of an *imperial city and appointed its governor, the burgrave. In 1192 the position passed to members of the *Hohenzollern family, who held it until 1427. Under their rule the city developed and in 1219 obtained a *charter of liberties. In 1256 N. joined the confederation of the cities of the Rhine, to which it remained connected until the end of the Middle Ages. N.'s central position in the German empire contributed to its prosperity in the 14th and 15th centuries. It was a centre of trade and its crafts were sold throughout the German provinces, and alongside the development of wealth and influence went the development of learning.

E. Kusch, *Nürnberg, Lebensbild einer Stadt* (1958).

The Altar of the Virgin *by Andrea Orcagna at Or San Michele, Florence*

O

OBADIA THE PROSELYTE (d. c. 1118) Born in Apulia, southern Italy, he studied theology and became a priest at the cathedral church of Bari in his native land. He came to the conclusion that the roots of Christianity lay in Judaism, and converted to the Jewish faith (c. 1092), and changed his name from Andrew to O. Aware that a Christian country could mean a trial and the death sentence, he left Bari and settled in Moslem Syria, first at Banias and later at Aleppo, where he died. After his conversion, O. was active in Jewish spiritual life, both as a scholar and as a contributor to the development of the liturgical chant.
N. Golb, *Proceedings of the American Academy for Jewish Research* (1962).

OBSERVANTINES (OBSERVANTS) A movement within the *Franciscan order that emerged in Italy in 1368, aiming to observe the original rule of St. *Francis.

OCHRIDA City in western *Macedonia. A *Byzantine provincial centre, it was settled by Daco-Roman elements – called Vlachs by the local Greeks – after the Romans abandoned Dacia. After a series of raids in the 8th century, Slavs settled in the city, and there converted to Christianity. Conquered by the *Bulgarians in the 9th century, O. flourished in the 10th as a cultural and economical centre of the Bulgarian empire, the capital of which alternated between *Tivorno and O. Its conquest in 1014 by Emperor *Basil II marked the fall of the first Bulgarian empire and the return of Byzantine hegemony in the Balkans. In 1187 a revolt by the *Vlachs and the Bulgarian elements in the area ended Byzantine domination at O. The autonomous status granted its archbishops by the patriarchs of Constantinople in the 13th century paved the way for the establishment of the Serbian patriarchate. In the 14th century, O. belonged to the *Serbian empire, but after the Battle of Kossovo (1386), it was conquered by the Turks. Its cathedral church is one of the most beautiful samples of Byzantine-Slavic architecture.
CMedH, IV.

OCKHAM (OCCAM), WILLIAM OF See WILLIAM OF OCKHAM.

ODILO Duke of *Bavaria (737-47). He opposed the penetration of *Frankish influence in Bavaria and struggled to maintain his duchy's independence. To reach his aims, he promoted the establishment of a Bavarian archbishopric at Augsburg, appointing the Anglo-Saxon missionary Victor as archbishop.

ODILO, St. (962-1048) Abbot of *Cluny (994-1048). He entered the monastery in 991, and soon became famous for his virtues. Three years later he was elected abbot. In that capacity, he proved an able administrator and leader, and showed a remarkable political understanding. Under his government, the Cluniac order rose from 37 houses to 65, its influence spreading throughout the Catholic world. O. travelled much in the interests of his order and the church, and maintained good relations with the popes, emperors and kings of France. He was active in spreading the *Peace and *Truce of God movement, and the relevant legislation was largely his work. He instituted the "All Souls' Day" ceremony, held in commemoration of the faithful deceased. The feast was first observed in the order and under his influence spread throughout the Catholic world.
L. Coté, *St. Odilon, un Moine de l'An Mille* (1949).

ODO, St. (879-942) Abbot of *Cluny (927-42). Son of a knight, he was born at Tours and brought up in the household of the dukes of Aquitaine. In 898 he became canon at Tours and then travelled for studies. In 909 he gave up his canonry and was admitted by St. *Berno to his monastery of Baume. After the foundation of Cluny, Berno put O. in charge of the school of Baume. In 972 O. succeeded Bermo as abbot of Cluny and, through his efforts, the monastery rose to its prominent position in the Catholic Church. He extended the authority of Cluny over other monasteries and won the support of the papacy for his activities. He also wrote a number of treatises on morals and the ideals of monastic life.
E. Amman, *Odon de Cluny* (1931).

ODO OF BAYEUX (1036-97) He was a half-brother of *William the Conqueror, who appointed him bishop of Bayeux, Normandy (c. 1050), despite his youth. His career was, however, that of a statesman and soldier: he fought at the Battle of *Hastings (1066), was appointed earl of Kent (1067), and was a trusted minister of William in England until 1082, when he fell in disgrace and was imprisoned for having planned a military expedition to Italy. On his release at the Conqueror's death, he returned to Kent, where he organized a rebellion against *William II Rufus, designed to put his other nephew, *Robert of Normandy, on the throne. Failing, he returned to Normandy and devoted his time to his church at Bayeux, where he rebuilt the cathedral. In 1096 he joined Robert on the *Crusade but died on the way at Palermo.
C. D. Douglas, *William the Conqueror* (1966).

ODO OF DUEIL See EUDES OF DUEIL.

ODO OF MEUNG (11th century) Botanist. Little is known about his life. Later authorities describe him as a student of plants and flowers; in 1287, the botanist *Rufinus attributed to him the authorship of the *Macer Floridus*, a description of flowers of northern France and the Low Countries which dates from the late 11th century.
A. C. Crombie, *Science in the Middle Ages* (1957).

ODO OF TOURNAI (11th century) Hermit. Member of a noble family of Tournai, Flanders, he inveighed against the social order and in the late 11th century elaborated the ideal of poverty as a moral virtue. He left the city, became a hermit and conducted a life of extreme poverty, despite the opposition of the bishop and the nobles, who feared lest his behaviour might serve as an example to others and disrupt the social order.

ODOACER (c. 434-93) King of *Italy (476). O. was a German chieftain, who entered Italy in 470 and became king of the *Heruli. Like other German chieftains, he joined the Roman army, but revolted against his general, Orestes, and defeated him in 476. After his victory, he entered Rome, deposed the last Roman emperor of the West, Romulus Augustulus, and, while acknowledging the overlordship of the Eastern emperor at Constantinople, he proclaimed himself ruler of Italy. His rule was liberal, but he opposed any attempts by the Byzantine emperors to interfere in Italy and, to assure his independence, invaded the Balkans. Failing to prevent the *Ostrogoths' invasion of Italy in 493, he tried to come to an understanding with their king, *Theodoric. He was murdered during a reception at Ravenna.
J. M. Wallace-Hadrill, *The Barbarian West* (1965).

OECUMENICAL COUNCILS See COUNCIL.

OFFA (d. 796) King of *Mercia (757-96). He seized the throne after a brief civil war and reorganized the Anglo-Saxon kingdom of Mercia, which became the most powerful realm in Britain during his reign. He gradually extended his dominions in England south of the Humber, by the conquest of East *Anglia and *Essex. In 776 he defeated the Kentish army at Oxford. In contrast to his direct rule over his domains north of the Thames, O. contented himself with imposing his overlordship upon the southern realms of *Wessex (779) and *Kent (785). Assuming the titles "King of the English" and "King of the Whole English Fatherland", O. was respected as an independent ruler by *Charlemagne and maintained good relations with the papacy. In his internal policy, he proved himself an able monarch, promoted trade and built fortifications, notable among which is the still extant dyke to defend his realm from Welsh attacks.
F. M. Stenton, *Anglo-Saxon England* (1947).

OGIER LE DANOIS French epic. Written in the 12th century in northern France, the poem deals with the adventures of a certain Ogier the Dane, one of *Charlemagne's knights, who entered into a long conflict with the emperor, fighting for his rights and justice. The second part of the poem relates O.'s saintly life in a monastery, after he had concluded that lay life is mere vanity. The epic reflects the feudal concept of the vassal's rights, legitimizing revolt to defend them.
U. T. Homes, *A History of Old French Literature* (1948).

OGODAI (1185-1241) Great khan of the *Mongols (1229-41). Third son of *Genghis-Khan, he succeeded his father and styled himself "great khan". O. resided at *Karakorum, which he embellished and made the real capital of the Mongol empire. He introduced a system of controls over the other members of his family, who ruled the various provinces and, according to his orders, resumed the campaigns launched by his father. His reign saw the continuation of attacks on China, the conquest of Russia by his nephew *Batu-khan, and the invasion of Poland and Hungary.
N. Prowden, *The Mongols* (1940).

OLAF I (1052-95) King of *Denmark (1086-95). His reign was a period of dynastic struggle, which divided the nobility and weakened the realm. Denmark lost its influence over the Obrodite Slavs, thus paving the way for German expansion in the northern part of the trans-Elbe territories.

OLAF II, Haakonsson (1370-87) King of *Denmark (1376) and Norway (1380). Son of *Haakon VI of Norway and *Margaret, heiress of Denmark, he reigned under the regency of his mother. His reign prepared the *Kalmar Union of Sweden, Denmark and Norway, realized after his death by Margaret. Denmark and Norway remained united until 1814.
L. Musset, *Les Peuples Scandinaves au Moyen Age* (1951).

OLAF I, Trygvesson (c. 694-1000) King of *Norway (995-1000). Born after the murder of his father, King Trygve, he was brought up in Russia and became a Viking adventurer. In 991 he entered the service of the Danish King *Sweyn I, whom he joined in his raids in England, but showed an independent spirit. In 995 he returned to Norway, was proclaimed king and introduced Christianity in his realm.
G. Jones, *The Vikings* (1968).

OLAF II, Haraldsson, St. (995-1030) King of *Norway (1016-1030). He assisted the English in their fight against the Danes, although he had earlier fought against the English as head of the Norse army in 1009-11. In 1013, during a stay in France, he converted to Christianity and, on becoming king, imposed the new faith on all his subjects with the help of English missionaries. The harshness of his methods provoked a revolt by the nobles, who turned to King *Canute the Great of Denmark and England and proclaimed him their king. Defeated, O. fled to Russia in 1029, but returned the following year, only to be killed at the Battle of Stiklestad. He was venerated as the patron saint of Norway.
G. Jones, *The Vikings* (1968).

OLAF III, Kyrre (the Pacific; d. 1093) King of *Norway (1066-93). Son of *Harold III, he joined his father in his invasion of England, where Harold was killed. O. concluded a peace treaty with King *Harold of England and returned to Norway, dedicating himself to the organization and pacification of the realm. On good relations with Pope *Gregory VII, he favoured the establishment of a church in Norway. He founded the city of *Bergen (1070), fostered the development of other Norwegian towns and promoted trade.
G. Jones, *The Vikings* (1968).

OLAF IV, Magnusson (d. 1115) King of *Norway from 1103. Son of King *Magnus II, he was associated with the kingship at his father's death, with his brothers Eystein and *Sigurd I. He dealt mainly with domestic affairs.

OLDENBURG City and county in northwestern Germany. The town is first mentioned in 1108 as·a *Saxon borough founded around a feudal castle. During the 12th century, the lords of O., who developed the town and promoted settlement in the area, were granted the countal title, officially confirmed by *Frederick Barbarossa in 1180. The city grew as a commercial centre and was granted a charter of liberties in 1345. In the 14th century the counts of O. became related with highly prominent families in northern Germany and Scandinavia, among them the royal dynasty of *Denmark. These relations influenced the election of Count *Christian as king of Denmark and the establishment of the O. dynasty, which was to reign in Denmark until 1863.

J. W. Thompson, *Feudal Germany* (1928).

OLEG (d. c. 912) Prince of *Kiev. He was the semi-legendary Viking chieftain, who followed *Rurik to *Novgorod and was probably his kinsman. At Rurik's death, he ruled Novgorod, but in 882 left it and conquered Smolensk and Kiev, where he established his capital. O. united the Slav tribes of the Dnieper Valley under his leadership and after a number of victories over the *Khazars, became the head of an important Russian principality, which included Kiev and Novgorod. In 907, he led an expedition against Constantinople and compelled the Byzantines to sign a trade agreement, which regulated commercial relations between the two countries (911).

G. Vernadsky, *Kievan Russia* (1953).

OLGA, St. (c. 890-969) Kievan princess. Widow of *Igor I, she became regent of *Kiev in 945 and continued her husband's policy, aiming to develop commercial relations with Byzantium. In 957, she went to Constantinople to negotiate a new commercial treaty and during her stay was converted to Orthodoxy. On her return, she attempted to convert the Russians to Christianity.

G. Vernadsky, *Kievan Russia* (1953).

OLGIERD Grand duke of *Lithuania (1341-77). Son of *Gedymin, he shared the government with his younger brother Kestutis, but was the effective ruler. O. continued his father's policy of southward expansion, conquering from the *Mongols the Dnieper Valley and thus extending his southern frontier to the Black Sea. He introduced a liberal government in his vast duchy, populated mainly by Slavs, but at the same time sought to maintain an effective and mobile army.

OLIM French judicial record. The O. (Latin: once) was a record kept on parchment scrolls by the clerks of the *Parliament of Paris, containing the parliament's charters and judgements from the middle of the 13th century on. It serves as an invaluable source for the history of France in the Middle Ages.

OLIVER (OLIVIER) A legendary figure in French medieval epics, O. was a loyal and close friend of the hero *Roland.

OLIVES, MOUNT OF The highest point of the mountain range east of *Jerusalem, separated from the city by the valley of Josaphat. The many Christian legends related with the mount made it renowned as a holy place in medieval society. From the 5th century the M. was one of the destinations of pilgrimages from western Europe to Palestine. In the 8th century a Catholic monastery was established on its peak, with monks coming mainly from the *Frankish kingdom and Germany. They maintained close relations with their countries of origin, and, until the end of the 11th century, were instrumental in diffusing information on the Holy Land throughout western Europe.

H. Vincent, P. M. Abel, *Jérusalem*, II (1914).

OLIVI, PETRUS JOANNIS (c. 1248-98) Leader of the Spiritual *Franciscans. Born in southern France, he entered the Franciscan order at the age of 12 and studied at Paris and probably also at Oxford. His zeal for the strict observance of the order's rule led him to be consulted in 1270 by Pope *Nicholas III about the Franciscan ideal of poverty. His ideas were initially attacked within the order and censured, but later accepted as orthodox. In 1287 he was appointed to lecture in the various Franciscan houses, where he disseminated his ideas.

B. Jansen, *Die Erkennislehre Olivis* (1921).

OMAR II Caliph (717-20). Member of the *Ummayad dynasty, he reigned in Damascus during a troubled period of dynastic strife. The great mosque at *Jerusalem, called Omar's mosque, was completed during his reign. Moslem tradition attributes the building to Caliph *Omar Ibn Al-Khattab, the conqueror of Jerusalem.

OMAR, ABU HAFSA IBN AL-KHATTAB (c. 581-644) Caliph (634-44). Member of a patrician family of Mecca, he was one of *Mohammad's first disciples, belonging to the inner circle around the prophet, which became the leadership of Islam after 622. O. distinguished himself in the battles which established Islam in Arabia. In 634 he was elected second caliph, enjoying universal prestige as friend of Mohammad, a devout Moslem and able leader. During his caliphate, the Arabs accomplished their great conquests, of Palestine, Syria, Egypt and Iraq, and had begun the conquest of Persia. The battles of the *Yarmuk and *Qadisiyah broke the military power of Byzantium and Persia, assuring Arab supremacy in the Middle East. O. appointed his generals as governors of the conquered provinces, while he continued to reside in the capital, Medina.

CHI.

OMAR IBN AL-AAS (d. 649) Arab general. He joined *Mohammad's army and distinguished himself in the battles of the Hedjaz. In the last years of the prophet's life, he commanded several raids in Palestine and Syria, where he distinguished himself for the rapidity of his movements. During the caliphate of *Omar, he was a commander in the Arab army, conquering parts of Syria, Palestine and Egypt. The campaign of Egypt, which he undertook with 4000 fighters and against the advice of the caliph, was the peak of his career. After mobilizing additional troops from among new converts to Islam, he conquered the country. He built a new city in Egypt, *Fustat, designed as a military camp, which replaced *Alexandria as the country's capital. O. conquered Alexandria in 642. Appointed governor of Egypt, he reorganized its administration (644) and laid the basis for its Islamization and Arabization.

CHI.

OMAR KHAYYAM (c. 1048-1123) *Persian poet and mathematician. Born at Nishapur, he was educated in his native city and at Samarkand, where he became renowned as an astronomer. The *Seljuk ruler of Persia, *Malik Shah, impressed by his vast knowledge, called him to his palace and commissioned him with reforming the calendar. In 1092, after the death of Malik Shah, O. left the palace, went on a pilgrimage to Mecca and returned to Nishapur, where he wrote his poetic work, the *Rubaiyat* (Quatrains), which made him one of the greatest poets of the Middle Ages. He died and was buried at Isfahan, where his tomb became a symbol of Persian identity. His calendar of 1079 was considered the most accurate until it was superseded by the 16th-century *Gregorian calendar.

E. Fitzgerald, *The Rubaiyat of Omar Khayyam* (ed.) (1956).

OMURTAG Tsar of the *Bulgarians (814-29). He consolidated Bulgarian authority in the Balkans, maintaining his independence from Byzantium. In 822 he inter-

le temple de Iherusalem · mahomet le roux · dambe ·

es anciennes histoires
dient que Eracles
qui fu monlt bon xp̄e
stien gouuernoit se
pire de romme · Mais
en son temps mahommet p̄noit
ia este qui fu messagier au deable ·
et fist entendant qu'il estoit p̄o
phete enuoie de dieu · En terre
Eracle estoit ia la desloiaute ⁊
fausse loy que il sema espandue
par toute la terre de oriant et
nommeement en Arabe · tellemēt
que les princes de la terre ne ne
oient en chose que sen seur enser
tnast ou admonnestast · Aincois
contraintnoient par force ⁊ par
espee tous seurs subtiez a obeir
auz commandemens mahomet
et a croire en sa loy · Quant Era
cles ost conquiz perse et oult
occiz Cosdroe qui estoit si puissat

foy il en emporta sa braie cuer
en thr̄lm̄ Auquel lieu il auoit
vint vn patriarche monlt prudo
me qui auoit nom Modestes
par le conseil duquel il faisoit
reffaire les eglises et ordonner
les sains lieux que les desloiaulx
princes de perse qui auoient
nom Cosdroes auoient destruiz
⁊ abatuz · Monlt y mettoit em
ses grant entente ⁊ grans coust
anges choses reparer · En de mē
tres quilz entendoient a ces cho
ses · homar filz katap qui est
prince dambe tiers apres ma
hommet vint en sa terre qui
a nom Palestine ast grant
plante de gent que toute sa
terre en estoit couuerte et p
prinst par force vne forteresse
qui a nom Ladre · Dist se
tnap pres damas et assailli

vened in Byzantine affairs, helping Emperor *Michael II to defend Constantinople against the rebellion of the general, Thomas the Sclavonian.

S. Runciman, *The First Bulgarian Empire* (1930).

ORANGE City in *Provence. One of the most important Roman centres in the province, it was devastated by the *Visigoths in the 5th century, but its fairs continued to be active. Its position made it the site of several councils of the Western Church, among them those of 441 and 529, where decisions concerning the organization of Christendom were taken. In 543, O. was annexed to the *Frankish kingdom and in the 9th century it became part of the kingdom of *Provence. In 1049, the city and its surroundings were made a county, which gradually became independent of the counts of Provence.

M. Demayeur, *Orange: Vie d'une Cité* (1962).

ORCAGNA, ANDREA (c. 1308-68) Florentine sculptor and architect. He studied in his native city and in 1354 was admitted to the stone masons' guild. Having won fame for his work at the Strozzi Chapel (1354-57), he was commissioned in 1357 as architect of the Duomo Cathedral of Florence, where he worked until 1367. In the meantime, he also planned the rebuilding of the Orvieto Cathedral.

E. Panofski, *Gothic Architecture and Scholasticism* (1957).

ORDEALS A juridical practice widely used in the Middle Ages, according to which an accused could prove his innocence by successfully undergoing an "ordeal", commonly of fire or water. Its origins emerged from Germanic tribal practices and, despite the opposition of the Church, which preferred the testimony methods, it remained in usage in the *feudal courts. Although the practise of O. began to diminish in the 13th century, it was never eliminated, being considered the expression of the "judgement of God" by the popular classes.

ORDERIC VITALIS (c. 1075-1143) Historian. Of Anglo-Norman origin, he was educated at Shrewsbury, England, and in 1085 was sent to Normandy to continue his studies at the abbey of St. Evroul, where he became a monk. His work at the abbey was copying ancient books, which developed his knowledge and understanding of history. In 1109 he began to write his *Historia ecclesiastica*, on which he worked until his death. The major part of the book is a contemporary narrative that is an invaluable source for the history of England, France and Normandy in the first half of the 12th century.

Works, ed. A. Le Provost, 5 vols. (1886-99).

ORDERS (Latin: ordo "status") The term, in its larger meaning, designated the three corporate bodies, also called *estates, into which medieval society was divided: the clergy, the nobility and the peasants. In a narrower sense, which became the common one, the term is related to the organization of the church and especially *monastic society. Monasteries which adopted a common rule were organized into O., such as the *Benedictine, Cluniac, *Cistercian and, from the 13th century, the *Mendicant O. The impact of monastic organization led to the foundation of military O. of knights, who fought for Christianity against *Islam, first in Palestine and later in Spain. The most famous of these O. were the *Hospitallers, the *Templars and the *Teutonic, in the Holy Land and the *Alcantara, *Calatrava and *San-

tiago in Spain. The military O. were richly endowed with land and revenues in western Europe. From the 13th century, they expanded to other areas, for example, the Teutonic order spread to *Prussia and the Baltic countries and the Hospitallers to *Rhodes and finally to *Malta. The term was later applied to chivalric associations that were founded in the 14th century, such as the O. of the *Garter, or the Golden Fleece, that lost all resemblance to the classical military O. O. in this case expressed a manner of life and behaviour, according to the social dignity of the higher nobility and the *chivalric ideals of the later Middle Ages.

S. Painter, *French Chivalry* (1940).

ORESME, NICHOLAS (1320-82) French philosopher and economist. After studying at Paris, he was appointed to several ecclesiastical offices, culminating in that of bishop of Lisieux (1377). He was also a counsellor to King *Charles V. His writings, in Latin and French, deal with politics, economics and natural science. Best known was his treatise on *coinage, *De l'origine, nature et mutations des monnayes*, also written in a Latin version, *De Monete*, which greatly influenced medieval economic theories. His *Livre du Ciel et du Monde* (On the Sky and the World), on planetary motion, anticipated some of Copernicus' theories.

Works, ed. M. L. Wolowski (1864);

C. Johnson, *Nicholas d'Oresme, De Moneta* (1956).

ORKHAN Ottoman sultan (1326-59). He was the second sultan of the Ottoman *Turks. After the death of his father, *Osman I, he pursued the attack against the *Byzantine empire, conquering successively Brussa (1326), Nicaea (1331) and Nicomedia (1337). He expelled the Byzantines from Anatolia and constituted a powerful state covering its northwestern part. In 1346 he became involved in Byzantine European affairs, as ally to Emperor *John VI, whose daughter Theodora he married. Ostensibly to help John, he led raids in the Balkans, conquering Gallipoli in 1354, and thus paving the way for the Turkish conquest of the Balkans. O. reorganized the Ottoman army on a more permanent basis.

P. Wittek, *The Rise of the Ottoman Empire* (1938).

ORLÉANS City in *France. The ancient Gallo-Roman city was conquered by *Clovis in 487 and annexed to the Frankish kingdom. Its favourable location in the centre of France made it an important city in the kingdom and, during the frequent divisions of the realm among the kings' sons, it was the capital of the southwestern realm. Under the *Carolingians (8th-9th centuries), O. was also an important centre of learning, its schools enjoying fame throughout the realm. At the end of the 9th century, the county of O. became part of the dominions of the Robertians and, as such, was incorporated into the "duchy of the Franks" (the future Ile de France). When *Hugh Capet became king of France in 987, he gave the major part of his duchy to his vassals, but maintained the county of O. under his direct administration and it was to remain a constituent part of the *Capetians' royal domain. A burgher uprising at the beginning of the 11th century was condemned as heresy and severely repressed by King *Robert the Pious in 1025. The continuous growth of the city, based both on the frequent sojourns of the kings and their administration and on trade development, made of O. an important provincial city, while its schools continued to enjoy prestige even after the foundation of *Paris Uni-

Caliph Omar orders the rebuilding of the Temple; illuminated manuscript

versity. In the 13th century, Roman Law, the teaching of which was prohibited at Paris, was taught at O., and, with the migration of Parisian teachers to O. in 1229, a temporary university was established in the city. Until the end of the 14th century, the city and its surroundings were directly administered by royal officers. This situation changed in 1392, when a duchy of O. was constituted for *Louis, the younger son of King *Charles V, who founded the house of O., as a cadet branch of the *Valois dynasty. Louis' eldest son (the future *Charles VII) was taken prisoner by the English at *Agincourt (1415) and, during his captivity, the city remained faithful to the dauphin, who became king in 1422. In 1429, O. was besieged by the English army and was delivered thanks to Joan of Arc's intervention.

E. Jarry, *Provinces et Pays de France* (1945).

ORSEOLO Venetian aristocratic family. The Os. became active in *Venice's political life in the 10th century, many of their members reaching the office of doge in the 10th-11th centuries. Their economic interests in Istria and Dalmatia influenced Venice's expansionist policy, manifested by the conquest of Dalmatia by Peter II O. in 999. The family's importance gradually declined after the 12th century.

H. Kretschmayr, *Geschichte von Venedig*, I (1905).

ORSINI Highly influential *Roman aristocratic family, first recorded in 998. Their importance grew in the 11th and 12th centuries, both by the extension of their territorial possessions in the city's surroundings and by their service at the papal court. With the election of an O., *Celestine III, as pope, the family became the adversaries of the anti-papal *Colonna. In the 13th century, they assumed the leadership of the pro-papal *Guelphs of Rome against Emperor *Frederick II, organizing a powerful army and extending their possessions in southern Latium. The family supported Pope *Boniface VIII as part of their fight against the Colonna, but after his death, were instrumental in the election of the French Pope *Clement V, in order to restore the peace.

J. Haller, *Das Papsttum*, II-IV (1953-55).

ORVIETO City in central *Italy, between Rome and Florence. Until the *Lombard conquest of Italy, the city followed the historical evolution of the country. In 588, it became a Lombard duchy which soon merged with that of *Spoleto. After *Charlemagne's conquest of Italy, it became a county (774). From the 9th century on, the counts were dependent on the margraves of *Tuscany; but became independent after the death of Marquess *Matilda (1115), when the city obtained a communal charter. O. maintained its independence until 1448, when it was annexed to the *Papal States. Its famous cathedral, a masterpiece of late Italian Gothic architecture, was built between 1290-1370. The mosaic decoration of the façade, its final stage, was designed by Andrea *Orcagna.

J. K. Hyde, *Society and Politics in Medieval Italy* (1973).

OSLO City in *Norway. Founded in 1050 by King *Harold Hardruler as a naval base in the southern part of the country, it became an important fortress, which assured royal supremacy in the face of revolts by local nobles. The city developed as a fishermen's harbour. The Akershus royal castle, one of the finest structures of lay Scandinavian architecture, was built in 1300.

G. Jones, *The Vikings* (1968).

OSMAN I (1259-1326) *Ottoman sultan (1281-1326). He was a Turkish chieftain, who inherited a small principality founded by the *Seljuk sultans of Konya at its northwestern marches. O. organized a powerful army and consolidated his principality. He attacked his Byzantine neighbours, gradually extending his control over several castles in the area. In 1290 he entitled himself sultan of the Turks. The Turkish state, adopting his name, became known as the Osman (or Ottoman) realm. In 1304 he attempted to conquer Gallipoli but, being decisively defeated by the *Catalan Company, he returned to Anatolia, where, avoiding major battles, he continued to increase his territories at the expense of the weakened Byzantine empire.

P. Wittek, *The Rise of the Ottoman Empire* (1938).

OSMUND, St. (d. 1099) Bishop of *Salisbury. Member of the countal family of Séez, he followed *William the Conqueror to England, becoming one of his chief aides and chancellor of his kingdom. He assisted William in the compilation of the *Domesday Book and was rewarded in 1078 with the bishopric of Salisbury. He devoted his last years to his ecclesiastical post and the organization of the diocese.

W. J. Torrance, *St. Osmund of Salisbury* (1920).

OSTROGOTHS The name of the *Gothic tribes who settled in the Ukraine in the 3rd century. After the fall

Ostrogothic fibula of gold-covered silver and jewels

of the *Hun empire in the 5th century, the O. recovered their independence, settled on the Danube, and launched their attacks on the Eastern Roman empire. Towards the end of the century they invaded and conquered Illyria and, under the leadership of their king, *Theodoric, penetrated Italy. In 493 they defeated the *Heruli and their king, *Odoacer, conquering his capital, Ravenna. The following year they completed the conquest of Italy, where *Theodoric founded a powerful state, based on collaboration between the local elements and the conquerors. Theodoric subsequently enlarged his realm by conquering Provence. Although he attempted to preserve the O.' ethnic character, the process of assimilation was already felt before his death. In 533 Byzantine Emperor *Justinian sent his general *Belisarius to Italy to overthrow the O.' realm. The O. offered fierce resistance and it was only in 555 that the Byzantine army, commanded by *Narses, was able to reconquer Italy. The O. were dispersed and assimilated either with the Italians, or, out of Italy, with other Germanic tribes.
J. M. Wallace-Hadrill, *The Barbarian West* (1965).

OSWALD, St. (605-42) King of *Northumbria (633-42). In 616, at the death of his father, he fled to Scotland, while the throne was seized by *Edwin. During his exile, he was converted to Christianity by the monks of *Iona. He returned to Northumbria after Edwin's death in 633. On becoming king, he devoted himself to converting his subjects with the help of Irish missionaries. Killed in battle by the pagan King *Penda of Mercia in 642, O. was venerated as a martyr.
F. M. Stenton, *Anglo-Saxon England* (1947).

OSWALD, St. Archbishop of York (972-92). A Dane by birth, he studied at Canterbury and at Fleury, France. He returned to England in 959 and dedicated himself to reforming the clergy and the monasteries, first as bishop of Worcester and later as archbishop of *York.
M. D. Knowles, *The Monastic Order in England* (1949).

OSWIN, St. King of *Deira (642-51). After the murder of his father in 634, he fled to Wessex, where he was brought up. He returned to Northumbria after the death of his cousin, St. *Oswald, and restored the kingdom of Deira, being its last king. Murdered during a conflict with another cousin, *Oswy, king of *Bernicia, he was venerated as a martyr.
F. M. Stenton, *AngloSaxon England* (1947).

OSWY (d. 670) King of *Northumbria (655-70). A cousin of St. *Oswald, he was proclaimed king of *Bernicia in 641, under the suzerainty of *Penda, king of Mercia. He remained faithful to his overlord, who supported him in his conflicts with his cousin, St. *Oswin, king of Deira. But when Penda invaded Bernicia in 655, he was killed by O.'s army at Winwaed, in modern Yorkshire. O. subsequently reunited Northumbria by annexing Deira. He also annexed a large part of *Mercia, but gave another part to Penda's son, becoming his overlord. He thus extended his influence to southern England, as far as the Thames. But in 657, when a revolt by the Mercian nobility compelled him to surrender his overlordship of Mercia, he dedicated his efforts to governing and bringing peace to Northumbria. Thus, at the Council of Whitby (664), over which he presided, he attempted to reconcile the *Celtic and *Anglo-Saxon churches.
F. M. Stenton, *Anglo-Saxon England* (1947).

Ostrogothic bronze belt buckle with jewels; 7th century

OTBERT (d. 1101) Bishop of *Liège. He was one of the most prominent members of the school of Liège in the second half of the 11th century. After being consecrated bishop, D. proved an able administrator and politician. His main achievement was his transformation of the Liège bishopric into a principality, by the acquisition, in 1096, of the castle of Bouillon and the domains of *Godfrey of Bouillon, when the latter left for the First *Crusade.
E. de Moreau, *Histoire de l'Eglise de Belgique* (1928).

OTHMAN (UTHMAN) IBN AFFAN (d. 656) Third caliph (644-56). Born into the *Ummayad family of Mecca, who originally resisted Islam, he was the first of the clan to accept *Mohammad, whose daughter, Raqia, he married. At *Omar's death, he was elected caliph, against the candidature of *Ali. O. resumed the expansionist wars of his predecessor, extending the frontiers of the Arab caliphate in north Africa and Asia. But unlike Omar, he left the wars entirely to his generals while he resided at *Medina, where he dedicated his efforts to religion and administration. He ordered that an official version of the *Koran be produced, under his personal supervision, and that the parchment containing variant versions be destroyed. (The Koran hitherto existed as various compilations of Mohammad's sayings, as noted by his pupils.) He reorganized the caliphate,

Otto II; 11th-century miniature

creating provincial governments, under a central administration. But he also practised nepotism, distributing the most important charges and largest incomes to members of his family, and neglecting the generals, who revolted in *Egypt and *Iraq in 650. In 656 he was murdered in his palace by a group of Egyptian rebels, probably supported by his rival Ali.

CHI.

OTHO OF LA ROCHE (d. 1234) Duke of *Athens (1205-25). Member of a noble family of the county of *Burgundy, he joined Boniface of *Montferrat on the Fourth *Crusade and, after the conquest of *Thessalonica, was appointed by Boniface lord of Athens. He conquered Athens and its neighbourhood, where he established a Frankish duchy. In 1225, he abdicated in favour of his son and returned to administer his native land.

W. Miller, *The Latins in Greece* (1908).

OTRIC (10th century) Scholar. The master of the school of Magdeburg, Germany, he reached fame as critic of the works of *Gerbert of Aurillac, especially his theories on the classification of knowledge. The dispute between them, in 980 at Ravenna, was one of the major intellectual discussions of the 10th century. See Pope *Sylvester II.

OTTO I, the Great (912-73) King of *Germany (936-73) and *Holy Roman emperor. Son of *Henry I, he was entrusted by his father with the government of the duchy of *Saxony, where he acquired political and military experience. After his election as king, he repressed a series of revolts by the dukes (936-41) and bestowed the dukedoms on his brothers and kinsmen. To limit the ducal powers, which were based on the tribal traditions still extant in Germany, he gave large territories within

the duchies to bishops and abbots, who were dependent directly on the king; he thus constituted a large ecclesiastical patrimony in Germany. Moreover, the bishops had to put their military resources at the king's disposal and to rely on him for support against the dukes. In 951 O. was called to intervene in Italy, where anarchy reigned and the ambitions of *Berengar II of Friuli endangered the papacy. During the campaign, he freed from prison Adelaide of Burgundy, widow of *Lothair of Provence, and married her. Having imposed his overlordship on Berengar, he returned to Germany to check a revolt by the Lotharingians. His decisive victory over the *Hungarians at *Lechfeld in 955, finally terminated their invasions, and the prestige he gained in Germany as a result of the event helped put an end to local revolts. In 962 he was recalled to Italy by Pope *John XII, whose authority was challenged both by Berengar and by rivals within Rome. On his arrival at Rome, he was crowned emperor by the pope, founding the *Holy Roman empire of the Germans. Soon after his imperial coronation, he began to exert full authority in Italy. He had Berengar exiled to Germany. When John refused to take on oath of obedience to him, O. convened a council at Rome in 963 which deposed the pope. Northern Italy was given a feudal structure, with a special chancery, dependent directly on the emperor. O., who reached the peak of his power and prestige, intervened in the affairs of other European countries and especially of France, where he held a delicate balance between King *Lothair and Duke *Hugh the Great. In 972 he sent Bishop *Liutprand of Cremona to Constantinople, to negotiate the marriage of his son and heir, *Otto II, with the Byzantine princess *Theophano.

Under O., imperial majesty was expressed not only by the exercise of authority, but also by Ottonian architecture and ornamentation and the flowering of culture. O. was a patron of the arts and letters, supported scholars and founded schools within the empire. His cultural activity led to the development of the "Ottonian Renaissance", which reached its highest expression under the reign of his grandson, *Otto III.

G. Tellenbach, *Otto der Grosse (Die grossen Deutschen, I)* (1956).

OTTO II (955-83) *Holy Roman emperor (973-83). Son of Otto I, he began his reign with the help of his mother, Adelaide, and had to face the revolt of his cousin, Duke *Henry II of Bavaria, who was supported by the dukes of Bohemia. Only in 978 was he able to repress the Bavarian revolt; the following year he obtained the submission of the dukes of Bohemia and Poland. After the pacification of Germany, he turned to Italy (980), fighting the Arabs, who had conquered Sicily and Apulia. Defeated in 982, he was in the midst of preparations for a new expedition when he died.

G. Barraclough, *The Origins of Modern Germany* (1951).

OTTO III (980-1002) *Holy Roman emperor (983-1002). During his minority, he reigned under the regencies of his mother *Theophano (983-91) and grandmother Adelaide (991-94), who, with the assistance of the best scholars of the period, among them *Gerbert of Aurrilac, educated him in the majestic spirit of the ancient Roman empire, which he was later to try to re-create. While Germany was pacified and governed by an experienced administration, faithful to the Ottonian

dynasty, imperial authority declined in Italy, where local princes, notably the *Crescentius family at Rome, manifested their independence. Reaching his majority, O. went to Italy in 996, deposed Pope *John XV, defeated the Crescentii, and installed his cousin, Bruno of Carinthia (*Gregory VI), as pope. At the same time, he appointed as archbishop of Ravenna his former tutor and friend, Gerbert. After O.'s return to Germany, another revolt broke out at Rome and the Crescentii expelled Gregory. O. returned to Italy in 998, and conquered Rome, which he made his capital. In 999, at the death of Gregory VI, O. appointed Gerbert pope (*Sylvester II). Gerbert agreed with O.'s idea of a "universal empire", superior to all kingdoms, four of which were already under the emperor's direct authority (Germany, Italy, Gaul-Lotharingia and the Slavs). In 1000, he made a pilgrimage to Gniezno, Poland, which he established as an archiepiscopal see. His direct rule at Rome brought him the opposition of the Roman aristocracy. He repressed a revolt in 1001, but died in 1002, shortly before the arrival of reinforcements from Germany to repress a second revolt led by the Crescentii.
R. Folz, *La Naissance du Saint-Empire* (1968).

OTTO IV, of Brunswick (1175-1218) *Holy Roman emperor (1208-12). Son of *Henry the Lion, duke of Saxony, he was brought up at the court of his uncle, King *Richard I of England, who appointed him earl of York in 1190. At the death of Emperor *Henry VI in 1198, the German opposition to the house of *Hohenstaufen elected him as their candidate to the imperial throne. Although O. obtained the support of Pope *Innocent III after acknowledging the papacy's territorial rights in central Italy, he had to struggle against his rival, *Philip of Swabia and it was not until 1208, when Philip was murdered, that he was recognized as emperor; he was crowned at Rome the following year. O. failed to honour all his commitments to the papacy and resumed the political aims of the Hohenstaufen in Italy, much to the chagrin of the pope, who excommunicated him in 1210, while an assembly of German princes at Nuremberg deposed him. O. returned to Germany in 1212 to reunite his supporters and, in order to appease the Hohenstaufen party, married Beatrice, daughter of Philip of Swabia. Despite his efforts and the help of his uncle, King *John of England, he failed to rally a significant number of supporters and *Frederick II was recognized as emperor. Defeated at the Battle of *Bouvines, O. was compelled to renounce the imperial throne. He was appointed duke of *Brunswick in 1215.
E. Kantorowicz, *Emperor Frederick II* (1931).

OTTO, St. (1062-1130) Bishop of *Bamberg (1102-30), the "Apostle of Pomerania". Of a noble Swabian family, he entered the service of Emperor *Henry IV before 1090 and became his chancellor in 1101. The neutral stance he adopted in the struggle between the empire and the papacy, made him eligible as a negotiator in the *Investiture contest which ended with the Concordat of *Worms (1122). In 1124 he went on a missionary journey to Pomerania, where he influenced the Slav tribes to convert to Christianity.
A. Zimmermann, *Der Heilige Otto von Bamberg* (1935).

OTTO OF FREISING (c. 1110-58) Margrave of Austria and historian. He was the son of *Leopold III and uncle of *Frederick Barbarossa. O. studied at Paris, entered the *Cistercian abbey of Morimond, Champagne,

The Four Nations' Empire of Otto III

in 1132, and became its abbot in 1136. In 1138 he was appointed bishop of Freising and reformed the diocese. O. introduced the study of Aristotle in Germany and was active at the imperial court. In 1148 he joined *Conrad III on the Second *Crusade. Important chiefly as a historian, he became famous for his two books *The Two Cities* and *The Deeds of Frederick Barbarossa*, which was continued by his pupil Rahewin. In the first book, of value primarily as a philosophy of history and drawing on St. *Augustine's *City of God*, O. regards all temporal history as a conflict between this world and the realm of God, envisaging their union in the Catholic Church as the continuation of the Roman empire.
Works, ed. and trans. C. C. Mierow, with biographical introduction (1928).

OTTO OF NORDHEIM (d. 1083) Feudal *Saxon leader. He entered the service of Emperor *Henry III and was one of the supporters of his widow, Agnes, who appointed him duke of Bavaria in 1161. Together with Archbishop Anno of Cologne, he was influential in the government of the German state during the minority of *Henry IV. When Henry reached his majority, O. secured the dismissal of the emperor's counsellor, *Adelbert of Bremen, in 1066. Accused of complicity in a plot against the emperor in 1070 he was deprived of the duchy of Bavaria and his fief of Nordheim. When he came to an agreement with Henry in 1072, he was restored to his lands in Saxony. But shortly afterwards, he led the Saxon revolts against the emperor, and in 1076 agreed to the election of *Rudolf of Swabia in opposition to Henry. A brave and skilful fighter, O. inflicted losses to Henry's forces, but Rudolf was killed in the battle.
G. Barraclough, *Origins of Modern Germany* (1951).

OTTO OF WITTELSBACH (c. 1120-83) Duke of Bavaria (1180-83). He was count palatine of the Rhine and one of the faithful princes of *Frederick Barbarossa in Germany. In 1180, after the banishment of *Henry the Lion, the emperor appointed him duke of Bavaria, where he founded the *Wittelsbach dynasty, destined to reign until 1918.

OTTOKAR (OTAKAR) I, of Premsyl (c. 1155-1230) Duke and king of *Bohemia (1192-1230). He began his reign in chaotic conditions and only in 1198, after the death of Emperor *Henry VI, who had had him deposed in 1193, was he able to govern effectively; He took advantage of the rivalry over the imperial title in Gemany to secure a large measure of autonomy for Bohemia, the *Premyslids' hereditary rights to the ducal title, and in 1212 also the royal title, which was conferred on him by *Frederick II. O. reorganized Bohemia after the civil wars, strengthened the central authority and promoted the development of towns.

E. Kantorowicz, *Emperor Frederick II* (1931).

OTTOKAR (OTAKAR) II (1230-78) King of *Bohemia (1253-78). Son of *Wenceslas III, he became duke of Moravia and in 1251 inherited the duchy of Austria. After his royal coronation at Prague in 1253, he was one of the most powerful princes in the *Holy Roman empire. In 1254 and 1266 he took part in the wars of the *Teutonic knights against the Prussian and Lithuanian tribes. During the Great Interregnum (1254-72) he became involved in the affairs of *Germany, attempting to increase his power. With a strong army and a series of alliances, he was able to conquer Styria and Carinthia in 1260, becoming the greatest prince in the Holy Roman empire and reigning over a German-Slav state that stretched from Silesia to the Adriatic. He aspired to the imperial throne, but his power posed a threat to the princes, who instead chose *Rudolf of Hapsburg in 1272. O. refused to recognize the election and in 1274 rose against Rudolf, who, at the Diet of Ratisbon, divested him of his rights to Austria, Styria and Carinthia. In the ensuing war, O. was defeated and the confiscated territories were granted to the house of *Hapsburg. His attempt to invade Austria in 1278 ended with his death at Dürnkrut.

G. Barraclough, *The Origins of Modern Germany* (1951).

OTTOMAN TURKS See TURKS, OTTOMAN.

OUEN, St. (610-84) Bishop of *Rouen. Member of a noble Frankish family, he served at the courts of *Clotaire II and *Dagobert I, and was chancellor of the latter. In 641 he became bishop of Rouen, was active in monastic reform and reached such great prestige, as to be called upon to mediate between the various kings of Neustria and Austrasia.

J. M. Wallace-Hadrill, *The Long-Haired Kings* (1963).

OURSCAMP Cistercian monastery in northern France. It became famous for its important library (1184) and its church, which reflected the principles of humility and modesty of the *Cisterian order.

OVIEDO City in northern *Spain. Founded in 757 around a small monastery, O. became the capital of the kingdom of *Asturias in 810. King *Alfonso II built a chapel there, destined to house his treasury, his relics and the archives of the realm. The chapel, named *Camera Sacra* (holy chamber). was rebuilt in the 12th century in a splendid Romanesque style.

OXFORD City in *England. In the 7th century it arose as a cattle market on the border of *Mercia and *Wessex. In the 8th century a borough grew around the shrine of St. *Frideswide, which attracted pilgrims as well as merchants, who came to its fairs. After the *Norman conquest of England a number of monasteries and *collegiate churches were established at O. Some of them developed monastic schools, the founding of which was attributed to *Alfred the Great. In the 12th century, O.'s inhabitants enjoyed the special peace of *William the Conqueror, which put them under the direct administration of royal officers.

In 1167, when *Henry II prohibited English students from studying at *Paris, a *Studium Generale*, the nucleus of the *university, was established at O. The institution gradually developed, its organization being completed in 1215, with the appointment of a chancellor as the head of the university by the bishop of Lincoln, in O. Already by 1230, O. housed one of the three most celebrated universities, the other two being those of *Bologna and Paris. Its reputation was based on theology, philosophy and science. The activity of Robert *Grosseteste gave the university its great prestige, while the patronage of King *Henry III enabled its masters and students to obtain various privileges in the city. The second half of the 13th century saw the founding of its first colleges, University, Merton and Balliol, which were followed by others during the 14th and 15th centuries. In the second half of the 14th century the university became a cêntre of religious non-conformism, influenced by the teaching of *Wycliffe and his colleagues at the university who disseminated his controversial views and founded the *Lollard movement.

H. Rashdall, ed. F. M. Powicke and A. B. Emden, *The Universities of Europe in the Middle Ages,* III (1936).

OXFORD, PROVISIONS OF (1285) An important constitutional document, issued by *Henry III to the barons of his realm. It confirmed the stipulations of the *Magna Charta and called for the establishment of a council, whose consent would be needed before the king could impose any new taxes. The O. was the nucleus of the English *parliament.

P

PADEBORN City in *Westphalia (northern Germany). Founded in 777 by *Charlemagne as a military camp and logistic base for his wars against the Saxons, P. gradually expanded and was made a bishopric in 805. The seignorial rights over the city and its surroundings, granted to the bishops by *Otto I, were the nucleus of its development as an episcopal principality, formally recognized by *Frederick Barbarossa in 1180.
J. W. Thompson, *Feudal Germany* (1928).

PADUA City in the *Venetia region, northern Italy. Conquered in 493 by the *Ostrogoths, it passed in 540 to the Byzantines, but the Ostrogoths reconquered it in 541 and held it until 563, when *Narses annexed it to his domains. The ancient Roman city was destroyed by the *Lombards in 601 and only a part of it was reconstructed around the cathedral. In 774, after his conquest of the Lombard kingdom, *Charlemagne made P. the seat of a county. In 897, Bishop Peter I, who fought

The basilica of S. Antonio, Padua built in the 13th century in combined Gothic and Byzantine styles

The Capella Palatina *in the Royal Palace, Palermo*

against the countal family, took the countal title, which remained that of his successors until 1125. With the establishment of communal institutions, P. became an autonomous city, governed by *Guelph families. Conquered in 1237 on behalf of Emperor *Frederick II, who gave it to his faithful general, the *Ghibelline leader *Ezzelino da Romano, P. remained under the Ghibellines until its fall in 1256, when the commune was restored. Internal divisions led to the rise of local tyrants, as well as to its dominion by various *condottieri* in the 14th century. P. was also the subject of dispute between the neighbouring states of *Milan and *Venice, until it was finally annexed to the latter in 1405.

The *university established at P. in 1222 became renowned, especially for its schools of law and medicine, which accommodated foreign scholars and students.

J. K. Hyde, *Society and Politics in Medieval Italy* (1973).

PALAEOLOGUS Imperial dynasty in *Byzantium. The Palaeologi were descendants of a noble family of *Constantinople which settled at *Nicaea in 1204, when the *Crusaders conquered the capital of the Byzantine empire. Its members held important positions in the government and the army of the empire of Nicaea. *Michael VIII P., who became emperor at Nicaea in 1258, founded the dynasty, reconquered Constantinople and restored the Byzantine empire, which was governed by the Palaeologi until the fall of Constantinople and its conquest by the Turks in 1453.

PALATINATE (PFALZ) County on the Rhine in *Germany. The name originated in the office of count palatine, an official entrusted with guarding the Roman emperor's palace. In the *Carolingian empire the counts palatine were officials with judicial and administrative responsibilities, and the territory under their jurisdiction became known as the P. The German kings, and later emperors, appointed faithful vassals to govern the P., which, located in central Germany, was of immense strategic importance. From the second half of the 12th century, the P. belonged to the *Wittelsbach dynasty and after 1180 was part of the duchy of Bavaria, while preserving its special status. The *Golden Bull of *Charles IV made the count of the P. one of the seven electors of the empire.

G. Barraclough, *The Origins of Modern Germany* (1951).

PALERMO Capital of *Sicily. The ancient Roman city continued to develop in the early Middle Ages as an important harbour of the Tyrrhenian Sea. Successively occupied by the *Vandals and the *Byzantines, P. was conquered by the *Aghlabid Arabs of north Africa in 829 and became the seat of Sicily's governor, entitled *Amir Al-Bahr* (The Lord of the Sea) and known by the island's inhabitants as *Amiral* (hence the origin of the modern term "admiral"). Arab domination ended in 1072, with the conquest of the city by the Norman chieftain *Roger of Hauteville, who was commissioned with the conquest by his brother *Robert Guiscard, and vested with the county of Sicily. After the death of his brother, Roger became the head of the family and founded a powerful state, the capital of which was established at P. Under his reign and that of Roger II, P. prospered and was embellished. The royal palace, built in the style of feudal castles, contained a splendid Romanesque chapel, which represents a synthesis of Byzantine, Arabic and Romanesque architecture and art. The development of the kingdom in the 12th and 13th centuries and the establishment of a large administration led to the growth of P., which became a cultural centre and the main place in western Europe where Greek and Arabic scientific and philosophical works were translated into Latin. In the middle of the 12th century, Roger II established P.'s silk industry, the first in western Europe, and the export of silk products contributed to P.'s prosperity. Under *Frederick II, the city became one of the richest and most brilliant centres of western Europe, with a court where Latin, Greek, Arabic, Hebrew, as well as the vernacular languages (Italian, French, German), were fluently spoken. The reign of French King *Charles of Anjou inaugurated a period of decline. His oppressive policies gave rise to an opposition in P. and the outbreak of the *Sicilian Vespers (1282), which ended with the expulsion of the French and the implantation of *Aragonese rule. P. became the capital of an insignificant kingdom, the monarchs of which resided in Aragon.

D. Mac Smith, *Medieval Sicily* (1968).

PALESTINE (HOLY LAND) Country on the eastern shore of the Mediterranean Sea and holy land for Jews, Christians and Moslems. In the early Middle Ages it belonged to the *Byzantine empire and was traditionally divided into three provinces. The city of *Jerusalem, because of its religious significance, was put under the authority of a patriarch. Under the reign of *Justinian, P. became the centre of Christian pilgrimages. With the spread of Christianity, the emperor encouraged the construction of churches and monasteries. His excessive repressions of Jewish and Samaritan revolts led to the desolation of inhabited areas. At the end of the 6th century, many Syriac Christians supported *Monophysitism and were in open conflict with the imperial administration. In 612 the country was attacked by the *Persians, met passively by Eastern Christians and supported actively by a Jewish revolt. Only in 629 was Emperor *Heraclius able to defeat *Chosroes II and restore Byzantine authority in the land, the southern frontiers of which became the target of raids by the Moslem Arabs of *Mohammad. The raids were intensified after 630 and Transjordan, which was given to vassal Arab chieftains, was conquered by the Moslems under the caliphate of *Abu Bakr. In 636, when the Byzantine army was defeated on the Yarmuk by Caliph *Omar, P. fell to the Arabs, with only its capital, *Caesarea, resisting until 642. Caesarea's capitulation marked the end of the Byzantine period.

The Arab conquest introduced demographic changes: most of the Greeks emigrated, while many Eastern Christians – although their religion was recognized by the conquerors as legal – converted to Islam and were gradually Arabized; those who maintained their faith were divided among several churches. On the other hand, Beduin of Hedjaz, as well as other Moslem inhabitants from various parts of the caliphate, settled in the land. The *Umayyad caliphs, who resided at nearby Damascus, changed P.'s administrative structure and created two new provinces: that of the Jordan, with Tiberias as capital, and that of Falastin, with the new city of *Ramlah as capital. A number of Jews were allowed to settle at Jerusalem, which was forbidden to them under the Romans and the Byzantines, but they were prohibited from praying on Mount Moriah, the site of the Temple, which, named *Haram al-Sherif*, was reserved for Moslem worship. Two mosques, the *Dome of the Rock and Al-Aksa, were built on the mount. Jerusalem was divided into three quarters, but remained a small and poor city. Under the *Abbasid caliphs of Baghdad, the real authority over the country was given to the governors of Egypt. The 9th century was a troubled period for P.: revolts and Beduin raids posed a constant threat to security on trade routes and had their impact on commerce. At the end of the century, widespread poverty instigated the emigration of active elements of all communities. The state of anarchy ceased after 970, when the *Fatimids conquered P. and annexed it to their caliphate of Egypt. With the exception of the reign of *Hakim, their rule was liberal and the coastal cities knew a period of prosperity, due to trade revival in the Mediterranean Sea, stimulated by the Fatimid government. The situation changed, however, in 1071, when the *Seljuks, who had conquered the Abbasid caliphate and Syria, penetrated P. and conquered its interior, while the coastal area remained in the hands of the Fatimids. This division of the small country into two enemy territories – which did not affect the peasants, who only changed their lords – created conditions of insecurity which were felt by pilgrims coming from western Europe. Their reports provoked the emergence of European public opinion in favour of conquering the Holy Land.

The *Crusades were rooted in various historical phenomena. The quest for the liberation of the Holy Land and of the church of the *Holy Sepulchre of Christ was only one aspect – albeit one that had tremendous impact on European public opinion. The study of the Bible by the clergy and monks, its quotation by preachers in their sermons, the representation of biblical scenes and the holy places in Romanesque cathedrals and churches, as well as the increased popularity of pilgrimages during the 11th century, made the Holy Land familiar to nobles and peasants alike, who seemed to know more about P. than about some of their neighbouring countries. (Chroniclers of the First Crusade relate that the participants, arriving before the walls of cities of the Danube Valley, asked: "Is that Jerusalem?") The Crusaders penetrated P. in the spring of 1099; they avoided the siege of the coastal cities and went directly to Ramlah, which was deserted, and prepared for the siege of Jerusalem. The holy city was conquered on 15 July 1099. Its Jewish population was exterminated, while the Moslems were expelled. Arriving at the church of the Holy Sepulchre, the crusaders had to solve the problem of whether to create a lay kingdom or an ecclesiastical state. The decision was made in favour of the latter when *Godfrey of Bouillon was chosen as advocate of the Holy Sepulchre. The death of Godfrey in 1100 and the election of his brother *Baldwin, count of *Edessa, as his successor, changed the situation. Baldwin took the royal title and founded the "Latin kingdom of Jerusalem".

The Crusader period was the only one in the history of P., from the destruction of Judaea and the foundation of the State of Israel, during which the political capital of the land was in P. itself. It therefore had a deeper impact than some of the other periods, when P. was a province, within a greater empire. Lasting from 1099 to 1291, the Crusader period is divided into two: the kingdom of Jerusalem until 1187, and that of *Acre, 1187-1291. The first period was one of expansion: after the failure of the Fatimid counter-attacks, Baldwin I completed the conquest of P., including southern Transjordan, and established a *feudal regime, modelled on west European practices, but lacking the peasant infrastructure and countryside settlements. To develop P.'s economy, he gave extensive privileges to Italian cities, which established *communes in the harbours and made P. the emporium of trade between East and West. He also allowed Jews to settle and work in the cities. This policy was continued by his successors, who fortified the land by building castles and fortresses, where the knights were settled, while the countryside remained populated by Arab peasants. The crusaders, however, were few in number and the combatants among them were unable to secure the defence of their realm. They were thus dependent on further crusades from Europe and on the recruitment of knights by the military *orders, the *Hospitallers and the newly-founded *Templars (1119). The shortage of manpower accounted for the Crusaders' defensive strategy that was based on castles, and for their continuous appeals to the West, when even a minor defeat was perceived as a disaster. In the middle of the 12th century, the kingdom of Jerusalem saw its great civil wars between *Baldwin III and his mother, *Melisande, which divided the nobility and contributed to the increase of its power. The Assize of *Amalric I, which granted the vassals the right to participate at the High Court, created the conditions for the institutionalization of an oligarchic republic ruled by nobles. A state of anarchy ensued, with the nobles divided into the moderates, who sought peaceful relations with the Moslem states, and the radicals, who preached continuous war. This, in conjunction with the radicalization of Moslem society under the rule of the *Zengid sultans. precipitated the kingdom's fall. After *Saladin united Egypt and Syria, he attacked the kingdom in 1177. Defeated at Montgisard, near Ramlah, he nonetheless persevered. Helped by the quarrels within the Crusaders' realm and by an adventurous expedition in the Red Sea which awakened the *Jihad spirit in the Moslem world, Saladin defeated and destroyed the Crusaders' army at *Hattin, in Galilee, in 1187, conquering the whole kingdom, with the exception of Tyre.

The disaster at Hattin precipitated the Third Crusade, led by Emperor *Frederick Barbarossa and the kings of England and France, *Richard I and *Philip II respectively. While Frederick died in Asia Minor, the other Crusaders reconquered Acre in 1191 and, under *Richard's command, recovered the coastal area between Acre and *Ascalon. Since the attempt to reconquer Jerusalem failed, the capital of the kingdom was established at Acre. P. was split up between the Crusader realm and that of the Ayyubids of Egypt and Damascus, among whom Saladin's empire was divided. The history of the kingdom of Acre is characterized by political instability, the limitation of royal power by the high court and by a total dependence on Europe. The various 13th-century Crusades brought some territorial additions and the means to prolong the survival of the kingdom. The "diplomatic" Crusade of *Frederick II in 1229 peacefully recovered a demilitarized Jerusalem, but also introduced civil war, which ended with the victory of the nobility, organized in the "commune" of St. *Andrew. The *Khwarizmian invasion of 1244 led to the loss of Jerusalem and to the Crusaders' disastrous defeat at Forbie, which limited the realm to most of Galilee and to the strip of land between Acre and *Jaffa. The Crusade of King *Louis IX of France (1247-52) had only one effect, the fortification of the cities, which put the realm entirely on the defensive. Meanwhile, the *Mamelukes, who replaced the Ayyubids as rulers of Egypt (1250), began to attack the realm. After *Baibars defeated the *Mongols at Ain-Jalud (1261), he turned against the Crusaders and began the systematic conquest of P. This the Mamelukes finally achieved with the fall of Acre in 1291.

The 13th century was also the period of a large Jewish immigration, both from western Europe and north Africa. Jewish settlements were again established, such as the Jewish quarter in Jerusalem. The influx of Jews was influenced by the messianic ideal of settling the country to bring salvation to the Jewish people.

The last period in the history of medieval P. was that of Mameluke domination. To prevent the return of the Crusaders, the Mamelukes completely devastated P.'s coastal area and its cities. The Mamelukes' conception of P. as only a corridor between Egypt and Syria led them to neglect its civil administration and to concentrate only on the fortification of strategic cities, such as Ramlah and Safed. The irrigation channels were gradually ruined in the 14th and 15th centuries, and the use of wood for military purposes destroyed the forests of the mountain area, radically changing its landscape. A notable exception was Jerusalem. Fortified by Baibars, Jerusalem saw a period of development, caused by its status of holy city for the three monotheistic religions. A Moslem high school (medersa) established at the entrance to the Haram al-Sherif, contributed to the development of the Moslem quarter of Jerusalem and to the settlement of prominent Arab families within its walls. At the Jewish quarter, populated by immigrants from various countries, new synagogues and schools sprang up. The Christian quarter also flourished, both because of the settlement there of Eastern Christians, Georgians and Armenians, and because of the establishment of monasteries of the Orthodox and Catholic churches.

CMedH, IV;
CHI;
J. Prawer, The Crusaders (1973).

PALLAVICINI, GUIDO (d. 1218) Margrave of Bodonitza (1205-18). Member of a Lombard baronial family, he took part in the Fourth *Crusade, as vassal of *Boniface of Montferrat. After the conquest of *Thessalonica, Boniface appointed him margrave of Bodonitza, Greece, which he conquered in 1205, together with the Thermopylae passes. He organized his principality according to the feudal customs of Lombardy.
W. Miller, The Latins in the East (1908).

PALLAVICINI, UBERTO (1197-1269) *Ghibelline leader in northern Italy. Member of a Lombard baronial family, he entered the service of Emperor *Frederick II in 1238 and, until 1254, commanded the imperial army in western Lombardy. In 1254 he seized power at Pavia, Cremona and Piacenza, forming one of the most powerful principalities in northern Italy. He gradually enlarged his possessions and in 1260, as "Captain General", he became the virtual lord of Milan. Defeated in 1265 by *Charles of Anjou, P. had to give up his office at Milan. His principality disintegrated after his death.
J. K. Hyde, Society and Politics in Medieval Italy (1973).

PALLIUM A circular band of white woollen material, with two hanging strips, worn around the shoulders by popes at liturgical services. In the early Middle Ages, popes used to present a P. to archbishops and bishops as a symbol of distinction. From the 9th century on, the "sending of the P." became institutionalized; an archbishop-designate had to announce his election to the pope, and, as a sign of recognition, and – from the late 11th century onwards – confirmation, the pope would send him the P.
EC, IX.

PAMPLONA City in northwestern *Spain. An ancient Ibero-Roman town, P. was conquered by the *Visigoths, but they did not rule it effectively and it became the capital of a petty *Basque principality. After the fall of the Visigothic kingdom (711) and the conquest of Spain by the Arabs, P. became the capital of a Christian principality, which resisted the Moslems and later became the kingdom of *Navarre. In 778 *Charlemagne attacked the city and destroyed its fortifications. In the 11th and 12th centuries P. flourished as an important station on the pilgrims' way to *Santiago de Compostela. From the 13th century on the city declined, following the decrease in importance of the realm of Navarre.

A. Castro, *The Structure of Spanish History* (1954).

PANDECTS The name of manuals containing interpretations of Roman *Law and used in medieval universities.

PANNONIA See HUNGARY.

PAPACY The name of the bishopric of *Rome, presided over by the pope as head of the Roman Catholic Church. Derived from the Latin word *pater,* which in popular usage of late classical Latin became *papa* (father), the term pope was first used by the faithful in addressing a priest. From the 5th century, when *Leo I claimed that the Roman bishop was the supreme leader in the church hierarchy, it became specifically used in the Western Church as the title of the bishops of Rome, while in the Greek Orthodox and Eastern Churches, it remained the title of any priest, regardless of rank.

As an institution, the P. emerged in the 5th century, mainly due to the fact that in the entire Western Roman empire, no patriarchal sees had been established, with the exception of that of Rome. The belief in its primacy among the other churches and the faithful was rooted in the Petrine doctrine, according to which the bishop of Rome is considered to be the successor of St. *Peter, who was appointed by Jesus Christ as Prince of the Apostles and his Vicar, and founded the Church of Rome. An important step in enhancing the position of the pope was taken by Pope *Gregory I the Great, who took it upon himself to confirm bishops, interpret *canon law and liturgical practices, and to confirm council decisions. He also laid down the basis for the temporal independence of the P., by founding the *Papal States. Theoretically, the P. never gave up its claim to universal authority over the faithful, and even a pope such as *Leo III, who was totally dependent on *Charlemagne, could claim that *Papa a nemine judicatur* (the pope could not be judged by any person or body, namely a council). But in practice its power was often limited. During the *Carolingian and *Ottonian periods, it was held that a pope needed the confirmation of the emperor after his election. Moreover, in the 10th and 11th centuries, popes were dependent on the heads of the Roman aristocracy, who used to appoint their own candidates to the papal see. This corruption led Emperors *Otto I, *Otto III and *Henry III to intervene in papal elections and to assure the promotion of more suitable candidates. Henry III even selected the pope from among highly-esteemed German bishops, thus introducing in Rome the *Cluniac reform, which was largely adopted by German bishops in the 11th century. This reform movement influenced the decision of the Lateran Council, convened by Pope *Nicholas II in 1059, to restrict papal elections to the college of *cardinals – which meant, in essence, that the P. was to be independent of lay control. Under his successors, and especially *Gregory VII, the P. developed a centralistic government of the Church, thereby inaugurating a long conflict with the *Holy Roman empire that was to

St. Peter blessing Pope Leo III and Charlemagne, Rome

Bronze statue of St. Peter at S. Pietro Basilica, Rome

last for almost two centuries (1077-1250). While the first phase of that struggle, the *Investiture contest, seemed to be only a technical dispute, involving the freedom of episcopal elections, the real issue was whether the emperor or the pope should dominate Christendom. During the conflict, the P. advanced a theocratic ideology, fully expressed in the thought and actions of *Innocent III, who claimed to be not only the Vicar of Christ, but also the Lord of the Catholic World. The conflict ended not only with the destruction of the Holy Roman empire and political anarchy in Italy and Germany, but also with the weakening of the P., which failed in its attempts to impose its authority over the sovereign monarchies in the West. The claims of *Boniface VIII to universal authority met with formal opposition from France, which secured control of the P. After his death, the P. was moved to *Avignon, where it remained from 1305 to 1378, a period named "the Babylonian captivity of the P.", and during which it was under the influence of French kings. The *Great Schism – which emerged at the end of the Avignon period when two popes were elected, at Rome and at Avignon, each contesting the legitimacy of the other – led to the decline of the P., to the rise of non-conformist theories – which ended with the Reformation, and to the elaboration, by theologians and ecclesiastical leaders, on the *Conciliar theory, according to which the council is superior to the P. The councils' failure to become executive bodies in the 15th century restored the primacy to the P., but its prestige largely declined and the popes of the second half of the 15th century were little more than Renaissance princes.

W. Ullman, *A Short History of the Papacy* (1972).

PAPAL STATES (Patrimonium Sancti Petri) The provinces belonging to the *papacy as its temporal demesne and under its sovereignty. They originate in the donations of several popes, in the 5th and 6th centuries, of their personal possessions in *Rome and its surroundings. Until the end of the 6th century those estates were considered private possessions, according to Roman law, and were exempt from taxes by imperial privileges. When the *Lombards approached Rome and the Byzantine exarch of Ravenna was unable to send an army to defend the city, Pope *Gregory I ordered that the Sign of St. *Peter be put on the walls of Rome (590), signifying the change of sovereignty. With this symbolical gesture he founded the P., giving Rome the public authority over the estates of the neighbourhood. With the abolition, in the 7th century, of the Byzantine duchy of Rome, its functions were inherited by the papacy, which consequently became the sovereign possessor of the province of *Latium. When the Church clashed with the Lombards in the 7th and 8th centuries, it was because of their efforts to conquer Italy, including the province of Rome. For this reason the popes appealed to the *Franks. In return for a papal confirmation of his royal title, *Pepin the Short issued in 754 a charter confirming papal territorial claims in Italy, including not only the ancient duchy of Rome, but also the remnants of the Byzantine lands of Ravenna and its surroundings, and a number of Lombard lands between Rome and the Po River. The area corresponds more or less with the traditional P. at the end of the Middle Ages. In 774 *Charlemagne confirmed his father's charter, but, using his title and quality of "Patrice of the

Romans", he undertook the administration of the state, which was incorporated in his empire. With the division and decline of the *Carolingian empire, the P. were legally returned to the papacy, but in reality only Latium was under papal rule, while the northern provinces were divided among local magnates. In the 10th century the process of feudalization spread through the P., and the aristocracy sought to impose its authority over the various fiefs, as well as over the papacy. In the second half of the 13th century, after the fall of *Frederick II, the popes began to recover their sovereignty by demanding and obtaining the homage of various *Guelph leaders in the provinces of Ravenna and Bologna. However, after the settlement of the papacy at *Avignon (1305), local lords and tyrants recovered their independence, and even in Rome republican trends were manifested to the point that little remained of the P. in Italy. On the other hand, Queen *Joan I of Naples, who was also the countess of Provence, donated to Pope *John XXII the full sovereignty of Avignon and its surroundings and a new papal state, containing the area of Avignon-Vaucluse, was established in southern France. In 1350 the Spanish cardinal *Albornoz was sent to Rome by Pope *Clement VI, as papal governor of the city and of the "Patrimony of St. Peter". He undertook to restore papal authority in the P. and defeated many of the local tyrants and other *signori*, recovering the major part of the P. in Italy. After the return of the papacy to Rome and the *Conciliar epoch of the first half of the 15th century, the process was continued by the popes and their captains, and the P. were reconstituted in Latium, Umbria, Ancona, Ravenna, Bologna and their respective provinces.

L. Duchesne, *Les Origines de l'Etat Pontifical au Moyen Age* (1912).

PARACLETE (Holy Spirit) Chapel founded in northwestern Champagne by *Abelard, who found refuge there in 1122. He lived and taught there until 1129, when he gave the place to his wife *Heloise, who, with other nuns, had been expelled from the abbey of Argenteuil. Heloise founded a nunnery at P., whose rule was written by Abelard himself and confirmed by Pope *Innocent II. When he died (1142), Abelard was buried at P.

P. Sikes, *Peter Abelard* (1932).

PARIS Capital of France. The Gallo-Roman city Lutetia Parisiorum, corresponded in the last century of the Western Roman empire to its central part, the island called the Cité. During the raids of the *Huns, led by *Attila, it was saved by St. *Geneviève, who from 453 has been the patron saint of the city. Conquered by the *Franks under *Clovis, it became one of the capitals of the *Merovingian realm, and especially of the *Neustrian kings. Some of these promoted its development, especially *Dagobert I, who took care of its *fairs. During this period, however, its main importance was religious, thanks to the growing cult of St. *Denis, and its bishops achieved power and prestige in the realm. Under the *Carolingians P. lost its status as the capital and was governed by counts. In the 8th and 9th centuries a number of great abbeys were established around the city, such as the abbeys of St. Geneviève and *St. Germain-des-Prés, and the abbey of St. Denis knew a period of great prosperity. Attacked in 887-88 by the *Normans, it was saved by its Robertian count *Eudes

who, after the abdication of *Charles the Fat, was elected king of France. His family created in the 10th
century a vast and powerful feudal principality, the
duchy of the Franks, between the Seine and Loire, with
P. as its centre. With the royal coronation of the last
duke, *Hugh Capet (987), P. recovered its position as
royal city, being the principal residence of the *Capetians, and continued to grow. Due to its position at the
cross-roads of commercial routes, it enjoyed economical
prosperity, and at the beginning of the 12th century
new quarters were built on the right and left banks of
the Seine. At the same time, with the development of
the royal administration under *Louis VI and *Louis
VII, P. became officially the capital of France and the
seat of the royal administration, established on the
island of the Cité, while the quarters on the right bank
of the Seine became the centre of commerce and crafts.
In the 12th century the city also became famous for the
schools of the cathedral of St. Geneviève and the newly-
founded abbey of *St. Victor, where masters such as
*William of Champeaux, *Abelard, *Hugh and *Richard
of St. Victor, *Adelard of Bath and *Peter Lombard
taught, attracting a multitude of students from all over
western Europe. Out of these schools, established
mainly on the left bank of the Seine, emerged during
the 12th century the *University of P., which became
the most famous in Europe. The students also settled
on the left bank and, being of different nationalities,
they could speak together only in Latin, with the result
that the quarter which grew during this century between
the abbeys of St. Germain-des-Prés, St. Geneviève and
St. Victor, was named the *Quartier Latin.* The expansion of the city reached its peak at the beginning of the
13th century, when the *Gothic cathedral of the Cité
was completed, and the royal palace on its opposite side
was enlarged, and King *Philip II ordered the building
of a new wall to contain the new quarters. Within, the
city retained its triple distinction of being a centre of
government and administration, commerce and scholarship. At that time the population of P. was between
50,000 and 80,000 inhabitants. P. knew a golden age
during the reign of *Louis IX, when it became one of
the greatest cities in Europe. Many noble families and
important abbots built palaces to live in during their
visits to the royal court, and one of the most beautiful
monuments of Gothic art, the *Sainte Chapelle, was built
by King Louis within the royal palace in the Cité.

Despite the crises and the *plagues of the 14th century and the *Hundred Years' War, P. continued to
grow and to expand, especially on the right bank.
*Charles V ordered the building of a new wall, which
marked a 100 per cent increase of the urban area in 150
years, a rate which was not matched by other European
cities of the age. With the greatly enlarged administration,
Charles V left the royal palace of the Cité to the *Parliament, and built a new royal palace on the right bank,
in the new aristocratic quarter, *Le Marais,* where several
noble families, including the princes of the dynasty,
built their palaces. Owing to its importance as royal
capital, P. never received the status of *commune and
was not allowed to have a city council. A royal provost
was appointed to administer the city and maintain
public order. On the other hand, the *guilds were allowed
to have their representative bodies and elected provosts;
the most important of these was the guild of the Seine

Paris in the 15th century, *by Jean Fouquet*

merchants, *les marchands d'eau,* whose provost claimed
a parallel position to the royal provost. With the revolt
of Etienne *Marcel (1358-60), an attempt was made to
compel the monarchy to recognize communal institutions in P. The suppression of the revolt by Charles V
ended the attempt. At the beginning of the 15th century the city went through a troubled period: the
struggle between the *Armagnacs and *Bourguignons
affected life in P., which suffered from violence and
disorder.

The University of P. was formed in the second half
of the 12th century out of a large number of schools,
many of them private establishments of the masters.
Its first institutional organization originated in the
obligation to obtain a teaching licence from the chancellor of the bishopric. To shorten the procedures and the
required examinations the masters created a corporation,
with the chancellor *Peter Comestor, who was a reputed
scholar, at its head. In 1200 King *Philip II granted the
corporation — entitled *Universitas Societas Magistrorum
et Scholarium* (The Universal Society of the Masters and
Scholars) — its privileges, forbidding the provost to
intervene in its affairs. Pope *Innocent III, a former
student at P., confirmed its statutes in 1208 and 1215,
and in 1229 *Gregory IX broadened its privileges after
a conflict between the bishop and the masters, who
migrated to *Orléans. As an institution the university
was organized in four "Nations": the French, Norman,
Picardian (and Low Countries) and English (including
Germans). The heads of the nations formed the collegiate
directory of the university and administered its properties. Another stage in the organization was the emergence

The English Parliament meeting at Westminster; from a 15th-century illuminated manuscript

of the faculties, whose number was limited to four: arts, medicine, law and theology, the last-named being the senior faculty. The difficulty of finding lodgings for students, and sometimes for foreign masters, led to the establishment of colleges, built by pious donations, and gradually the teaching activities were transferred to them. The most famous of the colleges was the *Sorbonne, containing the faculty of theology. The university had its heydey in the 13th century, when the most famous masters of all Europe taught there. Many were members of the *Mendicant orders, who used to teach in their own establishment. The *Dominicans, too, possessed a house in St. Jacques Street, hence the name of their college, the Jacobins. The introduction of the Mendicants into the university caused a long dispute between them and the other masters and ended with a papal decision in their favour. The crises of the 14th century and the *Hundred Years' War affected the university adversely, though the prestige of the faculty of theology remained high and rose even higher during the *Great Schism. The Sorbonne was consulted both by the church and the monarchy on various problems. At the beginning of the 15th century the university adopted theses on the *Conciliar authority which were largely followed by the church. The failure of the Conciliar movement, as well as the proliferation of

universities at the end of the Middle Ages caused the decline of the University of P. in the 15th century.

B. Maurel, *Paris, Ses origines, sa croissance, son histoire* (1932);

H. Rashdall, *The Universties of Europe in the Middle Ages*, I, ed. F. M. Powicke and A. B. Emden (1936).

PARIS, MATTHEW See MATTHEW PARIS.

PARISH (Greek: parrochia) Smallest subdivision in the *church, consisting of a community of the faithful served by a local church with its own priest. The organization of Ps. in the Middle Ages was a long and unequal process. In most of the main cities of Italy there were Ps. as early as the beginning of the Middle Ages. North of the Alps, the development took longer, because of the decline of the cities in the early Middle Ages and the existence of private chapels. Only in the 11th century did most European countries have organized Ps. in their urban societies. In the countryside they were formed in the 12th century. The P. church was the social centre of the community and the local cemetery was in its courtyard.

EC, XI.

PARLIAMENT Name given to representative assemblies from the 13th century on. It derives from the vernacular French, meaning a place where people speak. This popular term was nevertheless adopted by learned society, despite its pejorative sense. Two classical forms and characters of P. emerged in medieval society, the English and the French, while in other countries the name was given by modern historians out of convenience.

The English P. emerged during the reign of *Edward I, as an outgrowth of the councils of the barons and prelates, assembled after the giving of the *Magna Charta to deal with the affairs of the *community of the realm. To the prelates and barons, who were summoned by the king, Edward I used to add representatives of the knights of the shires and boroughs, who were summoned through the sheriffs. There was no rule about the assembling of a P., the number of its members, its agenda and the length of sessions. The main role of P. was to deal with the royal demands for taxes, and the king alone decided when and under what circumstances he wished to consult with the "community of the realm". Edwardian legislation, however, emphasized the function of consultation on public affairs. P. would be summoned to deal with one matter, and disperse after the reaching of conclusions. It also served as the feudal high *court, and therefore had also judicial prerogatives, reserved to its baronial part. English practice in the 14th century led to the division of P. into two assemblies, that of the Lords, representing the prelates and barons, and that of the Commoners (later "Commons"), being the representatives of the knights of the *shires and the *boroughs. As the king presided over the assembly of the Lords, the Commoners were allowed to elect a chairman who would serve as their speaker before the king and his council, a title that was preserved through the ages. In the 14th and 15th centuries the assemblies of the Lords dealt with political affairs and were also high courts of justice, even on occasion impeaching the royal counsellors, whereas the Commoners had to deal with financial and economic affairs. The English form of P., with representative assemblies of estates and free-men, was later adopted in European countries.

The French P., or *Parlement* was, on the contrary, an organ of royal authority. It grew out of the feudal high court of justice, where, during the reign of *Louis IX, professional lawyers (also called *legistes*) introduced legal procedures to replace equity. Gradually the king and the high nobility left the court, which became too specialized and professional, appointing among its professional members *procureurs* (English – proctors), to represent their interests. The P. of *Paris was the first French P. and its evolution in the 13th and 14th centuries influenced the organization of provincial Ps. Its court, headed by an appointed president, dealt with a great range of subjects and considered appeals to the royal justice. It adopted as procedure the *factum*, whereby the appellant had to present, through his counsellor, a written memoir, with the relevant documents; the *factum* remained in the archives, while the sentence was recorded in a special collection, the *olim*.

A. Marongiu, *Medieval Parliaments; A Comparative Study* (1969).

Christ in Majesty, *a Romanesque relief by Antelami at the cathedral of Parma, Italy*

The Baptistery of Parma by Antelami

PARLOIR AUX BOURGEOIS The term, meaning, in medieval French, "Parliament of Burghers", referred to a court of justice, established in Paris in the 13th century to deal with commercial cases. It was headed by a provost of the merchants who held an important rank in the city, to such an extent that from the end of the 13th century, he was considered an unofficial mayor.
F. Lot and R. Fawtier, *Histoire des Institutions Françaises au Moyen Age*, II (1958).

PARMA City in northern *Italy. Like the rest of the country, P. was successively ruled by *Heruli, *Ostrogoths, *Byzantines and *Lombards. It was conquered by *Charlemagne in 774, and in 807 was given by him to its bishops. In 1081 a feudal rising compelled Bishop Everard to renounce his temporal government and institute a countal one, which lasted until 1115, when a *commune was established in P. Under the communal statute the city prospered and became one of the most important stations on the road between Rome and Lombardy. Its prosperity was reflected in the artistic flowering of the city. The famous baptistery, designed by *Antelami in the Romanesque and Gothic style, was built at the end of the 13th century. At this time the rivalry between the leading local families caused the decline of the communal government, which collapsed in 1244, when Bernardo Rossi seized power in the city and established a seigniory. A devoted ally of Emperor *Frederick II, Rossi brought P. into the *Ghibelline camp, involving the city in the struggle between the papacy and the *Hohenstaufens. Even after the fall of the Hohenstaufens, the Rossi family remained the most influential power in P. and maintained their authority until the middle of the 14th century, when the city was conquered by the *Visconti of Milan.
T. Bazzi, *Storia di Parma* (1903).

PASCHAL I Pope (817-24). Member of the Roman family of Massimi, he was employed at the court of Pope *Leo III and was himself elected pope because of his saintly life. In 822, at the request of *Louis the Pious, he crowned *Lothair I emperor.

PASCHAL II (Ranier of San Lorenzo; c. 1050-1118) Pope from 1099. Born in Ravenna, he entered the *Cluniac monastery of San Lorenzo and in time became its abbot. In 1080, while on a visit to Rome, he attracted the attention of Pope *Gregory VII, who created him cardinal. He was elected pope after the death of *Urban II, and continued the *Gregorian reform. With the renewal of the *Investiture controversy, he stood firmly against *Henry IV and *Henry V. In 1106 he went to France to seek German allies against the emperor. During this journey he solved investiture procedures in England and France. In 1111, when Henry V came to Rome for the imperial coronation, P. refused to crown him and was taken prisoner. He was compelled to surrender to Henry's demands at Sutri, but the privilege was declared void by a council held at Lateran after his liberation in 1112.
W. Ullmann, *A Short History of the Papacy* (1972).

PASCHAL III (Guy of Crema; 1100-68) Antipope (1164-68). In 1159 he was among the leading opponents of the election of *Alexander III, and supported the candidature of the pro-imperial Cardinal Octavian. Upon Octavian's death, P. was elected antipope, supported by *Frederick Barbarossa. He never received recognition in the Catholic world.

PASCHAL CONTROVERSIES A series of disputes within the *Church, concerning the calculation of the date of Easter. The main disputes took place in the 3rd century, when it was formally decreed that Easter would always fall on Sunday. Also in 7th-century Britain, where the Celtic and Irish churches used an archaic method of computation, celebrating Easter a week before the Roman date, which was used by the Anglo-Saxons. This dispute lasted more than half a century, until the Roman custom was imposed on England in 669.
F. M. Stenton, *Anglo-Saxon England* (1947).

PASCHASIUS RADBERTUS, St. (785-860) Theologian. A monk at the monastery of Corbie in northern *France, his wide knowledge of theological sources impressed his abbot, Adalhard, whom he followed on a missionary journey to Saxony in 822. In 844, he was elected abbot, but resigned in 853, in order to devote himself to study. His most important work is a commentary on St. Matthew, written in 831 and revised in 844, entitled *De Corpore et Sanguine Domini* (On the Body and Blood of the Lord), for the instruction of the Saxon monks. It is the first doctrinal monograph on the *Eucharist. P. adopted a realistic view of the question, which was criticized by his contemporary *Rabanus Maurus. His treatise is also a polemical anti-Jewish work, and influenced the development of anti-Semitic ideas in western Europe.
PL, 120;
H. Peltier, *Paschase Radbert* (1938).

PASSAU City in western *Bavaria, on the Danube. Its growth began in the 8th century, when Duke *Odilo established a bishopric there, which became a base for missionary activity in the lands of the *Avars and the *Czechs. During the reign of *Charlemagne, P. became an important commercial centre, having an important share of the trade between the Frankish empire and the countries of the Danube. From the 10th century on, the bishops were granted the lordship of the city and, in 1217, Emperor *Frederick II granted them the status of Princes of the Empire.

PASSION, THE (Latin: passio "suffering") The term used to describe the sufferings of Christ during the final week of His earthly life, which came to be known as Holy Week, culminating on the eve of Easter. From the 4th century on, the gospels' narratives of P., which were recited in the churches during Holy Week, were accompanied by musical settings and choruses, both in the Greek and the Latin churches. From these liturgical representations there emerged in western Europe, beginning in the 10th century, a series of public representations and plays, held in the square before the church, in which the whole community participated. The performances often provoked violent attacks on the local Jews, some of whom were incorporated in the play. From the 13th century on, P. was the subject of an evolving dramatic form, with its own particular music and casting, especially in Germany. In 1388 *Philip of Mézières planned a new order of *chivalry, named after P., whose purpose was to bring back the Redeemer, by making peace among the Christian monarchs and undertaking a *Crusade.

D. K. Young, *Medieval Drama* (1936).

PASTOUREAUX Name given to a revolt of *peasants in France against the heavy taxation imposed on them. Led by a group of shepherds, after whom the movement was named, they demanded the return of King *Louis IX from the *Crusade, hoping he would bring them justice. The revolt was crushed in 1251 by the regent, Queen Blanche of Castile.

PATARINES *Milanese political-religious movement. The name was first used in the 11th century, when a movement demanding Catholic reform emerged in the Pataria quarter in Milan. Its roots, however, lay in the struggle of the burghers of the city against the power of the archbishops, beginning in 1045. The P., therefore, combined a religious ideology with a burghers' communal movement, whose aims were political. In 1061 they forced Archbishop Guy to abdicate and opposed the prerogative of Emperor *Henry IV to invest his successor. The P. were crushed *c.* 1075, but their ideology remained active in Milan and was expressed in the 12th century by a pro-papal, anti-imperial attitude.

C. Violante, *La Società Milanesa nell 11. sècolo* (1952)

PATRIARCH, PATRIARCHATE A hierarchical dignity in the Christian Church, whose origins date from the 4th century. At the Council of Constantinople of 381, four patriarchal sees were formally established: *Alexandria, *Antioch and *Rome, as apostolic foundations, and Constantinople, as the capital of the empire. In the 5th century the see of *Jerusalem was also elevated to the status of a P. The P. exercised administrative and moral authority and, until the 6th century, had no other powers than those of a bishop. In the theological disputes of the early Middle Ages, the Ps. played an important role, but their decisions had to be confirmed by the emperors and the councils of the Church. The

A Passion play; after a 16th-century woodcut

most important P. was that of Rome who, on the basis of the Petrine heritage, claimed authority over the entire Church (see *papacy), and that of Constantinople, who was supported by the Byzantine emperors, and claimed the title of Oecumenical P. and authority over his colleagues. The Arab conquest reduced the status of the Eastern P., and so did the establishment of the new P. of the dissident Eastern churches.

PATRICK, St. (c. 389-461) The so-called Apostle of *Ireland and its patron saint. Of Roman-British origin, he was captured by pirates at the age of 16 and sold as a slave in Ireland. Working on a ship he succeeded in escaping and returning to his family. Then he had a vision that made him resolve to evangelize Ireland. He first went to Gaul, where he studied and was ordained at Auxerre. In 431 he was sent to convert the Irish and began his missionary work, probably in Leinster. In 442 he visited Rome and accounted for his activities, having been consecrated bishop of Ireland. On his return in 444 he founded the cathedral of *Armagh, which became the centre of the Irish church. P. organized the scattered Christian communities in northern Ireland and made additional converts in other regions of the island. He encouraged the study of Latin and the development of a local clergy, rooted in the social system of the land. His cult, with many legendary episodes, became part of the Irish national religious and cultural heritage.

E. MacNeill, *St. Patrick, Apostle of Ireland* (1934).

PAUL I (700-67) Pope from 757. Of Roman origin, he was the principal adviser of *Stephen III and, after his death, was elected pope. Being in constant conflict with *Desiderius, king of the Lombards, P. relied on *Pepin the Short, king of the Franks, and gave him the title of "Patrice of the Romans", thereby hoping to involve him in the defence of the papacy.

PAUL OF AEGINA (c. 625-c. 690) Physician. He studied in Alexandria and there practised medicine. His main work, *Epitomae Medicae Libri Septem* (The Seven Books of Medical Epitome), is a summary of classical medicine. It was translated into Arabic and served as a manual for the study of *medicine for centuries.

D. Guthrie, *A History of Medicine* (1945).

PAUL THE DEACON (c. 720-800) Historian. Of noble Lombard descent, he was educated at the royal court of Pavia and in about 775, became monk at *Monte Cassino. In 782 he visited *Charlemagne and was well received at his court, where he remained until 786. While there he wrote a history of the bishops of Metz, as well as didactical works. After his return to Monte Cassino he undertook his most important work, the history of the Lombards, covering the period 668-744.

PAULICIANS A sect in the *Byzantine empire which was active in the 7th century, though its origins in Asia Minor were probably earlier. They upheld *Manichaean ideas and, in 684, were proclaimed heretics by the orthodox *Church and persecuted by the imperial government. Nevertheless, the P. continued to profess their dualistic doctrine. Some of them supported the Arab attacks on Asia Minor, hoping for the downfall of the Byzantine empire, which they considered the embodiment of evil, and eventually converted to Islam. Others diffused their teaching within the empire in the 8th and 9th centuries, and eventually established communities in Bulgaria, and influenced the *Albigenses in southern France.

S. Runciman, *The Medieval Manichee* (1951).

PAULINUS OF AQUILEIA, St. (726-802) Bishop of Aquileia. Born in Friuli, he became a reputed scholar. In 776 *Charlemagne summoned him to the royal court, where he became a prominent member of the palace academy, headed by *Alcuin. In 787 Charlemagne appointed him bishop of Aquileia, with the title of patriarch.

Works, *PL*, 99;

W. Ullmann, *The Carolingian Renaissance and the Idea of Kingship* (1969).

PAULINUS OF YORK, St. (d. 644) Bishop of *York. He was sent in 601 by Pope *Gregory I to England, to reinforce the mission of St. Augustine. In 625 he accompanied *Ethelburga of Kent to Northumbria, where she married King *Edwin. As a result of P.'s preaching, Edwin converted to Christianity. In 627 P. began the building of the cathedral of York, to serve as the religious centre of Northumbria. After Edwin's defeat by Cadwallon in 633 P. was compelled to flee, and spent the remainder of his life at Rochester.

PAULO NICOLETTI OF VENICE (d. 1429) Philosopher and scholar. He studied at Merton College, *Oxford, where he became acquainted with the scientific works of the Mertonian scholars, as well as with those of *William of Ockham. Later he settled in Padua and taught logic and physics at its university, developing ideas on geology.

F. D. Adams, *The Birth and Development of the Geological Sciences* (1938).

PAVIA City in *Lombardy, on the banks of the Po River. Devastated by *Attila in 452, P. was rebuilt by the *Ostrogoths at the beginning of the 6th century and became one of their centres in northern Italy. In 568 the Lombards conquered the city and made it the capital of their kingdom. Under Lombard rule, P. prospered and became an important cultural and politi-

cal centre. Conquered by *Charlemagne in 774, it was proclaimed the capital of the kingdom of Italy and the residence of Charlemagne's son *Pepin. Even after the fall of the *Carolingian empire P. was still considered as capital of the kingdom of Italy, and pretenders to the imperial crown would seize the city and be crowned there. In 952 it was conquered by *Otto I the Great and, after the establishment of the *Holy Roman empire, the seat of the chancery of Italy was established in P. In 1110 the city burghers proclaimed a commune. In 1154 Emperor *Frederick Barbarossa conquered the city, imposing an imperial governor. In the 13th century it became one of the fiefs of the principality of the *Pallavicini family, who lost it in 1268. After a short period of independence P. was conquered in 1315 by the *Visconti of Milan and united with the Milanese duchy. The annexation caused its trade to decline, while Milan prospered. Despite the establishment of a *university in 1361, P.'s importance declined.

J. K. Hyde, *Society and Politics in Medieval Italy* (1973).

PEACE OF GOD A social-religious movement which arose in western France in the 10th century as a reaction against *feudal disorder. The Church protected the movement and, in 987, a council assembled at Charroux decreed the P. among the Christians, threatening to excommunicate those who broke it. Bishops raised armies so as to impose respect for the P., with the result that they were able to enlarge their estates and the number of their vassals. However, the ideal of permanent, general peace was seen to be excessive, and in the 11th century the movement was transformed into the *Truce of God, forbidding attacks on clergy and non-combatants, and restricting warfare to certain seasons and three days a week. The movement, supported by the order of *Cluny, was widespread in France and Italy, countries where royal power was weak, whereas in Germany and England it was superseded by the imperial or royal peace. After its confirmation by the papacy in 1058, institutions of peace were established, among them special courts, where "justices of the peace" would settle conflicts so as to avoid feudal wars. Militias of the peace were organized to reinforce sentences against knights who were convicted of breaking the P. or the Truce. In the 12th century, with the revival of royal power in France, the kings used the institutions of the P. to reinforce their own authority. From 1156 on, the sovereign had the power to legislate the peace.

H. Hoffmann, *Gottesfried und Tregua Dei* (1964);

A. Grabois, *De la Trève de Dieu à la Paix du Roi* (1966).

PEARLS, POEM OF THE One of the oldest English poems, composed in the first half of the 15th century, praising the virtues of the perfect knight and the gentle lady. It was very popular among the English gentry throughout the 15th century.

PEASANTRY See AGRICULTURE and FEUDALISM.

PECKAM, JOHN (1225-92) Archbishop of *Canterbury from 1279. Born in Sussex, he joined the *Franciscan order in 1250 and studied at Oxford and Paris. In 1272 he returned to Oxford as a reputed theologian and taught there, until he was called to Rome and appointed lecturer of the sacred palace (1276). In 1279 he became archbishop of Canterbury, being the papal candidate against the will of King *Edward I, with whom, however, he was soon reconciled. He devoted his time to supervising the clergy and to raising its standards, and

Peasants at work under the supervision of the lord's bailiff; from Queen Mary's Psalter, 14th century

sought to abolish abuses. P. wrote several treatises on scientific problems, among them a theory of the planets, as well as theological works, such as his famous scholastic book, *Quaestiones Quodlibeta*.

D. L. Douie, *Archbishop Peckam* (1952).

PECS City in southwestern *Hungary. See of a bishopric established there in 1005 by King *Stephen I, it was one of the oldest urban centres in Hungary and, from the 13th century on, an important cultural centre. In 1367 King *Louis I of Anjou founded a university in P., the first in the kingdom of Hungary.

PEDRO See PETER.

PEERS (Latin: pares, French: pairs) Term used in feudal society to designate the vassals of a lord, who were considered equal amongst themselves. This equality, expressed only in the law, allowed them to sit as a council, and to judge, on behalf of the lord, any of their colleagues. The *chivalric ideals of the 12th century gave rise to the concept of peerage as a supreme council of the realm, presided over by the monarch, and the source of moral authority and good behaviour. From this idea, poets created the story of the 12 P. of *Charlemagne, or of King *Arthur, as an example of chivalric virtue. Indirectly, the idea was inspired by the 12 Apostles of Christ. Literary ideology praised the assembly of the P. as the highest representation of feudal morality, so that the lord was described as *primus inter pares* (the first among the peers). In the 13th century, a French institution came into being which combined the feudal court and the chivalric ideal, i.e., the P. of France, composed of six lay nobles (the dukes of Normandy, Aquitaine and Burgundy, and the counts of Flanders, Champagne and Toulouse) and six bishops. The development of *Parliament and the progress of the monarchy, which led to the annexation of the ancient feudal society to designate the vassals of a lord, who ceremonial prerogatives, especially at the king's coronation. In England the House of Lords was also named "The House of P."

PEGOLOTTI, FRANCESCO DI BALDUCCIO (d. 1340) A writer on economics. He was an agent of the Florentine commercial house of the *Bardi family, who was active between 1315-40. He travelled on behalf of his employers to London, Bruges and Antwerp, as well as to several Mediterranean countries. His fame rests on his book, *Prattica della Mercatura* (The Practice of Marketing), which is an accurate and original description of the trading methods of his time, as well as a treatise on the economics of the late 13th and early 14th century.

PEKING City in northern *China, one of its capitals. Until the period of the Kin empire (see *China), P. was a provincial centre, of strategic importance after the erection of the Great Wall. In the 12th and 13th centuries it became the imperial capital, especially of the northern empire. Conquered by *Genghis-Khan, it became the centre of the *Mongol khanate, and was known as Kambalek. After the establishment of the Mongol empire of China, P., as its capital, was developed and adorned. The Mongols built an inner city, forbidden to strangers, with palaces and gardens in the Chinese-Mongol style.

M. Prowden, *The Mongols* (1942).

PELAGIANISM Christian heresy in the 4th-6th centuries, according to which a man wins salvation by his own efforts, without the help of divine grace. The doctrine was attacked by the Catholic Church, which saw it endangering its role in the administration of sacraments as instruments of divine grace. Its chief opponent was St. *Augustine of Hippo, who brought about its condemnation in 415, later affirmed by Pope *Innocent I in 417. The remnants of the believers in P. retired to Spain, where they enjoyed a certain degree of liberty under the *Visigothic kings. The heresy disappeared in the 6th century.

J. Fergusson, *Pelagius* (1936).

PELAGIUS (PELAYO) (d. 737) Spanish Christian leader. Little is known about his origins and early career. After the fall of the *Visigothic kingdom of Spain and its conquest by the Arabs, he retired northwards and founded a Christian principality in the mountains of northern Spain. This became before his death the kingdom of *Asturias. P. was a popular figure in Spanish legend and a symbol of the resistance against the Islamic conquest.

A. Castro, *The Structure of Spanish History* (1954).

PELAGIUS (d. 1224) Cardinal of Albano and leader of the Fifth *Crusade. Appointed papal legate to the Crusade (1218), he arrived in the East and decided to attack Egypt. He besieged *Damietta, against the advice of King *John of Brienne, refusing to negotiate with the *Ayyubid sultan Al-Malik Al-Kamel, who offered to cede Jerusalem to the Crusaders if they would abandon Damietta. P. conquered the city, but his army was destroyed and sunk in the Nile when he decided to continue to Cairo (1221).

S. Runciman, *A History of the Crusades*, III (1953).

PELAGIUS I (c. 500-61) Pope from 556. A churchman who, from 535, was very active in the theological and political fields, he was elected pope on the recommendation of *Justinian, his protector. He devoted his pontificate to rebuilding Rome, where he acquired large possessions, destined to become the basis of the future *Papal States.

J. Haller, *Das Papsttum* (1949).

PELAGIUS II (520-90) Pope from 579. Elected after large areas of Italy were conquered by the *Lombards, he began his pontificate without the required imperial confirmation, creating a precedent. In 580 he created another precedent by appealing to the *Franks for help against the Lombards, when the hoped-for Byzantine reinforcements did not arrive. In 585 he turned again to Constantinople for help and sent the future *Gregory I to negotiate with Emperor *Mauricius. He died of the plague in 590.

W. Ullmann, *A Short History of the Papacy* (1972).

PELAGONIA, BATTLE OF (1259) Fought between the army of *Michael VIII Palaeologus and the Frankish lords of Greece, who tried to prevent the emperor of *Nicaea from invading Greece. The Byzantine army severely defeated the *Crusaders, whose army was decimated. Michael's victory opened his way to the reconquest of Constantinople in 1261.

PELOPONNESE (PELOPONNESUS) See MOREA.

PENANCE (Greek: poenitentia) In Christian religious practice a person who confessed a great sin had to make P. to purge himself. He could do so by undertaking some pious act, such as a *pilgrimage to a holy shrine, giving a donation to a religious institution, building a chapel, etc. From the 12th century participation in the *Crusades and the *Reconquista wars in Spain could also be undertaken as a P. People who could not participate in person, could make a monetary contribution instead. The practice opened the way to abuses, of which the most famous are the *indulgences, bought and sold at the end of the Middle Ages.

O. D. Watkins, *A History of Penance* (1920).

PENDA (d. 655) King of *Mercia. The last pagan king of Mercia, he is represented by Christian sources as a merciless ruler. His reign was the apex of Mercian greatness in Anglo-Saxon England. In 628 he defeated the army of *Wessex at Cirencester, and conquered the West Saxon realm. Then he turned to *Northumbria and in 632 defeated and killed its king, *Edwin, becoming

overlord of the realm. He imposed his authority over the Mercian lords and reorganized the kingdom before undertaking a campaign against East *Anglia, which he defeated and conquered in 645. In 655 he led a raid in Northumbria to suppress the revolt of his vassal, Edwy, but was killed at the Battle of Winwaed.

F. M. Stenton, *Anglo-Saxon England* (1947).

PEPIN I (803-38) King of *Aquitaine from 817. Son of *Louis the Pious, he was allotted the kingdom of Aquitaine when the empire was divided in 817. In 829-31 he took part in the revolt of his brothers *Lothair and *Louis the German, to prevent the granting of a kingdom to their half-brother, *Charles the Bald. Defeated, he returned to Aquitaine, where he died in his father's lifetime.

PEPIN II (c. 823-65) King of *Aquitaine (838-56). Son and heir of *Pepin I, he was unable to rule his kingdom, partly conquered by *Charles the Bald, until his victory at Angoulême in 844. In 851 Charles again invaded Aquitaine and P. took refuge in the castle of Sancho, duke of *Gascony, who in 852 turned him in to Charles. P. was deposed and sent to a monastery, but in 854, helped by the Aquitanian nobility, he escaped and returned to his kingdom. However, his rule, which was arbitrary, disappointed his vassals, who left his army and proclaimed Charles the Bald their king. P. escaped from his palace in 856 and led an unsettled life until his death.

A. Ausias, *L'Aquitaine Carolingienne* (1931).

PEPIN I (777-810) King of *Italy from 781. He was the second son of *Charlemagne, who made him king of Italy. After reaching maturity, P. was sent to *Pavia, was crowned and reigned on behalf of his father.

PEPIN I, of Landen (c. 580-640) *Mayor of the palace of *Austrasia. He was active in the political life of the *Frankish kingdom and enlarged his possessions in Austrasia, whose real master he became after the death of King *Dagobert I. P. is one of the ancestors of the *Carolingian dynasty.

PEPIN II, of Herstal (c. 640-714) *Mayor of the palace. Grandson of Pepin I and of *Arnulf of Metz, he was the wealthiest and most powerful lord in *Austrasia. He intervened in the affairs of *Neustria and, after his victory over *Ebroin (687), he became mayor of the palace of all the *Frankish kingdom and virtually governed the kingdom. P. supported the missionary activities of the Anglo-Saxon monks in Germany and especially in *Frisia, which he was preparing to conquer when he fell ill and died.

PEPIN III, the Short (714-68) *Mayor of the palace (741-51) and king of the *Franks (751-68). Son of *Charles Martel, he inherited his office together with his brother *Carloman, who left him the government and became a monk at *Monte Cassino. P., who was a close friend of St. *Boniface, whose missionary activity in Germany he supported, planned to take the royal title. With the support of the Church and of his vassals, and with the specific consent of the pope, he sent the last *Merovingian king, *Chilperic III, to a monastery, was hailed king and crowned by St. Boniface. In 753 he was anointed at Rheims by Pope *Stephen III, who needed his help against the *Lombards. In 754 he granted the pope territories in Italy, which became the *Papal States. P. continued his father's conquests in southern France, seizing *Languedoc from the Arabs and the Visigoths. In 767 he led an expedition to Italy, to help

the papacy against the Lombards. At his death he left
a strong realm, the most powerful in Europe.
R. Folz, *Le Couronnement Impérial de Charlemagne*
(1973).
PERCEVAL (PARSIFAL) Poem. Its original version
dates back to *Chrétien de Troyes, who composed it in
French in the framework of the *Arthurian romance. At
the beginning of the 13th century the German poet
*Wolfram of Eschenbach recast the story in his German
poem of this name, which is the best version of the
legend, describing the adventures of a perfect knight, P.,
in search of the Holy *Grail.
R. S. Loomis, *Arthurian Literature in the Middle Ages*
(1959).
PERCY Family of *Northumberland. Settled in northern England after the *Norman Conquest, the P. family
rose to a high position in the realm, being charged with the
defence of its northern frontiers against the *Scots.
Under *Edward III they were granted the earldom of
Northumbria. They began to play an important role in
English politics during the reign of *Richard II, when
Sir Henry Percy (1364-1403) was one of the leading
barons of England, and opposed *Henry IV.
K. L. MacFarlane, *The English Nobility* (1972).
PEREIASLAV City in the Ukraine, not far from Kiev.
Founded in the 10th century, it was a commercial
centre, its merchants trading with Kiev, Constantinople
and the *Khazarian principalities of eastern Ukraine. In
1054 a principality was established there by a branch of
the *Rurik family, which ruled P. until 1240, when it
was conquered by *Batu-khan.
G. Vernadsky, *Kievan Russia* (1953).
PÉRIGORD County in *Aquitaine. The county was
established in the 10th century and, thereafter, its
dynasty played an important role in the political life of
the duchy, taking advantage of its strategic position on
the main road between the capitals, *Poitiers and
Bordeaux. The counts of P. gradually increased their
territories. In the 13th century they benefited from the
constant conflicts between France and England by
changing sides.
E. Jarry, *Provinces et Pays de France* (1945).
PERPIGNAN City in southern France. It emerged in
the 10th century around the feudal castle of the counts
of *Roussillon and developed due to its position between *Catalonia and *Languedoc. In 1272 it was
annexed together with the county to the crown of
*Aragon and was, until 1344, the capital of *Majorca.
In the 14th century it was fortified, becoming an important royal military basis.
PERSIA Country in *Asia, which in the Middle Ages
occupied the whole Iranian plateau, the southern part
of present-day Turkestan and territories from the Indus
River to the Aral Sea. This geographical and ethno-
cultural area was made up of independent provinces,
which became united only at the beginning of the
Middle Ages. Its political development was to be shaped
by external factors.
History In the 5th century, P. was under the rule of
the *Sassanid dynasty, which inherited the partially
Hellenized empire of the Parthians. Its political power
remained concentrated in the west and its capital,
Ctesiphon, on the Tigris River, was merely a frontier
city. This orientation caused continuous clashes between
the Sassanids and Byzantium in the 5th and 6th centu-

ries because of the struggle for supremacy in Armenia
and, from the end of the 6th century, over Mesopotamia
and Syria. The Sassanids waged a long series of wars
against *Justinian, and their king, *Chosroes I, preserved himself successfully against the attacks of his generals,
to the point that both empires came to a peaceful
understanding, dividing their areas of influence in
*Armenia. In order to guard their southern borders
against raids of Arab tribes from the desert, the Sassanids
settled one of them, the Lakhmids, in the valley of the
Euphrates, creating a vassal principality, which allowed
them to concentrate their efforts to fight Byzantium.
*Chosroes II resumed the war against Emperor *Hera-
clius, which englobed all the Middle East, and exhausted
both empires. Allied with the Yemenite kingdom of
*Hemyar, he attacked, both on the sea, fighting
*Ethiopia – the Christian ally of Byzantium – and on
land; his army penetrated Asia Minor, conquered
Syria, part of Palestine including Jerusalem (614) and
penetrated into Egypt. The Byzantine effort and the
superiority of the combined Byzantine-Ethiopian fleet
assured the allies supremacy in the Persian Gulf, allowing them to attack Persia itself and to destroy the
kingdom of Hemyar. When Heraclius succeeded in
redressing the situation in 629 and in recovering his
provinces, the Sassanid empire was exhausted. It was
therefore easily defeated by the Arabs in 641, who
conquered P. (under the caliphates of *Omar and
*Othman).
The Battle of *Qadisiyah (641) put an end to the
independence of P. and to its ancient civilization. The
Moslem conquest, completed in 657 with the fall of
*Khorasan, was followed by the Islamization of the
country; the dualist Zoroastrian religion was not
recognized, like Christianity and Judaism, and conversion
to Islam was imposed by force of arms. Morevoer, the
written use of the Persian language was forbidden, and
Arabic – the language of the Koran and of liturgy –
became the official language. P. became a province
within the Arab caliphate, administrated from 661 by
governors and generals sent from the *Ummayad capital,
Damascus, who also pursued their expansion in central
Asia and towards *India, where the last Persian province,
Sind, was conquered in 704. Compelled to convert to
Islam, the Persians strongly resented Ummayad rule, and
as a sign of opposition to the government of Damascus,
they followed the *Shiite movement, becoming in their
great majority supporters of the heretical Moslem sect
and its Arab leaders, the *Abbasids.
The Abbasid revolution, preached by agents sent
from the Transjordan headquarters of the family,
emerged from P. and, besides the dissident Arabs and
the army of the eastern provinces won by the agents,
many Iranians were among its leaders. With the establishment of the new caliphate in Iraq, they were able to
become an influential body in the government of
*Baghdad (750), despite the decision of the Abbasid
caliphs to convert to *Sunnite Islam. While P. itself
remained a province within the caliphate and did not
reach independence, the institutions of the empire were
modelled by Persian officials on the traditions of
Sassanian administration. The impact of Persian culture and science was felt at the Academy of Baghdad,
which attracted many Persians to the new centre. Moreover, the proximity of Baghdad to P. gave an Eastern

orientation to the caliphate. Trade and industry were developed both in P. proper, in Khorasan and in *Transoxiana, with the peoples of the steppes, the *Khazars and even with Scandinavia and *Bolgar. The revival of P.'s prosperity was followed in the 9th century by the decline of the Abbasids, who were compelled to yield the real power to local families, some of them Iranians and some of *Turkish origin, under a nominal appointee of the caliph.

Most of these local dynasties never maintained power beyond the third generation, and the country fell into a state of anarchy and civil war, which emphasized the need for hired soldiers of Turkish stock. Divided into many rival principalities, P. became in the 10th century merely a geographical and cultural entity. However, the revival of the Persian language and culture was due to a Turkish factor, the sultanate of *Ghazni, which included Khorasan and Afghanistan. At the court of *Mahmud of Ghazni, towards the turn of the 10th and at the beginning of the 11th century, poets and writers, as well as artists produced works in Persian, but written, however, in Arabic script. When *Firdussi wrote his *Shah Nameh*, the epic story of the ancient Persian kings, the national feelings of the Persians and their pride in their millenary heritage found their expression and brought a revival of literary, philosophical and scientific creation in the Persian language.

The fall of the Ghaznavid empire opened the way to a new invasion of P. from central Asia, that of the *Seljuk Turks. Led by *Tughrul-Beg, they conquered P. between 1044 and 1155, putting an end to the petty local dynasties and uniting the country into a large empire, which included also Iraq, Syria and a great part of Anatolia. After the conquest period, which was completed in 1075, the Seljuks, who divided their empire among princes of the dynasty, established their centre in P., which knew, under *Malik Shah (whose capital was established at *Isfahan), a new period of prosperity and development. The Seljuks, who were Sunnites, had, however, to solve the problem of the religious unity in P., where *Ismaili Shiites had become active. One of their sects, the *Assassins, established their military centre in the castle of Alamuth (north of Teheran), bringing violence and murder as a political system in the country. The Seljuk sultans of the 12th century were unable to solve the Assassin problem, and, at the end of the 12th century, when the direct dynasty of the Seljuks of P. became extinct, the country fell into an anarchical state, which contrasted with its economic and cultural prosperity. In 1157, following the death of Sultan *Sanjar, Seljuk authority began to decline and in northern P. an Iranian-Turkish dynasty, the *Khwarizmians, concentrated around the Aral Sea, began to manifest their power, which reached its peak at the beginning of the 13th century, when *Muhammad Ala Ad-Din established their empire, while in southern and eastern P. local principalities began to be constituted.

The Mongol invasion of *Genghis-Khan and his general Subodai brought ruin and destruction to P. The majority of the cities were ravaged during the Mongol invasion (1220-21), and a great part of the population was killed. A part of the northern territories was entirely devastated and lost its Persian character, including ancient centres of civilization in Transoxiana. During the 13th century the Mongol threat continued to be felt, but the various principalities were too weak and divided among themselves to organize any kind of resistance. When the grandson of Genghis-Khan, *Hulagu, was ordered by his brother, the Great Khan *Mangu, to conquer P., in 1256, he did not find any difficulty in accomplishing this task and pursued his raid into Iraq, where he destroyed Baghdad and put an end to the Abbasid caliphate (1258) and to Syria. The conquest of P. by Hulagu and the division of the Mongol empire (c. 1261) into autonomous khanates ruled by the descendants of Genghis-Khan, gave P. its independence under the rule of the Mongol dynasty of Hulagu, the Il-khans. The latter converted to Islam c. 1280, and made P. the centre of their government, organizing the country and promoted the revival of its cities, crafts and trade, as well as agriculture. In the middle of the 14th century, P. had almost recovered, although the prosperity of the 11th and 12th centuries was not regained.

The Il-khans were overthrown in 1380 by *Timurleng (Tamerlane), who constituted his own realm with centralized power at Samarkand. In 1380-81 Tamerlane swept over Inan without meeting much opposition; the cities were again destroyed and desolation prevailed in P., which became part of the new Timurid empire. After the death of Timur, his sons divided the empire among themselves (1405) and P., which had become a poor and depopulated country, was divided among several branches of the Turkmen Timurid dynasty. Only some of its cities, such as Isfahan, Hamadan, reflected the remnants of its brillant civilization.

Civilization After the Sassanid period, P.'s civilization reflected the Moslem impact. While its ancient literary heritage was neglected until the end of the 10th century, and its religious traditions disappeared entirely, its artistic and scientific heritage was adopted by Islam and, through the Arab caliphate, diffused throughout the Moslem world. Moreover, Moslem P. took part, from the 8th century on, in the development of the philosophic and scientific activity in Arabic and, in certain fields, took the lead. This was, for example, the case of *Ibn Sinna (Avicenna), who, following Aristotelian philosophy, attempted in his works to develop a philosophic way of rationalization of the faith, and led the way to the emergence and development of medieval *Aristotelianism. In the same way, scholars contributed to the development of mathematics, physics and medicine, to which they brought also the results of their own Persian heritage. In fields such as astronomy, the achievements of ancient P., the methods of observation and measurement, were brought to medieval science by Persian scholars, who wrote in Arabic, like Al-*Biruni, in the 10th century.

The literary activity of P. revived at the end of the 10th century and is symbolized by the composition of the *Shah Nameh* (Book of Kings) by Firdussi. Medieval Persian literature flourished both in prose and poetry, although poetry occupied the central place. In the late 11th and the 12th century, among many others, two great names emerge: *Omar Khayyam and Al-*Hariri. Expressed first in the epic, following the national tradition, poetry also found its expression in the lyrical works of poets inspired by religious and other themes.

In the arts, the development of Persian architecture, with its light vaults, contrasting with the massive European columns and vaults, enabled the emergence of the Moslem style of building, represented in its original expression at Isfahan and by its greatest and most famous variant, in the *Alhambra palace at Granada in Spain.

A. J. Arbery (ed.), *The Legacy of Persia* (1953).

PERUGIA City in central *Italy. Conquered in 592 by the *Lombards, it became the capital of a duchy which was united in the 8th century with that of *Spoleto. In 774 *Charlemagne gave it to the papacy, according to the grant of *Pepin the Short and P. remained part of the *Papal States. In the 11th-14th centuries, a communal government was established in the city. At the end of the 14th century P. was the centre of the great artistic period which was known in the Renaissance as the Umbrian school.

PERUZZI The P. were one of the most ancient leading families of *Florence and in the 13th century they became the heads of the *Guelph party in the city. Their palace in the Santa Croce quarter of the city, fortified in 1284, was considered one of the most imposing lay buildings of 13th-century Italy. The P. entered the banking business *c.* 1275 and opened agencies in the major centres of western Europe, becoming the second bank in the West after the *Bardi company. At the beginning of the 14th century, they held an important share of the credit operations in England, France and Naples, as well as in other European centres. In 1330-37 King *Edward III of England requested more loans, needed for financing the *Hundred Years' War, but the P. Bank found it difficult to raise the money. In 1340 the bank went bankrupt and members of the family were arrested, while the French agency was confiscated by the royal government and its activities forbidden. The fall of the P. was felt in Florence in 1345, provoking a general crisis in the city and social unrest, which brought about a revolt of the smaller guilds, and their disappearance.

CEcH, II, III.

PER VENERABILEM *Decretal of Pope Innocent III. Issued in 1205 and addressed to *Philip II, king of France, it deals with the papal and royal prerogatives, stating that "the king of France has no superior within his kingdom". It is the first affirmation of the idea of royal sovereignty.

PEST City in *Hungary. Situated on the west bank of the Danube, opposite the royal capital of *Buda, it grew in the 11th-14th centuries as a commercial city.

PETAHYA OF RATISBON (12th century) Traveller. Born at Ratisbon in Bavaria, where he was educated at the already famous Jewish school, he undertook in *c.* 1170 to travel to Palestine, Syria and Iraq. The account of his travels, condensed in his book *Sibub* (Tour), is an important testimony of the Jewish communities of his times, especially in Palestine and Iraq.

Works, ed. A. Grünhutt (1914).

PETCHENEGS Common name of a group of *Turkish tribes, originating in central Asia. Before the 9th century they settled in the Ural Mountains area and, from this place, raided the *Khazars. In the 9th century they settled in the steppes of Ukraine and were the allies of the Russians against the Khazars. Repulsed by the latter westwards, they settled in the areas of modern western Ukraine and Rumania, reaching the Danube. In the 11th century their raids south of the Danube brought them into open conflict with the Byzantine empire. Defeated at the beginning of the 12th century by *Alexius Comnenus, they lost their power and were gradually assimilated by other tribes.

R. Grousset, *L'Empire des Steppes* (1945).

PETER, St. (Simon Peter) The foremost of the 12 apostles of Christ. His cult was widely spread in the Middle Ages among all Christian churches. The most important was, however, his cult at *Rome, as he was considered the founder of the Roman Church. In the early Middle Ages the papacy developed the Petrine doctrine, according to which the popes were the successors of P. and, as such, enjoyed his position as Vicar of Christ. On his tomb at Rome a church was built, which became one of the Roman cathedrals and every sign of allegiance to the pope had to be completed by a donation to P.'s church. In that respect, the *Papal States were considered P.'s patrimony and chapels and churches bearing his title were considered dependent directly on the papacy.

PETER I (c. 1070-1104) King of *Aragon (1094-1104). Immediately after acceding to the throne, he renewed the *Reconquista wars against the Moslems. In 1096 he conquered Huesca and made it his capital and, continuing his offensive, conquered Barbastro, doubling the area of his kingdom.

PETER II (1174-1213) King of *Aragon (1196-1213). Son of *Alfonso II, he inherited his father's rights in southern France and especially the seigniory of *Montpellier, which he annexed to his estates in 1204. During a visit to Rome in 1204 he recognized the kingdom of Aragon as a papal fief, held from *Innocent III. In 1212 he took part in the Battle of *Las Navas de Tolosa and, immediately after the victory, returned to southern France, where he was killed at the Battle of Muret.

A. Castro, *The Structure of Spanish History* (1954).

PETER III (1236-85) King of Aragon (1276-85). Married to Constance, daughter of *Manfred, king of Sicily; he inherited the *Hohenstaufen claims to the kingdom of Sicily and became the rival of *Charles of Anjou. In 1282 he supported the *Sicilian Vespers and was proclaimed king at Palermo. His policy brought him to war with France, during which he defeated the French army in the Pyrénées and suppressed the uprising of the nobility and burghers, who protested against the taxes imposed to finance his wars. He was compelled to reconfirm the privileges of the *Cortes.

PETER IV (1319-87) King of *Aragon (1336-87). Son of *Alfonso IV, his aim was to unite the Aragonese realms under his authority. In 1344 he reconquered the Balearic Islands and Roussillon, bringing the kingdom of *Majorca to its end and, towards the end of his reign, annexed *Sicily (1377) and the duchy of *Athens (1381), making Aragon a great Mediterranean power. In 1348 he crushed a revolt of nobles and imposed an authoritarian regime in the kingdom. Allied with *Henry of Trastamare, who claimed the throne of Castile, he fought in 1356-66 against *Peter the Cruel, king of Castile.

A. Castro, *The Structure of Spanish History* (1954).

PETER I Tsar of the *Bulgarians (927-69). Son and successor of *Simeon the Great, he continued his father's policy, aiming to establish a great *Bulgarian empire in the Balkans. His main achievement was the conquest of Serbia and the organization of the administration of the realm.

S. Runciman, *The First Bulgarian Empire* (1930).

PETER II, Assen Tsar of *Bulgaria (1185-97). In 1185 he led a revolt of the *Bulgarians at Tirnovo, proclaiming the independence of Bulgaria from Byzantine rule. He reigned together with his brother *John I Assen, who was the leader of the uprising at *Ochrida, and the principal figure of the joint kingship. P. was murdered by nobles in 1197.

PETER the Cruel (1334-69) King of *Castile from 1350. Son of *Alfonso XI, he established an authoritarian regime in the country, assisted by Moorish ministers and a hired army, while a part of the nobility, led by his half-brothers, opposed him. The leader of the opposition, his half-brother, *Henry of Trastamare, claimed the throne and appealed for support from Aragon and France, while P., who gave his daughter in marriage to John of Gaunt, duke of *Lancaster, addressed himself to *Edward, the Black Prince. During the years 1366-69, Castile was devastated by the mercenaries of the *Grandes Compagnies, led by Bertrand *Du Guesclin and, despite the victory of *Najera, won for him by the Black Prince, P. was defeated and killed at Montiel by Henry and the French coalition.

A. Castro, *The Structure of the Spanish History* (1954).

PETER King of *Croatia (1090-97). He was the last king of independent Croatia and fought against the Venetians in Dalmatia. In 1094 he established a bishopric at *Zagreb, his new capital. Following his death, in 1097, Croatia knew some years of disorder, before it was conquered by Hungary.

PETER I, of Lusignan (1329-69) King of *Cyprus from 1359. After his accession to the throne, he began to organize a new *Crusade. He travelled to France, attempting to recruit knights for his army. On his return journey he landed in *Armenia, where he captured two *Seljuk castles, and then turned to Egypt. In 1365 he conquered and plundered Alexandria, but was compelled by the *Mamelukes to retire. In 1369, while preparing a new expedition, he was murdered by one of his knights.

G. Hill, *A History of Cyprus* (1945).

PETER II, of Lusignan (1354-82) King of *Cyprus from 1369. Son of *Peter I, he was crowned in his boyhood. During his minority civil wars broke out in Cyprus, which were complicated by a war between *Venice and *Genoa. In 1373 the Genoese fleet captured Famagusta, the main harbour of the kingdom, without encountering resistance on the part of P.

PETER I (1320-67) King of *Portugal from 1357. In 1355 he rebelled against his father, *Alfonso IV, whom he accused of instigating the murder of his second wife, Ines (he had married her against the dynastic interests). As king, he had to deal with baronial uprisings and with the Castilian war between *Peter the Cruel and *Henry of Trastamare, claiming the rights of his first wife, Constance of Castile and their son, Ferdinand.

F. Livermore, *A History of Portugal* (1933).

PETER (PEIRE) CARDENAL (13th century) Provençal poet and troubadour. His verses, inspired by love of nature, were very popular in southern France.

H. Davenson, *Les Troubadours* (1960).

PETER COMESTOR (d. 1179) Biblical scholar. Born in Troyes, where he was a canon at the cathedral, he went to Paris in 1164, and was appointed chancellor of the cathedral. In that capacity he was responsible for the school system in the city. He wrote a *Historia Scholastica*, a history of learning from biblical times to his own. It became the standard work on the history of the Bible in the Middle Ages, and brought him fame as the greatest scholar of his time. As chancellor, he regulated studies at the Parisian schools, laying down the procedures of granting licences to the masters. Under his leadership the schools became a university.

Works, *PL*, 198;

B. Smalley, *The Study of the Bible in the Middle Ages* (1952).

PETER DAMIAN, St. (1007-72) Reformer and "doctor of the church". Born in Ravenna of poor parents, he was a swineherd until he was sent by a rich protector to study. In 1035 he entered the hermitage of *Fonte Avellana and became known for his extreme austerity. In 1057 he was created cardinal of Ostia and took a prominent part in the elaboration of the ecclesiastical reform, named the *Gregorian. His writings concern problems of monastic discipline and of the moral life. Other treatises of his deal with the problems of *simony and other abuses in the church. He also wrote on doctrinal matters, which earned him in 1828 the title of "doctor of the church" from Pope Leo XII.

Works, *PL*, 144-145;

R. Biron, *St. Pierre Damien* (1908).

PETER (PIERO) DELLA VIGNA (d. 1249) Poet and minister. Of humble origins, he won the heart of *Frederick II with his beautiful verse and was accepted at the court of Palermo. P. was a scholar, who wrote in a distinguished Latin style. Having won the confidence of the emperor, he became chancellor and was associated with his policy until 1249, when Frederick charged him with treason and had him blinded. P. committed suicide in prison. He is described by Dante in the *Divine Comedy*.

T. C. van Cleve, *The Emperor Frederick II of Hohenstaufen* (1972).

PETER DUBOIS (d. 1337) Political theorist. He was among the French jurists who supported King *Philip IV in his conflict with Pope *Boniface VIII. In his later years, becoming aware of the dangers of the conflict which opposed the kings of France and England, he called for a general *Crusade, and wrote a treatise *On the Recovery of the Holy Land*, wherein he expressed his political and religious ideas.

Works, ed., trans. V. Durant (1949).

PETER LOMBARD (1100-60) Bishop of *Paris from 1159. Born in Novara, Lombardy, he studied at Bologna, Rheims and Paris, and from 1140 taught at the cathedral school of Paris. Besides his commentaries on St. Paul, he wrote one of the most famous works of the century, *Summa Sententiarum* (1148-50), a *scholastic treatise, dealing with the trinity, creation, original sin, incarnation, the virtues and the Sacraments. Though criticized by some contemporaries, the book became the standard textbook of Catholic theology during the Middle Ages.

Works, *PL*, 191-192;

P. Delhaye, *Pierre Lombard, Sa Vie, Son Oeuvre, Sa Morale* (1961).

PETER MARTYR, St. (1205-52) Inquisitor. Born in Verona, he joined the *Dominican order in 1221 in Bologna, where he studied. It seems that he was prior of several houses of the order in northern Italy. In 1241 Pope *Gregory IX appointed him *inquisitor for

Page from the sermons of Peter Lombard

northern Italy, where he distinguished himself by his zeal and his conciliatory attitude towards heretics who repented. In 1251 he was murdered by bandits.
G. Meerseman, *Les Confréries de St. Pierre Martyr* (1951).

PETER NOLASCO, St. (c. 1189-1256) Founder of the Order of the Mercedarians. The data about his youth and early career are contradictory and doubtful. Settled in Aragon at the beginning of the 13th century, he was one of the tutors of King *James I. About 1230 he founded the Mercedarian order, whose aim was to ransom Christian prisoners from the *Saracens. To do this he travelled through the kingdoms of Valencia, Granada and north Africa.
EC, IX.

PETER ORSEOLO See ORSEOLO.

PETER OF AILLY See AILLY, PETER OF.

PETER OF BLOIS (1135-1212) Poet and scholar. He was secretary to King *Henry II of England, about whom he wrote admiringly. After Henry's death (1189), P. settled in Paris, where he taught grammar to English students. He wrote Latin poems and a manual of grammar, *Ars dictamina*. His collected letters are an important historical source.
C. H. Haskins, *The Twelfth-Century Renaissance* (1928).

PETER OF BRUYS (d. c. 1140) *Heretic. From 1110 he began to preach in southwestern France against the abuses of the ecclesiastical hierarchy, criticizing especially the Church's ownership of properties. Despite repeated condemnations he continued to preach, being supported by the masses. His adherents, the Petrobruysians, were fiercely attacked by *Peter the Venerable, abbot of Cluny, who wrote a treatise against their heresy.
K. Bols, *Die Kathärer* (1958).

PETER OF CELLE (1115-83) Bishop of Chartres from 1180. After a period of study at Paris, he joined the *Benedictine abbey of La Celle, whose abbot he became in 1150. A close friend of *John of Salisbury, he was active in the *Becket controversy, mobilizing French public opinion against King *Henry II. As his letters show, P. was one of the humanists of the 12th century.
J. Leclerq, *Pierre de La Celle* (1951).

PETER OF COURTENAY (c. 1167-1217) *Latin emperor of Constantinople (1217). Grandson of King *Louis VI of France, he was count of *Courtenay and, in 1216, inherited the county of Flanders. In 1217 he was called to Constantinople, proclaimed emperor and crowned at Rome by *Innocent III. He was captured during the siege of *Thessalonica, and murdered.

PETER (MAUCLERC) OF DREUX (1190-1250) Duke of *Brittany (1213-37). A member of a collateral branch of the *Capetian dynasty, he married Alice, the heiress of Brittany, and received its dukedom in 1213 from King *Philip II. He fought against the clergy and the vassals of the duchy, and became unpopular. In 1229 he revolted against the regent, *Blanche of Castile, and declared himself vassal of the English crown. Reconciled with the French crown in 1234, he was compelled by his vassals to surrender the duchy to his son (1337). His repeated conflicts with the clergy caused him to be excommunicated. However, in 1247 he accompanied *Louis IX to the *Crusade. He died of wounds in Egypt.
C. Petit-Dutaillis, *Feudal Monarchy in France and England* (1939).

PETER OF MONTREUIL (c. 1200-66) Architect. He was one of the most famous builders in the Gothic style. In 1231 he was commissioned to complete the abbey church of *St. Denis. He also worked at *St. Germain-des-Prés in Paris, and on the cathedral of Notre Dame. But his main work was the building of the *Sainte-Chapelle in the royal palace in Paris.
E. Male, *The Gothic Image* (1951).

PETER OF MORONE See CELESTINE V.

PETER OF PISA (d. c. 800) Grammarian. A native of Pisa, he became famous as a Latin grammarian. Called by *Charlemagne to join the palace academy, he was one of the most important figures of the *Carolingian Renaissance.

PETER OF POITIERS (d. 1205) Scholar. He studied in Paris under *Peter Lombard, and in the second half of the 12th century taught theology there, continuing his master's work.
C. H. Haskins, *The Twelfth-Century Renaissance* (1928).

PETER OF ROCHES (d. 1238) Regent of *England. Originally of Poitou, where he was baron of Roches, he joined the court of King *John in England. There he became a clergyman and, in 1205, became bishop of Winchester. In 1214 King John appointed him as chief justiciary, but he was extremely unpopular and had to resign in 1215. When the king died, P. became one of the regents of the realm and was charged with the education of the young king, *Henry III. His rivalry with *Hubert of Burgh marked the political life of England in the last years of the regency. Defeated in 1224, P. left England and accompanied Emperor *Frederick II on the Crusade of 1229, and attempted to reconcile him with Pope *Gregory IX. In 1231 he returned to England, and with the king's support renewed his struggle against Hubert of Burgh, bringing about his fall in 1232. His methods provoked baronial protest, and in 1234 Henry III was compelled to dismiss him.

F. M. Powicke, *Oxford History of England: The 13th Century* (1951).

PETER THE CANTOR (d. 1189) Scholar. He was one of the famous teachers at the episcopal school in Paris, where he taught theology. His works also contain many social and economical reflections concerning the social changes in the 12th century. He criticized the luxury of the episcopal palaces and upheld the simple way of life. He was one of the main *scholastics of the 12th century.

J. Baldwin, *Peter the Cantor* (1969).

PETER THE DEACON (1107-1159) Historian. He was a monk at *Monte Cassino, where he served as the abbey librarian. In 1138 he took up the chronicle of Monte Cassino, from the 11th century until his death.

PETER THE HERMIT (c. 1050-1115) Preacher and spiritual leader of the First *Crusade. Born in the region of Amiens, northern France, he became a hermit and probably visited Palestine as a pilgrim. After the proclamation of the crusade by Pope *Urban II at Clermont (1095), he left his hermitage and preached the crusade among the lower classes, winning a reputation as a highly eloquent speaker. In 1096 he led the "popular" crusade, that of the peasants, towards the valleys of the Rhine and Danube on its way to Jerusalem. The participants attacked the Jewish communities on their way and slaughtered many Jews. From Constantinople Emperor *Alexius I sent them into Asia Minor, where most of them were killed by the *Seljuk army at Nicaea. P. brought the survivors to the main army of *Godfrey of Bouillon (1097) and thereafter effaced himself and during the siege of Antioch attempted to escape and return to France. He did, however, enter Jerusalem with the army. In 1100 he returned to Europe and became prior of an *Augustinian house in Belgium.

Y. Le Febvre, *Pierre l'Hermite et la Croisade* (1946).

PETER THE VENERABLE (1092-1156) Abbot of *Cluny from 1122. Member of the noble family of Montboissier of central France, he became a monk at Cluny in 1109. After serving as prior at Vézelay, he was elected abbot of Cluny in 1122, when the monastery was in disorder. A skilled administrator with a gift for leadership, he imposed reform of the monks' way of life. He became one of the most powerful persons in the Catholic world and his support of Pope *Innocent II in 1130 rallied to him King *Louis VI, who respected P. He had friendly disputes with *Bernard of Clairvaux, his contemporary, but stood firm on his own principles. In 1140 he gave shelter at Cluny to Peter *Abelard, who was being persecuted by Bernard. He travelled in Spain on behalf of his order, entrusted with the re-establishment of Christianity in the reconquered provinces and ordered that the *Koran be translated into Latin for polemical purposes. The translation was finished in 1143, and enabled P. to write a treatise against Islam,

following those he had already written against the Jews and *Peter of Bruys. Together, these form the bulk of his literary work, which also includes a number of sermons and letters. His style was concise and he avoided allegorical speculations.

Works, *PL*, 189;

L. Leclercq, *Pierre le Vénérable* (1946).

PETER (PEIRE) VIDAL (13th century) Poet. Born in Languedoc, he wrote both in Occitanian French and in Provençal. His poems express a high lyrical feeling and are part of the "allegory of love" of the 13th century.

H. Davenson, *Les Troubadours* (1960).

PETER'S PENCE The popular name of a tax paid in England to the papacy. It was first undertaken and paid by King *Offa in 787, and continued to be raised by his successors. Renewed by *William the Conqueror in 1080, it was paid regularly until 1534, when Henry VIII abolished it.

W. E. Lunt, *Papal Revenues in the Middle Ages* (1934).

PETERBOROUGH Monastery on the southeastern border of *Mercia. Founded in 655, it was destroyed by the Danes in 870. The abbey was re-established in 970 and dedicated to St. Peter, and a borough grew around it. The church, begun in the Anglo-Saxon cruciform style, was completed in 1237 in the Gothic style, going through eight periods of construction. The Anglo-Saxon community survived the Norman conquest of 1066 and existed until 1154. Its monks wrote *The Anglo-Saxon Chronicle*, an annual summary of events in England, from the 10th century until 1154.

W. D. Sweeting, *The Cathedral Church of Peterborough* (1898).

PETIT, JEAN (1360-1411) French political theorist. He studied theology and *medicine, which he practised until the beginning of the 15th century, when he became one of the magistrates of the Parisian burghers and their spokesman. In 1407 he distinguished himself at the court for his speech condemning the *Great Schism and became one of the leaders of the *Bourguignon party in the city. In 1408 he publicly justified the murder of Duke *Louis of Orléans, the king's brother, proposing the concept of "reasons of state" as an excuse for political murders.

P. S. Lewis, *France in the 15th Century* (1968).

PETRARCH, FRANCESCO (1304-74) Italian poet and humanist. He spent a part of his youth at Carpentras, near Avignon, where his father settled after being exiled from Florence. He studied law at Montpellier (1319-23) and at Bologna (1323-25). In 1327 he first saw Laura, who was to inspire his most famous poems. From 1330 to 1337 he travelled through France, Germany and Italy, visiting scholars and copying classical manuscripts. Finally he settled to a life of solitude, in Vaucluse, where most of his important works were written. For his *Poems to Laura* and his epic *Africa,* on Scipio Africanus, he was crowned Poet Laureate in Rome, 1341. In 1342 he wrote a treatise *De Contemptu Mundi,* an imaginary dialogue with St. *Augustine, on the eternal life. In 1347 he joined the republican movement of *Cola di Rienzi and was received in Rome triumphantly. In 1350 began his famous friendship with *Boccaccio. After a short period of political activity and missions on behalf of the papacy, he retired to Padua, where he spent his life in meditation and writing. His religious nature often conflicted with his sensuous-

ness and love of fame and with his admiration for the pagan culture of antiquity. This explains the versatility of his work, from treatises and books of theological character, expressing views about the ephemerality of this world and in praise of the contemplative life, to the allegorical interpretation of secular poetry and human fate. He is a major forerunner of the Renaissance. Collected works, ed. (1926ff.);
E. H. R. Tatham, *Francesco Petrarca, his Life and Correspondence* (1925).

PETRUS HISPANUS See JOHN XXI.

PHILIP I (1052-1108) King of *France from 1060. Son of *Henry I, he began his reign under the regency of *Baldwin V, count of Flanders. He gave up trying to impose royal authority over the great vassals, who became practically independent, and concentrated on governing his own lands, between Paris and Orléans, reducing the petty vassals. He added some estates to the royal demesne, among them the viscounty of Bourges. In 1095 he was excommunicated for his illicit marriage with Bertrade of Montfort, the wife of *Fulk V, count of Anjou, but refused to submit to the church. The issue was settled in 1105, when the papacy needed P.'s support against Emperor *Henry V.
J. F. Lemarignier, *Le Gouvernement Royal aux Premiers Temps Capétiens* (1965).

PHILIP II, Augustus (1165-1223) King of *France from 1180. The son of *Louis VII and Adèle of Champagne, he was at first influenced by the counts of Champagne and Flanders, but before long began to use his political talents. In 1183 he expelled the Jews of Paris for financial reasons and recalled them after a while. He supported the revolts of the sons of *Henry II of England, and at the same time negotiated with him about a great Crusade. In 1189 he took part in the Third *Crusade, but immediately after the conquest of *Acre (1191) returned to France, to deal with the problem of the inheritance of *Flanders and secure the royal interests. He took advantage of the absence of King *Richard I of England in Palestine, and his captivity in Germany, to seize his French lands. But when Richard returned, P. was severely defeated at Freteval in 1194. He had to content himself with dealing with the Flemish problem. He received the county of Artois as his share of Flanders. At the same time he supported young *Arthur of Brittany against his uncle, King Richard. After Richard's death. P. supported Arthur's claims against his other uncle, John, creating an open conflict in the *Plantagenet dynasty.

In 1200, when John married Isabelle of Angoulême, P. summoned him to the royal court, to answer the charges of the *Lusignan family. When John refused to appear P. declared his French lands forfeit. He profited from John's political mistakes, and especially the murder of Arthur (1202), to invade *Normandy and conquer it. In 1206 he conquered the Loire lands of the Plantagenets, including the city of Tours, and their ancestral county of *Anjou. P. opposed any intervention by Pope *Innocent III in the conflict, claiming the rights of his sovereign kingship. In 1205 the pope was forced to acknowledge, in his decretal *Per Venerabilem*, that the "king of France has no superior in his kingdom". P. supported the crusade against the *Albigenses, but did not take part in it and left the task to the barons. He occupied himself with the organization of his newly-acquired lands, where he introduced the royal administration and annexed them to the royal domain. He allied himself with young *Frederick II, who claimed the empire against *Otto IV, King John's nephew. The issue was decided in 1214 at the Battle of *Bouvines, in Flanders. P.'s victory destroyed John's power and authority. At the same time another French army, commanded by Prince Louis, P.'s son and heir, was active on the Loire, defeating John's forces and preparing the conquest of *Poitou. These territorial gains wrought a radical change in western Europe, where France became the most powerful monarchy. P. was now able to impose his authority on the great barons of the realm and in the cities. He used the feudal law and procedures to weaken *feudalism and bring about its decline. In the last years of his reign, he changed his attitude towards the heretical south, allowing his son Louis to lead a new expedition against the *Albigenses. It ended with the establishment of a royal enclave in *Languedoc.
C. Petit-Dutaillis, *Feudal Monarchy in France and England* (1938).

PHILIP III, the Bold (1245-85) King of *France from 1270. The son of *Louis IX, he accompanied his father on the *Crusade of Tunis, where he was proclaimed king. In 1271 he annexed the large domains of his uncle, *Alphonse of Poitiers and, during the first years of his reign, devoted his efforts to their integration in the royal government. Influenced by his uncle, *Charles of Anjou, he supported his policy and, in 1284, invaded *Aragon unsuccessfully and died on his way back.

PHILIP IV, the Fair (1268-1314) King of France from 1285. He left the pursuit of Italian and Angevin affairs to his brother, *Charles of Valois, while he concentrated his efforts on governing the realm. He put through an administrative reform, designed to reinforce royal power and increase his revenues. He surrounded himself with legally-trained functionaries *(legistes)*. Many of these were clergymen who also held ecclesiastical dignities. These jurists helped to develop the doctrine of the sovereignty of the king of France, whom they defined in accordance with Roman law "as emperor in his kingdom". The implementation of these doctrines led to prolonged conflicts with *Edward I of England concerning Gascony, and in *Flanders, where the cities rose up against the French and, in 1302, defeated P.'s army at Courtrai. But his most difficult conflict was with Pope *Boniface VIII, who upheld the doctrine of the universal authority of the papacy. The conflict, which erupted in 1296 in connection with the taxation of the clergy, grew into a confrontation between the spiritual and lay authorities, with polemical publications of both sides and appeals to the public opinion in France. Some of the clergy, upholding the liberties of the *Gallican church, opposed the pope. In order to obtain support for his side, P. convened the *Estates General, as the organ of public opinion and the expression of the unity of the realm. He allied himself with the *Colonna family, the pope's enemies in Italy, and in 1303 sent his counsellor, *William of Nogaret, to the pope, to denounce his *Unam Sanctam. In *Anagni Boniface was assaulted by Colonna and P. was excommunicated. The pope's death created a new crisis which ended in 1305, when Archbishop Bertrand of Got, of Bordeaux, was elected Pope *Clement V, with P.'s consent. He

remained in the valley of the Rhône before the establishment of the papacy at *Avignon. Thus the conflict ended favourably for the king, and increased the French influence over the papacy. P. was concerned with the economic crisis, which began at the end of the 13th century, but neither he nor his counsellors saw its real causes, and tried to deal with it as a financial crisis. The royal administration did all it could to increase the revenues by heavier taxation, as well as by measures against foreigners, which were supposedly popular with the masses. P. took measures against Italian merchants and bankers and in 1306 expelled the *Jews from the kingdom, confiscating all their possessions. In 1308 he accused the Knights *Templars of using witchcraft, and after their conviction had the order abolished and confiscated its properties. But these measures could not solve the problem and P. issued new *coins, with a lesser ratio of gold. The depreciated money led to an anarchic increase in prices and accelerated the crisis. This was followed by an issue of good coins and speculative measures. P. was the last great *Capetian king of France.
J. P. Strayer, *Medieval Statescraft and the Perspectives of History* (1971).

PHILIP V, the Tall (1294-1322) King of *France from 1316. Second son of *Philip IV, he became king after the death of his brother, *Louis X and his infant nephew, *John I. An assembly of barons, clergymen and *Sorbonne doctors proclaimed his right to reign, denying the claim of his niece, Joan, on the grounds that "the crown of France cannot be transmitted by females". This created a precedent which was used later against P.'s own daughters and became the basis of the *Salic Law of the 16th century.
R. Cazelles, *La Royauté de Philippe VI de Valois* (1951).

PHILIP VI, of Valois (1293-1350) King of *France from 1328. Son of *Charles of Valois and grandson of *Philip III, he was proclaimed king at the death of *Charles IV, the last king of the direct Capetian dynasty. This necessitated the rejection of Charles' daughter's claim. His coronation was contested by King *Edward III of England, who claimed the crown as son of Isabella, daughter of *Philip IV. Thus a dynastic aspect was added to the conflict between England and France, which degenerated into the *Hundred Years' War (1337). P. began his reign with a victory over the Flemish at Cassel (1328), which restored French influence in *Flanders. But he was repeatedly defeated in the war with Edward III, beginning with the naval Battle of the Sluys, which destroyed the French navy. The Battle of *Crécy (1346) was a great disaster for France and allowed Edward to conquer Calais and to establish his dominion in Normandy. The last years of P.'s reign were marked by plagues, culminating with the *Black Death (1348-49).
R. Cazelles, *La Royauté de Philippe VI de Valois* (1951).

PHILIP I, of Courtenay (1243-83) Titular emperor of the *Latin empire of Constantinople (1273-83). Son of *Baldwin II, the last Latin emperor, he lived in Italy from 1261, and was proclaimed emperor after his father's death. Married to Beatrice, daughter of *Charles of Anjou, he secured the support of the king of Sicily for his claims, but never succeeded in making them good.
J. Longon, *Les Français d'Outre-Mer* (1946).

PHILIP II, of Anjou-Taranto (1280-1332) Titular emperor of the Latin empire of Constantinople (1313-32). Son of *Charles II, king of Naples, he married Catherine of Valois, granddaughter of Philip I, and inherited the claim to the Latin empire. Prince of Morea from 1307, he failed to realize his claims, and only weakened Byzantium, which was under attack by the Ottoman *Turks.

PHILIP III, of Anjou (1323-73) Titular emperor of the Latin empire of Constantinople (1364-73). Younger son of Philip II, he inherited the family's claims.

PHILIP BARDANES Emperor of Byzantium (711-13). Of Armenian origin, he was proclaimed emperor after the fall of *Justinian II. He was unable to defend the empire from the *Bulgarians who were threatening Constantinople, while the Arabs were advancing in Asia Minor, and was deposed by a military revolt.
CMedH, IV.

PHILIP OF ALSACE (1143-91) Count of *Flanders from 1168. He continued the reorganization of the county begun by his father, *Thierry, to strengthen his authority. His castle of *Ghent combined the style of the feudal fortresses and the new palaces of the Gothic period. In 1177 he led a *Crusade to Jerusalem, where he distinguished himself at the Battle of Montgisard. In 1180 he became regent during the minority of *Philip II, king of France, to whom he married his niece, Isabella of Hainault. He died in the siege of Acre during the Third Crusade.

PHILIP OF MÉZIÈRES (1327-1405) French writer. Born into a family of knights in northeastern France, he was brought up for a military career, and in 1345 followed Humbert II, dauphin of Viennois, on the Crusade. He remained in the East, and in 1360 became chancellor of *Peter I of Lusignan, king of Cyprus, whom he helped in his crusading projects. In 1373 he returned to France and was appointed counsellor by King *Charles V. After the king's death P. entered the *Celestine monastery in Paris, where he devoted his life to writing and to elaborating new plans for crusades and for the recovery of the kingdom of Jerusalem. His most famous book, *Le Songe du Vieil Pèlerin* (The Dream of the Old Pilgrim, 1389), is an account of his life and ideas and a mirror of 14th-century religious-chivalric ideals.
N. Jorga, *Philippe de Mézières et la Croisade au XIVe siècle* (1896).

PHILIP OF NOVARE (d. 1264) Historian and lawyer. Originally from Lombardy, he settled in the Latin kingdom of Jerusalem, where he was among the opponents of *Frederick II, and was compelled to take refuge in Cyprus. Besides poems and letters he wrote a chronicle of his times and compiled a code of feudal customs of the Latin East.
S. Runciman, *A History of the Crusades* (1953).

PHILIP OF ROUVRES (1346-61) Duke of *Burgundy from 1349. He was the last *Capetian duke of *Burgundy. He added the county of Burgundy, which belonged to the *Holy Roman empire, to the duchy.

PHILIP OF SWABIA (1178-1208) *Holy Roman emperor from 1198. The younger son of *Frederick Barbarossa, he was titled duke of Swabia by his brother, *Henry VI. In 1198, after Henry's death, P. was elected emperor by some of the princes, and was crowned at Mainz, despite the opposition of Pope *Innocent III, who supported *Otto of Brunswick. His reign was marked by a civil war in Germany, where he gradually enlarged his authority. In 1208 P. was recognized by the pope, who invited him to come to Rome for the imperial coronation. But before he completed his preparations for the journey, P. was murdered by the count palatine, *Otto of Wittelsbach, to whom he had refused to give his daughter in marriage.

G. Barraclough, *The Origins of Modern Germany* (1951).

PHILIP OF TRIPOLI (13th century) Scientific writer. Educated in France, he settled in Toledo, where he discovered the scientific writings of the Arabs. He translated some of them into Latin, especially works on *astronomy and *medicine.

C. H. Haskins, *Studies in Mediaeval Science* (1927).

PHILIP OF VITRY (1290-1361) Musician. He began his career as choir master in his native country of Champagne, and composed liturgical music. P. was among the theorists of the *Ars Nova,* the polyphonic *music.

J. Chailley, *Histoire musicale du Moyen Age* (1969).

PHILIP THE BOLD (1342-1404) Duke of *Burgundy and of the Low Countries from 1363. Son of *John II, king of France, he distinguished himself at the Battle of *Poitiers (1356), where he received the title the "Bold". In 1363 he was granted the duchy of Burgundy. By his marriage with Margaret, heiress of Flanders (1369), he inherited Artois, and in 1384 also became count of *Flanders, with a large number of estates in northeastern France. While he was very active in the royal court, where he and his brothers were regents, he used the French army to enlarge his possessions in the Low Countries, where he established the centre of his new state.

E. Perroy, *The Hundred Years' War* (1957).

PHOCAS Emperor of *Byzantium (602-10). He seized power by a military revolt and tried to govern the empire by concluding peace treaties for which he paid heavy tributes, such as with the *Avars in 604. The taxes imposed to provide the tributes made him unpopular and in 608, when King *Chosroes II of Persia invaded Asia Minor, he was able to conquer it without opposition. P. was deposed and murdered by *Heraclius. *CMedH,* IV.

PHOCAS *Byzantine dynasty. Originally from Cappadocia, Asia Minor, the family made its military reputation in the wars against the Arabs and the Bulgarians in the 9th and 10th centuries. The first P. to reach the imperial throne was *Nicephorus. In the 11th century the P. were among the leading noble families in the Byzantine empire.

PHOTIUS (810-95) Patriarch of *Constantinople (858-67 and 877-86). Of noble family, he entered the imperial service at Constantinople, where he won the friendship and protection of Emperor *Michael III. In 858, when Michael deposed Patriarch *Ignatius, P. was appointed patriarch. To secure papal recognition, Michael invited Pope *Nicholas I to send legates to Constantinople, where the question would be decided in a council. The legates' approval, however, was rejected by the pope in 862 and, at a council held in Rome the following year, he recognized Ignatius and excommunicated P. In 865 the crisis was almost settled, but then a dispute broke out about the new *Bulgarian Church. P. denounced the Latin missionaries in Bulgaria and contested the papal version of the word *Filioque in the creed. He also pronounced the pope deposed. With the accession of Emperor *Basil I to the imperial throne, the situation changed. The new emperor reinstated Ignatius in 867, and sent P. to a monastery. But papal intervention in Bulgaria reopened the conflict between Rome and Constantinople, and Ignatius was excommunicated by the pope (870). In 877, after Ignatius' death, P. was reappointed patriarch by imperial order. This led to a schism with Rome, which numerous councils failed to settle. Despite appearances, the quarrel expressed not personal views, but the accentuation of the theological conflict between the Orthodox and Catholic churches. This is proved by the separation of the churches after P. was deposed again, this time by Emperor *Leo VI, who sent him to a monastery where he died. P. was also a great scholar of encyclopedic knowledge. He wrote theological treatises, in defence of Greek Orthodox practices.

Works, *PG,* 101-104;

F. Dvornik, *The Photian Schism* (1948).

PHRYGIUM Cap worn by popes as symbol of their office. It was used until the 11th century, when it was replaced by the more regal tiara.

PIACENZA City in Lombardy, Italy. After the fall of the *Lombard kingdom in 774, P. was governed by Frankish counts. At the end of the 9th century the counts' power declined and feudal lords fought for dominion over the city, which in 997 fell to its bishops. P. became an important ecclesiastical centre which supported the papacy. In 1095 Pope *Urban II held a council in the city, gathering his Italian supporters. At the council the idea of a *Crusade was first proposed. In the 12th century P. became an independent commune, with a leading position in the *Lombard League. In the second half of the 14th century it was conquered by the *Visconti and annexed to Milan.

J. K. Hyde, *Society and Politics in Medieval Italy* (1973).

PIANO DEI CARPINI, GIOVANNI See JOHN OF PIANO CARPINI.

PIAST The name of the dynasty which founded the kingdom of *Poland in the 10th century, and reigned until it became extinct in 1370. The dynasty took its name from the first duke of Poland (c. 900), who united the *Slav tribes between the Oder and the Vistula under his rule.

PICARDY Province in northeastern *France. Conquered by the Salian *Franks in the 5th century, it was a central part of the Frankish kingdom in the reign of *Clovis. The assimilation of the Gallo-Roman and Frankish elements in the province produced a particular early French dialect. One of the last *Carolingian centres in France, P. was subdivided among several feudal lords, the city of *Laon remaining the capital of the kingdom until 987. The most important of P.'s feudal units was the county of *Vermandois, which was annexed to the royal domain by *Philip II in 1185. In the 15th century the major part of the province was under the domination of the dukes of *Burgundy. After the death of *Charles the Bold in 1477 it was reconquered by *Louis XI.

E. Jarry, *Provinces et Pays de France* (1946).

PICTS *Celtic tribe in Scotland. Never conquered by the Romans, their society was based on clans, led by military chieftains. In the 4th and 5th centuries they attacked Roman Britain. At the end of the 5th century

The Holy Land between Paradise and Hell; *from a 15th-century miniature*

they began to be ruled by kings. In the 6th century Irish monks came to Scotland and began to spread the Christian faith. At this time Scottish tribes from Ireland began to penetrate the southwestern part of the kingdom. In the 8th century the P. became fully absorbed by the Scots.

PIEDMONT (PIEMONTE) Province in northwestern *Italy. Until the 15th century it was divided among several feudal estates, and was dependent on the *Lombard kingdom (until 774), the *Carolingian (until the end of the 9th century) and the *Holy Roman empire. The most important of the feudalities was the march of *Montferrat. In the 15th century the counts of *Savoy conquered and annexed the various feudal principalities to their state.

PIERLEONI *Roman family. Its origins began with the conversion of a Jewish financial agent of Pope *Leo IX (1050). He took the name Pietro Leone in honour of St. Peter and of his pontifical patron. During the latter half of the 11th century the P. became politically powerful. Some of them commanded the city guard. Pietro P. joined the order of Cluny, became a cardinal – one of the most influential in the Catholic world – and in 1130 became Antipope *Anacletus II. The P. began to decline in the latter half of the 12th century.
G. Falco, *The Holy Roman Republic* (1967).

PIERS PLOWMAN Long allegorical English poem attributed to William *Langland (*c.* 1330-*c.* 1400). A religious work, with personifications of the Church, Truth, Reason, Fraud, Hunger, etc., it is written mostly in simple everyday language, yet is rich in allusions and scholarly sources. It has also served as a useful source of information on the everyday life and material culture of 14th-century rural England.
W. W. Skeat (ed.), *Piers Plowman (Ploughman)* (1886).

PILGRIMAGE Journey to a shrine or other holy place undertaken by pious Christians from the 4th century on, with the aim of winning salvation by contact with the sacred site. By the 6th century the practice had become well established in the Church. It was theologically rooted in the *Augustinian interpretation of the

Latin word *peregrinus* (stranger): it was applied to the believer who left all worldy affairs behind him to pursue his goal, ultimately the Kingdom of Heaven, thus becoming a stranger to the material preoccupations of his environment. A P. was undertaken as a pious deed, the pilgrim being, for the duration of his journey, a stranger to his family and social status. He wore simple clothes on his way, put up at the monasteries and ate the food of poverty. In later centuries members of the upper classes, who travelled with their retinues and baggage, took a few symbolic steps clothed in traditional pilgrim's garments. There were four kinds of P.: the local, by the people of a region to a shrine of local importance; the general and multi-national, like the P. to *Santiago de Compostela in northwestern Spain, which drew pilgrims from all Europe; *ad limina apostolorum,* to St. *Peter's tomb at Rome and to the papal audience; to Jerusalem and the *Holy Land. They increased after the 10th century, becoming mass manifestations in the 11th and 12th centuries. The P. to the Holy Land prepared the ground for the *Crusades, which were also viewed as a kind of P., and accustomed the European public to accounts of Palestine.

Under the influence of the Christian practice, as well as of the biblical Jewish custom of going to Jerusalem on the great feasts. Mohammad prescribed the Moslem P. to Mecca, the *Hajj,* which also continued the pagan Arabian tradition.
S. Heath, *Pilgrim Life in the Middle Ages* (1911).

PIPE ROLLS Financial accounts of the court of *Exchequer in England. Many of them are preserved and are an important source for the economical history of medieval England.

PISA City in *Tuscany, Italy, on the shores of the Tyrrhenian Sea. Its autonomy dates from the 5th century, although it continued to be influenced by political development in Tuscany. P. developed its maritime trade in the western Mediterranean, becoming the main city in Tuscany in the 9th century and one of the wealthiest in Italy. Already in the 10th century with the conquest of *Corsica its merchants began to build an

Pisa's leaning tower, cathedral and baptistery, built from the 11th to the 13th centuries

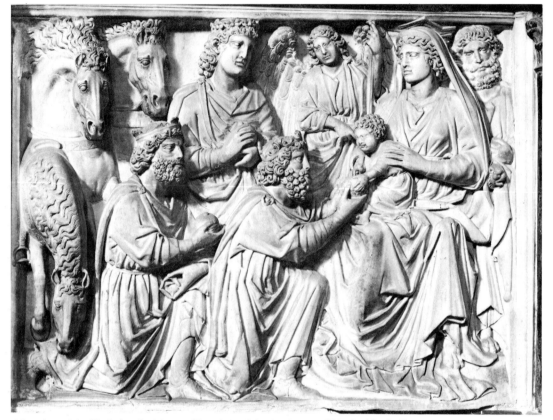

Adoration of the Magi; *detail of the marble pulpit of the Baptistery of Pisa by Nicola Pisano*

empire, and during the 11th century its navy, together with that of Genoa, seized *Sardinia from the Arabs; in 1163 P. provided assistance to the *Normans in their conquest of *Sicily. At the end of the 11th century the merchants of P. began to trade in the eastern Mediterranean, where they soon replaced *Amalfi. After the establishment of the Latin kingdom of Jerusalem, P. was prominent in the trade of Acre, after *Venice and *Genoa. The expansion of P. caused repeated conflicts with Genoa and with its Tuscan neighbours *Florence and *Lucca. These struggles affected its life in the 12th century, as they obliged the city to maintain a strong army, which was a financial burden. In the 13th century industry began to develop in the city, whose population increased. The establishment of the silk and *cloth industry changed the social structure of P. There were uprisings of the lower classes against the mercantile government, from which Genoa and Florence profited. In 1284 the fleet of P. was defeated and destroyed at Meloria, and the city lost the remnants of its former economic empire. Meantime the Florentine merchants and bankers competed with those of P. Its decline began at the beginning of the 14th century. The internecine struggles and the external defeats produced a state of anarchy in the city, which in 1348 fell under the rule of tyrants and military commanders. In 1406 P. surrendered to Florence and became part of the Florentine state, the future duchy of Tuscany.

At the height of its prosperity, in the 12th century, P. was an important cultural centre, which concentrated around its new cathedral, whose baptistery and famous tower made it one of the most beautiful monuments in Italy. Ecclesiastic councils were also held in the city.

The Council of P. in 1409, assembled to end the *Great Schism, opened the *Conciliar period in the history of the Church. It did not solve the problem of the double papacy, but decided on a new council, at *Constance, and urged both popes to abdicate before its opening. Consequently, as according to the decisions of the council the popes were already considered deposed, a third pope, *Alexander V, was elected.

J. K. Hyde, *Society and Politics in Medieval Italy* (1973).

PIUS I   Pope (1140-54). He was a native of Aquileia in northern Italy.

PLAGUE   See BLACK DEATH.

PLANTAGENET   English royal dynasty. Its name supposedly came from a nickname of *Geoffrey of Anjou, its founder, who wore a sprig of broom (*genista*) in his hat. The Ps. became connected with *England when Count Geoffrey married Matilda, daughter of King *Henry I, in 1128. The dynasty reigned continuously from the coronation of *Henry II in 1154, until 1399; after the death of *Richard II, it was continued by two collateral branches, the houses of *Lancaster and *York, who fought each other for the throne. The dynasty came to an end in 1485.

PLATEARIUS, MATTHEW (12th century) Botanist. Little is known about his life. He tought medicine at Salerno, where he studied the medicinal qualities of plants and herbs. His book, *Circa Instans,* contained a classification of plants, and became a leading authority in botany in the 12th century.
A. C. Crombie, *Medieval Science* (1957).

PLATO (d. 799) Abbot of *Studion. An eminent Greek Orthodox theologian, he became the most famous preacher in Constantinople in the second half of the 8th century. As abbot of the imperial monastery of Studion, a leading centre of Byzantine learning, he was involved in the political affairs of the day. In 795 he strongly opposed the divorce of *Constantine VI and his remarriage with a lady-in-waiting of his mother *Irene. Arrested by the emperor, P.'s imprisonment provoked a revolt of the monks at Constantinople and facilitated the seizing of power by Irene.
CMedH, IV.

PLATO OF TIVOLI (12th century) Translator. Originally from Rome, he studied in southern Italy and about 1120 went to Spain, where he became acquainted with Arab philosophical and scientific works. He settled in Toledo, Castile, where he translated Arabic works into Latin, being among the pioneers in the field.
C. H. Haskins, *Studies in Medieval Science* (1927).

PLATONISM The philosophical system based on the works of Plato of Athens, which was developed through the centuries at the Hellenistic academies of *Athens and *Alexandria. In the 2nd and 3rd centuries it was studied in Alexandria by the Fathers of the Church, such as Clement of Alexandria and Origen and was thereafter held in great esteem by the early Christian theologians. The influence of P. on the thought of St. *Augustine, made it the accepted philosophical method, by which the doctrine of the unity of the Church and the corporative concept of Christian society were explained. P. having become the sole method of learning in medieval Christian society, Aristotle was neglected and left to the *Moslem philosophers until the end of the 12th century. But even after the adoption of *Aristotelian thought in western universities and schools, many of its followers, like *Thomas of Aquinas, continued to be influenced by Platonic ideas. In the 15th century there was a revival of interest in Plato himself, as part of the humanist movement.
R. Klibansky, *The Platonist Tradition during the Middle Ages* (1939).

PLISKA City in Dobrudja, Bulgaria. Conquered by the *Bulgars in the 7th century, it became the first capital of the Bulgarian state in the Balkans. In 870 Tsar *Boris I, having accepted the Christian faith, decided to erase all traces of paganism and moved his capital from P. to Preslav. The city declined and finally disappeared.
S. Runciman, *The First Bulgarian Empire* (1930).

PODESTA The title of the highest magistrate in medieval Italian *communes, who often held the real power (*potestas* in Latin) in the city.

POITIERS City in western *France. In the last century of the Western Roman empire, and in the early Middle Ages, P. was one of the most important cultural centres in western Europe, where poets, thinkers and theologians gathered. Under the government of the *Franks, beginning in 507, the city became famous also for its monasteries, which attracted the devout from all over the kingdom. In 732 the Arabs entered the city, but were defeated in its vicinity by the army of *Charles Martel. The Battle of P. was represented as one of the greatest victories of Christendom, in which Europe was saved from "Moslem barbarity". This interpretation was developed in *Carolingian Europe, which prided itself on its civilization. In reality, in the 8th century the Arabs had a higher civilization than the *Franks; moreover, the "Arab army" had been a small unit, sent into Gaul for plunder. However, the impact of the battle was of major importance, being a decisive step in the rise of the *Carolingians, who were represented as the champions of Christianity, and helped to make the Franks the most powerful element in western Europe.

In the 9th century P. became the capital and cultural heart of the duchy of *Aquitaine. Its schools were developed, and by the 11th century were widely-known. At the beginning of the 12th century, under the active leadership of Duke *William IX, P. saw the rise of secular culture, represented by the poetry of the troubadours and by Romanesque art. The development of the city was continuous until 1137, and the presence of a ducal court accelerated its population growth. The marriages of *Eleanor of Aquitaine, first with King *Louis VII of France (1137) then with *Henry II of England (1152), led to the removal of the court and P. began to decline into a provincial town. During the 13th century *Alphonse of Poitiers, brother of *Louis IX, made the city an administrative centre, where the integration of the northern and western parts of Aquitaine, conquered by the French in 1223-44, was carried out. In 1356 P. was the site of one of the decisive battles of the *Hundred Years' War, when the Anglo-Gascon army, commanded by *Edward, the Black Prince, crushed the French army, led by King *John II, who was taken captive. P. remained under English domination until 1370, when Bertrand *Du Guesclin recaptured it for France.
G. Duby-R. Mandrou, *France, History and Civilization* (1968).

POITOU County in western France, whose capital was *Poitiers. In the 9th century the counts of P. became dukes of *Aquitaine and, until the 13th century, its history was involved with that of Aquitaine. In the 11th and 12th centuries some of the vassals of the counts of P. grew powerful and established feudal principalities. The most important of these were the lords of *Lusignan. In 1244 *Louis IX gave P. as apanage to his brother, Alphonse, who introduced French administrative systems and integrated it into the French royal demesne. After 1270 the county ceased to exist as a separate entity.

POLAND Kingdom in eastern Europe, between Germany and Russia. During the first centuries of the Middle Ages the territory was occupied by *Germanic tribes, who were migrating westwards and southwards. By the 7th century local *Slav tribes, of which the Poles (or *Polanii*), were the main ethnic group, became predominant and began to organize principalities. The main step towards political organization was made in the latter half of the 9th century, when a chieftain named *Piast united the Poles and founded a duchy. One of his descendants, *Mieszko I (*c.* 960-92) was the real founder of the state; he acknowledged the suzerainty of the *Holy Roman emperors, becoming a faithful vassal of *Otto I. During his reign Christianity spread through P., introduced by Bohemian missionaries, and a bishopric was established at *Gniezno, the capital. His successor, *Boleslaw the Brave (992-1025), aspired to independence; after the death of *Otto III (1002), he proclaimed himself king and conquered Pomerania, Silesia, Slovakia and Ruthenia. He also seized Bohemia, Moravia and Lusatia, but was forced by Emperor *Henry II to give them up. After the death of Boleslaw, the great Polish kingdom disintegrated, and the conquered territories were lost to the neighbouring states. The Piast kings concentrated on governing P. itself, founding new towns and struggling against nobles, whose character was still tribal. During the 11th century royal power declined, although some of the monarchs regained it for short periods. Only at the beginning of the 12th century was the kingdom reorganized by *Boleslaw III (1102-38), who introduced the *feudal system, and destroyed the last remnants of the tribal heritage. The division of the kingdom under his sons led to a state of anarchy and to the rise of powerful feudal principalities. On the western borders the German expansion swallowed up the territories east of the Elbe and crossed the Oder River. Begun in the 12th century, the process went on in the 13th century with the settlement of German colonists in Polish cities, where they monopolized the trade. In 1228 the *Teutonic Knights established themselves in *Prussia, and conquered parts of northern P. The *Mongol invasion, led by *Batu Khan in 1241, caused the political disruption of P. and ruined it economically. By the middle of the 13th century the kings of the Piast dynasty were in effect princes of *Cracow, while the kingdom fell into total anarchy, the nobles governing their estates and fighting among themselves as there was no central authority.

The 14th century was a period of Renaissance for P. In the reigns of *Wladyslaw IV and his son *Casimir III, the monarchy succeeded in regaining its authority, but only after many clashes with the nobles and the Teutonic Knights, and with the help of alliances with the neighbouring monarchs of *Hungary and *Lithuania. The reign of Casimir III (1333-70) was in that respect one of the most important in Polish history. He reorganized the constitution of the kingdom, issued the first code of law and established the high court of Cracow. To check the power of the nobility he based his authority on the cities, which were reorganized according to the German model of the *Magdeburg charter, and opened the towns to German and Jewish settlers, to stimulate economic development. He also improved the conditions of the peasantry and, in 1364, founded the University of Cracow, providing a cultural centre for the kingdom. His successor, *Louis I of Anjou, king of Hungary, had little interest in P., and in 1374 granted the nobles the Charter of Koszyce, which increased their privileges, exempting them from taxes and granting them the prerogative to elect the kings. His daughter, Jadwiga, elected in 1384, married Jagiello of Lithuania, who became king of Poland as *Wladyslaw II, and founded the *Jagiello dynasty. He was compelled to grant further privileges to the nobility, but his victory over the Teutonic Knights at Tannenberg (1410) endowed him with great prestige, and allowed him to exercise his royal authority over the nobility.
Cambridge History of Poland (1950).

POLENTA, DA Italian noble family which, under the leadership of Guido P., seized power in *Ravenna in 1275 and dominated the city until 1441. As captains and *condottieri*, they were also involved in the major power struggles in central and northern Italy. They fell from power when they lost Ravenna to Venice in 1441.

POLIGNAC, HOUSE OF *French noble family which became prominent in western France in the second half of the 13th century. In the early 14th century they secured hereditary rights to the viscounty of Polignac. They served in the French army during the *Hundred Years' War and in the 15th century rose to the ranks of the higher nobility.

POLO, MARCO (1254-1324) Venetian merchant and traveller. With his father and uncle he left Venice in 1271 for the *Mongol empire, where he remained some 17 years. During those years he travelled around China and saw most of its cities. He became the favourite of the khan and resided in his palace at Peking. From there he went to Persia, returning to Italy in 1297. Captured by the Genoese, he wrote an account of his travels and adventures during his imprisonment. His accurate description of Asia and China, as well as the court of Peking was the chief source of information on the East during the Middle Ages and the Renaissance.
M. Rugoff, *Marco Polo's Adventures in China* (1964).

POLOVTSY (CUMANS) *Turkish nomadic tribes. Originating in central Asia, they were pushed northwards in the 5th-8th centuries by other tribes. Some of them assimilated with the *Mongols, while others migrated in the 10th century to the southern Russian steppes, previously occupied by the *Khazars, who were defeated by the Russians and dispersed. They are mentioned in historical documents as having effectuated dangerous raids and rapid battles against the Byzantines, the Russians, the *Petchenegs and the Hungarians. Some of them settled in *Moldavia. In 1237, *Batu-Khan defeated their army, killed their *Bachman* (chief) and crushed their power. The P. thereafter merged with the *Golden Horde.
R. Grousset, *L'Empire des Steppes* (1945).

POMERANIA Region on the southern shore of the Baltic Sea lying between the Oder and the Wisla rivers. In the 5th century it was settled by Slavic Pomeranian tribes who divided the territory amongst themselves. Their history is obscure until the 10th century, when they are mentioned as paying tribute to *Mieszko I, duke of *Poland. His son and successor, *Boleslaw I, who conquered P. in 1000, opened it to Christian missionaries from Germany and founded in P. a bishopric, dependent on *Gniezno. The missionaries met with fierce resistance from the pagan tribes, who had united and established a principality. Only after 1107 did they succeed in Christianizing P. During the 12th century, western P. was Germanized, while eastern P. was conquered in 1225 by the *Teutonic knights and became known as Western Prussia. At the same time, the bishoprics of P. were made subject to the archbishop of *Magdeburg. On the other hand, Polish dukes continued to rule western P. In 1454, King *Casimir IV of Poland conquered eastern P. and annexed it to Poland.

PONTIGNY French *Cistercian abbey, founded in 1115. It was one of the four daughter-houses of *Cîteaux, its abbot holding a high position within the order. In the 12th century, the abbey enjoyed much

Marco Polo sails out of Venice; *from a 14th-century illuminated manuscript*

prestige throughout the Catholic world, and it was at P. that Thomas *Becket took refuge in 1164. Its monks expanded the Cistercian order, especially in Germany.

B. Mahn, *L'Ordre Cistercien et son gouvernement au XII*e *siècle* (1946).

POOR CLARES See CLARISSES.

POORE, RICHARD (d. 1237) Bishop of *Salisbury (1217-28). He built the new cathedral of Salisbury and elaborated the Constitutions of Salisbury which became a model for English diocese organization and rule. In 1228, he was transferred to the see of Durham, where he was active in organizing nunneries.

C. R. Cheney, *The English Synodals of the Thirteenth Century* (1941).

POPPO (11th century) Abbot of Stavelot. One of the main monastic reformers in *Belgium, he drew up a rule for his abbey that was inspired by the rule of *Cluny. Highly esteemed for his learning, P. contributed to the intellectual and cultural trend that developed in Liège at the time.

PORETE, MARGARET (d. c. 1390) Visionary. She joined the *Brethren of the Free Spirit, publicly professing that her soul was annihilated in God. Accused of heresy, she was convicted and burnt in Paris.

J. Russell, *The Heresy of the Free Spirit* (1973).

PORTO VENERE Harbour on the Ligurian coast of the Mediterranean Sea. Situated east of *Genoa, the ancient fishermen's harbour became in the 8th century one of the ports handling commerce between Europe and north Africa. It is mentioned in Frankish royal annals of 802 as the harbour where the ship bringing the presents sent by *Harun Al-Rashid to *Charlemagne arrived and was received by the imperial commander of the navy (*praefectus classis*). In the 12th century P. was conquered by Genoa and annexed to the Genoese state.

PORTUGAL Country in the western part of the Iberian peninsula. In the 5th century the region, hitherto occupied by the Romans, was overrun by the *Suevi, who conquered its northern part, the *Visigoths, the centre, and the *Vandals, who settled in the south. In the 6th century the Visigoths moved southwards and annexed all of P. to their kingdom of Spain. In 711-14 P. was conquered by the Arabs and incorporated into the *Ummayad caliphate of Córdoba. After the caliphate's fall in the 11th century, it was made subject to the kings of *Seville. In 1097 *Alfonso VI, king of Castile, conquered its northern part, and made it a county, vesting his son-in-law, Henry of Burgundy, with the countal title. The county became independent in 1109, and, pursuing the wars against the Moslems, expanded southwards. In 1139, Henry's son, *Alfonso I, was proclaimed king and thus established the new state of P. In 1148, he conquered Lisbon, with the help of English and Scandinavian Crusaders, and established the realm's southern frontier on the Tagus River. The second half of the 12th and beginning of the 13th century saw continued southward expansion at the expense of the Arabs, culminating in the conquest of *Algarve, the southernmost region of P. The 13th-century kings consecrated their efforts to organizing the kingdom and imposing royal authority on the church and the nobility. The kings were supported by the commoners, who were admitted in 1254 to the *Cortes* (representative assembly), to check the nobility. In 1280, King *Denis founded a university at Lisbon, which was later transferred to Coimbra. The 14th century saw P.'s involvement in the political affairs of Castile. Through intermarriages between members of the ruling dynasties of both realms, Castilian influence penetrated P., but was checked by the kings and the *Cortes*. The age of Portuguese expansion began towards the end of the century. The kings, taking advantage of the anarchy in north Africa, penetrated into *Morocco. The maritime expeditions that were organized along the African coast from 1415 on, inaugurated the era of geographical exploration. The Canaries, Madeira and the Azores were discovered during that century.

A. J. Livermore, *A History of Portugal* (1932).

POTOLSK City in western *Russia, situated on the Dvina River. It was first mentioned in 862 as a trade centre between *Novgorod and the Black Sea. In the second half of the 11th century it became the capital of a Russian principality, dependent on *Kiev. In the 13th and 14th centuries P. was an important centre of trade between Russia and the *Golden Horde, and the *Hanse. Conquered in the 14th century by *Gedymin, it became part of the *Lithuanian state.

M. Florinsky, *A History of Russia* (1957).

POZNAN City in western *Poland. It emerged from a 9th-century fortress, around which arose a borough, where various Polish tribes came to trade their goods. *Mieszko I establshed P. as the capital of Poland. The city developed in the 13th century as an important centre of trade with Germany and in 1253 was granted a communal charter modelled on that of *Magdeburg. German and Jewish influence became important in P. from the reign of *Casimir III.

Cambridge History of Poland (1950).

PRAEMUNIRE The title of statutes issued by English kings to protect their rights from encroachment by the *papacy; as such, they were part of an effort to assert royal sovereignty in *England. The first such statutes were issued in 1353, 1365 and 1393. That of 1353 forbade the appeal to the papal court of cases within the purview of the king's courts. That of 1393

forbade *excommunication or the issuance of a papal *bull without royal assent.

B. Lyon, *A Constitutional and Legal History of Medieval England* (1960).

PRAEPOSTINUS OF CREMONA (c. 1140-c. 1210) Theologian and preacher. He studied and later taught theology and law at Paris. In 1194 he became a prebendary at Mainz Cathedral and was an active preacher among the *Albigenses. In 1206 he was appointed chancellor of Paris *University. He wrote polemical treatises against heresies as well as interpretations of the symbolism of ecclesiastical offices. His works provide insight into the methods of teaching theology at Paris.

G. Lacombe, *La vie et les oeuvres de Prevosyin* (1927).

PRAGUE Capital of *Bohemia. Founded in the second half of the 9th century, as the seat of the ducal government of Bohemia, P. saw rapid growth. The bishopric established in the city in 973 assured its spiritual independence from the Bavarian church. The city thrived in the 12th and 13th centuries, becoming one of the wealthiest in Holy Roman empire. It saw the peak of its flowering in the 14th century, when the *Luxemburg emperors, who inherited the kingdom of Bohemia, made it their capital. As the virtual capital of the Holy Roman empire under *Charles IV, P. became a mixed Slav-German city, embellished under the emperor's personal supervision. In 1348 he founded the Caroline University, which soon became a spiritual and cultural centre of Bohemia. The activities of its scholars triggered the awakening of Bohemian nationalism. In 1349 the bishopric of P. was promoted to the rank of archbishopric. During the second half of the 14th century, P.'s economic prosperity attracted to the city settlers from Germany and Italy, as well as from Czech villages. At the beginning of the 15th century, P. and its university were the centre of the *Hussite movement. The continuous wars in the 15th century caused the city's decline and the emigration of foreign elements.

F. Graus, *Le mouvement urbain en Bohème médiévale* (1969).

PREBEND (Latin: praebaenda "stipend") A benefice assigned to *canons and other officials at a cathedral, destined to provide its holder with a fixed income. Until the 12th century the cathedral chapters and bishops decided on the number of Ps. to be granted and their amounts. From the 12th century the usage of assigning a. P. to a church official, who was also entrusted with temporal duties and thus received his salary indirectly, was repealed, except in the case of popes and kings. During the *Avignon period, the popes appointed the prebendaries and ordered the churches of the entire Catholic world to defray the costs of the Ps.

G. Barraclough, *Papal Provisions* (1935).

PRELATE Name given to the members of the upper hierarchy of the *church, including archbishops, bishops and abbots.

PRÉMONTRÉ Abbey in northern France, near Laon, founded in 1120 by St. *Norbert of Xanten. The rule he established for his community of *canons was modelled on that observed by full monastic communities. They were expected to serve parochial churches and to preach against heresy. The same year saw the founding of the Order of the Premonstratensian (from the Latin form of P.). Canons, which rapidly spread throughout western

The centre of Prague with buildings dating back to the 14th century

Europe. In England the Premonstratensians were called the "White Canons" after the colour of their habit.

H. M. Colvin, *The "White Canons" in England* (1951).

PREMYSLID The name of the first dynasty that ruled *Bohemia (*c.* 870-1306). According to tradition, P. was the first Czech leader who united the tribes of Bohemia, founded *Prague and established a principality. Under the Ps., Bohemia developed from a tribal principality lacking political structure, into a powerful kingdom that enjoyed virtual autonomy within the *Holy Roman empire.

PRESLAV City in eastern *Bulgaria and capital of the Bulgarian empire. Founded in the 9th century as Yeschi Stambolluk, its name was changed to P. after the Bulgarians converted to Christianity. In 970, Tsar *Simeon made it his capital, leaving the ancient pagan centre of *Pliska. P. remained the capital of the Bulgarian empire until its destruction by the Byzantine emperor, *Basil II.

PRESSBURG (modern Bratislava) City in Slovakia, in the *Hungarian kingdom. Founded as a borough by Slav settlers, who were subjected to Hungarian lords, it developed into a commercial centre on the Danube in the 9th century and gradually expanded. In 1291 its inhabitants were granted a charter, modelled on that of *Magdeburg, and, during the 14th century, German merchants settled there.

PRESTER JOHN Legendary Christian priest and king of a wealthy empire in the East, who allegedly defeated the *Moslems. The legend arose in the Christian world at the beginning of the *Crusader period and was popularized in the 13th century. It seems to be connected with a certain *Nestorian Turkish kingdom in central Asia or with the 13th-century *Mongol khans, many of whom were Nestorians. Some scholars relate the legend to the Christian *Ethiopian empire. Their theory, based on 15th-century Portuguese sources, does not take into account the fact that, in 1177, Pope *Alexander III, in response to a letter purporting to come from P., sent a reply to the "king of the Indies, the most holy priest", implying that P. was believed to be a ruler in Asia.

C. E. Nowell, *The Historical Prester John* (1953).

PREVOTS (Latin: praepositus "provost") Title given in the 12th century to French officials who were entrusted with administering estates belonging to the royal demesne. By extension, the title was given, from the 13th century, to royal agents administering a district.

PRIBISLAV Leader of the *Wends (12th century). He was one of the last chiefs of the Slav Wends, who inhabited the territory between the Elbe and Oder rivers. After he led a Wend uprising in 1147 against the implantation of German influence in his country a *Crusade against him was declared. Despite his general success against the Saxon Crusaders, he was compelled to cede the territory of *Brandenburg to *Albert the Bear in 1150.

J. W. Thompson, *Feudal Germany* (1928).

PRIEST (Greek: presbyteros "elder") In the early Christian *church, the term designated the community's leader, who directed its activities, such as prayers and common meals. With the development of the church and the institutionalization of bishops, priestly functions were split between the bishops and the Ps., the latter being subordinate to the former. The P. supervised the parish churches administering the *sacraments, namely, baptism, marriage and extreme unction, and conducting the prayers and the *Mass. From the 13th century on, with the introduction of the *Eucharist sacrament, the P. also heard confessions, granted absolution and administered the Eucharist. They were therefore regarded by the masses as the representatives of God, and, in that capacity, could intercede for divine grace.

E. O. James, *The Nature and Function of Priesthood* (1955).

PRIMAT D'ORLEANS See HUGH OF ORLEANS.

PRIMATE The title given to the archbishop of a primary see, usually the oldest bishopric in a realm. Thus, the archbishops of Canterbury were P. of England, those of Lyons of Gaul, those of Mainz of Germany and those of Toledo of Spain. It also designated certain individuals whom the popes entitled *primas ad personam*.

PRIVILEGE The private law that applied to a certain individual or a social body, who would benefit from it. The practice, originating in the system of legal pluralism (see *law) and instituted in the Germanic kingdoms after the fall of the Roman empire, became an essential component of *feudalism.

M. Bloch, *Feudal Society* (1955).

PRIVILEGIO DE LA UNION (The Privilege of the Union) Charter granted by King *Alfonso III to the union of nobles and townsmen at the *cortes (representative assembly) of 1287; which limited the kings' authority. The *cortes* was granted the right to appoint members of the royal council, and to depose the king and elect another.

PRIVILEGIO GENERAL (General Privilege) A concession the nobles of *Aragon wrested in 1283 from King *Peter III, whereby he promised to respect the ancient customs of the land, which forbade conviction without proper trial and the conscription of burghers for military service outside the kingdom. It also called for the inclusion of all classes of society in the royal *councils.

PRIVY SEAL Introduced in England by *Peter of Roches (c. 1220) as a means of enabling a king to control the government without consulting the *council, in which the barons secured a leading position, controlling the *exchequer and the chancery. The sealing of official documents by the king's P. remained a full royal prerogative.

B. Lyon, *Constitutional and Legal History of Medieval England* (1960).

PROCHEIRON A manual of legal studies issues by Byzantine Emperor *Basil I.

PROCOPIUS OF CAESAREA (6th century) Byzantine historian. Born in Caesarea in Palestine, he became secretary to *Belisarius in 527 and took part in the wars against the Persians, the Vandals and the Ostrogoths.

He supposedly lived at Constantinople in 542. P. wrote a history of Belisarius' wars and an account of the public buildings constructed during the reign of *Justinian, both of which are invaluable sources for this period.

Works, with Eng. trans., ed. H. B. Dewing, 7 vols. (1914-40).

PROCOPIUS OF GAZA (c. 475-538) Rhetorician and biblical exegete, he was the foremost figure in reviving Greek rhetoric in the "School of *Gaza" which flourished in the 5th and 6th centuries. His works consist of extracts of patristic exegesis, to which he added his own commentaries.

PRODROMOS (d. c. 1166) Byzantine writer and dramatist, famous during the *Comneni period; his plays were designed to honour and praise his patrons.

PROSPER OF AQUITAINE (c. 390-463) Theologian, poet and historian who became famous for his defence of St. *Augustine. He attempted to spread Augustine's teachings to monastic communities in Provence and Gaul, but they met with opposition, especially his doctrine on grace. While serving as secretary to Pope *Leo I (from 435), he versified excerpts of the works of the Church Fathers. He also wrote a history of his times, which is an important source for the decline of the Western Roman empire.

L. Valentin, *St. Prosper d'Aquitaine* (1900).

PROVENCE Region on the northern coast of the Mediterranean Sea, between the Rhône River and the Alps. Conquered at the beginning of the 5th century by the *Visigoths, it passed in 476 to the *Heruli and in 493 to the *Ostrogoths, who dominated it until the fall of their Italian kingdom. During this period, P. was a centre of the Christian church, and its monastery of Lérins was instrumental in spreading the classical heritage as well as Christianity. In the 6th century P. was annexed to the Frankish kingdom of Burgundy. It became part of the kingdom of *Lothair I in 843 and, at his death in 855, recovered its independence as the realm of Lothair's younger son, *Charles, who, however, was prevented from reigning by powerful nobles. In the late 9th century, the process of feudalization put the country in a state of anarchy, despite the fact that the royal title continued to exist and passed to the descendants of *Boso of Vienne. Primarily interested in the imperial crown and Italy, they neglected the realm, which was attacked and devastated by north African *Moslems. In the 10th century P. was ruled by *Burgundian kings as part of their kingdom of Arelate, named for Arles, the capital. As such, it was inherited by the *Holy Roman emperors. But the kings of Burgundy and the Holy Roman emperors had only nominal influence in the county. Until the end of the 12th century, the countal title − and the real authority − was contested by the counts of *Toulouse and those of *Barcelona, kings of Aragon since 1154, who finally managed to seize power. With the revival of trade in the Mediterranean Sea during the 12th century, Provençal cities' flourished. *Marseilles dominated commerce in the western Mediterranean, developing trade relations with Barcelona and *Genoa, but also directly with the Middle East; a colony of its merchants settled in the Latin kingdom of *Jerusalem. With the end of the Catalan countal dynasty in the mid-13th century, the county was inherited by *Charles of Anjou, brother of

King *Louis IX of France. He organized its administration and finances; established courts of justice, the highest being that of *Aix; and promoted the development of the cities and their economic interests, notably Marseilles and its maritime trade. He left P. in 1266, settling first at Naples and then at Palermo, while the county was governed by his officers. Because there were no grand baronies in P., its administration was able to maintain order. With the opening of trade relations with Naples. and the establishment of the papacy at *Avignon, P.'s prosperity increased, and by the 14th century the county was one of the wealthiest in western Europe.
P. Wolff (ed.), *La Provence (Horizons de France)* (1970).

PROVINS City in *Champagne (France). Originally a small town, it began to develop in the 11th century, when it became one of the sites of the *Fairs of Champagne, which attracted merchants from all over Europe. It soon became the third city of Champagne, in terms of population and economic activity. In the 12th and 13th centuries, the counts of Champagne erected walls around P. to protect the city and its fairs, the income from which constituted an important part of their revenue. The monumental tower, named the Tour de César, built in the 12th century, symbolized the growth and prosperity of the city and the countal authority. The mint established in P., produced the *coinage that was used in all of Champagne and its fairs and was one of the most widely-circulated currencies in western Europe. With an estimated 80,000 inhabitants in the mid-13th century, P. was one of the largest cities in western Europe, equal in size to *Paris. The economic crisis at the end of the 13th century and its repercussions in the 14th, affected the Fairs of Champagne and inaugurated a period of decline. By the end of the Middle Ages P. was a small provincial town with only its walls and the Tour de César attesting to its glorious past.
R. H. Bautier, *Les Foires de Champagne* (1935).

PROVISIONS OF OXFORD See OXFORD, PROVISIONS OF.

PRUDENTIUS, GALINDO (d. 861) Bishop of *Troyes. Of Spanish origin, he became chaplain at the court of *Louis the Pious and was promoted to the bishopric of Troyes (c. 843). A learned Augustinian, he entered a long dispute with *Hincmar of Rheims and John Scot *Erigena, concerning the interpretation of St. Augustine's theories. He also wrote a continuation of the *St. Bertin Annals* for the years 835-61, which is a valuable source for the period of disintegration of the *Carolingian empire.
W. Ullmann, *The Carolingian Renaissance and the Idea of Kingship* (1971).

PRUD'HOMME (Latin: probus homo "worthy man") In the 11th-13th centuries, the term designated a man who was deemed fit to testify at a court trial. From the 13th century on, it signified a gentleman and a worthy *knight.

PRUSSIA Region lying on the southern coast of the Baltic Sea, between the Vistula and Niemen rivers. It was inhabited from the 6th century by Prussian tribes, who were related to the *Lithuanians. Despite their contacts with Poland in the 11th and 12th centuries, they continued to preserve their tribal structure and pagan religion. But in 1220, with the approval of Emperor *Frederick II, *Teutonic knights, led by the grand master of the order, *Hermann of Salza, invaded and conquered P. Prussians were forcibly converted while those who resisted were murdered. The order brought German settlers to P., which became its centre and was governed by its officers. The knights enlarged their possessions during the 13th century, both along the Baltic towards *Livonia and *Pomerania, as well as southwards, conquering part of the Polish duchy of *Mazovia. The Germanization process and the *Hanse's economic activity brought prosperity and led to the establishment of new cities, which, in the 14th century, agitated for communal privileges. Conflict between the cities and the order weakened the latter and, in the early 15th century, Polish kings began to intervene in Prussian affairs. In 1410 *Jagiello defeated the knights at Tannenberg.
K. Gorski, *L'Ordre Theutonique* (1963).

PRZEMYSL City in southeastern *Poland. Founded on the ancient trade route between the West and Ruthenia and Russia in 1340, it became the centre of the royal administration in the area under King *Casimir III. P. received its *charter of liberties in 1389 and prospered at the end of the Middle Ages.
Cambridge History of Poland (1950).

PRZEMYSL (d. 1296) King of *Poland from 1295. As grand duke of Poznan from 1272, he succeeded in imposing stability and order in his duchy during a period of anarchy in Poland. He also managed to stem the rising tide of German cultural influence in his domain. At the initiative of Archbishop James Swinka, who had already complained before the pope that *Franciscans preached in German to the masses, P. was proclaimed king of Poland. He attempted to restore royal prerogatives, but encountered stiff opposition from the nobility and died before being able to achieve his aims.
Cambridge History of Poland (1950).

PRZEMYSLIDS See PREMYSLIDS.

PSALMS A book of the Old Testament, consisting of 150 poems, that was very popular in the Middle Ages

A page from the Utrecht Psalter, 13th century

among Jews and Christians alike. Verses of the P. were recited in private prayer or sung in liturgical service. It was also the subject of wide exegetical work by Christian and Jewish scholars; the symbolic and allegorical interpretations given to its form were an important basis for the development of medieval mysticism. The P. were widely disseminated, not only among ecclesiastical institutions, but also among lay society and especially royal and noble houses. The psalters were therefore artistically bound and richly ornamented by miniature paintings. The oldest psalter still extant dates from the 8th century. Those of the 9th century, such as the Psalter of *Charles the Bald, exemplify the fine artistic achievements of the *Carolingian Renaissance. Among the many psalters preserved, the Utrecht Psalter, that of Queen Ingeborg, wife of *Philip II of France, and especially the *Luttrell Psalter of the 14th century, are notable works of art. The latter portrays the various social classes and their occupations.

H. N. Snaith, *Studies in the Psalter* (1934);

H. Focillon, *Art de l'Occident*, 2nd ed. (1965).

PSELLUS, MICHAEL (1019-78) Byzantine writer and statesman. Appointed imperial secretary to *Michael V in 1041, he also served his successor, *Constantine IX. He was one of the leading personalities in the 11th-century revival of Byzantine classical culture, and in 1045 became professor of philosophy at the newly-founded *University of Constantinople. In 1054 he entered a monastery and divided his time between writing and appearances at the court. He wrote biblical exegeses, speeches, letters, poems, and treatises on a wide range of disciplines – philosophy, theology, law, grammar, *medicine and the natural sciences. His history of the empire, covering the years 976-1077, is an indispensable source for 11th-century Byzantium.

Eng. trans. E. R. A. Sewter (1954);

CMedH, IV.

PSKOV City in northwestern *Russia, conquered in the late 9th century by *Varangian Scandinavians of the Rurik clan. In 903 it was incorporated into the new Russian state of *Novgorod and developed into one of its most important commercial centres. A merchant uprising in 1136, aimed at effectuating P.'s independence from Novgorod, ended in a compromise, whereby the city was granted the right to establish a *veche,* corresponding to a city council. The *veche* was empowered to elect a prince, who was responsible for military defence. In the second half of the century, P. was the nucleus of a religious revival, which led to the establishment of monasteries in the area. Spared by the *Mongol conquest, P. was attacked and conquered in 1240 by the *Teutonic knights, but their defeat in 1242 by *Alexander Nevski compelled them to retreat. The walls and the castle that were destroyed in the battles were rebuilt in 1266, when P. again attained autonomy. The city became a republic in 1348, and remained thus until its annexation to Moscow in the early 16th century.

M. Florinsky, *A History of Russia* (1957).

PTOLEMAIC SYSTEM See GEOGRAPHY.

PUISET, HOUSE OF The name of a feudal family, originating in *Chartres, France. In the 11th and early 12th

century, they stirred uprisings that put the region between Paris and Chartres in a state of anarchy. Order was restored with their defeat and the destruction of their castle by *Louis VI in 1111. A number of them took part in the First *Crusade and settled in the Latin kingdom of Jerusalem, where they became counts of *Jaffa. In 1132, after an attempt to rise against the king, probably related with the romantic affair between Count Hugh and Queen *Melisande, they were expelled from the Crusaders' state and returned to Europe. Another branch, related to the counts of *Blois, settled in Anglo-Norman England, where *Hugh of Puiset (1125-91) became bishop of Durham and later was a counsellor to King *Richard.

G. V. Scammell, *Hugh of Puiset, Bishop of Durham* (1956).

PULANS (Latin: Pulani) Name given to the second generation in the Latin kingdom of *Jerusalem. Its origins and meanings are disputed; some scholars consider it pejorative, while others maintain that it was derived from their *Apulian origin. In the early 12th century marriages were arranged between Apulian woman and the *Crusaders in the Latin kingdom.

J. Prawer, *The Crusaders* (1973).

PULLEN, ROBERT (d. 1146) Theologian. He began teaching at Oxford in 1133, being one of the earliest known masters in the city. In 1135 he went to Paris, where he taught logic and theology. Called to Rome by Pope *Innocent II, he was created cardinal by the pope's successor, *Lucius II, in 1144. In 1145 he became chancellor of the papal court, where he used his influence against *Abelard's theses.

F. Courtney, *Cardinal Robert Pullen* (1954).

PURGATORY In Roman Catholic belief, P. designates the state of the souls of those who died in the grace of God but have yet to expiate their venial sins, before being admitted to heaven. P. can also refer to the place where the souls are purged. The early doctrine developed by the Church Fathers, was sanctioned by Pope *Gregory I and amplified in the 13th century by *Thomas Aquinas, who attacked the denial of P. by heretical sects, such as the *Albigenses and the *Waldenses. The official definitions of P. were adopted at the Council of *Lyons in 1274. At around the same time, *Dante contributed a literary picture of P. in his *Divine Comedy*.

EC, X.

PURVEYANCE The feudal right of the lord to stay in his vassal's home at the latter's expense for a stipulated number of days per year. The P. was one of the most unpopular feudal privileges and, from the 12th century on, it was generally commuted to a regular money payment.

M. Bloch, *Feudal Society* (1951).

PUY, LE City in central *France. The ancient Roman city of Anicium became famous as one of the most important centres of the cult of St. *Mary, who, according to visionaries, appeared on the bridge leading to the city to guide them on their way. The site attracted pilgrims from all over western Europe. The name of the city was changed to "the bridge of St. Mary" and, in the local dialect, Le Puy.

Q

QADISIYAH, BATTLE OF Fought in 637 between an Arab army, commanded by *Saad Ibn Abi-Waqqas, the Moslem governor of Iraq, and the Persians, under the command of Governor Rustem. Saad's victory allowed the Arabs to conquer *Ctesiphon, the capital of Sassanid *Persia, and was a decisive step towards the fall of the Persian empire.
CHI.

QALAWUN (Al-Mansur Saayf Al-Din Qulawun Al-Alfi; d. 1290) *Mameluke sultan of Egypt (1280-90). Beginning his career as a slave to the last *Ayyubid sultan, Al-Salih, he advanced through the ranks of the Mameluke hierarchy, to become sultan in 1280. He proved an energetic ruler, whose main concern was the establishment of Mameluke supremacy in *Syria, where he defeated the *Mongols and their allies, the *Armenians. Resuming *Baibars' policy, he conquered the *Crusaders' principality of *Tripoli in 1289, destroying the city and its harbour, to prevent the Crusaders from returning. He besieged *Acre shortly before his death.
CHI, II.

QANSUH AL-Gouri *Mameluke sultan of Egypt (1500-16). In the late 15th century he commanded the Egyptian army in battles over *Cyprus, which was dominated by Venice. He lost Syria, Palestine and part of Egypt to the Ottoman *Turks.

QILIJ ARSLAN I *Seljuk sultan (1092-1106). Son of *Suleiman, he reorganized the Seljuk sultanate in Asia Minor (Sultanate of *Rum), founded by his father, making it independent of the great Seljuk state, whose centre was in Persia. Defeated by the *Crusaders in 1097, he was compelled to surrender his capital, *Nicaea, to the Byzantines, and established his new capital in the city of Konya (Iconium), which gave its name to the kingdom.

QILIJ ARSLAN II *Seljuk sultan of Konya (1156-88). One of the most skilled 12th-century Islamic rulers, he was concerned about the rising power of the *Zengid dynasty in Syria and Iraq, as well as the recovery of territories in Asia Minor by the Comneni emperors of *Byzantium. He adopted a peaceful policy, attempting to strengthen his realm by taking advantage of conflicts among neighbouring powers. His decisive victory at Myriocephalum (1176) over *Manuel I Comnenus, who attacked Konya in an attempt to recover Asia Minor, assured Turkish domination of Anatolia.

QUADRIVIUM The name given to the four most advanced studies of the *seven liberal arts, comprising arithmetic, geometry, astronomy and music.

QUATRE FILS AYMON Twelfth-century French epic poem, belonging to the *Charlemagne cycle. It deals with the adventures of the four sons of Aymon, a prominent southern noble, who served *Charlemagne as skilled fighters and ideal knights.
U. T. Homes, *History of the Old French Literature* (1948).

QUEDLIMBURG City in eastern *Saxony. Founded as a ducal castle in 922 by King *Henry I, it became the residence of the kings of Germany in 930 and was a virtual capital of the Ottonian emperors.

QUERCY County in southwestern France. As part of *Aquitaine in the 9th century, it was a powerful feudal estate, dominated by a countal family, who acquired part of their resources from the development of trade at *Cahors, its principal city. In the 11th and 12th centuries, Q. was the subject of disputes between the dukes of Aquitaine and the counts of *Toulouse. It was finally ceded to the latter by the duke of Aquitaine and king of England, *Richard I, in 1230. In the 13th century Q. was a prosperous county, where merchants of Cahors invested their money in estates and used the profits for establishing banking houses. By the Treaty of Paris (1259), *Louis IX gave the lordship of Q. to *Henry III of England, who made the county part of his duchy of *Guienne. In the late 13th century French officers imposed royal authority in the area, which led to disputes, first diplomatic and then military, between England and France. Q. was given to England by the Treaty of *Bretigny (1360) but was recovered by France towards the end of the *Hundred Years' War.

QUIERZY (KIERZY) A *Carolingian royal palace in northeastern France, near *Laon, that was the site of important assemblies during the reign of *Charles the Bald. They include the synod of 849, at which *Hincmar condemned the teachings of *Gottschalk, and that of 875, at which Charles the Bald recognized the inheritance of *benefices, thus laying the juridical basis for the holding of fiefs.

QUO WARRANTO The title of a statute issued by *Edward I in 1290. It demanded to know by what warrant or right a baron possessed his private *court. Unless he could show a royal warrant, or prescriptive tenure prior to the accession of Richard I, his right to the court was invalid and he was deprived of it. The statute prevented the extension of feudal private justice.
B. Lyon, *A Constitutional and Legal History of Medieval England* (1960).

R

RABANUS MAURUS (Hrabanus Maurus; 776-856) Abbot of *Fulda and archbishop of Mainz (847-56), theologian and political thinker. A pupil of the famous scholar *Alcuin, he became the director of the monastic school of Fulda, which he developed into one of the most influential schools in Europe. Appointed abbot in 822, he made the monastery one of the greatest spiritual and cultural centres in the *Carolingian world. As archbishop of Mainz and head of the German church, he promoted the spread of Christianity and the education of missionaries for whom he composed a manual, *On the Formation of Clerics*. He also wrote commentaries on the Bible and the teachings of the Church Fathers, but became famous primarily for his encyclopedia of knowledge *De Universo*, based on *Etymologiae* by *Isidore of Seville. He was invited to pronounce his verdict on the controversies surrounding the teachings of *Gottschalk and *Paschasius Radbertus.
Works, *PL*, CVII-CXII;
E. F. Duckett, *Carolingian Portraits* (1964).
RADANITES See RHADANITES.
RADBOD (d. 719) King of *Frisia. Having united the various Frisian tribes, he allied himself with *Pepin II of Herstal, the mayor of the palace of *Austrasia. The alliance lapsed in 689 and, during the ensuing war, Pepin conquered western Frisia. While R. initially supported Anglo-Saxon missionary activity in his realm, he reverted to paganism at Pepin's death in 714 and reconquered western Frisia.
W. Levinson, *England and the Continent in the 8th Century* (1946).
RADEGUNDE, St. (518-87) Queen of the *Franks. Daughter of a Thuringian prince, she married *Clotaire I. Adopting a life of piety and virtue that put her at odds with the secular life of the court, she decided to leave her husband and enter a nunnery. The murder of her brother by Clotaire in 550 provided her with the pretext. She founded a monastery near Poitiers, where she devoted her life to prayer, study and charitable works. For her deeds, she was venerated as a saint at Poitiers.
F. Brittain, *St. Radegund, Patroness of Jesus College at Cambridge* (1925).
RADULF, RADULFUS See RALPH.
RAFFELSTETTEN Region in *Thuringia, containing, in the 9th century, an important trade route to the Slav countries. The *Carolingians established there a customs point to control trade and collect duties.
RAGUSA (modern Dubrovnik) City in *Dalmatia, on the Adriatic coast. It was ruled by *Byzantium after the fall of Rome. Defending itself against attacks by the *Croats in the 9th century, it remained under Byzantine rule until the 11th century, when it was the subject of disputes between Croatia and *Venice. The final conquest of the city by Venice marked the beginning of the

Illustration from Rabanus Maurus' encyclopedia

Venetian maritime empire (1082). Under Venetian rule until the 15th century and later as a tributary to Turkey, R. enjoyed virtual autonomy as a city-republic.
H. Kretschmayr, *Geschichte von Venedig* (1905).
RAHEWIN (d. c. 1165) Chronicler. He was a canon of the bishopric of Freising, where he became a confidant of the bishop, *Otto. After Otto's death, R. continued his chronicle on *Frederick Barbarossa, for the years 1156-60, but it does not preserve the high standard of Otto's work.
J. W. Thompson, *History of Historical Writing* (1943).
RAINULF OF AVERSA (d. 1045) Norman adventurer who established the first *Norman principality in Italy. According to tradition, he went to Jerusalem with a group of Norman pilgrims and visited St. Michael's shrine in Monte Gargano, Italy, on his return to Normandy. He allegedly was asked by an exiled Lombard noble to help him recover his lands lost to the Byzantines. In 1018, leading a band of Norman warriors, he returned to southern Italy to fight against the Byzantines. An opportunist, he switched allegiances several times, allying himself first with the duke of Naples, *Sergius IV, in return for which he obtained Aversa, then with Sergius' adversary, Pandulph III of Capua, and later with the latter's nephew, who led an uprising against his uncle. He was vested with the countal title of Aversa by *Conrad II in 1038.
F. Chalandon, *Histoire de la Domination Normande en Italie du Sud* (1908).
RALPH (RAOUL) GLABER See GLABER, RAOUL.

RALPH OF COGGESHALL (d. 1227) Chronicler. He was a monk at the *Cistercian abbey of Coggeshall, England, and in 1207 became its abbot. Because of poor health, he resigned his post in 1218, devoting himself to studying and writing history. He wrote a chronicle on his abbey, covering the years 1187-1224. His chronicle on the reign of *Henry II Plantagenet, for the years 1162-78, is an important source for the intermediate years of the English king's reign, including the *Becket affair.

L. A. Poole, *From Domesday Book to Magna Charta* (1953).

RALPH OF DICETO (d. 1206) Chronicler. Dean of St. Paul's at London, he was employed as cleric at the royal court during the reign of *Richard I. His book, *Imagines Historiarum*, is an official version of the history of England in the 12th century. Its last part, covering the years 1183-1202, is an important source for the last years of the reign of *Henry II and that of Richard I.

L. A. Poole, *From Domesday Book to Magna Charta* (1953).

RALPH OF VERMANDOIS (d. 1152) Count of *Vermandois. He served his cousin, *Louis VI, and in 1132 was appointed seneschal of France. At the beginning of the reign of *Louis VII, he became one of the most influential members of the court. His love affair with Petronilla, younger sister of Queen *Eleanor of Aquitaine, and his repudiation of his wife, daughter of *Theobald of Champagne, sparked a great feudal war, in which he obtained the full support of the king (1140-42). While Louis took part in the Second *Crusade, R. was regent of France, together with *Suger (1147-48).

C. Petit-Dutaillis, *Feudal Monarchy in France and England* (1938).

RAMIRO I First king of *Aragon (1035-63) and founder of its first royal dynasty. Son of *Sancho the Great, king of Navarre, he was granted the realm of Aragon at his father's death. He fought against the Moslems and conquered some of their territory.

RAMIRO II, the Monk (d. 1154) King of *Aragon (1134-37). As a monk, he was highly esteemed for his ascetic life. When his brother, *Alfonso I, died childless in 1134, he was proclaimed king and married Agnes of Aquitaine. In 1135, with the help of *Raymond Berengar IV, count of Barcelona, he crushed a revolt of the nobles, who wanted to share in the government. After the birth of his daughter, Petronilla, whom he promised as wife to the count of Barcelona, he abdicated and retired to his monastery, leaving the realm under the regency of his son-in-law.

A. Castro, *The Structure of Spanish History* (1954).

RAMLAH (RAMLEH) City in *Palestine, southeast of modern Tel Aviv-Jaffa. The only town founded in Palestine by the *Arabs, it was established in the 8th century on the trade route between Egypt and Damascus (*Via Maris*). Under the *Ummayad and *Abbasid caliphs, the city prospered as the commercial and administrative capital of Palestine. Conquered in 1099 by the *Crusaders, it served as a military base for the siege and conquest of Jerusalem. From 1099 it was the target of *Fatimid counter-attacks on the Crusaders and was devastated in 1102. Baldwin I appointed a Frankish lord to the city, which became part of the estates of the *Ibelin family in the 12th century and attracted many

Frankish settlers. A Romanesque-style cathedral was built in the middle of the 12th century. Conquered by *Saladin in 1187, R. remained under Moslem rule. Under the *Mamelukes it again became a provincial capital. The still-extant White Tower was built by the Mameluke sultan Baibars in the late 13th century as a minaret to the 8th-century Great Mosque, of which only ruins remain. A Mameluke castle was built in R. in the 14th century.

F. Abel, *Géographie de la Palestine* (1928),

RAMON LULL See LULL, RAYMOND.

RAMSEY Abbey in *England. The monastery was founded by *Benedictine monks in the 10th century and a small borough developed around it. After the *Norman Conquest (1066), it became one of the principal monasteries in the kingdom and was richly endowed with estates and revenues. Its collection of maps and archives are one of the best and most comprehensive sources for the administration of feudal estates and the social life in the villages.

A. Raftis, *The Estates of the Ramsey Abbey* (1965).

RANIERI (NERI) ACCIAJUOLI (d. 1394) Duke of *Athens (1388-94). Member of the Florentine Acciajuoli family, which became one of the most influential in 14th-century Italy. He was educated by his uncle, Nicolo (1310-65), grand seneschal of the kingdom of Naples, and it was through his influence that R. was admitted to the court and put in charge of relations with Greece. In 1378, he was involved in the wars between the Catalan and Navarrese Companies, which fought for the domination of Greece, and reached an influential position among the Franks of Greece. After the fall of the *Catalan Company, he became duke of Athens, where he founded a dynasty, destined to reign until 1456.

J. W. Miller, *The Latins in Greece* (1914).

RAOUL (RUDOLPH) (d. 936) King of *France (923-36). Member of the *Robertian family of northwestern France, he inherited the duchy of *Burgundy in 921 and, in 922, helped his father-in-law, *Robert I, to overthrow *Charles III, the Simple. In 923 he was elected king of France and crowned at *Soissons, but many magnates failed to recognize him as legitimate king. His reign was a period of continuous battles with the feudal nobility and especially with Herbert of Vermandois.

C. Petit-Dutaillis, *Feudal Monarchy in France and England* (1938).

RASPE, HENRY See HENRY RASPE.

RASHI (Rabbi Salomon ben Isaac; 1040-1105) Foremost medieval commentator on the *Bible and Talmud. Born at Troyes, where his family cultivated a vineyard, he was educated in the best Jewish schools of France and Lorraine. He pursued his studies at the famous Rhenish school of Judaism at Worms, where he was guided by the most renowned masters of his time and had access to the works of 10th- and 11th-century north African scholars. On returning to Troyes, he established his reputation as the best informed scholar on the Talmud and, already in his own lifetime, his works became an authority among Jewish communities. His use of his native language to explain certain obscure terms makes his works an important source for the study of Old French. His biblical commentaries, which synthesize the literal and figurative methods of interpretation, appeared in all editions of the Pentateuch.

The Byzantine-style basilica of S. Vitale, Ravenna, built in the 6th century

Those on the Talmud inaugurated a new phase in Talmudic exegesis and gave rise to the intellectual movement known as the *Tosafists, initiated by his grandchildren. His well-documented *responsa* – answers to religious and legal questions – were considered an authority in rabbinical jurisprudence.

Rashi, Memorial Volume, ed. S. W. Baron (1945).

RAT, RAAD See COUNCIL.

RATHERIUS (c. 887-974) Bishop of *Verona. Born near Liège, he became a monk at Lobbes. In 924, he travelled to Italy with his abbot. He was appointed bishop of Verona by King *Hugh in 931, but was removed from his post shortly afterwards. A man of great ambition, he became active in the political life of Germany, and was appointed bishop of Liège by *Otto I in 953 but was forced to resign in 955. After accompanying Otto to Rome in 962 for his imperial coronation, R. was re-elected bishop of Verona.

E. Amman, *L'Eglise au Pouvoir des Laiques* (1939).

RATISBON (REGENSBURG) City in *Bavaria. In 530, it became the capital of the Bavarian duchy, founded in the early 6th century. As an episcopal see from 739, it was an active religious and cultural centre. In the 9th century, it became the capital of the Carolingian kings and was known as the "royal city of R.". Trade with Bohemia and the Danube countries from the 10th cen-

tury transformed its character: new merchant quarters were built in the 11th and 12th centuries, when R. prospered and attracted many immigrants. In the 13th century, the merchants became the most powerful group in the city, obtaining in 1245 from *Frederick II a charter of liberties, which proclaimed R. an imperial free city.

H. Planitz, *Die deutsche Stadt im Mittelalter* (1964).

RAVENNA Strategically located on the Po River, the ancient Roman city in northern *Italy prospered in the early Middle Ages. From 402, it served as capital of the Western Roman emperors, and from 476 of the Ostrogothic kings *Odoacer and *Theodoric. Recovered by the *Byzantines in 540, R. became under *Justinian the capital and artistic centre of Italy. After the *Lombards conquered part of Italy, R. was made the seat of the exarchate of R. (the Byzantine possessions in Italy, governed by an exarch). Byzantine domination in R. ended in 752, when the exarchate fell to the Lombards. In 754 the Lombards were driven from R. by *Pepin, king of the Franks, who gave it to the papacy. As part of the *Papal States, R.'s archbishops were its lords on behalf of the popes. Visited frequently by the *Carolingian and *Ottonian emperors, R. continued to enjoy special status, both in the Papal States and in the *Holy Roman empire. The commune established in the city in the 13th century seized power in 1218; its head

entitled himself "duke". Conquered in 1240 by *Frederick II, R. remained under imperial domination until his death. Although papal sovereignty was formally restored in the late 13th century, the city was effectively ruled by a number of noble families, which quarrelled over the seigniory, until R. fell under the authority of Venice in 1438. Its churches, many of them with splendid mosaic decorations, reflect mainly Byzantine art, either directly (those of the 6th-8th centuries) or influences of (9th-12th centuries), but also Italian Gothic of the 13th and 14th centuries.
O. G. von Simson, *Sacred Fortress, Ravenna* (1948).

RAYMOND Archbishop of *Toledo (1125-51). He was reputed for his knowledge of Arabic. After his archiepiscopal consecration, he encouraged scholars of western Europe to study Arabic in Toledo. He thus became the patron of the famous school of translation, where scholars translated philosophical and scientific works from Arabic into Latin.
C. H. Haskins, *Studies in Mediaeval Science* (1927).

RAYMOND Name of seven counts of *Toulouse, in southern France, in the 10th-13th centuries. The frequency of the name induced historians to designate the feudal dynasty of Toulouse, which ruled the county of Toulouse and *Languedoc, as the Raymondine dynasty.

RAYMOND IV (c. 1041-1105) Count of *Toulouse from 1093. Heir of the St. Gilles branch of the countal dynasty, he inherited in 1063 the title of marquis of *Provence, where he was the rival of the counts of Barcelona. He was one of the leaders of the First *Crusade. He distinguished himself during the expedition and took part in the conquest of *Jerusalem, but refused the royal dignity there. In 1101 he founded the county of *Tripoli.
J. H. Hill and L. L. Hill, *Raymond IV of St. Gilles* (1959).

RAYMOND V (1130-94) Count of *Toulouse from 1149. He attempted to assert his domination in his vast principality against the rising feudal power of his vassals and the establishment of eeclesiastical seigniories. His efforts did not, however, bring the expected results because of the intervention of King *Louis VII of France who took the vassals under his protection (1159-66). R. was held in high esteem by the papacy, by the Byzantine emperors and by the leaders of the Latin principalities in the Middle East, who expected him to help them.
R. Wolff, *Horizons de France: Le Languedoc* (1965).

RAYMOND VI (1156-1222) Count of *Toulouse from 1194. His tolerant attitude to the *Albigenses aroused the criticism of the church and, in 1209, he joined the Albigensian Crusade in order to prove his Catholicism. In 1213 he opposed the attacks of the Crusaders, led by *Simon de Montfort, who had been established as viscount of *Béziers and Carcassonne, but R. was defeated at Muret. As one of the results of the battle, R. was deprived in 1215 of the county of Toulouse, granted to Simon by the Fourth Council of *Lateran. R. succeeded, however, in reconquering Toulouse and the major part of the county in 1218.
Z. Oldenburg, *The Albigensian Crusade* (1968).

RAYMOND VII (1197-1249) Count of *Toulouse from 1222. Son of *Raymond VI, he was the last member of the Raymondine dynasty of Toulouse. He began to re-establish his authority over several provinces lost by his father during the crusade against the *Albigenses and faced a new crusade, led by King *Louis VIII of France. By the Treaty of Meaux (1229), he was compelled to recognize royal rule at *Beaucaire – which deprived Toulouse of its maritime provinces – and to support the anti-Albigensian measures, including the *Inquisition. R.'s attempt to revolt in 1242 failed, and he had to agree to the marriage of his daughter and heiress, Joan, to King *Louis IX's brother, *Alphonse of Poitiers, who was granted the county after his death.
Z. Oldenburg, *The Albigensian Crusade* (1968).

RAYMOND Name of six counts of *Tripoli (Latin principality of *Crusaders). Among them, the most important were:
Raymond I Count 1101-05. The founder of the county. See *Raymond IV of St. Gilles, count of Toulouse.
Raymond III (c. 1140-87) Count from 1152. During his minority, the county was governed by King *Baldwin III, who arranged his marriage with the heiress of the principality of Galilee. R. thus became one of the most powerful barons of the Crusader states and he was even twice regent of the Latin kingdom of Jerusalem. He adopted a moderate policy, propounding that the Crusaders' interest lay in agreement with *Saladin. He opposed the radical policy of *Raynald of Châtillon, lord of Transjordan, and the proclamation of *Guy of Lusignan as king of Jerusalem. Wounded at *Hattin, he retired to Tripoli, where he died.
J. Baldwin, *Raymond III of Tripoli* (1936).

RAYMOND BERENGAR (RAMÓN BERENGUER) Name of four counts of *Barcelona and several counts of *Provence, in the 11th-13th centuries. Among them:
Raymond III (d. 1134) Count from 1089. He took an active part in the *Reconquista wars and enlarged his Catalan county with the conquest of Tarragona. At the same time he became involved in the feudal struggles in southern France, having inherited the county of *Provence and the lordship of *Carcassonne in *Languedoc.
Raymond IV The last independent count of Barcelona (1134-62). By his marriage with Petronilla, the heiress of *Aragon, he inherited the royal title, bringing about the union of Aragon and Barcelona.
A. Castro, *The Structure of Spanish History* (1954).

RAYMOND DU PUY Master of the *Hospitallers (1121-60). Upon attaining his position, R. changed the character of his order from one which merely tended the sick and defended hospitals into a military organization, following the example of the Templar knights. Under his rule, the Hospitallers grew and became the main armed force in the *Crusader states. R. was a close associate of Kings *Fulk of Anjou and *Baldwin III, and took part in the deliberations of the royal court. He also worked to establish the Hospitallers in newly-built fortresses, such as Beth-Jubrin, *Belvoir and others, in order to help defend the realm.
J. Rilley-Smith, *The Hospitallers in the Holy Land* (1967).

RAYMOND OF ARGUILERS Chronicler. He was one of the chaplains of *Raymond IV of St. Gilles, count of Toulouse, in the late 11th century and accompanied him on the First *Crusade. His chronicle of the Crusade, written in c. 1100, is an important eyewitness account of the event.
A. C. Krey, *The First Crusade* (1935).

Visigothic votive crowns made of gold and semi-precious stones; 7th century

San Marco Cathedral, Venice

RAYMOND OF BURGUNDY (d. 1106) Member of the countal house of *Burgundy. In the late 11th century, he took part in the *Reconquista* wars in Spain, where he married Urraca, daughter and heiress of King *Alfonso VI of Castile. After the marriage, he was made prince of *Galicia.

RAYMOND OF PEÑAFORT, St. (c. 1175-1275) Canonist. Born at Barcelona, where he studied and taught rhetoric and logic, he resigned in 1210 to study law at *Bologna. There he was made doctor in 1216 and lectured until 1222, when he entered the *Dominican order. In 1230, Pope *Gregory IX appointed him his confessor and commissioned him to codify papal *decretals. Completed in 1234, his compilation became the standard manual for canonists. During the same period, he wrote his *Summa de Poenitentia,* which profoundly influenced the development of the penitential system in the later Middle Ages. He returned to Spain in 1236, became general of the order in 1238, and revised its constitutions. He resigned his office in 1240, devoting his time to the conversion of Jews and Moslems. For that purpose, he founded schools of Hebrew and Arabic studies for missionaries. He was held in great esteem by his contemporaries.
T. M. Schwertner, *St. Raymond of Peñafort* (1935).

RAYMOND OF POITIERS (1099-1149) Prince of *Antioch (1136-49). Brother of Duke *William X of Aquitaine, he organized a private *Crusade after 1130 and settled at Antioch. By his marriage to Constance, heiress to the principality, he became prince of Antioch. His reign was a period of battles with the Byzantine emperor *John Comnenus, who attempted to extend Byzantine domination over Antioch. During the Second Crusade, R. tried unsuccessfully to persuade King *Louis VII of France to attack *Aleppo. Rumours about relations between R. and his niece, Queen *Eleanor of Aquitaine, might have influenced Louis' negative response and his departure to Jerusalem. R. was killed during a battle near Aleppo in 1149.
S. Runciman, *A History of the Crusades* (1953).

RAYMOND OF SEBONDE See SABUNDE, RAYMOND.

RAYNALD OF CHÂTILLON (d. 1187) Crusader leader. Born in Champagne, he took part in the Second Crusade and settled in 1147 at Antioch, where he served Prince *Raymond of Poitiers and, after his death, Princess Constance, whom he married in 1153. Prince of *Antioch (1153-60) and guardian of the infant heir *Bohemond III, he proved to be an authoritarian character and imposed his authority on the patriarch and the nobility. He adopted an aggressive policy towards his neighbours and especially King Thoros II of Lesser *Armenia, who defeated him. In 1157 he changed policy and, as ally of Thoros, attacked and devastated the Byzantine province of *Cyprus. Taken prisoner by *Nureddin in 1160, he remained captive until 1176. Released, he settled in Jerusalem, where he became one of the leaders of the radical faction of the nobility. His personal part in the Battle of Montgisard (1177), when he defeated *Saladin, brought him great prestige. By King *Baldwin IV's order, he married Stephanie, the heiress of Transjordan and made his new principality a basis for military activities against the Moslems. In 1182 he launched raids on the ports of the Red Sea and harassed shipping between Aden and Egypt, and

even threatened Mecca. A general Moslem holy war (*Jihad) was declared against him and his fleet was destroyed. R.'s policy, supported by part of the nobility of the Latin kingdom of Jerusalem, was opposed by the moderate faction, led by *Raymond III of Tripoli. His command of the Transjordanian castles, gave him, however, the possibility to act directly and, thus, precipitated the fall of the kingdom. Taken prisoner at the Battle of *Hattin he was put to death by Saladin.
G. Schlumberger, *Renaud de Châtillon* (1898).

RAYNALD (REGINALD) OF DASSEL (d. 1165) Chaplain of *Frederick Barbarossa he became his *chancellor in 1154. In 1156 he was promoted to the archiepiscopal see of *Cologne. R. was one of the most influential politicians of his age. He defined the principles of imperial supremacy expounded by Frederick Barbarossa at the Diet of *Besançon in 1156, and in 1158 at *Roncaglia.

RECCARED (d. 602) King of the *Visigoths (586-601). He converted in 589, together with his people, to Christianity, inaugurating a period of persecutions against the Arians and the *Jews in Spain. In 602 a revolt of the nobility brought about his deposition.

RECCESWINTH King of the *Visigoths (652-72). His reign was peaceful, which enabled him to devote himself to the building of churches and to a pious life. However, royal authority became weak during his reign and was challenged by the increasing power of the nobility and the bishops.

RECONQUISTA (Spanish: "the reconquest") Name given in the 11th century to the wars waged by the Christian realms in *Spain against the *Moslems, aiming to reconquer territories lost between 711 and 728. The name is linked with the whole process, which began in the 9th century and ended in 1492 with the conquest of *Granada. The expedition of *Charlemagne to Spain in 787 is considered as the beginning of the process of the R., but merely because of its literary and epic impact, as reflected in the *Chanson de *Roland*; actually, the expedition was not directed against the Moslems, but against Christian *Navarre. The wars waged from 901 by the *Franks of southern France against the Arabs of *Catalonia were the beginning of the R. process and, in 812, led to the establishment of the *march of Spain, as part of the *Carolingian empire. In the latter half of the 9th century, the kings of *Asturias took the initiative of the R. and enlarged their dominions by the conquest of *Galicia, and in the 10th century, of *León. At the same time, the establishment of the kingdom of Navarre caused the R. in northeastern Spain, resulting in the conquest of the upper Ebro provinces, where the kingdom of *Aragon was founded. A decisive step in the process, due both to the fall of the Arab caliphate of *Cordoba and a temporary union of the Christian realms under *Sancho III the Great of Navarre. During his reign, northern Spain was entirely reconquered. His sons, who reigned in *Castile, León and Aragon, continued during the 11th century the progress of the R., reaching the Tagus River and the lower valley of the Ebro. The conquest of Toledo in 1085 was the culmination of the achievements of the 11th century. The *Almoravide and *Almohade conquest in southern Spain brought the R. to a temporary halt, with the notable exception of the new kingdom of *Portugal.

York Minster, built in the 12th-15th centuries combining Gothic and Romanesque styles

The Battle of *Las Navas de Tolosa (1212) and the decisive victory of the Christian monarchs brought to an end the Almohade empire and opened the way for Christian penetration into southern Spain in the 13th century, with the conquest of Valencia, the Balearic Islands and Andalusia by the kings of Aragon and Castile. At the end of the 13th century, only the kingdom of *Granada remained Moslem. The R. was, however, interrupted in the 14th century, when the Christian realms had to face internal difficulties and dynastic struggles. The small conquests in the neighbourhood of Granada were poor achievements in comparison with the spectacular results of the 13th century. Only after the marriage of Isabella of Castile and Ferdinand of Aragon and the re-establishment of royal authority in the united kingdom, was the R. resumed and completed at Granada in 1492.

A. Castro, *The Structure of Spanish History* (1954).

REGALIA The term, used in the 11th-13th centuries, means the enfeoffment of the royal authority to the vassals. In practice, it concerned the rights of legislature, taxation and raising armies by the lord on his lands, which, in their majority had been acquired by usurpation; various charters legalized the facts, to the best interest of both the kingship and the lords.

M. Bloch, *Feudal Society* (1951).

REGENSBURG See RATISBON.

REGGIO DI CALABRIA City in *Calabria, southern Italy. Conquered in 411 by the *Visigoths, R. followed the fate of the province, especially under the rule of the *Byzantine dukes and the *Arabs of Sicily, who destroyed the city. R. was rebuilt, and became in the latter half of the 10th century the capital of the duchy and the centre of the monastic movement in Calabria. In 1060 *Robert Guiscard conquered the city, which became part of the *Norman kingdom of Sicily. In 1282, during the *Sicilian Vespers, the city remained faithful to *Charles of Anjou and from then onward belonged to the kingdom of Naples.

REGINALD OF PIPERNO (c. 1230-90) *Dominican friar. In 1259 he became the confessor and close companion of *Thomas Aquinas. He collected the writings of Thomas and, on the basis of his notes, compiled a supplement to the *Summa Theologiae*.

REGINO OF PRUM (d. 915) Historian. Of German noble origin, he became a monk at the *Benedictine abbey of Prum, where he studied theology and canon law. Between 892 and 899, he was the abbot of Prum, but was compelled to flee because of the intrigues of the monks. R. settled at St. Martin of *Tours, where he became the reformer of the community. He wrote a universal chronicle, which covered the period of the early church, until the end of the 9th century.

J. W. Thompson, *History of Historical Writing* (1943).

REICHENAU Monastery in Bavaria. Founded under *Charlemagne, it became during the reigns of *Louis the Pious and *Louis the German, one of the cultural centres of the *Carolingian Renaissance. An important school of historians developed at the abbey.

REINHART FUCHS See REYNARD THE FOX.

RELICS (Latin: reliquia "to relinquish") The word designates the mortal remains of a saint, which were venerated by the faithful. In the Christian Church, the first R. worshipped were the tombs of *martyrs and saints, and chapels and monasteries built over their graves,

Reliquary statue of St. Foy at the abbey of Conques

from the 4th century on. With the spread of Christianity in the West and the pilgrimages to the *Holy Land, the cult of R. was intensified. R. included also parts of clothes, worn or supposed to have been worn by saints, as well as other objects associated with them. At the same time, it became customary that a new church or monastery be given parts of the body of a saint. One of the oldest examples of such a dispersal of R. was that of St. *Nicholas of Bari, whose R. were sent to Bari (Italy) from Asia Minor in the 5th century, and were distributed in the whole West, where he became a very popular saint (Santa Claus). The most widely distributed were, however, R. of Christ. Besides bodily remains, such as his teeth, his garment, found at Jerusalem in the 8th century, and even thorns of his crown, were worshipped in the West. Donations of R. became in the 9th-13th centuries important religious activities and were reported in the *Acta Sanctorum*.

EC, XI.

RELIQUARY A vase or any other container, designed to preserve *relics in a church or chapel. Rs. were usually made of precious metals, such as gold or silver, artistically executed and decorated by goldsmiths. From the 11th century on, the use of *Limoges enamel was commonly used to adorn Rs. in the western churches.

H. Focillon, *Art de l'Occident* (1949).

REMIGIUS OF AUXERRE (c. 841-908) Theologian. He was master of the cathedral school of Auxerre, France, and one of the last scholars of the *Carolingian Renaissance. His works summed up the achievements of the 9th-century theological school of France and included also original contributions of his own.

REMIGIUS, St. (c. 438-c. 533) Bishop of *Rheims. He is known as the man who spread the Catholic faith to the *Franks and who, in full understanding with Queen *Clotilda, administered baptism to *Clovis (c. 497). In the following generations and, especially in the 9th century, his action was also represented as the coronation of the king, becoming the basis of the claim of the archbishops of Rheims to the privilege of crowning the kings of France.
J. M. Wallace-Hadrill, *The Long-Haired Kings* (1963).

RENNES City in western *Brittany. Conquered in the late 8th century by the *Franks, it became part of the *march of Brittany, established by *Charlemagne. With the establishment of the realm of Brittany by *Nominoë, R. was reconquered by the Bretons. In the 10th century, it became the centre of a county, whose rulers struggled for the domination of Brittany. From the beginning of the 11th century the counts of R. became dukes of Brittany. The city grew in the 12th-13th centuries, having benefited from the revival of trade. Due to the activity of some of its bishops, such as *Hildebert of Lavardin, *Marbodius and *Stephen of Fougères, it also became an important cultural centre, and Latin and French culture were introduced into the duchy. In the later Middle Ages, R. was the administrative and judicial centre of the duchy.
E. Durtelle de Saint-Sauveur, *Histoire de Bretagne* (1946).

RESPONSA The name given to rabbinical treatises, where, in the form of a *responsum* (answer to question put by an individual or a community), famous rabbis used to give an authoritative interpretation of Talmudic law. The R. were usually prepared at the rabbi's school, where the question was discussed in the light of the relevant passages of the Bible and Talmud, as well as former rabbinical decisions, and the conclusions were added to the whole discussion. The R. were already used by the Mesopotamian *gaonim and, from the 9th century on, also by Western scholars. The R. were collected and served as precedents for practical purposes, as well as the basis for exegetical and jurisprudential works. They are a valuable source for Jewish medieval history.
S. W. Baron, *A Religious and Social History of the Jews*, V (1958).

RETHEL County in eastern *France. Formed of a group of fiefs held in the 10th century by the lords of R. from the archbishops of *Rheims, in the 11th-12th centuries the county became a powerful feudal principality. The counts imposed full authority on their vassals and treated the archbishops as their subordinates. Following the campaigns of King *Louis VI against the archbishops (1106-12), royal authority was imposed in the region, depriving the archbishops of Rheims of their power. The countal title passed, by marriage and inheritance, to the counts of *Flanders in the 14th century and after 1385 to the dukes of *Burgundy. After the death of *Charles the Bold, R. was annexed by King *Louis XI to the lands of the crown of France.

RETRA Pagan shrine in the Slav territory situated between the Elbe and Oder rivers. In 983 the *Slav chieftains assembled there and united in a revolt against Emperor *Otto II and the German magnates, who had crossed the Elbe. The clash gained them the territories they had lost to *Otto I. However, once their victory

14th-century copper reliquary bust of St. Juliana

had been secured, the R. confederation ceased to exist.

REVAL City in *Estonia. In 1220 it was founded on the shores of the Baltic Sea by the *Hanse and became one of its most important colonies in the eastern part of the Baltic Sea. At the same time, R. became the see of a bishopric, active in the 13th and 14th centuries in the missionary and Germanization process of the country. In the second half of the 15th century, R. fell under the influence of Sweden.
H. Planitz, *Die deutsche Stadt im Mittelalter* (1954).

REYNARD THE FOX A popular cycle of poems, developed first in 13th-century France and England, which spread through western Europe. In Germany the poems revolved around "Reinhard Fuchs". The stories, in fable style, are both satirical and moralistic, dealing with the personification of a clever hero, represented by a fox (*Renart* in medieval French). The poets used the adventures and actions of R. to represent various social categories, and more particularly the peasants. The *Romans de Renard* became part of the entertainment of medieval society, especially that of the towns.
U. T. Holmes, *History of French Medieval Literature* (1948).

RHADANITES The name of a company of *Jewish merchants originally from Iraq or southern Persia, who played an important role in the development of trade in the late 9th and 10th centuries. The R. were active both in central Asia and eastern Europe, as well as in the Mediterranean, which was their main area of activity. They transported merchandise on their own vessels, calling at the ports of Spain, Provence and the Rhône Valley, Italy, Egypt and north Africa, carrying goods from harbour to harbour.
M. Gill, *On the Rhadanites' Origins* (1972).

RHAZES (Al-Razi; c. 865-c. 930) Moslem philosopher and physician. Born at Ray in Persia (hence his name),

The Sacred Order of Society. *Detail of a relief on the portal of the cathedral of Rheims*

he studied *medicine and practised at Ray and *Baghdad, where he was appointed member of the academy. His interests in *alchemy led him to study philosophy. His works, summing up his own experience and earlier medical works, became widely diffused and, in the 12th century, were translated into Latin, contributing towards the development of alchemy in western Europe.

A. C. Crombie, *Science in the Middle Ages* (1957).

RHEIMS City in northeastern *France. The ancient Gallo-Roman city was conquered by the *Franks in 483 and preserved its importance due to its episcopal see, whose activity during the episcopate of St. *Remigius brought about the conversion of the Franks to the Christian faith. In the 6th-8th centuries the city declined, and no major events occurred there during the Merovingian period. The coronation of *Pepin the Short (751-53) however, took place at R., as well as that of *Louis the Pious. Thus, the city became reputed as the royal coronation centre of French monarchs. In the middle of the 9th century, *Hincmar, archbishop of R., declared that only the coronations celebrated at R. were legitimate. With the decline of the *Carolingians, the feudal domination of R. was claimed in the 10th century by the counts of *Vermandois, but several energetic archbishops succeeded in seizing the countal authority of R., and became important feudal lords of the kingdom. In the 10th-12th centuries, the cathedral school of R. became one of the most important scholarly centres in western Europe thanks to *Gerbert of Aurillac, and one of the most reputed in France, attracting students from other regions of France. During the reign of *Louis IX, its Gothic cathedral, one of the most beautiful in France, was built.

La Ville, *Recueil de la Société Jean Bodin,* VI (1954).

RHENISH LEAGUE An economic confederation of the *German cities of the Rhine Valley, founded at the beginning of the 13th century. The political circumstances of the Great Interregnum of 1250-72, brought the cities to establish also a military organization, in order to ensure the "peace of the country", which lasted until the 15th century.

RHODES Island in the Aegean Sea. Belonging to the *Byzantine empire, R. was twice conquered by the *Arabs, between 653-58 and 717-18. Reconquered by the Byzantines, it served as an important naval base of the empire. *Leo III the Isaurian reconfirmed the ancient Rhodian maritime *law, as the maritime code of the empire. Conquered in 1204 by the participants of the Fourth *Crusade, R. fell under the influence of *Venice, but the Venetians were unable to consolidate their authority in the island, which changed hands until 1309, when the *Hospitallers made it their centre. The order fortified R. which became in the 14th century the main base of the Crusades against the Ottoman Turks. Despite their attempts in the 15th century, after the conquest of *Constantinople and Greece, the Ottomans did not succeed in conquering the island, before it was left by the knights in 1522.

J. Riley-Smith, *The Knights Hospitallers in the Holy Land and Rhodes* (1956).

RHODIAN SEA LAW See LAW.

RIALTO The name of one of the famous markets at *Venice, where merchandise imported from the East used to be sold to western merchants and traded in Italy and continental Europe. The prices negotiated at R. in the 12th-14th centuries were, in many ways, the basis for the international prices in western Europe.

In 1177 a peace agreement was reached at R. between Emperor *Frederick Barbarossa and Pope *Alexander III, which resulted in a temporary peace between the empire and the papacy.

RIBE City in southeastern *Jutland, Denmark. One of the most ancient Danish towns, R. was mentioned by historians since 862. From the 10th century, it was an active port and one of the royal residences, which led to the establishment of a royal administration in the city. It was granted municipal institutions only in the 16th century.

RICH, St. EDMUND See EDMUND OF ABINGTON.

RICHARD Name of two dukes of *Normandy in the late 10th and 11th century.

Richard II (d. 1076) led a Norman pilgrimage to Jerusalem (1018-20); some of his followers remained in southern Italy, where they founded the Norman principalities.

RICHARD (1209-72) Earl of *Cornwall. Younger brother of King *Henry III. He was brought up in the ideals of *chivalry and the romantic heritage of the *Arthurian legends. In 1240-41 he led a *Crusade, which added territories between *Ascalon and *Jerusalem to the Crusaders' kingdom. After the death of Emperor *Conrad IV (1254) he became candidate to the imperial crown, supported by the archbishop of Cologne. In order to win the German princes' favour, he needed money, which was provided by his brother. This policy led to baronial revolts in England and to the Provisions of *Oxford (1258), intended to prevent such expenses. R. never reigned in Germany.

N. Denholm-Young, *Richard of Cornwall* (1954).

RICHARD Count of Aversa (1047-78). A Norman adventurer, he arrived in southern Italy in 1045 and became the brother-in-law of *Robert Guiscard and heir to the county of Aversa after the death of *Rainulf of Aversa. He began his rule with the attempt to enlarge his territories north of *Naples. By changing alliances between Robert Guiscard and the papacy, R. succeeded in conquering *Capua and destroying the remnants of *Lombard domination in southern Italy.

F. Chalandon, *La Débuts de la Domination Normande en Sicile* (1908).

RICHARD Count of the Principate (1081-1112). Son of William, younger brother of *Robert Guiscard, R. became count of the Principate (in the northern part of the Norman state in southern Italy), where he imposed Norman customs on the local feudal system. In 1096 he took part in the First *Crusade, accompanying his cousin, *Bohemond of Taranto.

RICHARD I, the Lion-Hearted (Coeur de Lion; 1157-99) King of England from 1189. Son of *Henry II and *Eleanor of Aquitaine, he was given the duchy of *Aquitaine, his mother's inheritance. Educated as a French knight, as a warrior and an Aquitanian prince to love lyrical literature and the poetry of the *troubadours, he became one of the most colourful personalities of the latter half of the 12th century. In 1172 he was crowned duke of *Poitiers, where he established a brilliant court. R. rebelled several times against his father, together with his brothers, but was pardoned. After the death of his elder brother, *Henry the Young, he became heir to the throne. Allied with King *Philip II of France, he continued to conspire against Henry II until the latter's death. In 1189 he was crowned at London and, after a few months in England, during which time he imposed a tax on the kingdom, he left the administration of the realm in the hands of officers trained by his father. His ambition was to fulfil his vow to go to the *Crusade, together with Philip II, prompted by *Saladin's capture of Jerusalem.

He sailed in 1190 to Sicily, where his first conflict with Philip broke out and, on his way, conquered *Cyprus from its Byzantine ruler *Isaac Comnenus. He took a leading part in the siege of *Acre, where his military skills and courage earned him his title *Coeur de Lion*. But at the same time, he quarrelled with Philip of France and with Duke *Leopold of Austria, the leader of the German Crusaders after the death of *Frederick Barbarossa. After the conquest of *Acre, where he was the leading commander (1291), he advanced southwards, defeated Saladin at Arsuf and conquered *Jaffa; but his attempts to reconquer *Jerusalem failed. The treaty concluded between R. and Saladin in 1192 was the basis of the establishment of the second Crusader realm (see *Palestine).

On his way back, R. was captured by Leopold of Austria and kept in prison in Germany by Emperor *Henry VII, until a heavy ransom was collected in England. In the meantime, King Philip had seized *Vexin and attempted to fortify the French-Norman frontier. Released, R. attacked the French army and defeated it at *Freteval (1194). In 1196 he built the castle of *Château-Gaillard, to guard the Seine River and the Norman frontier. He then turned to Aquitaine, where he fought against vassals who, during his absence, had attempted to become autonomous and, during one of these battles was wounded and died in *Limousin.

As king of England, R. made no contribution to the government of the realm, which he left to his faithful *justiciar, *Hubert Walter. His sojourns were sporadic and related with the collection of taxes. The government and administration of the realm, however, proved very efficient and the country became accustomed to an administration based on the *Common Law.

J. Appleby, *England without Richard* (1968).

RICHARD II (1367-1400) King of *England (1377-99). Son of *Edward the Black Prince, he succeeded his grandfather, *Edward III. During his minority, the kingdom was ruled by his uncle *John of Gaunt, duke of *Lancaster. After reaching his majority, R. promoted favourites, such as the members of the De La *Pole family, who were detested by the nobility. John of Gaunt, who was a powerful figure in the kingdom, left for Spain in 1386 to pursue his own dynastic claims and the situation of the realm, troubled by the Peasants' Revolt of 1381, which had been repressed by Gaunt, deteriorated. Plots and revolts led to the loss of royal authority and prestige and in 1399, R. was deposed and put to death the next year.

J. M. Melsack, *The Oxford History of England: The Fourteenth Century* (1955).

RICHARD FITZNEALE See FITZNEALE, RICHARD.

RICHARD MARSHAL Earl of Pemboke. Son of *William Marshal, he was one of the leaders of the baronial opposition to King *Henry III in England. See *Simon de Montfort, earl of Leicester.

RICHARD OF CHICHESTER, St. (1197-1253) R. studied at Oxford and Paris. In 1235 he was appointed chancellor of the University of *Oxford, where his teachings on moral theology earned him great fame. In 1244 he was elected bishop of Chichester against the will of King *Henry III, who had supported another candidate and had been compelled by Pope *Innocent IV to consent to R.'s election. R. devoted himself to the administration of his diocese and issued new statutes. He was soon venerated for his great spiritual qualities; his cult emerged shortly after his death.

E. F. Jacob, *St. Richard of Chichester* (1950).

RICHARD OF CLARE (d. 1176) Earl of Pembroke. A member of the Clare family, established in England after the Norman Conquest, he served *Henry II, who made him earl of Pemboke and charged him in 1168 with the conquest of Ireland. R. conquered Dublin, which became the basis of the English rule in Ireland.

RICHARD OF DEVIZES (12th century) Chronicler. R. accompanied *Richard I to the *Crusade and wrote a detailed chronicle of the king's deeds until 1192. At that time he retired to the *Benedictine monastery of St. Swithun's at *Winchester. He composed the *Annals of Winchester* at the monastery prior to his death.

J. W. Thompson, *History of Historical Writing* (1943).

RICHARD OF HEXHAM (d. c. 1160) Chronicler. He composed a chronicle treating the early period of King *Stephen's reign in England. The work deals mainly with northern England.

RICHARD OF St. VICTOR (d. 1173) Theologian and exegete. He joined the school of *St. Victor at Paris, where he was one of *Hugh's pupils. From the middle of the 12th century, P. was one of the masters of the famous Parisian school. His exegetical works, among them a treatise on the Tabernacle, won him fame as a great biblical specialist; his treatise on the "Trinity", was an attempt to reconcile reason and faith.

B. Smalley, *The Study of the Bible in the Middle Ages* (1952).

RICHARD THE JUSTICIAR Duke of *Burgundy (887-921). He was the younger brother of *Boso of Vienne, from whom he inherited the county of Autun. Fighting against the Norman raids (888-89) he enlarged his domains, and founded the duchy of *Burgundy in the kingdom of France. He established his rule of law over the conglomeration of counties and seignories which became Burgundy, hence his title.

J. Richard, *Les Ducs de Bourgogne* (1953).

RICHEMONT, CONSTABLE OF See ARTHUR III, of Brittany.

RICHER (10th-11th centuries) Historian. He studied at the cathedral school of *Rheims (*c.* 980) under the direction of *Gerbert of Aurillac. Later he became a monk at the *St. Remi Abbey at Rheims. His historical work, written in the early 11th century, is a chronicle of France in the reign of the last *Carolingians (888-995), their decline and fall and the establishment of the *Robertian-*Capetian dynasty.

A. Pognon, *L'An Mille* (1954).

RIDDAH, WARS OF Name given to a series of religious and political revolts of *Arab tribes in 632-34, during the caliphate of *Abu Bakr, against the *Moslem government at *Medina. They began with the uprising of *Yemenite tribes against the authority of the caliph — the rebels claimed that their oath to *Mohammad was

intended for the Prophet personally. Some of the leaders of the R. proclaimed themselves prophets; the most important was Mussaylimah, who attempted to create a new religious sect. Abu Bakr sent his best general, *Khalid Ibn Al-Walid, to Yemen. He defeated Mussaylimah at Aqrabah (633), and reconquered Yemen.
CHI.

RIDWAN (d. 1112) sultan of *Aleppo. He tried unsuccessfully to prevent the conquest of *Antioch by the *Crusaders, and, at the beginning of the 12th century, to reconquer it. His failure led indirectly to the accession of the atabeg *Zengi.

RIEVAULX *Cistercian abbey in England, founded in the middle of the 12th century, which in the reigns of *Henry II and *Richard I became the centre of the order in England. In the later 12th century an important historical school flourished at the abbey. The cloister and its church were rebuilt in the 13th century in the Gothic style.
B. Mahn, *L'Ordre Cistercien et son Gouvernement* (1953).

RIGA City in Latvia (*Livonia). Founded at the beginning of the 13th century as a free city at the mouth of the Dvina River. R. was in confederation with the *Teutonic Order, and a centre of the Catholic faith in the Baltic countries. The headquarters of the German Order of the *Knights of the Sword of Livonia, it joined the *Hanseatic League in 1282. The authority over the city belonged, however, to the Teutonic Order (with which the Livonian knights had merged in 1237). They established their provincial centre in the city castle, rebuilt in 1328-40. The burghers were allowed to maintain their own institutions. Until the end of the Middle Ages, R. was the central port of the Hanseatic League in its trade with the Baltic countries, and with western Russia via the Dvina River. The city had a German political and cultural character.
H. Planitz, *Die deutsche Stadt im Mittelalter* (1954).

RIGORD (c. 1150-1207) Historian. In 1189 he gave up his career of physician at Paris, which he practised at the royal court and in the city, and became a monk at *St. Denis. There he became acquainted with the historical works of *Suger and other monks, and compiled a first draft of the chronicles of St. Denis, destined to become *Les Grandes Chroniques de France*. His most important work, entitled *Gesta Philippi Augusti* (The Deeds of Philip Augustus), a biography of *Philip II, was begun in 1190 and became the standard biography of that monarch.
H. Delaborde (ed.), *Les Chroniques de Rigord et de Philippe le Breton* (1890).

RIMINI City in northern *Italy, on the shores of the Adriatic Sea. Until the 9th century, R. shared the fate of the neighbouring provinces, especially *Ravenna. Claimed by the papacy, in the 9th-11th centuries the city was governed on its behalf by the archbishops of Ravenna. In 1115 a communal government was set up in the city, which became an independent republic. The city grew and prospered during the 12th century, but after 1220 was troubled by the civil wars between the *Ghibelline and *Guelph parties, which ended in 1239 with the establishment of a principality by *Malatesta di Veruccio. Under the rule of the Malatesta family, R. became one of the most important political centres of Italy and, from the beginning of the 15th century,

a leading cultural and artistical centre, where the Italian Renaissance was manifested.

RIPON Abbey in *Northumbria. Founded *c.* 650 by King Aldfrith of Northumbria, it was made up of a Celtic community which observed the rules of *Irish monasticism. Upon the king's attempt to compel the monks to adopt the Roman rite, the community was split in two, and in 661 a new congregation, which accepted the Roman customs, was established and began to spread the faith. R. became an important monastic and cultural centre in England until its destruction in the 10th century, during the wars between the *Danes and the Anglo-Saxons. In the 11th century the monastery was rebuilt, but did not regain its earlier importance.
F. M. Stenton, *Anglo-Saxon England* (1947).

RIPUARIAN FRANKS Eastern *Frankish tribes (as distinct from the *Salian Franks). In the 3rd century they settled on the Rhine, in the area of *Cologne and, during the 4th and 5th centuries, in the Moselle Valley. The R. remained Germanized and developed their own customs. Under *Clovis, they were united with the Salians, but preserved their own laws and traditions, from which *Austria derived its identity.
J. M. Wallace-Hadrill, *The Barbarian West* (1968).

RISHANGER (d. 1312) English chronicler. In 1271 he entered the abbey of *St. Albans, where he succeeded *Mathew Paris as historiographer. R. wrote a chronicle of the history of England, which covers the years 1259-1306 and is an important source on the reign of *Edward I.
J. W. Thompson, *History of Historical Writing* (1943).

ROBERT Earl of Chester (1080-1124). One of the most important barons of England during the reigns of *William the Conqueror, *William II and *Henry I. He completed the *Norman Conquest in the Welsh marches, and organized a powerful earldom in the northeastern part of the realm. His activities helped settle the area and promoted its economical development.
F. M. Stenton, *The First Century of English Feudalism* (1938).

ROBERT I, of Courtenay Latin emperor of *Constantinople (1221-28). Heir of *Philip of Courtenay, he was proclaimed emperor of Constantinople and had to face the beginning of the Byzantine conquest. He was unable to relieve *Thessalonica, and pitted his forces against the empire of *Nicaea, the *Bulgarians and the despotate of *Epirus.

ROBERT II, of Anjou-Naples Titular Latin emperor of *Constantinople.

ROBERT III Count of Artois. See ARTOIS, COUNTY.

ROBERT I (c. 865-923) King of *France from 922. Brother of the *Robertian King *Eudes, he helped him during his reign with his military skill. In 898 he inherited the whole principality of the Robertians between the Seine and the Loire, imposing his authority over the vassals and fighting against the *Normans, whom he defeated at Chartres in 911. With his increased power and prestige, R. was able to challenge the *Carolingian King *Charles III, considered a weak monarch by the magnates who elected him king in 922. R. defeated Charles' army at Soissons in 923, but was killed in the battle and the kingship passed to his son-in-law, *Raoul.
F. Lot, *Naissance de la France* (1947).

ROBERT II, the Pious (c. 970-1031) King of *France from 996. Son of *Hugh Capet, he was educated by *Gerbert of Aurillac at *Rheims. In 987 his father shared the throne with him, so as to avoid royal elections in France. He was at odds with the Church concerning his prohibited marriage with Berthe of Burgundy which was finally annulled. R. earned his title "the Pious" for his determined fight against heretical movements and especially the cruel repression of the heresy of *Orléans. In 1015 he conquered *Burgundy, which he claimed, but the magnates opposed the attempts to unify the royal counties of Paris and Orléans with the duchy of Burgundy. R. was compelled to enfeoff the duchy to his younger son *Hugh, the founder of the *Capetian line of dukes (1031-1360), but annexed Sens to the royal domain. He supported the order of *Cluny.
R. Pfister, *Le Règne de Robert le Pieux* (1899).

ROBERT II Count of *Flanders (1093-1109). He promoted the development of the Flemish cities and their trade. In 1096 he responded to the appeal of Pope *Urban II and became one of the principal leaders of the First *Crusade, taking part in its major events, including the conquest of Jerusalem.

ROBERT BRUCE (1274-1329) King of *Scotland from 1306. He claimed the Scottish crown against the wishes of King *Edward I of England, being supported by most of the Scottish nobles as the champion of national independence. After Edward's death (1307), R. openly revolted against English domination. In 1314 he conquered *Edinburgh and defeated *Edward II at *Bannockburn. R. allied Scotland with France, requiring its support against England. Adopting the English system of government, R. based his government on cooperation with the *Community of the Realm. He is one of the national heroes of *Scotland, glorified in Scottish national literature.
G. W. S. Barrow, *Robert Bruce and the Community of the Realm of Scotland* (1965).

ROBERT CURTHOSE (Courteheuse: "short boots"; c. 1054-1134) Duke of *Normandy (1087-1106). Eldest son of *William the Conqueror, he inherited the duchy of Normandy from his father. During his reign the Norman nobility became stronger and ducal authority declined. He participated in the First *Crusade until the conquest of Jerusalem, having sold the duchy to his brother, *William II of England. In 1100 he returned to Normandy and, at the death of William, attempted vainly to claim the English crown against his youngest brother *Henry I. The Anglo-Norman nobility revolted against him in Normandy and, in 1106, Henry I defeated R. at Tinchebray, conquered Normandy and held him captive until his death.
C. H. Haskins, *Norman Institutions* (1918).

ROBERT GROSSETESTE See GROSSETESTE.

ROBERT GUISCARD OF HAUTEVILLE (c. 1015-85) Duke of *Apulia from 1054. A member of the *Hauteville family of *Normandy, he went to southern Italy where he joined his brother and other Norman adventurers. By 1050 he was recognized as the virtual head of the Normans in *Calabria and *Apulia and the ally of the counts of Aversa. In 1153 he conquered *Benevento and took Pope *Leo IX prisoner, compelling him to recognize his title of duke of Apulia as vassal of the papacy. He became a faithful supporter of the papacy. Next, he conquered *Sicily, which he gave to his brother *Roger.

The Byzantine possessions in southern Italy became his in 1071 with the capture of Bari. R. was thus the founder of the Norman state of southern Italy, which he organized as a feudal monarchy. During his last years, he led raids against the Byzantines in *Albania and *Epirus.
R. Guillon, *La Domination Normande en Italie Méridionale* (1966).

ROBERT OF ARBRISSEL (c. 1047-1117) Hermit. In 1091 he retired to a solitary life in the woods of Anjou, but used to wander and preach. In 1098 many penitents gathered around him, and in 1101 he founded the monastery of *Fontevrault, whose spiritual director he remained until his death.
J. Walter, *Die ersten Wanderprediger Frankreichs* (1903).

ROBERT OF ARTOIS (1216-50) Second son of King *Louis VIII, he was given the county of *Artois as apanage in 1240. R. followed his brother *Louis IX on his *Crusade in Egypt and was killed at the Battle of *Mansurah.

ROBERT OF BURGUNDY See ROBERT II, the Pious.

ROBERT OF CLERMONT (1256-1318) He was the sixth son of King *Louis IX of France, who gave him the county of Clermont-in-Valois in northeastern France. By his marriage with Beatrix of Burgundy, lady of Bourbon, he was the founder of the dynasty of *Bourbon.

ROBERT OF COURÇON (c. 1160-1219) Theologian. He studied at Paris, together with the future Pope *Innocent III, and taught theology. In 1208 he became one of the leading masters of the university, and was created cardinal by his former fellow student. R. was appointed chancellor of the University of Paris and composed its statutes (1215).
P. Kibre, *The Scholarly Privileges of Mediaeval Universities* (1949).

ROBERT OF GLOUCESTER (c. 1260-1300) Historian. His chronicle, written in rhymed couplets, deals with early medieval English history. It includes a compilation of legendary stories; the last part, however, covering the 12th-13th centuries, is a genuine history. Written in Old English, much of its importance is linguistic.
J. W. Thompson, *History of Historical Writing* (1943).

ROBERT OF JUMIÈGES (d. 1055) Archbishop of *Canterbury (1051-52). Born in Normandy, he entered the monastery of Saint-Ouen at Rouen and in 1037 became abbot of Jumièges. Called by *Edward the Confessor to reform the Anglo-Saxon church, he was appointed in 1044 bishop of London and became one of the most influential counsellors of Edward, who made him archbishop of Canterbury, R. caused *Godwin, earl of Wessex, to be exiled. When the latter returned, R. was compelled to flee to Normandy. He died at Jumièges.
F. M. Stenton, *Anglo-Saxon England* (1947).

ROBERT OF MELUN (d. 1167) Philosopher. He studied at Paris and was one of the pupils of Peter *Abelard, but did not follow his master's non-conformist ideas. After 1140 he taught at the school of *St. Geneviève in Paris, becoming one of the principal Parisian teachers in the middle of the 12th century.
C. H. Haskins, *The Renaissance of the Twelfth Century* (1927).

ROBERT OF MOLESME, St. (1027-1111) Founder of
*Cîteaux. Monk and abbot at Molesme in Burgundy, he
reformed the monastery, imposing more austere behaviour. In 1098 he established a new, ascetic monastic
community at Cîteaux, but after its foundation was
compelled by the pope to return to Molesme.

ROBERT OF SORBON (d. 1256) Theologian. Born in
the village of Sorbon, in northeastern France, he studied
at Paris, where he became canon at the cathedral and
the personal confessor of King *Louis IX. He wrote a
treatise on "Conscience", but his most famous achievement was the foundation of the Parisian college, named
after him the *Sorbonne.
P. Glorieux, *Aux Origines de la Sorbonne* (1965).

ROBERT OF TORIGNY (1110-86) Historian. Member
of a noble Norman family, he entered the monastery of
Le Bec in 1128 and in 1149 became its prior. In 1154
he was elected abbot of *Mont-Saint-Michel. Beside his
administrative work and political activity at the court
of King *Henry II of England, he wrote chronicles,
which are among the most important sources for the
period between 1154-86.

ROBERT THE DEVIL (d. 1035) Duke of *Normandy
from 1026. He imposed a strong rule in Normandy,
where he oppressed the high nobility. In 1027 he was
invited to arbitrate a feudal conflict between King
*Robert the Pious and *Eudes, count of Blois. R. was
the father of *William the Conqueror.

ROBERT THE JERUSALEMITE (c. 1031-93) Count
of *Flanders from 1071. In 1085 he went on pilgrimage to *Jerusalem (hence his appellation). In 1090,
while in Constantinople on his way back, he served Emperor *Alexius I Comnenus in his wars against the
*Seljuks in Asia Minor. R. played an eminent part in
the development of the *Crusading idea.
S. Runciman, *A History of the Crusades,* I (1953).

ROBERT THE MONK (12th century) Historian. Little
is known about his life and career. He wrote a chronicle
of the First *Crusade, which is a valuable source for the
study of motives of the participants.
A. C. Krey, *The First Crusade* (1925).

ROBERT THE STRONG (le Fort; d. 866) Marquis of
*Neustria. He was one of the feudal adventurers who
rose during the reign of *Charles the Bald and acquired
counties and a great fortune. In 864 he fought against
Normans who penetrated the Loire Valley, and defended
Tours. Charles charged him with the defence of the
county between the Loire and Seine, where he acquired
direct rule over the counties of Tours and Paris. R.
fell in a battle near Tours, but his descendants reigned
in France. He was the founder of the *Robertian
(Capetian) dynasty.
F. Lot, *Naissance de la France* (1946).

ROBERT THE WISE (1278-1343) King of *Naples
from 1309. Son of *Charles II of Anjou, he was involved,
while heir to the throne, in the wars with *Aragon over
*Sicily. He took an active part in the negotiations which
led to the Treaty of *Caltabellotta (1302). His influence
at Rome became dominant after the death of Pope *Boniface VIII. After his coronation he continued to give
priority to Italian affairs, attempting to create a strong
Italian realm. In 1319 he defeated a north Italian coalition, led by the *Visconti of Milan, at the Battle of
Sesto and became the virtual ruler of large territories
in central Italy. He was neutral in the conflict between

Robin Hood, depicted in a 19th-century print

Pope *John XXII and Emperor *Louis of Bavaria, and
in 1330 was excommunicated by the pope, who appealed to *John of Luxemburg, king of Bohemia, to intervene in Italy. R. defeated John in 1236, and became the
leading figure in Italian politics. His failure to reconquer Sicily, however, was a blow to the *Angevins and
caused difficulties to the kingdom of *Naples and its
economy.
E. Léonard, *Les Angevins de Naples* (1933).

ROBERTIANS French dynasty, named after *Robert
the Strong. His sons, *Eudes and *Robert I, reigned in
France in 888-98 and 922-23. Their descendants were
dukes of the *Franks in the 10th century and, with the
accession of *Hugh Capet to the throne (987), became
known as the *Capetian dynasty.

ROBIN HOOD A legendary English hero, the subject
of several ballads, some of which were composed in the
14th century. The prototype of R. was created by popular legend in the 12th century — he is a robber, who attacks the agents of the new Norman establishment and
uses the spoils to help the poor peasants. While there
may not have been a historical basis for it, the prototype
is a composite figure of an Anglo-Saxon gentleman,
showing his reactions to the Norman Conquest and the
feudalization of England.
D. Stenton, *English Society in the Earlier Middle Ages
(1087-1307)* (1955).

ROCH, St. (1295-1327) Born at Montpellier, where he
probably studied medicine, R. became reputed and
venerated as a healer of the plague-stricken. During a
journey in Italy (*c.* 1320-25) it was reported that he
cured many victims of the plague by virtue of the sign
of the cross. He became venerated as a popular saint and
his cult spread rapidly in Italy and France.
M. Bessodes, *Saint Roch, Histoire et Légendes*
(1931).

ROCHESTER City in *Kent (*England), built around
an ancient Roman castle, it became an important centre

of the kingdom of Kent. In 604 it became an episcopal see, with a school, which became a missionary centre in the 8th century. *William the Conqueror made it the centre of a shire (1066-87). The city grew in the 12th-13th centuries and was granted a charter by *Henry III allowing the constitution of its local government. In the later Middle Ages the city was divided into two quarters, that of the bishopric, which had been granted the lordship already in the 11th century, and the borough. The distinction was suppressed in 1446, when *Henry VI abolished the episcopal seigniory and proclaimed R. a royal city.

RODERICK (d. 1198) King of Connaught (*Ireland, 1156-86). He was the last independent king of Ireland. In 1156 he inherited the crown of Connaught and had to fight against other claimants, before he was recognized "High King" of *Ireland in 1166. In 1170 he had to face an English invasion, commanded by *Richard of Clare, who conquered Dublin. After his failure to reconquer Dublin (1171) the Irish chieftains surrendered to the English. R. continued to fight until 1175, when he agreed to recognize the overlordship of *Henry II of England, and became his vassal for the kingdom of Connaught. In 1186 a plot in his own family dethroned him and compelled him to flee. In 1191 R. became a monk and died in obscurity in 1198.
A. L. Poole, *From Domesday Book to Magna Charta* (1951).

RODERICK OF BETICA (d. 711) King of *Visigothic Spain from 710. He was duke of Betica in southern Spain, and in 710 was elected king by the Visigothic nobility. Defeated in 711 by the Arab invaders, he was murdered while attempting to escape. R. was the last Visigothic king of Spain.

RODRIGO DIAZ DE VIVAR See CID.

ROGER (d. 1119) Prince of *Antioch from 1112. A nephew of *Tancred, whom he succeeded at *Antioch, he established a powerful government in the city and in 1115 consolidated it by his victory over the *Aleppo lords at Danith. His attempt to conquer Aleppo in 1119 failed and he was killed in the battle.

ROGER (d. 1139) Bishop of *Salisbury. He began his career as a clerk of King *Henry I and was promoted to the rank of chancellor of the kingdom. Henry also appointed him bishop of Salisbury. R. was a member of Henry's council and helped him to establish a centralized royal government and to impose the primacy of royal justice. In c. 1130 he acted as *justiciar of the realm.
B. Lyon, *A Constitutional and Legal History of Medieval England* (1960).

ROGER (1031-1101) Count of *Sicily from 1062. The youngest son of *Tancred, lord of Hauteville in Normandy, he went in 1157 to southern Italy to help his brother *Robert Guiscard. In 1062 he was charged with the conquest of *Sicily from the Arabs and was granted the title of count. In 1072 he conquered Palermo and began to organize the government of the island. After Robert's death, R. was considered by the members of the Hauteville family as the head of the house and his brother's heir in his capacity as overlord of *Norman Italy.
J. J. Norwich, *The Kingdom of the Sun* (1970).

ROGER II (1095-1154) King of *Sicily from 1130. He became count of *Sicily in 1105 and was the real suc-

cessor of *Roger I, whose reign he continued. Taking advantage of the weakness of his *Hauteville cousins to acquire their lands in southern Italy, he became in 1127 the head of a powerful state, with the title of duke of *Apulia, *Calabria and Sicily, which he governed from his capital, Palermo. In 1130 he was granted the royal title by the antipope *Anacletus II in return for his support. R. organized an efficient administration in his state, employing Byzantine and Arab officials and using their systems of government in the framework of Norman *feudalism. He built up a powerful army and navy which controlled the Mediterranean Sea. His power and influence caused Pope *Innocent II to recognize his royal title. In 1139 the organization of the kingdom, whose Constitutions of *Melfi became a model for western Europe, was completed. R. was the monarch of a flourishing state, able to resume the oriental policy of *Robert Guiscard. His court at Palermo was a meeting place of the Greek, Arab and Latin cultures, and one of the centres of the cultural Renaissance of the 12th century.
E. Curtis, *Roger II of Sicily and the Normans in Lower Italy* (1912);
J. J. Norwich, *The Kingdom of the Sun* (1970).

ROGER BORSA (c. 1060-1111) Younger son of *Robert Guiscard, he was designated by his father to inherit the duchy of *Apulia. As duke, his government was contested by his half-brother *Bohemond and by other members of the *Hauteville dynasty. From 1095 on he was recognized as duke, but the weakness of his rule led to uprisings of the Norman nobility and facilitated the establishment of the Sicilian supremacy among the Normans in southern Italy.

ROGER FITZOSBORN (11th century) Earl of Norfolk. A Norman baron, he accompanied *William the Conqueror to England in 1066. He displayed his worth by helping to conquer and organize the realm. Appointed earl of Norfolk, where his lands were concentrated, he attained a large degree of autonomy and led baronial revolts under *William II.
D. C. Douglas, *William the Conqueror and the Norman Conquest* (1965).

ROGER MORTIMER (1287-1330) Earl of March. He was one of the leaders of the opposition to *Edward II in England and was closely related to his wife, Isabelle of France.

ROGER OF HOVEDEN (d. 1201) Historian. Having studied at Durham, he taught theology at Oxford. In 1175 he entered the service of *Henry II, and continued under the reign of *Richard I, whom he accompanied on the *Crusade. He wrote a chronicle of the deeds of Henry II and Richard I, which is an official view and interpretation of the two reigns.
J. W. Thompson, *History of Historical Writing* (1943).

ROGER OF LORIA (c. 1245-1304) Admiral. Born at Loria (Italy), R. gained his naval experience in the service of *Genoa. In 1265-68 he attempted to prevent *Charles of Anjou's conquest of Sicily and from 1276 served *Peter III of Aragon. Active in the *Sicilian Vespers, he commanded the Aragonese-Sicilian fleet which defeated the Neapolitan ships at the Battle of Reggio (1283). In 1284 he was appointed grand admiral of Sicily and was the naval commander in the Vespers' wars (1285-1302), in which he defeated the French and Neapolitan fleets.
S. Runciman, *The Sicilian Vespers* (1958).

Roland calling for help and breaking his sword. Detail of a stained-glass window at the cathedral of Chartres

ROGER OF SALERNO (end 12th century) A surgeon who practised at Salerno and taught at the local school of *medicine, R. became the first important western man in his field. He summed up his experience in his treatise, *Practica Chirurgica*. R. was more greatly influenced by the Byzantine school of surgery of the 6th and 7th centuries than by that of the Arabs.
D. Guthrie, *A History of Medicine* (1945).

ROGER OF WENDOVER (d. 1236) Historian. His main work, the *Flores historarum* (Flowers of Histories), is a compilation of 12th-century English chronicles, covering the period until the death of *John Lackland. The last part, representing the years of the minority and youth of *Henry III, is an original contribution dealing not only with political history, but also with the social and intellectual aspects, including data on thought and science. In a sense, it was an early attempt to write a comprehensive history.
J. W. Thompson, *History of Historical Writing* (1943)

ROLAND, CHANSON DE The name of the most famous medieval French epic, dealing with the deeds of Roland, margrave of the Breton march, who fell in the Battle of *Roncesvalles (Roncevaux; 787). The poem depicted the historical Roland as the perfect knight, a relative of *Charlemagne, appointed by his sovereign to command the rear-guard of what was represented as the first great war against the Moslems in Spain. Together with his friend Olivier, another idealized knight, they save the main army by their sacrifice and courage, refusing to call for help and fighting until they fall. The first versions of the epic date from the 10th century; in the second part of the 11th it was so popular that it was read to the army of *William the Conqueror before the Battle of *Hastings (1066). The most complete version (preserved in the "Oxford Manuscript"), was probably composed in Normandy and dates from the reign of *Henry II Plantagenet. It was translated into several languages in the Middle Ages, among them Norse, under the title *Karla-Magnus Saga*.
R. Menendez-Pidal, *La Chanson de Roland* (1963).

ROLLE OF HAMPOLE, RICHARD (1295-1349) Hermit and mystic. R. studied theology at Oxford, but *c.* 1330 retired to Hampole. There he lived as a hermit, devoting his time to meditation and writing. He composed exegetical treatises on the Holy Books, explaining their mystical meaning, as well as poems in English and works of spiritual guidance.
D. Knowles, *The English Mystical Tradition* (1961).

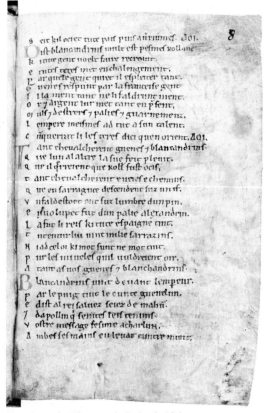

Page from the Chanson de Roland; *12th century*

ROLLO (d. 927) Duke of *Normandy from 911. He was the leader of the Scandinavian adventurers who settled at the end of the 9th century near the mouth of the Seine. In 911, after several raids in France, he compelled King *Charles III to recognize his leadership by the enfeoffment of Normandy. R. converted to the Catholic faith, imposed his authority over the other Norman chieftains and created the duchy of Normandy.

C. H. Haskins, *Norman Institutions* (1918).

ROLLS SERIES The name of a collection of chronicles and several documents relating to the history of medieval England, preserved by the "Master of the Rolls" (The British State Archives). The collection was published (in about 200 volumes) by 19th-century scholars.

ROMAGNA Province in northeastern *Italy. In 754 it was given by *Pepin the Short to the papacy, together with the other remnants of the exarchate of *Ravenna. Between the 9th and 15th century it was disputed between feudal princes, and in the 12th-13th between the papacy and the *Holy Roman empire. As a result, the cities became independent and, after the failure of the communal system, principalities were constituted in some of them, such as Ferrara, Modena, Parma. The name R. lost its political significance and is used only as a geographical designation.

ROMAN LAW See LAW.

ROMAN DE RENART See REYNARD THE FOX.

ROMANA MATER Bull of Pope *Boniface VIII (1297), issued in an attempt to reach a conciliation with King *Philip IV of France. The bull was addressed to the clergy and urged them to offer aid to their respective monarchs.

ROMANCE (ROMAN) A term which appears in the middle of the 12th century in the French-speaking countries (*France, *England, the Low Countries, *Lorraine), in reference to the first literary production in the vernacular. As the epic songs already had a name, *chansons de geste,* the word signified lyrical poetry and courtly stories. As a rule the R. was composed in verse. It reflects various aspects of *chivalric tradition and ideals, such as adventures, codes of behaviour and myths, combining religious and secular concepts. One of the most famous Rs. was the *Arthurian cycle. Another arose with the early classical traditions during the Renaissance of the 12th century, and concentrated on the person of Alexander the Great.

The first version of the *Roman d'Alexandre* appeared *c.* 1130. Classical themes were also used in the *Roman de Thèbes* and in a series of works about the war of Troy, which was a popular theme of medieval legends; among the Rs. inspired by Virgil's *Aeneid* was the *Roman d'Eneas,* while the *Roman de Troie* used the Homeric heritage.

Other mythological-historical Rs. are represented by the works of the Norman poet *Wace who, in the middle of the 12th century, wrote the *Roman de Brut,* which inspired the Arthurian literature, and the *Roman de Rou,* based on a mythical interpretation of the life and deeds of *Rollo, duke of Normandy, also represented as a 12th-century knight. The Arthurian themes, combined with other mythological elements, were the basis of the series of the Rs. of the Round Table, which became a subject of entertainment for the knightly society and chivalric feasts, representing ideals of perfect conduct.

The *Roman de la Rose* is the climax of the 13th-century R. Composed by two authors, *William of Lorris (*c.* 1236) and *John of Meung (*c.* 1275-80), it reflects 13th-century society with its division into classes and their ideals. The heroes are taken from the actual French feudal, ecclesiastical and urban *milieux.*

R. Bezzola, *Les Origines et la Formation de la Littérature Courtoise en Occident* (1944-63);

G. Cary, *The Medieval Alexander* (1956);

G. Paré, *Les Idées et les Lettres au XIIIᵉ siècle: le Roman de la Rose* (1947).

ROMANUS I, Lecapenus (d. 944) *Byzantine emperor from 920. He was a high dignitary at Constantinople and acted together with Empress *Theodora as regent after the death of *Basil I. Having married her in 920 he became emperor and, during the minority of *Constantine VII, governed the empire. Unable to deal with the military problems, he was compelled to accept the re-establishment of the *Bulgarian empire.

S. Runciman, *Emperor Romanus Lecapenus* (1932).

ROMANUS II (939-63) *Byzantine emperor from 959. Son of Constantine VII, he was a weak ruler, who left the real authority to *Nicephorus Phocas.

ROMANUS III, Argyrus (c. 970-1034) *Byzantine emperor from 1028. His reign over Byzantium marked the transition from the Macedonian dynasty to the *Comneni.

ROMANUS IV, Diogenes (d. 1072) Byzantine emperor (1068-71). Originally from Cappadocia in Asia Minor, he rose to a commanding position in the empire as general of the army of *Constantine X. After the emperor's death, he married his widow Eudocia (1068) and was proclaimed emperor. In 1070 he started his campaign against the *Seljuk Turks, to prevent them from invading Asia Minor. Defeated at *Menzikert, he was taken prisoner, while the Seljuks conquered Asia Minor. When he was released he found his stepson, *Michael VIII, reigning; he was blinded and exiled to Prote Island, where he died.
CMedH, IV.

ROME The capital of the Roman empire continued to be the most important centre of western Europe in the Middle Ages, when historians used to refer to it as *Civitas Aeterna* (The Eternal City), in contrast to the decline of many other cities and their devastation. One of the principal factors for this continuity was the establishment of the imperial capital of the West at *Ravenna, which left R. to the *papacy and to the emergence, from the middle of the 5th century, of its character as the centre of Christendom, the Roman Catholic Church. The *Heruli, *Ostrogoths and even *Byzantines, who inherited the Western Roman empire, did not establish their centre at Rome, but left it to the papacy and, between 550 and 590, to a Byzantine duke, a local official who was subordinate to the exarch of Ravenna. R. attracted pilgrims to the tomb of St. *Peter's and visitors to the papal court, which was not tied by any political allegiance to the Byzantine empire. From 590 this autonomy became independence with the establishment of the *Papal States by *Gregory I. A local administration was set up under the papal sovereignty. It was run by some aristocratic families under the authority of a "senator", the chief civil officer in the city. From 756 the papacy conferred on the Frankish kings, *Pepin the Short and *Charlemagne, the title of *Patricius Romanorum* (Patrice of the Romans), in return for their protection against the *Lombards. The title gave the Frankish kings authority over the city, which, however, continued to be the capital of the Papal States. In 800, with the imperial coronation of Charlemagne symbolizing the restoration of the Roman empire, the city became the capital of the empire. But the *Carolingian emperors did not reside in it, and its role as imperial capital was purely formal.

In the 9th century, with the decline of the Carolingian empire, the papacy undertook the defence of the city against external threats, especially the Arabs coming from north Africa. Among the works carried out were the *Citta' Leonina*, by Pope *Leo IX and the raising of an army, the militia of St. Peter's, by *John VIII. These measures, combined with the anarchy which prevailed in Italy, where various pretenders claimed the imperial crown, led to the feudalization of the area and the rise of aristocratic families, which came to dominate the city and even the papacy. At the end of the 9th century and during the first third of the 10th, the *Theophylactus family played a major role in Roman politics and ruled the papal see. After the revolution of 934, which ended the reign of *Marozia, their place was taken by the counts of *Tusculum. The establishment of the *Holy Roman empire by *Otto I in 962, put an end to the direct rule of the counts of Tusculum, but

during the minorities of the Ottonian emperors and their absences from R., the local families regained their influence. Such was the family of *Crescentius, whose rule lasted until 1106 and which led a Roman revolt against *Otto III. The situation changed only after the imperial coronation of *Henry III, who appointed German prelates to the papal see, in order to end its dependence on the Roman aristocracy. The German popes, educated in the spirit of the reform preached by the order of *Cluny, introduced the reform movement into R. and, in 1059, Pope *Nicholas II decreed the famous ordinance of papal elections, entrusting it solely to the *college of cardinals. The reform movement which culminated in the pontificate of *Gregory VII (1075-92), gave rise to a prolonged conflict with the empire — which lasted, with some interruptions, until 1250 — but at the same time hastened the centralization of the church government and the advent of the papal court as its centre of power. This in turn led to military intervention by the emperors. The papal court became an important administrative and financial power, whose activities benefited the city indirectly. By the middle of the 11th century the financial agents of the papacy were highly influential in the city, and the rise of the two important families of *Pierleone and *Frangipani, which dominated Roman politics for a hundred years, derived from their important positions in the papal court.

In the middle of the 12th century the city was affected by popular uprisings led by *Arnold of Brescia. Their suppression left the papal court in even greater control of the city. The court was dominated in part by ecclesiastical jurists, supported by the aristocratic families of *Colonna, *Gaetani and *Orsini, while the theocratical tendency of the papal government made R. also a political capital. The struggle against *Frederick II and the *Hohenstaufen dynasty made the papacy dependent on France, and strengthened the French party at the papal court, which supported *Charles of Anjou. The attempts of Pope *Boniface VIII to recover papal authority in the world brought him into direct conflict with King *Philip IV of France and, after his death, to the decline of the papacy (1303).

R. itself declined in the 14th century. When the papal court was established in *Avignon (1308-78), R. lost its position as the capital of the Catholic world. The influence of the Angevin kings of *Naples grew stronger, but at the same time, affected by the economic crisis, gave birth to a communal trend, which was supported by intellectuals led by *Cola de Rienzo, who sought to restore the ancient imperial traditions.

When the Spanish cardinal *Albornoz was sent to R. to restore order in the Papal States in 1350, it signalled the return of papal authority in the city. One of its results, however, was an intensified demand for the return of the popes to R., and in 1378, when some of the cardinals elected a pope in R., the Great Schism began. However, the city was now provided with a papal government, even if it enjoyed only limited obedience.
L. Homo, *Rome Médiévale* (1928).

ROMUALD OF SALERNO Bishop of *Salerno (1153-81) and chronicler. R. wrote a universal chronicle, which was famous due to his unique approach to historical events; as such, it is one of the finest chronicles of the 12th century. R.'s work dealt with the foundation and development of the Norman kingdom of Sicily, which he located within the larger framework of west European events of the 11th and 12th centuries.

J. W. Thompson, *History of Historical Writing* (1943).

ROMUALD, St. (950-1027) Founder of the *Camaldolese order. Born into a noble family of central Italy, he was destined for an ecclesiastical career. Highly respected by his contemporaries for his studies and piety, he gave up his functions in 1112 and retired to be a hermit at Camaldulo near Ravenna. There he founded a community of hermits.

RONCAGLIA, DIET OF (1058) Assembly held in the town of Roncaglia in northern Italy, presided over by Emperor *Frederick Barbarossa. There he decreed the restitution of the *regalia*, namely the imperial rights in Italy. This led to a conflict with the Lombard cities. Other decrees of the diet included the proclamation of the imperial peace and the privileges granted to the University of *Bologna, the first university privileges in the Middle Ages.

RONCESVALLES (RONCEVAUX) Valley in the western Pyrénées, serving as a passage between France and Spain. In 787 the army of *Charlemagne, having destroyed the walls of Pamplona, Navarre, was on its way back to the Frankish kingdom through R., when its rear-guard was attacked and destroyed by the *Basques, who set an ambush there. The blow was serious, as related by the contemporaries and according to the names of the high dignitaries killed there. The event caused through generations the emergence of epic legends, which were crystallized in the *Chanson de *Roland*. In the 11th century a chapel was built on the site, attracting pilgrims on their way to Spain.

ROOSEBEKE, BATTLE OF (1382) Fought between the French royal army, commanded by Duke *Philip the Bold of Burgundy, who came to help his father-in-law, *Louis II, count of *Flanders, and the Ghent rebels, led by Philip van *Artevelde. The French victory gave Philip virtual dominion over the Low Countries and was a step towards the creation of the *Burgundian state of the later Middle Ages.

ROSALIA, St. (d. 1160) Patron saint of *Palermo. Having received a strict religious education, she left her home at the age of 16, so as to avoid marriage, and settled on Mount Pellegrino, overlooking Palermo, where she lived in solitude. Venerated during her lifetime by the population, she was considered a martyr after her tragic death and her cult was celebrated in the city.

ROSARY A pious devotion of *Cistercian origin, which consisted of recitation of the Ave Maria prayers. Developed by St. *Dominic in the course of his preachings against the *Albigenses, it became the traditional devotion of the *Dominicans from the 13th century.

DTC, XIII.

ROSCELIN (d. 1125) Philosopher. He taught at *Tours in the second half of the 12th century, and developed a non-conformist philosophical method, leading to a logical interpretation of nature. Among his pupils was *Abelard. He was criticized and attacked by St. *Anselm of Canterbury and his teaching was condemned by the Church as heterodoxy.

E. Gilson, *History of Medieval Philosophy* (1952).

ROSE OF VITERBO, St. (1235-52) Born to a burgher family of Viterbo, R. joined the *Franciscan sisters at the age of ten, after experiencing a series of visions. In 1246, at the "command of St. Mary", she began to preach publicly against Emperor *Frederick II. In 1250 she retired to a cell in her father's house and became venerated for her asceticism. In 1457 the popular cult was followed by canonization. One of the most characteristic symbols of R.'s cult was the image of a saintly child as an expression of the divine presence in society.

ROSKILDE City in *Denmark. Founded in the late 10th century on a site which had been used as a harbour by the *Vikings in the 8th century, it became the capital of Denmark in 1020, when *Canute the Great established his court there. It remained the capital of the realm until 1416. From 1060 the city was the seat of a bishopric and the place where Denmark's monarchs were crowned and buried. R.'s Gothic cathedral was built in the 13th century.

ROSTISLAV Prince of Great *Moravia (846-70). He continued his family's efforts to unify the *Czechs and fought against *Louis the German and his son *Carloman, as well as against the spread of German influence in his principalities. For this reason, he encouraged the mission of St. *Cyril and Methodius.

ROSTOV City in northwestern *Russia. First mentioned as an urban centre in 862, it became in the 11th century the capital of one of the Russian principalities, dependent on Kiev. After the *Mongol conquest of Russia (1240), R. became one of the most important autonomous cities in northern Russia, until the rise of *Moscow. During this period, the city was embellished and a great cathedral was built in the 13th century in the Byzantine-Russian style. R. declined after 1380.

G. Vernadsky, *Medieval Russia* (1955).

ROTISLAV OF SMOLENSK Grand prince of *Kiev (1159-68). R. inherited the small Russian principality of Smolensk in 1132. He took advantage of the turmoil in *Russia after 1154 to extend his domination over *Novgorod and in 1159 he was recognized prince of Kiev. He thereby united almost all of Russia, with the exception of the newly-established principality of *Suzdal. During R.'s reign, the old centre of Kiev began to decline.

G. Vernadsky, *Kievan Russia* (1952).

ROUCY, LORDS OF Barons of northeastern *France who expanded their dominion by means of robbery and attacks on church property in the 10th and 11th centuries. Defeated by *Louis VI, they became integrated into the feudal system and contributed to the rise of the monarchy in France.

ROUEN City in northern France, the capital of *Normandy. The Gallo-Roman city of *Rotomagum* declined after the conquest of Gaul by the *Franks, though it remained an archiepiscopal see. Devastated during the 9th century by the *Normans, R. was finally conquered by them in 876, its situation at the mouth of the Seine attracting the Scandinavian sailors who used its harbour. In 911 the Norman count of R., *Rollo, who concluded the Treaty of Saint Claire-sur-Epte with King *Charles III of France, was recognized duke of Normandy, and under his lordship the city developed. Ducal institutions were established at R. during the 10th and 11th centuries, and the revival of northern sea trade brought prosperity. The harbour became an important link between the navigation along the Seine and the maritime routes. Much of the export of French

Medieval houses at Rouen, France

wines from the regions of Paris, Burgundy and Champagne passed through R. harbour. After the *Norman conquest of England (1066), its trade with England grew and became its predominant activity. In 1204 King *Philip II of France conquered R.; a royal bailiff was appointed to govern it and the city council was granted considerable powers. The prosperity of R. continued until the beginning of the *Hundred Years' War, which affected it adversely.

A. DeBoüard, *La Normandie (Histoire des Institutions Françaises au Moyen Age)* (1957).

ROUND TABLE See ROMANCE.

ROUSSILLON province in southern *France, on the Spanish border. Part of the *Visigothic kingdom since 462, R. was conquered *c.* 720 by the *Arabs and became their advance base for raids into Languedoc. In 750 *Pepin the Short conquered the province and annexed it to the kingdom of the *Franks. A count was appointed to rule it and a local dynasty governed the country until 865, when it was attached to the march of Spain. R. followed the fate of the Catalan counties related to *Barcelona and the kingdom of *Aragon. In 1278 it became part of the kingdom of *Majorca and its principal city, *Perpignan, was the capital of the realm until 1340, when R. was returned to the kingdom of Aragon. In 1480 *Louis IX acquired it for France.

P. Wolf, *Histoire du Languedoc* (1968).

RUDAKI, ABU ABDALLAH JA'AFAR IBN MUHAMMAD (*c.* 859-940) Persian poet. He is known as the earliest Moslem poet of *Persia. His poetry was essentially courtly, praising princes and high officials. He was the official poet at the court of the Samanid ruler Nasser II until 937, when he was disgraced and deprived of his possessions, ending his life in poverty.

RUDOLF I, of Hapsburg (1218-91) King of *Germany from 1273. In 1231 he became count of *Hapsburg, with extensive lands in Upper Alsace, the Aargau (northern and central Switzerland) and Breisgau. His faithful service to Emperors *Frederick II and *Conrad IV was rewarded by an extension of his territories, and by the Great Interregnum in *Germany he had become a powerful prince. In 1272 the German princes elected him emperor, despite the attempts of King *Ottokar II of Bohemia to win the election. The two clashed openly in 1274-76, and R. defeated *Ottokar, and gave the Austrian duchies (Austria, Styria and Carinthia) to his son *Albert, thus creating the basis of the *Hapsburg fortune. Ottokar's attempt to reconquer Austria failed in 1278. R. was the first German king who was not crowned at Rome and who concentrated his efforts on imposing his authority and the public peace in Germany.

G. Barraclough, *The Origins of Modern Germany* (1951).

RUDOLF I King of *Burgundy (888-912), member of the Welf family of Bavaria. In 888, when the *Carolingian empire of *Charles III the Fat fell, R. seized power in the Transjuran provinces of Burgundy (corresponding to present-day western Switzerland and Franche-Comté in France) and proclaimed himself king. All through his reign he expanded his rule southwards.

RUDOLF II King of *Burgundy (912-37). He continued the policy of his father, *Rudolf I, in building up a major realm between France and Germany. His success was due to his energy and to the weakness of the older kingdoms. In 921 he began to intervene in Italy, and was elected king and crowned the next year at Pavia. In 923 he defeated his rival, *Berenger I of Friuli, and founded a kingdom which contained both Burgundy and northern Italy. However, in Italy he was dependent on the support of the nobility. In 926, when the Italian opposition arose and a party supported the claims of *Hugh of Arles (Provence), R. was compelled to renounce the Italian throne and to return to Burgundy. In 933 an Italian movement calling him to resume the kingship brought R. to negotiate with Hugh, recognizing him as king of Italy and pretender to the imperial crown. In return, Hugh gave R. his kingdom of *Arles-Provence, which allowed R. to unite the Burgundies and establish his rule between the Juras and the Mediterranean Sea, as well as between the Saône and Rhône rivers and the Alps. His daughter Adelaide was married first to Hugh's son Lothair and later to *Otto I.
R. Poupardin, *Histoire du royaume de Bourgogne* (1912).

RUDOLF III King of Burgundy. See BURGUNDY.

RUDOLF OF HAPSBURG King of *Bohemia. See HAPSBURG, HOUSE OF.

RUDOLF OF SWABIA (d. 1080) Anti-emperor. He was duke of *Swabia and one of the heads of the German opposition to Emperor *Henry IV, being the ally of Pope *Gregory VII. In 1077 he was elected anti-king by the rebellious German princes, but was defeated by Henry and killed.

RUFINUS (d. c. 1161) He studied law at *Bologna and was one of the pupils of *Gratian. After his master's death he taught *canon law at Bologna and Paris, where he commented on Gratian's "Decree". His commentary, the *Summa*, was the beginning of a new juridical way to interpret canon law and influenced the canonists of the 12th and 13th centuries, who quoted it.
G. Le Bras, *Histoire de Collections Canoniques en Occident* (1932).

RUM A corruption in Arabic and Turkish of "Rome", denoting the *Byzantine empire. In addition, the *Seljuk sultanate which was established after 1071 in Asia Minor (its capital being Konya) was named the sultanate of R.

RUMELI-HISAR Castle near Constantinople, built by the Ottoman sultan *Bayazid I, in order to besiege the Byzantine capital. The castle is the first-known Ottoman fortification and its style was influenced by the *Seljuk works in Anatolia.

RUNNYMEDE Small island in the Thames, near London, where in 1215 King *John met the rebellious barons and issued the *Magna Charta.

RUPERT III, of Wittelsbach (1352-1410) Count of the *palatinate; emperor (1400-10). After the deposition of Emperor *Wenceslas of Luxemburg by the *electors, R. was elected emperor. In 1401 he attempted to conquer Bohemia, but was defeated and compelled to return to the Rhine area. His efforts to invade Italy in order to reassert imperial domination there also ended in failure; his army was severely defeated by the *Visconti of Milan. From 1402 until his death, R. concentrated his activities in the Rhine Valley.
G. Barraclough, *The Origins of Modern Germany* (1951).

RUPERT OF DEUTZ (c. 1070-1129) Abbot of the *Benedictine monastery of Deutz in Germany. One of the great conservative reformers of Benedictine monasticism, he opposed the new ascetic trends. His ideal was to bring about the salvation of Christian society by means of the monks' work at the *Opus Dei* (God's worship), which meant primarily prayer.
J. Leclercq, *La Spiritualité du Moyen Age* (1961).

RUPERT, St. (d. 718) Apostle of the *Bavarians. According to tradition, he was of *Merovingian descent, but this has not been proven. The bishop of *Worms, R. went to Bavaria in 695 and began his missionary activities. In 696 he founded and assumed leadership of the bishopric of *Salzburg.
J. M. Wallace-Hadrill, *The Barbarian West* (1965).

RUPRECHT See RUPERT III.

RURIK (d. 879) Scandinavian chieftain of the *Varangians and head of the Rus clan. He and his brothers led an army of Varangians and settled at *Novgorod (c. 869), whose lord he became. He founded a great principality which came to be known as *Russia. His life and deeds and their exact chronology remain obscure; reality and legend were combined in the historical writings of the later generations.

RURIKIDS The name of the dynasty which ruled *Russia from the end of the 9th century to 1614. *Rurik's descendants moved southwards from *Novgorod to *Kiev, which became their capital. In 1050 the dynasty was split into several principalities, under the overlordship of the princes of Kiev, who were considered as the heads of the house. In 1167 the principality of *Suzdal was established and became second to Kiev. After the *Mongol conquest of 1240, which destroyed the Kievan state, Suzdal became the main branch of the dynasty. In the 14th century the princes of *Moscow, descendants of the R. branch of Suzdol, became predominant and began to construct the Muscovite-Russian state.

RUSSIA Country in eastern Europe. In the 7th century the eastern *Slavs began to expand from the Pripet area along the rivers of eastern Europe and settled in the vast territory which had not been conquered by the *Khazars (in the south) and the *Bulgars (in the northeast). Gradually this group adopted a sedentary way of life, and became mainly agrarian, although some towns, such as *Novgorod and *Kiev, were founded and trade was begun with foreigners. The organization of this people remained primitive, however; descendants of chieftains became landowners, but no political organization was achieved until the arrival of Scandinavian merchant-adventurers, generally named the *Varangians.

In the 9th century these merchants became an important factor in the area, entering commercial relations with the Byzantine empire and the Abbasid caliphate. Some of them also entered the service of the empires, an example being the Varangian guard in Byzantium. Of these merchant-adventurers, the Rus clan, of Swedish origin, became influential in the northwestern part of the territory; during the second half of the 9th century they organized Slavonic tribes and established a principality and an army. Their soldiers marched down the Dnieper River, crossed the Black Sea and in 860 attacked *Constantinople. Accounts of the deeds of the Rus are mixed with legendary material, and, as a result, an accurate portrait of the emergence of R. remains partially obscure. The tradition of the 10th century relates that three Rus brothers, *Rurik, *Sinius and *Truvor landed at Novgorod in 875, where they founded a principality under the leadership of the first brother, whose descendants reigned in R. until 1613. After Rurik's death (879), they expanded southwards and, during the reign of *Oleg (c. 880- 912), Kiev was conquered and Constantinople was attacked and a favourable commercial treaty obtained (911). The new state extended from the Baltic to the Black Sea and incorporated the entire group of eastern Slavs, extending eastwards to the Don. During this process, the Scandinavian leadership became assimilated with the Slav nobility and became the largest Slav state.

Integration of the Russian state was achieved during the reign of *Igor, Oleg's son (912-45). In his last year he granted his wife *Olga ruling power, so that she continued his policy of commercial relations with Byzantium when she acted as regent for her infant child, *Svyatoslav. In 975, during a visit to Constantinople, Olga was baptized and thus Christianity began to penetrate into R. Svyatoslav, however, was a pagan. He renewed the Russian policy of expansion and in 968 invaded the Balkans, defeated the *Bulgarians and captured their capital of Preslav. He was compelled, however, to withdraw by Emperor *John Tzimisces, who had allied himself with the *Petchenegs (972). After a disputed succession, Svyatoslav's younger son *Vladimir (978-1015) acceded to the throne, accepted Christianity and made the orthodox faith the official religion of R. He organized the church and adopted the Byzantine culture in its Slavic form as the national culture. Kiev, with its churches and monasteries modelled in the Byzantine fashion, was often called the new Constantinople. Through his conversion, Vladimir ensured the continuation of commercial relations with Byzantium and, by his marriage to a Byzantine princess, acquired *Crimea. He began a holy war against the Khazars, which succeeded at the end of the century when their empire was destroyed. Vladimir had his sons appointed princes of key cities in the country; however, the lack of an order of succession led to civil war after his death. As a result of the turmoil, King *Boleslaw I of Poland was able to temporarily extend his rule to Kiev. But when *Yaroslav the Wise acceded to the throne (1019-54), Polish expansion was checked and R. reached its peak with regard to both domestic and foreign affairs. Kiev became a major European city, second only to Constantinople, as well as a famous cultural and art centre. Yaroslav issued the first Russian law, modelled after the Byzantine, granting the landed aristocracy (the boyars) a great deal of influence in the state. He also attempted to avoid future wars and conflicts over succession by establishing rules, according to which the princes of the dynasty would rotate, so that the senior member would always be prince of Kiev and thus the ruler of R. Yaroslav also played an important part in European affairs; his daughters were married to the kings of Norway, Hungary and France; his sons, to Byzantine and German princesses; his sister, to King *Casimir I of Poland, and he himself married a Swedish princess.

The death of Yaroslav led to dynastic quarrels despite his legislation, and the second half of the 11th century was marked by the rise of autonomous principalities ruled by his sons and their successors, while the authority of the princes of Kiev diminished. This destructive process was checked during the reign of *Vladimir Monomakh, who was chosen grand prince in 1113 and imposed his authority. However, after his death (1125), his sons renewed the dynastic disputes. One of the most important consequences of these struggles was the creation of the new principality of *Suzdal by Vladimir's youngest son, *Yuri Dolgoruki, who imposed his rule over the northeastern part of the country. In this same period, the city of Novgorod won its autonomy and established communal institutions, while the power of Kiev continued to diminish. The process was accentuated by the conquests of the *Polovtsy in the Ukrainian steppes, which closed off the trade routes in the Black Sea and made Kiev a frontier city. Thus, when the Suzdal princes were chosen grand princes in the second half of the 12th century, they refused to move to Kiev and governed R. from their own capital. The lack of a central power further increased the power of the princes, who were entirely disunited and openly effected their own policies. In 1223 a coalition of Russian princes, led by *Mstislav of Smolensk, was severely defeated by the *Mongols at Kalka. The defeat revealed the weakness of R., which no longer had a central authority. In 1238-40 *Batu- khan was able to destroy the remnants of ancient R., conquering Kiev and the southern part of the country and imposing his overlordship, together with the obligation to pay heavy tributes, upon the northern princes of Suzdal, *Ryazan, *Rostov and *Tver. The century which followed was one of the most difficult in Russian history. Kiev was destroyed and the *Golden Horde directly dominated the southern part of the country and indirectly ruled over the northern principalities, which owed them tribute and acknowledgement by the khan of every new prince. In addition, the dukes of *Lithuania conquered large territories of western R. between the Dvina and Dnieper rivers. Attempts of the *Teutonic knights to conquer Novgorod were, however, unsuccessful; thanks to the victories of *Alexander Nevski (1241), Novgorod maintained its independence and became the eastern centre of the *Hanse. The Mongol conquest of most of R. was also followed by a cultural decline. Following the destruction of Kiev, the religious centre was established at Vladimir in Suzdal; thus, isolated from Constantinople, the Russian church decayed and became characterized by piety and mysticism.

Reconstruction of R. was first undertaken by the princes of Suzdal from the second half of the 12th century. These rulers were less dependent upon the communal assemblies (the *veche*) of the cities and the boyars than the other princes of R. The hero of the 13th century, Alexander Nevski, who became grand prince of Vladimir-Suzdal (1246-63), was recognized as the head of the vassal Russian princes by the khans of the Golden Horde. He reorganized the principality, but was unable to secure acceptance of hereditary succession and the khans later appointed any prince they chose as leader of Vladimir-Suzdal. Alexander himself remained faithful to the tradition of his ancestors and created principalities for his sons. The petty principality of *Moscow was given to his youngest son, *Daniel, whose descendants made it into the centre of R.'s revival. Daniel's son, *Ivan I (1125-40) obtained the title of grand prince from the Mongols in 1328 in return for his promise to raise a greater tribute. Ivan used his position to impose authority over the other princes of the Suzdalian branch and his title became hereditary. The rise of the Muscovite princes in the 14th century began under the protection of the Mongols; however, they were able to take advantage of dynastic struggles within the Golden Horde to free themselves of Mongol overlordship. During the reign of *Dimitri Donskoi (1359-89), this policy was carried out successfully. While he agreed to adjudicate other Russian princes, such as those of Ryazan and Tver, on behalf of the khan, he himself strongly opposed the authority of the Golden Horde. When in 1380 he refused to pay tribute, a Mongol invasion resulted and was spectacularly defeated at *Kulikovo, an event which brought virtual independence to Moscow (1381). It was not the first Russian victory over Mongol armies, but it was the most important; the defeat of the Mongol army brought the Golden Horde to depend upon *Timur-leng, which enabled Dimitri's son, *Vasili I (1389-1425) to begin the reconquest of Russian territories.

G. Vernadsky, *Medieval Russia* (1953);
Idem, Kievan Russia (1952);
Idem, Russia Under the Mongols (1955).

RUSTICHELLO (ROSTICIANO) OF PISA (second half of the 13th century) Poet. Born in Pisa, he wrote romances modelled on French literature. Among them, his work on the knights of the *Round Table (1270) brought him great renown. Captured by the Genoese, he became the fellow prisoner of Marco *Polo in 1298-99. The latter dictated to him the tales of his adventures and he subsequently wrote a French version of Polo's journey in Mongol lands.

D. Waley, *The Later Middle Ages* (1972).

RUTEBEUF (d. c. 1285) French poet. Little is known about his life and origin. R. was a wandering poet who used satire to criticize society; an example of such is his *Renard le Bestourné*, a new genre of the *Reynard romances (1270). While at Paris, R. took part in the learned debates at the university between the friars and the secular masters, supporting the latter in 1277.

U. T. Holmes, *A History of French Medieval Literature* (1948).

RUTHENIA (Little Russia) *Russian principality founded in 1025, after the conquest of the area between the Carpathian Mountains and the Pripet River by *Vladimir the Great. In the second half of the 11th century it became the principality of *Galicia.

RUTLI, OATH OF (1291) The oath taken by the cantons of Schwyz and Uri to fight the *Hapsburgs. The act marked the first step in the foundation of the *Swiss Confederation.

RUYSBROECK, JAN VAN (1293-1381) Mystic. Born in Holland, R. was a highly-renowned preacher and was considered a master of the *devotio moderna* trend. His book, *Adornment of Spiritual Marriage*, is an attempt to explain the relations between the faithful and the divinity, perceived as a Catholic marriage. R. paved the way for the movement of the *Brethren of the Free Spirit. He had a considerable influence in the 14th century.

RUYSBROECK, WILLIAM OF (c. 1220-93) Born in the Netherlands, he joined the *Dominican order and was sent to Paris, where he was presented to King Louis IX. In 1253, Louis sent him at the head of an embassy to *Karakorum, in the hope that R. would be able to convert the great khan to the Christian faith and persuade him to initiate a *Crusade. R. wrote a diary of his journey in the *Mongol empire, which is the first western description of the Mongol state.

M. Prowden, *The Mongols* (1943).

RYAZAN City in central *Russia on the Oka River, southeast of Moscow. Founded c. 1100, it was also called *Pereiaslav and was ruled by a branch of the *Rurikid dynasty. The *Mongols destroyed the city in 1237 and it was rebuilt in the 14th century on a new site. The principality of R. rivalled *Moscow for predominance in Russia up until the Battle of *Kulikovo (1381), when the Muscovite victory over the *Golden Horde assured hegemony to the princes of Moscow. In 1521 R. was annexed to Moscow.

G. Vernadsky, *Medieval Russia* (1953).

S

SAAD IBN ABI WAQQAS (c. 600-70) *Arab general. At the age of 17, he left his family of Mecca for Medina, and became a follower of *Mohammad. He distinguished himself in the battles of *Hedjaz in Mohammad's lifetime and became one of the major Islamic generals. Sent to Iraq as commander-in-chief of the army by Caliph *Omar in 636, S. won the Battle of *Qadisiyah (637) and began the conquest of Sassanid *Persia. As governor of Iraq, he founded the city of *Kufa. Accused of tyranny, he was dismissed from his post, but remained a member of *Omar's council at *Medina. He was restored to the governorship in 645 by Caliph *Othman, but again met with resistance at Kufa. Opposing *Ali's claim to the caliphate in 657, he retired from public life.
CHI.

SAADIA GAON (882-942) Jewish leader, scholar and philosopher. Born in Egypt, he studied at Alexandria, where he became acquainted with the Arabic translation of Greek philosophical works. Already at the beginning of the 10th century, he became famous for his learning. In 905 he published, in the form of a letter, a polemical treatise against the *Karaites, that made him one of the leading scholars of Jewish orthodoxy. He left Egypt *c.* 910, and resided for a number of years first in Palestine and then at *Aleppo. In 921 he intervened in the dispute between the Jerusalem and Babylonian *gaonates on the Jewish calendar, opposing the Jerusalem school. His book, *On the Feasts* (923), put an end to the dispute and provided an authoritative method of calendrical computation. In 922, he settled in Baghdad, where he soon established his reputation as an outstanding scholar, and in 928 was appointed gaon (head) of the academy of Sura. He entered a series of conflicts with the *exilarch and other influential Jews of Baghdad, on the spiritual independence of the gaonate. In 934 he was compelled to flee and lived in seclusion to avoid persecution. During this period, he wrote his most important book, *Emunoth veDeoth* (Beliefs and Opinions), a classic of Judaism. In the book, the main subject of which is the nature of God v. the nature of man, S. reconciles his philosophical background with Talmudic scholasticism. Widely diffused among the Jewish communities, the book became an authority.
S. W. Baron, *A Social and Religious History of the Jews,* vols. IV, VI (1952-57).

SABAS, St. (Mar), (439-533) Monk. Native of Cappadocia, where he became a monk, he retired to the Judaean desert in *Palestine. The *lavra* (hermitage) he founded near the Dead Sea attracted many disciples and became known as the monastery of Mar Sabas. In 492, having declined an episcopal see, he was appointed superior of Palestinian monasticism.
J. Decarreaux, *Early Monasticism* (1970).

SABETAI DONOLO (913-82) Jewish physician and exegete. Born at Oria, in Byzantine Italy, to an important Jewish family, he studied medicine, as well as the Talmud. His knowledge of Hebrew, Greek, Latin and various Italian dialects, enabled him to become acquainted with the medical literature of the West and East. He wrote a medical manual in Hebrew, *The Book of Remedies,* based on the work of former authorities as well as his own experiments. He also wrote Talmudic treatises, where he adopted the views of *Saadia Gaon.
S. W. Baron, *A Social and Religious History of the Jews,* VI (1957).

SABODAI (SUBODAI) (d. 1244) One of the companions of *Genghis-Khan, he distinguished himself as a warrior and commander. In 1208-14, while Genghis invaded China, S. conquered Korea. In 1219 he commanded the army that pursued the remaining *Khwarizmians in *Khorasan and Persia. He entered Europe from the Caspian Sea area and in 1223 defeated the Russian army at Kalka. After pillaging the areas raided, he returned to the khan, who commissioned him with the education of his grandson, *Batu-khan. Together with Batu-khan he invaded Russia in 1237-41 and commanded the army that conquered and devastated Hungary. He reached Dalmatia, when he was recalled by Batu to accompany him to the *Kuraltai* of Karakorum. S. was a gifted general with unusual tactical skills.
H. Prowden, *The Mongols* (1942).

SACCHETTI, FRANCO (c. 1330-1400) Author. Born to a noble *Guelph family of Florence, he became a merchant and was involved in the public life of his city. He travelled in Italy and abroad, taking notes, which became the basis of his *Three Hundred Stories*, consisting of anecdotes and satires. His poems won him the title of the "best minor poet of 14th century Italy".

SACHSENSPIEGEL (German: The Saxon Mirror) A collection of feudal laws used mainly in *Saxony, which was compiled *c.* 1225 by Eike von Repgow. It represents the trends of German particularist law, opposed to the efforts of the *Hohenstaufen dynasty to establish an imperial code.

SACRAMENTS A term describing the mystical instruments by which divine grace was administered by the Church to the faithful. At the beginning of the Middle Ages the number of S. varied, and authorization to administer them was not fixed. For instance, in the Early Church, baptism and the common supper, at which the faithful consumed bread and wine symbolizing Christ's body and blood, were considered the principal S. Gradually, the number of S. was limited to seven, symbolizing the *Seven Virtues, but in practice the lay believer received only five of them in his lifetime. The doctrine of the S. and the right of priests to administer them

were elaborated and decreed at the Fourth Oecumenical Council of *Lateran (1215). From the 13th century on the S. ordinarily given in the Roman Catholic Church were: baptism, confirmation (at puberty, between 12-13 years), communion or *Eucharist, matrimony (and in the case of churchmen the ordination, whose administration was reserved to bishops), and extreme unction before death. The Eucharist was the subject of theological controversies concerning its character, and heretical sects denied it.
EC, XII.

SACROBOSCO (John of Hollywood; 13th century) Mathematician. Born at Hollywood (England), hence his nickname. He studied at Oxford and taught mathematics at Oxford and Paris. His treatise *De Sphaero*, became a standard text for the study of astronomy in the later Middle Ages.
A. C. Crombie, *Science in the Middle Ages* (1957).

SAFADIN (Al-Malik Al-Adin, Sayf Al-Din; 1143-1218) *Ayyubid sultan (1198-1218). He was active in the government of the empire of his brother *Saladin. As governor of Egypt (from 1182) and later Aleppo, he participated in Saladin's military and diplomatic activities. In 1193 he acted as regent for his nephew, Al-Aziz and, at the latter's death in 1198, became sultan of Egypt. Between 1200-02, he conquered Syria and, before his death, had virtually restored Saladin's empire.
CHI.

SAFFAH (Abu Al-Abbas Al-; d. 754) Caliph (749-54). In 749 he was proclaimed first *Abbasid caliph at Kufa. He defeated the *Ummayads in 750 and, after converting to *Sunnite Islam, pursued the members of the dethroned dynasty, killing them and their supporters.

SAFFARIDS Moslem dynasty in Persia (873-902). It was founded in *Khorasan by Yakub ibn Al-Layth Al-Saffar, a former merchant who organized a local militia of merchants and craftsmen to defend the trade. By 873 the S. had conquered the major part of Khorasan. Yakub died in 879 and was succeeded by his borther Amr. The dynasty reigned until 902, when Emir Amr was dethroned by the *Samanids.
CHI.

SAGA (sage "the tale") The name, of German-Scandinavian origin, given to popular tales and stories which glorify mythical and genuine heroes and their deeds. The S. was recited by poets, especially in the Scandinavian countries, and often included the singer's original additions. From the 12th century on, Ss. were set down in writing in authoritative texts, especially in Iceland and Norway. The *Norse Ss. are among the best and richest of this type of literature, which reached its peak in the 13th century. Besides *Viking mythology and the stories of the Scandinavian kings, heroes and adventurers, and personalities of general interest, such as *Charlemagne, were also subjects of Ss. In the case of Charlemagne, material was borrowed from the French *chansons de geste.*
G. Jones, *A History of the Vikings* (1969).

SAHEL (SAHL) BEN MATSLIYAH (10th century) Karaite scholar and preacher. Born in Persia, he settled at Jerusalem, where he became one of the leaders of the *Karaite community. He wrote polemical treatises against orthodox Judaism, charging its leaders, especially *Saadia Gaon, with materialism and careerism, and abandoning the fate of the Jewish settlement of Palestine. His

works were widely spread among Karaite communities.
Z. Ankori, *Karaites in Byzantium* (1957).

SAID IBN HUSAYN (ABDULLAH AL-MAHDI) Founder of the *Fatimid dynasty (909-34). He claimed to be a descendant of *Fatima and Mahdi of the *Ismailis. In 909 he arrived at Tunis and, having gained the support of the north African Shiites, settled at *Kairwan, which became his capital until the building of the new city of *Mahdia. He created a large state which extended from Morocco to the borders of Egypt.

SAINT ALBANS Monastery and town in England. The monastery was founded on the site of the martyrdom of St. Alban, the first Christian martyr of Britain (d. 304), by King *Offa of Mercia in the 8th century and a town grew up around it. The Norman abbey church that today is the cathedral was erected on the site of the 8th-century abbey in 1077 in Romanesque style and was completed in the 13th century in Gothic style. Under the Normans, the abbey flourished and was endowed with large estates. Its abbots played an important role in English history during the 12th and 13th centuries. In 1213 the first draft of the *Magna Charta was read to an assembly of barons and prelates at the abbey. Its fame in the 13th century was due to its historiographical school, illustrated by the works of *Matthew Paris. In 1381, during the Peasants' Revolt, the town was granted a municipal charter, but it was revoked after the revolt was quashed. During the Wars of the Roses, two important battles were fought at S.: that of 1455, when the *Lancastrian army was defeated and that of 1461, which ended with a *Yorkist defeat.
F. M. Powicke, *King Henry III and Prince Edward* (1947).

SAINT ANDREWS City in Scotland, founded around a Celtic monastery that was established in the 6th century and dedicated in the 8th to St. *Andrew, as patron saint of England. In 908 it became a bishopric and the ecclesiastical capital of Scotland. A new cathedral was built in the 12th century, while the city was granted the status of royal *borough in 1160. The university, the oldest in Scotland, was established as St. Mary's College in 1410.

SAINT ASAPH (LLANELLI) City in Wales. In the 12th century it became a bishopric. Its cathedral was dedicated to St. *Asaph, who was bishop there in the 6th century and was considered the apostle of the country. In the 13th century it was the centre of Welsh opposition to the English.

SAINT BERTIN Abbey in *Flanders. Founded in the 7th century, it was placed under the patronage of the *Merovingian kings and was richly endowed. *Charlemagne later introduced the *Benedictine rule there. During the 9th and 10th centuries the abbey flourished and became one of the most renowned cultural centres of Flanders; the counts of Flanders, who were its *advocates, used its lands to increase their power. The abbey was also an important centre of historical writing; the *Annals of S.* is one of the finest sources of the history of 9th- and 10th-century Carolingian France.

SAINT-CLAIR-SUR-EPTE See NORMANDY.

SAINT DENIS Monastery near Paris; one of the most famous in France. Founded in the 6th century over the tomb of St. *Denis, martyr and bishop of Paris (3rd century), it became an important site in the Frankish kingdom during the reign of *Dagobert. Many of the faithful were attracted to the tomb of the patron saint

The Resurrection; *early-Gothic sculpture on the portal of Saint Denis, Paris*

of the realm. Dagobert granted the monastery wide privileges as well as land near Paris. In addition, he had a large church built there to serve as the burial place of the *Merovingian kings. The *Carolingians continued to favour the monastery and *Charles Martel was buried there. Under *Charlemagne the abbey was richly endowed with land in various parts of the empire. *Fulrad, one of the leading personalities of the royal (and later imperial) government, was appointed its abbot. His influence enabled him to spread the cult of St. Denis so that it became one of the most popular in the empire. He also made the abbey into a cultural centre, where the cult of Denis was confused with that of *Dionysius the Aeropagite of Athens, who had lived in the 5th century and whose philosophical writings became known to the West at the beginning of the 9th century. Fulrad's disciple, *Hilduin, succeeded him as abbot and continued his master's activity. Under his rule, the abbey became one of the most important religious and cultural centres of 9th-century France, where personalities such as *Hincmar of Rheims and John Scot *Erigena expounded their teachings. During the 10th and 11th centuries S. declined; it was not until the appointment of Abbot *Adam (1096-1122) that it began to revive. At this time, actual and alleged connections between the monastery and the popular *Carolingian legend were reinforced and the story of the *pilgrimage of Charlemagne to Jerusalem was used to explain the origin of some of the abbey's relics. Adam founded a borough around the abbey, which became the centre of its economic activities, and established a fair, which was popular in the 12th-15th centuries. S. reached the peak of its fame during the abbacy of *Suger (1122-51), who completed Adam's work and built a new church, the first Gothic building in France. Under the patronage of the kings of France, S. became the royal place of worship and the history of the kingdom was set down there. The monastery continued to grow in importance and in the 13th century the abbey church was enlarged and became the royal necropolis of France.

F. M. McKormick, *The Abbey Church of St. Denis* (1962).

SAINT GALL Abbey, in northeastern *Switzerland. Founded in the 8th century on the site of St. *Gall's hermitage, the monastery and its school became one of the most important institutions in the empire of *Charlemagne. S. reached its greatest fame as a scholarly centre in the 9th and 10th centuries, when the school attracted monks and students from western Europe and when the first translations of the *Bible from Latin into German were carried out (see *Ekkehard of St. Gall). In the 12th century a city bearing the same name emerged around the monastery.

S. Gallen und ihre Stände in der europäischen Kulturgeschichte (various authors, Memorial Book; 1928).

SAINT-GERMAIN-DES-PRÉS Monastery in *Paris. One of the most famous abbeys of the medieval world, it was founded in the 6th century on the left bank of the Seine River and soon became a most highly venerated sanctuary in the *Merovingian kingdom. Through pious donations, it also became one of the richest institutions in the Frankish realm. Under *Charlemagne and *Louis the Pious, the abbots of S. played an active part in the imperial government. In the 9th century Abbot Irminon reorganized the seignory of the monastery

and the system of collecting revenues from peasants. In the 12th century S. became a scholarly centre and a borough, which became part of the *Quartier Latin, emerged. Although the borough was included within the walls of the city by King *Philip II in 1212, it continued to belong to the monastery until the end of the Middle Ages. The architectural plan of the abbey church of S. combines post-Carolingian, Romanesque and Gothic styles.

G. Lehoux, *Le bourg St. Germain* (1964).

SAINT-GILLES-DE-PROVENCE Monastery founded at the mouth of the Rhône River on the supposed site of the shrine of a legendary saint, *Egidius (or Giles), said to have been persecuted by the Visigoths. The monastic community had already existed in the 8th century, but was dispersed in the 9th, when the area was subjected to *Norman and Arab raids. Rebuilt in the 10th century, S. became an important pilgrimage centre, considered to hold the tomb of St. Egidius. The monastery's popularity led to the establishment of a town around it, and in the 11th century it housed an active harbour. The counts of *Toulouse encouraged the town's development and one of the family branches settled in the area, taking the title of counts of St. Gilles; in 1080, *Raymond of St. Gilles became count of Toulouse. He gave the monastery to the order of *Cluny, which introduced the monastic reform there.

SAINT JOHN, ORDER OF See HOSPITALLERS.

SAINT LAZARUS OF JERUSALEM, ORDER OF A religious order founded in 1120 to care for the lepers in the *Latin kingdom of Jerusalem. Like the *Hospitallers, the order also became a military one and the knights were employed in the defence of the kingdom, although they never reached the status of members of the major chilvalric orders. After 1187 S. ceased to be a military order and became known solely for the care it provided for lepers; at this time its work spread to the major part of western Europe, where hospitals were established near the larger cities. At the end of the Middle Ages houses for lepers were usually called "lazarets".

SAINT MARTIN Abbey in *Tours (France). Founded in the 5th century and dedicated to the cult of the patron saint of Gaul, the monastery came to be one of the most famous in western Europe. Richly endowed by the *Merovingians and *Carolingians, it also became a reputed scholarly centre when *Alcuin retired there as its abbot (796-804). In the 9th century the abbey declined and its rich possessions were surrendered to pay for the defence of the Loire Valley from *Norman raids. Several adventurers, such as Hugh the Abbot and *Robert the Strong, became its lay abbots during the reign of *Charles the Bald. The title of abbot was consequently removed from the monastic community, which came to be ruled by a prior, while it remained attached to the *Robertians and the *Capetians. From 987 to 1789 the title of abbot was held by the kings of France. In the 11th and 12th centuries control over the abbey was disputed between the counts of Blois and Anjou; the latter became most influential in 1041.

L. de Grandmaison, *St. Martin de Tours* (1892).

SAINT-OMER City in southern *Flanders. In the 11th century it became one of the most important centres of the cloth industry in northern Europe. The industrial *guilds that developed there became a model for crafts-

man associations in other European cities during the 12th and 13th centuries.
CEcH, III.

SAINT PETER'S OF ROME The church built on Vatican Hill over St. *Peter's grave, considered one of the four patriarchal churches of Rome. Until the 15th century it was subordinate to the *Lateran basilica, situated near the papal palace. Nevertheless, it was customary that certain festive prayers be celebrated by the popes at S., which was also the papal burial site. In 800, during Christmas mass, Pope *Leo III crowned *Charlemagne emperor there and that event created a precedent for other coronations. In the 9th century the church was fortified and, in order to protect it from Arab raids, Pope *Leo IV built the imposing *Leonine City. Additions were made to the church in the 12th century; these were erected above the original basilica, which remained a crypt. After the return of the papacy from *Avignon and the establishment of the papal court on Vatican Hill, S. became the main church of Rome.
G. Petrucci, The Four Patriarchal Cathedrals of Rome (1976).

SAINT-QUENTIN City in northeastern *France. In the 10th-12th centuries it was the capital of the feudal county of *Vermandois. In the 15th century it was the subject of dispute between the kings of France and the dukes of *Burgundy. Seized in 1468 by *Charles the Bold, it was recovered in 1477 after Charles' death by *Louis XI.

SAINT VICTOR Abbey of regular canons. It was founded in Paris on the left bank of the Seine River by *William of Champeaux (1108), who gave up his position as master of the cathedral school of Paris. The foundation and the rich endowment of the abbey were officially recognized in 1113, when William became bishop of Châlons-sur-Marne. Under his direction an important school was established within the abbey, whose scholars, known as the *Victorines, were among the most important theologians and exegetes in Paris. The school attracted students from all over western Europe. In the 13th century the Victorines became associated with the University of Paris.

SAINTE CHAPELLE A famous 13th-century Gothic structure, located in *Paris within the royal palace. King *Louis IX had it built to hold a relic he had brought from Constantinople, which was believed to be part of Christ's crown of thorns. The chapel is a two-storey building; its lower floor was occupied by court personnel, while the upper storey was the domain of the king, his family and the princes.
L. Grodecki, Les Vitraux de la Sainte-Chapelle de Paris (1962).

SAINTE GENEVIÈVE Abbey in *Paris on the left bank of the Seine River. S. was built on a hill, which became famous as the Mont Ste Geneviève. The abbey was already standing in the 6th century and was devoted to the cult of St. *Geneviève, patron saint of Paris. After a period of decline, it was given to a community of regular *canons, who devoted themselves to studies (11th century). From the beginning of the 12th century the abbey became the most important scholarly centre of Paris and was made famous by the teachings of Abelard. It grew to include an agglomeration of schools and colleges which developed into the University of Paris; the new settlement was known as the *Quartier Latin.

The Sainte Chapelle, Paris

The monastery was placed under the patronage of the kings of France, who had the right to recommend a candidate for the abbacy and were virtually responsible for the appointment.
M. Rashdall, History of Medieval Universities (F. M. Powicke and A. L. Emden eds.; 1936).

SAISSET, BERNARD (d. 1314) Bishop of Pamiers. A supporter of Pope *Boniface VIII, he was arrested in 1299 and brought to trial before the royal court of King *Philip IV of France for non-payment of dues owed by the clergy. His arrest aroused the pope's violent reaction, and caused him to publish his bull *Ausculta fili (1301), which was a warning to the king of France and raised the question of sovereignty.

SALADIN (Salah Al-Din Yussuf; 1138-93) Sultan of *Egypt and *Syria (1173-93). Of Kurdish origin, S. was the son of Al-Ayyub, minister of *Zengi and *Nureddin. In his youth S. entered the service of the Zengid ruler and distinguished himself as an army officer. In 1169 he was sent to Egypt as commander of a unit meant to aid the *Fatimids in their struggle against the invading *Crusaders, who had already approached Cairo. Thanks to his military success, S. was able to seize power in Egypt, having dethroned the last Fatimids. He was a virtually independent ruler, although he officially maintained his allegiance to *Nureddin. Upon the sultan's death, S. was entrusted with the guardianship of his sons, but he dethroned them and proclaimed himself sultan of Egypt and Syria (1173). The new state, however, was physically divided by the Latin kingdom of Jerusalem. It was S.'s aim to unite the two parts of his empire and this brought him to clash with the *Crusaders. His attempt to invade the kingdom of Jerusalem in 1177 was a failure; having been defeated at Montgisard near *Ramleh, he retreated to Egypt. Ironically, the attitude of the radical party of the Crusader nobility, and especially the policy of *Raynald of Châtillon, eventually allowed S. to achieve his aim. The Red Sea raid of Raynald in 1182 brought S. volunteers from the entire Moslem world and allowed him to dominate *Hedjaz and the territory from Yemen to the frontier of the *Transjordan principality of the Crusaders. From 1183 on, he annually besieged the castles of Transjordan and led raids into the Galilee. In 1187 S. succeeded in crushing the Crusader army at *Hattin. During the months of July and August he conquered the entire Latin kingdom, with the exception of the city of Tyre, defended by its lord, *Conrad of Montferrat. The loss of the realm of Jerusalem aroused western Europe and eventually led to the organization of the Third *Crusade. Unable to prevent the disembarkment of Crusaders on Palestinian soil and their reconquest of *Acre (1191), S. was determined to limit their achievements. He was nevertheless defeated by *Richard I of England at *Arsuf and was compelled to abandon the coastal area, having previously destroyed the city of *Ascalon. S. did, however, retain his hold on Jerusalem and in 1192 he agreed to a treaty with Richard which recognized the new kingdom of Acre and its territory as far as Jaffa. Upon S.'s death, the *Ayyubid empire was divided amongst the members of the dynasty and his younger brother, Al-Adil, became the leading ruler and the sultan of Egypt.

S. was praised by his contemporaries and later generations alike as the hero of Islam. He was noted for his numerous victories and the conquest of Jerusalem. A liberal ruler, he was reputed for his tolerance to the non-Moslem subjects in his realm. However, at the same time, he imposed *Sunnite Islam in the provinces of his empire. S. was unable to bring about the union of his state and was compelled to recognize provincial particularism and to appoint members of his family as governors. Even the union with Syria was no more than a personal unity and his other principalities, such as Damascus, Aleppo, Mosul and Hamah, preserved their local traditions and their feudal organization.
CHI.

SALADIN TITHE A tax imposed in 1187 by Kings *Philip II of France and *Henry II of England, with the consent of the papacy, intended to finance the Third *Crusade.

SALAMANCA City in León, Spain. Conquered by the Arabs in the 8th century, S. was one of their northern bases. In 1085 *Alfonso VI conquered and annexed it to the kingdom of León. The city developed in the 12th and 13th centuries. In 1254, *Alfonso X founded there a university, where astronomy became one of the main disciplines taught.
J. F. O'Callaghan, *A History of Medieval Spain* (1975).
SALERNO City in southern *Italy. The Roman city declined at the beginning of the Middle Ages. After its conquest by the *Lombards it became part of the duchy of *Benevento in 646. With the split of *Benevento in the 9th century, S. became an independent duchy, governed by a Lombard family (893-1057). Under the

rule of Gaimar II (901-46), the duchy was one of the most important political powers in southern Italy, but declined after his death when ducal authority was weakened by feudal lords. Conquered by *Robert Guiscard in 1057, S. became one of the main cities of the Norman realm of *Sicily. It was sacked in 1194 by *Henry VI, but was rebuilt during the reign of *Frederick II. From 1282, S. belonged to the kingdom of Naples. One of its most splendid monuments is the cathedral of San Matteo, built in the 10th-11th centuries in a style combining Byzantine and Italian Romanesque.

S. was famous in medieval western Europe for its medical school, established *c.* 1030. One of its founders, *Constantine the African, made it an important centre for disseminating Arab achievements in anatomy and medicine. Its physicians and teachers developed the experimental stage of anatomy. In 1224 it was licensed by Frederick II as the sole medical university in the kingdom of Naples.
J. Décarreaux, *Lombards, Moines et Normands en Italie Méridionale* (1974).
SALIC LAW The compilation of the legal traditions of the Salian *Franks, effectuated in the 6th-8th centuries.
SALICETO, WILLIAM OF (13th century) Surgeon. He studied and taught medicine at *Bologna and practised surgery. His book, *Cyrurgia* (1275), is considered the first west European manual of topographical anatomy, and includes conclusions from his own experience. S. also made a valuable contribution to the study of hernias.
D. Guthrie, *A History of Medicine* (1945).
SALIMBENE OF PARMA (1221-88) Historian. Born at Parma (Italy), he entered the Franciscan order in 1238. In 1247-49, he studied in France and, after his return, preached in most Italian cities. His *Cronica* (Chronicle), completed in 1287, is an important source for 13th-century Italy.
J. W. Thompson, *History of Historical Writing* (1943).
SALINGUERRA An aristocratic family of *Ferrara (Italy). They reached the height of their power in the 13th century, when they were the most important rivals of the *Este family. At the beginning of the 14th century they were defeated by the house of Este and lost their influence.
SALISBURY City in England, at the confluence of Wiley and Avon rivers. It was a famous *Anglo-Saxon ecclesiastical and commercial centre, which had its own mint in the 11th century. Under the Normans, it was an important administrative centre. In 1086, *William the Conqueror convened the vassals of his whole realm at S., requiring them to take an oath of fidelity to him as liege lord. The first cathedral was built by St. *Osmund in 1092 in Old Sarum (2.5 km north of S.), and rebuilt by Bishop *Roger (1107-39). Disputes between the wardens of the castle at Old Sarum and the bishopric there led to the transfer of the see to S. The still extant cathedral, with the highest spire in England, was founded in 1220.
SALISBURY, WILLIAM LONGSWORD (d. 1226) Illegitimate son of *Henry II, he was created earl of Salisbury by *Richard I. Soldier and politician, he played an important role during the reign of *John. In 1214 he commanded the English army at *Bouvines, where he was taken prisoner by *Philip II of France. Released in

1215, he joined the baronial opposition, but in 1216 returned to royal allegiance and served in the king's council during the minority of *Henry III.

J. C. Holt, *The Magna Charta* (1965).

SALOMON BEN ADERETH (Rashba; 1235-1310) Rabbi and spiritual leader of Spanish Jewry. Born at Barcelona, in his youth he was already a leading scholar of the Talmud. His commentaries made him famous, as reflected in his more than 3000 *responsa*, addressed to communities all over Europe. He opposed the study of philosophy, on the grounds that it might undermine the Jewish faith. Accordingly, he condemned the works of *Maimonides. His attitude, however, was largely opposed by other scholars, who continued the study of philosophy, and it sparked a heated controversy on the Maimonidean methods in 1285.

S. W. Baron, *A Social and Religious History of the Jews,* VIII (1959).

SALOMON BEN ISAAC See RASHI.

SALONIKA See THESSALONICA.

SALVATOR MUNDI (The Redeemer of the World) Title of a bull issued by *Boniface VIII in 1301, cancelling all privileges granted to *Philip IV, king of France.

SALZBURG City in medieval *Bavaria. Its origins are related with the missionary activity of St. *Rupert of Worms and the foundation of a monastery in 696. The city rose around the monastery, was made a bishopric in 739 and an archbishopric in 798, when *Charlemagne raised its bishop and his counsellor Arno to the rank of archbishop. In the 9th century the archbishops were granted the lordship of S. and built a powerful castle, Hohensalzburg, which dominated the city. In 1278 S. was promoted to the rank of principality of the *Holy Roman empire.

SAMANIDS Moslem dynasty in *Persia (902-1004). The S. were Iranians and originally from *Transoxiana, where they were landlords in Balkh. In 875 the family acquired the office of governors of Transoxiana on behalf of the *Abbasid caliphs of Baghdad. In 902 they defeated the *Saffarids and conquered *Khorasan, where they established a government loyal to the caliphate, but virtually independent. Like other Arab and Persian governors, they employed Turkish *Mamelukes in their army. The Turkish generals gained control of the army in the second half of the 10th century, and, as a result, the authority of the S. diminished. In 998 *Mahmud of Ghazni overthrew them. Attempts to maintain their authority in Balkh failed, and in 1004 the S. finally fell.

CHI.

SAMARKAND City in central Asia. Held by *Turkish tribes in the 6th century, it was conquered by the Arabs in 712. In the 8th-10th centuries S. developed into an important commercial and industrial centre, famous for its steel and rug industries. Under the rule of the *Samanids the city became a brilliant cultural and artistic centre. In 1220 it was destroyed by *Genghis-Khan, but during the 13th century the inhabitants who had managed to escape rebuilt it. S. reached the peak of its splendour during the reign of *Tamerlane, who made it his capital and promoted the building of sumptuous mosques.

SAMO Duke of *Moravia (*c.* 620-39). S. was a Frankish adventurer who, *c.* 620, arrived in the territories populated by *Slav tribes in the Elbe Valley. Having wandered some years between *Moravia and the middle course of the Elbe, as leader of a private army, he succeeded in uniting the various Slav tribes of the Elbe Valley and Bohemia and created a powerful state. In 630 he began his invasions of the eastern provinces of the Franks, successively defeating the armies sent against him. In 639, however, S. was defeated by a Franco-Thuringian army and killed in battle; his "state" fell upon his death.

J. M. Wallace-Hadrill, *The Barbarian West* (1965).

SAMSON BEN ABRAHAM OF SENS (d. c. 1216) Tosafist. He studied in the middle of the 12th century under *Jacob Tam and *Isaac of Dampierre and soon became an authority on Talmudic jurisprudence. By 1200 he was one of the greatest authorities on contemporary Judaism. In 1202 he pronounced his opposition to the works of *Maimonides, but expressed his veneration for his personality. He emigrated to Palestine *c.* 1211 and settled at Acre, where he died.

E. E. Urbach, *The Tossaphists* (1972).

SAMUEL (d. 1014) Tsar of the *Bulgarians (990-1014). Son of a provincial governor in Macedonia, S. restored the Bulgarian empire which had been destroyed by *John Tzimisces and established his capital at Preslav and Ochrida. His rule extended over large territories, including the major part of the Balkans and *Thessaly in Greece. Beginning in 1005 S. suffered attacks by Emperor *Basil II, who systematically defeated the Bulgarians and in 1014 destroyed most of his army, putting an end once again to the Bulgarian empire.

S. Runciman, *The First Bulgarian Empire* (1932).

SAMUEL BEN JEHUDAH IBN TIBBON (c. 1150-c. 1230) Jewish translator and physician. Born at Lunel, France, to a family already famous as translators of Jewish books from the Arabic into Hebrew, his main achievement was the translation of *Maimonides' *Guide for the Perplexed* into Hebrew (*c.* 1190). His text served as the basis for the Latin version of Maimonides' works and the polemics they aroused in the Jewish world in the 13th century. In the early 13th century he settled at Marseilles, where he practised medicine.

S. W. Baron, *A Social and Religious History of the Jews,* VIII (1959).

SAMUEL BEN MEIR HALEVI ABULAFIA (1320-61) Jewish leader at Toledo. As treasurer of King *Peter the Cruel of Castile, he reformed the kingdom's tax system. In 1360 he was disgraced and tortured to death. S. built the famous synagogue at Toledo, in a Jewish-Moorish style.

SAMUEL BEN MEIR OF RAMERUPT (Rashbam; c. 1080-1158) Jewish exegete. He studied under his grandfather, *Rashi, at Troyes. He was a spiritual leader of the community, but earned his living as sheep-farmer and wine grower. S. maintained close intellectual contacts with Christian scholars at Troyes and Paris, and his works influenced the *Victorines. His commentaries on the Bible and the Talmud are considered complementary to those of Rashi.

S. W. Baron, *A Social and Religious History of the Jews,* VI (1957).

SAMUEL HALEVI ABULAFIA (13th century) Scientist. Member of the famous Jewish Abulafia family of Toledo, he was employed by King *Alfonso X of Castile, for whom he built a water clock. At the request of the king, he translated from the Arabic into Castilian a manual on the manufacture and use of candle clocks.

The towers of San Gimignano, Tuscany

SAMUEL HANAGID HALEVI (Ibn Nagrela; 993-1055)
Scholar, poet, warrior and statesman. Born to a wealthy
Jewish family at Cordoba, he received a broad education in Hebrew and Arabic studies and was one of
the few specialists in Arab calligraphy. After the Berbers
sacked Cordoba (1013), he fled to Malaga, where he
was employed as secretary to the vizier of *Granada.
In *c.* 1020 he entered the service of Caliph Kasim ben
Hammud (1018-22) and in 1030 became vizier of the
kingdom of Granada, entrusted with directing political
and military affairs. From 1037 until his death, he was
virtually the head of the state, while the caliph reigned
only nominally. S. wrote Hebrew philological treatises
as well as poems, but his main work was an introduction
to the Talmud. He was also *nagid* (head) of the Jewish
community and, as such, established at his house a
**scriptorium*, where Talmud exemplars were copied
and diffused to the western communities.
S. W. Baron, *A Social and Religious History of the
Jews*, V-VI (1953-57).

SAN GERMANO, TREATY OF (1230) Agreement
concluded between *Frederick II, after his return from
the *Crusade, and Pope *Gregory IX. The pope consented to lift the emperor's excommunication on
the condition that the latter return the *Papal States.
In effect, the treaty made Frederick II master of Italy
and enabled him to concentrate his efforts upon subduing the *Lombard League.

SAN GIMIGNANO City in Tuscany, central Italy. It
reached a large measure of independence, in the 10th
century, when feudal families settled in the city and
created a feudal republic. S. was dominated by the imposing towers of 73 castles, 13 of them still extant. In
the 13th century, S. became an artistic centre; among
the major achievements was the *Palazzo del Popolo*
(1288-1323). The city was conquered by and annexed
to *Florence in 1354.
E. D. Hyde, *Politics and Society in Medieval Italy*
(1973).

SAN JUAN DELLA PEÑA *Cluniac monastery in Castile, Spain, founded in 1025. The monastery marked
the implantation of the order of Cluny in Spain, with
its two aims: (1) reconversion of the Christian population (the *Mozarabs*); (2) colonization activities in the
areas recovered.

SAN MARCO (Saint Mark's) Cathedral church of
*Venice. The history of the church is closely linked
with that of Venice and contains the shrine of the
city's patron saint. Situated in the centre of the political
life of the republic, the church grew in the 9th-12th
centuries from a small building into a great cathedral,
designed according to the Byzantine style and consecrated in 1094. The building's splendour was a result of
eastern influence, which had already become manifest in Italy in the form of the combination of Byzantine and Romanesque styles. In the case of S., the archi-

tectural design was a sign of greatness and was meant to assert Venetian claims to its own patriarchate.

O. Demus, *The Mosaics of the San-Marco Church* (1961).

SAN MARINO   Republic in the Apennines in central *Italy. It became famous in the 4th century, as the place where St. Marinus and a group of Christians took refuge to avoid persecution. In the 6th century an abbey was founded and around it a small lay community settled. During the wars that followed the fall of the *Carolingian empire in Italy (9th and 10th centuries), the commune built walls around the town and established its own defences. In the 15th century, a council of officers was appointed to govern the republic. Its isolation and mountain fortresses were important factors in S.'s continuous independence.

V. Rossi, *La Repubblica di San Marino* (1965).

SANCHO I, Ramirez (d. 1094)   King of Aragon (1063-94) and Navarre (as Sancho V, 1076-94). Son of *Ramiro I, S. allied himself with *Alfonso VI of Castile and fought against the Moslems. His conquests in the Ebro Valley doubled the territory of *Aragon. In 1076 he inherited the kingdom of Navarre, but the union remained a personal one and, after his death, the realms were again separated.

J. F. O'Callaghan, *A History of Medieval Spain* (1975).

SANCHO I   King of Castile. See SANCHO III, the Great.

SANCHO II   King of *Castile from 1065. His reign was marked by trouble with the local nobility, who supported his younger brother, *Alfonso VI, king of León. Alfonso succeeded S. in 1072, when the latter died without posterity.

SANCHO III   King of *Castile (1157-58). Son of *Alfonso VII, he died soon after he began his reign.

SANCHO IV   King of *Castile (1284-95). Second son of *Alfonso X, he was elected heir to the throne by the nobility, after the death of his elder brother *Ferdinand of La Cerda, against his father's will, who supported the rights of "La Cerda Infantes". S.'s reign was a period of dynastic conflict.

J. F. O'Callaghan, *A History of Medieval Spain* (1975).

SANCHO I   King of *Navarre (905-25). He founded the Garcia dynasty, destined to reign until 1234. His continuous wars against the Moslems created the climate for the *Reconquista wars. A Moslem retaliation in 924 led to the destruction of his capital, *Pamplona by *Abd Al-Rahman III, caliph of Córdoba.

SANCHO II (d. 1000)   King of *Navarre (970-94). His wars against the Moslems were unsuccessful and in 994, he abdicated in favour of his son Garcia.

SANCHO III, the Great (c. 965-1035)   King of *Navarre from 1000. After a series of successful wars against the Moslems, which culminated in his conquest of the upper Ebro Valley, he imposed his authority on the Christian states in northern Spain – *Asturias, *Galicia and *León – and created a powerful realm that extended as far as the Duero River and took the title "King of All Spain" (*c*. 1020). S. viewed his realm as a family patrimony, to be ruled by his sons and their descendants, with an "over-kingship" uniting them and commanding the *Reconquista wars. He thus created two new kingdoms, *Aragon and Castile (1028), which were to play a central role in Spanish history; they were given as heritage to his younger sons. The division of the empire after S.'s death and the ensuing fratricidal wars put

an end to his dream of an "over-kingship" and to Navarre's role as the centre of Spain.

J. F. O'Callaghan, *A History of Medieval Spain* (1975).

SANCHO IV   King of *navarre from 1054 to 1076. He devoted his efforts to the organization of the kingdom and the establishment of royal institutions.

SANCHO VI   King of *Navarre from 1150 to 1194. He recognized *Alfonso VII of Castile as his overlord and married Alfonso's daughter to prevent the division of his kingdom among his more powerful neighbours, *Aragon and *Castile.

SANCHO VII   King of *Navarre (1194-1234). Son of Sancho VI, he was the last Navarrese monarch of Spanish descent for almost 300 years; at his death, his nephew *Thibaut III of Champagne inherited the kingdom, which lost its importance.

SANCHO I (1154-1211)   King of *Portugal from 1185. He completed the *Reconquista process, with the conquest of *Algarve, establishing the final boundaries of Portugal. His efforts to assure his full independence, brought him into conflict with *Castile, and accounted for his consent to become a vassal of Pope *Innocent III in 1204.

SANCHO II   King of *Portugal from 1223 to 1245. He failed to impose his authority on the feudal nobility and was deposed by Pope *Innocent IV.

SANJAR   Sultan of the *Seljuks (1117-57). Third son of *Malik Shah, he succeeded his brother Muhammad. He was involved in a long series of wars with the *Khwarizmians and *Turkoman tribes in Turkestan. While he failed to attain full victory he was nonetheless able to avoid the disintegration of the empire. In the western provinces, he encouraged the promotion of *atabegs.

CHI.

SANTAREM   City in northern *Portugal. Capital of S. province under Arab rule in the 8th-10th centuries, it was conquered at the end of the 11th century by *Alfonso VI and became part of the county of Portugal. Captured by the *Almoravides in 1111, it became the capital of a Moslem principality and a fortified *Alcazar was built there. In 1147 the city was reconquered by the Portuguese and became a royal residence.

SANTA SOPHIA (HAGIA SOPHIA)   Cathedral church of *Constantinople, built and ornamented during the reign of *Justinian (528-65). The building, conceived in striking geometric form, represents the finest achievement of Byzantine *architecture. Furthermore, its sculptural and mosaic decorations became the model for Byzantine religious art.

SANTIAGO DE COMPOSTELA   City in northwestern Spain, in the province of *Galicia. Local traditions, which emerged in the 10th century and became more deeply rooted in the 11th, considered Compostela the burial site of St. James, the human "brother of Christ". According to the legend, the body of Patriarch James was taken from Jerusalem by his 12 disciples, who feared persecution, and was eventually brought to Compostela in the Far West, where by miracle the body was buried in a crypt. From the end of the 10th century the shrine attracted a great wave of pilgrimages from all over western Europe. Thus, S. became a major pilgrimage site, second in holiness only to *Jerusalem and *Rome. In the 11th and 12th centuries, hospices and abbeys were built along the "routes of St. James", the

Portal of the cathedral of Santiago de Compostela, Spain

main paths taken by the pilgrims. As a result, commerce was revived. The holiness of the pilgrimage site also was influential in recruiting knights from France for the *Reconquista* wars of Spain in the 11th and 12th centuries. During the pontificate of Diego Gelmirez, an attempt was made to compile the numerous traditions

and stories told to the pilgrims into an authoritative version, falsely attributed to Pope *Calixtus II (1119-23); on the basis of this work, the see of Compostela was promoted to the rank of archbishopric and a new cathedral was built. Eventually, the name of the city was changed to Santiago (St. James).

G. Hamilton, *The Routes to Compostela* (1961).

SANTIAGO, KNIGHTS OF Military order founded in 1164 and placed under the patronage of St. James of Compostela. Like the other two Spanish orders of *Alcántara and *Calatrava, the S. took the vow of chastity and pledged continuous warfare against the Moslems. They were especially active in the western part of the Iberian peninsula, holding frontier castles. In 1482 the knights were integrated by the King Ferdinand and Queen Isabella into the monarchic system of government.

SANUDO *Venetian aristocratic family which became prominent in the 13th century. Of its members, the most famous is the historian, Marino S. the Elder (*c.* 1270-1343). He travelled in the East for the affairs of the republic and visited Palestine at the beginning of the 14th century. On his return he advocated a new *Crusade and, for that purpose, wrote *The Book of the Secrets of the Faithful of the Holy Cross,* in which he elaborated a plan for the reconquest of the Holy Land, with detailed maps. In 1321 he dedicated his book to Pope *John XXII.

SARACENS Name given in the Middle Ages by western European scholarly and popular sources to the *Arabs and Moslems. It originally signified the Beduin tribe of *Sinai, *Banu Sara,* which was known to the monks of St. Catherine's Abbey, but it was eventually used to refer to all Arabs.

SARAGOSSA (ZARAGOZA) City in *Spain. Situated on the south bank of the Ebro River, it was conquered by the Arabs in 714 and became a provincial capital. In 754 its emirs proclaimed themselves subjects of the *Abbasids and were at constant war with the *Ummayad *Abd Al-Rakhman I. In 787 Emir Yussuf called *Charlemagne to help him, but the Ummayads emerged victorious and S. became part of the Ummayad caliphate of Cordoba. When the caliphate collapsed in 1031, the city became the capital of a *Taifa* kingdom. In 1118 *Alfonso I of Aragon conquered it and established there his capital.

E. Levi-Provençal, *Histoire de l'Espagne Musulmane* (1946).

SARDINIA Island in the western Mediterranean. Conquered in 477 by the *Vandals, and in 534 by the Byzantines, it fell in 711 to the Arabs, who sacked the island and imposed on its inhabitants a heavy annual tribute. The *Aghlabids conquered S. in the 9th century, and it remained under Moslem rule until 1046. In practice, however, S. was ruled by four hereditary *giudici* (governing judges), who enjoyed a large measure of independence in their respective provinces, provided that tribute to the Arab emir was regularly paid. In the 11th century S. was attacked by fleets of the Italian cities of *Pisa and *Genoa, who vied with each other for the overlordship and economic exploitation of the island. A compromise was reached at the end of the century, whereby Genoa received the northern and western parts, while Pisa obtained the southern and eastern. This solution did not prevent further conflicts in the 12th and

Interior of Santa Sophia, Constantinople

13th centuries. In 1239 *Frederick II made S. into a kingdom and gave it to his illegitimate son, *Enzo. At the same time, the cities developed and local government began to be introduced in urban centres; in 1241 Sassari was granted a communal charter. Enzo's reign, however, ended in 1248, when he was taken prisoner at *Bologna and the ancient rivalry between Pisa and Genoa was renewed. In 1284, the naval victory of the Genoese at Meloria, when Pisa lost its maritime power, brought the island under Genoese domination. In 1322, as a result of dynastic claims, the sovereignty of S. passed to *Aragon and King James II undertook its conquest (1326), completed only in 1348. Under the Aragonese, local *cortes, with a large degree of self-government, were established and feudal customs introduced. A general revolt against the Aragonese government (1386) culminated in the establishment of a local dynasty under the rule of Queen Eleanora of Arborea, who became the national hero of S. (d. 1421). She distinguished herself as warrior and military commander but also proved a wise and able administrator. In 1392, she issued the *Carta de Logu*, the first constitution of the island. After her death Sardinian unity collapsed, enabling Alfonso V to restore Aragonese rule and to continue the feudalization process.
M. Delane, *Sardinia* (1968).

SASSANIDS (226-651) The dynasty which ruled in *Persia until the Arab conquest.

SAVA, St. (1176-1235) Patron saint of *Serbia. Son of *Stephen Nemanja, he became a monk at Mount *Athos in 1191. Summoned by his brother, he returned to Serbia where he crowned him as Stephen I in 1217 and organized the Serbian church as independent of the Greek Orthodox.

SAVELLI *Roman aristocratic family which became influential in the 13th century when they were the

Chosroes II, Sassanid king of Persia, shown hunting; 7th-century silver plate decorated in relief

rivals of the *Colonna and *Orsini families. They provided two popes, *Honorius III and *Honorius IV.

SAVONA City in Liguria, northwestern *Italy. A feudal lordship, it was disputed in the 12th century by the Italian princes. Annexed by Genoa in 1146, it became the centre of Liguria.

SAVOY Alpine region between France and Italy. Known in the early Middle Ages as Sapaudia, it was settled by the *Burgundians in 443 and became part of their kingdom. In 534 it was conquered by the *Franks. Allotted to Emperor *Lothair by the Treaty of Verdun in 843, S. became part of the kingdom of Burgundy in 888. The feudalization process led to the growth of feudal dynasties, two of which took the countal title in the 10th century: the lords of *Genoa and the Humbertians. When the kingdom of Burgundy was annexed in 1032 to the *Holy Roman empire, the Humbertians rose in rank: in 1040, Humbert I was officially recognized count of S. and established his capital at Chambéry. His granddaughter Bertha married Emperor *Henry IV in 1066, while her brother, Count Peter, was appointed margrave of *Turin. At the end of the 11th century the house of S. embarked on a policy of territorial expansion in the Alpine region. The 12th and 13th centuries saw the annexation of counties and seignories in the upper Rhône Valley and in *Piedmont. Through marriages with the royal dynasties of France, England and Cyprus, the house of S. acquired much prestige throughout Europe. Blocked in the west by the French expansion in *Dauphiné, the counts of S. turned to Italy. Under the rule of Count Amadeus VI ("The Green Count", 1343-83), they became an important factor in Italy, their alliance being sought by *Venice, the *Visconti of Milan and other Italian lords. He completed the annexation of Piedmont and prepared to take over Nice, which, acquired by Amadeus VII (1383-91), gave S. a harbour in the Mediterranean. In 1416 Emperor *Sigismund granted Count Amadeus VIII (future Pope *Felix V) the ducal title. In 1430, S. was provided with a constitution, organizing its government and institutions.
E. L. Cox, *The Eagles of Savoy* (1974).

SAXONY Country in northern *Germany, between the Elbe and Rhine rivers. The territory was populated by tribes of Saxons, who settled there after the 5th-century migrations of other *Germanic tribes to the lands of the Roman empire. Some of the Saxon tribes later migrated to Britain, where they became assimilated with the neighbouring tribes of the Angles. The Saxons gradually developed a confederative organization, led by a king who was elected by the chieftains. This confederation was based on the social structures of the Germanic tribes. In the 8th century the Saxons resisted the activity of Catholic missionaries; this opposition brought St. *Boniface to rely upon the *Franks to continue his mission. Thus, after the coronation of *Pepin the Short (753), the Christianization of S. became a political issue which launched a long war between the Saxons and the Franks during the reign of *Charlemagne. The war lasted more than 30 years, ending only in 802 with the conquest of S. and its compulsory conversion to Christianity. *Widukind, the national leader of the Saxons, was captured and exiled to Neustria. Frankish domination was exercised from new urban centres, such as *Padeborn, *Fulda, and *Corvey, founded near bishoprics and abbeys. During the 9th century, the

country continuously developed; Bremen was founded and many new urban and rural settlements were established. The status of S., however, was as yet undefined; under Charlemagne and *Louis the Pious, several counts were appointed to administer the territories, while the frontier of the Elbe was entrusted to the margraves of the northern *march. In 843 S. was granted to *Louis the German, who constituted it as a separate kingdom which he intended for his son, *Louis.

At the end of the 9th century, the country finally received the status of duchy and a local dynasty imposed its rule, having been recognized in 911. When Duke *Henry the Wrangler was elected king of Germany, he decided to preserve the duchy as the territorial basis of his power, entrusting its administration to his elder son, *Otto I. After Otto's royal election in 936, he continued to act as duke of S. Under the Ottonians (10th century), S. knew economic and cultural prosperity, and the city of *Magdeburg became the base of German and Christian expansion eastwards. In the 11th century local princes were appointed as dukes of S. Saxon particularism became visibly pronounced under the reign of *Henry IV, when the majority of the revolts against imperial authority originated in that territory.

In 1125 Duke *Lothair of Supplinburg was elected emperor and enfeoffed the duchy to *Henry the Proud of the *Welf dynasty. Under the Welf dukes, S. reached its greatest prosperity and became the base of German colonization eastwards. Duke *Henry the Lion was the leader of that *Drang nach Osten* policy which led to the Germanization of the Slav areas between the Elbe and Oder rivers and to the foundation of the city of *Lübeck. As a result, Saxon influence spread both in Germany and in Europe to the point where it threatened the imperial authority of *Frederick Barbarossa. The emperor, taking advantage of Henry the Lion's failure to provide feudal service in Italy 1178, had him convicted and his Saxon fief confiscated (1180). The great duchy of S. was then divided into a number of units: the ducal title, together with territories in the southeastern part of the former duchy, were granted to *Bernard of Anhalt; the counties and marches east of the Elbe were proclaimed direct fiefs of the empire; and the city of Lübeck received the status of an imperial city. In the west, the Westphalian counties were granted to the archbishops of *Cologne, while the large ecclesiastical seigniories came under imperial authority. Henry the Lion, who was exiled to England, was ultimately allowed to retain his personal title of duke as well as his personal and family possessions at *Brunswick and Lüneburg. A number of counties in the southwestern part of the original duchy obtained their independence from ducal authorities and were constituted petty principalities.

The new duchy of S., organized at the end of the 12th and during the 13th century by the dynasty of Anhalt, became a noteworthy feudal principality in the later Middle Ages. Its importance was based on wealth from its mining industry and from trade with cities such as Dresden. In 1348 the dukes of S. were granted the status of prince-*electors of the empire.
G. Barraclough, *The Origins of Modern Germany* (1951).

SAYF AL-DIN Sultan of *Mosul (1145-76). Younger son of *Zengi, he was appointed heir of Mosul by his father. Under the influence of his elder brother, *Nureddin, S. modelled the organization of his state after that of Syria. In 1173, he sought the regency of his nephew Salih, but was defeated by *Saladin.

SCABINI (ÉCHEVINS) The term was applied to notable men of local communities and, from the 12th century, to members of municipal councils in Germany and France.

SCALIGER (DELLA SCALA) Family in *Verona, Italy. Leaders of the *Ghibelline party, they rose to prominence in the principality of *Ezzelino da Romano. After Ezzelino's death (1279), Mastino I seized power at *Verona (1259-77) and imposed the hereditary rule of his family on the feuding local families. The greatest member of the family was Cangrande (1291-1329), who became lord of Verona in 1311. He established a brilliant court in the city, where he offered protection to the poet *Dante. His military activities resulted in the foundation of a great principality in northeastern Italy, between Milan of the *Visconti and *Venice. An able politician, he became one of the most influential rulers of Italy. After his death, dynastic wars weakened the family and Verona.

SCANIA (SKÅNE) The southern part of *Sweden, which belonged in the Middle Ages to Denmark. The ecclesiastical metropole of *Lund was established there in the 12th century.

SCHILDBERGER, HANS-JOHANN (1380-1440) Traveller. He took part in the *Nicopolis Crusade (1396), where, taken prisoner by *Bayazid, he was reduced to slavery. Surrendered in 1401 to *Tamerlane, he was brought to central Asia, where he managed to escape and, after many years of travel in Asia, returned to Germany in 1427. He wrote an account of his adventures, with a description of the countries he visited.

SCHLESWIG Duchy. The area of S., south of the *Jutland peninsula, belonged to Denmark in the 9th century. It was conquered by the Germans under *Otto II and became a county within the duchy of *Saxony. Ceded in 1203 by Emperor *Conrad II to *Canute the Great, it developed in the late 11th and early 12th century into one of the most important principalities of Denmark, governed by members of the royal dynasty. It was conquered by *Henry the Lion, duke of Saxony, in 1149. and incorporated into his state. In the late Middle Ages, the area was the subject of disputes between the neighbouring counts of *Holstein and the *Hanse, which sought to prevent the emergence of a powerful regime in the duchy, close to its centre of *Lübeck.
L. Musset, *Les Peuples Scandinaves au Moyen Age* (1951).

SCHOLA CANTORUM A choir of priests and young clerics in the Roman Church who performed the liturgy from the 6th century. Pope *Gregory I, who reformed the liturgical chant, gave this group a primary role in the development of *Gregorian music.

SCHOLASTICISM The formal thought of medieval Christian Europe. Based on the assumption that all truth had already been expressed in patristic theology, Greek philosophy and Roman thought, the primary task of S. was to preserve the traditional teachings. Early S. was characterized by the collecting, interpreting and discussing of the works of ancient thinkers, notably St. *Augustine, *Plato and *Aristotle. It reached its apex in the 13th century, with the attempt to attain a comprehensive view of all truth, as exemplified in the work of Thomas *Aquinas. One of the founders of S. was

Memorial 15th-century statue of Cangrande Scaliger

the 6th-century scholar *Boethius, who, in his *The Consolation of Philosophy*, tried to reconcile faith with reason. In the 11th century, both St. *Anselm and *Berengar of Tours, and, a century later, Peter *Abelard, subscribed to Boethius' view of reason as the tool by which all mysteries of faith can be understood. On the other hand, Peter *Damian and Bernard of *Clairveaux, while extolling reason, also emphasized its limitations. At the same time, Aristotle's works, hitherto unknown to the West, were being translated into Latin. Aristotle became an authority on knowledge and commentaries on his work abounded. Instrumental in the spread of 13th-century Aristotelianism were Albertus *Magnus and his pupil, Thomas Aquinas. The late scholastic period was marked by a negation of what the earlier scholastic thinkers had laboured to achieve. Repudiating the attempt to bridge the gap between faith and reason, Duns *Scotus and William of *Ockham rejected Thomas Aquinas' rationalism and emphasized the necessity of faith in dealing with theological problems.
J. M. Baldwin, *The Scholastic Culture of the Middle Ages* (1971).

SCHWABENSPIEGEL (The Mirror of the Swabs) A compilation of German laws undertaken in the 13th century by the *Hohenstaufen lawmakers in reaction to the *Sachsenspiegel. The S. included imperial ordinances of *Frederick Barbarossa, *Henry VI and *Frederick II, as well as customary laws. The codification asserted the pre-eminence of the empire and of imperial legislation.

SCHWYZ See SWITZERLAND.

SCOT ERIGENA, JOHN See ERIGENA, JOHN SCOT.

SCOT, JOHN DUNS See DUNS, JOHN SCOT.

SCOTLAND Kingdom in the northern part of the British Isles. From the 5th century, it was inhabited by the *Picts, Scots, *Britons and *Angles, who eventually fused to form the Scottish kingdom. The Picts, believed to have been in the area since pre-Celtic times, occupied the region north of the Forth River; the Scots, who came from northern Ireland, colonized the Argyll region probably in the late 5th century; the Britons, who had settled in the south, lost southeast S. to the Angles in the early 7th century, but retained their kingdom of *Strathclyde in the southwest; the Angles, who migrated to S. from the 5th century, created the kingdom of *Northumbria from the Humber River to the Forth at around the 7th century. The *Irish monks who settled in S. introduced Christianity. Most famous is St. Columba, who came to Iona in 563 and converted the northern Scots. During the 8th century the fusion of the four ethnical elements was already evident, while political organization still remained at the tribal level; the clans, with their chieftains, were the common form of organization in the Highlands. The *Norman raids of the 9th century, mainly by the Norwegians, helped unify the tribal kingdoms. In 844 Kenneth MacAlpin, king of the Scots, also assumed the leadership of the Picts, and united the two groups into a permanent organization, the *Terra Scotiae*. In the 10th century, S. expanded southward, conquering the Lothian region containing *Edinburgh, while the ancient kingdom of Strathclyde was ceded to King *Malcolm of S. by *Edred of Wessex in 938. The second half of the 11th century saw the penetration of Anglo-Saxon cultural influence, instrumental in its spread having been the Saxon wife of King *Malcolm III, St. *Margaret. During the reign of *David I, Anglo-Norman families who immigrated to S. were granted large estates and offices, which led to the emergence of a form of *feudalism. Continuous wars with England accelerated the Anglicization process, especially after 1167, when the English King *Henry II compelled King *William the Lion to become his vassal. (It is not certain whether the vassalage applied to S. itself or to English lands south of the Tyne, held by the kings of S.)

The 13th century saw the cession of the *Hebrides by the Norwegians to S. under the Treaty of Perth (1266). At the death of *Alexander III (1286), who left no direct heir, a dynastic crisis put into question the independence of the realm. John *Balliol eventually won the support of King *Edward I of England, who, as overlord, arbitrated between the claimants. While Balliol agreed to pay homage to Edward for the kingdom of S., the Scottish barons imposed their own council to control the government and compelled their king to declare war on England (1295). Edward conquered S. and installed a government to rule on his behalf. But national resistance was to continue under the leadership of William *Wallace, despite Edward's annual campaigns in S. and the severe damage the country suffered as a result. After Wallace was executed in 1305, the anti-English movement was led by *Robert Bruce, who became the national hero of S. Allied with France, he inflicted a decisive defeat on *Edward II at *Bannockburn in 1314, thereby securing Scottish independence. The 14th century saw S.'s revival and development under the Robertian dynasty. The last vestiges of foreign domination came to an end in the 15th century, when the Okney Islands and Shetland were ceded to S. The foundation of a national university at *St. Andrews (1401) was an important manifestation of S.'s independence. The new dynasty that arose in the 15th century, the Stuarts, were faced with the problem of local particularism of the feudal nobility and clan chieftains. S.'s parliament was modelled on that of England, but, unlike the English House of Commons, it was made inoperative by the particularist elements and remained no more than the feudal court of the Scottish kings until the late 16th century. Moreover, the Stuart kings failed to assert their authority. Clashes between the kingship and the nobility weakened the realm in the second half of the 15th century. The penetration of English cultural influence notwithstanding, an important local culture developed. Based on the traditions of the Highland clans, it is exemplified by the ballads and the literary activity of minstrels. From the 14th century this tradition evolved into an important literary culture, whose leading figure was John Barbour (c. 1316-95), the author of the *Bruce poem*.

G. Barrow, *A History of Medieval Scotland* (1961).

SCOTTI Family of bankers in Piacenza, *Lombardy. They entered the money-lending business at the end of the 12th century and during the 13th created a banking house, whose affairs extended to France, England, Germany and Catalonia. In the 14th and 15th centuries they also seized power in their city.

SCRIPTORIUM The room in *Benedictine monasteries in which books were copied. In general, the manuscripts were dictated by one of the members of the congregation. In the 9th century the S. became common in most western abbeys and played a considerable role in the preservation of classical Latin works, as well as in the diffusion of books and study.

SCROPE, RICHARD (c. 1346-1405) Archbishop of York. Renowned for his scientific knowledge, he was appointed chancellor of the University of Cambridge in 1378. *Richard II, who employed him in his council, made him bishop of Coventry in 1386 and archbishop of *York in 1398. S. entered into conflict with *Henry IV in 1403, supporting the Northumbrian revolts and preaching against arbitrary royal role. He was arrested and sentenced to death in 1405.

J. Solloway, *Archbishop Scrope* (1928).

SCUTAGE (Latin: scutum; French: écuage) A tax imposed on knights as a substitute for military service. Originally, in the *Carolingian period, it had a pejorative connotation and was considered a fine paid by those who reneged upon their duty. In the 12th century the tax began to be thought of as a fiscal revenue of the crown. *Henry II of England used the S. to raise a mercenary army and to make the crown less dependent upon the feudal service of its knights.

Medieval Latin, samples of handwriting (See Scriptorium)

St. John the Evangelist, *from the Lambeth Bible*
(See Scriptorium)

SEDULIUS SCOTUS (9th century) Scholar, poet and
political thinker. Of Irish origin, he settled at Liège,
where he lived *c.* 848-58. His scholarly work includes
a series of commentaries on theological matters, the
Collectanea. In his treatise, *De Rectoribus Christianis*
(On Christian Rulers), he developed the idea of sacred
kingship, rooted in the biblical monarchy and adapted
to the reality of the 9th century.
W. W. Laistner, *Thought and Letters in Western Europe,
500-900* (1951).

SEGOVIA City in Castile, Spain. In 1079 *Alfonso VI
conquered it from the Moslems. Situated on the cross-
roads of trade routes in northern Spain, the city enjoyed
prosperity in the 12th and 13th centuries. It was a royal
residence in the 13th century, its palace having been
modelled on the Moslem *Alcazar.*

SELJUK (SALJUQ, SELDJUQ) Chieftain of a clan of
Oghuz *Turks, who served the *Samanids in the 10th
century. He organized his clan as one of the most
important Turkish military organizations, absorbing
warriors of the Black Turks.

SELJUK TURKS Dynasty ruling over Turkish tribes in
central Asia and considered to be descendants of *Seljuk.
Organized by *Tughril-beg (1037-63), they began systematically to conquer territories from the governors
of the eastern *Abbasid caliphs, whom they had
hitherto served. In 1037 Tugril-beg conquered Merv
and, defeating the *Ghaznavids, extended his realm

to *Khorasan and Persia. Seizing *Baghdad in 1055, he
was hailed by the caliph as a liberator and continued
his march westwards, where his army had already
invaded *Armenia in 1044. His nephew and successor,
*Alp Arslan I (1063-72), extended the conquests and in
1071 defeated the Byzantine army at *Menzikert,
capturing Emperor *Romanus IV. Under the rule of
his son *Malik Shah (1072-92), Seljuk expansion reached
its height. They conquered all of Anatolia and the city of
Nicaea, as well as most of Syria and Palestine, where
the *Fatimids were able to preserve only the coastal
area. Malik established his capital at *Isfahan in Persia,
while the western provinces, as well as Kirman, were
given as fiefs to members of the dynasty. He introduced
the feudal system of *Iqta'a, land given to governors
and their armies in lieu of salaries. Much of the organization of the empire was the work of the Persian vizier,
*Nizam Al-Mulk, who also promoted its cultural activity.
After Malik Shah's death, the empire began to show
signs of disintegration. Formally, Nizam's sons were still
recognized as the sole leaders of the Seljuk empire (1092-
1157) but their real authority was challenged by the
collateral princes who founded their own principalities
and fought amongst themselves. The rivalry between
*Sulaiman Ibn Qutlumish, governor of *Rum (Ana-
tolia), and his cousin, *Tutush of Syria, led to Sulaiman's
death at Aleppo (1092), and to the decline of both
principalities, facilitating in 1096-97 the *Crusader
penetration into Asia Minor and the conquest of Nicaea
and *Antioch. Moreover, the quarrels among Tutush's
sons, *Ridwan of Aleppo and *Duqaq of Damascus,
enabled the Crusaders to conquer *Jerusalem (1099).
In the early 12th century *Qilij-Arslan I established the
independent Seljuk sultanate of Rum at *Konya,
destined to last until 1307, while in Syria and Iraq the
Seljuk dynasties were replaced by the *atabegs who,
although they were appointed by the Seljuk sultans in
Persia, became virtually independent and constituted
their own states, notably at Damascus, Aleppo and
Mosul. After *Sanjar's death (1157) the sultanate of

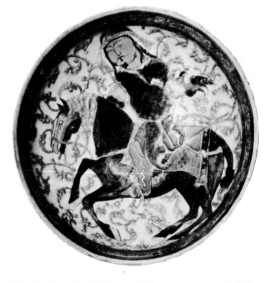

Seljuk prince depicted on a 12th-century ceramic dish

Persia fell to the *Turkomans and the *Khwarizmians, Seljuk power surviving only in the sultanate of *Rum. However, dynastic strife and Byzantine recovery under the Comneni in the 12th century posed a major threat to the Seljuk hold on Rum. The victory of Qilij-Arslan II at *Myriocephalon avoided the dissolution of the sultanate, but it was only during the reign of Kaykobad (1219-36) that the crisis was overcome and the sultanate knew a period of stability and prosperity. In the middle of the 13th century, a process of decline was precipitated by a series of Dervish revolts, followed by *Mongol invasions. *Hulagu-khan imposed a Mongol supervisor on the sultan, while various tribes, notably the *Ottomans and the Karamans, acquired independence. In 1302, the Mongol supervisor sentenced Sultan Kaykobad II (1297-1302) to death and the last Seljuk state was divided up into a large number of principalities, which were conquered in the 14th century by the Ottoman Turks.

CHI (1970).

SEMPACH, BATTLE OF (1386) Fought by the Swiss cantons against the *Hapsburgs. The Swiss victory assured the independence of the Confederation.

SENESCHAL The chief at the feudal court. He commanded the army in the lord's absence and was charged with administering justice. With the organization of feudal monarchies in the 11th century, the office was adopted by the royal court. However, when the S.'s power began to threaten royal authority, it was either restricted or abolished. In France, under *Philip II, the S. was the governor of the province situated near the boundaries of the realm.

M. Bloch, *Feudal Society* (1951).

SENIOR See LORD.

SENS City in France. The Gallo-Roman city of S. declined during the *Merovingian period, although an archiepiscopal see was established there and continued to be active. In the 9th century the county of S. belonged to the duchy of *Burgundy; in 1015 *Robert the Pious attached it to the royal demesne. The city's 12th-century cathedral is a beautiful example of Romanesque and Gothic architecture. S. remained a small provincial city until the end of the Middle Ages.

SEPHARDIM The Jewish communities of both Moslem and Christian Spain (Hebrew: *Sepharad*), which had a particular culture within *Judaism. The term, first found in biblical literature, came into common use in the 8th century, when the autonomous centre of *Andalusia was established. In general, the term was also used to include Jewish communities outside the Iberian peninsula which had an essentially Sephardi way of life. The main patterns of that way of life included a deep involvement in the cultures of the lands in which they lived and a good knowledge of Hebrew and of vernacular languages, such as Arabic and Castilian. Another characteristic feature of the S. was their acquaintance with the philosophical and scientific heritage of the ancient world and the wide use they made of their own spiritual works.

S. W. Baron, *A Social and Religious History of the Jewish People*, VI (1957).

SEPTIMANIA The province of *Languedoc.

SEPULCHRE, HOLY See HOLY SEPULCHRE.

SERBIA Country in the Balkan peninsula. Populated by the Serbs, a Slav tribe which in the 8th century settled in the territories between the Danube River and *Macedonia, it became a loose confederation of small principalities, governed by princes called *župans*, who fought amongst themselves. In the 9th-11th centuries, S. was dominated first by the *Bulgarian and then the *Byzantine empire. From 875, the Serbs were converted to Christian Orthodoxy. Under the Comneni, the *župans* of Skopje embarked on a process of unification. The founder of the realm, *Stephen Nemanja (1170-95) secured Serbian independence in 1180, but did not take the royal title. His son, *Stephen I (1196-1127), who continued his father's policy, was recognized king by Pope *Honorius III (1216), but preferred the Orthodox coronation rites administered by his brother St. *Sava. In 1219 he established an autonomous church and organized the realm according to Byzantine traditions, but preserved the Serbian custom of having an assembly of nobles and free-men, the *Sabor*. Under *Stephen IV Uroš (1243-76), the kingdom was reinforced, large territories being annexed in Macedonia and northern Epirus. But, after his death, S. was weakened by dynastic disputes that ended only in the middle of the 14th century, under *Stephen IX Dushan (1331-55), who was the founder of the Serbian empire. He extended his rule in *Epirus and *Bulgaria and aimed to create a Serbo-Byzantine state, able to defend itself against the *Turks. His death, near *Adrianople, prevented him from realizing his aims and further dynastic troubles facilitated the decline of S. Defeated at *Kossovo by the Turks in 1387, most of S. was made tributary to Turkey.

S. Setton-Watson, *A Short History of the Yugoslavs* (1938).

SERFDOM (SERVITIUM) The condition of the majority of *peasants in western Europe. S. was introduced in the 4th century and spread due to the decline of *slavery. A serf was attached to a *manor and owed particular duties to his *lord. Originally, such obligations included the donation of a substantial portion of the product of the serf's holding to the lord. In addition, the lord used the serf's labour for the cultivation of the demesne land and his services at the manor house. By the 10th century, however, the essential distinction between the serf and the free peasant lay in the fact that the serf had no freedom of movement, no legal rights in the courts, nor could he testify.

G. Duby, *The Agrarian Society in Western Europe* (1970).

SERGIUS (d. 636) Byzantine governor of Palestine. In 636 he organized the defence of the country against Arab attacks, but was defeated by *Omar at the Yarmuk Battle.

SERGIUS (d. 638) Patriarch of Constantinople (610-38). One of the most important personalities in the Byzantine empire of the early 7th century, he played an important role in the political events that brought *Heraclius to the imperial throne (610). Aware of the potential religious and political consequences of the *Monophysite controversy, he attempted to find a compromise formula, which would re-establish the religious unity of the Eastern Roman empire. He thus formulated the *Monothelite theory, which, while it was supported by Heraclius, was rejected by the Monophysites as well as by both the Greek Orthodox and Roman Catholic churches.

CMedH, IV.

SERGIUS I, St. (d. 701) Pope (687-701). Born of a *Syrian family which settled at Rome after the Arab conquest, he succeeded to the papacy only after a fierce struggle against two other contenders and with Byzantine support. During his pontificate, he introduced liturgical reforms.

SERGIUS II Pope (844-47). Of Roman origin, he was elected pope without imperial consent and, accordingly, was compelled to take an oath of fidelity to *Lothair I. He became very unpopular at *Rome, where he was accused of extorting money. His death prevented a crisis in the Roman Church.

SERGIUS III Pope (904-11). Born to a Roman family, he was dominated by *Theophylactus, whose daughter, *Marozia, was his mistress and bore him a son, the future Pope *John XI.

SERGIUS IV (Peter Buccaporci) Pope (1009-12). Member of a distinguished *Roman family, he became pope through the support of Count *Alberic of Tusculum. S. became renowned for his piety. In 1011 he issued a bull, calling for a holy war against the Moslems, thus developing the foundations of the future *Crusade ideology.
W. Ullmann, *A Short History of the Papacy* (1973).

SERGIUS, St. (1314-92) Russian mystic. Born at Rostov, he founded a monastery near Moscow dedicated to the Holy Trinity. The religious house contributed to the revival of Orthodox monasticism after the destruction of the religious centre of *Kiev during the Mongol invasions. S. was a gifted preacher, whose sermons had an important influence on popular and political circles. He helped unite the feuding Russian princes under the Great Prince *Dimitri Donskoi of Moscow. It was with S.'s spiritual support and encouragement that Donskoi led the Russian army in repelling a Mongol invasion. In his sermons, he described Russia as the Holy Land and the Russians as the Chosen People. S. helped make Moscow the new religious centre of Russia and, although he turned down the office of metropolitan, he was, in essence, the leader of the Russian Pravoslav Church.
N. Zernov, *St. Sergius, Builder of Russia* (1939).

SERRATA DEL GRAN CONSIGLIO (The Closing of the Great Council) An ordinance issued in 1296 at *Venice, which limited participation in the debates of the *Great Council to those members of the urban aristocracy whose families were already represented. Accordingly, the political life of Venice was restricted to a small number of aristocratic families which, through their domination of the Great Council, were able to control the executive authorities, including the doge.

SERVIENTES (SERGEANTS) The *lord's household servants, who were responsible for supervising the work of the peasants in the *manor and for leading them in wars. In the 11th century some S. were considered vassals of their lords and received land for their services; thus they became the upper strata of the peasantry.

SERVUS SERVORUM DEI (Latin: "the servant of God's servants") One of the titles of the popes. Introduced in the pontifical protocol by *Gregory I, it was an expression of papal humility, but also asserted the superiority of the pope as the servant of the apostles (God's servants).

SEVEN DEADLY SINS Established by the Fathers of the Church, they were: Pride, Covetousness, Lust, Envy, Gluttony, Anger and Sloth, and were condemned by Pope *Gregory I.
M. M. Bloomfield, *The Seven Deadly Sins* (1952).

SEVEN GIFTS OF THE HOLY GHOST They were: Wisdom, Understanding, Counsel, Fortitude, Knowledge, Piety and Fear of the Lord.
DTC. IV.

SEVEN LIBERAL ARTS, THE The medieval tradition of study, based on the doctrines of St. *Augustine and the teaching programmes of *Cassiodorus, adopted the Greek concept of liberal studies, on the condition that they be controlled by the Church. Thus, the S. were conceived as the essence of learning and their number was symbolically linked with the seven virtues. This interpretation was represented as the ideal at the beginning of the 13th century by the Norman scholar, *Hugh of Andely, in his famous book, *The Battle of the Seven Liberal Arts.* The S. were divided into two groups: the *Trivium,* consisting of grammar, dialectics and rhetoric, and the *Quadrivium,* which included arithmetic, geometry, astronomy and music.
H. Wiernszowski, *The Medieval Universities* (1968).

SEVEN SACRAMENTS See SACRAMENTS.

SEVEN VIRTUES They were: Faith, Hope, Charity, Justice, Prudence, Temperance and Fortitude. The first three were considered theological virtues and the others cardinal virtues.
DTC, XV.

SEVILLE City in Andalusia, *Spain. It was conquered by the *Vandals in the late 4th century and, after the collapse of their kingdom, it became in the middle of the 6th century the centre of Byzantine influence in Spain; in 580, it was conquered by the *Visigoths. The short period of *Byzantine domination made S. a centre of learning and of the transmission of the classical heritage, as personified a generation later by St. *Isidore of S. S. fell to the Arabs in 712 and became part of the caliphate of *Cordoba. With the fall of the caliphate (1031), an independent dynasty, the *Abbadids, established its authority at S., which became the capital of a powerful Moslem state. Annexed in 1088 to the *Almoravides' empire, S. became one of the most prosperous cities in southern Spain, and remained thus under their successors, the *Almohades. Its harbour became the most active in the West, with ships sailing to *Morocco. Its prosperity was reflected in the *Alcazar,* one of the greatest in Spain. Conquered by King *Ferdinand III of Castile in 1248, S. became one of the favourite royal residences in the later medieval Castile.
J. F. O'Callaghan, *A History of Medieval Spain* (1975).

SEWAL BOVILL (1206-58) Archbishop of *York (1252-58). He was dean of York Cathedral, where he served under Archbishop Walter Grey, whom he succeeded. He became famous for the dispute with Pope *Innocent IV over the privileges of the York see. Having accused the Pope of exactions, he was suspended in 1257.

SHAIZAR City in northern *Syria. In the 11th century it became the centre of an emirate, governed by the Arab family of Al-Munqidh. They managed to maintain their independence against the attacks of the *Fatimids and the *Seljuk Turks and a large degree of autonomy within *Saladin's empire. In the 12th century the court of S. became an important cultural centre, illustrated by the activity of *Usamah Ibn Munqidh.

SHEIKH AL JABAL (the old man of the mountains) See ASSASSINS.

SHERIFF The administrator of a *shire in England. During the *Anglo-Saxon period, the S. was an official whose main functions included the collection of revenues and the mobilization of the free peasants in case of war. After the *Norman Conquest, the institution was reformed to include the duties of the Norman viscount, the representative of the duke in the counties of the duchy. Thus, the S. became invested with judicial authority; he was responsible for dispensing royal justice in the shire, for maintaining order, for administering the royal direct possessions (as opposed to the lands enfeoffed to other vassals) and for collecting taxes. During the reigns of *Henry I and *Henry II the position of S. was firmly defined and set. It was customary to appoint Ss. from among vassals of the lesser nobility, who were thus dependent on the king. The S. presided over the assemblies of the shire and the *hundred and was responsible to the *justiciars and to the court of the *exchequer. With the establishment of the jury. he presided over this institution as well.
B. Lyon, *A Constitutional and Legal History of Medieval England* (1960).

SHERIRA GAON (c. 910-1006) *Gaon of Pumbedita (Mesopotamia). Member of the *exilarch's family, he was recognized as a scholar and in 968 became gaon, after a period in which the Academy of Pumbedita (situated in Baghdad since the preceding century) had undergone a crisis. S. reformed the academy and strengthened its authority over the Jewish communities spread over the world at a time when new centres of Jewish learning began to strive for autonomy. S. was reputed for his vast knowledge of the Talmud, as reflected in his *responsa*. In 987 he wrote the *Iggereth Rav Sharira Gaon* (The Letter of R. S. Gaon), a treatise on the history of Jewish learning, describing the Babylonian centre in particular.
S. W. Baron, *A Social and Religious History of the Jews*, VI (1957).

SHIITES Moslem sect, originally the supporters of *Ali, the son-in-law of *Mohammad. The sect originated due to certain political events – the clash between Ali and the *Ummayad family over the caliphate. After the death of Ali (661) Shiism emerged as a religious sect, opposed to the official interpretation of the *Hadith (the Islamic theology), and only accepting the *Koran. The S. gained support in *Persia, *Iraq and *Yemen and at the beginning of the 8th century were led by the members of the *Abbasid family. However, after the conversion of the Abbasid caliphs to *Sunnite Islam, the S. developed the concept of the hidden leader, who would eventually reveal himself (the *Mahdi*). The S. split into several sects, some of them radical, such as the *Karmatians of Eastern Arabia and the *Ismailis. In the 10th century, leadership of the sects passed to the *Fatimids, but their authority was not universally accepted and the radical S. continued their separate activity in the eastern part of the caliphate, making use of propaganda and even terror (*Assassins). Their power was diminished in the 12th century by the *Zengid sultans and was politically destroyed by the *Mongols in the 13th century. In Persia, however, their spiritual leader maintained authority over the population.
CHI.

SHIPS Due to the diversity of medieval civilization, a large variety of S. were used in the Middle Ages, only a portion of which had been part of the shipping industry in antiquity. S. were concentrated in the Mediterranean Sea; the main characteristic of these vessels was that they were flat-bottomed, adapted mainly for coastal navigation and offering larger quarters for cargo and passengers. Ancient (Greek and Roman) methods of shipbuilding continued to be used by the *Byzantines and *Vandals at the beginning of the Middle Ages and were further developed by the Islamized peoples in the 7th-10th centuries. From the 10th century on, modifications of such S. were used by the *Italian cities, mainly Amalfi, Pisa, Genoa and later Venice, while a slightly different form, the fishing boat, was found in most other countries. The Italian vessel, which was divided into a cargo hold and an upper deck meant for use by travellers, merchants and lords who occasionally sailed, was also adopted by other Christian maritime communities, especially *Catalonia, *Languedoc and *Provence. From the 13th century on, certain changes were made in shipbuilding to allow for navigation in the open sea; in particular, the sails were improved and an observation tower was added. In the northern seas, Roman methods of shipbuilding were maintained until the 8th century, but were gradually replaced by the construction of *Viking vessels. The latter underwent many modifications up to the 9th century due to the changeover from vessels meant for coastal navigation to the typical long and narrow boats designed to traverse the seas and even the ocean. A modified version of the Viking S. became commonly used in northern Europe, especially in England and Normandy and by members of the German *Hanse. Progress in river navigation led to the construction of flat river boats containing one hold.

Outside Europe, the boats of China and India sailed in the eastern seas and were used to ship cargo, for fishing and to transport passengers.
C. Singer, *A History of Medieval Technology* (1955).

SHIRAZ City in *Persia. One of the most famous centres of ancient Persia, S. declined after the Arab conquest (747). In the 9th century the dynasty of the Buwayhids (945-1055), which imposed its authority over the caliphate by appointing and dismissing rulers, established its capital in the city. As a result, S. became a Moslem-Persian cultural centre, rivalling *Baghdad. Under the *Mongols its prosperity continued, as the khans built palaces and mosques. During this period the city was also a reputed literary and art centre, where the Moslem form of the miniature was perfected.

SHIRE An administrative unit within the *English realm, corresponding to the continental county, but not to be confused with the earldom. The difference between the two had already been defined in the Anglo-Saxon period. The earldom was ruled by an *earl, while the S. belonged to the royal administration and was ruled by local assemblies presided over by a royal *sheriff. After the *Norman conquest, the Ss. represented territorial units while earldoms, with very few exceptions, included certain parts of several Ss. At this stage, the S. also became a social entity containing its own courts presided over by the sheriff of the free-men. Participation in these courts was limited to tenants or holders of an estate which rendered a minimum annual income of 20 pounds, corresponding to the revenue of a knight. From the 13th century on, representatives of *boroughs also participated in the S. courts. Thus, the S. became the essential unit of local government in England and, from the reign of *Edward I, provided the basic representation of the gentry and commons in the *Parliament.

B. Lyon, *A Constitutional and Legal History of Medieval England* (1960).

SHIRQUH, ASAD-AL-DIN (d. 1169) Moslem general. Of Kurdish origin, he was the uncle of *Saladin and served in *Nureddin's army in Syria. In 1168 he was sent to Egypt to help defend it against the *Crusaders. As a result he became vizier and the virtual ruler of the *Fatimid caliphate.

SHISHMAN (ŠISMAN) *Bulgarian dynasty (13th-14th centuries). Lords in eastern Bulgaria, they claimed the throne in 1246 and from 1271 assumed the royal title. Under their rule Bulgaria declined and in the 14th century became a vassal state of *Serbia. After 1371 the S. led the Bulgarian resistance against the *Turks, but were defeated at *Kossovo (1387). As a result, they lost their throne and realm to *Bayazid I.

SICARD (1160-1215) Bishop of *Cremona (1185-1215). Born at Cremona, S. was prepared for an ecclesiastical career. In *c.* 1179 he assisted Emperor *Frederick Barbarossa in Lombardy, proving himself politically able. Rewarded for his services, he was appointed canon of Mainz in 1183 and bishop of Cremona in 1185. S. maintained close relations with Frederick until the latter's death. In 1190-95 S. served *Henry VI and then devoted his time to the administration of his diocese. In 1212-13, at the request of Pope *Innocent III, he became active in promoting the imperial candidacy of *Frederick II. S. also wrote a chronicle which covered events up to 1213; his description of the *Crusade of Barbarossa became a classic.

P. Munz, *Frederick Barbarossa* (1957).

SICILIAN VESPERS A revolt against the authority of *Charles of Anjou which broke out in Sicily in 1282, with the help of King *Peter II of Aragon. The revolt was so named because it erupted at the hour of vespers. The S. was in reaction to the conquest of the island in 1266 and the fall of the *Hohenstaufen dynasty. It was led by counsellors and former ministers of King *Manfred, who remained faithful to his daughter, Constance, wife of the king of Aragon. Support among the local population did not materialize, however, until after a series of repressive actions taken by Charles, who favoured the merchants of Provence and used Sicily merely as a source of royal revenues. The Angevin government in the island fell and Charles' efforts to crush the uprising failed, despite the fact that he was supported by the papacy and by his nephew, King *Philip III of France. Peter II was proclaimed king of Sicily on the condition that he administer it according to its own laws, treating it as a separate realm.

S. Runciman, *The Sicilian Vespers* (1957).

SICILY Island in the Mediterranean Sea and medieval kingdom. In 442 S. was invaded by the *Vandals of north Africa and annexed to their realm. By means of the conquest, the Vandals cut off the wheat supply to Rome. In 535 *Belisarius conquered the island, which became a Byzantine province and prospered due to its location in the Mediterranean Sea. Byzantine rule lasted until the 9th century; in 827 the *Aghlabids of

Tunis invaded the island and began its conquest. As an Arab province, S. was provided with a government of emirs, presided over by the commander of the fleet (*emir al-bahr,* gradually changed to *amiral* by the population). During the period of Arab rule, Moslems settled in the island, and the ethnic, social and religious structure of the population became pluralistic, including Catholics, Greeks, Moslems and Jews. Commercial ties with Italy and western Europe and with north Africa and the Moslem world were strengthened and the city of *Palermo gradually gained international prestige. In order to restore Christian rule on the island and in accordance with agreements reached with Pope *Leo IX in 1154, the Norman leader, *Robert Guiscard, undertook the task of conquering S. He commissioned his younger brother, *Roger I, for that purpose, granting him the title of count of S. (1061-1101). Roger invaded the island in 1061; in 1070 he succeeded in capturing Palermo but conquest of the entire island was not achieved until 1091. In keeping with Robert's arrangements, S. became one of the fiefs of the Norman duchy of southern Italy. However, at the beginning of the 12th century, the senior branch of *Hauteville princes on the Continent proved themselves incapable of reigning; at the same time, Count *Roger II, the younger son of Roger I, extended his authority, conquering the Hauteville dominions and annexing them to his Sicilian state by 1127. In 1130, in return for his support to the papal candidacy of *Anacletus II, Roger was granted the title of king of S.

Roger II (1103-54) was one of the greatest monarchs of the Middle Ages. He founded a powerful state in southern Italy and was able to maintain his authority even when rebellious barons joined forces with Pope *Innocent II and Emperor *Lothair III (1133-35) and invaded the kingdom. Roger built up a powerful naval force and attacked north Africa, conquering the coastal area from *Tunis to *Tripoli. In the East he invaded the Byzantine empire, raiding *Athens and *Thebes and establishing his army in the Albanian area. Roger also proved himself to be an excellent organizer of his pluralistic regime. He allowed the Moslems of S., like the *Lombards in southern Italy, to observe their own laws, while seeing to it that the feudal customs of the Norman conquerors were respected. The royal chancery became a multilingual office, where documents were issued in Latin, Greek and Arabic. Roger modelled his government after the Byzantine system, instituting a non-feudal body of officials and magistrates, which allowed them wide powers. The *amiral* became the chief minister and an adaptation of the Byzantine *duana* administered the finances. In order to keep a firm hold on the power of the nobility, Roger compiled the *Catalogus Baronum,* in which their duties were set down. Roger's reign brought economic prosperity, especially to the cities. The capital, Palermo, developed tremendously and became the centre of a thriving silk industry, among others, as well as a commercial centre. Its wealth became legendary in the West; the revenues of the city alone in 1155 were greater than those of the whole kingdom of England. In terms of culture S. became the junction of East and West, where Greek and Arabic works were translated into Latin. Roger also encouraged the development of the arts. His palace in Palermo, containing the famous chapel, was built in a combination of Romanesque, Byzantine and Arabic styles. In addition, the new cathedral of *Monreale, near Palermo, was greatly praised by visitors.

Although S. remained the most organized and one of the most powerful states in Europe in the second half of the 12th century, Roger's death led to a certain decline. An important event at this time was the marriage of Roger's daughter, Constance, to *Henry VI (1188), heir to *Frederick Barbarossa; the alliance was intended to represent the peace established with the *Holy Roman empire after a century of enmity. It was not foreseen, however, that Constance would inherit the Sicilian throne since her nephew, King *William II, was young and expected to have immediate heirs of his own. Assured of peace in Italy, William decided to continue his grandfather's policy in the East by invading Byzantium (1185). He also prepared an expedition against Egypt, but died childless in 1192 before the plan could be carried out. Succession to the throne was disputed between *Tancred of Lecce, the illegitimate grandson of Roger II, and Henry VI, Constance's husband. Henry conquered S. in 1194 and established an administration of German *ministeriales, headed by *Markward of Anweiler. In 1197, when Henry died, Markward became regent for the infant heir, Frederick-Roger (*Frederick II), who in 1198 also lost his mother Constance. In accordance with feudal law (since the agreements of 1054), the pope, as overlord of the kingdom, became the guardian of the new king. *Innocent III took advantage of this privilege to encourage the separation of the Holy Roman empire. The events in Germany, however, made him change his mind and in 1212 he supported Frederick's candidacy.

Frederick, although born and educated at Palermo, was an Italian prince. His reign (1197-1250) marked the golden age of S. and in many ways was similar to that of Roger II. The court of Palermo once again became one of the most notable political and cultural centres of Europe; Frederick's tolerance of Christians, Moslems and Jews alike attracted men of all religions to his court. The continuous wars against the papacy in Italy did not affect the prosperity of the Sicilian kingdom nor the fidelity of the populace to Frederick. Frederick's rule was marked by a strongly centralized government; his legal code, the Constitutions of *Melfi (1231) reflected an enlightened absolutist regime. The king virtually became the sole source of authority and the governmental machinery, both on central and local levels, was transformed into a bureaucratic body of magistrates. The privileges of the nobility and of the cities were curtailed and strictly controlled by royal agents. Frederick's death dealt a serious blow to the kingdom, despite the fact that his illegitimate son, *Manfred (regent for his half-brother, 1250-54, and king 1254-66), continued to maintain authority. Manfred's claim to the throne was opposed by the papacy and, following the unsuccessful candidacy of Edmund, son of *Henry III of England, *Charles of Anjou, count of Provence and brother of King *Louis IX of France, was chosen king by Pope *Urban IV (1264). Charles' victories (1266, 1268) in S. not only instituted a dynastic change (coinciding with the death of Manfred and the murder of *Conradin) but also marked a new era in the history of the Sicilian kingdom.

Charles' reign outwardly appeared to be a continuation of the traditional policy of the Sicilian monarchy; Sicilian interests in the Mediterranean (Greece, the *Crusaders' states and north Africa) were looked after. However, Palermo ceased to be the true centre of the Sicilian realm, and Charles ruled from the northern provinces, so that the former capital's prosperity was sacrificed to the interests of the Provençal cities, such as *Marseilles. Bankers of *Lombardy and *Tuscany, who had financed Charles' conquest, were given vast incomes and leading positions within the kingdom. Thus, dissent against the Angevin government gradually developed and exploded in 1282 at Palermo, where the revolt of the *Sicilian Vespers marked the end of Angevin domination in the island. The Sicilian rebels then proclaimed *Peter III of Aragon king of S. The war that ensued lasted until 1302 and involved S., *Naples, *Aragon, *France and the papacy. The Angevin attempts to recover S., backed by the papacy and France, failed, although *Aragon and S. became separated and were ruled by two different branches of the house of Aragon. In 1302 the Peace of *Caltabellotta was reached, recognizing the separation of the kingdom of S. (also named "Trinacria") and Angevin Naples. The long war had destroyed the fruits of the work effected by Roger II and had brought both countries to decline. S. became politically subordinate to the Aragonese kingdom in the 14th and 15th centuries and was economically dominated by *Catalan interests. The *Black Death added its share to the kingdom's decline. Thus, when S. was reunited in 1409 with Aragon, it was a poor and backward province whose Norman and Hohenstaufen structures remained the only legacy of a glorious past.

J. J. Norwich, *The Normans in the South* (1967);
S. Runciman, *The Sicilian Vespers* (1957).

SIDON City in the coastal area of *Syria, which belonged to the first *Palestine province under the Byzantine administration. In 565 it was destroyed by an earthquake and was only partially rebuilt. The city was conquered by the Arabs in 638 and became part of the *Ummayad caliphate. S. remained a provincial town during the Arab period, but after its conquest by the *Fatimids (994) a local dynasty of emirs was established. Conquered in 1110 by the *Crusaders, it became the capital of one of the most important feudal baronies of the Latin kingdom of Jerusalem. A bishopric was established in the city, which became an ecclesiastical centre in the 13th century. In 1268 S. was conquered by the *Mamelukes and subsequently declined.

J. Prawer, *The Crusaders* (1973).

SIEGFRIED The legendary hero of the *Nibelungenlied.*

SIENA City in Tuscany, Italy. Part of the feudal principality of *Tuscany, S. gained its freedom at the beginning of the 12th century, but lords of southern Tuscany seized power in the city government. In 1147, after a short struggle, the guilds proclaimed the establishment of a republic and S. came under the rule of an aristocratic body of wealthy merchants. In the 13th century the city became one of the centres of international banking, thanks to the activities of the *Buonsignori. At this time it began to rival *Florence, and the two cities continued to struggle for supremacy in the later Middle Ages, S. being run by *Ghibellines. In the 14th century the city extended its domination over the southern part of Tuscany. In the second half of that century and until the beginning of the 15th, it became one of the most important centres of Italian painting. The Sienese school developed new styles of painting and adopted the colours and forms of Byzantine art.

D. Waley, *The Italian City Republics* (1969).

SIETE PARTIDAS The constitutional code of *Castile, issued by King *Alfonso X (1261).

SIGEBERT I (535-75) King of the *Franks (561-75). Son of *Clotaire I, S. ruled over Austrasia and established his capital at Metz, so as to be able to fight in Germany against the *Avars. In 566 he married the Visigothic princess, *Brunhilda, and consequently entered a series of conflicts with his brother, *Chilperic I, accused of the murder of Brunhilda's sister. S. was murdered by agents of *Fredegund; this act initiated a period of instability in the kingdom, mainly due to the revenge sought by Brunhilda (575-613).

J. M. Wallace-Hadrill, *The Long-Haired Kings* (1963).

SIGEBERT II (c. 601-56) King of the *Franks (634-56). Appointed by *Brunhilda, he was captured and murdered by *Clotaire II.

SIGEBERT III (631-56) King of the *Franks (634-56). S. was the son of *Dagobert I, who made him ruler of *Austrasia. During most of his reign, S. was under the tutelage of *Grimoald, mayor of the palace.

SIGEBERT OF GEMBLOUX (c. 1030-1112) Chronicler. Born in Brabant, he became a monk at the *Benedictine monastery of Gembloux and received a broad education at Liège. At the end of the 11th century he began to write a universal chronicle with the aim of explaining the common basis of Christian civilization in western Europe, as heir of Rome and the Bible. While he merely compiled the material dealing with the earlier periods, his selection of events marked a significant historiological approach. Furthermore, the account of contemporary events that he gave has been proved to be extremely accurate. S.'s *chronicle became an authoritative source utilized by many chroniclers of the 12th century.

J. W. Thompson, *History of Historical Writing* (1943).

SIGER OF BRABANT (c. 1235-82) Philosopher. S. studied at the University of Paris and became one of the most influential secular teachers there. His Aristotelian studies, influenced by *Averroist theories, led him to attempt to distinguish between theology and philosophy. In 1270 his teachings were condemned by Bishop Stephen Tempier of Paris and he was persecuted. Upon his refusal to recant, he was condemned (1277) and imprisoned.

G. Leff, *Paris and Oxford Universities in the 13th and 14th Centuries* (1972).

SIGISMUND, St. (d. 523) King of Burgundy (516-23). Son of *Gundobald, he was a pious Catholic monarch. Threatened by the sons of *Clovis, he allied himself with *Theodoric, king of the Ostrogoths, despite their religious differences. S. was captured in 523 by the Franks and he and his family were put to death by Clodomir. In addition, the *Burgundian realm was annexed to the Frankish kingdom. S. was venerated as a martyr and proclaimed a saint by the popular cult.

SIGISMUND OF LUXEMBURG (1368-1437) Younger brother of Emperor *Wenceslas, he became king of *Hungary by marriage in 1387. His interests, however, were concentrated in Germany, where he held an impor-

tant share of the territories belonging to the *Luxemburg dynasty, among them *Brandenburg. In 1411 he succeeded his brother as emperor. S. convened and presided over the Council of *Constance, where an attempt was made to put an end to the *Great Schism. He summoned John *Hus to the council, promising him his freedom; however, after Hus' condemnation, S. had him imprisoned and agreed to his burning as a heretic. From 1417 S. was one of the principal leaders of the anti-Hussite movement. When he became king of *Bohemia in 1419, he led the military activities against the radical *Hussites. S. was the last emperor of the Luxemburg dynasty, which became extinct upon his death.

G. Barraclough, *The Origins of Modern Germany* (1951).

SIGURD JORSALAFAR King of *Norway (1103-30). Son of *Magnus II, he reigned jointly with his brothers, whom he left to deal with internal affairs. S. became interested in the *Crusades and in 1107 gathered a powerful fleet for an expedition against the Moslems. After passing through England, France and northern Spain, he attacked the Moslems in Portugal (1108) and entered the Mediterranean. Well received by *Roger II of Sicily, S. arrived in Palestine in 1109 and provided King *Baldwin I with naval backing. In 1110 he conquered *Sidon. The following year S. returned to Norway, where he was given his nickname (Jerusalem-farer), and became involved in Scandinavian politics. S. actively worked to spread Christianity and fought in *Sweden for that purpose.

L. Musset, *Les Peuples Scandinaves au Moyen Age* (1951).

SILESIA Country on the upper Oder which was one of the central parts of the kingdom of *Poland from the latter's foundation at the end of the 10th century. In 1137 S. became a principality ruled by a branch of the *Piast dynasty, which refused to accept the overlordship of the Polish kings. In 1157 *Frederick Barbarossa attached S. to the *Holy Roman empire and the process of Germanization became accentuated in the country, especially in the cities; the dynasty itself lost its Slavic character and became assimilated with the neighbouring German princes. In 1354 *Charles IV annexed the country to his kingdom of Bohemia.

SIMEON (d. 927) Tsar of the *Bulgarians (893-927). Raised in Constantinople, S. was a fervent Christian. In order to remove all traces of paganism in Bulgaria, he moved his capital to Tirnovo, the see of the metropolitan. From the beginning of the 10th century, S. worked to reorganize his empire. He made Bulgaria religiously independent of Constantinople, creating an independent (autocephalous) patriarchate at Tirnovo.

S. Runciman, *The First Bulgarian Empire* (1930).

SIMEON (The New Theologian; 949-1022) *Byzantine mystic. S. was a high officer at the imperial court, where he was involved in political activity under the reign of *John Tzimisces. He left the court in 977 to become a monk at *Studios. In 980 he was appointed abbot of St. Mamas monastery in Constantinople. S. developed a new theological approach based on the Christocentrism of the world and on a mystical interpretation of revelation as the divine right.

CMedH, IV.

SIMEON OF DURHAM (c. 1060-1130) Historian. S. was one of the fathers of historical writing in the Anglo-

Norman kingdom. His main work consisted of a universal history, which he was encouraged to write by *Sigebert of Gembloux. The part dealing with the reign of *Henry I in England (1101-29) is an original contribution and a valuable source of English history at the beginning of the 12th century.

J. W. Thompson, *History of Historical Writing* (1943).

SIMEON STYLITES, St. (5th century) Hermit. In 433, while at Antioch, he took monastic vows. He then lived for 30 years on top of a pillar in total isolation. His figure became the symbol of ideal asceticism in the Middle Ages and was a favourite topic of moralists, both in the Greek Orthodox and Roman Catholic Churches.

SIMEON THE SUPERB (1316-53) Prince of *Moscow (1340-53). Recognized by the *Mongols as grand prince of the Russian principalities, he was given the task of raising the tribute due to the khans of the *Golden Horde. S. took advantage of his charge to increase his authority over the other Russian princes.

SIMON MAGUS (The Magician) See SIMONY.

SIMON OF MONTFORT (1150-1218) A member of the feudal family of Montfort, established at the frontier between the French royal demesne and *Normandy, he took part in the Crusade against the *Albigenses, and assumed military leadership in 1208. S. was notorious for his cruelty against the population of *Languedoc, executing innocents together with heretics. In 1209-10 he conquered the lands of the family of Trencavel, lords of Béziers, Albi and Carcassonne and became the feudal lord of a large principality in southern France. In 1213, after the Battle of *Muret and the deposition of Count *Raymond VI of Toulouse, he took the title of count of Toulouse, holding it until his death.

Z. Oldenburg, *The Albigensian Crusade* (1968).

SIMON OF MONTFORT (1208-65) Earl of Leicester. S. was a member of the branch of the Montfort family settled in England. He gained fame as the leader of the baronial opposition against *Henry III, whom he compelled in 1258 to issue the Provisions of *Oxford and whom he defeated in 1263 at *Lewes. S. headed the baronial government established in England between 1263-65.

F. M. Powicke, *The Thirteenth Century (Oxford History of England)* (1951).

SIMON OF SUDBURY (d. 1381) Archbishop of *Canterbury (1375-81). S. served at the papal court at *Avignon in the middle of the 14th century. In 1359 Pope *Innocent VI sent him on behalf of the papacy to *Edward II to assist in the peace negotiations with France (see *Hundred Years' War). His role in the *Brétigny treaty (1360) led Edward to appoint S. bishop of London in 1361; in 1375 *Richard II promoted him to the archbishopric of Canterbury. S. summoned *Wycliffe to his court in 1378 and charged him with heresy. In 1380 he became chancellor of England. He was killed in London during the Peasants' Revolt of the following year.

SIMONY Term denoting the sale of ecclesiastical office, named after Simon Magus, who attempted to buy spiritual powers. The practice of S. in the Roman Catholic Church was difficult to define in the Middle Ages, when appointment to office was usually accompanied by the donation of a gift to the authority (pope, emperor, king or prince) who had offered the position. This gift often became an annual allowance. Consequently, condemnation of S. remained a rhetorical one in the majority of cases, although the act was considered a sin. The *Gregorian reform (mid-11th- mid-12th century), however, took a firmer position against S. in an attempt to curb the interference of secular powers in ecclesiastical life. Despite the treatises written against S. and the repeated decrees, only a very limited number of bishops and clerks were openly accused of S. and deposed.

W. Ullmann, *A Short History of the Papacy* (1972).

SINAI, Mt. Mountain in the southern part of the peninsula lying between Egypt, Palestine and Saudi Arabia. From the 4th century Christian tradition accepted S. as the site of God's revelation to Moses and the giving of the Ten Commandments, as well as the refuge of the prophet Elijah. Consequently, monastic communities were established in the area. From the 6th century, when St. Catherine's Monastery was founded, these communities became subordinate to its abbot, who was often known as the patriarch of S. After the Arab conquest, S. belonged to the see of Alexandria and flourished as a scholarly-exegetical centre, as its library attests. The *Crusaders claimed sovereignty over the abbey in the 12th century and appointed Catholic abbots, who, however, resided in the Latin kingdom of Jerusalem.

SINBAD THE SAILOR Arabic popular tale of the 11th century and name of its hero. A sailor and adventurer, S. became the hero of numerous popular ballads and tales, united into a single story at Baghdad. The tales were based on the experiences of navigators during the *Abbasid period; hence, the story contains a popular description of various Asian countries S. was said to have visited.

R. Guillaume, *The Heritage of Islam* (1931).

SINIUS (9th century) *Varangian leader. S. was one of the Swedish chieftains who settled in Russia and raided Constantinople. According to Russian tradition, he was one of *Rurik's brothers and conquered *Novgorod (885) together with him.

SIS City in Cilicia in southeastern Anatolia and the capital of Lesser *Armenia.

SISEBUT King of the Visigoths (612-21). S. united the Iberian peninsula under *Visigothic rule by conquering tribal Cantabria (modern *Asturias) and by ending Byzantine domination in southern Spain. A fervent Catholic, he persecuted the *Jews and attempted to convert them to the Christian faith. S. also distinguished himself as one of the rare Germanic rulers who were writers; his book, a life of St. *Desiderius, was dedicated to *Isidore of Seville.

SIVAS City in Anatolia. Conquered by the *Seljuk Turks in 1071, it became a provincial capital of the Seljuk sultanate of *Konya. In the middle of the 13th century it was conquered by a Turkoman tribe and became the capital of an independent principality, which was destroyed by the Ottoman Turks under *Bayazid in 1392.

SKYLITZES, JOHN (11th century) Byzantine chronicler. S. received his education at the Academy of Constantinople and was employed at the imperial court, where he won the favour of *Constantine X Ducas and his son, *Michael VII. Promoted to high dignities, he had free access to the imperial archives. His chronicle, a continuation of *Theophanes' work, covers the years

The Gospel of St. John, from the Codex Sinaiticus, *a 4th-century manuscript found at Mount Sinai.*

811-1079 and is an excellent account of the Macedonian dynasty and the civil wars of the second half of the 11th century.

CMedH, IV.

SLAVERY Adopted from ancient times, when it had been the economic basis of the social structure, the character of S. changed in the various medieval societies, although it continued to work along traditional lines in Black Africa and in civilizations of the Far East. In the Moslem countries, its functions varied, and in Europe S. declined and eventually disappeared. This article will deal only with European and Islamic S.

The economic crisis of the 2nd century which led to the decline and fall of the Roman empire had been largely due to lack of war prisoners and a short supply of slaves. In the 4th and 5th centuries this type of labour became very expensive and, from the beginning of the Middle Ages, it became more profitable to use *serfs than to keep slaves. In addition, the teachings of the Church opposed the use of Christian slaves on moral and religious grounds. Consequently, S. gradually disappeared in western Europe, although it continued to persist to a limited extent until the 11th century and was generally practised in outlying regions, such as Anglo-Saxon England, Scandinavia and Spain. Slaves were originally brought from the Slavonic countries, where many of them had been captured by Scandinavians and sold at the markets, hence the origin of the term "slave" in the European languages. With the establishment of feudal practices and the conversion of the Slavs to the Christian faith, S. ceased to exist in Europe.

In the Moslem societies S. was practised on two different levels. Black Africans and captives were employed in the palaces or worked on the great estates. Peoples from the central Asian and European steppes, on the other hand, were mobilized into the army as *Mamelukes. This latter practice began in the 9th century, when the bulk of the Arab population of the caliphate was civilian. Although the Mamelukes (most being of Turkish stock) were considered slaves, they gradually reached commanding positions and eventually gained control of the caliphate and of the Moslem world (11th century).

M. Bloch, *Land and Work in Medieval Europe* (1968).

SLAVS The common name of a number of tribes of Indo-European origin, who were settled at the beginning of the Middle Ages in the Pripet area, west of the Dnieper River, towards the Carpathian Mountains.

After the great Germanic invasions, these tribes migrated westwards and southwards, having been dislodged from their original territory by the *Avars in the 6th and 7th centuries. They settled in the frontier areas of the Byzantine and German worlds. In the 7th century these people were divided into three main groups: the western S., including *Polish, *Bohemian and *Moravian tribes, as well as a group of tribes which settled between the Oder and Elbe rivers (Obodrites, Sorbs, Wends and Pomeranians); the southern S., who became partially assimilated with the *Bulgars (creating the Bulgarian people), and included the *Serbs, *Croats and *Slovenes who invaded the Balkan peninsula in the 8th century and reached Greece; and the eastern S., such as the Russians, Ukrainians and Ruthenes, who were organized by the Scandinavian *Varangians into the state of *Russia at the end of the 9th century. In the 9th century the S. began to become politically organized and founded their own states. The process of Christianization was begun at this time and was achieved in the 11th century by the Catholic and Orthodox missionaries.
L. Musset, *Les Invasions, Seconde Vague* (1968).

SLOVAKS Group of *Slav tribes, which settled south of the western chain of the Carpathian Mountains in the 7th century and became part of the *Avar realm. They later migrated towards the Danube River in the northern part of modern Hungary. After the collapse of the Avar empire, the S. became tributary to the Franks and, during the 9th century, to the *Moravian state. After the conquest of Pannonia by the *Hungarians, they were pushed northwards and came under the domination of Hungarian nobles.

SLOVENES *Slav tribes which settled in the southwestern part of the *Avar state in the 7th century. In the 8th-10th centuries their main settlements were in the eastern provinces of present-day Austria. The majority of S. were Germanized in the 11th and 12th centuries; only the southern group, located in present-day northwestern Yugoslavia, preserved their ethnic character. However, these southern S. were not politically organized and fell under the domination of *Frankish and Italian lords.

SLUIS, BATTLE OF Naval battle between the French and the English fleets at the beginning stages of the *Hundred Years' War. The English victory (1339) enabled *Edward I to establish English naval supremacy and to invade France.

SLUTER, CLAUS (c. 1345-1405) Sculptor. A native of the Low Countries S. became one of the leading personalities of the Flemish school of art of the second half of the 14th century. Employed by *Philip the Bold, duke of Burgundy, his most famous work was the dukes's tomb, installed in the Carthusian monastery of *Champmol (Burgundy), which became the leading piece of late Gothic sculpture.
W. Voge, *Bildhauer des Mittelalters* (1950).

SMARAGDUS (9th century) Scholar. Originally from Ireland, he settled in the *Carolingian empire and became abbot of Saint-Mihiel at Verdun in 819. S. wrote a treatise on Latin grammar and works commenting on the rule of St. *Benedict. He was considered one of the leading intellectuals during the reign of *Louis the Pious.
H. W. Laistner, *Thought and Letters in Western Europe, 500-900* (1947).

SMOLENSK City in central *Russia on the Dnieper River. Its location near the Valdai plateau, connecting the Baltic Sea routes to the Dnieper and the Black Sea, ensured S. prosperity in the 9th century. Between 890-900 it was conquered by the *Rurikids and became part of the principality of *Novgorod and, from the 10th century, of *Kiev. In the 12th century a principality, ruled by a cadet branch of the Rurikid dynasty, established itself in the city. When Kiev began to decline, the princes of S. played a more important role in Russian affairs; in 1223 they led the coalition organized to defend the country from the *Mongols, but were defeated at Kalka. From 1240 the principality came under the overlordship of the *Golden Horde and the princes of S. were forced to pay tribute to the khans. In 1398 the city was conquered by the *Lithuanians, who abolished the Rurikid principality
M. Florinsky, *A History of Russia* (1958).

SNORRI STURLUSON (1179-1241) Norwegian writer. Born in Norway, he lived in Iceland and became famous for his adaptations of the Norse *sagas. His main achievement, the *Heimskringla*, is a poetic biography of legendary and genuine Norse chieftains and heroes. The work was widely read in the Scandinavian countries in the 13th century and became a model of the genre.
D. M. Wilson and P. Foote, *The Viking Achievement* (1968).

SOFIA City in Bulgaria. The classical city of Serdica declined during the Middle Ages and its name and ethnic character changed in the 7th century, when it became the Slavic and Bulgarian town of S. The town became subordinate to new centres of the medieval *Bulgarian empire, such as *Tirnovo and *Ochrida; however, under the rule of the Šišman dynasty it became a provincial capital. In 1371 the *Ottoman Turks, commanded by Sultan *Murad I, conquered S., which became the Turkish capital of western Bulgaria.

SOISSONS City in France. After the collapse of the Western Roman empire, S. became the capital of a Roman principality in northern Gaul, under the rule of Syagrius. Conquered in 487 by *Clovis, it became one of the capitals of the Frankish realms in the 6th century but gradually declined and was reduced to the centre of a bishopric in northeastern France. In the 11th century the city began to recover and grow. In 1126 a commune was established and its character became a model for the communes of northeastern France. S. was famous as a centre of ecclesiastical councils, among them that of 1419, in which the works of *Abelard were condemned.
G. Bourgin, *Soissons et le groupe communal soissonnais* (1912).

SOKE (Latin: soca) Anglo-Saxon term denoting the free tenure of land (socage) by a peasant. The sokemen represented the upper strata of the English peasantry and were not constrained to serve their lords (in the majority of cases, the king). They did, however, owe them rent and lesser work duties. In the 11th century the sokemen formed a wealthy group in the village. With the *feudalization of England after the *Norman Conquest of 1066, they lost their privileged status but were not reduced to *serfdom and remained the upper class of the peasantry.
B. Lyon, *A Constitutional and Legal History of Medieval England* (1960).

SOLIDUS (Latin: "shilling") The gold coin commonly used in the Middle Ages. The S. was minted as the twentieth part of a pound of gold, but in general it was agreed that the pound be divided into 22 parts, two of which were the share of the *mint.

SOMERSET City in southwestern England. Annexed in the 7th century to *Wessex, it subsequently became an important centre of the Anglo-Saxon kingdom. After the *Norman Conquest the city continued to develop and a castle was built there in the 12th century and became the centre of an earldom.

SOPHRONIUS, St. (560-638) Patriarch of *Jerusalem. During the reign of Emperor *Heraclius, S. distinguished himself as one of the most radical defenders of Greek-Orthodox tenets in the religious disputes that split the *Byzantine empire. In 636, after the Byzantine defeat at the *Yarmuk River, he negotiated the surrender of Jerusalem to the Arabs and was promised the safety of the Christian population and their freedom to worship. *CMedH*, IV.

SORBON, ROBERT OF See ROBERT OF SORBON.

SORBONNE College at the University of Paris, founded between 1253-57 by *Robert of Sorbon, the chaplain of King *Louis IX. It was intended to provide students with the skills to develop theological thought. To establish the college, Robert bought property in the *Quartier Latin,* partly through royal donations, and their income was allotted to the regular budget of the hall and its chapel. By the end of the 13th century the college had become the most important school in the university and the centre of theological studies in the West. During the 14th century its prestige rose and the "Doctors of the S." were often consulted, as a corporate group, by popes and the kings of France on theological matters. Under the leadership of John *Gerson, the S. reached its height and the advice of its scholars on theological matters was considered orthodox. Moreover, the *Conciliar theory was elaborated in the college. P. Glorieux, *Aux Origines de la Sorbonne* (1967).

SPAHIS Ottoman cavalry, organized in the first half of the 14th century by Ala-al-Din, brother of Sultan *Orkhan. The S. was made up of specially-paid warriors who had already been trained. In the 14th and 15th centuries this cavalry earned the reputation of invincibility.

SPAIN In the major part of the Middle Ages, the term lost its political significance and simply denoted a geographical entity, identified with the Iberian peninsula. In the 5th century Roman domination in S. came to an end and the country was conquered by the *Visigoths, *Suevi and *Vandals. After the destruction and fall of the Vandal kingdom, part of *Andalusia was conquered by the *Byzantines (543). The Visigoths succeeded in reuniting S. by conquering the Suevi realm in 585 and recovering the Byzantine territories in 640. In 711, however, their kingdom fell and almost all of S. was conquered by the *Arabs, with the exception of the northern outlying regions, where Christian principalities were established in *Asturias and *Navarre. After the fall of the *Ummayad caliphate of Baghdad, an Ummayad dynasty established the caliphate of *Córdoba in S., which lasted until 1004. This period is considered the golden age of S. After the fall of the caliphate of Córdoba, independent Moslem principalities of the *Taifas were created, but these were unable to prevent the

foundation of the Christian realms of *Aragon, *Castile and *León. Nor could they maintain control over the counties of *Barcelona and *Portugal, which became Christian as a result of the *Reconquista wars. Thus, northern S., up to the Tago River, came under Christian domination. S. was invaded by the *Almoravides, who founded a strong Moslem, African-Andalusian empire, superseded in 1144 by the Almohades. Perpetuation of the *Reconquista* wars in the 13th century led to the Christian victory at *Las Navas de Tolosa (1211) and limited Moslem rule in S. to the kingdom of *Granada. The Spanish peninsula itself was divided into the petty kingdom of Navarre and the three greater realms of Aragon, Castile and Portugal. This division lasted until the end of the 15th century when Castile and Aragon were reunited under the kingship of Ferdinand and Isabella, who also conquered Granada. Portugal remained an independent realm, with its own language, culture and traditions.
E. G. Pears, *Spain* (1957).

SPALATO (SPLIT) City in *Dalmatia. Founded in 615 on the ruins of the ancient palace of Diocletian at Salona, the city became a Byzantine stronghold in Dalmatia. In the 9th century *Croatian princes established an independent principality there, annexed by *Tomislav I to the kingdom of Croatia. Conquered by *Hungary in 1133, the city continued to belong to that realm until 1420, when it was annexed to *Venice. However, economically speaking, it had fallen under Venetian domination long before its annexation.

SPECULUM REGALE (Konungs Skuggsja: The Royal Mirror) Anonymous *Norwegian encyclopedia of the 13th century. Compiled for the education of members of the royal family, it contains interesting descriptions of the earth, including physical phenomena, such as geysers and detailed geographical information.
D. Wilson and P. Foote, *The Viking Achievement* (1970).

SPECULUM VIRGINUM (Latin: Mirror of the Virgins) An anonymous treatise composed in the 12th century in the Rhine Valley, dealing with the piety and behaviour of nuns. It was widely circulated among the convents.

SPEYER (SPIRES) City in *Germany on the Rhine River. In the 5th century the Roman settlement was destroyed by the *Allemanni and was not rebuilt until the 8th century, when the *Carolingians restored it and *Charlemagne established a bishopric. In 843 S. was allotted to *Louis the German as part of Germany. S. was included in the duchy of *Franconia and became the centre of the western county of the *Conrads, who claimed the ducal title. Their descendants, the *Salian emperors, placed the city under the rule of the bishops and made it the centre of their dynasty. Its cathedral became the imperial burial place. In the 13th century S. grew thanks to the commercial development in the valley of the Rhine. Its burghers, who were in constant conflict with the bishops, joined the Confederation of the Rhine. In 1294 S. was granted the status of a free imperial city.
H. Planitz, *Die deutsche Stadt im Mittelalter* (1954).

SPINOLA Family in *Genoa. S. was one of the four noble families that dominated *Genoa in the 12th-14th centuries. According to family tradition, its members were descendants of Viscount Ido, the imperial governor of the provinces in the 10th century. In the 13th century, the S. were the leaders of the *Ghibellines in Genoa. They distinguished themselves as rulers, soldiers, diplomats, prelates and men of letters.

D. Waley, *The Italian City-Republics* (1969).

SPIRIT, THE HOLY According to the Christian doctrine of the Trinity, the divinity was composed of and indivisibly united by God, the Father, the Son and the S. Accordingly, the presence of the S. was considered by the Fathers of the Church and the *councils as the emanation of the divine in the human body. Thus, the S. was divine grace and its invocation was considered a condition for wise rule and good deeds. Decisions adopted unanimously were believed to be the voice of the S. Such a concept created difficulties even within the church, since the question as to who expressed the voice of the S. was not defined. The hierarchical view gave this prerogative to the pope and the patriarchs and, accordingly, to the superiors of the church establishment. However, in cases where ecclesiasts of equal authority expressed differing opinions, schisms often resulted. In the 12th century *Alexander III interpreted the voice of the majority (*sanior pars*, "the more sane part") as being the expression of the S. in papal elections.

DTC, V.

SPIRITUALISM The manner of life and thought adopted in accordance with the commands of the Holy *Spirit. Medieval man considered S. as detached from secular life, although a layman could reach a spiritual state through proper behaviour. Within the clerical society, observance of S. meant the assumption of a model life which would influence society. S. was largely practised by hermits and in the late Middle Ages by the mystic brotherhoods. It also led to the emergence of the Spiritual *Franciscans, who opposed the ecclesiastical order and were condemned.

SPOLETO City in central Italy. Up to the end of the 7th century S. was a town of little importance and its Roman antiquities were neglected. After the *Lombard conquest of Italy (585), however, it became a strategic part of the realm, thanks to its location along the main road between Ravenna and Rome, and between northern Italy and the southern Lombard territories of *Benevento. In accordance with its renewed importance, a *Lombard duchy was established in the city, threatening the power of Rome. In 774 S. became a *Frankish military centre and maintained its ducal status under the *Carolingians. At the end of the 9th century its dukes claimed the imperial crown. In the 10th century the ducal dynasty declined and the city fell to the rank of a provincial centre in the *Papal States.

D. Angelo, *La citta e il ducato di Spoleto* (1956).

STAINED GLASS Coloured pieces of glass, used in the ornamentation of church windows. The techniques of producing S. were already known and in practice at the end of the 11th century in the valley of the Meuse River. The work consisted of three stages: mineralogical production of colours and their isolation through the burning of wood and coal into liquid elements; the fusion of pieces of glass, between which were placed the necessary colours before the sheets became one solid entity; and the use of iron frameworks to divide larger pieces of glass within the windows. In the middle of the 12th century (1141-43) *Suger used S. to ornament the abbey church of Saint-Denis. The windows included

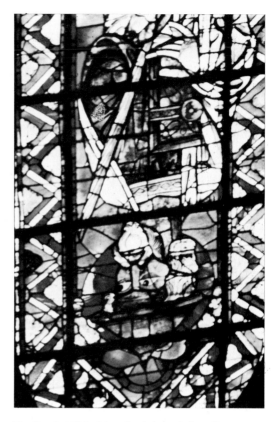

The Prophet Malachi; *stained-glass window, Bourges*

human figures and entire scenes based on biblical stories, achieved through exact use of colour and metallic background. The art of creating S. windows reached its peak in the Gothic style, especially in the cathedral of *Chartres, which became a model for other Gothic structures.

J. Harvey, *The Gothic World, 1100-1600* (1950).

STALLS The benches in the cathedrals and abbey churches used by the *canons and located around the master *altar.

STAMFORD Town in eastern *England. Nearby, at S. Bridge, *Harold of Wessex defeated the Norwegian invasion commanded by King *Harold in 1066. In the 13th century, S. became reputed for its fairs. In 1470, during the Wars of the Roses, the Lancastrians won a spectacular victory there.

STANISLAS (STANISLAW), St. (1030-79) Patron saint of Poland. Highly reputed for his piety, S. became bishop of *Cracow in 1071. He entered into bitter conflict with King *Boleslaw II, whom he admonished for his exactions. Boleslaw charged him with treason and in 1079 had him put to death. The murder launched a revolt in Poland, and S. became venerated as the patron saint of the country.

STAR, ORDER OF THE Founded in 1351 by King *John II, it was the first chivalric order in France. Its rule imposed a high standard of behaviour upon the knights, and included rules of warfare. A great part of the S.'s members were killed or taken prisoner at the Battle of *Poitiers (1356) refusing, in accordance with the order's rule, to retreat.

STATUTE OF MERTON Issued in 1236 by King *Henry III at the request of the barons, it required the *sheriffs to enclose those fields which were cultivated by the lords. While the statute limited the rights of the peasantry, it was an important factor in the development of sheep-raising and the production of wool, the main export of medieval England.

E. Carus-Wilson, *The English Wool Trade in the Middle Ages* (1954).

STATUTE OF THE LABOURERS (1351) Issued by the English Parliament in response to the shortage of manpower following the *Black Death, it decreed that no labourer could receive more than the wages that had been paid to him in 1346, prior to the pestilence. Although the parliament tried to bring down prices, this proved impossible to carry out and prices continued to follow the law of supply and demand, despite coercive acts passed in 1361. The statute created discontent among the labourers and eventually incited the Peasants' Revolt of 1381. The S. continued to be hated by the lower classes; one of the demands of the revolt of Jack Cade (1450) was for its abolition.

B. Wilkinson, *England in the Later Middle Ages* (1968).

STATUTE OF THE MERCHANTS (1285) Issued by *Edward I, in a separate meeting of the burgesses at the Parliament of Shrewsbury, it was intended to protect the English *merchants from foreign competition. The S. is considered the first act to have been passed by the House of Commons, even before its official existence.

STATUTE OF WALES (1284) Issued after the death of the Welsh leader, *Llewelyn, and his brother, David, it provided for the annexation of *Wales to the royal domain of England, its division into shires and the establishment of English law and administration of the principality.

F. M. Powicke, *Oxford History of England: The Thirteenth Century* (1953).

STATUTE OF YORK Issued in 1322, this ordinance established a distinction between king and kingship. According to the S., royal prerogatives could not be restricted since the kingship represented unlimited power. The king himself, however, was bound by the oath of coronation not to abuse the liberties granted him by his kingship.

STAUFEN See HOHENSTAUFEN.

STAURICIUS Byzantine emperor (811). Son of *Nicephorus I, he was recognized as emperor and reigned for several weeks. Because of rumours that he intended to alter the constitution of Byzantium and make the empire into a republic, S. was attacked and overthrown by his brother-in-law, *Michael I, and died of his wounds.

STAVELOT Abbey in Belgium. Founded in 651, it became a missionary centre of *Friesland. Under the *Carolingians the monastery and its school were culturally active, but gradually the influence of its monks declined. In the 13th century the abbey church was rebuilt in the Gothic style.

W. Legrand, *Stavelot* (1948).

STAVKIRKEN Scandinavian wooden churches, which were originally found only in Norway but which eventually appeared in other north European countries. The S. were built from long oak trees and had wooden roofs. They were adapted to the climate of northern Europe (12th-14th centuries).

P. Dubourg, *Les Stavkirken de la Norvège* (1966).

STENGEDINT Feudal tax paid in *Germany in the 11th-12th centuries by wealthy non-nobles to obtain freedom from service. The cities were able to free themselves of the tax as part of their urban *privileges.

H. Planitz, *Die deutsche Stadt im Mittelalter* (1954).

STEPHEN Name given to ten kings of *Serbia upon their coronation, replacing their baptismal names. A number of them are listed below:

Stephen Nemanja (d. 1200) Founder of the *Serbian kingdom (1170-96). Nemanja was one of the *župans* (princes) of the Serbs and in 1170 was recognized by the Byzantine emperor, *Manuel Comnenus, as grand *župan*. In 1180 he proclaimed his independence from Byzantium and began to unite the various principalities located in the valleys and mountains between the Danube and the Macedonian borders. His aim was realized in 1187 and the new state became a Balkan power. S. encouraged the development of trade and signed treaties with Venice and Ragusa. However, his religious convictions caused him to abdicate his throne and retire to a monastery on Mount Athos, where his son, *Sava, had already preceded him (1196).

F. Dvornik, *The Southern Slavs* (1942).

Stephen I, Nemanjŏ (d. 1228) King of Serbia (1196-(1227). Younger son of Stephen Nemanja, he was appointed grand *župan* by his father, upon the latter's decision to retire to a monastery. S. created a powerful kingdom in the western part of the Balkan peninsula. In 1217 Pope *Honorius III proclaimed him king but, due to his Orthodox feelings, he refused to accept a Catholic coronation and in 1219 was crowned by his brother *Sava, according to the Orthodox rite. S. established an autonomous Serbian Church. Following his father's example, he retired in 1227 to a monastery, where he died.

Stephen IV, Urosh (d. 1280) King of Serbia (1243-76). Third son of Stephen I Nemanja, he reigned after his brothers. S. reunited the Serbian realm after a period of internal troubles. He extended his domination into *Epirus and imposed overlordship upon the Bulgarian princes. S.'s attention was also directed to the development of his capital of Skopje, which became the centre of the Serbian national culture. In 1276 S. abdicated and retired to a monastery.

Stephen IX, Dushan (the Great; 1308-55) King (also entitled emperor) of Serbia (1331-55). S. spent his youth in exile at Constantinople, where he became aware of the decadence of the Byzantine empire. In 1331 he was crowned king and imposed his authority over *Bulgaria in the following year. Threatened in 1335 by the Angevin king, *Carobert of Hungary, he allied himself with *Venice, thereby preventing a Hungarian invasion of Serbia. This achievement allowed him to extend his rule over *Macedonia, *Epirus and *Thessaly (1342-45). His victories made S. conscious of the threat the *Ottoman Turks posed to the Balkans and the Byzantine empire and he therefore decided to rebuild the empire with the help of the Slavs. In 1246 S. was crowned emperor at Skopje and established an independent patriarchate of Serbia. In 1349 he issued a code of laws, named after himself, which reorganized the kingdom of Serbia. After a brief war against Hungary, which ended with the conquest of Belgrade (1354), S. mobilized a large army against the Turks and in 1355 conquered *Adrianople. He continued his march towards Constantinople, but died before achieving his aim. S. had given Serbia the widest frontiers in all its history; he is considered the national hero of Serbia.

F. Dvornik, *The Southern Slavs* (1942).

Stephen Lazorovish (d. 1427) King of Serbia (1389-1427). S. continued the Serbian resistance against the *Ottoman Turks, after having lost *Bulgaria to *Bayazid. At the beginning of the 15th century he was able to govern Serbia proper, despite the failure of the Crusade of *Nicopolis (1396), where much of his army was destroyed.

STEPHEN (c. 870-93) Patriarch of Constantinople. The younger son of Emperor *Basil I, he was appointed patriarch in 886 by his brother, *Leo VI, despite his youth. His term of office marked the spiritual decadence of the patriarchate of Constantinople.

STEPHEN (d. 1102) Count of Blois. S. married Adela, daughter of *William the Conqueror, and established his authority in France through an alliance with the kings of England. He imposed his rule over the counties of Troyes and Meaux and became one of the most powerful lords in France. In 1096 S. took part in the First *Crusade, but defected during the siege of *Antioch and returned to France. In 1101 he commanded a new crusade and was killed at the Battle of Ramlah. His younger son, *Stephen, became king of England.

STEPHEN II Pope (752-57). From an old Roman family, S. was concerned with the *Lombard threat and therefore continued the policy of Pope *Zacharias by allying himself with the *Carolingians. In 753 he crowned *Pepin the Short at Rheims and returned to Rome with a Frankish escort and a charter, *Privilegium Pipini*, containing Pepin's recognition of the *Papal States, including large territories between Rome and Ravenna.

W. Ullmann, *A Short History of the Medieval Papacy* (1973).

STEPHEN III (c. 720-72) Pope (768-72). A native of Sicily, S.'s papal election was opposed by aristocratic groups at Rome; he overcame such opposition by renewing the alliance with the *Franks. In 769 he assembled a council at Rome to determine the Catholic stand regarding the *Iconoclastic dispute in Byzantium. The council assumed a moderate position.

STEPHEN IV Pope (816-17). S. was one of the closest associates of *Leo III. Concerned with relations with the empire, he replaced lay imperial coronation, as had occurred in the case of *Louis the Pious, crowned by *Charlemagne, by the papal prerogative to crown emperors. For that purpose, he went to Rheims and crowned Louis again.

W. Ullmann, *The Growth of Papal Government in the Middle Ages* (1964).

STEPHEN V Pope (885-91). S. continued the dispute with Byzantium regarding *Photius and his doctrines. In Italy itself he tried to organize a coalition against the Moslems. Consequently he lent his support to Emperor *Basil I's efforts to reconquer southern Italy as well as to the imperial candidacy of *Guy of Spoleto.

STEPHEN VI Pope (896-97). His election was strongly opposed in Rome and resulted in an open revolt. Captured by rebels, S. was murdered in prison.

STEPHEN VII Pope (928-31). S.'s pontificate was deeply influenced by *Marozia, daughter of *Theophylactus and mistress of Rome. S. faithfully executed her orders, bringing the papacy to a state of decadence.

STEPHEN VIII Pope (938-42). S. was appointed by Count Alberic of *Tusculum, son of *Marozia, and faithfully executed his policy in Italy.

STEPHEN IX (Frederick of Lorraine; d. 1058) Pope (1057-58). Son of Duke Gozlin of Lower Lorraine, he accompanied Pope *Leo IX to Italy, where he became abbot of Monte Cassino. He was active in the circle working for church reform. His election as pope was effected without imperial consultation. S. supported his brother, Godfrey, margrave of *Tuscany, in his opposition to Emperor *Henry IV.

W. Ullmann, *A Short History of the Medieval Papacy* (1973).

STEPHEN I, St. (c. 959-1038) King of *Hungary (997-1038). Son of *Geza I, he adopted the Christian faith, making it the official religion of the kingdom in 1000. In the following year Pope Sylvester II, in acknowledgment of his conversion, sent him a royal crown, later named the "Crown of *St. Stephen", symbolizing Hungary's independence from the Holy Roman empire. S. also organized his realm and established its institutions.

C. A. Macartney, *Hungary – A History* (1962).

STEPHEN, St. (d. c. 35) The first Christian martyr. His cult was widely popular in the Middle Ages. Almost every medieval church had a chapel dedicated to his cult and many cathedrals were built in his name.

STEPHEN II (1101-31) King of *Hungary (1116-31). His reign was one of domestic tranquillity, enabling him to intervene in Russian affairs, as he sought to impose his lordship upon *Galicia.

STEPHEN III (1147-72) King of *Hungary (1162-72). S. was recognized by only part of the nobility, while another part supported his elder brother, proclaimed king as *Stephen IV. Only after his brother's death was he able to begin his personal reign (1165) and then was faced with the task of gaining authority over the nobility.

STEPHEN IV (1132-65) King of *Hungary (1163-65). Due to his rebellions, his hereditary rights to the throne were forfeited to his brother, *Stephen III (1162). An influential party within the nobility supported his claims, however, and brought about his royal proclamation in 1163. Defeated, he died in 1165.

STEPHEN V (1239-72) King of *Hungary. Married to a *Cumanian princess, S. was detested by the Magyar nobility, as he had brought Cumans to his court and entrusted them with high positions.

STEPHEN HARDING, St. (d. 1124) Abbot of *Cîteaux. Of English origin, he joined the monastery of Cîteaux founded by *Robert of Molesme and, after his retirement, became abbot. S. organized the *Cistercian order, wrote its rule and provided it with its own Bible, the so-called Bible of Cîteaux. The text he established by himself, after having consulted in 1108 a famous rabbi, one of *Rashi's pupils. S. also decided upon the foundation of the first four daughter-houses of Cîteaux, thus creating the structure of the order. After 1120 he resigned his position and spent the remainder of his life as an ascetic.

J. B. Mahn, *L'Ordre de Cîteaux et son Gouvernement* (1952).

STEPHEN LANGTON See LANGTON, STEPHEN.

STEPHEN OF BLOIS (c. 1097-1154) King of *England (1135-54). Son of Adela, the daughter of *William the Conqueror, and of Count Stephen of Blois, he was brought up in the court of his uncle, King *Henry I of England. In 1135, after Henry's death, the major part of the nobility chose S. as king, refusing to accept Henry's daughter, *Matilda. S.'s reign began with a long civil war, during which some of the most important barons changed parties in order to improve their situation and thus created a state of anarchy. S. was able to impose his authority after 1142, but he lost *Normandy to *Matilda's husband, *Geoffrey of Anjou, and was compelled to pass over some of the crown's power to various barons. The civil war ended in 1153 (Treaty of Winchester-Westminster) with S.'s agreement that, after his death, the crown of England would pass to Matilda's son *Henry Plantagenet.
C. A. Davies, *Stephen of Blois* (1964).

STEPHEN OF BURGUNDY A member of the ducal family of *Burgundy, he was one of the leaders of the *Crusade of 1101 and was distinguished for his bravery and prudence.

STEPHEN OF MURET (d. 1180) Founder of the order of *Grandmont. Born in Limousin (western France), he studied in France and Italy and was a hermit in Calabria before founding the order.

STEPHEN OF PISA (12th century) Translator. Born at Pisa, he was employed in its service and travelled in the Latin states of the Middle East on the city's behalf. In 1127, while at *Antioch, he translated the Arabic medical lexicon of Ali ibn Abbas into Latin. After his return to Europe, S. settled at *Salerno, where he translated scientific and medical treatises from Arabic into Latin.
C. H. Haskins, *Studies in Mediaeval Science* (1928).

STERLING BRIDGE, BATTLE OF (1297) Fought by the rebellious Scottish barons, under the command of William *Wallace, against the English army. The latter's defeat led *Edward I to concentrate all his power against *Scotland.

STETTIN City in *Pomerania, at the mouth of the Oder River. Founded by the Polish conquerors of Pomerania as an administrative and missionary centre, it was conquered by German *Crusaders in 1147 and annexed to the *Saxon duchy of *Henry the Lion. In 1180 it became the capital of the German principality of Pomerania.

STIGAND (d. 1072) Archbishop of Canterbury (1052-70). An Anglo-Saxon cleric, S. was counsellor to Earl *Godwin of Wessex, who had him appointed bishop of Elmham (1043) and archbishop of Canterbury (replacing the Norman *Robert of Jumièges). His appointment as archbishop was not recognized by the papacy and Robert continued to be considered the legitimate holder of that office. After the Norman Conquest *William the Conqueror deposed S. (1070).
F. M. Stenton, *Anglo-Saxon England* (1947).

STOCKHOLM Capital of *Sweden. The city originated from a fortification built in the 12th century at the mouth of Lake Mälaren. In 1252 the ruler of *Sweden, *Birger Jarl, founded a town around the fortress and established the political capital of his kingdom there. The religious and intellectual centre of Sweden remained at *Uppsala, however.
I. Andersen, *A History of Sweden* (1956).

STRALSUND, PEACE OF (1369) A treaty concluded between the *Hanse and *Waldemar IV, king of Denmark, Norway and Sweden, after the latter's defeat in the Hanse War of 1362-69. According to the S., the Hanse was restored to its former position in Denmark and Norway and its commercial privileges were enlarged. Another stipulation concerned the constitution of a national regency in *Sweden.

STRASSBURG (STRASBOURG) City in Alsace. The Roman city, Argentoratum, was conquered and destroyed in 451 by the *Huns. In the 6th century the site was settled by the *Allemanni, who Germanized the entire province and gave it its new name. Under the *Carolingians the city developed and became one of the most important commercial centres in the Rhine Valley. Due to its location at the crossroad between France and Germany, the city became the gathering place for several assemblies, the most famous among them being that of 840, in which *Louis the German and *Charles the Bald met with their respective vassals. Their agreement was followed by the public S. Oath, sworn in German by Charles and in French by Louis. The proclamation of the oath thus attested to the linguistic division of the Frankish kingdom. In 843 S. became part of the state of *Lothair and, as such, followed the destiny of *Lotharingia and in 925 was annexed to Germany, becoming part of the duchy of *Swabia. In 954 *Otto I made the city and its surroundings into an episcopal seigniory, detaching it from the county of Alsace and the duchy of Swabia. Due to the development of the city and the rise of the burghers in the 12th century, continuous conflicts arose with the city's bishops, who were compelled to enlarge the burghers' privileges. In 1201 S. obtained the status of a free imperial city within the episcopal seigniory. That arrangement, however, did not lessen the conflicts until the city's bishops retired to the castle of Saverne and the town reached full autonomy in 1262. At that time S. was one of the most developed of German cities and was a national literary and cultural centre under the rule of the local patriciate. The town's Gothic cathedral was a model of the period's art and sculpture. The city suffered from internal instability in the 14th century, when the craftsmen's guilds arose against the patriciate; although the former were able to seize the local government in 1332, struggles continued until a compromise was reached in 1482 (which lasted until 1648).
H. Planitz, *Die deutsche Stadt im Mittelalter* (1954).

STRATHCLYDE *Celtic kingdom in England. S. was organized by Britons following the *Anglo-Saxon invasion of England. The Britons fortified the principality situated between their lands and that of the Picts (present-day southwestern Scotland). S.'s history is marked by the constant warfare with *Northumbria (7th-9th centuries). Threatened by Danish invasions, especially after the conquest of Northumbria (857) and the Norwegian capture of large Scottish territories, the kings of S. preserved their independence by paying tribute to the Danes and by allying themselves with the Anglo-Saxon and Scottish princes. At the beginning of the 10th century the influence of *Wessex became paramount in the Celtic kingdom, which was reduced to vassalage by *Aethelstan (937). S. began to decline and, when King Edgar ceded it in 960 to *Malcolm of

Scotland, its integration within the realm of the Scots was rapidly effectuated.

F. M. Stenton, *Anglo-Saxon England* (1947).

STUDIOS One of the most famous monasteries of *Constantinople. From its foundation in 463, the monastic community of S. distinguished itself as among the most zealous defenders of Orthodoxy. Its school trained public functionaries and future prelates of the empire. During the *Iconoclastic conflict the monastery declined, as it was affected by the persecutions of the *Isaurians and by a lack of internal discipline. Reformed by *Theodore of Studios, who was appointed abbot in 799 and who introduced the rule of St. *Basil, the monastery again became an important centre in the empire. It served as a model for the organization of monastic institutions on Mount *Athos. The involvement of the monks in the political life of Byzantium was a constant factor in Byzantine history of the 9th-11th centuries, especially during crises, when the opposition of the monks of S. to certain emperors hastened their deposition. In 1204, upon the conquest of Constantinople by the *Crusaders, the monastery was destroyed; it was rebuilt under the *Palaeologi in 1290.

CMedH, IV.

STUDIUM GENERALE (Latin: the general teaching) An institution for the teaching of the *seven liberal arts which was established in most of western Europe in the 12th and 13th centuries. The S. was considered the progenitor of the medieval university.

H. Wiernszowski, *The Medieval Universities* (1968).

STURLA THORARDSON (1214-84) Icelandic poet. Nephew of *Snorri Storluson, he worked with his uncle and learned the technique of composing *sagas. He wrote the *Islendinga Saga* (Saga of the Icelanders), the most beautiful poetic account of the history and legends of the *Norse colonization of Iceland, Greenland and north America.

D. M. Wilson and P. Foote, *The Viking Achievement* (1968).

STYRIA *March and duchy in southeastern Germany. In the 6th-8th centuries, the area was part of the *Avar realm and populated by *Slav tribes (the Slovenes). Conquered in 788 by the Bavarians, it was annexed to the Frankish kingdom and *Charlemagne included it in the march of *Carinthia. Following the raids and domination of the Hungarians (*c.* 960), Germanization of the country was carried out by feudal lords, among whom the lords of Steyr became the most powerful. In 1050 Emperor *Henry III granted them the title of margrave and in 1180 *Frederick Barbarossa promoted S. to the rank of duchy. Upon the extinction of the Steyr family, the title was inherited by the *Babenberg dukes of *Austria and in 1278 S. became part of the *Hapsburg states.

F. Nabl, *Steiermark* (1960).

SUBIACO Monastery in Italy, near Rome. Founded *c.* 525 near the hermitage of St. *Benedict of Nursia, it became an important monastic centre in the 6th century. Certain future popes, such as *Gregory I, were educated there. A borough gradually grew around the monastery. In 1464 the first printing press of Italy was established in S. and the Roman print character originated there.

SUDA LEXICON An anonymous Byzantine encyclopedia compiled in the 11th century. It includes a number of biographies, and data on Greek philology.

SUDAN A large country located in the savannah areas of Africa, between the Sahara and the equator. Divided into western (near the Niger Valley) and eastern (between *Ethiopia and Egypt) parts, the country was populated by Negro tribes and located along the main African commercial routes. The *Arab conquest of Egypt and north Africa introduced Arab political and commercial influence in S. from the end of the 7th century. In addition, Islamization was begun and was especially effective in eastern S. The discovery and excavation of gold mines in S. from the beginning of the 8th century greatly contributed to the economic supremacy of the Moslem world up to the 11th century. S. also served as an important supplier of Negro *slaves, who became the main source of manpower in the centres of the caliphate. Moslem influence in western S. was weak and restricted to the northern outlying regions, where the *Almoravides settled in the 10th century. Eastern S., on the other hand, was organized within the caliphate and Arab tribes settled there, leading to the organization of Nubian tribes. Under the *Fatimids eastern S. was annexed to Egypt and its tribes made up a large part of the Fatimid army. Even after the fall of the Arab caliphates, S. was economically dependent on the Moslems, who exploited its gold, merchandise and manpower. The great empires of western S., *Ghana and *Mali attempted to acquire economic independence but, as they were isolated from Europe, could not achieve this aim.

R. Cornevin, *Etudes soudanaises* (1953).

SUEVI Germanic tribe. The S. invaded the Roman empire at the end of the 4th century, crossed the Rhine and, dislodged by the Burgundians, entered Gaul, where they were defeated by Roman generals. In 409 they reached Spain and settled in its northwestern part, corresponding to modern *Galicia and *Portugal and there founded their own kingdom. At the beginning of the 6th century they converted to the Catholic faith and began to assimilate with the local population. Their capital, Braga, became an important religious and cultural centre. After the extinction of their tribal royal dynasty, civil wars between chieftains weakened the S. kingdom, which was subsequently conquered by the *Visigoths.

J. M. Wallace-Hadrill, *The Barbarian West* (1965).

SUFFOLK, EARLS OF See POLE FAMILY.

SUFFRAGAN A *bishop who is hierarchically dependent on an archbishop. Since the 5th century all bishoprics of the Christian Church have been organized into provinces headed by the *metropolitan (in the West, archbishops) and, accordingly, every bishop is S. of a metropolitan. In the Catholic Church the pope has the prerogative of exempting a bishop from being a S.

SUFISM A mystical-ascetic trend in medieval *Islam. Under the influence of eastern Christian monasticism and its eremitic forms, S. emerged in the 8th century in *Syria, southern *Iraq and *Arabia. Christian influence, however, was limited to religious ascetic practices, and S. did not imply the breaking of family ties or eremitical retirement. The Sufis organized themselves into brotherhoods in the main cities of the Moslem world, where they gathered to study the holy texts and discuss their mystical meanings. The movement greatly expanded in the 9th century, when it reached Spain. Opposed by the *Sunnites, the Sufis were considered heterodox and were oppressed by the authorities. In the 11th century, however, the character of S. changed and a conciliatory theory of behaviour, elaborated by the thinker, Al-Rhazal, led to its recognition as a pious brotherhood within Islam.

J. W. Arnold, *The Preaching of Islam* (1935).

SUGER (1081-1151) French statesman and abbot of *Saint-Denis (1122-51). S. entered the Saint-Denis monastery while a child and studied at its school together with Prince Louis, the future King *Louis VI of France, whose intimate friend he became. S.'s administrative and political skills were noted by Abbot Adam, who employed him in various charges at the abbey and on its behalf. As a result, he established ties with the royal court, the papacy and most of the important feudal courts of northern France. In addition, he became counsellor to King Louis VI. In 1122 S. was elected abbot of Saint-Denis and worked to recover the monastery's possessions and to increase its prestige. For that purpose, he also gave strong support to the French monarchy. In response to the threat of a German invasion in 1124, he raised the *oriflamme*, the abbey's banner, which became the symbol of royal sovereignty and national solidarity. During the first years of the reign of King *Louis VII, S. retired from court and devoted all his efforts to his abbey. His administrative reform gave him the necessary funds to build the new abbey church of Saint-Denis, the first Gothic building, which he richly ornamented and which was consecrated in 1141. He also composed a biography of his late friend, Louis VI. Despite his retirement from public life, S. remained a reputed statesman, whose advice was sought by the most important personalities of his age. In 1144 S. was recalled to court, where he remained a faithful counsellor to the king. During the Second *Crusade, he was made regent of the realm and reorganized the royal finances and kept internal peace in that capacity.

M. Aubert, *Suger* (1945).

SULEIMAN *Umayyad caliph (715-17). S. was one of the last great Umayyad rulers of Islam. After his accession to the caliphate, S. attempted to renew the great conquests and mobilized a strong army and fleet. In 716 he besieged *Constantinople. The siege continued until his death, which marks the beginning of the decline of the Umayyads.

CHI.

SULEIMAN Ottoman sultan (1402-13). S. was one of the four sons of *Bayazid. When his father was captured by *Timur-leng, he seized power in the Balkan provinces, and upon Bayazid's death, he was proclaimed sultan at Adrianople. His accession was contested by his brothers, and during the subsequent wars the Turks lost *Thessalonica as well as other regions in the Balkans. S. was defeated and overthrown by his brother, *Muhammad I.

SULEIMAN IBN QUTLUMISH Seljuk sultan of *Rum (1077-85). Governor of the conquered territories in Anatolia, he was proclaimed sultan of Rum at *Nicaea and his title was recognized by the head of the *Seljuk empire, *Alp Arslan. S. established the capital of his state in Iconium (Konya). He was killed in 1085 while attempting to conquer *Aleppo.

SUNNA Moslem orthodoxy. Its tenets are based on the authorized version of the *Koran as established during the reign of Caliph *Uthman (d. 657), on the authoritative interpretation of the orthodox caliphs and on the exegesis (Hadith) of the *ulemas,* the religious wise men (or teachers). The S. was challenged by the *Shiites, the followers of *Ali, and the split in *Islam, which began as a political struggle between the Alids and the *Ummayads, turned into a religious controversy. The Sunnites gained influence when the *Abbasids converted in 750, bringing the great majority of the Arab population over to the Orthodox S. party. The theological centres of S., located in *Baghdad and Egypt, continued to develop Moslem thought even after the Hadith period of the 8th century. From the 10th century, theological learning was concentrated in the newly-founded *Al-Azhar academy at Cairo.

R. Guillaume, *The Legacy of Islam* (1952).

SURGERY See MEDICINE.

SUSCEPTUS (Latin: received) Term used in the 4th-7th centuries (adapted from the practices of the Late Roman empire), to denote a person received under the protection of a lord. It also referred to owners of smaller estates (later called *vassals and free-peasants), who were dependents of a lord.

F. L. Ganshof, *Feudalism* (1965).

SUSSEX Anglo-Saxon kingdom in southern England, between *Kent and *Wessex. According to Anglo-Saxon tradition, the kingship was established in S. after its conquest by the Saxons in 477. The same tradition relates the expansion of the realm in the 6th century. Data concerning the history of the 7th century are more accurate; S. was a small kingdom which managed to maintain its independence from Wessex. In 680 the realm was converted to the Christian faith. In 769 *Offa, king of Mercia, conquered S. and overthrew its kings; after 770 only local earls are mentioned. S. was annexed to Wessex in the 9th century and became a county in that realm.

F. M. Stenton, *Anglo-Saxon England* (1947).

SUTRI, CONCORDAT OF (1112) A treaty imposed by Emperor *Henry V upon Pope *Paschal II, his captive, as a settlement of the *Investiture controversy. According to its terms, renunciation of the lay investiture implied the abandonment of ecclesiastical lands. Denounced as extortion by the prelates, the act was abolished by a council summoned at Lateran in 1112.

SUZDAL *Russian principality, established in 1125 by the Kievan grand prince, *Vladimir Monomakh for his son, *Yuri Dolgoruki (1125-57), who brought Russian settlers to the northeastern part of the Kievan state. His son and heir, *Andrew Bogolyubski (1157-74) made the principality into a great power. He built a new capital, *Vladimir, near the city of S. and assembled a military force that enabled him to sack *Kiev in 1169. As a result, S. became the most powerful of the Russian principalities. In the newly-settled territories Andrew was not bound to respect the traditional privileges of the *veche,* the city councils of western Russia, and therefore imposed his authority over the nobility, the boyars. Discontented boyars had him murdered and his younger brother, *Vsevolod, was elected prince (1174-1212). S. reached the zenith of its power under Vsevolod. However, after his death, division of authority among his sons and the resulting civil wars weakened S. so that no attempt was made to resist *Mongol invasions. Raided in 1238, S. was reduced by *Batu-khan to the rank of vassal principality of the *Golden Horde. The princes of S. nevertheless continued their disputes until 1246, when the prestigious grandson of Vsevolod, *Alexander Nevski, famed for his victories over the *Swedes and the *Teutonic Knights, was called to the throne by the *Sobor* (the assembly of princes, clergy and boyars). Recognized as grand prince (1246-63) by the Mongols, he reorganized the principality and, as tributary prince of the Golden Horde, imposed the authority of Vladimir over the northern princes. Moreover, he made his capital into the new religious centre of Russia. After Alexander Nevski's death, dynastical struggles again divided S., which declined. In 1328 it was annexed by *Ivan I of Moscow, a member of a cadet branch of the Suzdalian dynasty.

G. Vernadsky, *Russia under the Mongols* (1955).

SUZERAIN The title given to the highest *lord of vassals, in many cases the king himself, although it was not specifically reserved for him and in no case implied any notion of sovereignty. Its practical implication was the highest lord to whom a vassal could appeal for justice.

F. L. Ganshof, *Feudalism* (1965).

SVATOPLUK (c. 830-94) Duke of Moravia (870-94). He was the successor of *Rostislav and the last of the great dukes of *Moravia. Having defeated *Louis the German in 871, he freed Moravia of *Carolingian overlordship. To halt the penetration of German influence, he supported the mission of St. *Methodius and entered into direct relations with the papacy.

SVERRE Cleric of the Faeroe Islands and king of *Norway (1177-1202). S. claimed to be a descendant of King *Sigurd. While cleric on the Faeroes, he became involved in Norwegian politics and in 1174 led the popular revolt of the *Birkebeiner* against *Magnus IV. After becoming Norwegian king, he opposed papal interference in his country's affairs and struggled with the ecclesiastical hierarchy of his realm in an attempt to integrate the local clergy in the national government. His anti-clerical policy won him great popularity, enabling him to resist the papacy and the bishops. S. was also interested in literature, especially in historical *sagas, and was a patron of poets.

L. Musset, *Les Peuples Scandinaves au Moyen Age* (1951).

SVYATOPOLK I Prince of *Kiev (1015-19). Son of St. *Vladimir, he was heir to the Kievan throne. His incompetence incited a dynastic war, as a result of which his brother, *Yaroslav the Wise, established his rule.

SVYATOPOLK II Prince of *Kiev (1097-1113). Involved in a long war of succession to the Kievan throne (1078-97), S. was recognized as prince at a conference held by the members of the *Rurikid dynasty at Lyubech in 1097. During his reign the authority and status of Kiev were considerably diminished.

SVYATOSLAV Prince of *Chernigov (1054-75). S. was made ruler of the principality of Chernigov by his father, *Yaroslav the Wise, and was second in rank of seniority after the prince of Kiev. S. attempted to conquer Kiev, but was defeated by his brothers, who demanded that he forfeit Chernigov; the decision, however, was never put into effect.

SVYATOSLAV (944-72) Prince of *Kiev (964-72). Son of *Igor (d. 945), he was proclaimed prince by his mother *Olga, who assumed the regency during his minority. S. defeated the *Khazars, who subsequently began to lose their authority during his reign. In 968 he allied himself with *Nicephorus Phocas, emperor of Byzantium, against the *Bulgarians. He invaded the Balkans and conquered eastern Bulgaria and its capital city of Preslav. Upon his refusal to surrender the conquered territories to the Byzantines, Emperor *John Tzimisces joined forces with the *Petchenegs and forced him to retreat. En route to Kiev, he was killed in a battle with the Petchenegs. S. was the last pagan prince of Russia.

G. Vernadsky, *Kievan Russia* (1951).

SWABIA (SCHWABEN) Duchy in southwestern Germany, whose territory roughly corresponded with the ancient province of *Alamania. It originates from a kingdom established in 845 by *Louis the German and intended for his son, *Charles the Fat. With *Arnulf's organization of the kingdom of Germany in the later years of the 9th century, S. became one of its duchies and was governed by appointed dukes. *Otto I had its bishoprics removed and created a new ducal dynasty, related to the *Saxon house. In the 11th century the duchy was troubled by civil wars and the power of the counts and several high lords grew until its reunification by *Rudolf of S. in 1060. However, Rudolf's opposition to *Henry IV renewed the internal troubles. In 1180 Henry appointed his relative, *Frederick of Hohenstaufen, as duke of S. and the country became the territorial basis of the *Hohenstaufen dynasty until the reign of *Frederick II (1212-50). At that time, the emperor, who felt no particular attachment to the duchy, granted large privileges to some of his greater vassals. Among them was *Rudolf of Hapsburg, who set up an important principality in southern S., which later became *Switzerland. The northern part of S. was divided into several counties and seignories. After the death of *Conrad IV, Frederick's son and heir, the ducal title was abolished and S. ceased to exist as a separate entity (1254).

J. W. Thompson, *Feudal Germany* (1928).

SWEDEN Kingdom in eastern Scandinavia. At the end of antiquity, the southern portion of its territory was inhabited by *Goths and other *Germanic tribes which later emigrated, while the north was settled by nomadic tribes of Finns. In the 4th century the Swedish realm was first constituted in the central area of Lake Mälar. This state was no more than a free confederation of chieftains who belonged to the *Thing, the sovereign assembly of the country. Despite its feeble structure, the Mälar kingdom introduced some order in central S. and enabled the merchants of Birka to develop and expand along the Baltic Sea into *Russia, where they exchanged goods in the 8th century with the *Khazars, *Moslems and Byzantines and were known as *Varangians. The Swedish kingdom became more firmly structured in the 9th century and a capital was established at *Uppsala, where German missionaries came to spread the Christian faith. During the same period, southern S. (Skäne) was conquered and annexed to *Denmark. Danish and Norwegian expansion led to constant conflicts in the 10th and 11th centuries, which consequently united the tribes. Their chieftains recognized the authority of the Uppsala kings at the beginning of the 11th century.

The 11th century was a period of territorial expansion and the kingdom of S. covered the entire country of the Swedes with the exception of Skäne. In 1020 the Christian faith began to penetrate the realm although Christianization was not achieved until the middle of the 12th century. In 1060 S. was weakened by a dynastic crisis and the *Thing* again became the most powerful institution in the country until the monarchy was restored in 1120, upon S.'s attack on *Sigurd, king of Norway. Rule was established (as well as official acceptance of Christianity) by *Eric IX the Saint (1156-60), but his murder led to anarchy once more. It was not until the middle of the 13th century, when *Birger Jarl took the title of regent and founded the dynasty of Folkung, that the kingship was restored. Birger built a new capital at *Stockholm, granted wide privileges to the *Hanse (which helped develop the Swedish cities), and began a policy of expansion into Finland. King *Magnus Ladulas (1275-90) introduced *feudalism to S., hoping, through the oath of homage, to destroy the power of the *Thing*; instead, the barons joined the *Thing* and reinforced its power, transforming it into an assembly of the nobility. In the 14th century the nobility gained overwhelming power in S. and royal authority declined. To counter the threat of the nobles, the kings allied themselves with other Scandinavian dynasties and formed the Union of *Kalmar under the rule of the Danish monarchy (1390). In accordance with the Union, the customs and privileges of S. were to be respected; however, as the Danes were virtually the most powerful and developed of the partners in the Union, they governed the other countries and exploited them. This situation incited the Swedish peasants and affected the mining industry. Subsequently, a popular revolt under the leadership of Engelbrekt (d. 1436) threatened Danish rule. The barons, however, aborted the rebellion and received the formal promise of King Eric of Pomerania to respect Swedish liberties.

I. Andersen, *A History of Sweden* (1956).

SWEYN (d. 1034) King of *Norway (1031-33). S. was appointed king by his father, *Canute the Great, who wished to create a semblance of Danish authority over Norway. S. was overthrown by a revolt of Norwegian nobles and died in Denmark.

SWEYN I, Forkbeard King of *Denmark (986-1014). Son of *Harald Bluetooth, S. rebelled against his father, who fled and died among the Slavs. S. reorganized the Danish monarchy and reinforced the country's power. From 994 he invaded *England several times and in 1003 began its conquest. In 1014 he added to his royal title that of king of England.

G. Jones, *A History of the Vikings* (1968).

SWEYN II, Estrithson King of *Denmark (1047-74). Proclaimed king by the Danish nobles who revolted against the rule of *Magnus of Norway, S. restored Denmark's independence. Due to his good relations with the papacy, he freed the Danish bishops of their allegiance to the archbishops of *Bremen and created a national church, directly obedient to the papal see.

SWEYN III King of Denmark (1146-57). His reign was marked by internal struggles concerning his right to the throne. Until 1152 S. shared the royal authority with his cousin, *Canute. In 1154 he was recognized as sole king by *Frederick Barbarossa. The civil wars continued,

however, until his defeat and death at the hands of *Waldemar the Great.

G. Jones, *A History of the Vikings* (1968).

SWEYN GODWINSON (d. 1052) Earl of *Oxford. S. was the eldest son of *Godwin of Wessex and through his father's influence, was appointed earl of Oxford in 1043 by *Edward the Confessor. After three years of administration, he was banished by the king, having seduced an abbess, and was compelled to flee to Denmark. His father had Edward recall S. in 1051, but the earl's behaviour caused him to be outlawed by the *witan in the following year. S. went on a pilgrimage to Jerusalem and died on his way back.

F. M. Stenton, *Anglo-Saxon England* (1947).

SWITZERLAND Country in central Europe. Its name derives from the community of free *peasants and shepherds of the valley of Schwyz, later (1291) to become the first canton of the Swiss Confederation. This community, whose origins are obscure, probably existed as early as the 10th century as one of the peasant groups settled in the duchy of *Swabia and ruled by feudal lords. With the organization of the *Hapsburg principality and its expansion toward the mountain areas south of the Aarau, the community of Schwyz, together with those of the valleys of Uri and Nidwalden, felt threatened by the *Hapsburg officers who came to collect taxes. The league formed in 1291 by these three communities, together with their revolt against *Albert of Austria, the son of *Rudolf of Hapsburg, marked the beginning of the Swiss Confederation. The victory of the cantons in 1315 against *Leopold of Austria was one of the most important steps toward the establishment of the new state, which included some cities, among them *Zurich and *Lucerne. During the 14th century the entire territory up to the Aar River was included in S., whose centre moved to *Bern, the capital of the greatest canton. The Battle of *Sempach assured the Swiss independence and the infantry of the cantons gained a great reputation and became an important military force in western Europe of the later Middle Ages.

See collective volume of the *Zeitschrift für Schweizerische Geschicht* (1961).

SYLVESTER I, St. Pope (314-25). Following Emperor *Constantine the Great's departure to the East, S. established the seat of the papacy on *Lateran Hill, in a villa which belonged to the imperial family and was granted him as a pious donation. In later centuries, he was alleged to have converted Constantine to the Christian faith, and the 8th-century forged document, the *Donation of Constantine, described him as the recipient of imperial authority in the West.

SYLVESTER II (Gerbert of Aurillac; 940-1003) Born in Auvergne in central France, Gerbert became a monk at Aurillac and was sent to Barcelona to study. There he acquired vast knowledge of Arab science and philosophy, as translated into Latin by local teachers. Upon completion of his studies, Gerbert settled at *Rheims, where he became the head of the cathedral school which consequently achieved great fame in Christian Europe. Besides his work at the cathedral, he also taught the future Emperor *Otto III and the future king of France, *Robert II. In compensation for his services, *Otto II appointed him abbot of *Bobbio, which enabled him to use the excellent Bobbio library for his works. In 987

Gerbert joined his archbishop, *Adalberon, in his support of *Hugh Capet and, after the latter's royal coronation, acted as his secretary. In 994 he attempted unsuccessfully to obtain the archbishopric of Rheims; he then settled in Italy, where Otto III appointed him archbishop of *Ravenna (996) and pope. In his papal dignity, S., together with the emperor, elaborated the ideology of the new Christian Roman empire and its universal supremacy. S. was also a reputed mathematician and in his earlier years developed the *abacus.

J. Havet, *Gerbert d'Aurillac, Pape Sylvestre II* (1904).

SYLVESTER III (c. 1000-46) Pope (1045). S. was elected pope after the Romans had overthrown Pope *Benedict IX. However, he did not succeed in gaining control of the papal see and was driven out by Benedict.

SYMMACHUS, St. (c. 450-514) Pope (498-514). His main efforts were directed towards maintaining his independence through a close relationship with the Ostrogothic king, *Theodoric. Aware of the king's strong Arian convictions, S. minimized the religious controversy with the Arians.

SYNAGOGUE (Greek: assembly house) The name given in Hellenistic Egypt in the 1st century BC to the *Jewish places of worship and learning, a translation of the Hebrew *beth ha-knesseth*. The term S. was adopted by Latin authors and passed into the major European languages, although in the Islamic East the Hebrew term, translated into Aramaean and Arabic, prevailed. The medieval S. was more than a house of worship and prayer; it was also the gathering place of the community, and included the local schools. Due to this function, the Middle German name of *schule* was adopted as well. The S. was generally a hall located in a larger building. Its spiritual function imposed certain requirements upon the arrangement of the building, particularly its interior, which had to include the ark containing the scrolls of the Pentateuch, the officiating clergyman's rostrum and a table for the reading of the scrolls. The benches or seats used by the congregation were arranged along the walls in Spain and the East, while in Europe the seats filled the central hall, like they did in churches. A gallery for women was also added to the main hall, either as a back room or a veiled *loggia* surrounding the hall. The interior of the S. was decorated with symbols of the faith, such as the tablets of the Ten Commandments and the Star of David. As a result of such developments, the medieval architecture of the S. became distinct from its classical prototype and, particularly in 10th-century Italy, the major medieval styles of construction (especially the Moslem and Carolingian-Romanesque) were adopted.

D. M. Cassutto, *Medieval Synagogues and Their Place in Art History* (1976).

SYRACUSE City and harbour in eastern *Sicily. At the beginning of the Middle Ages S. was the main port used to supply food to *Rome. Under *Byzantine domination (6th-9th centuries) it continued to be one of the most important cities of the island; however, after the *Arab conquest of 879 it declined and the economic and political activity of eastern Sicily gradually became concentrated in the neighbouring city of *Messina. In 1060 S. was invaded by the Normans.

SYRIA Country lying on the eastern part of the Mediterranean area, named after the city of Tyre (in Aramaic or Syriac, *Sour*), whose exact frontiers were never defined. At the end of antiquity, S. merely signified a cultural area populated by peoples speaking Syriac and extending from the frontiers of Asia Minor and the upper course of the Tigris River to the major part of Palestine. This territory, however, did not hold any administrative significance in the Roman and Byzantine empires. In *Byzantium, the Syrians were assimilated with the eastern Christians, whose cult language was also Syriac. After the Arab conquest (634-40) S. was made the centre of the new caliphate and in 661 *Muawiyah established *Damascus as its capital, bringing prosperity to the country. Islamization was especially strong in the Aleppo-Damascus areas, as well as in the cities, but affected some coastal cities and Palestine less, since the Christian-Syriac element was stronger there. With the rise of the *Abbasids in 750, S. was relegated to provincial status. There was a strong *Sunnite element at Damascus and minority groups of *Shiites were especially active in the north. At the end of the 10th century the western part of S. was conquered by the *Fatimids. Certain Arab principalities then reached a large degree of autonomy until their conquest by the *Seljuk Turks in 1071. At the end of the 11th century, under the nominal sovereignty of the Seljuk sultan of Persia, S. was divided into the principalities of *Aleppo, Hamah, Homs and *Damascus, each having its own monarchy. Due to the disunity of these entities, they were unable to prevent the penetration and establishment of the *Crusaders at *Antioch, *Edessa, Jerusalem (and all of *Palestine) and *Tripoli. Moreover, at the beginning of the 12th century they fell under the influence of the *atabegs, who inherited their power from the Seljuk princes and established their own states. One of those atabegs, *Zengi, reunited the principalities of Aleppo and *Mosul in 1028 and created a powerful state of northern S., which became a threat to the Crusaders; in 1144 he recovered Edessa. His son and heir, *Nureddin, took advantage of the failure of the Second Crusade to impose his authority upon the principalities of S. and in 1154, when he conquered Damascus, the country became united under his rule. Nureddin created new administrative structures in S., based on Sunnite Islam and its schools, and encouraged the Islamization of the countryside and the peasantry. He also adopted a policy of *jihad against the Crusaders, which was continued by his successor, *Saladin, the founder of the *Ayyubid dynasty. While Saladin maintained the unity of S. during his reign (1173-93), the country was divided among his relatives after his death and the earlier principalities were again established, their leaders fighting amongst themselves. Thus, S. fell without great difficulty when the *Mongols reached the country (1258). However, after the victory of *Baibars at Ayn Jalut, the major part of S. was conquered by the *Mamelukes, who made the country a military province. In 1321 the last Ayyubid principality of Hamah fell and S. completely lost its independence. *CHI;*

P. Hitti, *A History of Syria and Lebanon* (1947).

T

TABARI, ABU JAFAR MUHAMMAD, AL- (839-923) Chronicler. Born in *Tabaristan (Persia), he travelled in the countries belonging to the *Abbasid caliphate after studying Moslem law. He then settled at Baghdad (c. 880), where he taught law. T. is famous for his *Chronicle of the Prophets and Kings*, a historical essay on the Arab and Moslem past.

TABARISTAN Province in northern *Persia. In 818 a local dynasty which served the *Abbasid caliphs seized power and made it an autonomous principality. Inhabited by *Shiite radical sects, T. lacked stability from the second half of the 9th century. In the 11th century the *Ismailis became the most powerful factor in T., whose conquest by the *Seljuks (1058) failed to restore order. In the late 11th century it became the centre of the *Assassins, who seized the castle of Alamuth in 1092.
CHI.

TABORITES The radical wing of the *Hussites of Bohemia, named after the town of Tabor, which was their stronghold.

TAGLIACOZZO, BATTLE OF (1268) Battle in southern Italy, in which *Charles of Anjou finally defeated the *Hohenstaufen party, captured *Conradin and put him to death.

TAHIRIDS *Persian dynasty (820-72) founded at Merv (*Khorasan) by Tahir Ibn Hussayn (776-822), an Arab general who commanded the army in Khorasan and, after having served Caliphs *Harum Al-Rashid and *Mamun, became the governor of Syria. Sent to Khorasan to restore order, he seized power there and proclaimed his independence. His successors ruled Khorasan until 872, when they were overthrown by the *Saffarids.
CHI.

TAIFAS The Moslem principalities which arose at the beginning of the 11th century in *Spain and gained their independence after the fall of the caliphate of *Cordoba in 1031. Their leaders fought amongst themselves and brought Moslem Spain to a state of anarchy, which enabled the kings of *Castile and *Aragon to increase their possessions in northern Spain and allowed the *Almoravides to conquer the southern part of the country. The most important among the T. was the *Abbadid realm of Seville. (See *Andalusia).

TAILLE (Latin: tallia) Tax imposed by either the royal administration or the *feudal lords on the possessions or revenues of their non-noble subjects. Originally, the T. was arbitrarily imposed whenever the lord was in need of money; however, from the 13th century, its amount became fixed and the tax was collected annually.

TAILLEBOURG, BATTLE OF (1242) Fought between the Anglo-Gascon army of *Henry III, who claimed *Poitou, and the French army, led by King *Louis IX. The French victory caused the final retreat of the English from northern *Aquitaine and led to the establishment of the duchy of *Guienne near Bordeaux.

TAKKANOTH (Hebrew: rules, statutes) Ordinances issued by *Jewish communities, especially in western Europe, and approved by famous rabbis, which gave them religious authority. The T. concerned practical matters of everyday life within the community; they prescribed rules of conduct for relations between the Jews and the neighbouring authorities or population. The T. dealt with such areas as familial affairs (such as monogamy or absence of the husband), economic matters and social behaviour. The oldest known T. date from the 11th century and are attributed to *Gershom; they were adopted by all the European communities. The T. of the community of Troyes of 1095, dealing with fiscal affairs, are an example of community ordinances, sanctioned by *Rashi. In the 13th century the T. of the Rhenish communities were issued on behalf of a federation and were imposed upon all its members.
S. W. Baron, *The Jewish Community* (1945).

TAMERLANE See *TIMUR-LENG.

TAM, RABBENU See JACOB BEN MEIR TAM.

TANCHELM (d. 1115) Heretic. Originally from Flanders, he was probably a hermit who retired to the polders near *Antwerp. In 1112 he appeared in the city and began to preach against the established clergy, calling for piety. He was accompanied by 12 disciples and a woman, whom they considered the Virgin Mary. T. himself assumed the Christ figure. He was greatly successful at Antwerp and the neighbouring countryside. Condemned as a *heretic, he nevertheless continued his activities, preaching the simple life and denouncing the wealth of the church. Despite his murder in 1115, T.'s movement continued to flourish and spread in the Low Countries, mainly thanks to social tension. The order of the *Premonstratensians was created to fight the heresy, which was repressed c. 1130.
J. B. Russell, *Dissent and Reform in the Early Middle Ages* (1965).

TANCRED (d. 1112) Prince of *Galilee and *Antioch. Member of the *Hauteville house of southern Italy, he was the nephew of *Bohemond of Taranto, whom he accompanied on the First *Crusade. After the conquest of Antioch, he continued the march to *Jerusalem, joining the army of *Godfrey of Bouillon. In 1099 T. commanded units which effectuated raids around Jerusalem and, after its conquest, continued northwards, conquering *Tiberias. As vassal of Godfrey, he founded the principality of Galilee. In 1100 T. was the main leader of the siege of Haifa and its conquest. After

St. Lawrence and the Pilgrims; *carved pinewood relief, Tyrol, 15th century*

the death of Godfrey, he attempted, with the help of Patriarch *Daimbert, to accede to the throne. The election of *Baldwin I put T. in a delicate position. In 1102 he was called upon by his uncle to act as regent of Antioch; consequently he left Galilee and worked to establish the norhtern principality, fighting against Moslem *Aleppo. T. became a romantic figure of the crusading world.

H. Nicholson, *Tancred* (1941).

TANCRED OF HAUTEVILLE (11th century) *Norman baron. The father of *Robert Guiscard, who founded the Norman state of southern Italy and the *Hauteville dynasty.

TANCRED OF LECCE King of *Sicily (1190-94). The illegitimate son of Roger II, duke of *Apulia and the nephew of *William I, he was proclaimed king in 1190 by an influential noble party of Norman Sicily, which refused to recognize the claims of his aunt, Constance, fearing that her marriage to Emperor *Henry VI would bring Sicily under German rule. T., however, was unable to maintain his authority and in 1194 Sicily was conquered by Henry, who obtained the support of the baronial opposition.

TANNENBERG, BATTLE OF (1410) Fought between the *Poles and the *Teutonic Knights. The Polish victory diminished Teutonic domination in Prussia. The Poles called it the Battle of Grunwald.

TANNHÄUSER (1205-68) German poet. Member of an ancient Bavarian family, he was destined for a military career and in 1229 followed *Frederick II on the *Crusade. After his return to Germany, he gave up his military training and became a wandering poet. He wrote dance and love songs and lyric poetry on mytho-logical and pagan themes. T. became the hero of a popular legend, in which he is depicted as a lover of earthly pleasure who is refused absolution by Pope *Urban IV until his staff begins to bud, a symbol of divine grace. Wagner's opera *Tannhäuser* is based on the legend.

F. Tschirch, *Das Selbstverständnis des Mittelalterlichen Deutschen Dichters* (1964).

TARANTO City in *Apulia, southern Italy. Its history until the early 9th century is that of the province by the same name. In 927 it was conquered by the *Arabs and incorporated into the *Aghlabid state. Recovered by the *Byzantines in 967, it became an important commercial base. In 1063 *Robert Guiscard conquered the city and annexed it to his Norman state. Before his death, he established T. as a principality, for his son, *Bohemond (future prince of *Antioch). An important Crusader port from 1096, T. prospered under the reign of *Roger II. In the late 13th century, the principality was re-established as an *apanage for the younger branch of the *Anjou house of *Naples.

J. J. C. Norwich, *The Normans in the South* (1967).

TARASIUS (d. 806) Patriarch of *Constantinople (784-806). He was born in Athens and received a broad education. He followed Empress *Irene to Constantinople and served as secretary at the imperial court. In 784, Irene appointed him patriarch, despite the fact that he was a layman, and received the ecclesiastical orders only after his appointment. Supporting Irene's policies, T. opposed the *iconoclasts and proved an able religious leader. The wide support he enjoyed both in the church and in the state accounted for his retention of his post after Irene's fall.

CMedH, IV.

View of Taranto, Italy

TARIFA City in southern *Spain, near Gibraltar. Its strategic location on the straits between north Africa and Spain led to the building of a castle there in the 8th century. The city that grew up around the castle was fortified by the *Umayyad caliphs in the 10th century. Its conquest by the *Almoravides (1088) enabled the latter to dominate Spain. In the 13th and 14th centuries, T. belonged to the sultans of *Morocco.

TARIK (TARIQ) IBN-ZIYAD (d. 720) Moslem general. Of *Berber origin, he was the slave of Musa Ibn Nusayr, who freed him and employed him in his army in north Africa. Sent by Musa to invade Spain in 711, he crossed the straits, which bore his name ever since (*Jebel Al Tariq*, Gibraltar). He defeated the *Visigothic Kind *Roderick, conquered *Toledo and brought about the fall of the Visigothic kingdom.
CHI.

TARRAGONA City in eastern *Spain, south of the mouth of the Ebro River. After the fall of the Roman empire, T. declined, although it retained its archbishopric. Conquered by the Arabs in 614, it became a provincial capital and, in the 11th century, one of the *Taifa states. In 1092 *Raymond Berengar II, count of Barcelona, conquered T. and made it the religious centre of his state.

TARSUS City in *Cilicia (Asia Minor). Until the 7th century, T. was a famous *Byzantine cultural centre in Asia Minor, and enjoyed the prestige of being St. Paul's birthplace. Conquered in 613 by the *Persians, the city declined after its recovery by *Heraclius (629). Following the *Arab conquest of Syria (640), it became a military centre near the frontier. In 1073 it was conquered by the *Seljuks, but fell to the *Crusaders in 1097. In the 12th century it became part of the *Armenian state of Cilicia and Armenians settled there. In 1378 it was incorporated into the *Mameluke empire.

TASSILO Name of three dukes of *Bavaria in the 6th-8th centuries. The first was appointed duke by Frankish King *Childebert II (592), but managed to preserve his independence.

TASSILO III (742-94) Duke of *Bavaria (748-88). He tried to maintain his state's independence by a series of alliances with neighbouring powers, notably the *Avars, as well as by the support of the Bavarian church, which he granted large estates. To avoid a *Frankish conquest, urged by St. *Boniface, he became vassal of *Pepin the Short in 757. Frankish pressure continued under *Charlemagne, who, accusing him of breaking his oath of fidelity, forced him to surrender (784), deposed him (788) and annexed Bavaria. T. subsequently entered a monastery, where he died.
L. Halphen, *Charlemagne et l'Empire Carolingien* (1947).

TATARS, TARTARS See MONGOLS.

TAULER, JOHANN (1290-1399) German mystic. A native of Thuringia, he joined the *Dominican order and was a student of Meister *Eckhart. His thought was influenced by *Platonism and included some pantheistic ideas on the divinity. T. founded "The Friends of God", a group made up of laymen and ecclesiastics who hoped to reform the Church through restoration of the true Christian way of life. T. himself remained within the framework of Orthodoxy, but some of his pupils and followers paved the way for Martin Luther.
J. M. Clarke, *The Great German Mystics* (1949).

TAXATION T. in the Middle Ages was entirely different from the practices of the ancient world, although certain names of taxes persisted. A major change was that universal taxes were not collected and that certain groups could be exempted from payment. In *Islamic society, Moslems did not need to pay taxes, while in Christian Europe, the churches were given the same *privilege. During the early Middle Ages in western *Europe, payment in money was replaced by payment in produce or services. From the 7th century, it became customary that *vassals be freed from paying taxes, but owed their lord military service. It was not until the second half of the 11th century that direct monetary T. of the non-nobles began once again to be practised in some of the countries of western Europe and this process continued in the 12th and 13th centuries. The long period of non-monetary T., together with the foundation of *feudal structures, led to the imposition of indirect duties on goods, services and transactions. Such excises as the *teloneum*, the mill tax, etc., became customary taxes (the *consuetudines*) and were imposed on goods on a *pro rata* basis, which varied according to country and lord. Other indirect taxes, especially in the villages and manors, were imposed by the reeves, sergeants or bailiffs of the lords. With the exception of Norman *England, where royal T. was imposed from the conquest of 1066, there was no such T. in western Europe; until the end of the 13th century monarchs had to limit themselves to the collection of special contributions (aids) and to the revenues earned from their feudal estates. Eventually, however, the English and Sicilian practices were adopted by the royal courts and taxes, such as the *taille*, were imposed by royal officers. Even so, it was generally required that the monarch obtain the consent of his vassals before imposing taxes. The situation did, however, vary from state to state; in England, *Iceland and *Aragon T. became part of the actual *parliamentary practice, while in other countries, it was only nominally discussed in such assemblies as the *Estates-General or was even arbitrarily imposed.
CEcH, III.

TECHNOLOGY The fall of the Western Roman empire, together with the virtual disappearance of *slavery, brought on the cultural decline which characterized the beginning of the Middle Ages; on the other hand, it also led to a revival of T., necessary to solve the problems of a shortage of manpower, especially in the agrarian society. Two major innovations were achieved in western Europe by the 6th century: the three-field system of cultivation (*assolement*) which allowed better usage of land and the introduction of the water-*mill, which replaced human labour with natural energy. In the military domain, Oriental practices of horsemanship were adapted at the end of the 7th and the beginning of the 8th century in western Europe and led to the emergence of *chivalry. Another important stage in T. was made in the production of iron north of the Alps in the 9th century. The necessary heat for such production was obtained by burning wood in special caves, as the use of coal did not begin to spread until the 13th century. The iron which was produced was of fair quality and was primarily used for military purposes; however, it was also employed to improve the plough teams of the 10th and 11th centuries. This latter practice gradually spread in western Europe and iron was also adapted to carriages (*carruca) moved by animal power. In the 12th century the use of the wheel led to more technological advancements, such as the inventing of the windmill and the improvement of water-mills. Moreover, the use of the wheel in metallurgy enabled a better production of metal parts and pieces, needed either for masonry or for the manufacture of craftsmen's tools. The development of the textile industry was also facilitated by the use of the wheel (especially due to the invention of sewing machines). In addition, beginning in the 13th century, its use as a steering mechanism was employed in *mining. The progress made in *alchemy in the same century led to the development of chemical T., especially with regard to distillation and fermentation and to the creation of laboratories and heating systems. From the 13th century on, medieval T. was greatly dependent upon the achievements of the sciences, especially *mathematics, physics and chemistry, which allowed the adaptation of gunpowder, its manufacture in the 14th century in western Europe and its ballistic use. Despite the mechanical developments of the later Middle Ages, one of the most characteristic features of medieval T. was the use of manual labour, which remained predominant, even though sometimes assisted by animal, water or wind power.

C. Singer, *A History of Technology*, III (1954).

TEIA *Ostrogothic king in Italy (552). Elected king after *Totila's death, he was defeated and killed by the Byzantine general *Narses.

TELERIG Khan of the *Bulgars (770-86). His reign was a period of continuous wars with *Byzantium and the *Khazars. In 772 he was defeated, but renewed the war in 777. Defeated again by *Leo IV, he was compelled to submit and convert to Christianity.

TELETZ Khan of the *Bulgars (763-70). His reign, begun with a defeat by the Byzantines under *Constantine V (764), was a period of internal struggles that enfeebled the realm.

TELONEUM A tax on merchandise, imposed from the 6th century on, first in the kingdom of the *Franks and later on in the whole of western Europe, at bridges and cross-roads. The toll was imposed by royal agents (*vicarii*) who were responsible for road and bridge maintenance. With the feudalization of western society, the T. became a customary tax due the lords of the territories passed through by merchants marketing their wares. One of the most important motives behind the *communal organization of the 11th and 12th centuries was the desire to do away with seignorial T. stations.

F. L. Ganshof, *Feudalism* (1965).

TEMPLARS, KNIGHTS A military-religious order founded by *Hugh of Payns at Jerusalem in 1119. He and nine other knights swore at the site of the Temple (The *Dome of the Rock) to dedicate all their efforts to fighting the Moslems and defending the *Crusader kingdom of Jerusalem. At Hugh's request, *Bernard of Clairvaux wrote their rule in 1128 and the order was officially recognized by the papacy. The rule was inspired by Bernard's *Cistercian ideas. He praised the knights as the true representatives of *chivalry, devoted to holy war and observing the *monastic way of life. For that purpose, he wrote his treatise, *De laude novae militiae*. The order grew rapidly and was granted large properties in western Europe, whose incomes passed to the Crusader states in the East, where they kept fortresses and a permanent army. By the second half of the 12th century the knights also specialized in *banking affairs and supervised the transfer of funds to the Levant. In the major European cities, such as Paris and London, the T. held castles containing treasuries and these functioned as financial centres. In Palestine the knights adopted a radical and fanatic policy, which embarrassed the kingship and provoked the military response of Moslem leaders. In 1191 the order bought the island of *Cyprus, but being unable to pay the due sum, the island was given by *Richard I to *Guy of Lusignan. In the 13th century, the T. continued their military pursuits from their new castle of Château-Pèlerin (built in 1219), which became one of the most important fortresses of the kingdom, having its own harbour. The knights also owned the harbour at *Acre, the capital. In 1291, when Château-Pèlerin was conquered by the *Mamelukes, the T. returned to Europe, and Paris became their new centre. Their wealth caused them to be envied and they were subject to public attack. In 1308 King *Philip IV arrested them and charged them with *witchcraft. Their grand master, *James of Molay, was put to death, the order was abolished and their wealth was confiscated by the royal treasuries. In 1312 the Council of Vienne, summoned by Pope *Clement V, confirmed the abolishment of the order and decreed that their possessions be transferred to the *Hospitallers.

M. Melville, *L'Ordre des Templiers* (1948).

TEMUJIN See GENGHIS-KHAN.

TENANTS-IN-CHIEF The group of *English barons who held their fiefs directly from the crown. As such, they were justiciable only by the *peers at the king's court.

TENURE (Latin: tenura) The feudal concept of possession of land, whereby the vassal held his *fief from a lord, who held his estates from a higher lord, and so on. From this concept emerged the status of the nobility, which included those who possessed T., while the ownership of property was merely considered a sign of the non-noble class of free-men. In accordance with such assumptions, lawmen of the 14th century expressed the principle of sovereignty through the notion that the king holds his kingdom from God. The T. system was generally accompanied by the granting of "honours", such as the authority to govern.

TERBEL (c. 690-718) Khan of the *Bulgars (702-18). Successor of *Asperukh, he consolidated the implantation of the Bulgars in the Balkans. In 705, he helped *Justinian II to be restored at Byzantium. After the emperor's death, T. invaded Thrace and in 716 annexed to his realm territories south of the Balkan Mountains.

S. Runciman, *The First Bulgarian Empire* (1931).

TEUTONIC ORDER, KNIGHTS OF THE Order founded in 1198 by *Hermann of Salza and confirmed by Emperor *Henry IV. It was intended to be a fraternity of German crusading knights, as distinct from the French character of the orders of the *Hospitallers and the *Templars, and was placed under the patronage of St. Mary the Virgin. The order was patronized by *Frederick II in connection with its activities in the Holy Land as well as among the Slavs. In Palestine, the order was only partially successful. From their castle of *Montfort, in western Galilee, the T. ruled an important seigniory and were responsible for the defence of the area northeast of *Acre; however, they never reached any significant position in the Crusader kingdom and in 1268, when *Baibars conquered Montfort, their role in Palestine was ended. In Europe, on the other hand, the T. worked to spread the Catholic faith in *Hungary, but failed in the Carpathian marches. Consequently, Hermann of Salza turned northwards and in 1226 began the conquest of *Prussia, an area which was later to become the order's main base. The Prussians were annihilated or converted in the 13th century and the territory was Germanized through the settlement of a German populace (1285). The T. also gained control in *Livonia, heading an important state located on the southeastern coast of the Baltic Sea. Their attempt to penetrate Russia, however, failed after the defeat inflicted upon them by *Alexander Nevski at Lake Peipus (1243). In the 14th century, the T. were a powerful factor in eastern Europe; however, they had to answer to requests for freedom of the cities founded in the previous century by themselves and the *Hanse. Defeated by the Poles at *Tannenberg and Torun, they lost eastern *Pomerania and western Prussia in 1436 and were thereafter able to maintain their rule only in eastern Prussia around their stronghold of *Königsberg.

K. Gorski, *L'Ordre Teutonique* (1963).

THABIT IBN QURRAY (836-901) Scientist. Member of a prominent Arab family of Harran (Syria), he studied at Baghdad, where he became acquainted with Greek philosophical and scientific works. Appointed court astronomer at Baghdad, he attempted to create a mathematical system that would explain heaven's position in relation to humany destiny. His works were widely diffused in the 10th-12th centuries. See *astronomy.

THAILAND Kingdom in southeast *Asia. Its inhabitants, the Thais, originated in southern China and settled the territory of Siam in the 8th century. They retained their primitive tribal organization and, in the 11th and 12th centuries, were dominated by the *Khmers. Khmer rule had a deep influence on the social, religious and political evolution of the Thais, who, in the 13th century, organized into small principalities, under the overlordship of the Khmer emperors. In 1229 a northern principality imposed its rule on central T., creating the realm of Haripunjaya. Reaching independence from the Khmers in 1250, the Thais created a confederation of free principalities under the authority of the kings, who moved southwards. The second half of the thirteenth century was a period of struggle against the declining Khmer empire. Continuous wars led to a change in the Thais' political and social structure. The royal dynasty united the principalities, while a class of feudal warriors arose. The transformation was completed in 1292, with the establishment of the kingdom of T., based on an alliance of the kingship and the feudal lords. In the 14th century the Thais were converted to Buddhism, which became the official religion of the realm in 1405.

R. S. Le Hay, *Buddhism in Siam* (1938).

THAMAR Queen of *Georgia (1184-1212). Daughter of *George III, she is considered one of the greatest Georgian personalities in the 12th and 13th centuries. Under her reign, Georgia reached its zenith, expanding its authority over most of the Caucasus and developing a brilliant civilization. T. supported artists, writers and scientists, who gathered at her court.

THEBES City in *Greece, also known under its classical name of *Thebai*. Under *Byzantine rule, T. became an important centre of the silk industry and surpassed *Athens. In 1177 it was devastated by *Roger II of Sicily, who brought some of the Theban craftsmen to *Palermo and extended the manufacture of silk in the West. In 1205 T. was conquered by the participants in the Fourth *Crusade and became part of the Frankish duchy of *Athens. From the middle of the 13th century, the dukes resided at T., where a brilliant Franco-Italian court flourished until its decay in the 15th century.

THEMES The military provinces of the *Byzantine empire. Organized by *Leo III, the T. were established to provide efficient defence of the empire. The civil administrators of the provinces were responsible to a military governor, who commanded their armies, and the T. were obliged to provide the necessary resources for such military forces. The administration of justice remained, however, in civil hands so that military leaders were prevented from becoming too independent.

THEOBALD (d. 1161) Archbishop of *Canterbury (1139-61). A Norman monk, he was abbot of Le Bec before his promotion to the see of Canterbury. T. tried to emulate his predecessor *Lanfranc in setting up his moral authority. During the wars between *Stephen and *Matilda, he adopted a neutral stance, as part of his attempts to maintain the unity of the Church of England in a period of anarchy. In 1142, he proclaimed the *Truce of God in England in an effort to end the civil war.

A. Saltman, *Archbishop Theobald of Canterbury* (1960).

THEODAHAD King of the *Ostrogoths (534-36). His reign coincided with the *Byzantine invasion of Italy, which he was unable to prevent. Defeated in Apulia by *Belisarius, he died in 536.

THEODEBALD King of the *Franks (548-55). He reigned at Metz and was mainly concerned with the administration of his German provinces and the integration of *Thuringia.

THEODEBERT I (504-48) King of the *Franks (534-48). Son of *Thierry I. At his father's death, he was assigned *Austrasia. One of the most active *Merovingians of the 6th century, he took part in finalizing the conquest of Burgundy. In 539 he effectuated a long raid in Italy, where he defeated the *Ostrogoths and conquered the territories between the *Alps and the Danube.

J. M. Wallace-Hadrill, *The Long-Haired Kings* (1962).

THEODEBERT II (586-612) King of the *Franks (595-612). He was proclaimed king under the tutelage of his grandmother *Brunhilda. To free himself from Brunhilda's influence, he joined a revolt of *Austrasia's aristocracy in 599. In retaliation, she organized attacks against him that led to his capture and murder in 612.

THEODEMIR (d. 474) *Ostrogothic chieftain. He organized his tribe and after a victory against the *Gepids was recognized king by most of the Ostrogoths, whom he brought to Illiricum in the western Balkans. He left to his son, *Theodoric the Great, an organized kingdom with a powerful army.

THEODORA (500-47) *Byzantine empress. Raised to be an actress, she married *Justinian prior to his imperial accession. As empress, she proved to have great political skills, which enabled Justinian to overcome the

Niké insurrection. T. also had a leading part in the development of the Greek Orthodox Church and supported the *Monophysites. She patronized the revival of Byzantine art in the 6th century. T. shared imperial authority with her husband throughout her lifetime.
CMedH, IV.

THEODORA *Byzantine empress (842-56). Born to a family of officials in Paphlagonia, Asia Minor, she was chosen by Emperor *Theophilus as his wife in 838, in a beauty contest. She seized imperial power at her husband's death in the name of her three-year-old son, Michael III. In 843, she restored the cult of *icons, but opposed demands that she take measures against those who persecuted the iconoclasts. She suppressed the *Paulicians of Asia Minor. T. associated to her reign her brother Cesar Bardas, who eventually seized power, overthrew her in 856 and sent her to a monastery. The Greek Chruch gave her the title "Blessed".
CMedH, IV.

THEODORA *Byzantine empress (1028-56). Daughter of Emperor *Constantine VIII, she shared the throne with her sister Zoe. Her presence on the throne was an expression of her popularity and symbolized the perpetuation of the Macedonian dynasty in Constantinople. At her death the Macedonian dynasty became extinct.

THEODORE II, Pascario (d. 1222) *Byzantine emperor (1204-22). After the conquest of *Constantinople by the *Crusaders and the foundation of the Latin empire, T. settled at *Nicaea, where he proclaimed himself emperor, organizing his state in northwestern Asia Minor. While fighting the Latins and the rival despots of *Epirus, he devoted the major part of his reign to establishing a new administration at Nicaea and to developing his capital as a cultural centre in which the Byzantine heritage was preserved.
CMedH, IV.

THEODORE II, Ducas Lascaris (1222-58) *Byzantine emperor (1254-58). T. was proclaimed emperor at *Nicaea, but actual power was held by the general, *Michael Palaeologus, who rebelled, backed by most of the Byzantine army.

THEODORE I (d. 649) Pope (642-49). Born in Jerusalem; he was educated at Rome, where his family had settled, and joined the ecclesiastical orders. As pope, he opposed *Monothelitism and became popular for his generosity.

THEODORE II Pope (897). He was pope for 20 days. Concerned with rehabilitating the memory of Pope *Formosus, he ordered the pope's body to be retrieved from the Tiber and honourably buried. For that purpose he convened a synod to counter the earlier "Cadaver Synod", at which Formosus had been denounced posthumously and his corpse desecrated.

THEODORE ANGELUS Despot of *Epirus (1214-30). He succeeded his brother *Michael, and made *Epirus a powerful state, defeating the *Bulgarians and the *Frankish states of Greece. In 1224 he conquered the kingdom of *Thessalonica and annexed Durazzo, a large part of Albania, Thessaly and much of Macedonia. In 1230 he was defeated and killed by the king of the Bulgarians and the Vlachs, *John II Assen, who recovered part of the conquered territories.

THEODORE OF ANTIOCH (13th century) Scientist. Born at Antioch of mixed Syrian-Greek parentage, he entered the service of the *Ayyubids and was employed by Sultan Al-Kamil of Egypt as an interpreter. Sent to *Frederick II by Al-Kamil in 1226, T. joined the Sicilian court of *Palermo, where he distinguished himself as a translator of Greek and Arabic treatises on zoology.
C. H. Haskins, *Studies in Mediaeval Science* (1928).

THEODORE OF STUDIOS, St. (759-826) Abbot of Studios (799-826). One of the most influential monks at Constantinople and a very popular preacher, he was appointed abbot of *Studios by Empress *Irene. T. reorganized the prestigious monastery, where he introduced the *Basilian rule. He was esteemed in the learned circles of Byzantine society for his wide knowledge and his literary skills, as manifested in his sermons. Involved from 802 in the political life of the empire, he opposed the imperial courts' attempts to bring the Church under the control of secular authorities. His clashes with Emperors *Nicephorus I and *Leo V led to his exile. But following agitations by the monks at Constantinople, he was recalled by *Michael II (820). He led the opposition against the *iconoclasts, who were tolerated by the emperor.
CMedH, IV.

THEODORE OF TARSUS, St. (602-90) Archbishop of *Canterbury (669-90). Born at Tarsus and educated in Asia Minor, he settled in Rome. In 669 Pope Vitalian sent T. to England as archbishop of Canterbury, where he organized the dioceses and the ecclesiastical schools and assembled the first national synod at Hertford (673). At this council the organization of the Anglo-Saxon church was discussed.
F. M. Stenton, *Anglo-Saxon England* (1947).

THEODORIC THE GREAT (c. 455-526) King of the *Ostrogoths (474-526). T. was proclaimed king by the Ostrogothic chieftains of the northwestern part of the Balkan peninsula and attempted to expand into the Balkans. However, under the influence of the East Roman politicians, who were concerned with the fate of Constantinople, he altered his policy and in 493 invaded Italy, where he defeated and murdered *Odoacer, the king of the Heruli, at Ravenna. T. became king of Italy and enlarged his kingdom beyond the Alps, up to the Rhône River and the eastern part of modern Switzerland. He reached great international prestige, confirmed by a series of marriages with members of the reigning dynasties of the *Visigothic, *Frankish and *Thuringian realms, which raised him to the position of arbitration of conflicts in western Europe. In Italy he attempted to create a kingdom based on the Germanic traditions of his tribe and on the Roman cultural heritage. He appointed Italians to high dignities at his court for that purpose. Among his most distinguished counsellors were the philosopher, *Boethius, and the Roman lawyer and future monk, *Cassiodorus. However, T. displayed inconsistent behaviour and was wont to dismiss his counsellors and to charge them with various crimes; thus Boethius ended his life in prison, while Cassiodorus was exiled.
J. M. Wallace-Hadrill, *The Barbarian West* (1964).

THEODORIC Son of Strabo, *Ostrogothic chieftain. In 474 he challenged his cousin, *Theodoric the Great, for the kingship of the *Ostrogoths. The rivalry lasted until 478, when T. died.

THEODORIC I King of the *Visigoths (418-51). T. became king after the settlement of the Visigoths in southern Gaul and Spain and established his capital at *Toulouse. He dedicated his reign to the organization of his kingdom.

THEODORIC II King of the *Visigoths (453-66). He enlarged his territories in Spain and fought against the Gallo-Roman aristocracy, concentrated in *Auvergne, where he extended his possessions. His Arian policy caused him to be hated by the local populations of both Gaul and Spain.

THEODOSIUS III (d. 722) *Byzantine emperor (716-17). He was an obscure collector of imperial taxes in southwestern Asia Minor. Captured by sailors, he was brought to Constantinople and was proclaimed emperor by the rebelling troops against *Anastasius II. During his reign, the Ummayad Caliph *Suleiman besieged Constantinople. Deposed by *Leo III the Isaurian, he was sent to a monastery, where he died in obscurity.

THEODOTUS MELISSENOS Patriarch of *Constantinople (814-22). He began his career as officer at the imperial court. Appointed patriarch by Emperor *Leo V in order to impose imperial control on the Church, he was vehemently opposed by *Theodore of Studios.

THEODULF (c. 750-821) Bishop of *Orléans. Of Spanish-Gothic origin, T. settled in the empire of *Charlemagne in 788 and soon became reputed for his learning. Interested in education, T. was one of the most active members of the imperial cultural circle, where he also distinguished himself as a poet. Charlemagne appointed him bishop of Orléans, where he founded a school which later became famous. He was also a builder and restorer of churches.

G. Duckett, *The Carolingian Renaissance* (1958).

THEOLOGY The "science of God", as the term is literally interpreted, was considered in medieval civilization to be the philosophical study of religion and the search for the true faith. This study included exegetical works on the holy books, intended to provide an accurate interpretation of the texts. It also included the search for the divine path and revelation as well as for an explanation of faith as the link between man and the divinity. Monotheistic T. emphasized the omnipresence of divine grace in the universe, and cosmic phenomena were consequently considered topics of medieval theological study. The various schools of medieval theologians, be they Christian, Moslem or Jewish, differed with regard to approach and systems of study. The major split, however, was between the traditionalist school, based on the fundamental that faith is a precondition of understanding, and the rationalist, mainly *Aristotelians, who argued that understanding leads to firmer faith.

DTC.

THEOPHANES THE CONFESSOR (c. 758-818) Historian. A friend of *Theodore of Studios, he opposed the *iconoclastic legislation of *Leo V, who exiled him in 817. T. wrote an authoritative history of the Byzantine empire, covering the years 284-813.

CMedH, IV.

THEOPHANO Byzantine empress (959-69). Daughter of an inn-keeper, she won the affection of *Romanus II, son of Emperor *Constantine VII, who married her. At her instigation, Romanus poisoned his father, in order to accede to the imperial throne. T., however, took the real power, while Romanus lived in dissipation. At his death, she married *Nicephorus Phocas, who was

Interior of the church of Theodulf of Orleans

proclaimed emperor. The marriage was effectuated despite the admonition of prelates, who suspected T. of having poisoned her husband. Disappointed by Nicephorus' "Spartan" life, T. attempted to persuade his cousin, the General *John Tzimisces, to murder the emperor (969), promising to marry him and vest him with the imperial crown. The opposition against T., led by the patriarch, accused her publicly of adultery and crime. Tzimisces promptly repudiated T., banishing her to a nunnery.

CMedH, IV.

THEOPHANO (942-91) Empress of the *Holy Roman empire (973-91). Daughter of *Romanus II and *Theophano, she married *Otto II in 972, according to an agreement between *Otto I and *John Tzimisces. She made of her husband's Saxon court an important cultural centre, supporting theologians, scholars and artists. After Otto's death (983), she assumed the regency for her minor son, *Otto III, and until her death imposed imperial authority on Germany.

THEOPHILUS *Byzantine emperor (829-42). Son of *Michael II the Armorian, he was one of the chief

promoters of the Byzantine cultural renaissance. He reinforced *iconoclastic legislation, subjecting the monks to severe persecution. Allied with the *Khazars and the Spanish *Ummayads, he defeated an Abbasid army (938) and brought peace to the frontier regions. He also reorganized the administrative system, introduced financial reform, fortified the frontiers and embellished Constantinople with new palaces, where mechanical devices left a deep impression on foreign visitors.
CMedH, IV.

THEOPHILUS (11th-12th centuries) Monk. Little is known of his life and origin. T. probably came from the Rhine Valley and lived either in the area of Liège or *Utrecht, although historians have seriously considered other possibilities. His work, *Schedula diversarum artium*, probably written in the 12th century, is the first textbook on art technology and supplies data on numerous crafts, such as building, painting, sculpture and stained glass.
Works, ed. and trans. (1966).

THEOPHILUS THE PRIEST (7th century) *Byzantine physician. He wrote a treatise on diseases, in which he summed up the achievements of Greek, Roman and Byzantine *medicine. His book was used as a standard manual in Byzantium and southern Italy until the 11th century.
D. Guthrie, *A History of Medicine* (1945).

THEOPHYLACTUS (918-56) Patriarch of *Constantinople (933-56). Younger son of Emperor *Romanus I, he was appointed patriarch at the age of 15, to allow his father to directly control the Byzantine church.

THEOPHYLACTUS (9th-10th centuries) Senator of *Rome. Of a wealthy Roman family, he became the most influential person in the city (*c.* 900). He was appointed senator and, together with his wife, *Theodora, imposed a strong government not only on the city but also on the papacy. Their daughter *Marozia was the mistress of Pope *Sergius III. Sergius left full authority to T., who used his power to arbitrate between pretenders to the throne, as well as to appoint his own candidates to important posts at the papal court. After Sergius' death, he had his son appointed pope.
G. Fulco, *The Holy Roman Republic* (1962).

THESSALONICA (SALONIKA) City in the Byzantine empire and capital of the *Macedonian province. With the establishment of the empire, T. became one of its most important centres, second only to Constantinople. Its significance was largely a result of its harbour and its location at the cross-roads of the Balkan peninsula. In addition, T. was one of the most important centres of the Greek Orthodox Church, famous for its schools and monasteries. The *Slav and *Bulgarian invasions in the Balkans (8th-10th centuries) led to a certain decline in T., which was consequently cut off from its hinterland. However, under the reign of the Macedonian emperors, the city recovered its importance and became a military base for the wars against the Bulgarians. Its growth in the 11th and 12th centuries made T. the second most important city in the empire. In 1204-05 the city was conquered by the participants in the Fourth *Crusade and made into a kingdom for *Boniface of Montferrat, who failed, however, to be elected emperor of Constantinople. In principle, the kingdom of T. included the Frankish territories in Greece, but

neither Boniface nor his son, *Demetrius, were able to impose their authority beyond the surroundings of the capital, being primarily concerned with its defence against the Bulgarians, whose attacks weakened the kingdom. In 1224 the kingdom of T. fell and the city was conquered by the Comneni despots of *Epirus (1224-39). In 1239 Emperor *John Vatatzes of Nicaea, who had already been recognized as overlord in the city, conquered T. as part of his plan to recover Constantinople. The events of the 13th century led to the city's decline, although it continued to carry on trade with *Venice and *Genoa, and T. gradually became a mere provincial town in the 15th century.
CMedH, IV.

THIBAUT I, le Tricheur (908-78) Count of Blois. He took advantage of the anarchy in *France in the middle of the 10th century to establish a powerful principality, comprising the counties of *Blois, Chartres and Tours. An adventurer, robber and feudal lord, he imposed a rule of terror on the inhabitants of the Loire Valley and founded a dynasty that lasted until the 14th century.

THIBAUT II Count of Blois, Chartres and Tours (994-1004). He intervened in Champagne, where he inherited the county of Meaux and laid down the basis for his family's claims in *Burgundy.

THIBAUT III (1010-89) Count of *Blois (1037-89) and of *Champagne (as Thibaut I; 1063-89). T. was a firm adversary of King *Henry I of France and succeeded in isolating him in his demesne. Henry allied himself with *Geoffrey Martel, count of Anjou, whom he convinced to attack T. The Angevin conquest of *Tours (1044) was a considerable blow to T., but in 1063 he extended his domination in Champagne by conquering the county of *Troyes. At his death his principality was divided among his sons.

THIBAUT the Great (1093-1152) Count of *Blois (as Thibaut IV; 1102-52) and of *Champagne (as Thibaut II; 1125-52). Between 1108-20, T. was the most dangerous adversary of *Louis VI of France and a powerful ally of his uncle, *Henry I of England. The sudden death of Henry's son, William, in a storm, while sailing from Normandy to England, caused T. to change his attitude and he decided to put an end to feudal wars. He became pious, patronized monks and scholars and dedicated himself to the administration of his principality, paying special attention to *Champagne and its fairs (having inherited the county of Troyes in 1125). T. established his court at *Troyes, and Champagne, thus, became the centre of his principality. In 1135 he helped his brother, *Stephen, to obtain the crown of England. In 1140-42 a feudal conflict caused him to oppose King *Louis VII, who invaded Champagne; T. was supported by Pope *Innocent II and St. *Bernard of Clairvaux. The peace treaty reached in 1144 laid the basis for peaceful relations between the kingship and the house of Blois-Champagne in the second half of the 12th century.
G. Duby and R. Mandroux, *History of France* (1968).

THIBAUT V (d. 1191) Count of *Blois (1152-91). Younger son of *Thibaut the Great, he was granted the county of Blois. T. was an ally of *Louis VII, who appointed him *seneschal of France and adviser to his nephew, *Philip II.

THIBAUT III (1179-1201) Count of *Champagne (1197-1201). Involved in Spanish affairs before gaining the county of Champagne, he married Blanche, daughter of King *Sancho VI of Navarre.

THIBAUT IV (1201-53) Count of *Champagne and king of *Navarre (1234-53). T. was one of the most colourful personalities of 13th-century France. Feudal lord, perfect knight, adventurer and lyrical poet, he helped Queen *Blanche of Castile, towards whom he felt deep affection, during her regency in 1228-32. He also dedicated poetry to her. At the same time T. attempted to oppose the royal administration in Champagne, where he held a brilliant court. Having inherited the kingdom of Navarre in 1234, he assumed the royal title but was not particularly concerned with the realm, which his officers administered. In 1239 T. led a *Crusade in Palestine and conquered the territory between Ascalon and Jerusalem for the realm of *Acre.

THIERRY I (Theuderic I; d. 534) King of the *Franks (511-34). His father, *Clovis, made him ruler of the northeastern part of the Frankish realm. As the eldest brother, T. had considerable influence over the *Merovingian kingdom as a whole. However, he concentrated his efforts in Germany, where he fought against the *Thuringians.

THIERRY II (Theuderic II; 587-613) King of the Franks (595-613). Son of *Childebert II, he was assigned the kingdom of Burgundy and reigned under the tutelage of his grandmother, *Brunhilda. Her influence led him into constant wars with *Clotaire II of Neustria, who conquered Burgundy in 612. Brunhilda then proclaimed T. king of *Austrasia, having murdered *Theodebert II. T. himself was murdered in 613.
J. M. Wallace-Hadrill, *The Long-Haired Kings* (1962).

THIERRY III (Theuderic III; d. 690) King of the *Franks (673-90). T. was appointed king of *Neustria by *Ebroin, mayor of the palace. However, when he attempted to reign with the support of the nobility, Ebroin had him deposed (674), although he restored him to the throne in the following year. After the Battle of Tertry and Ebroin's death, T. came under the authority of *Pepin II, who proclaimed him king of all Frankish realms.

THIERRY IV (Theuderic IV; d. 737) King of the *Franks (721-37). Appointed king by *Charles Martel, his reign was nominal.

THIERRY OF ALSACE (1100-68) Count of Flanders (1128-68). In 1127 he claimed the right to Flanders, but King *Louis VI of France intervened and had his candidate, *William Clito (son of *Robert Curthose of Normandy and his ally against *Henry I of England), accepted. After Willima's collapse in 1128, however, T. received the title, enjoying the support of the cities. He promoted the county's economic activities and brought prosperity to Flanders. In 1156 T. annexed *Vermandois to the county through the marriage of his son *Philip, to Elisabeth, heiress of Vermandois.

THIERRY OF CHARTRES (d. 1151) Philosopher. Brother of *Bernard of Chartres, he became one of the most reputed teachers of the famous school of *Chartres and specialized in the teaching of the *seven liberal arts. In 1142 he became chancellor of the school, a position he held until his death. His *Heptateuchon* became the standard textbook of the seven liberal arts in the 12th century.
C. H. Haskins, *The Renaissance of the Twelfth Century* (1928).

THIETMAR OF MERSEBURG (975-1018) Chronicler. Son of Count Siegfried of Walbeck, he became bishop of Merseburg in 1009. He wrote a chronicle covering the reigns of *Henry I to *Henry II, which is especially important for the material provided about the rules of *Otto I, II and III.

THING The assembly of the barons in medieval *Sweden. It originated from the gatherings of chieftains in the 10th and 11th centuries, and their descendants continued to dominate it in the 12th century. Among its prerogatives were the elections of kings and the confirmation of ordinances. In the 13th century increasing royal power diminished its political importance.

THIONVILLE One of the estates of the *Carolingians in northeastern France. T. was one of *Charlemagne's favourite places of residence; it was there that he issued his *Capitularies.

THOMAS AQUINAS, St. (c. 1225-74) Philosopher and political thinker. Born at Aquino in Italy, he joined the *Dominican order in his youth and was sent to Paris to study. There he distinguished himself as an eminent student of *Albertus Magnus and was appointed master of philosophy at the university. T. rapidly gained fame as a great scholar; his methods of employing *Aristotelian philosophy for theological purposes, later known as the *Thomist system of study, earned him high regard. His writings represent voluminous work, among them his *Summa theologicae* (written 1266-74), the largest essay to deal with the whole of theology. T. distinguished between faith and reason, but only for scholastic purposes for the sake of stressing their interrelation. While his concepts have been criticized by some philosophers, they provide a complete picture of the theological achievements of the 13th century. T. also wrote the *Summa contra gentiles*, a treatise for Catholic missionaries in which he briefly presented the Christian faith. In his *De regimine principum* (On the Rule of Princes), he expressed his political views, distinguishing between the laws of nature, divine law and human law. Such a distinction brought him to the conclusion that the social establishment of his age was necessary in a Christian state. He also developed the idea that kingship was bound to the law, although the royal institution was to enjoy full authority within the legal framework. This legalistic view led him to distinguish between king and tyrant, whereby the latter had lost the grace of God. Consequently, the assassination of a tyrant monarch was approved, but only if he was first convicted by the Church.
J. Piper, *Einführung zu Thomas von Aquin* (1958).

THOMAS BECKET See BECKET, THOMAS.

THOMAS MOROSINI (d. 1211) Latin patriarch of Constantinople (1204-11). Member of the famous *Morosini family of Venice, he became a *Camaldolese monk. In 1204 he took part in the Fourth *Crusade and, after the conquest of *Constantinople, was elected Latin patriarch through Venetian influence. His attitude toward the Greek-Orthodox clergy, whom he attempted to bring to the obedience of the Catholic Church, created growing opposition to any collaboration with the Catholics and aroused strong enmity against the Latin conquerors.

THOMAS OF CELANO (c. 1190-1260) Hymnologist. Born at Celano in Italy, he wrote the music for some of the most famous religious hymns of the 13th century, among them the classical *Dies Irae*, which became one of the most popular interpretations of ecclesiastical music.

THOMAS OF ERCELDOUNE (Thomas the Rhymer; c. 1220-97) Poet. Born in Scotland, he wandered in his youth before settling in England in the middle of the 13th century. Acquainted with Authurian literature, he composed the romance of *Sir Tristram*, the English version of *Tristan et Iseult*. T. also prophesied events to occur in England in the high Middle Ages.

R. S. Loomis, *The Arthurian Literature in the Middle Ages* (1957).

THOMAS OF MARGA (9th century) Historian. T. was a *Nestorian Christian of northern Syria and entered a monastery near Mosul in 832. His scholarship attracted the attention of Patriarch Abraham, who appointed him his secretary in 837 and bishop of Marga in 850. In *c.* 840 T. wrote the *Book of Governors*, his historical work. Intended to be a history of his monastery, the first part of the book is important for the information it contains about the early history of the Nestorian church and about the development of its theological premises in the 4th-7th centuries.

W. Wright, *A Short History of Syriac Literature* (1894).

THOMAS OF MARLE (d. 1130) Feudal baron in northeastern France. Member of the lords of Coucy. T. was a notorious brigand, reputed for his cruelty. In 1096 he joined the First *Crusade as one of the leaders of the Peasants' Crusade and was known as one of the perpetrators of persecution of the Jews. His role in the East remains obscure, although a family tradition accredited him as the first knight to enter Jerusalem (see *Conqueste de Jérusalem*). After his return to France, T. continued his thieving activities and was twice excommunicated by the church. In 1130 King *Louis VI destroyed his castle and had him put to death.

THOMAS OF WOODSTOCK (1355-97) Duke of Gloucester. T. was the seventh son of *Edward III and, after the departure of his older brother, John of Gaunt, to Spain, he played an important role in the government of his nephew, *Richard II, who granted him the duchy of Gloucester (1385). In 1386 he entered into a bitter conflict with Richard's favourites, led by Michael De La *Pole, and became the leading "appellant" (accuser) of the king's friends. Supported by parliament, he seized the government and put some of Richard's advisers to death. In 1389 Richard dismissed him of his charge and sent him to Ireland as royal lieutenant (1392-97). Accused of treason, he was arrested in 1397 at Calais and murdered. His death precipitated Richard's own fall.

THOMISM The philosophical-theological system of *Thomas Aquinas and his followers. T. was sharply criticized by some of the rationalist philosophers, but enjoyed wide popularity among the *friars until the 15th century.

E. Gilson, *Le Thomisme* (1936).

THORESBY, JOHN (d. 1373) Archbishop of *York (1351-73). Cleric at the court of *Edward III, where he was master of the rolls, he became a close adviser of the king, who made him keeper of the privy seal in 1345 and chancellor in 1349. T. was an active negotiator with Scotland and France and was greatly responsible for arranging the Treaty of *Bretigny. After 1362 T. turned his attention solely to the administration of the archbishopric of York.

THORFINN KARLSEFNI (flourished 1002-07) *Viking explorer. He lived in *Iceland and from 1002 began to explore the western seas, sailing in the direction of the coasts of north America. In 1004 he led an expedition to north America and founded the first European settlement there, probably in Labrador. The colony was disbanded after a year.

G. Jones, *A History of the Vikings* (1968).

THORGEST (9th century) *Norse chieftain. T. landed in *Ireland *c.* 851, defeated local kings and founded a *Norwegian kingdom at *Dublin, which became one of the most important and richest Viking establishments.

THORISMUND King of the *Visigoths (451-53). Son of King *Theodoric I, he continued his father's hostile policy towards the Roman authorities in Gaul. He also increased Visigothic domination in *Auvergne.

THORN (TORUN) City in northern Poland. Founded in the 13th century by the *Teutonic Knights, it had a large Polish population. In 1410 it was conquered by *Jagiello and, in accordance with the treaty signed in the city (1411), annexed to Poland. In 1466 a new treaty with the Teutonic Knights was signed by King *Casimir IV, whereby the order surrendered western Prussia to Poland.

THURINGIA Country in central *Germany, named after the tribe of the Thuringians, who had settled there in the 5th century and established a principality. The tribe was able to maintain its independence despite Frankish attempts to conquer the land; until 526 they received the support of *Theodoric the Great, king of the Ostrogoths. In 530, however, dynastic conflicts weakened the principality and enabled its conquest by the *Franks in 541, who annexed T. to their realm. In the 8th century, T. became one of the bases of missionary activity in Germany and especially *Saxony. Governed by Frankish and local counts during the reigns of *Charlemagne, *Louis the Pious and *Louis the German, T. was attached to the duchy of *Franconia. In the 12th century the local dynasty was granted the title of landgraves and the country was separated from Franconia; *Frederick Barbarossa granted it the status of an imperial fief. The power of the landgrave grew in the 13th century, when they secured good relations with the kings of *Hungary and later with *Frederick II. In the 14th century T. was divided among several principalities, the most important of them becoming part of the duchy of Saxony. It prospered due to its rich mines.

J. W. Thompson, *Feudal Germany* (1928).

TIBERIAS City in *Galilee (Palestine). The Byzantine city of T. was conquered in 636 by the Arabs and became the capital of the northern part of Palestine (*Jund Al-Urdun*, "the province of the Jordan"). A prosperous city during the *Umayyad period (661-750), the city declined under the rule of the *Abbasids. Conquered in 1099 by the *Crusaders under the command of *Tancred, T. was fortified and became the capital of the principality of Galilee in the Latin kingdom of Jerusalem. In 1187, following his victory at *Hattin, *Saladin conquered the city. From the 13th century on, T. declined and became a small town limited to the area of the former Crusader fortifications. It was, however, one of the most important Jewish cities in Palestine.

TIBERIUS II *Byzantine emperor (578-82). One of the outstanding generals of the empire, he became regent in 574 as a result of the madness of *Justin II. In 578 he was proclaimed emperor and distinguished himself as an administrator. He was popular because he lowered taxes. T. continued *Justinian's policy of warring against the *Persians, whom he defeated in 575 and 581. However, his attention to the eastern frontier caused him to neglect the Danube border, where *Bulgars penetrated the Balkans.

CMedH, IV.

TIBERIUS III, Apsimar *Byzantine emperor (698-705). Commander of the fleet, he led a plot to overthrow Emperor *Leontius and thus became emperor, although he was considered a usurper by much of the civil nobility. T. fought against the Arabs on the borders of Asia Minor. In 705 he was dethroned and killed by *Justinian II.

TIBET Country in central Asia. Populated by Tibetan tribes, the majority of which were nomadic, the country fell under Chinese influence until the 7th century and was an area of strategic defence against the raids of *Huns and *Turks. In the 7th century the peoples of T. converted to Buddhism, imported from India. The tribal chieftains (*lamas*) became the religious heads of Tibetan Buddhism and fought for their independence from *China (8th century). In the same period they established commercial relations through *Afghanistan and *Transoxiana with the Abbasid caliphate, but opposed any attempts of Moslem penetration into the country. In the 11th century the political structures of T. evolved and a tribal confederation was established under the rule of an elected *dalai lama*. In 1253 T. was conquered by the *Mongol khan, *Kublai, who annexed it to his khanate of China. However, the country was granted a large degree of autonomy and was dominated by Buddhist monks.

R. B. Ekvall, *Tibet, the Closed Country* (1940).

TIHANY Monastery in *Hungary. Founded in the 11th century, it was richly endowed by King *Andrew I, who established a twin community of *Benedictine and Orthodox monks there and granted it large estates around Lake Balaton. T.'s abbey church was built in a combination of western (*Ottonian) and Byzantine styles of architecture.

TIMAR The Ottoman *Turkish fief. It was granted, as a modest income, to soldiers in payment for their services. The Timariotes (i.e., holders of T.) were among the most effective troops of the Ottoman army in the 14th century.

TIMUR-LENG (the lame Timur or Tamerlane; 1336-1405) *Mongol khan (1370-1405). Of Turkish or *Turkoman origin, T. distinguished himself in the service of the Mongol empire in central Asia and became governor of Transoxiana, where the descendants of *Genghis-Khan had begun to decline. In 1370 he seized power and was proclaimed khan of central Asia. T. mobilized a powerful Mongol-Turkish army and attacked *Persia. He renovated the territory and annexed it to his empire. In 1385 T. imposed his high authority over the khanate of the *Golden Horde and raided *India, destroying the kingdom of Delhi. In 1400 he invaded Anatolia and, at the Battle of *Ankara, crushed the Ottoman army (1401) and captured Sultan *Bayazid, whom he held prisoner in a cage until his death. T. created a powerful empire, but his life was devoted to destruction and he lacked the political skills of Genghis-Khan.

After his death, his empire was divided among his sons, who founded *Timurid dynasties in Persia, Transoxiana and India.

R. Grousset, *L'Empire des steppes* (1946).

TIMURIDS *Mongol-Turkish dynasties founded, in central Asia, India and *Persia, by the descendants of *Timur-leng (15th century). These groups constantly disputed possession of parts of the Timurid empire which eventually led to their fall. Among the T., the most important was the dynasty that ruled Persia (1405-1517); but even there civil wars brought poverty and ruin. Persia did not recover until 1447, when its rivals were overcome and a stabler government was established.

TINCHEBRAY, BATTLE OF (1107) Fought between King *Henry I of England, supported by the nobility of *Normandy, and *Robert Curthose, it led to the reunion of England and Normandy. Duke Robert was captured, deprived of his duchy and held prisoner in England by his brother until his death (1128).

TIRNOVO City in central *Bulgaria, chosen by Tsar *Simeon as capital of his realm in order to affirm his Christian way of life. Simeon also established the see of the autonomous Bulgarian patriarchate at T. T. remained the capital until the end of the 10th century.

TITHES (Latin: decima, French: dîme) The biblical tenth part of the harvest, which was due to the priests, was made into a medieval tax on agrarian produce to be paid to the Church. The T. are to be distinguished from *feudal taxes paid to ecclesiastical institutions, owners of estates and seigniories. The T. were due to the local bishop, but in the 9th-11th centuries ownership was often purchased or even usurped by powerful lay vassals. In certain cases, the T. were donated by their lay owners to abbeys.

M. Bloch, *Feudal Society* (1953).

TLEMCEN City in north Africa (western Algeria). Its history was linked with that of the surrounding area until the 11th century, when it became a religious centre of *Islam. Its mosques attracted many groups of pilgrims. The city grew under *Almoravide, *Almohade and *Marinid rule, but in the 14th century it began to rapidly decline.

TMUTOROKAN City in southern *Russia, on the eastern coast of the Azov Straits. Under *Byzantine and *Khazar domination, it became an important trading centre between the Black Sea and Crimea and between the north Caucasian and south Russian steppes. In the 9th century a small principality was established at T., which fell under the influence of the Kiev empire and in 1223 was destroyed by the *Mongols.

TODROS BEN JOSEPH HALEVI ABULAFIA (1225-c. 1285) *Kabbalist. Member of the distinguished Abulafia family of Toledo, he was the spiritual leader of the Jewish communities in Castile and became influential at the court of King *Alfonso X. T. was a prominent Kabbalist and attempted to combine the doctrines of the *Gnostic circles of *Gerona and *Castile. Although his work did not provide a coherent doctrine, it became the basis of later essays. T.'s mystical views brought him to the conclusion that the anti-Jewish persecutions of 1279 were the result of the sins of the Jews; he therefore urged his people, in a sermon in 1280, to become religiously observant and disassociate themselves from gentile women.

G. Scholem, *Major Trends in Jewish Mysticism* (1954).

TODROS BEN JUDAH ABULAFIA (1247-95) Poet.
His early life and work was dedicated to secular Hebrew
poetry. He also composed pieces for Jewish notables.
In 1280, during anti-Jewish persecution in Toledo, T.
was imprisoned; consequently, his behaviour changed
and he became moralistic. His poetry became religious
in nature. More than 1000 of his poems were collected
in a book he entitled *Gan Hameshalim ve-Hahidoth*
(A Garden of Legends and Riddles).

TOKHTAMYSH Khan of the *Golden Horde (1383-
95). T. was twice defeated by *Timur-leng in 1391 and
1395 and reduced to the status of vassalage. He was
the last monarch of the *Mongol empire in Russia. At
his death, two independent khanates of *Crimea and
Kazan were established, which diminished the power
of the Golden Horde.

TOLEDO City in *Spain. Situated on the Tago River
in the centre of the Iberian peninsula, T. was an important trade centre of Spain. The *Visigoths established
their capital at T. *c.* 520, following their defeat by the
*Franks and the loss of their capital at *Toulouse (507).
The city prospered and became the centre of the Catholic Church and the see of the archbishop *primate in
Spain. It was the site of a number of *councils which
regularly assembled. The council of 589 was one of the
most important due to the conversion of King *Reccared to the Catholic faith. In the 7th century the councils also had an important political and legislative impact on the kingdom. After the Arab conquest (714),
the political centre of the country moved southwards
to *Andalusia, but T. continued to be of economic
importance and crafts were established in addition to
its markets. In 1085 King *Alfonso VI of Castile conquered the city and made it his capital. Despite a brief
*Almoravide raid, T. remained a Castilian city. The 12th
century marked its golden age; it became one of the earliest industrial centres in western Europe, and was
especially famous for its steel industry. Moreover, T. became a centre for translations of Arabic philosophical
and scientific works into Latin; under the patronage of
Archbishop *Raymond, the school of translators
attracted intellectuals from numerous European
countries. T.'s powerful and prosperous Jewish community also played an important role in the cultural accomplishments of the 12th and 13th centuries and the
city became the centre of *Sephardi Jewish scholars.
The prolonged stays of the kings in the Andalusian
*Alcázars, as well as the civil wars of the 14th and 15th
centuries, led to the gradual decline of T. The city is
dominated by its Gothic cathedral, built in the 14th
century.
J. F. O'Callaghan, *A History of Medieval Spain* (1975).

TOMISLAV King of the *Croats (910-28). After a
period of anarchy and tribal wars, T. was recognized
as the leader of the Croats and, by unifying the northern and Dalmatian realms, he became the true founder
of the kingdom of Croatia. T. established relations with
the papacy and solved the religious dispute by uniting
his kingdom with Rome and the Catholic Church. In
920 he was recognized as king by Pope John X.

TORRE, DELLA Aristocratic family in Milan. Their
political rise is related to their leadership in the city's
*Guelph party and their opposition to Emperor *Fre-
derick II. In 1240 the head of the family, Pagano, was
recognized as the leader of Milan, a position that the

family maintained until 1278. In 1263 Filippo T. extended his authority over neighbouring cities and created
a strong principality. Napoleon T., however, had to face
the growing power of the *Ghibelline party in the city,
led by the rival family of *Visconti. Defeated in 1278,
he lost power and the family declined.
F. D. Hyde, *Society and Politics in Medieval Italy*
(1973).

TOSAFISTS (Supplementers) *Jewish authors of sup-
plementary religious treatises written in Germany and
France during the 11th-13th centuries. Their works
attained the authority of supplements to the Talmud,
as they up-dated and interpreted legislation, basing their
decisions on *gaonic and rabbinical sources. As distinct
from the sages of *Sephardi Jewry, the T. had no philosophical background.
S. W. Baron, *A Social and Religious History of the
Jewish People*, VI (1957).

TOTILA King of the *Ostrogoths (541-52). T. was the
last Ostrogothic king of Italy. From his accession to
the throne, he had to fight against the Byzantine general, *Narses, sent by *Justinian to conquer Italy. Defeated in 552 at Sena Gallica, T. was killed in the
Battle of Busta Gallorum.

TOULOUSE City in southern *France. Conquered in
416 by the *Visigoths, it became the capital of their
kingdom in Gaul and Spain until 507, when it was captured by *Clovis, king of the Franks. Under the *Merovingians the city declined and became an ecclesiastical
centre, being the see of a bishopric in the duchy and
(later) kingdom of *Aquitaine. In the 9th century T.
again became a political centre, this time under the
government of a Frankish count, *Bernard of Gothia
(*c.* 860). It became the heart of a large principality
which included southeastern Aquitaine and *Languedoc. In the 10th century the counts of T. attempted
to seize the ducal title of Aquitaine but were defeated
by the counts of *Poitiers. Consequently, they turned
to the Mediterranean area and became involved in dynastic struggles with the counts of *Barcelona over
Provence (11th-12th centuries). T. grew as an important
economic centre along the trade routes in southern
France; its municipal institutions (the consulate) were
established in accordance with Roman tradition. In the
13th century T. suffered from the *Albigensian wars. It
was conquered in 1213 by *Simon de Montfort and became the capital of the principality of *Raymond VII
in 1218, but lost its ascendancy over Languedoc. A
university was founded in the city in 1229 to provide
Catholic leadership for the province, and the influence
of the *Dominicans became paramount there. In 1249
T. was inherited by *Alphonse de Poitiers, the brother
of King *Louis IX of France. Alphonse introduced a new
administration, modelled after the royal administration
in northern France. In 1270, at the death of Alphonse,
T. was annexed to the royal demesne and governed by
royal officers, sent from Paris. As the centre of
Languedoc, an *estates-general and provincial parliament were established in the city, whose economic prosperity continued into the later Middle Ages.
J. Mundy, *Politics and Liberties at Toulouse* (1958).

TOURNAI City in *Flanders. In the middle of the 5th
century T. became the capital of a small realm of the
Salian *Franks. *Chilperic I (460-83) imposed his
authority over the other Salian realms, and, by his

death, T. had become a relatively important city and the capital of all Salian Franks. After the conquest of Gaul by *Clovis and the transfer of the kingship to the area between Soissons and Paris, T. declined. It remained a small town until the 9th century, when its bishops made it the ecclesiastical centre of the new county of Flanders. In the 10th-13th centuries the city grew, becoming one of the centres of the textile industry of Flanders. From the second half of the 12th century, some of the most distinguished scholars in western Europe were elected bishops of T., even though they were not native to the country; thanks to their activities, the prestige of the bishopric increased. However, any attempt to establish an ecclesiastical seigniory in the city was foiled by the counts of Flanders and opposed by the burghers, who were interested in commercial relations with the other Flemish towns and with the fairs of Champagne, where a good part of their fine drapery was sold. In the 14th and 15th centuries, T. became famous for its tapestries.

H. Pirenne, *The Early Democracies in the Low Countries* (1923).

TOURNAMENTS *Chivalric contests which were widespread in western Europe from the second half of the 12th century and consisted of duels and combat between knights. T. were part of chivalric education and were usually fought in honour of the grand ladies present at the chivalric court. While in some cases the battles were pursued until the death or serious injury of one party, rules of play were gradually adopted. Thus, the T. became a military exercise which had to end without bloodshed.

S. Painter, *French Chivalry* (1952).

TOURNUS Abbey in *Burgundy. Settled in 867 by the monks of St. Philibert, who fled from the *Norman invasion at the mouth of the Loire River, it was fortified in the 10th century to protect it from *Hungarian invasions. The abbey church, built within the fortifications in the 10th and 11th centuries, is one of the most interesting works of Romanesque art, especially its upper portion, built between 1060-80.

TOURS City in France on the Loire River. From the beginning of the Middle Ages, T. played an important strategic and economic role, due to its location along the cross-roads between northern and southern France and between the eastern and western provinces. Its religious tradition (St. *Martin, the patron saint of Gaul, was its bishop) also contributed to its importance, and popular gatherings were held at the saint's tomb in the monastery of *Marmoutier. Pilgrims from all over France were attracted to T. by tales about miracles accomplished at the shrine. In 732 the city was threatened by the Arabs, who were defeated at the famous Battle of *Poitiers, fought in its southern part. In the 9th century T. became a stronghold against *Norman raids and its count, *Robert the Strong, founded his dynasty there, later to reign in France. After the accession of *Hugh Capet to the throne, the city, with the exception of the seigniory of Marmoutier, which remained a royal enclave, became part of the fiefs of the house of *Blois. It remained in their possession until its conquest by *Geoffrey Martel in 1054, when it was annexed to the *Angevin principality. During the reign of *Henry II Plantagenet, T. became a key city in his empire and an important source of revenue, due to its

economic activities, the tolls imposed on the bridge over the Loire and the pilgrimages to *Santiago de Compostela (since T. was a major pilgrimage station for those worshippers coming from northern Europe in the 11th century). The city also developed as a scholarly and intellectual centre, thanks to the teachings of *Roscelin and the literary activity of Archbishop *Hildebert of Lavardin. In 1204 T. was conquered by *Philip II and annexed to the royal demesne. It continued to be an economic centre in the 13th-15th centuries, but lost its strategic importance. The local mint produced widely-used coins (the *livre tournois*), which rivalled other feudal and royal currencies and became the standard form of money in France at the end of the 13th century.

G. Duby and R. Maudron, *France, History and Society* (1969).

TOWNS At the beginning of the Middle Ages, with the decline of trade, the T. of western Europe lost much of their prosperity and the major portion of the former Roman cities simply remained episcopal centres. In the East (both *Byzantium and the *Moslem caliphate), on the other hand, urban life continued to be prominent. *Italy, in that respect, was an area of transit; thus, some of its cities continued to develop and grow, while others, especially in the northern and central parts of the country, followed the pattern of the West. In the later years of the 9th century, trade was renewed and the T. revived, although they were no longer political centres and their estates were settled by feudal lords. The status of T. rose in the 10th and 11th centuries; in addition to the development of existing cities, new *boroughs were founded around abbeys and at bridges or cross-roads. The exchange of agrarian produce and the sale of craftsmen's goods led to the establishment of markets and *fairs; these, too, aided in the development of T., as their economic role increased. During the first stage of their development, the urban communities were ruled by aldermen, but gradually, with the development of merchant and craft *guilds, the authority delegated to feudal or ecclesiastical lord was transferred to town councils composed of the leaders of the guilds and wealthy *merchants (11th and 12th centuries), and these began to struggle with the authorities for urban liberties. In the T. of Italy this struggle was aided by the settlement of the landed aristocracy and its assimilation with the wealthy merchants and craftsmen. The most common types of T. were the *cities (technically, T. with an episcopal see), boroughs, T. administered by a college of consuls (mainly in Italy and the Mediterranean area, where Roman traditions were preserved), and *communes.

J. Mundy and P. Riesenberg, *The Medieval Town* (1963).

TRANSPORTATION The decline of trade in the 5th-8th centuries affected T. The Roman roads were neglected and most travel was done by sea or river (see *ships). Land travel, limited within the great estates and their neighbourhood, was accomplished by chariots drawn by cattle. Organized systems of T. began to develop in Europe in the 9th century. The *Rhadanites introduced the system of sending vessels bearing merchandise from port to port. The Italian cities (*Amalfi, *Pisa, *Genoa) developed joint stock companies which chartered boats; at *Venice, the ships belonged to the republic and could be rented out to merchants. Venetian shipping of the 12th and 13th centuries was the most advanced system of organized T. in the Middle Ages. Land travel, on the other hand, despite improvements in the quality of chariots and cattle trucks, remained relatively undeveloped until the 13th century. At that time it was organized in the *Mongol empire and post stations, in which camels and horses could be rented, were established along the main trade roads. One of the main functions of the *Hanse authorities was to arrange T. for its members.

CEcH, III.

TRANSUBSTANTIATION A doctrine of the Catholic Church, according to which the bread and wine of the *Eucharist *Sacrament actually becomes the body and blood of Christ, although there is no physical change of appearance in the bread and wine. The view aroused long disputes concerning the change in substance. In 1215 it became the official doctrine of the Church, decreed by the Fourth *Lateran Council.

DTC, XV.

TRANSYLVANIA Principality situated between the Carpathian Mountains and belonging to *Hungary. Populated by Rumanians, who took refuge in the mountains after the fall of the Romans, T. was invaded and successively governed in the 5th-9th centuries by *Goths, *Gepids, *Huns, *Avars, *Slavs and *Bulgars. In the 10th century T. was conquered by the *Hungarians, some of whom settled there. In the 11th century the province was divided into seven counties, in accordance with the constitution of King *Stephen I (1003). The land was given to noble Hungarians, while the peasantry, both Hungarian and Rumanian, lost its freedom during the 12th century. From 1224, settlement was begun of German colonists originally from *Saxony, thus changing the rural character of the country and adding a third ethnic group to its population. At the end of the 13th century *Jewish settlers were established with royal permission. The counties were placed under the central government of a prince (*voivode*) who, from the beginning of the 14th century, acted as viceroy. The most famous among the *voivodes* was John *Hunyady (1440-56).

L. Makkay, *Histoire de la Transylvanie* (1946).

TRASAMUND (d. 523) King of the *Vandals (496-523). One of the most educated of the Germanic kings, T. studied at Constantinople, where he spent his youth. An ardent Arian, he persecuted the Catholic bishops of his realm (502). T.'s main concern was to halt a series of revolts in Mauretania, the western province of his kingdom, which he did by intervening in the affairs of the various nomadic tribes.

TRASTAMARE, DON HENRY See HENRY II, king of Castile.

TRAVE River in northern *Germany and the name of *Slavs who settled in the area. In 1147 the Ts. were defeated by Count Adolph of Holstein and Germanized.

TREBIZOND, EMPIRE OF Founded in 1204 in northeastern Anatolia, near the city and harbour of Trebizond. Its founder, *Alexius Comnenus, a cousin of the last *Byzantine emperor of the dynasty, had fled to T. where he was proclaimed emperor. During the first three years, he rivalled the emperor of Nicaea for legitimacy as the heir of the Byzantine throne. However, the empire's non-central location caused the Comneni, who reigned there until 1461, to concentrate themselves upon building and organizing their new state. Its political orientation was Asiatic and the emperors became involved in the affairs of *Georgia and the *Seljuks. Under the Comneni, T. became an important cultural centre containing a mixture of Greek-Byzantine, Armenian and Georgian cultures. In the middle of the 14th century T. reached the peak of its territorial expansion, dominating the entire area lying along the southern coast of the Black Sea, from Sinop to Georgia. In 1395 the *Ottoman sultan, *Bayazid I, conquered a large part of the Anatolian territories of the empire and imposed his overlordship. Despite the respite gained by the victories of *Timur-leng (1401), T. was unable to recover, and in 1461 the entire empire was conquered by the *Ottomans.

W. Miller, *The Empire of Trebizond* (1920).

TRÈS RICHES HEURES DE CHANTILLY One of the finest illuminated books of hours of the later 14th century, prepared for the duke of *Berry by the *Limburg brothers. It is preserved at the castle of Chantilly, hence its name.

TREUGA DEI See TRUCE OF GOD.

TREVET, NICHOLAS (d. 1328) Historian. T., a *Dominican friar, taught theology at Oxford. During the reign of *Edward II he became interested in history and tried to grasp its meaning and its educational value. Consequently, he compiled a history of *Six Reigns in England, 1135-1307*. The part covering the reign of *Edward I (1272-1307) is a valuable source of information.

J. W. Thompson, *History of Historical Writing* (1943).

TREVISO City in northeastern *Italy. Until the 13th century T. was a small town whose history was linked to that of the surrounding province. In 1236 it became the capital of a powerful march, ruled by *Ezzelino da Romano. During this period the city prospered and reached its cultural peak. In c. 1250 one of the first paper mills of western Europe was established there. After Ezzelino's death (1259), the *Scala lords of *Verona established their rule over T., but claim to the city was also disputed by *Venice and *Milan. The first part of the 14th century marked a period of perpetual war which ended only in 1338, when the city was annexed to Venice.

TRIAL The *legal and jurisdictional pluralism of the Middle Ages had its effect upon the justice system. Ts. varied according to jurisdiction and custom. Byzantine and Roman Catholic Ts. were based on legal evidence and procedure, as were the judicial systems of the Moslems and Jews. In feudal Europe, on the other hand, Germanic traditions played a role in Ts. Consequently, the accused had to prove his innocence. One way to do so was by his own oath before the assembly of free-men, or by those of his warrants. This manner of T. was common in the early and high Middle Ages. Another means of proving innocence was through combat; justice was on the side of the stronger party. From the 12th century on, the parties could substitute champions for themselves. The *ordeal was yet another means of conviction or vindication of the accused. T. by *jury developed in England from the reign of *Henry II and gradually spread to the Continent.

F. Kern, *Kingship and Law in the Middle Ages* (1939).

TRIBONIAN (d. c. 545) Legist. T. was the most important legist in the Byzantine empire in the 6th century and acted as legal adviser for *Justinian. He was chiefly responsible for the *Code of Justinian, the *Digest* and the *Institutes*.

TRIER (TRÈVES) City in the Moselle Valley in *Germany. After having served as a Roman capital, T. was burnt in 413 by the Ripuarian *Franks and, while a part of their realm, was merely a small town located around a cathedral church. In 490 T. was annexed by *Clovis to the Frankish kingdom. The city revived in the 9th century, when a number of abbeys established there attracted settlers and new *boroughs were built around the episcopal centre and on the former Roman walls. In the 10th century the archbishops became lords of the city; their court of the 10th and 11th centuries was an important centre of the *Ottonian Renaissance. The rise of T. was related to the growing political importance of its archbishops, who became, together with their colleagues of *Mainz and *Cologne, the three ecclesiastical *electors in Germany. In 1257 T. became the capital of the archiepiscopal principality, which extended in the 14th century over large territories west of the Rhine. The town also became the commercial centre of the region. Its growth led to uprisings on the part of the burghers (mid-late 13th century), who demanded municipal liberties. Their demands were only partially met when a municipal council was established in 1301 by archiepiscopal charter.

G. Barraclough, *The Origins of Modern Germany* (1951).

TRIESTE City in northeastern Italy. A small town under tribal and feudal rule during the early and high Middle Ages, T. was conquered by *Venice in 1202. During the 13th and 14th centuries its inhabitants often rebelled against Venetian domination. Conquered in 1382 by *Leopold of Austria, the city prospered as the main harbour of the Hapsburg states.

TRINITARIANS, ORDER OF Founded by a community of *Augustinian canons in 1198 in eastern France, the order was dedicated to the Holy Trinity. Its members followed an austere form of the Augustinian rule. Their chief cause in the 13th and 14th centuries was the liberation of captives.

DTC, XV.

TRIPOLI City in north Africa. In the 5th and 6th centuries it was disputed between the *Vandals and *Byzantines until its conquest in 532 by *Belisarius. Byzantine domination lacked stability, however, and during the reign of *Justinian the city was raided several times by nomadic tribes. In 645 it was conquered by the Arabs. In 1150 *Roger II of Sicily captured T., but Sicilian rule ended soon after his death.

CHI.

TRIPOLI City in Lebanon. The town was part of the *Byzantine empire until its conquest in 640 by the Arabs. Caliph *Muawiyah settled Moslems in the city and the process of Islamization was rapidly achieved. At the beginning of the 11th century T. fell under *Fatimid rule and was governed by an emir, responsible to the government of Cairo. In 1104 *Raymond IV of Saint-Gilles besieged it, after building the castle of Mont Pèlerin in the neighbourhood. The *Crusaders did not succeed in conquering T., however, until 1109, when it became the capital of an autonomous county, ruled by a collateral branch of the dynasty of *Toulouse, and was one of the three principal Crusader states. The constitution of the county was modelled after Occitanian and Provençal traditions. The main cities of the state, including T., Margat, Tortosa and Jebeil, were fortified. In the 13th century a *commune was established

in the city, whose Provençal counts were succeeded by the princes of *Antioch. In 1289 T. was conquered by the *Mamelukes.

J. Richard, *Le Comté de Tripoli sous les Croisés* (1943).

TRISTRAM AND ISEULT Romance. Based on a *Celtic tale, it became one of the most popular love stories in western Europe at the end of the 12th century. Dealing with the love between Tristram, the knight, and Iseult, the wife of King Mark, it posed the problem of passion and fate in the perspective of conjugal and knightly loyalty. Developed in French by *Béroul and in German by *Gottfried of Strasburg, the tale also had English versions in the 13th century. T. became part of the *chivalric tradition of the later Middle Ages.

M. A. Gist, *Love and War in the Middle English Romance* (1947).

TRIVIUM The three basic disciplines of the *seven liberal arts, which included grammar, rhetoric and dialectics.

TRONDHEIM (NIDAROS) City in *Norway. A small locality existed in the area in the 9th century and was the centre of the country of the *jarls* of Lade. In 997 King *Olaf I founded the city and made it his capital. The centre of missionary activity in Norway, T. became the see of the Norwegian archbishopric in 1152 and remained the capital of Norway until 1391. The city was also a medieval commercial centre.

L. Musset, *Les Peuples Scandinaves au Moyen Age*.

TROUBADOUR (trouvère) Wandering lyric poet. Originating in *Provence in the 11th century, the Ts. reached their highest popularity in 12th-century *Aquitaine, where they were active at the ducal court. Duke *William IX was himself a reputed T. The T. composed and sang his own songs, which generally focused on love or were ballads praising the glory of heroes. He was free to express personal emotions and sentiments. At the end of the 13th century the Ts. were replaced by the northern *minstrels.

H. Davenson, *La poèsie des Troubadours* (1961).

TROYES City in eastern France. Conquered by the *Franks in 483, it was the see of a bishopric under the *Merovingian dynasty. The seat of a county under the *Carolingians, it became part of the duchy of *Burgundy at the end of the 9th century but continued to be governed by the counts, who were made vassals of the dukes. In 1023 the county was inherited by the house of *Blois and was held by one of the members of the cadet branch. In the 12th century, however, its importance grew due to economic developments and the establishment of the fairs of *Champagne and, thus, it surpassed Blois. Accordingly, Count *Thibaut IV of Blois settled at T. and established the capital of Champagne there. Under his son, *Henry the Liberal, the court of T. became one of the most important and brilliant cultural and literary centres of western Europe. Thanks to works of *Chrétien de Troyes, it is considered the motherland of the French *romance. In the 13th century the city continued to develop and prosper, but with the decline of the fairs and the annexation of Champagne to the royal crown, it lost its importance and fell to the status of a provincial town. In 1420 the Treaty of T. between *Charles VI and *Henry V of England annulled the rights of Dauphin Charles and promised the inheritance of the crown of France to Henry, who married Charles' daughter, Catherine.

TRUCE OF GOD (Treuga Dei) A compromise decree established in the 11th century by the Church, which forbade combat during four days a week and during certain periods of the year. Pope *Urban II issued the legislation at the Council of *Clermont in 1095. See *Peace of God.

TRUVOR (9th century) *Varangian leader. One of the chieftains of the Rus clan, he was active in *Novgorod in the second half of the 9th century. According to Russian tradition, he was *Rurik's brother.

TSONG KHAPA (1355-1417) Religious leader in *Tibet. Educated to be a Buddhist monk, he founded a monastery at Lhasa and imposed an austere rule. This rule formed the basis for the Lamaist trend of Buddhism.
P. B. Ekvall, *Religious Observances in Tibet* (1964).

TUDELA City in *Spain. Conquered in 713 by the Arabs, it became a provincial capital in the 10th century. In 1114 *Alfonso I, king of Aragon, conquered and annexed T. to his realm. During the 12th century the city was fortified and its walls were built a great distance from the urban area, in order to allow the inclusion of rural lands; such an arrangement reflected the lack of security near the frontiers.

TU FU (712-70) *Chinese poet. According to stories about him, T. wandered in his youth, as his poetry was not appreciated. He was finally offered a position at the T'ang imperial court, where he stayed until 755. With the fall of the dynasty, T. was again reduced to poverty and ended his life as a wandering poet. His poetry is sensitive and expresses his feelings concerning human fate. He is considered one of the greatest Chinese poets, if not the greatest.
W. Hung, *Tu Fu, China's Greatest Poet* (1952).

TUGHRIL-BEG (d. 1063) *Seljuk sultan (1037-63) and the founder of the Seljuk empire. T. imposed his authority upon several Turkish tribes and in 1037 began the conquest of Persia and the *Abbasid caliphate. After the defeat of the *Ghaznavids, he captured *Khorasan (1040) and established his capital at *Nishapur. In 1051 he conquered *Isfahan and western Persia and invaded Iraq, where he defeated Arab tribes. In 1055 he gained *Baghdad. He allowed Caliph Al-Muqtadi to remain the Islamic spiritual leader and the formal sovereign of the city; however, the caliph was relieved of any real authority. T.'s new status was confirmed in a writ of 1058, which proclaimed him "king of the East and West".
CHI.

TULUI (d. 1245) Mongol khan. He was the fourth son of *Genghis-Khan and, after his father's death (1227), was appointed the lieutenant of his brother, *Ogadai, the new great khan. In 1230-32 he commanded an expedition to *China, where he destroyed the remnants of the Kin empire. At his death, he left his sons, *Mangu, *Kublai and *Hulagu in leading positions of the Mongol empire, sharing their power with their cousin, *Batu-khan.

TULUNID DYNASTY See AHMAD IBN TULUN.

TUNIS City in north Africa. Founded by the Arabs near the site of Carthage, it depended on the rulers of *Kairwan (8th-12th centuries) and became an important harbour of the *Aghlabids. In 1150 it was seized by *Roger II, and Sicilian influence was maintained until the middle of the 13th century. In 1217-20 T. became the scene of missionary activities on the part of the Franciscans. Following his conquest of *Sicily (1268), *Charles of Anjou attempted to restore Sicilian rule at T.; under his influence, his brother, *Louis IX of France, proclaimed a new *Crusade against the city. However, the plan failed upon Louis' death, which, together with the *Sicilian Vespers (1282), helped to ensure T.'s independence.

TURIN City in northwestern *Italy. The ancient city of Augusta Taurinorum declined after the fall of the Western empire. It was conquered by the *Lombards in 569, and the establishment of a Lombard duchy in the city led to its revival. Conquered in 774 by *Charlemagne, T. became the seat of a Frankish count; in the 9th century the dynasty seized power over the whole province and *Berengar I of Friuli granted its members the title of marquis. The dynasty became extinct in 1034 and there were struggles over the right to the lands. In 1048 Emperor *Henry III granted T. to the counts of *Savoy, who established the rule of a cadet branch there. In the 12th century the city was often troubled by wars in which emperors, counts, bishops and feudal lords took part. The guilds profited from the disorder, creating a commune which was granted a charter in 1139 by *Conrad III. In 1159 *Frederick Barbarossa gave the city to its bishops, enfeoffing them with the regalia. Episcopal rule lasted until 1225, when the city was attacked by the neighbouring lords of *Montferrat. The lords, however, were unable to establish a government and until 1276 the sovereignty of the city was disputed between them and *Charles of Anjou. The rivalry ended with *Thomas of Savoy's conquest of the city, which he annexed to his estates. Thomas brought peace to T., which prospered in the 14th and 15th centuries and became an important commercial centre. In 1404 a university was founded, making T. the intellectual centre of the Savoy principality.
D. Waley, *Cities and Principalities in later Medieval Italy* (1976).

TURKESTAN Steppe country in central *Asia. T. was populated by numerous nomadic *Turkish and *Turkoman tribes, which used the territory as a base for invasions into eastern Europe and the Middle East. It was also an important commercial centre lying along the main trade routes between the Far East, India, Persia and eastern Europe. Conquered by the *Mongols under *Genghis-Khan, T. was the centre of the White Horde, ruled by the descendants of Juchi, the eldest son of Genghis. In 1379 *Timur-leng annexed the area to his empire.

TURKOMANS A group of tribes in *Turkestan, mainly of Turkish origin. As distinct from the *Turks, the T. did not become politically organized and became part of numerous Iranian and Mongol civilizations. The men of the tribes served their more powerful neighbours, subsequently attacking them when able. Pushed by the *Khwarizmians and *Mongols, some of the T. invaded the *Seljuk states and settled in Anatolia, where they were assimilated by the Ottoman Turks. Another portion of T. was integrated into the Mongol empire. In the 15th century this group founded principalities in central Asia.
CHI.

TURKS An ethnical group of peoples originating in central *Asia, encompassing a number of individual tribes, known under different names from the 4th century. The most important of the Turkic peoples were the *Huns, the *Avars and the *Khazars (see individual entries). The nomadic T. spread over the steppes, from the borders of China in the Altai Mountains to the Black Sea, and from the Iranian borders of *Transoxiana to Mongolia, where they merged with Mongol tribes. In the 8th century Sunnite *Islam penetrated central Asia and part of the T., especially the Oghuz tribes, converted to the Moslem faith, but did not become part of the Arab caliphate. Some (known as *Mamelukes) entered the military service of the *Abbasids and of local governors in the eastern provinces of the caliphate during the 9th and 10th centuries. These soldiers rose to commanding positions and even founded dynasties, such as the *Ghaznavids who, under the rule of *Mahmud of Ghazni, established a powerful empire that extended from Afghanistan and Khorasan to Transoxiana and northwestern India.

The steppe tribes constituted two great confederations, the White and Black (Karakhan) T. At the beginning of the 11th century the Black T. became an important military power, controlling the main trading routes between Asia and Europe. Under the rule of a chieftain named Seljuk, the Black T. were united and began to dominate the peoples of the Oxus. Descendants of this tribe, the Seljuks, led by *Tughril-Beg, made a series of spectacular conquests in the 11th century, which transformed them into the masters of the Abbasid caliphate and brought them to *Nicaea, at the gates of Constantinople. The Seljuks lost much of their power in the 12th century and became no match for the Mongols, who destroyed their states.

Another group of T., the *Uighurs, merged with the Mongols and became an important element in their empire; in fact, their written language became the official tongue used by the chancery and their religion, *Nestorian Christianity, spread amongst the Mongols. In the 13th century the Uighurs played a secondary role in the Mongol empire, despite their influence; however, in the following century their importance gradually increased due to the decline of the dynasty of *Genghis-Khan. With the rise of *Timur-leng, the Uighurs attempted to rebuild the Mongol empire.

The most important group of T. were the Ottomans. This tribe was originally made up of cattle-herders, who, pushed by the *Khwarizmians and the Mongols, migrated to Anatolia and settled in the north-eastern marches of the sultanate of Konya in the middle of the 13th century. It appears that they founded a military-religious brotherhood, whose aim was to convert infidels. Due to the weakness of the Seljuks, they were able to gain independence in the second half of the 13th century and became a threat to the Byzantine empire. Under the rule of *Osman (1290-1326), who gave his name to his people, they openly attacked the Byzantines. They also began to extend their rule eastwards after the fall of the Seljuk realm of *Rum. In 1337 *Nicaea, Brusa and Nicomedia were conquered, putting an end to Byzantine domination in Asia Minor. Summoned by *John VI Cantacuzenus, the Ottomans entered Europe and conquered *Adrianople in 1357. They then turned against the *Serbs and using guns, defeated them in 1387 at *Kossovo. Under the rule of *Bayazid, they conquered Bulgaria,

defeated a European crusade at Nicopolis in 1396, besieged Constantinople and began the systematic conquest of Anatolia, fighting against the *Karamans, who ruled another Turkish principality. In 1401, at the Battle of Ankara, Bayazid was defeated and captured by *Timur-leng; during the following years, the Ottoman state was disorganized. However, the military organization, and particularly the fighting units of Timariotes (see *Timar) and *Spahis, remained strong and when *Muhammad I (1413-21) seized power, the empire was re-established and continued its conquests in the Balkans. Constantinople was again besieged and Hungarian attempts to organize a Crusade failed with the defeats of *Varna (1446) and the second Battle of Kossovo, which destroyed Serbia. Under Muhammad II the dream of the Ottoman empire was achieved: Constantinople was conquered in 1453, followed by *Morea (1460) and *Trebizond (1461).

P. Witteck, *The Rise of the Ottoman Empire* (1938).

TUSCANY Province in central Italy (ancient Etruria). Up to the 9th century the evolution of T. was dependent upon the main events in Italian history. However, with the fall of the *Carolingian empire, feudal families seized power and fought amongst themselves; the resultant anarchy caused the coastal area to fall under the power of the city of *Pisa, which established an independent maritime republic. In the 10th century the counts of *Canossa were able to impose their authority over T. and the neighbouring territories and founded a powerful march within the *Holy Roman empire. In 1051 *Godfrey of Lorraine, who had revolted against *Henry III, managed to flee to Italy. There he married the widow of Boniface of Canossa, the last Italian margrave of T., and thus became the guardian of the infant daughter, *Matilda. After Godfrey's death, Matilda ruled over T. together with a vast principality which extended to *Lombardy. She became a faithfull ally of Pope *Gregory VII against *Henry IV, and in 1078 offered him hospitality in her castle of Canossa, where the famous visit of the repentant emperor took place. In 1115, when Matilda died, T. collapsed and its cities gained their independence. Some of them, following the example of Pisa, proclaimed themselves republics; the most important among these were *Florence and *Siena, which eventually divided T. into two political units (14th century). The unity of T. was again realized in the second half of the 15th century, when the province fell under the authority of the Florentine government.

F. D. Hyde, *Politics and Society in Medieval Italy* (1973).

TUSCULUM Town in Latium, near Rome. Part of the *Papal States, the town and its estates were enfeoffed to a Roman family, which assumed the title of counts at the beginning of the 10th century. In 932 they imposed their authority in the city and soon became the patrons of the *papacy. In 962 *Otto I broke their power, but they maintained their fiefs and in 1015 regained their influence and took command over the papal see, appointing members of their family to the papal dignity. Their ultimate decline came when *Henry III selected popes from among German bishops and thereby curtailed their influence.

TUTUSH *Seljuk sultan of Syria (1079-95). The younger brother of *Malik Shah, he was commissioned by his brother to conquer Syria. Following a series of battles with the *Fatimids, T. conquered *Aleppo (1086) but lost the city as a result of a counter-offensive, which restored the coastal areas of Syria and Palestine to Fatimid control. Upon his brother's death (1092), T. attempted to seize power over the Seljuk empire and a civil war broke out in Persia. Defeated by his nephew, Barkiyarok, T. was killed. His sons continued to govern in Syria.

TVER Principality in central Russia (1209-1485). Ruled by a cadet branch of the *Rurikid dynasty, T. was sacked by the *Mongols in 1238. Its princes became tributary to the Golden Horde and, at the end of the 13th century, some of them were even appointed grand princes. In the 14th century the leaders of T. lost much of their importance, and in 1485 Ivan III annexed the principality to *Moscow.

TWELVE PEERS OF FRANCE See PEERS.

TWO SWORDS, DOCTRINE OF THE See GALASIUS, St.

TYLER, WAT (d. 1381) English rebel. Influenced by John *Ball, he left his work in Kent and organized a peasants' revolt in Kent and Essex against the king, nobility and church establishment. In the spring and summer of 1381 he led the revolt and seized London. However, the violence done by the rebels aroused the ire of the burghers, who rose up, killed T. and ended the revolt.

TYPUS Edict issued in 648 by the Byzantine emperor, *Constans II, forbidding religious controversies in the empire. The act aimed to achieve religious peace. Pope *Martin I opposed the T. as contrary to Orthodoxy; consequently, he was arrested, tried in Constantinople for political crimes and exiled to *Crimea. There he died in 655.

A. A. Vasiliev, *History of the Byzantine Empire* (1951).

TYRE City in Lebanon. Under Byzantine rule, its harbour was among the most important along the eastern coast of the Mediterranean. T. was also a major religious centre and its *metropolitans, first suffragans of the patriarchs of *Antioch, played an active role in the religious and political life of the empire. After the Arab conquest (638), the Greek population migrated and the city declined. In 1123 it was conquered by the *Crusaders, who had received naval support from *Venice. Consequently, the Italian power was granted one-third of the city, together with its harbour, second only to that of *Acre. In 1187, following the defeat at *Hattin, T. became the sole city of the Latin kingdom of Jerusalem to have resisted conquest by *Saladin, having been defended by *Conrad of Montferrat. It served as a base for the Third Crusade, in which part of the realm was restored. In the 13th century a *commune was established at T. and the main influence in the city was Venetian. The *glass industry of T. was gradually transferred to Italy and some of the workshops were moved to Murano, one of the islands north of Venice. Conquered by the *Mamelukes in 1291, the city declined in the later Middle Ages.

J. Prawer, *The Crusaders* (1973).

TYROL County in southern Germany, along the passes of the Alps. Part of the *Bavarian state in the early Middle Ages, T. became a distinct county within the duchy of Bavaria in the later 9th century. The local dynasty gradually extended its possessions and established a powerful government at Innsbruck. By the end of the 13th century the counts had established relations with the most important families of southern Germany and sought the ducal title. Upon the extinction of the dynasty at the death of Count Meinard (1338), the succession to T. was disputed between the houses of *Luxemburg and *Wittelsbach. The attempts of *Louis of Bavaria to secure the county for one of his sons incited the opposition of the Luxemburgs, widely supported by the German princes who feared an increase in Wittelsbach power. The compromise reached was only temporary. In 1363 Duke *Leopold of Austria secured the right to the county and annexed T. to the *Hapsburg estates.

J. W. Thompson, *Feudal Germany* (1928).

U

UBALDINI Feudal family from *Tuscany. Although supposedly of *Lombard origin, the family is first mentioned only in 1105, as lords of Mugello and the surrounding lands in the Tuscan-Emilian Apennine Mountains. They rose to eminence in the 13th century, mainly because of their control over the then oft-frequented trade route between Tuscany and the Romagna region.

Prominent members include Ubaldino della Pila (d. 1285), a *Ghibelline captain, his brother Ottaviano (d. 1272), bishop of Bologna and then cardinal, another Ottaviano, also bishop of Bologna (d. 1295), Straccia, bishop of Bologna (d. 1298) and Ruggeri, archbishop of Pisa (d. 1295).

P. Raina, *L'sscrizione degli Ubaldini e il suo autore, Archiv. Stor. Ital*, serie V, vol. XXXI.

UBALDO OF GUBBIO, St. (d. 1160) Born of a noble family at Gubbio in the Umbria region. An orphan since early childhood, he was educated at the local cathedral school and accepted as a regular canon by his uncle, the bishop of Gubbio. He became his successor in 1129 by decision of Pope *Honorius II, having been refused the bishopric of *Perugia a few years earlier. Famed for his devout life and endeavours to reform his church and pacify the civil strife in his hometown, he reputedly worked miracles after his death and was canonized by Pope *Celestine III in 1192. Amongst the local population he is held as a patron saint and protector against possession by the devil.

Vita di s. Ubaldo (1924).

UBAYDULLAH AL-MAHDI (d. 934) A leader of the *Ismaili revolutionary movement and founder of the *Fatimid empire in north Africa. After unsuccessful attempts at revolt against the orthodox *Abbasid caliphs in Syria, U. moved to north Africa, where he was imprisoned at Sijilmassa in the western Sahara. Freed in 909 by his successful adherents, he proclaimed himself Mahdi ("the guided one"), the rightful caliph (imam) by virtue of descent from *Fatima, daughter of Mohammad, and her husband *Ali, and established his capital at *Mahdia on the east coast of Tunisia, from where his successors conquered Egypt, *Mecca and Medina in the 10th century.

H. F. al-Hamdani, *On the Genealogy of Fatimid Caliphs* (1958).

UBERTI Leading noble Florentine family (12th-14th centuries). Spurning commercial enterprise, the U. were an early focal point of factional noble organization in Florence, leading in 1177 a civil war against a rival grouping of families. With the consolidation of the *Guelph and *Ghibelline parties, the U. became the natural leaders of the latter. After being exiled from the city upon Emperor *Frederick II's death and the rise of a democratic government (1250), Farinata degli U. led the Ghibelline forces to military victory and took over Florence (1260), saving it from destruction at the hands of his Sienese and imperial allies. After the collapse of the Ghibelline regime (1267) the family went into exile, continuing for many decades to plot its comeback.

UBERTINO OF *CASALE (c. 1259-c. 1329) Writer and a leader of the *Franciscan Spirituals. He studied theology in Paris. Returning to Italy (c. 1280-83), he came under the influence of mystic Joachimite teaching, notably of Petrus Joannis *Olivi. Preaching widely, he was for a time protected by the cardinals Napoleone *Orsini and Giacomo *Colonna, but was suspended in 1304 after attacking the established church as a "church of the flesh" and questioning the legality of papal elections. His *Arbor vitae crucifixae Jesu*, written in retirement, forcefully expresses the radical stance of the Franciscan Spirituals. Deeply involved in the dispute over the future of his order, U. was first transferred to the *Benedictine order, then prosecuted, but managed to flee Avignon, probably joining his comrades-in-belief at the court of *Louis IV the Bavarian. Details of his last years and death are unknown.

D. L. Douie, *The Nature and Effect of the Heresy of the Fratecelli* (1932).

UCLES Village in the Tagus Valley, east of *Toledo. A strategic place figuring already in the campaign of *Alfonso VI of Castile to win Toledo (1085), it was the site of a battle in which the *Almoravides routed Alfonso, his son Sancho dying in the battle (1108). Village and church were handed over by King *Alfonso VIII in 1174 to the Order of *Santiago, which built a monastery and fortress on the spot. During the early 13th century U. became the centre of the order and the main base for its military thrust into the Moslem territory to the south.

P. Quintero, *Ucles, residencia de la orden de Santiago* (1904).

UDALRIC OF BOHEMIA (d. 1304) Duke of *Bohemia from 1010, when his brother Duke Jaromir was driven out of Bohemia by *Boleslaw Chrobry of Poland. Trying to maintain a precarious balance between his feudal overlord, the German king and emperor, and his aggressive and powerful neighbour, the duke and later king of Poland, he took the latter's son and envoy prisoner (1013), but was deprived of his valuable hostage by King *Henry II of Germany. By 1031 U. fell foul of Emperor *Conrad II, when he refused to send troops for a campaign against Poland. Summoned to a diet at *Merseburg, he remained defiantly absent. Consequently, he was defeated in a short military campaign by the emperor's young son *Henry III, tried, condemned, banished and deprived of his lands (1033). Pardoned in 1034, U. attacked the lands of his reinstated brother Duke Jaromir and had him blinded, but died the same year while dining, probably from poison. He was succeeded by his able son Bratislav.

W. Wegener, *Böhmen, Mähren und das Reich im Hochmittelalter* (1959);

K. Richter, *Handbuch der Geschichte der böhmischen Länder*, I (1967).

UGOLINO DELLA GHERARDESCA (d. 1289) Pisan *Ghibelline leader and member of the great feudal family Gherardesca. A man of ruthless ambition, his plot to secure arbitrary power in Pisa was discovered and U. was exiled. Allying himself subsequently to the Florentines and the Luccese, who were then fighting the Pisans, he managed to reinstate himself in his hometown by force. Failing to achieve military victory over the Genoese and the Florentines, his rule turned into virtual tyranny. U. was overthrown by a conspiracy in 1288. His story and pitiful end (he and his sons and grandsons were starved to death in prison) are told in *Dante's *Inferno*.

UIGHUR TURKS A people of *Mongolian origin who replaced in 745 the eastern *Turks as the leading element of an empire stretching from the Altai Mountains and the Gobi Desert to the Amur River in the east. Their empire was centred on the town of Karabalghasun on the Orkon River, where their chief (khagan) resided, representing the confederation of the nine Uighur clans. The U. adopted *Manichaeism as a religion and developed peaceful relations with China, supplying war horses and receiving privileged access to the riches of China. Their empire was shattered in 840 by the arrival of another Turkish people, the nomadic Kirgiz. Withdrawing, the U. founded a new kingdom in eastern Turkistan and northwestern China with Khocho (modern Karakoja) as their capital. There they developed a remarkably high civilization based on religious tolerance and the use of written documents. After the Mongol conquest of 1250 the U. served their conquerors as scribes, thereby preserving their cultural heritage.

C. Mackerras, *The Uighur Empire, according to T'ang Dynastic Histories; A Study in Sino-Uighur Relations, 744-840* (1972).

ULM German town in *Swabia on the northern bank of the Danube where it is joined by the rivers Ill and Blon. First mentioned in 854 as a royal possession, it became in the 12th century a major basis for *Staufen expansion in Swabia and was established as a chartered town by *Frederick I. In the late Middle Ages it was one of the major free *imperial cities of Germany. Its economic prosperity was based on a thriving textile industry and on its location on important trade routes. The constitution was democratic as early as 1397, the *guilds having a majority of the Council seats. Protestant from 1530, U. had to submit to an aristocratic regime forced on it by the emperor (1548). With its hold on a large agricultural hinterland, U. was a major factor in the politics of the Swabian town leagues in the 14th century as well as a centre of regional self-government in the 16th century. It is still noted for the Gothic minster (1377), the town hall (1370) and other medieval and Renaissance buildings from its era of economic and political prosperity.

M. Huber, "Ulm", in *Würtembergisches Städtebuch* (1962).

ULPHILAS (c. 311-c. 382) The apostle and missionary of the *Goths. Of *Cappadocian origin, he seems to have had a Christian education and was made bishop of the yet heathen Visigoths, the lords of his Cappadocian people, by the Arian bishop of Constantinople, Eusebius of Nicomedia (341). Returning to his homeland, U. laboured at the Christianization of the Goths in face of growing persecution. Around 375 he led his congregation across the Danube into eastern Roman territory. Through U. the Christianity finally accepted by the Goths was of the Arian brand, which was consequently stamped as heretic. His second major achievement, instrumental to the conversion of the Goths, was his translation of the Bible into Gothic. For this purpose he constructed the first German script, the Gothic alphabet, from Greek and Latin letters. Besides fragments of his Old and New Testament translations, some theological writings of Arian character have been preserved.

G. Friedrichsen, *The Gothic Version of the Gospels* (1926);

K. D. Schmidt, *Die Bekehrung der Ostgermanen zum Christentum* (1939).

ULRICH, St. (c. 890-973) Bishop of *Augsburg. Son of a noble family, he was educated at the monastery of *St. Gallen and served subsequently as a cleric under his uncle, the bishop of Augsburg. Returning to manage his family estate near Zurich for a 15-year stretch, he was then made bishop of Augsburg (924). Attached to Emperor *Otto I by common aristocratic background, friendship and service, he was the prototype of the imperial bishop. Active as a high dignitary of the state as well as shepherd of his flock, he defended his city against the *Hungarians (955) and mediated between the emperor and his rebellious son. Highly esteemed, he was the first bishop to be solemnly canonized by a pope (993).

His life in: *Monumenta Germaniae Historica* (1841);

H. Kohl, *Bischop Ulrich von Augsburg* (1963).

UMAYYADS (Ummayads, Omayyads) An aristocratic and merchant clan who founded the first Moslem dynasty in *Syria (641-750) and a kingdom in *Spain (756-1031). Leaders of the pre-Moslem oligarchy at *Mecca, the U. opposed *Mohammad except for *Othman ibn Affan, who became caliph of the first Moslem empire (644). After the interlude of *Ali's caliphate, the U. again came to power with *Muawiya ibn Abu Sufyan, the governor of Syria and founder of the Sufyanid line of the family. Based by now in *Damascus, they expanded their empire to eastern Persian and rapidly changed some of the hallowed traditions of Arab tribalism. Their conception of the state was a secular one, drawing on the cooperation of the Syrian Christians, retaining the Byzantine and Persian administration and staff in the conquered provinces, and substituting hereditary succession for the tribal-elective nature of the *caliphate. They antagonized Arab national and religious sensitivities, which merged with Iraqi and Persian national resentment in the *Shiite movement. Combined with tribal civil wars amongst the Arabs and the premature deaths in the Sufyanid dynasty, Shiism brought about a shift of power to the Marwanid line of the U., beginning with *Marwan I (684-85). Under the rule of *Abd Al-Malik and Al-Walid I the empire reached its zenith, encompassing eastern Iran, *Transoxiana, the lower Indus Valley and *Visigothic Spain, but failing to take Constantinople (716). The policy of relative liberality towards other religions was dropped in favour of Islamization and Arabization in language, administration and coinage. The mass conversions in the period of the pietist *Omar II (717-20) added considerably to the religious opposition when the Arabizing policies were resumed after Omar's death. Consequent financial difficulties, military defeat (Poitiers 732, Anatolia 740) and the challenge of the Hashemite sect, culminating in major revolts in Syria, Iraq and *Khorasan (745-46), finally brought down the U. empire *Battle of the Great Zab River 750). *Abd al Rahman escaped the slaughter of his family by fleeing to Spain, where he founded the U. state of *Cordoba (756). Reaching brilliant heights of cultural achievement and political power, its rulers titled themselves caliphs in 929. The second U. state collapsed in 1031 from internal weakness and civil wars.

J. Wellhausen, *The Arab Kindgom and its Fall* (1973).

UNAM SANCTAM Papal bull issued in 1302 by *Boniface VIII asserting the supreme power of the pope. It was occasioned by the struggle between Boniface VIII and King *Philip IV of France over taxation of the clergy and the more general question of the loyalty of the French clergy. The bull is the culmination of a 200-year-long process, drawing together each and every argument in favour of papal supremacy raised since the beginning of the papal reform movement in the mid-11th century. The bull emphasizes the position of the pope as leader of the church as well as his duty to direct secular affairs towards religious goals. "It is necessary to salvation for every human creature to be subject to the Roman pontiff".

T. S. R. Boase, *Boniface VIII* (1933);

Text in H. Bettenson, ed., *Documents of the Christian Church* (1943).

UNCELEN (7th century) Duke of the Alamanni. A descendant of the royal family, he ruled Alamannia under the overlordship of the *Merovingian kings. He sought to gain independence from the Franks by intervening in 610 in the civil war between the Merovingian kings and by founding a "national" bishopric at Constance in 613. Thanks to his efforts, the dukes of Alamannia attained a greater degree of autonomy.

R. Folz, *Les Barbares* (1975).

UNCIAL SCRIPT A type of script developed in antiquity and used in the early Middle Ages (4th to 8th centuries), mainly for ecclesiastical texts, both in Greek and Latin. Its round forms are suited to pen-writing on parchment, a technique and material then becoming prevalent. The letters, which include capital, minuscule as well as characteristic uncial ones, are all of one size and contained within the upper and lower lines. The semi-U. is a variation using more cursive forms and leading to the pre-Carolingian script. Both types were used after the 8th century only for titling.

E. Chatelain, *Uncialis scriptura* (1901-02);

J. Stiennon, *Paléographie du Moyen Age* (1973).

UNCTION The religious process of anointing with consecrated oil. Originating from Jewish and pre-Christian sources, it is mentioned in the Old and New Testaments. In medieval practice, U. was used in and by the church for a number of different purposes. Anointing with oil and praying for the sick had developed by the 12th century from its original early medieval context as a measure of healing into the "Extreme U.", the *sacrament administered to the critically ill and the dying. U. is also part of the rites performed at the sacraments of baptism, confirmation and the ordination of priests, as well as in the consecration of churches, churchbells and altars. The anointing of kings was widely practised, both by rulers, to add a religious dimension to secular rule, and by the church, to emphasize its control over the kings. In all its variations, U. is seen as a physical process by which spiritual grace as well as physical gifts of well-being, success and power are bestowed.

A. Chavasse, *Etude sur l'onction des infirmes dans L'Eglise Latine du IIIe au XIe siècle* (1942);

B. Poschmann, *Penance and the Anointing of the Sick* (1964).

UNGER Second bishop of *Poznan (992-1012). Probably a former abbot of Memleben in *Saxony, he was appointed by the imperial government to head the bishopric of Poznan. As a missionary outpost, Poznan possessed a large measure of independence and was not incorporated into the newly-created archbishopric of *Gniezno, the primatial see of Poland. The Germans, for their part, claimed Poznan to be subject to the authority of the see of *Magdeburg. Thus U. became entangled in the Polish-German conflict of the period. The problem was accentuated by the fact that Poznan had been the Polish capital during part of *Miezko's reign. In the year 1000 U. opposed the appointment of Gaudentius as archbishop of Gniezno, as this curtailed his own rights. While taking his protest to Rome (c. 1003), he was kidnapped by German agents. He never reached his destination nor returned to his seat, which remained vacant until his death in 1012.

A. P. Vlasto, *The Entry of the Slavs into Christendom* (1970);

G. Sappok, *Die Anfänge des Bistums Posen und die Reihe seiner Bischöfe 968-1498* (1937).

UNIGENITUS Papal bull issued in 1343 by *Clement VII on the occasion of his jubilee. The bull canonized the teaching of Hugh of Saint-Cher (c. 1230) concerning *indulgences. Hugh related the current practice of granting indulgences to the church's treasury of merits and good deeds accumulated by Christ, the Virgin and the saints. By so doing Hugh returned to an early Christian notion of the union of all Christians in the mystical body of Christ, which was taken up by popes like *Boniface VIII in their efforts to achieve supreme rule. The principle expounded by Hugh was further developed by the *Scholastics of the 13th century, who rendered it into the final form in which it appears in the bull.

Text in H. Denzinger, *Enchiridon symbolorum 1025-1027* (1963);

J. E. Campbell, *Indulgences* (1953).

UNIVERSITY The institution of higher *education originated in the Middle Ages. Its full Latin name, *Universitas Societas Magistrorum et Scholarium* (The Universal Society of Teachers and Scholars) was abridged over the centuries, so that the adjective became the common noun. Up to the 12th century only two types of schools prevailed in western Europe, those of cathedrals and the monastic ones; however, a number of private schools, founded by distinguished teachers, emerged in the cities and attracted students interested in acquiring knowledge in specific subjects. Such was the school of law established by *Irnerius at Bologna, Italy, or that of Peter *Abelard, dedicated to philosophical-theological

A university classroom in Germany; 14th-century miniature

studies, at *Paris, France. *Bologna's school of law, which also offered the study of the *seven liberal arts, became famous in the middle of the 12th century. Students from all over western Europe formed a scholarly body which was not integrated in the city; thus it became necessary to draw up special regulations of the school's activities and the incorporation of the members. In 1158 Emperor *Frederick Barbarossa issued his charter, *Authentica Habita, granting the U. of Bologna self-rule and academic privileges, which included raising the status of the teachers and students to that of the clergy, so that they were exempt from lay jurisdiction. In later years a school of medicine was added to this U. Thus, the organization of the U. into these three schools, known as the *studium generale, became the standard model for Italian Us. of the 13th and 14th centuries.

The organization of the U. at Paris, which prevailed north of the Alps, was entirely different. The conflict involved with Abelard's teaching caused the canons of the Notre Dame Cathedral to decide in 1128 to exclude teachers and students from the cathedral's cloister. Consequently, a number of private schools, some of

which existed only as long as the lifetime of their famous teachers, were established on the left bank of the Seine, among them the famous school of Abelard. In the middle of the 12th century a multitude of students from all over Europe attended these schools, among them future popes and other influential persons. As a result, the new quarter in which the schools were situated became known as the *Quartier Latin*. Problems of organization and the incorporation of members, compulsory in the corporative structure of medieval cities, led to the creation of a body of teachers and students under the authority of the chancellor of the bishopric of Paris, who became the head of the U. (from 1176) and was given the authority to issue the *licentio docendi* (the licence to teach) to those persons who had passed the examinations and graduated as masters of art, canon law or theology. The confederation of teachers and students was officially recognized in 1200 by King *Philip II, who exempted it from lay jurisdiction. The U. established its own regulations in 1208 and 1213, approved by Pope *Innocent III. The academic body was divided into four *nationes, the French, Norman, Picardian and Anglo-German, as well as into four faculties (Arts, Law, Medicine and Theology) under their respective deans and ruled by a rector, who was elected by the assembly of the *natiures*. Conflicts between the U. and the bishops of Paris over the former's autonomy led to a long strike (1229-31), which was ended by the bull of Pope *Gregory IX, *Parens scientiarum*. This bull accorded academic freedom, but only in the sense of self-government but not that of liberty of thought and speech, which remained confined to the doctrinal boundaries of the Church. The solution of housing problems was beyond the power of the teachers. Consequently, *colleges emerged. Originally founded as pious *donationes* to provide housing for poor students, they also became study halls and thus changed the structure of the U. of Paris (13th century), which now contained a group of colleges, the most important among them being the *Sorbonne. An additional change was the penetration of the *friars into the teaching body of the U., despite the opposition of the secular teachers.

The construction of Paris and its structure were adopted at the beginning of the 13th century by the U. of *Oxford and spread to other institutions north of the Alps. In the 12th-14th centuries, the U. was the most important centre of thought and intellectual activity, whether in the fields of philosophy and theology, where scholastic methods were dominant, or in sciences, which were mainly dependent on Greek thought, obtained through Arabic translations, but which also fostered original observations and research. Despite the control and censures of ecclesiastical authorities, which led to condemnations and even imprisonments, non-conformist views prevailed and developed in the Us.; in certain cases, such as those of *Wycliffe at Oxford or *Hus at Prague, non-conformism led to open criticism of the ecclesiastical authorities and paved the way for the Reformation. The *Great Schism of the Church (1378-1416) and the *Conciliar period, in which the theologians were involved, caused the decline of the medieval Us. in the 15th century. New forms of thought, such as Humanism and the Renaissance, emerged but the structure of the U. remained unchanged until the scientific revolution of the 17th century.

H. Wiernszobski, *Medieval Universities* (1968).

UNSTRUT River in *Thuringia, the site of a battle (summer of 1075) between King *Henry IV of Germany, aided by most of the German ecclesiastical and secular princes, and the rebellious *Saxon nobles and peasants, allies of Pope *Gregory VII in his *Investiture struggle against Henry. The decisive military victory of the king followed by another invasion of Saxony in the autumn of the same year brought about the unconditional surrender of the Saxons. One of the casualties of the battle was Margrave Ernest, the *Babenberg ruler of *Austria.

Gebhardt, *Handbuch der deutschen Geschichte* (1973).

UNTERWALDEN Forest canton in central *Switzerland, divided geographically and politically by the Kernwald forest into eastern Obwalden and western Nidwalden. Its lands, owned by feudal and ecclesiastical lords, belonged politically to the *Hapsburgs. Their territorial expansion in *Lucerne and Unterwalden brought about the foundation of the "Everlasting League of 1291", of which *Schwyz, *Uri, Nidwalden and later

The Gothic 13th-century cathedral at Uppsala

Obwalden were part. Its two parts united by Hapsburg administrative measures (1304, 1309), U. took part in the victorious Battle of *Morgarten (1315) against *Leopold I of Hapsburg and became one of the founding members of the Swiss Confederation.

C. Gilliard, *A History of Switzerland* (1955).

UPPSALA The spiritual and educational capital of *Sweden since the Viking period. Old U.'s temple, the great centre of pagan worship, was described by *Adam of Bremen (*c.* 1070) as a magnificent place and formed the core of resistance to Christianization. Towards the end of the 11th century its strength declined and Old U. became the seat of a bishop and in 1164 the seat of the Swedish archbishop. The prestige of U. was enhanced by the presence of St. *Eric, the founder of one of the reigning dynasties.

In the 13th century the archbishop's seat was transferred to New U., less than two miles to the south, and its cathedral was begun *c.* 1260. The archbishop became a major factor in Swedish politics, his power based as much on spiritual prestige as on his control of huge landed wealth and large armed retinues.

N. Sundquis, ed., *Uppsala stads historia* (1953-58); I. Andersson, *A History of Sweden* (1956).

URBAN II (Odo of Lagery; c. 1042-99) Pope from 1088. Born at Châtillon-sur-Marne, he studied at Rheims under St. *Bruno, the founder of the Carthusian order, joined the monastery of *Cluny (*c.* 1070) and became its prior. He was made cardinal around 1080, and served Pope *Gregory VII as legate to Germany and France at the height of the *Investiture struggle (1084-85). Elected pope, he continued Gregory's line of ecclesiastical reform. A patron of the monastic movement, he convoked three synods (1095 *Piacenza and *Clermont, 1098 *Bari), among other things forbidding the clergy to render feudal oaths. His attempts to overcome the schism created by Emperor *Henry IV's reluctance to drop his antipope *Clement III met only with partial success. Urban did receive the allegiance of the church, but failed to oust Clement from Rome. Towards the secular rulers he pursued a more moderate line than Gregory VII, despite the many frictions caused by Henry IV's insistence on his antipope, the French King *Philip I's marital troubles and the tightening of royal control over the clergy of England and southern Italy. U.'s most important step was his call for the *Crusade (Clermont 1095), the results of which he did not live to see. His programme of reunion of the Latin and Greek Churches, of which the crusade was but one aspect, failed.

L. Paulot, *Un Pape français; Urbain II* (1903).

URBAN III (Uberto Crivelli; d. 1187) Pope from 1185. Archdeacon of Bourges, then of Milan, cardinal (1182), archbishop of *Milan (1185). Heir to the traditional hostility between papacy and empire, relations were further strained when Emperor *Frederick I married the heiress to the Norman kingdom of Sicily (1186). Full war broke out over the manning of an ecclesiastical post at Trier, and Frederick sent his son with an army into the *Papal States and had Urban closed in at *Verona. A new attempt by U. at negotiating a settlement was cut short by his death.

M. C. de Fischer-Reichenbach, *Urbain III et Barberousse* (1940).

URBAN IV (Jacques Pantaléon; c. 1200-64) Pope 1261-64. Born at Troyes, in Champagne, son of a shoemaker, he became a teacher of canon law and rose in ecclesiastical service in Laon and Liège, was legate in eastern Germany, archdeacon of Laon (1249), papal legate to the German princes (1251), bishop of Verdun (1253) and Latin patriarch of Jerusalem (1255). As pope, he drew the consequences of the long papal-imperial struggle over the kingdom of Sicily, dispossessed *Manfred, son of Emperor *Frederick II, and invited *Charles I of Anjou, younger brother of *Louis IX of France, to take over the Sicilian kingdom as a papal fief.

He interfered in the negotiations going on in Germany over the election of a successor to Frederick and sided with *Henry III of England in his struggle against the barons. His negotiations with Emperor *Michael VIII Palaeologus of Byzantium over ecclesiastical union were inconclusive. By his decision the Feast of *Corpus Christi became general usage in the Latin Church.

O. de Poli, *Le Pape Urbain IV* (1903).

URBAN V (Guillaume de Grimoard; c. 1310-70) Pope from 1362. U. was born at Grisac, Languedoc. He was a monk, and studied and taught canon law. Abbot of St. Germain, Auxerre (1352) and of St. Victor in Marseilles (1361), papal legate in Italy, he was a personality of high integrity and a serious matter-of-fact inclination, and is held to be the best of the *Avignon popes. In matters of ecclesiastical reform he fought against the evil of plural benefices. His initiative and support for a new crusade, which resulted in the short-lived conquest of *Alexandria by *Peter of Lusignan, king of Cyprus, as well as his efforts at ecclesiastical reunion with the Eastern Church (1369 recognition of the papacy by *John V Palaeologus) had no lasting effects. U.'s earnest attempt to return the papacy from *Avignon to Rome (1367) was foiled by the chronic state of war in

central Italy, and he returned to Avignon in 1370 where he died a few months later.

G. Mollat, *The Popes at Avignon* (1963).

URBAN VI (Bartolomeo Prignano; c. 1311-89) Pope from 1378. Born in Naples, he was archbishop of Acerenza (1363) and of Bari (1377), and chancellor to Pope *Gregory XI after the latter's return from *Avignon to Rome. U. was elected under strong popular pressure for an Italian pope, but the legality of his election was almost immediately doubted by the mostly French cardinals who had been antagonized by U.'s quick temper. Their return to Avignon and the election of a French antipope opened the *Great Schism. U.'s pontificate was marked by his unceasing struggle against the antipope, calling for crusades against the secular rulers supporting the antipope and employing torture and execution against the Italian cardinals who had advocated putting U. under tutelage because of his near-deranged behaviour.

W. Ullmann, *The Origins of the Great Schism* (1948); O. Prerorsky, *L'elezione di Urbano IV e l'insorgere dello scisma d'Occidente* (1960).

URBI ET ORBI ("for the town (of Rome) and the world") A phrase uttered by the first *cardinal *deacon while investing the newly-elected pope with his robe. Instituted in the papal elections decree of *Gregory X (1274), it expressed the integration of *Rome as the Petrine capital with the universal function and standing of the pope. No longer used in such a context, the phrase applies today to the papal benediction given on special occasions from the balcony of St. *Peter's in Rome as well as the *Lateran Basilica, which is called the "mother and head of all the churches of the town and the world".

URBINO Town in the march of *Ancona. Of Roman origin and a bishopric since the 6th century, it became part of the *Papal States by donation of *Pepin the Short (756). In the 12th century the town was disputed between the popes and the German emperors and their partisans in the city, the *Montefeltro family. The latter received U., first as a vicarate (1155) and in 1213 as a fief, thus becoming counts of U. Having turned *Guelph in the 14th century, the family was recalled by the citizens. In the 15th century the town developed and prospered and the Montefeltro, now dukes by papal grace, built up a Renaissance court and turned U. into a centre of arts and letters.

F. Ugolino, *Storia dei conti e duchi d'Urbino* (1859).

URGEL *Catalan county and its main town (Seo de Urgel) in the Spanish Pyrénées. A bishopric of U. is mentioned from the 6th century. In the 9th century it became part of the Spanish *march organized by the *Carolingians as a defence line against the Moslems. After the disintegration of the Carolingian empire, town and county were annexed by Wilfred the Hairy, count of *Barcelona (873-98), the founder of the Catalan dynasty, only to be given out again in the divisions of heritage following his death. In 1058 Raymond Berengar I, count of Barcelona, made himself feudal *suzerain of U. as well as of its neighbouring counties and, in the 12th century, it was joined to the kingdom of *Aragon as part of *Catalonia. In 1347 U. served as the base for Count Ghazni in his struggle against his brother, King *Peter IV of Aragon. U. seems to have been a centre of religious heterodoxy. In 792 its bishop Felix was forced to appear before a council to recant his *Adoptionist views. In the early 12th century many feudal lords from the diocese of U. were *Cathars, another proof of the strong connection between the French and the Spanish sides of the Pyrénées. Since the Treaty of *Corbeil (1258) the bishop of U. and the French count of Foix were joint overlords of *Andorra, the road to which starts from U.

J. F. O'Callaghan, *A History of Medieval Spain* (1975).

URI Forest canton in central *Switzerland. First mentioned in 732. The independent status of its *peasant communities in their inaccessible mountain valleys, having as overlord only the German king, was recognized by *Henry VII in 1231, when the region was formally joined to the empire, and again by *Rudolph of Hapsburg in 1274. A high state of inter-village organization is attested to by the existence of a common seal in 1243. Co-member of the Everlasting League of 1291, Uri took part in the victorious battles against the Austrians at *Morgarten (1315) and *Sempach (1386).

G. Guggenbühl, *Geschichte der schweizerischen Eidgenossenschaft*, 1 (1947).

URRACA (1077-1126) Queen of *León and *Castile. The widow of Count *Raymond of Burgundy, she succeeded her father *Alfonso VI as queen in 1109. The same year she was forced by the pressure of the Castilian nobles to marry Alfonso I of Aragon. U. was soon at open enmity with her husband, who at once estranged the Castilian magnates by his ambitions. The annulment of the marriage on grounds of consanguinity (1114) made no difference, as Alfonso did not relax his efforts for political control, stationing his soldiers in the town of her kingdom. At the same time U. had to thwart the attempts of her step-sister Theresa to form an independent principality in the county of *Portugal. In addition, Diego *Gelmirez, bishop and then archbishop of *Compostela, and the Galician nobles sought to dethrone U. in favour of her son Alfonso Ramirez, later *Alfonso VII of Castile. These struggles were complicated by urban-aristocratic and inter-aristocratic enmities as well as by the rivalry between the sees of Toledo and Compostela. The result was open civil war during U.'s reign, which was only somewhat relieved by her death in 1126.

J. F. O'Callaghan, *A History of Medieval Spain* (1975).

URTUKIDS (URTUQIDS, ORTOQIDS) *Turkoman dynasty in Syria and Iraq. Its founder, Urtuk ibn Aksab, entered the service of the *Seljuks and was one of the military leaders under *Tutush. In 1086 he was appointed governor of Jerusalem, and after his death (1092) the office was inherited by his sons. When the *Fatimids reconquered Jerusalem in 1096, the U. were given lands in *Iraq and northern *Syria, where they founded principalities. Active in the wars against the *Crusaders of *Antioch and *Edessa, their importance grew. The most important member of the dynasty, Ghazni, led the Seljuk counter-offensive against Antioch from 1102. In 1117 he became prince of *Aleppo until his death (1119). In the next generation the U. of northern Syria declined and were replaced by their *atabeg, *Zengi. The Iraqi branch, on the other hand, continued to govern a small principality until the 13th century.
CHI.

USAMA IBN MUNQUIDH (1095-1188) Courtier and man of letters. From a princely family in Schaizar,

Syria, he spent his life in the military, political and literary circles of *Damascus and *Cairo, taking a prominent part in many campaigns against the *Crusader states, as well as developing peaceful relations with some of the *Templars. Involved in the inter-Moslem wars and rivalries even more than in the fight against the infidels, he had to go into exile twice, losing his library of over 4000 manuscripts on the way from Cairo and having his Damascus home destroyed by the terrible earthquake of 1157. He spent his later years at the court of the *Urtukid Kara Arslan in literary work. A prolific writer, only some of his poetry and prose still exists, most of it in yet unedited manuscripts. His memoirs give a vivid picture of his time in peace and war, portraying Moslem society of Egypt and Syria as well as the Crusader states.

Biography and Texts in: H. Derenbourg, *Ousâma Ibn Mounkidh* (1889);
G. R. Potter, ed., *The Autobiography of Ousama* (1929).

USATGES OF BARCELONA Compilation of *Catalan feudal and public law dating from the 11th and 12th centuries. Drawing mainly from Germanic sources, its earlier nucleus includes various laws promulgated by Count *Raymond Berengar I on feudal matters, his recording of the basic feudal customs of Catalonia (c. 1058) and his compilation of public law (c. 1060). Additional texts relating to the *Peace and Truce of God were added. The whole work was given a new cast by the jurists in the service of *Raymond Berengar IV, who attempted to impose a concept of monarchical sovereignty upon the basically feudal character of the compilation. The U. became the fundamental law of Catalonia thereafter and, according to circumstances, a weapon in the cause of royal centralization of the maintenance of noble privileges.

E. N. van Kleffens, *Hispanic Law until the End of the Middle Ages* (1968).

USURY Initially, it meant exacting a charge for a loan. The medieval Church followed the Old Testament condemnation of oppressing the necessitous by the use of U. It strictly forbade U. to clergymen in the early Middle Ages, and to all Christians at the Third *Lateran *Council (1179), the Second Council of *Lyons (1274) and the Council of *Vienne (1311). At the last-named it was declared that anyone condoning U. should be treated as a heretic. Yet during the same period the rise of the money economy made the practice of U. much more widespread than before, causing an increasing demand for capital, both for personal purposes and for commercial ventures. The first problem was solved mainly by the existence of the *Jews, who were absolved from the ban on U. by the Fourth Lateran Council (1215). The need for commercial capital led to increasingly sophisticated ways of camouflaging the interest clauses in business contracts. At the same time *scholastic philosophy applied itself to the problem from a new perspective. Instead of focusing on the moral issues of the leader's motive and the debtor's plight, it analysed the debtor-creditor relationship itself. Basing itself on Roman legal concepts and the Aristotelian notion of interest founded on the "sterility" of money, scholasticism, led by *Thomas Aquinas, condemned U. on grounds of the nature of the loan itself. This left open the possibility of practising U. when certain circumstances, such as risk to capital, were weighty enough. Thus in response to strong pressures from lay society the Church adopted an increasingly liberal interpretation of U. allowing a wide range of exceptions, while maintaining at the same time its basic condemnation. The last step towards legitimization of U. was taken, when the Church authorized municipal pawnbrokers, the "Monte Pietatis", thus institutionalizing consumption credits to the poor after the expulsion of most Jewish communities in the 15th century.

E. Troeltsch, *The Social Teaching of the Christian Churches* (1950);

J. T. Noonan, *The Scholastic Analysis of Usury* (1957).

UTIGURS A *Hunnish-*Bulgarian tribe living on the eastern bank of the Sea of Azov. In the 6th century their formidable power and efficient organization brought them, together with their kinsmen, the Cotrigurs, to the attention of *Byzantium. When the Cotrigurs invaded the Balkans (551), Emperor *Justinian I cleverly used the U. to outmanoeuvre their cousins, bribing the khan, Sandilch, to attack the Cotrigurs from the rear (558). In 568 the weary U. succumbed to the *Turks, who expanded westwards under *Avar pressure. Although stripped of their old ruling class, the bulk of the U. seem to have survived and became the ethnic nucleus of the kingdom of Old Great *Bulgaria, which arose under Kubrat *c.* 584 around the lower Don River and south of the Caucasus Mountains, a territory previously occupied by the U.

S. Runciman, *A History of the First Bulgarian Empire* (1930).

UTRECHT Town and bishopric in the central Netherlands. Of pre-Roman origin, the site was continuously inhabited as a *Frisian and *Frankish fortress and market-place. It was handed over by *Pepin II to St. *Willibrord, who established his bishopric there (690). Captured by the *Normans in the 9th century, it was rebuilt by Bishop Balderik (918) and became a base of German imperial influence in the Rhine estuary. Richly endowed by the emperors, the bishops received in 1060 the countyship and built up a strong principality. In *c.* 1122 the burgher-town that had grown up adjacent to the bishop's city received a charter and began to construct its own walls. The major commercial and textile-producing centre since the 9th century, its social equilibrium of nobles, rich merchants and artisans was upset by the loss of economic leadership in the northern Netherlands in the late 13th century. With the victory of the guildsmen all citizens were obliged to join some *guild (1304-41). The guilds constituted the town's government and took over the struggle for independence from the bishop. Despite its losing ground economically, the late Middle Ages produced the still famous urban architecture, shaped by ring-canals, St. Martin's cathedral and sumptuous public and private buildings.

H. Pirenne, *Early Democracies in the Low Countries* (1963);

G. C. Labouchère, *The Medieval Churches of Utrecht.*

UTRECHT PSALTER A manuscript dating from *c.* 830 and belonging to the school of Rheims, coming probably from the monastery of Hautvilliers. Famous for its fine brush painting executed in the manner of pen-drawings, it illustrates the biblical text in a fresh and pertinent manner.

F. Wormald, *The Utrecht Psalter* (1953).

UZÈS Town and bishopric north of *Avignon, attested to since the 5th century. Although attached feudally to the count of *Toulouse, by 1065 its bishop acted as *suzerain for all practical purposes, rendering justice and minting money. The town had a *consular constitution and some measure of independence from the bishop, as attested by its right on tolls. In the 14th century it became the seat of a royal viscount, the rank of which was elevated in the 16th century to that of duke for the Crussol family.

C. Téraube, *Histoire d'Uzès* (1879).

V

VACARIUS, MASTER (c. 1120-c. 1200) Teacher and glossator of civil *law, born in Lombardy. He was trained as a civil lawyer at *Bologna, then went to England to act as legal adviser to the archbishop of *Canterbury (1146). The first to lecture on Roman law at *Oxford (1149), he wrote a textbook on the *Digest and *Code of Justinian, the so-called Liber Pauperum. Despite royal attempts to suppress the study of Roman law in England, V.'s lectures and works were a major success. He was subsequently employed as legal adviser and ecclesiastical judge in the archbishopric of *York, acting at the same time as an intermediary to the papal court. He also wrote Summa de matrimonio on the legal aspects of marriage (c. 1157) and De assumpto homine; Liber contra multiplices et varios errores (1177), a theological tract on the human nature of Christ.
F. de Zubeta (ed.), The Liber Pauperum of Vacarius (1927).

VADIUM, VADIMONIUM Early and high medieval legal term having three different, though related meanings: originally a pledge, then the object symbolizing the pledge and finally the symbolic act whereby the object is transferred from the debtor to the creditor, then to the warrantor and again to the debtor, making for a solemn confirmation of the debt; one of the terms denoting the fine paid by a culprit to the keeper of public peace in order to be readmitted to the peace; one of the terms denoting the money paid by a serf to his lord to obtain permission to marry.

VAGANTES The travelling students, scholars and clerics of the Middle Ages. They were the products of an ecclesiastical system in which not every cleric possessed a *benefice, and of the *universities, whose teachers moved easily from place to place, so that numbers of students followed them. Widespread from the late 12th century and sometimes developing into a real danger to law and order, the V. could not be controlled, despite the prohibitions issued from the mid-13th century by numerous synods. A by-product of the V. was their poetry, which is sometimes erroneously equated with that of the *Goliards. Usually written in Latin, it is characterized by groups of four consecutive rhyming lines. It dealt with the life of the V. as well as stressing the weaknesses of established ecclesiastical and laic society. Part of this poetry was in fact written by sedentary people, amongst them high church dignitaries (*Walter of Châtillon, Eraclius, *Henry of Avranches). Others were genuine wanderers catering to an educated and usually ecclesiastical public (Hugo of Orléans, the *Archipoeta). The most important collection of V. poetry is the *Carmina Burana.
H. Waddell, The Wandering Scholars (1961);
M. Bechthun, Beweggründe und Bedeutung des Vagantentums in der lateinischen Kirche des Mittelalters (1941).

VAHRAM (Philaretus Brachamius; 11th century) An *Armenian army commander under Emperor *Romanus IV who established Lesser Armenia, the first Armenian principality in exile, following the fall of *Cappadocia to the *Turks (after 1074). Together with his warlike followers, he created the independent state of Germanicea in Asia Minor and northern Syria. In addition, he ruled Melitene and *Edessa through his vassals while *Cilicia accepted his overlordship. In 1078 he was offered the rule of *Antioch. V. stabilized his position by making peace with the Eastern emperor, *Nicephorus III, whereby he also became the vassal of the *atabeg of *Mosul.
CMedH, IV (1964);
W. H. Rüdt-Callenberg, The Rupenides, Hethumides and Lusignans: the Structure of the Armeno-Cilician Dynasties (1963).

VAISON-LA-ROMAINE Bishopric and town in southern *France, north of Carpentras. An ancient Gallo-Roman village, it is mentioned as a bishopric from 450, when it became subject to the archbishopric of *Arles. Seat of numerous ecclesiastical councils in late antiquity, it was destroyed during the barbarian invasions but rebuilt in *Merovingian times, probably as a fortress, on the right bank of the Ouvèze River. During the 12th century the counts of *Toulouse built a castle on the left bank of the river overlooking and defending the new town. In 1229 the bishopric became independent, but in 1475 it was placed under the authority of the archbishopric of *Avignon. Its famous cathedral was built during the 11th and the 12th centuries.
J. Sautel, Vaison la Romaine, Sites, Histoire et Monuments (1953).

VAL D'ARAN Small town in southern France near Comminges, the seat of a bishopric and community belonging to the radical dualistic branch of *Catharism. The bishopric was founded by the great synod of European Cathars at St. Felix de Caraman (1167). Its first bishop was Raymond of Casals, who was mentioned only in 1167, its second, Raymond of Baimiac. After 1181 there is no more mention of either bishopric or community.
A. Borst, Die Katharer (1953).

VALDEMAR See WALDEMAR.

VAL-DES-DUNES Southeast of *Caen, it was the site of a battle (1047) in which William the Young, illegitimate son of Duke *Robert I of Normandy, acknowledged heir to his father and later *William I the Conqueror, king of England, defeated a rebellion of barons headed by his childhood companion Guy of Burgundy. Forced to flee after the outbreak of the rebellion, he sought help from his overlord, King *Henry I of France, and returned with the king and 3000 men to V., where he routed the rebels, driving many of them

Dish with Hispano-Moorish decoration, Valencia, c. 1420

into the Arne River. This victory was followed by a ten-year struggle in which Henry tried in vain to depose the now over-powerful William, instigating rebellions, and invading Normandy a number of times.

F. Barlow, *William I and the Norman Conquest* (1965).

VALENCIA Kingdom and its capital in eastern *Spain. Ruled by the *Visigoths from 413, it was conquered by the *Moslems in 714. Independent from 1021, the town became the capital of a Moorish principality after the distintegration of the caliphate of *Cordoba. The kingdom and town were attacked by *Ferdinand I of Castile (1065), causing it to relinquish its independence in favour of protection by the Moslem rulers of *Toledo. In 1094 it was captured by the *Cid, but in 1102 it was occupied by the *Almoravides after the town was set on fire by the retreating Christians. During the 30 years of Almoravide rule the city achieved partial independence and in 1041 became the seat of local potentates allied to the *Almohades. In 1238 the kingdom and city of V. passed into the ownership of *James I of Aragon, but a form of self-government persisted until 1707, including a separate administration, parliament and code of laws. In 1479 it was incorporated in the state of *Castile and Aragon. The city has been famous from antiquity for its agricultural products, mainly fruit, its fertility depending on highly-developed irrigation techniques. The Moors called V. "the town of joy". Its "Water Court", a tribunal of farmer-judges deciding on complicated questions of water-rights, is attested from the 10th century. V.'s prosperity continued under the frequent changes of government and is attested by its fine Romanesque, Gothic and Late Gothic architecture. The first printing press in Spain was set up there in 1474 and a *university was founded in 1501.

T. F. Glick, *Irrigation and Society in Medieval Valencia* (1970);

R. J. Burns, *Medieval Colonialism; Post-Crusade Exploitation of Islamic Valencia* (1975).

VALENCIENNES Town in northern *France at the confluence of the Escaut and Rônelle rivers. Mentioned in 691 as a *Merovingian *fiscus and in 695 as a merchant settlement, it was the site of *Charlemagne's first assembly (771). Situated in the border region between the *Holy Roman empire, *Flanders and *France, *Otto II made the region into a county as part of his military frontier with France. It was incorporated in Flanders (c. 1011), and then given to the counts of *Hainault (1047), who made it their capital. A centre of trade ((1050-70) statutes of the merchants' *guild) and the site of a textile industry (Charter of 1067), it was well located and was developed by the counts of Hainault. The town and region came under the rule of a branch of the *Burgundians (1418) and were incorporated in the lands of *Philip the Good (1433). A French attempt to conquer the town under *Louis XI failed.

H. Lancelin, *Histoire de Valenciennes depuis ses origines* (1934).

VALENTINIAN III (419-55) Western emperor (425-55). Born at *Ravenna to a patrician father who became emperor under the name of Constantius III, he married Eudoxia, daughter of Theodosius II (437), whose code of laws he brought to the West. More interested in sport than in running the empire, the real power was vested first with his mother Galla Placidia, then with the general *Aetius. V.'s reign was marked by the loss of Africa, Britain and large parts of Spain to the barbarians, but also by the victory of Aetius over *Attila (451). Fear and envy drove V. to have Aetius murdered (454), only to die one year later at the hands of the latter's followers.

Bury, *A History of the Later Roman Empire,* I (1923).

VALHALLA In the religion of the Germanic tribes, that place in the world beyond where the Valkyries serve drink to the fallen warriors. It was also considered the future site of the final battle between the forces of Good and Evil. The main source for these conceptions are two 9th-century poems, the *Songs of Eirik* and the *Song of Hakon.*

R. M. Derolez, *Götter und Mythen der Germanen* (1963).

VALLADOLID City in northwestern *Spain. An unimportant Moslem town, it was conquered by the Christians in the 10th century and in 1074 was given by King *Alfonso VI of Castile to Count Pedro Ansurez. The latter made V. his capital, lavishly endowing its church. It was the site of ecclesiastical councils (1124, 1137) and the residence of King *Alfonso VII, who authorized the holding of a yearly market. In 1208 it was incorporated into the crown lands by King *Alfonso VIII and remained the royal residence until the 14th century. The university, famous for its faculty of *medicine, was founded in the early 13th century and received a papal charter in 1346. In the 14th century it was the seat of the supreme law-courts of Castile and it housed numerous state assemblies (*cortes).

J. O. Callaghan, *A History of Medieval Spain* (1975).

VALOIS French dynasty deriving its name from the county of V. north of Paris. After being ruled by different families, it was taken over by a branch of the *Capetians (1076). After its extinction, King *Philip II Augustus made it part of the royal domain (1213). Used as an *apanage to the mother of *Louis IX

(1240) and to his son Jean Tristan (1268), in 1285 it was given by King *Philip III to his son Charles. The latter's son, who became king as *Philip VI (1328) founded the royal dynasty of the V. who ruled France directly until 1498 and, through its *Orléans and *Angoulême branches, until 1598. Under the V. the county became a possession of the duke of Orléans. It was elevated to the rank of a duchy in 1406.

G. Dodu, *Les Valois; Histoire d'une Maison royale* (1934);

J. Martin, *Les Valois* (1968).

VAN ARTEVELDE, JACOB (c. 1290-1345) Flemish popular leader. One of the rich *cloth merchants of *Ghent, in 1338 the cloth-workers and merchants made him captain of the town following the outbreak of the *Hundred Years' War between England and France. England had cut off the supply of raw wool to the Flemish textile industry after the count of *Flanders had sided with the French, thus causing widespread unemployment and hardship. In July 1338 V. managed to persuade England to recognize Flanders' neutrality and wool was again brought to the workshops. Under V.'s leadership, a trade league was formed between the rival towns of Ghent, *Bruges and *Ypres, and he succeeded for a time in maintaining the equilibrium between the warring merchant-entrepreneurs and the workers. In May 1345 the weavers rose against the merchants and shop-owners, causing V. to call in English help, which aroused popular feeling against him. He was killed in a mob uprising in July 1345, which brought back the rule of the count.

W. J. Ashley, *James and Philip van Artevelde* (1883);

H. S. Lucas, *The Low Countries and the Hundred Years' War* (1929).

VAN ARTEVELDE, PHILIP (1340-82) The son of Jacob *van Artevelde, landowner and wine merchant, he was made captain of Ghent in January 1382. Unable to persuade *Louis of Male, the count of Flanders, to lift a siege which closed down the town's cloth industry, he allied himself with the English and led the citizens against the count, taking *Bruges in May 1382. The army sent by *Charles VI of France to aid the count beat the Flemish decisively at the Battle of *Roosebeke November 1382. Philip was killed and his mutilated body exhibited on the rack.

VANDALS *Germanic tribe, founders of a kingdom in northern Africa. Originating from Denmark, they moved to Silesia and eastern *Poland, where their two main branches, the Silingi and Asdingi settled separately. Driven towards western Europe by the *Huns, they crossed France and entered *Spain (406-09). There the Silingi were attacked by the *Visigoths and almost totally wiped out in three years of fighting (415-18). Their remnants united with the Asdingi under Gunderic, who took the title of king. His brother and successor *Genseric moved his people, a force of 80,000 men, to north Africa (c. 428), where they were accepted most reluctantly by the Romans as allies. In 439 Genseric drove out the Romans and established an independent Vandal state with *Carthage as capital, which was recognized by the Romans in a treaty (442). Although expropriating and settling the lands around Carthage, the V. did retain Roman institutions in the rest of the country, but refrained from mixing with the local Catholic population, preserving their Arian brand of Christianity. From

north Africa they attacked and took the *Balearic Islands, *Sardinia, *Corsica and parts of *Sicily, venturing as far as *Rome, which they sacked in 455, thus incidentally creating the myth of Vandal lust for destruction. Under Genseric's successor their vigour waned and their rule grew lax; they abandoned the war and piracy which had previously been their main source of income. Their original persecution of Catholics changed into toleration and King *Hilderic established peaceful relations with *Byzantium, but was deposed by *Gelimer (530). This was used as a pretext for a Byzantine invasion of Africa in 533 under the general *Belisarius, who easily defeated the Vandal army. Most of the V. were made slaves. Thus, in one campaigning season the V. kingdom was completely destroyed.

R. A. G. Carson, *The Kingdom of the Vandals, History Today*, V (1955);

L. Schmidt, *Geschichte der Wandalen* (1942).

VANNES Town and bishopric in *Brittany, western France. Already settled in antiquity, it is mentioned as the seat of a bishop from the 5th century and as a centre of independent counts up to the *Frankish conquest. It won its independence again when *Nominoë, captain of *Armorica and ally of *Louis I, defeated King *Charles the Bald (845) and established a Breton duchy in which Vannes was included in 980. It was the meeting-place of the Breton *Estates (1425-1554) and the residence of Duke John of Brittany.

P. Thomas-Lacroix, *Vannes* (1949).

VARANGIANS (the sworn men) The name given by the Slavs and Byzantines to the *Viking adventurers from *Sweden who founded the states of *Novgorod and *Kiev in the 9th century. In the 10th century these pirates, warriors and merchants descended the Dnieper and Volga rivers in their fast ships, reaching the shores of the Black and Caspian seas, setting up trade-posts and plundering the towns of the Eastern empire as far as Athens.

In a more specific sense, the military *corps d'élite* of the Byzantine emperors was known as the Varangian guard. Founded by *Vladimir of Kiev in 988, it existed until the fall of Constantinople (1453). Originally composed of Kiev Norsemen and from the late 11th century of Normans and Saxons from England as well as other Scandinavians, they were feared for their ferocity and valued for their reliability. However, they were apt to try their hand at making and unmaking emperors.

VARENNES, JOHN OF (14th century) Preacher. His origin and early life are obscure. After a successful career as a popular preacher, V. accompanied the cardinal of Luxemburg to Avignon (c. 1376) and there became known as a mystic. In the last twenty years of the century, he frequently travelled to northern France, where he attacked the morality of French society, challenging both the aristocracy and the top hierarchy of the church. His sermons show him to be a fanatic who exaggerated in his zeal to inspire repentance. In 1392 he was brought before the archiepiscopal court of Rheims, but was released. V.'s behaviour is an example of the fanatical trends which emerged during the crisis of the Church..

J. Huizinga, *The Waning of the Middle Ages* (1923).

VASATICUM, VASSATICUM Medieval term denoting either *vassalage in general, the services of the vassal or the vassals of a lord as a body.

VASILI I (1371-1425) Grand prince of *Moscow after the death of his father (1389). He ruled a state much diminished by divisions of inheritance, but in general succeeded in strengthening his authority. Of the two great neighbouring powers, the *Tartar Golden Horde was checked in its expansion by internal weaknesses, and *Lithuanian ambitions were thwarted first by V.'s marriage to the ruler's daughter Sophia (1392) and then by a truce negotiated in 1408. Other neighbouring principalities such as *Nizhni-Novgorod, Muram, Wologoda and Welikij Ustpig were peacefully annexed. With *Novgorod there was almost continuous warfare (1397-1417), yielding little territorial gain but checking its expanson.
G. Vernadsky, *The History of Russia,* III (1953).

VASSAL (VASSALAGE) Term derived from the Celtic language, originally denoting a young boy. Increasingly, it came to signify the social link forged between the 9th and 14th centuries within the military and noble classes of medieval society. A V. is someone who, by a series of symbolic acts (*homage, *fidelity, the kiss) has become "someone else's man", committing himself to serve a master, in exchange for a *feudum, usually a landed estate. The relationship between V. and lord is parallel to, but not to be confused with, that between a *serf and landlord. In the conditions of the 9th and 10th centuries, vassalage was from the beginning geared towards organizing the potential and loyalty of the fighting class around the rulers, whether kings or local magnates, thus establishing the basically military nature of the vassal's service. This consisted first and foremost in doing duty as a mounted warrior (*auxilium), the duration of which was gradually restricted to 40 days. From the 13th century, however, feudal armies composed of vassals became obsolete, causing the rise of *mercenary armies. The other main service of the vassal was *consilium* (counsel), requiring the vassal's attendance at the lord's deliberative assemblies at his *court, which consequently developed into a permanent institution laying the basis for the *parliament. In the more settled conditions of life from the 11th century onwards, the originally personal relationship implied in vassalage gradually weakened as the material aspect of the *feudum* became more important; fiefs were inherited and the practice of multiple vassalage abounded. Thus vassalage as an instrument of social cohesion was abandoned in favour of new forms of social organization.
F. L. Ganshof, *Feudalism* (1964);
M. Bloch, *Feudal Society*, I (1965).

VATICAN The papal palace and residence in *Rome and in modern times the exterritorial city-state of the Church in Rome. On the Vatican Hill and Valley on the right bank of the Tiber River opposite the ancient city of Rome, there grew up a maze of ecclesiastical buildings centred around the tomb and basilica of St. *Peter and the early residence of the popes, the *Lateran palace. Parts of the Vatican palace itself were begun under *Innocent III, but the main building was erected under Pope *Nicholas III (1278). There was further construction in the 13th and 14th centuries, of which some mural paintings have been preserved. Building activity was stopped by the papal schism, but was resumed by *Nicholas V, whose grandiose plans, however, were only partly realized. The present structure and appearance of the Vatican is mainly the result of the immense building activities of the Renaissance popes. From *c.* 1200 the Vatican has also housed the Papal Archives, an inexhaustible source of historical documents.
A. A. de Marco, *The Tomb of St. Peter* (1964);
F. Ehrle-H. Egger, *Der vatikanische Palast in seiner Entwicklung bis zur Mitte des 15. Jahrhunderts* (1935).

VENANTIUS FORTUNATUS, St. Poet, hagiographer and bishop of *Poitiers. Born near Treviso *c.* 535, he died at Poitiers in 600. Following his studies at *Ravenna he became official poet at the court of King *Sigebert (565), with whom he travelled widely throughout *Merovingian Gaul. At Poitiers he met Queen *Radegunde (567) and entered her service and that of her daughter, an abbess, and between the three there developed an intensely productive literary and social relationship. After the death of the two women (*c.* 587) he continued his travels, meeting *Gregory of Tours, who encouraged him to publish his poetry. He became a priest and finally bishop of Poitiers (*c.* 599). During his lifetime, ten books of his religious poetry were published and he wrote numerous Lives of Saints. Not the most profound of poets, his main achievement lies in his description of Christian life during the harsh and brutal Merovingian era.
Works: *MGH Scriptores Rerum Merovingicarum,* 7, 1; *MGH, Auctores Antiquissimi,* 4;
S. A. Blomgren, *Studia Fortunatiana* (1933-34).

VENDOME Town and county on the Loire River in western *France. Of Gallic origin and centre of a rich agricultural area, the town rose to prominence at the beginning of the 11th century with the foundation of the *Benedictine abbey of the Holy Trinity, as a place of pilgrimage as well as a feudal centre for the county. In the 12th century the monastery prospered under the rule of its abbot, Geoffrey, a cardinal, while temporal jurisdiction remained in the hands of the powerful counts. In 1129 the town became English by the marriage of *Matilda, daughter of *Henry I of France, to *Geoffrey Plantagenet-Anjou, only to become part of the French royal domain with the confiscation of *John Lackland's possessions. In 1515 François I made it a duchy for Charles of Bourbon. It is still justly famous for its splendid Trinity church begun in the 12th century and completed in the 15th-16th centuries.
Simon, *Histoire du Vendôme et de ses environs* (1835).

VENICE City-state in northeastern *Italy. V. is the sole major city in Italy whose origins are medieval. In the 6th century, during the wars between *Byzantines and Ostrogoths, some of the population of the ancient Roman province of Veneti fled to the islands north of the mouth of the Po River and established communities of fishermen there. With the arrival of new settlers, who fled the *Lombard invasion of 568, a city was established and governed by a Byzantine general, with the rank of duke, who was subordinate to the exarch of Ravenna. From the middle of the 7th century local leaders were appointed to the ducal office, which entailed command of the fleet and the administration of the island's communities. In the 8th century the *Rialto group of islands became the focus of settlements and some of its important families became wealthy through their intermediary role in the commerce between Byzantium and northern Italy. In the 9th century the doges (dukes), who belonged to the Partecipazio clan of Rialto, adopted a policy of independence from Byzantium. In 840 the office of doge became elective; while in principle he was elected by the people, the right was actually exercised by a number of wealthy citizens, who became the core of the city's aristocratic government and sat in the council. The city developed in the 10th century and became the most important commercial factor in the Adriatic Sea. In 992 it became an ally of Byzantium against the Moslems in *Apulia. The defence of *Bari by the Venetian fleet in 1002 and the defeat it inflicted upon the Arab fleet in the southern Adriatic marked the rise of V.'s political power and the beginning of its expansion in the Adriatic Sea (11th century). The alliance with Byzantium was continued into the second half of the century in an attempt to halt the *Normans, who had conquered southern Italy. V. profited from the alliance, obtaining important commercial privileges at Constantinople in 1081. These rights gave the city a monopoly over the trade between the Byzantine capital and eastern Europe. One of the reasons for the emergence of the republic as a great maritime power lay in the organization of its resources and the creation of a maritime monopoly of the state; ships were built and owned by the state and the government was thereby also responsible for the organization of trade.

The 12th century marked a period of great expansion which led to the establishment of the Venetian empire. While the alliance with Byzantium and enmity with the Norman kingdom of *Sicily continued, V. established its supremacy in the Adriatic and conquered Istria and parts of Dalmatia. However, from the establishment of the Latin kingdom of *Jerusalem, the city became involved in the affairs of the Crusaders, receiving, together with *Genoa and *Pisa, large privileges in the Palestinian ports, especially at *Acre, where a quarter in the city became a Venetian commune. In 1122, the Venetian fleet defeated the *Fatimid fleet near *Ascalon and thus gained naval supremacy in the Mediterranean Sea; the victory led to the joint conquest (by V. and the Crusaders) of *Tyre in 1123. V. received a third of the city, as well as wider privileges at Acre, which made the commune a virtually independent state within the Crusader realm and provided it with a large share of the trade between the East and western Europe. The Balkan policy of *Manuel Comnenus, on the other hand, caused a rupture in Venetian relations with Byzantium. In 1171 the Venetian merchants in the empire were arrested and their goods were confiscated; this action provoked retaliations and attacks of Greek cities and incited V. to support the opponents of the Comneni. The enmity with Byzantium led V. to use its influence over the Crusaders to divert the Fourth Crusade (1202-05) to Constantinople. In addition, the Crusaders, dependent on Venetian naval services, conquered the city of Zara in Dalmatia (1202) for V. In 1204 the capital of the Byzantine empire was conquered as well. With the establishment of the new *Latin empire of Constantinople, V. received a "quarter and a half" of the territory. Its share consisted of an important base at Constantinople, including port and merchants' quarters, as well as the Greek islands and other bases in Greece, allowing it economic supremacy in the Mediterranean.

With the establishment of the Venetian empire in the East, fundamental changes were made in the republic's constitution. Basically, the city of V. governed the empire and remained primarily concerned with safeguarding its economic interests. This meant dominating the trade between East and West and competing with Genoa and Pisa. Certain eastern goods, such as spices, cloth and luxury items were not exported and foreign merchants came to the Rialto quarter, the new centre of international business, to acquire them. Establishments such as the *Fundacco dei Tedeschi* (The Germans' Market) enabled the trade of merchandise, whose prices were established at Rialto.

Changes were also effected in the administrative sphere. The council governing the city had been reformed in 1134 and wielded a large degree of control over the doges, who were elected for life but not on a hereditary basis. From 1230 this body (known as the Great Council) became the supreme organ of the republic. The duties of its 480 members, selected from the city wards, were to approve legislation and to elect officials, among them six ducal counsellors who assisted the doge. A senate, made up of 123 elected members, together with the doge and his counsellors, was set up as the chief legislative body of the state and its supreme court. In addition an elaborate system of courts provided judicial services, while the committee of the six *savii grandi* (high lords) acted as a supervisory body. The doge himself, who remained head of the government and represented the splendour and majesty of the republic, was elected in a complex manner by 41 electors chosen by lot and voting from the Great Council. V.'s constitution ensured that power would lie in the hands of the great aristocratic families, which also provided the provinces with governors. On the other hand, the system allowed the appointment of able persons to offices, while exercising effective control which prevented the rise of *tyrants and dynasties, as was the case in the other city-states of Italy. The city's constitution was further reformed at the end of the 13th and the beginning of the 14th century under Doge Pietro *Gradenico. In 1297 the *Serrata del Gran Consiglio* (The Closing of the Great Council) restricted membership of this body to families which had been members of the council since 1176. This measure, aided by the establishment in 1314 of a register of all births in the eligible families (The Golden Book), legalized the ruling oligarchy of the republic. In 1310, after the conspiracy of *Tiepolo, who attempted to seize the office of doge, a *Council of Ten was instituted and became the supreme body of the state, feared because of its secret proceedings.

One of the features of external Venetian affairs of the 13th century was its constant rivalry with Genoa. A war between the two states at *Acre (1254-56) ended in Genoa's defeat and its expulsion from the Crusader states. Genoa responded by allying itself with the empire of *Nicaea, and in 1261, when *Michael Palaeologus reconquered Constantinople, V. lost its privileged position in the city and its monopoly of trade with the Black Sea and the *Mongol empire, as well as some islands, such as *Chios, which became a Genoese possession. Doge Pietro Gradenico attempted to compensate for the losses by involvement in Italian politics, conquering *Treviso (1308). The rivalry with Genoa continued into the 14th century. Another war, begun in 1330 due to a dispute in the Black Sea, lasted for fifty years. After some initial Venetian victories, the republic was severely defeated in 1354 at Sapienza (Greece). Conflicts continued and Genoa imposed its influence over Cyprus. Allied with Hungary and Padua, the Genoese fleet raided the Adriatic in 1378 and attacked *Chioggia in the lagoon of V. The war of Chioggia came to an end with V.'s overwhelming victory, bringing about the decline of Genoa.

The foreign policy of the republic in the 15th century included two main aims: an attempt to mobilize western Europe against the Ottoman *Turks, with the aim of preserving Venetian possessions in Greece, and the conquest and annexation of northeastern Italy. The first goal was never realized due to the failure of the Crusades and the conquest of the Balkans by the Turks; the result was the loss of Venetian bases in Greece so that, after 1479. only Crete, the Ionian Islands and the duchy of Naxos remained in the city's possession (Cyprus was inherited in 1489). During the conquests, Greeks fleeing Byzantium sought refuge in V. and the city became one of the most brilliant centres of Greek studies. With regard to plans to conquer parts of Italy, mercenary *condottieri were hired to fight *Milan (1388-1432). During these wars *Padua, *Verona, *Vicenza and their territories were conquered and became part of a Venetian state established in northeastern Italy, which lasted until 1797.

G. Cracco, *Società e Stato nel Medioevo Veneziano* (1967).

VER Near *Compiegne, north of Paris. Site of a synod of the bishops of the Western kingdom (December 844), at which the ambitions of *Drogo, archbishop of Metz, to become apostolic vicar of the entire empire north of the Alps, and thereby receive almost absolute power, were refuted by the assembled bishops.

C. Pfister, *L'Archevêque de Metz Drogon, Mélanges Paul Fabre* (1902).

VERCELLI Town and bishopric in *Piedmont, northwestern Italy. Founded in pre-Roman times, it became a bishopric in 370 and the seat of a *Lombard duchy possessing the right of *coinage. In 899, it was captured by the *Hungarians, who slew Bishop Luithardo, the clergy and the entire population. At the end of the 10th century began the long history of fruitful cooperation between its bishops and the German emperors, when bishops Peter and Leo, the latter a German appointee by *Otto III, clashed with the powerful Margrave Arduin of Ivrea over the *immunity granted by the emperor. In 1014 V. was destroyed and its lands devastated by a league of Lombard magnates, but the revolt was suppressed by the imperial bishops led by the margrave of *Canossa (1016). In the early 11th century the feudal power of the bishops reached its peak, only to encounter increasing opposition from the citizens of the town, whose communal institutions are attested from the late 11th century. During the 12th century it was part of the *Lombard League, but *Guelph-Ghibelline factional strife within the city was rampant. In 1355 the independent commune was taken over by the *Visconti of *Milan and in 1427 passed into the hands of the house of *Savoy. The cathedral library houses the famous *Vercelli Codes,* a manuscript dating from the 10th century, believed to be the earliest extant Old English version of the Gospel. In 1338 a *studium generale* was established in the city.

VERDEN Town and bishopric in Lower *Saxony, on the Aller River, the site of the mass execution of 4500 rebellious Saxons by *Charlemagne (782). Mentioned as a fortress in documents from 810 onwards, it was the site of a merchant settlement (Wik) whose church became the centre of a bishopric in 849. *Otto I granted it the right of *coinage and holding markets, and the settlement developed into a permanent town. By 1235 it had freed itself from the bishop's tutelage, as is attested by its communal constitution. While the ecclesiastical authority of the bishopric extended over a wide area stretching up to the Elbe River in the east, its temporal rule was restricted to a smaller area.

E. Rundnagel, "Der Tag von Verde" in: *Historische Zeitschrift*, 160 (1939);

R. Drögereit, *Dom und Bistum Verden* (1970).

VERDUN Town and bishopric on the Meuse River in eastern *France. A Celtic settlement, the bishopric was first mentioned c. 350. From 511 the area was part of *Austrasia, the town itself belonging to the bishop. During the *Frankish period it grew into a trading centre of more than regional importance. It became famous for the treaty drawn up there in 843 by the three sons of Emperor *Louis I, which was intended to put an end to the ferocious warfare following the emperor's death (840). According to this treaty, *Lothair received Francia Media, an area running from the North Sea through parts of France and Germany to Switzerland and Italy; *Louis the German received the eastern and *Charles the Bald the western part of the Carolingian empire, the areas which subsequently developed into Germany and France. The treaty is usually viewed as the birth-certificate of the two countries, its text being written twice, in two languages resembling medieval German and French.

The town of V. was first part of Francia Media, and after 925 was incorporated with the rest of *Lorraine in the German empire. In the 13th century it became a free imperial city, a development which forced the bishop to move his seat.

L. Clouet, *Histoire de Verdun et des Verdunois* (1867-70).

VERE, ROBERT OF (1362-92) Ninth earl of *Oxford, favourite of *Richard II of England. Of royal descent, he succeeded his father as *earl and great *chamberlain (1371). On the accession of his close friend Richard, he became privy councellor, Knight of the *Garter (1377) and duke of *Ireland (1386). Hated for his power and somewhat frivolous influence on the king, he was the prime target for Richard's enemies in the nobility led by the duke of *Gloucester. When his army was beaten by the latter (1387) he went into exile in the Netherlands, where he died.

R. H. Jones, *The Royal Policy of Richard II: Absolutism in the Later Middle Ages* (1968).

VERMANDOIS French county in eastern *Picardy, named after the dispossessed Belgian tribe Viromandui. The *Carolingian *pagus Veromanduensis*, belonging, from the 9th century, to a branch of the Carolingians, developed into a powerful county headed by forceful personalities. Of these, Herbert I (d. 902) gave assistance to *Charles the Simple, when the latter sought the crown (893). His son Herbert II, however, was one of the greatest and most powerful enemies of the Carolingian king. In the 10th century, the counts were among the most powerful lords of northern France. After 1076 V. together with the county of *Valois passed into the ownership of Hugh, brother of Philip I of France. In 1186 *Eleanor ceded V. to King *Philip Augustus, who attached it to the royal domain as part of Picardy and created a bailiwick there.

M. Thiéry, *Histoires du Vermanois* (1895-97); H. Waquet, *Le Baillage du Ve aux XIIIe et XIVe siècles* (1919).

VERONA City in northeastern *Italy on the Adige River. One of the centres of the Roman empire, V. declined in the 5th century. In 489 it was conquered by *Theodoric the Great, king of the Ostrogoths, who was wont to reside in the local castle. Seized in 568 by the *Lombards, the city became the centre of a Lombard duchy in the 7th century. In 774 *Charlemagne established a march there. In the 9th and 10th centuries the *Carolingian margraves established relations with those of *Friuli and supported their claims to the imperial crown. After the expedition of *Otto I of Germany to Italy in 952, the march of V. was terminated and annexed as a county to the duchy of *Bavaria. Its bishops became directly dependent on the royal court. With the organization of the *Holy Roman empire at the end of the 10th century, V. became a county depending directly on the imperial court; however, no local dynasty arose and the counts, many of whom were Germans, were appointed by the emperors until 1164. At that date a *commune was established and chartered by *Frederick Barbarossa, who intended to make the city a base for his struggle against the *Lombard League. The episcopal seigniory, however, remained under the authority of the emperors. The establishment of a local government at V. led to rivalries, and civil war broke out in the city; the struggles between *Guelphs and *Ghibellines continued into the 13th century and the commune collapsed *c.* 1230. In 1232 V. was granted by *Frederick II to *Ezzelino da Romano and became part of his principality until his death in 1259. An attempt to restore self-government failed because of the rivalry between the guilds (1259-61) and the lordship of V. passed to the *Scaligeri (1261-1387). This period (14th century) marks the greatest epoch of Veronese history. The city became an important arts centre and. under the rule of Cangrande I, V. became the centre of a powerful principality between Milan and Venice. However, after his death it lost control over the neighbouring cities. In 1387 the city was conquered by the *Visconti of Milan, but was disputed by Venice. After passing back and forth from the authority of the two cities, V. was finally annexed by the latter (1405) and became the centre of Venice's Italian possessions. The Venetian government allowed the city's local institutions, led by noble families of V., to function.

P. Gazzola, *Verona* (1963).

VESPERS Church evening service and prayer. The name derives from the Latin term for the last hours of daylight. It developed out of the Jewish and early Christian blessing of the lamps which were lighted as evening came in. In addition, it denotes the evening sacrifice derived from the biblical burning of incense offered every evening in the temple. In the church, this evening sacrifice was changed into a hymn of praise in memory of the Calvary and the Last Supper. A distinctly Christian form of evening prayer existed from the 3rd century. The individual efforts of local churches and monasteries developed it into its present form, which consists of a brief introduction, five psalms, a short reading from the Scriptures, a hymn, the climax of the Magnificat, prayers for various purposes, a homily and concluding verses. As is seen from the *Benedictine rule, Vespers had almost reached its final form by the 6th century.

P. Salmon, *The Breviary through the Centuries* (1962).

VEXIN, VESQUESIN County in northern *France, west of Paris. A Carolingian *pagus*, when *Rollo was given *Normandy (911) it was divided into a Norman and French area, the former being included in Rollo's territory. In 1149 *Geoffrey of Anjou-Plantagenet gave Norman V. to *Louis VII of France in return for the latter's help in winning Normandy, but it returned to the *Plantagenets as a dowry in 1166. Conquered by *Philip II Augustus in 1193, it was incorporated in France (1196) and annexed to the royal domains. French V., in the 10th-century part of a feudal duchy together with Amiens and the Valois, was incorporated in the royal domains in 1077.

R. Fawtier, *The Capetian Kings of France* (1964).

VÉZELAY *Benedictine abbey in *Burgundy. Founded in 864 by Duke *Girart de Roussillon as a nunnery under direct papal authority, its nuns were replaced by monks in 877. The monastery was completely destroyed by the *Normans (886-87) and rebuilt on a slightly different site (888). Under the reforming abbot Geoffrey (1037), V. became a pilgrimage centre, due to the relics of *Mary Magdalene which it was reputed to contain. In 1058 it was put under the authority of *Cluny and in 1096 the construction of its beautiful church of La Madeleine was begun. During this period a legend emerged according to which the monastery's founder had been a pious slayer of the *Saracens. The fame claimed by V. made it a major centre in Burgundy, and *Bernard of Clairvaux chose to preach the Second *Crusade there (1146). During the same period V. had to cope with two serious attempts at revolt by its bourgeois subjects (1106 and 1152-55). Its subjection to Cluny's authority was abolished in 1159. Although the authenticity of its relics was certified by a papal bull from 1058, the "rediscovery" of Mary Magdalene's relics in *Provence led to a long, drawn-out and damaging struggle and consequently V. lost much of its attraction to pilgrims.

C. Porée, *L'Abbaye de Vézelay* (1930); R. B. C. Huygens, *Monumenta Vizeliacensia. Textes relatifs à l'histoire de l'abbaye de Vézelay* (1976).

VIA DOLOROSA The route in *Jerusalem along which Christ walked from the place of his judgement in the court of Pilate to Mount Calvary. Its "Stations of the Cross" symbolize the places where Jesus supposedly halted. In the late Middle Ages, under the influence of *Franciscan spirituality, the idea was taken up in the West to mark a series of stations in the naves of churches, or outdoors by the wayside, by means of some image representing the incidents of the original Way of the Cross where prayers were said. The Stations of the Cross, formerly seven in number, later became 14.

M. Adolfino, *La via crucis a Gerusalemme* (1974).

VIA EGNATIA The ancient road leading from *Durazzo to *Constantinople. Its last stretch to Constanti-

The Via Dolorosa, Jerusalem

nople was finished in the 4th century. Bypassing the Heliadic peninsula in its winding course over the Balkans, it was of utmost military importance to Byzantium. However, it became highly vulnerable once the line of the Danube had been broken, which occurred after the establishment of the *Bulgarian empire.

K. Milner, *Itineraria Romana* (1916).

VICAR Term of ancient Roman origin designating an official who acted in some special way for a superior. In secular usage in the *Frankish kingdom it denoted a royal official subordinate to a *count, or an official under direct supervision of the king. Later it was used to designate seignorial officials and manorial agents, and as a general term for one acting as proxy. The term was widely used in ecclesiastical matters, foremost as one of the titles of the *pope. The phrase was initially "V. of St. *Peter", but with the growth of papal authority in the Middle Ages it was changed to "V. of Jesus Christ", the former usage being forbidden in the 13th century. As such, the title gave expression to the papal claim to rule the world as immediate "V. of God" (*Boniface VIII). The term was also used in the title of temporary or permanent papal *legates. Archbishops and bishops could also be appointed Vs. in charge of a vacant see, or a bishop might act as vice-regent for an archbishop who bore the temporary title of V. Finally the term was used to denote various ecclesiastical officials acting in an office not regularly their own. The widespread use of the institution of V. is an indication of the bureaucratic element introduced by the Church and suggests the extent of the problem which arose out of the typically medieval bent towards treating offices as private possessions.

J. F. Niermeyer, *Mediae Latinitatis Lexicon Minus* (1976).

VICELIN, St. (d. 1154) Evangelizer of the *Wends, later bishop of Oldenburg. A cleric of the church of *Bremen, he was induced by *Adelbert his archbishop to preach amongst the *Wagrians (1126), where he could count on the active support of the Christian Duke Henry of Old Lübeck. Upon the latter's death (1127), V. found a new base for his missionary activity in the rural parish of Faldera on the Saxon-Slav border, where within a few years he built the convent of Neumünster. He made Emperor *Lothair III visit the country (1134) and had a fortress built to defend the newly-founded convent of Segeberg, thus stressing the close connection between Christianization and German expansion. In 1149 V. was put at the head of the revived bishopric of Oldenburg, but effective missionary activity among the Wagrians was possible only from *c.* 1150, when he withdrew his refusal to be invested by Duke *Henry the Lion.

G. Barraclough, *The Origins of Modern Germany* (1972).

VICH Town, county and bishopric in *Catalonia. An ancient settlement, called Ausona by the *Goths, it was destroyed and partly rebuilt by the *Saracens. Reconquered in the time of *Louis the Pious, powers of civil government were given to Count Borell and ecclesiastical matters were placed in the hands of the archbishop of *Narbonne. Captured once more by the Moors (826), V. finally became part of the lands of Wilfrid the Hairy, count of *Barcelona (873-98). The count founded the famous monastery of Ripoll (888) and obtained the consecration of a bishop of V. By 1054 the county was ruled by *Raymond Berengar I and in 1137 it became, together with the rest of the Catalan counties, part of the kingdom of *Aragon. However, the bishops and the Monacada family disputed the right of sovereignty over the city until 1315, when both sides ceded their rights to King *James II. Between 1089 and 1117 the bishops of V. exercised the rights of the archbishop of *Tarragona. The city is famous for its Gothic architecture.

J. F. O'Callaghan, *A History of Medieval Spain* (1975).

VICTOR II (Gebhart of Dollnstein-Hirschberg; d. 1057) Pope (1055-57). Born to Franconian-Swabian nobility and a relative of the imperial family, he was made bishop of Eichstätt (1042) and served as an esteemed counsellor of Emperor *Henry III. Having been appointed pope by the emperor in 1055, he retained his bishopric, while pressing for the continuation of papal reform. He made efforts in the direction of reform in southern France, where he held a number of synods (*Lyons in 1055; *Toulouse in 1056). He also worked hand in hand with the emperor, acting as the latter's caretaker in Italy, and was responsible for the administration of the duchy of *Spoleto in particular. On the death of Henry III, he ensured the coronation of *Henry IV and guided the caretaker-government of the new emperor's mother. His pontificate is usually considered the high-point of imperial-papal cooperation.

G. Tellenbach, *Church, State, and Christian Society at the Time of the Investiture Contest* (1959).

VICTOR III Pope (1086-87). A member of the ducal Lombard family of *Benevento, he was a hermit monk (*c.* 1047) and lived at the monasteries of St. Sophia in Benevento (1048-49) and *Monte Cassino (1055), becoming abbot of the latter in 1058. Known as Desiderius of Monte Cassino, literary production flowered under his rule and the daring reconstruction of the abbey was undertaken. V. was actively involved in the peace agreement worked out between Pope *Nicholas II and *Robert Guiscard, the south Italian leader of the Normans, being on good terms with the latter. For this feat he was made cardinal and papal vicar for the south Italian monasteries. After trying to evade the papal dignity for two years, he was finally consecrated in 1087. In ecclesiastical issues he took a militant reforming stand, but failed to reach a reconciliation with the excommunicated Emperor *Henry IV. He finally retired at Monte Cassino where he died.

H. K. Mann, *The Lives of the Popes in the Early Middle Ages*, VII.

VICTOR IV The name assumed by two antipopes:
Gregory Conti, antipope (March-May 1138). As cardinal, he was the tool of King *Roger II of Sicily and the *Pierleoni family in their struggle against Pope *Innocent II. He resigned his papal dignity under pressure from *Bernard of Clairvaux.
Ottavian of Monticelli, antipope (1159-64). A cardinal made pope by a minority of his peers in a disputed election where the majority had chosen *Alexander III. His armed followers forced Alexander to flee Rome. V. was backed by Emperor *Frederick I, but rejected by the majority of the European churches, including parts of the German church.

P. Kehr, *Zur Geschichte Victors IV, Neues Archiv* XLVI, 53-85.

VICTOR OF CARTHAGE (6th century) Historian. V. was bishop of Vita in north Africa and lived under *Vandal rule. In his history, he described the Vandal persecutions of the Catholic Church and used the term "vandalism".

M. L. W. Laister, *Thought and Letters in Western Europe* (1955).

VICTORINES Regular *canons and members of a theological school renowned for its special brand of spirituality. Founded in 1108 by *William of Champeaux, and closely associated with his theological teachings at Notre Dame cathedral school in Paris, the small community, under its first abbot Gilduin (1135-55), adopted the *Augustine rule augmented by its own *Book of Rules*. Living a life of dignified contemplation and including some pastoral activity, the V. took part in all the important intellectual ventures of the period, and their school attracted some of the best minds of the time, including *Hugh and *Richard of St. Victor, Andrew of Wigmore, Thomas Gallus, as well as a number of other thinkers. The V. adhered to the traditional theology of their time, but also attempted to create a synthesis between scholasticism and mysticism. Basing their beliefs on a symbolic interpretation of reality, they found the aim of science and life in the mystical theology of love and the mystical contemplation of God. The V. had a lasting influence on later theology, especially the *Franciscan school, and on late medieval mysticism.

Works: P. Wolff (ed. and trans.), *Die Viktoriner. Mystische Schriften* (1936);
F. Bonnard, *Histoire de l'Abbaye royale et de l'Ordre des Chanoines réguliers de Saint-Victoir* (1904-08).

VIDIMER (WIDIMIR) The name of three *Ostrogothic kings:
V., father to Widerich; he died in battle while fighting the *Alans and *Huns (*c.* 376).
V., who shared his kingship with two of his brothers, and took part in *Attila's campaign in Gaul. After the fall of the Hunnish empire (454), he took his people to *Pannonia and from there by way of Noricum to *Italy (*c.* 469). He was made military leader of Gaul by Emperor Anthemius and died in battle while attempting to rescue the latter from Ricimer (472).
V., son of the former king, was induced by Ricimer to lead his poeple to Gaul, where he assisted *Theodoric against Odoacer. In time the Ostrogoths were assimilated by the Western Goths.
CMedH, I.

VIDIN Town and fortress on the bank of the Danube in northeastern *Bulgaria. A strategic site of prime importance during the Middle Ages, it guarded the *Byzantine empire against the Bulgarians, but was lost to the latter in the mid-9th century. It became the centre of an independent Bulgarian principality under the despot Sisman, whose son Michael reunited it with Bulgaria when he was made emperor (1323). Michael's son, who received the town after 1344, restored its independence. In 1365 *Louis I of Hungary set up a "Province of the Bulgarians" with V. as its capital. After the Battle of *Nicopolis (1396) the town was occupied by the *Turks, and, as a result, the last remnant of the medieval Bulgarian state disappeared.
CMedH, 2nd ed. (1966).

VIENNA The capital city of *Austria. A Celtic and Roman settlement, it had a precarious existence as an ecclesiastical centre, threatened time and again by the nearby *Hungarians. Its earliest extant churches were founded in the 9th century. Around 1135 the place fell into the hands of the dukes of *Babenberg, who made it their residence (1156). It was first called a city (*civitas*) in 1137. Functioning as a place of residence and situated on the Danube, a major artery for the reviving trade, it developed considerably in the 12th century. New walls were built and churches erected, and in 1221 it received the right of staple from Duke *Leopold VI. Economic development was further heightened under the benevolent rule of King Premysl *Ottokar II of Bohemia (1251-76). In 1276 V. came into the hands of the *Hapsburgs and lost its status as a free imperial city after a series of futile uprisings against the new rulers. Nevertheless, the 14th century witnessed a demographic growth, which gave the artisan population an equal share of power (Statute of Council Elections 1396), and a new wave of building activity, from which only a few Gothic churches (such as St. Stephen) remain. The university was erected by Duke Rudolph IV in 1365. In 1438 V. began to serve as the residence of the Holy Roman emperors.

I. Barea, *Vienna* (1967).

VIENNE Town and archbishopric on the west bank of the Rhône in southern *France. A Celtic and Roman settlement, it became a bishopric in the 3rd century and an archbishopric *c.* 450, claiming primacy over all Gaul (in opposition to *Lyons). Conquered subsequently by the *Burgundians (438) and Franks (534), it was sacked by the *Lombards (558) and *Saracens (737). V. became part of the kingdom of *Provence when King *Charles the Bald gave the town to Count *Boso (869), who was subsequently proclaimed king of Provence. However, control over the city remained in the hands of the archbishop, whose legitimate rule was recognized when Emperor *Frederick I took possession of Provence and Burgundy (1157) in the name of his wife, Beatrice of *Burgundy, and thus realized the ancient German claim to the lands having once formed the kingdom of Media Francia. French claims over the city were realized in 1449, when V. was joined to the *Dauphiné, as part of France.

V. was the site of an important ecclesiastical council considered in the Western Church as *oecumenical. Convoked by Pope *Clement V under strong pressure from King *Philip the Fair, it met between October 1311 and May 1312. Yielding to the French king's demand, the council abolished the order of the *Templars by administrative decree, turning down, however, the French demand to bring Philip's late adversary, Pope *Boniface VIII, to trial for blasphemy. The council also dealt with struggles over apostolic poverty within the *Franciscan Order and legislated against the *Beguines.

M. Reymond, *Grenoble et Vienne* (1907);
G. Mollat, *The Popes at Avignon, 1305-1378* (1963).

VIET Empire in Indo-China. The peoples and tribes of Indo-China were under *Chinese domination in the early Middle Ages. After the fall of the Tang dynasty in 907, a series of revolts erupted in the country and V. tribes rose up against their Chinese governors. As a result, an independent state was established in Annam (939) by Ngo Quyen, who assumed the title of king of Champa. The kingdom continued to develop and grow in the 10th century, annexing small principalities in the north. Under the Li dynasty (1010-1225) the empire, whose capital was established near the site of modern Hanoi, was organized according to semi-feudal traditions and to the Chinese system of government. Divided into provinces governed by princes of the royal house, it was administered by a class of officials, trained as scholars and men of letters. In 1013 a general tax system was introduced, intended to be used to organize a powerful army, as well as for the construction of roads and the improvement of irrigation. The empire knew a period of economic prosperity and expansion southwards, as parts of the *Kmer empire fell under its domination. In 1257 the *Mongol army, led by *Kublai

Khan, invaded V., but was unable to conquer it. In 1258, however, the high authority of the *Peking government was recognized and the V. empire paid a tribute to the Mongols. Despite additional raids in 1285 and 1287, V. could not be conquered; however, the empire and its central government were considerably weakened. As a result, a long series of civil wars erupted in the 14th century, when feudalization of the provinces was begun, leading to peasants' revolts. In 1413 Chinese influence became dominant in the country, which lost its political independence and social stability. A peasants' revolt in Annam, led by Le Loy, broke out in 1428 and developed into a general rebellion against the Chinese authority; its success restored the independence of V. under the emperorship of Le Loy, who proclaimed an agrarian reform; the large estates were divided and the peasants were freed of their lords. At the end of the Middle Ages V. was an agrarian society based on a class of small landowners.

G. Maspero, *Le Royaume de Champa* (1928).

VIGILIUS Pope (537-55). Member of a distinguished *Roman family and deacon in 531, he was designated successor to Pope *Boniface II. His candidacy was withdrawn, however, in view of determined opposition from the Roman clergy (532) and V. was sent as papal representative to *Constantinople. There he secured the backing of Empress *Theodora. Upon his return to Rome he was elected pope in place of the deposed Silverius (537). Despite his previous accord with Constantinople, V. clashed with Emperor *Justinian over the treatment of the *Monophysites and was spirited away to Constantinople (545). He was held at the capital until he consented to change his position, but died on his way back to Rome (555).

L. Duchesne, *L'Eglise au VIe siècle* (1925).

VIKINGS The men who came out of Scandinavia, between the end of the 8th and the end of the 14th century to raid and settle overseas. At first, raids were headed by the younger sons of nobles who, having no hopes of receiving a share in the patrimony, led bands of armed followers in swift boats driven by sail and oars towards adventure, fame and plunder. From the latter half of the 9th century, however, Viking raids were carefully planned military operations led by men of high rank. Their strategy was to sail up the rivers and occupy fortified base camps, from which they launched inland raids for plunder and hostages. At some stage, however, the V. would settle down and occupy the conquered land, usually integrating quickly into the local population. After isolated raids, such as the plunder of the ancient monastic centre of *Lindisfarne (793), they started to stage yearly raids into *Ireland until they invaded the island and settled there (832-47). The fight between the Danish V. and the local Celts was only decided at the Battle of Clontarf (1014) in the latter's favour. *England was raided from 838 and invaded in 865-66. The V. quickly conquered eastern England, which became known as the *Danelaw. By 1016 King *Canute of Denmark and Norway ruled all of England, but the Viking element was assimilated by the Anglo-Saxon population even before the *Norman Conquest of 1066. In Continental Europe the story was similar. Their raids began in 810, the V. plundered the northern coast and infiltrated into the interior on the Elbe, Escaut, Rhine, Seine, Loire and Garonne rivers, generally meeting with no effective resistance. In fact, the anarchy spread by their devastation did much to bring down the *Carolingian empire. In 844 the V. reached *Seville from the sea and in 860 they gained Pisa, but they failed to make any impact on Moslem north Africa. Settling in *Normandy, they quickly adapted themselves to the Christian way of life (911-12) and to the feudal system.

They became a major factor in French politics, going out on new conquests in England and *Sicily in the 11th century. The *Swedish V. ventured into eastern and southeastern Europe, reaching as far as the Caspian Sea and establishing *Varangian principalities in Russia. The V. of *Norway sailed the northern Atlantic to *Iceland, *Greenland and North America, establishing islands in which they preserved their indigenous culture; such settlements continued to exist long after their fellow-V. in Russia, Europe and England had become part of the local cultures.

J. Brondsted, *The Vikings* (1960);
D. M. Wilson, *The Viking Achievement* (1970).

VILLA Derived from the Latin diminutive of *vicus* (village), it originally denoted a country house. During the Middle Ages the term was used to describe various forms of settlement. In the *Frankish period it was a general term covering any type of settlement, its meaning ranging from a single homestead to an entire village including its fields and pasture. In time it came to specifically denote the economic centre of a royal, ecclesiastical or noble estate, and by implication, a royal palace or residence. In its generic meaning of a jurisdictional area, the term was also applied to a castle, episcopal city and a certain part of the towns which had once been outside the nucleus of town life, having developed between the 8th and 11th centuries from merchant and artisan settlements. Thus V. came to denote a town in the juridical sense of possession of rights and privileges, but also signified the inhabitants of a town. In a parallel sense, it continued to be used to describe a village and its inhabitants.

J. F. Niermeyer, *Mediae Latinitatis Lexicon Minus* (1976).

VILLA FRANCA (VILLE FRANCHE) Type of medieval French and Dutch towns, and especially widespread in central France, characterized by a certain juridical status, as opposed to that of the *ville libre*. These towns enjoyed a certain degree of independence and were given a royal or seignorial privilege (*carta franchisiae*) containing a number of well-defined rights, such as a lowering of taxes, dispensation from military service, trade privileges, and the acceptance of the status of freemen of the individual townsmen. However, the V. did not possess autonomous self-government nor the right to administer justice themselves, but were conducted by a *prévôt* or some other official. The actual status of the V. differed from town to town. Newly-founded towns (*villes neuves*), especially royal ones, usually received the status of Vs., but lost the little weight their organs of self-government had by the end of the 13th century.

C. Petit-Dutaillis, *Les Communes Françaises* (1947).

VILLAIN (VILLEIN, VILLANUS) A medieval term having two distinct meanings. In *France, until the end of the 13th century, it designated a rural or urban non-noble. From the late 13th century, it was used to signify the free rural dweller, as opposed to the urban bourgeois and the rural *serf. The French V. depended to a large

Viking ship's figurehead; late 9th century

extent on the local administrator of justice, the *seigneur justicien*. He had to submit to a number of taxes and lordly privileges, compulsory labour and military service, as well as to royal taxes. He also had to fulfill the services and pay dues required of his land. Otherwise he was free, especially in movement, in stark contrast to the serf.

In *Norman England the term V. denoted the class of peasants which had enough land to support their families. This class emerged from the different Anglo-Saxon classes of free peasants. Originally their status was comparatively good, but gradually their services and dues to the landlords became undefined and their personal juridical status was assimilated to that of the serf. Taking advantage of the economic changes in the 14th century, the English V. managed to better his lot, and the institution was gradually replaced by a more rational landlord-peasant relationship.

M. Bloch, *Feudal Society*, I (1962);
G. Duby, *Rural Economy and Country Life in the Medieval West* (1968).

VILLANI, GIOVANNI (c. 1275-1348)   Chronicler. Member of a Florentine merchant family famous for its chroniclers. V. travelled widely in Italy, France and the Netherlands (c. 1304-12). Upon his return home he served in public offices as prior, officer of the mint, military commander and supervisor of fortifications. Involved in the collapse of the Buonaccorsi firm, he was harassed in his old age by prosecutions and a time in prison. He died of the *Black Death in 1348. His *History of Florence* or *Universal Chronicle,* covering biblical times up to the year of his death, is of utmost importance in the study of early Florentine history and the period he witnessed in person. His clear and simple style well suits his broad knowledge of affairs, his natural objectivity and his inquisitive mind. As a merchant with a bent for figures and politician living in a great city, his work heralds the advent of statistics in history. A continuation of the chronicle, although at a lower standard, was undertaken by V.'s brother, Matteo (d. 1363) and later by the latter's son Filippo, who brought it up to date to 1364.

Work: ed. *Magheri*, 8 vols. (1823);
P. H. Wicksteed (ed.), R. E. Selfe trans., *Selections from the First Nine Books of the Chronice Fiorentine* (1906).

VILLARD DE HONNECOURT (c. 1225-50)   French architect. Travelling widely, he moved from one building site to another, reaching as far as *Hungary (1245), yet almost none of his work is known. The little available information on V. comes from his sketchbook, containing 33 folios with line-drawings and a brief text in French. In these drawings he explored practical problems of design and craftsmanship, giving precise instructions for executing specific structures. V. also studied geometry at a higher level of abstraction, attempting to represent natural phenomena by lines and angles. These endeavours run parallel to the contemporary physicogeometric philosophy of *Robert Grosseteste and the *scholastic insights into the "whatness" of nature. However, there is no direct proof that the master-mason and architect was influenced by these intellectual ventures.

T. Bowie (ed.), *The Sketchbook of Villard de Honnecourt* (1959).

VILLEHARDOUIN, GEOFFROY DE (c. 1160-1213) Outstanding historian of the Fourth *Crusade. Probably born near *Troyes and a knight and official of the count of Champagne, he played a prominent role in the organization of the Fourth Crusade and in the diplomatic moves following the conquest of *Constantinople. Esteemed for his talents, he was made marshal of the Balkan mainland (Rumania) and placed at the head of some military ventures against the *Bulgarians. His *Conquête de Constantinople* is the first medieval historical work in Europe to be written in the vernacular, and is the paramount source for the study of the Fourth Crusade. The semi-poetic style of the work borrows heavily from the vocabulary of the French *chanson de geste.* V.'s selection and presentation of facts reflect the mentality of the French fighting knights, the backbone of the Crusades.

Work: M. R. B. Shaw trans., *Chronicles of the Crusades* (1976);
J. Dufournet, *Les Ecrivains de la IVᵉ Croissade: Villehardouin et Clori* (1973).

VILLEHARDOUIN, GEOFFROY (d. 1228)   Prince of *Morea. Nephew of his namesake, the chronicler, he was a participant in the Fourth *Crusade and went directly to Syria. Returning to share in the spoils of *Constantinople (1204), he was driven to Morea, which he and *William of Champlitte, together with 500 mounted fighters, conquered in a campaign lasting from spring to autumn of 1205. Upon William's death (1209), V. was acknowledged as prince of Morea (or Achaea), but had to accept the suzerainty of *Venice over part of his land. He organized his dominion into a feudal state based on 12 baronies held by the Latin conquerors, and established a great baronial parliament at his capital of Andravida. He clashed repeatedly with his Latin clergy over the taxing of their fiefs and fell several times under the ban of the Church. He was succeeded in 1228 by his able son, Geoffrey II.

CMedH, IV (1966);
J. Longnon, *Recherches sur la vie de Geoffroy de Villehardouin, suivies du Catalogue des Actes des Villehardouin* (1939).

VILLE LIBRE   A type of French medieval town which received full autonomy from its lord, usually through royal assistance. In the north of *France these towns were called *communes jurées*; in the south, *villes de consulat.* There were also towns whose juridical status approached that of a V., but not in all its aspects. In fact, from the end of the 13th century the French kings changed for all practical purposes the status of the V. to that of the *villa franca,* without the abolition of the old institutions, forms and titles.

C. Petit-Dutaillis, *Les communes françaises* (1947).

VILLE NEUVE   Term designating the villages founded in France in wild unoccupied areas between the mid-11th and mid-13th century. Part of the great movement of reclamation of cultivatable soil occasioned by demographic pressures brought the creation of new villages and with it a system of *manorial rights and monopolies more flexible and liberal to the peasant. The vast majority of Vs. were created through a deliberate act of the lord (king, count, castellan, monastery or urban community, in northern Italy). The settlement usually aimed at achieving, besides colonization, some political end, such as securing the safety of a road or frontier area, while the lord benefited from the financial advantages arising from the increase in tax-payers. In order to attract newcomers to waste lands, favourable conditions were granted in advance by written contract. Initial investments were financed by the lord, and consequently, the slowly accumulated wealth of the aristocracy came into circulation for the first time. Thus the V. marked a major social and economic innovation leading towards a more open system.

G. Duby, *Rural Economy and Country Life in the Medieval West* (1968).

VILNA   Bishopric and the capital city of *Lithuania. First mentioned in 1128, it became capital when Prince

*Gedymin moved his seat from Troki (1323). It was partially ruined by German knights on one of their periodical crusades against the heathen Lithuanian state (1383). Its period of temporal and ecclesiastical prosperity began with the destruction of its pagan temple, when Great Prince *Jagiello converted to Christianity upon his marriage to Jadwiga, queen of Poland (1386). After petitioning Pope Urban VI, a Roman Catholic bishopric of V. was established under the metropolitan of *Gneizno.

T. G. Chase, *The Story of Lithuania* (1946).

VINCENNES Town in northern *France near Paris and a traditional centre of the French monarchy. *Louis VII had a hunting lodge constructed at the nearby Bois de V. This structure was later enlarged and became a palace. Louis IX made the city famous as he used to pronounce justice under an oak in its woods. In 1329 V. was the site of an assembly of French barons and in 1330 a pact was signed there between *Edward III of England and *Charles IV of France, regulating the terms of the former's homage. The royal castle was sumptuously rebuilt under *Charles V (1379). During the *Hundred Years' War it was held for a period by the English and King *Henry V died there in 1422.

L. H. Cottineau, *Répertoire topobibliographique des abbayes et prieurés*, I (1935).

VINCENT, St. (MADELGAIRE) (d.677) Founder and abbot of Hautmont and Soignies. Born to a noble family in *Hainault, he led a group of missionaries on a journey to Ireland. Upon his return to his native country, he founded the monastery of Hautmont (c. 642) and entered it as a monk. The monastery became the centre of spiritual comfort for the nobility of the region. In search of greater seclusion, V. later founded a new monastery at Soignies (c. 670).

Lalieu, *Vie de St. Vincent Madelgaire et de Ste.*

Wandrau, son épouse, princes et patrons du Hainaut (1886).

VINCENT FERRER, St. (c. 1350-1419) Son of an Englishman married to a Spanish woman, he joined the *Dominicans (1367) and quickly became a renowned preacher, especially active among Jews and Moslems. Partisan of *Benedict XIII in the papal schism, he became the latter's counsellor and confessor at *Avignon. Leaving Avignon in 1399, V. returned to preaching, attracting huge crowds of *flagellant penitents who followed him from place to place. His reputation as a wonderworker increased the appeal of his impassioned warnings of impending doom. He was also instrumental in ending the papal schism when he withdrew his support of Benedict XIII. Death overtook him on yet another preaching tour, at Vannes in *Brittany. He was canonized in 1455.

H. Ghéon, *St. Vincent Ferrer* (1939);

M. Catherine, *Angel of the Judgement: Life of Vincent Ferrer* (1954).

VINCENT OF BEAUVAIS (c. 1190-c. 1264) Encyclopedist. Probably a member of the *Dominican house at *Paris (1215-20) and at *Beauvais, he was employed as reader at the monastery of Royaumont near Paris (c. 1240-60), where he came in contact with members of the family of King *Louis IX. Apart from some smaller works evidently written in connection with the royal family, he is known for his extensive work, *Speculum Majus* (The Great Mirror). Designed and executed in the

The 14th-century royal castle-keep at Vincennes

encyclopedic tradition, it is a great compendium of all the knowledge of the Middle Ages. It comprises three parts: the *Speculum Naturale* on natural history, an extensive commentary on the biblical story of Creation; the *Speculum Doctrinale* which sums up scholastic knowledge on philosophy, the humanities, law, mechanics, mathematics and medicine; and the *Speculum Historiale,* which deals with sacred and secular history up to the crusade of King *Louis IX (1250). The compendium is written according to the scholastic method of quoting earlier authorities; however, the scope of the work is very extensive for a one-man enterprise. Despite the lack of originality, the "Great Mirror" stands out as a monument to a great mind.

A. L. Gabriel, *The Educational Ideas of Vincent of Beauvais* (1962);

A. Steiner (ed.), *De eruditione filiorum nobilium* (1938).

VINLAND A region on the east coast of North America discovered by Norse colonists from *Greenland in the early 11th century. Information about this venture comes from three *Icelandic sagas, recorded in the 14th century, which mention two distinct settlement attempts. V. was discovered c. 992 by *Leif, son of *Eric the Red, colonizer of Greenland. His voyage was followed up by his brother Thorvald, who attempted to settle in the newly found land. However, he failed to establish a permanent settlement, and the second attempt of the Icelander Thorfinn Karlsefni (1003) was equally unsuccessful. Although conditions were suitable for hunting and raising cattle, the settlers suffered heavy casualties from hostile natives, probably Eskimos, and the settlements were abandoned. The exact location of Leif's discovery and the subsequent settlement attempts have not yet been determined. The place is usually identified with Labrador, Newfoundland and Nova Scotia regions, but the area north of the St. Lawrence River has also been suggested.

R. A. Shelton, *The Vinland Maps and the Tartar Relation* (1965);

M. Magnusson-H. Palsson, trans., *The Vinland Sagas*; *the Norse Discovery of America* (1970).

VIRGIL OF SALZBURG, St. (d. 784) Born in Ireland, where he became a monk, he went abroad and became abbot at *Salzburg (c. 740), with jurisdiction over the local Christians. Of a somewhat difficult character, he clashed with his superior, St. *Boniface of Crediton at Mainz, and was twice sent to Rome. On the first occasion, Pope *Zachary decided in his favour, but on the second he was severely censured by the pope for his cosmological speculations. However, it is by no means clear what V.'s ideas really were. Possessing a good education and active and successful as a missionary, he was eventually made bishop of Salzburg. He was particularly active in the Christianization of the province of *Carinthia.

P. Karner, *Die Heiligen und Seligen Salzburgs* (1913).

VISBY Town and bishopric on the island of Gotland in the Baltic Sea. The site of a pagan temple and a centre of trade as far back as prehistoric times, it was the centre of a thriving community of *Viking merchants organized in a brotherhood cult. Its prosperity depended on Asian trade passing through the island on its way from *Novgorod. The Scandinavian section of the population became eclipsed and eventually displaced by the penetration of German merchants beginning in the late 12th century. These traders organized themselves in the 13th century into the "Community of German Visitors to Gotland", which became the nucleus for the German *Hanse, and brought a period of extraordinary prosperity to the town. V.'s walls were strengthened by massive new fortifications which enlarged the town considerably (end of the 13th century) and a great many churches were built for the religious orders which settled in the town. The end of V.'s heyday was heralded by the slow decline in the fortunes of the German Hanse in the 14th century, and in 1361 V. was conquered by *Waldemar IV of Denmark.

P. Dollinger, *The German Hanse* (1970).

VISCONTI Italian family, leaders and princes of the town and duchy of *Milan from 1277 to 1447. A feudal family from northern Italy claiming descent from the *Lombard kings, the V. had been prominent in Milan in the late 11th century as partisans of *Henry IV. From the struggle for power between the great Milanese families, the V. emerged supreme under Archbishop Ottone. Before his death (1295) he ensured the election of his nephew Matteo as "captain of the people". After a brief interlude of rule by the rival *Della Torre family (1302-10) Matteo was re-established as imperial vicar by Emperor *Henry VII. He laid .the foundation for the duchy of Milan by bringing a number of neighbouring towns under his rule. When a clash with the papacy became imminent, Matteo abdicated in favour of his son Galeazzo (1322). Again relying on imperial connections, Galeazzo defeated a papal army with the aid of Emperor *Louis the Bavarian (1324). In the meantime, V. power was steadily extended through voluntary submission, intrigue, marriage and occasionally by conquest. By the time of Archbishop Giovanni V.'s death (1354) the family was ruling over 15 major towns besides Milan, covering the whole of northern Italy with the exceptions of *Piedmont, *Verona, *Mantua, *Ferrara and *Venice. The V. thereby attained a level of power where they were no longer mere tools in the hands of outside factors such as the emperor. Galeazzo II, ruler of *Pavia, married his daughter to the son of King *Edward III of England and his son Gian Galeazzo to the daughter of King *John of France. Gian Galeazzo gradually emerged as the sole ruler of all the Milanese territories after a period when the lord was divided up (1385). He bought the title of duke from Emperor *Wenceslas IV for 100,000 florins. Based on his fabulous wealth and a highly-developed bureaucratic government, he won town after town and region after region and nothing seemed to be able to halt the subjection of all of Italy. Galeazzo died of the *Black Death while besieging *Florence (1402), and his vast territories were bequeathed to his two sons. Upon the death of the last male V., Filippo Maria, the duchy passed into the hands of his son-in-law, the *condottiere* general Francesco Sforza (1447).

D. Muir, *A History of Milan under the Visconti* (1924);

C. Santoro (ed.), *La politica finanziaria di Visconti* (1976).

VISIGOTHS (WEST GOTHS) That part of the nomadic *Gothic people that settled *c.* 230 to the north of the Black Sea, establishing their own separate monarchy. By 238 they had begun to raid the Eastern Roman empire. Between 341 and 380 they were partly Christianized by *Ulphilas but the aristocracy remained pagan. They were driven by the *Huns into the Roman empire and settled under Fritigern in Thrace (376). In 377 they re-

The city-wall of Visby, built in the 13th century

volted against the conditions forced upon them and wiped out an imperial army under Valens at *Adrianople (378). They were stopped on the way to *Constantinople by *Theodore and wandered about the Balkan peninsula. Several truces were quickly broken and in 397 they made themselves masters of Illyria under *Alaric I. During these wanderings they were converted to Arian Christianity. Having devastated the western half of the Balkans, Alaric took his army and people into Italy (401) and sacked Rome (410). By 412 the V. had reached Gaul and settled under King *Athaulf in *Aquitaine. There his successors, *Wallia and *Theodoric I, created the kingdom of *Toulouse. The Gothic leaders became a landed aristocracy and the army fought for Rome against *Attila (451) and in Spain. Under *Euric, the Gothic state reached the height of its power and consolidated its conquests in Spain and southern France. After the disastrous defeat at the hands of the *Franks under *Clovis at *Vouille (507), and following the suppression of Arianism in Gaul, the V. undertook a mass exodus from Aquitaine to Old *Castile. There they extended their previous conquests and created the kingdom of *Toledo (after 554), which lasted until the Islamic invasion of 711. *Leovigild wiped out the *Suevi kingdom in *Galicia (585) and the *Byzantine conclave in the south was conquered by *Sisebut (612-21). Basque separatism was dealt with more or less effectively. Aside from the merciless persecution of the substantial Jewish population, the V., after accepting Catholicism (587), joined with the indigenous population to form a common culture and political-legal system. The only barbaric kingdom to favour intellectual life, they profited from the experience of the clergy, whom they persuaded to serve the state. The councils of Toledo, which were both political and ecclesiastical, put the talents of the clergy at the service of a monarchy becoming more and more Spanish in nature, up to the downfall of the V. kingdom.

L. Musset, *The Germanic Invasions* (1975).

VISITATION A formal periodical visit paid by a superior authority to an institution or district for purpose of investigation, examination and the like. In the Middle Ages it was used mainly in ecclesiastical bodies. Originally only the duty of the higher officials of the secular *church, such as archbishops, bishops and archdeacons, the practice of V. eventually became widespread in the monastic establishments as well. In the isolated abbeys of the first half of the Middle Ages, which were for long periods more like high-class hostels for the aristocracy than places of piety, the enforcement of discipline and moral standards could often be effected only by outsiders with full powers of coercion.

R. W. Southern, *Western Society and the Church in the Middle Ages* (1970).

VITALIAN (d. 672) Pope (657-72). V. inherited a conflict between the Eastern Church and the papacy which had begun over the *Monothelite controversy between Pope *Martin I and the Eastern emperor *Constans II. In an attempt to restore friendly relations, V. dispatched letters which announced his election without mentioning the controversial Monothelite issue, and made efforts to accommodate Constans upon the latter's visit to Rome (663). After the emperor's death (668) V. supported his heir, but took a more determined stand against Monothelitism. The pope also

sent *Theodore of Tarsus to England as archbishop of *Canterbury.

H. K. Mann, *The Lives of the Popes in the Early Middle Ages*, I (1902).

VITALIS OF SAVIGNY, St. (c. 1060-1122)   Norman monk. He became priest and chaplain to Robert of Mortain, brother of *William I the Conqueror. In search of religious perfection, he withdrew to the hermit colony of the forest of Craon (1095). Although leading an ascetic life, he also took care of the needs of the surrounding population, which was composed of many outlaws and bandits. In 1112 he founded the monastery of Savigny and between 1105 and 1120 the nunnery at Mortain, of which his sister, St. Adeline, became abbess.

VITERBO Town and bishopric in southern *Tuscany northwest of Rome. An old Roman settlement, it was fortified by the Lombard king *Desiderius. It was in the centre of the territory given by Countess *Matilda of Tuscany to the papacy as the "patrimony of St. Peter" (1115). Blessed with a pleasant climate and a most beautiful landscape, it became the second capital and summer residence of the popes in the 13th century. *Eugenius III had moved his seat to V. in 1145, after the citizens of Rome had established a senate of their own. During the great struggles between emperors and popes, the town witnessed numerous dramatic events. It was the scene of a meeting between *Otto IV and *Innocent III (1209), the latter opposed to the future emperor's Italian plans. In 1232 the Romans, after having driven out *Gregory IX, tried to subject V. to their rule and were made to retreat only by an imperial army. By 1241 relations between pope and emperor were at their worst, and imperial troops took the greater part of the papal state, including V. In 1266 a treaty was signed at V. between *Charles of Anjou and William II of Villehardouin, prince of the Frankish state of Achaia; it granted Achaia to Charles in exchange for military and financial help against the *Byzantines. The almost continuous presence of popes in the city resulted in the construction of a great many ecclesiastical buildings and palaces. Popes Urban IV, Gregory X, John XXI, Nicholas III and Martin IV were elected at V. and Popes Alexander IV, Clement IV, Adrian V and John XXI died there.

G. Signorelli, *Viterbo nella storia della Chiesa*, 2 vols. (1907-40).

VITIGES (d. 543)   King of the *Ostrogoths (536-40). A distinguished warrior, he was elected king in place of the incompetent *Theodehad when a *Byzantine army under *Belisarius landed in Italy and seized *Naples and *Rome. With considerable skill V. checked an invasion of the *Franks by the cession of *Provence, allowing him to proceed with united forces to besiege Rome. Exhausting his army in futile efforts against Belisarius' superior generalship, V. withdrew. By 539 he was pressed on every side and shut himself up in *Ravenna. He consented to abdicate in favour of Belisarius and was taken to Constantinople (530). There he was honoured with the title of patrician and a secure income, granted until his death in 543.

CMedH, II (1913);

L. Musset, *The Germanic Invasions* (1975).

VITOVT (1392-1430)   Grand duke of *Lithuania. After forcing his uncle *Jagiello, king of Poland and Lithuania, to recognize him as grand prince of the latter,

he secured for his country a most important role in east European political affairs. By 1396 *Moldavia, *Wallachia and Bessarabia were forced to recognize his suzerainty. Although defeated decisively by the *Mongols on the banks of the Vorskla (1399), he continued to interfere in the affairs of the *Golden Horde through friendly khans. In 1410 he personally led his army in the crucial Battle of *Tannenberg, where the joint forces of Poland and Lithuania crushed the *Teutonic knights. Were it not for the defeat by the Mongols, this man of ambition and foresight might have asserted the power of Lithuania over both Moscow and Poland.
G. Vernadsky, *The Mongols and Russia* (1953);
J. Pfitzner, *Grossfürst Witold von Litauen als Staatsmann* (1930).

VITTORIA A town built by *Frederick II beside *Parma, which he had sworn to raze to the ground after it had revolted against him (1248). A fortified camp, V. was laid out according to plan; a canal brought water to it and mills were erected on the artificial river. Coins were minted bearing the emperor's head on one side and a picture of the town on the other. Frederick installed himself, together with his court, in the new town, where he felt safe for the winter, and settled down to starve Parma into surrender. On 18 February 1248, while Frederick was out hawking, V. was assaulted at the most distant point from the besieged city by the Parmesans and taken by surprise. About 3000 of its defenders were made prisoners, the immense imperial treasure was captured and the new town went up in flames. Recalled by the alarm bells, Frederick cut his way through enemy lines, sword in hand, but was too late. Followed by a few knights, he withdrew to *Cremona to await fresh troops from *Sicily.
E. Kantorowicz, *Frederick the Second 1194-1250* (1957).

VIVARIUM Monastery founded in 555 together with a twin anchorite settlement by *Cassiodorus off the Gulf of Squillace in *Calabria. Intended to be a place of systematic biblical study, it was equipped by the founder with an extensive library and a *scriptorium; and included a curriculum embracing theological as well as secular studies. Cassiodorus, although no monk himself, took part in the religious services as patron. After his death intellectual activity at V. declined. However, the inclusion of liberal arts in the curriculum and the existence of secular works in the library had most important consequences. Since the monks devoted themselves not only to study, but also to the copying of manuscripts, they were responsible for the preservation of much of the ancient culture.
A. Momigliano, *Cassiodorus and Italian Culture of his Time* (1955).

VLACHS The name given by the *Byzantines and *Slavs to the Rumanian people. The subject of heated controversies, the V. were thought by Rumanian historians to be descendants of Roman colonists settled in the 2nd century in Illyria, while Hungarian historians believed them to be nomadic shepherds from south of the Danube. Whatever their origin, the V. played a prominent role in a number of political entities from the 12th century. The more important of these were the Bulgaro-Vlach empire north of the Danube (1185-1257), Megalovlachia in the mountains of Thessaly (second half of the 11th century to 1393), the principality of *Wallachia between the southern Carpathians and the principality of *Moldavia.
CMedH, IV (1966).

VLADIMIR Town in Russia. Founded in 1108 by *Vladimir II Monomakh, it became capital and lent its name to the principality of *Suzdal under *Andrei Bogolubski (1157), who made it the strongest of the Russian states and added *Kiev to his rule. It became a grand duchy and formally sovereign in Russia under *Vsevolod III Big-Nest. Although progressively weakened by apportionment of inheritance claims after 1216, it nevertheless remained a formidable power. This was recognized by the Mongols under *Batu-khan, who made Jaroslav grand prince of all Russia. Family feuds brought a steep decline in power after the death of *Alexander Nevski (1263) and V. had to yield to *Tver and *Moscow. Containing elements from both East and West, the town's architecture and school of painting greatly influenced the Russian culture. V. was destroyed by the Tartars (in 1238, and again in 1293), but was rapidly restored. In the 15th century it sank to the rank of a minor regional centre.
G. Vernadsky, *Kievan Russian* (1948);
Idem, The Mongols and Russia (1953).

VLADIMIR OF KIEV, St. (955-1015) Ruler of *Kiev (980-1015) said to have introduced Christianity to Russia. Coming to power as *Byzantine influence under *Basil II was strongly felt in the kingdom, he saved the latter from military defeat by the rebellious Bardas *Phocas when he rushed into Byzantium with an army of 6000 (989). In return, V. received the hand of the emperor's sister Anna, an unprecedented honour, promised fealty and received baptism. Taking his new religion to heart, he sometimes sought to impose it by force upon his people. In the main, however, Kiev and its borderlands were Christianized by Greek missionaries, to whom he gave wholehearted support. Later he and his Christian grandmother *Olga were revered as saints, becoming the subject of folklore and heroic poems.
N. de Baumgarten, *Saint Vladimir et la conversion de la Russie* (1932);
G. Vernadsky, *Kievan Russia* (1948).

VLADIMIR II, Monomakh (1053-1125) Prince of Tsernigov (1078-94), and of Pereiaslav, grand prince of *Kiev (1113-25). Son of *Vsevolod and maternal grandson of the Eastern emperor *Constantine IX Monomachos. He organized the defence of the Kievan principalities, waging a number of successful campaigns against the *Cumans and drawing the princes together. Popular with the lower classes, he ascended the Kievan throne after heavy rioting with obvious undertones of social revolution on his behalf, and restored the threatened social order. His *Instruction*, a treatise on statesmanship with biographical notes written by him for his sons, presents him as a man of dignity and Christian humility.
G. Vernadsky, *Kievan Russia* (1948).

VLASTIMIR OF SERBIA Chieftain and king of the *Serbian tribes in western *Macedonia (c. 840). In uniting the tribes, he was helped by the feeling of resentment aroused by the expansion of the first *Bulgarian empire into the Serbian lands. He was urged on by his nominal suzerain, the *Byzantine emperor. In 839 the Bulgarians invaded Serbia, but were defeated by V. after a three-year struggle. In 852 V.'s sons took the initiative and again defeated the Bulgarians, taking prisoner the son of *Boris and 12 great nobles and forcing Boris to ask for peace. Through these victories V. and his sons were able to preserve Serbian independence and check Bulgarian expansion, which was well taken advantage of by Byzantium in preparing its defence against Bulgaria.

CMedH, IV;
A. P. Vlasto, *The Entry of the Slavs into Christendom* (1970).

VOJVODINA Province between the Danube and the Carpathian Mountains. In the 4th-7th centuries it was used by Germanic, Mongol-Altaic and Slavic tribes as a passageway for their invasions to the west and south. From the 6th century Slavic tribes settled in the area under the rule of the *Avars. In the 10th century V. was conquered by the Hungarians and annexed to their kingdom. In the 12th century the territory, ruled by several families of counts, became a march. It was placed under the authority of a prince related to the royal dynasty, who took the Slav title of *voivode* (similar to margrave), from which the province took its name.

VOLHYNIA A region in southwestern Russia. It had been inhabited in ancient times and in the early Middle Ages by the Volhynians and the Buzhans, both eastern Slav tribes. In the 9th century the region came under the rule of descendants of the Varangian leader, *Rurik. From 1241 it had to recognize the overlordship of the *Tartar *Golden Horde, as did the rest of the Kievan principalities. In 1336, upon the long southward thrust of Grand Prince *Gedymin of Lithuania to the Black Sea, V. became part of the Lithuanian state.

G. Vernadsky, *Ancient Russia* (1943).

VOUILLE (VOCLADIS) Site of a battle in the neighbourhood of *Poitiers between the *Visigoths under *Alaric II and the Salian *Franks under *Clovis (507). In his expansionist drive to win all of Gaul, Clovis appealed to the religious sentiments of the *Ripuarian Franks and the *Burgundians and secured their support for a concerted attack on the *Arian Visigoths. The heroic resistance of the Goths was to no avail and Alaric was slain by Clovis himself. The Franks took over the greater part of Gothic Gaul, leaving the Visigoths only a district between the Cevennes Mountains, the Rhône and the sea, with its capital at *Narbonne.

CMedH, II;
"The Settlement of the Visigoths in Southern Gaul," in *Journal of Roman Studies*, 46 (1956).

VOX IN EXCELSO A papal bull issued in 1311 by *Clement V, which formally dissolved the order of *Templars, on suspicion of heresy. It ordered that their property pass to the *Hospitallers.

VSEVOLOD Prince of Pereiaslav (1054-93). Younger son of *Yaroslav the Wise, he was assigned the principality of Pereiaslav by his father as part of the plan by which succession in Kievan *Russia would be regulated. From 1078 to his death, he was a key figure in the Russian dynastic wars, supporting his nephew, *Svyatopolk.

VRATISLAV II Duke of Bohemia (1061-92); king of Bohemia (1085-92), V. continued the tradition of a close association with Germany. In return for his participation in Emperor *Henry IV's Italian campaigns, he was rewarded with the title of king at the imperial assembly at *Mainz (1085) and given the Mark of *Meissen. Largely for political reasons, he founded or restored a Moravian see at *Olmutz. For family and political reasons he made his troublesome brother, Jaromir, bishop of *Prague (1068). Unable to discipline him, he was eventually forced to send Jaromir to Rome (1073).

CMedH, VI.

VSEVOLOD BIG-NEST Grand prince of *Vladimir (1176-1212), so-called because of his many sons. Coming to power after the death of *Andrei Bogolubski (1174) and subsequent to a two-year struggle against other contenders, V.'s reign marks the height of the power of the grand prince of Vladimir. He forced his nearest neighbours, the princes of Murom and Ryazan, to become his vassals and severely repressed their efforts to achieve independence. Thus the nucleus of an upper Volga state was formed. After V.'s death the land was divided between his many sons, and its unity was restored only after two centuries of arduous work by the rulers of *Moscow.

G. Vernadsky, *Kievan Russia* (1948).

VULGATE The Latin version of the Bible in general use in the medieval West, as translated for the most part by St. *Jerome. Due to the great textual disparity between the versions in use in the 4th century, Jerome translated and revised from the Greek Septuagint and Hebrew versions long sections of the Old Testament as well as the Gospels. His product was recognized as superior to older versions, and in the 6th century his books were collected into one Bible, whose widespread popularity earned it the name Vulgata ("in general use"). This included Jerome's translation of the Hebrew Bible (except for the Psalter), the so-called Gallican Psalter, his translation of Tobit and Judith, older versions of the rest of the Old Testament in Old Latin, Jerome's revision of the Gospels and revised texts of the rest of the New Testament. Mention of such a complete Bible in one book was first given by *Cassiodorus. In the Middle Ages various attempts were made to improve and standardize the V. text, notably by *Alcuin and *Theodulf of Orléans, as well as by the University of *Paris in the 13th century. At the Council of Trent (1646) the V. was pronounced the only authentic Latin text of the Scriptures.

The Cambridge History of the Bible (1970).

VYACHESLAV Name of two medieval Russian princes. V. I, son of *Yaroslav the Wise (1036-54), was given the city of *Smolensk by his father, while his four brothers received other towns, one being *Kiev, the ruler of which was also vested with the state of Kievan Russia as a whole. V. II, younger son of *Vladimir II Monomakh, ruled the principality of Turov after his father's death (1125), while his elder brother, *Mstislav I, became prince of Kiev.

G. Vernadsky, *Kievan Russia* (1948).

W

WACE, ROBERT (c. 1100-c. 1175) Poet and chronicler. Born in Jersey to a noble family, he was educated for the church and sent to study at *Caen and *Paris. Returning to Caen (c. 1130), he was employed as reader by King *Henry I and later became a canon (c. 1160). W. was friendly with King *Henry II, who granted him a prebend in the church of *Bayeux. He wrote a few lives of saints and two metrical chronicles in Norman French. The *Roman de Brut* (known also as *Geste des Bretons*) was completed in 1155 and dedicated to *Eleanor of Aquitaine. It is a free translation of the Latin *Historia Britonum* by *Geoffrey of Monmouth. The *Roman du Rou* (*Geste des Normanz*), a chronicle of the *Norman dukes, was written in 1160-62, and is based on the chronicles of Dudo and *William of Jumièges. It was dedicated to Henry II.
G. Jones (introd.), *Arthurian Chronicles of Wace and Layamon* (1976);
J. H. Philpot, *Maistre Wace, a Pioneer in Two Literatures* (1925).

WACHO (WACCHO) King of the *Lombards (c. 510-39) in Austria, north of the Danube. W. rose to the royal throne after murdering his uncle Tato. Foiling the attempts of Tato's heirs to recover their rightful rule, he made an alliance with Emperor *Justinian against the neighbouring tribe of the *Gepids (539). As a consequence, he refused to join in the attack on the Byzantines planned by the Goth *Vitiges in Italy. He married his daughters to a *Frankish king and the duke of *Bavaria, while he himself married daughters of the kings of neighbouring tribes.
J. Werner, "Die Langobarden" in: *Pannonien, Abhandlungen der Bayerischen Akademie der Wissenschaften, Phil.-hist. Klasse,* N.F. 55A (1962).

WAGRIANS Slav tribe in northeastern *Germany. In the 10th and 11th centuries they were attacked by the *Danes, coming from Schleswig, but managed to defend themselves and to maintain their independence until the middle of the 12th century. In 1147 they were defeated by the Saxon army of *Henry the Lion and rapidly Germanized.

WAIFAR (WAIFRE) Duke of *Aquitaine (745-68). W. was the son and successor of Duke *Hunald. He granted asylum to Grippon, the brother of *Pepin, whom the latter had despoiled. War broke out and was fought fiercely for 17 years. Pepin devastated Aquitaine in yearly campaigns of plunder, and W. adopted a strategy of scorched earth. Before the superior power of the Franks, W. retreated into the mountains of Dordogne and afterwards into the strongholds of *Auvergne. The war was brought to an end when the indomitable W. was assassinated in the forest of *Ver in *Perigord.
F. Funck-Bretano, *The National History of France,* V (1927).

WALAFRID STRABO (c. 808-49) German monk, poet and theologian. A Swabian of humble origin, he was educated at *Reichenau under Tatto and *Wettin and later at *Fulda, where he was a pupil of *Hrabanus Maurus. He became tutor to *Charles the Bald, who made him abbot of Reichenau in 838. He had to flee from his monastery after taking the side of *Lothair (840), but was reinstated in 842. He died while on an embassy for Charles the Bald. Of his work, his very personal poems deal with spiritual tempests (*Visio Wettini*), the joys and uses of gardening (*Hortulus*) and the poet and his inner voice (*De imagine Tetricii*). He also wrote rhymed and prose lives of several saints. Of his theological works the most important is the great *Glossa ordinaria,* a commentary on the Scriptures which remained the medieval and early modern textbook in its field. W. also revised *Einhard's *Life of Charlemagne.*
PL, CXIII, CXIV;
R. Payne, trans., *Hortulus* (1966);
Life: E. S. Duckett, *Carolingian Portraits* (1969).

WALBURGA, St. (d. c. 779) Born in *Wessex and a nun of Winborne, she joined the mission of St. *Boniface of Crediton at Mainz together with her brothers, the monks St. *Willibald and Winebald. In 761 she succeeded the latter as head of the male and female Benedictine monasteries at Heidenheim near *Augsburg, directing them until her death. Her grave at Eichstädt became a popular centre of pilgrimage on account of the miraculous oil said to flow from it. After her death she seems to have been confused with Waldborg, a godess of fertility. Her name became associated with witchcraft and the first night of May is called Walpurgis Night, when the witches of Germany are said to congregate in the Harz Mountains as is related in Goethe's *Faust.*
C. H. Talbot, *The Anglo-Saxon Missionaries in Germany* (1954).

WALCHER OF MALVERN Monk and prior of Malvern, and scientist. Interested in astronomy, he acquired an *astrolabe with which he observed eclipses in Italy (1091) and England (1092), using his findings to establish lunar tables. Around 1110 he met the renowned physician and astronomer Pedro Alfonso, an apostate Jew, who relayed to him his vast practical experience. W.'s knowledge is reflected in his treatise *Of the Dragon,* in which he describes methods for forecasting eclipses and for calculating the position of the sun, the moon and its "nodes" (the points of intersection in its orbit with the angle of the equator). The works of W. and *Adelhard of Bath, another pupil of Pedro Alfonso, began a scientific tradition in England, which reached its apogee in the 13th century with Robert *Grosseteste and Roger *Bacon.
A. C. Crombie, *Augustine to Galileo, the History of Science, A.D. 400-1650* (1952).

Interior of the Norman cathedral of Winchester, England

WALDEBERT Abbot of Luxeuil (620-32). Born to an eminent Frankish family, he entered the Irish monastery of Luxeuil, where he gained the respect of St. Columban. Upon becoming abbot, he introduced the *Benedictine rule to the monastery. W. was also one of the counsellors of King *Dagobert.

WALDEMAR I, the Great (1132-82) King of *Denmark (1157-82). Heir to the ancient royal line of Denmark and son of *Canute Lavard, he was one of the three contenders to the throne upon the death of King Eric Lam (1147). By 1157 he had beaten his rivals and became the undisputed ruler. He fought the *Wendish pirates of Rügen for ten years, and in 1169 took the island, destroying their heathen idol and Christianizing the Wends at the point of the sword (1169). In his relations with Germany, W. acknowledged the suzerainty of Emperor *Frederick I in 1162, depending on his help against his aggressive German neighbours, led by *Henry the Lion. After the latter's fall (1180) and the strengthening of W.'s rule, relations were put on a more equal level. The two met in 1182 in the presence of their respective armies and arranged a double marriage between their children. An uprising of the *Scanian provinces in protest of heavy taxation was put down by W.'s minister Absalon, bishop of *Roskilde (1181).
J. H. S. Birch, *Denmark in History* (1938).

WALDEMAR II, the Conqueror (1170-1241) King of *Denmark (1202-41). Second son of *Waldemar I and duke of *Schleswig, he succeeded his brother *Canute VI in 1202. Having already conquered *Holstein, *Otto IV recognized his suzerainty over the German lands north of the Elbe River, including the important trade centre of *Lübeck. In return, W. recognized Otto as German emperor. W.'s hold over these lands was strengthened by the support he received from Pope *Innocent III, whom he had pleased by leading crusades against the heathen Estonians (1206) and *Pomeranians (1210). In 1215 W. easily foiled an attempt to recover Northalbingia. At the height of his power in 1223, he and his sons were kidnapped by his guest, Count Henry of *Schwerin. He was released only after having paid a heavy ransom and surrendering Northalbingia and all his *Wendish conquests (1225). He was subsequently defeated at the Battle of Bornhöved in 1227, but was able to retain the greater part of Danish Estonia by the Compact of Stensby (1238). Towards the end of his rule the great codification of Danish laws (the Jutland Code) was completed.
J. H. S. Birch, *Denmark in History* (1938).

WALDEMAR IV King of *Denmark (1340-75). The youngest son of *Christopher II of Denmark, he was brought up at the court of Emperor *Louis of Bavaria. After his election as king, he laboured for seven years to reunite the Danish state. He was assisted in his struggle by the emperor and the *Hanseatic towns, whose privileges he acknowledged. His fantastic plan to claim and invade England in league with France was foiled by rebellions of Jutish nobles, which he put down in 1357. His conquest of *Scania (1361), the centre of a great fishing industry, brought W. into conflict with the Hanse towns. War broke out in 1361, when W. took *Visby. At the battle near Helsingborg he decisively defeated a united Hanseatic-Swedish fleet. He averted a general attack by the Hanse and rebellious Danish nobles (1368) through diplomatic measures. The peace

settlement (1370) was humiliating, but W. managed to prevent the implementation of most of its clauses.
J. H. S. Birch, *Denmark in History* (1938).

WALDEMAR OF SWEDEN King (1250-67). Son of Burger Jar and nephew of *Eric Ericsson, he was elected king at the latter's death and founded the Folkungs dynasty. He ruled jointly with his father until the latter's death (1266). Soon afterwards he was overthrown as a result of a quarrel with his younger brother, *Magnus Ladulas, who was elected to the throne with the support of *Denmark. The quarrel was dramatized in the *Chronicle of Eric,* with particular stress on W.'s questionable liaison with his wife's sister, Jutta of Denmark. During his reign the power of central government increased, and close contact with the other Scandinavian kingdoms was maintained.
I. Andersson, *A History of Sweden* (1956).

WALDENSES (WALDENSIAN HERESY) A sect that developed when the poor of *Lyons, followers of Peter *Waldo, were denounced as *heretics (1184). Joined by a group of *Milanese wool workers, the so-called *Humiliati or Poor Lombards, the Waldensian movement spread rapidly through the cities of the southern French-German borderlands and the Alpine valleys of *Savoy, *Dauphiné and *Piedmont. Unable to reconcile the different views on the Waldensian tradition and the proper relationship to the Church and its *sacraments, the movement split into numerous sects, some of which became reconciled with the Church in the early 13th century. Among the latter were the groups revolving around Durandus of Huesca and Bernard Prim. The W. proper were driven by growing harassment into an ever more radical stance, escalating their criticism of the abuses of the Church into a denial of the Church's spiritual role in the process of salvation. Thus they negated most of the sacraments, the role of the priest, devotion to the saints, *indulgences, in short the whole apparatus of salvation in the hands of the Church. In this respect they strongly differed from other movements of apostolic poverty that arose in the same period, such as the *Franciscans. On the other hand, the W. remained basically Christian in their religious beliefs, as opposed to the equally widespread dualist heresy of the *Cathars. Wherever they took root, the W. developed some rudimentary organization usually comprising a large body of faithful and a smaller group of ministers. While in some areas bishops, priests and deacons were appointed, the movement never attained the interregional and international stage of organization of the Cathars. In addition, there was a clear dividing line between the more radical and socially revolutionary Italian wing and the French wing, influenced more by Waldo's spiritual teaching. Of all the numerous Waldensian communities, only the ones in the secluded mountain valleys of Piedmont and Savoy survived repression and persecution at the hands of secular and ecclesiastical authorities during the 13th-15th centuries.
W. L. Wakefield, *Heresy, Crusade and Inquisition in Southern France, 1100-1250* (1974);
H. C. Lea, *A History of the Inquisition of the Middle Ages,* 3 vols. (1888).

WALDO, PETER (d. 1216) Founder of the heretical *Waldensian sect. A wealthy merchant of *Lyons, he underwent a spiritual process similar to the one experienced by St. *Francis of Assisi. In his desire to acquire a deeper knowledge of the Scriptures, he had translations of the Gospels and other biblical and *patristic books made for him (*c.* 1170). Striving to attain Christian perfection and salvation, he followed the call of Christ and left his family, distributing his possessions among the poor and taking the vow of poverty (1176). W. found followers among the poor of Lyons, and established a confraternity for the practice of apostolic poverty, which was approved by Pope *Alexander III. Equipped with a translation of the New Testament in Provençal, W. and his followers set out to preach the doctrine of Christ in the streets, explaining the Scriptures as they understood it. This led to a papal censure, prohibiting them to preach without the permission of the bishops (1179), which was defied by W. on grounds of his moral consciousness. As a result, he and his followers were included among the heretics excommunicated by Pope *Lucius III at the Council of *Verona (1184). After the condemnation and the onset of persecution, W.'s circumstances are unknown, except for the fact that he fled to Bohemia, where he died in 1216.

W. L. Wakefield, *Heresy, Crusade and Inquisition in Southern France, 1100-1250* (1974);

M. Martini, *Pierre Valdo, Le Pauvre de Lyon: L'Epopée Vaudoise* (1961).

WALES Province in *Britain. After the Roman withdrawal from Britain in the early Middle Ages, W. was ruled by *Celtic princes, whose power was increasingly curtailed by Saxon expansion (577 Battle of Durham, 613 Battle of Chester). In the late 9th century *Viking naval raids and *Mercian territorial aggression were stemmed by Roderick the Great (Rhodri Mawr) (d. 877). Under his sons W. was divided into three principalities based on tribal entities, and the leadership of the whole country was vested in the princes of Gwynedd. Llewelyn ap Seissylt (d. 1002) managed to unite all of W. under his rule, but the country was again divided at the instigation of *Harold, earl of Wessex. Following the *Norman Conquest of England, southern W. was conquered by Robert Fitz-Hamon, earl of Gloucester. Further Norman inroads were met successfully by Griffith ap Rhys at the Battle of Cardigan (1136), to be followed by a peace treaty upon the accession of King *Henry II. The division of the independent parts of W. between the houses of Gwynedd and Dynevor was ended in 1196, when the former became undisputed overlords of the entire country. Llewelyn the Great (d. 1240) succeeded on the whole in maintaining a precarious independence from his feudal overlords, the kings of England, while fighting at the same time rebellious Welsh chieftains. He failed to preserve the ecclesiastical independence of the four Welsh sees, which were finally made subject to the archbishop of *Canterbury (1203). His nephew Llewelyn allied himself with *Simon de Montfort-Leicester and the rebellious English barons and was defeated by King *Edward (1282). Welsh independence was lost and the whole country became the *apanage of the English crown prince. English colonists were planted in the towns and granted far-reaching privileges, while development of the countryside was severely hampered. During the period of unrest following the usurpation of the English crown by *Henry IV, popular discontent in W. found its expression. The Welsh population was led by the princely adventurer Owen Glendower, who defeated all English

forces and ruled W. in the years 1402-08. After his mysterious disappearance (1408) the country fell again into the possession of the English king and settlers. Only with the rise of Henry Tudor (1485), which was achieved mainly by the help of the Welsh magnate Sir Rhys ap Thomas, did W. become truly integrated into the English realm.

A. W. Wade-Evans, *The Emergence of England and Wales* (1959).

WALID Name of two *Ummayad caliphs:

Walid ben Abd Al-Malik Ruled 705-15 and known for his religious fervour and extensive construction activities. He confiscated the basilica of St. John the Baptist in *Damascus and turned it into a magnificent mosque. Under his rule the administration was taken out of the hands of the Syrian Christians. The Arab empire expanded through conquest to its greatest extent, reaching from Transoxiana to Spain.

Walid ben Yazid Ruled 743-44. An artistic and cultivated man, he was something of a libertine. He is known for his fantastic project of building the grand palace of Mshatta in the middle of the desert, with all the refinements of civilization. His cruel and capricious behaviour caused Syria, up till then the basis of Ummayad strength, to rise against him and he was killed in a rebellion, which brought about the end of Ummayad rule.

J. Wellhausen, *The Arab Kingdom and its Fall* (1973).

WALLACE, WILLIAM (c. 1270-1305) Rebel and national hero of *Scotland. Of noble descent, he killed a young Englishman for insulting him and was declared an outlaw. Starting a guerilla war from his hideaway, he was joined by patriotic nobles and enlarged the scope of his operations. When a large English army frightened off his followers, who asked for peace (1297), he built up a new army to the north of the Firth of Forth. He destroyed an English army near Abbey Craig (September 1297), drove the English out of Scotland and was elected guardian of Scotland. In 1298 a new invading army led by King *Edward met and defeated W.'s forces at Falkirk. After the submission of the Scottish nobles (*c.* 1303) W. continued to conduct desultory raids, but was captured, taken to London, tried as a traitor and executed (August 1305).

J. Fergusson, *William Wallace, Guardian of Scotland* (1938).

WALLACHIA Name given to two political entities populated by the *Vlachs. In the second *Bulgarian empire the province of *Thessaly was inhabited by great numbers of Vlachs and became known as Great W., while *Epirus was known as Upper W. At the beginning of the 14th century (1324) a large state developed south of the Carpathian Mountains under the *voivode Basaraba. He began the struggle for emancipation from *Hungarian overlordship by surrounding and destroying a Hungarian army under King *Charles II (1336). This was followed by another victory in 1369. Liberation from the Catholic Hungarian rule ensured the establishment of the Orthodox Church and in 1359 the *patriarch of Constantinople appointed a metropolitan with his seat at Arges. Slavonic became the official language of administration and the church. The political institutions and the concept of the ruler were modelled on *Byzantine autocratic lines, but in practice the nobility had a powerful influence both on the peasants and on national politics.

From the late 14th century warring factions of nobles became involved with both the Turks and the Hungarians. The rivalry of the two great powers in the area resulted in a constant change of rulers and fierce civil war in W. With the decline of Hungarian power, Ottoman control over W. was gradually extended. The area became a vassal state, although it preserved its institutions and avoided Turkish colonization and conversion to Islam. Thus in the 19th century the unification of W. and its twin sister *Moldavia into a modern Rumanian state occurred without major convulsions.
CMedH, IV.

WALLIA King of the *Visigoths (415-19). He became king after the murder of *Athaulf. His efforts to break the Roman siege of the Visigoth-ruled Spanish province of Tarraconensis and to migrate with his people to Africa miscarried (416). W. was forced into a treaty with the Romans, whereby the Goths, in return for a supply of 600,000 measures of grain, undertook to free Galla Placidia, an imperial hostage, and to reconquer Spain from the *Vandals, *Alans and *Suevi. After fierce and prolonged fighting, the Silingian Vandals and then the Alans were decisively beaten (416-18). However, W. was called back by the Romans from his attack on the remaining foes in Spain, as he seemed to have become too powerful. The Goths were assigned land in the province of Aquitanica Secunda (418) and shortly afterwards W. died, to be succeeded by Theodoric I.
E. A. Thompson, *The Goths in Spain* (1969).

WALLINGFORD Town on the west bank of the Thames, west of London. W. was a fortified site prior to the *Norman Conquest and the largest *borough in Berkshire during the 11th century, as indicated in the *Domesday Book. Its importance stemmed from its location on the main road between London and *Gloucester. A large new castle was built there by the Normans. The town was the centre of resistance against King *Stephen for 14 years and the site of a treaty (1153) between Stephen and the future King *Henry II. In 1155 Henry II held a council there, at which he made the magnates swear *homage to him and his infant sons. The town itself had a market, several fairs and a guild of merchants and was favoured by royal privileges. The deflection of the London-Gloucester traffic resulting from the erection of two new bridges near Abingdon in the early 15th century brought about the economic decline of the town.
T. K. Hedges, *The History of Wallingford* (1881).

WALLOONS Ethnic group situated in northeastern Gaul and particularly in the Meuse Valley. Of Gallo-Roman origin, they maintained their ethnic and linguistic character despite the *Frankish conquest. In the 8th-9th centuries, they even assimilated the Frankish populace into their midst and created a French-speaking group among the Germanic dialects. In the 11th century they developed their own civilization, based on oral traditions and expressed in art as well as in written Latin works.

WALSINGHAM, THOMAS (c. 1360-c. 1422) English chronicler and monk. He was a scriptor in the monastery of *St. Albans, prior of the cell of Wymondham (1394) and again monk at St. Albans, where he died. Between 1380 and 1394 he wrote the *Chronica maiora*, a continuation of *Matthew Paris' *Great Chronicle*, and the *Gesta Abbatum*, a history of the abbots of St. Albans. At Wymondham he completed a condensed version of his chronicle, and back at St. Albans he wrote his greatest work, the *St. Albans Chronicle*. His work is an important source of Anglo-Norman and ecclesiastical history up to 1419.
V. H. Galbraith (ed.), *St. Albans' Chronicle* (1937).

WALTER I, of Brienne Duke of *Athens (1301-11). Member of the French counts of *Brienne, he inherited the duchy of Athens in 1301. In 1310 he hired the *Catalan Company to conquer Thessaly for him. Having failed to pay for their services, he was killed by the company in the following year.

WALTER II, of Brienne Count of *Brienne and titular duke of Athens (1311-56). Son of *Walter I, he was educated in Italy, where he became a *condottiere. In 1324 he became active in Florentine affairs. In 1342 W. supported a popular revolt at *Florence and became master of the city until the following year, when the aristocratic party returned to power. W. then went to France to govern his ancestral county in Champagne and entered the service of King *John II. He was killed at the Battle of *Poitiers in 1356.

WALTER MAP (c. 1140-c. 1209) Cleric and satirical writer. W. descended from a family of Welsh origin which was employed by King *Henry II of England. He studied at *Paris and was himself employed by the king as roving justice and envoy to Pope *Alexander III. At the Third *Lateran Council he was assigned to argue against the *Waldenses (1179). He rose rapidly in the ranks of the English church, becoming chancellor of *Lincoln (1186), canon of *St. Paul's Church in London (1192), archdeacon of *Oxford (1197) and canon of Hereford. He failed, however, to obtain the bishopric of Hereford (1199). Possessing an intimate knowledge of ecclesiastical and royal affairs, he wrote *De nugis curialium*, a collection of all sorts of gossip, legends and inside information. He directed his biting satire at all lay and ecclesiastical institutions, high-ranking personalities and even his own Welsh people.
Works: M. R. James trans., E. S. Hartland (ed.) (1923); *DNB*, XII.

WALTER OF CHÂTILLON (d. c. 1204) French poet of the late 12th century. A native of Lille, he studied at *Paris under Etienne of Beauvais, and at *Rheims, and taught at the school of Châtillon. Later he studied law at *Bologna. He served King *Henry II of England and, upon his return to France, was appointed secretary to the archbishop of Rheims. He is the author of a Latin poem written in 1184 on Alexander the Great (*Alexandreis, sive Gesta Alexandri Magni*), which was very highly thought of in his time. His moral and satirical lyrical works, noted for their attacks on the higher clergy, were also of influence. Other works of his include an anti-Jewish treatise and a tract on the Holy Trinity.
K. Strecker (ed.), *Die Lieder Walter von Chatillons in der Handschrift 351 von St. Omer* (1925).

WALTER OF COINCY (c. 1177-1236) French poet and monk. He entered the monastery of Saint-Medard in 1193, then served as prior of Vic-sur-Aisne (1214-33) and prior of Saint-Medard. He is best known for his great *Miracles Notre Dame* written in 1218-27, a description of a series of miraculous events taken from several Latin prose works and translated and recast into vernacular French verse. A Life of St. Christine and the moral poem *De la chastee as nonains,* addressed to the nuns of Notre Dame at *Soissons, can undoubtedly be attributed to him.

A. P. Ducrot-Granderyne, *Etudes sur les "Miracles de Notre Dame" de Gautier de Coincy* (1932).

WALTER OF COVENTRY Chronicler and monk living in the province of *York at the end of the 13th century, known only because of his work, the *Memoriale fratris Walteri de Coventria.* This historical compilation was written between 1293 and 1307. Only its second part, which deals with the history of England from 1002 to 1225, is of particular value. Of special, almost unique, interest is that part which covers the reign of *John Lackland. Other historical works have erroneously been ascribed to W.

Work: W. Stubbs (ed.), *Rolls Series,* 2 vols. (1872-73);
J. Taylor, *Medieval Historical Writing in Yorkshire* (1961).

WALTER OF HENLEY (c. 1250) An English friar who became famous due to his book, **Housebondrie,* a manual of estate management including detailed descriptions of the agrarian methods of his age. The work became a handbook in the later Middle Ages and is considered the best of its kind in the 13th and 14th centuries.

G. Duby, *Rural Economy and Country Life in the Medieval West* (1968).

WALTER OF ODINGTON Probably identical with Walter of Evesham; mathematician and music theorist of the 14th century, active at *Oxford. He was author of *De speculatione musicae,* where for the first time the concept of consonancy is developed. The six parts of the book treat proportional relations, intervals, poetic meters, instruments, plain-chant and notation. W. also described the various forms of polyphonic music existing around 1300, indicating the existence of English usages distinct from but influenced by Continental forms, in particular those of Notre Dame.

Works: H. Coussemaher, *Scriptorium de musica medii aevi, n.s.,* I (1864);
N. Slonimsky (ed.), *Baker's Biographical Dictionary of Musicians* (1958).

WALTER OF PALERMO (d. c. 1188) Sicilian ecclesiastic. An Englishman, he was sent by *Henry II as tutor for young *William II of Sicily, whom Henry intended to marry to his daughter Joanna. W. was later made archdeacon of Cefalu, dean of Girgenti and in 1168, against the will of the canons, archbishop of *Palermo. His elevation was upheld by Pope *Alexander III against the protests of the canons and a court party headed by the queen. W. became one of the chief ministers of the kingdom and replaced Matthew as chancellor. He was actively involved in the question of the succession of *Henry VI of Germany.
DNB, XX.

WALTER OF ROUEN (COUTAINCES) (1140-1207) English ecclesiastic and statesman, chancellor of *Rouen (1173), vice-chancellor of England (1175), archdeacon of Oxford, bishop of Lincoln (1182) and, with the help of *Henry II, archbishop of *Rouen (1184). He embarked with Richard I on the Third *Crusade (1189), but was sent back to investigate charges brought against his enemy, the chancellor *William Longchamp. After the latter's dismissal he was made chief justiciar and head of government, a post he filled until 1193, when he was replaced by *Hubert Walter. He also played a part in the struggles over *Normandy after Richard's death, and cooperated with the French after their conquest of the duchy (1204).
J. T. Appleby, *England without Richard* (1960).

WALTER OF SAINT-VICTOR (d. after 1180) Philosopher, mystic and theologian. Prior of the house of *St. Victor and author of a celebrated polemic, *Contra quatuor labyrinthos Franciae,* against the four masters of scholastics of his period, *Abelard, *Gilbert de la Porrée, *Peter Lombard and *Peter of Poitiers. The treatise is a violent attack on the dialectic method in theology and its argument stemmed from the mystic trend inherent in the *Victorine school. By his very violence W. defeated his own purpose, failing utterly to stem the tide of scholasticism in religious thought.
R. Glorieux (ed.), "Le Contra quattuor labyrinthos Franciae de Gauthier de Saint-Victor", in: *Archive d'histoire doctrinale et littéraire du Moyen Age* (1952).

WALTER THE PENNILESS (Sans Avoir; d. 1096) A French knight and one of the leaders of the "People's Crusade" of 1096. Lacking the patience to await the arrival of the rest of the Crusaders under their main leader *Peter the Hermit, W., his uncle and his three brothers set out from *Cologne with a few thousand compatriots. Passing into *Byzantine territory at *Belgrade, his followers began to pillage the countryside. Several of his men were killed in a fight and others were burnt alive in a church. Pushing on to Nish, the provincial capital, the Crusaders were well received and fed, and subsequently sent under escort to *Constantinople. There they were joined after a month by the main body of the crusade under Peter. W. was killed with the rest of the army on 21 October 1096 in a Turkish ambush near Civetot.
S. Runciman, *A History of the Crusades* (1951).

WALTER VON DER VOGELWEIDE (c. 1170-1228) German poet. Probably of *Tyrolian origin and of noble birth, he spent some time at the court of Duke *Frederick I Babenberg at *Vienna. There he learned the art of poetry from *Reinmar the Elder and was patronized by the duke. Upon the latter's death (1198) he became a roving poet and minstrel. His strong views and biting verse prevented him from residing for very long at any single place, such as the courts of the duke of *Carinthia, of the landgrave of *Thuringia and of the count of *Meissen. W. took part in the public struggles and polemics between the partisans of *Otto IV and *Frederick II, supporting first the former and then the latter. Only about 1224 does he seem to have settled down on a fief in *Franconia given to him by the Emperor Frederick II. The true value of W.'s poetry lies in its freshness and beauty as much or even more than in its political and contemporaneous content. Some of his love poems are among the most poignant and spontaneous to be produced in the Middle Ages. In his later years W. turned to religious and didactic themes.
F. Maurer (ed.), *Die Lieder des Walter von Vogelweide* (1955-56);
M. O. Walshe, *Medieval German Literature: A Survey* (1962).

WAMBA King of the *Visigoths in *Spain (672-80). Elected as successor to King *Recceswinth, W.'s reign was marked by constant warfare. He suppressed revolts by the Vasnens and by a general named Paulus, who was in league with dignitaries from *Tarragona, *Nîmes and *Narbonne. W. also drove back Moslem invaders who had occupied the southern coast of Spain around the town of *Algeciras, destroying their fleet. In 673 he enacted a controversial law of compulsory military service which deprived all deserters and all those who refused to serve in the army of the right to bear witness in court, thus arousing resentment among the nobility. Despite his military prestige and acknowledged statesmanship, W. became the victim of a conspiracy led by the noble Erwig and the metropolitan of *Toledo, and was forced to retire to a monastery.

E. A. Thompson, *The Goths in Spain* (1969).

WANG-KHAN The Chinese name given to Toghrul, the Christian chief of the Keraits, who is often identified with *Prester John. He was dethroned by a revolt of his kinsmen and restored to the throne by *Genghis-Khan (1197). Together they campaigned against neighbouring tribes and by 1202 had established their mastery over nomadic Asia. Their mutual loyalty was shaken by the shabby conduct of the ageing and feeble W., and finally broken by his refusal to give his daughter to the eldest son of Genghis. War broke out and, after initially indecisive clashes, W. gained the upper hand (1203). However, the coalition of tribes formed by W.'s sons fell to pieces and a surprise attack by Genghis on the Kerait forces ended in total victory. W. fled to the Naiman country, where he was killed by a frontier guard. His people became dispersed among Mongol settlements.

J. J. Saunders, *The History of the Mongol Conquests* (1971).

WAQIDI IBN 'UTHMAN, AL- (c. 747-c. 823) Arab historian. In 797 W. served as a guide to *Harun Al-Rashid on the ruler's pilgrimage to Medina, W.'s birthplace. In 807 he fled to Harun's court and was later made judge by Caliph Al-*Mamun. W.'s main work is the *Kitab al-Maghazi*, a biography of *Mohammad. It is a collection of unrelated monographs concerning different aspects of the prophet's life. W. based his work on the biography of Ibn Ishak, but made important additions in terms of chronology. Other works by W. are preserved only in the writings of later authors.

Works: Wellhausen (ed.), *Mohammed in Medina* (1882).

WAR The Middle Ages was a period of continuous W., due to tribal traditions (Germanic, Arabic, Turco-Altaic and Mongol) and to the development of the ideas of holy W. This entry will deal with the development of the ideology of the concept and its social impact, as well as with medieval warfare. Particular Ws. are treated either in separate entries (e.g., The *Hundred Years' War) or in the historical surveys of states and persons.

In the Germanic and Turkish tribes W. was one of the legitimate occupations, so much so that a peaceful period could lead the young members of the tribe (the warriors) to renounce their *fidelity to their chieftains and to enter the service of a more active leader. Thus, W. was endemic to the kingdoms established in the early Middle Ages, and when there was no foreign enemy, civil Ws. were pursued, despite the opposition of the Church, which adopted the concept of *pax romana*. At the same time, the warrior tradition of the Arab tribes led to the elaboration of the Islamic theory of spreading the faith of Mohammad by the sword, and this idea was behind the great Ws.

of conquest of the 7th century. The process of settlement in both Arab and Germanic societies of the 8th century caused the ancient customs to be neglected. The urbanized society in the East came to hire mercenaries, while the agrarian societies of the West found warfare to be harmful to agricultural development and so the warriors' class became restricted to tenants of estates, who had no work obligations and were therefore able to dedicate their time to fighting, which became an aristocratic occupation. In the second half of the 8th century, thanks to the influence of the Church, "Christian peace" (*pax christiana*) was imposed among the faithful and W. was directed, as a holy duty, towards the defence and diffusion of Christianity. Thus, the Latin terms, *bellum* (W.) and *pax* (peace), were only used with respect to pagans, non-Christians, or Christians convicted of a felony or excommunicated. This doctrine developed gradually in the 9th-11th centuries and from it evolved the idea of the *Crusade and the *Reconquista Ws. in Spain. Feudal conflicts did develop, however, and fighting was referred to by the use of Germanic terms, such as *werra, guerra, guerre* and *gwere,* from which derived the English term. Such Ws. were not considered legitimate and could not be ended by a *pax*; the term used to denote their settlement was the Germanic *treuga* or *trevia,* from which is derived the modern "truce". The distinction between legitimate holy W. and illegitimate feudal struggles prevailed in western Europe until the end of the 13th century; and the doctrine was given its greatest backing by the *Peace and Truce of God. W., however, could not be completely prevented; warfare became the ethos of the nobility, as is apparent in the concepts of *feudalism, and was developed by chivalric creeds and behaviour. Yet, the doctrine of peaceful relations among Christians had its effect on the combat itself; parties involved would attempt to blame their adversary as responsible for initiating the battle, either by aggression, or by breaking treaties of faith or committing a felony. Thus, the *casus belli* became an important factor in international relations from the 12th century on, despite the fact that the chivalric ethos continued to hail the perfect warrior, who was to set an example for the upper classes.

In the Moslem world the ideology of the holy W. continued to flourish, although the social transformation of Arab society gave primacy to the religious leadership of the *Abbasid caliphs and to the Arab *uleimah* (scholars), as well as to the civil society. Berber and Turkish warriors were hired to serve in the army and their status of *Mamelukes (slaves), showed them to be considered a lower class. However, from the 9th century, their importance grew until they eventually governed the Moslem world, confining the Arabs to religious and civil offices; this evolution was crystallized by the successive rise of the *Seljuks, *Ayyubids, Mamelukes and Ottoman *Turks.

Medieval western warfare was characterized by the rising importance of the cavalry. The Roman legion, based on infantry, collapsed at the Battle of *Adrianople (375), when mounted *Goths won a decisive victory; at this time soldiers did not yet fight mounted and their horses served mainly for purposes of transportation. Technological developments in the 7th and 8th centuries, as well as the adaptation, via the *Huns and Avars, of Chinese methods, led to mounted battles; the Battle of *Poitiers in 732 was among the first to be fought by cavalry. No peasant was able to procure the horses, scuts, lances and armour necessary for the new art of warfare, nor did he have the time to spend for training; therefore mounted warfare was necessarily limited to the aristocracy, granted with *benefices and *fiefs for that purpose. The peasantry ceased to be actively involved in W. and the nature of the new type of warfare led to the establishment of chivalry.

Mounted warfare, although it became popular, certainly did not become exclusive; it was basically used in open fields, but was not practised in the defence of castles and city walls, nor in sieges, where the infantry, made up of peasants and burghers, was used (although considered subsidiary to chivalry). An important change occurred in the concept of warfare in the second half of the 13th century, when the Ws. between the English and Welsh proved to *Edward I the importance of the Welsh archers, armed with *longbows, who successfully kept off the English knights. The introduction of archers equipped with longbows into the English army led to crushing defeats of the French chivalry at the battles of *Crécy and Poitiers in the Hundred Years' War. Moreover, the use of gunpowder and of the first *cannons in the 14th century dealt a serious blow to chivalric warfare; from the second half of the 14th century battles were decided by artillery, despite the fact that it was not yet perfected and had not attained ballistic precision. Until the end of the 15th century, however, the new corps of infantry (in which Swiss warriors excelled) and artillery remained secondary in rank to the cavalry, considered the occupation of noble warriors.

C. Oman (ed. W. Beeler), *The Art of War in the Middle Ages* (1952).

WARANTIA Feudal legal term meaning the obligation to produce guarantors by a person charged with a crime, both to assure his appearance at the *trial and to prove his innocence. These guarantors generally included the accused's *lord and members of his family, when he was a noble, or the reeve and a group of notable free-men. A man without W. could be outlawed. Its practice imposed the feudalization of society.

F. L. Ganshof, *Feudalism* (1965).

WARDROBE The place in *feudal courts where the *lords kept their precious objects, jewellery and valuable garments. With the establishment of feudal monarchies in the 11th and 12th centuries, the W. became part of the treasury. In England it was controlled by the *exchequer until the 13th century. During the minority of *Henry III it was organized as an independent body, becoming the king's private treasury; thus. its revenues and expenditures were not controlled by the exchequer nor the baronage. The W., however, lost its importance in the 14th century.

B. Lyon, *A Constitutional and Legal History of Medieval England* (1960).

WAWEL The cathedral of *Cracow (Poland). From the 14th century, it was the main church of Poland and the site of royal coronations. As such, W. became a symbol of national independence and unity.

WAZO OF LIÈGE (c. 980-1048) Bishop and early exponent of the *Gregorian reform. Educated at the schools of *Lobbes, *Liège and *Chartres, he became

Late medieval armour in steel, leather and velvet

master of the cathedral of Liège (1008) and bishop (1042). Although a loyal supporter of the emperor in political matters, he dared to challenge *Henry III and pronounced the deposition of Pope *Gregory VI (1046) as unlawful. W. stressed the division between spiritual and secular authority and the superiority of the ecclesiastical *unction over the kingly one. Such views by an otherwise typical exponent of the imperial bishopric point to a ripening of reformist opinions among the high clergy even before *Gregory VII.

E. Hörschelmann, *Bischof Wazo von Lüttich und seine Bedeutung für den Beginn des Investiturstreites* (1955).

WEIBLINGEN Town in *Württemberg, Germany, near Stuttgart, and name of a castle, which passed from the property of the *Carolingian kings into the hands of the dukes of *Swabia. It became the home of the *Hohenstaufen family and the name was used as their battle cry. As such it was first used at the siege of Weinsberg on the Neckar River (1140). In the Italian struggles of the 12th century this battle cry was adopted by the pro-imperial forces, who corrupted it into *Ghibelline. This became the term by which the pro-imperial enemies of the Italian *Guelphs were called.

G. Barraclough, *The Origins of Modern Germany* (1972).

WELF Family of *Bavaria. A German noble dynasty, whose earliest documented member, Count Welf I (d. *c.* 820) lived in Bavaria during the *Carolingian period. He married his daughter Judith to Emperor *Louis the Pious and his other daughter Emma to King *Louis the German. His son Conrad (d. 863) became the first of the Upper *Burgundian kings. Welf III (d. 1055) was enfeoffed with the duchy of *Carinthia and the march of *Verona. Welf IV (*c.* 1035-1101), son of Margrave Azzo II of *Este, founded the junior W. line and was given the duchy of Bavaria by *Henry IV. Upon the death of Welf V (1120), the entire property and holdings of the W. family came into the hands of his brother, *Henry the Black, who already held by marriage half of the lands of the *Billung dukes. Henry's son, *Henry the Proud, married the daughter of Emperor *Lothair III and was made heir to the emperor's property in *Brunswick, Supplinburg and the northern Rhine area. He was also granted the duchy of Saxony. This position of power brought the Ws. into conflict with the *Hohenstaufen emperors. *Henry the Lion's rebellion was put down by Emperor *Frederick I and he was expelled from his duchies. The Ws. were left with their property around Brunswick and Lüneburg, which was elevated in 1235 to the duchy of Brunswick-Lüneburg. In later times descendants of the Ws. also ruled the kingdom of Hanover and, between 1714 and 1837, *Britain and *Ireland.
E. König (ed.), *Historia Welforum* (1938).

WELF VI, of Tuscany (1115-91) The son of Duke *Henry the Black, he held the *Welf property in *Swabia and represented the Welf duchy of *Bavaria after the death of his brother *Henry the Proud (1139). His rebellion against King *Conrad III failed (1150), but he was on good terms with the king's successor, Emperor *Frederick I, who enfeoffed him with the duchy of *Spoleto and the margravate of *Tuscany. He later fell out with the emperor over his backing of Pope *Alexander III. Broken by the death of his only son, Welf VII (1167), he resigned his Italian holdings (1174). On strained terms with his nephew, *Henry the Lion, and constantly in need of funds, he sold his extensive Swabian property to the emperor.
S. Adler, *Herzog Welf VI und sein Sohn* (1881).

WELLS Episcopal city in Somerset, *England, known mostly for its ecclesiastical history and cathedral. One of the most important towns in Saxon times, it included a religious house founded in 704 and was made a bishop's seat by King *Edward the Elder (*c.* 905). The removal of the bishopric to Bath (*c.* 1091) caused a prolonged struggle between the clergy of both towns, which was ended in 1139 by a compromise solution. W. became a *borough owned by the bishops (prior to 1160). Several *charters of privileges granted to the city by the bishops and by the kings from *John to *Henry V are extant. The town was allowed a number of fairs, at which locally-made cloth was sold. W. was represented in parliament from 1295. Its cathedral, built between 1171 and 1242, is held to be one of the most magnificent in England, mainly because of the over 600 mostly life-size statues and reliefs of great artistic quality which decorate its 46 m-wide west front.
D. O. Shilton, *Wells City Charters* (1932);
H. E. Reynolds, *Wells Cathedral; Its Foundation, Constitutional History and Statutes* (1892).

WENCESLAS, St. (d. 929) Duke of *Bohemia from 921. Influenced by his grandmother St. Ludmila, who was murdered by pro-pagan elements in the nobility, he adopted a pro-Christian policy. Importing clergy, books and relics from Germany to assist him in the Christianization of his duchy, his pro-German attitude reached its culmination in 929, when he surrendered without resistance to a German expedition to *Prague under *Henry I. This provoked a national-religious reaction led by the nobles who instigated his brother, *Boleslav I, to murder him. Waylaid by Boleslav on his way to church, he was killed at the church door. Although his death was only remotely connected with religion, he was held to be a martyr and became ironically enough the national hero of Bohemia.
F. Dvornik, *The Life of Saint Wenceslas* (1929).

WENCESLAS I (1230-53) King. Son of *Ottokar I, he acceded to the throne at his father's death. His reign was marked by a struggle over *Austria. In league with *Bela IV of Hungary and Otto of Bavaria, W. invaded Austria in 1237, but was reconciled with its duke *Frederick of Babenberg, at the instigation of the papal Curia. By 1241 *Moravia was invaded and laid to waste by the *Tartars, but Bohemia was saved by W.'s military feats. In 1246 W. tried his hand again in Austria, marrying his son Vladislav to the niece of Frederick of Babenberg, but the plan miscarried due to Vladislav's death (1247). A military invasion in 1250 was equally unfruitful. Upon W.'s death in 1253, not one of Bohemia's problems had been solved.
CMedH, VI.

WENCESLAS II King of *Bohemia (1278-1305); king of *Poland (1300-05). Son of *Ottokar II, he became king of Bohemia at the age of seven and his minority ended in 1282. Led by his powerful minister and father-in-law, Zavis of Falkenstein, W. began to lay claim to the lands taken from his father. By 1300 he had become king of Poland, and in 1301 he gained the crown of Hungary for his 12-year-old son, *Wenceslas III. He overcame papal and German resistance by forming an alliance with King *Philip IV of France (1303) and entering into relations with England. When the Hungarian nobles withdrew their support for his son, he entered Hungary with a large army and brought back the child and the crown insignia. In internal affairs W. greatly encouraged growth of the towns and the exploitation of the mineral resources. W. reformed the *coinage system by the issue of the *groschen* of Prague (1300). Under his guidance a famous mining code was compiled, but his greater project of having a written code of laws drawn up was not put into operation.
CMedH, VI.

WENCESLAS III King of *Hungary (1301-06); king of Bohemia (1305-06). Son of *Wenceslas II, he succeeded his father at the age of 17. He concluded a peace treaty with King *Albert, according to which he ceded the disputed provinces of Eger and Meissen and received a solemn confirmation of the traditional liberties and rights of *Bohemia. He gave up a hopeless struggle for *Hungary, and handed over his claims to Otto of Bavaria. His plans to regain *Poland were cut short by his murder at the hand of an unknown assassin (1306). He was the last male of the *Premyslid dynasty.
CMedH, VI.

WENCESLAS IV, of Luxemburg (1361-1419) Son of Emperor *Charles IV, he was elected king of the Romans (1376) and became emperor, king of *Germany and king of *Bohemia at his father's death (1378). His rule was troubled by the *Great Schism, the conflict with *Burgundian power in the west of the empire, and clashes with almost every political and social force in his lands, which were accentuated by his rash and overbearing temperament. His attempts at bridging the papal schism caused Pope *Boniface IX to ally himself with *Rupert, W.'s German enemy. The emperor angered the German princes by his failure to protect the western frontier and antagonized the German towns, when their leagues were suppressed by the general Peace of Eger (1389). Thus, in 1400 he was deposed as German king by some of the electors. In Bohemia W. clashed with the archbishop John of Jenstein (1393) and the latter allied himself with the dissatisfied nobles. W. prevailed for a time, but rebellion again broke out after his deposition in Germany (1402). In 1410 he resigned the claim to the imperial title to his brother *Sigismund and devoted himself to Bohemia, failing however to disentangle the thorny *Hussite problem.
G. Barraclough, *The Origins of Modern Germany* (1972).

WENDS The collective name given to several northwestern *Slavonic tribes who settled in the 6th-8th centuries east of the Elbe and Saale Rivers. They included the Sorbs, Obrodrites, *Lusatians, Veletians, Pomeranians Wagrians and others. In the 9th century they were organized in loose federations containing a firm tribal and clan structure. The missionary efforts directed at them from Germany had little impact, but in the 10th century the Saxon emperors of Germany inaugurated a new policy of Christianizing by the sword. This policy was reinforced, beginning in the 11th century, by the overpowering influence of German traders and colonists. Violent rebellions by the still pagan tribes (983, 1066) produced only a temporary halt to German conquest. In 1147 a special crusade was preached by *Bernard of Clairvaux in terms of "convert or extirpate". By the late 12th century the pagan spirit was broken and the W. were swallowed up in the tide of German colonization.
A. P. Vlasto, *The Entry of the Slavs into Christendom* (1970).

WERGELD (WERGILD) The Germanic term for the compensation paid by a murderer to the relatives of the victim. Part of early Germanic customary law, it represented the substitution of compensation for the blood feud, and as such its appearance clearly signifies the rise of the authority of the community. In the codifications of tribal laws of the early Middle Ages, the rates of W. were meticulously graded according to the social rank of the murdered person. Thus they provide a rare source of information regarding social structure. With the decline of tribal forms of social organization, such as an evaluation fell into disuse, surviving only in some isolated and conservative regions, such as *Frisia and parts of *Spain. The compensation for injury and murder was henceforth determined in each particular case through agreement, arbitration, or judicial decision.
B. S. Philpotts, *Kindred and Clan in the Middle Ages and After* (1913);
M. Bloch, *Feudal Society* (1961).

WESSEX A kingdom of Anglo-Saxon *Britain. Legend aside, the origins of W. seem to have lain in the convergence of two migratory groups of West-Saxon expansion and settlement, one from the upper Thames and the other from the coast of Hampshire. Their progress towards the west was opposed by the Britons of *Devon in a series of battles between the beginning of the 6th century and 577 (Battle of Durham). The last battle gave the Saxons possession of the Roman cities of Cirencester, *Gloucester and Bath and also gave them access to the west coast, thereby cutting off the Britons of Cornwall from those of *Wales. After a halt at the beginning of the 7th century, probably caused by clashes with the *Mercian king *Penda, and marked by the construction of a rampart (the Wansdyke), expansion began again *c.* 650 under Cenwalh. It took two generations to defeat the *Celts of Somerset and Devon, many of whom were driven across the Channel to *Brittany.

By the end of the 7th century a considerable part of Devonshire as well as the whole of Somerset and Dorset seem to have been in the hands of the kings of W. It appears that, at first, the expansion of W. was too rapid in terms of its available manpower (hence the numerous setbacks attested in the sources and a certain slowness in the early settlement of central Hampshire and Wiltshire). After a period of unstable government and violent internal struggles between various contenders for the throne, W. expanded again under King *Egbert, who overthrew the Mercian king Beornwulf (825). He established the supremacy of the West Saxons and annexed *Sussex, Surrey, *Kent and *Essex. Upon his death (839) the enlarged kingdom was divided, but was united again by *Ethelbert (858). *Alfred the Great defeated the great *Danish invasion of his realm (878) and by 886, upon the extinction of the line of the Mercian kings, his authority was recognized in all parts of England not under Danish rule. From this point on, the history of W. corresponds with the history of England.
W. G. Haskins, *The Westward Expansion of Wessex* (1960).

WESTMINSTER *Benedictine abbey on the northern bank of the Thames in London. Probably the site of a monastery destroyed during the *Danish raids, it was founded or refounded by St. *Dunstan of Canterbury (*c.* 958). Lying in the area belonging to the royal palace, it was rebuilt and endowed by *Edward the Confessor, who was also buried there, as were many of his successors to the English throne. Thus a tradition was founded of royal patronage and of the abbey's connection to the nerve centre of English politics. From the time of *Harold II and *William the Conqueror, coronations of kings were held at the abbey, the royal treasure was kept and parliaments held there and its abbots were employed as royal clerks and ambassadors. Its first great abbot was Gilbert Crispin (1085-1117), who established a standard of learning unachieved in later periods. In the 13th and 14th centuries there seems to have been a steady decline in discipline, and Abbot Simon Langham (1349-62) laboured hard to restore the abbey to its former state. Of the 80 monks of the late 11th century there remained 40 to 50 after Langham's reform, a high number by late medieval standards.
L. E. Tanner, *History and Treasures of Westminster* (1909).

Westminster Abbey, London

WESTPHALIA Region in northwestern *Germany. Part of the large plain inhabited in the early Middle Ages by the confederation of Germanic tribes known as the *Saxons, it became the target of missionary activities from the end of the 7th century. Christianization was only achieved by the forceful conversion of the Saxons at the hands of *Charlemagne. With the ascension of the Saxon emperors and the foundation of a new Saxon duchy under *Herman Billung (919) W. was retained by the king as crown-land. After the extinction of the Saxon dynasty the many local lords, secular as well as ecclesiastical ones, increased their power, and the house of *Billung secured top rank. By 1124 the most prominent of these lords had died out and in 1142 the duchy and inheritance of the lords were united in the hands of the Welf, *Henry the Lion. Countering the ambitions of the archbishop of *Cologne, he re-established the ducal power in W. The totality of his power was rivaled only by that of Emperor *Frederick I. After the trial and fall of Henry (1180), the Sauerland, the southern Westphalian lands, were conferred as the duchy of W. on the archbishop of Cologne, under whose rule it continued to exist as an independent state until 1803. It possessed its own political and administrative institutions and a capital, first at Arnsberg and, from 1434, at Werl.
F. Uhlborn, "Der Westen", in: F. Uhlborn, W. Schlesinger, *Die deutschen Territorien;*
Gebhardt, *Handbuch der deutschen Geschichte,* 9th ed. (1974).

WETTIN German noble family, founded by Diedrich (d. 982), whose sons made the former *Wendish county of W. on the eastern bank of the Saale their home. The descendants of Dedo I (d. 1009) distinguished themselves in prolonged warfare on Germany's eastern border and Henry I became margrave of *Meissen (1089). Conrad I (d. 1156) was granted in addition lower *Lusatia (1135) by privilege of Emperor *Lothair II. By the time of Henry I the Illustrious (c. 1221-88) the extent of W. possessions had reached its peak, stretching from the Oder to the Werra and from the Erzgebirge to the Harz Mountains. Moreover, the family's original status as margraves was changed by the emperor's grace from the time of the *Investiture struggle into that of independent and sovereign rulers. In the later Middle Ages the Ws. of Meissen were one of the three or four great dynasties of eastern Germany, deriving their strength from their rich mining resources, their leadership in the development and colonization of the Slavonic east and the absence of imperial authority.
W. Schlesinger, "Der Osten", in: F. Uhlborn, *Wettin;*
Schlesinger, *Die deutschen Territorien;*
Gebhardt, *Handbuch der deutschen Geschichte,* 9th paperback ed. (1974);
G. Barraclough, *The Origins of Modern Germany* (1972).

WEXFORD Town and county in the province of *Leinster, Ireland. Inhabited by the *Danes in the 12th century, it was the gateway through which the English began their conquest of Ireland, after the deposed king of Leinster had appealed for the help of *Henry II of England. W. was the first town to be captured by Robert Fitzstephen (May 1169) and became a colony settled by descendants of English soldiers taking part in the conquest. Town and county were first in the hands of the conquerors Fitzstephen and Fitzgerald, then of Strongbow, and later passed to the Talbot family. In 1318 the town received a charter, which was extended in 1411 by *Henry IV, and sent two members to Parliament.
A. J. Otway-Ruthven, *A History of Medieval Ireland* (1968).

WHITBY Benedictine abbey and town on the coast of Yorkshire, England, founded c. 657 as a double monastery by the king of Northumberland. Under its first abbess, St. Hilda, W. became quite famous. An ecclesiastical council on the Easter controversy was held there in 664. The monastery was destroyed c. 867 by the *Danes, but the site was repopulated by a Danish colony, which in turn was laid to waste in the course of the *Norman Conquest. The monastery was re-founded and richly endowed by William de Percy, who appointed Reinfrid of Evesham as prior. It received a *charter of privileges from *William the Conqueror, which was extended and confirmed by *Henry I. The latter raised the priory to the rank of abbey. Due to conflicting privileges granted to the abbey and the burgesses at the beginning of the 12th century, a bitter struggle ensued over the status of the town, which was resolved in the 14th century by a judgement in favour of the abbey. W. being a port town, the population made its living by fishing, salting and selling herrings.
D. Knowles, *The Monastic Order in England* (1950).

WHITBY, SYNOD OF The first council of the Anglo-Saxon church, held in 664 after the conversion of

*Oswiu, king of Northumbria, to the Roman Catholic faith. The council symbolized the victory of the Roman Catholic mission among the Anglo-Saxons and the defeat of the Celtic Church.

WICHING (d. after 889) Bishop of Neutra in *Moravia. Of Swabian origin, he was sent to work as a missionary in Moravia and Hungary and, supported by *Svyatopluk of Moravia, became bishop of Neutra. As such, he came under the authority of the Greek metropolitan of *Pannonia and Moravia, St. *Methodius. On the latter's death (885), W. was appointed by the pope as administrator of the metropolis and became instrumental in obtaining Moravian adherence to the Western rite by ousting Greek priests and the Slavonic liturgy. After falling out with his protector, he joined the court of King *Arnulf at Regensburg (893) and was appointed bishop of *Passau. He failed to secure the recognition of his superior, the archbishop of Salzburg. Further information about W. is not known.

F. Dvornik, *The Slavs. Their Early History and Civilization* (1956).

WIDUKIND (d. c. 807) *Saxon noble of Westphalian origin and leader of his people against *Charlemagne. In 777 he went into exile in *Denmark, but returned in 778 to lead the Saxons on raids along the Rhine, reaching as far as *Fulda. Fleeing again after the Frankish victory at Laisa and the blood-bath of *Verden (782), he returned once again to organize a Saxon resistance, drawing other pagan people, such as the *Wends and *Frisians, into the struggle against Frankish expansion. By 785 Charlemagne had changed his tactics and began personal negotiations with W. at Attigny. These were climaxed by the Saxon's festive baptism, with Charlemagne acting as sponsor and conferring precious gifts on W. In fact, no mention is made of W. in the later Saxon revolts. He is reputed to have occupied an influential position with his people and in later periods many legends revolved around his figure and he became something of a national Saxon hero.

M. Lintzel, "Widukind", in: *Westfalische Lebensbilder,* V, 1 (1935).

WIDUKIND OF CORVEY *Saxon historian and monk of the 10th century. His *History of the Saxons* was written around 968 and deals with the origins of his people, devoting much space to the rise of the Saxon imperial dynasty and especially to the reign of *Otto the Great, for which he remains one of the authoritative sources. Despite his acquaintance with and imitation of Sallust, his style is often heavy and sometimes barely understandable. Shut up in his monastery, his outlook was quite narrow and he knew of little else other than his people and king.

Works: P. Hirsch trans., *Sächsische Geschichten* (1931).

WIELICZKA A famous salt mine in *Poland, its deposits became one of the most important economic resources of the kingdom from the 13th century. Increased production was enabled by the introduction of new mining methods adapted from those used in coal mines (14th century), such as protected galleries. The salt from W. was distributed by the *Hanse to the countries of western Europe.

WIHMORE The northern part of *Saxony, located between the lower courses of the Weser and Elbe rivers. W. was famous as the centre of the Saxon resistance against *Charlemagne in 792-803. Despite mass deporta-

tions, the warriors of W. fought until they were allowed to participate in the assemblies led by the Frankish counts. An important part of the lands of W. was granted to the new bishopric of Bremen.

WILCHARIUS (WILCHER) Archbishop of Sens (769-78). One of the firmest supporters of *Charlemagne in his struggle against Carloman, he became the king's main counsellor until his death. His influence in the organization of the *Lombard kingdom was paramount (774-75).

WILFRID, St. (634-c. 709) Bishop of *York. Born in *Northumbria, he was educated at the monastery of *Lindisfarne, later spending some years at *Lyons and *Rome, where he learned to appreciate the practices of the Roman Church. As abbot of *Ripon, he was instrumental in introducing these practices into northern England (664), where previously the Irish tradition had been prevalent. As bishop of York (669), he was the first Englishman to appeal to Rome over the division of his bishopric by the archbishop of *Canterbury. The papal decision in his favour caused him to be persecuted by King Egfrid, from whom he took refuge in Selsey, Sussex. From there he attempted to Christianize the heathen South Saxons, until recalled to the north (686) to direct the see of Hexham from Ripon monastery.

W. Levison, *England and the Continent in the 8th Century* (1946);

E. S. Duckett, *Anglo-Saxon Saints and Scholars* (1947).

WILLEHAD, St. (d. 789) Priest and missionary to the *Saxons. Of Northumbrian origin, in *c.* 767 he was sent by a Northumbrian synod under King Alfred as a missionary to North *Frisia, where he established his base at Dokkum. He also lived for a while at the monastery of *Echternach, Luxemburg, until called upon by *Charmagne to lead the mission to the Old Saxons between the lower Weser and the Elbe Rivers. After various setbacks, he was consecrated as their bishop (787) and established his see at *Bremen, where he died two years later.

J. Gommach, *Dictionary of Christian Biography,* IV (1887).

WILLIAM I, the Conqueror (c. 1027-87) Duke of *Normandy and first Norman king of *England, born at Falaise. The illegitimate son of Duke Robert I of Normandy, he became duke of Normandy in 1035. His minority years saw extreme feudal disorder, to which he put an end in a series of energetic campaigns against rebellious barons, beginning in 1042 and ending with the victory of Val-ès-Dunes (1047). In the following two decades W. countered outside threats by defeating the French and the *Angevins (at Mortimer in 1054; at Varaville in 1057) and extending his rule to *Maine (1063) and *Brittany (1064). He disregarded a papal prohibition and married his relative Matilda, daughter of *Baldwin V of Flanders (*c.* 1053). He later obtained a dispensation from Pope *Nicholas II (1059). The pretext for his invasion of England (1066) was a vague promise to receive the English crown made to W. by *Edward the Confessor, and was executed with papal blessing.

After the victory at *Hastings W. totally subjected England during five years of intermittent warfare, but had to put down a new rebellion in 1075. He created a centralized state in England based on a clearly de-

William the Conqueror sending messengers to prepare the expedition to England; detail from the Bayeux tapestry

fined feudal hierarchy, whose various levels were under the king's control. The old nobility was replaced by Normans and royal government was brought in touch with the peasant class of society, as attested in the *Domesday Book. W. instituted strict supervision of the clergy, vigorously rejecting papal claims to overlordship. Yet he largely deputed the governing of England to Archbishop *Lanfranc and spent most of his years after 1072 in Normandy. W. is not only known as one of the greatest soldiers of the Middle Ages and as a strict, energetic and ruthless ruler with a clear vision of his aims, but also as a generous and pious man.

D. C. Douglas, *William the Conqueror* (1964).

WILLIAM II, Rufus (b. c. 1056) King of *England (1087-1100). The third and favourite son of *William I, the Conqueror, he was made heir of England. After suppressing a rebellion of *Norman nobles in league with his brother, Robert of Normandy, he invaded his brother's realm with only partial success (1090 and 1094), but managed to gain hold of Normandy when Robert set out on the *Crusade (1096). He also recovered *Maine (1098-99) and made plans to invade *Vexin. In *Scotland he put Edgar on the throne, but failed to make headway in *Wales. In England he became infamous for his ruthless financial extortions and clashed with *Anselm of Canterbury over the control of the church. Strong-willed and energetic, yet no leader, W. was an unpopular ruler. He was killed in the New Forest by an arrow from an unknown hand.

E. A. Freeman, *The Reign of William Rufus and the Accession of Henry I* (1882);

H. W. C. Davis, *England under the Normans and Angevins, 1066-1272* (1949).

WILLIAM the Lion (b. 1143) King of *Scotland (1165-1214). He became king on the death of his brother, *Malcolm IV, and his reign was marked by the effort to retain the independence of Scotland. Thus he entered into a treaty of alliance with *Louis VII of France (1168) and interfered in the revolt against *Henry II of England (1173). Taken prisoner (1174), he secured his release by consenting to the Treaty of Falaise, which assured English suzerainty. In 1198 *Richard I gave up his claims over Scotland in exchange

of a payment of 10,000 marks. After the accession of King *John war seemed imminent in 1199 and again in 1209. On both occasions peace was preserved by negotiations and English suzerainty was acknowledged with major reservations. W. clashed with Pope *Alexander III over the appointment of the bishop of St. Andrews, but in 1188 a papal bull was secured which freed the Scottish Church from the claims of the English archbishop. W. asserted his authority by subduing the practically independent chieftains of outlying regions. His royal privileges furthered the development of towns.

A. M. Mackenzie, *Foundations of Scotland* (1938);

A. A. M. Duncan, *Scotland, The Making of the Kingdom* (1978).

WILLIAM I, the Bad King of *Sicily (1154-66). His unflattering title was probably not merited, but this man of mediocre qualities was, in fact, overshadowed by his father, *Roger II. Upon his accession, W.'s rule was threatened by a revolt of nobles and a Greek invasion of *Bari and *Brindisi, as well as by political resistance on the part of Pope *Adrian IV and Emperor *Frederick I. In 1156 W. obtained papal confirmation of his rule and put an end to *Byzantine aggression by military action and a peace treaty (1158). However, by 1160 the Sicilian lands in Africa were lost to the *Almohades. The powerful minister *Maio of Bari was murdered in 1160, when a new aristocratic rebellion broke out, but W. himself was rescued by the army and crushed the rebels in a short campaign. His later years were, on the whole, peaceful ones.

B. Mack Smith, *A History of Sicily*, I (1969).

WILLIAM II, the Good King of *Sicily (1166-89), son of *William I. After the end of his mother's regency (1177), he was married to Joan, daughter of *Henry II of England. He secured peace with the Western empire by marrying his aunt Constance, daughter of *Roger II, to *Frederick I's son, the future Emperor *Henry VI. He then commenced an ambitious foreign policy of military aggression. After having failed in 1174 against *Saladin's forces near *Alexandria, W. turned against the Byzantines. In 1185 Sicilian forces took *Durazzo and *Thessalonica, but were defeated in the same year and a peace agreement was arranged. W.'s last venture was his plan to lead the Third *Crusade, in anticipation of which his admiral Margarito cleared the eastern Mediterranean of Moslem fleets, but the campaign was cut short by W.'s death in 1189.

B. Mack Smith, *A History of Sicily,* I (1969).

WILLIAM III King of *Sicily (1194). He succeeded his father *Tancred while still a boy. However, the government of Sicily, which was vested in the hands of the queen-dowager, had no chance of resisting the invasion of Emperor *Henry VI (1194). W. and his family surrendered under the promise of safe-conduct, but were directly imprisoned. The details of W.'s unfortunate death were obscured; he was, in all probability, murdered.

D. Mack Smith, *A History of Sicily,* I (1969).

WILLIAM I, the Pious Duke of *Aquitaine (909-18). Son of *Bernard Plantevelue, he inherited large principalities in Toulouse, Auvergne and Mâcon, as well as the title of count of Toulouse in 886. W. was involved in a struggle with the counts of *Poitiers over the domination of *Aquitaine; the conflict ended in 909, when W. inherited the county of Poitiers and assumed the ducal title. In 910 he founded the monastery of *Cluny and granted it his estates in the county of Mâcon. This act earned him the cognomen "the Pious". At W.'s death, the county of Toulouse and the duchy of Aquitaine, including the lands of Auvergne and Poitiers, were divided amongst his sons.

L. Auzias, *L'Aquitaine Carolingienne* (1931).

WILLIAM III Duke of *Aquitaine (951-63). W. inherited Aquitaine at a time when the duchy was in a state of anarchy. Consequently, *Hugh the Great, duke of the Franks, was able to obtain from King *Louis IV enfeoffment to the ducal title. W. fought both against Hugh and the claims of his relatives, the counts of Toulouse, and succeeded in retaining his title. He made *Poitiers the capital of the duchy.

WILLIAM IV, the Great (c. 960-1030) Duke of *Aquitaine (989-1030). One of the great warriors and organizers of his time, W. imposed his authority over his vassals after a long series of battles. With the intention of setting down a code of their obligations to him, W. requested the advice of *Fulbert, bishop of Chartres, questioning the meaning of the feudal oath (c. 1020). Fulbert's answer was the first document to treat *homage as a mutual link between lord and vassal. W. was also a patron of artists and scholars and, thanks to him, the school of Poitiers became one of the most renowned in France.

J. Dhondt, *La naissance des Principautés territoriales en France* (1948).

WILLIAM VIII (1027-86) Duke of *Aquitaine (1058-86). W. annexed *Gascony to *Aquitaine after defeating the lords of *Armagnac (1060). He then reformed the administrative system of Aquitaine, increasing the ducal power. On two separate occasions (1063 and 1080), he took part in the *Reconquista wars in Spain.

WILLIAM IX (1071-1127) Duke of *Aquitaine (1086-1127). One of the most colourful figures of medieval civilization, W. was a prince, adventurer and poet. He twice attempted to annex *Toulouse (1098, 1119) and managed to conquer the city, but was unable to maintain his authority there. In 1101 he took part in the *Crusade of *Stephen of Blois. His love affair with the beautiful Maubegeon, wife of the viscount of Châtellerault, whom he publicly entertained at his court, brought papal excommunication, but W. continued to write his love poems, which he often recited and sang as well. W., known as "the first troubadour", assembled poets and troubadours at his court of *Poitiers, which became a brilliant centre of secular culture.

H. Davenson, *Les Troubadours* (1964).

WILLIAM X (1099-1137) Duke of *Aquitaine (1127-37). W. was the last of his dynasty to be duke of Aquitaine. Like his father, *William IX, he was a patron of *troubadours and maintained a brilliant court at *Poitiers. In 1137 he made a pilgrimage to Santiago de Compostela and died there. He left his daughter, *Eleanor, under the guardianship of *Louis VI of France, who married her to his son, the future *Louis VII.

WILLIAM IV, the Elder Marquis of *Montferrat (1155-90). Prince of the *Holy Roman empire, he increased his principality by conquering large parts of *Piedmont. A faithful ally of *Frederick Barbarossa in Italy, he fought against the *Lombard League.

WILLIAM VII, the Great (1235-92) Marquis of *Montferrat (1259-92). W. inherited his family's claims in Lombardy; in 1254 he became a *condottiere, serving several Italian cities and virtually imposing his rule there. He continued these practices even after becoming marquis and held the office of *podesta in Turin, Ivrea and Crema. For the sake of personal interests, he became a *Guelph in 1265, allowing *Charles of Anjou to infiltrate Italy. In 1276, however, he severed his alliance with Charles and became his adversary in northern Italy, where he attempted to create a powerful state of Piedmont and Lombardy (1278-90). Assuming the title of captain of the people, he seized power in Milan, Pavia, Novara, Vercelli, Como, Casale, Alessandria, Verona and Mantua and became the leader of the *Ghibellines in Italy. Local rivalries and the continued struggle with the Angevins and the Guelphs exhausted his resources, and at his death his state fell apart and the dream of Italian unity remained unfulfilled. W.'s main achievement was the disbanding of the communal system, which allowed the rise of principalities in the 14th century.

D. Waley, *The Italian City-States* (1972).

WILLIAM I, Longsword Duke of *Normandy (932-42). Son of *Rollo, he succeeded in unifying Normandy by conquering its western part (933). He organized the new duchy, which he based on a strong central authority. He removed the counts and appointed his officers to command the castles and administer justice. W. was murdered (942) by a vassal whom he had offended.

C. H. Haskins, *Norman Institutions* (1918).

WILLIAM II Duke of Normandy. See WILLIAM THE CONQUEROR.

WILLIAM AETHELING (ADELING) (1102-20) The only legitimate son of *Henry I of England, he served his father mostly through the marital arrangements made for him. His betrothal to the daughter of *Fulk V, the powerful count of Anjou, in 1113 put an end to France's attempts to confine Henry's power within *Normandy. A war in Normandy ended with Henry's victory at Bremule (1119) a few weeks after the marriage was consecrated. In the following year W. acted as his father's deputy in England and was made duke of Normandy. He died in 1120 in a shipwreck.

F. Barlow, *The Feudal King of England* (1955).

WILLIAM BONNE-ÂME Archbishop of Rouen (1078-1109). One of the closest friends of *William the Conqueror, he was influential in the Anglo-Norman kingdom until the monarch's death. In 1092 he persuaded *Anselm to accept the archbishopric of Canterbury. W. organized the Norman church and struggled for its autonomy.

WILLIAM CLITO (1101-28) Son of *Robert Curthose, duke of *Normandy, the young boy became a hostage after his father's defeat and capture by *Henry I of England (1106). He was released and taken to France, where he was used by *Louis VI as a symbol to rally the Norman barons against Henry. Thus W.'s claim to the duchy of Normandy furnished the pretext for two rebellions in Normandy (1112-20 and 1123) instigated by France, which were put down by the English king. In *c.* 1122 W. received the county of *Maine through his marriage to Sybil, daughter of *Fulk of Anjou, but Henry had the pope annul the union on grounds of consanguinity. In 1127 W. obtained from Louis VI the hand of Joan of Montferrat and the county of *Flanders. His rigid government incited a rebellion headed by *Thierry of Alsace and in one of the campaigns he received a fatal wound. After that Henry's power was no longer disputed.
CMedH, V.

WILLIAM DES ROCHES (13th century) Seneschal of *Anjou. W. was an eminent baron in *Poitou and wielded great influence during the reign of *Richard I. In 1199, at the king's death, he was one of the firmest supporters of *Arthur's claim to the English throne. A declared enemy of *John Lackland, he joined *Philip II of France and helped him to conquer the Loire Valley in 1204. Appointed royal seneschal of Anjou, he served the French government.

WILLIAM LONGCHAMP (d. 1197) Chancellor of England and bishop of *Ely. He started his career as official to *Henry II's son, *Geoffrey, at Rouen, but soon switched his allegiance to *Richard, who made him chancellor of the duchy of *Aquitaine. A shrewd ambassador, he ruined Henry II's attempts to make peace with *Philip Augustus of France (1189). On Richard's accession he became chancellor of the kingdom and bishop of Ely (1189). In 1190 he was made papal legate. However, he made many enemies and was expelled from the kingdom after a general uprising during the king's absence. In 1193 he joined Richard in Germany, and, for the remainder of the king's reign, was employed on confidential and diplomatic missions all over Europe.
J. H. Round, *The Commune of London and other Studies* (1899).

WILLIAM MARSHAL (c. 1146-1219) First earl of Pembroke; English warrior and statesman. A younger son of John (FitzGilbert) the Marshal (d. 1165), he entered the household and service of his uncle, Earl Patrick of Salisbury, at the age of 19. Already an accomplished soldier, he became guardian of Henry, eldest son of *Henry II (1170). In 1187 he entered the king's service, fighting for him until the king's death in 1189. By that time he was regarded as the foremost knight of his time and *Richard I had him perform his knighting ceremony. During Richard's absence on the *Crusade (1190-94) W., together with *William Longchamp and three other barons, formed the council of regency. Steadfastly loyal to Richard during the latter's captivity, W. assisted the succession of *John after the king's death and was formally recognized as earl of Pembroke (1199).

This title and the extensive lands attached to it W. had received from his wife Isabel, the heiress of *Richard of Clare. From 1200 to 1207 he fought in England and Normandy, and until 1213 he spent his time attending to his vast lordship of *Leinster in Ireland, as well as rallying the Irish nobles to King John's cause. He stood by the king during the latter's darkest moments at *Runnymede (1215). In the period of civil war after John's death, W. served as guardian of England and defeated the rebellious barons and Louis of France (later *Louis VIII), preserving the unity of country and crown for John's son, *Henry III. He showed wise restraint by granting an amnesty and restoring normal government. His actions during his long public career were characterized by the highest sense of honour and responsibility to his king and country.
J. Crosland, *William the Marshal: The Last Great Feudal General* (1962).

WILLIAM OF AUVERGNE (d. 1249) Philosopher and theologian. W. studied at *Paris and became a teacher of arts and theology (*c.* 1220). In 1228 he became bishop of Paris, but continued to show a keen interest in higher studies and the university. He is the author of several works on practical theology (*De virtutibus, De moribus, De sacramentis*) and philosophy (*De universo, De anima*). His *De immortalitate animae* is a re-write of a treatise by Dominicus *Gundissalinus bearing the same title. In philosophy and theology his main concern was the reconciliation of *Aristotelian thought and method with the Christian dogma derived from the *Augustinian tradition. He also paid much attention to the heresy of *Catharism and to refuting the Arabic doctrine of the eternity of the world. His main importance lies in his efforts to purge Aristotelian works of Arabic additions. Thus he prepared the way for the full assimilation of ancient philosophy in Christian thought.
A. Masnovo, *Da Guglielmo d'Auvergne a San Tomaso d'Aquino*, 3 vols. (1945-46).

WILLIAM OF AUXERRE (13th century) Teacher of theology at *Paris. Student at Paris under *Praepositinus of Cremona, he became headmaster and then archdeacon of *Beauvais. He was among the committee of three theologians appointed by Pope *Gregory IX in 1231 to prepare a new edition of *Aristotle's natural scientific and metaphysical works. Such a work had become a necessity after the ban of 1210. W. was the author of a *Summa aurea*, which, although greatly influenced by the work of *Peter Lombard, holds a place of honour as one of the first *Summas* to be composed after the introduction of Aristotelianism. W. taught John of Treviso, one of the first theologians of the *Dominican order. Perhaps for this reason the *Franciscan *Salimbene commented that W., although a great logician and polemist, was a totally inadequate preacher who did not know what he was saying.
C. Ottaviano, *Guglielmo d'Auxerre. La vita, le opere, il pensiero* (1929).

WILLIAM OF CHAMPEAUX (c. 1070-1121) Philosopher and theologian. A student of *Anselm of Laon, he became teacher at the cathedral school of *Paris (1103). His extremely realistic position on the question of *Universals was devastatingly criticized by *Abelard, and W. had to abandon his teaching position (1108).

Retreating to the abbey of St. Victor, he continued to lecture, and seems to have had a major influence on the mystical thought of the *Victorines. In 1113 he was made bishop of Châlons-sur-Marne. Besides being an outstanding spokesman of conservative orthodoxy, he enjoyed a great reputation for learning and sanctity and was sent by the king to address *Henry V of Germany on the issue of *Investiture. W.'s main contribution to philosophy lies in his creationist doctrine expounded in *De origine animae*. In this work he maintains that each and every human soul originates from the creative act of God.

G. Lefevre, *Les Variations de Guillaume de Champeaux et la Question des Universaux* (1898).

WILLIAM OF CHAMPLITTE (d. 1209) Latin conqueror in *Greece. Grandson of Count Hugh I of Champagne, he was one of the participants in the Fourth *Crusade. He met his friend Geoffrey of *Villehardouin (of Morea) at Nauplia in 1204, and the two set out in the spring of 1205 to conquer *Morea in the western Peloponnese. After a fierce battle against regional forces and *Michael Ducas of Epirus, the campaign came to an end in the late autumn of the same year. The two conquerors had started to build a state of their own, when W. left in 1209 to claim the inheritance of his elder brother in *Burgundy. A nephew whom he put in charge of his conquests died shortly afterwards and Geoffrey became the sole ruler of the principality after W.'s death in the same year.

CMedH, IV.

WILLIAM OF CONCHES (c. 1100-54) Philosopher and theologian. A pupil of *Bernard of Chartres, he became tutor to *Henry Plantagenet (c. 1122) and teacher of theology in *Paris. he expounded Platonic realism and humanism and was interested in natural science, all elements which distinguished the school of *Chartres. He was later accused of heresy because of his treatment of the ancient gods. The allegorical and moral role played by the ancient gods in his *World Philosophy* (*De Philosophia Mundi*) could and was too easily applied to the Christian God and his saints. W. also wrote glosses on Plato's *Timeus* and a commentary on *Boethius' *Consolations of Philosophy*. He was interested in medicine and was one of the first medieval Christian philosophers to take advantage of the medical and philosophical works of the Arabs, translated by *Constantine the African.

T. Gregory, *Anima Mundi: La filosofia di Guglielmo di Conches e la scuola di Chartres* (1955).

WILLIAM OF HAUTEVILLE (Iron Arm; d. 1046) Norman soldier and adventurer. Eldest of the 12 sons of *Tancred of Hauteville, he and his brothers, *Drogo and Humphrey, were the first of the family to make a career as soldiers of fortune in southern Italy. After responding to a call for reinforcements by the Norman *Rainulf of Aversa (c. 1035), W. became captain of the Norman army that, in league with the *Lombards, conquered *Apulia. By 1042 he called himself count of Apulia. In 1044 he and his formal overlord, the Lombard Gaimar of Salerno, invaded *Calabria and W. emerged as the most powerful leader in southern Italy. He was succeeded after his death by Drogo and, a few years later, by another brother, *Robert Guiscard.

E. Curtis, *Roger of Sicily and the Normans in Lower Italy, 1016-1154* (1912).

WILLIAM OF HIRSAU (d. 1091) Benedictine abbot of *Hirsau. A child oblate and later monk at St. Emmeran in *Regensburg, he was appointed abbot of Hirsau c. 1070. He obtained from Pope *Gregory VII a privilege of exemption from the bishop's authority, putting the monastery directly under the pope (1075). A devoted follower of Gregory, he became the leading partisan and spokesman of the pope's programme of ecclesiastical reform in Germany. He adopted the customs of *Cluny for his abbey, thereby introducing them into Germany, and instituted a new category of monks, the lay brothers (*fratres exteriores*) employed in manual labour. This innovation constituted a major break for the poorer classes, who until then had almost no chance of entering the aristocratic Benedictine monasteries. W. was the author of several treatises on astronomy and music, written at Regensburg. In his later years, however, he reversed his previously positive attitude towards the worth of secular science.

H. Jacobs, *Die Hirsauer* (1961).

WILLIAM OF HOLLAND (1227-56) Count of *Holland (1233-56); *German king (1247-56). After the death of his father, Count Floris IV, at a tournament (1233), he became count, with the government vested in the hands of his two uncles. In 1247, at the age of 19, he was chosen by Pope *Innocent IV as king of Germany in place of the excommunicated *Frederick II. For his coronation he had to besiege the imperial city of *Aix-la-Chapelle for half a year, and only after Frederick's death (1250) did he succeed in winning a degree of allegiance in Germany. He was recognized by the dukes of *Brunswick, *Saxony and *Brandenburg (1252) when he married a daughter of Otto of Brunswick. Upon the death of *Conrad IV the *imperial cities, until then the staunchest supporters of the *Hohenstaufen, recognized W. as king. At a diet at *Worms (February 1255) he placed himself at the head of the Great *Rhenish League and seemed on the verge of becoming a true leader of Germany. However, much of his time and energy was taken up by indecisive struggles in Holland, where he died in a campaign against the *Frisians.

O. Hintze, *Das Königtum Wilhelms von Holland* (1885).

WILLIAM OF JUMIÈGES (Calculus; d. c. 1090) Historian. Apparently a Norman by birth, he was a monk at the royal abbey of Jumièges in *Normandy. W. is the author of the *Historia Normannorum* in eight volumes, of which the first seven were written by W. and cover the history of the Norman people from 851 to 1087. Part of the work is based on the *Historia* of Dudon of St. Quentin, but W. corrected many of the more dubious passages of his predecessor. The last book of the work was written by an anonymous author and updates the story to the year 1137. The whole work is a chief authority for Norman history and was extensively used by *Ordericus Vitalis and Thomas *Walsingham.

Works, ed. J. Marx (1914).

WILLIAM OF LORRIS (d. 1240) French poet. W. was the author of the earlier section of the *Roman de la Rose*. Nothing is known about him except the fact that he lived in the region of the Loiret. His part of the work, the first 4500 lines, is characterized by the extraordinary vividness and beauty of his language. His technique of allegorical presentation was an innovation for his time, and became the model for later works.

L. Jarry, *Guillaume de Lorris et le Testament d'Alphonse de Poitiers* (1881).

WILLIAM OF MACHAUT (1284-1377) French poet and musician. Son of a noble family of *Champagne, he entered the service of *John of Luxemburg, king of Bohemia, as secretary (*c.* 1316). For 30 years he accompanied the king, taking part in his campaigns in *Poland and *Russia. At the request of his lord, W. was granted several benefices. Upon the death of John at the Battle of *Crecy (1346), W. was taken into the household of Bonne of Luxemburg, duchess of *Normandy. Upon her death (1349) he became secretary to the duke and when the latter's son became king as *Charles V (1350), W. was made royal notary. W. composed a great number of poems in all literary genres, as well as a substantial amount and variety of music, including motets, ballads, bawdy *chansons* and a Mass in four parts which was performed at Rheims on the occasion of Charles V's coronation.

Works: E. Hoepffner (ed.) (1908).

WILLIAM OF MALMESBURY (c. 1080-c. 1143) English historian. He was educated at the monastery of *Malmesbury, where he spent the greater part of his life as monk and librarian, turning down the abbacy offered to him (1140). As a writer, he aspired to produce an account of English history of the same calibre as *Bede. His main works are the *Gesta regum* (Deeds of the Kings, *c.* 1120), whose five books cover (in the final edition of *c.* 1140) the years 449-1127 and are based on a great many sources. The *Gesta pontificum* gives an account of the English sees from their beginnings to about 1120 and became the source for all later histories of the English church. W.'s *Historia novella* (*c.* 1140) is an annalistic continuation of the *Gesta regum* and deals mainly with the reign of *Stephen. Despite some flaws in his chronology and his habit of breaking off his story to relate some irrelevant anecdote, W. is considered the best English historian of his time, mainly for his shrewd judgement of persons and events.

Works: K. R. Potter trans., *Historia novella* (1955);
J. Stevenson (ed.), *The History of the Kings of England* (1854).

WILLIAM OF MOERBEKE (c. 1215-86) Translator and scholar. Of Belgian origin and a member of the *Dominican order, he was one of the true cosmopolitans of the Middle Ages. He resided at the papal court at *Viterbo (1268), appeared at the Council of *Lyons (1274) and occupied from 1277 until his death the see of the archbishop of *Corinth. W. was the most important translator of Aristotle from the Greek into Latin. Through his translation of Proclus' *Theological Elements,* W. wielded a tangible influence over the neo-Platonic philosophical movement. He also translated several mathematical treatises of the ancient Greeks, including one by Archimedes.

M. Grabmann, *Guglielmo di Moerbeke, O.P., il traduttore delle opere di Aristotele* (1946).

WILLIAM OF NANGIS (NANCY) (d. c. 1300) French chronicler. A monk at *Saint Denis, Paris, he was appointed keeper of manuscripts at the library of his abbey (*c.* 1285). Thus it is not surprising that W.'s historical works are mostly compilations from earlier authors. His *Chronicle,* covering the period from the creation of the world until 1300, is entirely based on *Sigebert of Gembloux and others for the period

prior to 1113. He condensed his material for the years 845-1300 into a summary called *Chronicon abbreviatum regum Francorum.* Other works of his include biographies of *Louis VIII, *Louis IX and *Philip III.

Work: H. Gerand (ed.), 2 vols. (1843).

WILLIAM OF NEWBURGH (Willelmus Parvus; 1136-98) English chronicler. A native of Bridlington, Yorkshire, he entered the *Augustinian priory of Newburgh, Yorkshire as a boy. He later became canon there. W. is the author of the *Historia rerum anglicarum,* a work in five volumes which covers the period 1066-1198. Although little factual information is original, the value of the work lies in the author's intelligent use of earlier sources and most of all in his impartiality and sound judgement of men and their actions. Belonging to the sober tradition founded by *Bede, W. spurned the mythical brand of historical writing of *Geoffrey of Monmouth and is viewed today as one of the founding fathers of historical criticism.

Work: J. Stevenson, ed. and trans., in: *The Church Historians of England,* IV (1857);
J. Taylor, *Medieval Historical Writing in Yorkshire* (1961).

WILLIAM OF NOGARET (c. 1265-1313) Lawyer and minister of King *Philip IV of France. Member of the royal council from 1296 and keeper of the seal (1307), he was the king's most powerful and influential adviser after the death of Peter *Flotte. W. was the driving force in the struggle against Pope *Boniface VIII. Together with Sciarra *Colonna he led the troops that nearly succeeded in kidnapping the pope at *Anagni (1303). He was backed by his king despite his excommunication (1304, lifted in 1311) and directed the proceedings against the *Templars with utter brutality (1308). He also prepared the trial of the late Boniface, charged with heresy (1310). A man of bourgeois origin and a loyal follower of the king, he was an outstanding example of the new brand of royal lawyers. Holding a firm belief and personal interest in the superiority of the king's office, he affirmed that the king's interests were identical with those of the nation and the faith.

M. Melville, "Guillaume de Nogaret et Philip le Bel", in: *Revue d'Histoire de l'Eglise de France,* 36 (1950).

WILLIAM OF NORWICH, St. (d. 1144) The mutilated body of this 12-year-old boy was found in a wood outside *Norwich. In 1149 it was alleged that he had been the victim of murder by *Jews, who were supposed to have tortured and crucified him. Although the authorities did not seem to have given credit to the story, the populace did, and W. was venerated locally as a martyr. This is the first recorded accusation of blood libel against Jews, feeding on popular anti-Semitism, and on a diabolic image of the Jews, who were supposed to have expressed their ancient anger against Jesus by abducting and killing innocent children to use their blood for the baking of Passover bread.

C. Roth, *The Ritual Murder Libel and the Jews* (1935).

WILLIAM OF OCKHAM (OCCAM) (c. 1285-1349) Theologian and philosopher. A native of England, W. entered the *Franciscan order in his youth. He later became a student of theology and lecturer at Oxford University; he was especially noted for his commentary on Peter *Lombard's *Sentences,* which differed somewhat from accepted beliefs. Consequently, his views were attacked by the university chancellor and he was forced to leave Oxford without completing his master's degree.

W.'s teachings were firmly rooted in logic. A late Scholastic thinker and considered to be the founder of the *Nominalist school, he believed in man's basic reason and human nature while never denying the omnipotence of God. His views were attacked and his teachings were ordered to be examined by Pope *John XXII; however, his work was never officially condemned.

In 1328 W. supported the Spiritual Franciscans. He also assumed a firm position regarding the ideal of Christian poverty, a stand which was at odds with that of the papacy. As a result, he entered a long dispute with the pope, whose power he believed should be curtailed. W. was the author of numerous treatises attacking the papacy and he took the side of the excommunicated emperor of Bavaria, *Louis IV, following him to Munich in 1330. It was at this time that W. himself was excommunicated. In 1339 W. defended the right of King *Edward III of England to impose taxes on ecclesiastic property.

W. is well known for his writings, which centred on both metaphysical and political issues. One of his most extensive works is the Opus nonaginta dierum (1330). He died in a Franciscan convent in Munich in 1349.

WILLIAM OF POITIERS (c. 1020-90) Norman chronicler. Of noble origin, he was active as a soldier, studied at Poitiers and became chaplain to Duke *William I, the Conqueror. He was then made archdeacon of Lisieux. W. was the author of a highly eulogistic biography of William the Conqueror, the Gesta Guilelmi II ducis Normannorum. Written in 1071-77, its extant parts cover the years 1047-68. Despite his personal acquaintance with the subject and his relation to the eyewitness acounts of others, W.'s work must be viewed sceptically because of the author's bias.
Works: F. Maseres (ed.) (1807).

WILLIAM OF RHEIMS (1135-1202) French high ecclesiastic, also known as the "Cardinal of Champagne", and as W. "with the White Hands". Fourth son of *Thibaut II the Great, count of Blois and Champagne, he was furthered by St. *Bernard of Clairvaux and became bishop of *Chartres (1165) and archbishop of *Sens (1168), resigning his first bishopric only in 1176. In 1168 he was chosen by Pope *Alexander III as *legate to intervene in the conflict between Thomas *Becket and *Henry II. In 1176 he became archbishop of *Rheims and three years later crowned *Philip II Augustus. Out of favour at the outset of the latter's reign, he went to Rome, where he was made cardinal (1180). He was soon restored to the king's favour and became a member of his council. W. served as head of the caretaker government at the time of the king's *crusade (1190-91). In 1193 he annulled the marriage of Philip Augustus to Ingelborg, for which he was severely censured by the pope.

WILLIAM OF SAINT-THIERRY (c. 1085-1148) Mystic and theologian. Of a noble French family, he was educated at the *Benedictine monastery of St. Nicaise at *Rheims. He became abbot of St. Thierry near Rheims in 1119 and played a prominent part in the first general chapter of the Benedictines at St. Médard (1140). In 1145 he resigned his dignity as abbot and withdrew to the *Cistercian abbey at Signy to lead a life of retirement and contemplation. W. is known for his corres-

pondence with his close friend, St. *Bernard of Clairvaux. He also wrote a number of theological works of a mystic and contemplative nature. W. was the first to lead a public polemic against *Abelard in his Dispute against Abelard and his reply to the theologian's apology. He also disputed *William of Conches' views on the trinity in his On the Errors of William of Conches.
Works: PL, 89 (1885);
E. Gilson, The Mystical Theology of St. Bernard (1940).

WILLIAM OF TYRE (c. 1130-90) Historian of the *Crusaders in the Holy Land. Probably the son of a noble French family and a native of *Palestine, he studied in Europe and returned home to be appointed archdeacon of *Tyre (1167). In 1170 he became tutor to the future king, Baldwin IV, and, after the latter's accession, was made chancellor of the kingdom of *Jerusalem (1174) and archbishop of Tyre (1175). W. travelled to Europe several times to call for military help for the beleaguered kingdom. Proficient in Greek, Latin and Arabic and possessing an enquiring mind, W. is the chief authority for the history of the Latin kingdom in Palestine. His General History of the Crusades and the Kingdom of Jerusalem was written between 1169 and 1173 and its 23 volumes are based on earlier sources, official documents and W.'s personal experience. He also wrote an account of the *Lateran Council of 1179 and a History of the Eastern Kings, fragments of which were preserved by *James of Vitry.
Work: trans. E. A. Babcock, A History of the Deeds done beyond the Sea (1943);
B. C. Schwinger, Kreuzzugsideologie und Toleranz, Studien zu Wilhelm v. Tyrus (1977).

WILLIAM OF VALENCE (d. 1296) English military leader. A half-brother of King *Henry III, he became a prominent member of the royal court after his arrival in England (1247). Attacked by the baronial opposition, he was forced to leave the country (1258), but returned in 1261 to lead the royal army against *Simon of Montfort (1264, at the Battle of Lewes; 1265 at the Battle of Evesham). He became *Edward's general and accompanied him to the Holy Land, fighting in *Aquitaine and in campaigns of southern *Wales. Upon his death at *Bayonne he was recognized, despite his foreign origin, as a respected leader of the baronage and a military commander of high repute.
F. R. Lewis, "William de Valence", in:
Aberystwyth Studies 13 (1934), 14 (1936).

WILLIAM OF WYKEHAM (1324-1404) Bishop of *Winchester and chancellor of England. He was educated at Winchester and became secretary to the constable of Winchester Castle. He was called to the attention of King *Edward III and in 1356 became one of the king's clerks and supervisor of construction work at the castle of *Windsor. In the following years he accumulated benefice after benefice and was keeper of a dozen royal castles and manors, working feverishly to improve their fortifications in anticipation of a French invasion. W. was made keeper of the privy seal (1364), bishop of Winchester (1366) and chancellor (1367). However, he became the victim of the hunt for scapegoats for the reverses in the war in France and had to resign the chancellorship (1372). W. was restored to favour on the accession of *Richard II (1389). He is famous for founding the New College at *Oxford, and St. Mary's

Idealized statue of William Tell and his son

Grammar School at Winchester, both of which he generously endowed.

G. H. Moberley, *Life of William of Wykeham* (1893).

WILLIAM OF YORK, St. (William Fitzherbert; d. 1154) Probably a nephew of King *Stephen of England, he served as treasurer of York cathedral and in 1140 was elected archbishop of York. His election was challenged by the *Cistercian monks of the province on grounds of *simony and undue royal influence. Although Pope *Innocent II upheld the election and W. was consecrated in 1143, *Bernard of Clairvaux vehemently supported the cause of his fellow Cistercians in York and W. was suspended by Pope *Eugenius III and finally deposed (1147). After he had lived for a time in dignified retirement at the court of his influential uncle, the bishop of *Winchester and papal legate, *Henry of Blois, the death of his chief opponents and the intervention of his uncle finally won his reinstatement by Pope *Anastasius IV (1154). W., however, died within a few months, possibly from poison.

R. L. Poole, *The Appointment and Deprivation of St. William, Archbishop of York,* in: Engl. Hist. Rev. 45 (1930).

WILLIAM TELL The legendary hero of the early 14th-century struggle of the *Swiss cantons, which sought emancipation from Austrian domination. As leader of the canton of *Uri, he refused to obey an order issued by Gessler, the tyrannical Austrian bailiff, demanding the payment of homage to a cap hung in the town square of Altdorf. As punishment, Gessler forced W.

to endanger the life of his son by shooting an arrow at an apple placed on the child's head. Although W. succeeded, he was arrested for having insulted the bailiff; however, he managed to escape while he and his escort were crossing Lake Lucerne. At an ambush at a narrow pass (the Hollow Way near Küsnacht) W. killed Gessler and emerged as the leader of the Swiss military struggle against Austria. Although no historical proof has been found up to now to verify the tale, which first appeared in late 15th-century ballads, this has not prevented W. from emerging as a hero of liberty.

H. Fehr, *Die Entstehung der Schweizer Eidgenossenschaft* (1929).

WILLIAM THE BRETON (c. 1160-c. 1225) Chronicler and poet. Educated at Mantes and at *Paris, he was appointed chaplain to King *Philip Augustus of France and teacher to the king's bastard son. He is the author of the Latin poem, *Philippide,* a laudatory discourse to his king, extant in three versions, all of which were written by himself. His second work, the *Gesta Philippi II regis Francorum,* deals with the same topic in a similar manner. It is basically a condensation of the work of *Rigord, to which W. added an account of the king's deeds in the years 1207-20. Both works are important because of the author's personal knowledge of the events related.

H. F. Delaborde (ed.), *Oeuvres de Rigord et de Guillaume Le Breton* (1882).

WILLIAM THE GREAT, St. (c. 755-812) Count of *Narbonne, marquis of *Gothia and *Spain (790-806). Related to the *Carolingian dynasty through his mother, Alda, daughter of *Charles Martel, W. was appointed by his cousin, *Charlemagne, as commander of the Frankish army in the wars against the Moslems in Spain. In 801 he conquered Barcelona. Under the influence of his friend, St. *Benedict of Aniane, W. founded the abbey of Gellone, where he retired in 806 and died a saint; the abbey was then named after him, St. Guilhem-du-Désert. W.'s figure became immortalized as the epic hero, *Guillaume d'Orange.

WILLIBALD, St. (700-86) Missionary and traveller. Descended from a noble Anglo-Saxon family and related to St. *Boniface, he made a pilgrimage to Rome in 722. Between 724-30, he also travelled to the holy places in Palestine and visited the countries of the eastern Mediterranean. Upon his return he became a monk at *Monte Cassino, but upon the request of St. Boniface Pope *Gregory III sent him as a missionary to Germany in 740. Appointed bishop of Eichstätt, W. consolidated Christianity in Franconia. W. was venerated and considered a saint during his lifetime.

W. Levison, *England and the Continent in the 8th Century* (1946).

WILLIBRORD, St. (658-739) Missionary and bishop of *Utrecht. Son of an English magnate, he was educated at the monastery of *Ripon and went to Ireland (678), where he was ordained a priest (688). Under the protection of *Pepin of Herstal he arrived with some other Englishmen in Frankish *Frisia (690) to Christianize the country. Consecrated as archbishop of the Frisians by Pope St. *Sergius I (695), he made Utrecht his centre, also founding the monastery of Echternach (Luxemburg) as a second missionary base for the growing English colony on the Continent. His achievements were threatened for a time by a revolt of the *Frisians against their Frankish masters (715-19), but W. subsequently managed to venture as far as *Denmark and *Thuringia on further missions. A *Calendar of his, containing several autobiographical lines, is preserved at the National Library in Paris.

A. Grieve, *Willibrord, Missionary in the Netherlands* (1923).

WILLIGIS, St. (d. 1011) Imperial *chancellor and archbishop of *Mainz. Born at Schöningen in *Brunswick of humble origin, from 975 he served the emperors *Otto II, *Otto III and *Henry II as imperial chancellor. During the struggle of the first years of Otto III's minority (983-86), he played an important role in preserving the dynastic unity of Germany, rallying the princes in support of the rule of the king's mother *Theophano. His later years were marred by a protracted struggle with *Bernard of Hildesheim over jurisdiction over the rich nunnery of *Gandersheim, which ended when W., under strong pressure from Henry II, withdrew his claims (1007).

H. Böhner, *Willigis von Mainz* (1895);
E. N. Johnson, *The Secular Activities of the German Episcopate, 919-1024* (1932).

WINCHELSEY, ROBERT OF (d. 1313) Archbishop of *Canterbury. Student and teacher at *Paris, and *Oxford, where he later became rector and chancellor, archdeacon of Essex and archbishop of Canterbury (from 1293). A stalwart upholder of the privileges of the clergy and a partisan of Pope *Boniface VIII, he clashed with King *Edward I over royal taxation of the clergy (1297). Despite a reconciliation (July 1297), the quarrel was renewed when W. joined the barons at the parliament of *Lincoln (1301). In 1305 Edward had his friend, the new pope, *Clement V, suspend W., who went into exile. Reinstated in 1308, W. joined the barons in their struggle against *Edward II, making frequent use of spiritual weapons. Despite his personal life of sanctity and asceticism, he is known foremost as a politician.

F. M. Powicke, *The Thirteenth Century: 1216-1307* (1962).

WINCHESTER City in Hampshire, *England. A Celtic and Roman settlement, it became the capital of the kingdom of *Wessex and the seat of a bishop (635). It also served for a time as the capital of England. W. was the burial place of several kings and the site of *Edward the Confessor's coronation (1043). King *Alfred the Great established W. as a centre of study and education. After the *Norman Conquest W. retained its connection to royalty, and its proximity to the New Forest and the port of Southampton made it even more attractive to the Norman kings. Its economy was based on trade and a developed wool industry. In addition to its merchants' guild, documented since the early Norman period, and the thriving St. Giles's Fair, W. possessed a great Jewish community. From early times, probably since the Saxon period, W. was allowed self-government, and this privilege was reaffirmed by successive kings. The area surrounding the city, however, belonged to the jurisdiction of the bishop. W.'s prosperity came to a peak at the beginning of the 12th century, but the city started its decline in the reign of King *Stephen, when the city was burnt. It suffered heavily from the loss of Normandy to France, which deprived W. of its favourable position with regard to the Continental pos-

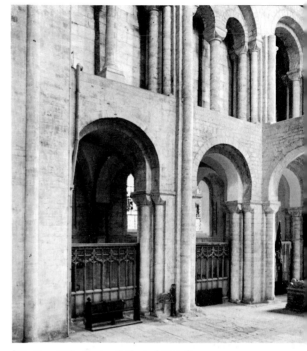

Interior of Winchester Cathedral (detail)

sessions of the English kings. It was also harmed by the relocation of the wool trade to the east of England, as well as from the loss of the wine trade following Southhampton's sack (1338). W. is famous for its Norman cathedral, one of the largest in England, and the College of St. Mary, founded by *William of Wykeham.

M. D. Lobel (ed.), *Historic Towns,* II (1970).

WINCHESTER, BIBLE OF The most outstanding product of 12th-century book illumination, it was written and painted in the Old Minster at *Winchester in the late 12th century. Its beautiful miniatures are distinguished by a fine sense of composition, good proportions, and extraordinarily rich and beautiful colours, in which deep dark tones predominate. The splendid historiated capitals contain human figures, dogs' heads, grotesques and luxurious foliage. No less than five artists, with highly individual styles, worked for several decades on the illumination of the two stately volumes, and even so the project was left unfinished.

W. Oakeshott, *The Artists of the Winchester Bible* (1945).

WINDESHEIM *Augustinian monastery in Holland and chief house of a congregation of regular canons. W. was founded *c.* 1386 by a group of disciples of Gerard *Groote, at a time when the movement of the *Brethren of the Common Life came under heavy attack from the *mendicant orders. Under Florence Radewyns the group adopted the usages of the Augustinian canons and erected a monastery and church at W. Under the second prior, Johan Vos (1391-1424), the number of monks greatly increased and many new houses were founded. At the height of its prosperity towards the end of the 15th century, the congregation numbered 86 houses of canons and 16 of nuns. Their organizational structure was modelled on the *Carthusian order.

J. G. R. Acquoy, *Het klooster te Windesheim en zijn invloed* (1875-80).

WINDSOR Town and castle on the Thames in Berkshire and one of the centres of English royalty since the Middle Ages. The site of a Roman settlement, Old W. was a royal residence under *Edward the Confessor, who granted it to *Westminster Abbey. *William I recovered it in exchange for two manors and erected the castle and manor of New W. Out of the latter, the town of W. was to grow. At W. Castle the Norman kings held their courts and assembled their councils. It was extended by *Henry III, and its sumptuous chapel, built under *Edward IV, served as the headquarters of the Knights of the *Garter.

R. R. Tighe-J. E. Davis, *Annals of Windsor: A History of the Castle and Town* (1858).

WINIFRED, St. British gentlewoman who lived in the 7th century. There are no reliable details about her life. According to a late medieval legend she was the niece of St. Beuno, who brought her back to life after she had been killed by an amorous noble whose attentions she had repulsed. At the place of her reputed death and resurrection a spring was said to have appeared, which was called W.'s Well and became a centre of pilgrimage.

P. Metcalf, *Life of St. Winifrede* (1712) (ed. H. Thurston; 1917).

WINKELRIED, ARNOLD VON *Swiss hero. Probably a member of a knightly family from Stans in Unterwalden, he is reputed to have been responsible for the victory of the Swiss cantons against the Austrians at the Battle of *Sempach (1386). At a critical moment, when the Swiss had failed to break the ranks of the massed Austrian knights, W. is said to have commended his wife and children to the care of his comrades. Then, rushing to the Austrian ranks, he opened a breach at the price of his own life. Historical criticism, however, has questioned the veracity of this account.

P. Zweifel, *Über die Schlacht von Sempach, zur Aufklärung der Winkelriedfrage* (1927).

WIPO (d. c. 1046) Historian. A native of Burgundy, he was chaplain to Emperor *Conrad II, whose biography in chronicle form, the *Gesta Chuonradi II imperatoris*, he presented to Conrad's son Henry II in 1046. Although a gifted writer not given to flattery, his history is handicapped by the lack of a general outlook common to his age. His other works include a book of maxims (*c.* 1027) and a eulogy of Emperor Henry mixed with earnest exhortations (*c.* 1041). He also wrote a lament on Conrad's death and a liturgical Easter sequence, the *Victimae paschali laudes*.

Works: R. Buchner (ed.), *Quellen des 9. und 11. Jahrhunderts zur Geschichte der hamburgischen Kirche und des Reiches* (1961).

WISMAR German town in *Mecklenburg on the Baltic coast. First colonized by German settlement in the Slavonic east, it was the site of a merchant community, whose citizens had belonged to the merchant guilds of *Novgorod, *Riga and *Visby as far back as 1200. The town received a charter according to the law of *Lübeck in 1226, which set up its organs of self-government. In 1293 W. joined with Rostock, Lübeck, Greifswald and Stralsund to form an association. In

the 14th century W. was an important *Hanse town, its economy based on an important textile industry, an expanding brewery and, of course, the Baltic trade. Although badly hit by the plague in 1276, the town remained fairly prosperous even after the decline of the Hanse. It remained politically independent of the princes of Mecklenburg until the 16th century.

F. Techen, *Geschichte der Seestadt Wismar* (1929).

WISSEMBURG Benedictine abbey in *Austrasia. Founded in 660, W. played an active role in the spread of Christianity in Franconia and Thuringia. The episcopal see of Erfurt was founded by its monks.

WITAN (WITENAGEMOT) The *Council of *Anglo-Saxon kings. It probably developed out of the folkmoot, in which all free-men had the right to appear, and was to be found in each of the larger kingdoms of the 7th and 8th centuries. With the unification of Anglo-Saxon England in the early 9th century there was one W. for the whole country. Convoked on occasions of special importance, its members declared their approval or rejection of proposals put to them. Made up of the king, his sons, bishops, abbots, under-kings, *aldermen of the *shires, and a growing number of nominees of the king, the power of the W. gradually decreased. Under the feudal regime of the Norman kings the institution fell into disuse.

T. J. Oleson, *Witenagemot in the Reign of Edward the Confessor* (1955).

WITCHCRAFT During the Middle Ages, magical experiences and behaviour were condemned as superstitions and the work of the devil by the authorized religious authorities. However, compromises were made, especially in western Europe, and the practices of the Christianized Germanic cults were accepted. Thus, certain supernatural practices could be viewed as miracles accomplished for the glory of the faith, and these were closely related to the cult of the *saints. Other magical enterprises, such as those related to *alchemy, were also accepted as legitimate. Moreover, popular medicine became based on herbal preparations made by good witches (*bella-donna* or *sage-femme*). Up to the 13th century witches, who prepared love potions for knights and members of the aristocracy, were referred to, without negative connotations, in medieval literature. In many cases these witches were considered a marginal group of society, like the hermits. However, where W. was seen as challenging, directly or indirectly, the authority of the Church, it was condemned as a *heresy. Beginning in the 14th century, when the study of medicine and pharmaceuticals was incorporated in the universities, a sharper distinction was made and W. was denounced as magic intended to prevent the salvation of souls. Accordingly, persecution of witches was decreed by Pope *John XXII in 1328 and investigations were carried out by the *Inquisition.

J. B. Russell, *Witchcraft in the Middle Ages* (1972).

WITELO (c. 1230-78) Polish mathematician and philosopher. A native of *Silesia, he studied philosophy and science at *Padua (*c.* 1260-68). At Viterbo he became friendly with *William of Moerbeke, the translator of scientific works to whom he dedicated his major extant work, the *Perspectiva* (On Optics). This work had a great influence on later scientists and became something of a textbook. It is based, to a large extent, on the Arabic scholar *Alhasan, but incorporates some of W.'s empirical experiments. Its psychological basis is close to modern theories of association and the subconscious and its philosophy is neo-Platonic.

A. C. Crombie, *Robert Grosseteste and the Origins of Experimental Science* (1953).

WITHAM A county in Somerset, *England, as well as the name of the country's first *Carthusian foundation, situated near Frome, Somerset. The monastery was founded *c.* 1178 by *Henry II as part of his expiation for the death of St. *Thomas Becket. After initial setbacks it came under the priorship of St. Hugh of Avahen (1180), who improved its temporal and spiritual conditions and attracted new converts to its exacting discipline. By the time of St. Hugh's death (1200) its foundations had been firmly laid and it continued to fulfil the ideals of Carthusianism.

E. M. Thompson, *A History of the Somerset Carthusians* (1895).

WITHIMER See VIDIMER.

WITIGIS King of the *Ostrogoths (536-41). After the Byzantine general, *Belisarius, arrived in Italy and secured his initial victories, W. was elected by the Ostrogothic nobles as king and led the defence against the Byzantines. He besieged Belisarius at Rome, and, after inflicting serious damage upon the city, and especially its aqueducts, W. forced the general to retreat.

WITTELSBACH Noble German family and dukes of *Bavaria from 1180. They stem from Luitpold, duke of Bavaria (d. 907), whose descendants lost the duchy in the mid-10th century and became known as the counts of Scheyern. Otto V was made count *palatine in Bavaria and moved the family's residence to the castle of W. His son, Otto VI, was a close associate of Emperor *Frederick I and was rewarded for his services in Italy with the duchy of Bavaria, taken from *Henry the Lion in 1180. Taking advantage of the continuing Staufen-Welf conflict and the extinction of several great families, the Ws. succeeded in building a comparatively highly integrated state in Bavaria. Their power was diminished only by the existence of the territories of *Salzburg, the *Hohenzollern and the city of Nuremberg. In 1214 they became count palatine of the Rhine. Louis II the Stern, a member of the family, was a candidate for the German crown (1273) and in 1314 another member became King *Louis IV. In 1329 the Ws. split into two branches. Louis IV's descendants ruled Bavaria (until 1918), while his nephews received the Rhine Palatinate and soon after became electoral princes.

M. Spindler, *Die Anfänge des bayerischen Landesfürstentums* (1937).

WLADYSLAW I (1260-1333) Called Lokietek the Short, king of *Poland (1296-1333). V. had been prince of Cujavia when he was elected king by the nobles of Great Poland. When the nobles switched their allegiance to *Wenceslas of Bohemia (1300), V. recruited the support of Pope *Boniface VIII and of Hungary. After Wenceslas' death (1305), V. made himself ruler of Little Poland and by 1314 he also ruled Great Poland. In 1320 he had himself crowned at *Cracow. He had to overcome the resistance of the German-populated towns and the clergy whom he proposed to tax. He saddled himself and his successors with the *Teutonic Knights, whom he called in to wrest *Danzig from the margraves of *Brandenburg. Consequently he was forced to wage a bloody war lasting from 1327 to 1333, which

involved all the major powers of central Europe. During his reign, the country's internal needs had been almost totally neglected, but at the time of his death, the Polish realm had been restored.

O. Halecki, *A History of Poland* (1976).

WOLDEMAR OF BRANDENBURG (c. 1281-1319) Margrave of *Brandenburg. The youngest son of Margrave Conrad I, he was co-ruler of Brandenburg together with Otto IV. After the latter's death (1308), he became the central figure of both the senior and the junior branches of the house of the Ascanians whose possessions he united after 1317 in his hands. He fought against *Danish expansion without visible results. After the death of his nephew and heir, Heinrich (1320), a fake W. appeared, pretending to return from a long pilgrimage. He won much support and was enfeoffed with Brandenburg by Emperor *Charles IV (1348). In 1350 the fraud was detected.

H. Krabbo, "Woldemar von Brandenburg", in: *Brandenburgica.*

WOLFGANG, St. (c. 925-94) Bishop of *Regensburg. Born in *Swabia, he was educated at the abbey of *Reichenau and later became a teacher at the cathedral schools of *Würzburg and *Trier. In 964 he joined the monastery of Einsiedeln. Sent by Bishop Pilgrim of Passau to Christianize Hungary, he failed to achieve substantial progress. Upon his return to Germany, he was made bishop of Regensburg (972), from where the colonization and Christianization of the *Bohemian Forest across the Danube were carried out. He was also for a time tutor to the future emperor *Henry II.

G. Barraclough, *The Origins of Modern Germany* (1972).

WOLFRAM OF ESCHENBACH (d. after 1216) One of the greatest medieval German poets. A native of *Bavaria and belonging to the petty nobility, he led the life of a wanderer. After 1203 he sojourned repeatedly at the *Minnesinger* court of Landgrave Hermann of Thuringia. W. left two long epic poems, *Parzival* and *Willehalm* as well as a few fragments titled *Titurel* and a group of love poems called *Tagelieder*. His *Parzival*, by far the most important work, was composed between 1200 and 1216, and is of a very different character to other medieval works treating the same topic. Although obviously drawing from an as yet unidentified French source, W. introduced historical details not found in earlier sources. Above all, he gave a deep spiritual meaning to the subject, and his moral radically departs from the one found in other versions. In place of ascetic celibacy and retirement from the world, he upholds chaste marriage and fulfilment of worldly duty.

Parzifal, trans. and introd. E. H. Zeydel (1951).

WOMEN Medieval society adopted an ambivalent attitude towards W., based both on Roman law and Germanic traditions. Accordingly, W. were deprived of legal status and could not appear in court or govern, due to their inability to wage combat. Legally, W. were placed under the authority of their father or husband, while a widow came under the protection of a guardian (virtually a second husband) if her sons were still minors. In actual practice, many W. wielded great influence and had authority over large fields of activity, especially in the economic sphere. In the early Middle Ages the lady was largely responsible for managing the estate; officers in charge of administering the manorial economy, especially the *chamberlains, were under her authority. Moreover, W. were given the duties of running the household, educating the children and being the mistresses of the *castle (or home, in the case of non-nobles). In certain instances, W. were openly allowed to have a share in the government, such as was the case of *Theodora, the wife of *Justinian. They also could be regents and certain W., such as *Irene of Byzantium, or *Brunhilda of the Frankish kingdom, ruled their own countries. Up to the 14th century it was generally agreed that W. could transmit inheritance rights of estates or titles but only on the condition "that an heir of a better sex did not exist". In such cases, with the exception of the territories belonging to the *Holy Roman empire, W. could administer justice. The French dynastic crisis of 1315-28, when the three sons of *Philip IV all left daughters, caused the decision to be reached that the crown of France could not be inherited through W. This law, later known as the *Salian law and enforced only in France, was contested during the 14th century, both by descendants of the granddaughters of Philip IV and by the kings of England, descendants of Philip through his daughter, Isabelle.

W. also played an important role in medieval culture and especially in the development of *chivalry. From the 12th century, the lady was in charge of providing the first stage in the education of the future knight and was the central figure in the chivalric court. Hailed by poets, and especially by the *troubadours and *minstrels, she was responsible for setting down conduct at the court: in c. 1160 *Andreas Capellanus distinguished between W. of noble and non-noble birth, laying down rules of love and behaviour in accordance with the social classes. A patroness of poets and artists, the feudal lady was largely responsible for the emergence and development of the secular culture; *tournaments were held under her patronage, and knights fought in her honour. The *courts of love, merely in the platonic sense of the word, praised the character and beauty of ladies and had an impact on certain forms of art, such as tapestry, where W. were represented as the objects of platonic love and no longer as models of the Virgin or of saints. The chivalric orders of the 14th and 15th centuries emphasized proper conduct towards W., and such rules became part of the gentry's behavioural code.

Within the church, W. were excluded from the priesthood and generally did not take part in scholarly activities. On the other hand, they played an important role as abbesses in the ecclesiastical hierarchy and in spiritual and mystical trends. In the 13th-15th centuries many of them were venerated as saints.

S. M. Stuart, *Women in Medieval Society* (1976).

WORCESTER Town and bishopric on the Severn in Worcestershire, *England. Probably the site of a Celtic-Roman settlement, its documented history begins with the foundation of the episcopal see c. 680 and the establishment of the same in 780. By 983 a monastic cathedral had been built, and was rebuilt by Bishop *Wulfstan after the *Norman Conquest according to Norman design. The canonization of Wulfstan brought many pilgrims to W. and wealth to its monks. The secular town was founded during the reign of King *Alfred by the bishop. Its location on the *Welsh border made W. a much-frequented stopping place for the English

kings. It suffered under the rule of *Stephen, who had it burnt down. *Richard I granted the town to the burgesses as a fee-estate for 24 pounds sterling (1189) and *Henry III extended its privileges, granting it a merchants' guild and exemption from taxation. Its economy was based on the production of wool and is attested to as early as 1203. The town features a number of medieval ecclesiastical buildings besides the cathedral.

WORMS German episcopal city on the left bank of the Rhine. A prehistorical and Roman settlement, it continued to exist during the early Middle Ages on account of its strategic position at a major cross-road. A bishopric from 346, it became the capital of the *Burgundians (413) and the centre of their uprising against the Romans. The destruction of the kingdom and its capital by the *Huns (436) is the subject of the famous *Nibelungenlied*. After the defeat of the Huns by *Aetius, W. was incorporated by the *Alemanni and c. 500 by the *Franks. Around 600 the episcopal seat was re-established. Under the Frankish kings W. became one of the most important cities in the kingdom and housed a royal palace built in the 8th century. Its greatest development occurred in the period of the German emperors, under whom the power of the bishops gradually increased. The bishops acquired extensive lands and the title and power of count (979). The foundations of their territorial power were laid by Bishop *Burchard I (1000-1125). However, the burgher element of W. was also strengthened, due to the *Investiture controversy, in which the citizens fought at the side of Emperor *Henry

The Romanesque 12th-century cathedral of Worms

IV against bishop and pope. Subsequent imperial privileges (in 1156 and 1184) established the town's independence from the bishop, making it the first of the free *imperial cities. Later attempts by the bishops to turn back the clock failed, and the town's status as subject only to the emperor was again acknowledged in 1273. W., together with *Mainz and *Spires, was a founding member of the *Rhenish Town League (1254). It was the site of a great number of meetings of emperors and princes, over a 100 of which took place between the 8th and the 16th century. Among them, the most famous is the one that led to the Concordat of W. (1122), which ended the *Investiture controversy. At the imperial diet at W. in 1495 *Maximilian I proclaimed his "perpetual peace" and at the diet of 1521 Luther appeared in front of Germany's leaders. W. has been the home of the most ancient Jewish community of Germany. It possesses a host of Romanesque and Gothic buildings.

H. Boos, *Geschichte der rheinischen Städtekultur mit besonderer Berücksichtigung der Stadt Worms,* 4 vols. (1897-1901).

WULFHERE (d. 675) King of the *Mercians. Younger son of King *Penda, he survived his father's defeat (655) and came out of hiding to become king when the Mercians threw off the supremacy of Oswio, king of *Northumbria. W. energetically furthered the spread of Christianity. He expanded his territory by military action against Northumbria and *Wessex and became *bretwalda* (ruler of Britain) or overlord and military leader of all the English kingdoms. He was succeeded by his brother, *Ethelred.

F. Stenton, *Anglo-Saxon England* (1947).

WULFRIC, St. (d. 1154) Hermit. An Anglo-Saxon priest, he retired to Somerset in 1125 and lived in complete isolation. W. became the object of a widespread popular cult in medieval *England; miracles and prophecies were attributed to him, although he was never canonized.

D. Knowles, *Saints and Scholars in Medieval England* (1968).

WULFSTAN OF WORCESTER, St. (c. 1009-95) Educated at the monasteries of Evesham and Peterborough, he joined the monastery of *Worcester, eventually becoming its prior. Successful at improving discipline and the material situation of his monastery and known for his pastoral concern, he was elected bishop of Worcester (1062). One of the churchmen who submitted to *William I the Conqueror in 1066, he was allowed to remain bishop after the Norman Conquest, aiding in the compilation of the *Domesday Book and supporting William against the rebellious barons (1075). In his personal life, he maintained a monastic routine. He became famous for his fight against the slave trade, and succeeded in stopping the Bristol merchants from selling slaves to *Ireland.

J. W. Lamb, *St. Wulstan, Prelate and Patriot* (1933); F. Barlow, *The English Church 1000-1066: A Constitutional History* (1963).

WULFSTAN OF YORK (d. 1023) Archbishop of *York (from 1003), also bishop of *Worcester (1003-16). W. is commonly held to be the author of a homily in alliterative English prose. An appeal to all classes to repent in the prospect of the imminent day of judgement, it is a first-class source of the desperate condition of England in the year of King *Ethelred II's expulsion (1013). The social principles found in W.'s treatise, especially concerning the abuses of the rights of freemen, were taken up in subsequent legislation, particularly that of *Canute the Great.

D. Whitelock, "Archbishop Wulfstan, Homilist and Statesman", *Transactions of the Royal Historical Society* (1942).

WÜRTTEMBERG Area, county and (from 1495) duchy in southwestern *Germany. A Roman dominion from the 1st century, it was conquered in the 3rd century by the *Alemanni. The latter were vanquished by the *Franks under *Clovis (496) and the area of W. became part of the Frankish empire and was governed by a count. In the 9th century the overlordship of W. and most of its lands were given to the dukes of *Swabia. The counts of W. began under the family of Conrad von Bertelsbach (c. 1080), who named himself after his ancestral castle of W. near Stuttgart. Possessing the countyship over large, but fragmented, family possessions in the Rem and Neckar Valleys, his descendants took advantage of the decline of the *Hohenstaufen, to whom the duchy of Swabia belonged, to extend their lands. The first acquisition of the W. counts, the county of Urach, doubled their territory (c. 1260). There they came into conflict with the *Hapsburgs, whose representative, King *Rudolf I, forced them to give up the strategic town of *Ulm. While giving way in the south, Count Eberhard (d. 1325) succeeded in the north and northwest and acquired, in the early 14th century, possession after possession. In 1321 Stuttgart became the residence of the counts of W. and in accordance with the "Law of the Household" (1361), an institutional base was laid for a strictly organized territorial state. Victorious in the war against the town league (1388) and against the nobility, the counts of the 15th century brought W. to the rank of a German power.

K. Weller, *Württenbergische Geschichte* (1963).

WÜRZBURG Town and bishopric in *Franconia, Germany. The site of a nearby Roman fort, W. is first mentioned in 704, and the diocese was established in 741 by St. *Boniface. The church was granted extensive gifts of land c. 752, as well as immunity and secular jurisdiction. This was the first of many royal and imperial privileges, which gradually established the ducal authority of the bishops over eastern Franconia, recognized formally in 1168. Their ducal status involved the bishops in each and every political struggle of medieval Germany. As early as the 11th century the burghers had clashed with their bishop, whose residence in the overpowering fortress of Leistenberg, high above the burghers' town, aggravated their feeling of resentment. First steps towards freeing the town from the bishop's tutelage were made during the *Investiture controversy, but the town's aspirations were checked in the time of Emperor *Frederick I. After the emperor's death W. joined the *Rhenish town league as an independent city. Bishop Gerhard von Schwarzburg defeated the burghers at the Battle of Bergstein (1400) and put an end to the town's independence.

T. Kramer (ed.), *Quellen und Forschungen zur Geschichte des Hochstiftes Würzburg* (1948).

WYCLIFFE, JOHN (c. 1330-84) English theologian and reformer. A native of Yorkshire, he studied at Oxford, where he became a fellow of Merton College

(1356) and master of Balliol (1360-61). In 1365-67 he was the warden of Canterbury Hall, but was expelled by Archbishop Simon Langton and lived at Queen's College until 1380. After 1371 W. was employed by *Edward, the Black Prince, and *John of Gaunt and represented them before the papal court. He soon became reputed as a philosopher and, reacting against the prevailing scepticism of thought at Oxford, returned to the realism of St. *Augustine and Robert *Grosseteste. His philosophical beliefs led him to compose a series of commentaries on the Bible, in which he distinguished between the eternal, ideal concept of the Church and the material one. In 1376 he published his *De civili dominio,* in which he maintained that secular and ecclesiastical authority depended on grace and that clergy not in a state of grace could therefore have their endowments withdrawn by the civil power. This non-conformist attitude was condemned in 1377 by Pope *Gregory XI. W., however, continued to express his ideas in a series of treatises, emphasizing the primacy of the Bible as the sole source of doctrine and claiming that the authority of the pope lacked scriptural justification. In 1380 he elaborated a new theory of the *eucharist, attacking the doctrine of *transubstantiation. This theory was publicly condemned by the university in 1381. W. refused to recant and his attitude became connected with the *peasants' revolt, erroneously attributed to his teachings. In 1832 a number of his followers were condemned, while he had to retire to Lutterworth. There he revised his works and wrote a series of pamphlets attacking his enemies. His disciples, known as the *Lollards, continued W.'s activity after his death. His writings wielded great influence on later reformers and non-conformists, such as John *Hus.

K. B. MacFarlane, *John Wycliffe and the Beginnings of English Non-Conformity* (1952).
C.Med.H., VII.

Seal of Archbishop William of Tyre

X

XANTEN City in the Rhine Valley. In the late 4th and during the 5th century it was the centre of the Ripuarian *Franks. From the 6th century it became one of the residences of the *Merovingians and declined gradually. Annexed to the principality of the archbishops of *Trier, X. became an active provincial town in the 12th century.

XILIPHINUS, JOHN (c. 1010-75) Patriarch of *Constantinople (1063-75). X. was considered one of the most learned persons of the Byzantine empire in the 11th century, the period of its great cultural development.

A jurist, he taught at the imperial school of law at Constantinople and in 1045 became its head. Under the patronage of *Constantine IX, he took an active part in the reorganization of the Academy of Constantinople and also distinguished himself as a philosopher. In 1054, after Constantine's death, he retired from public life and became a monk. His writings in the defence of the Greek-Orthodox tradition prompted Emperor *Constantine X to appoint him patriarch. X. vigorously opposed attempts of reunion with Rome.

CMedH, IV.

Y

YAQUBI, AHMAD IBN ABU YAQUB IBN JAFFAR IBN WAHB IBN WADIH, AL- (d. 897) Arab historian. Born in *Persia, he lived in *Khorasan under the patronage of the *Tahirids until 873 and began his great historical work there. After the dynasty's fall, he was exiled and travelled to India and the Maghreb, before settling in Egypt, where he completed his *History of the World* and wrote an account of the countries he visited. The history is divided into two parts; the non-Islamic and pre-Islamic period and that of the Moslem world. The latter is an important source for the rise of Islam and the foundation of the caliphate.

YAQUT (1179-1229) *Arab geographer. Born in *Mosul, Iraq, he travelled to various Moslem countries and served *Saladin and the *Ayyubids. He wrote (c. 1225) one of the most accurate accounts of the Moslem world, desribing the various cities, peoples and their folklore.

YARMUK River in *Palestine, on the banks of which (southeast of the Sea of Galilee) a decisive battle was fought between the *Byzantines and the *Arabs (636). Although tired after the great war against Persia, and disorganized after a series of defeats in Palestine and Syria, the troops of Emperor *Heraclius, led by Theodore Trithyrius, managed to hold a position on the Y. There they were met by a large contingent of *Monophysite Arabs under the Armenian prince, Vahan. On 20 August 636, in a blinding sandstorm, the battle against the Arabs was begun, in the midst of which the Christian Arabs went over to the enemy. The Moslem victory was complete; Palestine and Syria were opened to the Arabs and Heraclius left the Byzantine East.
CMedH, II.

YAROPOLK I Prince of *Kiev (972-77). Eldest son of *Svyatoslav, he held Kiev at his father's death but had to accept his father's general, Svereld, as co-ruler. The latent conflict between Y. and his brothers *Oleg and *Vladimir broke out in a savage war (976), in which Oleg was defeated and killed and Vladimir fled to Scandinavia. Y., who was married to a Greek Christian, became sole ruler of *Russia, and during his brief reign the Christian party had the ascendancy. He was, however, betrayed by his chief councellor, Blud, who advised him to negotiate with Vladimir. Y. agreed and was treacherously murdered by his brother's *Varangian supporters.
G. Vernadsky, *Kievan Russia* (1948).

YAROSLAV THE WISE Grand prince of Kievan *Russia (1036-54). The ablest son of *Vladimir and ruler of *Novgorod at his father's death (1015), he fought his brothers *Svyatopolk and *Mstislav. In 1024 he reached an agreement of partition with the latter. Together, the brothers fought the Poles, and after Mstislav's death (1036) Y. became the undisputed sovereign of the whole of Russia and assumed the title of *kagan*. Y. made

Kiev his capital and established its church of *St. Sophia as an important institution of learning (1045). Relations between the Russian Church and the patriarch of Constantinople were normalized by an agreement (c. 1038), according to which the *metropolitan of Kiev was to be ordained by the patriarch. Following the murder of some Russian merchants in Constantinople (1042), Y. placed his son Vladimir at the head of a large naval force sent to attack Byzantine territory, but the venture miscarried (1043). A new crisis in ecclesiastical relations with Byzantium (1051) led to the independent election of Hilary as metropolitan of Kiev.

YARROW AND WEARMOUTH Twin *Benedictine monasteries founded near the Wear River in Durham, in 674 and 684 respectively, by St. *Benedict Biscop on land given him by Egfrid, king of *Northumbria. Benedict dedicated W. to St. *Peter and Y. to St. Paul, and brought workmen from France to build a church at the former in the Roman fashion, equipped with the latest trappings of civilized luxury. The place became the cradle of English art and a main centre for education and literature. *Bede received his early education there. Y. and W. greatly suffered at the hands of the Danes (c. 860) and after the Norman Conquest, at the hands of *Malcolm of Scotland. Restored, they became subordinate to the cathedral priory at Durham.

YAZID I *Ummayad caliph (680-83). Son of *Muawiyah, he distinguished himself as a military commander under his father, when he took part in the conquest of *Syria. In 669 he commanded the Moslem forces sent by his father to lay siege to Constantinople. Proclaimed caliph in 680, he had to face a revolt both in *Iraq, where Ali's son, *Al-Husayn, was appointed caliph, and at Mecca, where Abdallah Ibn Az-Zubair rose against him in 683 (see *Arabia). Y. defeated and killed Al-Husayn at Kerbala. With a powerful army he marched into *Hedjaz in 683 and burned Mecca, but revolts against him continued until 692.
CHI.

YEHIEL BEN JOSEPH OF PARIS (d. c. 1265) French Jewish scholar. A student of Judah ben Isaac, he succeeded his teacher as head of the Paris *yeshiva* (Talmud academy). Y. was renowned among Jews and non-Jews alike both for his scholarship and his upright character. He was the leading Jewish protagonist in the famous Disputation of Paris (1240) regarding the status of the Talmud. When copies of the Talmud were publicly burnt as a result of the disputation, Y. continued to teach his students, apparently from memory. He emigrated with a large number of disciples to the Holy Land c. 1260 and settled at *Acre, then in the hands of the Crusaders. There he continued to head an academy.

YEMEN Country in southwest *Arabia. It was united in the late 4th century by the Hemyar dynasty, which accepted Judaism during the same period, their kings claiming to be descendants of King Solomon and the Queen of Sheba. Y. became a powerful kingdom controlling the Red Sea trade. Its civilization developed in the 5th century under the influence of Hellenistic traditions and the Jewish faith. Allied with the Persians against the Byzantines, the Hemyar kingdom was attacked by the Christian *Ethiopians and fell in 550, when Y. was annexed to Ethiopia; Christianity was introduced, but apparently was received only superficially. In 570, *Chosroes I of Persia conquered Y. Repeated wars led to the decline of the Hemyar civilization and to the desolation of southern Y. When Persian domination collapsed in 620, small, independent tribal realms were established. They failed, however, to resist invasions by Beduin, who introduced Islam. Y. was annexed to the caliphate of *Abu Bakr in 633. Tribal traditions, however, remained strong, with particularist trends facilitating *Shiite expansion in Y. after 680. The last vestiges of dependence on the caliphate disappeared in 820, when independent realms were established in the south and the north. In 893, after the *Karmatian invasions, the Zayid dynasty established its rule at Saada. During the 10th century the Saydites united Y., which became a moderate Shiite kingdom. Tribal separatism, however, continued to exert pressure on the dynasty and in the 12th century Y. lapsed into anarchy. While the tribes continued their endemic wars, the merchants of Aden, who were interested in developing their trade with Egypt and India, created an autonomous city-state, governed by their local *radi*. In 1174 they appealed to *Saladin to impose order in Y. Saladin's intervention brought the country under the overlordship of the *Ayyubids (1174-1229), who managed to put an end to the civil wars. At the same time, the *Sunnite Rassulids, local officers appointed by the Ayyubids, rose to power, and proclaimed their independence in 1228. Under the Rassulid dynasty (1228-1446), Y. knew one of its most prosperous periods, as a result of intensive trade with the Far East and east Africa. Revenues from trade created a class of wealthy families, which patronized the arts and crafts and the cloth industry.

YORK City and bishopric, later archbishopric, in Yorkshire, *England. A British settlement and the northernmost centre of the Romans in England, it was the seat of a bishop in 314. The early Christian settlement was destroyed by the *Saxons and restored for a few years under St. *Paulinus (625-33) and again by St. *Wilfrid in 664. Egbert, brother of King Edbert of *Northumbria, established Y. as an archbishopric in 735. Under him and *Alcuin it became one of the most celebrated educational centres in Europe. However, the independence of the archbishopric was far from definitive. From 1071 to c. 1350 there was an intermittent struggle with the archbishop of *Canterbury. Marked by conflicting papal decisions, it finally ended with a compromise establishing Y. on a practically equal, but formally slightly lower, level.

The town served as the centre of a *Norse kingdom in the Danish period, and played a prominent part in the uprising of northern England against *William I, for which it was put to the torch. Its first extant charter was granted by *Henry II, but it actually refers to prvileges granted from *Henry I's time, with the addi-

tion of the right to a merchants' guild. *Richard I granted exemption from paying toll (1194) and *John granted the city to the burghers at a fee-farm of 160 pounds sterling per year. In the late 14th century Y. was self-ruled by a lord mayor and aldermen, and, by the *charter of 1396 the city was made into a county and given the power to elect two sheriffs. A long struggle between the citizens and the abbey of St. Mary over the jurisdiction of a suburb was settled in 1353 in favour of the former. From the 11th century Y. was an important commercial centre and its weavers' guild was chartered by Henry II. It also possessed a large and thriving Jewish community, which was the victim of a pogrom in 1190. After taking refuge in the royal castle, most of the Jews committed suicide rather than fall into the hands of the rabble. The city possesses a number of fine medieval buildings, first and foremost a cathedral dedicated to St. Peter and commonly called the "Minster". It occupies the site of the church founded by *Edwin.

G. E. Aylmer *et al.*, ed., *A History of York Minster* (1978)

YUNNAN Province in southern *China. Although it was always part of the Chinese empire, Y. comprised a complexity of ethnic and religious groups which, between the 8th and 14th centuries, posed a barrier to Chinese attempts to control the region. The autonomous *Thais revolted several times before they were pushed southwards, while other Y. tribes invaded Indo-China. Buddhist revolts against the Tang dynasty (9th century) continued for over a century, until the dynasty's fall in 960. The immigration of *Moslems and *Nestorians exacerbated interracial tension and led to continuous civil and religious wars. In 1257, Y. was conquered by the *Mongols, who devastated the province and exploited its resources.

YURI DOLGORUKI OF SUZDAL (1125-57) He was the youngest son of *Vladimir Monomakh, prince of *Kiev, who, in 1125, constituted for him the principality of *Suzdal, then in northeastern Russia. Y. devoted his efforts to developing his new principality, founding its capital at Vladimir and bringing in colonists from the populated areas of the southwest. His achievements were destined to be of great historical importance in the 13th century, when Suzdal became the new centre of *Russia after Kiev was conquered by the Mongols. Taking advantage of the decline of the Kievan branch of the dynasty, he was recognized grand prince of Kiev (1154), but continued to reside at Suzdal, his power base.

YUSUF IBN TASHFIN *Almoravide sultan (1061-1106). Elected sultan in 1061, when the *Almoravides were concentrated in the Sahara, he expanded his domain by conquering *Morocco (1061-69). In 1062, he founded the city of Marrakesh and made it his capital. Called by the *Abbadids of Seville to help the Moslems of Spain after *Alfonso VI of Castile conquered Toledo, Y. invaded Spain in 1085 and the following year defeated the Castilian army at *Zallaca. He then annexed the Moslem Spanish emirates to his empire.
CHI

YZIASLAV Prince of *Kiev (1054-78). Eldest son of *Yaroslav the Wise, he inherited Kiev. His reign was marked by revolts at Kiev, that were supported by his brother *Svyatoslav of Chernigov. Only after 1071 was he able to return to Kiev and rule over his principality.

Z

ZACCARIA, BENEDETTO (c. 1240-1307) Genoese admiral and adventurer. Famous for his defence of *Chios (1262-70), he was appointed commander of the Genoese fleet in the Aegean Sea. He maintained close relations with Byzantine Emperor *Michael Palaeologus, who named him his representative in Italy. After having served *Genoa and *Byzantium, he entered the service of *Aragon, and in 1302 was hired by King *Philip IV of France to command the French fleet against England.

ZACHARIAS, St. (d. 752) A *Calabrian Greek by birth, he was elected pope in 741. The last Greek pope for almost 700 years, his pontificate symbolizes the widening rift between Eastern and Western Christianity, and the political consequences which followed. He suffered the loss of the ecclesiastical provinces of Calabria and Sicily, which included huge papal estates, when the Byzantine emperor ordered a redistribution of the church's provinces in favour of Constantinople. At the same time he faced the political realities in the West, coming to terms with the aggressive *Lombard king Luitprand, thus preparing the way for the imperial coronation of *Charlemagne and the siding of the papacy with the Carolingians at the expense of Byzantium. He also denounced Byzantine *iconoclasm. His attempt to bridge the cultural gap between East and West by translating the "Dialogues" of his predecessor Gregory I into Greek had no practical consequences.
H. K. Mann, *The Lives of the Popes in the Early Middle Ages from 590 to 1304* (1902).

ZAHRAWI, AL- (d. 1013) Moslem surgeon. He was one of the greatest physicians in Moslem Spain. In the late 10th century he practised dissections, developing this field of medical science. His treatise on surgery, summing up his experience, was translated into Latin and used as a standard manual in western schools of *medicine in the 11th and 12th centuries.

ZÄHRINGEN Noble family of southwest Germany, whose name derived from the castle and village of Z. near *Freiburg-im Breisgau. The family stemmed from the *Alamanni ducal house of the Agilolfing. Based at their substantial holdings around Villingen, they slowly enlarged their control over neighbouring territories and gained titles. Berthold I. (d. 1078) became titular duke of *Carinthia (1053) and margrave of *Verona (1061) in exchange for surrendering to the *Hohenstaufen his claim to the duchy of *Swabia. During the *Investiture controversy the Z. were partisans of the pope and strengthened their hold on *Zurich (1097) and on extensive lands in western Switzerland. Conrad (d. 1152) inherited some land in *Burgundy and was appointed in 1127 rector of the kingdom of *Arles by Emperor *Lothair III. When *Frederick I assumed the regalian rights in Burgundy (1169), the Z. were compensated by extensive rights of advocacy in the bishoprics of *Geneva, *Lausanne and Sitten, but retained a cool relationship with the Hohenstaufen. At the end of the 11th century the Z. divided into two branches, the margraves of *Baden and the dukes of Z. The latter built up a highly integrated territory in the Schwartzwald region and Switzerland, which, together with the *Norman kingdom in southern Italy, has been called the first modern state of the Middle Ages. Such a strong consolidation was achieved by a shrewd policy of advocacy over churches and monasteries, through the construction of castles and towns in strategic sites and by planned colonization of virgin land. At the death of the childless Berthold V (1218), the main ducal line became extinct and the Z. state was divided up.
G. Barraclough, *The Origins of Modern Germany* (1972); T. Mayer, *Der Staat der Herzöge von Z.* (1935).

ZALLACA, BATTLE OF (1086) Fought between the Castilian army of *Alfonso VI and the *Almoravides, commanded by *Yussuf Ibn Tashfin, who inflicted a crushing defeat on the Christians in Spain. The battle culminated in the Castilian retreat to the Tagus River and Almoravide domination in Moslem Spain.

ZEELAND County in the Low Countries. Occupying the region between the estuaries of the Meuse and Schelde rivers, it was created in the 12th century on land reclaimed from the North Sea, hence its name, meaning "sea land". A countal dynasty related to the counts of *Holland established its power in Z. In the 14th century, the countal title passed to the *Wittelsbach dynasty and, by a series of marriages, *Philip the Good annexed Z. to the *Burgundian state in 1419.

ZENGI, IMAD AL-DIN (1084-1146) The son of a Turkish officer, who served the *Seljuk dynasty at *Aleppo, he fled from the city after his father's murder in 1094. Brought up in Persia, he entered the service of the Seljuks and was appointed *atabeg first of Basra in southern Iraq and, in 1128, of *Mosul, where he seized power. He conquered *Aleppo in 1130, and imposed his authority on the Turkish and Arab princes in northern Syria and northern Iraq, calling on them to join in the holy war against the *Crusaders. His conquest of *Edessa represented Islam's first important counter-offensive against the Crusaders. Z. intended to enlarge his powerful state to include all of Syria, but never achieved his goal.
CHI.

ZENGIDS (ZENGHIDS) Dynasty founded by *Zengi, which ruled *Syria and northern *Iraq in the 12th century. Its most important sultan was Zengi's son and heir, *Nureddin (1146-73), who united Syria under his rule. After his death, the dynasty declined and *Saladin inherited its lands.

ZENO Eastern Roman emperor (474-75; 476-91). A chieftain of the *Isaurians, originally called Tarasicodissa,

he appeared with his army at *Constantinople at the invitation of Emperor *Leo, who was hard pressed by the *Goths (466). There he married the emperor's daughter, Ariadne and changed his name to Z. In 474 he became co-ruler and, later in the same year, emperor. However, the rule of the Isaurian soldiers and administrators, who were regarded by the Byzantines as foreigners, led to a rebellion, which forced Z. to take refuge in Isauria (475). Due to the misrule of his successor Basilius, Z. managed to make an uncontested come-back (476). Under his rule the Eastern empire was rid of the *Ostrogoths, but had to bear with a long war between Z. and his former generals. In ecclesiastical matters Z. tried to arrange a compromise solution on the *Monophysite question, and published the "Henotikon" (482). This edict of union only inflamed both the eastern Monophysites and their opponents in Byzantium.
G. Ostrogorsky, *History of the Byzantine State* (1968).

ZESLAV (ZDESLAV) Duke of the *Croats (867-79). Adopting a policy designed to achieve Croatian independence, he rejected the overlordship of *Carolingian King *Louis the German in 876. To maintain his power, he became an ally to Byzantine Emperor *Basil I. His attitude led to the rise of an anti-Byzantine movement among the Croats and to his deposition in a plot led by his rival, *Branimir, in 879.

ZITA, St. (d. 1278) Spending her life as a domestic servant in the household of Fatinelli, a well-to-do weaver of *Lucca, she became a model of devoted service, after initial tensions winning the trust of her employer and her fellow-servants, and caring for the poor, to whom she distributed her food. Having acquired a reputation for saintliness, she was able to spend her later years in the performance of good deeds, visiting the sick and comforting prisoners. Through her supernatural manifestations and her devout life-style she became a celebrity and at her death she was popularly acclaimed a saint. Since then she has been regarded as the patron saint of domestic servants.
A. Butler, *The Lives of the Saints*, rev. ed. (1956).

ŽIŽKA, JAN (c. 1376-1424) *Hussite military leader. Born to a noble family, he lost an eye in the Bohemian civil wars during the reign of *Wenceslas IV. A zealous follower of *Hus, he was at the head of those men who threw the Prague town councillors out of the town hall windows (1419). Z. joined the Hussites at *Tabor, where he organized their new army. In 1420 he defeated the German army of *Sigismund at Vitkov, and continued to fight off the subsequent invasion forces in 1421 and 1422. While fighting against the Bohemian partisans of Sigismund and the adherents to the Roman rite, he lost the use of his remaining eye in battle. Despite internal dissensions he led the forces of Tabor against those of *Prague (1423). In the summer of the same year Z. undertook a daring invasion of *Hungary, which failed only because of the numerical superiority of Sigismund's forces. After beating the Utraquist nobles and the forces of Prague again (1424), Z. prepared an attack on *Moravia, but died before realizing his plans.
F. G. Heymann, *John Žižka and the Hussite Revolution* (1955).

ZLATA KORUNA *Benedictine monastery in southern Bohemia. Founded by *Ottokar I in the early 13th century, Z. became the symbol of Bohemian kingship and was richly endowed. The seizure of the abbey

and its estates by the *Hussites in 1419-20 created a precedent for the confiscation of church properties.

ZONARAS, JOHN (1042-c. 1130) Byzantine civil servant and chronicler. During the reign of *John II, following a career as commander of the imperial bodyguard, private secretary to *Alexius I Comnenus and first secretary of the imperial chancery, Z. became a monk at Hagia Glykeria. Z. wrote a world history in 18 volumes, which extends from the creation of the world to 1118. He based his work on earlier sources, such as Josephus and Dio Cassius for the Roman period. The chief importance of his work lies in its preservation of the first 200 books of Cassius' work which would otherwise have been lost, as well as in his independent approach. Z. also wrote several theological works.
C. Krumbacher, *Geschichte der byzantinischen Literatur* (1897).

ZUG (ZOUG) Canton and its capital in central *Switzerland. The town is first mentioned in a document of 1240 as a fortified place. The town and district (the Ausser Amt) became Austrian by purchase in 1273 and were each governed by a *Hapsburg bailiff. In 1352 both independently became members of the Swiss confederation, but were forced in the same year to acknowledge the Hapsburgs as lords. However, in 1364 Z. joined in the league of the Swabian cities and shared in the victory of *Sempach. By 1389 the Hapsburgs had renounced all their claims, and their formal overlordship was ended in 1415. At the beginning of the 15th century the town and the region quarreled over the privilege of keeping the banner and seal of Z.; the matter was settled in 1414 in favour of the town. In the 15th century the town acquired territories to the north and the west.
E. Gruber, *Geschichte des Kantons Zug* (1968).

ZURICH Town and canton in northeastern *Switzerland. A Celtic-Roman settlement, the town of Z. arose in the 9th century out of the union of a royal palace with its tenants, the tenants of two churches (the Grossmünster and Fraumünster) and a community of free *Alamanni. The sovereign rights over the settlement were granted consecutively to the counts of Lenzburg, the dukes of *Zähringen and (1218) to the burghers, whereby the town became a free *imperial city. The administration of Z., which had been in the hands of the abbess of Fraumünster passed in the 13th century to the city council. By 1304 this body, made up of the representatives of the patrician families, was ruling the city for all practical purposes. In 1336 the craftsmen were allowed a share in town government. Z. was a founding member of the Swiss confederation, but pursued an ambiguous policy vis-à-vis the confederation and the *Hapsburgs until c. 1380, when the guilds gained the majority in the town executive. In the 14th and 15th centuries Z. acquired considerable lands and by 1400 it had become completely independent of the German empire.
A. Langiader, *Geschichte von Stadt und Landschaft Zürich*, 2 vols. (1945).

ZWENTIBOLD King of *Lotharingia (888-99). An illegitimate son of Emperor *Arnulf, he was proclaimed king by his father, who thereby sought to impose his authority over the rebellious feudal nobles in Lotharingia. But Z. failed to assert his power and, with his death, *Carolingian control over *Lotharingia ended.
E. Hlawitschka, *Lotharingien und das Reich* (1968).

MAPS

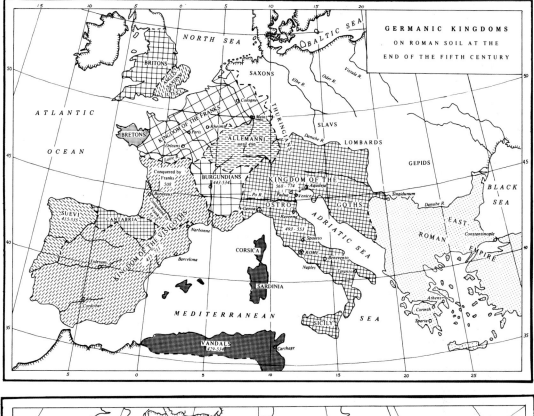

GERMANIC KINGDOMS
ON ROMAN SOIL AT THE
END OF THE FIFTH CENTURY

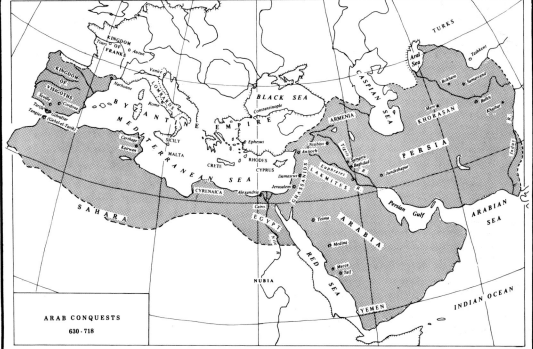

ARAB CONQUESTS
630 - 718

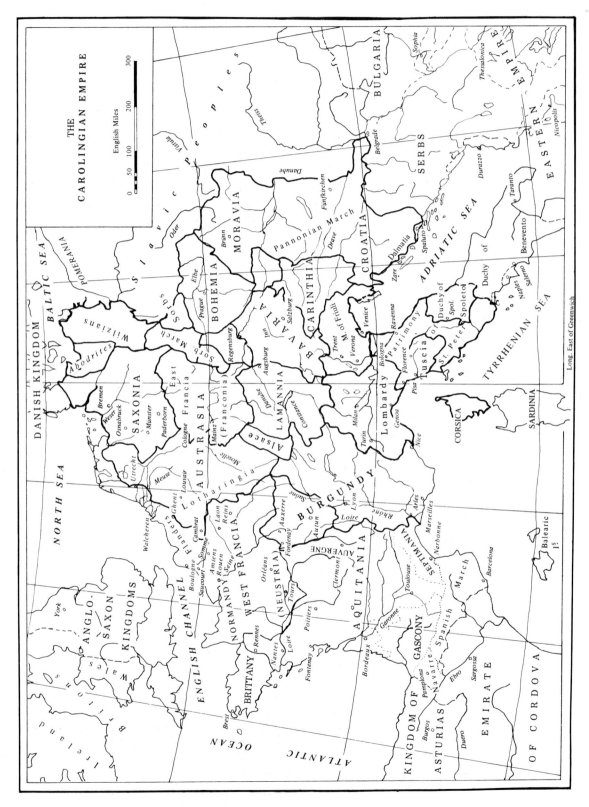

THE CAROLINGIAN EMPIRE

English Miles

0   50   100   200   300

Long. East of Greenwich

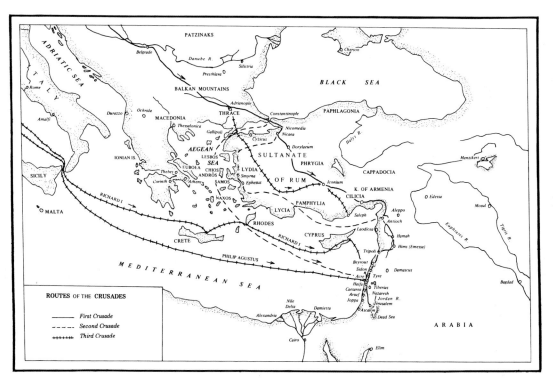

ROUTES OF THE CRUSADES

————— First Crusade
– – – – – Second Crusade
+++++++ Third Crusade

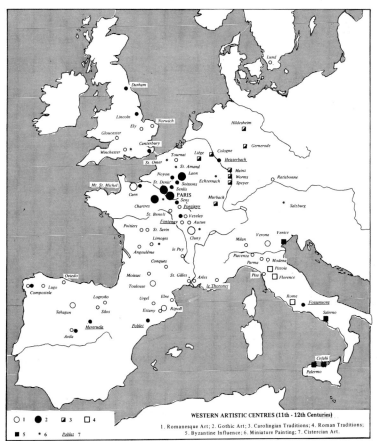

WESTERN ARTISTIC CENTRES (11th - 12th Centuries)

1. Romanesque Art; 2. Gothic Art; 3. Carolingian Traditions; 4. Roman Traditions;
5. Byzantine Influence; 6. Miniature Painting; 7. Cistercian Art.

○ 1   ● 2   ▨ 3   ▢ 4
■ 5   * 6   *Poblet* 7

**THE HOLY ROMAN EMPIRE
UNDER THE
HOHENSTAUFEN**

—— Boundary of the
Holy Roman Empire

CHRONOLOGICAL TABLE

Date/Century	Western Europe	Eastern Europe	Moslem World	Far East and Africa	Society, Economy, Arts, Letters and Science
395	Division of the Roman Empire			Gupta Empire in India.	
406	Vandals and Suevi cross the Rhine.			Wei dynasty in N. China.	
410	Alaric and the Visigoths conquer Rome.	Ostrogothic raids in the Balkans.			
412-30	St. Augustine's activity.			Buddhist penetration in China.	
430	Conquest of N. Africa by the Vandals.				
c. 450	Invasions of the Huns. St. Patrick in Ireland. Visigothic kingdom in Gaul and Spain. Vandal raids in Italy.	Council of Chalcedon.			W. Mediterranean navigation obstructed by the Vandals. Chinese characters adopted in Japan.
476	Fall of the Western Roman Empire.	Organization of the Byzantine Empire.		Fall of the Gupta Empire in India.	
483-511	Clovis and Frankish Kingdom of Gaul. Conversion of Franks to Christianity.		Hemyar Kingdom in Yemen.		
493-526	Theodoric and Ostrogothic Kingdom in Italy.				
527-65	Benedictine monastery at Monte Cassino (c. 530).	Reign of Justinian; wars against Persians and Byzantine reconquest of Italy, N. Africa and S. Spain; codification of Roman law.	Sassanids rule in Persian Empire and S. Arabia.		
6th cent.	Anglo-Saxon realms in Britain.				Pre-feudal economy in W. Europe.
568	Lombard conquest of Italy.	The Avar Kingdom.			
590-604	Gregory the Great and Papal State at Rome; St. Augustine at Canterbury.				
610-41		Reign of Heraclius.		Feudalism in Japan.	
618			Mohammed at Mecca.	Tang dynasty in China.	Isidore of Seville in Spain.
622			The Hegira; Mohammed at Medina; emergence of Islam.		
634-50		Loss of Syria, Palestine and Egypt.	Middle East conquered by the Arabs.		
630-700	Mayors of the palace in the Frankish kingdom.			Chinese expansion in E. Asia.	Emergence of feudalism in W. Europe.
660			Umayyad Caliphate; Arab conquest of N. Africa and Khorasan.		Cultural awakening in China and Japan.
711			Arab conquest of Spain.		
717	Charles Martel mayor of the palace.	Siege of Constantinople by the Arabs.			Bede the Venerable in England.
8th cent.	Mercian domination in England.	Iconoclastic Controversy at Byzantium. Bulgarian settlement in the Balkans. The Khazar Empire in the Russian steppes.		Chinese-Arab encounters.	Gold mines in the Arab Caliphate. Rise of Moslem philosophy and science in Egypt, Syria and Persia.
732	Battle of Poitiers.				Economic prosperity of Asia and E. Europe.
750			The Abbasid Caliphate.	Beginning of Tang decline in China.	
751	Pepin the Short, King of the Franks.		Arab conquest of Central Asia.		
762			Foundation of Baghdad.	The Java Empire.	
					Buddhist books printed in Japan.
768	Charlemagne, King of the Franks.				

TABLE 742

Date/Century	Western Europe	Eastern Europe	Moslem World	Far East and Africa	Society, Economy, Arts, Letters and Science
774	Charlemgane conquers Lombardy.				Baghdad cultural centre.
778	Battle of Roncesvalles.			Civil wars in China.	
782				The Fujiwara period in Japan.	Settlement of Alcuin in Gaul.
800	Imperial coronation of Charlemagne.	Irene, Empress of Byzantium.	Harun Al-Rashid, Caliph.	Foundation of the Khmer Empire.	Carolingian Renaissance.
9th cent.	Norman invasions in W. Europe. Moslem raids and conquests in S.W. Europe.	Civil wars in Byzantium. Conversion of Slavs and Bulgarians.	Decline of the Abbasids and rise of local dynasties in Persia and N. Africa.	Persecution of Buddhists in China.	Agrarian-feudal economy in W. Europe.
843	Treaty of Verdun; division of the Carolingian Empire. Foundation of Citta Leonina by Leo IV.		Turks enter the service of the Caliphate.		
858	Danish conquest of England.			Ghana Empire in Africa.	
871	Alfred the Great, King of Wessex.	The Photian schism in Byzantium. Mission of Cyril and Methodius.	Tulunid dynasty in Egypt. Samanid dynasty in Khorasan.		
875		Rurik founds a Russian state at Novgorod.			Feudalism as political system in W. Europe; heredity of fiefs.
885		Establishment of the realm of Georgia.	Karmatian revolts.		
888	Final division of the Carolingian Empire.			Chonda Empire in India. Foundation of Angkor.	The Golden Age in Moslem Spain.
893		Simeon, Tsar of the Bulgarians.			End of the Carolingian Renaissance.
900-55	Hungarian invasions.	Macedonian dynasty at Byzantium. Kiev, capital of Russia.	Rise of the Fatimids in N. Africa. Karmatian Kingdom in Arabia.	Division of China into Five Empires.	Confucian civilization in China. Death of Tabari.
955	Victory of Otto I at Lechfield.				
960				Sung dynasty in China.	Flowering of Arab science.
962	Imperial coronation of Otto I (Holy Roman Empire.				
969			Fatimids conquer Egypt.		
972				India divided into small kingdoms.	Gerbert's teaching at Rheims.
976		Basil II, Emperor of Byzantium.			The Ottonian Renaissance.
987	Hugh Capet, King of France.				Scholarly centre at Liège.
989	Movement of Peace of God.	Conversions of Stephen of Hungary and Vladimir of Kiev to Christianity.	Mahmud of Ghazna and his Empire.	N.W. India conquered by Moslems.	Al-Azhar University at Cairo.
998	Imperial ideology of Otto II.				
1010					Revival of trade in Italy. Shah-Nama and revival of Persia.
1014-18		Basil II conquers Bulgaria.			Byzantine literary renaissance. Communal movement in N. Italy.
1015-35	Northern Empire of Canute the Great.	Byzantine conquest of Armenia.		China governed by scholars.	Medical school at Salerno.
1044-77	Reform of the Papacy. Norman principalities in S. Italy.		Seljuk conquest of the Abbasid Caliphate.	Feudal wars in Japan.	Scholarly revival in W. Europe.
1054	Final separation between Catholic and Orthodox Churches.				
1055			Toghrul-beg takes over Baghdad.		Romanesque art in W. Europe.
1066	Norman Conquest of England.				

Date/Century	Western Europe	Eastern Europe	Moslem World	Far East and Africa	Society, Economy, Arts, Letters and Science
1071		Battle of Menzikert; Seljuk conquest of Asia Minor.			Expansion of Venetian trade in E. Mediterranean Sea.
1077	Gregory VII and Henry IV at Canossa.				
1085	Conquest of Toledo by Alfonso VI of Castile.		Organization of the Assassins.		Development of trade in W. Europe.
1086			The Almoravides in Spain.	Rise of the Burman Empire.	Flowering of Buddhist art.
1088					Rashi at Troyes; Jewish exegesis. Roman law taught at Bologna by Irnerius.
1095	Urban II's call to the Crusade.		Division of the Seljuk Empire.		
1096-1125		Zenith of Kievan Russia.			William IX of Aquitaine and the troubadours.
1099			Conquest of Jerusalem by the Crusaders.		
1100				Unification of China by Hwei-Tsong.	Flourishing of Arab science in Spain.
1100-40			Decline of the Seljuks and rise of the Atabeg dynasties.		Italian domination of the Mediterranean. Teaching of Abelard at Paris.
1115	Bernard of Clairvaux's activity.			Prosperity of the Khmer Empire.	Romanesque art in W. Europe.
1122	Concordat of Worms.				
1124-36	Communal movement in France and England.	Foundation of Suzdal in Russia.			Chivalric civilization in W. Europe.
1128	The rule of the Templars.		Zengi, ruler of Mosul.	Nanking capital of China.	Toledo school of translators from the Arabic into Latin.
c. 1140				Decline of India.	Rise of urban society in the West.
1143	Foundation of Lübeck.				Decree of Gratian.
1144			Conquest of Edessa by Zengi.		Gothic art in W. Europe.
1147	Second Crusade.	Manuel Comnenus and Byzantine revival.		Kin dynasty in China. Expansion of Vietnam in Indochina.	
1152-90	Frederick Barbarossa, Emperor.				Ibn-Rushd (Averroes) and Maimonides.
1154-89	Henry II, King of England.		Unification of Syria by Nureddin.		
1162-82					Chrétien de Troyes; rise of cultural centre of Champagne.
1170	Murder of Thomas Becket.				
1171		Venetians halted at Constantinople.	Saladin ends Fatimid rule in Egypt.	Shogunate in Japan.	Parisian scholarly centre.
1173-94			Saladin, Sultan of Egypt and Syria.		Zenith of the 12th-cent. Renaissance.
1180-1223	Philip II, King of France.	Death of Manuel Comnenus.			
1187		Stephen Nemanja founds Serbian Kingdom.	Battle of Hattin; fall of Jerusalem.		
1189-92			Third Crusade; conquest of Cyprus.		
1196				Genghis-Khan and emergence of the Mongol Emp.	
1198-1216	Innocent III, Pope.				
1202-06	French conquest of Normandy and Anjou.				The German Hanse.
1204		Conquest of Constantinople by Fourth Crusade and Venetians. Byzantine Empire of Nicaea.	Khwarizmian Empire in Persia.		Rise of the Venetian Empire in Greece.

TABLE

744

Date/Century	Western Europe	Eastern Europe	Moslem World	Far East and Africa	Society, Economy, Arts, Letters and Science
1207				Union of Mongol and Turkish tribes under Genghis-Khan.	
1208	Albigensian Crusade.				
1209	First Franciscan brotherhood.			First raid of Genghis-Khan in China.	
1212			Battle of Las Navas de Tolosa.		
1214	Battle of Bouvines; Frederick II, Emperor.		Decline of the Almohades.		
1215	Magna Charta in England.			Organization of the Mongol Empire.	Statutes of the University of Paris.
1216-18			Division of the Ayyubid Empire.	Mongol conquest of N. China.	Foundation of the University of Oxford.
1220-23				Mongol conquest of Persia. Moslem Sultanate of Delhi.	Robert Grosseteste at Oxford.
1223		Battle of Kalka; Mongol raid in Russia.		Foundation of Karakorum.	Decline of feudal economy.
1226-70	Louis IX, King of France.	Decline of the Latin Emp. of Constantinople.			Flowering of French culture.
1227				Death of Genghis-Khan; unity of the Mongol Emp.	
1229			Frederick II's Crusade.		Papal privileges to University of Paris.
1231	Constitution of Melfi, Sicily; Frederick II master of Italy.				Hanse expansion in the Baltic Sea.
c. 1236					The *Roman de la Rose*.
1237-41	War between Papacy and Frederick II.	Conquest of Russia by Batu-Khan. Mongol raids in Poland and Hungary. Establishment of the Golden Horde.			Issuance of paper currency by the Mongols in China; international trade dominated by the Mongols.
1243		Alexander Newski, lord of Novgorod.	Seljuk state destroyed by the Mongols.		Flowering of Gothic art.
1244			The Khwarizmians destroy Jerusalem.		Albert the Great; progress of science.
1248			Louis IX's Crusade.		
1249			The Mamelukes seize power in Egypt.	Prosperity of Karakorum.	Disputes between seculars and friars at the Paris University.
1250	Death of Frederick II; the Great Interregnum in Germany.				Emission of the gold florin at Florence; prosperity of Italian banks.
1258	Provisions of Oxford in England.		Mongol conquest of Baghdad and abolition of the Caliphate.	Mongol conquest of China; the Khanate of Persia.	Foundation of the Sorbonne. Niccolo Pisano.
1261		Constantinople reconquered by Michael Palaeologus.	Baibars' victory at Ain-Jalut. Decline of the Crusaders.	Mongol dynasty (Yuan) in China founded by Kublai Khan.	The *Boke of Housebondrie*. Building of Peking's "Inner City".
1263-70	Failure of barons' rebellions in England.				Thomas of Aquinas at Paris; Roger Bacon; Siger of Brabant.
1266	Conquest of Sicily by Charles of Anjou.				
1282	Sicilian Vespers.			Mongols fail to conquer Java.	
1284			Rise of Ottoman Turks in Anatolia.	MOngols fail to conquer Japan.	Battle of Melonia; decline of Pisa. Genoese supremacy in the Mediterranean.
1291	Swiss confederation.	Rise of Lithuania.	Fall of Acre; end of the Crusader Kingdom.	Assimilation of the Mongols in China.	
1298-1303	Conflict between Philip IV and Pope Boniface VIII.	The Catalan Company.	Fall of the Seljuk Sultanate of Rum.		Giotto.
1305-78	The Papacy at Avignon.				Economic crisis in W. Europe; bankruptcies.

Date/Century	Western Europe	Eastern Europe	Moslem World	Far East and Africa	Society, Economy, Arts, Letters and Science
1308	Suppression of the Templars.				Dante.
1315					Epidemics in W. Europe. and social unrest. William of Ockham at Oxford.
1327	Edward III, King of England.	Civil war at Byzantium.			Marsilius of Padua.
1328	Philip VI of Valois, King of France.	Rise of the Moscow principality.			Epidemics in Italy.
1337	Beginning of the Hundred Years' War.	Decline of the Frankish states in Greece.			Social unrest in Flanders Mystical trends in W. Europe.
1341	Cola di Rienzo and the Republic at Rome.		Ottoman Turks masters of W. Anatolia.		Petrarch.
1346	Battle of Crécy.			Merinid dynasty in Morocco.	Advancement in surgery; Fall of the Bardi Company.
1347	Conquest of Calais by the English.				The Black Death.
1354		Gallipoli conquered by the Ottomans.		S. China revolts against Yuan.	Foundation of the University of Prague.
1355		Death of Stephen Dushan of Serbia.			Chivalric orders in the West.
1356	Battle of Poitiers. The Golden Bull in Germany.		Mameluke Empire at its height.		Spread of use of gunpowder. The artistic centre of Siena.
1358	Revolts in France.			Mali Emp. in Black Africa.	
1360	Treaty of Brétigny between England and France.				
1362		Adrianople conquered by the Ottomans.		Decline of Yuan in China.	
1368				Ming dynasty in China.	
1378	Beginning of the Great Schism.				John Wycliffe's activities in England.
1380	Peace of Stralsund.	Dimitri Donskoi defeats Mongols at Kulikovo.	Empire of Timur-Leng.		Genoese domination in Cyprus. Domination of Hanse in Northern Seas.
1381	Peasants' revolt in England.	Muscovite domination in Russia.			
1389	The Visconti at Milan.	Battle of Kossovo; Ottoman conquest of the Balkans.			Flowering of N. French and Flemish art.
1397	The Union of Kalmar.	Failure of the Nicopolis Crusade.		Discovery of the Canary Islands.	John Hus rector of University of Prague.
1402	Beginning of the Conciliar movement.		Timur-Leng's victory over Bayazid.	Peasants' Empire of Vietnam.	Ghiberti and pre-Renaissance in Italy.
1409	Council of Pisa.	Decline of the Golden Horde.	Anarchy in the Turkish and Mongol empires.		
1410	Armagnac-Burgundian quarrel in France.	Polish victory over Teutonic Knights at Tannenberg.		The Timurids in India.	
1415	Battle of Agincourt; burning of Hus at Constance.			Portuguese conquest of Ceuta. Anarchy in N. Africa.	
1420	Treaty of Troyes.	Hussite revolt in Bohemia.	Reorganization		The fairs of Lyons; prosperity of W. Europe.
1425					The Golden Fleece Order. Thomas à Kempis.
1429	Joan of Arc and awakening of French national feeling.				Burgundian civilization at its height. Humanism in Italy.

INDEX

INDEX OF PERSONS, TERMS AND SUBJECTS
WHICH ARE NOT TITLES OF ENTRIES IN THE ENCYCLOPEDIA

A

Aachen → Aix-la-Chapelle
Abba Graeca → Belgrade
Abbad Al Mutalid → Abbadids
Abbaye aux Dames → Caen
Abbaye aux Hommes → Caen
Abdallah Ibn Al-Zubair → Abd Al-Malik Ibn Marwan; Arabia
Abraham ben David → Catalan World Atlas
Abu Al-Faraj → Bar Hebraeus
Abu Ma'shar → Albumassar
Abu Muslim → Abu Al-Abbas, Al Saffah
Acciajuoli family → Ranieri (Neri) Acciajuoli
Achaio → Greece; Moria
Adalbert of Prague → Boleslav II
Adam Scotus → Dryburgh; Prémontré
Adelaide of Burgundy → Otto I of Germany
Adèle of Champagne → Champagne; Philip II of France
Adèle of Flanders → Charles the Good of France
Aden → Yemen
Adington, Battle of → Alfred the Great
Adolf of Holstein → Hamburg; Holstein
Aelia Capitolina → Jerusalem
Aetius → Burgundians
Afonso (kings of Portugal) → Alfonso
Agio → Banking
Agnes of Poitou → Henry IV (Holy Roman Emperor)
Aidan St. → Lindisfarne Island

Alarcos → Alfonso VIII; Cuenca, Battle of
Al-Ayyub, Emir → Kurdistan
Albategnius → Battani, Mohammed ben Gebir, Al
Albert I of Austria → Albert of Hapsburg
Albertus Magnus → Albert the Great
Albret, House of → Gascony; Buch, Capitals of
Aldfrith, king of Northumbria → Ripon
Alexiad → Anna Comemna; Byzantium (Literature)
Alfabarius → Farabi
Alfasi → Isaac ben Jacob Alfasi
Algazel → Ghazzali, Al
Alice of Brittany → Peter of Dreux
Ali Harari → Kurdistan
Alixandre, Roman d' → Alexander of Bernai
Alkadar → Alfonso VI.
Al Mamun → Alfonso VI.
Amal → Arabs
Amida → Diyarbakir
Andernach → Frederick, Archbishop of Cologne
Anders Sunesen → Danemark
Angelo Corer → Gregory XII
Angkor → Khmer
Anglia → England
Angora → Mongols
Anhalt → Albert the Bear; Saxony
Annals of Aura → Ekkehard of Aura; Herman the Lame
Anselm of Luca → Alexander II, Pope

Appollonius of Perge → Arabs
Arabesque → Abbasids; Art, Islamic
Ard Macha → Armagh
Arelate → Arles; Burgundy; Provence
Argenteuil → Heloise
Ariadne → Anastasius I, Emperor
Arianism → Church; Reccared
Aribal → Art, Pre-Columbian
Armor → Armorica
Arti → Florence
Ascelin → Adalberon of Laon
Ashot III → Armenia
Assolement → Agriculture
Assyrian Christians → Church (Eastern)
Aubert Etienne → Innocent IV, Pope
Audaghost → Ghana; Mauritania
Ausona → Vich
Austria → Carniola
Authentica Habita → Bologna; Frederick Barbarossa
Autodafé → Inquisition
Autun → Burgundy
Autrecourt, Nicholas → Bradwardine, Thomas
Avempace → Ibn Bajjah
Aversa, Counts → Gaeta
Avesnes, Counts of → Holland
Avicebron → Gabirol, Solomon ben Juddah, ibn
Aybeg → Bahrites
Aymeri of Cyprus → Henry II, K. of Cyprus
Ayyub Ibn Shaddi Ibn Marwan → Ayyubids
Axum Kingdom → Ethiopia

B

arlam of Mt. Athos → Hesychasts
ccalarius → Bachelor
.don, Battle of Mount → England
gratians → Armenia
lian the Old → Ibelin
indinelli → Alexander III, Pope;
  Frederick I Barbarossa
.arbary → Berbers; Maghreb
irka-Khan → Golden Horde
.arons' Inquest → Catalogus Baronus
Baruth → Beirut
Battle of the Thirty → Beaumanoir,
  John of
Bearn → Gascogne; Gaston III of
  Foix
.eatrice of Tuscany → Henry VI
  f England
ort, Peter Roger of → Gregory
  Pope
  ium → Benefice
  i → Hainault
  → War
  i → India
  garia of Navarre → Fontevrault;
  .chard Coeur de Lion
  .agarius → Berengar of Tours
ertha → Charlemagne
Bertrade of Montfort → Fulk IV of
  Anjou; Philip I, K. of France
Bertrand of Got → Clement V, Pope;
  Philip IV the Fair
Besançon, Diet of → Frederick I
  Barbarossa; Germany
Bigorre County → Gaston VII
Bill of exchange → Fairs; Commerce
Black Prince → Edward, the Black
  Prince
Blanche of Navarre → Champagne;
  Thibaut III
Blood libel → Blois; Lincoln; William
  of Norwich
Boabdil → Granada
Boethius of Denmark → Denmark
Boiars → Novgorod
Bojars → Moldavia
Bonacolso family → Mantua
Bona fide → Fides
"Book of the Popes" → Liber Pontifi-
  calis
Boru, Brian → Limerick
Bourgeois du Roi → Commune
Braga → Suevi
Brahmanism → India
Bretagne → Armorica; Celts
Brotherhood of the Rosary → Rosary
Bruno of Carinthia → Gregory V;
  Otto III
Buddhism → India; Japan; Thailand
Burghers of Calais → Calais; Eustache
  of Saint-Pierre
Busta Gallorum, Battle of → Totila,
  K. of the Ostrogoths

Butchers' Guild → Buccelari; Caboche, Jean
Byblos → Gibelet

C

Caffa (Kaffa) → Crimea; Genoa;
  Golden Horde
Caliph → Islam
Campagna → Genoa
Campin, Robert → Flemalle, Master of
Candia → Crete
Cantabria → Asturias; Sisebut
Canterbury Tales → Chaucer, Geof-
  frey; England
Capitals of Buch → Buch
Capitano → Florence
Capitulary of Herstal → Charle-
  magne; Herstal
Cardigan, Battle of → Wales
Caro, Joseph → Joseph Karo ben
  Ephraim
Carobert → Charles I of Anjou
"Caroline Books," → Libri Carolini
Carpathian Mountains → Galicia
Castrum → Chester
Catelinius → John III, Pope
Cathay → China
Catherine of France → France;
  Henry V of England
Catherine of Gaunt → Henry III of
  Castile; Peter the Cruel
Cencio Sarelli → Honorius III, Pope
Centenarius → Hundred
Ceremonies → Constantine VII
Chartreuse, Great → Guigues I
Chastelain, George → Historiography
Château-Pèlerin → Templars, Knights
Cheirokitias → Cyprus
Childermas → Innocents' Day
Chinghazids → Abragha; Genghis-
  Khan
Chioggia → Genoa
Chronicles of Bohemia → Cosmas of
  Prague
Chronicle of William of Tyre → His-
  toire d'Eracles
Chronographia → Guy of Bazoches
Cilicia → Frederick I Barbarossa
Clarence, Duke of → Lionel
Clontarf, Battle of → Vikings
Codex Theodosius → Byzantium
Comes → Count; Comitatus
Comminges, Counts of → Gascony;
  Gaston III
Communion → Eucharist
Commynes, Philip de → Historio-
  graphy
Conan IV → Brittany
Confederation of the Rhine →
  Fairs; Germany
Connétable → Constable
Conradin → Conrad V

Constance of Antioch → Raymond
  of Poitiers; Raynald of Châtillon
Constance of Castile → Peter I of
  Portugal
Constance (I) of Sicily → Frederick I
  Barbarossa; Frederick II; Henry
  IV; Holy Roman Empire; Mark-
  ward of Anweiler; Tancred of
  Lecce; William II the Good
Constance (II) of Sicily → Manfred
  of Hohenstaufen; Peter III of
  Aragon; Sicilian Vespers
Corbeil, Treaty of → Cerdagne;
  James the Conqueror of Aragon;
  Louis IX of France
Corvée → Corvada; Famulus
Cossa, Baldassare → John XXIII, Pope
Consuetudines → Taxation
Cosmographia → Bernard Silvestris;
  Guy of Bazoches
"Council of the 39" → Ghent
Court of Burghers → Acre
Creed of Athanasius → Athanasius, St.
Credo ut intelligam → Anselm of
  Canterbury
Crescenti family → John XIX, Pope
Crucessignati → Crusades
Csetiphon → Persia
Cuenca, Battle of → Castile
Currency → Abacus; Coinage
"Cycle of Godfrey of Bouillon" →
  Crusade; Cycle of poems; Chan-
  son de geste; Godefrey of Bouillon
Cynegils, King → Birinus, St.
Czechoslovakia → Bohemia; Caslav

D

Datini family → Banking, Book-
  keeping
Dauphin → Dauphiné
Day of Wrath → Dies Irae
Death → Dance of Death
Decameron → Boccacio, Giovanni
Decapolis → Alsace
Deccan → India
De civitate Dei → Augustine, St.
De contemptie Mundie → Bernard
  of Cluny
De divisione naturae → Erigena;
  John Scot
Defence (fortifications) → Castle;
  China; Danewerk
De imago Mundi → Ailly, Pierre d'
Desiderius of Monte Cassino → Victor
  III, Pope
Deying → Cloth manufacture; Com-
  positiones ad tigenda
Dictatus Papae → Henry IV; Gregory
  VII
Diet of Roncaglia → Bulgarus
Digenis Akritas → Byzantium (Litera-
  ture)

Dirk (Frisian leader) → Holland
Divina Commedia → Dante
Diwan → Abu Nuwas; Al Hasan Ibn Hani; Arabs; Hafiz, Shams Al-Din Muhammad; Hebrew
Djihlal → Druzes
Djizya → Dhimmi
Doge → Venice
Donald IV of Scotland → Malcolm I
Drang nach Osten (The March Eastwards) → Germany; Henry XII; Saxony
Dreux, house of → Britanny
Dualism → Albigenses; Bogomiles; Manichaeism
Duana → Sicily
Dublin → Ireland
Duncan I (k. of the Scots) → Macbeth; Malcom III

E

Eadred of Mercia → Edgar the Peaceful
Eadwig, k. of Wessex → Edgar
Ealhmund of Wessex → Egbert the Great
Ecclesia → Church, *Libertas*
Edward the Martyr → Ethelred II
Egbert of Kent → Ethelwulf
Eger, Peace of → Wenceslas IV
Eike von Repgow → *Sachsenspiegel*
Eleonora of Arborea → Sardinia
Eleonora of Provence → Henry III of England
Elipandus → Adoptionism
Emilia → Italy
Emir Al Bahr → Aghlabids
Epirus → Byzantium; Greece
Erispoë → Brittany
Erwig → Wamba
Eskisehir → Dorylaeum
Esztergom → Gran
Ethelburga, St. → Paulinus of York
Ethelreda, St. → Ely, Isle of
Etymologies → Braulio; Geography; Isidore of Seville
Eudoxia, Empress → Arcadius; Chrisostom, John; Hilderic; Huneric
Evesham, Battle of → Bohum

F

Factum → Parliament
Faeroe Islands → Haakon IV; Harold I of Norway
Falaise, Treaty of → William the Lion of Scotland
Falconry → *De Arte venandi cum Avibus;* Frederick II; Hunting; Lopez de Ayala
Famagusta → Cyprus

Farae → Lombards
Fargani, Al → Geography
Felicitas Julia → Lisbon
Ferrers, Earls of → Derbyshire
Fieschi, Sinibaldo → Innocent IV
Filastin → Ascalon
Filiangeri → Andrew. St.
Foederati → Burgundians; Germans
Foucault, Guy → Clement IV, Pope
Fraga, Battle of → Aragon
Franche-Comté → Besançon; Burgundy; Eudes IV
Franchise → Charters of franchise; towns
Francia → France; Franks
Francia Media → Lothair I; Verdun
Francia Orientalis → Germany
Free-men → Colonate; Feudalism; Fidelity; Hospites; *Munderburium*
Free-peasants → *Mansus*
Fuero → Aragon; Castile
Fulbert, Canon → Abelard, Peter; Heloise
Fundacco → *Comitatus*

G

Gaiseric → Genseric
Galilee → Architecture
Gallia → Gaul
Gallia Placida → Valentinian III, Pope
Garcia dynasty → Sancho I, king of Navarre
Gascony → Aquitaine
Gâtinais → Geoffrey, counts of Anjou
Gau → *Comitatus*
Gebel → Djebal
Gediminas → Gedymin
Gelati Monastery → Georgia
Gelnhausen, Diet of → Germany
Genealogy → Historiography
Genesaret Lake → Galilee
Genizah → Cairo; Commerce
George Palmas → Hesychasts
Gerald of Wales → Giraldus Cambrensis
Gerard of Bologna → Lucius II, Pope
Gerard of Châtenois → Lorraine
Gerardus Magnus → Groote, Geert of
Gerbert of Aurillac → Catalonia; Sylvester II, Pope
Gerhard → Nicholas II, Pope
Geste → *Chanson de geste*
Gesuati brothers → Colombini, Giovanni
Gethica → Jordanus
Ghana, Empire of → Africa
Ghazanids → Arabs
Ghebhart of Dollnstein-Hirschberg → Victor II, Pope
Gilbertine Order → Gilbert of Sempringham

Gildas → Arthur
Giorgio family → Bodonitza
Giovanni Gaetano Orsini → Nicholas III, Pope
Girolamo Masci → Nicholas IV, Pope
Giudici → Sardinia
Giudoni, Gregorio Papareschi → Innocent II, Pope
Glycerius → Gundobald
Goldsmiths → Limoges
Gonfaloniere → Florence
Got, Bertrand de → Clement V, Pope
Gothia → Languedoc
Gothic Flamboyant → Architecture; Bourges
Gottfried → Hedeby
Gregorian reform → Church
Gregory Conti → Victor IV, Antipope
Gregory of Nyssa → Byzantium (Literature)
Gregory the Illuminator → Armenia
Guigues → Dauphiné
Grimaldi family → Monaco
Grodno → Lithuania
Guibert of Ravina → Clement III, Pope
Guide for the Perplexed → Maimonides; Samuel Ibn Tibbon
Guidebook to the Duties of the Heart → Bahya Ibn Paquda
Guido of Vienne → Calixtus II, Pope
Guillaume de Grimoald → Urban V, Pope
Guillelm of Aquitaine → Aquitaine, William
Gundioc → Chilperic; Gundobald
Guntaric → Burgundians
Gupta Empire → India
Guy of Crema → Paschal III, Pope

H

Habichtsburg → Hapsburg
Hadith → Arabs; Islam
Hajj → Islam; Kaaba; Mecca
Haly Abbas → Medicine
Han dynasty → China
Hanbalik → Peking
Hanseatic League → Hanse
Hasan-i-Sabbah → Assassins
Havn → Absalom of Lund; Copenhagen
Helinand of Froidmont → Historiography
Hemming → Denmark
Hemyar → Ethiopia; Yemen
Hennequin (Pol, Hermann, Jan) → Limburg Brothers
Henry II of Brabenberg → Austria
Henry of Suza → Hostiensis
Heregeld → Danegeld
Hidalgo → Aragon; Castile
Hilda, St. → Whitby

Hildebrand → Gregory VII
Historia Occidentalis → James of Vitry
Historia Orientalis → James of Vitry
Hochdeutsch → Germany (Language)
Hof → Denmark
Holyrood Abbey → Edinburgh
Hugh of Lacy → Dublin
Hugo Primas → Hugh of Orléans
Huesca → Aragon
Humbertian dynasty → Savoy

I

Iberian Peninsula → Portugal; Spain
Ibn Batutta → Africa; Arabs
Ibn Ezra, Abraham → Abraham Ibn Ezra
Ibn Nagrela → Samuel Hanagid Halevi
Ibn Tumart → Almohades; Almoravides
Iconium → Konya
Idrissi → Al-Idrissi
Idrissids → Aghlabids; Morocco
Ifriqyia → Africa; Aghlabids; Constantine; Kairwan
Imam → Abbasids
Imago Mundi → Honorius Augustodunensis
Indolent kings → Clovis II
Infidels → *Dhimmis*
"Inner City" → China
Interregnum → Franconia; Germany; Rhenisch League
Isabel of Clare → William Marshall
Isabella of Angoulême → Angoulême; Hugh of Lusignan
Isabella (Isabeau) of Bavaria → Charles VI; Louis, duke of Orléans
Isabella of Brienne → Frederick II; John of Brienne
Isabella of France → Despenser
Isabella of Montferrat → Aquitaine; Henry of Champagne

J

Jacopo Capocci → James of Vitterbo
Jacques d'Euse → John XXII, Pope
Jacques Pantaléon → Urban IV, Pope
Jadwiga of Poland → Jagiello; Lithuania; Vilna
James, St. → Santiago de Compostela
James of Edessa → Geography
Jihad → *Gihad*
Joachinism → Joachim of Fiore
Joan I of Anjou → Charles of Calabria
Joan of Baumont → Burchard d'Avesnes
Joan of Flanders → Ferrand of Portugal; Flanders
Joan of Montferrat → William Clito

Joan of Navarre → Champagne; Charles I of Navarre; Philip IV the Fair; Philip I the Tall
Joan of Toulouse → Alphonse of Poitiers; Raymond VII
John Gratian → Gregory VI, Pope
John Le Charlier → Gerson
John of Tepla → Germany (Literature)
John, Order of St. → Hospitaller Knights
John of Seville → John of Spain
Jubilaeum → Holy Year
Junker → Chivalry

K

Kadi → Abbadids; Alcade
Kagan → Yaroslav the Wise
Kalka → Mstislav the Brave; Smolensk
Kambalek → Peking
Karabalghasun → Uighur Turks
Karakhan → Turks
Karakorum → Genghis Khan; Mongols
Karelia → Finland
Khalji sultans → Delhi
Khanafites → Abu Khanifa
Khocho → Uighur Turks
Kin → China
Knights' Alphabet → Georgia
Knights of Malta → Hospitaller Knights
Knut → Canuta
Konya → Osman 1; Seljuks; Qilij Arslan I
Kossovo, Battle of → Bulgari; Byzantium; Fire-arms; Ochrida
Kotuz, Sultan → Damascus
Kovno → Lithuania
Kuraltai → Hulagu
Kuzari → Jehudah Halevi

L

Laeliarts → Matins of Bruges
Lama → Tibet
Landesfrieden → Charles III of Germany; Commerce
Landrecht → Law
Lapis philosophorum → Alchemy
Laskarids → Byzantium; Nicaea, Empire of
Las Navas de Tortosa, Battle of → Alphonso VIII; Almohades; Morocco; *Reconquista*
Latifundia → Feudalism
Lavra → Abbey; Athos, Mount; Sabas, St.
Lazarists → Hospitals
Letter of credit → Banking; Fairs
Legenda Aura → *Acta Sanctorum*; Golden Legend; Jacob of Voragine
Legistes → Parliament; Philip IV of France

Lehnrecht → Law
Leonardo of Pisa → Algebra
Leudes → Clovis
Li dynasty → Viet
Libourne, Battle of → Aquitaine
Liguria → Genoa; Italy
Limes Germaniae → Germans
Liutgard → Conrad the Red; Franconia
Llanelwy → Asaph, St.
Llanelwy the Great → Wales
Loire River → Anjou
Low Countries → Belgium

M

Magister militum → Arbogast
Magyars → Hungary
Maharam → Meir ben Baruch of Rothenburg
Mahdi → Almohades; Almoravides; Fatimids
Mahonna → Chios; Giustiniani
Maine → Anjou
Maistre Petit → David Kimhi
Mallus → Jury trial
Mande H. → *Devotio Moderna*
Manes → Manichaean heresy
Manoello Romano → Emmanuel ben Salomon
Mansa-Musa → Mali
Mansi → Chivalry; Feudalism
Margaret of Angoulême → Anjou; John Lackland
Margaret of Bearn → Gaston VII
Margaret of Beaumont → Burchard d'Avesnes
Margaret of Flanders → Burgundy; Louis of Male
Margaret of Gloucester → Gaveston, Piers
Margaret of Holland → Hainault
Margrave → March
Marinids → Fez; Morocco
Marinus → Martin III, Pope
Marinus, St. → San Marino
Marquis → March
Maro, St. → Maronites
Marrakech → Almoravides; Morocco
Marsan → Gaston VII of Bearn
Mary of Burgundy → Champagne
Mary of Montferrat → John of Brienne
Mary of Montpellier → James I of Aragon
Mary of Scotland → Eustace of Boulogne-
Maud, Empress → Matilda of England
Mayan Art → Art
Mayer of Rothenberg → Asher bar Jehiel
Medersa → Education
Meloria, Battle of → Genoa; Pisa; Sardinia

Mercedarian Order → Peter Nolasco
Mercurius → John II, Pope
Merlin → Geoffrey of Monmouth
Mesrob, St. → Armenia
Messianism → Gog and Magog; Milleniarism
Michaelmas → Michael the Archangel
Migliorati, Cosimo → Innocent III, Pope
Ming dynasty → China
Minnesinger → Germany (Literature)
Military service → Expeditio; Feudalism; Fyrd
Minor friars → Frances of Assisi
Minting → Coinage
Monacada family → Vich
"Monte Pietatis" → Usury
Montgisard, Battle of → Raynald of Châtillon
Morgain → Arthur
Moriscos → Malaga
Mortmain → De viris religiosi
Moses de Leon → Kabbalah
Muret, Battle of → Albigenses
Mynyw → David, St.

N

Navarete, Battle of → Najera
Negroponte → Euobea; Greece
Netherlands → Frisia
Nicholas of Hereford → Lollards
Niger River → Mali
Nike Riots → Byzantium; Justinian I; Narses
Nizamyah → Baghdad
Nonnos → Byzantium (Literature)
Nordmark → Brandenburg
Nuns → Speculum Virginum

O

Occitanian (langue d'Oc) → Bernard of Ventadour; France; Gascony; Peter Vidal
Octavian → John XII, Pope
Odo of Chartres → Dreux
Odo of Lagerey → Urban II, Pope
Odo of La Roche → Greece; Guy II of La Roche
Oghuz tribes → Turks
Opus Dei → Benedict of Nursia
Ordainers (ordinances) → Gaveston, Piers; Edward II
Oriflame → Suger
Orkney Islands → Harold I of Norway
Orosius → Geography
Ottavian of Monticelli → Victor IV, Antipope
Otto the Illustrious (of Saxony) → Henry I
Oviedo → Asturias

P

Pagus → Brabant; Brienne
Pannonia → Arpad; Hungary
Pax christiana → War
Pax romana → War
Pembroke, Earls of → Richard of Clare; Richard Marshal
Peasant revolts → Enclosure; Great Revolt; Hundred Years' War; Jacqueries; Pastoureaux; Statutes of the Labourers; Tyler, Wyat
Penthievre, House of → Brittany
Perth, Treaty of → Scotland
Peter Hispanus → John XII, Pope
Peter Juliani → John XII, Pope
Peter of Tarentaise → Innocent V
Peter Philarges → Alexander V
Petrine doctrine → Peter, St.
Petronilla of Aragon → Aragon; Raymond Berengar IV, count of Barcelona; Ralph of Vermandois; Ramiro II
Philagatus, Giovanni → John XVI
Piast principality → Breslau
Piedpowders, Court of → Fairs
Pisides, George → Byzantium (Literature)
Pitres, Assembly of → Bernard Plantevelne
"Photian Schism" → Byzantium
Poitiers, Battle of (732) → Charles Martel; France; Franks; War
Poitiers, Battle of (1356) → France; Gaston III; John II of France; Charles V of France; Charles II of France; Charny, Geoffrey of; Edward III of England; Grandes Compagnies; Hundred Years' War; Walter II of Brienne
Placetum → Capitulary; Jury trial
Prebend → Canon
Ptolemaic system → Geography
Ptolemais → Acre
Pumbedita → David Ben Zakkai; Gaon; Hai Gaon
Punjab → India

Q

Quraish → Abu Sufyan; Arabia

R

Rabad → Abraham ben David of Posquières
Radak → David Kimhi
Radbot → Hapsburg
Radewijns, F. → Devotio Moderna
Rajastan → India
Rajputana empire → India

Rambam → Maimonides, Moses
Ranier of San Lorenzo → Paschal II, Pope
Raoul de Cambrai → Herbert II of Vermandois
Raynald de Segni → Alexander IV, Pope
Rashbam → Samuel ben Meir of Ramerupt
Rassulids → Yemen
Reeve → Cattle; Taxation; Warrantia
Rhine Valley → Imperial cities; Palatinate
Rialto, Peace of → Alexander III
Riba → Isaac ben Asher Halevi
Ribat → Almoravides
Ribemont, Treaty of → Louis II of Germany
Ricimer → Gundobald
Reggio, Battle of → Roger of Loria
Robert of Genoa → Clement VII, Pope
Roger Peter → Clement VI, Pope
Rolando Bandinelli → Alexander III, Pope
Roman de la Rose → Allegory; John of Meung; William of Lorris
Romanus of Tusculum → John XIX, Pope
Rosary Brotherhood → Dominic St.
Rudolieb → Germany (Literature)
Rufinus → Herbals
Rupenids (dynasty) → Armenia

S

Sahel Ibn Bishar → Astrology
Saint-Jean-d'Acre → Acre
Saints, lives of → Acta Sanctorum; Golden Legend
Samson, St. → Brittany
Samurai → Japan
Sancho V of Navarre → Sancho I Ramirez of Aragon
Santa Claus → Nicholas, St.
Sapandia → Savoy
Sapienza, Battle of → Venice
Sarai → Golden Horde
Satawhana dynasty → India
Savelli, Cencio → Honorius III, Pope
Savelli, Giacomo → Honorius IV, Pope
Savoy, House of → Geneva
Sayf Al-Dawlah → Aleppo; Hamanids
Scannabecchi, Lambert → Honorius II, Pope
Schleswig → Denmark; Germany
Schulteiss → Agriculture
Scribe → Chancery
Segni, Lotaris → Innocent III, Pope
Segni, Raynald → Alexander IV, P
Segni, Ugolino → Gregory IX, P
Shetland Islands → Harold I of N
Shogun → Japan

Silk industry → Palermo; Thebes
Simon of Brie → Martin IV, Pope
Skäne → Lund; Sweden
Sluys, Battle of → Philip IV of Valois
Sobor → Suzdal
Social classes → Estates
Solde → *Condottieri*
Solomon ben Isaac → Rashi
Solomonic dynasty → Ethiopia
Spirituals → Franciscans; Fraticelli
Stephen of Fougères → Brittany
Straslund, Peace of → Hanse
Styria → Hapsburg
St. Clair-on-Epte, Treaty → Rouen;
   Rollo
Sundiata → Mali
Sunesen, Anders → Denmark
Sung dynasty → China
Supplinbury → Lothair III
"Swan Knight" → Godfrey of Bouillon
 wei → China
ybil of Anjou → William Clito
ybil of Jerusalem → Baldwin IV;
   Bohemond VI
Synod of Perpignan → Benedict XIII
Syriac rite → Maronites

T

Tagliacozzo, Battle of → Conrad V
Tahir Ibn Hussayn → Tahirids
Tamarán → Alfonso VII; Ferdinand I
Tang dynasty → China; Viet; Yunnan
Tarasicodissa → Zeno
Temuchin → Genghis Khan
Terra Scotiae → Scotland
Thanes → Anglo-Saxons
Theodora Comemna → Baldwin III;
   Manuel I; Michael III
Thomas à Kempis → *Devotio Moderna*
Thousand and One Tales → Abba-
   sids; Arabs; Harun Al Rashid

Thorkel I → Dublin
Tiel → Dorestad
Tiflis → Georgia
Timbuctu → Ghana; Mali
Time, measuring → Bells
Tirnoro → Bulgari
Toghrul → Wang-Khan
Tokhtamysh → Dimitri Donskoi;
   Tamerlane
Torri → Florence
Trencavel → Beziers; Languedoc;
   Simon of Montfort
Tusculum family → Benedict VIII;
   Benedict IX; Benedict X

U

Ubaldo Allucingoli → Lucius III,
   Pope
Uberto Crivelli → Urban III, Pope
'Ukkal → Druzes
Ulemas → Arabs; Islam; *Sunna;*
   War
Ultraquists → Hussites
Universal Chronicle → Burchard of
   Ursberg
Ushbuna, Al → Lisbon

V

Valachia → Wallachia
Valdemar (kings of Denmark) → Wal-
   demar
Val-ès-Dunes, Battle of → William the
   Conqueror
Vascones → Basques
Vasus casatus → *Casamentum*
Via Maris → Gaza; Ramlah
Vilayeth → Catalonia
Veche → Pskov; Russia; Suzdal

Visconti, Tebaldo → Gregory X,
   Pope
Vivaldi → Doria, Theodosio
Verdun, Treaty of → Louis the
   German
Vojvod → Moldavia; Transylvania

W

Wali → Barcelona
Waltharius → Ekkehard of St. Gall
Waqf → Almohades
Watassi → Morocco
Water Court → Valencia
Wei kingdom → China
Welf II → Henry IX of Bavaria
Westminster, Statute of → *De donis
   conditionalibus*
Wilfrid of Saxony → Henry IX of
   Bavaria
William VIII → Guy-Geoffrey of
   Aquitaine

Y

Yabgu → Khazars
Yamato Empire → Japan
Yatrib → Medina
Yngling dynasty → Harold I of Norway

Z

Zab River, Battle of the → Umayyad
Zagwe dynasty → Ethiopia
Zayd → Arabia; Yemen
Zeeland → Hainault
Zirids → Algiers; Berbers; Kairwan
Zohar → Kabbalah
Zupan → Stephen (kings of Serbia)

ACKNOWLEDGMENTS

The Publishers wish to express their thanks to the following museums, libraries and other institutions from whose collections works have been reproduced:

Fratelli Alinari, S.P.A., Florence 96, 109, 129 (bottom), 236, 336, 396, 531, 569 (bottom), 590, 664; The Bettmann Archive, Inc., New York 13, 31, 67 (top), 78, 83, 122 (top), 122 (bottom), 124 (top), 124 (bottom), 129 (top), 155, 205, 221 (top), 221)bottom), 226, 267, 279, 286, 290, 329, 348, 368, 461, 471, 499, 514 (top), 514 (bottom), 515 (top), 515 (bottom), 518 (top), 518 (bottom), 527, 531 (top), 575, 601, 617, 699, 706, 725; Biblioteca Medicea Laurenziana, Florence 196; Bibliothèque Municipale de Reims 256; Bibliothèque Nationale, Paris 6, 141, 384; Bodleian Library, Oxford 517, 593; Reproduced by permission of the British Library, London 204 (Add. MS 42130 ff. 206 v, 207), 217 (Egerton 1894, f. 2v), 218 (Royal MS15 EIII, f269), 249 (Royal MS 18 E.i.f.165), 376 (Royal MS15 E.ii, f.265), 419 (Royal MS 2B, vii, f.150v), 493 (Add. MS42130, f.158), 525 (Add. MS42130, f.181), 572 (Harley 1319, f. 57), 577 (Roy. MS 2B, vii, f.78v); Elsevier Publishing Projects, Amsterdam 1, 2, 4, 11, 26, 27, 29, 38, 41, 45, 46, 62, 63, 64, 65 (top), 65 (bottom), 66 (top), 66 (bottom), 67 (bottom), 68, 73 (bottom), 74 (bottom), 75 (top), 76 (top), 76 (bottom), 81, 84, 94, 95, 97, 103, 113, 115, 116, 118 (top), 118 (bottom), 119, 131, 144, 149, 150, 159, 161, 163, 164, 166, 168, 171, 180, 194-195, 197, 206, 209, 216, 219, 225, 237, 240, 254, 255, 260, 265, 273, 274, 291, 305, 313, 315 (top), 318, 324, 325, 326, 331, 344, 346, 360, 367, 400 (top), 400 (bottom), 401, 421, 447, 453, 454-455, 456, 462, 464, 468, 470, 491, 494, 513, 521, 522-523, 524, 528, 533, 534, 540, 542, 550, 559, 562, 563, 569 (top), 573, 574, 588, 589, 595, 597, 600, 603, 606-607, 608, 619, 620, 623, 631, 636 (top), 641, 642 (top), 650, 653, 668, 684, 685, 701, 702, 716, 724, 728, 730; Hirmer Verlag, Münich 12, 74 (top), 75 (bottom), 98, 210, 235, 388, 402-403, 407, 605, 612, 629, 636 (bottom); Jerusalem Publishing House, Ltd. 18, 42, 91 (top), 91 (bottom), 160, 250, 255, 271, 307, 343, 378, 411, 440, 445, 446, 502, 510, 544, 637, 696, 732; Jewish National and University Library, Jerusalem 498; The Metropolitan Museum of Art, New York 121, 158, 200, 215, 218, 239, 321, 356, 363, 420, 428, 486, 487, 510 (bottom), 529, 560, 561, 571, 611, 642, 662, 690, 713; Musée Condé, Chantilly 559; Musée de Dijon 143; Musée des Monuments Français 249; Musée des Tapisseries, Angers 50 (bottom); Musée Marmottan, Paris 404; Museo Nazionale del Bargello, Florence 292; National Gallery, London 315 (bottom); Palazzo Publico di Siena 486 (bottom); Sarajevo National Museum 380; Galleria degli Uffizi, Florence 509; Universitätsbibliotek, Heidelberg 193; By courtesy of the Victoria and Albert Museum, London 314; La Ville de Bayeux 718.

The Publishers have attempted to observe the legal requirements with respect to copyrights. However, in view of the large number of illustrations included in this volume, the Publishers wish to apologize in advance for any involuntary omissions or errors and invite persons or bodies concerned to write to the Publishers.